BARTLETT'S FAMILIAR QUOTATIONS

BARTLETT'S FAMILIAR QUOTATIONS

A collection of passages, phrases, and proverbs traced
to their sources in ancient and modern literature

EIGHTEENTH EDITION

JOHN BARTLETT

GEOFFREY O'BRIEN, GENERAL EDITOR

Little, Brown and Company
NEW YORK · BOSTON · LONDON

Little, Brown and Company
Hachette Book Group
237 Park Avenue, New York, NY 10017
littlebrown.com

First Edition Published 1855
First Little, Brown Edition Published 1863
Eighteenth Edition Published October 2012
First Printing

Little, Brown and Company is a division of Hachette Book Group, Inc., and is celebrating its
175th anniversary in 2012. The Little, Brown name and logo are trademarks of Hachette Book Group, Inc.

LIBRARY OF CONGRESS CATALOGING-IN-PUBLICATION DATA
Bartlett, John, 1820–1905.
Bartlett's familiar quotations: a collection of passages, phrases, and proverbs
traced to their sources in ancient and modern literature / John Bartlett;
edited by Geoffrey O'Brien.—18th ed., rev. and enl.
p.   cm.
Includes indexes.
ISBN 978-0-316-01759-6
1. Quotations, English.   I. Geoffrey O'Brien.   II. Little, Brown and Company.   III. Title.
PN6081.B27 2012
808.88'2—dc23   2012019870

HML

PRINTED IN THE UNITED STATES OF AMERICA

CONTENTS

PREFACE TO THE EIGHTEENTH EDITION

WHEN THE BOOKSELLER JOHN BARTLETT PUBLISHED HIS COLLECTION OF FAMILIAR QUOTATIONS IN 1855, IT WAS ALREADY THE CULMINATION OF A LONG PROCESS OF compiling and sifting. An early reader with an extraordinarily retentive memory, Bartlett, born in Plymouth, Massachusetts, in 1820, had for years kept a commonplace book in which he noted those "passages, phrases, and proverbs" that he had a penchant for collecting. The privately printed 1855 edition was only 258 pages long; by the time of his death in 1905, he had overseen nine editions, and his commonplace book had taken its place as an indispensable reference.

Bartlett's original *Familiar Quotations* registered the essential influences of his culture: the Bible and Shakespeare above all, flanked by an array of chiefly British writers. Bartlett's range may have been narrow, but within it his tastes were solid, and his work has provided an unshakeable foundation for the extensive revisions and additions of the editors who have followed him. The apparent modesty of the sentence by Montaigne that Bartlett affixed to the title page of the seventh edition (1876) — "I have gathered a posie of other men's flowers, and nothing but the thread that binds them is mine own" — doubtless conceals pride in the characteristic aptness of the choice. The book as it evolved under his care became a sort of history of thought and expression, a way for a reader to sail rapidly over centuries and pass them in review. Bartlett knew that *familiar* is not a word that can be easily defined — "what is familiar to one class of readers may be quite new to another" — and acknowledged that "it has been thought better to incur the risk of erring on the side of fullness." In taking that risk he created not merely a reference work but a unique anthology, a book that can be read straight through, a graph of the thought of centuries spread out like an entrancing scroll.

John Bartlett's achievement was singular, and it has continued to inspire the editors who have followed him. *Bartlett's Familiar Quotations* has always been, and will remain, a work in progress. Such a book must change over time to reflect not only what has been newly written or said but to take note of how the past changes as well, always renewing itself as new readers and observers uncover fresh perspectives and areas of interest. It is not so much like walking through a museum of fixed exhibits as of tuning in to a millennia-old conversation and picking up, each time, slightly different clusters of fragments and piecing together a slightly different story. The voices resonating in that echo chamber are also talking to one another, and so *Bartlett's* is also a map of interconnections and variants. Quotations respond to quotations, to affirm them or turn them inside out or perhaps to drown them. One way or another, the conversation sustains itself over vast stretches of time — from the Sumerian Gilgamesh epic to the newly minted sound bites of the Internet era — even as it suffers interruption from the intrusions and catastrophes of history.

One thing that has changed significantly is the range of source materials on which *Bartlett's* draws. A work that was once dominated by scripture, classical literature, and poetry has opened itself to the multiple voices of mass journalism, recording, movies, radio and television broadcasting, and now the Internet. The digital era offers opportunities that are both exhilarating and overwhelming; we can see a phrase traveling from place to place virtually before our eyes, and we can get a quantitative sense of how widely and quickly it has traveled. Millions of words are captured that would once have disappeared into the wind. But the age of recording is also the age of ephemerality. The familiar quotations of last year are for the most part well on their way to oblivion. A new edition of *Bartlett's* must gamble on the newest utterances, but only a future editor will be in a position to measure how long-lasting any of them proves.

Many voices appear in *Bartlett's* for the first time in this eighteenth edition, some the expected brand-new ones — Barack Obama, Anne Carson, David Foster Wallace, Sonia Sotomayor, Steve Jobs, Sarah Palin, Warren Buffett, *The Sopranos, South Park* — and others from the recent and not-so-recent past whose phrases continue to pervade and sometimes transform the culture. As in any era, but now at a faster rate than ever, catchphrases from many different corners — whether "the anxiety of influence" or "wardrobe malfunction" or "the male gaze" or "the age of mechanical reproduction" or "gonzo journalism" — find their way into the main corridors of speech.

This edition expands its international coverage, incorporating important writers from Europe, Asia, Africa, and Latin America, and elsewhere, from Wang Wei and Ibn Khaldun to Wislawa Szymborska and Orhan Pamuk. It adds the words of over a hundred women. It offers a richer gathering of memorable verbal expression by artists of many kinds (painters, musicians, photographers, architects, filmmakers) and draws more heavily on novelists as varied as Dostoevsky and Elmore Leonard. It acknowledges that the words of songwriters — from Johnny Mercer, Willie Dixon, and Leonard Cohen to Madonna, Grandmaster Flash, and Kurt Cobain — have an unequaled reach and influence. But here will be found as well astronauts and entrepreneurs, athletes and physicists, rappers, federal judges, deconstructionists, and otherwise almost unknown figures who have given utterance to phrases that continue to make inroads as only the most eloquent or startling or suggestive or even unsettling quotations can.

I must gratefully acknowledge the suggestions of many consultants, friends, and colleagues whose guidance has been invaluable in the preparation of this edition. They include Tracy Behar, Susanna Brougham, Devin Dougherty, Evan Eisenberg,

Peggy Freudenthal, Katherine Isaacs, Kent Jones, Katherine Kiger, Cynthia Lindlof, Barbara Necol, Michael Neibergall, Heather O'Brien, Flaminia Ocampo, Janet Malcolm, Pamela Marshall, Jonathan Miller, Laura Miller, Albert Mobilio, Jed Perl, Robert Polito, Kathryn Rogers, Luc Sante, Harold Schechter, Jill Schoolman, and Drake Stutesman. I owe a special debt to James Gibbons, who participated extensively in every phase of this project, helping to enlarge its scope in many free-ranging discussions and enriching its contents by uncovering a wide array of memorable contributions.

GEOFFREY O'BRIEN
New York, New York

GUIDE TO THE USE OF
BARTLETT'S FAMILIAR QUOTATIONS

· BASIC INFORMATION ·

AUTHORS APPEAR CHRONOLOGICALLY IN THE ORDER OF THEIR BIRTH DATES; AUTHORS BORN IN THE SAME YEAR ARE ARRANGED ALPHABETICALLY. The quotations for each author are generally in chronological order according to the date of publication (in some instances according to the date of composition). Poetry generally precedes prose for authors who wrote both.

Anonymous quotations are located as follows: early miscellaneous and Latin quotations are placed at about 670 C.E. General anonymous quotations begin immediately after the last dated author and are arranged in roughly chronological order (the precise dates of origin often being unknown). Specific groupings of anonymous quotations—African, Ballads, Cowboy Songs, and so on—follow the general Anonymous section in alphabetical order according to the heading.

A document without a specific author appears near the people with whom it is associated; for example, the Constitution of the United States (1787) appears among its creators, such as George Washington (born in 1732), John Adams (1735), James Madison (1751), and Alexander Hamilton (1755).

To find a particular author, consult the Index of Authors, page xv; to find a particular quotation, consult the Index, page 901. For information on the arrangement and use of the index, see below.

· QUOTATION SOURCES ·

Each quotation has a source line supplying title, date if known (most often that of publication), and other information the reader might find helpful. In the quotations from the Bible and from Shakespeare, the page headings provide blanket sources for the quotations on the particular page, while the source lines provide only chapter and verse or act, scene, and line references.

· FOOTNOTES ·

The footnotes supply information about a quotation, such as the original text of a translated quotation, the name of a translator, background comments for the quotation, and other quotations related in phrase or content to the footnoted quotation.

· INDEX OF AUTHORS ·

The Index of Authors provides birth and death dates and the page number for the quotations by each author, as well as the page numbers for any additional quotations by that author in the footnotes. When an author is better known by a name other than his or her given name, the author is listed under the more familiar name, with the given name provided in square brackets—for example, Bill [William Jefferson] Clinton. Bracketed parts of a name as listed in this index are those not used in the author's typical "signature"—for example, T[homas] S[tearns] Eliot. The Index of Authors also lists many pseudonyms, with cross-references from the less familiar name to the more familiar—for example, Karen Blixen is cross-referred to Isak Dinesen, the pseudonym under which she wrote. Authors who are quoted only in footnotes have their full names and birth and death dates given in the footnotes.

To find a particular book of the Bible, see the Bible entry, where the books are listed alphabetically. The same is true for Shakespeare; to find any work by Shakespeare, consult the Shakespeare entry. Anonymous quotations are listed under the heading "Anonymous," as well as by specific groupings, such as Ballads (Anonymous), Cowboy Songs (Anonymous), and so on.

· INDEX ·

The *Bartlett's* index is arranged by keywords, not topics. The keywords are spelled according to *Webster's Tenth New Collegiate Dictionary* and *Webster's Third New International Dictionary*. The spelling and capitalization in the index entry are those of the quotation. Some older or variant spellings are indexed, as are "made" words, such as "hitherandthithering," "slithy," acronyms, and dialectal words. Compound expressions not found in *Webster's* are sometimes indexed: the hyphenated form "good-night," for example, is so indexed to allow grouping under this key expression rather than under "good" and "night." ("Human" and "being," however, are separately indexed.) Compound names, such as "Long Island," "South Vietnam," "United States," are indexed as one word. Elided letters found in many quotations (such as *'d* for *ed*) are supplied in the index entries. Quotations from other languages generally are indexed, usually at a keyword specific to the other language, but sometimes at a keyword that is also in English; see, for example, the entries at "Bourgeois."

Alphabetization of keywords is word-for-word, not letter-by-letter. Thus, "New Zealand" precedes "Newborn." The order of plural and possessive keywords is from singular possessive to plural to plural possessive: for example, *Lover's, Lovers, Lovers'*.

The number at the end of each index entry shows the page on which the quotation starts and the number of the quotation on the page — 224:4, for example, is the fourth quotation on page 224. Entries for footnote quotations are cited by page and note number, such as 224:*n*2 for the second footnote on page 224.

The index entry line is usually a short form of the indexed phrase, and the words in general appear in the same order, with the keyword abbreviated unless it starts the entry, in which case it is supplied by the keyword itself. Index entry lines are alphabetized, with articles, prepositions, and conjunctions included.

> Hope, all h. abandon ye who enter here, 128:6
> > Americans h. of world, 321:19
> > animated by faith and h., 307:16
> > is waking dream, 77:6
> > the thing with feathers, 508:12
> > to see Pilot, 456:6

Occasionally words not in the actual quotations are supplied in the index entries to make the entries clear.

Readers who cannot find a particular quotation under one keyword are advised to scan any keyword entry in its entirety, since there are many ways of indexing one phrase, or to try other keywords.

KATHRYN ROGERS

INDEX OF AUTHORS

BARTLETT'S
FAMILIAR
QUOTATIONS

FAMILIAR QUOTATIONS

The Song of the Harper[1]
2600? B.C.E.

1 There is no one who can return from there,
   To describe their nature, to describe their dissolution,
   That he may still our desires,
   Until we reach the place where they have gone.
                                                    St. 5

2 Remember: it is not given to man to take his goods
      with him.
   No one goes away and then comes back.
                                                   St. 10

Ptahhotep
Twenty-fourth century B.C.E.

3   Teach him what has been said in the past; then he
will set a good example to the children of the magistrates, and judgment and all exactitude shall enter
into him. Speak to him, for there is none born wise.
          The Maxims of Ptahhotep,[2] introduction

4   Do not be arrogant because of your knowledge,
but confer with the ignorant man as with the
learned. . . . Good speech is more hidden than malachite, yet it is found in the possession of women slaves
at the millstones.
                    The Maxims of Ptahhotep, no. 1

5   Follow your desire as long as you live and do not
perform more than is ordered; do not lessen the time
of following desire, for the wasting of time is an
abomination to the spirit. . . . When riches are gained,
follow desire, for riches will not profit if one is sluggish.   *The Maxims of Ptahhotep, 11*

6   One who is serious all day will never have a good
time, while one who is frivolous all day will never
establish a household.
                       The Maxims of Ptahhotep, 25

7   Be cheerful while you are alive.
                       The Maxims of Ptahhotep, 34

The Teaching for Merikare[3]
c. 2135–2040 B.C.E.

8   Do justice, that you may live long upon earth.
Calm the weeper, do not oppress the widow, do not
oust a man from his father's property, do not degrade
magnates from their seats. Beware of punishing
wrongfully; do not kill, for it will not profit you.
                                              Parable 8

9   Instill the love of you into all the world, for a good
character is what is remembered.   *Parable 24*

The Book of the Dead
c. 1700–1000 B.C.E.

10 Hail to you gods . . .
   On that day of the great reckoning.
   Behold me, I have come to you,
   Without sin, without guilt, without evil,
   Without a witness against me,
   Without one whom I have wronged. . . .
   Rescue me, protect me,
   Do not accuse me before the great god!

   I am one pure of mouth, pure of hands.
                        The Address to the Gods[4]

Love Songs of the New Kingdom
c. 1550–1080 B.C.E.

11 My love for you is mixed throughout my body . . .

   So hurry to see your lady,
   like a stallion on the track,
   or like a falcon swooping down to its papyrus marsh.

   Heaven sends down the love of her
   as a flame falls in the hay.   *Song[5] no. 2*

12 The voice of the wild goose,
   caught by the bait, cries out.

---

[1]From the tomb of King Inyotef.
Translated by WILLIAM KELLY SIMPSON.
[2]Translated by R. O. FAULKNER.

[3]A treatise on kingship addressed by a king of Heracleopolis,
whose name is lost, to his son and successor, Merikare.
   Translated by R. O. FAULKNER.
[4]Translated by MIRIAM LICHTHEIM.
[5]All songs translated by WILLIAM KELLY SIMPSON.

Love of you holds me back,
and I can't loosen it at all....

I did not set my traps today;
love of you has thus entrapped me.   *Song no. 10*

1 Sweet pomegranate wine in my mouth
is bitter as the gall of birds.

But your embraces
alone give life to my heart;
may Amun give me what I have found
for all eternity.   *Song no. 12*

Suti and Hor[1]
Fifteenth–fourteenth centuries B.C.E.

2 Creator uncreated.
Sole one, unique one, who traverses eternity,
Remote one, with millions under his care;
Your splendor is like heaven's splendor.
    First Hymn to the Sun God

3 Beneficent mother of gods and men ...
Valiant shepherd who drives his flock,
Their refuge, made to sustain them....
He makes the seasons with the months,
Heat as he wishes, cold as he wishes....
Every land rejoices at his rising,
Every day gives praise to him.
    Second Hymn to the Sun God

The Great Hymn to the Aten[2]
c. 1350 B.C.E.

4 Splendid you rise in heaven's lightland,
O living Aten, creator of life!   *St. 1*

5 When you set in western lightland,
Earth is in darkness as if in death.   *St. 2*

6 Every lion comes from its den,
All the serpents bite;
Darkness hovers, earth is silent,
As their maker rests in lightland.

Earth brightens when you dawn in lightland,
When you shine as Aten of daytime;
As you dispel the dark,
As you cast your rays,
The Two Lands are in festivity.
Awake they stand on their feet,
You have roused them.   *St. 2, 3*

7 The entire land sets out to work,
All beasts browse on their herbs;
Trees, herbs are sprouting,
Birds fly from their nests ...
Ships fare north, fare south as well,
Roads lie open when you rise;
The fish in the river dart before you,
Your rays are in the midst of the sea.   *St. 3*

8 How many are your deeds,
Though hidden from sight,
O Sole God beside whom there is none!
You made the earth as you wished, you alone.   *St. 5*

The Epic of Gilgamesh
c. 1300–c. 1000 B.C.E.

9   From the days of old there is no permanence.
The sleeping and the dead, how alike they are, they
are like a painted death. What is there between the
master and the servant when both have fulfilled their
doom?[3]   *Sec. 4, The Search for the Everlasting Life*

I Ching[4]
[The Book of Changes]
c. Twelfth century B.C.E.

10   The mountain rests on the earth: the image of
Splitting Apart. Thus those above can ensure their
position only by giving generously to those below.
    Bk. I, ch. 23, Po / Splitting Apart

11   Fire in the lake: the image of Revolution.
    I, 49, Ko / Revolution (Molting)

12   Wind over lake: the image of Inner Truth.
    I, 61, Chung Fu / Inner Truth

Amenemope
c. Eleventh century B.C.E.

13 Beginning of the teaching for life,
The instructions for well-being ...
Knowing how to answer one who speaks,
To reply to one who sends a message.
    The Instruction of Amenemope,[5] *prologue*

14 The truly silent, who keeps apart,
He is like a tree grown in a meadow.
It greens, it doubles its yield,
It stands in front of its lord.

---

[1]Architects to Amenhotep III (reigned c. 1411–1375 B.C.E.).
Translated by MIRIAM LICHTHEIM.

[2]Aten is the Egyptian sun god, which came to be worshipped as the
sole creator god. Translated by MIRIAM LICHTHEIM.

---

[3]Translated by N. K. SANDARS.

[4]Translated from Chinese into German by RICHARD WILHELM, and
into English by CARY F. BAYNES.

[5]Translated by MIRIAM LICHTHEIM.

Its fruit is sweet, its shade delightful,
Its end comes in the garden.

The Instruction of Amenemope, ch. 4

1 Better is poverty in the hand of the god,
Than wealth in the storehouse;
Better is bread with a happy heart
Than wealth with vexation.[1]

The Instruction of Amenemope, 6

2 Do not set your heart on wealth . . .
Do not strain to seek increase,
What you have, let it suffice you.
If riches come to you by theft,
They will not stay the night with you. . . .
They made themselves wings like geese,
And flew away to the sky.

The Instruction of Amenemope, 7

The Holy Bible[2]
The Old Testament[3]

3 In the beginning God created the heaven and the earth.

And the earth was without form, and void; and darkness was upon the face of the deep. And the Spirit of God moved upon the face of the waters.

And God said, Let there be light:[4] and there was light.

The First Book of Moses, Called Genesis,
chapter 1, verses 1–3

4 And the evening and the morning were the first day.   *1:5*

5 And God saw that it was good.   *1:10*

6 And God said, Let us make man in our image, after our likeness.   *1:26*

7 Male and female created he them.   *1:27*

8 Be fruitful, and multiply, and replenish the earth, and subdue it: and have dominion over the fish of the sea, and over the fowl of the air, and over every living thing that moveth upon the earth.   *1:28*

9 And on the seventh day God ended his work which he had made.   *2:2*

10 And the Lord God formed man of the dust of the ground, and breathed into his nostrils the breath of life; and man became a living soul.   *2:7*

11 And the Lord God planted a garden eastward in Eden.   *2:8*

12 The tree of life also in the midst of the garden.   *2:9*

13 But of the tree of the knowledge of good and evil, thou shalt not eat of it: for in the day that thou eatest thereof thou shalt surely die.   *2:17*

14 It is not good that the man should be alone; I will make him an help meet for him.   *2:18*

15 And the Lord God caused a deep sleep to fall upon Adam, and he slept: and he took one of his ribs, and closed up the flesh instead thereof.

And the rib, which the Lord God had taken from man, made he a woman.   *2:21–22*

16 Bone of my bones, and flesh of my flesh.   *2:23*

17 Therefore shall a man leave his father and his mother, and shall cleave unto his wife: and they shall be one flesh.

And they were both naked, the man and his wife, and were not ashamed.   *2:24–25*

18 Now the serpent was more subtile than any beast of the field.   *3:1*

19 Your eyes shall be opened, and ye shall be as gods, knowing good and evil.   *3:5*

20 And they sewed fig leaves together, and made themselves aprons.[5]

And they heard the voice of the Lord God walking in the garden in the cool of the day.   *3:7–8*

21 The woman whom thou gavest to be with me, she gave me of the tree, and I did eat.   *3:12*

22 What is this that thou hast done? And the woman said, The serpent beguiled me, and I did eat.

And the Lord God said unto the serpent, Because thou hast done this, thou art cursed above all cattle, and above every beast of the field; upon thy belly shalt thou go, and dust shalt thou eat all the days of thy life.   *3:13–14*

23 And I will put enmity between thee and the woman, and between thy seed and her seed; it shall bruise thy head, and thou shalt bruise his heel.   *3:15*

24 In sorrow thou shalt bring forth children.   *3:16*

---

[1]Better a dry crust with peace and quiet than a house full of feasting, with strife. — *Proverbs 17:1* (NIV)

See Aesop, 59:1.

[2]Bible quotations are from the Authorized (King James) Version [1611]. Numbers in Bible citations represent chapter and verse. The oldest part of the Bible, Song of the Sea (*Exodus 15:1–18; see 8:4–8:7*), dates from the tenth century B.C.E., the era of Solomon, but the material used by the author (called J, or the Yahwist) was much older. Next oldest is the Song of Deborah (*Judges 5:1–12, 10:8–10:9*).

[3]The Hebrew Scriptures. The first five books (the Pentateuch, or the five books of Moses) are the Jewish Torah.

[4]Fiat lux. — *The Vulgate* [fourth-century Latin translation of the Bible from Hebrew and Aramaic texts]

[5]The Geneva Bible [1560] was known sometimes as the Breeches Bible because in this passage "aprons" is rendered as "breeches."

1   In the sweat of thy face shalt thou eat bread, till thou return unto the ground; for out of it wast thou taken: for dust thou art, and unto dust shalt thou return.

And Adam called his wife's name Eve; because she was the mother of all living.   *Genesis 3:19–20*

2   So he drove out the man: and he placed at the east of the garden of Eden cherubims, and a flaming sword which turned every way, to keep the way of the tree of life.   *3:24*

3   And Abel was a keeper of sheep, but Cain was a tiller of the ground.   *4:2*

4   Am I my brother's keeper?   *4:9*

5   The voice of thy brother's blood crieth unto me from the ground.   *4:10*

6   A fugitive and a vagabond shalt thou be in the earth.   *4:12*

7   My punishment is greater than I can bear.   *4:13*

8   And the Lord set a mark upon Cain.   *4:15*

9   And Cain went out from the presence of the Lord, and dwelt in the land of Nod.   *4:16*

10   Jabal: he was the father of such as dwell in tents.   *4:20*

11   Jubal: he was the father of all such as handle the harp and organ.   *4:21*

12   Tubal-cain, an instructor of every artificer in brass and iron.   *4:22*

13   And Enoch walked with God.   *5:24*

14   And all the days of Methuselah were nine hundred sixty and nine years.   *5:27*

15   And Noah begat Shem, Ham, and Japheth.   *5:32*

16   There were giants in the earth in those days... mighty men which were of old, men of renown.   *6:4*

17   Make thee an ark of gopher wood.   *6:14*

18   And of every living thing of all flesh, two of every sort shalt thou bring into the ark.   *6:19*

19   And the rain was upon the earth forty days and forty nights.   *7:12*

20   But the dove found no rest for the sole of her foot.   *8:9*

21   And, lo, in her mouth was an olive leaf pluckt off.   *8:11*

22   For the imagination of man's heart is evil from his youth.   *8:21*

23   While the earth remaineth, seedtime and harvest, and cold and heat, and summer and winter, and day and night shall not cease.   *8:22*

24   Whoso sheddeth man's blood, by man shall his blood be shed: for in the image of God made he man.   *9:6*

25   I do set my bow in the cloud, and it shall be for a token of a covenant between me and the earth.   *9:13*

26   Even as Nimrod the mighty hunter before the Lord.   *10:9*

27   Therefore is the name of it called Babel; because the Lord did there confound the language of all the earth.   *11:9*

28   Let there be no strife, I pray thee, between me and thee ... for we be brethren.   *13:8*

29   Abram dwelled in the land of Canaan, and Lot dwelled in the cities of the plain, and pitched his tent toward Sodom.   *13:12*

30   In a good old age.   *15:15*

31   His [Ishmael's] hand will be against every man, and every man's hand against him.   *16:12*

32   Thy name shall be Abraham; for a father of many nations have I made thee.   *17:5*

33   My Lord, if now I have found favor in thy sight, pass not away, I pray thee, from thy servant.   *18:3*

34   But his [Lot's] wife looked back from behind him, and she became a pillar of salt.   *19:26*

35   My son, God will provide himself a lamb for a burnt offering.   *22:8*

36   Behold behind him a ram caught in a thicket by his horns.   *22:13*

37   Esau was a cunning hunter, a man of the field; and Jacob was a plain man, dwelling in tents.   *25:27*

38   And he [Esau] sold his birthright unto Jacob. Then Jacob gave Esau bread and pottage of lentils.   *25:33–34*

39   The voice is Jacob's voice, but the hands are the hands of Esau.   *27:22*

40   Thy brother came with subtilty, and hath taken away thy blessing.   *27:35*

41   He [Jacob] dreamed, and behold a ladder set up on the earth, and the top of it reached to heaven: and behold the angels of God ascending and descending on it.   *28:12*

42   Surely the Lord is in this place; and I knew it not.   *28:16*

43   This is none other but the house of God, and this is the gate of heaven.   *28:17*

44   Jacob served seven years for Rachel; and they seemed unto him but a few days, for the love he had to her.   *29:20*

1   And Laban said, This heap [of stones] is a witness between me and thee this day. Therefore was the name of it called Galeed;

And Mizpah; for he said, The Lord watch between me and thee, when we are absent one from another.

31:48–49

2   And Jacob was left alone; and there wrestled a man with him until the breaking of the day.   *32:24*

3   I will not let thee go, except thou bless me.

32:26

4   And Jacob called the name of the place Peniel: for I have seen God face to face, and my life is preserved.

32:30

5   Behold, this dreamer cometh.   *37:19*

6   They stript Joseph out of his coat, his coat of many colors.   *37:23*

7   The Lord made all that he did to prosper in his hand.   *39:3*

8   And she [Potiphar's wife] caught him by his garment, saying, Lie with me: and he left his garment in her hand, and fled, and got him out.   *39:12*

9   The seven good kine are seven years; and the seven good ears are seven years: the dream is one.

And the seven thin and ill-favored kine that came up after them are seven years; and the seven empty ears blasted with the east wind shall be seven years of famine.   *41:26–27*

10   Then shall ye bring down my gray hairs with sorrow to the grave.   *42:38*

11   But Benjamin's mess was five times so much as any of theirs.   *43:34*

12   Wherefore have ye rewarded evil for good?

44:4

13   God forbid.   *44:7*

14   The man in whose hand the cup is found, he shall be my servant.   *44:17*

15   And he fell upon his brother Benjamin's neck, and wept; and Benjamin wept upon his neck.   *45:14*

16   And ye shall eat the fat of the land.   *45:18*

17   And they came into the land of Goshen.   *46:28*

18   But I will lie with my fathers, and thou shalt carry me out of Egypt, and bury me in their buryingplace. And he said, I will do as thou hast said.   *47:30*

19   Unstable as water, thou shalt not excel.   *49:4*

20   I have waited for thy salvation, O Lord.   *49:18*

21   Unto the utmost bound of the everlasting hills.

49:26

22   Now there arose up a new king over Egypt, which knew not Joseph.

The Second Book of Moses, Called Exodus 1:8

23   She took for him an ark of bulrushes, and daubed it with slime and with pitch.   *2:3*

24   I have been a stranger in a strange land.   *2:22*

25   Behold, the bush burned with fire, and the bush was not consumed.   *3:2*

26   Put off thy shoes from off thy feet, for the place whereon thou standest is holy ground.   *3:5*

27   And Moses hid his face; for he was afraid to look upon God.   *3:6*

28   A land flowing with milk and honey.   *3:8*

29   And God said unto Moses, I AM THAT I AM.

3:14

30   I am slow of speech, and of a slow tongue.   *4:10*

31   Let my people go.   *5:1*

32   Ye shall no more give the people straw to make brick.   *5:7*

33   Thou shalt say unto Aaron, Take thy rod, and cast it before Pharaoh, and it shall become a serpent.   *7:9*

34   They [Pharaoh's wise men] cast down every man his rod, and they became serpents: but Aaron's rod swallowed up their rods.

And he hardened Pharaoh's heart.   *7:12–13*

35   This is the finger of God.   *8:19*

36   Darkness which may be felt.   *10:21*

37   Yet will I bring one plague more upon Pharaoh, and upon Egypt.   *11:1*

38   Your lamb shall be without blemish.   *12:5*

39   And they shall eat the flesh in that night, roast with fire, and unleavened bread; and with bitter herbs they shall eat it.   *12:8*

40   And thus shall ye eat it; with your loins girded, your shoes on your feet, and your staff in your hand; and ye shall eat it in haste: it is the Lord's passover.

For I will pass through the land of Egypt this night, and will smite all the firstborn in the land of Egypt, both man and beast; and against all the gods of Egypt I will execute judgment: I am the Lord.

12:11–12

41   This day [Passover] shall be unto you for a memorial; and ye shall keep it a feast to the Lord throughout your generations.   *12:14*

42   Seven days shall ye eat unleavened bread.   *12:15*

43   There was a great cry in Egypt; for there was not a house where there was not one dead.   *12:30*

1   Remember this day, in which ye came out from Egypt, out of the house of bondage.   *Exodus 13:3*

2   And the Lord went before them by day in a pillar of a cloud, to lead them the way; and by night in a pillar of fire, to give them light.   *13:21*

3   And the children of Israel went into the midst of the sea upon the dry ground: and the waters were a wall unto them on their right hand, and on their left.   *14:22*

4   I will sing unto the Lord, for he hath triumphed gloriously: the horse and his rider hath he thrown into the sea.

   The Lord is my strength and song, and he is become my salvation.   *15:1–2*

5   The Lord is a man of war.   *15:3*

6   Thy right hand, O Lord, is become glorious in power: thy right hand, O Lord, hath dashed in pieces the enemy.   *15:6*

7   Thou sentest forth thy wrath, which consumed them as stubble.

   And with the blast of thy nostrils the waters were gathered together, the floods stood upright as an heap, and the depths were congealed in the heart of the sea.   *15:7–8*

8   Would to God we had died by the hand of the Lord in the land of Egypt, when we sat by the flesh-pots, and when we did eat bread to the full.   *16:3*

9   It is manna.   *16:15*

10   I am the Lord thy God.   *20:2*[1]

11   Thou shalt have no other gods before me.

   Thou shalt not make unto thee any graven image.   *20:3–4*

12   For I the Lord thy God am a jealous God, visiting the iniquity of the fathers upon the children unto the third and fourth generation of them that hate me;

   And showing mercy unto thousands of them that love me, and keep my commandments.

   Thou shalt not take the name of the Lord thy God in vain.   *20:5–7*

13   Remember the sabbath day, to keep it holy.

   Six days shalt thou labor, and do all thy work:

   But the seventh day...thou shalt not do any work.   *20:8–10*

14   Honor thy father and thy mother: that thy days may be long upon the land which the Lord thy God giveth thee.

Thou shalt not kill.

Thou shalt not commit adultery.

Thou shalt not steal.

Thou shalt not bear false witness against thy neighbor.

Thou shalt not covet thy neighbor's house, thou shalt not covet thy neighbor's wife, nor his manservant, nor his maidservant, nor his ox, nor his ass, nor any thing that is thy neighbor's.   *20:12–17*

15   But let not God speak with us, lest we die.   *20:19*

16   He that smiteth a man, so that he die, shall be surely put to death.   *21:12*

17   Eye for eye, tooth for tooth, hand for hand, foot for foot.   *21:24*

18   Behold, I send an Angel before thee, to keep thee in the way.   *23:20*

19   A stiffnecked people.   *32:9*

20   Who is on the Lord's side? let him come unto me.   *32:26*

21   Thou canst not see my face: for there shall no man see me, and live.   *33:20*

22   And he [Moses] was there with the Lord forty days and forty nights; he did neither eat bread, nor drink water. And he wrote upon the tables the words of the covenant, the ten commandments.   *34:28*

23   Whatsoever parteth the hoof, and is cloven-footed, and cheweth the cud, among the beasts, that shall ye eat.

   The Third Book of Moses, Called Leviticus 11:3

24   And the swine...is unclean to you.

   Of their flesh shall ye not eat.   *11:7–8*

25   Let him go for a scapegoat into the wilderness.   *16:10*

26   And when ye reap the harvest of your land, thou shalt not wholly reap the corners of thy field, neither shalt thou gather the gleanings of thy harvest.

   And thou shalt not glean thy vineyard, neither shalt thou gather every grape of thy vineyard; thou shalt leave them for the poor and stranger.   *19:9–10*

27   Thou shalt not go up and down as a talebearer among thy people.   *19:16*

28   Thou shalt love thy neighbor as thyself.[2]   *19:18*

---

[1] *Exodus 20:2–17* contains the Ten Commandments (the Decalogue), which, according to scripture, Moses received from God on Mount Sinai.

[2] Also in *Matthew 19:19* and *22:39, 35:13; Mark 12:31* and *33; Romans 13:9; Galatians 5:14; James 2:8.*

1   Ye shall hallow the fiftieth year, and proclaim liberty throughout all the land unto all the inhabitants thereof:[1] it shall be a jubilee unto you.   *25:10*

2   The Lord bless thee, and keep thee:
    The Lord make his face shine upon thee, and be gracious unto thee:
    The Lord lift up his countenance upon thee, and give thee peace.
    *The Fourth Book of Moses, Called
    Numbers 6:24–26*

3   Sent to spy out the land.   *13:16*

4   And your children shall wander in the wilderness forty years.   *14:33*

5   Moses lifted up his hand, and with his rod he smote the rock twice: and the water came out abundantly.   *20:11*

6   He whom thou blessest is blessed.   *22:6*

7   The Lord opened the mouth of the ass, and she said unto Balaam, What have I done unto thee?   *22:28*

8   Let me die the death of the righteous, and let my last end be like his!   *23:10*

9   God is not a man, that he should lie.   *23:19*

10 What hath God wrought![2]   *23:23*

11 How goodly are thy tents, O Jacob, and thy tabernacles, O Israel!   *24:5*

12 Be sure your sin will find you out.   *32:23*

13 I call heaven and earth to witness.
    *The Fifth Book of Moses, Called
    Deuteronomy 4:26*

14 Hear, O Israel: The Lord our God is one Lord.   *6:4*

15 Thou shalt love the Lord thy God with all thine heart, and with all thy soul, and with all thy might.
    And these words, which I command thee this day, shall be in thine heart:
    And thou shalt teach them diligently unto thy children.   *6:5–7*

16 Ye shall not tempt the Lord your God.   *6:16*

17 The Lord thy God hath chosen thee to be a special people unto himself.   *7:6*

18 Man doth not live by bread only,[3] but by every word that proceedeth out of the mouth of the Lord doth man live.   *8:3*

19 For the Lord thy God bringeth thee into a good land.   *8:7*

20 A land of wheat, and barley, and vines, and fig trees, and pomegranates; a land of oil olive, and honey;
    A land wherein thou shalt eat bread without scarceness, thou shalt not lack any thing in it; a land whose stones are iron, and out of whose hills thou mayest dig brass.   *8:8–9*

21 A dreamer of dreams.   *13:1*

22 The wife of thy bosom.   *13:6*

23 The poor shall never cease out of the land.   *15:11*

24 Thou shalt not move a sickle unto thy neighbor's standing corn.   *23:25*

25 Thou shalt not muzzle the ox when he treadeth out the corn.   *25:4*

26 And thou shalt become an astonishment, a proverb, and a byword, among all nations.   *28:37*

27 In the morning thou shalt say, Would God it were even! and at even thou shalt say, Would God it were morning!   *28:67*

28 The secret things belong unto the Lord our God.   *29:29*

29 I have set before you life and death, blessing and cursing: therefore choose life, that both thou and thy seed may live.   *30:19*

30 He is the Rock, his work is perfect: for all his ways are judgment: a God of truth.   *32:4*

31 Jeshurun waxed fat, and kicked.   *32:15*

32 As thy days, so shall thy strength be.   *33:25*

33 The eternal God is thy refuge, and underneath are the everlasting arms.   *33:27*

34 No man knoweth of his [Moses'] sepulcher unto this day.   *34:6*

35 Be strong and of a good courage; be not afraid, neither be thou dismayed: for the Lord thy God is with thee whithersoever thou goest.
    The Book of Joshua 1:9

36 And the priests that bare the ark of the covenant of the Lord stood firm on dry ground in the midst of Jordan, and all the Israelites passed over on dry ground, until all the people were passed clean over Jordan.   *3:17*

37 Mighty men of valor.   *6:2*

38 And it came to pass, when the people heard the sound of the trumpet, and the people shouted with a great shout, that the wall fell down flat, so that the people went up into the city [Jericho].   *6:20*

---

[1]From "proclaim" through "thereof": inscription on the Liberty Bell, Philadelphia [1751].

[2]Quoted by Samuel F. B. Morse in the first telegraph message he sent to his partner, Alfred Vail, from Washington to Baltimore [May 24, 1844].

[3]Man shall not live by bread alone. — *Matthew 4:4*

1   His fame was noised throughout all the country.
Joshua 6:27

2   Hewers of wood and drawers of water.   *9:21*

3   Sun, stand thou still upon Gibeon; and thou, Moon, in the valley of Ajalon.   *10:12*

4   Old and stricken in years.   *13:1*

5   I am going the way of all the earth.   *23:14*

6   They shall be as thorns in your sides.
The Book of Judges 2:3

7   Then Jael, Heber's wife, took a nail of the tent, and took an hammer in her hand, and went softly unto him [Sisera], and smote the nail into his temples, and fastened it into the ground; for he was fast asleep, and weary: so he died.   *4:21*

8   I Deborah arose . . . I arose a mother in Israel.   *5:7*

9   Awake, awake, Deborah: awake, awake, utter a song: arise, Barak, and lead thy captivity captive.   *5:12*

10   The stars in their courses fought against Sisera.   *5:20*

11   She [Jael] brought forth butter in a lordly dish.   *5:25*

12   At her feet he bowed, he fell, he lay down: at her feet he bowed, he fell: where he bowed, there he fell down dead.   *5:27*

13   The mother of Sisera looked out at a window, and cried through the lattice, Why is his chariot so long in coming? why tarry the wheels of his chariots?   *5:28*

14   Have they not divided the prey; to every man a damsel or two?   *5:30*

15   The sword of the Lord, and of Gideon.   *7:18*

16   Is not the gleaning of the grapes of Ephraim better than the vintage of Abiezer?   *8:2*

17   Say now Shibboleth: and he said Sibboleth: for he could not frame to pronounce it right.   *12:6*

18   There was a swarm of bees and honey in the carcass of the lion.   *14:8*

19   Out of the eater came forth meat, and out of the strong came forth sweetness.   *14:14*

20   If ye had not plowed with my heifer, ye had not found out my riddle.   *14:18*

21   He smote them hip and thigh.   *15:8*

22   With the jawbone of an ass . . . have I slain a thousand men.   *15:16*

23   The Philistines be upon thee, Samson.   *16:9*

24   The Philistines took him [Samson], and put out his eyes, and brought him down to Gaza, and bound him with fetters of brass; and he did grind in the prison house.   *16:21*

25   Strengthen me, I pray thee, only this once, O God, that I may be . . . avenged of the Philistines for my two eyes.   *16:28*

26   So the dead which he slew at his death were more than they which he slew in his life.   *16:30*

27   From Dan even to Beersheba.   *20:1*

28   All the people arose as one man.   *20:8*

29   In those days there was no king in Israel: every man did that which was right in his own eyes.   *21:25*

30   Whither thou goest, I will go; and where thou lodgest, I will lodge: thy people shall be my people, and thy God my God.   *The Book of Ruth 1:16*

31   Let me glean and gather after the reapers among the sheaves.   *2:7*

32   Go not empty unto thy mother in law.   *3:17*

33   In the flower of their age.
The First Book of Samuel 2:33

34   The Lord called Samuel: and he answered, Here am I.   *3:4*

35   Speak, Lord; for thy servant heareth.   *3:9*

36   Be strong, and quit yourselves like men.   *4:9*

37   And she named the child Ichabod, saying, The glory is departed from Israel: because the ark of God was taken.   *4:21*

38   Is Saul also among the prophets?   *10:11*

39   God save the king.   *10:24*

40   A man after his own heart.   *13:14*

41   Every man's sword was against his fellow.   *14:20*

42   But Jonathan heard not when his father charged the people with the oath: wherefore he put forth the end of the rod that was in his hand, and dipped it in an honeycomb, and put his hand to his mouth; and his eyes were enlightened.   *14:27*

43   For the Lord seeth not as man seeth; for man looketh on the outward appearance, but the Lord looketh on the heart.   *16:7*

44   I know thy pride, and the naughtiness of thine heart.   *17:28*

45   Let no man's heart fail because of him [Goliath].   *17:32*

46   Go, and the Lord be with thee.   *17:37*

1   And he [David]...chose him five smooth stones out of the brook.   *17:40*

2   So David prevailed over the Philistine with a sling and with a stone.   *17:50*

3   Saul hath slain his thousands, and David his ten thousands.   *18:7*

4   And Jonathan...loved him [David] as he loved his own soul.   *20:17*

5   Wickedness proceedeth from the wicked.   *24:13*

6   I have played the fool.   *26:21*

7   Tell it not in Gath, publish it not in the streets of Askelon.   *The Second Book of Samuel 1:20*

8   Saul and Jonathan were lovely and pleasant in their lives, and in their death they were not divided: they were swifter than eagles, they were stronger than lions.   *1:23*

9   How are the mighty fallen in the midst of the battle!   *1:25*

10   Thy love to me was wonderful, passing the love of women.

How are the mighty fallen, and the weapons of war perished!   *1:26–27*

11   Abner...smote him under the fifth rib.   *2:23*

12   Know ye not that there is a prince and a great man [Abner] fallen this day in Israel?   *3:38*

13   And David and all the house of Israel played before the Lord on all manner of instruments made of fir wood, even on harps, and on psalteries, and on timbrels, and on cornets, and on cymbals.   *6:5*

14   Uzzah put forth his hand to the ark of God, and took hold of it...and the anger of the Lord was kindled against Uzzah.   *6:6*

15   David danced before the Lord.   *6:14*

16   Tarry at Jericho until your beards be grown.   *10:5*

17   Set ye Uriah in the forefront of the hottest battle.   *11:15*

18   The poor man had nothing, save one little ewe lamb.   *12:3*

19   Thou art the man.   *12:7*

20   Now he is dead, wherefore should I fast? Can I bring him back again? I shall go to him, but he shall not return to me.   *12:23*

21   For we must needs die, and are as water spilt on the ground, which cannot be gathered up again.   *14:14*

22   Would God I had died for thee, O Absalom, my son, my son!   *18:33*

23   The Lord is my rock, and my fortress, and my deliverer.   *22:2*

24   David the son of Jesse...the sweet psalmist of Israel.   *23:1*

25   Went in jeopardy of their lives.   *23:17*

26   A wise and an understanding heart.
The First Book of the Kings 3:12

27   Many, as the sand which is by the sea in multitude.   *4:20*

28   Judah and Israel dwelt safely, every man under his vine and under his fig tree.   *4:25*

29   He [Solomon] spake three thousand proverbs: and his songs were a thousand and five.   *4:32*

30   The wisdom of Solomon.   *4:34*

31   So that there was neither hammer nor axe nor any tool of iron heard in the house,[1] while it was in building.   *6:7*

32   A proverb and a byword among all people.   *9:7*

33   When the queen of Sheba heard of the fame of Solomon...she came to prove him with hard questions.   *10:1*

34   The half was not told me: thy wisdom and prosperity exceedeth the fame which I heard.   *10:7*

35   Once in three years came the navy of Tharshish, bringing gold, and silver, ivory, and apes, and peacocks.   *10:22*

36   King Solomon loved many strange women.   *11:1*

37   My father hath chastised you with whips, but I will chastise you with scorpions.   *12:11*

38   To your tents, O Israel.   *12:16*

39   He [Elijah] went and dwelt by the brook Cherith, that is before Jordan.   *17:5*

40   And the ravens brought him bread and flesh in the morning, and bread and flesh in the evening; and he drank of the brook.   *17:6*

41   An handful of meal in a barrel, and a little oil in a cruse.   *17:12*

42   And the barrel of meal wasted not, neither did the cruse of oil fail.   *17:16*

43   How long halt ye between two opinions?   *18:21*

---

[1]Solomon's temple (the house of the Lord).

1   Either he [Baal] is talking, or he is pursuing, or he is in a journey, or peradventure he sleepeth, and must be awaked.   *I Kings 18:27*

2   There ariseth a little cloud out of the sea, like a man's hand.   *18:44*

3   And he girded up his loins, and ran before Ahab.   *18:46*

4   But the Lord was not in the wind: and after the wind an earthquake; but the Lord was not in the earthquake:
And after the earthquake a fire; but the Lord was not in the fire: and after the fire a still small voice.
19:11–12

5   Let not him that girdeth on his harness boast himself as he that putteth it off.   *20:11*

6   Hast thou found me, O mine enemy?   *21:20*

7   The dogs shall eat Jezebel by the wall of Jezreel.
21:23

8   But there was none like unto Ahab, which did sell himself to work wickedness in the sight of the Lord, whom Jezebel his wife stirred up.   *21:25*

9   I saw all Israel scattered upon the hills, as sheep that have not a shepherd.   *22:17*

10   Feed him [Micajah] with bread of affliction, and with water of affliction, until I come in peace.   *22:27*

11   There appeared a chariot of fire, and horses of fire, and parted them both asunder; and Elijah went up by a whirlwind into heaven.
The Second Book of the Kings 2:11

12   The chariot of Israel, and the horsemen thereof. And he saw him no more.   *2:12*

13   He [Elisha] took up also the mantle of Elijah.
2:13

14   There is death in the pot.   *4:40*

15   Is thy servant a dog, that he should do this great thing?   *8:13*

16   What hast thou to do with peace? turn thee behind me.   *9:18*

17   The driving is like the driving of Jehu the son of Nimshi; for he driveth furiously.   *9:20*

18   Jezebel heard of it; and she painted her face, and tired her head, and looked out at a window.   *9:30*

19   The angel of the Lord went out, and smote in the camp of the Assyrians an hundred fourscore and five thousand: and when they arose early in the morning, behold, they were all dead corpses.
So Sennacherib king of Assyria departed.
19:35–36

20   Set thine house in order.   *20:1*

21   I will wipe Jerusalem as a man wipeth a dish, wiping it, and turning it upside down.   *21:13*

22   His mercy endureth for ever.
The First Book of the Chronicles 16:41

23   The Lord searcheth all hearts, and understandeth all the imaginations of the thoughts.   *28:9*

24   Thine, O Lord, is the greatness, and the power, and the glory, and the victory, and the majesty: for all that is in the heaven and in the earth is thine; thine is the kingdom, O Lord, and thou art exalted as head above all.   *29:11*

25   For all things come of thee, and of thine own have we given thee.   *29:14*

26   Our days on the earth are as a shadow.   *29:15*

27   He [David] died in a good old age, full of days, riches, and honor.   *29:28*

28   They which builded on the wall, and they that bare burdens, with those that laded, every one with one of his hands wrought in the work, and with the other hand held a weapon.
The Book of Nehemiah 4:17

29   And he [Ezra] read therein before the street that was before the water gate from the morning until midday, before the men and the women, and those that could understand; and the ears of all the people were attentive unto the book of the law.   *8:3*

30   Thou art a God ready to pardon, gracious and merciful, slow to anger, and of great kindness.   *9:17*

31   Mordecai rent his clothes, and put on sackcloth with ashes.   *The Book of Esther 4:1*

32   The man whom the king delighteth to honor.
6:6

33   They hanged Haman on the gallows.   *7:10*

34   One that feared God, and eschewed evil.
The Book of Job 1:1

35   Satan came also.   *1:6*

36   And the Lord said unto Satan, Whence comest thou? Then Satan answered the Lord, and said, From going to and fro in the earth, and from walking up and down in it.   *1:7*

37   Doth Job fear God for nought?   *1:9*

38   And I only am escaped alone to tell thee.   *1:15*

39   Naked came I out of my mother's womb, and naked shall I return thither: the Lord gave, and the Lord hath taken away; blessed be the name of the Lord.   *1:21*

1 Skin for skin, yea, all that a man hath will he give for his life. *2:4*

2 Curse God, and die. *2:9*

3 Let the day perish wherein I was born, and the night in which it was said, There is a man child conceived. *3:3*

4 For now should I have lain still and been quiet, I should have slept: then had I been at rest,
With kings and counsellors of the earth, which built desolate places for themselves. *3:13–14*

5 There the wicked cease from troubling; and there the weary be at rest. *3:17*

6 Who ever perished, being innocent? or where were the righteous cut off? *4:7*

7 Fear came upon me, and trembling. *4:14*

8 Then a spirit passed before my face; the hair of my flesh stood up. *4:15*

9 Shall mortal man be more just than God? shall a man be more pure than his maker? *4:17*

10 Wrath killeth the foolish man, and envy slayeth the silly one. *5:2*

11 Man is born unto trouble, as the sparks fly upward. *5:7*

12 He taketh the wise in their own craftiness. *5:13*

13 For thou shalt be in league with the stones of the field: and the beasts of the field shall be at peace with thee. *5:23*

14 Thou shalt come to thy grave in a full age, like as a shock of corn cometh in in his season. *5:26*

15 How forcible are right words! *6:25*

16 My days are swifter than a weaver's shuttle, and are spent without hope. *7:6*

17 He shall return no more to his house, neither shall his place know him any more. *7:10*

18 I would not live alway: let me alone: for my days are vanity. *7:16*

19 But how should man be just with God? *9:2*

20 The land of darkness and the shadow of death. *10:21*

21 Canst thou by searching find out God? *11:7*

22 And thine age shall be clearer than the noonday. *11:17*

23 No doubt but ye are the people, and wisdom shall die with you. *12:2*

24 The just upright man is laughed to scorn. *12:4*

25 But ask now the beasts, and they shall teach thee; and the fowls of the air, and they shall tell thee:
Or speak to the earth, and it shall teach thee; and the fishes of the sea shall declare unto thee. *12:7–8*

26 With the ancient is wisdom; and in length of days understanding. *12:12*

27 He discovereth deep things out of darkness, and bringeth out to light the shadow of death. *12:22*

28 Though he slay me, yet will I trust in him. *13:15*

29 Man that is born of a woman is of few days, and full of trouble.
He cometh forth like a flower, and is cut down: he fleeth also as a shadow, and continueth not. *14:1–2*

30 But man dieth, and wasteth away: yea, man giveth up the ghost, and where is he? *14:10*

31 If a man die, shall he live again? *14:14*

32 Should a wise man utter vain knowledge, and fill his belly with the east wind? *15:2*

33 Miserable comforters are ye all. *16:2*

34 My days are past. *17:11*

35 I have said to corruption, Thou art my father: to the worm, Thou art my mother, and my sister. *17:14*

36 The king of terrors. *18:14*

37 I am escaped with the skin of my teeth. *19:20*

38 Oh that my words were now written! oh that they were printed in a book! *19:23*

39 I know that my redeemer liveth, and that he shall stand at the latter day upon the earth:[1]
And though, after my skin, worms destroy this body, yet in my flesh shall I see God. *19:25–26*

40 Seeing the root of the matter is found in me. *19:28*

41 Though wickedness be sweet in his mouth, though he hide it under his tongue. *20:12*

42 Suffer me that I may speak; and after that I have spoken, mock on. *21:3*

43 Shall any teach God knowledge? *21:22*

44 They are of those that rebel against the light. *24:13*

45 The womb shall forget him; the worm shall feed sweetly on him; he shall be no more remembered. *24:20*

---

[1] *Book of Common Prayer, Burial of the Dead, anthem.*

1   Yea, the stars are not pure in his sight.
How much less man, that is a worm? and the son of man, which is a worm?   *Job 25:5–6*

2   But where shall wisdom be found? and where is the place of understanding?   *28:12*

3   The land of the living.   *28:13*

4   The price of wisdom is above rubies.   *28:18*

5   Behold, the fear of the Lord, that is wisdom; and to depart from evil is understanding.   *28:28*

6   I caused the widow's heart to sing for joy.   *29:13*

7   I was eyes to the blind, and feet was I to the lame.   *29:15*

8   I know that thou wilt bring me to death, and to the house appointed for all living.   *30:23*

9   I am a brother to dragons, and a companion to owls.   *30:29*

10   My desire is, that the Almighty would answer me, and that mine adversary had written a book.   *31:35*

11   Great men are not always wise.   *32:9*

12   For I am full of matter, the spirit within me constraineth me.   *32:18*

13   One among a thousand.   *33:23*

14   Far be it from God, that he should do wickedness.   *34:10*

15   He multiplieth words without knowledge.   *35:16*

16   Fair weather cometh out of the north.   *37:22*

17   Then the Lord answered Job out of the whirlwind, and said,
Who is this that darkeneth counsel by words without knowledge?
Gird up now thy loins like a man.   *38:1–3*

18   Where wast thou when I laid the foundations of the earth? declare, if thou hast understanding.   *38:4*

19   The morning stars sang together, and all the sons of God shouted for joy.   *38:7*

20   Hitherto shalt thou come, but no further: and here shall thy proud waves be stayed.   *38:11*

21   Hast thou entered into the springs of the sea? or hast thou walked in the search of the depth?   *38:16*

22   Hath the rain a father? or who hath begotten the drops of dew?   *38:28*

23   Canst thou bind the sweet influences of Pleiades, or loose the bands of Orion?   *38:31*

24   Canst thou guide Arcturus with his sons?   *38:32*

25   Who can number the clouds in wisdom? or who can stay the bottles of heaven?   *38:37*

26   Hast thou given the horse strength? hast thou clothed his neck with thunder?   *39:19*

27   He paweth in the valley, and rejoiceth in his strength: he goeth on to meet the armed men.   *39:21*

28   He swalloweth the ground with fierceness and rage; neither believeth he that it is the sound of the trumpet.
He saith among the trumpets, Ha, ha; and he smelleth the battle afar off, the thunder of the captains, and the shouting.   *39:24–25*

29   Doth the eagle mount up at thy command, and make her nest on high?
She dwelleth and abideth on the rock, upon the crag of the rock, and the strong place.
From thence she seeketh the prey, and her eyes behold afar off.
Her young ones also suck up blood: and where the slain are, there is she.   *39:27–30*

30   Behold, I am vile; what shall I answer thee?   *40:4*

31   Behold now behemoth, which I made with thee; he eateth grass as an ox.   *40:15*

32   Canst thou draw out leviathan with a hook?   *41:1*

33   Who can open the doors of his face? his teeth are terrible round about.
His scales are his pride, shut up together as with a close seal.   *41:14–15*

34   His heart is as firm as a stone; yea as hard as a piece of the nether millstone.   *41:24*

35   He maketh the deep to boil like a pot.   *41:31*

36   Upon earth there is not his like, who is made without fear.   *41:33*

37   He is a king over all the children of pride.   *41:34*

38   I have heard of thee by the hearing of the ear: but now mine eye seeth thee.   *42:5*

39   So the Lord blessed the latter end of Job more than his beginning.   *42:12*

40   Blessed is the man that walketh not in the counsel of the ungodly, nor standeth in the way of sinners, nor sitteth in the seat of the scornful.
But his delight is in the law of the Lord; and in his law doth he meditate day and night.
And he shall be like a tree planted by the rivers of water, that bringeth forth his fruit in his season; his leaf also shall not wither; and whatsoever he doeth shall prosper.
The ungodly are not so: but are like the chaff which the wind driveth away.
The Book of Psalms 1:1–4

1 Why do the heathen rage, and the people imagine a vain thing? *2:1*

2 Blessed are all they that put their trust in him. *2:12*

3 Lord, lift thou up the light of thy countenance upon us. *4:6*

4 I will both lay me down in peace, and sleep. *4:8*

5 Out of the mouth of babes and sucklings hast thou ordained strength, because of thine enemies; that thou mightest still the enemy and the avenger.

When I consider thy heavens, the work of thy fingers, the moon and the stars, which thou hast ordained;

What is man, that thou art mindful of him? and the son of man, that thou visitest him?

For thou hast made him a little lower than the angels. *8:2–5*

6 How excellent is thy name in all the earth. *8:9*

7 Flee as a bird to your mountain. *11:1*

8 How long wilt thou forget me, O Lord? *13:1*

9 The fool hath said in his heart, There is no God. *14:1 and 53:1*

10 Lord, who shall abide in thy tabernacle? who shall dwell in thy holy hill? *15:1*

11 He that sweareth to his own hurt, and changeth not. *15:4*

12 The lines are fallen unto me in pleasant places; yea, I have a goodly heritage. *16:6*

13 Keep me as the apple of the eye, hide me under the shadow of thy wings. *17:8*

14 He rode upon a cherub, and did fly: yea, he did fly upon the wings of the wind. *18:10*

15 The heavens declare the glory of God; and the firmament showeth his handiwork.

Day unto day uttereth speech, and night unto night showeth knowledge. *19:1–2*

16 Their line is gone out through all the earth, and their words to the end of the world. In them hath he set a tabernacle for the sun,

Which is as a bridegroom coming out of his chamber, and rejoiceth as a strong man to run a race.

His going forth is from the end of the heaven, and his circuit unto the ends of it: and there is nothing hid from the heat thereof. *19:4–6*

17 The judgments of the Lord are true and righteous altogether.

More to be desired are they than gold, yea, than much fine gold: sweeter also than honey and the honeycomb. *19:9–10*

18 Cleanse thou me from secret faults. *19:12*

19 Let the words of my mouth, and the meditation of my heart, be acceptable in thy sight, O Lord, my strength, and my redeemer. *19:14*

20 Thou hast given him his heart's desire. *21:2*

21 My God, my God, why hast thou forsaken me?[1] why art thou so far from helping me, and from the words of my roaring? *22:1*

22 They part my garments among them, and cast lots upon my vesture. *22:18*

23 The Lord is my shepherd; I shall not want.

He maketh me to lie down in green pastures: he leadeth me beside the still waters.

He restoreth my soul: he leadeth me in the paths of righteousness for his name's sake.

Yea, though I walk through the valley of the shadow of death, I will fear no evil: for thou art with me; thy rod and thy staff they comfort me.

Thou preparest a table before me in the presence of mine enemies: thou anointest my head with oil; my cup runneth over.

Surely goodness and mercy shall follow me all the days of my life: and I will dwell in the house of the Lord for ever. *23*

24 The earth is the Lord's, and the fullness thereof; the world, and they that dwell therein.

For he hath founded it upon the seas, and established it upon the floods.

Who shall ascend into the hill of the Lord? or who shall stand in his holy place?

He that hath clean hands, and a pure heart; who hath not lifted up his soul unto vanity, nor sworn deceitfully. *24:1–4*

25 Lift up your heads, O ye gates; and be ye lift up, ye everlasting doors; and the King of glory shall come in. *24:7*

26 Who is this King of glory? The Lord of hosts, he is the King of glory. *24:10*

27 The Lord is my light[2] and my salvation; whom shall I fear? the Lord is the strength of my life; of whom shall I be afraid? *27:1*

28 Though an host should encamp against me, my heart shall not fear: though war should rise against me, in this will I be confident. *27:3*

29 The Lord is my strength and my shield. *28:7*

30 Worship the Lord in the beauty of holiness. *29:2*

---

[1]This was the psalm Jesus recited on the cross, according to *Matthew 27:46*, 36:20.

[2]Dominus illuminatio mea. — *The Vulgate.* Motto of Oxford University.

1   Weeping may endure for a night, but joy cometh in the morning.   *Psalms 30:5*

2   I am forgotten as a dead man out of mind: I am like a broken vessel.   *31:12*

3   My times are in thy hand.   *31:15*

4   From the strife of tongues.   *31:20*

5   Sing unto him a new song; play skillfully with a loud noise.   *33:3*

6   O taste and see that the Lord is good.   *34:8*

7   Keep thy tongue from evil, and thy lips from speaking guile.

Depart from evil, and do good; seek peace, and pursue it.   *34:13–14*

8   Rescue my soul from their destructions, my darling from the lions.   *35:17*

9   How excellent is thy lovingkindness, O God!   *36:7*

10   The meek shall inherit the earth.   *37:11*

11   I have been young, and now am old; yet have I not seen the righteous forsaken, nor his seed begging bread.   *37:25*

12   I have seen the wicked in great power, and spreading himself[1] like a green bay tree.   *37:35*

13   Mark the perfect man, and behold the upright: for the end of that man is peace.   *37:37*

14   For thine arrows stick fast in me, and thy hand presseth me sore.   *38:2*

15   I said, I will take heed to my ways, that I sin not with my tongue.   *39:1*

16   My heart was hot within me, while I was musing the fire burned.   *39:3*

17   Lord, make me to know mine end, and the measure of my days, what it is; that I may know how frail I am.   *39:4*

18   Every man at his best state is altogether vanity.   *39:5*

19   Surely every man walketh in a vain show: surely they are disquieted in vain: he heapeth up riches, and knoweth not who shall gather them.   *39:6*

20   For I am a stranger with thee, and a sojourner, as all my fathers were.

O spare me, that I may recover strength, before I go hence, and be no more.   *39:12–13*

21   As the hart panteth after the water brooks, so panteth my soul after thee, O God.

My soul thirsteth for God, for the living God.   *42:1–2*

22   Why art thou cast down, O my soul? and why art thou disquieted in me?   *42:5*

23   Deep calleth unto deep.   *42:7*

24   My tongue is the pen of a ready writer.   *45:1*

25   The king's daughter is all glorious within.   *45:13*

26   God is our refuge and strength, a very present help in trouble.

Therefore will we not fear, though the earth be removed, and though the mountains be carried into the midst of the sea.   *46:1–2*

27   There is a river, the streams whereof shall make glad the city of God, the holy place of the tabernacles of the most High.

God is in the midst of her; she shall not be moved: God shall help her, and that right early.   *46:4–5*

28   Be still, and know that I am God.   *46:10*

29   Every beast of the forest is mine, and the cattle upon a thousand hills.   *50:10*

30   I was shapen in iniquity; and in sin did my mother conceive me.   *51[2]:5*

31   Purge me with hyssop, and I shall be clean: wash me, and I shall be whiter than snow.   *51:7*

32   Create in me a clean heart, O God; and renew a right spirit within me.   *51:10*

33   And take not thy holy spirit from me.   *51:11*

34   Open thou my lips; and my mouth shall show forth thy praise.   *51:15*

35   A broken and a contrite heart, O God, thou wilt not despise.   *51:17*

36   Oh that I had wings like a dove! for then would I fly away, and be at rest.   *55:6*

37   We took sweet counsel together.   *55:14*

38   The words of his mouth were smoother than butter, but war was in his heart: his words were softer than oil, yet were they drawn swords.   *55:21*

39   They are like the deaf adder that stoppeth her ear;

Which will not hearken to the voice of charmers, charming never so wisely.   *58:4–5*

---

[1]Flourishing. — *Book of Common Prayer, Psalm 37:37*

[2]This psalm is known as the Miserere from its opening word in the *Vulgate*. The first line is: Have mercy upon me, O God.

1　Thou hast showed thy people hard things: thou hast made us to drink the wine of astonishment.

60:3

2　Moab is my washpot; over Edom will I cast out my shoe: Philistia, triumph thou because of me.　*60:8*

3　Lead me to the rock that is higher than I.　*61:2*

4　He only is my rock and my salvation: he is my defense; I shall not be moved.　*62:6*

5　Thou renderest to every man according to his work.　*62:12*

6　My soul thirsteth for thee, my flesh longeth for thee in a dry and thirsty land, where no water is.

63:1

7　Thou crownest the year with thy goodness.

65:11

8　Make a joyful noise unto God, all ye lands.

66:1

9　We went through fire and through water.　*66:12*

10　God setteth the solitary in families.　*68:6*

11　Cast me not off in the time of old age; forsake me not when my strength faileth.　*71:9*

12　He shall come down like rain upon the mown grass: as showers that water the earth.　*72:6*

13　His enemies shall lick the dust.　*72:9*

14　His name shall endure for ever.　*72:17*

15　A stubborn and rebellious generation.　*78:8*

16　Man did eat angels' food.　*78:25*

17　But ye shall die like men, and fall like one of the princes.　*82:7*

18　How amiable are thy tabernacles, O Lord of hosts!

84:1

19　They go from strength to strength.　*84:7*

20　A day in thy courts is better than a thousand. I had rather be a doorkeeper in the house of my God, than to dwell in the tents of wickedness.　*84:10*

21　Mercy and truth are met together; righteousness and peace have kissed each other.　*85:10*

22　Lord, why castest thou off my soul? why hidest thou thy face from me?　*88:14*

23　Lord, thou hast been our dwelling place in all generations.

Before the mountains were brought forth, or ever thou hadst formed the earth and the world, even from everlasting to everlasting, thou art God.

Thou turnest man to destruction; and sayest, Return, ye children of men.

For a thousand years in thy sight are but as yesterday when it is past, and as a watch in the night.

Thou carriest them away as with a flood; they are as a sleep: in the morning they are like grass which groweth up.

In the morning it flourisheth, and groweth up; in the evening it is cut down, and withereth.　*90:1–6*

24　We spend our years as a tale that is told.　*90:9*

25　The days of our years are threescore years and ten; and if by reason of strength they be fourscore years, yet is their strength labor and sorrow; for it is soon cut off, and we fly away.　*90:10*

26　So teach us to number our days, that we may apply our hearts unto wisdom.　*90:12*

27　Establish thou the work of our hands upon us; yea, the work of our hands establish thou it.　*90:17*

28　He that dwelleth in the secret place of the most High shall abide under the shadow of the Almighty.

I will say of the Lord, He is my refuge and my fortress: my God; in him will I trust.

Surely he shall deliver thee from the snare of the fowler, and from the noisome pestilence.

He shall cover thee with his feathers, and under his wings shalt thou trust: his truth shall be thy shield and buckler.

Thou shalt not be afraid for the terror by night; nor for the arrow that flieth by day.

Nor for the pestilence that walketh in darkness; nor for the destruction that wasteth at noonday.

A thousand shall fall at thy side, and ten thousand at thy right hand; but it shall not come nigh thee.

91:1–7

29　He shall give his angels charge over thee, to keep thee in all thy ways.

They shall bear thee up in their hands, lest thou dash thy foot against a stone.

Thou shalt tread upon the lion and adder: the young lion and the dragon shalt thou trample under feet.　*91:11–13*

30　The righteous shall flourish like the palm tree: he shall grow like a cedar in Lebanon.　*92:12*

31　Mightier than the noise of many waters.　*93:4*

32　O come, let us sing unto the Lord: let us make a joyful noise to the rock of our salvation.

Let us come before his presence with thanksgiving, and make a joyful noise unto him with psalms.

For the Lord is a great God, and a great King above all gods.

In his hand are the deep places of the earth: the strength of the hills is his also.

The sea is his, and he made it: and his hands formed the dry land.

O come, let us worship and bow down: let us kneel before the Lord our maker.

For he is our God; and we are the people of his pasture, and the sheep of his hand.   *Psalms 95:1–7*

1   O sing unto the Lord a new song.   *96:1*

2   The Lord reigneth; let the earth rejoice.   *97:1*

3   Make a joyful noise unto the Lord, all ye lands.

Serve the Lord with gladness: come before his presence with singing.

Know ye that the Lord he is God: it is he that hath made us, and not we ourselves; we are his people, and the sheep of his pasture.

Enter into his gates with thanksgiving, and into his courts with praise: be thankful unto him, and bless his name.

For the Lord is good; his mercy is everlasting; and his truth endureth to all generations.   *100*

4   My days are consumed like smoke.   *102:3*

5   I watch, and am as a sparrow alone upon the house top.   *102:7*

6   As the heaven is high above the earth, so great is his mercy toward them that fear him.   *103:11*

7   As for man, his days are as grass: as a flower of the field, so he flourisheth.

For the wind passeth over it, and it is gone; and the place thereof shall know it no more.   *103:15–16*

8   Who layeth the beams of his chambers in the waters: who maketh the clouds his chariot: who walketh upon the wings of the wind.   *104:3*

9   Wine that maketh glad the heart of man.   *104:15*

10   The cedars of Lebanon.   *104:16*

11   He appointed the moon for seasons: the sun knoweth his going down.

Thou makest darkness, and it is night: wherein all the beasts of the forest do creep forth.

The young lions roar after their prey, and seek their meat from God.

The sun ariseth, they gather themselves together, and lay them down in their dens.

Man goeth forth unto his work and to his labor until the evening.

O Lord, how manifold are thy works! in wisdom hast thou made them all: the earth is full of thy riches.

So is this great and wide sea, wherein are things creeping innumerable, both small and great beasts.

There go the ships: there is that leviathan, whom thou hast made to play therein.

These wait all upon thee; that thou mayest give them their meat in due season.   *104:19–27*

12   The people asked, and he brought quails, and satisfied them with the bread of heaven.   *105:40*

13   Such as sit in darkness and in the shadow of death.   *107:10*

14   They that go down to the sea in ships, that do business in great waters.   *107:23*

15   They mount up to the heaven, they go down again to the depths.   *107:26*

16   They reel to and fro, and stagger like a drunken man, and are at their wit's end.   *107:27*

17   For I am poor and needy, and my heart is wounded within me.

I am gone like the shadow when it declineth: I am tossed up and down as the locust.   *109:22–23*

18   Thou hast the dew of thy youth.   *110:3*

19   The fear of the Lord is the beginning of wisdom.   *111:10*

20   From the rising of the sun unto the going down of the same the Lord's name is to be praised.   *113:3*

21   The mountains skipped like rams, and the little hills like lambs.   *114:4*

22   They have mouths, but they speak not: eyes have they, but they see not.

They have ears, but they hear not.   *115:5–6*

23   I said in my haste, All men are liars.   *116:11*

24   Precious in the sight of the Lord is the death of his saints.   *116:15*

25   The stone which the builders refused is become the head stone of the corner.   *118:22*

26   This is the day which the Lord hath made.   *118:24*

27   Blessed be he that cometh in the name of the Lord.   *118:26*

28   Thy word is a lamp unto my feet, and a light unto my path.   *119:105*

29   I am for peace: but when I speak, they are for war.   *120:7*

30   I will lift up mine eyes unto the hills, from whence cometh my help.

My help cometh from the Lord, which made heaven and earth.

He will not suffer thy foot to be moved: he that keepeth thee will not slumber.

Behold, he that keepeth Israel shall neither slumber nor sleep.

The Lord is thy keeper: the Lord is thy shade upon thy right hand.

The sun shall not smite thee by day, nor the moon by night.

The Lord shall preserve thee from all evil: he shall preserve thy soul.

The Lord shall preserve thy going out and thy coming in from this time forth, and even for evermore.   *121*

1   I was glad when they said unto me, Let us go into the house of the Lord.   *122:1*

2   Peace be within thy walls, and prosperity within thy palaces.   *122:7*

3   They that sow in tears shall reap in joy.

He that goeth forth and weepeth, bearing precious seed, shall doubtless come again with rejoicing, bringing his sheaves with him.   *126:5–6*

4   Except the Lord build the house, they labor in vain that build it: except the Lord keep the city, the watchman waketh but in vain.   *127:1*

5   He giveth his beloved sleep.   *127:2*

6   As arrows are in the hand of a mighty man; so are children of the youth.

Happy is the man that hath his quiver full of them.   *127:4–5*

7   Out of the depths have I cried unto thee, O Lord.   *130:1*

8   My soul waiteth for the Lord more than they that watch for the morning.   *130:6*

9   I will not give sleep to mine eyes, or slumber to mine eyelids.   *132:4*

10   Behold, how good and how pleasant it is for brethren to dwell together in unity!   *133:1*

11   By the rivers of Babylon, there we sat down, yea, we wept, when we remembered Zion.

We hanged our harps upon the willows in the midst thereof.

For there they that carried us away captive required of us a song; and they that wasted us required of us mirth, saying, Sing us one of the songs of Zion.

How shall we sing the Lord's song in a strange land?

If I forget thee, O Jerusalem, let my right hand forget her cunning.

If I do not remember thee, let my tongue cleave to the roof of my mouth.   *137:1–6*

12   O Lord, thou hast searched me, and known me.

Thou knowest my downsitting and mine uprising; thou understandest my thought afar off.   *139:1–2*

13   Whither shall I go from thy Spirit? or whither shall I flee from thy presence?

If I ascend up into heaven, thou art there: if I make my bed in hell, behold, thou art there.

If I take the wings of the morning, and dwell in the uttermost parts of the sea;

Even there shall thy hand lead me, and thy right hand shall hold me.   *139:7–10*

14   The darkness and the light are both alike to thee.   *139:12*

15   I am fearfully and wonderfully made.   *139:14*

16   They have sharpened their tongues like a serpent.   *140:3*

17   Thou openest thine hand, and satisfiest the desire of every living thing.   *145:16*

18   The Lord is nigh unto all them that call upon him, to all that call upon him in truth.   *145:18*

19   Put not your trust in princes.   *146:3*

20   He telleth the number of the stars; he calleth them all by their names.   *147:4*

21   Praise him with the sound of the trumpet: praise him with the psaltery and harp.

Praise him with the timbrel and dance: praise him with stringed instruments and organs.

Praise him upon the loud cymbals: praise him upon the high sounding cymbals.

Let every thing that hath breath praise the Lord.   *150:3–6*

22   To give subtilty to the simple, to the young man knowledge and discretion.   *The Proverbs 1:4*

23   My son, if sinners entice thee, consent thou not.   *1:10*

24   Wisdom crieth without; she uttereth her voice in the streets.   *1:20*

25   Length of days is in her right hand; and in her left hand riches and honor.   *3:16*

26   Her ways are ways of pleasantness, and all her paths are peace.   *3:17*

27   Be not afraid of sudden fear.   *3:25*

28   Wisdom is the principal thing; therefore get wisdom: and with all thy getting get understanding.   *4:7*

29   The path of the just is as the shining light, that shineth more and more unto the perfect day.   *4:18*

30   Keep thy heart with all diligence; for out of it are the issues of life.   *4:23*

31   The lips of a strange woman drop as a honeycomb, and her mouth is smoother than oil:

But her end is bitter as wormwood, sharp as a two-edged sword.   *5:3–4*

32   Go to the ant, thou sluggard; consider her ways, and be wise:

Which having no guide, overseer, or ruler,

Provideth her meat in the summer, and gathereth her food in the harvest.   *Proverbs 6:6–8*

1   Yet a little sleep, a little slumber, a little folding of the hands to sleep:

So shall thy poverty come as one that traveleth, and thy want as an armed man.   *6:10–11*

2   Lust not after her beauty in thine heart; neither let her take thee with her eyelids.   *6:25*

3   Can a man take fire in his bosom, and his clothes not be burned?

Can one go upon hot coals, and his feet not be burned?   *6:27–28*

4   Jealousy is the rage of a man: therefore he will not spare in the day of vengeance.   *6:34*

5   He goeth after her straightway, as an ox goeth to the slaughter.   *7:22*

6   I love them that love me; and those that seek me early shall find me.   *8:17*

7   Wisdom hath built her house, she hath hewn out her seven pillars.   *9:1*

8   Reprove not a scorner, lest he hate thee: rebuke a wise man, and he will love thee.   *9:8*

9   Stolen waters are sweet, and bread eaten in secret is pleasant.   *9:17*

10   A wise son maketh a glad father: but a foolish son is the heaviness of his mother.   *10:1*

11   Blessings are upon the head of the just: but violence covereth the mouth of the wicked.

The memory of the just is blessed: but the name of the wicked shall rot.   *10:6–7*

12   Hatred stirreth up strifes: but love covereth all sins.   *10:12*

13   In the multitude of counsellors there is safety.
He that is surety for a stranger shall smart for it.   *11:14–15*

14   As a jewel of gold in a swine's snout, so is a fair woman which is without discretion.   *11:22*

15   He that trusteth in his riches shall fall.   *11:28*

16   He that troubleth his own house shall inherit the wind.   *11:29*

17   A virtuous woman is a crown to her husband.   *12:4*

18   A righteous man regardeth the life of his beast: but the tender mercies of the wicked are cruel.   *12:10*

19   The way of a fool is right in his own eyes.   *12:15*

20   Hope deferred maketh the heart sick.   *13:12*

21   The way of transgressors is hard.   *13:15*

22   The desire accomplished is sweet to the soul.   *13:19*

23   He that spareth his rod hateth his son: but he that loveth him chasteneth him betimes.   *13:24*

24   Fools make a mock at sin.   *14:9*

25   The heart knoweth his own bitterness; and a stranger doth not intermeddle with his joy.   *14:10*

26   Even in laughter the heart is sorrowful.   *14:13*

27   The prudent man looketh well to his going.   *14:15*

28   In all labor there is profit: but the talk of the lips tendeth only to penury.   *14:23*

29   Righteousness exalteth a nation.   *14:34*

30   A soft answer turneth away wrath.   *15:1*

31   A merry heart maketh a cheerful countenance: but by sorrow of the heart the spirit is broken.   *15:13*

32   He that is of a merry heart hath a continual feast.
Better is little with the fear of the Lord, than great treasure, and trouble therewith.
Better is a dinner of herbs where love is, than a stalled ox and hatred therewith.   *15:15–17*

33   A wrathful man stirreth up strife: but he that is slow to anger appeaseth strife.   *15:18*

34   A word spoken in due season, how good is it!   *15:23*

35   Before honor is humility.   *15:33 and 18:12*

36   A man's heart deviseth his way: but the Lord directeth his steps.   *16:9*

37   Pride goeth before destruction, and an haughty spirit before a fall.   *16:18*

38   The hoary head is a crown of glory, if it be found in the way of righteousness.
He that is slow to anger is better than the mighty; and he that ruleth his spirit than he that taketh a city.   *16:31–32*

39   Whoso mocketh the poor reproacheth his Maker.   *17:5*

40   He that repeateth a matter separateth very friends.   *17:9*

41   Whoso rewardeth evil for good, evil shall not depart from his house.   *17:13*

42   A merry heart doeth good like a medicine.   *17:22*

43   He that hath knowledge spareth his words: and a man of understanding is of an excellent spirit.
Even a fool, when he holdeth his peace, is counted wise.   *17:27–28*

1 A fool's mouth is his destruction. *18:7*

2 A wounded spirit who can bear? *18:14*

3 A brother offended is harder to be won than a strong city: and their contentions are like the bars of a castle. *18:19*

4 Whoso findeth a wife findeth a good thing. *18:22*

5 A man that hath friends must show himself friendly: and there is a friend that sticketh closer than a brother. *18:24*

6 Wealth maketh many friends. *19:4*

7 A foolish son is the calamity of his father: and the contentions of a wife are a continual dropping. *19:13*

8 He that hath pity upon the poor lendeth unto the Lord. *19:17*

9 Wine is a mocker, strong drink is raging. *20:1*

10 It is an honor for a man to cease from strife: but every fool will be meddling. *20:3*

11 Even a child is known by his doings, whether his work be pure, and whether it be right.
The hearing ear, and the seeing eye, the Lord hath made even both of them. *20:11–12*

12 It is naught, it is naught, saith the buyer: but when he is gone his way, then he boasteth. *20:14*

13 Bread of deceit is sweet to a man; but afterwards his mouth shall be filled with gravel. *20:17*

14 Meddle not with him that flattereth with his lips. *20:19*

15 It is better to dwell in a corner of the housetop, than with a brawling woman in a wide house. *21:9 and 25:24*

16 A good name is rather to be chosen than great riches. *22:1*

17 Train up a child in the way he should go; and when he is old, he will not depart from it. *22:6*

18 The borrower is servant to the lender. *22:7*

19 Bow down thine ear, and hear the words of the wise, and apply thine heart unto my knowledge.
For it is a pleasant thing if thou keep them within thee; they shall withal be fitted in thy lips. *22:17–18*

20 Have I not written to thee excellent things in counsels and knowledge,
That I might make thee know the certainty of the words of truth; that thou mightest answer the words of truth to them that send unto thee? *22:20–21*

21 Rob not the poor, because he is poor: neither oppress the afflicted in the gate. *22:22*

22 Remove not the ancient landmark. *22:28*

23 Seest thou a man diligent in his business? He shall stand before kings. *22:29*

24 Put a knife to thy throat, if thou be a man given to appetite. *23:2*

25 Labor not to be rich: cease from thine own wisdom. *23:4*

26 Riches certainly make themselves wings; they fly away as an eagle toward heaven. *23:5*

27 As he thinketh in his heart, so is he. *23:7*

28 The drunkard and the glutton shall come to poverty: and drowsiness shall clothe a man with rags. *23:21*

29 Despise not thy mother when she is old. *23:22*

30 Look not thou upon the wine when it is red, when it giveth his color in the cup, when it moveth itself aright.
At the last it biteth like a serpent, and stingeth like an adder. *23:31–32*

31 A wise man is strong; yea, a man of knowledge increaseth strength. *24:5*

32 If thou faint in the day of adversity, thy strength is small. *24:10*

33 A word fitly spoken is like apples of gold in pictures of silver. *25:11*

34 If thine enemy be hungry, give him bread to eat; and if he be thirsty, give him water to drink:
For thou shalt heap coals of fire upon his head. *25:21–22*

35 As cold waters to a thirsty soul, so is good news from a far country. *25:25*

36 For men to search their own glory is not glory. *25:27*

37 Answer a fool according to his folly. *26:5*

38 As a dog returneth to his vomit, so a fool returneth to his folly.
Seest thou a man wise in his own conceit? There is more hope of a fool than of him.
The slothful man saith, There is a lion in the way; a lion is in the streets. *26:11–13*

39 Whoso diggeth a pit shall fall therein: and he that rolleth a stone, it will return upon him. *26:27*

40 Boast not thyself of tomorrow; for thou knowest not what a day may bring forth. *27:1*

41 Let another man praise thee, and not thine own mouth. *27:2*

1   Open rebuke is better than secret love.
Faithful are the wounds of a friend; but the kisses of an enemy are deceitful.   *Proverbs 27:5–6*

2   To the hungry soul every bitter thing is sweet.   *27:7*

3   Better is a neighbor that is near than a brother far off.   *27:10*

4   Iron sharpeneth iron; so a man sharpeneth the countenance of his friend.   *27:17*

5   The wicked flee when no man pursueth: but the righteous are bold as a lion.   *28:1*

6   He that maketh haste to be rich shall not be innocent.   *28:20*

7   He that trusteth in his own heart is a fool.   *28:26*

8   He that giveth unto the poor shall not lack.   *28:27*

9   A fool uttereth all his mind.   *29:11*

10   Where there is no vision, the people perish.   *29:18*

11   A man's pride shall bring him low: but honor shall uphold the humble in spirit.   *29:23*

12   Give me neither poverty nor riches.   *30:8*

13   Accuse not a servant unto his master.   *30:10*

14   There be three things which are too wonderful for me, yea, four which I know not:
The way of an eagle in the air; the way of a serpent upon a rock; the way of a ship in the midst of the sea; and the way of a man with a maid.   *30:18–19*

15   Give strong drink unto him that is ready to perish, and wine unto those that be of heavy hearts.
Let him drink, and forget his poverty, and remember his misery no more.   *31:6–7*

16   Who can find a virtuous woman? for her price is far above rubies.
The heart of her husband doth safely trust in her.   *31:10–11*

17   Her husband is known in the gates, when he sitteth among the elders of the land.   *31:23*

18   Strength and honor are her clothing.   *31:25*

19   In her tongue is the law of kindness.
She looketh well to the ways of her household, and eateth not the bread of idleness.
Her children arise up, and call her blessed.   *31:26–28*

20   Many daughters have done virtuously, but thou excellest them all.
Favor is deceitful, and beauty is vain: but a woman that feareth the Lord, she shall be praised.

Give her of the fruit of her hands; and let her own works praise her in the gates.   *31:29–31*

21   Vanity of vanities, saith the Preacher, vanity of vanities; all is vanity.
What profit hath a man of all his labor which he taketh under the sun?
One generation passeth away, and another generation cometh: but the earth abideth for ever.
The sun also ariseth.   *Ecclesiastes; or, The Preacher 1:2–5*

22   All the rivers run into the sea; yet the sea is not full.   *1:7*

23   The eye is not satisfied with seeing, nor the ear filled with hearing.   *1:8*

24   The thing that hath been, it is that which shall be; and that which is done is that which shall be done: and there is no new thing under the sun.   *1:9*

25   There is no remembrance of former things; neither shall there be any remembrance of things that are to come with those that shall come after.   *1:11*

26   I have seen all the works that are done under the sun; and, behold, all is vanity and vexation of spirit.
That which is crooked cannot be made straight: and that which is wanting cannot be numbered.   *1:14–15*

27   In much wisdom is much grief: and he that increaseth knowledge increaseth sorrow.   *1:18*

28   Wisdom excelleth folly, as far as light excelleth darkness.   *2:13*

29   One event happeneth to them all.   *2:14*

30   How dieth the wise man? as the fool.   *2:16*

31   To every thing there is a season, and a time to every purpose under the heaven.
A time to be born, and a time to die; a time to plant, and a time to pluck up that which is planted;
A time to kill, and a time to heal; a time to break down, and a time to build up;
A time to weep, and a time to laugh; a time to mourn, and a time to dance;
A time to cast away stones, and a time to gather stones together; a time to embrace, and a time to refrain from embracing;
A time to get, and a time to lose; a time to keep, and a time to cast away;
A time to rend, and a time to sew; a time to keep silence, and a time to speak;
A time to love, and a time to hate; a time of war, and a time of peace.   *3:1–8*

32   Wherefore I praised the dead which are already dead more than the living which are yet alive.   *4:2*

1　Better is a handful with quietness, than both the hands full with travail and vexation of spirit.　*4:6*

2　A threefold cord is not quickly broken.　*4:12*

3　Better is a poor and a wise child than an old and foolish king.　*4:13*

4　God is in heaven, and thou upon earth: therefore let thy words be few.　*5:2*

5　Better is it that thou shouldest not vow, than that thou shouldest vow and not pay.　*5:5*

6　The sleep of a laboring man is sweet . . . but the abundance of the rich will not suffer him to sleep.　*5:12*

7　As he came forth of his mother's womb, naked shall he return to go as he came, and shall take nothing of his labor, which he may carry away in his hand.　*5:15*

8　A good name is better than precious ointment; and the day of death than the day of one's birth.　*7:1*

9　It is better to go to the house of mourning, than to go to the house of feasting.　*7:2*

10　The heart of the wise is in the house of mourning; but the heart of fools is in the house of mirth.　*7:4*

11　As the crackling of thorns under a pot, so is the laughter of the fool.　*7:6*

12　Better is the end of a thing than the beginning thereof.　*7:8*

13　In the day of prosperity be joyful, but in the day of adversity consider.　*7:14*

14　Be not righteous over much.　*7:16*

15　There is not a just man upon earth, that doeth good, and sinneth not.　*7:20*

16　And I find more bitter than death the woman, whose heart is snares and nets, and her hands as bands.　*7:26*

17　One man among a thousand have I found; but a woman among all those have I not found.　*7:28*

18　God hath made man upright; but they have sought out many inventions.　*7:29*

19　There is no discharge in that war.　*8:8*

20　A man hath no better thing under the sun, than to eat, and to drink, and to be merry.[1]　*8:15*

21　A living dog is better than a dead lion.

---

[1]See *Isaiah 22:13*, 25:29, and *Luke 12:19*, 38:3.

For the living know that they shall die: but the dead know not any thing, neither have they any more a reward; for the memory of them is forgotten.　*9:4–5*

22　Whatsoever thy hand findeth to do, do it with thy might; for there is no work, nor device, nor knowledge, nor wisdom, in the grave, whither thou goest.　*9:10*

23　I returned, and saw under the sun, that the race is not to the swift, nor the battle to the strong, neither yet bread to the wise, nor yet riches to men of understanding, nor yet favor to men of skill; but time and chance happeneth to them all.

For man also knoweth not his time: as the fishes that are taken in an evil net, and as the birds that are caught in the snare; so are the sons of men snared in an evil time, when it falleth suddenly upon them.　*9:11–12*

24　A feast is made for laughter, and wine maketh merry: but money answereth all things.　*10:19*

25　A bird of the air shall carry the voice, and that which hath wings shall tell the matter.　*10:20*

26　Cast thy bread upon the waters: for thou shalt find it after many days.　*11:1*

27　He that observeth the wind shall not sow; and he that regardeth the clouds shall not reap.　*11:4*

28　In the morning sow thy seed, and in the evening withhold not thine hand.　*11:6*

29　Rejoice, O young man, in thy youth.　*11:9*

30　Remember now thy Creator in the days of thy youth, while the evil days come not, nor the years draw nigh, when thou shalt say, I have no pleasure in them;

While the sun, or the light, or the moon, or the stars, be not darkened, nor the clouds return after the rain:

In the day when the keepers of the house shall tremble, and the strong men shall bow themselves, and the grinders cease because they are few, and those that look out of the windows be darkened,

And the doors shall be shut in the streets, when the sound of the grinding is low, and he shall rise up at the voice of the bird, and all the daughters of music shall be brought low.　*12:1–4*

31　The almond tree shall flourish, and the grasshopper shall be a burden, and desire shall fail; because man goeth to his long home, and the mourners go about the streets:

Or ever the silver cord be loosed, or the golden bowl be broken, or the pitcher be broken at the fountain, or the wheel broken at the cistern.

Then shall the dust return to the earth as it was: and the spirit shall return unto God who gave it.　*12:5–7*

1   The words of the wise are as goads, and as nails fastened by the masters of assemblies.

Ecclesiastes 12:11

2   Of making many books there is no end; and much study is a weariness of the flesh.

Let us hear the conclusion of the whole matter: Fear God, and keep his commandments: for this is the whole duty of man.

For God shall bring every work into judgment, with every secret thing, whether it be good, or whether it be evil.

12:12–14

3   The song of songs, which is Solomon's.

The Song of Solomon 1:1

4   I am black, but comely, O ye daughters of Jerusalem, as the tents of Kedar, as the curtains of Solomon.

1:5

5   O thou fairest among women.

1:8

6   I am the rose of Sharon, and the lily of the valleys.

2:1

7   As the apple tree among the trees of the wood, so is my beloved among the sons.

2:3

8   His banner over me was love.

Stay me with flagons, comfort me with apples: for I am sick of love.

2:4–5

9   Rise up, my love, my fair one, and come away.

For, lo, the winter is past, the rain is over and gone;

The flowers appear on the earth; the time of the singing of birds is come, and the voice of the turtle is heard in our land.

2:10–12

10   Take us the foxes, the little foxes, that spoil the vines: for our vines have tender grapes.

2:15

11   Until the day break, and the shadows flee away.

2:17 and 4:6

12   By night on my bed I sought him whom my soul loveth: I sought him, but I found him not.

3:1

13   Thy two breasts are like two young roes that are twins, which feed among the lilies.

4:5

14   Thou art all fair, my love; there is no spot in thee.

4:7

15   How much better is thy love than wine!

4:10

16   Awake, O north wind; and come, thou south; blow upon my garden, that the spices thereof may flow out. Let my beloved come into his garden, and eat his pleasant fruits.

4:16

17   My beloved put in his hand by the hole of the door, and my bowels were moved for him.

5:4

18   His mouth is most sweet: yea, he is altogether lovely. This is my beloved, and this is my friend, O daughters of Jerusalem.

5:16

19   Who is she that looketh forth as the morning, fair as the moon, clear as the sun, and terrible as an army with banners?

6:10

20   Return, return, O Shulamite.

6:13

21   Thy belly is like a heap of wheat set about with lilies.

7:2

22   Thy neck is as a tower of ivory.

7:4

23   Like the best wine... that goeth down sweetly, causing the lips of those that are asleep to speak.

7:9

24   I am my beloved's, and his desire is toward me.

7:10

25   Set me as a seal upon thine heart, as a seal upon thine arm: for love is strong as death; jealousy is cruel as the grave.

8:6

26   Many waters cannot quench love, neither can the floods drown it.

8:7

27   Make haste, my beloved, and be thou like to a roe or to a young hart upon the mountains of spices.

8:14

28   The ox knoweth his owner, and the ass his master's crib.

The Book of the Prophet Isaiah 1:3

29   The whole head is sick, and the whole heart faint.

1:5

30   As a lodge in a garden of cucumbers.

1:8

31   Bring no more vain oblations.

1:13

32   Learn to do well; seek judgment, relieve the oppressed, judge the fatherless, plead for the widow.

Come now, and let us reason together... though your sins be as scarlet, they shall be as white as snow.

1:17–18

33   They shall beat their swords into plowshares, and their spears into pruninghooks: nation shall not lift up sword against nation, neither shall they learn war any more.[1]

2:4

34   In that day a man shall cast his idols... to the moles and to the bats.

2:20

35   Cease ye from man, whose breath is in his nostrils.

2:22

36   The stay and the staff, the whole stay of bread, and the whole stay of water.

3:1

37   What mean ye that ye beat my people to pieces and grind the faces of the poor?

3:15

---

[1]Also in *Joel 3:10* and *Micah 4:3*.

1   Walk with stretched forth necks and wanton eyes, walking and mincing as they go, and making a tinkling with their feet.   *3:16*

2   In that day seven women shall take hold of one man.   *4:1*

3   My wellbeloved hath a vineyard in a very fruitful hill.   *5:1*

4   And he looked for judgment, but behold oppression; for righteousness, but behold a cry.

Woe unto them that join house to house, that lay field to field, till there be no place, that they may be placed alone in the midst of the earth!   *5:7–8*

5   Woe unto them that rise up early in the morning, that they may follow strong drink.   *5:11*

6   Woe unto them that draw iniquity with cords of vanity, and sin as it were with a cart rope.   *5:18*

7   Woe unto them that call evil good, and good evil.   *5:20*

8   I saw also the Lord sitting upon a throne, high and lifted up, and his train filled the temple.

Above it stood the seraphims: each one had six wings; with twain he covered his face, and with twain he covered his feet, and with twain he did fly.   *6:1–2*

9   Holy, holy, holy, is the Lord of hosts: the whole earth is full of his glory.   *6:3*

10   Woe is me! for I am undone; because I am a man of unclean lips, and I dwell in the midst of a people of unclean lips: for mine eyes have seen the King, the Lord of hosts.   *6:5*

11   I heard the voice of the Lord, saying, Whom shall I send, and who will go for us? Then said I, Here am I; send me.   *6:8*

12   Then said I, Lord, how long?   *6:11*

13   Behold, a virgin shall conceive, and bear a son, and shall call his name Immanuel.   *7:14*

14   For a stone of stumbling and for a rock of offense.   *8:14*

15   The people that walked in darkness have seen a great light: they that dwell in the land of the shadow of death, upon them hath the light shined.   *9:2*

16   For unto us a child is born, unto us a son is given: and the government shall be upon his shoulder: and his name shall be called Wonderful, Counsellor, The mighty God, The everlasting Father, The Prince of Peace.

Of the increase of his government and peace there shall be no end.   *9:6–7*

17   The ancient and honorable, he is the head.   *9:15*

18   And there shall come forth a rod out of the stem of Jesse, and a Branch shall grow out of his roots:

And the Spirit of the Lord shall rest upon him, the spirit of wisdom and understanding, the spirit of counsel and might, the spirit of knowledge and of the fear of the Lord.   *11:1–2*

19   The wolf also shall dwell with the lamb, and the leopard shall lie down with the kid; and the calf and the young lion and the fatling together; and a little child shall lead them.

And the cow and the bear shall feed; their young ones shall lie down together: and the lion shall eat straw like the ox.

And the suckling child shall play on the hole of the asp, and the weaned child shall put his hand on the cockatrice' den.

They shall not hurt nor destroy in all my holy mountain: for the earth shall be full of the knowledge of the Lord, as the waters cover the sea.   *11:6–9*

20   For the Lord JEHOVAH is my strength and my song; he also is become my salvation.   *12:2*

21   And I will punish the world for their evil, and the wicked for their iniquity; and I will cause the arrogancy of the proud to cease, and will lay low the haughtiness of the terrible.   *13:11*

22   How art thou fallen from heaven, O Lucifer, son of the morning!   *14:12*

23   Is this the man that made the earth to tremble, that did shake kingdoms.   *14:16*

24   The nations shall rush like the rushing of many waters.   *17:13*

25   And they shall fight every one against his brother.   *19:2*

26   The burden of the desert of the sea. As whirlwinds in the south pass through; so it cometh from the desert, from a terrible land.   *21:1*

27   Babylon is fallen, is fallen; and all the graven images of her gods he hath broken unto the ground.   *21:9*

28   Watchman, what of the night?   *21:11*

29   Let us eat and drink; for tomorrow we shall die.[1]   *22:13*

30   I will fasten him as a nail in a sure place.   *22:23*

31   Whose merchants are princes.   *23:8*

32   As with the maid, so with her mistress.   *24:2*

33   For thou hast been a strength to the poor, a strength to the needy in his distress.   *25:4*

---

[1]See *Ecclesiastes 8:15*, 23:20, and *Luke 12:19*, 38:3.

1   A feast of fat things, a feast of wines on the lees.
Isaiah 25:6

2   He will swallow up death in victory; and the Lord God will wipe away tears from off all faces.   *25:8*

3   Open ye the gates, that the righteous nation which keepeth the truth may enter in.
Thou wilt keep him in perfect peace, whose mind is stayed on thee.   *26:2–3*

4   Awake and sing, ye that dwell in dust.   *26:19*

5   Hide thyself as it were for a little moment, until the indignation be overpast.   *26:20*

6   Leviathan that crooked serpent . . . the dragon that is in the sea.   *27:1*

7   For precept must be upon precept, precept upon precept; line upon line, line upon line; here a little, and there a little.   *28:10*

8   We have made a covenant with death, and with hell are we at agreement.   *28:15*

9   It shall be a vexation only to understand the report.   *28:19*

10   They are drunken, but not with wine; they stagger, but not with strong drink.   *29:9*

11   Their strength is to sit still.
Now go, write it before them in a table, and note it in a book, that it may be for the time to come for ever and ever.   *30:7–8*

12   The bread of adversity, and the water of affliction.   *30:20*

13   This is the way, walk ye in it.   *30:21*

14   Behold, a king shall reign in righteousness.   *32:1*

15   And a man shall be as an hiding place from the wind, and a covert from the tempest; as rivers of water in a dry place, as the shadows of a great rock in a weary land.   *32:2*

16   An habitation of dragons, and a court for owls.   *34:13*

17   The desert shall rejoice, and blossom as the rose.   *35:1*

18   Then the eyes of the blind shall be opened, and the ears of the deaf shall be unstopped.
Then shall the lame man leap as an hart, and the tongue of the dumb sing.   *35:5–6*

19   Sorrow and sighing shall flee away.   *35:10*

20   Thou trustest in the staff of this broken reed.   *36:6*

21   Incline thine ear, O Lord, and hear.   *37:17*

22   I shall go softly all my years in the bitterness of my soul.   *38:15*

23   Comfort ye, comfort ye my people.   *40:1*

24   Speak ye comfortably to Jerusalem, and cry unto her, that her warfare is accomplished, that her iniquity is pardoned: for she hath received of the Lord's hand double for all her sins.
The voice of him that crieth in the wilderness, Prepare ye the way of the Lord, make straight in the desert a highway for our God.   *40:2–3*

25   Every valley shall be exalted, and every mountain and hill shall be made low: and the crooked shall be made straight, and the rough places plain.   *40:4*

26   The voice said, Cry. And he said, what shall I cry? All flesh is grass, and all the goodliness thereof is as the flower of the field.   *40:6*

27   The grass withereth, the flower fadeth; but the word of our God shall stand for ever.   *40:8*

28   Get thee up into the high mountain . . . say unto the cities of Judah, Behold your God!   *40:9*

29   He shall feed his flock like a shepherd: he shall gather the lambs with his arm, and carry them in his bosom, and shall gently lead those that are with young.   *40:11*

30   The nations are as a drop of a bucket, and are counted as the small dust of the balance.   *40:15*

31   Have ye not known? have ye not heard? hath it not been told you from the beginning?   *40:21*

32   They that wait upon the Lord shall renew their strength; they shall mount up with wings as eagles; they shall run, and not be weary, and they shall walk, and not faint.   *40:31*

33   They helped every one his neighbor; and every one said to his brother, Be of good courage.   *41:6*

34   A bruised reed shall he not break, and the smoking flax shall he not quench.   *42:3*

35   Shall the clay say to him that fashioneth it, What makest thou?   *45:9*

36   Behold, I have refined thee, but not with silver; I have chosen thee in the furnace of affliction.   *48:10*

37   O that thou hadst hearkened to my commandments! then had thy peace been as a river, and thy righteousness as the waves of the sea.   *48:18*

38   There is no peace, saith the Lord, unto the wicked.   *48:22*

39   Therefore the redeemed of the Lord shall return, and come with singing unto Zion.   *51:11*

1   Thou hast drunken the dregs of the cup of trembling.   *51:17*

2   Therefore hear now this.   *51:21*

3   How beautiful upon the mountains are the feet of him that bringeth good tidings, that publisheth peace.   *52:7*

4   They shall see eye to eye.   *52:8*

5   He is despised and rejected of men; a man of sorrows, and acquainted with grief.   *53:3*

6   Surely he hath borne our griefs, and carried our sorrows.   *53:4*

7   All we like sheep have gone astray.   *53:6*

8   He is brought as a lamb to the slaughter.   *53:7*

9   Ho, everyone that thirsteth, come ye to the waters.   *55:1*

10   Behold, I have given him for a witness to the people, a leader and commander to the people.   *55:4*

11   Let the wicked forsake his way, and the unrighteous man his thoughts.   *55:7*

12   For my thoughts are not your thoughts, neither are your ways my ways, saith the Lord.   *55:8*

13   Peace to him that is far off, and to him that is near.   *57:19*

14   Arise, shine; for thy light is come, and the glory of the Lord is risen upon thee.   *60:1*

15   A little one shall become a thousand, and a small one a strong nation.   *60:22*

16   Give unto them beauty for ashes, the oil of joy for mourning, the garment of praise for the spirit of heaviness.   *61:3*

17   I have trodden the winepress alone; and of the people there was none with me: for I will tread them in mine anger, and trample them in my fury; and their blood shall be sprinkled upon my garments, and I will stain all my raiment.   *63:3*

18   All our righteousnesses are as filthy rags; and we all do fade as a leaf.   *64:6*

19   We all are the work of thy hand.   *64:8*

20   I am holier than thou.   *65:5*

21   For, behold, I create new heavens and a new earth.   *65:17*

22   And they shall build houses, and inhabit them; and they shall plant vineyards, and eat the fruit of them.
They shall not build, and another inhabit; they shall not plant, and another eat.   *65:21–22*

23   As one whom his mother comforteth, so will I comfort you.   *66:13*

24   They were as fed horses in the morning: every one neighed after his neighbor's wife.
The Book of the Prophet Jeremiah 5:8

25   Hear now this, O foolish people, and without understanding; which have eyes, and see not; which have ears, and hear not.   *5:21*

26   But this people hath a revolting and a rebellious heart.   *5:23*

27   Saying, Peace, peace; when there is no peace.
6:14 and 8:11

28   Stand ye in the ways, and see, and ask for the old paths, where is the good way, and walk therein.
6:16

29   Amend your ways and your doings.
7:3 and 26:13

30   The harvest is past, the summer is ended, and we are not saved.   *8:20*

31   Is there no balm in Gilead?   *8:22*

32   Oh that I had in the wilderness a lodging place of wayfaring men!   *9:2*

33   Thus saith the Lord, Let not the wise man glory in his wisdom, neither let the mighty man glory in his might, let not the rich man glory in his riches:
But let him that glorieth glory in this, that he understandeth and knoweth me.   *9:23–24*

34   Can the Ethiopian change his skin, or the leopard his spots?   *13:23*

35   Our backslidings are many; we have sinned against thee.   *14:7*

36   Her sun is gone down while it was yet day.   *15:9*

37   A man of strife and a man of contention.   *15:10*

38   The sin of Judah is written with a pen of iron, and with the point of a diamond.   *17:1*

39   Cursed be the man that trusteth in man, and maketh flesh his arm, and whose heart departeth from the Lord.
For he shall be like the heath in the desert, and shall not see when good cometh; but shall inhabit the parched places in the wilderness, in a salt land and not inhabited.
Blessed is the man that trusteth in the Lord, and whose hope the Lord is.
For he shall be as a tree planted by the waters, and that spreadeth out her roots by the river, and shall not see when heat cometh, but her leaf shall be green; and shall not be careful in the year of drought, neither shall cease from yielding fruit.   *17:5–8*

1   The heart is deceitful above all things, and desperately wicked: who can know it?   *Jeremiah 17:9*

2   As the partridge sitteth on eggs, and hatcheth them not; so he that getteth riches, and not by right, shall leave them in the midst of his days, and at his end shall be a fool.   *17:11*

3   Thou art my hope in the day of evil.   *17:17*

4   O earth, earth, earth, hear the word of the Lord.   *22:29*

5   A curse, and an astonishment, and a hissing, and a reproach.   *29:18*

6   The fathers have eaten a sour grape, and the children's teeth are set on edge.   *31:29*

7   With my whole heart and with my whole soul.   *32:41*

8   And seekest thou great things for thyself? seek them not.   *45:5*

9   How doth the city sit solitary, that was full of people! how is she become as a widow!
The Lamentations of Jeremiah 1:1

10   She weepeth sore in the night, and her tears are on her cheeks: among all her lovers she hath none to comfort her.   *1:2*

11   Is it nothing to you, all ye that pass by? behold, and see if there be any sorrow like unto my sorrow.   *1:12*

12   Remembering mine affliction and my misery, the wormwood and the gall.   *3:19*

13   It is good for a man that he bear the yoke in his youth.   *3:27*

14   As it were a wheel in the middle of a wheel.
The Book of the Prophet Ezekiel 1:16

15   As is the mother, so is her daughter.   *16:44*

16   The king of Babylon stood at the parting of the way.   *21:21*

17   The valley...was full of bones...and lo, they were very dry.   *37:1–2*

18   Can these bones live?   *37:3*

19   O ye dry bones, hear the word of the Lord.   *37:4*

20   Every man's sword shall be against his brother.   *38:21*

21   His legs of iron, his feet part of iron and part of clay.   *The Book of Daniel 2:33*

22   Shadrach, Meshach, and Abednego, fell down bound into the midst of the burning fiery furnace.   *3:23*

23   Nebuchadnezzar...was driven from men, and did eat grass as oxen.   *4:33*

24   Belshazzar the king made a great feast to a thousand of his lords.   *5:1*

25   And this is the writing that was written, MENE, MENE, TEKEL, UPHARSIN.
This is the interpretation of the thing: MENE; God hath numbered thy kingdom, and finished it.
TEKEL; Thou art weighed in the balances, and art found wanting.
PERES; Thy kingdom is divided, and given to the Medes and Persians.   *5:25–28*

26   According to the law of the Medes and Persians, which altereth not.   *6:12*

27   They brought Daniel, and cast him into the den of lions.   *6:16*

28   So Daniel was taken up out of the den, and no manner of hurt was found upon him, because he believed in his God.   *6:23*

29   The Ancient of days.   *7:9 and 7:13*

30   Many shall run to and fro, and knowledge shall be increased.   *12:4*

31   Ye are the sons of the living God.   *Hosea 1:10*

32   Like people, like priest.   *4:9*

33   After two days will he revive us: in the third day he will raise us up, and we shall live in his sight.   *6:2*

34   He shall come unto us as the rain, as the latter and former rain unto the earth.   *6:3*

35   For I desired mercy, and not sacrifice; and the knowledge of God more than burnt offerings.   *6:6*

36   They have sown the wind, and they shall reap the whirlwind.   *8:7*

37   Ye have plowed wickedness, ye have reaped iniquity.   *10:13*

38   I drew them with...bands of love.   *11:4*

39   I have multiplied visions, and used similitudes, by the ministry of the prophets.   *12:10*

40   I will ransom them from the power of the grave; I will redeem them from death: O death, I will be thy plagues; O grave, I will be thy destruction.[1]   *13:14*

41   Your old men shall dream dreams, your young men shall see visions.   *Joel 2:28*

42   Multitudes in the valley of decision.   *3:14*

[1]See *Isaiah 25:8*, 26:2, and *I Corinthians 15:54*, 43:9.

1   They sold the righteous for silver, and the poor for a pair of shoes.   *Amos 2:6*

2   Can two walk together, except they be agreed?   *3:3*

3   Woe to them that are at ease in Zion.   *6:1*

4   And Jonah was in the belly of the fish three days and three nights.   *Jonah 1:17*

5   What doth the Lord require of thee, but to do justly, and to love mercy, and to walk humbly with thy God?   *Micah 6:8*

6   The faces of them all gather blackness.[1]   *Nahum 2:10*

7   Write the vision, and make it plain upon tables, that he may run that readeth it.   *Habakkuk 2:2*

8   The stone shall cry out of the wall, and the beam out of the timber shall answer it.   *2:11*

9   The Lord is in his holy temple: let all the earth keep silence before him.   *2:20*

10   Your fathers, where are they? And the prophets, do they live forever?   *Zechariah 1:5*

11   I have spread you abroad as the four winds of the heaven.   *2:6*

12   Not by might, nor by power, but by my spirit, saith the Lord of hosts.   *4:6*

13   For who hath despised the day of small things?   *4:10*

14   Behold, thy King cometh unto thee . . . lowly, and riding upon an ass.   *9:9*

15   Prisoners of hope.   *9:12*

16   So they weighed for my price thirty pieces of silver.   *11:12*

17   What are these wounds in thine hands? . . . Those with which I was wounded in the house of my friends.   *13:6*

18   Have we not all one father? hath not one God created us?   *Malachi 2:10*

19   Behold, I will send my messenger, and he shall prepare the way before me.   *3:1*

20   Behold, the day cometh, that shall burn as an oven.   *4:1*

21   Unto you that fear my name shall the Sun of righteousness arise with healing in his wings.   *4:2*

22   Behold, I will send you Elijah the prophet before the coming of the great and dreadful day of the Lord.   *4:5*

The Apocrypha[2]

23   And when they are in their cups, they forget their love both to friends and brethren, and a little after draw out swords.   *I Esdras 3:22*

24   Great is Truth, and mighty above all things.[3]   *4:41*

25   What is past I know, but what is for to come I know not.   *II Esdras 4:46*

26   Now therefore keep thy sorrow to thyself, and bear with a good courage that which hath befallen thee.   *10:15*

27   I shall light a candle of understanding in thine heart, which shall not be put out.   *14:25*

28   If thou hast abundance, give alms accordingly: if thou have but a little, be not afraid to give according to that little.   *Tobit 4:8*

29   Put on her garments of gladness.   *Judith 10:3*

30   The ear of jealousy heareth all things.   *The Wisdom of Solomon 1:10*

31   Our time is a very shadow that passeth away.   *2:5*

32   Let us crown ourselves with rosebuds, before they be withered.[4]   *2:8*

33   For God created man to be immortal, and made him to be an image of his own eternity.

Nevertheless through envy of the devil came death into the world.   *2:23–24*

34   The souls of the righteous are in the hand of God, and there shall no torment touch them.

In the sight of the unwise they seemed to die: and their departure is taken for misery,

And their going from us to be utter destruction: but they are in peace.

For though they be punished in the sight of men, yet is their hope full of immortality.

---

[1]The faces of them all are as the blackness of a kettle. — *Douay Bible* [1609]

[2]The Apocrypha (The Hidden Books) is a term for a set of ancient Jewish writings that are not a part of Hebrew scripture. Some of these writings are considered deuterocanonical by the Roman Catholic Church; others, by various branches of the Eastern Orthodox Church. Most are included in the Septuagint, the Greek version of the Hebrew Bible.

[3]Magna est veritas et praevalet. — *The Vulgate, Book III* (non-canonical)

[4]See Horace, 96:11; Ronsard, 150:8; Spenser, 160:9; and Herrick, 241:4.

And having been a little chastised, they shall be greatly rewarded: for God proved them, and found them worthy for himself. *Solomon 3:1–5*

1 They that put their trust in him shall understand the truth. *3:9*

2 Even so we in like manner, as soon as we were born, began to draw to our end. *5:13*

3 For the hope of the ungodly is like dust that is blown away with the wind . . . and passeth away as the remembrance of a guest that tarrieth but a day. *5:14*

4 For the very true beginning of her [wisdom] is the desire of discipline; and the care of discipline is love. *6:17*

5 And when I was born, I drew in the common air, and fell upon the earth, which is of like nature; and the first voice which I uttered was crying, as all others do. *7:3*

6 All men have one entrance into life, and the like going out. *7:6*

7 The light that cometh from her [wisdom] never goeth out. *7:10*

8 Who can number the sand of the sea, and the drops of rain, and the days of eternity?
*The Wisdom of Jesus the Son of Sirach,
or Ecclesiasticus, 1:2*

9 To whom hath the root of wisdom been revealed? *1:6*

10 For the Lord is full of compassion and mercy, long-suffering, and very pitiful, and forgiveth sins, and saveth in time of affliction. *2:11*

11 The greater thou art, the more humble thyself. *3:18*

12 Many are in high place, and of renown: but mysteries are revealed unto the meek. *3:19*

13 Seek not out the things that are too hard for thee, neither search the things that are above thy strength. *3:21*

14 Be not curious in unnecessary matters: for more things are showed unto thee than men understand. *3:23*

15 Profess not the knowledge . . . that thou hast not. A stubborn heart shall fare evil at the last. *3:25–26*

16 Defraud not the poor of his living, and make not the needy eyes to wait long. *4:1*

17 Wisdom exalteth her children, and layeth hold of them that seek her.
He that loveth her loveth life. *4:11–12*

18 Observe the opportunity. *4:20*

19 Be not as a lion in thy house, nor frantic among thy servants.
Let not thine hand be stretched out to receive, and shut when thou shouldest repay. *4:30–31*

20 Set not thy heart upon thy goods; and say not, I have enough for my life. *5:1*

21 Winnow not with every wind, and go not into every way. *5:9*

22 Let thy life be sincere. *5:11*

23 Be not ignorant of any thing in a great matter or a small. *5:15*

24 If thou wouldest get a friend, prove him first. *6:7*

25 A faithful friend is a strong defense: and he that hath found such an one hath found a treasure. *6:14*

26 A faithful friend is the medicine of life. *6:16*

27 If thou seest a man of understanding, get thee betimes unto him, and let thy foot wear the steps of his door. *6:36*

28 Whatsoever thou takest in hand, remember the end, and thou shalt never do amiss. *7:36*

29 Rejoice not over thy greatest enemy being dead, but remember that we die all. *8:7*

30 Miss not the discourse of the elders. *8:9*

31 Forsake not an old friend; for the new is not comparable to him: a new friend is as new wine; when it is old, thou shalt drink it with pleasure. *9:10*

32 Pride is hateful before God and man. *10:7*

33 He that is today a king tomorrow shall die. *10:10*

34 Pride was not made for men, nor furious anger for them that are born of a woman. *10:18*

35 Be not overwise in doing thy business. *10:26*

36 Many kings have sat down upon the ground; and one that was never thought of hath worn the crown. *11:5*

37 In the day of prosperity there is a forgetfulness of affliction: and in the day of affliction there is no more remembrance of prosperity. *11:25*

38 Judge none blessed before his death. *11:28*

39 A friend cannot be known in prosperity: and an enemy cannot be hidden in adversity. *12:8*

40 He that toucheth pitch shall be defiled therewith. *13:1*

41 How agree the kettle and the earthen pot together? *13:2*

1   All flesh consorteth according to kind, and a man will cleave to his like.   *13:16*

2   A rich man beginning to fall is held up of his friends: but a poor man being down is thrust also away by his friends.   *13:21*

3   The heart of a man changeth his countenance, whether it be for good or evil.   *13:25*

4   So is a word better than a gift.   *18:16*

5   Be not made a beggar by banqueting upon borrowing.   *18:33*

6   He that contemneth small things shall fall by little and little.   *19:1*

7   Whether it be to friend or foe, talk not of other men's lives.   *19:8*

8   A man's attire, and excessive laughter, and gait, show what he is.   *19:30*

9   A tale out of season [is as] music in mourning.   *22:6*

10   I will not be ashamed to defend a friend.   *22:25*

11   All wickedness is but little to the wickedness of a woman.   *25:19*

12   The discourse of fools is irksome.   *27:13*

13   Many have fallen by the edge of the sword: but not so many as have fallen by the tongue.   *28:18*

14   Better is the life of a poor man in a mean cottage, than delicate fare in another man's house.   *29:22*

15   There is no riches above a sound body.   *30:16*

16   Gladness of the heart is the life of a man, and the joyfulness of a man prolongeth his days.   *30:22*

17   Envy and wrath shorten the life, and carefulness bringeth age before the time.   *30:24*

18   Watching for riches consumeth the flesh, and the care thereof driveth away sleep.   *31:1*

19   Let thy speech be short, comprehending much in few words.   *32:8*

20   Consider that I labored not for myself only, but for all them that seek learning.   *33:17*

21   Leave not a stain in thine honor.   *33:22*

22   Let the counsel of thine own heart stand.   *37:13*

23   Honor a physician with the honor due unto him for the uses which ye may have of him: for the Lord hath created him.   *38:1*

24   When the dead is at rest, let his remembrance rest; and be comforted for him, when his spirit is departed from him.   *38:23*

25   How can he get wisdom . . . whose talk is of bullocks?   *38:25*

26   Let us now praise famous men, and our fathers that begat us.   *44:1*

27   All these were honored in their generations, and were the glory of their times.

There be of them, that have left a name behind them, that their praises might be reported.

And some there be, which have no memorial; who are perished, as though they had never been; and are become as though they had never been born; and their children after them.   *44:7–9*

28   Their bodies are buried in peace; but their name liveth for evermore.   *44:14*

29   His word burned like a lamp.   *48:1*

30   O all ye works of the Lord, bless ye the Lord: praise him and exalt him above all for ever.
The Song of the Three Holy Children 35

31   Daniel had convicted them of false witness by their own mouth.   *The History of Susanna 61*

32   It is a foolish thing to make a long prologue, and to be short in the story itself.
The Second Book of the Maccabees 2:32

33   When he was at the last gasp.   *7:9*

34   Speech finely framed delighteth the ears.   *15:39*

The New Testament[1]

35   Behold, a virgin shall be with child, and shall bring forth a son, and they shall call his name Emmanuel, which being interpreted is, God with us.
The Gospel According to Saint Matthew 1:23

36   Now when Jesus was born in Bethlehem of Judaea in the days of Herod the king, behold, there came wise men from the east to Jerusalem,

Saying, Where is he that is born King of the Jews? for we have seen his star in the east, and are come to worship him.   *2:1–2*

37   They saw the young child with Mary his mother, and fell down, and worshipped him: and . . . they presented unto him gifts; gold, and frankincense, and myrrh.

And being warned of God in a dream that they should not return to Herod, they departed into their own country another way.   *2:11–12*

---

[1]The earliest Christian writings [c. 50–c. 64 C.E.] are the Letters (Epistles) of Paul the Apostle. The Gospels were written later, between the years 70 and 100.

1   Out of Egypt have I called my son.

Matthew 2:15

2   Rachel weeping for her children, and would not be comforted, because they are not.   *2:18*

3   He shall be called a Nazarene.   *2:23*

4   Repent ye: for the kingdom of heaven is at hand.   *3:2*

5   The voice of one crying in the wilderness, Prepare ye the way of the Lord, make his paths straight.   *3:3*

6   And his meat was locusts and wild honey.   *3:4*

7   O generation of vipers, who hath warned you to flee from the wrath to come?   *3:7*

8   Now also the axe is laid unto the root of the trees: therefore every tree which bringeth not forth good fruit is hewn down, and cast into the fire.   *3:10*

9   The Spirit of God descending like a dove.   *3:16*

10   This is my beloved Son, in whom I am well pleased.   *3:17*

11   And when he had fasted forty days and forty nights, he was afterward an hungred.   *4:2*

12   The people which sat in darkness saw great light.   *4:16*

13   Follow me, and I will make you fishers of men.   *4:19*

14   Blessed are the poor in spirit: for theirs is the kingdom of heaven.

Blessed are they that mourn: for they shall be comforted.

Blessed are the meek: for they shall inherit the earth.

Blessed are they which do hunger and thirst after righteousness: for they shall be filled.

Blessed are the merciful: for they shall obtain mercy.

Blessed are the pure in heart: for they shall see God.

Blessed are the peacemakers: for they shall be called the children of God.

Blessed are they which are persecuted for righteousness' sake: for theirs is the kingdom of heaven.

Blessed are ye, when men shall revile you, and persecute you, and shall say all manner of evil against you falsely, for my sake.   *5:3–11*[1]

15   Ye are the salt of the earth: but if the salt have lost his savor, wherewith shall it be salted?   *5:13*

16   Ye are the light of the world. A city that is set on an hill cannot be hid.

Neither do men light a candle, and put it under a bushel, but on a candlestick; and it giveth light unto all that are in the house.

Let your light so shine before men, that they may see your good works, and glorify your Father which is in heaven.

Think not that I am come to destroy the law, or the prophets: I am not come to destroy, but to fulfill.   *5:14–17*

17   Till heaven and earth pass, one jot or one tittle shall in no wise pass from the law, till all be fulfilled.   *5:18*

18   Whosoever looketh on a woman to lust after her hath committed adultery with her already in his heart.

And if thy right eye offend thee, pluck it out, and cast it from thee: for it is profitable for thee that one of thy members should perish, and not that thy whole body should be cast into hell.

And if thy right hand offend thee, cut it off.   *5:28–30*

19   Swear not at all; neither by heaven; for it is God's throne:

Nor by the earth; for it is his footstool.   *5:34–35*

20   Resist not evil: but whosoever shall smite thee on thy right cheek, turn to him the other also.   *5:39*

21   Love your enemies, bless them that curse you, do good to them that hate you, and pray for them which despitefully use you, and persecute you.   *5:44*

22   He maketh his sun to rise on the evil and on the good, and sendeth rain on the just and on the unjust.   *5:45*

23   Be ye therefore perfect, even as your Father which is in heaven is perfect.   *5:48*

24   When thou doest alms, let not thy left hand know what thy right hand doeth.   *6:3*

25   After this manner therefore pray ye: Our Father which art in heaven, Hallowed be thy name.

Thy kingdom come. Thy will be done in earth, as it is in heaven.

Give us this day our daily bread.

And forgive us our debts, as we forgive our debtors.[2]

And lead us not into temptation, but deliver us from evil: For thine is the kingdom, and the power, and the glory, for ever. Amen.   *6:9–13*

---

[1]These verses are referred to as the Beatitudes. Chapters 5–7 of the book of Matthew are known as the Sermon on the Mount.

[2]These verses are known as the Lord's Prayer. In some prayer books this verse is rendered as: And forgive us our trespasses, as we forgive those who trespass against us.

1 Lay not up for yourselves treasures upon earth, where moth and rust doth corrupt, and where thieves break through and steal:

But lay up for yourselves treasures in heaven.
6:19–20

2 For where your treasure is, there will your heart be also.   *6:21*

3 The light of the body is the eye.   *6:22*

4 If therefore the light that is in thee be darkness, how great is that darkness!   *6:23*

5 No man can serve two masters: for either he will hate the one, and love the other; or else he will hold to the one, and despise the other. Ye cannot serve God and mammon.   *6:24*

6 Is not the life more than meat, and the body than raiment?

Behold the fowls of the air: for they sow not, neither do they reap, nor gather into barns.   *6:25–26*

7 Which of you by taking thought can add one cubit unto his stature?   *6:27*

8 Consider the lilies of the field, how they grow; they toil not, neither do they spin.   *6:28*

9 Even Solomon in all his glory was not arrayed like one of these.   *6:29*

10 Seek ye first the kingdom of God, and his righteousness; and all these things shall be added unto you.   *6:33*

11 Take therefore no thought for the morrow: for the morrow shall take thought for the things of itself. Sufficient unto the day is the evil thereof.   *6:34*

12 Judge not, that ye be not judged.   *7:1*

13 With what measure ye mete, it shall be measured to you again.

And why beholdest thou the mote that is in thy brother's eye, but considerest not the beam that is in thine own eye?   *7:2–3*

14 Thou hypocrite, first cast out the beam out of thine own eye.   *7:5*

15 Neither cast ye your pearls before swine.   *7:6*

16 Ask, and it shall be given you; seek, and ye shall find; knock, and it shall be opened unto you.   *7:7*

17 Or what man is there of you, whom if his son ask bread, will he give him a stone?   *7:9*

18 Therefore all things whatsoever ye would that men should do to you, do ye even so to them: for this is the law and the prophets.[1]   *7:12*

---

[1] The Golden Rule. Common form: Do unto others as you would have others do unto you.

See Confucius, 61:20; Aristotle, 77:12; Hillel, 102:27; and the Earl of Chesterfield, 298:5.

19 Wide is the gate, and broad is the way, that leadeth to destruction, and many there be which go in thereat:

Because strait is the gate, and narrow is the way, which leadeth unto life, and few there be that find it.
7:13–14

20 Beware of false prophets, which come to you in sheep's clothing, but inwardly they are ravening wolves.   *7:15*

21 Ye shall know them by their fruits. Do men gather grapes of thorns, or figs of thistles?   *7:16*

22 By their fruits ye shall know them.   *7:20*

23 Not every one that saith unto me, Lord, Lord, shall enter into the kingdom of heaven; but he that doeth the will of my Father which is in heaven.   *7:21*

24 [The house] fell not: for it was founded upon a rock.   *7:25*

25 A foolish man, which built his house upon the sand.   *7:26*

26 But the children of the kingdom shall be cast out into outer darkness: there shall be weeping and gnashing of teeth.   *8:12*

27 The foxes have holes, and the birds of the air have nests; but the Son of man hath not where to lay his head.   *8:20*

28 Follow me; and let the dead bury their dead.
8:22

29 Why are ye fearful, O ye of little faith?   *8:26*

30 He saw a man, named Matthew, sitting at the receipt of custom.   *9:9*

31 They that be whole need not a physician, but they that are sick.   *9:12*

32 I am not come to call the righteous, but sinners to repentance.   *9:13*

33 Can the children of the bridechamber mourn, as long as the bridegroom is with them?   *9:15*

34 Neither do men put new wine into old bottles.
9:17

35 The maid is not dead, but sleepeth.   *9:24*

36 The harvest truly is plenteous, but the laborers are few.   *9:37*

37 Go rather to the lost sheep of the house of Israel.   *10:6*

38 Freely ye have received, freely give.   *10:8*

39 Whosoever shall not receive you, nor hear your words, when ye depart out of that house or city, shake off the dust of your feet.   *10:14*

1   Be ye therefore wise as serpents, and harmless as doves.   *Matthew 10:16*

2   Ye shall be hated of all men for my name's sake.   *10:22*

3   The disciple is not above his master, nor the servant above his lord.   *10:24*

4   Are not two sparrows sold for a farthing? and one of them shall not fall on the ground without your Father.

But the very hairs of your head are all numbered.   *10:29–30*

5   I came not to send peace, but a sword.   *10:34*

6   He that taketh not his cross, and followeth after me, is not worthy of me.

He that findeth his life shall lose it: and he that loseth his life for my sake shall find it.   *10:38–39*

7   He that hath ears to hear, let him hear.   *11:15*

8   The Son of man came eating and drinking, and they say, Behold a man gluttonous, and a winebibber, a friend of publicans and sinners. But wisdom is justified of her children.   *11:19*

9   Come unto me, all ye that labor and are heavy laden, and I will give you rest.

Take my yoke upon you, and learn of me; for I am meek and lowly in heart: and ye shall find rest unto your souls.

For my yoke is easy, and my burden is light.   *11:28–30*

10   He that is not with me is against me.   *12:30*

11   The tree is known by his fruit.   *12:33*

12   Out of the abundance of the heart the mouth speaketh.   *12:34*

13   Behold, a greater than Solomon is here.   *12:42*

14   Some seeds fell by the way side.   *13:4*

15   Because they had no root, they withered away.   *13:6*

16   But other fell into good ground, and brought forth fruit, some an hundredfold, some sixtyfold, some thirtyfold.   *13:8*

17   The care of this world, and the deceitfulness of riches.   *13:22*

18   The kingdom of heaven is like to a grain of mustard seed.   *13:31*

19   Pearl of great price.   *13:46*

20   The kingdom of heaven is like unto a net, that was cast into the sea, and gathered of every kind.   *13:47*

21   Is not this the carpenter's son?   *13:55*

22   A prophet is not without honor, save in his own country.   *13:57*

23   [Salome] the daughter of Herodias danced before them, and pleased Herod.   *14:6*

24   Give me here John Baptist's head in a charger.   *14:8*

25   We have here but five loaves, and two fishes.   *14:17*

26   And they did all eat, and were filled: and they took up of the fragments that remained twelve baskets full.   *14:20*

27   And in the fourth watch of the night Jesus went unto them, walking on the sea.   *14:25*

28   Be of good cheer; it is I; be not afraid.   *14:27*

29   O thou of little faith, wherefore didst thou doubt?   *14:31*

30   Of a truth thou art the Son of God.   *14:33*

31   Not that which goeth into the mouth defileth a man; but that which cometh out of the mouth, this defileth a man.   *15:11*

32   They be blind leaders of the blind. And if the blind lead the blind, both shall fall into the ditch.   *15:14*

33   The dogs eat of the crumbs which fall from their masters' table.   *15:27*

34   When it is evening, ye say, It will be fair weather: for the sky is red.   *16:2*

35   The signs of the times.   *16:3*

36   Thou art the Christ, the Son of the living God.   *16:16*

37   Thou art Peter, and upon this rock I will build my church; and the gates of hell shall not prevail against it.

And I will give unto thee the keys of the kingdom of heaven.   *16:18–19*

38   Get thee behind me, Satan.   *16:23*

39   Whosoever will save his life shall lose it: and whosoever will lose his life for my sake shall find it.

For what is a man profited, if he shall gain the whole world, and lose his own soul?   *16:25–26*

40   Except ye be converted, and become as little children, ye shall not enter into the kingdom of heaven.   *18:3*

41   He rejoiceth more of that sheep, than of the ninety and nine which went not astray.   *18:13*

42   Where two or three are gathered together in my name, there am I in the midst of them.   *18:20*

1   Until seventy times seven.   *18:22*

2   What therefore God hath joined together, let not man put asunder.   *19:6*

3   If thou wilt be perfect, go and sell that thou hast, and give to the poor, and thou shalt have treasure in heaven.   *19:21*

4   It is easier for a camel to go through the eye of a needle, than for a rich man to enter into the kingdom of God.   *19:24*

5   Many that are first shall be last; and the last shall be first.   *19:30*

6   Borne the burden and heat of the day.   *20:12*

7   Is it not lawful for me to do what I will with mine own?   *20:15*

8   Overthrew the tables of the moneychangers.   *21:12*

9   My house shall be called the house of prayer; but ye have made it a den of thieves.   *21:13*

10   They made light of it.   *22:5*

11   Many are called, but few are chosen.   *22:14*

12   Render therefore unto Caesar the things which are Caesar's; and unto God the things that are God's.   *22:21*

13   Thou shalt love the Lord thy God with all thy heart, and with all thy soul, and with all thy mind.
This is the first and great commandment.
And the second is like unto it, Thou shalt love thy neighbor as thyself.[1]
On these two commandments hang all the law and the prophets.   *22:37–40*

14   Whosoever shall exalt himself shall be abased; and he that shall humble himself shall be exalted.   *23:12*

15   Woe unto you, scribes and Pharisees, hypocrites! for ye pay tithe of mint and anise and cumin.   *23:23*

16   Blind guides, which strain at a gnat, and swallow a camel.   *23:24*

17   Whited sepulchers, which indeed appear beautiful outward, but are within full of dead men's bones.   *23:27*

18   O Jerusalem, Jerusalem, thou that killest the prophets, and stonest them which are sent unto thee, how often would I have gathered thy children together, even as a hen gathereth her chickens under her wings, and ye would not!   *23:37*

---

[1]See *Leviticus 19:18,* 8:28. Also *Mark 12:31* and *33, Romans 13:9, Galatians 5:14,* and *James 2:8.*

19   Ye shall hear of wars and rumors of wars: see that ye be not troubled: for all these things must come to pass, but the end is not yet.
For nation shall rise against nation.   *24:6–7*

20   Abomination of desolation.   *24:15*

21   Wheresoever the carcase is, there will the eagles be gathered together.   *24:28*

22   And he shall send his angels with a great sound of a trumpet.   *24:31*

23   Heaven and earth shall pass away, but my words shall not pass away.   *24:35*

24   The one shall be taken, and the other left.   *24:40*

25   Then shall the kingdom of heaven be likened unto ten virgins, which took their lamps, and went forth to meet the bridegroom.
And five of them were wise, and five were foolish.   *25:1–2*

26   Well done, thou good and faithful servant . . . enter thou into the joy of thy lord.   *25:21*

27   Unto every one that hath shall be given, and he shall have abundance: but from him that hath not shall be taken away even that which he hath.   *25:29*

28   Cast ye the unprofitable servant into outer darkness.   *25:30*

29   And before him shall be gathered all nations: and he shall separate them one from another, as a shepherd divideth his sheep from the goats.   *25:32*

30   For I was an hungred, and ye gave me meat: I was thirsty, and ye gave me drink: I was a stranger, and ye took me in:
Naked, and ye clothed me: I was sick, and ye visited me: I was in prison, and ye came unto me.   *25:35–36*

31   Inasmuch as ye have done it unto one of the least of these my brethren, ye have done it unto me.   *25:40*

32   There came unto him [Jesus] a woman having an alabaster box of very precious ointment, and poured it on his head, as he sat at meat.   *26:7*

33   To what purpose is this waste?   *26:8*

34   For ye have the poor always with you; but me ye have not always.   *26:11*

35   What will ye give me, and I will deliver him unto you? And they covenanted with him for thirty pieces of silver.   *26:15*

36   My time is at hand.   *26:18*

37   Verily I say unto you, that one of you shall betray me.   *26:21*

1   And they were exceeding sorrowful, and began every one of them to say unto him, Lord, is it I?
Matthew 26:22

2   It had been good for that man [Judas] if he had not been born.   *26:24*

3   Jesus took bread, and blessed it, and brake it, and gave it to the disciples, and said, Take, eat; this is my body.
    And he took the cup, and gave thanks, and gave it to them, saying, Drink ye all of it;
    For this is my blood of the new testament, which is shed for many for the remission of sins.
    But I say unto you, I will not drink henceforth of this fruit of the vine, until that day when I drink it new with you in my Father's kingdom.
26:26–29

4   My soul is exceeding sorrowful, even unto death.
26:38

5   O my Father, if it be possible, let this cup pass from me: nevertheless, not as I will, but as thou wilt.   *26:39*

6   Could ye not watch with me one hour?
    Watch and pray, that ye enter not into temptation: the spirit indeed is willing, but the flesh is weak.
26:40–41

7   Behold, the hour is at hand, and the Son of man is betrayed into the hands of sinners.   *26:45*

8   He came to Jesus, and said, Hail, Master; and kissed him.   *26:49*

9   All they that take the sword shall perish with the sword.   *26:52*

10   Thy speech bewrayeth thee.   *26:73*

11   Then began he to curse and to swear, saying, I know not the man. And immediately the cock crew.
    And Peter remembered the word of Jesus . . . Before the cock crow, thou shalt deny me thrice.[1] And he went out, and wept bitterly.
26:74–75

12   The potter's field, to bury strangers in.   *27:7*

13   Have thou nothing to do with that just man.
27:19

14   Let him be crucified.   *27:22*

15   [Pilate] took water, and washed his hands before the multitude, saying, I am innocent of the blood of this just person: see ye to it.   *27:24*

16   His blood be on us, and on our children.   *27:25*

17   A place called Golgotha, that is to say, a place of a skull.   *27:33*

18   This is Jesus the King of the Jews.   *27:37*

19   He saved others; himself he cannot save.
27:42

20   Eli, Eli, lama sabachthani? that is to say, My God, my God, why hast thou forsaken me?[2]   *27:46*

21   And, behold, the veil of the temple was rent in twain from the top to the bottom; and the earth did quake, and the rocks rent.   *27:51*

22   His countenance was like lightning, and his raiment white as snow.   *28:3*

23   Go ye therefore, and teach all nations, baptizing them in the name of the Father, and of the Son, and of the Holy Ghost.   *28:19*

24   Lo, I am with you alway, even unto the end of the world.   *28:20*

25   There cometh one mightier than I [John the Baptist] after me, the latchet of whose shoes I am not worthy to stoop down and unloose.
The Gospel According to Saint Mark 1:7

26   Arise, and take up thy bed, and walk.   *2:9*

27   The sabbath was made for man, and not man for the sabbath.   *2:27*

28   If a house be divided against itself, that house cannot stand.   *3:25*

29   The earth bringeth forth fruit of herself; first the blade, then the ear, after that the full corn in the ear.
4:28

30   What manner of man is this?   *4:41*

31   My name is Legion: for we are many.   *5:9*

32   And the unclean spirits went out, and entered the swine: and the herd ran violently down a steep place into the sea . . . and were choked in the sea.   *5:13*

33   Clothed, and in his right mind.   *5:15*

34   My little daughter lieth at the point of death.
5:23

35   Knowing in himself that virtue had gone out of him.   *5:30*

36   I see men as trees, walking.   *8:24*

37   Lord, I believe; help thou mine unbelief.   *9:24*

38   Suffer the little children to come unto me, and forbid them not; for of such is the kingdom of God.   *10:14*

---

[1]This night, before the cock crow, thou shalt deny me thrice. — *Matthew 26:34*

[2]See *Psalm 22:1*, 15:21.

1. Which devour widows' houses, and for a pretense make long prayers. *12:40*

2. And there came a certain poor widow, and she threw in two mites. *12:42*

3. Watch ye therefore: for ye know not when the master of the house cometh, at even, or at midnight, or at the cockcrowing, or in the morning:
Lest coming suddenly he find you sleeping. *13:35–36*

4. He is risen. *16:6*

5. Go ye into all the world, and preach the gospel to every creature. *16:15*

6. Hail, thou that art highly favored, the Lord is with thee: blessed art thou among women.
The Gospel According to Saint Luke 1:28

7. For with God nothing shall be impossible. *1:37*

8. Blessed is the fruit of thy womb. *1:42*

9. My soul doth magnify the Lord. *1:46*

10. For he hath regarded the low estate of his handmaiden: for, behold, from henceforth all generations shall call me blessed. *1:48*

11. He hath scattered the proud in the imagination of their hearts.
He hath put down the mighty from their seats, and exalted them of low degree. *1:51–52*

12. He hath filled the hungry with good things; and the rich he hath sent empty away. *1:53*

13. Blessed be the Lord God of Israel; for he hath visited and redeemed his people. *1:68*

14. As he spake by the mouth of his holy prophets, which have been since the world began:
That we should be saved from our enemies, and from the hand of all that hate us. *1:70–71*

15. Through the tender mercy of our God; whereby the dayspring from on high hath visited us,
To give light to them that sit in darkness and in the shadow of death. *1:78–79*

16. And she brought forth her firstborn son, and wrapped him in swaddling clothes, and laid him in a manger; because there was no room for them in the inn. *2:7*

17. There were in the same country shepherds abiding in the field, keeping watch over their flock by night.
And, lo, the angel of the Lord came upon them, and the glory of the Lord shone round about them: and they were sore afraid.
And the angel said unto them, Fear not: for, behold, I bring you good tidings of great joy, which shall be to all people.
For unto you is born this day in the city of David a Savior, which is Christ the Lord. *2:8–11*

18. Glory to God in the highest, and on earth peace, good will toward men. *2:14*

19. Lord, now lettest thou thy servant depart in peace. *2:29*

20. A light to lighten the Gentiles, and the glory of thy people Israel. *2:32*

21. Wist ye not that I must be about my Father's business? *2:49*

22. Jesus increased in wisdom and stature, and in favor with God and man. *2:52*

23. [The devil] showed unto him all the kingdoms of the world in a moment of time. *4:5*

24. For it is written, He shall give his angels charge over thee, to keep thee:
And in their hands they shall bear thee up, lest at any time thou dash thy foot against a stone. *4:10–11*

25. Physician, heal thyself. *4:23*

26. Woe unto you, when all men shall speak well of you! *6:26*

27. Her sins, which are many, are forgiven; for she loved much. *7:47*

28. And he said to the woman, Thy faith hath saved thee; go in peace. *7:50*

29. Nothing is secret, that shall not be made manifest. *8:17*

30. No man, having put his hand to the plow, and looking back, is fit for the kingdom of God. *9:62*

31. Nor scrip, nor shoes. *10:4*

32. Peace be to this house. *10:5*

33. The laborer is worthy of his hire. *10:7*

34. I beheld Satan as lightning fall from heaven. *10:18*

35. Many prophets and kings have desired to see those things which ye see, and have not seen them; and to hear those things which ye hear, and have not heard them. *10:24*

36. A certain man went down from Jerusalem to Jericho, and fell among thieves. *10:30*

37. A certain Samaritan . . . had compassion on him. *10:33*

38. Go, and do thou likewise. *10:37*

39. But Martha was cumbered about much serving. *10:40*

1   But one thing is needful: and Mary hath chosen that good part, which shall not be taken away from her.   *Luke 10:42*

2   This is an evil generation: they seek a sign.   *11:29*

3   Soul, thou hast much goods laid up for many years; take thine ease, eat, drink, and be merry.   *12:19*

4   Thou fool, this night thy soul shall be required of thee.   *12:20*

5   Let your loins be girded about, and your lights burning.   *12:35*

6   For unto whomsoever much is given, of him shall be much required: and to whom men have committed much, of him they will ask the more.   *12:48*

7   The poor, and the maimed, and the halt, and the blind.   *14:21*

8   Which of you, intending to build a tower, sitteth not down first, and counteth the cost, whether he have sufficient to finish it?   *14:28*

9   Rejoice with me; for I have found my sheep which was lost.   *15:6*

10   [The prodigal son] wasted his substance with riotous living.   *15:13*

11   Bring hither the fatted calf, and kill it.   *15:23*

12   For this my son was dead, and is alive again; he was lost, and is found.   *15:24*

13   Son, thou art ever with me, and all that I have is thine.   *15:31*

14   What shall I do?...I cannot dig; to beg I am ashamed.   *16:3*

15   The children of this world are in their generation wiser than the children of light.   *16:8*

16   He that is faithful in that which is least is faithful also in much: and he that is unjust in the least is unjust also in much.   *16:10*

17   The beggar died, and was carried by the angels into Abraham's bosom.   *16:22*

18   Between us and you there is a great gulf fixed.   *16:26*

19   It were better for him that a millstone were hanged about his neck, and he cast into the sea.   *17:2*

20   The kingdom of God is within you.   *17:21*

21   Remember Lot's wife.   *17:32*

22   Two men went up into the temple to pray; the one a Pharisee, and the other a publican.   *18:10*

23   God, I thank thee, that I am not as other men are.   *18:11*

24   God be merciful to me a sinner.   *18:13*

25   Out of thine own mouth will I judge thee.   *19:22*

26   If these should hold their peace, the stones would immediately cry out.   *19:40*

27   He is not a God of the dead, but of the living.   *20:38*

28   In your patience possess ye your souls.   *21:19*

29   The Son of man coming in a cloud with power and great glory.   *21:27*

30   This do in remembrance of me.   *22:19*

31   Not my will, but thine, be done.   *22:42*

32   For if they do these things in a green tree, what shall be done in the dry?   *23:31*

33   The place, which is called Calvary.   *23:33*

34   Father, forgive them; for they know not what they do.   *23:34*

35   Lord, remember me when thou comest into thy kingdom.   *23:42*

36   To day shalt thou be with me in paradise.   *23:43*

37   Father, into thy hands I commend my spirit.   *23:46*

38   He gave up the ghost.   *23:46*

39   He was a good man, and a just.   *23:50*

40   Why seek ye the living among the dead?   *24:5*

41   Their words seemed to them as idle tales.   *24:11*

42   Did not our heart burn within us, while he talked with us?   *24:32*

43   The Lord is risen indeed.   *24:34*

44   In the beginning was the Word, and the Word was with God, and the Word was God.
The Gospel According to Saint John 1:1

45   And the light shineth in darkness; and the darkness comprehended it not.   *1:5*

46   There was a man sent from God, whose name was John.   *1:6*

47   The true Light, which lighteth every man that cometh into the world.   *1:9*

48   The Word was made flesh, and dwelt among us... full of grace and truth.   *1:14*

49   No man hath seen God at any time.   *1:18*

50   Behold the Lamb of God, which taketh away the sin of the world.   *1:29*

1　Can there any good thing come out of Nazareth? *1:46*

2　Hereafter ye shall see heaven open, and the angels of God ascending and descending upon the Son of man. *1:51*

3　Woman, what have I to do with thee? mine hour is not yet come. *2:4*

4　The water that was made wine. *2:9*

5　This beginning of miracles did Jesus in Cana of Galilee, and manifested forth his glory; and his disciples believed on him. *2:11*

6　When he had made a scourge of small cords, he drove them all out of the temple. *2:15*

7　Make not my Father's house an house of merchandise. *2:16*

8　Except a man be born again, he cannot see the kingdom of God. *3:3*

9　The wind bloweth where it listeth, and thou hearest the sound thereof, but canst not tell whence it cometh, and whither it goeth: so is every one that is born of the Spirit. *3:8*

10　How can these things be? *3:9*

11　God so loved the world, that he gave his only begotten Son, that whosoever believeth in him should not perish, but have everlasting life. *3:16*

12　There cometh a woman of Samaria to draw water: Jesus saith unto her, Give me to drink. *4:7*

13　The hour cometh, and now is, when the true worshippers shall worship the Father in spirit and in truth. *4:23*

14　He was a burning and a shining light. *5:35*

15　Search the scriptures. *5:39*

16　What are they among so many? *6:9*

17　Gather up the fragments that remain, that nothing be lost. *6:12*

18　I am the bread of life: he that cometh to me shall never hunger; and he that believeth on me shall never thirst. *6:35*

19　It is the spirit that quickeneth; the flesh profiteth nothing. *6:63*

20　Judge not according to the appearance. *7:24*

21　Never man spake like this man. *7:46*

22　He that is without sin among you, let him first cast a stone at her. *8:7*

23　Neither do I condemn thee: go, and sin no more. *8:11*

24　I am the light of the world: he that followeth me shall not walk in darkness, but shall have the light of life. *8:12*

25　The truth shall make you free. *8:32*

26　Ye are of your father the devil . . . there is no truth in him. . . . he is a liar, and the father of it. *8:44*

27　I must work the works of him that sent me, while it is day: the night cometh, when no man can work. *9:4*

28　Whether he be a sinner or no, I know not: one thing I know, that, whereas I was blind, now I see. *9:25*

29　I am the door. *10:9*

30　I am come that they might have life, and that they might have it more abundantly. *10:10*

31　I am the good shepherd: the good shepherd giveth his life for the sheep. *10:11*

32　Other sheep I have, which are not of this fold. *10:16*

33　I am the resurrection, and the life: he that believeth in me, though he were dead, yet shall he live:
And whosoever liveth and believeth in me shall never die. *11:25–26*

34　Jesus wept. *11:35*

35　It is expedient for us, that one man should die for the people. *11:50*

36　Then saith one of his disciples, Judas Iscariot, Simon's son, which should betray him,
Why was not this ointment sold for three hundred pence, and given to the poor? *12:4–5*

37　Yet a little while is the light with you. Walk while ye have the light, lest darkness come upon you. *12:35*

38　That thou doest, do quickly. *13:27*

39　A new commandment I give unto you, That ye love one another. *13:34*

40　Let not your heart be troubled: ye believe in God, believe also in me.
In my Father's house are many mansions: if it were not so, I would have told you. I go to prepare a place for you. *14:1–2*

41　I will come again, and receive you unto myself; that where I am, there ye may be also. *14:3*

42　I am the way, the truth, and the life. *14:6*

43　I will not leave you comfortless. *14:18*

44　Peace I leave with you, my peace I give unto you: not as the world giveth, give I unto you. Let not your heart be troubled, neither let it be afraid. *14:27*

1   Greater love hath no man than this, that a man lay down his life for his friends.   *John 15:13*

2   Ye have not chosen me, but I have chosen you.   *15:16*

3   Whither goest thou?[1]   *16:5*

4   Ask, and ye shall receive, that your joy may be full.   *16:24*

5   Be of good cheer; I have overcome the world.   *16:33*

6   Pilate saith unto him, What is truth?   *18:38*

7   Now Barabbas was a robber.   *18:40*

8   Behold the man![2]   *19:5*

9   Woman, behold thy son!   *19:26*

10   It is finished.   *19:30*

11   Touch me not.[3]   *20:17*

12   Then saith he to Thomas ... be not faithless, but believing.   *20:27*

13   Blessed are they that have not seen, and yet have believed.   *20:29*

14   Suddenly there came a sound from heaven as of a rushing mighty wind.   *The Acts of the Apostles 2:2*

15   There appeared unto them cloven tongues like as of fire, and it sat upon each of them.
     And they were all filled with the Holy Ghost, and began to speak with other tongues.   *2:3–4*

16   Silver and gold have I none; but such as I have give I thee.   *3:6*

17   And distribution was made unto every man according as he had need.   *4:35*

18   If this counsel or this work be of men, it will come to nought:
     But if it be of God, ye cannot overthrow it.   *5:38–39*

19   Thy money perish with thee.   *8:20*

20   In the gall of bitterness, and in the bond of iniquity.   *8:23*

21   Saul, yet breathing out threatenings and slaughter against the disciples of the Lord.   *9:1*

22   Saul, Saul, why persecutest thou me?   *9:4*

23   It is hard for thee to kick against the pricks.   *9:5*

24   He is a chosen vessel unto me.   *9:15*

25   Immediately there fell from his eyes as it had been scales.   *9:18*

26   What God hath cleansed, that call not thou common.   *10:15*

27   God is no respecter of persons.   *10:34*

28   The gods are come down to us in the likeness of men.   *14:11*

29   We also are men of like passions with you.   *14:15*

30   Come over into Macedonia, and help us.   *16:9*

31   Certain lewd fellows of the baser sort.   *17:5*

32   Ye men of Athens, I perceive that in all things ye are too superstitious.
     For as I passed by, and beheld your devotions, I found an altar with this inscription, TO THE UNKNOWN GOD.   *17:22–23*

33   God that made the world, and all things therein, seeing that he is Lord of heaven and earth, dwelleth not in temples made with hands;
     Neither is worshipped with men's hands, as though he needed any thing, seeing he giveth to all life, and breath, and all things;
     And hath made of one blood all nations of men for to dwell on all the face of the earth.   *17:24–26*

34   For in him we live, and move, and have our being; as certain also of your own poets have said, For we are also his offspring.   *17:28*

35   Your blood be upon your own heads.   *18:6*

36   And Gallio, cared for none of those things.   *18:17*

37   Mighty in the Scriptures.   *18:24*

38   We have not so much as heard whether there be any Holy Ghost.   *19:2*

39   All with one voice about the space of two hours cried out, Great is Diana of the Ephesians.   *19:34*

40   It is more blessed to give than to receive.   *20:35*

41   I [Paul] am ... a Jew of Tarsus, a city in Cilicia, a citizen of no mean city.   *21:39*

42   Brought up in this city at the feet of Gamaliel.   *22:3*

43   And the chief captain answered, With a great sum obtained I this freedom. And Paul said, But I was free born.   *22:28*

44   God shall smite thee, thou whited wall.   *23:3*

45   Revilest thou God's high priest?   *23:4*

46   I [Paul] am a Pharisee, the son of a Pharisee.   *23:6*

---

[1]Quo vadis? — *The Vulgate*

[2]Ecce homo. — *The Vulgate*

[3]Noli me tangere. — *The Vulgate*

1 A conscience void of offense toward God, and toward men. *24:16*

2 When I have a convenient season, I will call for thee. *24:25*

3 I appeal unto Caesar. *25:11*

4 Paul, thou art beside thyself; much learning doth make thee mad. *26:24*

5 I am not mad...but speak forth the words of truth and soberness. *26:25*

6 For this thing was not done in a corner. *26:26*

7 Almost thou persuadest me to be a Christian. *26:28*

8 Wherein thou judgest another, thou condemnest thyself.

The Epistle of Paul the Apostle to the Romans 2:1

9 These, having not the law, are a law unto themselves. *2:14*

10 The things that are more excellent. *2:18*

11 Where no law is, there is no transgression. *4:15*

12 Who against hope believed in hope. *4:18*

13 Where sin abounded, grace did much more abound. *5:20*

14 Death hath no more dominion over him. *6:9*

15 I speak after the manner of men. *6:19*

16 The wages of sin is death; but the gift of God is eternal life. *6:23*

17 The good that I would I do not: but the evil which I would not, that I do. *7:19*

18 Who shall deliver me from the body of this death? *7:24*

19 Heirs of God, and joint-heirs with Christ. *8:17*

20 For we know that the whole creation groaneth and travaileth in pain together until now. *8:22*

21 All things work together for good to them that love God. *8:28*

22 For whom he did foreknow, he also did predestinate to be conformed to the image of his Son, that he might be the firstborn among many brethren.
Moreover whom he did predestinate, them he also called: and whom he called, them he also justified: and whom he justified, them he also glorified. *8:29–30*

23 If God be for us, who can be against us? *8:31*

24 Who shall lay any thing to the charge of God's elect? It is God that justifieth. *8:33*

25 Who shall separate us from the love of Christ? *8:35*

26 Neither death, nor life, nor angels, nor principalities, nor powers, nor things present, nor things to come,
Nor height, nor depth, nor any other creature, shall be able to separate us from the love of God, which is in Christ Jesus our Lord. *8:38–39*

27 Hath not the potter power over the clay, of the same lump to make one vessel unto honor, and another unto dishonor? *9:21*

28 For who hath known the mind of the Lord? *11:34*

29 I beseech you therefore, brethren...that ye present your bodies a living sacrifice, holy, acceptable unto God, which is your reasonable service. *12:1*

30 Let love be without dissimulation. *12:9*

31 Be kindly affectioned one to another with brotherly love. *12:10*

32 Given to hospitality. *12:13*

33 Be not wise in your own conceits.
Recompense to no man evil for evil. *12:16–17*

34 If it be possible, as much as lieth in you, live peaceably with all men. *12:18*

35 Vengeance is mine; I will repay, saith the Lord. *12:19*

36 Be not overcome of evil, but overcome evil with good. *12:21*

37 The powers that be are ordained of God. *13:1*

38 Render therefore to all their dues: tribute to whom tribute is due; custom to whom custom; fear to whom fear; honor to whom honor.
Owe no man anything, but to love one another. *13:7–8*

39 Love is the fulfilling of the law. *13:10*

40 The night is far spent, the day is at hand: let us therefore cast off the works of darkness, and let us put on the armor of light.
Let us walk honestly, as in the day; not in rioting and drunkenness, not in chambering and wantonness, not in strife and envying.
But put ye on the Lord Jesus Christ, and make not provision for the flesh, to fulfil the lusts thereof.[1] *13:12–14*

41 Doubtful disputations. *14:1*

---

[1] See Saint Augustine, 116:5, and note.

1   Let every man be fully persuaded in his own mind.
Romans 14:5

2   For none of us liveth to himself, and no man dieth to himself.

For whether we live, we live unto the Lord; and whether we die, we die unto the Lord: whether we live therefore, or die, we are the Lord's.   *14:7–8*

3   Let us therefore follow after the things which make for peace.   *14:19*

4   We then that are strong ought to bear the infirmities of the weak, and not to please ourselves.
15:1

5   God hath chosen the foolish things of the world to confound the wise; and God hath chosen the weak things of the world to confound the things which are mighty.

The First Epistle of Paul the Apostle
to the Corinthians 1:27

6   As it is written,[1] Eye hath not seen, nor ear heard.
2:9

7   I have planted, Apollos watered; but God gave the increase.   *3:6*

8   We are laborers together with God: ye are God's husbandry.   *3:9*

9   Every man's work shall be made manifest: for the day shall declare it, because it shall be revealed by fire; and the fire shall try every man's work of what sort it is.   *3:13*

10   For the temple of God is holy, which temple ye are.   *3:17*

11   We are made a spectacle unto the world, and to angels, and to men.   *4:9*

12   Absent in body, but present in spirit.   *5:3*

13   A little leaven leaveneth the whole lump.   *5:6*

14   For even Christ our Passover is sacrificed for us.
5:7

15   It is better to marry than to burn.   *7:9*

16   The fashion of this world passeth away.   *7:31*

17   Knowledge puffeth up, but charity edifieth.   *8:1*

18   I am made all things to all men.   *9:22*

19   Know ye not that they which run in a race run all, but one receiveth the prize?   *9:24*

20   Let him that thinketh he standeth take heed lest he fall.   *10:12*

21   All things are lawful for me, but all things are not expedient.   *10:23*

22   The earth is the Lord's, and the fullness thereof.
10:26

23   If a woman have long hair, it is a glory to her.
11:15

24   Take, eat: this is my body, which is broken for you: this do in remembrance of me.   *11:24*

25   This cup is the new testament in my blood: this do ye, as oft as ye drink it, in remembrance of me.
11:25

26   Though I speak with the tongues of men and of angels, and have not charity,[2] I am become as sounding brass, or a tinkling cymbal.   *13:1*

27   Though I have all faith, so that I could remove mountains, and have not charity, I am nothing.

And though I bestow all my goods to feed the poor, and though I give my body to be burned, and have not charity, it profiteth me nothing.

Charity suffereth long, and is kind; charity envieth not; charity vaunteth not itself, is not puffed up.
13:2–4

28   Beareth all things, believeth all things, hopeth all things, endureth all things.

Charity never faileth.   *13:7–8*

29   We know in part, and we prophesy in part.

But when that which is perfect is come, then that which is in part shall be done away.

When I was a child, I spake as a child, I understood as a child, I thought as a child: but when I became a man, I put away childish things.

For now we see through a glass, darkly; but then face to face: now I know in part; but then shall I know even as also I am known.

And now abideth faith, hope, charity, these three; but the greatest of these is charity.   *13:9–13*

30   If the trumpet give an uncertain sound, who shall prepare himself to the battle?   *14:8*

31   Let all things be done decently and in order.
14:40

32   And last of all he was seen of me also, as of one born out of due time.

For I am the least of the apostles, that am not meet to be called an apostle, because I persecuted the church of God.

But by the grace of God I am what I am.
15:8–10

---

[1] Men have not heard, nor perceived by the ear, neither hath the eye seen. — *Isaiah 64:4*

[2] In most newer translations "charity" throughout this chapter is translated as "love" — the love of humanity in the sense of the Greek *agapē* and the Latin *caritas*.

1   But now is Christ risen from the dead, and become the firstfruits of them that slept.

For since by man came death, by man came also the resurrection of the dead.

For as in Adam all die, even so in Christ shall all be made alive.   *15:20–22*

2   The last enemy that shall be destroyed is death.
                                                        15:26

3   Evil communications corrupt good manners.
                                                        15:33

4   Thou fool, that which thou sowest is not quickened, except it die.   *15:36*

5   One star differeth from another star in glory.
                                                        15:41

6   It is sown in corruption; it is raised in incorruption.   *15:42*

7   The first man is of the earth, earthy.   *15:47*

8   Behold, I show you a mystery; We shall not all sleep, but we shall all be changed,

In a moment, in the twinkling of an eye, at the last trump: for the trumpet shall sound, and the dead shall be raised incorruptible, and we shall be changed.

For this corruptible must put on incorruption, and this mortal must put on immortality.   *15:51–53*

9   Death is swallowed up in victory.

O death, where is thy sting? O grave, where is thy victory?   *15:54–55*

10   Watch ye, stand fast in the faith, quit you like men, be strong.   *16:13*

11   If any man love not the Lord Jesus Christ, let him be Anathema Maranatha.   *16:22*

12   Not of the letter, but of the spirit: for the letter killeth, but the spirit giveth life.

*The Second Epistle of Paul the Apostle
to the Corinthians 3:6*

13   Seeing then that we have such hope, we use great plainness of speech.   *3:12*

14   The things which are seen are temporal; but the things which are not seen are eternal.   *4:18*

15   We walk by faith, not by sight.   *5:7*

16   Now is the accepted time.   *6:2*

17   By honor and dishonor, by evil report and good report.   *6:8*

18   As having nothing, and yet possessing all things.
                                                        6:10

19   God loveth a cheerful giver.   *9:7*

20   Though I be rude in speech.   *11:6*

21   For ye suffer fools gladly, seeing ye yourselves are wise.   *11:19*

22   Forty stripes save one.   *11:24*

23   A thorn in the flesh.   *12:7*

24   My strength is made perfect in weakness.
                                                        12:9

25   The grace of the Lord Jesus Christ, and the love of God, and the communion of the Holy Ghost, be with you all.   *13:14*

26   The right hands of fellowship.
*The Epistle of Paul the Apostle
to the Galatians 2:9*

27   Weak and beggarly elements.   *4:9*

28   It is good to be zealously affected always in a good thing.   *4:18*

29   Ye are fallen from grace.   *5:4*

30   For the flesh lusteth against the Spirit, and the Spirit against the flesh: and these are contrary the one to the other: so that ye cannot do the things that ye would.   *5:17*

31   The fruit of the Spirit is love, joy, peace, longsuffering, gentleness, goodness, faith,

Meekness, temperance.   *5:22–23*

32   Every man shall bear his own burden.   *6:5*

33   Be not deceived; God is not mocked: for whatsoever a man soweth, that shall he also reap.   *6:7*

34   Let us not be weary in well doing.   *6:9*

35   To be strengthened with might by his Spirit in the inner man.
*The Epistle of Paul the Apostle
to the Ephesians 3:16*

36   Carried about with every wind of doctrine.   *4:14*

37   We are members one of another.

Be ye angry, and sin not: let not the sun go down upon your wrath.   *4:25–26*

38   Speaking to yourselves in psalms and hymns and spiritual songs, singing and making melody in your heart to the Lord.   *5:19*

39   Put on the whole armor of God.   *6:11*

40   For we wrestle not against flesh and blood, but against principalities, against powers, against the rulers of the darkness of this world, against spiritual wickedness in high places.

Wherefore take unto you the whole armor of God, that ye may be able to withstand in the evil day, and having done all, to stand.   *6:12–13*

1   To live is Christ, and to die is gain.
    The Epistle of Paul the Apostle to the Philippians 1:21

2   Work out your own salvation with fear and trembling.   *2:12*

3   For it is God which worketh in you both to will and to do of his good pleasure.   *2:13*

4   This one thing I do, forgetting those things which are behind, and reaching forth unto those things which are before,
    I press toward the mark.   *3:13–14*

5   Whose end is destruction, whose God is their belly, and whose glory is in their shame, who mind earthly things.   *3:19*

6   The peace of God, which passeth all understanding, shall keep your hearts and minds through Christ Jesus.   *4:7*

7   Whatsoever things are true, whatsoever things are honest, whatsoever things are just, whatsoever things are pure, whatsoever things are lovely, whatsoever things are of good report; if there be any virtue, and if there be any praise, think on these things.   *4:8*

8   I have learned, in whatsoever state I am, therewith to be content.   *4:11*

9   By him were all things created, that are in heaven, and that are in earth, visible and invisible . . . all things were created by him, and for him:
    And he is before all things, and by him all things consist.
    The Epistle of Paul the Apostle to the Colossians 1:16–17

10   Touch not; taste not; handle not.   *2:21*

11   Set your affection on things above, not on things on the earth.   *3:2*

12   Where there is neither Greek nor Jew, circumcision nor uncircumcision, Barbarian, Scythian, bond nor free: but Christ is all, and in all.   *3:11*

13   Fathers, provoke not your children to anger, lest they be discouraged.   *3:21*

14   Let your speech be alway with grace, seasoned with salt.   *4:6*

15   Luke, the beloved physician.   *4:14*

16   Labor of love.
    The First Epistle of Paul the Apostle to the Thessalonians 1:3

17   Study to be quiet, and to do your own business.   *4:11*

18   The day of the Lord so cometh as a thief in the night.   *5:2*

19   Ye are all the children of light, and the children of the day: we are not of the night, nor of darkness.   *5:5*

20   Putting on the breastplate of faith and love; and for an helmet, the hope of salvation.   *5:8*

21   Pray without ceasing.   *5:17*

22   Prove all things; hold fast that which is good.   *5:21*

23   The law is good, if a man use it lawfully.
    The First Epistle of Paul the Apostle to Timothy 1:8

24   Christ Jesus came into the world to save sinners; of whom I am chief.   *1:15*

25   For if a man know not how to rule his own house, how shall he take care of the church of God?   *3:5*

26   Not greedy of filthy lucre.   *3:8*

27   Speaking lies in hypocrisy; having their conscience seared with a hot iron.   *4:2*

28   Every creature of God is good, and nothing to be refused, if it be received with thanksgiving.   *4:4*

29   Refuse profane and old wives' fables.   *4:7*

30   Let them learn first to show piety at home.   *5:4*

31   But if any provide not for his own, and specially for those of his own house, he hath denied the faith, and is worse than an infidel.   *5:8*

32   They learn to be idle, wandering about from house to house; and not only idle, but tattlers also and busybodies, speaking things which they ought not.   *5:13*

33   Drink no longer water, but use a little wine for thy stomach's sake.   *5:23*

34   We brought nothing into this world, and it is certain we can carry nothing out.   *6:7*

35   The love of money is the root of all evil.[1]   *6:10*

36   Fight the good fight of faith, lay hold on eternal life.   *6:12*

37   Rich in good works.   *6:18*

38   O Timothy, keep that which is committed to thy trust, avoiding profane and vain babblings, and oppositions of science falsely so called.   *6:20*

39   For God hath not given us the spirit of fear; but of power, and of love, and of a sound mind.
    The Second Epistle of Paul the Apostle to Timothy 1:7

40   A workman that needeth not to be ashamed.   *2:15*

---

[1]Radix malorum est cupiditas. — CHAUCER, *The Canterbury Tales, The Pardoner's Prologue, l. 6*

1   Be instant in season, out of season.   *4:2*

2   I have fought a good fight, I have finished my course, I have kept the faith.   *4:7*

3   The Lord reward him according to his works.   *4:14*

4   Unto the pure all things are pure.
The Epistle of Paul to Titus 1:15

5   Making mention of thee always in my prayers.
The Epistle of Paul to Philemon 1:4

6   Who maketh his angels spirits, and his ministers a flame of fire.
The Epistle of Paul the Apostle to the Hebrews 1:7

7   The word of God is quick, and powerful, and sharper than any two-edged sword, piercing even to the dividing asunder of soul and spirit, and of the joints and marrow, and is a discerner of the thoughts and intents of the heart.   *4:12*

8   Strong meat belongeth to them that are of full age.   *5:14*

9   They crucify to themselves the Son of God afresh, and put him to an open shame.   *6:6*

10   Without shedding of blood is no remission.   *9:22*

11   Faith is the substance of things hoped for, the evidence of things not seen.   *11:1*

12   Wherefore seeing we also are compassed about with so great a cloud of witnesses . . . let us run with patience the race that is set before us,
Looking unto Jesus the author and finisher of our faith.   *12:1–2*

13   Whom the Lord loveth he chasteneth.   *12:6*

14   The spirits of just men made perfect.   *12:23*

15   Let brotherly love continue.
Be not forgetful to entertain strangers: for thereby some have entertained angels unawares.   *13:1–2*

16   The Lord is my helper, and I will not fear what man shall do unto me.   *13:6*

17   Jesus Christ the same yesterday, and to day, and for ever.   *13:8*

18   For here have we no continuing city, but we seek one to come.   *13:14*

19   To do good and to communicate forget not: for with such sacrifices God is well pleased.   *13:16*

20   Let patience have her perfect work, that ye may be perfect and entire, wanting nothing.
If any of you lack wisdom, let him ask of God.
The General Epistle of James 1:4–5

21   Blessed is the man that endureth temptation: for when he is tried, he shall receive the crown of life.   *1:12*

22   Every good gift and every perfect gift is from above, and cometh down from the Father of lights, with whom is no variableness, neither shadow of turning.   *1:17*

23   Be swift to hear, slow to speak, slow to wrath:
For the wrath of man worketh not the righteousness of God.   *1:19–20*

24   Be ye doers of the word, and not hearers only.   *1:22*

25   Unspotted from the world.   *1:27*

26   As the body without the spirit is dead, so faith without works is dead also.   *2:26*

27   How great a matter a little fire kindleth!   *3:5*

28   The tongue can no man tame; it is an unruly evil.   *3:8*

29   This wisdom descendeth not from above, but is earthly, sensual, devilish.   *3:15*

30   Resist the devil, and he will flee from you.   *4:7*

31   What is your life? It is even a vapor, that appeareth for a little time, and then vanisheth away.   *4:14*

32   Be patient therefore, brethren, unto the coming of the Lord. Behold, the husbandman waiteth for the precious fruit of the earth, and hath long patience for it, until he receive the early and latter rain.   *5:7*

33   Ye have heard of the patience of Job.   *5:11*

34   The effectual fervent prayer of a righteous man availeth much.   *5:16*

35   Hope to the end.
The First Epistle General of Peter 1:13

36   The Father, who without respect of persons judgeth according to every man's work.   *1:17*

37   All flesh is as grass, and all the glory of man as the flower of grass. The grass withereth, and the flower thereof falleth away:
But the word of the Lord endureth for ever.   *1:24–25*

38   Abstain from fleshly lusts, which war against the soul.   *2:11*

39   Honor all men. Love the brotherhood. Fear God. Honor the king.   *2:17*

40   Ornament of a meek and quiet spirit.   *3:4*

41   Giving honor unto the wife, as unto the weaker vessel.   *3:7*

1   Charity shall cover the multitude of sins.

I Peter 4:8

2   A crown of glory that fadeth not away.   *5:4*

3   Be sober, be vigilant; because your adversary the devil, as a roaring lion, walketh about, seeking whom he may devour.   *5:8*

4   And the day star arise in your hearts.
The Second Epistle General of Peter 1:19

5   The dog is turned to his own vomit again.   *2:22*

6   God is light, and in him is no darkness at all.
The First Epistle General of John 1:5

7   If we say that we have no sin, we deceive ourselves, and the truth is not in us.   *1:8*

8   If any man sin, we have an advocate with the Father, Jesus Christ the righteous:

And he is the propitiation for our sins: and not for ours only, but also for the sins of the whole world.   *2:1–2*

9   He is antichrist, that denieth the Father and the Son.   *2:22*

10   Whoso hath this world's good, and seeth his brother have need, and shutteth up his bowels of compassion from him, how dwelleth the love of God in him?   *3:17*

11   He that loveth not, knoweth not God; for God is love.   *4:8*

12   There is no fear in love; but perfect love casteth out fear.   *4:18*

13   Raging waves of the sea, foaming out their own shame; wandering stars, to whom is reserved the blackness of darkness for ever.
The General Epistle of Jude 13

14   I John, who also am your brother, and companion in tribulation, and in the kingdom and patience of Jesus Christ, was in the isle that is called Patmos, for the word of God, and for the testimony of Jesus Christ.
The Revelation of Saint John the Divine 1:9

15   What thou seest, write in a book, and send it unto the seven churches which are in Asia.   *1:11*

16   And being turned, I saw seven golden candlesticks.   *1:12*

17   His feet like unto fine brass, as if they burned in a furnace; and his voice as the sound of many waters.   *1:15*

18   When I saw him, I fell at his feet as dead.   *1:17*

19   I am he that liveth, and was dead; and, behold, I am alive for evermore, Amen; and have the keys of hell and of death.   *1:18*

20   I have somewhat against thee, because thou hast left thy first love.   *2:4*

21   To him that overcometh will I give to eat of the tree of life.   *2:7*

22   Be thou faithful unto death, and I will give thee a crown of life.   *2:10*

23   He shall rule them with a rod of iron.   *2:27*

24   I will give him the morning star.   *2:28*

25   I will not blot out his name out of the book of life.   *3:5*

26   I know thy works, that thou art neither cold nor hot: I would thou wert cold or hot.

So then because thou art lukewarm, and neither cold nor hot, I will spew thee out of my mouth.   *3:15–16*

27   Behold, I stand at the door, and knock.   *3:20*

28   The first beast was like a lion, and the second beast like a calf, and the third beast had a face as a man, and the fourth beast was like a flying eagle.

And the four beasts had each of them six wings about him; and they were full of eyes within: and they rest not day and night, saying, Holy, holy, holy, Lord God Almighty, which was, and is, and is to come.   *4:7–8*

29   Thou hast created all things, and for thy pleasure they are and were created.   *4:11*

30   A book . . . sealed with seven seals.   *5:1*

31   He went forth conquering, and to conquer.   *6:2*

32   Behold a pale horse: and his name that sat on him was Death, and Hell followed with him.   *6:8*

33   Four angels standing on the four corners of the earth, holding the four winds of the earth.   *7:1*

34   Hurt not the earth, neither the sea, nor the trees.   *7:3*

35   All nations, and kindreds, and people, and tongues.   *7:9*

36   These are they which came out of great tribulation, and have washed their robes, and made them white in the blood of the lamb.   *7:14*

37   They shall hunger no more, neither thirst any more; neither shall the sun light on them, nor any heat.   *7:16*

38   The name of the star is called Wormwood.   *8:11*

39   The kingdoms of this world are become the kingdoms of our Lord and of his Christ.   *11:15*

1   There was war in heaven: Michael and his angels fought against the dragon; and the dragon fought and his angels,

    And prevailed not.   *12:7–8*

2   The great dragon was cast out, that old serpent, called the Devil, and Satan, which deceiveth the whole world.   *12:9*

3   No man might buy or sell, save he that had the mark, or the name of the beast.   *13:17*

4   The voice of many waters.   *14:2*

5   Babylon is fallen, is fallen, that great city.   *14:8*

6   Blessed are the dead which die in the Lord . . . that they may rest from their labours.   *14:13*

7   And he gathered them together into a place called in the Hebrew tongue Armageddon.   *16:16*

8   He is Lord of lords, and King of kings.   *17:14*

9   He treadeth the winepress of the fierceness and wrath of Almighty God.   *19:15*

10   Another book was opened, which is the book of life.   *20:12*

11   I saw a new heaven and a new earth: for the first heaven and the first earth were passed away; and there was no more sea.

    And I John saw the holy city, new Jerusalem, coming down from God out of heaven, prepared as a bride adorned for her husband.   *21:1–2*

12   God shall wipe away all tears from their eyes; and there shall be no more death, neither sorrow, nor crying, neither shall there be any more pain: for the former things are passed away.   *21:4*

13   There shall be no night there.   *22:5*

14   He that is unjust, let him be unjust still: and he which is filthy, let him be filthy still: and he that is righteous, let him be righteous still: and he that is holy, let him be holy still.

    And, behold, I come quickly.   *22:11–12*

15   I am Alpha and Omega, the beginning and the end, the first and the last.   *22:13*

The Roman Missal[1]

16   Introibo ad altare Dei [I will go in to the altar of God].   *Antiphon*

17   Mea culpa, mea culpa, mea maxima culpa [Through my fault, through my fault, through my most grievous fault].   *Confession of Sins*

18   Dominus vobiscum [The Lord be with you].
Et cum spiritu tuo [And with your spirit].
     Antiphon

19   Requiem aeternam dona eis, Domine: et lux perpetua luceat eis [Eternal rest give them, O Lord: and let perpetual light shine upon them].
    Mass for the Dead

20   Dies irae, dies illa / Solvet saeclum in favilla / Teste David cum Sibylla [Day of wrath, that day, the earth will dissolve in ashes, as David and the Sibyl say].[2]   *Mass for the Dead*

21   Kyrie eleison [Lord, have mercy on us].
    Kyrie

22   Gloria in excelsis Deo. Et in terra pax hominibus bonae voluntatis [Glory to God in the highest. And on earth peace to men of good will].   *Gloria*

23   Agnus Dei, qui tollis peccata mundi, miserere nobis; Agnus Dei, qui tollis peccata mundi, miserere nobis; Agnus Dei, qui tollis peccata mundi, dona nobis pacem [Lamb of God, who takes away the sins of the world, have mercy on us; Lamb of God, who takes away the sins of the world, give us peace].
    Communion

24   Hoc est enim Corpus meum [For this is My Body].   *Consecration*

25   Hic est enim calix Sanguinis mei, novi et aeterni testamenti: mysterium fidei: qui pro vobis et pro multis effundetur in remissionem peccatorum [For this is the chalice of My Blood, of the new and eternal covenant; the mystery of faith; which shall be shed for you and for many unto the forgiveness of sins].
    Consecration

26   O felix culpa, quae talem ac tantum meruit habere Redemptorem [O happy fault, which has deserved to have such and so mighty a Redeemer].[3]
    Exsultet on Holy Saturday

The Book of Common Prayer [American][4]

27   Movable feasts.   *Tables and Rules, p. xxxi*

28   Christ is risen. The Lord is risen indeed.
    Morning Prayer, Easter, p. 5

---

[1]The Latin liturgy, regularly used by Catholics until 1964.

[2]Attributed to Thomas of Celano (c. 1185–c. 1255).

[3]Attributed to Saint Augustine and Saint Ambrose.

[4]The Book of Common Prayer of the American Episcopal Church derives from the English Book of Common Prayer; see 49:22–25. First published in 1789, the American version was revised in 1892, 1928, and 1979. *Bartlett's* draws from the 1928 edition, much of which is retained in Rite One of the 1979 BCP.

1   The Scripture moveth us, in sundry places, to acknowledge and confess our manifold sins and wickedness.
Morning Prayer, Minister's Opening Words, p. 5

2   We have erred, and strayed from thy ways like lost sheep.   *Morning Prayer, A General Confession, p. 6*

3   We have left undone those things which we ought to have done; And we have done those things which we ought not to have done.
Morning Prayer, A General Confession, p. 6

4   Have mercy upon us, miserable offenders.
Morning Prayer, A General Confession, p. 6

5   Who desireth not the death of a sinner, but rather that he may turn from his wickedness and live.
Morning Prayer, The Declaration of Absolution, p. 7

6   Let us come before his presence with thanksgiving; and show ourselves glad in him with psalms.   *Morning Prayer, Venite, p. 9*

7   In his hand are all the corners of the earth; and the strength of the hills is his also.
The sea is his, and he made it; and his hands prepared the dry land.   *Morning Prayer, Venite, p. 9*

8   Glory be to the Father, and to the Son, and to the Holy Ghost;
As it was in the beginning, is now, and ever shall be, world without end. Amen.
Morning Prayer, Gloria Patri, p. 9

9   We praise thee, O God.[1]
Morning Prayer, Te Deum, p. 10

10   The noble army of martyrs.
Morning Prayer, Te Deum, p. 10

11   I believe in God the Father Almighty, Maker of heaven and earth:
And in Jesus Christ his only Son our Lord: Who was conceived by the Holy Ghost, Born of the Virgin Mary: Suffered under Pontius Pilate, Was crucified, dead, and buried: He descended into hell; The third day he rose again from the dead: He ascended into heaven, And sitteth on the right hand of God the Father Almighty: From thence he shall come to judge the quick and the dead.
I believe in the Holy Ghost: The holy Catholic Church; The Communion of Saints: The Forgiveness of sins: The Resurrection of the body: And the Life everlasting.   *Morning Prayer, Apostles' Creed, p. 15*

12   Begotten of his Father before all worlds, God of God, Light of Light, Very God of very God;

Begotten, not made; Being of one substance with the Father; By whom all things were made: Who for us men and for our salvation came down from heaven, And was incarnate by the Holy Ghost of the Virgin Mary, And was made man.
Morning Prayer, Nicene Creed, p. 16

13   O God, who art the author of peace and lover of concord, in knowledge of whom standeth our eternal life, whose service is perfect freedom; Defend us thy humble servants in all assaults of our enemies.
Morning Prayer, A Collect for Peace, p. 17

14   O God, the Creator and Preserver of all mankind, we humbly beseech thee for all sorts and conditions of men; that thou wouldest be pleased to make thy ways known unto them, thy saving health unto all nations.   *Morning Prayer, A Prayer for All Conditions of Men, p. 18*

15   We commend to thy fatherly goodness all those who are any ways afflicted, or distressed, in mind, body, or estate.
Morning Prayer, A Prayer for All Conditions of Men, p. 19

16   We, thine unworthy servants, do give thee most humble and hearty thanks for all thy goodness and loving-kindness to us, and to all men; We bless thee for our creation, preservation, and all the blessings of this life; but above all, for thine inestimable love in the redemption of the world by our Lord Jesus Christ; for the means of grace, and for the hope of glory.   *Morning Prayer, A General Thanksgiving, p. 19*

17   Almighty God, who . . . dost promise that when two or three are gathered together in thy Name thou wilt grant their requests; Fulfill now, O Lord, the desires and petitions of thy servants, as may be most expedient for them.
Morning Prayer, A Prayer of Saint Chrysostom, p. 20

18   Lighten our darkness, we beseech thee, O Lord; and by thy great mercy defend us from all perils and dangers of this night.
Evening Prayer, A Collect for Aid Against Perils, p. 31

19   From all blindness of heart, from pride, vainglory, and hypocrisy; from envy, hatred, and malice, and all uncharitableness,
Good Lord, deliver us.   *The Litany, p. 54*

20   From all the deceits of the world, the flesh, and the devil.   *The Litany, p. 54*

21   From battle and murder, and from sudden death.
The Litany, p. 54

---

[1]Te Deum laudamus.

1   Give to all nations unity, peace, and concord.
The Litany, p. 56

2   The kindly fruits of the earth.
The Litany, p. 57

3   Almighty God, unto whom all hearts are open, all desires known, and from whom no secrets are hid; Cleanse the thoughts of our hearts by the inspiration of thy Holy Spirit, that we may perfectly love thee, and worthily magnify thy holy Name.
Holy Communion, The Collect, p. 67

4   Ye who do truly and earnestly repent you of your sins, and are in love and charity with your neighbors, and intend to lead a new life.
Holy Communion, To those who come to receive the Holy Communion, p. 75

5   We acknowledge and bewail our manifold sins and wickedness, Which we, from time to time, most grievously have committed, By thought, word, and deed, Against thy Divine Majesty, Provoking most justly thy wrath and indignation against us. We do earnestly repent, And are heartily sorry for these our misdoings; The remembrance of them is grievous unto us; The burden of them is intolerable.
Holy Communion, General Confession, p. 75

6   Therefore with Angels and Archangels, and with all the company of heaven, we laud and magnify thy glorious Name; evermore praising thee.
Holy Communion, Proper Preface, p. 77

7   And here we offer and present unto thee, O Lord, our selves, our souls and bodies, to be a reasonable, holy, and living sacrifice unto thee.
Holy Communion, The Invocation, p. 81

8   The Peace of God, which passeth all understanding, keep your hearts and minds in the knowledge and love of God, and of his Son Jesus Christ our Lord.   *Holy Communion, Blessing, p. 84*

9   Miserable sinners.
Holy Communion, The Exhortations, p. 86

10   Read, mark, learn, and inwardly digest [the Scriptures].   *The Second Sunday in Advent, The Collect, p. 92*

11   Dost thou, therefore, in the name of this Child, renounce the devil and all his works, the vain pomp and glory of the world, with all covetous desires of the same, and the sinful desires of the flesh, so that thou wilt not follow, nor be led by them?
Holy Baptism, To the Godfathers and Godmothers, p. 276

12   An outward and visible sign of an inward and spiritual grace.
Offices of Instruction, Questions on the Sacraments, p. 292

13   Is not by any to be entered into unadvisedly or lightly; but reverently, discreetly, advisedly, soberly, and in the fear of God.
Solemnization of Matrimony, p. 300

14   If any man can show just cause, why they may not lawfully be joined together, let him now speak, or else hereafter for ever hold his peace.
Solemnization of Matrimony, p. 300

15   Wilt thou ... forsaking all others, keep thee only unto [him; her], so long as ye both shall live?
Solemnization of Matrimony, p. 301

16   To have and to hold from this day forward, for better for worse, for richer for poorer, in sickness and in health, to love and to cherish, till death us do part.
Solemnization of Matrimony, p. 301

17   With this Ring I thee wed.
Solemnization of Matrimony, p. 302

18   Those whom God hath joined together let no man put asunder.
Solemnization of Matrimony, p. 303

19   In the midst of life we are in death.
Burial of the Dead, p. 332

20   Earth to earth, ashes to ashes, dust to dust; in sure and certain hope of the Resurrection unto eternal life.
Burial of the Dead, p. 333

21   The iron entered into his soul.
The Psalter, Psalm 105:18, p. 471

The Book of Common Prayer [English][1]

22   Give peace in our time, O Lord.
Morning Prayer, Versicles

23   Grant that the old Adam in this Child may be so buried, that the new man may be raised up in him.
Public Baptism of Infants, Blessing on the Child

24   To love, cherish, and to obey.
Solemnization of Matrimony

25   With all my worldly goods I thee endow.
Solemnization of Matrimony

---

[1]THOMAS CRANMER [1489–1556] compiled the first official Anglican prayer book [1549], which was known as The Prayer Book of Edward VI and was twice revised [1552, 1559]. The present English Book of Common Prayer was published in 1662. Various alternative prayer books are also widely used in the Church of England.

The Upanishads[1]

c. 800–500 B.C.E.

1 Lead me from the unreal to the real!
Lead me from darkness to light!
Lead me from death to immortality![2]

Brihadaranyaka Upanishad, 1.3.28

2   This Self is the honey of all beings, and all beings are the honey of this Self.[3]

Brihadaranyaka, 2.5.14

3   The gods love the obscure and hate the obvious.[3]

Brihadaranyaka, 4.2.2

4   Da da da[4] (that is) Be subdued, Give, Be merciful.[2]

Brihadaranyaka, 5.2.3

5 If the slayer thinks he slays,
If the slain thinks he is slain,
Both these do not understand:
He slays not, is not slain.[5]

Katha Upanishad, 2.19

6   Om.[6]

Passim

7   Shanti.[7]

Passim

8   The little space within the heart is as great as this vast universe. The heavens and the earth are there, and the sun, and the moon, and the stars; fire and lightning and winds are there; and all that now is and all that is not: for the whole universe is in Him [Atman, the Spirit] and He dwells within our heart.[8]

Chandogya Upanishad, 8.1

Homer

c. 700 B.C.E.

9   Sing, goddess, the wrath of Peleus' son Achilles, a destroying wrath which brought upon the Achaeans myriad woes, and sent forth to Hades many valiant souls of heroes.

The Iliad, bk. I, l. 1

---

[1]Ancient sacred Hindu texts written in Sanskrit.

[2]Translated by F. MAX MÜLLER.

[3]Translated by R. C. ZAEHNER.

[4]The voice of the thunder. The full Sanskrit is: Da da da iti. Damyata datta dayadhvamiti.
"Datta, dayadhvam, damyata" (Give, sympathize, control).— T. S. ELIOT, *The Waste Land, note to line 401*
See T. S. Eliot, 676:17.

[5]See Ralph Waldo Emerson, 425:4.

[6]Om is a sacred syllable used especially to begin and end a scriptural recitation.

[7]Shanti means "peace." T. S. Eliot, in his note to line 434 of *The Waste Land,* says, " 'The Peace which passeth understanding' is our equivalent to this word."

[8]Translated by JUAN MASCARÓ.

---

10   And the plan of Zeus was being accomplished.

Iliad, I, l. 5

11   A dream, too, is from Zeus.   *Iliad, I, l. 63*

12   He knew the things that were and the things that would be and the things that had been before.

Iliad, I, l. 70

13   If you are very valiant, it is a god, I think, who gave you this gift.   *Iliad, I, l. 178*

14   Speaking, he addressed her with winged words.

Iliad, I, l. 201

15   Whoever obeys the gods, to him they particularly listen.   *Iliad, I, l. 218*

16   From his [Nestor's] tongue flowed speech sweeter than honey.   *Iliad, I, l. 249*

17   Rosy-fingered dawn appeared, the early-born.

Iliad, I, l. 477 and elsewhere

18   The son of Kronos [Zeus] spoke, and bowed his dark brow, and immortal locks fell forward from the lord's deathless head, and he made great Olympus tremble.   *Iliad, I, l. 528*

19   The Olympian is a difficult foe to oppose.

Iliad, I, l. 589

20   Unquenchable laughter arose among the blessed gods.[9]   *Iliad, I, l. 599*

21   A councilor ought not to sleep the whole night through, a man to whom the populace is entrusted, and who has many responsibilities.   *Iliad, II, l. 24*

22   Proud is the spirit of Zeus-fostered kings — their honor comes from Zeus, and Zeus, god of council, loves them.   *Iliad, II, l. 196*

23   A multitude of rulers is not a good thing. Let there be one ruler, one king.   *Iliad, II, l. 204*

24   He [Thersites] was the ugliest man who came to Ilium.   *Iliad, II, l. 216*

25   I could not tell nor name the multitude, not even if I had ten tongues, ten mouths, not if I had a voice unwearying and a heart of bronze were in me.

Iliad, II, l. 488

26   Yet with his powers of augury he [Chromis] did not save himself from dark death.   *Iliad, II, l. 859*

27   The glorious gifts of the gods are not to be cast aside.   *Iliad, III, l. 65*

28   Young men's minds are always changeable, but when an old man is concerned in a matter, he looks both before and after.   *Iliad, III, l. 108*

---

[9]Also in *The Odyssey, bk. VIII, l. 326.*

1 Like cicadas, which sit upon a tree in the forest and pour out their piping voices, so the leaders of the Trojans were sitting on the tower. *Iliad, III, l. 151*

2 There is no reason to blame the Trojans and the well-greaved Achaeans that for such a woman [Helen] they long suffer woes. *Iliad, III, l. 156*

3 Words like winter snowflakes. *Iliad, III, l. 222*

4 The sun, which sees all things and hears all things. *Iliad, III, l. 277*

5 Son of Atreus, what manner of speech has escaped the barrier of your teeth? *Iliad, IV, l. 350*

6 Far away in the mountains a shepherd hears their [the warriors'] thundering. *Iliad, IV, l. 455*

7 He lives not long who battles with the immortals, nor do his children prattle about his knees when he has come back from battle and the dread conflict. *Iliad, V, l. 407*

8 Not at all similar are the race of the immortal gods and the race of men who walk upon the earth. *Iliad, V, l. 441*

9 Great-hearted Stentor with brazen voice, who could shout as loud as fifty other men. *Iliad, V, l. 785*

10 He [Axylus] was a wealthy man, and kindly to his fellow men; for dwelling in a house by the side of the road, he used to entertain all comers.[1] *Iliad, VI, l. 14*

11 A generation of men is like a generation of leaves: the wind scatters some leaves upon the ground, while others the burgeoning wood brings forth — and the season of spring comes on. So of men one generation springs forth and another ceases. *Iliad, VI, l. 146*

12 Always to be bravest and to be preeminent above others. *Iliad, VI, l. 208*

13 Victory shifts from man to man. *Iliad, VI, l. 339*

14 May men say, "He is far greater than his father," when he returns from battle. *Iliad, VI, l. 479*

15 Smiling through tears. *Iliad, VI, l. 484*

16 Attach a golden chain from heaven, and all of you take hold of it, you gods and goddesses, yet would you not be able to drag Zeus the most high from heaven to earth. *Iliad, VIII, l. 19*

17 Hades is relentless and unyielding. *Iliad, IX, 1. 158*

18 Hateful to me as the gates of Hades is that man who hides one thing in his heart and speaks another. *Iliad, IX, l. 312*

19 Even when someone battles hard, there is an equal portion for one who lingers behind, and in the same honor are held both the coward and the brave man; the idle man and he who has done much meet death alike. *Iliad, IX, l. 318*

20 To be both a speaker of words and a doer of deeds. *Iliad, IX, l. 443*

21 Prayers are the daughters of mighty Zeus, lame and wrinkled and slanting-eyed. *Iliad, IX, l. 502*

22 A companion's words of persuasion are effective. *Iliad, XI, l. 793*

23 It was built against the will of the immortal gods, and so it did not last for long. *Iliad, XII, l. 8*

24 The single best augury is to fight for one's country. *Iliad, XII, l. 243*

25 There is a strength in the union even of very sorry men. *Iliad, XIII, l. 237*

26 There is a fullness of all things, even of sleep and of love. *Iliad, XIII, l. 636*

27 You will certainly not be able to take the lead in all things yourself, for to one man a god has given deeds of war, and to another the dance, to another the lyre and song, and in another wide-sounding Zeus puts a good mind. *Iliad, XIII, l. 729*

28 It is not possible to fight beyond your strength, even if you strive. *Iliad, XIII, l. 787*

29 She [Aphrodite] spoke and loosened from her bosom the embroidered girdle of many colors into which all her allurements were fashioned. In it was love and in it desire and in it blandishing persuasion which steals the mind even of the wise. *Iliad, XIV, l. 214*

30 Sleep, the brother of Death.[2] *Iliad, XIV, l. 231 and XVI, l. 672*

31 Ocean, who is the source of all. *Iliad, XIV, l. 246*

32 The hearts of the noble may be turned [by entreaty]. *Iliad, XV, l. 203*

33 It is not unseemly for a man to die fighting in defense of his country.[3] *Iliad, XV, l. 496*

---

[1]He held his seat; a friend to human race. / Fast by the road, his ever-open door / Obliged the wealthy and relieved the poor. — ALEXANDER POPE, *translation of The Iliad* [1715]

[2]Sleep, the brother of Death. — HESIOD, *The Theogony, l. 756*
Sleep, Death's twin-brother. — TENNYSON, *In Memoriam, pt. 68, st. 1*

[3]See Horace, 96:26, and Wilfred Owen, 699:5.

1   Of men who have a sense of honor, more come through alive than are slain, but from those who flee comes neither glory nor any help.   *Iliad, XV, l. 563*

2   The outcome of the war is in our hands; the outcome of words is in the council.   *Iliad, XVI, l. 630*

3   But he, mighty man, lay mightily in the whirl of dust, forgetful of his horsemanship.
Iliad, XVI, l. 775

4   Once harm has been done, even a fool understands it.   *Iliad, XVII, l. 32*

5   The most preferable of evils.[1]   *Iliad, XVII, l. 105*

6   Surely there is nothing more wretched than a man, of all the things which breathe and move upon the earth.   *Iliad, XVII, l. 446*

7   Sweeter it [wrath] is by far than the honeycomb dripping with sweetness, and spreads through the hearts of men.   *Iliad, XVIII, l. 109*

8   I too shall lie in the dust when I am dead, but now let me win noble renown.   *Iliad, XVIII, l. 120*

9   Zeus does not bring all men's plans to fulfillment.   *Iliad, XVIII, l. 328*

10   The Erinyes, who exact punishment of men underground if one swears a false oath.
Iliad, XIX, l. 259

11   Not even Achilles will bring all his words to fulfillment.   *Iliad, XX, l. 369*

12   Miserable mortals who, like leaves, at one moment flame with life, eating the produce of the land, and at another moment weakly perish.   *Iliad, XXI, l. 463*

13   It is entirely seemly for a young man killed in battle to lie mangled by the bronze spear. In his death all things appear fair. But when dogs shame the gray head and gray chin and nakedness of an old man killed, it is the most piteous thing that happens among wretched mortals.   *Iliad, XXII, l. 71*

14   Then the father held out the golden scales, and in them he placed two fates of dread death.
Iliad, XXII, l. 209

15   There are no compacts between lions and men, and wolves and lambs have no concord.
Iliad, XXII, l. 262

16   By the ships there lies a dead man, unwept, unburied: Patroclus.   *Iliad, XXII, l. 386*

17   Remembering this, he [Achilles] wept bitterly, lying now on his side, now on his back, now on his face.   *Iliad, XXIV, l. 9*

18   The fates have given mankind a patient soul.
Iliad, XXIV, l. 49

19   Thus have the gods spun the thread for wretched mortals: that they live in grief while they themselves are without cares; for two jars stand on the floor of Zeus of the gifts which he gives, one of evils and another of blessings.
Iliad, XXIV, l. 525

20   Tell me, muse, of the man of many resources who wandered far and wide after he sacked the holy citadel of Troy, and he saw the cities and learned the thoughts of many men, and on the sea he suffered in his heart many woes.
The Odyssey, bk. I, l. 1

21   By their own follies they perished, the fools.
Odyssey, I, l. 7

22   Look now how mortals are blaming the gods, for they say that evils come from us, but in fact they themselves have woes beyond their share because of their own follies.   *Odyssey, I, l. 32*

23   Surely these things lie on the knees of the gods.[2]   *Odyssey, I, l. 267*

24   You ought not to practice childish ways, since you are no longer that age.   *Odyssey, I, l. 296*

25   For rarely are sons similar to their fathers: most are worse, and a few are better than their fathers.
Odyssey, II, l. 276

26   Gray-eyed Athena sent them a favorable breeze, a fresh west wind, singing over the wine-dark sea.
Odyssey, II, 420

27   A young man is embarrassed to question an older one.   *Odyssey, III, l. 24*

28   All men have need of the gods.   *Odyssey, III, l. 48*

29   The minds of the everlasting gods are not changed suddenly.   *Odyssey, III, l. 147*

30   A small rock holds back a great wave.
Odyssey, III, l. 296

31   No mortal could vie with Zeus, for his mansions and his possessions are deathless.
Odyssey, IV, l. 78

32   She [Helen] threw into the wine which they were drinking a drug which takes away grief and passion and brings forgetfulness of all ills.
Odyssey, IV, l. 220

---

[1]Of two evils, the least should be chosen. — CICERO, *De Officiis (On Moral Duties), bk. III, ch. 1*

Of harmes two, the lesse is for to chese. — CHAUCER, *Troilus and Criseyde, bk. II, l. 470*

Of two evils the less is always to be chosen. — THOMAS À KEMPIS, *Imitation of Christ, bk. III, ch. 12*

---

[2]Also familiar as: In the lap of the gods.

1   The immortals will send you to the Elysian plain at the ends of the earth, where fair-haired Rhadamanthys is. There life is supremely easy for men. No snow is there, nor ever heavy winter storm, nor rain, and Ocean is ever sending gusts of the clear-blowing west wind to bring coolness to men.

Odyssey, IV, l. 563

2   Olympus, where they say there is an abode of the gods, ever unchanging: it is neither shaken by winds nor ever wet with rain, nor does snow come near it, but clear weather spreads cloudless about it, and a white radiance stretches above it.[1]

Odyssey, VI, l. 42

3   May the gods grant you all things which your heart desires, and may they give you a husband and a home and gracious concord, for there is nothing greater and better than this — when a husband and wife keep a household in oneness of mind, a great woe to their enemies and joy to their friends, and win high renown.   *Odyssey, VI, l. 180*

4   All strangers and beggars are from Zeus, and a gift, though small, is precious.

Odyssey, VI, l. 207

5   Their ships are swift as a bird or a thought.

Odyssey, VII, l. 36

6   We are quick to flare up, we races of men on the earth.   *Odyssey, VII, l. 307*

7   So it is that the gods do not give all men gifts of grace — neither good looks nor intelligence nor eloquence.   *Odyssey, VIII, l. 167*

8   Evil deeds do not prosper; the slow man catches up with the swift.   *Odyssey, VIII, l. 329*

9   Even if you gods, and all the goddesses too, should be looking on, yet would I be glad to sleep with golden Aphrodite.

Odyssey, VIII, l. 341

10   Among all men on the earth bards have a share of honor and reverence, because the muse has taught them songs and loves the race of bards.

Odyssey, VIII, l. 479

11   Thus she spoke; and I longed to embrace my dead mother's ghost. Thrice I tried to clasp her image, and thrice it slipped through my hands, like a shadow, like a dream.[2]   *Odyssey, XI, l. 204*

12   They strove to pile Ossa on Olympus, and on Ossa Pelion with its leafy forests, that they might scale the heavens.[3]   *Odyssey, XI, l. 315*

13   There is a time for many words, and there is also a time for sleep.   *Odyssey, XI, l. 379*

14   There is nothing more dread and more shameless than a woman who plans such deeds in her heart as the foul deed which she plotted when she contrived her husband's murder.   *Odyssey, XI, l. 427*

15   In the extravagance of her evil she has brought shame both on herself and on all women who will come after her, even on one who is virtuous.

Odyssey, XI, l. 432

16   Therefore don't you be gentle to your wife either. Don't tell her everything you know, but tell her one thing and keep another thing hidden.

Odyssey, XI, l. 441

17   There is no more trusting in women.

Odyssey, XI, l. 456

18   I should rather labor as another's serf, in the home of a man without fortune, one whose livelihood was meager, than rule over all the departed dead.

Odyssey, XI, l. 489

19   Friends, we have not till now been unacquainted with misfortunes.   *Odyssey, XII, l. 208*

20   It is tedious to tell again tales already plainly told.

Odyssey, XII, l. 452

21   The wine urges me on, the bewitching wine, which sets even a wise man to singing and to laughing gently and rouses him up to dance and brings forth words which were better unspoken.

Odyssey, XIV, l. 463

22   It is equally wrong to speed a guest who does not want to go, and to keep one back who is eager. You ought to make welcome the present guest, and send forth the one who wishes to go.   *Odyssey, XV, l. 72*

23   Even his griefs are a joy long after to one that remembers all that he wrought and endured.

Odyssey, XV, l. 400

24   God always pairs off like with like.

Odyssey, XVII, l. 218

25   Bad herdsmen ruin their flocks.

Odyssey, XVII, l. 246

---

[1]The majesty of the gods is revealed, and their peaceful abodes, which neither the winds shake nor clouds soak with showers, nor does the snow congealed with biting frost besmirch them with its white fall, but an ever cloudless sky vaults them over, and smiles with light bounteously spread abroad. — LUCRETIUS, *De Rerum Natura (On the Nature of Things), bk. III, l. 18*

[2]See Virgil, 94:18.

[3]Then the omnipotent Father with his thunder made Olympus tremble, and from Ossa hurled Pelion. — OVID, *Metamorphoses, bk. I, l. 154*

I would have you call to mind the strength of the ancient giants, that undertook to lay the high mountain Pelion on the top of Ossa, and set among those the shady Olympus. — FRANÇOIS RABELAIS, *Works, bk. IV* [1548], *ch. 38*

1   Wide-sounding Zeus takes away half a man's worth on the day when slavery comes upon him.
Odyssey, XVII, l. 322

2   Then dark death seized Argus, as soon as he had seen Odysseus in the twentieth year.
Odyssey, XVII, l. 326

3   The gods, likening themselves to all kinds of strangers, go in various disguises from city to city, observing the wrongdoing and the righteousness of men.
Odyssey, XVII, l. 485

4   Nothing feebler than a man does the earth raise up, of all the things which breathe and move on the earth, for he believes that he will never suffer evil in the future, as long as the gods give him success and he flourishes in his strength; but when the blessed gods bring sorrows too to pass, even these he bears, against his will, with steadfast spirit, for the thoughts of earthly men are like the day which the father of gods and men brings upon them.   *Odyssey, XVIII, l. 130*

5   Men flourish only for a moment.
Odyssey, XIX, l. 328

6   Dreams surely are difficult, confusing, and not everything in them is brought to pass for mankind. For fleeting dreams have two gates: one is fashioned of horn and one of ivory. Those which pass through the one of sawn ivory are deceptive, bringing tidings which come to nought, but those which issue from the one of polished horn bring true results when a mortal sees them.   *Odyssey, XIX, l. 560*

7   Endure, my heart: you once endured something even more dreadful.   *Odyssey, XX, l. 18*

8   Your heart is always harder than a stone.
Odyssey, XXIII, l. 103

9   Therefore the fame of her excellence will never perish, and the immortals will fashion among earthly men a gracious song in honor of faithful Penelope.
Odyssey, XXIV, l. 196

Hesiod
fl. c. 700 B.C.E.

10   With the muses of Helicon let us begin our singing.   *The Theogony, l. 1*

11   They once taught Hesiod beauteous song, when he was shepherding his sheep below holy Helicon.
Theogony, l. 22

12   We know how to speak many falsehoods which resemble real things, but we know, when we will, how to speak true things.   *Theogony, l. 27*

13   On his tongue they pour sweet dew, and from his mouth flow gentle words.   *Theogony, l. 83*

14   Love, who is most beautiful among the immortal gods, the melter of limbs, overwhelms in their hearts the intelligence and wise counsel of all gods and all men.   *Theogony, l. 120*

15   From their eyelids as they glanced dripped love.
Theogony, l. 910

16   There was not after all a single kind of strife, but on the earth there are two kinds: one of them a man might praise when he recognized her, but the other is blameworthy.   *Works and Days, l. 11*

17   Potter bears a grudge against potter, and craftsman against craftsman, and beggar is envious of beggar, and bard of bard.   *Works and Days, l. 25*

18   Fools, they do not even know how much more is the half than the whole.   *Works and Days, l. 40*

19   Often an entire city has suffered because of an evil man.   *Works and Days, l. 240*

20   He harms himself who does harm to another, and the evil plan is most harmful to the planner.
Works and Days, l. 265

21   Badness you can get easily, in quantity: the road is smooth, and it lies close by. But in front of excellence the immortal gods have put sweat, and long and steep is the way to it, and rough at first. But when you come to the top, then it is easy, even though it is hard.   *Works and Days, l. 287*

22   A bad neighbor is a misfortune, as much as a good one is a great blessing.   *Works and Days, l. 346*

23   Do not seek evil gains; evil gains are the equivalent of disaster.   *Works and Days, l. 352*

24   If you should put even a little on a little, and should do this often, soon this too would become big.   *Works and Days, l. 361*

25   At the beginning of a cask and at the end take your fill; in the middle be sparing.   *Works and Days, l. 368*

26   The dawn speeds a man on his journey, and speeds him too in his work.   *Works and Days, l. 579*

27   Observe due measure, for right timing is in all things the most important factor.   *Works and Days, l. 694*

28   Gossip is mischievous, light and easy to raise, but grievous to bear and hard to get rid of. No gossip ever dies away entirely, if many people voice it: it too is a kind of divinity.   *Works and Days, l. 761*

Archilochus
Early seventh century B.C.E.

29   I have saved myself—what care I for that shield? Away with it! I'll get another one no worse.
Fragment 6

1   Old women should not seek to be perfumed.
From PLUTARCH, *Lives, Pericles*[1]

2   The fox knows many things, but the hedgehog knows one big thing.[2]   *Fragment 103*

Mimnermus
c. 650–c. 590 B.C.E.

3   What life is there, what delight, without golden Aphrodite?[3]   *Fragment 1*

The Seven Sages[4]
c. 650–c. 550 B.C.E.

4   Know thyself.
Inscription at the Delphic Oracle.
From PLUTARCH, *Morals*

5   Hesiod might as well have kept his breath to cool his pottage.[5]
PERIANDER. *From* PLUTARCH, *Morals,*
The Banquet of the Seven Wise Men,
sec. 14

6   Every one of you hath his particular plague, and my wife is mine; and he is very happy who hath this only.
PITTACUS. *From* PLUTARCH, *Morals,*
On the Tranquillity of the Mind

7   Nothing too much.[6]
From DIOGENES LAERTIUS,
Lives of Eminent Philosophers, bk. I, sec. 63

8   Do not speak ill of the dead.[7]
From DIOGENES LAERTIUS,
Lives of Eminent Philosophers, I, 70

9   Not even the gods fight against necessity.
From DIOGENES LAERTIUS,
Lives of Eminent Philosophers, I, 77

10   Know the right moment.[8]
From DIOGENES LAERTIUS,
Lives of Eminent Philosophers, I, 79

11   Rule will show the man.
BIAS. *From* ARISTOTLE,
Nicomachean Ethics, bk. V, ch. 1

Solon
c. 638–c. 559 B.C.E.

12   Many evil men are rich, and good men poor, but we shall not exchange with them our excellence for riches.   *Fragment 4*

13   Poets tell many lies.   *Fragment 21*

14   I grow old ever learning many things.
Fragment 22

15   Speech is the image of actions.
From DIOGENES LAERTIUS,
Lives of Eminent Philosophers, bk. I, sec. 58

16   Let us sacrifice to the Muses.
From PLUTARCH, *Morals,*
The Banquet of the Seven Wise Men

17   Until he is dead, do not yet call a man happy, but only lucky.
From HERODOTUS,[9] *The Histories, bk. I, ch. 32*

Stesichorus
c. 630–c. 555 B.C.E.

18   This tale is not true: you [Helen] did not even board the well-benched ships, and you did not go to the citadel of Troy.[10]   *From* PLATO, *Phaedrus, sec. 243*

Alcaeus
c. 625–c. 575 B.C.E.

19   Wine, dear boy, and truth.[11]   *Fragment 66*

20   Wine is a peep-hole on a man.[11]
Fragment 104

21   Let us run into a safe harbor.   *Fragment 120*

---

[1]The "Dryden translation," edited by A. H. CLOUGH.

[2]As phrased by ISAIAH BERLIN. See 757:14.
The fox has many tricks, and the hedgehog has only one, but that is the best of all. — ERASMUS, *Adagia.*

[3]Translated by DOUGLAS E. GERBER.

[4]Sayings throughout antiquity were variously attributed to the figures known as The Seven Sages. The list is commonly given as Thales, Solon, Periander, Cleobulus, Chilon, Bias, Pittacus. See Solon, 55:12.

[5]Spare your breath to cool your porridge. — FRANÇOIS RABELAIS, *Works, bk. V* [1552], *ch. 28*

[6]See Terence, 85:13; Horace, 95:17 and 96:22; Lucan, 106:11; and Anonymous: Latin, 121:1.

[7]The Latin form: De mortuis nil nisi bonum [Of the dead, nothing but good].

[8]Occasionem cognosce.

[9]Herodotus attributed these words to Solon.

[10]Stesichorus allegedly went blind after writing an account of Helen's perfidy to Menelaus in his *Helen,* but he was cured after he composed a palinode denying that Helen ever went to Troy and blaming Homer for the story.

[11]Earliest references to what became the proverb "in vino veritas," "in wine is truth," which was known to Plato (*Symposium, pt. 2, sec. 217*) and to Pliny the Elder (*Natural History, bk. XIV, sec. 141*).
See Anonymous: Latin, 120:29.

Anacharsis

fl. c. 600 B.C.E.

1   [On learning that the sides of a ship were four fingers thick:] The passengers are just that distance from death.[1]

> From DIOGENES LAERTIUS,
> *Lives of Eminent Philosophers*,
> *bk. 1, Anacharsis, sec. 5*

2   [Anacharsis] laughed at him [Solon] for imagining the dishonesty and covetousness of his countrymen could be restrained by written laws, which were like spiders' webs, and would catch, it is true, the weak and poor, but easily be broken by the mighty and rich.   *From PLUTARCH, Lives, Solon*

3   In Greece wise men speak and fools decide.[2]

> *From PLUTARCH, Lives, Solon*

Sappho[3]

fl. c. 612 B.C.E.

4   Deathless Aphrodite on your rich-wrought throne.[4]   *Fragment 1*

5   Equal to the gods seems to me that man who sits facing you and hears you nearby sweetly speaking and softly laughing. This sets my heart to fluttering in my breast, for when I look on you a moment, then can I speak no more, but my tongue falls silent, and at once a delicate flame courses beneath my skin, and with my eyes I see nothing, and my ears hum, and a cold sweat bathes me, and a trembling seizes me all over, and I am paler than grass, and I feel that I am near to death.   *Fragment 2*

6   The stars about the lovely moon hide their shining forms when it lights up the earth at its fullest.

Fragment 4

7   I loved you once long ago, Athis . . . you seemed to me a small, ungainly child.

Fragments 40–41

8   The moon has set, and the Pleiades; it is midnight, and time passes, and I sleep alone.[5]

Fragment 94

---

[1]"How thick do you judge the planks of our ship to be?" "Some two good inches and upward," returned the pilot. "It seems, then, we are within two fingers' breadth of damnation." — FRANÇOIS RABELAIS, *Works, bk. IV* [1548], *ch. 23*

[2]Literally: Anacharsis said [to Solon] that in Greece wise men spoke and fools decided.

[3]Some say there are nine Muses: but they're wrong. / Look at Sappho of Lesbos; she makes ten. — PLATO, epigram 9.506, translated by PETER JAY in his edition of *The Greek Anthology*.

[4]Or "with your intricate charms."

[5]See A. E. Housman, 576:1.

9   Sweet mother, I cannot ply the loom, vanquished by desire for a youth through the work of soft Aphrodite.   *Fragment 114*

10   As an apple reddens on the high bough; high atop the highest bough the apple pickers passed it by — no, not passed it by, but they could not reach it.[6]   *Fragment 116*

11   Hesperus, you herd homeward whatever Dawn's light dispersed: you herd sheep — herd goats — herd children home to their mothers.[7]

Fragment 120

Lao-tzu

c. 604 – c. 531 B.C.E.

12 The Tao [Way] that can be told of is not the eternal Tao;
The name that can be named is not the eternal name.
The Nameless is the origin of Heaven and Earth;
The Named is the mother of all things.
Therefore let there always be non-being, so we may see their subtlety,
And let there always be being, so we may see their outcome.
The two are the same,
But after they are produced, they have different names.
They both may be called deep and profound.
Deeper and more profound,
The door of all subtleties!

The Way of Lao-tzu,[8] ch. 1

13 When the people of the world all know beauty as beauty,
There arises the recognition of ugliness.
When they all know the good as good,
There arises the recognition of evil.

The Way of Lao-tzu, 2

14 In the government of the sage,
He keeps their hearts vacuous,
Fills their bellies,
Weakens their ambitions,
And strengthens their bones,
He always causes his people to be without knowledge [cunning] or desire,
And the crafty to be afraid to act.

The Way of Lao-tzu, 3

---

[6]Describing a young girl before marriage.

[7]Translated by MARY BARNARD.

[8]Translated by WING-TSIT CHAN unless otherwise noted.

1 Heaven and Earth are not humane.
They regard all things as straw dogs.[1]
The Way of Lao-tzu, 5

2 The spirit of the valley never dies.
It is called the subtle and profound female.
The gate of the subtle and profound female
Is the root of Heaven and Earth.
It is continuous, and seems to be always existing.
Use it and you will never wear it out.
The Way of Lao-tzu, 6

3 The best [man] is like water.
Water is good; it benefits all things and does not
compete with them.
It dwells in [lowly] places that all disdain.
This is why it is so near to Tao.
The Way of Lao-tzu, 8

4 To produce things and to rear them,
To produce, but not to take possession of them,
To act, but not to rely on one's own ability,
To lead them, but not to master them —
This is called profound and secret virtue.
The Way of Lao-tzu, 10

5 He who loves the world as his body may be entrusted
with the empire.
The Way of Lao-tzu, 13

6 We look at it [Tao] and do not see it;
Its name is The Invisible.
We listen to it and do not hear it;
Its name is The Inaudible.
We touch it and do not find it;
Its name is The Subtle [formless].
The Way of Lao-tzu, 14

7 It is The Vague and Elusive.
Meet it and you will not see its head.
Follow it and you will not see its back.
The Way of Lao-tzu, 14

8 Manifest plainness,
Embrace simplicity,
Reduce selfishness,
Have few desires.
The Way of Lao-tzu, 19

9 Abandon learning and there will be no sorrow.
The Way of Lao-tzu, 20

10 To yield is to be preserved whole.
To be bent is to become straight.
To be empty is to be full.
To be worn out is to be renewed.
To have little is to possess.
To have plenty is to be perplexed.
The Way of Lao-tzu, 22

11 He who knows others is wise;
He who knows himself is enlightened.
The Way of Lao-tzu, 33

12 [The sage] never strives himself for the great, and
thereby the great is achieved.
The Way of Lao-tzu, 34

13 Tao invariably takes no action, and yet there is
nothing left undone.
Reversion is the action of Tao.
Weakness is the function of Tao.
All things in the world come from being.
And being comes from non-being.
The Way of Lao-tzu, 40

14 The softest things in the world overcome the hardest
things in the world.
Non-being penetrates that in which there is no space.
Through this I know the advantage of taking no
action.   *The Way of Lao-tzu, 43*

15 There is no calamity greater than lavish desires.
There is no greater guilt than discontentment.
And there is no greater disaster than greed.
The Way of Lao-tzu, 46

16 One may know the world without going out of
doors.
One may see the Way of Heaven without looking
through the windows.
The further one goes, the less one knows.[2]
Therefore the sage knows without going about,
Understands without seeing,
And accomplishes without any action.
The Way of Lao-tzu, 47

17 He who possesses virtue in abundance
May be compared to an infant.
The Way of Lao-tzu, 55

18 He who knows does not speak.
He who speaks does not know.
The Way of Lao-tzu, 56

19 The more laws and order are made prominent,
The more thieves and robbers there will be.
The Way of Lao-tzu, 57

20 Tao is the storehouse of all things.
It is the good man's treasure and the bad man's
refuge.   *The Way of Lao-tzu, 62*

21 A journey of a thousand miles must begin with a
single step.[3]   *The Way of Lao-tzu, 64*

22 I have three treasures. Guard and keep them:
The first is deep love,
The second is frugality,

---

[1]Straw dogs were used in sacrifices and then discarded.

[2]I.e., the more one studies, the further one is from the Tao.
[3]Traditional

And the third is not to dare to be ahead of the
  world.
Because of deep love, one is courageous.
Because of frugality, one is generous.
Because of not daring to be ahead of the world, one
  becomes the leader of the world.
> *The Way of Lao-tzu, 67*

1 When armies are mobilized and issues joined,
The man who is sorry over the fact will win.
> *The Way of Lao-tzu, 69*

2 To know that you do not know is the best.
To pretend to know when you do not know is a
  disease.
> *The Way of Lao-tzu, 71*

3 Heaven's net is indeed vast.
Though its meshes are wide, it misses nothing.
> *The Way of Lao-tzu, 73*

4 To undertake executions for the master executioner
[Heaven] is like hewing wood for the master
  carpenter.
Whoever undertakes to hew wood for the master
  carpenter rarely escapes injuring his own hands.
> *The Way of Lao-tzu, 74*

5 The Way of Heaven has no favorites.
It is always with the good man.
> *The Way of Lao-tzu, 79*

6 Let there be a small country with few people....
Though neighboring communities overlook one
    another and the crowing of cocks and barking of
    dogs can be heard,
Yet the people there may grow old and die without
    ever visiting one another.
> *The Way of Lao-tzu, 80*

Epimenides
Sixth century B.C.E.

7   All Cretans are liars.   *Attributed*

Pythagoras
c. 582–500 B.C.E.

8   Friends share all things.
> From DIOGENES LAERTIUS, *Lives of
> Eminent Philosophers,*[1] *bk. VIII,
> sec. 10*

9   Don't eat your heart.
> From DIOGENES LAERTIUS, *Lives of
> Eminent Philosophers, VIII, 17*

---

[1]Translated by R. D. HICKS (Loeb Classical Library).

10   Reason is immortal, all else mortal.
> From DIOGENES LAERTIUS,
> *Lives of Eminent Philosophers, VIII, 30*

Ibycus[2]
fl. c. 580 B.C.E.

11   There is no medicine to be found for a life which
has fled.
> *Fragment 23*

12   An argument needs no reason, nor a friendship.
> *Fragment 40*

Aesop[3]
fl. c. 550 B.C.E.

13   The lamb...began to follow the Wolf in the
Sheep's clothing.
> *The Wolf in Sheep's Clothing*

14   Appearances are deceptive.
> *The Wolf in Sheep's Clothing*

15   Do not count your chickens before they are
hatched.[4]   *The Milkmaid and Her Pail*

16   I am sure the grapes are sour.[5]
> *The Fox and the Grapes*

17   Little friends may prove great friends.
> *The Lion and the Mouse*

18   Slow and steady wins the race.[6]
> *The Hare and the Tortoise*

19   Familiarity breeds contempt.[7]
> *The Fox and the Lion*

20   The boy cried "Wolf, wolf!" and the villagers came
out to help him.[6]
> *The Shepherd Boy and the Wolf*

---

[2]The phrase *the cranes of Ibycus* derives from the legend that Ibycus
was murdered at sea and his murderers were discovered through
cranes that followed the ship. The phrase became a term for the
agency of the gods in revealing crime.

[3]Animal fables from before Aesop's time and after were attributed
to him. The first collection was made two hundred years after his
death. Unless otherwise noted, the quotations derive from
retellings by JOSEPH JACOBS. See also Jean de La Fontaine, 266.

[4]To swallow gudgeons ere they're catched / And count their
chickens ere they're hatched. — SAMUEL BUTLER [1612–1680],
Hudibras, pt. II, canto III, l. 923

[5]The fox, when he cannot reach the grapes, says they are not ripe.
— GEORGE HERBERT, *Jacula Prudentum*
"They are too green," he said, "and only good for fools." — JEAN
DE LA FONTAINE, *Fables, bk. III, fable 11, The Fox and the Grapes*

[6]Traditional.

[7]Familiarity breeds contempt — and children. — MARK TWAIN,
Notebooks [1935]

1   A crust eaten in peace is better than a banquet partaken in anxiety.[1]
The Town Mouse and the Country Mouse

2   Borrowed plumes.
The Jay and the Peacock

3   It is not only fine feathers that make fine birds.
The Jay and the Peacock

4   People often grudge others what they cannot enjoy themselves.
The Dog in the Manger

5   It is thrifty to prepare today for the wants of tomorrow.
The Ant and the Grasshopper

6   Be content with your lot; one cannot be first in everything.   *Juno and the Peacock*

7   A huge gap appeared in the side of the mountain. At last a tiny mouse came forth.[2]
The Mountain in Labor

8   Any excuse will serve a tyrant.
The Wolf and the Lamb

9   Beware lest you lose the substance by grasping at the shadow.   *The Dog and the Shadow*

10   Who shall bell the cat?
The Rats and the Cat

11   I will have nought to do with a man who can blow hot and cold with the same breath.
The Man and the Satyr

12   Thinking to get at once all the gold the goose could give, he killed it and opened it only to find — nothing.   *The Goose with the Golden Eggs*

13   Put your shoulder to the wheel.
Hercules and the Wagoner

14   The gods help them that help themselves.[3]
Hercules and the Wagoner

15   We would often be sorry if our wishes were gratified.[4]   *The Old Man and Death*

16   Union gives strength.
The Bundle of Sticks

17   While I see many hoof-marks going in, I see none coming out.... It is easier to get into the enemy's toils than out again.
The Lion, the Fox, and the Beasts

18   The haft of the arrow had been feathered with one of [the eagle's] own plumes.... We often give our enemies the means for our own destruction.[5]
The Eagle and the Arrow

Theognis
fl. c. 545 B.C.E.

19   One finds many companions for food and drink, but in a serious business a man's companions are very few.   *Elegies, l. 115*

20   Even to a wicked man a divinity gives wealth, Cyrnus, but to few men comes the gift of excellence.   *Elegies, l. 149*

21   Surfeit begets insolence, when prosperity comes to a bad man.   *Elegies, l. 153*

22   Adopt the character of the twisting octopus, which takes on the appearance of the nearby rock. Now follow in this direction, now turn a different hue.   *Elegies, l. 215*

23   The best of all things for earthly men is not to be born and not to see the beams of the bright sun; but if born, then as quickly as possible to pass the gates of Hades, and to lie deep buried.
Elegies, l. 425

24   No man takes with him to Hades all his exceeding wealth.   *Elegies, l. 725*

25   Bright youth passes swiftly as a thought.
Elegies, l. 985

---

[1]Traditional.

[2]A mountain was in labor, sending forth dreadful groans, and there was in the region the highest expectation. After all, it brought forth a mouse. — PHAEDRUS, *Fables, bk. IV, fable 22, l. 1*

[3]God loves to help him who strives to help himself. — AESCHYLUS, *Fragment 223*

Heaven helps not the men who will not act. — SOPHOCLES, *Fragment 288*

Try first thyself, and after call in God; / For to the worker God himself lends aid. — EURIPIDES, first version of *Hippolytus, fragment 435*

Help thyself, and God will help thee. — GEORGE HERBERT, *Jacula Prudentum*

God helps those who help themselves. — ALGERNON SIDNEY, *Discourses on Government, ch. 2, sec. 23,* and BENJAMIN FRANKLIN, *Poor Richard's Almanac* [1736]

[4]Granting our wish one of Fate's saddest jokes is! — JAMES RUSSELL LOWELL, *Two Scenes from the Life of Blondel* [1863], sc. II, st. 2

Beware, my lord! Beware lest stern Heaven hate you enough to hear your prayers! — ANATOLE FRANCE, *The Crime of Sylvestre Bonnard, pt. II, ch. 4*

When the gods wish to punish us they answer our prayers. — OSCAR WILDE, *An Ideal Husband* [1895], *act II*

[5]So in the Libyan fable it is told / That once an eagle, stricken with a dart, / Said, when he saw the fashion of the shaft, / "With our own feathers, not by others' hands, / Are we now smitten." — AESCHYLUS, *Fragment 135*

That eagle's fate and mine are one, / Which on the shaft that made him die / Espied a feather of his own, / Wherewith he wont to soar so high. — EDMUND WALLER, *To a Lady Singing a Song of His Composing*

Anacreon

c. 570–c. 480 B.C.E.

1   Bring water, bring wine, boy! Bring flowering garlands to me! Yes, bring them, so that I may try a bout with love.   *Fragment 27*

2   I both love and do not love, and am mad and am not mad.   *Fragment 79*

3   War spares not the brave, but the cowardly.
    Epigram from the Greek Anthology

Xenophanes

c. 570–c. 475 B.C.E.

4   Homer and Hesiod attributed to the gods everything that is a shame and a reproach among men.
                                                         Fragment 11

5   If cattle and horses, or lions, had hands, or were able to draw with their feet and produce the works which men do, horses would draw the forms of gods like horses, and cattle like cattle, and they would make the gods' bodies the same shape as their own.
                                                         Fragment 15

6   One god, greatest among gods and men, similar to mortals neither in shape nor even in thought.
                                                         Fragment 23

7   It takes a wise man to recognize a wise man.
    From *Diogenes Laertius*, *Lives of Eminent Philosophers, bk. IX*

Simonides

c. 556–468 B.C.E.

8   It is hard to be truly excellent, four-square in hand and foot and mind, formed without blemish.
                                                          Fragment 4

9   The city is teacher of the man.[1]   *Fragment 53*

10 Fighting in the forefront of the Greeks, the Athenians crushed at Marathon the might of the gold-bearing Medes.   *Fragment 88*

11 Go tell the Spartans, thou who passest by,
    That here, obedient to their laws, we lie.[2]
                                                         Fragment 92

12 If to die honorably is the greatest
    Part of virtue, for us fate's done her best.

---

[1]Translated by David A. Campbell.

[2]Translated by W. L. Bowles.
    Epitaph for the Lacedaemonian [Spartan] king Leonidas and his small force at Thermopylae, who all died fighting to hold the pass against the invading Persian army [480 B.C.E.].

Because we fought to crown Greece with freedom
We lie here enjoying timeless fame.
                            For the Athenian Dead at Plataia[3]

13 We did not flinch but gave our lives to save
    Greece when her fate hung on a razor's edge.
                                Cenotaph at the Isthmos[3]

14 Painting is silent poetry, and poetry painting that speaks.
    From *Plutarch*, *Morals*,
    De Gloria Atheniensium, III, 346

Confucius
[K'ung Fu-zi, K'ung the Master]

551–479 B.C.E.

15 A young man's duty is to behave well to his parents at home and to his elders abroad.
                                                     Analects,[4] *1:6*

16 A man who
    Treats his betters as betters,
    Wears an air of respect,
    Who into serving father and mother
    Knows how to put his whole strength,
    Who in the service of his prince will lay down his life,
    Who in intercourse with friends is true to his word — others may say of him that he still lacks education, but I for my part should certainly call him an educated man.   *Analects, 1:7*

17 First and foremost he must learn to be faithful to his superiors, to keep promises, to refuse the friendship of all who are not like him. And if he finds he has made a mistake, then he must not be afraid of admitting the fact and amending his ways.   *Analects, 1:8*

18 He who rules by moral force is like the pole-star, which remains in its place while all the lesser stars do homage to it.   *Analects, 2:1*

19 He who learns but does not think, is lost. He who thinks but does not learn is in great danger.
                                                      Analects, 2:15

20 What is over and done with, one does not discuss. What has already taken its course, one does not criticize; what already belongs to the past, one does not censure.   *Analects, 3:21*

21 I for my part have never yet seen one who really cared for Goodness, nor one who really abhorred wickedness. One who really cared for Goodness would never let any other consideration come first. One who abhorred wickedness would be so constantly doing

---

[3]Translated by Peter Jay in his edition of *The Greek Anthology*.
[4]Translated by Arthur Waley.

Good that wickedness would never have a chance to get at him. *Analects, 4:6*

1 In the morning, hear the Way; in the evening, die content! *Analects, 4:8*

2 In the presence of a good man, think all the time how you may learn to equal him. In the presence of a bad man, turn your gaze within! *Analects, 4:17*

3 Moral force never dwells in solitude; it will always bring neighbors. *Analects, 4:25*

4 He who seeks only coarse food to eat, water to drink, and bent arm for pillow, will without looking for it find happiness to boot. Any thought of accepting wealth and rank by means that I know to be wrong is as remote from me as the clouds that float above. *Analects, 7:15*

5 I for my part am not one of those who have innate knowledge. I am simply one who loves the past and who is diligent in investigating it. *Analects, 7:19*

6 Is Goodness indeed so far away? If we really wanted Goodness, we should find that it was at our very side. *Analects, 7:29*

7 Till you have learned to serve men, how can you serve ghosts? Till you know about the living, how are you to know about the dead? *Analects, 11:11*

8 To go too far is as bad as not to go far enough. *Analects, 11:15*

9 He who is influenced neither by the soaking in of slander nor by the assault of denunciation may indeed be called illumined. *Analects, 12:6*

10 You are there to rule, not to slay. If you desire what is good, the people will at once be good. The essence of the gentleman is that of wind; the essence of small people is that of grass. And when a wind passes over the grass, it cannot choose but bend. *Analects, 12:19*

11 The Duke of Shê asked about government. The Master said, When the near approve and the distant approach. *Analects, 13:16*

12 Imperturbable, resolute, tree-like, slow to speak — such a one is near to Goodness. *Analects, 13:27*

13 The knight of the Way who thinks only of sitting quietly at home is not worthy to be called a knight. *Analects, 14:3*

14 Do not be too ready to speak of it [Goodness], lest the doing of it should prove to be beyond your powers. *Analects, 14:21*

15 A gentleman is ashamed to let his words outrun his deeds. *Analects, 14:29*

16 Meet resentment with upright dealing and meet inner power with inner power. *Analects, 14:36*

17 Neither the knight who has truly the heart of a knight nor the man of good stock who has the qualities that belong to good stock will ever seek life at the expense of Goodness; and it may be that he has to give his life in order to achieve Goodness. *Analects, 15:8*

18 He who will not worry about what is far off will soon find something worse than worry close at hand. *Analects, 15:11*

19 The demands that a gentleman makes are upon himself; those that a small man makes are upon others. *Analects, 15:20*

20 Never do to others what you would not like them to do to you.[1] *Analects, 15:23*

21 He whose wisdom brings him into power, needs Goodness to secure that power. Else, though he get it, he will certainly lose it. *Analects, 15:32*

22 Goodness is more to the people than water and fire. I have seen men lose their lives when "treading upon" water and fire;[2] but I have never seen anyone lose his life through "treading upon" Goodness. *Analects, 15:34*

23 By nature, near together; by practice far apart. *Analects, 17:2*

24 Tzu-chang asked Master K'ung about Goodness. Master K'ung said, He who could put the Five into practice everywhere under Heaven would be Good. Tzu-chang begged to hear what these were. The Master said, Courtesy, breadth, good faith, diligence, and clemency. *Analects, 17:6*

25 He who does not understand the will of Heaven cannot be regarded as a gentleman. He who does not know the rites cannot take his stand. He who does not understand words, cannot understand people. *Analects, 20:3*

Heraclitus
c. 540–c. 480 B.C.E.

26 All is flux, nothing stays still.
*From DIOGENES LAERTIUS,
Lives of Eminent Philosophers, bk. IX,
sec. 8, and PLATO, Cratylus, sec. 402A*

27 Nothing endures but change.
*From DIOGENES LAERTIUS,
Lives of Eminent Philosophers, IX,
8, and PLATO, Cratylus, 402A*

---

[1]See *Matthew 7:12*, 33:18; Aristotle, 77:12; Hillel, 102:27; and the Earl of Chesterfield, 298:5.

[2]These refer to rites of purification and rainmaking.

1   It is wise to listen, not to me but to the Word, and to confess that all things are one.

On the Universe,[1] fragment 1

2   Nature is wont to hide herself.

On the Universe, 10

3   Much learning does not teach understanding.

On the Universe, 16

4   This world . . . ever was, and is, and shall be, ever-living Fire, in measures being kindled and in measures going out.   *On the Universe, 20*

5   God is day and night, winter and summer, war and peace, surfeit and hunger.   *On the Universe, 36*

6   You could not step twice into the same rivers;[2] for other waters are ever flowing on to you.

On the Universe, 41

7   The opposite is beneficial; from things that differ comes the fairest attunement; all things are born through strife.   *On the Universe, 46*

8   Couples are wholes and not wholes, what agrees disagrees, the concordant is discordant. From all things one and from one all things.

On the Universe, 59

9   The road up and the road down is one and the same.   *On the Universe, 69*

10   Man, like a light in the night, is kindled and put out.   *On the Universe, 77*

11   For when is death not within ourselves? . . . Living and dead are the same, and so are awake and asleep, young and old.   *On the Universe, 78*

12   The people should fight for their law as for a wall.   *On the Universe, 100*

13   It is better to hide ignorance, but it is hard to do this when we relax over wine.

On the Universe, 108

14   A man's character is his fate.

On the Universe, 121

Themistocles

c. 528–c. 462 B.C.E.

15   Tuning the lyre and handling the harp are no accomplishments of mine, but rather taking in hand a city that was small and inglorious and making it glorious and great.

From PLUTARCH, Lives, Themistocles, sec. 2

16   The wooden wall is your ships.[3]

From PLUTARCH, Lives, Themistocles, 10

17   Strike, but hear me.[4]

From PLUTARCH, Lives, Themistocles, 11

18   [Of his son:] The boy is the most powerful of all the Hellenes; for the Hellenes are commanded by the Athenians, the Athenians by myself, myself by the boy's mother, and the mother by her boy.

From PLUTARCH, Lives, Themistocles, 18

19   [Of two suitors for his daughter's hand:] I choose the likely man in preference to the rich man; I want a man without money rather than money without a man.   *From PLUTARCH, Lives, Themistocles, 18*

20   I have with me two gods, Persuasion and Compulsion.[5]   *From PLUTARCH, Lives, Themistocles, 21*

21   The speech of man is like embroidered tapestries, since like them this too has to be extended in order to display its patterns, but when it is rolled up it conceals and distorts them.

From PLUTARCH, Lives, Themistocles, 29

22   He who commands the sea has command of everything.

From CICERO, Ad Atticum (Letters to Atticus), bk. X, letter 8

23   [Upon being asked whether he would rather be Achilles or Homer:] Which would you rather be — a victor in the Olympic games, or the announcer of the victor?   *From PLUTARCH, Apothegms, Themistocles*

Aeschylus

525–456 B.C.E.

24   I would far rather be ignorant than knowledgeable of evils.   *The Suppliants, l. 453*

25   "Reverence for parents" stands written among the three laws of most revered righteousness.

The Suppliants, l. 707

26   His resolve is not to seem, but to be, the best.

The Seven Against Thebes [467 B.C.E.], l. 592

27   I pray the gods some respite from the weary task of this long year's watch that lying on the Atreidae's roof on bended arm, doglike, I have kept, marking

---

[1]Translated by W. H. S. JONES (Loeb Classical Library).

[2]Usually quoted as: river.

[3]This was Themistocles' interpretation to the Athenians in 480 B.C.E. of the second oracle at Delphi: "Safe shall the wooden wall continue for thee and thy children." The account appears in full in HERODOTUS, *Histories, bk. VII, ch. 141–143.*

[4]Said in reply to Eurybiades, commander of the Spartan fleet, when he raised his staff as though to strike.

[5]Said to the Andrians, when demanding money from them, to which they replied that they already had two great gods, Penury and Powerlessness, who hindered them from giving him money.

the conclave of all the night's stars, those potentates blazing in the heavens that bring winter and summer to mortal men, the constellations, when they wane, when they rise. *Agamemnon [458 B.C.E.], l. 1*

1 A great ox stands on my tongue.[1]
Agamemnon, l. 36

2 He who learns must suffer. And even in our sleep pain that cannot forget falls drop by drop upon the heart, and in our own despair, against our will, comes wisdom to us by the awful grace of God.
Agamemnon, l. 177

3 She [Helen] brought to Ilium her dowry, destruction. *Agamemnon, l. 406*

4 It is in the character of very few men to honor without envy a friend who has prospered.
Agamemnon, l. 832

5 Only when man's life comes to its end in prosperity can one call that man happy.
Agamemnon, l. 928

6 Alas, I am struck a deep mortal blow!
Agamemnon, l. 1343

7 Death is better, a milder fate than tyranny.
Agamemnon, l. 1364

8 Zeus, first cause, prime mover; for what thing without Zeus is done among mortals?
Agamemnon, l. 1485

9 Do not kick against the pricks.
Agamemnon, l. 1624

10 I know how men in exile feed on dreams of hope. *Agamemnon, l. 1668*

11 Good fortune is a god among men, and more than a god. *The Libation Bearers [458 B.C.E.], l. 59*

12 Destiny waits alike for the free man as well as for him enslaved by another's might.
The Libation Bearers, l. 103

13 For a deadly blow let him pay with a deadly blow: it is for him who has done a deed to suffer.
The Libation Bearers, l. 312

14 What is pleasanter than the tie of host and guest? *The Libation Bearers, l. 702*

15 Myriad laughter of the ocean waves.
Prometheus Bound, l. 89

16 For somehow this is tyranny's disease, to trust no friends. *Prometheus Bound, l. 224*

17 Words are the physicians of a mind diseased.
Prometheus Bound, l. 378

18 Time as he grows old teaches all things.
Prometheus Bound, l. 981

19 God's mouth knows not how to speak falsehood, but he brings to pass every word.
Prometheus Bound, l. 1030

20 On me the tempest falls. It does not make me tremble. O holy Mother Earth, O air and sun, behold me. I am wronged.[2]
Prometheus Bound, l. 1089

Pindar
c. 518–c. 438 B.C.E.

21 Water is best. But gold shines like fire blazing in the night, supreme of lordly wealth.
Olympian Odes, no. I, l. 1

22 The days that are still to come are the wisest witnesses. *Olympian Odes, I, l. 51*

23 If any man hopes to do a deed without God's knowledge, he errs.
Olympian Odes, I, l. 104

24 Do not peer too far. *Olympian Odes, I, l. 184*

25 I have many swift arrows in my quiver which speak to the wise, but for the crowd they need interpreters. The skilled poet is one who knows much through natural gift, but those who have learned their art chatter turbulently, vainly, against the divine bird of Zeus. *Olympian Odes, II, l. 150*

26 I will not steep my speech in lies; the test of any man lies in action.[3] *Olympian Odes, IV, l. 27*

27 The issue is in God's hands.
Olympian Odes, XIII, l. 147

28 Zeus, accomplisher, to all grant grave restraint and attainment of sweet delight.
Olympian Odes, XIII, last line

29 Seek not, my soul, the life of the immortals; but enjoy to the full the resources that are within thy reach. *Pythian Odes, no. III, l. 109*

30 They say that this lot is bitterest: to recognize the good but by necessity to be barred from it.
Pythian Odes, IV, l. 510

31 Creatures of a day, what is a man? What is he not? Mankind is a dream of a shadow. But when a god-given brightness comes, a radiant light rests on men, and a gentle life.
Pythian Odes, VIII, l. 135

---

[1] A proverbial expression of uncertain origin for enforced silence.

[2] Translated by EDITH HAMILTON.

[3] Translated by RICHMOND LATTIMORE.

1   When toilsome contests have been decided, good cheer is the best physician, and songs, the sage daughters of the Muses, soothe with their touch.
Nemean Odes, no. IV, l. 1

2   Words have a longer life than deeds.
Nemean Odes, IV, l. 10

3   Not every truth is the better for showing its face undisguised; and often silence is the wisest thing for a man to heed.   *Nemean Odes, V, l. 30*

4   One race there is of men, one of gods, but from one mother we both draw our breath.
Nemean Odes, VI, l. 1

5   If one but tell a thing well, it moves on with undying voice, and over the fruitful earth and across the sea goes the bright gleam of noble deeds ever unquenchable.   *Isthmian Odes, no. IV, l. 67*

6   It is not possible with mortal mind to search out the purposes of the gods.   *Fragment 61*

7   O bright and violet-crowned and famed in song, bulwark of Greece, famous Athens, divine city!
Fragment 76

8   Unsung, the noblest deed will die.[1]   *Fragment 120*

9   What is God? Everything.   *Fragment 140d*

10   Hope, which most of all guides the changeful mind of mortals.   *Fragment 214*

Anaxagoras
c. 500–428 B.C.E.

11   The descent to Hades is the same from every place.[2]
From DIOGENES LAERTIUS, Lives of Eminent Philosophers, bk. 2, sec. 6

The Pali Canon[3]
c. 500–c. 250 B.C.E.[4]

12   All that is comes from the mind; it is based on the mind, it is fashioned by the mind.[5]
Suttapitaka. Dhammapada, ch. 1, verse 1

13   Avoid what is evil; do what is good; purify the mind — this is the teaching of the Awakened One [Buddha].[5]
Suttapitaka. Dhammapada, 14:183

14   Better to live alone; with a fool there is no companionship. With few desires live alone and do no evil, like an elephant in the forest roaming at will.
Suttapitaka. Dhammapada, 23:330

15   Be lamps [or islands] unto yourselves. Be a refuge unto yourselves. Do not turn to any external refuge. Hold fast to the teaching [dhamma] as a lamp.[5]
Suttapitaka. Mahaparinibbana-sutta, 2:33

16   Decay is inherent in all component things! Work out your salvation with diligence.
Suttapitaka. Mahaparinibbana-sutta, 6:10

17   The law that I have preached . . . and the discipline that I have established, will be your master after my disappearance.[5]
Suttapitaka. Digha Nikaya, II

18   This noble eightfold path . . . right views, right aspirations, right speech, right conduct, right livelihood, right effort, right mindfulness, and right contemplation.[6]
Suttapitaka. Dhammacakkappavattanasutta, verse 4

19   The wise and moral man
Shines like a fire on a hilltop,
Making money like the bee,
Who does not hurt the flower.[7]
Suttapitaka. Singalavada-sutta, Digha Nikaya, 3:180

20   I go for refuge to the Buddha.
I go for refuge to the Doctrine.
I go for refuge to the Order [of monks].
Traditional (liturgical), passim

21   We are what we think, having become what we thought.[8]
Ten Twin Verses, no. 1

22   For hatred does not cease by hatred at any time; hatred ceases by love — this is an old rule.[9]
Twin Verses, no. 5

Pericles[10]
c. 495–429 B.C.E.

23   Wait for that wisest of all counselors, Time.
From PLUTARCH, Lives, Pericles, sec. 18

---

[1]See Horace, 97:14, and Pope, 296:19.
[2]Translated by C. D. YONGE.
[3]The sacred scriptures of Theravada Buddhists.
[4]Ancient Indian literary chronology is conjectural.
[5]Translated by JAN NATTIER-BARBARO.

[6]Translated by T. W. RHYS DAVIDS and H. OLDENBERG.
[7]Translated by WILLIAM THEODORE DE BARY.
A text addressed — exceptionally in the early Buddhist literature — to laity rather than monks.
[8]Translated by PURUSHOTTAMA LAL.
[9]Translated by F. MAX MÜLLER.
[10]See Thucydides, *Funeral Oration of Pericles*, 71:14–72:5.

1   Trees, though they are cut and lopped, grow up again quickly, but if men are destroyed, it is not easy to get them again.

From PLUTARCH, *Lives, Pericles, 33*

Sophocles[1]

c. 495–406 B.C.E.

2 Silence gives the proper grace to women.

Ajax, l. 293

3 Nobly to live, or else nobly to die,
Befits proud birth.[2]   *Ajax, l. 480*

4   Of all human ills, greatest is fortune's wayward tyranny.[2]   *Ajax, l. 486*

5 For kindness begets kindness evermore,
But he from whose mind fades the memory
Of benefits, noble is he no more.[2]   *Ajax, l. 522*

6 Sleep that masters all.   *Ajax, l. 675*

7 I, whom proof hath taught of late
How so far only should we hate our foes
As though we soon might love them, and so far
Do a friend service as to one most like
Someday to prove our foe, since oftenest men
In friendship but a faithless haven find.[3]   *Ajax, l. 678*

8 Men of ill judgment oft ignore the good
That lies within their hands, till they have lost it.[2]

Ajax, l. 964

9 It is not righteousness to outrage
A brave man dead, not even though you hate him.

Ajax, l. 1344

10 For God hates utterly
The bray of bragging tongues.

Antigone[4] *[c. 442 B.C.E.], l. 123*

11   Our ship of state, which recent storms have threatened to destroy, has come safely to harbor at last.

Antigone, l. 163

12   I have nothing but contempt for the kind of governor who is afraid, for whatever reason, to follow the course that he knows is best for the State; and as for the man who sets private friendship above the public welfare — I have no use for him, either.

Antigone, l. 181

13   Nobody likes the man who brings bad news.[5]

Antigone, l. 277

14   Money: There's nothing in the world so demoralizing as money.   *Antigone, l. 295*

15   How dreadful it is when the right judge judges wrong!   *Antigone, l. 323*

16 Numberless are the world's wonders, but none
More wonderful than man.

Antigone, l. 333 (Ode I)

17 It is a good thing
To escape from death, but it is not great pleasure
To bring death to a friend.   *Antigone, l. 437*

18 But all your [Creon's] strength is weakness itself against
The immortal unrecorded laws of God.
They are not merely now: they were and shall be
Forever, beyond man utterly.

Antigone, l. 452

19 Grief teaches the steadiest minds to waver.

Antigone, l. 563

20 All that is and shall be,
And all the past, is his [Zeus's].

Antigone, l. 611 (Ode II)

21 Show me the man who keeps his house in hand,
He's fit for public authority.   *Antigone, l. 660*

22 Anarchy, anarchy! Show me a greater evil!
This is why cities tumble and the great houses rain down,
This is what scatters armies!   *Antigone, l. 672*

23 Reason is God's crowning gift to man.

Antigone, l. 684

24 The ideal condition
Would be, I admit, that men should be right by instinct;
But since we are all likely to go astray,
The reasonable thing is to learn from those who can teach.   *Antigone, l. 720*

25 Love, unconquerable,
Waster of rich men, keeper
Of warm lights and all-night vigil
In the soft face of a girl:
Sea-wanderer, forest-visitor!
Even the pure immortals cannot escape you,
And mortal man, in his one day's dusk,
Trembles before your glory.

Antigone, l. 781 (Ode III)

26 Wisdom outweighs any wealth.

Antigone, l. 1050

---

[1]Sophocles said he drew men as they ought to be, and Euripides as they were. — ARISTOTLE, *Poetics, ch. 25*

[2]Translated by R. C. TREVELYAN.

[3]They love as though they will someday hate and hate as though they will someday love. — ARISTOTLE quoting BIAS [sixth century B.C.E.], *Rhetoric, bk. II, ch. 13*
Translated by R. C. TREVELYAN.
See Publilius Syrus, 100:8.

[4]Translated by DUDLEY FITTS and ROBERT FITZGERALD.

[5]Don't shoot the messenger. — *Saying*

1 There is no happiness where there is no wisdom;
No wisdom but in submission to the gods.
Big words are always punished,
And proud men in old age learn to be wise.
Antigone, l. 1347, closing lines

2 Ships are only hulls, high walls are nothing,
When no life moves in the empty passageways.
Oedipus Rex[1] *[c. 430 B.C.E.], l. 56*

3 How dreadful knowledge of the truth can be
When there's no help in truth!
Oedipus Rex, l. 316

4 The tyrant is a child of Pride
Who drinks from his great sickening cup
Recklessness and vanity,
Until from his high crest headlong
He plummets to the dust of hope.[2]
Oedipus Rex, l. 872

5 The greatest griefs are those we cause ourselves.
Oedipus Rex, l. 1230

6 Time eases all things.   *Oedipus Rex, l. 1515*

7 Look upon Oedipus
This is the king who solved the famous riddle [of the
Sphinx].[3]   *Oedipus Rex, l. 1524*

8 Let every man in mankind's frailty
Consider his last day; and let none
Presume on his good fortune until he find
Life, at his death, a memory without pain.
Oedipus Rex, l. 1529

9   A prudent mind can see room for misgiving, lest
he who prospers should one day suffer reverse.
Trachiniae (Women of Trachis)
[c. 430 B.C.E.], l. 296

10   They are not wise, then, who stand forth to buffet
against Love; for Love rules the gods as he will,
and me.   *Trachiniae, l. 441*

11   Knowledge must come through action; you can
have no test which is not fanciful, save by trial.
Trachiniae, l. 592

12   Rash indeed is he who reckons on the morrow, or
haply on days beyond it; for tomorrow is not, until
today is past.   *Trachiniae, l. 943*

13 Death is not the worst; rather, in vain
To wish for death, and not to compass it.
Electra [c. 418 B.C.E.], l. 1008

14 War never slays a bad man in its course,
But the good always![4]
Philoctetes [409 B.C.E.], l. 436

15 Stranger in a strange country.
Oedipus at Colonus[5] *[c. 406 B.C.E.], l. 184*

16 The good befriend themselves.
Oedipus at Colonus, l. 309

17   The immortal
Gods alone have neither age nor death!
All other things almighty Time disquiets.
Oedipus at Colonus, l. 607

18 Athens, nurse of men.
Oedipus at Colonus, l. 701

19 Not to be born surpasses thought and speech.
The second best is to have seen the light
And then to go back quickly whence we came.
Oedipus at Colonus, l. 1224

20   One word
Frees us of all the weight and pain of life:
That word is love.   *Oedipus at Colonus, l. 1616*

21 It made our hair stand up in panic fear.
Oedipus at Colonus, l. 1625

22 A remedy too strong for the disease.
Tereus, fragment 514[6]

23 Sons are the anchors of a mother's life.
Phaedra, fragment 612

24 To him who is in fear everything rustles.
Acrisius, fragment 58

25 No falsehood lingers on into old age.
Acrisius, fragment 59

26 No man loves life like him that's growing old.
Acrisius, fragment 64

27 A woman's vows I write upon the wave.
Unknown Drama, fragment 694

---

[1]Translated by DUDLEY FITTS and ROBERT FITZGERALD.

[2]Pride will have a fall. — *English proverb* [c. 1509]
A variant is: Pride goeth before a fall.
Pride goeth before, and shame cometh behind. — *Treatise of a Gallant* [c. 1510]
Pride will have a fall; / For pride goeth before and shame cometh after. — JOHN HEYWOOD, *Proverbs, pt. I, ch. 10*
See *Proverbs 16:18, 20:37.*

[3]The riddle of the Sphinx: What creature walks in the morning on four feet, at noon upon two, and at evening upon three? Oedipus solved it: Man as a baby crawls on hands and knees, then strides erect on his feet, and in old age walks with a staff. The Sphinx, a monster with a woman's head and bust and a lion's body with wings, waylaid passers on the road to Thebes to propound the riddle, destroying anyone who failed to guess the answer. Oedipus solved the riddle, the Sphinx destroyed herself, and the grateful Thebans made him king.

[4]Translated by SIR GEORGE YOUNG.

[5]Translated by ROBERT FITZGERALD.

[6]The fragments are from the Everyman edition of *The Dramas of Sophocles.*

Empedocles

c. 490–c. 430 B.C.E.

1   At one time through love all things come together into one, at another time through strife's hatred they are borne each of them apart.   *Fragment 17*

2   The blood around men's heart is their thinking.
     Fragment 105

Euripides[1]

c. 485–406 B.C.E.

3 Never say that marriage has more of joy than pain.
     Alcestis[2] *[438 B.C.E.], l. 238*

4   A second wife
is hateful to the children of the first;
a viper is not more hateful.   *Alcestis, l. 309*

5 A sweet thing, for whatever time,
to revisit in dreams the dear dead we have lost.
     Alcestis, l. 355

6 Oh, if I had Orpheus' voice and poetry
with which to move the Dark Maid and her Lord,
I'd call you back, dear love, from the world below.
I'd go down there for you. Charon or the grim
King's dog could not prevent me then
from carrying you up into the fields of light.
     Alcestis, l. 358

7 Light be the earth upon you, lightly rest.
     Alcestis, l. 462

8   God, these old men!
How they pray for death! How heavy
they find this life in the slow drag of days!
And yet, when Death comes near them,
You will not find one who will rise and walk with him,
     not one whose years are still a burden to him.
     Alcestis, l. 669

9 You love the daylight: do you think your
father does not?   *Alcestis, l. 691*

10 Dishonor will not trouble me, once I am dead.
     Alcestis, l. 726

11 Today's today. Tomorrow, we may be
ourselves gone down the drain of Eternity.
     Alcestis, l. 788

12 O mortal man, think mortal thoughts!
     Alcestis, l. 799

13 My mother was accursed the night she bore me,
and I am faint with envy of all the dead.
     Alcestis, l. 865

14 You were a stranger to sorrow: therefore Fate
has cursed you.   *Alcestis, l. 927*

15 I have found power in the mysteries of thought,
exaltation in the chanting of the Muses;
I have been versed in the reasonings of men;
but Fate is stronger than anything I have known.
     Alcestis, l. 962

16 Time cancels young pain.   *Alcestis, l. 1085*

17 Slight not what's near through aiming at
what's far.   *Rhesus [c. 435 B.C.E.], l. 482*

18 There is no benefit in the gifts of a bad man.
     Medea[3] *[431 B.C.E.], l. 618*

19 When love is in excess it brings a man no honor
nor any worthiness.   *Medea, l. 627*

20 What greater grief than the loss of one's
native land.   *Medea, l. 650*

21 I know indeed what evil I intend to do,
but stronger than all my afterthoughts is my fury,
fury that brings upon mortals the greatest evils.
     Medea, l. 1078

22 We know the good, we apprehend it clearly,
but we can't bring it to achievement.
     Hippolytus[4] *[428 B.C.E.], l. 380*

23 There is one thing alone
that stands the brunt of life throughout its course:
a quiet conscience.   *Hippolytus, l. 426*

24 In this world second thoughts, it seems, are best.[5]
     Hippolytus, l. 435

25 Love distills desire upon the eyes,
love brings bewitching grace into the heart
of those he would destroy.
I pray that love may never come to me
with murderous intent,
in rhythms measureless and wild.
Not fire nor stars have stronger bolts
than those of Aphrodite sent
by the hand of Eros, Zeus's child.
     Hippolytus, l. 525

---

[1] All Greece is his monument, though his grave / Lies in Macedon, refuge of his last days. / Hellas of Hellas, Athens his land, who gave / so much joy by his art, whom so many praise. — THUCYDIDES, *Euripides;* translated by PETER JAY in his edition of *The Greek Anthology*

Sophocles said he drew men as they ought to be, and Euripides as they were. — ARISTOTLE, *Poetics, ch. 25*

[2] Translated by DUDLEY FITTS and ROBERT FITZGERALD.

[3] Translated by REX WARNER.

[4] Translated by DAVID GRENE unless otherwise noted.

[5] Second thoughts, they say, are best. — JOHN DRYDEN, *The Spanish Friar, act II, sc. ii*

Is it so true that second thoughts are best? — ALFRED, LORD TENNYSON, *Sea Dreams* [1864]

1 My tongue swore, but my mind was still unpledged.
Hippolytus, l. 612

2 Would that I were under the cliffs, in the secret
hiding-places of the rocks,
that Zeus might change me to a winged bird.
Hippolytus, l. 732

3 I would win my way to the coast,
apple-bearing Hesperian coast
of which the minstrels sing,
where the Lord of the Ocean
denies the voyager further sailing,
and fixes the solemn limit of Heaven
which giant Atlas upholds.
There the streams flow with ambrosia
by Zeus's bed of love,
and holy Earth, the giver of life,
yields to the gods rich blessedness.[1]
Hippolytus, l. 742

4   In a case of dissension, never dare to judge till
you've heard the other side.
*Heraclidae[2] [The Children of Heracles,
c. 428 B.C.E.] (quoted by* ARISTOPHANES,
Wasps)

5   Leave no stone unturned.
Heraclidae

6   I care for riches, to make gifts
To friends, or lead a sick man back to health
With ease and plenty. Else small aid is wealth
For daily gladness; once a man be done
With hunger, rich and poor are all as one.
Electra[1] [413 B.C.E.], l. 427

7   A coward turns away, but a brave man's choice is
danger.
Iphigenia in Tauris[2] [c. 412 B.C.E.], l. 114

8   The day for honest men, the night for thieves.
Iphigenia in Tauris, l. 1026

9   Mankind...possesses two supreme blessings.
First of these is the goddess Demeter, or Earth —
whichever name you choose to call her by. It was she
who gave to man his nourishment of grain. But after
her there came the son of Semele, who matched her
present by inventing liquid wine as his gift to man.
For filled with that good gift, suffering mankind forgets its grief; from it comes sleep; with it oblivion of
the troubles of the day. There is no other medicine
for misery.
*The Bacchae (Bacchants)[3]
[c. 407 B.C.E.], l. 274*

---

[1]Translated by GILBERT MURRAY.
[2]Translated by RICHARD LATTIMORE.
[3]Translated by WILLIAM ARROWSMITH.

10   Talk sense to a fool and he calls you foolish.
The Bacchae, l. 480

11   Slow but sure moves the might of the gods.
The Bacchae, l. 882

12 What is wisdom? What gift of the gods
is held in glory like this:
to hold your hand victorious
over the heads of those you hate?
Glory is precious forever.   *The Bacchae, l. 877*

13 Humility, a sense of reverence before the sons of
        heaven —
of all the prizes that a mortal man might win,
these, I say, are wisest; these are best.
The Bacchae, l. 1150

14   Yet do I hold that mortal foolish who strives
against the stress of necessity.
Mad Heracles, l. 281

15   The company of just and righteous men is better
than wealth and a rich estate.
Aegeus,[4] fragment 7

16   A bad beginning makes a bad ending.
Aeolus,[4] fragment 32

17   Time will explain it all. He is a talker, and needs no
questioning before he speaks.
Aeolus, fragment 38

18   The nobly born must nobly meet his fate.[5]
Alcymene,[4] fragment 100

19   Man's best possession is a sympathetic wife.
Antigone,[4] fragment 164

20 When good men die their goodness does not perish,
But lives though they are gone. As for the bad,
All that was theirs dies and is buried with them.
Temenidae,[6] fragment 734

21 An old man weds a tyrant, not a wife.[7]
Phoenix (quoted by ARISTOPHANES,
Thesmophoriazusae), fragment 413

22   Every man is like the company he is wont to
keep.[8]
Phoenix (quoted by ARISTOPHANES,
Thesmophoriazusae), fragment 809

---

[4]Translated by MORRIS HICKEY MORGAN.

[5]If there be any good in nobility, I judge it to be only this, that it
imposeth a necessity upon those which are noble, not to suffer their
nobility to degenerate from the virtue of their ancestors. —
BOETHIUS, *The Consolation of Philosophy, bk. III, prose 6, l. 25*

[6]Translated by MORRIS HICKEY MORGAN. The Temenidae are a
mythic people said to be ancestors of Alexander the Great.

[7]Translated by BENJAMIN BICKLEY ROGERS.

[8]Translated by MORRIS HICKEY MORGAN.
Familiar form: A man is known by the company he keeps.

1 Who knows but life be that which men call death,
And death what men call life?

Phrixus,[1] *fragment 830*

2   The gods
Visit the sins of the fathers upon the children.[2]

Phrixus, fragment 970

3   Those whom God wishes to destroy, he first makes mad.[3]   *Fragment*

4   These men won eight victories over the Syracusans when the favor of the gods was equal for both sides.   *Epitaph for the Athenians Slain in Sicily*

Herodotus
c. 485–c. 425 B.C.E.

5   Men trust their ears less than their eyes.

The Histories,[4] *bk. I, ch. 8*

6   A woman takes off her claim to respect along with her garments.   *Histories, I, 8*

7   In peace, children inter their parents; war violates the order of nature and causes parents to inter their children.   *Histories, I, 87*

8   [The Persians] deliberate about the gravest matters when they are drunk.   *Histories, I, 133*

9   It was a kind of Cadmean victory.[5]

Histories, I, 166

10   For great wrongdoing there are great punishments from the gods.   *Histories, II, 120*

11   If a man insisted always on being serious, and never allowed himself a bit of fun and relaxation, he would go mad or become unstable without knowing it.   *Histories, II, 173*

12   It is better to be envied than pitied.

Histories, III, 52

13   Envy is born in a man from the start.

Histories, III, 80

14   Force has no place where there is need of skill.

Histories, III, 127

15   From the foot, Hercules.[6]   *Histories, IV, 82*

16   It is the gods' custom to bring low all things of surpassing greatness.[7]   *Histories, VII, 10*

17   Haste in every business brings failures.

Histories, VII, 10

18   When life is so burdensome, death has become for man a sought-after refuge.   *Histories, VII, 46*

19   Circumstances rule men; men do not rule circumstances.   *Histories, VII, 49*

20   Great deeds are usually wrought at great risks.

Histories, VII, 50

21   Not snow, no, nor rain, nor heat, nor night keeps them from accomplishing their appointed courses with all speed.[8]   *Histories, VIII, 98*

22   The king's might is greater than human, and his arm is very long.   *Histories, VIII, 140*

23   This is the bitterest pain among men, to have much knowledge but no power.   *Histories, IX, 16*

24   In soft regions are born soft men.

Histories, IX, 122

Protagoras
c. 485–c. 410 B.C.E.

25   Man is the measure of all things.

Fragment 1

26   There are two sides to every question.

From DIOGENES LAERTIUS,
Lives of Eminent Philosophers,
bk. IX, sec. 51

---

[1]Translated by MORRIS HICKEY MORGAN.

[2]For the sins of your fathers you, though guiltless, must suffer. — HORACE, *Odes, bk. III, no. vi, l. 1*

The sins of the father are to be laid upon the children. — SHAKESPEARE, *The Merchant of Venice, act III, sc. v, l. 1*

[3]In Boswell's *Life of Johnson* [1791], *vol. II, pp. 442–443* (Everyman edition), this is quoted as a saying which everybody repeats but nobody knows where to find.

Whom Fortune wishes to destroy she first makes mad. — PUBLILIUS SYRUS, *Maxim 911*

When falls on man the anger of the gods, / First from his mind they banish understanding. — LYCURGUS [fl. 820 B.C.E.]

For those whom God to ruin has designed, / He fits for fate, and first destroys their mind. — JOHN DRYDEN, *The Hind and the Panther, pt. III, l. 1093*

Whom the Gods would destroy they first make mad. — HENRY WADSWORTH LONGFELLOW, *The Masque of Pandora* [1875], *pt. VI*

[4]Translated by A. D. GODLEY, with adaptations.

[5]Polyneices and Eteocles, sons of Oedipus and descendants of Cadmus, fought for the possession of Thebes and killed each other. Hence, in a Cadmean victory, victor and vanquished suffer alike.

See also Pyrrhus, 82:10 ("Pyrrhic victory").

[6]Ex pede, Herculem. From AULUS GELLIUS [c. 123–165] (*Attic Nights, bk. I, sec. 1*), who tells how Pythagoras deduced the stature of Hercules from the length of his foot.

See Anonymous: Latin 120:21.

[7]It is the lofty pine that by the storm / Is oftener tossed; towers fall with heavier crash / Which higher soar. — HORACE, *Odes, bk. II, no. x, l. 9*

The bigger they come, the harder they fall. — *Boxing expression attributed to ROBERT FITZSIMMONS* [1862–1917] *and to JOHN L. SULLIVAN* [1858–1918]; *probably predates both*

[8]Neither snow, nor rain, nor heat, nor gloom of night stays these couriers from the swift completion of their appointed rounds. — *Inscription, New York City General Post Office, adapted from HERODOTUS by architect William Kendall* [1913]

Agis

Fifth century B.C.E.

1   The Lacedemonians are not wont to ask how many the enemy are, but where they are.

From PLUTARCH, *Apothegms, Agis*

Socrates[1]

469–399 B.C.E.

2   Often when looking at a mass of things for sale, he would say to himself, "How many things I have no need of!"

From DIOGENES LAERTIUS,
Lives of Eminent Philosophers, bk. II, sec. 25

3   Having the fewest wants, I am nearest to the gods.

From DIOGENES LAERTIUS,
Lives of Eminent Philosophers, II, 27

4   There is only one good, knowledge, and one evil, ignorance.

From DIOGENES LAERTIUS,
Lives of Eminent Philosophers, II, 31

5   My divine sign indicates the future to me.

From DIOGENES LAERTIUS,
Lives of Eminent Philosophers, II, 32

6   I know nothing except the fact of my ignorance.[2]

From DIOGENES LAERTIUS,
Lives of Eminent Philosophers, II, 32

7   Bad men live that they may eat and drink, whereas good men eat and drink that they may live.[3]

From PLUTARCH, *Morals, How a Young
Man Ought to Hear Poems, 4*

8   I am not an Athenian or a Greek, but a citizen of the world.   *From* PLUTARCH, *Morals, On Banishment*

9   Crito, I owe a cock to Asclepius; will you remember to pay the debt?

From PLATO, *Phaedo (Socrates' last words)*

Democritus

c. 460–c. 370 B.C.E.

10   Whatever a poet writes with enthusiasm and a divine inspiration is very fine.   *Fragment 18*

---

[1]Much of Plato, especially in the *Apology* and *Phaedo,* is thought to be direct quotation from Socrates. See Plato, 74:12.

[2]See Milton, 260:5.

[3]He used to say that other men lived to eat, but that he ate to live.
— DIOGENES LAERTIUS, *Lives of Eminent Philosophers, Socrates, sec. 14*
We must eat to live, and not live to eat. — MOLIÈRE, *The Miser, act III, sc. v*

11   In truth we know nothing, for truth lies in the depth.   *Fragment 117*

12   By convention there is color, by convention sweetness, by convention bitterness, but in reality there are atoms and space.   *Fragment 125*

13   Word is a shadow of deed.   *Fragment 145*

Hippocrates

c. 460–377 B.C.E.

14   I swear by Apollo Physician, by Asclepius, by Health, by Panacea, and by all the gods and goddesses, making them my witnesses, that I will carry out, according to my ability and judgment, this oath and this indenture. . . . I will use treatment to help the sick according to my ability and judgment, but never with a view to injury and wrongdoing. Neither will I administer a poison to anybody when asked to do so, nor will I suggest such a course. Similarly, I will not give to a woman a pessary to cause abortion. I will keep pure and holy both my life and my art. . . . In whatsoever houses I enter, I will enter to help the sick, and I will abstain from all intentional wrongdoing and harm, especially from abusing the bodies of man or woman, bond or free. And whatsoever I shall see or hear in the course of my profession in my intercourse with men, if it be what should not be published abroad, I will never divulge, holding such things to be holy secrets. Now if I carry out this oath, and break it not, may I gain forever reputation among all men for my life and for my art.

The Physician's Oath[4]

15   As to diseases make a habit of two things — to help, or at least, to do no harm.[5]

Epidemics, bk. I, ch. 11

16   Healing is a matter of time, but it is sometimes also a matter of opportunity.   *Precepts,*[6] *ch. 1*

17   Time is that wherein there is opportunity, and opportunity is that wherein there is no great time.

Precepts, 1

18   Sometimes give your services for nothing, calling to mind a previous benefaction or present satisfaction. And if there be an opportunity of serving one who is a stranger in financial straits, give full assistance to all such. For where there is love of man, there is also love of the art. For some patients, though conscious that their condition is perilous, recover their health simply through their contentment with the

---

[4]Translated by W. H. S. JONES (Loeb Classical Library).

[5]Often cited in Latin: primum non nocere.
See Florence Nightingale, 489:6.

[6]Translated by W. H. S. JONES (Loeb Classical Library).

goodness of the physician. And it is well to superintend the sick to make them well, to care for the healthy to keep them well, also to care for one's own self, so as to observe what is seemly.   *Precepts, 6*

1   Opposites are cures for opposites.
Breaths, bk. I

2   Medicine is the most distinguished of all the arts, but through the ignorance of those who practice it, and of those who casually judge such practitioners, it is now of all the arts by far the least esteemed.
Law, bk. I

3   There are in fact two things, science and opinion; the former begets knowledge, the latter ignorance.
Law, IV

4   Idleness and lack of occupation tend — nay are dragged — towards evil.   *Decorum, bk. I*

5   A wise man should consider that health is the greatest of human blessings, and learn how by his own thought to derive benefit from his illnesses.
Regimen in Health,[1] *bk. IX*

6   Life is short, the art long,[2] opportunity fleeting, experiment treacherous, judgment difficult.
Aphorisms,[1] *sec. I, 1*

7   For extreme diseases extreme strictness of treatment is most efficacious.   *Aphorisms, I, 6*

8   Many admire, few know.
Regimen,[1] *bk. I, sec. 24*

9   Male and female have the power to fuse into one solid, both because both are nourished in both and because soul is the same thing in all living creatures, although the body of each is different.
Regimen, I, 28

10   Prayer indeed is good, but while calling on the gods a man should himself lend a hand.
Regimen, IV, 87

Thucydides
c. 460–400 B.C.E.

11   Thucydides, an Athenian, wrote the history of the war between the Peloponnesians and the Athenians; he began at the moment that it broke out, believing that it would be a great war, and more memorable than any that had preceded it.
The History of the Peloponnesian War[3]
[431–413 B.C.E.], bk. I, sec. 1

---

[1]Translated by W. H. S. Jones (Loeb Classical Library).

[2]*Vita brevis est, ars longa.* — Seneca, *De Brevitate Vitae (On the Shortness of Life), ch. I, sec. 1*

[3]Translated by Richard Livingstone unless otherwise noted.

12   With reference to the narrative of events, far from permitting myself to derive it from the first source that came to hand, I did not even trust my own impressions, but it rests partly on what I saw myself, partly on what others saw for me, the accuracy of the report being always tried by the most severe and detailed tests possible. My conclusions have cost me some labor from the want of coincidence between accounts of the same occurrences by different eyewitnesses, arising sometimes from imperfect memory, sometimes from undue partiality for one side or the other. The absence of romance in my history will, I fear, detract somewhat from its interest; but I shall be content if it is judged useful by those inquirers who desire an exact knowledge of the past as an aid to the interpretation of the future, which in the course of human things must resemble if it does not reflect it. My history has been composed to be an everlasting possession, not the showpiece of an hour.   *Peloponnesian War, I, 22*

13   The great wish of some is to avenge themselves on some particular enemy, the great wish of others to save their own pocket. Slow in assembling, they devote a very small fraction of the time to the consideration of any public object, most of it to the prosecution of their own objects. Meanwhile each fancies that no harm will come of his neglect, that it is the business of somebody else to look after this or that for him; and so, by the same notion being entertained by all separately, the common cause imperceptibly decays.   *Peloponnesian War, I, 141*

14   Our constitution is named a democracy, because it is in the hands not of the few but of the many. But our laws secure equal justice for all in their private disputes, and our public opinion welcomes and honors talent in every branch of achievement, not for any sectional reason but on grounds of excellence alone. And as we give free play to all in our public life, so we carry the same spirit into our daily relations with one another.... Open and friendly in our private intercourse, in our public acts we keep strictly within the control of law. We acknowledge the restraint of reverence; we are obedient to whomsoever is set in authority, and to the laws, more especially to those which offer protection to the oppressed and those unwritten ordinances whose transgression brings admitted shame.
Peloponnesian War, II, 37
(Funeral Oration of Pericles)

15   We are lovers of beauty without extravagance, and lovers of wisdom without unmanliness. Wealth to us is not mere material for vainglory but an opportunity for achievement; and poverty we think it no disgrace to acknowledge but a real degradation to make no effort to overcome.   *Peloponnesian War, II, 40*

1   But the bravest are surely those who have the clearest vision of what is before them, glory and danger alike, and yet notwithstanding go out to meet it.
Peloponnesian War, II, 40

2   We secure our friends not by accepting favors but by doing them.[1]
Peloponnesian War, II, 40

3   In a word I claim that our city as a whole is an education to Greece.
Peloponnesian War, II, 41

4   Fix your eyes on the greatness of Athens as you have it before you day by day, fall in love with her, and when you feel her great, remember that this greatness was won by men with courage, with knowledge of their duty, and with a sense of honor in action ... So they gave their bodies to the commonwealth and received, each for his own memory, praise that will never die, and with it the grandest of all sepulchers, not that in which their mortal bones are laid, but a home in the minds of men, where their glory remains fresh to stir to speech or action as the occasion comes by. For the whole earth is the sepulcher of famous men; and their story is not graven only on stone over their native earth, but lives on far away, without visible symbol, woven into the stuff of other men's lives. For you now it remains to rival what they have done and, knowing the secret of happiness to be freedom and the secret of freedom a brave heart, not idly to stand aside from the enemy's onset.
Peloponnesian War, II, 43

5   Great is the glory of the woman who occasions the least talk among men, whether of praise or of blame.   *Peloponnesian War, II, 45*

6   We should realize that a city is better off with bad laws, so long as they remain fixed, than with good laws that are constantly being altered, that lack of learning combined with sound common sense is more helpful than the kind of cleverness that gets out of hand, and that as a general rule states are better governed by the man in the street than by intellectuals.[2]
Peloponnesian War, III, 37
(Address of Cleon to the Athenians)

7   You know as well as we do that right, as the world goes, is only in question between equals in power, while the strong do what they can and the weak suffer what they must.[3]
Peloponnesian War, V, 17

8   Men make the city, and not walls or ships without men in them.
Peloponnesian War, VII, 77
(Address of Nicias to the Athenians at Syracuse)

9   This was the greatest event in the war, or, in my opinion, in Greek history; at once most glorious to the victors and most calamitous to the conquered. They were beaten at all points and altogether; their sufferings in every way were great. They were totally destroyed — their fleet, their army, everything — and few out of many returned home. So ended the Sicilian expedition.
Peloponnesian War, VIII, 87

Aristophanes
c. 450–385 B.C.E.

10 For then, in wrath, the Olympian Pericles
Thundered and lightened, and confounded Hellas
Enacting laws which ran like drinking songs.[4]
Acharnians [425 B.C.E.], l. 530

11 When men drink, then they are rich and successful
and win lawsuits and are happy and help their
friends.
Quickly, bring me a beaker of wine, so that I may wet
my mind and say something clever.
Knights [424 B.C.E.], ll. 92–95

12 You have all the characteristics of a popular politician:
a horrible voice, bad breeding, and a vulgar
manner.   *Knights, l. 217*

13 To make the worse appear the better reason.
Clouds [423 B.C.E.], l. 114 and elsewhere

14 Haven't you sometimes seen a cloud that looked like
a centaur?
Or a leopard perhaps? Or a wolf? Or a bull?[5]
Clouds, l. 346

15 Old men are children for a second time.
Clouds, l. 1417

16 This is what extremely grieves us, that a man who
never fought
Should contrive our fees to pilfer, one who for his
native land
Never to this day had oar, or lance, or blister in his
hand.
Wasps[4] [422 B.C.E.], l. 1117

17 You cannot teach a crab to walk straight.
Peace [421 B.C.E.], l. 1083

---

[1] Rather by conferring than by accepting favors, they [the Romans] established friendly relations. — SALLUST, *The War with Catiline, sec. 6*

[2] Translated by REX WARNER.

[3] Translated by RICHARD CRAWLEY.

---

[4] Translated by BENJAMIN BICKLEY ROGERS (Loeb Classical Library).

[5] Translated by DUDLEY FITTS.

1 [On the nightingale:] Lord Zeus, listen to the little bird's voice; he has filled the whole thicket with honeyed song.

Birds [414 B.C.E.], l. 223

2 Bringing owls to Athens.

Birds, l. 301

3 The wise learn many things from their enemies.

Birds, l. 375

4 Full of wiles, full of guile, at all times, in all ways, Are the children of Men.[1]

Birds, l. 451

5 Mankind, fleet of life, like tree leaves, weak creatures of clay, unsubstantial as shadows, wingless, ephemeral, wretched, mortal and dreamlike.

Birds, l. 685

6 Somewhere, what with all these clouds, and all this air,
There must be a rare name, somewhere . . . How do you like "Cloud-Cuckoo-Land"?[1]

Birds, l. 817

7 Halcyon days.[2]

Birds, l. 1594

8 A woman's time of opportunity is short, and if she doesn't seize it, no one wants to marry her, and she sits watching for omens.

Lysistrata [411 B.C.E.], l. 596

9 There is no animal more invincible than a woman, nor fire either, nor any wildcat so ruthless.

Lysistrata, l. 1014

10 These impossible women! How they do get around us!
The poet was right: can't live with them, or without them![1]

Lysistrata, l. 1038

11 Under every stone lurks a politician.[3]

Thesmophoriazusae (Women of the Festival) [410 B.C.E.], l. 530

12 There's nothing worse in the world than shameless woman — save some other woman.

Thesmophoriazusae, l. 531

13 Shall I crack any of those old jokes, master, At which the audience never fail to laugh?

Frogs[1] [405 B.C.E.], l. 1

14 Brekekekex, ko-ax, ko-ax.

Frogs, l. 209 and elsewhere

15 A savage-creating stubborn-pulling fellow, Uncurbed, unfettered, uncontrolled of speech, Unperiphrastic, bombastiloquent.[4]

Frogs, l. 837

16 High thoughts must have high language.

Frogs, l. 1058

17 Who knows whether living is dying, and breathing Is eating, and sleeping is a wool blanket?

Frogs, l. 1477

18 I am amazed that anyone who has made a fortune should send for his friends.

Plutus [c. 388 B.C.E.], l. 340

19 Even if you persuade me, you won't persuade me.

Plutus, l. 600

20 A man's homeland is wherever he prospers.

Plutus, l. 1151

Agathon

c. 448–400 B.C.E.

21 This only is denied to God: the power to undo the past.

From Aristotle, Nicomachean Ethics, bk. VI, ch. 2

Agesilaus

444–400 B.C.E.

22 If all men were just, there would be no need of valor. *From Plutarch, Lives, Agesilaus, sec. 23*

23 It is circumstance and proper timing that give an action its character and make it either good or bad.

From Plutarch, Lives, Agesilaus, 36

Xenophon

c. 430–c. 355 B.C.E.

24 Apollo said that everyone's true worship was that which he found in use in the place where he chanced to be.

Recollections of Socrates, bk. I, ch. 3, sec. 1

25 The sea! The sea![5]

Anabasis, bk. IV, ch. 7, sec. 24

26 I knew my son was mortal.[6]

From Diogenes Laertius, Lives of Eminent Philosophers, bk. II, sec. 55

---

[1]Translated by Dudley Fitts.

[2]The appellation of Halcyon days, which was applied to a rare and bloodless week of repose. — Edward Gibbon, *History of the Decline and Fall of the Roman Empire*, ch. 48

[3]A play on the proverb: Under every stone lurks a scorpion.

[4]Refers to Aeschylus.

[5]Thalatta! Thalatta! / Hail to thee, O Sea, ageless and eternal! — Heinrich Heine, *The North Sea*, cycle 2, Greeting to the Sea, st. 1

[6]When his son was killed in battle.

Zeuxis
fl. 400 B.C.E.

1   Criticism comes easier than craftsmanship.
From PLINY THE ELDER, *Natural History*

Plato[1]
c. 428–348 B.C.E.

2   We who of old left the booming surge of the Aegean lie here in the mid-plain of Ecbatana: farewell, renowned Eretria once our country; farewell, Athens nigh to Euboea; farewell, dear sea.[2]
Epitaph from The Greek Anthology

3   Beloved Pan, and all ye other gods who haunt this place, give me beauty in the inward soul; and may the outward and inward man be at one. May I reckon the wise to be the wealthy, and may I have such a quantity of gold as none but the temperate can carry.
Phaedrus, sec. 279

4   Friends have all things in common.
Phaedrus, 279

5   And the true order of going, or being led by another, to the things of love, is to begin from the beauties of earth and mount upwards for the sake of that other beauty, using these steps only, and from one going on to two, and from two to all fair forms to fair practices, and from fair practices to fair notions, until from fair notions he arrives at the notion of absolute beauty, and at last knows what the essence of beauty is.
Symposium, sec. 211

6   Beholding beauty with the eye of the mind, he will be enabled to bring forth, not images of beauty, but realities (for he has hold not of an image but of a reality), and bringing forth and nourishing true virtue to become the friend of God and be immortal, if mortal man may.
Symposium, 212

7   Socrates is a doer of evil, who corrupts the youth; and who does not believe in the gods of the state, but has other new divinities of his own. Such is the charge.
Apology, sec. 24

8   The life which is unexamined is not worth living.
Apology, 38

9   Either death is a state of nothingness and utter unconsciousness, or, as men say, there is a change and migration of the soul from this world to another... Now if death be of such a nature, I say that to die is to gain; for eternity is then only a single night.
Apology, 40

10   No evil can happen to a good man, either in life or after death.
Apology, 41

11   The hour of departure has arrived, and we go our ways — I to die, and you to live. Which is better God only knows.
Apology, 42

12   Man is a prisoner who has no right to open the door of his prison and run away...A man should wait, and not take his own life until God summons him.
Phaedo,[3] sec. 62

13   Must not all things at the last be swallowed up in death?
Phaedo, 72

14   Will you not allow that I have as much of the spirit of prophecy in me as the swans? For they, when they perceive that they must die, having sung all their life long, do then sing more lustily than ever, rejoicing in the thought that they are going to the god they serve.[4]
Phaedo, 85

15   The partisan, when he is engaged in a dispute, cares nothing about the rights of the question, but is anxious only to convince his hearers of his own assertions.
Phaedo, 91

16   False words are not only evil in themselves, but they infect the soul with evil.
Phaedo, 91

17   The soul takes nothing with her to the other world but her education and culture; and these, it is said, are of the greatest service or of the greatest injury to the dead man, at the very beginning of his journey thither.
Phaedo, 107

18   He who is of a calm and happy nature will hardly feel the pressure of age, but to him who is of an opposite disposition youth and age are equally a burden.
The Republic, bk. I, sec. 329–D

19   No physician, insofar as he is a physician, considers his own good in what he prescribes, but the good of his patient; for the true physician is also a ruler having the human body as a subject, and is not a mere moneymaker.
Republic, I, 342–D

20   When there is an income tax, the just man will pay more and the unjust less on the same amount of income.
Republic, I, 343–D

---

[1]Translated by BENJAMIN JOWETT unless otherwise noted.

Asclepius cured the body: to make men whole / Phoebus sent Plato, healer of the soul. — *On Plato's Grave*, anonymous inscription translated by WILLIAM J. PHILBIN in *The Greek Anthology* edited by PETER JAY

[2]On the Eretrian exiles settled in Persia by Darius. Translated by J. W. MACKAIL.

---

[3]See Socrates, 70: *n* 1.

[4]The jalous swan, ayens his deth that singeth. — CHAUCER, *The Parliament of Fowls, l. 342*

I will play the swan and die in music. — SHAKESPEARE, *Othello, act V, sc. ii, l. 245*

1   Mankind censure injustice fearing that they may be the victims of it, and not because they shrink from committing it.   *Republic, I, 344–C*

2   The beginning is the most important part of the work.[1]   *Republic, I, 377–B*

3   The judge should not be young; he should have learned to know evil, not from his own soul, but from late and long observation of the nature of evil in others: knowledge should be his guide, not personal experience.   *Republic, III, 409–B*

4   Everything that deceives may be said to enchant.   *Republic, III, 413–C*

5   How, then, might we contrive . . . one noble lie to persuade if possible the rulers themselves, but failing that the rest of the city?[2]   *Republic, III, 414–C*

6   Wealth is the parent of luxury and indolence, and poverty of meanness and viciousness, and both of discontent.   *Republic, IV, 422–A*

7   The direction in which education starts a man will determine his future life.   *Republic, IV, 425–B*

8   What is the prime of life? May it not be defined as a period of about twenty years in a woman's life, and thirty in a man's?   *Republic, V, 460–E*

9   Until philosophers are kings, or the kings and princes of this world have the spirit and power of philosophy, and political greatness and wisdom meet in one, and those commoner natures who pursue either to the exclusion of the other are compelled to stand aside, cities will never have rest from their evils — no, nor the human race, as I believe — and then only will this our State have a possibility of life and behold the light of day.   *Republic, V, 473–C*

10   Let there be one man who has a city obedient to his will, and he might bring into existence the ideal polity about which the world is so incredulous.   *Republic, V, 502–B*

11   Behold! human beings living in an underground den. . . . Like ourselves . . . they see only their own shadows, or the shadows of one another, which the fire throws on the opposite wall of the cave.   *Republic, VII, 515–B*

12   Astronomy compels the soul to look upwards and leads us from this world to another.   *Republic, VII, 529*

13   I have hardly ever known a mathematician who was capable of reasoning.   *Republic, VII, 531–E*

14   Solon was under a delusion when he said that a man when he grows old may learn many things — for he can no more learn much than he can run much; youth is the time for any extraordinary toil.   *Republic, VII, 536–D*

15   Bodily exercise, when compulsory, does no harm to the body; but knowledge which is acquired under compulsion obtains no hold on the mind.   *Republic, VII, 536–E*

16   Let early education be a sort of amusement; you will then be better able to find out the natural bent.   *Republic, VII, 537*

17   Oligarchy: A government resting on a valuation of property, in which the rich have power and the poor man is deprived of it.   *Republic, VIII, 550–C*

18   Democracy, which is a charming form of government, full of variety and disorder, and dispensing a sort of equality to equals and unequals alike.   *Republic, VIII, 558–C*

19   Democracy passes into despotism.[3]   *Republic, VIII, 562–A*

20   The people have always some champion whom they set over them and nurse into greatness . . . This and no other is the root from which a tyrant springs; when he first appears he is a protector.   *Republic, VIII, 565–C*

21   In the early days of his power, he is full of smiles, and he salutes everyone whom he meets.   *Republic, VIII, 566–D*

22   When the tyrant has disposed of foreign enemies by conquest or treaty, and there is nothing to fear from them, then he is always stirring up some war or other, in order that the people may require a leader.   *Republic, VIII, 566–E*

23   There are three arts which are concerned with all things: one which uses, another which makes, a third which imitates them.   *Republic, X, 601–D*

24   No human thing is of serious importance.   *Republic, X, 604–C*

25   The soul of man is immortal and imperishable.   *Republic, X, 608–D*

26   If a person shows that such things as wood, stones, and the like, being many are also one, we admit that he shows the coexistence of the one and many, but he does not show that the many are one or the one many; he is uttering not a paradox but a truism.   *Parmenides, sec. 129*

---

[1]Proverbial. Also in PLATO, *Laws, VI, 2.*

[2]Translated by PAUL SHOREY (Loeb Classical Library).

[3]Translated by FRANCIS CORNFORD.

1   The absolute natures or kinds are known severally by the absolute idea of knowledge.   *Parmenides, 134*

2   If a man, fixing his attention on these and the like difficulties, does away with ideas of things and will not admit that every individual thing has its own determinate idea which is always one and the same, he will have nothing on which his mind can rest; and so he will utterly destroy the power of reasoning.
Parmenides, 135

3   You cannot conceive the many without the one.
Parmenides, 166

4   Let us affirm what seems to be the truth, that, whether one is or is not, one and the others in relation to themselves and one another, all of them, in every way, are and are not, and appear to be and appear not to be.   *Parmenides, 166*

5   Well, my art of midwifery is in most respects like theirs; but differs, in that I attend men and not women, and I look after their souls when they are in labor, and not after their bodies: and the triumph of my art is in thoroughly examining whether the thought which the mind of the young man brings forth is a false idol or a noble and true birth.
Theaetetus, sec. 150

6   He [the philosopher] does not hold aloof in order that he may gain a reputation; but the truth is, that the outer form of him only is in the city: his mind, disdaining the littlenesses and nothingnesses of human beings, is "flying all abroad" as Pindar says, measuring earth and heaven and the things which are under and on the earth and above the heaven, interrogating the whole nature of each and all in their entirety, but not condescending to anything which is within reach.   *Theaetetus, 173*

7   I would have you imagine, then, that there exists in the mind of man a block of wax, which is of different sizes in different men; harder, moister, and having more or less of purity in one than another, and in some of an intermediate quality. . . . Let us say that this tablet is a gift of Memory, the mother of the Muses; and that when we wish to remember anything which we have seen, or heard, or thought in our own minds, we hold the wax to the perceptions and thoughts, and in that material receive the impression of them as from the seal of a ring; and that we remember and know what is imprinted as long as the image lasts; but when the image is effaced, or cannot be taken, then we forget and do not know.   *Theaetetus, 191*

8   Let us now suppose that in the mind of each man there is an aviary of all sorts of birds — some flocking together apart from the rest, others in small groups, others solitary, flying anywhere and everywhere. . . . We may suppose that the birds are kinds of knowledge, and

that when we were children, this receptacle was empty; whenever a man has gotten and detained in the enclosure a kind of knowledge, he may be said to have learned or discovered the thing which is the subject of the knowledge: and this is to know.   *Theaetetus, 197*

9   The greatest penalty of evildoing — namely, to grow into the likeness of bad men.   *Laws, sec. 728*

10   Of all the animals, the boy is the most unmanageable.   *Laws, 808*

11   You are young, my son, and, as the years go by, time will change and even reverse many of your present opinions. Refrain therefore awhile from setting yourself up as a judge of the highest matters.   *Laws, 888*

12   And this which you deem of no moment is the very highest of all: that is whether you have a right idea of the gods, whereby you may live your life well or ill.   *Laws, 888*

13   Not one of them who took up in his youth with this opinion that there are no gods ever continued until old age faithful to his conviction.   *Laws, 888*

Iphicrates
c. 419–348 B.C.E.

14 My family history begins with me, but yours ends with you.[1]
From PLUTARCH, Apothegms, Iphicrates

Phocion
c. 402–317 B.C.E.

15   Have I inadvertently said some evil thing?[2]
From PLUTARCH, Apothegms, Phocion, sec. 10

16   The good have no need of an advocate.
From PLUTARCH, Apothegms, Phocion, 10

Diogenes the Cynic
c. 400–c. 325 B.C.E.

17   [When asked by Alexander if he wanted anything:] Stand a little out of my sun.
From PLUTARCH, Lives, Alexander, sec. 14

18   Plato having defined man to be a two-legged animal without feathers, Diogenes plucked a cock

---

[1]Iphicrates, a shoemaker's son who became a famous general, said this to Harmodius of distinguished ancestry when he reviled him for his mean birth.

Curtius Rufus seems to be descended from himself. — TIBERIUS [42 B.C.E.–37 C.E.]. From TACITUS, *Annals, bk. XI, sec. 21*

[2]Said when an opinion he delivered pleased the people.

and brought it into the Academy, and said, "This is Plato's man."[1] On which account this addition was made to the definition: "With broad flat nails."

> From DIOGENES LAERTIUS, *Lives of Eminent Philosophers, Diogenes, sec. 6*

1   [When asked what was the proper time for supper:] If you are a rich man, whenever you please; and if you are a poor man, whenever you can.[2]

> From DIOGENES LAERTIUS,
> *Lives of Eminent Philosophers, Diogenes, 6*

2   I am looking for an honest man.[3]

> From DIOGENES LAERTIUS,
> *Lives of Eminent Philosophers, Diogenes, 6*

3   The sun too penetrates into privies, but is not polluted by them.[4]

> From DIOGENES LAERTIUS,
> *Lives of Eminent Philosophers, Diogenes, 6*

Antiphanes

c. 388–c. 311 B.C.E.

4   We must have richness of soul.

> *Greek Comic Fragments, no. 570*

Aristotle[5]

384–322 B.C.E.

5   Liars when they speak the truth are not believed.

> From DIOGENES LAERTIUS,
> *Lives of Eminent Philosophers, bk. V, sec. 17*

6   Hope is a waking dream.

> From DIOGENES LAERTIUS,
> *Lives of Eminent Philosophers, V, 18*

7   What soon grows old? Gratitude.

> From DIOGENES LAERTIUS,
> *Lives of Eminent Philosophers, V, 18*

8   Beauty is the gift of God.

> From DIOGENES LAERTIUS,
> *Lives of Eminent Philosophers, V, 19*

9   Educated men are as much superior to uneducated men as the living are to the dead.

> From DIOGENES LAERTIUS,
> *Lives of Eminent Philosophers, V, 19*

10   What is a friend? A single soul dwelling in two bodies.[6]

> From DIOGENES LAERTIUS,
> *Lives of Eminent Philosophers, V, 20*

11   I have gained this by philosophy: that I do without being commanded what others do only from fear of the law.[7]

> From DIOGENES LAERTIUS,
> *Lives of Eminent Philosophers, V, 21*

12   We should behave to our friends as we would wish our friends to behave to us.[8]

> From DIOGENES LAERTIUS,
> *Lives of Eminent Philosophers, V, 21*

13   Education is the best provision for old age.

> From DIOGENES LAERTIUS,
> *Lives of Eminent Philosophers, V, 21*

14   If purpose, then, is inherent in art, so is it in Nature also. The best illustration is the case of a man being his own physician, for Nature is like that — agent and patient at once.

> *Physics,*[9] *bk. II, ch. 8*

15   Time crumbles things; everything grows old under the power of Time and is forgotten through the lapse of Time.

> *Physics, IV, 12*

16   The least initial deviation from the truth is multiplied later a thousandfold.

> *On the Heavens, bk. I, ch. 5*

17   In all things of nature there is something of the marvelous.

> *On the Parts of Animals, bk. I, ch. 5*

18   All men by nature desire knowledge.

> *Metaphysics, bk. I, ch. 1*

19   The final cause, then, produces motion through being loved.

> *Metaphysics, I, 7*

---

[1]Seeing that the human race falls into the same classification as the feathered creatures, we must divide the biped class into featherless and feathered. — PLATO, *The Statesman, sec. 266–E*

[2]The rich when he is hungry, the poor when he has anything to eat. — FRANÇOIS RABELAIS, *Works, bk. IV* [1548], *ch. 64*

[3]Attributed also to AESOP.

[4]The spiritual virtue of a sacrament is like light: although it passes among the impure, it is not polluted. — SAINT AUGUSTINE, *Homilies on the Gospel of John, tractate 5, sec. 15*

The sun shineth upon the dunghill, and is not corrupted. — LYLY, *Euphues, Arber's reprint, p. 43*

The sun, which passeth through pollutions and itself remains as pure as before. — FRANCIS BACON, *Advancement of Learning, bk. II, sec. 1*

Truth is as impossible to be soiled by any outward touch as the sunbeam. — JOHN MILTON, *The Doctrine and Discipline of Divorce*

[5]From *The Basic Works of Aristotle,* edited by RICHARD MCKEON, unless otherwise noted.

[6]Andrágathos, my soul's half. — MELEAGER, *Epigram*

[7]Also attributed to Xenocrates [396–314 B.C.E.] by Cicero.

[8]See *Matthew 7:12,* 33:18; Confucius 61:20; Hillel, 102:27; and the Earl of Chesterfield, 298:5.

[9]Translated by PHILIP H. WICKSTEED and FRANCIS CORNFORD (Loeb Classical Library).

1 The actuality of thought is life.

Metaphysics, XII, 7

2 It is of itself that the divine thought thinks (since it is the most excellent of things), and its thinking is a thinking on thinking. *Metaphysics, XII, 9*

3 Every science and every inquiry, and similarly every activity and pursuit, is thought to aim at some good. *Nicomachean Ethics, bk. I, ch. 1*

4 While both [Plato and truth] are dear, piety requires us to honor truth above our friends.[1]

Nicomachean Ethics, I, 6

5 One swallow does not make a summer.[2]

Nicomachean Ethics, I, 7

6 For the things we have to learn before we can do them, we learn by doing them.

Nicomachean Ethics, II, 1

7 It is possible to fail in many ways... while to succeed is possible only in one way (for which reason also one is easy and the other difficult — to miss the mark easy, to hit it difficult). *Nicomachean Ethics, II, 6*

8 We must as second best... take the least of the evils. *Nicomachean Ethics, II, 9*

9 A man is the origin of his action.

Nicomachean Ethics, III, 3

10 Without friends no one would choose to live, though he had all other goods.

Nicomachean Ethics, VIII, 1

11 To be conscious that we are perceiving or thinking is to be conscious of our own existence.

Nicomachean Ethics, IX, 9

12 To enjoy the things we ought and to hate the things we ought has the greatest bearing on excellence of character. *Nicomachean Ethics, X, 1*

13 If happiness is activity in accordance with excellence, it is reasonable that it should be in accordance with the highest excellence.

Nicomachean Ethics, X, 7

14 We make war that we may live in peace.

Nicomachean Ethics, X, 7

15 With regard to excellence, it is not enough to know, but we must try to have and use it.

Nicomachean Ethics, X, 9

16 Man is by nature a political animal.

Politics, bk. I, ch. 2

17 Nature does nothing uselessly.[3] *Politics, I, 2*

18 He who is unable to live in society, or who has no need because he is sufficient for himself, must be either a beast or a god. *Politics, I, 2*

19 The two qualities which chiefly inspire regard and affection [are] that a thing is your own and that it is your only one. *Politics, II, 4*

20 It is the nature of desire not to be satisfied, and most men live only for the gratification of it. The beginning of reform is not so much to equalize property as to train the noble sort of natures not to desire more, and to prevent the lower from getting more.

Politics, II, 7

21 Even when laws have been written down, they ought not always to remain unaltered. *Politics, II, 8*

22 Again, men in general desire the good, and not merely what their fathers had. *Politics, II, 8*

23 They should rule who are able to rule best.

Politics, II, 11

24 A state is not a mere society, having a common place, established for the prevention of mutual crime and for the sake of exchange.... Political society exists for the sake of noble actions, and not of mere companionship. *Politics, III, 9*

25 If liberty and equality, as is thought by some, are chiefly to be found in democracy, they will be best attained when all persons alike share in the government to the utmost. *Politics, IV, 4*

26 The best political community is formed by citizens of the middle class. *Politics, IV, 11*

27 Democracy arises out of the notion that those who are equal in any respect are equal in all respects; because men are equally free, they claim to be absolutely equal. *Politics, V, 1*

28 Inferiors revolt in order that they may be equal, and equals that they may be superior. Such is the state of mind which creates revolutions. *Politics, V, 2*

29 In revolutions the occasions may be trifling but great interests are at stake. *Politics, V, 3*

30 Well begun is half done.[4] *Politics, V, 4*

31 The basis of a democratic state is liberty.

Politics, VI, 2

32 Law is order, and good law is good order.

Politics, VII, 4

---

[1]Amicus Plato, sed magis amica veritas [Plato is dear to me, but dearer still is truth]. Adapted from a medieval life of Aristotle.

[2]One swallow maketh not summer. — JOHN HEYWOOD, *Proverbs*, pt. II, ch. 5

One swallow makes a summer. — ROBERT LOWELL, *Fall 1961*

---

[3]God and nature do nothing uselessly. — ARISTOTLE, *On the Heavens, bk. I, ch. 4*

[4]Aristotle is quoting a proverb.

1   Evils draw men together.

Rhetoric, bk. I, ch. 6

2   It is this simplicity that makes the uneducated more effective than the educated when addressing popular audiences. *Rhetoric, II, 22*

3   A tragedy is the imitation of an action that is serious and also, as having magnitude, complete in itself . . . with incidents arousing pity and fear, wherewith to accomplish its catharsis of such emotions.

Poetics, ch. 6

4   A whole is that which has beginning, middle, and end. *Poetics, 7*

5   Poetry is something more philosophic and of graver import than history, since its statements are of the nature of universals, whereas those of history are singulars. *Poetics, 9*

6   A likely impossibility is always preferable to an unconvincing possibility. *Poetics, 24*

7   Misfortune shows those who are not really friends.[1] *Eudemian Ethics, bk. VII, ch. 2*

Demosthenes
c. 384–322 B.C.E.

8   Every advantage in the past is judged in the light of the final issue. *First Olynthiac, sec. 11*

9   Nothing is easier than self-deceit. For what each man wishes, that he also believes to be true.[2]

Third Olynthiac, sec. 19

10   You cannot have a proud and chivalrous spirit if your conduct is mean and paltry; for whatever a man's actions are, such must be his spirit.

Third Olynthiac, 33

11   I decline to buy repentance at the cost of ten thousand drachmas.[3]

From AULUS GELLIUS, Noctes Atticae (Attic Nights), bk. I, ch. 8

Antigonus
c. 382–301 B.C.E.

12   But how many ships do you reckon my presence to be worth?[4]

From PLUTARCH, Apothegms, Antigonus

---

[1]In prosperity it is very easy to find a friend, but in adversity it is the most difficult of all things. — EPICTETUS [c. 55–135 C.E.], *Fragment 127*

[2]See Julius Caesar, 88:22.

[3]In reply to the courtesan Laïs.

[4]His pilot had told him that the enemy outnumbered him in ships.

13   [When described by Hermodotus as "Son of the Sun":] My valet is not aware of this.

From PLUTARCH, Apothegms, Antigonus

Mencius [Meng-tzu]
372–289 B.C.E.

14   When one by force subdues men, they do not submit to him in heart. They submit, because their strength is not adequate to resist.

Works,[5] bk. II, pt. 1, ch. 3, v. 2

15   There is no attribute of the superior man greater than his helping men to practice virtue.

Works, II, 1:8.5

16   The superior man will not manifest either narrow-mindedness or the want of self-respect.

Works, II, 1:9.3

17   The root of the kingdom is in the state. The root of the state is in the family. The root of the family is in the person of its head. *Works, IV, 1:5*

18   The people turn to a benevolent rule as water flows downwards, and as wild beasts fly to the wilderness. *Works, IV, 1:9.2*

19   Benevolence is the tranquil habitation of man, and righteousness is his straight path.

Works, IV, 1:10.2

20   The path of duty lies in what is near, and man seeks for it in what is remote. *Works, IV, 1:11*

21   Sincerity is the way of Heaven. *Works, IV, 1:12.2*

22   There are three things which are unfilial, and to have no posterity is the greatest of them.

Works, IV, 1:26.1

23   Men must be decided on what they will not do, and then they are able to act with vigor in what they ought to do. *Works, IV, 2:8*

24   The great man does not think beforehand of his words that they may be sincere, nor of his actions that they may be resolute — he simply speaks and does what is right. *Works, IV, 2:11*

25   The great man is he who does not lose his child's-heart. *Works, IV, 2:12*

26   Friendship with a man is friendship with his virtue, and does not admit of assumptions of superiority.

Works, IV, 2:13.1

27   The tendency of man's nature to good is like the tendency of water to flow downwards.

Works, VI, 1:2.2

---

[5]Translated by JAMES LEGGE.

1   From the feelings proper to it, [man's nature] is constituted for the practice of what is good.
Works, VI, 1:6.5–6

2   Benevolence, righteousness, propriety, and knowledge are not infused into us from without.
Works, VI, 1:6.7

3   Benevolence is man's mind, and righteousness is man's path.   *Works, VI, 1:11.1*

4   The great end of learning is nothing else but to seek for the lost mind.   *Works, VI, 1:11.4*

5   All men have in themselves that which is truly honorable. Only they do not think of it.
Works, VI, 1:17.1

6   When Heaven is about to confer a great office on any man, it first exercises his mind with suffering, and his sinews and bones with toil.   *Works, VI, 2:15.2*

7   Is it only the mouth and belly which are injured by hunger and thirst? Men's minds are also injured by them.   *Works, VII, 1:27.1*

8   The people are the most important element in a nation; the spirits of the land and grain are next; the sovereign is the lightest.   *Works, VII, 2:14.1*

Chuang-tzu
369–286 B.C.E.

9   For all men strive to grasp what they do not know, while none strive to grasp what they already know; and all strive to discredit what they do not excel in, while none strive to discredit what they do excel in. This is why there is chaos.[1]
Opening Trunks; or,
A Protest Against Civilization

10   Great understanding is broad and unhurried; little understanding is cramped and busy. Great words are clear and limpid; little words are shrill and quarrelsome.   *Discussion on Making All Things Equal*[2]

11   Joy, anger, grief, delight, worry, regret, fickleness, inflexibility, modesty, willfulness, candor, insolence — music from empty holes, mushrooms springing up in dampness, day and night replacing each other before us, and no one knows where they sprout from. Let it be! Let it be!
Discussion on Making All Things Equal

12   People suppose that words are different from the peeps of baby birds, but is there any difference, or isn't there?
Discussion on Making All Things Equal

13   All men know the use of the useful, but nobody knows the use of the useless!   *In the World of Men*[2]

14   He who delights in bringing success to things is not a sage; he who has affections is not benevolent; he who looks for the right time is not a worthy man; he who cannot encompass both profit and loss is not a gentleman; he who thinks of conduct and fame and misleads himself is not a man of breeding; and he who destroys himself and is without truth is not a user of men.   *The Great and Venerable Teacher*[2]

15   Be cautious of what is within you; block off what is outside you, for much knowledge will do you harm.   *Let It Be, Leave It Alone*[2]

Sun-tzu
c. Fourth century B.C.E.

16   A military operation involves deception. Even though you are competent, appear to be incompetent. Though effective, appear to be ineffective.
The Art of War.[3] *Strategic Assessments*

17   Victorious warriors win first and then go to war, while defeated warriors go to war first and then seek to win.   *Art of War. Strategic Assessments*

18   The best victory is when the opponent surrenders of its own accord before there are any actual hostilities. . . . It is best to win without fighting.
Art of War. Planning a Siege

19   Be extremely subtle, even to the point of formlessness. Be extremely mysterious, even to the point of soundlessness. Thereby you can be the director of the opponent's fate.
Art of War. Emptiness and Fullness

Pytheas
fl. 330 B.C.E.

20   They smell of the lamp.[4]
From PLUTARCH, *Lives, Demosthenes, sec. 8*

Alexander the Great
356–323 B.C.E.

21   [At Achilles' tomb:] O fortunate youth, to have found Homer as the herald of your glory!
From CICERO, *Pro Archia*
(In Defense of the Poet Archias), sec. 24

---

[1]Translated by LIN YUTANG.
[2]Translated by BURTON WATSON.

[3]Translated by THOMAS CLEARY.
[4]Pytheas refers to the orations of Demosthenes, who worked in an underground cave lit only by a lamp.

1   If I were not Alexander, I would be Diogenes.
From PLUTARCH, *Lives,*
Alexander, sec. 14

Apelles
fl. 325 B.C.E.

2   Not a day without a line.[1]
Proverbial from PLINY THE ELDER,
Natural History, bk. XXXV, ch. 36

3   A cobbler should not judge above his last.[2]
Proverbial from PLINY THE ELDER,
Natural History, XXXV, 85

Menander
c. 342–292 B.C.E.

4   We live, not as we wish to, but as we can.
Lady of Andros, fragment 50[3]

5   Riches cover a multitude of woes.
The Boeotian Girl, fragment 90

6   Whom the gods love dies young.[4]
The Double Deceiver, fragment 125

7   The man who has never been flogged has never been taught.[5]
The Girl Who Gets Flogged, fragment 422

8   This is living, not to live unto oneself alone.
The Brothers in Love, fragment 508

9   Deus ex machina [A god from the machine].[6]
The Woman Possessed with a Divinity,
fragment 227

10   I call a fig a fig, a spade a spade.[7]
Unidentified fragment 545

11   Marriage, if one will face the truth, is an evil, but a necessary evil.[8]   *Unidentified fragment 651*

12   The man who runs may fight again.[9]
Monostikoi (Single Lines)

13   Conscience is a God to all mortals.
Monostikoi (Single Lines)

Epicurus
341–270 B.C.E.

14   Death is nothing to us, since when we are, death has not come, and when death has come, we are not.
From DIOGENES LAERTIUS,
Lives of Eminent Philosophers, bk. X, sec. 125

15   Pleasure is the beginning and the end of living happily.
From DIOGENES LAERTIUS,
Lives of Eminent Philosophers, X, 128

16   It is impossible to live pleasurably without living wisely, well, and justly, and impossible to live wisely, well, and justly without living pleasurably.
From DIOGENES LAERTIUS,
Lives of Eminent Philosophers, X, 140

Theophrastus
d. 278 B.C.E.

17   Time is the most valuable thing a man can spend.[10]
From DIOGENES LAERTIUS,
Lives of Eminent Philosophers, bk. V, sec. 40

Zeno
335–263 B.C.E.

18   [When asked, "What is a friend?"] Another I.[11]
From DIOGENES LAERTIUS,
Lives of Eminent Philosophers, bk. VII, sec. 23

---

[1]Nulla dies sine linea.

[2]Ne supra crepidam sutor iudicaret.
The more common rendering is: Cobbler, stick to your last.

[3]All fragments translated by F. C. ALLINSON (Loeb Classical Library).

[4]Also in PLAUTUS, *Bacchides,* act IV, sc. vii, l. 816.
Those that God loves do not live long. — GEORGE HERBERT, *Jacula Prudentum*
Heaven gives its favorites — early death. — LORD BYRON, *Childe Harold, canto IV* [1818], st. 102

[5]They spare the rod and spoil the child. — RALPH VENNING [c. 1621–1674], *Mysteries and Revelations* [1649]

[6]Also in LUCIAN, *Hermotimus, sec. 86.*

[7]Also attributed to Aristophanes by LUCIAN, *The Way to Write History, sec. 41.*
The Macedonians are a rude and clownish people that call a spade a spade. — PLUTARCH, *Apothegms, Philip of Macedon*
I think it good plain English, without fraud, To call a spade a spade, a bawd a bawd. — JOHN TAYLOR [1580–1653], *A Kicksey Winsey* [1619]

[8]Marriage is an evil that most men welcome. — *Monostikoi (Single Lines)*
Motto of *The Spectator* [December 29, 1711].

[9]He who flees will fight again. — TERTULLIAN, *De Fuga in Persecutione (On Fleeing Persecution), ch. 10*
That same man that runneth away / May again fight another day. — ERASMUS, *Apothegms* [1542]
Celuy qui fuit de bonne heure / Peut combattre derechef / [Who flies in good time / Can fight anew]. — ANONYMOUS [1594]; *translated from* VARRO, *Saturae Menippeae (Menippean Satires)*
For he who fights and runs away / May live to fight another day; / But he who is in battle slain / Can never rise and fight again. — OLIVER GOLDSMITH, *The Art of Poetry on a New Plan* [1761]
A version similar to Goldsmith's appears in JAMES RAY [fl. 1745], *Compleat History of the Rebellion* [1752].

[10]Nothing is so dear and precious as time. — FRANÇOIS RABELAIS, *Works, bk. V* [1564], *ch. 5*

[11]Alter ego.

1   The goal of life is living in agreement with nature.

> *From* DIOGENES LAERTIUS,
> *Lives of Eminent Philosophers, VII, 87*

Cleanthes
c. 330–232 B.C.E.

2   For we are your offspring.

> *Hymn to Zeus, l. 4*

3   Lead me, Zeus, and you, Fate, wherever you have assigned me. I shall follow without hesitation; but even if I am disobedient and do not wish to, I shall follow no less surely.

> *From* EPICTETUS, *Enchiridion, sec. 53*

Euclid
fl. 300 B.C.E.

4   Q.E.D. [Quod erat demonstrandum: Which was to be proved.]

> *Elements, bk. I, proposition 5*[1]

5   [To Ptolemy I:] There is no royal road to geometry.[2]

> *From* PROCLUS,
> *Commentary on Euclid, prologue*

Bion
c. 325–c. 255 B.C.E.

6   Old age is the harbor of all ills.

> *From* DIOGENES LAERTIUS,
> *Lives of Eminent Philosophers,*
> *bk. IV, sec. 47*

7   Wealth is the sinews of affairs.

> *From* DIOGENES LAERTIUS,
> *Lives of Eminent Philosophers, IV, 48*

8   The road to Hades is easy to travel.[3]

> *From* DIOGENES LAERTIUS,
> *Lives of Eminent Philosophers, IV, 49*

9   Though boys throw stones at frogs in sport, the frogs do not die in sport, but in earnest.

> *From* PLUTARCH, *Morals,*
> *On Water and Land Animals, 7*

Pyrrhus
c. 318–272 B.C.E.

10   Another such victory over the Romans, and we are undone.[4]

> *From* PLUTARCH, *Lives, Pyrrhus, sec. 21*

Aratus
c. 315–240 B.C.E.

11   From Zeus let us begin, whom we mortals never leave unnamed: full of Zeus are all streets and all gathering places of men, and full are the sea and harbors. Everywhere we all have need of Zeus. For we are also his offspring.   *Phaenomena, sec. 1*

Theocritus
c. 310–250 B.C.E.

12 Sweet is the whispering music of yonder pine that sings.

> *Idylls,*[5] *no. I*

13 Our concern be peace of mind: some old crone let us seek,
To spit on us for luck and keep unlovely things afar.

> *Idylls, VII*

14 Cicala to cicala is dear, and ant to ant,
And kestrels dear to kestrels, but to me the Muse and song.   *Idylls, IX*

15 The frog's life is most jolly, my lads; he has no care
Who shall fill up his cup; for he has drink enough to spare.   *Idylls, X*

16   Verily great grace may go
With a little gift; and precious are all things that come from friends.

> *Idylls, XXVIII*

Callimachus
c. 300–240 B.C.E.

17   Big book, big bore.[6]

> *From The Greek Anthology,*
> PETER JAY, *ed., introduction to Callimachus*

18 You're[7] walking by the tomb of Battiades,
Who knew well how to write poetry, and enjoy

---

[1]Proposition 5, too difficult for many students to pass beyond, became known as the asses' bridge [pons asinorum].

[2]Often quoted as: There is no royal road to learning.

[3]A passage broad, / Smooth, easy, inoffensive, down to Hell. — MILTON, *Paradise Lost, bk. II, l. 432*

[4]Pyrrhus, king of Epirus, refers to the dearly bought victory at Asculum, 280 B.C.E. Hence the phrase: Pyrrhic victory. See also Herodotus, 69:9 ("Cadmean victory").

[5]Translated by R. C. TREVELYAN.

[6]In reference to the traditional epics.

[7]Callimachus.

Laughter at the right moment, over the wine.
> *From The Greek Anthology,*
> PETER JAY, *ed., no. 150,*
> *On Himself*[1]

1 Someone spoke of your death, Heraclitus.[2] It
    brought me
Tears, and I remembered how often together
We ran the sun down with talk . . . somewhere
You've long been dust, my Halicarnassian friend.
But your *Nightingales* live on. Though the Death-
    world
Claws at everything, it will not touch them.[1]
> *From The Greek Anthology,*
> PETER JAY, *ed., no. 152*

Leonidas of Tarentum
c. 290–c. 220 B.C.E.

2 Far from Italy, far from my native Tarentum
I lie; and this is the worst of it — worse than death.
An exile's life is no life. But the Muses loved me.
For my suffering they gave me a honeyed gift:
My name survives me. Thanks to the sweet
    Muses
Leonidas will echo throughout all time.[3]
> *From The Greek Anthology,*
> PETER JAY, *ed., no. 189*

3 The season of ships is here,
The west wind and the swallows;
Flowers in the fields appear,
And the ocean of hills and hollows
Has calmed its waves and is clear.
Free that anchor and chain!
Set your full canvas flying,
O men in the harbor lane:
It is I, Priapus, crying.
Sail out on your trades again![4]
> *From The Greek Anthology,*
> PETER JAY, *ed., no. 197*

Archimedes
c. 287–212 B.C.E.

4 Eureka! [I have found it!][5]
> *From* VITRUVIUS POLLIO
> [*first century* B.C.E.],
> *De Architectura, bk. IX, sec. 10*

5 Give me where to stand, and I will move the
earth.[6]
> *From* PAPPUS OF ALEXANDRIA,
> *Collectio, bk. VIII, prop. 10, sec. 11*

Quintus Fabius Maximus
c. 275–203 B.C.E.

6 To be turned from one's course by men's opinions, by blame, and by misrepresentation shows a
man unfit to hold an office.
> *From* PLUTARCH, *Lives, Fabius Maximus, sec. 5*

Lacydes
fl. c. 241 B.C.E.

7 [When asked late in life why he was studying geometry:] If I should not be learning now, when should
I be?
> *From* DIOGENES LAERTIUS,
> *Lives of Eminent Philosophers, Lacydes, sec. 5*

Titus Maccius Plautus
254–184 B.C.E.

8 What is yours is mine, and all mine is yours.
> *Trinummus (A Three-Bob Day),*[7]
> *act II, sc. ii, l. 48*

9 Not by age but by character is wisdom acquired.
> *Trinummus, II, ii, l. 88*

10 In the one hand he is carrying a stone, while he
shows the bread in the other.
> *Aulularia (The Pot of Gold), act II, sc. ii, l. 18*

11 Consider the little mouse, how sagacious an
animal it is which never entrusts its life to one hole
only.[8] *Truculentus (The Churl), act IV, sc. iv, l. 15*

12 No guest is so welcome in a friend's house that he
will not become a nuisance after three days.[9]
> *Miles Gloriosus (The Braggart Soldier),*
> *act III, sc. i, l. 144*

---

[1]Translated by PETER JAY.

[2]Elegiac poet from Halicarnassus, author of a collection of poems, *Nightingales,* and a friend of Callimachus.

[3]Translated by FLEUR ADCOCK.

[4]Translated by CLIVE SANSOM.

[5]On discovery of a method to test the purity of gold.

[6]Said with reference to the lever.

[7]Translated by PAUL NIXON.

[8]I holde a mouses herte nat worth a leek / That hath but oon hole for to sterte to, / And if that faille, thanne is al ydo. — CHAUCER, *The Canterbury Tales, The Wife of Bath's Prologue, l. 572*

The mouse that hath but one hole is quickly taken. — GEORGE HERBERT, *Jacula Prudentum*

The mouse that always trusts to one poor hole / Can never be a mouse of any soul. — ALEXANDER POPE, *The Wife of Bath: Her Prologue* [1713], *l. 298*

[9]Fish and guests in three days are stale. — JOHN LYLY, *Euphues*

Fish and visitors stink in three days. — BENJAMIN FRANKLIN, *Poor Richard's Almanac* [1736], *January*

1   No man is wise enough by himself.
Miles Gloriosus, III, iii, l. 885

2   Nothing is there more friendly to a man than a friend in need.[1]   *Epidicus, act III, sc. iii, l. 44*

3   Things which you do not hope happen more frequently than things which you do hope.[2]
Mostellaria (The Ghost), act I, sc. iii, l. 40

4   To blow and swallow at the same moment is not easy.   *Mostellaria, III, ii, l. 104*

5   Practice yourself what you preach.[3]
Asinaria (Asses Galore), act III, sc. iii, l. 644

Maharbal [Barca the Carthaginian]
fl. 210 B.C.E.

6   You know how to win a victory, Hannibal, but not how to use it.[4]
From LIVY, History, bk. XXII, ch. 51

Bhagavad Gita[5]
250 B.C.E.– 250 C.E.[6]

7 For certain is death for the born
And certain is birth for the dead;
Therefore over the inevitable
Thou shouldst not grieve.[7]   *Chapter 2, verse 27*

8 This embodied [soul] is eternally unslayable
In the body of everyone, son of Bharata;
Therefore all beings
Thou shouldst not mourn.
Likewise having regard for thine own
        [caste] duty
Thou shouldst not tremble;
For another, better thing than a fight required of
        duty
Exists not for a warrior.   *2:30*

9 On action alone be thy interest,
Never on its fruits.

---

[1] A friend in need is a friend indeed. — WILLIAM CAREW HAZLITT [1834–1913] editor, *English Proverbs and Proverbial Phrases* [1882], p. 14

[2] The unexpected always happens. — *Common saying*

[3] Facias ipse quod faciamus suades.

[4] Vincere scis, Hannibal, victoria uti nescis.
Maharbal was commander of cavalry under Hannibal, who had insisted on a day's rest for the army after the victory at Cannae [216 B.C.E.], thereby enabling the enemy to recoup.

[5] Ancient Hindu scriptures written in Sanskrit. The title means Song of God.

[6] Ancient Indian literary chronology is conjectural. The dates given are approximate.

[7] Translated by ANNIE BESANT.

Let not the fruits of action be thy motive,
Nor be thy attachment to inaction.[8]   *2:47*

10 Better one's own duty, [though] imperfect,
Than another's duty well performed.[9]
3:35 and 18:47

11 In whatsoever way any come to Me,
In that same way I grant them favor.[9]   *4:11*

12 Who sees Me in all,
And sees all in Me,
For him I am not lost,
And he is not lost for Me.[9]   *6:30*

13   If the radiance of a thousand suns were to burst forth at once in the sky, that would be like the splendor of the Mighty One [Krishna].[10]
11:12

14 I am mighty, world-destroying Time.
11:32

Quintus Ennius
239–169 B.C.E.

15   No sooner said than done — so acts your man of worth.   *Annals, bk. 9 (quoted by PRISCIANUS)*

16   By delaying he preserved the state.
From CICERO, De Senectute (On Old Age), ch. IV, sec. 10

17   Let no one pay me honor with tears, nor celebrate my funeral rites with weeping.
From CICERO, De Senectute, XX, 73

18   The ape, vilest of beasts, how like to us.[11]
From CICERO, De Natura Deorum (On the Nature of the Gods), bk. I, ch. 35

19   No one regards what is before his feet; we all gaze at the stars.
Iphigenia. From CICERO, De Divinatione, bk. II, ch. 13

20   Whom they fear they hate.
Thyestes. From CICERO, De Officiis (On Moral Duties), bk. II, ch. 7

---

[8] Translated by F. EDGERTON.
At the moment which is not of action or inaction / You can receive this: "on whatever sphere of being / The mind of a man may be intent / At the time of death" — that is the one action / (And the time of death is every moment) / Which shall fructify in the lives of others: / And do not think of the fruit of action, / Fare forward. — T. S. ELIOT, *Four Quartets, The Dry Salvages, pt. III*

[9] Translated by F. EDGERTON.

[10] Translated by SWAMI NIKHILANANDA.
See J. Robert Oppenheimer, 739:n3.

[11] Simia quam similis, turpissima bestia, nobis!

Marcus Porcius Cato
[Cato the Elder, Cato the Censor]
234–149 B.C.E.

1 A farm is like a man — however great the income, if there is extravagance but little is left.
On Agriculture,[1] *bk. I, sec. 6*

2 Even though work stops, expenses run on.
On Agriculture, XXXIX, 2

3 It is a hard matter, my fellow citizens, to argue with the belly, since it has no ears.[2]
From PLUTARCH, *Lives, Cato, sec. 8*

4 Wise men profit more from fools than fools from wise men; for the wise men shun the mistakes of fools, but fools do not imitate the successes of the wise.
From PLUTARCH, *Lives, Cato, 9*

5 I would much rather have men ask why I have no statue, than why I have one.
From PLUTARCH, *Lives, Cato, 19*

6 Carthage must be destroyed.[3]
From PLUTARCH, *Lives, Cato, 27*

7 Grasp the subject, the words will follow.[4]
From GAIUS JULIUS VICTOR
[fourth century B.C.E.*],*
Ars Rhetorica, ch. II, sec. 1

8 An orator is a good man who is skilled in speaking.
From SENECA THE ELDER *[c. 45* B.C.E.*–40* C.E.*],*
Controversiae, I, Preface, and elsewhere

Caecilius Statius
220–168 B.C.E.

9 He plants trees to benefit another generation.[5]
Synephebi (Fellow Youths).
Quoted by CICERO *in*
De Senectute (On Old Age), sec. VII

---

[1]Translated by WILLIAM D. HOOPER, revised by HARRISON BOYD ASH (Loeb Classical Library).

[2]The belly has no ears nor is it to be filled with fair words. — FRANÇOIS RABELAIS, *Works, bk. IV* [1548], *ch. 67*

[3]Delenda est Carthago.
These words were added to every speech Cato made in the senate, preceded by *ceterum censeo* [in my opinion].

[4]Rem tene; verba sequentur.

[5]Serit arbores quae alteri seculo prosint.
He that plants trees loves others beside himself. — THOMAS FULLER [1654–1734], *Gnomologia* [1732]
A man does not plant a tree for himself; he plants it for posterity.
— ALEXANDER SMITH, *Dreamthorp. Books and Gardens*

Polybius
fl. c. 200–c. 118 B.C.E.

10 From this point onwards history becomes an organic whole: the affairs of Italy and of Africa are connected with those of Asia and of Greece, and all events bear a relationship and contribute to a single end.[6]
History, bk. I, sec. 3

11 Those who know how to win are much more numerous than those who know how to make proper use of their victories.
History, X, 36

12 There is no witness so dreadful, no accuser so terrible as the conscience that dwells in the heart of every man.
History, XVIII, 43

Terence[7] [Publius Terentius Afer]
c. 190–159 B.C.E.

13 Moderation in all things.[8]
Andria (The Lady of Andros), l. 61

14 Hence these tears.[9]
Andria, l. 126

15 Lovers' quarrels are the renewal of love.[10]
Andria, l. 555

16 Charity begins at home.[11]
Andria, l. 635

17 I am a man: nothing human is alien to me.[12]
Heauton Timoroumenos
(The Self-Tormentor), l. 77

18 Draw from others the lesson that may profit yourself.[13]
Heauton Timoroumenos, l. 221

---

[6]Translated by IAN SCOTT-KILVERT.

[7]Translated by JOHN SARGEAUNT (Loeb Classical Library), with occasional adaptations.

[8]See The Seven Sages, 55:7; Horace, 95:17 and 96:22; Lucan, 106:11, and Anonymous: Latin, 121:1.

[9]Hinc illae lacrimae.
The phrase is proverbial for "That's the cause of it," and was often quoted, by Horace in *Epistles, bk. I, epistle xix, l. 41,* and by others.
Hence rage and tears [Inde irae et lacrimae]. — JUVENAL, *Satires, bk. I, l. 168*

[10]Amantium irae amoris integratio est.
The anger of lovers renews the strength of love. — PUBLILIUS SYRUS, *Maxim 24*
The falling out of faithful friends renewing is of love. — RICHARD EDWARDS [c. 1523–1566], *The Paradise of Dainty Devices* [1576]
Let the falling out of friends be a renewing of affection. — JOHN LYLY, *Euphues*
The falling out of lovers is the renewing of love. — ROBERT BURTON, *Anatomy of Melancholy, pt. III, sec. 2*

[11]Proxumus sum egomet mihi.

[12]Homo sum: humani nil a me alienum puto. Quoted by CICERO in *De Officiis, bk. I, sec. 30.*
I consider nothing human as alien to myself. — CARSON MCCULLERS, *The Heart Is a Lonely Hunter* [1940], *pt. 2, ch. 6*
By tradition, a favorite maxim of KARL MARX.

[13]Periculum ex aliis facito tibi quod ex usu siet. (A saying.)

1   Nothing is so difficult but that it may be found out by seeking.[1]   *Heauton Timoroumenos, l. 675*

2   Some people ask, "What if the sky were to fall?"[2]   *Heauton Timoroumenos, l. 719*

3   Extreme law is often extreme injustice.[3]   *Heauton Timoroumenos, l. 796*

4   There is nothing so easy but that it becomes difficult when you do it reluctantly.   *Heauton Timoroumenos, l. 805*

5   While there's life, there's hope.   *Heauton Timoroumenos, l. 981*

6   In fact, nothing is said that has not been said before.   *Eunuchus (The Eunuch), l. 41 (Prologue)*

7   I have everything, yet have nothing; and although I possess nothing, still of nothing am I in want.   *Eunuchus, l. 243*

8   There are vicissitudes in all things.   *Eunuchus, l. 276*

9   I don't care one straw.[4]   *Eunuchus, l. 411*

10   He is wise who tries everything before arms.   *Eunuchus, l. 789*

11   I know the disposition of women: when you will, they won't; when you won't, they set their hearts upon you of their own inclination.   *Eunuchus, l. 812*

12   I took to my heels as fast as I could.   *Eunuchus, l. 844*

13   Fortune helps the brave.[5]   *Phormio, l. 203*

14   So many men, so many opinions; every one his own way.[6]   *Phormio, l. 454*

15   I bid him look into the lives of men as though into a mirror, and from others to take an example for himself.   *Adelphoe (The Brothers), l. 415*

Huai-nan Tzu[7]
[The Creation of the Universe]
Second century B.C.E.

16   Before heaven and earth had taken form all was vague and amorphous. Therefore it was called the Great Beginning. The Great Beginning produced emptiness and emptiness produced the universe.... The combined essences of heaven and earth became the yin and yang, the concentrated essences of the yin and yang became the four seasons, and the scattered essences of the four seasons became the myriad creatures of the world.   *Huai-nan Tzu, 3:1a*

Lucius Accius
170–86 B.C.E.

17   Let them hate, so long as they fear.[8]   *Fragment*

Han Wu-ti[9]
157–87 B.C.E.

18   The sound of her silk skirt has stopped.
On the marble pavement dust grows.
Her empty room is cold and still.
Fallen leaves are piled against the doors.
    Longing for that lovely lady
How can I bring my aching heart to rest?
    On the death of his mistress[10]

Marcus Terentius Varro
116–27 B.C.E.

19   The longest part of the journey is said to be the passing of the gate.   *On Agriculture (De Re Rustica),*[11] *bk. I, sec. ii, l. 6*

---

[1]Nil tam difficile est quin quaerendo investigari possiet.

[2]Quid si nunc caelum ruat?
Some ambassadors from the Celtae, being asked by Alexander what in the world they dreaded most, answered, that they feared lest the sky should fall upon them. — FLAVIUS ARRIANUS [c. 100–170], *Campaigns of Alexander, bk. I, ch. 4*

[3]Ius summum saepe summa est malitia.
Extreme law, extreme injustice, is now become a stale proverb in discourse. — CICERO, *De Officiis, bk. I, sec. 33*
Extreme justice is often injustice. — JEAN RACINE, *La Thébaïde* [1664], *act IV, sc. iii*
Mais l'extrême justice est une extrême injure. — VOLTAIRE, *Oedipe* [1718], *act III, sc. iii*

[4]Ego non flocci pendere.
Nor do they care a straw. — CERVANTES, *Don Quixote, pt. I, bk. III, ch. 9*

[5]Pliny the Younger says (*Letters, bk. VI, no. 16*) that Pliny the Elder said this during the eruption of Vesuvius: "Fortune favors the brave."

[6]Quot homines tot sententiae: suo quoque mos.
So many heads so many wits. — JOHN HEYWOOD, *Proverbs, pt. I, ch. 2*
So many men so many minds. — GEORGE GASCOIGNE [c. 1525–1577], *The Glass of Government* [1575]

[7]From *Sources of Chinese Tradition* [1960], edited by WILLIAM THEODORE DE BARY.
Huai-nan Tzu is from the scholarly court of Liu An (d. 122 B.C.E.), prince of Huai-nan.

[8]Oderint dum metuant.
From a lost tragedy. Frequently cited by Cicero and others. Suetonius (*Lives of the Caesars, Gaius Caligula, sec. 30*) says that the emperor Caligula was fond of quoting it.

[9]Sixth emperor of the Han dynasty.

[10]Translated by ARTHUR WALEY.

[11]Translated by WILLIAM D. HOOPER, revised by HARRISON BOYD ASH (Loeb Classical Library).

1   Not all who own a harp are harpers.
On Agriculture, II, i, 3

2   It was divine nature which gave us the country, and man's skill that built the cities.[1]
On Agriculture, III, i, 4

Marcus Licinius Crassus
fl. 70 B.C.E.

3   Those who aim at great deeds must also suffer greatly.   *From* PLUTARCH, *Lives, Crassus, ch. 26*

Meleager
First century B.C.E.

4   Farewell, Morning Star, herald of dawn, and quickly come again as the Evening Star, bringing secretly her whom thou takest away.[2]
Epigram from the Greek Anthology

Marcus Tullius Cicero
106–43 B.C.E.

5   How long, Catiline, will you abuse our patience?[3]
In Catilinam (Against Catiline), oration I, ch. 1

6   O tempora! O mores! [Oh the times! The customs!]   *In Catilinam, I, 2*

7   He has departed, withdrawn, gone away, broken out.[4]   *In Catilinam, II, 1*

8   I am a Roman citizen.[5]
In Verrem (Against Gaius Verres), oration V, ch. 57

9   Law stands mute in the midst of arms.[6]
Pro Milone (In Defense of Milo), sec. 11

10   Cui bono? [To whose advantage?][7]
Pro Milone, 32

11   These studies are a spur to the young, a delight to the old; an ornament in prosperity, a consoling refuge in adversity; they are pleasure for us at home, and no burden abroad; they stay up with us at night, they accompany us when we travel, they are with us in our country visits.
Pro Archia Poeta (In Defense of the Poet Archias), sec. 16

12   Leisure with dignity.[8]
Pro Publio Sestio (In Defense of Publius Sestius), sec. 98

13   History is the witness that testifies to the passing of time; it illumines reality, vitalizes memory, provides guidance in daily life, and brings us tidings of antiquity.
De Oratore (On Oratory), bk. II, ch. IX, sec. 36

14   The first law for the historian is that he shall never dare utter an untruth. The second is that he shall suppress nothing that is true. Moreover, there shall be no suspicion of partiality in his writing, or of malice.
De Oratore, II, XV, 62

15   The freedom of poetic license.[9]
De Oratore, III, XXXVIII, 153

16   If a man aspires to the highest place, it is no dishonor to him to halt at the second, or even at the third.   *Orator (The Accomplished Speaker), sec. 4*

17   For just as some women are said to be handsome though without adornment, so this subtle manner of speech, though lacking in artificial graces, delights us.   *Orator, 78*

18   Nothing quite new is perfect.
Brutus (History of Famous Orators), sec. 71

19   There were poets before Homer.   *Brutus, 71*

20   The aim of forensic oratory is to teach, to delight, to move.
De Optimo Genere Oratorum (The Best Kind of Orator), sec. 16

21   The dregs of Romulus.[10]
Ad Atticum (To Atticus), bk. II, letter 1

22   While there's life, there's hope.[11]
Ad Atticum, IX, 10

23   What is more agreeable than one's home?[12]
Ad Familiares (To Friends), bk. IV, letter 8

24   I like myself, but I won't say I'm as handsome as the bull that kidnapped Europa.
De Natura Deorum (On the Nature of the Gods), bk. I, sec. 78

---

[1]Divina natura dedit agros, ars humana aedificavit urbes.

[2]Translated by J. W. MACKAIL.

[3]Quo usque, Catilina, abutere patientia nostra?

[4]Abiit, excessit, evasit, erupit.
Depart — be off — excede — evade — erump! — OLIVER WENDELL HOLMES, *The Autocrat of the Breakfast-Table, Aestivation, ch. 2*

[5]Civis Romanus sum.

[6]Silent enim leges inter arma.

[7]In full: Cui bono fuerit? [To whose advantage was it?]

[8]Cum dignitate otium.

[9]Poetarum licentiae liberiora.

[10]In Romuli faece. That is, the lowest order of society.

[11]Dum anima est, spes est.

[12]Quae est domestica sede iucundior?

1   It was ordained at the beginning of the world that certain signs should prefigure certain events.
De Divinatione, bk. I, sec. 118

2   There is nothing so ridiculous but some philosopher has said it.   *De Divinatione, II, 119*

3   I would rather be wrong with Plato than right with such men as these [the Pythagoreans].
Tusculanae Disputationes (Tusculan Disputations), bk. I, sec. 17

4   O philosophy, you leader of life.[1]
Tusculanae Disputationes, V, 2

5   Socrates was the first to call philosophy down from the heavens and to place it in cities, and even to introduce it into homes and compel it to inquire about life and standards and goods and evils.
Tusculanae Disputationes, V, 4

6   The highest good.[2]
De Officiis (On Moral Duties), bk. I, sec. 2

7   Let arms yield to the toga, the laurel crown to praise.[3]   *De Officiis, I, 22*

8   Never less idle than when wholly idle, nor less alone than when wholly alone.   *De Officiis, III, 1*

9   Rome, fortunately natal 'neath my consulship![4]
De Consultatu Suo (On His Consulship)

10   The people's good is the highest law.[5]
De Legibus (On the Laws), bk. III, sec. 3

11   He used to raise a storm in a teapot.[6]
De Legibus, III, 16

12   Let the punishment match the offense.[7]
De Legibus, III, 20

13   The shifts of Fortune test the reliability of friends.   *De Amicitia (On Friendship), ch. XVII*

14   A friend is, as it were, a second self.
De Amicitia, XXI

15   Give me a young man in whom there is something of the old, and an old man with something of the young: guided so, a man may grow old in body, but never in mind.   *De Senectute (On Old Age), sec. XI*

16   Old men are garrulous by nature.
De Senectute, XVI

17   Old age: the crown of life, our play's last act.
De Senectute, XXIII

18   Endless money forms the sinews of war.[8]
Philippics, oration V, sec. 5

Pompey [Gnaeus Pompeius]
106–48 B.C.E.

19   More worship the rising than the setting sun.[9]
From PLUTARCH, *Lives, Pompey, sec. 14*

20   A dead man cannot bite.
From PLUTARCH, *Lives, Pompey, 77*

[Gaius] Julius Caesar
100–44 B.C.E.

21   All Gaul is divided into three parts.[10]
De Bello Gallico (The Gallic Wars),[11] *bk. I, sec. 1*

22   Men willingly believe what they wish.[12]
De Bello Gallico, III, 18

23   I love treason but hate a traitor.[13]
From PLUTARCH, *Lives, Romulus, sec. 17*

24   I wished my wife to be not so much as suspected.[14]

From PLUTARCH, *Lives, Caesar, sec. 10*

---

[1]O vitae philosophia dux.

[2]Summum bonum.
The nature of the good and the highest good. — HORACE, *Satires, bk. II, no. vi, l. 76*
See Lucretius, 90:21.

[3]Cedant arma togae, concedat laurea laudi.
He is quoting from his own poem *De suis temporibus, bk. III.*

[4]O fortunatam natam me consule Romam!
The verse is quoted disparagingly by Juvenal (*Satire X, l. 122*), Quintilian (*bk. XI, ch. 1, sec. 24*), and others.

[5]Salus populi suprema est lex.

[6]Excitabat enim fluctus in simpulo.
A tempest in a teapot. — *Proverb*

[7]Noxiae poena par esto.
See W. S. Gilbert, 527:15.

[8]He who first called money the sinews of business seems to have spoken with special reference to the affairs of war. — PLUTARCH, *Lives, Cleomenes, sec. 27*
Neither is money the sinews of war (as it is trivially said).
— FRANCIS BACON, *Essays. Of the True Greatness of Kingdoms*
Money is the sinew of love as well as of war. — THOMAS FULLER [1654–1734], *Gnomonologia* [1732], *no. 3442*

[9]Addressed to Sulla.

[10]Gallia est omnis divisa in partes tres.

[11]Translated by W. A. McDEVITTE and W. S. BOHN.

[12]Fere libenter homines id quod volunt credunt.
See Demosthenes, 79:9.

[13]Princes in this case do hate the traitor, though they love the treason. — SAMUEL DANIEL, *Tragedy of Cleopatra* [1594], *act IV, sc. i*
This principle is old, but true as fate, / Kings may love treason, but the traitor hate. — THOMAS DEKKER, *The Honest Whore, pt. I* [1604], *act IV, sc. iv*
Though I love the treason, I hate the traitor. — SAMUEL PEPYS, *Diary, March 7, 1667*

[14]Caesar's wife must be above suspicion. — *Traditional saying*

1   I had rather be the first man among these fellows than the second man in Rome.
From PLUTARCH, *Lives, Caesar, 11*

2   The die is cast.[1]
From PLUTARCH, *Lives, Caesar, 32*

3   Go on, my friend, and fear nothing; you carry Caesar and his fortune in your boat.
From PLUTARCH, *Lives, Caesar, 38*

4   The Ides of March have come.
From PLUTARCH, *Lives, Caesar, 63*

5   [In answer to a question as to what sort of death was the best:] A sudden death.
From PLUTARCH, *Lives, Caesar, 63*

6   I came, I saw, I conquered.[2]
From SUETONIUS, *Lives of the Caesars, Julius, sec. 37*

7   You also, Brutus my son.[3]
From SUETONIUS, *Lives of the Caesars, Julius, 82*

8   It is not these well-fed long-haired men that I fear, but the pale and the hungry-looking.[4]
From PLUTARCH, *Lives, Antony, sec. 11*

Lucretius
[Titus Lucretius Carus]
99–55 B.C.E.

9   Mother of Aeneas and his race, darling of men and gods, nurturing Venus.
De Rerum Natura (On the Nature of Things),[5] *bk. I, l. 1 (Invocation)*

10   For thee the wonder-working earth puts forth sweet flowers.
De Rerum Natura, I, l. 7

11   The lively power of his mind prevailed, and forth he marched far beyond the flaming walls of the heavens,[6] as he traversed the immeasurable universe in thought and imagination.
De Rerum Natura, I, l. 72

12   Such evil deeds could religion prompt.[7]
De Rerum Natura, I, l. 101

13   Nothing can be created from nothing.[8]
De Rerum Natura, I, l. 155

14   The first beginnings of things cannot be distinguished by the eye.   *De Rerum Natura, I, l. 268*

15   The ring on the finger becomes thin beneath by wearing, the fall of dripping water hollows the stone.[9]   *De Rerum Natura, I, l. 312*

16   Nature works by means of bodies unseen.
De Rerum Natura, I, l. 328

17   Material objects are of two kinds, atoms and compounds of atoms. The atoms themselves cannot be swamped by any force, for they are preserved indefinitely by their absolute solidity.[10]
De Rerum Natura, I, l. 518

18   On a dark theme I trace verses full of light, touching all the muses' charm.[11]
De Rerum Natura, I, l. 933

19   Truths kindle light for truths.
De Rerum Natura, I, l. 1117

20   Pleasant it is, when over a great sea the winds trouble the waters, to gaze from shore upon another's great tribulation: not because any man's troubles are a delectable joy, but because to perceive what ills you are free from yourself is pleasant.[12]
De Rerum Natura, II, l. 1

---

[1]Iacta alea est. Proverb quoted by Caesar as he crossed the Rubicon.
Also in SUETONIUS, *Lives of the Caesars, Julius.*

[2]Veni, vidi, vici. Inscription displayed in Caesar's Pontic triumph.
Also in PLUTARCH, *Apothegms, Caesar Augustus.*

[3]Et tu, Brute. Suetonius reports that Caesar said this in Greek.

[4]The reference is to Brutus and Cassius.

[5]Translated by W. H. D. ROUSE (Loeb Classical Library), with adaptations, unless noted otherwise.

[6]Flammantia moenia mundi.

[7]Tantum religio potuit suadere malorum.
The reference is to Agamemnon's sacrifice of his daughter Iphigenia.
Translated by CYRIL BAILEY.

[8]Nil posse creari de nilo.

[9]Anulus in digito subter tenuatur habendo, / Stilicidi casus lapidem cavat.
See also the concluding lines of *Book IV*:
Nonne vides etiam guttas in saxa cadentis / Umoris longo in spatio pertundere saxa? [Do you not see that even drops of water falling upon a stone in the long run beat a way through the stone?]
Drops of water hollow out a stone, a ring is worn thin by use. — OVID, *Ex Ponto, bk. IV, letter 10, l. 5*
Also in PLUTARCH, *Morals, Of the Training of Children.*
The drop of rain maketh a hole in the stone, not by violence, but by oft falling. — HUGH LATIMER, *Seventh Sermon Before Edward VI* [1549]
The soft droppes of rain perce the hard marble. — JOHN LYLY, *Euphues*
And drizling drops that often doe redound, / The firmest flint doth in continuance wear. — EDMUND SPENSER, *Amoretti, sonnet 18*

[10]Translated by R. E. LATHAM.

[11]Translated by CYRIL BAILEY.

[12]It is a pleasure to stand upon the shore, and to see ships tost upon the sea: a pleasure to stand in the window of a castle, and to see a battle and the adventures thereof below: but no pleasure is comparable to the standing upon the vantage ground of truth . . . and to see the errors, and wanderings, and mists, and tempests, in the vale below. — FRANCIS BACON, *Essays. Of Truth*

1   O miserable minds of men! O blind hearts! In what darkness of life, in what great dangers ye spend this little span of years![1]   *De Rerum Natura, II, l. 14*

2   Life is one long struggle in the dark.
De Rerum Natura, II, l. 54

3   Thus the sum of things is ever being renewed, and mortals live dependent one upon another. Some nations increase, others diminish, and in a short space the generations of living creatures are changed and like runners pass on the torch of life.[2]
De Rerum Natura, II, l. 75

4   So far as it goes, a small thing may give analogy of great things, and show the tracks of knowledge.
De Rerum Natura, II, l. 123

5   All things must needs be borne on through the calm void, moving at equal rate with unequal weights.[3]   *De Rerum Natura, II, l. 238*

6   Never trust her at any time when the calm sea shows her false alluring smile.
De Rerum Natura, II, l. 558

7   What once sprung from the earth sinks back into the earth.[3]   *De Rerum Natura, II, l. 999*

8   That fear of Acheron be sent packing which troubles the life of man from its deepest depths, suffuses all with the blackness of death, and leaves no delight clean and pure.   *De Rerum Natura, III, l. 37*

9   So it is more useful to watch a man in times of peril, and in adversity to discern what kind of man he is; for then at last words of truth are drawn from the depths of his heart, and the mask is torn off, reality remains.   *De Rerum Natura, III, l. 55*

10   For as children tremble and fear everything in the blind darkness, so we in the light sometimes fear what is no more to be feared than the things children in the dark hold in terror and imagine will come true.
De Rerum Natura, III, l. 87

11   A tree cannot grow in the sky, nor clouds be in the deep sea, nor fish live in the fields, nor can blood be in sticks nor sap in rocks.   *De Rerum Natura, III, l. 784*

12   Therefore death is nothing to us, it matters not one jot, since the nature of the mind is understood to be mortal.[4]   *De Rerum Natura, III, l. 830*

13   When immortal Death has taken mortal life.[5]
De Rerum Natura, III, l. 869

14   Why dost thou not retire like a guest sated with the banquet of life, and with calm mind embrace, thou fool, a rest that knows no care?[3]
De Rerum Natura, III, l. 938

15   By protracting life, we do not deduct one jot from the duration of death.
De Rerum Natura, III, l. 1087

16   What is food to one, is to others bitter poison.[6]
De Rerum Natura, IV, l. 637

17   From the heart of this fountain of delights wells up some bitter taste to choke them even amid the flowers.[3]
De Rerum Natura, IV, l. 1133

18   But if one should guide his life by true principles, man's greatest riches is to live on a little with contented mind; for a little is never lacking.
De Rerum Natura, V, l. 1117

19   Men are eager to tread underfoot what they have once too much feared.
De Rerum Natura, V, l. 1140

20   Violence and injury enclose in their net all that do such things, and generally return upon him who began.
De Rerum Natura, V, l. 1152

21   [Epicurus] set forth what is the highest good, towards which we all strive, and pointed out the past, whereby along a narrow track we may strain on towards it in a straight course.[7]
De Rerum Natura, VI, l. 26

22   [The people] were given over in troops to disease[8] and death.
De Rerum Natura, VI, l. 1144

Gaius Valerius Catullus
87–c. 54 B.C.E.

23   To whom am I to present my pretty new book, freshly smoothed off with dry pumice stone? To you,

---

[1]Translated by CYRIL BAILEY.
Insensate care of mortals! Oh how false the argument which makes thee downward beat thy wings. — DANTE, *Divine Comedy, Paradiso, canto XI, l. 1*

[2]Et quasi cursores vitae lampada tradunt.

[3]Translated by CYRIL BAILEY.

[4]Nil igitur mors est ad nos neque pertinet hilum, / Quandoquidem natura animi mortalis habetur.

[5]Mortalem vitam mors cum immortalis ademit.
Translated by CYRIL BAILEY.

[6]Ut quod ali cibus est aliis fuat acre venenum.
What's one man's poison, signor, / Is another's meat or drink. — BEAUMONT AND FLETCHER, *Love's Cure* [1647], *act III, sc. ii*
One man's meat is another man's poison. — OSWALD DYKES [fl. c. 1709], *English Proverbs* [1709]

[7]Translated by CYRIL BAILEY.
The highest good [summum bonum]. See Cicero 88:6.

[8]The devastating Athenian plague [430 B.C.E.] described by Thucydides.

Cornelius: for you used to think that my trifles were worth something, long ago.   *Carmina,*[1] *poem I, l. 1*

1   May it live and last for more than one century.
    Carmina, I, l. 10

2   Mourn, ye Graces and Loves, and all you whom the Graces love. My lady's sparrow is dead, the sparrow, my lady's pet.[2]   *Carmina, III, l. 1*

3   Now he goes along the dark road, thither whence they say no one returns.   *Carmina, III, l. 11*

4   But these things are past and gone.[3]
    Carmina, IV, l. 25

5   Let us live and love, my Lesbia, and value at a penny all the talk of crabbed old men. Suns may set and rise again: for us, when our brief light has set, there's the sleep of perpetual night. Give me a thousand kisses.[4]   *Carmina, V, l. 1*

6   Poor Catullus, you should cease your folly.
    Carmina, VIII, l. 1

7   But you, Catullus, be resolved and firm.
    Carmina, VIII, l. 19

8   And let her not look to find my love, as before; my love, which by her fault has dropped like a flower on the meadow's edge, when it has been touched by the plow passing by.   *Carmina, XI, l. 21*

9   Over head and heels.[5]   *Carmina, XX, l. 9*

10   Ah, what is more blessed than to put cares away!
    Carmina, XXXI, l. 7

11   Whatever it is, wherever he is, whatever he is doing, he smiles: it is a malady he has, neither an elegant one as I think, nor in good taste.
    Carmina, XXXIX, l. 6

12   There is nothing more silly than a silly laugh.
    Carmina, XXXIX, l. 16

13   Oh this age! How tasteless and ill-bred it is!
    Carmina, XLIII, l. 8

14   Now spring brings back balmy warmth.[6]
    Carmina, XLVI, l. 1

15   Catullus, the worst of all poets, gives you [Marcus Tullius] his warmest thanks; he being as much

the worst of all poets as you are the best of all patrons.   *Carmina, XLIX, l. 4*

16   He seems to me to be equal to a god, he, if it may be, seems to surpass the very gods, who sitting opposite you again gazes at you and hears you sweetly laughing.   *Carmina, LI, l. 1*

17   What an eloquent manikin![7]
    Carmina, LIII, l. 5

18   I would see a little Torquatus, stretching his baby hands from his mother's lap, smile a sweet smile at his father with lips half parted.
    Carmina, LXI, l. 216

19   The evening is come; rise up, ye youths. Vesper from Olympus now at last is just raising his long-looked-for light.   *Carmina, LXII, l. 1*

20   What is given by the gods more desirable than the fortunate hour?[8]   *Carmina, LXII, l. 30*

21   Not unknown am I to the goddess [Venus] who mingles with her cares a sweet bitterness.
    Carmina, LXVIII, l. 17

22   It is not fit that men should be compared with gods.   *Carmina, LXVIII, l. 141*

23   What a woman says to her ardent lover should be written in wind and running water.
    Carmina, LXX, l. 3

24   Leave off wishing to deserve any thanks from anyone, or thinking that anyone can ever become grateful.   *Carmina, LXXIII, l. 1*

25   If a man can take any pleasure in recalling the thought of kindnesses done.   *Carmina, LXXVI, l. 1*

26   It is difficult suddenly to lay aside a long-cherished love.   *Carmina, LXXVI, l. 13*

27   O ye gods, grant me this in return for my piety.
    Carmina, LXXVI, l. 26

28   I hate and I love. Why I do so, perhaps you ask. I know not, but I feel it and I am in torment.[9]
    Carmina, LXXXV, l. 1

29   Wandering through many countries and over many seas, I come, my brother, to these sorrowful obsequies, to present you with the last guerdon of death, and speak, though in vain, to your silent ashes.
    Carmina, CI, l. 1

30   And forever, O my brother, hail and farewell![10]
    Carmina, CI, l. 10

---

[1]Translated by FRANCIS CORNFORD (Loeb Classical Library).

[2]Passer, deliciae meae puellae.
This is also the opening line of *Carmina, poem II.*

[3]Sed haec prius fuere.

[4]Vivamus, mea Lesbia, atque amemus . . . / Soles occidere et redire possunt: / Nobis cum semel occidit brevis lux / Nox est perpetua una dormienda. / Da mi basia mille.

[5]Per caputque pedesque.

[6]Iam ver egelidos refert tepores.

---

[7]Salaputium disertum!

[8]Quid datur a divis felici optatius hora?

[9]Odi et amo. Quare id faciam, fortasse requiris. / Nescio, sed fieri sentio et excrucior.

[10]Atque in perpetuum, frater, ave atque vale.

1   But you shall not escape my iambics.[1]

Fragment

Sallust
[Gaius Sallustius Crispus]
86–34 B.C.E.

2   All our power lies in both mind and body; we employ the mind to rule, the body rather to serve; the one we have in common with the Gods, the other with the brutes.

The War with Catiline[2] *[c. 42 B.C.E.], sec. 1*

3   The renown which riches or beauty confer is fleeting and frail; mental excellence is a splendid and lasting possession.

The War with Catiline, 1

4   Covetous of others' possessions, he [Catiline] was prodigal of his own.[3]

The War with Catiline, 5

5   Ambition drove many men to become false; to have one thought locked in the breast, another ready on the tongue.

The War with Catiline, 10

6   In truth, prosperity tries the souls even of the wise.[4]   *The War with Catiline, 11*

7   Thus in the highest position there is the least freedom of action.[5]

The War with Catiline, 51

8   On behalf of their country, their children, their altars, and their hearths.[6]

The War with Catiline, 59

9   The soul is the captain and ruler of the life of mortals.[7]

The War with Jugurtha[2] *[c. 40 B.C.E.], sec. 1*

10   The splendid achievements of the intellect, like the soul, are everlasting.

The War with Jugurtha, 2

11   A city for sale and soon to perish if it finds a buyer![8]   *The War with Jugurtha, 35*

12   Punic faith.[9]   *The War with Jugurtha, 108*

---

13   Experience has shown that to be true which Appius[10] says in his verses, that every man is the architect of his own fortune.[11]

Speech to Caesar on the State,[12] *sec. 1*

Virgil
[Publius Vergilius Maro]
70–19 B.C.E.

14   A god has brought us this peace.

Eclogues, no. I, l. 6

15   To compare great things with small.

Eclogues, I, l. 23

16   Happy old man![13]   *Eclogues, I, l. 46*

17   Ah Corydon, Corydon, what madness has caught you?   *Eclogues, II, l. 69*

18   With Jove I begin.[14]   *Eclogues, III, l. 60*

19   A sad thing is a wolf in the fold, rain on ripe corn, wind in the trees, the anger of Amaryllis.

Eclogues, III, l. 80

20   A snake lurks in the grass.[15]

Eclogues, III, l. 93

21   Let us raise a somewhat loftier strain![16]

Eclogues, IV, l. 1

22   The great cycle of the ages is renewed. Now Justice returns, returns the Golden Age; a new generation now descends from on high.[17]   *Eclogues, IV, l. 5*

23   We have made you [Priapus] of marble for the time being.   *Eclogues, VII, l. 35*

24   We are not all capable of everything.[18]

Eclogues, VIII, l. 63

---

[1]At non effugies meos iambos.

[2]Translated by J. C. Rolfe (Loeb Classical Library).

[3]Alieni appetens, sui profusus.

[4]Quippe secundae res sapientium animos fatigant.

[5]Ita in maxima fortuna minima licentia est.

[6]Pro patria, pro liberis, pro aris atque focis suis.

[7]Dux atque imperator vitae mortalium animus est.

[8]Jugurtha's remark as he looked back at Rome upon being ordered by the senate to leave Italy.

[9]Punica fide (treachery).

[10]Appius Claudius Caecus, consul in 307 B.C.E., the earliest Roman writer known to us.

[11]His own character is the arbiter of everyone's fortune. — Publilius Syrus, *Maxim 283*

The brave man carves out his fortune, and every man is the son of his own works. — Cervantes, *Don Quixote, pt. I, bk. I, ch. 4*

[12]Translated by J. C. Rolfe (Loeb Classical Library).

[13]Fortunate senex.

[14]Ab Iove principium.

[15]Latet anguis in herba.

[16]Paulo maiora canamus!

[17]Magnus ab integro saeclorum nascitur ordo. / Iam redit et Virgo, redeunt Saturnia regna; / Iam nova progenies caelo demittitur alto.

Interpreted by the Middle Ages as a prophecy of the birth of Christ. Dante cites the lines in *Purgatorio, canto XXII, l. 70.*

A phrase altered from the first line (Novus ordo seclorum) appears on the reverse of the Great Seal of the United States of America. Virgil's Latin is the source of other mottoes of the Great Seal.

See Virgil, 93:10 and 95:13.

[18]Non omnia possumus omnes.

1   Draw Daphnis from the town, my songs, draw Daphnis home.   *Eclogues, VIII, l. 68*

2   Hylax barks in the doorway.
Eclogues, VIII, l. 107

3   Your descendants shall gather your fruits.[1]
Eclogues, IX, l. 50

4   Time bears away all things, even our minds.
Eclogues, IX, l. 51

5   Let us go singing as far as we go: the road will be less tedious.   *Eclogues, IX, l. 64*

6   This last labor grant me, O Arethusa.
Eclogues, X, l. 1

7   What if Amyntas is dark? Violets are dark, too, and hyacinths.   *Eclogues, X, l. 38*

8   Love conquers all things; let us too surrender to Love.[2]   *Eclogues, X, l. 69*

9   Utmost [farthest] Thule.[3]   *Georgics, no. I, l. 30*

10   Look with favor upon a bold beginning.[4]
Georgics, I, l. 40

11   O farmers, pray that your summers be wet and your winters clear.
Georgics, I, l. 100

12   Practice and thought might gradually forge many an art.   *Georgics, I, l. 133*

13   Thrice they tried to pile Ossa on Pelion, yes, and roll up leafy Olympus upon Ossa; thrice the Father of Heaven split the mountains apart with his thunderbolt.   *Georgics, I, l. 281*

14   Frogs in the marsh mud drone their old lament.
Georgics, I, l. 378

15   Not every soil can bear all things.
Georgics, II, l. 109

16   Ah too fortunate farmers, if they knew their own good fortune!   *Georgics, II, l. 458*

17   May the countryside and the gliding valley streams content me. Lost to fame, let me love river and woodland.   *Georgics, II, l. 485*

18   Happy the man who could search out the causes of things.[5]   *Georgics, II, l. 490*

19   And no less happy he who knows the rural gods.[6]   *Georgics, II, l. 493*

20   This life the old Sabines knew long ago; Remus knew it, and his brother.   *Georgics, II, l. 532*

21   The best day . . . is the first to flee.[7]
Georgics, III, l. 66

22   Years grow cold to love.   *Georgics, III, l. 97*

23   Time is flying never to return.[8]
Georgics, III, l. 284

24   All aglow is the work.[9]   *Georgics, IV, l. 169*

25   A sudden madness came down upon the unwary lover [Orpheus] — forgivable, surely, if Death knew how to forgive.   *Georgics, IV, l. 488*

26   Sweet Parthenope nourished me, flourishing in studies of ignoble ease.[10]   *Georgics, IV, l. 563*

27   I who once played shepherds' songs and in my brash youth sang of you, O Tityrus, beneath the spreading beech.[11]   *Georgics, IV, l. 565*

28   Of arms and the man I sing.[12]   *Aeneid, bk. I, l. 1*

29   Can heavenly minds yield to such rage?
Aeneid, I, l. 11

30   So vast was the struggle to found the Roman state.   *Aeneid, I, l. 33*

31   Night, pitch-black, lies upon the deep.
Aeneid, I, l. 89

32   O thrice and four times blessed![13]   *Aeneid, I, l. 94*

33   Fury provides arms.   *Aeneid, I, l. 150*

34   You have suffered worse things; God will put an end to these also.   *Aeneid, I, l. 199*

35   Perhaps someday it will be pleasant to remember even this.[14]   *Aeneid, I, l. 203*

---

[1] Carpent tua poma nepotes.

[2] Omnia vincit amor: et nos cedamus amori.

[3] Ultima Thule.
The phrase, designating a far-off land, has been in use since the Greek mariner Pytheas discovered in the fourth century B.C.E. an island he named Thule six days north of England, thought to be Iceland.

[4] Audacibus annue coeptis.
This phrase also (see 92:*n*17) was adapted for use on the reverse of the Great Seal of the United States of America: Annuit coeptis. See Virgil, 95:*n*5, for the Latin on the face of the Great Seal.

[5] Felix qui potuit rerum cognoscere causas.
The reference is apparently to Lucretius (see 89:9–90:22).

[6] Fortunatus et ille deos qui novit agrestis.

[7] Optima . . . dies . . . prima fugit.

[8] Fugit inreparabile tempus.

[9] Fervet opus.

[10] Me . . . dulcis alebat / Parthenope, studiis florentem ignobilis otii.
Parthenope: ancient name of Naples.

[11] Tityrus is also referred to in *Eclogues, no. I, l. 1*.

[12] Arma virumque cano.
Arms and the Man. — GEORGE BERNARD SHAW, *title of play* [1898]
See John Dryden, 274:13.

[13] O terque quaterque beati!

[14] Forsan et haec olim meminisse iuvabit.

1　The organizer a woman.[1]　*Aeneid, I, l. 364*

2　Her walk revealed her as a true goddess.
Aeneid, I, l. 405

3　How happy those whose walls already rise!
Aeneid, I, l. 437

4　Here are the tears of things; mortality touches the heart.[2]　*Aeneid, I, l. 462*

5　I make no distinction between Trojan and Tyrian.　*Aeneid, I, l. 574*

6　A mind aware of its own rectitude.[3]
Aeneid, I, l. 604

7　As long as rivers shall run down to the sea, or shadows touch the mountain slopes, or stars graze in the vault of heaven, so long shall your honor, your name, your praises endure.　*Aeneid, I, l. 607*

8　I have known sorrow and learned to aid the wretched.　*Aeneid, I, l. 630*

9　Unspeakable, O Queen, is the sorrow you bid me renew.　*Aeneid, II, l. 3*

10　Whatever it is, I fear Greeks even when they bring gifts.[4]　*Aeneid, II, l. 49*

11　From a single crime know the nation.
Aeneid, II, l. 65

12　I shudder to say it.[5]　*Aeneid, II, l. 204*

13　O fatherland, O Ilium home of the gods, O Troy walls famed in battle!　*Aeneid, II, l. 241*

14　We have been Trojans; Troy has been.
Aeneid, II, l. 325

15　There is but one safety to the vanquished — to hope not safety.　*Aeneid, II, l. 354*

16　Our foes will provide us with arms.
Aeneid, II, l. 391

17　The gods thought otherwise.[6]　*Aeneid, II, l. 428*

18　Thrice would I have thrown my arms about her neck, and thrice the ghost embraced fled from my grasp: like a fluttering breeze, like a fleeting dream.[7]　*Aeneid, II, l. 793*

19　O accurst craving for gold!　*Aeneid, III, l. 57*

20　Rumor flies.[8]　*Aeneid, III, l. 121*

21　I feel again a spark of that ancient flame.[9]
Aeneid, IV, l. 23

22　Deep in her breast lives the silent wound.
Aeneid, IV, l. 67

23　A woman is always a fickle, unstable thing.[10]
Aeneid, IV, l. 569

24　Thus, thus, it is joy to pass to the world below.[11]　*Aeneid, IV, l. 660*

25　Naked in death upon an unknown shore.
Aeneid, V, l. 871

26　Yield not to evils, but attack all the more boldly.
Aeneid, VI, l. 95

27　It is easy to go down into Hell; night and day, the gates of dark Death stand wide; but to climb back again, to retrace one's steps to the upper air — there's the rub, the task.[12]　*Aeneid, VI, l. 126*

28　Faithful Achates.[13]
Aeneid, VI, l. 158 and elsewhere

29　Death's brother, Sleep.　*Aeneid, VI, l. 278*

30　Unwillingly I left your land, O Queen.[14]
Aeneid, VI, l. 460

31　Had I a hundred tongues, a hundred mouths, a voice of iron and a chest of brass, I could not tell all the forms of crime, could not name all the types of punishment.　*Aeneid, VI, l. 625*

32　That happy place, the green groves of the dwelling of the blest.　*Aeneid, VI, l. 638*

33　The spirit within nourishes, and the mind, diffused through all the members, sways the mass and mingles with the whole frame.　*Aeneid, VI, l. 726*

34　Each of us bears his own Hell.　*Aeneid, VI, l. 743*

35　Others, I take it, will work better with breathing bronze and draw living faces from marble; others will

---

[1]Dux femina facti.

[2]Sunt lacrimae rerum et mentem mortalia tangunt.

[3]The mind, conscious of rectitude, laughed to scorn the falsehood of report. — OVID, *Fasti, bk. IV, l. 311*

[4]Quidquid id est, timeo Danaos et dona ferentis.

[5]Horresco referens.

[6]Dis aliter visum.

[7]Virgil here translates HOMER, *Odyssey, bk. XI, l. 204*. See 53:11.

[8]Fama volat.

[9]Agnosco veteris vestigia flammae.

[10]Varium et mutabile semper femina.
Woman often changes; foolish the man who trusts her. — FRANCIS I OF FRANCE, written by him with his ring on a window of the château of Chambord (PIERRE DE BRANTÔME [d. 1614], *Oeuvres, vol. VII*)
La donna è mobile. — FRANCESCO MARIA PIAVE [1810–1879], *libretto of Verdi's Rigoletto, Duke's song*

[11]Sic, sic, iuvat ire sub umbras.

[12]Facilis descensus Averni: / Noctes atque dies patet atri ianua Ditis; / Sed revocare gradum superasque evadere ad auras, / Hoc opus, hic labor est.

[13]Fidus Achates. Proverbial for a trusted friend; Achates was the faithful comrade of Aeneas.

[14]Aeneas to the ghost of Dido, who had killed herself when he left her.

plead at law with greater eloquence, or measure the pathways of the sky, or forecast the rising stars. Be it your concern, Roman, to rule the nations under law (this is your proper skill) and establish the way of peace; to spare the conquered and put down the mighty from their seat.   *Aeneid, VI, l. 847*

1   Give me handfuls of lilies to scatter.[1]
Aeneid, VI, l. 883

2   There are two gates of Sleep. One is of horn, easy of passage for the shades of truth; the other, of gleaming white ivory, permits false dreams to ascend to the upper air.   *Aeneid, VI, l. 893*

3   Prayed to the Genius of the place.
Aeneid, VII, l. 136

4   We descend from Jove; in ancestral Jove Troy's sons rejoice.   *Aeneid, VII, l. 219*

5   If I cannot bend Heaven, I shall move Hell.
Aeneid, VII, l. 312

6   An old story, but the glory of it is forever.
Aeneid, IX, l. 79

7   To have died once is enough.   *Aeneid, IX, l. 140*

8   I cannot bear a mother's tears.
Aeneid, IX, l. 289

9   Good speed to your youthful valor, boy! So shall you scale the stars![2]   *Aeneid, IX, l. 641*

10   Fortune favors the brave.[3]   *Aeneid, X, l. 284*

11   Believe one who has proved it. Believe an expert.[4]   *Aeneid, XI, l. 283*

12   His limbs were cold in death; his spirit fled with a groan, indignant, to the shades below.
Aeneid, XII, l. 951

13   One composed of many.[5]
Minor Poems. Moretum (Rustic Dinner), l. 104

14   Death twitches my ear. "Live," he says; "I am coming."
Minor Poems. Copa (Dancing Girl), l. 38

Horace [Quintus Horatius Flaccus]
65–8 B.C.E.

15   How comes it, Maecenas, that no man living is content with the lot that either his choice has given him, or chance has thrown in his way, but each has praise for those who follow other paths?
Satires, bk. I [35 B.C.E.], no. i, l. 1

16   The story's about you.[6]   *Satires, I, i, l. 69*

17   There is measure in all things.[7]   *Satires, I, i, l. 106*

18   We rarely find anyone who can say he has lived a happy life, and who, content with his life, can retire from the world like a satisfied guest.
Satires, I, i, l. 117

19   And all that tribe.[8]   *Satires, I, ii, l. 2*

20   The limbs of a dismembered poet.[9]
Satires, I, iv, l. 62

21   A man without a flaw.[10]   *Satires, I, v, l. 32*

22   As crazy as hauling timber into the woods.
Satires, I, x, l. 34

23   Simplicity and charm.[11]   *Satires, I, x, l. 44*

24   This used to be among my prayers[12] — a piece of land not so very large, which would contain a garden, and near the house a spring of ever-flowing water, and beyond these a bit of wood.
Satires, II [30 B.C.E.], vi, l. 1

25   O nights and feasts of the gods![13]
Satires, II, vi, l. 65

26   In Rome you long for the country; in the country — oh inconstant! — you praise the distant city to the stars.   *Satires, II, vii, l. 28*

27   Happy the man who far from schemes of business, like the early generations of mankind, works his ancestral acres with oxen of his own breeding, from all usury free.   *Epodes [c. 29 B.C.E.], no. II, st. 1*

28   You ask me why a soft numbness diffuses all my inmost senses with deep oblivion, as though with thirsty throat I'd drained the cup that brings the sleep of Lethe.   *Epodes, XIV, st. 1*

---

[1] Quoted by DANTE in *The Divine Comedy, Purgatorio,* canto XXX, l. 21.

[2] Macte nova virtute, puer, sic itur ad astra.

[3] Audentes fortuna iuvat.

[4] Experto credite.
Believe an expert; believe one who has had experience. — SAINT BERNARD, *Epistle 106*
Believe the experienced Robert. Believe Robert, who has tried it. — ROBERT BURTON, *Anatomy of Melancholy, Introduction*

[5] E pluribus unus.
Adapted (E pluribus unum) for the motto on the face of the Great Seal of the United States, adopted June 20, 1782. For the Latin on the reverse of the Great Seal, see Virgil, 92:n17 and 93:n4.

[6] De te fabula.

[7] Est modus in rebus.
See The Seven Sages, 55:7; Terence, 85:13; Horace, 96:22; Lucan, 106:11; and Anonymous: Latin, 121:1.

[8] Hoc genus omne.

[9] Disiecti membra poetae.
The reference is to Orpheus torn apart by the Maenads.

[10] Ad unguem factus homo.

[11] Molle atque facetum. This refers to Virgil's poetry.

[12] Hoc erat in votis.

[13] O noctes cenaeque deum!

1   But if you name me among the lyric bards, I shall strike the stars with my exalted head.
Odes, bk. I [23 B.C.E.], no. i, last lines

2   The half of my own soul.[1]   *Odes, I, iii, l. 8*

3   No ascent is too steep for mortals. Heaven itself we seek in our folly.
Odes, I, iii, l. 37

4   Pale Death with impartial tread beats at the poor man's cottage door and at the palaces of kings.
Odes, I, iv, l. 13

5   Life's brief span forbids us to enter on far-reaching hopes.[2]   *Odes, I, iv, l. 15*

6   What slender youth, bedewed with liquid odors, Courts thee on roses in some pleasant cave, Pyrrha? For whom bind'st thou In wreaths thy golden hair, Plain in thy neatness?[3]
Odes, I, v, l. 1

7   Never despair.[4]   *Odes, I, vii, l. 27*

8   Tomorrow once again we sail the Ocean Sea.[5]
Odes, I, vii, last line

9   Leave all else to the gods.[6]
Odes, I, ix, l. 9

10   Cease to ask what the morrow will bring forth, and set down as gain each day that Fortune grants.
Odes, I, ix, l. 13

11   Seize the day, put no trust in the morrow![7]
Odes, I, xi, last line

12   Happy, thrice happy and more, are they whom an unbroken bond unites and whose love shall know no sundering quarrels so long as they shall live.
Odes, I, xiii, l. 17

13   O fairer daughter of a fair mother![8]
Odes, I, xvi, l. 1

14   The pure in life and free from sin.[9]
Odes, I, xxii, l. 1

15   Grant me, sound of body and of mind, to pass an old age lacking neither honor nor the lyre.
Odes, I, xxxi, last lines

16   A grudging and infrequent worshipper of the gods.[10]   *Odes, I, xxxiv, l. 1*

17   Now is the time for drinking, now the time to beat the earth with unfettered foot.[11]
Odes, I, xxxvii, l. 1

18   Persian luxury, boy, I hate.[12]
Odes, I, xxxviii, l. 1

19   Cease your efforts to find where the last rose lingers.[13]
Odes, I, xxxviii, l. 3

20   In adversity remember to keep an even mind.[14]
Odes, II [23 B.C.E.], iii, l. 1

21   We are all driven into the same fold.[15]
Odes, II, iii, l. 25

22   Whoever cultivates the golden mean[16] avoids both the poverty of a hovel and the envy of a palace.
Odes, II, x, l. 5

23   It is the mountaintop that the lightning strikes.
Odes, II, x, l. 11

24   Nor does Apollo always stretch the bow.[17]
Odes, II, x, l. 19

25   I hate the common herd of men and keep them afar. Let there be sacred silence: I, the Muses' priest, sing for girls and boys songs not heard before.
Odes, III [23 B.C.E.], i, l. 1

26   It is sweet and honorable to die for one's country.[18]   *Odes, III, ii, l. 13*

27   The man who is tenacious of purpose in a rightful cause is not shaken from his firm resolve by the frenzy of his fellow citizens clamoring for what is wrong, or by the tyrant's threatening countenance.
Odes, III, iii, l. 1

28   Force without wisdom falls of its own weight.
Odes, III, iv, l. 65

---

[1]Animae dimidium meae.
The reference is to Virgil.

[2]Vitae summa brevis spem nos vetat incohare longam.

[3]Simplex munditiis.
Translated by JOHN MILTON.

[4]Nil desperandum.

[5]Cras ingens iterabimus aequor.
Translated by S. E. MORISON.

[6]Permitte divis cetera.

[7]Carpe diem, quam minimum credula postero.
See *The Wisdom of Solomon 2:8*, 29:32; Ronsard, 150:8; Spenser, 160:9; and Herrick, 241:4.

[8]O matre pulchra filia pulchrior.

[9]Integer vitae scelerisque purus.

---

[10]Parcus deorum cultor et infrequens.

[11]Nunc est bibendum, nunc pede libero / Pulsanda tellus.
Ode on the death of Cleopatra.

[12]Persicos odi, puer, apparatus.

[13]Mitte sectari, rosa quo locorum / Sera moretur.

[14]Aequam memento rebus in arduis / Servare mentem.

[15]Omnes eodem cogimur.

[16]Auream quisquis mediocritatem / Diliget.
Keep the golden mean. — PUBLILIUS SYRUS, *Maxim 1072*

[17]Neque semper arcum / Tendit Apollo.

[18]Dulce et decorum est pro patria mori.
See Homer, 51:33, and Wilfred Owen, 699:5.

1   Our sires' age was worse than our grandsires'. We their sons are more worthless than they: so in our turn we shall give the world a progeny yet more corrupt.   *Odes, III, vi, l. 46*

2   Skilled in the works of both languages.
Odes, III, viii, l. 5

3   With you I should love to live, with you be ready to die.[1]
Odes, III, ix, last line

4   Gloriously perjured,[2] a maiden famous to all time.[3]
Odes, III, xi, l. 35

5   O fount Bandusian, more sparkling than glass.[4]
Odes, III, xiii, l. 1

6   I would not have borne this in my hot youth when Plancus was consul.[5]   *Odes, III, xiv, l. 27*

7   A pauper in the midst of wealth.[6]
Odes, III, xvi, l. 28

8   He will through life be master of himself and a happy man who from day to day can have said, "I have lived: tomorrow the Father may fill the sky with black clouds or with cloudless sunshine."[7]
Odes, III, xxix, l. 41

9   I have built a monument more lasting than bronze.[8]
Odes, III, xxx, l. 1

10   I shall not wholly die.[9]
Odes, III, xxx, l. 6

11   I am not what I was in the reign of the good Cinara. Forbear, cruel mother of sweet loves.[10]
Odes, IV [13 B.C.E.], i, l. 3

12   The centuries roll back to the ancient age of gold.
Odes, IV, ii, l. 39

13   We are but dust and shadow.
Odes, IV, vii, l. 16

14   Many brave men lived before Agamemnon; but all are overwhelmed in eternal night, unwept, unknown, because they lack a sacred poet.[11]
Odes, IV, ix, l. 25

15   It is not the rich man you should properly call happy, but him who knows how to use with wisdom the blessings of the gods, to endure hard poverty, and who fears dishonor worse than death, and is not afraid to die for cherished friends or fatherland.
Odes, IV, ix, l. 45

16   It is sweet to let the mind unbend on occasion.
Odes, IV, xii, l. 27

17   I am not bound over to swear allegiance to any master; where the storm drives me I turn in for shelter.
Epistles, bk. I [c. 20 B.C.E.], epistle i, l. 14

18   To flee vice is the beginning of virtue, and to have got rid of folly is the beginning of wisdom.
Epistles, I, i, l. 41

19   Make money, money by fair means if you can, if not, by any means money.[12]   *Epistles, I, i, l. 66*

20   The people are a many-headed beast.[13]
Epistles, I, i, l. 76

21   He who has begun has half done. Dare to be wise; begin!   *Epistles, I, ii, l. 40*

22   The covetous man is ever in want.
Epistles, I, ii, l. 56

23   Anger is a short madness.
Epistles, I, ii, l. 62

---

[1]Tecum vivere amem, tecum obeam libens.

[2]Splendide mendax.
Chosen by Swift as Gulliver's motto.

[3]Hypermestra.

[4]O fons Bandusiae splendidior vitro.

[5]In my hot youth, when George the Third was king. — LORD BYRON, *Don Juan, canto 1, st. 212*

[6]Magnus inter opes inops.

[7]Ille potens sui / Laetusque deget, cui licet in diem / Dixisse "Vixi: cras vel atra / Nube polum pater occupato / Vel sole puro."

[8]Exegi monumentum aere perennius.

[9]Non omnis moriar.

[10]Non sum qualis eram bonae / Sub regno Cinarae. Desine, dulcium / Mater saeva Cupidinum.
Mater saeva Cupidinum. — HORACE, *Odes, bk. I, no. xix, l. 1*

[11]How many, famous while they lived, are utterly forgotten for want of writers! — BOETHIUS, *The Consolation of Philosophy, bk. II, prose 7, l. 45*
Brave men were living before Agamemnon / And since, exceeding valorous and sage, / A good deal like him too, but quite the same none; / But then they shone not on the poet's page. — LORD BYRON, *Don Juan, canto I, st. 5*
See Pindar, 64:8, and Alexander Pope, 296:19.

[12]Get money; still get money, boy, no matter by what means. — BEN JONSON, *Every Man in His Humour, act II, sc. iii*

[13]Belua multorum es capitum.
Plato describes the multitude as a "great strong beast." — *The Republic, bk. VI, sec. 493–B*
The multitude of the gross people, being a beast of many heads. — ERASMUS, *Adagia, no. 122*
O weak trust of the many-headed multitude. — PHILIP SIDNEY, *Arcadia, bk. II*
The beast of many heads, the staggering multitude. — MARSTON AND WEBSTER, *The Malcontent* [1604], *act III, sc. iii*
If there be any among those common objects of hatred I do contemn and laugh at, it is that great enemy of reason, virtue, and religion, the multitude . . . one great beast and a monstrosity more prodigious than Hydra. — THOMAS BROWNE, *Religio Medici, pt. II, sec. 1*
Sir, your people is a great beast. — *Attributed to* ALEXANDER HAMILTON

1   Think to yourself that every day is your last; the hour to which you do not look forward will come as a welcome surprise. As for me, when you want a good laugh, you will find me, in a fine state, fat and sleek, a true hog of Epicurus' herd.

Epistles, I, iv, l. 13

2   You may drive out Nature with a pitchfork, yet she still will hurry back.   *Epistles, I, iv, l. 24*

3   They change their clime, not their disposition, who run across the sea.   *Epistles, I, xi, l. 27*

4   He is not poor who has enough of things to use. If it is well with your belly, chest and feet, the wealth of kings can give you nothing more.

Epistles, I, xii, l. 4

5   Harmony in discord.[1]   *Epistles, I, xii, l. 19*

6   For joys fall not to the rich alone, nor has he lived ill, who from birth to death has passed unknown.

Epistles, I, xvii, l. 9

7   It is not everyone that can get to Corinth.[2]

Epistles, I, xvii, l. 36

8   Once a word has been allowed to escape, it cannot be recalled.[3]

Epistles, I, xviii, l. 71

9   It is your concern when your neighbor's wall is on fire.   *Epistles, I, xviii, l. 84*

10   No poems can please for long or live that are written by water-drinkers.   *Epistles, I, xix, l. 2*

11   O imitators, you slavish herd!

Epistles, I, xix, l. 19

12   And seek for truth in the groves of Academe.[4]

Epistles, II [14 B.C.E.], ii, l. 45

13   Barefaced poverty drove me to writing verses.

Epistles, II, ii, l. 51

14   The years as they pass plunder us of one thing after another.   *Epistles, II, ii, l. 55*

15   I have to submit to much in order to pacify the touchy tribe of poets.[5]   *Epistles, II, ii, l. 102*

16   "Painters and poets," you say, "have always had an equal license in bold invention." We know; we claim the liberty for ourselves and in turn we give it to others.

Epistles, III (Ars Poetica) [c. 15 B.C.E.], l. 9

17   It was a wine jar when the molding began: as the wheel runs round why does it turn out a water pitcher?   *Epistles, III, l. 21*

18   It is when I struggle to be brief that I become obscure.   *Epistles, III, l. 25*

19   Scholars dispute and the case is still before the courts.[6]   *Epistles, III, l. 78*

20   Foot-and-a-half-long words.[7]   *Epistles, III, l. 97*

21 If you wish me to weep, you yourself
Must first feel grief.[8]   *Epistles, III, l. 102*

22   Taught or untaught, we all scribble poetry.

Epistles, III, l. 117

23   The mountains will be in labor, and a ridiculous mouse will be brought forth.[9]   *Epistles, III, l. 139*

24   From the egg.[10]   *Epistles, III, l. 147*

25   In the midst of things.[11]   *Epistles, III, l. 148*

26   A praiser of past time.[12]   *Epistles, III, l. 173*

27   Let a play have five acts, neither more nor less.

Epistles, III, l. 189

28   Turn the pages of your Greek models night and day.   *Epistles, III, l. 268*

29   He wins every hand who mingles profit with pleasure, by delighting and instructing the reader at the same time.   *Epistles, III, l. 343*

30   Sometimes even good old Homer nods.[13]

Epistles, III, l. 359

---

[1]Concordia discors.

[2]A rendering of a Greek proverb, "It's not everyone that can make the voyage to Corinth," which referred to the expense of the life there.

There is but one road that leads to Corinth. — WALTER PATER, *Marius the Epicurean*, ch. 24

[3]Semel emissum volat irrevocabile verbum.

The written word, unpublished, can be destroyed, but the spoken word can never be recalled. — HORACE, *Ars Poetica* [c. 8 B.C.E.], *l. 389*

It is as easy to recall a stone thrown violently from the hand as a word which has left your tongue. — MENANDER, *Fragment 1092K*

Four things come not back: the spoken word; the sped arrow; time past; the neglected opportunity. — OMAR IBN AL-HALIF, *Aphorism*

A word once spoken revoked cannot be. — ALEXANDER BARCLAY [c. 1475–1552], *The Ship of Fools* [1509]

Thoughts unexpressed may sometimes fall back dead; / But God Himself can't kill them when they're said. — WILL CARLETON [1845–1912], *The First Settler's Story* [1881], st. 21

[4]Atque inter silvas Academi quaerere verum.

[5]Genus irritabile vatum.

[6]Grammatici certant et adhuc sub iudice lis est.

[7]Sesquipedalia verba.

[8]Si vis me flere, dolendum est / Primum ipsi tibi.

[9]Parturient montes, nascetur ridiculus mus.

[10]Ab ovo.

Helen, the cause of the Trojan War, sprang from an egg engendered by Leda and the Swan (Zeus).

[11]In medias res.

[12]Laudator temporis acti.

[13]Quandoque bonus dormitat Homerus.

Homer himself, in a long work, may sleep. — ROBERT HERRICK, *Hesperides. To the Generous Reader*

1   As in painting, so in poetry.[1]   *Epistles, III, l. 361*

2   He has defiled his father's grave.
                                    Epistles, III, l. 471

Augustus Caesar
63 B.C.E.–14 C.E.

3   Quintilius Varus, give me back my legions![2]
    From SUETONIUS,
    Lives of the Caesars, Augustus, sec. 23

4   More haste, less speed.[3]
    From SUETONIUS,
    Lives of the Caesars, Augustus, 25

5   Well done is quickly done.[4]
    From SUETONIUS,
    Lives of the Caesars, Augustus, 25

6   I found Rome a city of bricks and left it a city of marble.
    From SUETONIUS,
    Lives of the Caesars, Augustus, 28

7   After this time I surpassed all others in authority, but I had no more power than the others who were also my colleagues in office.
    Res Gestae Divi Augusti
    (The Deeds of the Divine Augustus),
    bk. I, sec. 34

8   Young men, hear an old man to whom old men hearkened when he was young.
    From PLUTARCH, *Apothegms, Caesar Augustus*

Livy [Titus Livius]
59 B.C.E.–17 C.E.

9   We can endure neither our evils nor their cures.[5]   *History, prologue*

10   The study of history is the best medicine for a sick mind.[6]   *History, prologue*

11   Better late than never.[7]   *History, bk. IV, sec. 23*

12   Beyond the Alps lies Italy.[8]   *History, XXI, 30*

13   Our ancestors refused to allow any woman to transact even private business without a guardian to represent her; women had to be under the control of fathers, brothers, or husbands. But we (heaven preserve us!) are now allowing them even to take part in politics, and actually to appear in the Forum and to be present at our meetings and assemblies! ... Give a free rein to their undisciplined nature, to this untamed animal, and then expect them to set a limit on their own license![9]   *History, XXXIV, 2*

Publilius Syrus[10]
First century B.C.E.

14   As men, we are all equal in the presence of death.
    Maxim 1

15   He doubly benefits the needy who gives quickly.
    Maxim 6

16   To do two things at once is to do neither.
    Maxim 7

17   A god could hardly love and be wise.[11]
    Maxim 25

18   The loss which is unknown is no loss at all.
    Maxim 38

19   A good reputation is more valuable than money.   *Maxim 108*

20   Many receive advice, few profit by it.   *Maxim 149*

21   While we stop to think, we often miss our opportunity.   *Maxim 185*

22   For a good cause, wrongdoing is virtuous.[12]
    Maxim 244

23   You should hammer your iron when it is glowing hot.[13]   *Maxim 262*

24   What is left when honor is lost?   *Maxim 265*

25   Fortune is not satisfied with inflicting one calamity.   *Maxim 274*

26   When Fortune is on our side, popular favor bears her company.   *Maxim 275*

---

[1]Ut pictura poesis.

[2]Quintili Vare, legiones redde!

[3]A Greek proverb, a familiar rendering of which is the Latin Festina lente.

[4]A Latin proverb: Sat celeriter fieri quidquid fiat satis bene. See Publilius Syrus, 99:15, and Anonymous: Latin, 120:7.

[5]The two reasons for writing a history.

[6]Translated by AUBREY DE SÉLINCOURT.

[7]Potius sero quam numquam.
It is better to learn late than never. — PUBLILIUS SYRUS, *Maxim 864*

[8]In conspectu Alpes habeant, quarum alterum latus Italiae sit.
Au-delà des Alpes est l'Italie. — NAPOLEON [1797]

[9]Translated by HENRY BETTENSON.

[10]Commonly called Publius, but spelled Publilius by Pliny in his *Natural History, bk. 35, sec. 199.* Translated mainly by DARIUS LYMAN. The numbers are those of the translator.

[11]It is impossible to love and be wise. — FRANCIS BACON, *Essays. Of Love*

[12]Honesta turpitudo est pro causa bona.

[13]Strike while the iron is hot. — FRANÇOIS RABELAIS, *Gargantua and Pantagruel, bk. II, ch. 31*
When the iron is hot, strike. — JOHN HEYWOOD, *Proverbs, pt. I, ch. 2*
Nothing like striking while the iron is hot. — CERVANTES, *Don Quixote, pt. II, bk. IV, ch. 71*

1　When Fortune flatters, she does it to betray.
Maxim 277

2　Fortune is like glass — the brighter the glitter, the more easily broken. *Maxim 280*

3　It is more easy to get a favor from Fortune than to keep it. *Maxim 282*

4　There are some remedies worse than the disease.[1] *Maxim 301*

5　A cock has great influence on his own dunghill.[2] *Maxim 357*

6　Anyone can hold the helm when the sea is calm.
Maxim 358

7　The bow too tensely strung is easily broken.
Maxim 388

8　Treat your friend as if he might become an enemy.[3] *Maxim 402*

9　No pleasure endures unseasoned by variety.
Maxim 406

10　The judge is condemned when the criminal is absolved.[4] *Maxim 407*

11　Practice is the best of all instructors.[5] *Maxim 439*

12　He who is bent on doing evil can never want occasion. *Maxim 459*

13　Never find your delight in another's misfortune. *Maxim 467*

14　It is a bad plan that admits of no modification.
Maxim 469

15　The fear of death is more to be dreaded than death itself. *Maxim 511*

16　A rolling stone gathers no moss.[6] *Maxim 524*

17　Never promise more than you can perform.
Maxim 528

18　No one should be judge in his own case.[7]
Maxim 545

19　Necessity knows no law except to prevail.[8]
Maxim 553

20　Nothing can be done at once hastily and prudently. *Maxim 557*

21　We desire nothing so much as what we ought not to have. *Maxim 559*

22　It is only the ignorant who despise education.
Maxim 571

23　Do not turn back when you are just at the goal.[9]
Maxim 580

24　No man is happy who does not think himself so.[10]
Maxim 584

25　Never thrust your own sickle into another's corn.[11] *Maxim 593*

26　You cannot put the same shoe on every foot.
Maxim 596

27　Every day should be passed as if it were to be our last. *Maxim 633*

28　Money alone sets all the world in motion.
Maxim 656

29　You should go to a pear tree for pears, not to an elm.[12] *Maxim 674*

30　It is a very hard undertaking to seek to please everybody. *Maxim 675*

31　Look for a tough wedge for a tough log.
Maxim 723

32　Pardon one offense, and you encourage the commission of many. *Maxim 750*

33　No one knows what he can do till he tries.
Maxim 786

---

[1]Marius said, "I see the cure is not worth the pain." — PLUTARCH, *Lives, Caius Marius*

The remedy is worse than the disease. — FRANCIS BACON, *Essays. Of Seditions*

I find the medicine worse than the malady. — BEAUMONT AND FLETCHER, *Love's Cure* [1647], *act III, sc. ii*

[2]Every cock is proud on his own dunghill. — JOHN HEYWOOD, *Proverbs, pt. I, ch. 2*

[3]Treat your friend as if he will one day be your enemy, and your enemy as if he will one day be your friend. — LABERIUS [105–43 B.C.E.], *Fragment*

See Sophocles, 65:7.

[4]Iudex damnatur ubi nocens absolvitur. — *Motto adopted for the Edinburgh Review*

[5]Practice makes perfect. — *Proverb*

The saying "Practice is everything" is Periander's. — DIOGENES LAERTIUS, *Lives of Eminent Philosophers, Periander, sec. 6*

[6]The rolling stone never gathereth mosse. — JOHN HEYWOOD, *Proverbs, pt. I, ch. 2*

The stone that is rolling can gather no moss. — THOMAS TUSSER, *A Hundred Good Points of Husbandry. Housewifely Admonitions*

[7]It is not permitted to the most equitable of men to be a judge in his own cause. — BLAISE PASCAL, *Pensées, sec. 2, ch. 82*

[8]Proverbial; attributed to Syrus.

Necessity gives the law and does not itself receive it. — *Maxim 399*

[9]When men are arrived at the goal, they should not turn back. — PLUTARCH, *Morals, Of the Training of Children*

[10]No man can enjoy happiness without thinking that he enjoys it. — SAMUEL JOHNSON, *The Rambler* [1750–1752]

[11]Did thrust as now in others' corn his sickle. — DU BARTAS, *Divine Weeks and Works, Second Week, pt. 2*

Not presuming to put my sickle in another man's corn. — NICHOLAS YONGE [d. 1619], *Musica Transalpina, Epistle Dedicatory* [1588]

[12]You may as well expect pears from an elm. — CERVANTES, *Don Quixote, pt. II, bk. IV, ch. 40*

1   It is vain to look for a defense against lightning.
Maxim 835

2   Everything is worth what its purchaser will pay for it.
Maxim 847

3   Better be ignorant of a matter than half know it.
Maxim 865

4   Prosperity makes friends, adversity tries them.
Maxim 872

5   Let a fool hold his tongue and he will pass for a sage.
Maxim 914

6   You need not hang up the ivy branch over the wine that will sell.[1]
Maxim 968

7   It is a consolation to the wretched to have companions in misery.
Maxim 995

8   Unless degree is preserved, the first place is safe for no one.
Maxim 1042

9   I have often regretted my speech, never my silence.[2]
Maxim 1070

10   Speech is a mirror of the soul: as a man speaks, so is he.
Maxim 1073

Dionysius of Halicarnassus
c. 54–c. 7 B.C.E.

11   The contact with manners then is education; and this Thucydides appears to assert when he says history is philosophy learned from examples.
Ars Rhetorica, ch. XI, sec. 2

Sextus Propertius
c. 54 B.C.E.–2 C.E.

12   Never change when love has found its home.
Elegies, bk. I, elegy i, l. 36

13   The seaman's story is of tempest, the plowman's of his team of bulls; the soldier tells his wounds, the shepherd his tale of sheep.   *Elegies, II, i, l. 43*

14   Let each man pass his days in that wherein his skill is greatest.
Elegies, II, i, l. 46

15   What though strength fails? Boldness is certain to win praise. In mighty enterprises, it is enough to have had the determination.[3]   *Elegies, II, x, l. 5*

16   Let no one be willing to speak ill of the absent.[4]
Elegies, II, xix, l. 32

17   Absence makes the heart grow fonder.[5]
Elegies, II, xxxiii, l. 43

18   There is something beyond the grave; death does not end all, and the pale ghost escapes from the vanquished pyre.[6]   *Elegies, IV, vii, l. 1*

Albius Tibullus
c. 54–c. 19 B.C.E.

19   May I look on you when my last hour comes; may I hold you, as I sink, with my failing hand.[7]
Elegies, bk. I, elegy i, l. 59

20   Jupiter laughs at the perjuries of lovers.[8]
Elegies, III, vi, l. 49

Ovid
[Publius Ovidius Naso]
43 B.C.E.–c. 18 C.E.

21   I have faith that yields to none, and ways without reproach, and unadorned simplicity, and blushing modesty.
Amores (The Loves), bk. I, poem iii, l. 13

22   The rest who does not know?[9]   *Amores, I, v, l. 25*

23   Every lover is a warrior, and Cupid has his camps.[10]
Amores, I, ix, l. 1

24   Run slowly, horses of the night.[11]
Amores, I, xiii, l. 39

---

[1]Good wine needs no bush. — SHAKESPEARE, *As You Like It,* epilogue, l. 4
  Good wine needs neither bush nor preface / To make it welcome. — WALTER SCOTT, *Peveril of the Peak* [1822], *ch. 4*
  Bush . . . *archaic:* a bunch of ivy formerly hung outside a tavern to indicate wine for sale. — *Merriam-Webster's Collegiate Dictionary* (10th ed.) [1998]
  I.e., good wine needs no advertising.

[2]Simonides said that "he never repented that he held his tongue, but often that he had spoken." — PLUTARCH, *Morals, Rules for the Preservation of Health*

[3]Quod si deficiant vires, audacia certe / Laus erit: in magnis et voluisse sat est.

[4]Absenti nemo non nocuisse velit.

[5]Semper in absentes felicior aestus amantes.

[6]Our souls survive this death. — OVID, *Metamorphoses, bk. XV, l. 158*

[7]Te spectem, suprema mihi cum venerit hora. / Te teneam moriens deficiente manu.

[8]Periuria ridet amantum Iupiter.
  Also in OVID, *Ars Amatoria, bk. I, l. 633*
  And Jove but laughs at lovers' perjury. — JOHN DRYDEN, *Palamon and Arcite* [1680], *bk. II, l. 758,* and *Amphitryon, act I, sc. ii*

[9]Cetera quis nescit?

[10]Love is a kind of warfare. — OVID, *Ars Amatoria, bk. II, l. 233*
  A batallas de amor campo de pluma [A field of feathers for the strife of love]. — LUIS DE GÓNGORA Y ARGOTE, *Soledad* [1613], *pt. I*

[11]At si, quem malis, Cephalum complexa teneres, / Clamares "lente currite noctis equi."
  See Christopher Marlowe, 169:4.

1 Stay far hence, far hence, you prudes![1]
Amores, II, i, l. 3

2 So I can't live either without you or with you.[2]
Amores, III, xi, l. 39

3 They come to see; they come that they themselves may be seen.[3]
Ars Amatoria (The Art of Love), bk. I, l. 99

4 It is convenient that there be gods, and, as it is convenient, let us believe there are.[4]
Ars Amatoria, I, l. 637

5 To be loved, be lovable. *Ars Amatoria, II, l. 107*

6 Nothing is stronger than habit.
Ars Amatoria, II, l. 345

7 Perhaps too my name will be joined to theirs[5] [the names of famous poets]. *Ars Amatoria, III, l. 339*

8 Now there are fields of corn where Troy once was.
Heroides (Letters from Heroines), letter I, l. 53

9 [Chaos] A rough, unordered mass of things.[6]
Metamorphoses, bk. I, l. 7

10 Your lot is mortal: not mortal is what you desire. *Metamorphoses, II, l. 56*

11 You will be safest in the middle.[7]
Metamorphoses, II, l. 137

12 I am Actaeon: recognize your master![8]
Metamorphoses, III, l. 230

13 The cause is hidden, but the result is well known.[9] *Metamorphoses, IV, l. 287*

14 We can learn even from our enemies.[10]
Metamorphoses, IV, l. 428

15 I see and approve better things, but follow worse.[11] *Metamorphoses, VII, l. 20*

16 The gods have their own rules.[12]
Metamorphoses, IX, l. 500

17 Time the devourer of all things.[13]
Metamorphoses, XV, l. 234

18 And now I have finished a work that neither the wrath of love, nor fire, nor the sword, nor devouring age shall be able to destroy. *Metamorphoses, XV, l. 871*

19 Resist beginnings; the prescription comes too late when the disease has gained strength by long delays. *Remedia Amoris (Cures for Love), l. 91*

20 Love yields to business. If you seek a way out of love, be busy; you'll be safe then.[14]
Remedia Amoris, l. 143

21 Poetry comes fine-spun from a mind at peace.
Tristia, bk. I, poem i, l. 39

22 So long as you are secure you will count many friends; if your life becomes clouded you will be alone. *Tristia, I, ix, l. 5*

23 He who lives well, lives hidden.[15]
Tristia, III, iv, 25

24 Whatever I tried to write was verse.
Tristia, IV, x, l. 26

25 It is annoying to be honest to no purpose.
Epistulae Ex Ponto (Black Sea Letters), bk. II, letter iii, l. 14

26 Note too that a faithful study of the liberal arts humanizes character and permits it not to be cruel.
Epistulae Ex Ponto, II, ix, l. 47

Hillel

fl. 30 B.C.E.–10 C.E.

27 What is hateful to you do not do to your neighbor. That is the whole Torah. The rest is commentary.[16] *From Talmud. Shabbath*

28 God says: If you come to My House, I will come to yours. *From Talmud. Sukkah*[17]

29 If I am not for myself, who is for me? And when I am for myself, what am I? And if not now, when?
From Talmud. The Wisdom of the Fathers[18]

---

[1]Procul hinc, procul este, severi!

[2]Sic ego nec sine te nec tecum vivere possum.

[3]Spectatum veniunt, veniunt spectentur ut ipsae.
And for to se, and eek for to be seye. — CHAUCER, *The Canterbury Tales, The Wife of Bath's Prologue, l. 552*
To see and to be seen. — BEN JONSON, *Epithalamion, st. 3, l. 4*

[4]See Voltaire, 299:27.

[5]Forsitan et nostrum nomen miscebitur istis.

[6]Rudis indigestaque moles.

[7]Medio tutissimus ibis.

[8]Actaeon ego sum, dominum cognoscite vestrum!

[9]Causa latet, vis est notissima.

[10]Fas est et ab hoste doceri. Imitated from ARISTOPHANES, *The Birds, l. 370:* People before this have learned from their enemies.

[11]Video meliora, proboque, deteriora sequor.
I know and love the good, yet, ah! the worst pursue. —
PETRARCH, *sonnet 225, canzone 21, To Laura in Life*

[12]Sunt superis sua iura.

[13]Tempus edax rerum.

[14]Qui finem quaeris amoris / Cedit amor rebus; res age, tutus eris.

[15]Bene qui latuit, bene vixit.
This was adopted by Descartes as his motto.

[16]See *Matthew 7:12,* 33:18; Confucius, 61:20; Aristotle, 77:12; and The Earl of Chesterfield, 298:5. See also Talmud, 117:*n4.*

[17]Translated by ISRAEL W. SLOTKIN.

[18]Translated by JACOB NEUSNER.

1 The more flesh, the more worms. The more possessions, the more worry.
From Talmud. The Wisdom of the Fathers

Phaedrus

fl. c. 8 C.E.

2 Submit to the present evil, lest a greater one befall you.
Fables,[1] *bk. I, fable 2, l. 31*

3 It has been related that dogs drink at the river Nile running along, that they may not be seized by the crocodiles.[2]
Fables, I, 25, l. 3

4 Come of it what may, as Sinon said.
Fables, III, prologue, l. 27

5 Things are not always what they seem.[3]
Fables, IV, 2, l. 5

6 To add insult to injury.
Fables, V, l. 3

7 Once lost, Jupiter himself cannot bring back opportunity.[4]
Fables, VII, l. 4

Lucius Annaeus Seneca[5]

c. 4 B.C.E.–65 C.E.

8 What fools these mortals be.[6]
Epistles, letter 1, l. 3

9 It is not the man who has too little, but the man who craves more, that is poor.
Epistles, 2, l. 2

10 Live among men as if God beheld you; speak to God as if men were listening.
Epistles, 10, l. 5

11 The best ideas are common property.
Epistles, 12, l. 11

12 Men do not care how nobly they live, but only how long, although it is within the reach of every man to live nobly, but within no man's power to live long.
Epistles, 22, l. 17

13 A great pilot can sail even when his canvas is rent.
Epistles, 30, l. 3

14 Man is a reasoning animal.
Epistles, 41, l. 8

15 It is quality rather than quantity that matters.
Epistles, 45, l. 1

16 You can tell the character of every man when you see how he receives praise.
Epistles, 52, l. 12

17 Not lost, but gone before.[7]
Epistles, 63, l. 16

18 All art is but imitation of nature.
Epistles, 65, l. 3

19 It is a rough road that leads to the heights of greatness.
Epistles, 84, l. 13

20 The pilot . . . who has been able to say, "Neptune, you shall never sink this ship except on an even keel," has fulfilled the requirements of his art.[8]
Epistles, 85, l. 33

21 I was shipwrecked before I got aboard.
Epistles, 87, l. 1

22 It is better, of course, to know useless things than to know nothing.
Epistles, 88, l. 45

23 We are mad, not only individually, but nationally. We check manslaughter and isolated murders; but what of war and the much vaunted crime of slaughtering whole peoples?
Epistles, 95, l. 30

24 A great step towards independence is a good-humored stomach, one that is willing to endure rough treatment.
Epistles, 123, l. 3

25 Fire is the test of gold; adversity, of strong men.
Moral Essays. On Providence, ch. 5, sec. 9

26 Time discovers truth.[9]
Moral Essays. On Anger, 2, 22

27 Whom they have injured they also hate.[10]
Moral Essays. On Anger, 2, 33

---

[1]Translated by HENRY THOMAS RILEY.

[2]"To treat a thing as the dogs do the Nile" was a common proverb, signifying superficial treatment.

[3]Non semper ea sunt quae videntur.

[4]Opportunity knocks only once. — *Proverb*

[5]Translated by R. M. GUMMERE, J. W. BASORE, W. H. D. ROUSE, and F. J. MILLER (Loeb Classical Library).

[6]Tanta stultitia mortalium est.

[7]Non amittuntur, sed praemittuntur.
Not dead, but gone before. — SAMUEL ROGERS, *Human Life*

[8]The mariner of old said thus to Neptune in a great tempest, "O God! thou mayest save me if thou wilt, and if thou wilt, thou mayest destroy me; but whether or no, I will steer my rudder true." — MONTAIGNE, *Essays, bk. II, ch. 16*

[9]Veritatem dies aperit. Omnia tempus revelat [Time reveals all]. — TERTULLIAN, *Apologeticum, sec. 7*
Time reveals all things. — ERASMUS, *Adagia*

[10]It is human nature to hate those whom you have injured. — TACITUS, *Agricola, sec. 42*
Chi fa ingiuria non perdona mai [He never pardons those he injures]. — *Italian proverb*
The offender never pardons. — GEORGE HERBERT, *Jacula Prudentum*
Forgiveness to the injured does belong; / But they ne'er pardon who have done the wrong. — JOHN DRYDEN, *The Conquest Of Granada, pt. II, act I, sc. ii*

1   There is no great genius without some touch of madness.[1]
> *Moral Essays. On the Tranquillity of the Mind, 17, 10*

2   A great fortune is a great slavery.
> *Moral Essays. To Polybius on Consolation, 6, 5*

3   Wherever the Roman conquers, there he dwells.
> *Moral Essays. To Helvia on Consolation, 7, 7*

4   You roll my log, and I will roll yours.
> *Apocolocyntosis Divi Claudi (The Gourdification of The Divine Claudius), sec. 9*

5   Do you seek Alcides' equal? None is, except himself.[2]
> *Hercules Furens (Mad Hercules), act I, sc. i, l. 84*

6   Successful and fortunate crime is called virtue.
> *Hercules Furens, I, i, l. 255*

7   An age will come after many years when the Ocean will loose the chains of things, and a huge land lie revealed; when Tiphys[3] will disclose new worlds and Thule no more be the ultimate.[4]
> *Medea, II, ii, l. 374*

8   A good mind possesses a kingdom.
> *Thyestes, l. 380*

Marcus Manilius
First century C.E.

9   [Human reason] freed men's minds from wondering at portents by wresting from Jupiter his bolts and power of thunder, and ascribing to the winds the noise and to the clouds the flame.[5]
> *Astronomica,[6] bk. I, l. 102*

10   Who could know heaven save by heaven's gift and discover God save one who shares himself in the divine?
> *Astronomica, II, l. 115*

Caligula
[Gaius Caesar]
12–41 C.E.

11   Strike so that he may feel he is dying.[7]
> *From* SUETONIUS, *Lives of the Caesars, Caligula, sec. 30*

12   Would that the Roman people had a single neck [to cut off their head].[8]
> *From* SUETONIUS, *Lives of the Caesars, Caligula, 30*

Pliny the Elder
[Gaius Plinius Secundus]
23–79 C.E.

13   In comparing various authors with one another, I have discovered that some of the gravest and latest writers have transcribed, word for word, from former works, without making acknowledgment.
> *Natural History, bk. I, dedication, sec. 22*

14   Everything is soothed by oil, and this is the reason why divers send out small quantities of it from their mouths, because it smooths every part which is rough.[9]
> *Natural History, II, 234*

15   It is far from easy to determine whether she [Nature] has proved to man a kind parent or a merciless stepmother.[10]
> *Natural History, VII, 1*

---

[1]An ancient commonplace, which Seneca says he quotes from ARISTOTLE, *Problemata, 30, 1:* "No excellent soul is exempt from a mixture of madness." It is also in PLATO, *Phaedrus, sec. 245-A.*

Good sense travels on the well-worn paths; genius, never. And that is why the crowd, not altogether without reason, is so ready to treat great men as lunatics. — CESARE LOMBROSO [1836–1909], *The Man of Genius* [1891], *preface*

[2]And but herself admits no parallel. — PHILIP MASSINGER, *Duke of Milan, act IV, sc. iii*

None but himself can be his parallel. — LEWIS THEOBALD [1688–1744], *The Double Falsehood* [1727]

[3]Jason's pilot.

[4]Venient annis / Saecula seris, quibus Oceanus / Vincula rerum laxet, et ingens / Pateat tellus, Tiphysque novos / Detegat orbes nec sit terris / Ultima Thule.

Translated by S. E. MORISON.

As one much addicted to prophecies, and who had already voyaged beyond Thule (Iceland), Columbus was much impressed by the passage in Seneca's *Medea.* — S. E. MORISON, *Admiral of the Ocean Sea* [1942], *vol. I, ch. 6*

Next to these lines from *Medea* in an early edition of Seneca's tragedies that belonged to Columbus's son Ferdinand, there is this annotation in the son's hand: Haec profetia impleta est per patrem meum . . . almirantem anno 1492 [The prophecy was fulfilled by my father the Admiral in the year 1492]. — S. E. MORISON, *Admiral of the Ocean Sea* [1942], *vol. I, ch. 6*

---

[5]Cur imbres ruerent, ventosque causa moveret pervidit, solvitque animis miracula rerum eripuitque Jovi fulmen viresque tonandi et sonitum ventis concessit, nubibus ignem.

See Shakespeare, 219:32, and Benjamin Franklin, 301:*n*3.

[6]Translated by G. P. GOULD (Loeb Classical Library).

[7]Ita feri ut se mori sentiat.

Translated by J. C. ROLFE (Loeb Classical Library).

[8]Utinam populus Romanus unam cervicem haberet.

[9]Why does pouring oil on the sea make it clear and calm? Is it for that the winds, slipping the smooth oil, have no force, nor cause any waves? — PLUTARCH, *Morals, Natural Questions, sec. 9*

Bishop Adain [651] gave to a company about to take a journey by sea "some holy oil, saying, 'I know that when you go abroad you will meet with a storm and contrary wind; but do you remember to cast this oil I give you into the sea, and the wind shall cease immediately.' " — BEDE, *Ecclesiastical History, bk. III, ch. 14*

[10]To man the earth seems altogether / No more a mother, but a stepdame rather. — DU BARTAS, *Divine Weeks and Works, First Week, Third Day*

1 Man alone at the very moment of his birth, cast naked upon the naked earth, does she abandon to cries and lamentations.[1]
Natural History, VII, 2

2 To laugh, if but for an instant only, has never been granted to man before the fortieth day from his birth, and then it is looked upon as a miracle of precocity.
Natural History, VII, 2

3 Man is the only one that knows nothing, that can learn nothing without being taught. He can neither speak nor walk nor eat, and in short he can do nothing at the prompting of nature only, but weep.
Natural History, VII, 4

4 With man, most of his misfortunes are occasioned by man. *Natural History, VII, 5*

5 Indeed, what is there that does not appear marvelous when it comes to our knowledge for the first time? How many things, too, are looked upon as quite impossible until they have been actually effected? *Natural History, VII, 6*

6 The human features and countenance, although composed of but some ten parts or little more, are so fashioned that among so many thousands of men there are no two in existence who cannot be distinguished from one another.[2]
Natural History, VII, 8

7 There is always something new out of Africa.[3]
Natural History, VIII, 17

8 When a building is about to fall down, all the mice desert it.[4] *Natural History, VIII, 103*

9 The best plan is to profit by the folly of others.
Natural History, XVIII, 31

10 With a grain of salt.[5] *Natural History, XXIII, 8*

11 Why is it that we entertain the belief that for every purpose odd numbers are the most effectual?[6]
Natural History, XXVIII, 23

Persius
[Aulus Persius Flaccus]
34–62 C.E.

12 The stomach is the teacher of the arts and the dispenser of invention.[7] *Satires, prologue, l. 10*

13 Tell, priests, what is gold doing in a holy place?
Satires, no. II, l. 69

14 Let them look upon virtue and pine because they have lost her. *Satires, III, l. 38*

15 Meet the disease at its first stage.[8]
Satires, III, l. 64

Gaius Petronius
[Petronius Arbiter]
d. c. 66 C.E.

16 He has joined the great majority.[9]
Satyricon, sec. 42

17 A man who is always ready to believe what is told him will never do well. *Satyricon, 43*

18 One good turn deserves another.
Satyricon, 45

19 A man must have his faults. *Satyricon, 45*

20 I have seen with my own eyes the Sybil of Cumae hanging in a jar, and when the boys asked her, "What do you want?" she answered, "I want to die."[10]
Satyricon, 48

21 Not worth his salt. *Satyricon, 57*

22 My heart was in my mouth. *Satyricon, 62*

23 Beauty and wisdom are rarely conjoined.
Satyricon, 94

24 The studied spontaneity of Horace.[11]
Satyricon, 118

[1]He is born naked, and falls a-whining at the first. — ROBERT BURTON, *Anatomy of Melancholy, pt. I, sec. 2, member 3, subsec. 10*

[2]It is the common wonder of all men, how among so many millions of faces there should be none alike. — THOMAS BROWNE, *Religio Medici, pt. II, sec. 2*
Of a thousand shavers, two do not shave so much alike as not to be distinguished. — SAMUEL JOHNSON [1777]; from BOSWELL, *Life of Johnson, vol. II, p. 120* (Everyman edition)

[3]Ex Africa semper aliquid novi.
Quoted as a Greek proverb.

[4]Compare the modern proverb: Rats desert a sinking ship.

[5]Cum grano salis.
Pompey's antidote against poison was "to be taken fasting, a grain of salt being added."

[6]The god delights in an odd number. — VIRGIL, *Eclogues, no. VIII, l. 75*

[7]Magister artis ingenique largitor venter.
Necessity, mother of invention. — WILLIAM WYCHERLEY, *Love in a Wood* [1671], *act III, sc. iii*
Art imitates Nature, and necessity is the mother of invention. — RICHARD FRANCK [c. 1624–1708], *Northern Memoirs* [written 1658, published 1694]
Sheer necessity—the proper parent of an art so nearly allied to invention. — R. B. SHERIDAN, *The Critic, act I, sc. ii*

[8]Venienti occurrite morbo.
A stitch in time saves nine. — *Proverb*

[9]Abiit ad plures.

[10]Epigraph to *The Waste Land* by T. S. ELIOT. Translated from the Latin and Greek as per Eliot's original footnote.
This sibyl of Greek myth asked Apollo to let her live for years equal in number to the grains of sand she could hold in her hand. She forgot, however, to ask for enduring youth.

[11]Horatii curiosa felicitas.

Quintilian
[Marcus Fabius Quintilianus]
c. 35–c. 100 C.E.

1   We give to necessity the praise of virtue.[1]
Institutio Oratoria, bk. I,
ch. 8, sec. 14

2   A liar should have a good memory.[2]
Institutio Oratoria, IV, 2, 91

3   For it is feeling and force of imagination that makes us eloquent.[3]
Institutio Oratoria, X, 7, 15

4   Those who wish to appear wise among fools, among the wise seem foolish.[4]
Institutio Oratoria, X, 7, 21

Flavius Josephus
[Joseph ben Matthias]
37–95? C.E.

5   Everyone ought to worship God according to his own inclinations, and not to be constrained by force.   *Life*,[5] *ch. 23*

6   While I am alive I shall never be in such slavery as to forgo my own kindred, or forget the laws of our forefathers.
The Wars of the Jews,[5]
bk. VI, ch. 8

Eleazar ben Jair
d. 73 C.E.

7   Let us spare nothing but our provisions. For they will be a testimonial when we are dead, that we were not subdued for want of necessaries; but that,

according to our original resolution, we have preferred death before slavery.
Speech at Masada. From JOSEPHUS,
The Wars of the Jews,[5] *bk. VII, ch. 8*

Nero
[Lucius Domitius Ahenobarbus]
37–68 C.E.

8   What an artist dies with me![6]
From SUETONIUS, *Lives of the Caesars,*
Nero, sec. 49

Lucan
39–65 C.E.

9   If the victor had the gods on his side, the vanquished had Cato.[7]   *The Civil War, bk. I, l. 128*

10   There stands the shadow of a glorious name.[8]
The Civil War, I, l. 135

11   Keep to moderation, keep the end in view, follow nature.[9]   *The Civil War, II, l. 381*

12   Thinking nothing done while anything remained to be done.[10]   *The Civil War, II, l. 657*

13   More was lost than mere life and existence.[11]
The Civil War, VII, l. 639

14   We all praise fidelity; but the true friend pays the penalty when he supports those whom Fortune crushes.   *The Civil War, VIII, l. 485*

15   A name illustrious and revered by nations.[12]
The Civil War, IX, l. 203

16   Is the dwelling place of God anywhere but in the earth and sea, the air and sky, and virtue? Why seek we further for deities? Whatever you see, whatever you touch, that is Jupiter.   *The Civil War, IX, l. 578*

17   The very ruins have been destroyed.[13]
The Civil War, IX, l. 969

---

[1] Seize the opportunity, I beg, and make a virtue of necessity [fac de necessitate virtutem]. — SAINT JEROME, *Letter 54*

Thus maketh vertue of necessitee. — CHAUCER, *Troilus and Criseyde, bk. IV, l. 1586*

Make a virtue of necessity. — ROBERT BURTON, *Anatomy of Melancholy, pt. III, sec. 3, member 4, subsec. I*

[2] He who has not a good memory should never take upon him the trade of lying. — MONTAIGNE, *Essays, bk. I, ch. 9, Of Liars*

Il faut bonne mémoire, après qu'on a menti [You must have a good memory after you have lied]. — PIERRE CORNEILLE, *Le Menteur, act IV, sc. v*

Liars ought to have good memories. — ALGERNON SIDNEY, *Discourses on Government, ch. 2, sec. 15*

[3] Pectus est enim, quod disertos facit.

[4] A fool with judges, amongst fools a judge. — WILLIAM COWPER, *Conversation, l. 298*

[5] Translated by WILLIAM WHISTON.

[6] Qualis artifex pereo!

[7] Victrix causa deis placuit, sed victa Catoni.

[8] Stat magni nominis umbra.

[9] Servare modum, finemque tenere, / Naturamque sequi.
See The Seven Sages, 55:7; Terence, 85:13; Horace, 95:17 and 96:22; and Anonymous: Latin, 121:1.

[10] The reference is to Caesar.

[11] Plus est quam vita salusque / Quod perit.

[12] Clarum et venerabile nomen / Gentibus.
Cato's tribute to the fallen Pompey.

[13] Etiam periere ruinae.
The reference is to Troy.

Longinus
First century C.E.

1   It frequently happens that where the second line is sublime, the third, in which he [Lucan] meant to rise still higher, is perfect bombast.   *On the Sublime, sec. 3*

2   Sublimity is the echo of a noble mind.
                    On the Sublime, 9

3   In the Odyssey one may liken Homer to the setting sun, of which the grandeur remains without the intensity.   *On the Sublime, 9*

Martial
[Marcus Valerius Martialis]
c. 40–c. 104 C.E.

4   My poems are naughty, but my life is pure.[1]
          Epigrams,[2] *bk. I, poem 4, l. 8*

5   Tomorrow's life is too late. Live today.
             Epigrams, I, 15, l. 12

6   Some good, some so-so, and lots plain bad: that's how a book of poems is made, my friend.
             Epigrams, I, 16, l. 1

7   I don't like you, Sabidius, I can't say why; But I can say this: I don't like you, Sabidius.[3]
             Epigrams, I, 32, l. 1

8   Stop abusing my verses, or publish some of your own.   *Epigrams, I, 91, l. 2*

9   Conceal a flaw, and the world will imagine the worst.   *Epigrams, III, 42, l. 4*

10   The bee is enclosed, and shines preserved in amber, so that it seems enshrined in its own nectar.[4]
             Epigrams, IV, 32, l. 1

11   They praise those verses, yes, but read something else.   *Epigrams, IV, 49, l. 10*

12   You ask what a nice girl will do? She won't give an inch, but she won't say no.   *Epigrams, IV, 71, l. 6*

13   Our days pass by, and are scored against us.[5]
             Epigrams, V, 20, l. 13

14   A man who lives everywhere lives nowhere.
            Epigrams, VII, 73, l. 6

15   You puff the poets of other days,
The living you deplore.
Spare me the accolade: your praise
Is not worth dying for.
             Epigrams, VIII, 69, l. 1

16   Virtue extends our days: he lives two lives who relives his past with pleasure.   *Epigrams, X, 23, l. 8*

17   Neither fear your death's day nor long for it.
             Epigrams, X, 47, l. 13

18   You're obstinate, pliant, merry, morose, all at once. For me there's no living with you, or without you.[6]   *Epigrams, XII, 46, l. 1*

19   The country in town.[7]   *Epigrams, XII, 57, l. 21*

20   I know these are nothing.[8]
             Epigrams, XIII, 2, l. 8

Titus Vespasianus
c. 41–81 C.E.

21   Friends, I have lost a day.[9]
  From SUETONIUS, *Lives of the Caesars, Titus, sec. 8*

Plutarch
46–120 C.E.

22   As geographers, Sosius, crowd into the edges of their maps parts of the world which they do not know about, adding notes in the margin to the effect that beyond this lies nothing but sandy deserts full of wild beasts, and unapproachable bogs.[10]
     Lives, Aemilius Paulus, sec. 5

23   A Roman divorced from his wife, being highly blamed by his friends, who demanded, "Was she not chaste? Was she not fair? Was she not fruitful?" holding out his shoe, asked them whether it was not new and well made. "Yet," added he, "none of you can tell where it pinches me."[11]
      Lives, Aemilius Paulus, 29

---

[1]Lasciva est nobis pagina, vita proba.

[2]Translated by DUDLEY FITTS.

[3]See Tom Brown, 282:23.

[4]Whence we see spiders, flies, or ants entombed preserved forever in amber, a more than royal tomb. — FRANCIS BACON, *Historia Vitae et Mortis* [1623], *Sylva Sylvarum, cent. I, exper. 100*
I saw a fly within a bead / Of amber cleanly buried. — ROBERT HERRICK, *Hesperides. The Amber Bead*

[5]Nobis pereunt et imputantur.

[6]Difficilis facilis iucundus acerbus es idem: / Nec tecum possum vivere nec sine te.

[7]Rus in urbe.

[8]Nos haec novimus esse nihil.
Said of his own poems. The phrase was used by John Gay as an epigraph for *The Beggar's Opera.*

[9]Amici, diem perdidi.

[10]So geographers, in Afric maps, / With savage pictures fill their gaps, / And o'er unhabitable downs / Place elephants for want of towns. — JONATHAN SWIFT, *On Poetry, A Rhapsody*

[11]The wearer knows where the shoe wrings. — GEORGE HERBERT, *Jacula Prudentum*
I can tell where my own shoe pinches me. — CERVANTES, *Don Quixote, pt. I, bk. IV, ch. 5*

1   Where the lion's skin will not reach, you must patch it out with the fox's.[1]

Lives, Lysander, sec. 7

2   Perseverance is more prevailing than violence; and many things which cannot be overcome when they are together, yield themselves up when taken little by little.   *Lives, Sertorius, sec. 16*

3   Medicine, to produce health, has to examine disease; and music, to create harmony, must investigate discord.   *Lives, Demetrius, sec. 1*

4   The very spring and root of honesty and virtue lie in good education.

Morals, On the Training of Children

5   It is wise to be silent when occasion requires, and better than to speak, though never so well.[2]

Morals, On the Training of Children

6   An old doting fool, with one foot already in the grave.

Morals, On the Training of Children

7   He is a fool who leaves things close at hand to follow what is out of reach.[3]

Morals, On Garrulity

8   All men whilst they are awake are in one common world; but each of them, when he is asleep, is in a world of his own.[4]   *Morals, On Superstition*

9   Spintharus, speaking in commendation of Epaminondas, says he scarce ever met with any man who knew more and spoke less.

Morals, On Hearing, sec. 6

10   Antiphanes said merrily that in a certain city the cold was so intense that words were congealed as soon as spoken, but that after some time they thawed and became audible; so that the words spoken in winter were articulated next summer.

Morals, On Man's Progress in Virtue

11   When the candles are out all women are fair.[5]

Morals, Conjugal Precepts

12   Like watermen, who look astern while they row the boat ahead.[6]

Morals, Whether 'Twas Rightfully Said, Live Concealed

13   The great god Pan is dead.

Morals, Why the Oracles Cease to Give Answers

14   I am whatever was, or is, or will be; and my veil no mortal ever took up.[7]   *Morals, On Isis and Osiris*

15   For to err in opinion, though it be not the part of wise men, is at least human.

Morals, Against Colotes

16   Pythagoras, when he was asked what time was, answered that it was the soul of this world.

Morals, Platonic Questions

Epictetus
c. 55–135 C.E.

17   When you close your doors, and make darkness within, remember never to say that you are alone, for you are not alone;[8] nay, God is within, and your genius is within. And what need have they of light to see what you are doing?

Discourses,[9] bk. I, ch. 14

18   No thing great is created suddenly, any more than a bunch of grapes or a fig. If you tell me that you desire a fig, I answer you that there must be time. Let it first blossom, then bear fruit, then ripen.

Discourses, I, 15

19   Any one thing in the creation is sufficient to demonstrate a Providence to a humble and grateful mind.   *Discourses, I, 16*

20   Were I a nightingale, I would sing like a nightingale; were I a swan, like a swan. But as it is, I am a rational being, therefore I must sing hymns of praise to God.   *Discourses, I, 16*

21   Appearances to the mind are of four kinds. Things either are what they appear to be; or they neither are, nor appear to be; or they are, and do not appear to be; or they are not, and yet appear to be. Rightly to aim in all these cases is the wise man's task.   *Discourses, I, 27*

---

[1]The prince must be a lion, but he must also know how to play the fox. — MACHIAVELLI, *The Prince*

[2]Closed lips hurt no one, speaking may. — CATO, *On Agriculture, bk. I, distich 12*

[3]Better one bird in hand than ten in the wood. — JOHN HEYWOOD, *Proverbs, pt. I, ch. 2*

One bird in the hand is worth two in the wood. — THOMAS LODGE, *Rosalynde*

A bird in hand is worth two in the bush. — CERVANTES, *Don Quixote, pt. I, bk. IV, ch. 4*

A feather in hand is better than a bird in the air. — GEORGE HERBERT, *Jacula Prudentum*

[4]A saying attributed to Heraclitus.

[5]When all candles be out, all cats be gray. — JOHN HEYWOOD, *Proverbs, pt. I, ch. 5*

[6]Like rowers, who advance backward. — MONTAIGNE, *Essays, Of Profit and Honor, bk. III, ch. I*

Like the watermen that row one way and look another. — ROBERT BURTON, *Anatomy of Melancholy, Democritus to the Reader*

[7]I am the things that are, and those that are to be, and those that have been. No one ever lifted my skirts; the fruit which I bore was the sun. — PROCLUS [c. 411–485], *On Plato's Timaeus* (inscription in the temple of Neith at Sais, in Egypt)

[8]Though in a wilderness, a man is never alone. — THOMAS BROWNE, *Religio Medici, p. 82* (Everyman edition)

[9]Translated by W. A. OLDFATHER (Loeb Classical Library).

1　Only the educated are free.

Discourses, II, 1

2　Shall I show you the sinews of a philosopher? "What sinews are those?" — A will undisappointed; evils avoided; powers daily exercised; careful resolutions; unerring decisions.　*Discourses, II, 8*

3　What is the first business of one who practices philosophy? To get rid of self-conceit. For it is impossible for anyone to begin to learn that which he thinks he already knows.　*Discourses, II, 17*

4　Be not swept off your feet by the vividness of the impression, but say, "Impression, wait for me a little. Let me see what you are and what you represent. Let me try you."　*Discourses, II, 18*

5　First say to yourself what you would be; and then do what you have to do.

Discourses, III, 23

6　Remember that you ought to behave in life as you would at a banquet. As something is being passed around it comes to you; stretch out your hand, take a portion of it politely. It passes on; do not detain it. Or it has not come to you yet; do not project your desire to meet it, but wait until it comes in front of you. So act toward children, so toward a wife, so toward office, so toward wealth.

The Encheiridion,[1] *15*

7　Where do you suppose he got that high brow?

The Encheiridion, 22

Juvenal
[Decimus Junius Juvenalis]
c. 55–c. 130 C.E.

8　It is hard not to write satire.[2]　*Satire I, l. 30*

9　Honesty is praised and starves.[3]

Satire I, l. 74

10　If nature refuses, indignation will produce verses.[4]　*Satire I, l. 79*

11　All the doings of mankind, their wishes, fears, anger, pleasures, joys, and varied pursuits, form the motley subject of my book.

Satire I, l. 85

12　Censure pardons the raven, but is visited upon the dove.[5]　*Satire II, l. 63*

13　No one becomes depraved in a moment.[6]

Satire II, l. 83

14　Grammarian, rhetorician, geometrician, painter, trainer, soothsayer, rope-dancer, physician, magician — he knows everything. Tell the hungry little Greek to go to heaven; he'll go.　*Satire III, l. 76*

15　Bitter poverty has no harder pang than that it makes men ridiculous.[7]　*Satire III, l. 152*

16　It is not easy for men to rise whose qualities are thwarted by poverty.　*Satire III, l. 164*

17　We all live in a state of ambitious poverty.

Satire III, l. 182

18　A rare bird on earth, comparable to a black swan.[8]　*Satire VI, l. 165*

19　I wish it, I command it. Let my will take the place of reason.[9]　*Satire VI, l. 223*

20　We are now suffering the evils of a long peace. Luxury, more deadly than war, broods over the city, and avenges a conquered world.[10]　*Satire VI, l. 292*

21　But who is to guard the guards themselves?[11]

Satire VI, l. 347

22　An inveterate and incurable itch for writing besets many, and grows old in their sick hearts.

Satire VII, l. 51

23　Count it the greatest sin to prefer life to honor, and for the sake of living to lose what makes life worth having.[12]　*Satire VIII, l. 83*

24　The people that once bestowed commands, consulships, legions, and all else, now concerns itself no more, and longs eagerly for just two things — bread and circuses![13]　*Satire X, l. 79*

25　Put Hannibal in the scales.[14]　*Satire X, l. 147*

26　You should pray for a sound mind in a sound body.[15]　*Satire X, l. 356*

---

[1]Translated by W. A. OLDFATHER (Loeb Classical Library).

[2]Difficile est saturam non scribere.
Translated by G. G. RAMSAY (Loeb Classical Library).

[3]Probitas laudatur et alget.

[4]Si natura negat, facit indignatio versum.

[5]Dat veniam corvis, vexat censura columbas.

[6]Nemo repente fuit turpissimus.
Translated by GILBERT HIGHET.

[7]Nil habet infelix paupertas durius in se / Quam quod ridiculos homines facit.

[8]Rara avis in terris nigroque simillima cycno.

[9]Hoc volo, sic iubeo, sit pro ratione voluntas.

[10]Nunc patimur longae pacis mala, saevior armis / Luxuria incubuit victumque ulciscitur orbem.

[11]Sed quis custodiet ipsos / Custodes?
What an absurd idea — a guardian to need a guardian! — PLATO, *The Republic, bk. III, 403–E*

[12]Summum crede nefas animam praeferre pudori, / Et propter vitam vivendi perdere causas.

[13]Panem et circenses.

[14]Expende Hannibalem.

[15]Mens sana in corpore sano.

1 For revenge is always the delight of a mean spirit, of a weak and petty mind! You may immediately draw proof of this — that no one rejoices more in revenge than a woman. *Satire XIII, l. 189*

2 The greatest reverence is due the young.[1] *Satire XIV, l. 47*

Cornelius Tacitus
c. 56–c. 120 C.E.

3 The images of the most illustrious families . . . were carried before it [the bier of Julia]. Those of Brutus and Cassius were not displayed; but for that reason they shone with preeminent luster. *Annals,[2] bk. III, sec. 76*

4 He had talents equal to business, and aspired no higher. *Annals, VI, 39*

5 What is today supported by precedents will hereafter become a precedent. *Annals, XI, 24*

6 The man who gave them their name, Christus, had been executed during the rule of Tiberius by the [prefect] Pontius Pilatus. The pernicious superstition had been temporarily suppressed, but it was starting to break out again, not just in Judaea, the starting point of the curse, but in Rome as well, where all that is abominable and shameful in the world flows together and gains popularity. And so, at first, those who confessed were apprehended, and subsequently, on the disclosures they made, a huge number were found guilty — more because of their hatred of mankind than because they were arsonists.[3] *Annals, XV, 44*

7 [Of Petronius:] Nero . . . looked up to him as a decisive authority in matters of taste.[4] *Annals, XVI, 18*

8 It is the rare fortune of these days that one may think what one likes and say what one thinks. *Histories, bk. I, 1*

9 [Of Servius Galba:] He seemed more important than a private citizen while he was a private citizen, and in the opinion of all he was capable of rule — if he had not ruled. *Histories, I, 49*

10 The desire for glory clings even to the best men longer than any other passion.[5] *Histories, IV, 6*

11 The gods are on the side of the stronger.[6] *Histories, IV, 17*

12 Whatever is unknown is taken for marvelous;[7] but now the limits of Britain are laid bare. *Agricola, sec. 30*

13 Where they make a desert, they call it peace.[8] *Agricola, 30*

14 Think of your forefathers and posterity.[9] *Agricola, 32*

15 Fortune favored him . . . in the opportune moment of his death. *Agricola, 45*

Pliny the Younger
[Gaius Plinius Caecilius Secundus]
c. 61–c. 112 C.E.

16 Modestus said of Regulus that he was "the biggest rascal that walks upon two legs." *Letters, bk. I, letter 5*

17 There is nothing to write about, you say. Well then, write and let me know just this — that there is nothing to write about; or tell me in the good old style if you are well. That's right. I am quite well. *Letters, I, 11*

18 An object in possession seldom retains the same charm that it had in pursuit.[10] *Letters, II, 15*

19 He [Pliny the Elder] used to say that "no book was so bad but some good might be got out of it."[11] *Letters, III, 5*

20 This expression of ours, "Father of a family."[12] *Letters, V, 19*

21 That indolent but agreeable condition of doing nothing.[13] *Letters, VIII, 9*

22 His only fault is that he has no fault.[14] *Letters, IX, 26*

---

[1]Maxima debetur puero reverentia.

[2]Translation from the Talboys edition.

[3]Translated by J. C. YARDLEY.

[4]Elegantiae arbiter [Arbiter of taste].

[5]See Milton, 253:6.

---

[6]Deos fortioribus adesse.

[7]Omne ignotum pro magnifico est.

[8]Calgacus, addressing the Britons at the battle of the Grampians, referring to the Romans.

[9]Et maiores vestros et posteros cogitate.

[10]It has been a thousand times observed, and I must observe it once more, that the hours we pass with happy prospects in view are more pleasing than those crowned with fruition — OLIVER GOLDSMITH, *The Vicar of Wakefield, ch. 10*

[11]"There is no book so bad," said the bachelor, "but something good may be found in it." — CERVANTES, *Don Quixote, pt. II, ch. 3*

[12]Paterfamilias.

[13]Dolce far niente [Sweet doing-nothing]. — *Italian proverb*

[14]The greatest of faults, I should say, is to be conscious of none. — THOMAS CARLYLE, *On Heroes and Hero Worship. The Hero as Prophet*

Suetonius
[Gaius Suetonius Tranquillus]
c. 69–c. 140 C.E.

1   Hail, Emperor, we who are about to die salute you.[1]   *Lives of the Caesars, Claudius, sec. 21*

Hadrian
[Publius Aelius Hadrianus]
76–138 C.E.

2   Little soul, wandering, gentle guest and companion of the body, into what places will you now go, pale, stiff, and naked, no longer sporting as you did![2]
Ad Animam Suam
(Hadrian's Address to His Soul)

Chang Heng
78–139 C.E.

3   Heaven is like an egg, and the earth is like the yolk of the egg.[3]   *Saying*

Lucius Annaeus Florus
fl. 125 C.E.

4   Each year new consuls and proconsuls are made; but not every year is a king or a poet born.[4]
De Qualitate Vitae (The Quality of Life),
fragment 8

Ptolemy
[Claudius Ptolemaeus]
c. 100–178

5   Everything that is hard to attain is easily assailed by the generality of men.   *Tetrabiblos,[5] bk. I, sec. 1*

6   The length of life takes the leading place among inquiries about events following birth.
Tetrabiblos, III, 10

7   As material fortune is associated with the properties of the body, so honor belongs to those of the soul.   *Tetrabiblos, IV, 1*

Marcus Aurelius Antoninus
121–180

8   This Being of mine, whatever it really is, consists of a little flesh, a little breath, and the part which governs.   *Meditations,[6] II, 2*

9   You will find rest from vain fancies if you perform every act in life as though it were your last.
Meditations, II, 5

10   Remember that no man loses other life than that which he lives, nor lives other than that which he loses.   *Meditations, II, 14*

11   Each thing is of like form from everlasting and comes round again in its cycle.
Meditations, II, 14

12   The longest-lived and the shortest-lived man, when they come to die, lose one and the same thing.
Meditations, II, 14

13   As for life, it is a battle and a sojourning in a strange land; but the fame that comes after is oblivion.   *Meditations, II, 17*

14   Never esteem anything as of advantage to you that will make you break your word or lose your self-respect.   *Meditations, III, 7*

15   By a tranquil mind I mean nothing else than a mind well ordered.   *Meditations, IV, 3*

16   The universe is change; our life is what our thoughts make it.   *Meditations, IV, 3*

17   How much time he gains who does not look to see what his neighbor says or does or thinks, but only at what he does himself, to make it just and holy.
Meditations, IV, 18

18   Whatever is in any way beautiful hath its source of beauty in itself, and is complete in itself; praise forms no part of it. So it is none the worse nor the better for being praised.
Meditations, IV, 20

19   All that is harmony for you, my Universe, is in harmony with me as well. Nothing that comes at the right time for you is too early or too late for me. Everything is fruit to me that your seasons bring, Nature. All things come of you, have their being in you, and return to you.
Meditations, IV, 23

---

[1]Ave, Caesar, morituri te salutamus.

[2]Animula vagula blandula, / Hospes comesque corporis, / Quae nunc abibis in loca / Pallidula rigida nudula, / Nec ut soles dabis iocosi.

Amelette Ronsardelette, / mignonelette doucelette, / très chère hostesse de mon corps, / tu descens là bas foibelette, / pasle, maigrelette, seulette, / dans le froid Royaulme des mors. — Pierre de Ronsard, *A son âme* [dictated on his deathbed, December 27, 1585]

[3]Edited by William Theodore de Bary.

[4]From this derived the proverb: Poeta nascitur, non fit (The poet is born, not made).

[5]Translated by F. E. Robbins (Loeb Classical Library).

[6]Translated by Morris Hickey Morgan, with some adaptations.

1 "Let your occupations be few," says the sage,[1] "if you would lead a tranquil life."

Meditations, IV, 24

2 Love the little trade which you have learned, and be content with it. *Meditations, IV, 31*

3 All is ephemeral — fame and the famous as well.

Meditations, IV, 35

4 Search men's governing principles, and consider the wise, what they shun and what they cleave to.

Meditations, IV, 38

5 Time is a sort of river of passing events, and strong is its current; no sooner is a thing brought to sight than it is swept by and another takes its place, and this too will be swept away. *Meditations, IV, 43*

6 All that happens is as usual and familiar as the rose in spring and the crop in summer.

Meditations, IV, 44

7 Mark how fleeting and paltry is the estate of man — yesterday in embryo, tomorrow a mummy or ashes. So for the hairsbreadth of time assigned to thee, live rationally, and part with life cheerfully, as drops the ripe olive, extolling the season that bore it and the tree that matured it.

Meditations, IV, 48

8 In the morning, when you are sluggish about getting up, let this thought be present: "I am rising to a man's work." *Meditations, V, 1*

9 A man makes no noise over a good deed, but passes on to another as a vine to bear grapes again in season. *Meditations, V, 6*

10 Nothing happens to anybody which he is not fitted by nature to bear. *Meditations, V, 18*

11 Live with the gods. *Meditations, V, 27*

12 The controlling intelligence understands its own nature, and what it does, and whereon it works.

Meditations, VI, 5

13 What is not good for the swarm is not good for the bee. *Meditations, VI, 54*

14 One universe made up of all that is; and one God in it all, and one principle of being, and one law, the reason, shared by all thinking creatures, and one truth. *Meditations, VII, 9*

15 It is man's peculiar duty to love even those who wrong him. *Meditations, VII, 22*

16 Very little is needed to make a happy life.

Meditations, VII, 67

17 To change your mind and to follow him who sets you right is to be nonetheless the free agent that you were before. *Meditations, VIII, 16*

18 Think not disdainfully of death, but look on it with favor; for even death is one of the things that Nature wills.

Meditations, IX, 3

19 A wrongdoer is often a man who has left something undone, not always one who has done something. *Meditations, IX, 5*

20 Blot out vain pomp; check impulse; quench appetite; keep reason under its own control.

Meditations, IX, 7

21 Whatever may befall you, it was preordained for you from everlasting.

Meditations, X, 5

Galen
129–199

22 The chief merit of language is clearness, and we know that nothing detracts so much from this as do unfamiliar terms.

On the Natural Faculties,[2] *bk. I, sec. 2*

23 It was, of course, a grand and impressive thing to do, to mistrust the obvious, and to pin one's faith in things which could not be seen!

On the Natural Faculties, I, 13

24 Praxiteles and Phidias . . . were unable to . . . reach and handle all portions of the material. It is not so, however, with nature. Every part of a bone she makes bone, every part of the flesh she makes flesh, and so with fat and all the rest; there is no part she has not touched, elaborated, and embellished.

On the Natural Faculties, II, 3

25 That which *is* grows, while that which *is not* becomes.

On the Natural Faculties, II, 3

The Diamond Sutra
[Vajracchedika]
Second century C.E.

26 Thus shall ye think of all this fleeting world:
 A star at dawn, a bubble in a stream;
 A flash of lightning in a summer cloud,
 A flickering lamp, a phantom, and a dream.[3]

Attributed to Nagarjuna

---

[1]Democritus, *Fragment 3;* also quoted by Seneca in the essay *On Anger, ch. 3, sec. 6,* and in the letter *On the Happy Life, sec. 13.*

[2]Translated by Arthur J. Brock (Loeb Classical Library).
[3]Translated by Kenneth Saunders.

Diogenes Laertius
fl. c. 200

1   Time is the image of eternity.
Lives of Eminent Philosophers,
Plato, bk. III, sec. 73

2   There is a written and an unwritten law. The one
by which we regulate our constitutions in our cities
is the written law; that which arises from custom is the
unwritten law.
Lives of Eminent Philosophers, Plato, III, 86

Tabula Smaragdina [Emerald Tablet]
Second or third century C.E.

3   Whatever is below is like that which is above, and
whatever is above is like that which is below, to
accomplish the miracles of one thing.[1]
Attributed to Hermes Trismegistus

Clement of Alexandria
c. 150–c. 215

4   To write all things in a book is to leave a sword in
the hands of a child.[2]
The Stromata (Miscellanies), bk. 1

Tertullian
[Quintus Septimius Tertullianus]
c. 160–240

5   O witness of the soul naturally Christian.
Apologeticum, sec. 17

6   See how these Christians love one another.[3]
Apologeticum, 39

7   We multiply whenever we are mown down by you;
the blood of Christians is seed.[4]   *Apologeticum, 50*

8   Man is one name belonging to every nation upon
earth. In them all is one soul though many tongues.
Every country has its own language, yet the subjects
of which the untutored soul speaks are the same
everywhere.
De Testimonio Animae (Testimony of the Soul)

9   Mother Church.[5]
Ad Martyras (To the Martyrs), sec. 1

10   Truth persuades by teaching, but does not teach
by persuading.
Adversus Valentinianos
(Against the Valentinians), sec. 1

11   Truth does not blush.[6]
Adversus Valentinianos, 3

12   It is to be believed because it is absurd.[7]
De Carne Christi (On the Flesh of Christ), sec. 5

13   It is certain because it is impossible.[8]
De Carne Christi, 5

14   Out of the frying pan into the fire.[9]
De Carne Christi, 6

15   One man's religion neither harms nor helps
another man.
Ad Scapulam (To Scapula [the name of
a proconsul]), 2

16   It is certainly no part of religion to compel religion.   *Ad Scapulam, 2*

17   I must dispel vanity with vanity.
Adversus Marcionem (Against Marcion),
IV, 30

18   What has Athens to do with Jerusalem?[10]
De Praescriptione Haereticorum
(Prescription Against Heretics),
ch. 7, sec. 9

Fragments from the Gospel of Thomas
Third century

19   Jesus saith, Wherever there are two, they are not
without God, and wherever there is one alone, I say,

---

[1]Often cited as: As above, so below.

[2]As quoted by JORGE LUIS BORGES in *Other Inquisitions*, translated
into English by RUTH L. C. SIMMS.

[3]Tertullian is sarcastically repeating what the enemies of
Christianity are saying.

[4]Plures efficimur, quoties metimur a vobis; semen est sanguis
christianorum.
This is often rendered as: The blood of the martyrs is the seed of
the Church.
The Church of Christ has been founded by shedding its own
blood, not that of others; by enduring outrage, not by inflicting it.
Persecutions have made it grow; martyrdoms have crowned it.
— SAINT JEROME, *Letter 82*
The blood of martyrs is the seed of Christians. — LAURENS
BEYERLINCK [1578–1627], *Magnum Theatrum Vitae Humanorum*
[1665]
The seed of the Church, I mean the blood of primitive martyrs. —
THOMAS FULLER [1608–1661], *Church History of Britain* [1655],
pt. IV, bk. I

[5]Domina mater ecclesia.

[6]Veritas non erubescit.

[7]Prorsus credibile est, quia ineptum est.

[8]Certum est, quia impossibile est.
This is called Tertullian's rule of faith. It is sometimes rendered as:
Credo quia impossibile [I believe because it is impossible]. Saint
Augustine expresses the same idea in *Confessions, bk. VI, ch. 5, sec. 7.*

[9]De calcaria in carbonarium.
Leap out of the frying pan into the fire. — JOHN HEYWOOD,
Proverbs, pt. II, ch. 5

[10]Quid ergo Athenis et Hierosolymis?

I am with him. Raise the stone, and there thou shalt find Me, cleave the wood and there am I.

The Oxyrhynchus Papyri,[1] pt. I, no. 1,
Sayings of Jesus, fifth saying

1   Jesus saith, Ye ask who are those that draw us to the kingdom, if the kingdom is in Heaven? . . . The fowls of the air, and all beasts that are under the earth or upon the earth, and the fishes of the sea, these are they which draw you, and the kingdom of Heaven is within you.

Oxyrhynchus Papyri, 4, no. 654,
New Sayings of Jesus, second saying

Saint Cyprian
d. 258

2   He cannot have God for his father who has not the Church for his Mother.[2]

De Unitate Ecclesiae (On Church Unity)
[251], ch. 6

3   There is no salvation outside the Church.[3]

Letter 73 [c. 256]

Plotinus
205–270

4   All things are filled full of signs, and it is a wise man who can learn about one thing from another.

Enneads,[4] bk. II, treatise iii, sec. 7

5   One principle must make the universe a single complex living creature, one from all.

Enneads, II, iii, 8

Longus
Third century?

6   There was never any yet that wholly could escape love, and never shall there be any, never so long as beauty shall be, never so long as eyes can see.

Daphnis and Chloe, proem, ch. 2

7   He is so poor that he could not keep a dog.

Daphnis and Chloe, 15

Constantine [Flavius Valerius Aurelius Constantinus]
c. 285–337

8   In this sign shalt thou conquer.[5]

From EUSEBIUS, *Life of Constantine,*
bk. I, ch. 28

Julian [the Apostate] [Flavius Claudius Julianus]
332–363

9   You have conquered, Galilean.[6]

From THEODORET, *Church History,*
bk. III, ch. 20

Saint Ambrose
c. 340–397

10   When you are at Rome live in the Roman style; when you are elsewhere live as they live elsewhere.[7]

Ambrose's advice to Saint Augustine.
From JEREMY TAYLOR, *Ductor Dubitantium*
(The Rule of Conscience) [1660],
pt. I, bk. 1, rule 5

Saint Jerome
c. 342–420

11   The friendship that can cease has never been real.   *Letter 3*[8]

12   It is easier to mend neglect than to quicken love.   *Letter 7*

13   Love knows nothing of order.   *Letter 7*

14   The fact is that my native land is a prey to barbarism, that in it men's only God is their belly, that they live only for the present, and that the richer a man is the holier he is held to be.   *Letter 7*

---

[1]Translated and edited by BERNARD P. GRENFELL and ARTHUR H. HUNT, who also discovered the papyri.

[2]Habere non potest deum patrem qui ecclesiam non habet matrem.

[3]Salus extra ecclesiam non est.
Quoted by Saint Augustine in *De Baptismo,* hence sometimes attributed to him.

[4]Translated by A. H. ARMSTRONG (Loeb Classical Library).

[5]In hoc signo vinces.
The alleged words of Constantine's vision before his battle with Maxentius at Saxa Rubra, near Rome [312].

[6]Vicisti, Galilaee.
The Latin translation of the alleged dying words of the emperor.

[7]Cum fueris Romae, Romano vivito more; / Cum fueris alibi, vivito sicut ibi.
My mother, having joined me at Milan, found that the church there did not fast on Saturdays as at Rome, and was at a loss what to do. I consulted Saint Ambrose, of holy memory, who replied, "When I am at Rome, I fast on a Saturday; when I am at Milan, I do not. Follow the custom of the church where you are." — SAINT AUGUSTINE, *Epistle to Januarius (epistle 2), sec. 18.* Also *Epistle to Casualanus (epistle 36), sec. 32*
When in Rome, do as the Romans do. — *Proverb*

[8]Works of Jerome translated by W. H. FREMANTLE unless otherwise noted.

1   An unstable pilot steers a leaking ship, and the blind is leading the blind straight to the pit. The ruler is like the ruled.   *Letter 7*

2   No athlete is crowned but in the sweat of his brow.   *Letter 14*

3   If there is but little water in the stream, it is the fault, not of the channel, but of the source.   *Letter 17*

4   You are a Ciceronian, not a Christian.[1]   *Letter 22*

5   It is idle to play the lyre for an ass.[2]   *Letter 27*

6   The line, often adopted by strong men in controversy, of justifying the means by the end.   *Letter 48*

7   Do not let your deeds belie your words, lest when you speak in church someone may say to himself, "Why do you not practice what you preach?"[3]   *Letter 48*

8   Avoid, as you would the plague, a clergyman who is also a man of business.[4]   *Letter 52*

9   A fat paunch never breeds fine thoughts.[5]   *Letter 52*

10   That clergyman soon becomes an object of contempt who being often asked out to dinner never refuses to go.   *Letter 52*

11   It is worse still to be ignorant of your ignorance.   *Letter 53*

12   Even brute beasts and wandering birds do not fall into the same traps or nets twice.[6]   *Letter 54*

13   The face is the mirror of the mind, and eyes without speaking confess the secrets of the heart.   *Letter 54*

14   The scars of others should teach us caution.   *Letter 54*

15   I have always revered not crude verbosity but holy simplicity.[7]   *Letter 57*

16   When the stomach is full, it is easy to talk of fasting.   *Letter 58*

17   The Roman world is falling,[8] yet we hold our heads erect instead of bowing our necks.   *Letter 60*

18   Every day we are changing, every day we are dying, and yet we fancy ourselves eternal.   *Letter 60*

19   Early impressions are hard to eradicate from the mind. When once wool has been dyed purple, who can restore it to its previous whiteness?   *Letter 107*

20   Christians are not born but made.[9]   *Letter 107*

21   The tired ox treads with a firmer step.[10]   *Letter 112*

22   For they wished to fill the winepress of eloquence not with the tendrils of mere words but with the rich grape juice of good sense.   *Letter 125*

23   The privileges of a few do not make common law.[11]   *Exposition on Jona*

24   Never look a gift horse in the mouth.[12]   *On the Epistle to the Ephesians*

Saint John Chrysostom
c. 345–407

25   Hell is paved with priests' skulls.   *De Sacerdotio (On the Priesthood) [c. 390]*

26   No one can harm the man who does himself no wrong.[13]   *Letter to Olympia*

Vegetius
[Flavius Vegetius Renatus]
fl. c. 375

27   Let him who desires peace prepare for war.[14]   *De Rei Militari (Concerning Military Matters), bk. III, prologue*

Saint Augustine
354–430

28   The weakness of little children's limbs is innocent, not their souls.   *Confessions [397–401], bk. I, ch. 7*

---

[1]This was addressed to Jerome in a dream by Christ the Judge, censuring him for loving the classics more than the Fathers.

[2]A Greek proverb frequently quoted by Jerome.

[3]Cur ergo haec ipse non facis?

[4]Translated by F. A. WRIGHT (Loeb Classical Library).

[5]This is a Greek proverb.
Fat paunches have lean pates, and dainty bits / Make rich the ribs, but bankrupt quite the wits. — SHAKESPEARE, *Love's Labour's Lost*, act I, sc. i, l. 26

[6]Translated by F. A. WRIGHT (Loeb Classical Library).

[7]Venerationi mihi semper fuit non verbosa rusticas sed sancta simplicitas.

---

[8]Romanus orbis ruit.

[9]Fiunt, non nascuntur Christiani.

[10]An old Roman proverb quoted by Saint Jerome to Saint Augustine.

[11]Privilegia paucorum non faciunt legem.

[12]Noli equi dentes inspicere donati.

[13]No one is injured save by himself. — ERASMUS, *Adagia*

[14]Qui desiderat pacem, praeparet bellum.

1　To Carthage I came, where all about me resounded a caldron of dissolute loves.

Confessions, III, 1

2　I was in love with loving.　*Confessions, III, 1*

3　In the usual course of study I had come to a book of a certain Cicero.　*Confessions, III, 4*

4　Give me chastity and continence, but not just now.　*Confessions, VIII, 7*

5　Take up, read! Take up, read![1]

Confessions, VIII, 12

6　What then is time? Provided that no one asks me, I know. If I want to explain it to an inquirer, I do not know.　*Confessions, XI*

7　Too late I loved you, O Beauty ever ancient and ever new! Too late I loved you! And, behold, you were within me, and I out of myself, and there I searched for you.　*Confessions, X, 27*

8　Give what you command, and command what you will.　*Confessions, X, 29*

9　Hear the other side.[2]

De Duabus Animabus
(Concerning Two Souls), ch. XIV

10　I would not have believed the gospel had not the authority of the Church moved me.

Against the Epistle of Manichaeus,
Called Fundamenti [c. 397], ch. 5

11　Necessity has no law.

Soliloquiorum. Animae ad Deum
[c. 410], 2

12　We make a ladder of our vices, if we trample those same vices underfoot.

Sermons, no. 3

13　Anger is a weed; hate is the tree.

Sermons, 58

14　The dove loves when it quarrels; the wolf hates when it flatters.　*Sermons, 64*

15　Rome has spoken; the case is closed.[3]

Sermons, 131

16　He who created you without you will not justify you without you.　*Sermons, 169*

17　The most glorious city of God.

The City of God [415], vol. I, preface

18　Our time for this life is nothing other than a race to death.

The City of God, vol. XIII, ch. 10

19　Two cities have been formed by two loves: the earthly by the love of self, even to the contempt of God; the heavenly by the love of God, even to the contempt of self.

The City of God, XIV, ch. 28

20　For what is that which we call evil but the absence of good?　*Enchiridion [after 420], pt. XI*

T'ao Chien
365–427

21 I built my hut in a zone of human habitation,
Yet near me there sounds no noise of horse or coach.
　Would you know how that is possible?
A heart that is distant creates a wilderness around it.[4]

Untitled poem

22 I have done my plowing:
I have sown my seed.
Again I have time to sit and read my books.[4]

Reading the Book of Hills and Seas

Saint Vincent of Lérins
d. c. 450

23　[That faith is catholic] which has been believed always, everywhere, and by all.[5]

Commonitorium, ch. 2

Saint Remy
[Remigius]
c. 438–c. 533

24　Henceforward burn what thou hast worshipped, and worship what thou hast burned.

Said to Clovis at his baptism [496]

Clovis
466–511

25　God of Clotilda,[6] if you grant me victory I shall become a Christian.[7]

Legendary vow before battle

---

[1]Tolle lege, tolle lege.
　What the bell seemed to say to Augustine at the moment of his conversion. When he opened the Bible, his eyes fell on *Romans 13:12–14,* 41:40.

[2]Audi partem alteram.

[3]Roma locuta est; causa finita est.

---

[4]Translated by ARTHUR WALEY.

[5]Quod semper, quod ubique, quod ab omnibus creditum est.
The definition of the traditional articles of faith.

[6]Saint Clotilda, wife of Clovis.

[7]Clovis defeated the Alemanni in 496, and following his vow was baptized with three thousand followers by Saint Remy at Rheims.

Saint Benedict
480–543

1   We are therefore about to establish a school of the Lord's service in which we hope to introduce nothing harsh or burdensome.
Rule of Saint Benedict, prologue

Boethius
[Anicius Manlius Severinus]
480–524

2   For in all adversity of fortune, it is the most unhappy kind of misfortune to have been happy.
The Consolation of Philosophy,[1] *bk. II, prose 4, l. 4*

3   Who hath so entire happiness that he is not in some part offended with the condition of his estate?
The Consolation of Philosophy, II, prose 4, l. 41

4   Nothing is miserable but what is thought so, and contrariwise, every estate is happy if he that bears it be content.
The Consolation of Philosophy, II, prose 4, l. 64

5 From thee, great God, we spring, to thee we tend — Path, motive, guide, original and end.[2]
The Consolation of Philosophy, III, verse 9, l. 27

6   Who can give law to lovers? Love is a greater law to itself.
The Consolation of Philosophy, III, verse 12, l. 47

Pope Gregory I
540–604

7   [They answered that they were called Angles.] It is well, for they have the faces of angels, and such should be the co-heirs of the angels in heaven.[3]
From BEDE, *Ecclesiastical History of the English People, bk. II, ch. 1*

The Talmud[4]
compiled c. sixth century

8   The day is short, the labor long, the workers are idle, and reward is great, and the Master is urgent.
Mishna. The Wisdom of the Fathers

9   Whoever destroys a single life is as guilty as though he had destroyed the entire world; and whoever rescues a single life earns as much merit as though he had rescued the entire world.   *Mishna. Sanhedrin*

Ali ibn-Abi-Talib[5]
c. 602–661

10 He who has a thousand friends has not a friend to
   spare,
And he who has one enemy will meet him
   everywhere.   *A Hundred Sayings*

The Koran[6]

11 In the Name of God, the Merciful, the
   Compassionate.

Praise belongs to God, the Lord of all Being,
the All-merciful, the All-compassionate,
the Master of the Day of Doom.

Thee only we serve; to Thee alone we pray for succor.
Guide us in the straight path,
the path of those whom Thou hast blessed,
not of those against whom Thou art wrathful,
nor of those who are astray.   *Sura 1*

12   Do not veil the truth with vanity, nor conceal the truth wittingly.   *2:42*

13   We believe in God, and in that which has been sent down on us and sent down on Abraham, Ishmael, Isaac and Jacob, and the Tribes, and that which was given to Moses and Jesus and the Prophets, of their Lord; we make no division between any of them, and to Him we surrender.[7]   *2:135–136*

---

[1]Translated by H. F. STEWART and E. K. RAND, unless otherwise noted.

[2]Translated by SAMUEL JOHNSON, and used as motto to *The Rambler, no. 7* [1750].

[3]Often quoted "Non Angli sed angeli" (Not Angles but angels), these are by tradition the words of Pope Gregory when he beheld two English slaves in a Roman slave market.

[4]The Talmud is a collection of rabbinic discourses concerning Jewish law, customs, and history. Its two main sections are the Mishna and the Gemara.

[5]Ali ibn-Abi-Talib, son-in-law of Muhammad and fourth caliph, who was called the Lion of God, was murdered in 661.

[6]Also spelled Qur'an, Quran. Muslims believe the Koran was revealed by God to the prophet Muhammad [c. 570–632].
   The word Koran, derived from *karaa, to read,* signifies in Arabic "the reading," or rather, "that which ought to be read." . . . The Koran is divided into 114 larger portions of very unequal length, which we call chapters, but the Arabians *sowar,* in the singular *sura.*
— GEORGE SALE, *The Koran* [1734], *Preliminary Discourse, sec. III*
   Translated by A. J. ARBERRY [1955].

[7]"Surrender" is the literal translation of the word Islam.

1   A believing slave is better than an idolater, even though ye admire him.   *2:221*

2   God will not take you to task for vain words in your oaths, but He will take you to task for what your hearts have earned.   *2:225*

3   Wherever you may be, death will overtake you, though you should be in raised-up towers.   *4:80*

4   I [Muhammad] have no power to profit for myself except as God will . . . I am only a warner, and a bearer of good tidings to a people who believe.   *7:188*

5   God is enough for me: there is no God but He. In Him I have put my trust.   *9:129*

6   In the alternation of night and day, and what God has created in the heavens and the earth — surely there are signs for a god-fearing people.   *10:6*

7   Surely God wrongs not men anything, but themselves men wrong.   *10:44*

8   Not so much as the weight of an ant in earth or heaven escapes from thy Lord.   *10:61*

9   God changes not what is in a people, until they change what is in themselves.   *13:11*

10   We [God] have sent no messenger save with the tongue of his people, that he might make clear to them.   *14:4*

11   A good word is as a good tree — its roots are firm, and its branches are in heaven; it gives its produce every season by the leave of its Lord. . . . And the likeness of a corrupt word is as a corrupt tree — uprooted from the earth. . . . God confirms those who believe with the firm word, in the present life and in the world to come; and God leads astray the evildoers; and God does what He will.   *14:24–27*

12   The only thing We [God] say to a thing, when We desire it, is that We say to it, "Be," and it is.   *16:40*

13   Set not up with God another god, or thou wilt sit condemned and forsaken. The Lord has decreed you shall not serve any but Him, and be good to parents . . . speak unto them words respectful, and lower to them the wing of humbleness out of mercy and say, "My Lord, have mercy upon them, as they raised me up when I was little."   *17:23–24*

14   Walk not on the earth exultantly; certainly thou wilt never tear the earth open, nor attain the mountains in height.   *17:37*

15   They will question thee concerning the soul. Say: "The spirit is the concern of my Lord, and you have been given of knowledge nothing except a little."   *17:85*

16   They say: "We will not believe thee till thou makest a spring to gush forth from the earth for us, or . . . bringest God and the angels as a surety." . . . And naught prevented men from believing when the guidance came to them, but that they said, "Has God sent forth a mortal as Messenger?" Say: "Had there been in the earth angels walking at peace, We would have sent down upon them out of heaven an angel as Messenger."   *17:90–95*

17   And do not say, regarding anything, "I am going to do that tomorrow," but only, "If God will."[1]   *18:23–24*

18   Wealth and children are the adornment of this present world; but the abiding things, the deeds of righteousness, are better with God in reward, and better in hope.   *18:46*

19   Man says, "What, when I am dead shall I then be brought forth alive?" Will not man remember that We created him aforetime, when he was nothing?   *19:66–67*

20   Have not the unbelievers then beheld that the heavens and the earth were a mass all sewn up, and then We unstitched them and of water fashioned every living thing? Will they not believe?   *21:30*

21   O men, if you are in doubt as to the Resurrection, surely We created you of dust, then of a sperm drop, then of a blood clot, then of a lump of flesh. . . . And thou beholdest the earth blackened; then, when We send down water upon it, it quivers, and swells, and puts forth herbs of every joyous kind.   *22:5*

22   We [God] charge not any soul save to its capacity.   *23:62*

23   God is the light of the heavens and of the earth. His light is like a niche in which is a lamp — the lamp encased in glass — the glass, as it were, a glistening star. From a blessed tree it is lighted, the olive neither from the East nor of the West, whose oil would well nigh shine out, even though fire touched it not. It is light upon light. God guideth whom He will to His light, and God setteth forth parables to men.[2]   *24:35*

24   As for the unbelievers, their works are as a mirage in a spacious plain which the man athirst supposes to be water, till, when he comes to it, he finds it is nothing; there indeed he finds God, and He pays him his account in full; and God is swift at the reckoning.

Or they are as shadows upon a sea obscure, covered by a billow above which is a billow, above which are clouds, shadows piled upon one another; when he puts forth his hand, wellnigh he cannot see it. And to whomsoever God assigns no light, no light has he.   *24:39–40*

---

[1] In Arabic: Inshallah.
[2] Adapted.

1 Thou shalt see the mountains that thou supposest fixed, passing by like clouds. *27:88*

2 Thou truly canst not guide whom thou lovest; but God guideth whom He will; and He best knoweth those who yield to guidance.[1] *28:55*

3 The present life is naught but a diversion and a sport; surely the Last Abode is Life, did they but know. *29:64*

4 Whosoever submits his will to God and performs good deeds, has laid hold of the most firm handle, and unto God is the issue of all affairs. *31:22*

5 Though all the trees in the earth were pens, and the sea — and seven seas after it to replenish it, yet would the Words of God not be spent. *31:27*

6 We offered this trust[2] to the heavens and the earth and the mountains, but they refused to carry it and were afraid of it; and man carried it. Surely he is sinful, very foolish. *33:72*

7 He makes the night to enter into the day and makes the day to enter into the night, and He has subjected the sun and the moon, each of them, to a stated term. *31:13*

8 So today no soul shall be wronged anything, and you shall not be recompensed, except according to what you have been doing. *36:54*

9 They say, "There is nothing but our present life; we die, and we live, and nothing but Time destroys us." Of that they have no knowledge; they merely conjecture. *45:24*

10 O believers, let not any people scoff at another people who may be better than they; . . . And find not fault with one another, neither revile one another. *49:10–13*

11 The Bedouins say, "We believe." Say: "You do not believe; rather say, 'We surrender,'; for belief has not yet entered your hearts." *49:14*

12 We [God] created Man, and We know what his soul whispers within him; and We are nearer to him than his jugular vein. *50:16*

13 O tribe of [spirits] and of men, if you are able to pass through the confines of heaven and earth, pass through them! You shall not pass through them except with [the Lord's] authority. *55:33*

14 He is the First and the Last, the Outward and the Inward; He has knowledge of everything. *57:3*

15 Let every soul consider what it has forwarded for the morrow. And fear God: God is aware of the things you do. *59:18*

16 What, is he who walks prone upon his face better guided than he who walks upright on a straight path? *67:22*

17 Man shall be a clear proof against himself, even though he offer his excuses. *75:14*

18 Recite: In the name of thy Lord who created, Created Man of a blood clot. Recite: And thy Lord is the most Generous, who taught by the Pen, Taught Man that he knew not. *96:1–5*

19 Whoso has done an atom's weight of good shall see it; and whoso has done an atom's weight of evil shall see it. *99:7–8*

20 Say: "He is God, One God, the Everlasting Refuge, who has not begotten, and has not been begotten, and equal to Him is not anyone." *112*

Anonymous: Early Miscellaneous

21 Whatever kind of word thou speakest the like shalt thou hear. *The Greek Anthology,*[3] *bk. IX, 382*

22 Envy slays itself by its own arrows. *The Greek Anthology, X, 111*

23 Give a sop to Cerberus. *Greek and Roman saying*

24 Give me today, and take tomorrow. *Quoted, and condemned, by Saint Chrysostom*

25 Death is afraid of him because he has the heart of a lion. *Arab proverb*

26 I came to the place of my birth, and cried, "The friends of my youth, where are they?" And echo answered, "Where are they?" *Arab saying*

27 If only, when one heard
That Old Age was coming
One could bolt the door,
Answer "Not at home"
And refuse to meet him! *Kokinshu (Collection of Ancient and Modern Poems)*[4] *[905]*

Anonymous: Latin

28 Ab urbe condita [Since the founding of the city (Rome)]. *Saying*

---

[1]Translated by J. M. RODWELL.

[2]The message conveyed in the Koran.

[3]Translated by W. R. PATON (Loeb Classical Library).

[4]Translated by ARTHUR WALEY.

1   Absit omen [May it not be an omen].   *Saying*

2   Acta est fabula [The play is over].
    *Said at ancient dramatic performances
    and quoted by Augustus on his deathbed*

3   Actus non facit reum, nisi mens sit rea [The act is
    not criminal unless the intent is criminal].
    Legal maxim

4   Ad astra per aspera [To the stars through hard-
    ships].   *Proverb*

5 Adeste, fideles,
    Laeti triumphantes;
    Venite, venite in Bethlehem.

    [O come, all ye faithful,
    Joyful and triumphant,
    O come ye, O come ye to Bethlehem.]
    Hymn [eighteenth century]

6   Anno aetatis suae . . . [In the year of his age].
    Phrase

7   Bis dat qui cito dat [He gives twice who gives
    promptly].[1]   *Saying*

8   Cave ab homine unius libri [Beware the man of
    one book].
    Quoted by ISAAC D'ISRAELI *[1766–1848]
    in* Curiosities of Literature *[1791–1793]*

9   Cave canem [Beware of the dog].   *Proverb*

10   Caveat emptor [Let the buyer beware].   *Proverb*

11   Cras amet qui nunquam amavit quique amavit cras
    amet [Tomorrow let him love who has never loved
    and tomorrow let him who has loved love].
    Pervigilium Veneris (The Vigil of Venus)
    [c. 350], refrain

12   Cucullus non facit monachum [The cowl does not
    make a monk].[2]   *Medieval proverb*

13   Cuius regio eius religio [He who controls the area
    controls the religion].   *Proverb*

14   De gustibus non disputandum [There is no
    accounting for tastes].   *Proverb*

15   De minimis non curat lex [The law is not con-
    cerned with trifles].   *Legal maxim*

16   Deus vult [God wills it].
    Motto of the Crusades [1095]

17   Dis manibus sacrum[3] [Sacred to the departed
    spirit(s)].   *Tombstone inscription*

18   Divide et impera [Divide and rule].
    Ancient political maxim cited by MACHIAVELLI

19   Errare humanum est [To err is human].   *Saying*

20   Et in Arcadia ego [I too am in Arcadia].[4]
    *Inscription on a tomb in a painting
    [c. 1623] by* GUERCINO *[1591–1666]*

21   Ex ungue leonem [From his claw one can tell a
    lion].[5]   *Saying*

22   Fiat justitia ruat coelum [Let justice be done
    though heaven should fall].[6]
    Proverb, sometimes attributed to
    LUCIUS CALPURNIUS PISO CAESONINUS
    [d. 43 B.C.E.*]*

23   Finis coronat opus [The end crowns the work].
    Saying

24   Flagrante delicto ["Red-handed"].   *Saying*

25   Fluctuat nec mergitur [It tosses but doesn't
    sink].   *Saying*

26 Gaudeamus igitur,
    Iuvenes dum sumus.
    [Let us live then and be glad
    While young life is before us.]
    Students' song [c. 1267]

27   Habeas corpus [You are to produce the person[7]].
    Legal phrase

28   Hannibal ad portas [Hannibal is at the gates]!
    Saying

29   In vino veritas [In wine is truth].
    Proverb quoted by PLATO, Symposium,
    sec. 217

30   Ipse dixit [He himself said it].   *Phrase of "proof"*

31   Ius est ars boni et aequi [Legal justice is the art of
    the good and the fair].   *Saying*

32   Mater artium necessitas [Necessity is the mother
    of invention].   *Saying*

33   Mors ultima ratio [Death is the final accounting].
    Saying

34   Nemo me impune lacessit [No one provokes me
    with impunity].
    Motto of the Crown of Scotland

---

[1]See Augustus Caesar, 99:5, and Publilius Syrus, 99:15.

[2]It takes more than a hood and sad eyes to make a monk. —
Albanian proverb

[3]Abbreviated DMS.

[4]That is: Even in Arcadia there am I [Death].

[5]Literally: From the claw a lion.
See Herodotus, 69:15.

[6]Also familiar as: Fiat justitia et ruant coeli [Let justice be done
though the heavens fall].
   And as: Fiat justitia et pereat mundus [Let justice be done though
the world perish].

[7]The person of the accused.

1 Nihil nimis [Nothing in excess].[1]   *Saying*

2 Non multa sed multum [Not many but much].[2]
Proverb

3 Orate est laborare, laborare est orare [To pray is to work, to work is to pray].
Ancient motto of the Benedictine order

4 Parvis e glandibus quercus [Tall oaks from little acorns grow].   *Saying*

5 Pereant qui nostra ante nos dixerunt [May they perish who have used our words before us].   *Saying*

6 Piscem natare doces [You're teaching a fish to swim].   *Saying*

7 Post coitum omne animal triste [Every creature is sad after coitus].   *Saying*

8 Post hoc, ergo propter hoc [After this, therefore because of this].   *Definition of fallacy in logic*

9 Primus inter pares [First among equals].   *Saying*

10 Pro bono publico [For the public good].
Saying

11 Quos [or Quem] deus vult perdere prius dementat [Those whom God wishes to destroy, he first makes mad].   *Saying*

12 Requiescat in pace[3] [May he rest in peace; May she rest in peace].   *Saying*

13 Res iudicata pro veritate habetur [A matter that has been legally decided is considered true].
Legal maxim

14 Ruat coelum, fiat voluntas tua [Though heaven should fall, let thy will be done].   *Proverb*

15 Semper fidelis [Ever faithful].   *Saying*

16 Sic semper tyrannis[4] [Thus always to tyrants].
Saying

17 Sit tibi terra levis[5] [May the earth rest lightly on you].   *Tombstone inscription*

18 Summum ius summa iniuria [Extreme justice is extreme injustice].[6]
Legal maxim cited by CICERO *in De Officiis, bk. I, sec. 33*

---

[1]Also quoted as: Ne quid nimis.
See The Seven Sages, 55:7; Terence, 85:13; Horace, 95:17 and 96:22; and Lucan, 106:11.
[2]That is: Not quantity but quality.
[3]Abbreviated RIP.
[4]Motto of Virginia.
[5]Abbreviated STTL.
[6]That is: Extreme legal justice.

19 Tempora mutantur, nos et mutamur in illis [Times change, and we change with them too].[7]
From the Epigrammata [1615] of JOHN OWEN *[c. 1564–1622]*

20 Testis unus testis nullus [A single witness is no witness].   *Legal maxim*

21 Ubi bene ibi patria [Where one is happy, there's one's homeland].   *Saying*

22 Urbi et orbi [To the city[8] and to the world].
Apostolic blessing

23 Vade in pace [Go in peace].
End of confessional absolution

24 Vae victis [Woe to the conquered]!
From LIVY, *History, bk. V, sec. 48, as said by Brennus to the Romans*

25 Volenti non fit iniuria [To a person who consents no injustice is done].   *Legal maxim*

[Kakinomoto no] Hitomaro
c. 662–710

26 Though I grieve, there is no help;
Vainly I long to see her.
Men tell me that my wife is
In the mountains of Hagai —
Thither I go,
Toiling along the stony path;
But it avails me not,
For of my wife, as she lived in this world,
I find not the faintest shadow.[9]
The Manyôshu [late eighth century], bk. 2, poem 210-2

Bede
[Venerable Bede]
c. 672–c. 735

27 No reptiles are found there [in Ireland], and no snake can live there; for, though often carried thither out of Britain, as soon as the ship comes near the shore, and the scent of the air reaches them, they die.
Ecclesiastical History of the English People, bk. I, ch. 1

28 One day some merchants who had recently arrived in Rome displayed their many wares in the

---

[7]Also quoted by RAPHAEL HOLINSHED [1529–1580] in *Chronicles of England* [1578].
[8]Rome.
[9]Translated by the JAPANESE CLASSICS TRANSLATION COMMITTEE.

marketplace. Among the crowd who thronged to buy was Gregory, who saw among other merchandise some boys exposed for sale. These had fair complexions, fine-cut features and beautiful hair. Looking at them with interest, he enquired from what country and what part of the world they came. "They come from the island of Britain," he was told. . . . "What is the name of this race?" "They are called Angles," he was told. "That is appropriate," he said, "for they have angelic faces."[1]

Ecclesiastical History of the English People, II, 1

1   The present life of man, O king, seems to me, in comparison of that time which is unknown to us, like to the swift flight of a sparrow through the room wherein you sit at supper in winter, with your commanders and ministers, and a good fire in the midst, whilst the storms of rain and snow prevail abroad; the sparrow, I say, flying in at one door, and immediately out at another, whilst he is within, is safe from the wintry storm; but after a short space of fair weather, he immediately vanishes out of your sight, into the dark winter from which he had emerged. So this life of man appears for a short space, but of what went before, or what is to follow, we are utterly ignorant.

Ecclesiastical History of the English People, II, 13

Saint John of Damascus
c. 675–c. 749

2   God is a sea of infinite substance.[2]
De Fide Orthodoxa (On the Orthodox Faith), bk. I, ch. 9

Li Po
701–762

3   Drunk we lie down in empty hills,
heaven and earth our quilt and pillow.[3]
A Night with a Friend

Wang Wei
701–761

4   Empty hills, no one in sight,
only the sound of someone talking;
late sunlight enters the deep wood,
shining over the green moss again.[3]   *Deer Fence*

Alcuin
c. 732–804

5   The voice of the people is the voice of God.[4]
Letter to Charlemagne [800 C.E.]

6   Here halt, I pray you, make a little stay,
O wayfarer, to read what I have writ,
And know by my fate what thy fate shall be.
What thou art now, wayfarer, world renowned,
I was: what I am now, so shall thou be.
The world's delight I followed with a heart
Unsatisfied: ashes am I, and dust.   *His own epitaph*[5]

7   Alcuin was my name: learning I loved.
His own epitaph

Han-Shan
Eighth or ninth century

8   Slowly consumed, like fire down a candle;
Forever flowing, like a passing river.
Now, morning, I face my lone shadow:
Suddenly my eyes are bleared with tears.[6]
Cold Mountain Poems, no. 10

Ono no Komachi
Ninth century

9   The flowers withered,
Their color faded away,
While meaninglessly
I spent my days in the world
And the long rains were falling.
Kokinshu (Collection of Ancient and Modern Poems)[7] *[905]*

10   This night of no moon
There is no way to meet him.
I rise in longing—
My breast pounds, a leaping flame,
My heart is consumed in fire.   *Kokinshu*

Ching Hao
fl. 925

11   There are Six Essentials in painting. The first is called *spirit;* the second, *rhythm;* the third, *thought;* the fourth, *scenery;* the fifth, the *brush;* and the last is the *ink.*   *Notes on Brushwork*[8]

---

[1] Translated by Leo Sherley-Price.

[2] This is the most frequently quoted definition of God in the Middle Ages. It is based on Saint Gregory of Nazianzus [c. 330–390], *Oration 38.*

[3] Translated by Burton Watson.

[4] Vox populi vox Dei.

[5] Translated by Helen Waddell.

[6] Translated by Gary Snyder.

[7] Translated by Donald Keene.

[8] Translated by Shio Sakanishi.

1 Resemblance reproduces the formal aspect of objects, but neglects their spirit; truth shows the spirit and substance in like perfection.

Notes on Brushwork

Murasaki Shikibu
c. 978–c. 1031

2 [The art of the novel] happens because the story-teller's own experience of men and things, whether for good or ill — not only what he has passed through himself, but even events which he has only witnessed or been told of — has moved him to an emotion so passionate that he can no longer keep it shut up in his heart.

The Tale of Genji [c. 1000][1]

3 Anything whatsoever may become the subject of a novel, provided only that it happens in this mundane life and not in some fairyland beyond our human ken.

The Tale of Genji

The Primary Chronicle[2]
1040–1118

4 The Chuds, the Slavs, and the Krivchians then said to the peoples of Rus: "Our whole land is great and rich, but there is no order in it. Come to rule and reign over us."

*Annal for the years 860–862:
Invitation of the Varangians to Novgorod*

5 It is the Russians' joy to drink; we cannot do without it.

*Annal for the year 987: Vladimir's
Christianization of Russia*

Saint Anselm
c. 1033–1109

6 God is that, the greater than which cannot be conceived.[3]

Proslogion, ch. 3

Wei T'ai
Eleventh century

7 Poetry presents the thing in order to convey the feeling. It should be precise about the thing and reticent about the feeling, for as soon as the mind responds and connects with the thing the feeling shows in the words; this is how poetry enters deeply into us.[4]

From Poems of the Late T'ang [1965]

Abu Muhammad al-Kasim al-Hariri
1054–1122

8 We praise Thee, O God,
For whatever perspicuity of language Thou hast
        taught us
And whatever eloquence Thou hast inspired us with.

Makamat. Prayer

Peter Abelard
1079–1142

9 O what their joy and their glory must be,
Those endless sabbaths the blessed ones see![5]

Hymnus Paraclitensis

10 Against the disease of writing one must take special precautions, since it is a dangerous and contagious disease.

Letter 8, Abelard to Heloise

Saint Bernard
1091–1153

11 You will find something more in woods than in books. Trees and stones will teach you that which you can never learn from masters.

Epistle 106

12 I have liberated my soul.[6]

Epistle 371

13 Hell is full of good intentions or desires.[7]

*Attributed. From SAINT FRANCIS DE SALES
[1567–1622], Letter 74*

---

[1]Translated by ARTHUR WALEY.

[2]The earliest of the Russian chronicles or annals, begun in 1040 and continued through 1118 by various annalists, gives the record of Russian history since 852. It was copied several times and incorporated into later chronicles. These quotations are from the Laurentian version, copied in 1377, translated by SAMUEL CROSS.

[3]This is commonly referred to as the ontological argument for the existence of God, and derives from Saint Augustine, *On Christian Doctrine*, bk. I, ch. 7. It is also to be found in René Descartes, *Third Meditation*.

---

[4]Translated by A. C. GRAHAM.

[5]O quanta qualia sunt illa sabbata, / Quae semper celebrat superna curia.

Translated by JOHN MASON NEALE.

[6]Liberavi animam meam.

[7]Hell is full of good meanings and wishings. — GEORGE HERBERT, *Jacula Prudentum, no. 170*

Hell is paved with good intentions. — JOHN RAY [1627–1705], *English Proverbs* [1670]

Hell is paved with good intentions, not with bad ones. — GEORGE BERNARD SHAW, *Man and Superman. Maxims for Revolutionists*

Heloise
c. 1098–c. 1164

1 Riches and power are but gifts of blind fate, whereas goodness is the result of one's own merits.

Letter 2, Heloise to Abelard

Song of Roland
Eleventh century

2 Friend Roland, sound your horn.[1]

La Chanson de Roland, l. 1070

3 Roland is valorous and Oliver is wise.[2]

La Chanson de Roland, l. 1093

Poem of the Cid[3]
Twelfth century

4 Were his lord but worthy, God, how fine a vassal.

l. 20

5 Thus parted the one from the others as the nail from the flesh.

l. 375

6 Who serves a good lord lives always in luxury.

l. 850

Bernard of Chartres
c. 1100

7 We are like dwarfs on the shoulders of giants, so that we can see more than they, and things at a greater distance, not by virtue of any sharpness of sight on our part, or any physical distinction, but because we are carried high and raised up by their giant size.[4]

Cited in JOHN OF SALISBURY *[c. 1115–1176], The Metalogicon [1159], bk. 3, ch. 4*

Frederick I [Barbarossa]
c. 1122–1190

8 An emperor is subject to no one but God and Justice.

From JULIUS WILHELM ZINCGREF *[1591–1635], Apophthegmata [1626], bk. I*

Averroës [Ibn Rushd]
1126–1198

9 Knowledge is the conformity of the object and the intellect.

Tahafut-ul-Tahafut (Destruction of Destruction)

Henry II
1133–1189

10 Who will free me from this turbulent priest?[5]

Attributed

Maimonides [Moses ben Maimon]
1135–1204

11 Anticipate charity by preventing poverty; assist the reduced fellowman, either by a considerable gift, or a sum of money, or by teaching him a trade, or by putting him in the way of business, so that he may earn an honest livelihood, and not be forced to the dreadful alternative of holding out his hand for charity. This is the highest step and the summit of charity's golden ladder.

Charity's Eight Degrees

12 Astrology is a disease, not a science.

Laws of Repentance [1170–1180]

13 When I find the road narrow, and can see no other way of teaching a well-established truth except by pleasing one intelligent man and displeasing ten thousand fools — I prefer to address myself to the one man.[6]

The Guide for the Perplexed [1190]. Introduction

14 The spiritual perfection of man consists in his becoming an intelligent being — one who knows all that he is capable of learning.

The Guide for the Perplexed, pt. I, ch. 3

15 In the realm of Nature there is nothing purposeless, trivial, or unnecessary.

The Guide for the Perplexed, I, 15

---

[1]Compagnon Roland, sonnez de votre oliphant.

[2]Roland est preux et Oliver est sage.

A Roland for an Oliver — i.e., a blow for a blow, tit for tat, referring to the drawn combat between Roland and Oliver.

[3]Translated by W. S. MERWIN.

[4]By tradition, a biblical image in a stained-glass window in the cathedral of Chartres inspired these words.

See Isaac Newton, 279:11.

Translation based on Clement Webb's Latin edition.

A dwarf standing on the shoulders of a giant may see farther than a giant himself. — ROBERT BURTON, *Anatomy of Melancholy, Democritus to the Reader*

A Dwarf on a Giant's shoulder sees farther of the two. — GEORGE HERBERT, *Jacula Prudentum*

The Dwarf sees farther than the Giant, when he has the Giant's shoulders to mount on. — SAMUEL TAYLOR COLERIDGE, *The Friend, issue 15* [November 30, 1809]

[5]Thomas à Becket.

[6]Translated by M. FRIEDLANDER.

1   The foundation of our faith is the belief that God created the Universe from nothing; that time did not exist previously, but was created.

The Guide for the Perplexed,
II, 30

2   Thou has endowed man with the wisdom to relieve the suffering of his brother, to recognize his disorders, to extract the healing substances, to discover their powers and to apply them to suit every ill.

Attributed

Walter Map [Mapes]
c. 1140–c. 1210

3   I intend to die in a tavern; let the wine be placed near my dying mouth,[1] so that when the choirs of angels come, they may say, "God be merciful to this drinker!"

De Nugis Curialium (Courtiers' Trifles)

Alain de Lille
[Alanus de Insulis]
d. 1202

4   Do not hold as gold all that shines as gold.[2]

Parabolae

Kamo no Chōmei
1153–1216

5   The flow of the river is ceaseless and its water is never the same. The bubbles that float in the pools, now vanishing, now forming, are not of long duration: so in the world are man and his dwellings.... [People] die in the morning, they are born in the evening, like foam on the water.

Hojoki (An Account of My Hut)[3] *[1212]*

---

[1]Meum est propositum in taberna mori; / Vinum sit appositum morientis ori.

[2]Non teneas aurum totum quod splendet ut aurum.

Hyt is not al gold that glareth. — CHAUCER, *The House of Fame, bk. I, l. 272*

But al thyng which that shineth as the gold / Nis nat gold, as that I have herd it told. — CHAUCER, *The Canterbury Tales, The Canon's Yeoman's Tale, l. 962*

All is not gold that outward showeth bright. — JOHN LYDGATE [c. 1370–c. 1451], *On the Mutability of Human Affairs*

Non omne quod fulget est aurum. — GABRIEL BIEL [c. 1420–1495], *Expositio Canonis Messe, lecture 77*, derived from WILLIAM OF AUVERGNE [d. 1249]

All that glisters is not gold — / Often have you heard that told. — SHAKESPEARE, *The Merchant of Venice, act II, sc. vii, l. 65*

[3]Translated by DONALD KEENE.

Walther von der Vogelweide
c. 1170–c. 1230

6 Now the summer came to pass
And flowers through the grass
Joyously sprang,
While all the tribes of birds sang.[4]   *Dream Song, st. 1*

7 The sun no longer shows
His face; and treason sows
His secret seeds that no man can detect;
Fathers by their children are undone;
The brother would the brother cheat;
And the cowled monk is a deceit...
Might is right, and justice there is none.[5]

Millennium

Eike von Repgow
fl. c. 1220

8   Who comes first, grinds first.[6]

Sachsenspiegel (Saxon Mirror) [1219–1233]

Saint Francis of Assisi[7]
c. 1181–1226

9 Praise to thee, my Lord, for all thy creatures,
Above all Brother Sun
Who brings us the day and lends us his light.

The Song of Brother Sun and of
All His Creatures [1225]

10 Love is he, radiant with great splendor,
And speaks to us of Thee, O Most High.

The Song of Brother Sun and
of All His Creatures

11   Where there is charity and wisdom, there is neither fear nor ignorance. Where there is patience and humility, there is neither anger nor vexation. Where there is poverty and joy, there is neither greed nor avarice. Where there is peace and meditation, there is neither anxiety nor doubt.

The Counsels of the Holy Father
Saint Francis. Admonition 27

12   Lord, make me an instrument of Your peace. Where there is hatred let me sow love; where there is injury, pardon; where there is doubt, faith; where there is despair, hope; where there is darkness, light; and where there is sadness, joy.

---

[4]Dô der sumer komen was, / Und die blumen dur daz gras / Wünneclâchen sprungen, / Aedâ die vogele sungen.

[5]Translated by JETHRO BITHELL.

[6]Familiar as: First come first served.
A rule to determine the order by which a miller would grind corn.

[7]Translated by LEO SHERLEY-PRICE.

O divine Master, grant that I may not so much seek to be consoled as to console; to be understood as to understand; to be loved as to love. For it is in giving that we receive; it is in pardoning that we are pardoned; and it is in dying that we are born to eternal life.

Attributed

1   I have sinned against my brother the ass.

Dying words

Arnaud-Amaury
d. 1225

2   Kill them all. God will recognize his own.[1]
Said during a massacre of those considered heretics in Béziers [1209]

Jalal Al-Din Rumi
1207–1273

3 This poetry. I never know what I'm going to say.
I don't plan it.
When I'm outside the saying of it,
I get very quiet and rarely speak at all.
Who Says Words with My Mouth[2]

Magna Carta
1215

4   No freeman shall be taken, or imprisoned, or outlawed, or exiled, or in any way harmed, nor will we go upon him nor will we send upon him, except by the legal judgment of his peers or by the law of the land.
Clause 39

5   To none will we sell, to none deny or delay, right or justice.
Clause 40

Saint Bonaventure
c. 1217–1274

6   An example from the monkey: The higher it climbs, the more you see of its behind.[3]
Conferences on the Gospel of John

Roger Bacon
c. 1220–c. 1292

7   If in other sciences we should arrive at certainty without doubt and truth without error, it behooves us to place the foundations of knowledge in mathematics.
Opus Majus (The Greater Work),[4]
bk. I, ch. 4

Shih Nai-An
Thirteenth century

8   A man should not marry after thirty years of age; should not enter the government service after the age of forty; should not have any more children after the age of fifty; and should not travel after the age of sixty. That is because the proper time for those things has passed.[5]
Water Margin, vol. 1, introduction

Alfonso X
[Alfonso the Wise]
1221–1284

9   Had I been present at the creation, I would have given some useful hints for the better ordering of the universe.
Attributed

Rutebeuf
d. 1285

10 What became of the friends I had
With whom I was always so close
And loved so dearly?
La Complainte Rutebeuf

11   Friendship is dead:
They were friends who go with the wind,
And the wind was blowing at my door.
La Complainte Rutebeuf

Saint Thomas Aquinas
c. 1225–1274

12 Sing, my tongue, the Savior's glory,
Of His Flesh the mystery sing;

---

[1]Attributed to Arnaud by the Cistercian writer Caesarius of Heisterbach [c. 1180–c. 1240]: Caedite eos. Novit enim Dominus qui sunt eius.

[2]Translated by John Moyne and Coleman Barks.

[3]Exemplum de simia, quae, quanto plus ascendit, tanto plus apparent posteriora eius.
Translated by the Rev. Walter J. Burghardt, S.J.

---

[4]Translated by Robert Burke.

[5]Translated by J. H. Jackson.

Of the Blood, all price exceeding,
Shed by our immortal King.[1]
> *Pange, Lingua (hymn for Vespers on
> the Feast of Corpus Christi), st. 1*

1 Down in adoration falling,
Lo! the sacred Host we hail;
Lo! o'er ancient forms departing,
Newer rites of grace prevail;
Faith for all defects supplying,
Where the feeble senses fail.
> *Pange, Lingua, st. 5 (Tantum Ergo)*

2 Thus Angels' Bread is made
The Bread of man today:
The Living Bread from Heaven
With figures doth away:
O wondrous gift indeed!
The poor and lowly may
Upon their Lord and Master feed.[2]
> *Sacris Solemniis Juncta Sint Gaudia
> (Matins hymn for Corpus Christi),
> st. 6 (Panis Angelicus)*

3 O saving Victim, opening wide
The gate of heaven to man below,
Our foes press on from every side,
Thine aid supply, Thy strength bestow.[3]
> *Verbum Supernum Prodiens (hymn for
> Lauds on Corpus Christi), st. 5
> (O Salutaris Hostia)*

4 Lord Jesu, blessed Pelican.[4]
> *Adoro Te Devote (hymn appointed for the
> Thanksgiving after Mass), st. 6
> (Pie Pellicane Jesu Domine)*

5 Three things are necessary for the salvation of man: to know what he ought to believe; to know what he ought to desire; and to know what he ought to do.   *Two Precepts of Charity [1273]*

6 Concerning perfect blessedness which consists in a vision of God.[5]
> *Summa Theologica [1273], pt. 1 of Pt. II, question 3*

7 Law: an ordinance of reason for the common good, made by him who has care of the community.
> *Summa Theologica, pt. 1 of Pt. II, question 90*

8 In order that the happiness of the saints may be more delightful to them and that they may render more copious thanks to God for it, they are allowed to see perfectly the sufferings of the damned.[6]
> *Summa Theologica, supplement to Pt. III,
> question 94*

9 Reason in man is rather like God in the world.
> *Opuscule 11, De Regno*

Meister Eckhart
[Eckhart von Hochheim]
c. 1260–c. 1327

10 In silence man can most readily preserve his integrity.   *Directions for the Contemplative Life*

11 The more wise and powerful a master, the more directly is his work created, and the simpler it is.
> *Of the Eternal Birth*

12 One must not always think so much about what one should do, but rather what one should be. Our works do not ennoble us; but we must ennoble our works.   *Work and Being*

13 If the soul knows God in creatures, night falls. If it sees how they have their being in God, morning breaks. But if it sees the Being that is in God himself alone, it is high noon! See! This is what one ought to desire with mad fervor—that all his life should become Being.[7]
> *Sermons. Being Is More than Life*

14 The eye in which I see God is the same eye in which God sees me. My eye and God's eye are one seeing, one knowing, and one loving.[8]
> *German Sermons. Sermon 12*

Dante Alighieri
1265–1321

15 In that part of the book of my memory before which is little that can be read, there is a rubric, saying, "Incipit Vita Nova [The new life begins]."
> *La Vita Nuova[9] [1293]*

---

[1]Pange, lingua, gloriosi / Corporis mysterium / Sanguinisque pretiosi, / Quem in mundi pretium / Fructus ventris generosi / Rex effudit gentium.
 Translated by EDWARD CASWALL.
 Pange, lingua, gloriosi proelium certáminis [Sing, my tongue, the glorious battle]. — SAINT VENANTIUS FORTUNATUS [c. 530–c. 610], bishop of Poitiers

[2]Translated by J. D. CHAMBERS.

[3]Translated by EDWARD CASWALL.

[4]The pelican was once believed to wound itself and feed its young with its own blood. It became a symbol of the selfless sacrifice of Jesus on the cross.
 LAERTES: I'll ope wide my arms; / And like the kind life-rendering pelican, / Repast them with my blood. — SHAKESPEARE, *Hamlet, act IV, sc. v, l. 146.*

[5]Probably the origin of the phrase: beatific vision.

[6]Translated by FATHERS OF THE ENGLISH DOMINICAN PROVINCE.

[7]Translated by RAYMOND BERNARD BLAKNEY.

[8]Translated by FRANK TOBIN.

[9]Translated by DANTE GABRIEL ROSSETTI.

1 Love hath so long possessed me for his own
And made his lordship so familiar.
La Vita Nuova

2 Love with delight discourses in my mind
Upon my lady's admirable gifts . . .
Beyond the range of human intellect.
Il Convito (The Banquet),[1] *treatise 3, l. 1*

3 In the middle of the journey of our life I came to myself within a dark wood where the straight way was lost.[2]
The Divine Comedy [c. 1310–1321].
Inferno,[3] *canto I, l. 1*

4 And as he, who with laboring breath has escaped from the deep to the shore, turns to the perilous waters and gazes.
The Divine Comedy. Inferno, I, l. 22

5 Thou [Virgil] art my master and my author, thou art he from whom alone I took the style whose beauty has done me honor.
The Divine Comedy. Inferno, I, l. 85

6 All hope abandon, ye who enter here![4]
The Divine Comedy. Inferno, III, l. 9

7 Here must all distrust be left behind; all cowardice must be ended.
The Divine Comedy. Inferno, III, l. 14

8 There sighs, lamentations and loud wailings resounded through the starless air, so that at first it made me weep; strange tongues, horrible language, words of pain, tones of anger, voices loud and hoarse, and with these the sound of hands, made a tumult which is whirling through that air forever dark, as sand eddies in a whirlwind.
The Divine Comedy. Inferno, III, l. 22

9 This miserable state is borne by the wretched souls of those who lived without disgrace and without praise.   *The Divine Comedy. Inferno, III, l. 34*

10 Let us not speak of them; but look, and pass on.[5]   *The Divine Comedy. Inferno, III, l. 51*

11 These wretches, who never were alive.
The Divine Comedy. Inferno, III, l. 64

12 Into the eternal darkness, into fire and into ice.[5]
The Divine Comedy. Inferno, III, l. 87

13 Without hope we live in desire.
The Divine Comedy. Inferno, IV, l. 42

14 I came into a place void of all light, which bellows like the sea in tempest, when it is combated by warring winds.[6]
The Divine Comedy. Inferno, V, l. 28

15 As in the cold season their wings bear the starlings along in a broad, dense flock, so does that blast the wicked spirits. Hither, thither, downward, upward, it drives them.[7]
The Divine Comedy. Inferno, V, l. 40

16 Love, which is quickly kindled in the gentle heart, seized this man for the fair form that was taken from me, and the manner still hurts me. Love, which absolves no beloved one from loving, seized me so strongly with his charm that, as thou seest, it does not leave me yet.
The Divine Comedy. Inferno, V, l. 100

17 What sweet thoughts, what longing led them to the woeful pass.[6]
The Divine Comedy. Inferno, V, l. 113

18 There is no greater sorrow
Than to be mindful of the happy time
In misery.[8]
The Divine Comedy. Inferno, V, l. 121

19 Galeotto was the book and he that wrote it; that day we read in it no farther.[9]
The Divine Comedy. Inferno, V, l. 137

20 I fell as a dead body falls.
The Divine Comedy. Inferno, V, last line

21 Pride, Envy, and Avarice are the three sparks that have set these hearts on fire.
The Divine Comedy. Inferno, VI, l. 74

22 But when thou shalt be in the sweet world, I pray thee bring me to men's memory.
The Divine Comedy. Inferno, VI, l. 88

23 Ye that are of good understanding, note the doctrine that is hidden under the veil of the strange verses!
The Divine Comedy. Inferno, IX, l. 61

24 Already I had fixed my look on his; and he rose upright with breast and countenance, as if he entertained great scorn of Hell.[6]
The Divine Comedy. Inferno, X, l. 34

---

[1] Translated by Charles Lyell.
The first line is also in *The Divine Comedy, Purgatorio, canto II, l. 112.*

[2] Nel mezzo del cammin di nostra vita / Mi ritrovai per una selva oscura, / Che la diritta via era smarrita.

[3] Translated by John D. Sinclair unless otherwise noted.

[4] Lasciate ogni speranza, voi ch'entrate.
Traditional translation.

[5] Translated by John Aitken Carlyle.

---

[6] Translated by John Aitken Carlyle.

[7] Di qua, di là, di giù, di su li mena.

[8] Nessun maggior dolore / Che ricordarsi del tempo felice / Nella miseria.
Translated by Henry Wadsworth Longfellow.

[9] Galeotto fu il libro e chi lo scrisse: / Quel giorno più non vi leggemmo avante.

1 Necessity brings him [Dante] here, not pleasure. *The Divine Comedy. Inferno, XII, l. 87*

2 If thou follow thy star, thou canst not fail of a glorious haven.
The Divine Comedy. Inferno, XV, l. 55

3 So my conscience chide me not, I am ready for Fortune as she wills.
The Divine Comedy. Inferno, XV, l. 91

4 He listens well who takes notes.
The Divine Comedy. Inferno, XV, l. 99

5 A fair request should be followed by the deed in silence. *The Divine Comedy. Inferno, XXIV, l. 77*

6 Consider your origin; you were not born to live like brutes, but to follow virtue and knowledge.
The Divine Comedy. Inferno, XXVI, l. 118

7 If I thought my answer were to one who would ever return to the world, this flame should stay without another movement; but since none ever returned alive from this depth, if what I hear is true, I answer thee without fear of infamy.
The Divine Comedy. Inferno, XXVII, l. 60

8 And thence we came forth, to see again the stars.[1] *The Divine Comedy. Inferno, XXXIV, l. 139*

9 To run over better waters the little vessel of my genius now hoists her sails, as she leaves behind her a sea so cruel.
The Divine Comedy. Purgatorio,[2] I, l. 1

10 He goes seeking liberty, which is so dear, as he knows who for it renounces life.
The Divine Comedy. Purgatorio, I, l. 71

11 O conscience, upright and stainless, how bitter a sting to thee is a little fault!
The Divine Comedy. Purgatorio, III, 1. 8

12 For to lose time is most displeasing to him who knows most.
The Divine Comedy. Purgatorio, III, 1. 78

13 The Infinite Goodness has such wide arms that it takes whatever turns to it.
The Divine Comedy. Purgatorio, III, l. 121

14 Unless, before then, the prayer assist me which rises from a heart that lives in grace: what avails the other, which is not heard in heaven?
The Divine Comedy. Purgatorio, IV, l. 133

15 "Why is thy mind so entangled," said the Master [Virgil], "that thou slackenest thy pace? What is it to thee what they whisper there? Come after me and let the people talk. Stand like a firm tower that never shakes its top for blast of wind."
The Divine Comedy. Purgatorio, V,[3] l. 10

16 Go right on and listen as thou goest.
The Divine Comedy. Purgatorio, V, l. 45

17 [Beatrice] who shall be a light between truth and intellect. *The Divine Comedy. Purgatorio, VI, l. 45*

18 It was now the hour that turns back the longing of seafarers and melts their hearts, the day they have bidden dear friends farewell, and pierces the new traveler with love if he hears in the distance the bell that seems to mourn the dying day.
The Divine Comedy. Purgatorio, VIII,[3] l. 1

19 Give us this day the daily manna, without which, in this rough desert, he backward goes, who toils most to go on.
The Divine Comedy. Purgatorio, XI, l. 13

20 Worldly renown is naught but a breath of wind, which now comes this way and now comes that, and changes name because it changes quarter.
The Divine Comedy. Purgatorio, XI, l. 100

21 O human race, born to fly upward, wherefore at a little wind dost thou so fall?
The Divine Comedy. Purgatorio, XII, l. 95

22 To a greater force, and to a better nature, you, free, are subject, and that creates the mind in you, which the heavens have not in their charge. Therefore if the present world go astray, the cause is in you, in you it is to be sought.
The Divine Comedy. Purgatorio, XVI, l. 79

23 Everyone confusedly conceives of a good in which the mind may be at rest, and desires it; wherefore everyone strives to attain to it.
The Divine Comedy. Purgatorio, XVII, l. 127

24 Love kindled by virtue always kindles another, provided that its flame appear outwardly.
The Divine Comedy. Purgatorio, XXII, l. 10

25 Less than a drop of blood remains in me that does not tremble; I recognize the signals of the ancient flame.[4]
The Divine Comedy. Purgatorio, XXX, l. 46

26 But so much the more malign and wild does the ground become with bad seed and untilled, as it has the more of good earthly vigor.
The Divine Comedy. Purgatorio, XXX, l. 118

---

[1]E quindi uscimmo a riveder le stelle.

[2]Translated by CHARLES ELIOT NORTON unless otherwise noted.

[3]Translated by JOHN D. SINCLAIR.

[4]Men che dramma / Di sangue m'è rimaso, che no tremi; / Conosco i segni dell' antica fiamma.

1   Pure and disposed to mount unto the stars.[1]
> *The Divine Comedy. Purgatorio,*
> *XXXIII, l. 145*

2   The glory of Him who moves everything penetrates through the universe, and is resplendent in one part more and in another less.
> *The Divine Comedy. Paradiso,[2] I, l. 1*

3   A great flame follows a little spark.
> *The Divine Comedy. Paradiso, I, l. 34*

4   And in His will is our peace.[3]
> *The Divine Comedy. Paradiso, III, l. 85*

5   The greatest gift that God in His bounty made in creation, and the most conformable to His goodness, and that which He prizes the most, was the freedom of the will, with which the creatures with intelligence, they all and they alone, were and are endowed.
> *The Divine Comedy. Paradiso, V, l. 19*

6   Thou shalt prove how salt is the taste of another's bread and how hard is the way up and down another man's stairs.
> *The Divine Comedy. Paradiso,*
> *XVII, l. 58*

7   Overcoming me with the light of a smile, she [Beatrice] said to me: "Turn and listen, for not only in my eyes is Paradise."
> *The Divine Comedy. Paradiso,*
> *XVIII, l. 19*

8   Therefore the sight that is granted to your world penetrates within the Eternal Justice as the eye into the sea; for though from the shore it sees the bottom, in the open sea it does not, and yet the bottom is there but the depth conceals it.
> *The Divine Comedy. Paradiso, XIX, l. 73*

9   The experience of this sweet life.[4]
> *The Divine Comedy. Paradiso, XX, l. 47*

10   Like the lark that soars in the air, first singing, then silent, content with the last sweetness that satiates it, such seemed to me that image, the imprint of the Eternal Pleasure.
> *The Divine Comedy. Paradiso, XX, l. 73*

11   The night that hides things from us.
> *The Divine Comedy. Paradiso, XXIII, l. 3*

12   With the color that paints the morning and evening clouds that face the sun I saw then the whole heaven suffused.
> *The Divine Comedy. Paradiso, XXVII, l. 28*

13   The Love that moves the sun and the other stars.[5]
> *The Divine Comedy. Paradiso, XXXIII, l. 145*

Yoshida Kenkō
1283?–1350?

14   The pleasantest of all diversions is to sit alone under the lamp, a book spread out before you, and to make friends with people of a distant past you have never known.[6]
> *Tsurezuregusa (Essays in Idleness)*
> *[c. 1330], ch. 13*

William of Occam
[Ockham]
c. 1285–c. 1349

15   Entities should not be multiplied unnecessarily.[7]
> *Quodlibeta Septem (Seven Quodlibetal*
> *Questions) [c. 1320]*

Philip VI
[Philip of Valois]
1293–1350

16   He who loves me, let him follow me.[8]
> *Attributed*

Petrarch
[Francesco Petrarca]
1304–1374

17   Who overrefines his argument brings himself to grief.
> *To Laura in Life [c. 1327], canzone 11*

18   A good death does honor to a whole life.
> *To Laura in Death, 16*

19   To be able to say how much you love is to love but little.
> *To Laura in Death, 137*

20   Rarely do great beauty and great virtue dwell together.
> *De Remediis (Remedies for Fortune*
> *Fair and Foul) [1354], bk. II*

---

[1] Puro e disposto a salire alle stelle.

[2] Translated by JOHN D. SINCLAIR.

[3] E'n la sua volontade e nostra pace.

[4] L'esperienza di questa dolce vita.

---

[5] L'amor che muove il sole e l'altre stelle.

[6] Translated by DONALD KEENE.

[7] Translated [seventeenth century] by JOHN PONCE of Cork. The axiom became known as Occam's Razor.

[8] Qui m'aime me suive.

Edward III
1312–1377

1   Honi soit qui mal y pense [Shame on anyone who thinks evil of it].
Motto of the Order of the Garter [1349]

2   Let the boy win his spurs.
Said of the Black Prince at the battle of Crécy [1345]

Giovanni Boccaccio
1313–1375

3   In this extremity of our city's suffering and tribulation the revered authority of laws, human and divine, was abased and all but totally dissolved, for lack of those who should have administered and enforced them, most of whom, like the rest of the citizens, were either dead or sick, or so hard pressed for servants that they were unable to execute any office; whereby every man was free to do what was right in his own eyes.[1]
The Decameron [1349–1351], First Day

John Barbour
c. 1316–1395

4   Freedom all solace to man gives;
He lives at ease that freely lives.
The Bruce [c. 1375], l. 227

William of Wykeham
1324–1404

5   Manners maketh man.
Motto of his two foundations, Winchester College and New College, Oxford

William Langland
c. 1330–c. 1400

6   In a summer season when soft was the sun.
The Vision of Piers Plowman [1362–1390]

7   A fair field full of folk found I there.
The Vision of Piers Plowman

8   Who will bell the cat?
The Vision of Piers Plowman

John Wycliffe
c. 1330–1384

9   I believe that in the end the truth will conquer.
To the Duke of Lancaster [1381].
From J. R. GREEN, A Short History of the English People [1874], ch. 5

Ibn Khaldûn
1332–1406

10   Man is a child of the customs and the things he has become used to. He is not the product of his natural disposition and temperament. The conditions to which he has become accustomed, until they have become for him a quality of character and matters of habit and custom, have replaced his natural disposition.
The Muqaddimah[2] *[1377], bk. I, ch. 2*

11   It should be known that at the beginning of a dynasty, taxation yields a large revenue from small assessments. At the end of a dynasty, taxation yields a small revenue from large assessments.
The Muqaddimah, I, 3

Jean Froissart
c. 1337–c. 1405

12   At least a third of all the people in the world died.[3]
Chronicles [1373]. On the Black Plague

Julian of Norwich[4]
c. 1342–after 1416

13   Just because I am a woman, must I therefore believe that I must not tell you about the goodness of God, when I saw at the same time both his goodness and his wish that it should be shown?
Revelations of Divine Love, The Short Text [c. 1373], ch. 7

14   It behoved that there should be sin; but all shall be well, and all shall be well, and all manner of thing shall be well.[5]
Revelations of Divine Love, The Long Text [c. 1373–c. 1393], ch. 27

---

[2]Translated by FRANZ ROSENTHAL.

[3]Translated by GEOFFREY BRERETON.

[4]The identity of this woman writer is unknown. She is known by this name, taken from St. Julian's Church, Norwich, England.

[5]Sin is Behovely . . . —T. S. ELIOT, *Four Quartets. Little Gidding, pt. III*

---

[1]Translated by J. M. RIGG.

1   He said not "Thou shalt not be tempested, thou
shalt not be travailed, thou shalt not be dis-eased";
but he said, "Thou shalt not be overcome."
Revelations of Divine Love, 68

Geoffrey Chaucer

c. 1343–1400

2 Soun ys noght but eyr ybroken,
And every speche that ys spoken,
Lowd or pryvee, foul or fair,
In his substaunce ys but air.
The House of Fame[1] *[1374–1385],*
bk. II, l. 765

3   Venus clerk, Ovide,
That hath ysowen wonder wide
The grete god of Loves name.
The House of Fame, III, 1. 1487

4 Hard is the herte that loveth nought
In May.
The Romaunt of the Rose
[c. 1380], l. 85

5 For nakid as a worm was she.
The Romaunt of the Rose, l. 454

6 As round as appil was his face.
The Romaunt of the Rose, l. 819

7 The lyf so short, the craft so long to lerne,
Th' assay so hard, so sharp the conquerynge.
The Parliament of Fowls
[1380–1386], l. 1

8 For out of olde feldes, as men seyth,
Cometh al this newe corn fro yer to yere;[2]
And out of olde bokes, in good feyth,
Cometh al this newe science that men lere.
The Parliament of Fowls, l. 22

9 Nature, the vicaire of the almyghty lorde.
The Parliament of Fowls, l. 379

10 Now welcome, somer, with thy sonne softe,
That hast this wintres wedres overshake.
The Parliament of Fowls, l. 680

11 But the Troian gestes, as they felle,
In Omer, or in Dares, or in Dite,
Whoso that kan may rede hem as they write.
Troilus and Criseyde [c. 1385],
bk. I, l. 145

12 If no love is, O God, what fele I so?
And if love is, what thing and which is he?
If love be good, from whennes cometh my woo?
Troilus and Criseyde, I, l. 400
(Canticus Troili)

13 Unknowe, unkist, and lost, that is unsought.
Troilus and Criseyde, I, l. 809

14 O wynd, o wynd, the weder gynneth clere.
Troilus and Criseyde, II, l. 2

15 Til crowes feet be growen under youre yë.
Troilus and Criseyde, II, l. 403

16   Lord, this is an huge rayn!
This were a weder for to slepen inne!
Troilus and Criseyde, III, 1. 656

17 For I have seyn, of a ful misty morwe
Folowen ful often a myrie someris day.
Troilus and Criseyde, III, l. 1060

18 Right as an aspes leef she gan to quake.
Troilus and Criseyde, III, l. 1200

19 For of fortunes sharpe adversitee
The worste kynde of infortune is this,
A man to han ben in prosperitee,
And it remembren, whan it passed is.
Troilus and Criseyde, III, l. 1625

20 Oon ere it herde, at tothir out it wente.[3]
Troilus and Criseyde, IV, l. 434

21 But manly sette the world on six and sevene;[4]
And if thow deye a martyr, go to hevene!
Troilus and Criseyde, IV, l. 622

22 For tyme ylost may nought recovered be.
Troilus and Criseyde, IV, l. 1283

23   They take it wisly, faire, and softe.[5]
Troilus and Criseyde, V, l. 347

24 For he that naught n' assaieth, naught n' acheveth.
Troilus and Criseyde, V, l. 784

25 That Paradis stood formed in her yën.
Troilus and Criseyde, V, l. 817

26 Trewe as stiel.   *Troilus and Criseyde, V, l. 831*

27   This sodeyn Diomede.
Troilus and Criseyde, V, l. 1024

---

[1]Works by Chaucer edited by F. N. Robinson.

[2]John Bartlett quoted this line at the head of his preface to the ninth edition of *Bartlett's Familiar Quotations* [1891].

[3]Commonly quoted: In one ear and out the other.

[4]All is uneven, / And everything is left at six and seven. — Shakespeare, *Richard II, act II, sc. ii, l. 120*

Things going on at sixes and sevens. — Oliver Goldsmith, *The Good-Natur'd Man, act I*

[5]The proverb is: Fair and softly goes far.

1 Ye, fare wel al the snow of ferne yere![1]
    Troilus and Criseyde, V, l. 1176

2 Ek gret effect men write in place lite;
    Th' entente is al, and nat the lettres space.
    Troilus and Criseyde, V, l. 1629

3 Go, litel bok, go, litel myn tragedye.[2]
    Troilus and Criseyde, V, l. 1786

4 O yonge, fresshe folkes, he or she,
    In which that love up groweth with youre age,
    Repeyreth hom fro worldly vanyte.
    Troilus and Criseyde, V, l. 1835

5 O moral Gower, this book I directe
    To the.
    Troilus and Criseyde, V, l. 1856

6   Whan that the month of May
    Is comen, and that I here the foules synge,
    And that the floures gynnen for to sprynge,
    Farewel my bok, and my devocioun!
    The Legend of Good Women [c. 1386], l. 36

7 That, of al the floures in the mede,
    Thanne love I most thise floures white and rede,
    Swiche as men callen daysyes in our toun.
    The Legend of Good Women, l. 41

8 Whan that Aprille with his shoures soote
    The droghte of March hath perced to the roote.
    The Canterbury Tales [c. 1387]. Prologue, l. 1

9 And smale foweles maken melodye,
    That slepen al the nyght with open yë,
    (So priketh hem nature in hit corages);
    Thanne longen folk to goon on pilgrimages.
    The Canterbury Tales. Prologue, l. 9

10 He was a verray, parfit gentil knyght.
    The Canterbury Tales. Prologue, l. 72

11 He was as fressh as is the month of May.
    The Canterbury Tales. Prologue, l. 92

12 He koude songes make and wel endyte.
    The Canterbury Tales. Prologue, l. 95

---

[1]See Villon, 138:19.

[2]Off with you down where you want to go. — HORACE, *Epistles, bk. I, epistle xx, l. 5*

Little book, you will go without me — I don't mind — to the city. — OVID, *Tristia, bk. I, poem i, l. 1*

Vade salutatum pro me, liber [Go forth, my book, to bear my greetings]. — MARTIAL, *Epigrams, bk. I, no. 70*

Go now, my little book, to every place / Where my first pilgrim has but shown his face. — JOHN BUNYAN, *The Pilgrim's Progress, Apology*

Go, little Book! From this my solitude / I cast thee on the Waters — go thy ways. — SOUTHEY, *Lay of the Laureate* [1815], *L'Envoi*

These lines of Southey's and the next two were quoted by BYRON in *Don Juan, canto I, st. 222:* The four first rhymes are Southey's, every line: / For God's sake, reader! take them not for mine!

Go, little book, and wish to all / Flowers in the garden, meat in the hall. — R. L. STEVENSON, *Underwoods. Envoy*

13 Curteis he was, lowely, and servysable,
    And carf biforn his fader at the table.
    The Canterbury Tales. Prologue, l. 99

14 Ful weel she soong the service dyvyne,
    Entuned in hir nose ful semely;
    And Frenssh she spak ful faire and fetisly,
    After the scole of Stratford atte Bowe
    For Frenssh of Parys was to hir unknowe.
    The Canterbury Tales. Prologue, l. 122

15 She wolde wepe, if that she saugh a mous
    Kaught in a trappe, if it were deed or bledde.
    The Canterbury Tales. Prologue, l. 144

16 And theron heng a brooch of gold ful sheene,
    On which ther was first write a crowned *A,*
    And after *Amor vincit omnia.*
    The Canterbury Tales. Prologue, l. 160

17 His palfrey was as broun as is a berye.
    The Canterbury Tales. Prologue, l. 207

18 A Frere ther was, a wantowne and a merye.
    The Canterbury Tales. Prologue, l. 208

19 He knew the tavernes wel in every toun.
    The Canterbury Tales. Prologue, l. 240

20 Somwhat he lipsed, for his wantownesse,
    To make his Englissh sweete upon his tonge.
    The Canterbury Tales. Prologue, l. 264

21 A Clerk ther was of Oxenford also.
    The Canterbury Tales. Prologue, l. 285

22 As leene was his hors as is a rake.
    The Canterbury Tales. Prologue, l. 287

23 For hym was levere have at his beddes heed
    Twenty bookes, clad in blak or reed,
    Of Aristotle and his philosophie,
    Than robes riche, or fithele, or gay sautrie,
    But al be that he was a philosophre,
    Yet hadde he but litel gold in cofre.
    The Canterbury Tales. Prologue, l. 293

24 And gladly wolde he lerne, and gladly teche.
    The Canterbury Tales. Prologue, l. 308

25 Nowher so bisy a man as he ther nas,
    And yet he semed bisier than he was.
    The Canterbury Tales. Prologue, l. 321

26 For he was Epicurus owene sone.
    The Canterbury Tales. Prologue, l. 336

27 It snewed in his hous of mete and drynke.
    The Canterbury Tales. Prologue, l. 345

28   He was a good felawe.
    The Canterbury Tales. Prologue, l. 395

29 His studie was but litel on the Bible.
    The Canterbury Tales. Prologue, l. 438

1 For gold in phisik is a cordial,
Therefore he lovede gold in special.
The Canterbury Tales. Prologue, l. 443

2 She was a worthy womman al hit lyve,
Housbondes at chirche dore she hadde fyve.
The Canterbury Tales. Prologue, l. 459

3 This noble ensample to his sheep he yaf,
That first he wroghte, and afterward he taughte.
The Canterbury Tales. Prologue, 1. 496

4 If gold ruste, what shal iren do?
The Canterbury Tales. Prologue, l. 500

5 But Cristes loore and his apostles twelve
He taughte, but first he folwed it hymselve.
The Canterbury Tales. Prologue, l. 527

6 And yet he hadde a thombe of gold.[1]
The Canterbury Tales. Prologue, l. 563

7 That hadde a fyr-reed cherubynnes face.
The Canterbury Tales. Prologue, l. 624

8 Wel loved he garleek, oynons, and eek lekes,
And for to drynken strong wyn, reed as blood.
The Canterbury Tales. Prologue, l. 634

9 And whan that he wel dronken hadde the wyn,
Than wolde he speke no word but Latyn.
The Canterbury Tales.
Prologue, l. 637

10 Whoso shal telle a tale after a man,
He moot reherce as ny as evere he kan
Everich a word, if it be in his charge,
Al speke he never so rudeliche and large,
Or ellis he moot telle his tale untrewe,
Or feyne thyng, or fynde wordes new.
The Canterbury Tales.
Prologue, l. 731

11 For May wol have no slogardie anyght.
The sesoun priketh every gentil herte,
And maketh hym out of his slep to sterte.
The Canterbury Tales.
The Knight's Tale, l. 1042

12 Ech man for hymself.
The Canterbury Tales.
The Knight's Tale, l. 1182

13 The bisy larke, messager of day.
The Canterbury Tales.
The Knight's Tale, l. 1491

14 May, with alle thy floures and thy grene,
Welcome be thou, faire, fresshe May.
The Canterbury Tales.
The Knight's Tale, l. 1510

15 That "feeld hath eyen, and the wode hath eres."[2]
The Canterbury Tales.
The Knight's Tale, l. 1522

16 Now up, now doun, as boket in a welle.
The Canterbury Tales. The Knight's Tale, l. 1533

17 For pitee renneth soone in gentil herte.
The Canterbury Tales. The Knight's Tale, l. 1761

18   Cupido,
Upon his shuldres wynges hadde he two;
And blynd he was, as it is often seene;
A bowe he bar and arwes brighte and kene.
The Canterbury Tales. The Knight's Tale, l. 1963

19 The smylere with the knyf under the cloke.
The Canterbury Tales. The Knight's Tale, l. 1999

20 Up roos the sonne, and up roose Emelye.
The Canterbury Tales. The Knight's Tale, l. 2273

21 Myn be the travaille, and thyn be the glorie!
The Canterbury Tales. The Knight's Tale, l. 2406

22 And was al his chiere, as in his herte.
The Canterbury Tales. The Knight's Tale, l. 2683

23 What is this world? what asketh men to have?
Now with his love, now in his colde grave
Allone, withouten any compaignye.
The Canterbury Tales. The Knight's Tale, l. 2777

24 This world nys but a thurghfare ful of wo,
And we been pilgrymes, passing to and fro.
Deeth is an ende of every worldly soore.
The Canterbury Tales. The Knight's Tale, l. 2847

25 Jhesu Crist, and seiynte Benedight,
Blesse this hous from every wikked wight.
The Canterbury Tales.
The Miller's Tale, 1. 3483

26 And broghte of myghty ale a large quart.
The Canterbury Tales.
The Miller's Tale, l. 3497

27 "Tehee!" quod she, and clapte the wyndow to.
The Canterbury Tales.
The Miller's Tale, l. 3740

28 Yet in our asshen olde is fyr yreke.
The Canterbury Tales.
The Reeve's Prologue, l. 3882

---

[2]The proverb also occurs in the Latin form: Campus habet lumen, et habet nemus auris acumen [The field has sight, and the wood a sharp ear].
   Wode has erys, felde has sigt. — *King Edward and the Shepherd, MS* [c. 1300]
   Fields have eyes and woods have ears. — JOHN HEYWOOD, *Proverbs, pt. II, ch. 5*
   Walls have ears. — CERVANTES, *Don Quixote, pt. II, ch. 48*
   Woods have tongues / As walls have ears. — TENNYSON, *Idylls of the King. Balin and Balan, l. 522*

---

[1]In allusion to the proverb: An honest miller hath a golden thumb.

1 The gretteste clerkes been noght the wisest men.
The Canterbury Tales.
The Reeve's Tale, l. 4054

2 Thurgh thikke and thurgh thenne.[1]
The Canterbury Tales.
The Reeve's Tale, l. 4066

3 So was hir joly whistle wel ywet.
The Canterbury Tales.
The Reeve's Tale, l. 4155

4 She is mirour of alle curteisye.[2]
The Canterbury Tales.
The Man of Law's Tale, l. 166

5 For in the sterres, clerer than is glas,
Is writen, God woot, whoso koude it rede,
The deeth of every man.
The Canterbury Tales.
The Man of Law's Tale, l. 194

6 Sathan, that evere us waiteth to bigile.
The Canterbury Tales.
The Man of Law's Tale, l. 582

7 But, Lord Crist! whan that it remembreth me
Upon my yowthe, and on my jolitee,
It tikleth me aboute myn herte roote.
Unto this day it dooth myn herte boote
That I have had my world as in my tyme.
The Canterbury Tales.
The Wife of Bath's Prologue, l. 469

8 In his owene grece I made hym frye.[3]
The Canterbury Tales.
The Wife of Bath's Prologue, l. 487

9 By God! in erthe I was his purgatorie,
For which I hope his Soule be in glorie.
The Canterbury Tales.
The Wife of Bath's Prologue, l. 489

10   What thyng we may nat lightly have,
Thereafter wol we crie al day and crave.
The Canterbury Tales.
The Wife of Bath's Prologue, l. 517

11 Greet prees at market maketh deere ware,
And to greet cheep is holde at litel prys.
The Canterbury Tales.
The Wife of Bath's Prologue, l. 522

12 But yet I hadde alwey a coltes tooth.
Gat-toothed I was, and that bicam me weel.
The Canterbury Tales. The Wife of Bath's
Prologue, l. 601

13   A womman cast hir shame away,
Whan she cast of hir smok.
The Canterbury Tales. The Wife of Bath's
Prologue, l. 782

14 As thikke as motes in the sonne-beem.
The Canterbury Tales.
The Wife of Bath's Tale, l. 868

15 "My lige lady, generally," quod he,
"Wommen desiren have sovereynetee
As well over hir housbond as hir love."
The Canterbury Tales.
The Wife of Bath's Tale, l. 1037

16 Looke who that is moost vertuous alway,
Pryvee and apert, and most entendeth ay
To do the gentil dedes that he kan;
Taak hym for the grettest gentil man.
The Canterbury Tales.
The Wife of Bath's Tale, l. 1113

17 That he is gentil that dooth gentil dedis.
The Canterbury Tales.
The Wife of Bath's Tale, l. 1170

18 For thogh we slepe, or wake, or rome, or ryde,
Ay fleeth the tyme, it nyl no man abyde.
The Canterbury Tales. The Clerk's Tale, l. 118

19 Ye been oure lord, dooth with youre owene thyng
Right as yow list.
The Canterbury Tales. The Clerk's Tale, l. 652

20 Love is noght oold as whan that it is newe.
The Canterbury Tales. The Clerk's Tale, l. 857

21   This flour of wyfly pacience.
The Canterbury Tales. The Clerk's Tale, l. 919

22 O stormy peple! unsad and evere untrewe!
The Canterbury Tales. The Clerk's Tale, l. 995

23 No wedded man so hardy be t'assaille
His wyves pacience, in trust to fynde
Grisildis, for in certein he shal faille!
The Canterbury Tales. The Clerk's Tale, l. 1180

24   It is no childes pley
To take a wyf withouten avysement.
The Canterbury Tales.
The Merchant's Tale, l. 1530

25 For love is blynd.[4]
The Canterbury Tales.
The Merchant's Tale, l. 1598

---

[1]Through thick and thin. — Du Bartas, *Divine Weeks and Works, Second Week, Fourth Day*

[2]Call him bounteous Buckingham, / The mirror of all courtesy. — Shakespeare, *Henry VIII, act II, sc. i, l. 52*

[3]Proverbial.
Fryeth in her own grease. — John Heywood, *Proverbs, pt. I, ch. 11*
The best way were to entertain him with hope, till the wicked fire of lust have melted him in his own grease. — Shakespeare, *The Merry Wives of Windsor, act II, sc. i, l. 69*

---

[4]Proverbial.

1   My wit is thynne.
       The Canterbury Tales. The Merchant's Tale,
       l. 1682

2 Ther nys no werkman, whatsoevere he be,
  That may bothe werke wel and hastily;
  This wol be doon at leyser parfitly.
       The Canterbury Tales.
       The Merchant's Tale, l. 1832

3 Therfore bihoveth hire a ful long spoon
  That shal ete with a feend.[1]
       The Canterbury Tales. The Squire's Tale, l. 602

4 Men loven of propre kynde newefangelnesse.
       The Canterbury Tales. The Squire's Tale,
       l. 610

5   Fy on possessioun
  But if a man be vertuous withal.
       The Canterbury Tales. The Squire's Tale, l. 686

6 Pacience is an heigh vertu, certeyn.
       The Canterbury Tales. The Franklin's Tale, l. 773

7 Servant in love and lord in marriage.
       The Canterbury Tales. The Franklin's Tale, l. 793

8 It is agayns the proces of nature.
       The Canterbury Tales.
       The Franklin's Tale, l. 1345

9 Trouthe is the hyeste thyng that men may kepe.
       The Canterbury Tales.
       The Franklin's Tale, l. 1479

10 For dronkenesse is verray sepulture
   Of mannes wit and his discrecioun.
       The Canterbury Tales. The Pardoner's Tale, l. 558

11 Mordre wol out, certeyn, it wol nat faille.[2]
       The Canterbury Tales. The Prioress's Tale, l. 1766

12 This may wel be rym dogerel.
       The Canterbury Tales.
       Chaucer's Tale of Sir Thopas, l. 2115

13 Ful wys is he that kan hymselven knowe!
       The Canterbury Tales. The Monk's Tale, l. 3329

---

[1]Proverbial.
  He must have a long spoon that must eat with the devil. —
SHAKESPEARE, *The Comedy of Errors, act IV, sc. iii, l. 64*
  [2]Proverbial.
  How easily murder is discovered! — SHAKESPEARE, *Titus Andronicus, act II, sc. iii, l. 287*
  Truth will come to light; murder cannot be hid long. — SHAKESPEARE, *The Merchant of Venice, act II, sc. ii, l. 86*
  Murder, though it have no tongue, will speak / With most miraculous organ. — SHAKESPEARE, *Hamlet, act II, sc. ii, l. 630*
  Murder will out. — CERVANTES, *Don Quixote, pt. I, bk. III, ch. 8*
  Carcasses bleed at the sight of the murderer. — ROBERT BURTON, *Anatomy of Melancholy, pt. I, sec. I, member 2, subsec. 5*
  Other sins only speak; murder shrieks out. — JOHN WEBSTER, *The Duchess of Malfi, act IV, sc. ii*

14 He was of knyghthod and of fredom flour.
       The Canterbury Tales. The Monk's Tale, l. 3832

15 For whan a man hath over-greet a wit,
   Ful oft hym happeth to mysusen it.
       The Canterbury Tales.
       The Canon Yeoman's Prologue, l. 648

16 My sone, keep wel thy tonge, and keep thy freend.
       The Canterbury Tales. The Manciple's Tale, l.
       319

17 Thing that is seyd is seyd; and forth it gooth.
       The Canterbury Tales. The Manciple's Tale, l.
       355

18 For the proverbe seith that "manye smale maken a
   greet."[3]
       The Canterbury Tales. The Parson's Tale, l. 361

19 Reule wel thyself, that other folk canst rede.
   And trouthe thee shal delivere, it is no drede.
       Truth [c. 1390], l. 6

20 The wrastling for this world axeth a fal.
       Truth, l. 16

The Cloud of Unknowing
Late fourteenth century

21   A short prayer pierces heaven.

Christine de Pisan
1363–c. 1434

22   I could hardly find a book on morals where, even
before I had read it in its entirety, I did not find several chapters or certain sections attacking women,
no matter who the author was.... I finally decided
that God formed a vile creature when He made
woman, and I wondered how such a worthy artisan
could have deigned to make such an abominable
work which, from what they say, is the vessel as well
as the refuge and abode of every evil and vice.[4]
       The Book of the City of Ladies [1405],
       pt. 1, sec. 1

Zeami Motokiyo
1363–1443

23   Dancing and singing, movements on the stage,
and the different types of miming are all acts performed by the body. Moments of "no action" occur
in between.... The actions before and after an interval

---

[3]The proverb goes back to Saint Augustine.
  Many small make a great. — JOHN HEYWOOD, *Proverbs, pt. I, ch. 11*
[4]Translated by E. J. RICHARDS.

of "no action" must be linked by entering the state of mindlessness in which the actor conceals even from himself his own intent.[1]

The One Mind Linking All Powers

John Huss [Jan Hus]
c. 1372–1415

1   O holy simplicity![2]   *Last words, at the stake*

Margery Kempe
c. 1373–1438

2   Patience is more worthy than miracle-working.
The Book of Margery Kempe [1438]

Thomas à Kempis
1380–1471

3   Sic transit gloria mundi [So passes away the glory of this world].[3]
Imitation of Christ [c. 1420], bk. I, ch. 3

4   Be not angry that you cannot make others as you wish them to be, since you cannot make yourself as you wish to be.   *Imitation of Christ, I, 16*

5   Man proposes, but God disposes.[4]
Imitation of Christ, I, 19

6   What canst thou see elsewhere which thou canst not see here? Behold the heaven and the earth and all the elements; for of these are all things created.
Imitation of Christ, I, 20

7   No man ruleth safely but he that is willingly ruled.   *Imitation of Christ, I, 20*

8   And when he is out of sight, quickly also is he out of mind.[5]   *Imitation of Christ, I, 23*

---

[1]Translated by RYUSAKU TSUNODA and DONALD KEENE. On the aesthetic principle of Noh.

[2]O sancta simplicitas!

[3]These words are used in the crowning of the pope.

[4]Homo proponet et Deus disponit. — WILLIAM LANGLAND, *The Vision of Piers Plowman, l. 13,994* [1550 edition]
Man appoints, and God disappoints. — CERVANTES, *Don Quixote, pt. II, bk. IV, ch. 55*

[5]Fer from eze, fer from herte, / Quoth Hendyng. — HENDYNG [1272–1307], *Proverbs, MS*
Out of sight, out of mind. — BARNABE GOOGE [1540–1594], *Eglogs* [1563], title of poem
And out of mind as soon as out of sight. — FULKE GREVILLE, *Sonnet 56*
I do perceive that the old proverbs be not always true, for I do find that the absence of my Nath. doth breed in me the more continual remembrance of him. — LADY ANN BACON [1528–1610], *letter to Lady Jane Cornwallis*

9   O that we had spent but one day in this world thoroughly well!
Imitation of Christ, I, 23

10   First keep the peace within yourself, then you can also bring peace to others.
Imitation of Christ, II, 3

11   Love is swift, sincere, pious, pleasant, gentle, strong, patient, faithful, prudent, long-suffering, manly and never seeking her own; for wheresoever a man seeketh his own, there he falleth from love.
Imitation of Christ, III, 5

Charles d'Orléans
1394–1465

12   I am dying of thirst by the side of the fountain.[6]
Ballades, no. 2

13   The season has shed its mantle of wind and chill and rain.[7]   *Rondeaux, no. 63*

14 All by myself, wrapped in my thoughts,
And building castles in Spain and in France.[8]
Rondeaux, 109

John Fortescue
c. 1395–c. 1479

15   Much cry and no wool.[9]
De Laudibus Legum Angliae
(In Praise of English Law) [1471], ch. 10

16   Comparisons are odious.[10]
De Laudibus Legum Angliae, 19

Leon Battista Alberti
1404–1472

17   Painting contains a divine force which not only makes absent men present, as friendship is said to do, but moreover makes the dead seem almost alive.[11]   *On Painting [1435]*

---

[6]Je meurs de soif auprès de la fontaine.

[7]Le temps a laissé son manteau / De vent, de froidure et de pluie.

[8]Translated by NORBERT GUTERMAN.
Thou shalt make castels thanne in Spayne, / And dreme of joye, all but in vayne. — JEAN DE MEUN [13th cent.], *The Romaunt of the Rose* [c. 1277], *fragment B, l. 2573,* translated by CHAUCER

[9]A great cry, but little wool. — CERVANTES, *Don Quixote, pt. II, bk. III, ch. 13*
All cry and no wool. — SAMUEL BUTLER [1612–1680], *Hudibras, pt. I, canto I, l. 852*

[10]This was a well-known phrase in the fourteenth century, and has been repeated by many, including Lydgate, Shakespeare, and Swift.

[11]Translated by JOHN R. SPENCER.

Sir Thomas Malory

d. 1471

1   The noble history of the Sangreal,[1] and of the most renowned Christian king...King Arthur.
Le Morte d'Arthur [1485].
Preface by WILLIAM CAXTON [c. 1422–1491],
the first English printer

2   Whoso pulleth out this sword of this stone and anvil, is rightwise king born of all England.
Le Morte d'Arthur, bk. I, ch. 5

3   And with that the king saw coming toward him the strangest beast that ever he saw or heard of; so the beast went to the well and drank, and the noise was in the beast's belly like unto the questing of thirty couple hounds; but all the while the beast drank there was no noise in the beast's belly: and therewith the beast departed with a great noise....Pellinore, that time king, followed the questing beast.
Le Morte d'Arthur, I, 19

4   In the midst of the lake Arthur was ware of an arm clothed in white samite, that held a fair sword in that hand.   *Le Morte d'Arthur, I, 25*

5   Always Sir Arthur lost so much blood that it was marvel he stood on his feet, but he was so full of knighthood that knightly he endured the pain.
Le Morte d'Arthur, IV, 9

6   What, nephew, said the king, is the wind in that door?   *Le Morte d'Arthur, VII, 34*

7   The joy of love is too short, and the sorrow thereof, and what cometh thereof, dureth over long.   *Le Morte d'Arthur, X, 56*

8   It is his day.   *Le Morte d'Arthur, X, 70*

9   The month of May was come, when every lusty heart beginneth to blossom, and to bring forth fruit; for like as herbs and trees bring forth fruit and flourish in May, in likewise every lusty heart that is in any manner a lover, springeth and flourisheth in lusty deeds. For it giveth unto all lovers courage, that lusty month of May.
Le Morte d'Arthur, XVIII, 25

10   All ye that be lovers call unto your remembrance the month of May, like as did Queen Guenever, for whom I make here a little mention, that while she lived she was a true lover, and therefore she had a good end.   *Le Morte d'Arthur, XVIII, 25*

11   Such a fellowship of good knights shall never be together in no company.
Le Morte d'Arthur, XX, 9

12   I shall curse you with book and bell and candle.[2]
Le Morte d'Arthur, XXI, 1

13   Through this man [Launcelot] and me [Guenever] hath all this war been wrought, and the death of the most noblest knights of the world; for through our love that we have loved together is my most noble lord slain.
Le Morte d'Arthur, XXI, 9

14   For as well as I have loved thee, mine heart will not serve me to see thee, for through thee and me is the flower of kings and knights destroyed.
Le Morte d'Arthur, XXI, 9

15   Thou were the meekest man and the gentlest that ever ate in hall among ladies. And thou were the sternest knight to thy mortal foe that ever put spear in the rest.   *Le Morte d'Arthur, XXI, 13*

16   Yet some men say in many parts of England that King Arthur is not dead, but had by the will of our Lord Jesu into another place. And men say that he shall come again and he shall win the Holy Cross. Yet I will not say that it shall be so, but rather I will say, Here in this world he changed his life. And many men say that there is written upon his tomb this verse: *Hic iacet Arthurus, rex quondam, rexque futurus* [Here lies Arthur, the once and future king].
Le Morte d'Arthur, XXXI, 7

Henry VI

1421–1471

17 Kingdoms are but cares,
State is devoid of stay;
Riches are ready snares,
And hasten to decay.
From SIR JOHN HARINGTON,
Nugae Antiquae (Old Trifles) [1769]

François Villon

1431–c. 1465

18 Ah God! Had I but studied
In the days of my foolish youth.[3]
Le Grand Testament, 26

19 But where are the snows of yesteryear?[4]
Le Grand Testament. Ballade des Dames
du Temps Jadis (Ladies of the Past)

---

[1]The Holy Grail.

[2]The reference is to the ceremony of excommunication, performed with bell, book, and candle.

[3]Hé Dieu! si j'eusse étudié / Au temps de ma jeunesse folle.

[4]Mais où sont les neiges d'antan?
Translated by DANTE GABRIEL ROSSETTI.
See Chaucer, 133:1.

1 In this faith I will to live and die.
> *Le Grand Testament. Ballade de l'Homage
> à Notre Dame*

2 There's no good speech save in Paris.[1]
> *Le Grand Testament. Ballade des Femmes de Paris*

3 But pray God that he absolve us all![2]   *Codicile*

4 I know all except myself.[3]
> *Ballade des Menus Propos (Small Talk)*

Jorge Manrique
1440–1479

5　　　　　Let the dozing soul remember,
let the mind awake and revive
　　　by contemplating
how our life goes by so swiftly
and how our death comes near
　　　so silently;
how quickly pleasure fades,
and how when it is recalled
　　　it give us pain,
how we seem always to think
that times past must have been better
　　　than today.
> *Verses Written on the Death of His Father*[4]
> *[1476], st. 1*

Aldus Manutius
1449–1515

6　Talk of nothing but business, and dispatch that
business quickly.
> *Placard on the door of the Aldine Press,
> Venice, established about 1490*

Christopher Columbus
1451–1506

7　Here the people could stand it no longer and
complained of the long voyage; but the Admiral
cheered them as best he could, holding out good
hope of the advantages they would have. He added
that it was useless to complain, he had come [to go]
to the Indies, and so had to continue it until he found
them, with the help of Our Lord.
> *Journal of the First Voyage,*[5] *October 10, 1492*

8　At two hours after midnight appeared the land, at
a distance of 2 leagues. They handed all sails and set
the *treo,* which is the mainsail without bonnets, and
lay-to waiting for daylight Friday, when they arrived
at an island of the Bahamas that was called in the
Indians' tongue Guanahaní [San Salvador].
> *Journal of the First Voyage, October 12, 1492*

9　The two Christians met on the way many people
who were going to their towns, women and men,
with a firebrand in the hand, [and] herbs to drink the
smoke thereof, as they are accustomed.[6]
> *Journal of the First Voyage, November 6, 1492*

10　And I say that Your Highnesses ought not to consent that any foreigner does business or sets foot here,
except Christian Catholics, since this was the end and
the beginning of the enterprise, that it should be for
the enhancement and glory of the Christian religion,
nor should anyone who is not a good Christian come
to these parts.
> *Journal of the First Voyage, November 27, 1492*

11　And they know neither sect nor idolatry, with the
exception that all believe that the source of all power
and goodness is in the sky, and they believe very
firmly that I, with these ships and people, came from
the sky, and in this belief they everywhere received
me, after they had overcome their fear.
> *Letter to the Sovereigns on the First Voyage,
> February 15–March 4, 1493*[7]

12　I have always read that the world, both land and
water, was spherical, as the authority and researches
of Ptolemy and all the others who have written on
this subject demonstrate and prove, as do the eclipses
of the moon and other experiments that are made
from east to west, and the elevation of the North Star
from north to south.
> *Letter to the Sovereigns on the Third Voyage,
> October 18, 1498*[8]

13　I should be judged as a captain who went from
Spain to the Indies to conquer a people numerous
and warlike, whose manners and religion are very different from ours, who live in sierras and mountains,
without fixed settlements, and where by divine will I
have placed under the sovereignty of the King and
Queen our Lords, an Other World, whereby Spain,
which was reckoned poor, is become the richest of
countries.
> *Letter to Doña Juana de Torres, October 1500*[9]

---

[1] Il n'est bon bec que de Paris.

[2] Mais priez Dieu que tous nous veuille absoudre.

[3] Je connais tout, fors que moi-même.

[4] Translated by EDITH GROSSMAN.

[5] BARTOLOMÉ DE LAS CASAS [1474–1566] made an abstract of
Columbus's *Journal of the First Voyage (El Libro de la Primera Navega-
ción),* which is the nearest thing to an original journal that we have.
Translated by SAMUEL ELIOT MORISON.

---

[6] Likely the first certain reference in history to smoking tobacco.

[7] This letter, among the oldest documents depicting the Americas,
describes the scenery and the native people of what came to be called
Hispaniola.

[8] Translated by SAMUEL ELIOT MORISON and MILTON ANASTOS.

[9] Columbus is returning from the Indies as a prisoner.

1   I came to serve you at the age of 28 and now I have not a hair on me that is not white, and my body is infirm and exhausted. All that was left to me and my brothers has been taken away and sold, even to the cloak that I wore, without hearing or trial, to my great dishonor.

Lettera Rarissima to the Sovereigns, July 7, 1503 (Fourth Voyage)[1]

Leonardo da Vinci
1452–1519

2   Man and the animals are merely a passage and channel for food, a tomb for other animals, a haven for the dead, giving life by the death of others, a coffer full of corruption.

The Notebooks[2] *[1508–1518], vol. I, ch. 1*

3   Intellectual passion drives out sensuality.

The Notebooks, I, 1

4   Life well spent is long.   *The Notebooks, I, 1*

5   Shun those studies in which the work that results dies with the worker.   *The Notebooks, I, 1*

6   Whoever in discussion adduces authority uses not intellect but rather memory.   *The Notebooks, I, 2*

7   Iron rusts from disuse; stagnant water loses its purity and in cold weather becomes frozen; even so does inaction sap the vigor of the mind.

The Notebooks, I, 2

8   Savage is he who saves himself.

The Notebooks, I, 2

9   It is easier to resist at the beginning than at the end.   *The Notebooks, I, 2*

10   Necessity is the mistress and guardian of nature.

The Notebooks, I, 2

11   Human subtlety...will never devise an invention more beautiful, more simple or more direct than does nature, because in her inventions nothing is lacking, and nothing is superfluous.   *The Notebooks, I, 3*

12   Mechanics is the paradise of the mathematical sciences because by means of it one comes to the fruits of mathematics.   *The Notebooks, I, 20*

13   O speculators about perpetual motion, how many vain chimeras have you created in the like quest? Go and take your place with the seekers after gold.

The Notebooks, II, 25

14   O neglectful Nature, wherefore art thou thus partial, becoming to some of thy children a tender and

---

[1]Translated by MILTON ANASTOS.
[2]Translated by EDWARD MACCURDY.

benignant mother, to others a most cruel and ruthless stepmother? I see thy children given into slavery to others without ever receiving any benefit, and in lieu of any reward for the services they have done for them they are repaid by the severest punishments.

The Notebooks, II, 45

15   The Medici created and destroyed me.

The Notebooks, II, 46

Amerigo Vespucci
1454–1512

16   Those new regions [America] which we found and explored with the fleet...we may rightly call a New World...a continent more densely peopled and abounding in animals than our Europe or Asia or Africa; and, in addition, a climate milder than in any other region known to us.[3]

*Letter called Mundus Novus [1503]
to Lorenzo Pier Francesco de' Medici*

Sebastian Brant
c. 1458–1521

17   The world wants to be deceived.

The Ship of Fools (Das Narrenschiff) [1494]

John Skelton
c. 1460–1529

18 I say, thou mad March hare.[4]

Replication Against Certain Young Scholars

19 He ruleth all the roost.[5]

Why Come Ye Not to Court, l. 198

20 The wolf from the door.[6]

Why Come Ye Not to Court, l. 1531

21   Old proverb says,
That bird is not honest

---

[3]Translated by G. T. NORTHUP.
This, and a letter of Vespucci to his friend Pier Soderini [1504], led geography professor Martin Waldseemüller to credit Vespucci with discovering "a fourth part of the world" and to issue a map [1507] with a bold AMERICA on the continent now called South America. Vespucci had invented a voyage of 1497, a year before Columbus's Third Voyage, which reached the mainland of South America.

[4]Mad as a March hare. — JOHN HEYWOOD, *Proverbs, pt. II, ch. 5*
[5]Rule the rost. — JOHN HEYWOOD, *Proverbs, pt. I, ch. 5*
Rules the roast. — JONSON, CHAPMAN, MARSTON, *Eastward Ho* [1605], *act II, sc. ii*
Her that ruled the rost. — THOMAS HEYWOOD, *History of Women* [ed. 1624]

[6]To keep the wolf from the door. — JOHN HEYWOOD, *Proverbs, pt. II, ch. 7*

That filleth his own nest.[1]

Poems Against Garnesche

1 Maid, widow, or wife. *Philip Sparrow*

2 Merry Margaret,
  As midsummer flower,
  Gentle as falcon
  Or hawk of the tower. *To Mistress Margaret Hussey*

Giovanni Pico della Mirandola
1463–1494

3   We have made thee neither of heaven nor of earth, neither mortal nor immortal, so that with freedom of choice and with honor, as though the maker and molder of thyself, thou mayest fashion thyself in whatever shape thou shalt prefer. Thou shalt have the power to degenerate into the lower forms of life, which are brutish. Thou shalt have the power, out of thy soul's judgment, to be reborn into the highest forms, which are divine.[2]

On the Dignity of Man [1496]

William Dunbar
c. 1465–c. 1530

4 London, thou art the flower of Cities all.

London, refrain

5 Gem of all joy, jasper of jocundity.

London, st. 3

6 I that in heill wes and gladnes
  Am trublit now with gret seiknes
  And feblit with infermite:
  Timor Mortis conturbat me.[3]

*Lament for the Makaris[4] [c. 1508],
refrain*

7 Our plesance here is all vain glory,
  This false world is but transitory.

Lament for the Makaris, st. 2

8 O reverend Chaucere, rose of rethoris all,
  As in oure tong ane flour imperiall,
     That raise in Britane evir, quho redis rycht,
  Thou beris of makaris the triumph riall.[5]

The Goldyn Targe [c. 1508], l. 253

9 Yisterday fair up sprang the flouris,
  This day thai are all slane with schouris;
     And fowles in forrest that sang cleir
     Now walkis with a drery cheir;
  Full caild are baith thair beddis and bouris.

I seik about this warld unstabille, st. 3

Desiderius Erasmus
c. 1466–1536

10   In the country of the blind the one-eyed man is king.[6] *Adagia [1500]*

11   It is folly alone that stays the fugue of Youth and beats off louring Old Age.

The Praise of Folly [1509]

12   They may attack me with an army of six hundred syllogisms; and if I do not recant, they will proclaim me a heretic. *The Praise of Folly*

Niccolò Machiavelli[7]
1469–1527

13   There is nothing more difficult to take in hand, more perilous to conduct, or more uncertain in its success, than to take the lead in the introduction of a new order of things. *The Prince[8] [1532], ch. 6*

14   Since love and fear can hardly exist together, if we must choose between them, it is far safer to be feared than loved. *The Prince, 8*

15   The chief foundations of all states, new as well as old or composite, are good laws and good arms; and as there cannot be good laws where the state is not well armed, it follows that where they are well armed they have good laws. *The Prince, 12*

16   A prince should therefore have no other aim or thought, nor take up any other thing for his study, but war and its organization and discipline, for that is the only art that is necessary to one who commands. *The Prince, 14*

17   Among other evils which being unarmed brings you, it causes you to be despised.

The Prince, 14

---

[1]It is a foul bird that filleth his own nest. — JOHN HEYWOOD, *Proverbs, pt. II, ch. 5*

[2]Translated by ELIZABETH LIVERMORE FORBES.

[3]Fear of Death troubles me.

[4]Makers, meaning poets.

[5]O reverend Chaucer, rose of rhetoricians all, / as in our tongue a flower imperial / that rose in Britain ever, who reads aright, / thou bearest of poets the triumph royal.

[6]In regione caecorum rex est luscus.

In the country of the blind the one-eyed man is king; I passed for a good teacher, because the rest in town were bad. — JEAN-JACQUES ROUSSEAU, *Confessions, pt. I, bk. 5*

[7]Every Country hath its Machiavel. — THOMAS BROWNE, *Religio Medici, pt. I, sec. 20*

Out of his surname they have coined an epithet for a knave, and out of his Christian name a synonym for the Devil. — THOMAS BABINGTON MACAULAY, *On Machiavelli [1827]*

[8]Translated by W. K. MARRIOTT.

1 Many have imagined republics and principalities which have never been seen or known to exist in reality; for how we live is so far removed from how we ought to live, that he who abandons what is done for what ought to be done, will rather bring about his own ruin than his preservation. *The Prince, 15*

2 A prince being thus obliged to know well how to act as a beast must imitate the fox and the lion, for the lion cannot protect himself from traps, and the fox cannot defend himself from wolves. One must therefore be a fox to recognize traps, and a lion to frighten wolves. *The Prince, 17*

3 When neither their property nor their honor is touched, the majority of men live content.
The Prince, 19

4 There are three classes of intellects: one which comprehends by itself; another which appreciates what others comprehend; and a third which neither comprehends by itself nor by the showing of others; the first is the most excellent, the second is good, the third is useless. *The Prince, 22*

5 There is no other way of guarding oneself against flattery than by letting men understand that they will not offend you by speaking the truth; but when everyone can tell you the truth, you lose their respect.
The Prince, 23

6 God is not willing to do everything, and thus take away our free will and that share of glory which belongs to us. *The Prince, 26*

7 Whoever desires to found a state and give it laws, must start with assuming that all men are bad and ever ready to display their vicious nature, whenever they may find occasion for it.
Discourse upon the First Ten Books of Livy,
bk. I, ch. 3

8 The people resemble a wild beast, which, naturally fierce and accustomed to live in the woods, has been brought up, as it were, in a prison and in servitude, and having by accident got its liberty, not being accustomed to search for its food, and not knowing where to conceal itself, easily becomes the prey of the first who seeks to incarcerate it again.
Discourse upon the First Ten Books of Livy,
I, 16

9 He who establishes a tyranny and does not kill Brutus, and he who establishes a democratic regime and does not kill the sons of Brutus, will not last long.[1]
Discourse upon the First Ten Books of Livy,
III, 3

---

[1]Translated by Leslie J. Walker, S.J.

Nanak Dev Ji
1469–1539

10 There is no Hindu, there is no Muslim.
Attributed; first announcement of Sikh doctrine

Charles VIII
1470–1498

11 This is our gracious will.[2]
Royal Order of March 12, 1497

Albrecht Dürer
1471–1528

12 The Creator fashioned men once and for all as they *must* be, and I hold that the perfection of form and beauty is contained in the sum of all men.[3]
Four Books of Human Proportions [1528]

Nicholas Copernicus
1473–1543

13 Finally we shall place the Sun himself at the center of the Universe. All this is suggested by the systematic procession of events and the harmony of the whole Universe, if only we face the facts, as they say, "with both eyes open."
De Revolutionibus Orbium Coelestium
(On the Revolutions of the Heavenly Spheres)[4]
[1543]

Ludovico Ariosto
1474–1533

14 Nature made him, and then broke the mold.[5]
Orlando Furioso [1532], canto X, st. 84

Michelangelo [Buonarroti]
1475–1564

15 The more the marble wastes, the more the statue grows. *Sonnet*

16 If it be true that any beautiful thing raises the pure and just desire of man from earth to God, the eternal fount of all, such I believe my love. *Sonnet*

---

[2]Tel est notre bon plaisir.
[3]Translated by William Martin Conway.
[4]Translated by John F. Dobson.
[5]Natura il fece, e poi ruppe la stampa.

1 The power of one fair face makes my love sublime,
for it has weaned my heart from low desires.   *Sonnet*

2 I live and love in God's peculiar light.   *Sonnet*

Sir Thomas More[1]
1478–1535

3 They wonder much to hear that gold, which in itself is so useless a thing, should be everywhere so much esteemed, that even men for whom it was made, and by whom it has its value, should yet be thought of less value than it is.
Utopia [1516]. Of Jewels and Wealth

4 They have no lawyers among them, for they consider them as a sort of people whose profession it is to disguise matters.
Utopia. Of Law and Magistrates

5 Plato by a goodly similitude declareth, why wise men refrain to meddle in the commonwealth. For when they see the people swarm into the streets, and daily wet to the skin with rain, and yet cannot persuade them to go out of the rain,[2] they do keep themselves within their houses, seeing they cannot remedy the folly of the people.
Utopia. Concerning the Best State of a Commonwealth

6 A little wanton money, which burned out the bottom of his purse.
Works [c. 1530]

7 This is a fair tale of a tub told of his election.[3]
Confutation of Tyndale's Answers [1532]

8 For men use, if they have an evil turn, to write it in marble: and whoso doth us a good turn we write it in dust.
Richard III and His Miserable End [1543]

9 See me safe up, and for my coming down let me shift for myself.
On ascending the scaffold. From WILLIAM ROPER *[c. 1496–1578], Life of Sir Thomas More [published 1626]*

10 This hath not offended the king.
As he drew his beard aside upon placing his head on the block. From FRANCIS BACON, *Apothegms, no. 22*

Robert Whittinton
c. 1480–c. 1530

11 [Sir Thomas] More is a man of angel's wit and singular learning; I know not his fellow. For where is the man of that gentleness, lowliness and affability? And as time requireth, a man of marvelous mirth and pastimes; and sometimes of as sad a gravity; a man for all seasons.
Passage composed for schoolboys to put into Latin

Robert Henryson
fl. 1480

12 The firmament payntit with sternis cleir
From eist to west rolland in cirkill round,
And everilk planet in his proper spheir,
In moving makand harmonie and sound;
The fyre, the air, the watter, and the ground —
Till understand it is aneuch, I wis,
That God in all His werkis wittie is.
The Morall Fabillis of Esope the Phrygian. The Preiching of the Swallow, l. 1658

Martin Luther
1483–1546

13 If it were an art to overcome heresy with fire, the executioners would be the most learned doctors on earth.
To the Christian Nobility of the German States [1520]

14 Here I stand; I can do no other. God help me. Amen.[4]
Speech at the Diet of Worms [April 18, 1521]

15 The mad mob does not ask how it could be better, only that it be different. And when it then becomes worse, it must change again. Thus they get bees for flies, and at last hornets for bees.
Whether Soldiers Can Also Be in a State of Grace [1526]

16 A mighty fortress is our God,
A bulwark never failing.
Our helper He amid the flood
Of mortal ills prevailing.[5]   *Ein' Feste Burg [1529]*

---

[1]Canonized [1935] by Pope Pius XI.

[2]In the modern phrase: Not sense enough to come in out of the rain.

[3]A tale of a tub is a cock-and-bull story. Jonson used it as the title of a comedy [1633], and Swift as the title of a satire [1696].

[4]Hier stehe ich, ich kann nicht anders. Gott helfe mir. Amen.
Inscribed on his monument at Worms.
Also translated as: Here I stand, I cannot do otherwise. And: God helping me, I can do no other.

[5]Ein' feste burg is unser Gott, / ein gute wehr und waffen. / Er hilft uns frei aus aller not, / die uns itzt hat betroffen.
Translated by FREDERICK HENRY HEDGE.
Great God! there is no safety here below; / Thou art my fortress, thou that seem'st my foe. — FRANCIS QUARLES, *Divine Poems* [1633]

1   What can only be taught by the rod and with blows will not lead to much good; they will not remain pious any longer than the rod is behind them.
The Great Catechism. Second Command [1529]

2   Peace is more important than all justice; and peace was not made for the sake of justice, but justice for the sake of peace.   *On Marriage [1530]*

3   Justice is a temporary thing that must at last come to an end; but the conscience is eternal and will never die.   *On Marriage*

4   Superstition, idolatry, and hypocrisy have ample wages, but truth goes a-begging.
Table Talk [1569]

5   For where God built a church, there the Devil would also build a chapel.[1] . . . Thus is the Devil ever God's ape.   *Table Talk*

6   The Mass is the greatest blasphemy of God, and the highest idolatry upon earth, an abomination the like of which has never been in Christendom since the time of the Apostles.   *Table Talk*

7   There is no more lovely, friendly and charming relationship, communion or company than a good marriage.   *Table Talk*

8   A theologian is born by living, nay dying and being damned, not by thinking, reading, or speculating.   *Table Talk*

9   Reason is the greatest enemy that faith has: it never comes to the aid of spiritual things, but — more frequently than not — struggles against the divine Word, treating with contempt all that emanates from God.   *Table Talk*

10   If I had heard that as many devils would set on me in Worms as there are tiles on the roofs, I should nonetheless have ridden there.
Works [1745], XVI, 14

11   It makes a difference whose ox is gored.
Works [1854], LXII

Hernán Cortés
[Hernando Cortez]
1485–1547

12   [The Aztecs] said that by no means would they give themselves up, for as long as one of them was left he would die fighting, and that we would get nothing of theirs because they would burn everything or throw it into the water.
Third Dispatch [May 15, 1522].
To Charles V

Hugh Latimer
c. 1485–1555

13   Be of good comfort, Master Ridley, and play the man. We shall this day light such a candle, by God's grace, in England, as I trust shall never be put out.
To Nicholas Ridley [1500–1555] as they were being burned alive at Oxford for heresy [October 16, 1555]. From JOHN FOXE *[1516–1587], The Book of Martyrs [1563], vol. II*

Pope Julius III
1487–1555

14   Do you not know, my son, with what little understanding the world is ruled?[2]
To a Portuguese monk who sympathized with the pope's burdens of office

Jacques Cartier
1491–1557

15   I am rather inclined to believe that this is the land God gave to Cain.[3]   *La Première Relation*

Saint Ignatius of Loyola
1491–1556

16 Teach us, good Lord, to serve Thee as Thou deservest:
To give and not to count the cost;
To fight and not to heed the wounds;
To toil and not to seek for rest;
To labor and not ask for any reward
Save that of knowing that we do Thy will.
Prayer for Generosity [1548]

17   Almost the whole life of religious bodies lies in the maintenance of their first fervor.
Scintillae Ignatianae (Thoughts of Ignatius)[4] [compiled 1712]

---

[1]Where God hath a temple, the Devil will have a chapel. — ROBERT BURTON, *Anatomy of Melancholy, pt. III, sec. 4, member I, subsec. 1*
  No sooner is a temple built to God but the Devil builds a chapel hard by. — GEORGE HERBERT, *Jacula Prudentum*

[2]An nescis, mi fili, quantilla prudentia mundus regatur?

[3]J'estime mieux que autrement, que c'est la terre que Dieu donna à Caïn.
  Upon discovering the bleak shore of the Gulf of St. Lawrence, today's Labrador and Quebec [summer 1534].

[4]Compiled by the Hungarian Jesuit GABRIEL HEVENSI.
Translated by ALAN G. McDOUGALL.

Bernal Díaz del Castillo
c. 1492–c. 1581

1   To me it appears that the names of those[1] ought to be written in letters of gold, who died so cruel a death, for the service of God and His Majesty, to give light to those who were in darkness, and to procure wealth which all men desire.[2]

The True History of the Conquest of New Spain (Historia Verdadera de la Conquista de la Nueve España) [1800], pt. II, ch. 10

Paracelsus [Theophrastus Bombast von Hohenheim]
c. 1493–1541

2   Every experiment is like a weapon which must be used in its particular way — a spear to thrust, a club to strike. Experimenting requires a man who knows when to thrust and when to strike, each according to need and fashion.[3]

Surgeon's Book (Chirurgische Bucher) [1605]

Francis [François] I
1494–1547

3   All is lost save honor.[4]

Letter to his mother after his defeat at Pavia [February 23, 1525]

François Rabelais
c. 1494–1553

4   Break the bone and suck out the substantific marrow.

Gargantua and Pantagruel,[5] bk. I [1532], prologue

5   To laugh is proper to man.[6]

Gargantua and Pantagruel, I, Rabelais to the Reader

6   Appetite comes with eating[7] . . . but the thirst goes away with drinking.

Gargantua and Pantagruel, I, ch. 5

7   War begun without good provision of money beforehand for going through with it is but as a breathing of strength and blast that will quickly pass away. Coin is the sinews of war.

Gargantua and Pantagruel, I, 46

8   How shall I be able to rule over others, that have not full power and command of myself?[8]

Gargantua and Pantagruel, I, 52

9   Do what thou wilt.[9]

Gargantua and Pantagruel, I, 57

10   Wisdom entereth not into a malicious mind, and science without conscience is but the ruin of the soul.

Gargantua and Pantagruel, II [1534], 8

11   Subject to a kind of disease, which at that time they called lack of money.

Gargantua and Pantagruel, II, 16

12   So much is a man worth as he esteems himself.

Gargantua and Pantagruel, II, 29

13   This flea which I have in mine ear.

Gargantua and Pantagruel, III [1545], 31

14   Oh thrice and four times happy those who plant cabbages!

Gargantua and Pantagruel, IV [1548], 18

15   Which was performed to a T.[10]

Gargantua and Pantagruel, IV, 41

16   We will take the good will for the deed.[11]

Gargantua and Pantagruel, IV, 49

---

[1]The five hundred and fifty soldiers who came to Mexico with Cortés [1519], all but five of whom were dead at the time Díaz was writing [1568].

[2]Translated by MAURICE KEATINGE.

[3]Translated by HENRY M. PACHTER.

[4]Tout est perdu fors l'honneur.
The actual words written were: De toutes choses ne m'est demeuré que l'honneur et la vie qui est sauvé. The letter is in JACQUES-ANTOINE DULAURE [1755–1835], *Histoire Civile, Physique, et Morale de Paris* [1821–1825].

[5]Translated by SIR THOMAS URQUHART and PETER ANTHONY MOTTEUX [1653–1694].

[6]Pour ce que rire est le propre de l'homme.

[7]My appetite comes to me while eating. — MONTAIGNE, *Essays, bk. III, ch. 9*

[8]He is most powerful who has power over himself. — SENECA, *Epistles, letter 90, l. 34*

[9]Fais ce que voudras.

[10]We could manage this matter to a T. — LAURENCE STERNE, *Tristram Shandy, bk. II, ch. 5*
You see they'd have fitted him to a T. — SAMUEL JOHNSON; from BOSWELL, *Life of Johnson* [1791]
You will find it shall echo my speech to a T. — THOMAS MOORE, *Address for the Opening of the New Theatre of St. Stephen*

[11]The will for deed I do accept. — DU BARTAS, *Divine Weeks and Works, Second Week, Third Day, pt. 2*
You must take the will for the deed. — JONATHAN SWIFT, *Polite Conversation, Dialogue 2*

1   Speak the truth and shame the Devil.[1]
    Gargantua and Pantagruel, V [1552],
    author's prologue

2   Plain as a nose in a man's face.[2]
    Gargantua and Pantagruel, V, author's prologue

3   Like hearts of oak.
    Gargantua and Pantagruel, V, author's prologue

4   Go hang yourselves [critics]...you shall never want rope enough.[3]
    Gargantua and Pantagruel, V, author's prologue

5   Looking as like...as one pea does like another.[4]
    Gargantua and Pantagruel, V, 2

6   It is meat, drink, and cloth to us.
    Gargantua and Pantagruel, V, 7

7   I am going to seek a grand perhaps; draw the curtain, the farce is played.[5]
    Alleged last words. From PETER LE MOTTEUX
    [1653–1694], Life of Rabelais [1694]

John Heywood

c. 1497–c. 1580

8 All a green willow, willow, willow,
  All a green willow is my garland.
                    The Green Willow[6]

9 The loss of wealth is loss of dirt,
  As sages in all times assert;
  The happy man's without a shirt.

                    Be Merry Friends

10 Let the world slide,[7] let the world go;
   A fig for care, and a fig for woe!
   If I can't pay, why I can owe,
   And death makes equal the high and low.
                    Be Merry Friends

11   Haste maketh waste.[8]   *Proverbs*[9] *[1546], pt. I, ch. 2*

12   Good to be merry and wise.   *Proverbs, I, 2*

13   Look ere ye leap.[10]   *Proverbs, I, 2*

14   While between two stools my tail go to the ground.[11]   *Proverbs, I, 2*

15   The fat is in the fire.   *Proverbs, I, 3*

16   When the sun shineth, make hay.   *Proverbs, I, 3*

17   The tide tarrieth no man.[12]   *Proverbs, I, 3*

18 And while I at length debate and beat the bush,
   There shall step in other men and catch the birds.[13]
                    Proverbs, I, 3

19   Wedding is destiny,
   And hanging likewise.[14]   *Proverbs, I, 3*

20   Happy man, happy dole.[15]   *Proverbs, I, 3*

21   God never send'th mouth but he sendeth meat.[16]   *Proverbs, I, 4*

---

[1]While you live, tell truth and shame the devil! — SHAKESPEARE, *Henry IV, pt. I, act III, sc. i, l. 62*

I'd tell the truth, and shame the devil. — OLIVER GOLDSMITH; from BOSWELL, *Life of Johnson, vol. I, p. 460* (Everyman edition)

Truth being truth, / Tell it and shame the devil. — ROBERT BROWNING, *The Ring and the Book, bk. III, The Other Half-Rome*

[2]As clear and as manifest as the nose in a man's face. — ROBERT BURTON, *Anatomy of Melancholy, pt. III, sec. 3, member 4, subsec. 1*

[3]They were suffered to have rope enough till they had haltered themselves. — THOMAS FULLER [1608–1661], *The Historie of the Holy Warre* [1639], *bk. 5, ch. 7*

Give a man enough rope and he'll hang himself. — *Proverb*

[4]As like as one pease is to another. — JOHN LYLY, *Euphues*

They say we are / Almost as like as eggs. — SHAKESPEARE, *The Winter's Tale, act I, sc. ii, l. 130*

As one egg is like another. — CERVANTES, *Don Quixote, pt. II, bk. III, ch. 14*

[5]Je m'en vais chercher un grand peut-être; tirez le rideau, la farce est jouée.

His religion, at best, is an anxious wish; like that of Rabelais, "a great Perhaps." — THOMAS CARLYLE, *Essays, Burns* [1828]

The grand perhaps. — ROBERT BROWNING, *Bishop Blougram's Apology*

[6]The earliest known of the "willow" songs (see Shakespeare, 210:8).

[7]Let the world slide. — *Towneley Mysteries* [1420]

Let the world slide. — SHAKESPEARE, *The Taming of the Shrew, induction, sc. i, l. 6*

[8]In wikked haste is no profit. — CHAUCER, *The Canterbury Tales, Melibee, sec. 2240*

[9]John Heywood's *Proverbs*, first printed in 1546, is the earliest collection of English colloquial sayings. The selection here given is from the edition of 1874 (a reprint of 1598), edited by JULIAN SHARMAN.

[10]Thou shouldst have looked before thou hadst leapt. — JONSON, CHAPMAN, MARSTON, *Eastward Ho* [1605], *act V, sc. i*

[11]Between two stools one sits on the ground. — *Les Proverbes del Vilain, MS Bodleian* [c. 1303]

[12]Time nor tide tarrieth no man. — ROBERT GREENE, *Disputations* [1592]

Hoist up sail while gale doth last, / Tide and wind stay no man's pleasure. — ROBERT SOUTHWELL, *St. Peter's Complaint* [1595]

Nae man can tether time or tide. — ROBERT BURNS, *Tam o' Shanter*

[13]It is this proverb which Henry V is reported to have uttered at the siege of Orléans: Shall I beat the bush and another take the bird?

[14]Hanging and wiving go by destiny. — *The Schole-hous for Women* [1541]

Marriage and hanging go by destiny; matches are made in heaven. — ROBERT BURTON, *Anatomy of Melancholy, pt. III, sec. 2, member 5, subsec. 5*

[15]Happy man be his dole. — SHAKESPEARE, *The Merry Wives of Windsor, act III, sc. iv, l. 68,* and *The Winter's Tale, act I, sc. ii, l. 163*

[16]God sendeth and giveth both mouth and the meat. — THOMAS TUSSER, *A Hundred Good Points of Husbandry. Good Husbandly Lessons, verse 1*

God sends meat, and the Devil sends cooks. — JOHN TAYLOR [1580–1653], *Works* [1630], *vol. II, p. 85*

The holy prophet Zoroaster said, / The Lord who made thy teeth shall give thee bread. — *Persian couplet*

1   A hard beginning maketh a good ending.

Proverbs, I, 4

2   Like will to like.   *Proverbs, I, 4*

3   More afraid than hurt.   *Proverbs, I, 4*

4   Nothing is impossible to a willing heart.

Proverbs, I, 5

5   Let the world wag, and take mine ease in mine inn.   *Proverbs, I, 5*

6   Hold their noses to grindstone.

Proverbs, I, 5

7   Cut my coat after my cloth.   *Proverbs, I, 8*

8   The nearer to the church, the further from God.[1]   *Proverbs, I, 9*

9   Now for good luck, cast an old shoe after me.

Proverbs, I, 9

10   Better is to bow than break.[2]

Proverbs, I, 9

11   It hurteth not the tongue to give fair words.[3]

Proverbs, I, 9

12   Two heads are better than one.

Proverbs, I, 9

13   To tell tales out of school.   *Proverbs, I, 10*

14   To hold with the hare and run with the hound.

Proverbs, I, 10

15   Neither fish nor flesh, nor good red herring.

Proverbs, I, 10

16   All is well that ends well.[4]   *Proverbs, I, 10*

17   Of a good beginning cometh a good end.[5]

Proverbs, I, 10

18   When the steed is stolen, shut the stable door.[6]

Proverbs, I, 10

19   She looketh as butter would not melt in her mouth.   *Proverbs, I, 10*

20   Ill weed groweth fast.[7]   *Proverbs, I, 10*

21   Beggars should be no choosers.

Proverbs, I, 10

22   Merry as a cricket.   *Proverbs, I, 11*

23   To rob Peter and pay Paul.[8]   *Proverbs, I, 11*

24 A man may well bring a horse to the water,
But he cannot make him drink without he will.[9]

Proverbs, I, 11

25   Rome was not built in one day.

Proverbs, I, 11

26   Ye have many strings to your bow.[10]

Proverbs, I, 11

27   Children learn to creep ere they can learn to go.

Proverbs, I, 11

28   Better is half a loaf than no bread.   *Proverbs, I, 11*

29   Nought venture nought have.   *Proverbs, I, 11*

30   Children and fools cannot lie.[11]   *Proverbs, I, 11*

31   All is fish that cometh to net.[12]   *Proverbs, I, 11*

32   Who is worse shod than the shoemaker's wife?[13]   *Proverbs, I, 11*

33   One good turn asketh another.   *Proverbs, I, 11*

34   A dog hath a day.   *Proverbs, I, 11*

35   A hair of the dog that bit us.[14]   *Proverbs, I, 11*

36   But in deed,
A friend is never known till a man have need.

Proverbs, I, 11

---

[1]Qui est près de l'église est souvent loin de Dieu [He who is near the Church is often far from God]. — *Les Proverbes Communs* [c. 1500]

[2]Rather to bow than break is profitable: / Humility is a thing commendable. — *The Moral Proverbs of Cristyne* [1390]

[3]Fair words never hurt the tongue. — JONSON, CHAPMAN, MARSTON, *Eastward Ho* [1605], *act IV, sc. i*

[4]Si finis bonus est, totum bonum erit [If the end is good, all will be good]. — *Gesta Romanorum (Deeds of the Romans)* [1472], *tale 67*

[5]Who that well his warke beginneth, / The rather a good end he winneth. — JOHN GOWER [c. 1325–1408], *Confessio Amantis (The Lover's Confession)* [c. 1386–1390]

[6]Quant le cheval est emblé dounke ferme fols l'estable [When the horse has been stolen, the fool shuts the stable]. — *Les Proverbes del Vilain, MS Bodleian* [c. 1303]

[7]Ewyl weed ys sone y-growe. — *MS Harleian* [c. 1490]
Great weeds do grow apace. — SHAKESPEARE, *Richard III, act II, sc. iv, l. 13*
An ill weed grows apace. — GEORGE CHAPMAN, *An Humorous Day's Mirth* [1599]

[8]Give not Saint Peter so much, to leave Saint Paul nothing. — GEORGE HERBERT, *Jacula Prudentum*
"To rob Peter and pay Paul" is said to have had its origin in the reign of Edward VI when the lands of St. Peter at Westminster were appropriated to raise money for the repair of St. Paul's in London.
The French form of the proverb is: Découvrir saint Pierre pour couvrir saint Paul.

[9]You may bring a horse to the river, but he will drink when and what he pleaseth. — GEORGE HERBERT, *Jacula Prudentum*

[10]Two strings to his bow. — RICHARD HOOKER, *Laws of Ecclesiastical Polity, bk. V* [1597], *ch. 80*

[11]'Tis an old saw, children and fools speak true. — JOHN LYLY, *Endymion* [1591]

[12]All's fish they get that cometh to net. — THOMAS TUSSER, *A Hundred Good Points of Husbandry. February Abstract*

[13]Him that makes shoes go barefoot himself. — ROBERT BURTON, *Anatomy of Melancholy, Democritus to the Reader*

[14]Old recipe books advised that an inebriate should drink sparingly in the morning some of the same kind of liquor which he had drunk to excess the night before.

1 Burnt child fire dreadeth.[1] *Proverbs, II, 2*

2 There is no fool to the old fool.[2] *Proverbs, II, 2*

3 A woman hath nine lives like a cat. *Proverbs, II, 4*

4 A penny for your thought. *Proverbs, II, 4*

5 You cannot see the wood for the trees.
Proverbs, II, 4

6 You stand in your own light. *Proverbs, II, 4*

7 Tit for tat.[3] *Proverbs, II, 4*

8 Three may keep counsel, if two be away.[4]
Proverbs, II, 5

9 Small pitchers have wide ears.[5] *Proverbs, II, 5*

10 Many hands make light work. *Proverbs, II, 5*

11 Out of God's blessing into the warm sun.[6]
Proverbs, II, 5

12 There is no fire without some smoke.[7]
Proverbs, II, 5

13 A cat may look on a king. *Proverbs, II, 5*

14   Much water goeth by the mill
That the miller knoweth not of.[8] *Proverbs, II, 5*

15 He must needs go whom the devil doth drive.
Proverbs, II, 7

16 Set the cart before the horse. *Proverbs, II, 7*

17 The more the merrier. *Proverbs, II, 7*

18   Be the day never so long,
Evermore at last they ring to even-song.[9]
Proverbs, II, 7

19 The moon is made of a green cheese.[10]
Proverbs, II, 7

20 I know on which side my bread is buttered.
Proverbs, II, 7

21 An ill wind that bloweth no man to good.[11]
Proverbs, II, 9

22 For when I gave you an inch, you took an ell.[12]
Proverbs, II, 9

23 Would ye both eat your cake and have your
cake?[13] *Proverbs, II, 9*

24 Every man for himself and God for us all.[14]
Proverbs, II, 9

25 Though he love not to buy the pig in the
poke.[15] *Proverbs, II, 9*

26 This hitteth the nail on the head.
Proverbs, II, 11

27 Enough is as good as a feast. *Proverbs, II, 11*

Charles V
1500–1558

28 Iron hand in a velvet glove.
Attributed. From THOMAS CARLYLE,
Latter-Day Pamphlets, no. 11

29 You have built here what you, or anyone else,
might have built anywhere; to do so you have
destroyed what was unique in the world.
*On the building of a cathedral inside
the great mosque of Cordoba [1526]*

30 I make war on the living, not on the dead.
*Said when advised to hang Luther's corpse
on the gallows [1546]*

31 I speak Spanish to God, Italian to women, French
to men, and German to my horse.[16] *Attributed*

---

[1]Brend child fur dredth, / Quoth Hendyng. — HENDYNG [1272–1307], *Proverbs, MS*

[2]There is no fool like an old fool. — JOHN LYLY, *Mother Bombie, act IV, sc. ii,* and in frequent use thereafter

[3]This is a corruption of *Tant pour tant.*

[4]Two may keep counsel when the third's away. — SHAKESPEARE, *Titus Andronicus, act IV, sc. ii, l. 145*
Three can hold their peace if two be away. — GEORGE HERBERT, *Jacula Prudentum*

[5]Pitchers have ears. — SHAKESPEARE, *The Taming of the Shrew, act IV, sc. iv, l. 52,* and *Richard III, act II, sc. iv, l. 37*
Little pitchers have wide ears. — GEORGE HERBERT, *Jacula Prudentum*

[6]Thou shalt come out of a warm sun into God's blessing.
— JOHN LYLY, *Euphues*
Thou out of Heaven's benediction com'st / To the warm sun.
— SHAKESPEARE, *King Lear, act II, sc. ii, l. 168*

[7]There can no great smoke arise, but there must be some fire.
— JOHN LYLY, *Euphues*

[8]More water glideth by the mill / Than wots the miller of.
— SHAKESPEARE, *Titus Andronicus, act II, sc. i, l. 85*
The miller sees not all the water that goes by his mill. — ROBERT BURTON, *Anatomy of Melancholy, pt. III, sec. 3, member 4, subsec. 1*

[9]Be the day short or never so long, / At length it ringeth to evensong. — *Quoted at the stake by George Tankerfield [1555].* From JOHN FOXE [1516–1587], *The Book of Martyrs* [1563], *ch. 7*

[10]They would make me believe that the moon was made of green cheese. — JOHN FRITH [1503–1533], *A Pistle to the Christian Reader* [1529]

[11]Except wind stands as never it stood, / It is an ill wind turns none to good. — THOMAS TUSSER, *A Description of the Properties of Winds*
Falstaff. What wind blew you hither, Pistol?
Pistol. Not the ill wind which blows no man to good. — SHAKESPEARE, *Henry IV, Part II, act V, sc. iii, l. 87*

[12]Give an inch, he'll take an ell. — THOMAS DEKKER and JOHN WEBSTER, *The Famous History of Sir Thomas Wyat* [1607]

[13]Wouldst thou both eat thy cake and have it? — GEORGE HERBERT, *The Temple. The Size l. 18*

[14]Every man for himself, his own ends, the Devil for all. — ROBERT BURTON, *Anatomy of Melancholy, pt. III, sec. 1, member 3*

[15]For buying or selling of pig in a poke. — THOMAS TUSSER, *A Hundred Good Points of Husbandry. September Abstract*

[16]Je parle espagnol à Dieu, italien aux femmes, français aux hommes, et allemand à mon cheval.

Pope Gregory XIII
1502–1585

1   To the greater glory of God.[1]
From The Canons and Decrees of the
Council of Trent [1542–1560]

Sir Thomas Wyatt
c. 1503–1542

2 Forget not yet the tried intent
Of such a truth as I have meant;
My great travail so gladly spent,
Forget not yet!

Forget Not Yet

3 My lute, awake! perform the last
Labor that thou and I shall waste,
And end that I have now begun;
For when this song is sung and past,
My lute, be still, for I have done.
The Lover Complaineth the Unkindness
of His Love

4 They flee from me, that sometime did me seek
With naked foot, stalking in my chamber.
The Lover Showeth How He Is Forsaken
of Such as He Sometime Enjoyed

5 And graven with diamonds in letters plain
There is written her fair neck round about:
Noli me tangere, for Caesar's I am,
And wild for to hold, though I seem tame.
Whoso List to Hunt

John Calvin
1509–1564

6   There is no medium between the two things: the
earth must either be worthless in our estimation, or
keep us enslaved by an intemperate love of it.
Institutes of the Christian Religion[2] [1536],
bk. III, ch. 9, sec. 2

7   If we see a funeral, or walk among graves, as the
image of death is then present to the eye, I admit
we philosophize admirably on the vanity of life. We
do not indeed always do so, for those things often
have no effect upon us at all. But, at the best, our philosophy is momentary. It vanishes as soon as we turn
our back, and leaves not the vestige of remembrance
behind; in short, it passes away, just like the applause
of a theatre at some pleasant spectacle.
Institutes of the Christian Religion,
III, 9, 2

John Bradford
c. 1510–1555

8   The familiar story, that, on seeing evildoers taken
to the place of execution, he was wont to exclaim:
"But for the grace of God there goes John Bradford,"
is a universal tradition, which has overcome the lapse
of time.
Biographical notice,
Parker Society edition,
The Writings of John Bradford
[1853]

Sir Thomas Vaux
1510–1556

9 Companion none is like
Unto the mind alone;
For many have been harmed by speech,
Through thinking, few or none.
Of a Contented Mind
[1557]

10 But age, with his stealing steps,
Hath claw'd me in his clutch.[3]
The Aged Lover Renounceth Love,
st. 3

Giorgio Vasari
1511–1574

11   The contours of its legs are extremely beautiful,
along with the splendid articulations and grace of its
flanks; a sweeter and more graceful pose has never
been seen that could equal it, nor have feet, hands,
and a head ever been produced which so well match
all the other parts of the body in skill of workmanship
or design. To be sure, anyone who sees this statue
need not be concerned with seeing any other piece
of sculpture done in our times or in any other period
by any other artist.
The Lives of the Artists[4] [1550].
Michelangelo

Richard Grafton
c. 1513–1572

12 Thirty days hath November,
April, June, and September,

---

[1]Ad maiorem Dei gloriam. Motto of the Society of Jesus.
[2]Translated by HENRY BEVERIDGE.

[3]Quoted by First Clown in SHAKESPEARE, *Hamlet,* act V, sc. i, l. 77.
[4]On Michelangelo's *David.*
Translated by JULIA CONAWAY BONDANELLA and PETER BONDA-
NELLA.

February hath twenty-eight alone,
And all the rest have thirty-one.[1]
Chronicles of England
[1562]

John Knox
c. 1513–1572

1 The First Blast of the Trumpet Against the Monstrous Regiment [Regimen] of Women.
Title of pamphlet [1558]

2 A man with God is always in the majority.[2]
Inscription on Reformation Monument,
Geneva, Switzerland

Saint Teresa of Ávila
1515–1582

3 In ecstasy come true revelations, great favors, and visions, all of which help to humble and strengthen the soul, to make it despise the things of this life, and more clearly realize the greatness of the reward that the Lord reserves for those who serve him.
The Life of Saint Teresa of Ávila[3]
[c. 1565], ch. 21

4 Alas, O Lord, to what a state dost Thou bring those who love thee! Yet these sufferings are as nothing compared to the reward Thou wilt give for them.
The Interior Castle[4] [1577],
The Sixth Mansions, ch. 11,
sec. 6

Mary Tudor [Mary I]
1516–1558

5 When I am dead and opened, you shall find "Calais" lying in my heart.
From RAPHAEL HOLINSHED,
Chronicles [1577],
vol. 4

Joachim du Bellay
1522–1560

6 Happy he who like Ulysses has made a glorious voyage.[5]
Les Regrets [1559], sonnet 31

Pierre de Ronsard
1524–1585

7 When you are old, at evening candlelit,
Beside the fire bending to your wool,
Read out my verse and murmur, "Ronsard writ
This praise for me when I was beautiful."[6]
Sonnets pour Hélène, vol. II, no. 42

8 Live now, believe me, wait not till tomorrow;
Gather the roses of life today.[7]
Sonnets pour Hélène, II, 42

9 Sweetheart, come see if the rose
Which at morning began to unclose
Its damask gown to the sun
Has not lost, now the day is done,
The folds of its damasked gown
And its colors so like your own.
Odes [1553]. À Cassandre[8]

10 Harvest, oh! harvest your hour
While life is abloom with youth!
For age with bitter ruth
Will fade your beauty's flower.[9]
Odes. À Cassandre, last lines

Thomas Tusser
c. 1524–1580

11 At Christmas play and make good cheer,
For Christmas comes but once a year.
A Hundred Good Points of Husbandry
[1557]. The Farmer's Daily Diet

---

[1] Thirty days hath September, / April, June, and November; / All the rest have thirty-one, / Excepting February alone, / Which hath but twenty-eight, in fine, / Till leap year gives it twenty-nine. — *Common in the New England states*
Compare the old Latin class mnemonic:
In March, July, October, May, / The Ides are on the fifteenth day, / The Nones the seventh: all other months besides / Have two days less for Nones and Ides.

[2] *Un homme avec Dieu est toujours dans la majorité.*
See Wendell Phillips, 458:11.

[3] Translated by J. M. COHEN.

[4] Translated by BENEDICT ZIMMERMAN.

[5] *Heureux qui, comme Ulysse, a fait un beau voyage.*

[6] *Quand vous serez bien vieille, au soir à la chandelle, / Assise auprès du feu, dévidant et filant, / Direz, chantant mes vers, en vous émerveillant: / "Ronsard me célébrait du temps que j'étais belle."*
Translated by HUMBERT WOLFE.
See the adaptation by Yeats: When you are old and gray and full of sleep, 591:5.

[7] *Vivez, si m'en croyez, n'attendez à demain: / Cueillez dès aujourd'hui les roses de la vie.*
See *The Wisdom of Solomon 2:8*, 29:32; Horace, 96:11; Spenser, 160:9; and Herrick, 241:4.

[8] *Mignonne, allons voir si la rose / Qui, ce matin, avoit déclose / Sa robe de pourpre au soleil, / A point perdu, cette vesprée / Les plis de sa robe pourprée / Et son teint au vôtre pareil.*
Translated by CURTIS HIDDEN PAGE.

[9] *Cueillez, cueillez votre jeunesse: / Comme à cette fleur, la vieillesse / Fera ternir votre beauté.*

1 Such mistress, such Nan,
Such master, such man.[1]
A Hundred Good Points of Husbandry.
April's Abstract

2 Sweet April showers
Do spring May flowers.
A Hundred Good Points of Husbandry.
April's Husbandry

Gabriel Meurier
1530–1601

3 He who excuses himself accuses himself.[2]
Trésor des Sentences

William Stevenson
c. 1530–1575

4 Back and side go bare, go bare,
Both foot and hand go cold;
But, belly, God send thee good ale enough,
Whether it be new or old.
Gammer Gurton's Needle [1566],
act II, drinking song, refrain

Henri Estienne
c. 1531–1598

5 Si jeunesse savait, si vieillesse pouvait [If youth but knew, if old age but could].
Les Prémices [1594]

6 God tempers the wind to the shorn lamb.[3]
Les Prémices

Elizabeth I
1533–1603

7 I know I have the body of a weak and feeble woman, but I have the heart and stomach of a king, and of a king of England too; and think foul scorn that Parma or Spain, or any prince of Europe, should dare to invade the borders of my realm.
Speech to the troops at Tilbury on the
approach of the Armada [1588]

8 I am your anointed Queen. I will never be by violence constrained to do anything. I thank God I am endued with such qualities that if I were turned out

of the Realm in my petticoat I were able to live in any place in Christendom.
From FREDERICK CHAMBERLIN [1870–1943],
Sayings of Queen Elizabeth [1923]

9 I will make you shorter by the head.
From CHAMBERLIN, Sayings of Queen Elizabeth

10 The daughter of debate, that eke discord doth sow.[4] *From CHAMBERLIN, Sayings of Queen Elizabeth*

11 [To the Countess of Nottingham] God may forgive you, but I never can.
From DAVID HUME, History of England
[1754–1762], vol. II, ch. 7

12 Though God hath raised me high, yet this I count the glory of my crown: that I have reigned with your loves. *The Golden Speech [1601]*

13 Semper eadem [Ever the same]. *Motto*

14 'Twas God the word that spake it,
He took the Bread and brake it;
And what the word did make it,
That I believe, and take it.[5]
From SAMUEL CLARKE [1599–1682],
Marrow of Ecclesiastical History [ed. 1675],
pt. II, Life of Queen Elizabeth

15 Must! Is *must* a word to be addressed to princes? Little man, little man!
On her deathbed, to Robert Cecil,
her principal secretary [March 24, 1603]

Michel Eyquem de Montaigne
1533–1592

16 I want to be seen here in my simple, natural, ordinary fashion, without straining or artifice; for it is myself that I portray . . . I am myself the matter of my book.[6] *Essays,[7] bk. I [1580], To the Reader*

17 Truly man is a marvelously vain, diverse, and undulating object. It is hard to found any constant and uniform judgment on him.[8] *Essays, I, ch. 1*

---

[1] Tel maître, tel valet. — *Attributed to* PIERRE TERRÀIL, SEIGNEUR DE BAYARD [c. 1473–1524], *known as the* CHEVALIER BAYARD

[2] Qui s'excuse, s'accuse.

[3] Dieu mesure le froid à la brebis tondue.

[4] Mary, Queen of Scots [1542–1587].

[5] Answer on being asked her opinion of Christ's presence in the Sacrament.

[6] Je veux qu'on m'y voit en ma façon simple, naturelle, et ordinaire, sans étude et artifice; car c'est moi que je peins . . . Je suis moi-même la matière de mon livre.

[7] Books I and II of the *Essays* were published in 1580; republished [1588] with the addition of book III and with many interpolations in books I and II; the whole republished posthumously [1595], incorporating material based on Montaigne's marginal annotations in the 1588 edition.
Translated by DONALD M. FRAME unless otherwise noted.

[8] Certes, c'est un subject [sic] merveilleusement vain, divers, et ondoyant, que l'homme. Il est malaisé d'y fonder jugement constant et uniforme.

1   The thing I fear most is fear.[1]   *Essays, I, 18*

2   I want death to find me planting my cabbages.[2]
  Essays, I, 20

3   He who would teach men to die would teach them to live.[3]   *Essays, I, 20*

4   Live as long as you please, you will strike nothing off the time you will have to spend dead.
  Essays, I, 20

5   Wherever your life ends, it is all there. The advantage of living is not measured by length, but by use; some men have lived long, and lived little; attend to it while you are in it. It lies in your will, not in the number of years, for you to have lived enough.
  Essays, I, 20

6   I do not speak the minds of others except to speak my own mind better.   *Essays, I, 26*

7   Since I would rather make of him [the child] an able man than a learned man, I would also urge that care be taken to choose a guide [tutor] with a well-made rather than a well-filled head.[4]
  Essays, I, 26

8   If you press me to say why I loved him, I can say no more than it was because he was he and I was I.[5]   *Essays, I, 28*

9   Nothing is so firmly believed as what is least known.   *Essays, I, 32*

10   A man of understanding has lost nothing, if he has himself.[6]   *Essays, I, 39*

11   We must reserve a back shop all our own,[7] entirely free, in which to establish our real liberty and our principal retreat and solitude.
  Essays, I, 39

12   The greatest thing in the world is to know how to belong to oneself.[8]   *Essays, I, 39*

13   It is a thorny undertaking, and more so than it seems, to follow a movement so wandering as that of our mind, to penetrate the opaque depths of its innermost folds, to pick out and immobilize the innumerable flutterings that agitate it.[9]
  Essays, II [1580], 6

14   My trade and my art is living.[10]
  Essays, II, 6

15   The easy, gentle, and sloping path . . . is not the path of true virtue. It demands a rough and thorny road.   *Essays, II, 11*

16   When I play with my cat, who knows if I am not a pastime to her more than she is to me?
  Essays, II, 12

17   The souls of emperors and cobblers are cast in the same mold. . . . The same reason that makes us bicker with a neighbor creates a war between princes.
  Essays, II, 12

18   Their [the Skeptics'] way of speaking is: "I settle nothing. . . . I do not understand it. . . . Nothing seems true that may not seem false." Their sacramental word is Επεχω, which is to say, I suspend my judgment.[11]   *Essays, II, 12*

19   This notion [skepticism] is more clearly understood by asking "What do I know?"[12]
  Essays, II, 12

20   Man is certainly crazy. He could not make a mite, and he makes gods by the dozen.[13]
  Essays, II, 12

21   What of a truth that is bounded by these mountains and is falsehood to the world that lives beyond?[14]
  Essays, II, 12

---

[1]C'est de quoi j'ai le plus de peur que la peur.

[2]Je veux que la mort me trouve plantant mes choux.

[3]I have taught you, my dear flock, for above thirty years how to live, and I will show you in a very short time how to die. — SIR EDWIN SANDYS [1561–1629], *Anglorum Speculum*
  Teach him how to live, / And, oh still harder lesson! how to die. — BEILBY PORTEUS [1731–1808], *Death* [1759], *l. 316*

[4]Plutôt la tête bien faite que bien pleine.

[5]Parce que c'était lui; parce que c'était moi.
  Translated by CHARLES COTTON, revised by WILLIAM CAREW HAZLITT.

[6]L'homme d'entendement n'a rien perdu, s'il a soi-même.

[7]Il se faut réserver une arrière boutique toute nôtre.

[8]La plus grande chose du monde, c'est de savoir être à soi.

[9]C'est une épineuse entreprise, et plus qu'il ne semble, de suivre une allure si vagabonde que celle de nôtre esprit; de pénétrer les profondeurs opaques de ses replis internes; de choisir et arrêter tant de menus de ses agitations.

[10]Mon métier et mon art, c'est vivre.

[11]Je suspends mon jugement.
  Translated by E. J. TRECHMANN.
  Greek word (*epecho*) inscribed in Montaigne's library. — MAURICE RAT, *Oeuvres Complètes de Montaigne, note*
  This is one of a dozen maxims from Sextus Empiricus, third-century Greek philosopher, which together with biblical and Latin quotations comprise the fifty-seven sentences painted on the roof bays of Montaigne's library. About two-thirds of the sentences are in *Apologie de Raimond Sebond* (chapter 12 of book II of the *Essays*).

[12]Que sais-je?
  Translated by E. J. TRECHMANN.
  This phrase appeared on a medal of Montaigne's, which showed also his coat of arms and the collar of the order of Saint Michael, and on the reverse side a pair of scales in perfect balance, the date [1576], his age (forty-two), and the Skeptics' motto Επεχω (see Montaigne, 152:18).

[13]L'homme est bien insensé. Il ne saurait forger un ciron, et forge des Dieux à douzaines.

[14]Quelle vérité que ces montagnes bornent, qui est mensonge qui se tient au delà?

1   Those who have compared our life to a dream were right. . . . We sleeping wake, and waking sleep.[1]
Essays, II, 12

2   How many valiant men we have seen to survive their own reputation!   *Essays, II, 16*

3   We are, I know not how, double in ourselves, so that what we believe we disbelieve and cannot rid ourselves of what we condemn.
Essays, II, 16

4   A man may be humble through vainglory.
Essays, II, 17

5   I find that the best goodness I have has some tincture of vice.   *Essays, II, 20*

6   Saying is one thing and doing is another.
Essays, II, 31

7   There were never in the world two opinions alike, any more than two hairs or two grains. Their most universal quality is diversity.   *Essays, II, 37*

8   I will follow the good side right to the fire, but not into it if I can help it.   *Essays, III [1595], 1*

9   I speak the truth, not my fill of it, but as much as I dare speak; and I dare to do so a little more as I grow old.   *Essays, III, 1*

10   Few men have been admired by their own households.   *Essays, III, 1*

11   Every man bears the whole stamp of the human condition.[2]   *Essays, III, 1*

12   It [marriage] happens as with cages: the birds without despair to get in, and those within despair of getting out.[3]   *Essays, III, 5*

13   Everyone recognizes me in my book, and my book in me.   *Essays, III, 5*

14   It takes so much to be a king that he exists only as such. That extraneous glare that surrounds him hides him and conceals him from us; our sight breaks and is dissipated by it, being filled and arrested by this strong light.   *Essays, III, 7*

15   Our wisdom and deliberation for the most part follow the lead of chance.[4]
Essays, III, 8

16   Not because Socrates said so, but because it is in truth my own disposition — and perchance to some excess — I look upon all men as my compatriots, and embrace a Pole as a Frenchman, making less account of the national than of the universal and common bond.[5]   *Essays, III, 9*

17   There is no man so good that if he placed all his actions and thoughts under the scrutiny of the laws, he would not deserve hanging ten times in his life.
Essays, III, 9

18   I have seen no more evident monstrosity and miracle in the world than myself.   *Essays, III, 11*

19   I have here only made a nosegay of culled flowers, and have brought nothing of my own but the thread that ties them together.[6]
Essays, III, 12

20   It is more of a job to interpret the interpretations than to interpret the things, and there are more books about books than about any other subject: we do nothing but write glosses about each other.
Essays, III, 13

21   For truth itself does not have the privilege to be employed at any time and in every way; its use, noble as it is, has its circumscriptions and limits.
Essays, III, 13

22   No matter that we may mount on stilts, we still must walk on our own legs. And on the highest throne in the world, we still sit only on our own bottom.[7]   *Essays, III, 13*

23   Let us give Nature a chance; she knows her business better than we do.   *Essays, III, 13*

---

[1]Ceux qui ont apparié notre vie à un songe ont eu de la raison . . . Nous veillons dormants et veillants dormons.
Translated by E. J. TRECHMANN.

[2]Chaque homme porte la forme, entière de l'humaine condition. Translated by CHARLES COTTON, revised by WILLIAM CAREW HAZLITT.

[3]Translated by CHARLES COTTON, revised by WILLIAM CAREW HAZLITT.
I myself have loved a lady and pursued her with a great deal of under-age protestation, whom some three or four gallants . . . would have been glad to have been rid of. 'Tis just like a summer bird-cage in a garden: the birds that are without despair to get in, and the birds that are within . . . fear they shall never get out. — JOHN WEBSTER, *The White Devil, act I, sc. ii*
Wedlock, indeed, hath oft comparèd been / To public feasts, where meet a public rout — / Where they that are without would fain go in, / And they that are within would fain go out. — SIR JOHN DAVIES [1569–1626], *A Contention* [1602]

[4]Although men flatter themselves with their great actions, they are not so often the result of great design as of chance. — LA ROCHEFOUCAULD, *Maxim 57*

[5]Translated by CHARLES COTTON, revised by WILLIAM CAREW HAZLITT.

[6]Translated by CHARLES COTTON, revised by WILLIAM CAREW HAZLITT.
John Bartlett used this passage as an epigraph for the fourth edition of *Bartlett's Familiar Quotations* [1864].
I am but a gatherer and disposer of other men's stuff, at my best value. — SIR HENRY WOTTON [1568–1639], *The Elements of Architecture* [1624], *preface*

[7]Si, avons nous beau monter sur des échasses, car sur des échasses encore faut-il marcher de nos jambes. Et au plus élevé trône du monde, si ne sommes assis que sur notre cul.
Translated by WALTER KAISER.

William I
[William the Silent]
1533–1584

1 My God, have mercy on my soul and on my poor people.[1]
> *Last words as he fell under an assassin's bullets*

William Butler
1535–1618

2 It is unseasonable and unwholesome in all months that have not an *r* in their name to eat an oyster.
> *Dyet's Dry Dinner [1599]*

Sir Humphrey Gilbert
c. 1539–1583

3 We are as near to heaven by sea as by land![2]
> *From* RICHARD HAKLUYT *[c. 1552–1616],*
> *Voyages, vol. III [1600]*

Saint John of the Cross
[San Juan de la Cruz]
1542–1591

4 The spring that brims and ripples oh I know in dark of night.[3]
> *Song of the Soul Whose Pleasure Is in*
> *Knowing God by Faith [c. 1578]*

5 The Dark Night of the Soul.
> *Title of treatise[4] [c. 1583]*

6   O night that joined
Beloved and lover
Lover into beloved transformed[5]
> *The Dark Night*

Mary Stuart
[Mary, Queen of Scots]
1542–1587

7 In my end is my beginning.   *Motto*

8 O Lord my God, I have trusted in thee;
O Jesu my dearest one, now set me free.
In prison's oppression, in sorrow's obsession,
I weary for thee.
With sighing and crying bowed down as dying,
I adore thee, I implore thee, set me free![6]
> *Prayer written in her Book of Devotion*
> *before her execution*

Jan Zamoyski
1542–1605

9 The king reigns, but does not govern.[7]
> *Speech in the Polish Parliament [1605],*
> *referring to King Sigismund III*

Sir Edward Dyer
1543–1607

10 My mind to me a kingdom is;
Such present joys therein I find
That it excels all other bliss
That earth affords or grows by kind:
Though much I want which most would have,
Yet still my mind forbids to crave.
> *Rawlinson Poetry MS 85,[8] p. 17*

Guillaume de Salluste, Seigneur Du Bartas
1544–1590

11 For where's the state beneath the firmament
That doth excel the bees for government?
> *Divine Weeks and Works [1578],*
> *First Week, Fifth Day, pt. 1*

12 Or almost like a spider, who, confined
In her web's center, shakt with every wind,

---

[1]Mon Dieu, ayez pitié de mon âme et de mon pauvre peuple.

[2]The way to heaven out of all places is of like length and distance. — SIR THOMAS MORE, *Utopia*
 Gilbert called out these words from his pinnace, the *Squirrel*, to the captain of another vessel during their return voyage from Newfoundland to England. Gilbert held a book, likely More's *Utopia* and the inspiration for his utterance. The *Squirrel* and all on board were lost at sea that night [August 1583].
 "Do not fear! Heaven is as near," / He said, "by water as by land!" — HENRY WADSWORTH LONGFELLOW, *Sir Humphrey Gilbert* [1849], *st. 6*

[3]Que bien se yo la fonte que mana y corre / aunque es de noche.
 Translated by JOHN FREDERICK NIMS.

[4]The title is taken from the earlier poem quoted in 154:4.

[5]O noche que juntaste / Amado con amada / Amada en el amado transformada.
 Translated by JOHN FREDERICK NIMS.

[6]O Domine Deus! speravi in te; / O care mi Jesu! nunc libera me. / In dura catena, in misera poena, / Disidero te. / Languendo, gemendo, et genuflectendo, / Adoro, imploro, ut liberes me!
 Translated by ALGERNON CHARLES SWINBURNE.

[7]Adolphe Thiers adopted the epigram as the motto for his journal *Le National*.

[8]This poem became popular as a song, altered thus:
 My mind to me a kingdom is; / Such perfect joy therein I find, / As far exceeds all earthly bliss / That God and Nature hath assigned. / Though much I want that most would have, / Yet still my mind forbids to crave. — WILLIAM BYRD [1543–1623], *Psalms, Sonnets, and Songs of Sadness and Piety* [1588]

Moves in an instant if the buzzing fly
Stir but a string of her lawn canapie.[1]
Divine Weeks and Works, First Week,
Sixth Day

1 Living from hand to mouth.
Divine Weeks and Works, Second Week,
First Day, pt. 4

2 In the jaws of death.[2]
Divine Weeks and Works, Second Week,
First Day, pt. 4

3   My lovely living boy,
My hope, my hap, my love, my life, my joy.[3]
Divine Weeks and Works, Second Week,
Fourth Day, pt. 2

4 Out of the book of Nature's learned breast.[4]
Divine Weeks and Works, Second Week,
Fourth Day, pt. 2

5 Flesh of thy flesh, nor yet bone of thy bone.
Divine Weeks and Works, Second Week,
Fourth Day, pt. 2

William Gilbert
1544–1603

6   Philosophy is for the few.[5]
De Magnete (On the Magnet) [1600]

7   In the discovery of secret things and in the investigation of hidden causes, stronger reasons are
obtained from sure experiments and demonstrated
arguments than from probable conjectures and the
opinions of philosophical speculators of the common
sort.[5]

De Magnete

Miguel de Cervantes
1547–1616

8   You are a king by your own fireside, as much as
any monarch in his throne.
Don Quixote de la Mancha [1605–1615],[6]
author's preface, p. xix

9   I was so free with him as not to mince the matter.
Don Quixote, preface, p. xx

10   They can expect nothing but their labor for their
pains.[7]
Don Quixote, preface, p. xxiii

11   Time out of mind.[8]
Don Quixote, pt. I [1605], bk. I, ch. 1, p. 4

12   Which I have earned with the sweat of my
brows.   *Don Quixote, pt. I, I, 4, p. 22*

13   By a small sample we may judge of the whole
piece.   *Don Quixote, pt. I, I, 4, p. 25*

14   Put you in this pickle.[9]
Don Quixote, pt. I, I, 5, p. 30

15   Can we ever have too much of a good thing?
Don Quixote, pt. I, I, 6, p. 37

16   I don't know that ever I saw one in my born
days.   *Don Quixote, pt. I, II, 2, p. 57*

17   Those two fatal words, Mine and Thine.
Don Quixote, pt. I, II, 3, p. 63

18   And had a face like a benediction.
Don Quixote, pt. I, II, 4, p. 69

19   There's not the least thing can be said or done,
but people will talk and find fault.[10]
Don Quixote, pt. I, II, 4, p. 70

20   Without a wink of sleep.
Don Quixote, pt. I, II, 4, p. 72

21   Fortune leaves always some door open to come at
a remedy.
Don Quixote, pt. I, III, 1, p. 94

22   Thank you for nothing.
Don Quixote, pt. I, III, 1, p. 94

---

[1]Much like a subtle spider which doth sit / In middle of her web, which spreadeth wide; / If aught do touch the utmost thread of it / She feels it instantly on every side. — Sir John Davies [1569–1626], *The Immortality of the Soul* [1599]

Our souls sit close and silently within, / And their own webs from their own entrails spin; / And when eyes meet far off, our sense is such / That, spider-like, we feel the tenderest touch. — John Dryden, *Marriage à la Mode* [1673], act II, sc. i

The spider's touch, how exquisitely fine! / Feels at each thread, and lives along the line. — Alexander Pope, *An Essay on Man,* epistle I, l. 217

[2]Out of the jaws of death. — Shakespeare, *Twelfth-Night,* act III, sc. iv, l. 396

[3]My fair son! / My life, my joy, my food, my all the world! — Shakespeare, *King John,* act III, sc. iv, l. 103

[4]The physician, [Paracelsus] said, must read Nature's book, and to do so must walk over the leaves. — Margaret L. Lee, introduction to *Browning's Paracelsus* [1909], citing the preface to *Paragranum* by Paracelsus

[5]Translated by P. F. Mottelay.

[6]Translated [1700–1703] by Peter Anthony Motteux. Page numbers are those of the Modern Library Giant edition.

[7]Nothing is to be gotten without pains (labor). — *Proverb*

[8]Time out o' mind. — Shakespeare, *Romeo and Juliet,* act I, sc. iv, l. 70

[9]How cam'st thou in this pickle? — Shakespeare, *The Tempest,* act V, sc. i, l. 281

[10]Do you think you could keep people from talking? — Molière, *Tartuffe,* act I, sc. viii

Take wife, or cowl; ride you, or walk: / Doubt not but tongues will have their talk. — Jean de La Fontaine, *The Miller, His Son, and the Donkey* [1694]

1 To give the devil his due.
Don Quixote, pt. I, III, 3, p. 111

2 You're leaping over the hedge before you come to the stile. *Don Quixote, pt. I, III, 4, p. 117*

3 Paid him in his own coin.
Don Quixote, pt. I, III, 4, p. 119

4 The famous Don Quixote de la Mancha, otherwise called the Knight of the Sorrowful Countenance.[1] *Don Quixote, pt. I, III, 5, p. 126*

5 You are come off now with a whole skin.
Don Quixote, pt. I, III, 5, p. 127

6 Fear is sharp-sighted, and can see things underground, and much more in the skies.
Don Quixote, pt. I, III, 6, p. 131

7 A finger in every pie.[2]
Don Quixote, pt. I, III, 6, p. 133

8 No better than she should be.[3]
Don Quixote, pt. I, III, 6, p. 133

9 That's the nature of women . . . not to love when we love them, and to love when we love them not.
Don Quixote, pt. I, III, 6, p. 133

10 You may go whistle for the rest.
Don Quixote, pt. I, III, 6, p. 134

11 Why do you lead me a wild-goose chase?
Don Quixote, pt. I, III, 6, p. 136

12 Experience, the universal Mother of Sciences.
Don Quixote, pt. I, III, 7, p. 140

13 Give me but that, and let the world rub, there I'll stick. *Don Quixote, pt. I, III, 7, p. 148*

14 Sing away sorrow, cast away care.
Don Quixote, pt. I, III, 8, p. 153

15 Of good natural parts, and of a liberal education. *Don Quixote, pt. I, III, 8, p. 154*

16 Let every man mind his own business.
Don Quixote, pt. I, III, 8, p. 157

17 Those who'll play with cats must expect to be scratched. *Don Quixote, pt. I, III, 8, p. 159*

18 'Tis the part of a wise man to keep himself today for tomorrow, and not venture all his eggs in one basket. *Don Quixote, pt. I, III, 9, p. 162*

19 The ease of my burdens, the staff of my life.
Don Quixote, pt. I, III, 9, p. 163

20 Within a stone's throw of it.
Don Quixote, pt. I, III, 9, p. 170

21 The very remembrance of my former misfortune proves a new one to me.
Don Quixote, pt. I, III, 10, p. 174

22 Absence, that common cure of love.
Don Quixote, pt. I, III, 10, p. 177

23 From pro's and con's they fell to a warmer way of disputing.
Don Quixote, pt. I, III, 10, p. 181

24 Little said is soon amended.[4]
Don Quixote, pt. I, III, 10, p. 184

25 Thou hast seen nothing yet.
Don Quixote, pt. I, III, 11, p. 190

26 Between jest and earnest.
Don Quixote, pt. I, III, 11, p. 190

27 My love and hers have always been purely Platonic. *Don Quixote, pt. I, III, 11, p. 192*

28 'Tis ill talking of halters in the house of a man that was hanged. *Don Quixote, pt. I, III, 11, p. 195*

29 My memory is so bad that many times I forget my own name! *Don Quixote, pt. I, III, 11, p. 195*

30 'Twill grieve me so to the heart that I shall cry my eyes out. *Don Quixote, pt. I, III, 11, p. 197*

31 Ready to split his sides with laughing.
Don Quixote, pt. I, III, 13, p. 208

32 My honor is dearer to me than my life.
Don Quixote, pt. I, IV, 1, p. 226

33 On the word of a gentleman, and a Christian.
Don Quixote, pt. I, IV, 1, p. 236

34 Let us forget and forgive injuries.
Don Quixote, pt. I, IV, 3, p. 254

35 I must speak the truth, and nothing but the truth. *Don Quixote, pt. I, IV, 3, p. 255*

36 Here's the devil-and-all to pay.
Don Quixote, pt. I, IV, 10, p. 319

37 I begin to smell a rat.
Don Quixote, pt. I, IV, 10, p. 319

38 The proof of the pudding is in the eating.
Don Quixote, pt. I, IV, 10, p. 322

39 Let none presume to tell me that the pen is preferable to the sword. *Don Quixote, pt. I, IV, 10, p. 325*

---

[1]El Caballero de la Triste Figura.
Translated by Tobias Smollett.

[2]No pie was baked at Castlewood but her little finger was in it. — William Makepeace Thackeray, *The Virginians*, ch. 5

[3]An old proverb.
You are no better than you should be. — Beaumont and Fletcher, *The Coxcomb* [1647], *act IV, sc. iii*

---

[4]Often rendered: Least said soonest mended.

1 There's no striving against the stream; and the weakest still goes to the wall.
Don Quixote, pt. I, IV, 20, p. 404

2 The bow cannot always stand bent, nor can human frailty subsist without some lawful recreation. *Don Quixote, pt. I, IV, 21, p. 412*

3 It is not the hand but the understanding of a man that may be said to write.[1]
Don Quixote, pt. II [1615], III, author's preface, p. 441

4 When the head aches, all the members partake of the pains.[2] *Don Quixote, pt. II, III, 2, p. 455*

5 Youngsters read it [Don Quixote's story], grown men understand it, and old people applaud it.
Don Quixote, pt. II, III, 3, p. 464

6 History is in a manner a sacred thing, so far as it contains truth; for where truth is, the supreme Father of it may also be said to be, at least, inasmuch as concerns truth. *Don Quixote, pt. II, III, 3, p. 465*

7 Every man is as Heaven made him, and some times a great deal worse.
Don Quixote, pt. II, III, 4, p. 468

8 There's no sauce in the world like hunger.
Don Quixote, pt. II, III, 5, p. 473

9 He casts a sheep's eye at the wench.
Don Quixote, pt. II, III, 5, p. 474

10 I ever loved to see everything upon the square.
Don Quixote, pt. II, III, 5, p. 475

11 Neither will I make myself anybody's laughing-stock. *Don Quixote, pt. II, III, 5, p. 475*

12 Journey over all the universe in a map, without the expense and fatigue of traveling, without suffering the inconveniences of heat, cold, hunger, and thirst.
Don Quixote, pt. II, III, 6, p. 479

13 Presume to put in her oar.
Don Quixote, pt. II, III, 6, p. 480

14 The fair sex.[3] *Don Quixote, pt. II, III, 6, p. 480*

15 A little in one's own pocket is better than much in another man's purse. 'Tis good to keep a nest egg. Every little makes a mickle.
Don Quixote, pt. II, III, 7, p. 486

16 Remember the old saying, "Faint heart ne'er won fair lady." *Don Quixote, pt. II, III, 10, p. 501*

17 Forewarned forearmed.
Don Quixote, pt. II, III, 10, p. 502

18 As well look for a needle in a bottle of hay.[4]
Don Quixote, pt. II, III, 10, p. 502

19 Are we to mark this day with a white or a black stone? *Don Quixote, pt. II, III, 10, p. 502*

20 I'll turn over a new leaf.
Don Quixote, pt. II, III, 13, p. 524

21 He's [Don Quixote's] a muddled fool, full of lucid intervals. *Don Quixote, pt. II, III, 18, p. 556*

22 There are only two families in the world, the Haves and the Have-Nots.
Don Quixote, pt. II, III, 20, p. 574

23 He preaches well that lives well, quoth Sancho; that's all the divinity I understand.
Don Quixote, pt. II, III, 20, p. 575

24 Love and War are the same thing, and stratagems and policy are as allowable in the one as in the other. *Don Quixote, pt. II, III, 21, p. 580*

25 A private sin is not so prejudicial in this world as a public indecency. *Don Quixote, pt. II, III, 22, p. 582*

26 There is no love lost, sir.
Don Quixote, pt. II, III, 22, p. 582

27 Come back sound, wind and limb.
Don Quixote, pt. II, III, 22, p. 587

28 Patience, and shuffle the cards.[5]
Don Quixote, pt. II, III, 23, p. 592

29 Tell me thy company, and I'll tell thee what thou art. *Don Quixote, pt. II, III, 23, p. 594*

30 Tomorrow will be a new day.
Don Quixote, pt. II, III, 26, p. 618

31 I can see with half an eye.
Don Quixote, pt. II, III, 29, p. 632

32 Great persons are able to do great kindnesses.
Don Quixote, pt. II, III, 32, p. 662

33 Honesty's the best policy.[6]
Don Quixote, pt. II, III, 33, p. 666

---

[1]Cervantes's left hand was maimed for life by gunshot wounds in the battle of Lepanto.

[2]When the head is not sound, the rest cannot be well. — Du Bartas, *Divine Weeks and Works*

For let our finger ache, and it indues / Our other healthful members ev'n to that sense / Of pain. — Shakespeare, *Othello*, act III, sc. iv, l. 145

[3]That sex which is therefore called fair. — Sir Richard Steele, *The Spectator, no. 302* [February 15, 1712]

[4]A needle in a haystack.

[5]But patience, cousin, and shuffle the cards, till our hand is a stronger one. — Walter Scott, *Quentin Durward* [1823], *ch. 8*

Men disappoint me so, I disappoint myself so, yet courage, patience, shuffle the cards. — Margaret Fuller, *Letter to the Reverend W. H. Channing* [February 21, 1841]

[6]I hold the maxim no less applicable to public than to private affairs, that honesty is always the best policy. — George Washington, *Farewell Address* [1796]

1   An honest man's word is as good as his bond.
Don Quixote, pt. II, IV, 34, p. 674

2   A blot in thy scutcheon to all futurity.
Don Quixote, pt. II, IV, 35, p. 681

3   Good wits jump;[1] a word to the wise is enough.
Don Quixote, pt. II, IV, 37, p. 692

4   What a man has, so much he's sure of.
Don Quixote, pt. II, IV, 38, p. 725

5   The pot calls the kettle black.
Don Quixote, pt. II, IV, 38, p. 727

6   Mum's the word.[2]
Don Quixote, pt. II, IV, 44, p. 729

7   I shall be as secret as the grave.
Don Quixote, pt. II, IV, 62, p. 862

8   Now blessings light on him that first invented this same sleep! It covers a man all over, thoughts and all, like a cloak;[3] 'Tis meat for the hungry, drink for the thirsty, heat for the cold, and cold for the hot. 'Tis the current coin that purchases all the pleasures of the world cheap; and the balance that sets the king and the shepherd, the fool and the wise man even.
Don Quixote, pt. II, IV, 68, p. 898

9   The ass will carry his load, but not a double load; ride not a free horse to death.
Don Quixote, pt. II, IV, 71, p. 917

10   He . . . got the better of himself, and that's the best kind of victory one can wish for.
Don Quixote, pt. II, IV, 72, p. 924

11   Every man was not born with a silver spoon in his mouth.   *Don Quixote, pt. II, IV, 73, p. 926*

12   Ne'er look for birds of this year in the nests of the last.   *Don Quixote, pt. II, IV, 74, p. 933*

13   There is a strange charm in the thoughts of a good legacy, or the hopes of an estate, which wondrously alleviates the sorrow that men would otherwise feel for the death of friends.
Don Quixote, pt. II, IV, 74, p. 934

14 For if he like a madman lived,
At least he like a wise one died.
Don Quixote, pt. II, IV, 74, p. 935
(Don Quixote's epitaph)

15   Don't put too fine a point to your wit for fear it should get blunted.   *The Little Gypsy (La Gitanilla)*

---

[1]Great wits jump. — LAURENCE STERNE, *Tristram Shandy, vol. III, ch. 9*

[2]Cry "mum." — SHAKESPEARE, *The Merry Wives of Windsor, act V, sc. ii, l. 6*

[3]"God's blessing," said Sancho Panza, "be upon the man who first invented this self-same thing called sleep; it covers a man all over like a cloak." — LAURENCE STERNE, *Tristram Shandy, vol. IV, ch. 15*

Giordano Bruno
1548–1600

16   Time takes all and gives all.
The Candle Bearer[4] [1582], dedication

17   It is Unity that doth enchant me. By her power I am free though thrall, happy in sorrow, rich in poverty, and quick even in death.
On the Infinite Universe and Worlds[5] [1584], introductory epistle

18   Our bodily eye findeth never an end, but is vanquished by the immensity of space.
On the Infinite Universe and Worlds, fifth dialogue

19   There is in the universe neither center nor circumference.
On the Infinite Universe and Worlds, fifth dialogue

Charles IX
1550–1574

20   Horses and poets should be fed, not overfed.[6]
Saying

Sir Edward Coke
1552–1634

21   Reason is the life of the law; nay, the common law itself is nothing else but reason . . . The law, which is perfection of reason.   *First Institute [1628]*

22   The gladsome light of jurisprudence.
First Institute, epilogue

23   For a man's house is his castle, *et domus sua cuique tutissimum refugium.*[7]
Third Institute [1644]

24   The house of everyone is to him as his castle and fortress, as well for his defense against injury and violence as for his repose.   *Semayne's Case. 5 Report 91*

25   They [corporations] cannot commit treason, nor be outlawed nor excommunicate, for they have no souls.   *Case of Sutton's Hospital. 10 Report 32*

26   Magna Carta is such a fellow that he will have no sovereign.
Debate in the Commons [May 17, 1628]

---

[4]Translated by J. B. HALLE.

[5]Translated by DOROTHEA SINGER.

[6]Equi et poetae alendi, non saginandi.

[7]One's home is the safest refuge to everyone. — *Pandects (Digest of Roman Law)* [533], *lib. II, tit. IV, De in Ius Vocando*

I in mine own house am an emperor / And will defend what's mine. — PHILIP MASSINGER, *The Roman Actor, act I, sc. ii*

1 Six hours in sleep, in law's grave study six,
Four spend in prayer, the rest on Nature fix.[1]
Translation quoted by COKE.
From The Pandects (Digest of Justinian).
De in Ius Vocando

Sir Walter Ralegh
c. 1552–1618

2 Like to an hermit poor in place obscure,
I mean to spend my days of endless doubt,
To wail such woes as time cannot recure,
Where none but Love shall ever find me out.

The Phoenix Nest [1593]. Sonnet

3 As you came from the holy land
Of Walsinghame,
Met you not with my true Love
By the way as you came?
As You Came from the Holy Land
[c. 1599], st. 1

4 But true love is a durable fire,
In the mind ever burning,
Never sick, never old, never dead,
From itself never turning.
As You Came from the Holy Land, st. 11

5 If all the world and love were young,
And truth in every shepherd's tongue,
These pretty pleasures might me move
To live with thee, and be thy love.
The Nymph's Reply to the Passionate Shepherd[2]
(printed in England's Helicon) [1600], st. 1

6 Fain would I climb, yet fear I to fall.
Written on a windowpane[3]

7 Our passions are most like to floods and streams,
The shallow murmur, but the deep are dumb.[4]
Sir Walter Ralegh to the Queen [c. 1599], st. 1

8 Silence in love bewrays more woe
Than words, though ne'er so witty;
A beggar that is dumb, you know,
Deserveth double pity.
Sir Walter Ralegh to the Queen, st. 5

9 Go, Soul, the body's quest,
Upon a thankless arrant:
Fear not to touch the best,
The truth shall be thy warrant:
Go, since I needs must die,
And give the world the lie.
The Lie (printed in FRANCIS DAVISON,
Poetical Rhapsody) [1608; manuscript
copy traced to 1595], st. 1

10 Give me my scallop shell of quiet,
My staff of faith to walk upon,
My scrip of joy, immortal diet,
My bottle of salvation,
My gown of glory, hope's true gage
And thus I'll take my pilgrimage.
Diaphantus [1604].
The Passionate Man's Pilgrimage

11 Methought I saw the grave where Laura lay.
Verses to Edmund Spenser

12 Shall I, like a hermit, dwell
On a rock or in a cell? *Poem*

13 [History] hath triumphed over time, which besides
it nothing but eternity hath triumphed over.
History of the World [1614], preface

14 Whosoever, in writing a modern history, shall
follow truth too near the heels, it may haply strike out
his teeth. *History of the World, preface*

15 O eloquent, just, and mighty Death! whom none
could advise, thou hast persuaded; what none hath
dared, thou hast done; and whom all the world hath
flattered, thou only hast cast out of the world and
despised. Thou hast drawn together all the far-
stretched greatness, all the pride, cruelty, and ambition of man, and covered it all over with these two
narrow words, *Hic jacet!*
History of the World, bk. V, pt. I,
ch. 6, conclusion

16 Even such is time, that takes in trust
Our youth, our joys, our all we have,
And pays us but with age and dust;
Who in the dark and silent grave,
When we have wandered all our ways,
Shuts up the story of our days.
And from which earth, and grave, and dust,
The Lord shall raise me up, I trust.
A version of one of his earlier poems,
found at his death in his Bible in the
Gatehouse at Westminster

---

[1]Seven hours to law, to soothing slumber seven; / Ten to the world allot, and all to heaven. — SIR WILLIAM JONES [1746–1794]

[2]An answer to CHRISTOPHER MARLOWE, *The Passionate Shepherd to His Love* (see 168:4).

[3]Under this Queen Elizabeth wrote, "If thy heart fails thee, climb not at all." — THOMAS FULLER [1608–1661], *Worthies of England* [1662]

[4]Altissima quaeque flumina minimo sono labi [The deepest rivers flow with the least sound]. — QUINTUS CURTIUS [first century C.E.], *Life of Alexander the Great, bk. VII, ch. 4, sec. 13*
   Where the stream runneth smoothest, the water is deepest. — JOHN LYLY, *Euphues and His England*
   Smooth runs the water where the brook is deep. — SHAKESPEARE, *Henry VI, Part II, act III, sc. i, l. 53*
   Take heed of still waters, the quick pass away. — GEORGE HERBERT, *Jacula Prudentum*

Edmund Spenser
1552–1599

1 To kirk the nearer, from God more far,
Has been an old-said saw.
And he that strives to touch the stars,
Oft stumbles at a straw.
The Shepherd's Calendar [1579]. July, l. 97

2 Fierce wars and faithful loves shall moralize my
song.[1]
The Faerie Queene [1590], introduction, st. 1

3 A gentle knight was pricking on the plain.
The Faerie Queene, bk. I, canto 1, st. 1

4 A bold bad man.　　*The Faerie Queene, I, 1, st. 37*

5　　　　Her angel's face
As the great eye of heaven shined bright,
And made a sunshine in the shady place.
The Faerie Queene, I, 3, st. 4

6 Ay me, how many perils do enfold
The righteous man, to make him daily fall.[2]
The Faerie Queene, I, 8, st. 1

7 Sleep after toil, port after stormy seas,
Ease after war, death after life does greatly please.[3]
The Faerie Queene, I, 9, st. 40

8 All for love, and nothing for reward.
The Faerie Queene, II, 8, st. 2

9 Gather therefore the Rose, whilst yet is prime,
For soon comes age, that will her pride deflower:
Gather the Rose of love, whilst yet is time.[4]
The Faerie Queene, II, 12, st. 75

10 Her birth was of the womb of morning dew.[5]
The Faerie Queene, III, 6, st. 3

11　　　Roses red and violets blue,
And all the sweetest flowers, that in the forest grew.
The Faerie Queene, III, 6, st. 6

12 All that in this delightful garden grows,
Should happy be, and have immortal bliss.
The Faerie Queene, III, 6, st. 41

13 And painful pleasure turns to pleasing pain.
The Faerie Queene, III, 10, st. 60

14 How over that same door was likewise writ,

Be bold, be bold, and everywhere *Be bold*.
The Faerie Queene, III, 11, st. 54

15 Another iron door, on which was writ,
Be not too bold.[6]　　*The Faerie Queene, III, 11, st. 54*

16 Dan Chaucer, well of English undefiled,
On Fame's eternal beadroll worthy to be filed.
The Faerie Queene, IV [1596], 2, st. 32

17 For all that nature by her mother wit
Could frame in earth.
The Faerie Queene, IV, 10, st. 21

18 Ill can he rule the great, that cannot reach the
small.　　　*The Faerie Queene, V, 2, st. 43*

19 Who will not mercy unto others show,
How can he mercy ever hope to have?
The Faerie Queene, VI, 1, st. 42

20 The gentle mind by gentle deeds is known.
For a man by nothing is so well bewrayed,
As by his manners.　　*The Faerie Queene, VI, 3, st. 1*

21 That here on earth is no sure happiness.
The Faerie Queene, VI, 11, st. 1

22　　　　The ever-whirling wheel
Of Change; the which all mortal things doth sway.
The Faerie Queene, VII, 6, st. 1

23 Wars and alarums unto nations wide.
The Faerie Queene, VII, 6, st. 3

24 But times do change and move continually.
The Faerie Queene, VII, 6, st. 47

25 For deeds do die, however nobly done,
And thoughts of men do as themselves decay,
But wise words taught in numbers for to run,
Recorded by the Muses, live for ay.
The Ruines of Time [1591], l. 400

26 Full little knowest thou that hast not tried,
What hell it is, in suing long to bide:
To lose good days, that might be better spent;
To waste long nights in pensive discontent;
To speed today, to be put back tomorrow;
To feed on hope, to pine with fear and sorrow.
Mother Hubberd's Tale [1591], l. 895

27 What more felicity can fall to creature,
Than to enjoy delight with liberty.
*Muiopotmos; or, The Fate of the
Butterfly [1591], l. 209*

---

[1]And moralized his song. — ALEXANDER POPE, *Epistle to Dr. Arbuthnot, l. 340*

[2]Ay me! what perils do environ / The man that meddles with cold iron! — SAMUEL BUTLER [1612–1680], *Hudibras, pt. 1, canto III, l. 1*

[3]These lines are cut on Joseph Conrad's gravestone at Canterbury.

[4]See *The Wisdom of Solomon 2:8, 29:32; Horace, 96:11; Ronsard, 150:8; and Herrick, 241:4.*

[5]The dew of thy birth is of the womb of the morning. — *Book of Common Prayer, Psalter, Psalm 110:3*

---

[6]Jockey of Norfolk, be not too bold, / For Dickon thy master is bought and sold. — SHAKESPEARE, *Richard III, act V, sc. iii, l. 305*
　Forbear, said I: be not too bold. / Your fleece is white but 'Tis too cold. — RICHARD CRASHAW, *Hymn of the Nativity, l. 50*
　Write on your doors the saying wise and old, / "Be bold! be bold!" and everywhere — "Be bold; / Be not too bold!" — HENRY WADSWORTH LONGFELLOW, *Morituri Salutamus*

1 I hate the day, because it lendeth light
  To see all things, and not my love to see.
  Daphnaida [1591], l. 407

2 Death slew not him, but he made death his ladder to
  the skies.
  An Epitaph upon Sir Philip Sidney [1591], l. 20

3 Though last not least.[1]
  Colin Clouts Come Home Again [1595], l. 144

4 Tell her the joyous time will not be stayed
  Unlesse she do him by the forelock take.[2]
  Amoretti [1595]. Sonnet 70

5 The woods shall to me answer, and my Echo ring.
  Epithalamion [1595], l. 18

6 Ah! when will this long weary day have end,
  And lend me leave to come unto my love?
  Epithalamion, l. 278

7 For of the soul the body form doth take:
  For soul is form, and doth the body make.
  Hymn in Honor of Beauty [1596], l. 132

8 For all that fair is, is by nature good;
  That is a sign to know the gentle blood.
  Hymn in Honor of Beauty, l. 139

9 Sweet Thames! run softly, till I end my Song.[3]
  Prothalamion [1596], refrain

10 I was promised on a time
  To have reason for my rhyme;
  From that time unto this season,
  I received nor rhyme nor reason.
  Lines on his promised pension.
  From THOMAS FULLER [1608–1661],
  Worthies of England [1662]

John Florio
c. 1553–1625

11 England is the paradise of women, the purgatory
  of men, and the hell of horses.   *Second Frutes [1591]*

Henri IV [Henry of Navarre]
1553–1610

12 I want there to be no peasant in my realm so poor
  that he will not have a chicken in his pot every
  Sunday.   *Attributed*

13 Paris is well worth a Mass.[4]   *Attributed*[5]

14 The wisest fool in Christendom [James I of Eng-
  land].   *Attributed*[5]

Fulke Greville, Lord Brooke
1554–1628

15 Oh wearisome condition of humanity!
  Born under one law, to another bound.
  Mustapha [1609], act V, sc. iv

16 Fulke Greville, Servant to Queen Elizabeth,
  Councillor to King James, and Friend to Sir Philip
  Sidney.

  Epitaph on his monument in Warwick

Richard Hooker
c. 1554–1600

17 Of Law there can be no less acknowledged than
  that her seat is the bosom of God, her voice the harmony of the world. All things in heaven and earth
  do her homage — the very least as feeling her care,
  and the greatest as not exempted from her power.
  Laws of Ecclesiastical Polity [1593], bk. 1

18 That to live by one man's will became the cause of
  all men's misery.   *Laws of Ecclesiastical Polity, 1*

John Lyly
c. 1554–1606

19 Be valiant, but not too venturous. Let thy attire be
  comely, but not costly.
  Euphues: The Anatomy of Wit [1579].
  Arber's reprint, p. 39

20 Delays breed dangers.[6]
  Euphues: The Anatomy of Wit.
  Arber's reprint, p. 65

21 It seems to me (said she) that you are in some
  brown study.
  Euphues: The Anatomy of Wit. Arber's reprint, p. 80

22 Many strokes overthrow the tallest oaks.[7]
  Euphues: The Anatomy of Wit.
  Arber's reprint, p. 81

---

[1]The last, not least in honor or applause. — ALEXANDER POPE, *The Dunciad, bk. IV, l. 577*

[2]Take Time by the forelock. — THALES [one of the SEVEN SAGES; c. 640–c. 546 B.C.E.]

[3]Sweet Thames, run softly till I end my song, / Sweet Thames, run softly, for I speak not loud or long. — T. S. ELIOT, *The Waste Land, pt. III*

[4]Paris vaut bien une messe.

[5]Attributed also to Henri's minister, Duc de Sully.

[6]Periculum in mora. — *Latin proverb*
All delays are dangerous in war. — JOHN DRYDEN, *Tyrannic Love* [1669], *act I, sc. i*

[7]Many strokes, though with a little axe, / Hew down and fell the hardest-timber'd oak. — SHAKESPEARE, *Henry VI, pt. III, act II, sc. i, l. 54*

1   Let me stand to the main chance.
Euphues: The Anatomy of Wit.
Arber's reprint, p. 104

2   It is a world to see.
Euphues: The Anatomy of Wit.
Arber's reprint, p. 116

3   Go to bed with the lamb, and rise with the lark.[1]
Euphues and His England [1580], p. 229

4   A comely old man as busy as a bee.
Euphues and His England, p. 252

5   Your eyes are so sharp that you cannot only look through a millstone, but clean through the mind.
Euphues and His England, p. 289

6   I am glad that my Adonis hath a sweet tooth in his head.
Euphues and His England, p. 308

7   A rose is sweeter in the bud than full-blown.[2]
Euphues and His England, p. 314

8 Cupid and my Campaspe played
At cards for kisses: Cupid paid.
Alexander and Campaspe [1584],
act III, sc. v

9 How at heaven's gates she claps her wings,
The morn not waking till she sings.
Alexander and Campaspe, V, i

10 Night hath a thousand eyes.
Maides Metamorphosis, III, 1

11   Marriages are made in heaven and consummated on earth.[3]   *Mother Bombie [1590], act IV, sc. i*

Sir Philip Sidney
1554–1586

12   High-erected thoughts seated in the heart of courtesy.
Arcadia [written 1580], bk. I

13   My dear, my better half.   *Arcadia, III*

14 My true-love hath my heart, and I have his,
By just exchange one for the other given:
I hold his dear, and mine he cannot miss,
There never was a better bargain driven.
Arcadia, song

15 Ring out your bells! Let mourning shows be spread!

For Love is dead.   *Sonnet*

16 Leave me, O Love, which reachest but to dust,
And thou, my mind, aspire to higher things;
Grow rich in that which never taketh rust:
Whatever fades, but fading pleasure brings.
Sonnet

17 Sweet food of sweetly uttered knowledge.
The Defense of Poesy [written c. 1580]

18   He cometh unto you with a tale which holdeth children from play, and old men from the chimney corner.
The Defense of Poesy

19   I never heard the old song of Percy and Douglas that I found not my heart moved more than with a trumpet.   *The Defense of Poesy*

20 "Fool!" said my muse to me, "look in thy heart, and write."   *Astrophel and Stella [1591], I*

21 With how sad steps, O Moon, thou climb'st the skies!
How silently, and with how wan a face!
Astrophel and Stella, XXXI

22 Have I caught my heav'nly jewel.[4]
Astrophel and Stella, second song

23   Thy necessity[5] is yet greater than mine.
Said on the battlefield of Zutphen
[September 22, 1586] on giving
his water bottle to a dying soldier

François de Malherbe[6]
1555–1628

24   And a rose, she lived as roses do, the space of a morn.[7]   *Consolation à Monsieur du Périer [1599]*

25   What Malherbe writes will endure forever.
Sonnet à Louis XIII [1624]

Philip Nicolai
1556–1608

26 Wake, awake, for night is flying:
The watchmen on the heights are crying.[8]
Hymn [1597]

---

[1]To rise with the lark and go to bed with the lamb. — Nicholas Breton [c. 1553–c. 1625], *Court and Country* [1618]

[2]The rose is fairest when 'tis budding new. — Walter Scott, *The Lady of the Lake*, canto III, st. I

[3]Les mariages se font au ciel, et se consoment sur la terre. — *French proverb*
  If marriages / Are made in heaven, they should be happier.— Thomas Southerne [1660–1746], *The Fatal Marriage* [1694]

[4]Quoted by Shakespeare in *The Merry Wives of Windsor*, act III, sc. iii, l. 45.

[5]More often quoted as: Thy need.

[6]See Boileau-Despréaux, 278:2.

[7]Et rose, elle a vécu ce que vivent les roses, / L'espace d'un matin.

[8]Wachet auf, ruft uns die Stimme.
Translated by Catherine Winkworth.

George Peele
1556–1596

1 Fair and fair, and twice so fair,
  As fair as any may be.
> *The Arraignment of Paris [1584]*

2 My merry, merry, merry roundelay
  Concludes with Cupid's curse:
  They that do change old love for new,
  Pray gods, they change for worse!
> *The Arraignment of Paris*

3 His golden locks time hath to silver turned;
  O time too swift, O swiftness never ceasing!
  His youth 'gainst time and age hath ever spurned,
  But spurned in vain; youth waneth by increasing.
> *Polyhymnia [1590]. Farewell to Arms, st. 1*

4 His helmet now shall make a hive for bees,
  And lovers' sonnets turned to holy psalms,
  A man-at-arms must now serve on his knees,
  And feed on prayers, which are age his alms.
> *Polyhymnia. Farewell to Arms, st. 2*

5 Hot sun, cool fire, tempered with sweet air,
  Black shade, fair nurse, shadow my white hair,
  Shine sun, burn fire, breathe air, and ease me,
  Black shade, fair nurse, shroud me and please me.
> *The Love of King David and Fair Bethsabe [published 1599]*

Thomas Kyd
1558–1594

6 What outcries call me from my naked bed?
> *The Spanish Tragedy [1594], act II, sc. v, l. 1*

7 O eyes, no eyes, but fountains fraught with tears;
  O life, no life, but lively form of death;
  O world, no world, but mass of public wrongs,
  Confused and filled with murder and misdeeds.
> *The Spanish Tragedy, III, ii, l.1*

8 Why then I'll fit you, say no more.
  When I was young, I gave my mind
  And plied myself to fruitless poetry:
  Which though it profit the professor naught
  Yet it is passing pleasing to the world.
> *The Spanish Tragedy, IV, ii, l. 70*

Thomas Lodge
c. 1558–1625

9 Love in my bosom like a bee
  Doth suck his sweet.   *Rosalynde [1590]*

10   Devils are not so black as they are painted.
> *A Margarite of America [1596]*

Chidiock Tichborne
c. 1558–1586

11 My prime of youth is but a frost of cares;
  My feast of joy is but a dish of pain;
  My crop of corn is but a field of tares;
  And all my good is but vain hope of gain:
  The day is past, and yet I saw no sun;
  And now I live, and now my life is done.[1]
> *Tichborne's Elegy [1586]*

George Chapman
c. 1559–1634

12 Promise is most given when the least is said.
> *Hero and Leander [1598]*

13   Young men think old men are fools; but old men
  know young men are fools.
> *All Fools [1605], act V, sc. i*

14   Keep thy shop, and thy shop will keep thee. Light
  gains make heavy purses.[2]
> *Eastward Ho[3] [1605], act I, sc. i*

15   I will neither yield to the song of the siren nor the
  voice of the hyena, the tears of the crocodile[4] nor the
  howling of the wolf.
> *Eastward Ho, V, i*

16 For one heat, all know, doth drive out another,
  One passion doth expel another still.
> *Monsieur d'Olive [1606], act V, sc. i*

17 Speed his plow.[5]
> *Bussy d'Ambois [1607], act I, sc. i*

18   So our lives
  In acts exemplary, not only win
  Ourselves good names, but doth to others give
  Matter for virtuous deeds, by which we live.
> *Bussy d'Ambois, I, i*

19 Who to himself is law no law doth need,
  Offends no law, and is a king indeed.
> *Bussy d'Ambois, II, i*

20 Give me a spirit that on this life's rough sea
  Loves t' have his sails filled with a lusty wind,
  Even till his sail-yards tremble, his masts crack,

---

[1]Tichborne was beheaded for an attempt on Queen Elizabeth's life.

[2]Quoted by BENJAMIN FRANKLIN in *Poor Richard's Almanac* [1735], *June.*

[3]By Chapman, Jonson, and Marston.

[4]These crocodile tears. — ROBERT BURTON, *Anatomy of Melancholy,* pt. III, sec. 2, member 2, subsec. 4
  She's false, false as the tears of crocodiles. — SIR JOHN SUCKLING, *The Sad One* [produced posthumously in 1659], act IV, sc. v

[5]Usually quoted: Speed the plow.

And his rapt ship run on her side so low
That she drinks water, and her keel plows air.
                                    The Conspiracy of Charles,
                                    Duke of Byron [1608], act III, sc. i

1 We have watered our horses in Helicon.
                                    May-Day [1611], act III, sc. iii

Robert Greene
c. 1560–1592

2 Sweet are the thoughts that savor of content;
The quiet mind is richer than a crown.
                                    Farewell to Folly [1591], st. 1

3   For there is an upstart crow, beautified with our
feathers, that with his tiger's heart wrapped in a
player's hide, supposes he is as well able to bumbast
out a blank verse as the best of you; and being an
absolute *Johannes fac totum*, is in his own conceit the
only Shake-scene in a country.[1]
                                    The Groatsworth of Wit [1592]

4 Hangs in the uncertain balance of proud time.
                                    Friar Bacon and Friar Bungay
                                    [acted 1594], act III

5 Hell's broken loose.
                                    Friar Bacon and Friar Bungay, IV

Francis Bacon[2]
1561–1626

6   I have taken all knowledge to be my province.
                                    Letter to Lord Burleigh [1592]

7   The monuments of wit survive the monuments of
power.   *Essex's Device [1595]*

8   Knowledge is power [*Nam et ipsa scientia potestas
est*].[3]   *Meditationes Sacrae [1597]. De Haeresibus*

9   For all knowledge and wonder (which is the seed
of knowledge) is an impression of pleasure in itself.
                                    The Advancement of Learning [1605], bk. I, i, 3

10   Time, which is the author of authors.
                                    The Advancement of Learning, I, iv, 12

11   If a man will begin with certainties, he shall end in
doubts; but if he will be content to begin with doubts
he shall end in certainties.
                                    The Advancement of Learning, I, v, 8

12   *Antiquitas saeculi juventus mundi.*[4] These times
are the ancient times, when the world is ancient, and
not those which we account ancient *ordine retro-
grado*, by a computation backward from our-
selves.[5]   *The Advancement of Learning, I, v, 8*

13   [Knowledge] is a rich storehouse for the glory of
the Creator and the relief of man's estate.
                                    The Advancement of Learning, I, v, 11

14   It [Poesy] was ever thought to have some participation of divineness, because it doth raise and erect
the mind by submitting the shows of things to the
desires of the mind.
                                    The Advancement of Learning, II, iv, 2

15   They are ill discoverers that think there is no land,
when they can see nothing but sea.
                                    The Advancement of Learning, II, vii, 5

16   But men must know that in this theater of man's
life it is reserved only for God and angels to be lookers
on.   *The Advancement of Learning, II, xx, 8*

17   We are much beholden to Machiavel and others,
that write what men do, and not what they ought to
do.   *The Advancement of Learning, II, xxi, 9*

18   There are and can be only two ways of searching
into and discovering truth. The one flies from the
senses and particulars to the most general axioms . . .
this way is now in fashion. The other derives axioms
from the senses and particulars, rising by a gradual
and unbroken ascent, so that it arrives at the most
general axioms last of all. This is the true way, but as
yet untried.   *Novum Organum*[6] *[1620]*

19   There are four classes of Idols which beset men's
minds. To these for distinction's sake I have assigned
names — calling the first class, Idols of the Tribe; the
second, Idols of the Cave; the third, Idols of the
Market-Place; the fourth, Idols of the Theater.
                                    Novum Organum, aphorism 39

20   The human understanding is like a false mirror,
which, receiving rays irregularly, distorts and discolors

---

[1]First known literary reference to Shakespeare.

[2]If parts allure thee, think how Bacon shined, / The wisest,
brightest, meanest of mankind. — ALEXANDER POPE, *Essay on Man,*
epistle IV, l. 281

[3]Knowledge is more than equivalent to force. — SAMUEL JOHNSON,
Rasselas, ch. 13

[4]The age of antiquity is the youth of the world.

[5]As in the little, so in the great world, reason will tell you that old
age or antiquity is to be accounted by the farther distance from the
beginning and the nearer approach to the end — the times wherein
we now live being in propriety of speech the most ancient since the
world's creation. — GEORGE HAKEWILL [1578–1649], *An Apologie*
or Declaration of the Power and Providence of God in the
Government of the World [1627]

For as old age is that period of life most remote from infancy, who
does not see that old age in this universal man ought not to be sought
in the times nearest his birth, but in those most remote from it? —
BLAISE PASCAL, *Preface to the Treatise on the Vacuum* [1647]

We are Ancients of the earth, / And in the morning of the
times. — TENNYSON, *The Day Dream, L'Envoi*

[6]"The New Organon," referring to Aristotle's *Organon*, which lays
out his system of logic.

the nature of things by mingling its own nature with it. *Novum Organum, aphorism 41*

1 Nature, to be commanded, must be obeyed. *Novum Organum, aphorism 129*

2 I do plainly and ingenuously confess that I am guilty of corruption, and do renounce all defense. I beseech your Lordships to be merciful to a broken reed.
On being charged by Parliament with corruption in office [1621]

3 Lucid intervals and happy pauses.
History of King Henry VII [1622], III

4 Nothing is terrible except fear itself.[1]
De Augmentis Scientiarum, bk. II, Fortitudo [1623]

5 Riches are a good handmaid, but the worst mistress. *De Augmentis Scientiarum, II, Antitheta*

6 Hope is a good breakfast, but it is a bad supper.
Apothegms [1624], no. 36

7 Like strawberry wives, that laid two or three great strawberries at the mouth of their pot, and all the rest were little ones. *Apothegms, 54*

8 Alonso of Aragon was wont to say in commendation of age, that age appears to be best in four things — old wood best to burn, old wine to drink, old friends to trust, and old authors to read.
Apothegms, 97

9 Cosmus, Duke of Florence, was wont to say of perfidious friends, that "We read that we ought to forgive our enemies; but we do not read that we ought to forgive our friends." *Apothegms, 206*

10 My essays . . . come home to men's business and bosoms. *Essays*[2] *[1625], dedication*

11 What is truth? said jesting Pilate, and would not stay for an answer. *Essays. Of Truth*

12 No pleasure is comparable to the standing upon the vantage-ground of truth. *Essays. Of Truth*

13 Men fear death as children fear to go in the dark; and as that natural fear in children is increased with tales, so is the other. *Essays. Of Death*

14 Revenge is a kind of wild justice, which the more man's nature runs to, the more ought law to weed it out. *Essays. Of Revenge*

15 Prosperity is the blessing of the Old Testament; adversity is the blessing of the New.
Essays. Of Adversity

16 Prosperity is not without many fears and distastes; and adversity is not without comforts and hopes.
Essays. Of Adversity

17 Prosperity doth best discover vice, but adversity doth best discover virtue. *Essays. Of Adversity*

18 Virtue is like precious odors — most fragrant when they are incensed or crushed.[3]
Essays. Of Adversity

19 He that hath wife and children hath given hostages to fortune; for they are impediments to great enterprises, either of virtue or mischief.
Essays. Of Marriage and Single Life

20 Wives are young men's mistresses, companions for middle age, and old men's nurses.
Essays. Of Marriage and Single Life

21 A good name is like a precious ointment; it filleth all around about, and will not easily away; for the odors of ointments are more durable than those of flowers. *Essays. Of Praise*

22 In charity there is no excess.
Essays. Of Goodness and Goodness of Nature

23 If a man be gracious and courteous to strangers, it shows he is a citizen of the world, and that his heart is no island cut off from other lands, but a continent that joins to them.
Essays. Of Goodness and Goodness of Nature

24 The desire of power in excess caused the angels to fall; the desire of knowledge in excess caused man to fall.[4]
Essays. Of Goodness and Goodness of Nature

25 Money is like muck, not good except it be spread. *Essays. Of Seditions and Troubles*

26 I had rather believe all the fables in the legends and the Talmud and the Alcoran, than that this universal frame is without a mind. *Essays. Of Atheism*

27 A little philosophy inclineth man's mind to atheism, but depth in philosophy bringeth men's minds about to religion.[5] *Essays. Of Atheism*

28 Travel, in the younger sort, is a part of education; in the elder, a part of experience. He that traveleth

---

[1] Nil terribile nisi ipse timor.

[2] First edition, 1597; first complete edition, 1625.

[3] As aromatic plants bestow / No spicy fragrance while they grow; / But crushed or trodden to the ground, / Diffuse their balmy sweets around. — OLIVER GOLDSMITH, *The Captivity* [1764], *act I*

[4] Pride still is aiming at the blest abodes; / Men would be angels, angels would be gods. / Aspiring to be gods if angels fell, / Aspiring to be angels men rebel. — ALEXANDER POPE, *Essay on Man, epistle I, l. 125*

[5] A little skill in antiquity inclines a man to Popery; but depth in that study brings him about again to our religion. — THOMAS FULLER [1608–1661], *The Holy State and the Profane State. The True Church Antiquary*

into a country before he hath some entrance into the language, goeth to school, and not to travel.
Essays. Of Travel

1   Princes are like to heavenly bodies, which cause good or evil times, and which have much veneration but no rest.   *Essays. Of Empire*

2   Fortune is like the market, where many times, if you can stay a little, the price will fall.
Essays. Of Delays

3   Nothing doth more hurt in a state than that cunning men pass for wise.   *Essays. Of Cunning*

4   Be so true to thyself, as thou be not false to others.
Essays. Of Wisdom for a Man's Self

5   It is the nature of extreme self-lovers, as they will set an house on fire, and it were but to roast their eggs.
Essays. Of Wisdom for a Man's Self

6   It is the wisdom of the crocodiles, that shed tears when they would devour.
Essays. Of Wisdom for a Man's Self

7   He that will not apply new remedies must expect new evils; for time is the greatest innovator.
Essays. Of Innovations

8   Cure the disease and kill the patient.
Essays. Of Friendship

9   Riches are for spending.   *Essays. Of Expense*

10   There is a wisdom in this beyond the rules of physic. A man's own observation, what he finds good of and what he finds hurt of, is the best physic to preserve health.
Essays. Of Regimen of Health

11   Nature is often hidden; sometimes overcome; seldom extinguished.
Essays. Of Nature in Men

12   If a man look sharply and attentively, he shall see Fortune; for though she is blind, she is not invisible.[1]   *Essays. Of Fortune*

13   Chiefly the mold of a man's fortune is in his own hands.   *Essays. Of Fortune*

14   There is no excellent beauty that hath not some strangeness in the proportion.   *Essays. Of Beauty*

15   God Almighty first planted a garden.[2]
Essays. Of Gardens

16   He that commands the sea is at great liberty, and may take as much and as little of the war as he will.[3]
Essays. Of the True Greatness of Kingdoms

17   Some books are to be tasted, others to be swallowed, and some few to be chewed and digested.
Essays. Of Studies

18   Reading maketh a full man, conference a ready man, and writing an exact man.   *Essays. Of Studies*

19   Histories make men wise; poets, witty; the mathematics, subtile; natural philosophy, deep; moral, grave; logic and rhetoric, able to contend.
Essays. Of Studies

20   The greatest vicissitude of things amongst men is the vicissitude of sects and religions.
Essays. Of Vicissitude of Things

21   I bequeath my soul to God...My body to be buried obscurely. For my name and memory, I leave it to men's charitable speeches, and to foreign nations, and the next age.   *From his will [1626]*

22 The world's a bubble, and the life of man
Less than a span.   *The World [1629]*

23 Who then to frail mortality shall trust
But limns on water, or but writes in dust.   *The World*

24 What then remains but that we still should cry
For being born, and, being born, to die?   *The World*

Luis de Góngora y Argote
1561–1627

25   All that lasts of love is its poison.[4]
Sonnet LXXXII [1584]

Sir John Harington
1561–1612

26 Treason doth never prosper: what's the reason?
For if it prosper, none dare call it treason.
Epigrams. Of Treason

Robert Southwell
c. 1561–1595

27 Times go by turns, and chances change by course,
From foul to fair, from better hap to worse.
Times Go by Turns [c. 1595], st. 1

---

[1] Fortune is painted blind, with a muffler afore her eyes, to signify to you that Fortune is blind. — SHAKESPEARE, *King Henry V, act III, sc. vi, l. 31*

[2] Gardens were before gardeners, and but some hours after the earth. — THOMAS BROWNE, *The Garden of Cyrus, ch. 1*

[3] He that is master of the sea, may, in some sort, be said to be Master of every country; at least such as are bordering on the sea. For he is at liberty to begin and end War, where, when, and on what terms he pleaseth, and extend his conquests even to the Antipodes. — JOSEPH GANDER [fl. c. 1703], *The Glory of Her Sacred Majesty Queen Anne in the Royal Navy* [1703]

[4] Solo del amor queda el veneno.

1 As I in hoary winter night stood shivering in the
    snow,
    Surprised was I with sudden heat which made my
        heart to glow;
    And lifting up a fearful eye to view what fire was near
    A pretty Babe all burning bright did in the air
        appear.   *The Burning Babe [written c. 1595]*

2 With this he vanished out of sight, and swiftly shrunk
    away,
    And straight I called unto mind that it was Christmas
    Day.   *The Burning Babe*

Samuel Daniel
c. 1562–1619

3 Care-charmer Sleep, son of the sable Night,
    Brother to Death, in silent darkness born.
                        Sonnets to Delia [1592], no. XLV

4 Let others sing of knights and paladins
    In aged accents and untimely words.
                                Sonnets to Delia, XLVI

5 These are the arks, the trophies, I erect,
    That fortify thy name against old age.
                                Sonnets to Delia, XLVI

6 This is the thing that I was born to do.
                    *Musophilus, or Defense of All Learning
                    [1602–1603], st. 100*

Lope de Vega
1562–1635

7   Harmony is pure love, for love is complete agree-
    ment.
                    *Fuenteovejuna (The Sheep Well)[1]
                    [c. 1613], act I, l. 381*

8   Except for God, the King's our only lord.
                        Fuenteovejuna, I, l. 1701

Michael Drayton
1563–1631

9 Fair stood the wind for France.
                The Ballad of Agincourt [1606], st. 1

10 O, when shall Englishmen
    With such acts fill a pen,
    Or England breed again
    Such a King Harry?
                    The Ballad of Agincourt, st. 15

11 Since there's no help, come let us kiss and part —
    Nay, I have done: you get no more of me,
    And I am glad, yea glad with all my heart,

That thus so cleanly I myself can free.
    Shake hands forever, cancel all our vows,
    And when we meet at any time again,
    Be it not seen in either of our brows
    That we one jot of former love retain.
                                Poems [1619]. Idea

12 The coast was clear.   *Nymphidia [1627]*

13 Had in him those brave translunary things
    That the first poets had.
                    *Said of CHRISTOPHER MARLOWE.
                    To Henry Reynolds,
                    Of Poets and Poesy [1627]*

14 For that fine madness still he did retain
    Which rightly should possess a poet's brain.
                    *Said of MARLOWE. To Henry Reynolds,
                    Of Poets and Poesy*

Galileo Galilei
1564–1642

15   Philosophy is written in this grand book — I mean
    the universe — which stands continually open to our
    gaze, but it cannot be understood unless one first
    learns to comprehend the language and interpret the
    characters in which it is written. It is written in the
    language of mathematics, and its characters are trian-
    gles, circles, and other geometrical figures, without
    which it is humanly impossible to understand a single
    word of it; without these, one is wandering about in a
    dark labyrinth.
                    Il Saggiatore (The Assayer)[2] [1623]

16   But it does move![3]
                                    Attributed

17   Facts which at first seem improbable will, even on
    scant explanation, drop the cloak which has hidden
    them and stand forth in naked and simple beauty.
                    *Dialogues Concerning Two New Sciences[4]
                    [1638], Day 1*

Christopher Marlowe
1564–1593

18 Our swords shall play the orators for us.
                    *Tamburlaine the Great [c. 1587],
                    pt. I, l. 328*

19 Accurst be he that first invented war.
                    Tamburlaine the Great, I, l. 664

---

[1]Translated by ANGEL FLORES and MURIEL KITTEL.

[2]Translated by STILLMAN DRAKE and C. D. O'MALLEY.
[3]E pur si muove!
    Alleged to have been whispered by Galileo after recanting before
the Inquisition his claim that the earth revolved around the sun.
[4]Translated by HENRY CREW and ALFONSO DE SALVIO.

1 Is it not passing brave to be a king,
   And ride in triumph through Persepolis?
   Tamburlaine the Great, I, l. 758

2 Nature that framed us of four elements,
   Warring within our breasts for regiment,
   Doth teach us all to have aspiring minds:
   Our souls, whose faculties can comprehend
   The wondrous Architecture of the world:
   And measure every wandering planet's course,
   Still climbing after knowledge infinite,
   And always moving as the restless Spheres,
   Will us to wear ourselves and never rest,
   Until we reach the ripest fruit of all,
   That perfect bliss and sole felicity,
   The sweet fruition of an earthly crown.
   Tamburlaine the Great, I,
   l. 869

3 Tamburlaine, the Scourge of God, must die.
   Tamburlaine the Great, I,
   l. 4641

4 Come live with me, and be my love;
   And we will all the pleasures prove
   That valleys, groves, hills, and fields,[1]
   Woods or steepy mountain yields.
   The Passionate Shepherd to His Love
   [c. 1589]

5 By shallow rivers, to whose falls
   Melodious birds sing madrigals.[2]
   The Passionate Shepherd to His Love

6 And I will make thee beds of roses
   And a thousand fragrant posies.[2]
   The Passionate Shepherd to His Love

7 I count religion but a childish toy,
   And hold there is no sin but ignorance.
   The Jew of Malta [c. 1589],
   prologue

8 Infinite riches in a little room.[3]
   The Jew of Malta, act I, sc. i

9 Excess of wealth is cause of covetousness.
   The Jew of Malta, I, ii

10   Now will I show myself to have more of the serpent than the dove; that is, more knave than fool.
   The Jew of Malta, II, iii

11 *Friar Barnadine:* Thou hast committed —
   Barabas: Fornication — but that was in another
      country;
   And besides, the wench is dead.
   The Jew of Malta, IV, i

12 My men, like satyrs grazing on the lawns,
   Shall with their goat feet dance the antic hay.
   Edward II [1593], act I, sc. i

13 Judge you the rest; being tired she bade me kiss;
   Jove send me more such afternoons as this!
   Ovid's Elegies [1596], bk. 1, no. 5

14 Who ever loved that loved not at first sight?[4]
   Hero and Leander [1598]

15 Like untuned golden strings all women are,
   Which long time lie untouched, will harshly jar.
   Vessels of brass oft handled brightly shine.
   Hero and Leander

16 Live and die in Aristotle's works.
   The Tragical History of Doctor Faustus
   [1604], act I, sc. i

17 Unhappy spirits that fell with Lucifer,
   Conspired against our God with Lucifer,
   And are forever damned with Lucifer.
   The Tragical History of Doctor Faustus, I, iii

18 Why this is hell, nor am I out of it:
   Think'st thou that I who saw the face of God,
   And tasted the eternal joys of Heaven,
   Am not tormented with ten thousand hells,
   In being deprived of everlasting bliss?
   The Tragical History of Doctor Faustus, I, iii

19 Hell hath no limits, nor is circumscribed
   In one self place; for where we are is hell,
   And where hell is there must we ever be.
   The Tragical History of Doctor Faustus, II, i

20   When all the world dissolves,
   And every creature shall be purified,
   All places shall be hell that is not Heaven.
   The Tragical History of Doctor Faustus, II, i

21 Was this the face that launched a thousand
      ships,
   And burnt the topless towers of Ilium?[5]
   Sweet Helen, make me immortal with a kiss.
   Her lips suck forth my soul;[6] see, where it flies!
   The Tragical History of Doctor Faustus, V, i

---

[1]Also given as: Hills and valleys, dales, and fields.

[2]To shallow rivers, to whose falls / Melodious birds sing madrigals; / There will we make our peds of roses, / And a thousand fragrant posies. — SHAKESPEARE, *The Merry Wives of Windsor, act III, sc. i, l. 17*

[3]Here lyeth muche rychnesse in lytell space. — JOHN HEYWOOD, *The Foure PP* [1521–1525]

[4]Quoted in SHAKESPEARE, *As You Like It, act III, sc. v, l. 82.*
None ever loved but at first sight they loved. — GEORGE CHAPMAN, *The Blind Beggar of Alexandria* [1598]

[5]Was this fair face the cause, quoth she, / Why the Grecians sacked Troy? — SHAKESPEARE, *All's Well That Ends Well, act I, sc. iii, l. 75*

[6]Once he drew / With one long kiss my whole soul through / My lips. — TENNYSON, *Fatima* [1833], *st. 3*

1 Oh, thou art fairer than the evening air
Clad in the beauty of a thousand stars.
The Tragical History of Doctor Faustus,
V, i

2   Pray for me! and what noise soever ye hear, come
not unto me, for nothing can rescue me.
The Tragical History of Doctor Faustus,
V, ii

3 Now hast thou but one bare hour to live,
And then thou must be damned perpetually!
Stand still, you ever-moving spheres of Heaven,
That time may cease, and midnight never come.
The Tragical History of Doctor Faustus,
V, ii

4 *O lente, lente currite noctis equi:*[1]
[Slowly, slowly run, O horses of the night:]
The stars move still, time runs, the clock will strike,
The Devil will come, and Faustus must be damned.
O, I'll leap up to my God! Who pulls me down?
See, see where Christ's blood streams in the
firmament!
One drop would save my soul — half a drop: ah, my
Christ!
The Tragical History of Doctor Faustus, V, ii

5 O soul, be changed into little waterdrops,
And fall into the ocean — ne'er to be found.
My God! my God! look not so fierce on me!
The Tragical History of Doctor Faustus,
V, ii

6 I'll burn my books!
The Tragical History of Doctor Faustus,
V, ii

7 Cut is the branch that might have grown full straight,
And burned is Apollo's laurel bough,
That sometime grew within this learned man.
The Tragical History of Doctor Faustus, V, iii

Matthew Roydon
c. 1564–c. 1622

8 You knew — who knew not Astrophil?
The Phoenix Nest [1593]; An Elegy,
or Friend's Passion for His Astrophil
(on the death of Sir Philip Sidney)

9 A sweet attractive kind of grace,
A full assurance given by looks,
Continual comfort in a face,
The lineaments of Gospel books;
I trow that countenance cannot lie.
Whose thoughts are legible in the eye.
The Phoenix Nest

William Shakespeare[2]
1564–1616

10 Hung be the heavens with black, yield day to
night!
King Henry VI, Part I [1589–1590],
act I, sc. i, l. 1

11 Fight till the last gasp.   *I, ii, l. 127*

12 Expect Saint Martin's summer, halcyon days.
I, ii, l. 131

13 Glory is like a circle in the water,
Which never ceaseth to enlarge itself,
Till by broad spreading it disperse to nought.
I, ii, l. 133

14   Unbidden guests
Are often welcomest when they are gone.   *II, ii, l. 55*

15 Between two hawks, which flies the higher pitch;
Between two dogs, which hath the deeper mouth;
Between two blades, which bears the better temper;
Between two horses, which doth bear him best;
Between two girls, which hath the merriest eye;
I have perhaps, some shallow spirit of judgment;
But in these nice sharp quillets of the law,
Good faith, I am no wiser than a daw.   *II, iv, l. 12*

16 I'll note you in my book of memory.   *II, iv, l. 101*

17 Just death, kind umpire of men's miseries.
II, v, l. 29

18 Chok'd with ambition of the meaner sort.
II, v, l. 123

19 Delays have dangerous ends.   *III, ii, l. 33*

20 Of all base passions, fear is most accurs'd.
V, ii, l. 18

21 She's beautiful and therefore to be woo'd,
She is a woman, therefore to be won.   *V, iii, l. 78*

22 For what is wedlock forced, but a hell,
An age of discord and continual strife?
Whereas the contrary bringeth bliss,
And is a pattern of celestial peace.   *V, v, l. 62*

23 'Tis not my speeches that you do mislike,
But 'tis my presence that doth trouble ye.
Rancor will out.
King Henry VI, Part II [1590–1591],
act I, sc. i, l. 141

24 Could I come near your beauty with my nails
I'd set my ten commandments in your face.
I, iii, l. 144

---

[1] See Ovid, 101:24.

[2] From the text edited by W. J. CRAIG. For the dating and sequence
of the plays and poems see E. K. CHAMBERS, *William Shakespeare,*
and JAMES G. McMANAWAY, "Recent Studies in Shakespeare's
Chronology."

1 Blessed are the peacemakers on earth.
King Henry VI, Part II, II, i, l. 34

2 Now, God be prais'd, that to believing souls
Gives light in darkness, comfort in despair!   *II, i, l. 66*

3 God defend the right!   *II, iii, l. 55*

4 Sometimes hath the brightest day a cloud;
And after summer evermore succeeds
Barren winter, with his wrathful nipping cold:
So cares and joys abound, as seasons fleet.   *II, iv, l. 1*

5 Now 'tis the spring, and weeds are shallow-rooted;
Suffer them now and they'll o'ergrow the garden.
III, i, l. 31

6   In thy face I see
The map of honor, truth, and loyalty.   *III, i, l. 202*

7 What stronger breastplate than a heart untainted!
Thrice is he arm'd that hath his quarrel just,
And he but naked, though lock'd up in steel,
Whose conscience with injustice is corrupted.
III, ii, l. 232

8 He dies, and makes no sign.   *III, iii, l. 29*

9 Forbear to judge, for we are sinners all.
Close up his eyes, and draw the curtain close;
And let us all to meditation.   *III, iii, l. 31*

10 The gaudy, blabbing, and remorseful day
Is crept into the bosom of the sea.   *IV, i, l. 1*

11 Small things make base men proud.   *IV, i, l. 106*

12 True nobility is exempt from fear.   *IV, i, l. 129*

13   I will make it felony to drink small beer.
IV, ii, l. 75

14   The first thing we do, let's kill all the lawyers.
IV, ii, l. 86

15   Is not this a lamentable thing, that of the skin of
an innocent lamb should be made parchment? that
parchment, being scribbled o'er, should undo a man?
IV, ii, l. 88

16   Adam was a gardener.   *IV, ii, l. 146*

17   Thou hast most traitorously corrupted the youth
of the realm in erecting a grammar-school; and
whereas, before, our forefathers had no other books
but the score and the tally, thou hast caused printing
to be used; and, contrary to the king, his crown, and
dignity, thou hast built a paper-mill.   *IV, vii, l. 35*

18 Beggars mounted run their horse to death.[1]
*King Henry VI, Part III [1590–1591],
act I, sc. iv, l. 127*

19 O tiger's heart wrapp'd in a woman's hide!
I, iv, l. 137

20 To weep is to make less the depth of grief.   *II, i, l. 85*

21 The smallest worm will turn being trodden on.
II, ii, l. 17

22   Didst thou never hear
That things ill got had ever bad success?   *II, ii, l. 45*

23 Thou [Death] setter up and plucker down of
kings.[2]   *II, iii, l. 37*

24 And what makes robbers bold but too much lenity?
II, vi, l. 22

25 My crown is in my heart, not on my head;
Not deck'd with diamonds and Indian stones,
Nor to be seen: my crown is call'd content;
A crown it is that seldom kings enjoy.   *III, i, l. 62*

26   'Tis a happy thing
To be the father unto many sons.   *III, ii, l. 104*

27 Like one that stands upon a promontory,
And spies a far-off shore where he would tread,
Wishing his foot were equal with his eye.
III, ii, l. 135

28   Yield not thy neck
To fortune's yoke, but let thy dauntless mind
Still ride in triumph over all mischance.
III, iii, l. 16

29 For how can tyrants safely govern home,
Unless abroad they purchase great alliance?
III, iii, l. 69

30 Having nothing, nothing can he lose.   *III, iii, l. 152*

31 Hasty marriage seldom proveth well.   *IV, i, l. 18*

32 What fates impose, that men must needs abide;
It boots not to resist both wind and tide.
IV, iii, l. 57

33 Now join your hands, and with your hands your
hearts.   *IV, vi, l. 39*

34 For many men that stumble at the threshold
Are well foretold that danger lurks within.
IV, vii, l. 11

35 A little fire is quickly trodden out,
Which, being suffer'd, rivers cannot quench.
IV, viii, l. 7

36   When the lion fawns upon the lamb,
The lamb will never cease to follow him.
IV, viii, l. 49

37   What is pomp, rule, reign, but earth and dust?

---

[1]Set a beggar on horseback and he will ride a gallop. — ROBERT
BURTON, *Anatomy of Melancholy, pt. II, sec. 2, member 2*
   Set a beggar on horseback, and he'll outride the Devil. — HENRY
GEORGE BOHN [1796–1884], *Foreign Proverbs, German* [1855]

---

[2]Proud setter up and puller down of kings. — *King Henry VI, Part
III, act III, sc. iii, l. 157*

And, live we how we can, yet die we must.

V, ii, l. 27

1 What though the mast be now blown overboard,
  The cable broke, the holding anchor lost,
  And half our sailors swallow'd in the flood?
  Yet lives our pilot still.   *V, iv, l. 3*

2 So part we sadly in this troublous world,
  To meet with joy in sweet Jerusalem.
                                       V, v, l. 7

3 Men ne'er spend their fury on a child.   *V, v, l. 57*

4 He's sudden if a thing comes in his head.   *V, v, l. 86*

5 Suspicion always haunts the guilty mind;
  The thief doth fear each bush an officer.   *V, vi, l. 11*

6 This word "love," which greybeards call divine.
                                       V, vi, l. 81

7 Bid me discourse, I will enchant thine ear.
              Venus and Adonis [1592], l. 145

8 Love is a spirit all compact of fire,
  Not gross to sink, but light, and will aspire.   *l. 149*

9 "Fondling," she saith, "since I have hemm'd thee
       here
  Within the circuit of this ivory pale,
  I'll be a park, and thou shalt be my deer;
  Feed where thou wilt, on mountain, or in dale:
      Graze on my lips, and if those hills be dry,
      Stray lower, where the pleasant fountains lie."
                                       l. 229

10 O! what a war of looks was then between them.
                                       l. 355

11 Like a red morn, that ever yet betoken'd
  Wrack to the seaman, tempest to the field.   *l. 453*

12 The owl, night's herald.   *l. 531*

13 Love comforteth like sunshine after rain.   *l. 799*

14 For he being dead, with him is beauty slain,
  And, beauty dead, black chaos comes again.   *l. 1019*

15 The grass stoops not, she treads on it so light.
                                       l. 1028

16 Now is the winter of our discontent
  Made glorious summer by this sun of York.
       King Richard III [1592–1593],
          act I, sc. i, l. 1

17 Grim-visag'd war hath smooth'd his wrinkled
       front.   *I, i, l. 9*

18 He capers nimbly in a lady's chamber
  To the lascivious pleasing of a lute.   *I, i, l. 12*

19 This weak piping time of peace.   *I, i, l. 24*

20 No beast so fierce but knows some touch of pity.
                                       I, ii, l. 71

21 Look, how my ring encompasseth thy finger,
  Even so thy breast encloseth my poor heart;
  Wear both of them, for both of them are thine.
                                       I, ii, l. 204

22 Was ever woman in this humor woo'd?
  Was ever woman in this humor won?   *I, ii, l. 229*

23   The world is grown so bad
  That wrens make prey where eagles dare not perch.
                                       I, iii, l. 70

24 The day will come that thou shalt wish for me
  To help thee curse this pois'nous bunch-back'd
       toad.   *I, iii, l. 245*

25 And thus I clothe my naked villany
  With odd old ends stol'n forth of holy writ,
  And seem a saint when most I play the devil.
                                       I, iii, l. 336

26 Talkers are no good doers.   *I, iii, l. 351*

27 O, I have pass'd a miserable night,
  So full of ugly sights, of ghastly dreams,
  That, as I am a Christian faithful man,
  I would not spend another such a night,
  Though 'twere to buy a world of happy days.
                                       I, iv, l. 2

28 Lord, Lord! methought what pain it was to drown:
  What dreadful noise of water in mine ears!
  What sights of ugly death within mine eyes!
  Methought I saw a thousand fearful wracks;
  A thousand men that fishes gnaw'd upon.   *I, iv, l. 21*

29 The kingdom of perpetual night.   *I, iv, l. 47*

30 Sorrow breaks seasons and reposing hours,
  Makes the night morning, and the noontide night.
                                       I, iv, l. 76

31 A parlous boy.   *II, iv, l. 35*

32 So wise so young, they say, do never live long.[1]
                                       III, i, l. 79

33 Off with his head!   *III, iv, l. 75*

34 Lives like a drunken sailor on a mast;
  Ready with every nod to tumble down
  Into the fatal bowels of the deep.   *III, iv, l. 98*

35 I am not in the giving vein today.   *IV, ii, l. 115*

36 The sons of Edward sleep in Abraham's bosom.
                                       IV, iii, l. 38

37 A grievous burden was thy birth to me;
  Tetchy and wayward was thy infancy.   *IV, iv, l. 168*

---

[1]A little too wise, they say, do ne'er live long. — THOMAS
MIDDLETON, *The Phoenix* [1603–1604], *act I, sc. i*

1 An honest tale speeds best being plainly told.
King Richard III, IV, iv, l. 359

2 Harp not on that string. *IV, iv, l. 365*

3 Relenting fool, and shallow changing woman!
IV, iv, l. 432

4 Is the chair empty? is the sword unsway'd?
Is the king dead? the empire unpossess'd?
IV, iv, l. 470

5 True hope is swift, and flies with swallow's wings;
Kings it makes gods, and meaner creatures kings.
V, ii, l. 23

6 The king's name is a tower of strength. *V, iii, l. 12*

7 Give me another horse! bind up my wounds!
V, iii, l. 178

8 O coward conscience, how dost thou afflict me!
V, iii, l. 180

9 My conscience hath a thousand several tongues,
And every tongue brings in a several tale,
And every tale condemns me for a villain.
V, iii, l. 194

10 Conscience is but a word that cowards use,
Devis'd at first to keep the strong in awe.
V, iii, l. 310

11 A horse! a horse! my kingdom for a horse! *V, iv, l. 7*

12 I have set my life upon a cast,
And I will stand the hazard of the die.
I think there be six Richmonds in the field. *V, iv, l. 9*

13 The pleasing punishment that women bear.
*The Comedy of Errors [1592–1594],
act I, sc. i, l. 46*

14 For we may pity, though not pardon thee. *I, i, l. 97*

15 Why, headstrong liberty is lash'd with woe.
There's nothing situate under heaven's eye
But hath his bound, in earth, in sea, in sky.
II, i, l. 15

16 Every why hath a wherefore.[1] *II, ii, l. 45*

17 There's no time for a man to recover his hair that
grows bald by nature. *II, ii, l. 74*

18 What he hath scanted men in hair, he hath given
them in wit. *II, ii, l. 83*

19 Small cheer and great welcome makes a merry
feast. *III, i, l. 26*

20 There is something in the wind. *III, i, l. 69*

21 We'll pluck a crow together. *III, i, l. 83*

22 For slander lives upon succession,
Forever housed where it gets possession.
III, i, l. 105

23 Be not thy tongue thy own shame's orator.
III, ii, l. 10

24 Ill deeds are doubled with an evil word.
III, ii, l. 20

25 A back-friend, a shoulder-clapper. *IV, ii, l. 37*

26 The venom clamors of a jealous woman
Poison more deadly than a mad dog's tooth.
V, i, l. 69

27 Unquiet meals make ill digestions. *V, i, l. 74*

28 One Pinch, a hungry lean-fac'd villain,
A mere anatomy, a mountebank,
A threadbare juggler, and a fortune-teller,
A needy, hollow-ey'd, sharp-looking wretch,
A living-dead man. *V, i, l. 238*

29 Beauty itself doth of itself persuade
The eyes of men without an orator.
The Rape of Lucrece [1593–1594], l. 29

30 This silent war of lilies and of roses,
Which Tarquin view'd in her fair face's field. *l. 71*

31 One for all, or all for one we gage. *l. 144*

32 Who buys a minute's mirth to wail a week?
Or sells eternity to get a toy?
For one sweet grape who will the vine destroy?
l. 213

33 Extreme fear can neither fight nor fly. *l. 230*

34 All orators are dumb when beauty pleadeth. *l. 268*

35 Time's glory is to calm contending kings,
To unmask falsehood and bring truth to light.
l. 939

36 For greatest scandal waits on greatest state. *l. 1006*

37 To see sad sights moves more than hear them told.
l. 1324

38 Cloud-kissing Ilion. *l. 1370*

39 Lucrece swears he did her wrong.[2] *l. 1462*

40 Sweet mercy is nobility's true badge.
*Titus Andronicus [1593–1594],
act I, sc. i, l. 119*

41 These words are razors to my wounded heart.
I, i, l. 314

42 He lives in fame that died in virtue's cause.
I, i, l. 390

---

[1]For every why he had a wherefore. — SAMUEL BUTLER [1612–1680], *Hudibras, pt. I, canto 1, l. 132*

[2]Some villain hath done me wrong. — *King Lear, act I, sc. ii, l. 186*

1 These dreary dumps.[1]   *I, i, l. 391*

2 The eagle suffers little birds to sing,
And is not careful what they mean thereby.
IV, iv, l. 82

3 Tut! I have done a thousand dreadful things
As willingly as one would kill a fly.   *V, i, l. 141*

4   I'll not budge an inch.
*The Taming of the Shrew [1593–1594],
induction, sc. i, l. 13*

5 And if the boy have not a woman's gift
To rain a shower of commanded tears,
An onion will do well for such a shift.   *i, l. 124*

6 No profit grows where is no pleasure ta'en;
In brief, sir, study what you most affect.
act I, sc. i, l. 39

7   There's small choice in rotten apples.   *I, i, l. 137*

8 To seek their fortunes further than at home,
Where small experience grows.   *I, ii, l. 51*

9 I come to wive it wealthily in Padua.   *I, ii, l. 75*

10   Nothing comes amiss, so money comes withal.
I, ii, l. 82

11 And do as adversaries do in law,
Strive mightily, but eat and drink as friends.
I, ii, l. 281

12 I must dance barefoot on her wedding day,
And, for your love to her, lead apes in hell.
II, i, l. 33

13 Asses are made to bear, and so are you.   *II, i, l. 200*

14 Kiss me, Kate, we will be married o' Sunday.
II, i, l. 318

15 Old fashions please me best.   *III, i, l. 81*

16 Who woo'd in haste and means to wed at leisure.
III, ii, l. 11

17 Such an injury would vex a very saint.   *III, ii, l. 28*

18   A little pot and soon hot.   *IV, i, l. 6*

19 Sits as one new-risen from a dream.   *IV, i, l. 189*

20 This is a way to kill a wife with kindness.   *IV, i, l. 211*

21 Kindness in women, not their beauteous looks,
Shall win my love.   *IV, ii, l. 41*

22 Our purses shall be proud, our garments poor:
For 'tis the mind that makes the body rich;
And as the sun breaks through the darkest clouds,
So honor peereth in the meanest habit.
IV, iii, l. 173

23 Forward, I pray, since we have come so far,
And be it moon, or sun, or what you please.
And if you please to call it a rush-candle,
Henceforth I vow it shall be so for me.   *IV, v, l. 12*

24 He that is giddy thinks the world turns round.
V, ii, l. 20

25 A woman mov'd is like a fountain troubled,
Muddy, ill-seeming, thick, bereft of beauty.
V, ii, l. 143

26 Such duty as the subject owes the prince,
Even such a woman oweth to her husband.
V, ii, l. 156

27 Home-keeping youth have ever homely wits.
*The Two Gentlemen of Verona [1594],
act I, sc. i, l. 2*

28 *Julia:* They do not love that do not show their love.
Lucetta: O! they love least that let men know their
love.   *I, ii, l. 31*

29 O! how this spring of love resembleth
The uncertain glory of an April day!   *I, iii, l. 84*

30 O jest unseen, inscrutable, invisible,
As a nose on a man's face, or a weathercock on a
steeple!   *II, i, l. 145*

31 He makes sweet music with th' enamell'd stones.
II, vii, l. 28

32 That man that hath a tongue, I say, is no man,
If with his tongue he cannot win a woman.
III, i, l. 104

33 Except I be by Silvia in the night,
There is no music in the nightingale.   *III, i, l. 178*

34 Who is Silvia? what is she,
That all our swains commend her?
Holy, fair, and wise is she;
The heaven such grace did lend her,
That she might admired be.   *IV, ii, l. 40*

35 Alas, how love can trifle with itself!   *IV, iv, l. 190*

36 Black men are pearls in beauteous ladies' eyes.
V, ii, l. 12

37 How use doth breed a habit in a man!   *V, iv, l. 1*

38 Spite of cormorant devouring Time.
*Love's Labour's Lost [1594–1595],
act I, sc. i, l. 4*

39 Make us heirs of all eternity.   *I, i, l. 7*

40 Why, all delights are vain; but that most vain
Which, with pain purchas'd doth inherit pain.
I, i, l. 72

41 Light seeking light doth light of light beguile.
I, i, l. 77

---

[1]And doleful dumps the mind oppress. — *Romeo and Juliet, act
IV, sc. v, l. 130*

1 Study is like the heaven's glorious sun,
That will not be deep-search'd with saucy looks;
Small have continual plodders ever won,
Save base authority from others' books.
These earthly godfathers of heaven's lights
That give a name to every fixed star,
Have no more profit of their shining nights
Than those that walk and wot not what they are.
Love's Labour's Lost, I, i, l. 84

2 At Christmas I no more desire a rose
Than wish a snow in May's newfangled mirth;
But like of each thing that in season grows.
I, i, l. 105

3 And men sit down to that nourishment which is
called supper. *I, i, l. 237*

4 That unlettered small-knowing soul. *I, i, l. 251*

5 A child of our grandmother Eve, a female; or, for
thy more sweet understanding, a woman. *I, i, l. 263*

6 Affliction may one day smile again; and till then,
sit thee down, sorrow! *I, i, l. 312*

7 Devise, wit; write, pen; for I am for whole volumes
in folio. *I, ii, l. 194*

8 Beauty is bought by judgment of the eye,
Not utter'd by base sale of chapmen's tongues.
II, i, l. 15

9 A merrier man,
Within the limit of becoming mirth,
I never spent an hour's talk withal. *II, i, l. 66*

10 Your wit's too hot, it speeds too fast, 'twill tire.
II, i, l. 119

11 Warble, child; make passionate my sense of
hearing. *III, i, l. 1*

12 Remuneration! O! that's the Latin word for three
farthings. *III, i, l. 143*

13 A very beadle to a humorous sigh. *III, i, l. 185*

14 This wimpled, whining, purblind, wayward boy,
This senior-junior, giant-dwarf, Dan Cupid;
Regent of love-rimes, lord of folded arms,
The anointed sovereign of sighs and groans,
Liege of all loiters and malcontents. *III, i, l. 189*

15 He hath not fed of the dainties that are bred of a
book; he hath not eat paper, as it were; he hath not
drunk ink. *IV, ii, l. 25*

16 Many can brook the weather that love not the
wind. *IV, ii, l. 34*

17 You two are book-men. *IV, ii, l. 35*

18 These are begot in the ventricle of memory, nourished in the womb of pia mater, and delivered upon
the mellowing of occasion. *IV, ii, l. 70*

19 By heaven, I do love, and it hath taught me to
rime, and to be melancholy. *IV, iii, l. 13*

20 For where is any author in the world
Teaches such beauty as a woman's eye?
Learning is but an adjunct to ourself. *IV, iii, l. 312*

21 But love, first learned in a lady's eyes,
Lives not alone immured in the brain. *IV, iii, l. 327*

22 It adds a precious seeing to the eye. *IV, iii, l. 333*

23 As sweet and musical
As bright Apollo's lute, strung with his hair;
And when Love speaks, the voice of all the gods
Makes heaven drowsy with the harmony.
IV, iii, l. 342

24 From women's eyes this doctrine I derive:
They sparkle still the right Promethean fire;
They are the books, the arts, the academes,
That show, contain, and nourish all the world.
IV, iii, l. 350

25 He draweth out the thread of his verbosity finer
than the staple of his argument. *V, i, l. 18*

26 *Moth:* They have been at a great feast of languages,
and stolen the scraps.
Costard: O! they have lived long on the almsbasket
of words. I marvel thy master hath not eaten thee for
a word; for thou art not so long by the head as *honor-
ificabilitudinitatibus:* thou art easier swallowed than
a flap-dragon. *V, i, l. 39*

27 In the posteriors of this day, which the rude multitude call the afternoon. *V, i, l. 96*

28 Taffeta phrases, silken terms precise,
Three-pil'd hyperboles, spruce affectation,
Figures pedantical. *V, ii, l. 407*

29 Let me take you a button-hole lower.
V, ii, l. 705

30 The naked truth of it is, I have no shirt.
V, ii, l. 715

31 A jest's prosperity lies in the ear
Of him that hears it, never in the tongue
Of him that makes it. *V, ii, l. 869*

32 When daisies pied and violets blue,
And lady-smocks all silver-white,
And cuckoo-buds of yellow hue
Do paint the meadows with delight,
The cuckoo then, on every tree,
Mocks married men; for thus sings he,
Cuckoo;
Cuckoo, cuckoo: O word of fear,
Unpleasing to a married ear! *V, ii, l. 902*

33 When icicles hang by the wall,
And Dick the shepherd blows his nail,

And Tom bears logs into the hall,
And milk comes frozen home in pail,
When blood is nipp'd and ways be foul,
Then nightly sings the staring owl,
    Tu-who;
Tu-whit, tu-who — a merry note,
While greasy Joan doth keel the pot.   *V, ii, l. 920*

1 When all aloud the wind doth blow,
And coughing drowns the parson's saw,
And birds sit brooding in the snow,
And Marian's nose looks red and raw,
When roasted crabs hiss in the bowl.   *V, ii, l. 929*

2   The words of Mercury are harsh after the songs of Apollo.   *V, ii, l. 938*

3 For new-made honor doth forget men's names.
    King John [1594–1596], act I, sc. i, l. 187

4 Sweet, sweet, sweet poison for the age's tooth.
    I, i, l. 213

5 Bearing their birthrights proudly on their backs,
To make a hazard of new fortunes here.   *II, i, l. 70*

6 For courage mounteth with occasion.   *II, i, l. 82*

7   The hare of whom the proverb goes,
Whose valor plucks dead lions by the beard.[1]
    II, i, l. 137

8 Saint George, that swing'd the dragon, and e'er since
Sits on his horse back at mine hostess' door.
    II, i, l. 288

9 He is the half part of a blessed man,
Left to be finished by such a she;
And she a fair divided excellence,
Whose fullness of perfection lies in him.   *II, i, l. 437*

10 'Zounds! I was never so bethump'd with words
Since I first call'd my brother's father dad.
    II, i, l. 466

11 Mad world! mad kings, mad composition!
    II, i, l. 561

12 That smooth-fac'd gentleman, tickling Commodity,
Commodity, the bias of the world.   *II, i, l. 573*

13 I will instruct my sorrows to be proud;
For grief is proud and makes his owner stoop.
    III, i, l. 68

14 Thou wear a lion's hide! doff it for shame,
And hang a calf's-skin on those recreant limbs.
    III, i, l. 128

15 The sun's o'ercast with blood: fair day, adieu!
Which is the side that I must go withal?

---

[1]So hares may pull dead lions by the beard. — THOMAS KYD, *The Spanish Tragedy, act I, sc. ii, l. 172*

I am with both: each army hath a hand;
And in their rage, I having hold of both,
They whirl asunder and dismember me.   *III, i, l. 326*

16 Bell, book, and candle shall not drive me back.
    III, iii, l. 12

17 Look, who comes here! a grave unto a soul.
    III, iv, l. 17

18 Death, death: O, amiable lovely death!   *III, iv, l. 25*

19 Grief fills the room up of my absent child,
Lies in his bed, walks up and down with me,
Puts on his pretty looks, repeats his words,
Remembers me of all his gracious parts,
Stuffs out his vacant garments with his form.
    III, iv, l. 93

20 Life is as tedious as a twice-told tale,
Vexing the dull ear of a drowsy man.   *III, iv, l. 108*

21 When Fortune means to men most good,
She looks upon them with a threatening eye.
    III, iv, l. 119

22 A scepter snatch'd with an unruly hand
Must be as boisterously maintain'd as gain'd;
And he that stands upon a slippery place
Makes nice of no vile hold to stay him up.
    III, iv, l. 135

23 As quiet as a lamb.   *IV, i, l. 80*

24 To gild refined gold, to paint the lily,
To throw a perfume on the violet,
To smooth the ice, or add another hue
Unto the rainbow, or with taper-light
To seek the beauteous eye of heaven to garnish,
Is wasteful and ridiculous excess.   *IV, ii, l. 11*

25 And oftentimes excusing of a fault
Doth make the fault the worse by the excuse.
    IV, ii, l. 30

26 We cannot hold mortality's strong hand.
    IV, ii, l. 82

27 There is no sure foundation set on blood,
No certain life achiev'd by others' death.
    IV, ii, l. 104

28 Make haste; the better foot before.   *IV, ii, l. 170*

29 Another lean unwash'd artificer.   *IV, ii, l. 201*

30 How oft the sight of means to do ill deeds
Makes ill deeds done!   *IV, ii, l. 219*

31 Heaven take my soul, and England keep my bones!
    IV, iii, l. 10

32 I am amaz'd, methinks, and lose my way
Among the thorns and dangers of this world.
    IV, iii, l. 140

1 Unthread the rude eye of rebellion,
 And welcome home again discarded faith.
 King John, V, iv, l. 11

2 The day shall not be up so soon as I,
 To try the fair adventure of tomorrow.   *V, v, l. 21*

3   'Tis strange that death should sing.
 I am the cygnet to this pale faint swan,
 Who chants a doleful hymn to his own death.
 V, vii, l. 20

4 Now my soul hath elbow-room.   *V, vii, l. 28*

5   I do not ask you much:
 I beg cold comfort.   *V, vii, l. 41*

6 This England never did, nor never shall,
 Lie at the proud foot of a conqueror.   *V, vii, l. 112*

7 Come the three corners of the world in arms,
 And we shall shock them. Nought shall make us rue,
 If England to itself do rest but true.   *V, vii, l. 116*

8 The purest treasure mortal times afford
 Is spotless reputation.
 *King Richard II [1595], act I,
 sc. i, l. 177*

9 Mine honor is my life; both grow in one;
 Take honor from me, and my life is done.   *I, i, l. 182*

10 We were not born to sue, but to command.
 I, i, l. 196

11 The daintiest last, to make the end most sweet.
 I, iii, l. 68

12 Truth hath a quiet breast.   *I, iii, l. 96*

13 How long a time lies in one little word!   *I, iii, l. 213*

14 Things sweet to taste prove in digestion sour.
 I, iii, l. 236

15 Must I not serve a long apprenticehood
 To foreign passages, and in the end,
 Having my freedom, boast of nothing else
 But that I was a journeyman to grief?   *I, iii, l. 271*

16 All places that the eye of heaven visits
 Are to a wise man ports and happy havens.
 Teach thy necessity to reason thus;
 There is no virtue like necessity.
 Think not the king did banish thee,
 But thou the king.   *I, iii, l. 275*

17 For gnarling sorrow hath less power to bite
 The man that mocks at it and sets it light.
 I, iii, l. 292

18 O! who can hold a fire in his hand
 By thinking on the frosty Caucasus?
 Or cloy the hungry edge of appetite
 By bare imagination of a feast?

Or wallow naked in December snow
 By thinking on fantastic summer's heat?
 O, no! the apprehension of the good
 Gives but the greater feeling to the worse.   *I, iii, l. 294*

19 Where'er I wander, boast of this I can,
 Though banish'd, yet a true-born Englishman.
 I, iii, l. 308

20   The tongues of dying men
 Enforce attention like deep harmony.   *II, i, l. 5*

21 The setting sun, and music at the close,
 As the last taste of sweets, is sweetest last,
 Writ in remembrance more than things long past.
 II, i, l. 12

22 Report of fashions in proud Italy,
 Whose manners still our tardy apish nation
 Limps after in base imitation.   *II, i, l. 21*

23 For violent fires soon burn out themselves;
 Small showers last long, but sudden storms are
   short.   *II, i, l. 34*

24 This royal throne of kings, this scepter'd isle,
 This earth of majesty, this seat of Mars,
 This other Eden, demi-paradise,
 This fortress built by Nature for herself
 Against infection and the hand of war,
 This happy breed of men, this little world,
 This precious stone set in the silver sea,
 Which serves it in the office of a wall,
 Or as a moat defensive to a house,
 Against the envy of less happier lands,
 This blessed plot, this earth, this realm, this England,
 This nurse, this teeming womb of royal kings,
 Fear'd by their breed and famous by their birth.
 II, i, l. 40

25 England, bound in with the triumphant sea,
 Whose rocky shore beats back the envious siege
 Of watery Neptune.   *II, i, l. 61*

26 That England, that was wont to conquer others,
 Hath made a shameful conquest of itself.   *II, i, l. 65*

27 The ripest fruit first falls.   *II, i, l. 154*

28 Each substance of a grief hath twenty shadows.
 II, ii, l. 14

29 I count myself in nothing else so happy
 As in a soul remembering my good friends.   *II, iii, l. 46*

30 Evermore thanks, the exchequer of the poor.
 II, iii, l. 65

31 Grace me no grace, nor uncle me no uncle.
 II, iii, l. 87

32 The caterpillars of the commonwealth,
 Which I have sworn to weed and pluck away.
 II, iii, l. 166

1 Things past redress are now with me past care.
II, iii, l. 171

2 I see thy glory like a shooting star
Fall to the base earth from the firmament.
II, iv, l. 19

3 Eating the bitter bread of banishment.   *III, i, l. 21*

4 Not all the water in the rough rude sea
Can wash the balm from an anointed king.
III, ii, l. 54

5 O! call back yesterday, bid time return.   *III, ii, l. 69*

6 The worst is death, and death will have his day.
III, ii, l. 103

7   Of comfort no man speak:
Let's talk of graves, of worms, and epitaphs;
Make dust our paper, and with rainy eyes
Write sorrow on the bosom of the earth;
Let's choose executors and talk of wills.
III, ii, l. 144

8 And nothing can we call our own but death,
And that small model of the barren earth
Which serves as paste and cover to our bones.
For God's sake, let us sit upon the ground
And tell sad stories of the death of kings:
How some have been depos'd, some slain in war,
Some haunted by the ghosts they have depos'd,
Some poison'd by their wives, some sleeping kill'd;
All murder'd: for within the hollow crown
That rounds the mortal temples of a king
Keeps Death his court.
III, ii, l. 152

9 Comes at the last, and with a little pin
Bores through his castle wall, and farewell king!
III, ii, l. 169

10   He is come to open
The purple testament of bleeding war.
III, iii, l. 93

11   O! that I were as great
As is my grief, or lesser than my name,
Or that I could forget what I have been,
Or not remember what I must be now.
III, iii, l. 136

12 I'll give my jewels for a set of beads,
My gorgeous palace for a hermitage,
My gay apparel for an almsman's gown.
III, iii, l. 147

13 And my large kingdom for a little grave,
A little little grave, an obscure grave.
III, iii, l. 153

14   And there at Venice gave
His body to that pleasant country's earth,

And his pure soul unto his captain Christ,
Under whose colors he had fought so long.
IV, i, l. 97

15 Peace shall go sleep with Turks and infidels.
IV, i, l. 139

16 So Judas did to Christ: but he, in twelve,
Found truth in all but one; I, in twelve thousand,
none.
God save the king! Will no man say, amen?
IV, i, l. 170

17 Now is this golden crown like a deep well
That owes two buckets filling one another;
The emptier ever dancing in the air,
The other down, unseen and full of water:
That bucket down and full of tears am I,
Drinking my griefs, whilst you mount up on high.
IV, i, l. 184

18 You may my glories and my state depose,
But not my griefs; still am I king of those.
IV, i, l. 192

19   Some of you with Pilate wash your hands,
Showing an outward pity.   *IV, i, l. 239*

20 A mockery king of snow.   *IV, i, l. 260*

21 As in a theater, the eyes of men,
After a well-grac'd actor leaves the stage,
Are idly bent on him that enters next,
Thinking his prattle to be tedious.   *V, ii, l. 23*

22   How sour sweet music is
When time is broke and no proportion kept!
So is it in the music of men's lives.   *V, v, l. 42*

23 I wasted time, and now doth time waste me;
For now hath time made me his numbering clock:
My thoughts are minutes.   *V, v, l. 49*

24 This music mads me: let it sound no more.
V, v, l. 61

25 Mount, mount, my soul! thy seat is up on high,
Whilst my gross flesh sinks downward, here to die.
V, v, l. 112

26 To live a barren sister all your life,
Chanting faint hymns to the cold fruitless moon.
A Midsummer-Night's Dream
[1595–1596], act I, sc. i, l. 72

27   For aught that I could ever read,
Could ever hear by tale or history,
The course of true love never did run smooth.
I, i, l. 132

28 Swift as a shadow, short as any dream,
Brief as the lightning in the collied night,
That, in a spleen, unfolds both heaven and earth,
And ere a man hath power to say, "Behold!"

The jaws of darkness do devour it up:
So quick bright things come to confusion.

A Midsummer-Night's Dream, I, i, l. 144

1 Love looks not with the eyes, but with the mind,
And therefore is wing'd Cupid painted blind.[1]

I, i, l. 234

2 The most lamentable comedy, and most cruel death of Pyramus and Thisby. *I, ii, l. 11*

3 Masters, spread yourselves. *I, ii, l. 16*

4 This is Ercles' vein, a tyrant's vein. *I, ii, l. 43*

5 I'll speak in a monstrous little voice. *I, ii, l. 55*

6 I am slow of study. *I, ii, l. 70*

7 That would hang us, every mother's son.

I, ii, l. 81

8 I will aggravate my voice so that I will roar you as gently as any sucking dove; I will roar you as 'twere any nightingale. *I, ii, l. 85*

9 A proper man, as one shall see in a summer's day; a most lovely, gentleman-like man. *I, ii, l. 89*

10 Over hill, over dale,
Thorough bush, thorough brier,
Over park, over pale,
Thorough flood, thorough fire. *II, i, l. 2*

11 I must go seek some dew drops here,
And hang a pearl in every cowslip's ear. *II, i, l. 14*

12 I am that merry wanderer of the night.
I jest to Oberon, and make him smile
When I a fat and bean-fed horse beguile,
Neighing in likeness of a filly foal:
And sometimes lurk I in a gossip's bowl,
In very likeness of a roasted crab. *II, i, l. 43*

13 Ill met by moonlight, proud Titania. *II, i, l. 60*

14 These are the forgeries of jealousy. *II, i, l. 81*

15 Since once I sat upon a promontory,
And heard a mermaid on a dolphin's back
Uttering such dulcet and harmonious breath,
That the rude sea grew civil at her song,
And certain stars shot madly from their spheres
To hear the sea-maid's music. *II, i, l. 149*

16 And the imperial votaress passed on,
In maiden meditation, fancy-free.
Yet mark'd I where the bolt of Cupid fell:
It fell upon a little western flower,
Before milk-white, now purple with love's wound,
And maidens call it, Love-in-idleness. *II, i, l. 163*

---

[1] I have heard of reasons manifold / Why Love must needs be blind, / But this the best of all I hold / His eyes are in his mind. — SAMUEL TAYLOR COLERIDGE, *Reason for Love's Blindness* [1828]

17 I'll put a girdle round about the earth
In forty minutes. *II, i, l. 175*

18 For you in my respect are all the world:
Then how can it be said I am alone,
When all the world is here to look on me? *II, i, l. 224*

19 I know a bank whereon the wild thyme blows,
Where oxlips and the nodding violet grows
Quite over-canopied with luscious woodbine,
With sweet musk-roses, and with eglantine:
There sleeps Titania some time of the night,
Lull'd in these flowers with dances and delight;
And there the snake throws her enamell'd skin,
Weed wide enough to wrap a fairy in. *II, i, l. 249*

20 Some to kill cankers in the musk-rose buds,
Some war with rere-mice for their leathern wings,
To make my small elves coats. *II, ii, l. 3*

21 The clamorous owl, that nightly hoots, and wonders
At our quaint spirits. *II, ii, l. 6*

22 You spotted snakes with double tongue,
Thorny hedge-hogs, be not seen;
Newts, and blind-worms, do no wrong;
Come not near our fairy queen. *II, ii, l. 9*

23 Night and silence! who is here?
Weeds of Athens he doth wear. *II, ii, l. 70*

24 As a surfeit of the sweetest things
The deepest loathing to the stomach brings.

II, ii, l. 137

25 To bring in — God shield us! — a lion among ladies, is a most dreadful thing; for there is not a more fearful wild-fowl than your lion living. *III, i, l. 32*

26 A calendar, a calendar! look in the almanack; find out moonshine. *III, i, l. 55*

27 Bless thee, Bottom! bless thee! thou art translated. *III, i, l. 124*

28 Lord, what fools these mortals be! *III, ii, l. 115*

29 So we grew together,
Like to a double cherry, seeming parted,
But yet an union in partition;
Two lovely berries molded on one stem.

III, ii, l. 208

30 Though she be but little, she is fierce. *III, ii, l. 325*

31 I have a reasonable good ear in music: let us have the tongs and the bones. *IV, i, l. 32*

32 Truly, a peck of provender: I could munch your good dry oats. Methinks I have a great desire to a bottle of hay: good hay, sweet hay, hath no fellow.

IV, i, l. 36

33 I have an exposition of sleep come upon me.

IV, i, l. 44

1 My Oberon! what visions have I seen!
Methought I was enamor'd of an ass.   *IV, i, l. 82*

2   I never heard
So musical a discord, such sweet thunder.
                                          IV, i, l. 123

3   I have had a dream, past the wit of man to say what
dream it was.   *IV, i, l. 211*

4   The eye of man hath not heard, the ear of man
hath not seen, man's hand is not able to taste, his
tongue to conceive, nor his heart to report, what my
dream was.   *IV, i, l. 218*

5   Eat no onions nor garlic, for we are to utter sweet
breath.   *IV, ii, l. 44*

6 The lunatic, the lover, and the poet,
Are of imagination all compact:
One sees more devils than vast hell can hold,
That is, the madman; the lover, all as frantic,
Sees Helen's beauty in a brow of Egypt:
The poet's eye, in a fine frenzy rolling,
Doth glance from heaven to earth, from earth to
    heaven;
And, as imagination bodies forth
The forms of things unknown, the poet's pen
Turns them to shapes, and gives to airy nothing
A local habitation and a name.
Such tricks hath strong imagination,
That, if it would but apprehend some joy,
It comprehends some bringer of that joy;
Or in the night, imagining some fear,
How easy is a bush suppos'd a bear!   *V, i, l. 7*

7 But all the story of the night told over,
And all their minds transfigur'd so together,
More witnesseth than fancy's images,
And grows to something of great constancy,
But, howsoever, strange and admirable.
                                          V, i, l. 23

8 Very tragical mirth.   *V, i, l. 57*

9 The true beginning of our end.[1]   *V, i, l. 111*

10   The best in this kind are but shadows.
                                          V, i, l. 215

11   A very gentle beast, and of a good conscience.
                                          V, i, l. 232

12   All that I have to say, is, to tell you that the lant-
horn is the moon; I, the man in the moon; this
thorn-bush, my thorn-bush; and this dog, my dog.
                                          V, i, l. 263

13   Well roared, Lion.   *V, i, l. 272*

14   This passion, and the death of a dear friend, would
go near to make a man look sad.   *V, i, l. 295*

15   With the help of a surgeon, he might yet recover,
and prove an ass.   *V, i, l. 318*

16   No epilogue, I pray you, for your play needs no
excuse. Never excuse.   *V, i, l. 363*

17 The iron tongue of midnight hath told twelve;
Lovers, to bed; 'tis almost fairy time.   *V, i, l. 372*

18 If we shadows have offended,
Think but this, and all is mended,
That you have but slumber'd here
While these visions did appear.   *V, ii, l. 54*

19 A pair of star-cross'd lovers.
         Romeo and Juliet [1595–1596], prologue, l. 6

20 Saint-seducing gold.   *act I, sc. i, l. 220*

21   One fire burns out another's burning,
One pain is lessen'd by another's anguish.   *I, ii, l. 47*

22 I will make thee think thy swan a crow.   *I, ii, l. 92*

23 For I am proverb'd with a grandsire phrase.
                                          I, iv, l. 37

24 We burn daylight.   *I, iv, l. 43*

25 O! then, I see, Queen Mab hath been with you! . . .
She is the fairies' midwife, and she comes
In shape no bigger than an agate-stone
On the forefinger of an alderman,
Drawn with a team of little atomies
Athwart men's noses as they lie asleep.   *I, iv, l. 53*

26   True, I talk of dreams,
Which are the children of an idle brain,
Begot of nothing but vain fantasy.   *I, iv, l. 97*

27 For you and I are past our dancing days.[2]   *I, v, l. 35*

28 It seems she hangs upon the cheek of night
Like a rich jewel in an Ethiop's ear;
Beauty too rich for use, for earth too dear!   *I, v, l. 49*

29 My only love sprung from my only hate!
Too early seen unknown, and known too late!
                                          I, v, l. 142

30 Young Adam Cupid, he that shot so trim
When King Cophetua lov'd the beggarmaid.
                                          II, i, l. 13

31 He jests at scars, that never felt a wound.
But, soft! what light through yonder window breaks?
It is the east, and Juliet is the sun!   *II, ii, l. 1*

32 She speaks, yet she says nothing.   *II, ii, l. 12*

---

[1] I see the beginning of my end. — PHILIP MASSINGER, *The Virgin Martyr* [1622], *act III, sc. iii*

[2] My dancing days are done. — BEAUMONT AND FLETCHER, *The Scornful Lady, act V, sc. iii*

1 See! how she leans her cheek upon her hand:
  O! that I were a glove upon that hand,
  That I might touch that cheek.
  Romeo and Juliet, II, ii, l. 23

2 O Romeo, Romeo! wherefore art thou Romeo?[1]
  Deny thy father, and refuse thy name;
  Or, if thou wilt not, be but sworn my love,
  And I'll no longer be a Capulet.   *II, ii, l. 33*

3 What's in a name? that which we call a rose
  By any other name would smell as sweet.   *II, ii, l. 43*

4 For stony limits cannot hold love out.   *II, ii, l. 67*

5   At lovers' perjuries,
  They say, Jove laughs.   *II, ii, l. 92*

6 In truth, fair Montague, I am too fond.   *II, ii, l. 98*

7   I'll prove more true
  Than those that have more cunning to be strange.
  II, ii, l. 100

8 *Romeo:* Lady, by yonder blessed moon I swear
  That tips with silver all these fruit-tree tops —
  Juliet: O! swear not by the moon, the inconstant
    moon,
  That monthly changes in her circled orb,
  Lest that thy love prove likewise variable.
  II, ii, l. 107

9   Do not swear at all;
  Or, if thou wilt, swear by thy gracious self,
  Which is the god of my idolatry.   *II, ii, l. 112*

10 It is too rash, too unadvis'd, too sudden;
  Too like the lightning, which doth cease to be
  Ere one can say it lightens.   *II, ii, l. 118*

11 This bud of love, by summer's ripening breath,
  May prove a beauteous flower when next we meet.
  II, ii, l. 121

12 Love goes toward love, as schoolboys from their
    books;
  But love from love, toward school with heavy
    looks.   *II, ii, l. 156*

13   O! for a falconer's voice,
  To lure this tassel-gentle back again.   *II, ii, l. 158*

14 How silver-sweet sound lovers' tongues by night,
  Like softest music to attending ears!   *II, ii, l. 165*

15   I would have thee gone;
  And yet no further than a wanton's bird,
  Who lets it hop a little from her hand,
  Like a poor prisoner in his twisted gyves,
  And with a silk thread plucks it back again,
  So loving-jealous of his liberty.   *II, ii, l. 176*

16 Good night, good night! parting is such sweet
    sorrow,
  That I shall say good night till it be morrow.
  II, ii, l. 184

17 Virtue itself turns vice, being misapplied;
  And vice sometime's by action dignified.   *II, iii, l. 21*

18 Care keeps his watch in every old man's eye,
  And where care lodges, sleep will never lie.
  II, iii, l. 35

19 Wisely and slow; they stumble that run fast.
  II, iii, l. 94

20   One, two, and the third in your bosom.
  II, iv, l. 24

21   O flesh, flesh, how art thou fishified!   *II, iv, l. 41*

22   The very pink of courtesy.   *II, iv, l. 63*

23   A gentleman, nurse, that loves to hear himself talk,
  and will speak more in a minute than he will stand to
  in a month.   *II, iv, l. 156*

24 These violent delights have violent ends.   *II, vi, l. 9*

25 Therefore love moderately; long love doth so;
  Too swift arrives as tardy as too slow.   *II, vi, l. 14*

26   Thy head is as full of quarrels as an egg is full of
  meat.[2]   *III, i, l. 23*

27   A word and a blow.   *III, i, l. 44*

28   No, 'tis not so deep as a well, nor so wide as a
  church door; but 'tis enough, 'twill serve: ask for me
  tomorrow, and you shall find me a grave man.
  III, i, l. 101

29   A plague o' both your houses!
  They have made worms' meat of me.   *III, i, l. 112*

30 O! I am Fortune's fool.   *III, i, l. 142*

31 Gallop apace, you fiery-footed steeds,
  Towards Phoebus' lodging.   *III, ii, l. 1*

32   When he shall die,
  Take him and cut him out in little stars,
  And he will make the face of heaven so fine
  That all the world will be in love with night,
  And pay no worship to the garish sun.
  III, ii, l. 21

33   He was not born to shame:
  Upon his brow shame is asham'd to sit.   *III, ii, l. 91*

34 Adversity's sweet milk, philosophy.   *III, iii, l. 54*

35   Hang up philosophy!
  Unless philosophy can make a Juliet.   *III, iii, l. 56*

---

[1] *Huncamunca:* O Tom Thumb! Tom Thumb! wherefore art thou Tom Thumb? — Henry Fielding, *Tom Thumb, act II, sc. iii*

[2] It's as full of good-nature as an egg's full of meat. — Richard Brinsley Sheridan, *A Trip to Scarborough* [1777], *act III, sc. iv*

1 The lark, the herald of the morn.   *III, v, l. 6*

2 Night's candles are burnt out, and jocund day
Stands tiptoe on the misty mountaintops.   *III, v, l. 9*

3 Thank me no thankings, nor proud me no prouds.
III, v, l. 153

4 Is there no pity sitting in the clouds,
That sees into the bottom of my grief?   *III, v, l. 198*

5 Past hope, past cure, past help!   *IV, i, l. 45*

6 'Tis an ill cook that cannot lick his own fingers.
IV, ii, l. 6

7 *Apothecary:* My poverty, but not my will, consents.
Romeo: I pay thy poverty, and not thy will.   *V, i, l. 75*

8   The strength
Of twenty men.   *V, i, l. 78*

9 The time and my intents are savage-wild,
More fierce and more inexorable far
Than empty tigers or the roaring sea.   *V, iii, l. 39*

10 Tempt not a desperate man.   *V, iii, l. 59*

11 One writ with me in sour misfortune's book.
V, iii, l. 82

12 How oft when men are at the point of death
Have they been merry!   *V, iii, l. 88*

13   Beauty's ensign yet
Is crimson in thy lips and in thy cheeks,
And death's pale flag is not advanced there.
V, iii, l. 94

14   O! here
Will I set up my everlasting rest,
And shake the yoke of inauspicious stars
From this world-wearied flesh. Eyes, look your last!
Arms, take your last embrace!   *V, iii, l. 109*

15   O true apothecary!
Thy drugs are quick.   *V, iii, l. 119*

16 See what a scourge is laid upon your hate,
That heaven finds means to kill your joys with love.
V, iii, l. 292

17 For never was a story of more woe
Than this of Juliet and her Romeo.   *V, iii, l. 309*

18 So shaken as we are, so wan with care.
*King Henry IV, Part I [1596–1597],
act I, sc. i, l. 1*

19   In those holy fields
Over whose acres walk'd those blessed feet
Which fourteen hundred years ago were nail'd
For our advantage on the bitter cross.   *I, i, l. 24*

20   Unless hours were cups of sack, and minutes
capons, and clocks the tongues of bawds, and dials

the signs of leaping-houses, and the blessed sun himself a fair hot wench in flame-color'd taffeta, I see no reason why thou shouldst be so superfluous to demand the time of the day.   *I, ii, l. 7*

21   Diana's foresters, gentlemen of the shade, minions of the moon.   *I, ii, l. 29*

22   A purse of gold most resolutely snatched on Monday night and most dissolutely spent on Tuesday morning.   *I, ii, l. 38*

23   Thy quips and thy quiddities.   *I, ii, l. 51*

24   So far as my coin would stretch; and where it would not, I have used my credit.   *I, ii, l. 61*

25   Old father antick the law.   *I, ii, l. 69*

26   I am as melancholy as a gib cat, or a lugged bear.   *I, ii, l. 82*

27   I would to God thou and I knew where a commodity of good names were to be bought.   *I, ii, l. 92*

28   O! thou hast damnable iteration, and art indeed able to corrupt a saint.   *I, ii, l. 101*

29   Now am I, if a man should speak truly, little better than one of the wicked.   *I, ii, l. 105*

30   'Tis my vocation, Hal; 'tis no sin for a man to labor in his vocation.   *I, ii, l. 116*

31   There's neither honesty, manhood, nor good fellowship in thee.   *I, ii, l. 154*

32   Well then, once in my days I'll be a madcap.
I, ii, l. 158

33 I know you all, and will a while uphold
The unyok'd humor of your idleness:
Yet herein will I imitate the sun,
Who doth permit the base contagious clouds
To smother up his beauty from the world,
That when he please again to be himself,
Being wanted, he may be more wonder'd at,
By breaking through the foul and ugly mists
Of vapors that did seem to strangle him.
If all the year were playing holidays,
To sport would be as tedious as to work.   *I, ii, l. 217*

34 You tread upon my patience.   *I, iii, l. 4*

35 Came there a certain lord, neat, and trimly dress'd,
Fresh as a bridegroom; and his chin new-reap'd,
Show'd like a stubble-land at harvest-home:
He was perfumed like a milliner,
And 'twixt his finger and his thumb he held
A pouncet-box, which ever and anon
He gave his nose and took 't away again.   *I, iii, l. 33*

36 And as the soldiers bore dead bodies by,
He call'd them untaught knaves, unmannerly,
To bring a slovenly unhandsome corpse

Betwixt the wind and his nobility.
King Henry IV, Part I, I, iii, l. 42

1 So pester'd with a popinjay. *I, iii, l. 50*

2 God save the mark! *I, iii, l. 56*

3 To put down Richard, that sweet lovely rose,
And plant this thorn, this canker, Bolingbroke.
I, iii, l. 176

4 Or sink or swim. *I, iii, l. 194*

5 O! the blood more stirs
To rouse a lion than to start a hare! *I, iii, l. 197*

6 By heaven methinks it were an easy leap
To pluck bright honor from the pale-fac'd moon,
Or dive into the bottom of the deep,
Where fathom-line could never touch the
     ground,
And pluck up drowned honor by the locks.
I, iii, l. 201

7 Why, what a candy deal of courtesy
This fawning greyhound then did proffer me!
I, iii, l. 251

8 I know a trick worth two of that. *II, i, l. 40*

9 If the rascal have not given me medicines to make
me love him, I'll be hanged. *II, ii, l. 20*

10 I'll starve ere I'll rob a foot further. *II, ii, l. 24*

11 It would be argument for a week, laughter for a
month, and a good jest forever. *II, ii, l. 104*

12 Falstaff sweats to death
And lards the lean earth as he walks along.
II, ii, l. 119

13 Out of this nettle, danger, we pluck this flower,
safety. *II, iii, l. 11*

14 I could brain him with his lady's fan. *II, iii, l. 26*

15 Constant you are,
But yet a woman: and for secrecy,
No lady closer; for I well believe
Thou wilt not utter what thou dost not know;
And so far will I trust thee, gentle Kate. *II, iii, l. 113*

16 A Corinthian, a lad of mettle, a good boy. *II, iv, l. 13*

17 I am not yet of Percy's mind, the Hotspur of the
North; he that kills me some six or seven dozen of
Scots at a breakfast, washes his hands, and says to his
wife, "Fie upon this quiet life! I want work."
II, iv, l. 116

18 A plague of all cowards, I say. *II, iv, l. 129*

19 There live not three good men unhanged in England, and one of them is fat and grows old.
II, iv, l. 146

20 You care not who sees your back: call you that
backing of your friends? A plague upon such
backing! *II, iv, l. 168*

21 I have peppered two of them.... I tell thee what,
Hal, if I tell thee a lie, spit in my face, call me horse.
II, iv, l. 216

22 Give you a reason on compulsion! if reasons were
as plenty as blackberries, I would give no man a
reason upon compulsion, I. *II, iv, l. 267*

23 Mark now, how a plain tale shall put you down.
II, iv, l. 285

24 What doth gravity out of his bed at midnight?
II, iv, l. 328

25 A plague of sighing and grief! it blows a man up
like a bladder. *II, iv, l. 370*

26 I must speak in passion, and I will do it in King
Cambyses' vein. *II, iv, l. 429*

27 That reverend vice, that gray iniquity, that father
ruffian, that vanity in years. *II, iv, l. 505*

28 If sack and sugar be a fault, God help the wicked!
If to be old and merry be a sin, then many an old host
that I know is damned: if to be fat be to be hated,
then Pharaoh's lean kine are to be loved.
II, iv, l. 524

29 Banish plump Jack, and banish all the world.
II, iv, l. 534

30 Play out the play. *II, iv, l. 539*

31 O, monstrous! but one half-penny-worth of bread
to this intolerable deal of sack! *II, iv, l. 597*

32 Diseased nature oftentimes breaks forth
In strange eruptions. *III, i, l. 27*

33 I am not in the roll of common men. *III, i, l. 43*

34 *Glendower:* I can call spirits from the vasty deep.
Hotspur: Why, so can I, or so can any man;
But will they come when you do call for them?
III, i, l. 53

35 I had rather be a kitten and cry mew,
Than one of these same meter ballad-mongers.
III, i, l. 128

36 Mincing poetry:
'Tis like the forc'd gait of a shuffling nag.
III, i, l. 133

37 But in the way of bargain, mark you me,
I'll cavil on the ninth part of a hair. *III, i, l. 138*

38 A deal of skimble-skamble stuff. *III, i, l. 153*

39 I understand thy kisses and thou mine,
And that's a feeling disputation. *III, i, l. 204*

1 *Lady Percy:* . . . Lie still, ye thief, and hear the lady sing in Welsh.

Hotspur: I had rather hear Lady, my brach, howl in Irish.   *III, i, l. 238*

2 A good mouth-filling oath.   *III, i, l. 258*

3 They surfeited with honey and began
To loathe the taste of sweetness, whereof a little
More than a little is by much too much.   *III, ii, l. 71*

4 He was but as the cuckoo is in June,
Heard, not regarded.   *III, ii, l. 75*

5 My near'st and dearest enemy.   *III, ii, l. 123*

6 The end of life cancels all bands.   *III, ii, l. 157*

7 And I have not forgotten what the inside of a church is made of, I am a peppercorn, a brewer's horse.   *III, iii, l. 8*

8 Company, villanous company, hath been the spoil of me.   *III, iii, l. 10*

9 I have more flesh than another man, and therefore more frailty.   *III, iii, l. 187*

10 The very life-blood of our enterprise.   *IV, i, l. 28*

11 Were it good
To set the exact wealth of all our states
All at one cast? to set so rich a main
On the nice hazard of one doubtful hour?
                                                                  IV, i, l. 45

12 Baited like eagles having lately bath'd . . .
As full of spirit as the month of May,
And gorgeous as the sun at midsummer.   *IV, i, l. 99*

13 I saw young Harry, with his beaver on.   *IV, i, l. 104*

14 To turn and wind a fiery Pegasus
And witch the world with noble horsemanship.
                                                                  IV, i, l. 109

15 Worse than the sun in March
This praise doth nourish agues.   *IV, i, l. 111*

16 Doomsday is near; die all, die merrily.   *IV, i, l. 134*

17 The cankers of a calm world and a long peace.
                                                                  IV, ii, l. 32

18 Tut, tut, good enough to toss; food for powder, food for powder; they'll fill a pit as well as better.
                                                                  IV, ii, l. 72

19 To the latter end of a fray and the beginning of a feast
Fits a dull fighter and a keen guest.   *IV, ii, l. 86*

20 Greatness knows itself.   *IV, iii, l. 74*

21 I could be well content
To entertain the lag-end of my life
With quiet hours.   *V, i, l. 23*

22 Rebellion lay in his way, and he found it.   *V, i, l. 28*

23 Never yet did insurrection want
Such water-colors to impaint his cause.   *V, i, l. 79*

24 I would it were bed-time, Hal, and all well.
                                                                  V, i, l. 126

25 Honor pricks me on. Yea, but how if honor prick me off when I come on? how then? Can honor set to a leg? No. Or an arm? No. Or take away the grief of a wound? No. Honor hath no skill in surgery then? No. What is honor? a word. What is that word, honor? Air. A trim reckoning! Who hath it? he that died o' Wednesday. Doth he feel it? No. Doth he hear it? No. It is insensible then? Yea, to the dead. But will it not live with the living? No. Why? Detraction will not suffer it. Therefore I'll none of it: honor is a mere scutcheon; and so ends my catechism.
                                                                  V, i, l. 131

26 Suspicion all our lives shall be stuck full of eyes;
For treason is but trusted like the fox.   *V, ii, l. 8*

27 Let me tell the world.[1]   *V, ii, l. 65*

28 The time of life is short;
To spend that shortness basely were too long.
                                                                  V, ii, l. 81

29 Two stars keep not their motion in one sphere.
                                                                  V, iv, l. 65

30 But thought's the slave of life, and life time's fool;
And time, that takes survey of all the world,
Must have a stop. O! I could prophesy,
But that the earthy and cold hand of death
Lies on my tongue.   *V, iv, l. 81*

31 This earth, that bears thee dead,
Bears not alive so stout a gentleman.   *V, iv, l. 92*

32 Thy ignominy sleep with thee in the grave,
But not remember'd in thy epitaph!   *V, iv, l. 100*

33 I could have better spar'd a better man.   *V, iv, l. 104*

34 The better part of valor is discretion.[2]   *V, iv, l. 120*

35 Full bravely hast thou flesh'd
Thy maiden sword.   *V, iv, l. 132*

36 Lord, Lord, how this world is given to lying!
                                                                  V, iv, l. 148

37 I'll purge, and leave sack, and live cleanly.
                                                                  V, iv, l. 168

38 Your mind is tossing on the ocean.
*The Merchant of Venice [1596–1597],
act I, sc. i, l. 8*

---

[1] I'll tell the world. — *Measure for Measure, act II, sc. iv, l. 154*
Ay, tell the world! — ROBERT BROWNING, *Paracelsus* [1835], *pt. II*

[2] It showed discretion the best part of valor. — BEAUMONT AND FLETCHER, *A King and No King, act II, sc. iii*

1 My ventures are not in one bottom trusted,
Nor to one place.
The Merchant of Venice, I, i, l. 42

2 Nature hath fram'd strange fellows in her time.
I, i, l. 51

3 You have too much respect upon the world:
They lose it that do buy it with much care. *I, i, l. 74*

4 I hold the world but as the world, Gratiano;
A stage where every man must play a part,
And mine a sad one. *I, i, l. 77*

5 Why should a man, whose blood is warm within,
Sit like his grandsire cut in alabaster? *I, i, l. 83*

6 There are a sort of men whose visages
Do cream and mantle like a standing pond. *I, i, l. 88*

7   I am Sir Oracle,
And when I ope my lips let no dog bark! *I, i, l. 93*

8   I do know of these,
That therefore only are reputed wise
For saying nothing. *I, i, l. 95*

9 Fish not, with this melancholy bait,
For this fool-gudgeon, this opinion. *I, i, l. 101*

10   Gratiano speaks an infinite deal of nothing, more
than any man in all Venice. His reasons are as two
grains of wheat hid in two bushels of chaff: you shall
seek all day ere you find them, and, when you have
them, they are not worth the search. *I, i, l. 114*

11 In my school-days, when I had lost one shaft,
I shot his fellow of the selfsame flight
The selfsame way with more advised watch,
To find the other forth, and by adventuring both,
I oft found both. *I, i, l. 141*

12   They are as sick that surfeit with too much as they
that starve with nothing. *I, ii, l. 5*

13   Superfluity comes sooner by white hairs, but com-
petency lives longer. *I, ii, l. 9*

14   If to do were as easy as to know what were good to
do, chapels had been churches, and poor men's cottages princes' palaces. *I, ii, l. 13*

15   The brain may devise laws for the blood, but a hot
temper leaps o'er a cold decree. *I, ii, l. 19*

16   He doth nothing but talk of his horse. *I, ii, l. 43*

17   I fear he will prove the weeping philosopher when
he grows old, being so full of unmannerly sadness in
his youth. *I, ii, l. 51*

18   God made him, and therefore let him pass for a
man. *I, ii, l. 59*

19   When he is best, he is a little worse than a man,
and when he is worst, he is little better than a beast.
I, ii, l. 93

20   I dote on his very absence. *I, ii, l. 118*

21   Ships are but boards, sailors but men: there be
land-rats and water-rats, land-thieves and water-
thieves. *I, iii, l. 22*

22   Yes, to smell pork; to eat of the habitation which
your prophet the Nazarite[1] conjured the devil into.
I will buy with you, sell with you, talk with you, walk
with you, and so following; but I will not eat with
you, drink with you, nor pray with you. What news
on the Rialto? *I, iii, l. 34*

23 How like a fawning publican he looks!
I hate him for he is a Christian. *I, iii, l. 42*

24 If I can catch him once upon the hip,
I will feed fat the ancient grudge I bear him.
I, iii, l. 47

25   Cursed be my tribe,
If I forgive him! *I, iii, l. 52*

26 The devil can cite Scripture for his purpose.
I, iii, l. 99

27 A goodly apple rotten at the heart.
O, what a goodly outside falsehood hath!
I, iii, l. 102

28 For sufferance is the badge of all our tribe.
You call me misbeliever, cut-throat dog,
And spet upon my Jewish gaberdine. *I, iii, l. 111*

29 Shall I bend low, and in a bondman's key,
With bated breath, and whispering humbleness,
Say this. *I, iii, l. 124*

30   I'll seal to such a bond,
And say there is much kindness in the Jew.
I, iii, l. 153

31 O father Abram! what these Christians are,
Whose own hard dealing teaches them suspect
The thoughts of others. *I, iii, l. 161*

32 I like not fair terms and a villain's mind. *I, iii, l. 180*

33 Mislike me not for my complexion,
The shadow'd livery of the burnish'd sun. *II, i, l. 1*

34   O heavens! this is my true-begotten father.
II, ii, l. 36

35   An honest, exceeding poor man. *II, ii, l. 54*

36   The very staff of my age, my very prop. *II, ii, l. 71*

37   It is a wise father that knows his own child.
II, ii, l. 83

38 And the vile squealing of the wry-neck'd fife. *II, v, l. 30*

39   Who riseth from a feast
With that keen appetite that he sits down? *II, vi, l. 8*

---

[1]That hee shall be called a Nazarite. — The Geneva Bible [1557–
1560], *Matthew 2:23*

The Geneva version of the Bible is the one Shakespeare was familiar
with.

1 But love is blind, and lovers cannot see
The pretty follies that themselves commit.
II, vi, l. 36

2 Must I hold a candle to my shames?   *II, vi, l. 41*

3   Men that hazard all
Do it in hope of fair advantages:
A golden mind stoops not to shows of dross.
II, vii, l. 18

4 Young in limbs, in judgment old.   *II, vii, l. 71*

5 My daughter! O my ducats! O my daughter!
Fled with a Christian! O my Christian ducats!
Justice! the law! my ducats, and my daughter!
A sealed bag, two sealed bags of ducats,
Of double ducats, stol'n from me by my daughter!
II, viii, l. 15

6 The fool multitude, that choose by show.
II, ix, l. 26

7   I will not jump with common spirits
And rank me with the barbarous multitude.
II, ix, l. 32

8   Let none presume
To wear an undeserved dignity.
O! that estates, degrees, and offices
Were not deriv'd corruptly, and that clear honor
Were purchas'd by the merit of the wearer.
II, ix, l. 39

9 Some there be that shadows kiss;
Such have but a shadow's bliss.   *II, ix, l. 66*

10   Let him look to his bond.   *III, i, l. 49*

11   I am a Jew. Hath not a Jew eyes? hath not a Jew
hands, organs, dimensions, senses, affections, passions?   *III, i, l. 62*

12   If you prick us, do we not bleed? if you tickle us,
do we not laugh? if you poison us, do we not die? and
if you wrong us, shall we not revenge?   *III, i, l. 65*

13   The villainy you teach me I will execute, and it
shall go hard but I will better the instruction.
III, i, l. 76

14   I would not have given it for a wilderness of monkeys.   *III, i, l. 130*

15 There's something tells me, but it is not love,
I would not lose you; and you know yourself,
Hate counsels not in such a quality.   *III, ii, l. 4*

16   Makes a swanlike end,
Fading in music.   *III, ii, l. 44*

17 Tell me where is fancy bred,
Or in the heart or in the head?
How begot, how nourished?
Reply, reply.   *III, ii, l. 63*

18 In law, what plea so tainted and corrupt
But, being season'd with a gracious voice,
Obscures the show of evil?   *III, ii, l. 75*

19 There is no vice so simple but assumes
Some mark of virtue on his outward parts.
III, ii, l. 81

20 The seeming truth which cunning times put on
To entrap the wisest.   *III, ii, l. 100*

21 How all the other passions fleet to air,
As doubtful thoughts, and rash-embrac'd despair,
And shuddering fear, and green-ey'd jealousy.
III, ii, l. 108

22 An unlesson'd girl, unschool'd, unpractic'd;
Happy in this, she is not yet so old
But she may learn.   *III, ii, l. 160*

23 Here are a few of the unpleasant'st words
That ever blotted paper.
III, ii, l. 252

24 Thou call'dst me dog before thou hadst a cause,
But, since I am a dog, beware my fangs.   *III, iii, l. 6*

25   Thus when I shun Scylla, your father, I fall into
Charybdis, your mother.[1]   *III, v, l. 17*

26 Some men there are love not a gaping pig;
Some, that are mad if they behold a cat.   *IV, i, l. 47*

27 A harmless necessary cat.   *IV, i, l. 55*

28 *Bassanio:* Do all men kill the things they do not love?
Shylock: Hates any man the thing he would not kill?
IV, i, l. 66

29 What! wouldst thou have a serpent sting thee
twice?   *IV, i, l. 69*

30   The weakest kind of fruit
Drops earliest to the ground.   *IV, i, l. 115*

31 To hold opinion with Pythagoras,
That souls of animals infuse themselves
Into the trunks of men.[2]   *IV, i, l. 131*

32   I never knew so young a body with so old a
head.[3]   *IV, i, l. 163*

---

[1]Scylla to port, and on our starboard beam Charybdis, dire gorge of the salt sea tide. — HOMER, *Odyssey, bk. XII, l. 232*
Scylla guards the right side; implacable Charybdis the left. — VIRGIL, *Aeneid, bk. III, l. 420*
Incidis in Scyllam cupiens vitare Charybdim [You fall into Scylla in seeking to avoid Charybdis]. — PHILIPPE GUALTIER [fl. c. 1300], *Alexandreis* [c. 1300], *bk. V, l. 301*

[2]*Clown:* What is the opinion of Pythagoras concerning wild fowl? / *Malvolio:* That the soul of our grandam might haply inhabit a bird. — *Twelfth-Night, act IV, sc. ii, l. 55*

[3]He is young, but take it from me, a very staid head. — THOMAS WENTWORTH, EARL OF STRAFFORD [1593–1641], *Letter commending the Earl of Ormond to Charles I for appointment as councilor*

1 The quality of mercy is not strain'd,
It droppeth as the gentle rain from heaven
Upon the place beneath: it is twice bless'd;
It blesseth him that gives and him that takes:
'Tis mightiest in the mightiest; it becomes
The throned monarch better than his crown;
His scepter shows the force of temporal power,
The attribute to awe and majesty,
Wherein doth sit the dread and fear of kings;
But mercy is above this sceptered sway,
It is enthroned in the hearts of kings,
It is an attribute to God himself,
And earthly power doth then show likest God's
When mercy seasons justice. Therefore, Jew,
Though justice be thy plea, consider this,
That in the course of justice none of us
Should see salvation: we do pray for mercy,
And that same prayer doth teach us all to render
The deeds of mercy.
The Merchant of Venice, IV, i, l. 184

2 To do a great right, do a little wrong.   *IV, i, l. 216*

3 A Daniel come to judgment! yea, a Daniel!
IV, i, l. 223

4 How much more elder art thou than thy looks!
IV, i, l. 251

5 Is it so nominated in the bond?   *IV, i, l. 260*

6 'Tis not in the bond.   *IV, i, l. 263*

7 For herein Fortune shows herself more kind
Than is her custom: it is still her use
To let the wretched man outlive his wealth,
To view with hollow eye and wrinkled brow
An age of poverty.   *IV, i, l. 268*

8   I have a daughter;
Would any of the stock of Barabbas
Had been her husband rather than a Christian!
IV, i, l. 296

9 An upright judge, a learned judge!   *IV, i, l. 324*

10 Now, infidel, I have thee on the hip.   *IV, i, l. 334*

11 A Daniel, still say I; a second Daniel!
I thank thee, Jew, for teaching me that word.
IV, i, l. 341

12 You take my house when you do take the prop
That doth sustain my house; you take my life
When you do take the means whereby I live.
IV, i, l. 376

13 He is well paid that is well satisfied.   *IV, i, l. 416*

14 *Lorenzo:* The moon shines bright: in such a night as
this . . .
Troilus methinks mounted the Troyan walls,
And sigh'd his soul toward the Grecian tents,
Where Cressid lay that night.

Jessica:
In such a night
Did Thisbe fearfully o'ertrip the dew,
And saw the lion's shadow ere himself,
And ran dismay'd away.
Lorenzo:
In such a night
Stood Dido with a willow in her hand
Upon the wild sea-banks, and waft her love
To come again to Carthage.
Jessica:
In such a night
Medea gather'd the enchanted herbs
That did renew old Aeson.   *V, i, l. 1*

15 How sweet the moonlight sleeps upon this bank!
Here we will sit, and let the sounds of music
Creep in our ears: soft stillness and the night
Become the touches of sweet harmony.
Sit, Jessica: look, how the floor of heaven
Is thick inlaid with patines of bright gold:
There's not the smallest orb which thou behold'st
But in his motion like an angel sings,
Still quiring to the young-eyed cherubins.
Such harmony is in immortal souls;
But, whilst this muddy vesture of decay
Doth grossly close it in, we cannot hear it.   *V, i, l. 54*

16 I am never merry when I hear sweet music.
V, i, l. 69

17 The man that hath no music in himself,
Nor is not mov'd with concord of sweet sounds,
Is fit for treasons, stratagems, and spoils;
The motions of his spirit are dull as night,
And his affections dark as Erebus:
Let no such man be trusted.   *V, i, l. 83*

18 How far that little candle throws his beams!
So shines a good deed in a naughty world.   *V, i, l. 90*

19 How many things by season season'd are
To their right praise and true perfection!   *V, i, l. 107*

20 This night methinks is but the daylight sick.
V, i, l. 124

21 A light wife doth make a heavy husband.   *V, i, l. 130*

22 These blessed candles of the night.   *V, i, l. 220*

23   I will make a Star Chamber matter of it.
The Merry Wives of Windsor
[1597; revised 1600–1601], act I, sc. i, l. 2

24   She has brown hair, and speaks small like a
woman.   *I, i, l. 48*

25   Seven hundred pounds and possibilities is goot
gifts.   *I, i, l. 65*

26   I had rather than forty shillings I had my Book of
Songs and Sonnets here.   *I, i, l. 205*

1 "Convey," the wise it call. "Steal"' foh! a fico for the phrase!   *I, iii, l. 30*

2 I am almost out at heels.   *I, iii, l. 32*

3 Thou art the Mars of malcontents.
                                               I, iii, l. 111

4 Here will be an old abusing of God's patience and the king's English.   *I, iv, l. 5*

5 Dispense with trifles.   *II, i, l. 47*

6 Faith, thou hast some crotchets in thy head now.   *II, i, l. 158*

7 Why, then the world's mine oyster,
Which I with sword will open.   *II, ii, l. 2*

8 This is the short and the long of it.
                                               II, ii, l. 62

9 Like a fair house built upon another man's ground.   *II, ii, l. 229*

10 Better three hours too soon than a minute too late.   *II, ii, l. 332*

11 I cannot tell what the dickens his name is.
                                               III, ii, l. 20

12 He capers, he dances, he has eyes of youth, he writes verses, he speaks holiday, he smells April and May.   *III, ii, l. 71*

13 O, what a world of vile ill-favor'd faults
Looks handsome in three hundred pounds a year!
                                               III, iv, l. 32

14 A woman would run through fire and water for such a kind heart.   *III, iv, l. 106*

15 As good luck would have it.[1]   *III, v, l. 86*

16 A man of my kidney.   *III, v, l. 119*

17 [He] curses all Eve's daughters, of what complexion soever.   *IV, ii, l. 24*

18 Wives may be merry, and yet honest too.
                                               IV, ii, l. 110

19 This is the third time; I hope good luck lies in odd numbers.... There is divinity in odd numbers, either in nativity, chance or death.
                                               V, i, l. 2

20 Better a little chiding than a great deal of heart-break.   *V, iii, l. 10*

21   Rumor is a pipe
Blown by surmises, jealousies, conjectures,
And of so easy and so plain a stop
That the blunt monster with uncounted heads,

The still-discordant wavering multitude,
Can play upon it.
       *King Henry IV, Part II [1598],
       induction, l. 15*

22 Even such a man, so faint, so spiritless,
So dull, so dead in look, so woe-begone,
Drew Priam's curtain in the dead of night,
And would have told him half his Troy was burn'd.
                                               act I, sc. i, l. 70

23 Yet the first bringer of unwelcome news
Hath but a losing office, and his tongue
Sounds ever after as a sullen bell,
Remember'd knolling a departing friend.   *I, i, l. 100*

24 I am not only witty in myself, but the cause that wit is in other men.   *I, ii, l. 10*

25 A rascally yea-forsooth knave.   *I, ii, l. 40*

26 You lie in your throat.   *I, ii, l. 97*

27 Your lordship, though not clean past your youth, hath yet some smack of age in you, some relish of the saltness of time.   *I, ii, l. 112*

28 It is the disease of not listening, the malady of not marking, that I am troubled withal.   *I, ii, l. 139*

29 I am as poor as Job, my lord, but not so patient.
                                               I, ii, l. 145

30 We that are in the vaward of our youth.
                                               I, ii, l. 201

31 Have you not a moist eye, a dry hand, a yellow cheek, a white beard, a decreasing leg, an increasing belly?   *I, ii, l. 206*

32 Every part about you blasted with antiquity.
                                               I, ii, l. 210

33 For my voice, I have lost it with hollaing and singing of anthems.   *I, ii, l. 215*

34 It was always yet the trick of our English nation, if they have a good thing, to make it too common.
                                               I, ii, l. 244

35 I were better to be eaten to death with rust than to be scoured to nothing with perpetual motion.
                                               I, ii, l. 249

36 I can get no remedy against this consumption of the purse: borrowing only lingers and lingers it out, but the disease is incurable.   *I, ii, l. 267*

37   Who lin'd himself with hope,
Eating the air on promise of supply.   *I, iii, l. 27*

38 A habitation giddy and unsure
Hath he that buildeth on the vulgar heart. *I, iii, l. 89*

39 Past and to come seem best; things present worst.
                                               I, iii, l. 108

---

[1] As ill luck would have it. — CERVANTES, *Don Quixote, pt. I, bk. I, ch. 2*

1 A poor lone woman.
King Henry IV, Part II, II, i, l. 37

2 Away, you scullion! you rampallian! you fustilarian! I'll tickle your catastrophe. *II, i, l. 67*

3 He hath eaten me out of house and home.
II, i, l. 82

4 Let the end try the man. *II, ii, l. 52*

5 Thus we play the fools with the time, and the spirits of the wise sit in the clouds and mock us.
II, ii, l. 155

6 He was indeed the glass
Wherein the noble youth did dress themselves.
II, iii, l. 21

7 And let the welkin roar. *II, iv, l. 181*

8 Is it not strange that desire should so many years outlive performance? *II, iv, l. 283*

9 O sleep! O gentle sleep![1]
Nature's soft nurse, how have I frighted thee,
That thou no more wilt weigh my eyelids down
And steep my senses in forgetfulness? *III, i, l. 5*

10 With all appliances and means to boot. *III, i, l. 29*

11 Uneasy lies the head that wears a crown.
III, i, l. 31

12 O God! that one might read the book of fate.
III, i, l. 45

13 There is a history in all men's lives. *III, i, l. 80*

14 Death, as the Psalmist saith, is certain to all; all shall die. *III, ii, l. 41*

15 We have heard the chimes at midnight.
III, ii, l. 231

16 A man can die but once; we owe God a death.
III, ii, l. 253

17 We see which way the stream of time doth run
And are enforc'd from our most quiet sphere
By the rough torrent of occasion. *IV, i, l. 70*

18 We ready are to try our fortunes
To the last man. *IV, ii, l. 43*

19 I may justly say with the hook-nosed fellow of Rome, "I came, saw, and overcame." *IV, iii, l. 44*

20 O polish'd perturbation! golden care!
That keep'st the ports of slumber open wide
To many a watchful night! *IV, v, l. 22*

21 See, sons, what things you are!
How quickly nature falls into revolt
When gold becomes her object! *IV, v, l. 63*

22 Thy wish was father, Harry, to that thought!
IV, v, l. 91

23 Before thy hour be ripe. *IV, v, l. 95*

24 Commit
The oldest sins the newest kind of ways. *IV, v, l. 124*

25 His cares are now all ended. *V, ii, l. 3*

26 This is the English, not the Turkish court;
Not Amurath an Amurath succeeds,
But Harry Harry. *V, ii, l. 47*

27 I know thee not, old man: fall to thy prayers;
How ill white hairs become a fool and jester!
V, v, l. 52

28 Master Shallow, I owe you a thousand pound.
V, v, l. 78

29 O! for a Muse of fire, that would ascend
The brightest heaven of invention!
King Henry V [1598–1599], chorus, l. 1

30 Or may we cram
Within this wooden O the very casques
That did affright the air at Agincourt? *chorus, l. 12*

31 Consideration like an angel came,
And whipp'd the offending Adam out of him.
act I, sc. i, l. 28

32 Hear him debate of commonwealth affairs,
You would say it hath been all in all his study.
I, i, l. 41

33 Turn him to any cause of policy,
The Gordian knot of it he will unloose,
Familiar as his garter; that, when he speaks,
The air, a charter'd libertine, is still. *I, i, l. 45*

34 Therefore doth heaven divide
The state of man in divers functions,
Setting endeavor in continual motion;
To which is fixed, as an aim or butt,
Obedience: for so work the honeybees,
Creatures that by a rule in nature teach
The act of order to a peopled kingdom. *I, ii, l. 183*

35 The singing masons building roofs of gold.
I, ii, l. 198

36 Many things, having full reference
To one consent, may work contrariously;
As many arrows, loosed several ways,
Fly to one mark; as many ways meet in one town;
As many fresh streams meet in one salt sea;
As many lines close in the dial's center;
So may a thousand actions, once afoot,
End in one purpose, and be all well borne
Without defeat. *I, ii, l. 205*

37 'Tis ever common
That men are merriest when they are from home.
I, ii, l. 271

---

[1]Sleep, most gentle sleep. — OVID, *Metamorphoses, bk. II, l. 624*

1 Now all the youth of England are on fire,
And silken dalliance in the wardrobe lies.
II, chorus, l. 1

2 O England! model to thy inward greatness,
Like little body with a mighty heart,
What mightst thou do, that honor would thee do,
Were all thy children kind and natural!
II, chorus, l. 16

3 That's the humor of it.   *II, i, l. 63*

4   He's [Falstaff's] in Arthur's bosom, if ever man
went to Arthur's bosom. A' made a finer end and
went away an it had been any christom child; a' parted
even just between twelve and one, even at the turning
o' the tide: for after I saw him fumble with the sheets
and play with flowers and smile upon his fingers'
ends, I knew there was but one way; for his nose was
as sharp as a pen, and a' babbled of green fields.
II, iii, l. 11

5   As cold as any stone.   *II, iii, l. 26*

6 Trust none;
For oaths are straws, men's faiths are wafer-cakes,
And hold-fast is the only dog, my duck.   *II, iii, l. 53*

7 Once more unto the breach, dear friends, once more;
Or close the wall up with our English dead!
In peace there's nothing so becomes a man
As modest stillness and humility:
But when the blast of war blows in our ears,
Then imitate the action of the tiger;
Stiffen the sinews, summon up the blood,
Disguise fair nature with hard-favor'd rage;
Then lend the eye a terrible aspect.   *III, i, l. 1*

8 And sheath'd their swords for lack of argument.
III, i, l. 21

9 I see you stand like greyhounds in the slips,
Straining upon the start. The game's afoot:
Follow your spirit; and, upon this charge
Cry "God for Harry! England and Saint George!"
III, i, l. 31

10   I would give all my fame for a pot of ale, and
safety.   *III, ii, l. 14*

11   Men of few words are the best men.   *III, ii, l. 40*

12   He will maintain his argument as well as any military man in the world.   *III, ii, l. 89*

13   I know the disciplines of wars.   *III, ii, l. 156*

14 I thought upon one pair of English legs
Did march three Frenchmen.   *III, vi, l. 161*

15 We are in God's hand.   *III, vi, l. 181*

16   That island of England breeds very valiant creatures: their mastiffs are of unmatchable courage.
III, vii, l. 155

17   Give them great meals of beef and iron and steel,
they will eat like wolves and fight like devils.
III, vii, l. 166

18 The hum of either army stilly sounds,
That the fix'd sentinels almost receive
The secret whispers of each other's watch:
Fire answers fire, and through their paly flames
Each battle sees the other's umber'd face:
Steed threatens steed, in high and boastful neighs
Piercing the night's dull ear; and from the tents
The armorers, accomplishing the knights,
With busy hammers closing rivets up,
Give dreadful note of preparation.   *IV, chorus, l. 5*

19 A little touch of Harry in the night.   *IV, chorus, l. 47*

20 There is some soul of goodness in things evil,
Would men observingly distill it out.   *IV, i, l. 4*

21   Every subject's duty is the king's; but every subject's soul is his own.   *IV, i, l. 189*

22   What infinite heart's ease
Must kings neglect that private men enjoy!
And what have kings that privates have not too,
Save ceremony, save general ceremony?
And what art thou, thou idol[1] ceremony?
What kind of god art thou, that suffer'st more
Of mortal griefs than do thy worshippers?
What are thy rents? what are thy comings-in?
O ceremony! show me but thy worth.   *IV, i, l. 256*

23 'Tis not the balm, the scepter and the ball,
The sword, the mace, the crown imperial,
The intertissued robe of gold and pearl,
The farced title running 'fore the king,
The throne he sits on, nor the tide of pomp
That beats upon the high shore of this world,
No, not all these, thrice-gorgeous ceremony,
Not all these, laid in bed majestical,
Can sleep so soundly as the wretched slave,
Who with a body fill'd and vacant mind
Gets him to rest, cramm'd with distressful bread.
IV, i, l. 280

24 O God of battles! steel my soldiers' hearts;
Possess them not with fear; take from them now
The sense of reckoning, if the opposed numbers
Pluck their hearts from them.   *IV, i, l. 309*

25 But if it be a sin to covet honor,
I am the most offending soul alive.   *IV, iii, l. 28*

26 This day is call'd the feast of Crispian:
He that outlives this day, and comes safe home,
Will stand a tip-toe when this day is nam'd.
And rouse him at the name of Crispian.
IV, iii, l. 40

---

[1]Sometimes rendered: idle.

1 We few, we happy few, we band of brothers;
For he today that sheds his blood with me
Shall be my brother.   *King Henry V, IV, iii, l. 60*

2   The saying is true, "The empty vessel makes the greatest sound."   *IV, iv, l. 72*

3   There is occasions and causes why and wherefore in all things.   *V, i, l. 3*

4   By this leek, I will most horribly revenge. I eat and eat, I swear.   *V, i, l. 49*

5   All hell shall stir for this.   *V, i, l. 72*

6   The naked, poor, and mangled Peace,
Dear nurse of arts, plenties, and joyful births.
              V, ii, l. 34

7   Grow like savages — as soldiers will,
That nothing do but meditate on blood.   *V, ii, l. 59*

8   For these fellows of infinite tongue, that can rime themselves into ladies' favors, they do always reason themselves out again.   *V, ii, l. 162*

9   My comfort is, that old age, that ill layer-up of beauty, can do no more spoil upon my face.
              V, ii, l. 246

10   O Kate! nice customs curtsy to great kings.
              V, ii, l. 291

11   He hath indeed better bettered expectation than you must expect of me to tell you how.
     *Much Ado About Nothing [1598–1600],
     act I, sc. i, l. 15*

12   How much better is it to weep at joy than to joy at weeping!   *I, i, l. 28*

13   A very valiant trencher-man.   *I, i, l. 52*

14   There's a skirmish of wit between them.
              I, i, l. 64

15   He wears his faith but as the fashion of his hat.
              I, i, l. 76

16   I see, lady, the gentleman is not in your books.
              I, i, l. 79

17   What! my dear Lady Disdain, are you yet living?
              I, i, l. 123

18   Shall I never see a bachelor of threescore again?
              I, i, l. 209

19   In time the savage bull doth bear the yoke.
              I, i, l. 271

20   Benedick the married man.   *I, i, l. 278*

21   I could not endure a husband with a beard on his face: I had rather lie in the woollen.   *II, i, l. 31*

22   As merry as the day is long.   *II, i, l. 52*

23   Would it not grieve a woman to be over-mastered with a piece of valiant dust? to make an account of her life to a clod of wayward marl?   *II, i, l. 64*

24   I have a good eye, uncle: I can see a church by daylight.   *II, i, l. 86*

25   Speak low, if you speak love.   *II, i, l. 104*

26 Friendship is constant in all other things
Save in the office and affairs of love:
Therefore all hearts in love use their own tongues;
Let every eye negotiate for itself
And trust no agent.   *II, i, l. 184*

27   She speaks poniards, and every word stabs: if her breath were as terrible as her terminations, there were no living near her; she would infect to the north star.   *II, i, l. 257*

28   Silence is the perfectest herald of joy: I were but little happy, if I could say how much.   *II, i, l. 319*

29   It keeps on the windy side of care.[1]   *II, i, l. 328*

30   There was a star danced, and under that was I born.   *II, i, l. 351*

31   I will tell you my drift.[2]   *II, i, l. 406*

32   He was wont to speak plain and to the purpose.
              II, iii, l. 19

33 Sigh no more, ladies, sigh no more.
Men were deceivers ever;
One foot in sea, and one on shore,
To one thing constant never.   *II, iii, l. 65*

34   Sits the wind in that corner?   *II, iii, l. 108*

35   Bait the hook well: this fish will bite.
              II, iii, l. 121

36   Shall quips and sentences and these paper bullets of the brain awe a man from the career of his humor? No; the world must be peopled. When I said I would die a bachelor, I did not think I should live till I were married.   *II, iii, l. 260*

37   From the crown of his head to the sole of his foot, he is all mirth.   *III, ii, l. 9*

38   He hath a heart as sound as a bell, and his tongue is the clapper; for what his heart thinks his tongue speaks.   *III, ii, l. 12*

39   Everyone can master a grief but he that has it.
              III, ii, l. 28

40   Are you good men and true?   *III, iii, l. 1*

41   To be a well-favored man is the gift of fortune; but to write and read comes by nature.   *III, iii, l. 14*

---

[1] The windy side of the law. — *Twelfth-Night, act III, sc. iv, l. 183*
[2] We know your drift. — *Coriolanus, act III, sc. iii, l. 114*

1   If they make you not then the better answer, you may say they are not the men you took them for.
III, iii, l. 49

2   The fashion wears out more apparel than the man.   *III, iii, l. 147*

3   A good old man, sir; he will be talking: as they say, When the age is in, the wit is out.   *III, v, l. 36*

4   Of what men dare do! what men may do! what men daily do, not knowing what they do! *IV, i, l. 19*

5 O! what authority and show of truth
Can cunning sin cover itself withal.   *IV, i, l. 35*

6   For it so falls out
That what we have we prize not to the worth
Whiles we enjoy it, but being lack'd and lost,
Why, then we rack the value, then we find
The virtue that possession would not show us
Whiles it was ours.   *IV, i, l. 219*

7   Masters, it is proved already that you are little better than false knaves, and it will go near to be thought so shortly.   *IV, ii, l. 23*

8   Flat burglary as ever was committed. *IV, ii, l. 54*

9   Thou wilt be condemned into everlasting redemption for this.   *IV, ii, l. 60*

10   O that he were here to write me down an ass!
IV, ii, l. 80

11 Patch griefs with proverbs.   *V, i, l. 17*

12 Charm ache with air and agony with words.
V, i, l. 26

13 For there was never yet philosopher
That could endure the toothache patiently. *V, i, l. 35*

14 Some of us will smart for it.   *V, i, l. 108*

15   What though care killed a cat,[1] thou hast mettle enough in thee to kill care.   *V, i, l. 135*

16   I was not born under a riming planet. *V, ii, l. 40*

17   The trumpet of his own virtues.   *V, ii, l. 91*

18 Done to death by slanderous tongues.   *V, iii, l. 3*

19   A surgeon to old shoes.
Julius Caesar [1599], act I, sc. i, l. 26

20   As proper men as ever trod upon neat's leather.
I, i, l. 27

21 Have you not made a universal shout,
That Tiber trembled underneath her banks,

To hear the replication of your sounds
Made in her concave shores?   *I, i, l. 48*

22 Beware the ides of March.   *I, ii, l. 18*

23 Set honor in one eye and death i' the other,
And I will look on both indifferently.   *I, ii, l. 86*

24 Well, honor is the subject of my story.
I cannot tell what you and other men
Think of this life; but, for my single self,
I had as lief not be as live to be
In awe of such a thing as I myself.   *I, ii, l. 92*

25 Stemming it with hearts of controversy. *I, ii, l. 109*

26 Why, man, he doth bestride the narrow world
Like a Colossus; and we petty men
Walk under his huge legs, and peep about
To find ourselves dishonorable graves.
Men at some time are masters of their fates:
The fault, dear Brutus, is not in our stars,
But in ourselves, that we are underlings. *I, ii, l. 134*

27 Upon what meat doth this our Caesar feed,
That he is grown so great?   *I, ii, l. 148*

28 Let me have men about me that are fat;
Sleek-headed men and such as sleep o' nights.
Yond Cassius has a lean and hungry look;
He thinks too much: such men are dangerous.
I, ii, l. 191

29   He reads much;
He is a great observer, and he looks
Quite through the deeds of men.   *I, ii, l. 200*

30 Seldom he smiles, and smiles in such a sort
As if he mock'd himself, and scorn'd his spirit
That could be mov'd to smile at anything.
I, ii, l. 204

31 But, for my own part, it was Greek to me.[2]
I, ii, l. 288

32   Yesterday the bird of night did sit,
Even at noonday, upon the marketplace,
Hooting and shrieking.   *I, iii, l. 26*

33 So every bondman in his own hand bears
The power to cancel his captivity.   *I, iii, l. 101*

34 O! he sits high in all the people's hearts:
And that which would appear offense in us,
His countenance, like richest alchemy,
Will change to virtue and to worthiness. *I, iii, l. 157*

35 The abuse of greatness is when it disjoins
Remorse from power.   *II, i, l. 18*

36   'Tis a common proof,
That lowliness is young ambition's ladder,

---

[1]Let care kill a cat, / We'll laugh and grow fat. — *Shirburn Ballads* [1585], *no. 91*

Hang sorrow, care'll kill a cat. — BEN JONSON, *Every Man in His Humour, act I, sc. i*

---

[2]This geare is Greeke to me. — GEORGE GASCOIGNE [c. 1525–1577], *Supposes* [1566], *act I, sc. i*

Whereto the climber-upward turns his face;
But when he once attains the upmost round,
He then unto the ladder turns his back,
Looks in the clouds, scorning the base degrees
By which he did ascend.

Julius Caesar, II, i, l. 21

1 Therefore think him as a serpent's egg
Which, hatch'd, would, as his kind, grow
    mischievous,
And kill him in the shell.   *II, i, l. 32*

2 Between the acting of a dreadful thing
And the first motion, all the interim is
Like a phantasma, or a hideous dream:
The genius and the mortal instruments
Are then in council; and the state of man,
Like to a little kingdom, suffers then
The nature of an insurrection.   *II, i, l. 63*

3   O conspiracy!
Sham'st thou to show thy dangerous brow by night,
When evils are most free?   *II, i, l. 77*

4 Let's carve him as a dish fit for the gods,
Not hew him as a carcass fit for hounds.   *II, i, l. 173*

5 But when I tell him he hates flatterers,
He says he does, being then most flattered.

II, i, l. 207

6 Enjoy the honey-heavy dew of slumber.   *II, i, l. 230*

7   Dwell I but in the suburbs
Of your good pleasure?   *II, i, l. 285*

8 You are my true and honorable wife,
As dear to me as are the ruddy drops
That visit my sad heart.   *II, i, l. 288*

9 Think you I am no stronger than my sex,
Being so father'd and so husbanded?   *II, i, l. 296*

10 When beggars die there are no comets seen;
The heavens themselves blaze forth the death of
    princes.   *II, ii, l. 30*

11 Cowards die many times before their deaths;
The valiant never taste of death but once.
Of all the wonders that I yet have heard,
It seems to me most strange that men should fear;
Seeing that death, a necessary end,
Will come when it will come.   *II, ii, l. 32*

12 Antony, that revels long o' nights.   *II, ii, l. 116*

13 How hard it is for women to keep counsel!

II, iv, l. 9

14 But I am constant as the northern star,
Of whose true-fix'd and resting quality
There is no fellow in the firmament.   *III, i, l. 60*

15 Speak, hands, for me!   *III, i, l. 76*

16 Et tu, Brute?   *III, i, l. 77*

17 Some to the common pulpits, and cry out,
"Liberty, freedom, and enfranchisement!"

III, i, l. 79

18   How many ages hence
Shall this our lofty scene be acted o'er,
In states unborn and accents yet unknown!

III, i, l. 111

19 O mighty Caesar! dost thou lie so low?
Are all thy conquests, glories, triumphs, spoils,
Shrunk to this little measure?   *III, i, l. 148*

20 The choice and master spirits of this age.

III, i, l. 163

21 Though last, not least in love.   *III, i, l. 189*

22 O! pardon me, thou bleeding piece of earth,
That I am meek and gentle with these butchers;
Thou art the ruins of the noblest man
That ever lived in the tide of times.   *III, i, l. 254*

23 Cry "Havoc!" and let slip the dogs of war.

III, i, l. 273

24   Romans, countrymen, and lovers! hear me for my
cause; and be silent, that you may hear.   *III, ii, l. 13*

25   Not that I loved Caesar less, but that I loved
Rome more.   *III, ii, l. 22*

26   As he was valiant, I honor him; but, as he was
ambitious, I slew him.   *III, ii, l. 27*

27   If any, speak; for him have I offended. I pause for a
reply.   *III, ii, l. 36*

28 Friends, Romans, countrymen, lend me your ears;
I come to bury Caesar, not to praise him.
The evil that men do lives after them,
The good is oft interred with their bones.

III, ii, l. 79

29 For Brutus is an honorable man;
So are they all, all honorable men.   *III, ii, l. 88*

30 When that the poor have cried, Caesar hath wept;
Ambition should be made of sterner stuff.   *III, ii, l. 97*

31 O judgment! thou art fled to brutish beasts,
And men have lost their reason.   *III, ii, l. 110*

32 But yesterday the word of Caesar might
Have stood against the world; now lies he there,
And none so poor to do him reverence.

III, ii, l. 124

33 If you have tears, prepare to shed them now.

III, ii, l. 174

34 See what a rent the envious Casca made.   *III, ii, l. 180*

35 This was the most unkindest cut of all.   *III, ii, l. 188*

1   Great Caesar fell.
O! what a fall was there, my countrymen;
Then I, and you, and all of us fell down,
Whilst bloody treason flourish'd over us.
III, ii, l. 194

2 What private griefs they have, alas! I know not.
III, ii, l. 217

3 I come not, friends, to steal away your hearts:
I am no orator, as Brutus is;
But, as you know me all, a plain blunt man.
III, ii, l. 220

4 For I have neither wit, nor words, nor worth,
Action, nor utterance, nor the power of speech,
To stir men's blood: I only speak right on.
III, ii, l. 225

5   Put a tongue
In every wound of Caesar, that should move
The stones of Rome to rise and mutiny.
III, ii, l. 232

6 When love begins to sicken and decay,
It useth an enforced ceremony.
There are no tricks in plain and simple faith.
IV, ii, l. 20

7 An itching palm.   *IV, iii, l. 10*

8 I had rather be a dog, and bay the moon,
Than such a Roman.   *IV, iii, l. 27*

9 I'll use you for my mirth, yea, for my laughter,
When you are waspish.   *IV, iii, l. 49*

10 There is no terror, Cassius, in your threats;
For I am arm'd so strong in honesty
That they pass by me as the idle wind,
Which I respect not.   *IV, iii, l. 66*

11 A friend should bear his friend's infirmities,
But Brutus makes mine greater than they are.
IV, iii, l. 85

12   All his faults observ'd,
Set in a notebook, learn'd, and conn'd by rote.
IV, iii, l. 96

13 There is a tide in the affairs of men,
Which, taken at the flood, leads on to fortune;
Omitted, all the voyage of their life
Is bound in shallows and in miseries.
IV, iii, l. 217

14 We must take the current when it serves,
Or lose our ventures.   *IV, iii, l. 222*

15 The deep of night is crept upon our talk,
And nature must obey necessity.   *IV, iii, l. 225*

16 But for your words, they rob the Hybla bees,
And leave them honeyless.   *V, i, l. 34*

17 Forever, and forever, farewell, Cassius!
If we do meet again, why, we shall smile;
If not, why then, this parting was well made.
V, i, l. 117

18   O! that a man might know
The end of this day's business, ere it come.
V, i, l. 123

19 O Julius Caesar! thou art mighty yet!
Thy spirit walks abroad, and turns our swords
In our own proper entrails.   *V, iii, l. 94*

20 The last of all the Romans, fare thee well!
V, iii, l. 99

21 This was the noblest Roman of them all.   *V, v, l. 68*

22 His life was gentle, and the elements
So mix'd in him that Nature might stand up
And say to all the world, "This was a man!"
V, v, l. 73

23   What's the new news at the new court?
As You Like It [1599–1600], act I, sc. i, l. 103

24   Fleet the time carelessly, as they did in the golden
world.   *I, i, l. 126*

25   Always the dullness of the fool is the whetstone of
the wits.   *I, ii, l. 59*

26   The little foolery that wise men have makes a great
show.   *I, ii, l. 97*

27   Well said: that was laid on with a trowel.
I, ii, l. 113

28   Your heart's desires be with you!   *I, ii, l. 214*

29 One out of suits with fortune.   *I, ii, l. 263*

30 My pride fell with my fortunes.   *I, ii, l. 269*

31 Hereafter, in a better world than this,
I shall desire more love and knowledge of you.
I, ii, l. 301

32 Heavenly Rosalind!   *I, ii, l. 306*

33   O, how full of briers is this working-day world!
I, iii, l. 12

34 Beauty provoketh thieves sooner than gold.
I, iii, l. 113

35 We'll have a swashing and a martial outside,
As many other mannish cowards have.   *I, iii, l. 123*

36 Hath not old custom made this life more sweet
Than that of painted pomp? Are not these woods
More free from peril than the envious court?
II, i, l. 2

37 Sweet are the uses of adversity,
Which, like the toad, ugly and venomous,
Wears yet a precious jewel in his head;

And this our life exempt from public haunt,
Finds tongues in trees, books in the running brooks,
Sermons in stones, and good in everything.
As You Like It, II, i, l. 12

1   The big round tears
Cours'd one another down his innocent nose
In piteous chase.   *II, i, l. 38*

2 Sweep on, you fat and greasy citizens.   *II, i, l. 55*

3   And He that doth the ravens feed,
Yea, providently caters for the sparrow,
Be comfort to my age!   *II, iii, l. 43*

4 Though I look old, yet I am strong and lusty;
For in my youth I never did apply
Hot and rebellious liquors in my blood.
II, iii, l. 47

5 Therefore my age is as a lusty winter,
Frosty, but kindly.   *II, iii, l. 52*

6 Thou art not for the fashion of these times,
Where none will sweat but for promotion.
II, iii, l. 59

7   Ay, now am I in Arden; the more fool I: when I
was at home, I was in a better place: but travelers
must be content.   *II, iv, l. 16*

8 If you remember'st not the slightest folly
That ever love did make thee run into,
Thou hast not lov'd.   *II, iv, l. 34*

9   We that are true lovers run into strange capers.
II, iv, l. 53

10   I shall ne'er be ware of mine own wit, till I break
my shins against it.   *II, iv, l. 59*

11 Under the greenwood tree
Who loves to lie with me,
And turn his merry note
Unto the sweet bird's throat,
Come hither, come hither, come hither:
Here shall he see
No enemy
But winter and rough weather.   *II, v, l. 1*

12   I can suck melancholy out of a song as a weasel
sucks eggs.   *II, v, l. 12*

13 Who doth ambition shun,
And loves to live i' the sun,
Seeking the food he eats,
And pleas'd with what he gets.   *II, v, l. 38*

14   I met a fool i' the forest,
A motley fool.   *II, vii, l. 12*

15 And then he drew a dial from his poke,
And, looking on it with lack-luster eye,
Says very wisely, "It is ten o'clock;

Thus may we see," quoth he, "how the world
wags."[1]   *II, vii, l. 20*

16 And so, from hour to hour we ripe and ripe,
And then from hour to hour we rot and rot,
And thereby hangs a tale.   *II, vii, l. 26*

17 My lungs began to crow like chanticleer,
That fools should be so deep-contemplative,
And I did laugh sans intermission
An hour by his dial.   *II, vii, l. 30*

18 Motley's the only wear.   *II, vii, l. 34*

19   If ladies be but young and fair,
They have the gift to know it.   *II, vii, l. 37*

20   I must have liberty
Withal, as large a charter as the wind,
To blow on whom I please.   *II, vii, l. 47*

21 The "why" is plain as way to parish church.
II, vii, l. 52

22   But whate'er you are
That in this desert inaccessible,
Under the shade of melancholy boughs,
Lose and neglect the creeping hours of time;
If ever you have look'd on better days,
If ever been where bells have knoll'd to church,
If ever sat at any good man's feast,
If ever from your eyelids wip'd a tear,
And know what 'tis to pity, and be pitied,
Let gentleness my strong enforcement be.
II, vii, l. 109

23 True is it that we have seen better days.   *II, vii, l. 120*

24 Oppress'd with two weak evils, age and hunger.
II, vii, l. 132

25   All the world's a stage,[2]
And all the men and women merely players:
They have their exits and their entrances;
And one man in his time plays many parts,
His acts being seven ages. At first the infant,
Mewling and puking in the nurse's arms.
And then the whining school-boy, with his satchel,
And shining morning face, creeping like snail
Unwillingly to school. And then the lover,
Sighing like furnace, with a woful ballad
Made to his mistress' eyebrow. Then a soldier,
Full of strange oaths, and bearded like the pard,
Jealous in honor, sudden and quick in quarrel,
Seeking the bubble reputation
Even in the cannon's mouth. And then the justice,

---

[1] So wags the world. — WALTER SCOTT, *Ivanhoe*, *ch. 37*

[2] The world's a theater, the earth a stage, / Which God and Nature
do with actors fill. — THOMAS HEYWOOD, *Apology for Actors* [1612]
The world's a stage on which all the parts are played. — THOMAS
MIDDLETON, *A Game of Chess* [1624], *act V, sc. i*

In fair round belly with good capon lin'd,
With eyes severe, and beard of formal cut,
Full of wise saws and modern instances;
And so he plays his part. The sixth age shifts
Into the lean and slipper'd pantaloon,
With spectacles on nose and pouch on side,
His youthful hose well sav'd, a world too wide
For his shrunk shank; and his big manly voice,
Turning again toward childish treble, pipes
And whistles in his sound. Last scene of all,
That ends this strange eventful history,
Is second childishness and mere oblivion,
Sans teeth, sans eyes, sans taste, sans everything.

II, vii, l. 139

1 Blow, blow, thou winter wind,
Thou art not so unkind
As man's ingratitude. *II, vii, l. 174*

2 These trees shall be my books. *III, ii, l. 5*

3 The fair, the chaste, and unexpressive she.

III, ii, l. 10

4 It goes much against my stomach. Hast any philosophy in thee, shepherd? *III, ii, l. 21*

5 He that wants money, means, and content, is without three good friends. *III, ii, l. 25*

6 I am a true laborer: I earn that I eat, get that I wear, owe no man hate, envy no man's happiness, glad of other men's good, content with my harm.

III, ii, l. 78

7 From the east to western Ind,
No jewel is like Rosalind. *III, ii, l. 94*

8 This is the very false gallop of verses.

III, ii, l. 120

9 Let us make an honorable retreat; though not with bag and baggage, yet with scrip and scrippage.

III, ii, l. 170

10 O, wonderful, wonderful, and most wonderful, wonderful! and yet again wonderful! and after that, out of all whooping. *III, ii, l. 202*

11 Answer me in one word. *III, ii, l. 238*

12 Do you not know I am a woman? when I think, I must speak. *III, ii, l. 265*

13 I do desire we may be better strangers.

III, ii, l. 276

14 *Jaques:* What stature is she of?
Orlando: Just as high as my heart. *III, ii, l. 286*

15 Time travels in divers paces with divers persons. I'll tell you who Time ambles withal, who Time trots withal, who Time gallops withal, and who he stands still withal. *III, ii, l. 328*

16 Every one fault seeming monstrous till his fellow fault came to match it. *III, ii, l. 377*

17 Everything about you demonstrating a careless desolation. *III, ii, l. 405*

18 Truly, I would the gods had made thee poetical.

III, iii, l. 16

19 The wounds invisible
That love's keen arrows make. *III, v, l. 30*

20 Down on your knees,
And thank heaven, fasting, for a good man's love.

III, v, l. 57

21 Sell when you can, you are not for all markets.

III, v, l. 60

22 I am falser than vows made in wine. *III, v, l. 73*

23 It is a melancholy of mine own, compounded of many simples, extracted from many objects, and indeed the sundry contemplation of my travels, which, by often rumination, wraps me in a most humorous sadness. *IV, i, l. 16*

24 I had rather have a fool to make me merry than experience to make me sad. *IV, i, l. 28*

25 Farewell, Monsieur Traveler: look you lisp, and wear strange suits, disable all the benefits of your own country, be out of love with your nativity, and almost chide God for making you that countenance you are; or I will scarce think you have swam in a gondola.

IV, i, l. 35

26 I'll warrant him heart-whole. *IV, i, l. 51*

27 Men have died from time to time, and worms have eaten them, but not for love. *IV, i, l. 110*

28 Forever and a day. *IV, i, l. 151*

29 Men are April when they woo, December when they wed: maids are May when they are maids, but the sky changes when they are wives. *IV, i, l. 153*

30 My affection hath an unknown bottom, like the bay of Portugal. *IV, i, l. 219*

31 The horn, the horn, the lusty horn
Is not a thing to laugh to scorn. *IV, ii, l. 17*

32 Chewing the food of sweet and bitter fancy.

IV, iii, l. 103

33 "So so," is good, very good, very excellent good: and yet it is not; it is but so so. *V, i, l. 30*

34 The fool doth think he is wise, but the wise man knows himself to be a fool. *V, i, l. 35*

35 No sooner met, but they looked; no sooner looked but they loved; no sooner loved but they

sighed; no sooner sighed but they asked one another the reason; no sooner knew the reason but they sought the remedy.   *As You Like It, V, ii, l. 37*

1   But, O! how bitter a thing it is to look into happiness through another man's eyes!   *V, ii, l. 48*

2 It was a lover and his lass,
With a hey, and a ho, and a hey nonino,
That o'er the green corn-field did pass,
In the spring time, the only pretty ring time,
When birds do sing, hey ding a ding, ding;
Sweet lovers love the spring.   *V, iii, l. 18*

3   Here comes a pair of very strange beasts, which in all tongues are called fools.   *V, iv, l. 36*

4   An ill-favored thing, sir, but mine own.[1]   *V, iv, l. 60*

5   Rich honesty dwells like a miser, sir, in a poor house, as your pearl in your foul oyster.   *V, iv, l. 62*

6   "The retort courteous" . . . "the quip modest." . . . "the reply churlish." . . . "the reproof valiant . . . "the countercheck quarrelsome." . . . "the lie circumstantial," and "the lie direct."   *V, iv, l. 75*

7   Your "if" is the only peacemaker; much virtue in "if."   *V, iv, l. 108*

8   He uses his folly like a stalking horse, and under the presentation of that he shoots his wit.   *V, iv, l. 112*

9 For this relief much thanks; 'tis bitter cold,
And I am sick at heart.
        Hamlet [1600–1601], act I, sc. i, l. 8

10 Not a mouse stirring.   *I, i, l. 10*

11 Thou art a scholar; speak to it, Horatio.   *I, i, l. 42*

12 But in the gross and scope of my opinion,
This bodes some strange eruption to our state.
        I, i, l. 68

13   Whose sore task
Does not divide the Sunday from the week.
        I, i, l. 75

14   This sweaty haste
Doth make the night joint-laborer with the day.
        I, i, l. 77

15 In the most high and palmy state of Rome,
A little ere the mightiest Julius fell,
The graves stood tenantless and the sheeted dead
Did squeak and gibber in the Roman streets.
        I, i, l. 113

16 And then it started like a guilty thing
Upon a fearful summons.   *I, i, l. 148*

17 The cock, that is the trumpet to the morn.
        I, i, l. 150

18 Whether in sea or fire, in earth or air,
The extravagant and erring spirit hies
To his confine.   *I, i, l. 153*

19 It faded on the crowing of the cock.
Some say that ever 'gainst that season comes
Wherein our Savior's birth is celebrated,
The bird of dawning singeth all night long;
And then, they say, no spirit can walk abroad;
The nights are wholesome; then no planets strike,
No fairy takes, nor witch hath power to charm,
So hallow'd and so gracious is the time.   *I, i, l. 157*

20 But, look, the morn in russet mantle clad,
Walks o'er the dew of yon high eastern hill.   *I, i, l. 166*

21 The memory be green.   *I, ii, l. 2*

22 With one auspicious and one dropping eye,
With mirth in funeral and with dirge in marriage,
In equal scale weighing delight and dole.   *I, ii, l. 11*

23 So much for him.   *I, ii, l. 25*

24 A little more than kin, and less than kind.   *I, ii, l. 65*

25 Thou know'st 'tis common; all that live must die,
Passing through nature to eternity.   *I, ii, l. 72*

26 Seems, madam! Nay, it is; I know not "seems."
'Tis not alone my inky cloak, good mother,
Nor customary suits of solemn black.   *I, ii, l. 76*

27 But I have that within which passeth show;
These but the trappings and the suits of woe.
        I, ii, l. 85

28   To persever
In obstinate condolement is a course
Of impious stubbornness; 'tis unmanly grief:
It shows a will most incorrect to heaven,
A heart unfortified, a mind impatient.   *I, ii, l. 92*

29 O! that this too too solid[2] flesh would melt,
Thaw and resolve itself into a dew;
Or that the Everlasting had not fix'd
His canon 'gainst self-slaughter! O God! O God!
How weary, stale, flat, and unprofitable
Seem to me all the uses of this world.   *I, ii, l. 129*

30   Things rank and gross in nature
Possess it merely. That it should come to this!
        I, ii, l. 136

31 So excellent a king; that was, to this,
Hyperion to a satyr; so loving to my mother
That he might not beteem the winds of heaven
Visit her face too roughly.   *I, ii, l. 139*

---

[1]"A poor thing but mine own" is the popular version.

[2]Alternative readings are "sallied" and "sullied."

1
    Why, she would hang on him,
As if increase of appetite had grown
By what it fed on.   *I, ii, l. 143*

2 Frailty, thy name is woman!   *I, ii, l. 146*

3 Like Niobe, all tears.   *I, ii, l. 149*

4 A beast, that wants discourse of reason.   *I, ii, l. 150*

5 It is not nor it cannot come to good.   *I, ii, l. 158*

6 A truant disposition.   *I, ii, l. 169*

7 Thrift, thrift, Horatio! the funeral bak'd meats
Did coldly furnish forth the marriage tables.
Would I had met my dearest foe in heaven
Ere I had ever seen that day.   *I, ii, l. 180*

8 In my mind's eye, Horatio.   *I, ii, l. 185*

9 He was a man, take him for all in all,
I shall not look upon his like again.   *I, ii, l. 187*

10 Season your admiration for a while.   *I, ii, l. 192*

11 In the dead vast and middle of the night.   *I, ii, l. 198*

12 Armed at points exactly, cap-a-pe.   *I, ii, l. 200*

13
    Distill'd
Almost to jelly with the act of fear.   *I, ii, l. 204*

14 A countenance more in sorrow than in anger.   *I, ii, l. 231*

15 *Hamlet:*   His beard was grizzled, no?
Horatio: It was, as I have seen it in his life,
A sable silver'd.   *I, ii, l. 239*

16 Give it an understanding, but no tongue.   *I, ii, l. 249*

17
    All is not well;
I doubt some foul play.   *I, ii, l. 254*

18
    Foul deeds will rise,
Though all the earth o'erwhelm them, to men's
    eyes.   *I, ii, l. 256*

19 The chariest maid is prodigal enough
If she unmask her beauty to the moon;
Virtue itself 'scapes not calumnious strokes;
The canker galls the infants of the spring
Too oft before their buttons be disclos'd,
And in the morn and liquid dew of youth
Contagious blastments are most imminent.
   I, iii, l. 36

20 Do not, as some ungracious pastors do,
Show me the steep and thorny way to heaven,
Whiles, like a puff'd and reckless libertine,
Himself the primrose path of dalliance treads,
And recks not his own rede.[1]   *I, iii, l. 47*

21 Give thy thoughts no tongue.   *I, iii, l. 59*

22 Be thou familiar, but by no means vulgar;
Those friends thou hast, and their adoption tried,
Grapple them to thy soul with hoops of steel.
   I, iii, l. 61

23
    Beware
Of entrance to a quarrel, but, being in,
Bear 't that th' opposed may beware of thee.
Give every man thy ear, but few thy voice;
Take each man's censure, but reserve thy judgment.
Costly thy habit as thy purse can buy,
But not express'd in fancy; rich, not gaudy;
For the apparel oft proclaims the man.   *I, iii, l. 65*

24 Neither a borrower, nor a lender be;
For loan oft loses both itself and friend,
And borrowing dulls the edge of husbandry.
This above all: to thine own self be true,
And it must follow, as the night the day,
Thou canst not then be false to any man.
   I, iii, l. 75

25
    'Tis in my memory lock'd,
And you yourself shall keep the key of it.   *I, iii, l. 85*

26
    You speak like a green girl,
Unsifted in such perilous circumstance.   *I, iii, l. 101*

27 Springes to catch woodcocks.   *I, iii, l. 115*

28 When the blood burns, how prodigal the soul
Lends the tongue vows.   *I, iii, l. 116*

29 Be somewhat scanter of your maiden presence.
   I, iii, l. 121

30 The air bites shrewdly.   *I, iv, l. 1*

31 But to my mind, — though I am native here
And to the manner born — it is a custom
More honor'd in the breach than the observance.
   I, iv, l. 14

32 Angels and ministers of grace defend us!   *I, iv, l. 39*

33 Be thy intents wicked or charitable,
Thou com'st in such a questionable shape
That I will speak to thee.   *I, iv, l. 42*

34
    What may this mean,
That thou, dead corse, again in complete steel
Revisit'st thus the glimpses of the moon,
Making night hideous;[2] and we fools of nature
So horridly to shake our disposition
With thoughts beyond the reaches of our souls?
   I, iv, l. 51

35 I do not set my life at a pin's fee.   *I, iv, l. 65*

---

[1]Wel oghte a preest ensample for to yive. / By his clennesse, how that his sheep shold live. — CHAUCER, *The Canterbury Tales, The Prologue, l. 504*

And may ye better reck the rede, / Than ever did th' adviser. — ROBERT BURNS, *Epistle to a Young Friend*

---

[2]And makes night hideous. — ALEXANDER POPE, *The Dunciad, bk. III, l. 166*

1   The dreadful summit of the cliff
That beetles o'er his base into the sea.

Hamlet, I, iv, l. 70

2   My fate cries out,
And makes each petty artery in this body
As hardy as the Nemean lion's nerve.   *I, iv, l. 81*

3   Unhand me, gentlemen,
By heaven! I'll make a ghost of him that lets me.

I, iv, l. 84

4 Something is rotten in the state of Denmark.

I, iv, l. 90

5 I could a tale unfold whose lightest word
Would harrow up thy soul, freeze thy young blood,
Make thy two eyes, like stars, start from their spheres,
Thy knotted and combined locks to part,
And each particular hair to stand an end,
Like quills upon the fretful porpentine.   *I, v, l. 15*

6 Murder most foul, as in the best it is.   *I, v, l. 27*

7 And duller shouldst thou be than the fat weed
That rots itself in ease on Lethe wharf.   *I, v, l. 32*

8   O my prophetic soul!
My uncle!   *I, v, l. 40*

9 O Hamlet! what a falling-off was there.   *I, v, l. 47*

10 But virtue, as it never will be mov'd,
Though lewdness court it in a shape of heaven,
So lust, though to a radiant angel link'd,
Will sate itself in a celestial bed,
And prey on garbage.   *I, v, l. 53*

11 In the porches of mine ears.   *I, v, l. 63*

12 Cut off even in the blossoms of my sin,
Unhousel'd, disappointed, unanel'd,
No reckoning made, but sent to my account
With all my imperfections on my head.   *I, v, l. 76*

13   Leave her to heaven,
And to those thorns that in her bosom lodge,
To prick and sting her.   *I, v, l. 86*

14 The glowworm shows the matin to be near,
And 'gins to pale his uneffectual fire.   *I, v, l. 89*

15   While memory holds a seat
In this distracted globe. Remember thee!
Yea, from the table of my memory
I'll wipe away all trivial fond records.   *I, v, l. 96*

16 Within the book and volume of my brain.

I, v, l. 103

17 O villain, villain, smiling, damned villain!
My tables — meet it is I set it down,
That one may smile, and smile, and be a villain;
At least I'm sure it may be so in Denmark.

I, v, l. 106

18 There's ne'er a villain dwelling in all Denmark,
But he's an arrant knave.   *I, v, l. 123*

19 There are more things in heaven and earth, Horatio,
Than are dreamt of in your philosophy.   *I, v, l. 166*

20 To put an antic disposition on.   *I, v, l. 172*

21 Rest, rest, perturbed spirit!   *I, v, l. 182*

22 The time is out of joint; O cursed spite,
That ever I was born to set it right!   *I, v, l. 188*

23 Your bait of falsehood takes this carp of truth;
And thus do we of wisdom and of reach,
With windlasses and with assays of bias,
By indirections find directions out.   *II, i, l. 63*

24 Ungarter'd, and down-gyved to his ankle.   *II, i, l. 80*

25 This is the very ecstasy of love.   *II, i, l. 102*

26 Brevity is the soul of wit.   *II, ii, l. 90*

27 More matter, with less art.   *II, ii, l. 95*

28 That he is mad, 'tis true; 'tis true 'tis pity;
And pity 'tis 'tis true.   *II, ii, l. 97*

29   Find out the cause of this effect,
Or rather say, the cause of this defect,
For this effect defective comes by cause.   *II, ii, l. 101*

30 Doubt thou the stars are fire;
Doubt that the sun doth move;
Doubt truth to be a liar;
But never doubt I love.   *II, ii, l. 115*

31   *Polonius:* Do you know me, my lord?
Hamlet: Excellent well; you are a fishmonger.

II, ii, l. 173

32   To be honest, as this world goes, is to be one man
picked out of ten thousand.   *II, ii, l. 179*

33   *Hamlet:* For if the sun breed maggots in a dead
dog, being a god[1] kissing carrion, — Have you a
daughter?
Polonius: I have, my lord.
Hamlet: Let her not walk i' the sun.   *II, ii, l. 183*

34   Still harping on my daughter.   *II, ii, l. 190*

35   *Polonius:* What do you read, my lord?
Hamlet: Words, words, words.   *II, ii, l. 195*

36   They have a plentiful lack of wit.   *II, ii, l. 204*

37   Though this be madness, yet there is method
in 't.   *II, ii, l. 211*

38   These tedious old fools!   *II, ii, l. 227*

39   The indifferent children of the earth.   *II, ii, l. 235*

---

[1]In some editions: good.

1   Happy in that we are not over happy.

                                                  II, ii, l. 236

2   There is nothing either good or bad, but thinking makes it so.   *II, ii, l. 259*

3   O God! I could be bounded in a nutshell, and count myself a king of infinite space, were it not that I have bad dreams.   *II, ii, l. 263*

4   Beggar that I am, I am even poor in thanks.

                                                  II, ii, l. 286

5   This goodly frame, the earth, seems to me a sterile promontory; this most excellent canopy, the air, look you, this brave o'erhanging firmament, this majestical roof fretted with golden fire, why, it appears no other thing to me but a foul and pestilent congregation of vapors. What a piece of work is a man! How noble in reason! how infinite in faculty! in form, in moving, how express and admirable! in action how like an angel! in apprehension how like a god!   *II, ii, l. 317*

6   And yet, to me, what is this quintessence of dust? man delights not me; no, nor woman neither.

                                              II, ii, l. 328

7   There is something in this more than natural, if philosophy could find it out.   *II, ii, l. 392*

8   I am but mad north-northwest: when the wind is southerly I know a hawk from a handsaw.[1]

                                              II, ii, l. 405

9   They say an old man is twice a child.   *II, ii, l. 413*

10 One fair daughter and no more,
The which he loved passing well.   *II, ii, l. 435*

11   Come, give us a taste of your quality.   *II, ii, l. 460*

12   The play, I remember, pleased not the million; 'twas caviare to the general.   *II, ii, l. 465*

13   They are the abstracts and brief chronicles of the time: after your death you were better have a bad epitaph than their ill report while you live.

                                              II, ii, l. 555

14   Use every man after his desert, and who should 'scape whipping?   *II, ii, l. 561*

15 O! what a rogue and peasant slave am I.   *II, ii, l. 584*

16 What's Hecuba to him or he to Hecuba,
That he should weep for her?   *II, ii, l. 593*

17 Who calls me villain? breaks my pate across?
Plucks off my beard and blows it in my face?

                                              II, ii, l. 607

---

[1] The *hawk* was a basic tool of the plasterer and the *handsaw* a basic tool of the carpenter. — *Morris Dictionary of Word and Phrase Origins* [1977]

18 But I am pigeon-liver'd, and lack gall
To make oppression bitter.   *II, ii, l. 613*

19   The play's the thing
Wherein I'll catch the conscience of the king.

                                              II, ii, l. 641

20   With devotion's visage
And pious action we do sugar o'er
The devil himself.   *III, i, l. 47*

21 To be, or not to be: that is the question:
Whether 'tis nobler in the mind to suffer
The slings and arrows of outrageous fortune,
Or to take arms against a sea of troubles,
And by opposing end them? To die: to sleep;
No more; and, by a sleep to say we end
The heartache and the thousand natural shocks
That flesh is heir to, 'tis a consummation
Devoutly to be wish'd. To die, to sleep;
To sleep: perchance to dream: ay, there's the rub;
For in that sleep of death what dreams may come
When we have shuffled off this mortal coil,
Must give us pause. There's the respect
That makes calamity of so long life;
For who would bear the whips and scorns of time,
The oppressor's wrong, the proud man's contumely,
The pangs of dispriz'd love, the law's delay,
The insolence of office, and the spurns
That patient merit of the unworthy takes,
When he himself might his quietus make
With a bare bodkin? who would fardels bear,
To grunt and sweat under a weary life,
But that the dread of something after death,
The undiscover'd country from whose bourn
No traveler returns, puzzles the will,
And makes us rather bear those ills we have
Than fly to others that we know not of?
Thus conscience does make cowards of us all;
And thus the native hue of resolution
Is sicklied o'er with the pale cast of thought,
And enterprises of great pith and moment
With this regard their currents turn awry,
And lose the name of action.   *III, i, l. 56*

22   Nymph, in thy orisons
Be all my sins remember'd.   *III, i, l. 89*

23   To the noble mind
Rich gifts wax poor when givers prove unkind.

                                              III, i, l. 100

24   Get thee to a nunnery.   *III, i, l. 124*

25   What should such fellows as I do crawling between heaven and earth? We are arrant knaves, all.

                                              III, i, l. 128

26   Be thou as chaste as ice, as pure as snow, thou shalt not escape calumny.   *III, i, l. 142*

1   I have heard of your paintings too, well enough; God has given you one face, and you make yourselves another.   *Hamlet, III, i, l. 150*

2   O! what a noble mind is here o'erthrown: The courtier's, soldier's, scholar's, eye, tongue, sword.   *III, i, l. 159*

3   The glass of fashion and the mould of form, The observ'd of all observers!   *III, i, l. 162*

4   Now see that noble and most sovereign reason, Like sweet bells jangled, out of tune and harsh.   *III, i, l. 166*

5   O! woe is me, To have seen what I have seen, see what I see!   *III, i, l. 169*

6   Speak the speech, I pray you, as I pronounced it to you, trippingly on the tongue; but if you mouth it, as many of your players do, I had as lief the towncrier spoke my lines. Nor do not saw the air too much with your hand, thus; but use all gently: for in the very torrent, tempest, and — as I may say — whirlwind of passion, you must acquire and beget a temperance, that may give it smoothness. O! it offends me to the soul to hear a robustious periwigpated fellow tear a passion to tatters, to very rags, to split the ears of the groundlings, who for the most part are capable of nothing but inexplicable dumbshows and noise: I would have such a fellow whipped for o'erdoing Termagant; it out-herods Herod.   *III, ii, l. 1*

7   Suit the action to the word, the word to the action; with this special observance, that you o'erstep not the modesty of nature.   *III, ii, l. 20*

8   To hold, as 'twere, the mirror up to nature; to show virtue her own feature, scorn her own image, and the very age and body of the time his form and pressure.   *III, ii, l. 25*

9   I have thought some of nature's journeymen had made men and not made them well, they imitated humanity so abominably.   *III, ii, l. 38*

10   No; let the candied tongue lick absurd pomp, And crook the pregnant hinges of the knee Where thrift may follow fawning.   *III, ii, l. 65*

11   A man that fortune's buffets and rewards Hast ta'en with equal thanks.   *III, ii, l. 72*

12   They are not a pipe for fortune's finger To sound what stop she please. Give me that man That is not passion's slave, and I will wear him In my heart's core, ay, in my heart of heart, As I do thee. Something too much of this.   *III, ii, l. 75*

13   My imaginations are as foul As Vulcan's stithy.   *III, ii, l. 88*

14   The chameleon's dish: I eat the air, promisecrammed; you cannot feed capons so.   *III, ii, l. 98*

15   Nay, then, let the devil wear black, for I'll have a suit of sables.   *III, ii, l. 138*

16   There's hope a great man's memory may outlive his life half a year.   *III, ii, l. 141*

17   Marry, this is miching mallecho; it means mischief.   *III, ii, l. 148*

18   *Ophelia:* 'Tis brief, my lord. *Hamlet:* As woman's love.   *III, ii, l. 165*

19   Where love is great, the littlest doubts are fear; When little fears grow great, great love grows there.   *III, ii, l. 183*

20   Wormwood, wormwood.   *III, ii, l. 193*

21   The lady doth protest too much, methinks.   *III, ii, l. 242*

22   Let the galled jade wince, our withers are unwrung.   *III, ii, l. 256*

23   Why, let the stricken deer go weep, The hart ungalled play; For some must watch, while some must sleep: So runs the world away.   *III, ii, l. 287*

24   You would pluck out the heart of my mystery.   *III, ii, l. 389*

25   Do you think I am easier to be played on than a pipe?   *III, ii, l. 393*

26   *Hamlet:* Do you see yonder cloud that's almost in shape of a camel? *Polonius:* By the mass, and 'tis like a camel, indeed. *Hamlet:* Methinks it is like a weasel. *Polonius:* It is backed like a weasel. *Hamlet:* Or like a whale? *Polonius:* Very like a whale.   *III, ii, l. 400*

27   They fool me to the top of my bent.   *III, ii, l. 408*

28   By and by is easily said.   *III, ii, l. 411*

29   'Tis now the very witching time of night, When churchyards yawn and hell itself breathes out Contagion to this world.   *III, ii, l. 413*

30   I will speak daggers to her, but use none.   *III, ii, l. 421*

31   O! my offense is rank, it smells to heaven; It hath the primal eldest curse upon 't; A brother's murder!   *III, iii, l. 36*

32   Now might I do it pat, now he is praying; And now I'll do 't: and so he goes to heaven; And so I am reveng'd.   *III, iii, l. 73*

33   With all his crimes broad blown, as flush as May.   *III, iii, l. 81*

1 My words fly up, my thoughts remain below:
Words without thoughts never to heaven go.
III, iii, l. 97

2   How now! a rat? Dead, for a ducat, dead!
III, iv, l. 23

3 False as dicers' oaths.   *III, iv, l. 45*

4 A rhapsody of words.   *III, iv, l. 48*

5 See, what a grace was seated on this brow;
Hyperion's curls, the front of Jove himself,
An eye like Mars, to threaten and command,
A station like the herald Mercury
New-lighted on a heaven-kissing hill,
A combination and a form indeed,
Where every god did seem to set his seal,
To give the world assurance of a man.
III, iv, l. 55

6   At your age
The heyday in the blood is tame, it's humble.
III, iv, l. 68

7 O shame! where is thy blush? Rebellious hell,
If thou canst mutine in a matron's bones,
To flaming youth let virtue be as wax,
And melt in her own fire: proclaim no shame
When the compulsive ardor gives the charge,
Since frost itself as actively doth burn,
And reason panders will.   *III, iv, l. 82*

8 A king of shreds and patches.   *III, iv, l. 102*

9 Lay not that flattering unction to your soul.
III, iv, l. 145

10   Confess yourself to heaven;
Repent what's past; avoid what is to come.
III, iv, l. 149

11 For in the fatness of these pursy times
Virtue itself of vice must pardon beg.   *III, iv, l. 153*

12 Assume a virtue, if you have it not.   *III, iv, l. 160*

13   Refrain tonight;
And that shall lend a kind of easiness
To the next abstinence: the next more easy;
For use almost can change the stamp of nature.
III, iv, l. 165

14 I must be cruel only to be kind.   *III, iv, l. 178*

15 For 'tis the sport to have the enginer
Hoist with his own petar.   *III, iv, l. 206*

16   Diseases desperate grown
By desperate appliance are relieved,
Or not at all.   *IV, iii, l. 9*

17   A man may fish with the worm that hath eat of a
king, and eat of the fish that hath fed of that worm.
IV, iii, l. 29

18 We go to gain a little patch of ground
That hath in it no profit but the name.   *IV, iv, l. 18*

19 How all occasions do inform against me,
And spur my dull revenge! What is a man,
If his chief good and market of his time
Be but to sleep and feed? a beast, no more.
Sure he that made us with such large discourse,
Looking before and after, gave us not
That capability and godlike reason
To fust in us unus'd.   *IV, iv, l. 32*

20   Some craven scruple
Of thinking too precisely on the event.   *IV, iv, l. 40*

21   Rightly to be great
Is not to stir without great argument,
But greatly to find quarrel in a straw
When honor's at the stake.   *IV, iv, l. 53*

22 So full of artless jealousy is guilt,
It spills itself in fearing to be spilt.   *IV, v, l. 19*

23 How should I your true love know
From another one?
By his cockle hat and staff,
And his sandal shoon.[1]   *IV, v, l. 23*

24 He is dead and gone, lady,
He is dead and gone;
At his head a grass-green turf
At his heels a stone.   *IV, v, l. 29*

25   We know what we are, but know not what we
may be.   *IV, v, l. 43*

26   Come, my coach! Good night, ladies; good night,
sweet ladies; good night, good night.   *IV, v, l. 72*

27 When sorrows come, they come not single spies,
But in battalions.[2]   *IV, v, l. 78*

28   We have done but greenly,
In hugger-mugger to inter him.   *IV, v, l. 84*

29 There's such divinity doth hedge a king,
That treason can but peep to what it would.
IV, v, l. 123

30   There's rosemary, that's for remembrance . . . and
there is pansies, that's for thoughts.   *IV, v, l. 174*

31   O! you must wear your rue with a difference.
There's a daisy; I would give you some violets, but
they withered all when my father died.
IV, v, l. 181

---

[1]Ophelia is quoting a version of a poem by Walter Ralegh.

[2]One woe doth tread upon another's heel, / So fast they follow. — *Hamlet, act IV, sc. vii, l. 164*

Thus woe succeeds a woe, as wave a wave. — ROBERT HERRICK, *Sorrows Succeed* [1648]

Woes cluster; rare are solitary woes; / They love a train, they tread each other's heel. — EDWARD YOUNG, *Night Thoughts, Night III, l. 63*

1 A very riband in the cap of youth.

Hamlet, IV, vii, l. 77

2   Nature her custom holds,
Let shame say what it will.   *IV, vii, l. 188*

3   There is no ancient gentlemen but gardeners, ditchers, and grave-makers; they hold up Adam's profession.   *V, i, l. 32*

4   Cudgel thy brains no more about it.   *V, i, l. 61*

5   Has this fellow no feeling of his business, that he sings at grave-making?   *V, i, l. 71*

6   Custom hath made it in him a property of easiness.   *V, i, l. 73*

7   A politician . . . one that would circumvent God.

V, i, l. 84

8   Why may not that be the skull of a lawyer? Where be his quiddities now, his quillets, his cases, his tenures, and his tricks?   *V, i, l. 104*

9   One that was a woman, sir; but, rest her soul, she's dead.   *V, i, l. 145*

10   How absolute the knave is! we must speak by the card, or equivocation will undo us.   *V, i, l. 147*

11   The age is grown so picked that the toe of the peasant comes so near the heel of the courtier, he galls his kibe.   *V, i, l. 150*

12   Alas! poor Yorick. I knew him, Horatio; a fellow of infinite jest, of most excellent fancy; he hath borne me on his back a thousand times; and now, how abhorred in my imagination it is! my gorge rises at it. Here hung those lips that I have kissed I know not how oft. Where be your gibes now? your gambols? your songs? your flashes of merriment, that were wont to set the table on a roar? Not one now, to mock your own grinning? quite chapfallen? Now get you to my lady's chamber, and tell her, let her paint an inch thick, to this favor she must come; make her laugh at that.   *V, i, l. 201*

13   To what base uses we may return, Horatio! Why may not imagination trace the noble dust of Alexander, till he find it stopping a bung-hole?

V, i, l. 222

14 Imperious Caesar, dead and turn'd to clay,
Might stop a hole to keep the wind away. *V, i, l. 235*

15   Lay her i' the earth;
And from her fair and unpolluted flesh
May violets spring!   *V, i, l. 260*

16 A ministering angel shall my sister be. *V, i, l. 263*

17 Sweets to the sweet: farewell!   *V, i, l. 265*

18 I thought thy bride-bed to have deck'd, sweet maid,
And not have strew'd thy grave.   *V, i, l. 267*

19 Though I am not splenetive and rash
Yet have I in me something dangerous.   *V, i, l. 283*

20 I lov'd Ophelia: forty thousand brothers
Could not, with all their quantity of love,
Make up my sum.   *V, i, l. 291*

21   Nay, an thou'lt mouth,
I'll rant as well as thou.   *V, i, l. 305*

22 Let Hercules himself do what he may,
The cat will mew and dog will have his day.

V, i, l. 313

23 There's a divinity that shapes our ends,
Rough-hew them how we will.   *V, ii, l. 10*

24 I once did hold it, as our statists do,
A baseness to write fair.   *V, ii, l. 33*

25 It did me yeoman's service.   *V, ii, l. 36*

26   Not a whit, we defy augury; there's a special providence in the fall of a sparrow. If it be now, 'tis not to come; if it be not to come, it will be now; if it be not now, yet it will come: the readiness is all. *V, ii, l. 232*

27 A hit, a very palpable hit.   *V, ii, l. 295*

28   This fell sergeant, death,
Is strict in his arrest.   *V, ii, l. 350*

29 Report me and my cause aright.   *V, ii, l. 353*

30 I am more an antique Roman than a Dane.

V, ii, l. 355

31 O God! Horatio, what a wounded name,
Things standing thus unknown, shall live behind me.
If thou didst ever hold me in thy heart,
Absent thee from felicity awhile,
And in this harsh world draw thy breath in pain,
To tell my story.   *V, ii, l. 358*

32 The rest is silence.   *V, ii, l. 372*

33 Now cracks a noble heart. Good night, sweet prince,
And flights of angels sing thee to thy rest!

V, ii, l. 373

34   O proud death!
What feast is toward in thine eternal cell?

V, ii, l. 378

35 Property was thus appall'd,
That the self was not the same;
Single nature's double name
Neither two nor one was call'd.
The Phoenix and the Turtle [1601], l. 37

36 Reason, in itself confounded,
Saw division grow together.   *l. 41*

37 The chance of war.
*Troilus and Cressida [1601–1602],
prologue, l. 31*

1   I have had my labor for my travail.

act I, sc. i, l. 73

2   Women are angels, wooing:
Things won are done; joy's soul lies in the doing.

I, ii, l. 310

3 Men prize the thing ungain'd more than it is.

I, ii, l. 313

4   The sea being smooth,
How many shallow bauble boats dare sail
Upon her patient breast.   *I, iii, l. 34*

5 The heavens themselves, the planets, and this center
Observe degree, priority, and place,
Insisture, course, proportion, season, form,
Office, and custom, in all line of order.   *I, iii, l. 85*

6   O! when degree is shaked,
Which is the ladder to all high designs,
The enterprise is sick.   *I, iii, l. 101*

7 Take but degree away, untune that string,
And, hark! what discord follows; each thing meets
In mere oppugnancy: the bounded waters
Should lift their bosoms higher than the shores,
And make a sop of all this solid globe.   *I, iii, l. 109*

8 Then everything includes itself in power,
Power into will, will into appetite;
And appetite, a universal wolf,
So doubly seconded with will and power,
Must make perforce a universal prey,
And last eat up himself.   *I, iii, l. 119*

9 Like a strutting player, whose conceit
Lies in his hamstring, and doth think it rich
To hear the wooden dialogue and sound
'Twixt his stretch'd footing and the scaffoldage.

I, iii, l. 153

10 And in such indexes, although small pricks
To their subsequent volumes, there is seen
The baby figure of the giant mass
Of things to come.   *I, iii, l. 343*

11   Who wears his wit in his belly, and his guts in his
head.   *II, i, l. 78*

12   Modest doubt is call'd
The beacon of the wise, the tent that searches
To the bottom of the worst.   *II, ii, l. 15*

13   'Tis mad idolatry
To make the service greater than the god.   *II, ii, l. 56*

14   He that is proud eats up himself; pride is his own
glass, his own trumpet, his own chronicle.

II, iii, l. 165

15 I am giddy, expectation whirls me round.
The imaginary relish is so sweet
That it enchants my sense.   *III, ii, l. 17*

16   Words pay no debts.   *III, ii, l. 56*

17   To fear the worst oft cures the worse.

III, ii, l. 77

18   All lovers swear more performance than they are
able, and yet reserve an ability that they never perform; vowing more than the perfection of ten and
discharging less than the tenth part of one.

III, ii, l. 89

19   For to be wise, and love,
Exceeds man's might; that dwells with gods above.

III, ii, l. 163

20 If I be false, or swerve a hair from truth,
When time is old and hath forgot itself,
When waterdrops have worn the stones of Troy,
And blind oblivion swallow'd cities up.
And mighty states characterless are grated
To dusty nothing, yet let memory,
From false to false, among false maids in love
Upbraid my falsehood! when they have said "as false
As air, as water, wind, or sandy earth,
As fox to lamb, as wolf to heifer's calf,
Pard to the hind, or stepdame to her son";
Yea, let them say, to stick the heart of falsehood,
"As false as Cressid."   *III, ii, l. 191*

21 Time hath, my lord, a wallet at his back,
Wherein he puts alms for oblivion.   *III, iii, l. 145*

22   Perseverance, dear my lord,
Keeps honor bright: to have done, is to hang
Quite out of fashion, like a rusty mail
In monumental mockery.   *III, iii, l. 150*

23 For honor travels in a strait so narrow
Where one but goes abreast.   *III, iii, l. 154*

24   Time is like a fashionable host,
That slightly shakes his parting guest by the hand,
And with his arms outstretch'd, as he would fly,
Grasps in the comer: welcome ever smiles,
And farewell goes out sighing.   *III, iii, l. 168*

25   Beauty, wit,
High birth, vigor of bone, desert in service,
Love, friendship, charity, are subjects all
To envious and calumniating time.
One touch of nature makes the whole world kin.

III, iii, l. 171

26 And give to dust that is a little gilt
More laud than gilt o'er-dusted.   *III, iii, l. 178*

27 My mind is troubled, like a fountain stirr'd;
And I myself see not the bottom of it.   *III, iii, l. 314*

28   You do as chapmen do,
Dispraise the thing that you desire to buy.

IV, i, l. 75

1 As many farewells as be stars in heaven.
Troilus and Cressida, IV, iv, l. 44

2 And sometimes we are devils to ourselves
When we will tempt the frailty of our powers,
Presuming on their changeful potency. *IV, iv, l. 95*

3 The kiss you take is better than you give. *IV, v, l. 38*

4   Fie, fie upon her!
There's language in her eye, her cheek, her lip,
Nay, her foot speaks; her wanton spirits look out
At every joint and motive of her body. *IV, v, l. 54*

5 What's past and what's to come is strew'd with husks
And formless ruin of oblivion. *IV, v, l. 165*

6   The end crowns all,
And that old common arbitrator, Time,
Will one day end it. *IV, v, l. 223*

7 Words, words, mere words, no matter from the
       heart. *V, iii, l. 109*

8 Hector is dead; there is no more to say. *V, x, l. 22*

9   O world! world! world! thus is the poor agent
despised. *V, x, l. 36*

10 If music be the food of love,[1] play on;
Give me excess of it, that, surfeiting,
The appetite may sicken, and so die.
That strain again! it had a dying fall:
O! it came o'er my ear like the sweet sound
That breathes upon a bank of violets,
Stealing and giving odor!
Twelfth-Night [1601–1602], act I, sc. i, l. 1

11 O spirit of love! how quick and fresh art thou,
That, notwithstanding thy capacity
Receiveth as the sea, nought enters there,
Of what validity and pitch soe'er,
But falls into abatement and low price,
Even in a minute: so full of shapes is fancy,
That it alone is high fantastical. *I, i, l. 9*

12 When my tongue blabs, then let mine eyes not see.
I, ii, l. 61

13   I am sure care's an enemy to life. *I, iii, l. 2*

14   Let them hang themselves in their own straps.
I, iii, l. 13

15   I am a great eater of beef, and I believe that does
harm to my wit. *I, iii, l. 92*

16   Wherefore are these things hid? *I, iii, l. 135*

17   Is it a world to hide virtues in? *I, iii, l. 142*

18   God give them wisdom that have it; and those that
are fools, let them use their talents. *I, v, l. 14*

19   One draught above heat makes him a fool, the
second mads him, and a third drowns him.
I, v, l. 139

20 'Tis beauty truly blent, whose red and white
Nature's own sweet and cunning hand laid on:
Lady, you are the cruel'st she alive,
If you will lead these graces to the grave
And leave the world no copy. *I, v, l. 259*

21 Make me a willow cabin at your gate,
And call upon my soul within the house. *I, v, l. 289*

22 Holla your name to the reverberate hills,
And make the babbling gossip of the air
Cry out, "Olivia!" *I, v, l. 293*

23 Farewell, fair cruelty. *I, v, l. 309*

24 O mistress mine! where are you roaming?
II, iii, l. 42

25 Journeys end in lovers meeting,
Every wise man's son doth know. *II, iii, l. 46*

26 What is love? 'tis not hereafter;
Present mirth hath present laughter.
What's to come is still unsure:
In delay there lies no plenty;
Then come kiss me, sweet and twenty,
Youth's a stuff will not endure. *II, iii, l. 50*

27   He does it with a better grace, but I do it more
natural. *II, iii, l. 91*

28   Is there no respect of place, persons, nor time, in
you? *II, iii, l. 100*

29   *Sir Toby:* Dost thou think, because thou art virtuous, there shall be no more cakes and ale?
     Clown: Yes, by Saint Anne; and ginger shall be hot
i' the mouth too. *II, iii, l. 124*

30   The devil a puritan that he is, or anything constantly but a time-pleaser; an affectioned ass.
II, iii, l. 161

31   My purpose is, indeed, a horse of that color.[2]
II, iii, l. 184

32 These most brisk and giddy-paced times. *II, iv, l. 6*

33   If ever thou shalt love,
In the sweet pangs of it remember me;
For such as I am all true lovers are:
Unstaid and skittish in all motions else
Save in the constant image of the creature
That is belov'd. *II, iv, l. 15*

34   Let still the woman take
An elder than herself, so wears she to him,
So sways she level in her husband's heart:

---

[1] Is not music the food of love? — RICHARD BRINSLEY SHERIDAN, *The Rivals, act II, sc. i*

[2] A play on "a horse of a different color."

For, boy, however we do praise ourselves,
Our fancies are more giddy and unfirm,
More longing, wavering, sooner lost and worn,
Than women's are.   *II, iv, l. 29*

1 Then, let thy love be younger than thyself,
Or thy affection cannot hold the bent;
For women are as roses, whose fair flower
Being once display'd, doth fall that very hour.
                                      II, iv, l. 36

2 The spinsters and the knitters in the sun,
And the free maids that weave their thread with
        bones,
Do use to chant it: it is silly sooth,
And dallies with the innocence of love,
Like the old age.   *II, iv, l. 44*

3 Come away, come away, death,
And in sad cypress let me be laid;
Fly away, fly away, breath;
I am slain by a fair cruel maid.   *II, iv, l. 51*

4 *Duke:*   And what's her history?
Viola: A blank, my lord. She never told her love,
But let concealment, like a worm i' the bud,
Feed on her damask cheek: she pin'd in thought,
And with a green and yellow melancholy,
She sat like Patience on a monument,
Smiling at grief.   *II, iv, l. 112*

5 I am all the daughters of my father's house,
And all the brothers too.   *II, iv, l. 122*

6   Here comes the trout that must be caught with
tickling.   *II, v, l. 25*

7 I may command where I adore.   *II, v, l. 116*

8   Be not afraid of greatness: some are born great,
some achieve greatness, and some have greatness
thrust upon them.   *II, v, l. 159*

9   Remember who commended thy yellow stockings, and wished to see thee ever cross-gartered.
                                      II, v, l. 168

10   Foolery, sir, does walk about the orb like the sun;
it shines everywhere.   *III, i, l. 44*

11 This fellow's wise enough to play the fool,
And to do that well craves a kind of wit.   *III, i, l. 68*

12 Music from the spheres.[1]   *III, i, l. 122*

13 How apt the poor are to be proud.
                                      III, i, l. 141

14 Then westward-ho!   *III, i, l. 148*

15 O! what a deal of scorn looks beautiful
In the contempt and anger of his lip.   *III, i, l. 159*

16 Love sought is good, but giv'n unsought is better.
                                      III, i, l. 170

17   You will hang like an icicle on a Dutchman's
beard.   *III, ii, l. 30*

18   Let there be gall enough in thy ink.
                                      III, ii, l. 54

19   Laugh yourselves into stitches.   *III, ii, l. 75*

20   I think we do know the sweet Roman hand.
                                      III, iv, l. 31

21   This is very midsummer madness.   *III, iv, l. 62*

22   More matter for a May morning.   *III, iv, l. 158*

23   He's a very devil.   *III, iv, l. 304*

24 Out of my lean and low ability
I'll lend you something.   *III, iv, l. 380*

25 I hate ingratitude more in a man
Than lying, vainness, babbling drunkenness,
Or any taint of vice whose strong corruption
Inhabits our frail blood.   *III, iv, l. 390*

26   As the old hermit of Prague, that never saw pen
and ink, very wittily said to a niece of King Gorboduc,
"That, that is, is."   *IV, ii, l. 14*

27   I say there is no darkness but ignorance, in which
thou art more puzzled than the Egyptians in their
fog.   *IV, ii, l. 47*

28   Thus the whirligig of time brings in his revenges.
                                      V, i, l. 388

29 When that I was and a little tiny boy,
With hey, ho, the wind and the rain;
A foolish thing was but a toy,
For the rain it raineth every day.[2]   *V, i, l. 404*

30   Love all, trust a few,
Do wrong to none: be able for thine enemy
Rather in power than use, and keep thy friend
Under thy own life's key: be check'd for silence,
But never tax'd for speech.
        All's Well That Ends Well [1602–1604],
        act I, sc. i, l. 74

31   It were all one
That I should love a bright particular star
And think to wed it, he is so above me.   *I, i, l. 97*

32 The hind that would be mated by the lion
Must die for love.   *I, i, l. 103*

---

[1]The music of the spheres. — *Pericles, act V, sc. i, l. 231*
    A reference to the Pythagorean idea (sixth century B.C.E.) that the stars and planets in movement created music, since their motion is governed by mathematical equations that correspond to musical tones.

---

[2]Parodied by the Fool in *King Lear*, 211:31.

1 My friends were poor, but honest.[1]
All's Well That Ends Well, I, iii, l. 203

2 Oft expectation fails, and most oft there
Where most it promises. *II, i, l. 145*

3 They say miracles are past. *II, iii, l. 1*

4 A young man married is a man that's marr'd.
II, iii, l. 315

5 The web of our life is of a mingled yarn, good and
ill together. *IV, iii, l. 83*

6 There's place and means for every man alive.
IV, iii, l. 379

7 All's well that ends well: still the fine's the crown;
Whate'er the course, the end is the renown.
IV, iv, l. 35

8 I am a man whom Fortune hath cruelly scratched.
V, ii, l. 28

9 Praising what is lost
Makes the remembrance dear. *V, iii, l. 19*

10 The inaudible and noiseless foot of time. *V, iii, l. 41*

11 Love that comes too late,
Like a remorseful pardon slowly carried. *V, iii, l. 57*

12 All impediments in fancy's course
Are motives of more fancy. *V, iii, l. 216*

13 Good counselors lack no clients.
Measure for Measure [1604], act I, sc. ii, l. 115

14 And liberty plucks justice by the nose. *I, iii, l. 29*

15 I hold you as a thing ensky'd and sainted. *I, iv, l. 34*

16 A man whose blood
Is very snow-broth; one who never feels
The wanton stings and motions of the sense.
I, iv, l. 57

17 Our doubts are traitors,
And make us lose the good we oft might win,
By fearing to attempt. *I, iv, l. 78*

18 We must not make a scarecrow of the law,
Setting it up to fear the birds of prey,
And let it keep one shape, till custom make it
Their perch and not their terror. *II, i, l. 1*

19 The jury, passing on the prisoner's life,
May in the sworn twelve have a thief or two
Guiltier than him they try. *II, i, l. 19*

20 Some rise by sin, and some by virtue fall. *II, i, l. 38*

21 Great with child, and longing...for stewed
prunes. *II, i, l. 94*

22 This will last out a night in Russia,
When nights are longest there. *II, i, l. 144*

23 His face is the worst thing about him. *II, i, l. 167*

24 Condemn the fault, and not the actor of it?
II, ii, l. 37

25 No ceremony that to great ones 'longs,
Not the king's crown, nor the deputed sword,
The marshal's truncheon, nor the judge's robe,
Become them with one half so good a grace
As mercy does. *II, ii, l. 59*

26 The law hath not been dead, though it hath slept.
II, ii, l. 90

27 O! it is excellent
To have a giant's strength, but it is tyrannous
To use it like a giant. *II, ii, l. 107*

28 But man, proud man,
Drest in a little brief authority,
Most ignorant of what he's most assur'd,
His glassy essence, like an angry ape,
Plays such fantastic tricks before high heaven
As make the angels weep. *II, ii, l. 117*

29 That in the captain's but a choleric word,
Which in the soldier is flat blasphemy. *II, ii, l. 130*

30 It oft falls out,
To have what we would have, we speak not what we
mean. *II, iv, l. 118*

31 The miserable have no other medicine
But only hope. *III, i, l. 2*

32 Be absolute for death. *III, i, l. 5*

33 A breath thou art,
Servile to all the skyey influences. *III, i, l. 8*

34 Thou hast nor youth nor age;
But, as it were, an after-dinner's sleep,
Dreaming on both; for all thy blessed youth
Becomes as aged, and doth beg the alms
Of palsied eld; and when thou art old and rich,
Thou hast neither heat, affection, limb, nor beauty,
To make thy riches pleasant. *III, i, l. 32*

35 The sense of death is most in apprehension,
And the poor beetle, that we tread upon,
In corporal sufferance finds a pang as great
As when a giant dies. *III, i, l. 76*

36 If I must die,
I will encounter darkness as a bride,
And hug it in my arms. *III, i, l. 81*

37 The cunning livery of hell. *III, i, l. 93*

38 Ay, but to die, and go we know not where;
To lie in cold obstruction and to rot;
This sensible warm motion to become

---

[1]Though I be poor, I'm honest. — THOMAS MIDDLETON, *The Witch* [c. 1627], *act III, sc. ii*

A kneaded clod; and the delighted spirit
To bathe in fiery floods, or to reside
In thrilling region of thick-ribbed ice;
To be imprison'd in the viewless winds,
And blown with restless violence round about
The pendant world.   *III, i, l. 116*

1 The weariest and most loathed worldly life
That age, ache, penury, and imprisonment
Can lay on nature is a paradise
To what we fear of death.   *III, i, l. 127*

2   The hand that hath made you fair hath made you
good.   *III, i, l. 182*

3   Virtue is bold, and goodness never fearful.
                                      III, i, l. 214

4   There, at the moated grange, resides this dejected
Mariana.[1]   *III, i, l. 279*

5   This news is old enough, yet it is every day's
news.   *III, ii, l. 249*

6 He, who the sword of heaven will bear
Should be as holy as severe.   *III, ii, l. 283*

7 O, what may man within him hide,
Though angel on the outward side!   *III, ii, l. 293*

8 Take, O take those lips away,
That so sweetly were forsworn;
And those eyes, the break of day,
Lights that do mislead the morn:
But my kisses bring again, bring again,
Seals of love, but seal'd in vain, seal'd in vain.[2]
                                      IV, i, l. 1

9   Music oft hath such a charm
To make bad good, and good provoke to harm.
                                      IV, i, l. 16

10   Every true man's apparel fits your thief.
                                      IV, ii, l. 46

11   The old fantastical duke of dark corners.
                                      IV, iii, l. 167

12   I am a kind of burr; I shall stick. *IV, iii, l. 193*

13 We would, and we would not.   *IV, iv, l. 37*

14 A forted residence 'gainst the tooth of time
And razure of oblivion.   *V, i, l. 12*

15   Truth is truth
To the end of reckoning.   *V, i, l. 45*

16 Neither maid, widow, nor wife.   *V, i, l. 173*

17 Haste still pays haste, and leisure answers leisure,
Like doth quit like, and Measure still for Measure.
                                      V, i, l. 411

18 They say best men are molded out of faults,
And, for the most, become much more the better
For being a little bad.   *V, i, l. 440*

19 What's mine is yours, and what is yours is mine.
                                      V, i, l. 539

20 Horribly stuff'd with epithets of war.
          Othello [1604–1605], act I, sc. i, l. 14

21 A fellow almost damn'd in a fair wife.   *I, i, l. 21*

22 The bookish theoric.   *I, i, l. 24*

23 We cannot all be masters.   *I, i, l. 43*

24 And when he's old, cashier'd.   *I, i, l. 48*

25 In following him, I follow but myself. *I, i, l. 58*

26 But I will wear my heart upon my sleeve
For daws to peck at.   *I, i, l. 64*

27   An old black ram
Is tupping your white ewe.   *I, i, l. 88*

28   You are one of those that will not serve God if the
devil bid you.   *I, i, l. 108*

29   Your daughter and the Moor are now making the
beast with two backs.   *I, i, l. 117*

30 Keep up your bright swords, for the dew will rust
them.   *I, ii, l. 59*

31 The wealthy curled darlings of our nation.
                                      I, ii, l. 68

32   The bloody book of law
You shall yourself read in the bitter letter
After your own sense.   *I, iii, l. 67*

33   Rude am I in my speech,
And little bless'd with the soft phrase of peace.
                                      I, iii, l. 81

34   Little shall I grace my cause
In speaking for myself. Yet, by your gracious patience,
I will a round unvarnish'd tale deliver
Of my whole course of love.   *I, iii, l. 88*

35   A maiden never bold;
Of spirit so still and quiet, that her motion
Blush'd at herself.   *I, iii, l. 94*

36 Still question'd me the story of my life
From year to year, the battles, sieges, fortunes
That I have pass'd.   *I, iii, l. 129*

37 Wherein I spake of most disastrous chances,
Of moving accidents by flood and field,

---

[1]"Mariana in the moated grange." — *Motto used by* Tennyson *for
the poem* Mariana; *see* 450:7.

[2]This song occurs in act V, sc. ii, of John Fletcher's *Bloody Brother*
[c. 1616], with an additional stanza:
    Hide, O hide those hills of snow, / Which thy frozen bosom
bears, / On whose tops the pinks that grow / Are of those that
April wears! / But first set my poor heart free, / Bound in those icy
chains by thee.

Of hair-breadth 'scapes i' the imminent deadly breath. *Othello, I, iii, l. 134*

1 Hills whose heads touch heaven. *I, iii, l. 141*

2 And of the Cannibals that each other eat,
The Anthropophagi, and men whose heads
Do grow beneath their shoulders. *I, iii, l. 143*

3   My story being done,
She gave me for my pains a world of sighs:
She swore, in faith, 'twas strange, 'twas passing strange;
'Twas pitiful, 'twas wondrous pitiful:
She wish'd she had not heard it, yet she wish'd
That heaven had made her such a man; she thank'd me,
And bade me, if I had a friend that lov'd her,
I should but teach him how to tell my story,
And that would woo her. Upon this hint I spake:
She lov'd me for the dangers I had pass'd,
And I lov'd her that she did pity them.
This only is the witchcraft I have us'd. *I, iii, l. 158*

4 I do perceive here a divided duty. *I, iii, l. 181*

5 To mourn a mischief that is past and gone
Is the next way to draw new mischief on. *I, iii, l. 204*

6 The robb'd that smiles steals something from the thief. *I, iii, l. 208*

7   Our bodies are our gardens, to the which our wills are gardeners. *I, iii, l. 324*

8   Put money in thy purse. *I, iii, l. 345*

9   The food that to him now is as luscious as locusts, shall be to him shortly as bitter as coloquintida. *I, iii, l. 354*

10 Framed to make women false. *I, iii, l. 404*

11 The enchafed flood. *II, i, l. 17*

12 One that excels the quirks of blazoning pens. *II, i, l. 63*

13   You are pictures out of doors,
Bells in your parlors, wildcats in your kitchens,
Saints in your injuries, devils being offended,
Players in your housewifery, and housewives in your beds. *II, i, l. 109*

14 For I am nothing if not critical. *II, i, l. 119*

15 I am not merry, but I do beguile
The thing I am by seeming otherwise. *II, i, l. 122*

16 She that was ever fair and never proud,
Had tongue at will and yet was never loud. *II, i, l. 148*

17 *Iago:* To suckle fools and chronicle small beer.
Desdemona: O most lame and impotent conclusion! *II, i, l. 160*

18   You may relish him more in the soldier than in the scholar. *II, i, l. 165*

19   If it were now to die,
'Twere now to be most happy. *II, i, l. 192*

20   Base men being in love have then a nobility in their natures more than is native to them. *II, i, l. 218*

21 Egregiously an ass. *II, i, l. 321*

22   I have very poor and unhappy brains for drinking. *II, iii, l. 34*

23 Potations pottle deep. *II, iii, l. 57*

24   Well, God's above all; and there be souls must be saved, and there be souls must not be saved. *II, iii, l. 106*

25 Silence that dreadful bell! it frights the isle
From her propriety. *II, iii, l. 177*

26 But men are men; the best sometimes forget. *II, iii, l. 243*

27 Thy honesty and love doth mince this matter. *II, iii, l. 249*

28   Reputation, reputation, reputation! O! I have lost my reputation. I have lost the immortal part of myself, and what remains is bestial. *II, iii, l. 264*

29   Reputation is an idle and most false imposition; oft got without merit, and lost without deserving. *II, iii, l. 270*

30   O thou invisible spirit of wine! if thou hast no name to be known by, let us call thee devil! *II, iii, l. 285*

31   O God! that men should put an enemy in their mouths to steal away their brains; that we should, with joy, pleasance, revel, and applause, transform ourselves into beasts. *II, iii, l. 293*

32   Good wine is a good familiar creature if it be well used. *II, iii, l. 315*

33 Play the villain. *II, iii, l. 345*

34 How poor are they that have not patience!
What wound did ever heal but by degrees? *II, iii, l. 379*

35 Excellent wretch! Perdition catch my soul
But I do love thee! and when I love thee not,
Chaos is come again. *III, iii, l. 90*

36 Men should be what they seem. *III, iii, l. 126*

1   Speak to me as to thy thinkings,
As thou dost ruminate, and give thy worst of
        thoughts
The worst of words.   *III, iii, l. 131*

2 Good name in man and woman, dear my lord,
Is the immediate jewel of their souls:
Who steals my purse steals trash; 'tis something,
        nothing;
'Twas mine, 'tis his, and has been slave to thousands;
But he that filches from me my good name
Robs me of that which not enriches him,
And makes me poor indeed.
                              III, iii, l. 155

3   O! beware, my lord, of jealousy;
It is the green-ey'd monster which doth mock
The meat it feeds on; that cuckold lives in bliss
Who, certain of his fate, loves not his wronger;
But, O! what damned minutes tells he o'er
Who dotes, yet doubts; suspects, yet soundly loves!
                              III, iii, l. 165

4 Poor and content is rich, and rich enough.
                              III, iii, l. 172

5 Think'st thou I'd make a life of jealousy,
To follow still the changes of the moon
With fresh suspicions? No; to be once in doubt
Is once to be resolved.   *III, iii, l. 177*

6 I humbly do beseech you of your pardon
For too much loving you.
                              III, iii, l. 212

7   If I do prove her haggard,
Though that her jesses were my dear heart-strings,
I'd whistle her off and let her down the wind,
To prey at fortune.   *III, iii, l. 260*

8   I am declin'd
Into the vale of years.   *III, iii, l. 265*

9   O curse of marriage!
That we can call these delicate creatures ours,
And not their appetites. I had rather be a toad,
And live upon the vapor of a dungeon,
Than keep a corner in the thing I love
For others' uses.   *III, iii, l. 268*

10   Trifles light as air
Are to the jealous confirmations strong
As proofs of holy writ.   *III, iii, l. 323*

11   Not poppy, nor mandragora,
Nor all the drowsy syrups of the world,
Shall ever medicine thee to that sweet sleep
Which thou ow'dst yesterday. *III, iii, l. 331*

12 He that is robb'd, not wanting what is stol'n,
Let him not know 't and he's not robb'd at all.
                              III, iii, l. 343

13   O! now, forever
Farewell the tranquil mind; farewell content!
Farewell the plumed troop and the big wars
That make ambition virtue! O, farewell!
Farewell the neighing steed, and the shrill trump,
The spirit-stirring drum, the ear-piercing fife,
The royal banner, and all quality,
Pride, pomp, and circumstance of glorious war!
And, O you mortal engines, whose rude throats
The immortal Jove's dread clamors counterfeit,
Farewell! Othello's occupation's gone!
                              III, iii, l. 348

14 Be sure of it; give me the ocular proof. *III, iii, l. 361*

15   No hinge nor loop
To hang a doubt on.   *III, iii, l. 366*

16 On horror's head horrors accumulate. *III, iii, l. 371*

17   Take note, take note, O world!
To be direct and honest is not safe. *III, iii, l. 378*

18 But this denoted a foregone conclusion.
                              III, iii, l. 429

19   Swell, bosom, with thy fraught,
For 'tis of aspics' tongues! *III, iii, l. 450*

20   Like to the Pontick sea,
Whose icy current and compulsive course
Ne'er feels retiring ebb, but keeps due on
To the Propontic and the Hellespont,
Even so my bloody thoughts, with violent pace,
Shall ne'er look back, ne'er ebb to humble love,
Till that a capable and wide revenge
Swallow them up.   *III, iii, l. 454*

21 Our new heraldry is hands not hearts. *III, iv, l. 48*

22 But jealous souls will not be answer'd so;
They are not ever jealous for the cause,
But jealous for they are jealous; 'tis a monster
Begot upon itself, born on itself. *III, iv, l. 158*

23   'Tis the strumpet's plague
To beguile many and be beguil'd by one.
                              IV, i, l. 97

24 They laugh that win.   *IV, i, l. 123*

25 My heart is turned to stone; I strike it, and it hurts
my hand. O! the world hath not a sweeter creature;
she might lie by an emperor's side and command him
tasks.   *IV, i, l. 190*

26 O, she will sing the savageness out of a bear.
                              IV, i, l. 198

27 But yet the pity of it, Iago! O! Iago, the pity of it,
Iago!   *IV, i, l. 205*

28   Is this the noble nature
Whom passion could not shake? whose solid virtue

The shot of accident nor dart of chance
Could neither graze nor pierce?
Othello, IV, i, l. 276

1 I understand a fury in your words,
But not the words.   *IV, ii, l. 31*

2 Steep'd me in poverty to the very lips.   *IV, ii, l. 49*

3   But, alas! to make me
A fixed figure for the time of scorn
To point his slow and moving finger at.   *IV, ii, l. 52*

4 Patience, thou young and rose-lipp'd cherubin.
IV, ii, l. 62

5   O thou weed!
Who art so lovely fair and smell'st so sweet
That the sense aches at thee, would thou hadst ne'er
          been born.   *IV, ii, l. 66*

6 O heaven! that such companions thou'dst unfold,
And put in every honest hand a whip
To lash the rascals naked through the world.
IV, ii, l. 141

7   Unkindness may do much;
And his unkindness may defeat my life,
But never taint my love.   *IV, ii, l. 159*

8 The poor soul sat sighing by a sycamore tree,
Sing all a green willow;
Her hand on her bosom, her head on her knee,
Sing willow, willow, willow.[1]   *IV, iii, l. 41*

9 It makes us, or it mars us.   *V, i, l. 4*

10 Every way makes my gain.   *V, i, l. 14*

11 He hath a daily beauty in his life.   *V, i, l. 19*

12   This is the night
That either makes me or fordoes me quite.
V, i, l. 128

13 And smooth as monumental alabaster.   *V, ii, l. 5*

14 Put out the light, and then put out the light:
If I quench thee, thou flaming minister,
I can again thy former light restore,
Should I repent me; but once put out thy light,
Thou cunning'st pattern of excelling nature,
I know not where is that Promethean heat
That can thy light relume.   *V, ii, l. 7*

15 It is the very error of the moon;
She comes more near the earth than she was wont,
And makes men mad.   *V, ii, l. 107*

16 She was as false as water.   *V, ii, l. 132*

17 Curse his better angel from his side,
And fall to reprobation.   *V, ii, l. 206*

---

[1] See John Heywood, 146:8 and note.

18 Here is my journey's end, here is my butt,
And very sea-mark of my utmost sail.
V, ii, l. 266

19 An honorable murderer, if you will;
For nought I did in hate, but all in honor.
V, ii, l. 293

20 I have done the state some service, and they know 't;
No more of that. I pray you, in your letters,
When you shall these unlucky deeds relate,
Speak of me as I am; nothing extenuate,
Nor set down aught in malice: then, must you speak
Of one that lov'd not wisely but too well;
Of one not easily jealous, but, being wrought,
Perplex'd in the extreme; of one whose hand,
Like the base Indian, threw a pearl away
Richer than all his tribe; of one whose subdu'd eyes
Albeit unused to the melting mood,
Drop tears as fast as the Arabian trees
Their med'cinable gum.   *V, ii, l. 338*

21   In Aleppo once,
Where a malignant and a turban'd Turk
Beat a Venetian and traduc'd the state,
I took by the throat the circumcised dog,
And smote him thus.   *V, ii, l. 354*

22   My love's
More richer than my tongue.
King Lear [1605], act I, sc. i, l. 79

23   Now, our joy,
Although our last, not least.   *I, i, l. 84*

24 Nothing will come of nothing.   *I, i, l. 92*

25   Mend your speech a little,
Lest you may mar your fortunes.   *I, i, l. 96*

26 *Lear:* So young, and so untender?
Cordelia: So young, my lord, and true.   *I, i, l. 108*

27 Come not between the dragon and his wrath.
I, i, l. 124

28 Kill thy physician, and the fee bestow
Upon the foul disease.   *I, i, l. 166*

29   I want that glib and oily art
To speak and purpose not.   *I, i, l. 227*

30 A still-soliciting eye.   *I, i, l. 234*

31 Time shall unfold what plighted cunning hides;
Who covers faults, at last shame them derides.
I, i, l. 282

32   The infirmity of his age.   *I, i, l. 296*

33 Who in the lusty stealth of nature take
More composition and fierce quality
Than doth, within a dull, stale, tired bed,
Go to the creating a whole tribe of fops.   *I, ii, l. 11*

1 Now, gods, stand up for bastards!   *I, ii, l. 22*

2   We have seen the best of our time: machinations, hollowness, treachery, and all ruinous disorders, follow us disquietly to our graves.   *I, ii, l. 125*

3   This is the excellent foppery of the world, that, when we are sick in fortune, — often the surfeit of our own behavior, — we make guilty of our disasters the sun, the moon, and the stars; as if we were villains by necessity, fools by heavenly compulsion, knaves, thieves, and treachers by spherical predominance, drunkards, liars, and adulterers by an enforced obedience of planetary influence.   *I, ii, l. 129*

4   Edgar —
   [*Enter Edgar*]
and pat he comes, like the catastrophe of the old comedy: my cue is villainous melancholy, with a sigh like Tom o' Bedlam.   *I, ii, l. 149*

5   *Lear:* Dost thou know me, fellow?
   Kent: No, sir, but you have that in your countenance which I would fain call master.
   Lear: What's that?
   Kent: Authority.   *I, iv, l. 28*

6   That which ordinary men are fit for, I am qualified in, and the best of me is diligence.   *I, iv, l. 36*

7   Truth's a dog must to kennel; he must be whipped out when Lady the brach may stand by the fire and stink.   *I, iv, l. 125*

8 Have more than thou showest,
Speak less than thou knowest,
Lend less than thou owest.   *I, iv, l. 132*

9   Can you make no use of nothing, nuncle?
   I, iv, l. 144

10 Ingratitude, thou marble-hearted fiend,
More hideous, when thou show'st thee in a child,
Than the sea-monster.   *I, iv, l. 283*

11 How sharper than a serpent's tooth it is
To have a thankless child!   *I, iv, l. 312*

12 Striving to better, oft we mar what's well.
   I, iv, l. 371

13   The son and heir of a mongrel bitch.   *II, ii, l. 23*

14 I have seen better faces in my time
Than stands on any shoulder that I see
Before me at this instant.   *II, ii, l. 99*

15 A good man's fortune may grow out at heels.
   II, ii, l. 164

16 Fortune, good night, smile once more; turn thy
   wheel!   *II, ii, l. 180*

17 *Hysterica passio!* down, thou climbing sorrow!
Thy element's below.   *II, iv, l. 57*

18 That sir which serves and seeks for gain,
And follows but for form,
Will pack when it begins to rain,
And leave thee in the storm.   *II, iv, l. 79*

19 Nature in you stands on the very verge
Of her confine.   *II, iv, l. 149*

20 Necessity's sharp pinch!   *II, iv, l. 214*

21   Our basest beggars
Are in the poorest thing superfluous:
Allow not nature more than nature needs,
Man's life is cheap as beast's.   *II, iv, l. 267*

22 Let not women's weapons, waterdrops,
Stain my man's cheeks!   *II, iv, l. 280*

23 I have full cause of weeping, but this heart
Shall break into a hundred thousand flaws
Or ere I'll weep. O fool! I shall go mad.
   II, iv, l. 287

24 Blow, winds, and crack your cheeks! rage! blow!
You cataracts and hurricanoes, spout
Till you have drench'd our steeples, drown'd the
   cocks!
You sulphurous and thought-executing fires,
Vaunt-couriers to oak-cleaving thunderbolts,
Singe my white head! And thou, all-shaking thunder,
Strike flat the thick rotundity o' the world!
Crack nature's molds, all germens spill at once
That make ingrateful man!   *III, ii, l. 1*

25 I tax not you, you elements, with unkindness.
   III, ii, l. 16

26 A poor, infirm, weak, and despis'd old man.
   III, ii, l. 20

27   There was never yet fair woman but she made mouths in a glass.   *III, ii, l. 35*

28 I will be the pattern of all patience.   *III, ii, l. 37*

29   I am a man
More sinn'd against than sinning.   *III, ii, l. 59*

30 The art of our necessities is strange,
That can make vile things precious.   *III, ii, l. 70*

31 He that has and a little tiny wit,
With hey, ho, the wind and the rain,
Must make content with his fortunes fit,
Though the rain it raineth every day.[1]   *III, ii, l. 76*

32 O! that way madness lies; let me shun that.
   III, iv, l. 21

33 Poor naked wretches, wheresoe'er you are,
That bide the pelting of this pitiless storm,

---

[1]See *Twelfth-Night*, 205:29.

How shall your houseless heads and unfed sides,
Your loop'd and window'd raggedness, defend you
From seasons such as these? O! I have ta'en
Too little care of this. Take physic, pomp;
Expose thyself to feel what wretches feel,
That thou mayst shake the superflux to them,
And show the heavens more just.

King Lear, III, iv, l. 28

1 Pillicock sat on Pillicock-hill:
Halloo, halloo, loo, loo!   *III, iv, l. 75*

2   Out-paramoured the Turk.   *III, iv, l. 91*

3   Is man no more than this? Consider him well.
Thou owest the worm no silk, the beast no hide, the
sheep no wool, the cat no perfume. Ha! here's three
on 's are sophisticated; thou art the thing itself; unaccommodated man is no more but such a poor, bare,
forked animal as thou art. Off, off, you lendings!
Come; unbutton here.   *III, iv, l. 105*

4   'Tis a naughty night to swim in.
III, iv, l. 113

5   The green mantle of the standing pool.
III, iv, l. 137

6 But mice and rats and such small deer
Have been Tom's food for seven long year.
III, iv, l. 142

7 The prince of darkness is a gentleman.[1]
III, iv, l. 147

8 Poor Tom's a-cold.   *III, iv, l. 151*

9 Child Rowland to the dark tower came,[2]
His word was still, Fie, foh, and fum,
I smell the blood of a British man.   *III, iv, l. 185*

10   He's mad that trusts in the tameness of a wolf, a
horse's health, a boy's love, or a whore's oath.
III, vi, l. 20

11   The little dogs and all,
Tray, Blanch, and Sweetheart, see, they bark at me.
III, vi, l. 65

12   Is there any cause in nature that makes these hard
hearts?   *III, vi, l. 81*

13 I am tied to the stake, and I must stand the course.
III, vii, l. 54

14 Out, vile jelly!   *III, vii, l. 83*

15 The lowest and most dejected thing of fortune.
IV, i, l. 3

---

[1]The Devil is a gentleman. — PERCY BYSSHE SHELLEY, *Peter Bell the Third*, pt. II, st. 2

[2]Child Roland to the dark tower came. — WALTER SCOTT, *The Bridal of Triermain* [1813]
Dauntless the slug-horn to my lips I set, / And blew. — ROBERT BROWNING, *Childe Roland to the Dark Tower Came* [1855], st. 34

16   The worst is not,
So long as we can say, "This is the worst."
IV, i, l. 27

17 As flies to wanton boys, are we to the gods;
They kill us for their sport.   *IV, i, l. 36*

18 You are not worth the dust which the rude wind
Blows in your face.   *IV, ii, l. 30*

19 She that herself will sliver and disbranch
From her material sap, perforce must wither
And come to deadly use.   *IV, ii, l. 34*

20 Wisdom and goodness to the vile seem vile;
Filths savor but themselves.   *IV, ii, l. 38*

21 Tigers, not daughters.   *IV, ii, l. 39*

22   It is the stars,
The stars above us, govern our conditions.
IV, iii, l. 34

23 Our foster-nurse of nature is repose.   *IV, iv, l. 12*

24   How fearful
And dizzy 'tis to cast one's eyes so low!
The crows and choughs that wing the midway air
Show scarce so gross as beetles; halfway down
Hangs one that gathers samphire, dreadful trade!
Methinks he seems no bigger than his head.
The fishermen that walk upon the beach
Appear like mice, and yond tall anchoring bark
Diminish'd to her cock, her cock a buoy
Almost too small for sight. The murmuring surge,
That on the unnumber'd idle pebbles chafes,
Cannot be heard so high.   *IV, vi, l. 12*

25   Nature's above art in that respect.   *IV, vi, l. 87*

26 Ay, every inch a king.   *IV, vi, l. 110*

27   The wren goes to 't, and the small gilded fly
Does lecher in my sight.
Let copulation thrive.   *IV, vi, l. 115*

28   Give me an ounce of civet, good apothecary, to
sweeten my imagination.   *IV, vi, l. 133*

29   A man may see how this world goes with no eyes.
Look with thine ears: see how yond justice rails upon
yon simple thief. Hark, in thine ear: change places;
and, handy-dandy, which is the justice, which is the
thief?   *IV, vi, l. 154*

30 Through tatter'd clothes small vices do appear;
Robes and furr'd gowns hide all. Plate sin with gold,
And the strong lance of justice hurtless breaks;
Arm it in rags, a pigmy's straw does pierce it.
IV, vi, l. 169

31   Get thee glass eyes;
And, like a scurvy politician, seem
To see the things thou dost not.   *IV, vi, l. 175*

1 When we are born, we cry that we are come
  To this great stage of fools.   *IV, vi, l. 187*

2 Then, kill, kill, kill, kill, kill, kill!   *IV, vi, l. 192*

3   Mine enemy's dog,
  Though he had bit me, should have stood that night
  Against my fire.   *IV, vii, l. 36*

4 Thou art a soul in bliss; but I am bound
  Upon a wheel of fire, that mine own tears
  Do scald like molten lead.   *IV, vii, l. 46*

5 I am a very foolish fond old man,
  Fourscore and upward, not an hour more or less;
  And, to deal plainly,
  I fear I am not in my perfect mind.   *IV, vii, l. 60*

6 Pray you now, forget and forgive.   *IV, vii, l. 84*

7   Men must endure
  Their going hence, even as their coming hither:
  Ripeness is all.   *V, ii, l. 9*

8   Come, let's away to prison;
  We two alone will sing like birds i' the cage:
  When thou dost ask me blessing, I'll kneel down,
  And ask of thee forgiveness: so we'll live,
  And pray, and sing, and tell old tales, and laugh
  At gilded butterflies, and hear poor rogues
  Talk of court news; and we'll talk with them too,
  Who loses and who wins; who's in, who's out;
  And take upon's the mystery of things,
  As if we were God's spies: and we'll wear out,
  In a wall'd prison, packs and sets of great ones
  That ebb and flow by the moon.   *V, iii, l. 8*

9 Upon such sacrifices, my Cordelia,
  The gods themselves throw incense.   *V, iii, l. 20*

10 The gods are just, and of our pleasant vices
  Make instruments to plague us.   *V, iii, l. 172*

11 The wheel is come full circle.   *V, iii, l. 176*

12 Howl, howl, howl, howl! O! you are men of stones:
  Had I your tongues and eyes, I'd use them so
  That heaven's vaults should crack. She's gone
      forever.   *V, iii, l. 259*

13   Her voice was ever soft,
  Gentle and low, an excellent thing in woman.
                                                   V, iii, l. 274

14 And my poor fool is hang'd! No, no, no life!
  Why should a dog, a horse, a rat, have life,
  And thou no breath at all? Thou'lt come no more,
  Never, never, never, never, never!
  Pray you, undo this button.   *V, iii, l. 307*

15 Vex not his ghost: O! let him pass; he hates him
  That would upon the rack of this tough world
  Stretch him out longer.   *V, iii, l. 315*

16 The weight of this sad time we must obey;
  Speak what we feel, not what we ought to say.
  The oldest hath borne most: we that are young,
  Shall never see so much, nor live so long.
                                                   V, iii, l. 325

17 'Tis not enough to help the feeble up,
  But to support him after.
      Timon of Athens [1605–1608], act I, sc. i, l. 108

18 I call the gods to witness.   *I, i, l. 138*

19 I wonder men dare trust themselves with men.
                                                   I, ii, l. 45

20 Here's that which is too weak to be a sinner,
  Honest water, which ne'er left man i' the mire.[1]
                                                   I, ii, l. 60

21 Immortal gods, I crave no pelf;
  I pray for no man but myself:
  Grant I may never prove so fond,
  To trust man on his oath or bond.   *I, ii, l. 64*

22 Men shut their doors against a setting sun.
                                                   I, ii, l. 152

23   Every man has his fault, and honesty is his.
                                                   III, i, l. 30

24 Nothing emboldens sin so much as mercy.
                                                   III, v, l. 3

25 You fools of fortune, trencher-friends, time's flies.
                                                   III, vi, l. 107

26 We have seen better days.   *IV, ii, l. 27*

27 O! the fierce wretchedness that glory brings us.
                                                   IV, ii, l. 30

28 I am Misanthropos, and hate mankind.
                                                   IV, iii, l. 53

29 Life's uncertain voyage.   *V, i, l. 207*

30 *First Witch:* When shall we three meet again
  In thunder, lightning, or in rain?
  Second Witch: When the hurlyburly's done,
  When the battle's lost and won.
              Macbeth [1606], act 1, sc. i, l. 1

31 Fair is foul, and foul is fair:
  Hover through the fog and filthy air.   *I, i, l. 12*

32 Banners flout the sky.   *I, ii, l. 50*

33 A sailor's wife had chestnuts in her lap,
  And munch'd, and munch'd, and munch'd: "Give
      me," quoth I:
  "Aroint thee, witch!" the rump-fed ronyon cries.
                                                   I, iii, l. 4

---

[1]Inscribed on the drinking fountain in the market square of Stratford-on-Avon.

1 Sleep shall neither night nor day
Hang upon his pent-house lid.

Macbeth, I, iii, l. 19

2 Dwindle, peak, and pine. *I, iii, l. 23*

3 The weird sisters, hand in hand,
Posters of the sea and land,
Thus do go about, about:
Thrice to thine, and thrice to mine,
And thrice again, to make up nine.
Peace! The charm's wound up. *I, iii, l. 32*

4 So foul and fair a day I have not seen. *I, iii, l. 38*

5 If you can look into the seeds of time,
And say which grain will grow and which will not,
Speak. *I, iii, l. 58*

6 And to be king
Stands not within the prospect of belief. *I, iii, l. 73*

7 The earth hath bubbles, as the water has,
And these are of them. *I, iii, l. 79*

8 Or have we eaten on the insane root
That takes the reason prisoner? *I, iii, l. 84*

9 And oftentimes, to win us to our harm,
The instruments of darkness tell us truths,
Win us with honest trifles, to betray 's
In deepest consequence. *I, iii, l. 123*

10 As happy prologues to the swelling act
Of the imperial theme. *I, iii, l. 128*

11 I am Thane of Cawdor:
If good, why do I yield to that suggestion
Whose horrid image doth unfix my hair
And make my seated heart knock at my ribs,
Against the use of nature? Present fears
Are less than horrible imaginings. *I, iii, l. 134*

12 If chance will have me king, why, chance may crown me,
Without my stir. *I, iii, l. 143*

13 Come what come may,
Time and the hour runs through the roughest day.

I, iii, l. 146

14 Nothing in his life
Became him like the leaving it; he died
As one that had been studied in his death
To throw away the dearest thing he ow'd,
As 'twere a careless trifle. *I, iv, l. 7*

15 There's no art
To find the mind's construction in the face:
He was a gentleman on whom I built
An absolute trust. *I, iv, l. 11*

16 Glamis thou art, and Cawdor; and shalt be
What thou art promis'd. Yet do I fear thy nature;

It is too full o' the milk of human kindness[1]
To catch the nearest way. *I, v, l. 16*

17 The raven himself is hoarse
That croaks the fatal entrance of Duncan
Under my battlements. Come, you spirits
That tend on mortal thoughts! unsex me here,
And fill me from the crown to the toe top full
Of direst cruelty; make thick my blood,
Stop up the access and passage to remorse,
That no compunctious visitings of nature
Shake my fell purpose, nor keep peace between
The effect and it! Come to my woman's breasts,
And take my milk for gall, you murdering
ministers. *I, v, l. 38*

18 Nor heaven peep through the blanket of the dark,
To cry, "Hold, hold!" *I, v, l. 54*

19 Your face, my thane, is as a book where men
May read strange matters. *I, v, l. 63*

20 Look like the innocent flower,
But be the serpent under 't. *I, v, l. 66*

21 *Duncan:* This castle hath a pleasant seat; the air
Nimbly and sweetly recommends itself
Unto our gentle senses.
Banquo: This guest of summer,
The temple-haunting martlet, does approve
By his lov'd mansionry that the heaven's breath
Smells wooingly here: no jutty, frieze,
Buttress, nor coign of vantage, but this bird
Hath made his pendent bed and procreant cradle:
Where they most breed and haunt, I have observ'd
The air is delicate. *I, vi, l. 1*

22 If it were done when 'tis done, then 'twere well
It were done quickly; if the assassination
Could trammel up the consequence, and catch
With his surcease success; that but this blow
Might be the be-all and the end-all here,
But here, upon this bank and shoal of time,
We'd jump the life to come. *I, vii, l. 1*

23 This even-handed justice. *I, vii, l. 10*

24 Besides, this Duncan
Hath borne his faculties so meek, hath been
So clear in his great office, that his virtues
Will plead like angels trumpet-tongu'd against
The deep damnation of his taking-off;
And pity, like a naked new-born babe,
Striding the blast, or heaven's cherubin, hors'd
Upon the sightless couriers of the air,
Shall blow the horrid deed in every eye,

---

[1]The thunder of your words has soured the milk of human kindness in my heart. — RICHARD BRINSLEY SHERIDAN, *The Rivals*, act III, sc. iv

That tears shall drown the wind. I have no spur
To prick the sides of my intent, but only
Vaulting ambition, which o'erleaps itself
And falls on the other.   *I, vii, l. 16*

1   I have bought
Golden opinions from all sorts of people.
                                                     I, vii, l. 32

2 Letting "I dare not" wait upon "I would,"
Like the poor cat i' the adage.   *I, vii, l. 44*

3 I dare do all that may become a man;
Who dares do more is none.   *I, vii, l. 46*

4   Nor time nor place
Did then adhere.   *I, vii, l. 51*

5   I have given suck, and know
How tender 'tis to love the babe that milks me:
I would, while it was smiling in my face,
Have pluck'd my nipple from his boneless gums,
And dash'd the brains out, had I so sworn as you
Have done to this.
                                                     I, vii, l. 54

6 *Macbeth:* If we should fail —
Lady Macbeth: We fail!
But screw your courage to the sticking-place,
And we'll not fail.   *I, vii, l. 59*

7 Memory, the warder of the brain.   *I, vii, l. 65*

8 Away, and mock the time with fairest show:
False face must hide what the false heart doth
        know.   *I, vii, l. 81*

9 The moon is down.   *III i, l. 2*

10   There's husbandry in heaven;
Their candles are all out.   *II, i, l. 4*

11   Merciful powers!
Restrain in me the cursed thoughts that nature
Gives way to in repose.   *II, i, l. 7*

12   Shut up
In measureless content.   *II, i, l. 16*

13 Is this a dagger which I see before me,
The handle toward my hand? Come, let me clutch
        thee:
I have thee not, and yet I see thee still.
Art thou not, fatal vision, sensible
To feeling as to sight? or art thou but
A dagger of the mind, a false creation,
Proceeding from the heat-oppressed brain?
                                                     II, i, l. 33

14   Now o'er the one half-world
Nature seems dead, and wicked dreams abuse
The curtain'd sleep; witchcraft celebrates
Pale Hecate's offerings.   *II, i, l. 49*

15   Thou sure and firm-set earth,
Hear not my steps, which way they walk, for fear
The very stones prate of my whereabout.   *II, i, l. 56*

16   The bell invites me.
Hear it not, Duncan; for it is a knell
That summons thee to heaven or to hell.
                                                     II, i, l. 62

17 It was the owl that shriek'd, the fatal bellman,
Which gives the stern'st good-night.   *II, ii, l. 4*

18   The attempt and not the deed
Confounds us.   *II, ii, l. 12*

19   Had he not resembled
My father as he slept I had done 't.   *II, ii, l. 14*

20 I had most need of blessing, and "Amen"
Stuck in my throat.   *II, ii, l. 33*

21 Methought I heard a voice cry "Sleep no more!
Macbeth does murder sleep," the innocent sleep,
Sleep that knits up the ravell'd sleave of care,
The death of each day's life, sore labor's bath,
Balm of hurt minds, great nature's second course,
Chief nourisher in life's feast.   *II, ii, l. 36*

22 Glamis hath murder'd sleep, and therefore Cawdor
Shall sleep no more, Macbeth shall sleep no more!
                                                     II, ii, l. 43

23   Infirm of purpose!
Give me the daggers. The sleeping and the dead
Are but as pictures; 'tis the eye of childhood
That fears a painted devil.   *II, ii, l. 53*

24 Will all great Neptune's ocean wash this blood
Clean from my hand? No, this my hand will rather
The multitudinous seas incarnadine,
Making the green one red.   *II, ii, l. 61*

25   The primrose way to the everlasting bonfire.
                                                     II, iii, l. 22

26   It [drink] provokes the desire, but it takes away
the performance.   *II, iii, l. 34*

27 The labor we delight in physics pain.   *II, iii, l. 56*

28 Confusion now hath made his masterpiece!
Most sacrilegious murder hath broke ope
The Lord's anointed temple, and stole thence
The life o' the building!   *II, iii, l. 72*

29 Shake off this downy sleep, death's counterfeit.
                                                     II, iii, l. 83

30 Had I but died an hour before this chance
I had liv'd a blessed time; for, from this instant,
There's nothing serious in mortality,
All is but toys; renown and grace is dead,
The wine of life is drawn, and the mere lees
Is left this vault to brag of.   *II, iii, l. 98*

1 Who can be wise, amaz'd, temperate and furious,
Loyal and neutral, in a moment? No man.
Macbeth, II, iii, l. 115

2 To show an unfelt sorrow is an office
Which the false man does easy.   *II, iii, l. 143*

3 A falcon, towering in her pride of place,
Was by a mousing owl hawk'd at and kill'd.
II, iv, l. 12

4 I must become a borrower of the night
For a dark hour or twain.   *III, i, l. 27*

5   To be thus is nothing;
But to be safely thus.   *III, i, l. 48*

6 *Murderer:*   We are men, my liege.
Macbeth: Ay, in the catalogue ye go for men.
III, i, l. 91

7   I am one, my liege,
Whom the vile blows and buffets of the world
Have so incens'd that I am reckless what
I do to spite the world.   *III, i, l. 108*

8 So weary with disasters, tugg'd with fortune,
That I would set my life on any chance,
To mend it or be rid on 't.   *III, i, l. 112*

9   Things without all remedy
Should be without regard: what's done is done.
III, ii, l. 11

10 We have scotch'd the snake, not kill'd it.   *III, ii, l. 13*

11   Duncan is in his grave;
After life's fitful fever he sleeps well;
Treason has done his worst: nor steel, nor poison,
Malice domestic, foreign levy, nothing
Can touch him further.   *III, ii, l. 22*

12 Then be thou jocund. Ere the bat hath flown
His cloister'd flight, ere, to black Hecate's summons
The shard-borne beetle with his drowsy hums
Hath rung night's yawning peal, there shall be done
A deed of dreadful note.   *III, ii, l. 40*

13   Come, seeling night,
Scarf up the tender eye of pitiful day,
And with thy bloody and invisible hand
Cancel and tear to pieces that great bond
Which keeps me pale! Light thickens, and the crow
Makes wing to the rooky wood.
III, ii, l. 46

14 Now spurs the lated traveler apace
To gain the timely inn.   *III, iii, l. 6*

15 But now I am cabin'd, cribb'd, confin'd, bound in
To saucy doubts and fears.   *III, iv, l. 24*

16 Now good digestion wait on appetite,
And health on both!   *III, iv, l. 38*

17 Thou canst not say I did it: never shake
Thy gory locks at me.   *III, iv, l. 50*

18 The air-drawn dagger.   *III, iv, l. 62*

19 I drink to the general joy of the whole table.
III, iv, l. 89

20   What man dare, I dare:
Approach thou like the rugged Russian bear,
The arm'd rhinoceros, or the Hyrcan tiger;
Take any shape but that, and my firm nerves
Shall never tremble.   *III, iv, l. 99*

21   Hence, horrible shadow!
Unreal mockery, hence!   *III, iv, l. 106*

22 Stand not upon the order of your going,
But go at once.   *III, iv, l. 119*

23 It will have blood, they say; blood will have blood:
Stones have been known to move and trees to
speak.   *III, iv, l. 122*

24 *Macbeth:*   What is the night?
Lady Macbeth: Almost at odds with morning, which is
which.   *III, iv, l. 126*

25   I am in blood
Stepp'd in so far, that, should I wade no more,
Returning were as tedious as go o'er.
III, iv, l. 136

26 Double, double toil and trouble;
Fire burn and cauldron bubble.   *IV, i, l. 10*

27 Eye of newt, and toe of frog,
Wool of bat, and tongue of dog.   *IV, i, l. 14*

28 Finger of birth-strangled babe,
Ditch-deliver'd by a drab.   *IV, i, l. 30*

29 By the pricking of my thumbs,
Something wicked this way comes.
Open, locks,
Whoever knocks!   *IV, i, l. 44*

30 How now, you secret, black, and midnight hags!
IV, i, l. 48

31 A deed without a name.   *IV, i, l. 49*

32 Be bloody, bold, and resolute; laugh to scorn
The power of man, for none of woman born
Shall harm Macbeth.   *IV, i, l. 79*

33 But yet I'll make assurance double sure,
And take a bond of fate.   *IV, i, l. 83*

34 Macbeth shall never vanquish'd be until
Great Birnam wood to high Dunsinane hill
Shall come against him.[1]   *IV, i, l. 92*

---

[1]Till Birnam wood remove to Dunsinane / I cannot taint with
fear. — *Macbeth, act V, sc. iii, l. 2*

1 Show his eyes, and grieve his heart;
 Come like shadows, so depart.   *IV, i, l. 110*

2 What! will the line stretch out to the crack of
   doom?   *IV, i, l. 117*

3   When our actions do not,
 Our fears do make us traitors.   *IV, ii, l. 3*

4 He wants the natural touch.   *IV, ii, l. 9*

5 Angels are bright still, though the brightest fell.
                                         IV, iii, l. 22

6 Pour the sweet milk of concord into hell,
 Uproar the universal peace, confound
 All unity on earth.   *IV, iii, l. 98*

7 Give sorrow words; the grief that does not speak
 Whispers the o'er-fraught heart and bids it break.
                                         IV, iii, l. 209

8   All my pretty ones?
 Did you say all? O hell-kite! All?
 What! all my pretty chickens and their dam
 At one fell swoop?   *IV, iii, l. 216*

9 *Malcolm:* Dispute it like a man.
 Macduff: I shall do so;
 But I must also feel it as a man:
 I cannot but remember such things were,
 That were most precious to me.   *IV, iii, l. 219*

10   Out, damned spot! out, I say!   *V, i, l. 38*

11   Fie, my lord, fie! a soldier, and afeard?   *V, i, l. 40*

12   Who would have thought the old man to have had
 so much blood in him?   *V, i, l. 42*

13   The Thane of Fife had a wife: where is she now?
                                         V, i, l. 46

14   All the perfumes of Arabia will not sweeten this
 little hand.   *V, i, l. 56*

15 Those he commands move only in command,
 Nothing in love; now does he feel his title
 Hang loose about him, like a giant's robe
 Upon a dwarfish thief.   *V, ii, l. 19*

16 The devil damn thee black, thou cream-fac'd loon!
 Where gott'st thou that goose look?   *V, iii, l. 11*

17 Thou lily-liver'd boy.   *V, iii, l. 15*

18 I have liv'd long enough: my way of life
 Is fall'n into the sere, the yellow leaf;
 And that which should accompany old age,
 As honor, love, obedience, troops of friends,
 I must not look to have; but, in their stead,
 Curses, not loud but deep, mouth-honor, breath,
 Which the poor heart would fain deny, and dare
   not.   *V, iii, l. 22*

19 *Macbeth:* Canst thou not minister to a mind diseas'd,
 Pluck from the memory a rooted sorrow,
 Raze out the written troubles of the brain,
 And with some sweet oblivious antidote
 Cleanse the stuff'd bosom of that perilous stuff
 Which weighs upon the heart?
 Doctor: Therein the patient
 Must minister to himself.
 Macbeth: Throw physic to the dogs; I'll none of it.
                                         V, iii, l. 40

20 I would applaud thee to the very echo,
 That should applaud again.   *V, iii, l. 53*

21 Hang out our banners on the outward walls;
 The cry is still, "They come"; our castle's strength
 Will laugh a siege to scorn.   *V, v, l. 1*

22   My fell of hair
 Would at a dismal treatise rouse and stir
 As life were in 't. I have supp'd full with horrors.
                                         V, v, l. 11

23 She should have died hereafter;
 There would have been a time for such a word.
 Tomorrow, and tomorrow, and tomorrow,
 Creeps in this petty pace from day to day,
 To the last syllable of recorded time;
 And all our yesterdays have lighted fools
 The way to dusty death. Out, out, brief candle!
 Life's but a walking shadow, a poor player
 That struts and frets his hour upon the stage,
 And then is heard no more; it is a tale
 Told by an idiot, full of sound and fury,
 Signifying nothing.   *V, v, l. 17*

24 I 'gin to be aweary of the sun,
 And wish the estate o' the world were now
   undone.   *V, v, l. 49*

25   Blow, wind! come, wrack!
 At least we'll die with harness on our back.
                                         V, v, l. 51

26 Why should I play the Roman fool; and die
 On mine own sword?   *V, vii, l. 30*

27 I bear a charmed life.   *V, vii, l. 41*

28   Macduff was from his mother's womb
 Untimely ripp'd.   *V, vii, l. 44*

29 And be these juggling fiends no more believ'd,
 That palter with us in a double sense;
 That keep the word of promise to our ear
 And break it to our hope.   *V, vii, l. 48*

30 Live to be the show and gaze o' the time.
                                         V, vii, l. 53

31   Lay on, Macduff,
 And damn'd be him that first cries, "Hold,
   enough!"   *V, vii, l. 62*

1   You shall see in him
The triple pillar of the world transform'd
Into a strumpet's fool.
     Antony and Cleopatra [1606–1607],
    act 1, sc. i, l. 12

2 There's beggary in the love that can be reckon'd.
            I, i, l. 15

3 Let Rome in Tiber melt, and the wide arch
Of the rang'd empire fall! Here is my space.
Kingdoms are clay.
            I, i, l. 33

4 In nature's infinite book of secrecy
A little I can read.
            I, ii, l. 11

5 I love long life better than figs.
            I, ii, l. 34

6   On the sudden
A Roman thought hath struck him.
            I, ii, l. 90

7 Eternity was in our lips and eyes,
Bliss in our brows bent.
            I, iii, l. 35

8   Good now, play one scene
Of excellent dissembling, and let it look
Like perfect honor.
            I, iii, l. 78

9 O! my oblivion is a very Antony,
And I am all forgotten.
            I, iii, l. 90

10 Give me to drink mandragora. . . .
That I might sleep out this great gap of time
My Antony is away.
            I, v, l. 4

11 O happy horse, to bear the weight of Antony!
            I, v, l. 21

12 The demi-Atlas of this earth, the arm
And burgonet of men.
            I, v, l. 23

13 Where's my serpent of old Nile?   *I, v, l. 25*

14 A morsel for a monarch.   *I, v, l. 31*

15 My man of men.   *I, v, l. 71*

16   My salad days,
When I was green in judgment.
            I, v, l. 73

17   We, ignorant of ourselves,
Beg often our own harms, which the wise powers
Deny us for our good; so find we profit
By losing of our prayers.
            II, i, l. 5

18   Epicurean cooks
Sharpen with cloyless sauce his appetite. *II, i, l. 24*

19 No worse a husband than the best of men.
            II, ii, l. 135

20 The barge she sat in, like a burnish'd throne,
Burn'd on the water; the poop was beaten gold,
Purple the sails, and so perfumed, that
The winds were love-sick with them; the oars were
    silver,

Which to the tune of flutes kept stroke, and made
The water which they beat to follow faster,
As amorous of their strokes. For her own person,
It beggar'd all description.   *II, ii, l. 199*

21 Age cannot wither her, nor custom stale
Her infinite variety; other women cloy
The appetites they feed, but she makes hungry
Where most she satisfies; for vilest things
Become themselves in her, that the holy priests
Bless her when she is riggish.   *II, ii, l. 243*

22 I have not kept my square, but that to come
Shall all be done by the rule.   *II, iii, l. 6*

23   I will to Egypt
And though I make this marriage for my peace,
I' the East my pleasure lies.   *II, iii, l. 38*

24   Music, moody food
Of us that trade in love.   *II, v, l. 1*

25 Though it be honest, it is never good
To bring bad news.   *II, v, l. 85*

26 He will to his Egyptian dish again. *II, vi, l. 133*

27 Come, thou monarch of the vine,
Plumpy Bacchus, with pink eyne! *II, vii, l. 120*

28   Ambition,
The soldier's virtue.   *III, i, l. 22*

29 Celerity is never more admir'd
Than by the negligent.   *III, vii, l. 24*

30   We have kiss'd away
Kingdoms and provinces.   *III, viii, l. 17*

31   He wears the rose
Of youth upon him.   *III, xi, l. 20*

32   Men's judgments are
A parcel of their fortunes, and things outward
Do draw the inward quality after them,
To suffer all alike.   *III, xi, l. 31*

33 I found you as a morsel, cold upon
Dead Caesar's trencher.   *III, xi, l. 116*

34 Let's have one other gaudy night. *III, xi, l. 182*

35 Now he'll outstare the lightning. To be furious
Is to be frighted out of fear.   *III, xi, l. 194*

36 To business that we love we rise betime,
And go to 't with delight.   *IV, iv, l. 20*

37 O infinite virtue! com'st thou smiling from
The world's great snare uncaught? *IV, viii, l. 17*

38 The shirt of Nessus is upon me.   *IV, x, l. 56*

39 Sometimes we see a cloud that's dragonish;
A vapor sometime like a bear or lion,
A tower'd citadel, a pendant rock,

A forked mountain, or blue promontory
With trees upon 't. *IV, xii, l. 2*

1 Unarm, Eros; the long day's task is done,
And we must sleep. *IV, xii, l. 35*

2   But I will be
A bridegroom in my death, and run into 't
As to a lover's bed. *IV, xii, l. 99*

3   O sun!
Burn the great sphere thou mov'st in; darkling stand
The varying shore o' the world. *IV, xiii, l. 10*

4 I am dying, Egypt, dying; only
I here importune death awhile, until
Of many thousand kisses the poor last
I lay upon thy lips. *IV, xiii, l. 18*

5 O! wither'd is the garland of the war,
The soldier's pole is fall'n; young boys and girls
Are level now with men; the odds is gone,
And there is nothing left remarkable
Beneath the visiting moon.
        IV, xiii, l. 64

6 Let's do it after the high Roman fashion,
And make death proud to take us. *IV, xiii, l. 87*

7   And it is great
To do that thing that ends all other deeds,
Which shackles accidents, and bolts up change.
        V, ii, l. 4

8 His legs bestrid the ocean; his rear'd arm
Crested the world; his voice was propertied
As all the tuned spheres, and that to friends;
But when he meant to quail and shake the orb,
He was as rattling thunder. For his bounty,
There was no winter in 't, an autumn 'twas
That grew the more by reaping; his delights
Were dolphin-like, they show'd his back above
The element they liv'd in; in his livery
Walk'd crowns and crownets, realms and islands were
As plates dropp'd from his pocket. *V, ii, l. 82*

9   The bright day is done,
And we are for the dark. *V, ii, l. 192*

10   The quick comedians
Extemporally will stage us, and present
Our Alexandrian revels. Antony
Shall be brought drunken forth, and I shall see
Some squeaking Cleopatra boy my greatness
I' the posture of a whore. *V, ii, l. 215*

11 A woman is a dish for the gods, if the devil dress
her not. *V, ii, l. 274*

12   I wish you joy of the worm. *V, ii, l. 280*

13   I have
Immortal longings in me. *V, ii, l. 282*

14 Husband, I come. *V, ii, l. 289*

15 If thou and nature can so gently part,
The stroke of death is as a lover's pinch,
Which hurts, and is desir'd. *V, ii, l. 296*

16 Dost thou not see my baby at my breast,
That sucks the nurse asleep? *V, ii, l. 311*

17 Now boast thee, death, in thy possession lies
A lass unparallel'd. *V, ii, l. 317*

18 *First Guard:* . . . Charmian, is this well done?
Charmian: It is well done, and fitting for a princess
Descended of so many royal kings.[1] *V, ii, l. 327*

19 As she would catch another Antony
In her strong toil of grace. *V, ii, l. 348*

20   The gods sent not
Corn for the rich men only.
   Coriolanus [1607–1608], act 1, sc. i, l. 213

21   They threw their caps
As they would hang them on the horns o' the moon,
Shouting their emulation. *I, i, l. 218*

22 All the yarn she spun in Ulysses' absence did but
fill Ithaca full of moths. *I, iii, l. 93*

23 Nature teaches beasts to know their friends.
        II, i, l. 6

24 A cup of hot wine with not a drop of allaying
Tiber in 't. *II, i, l. 52*

25 My gracious silence, hail! *II, i, l. 194*

26 He himself stuck not to call us the many-headed
multitude. *II, iii, l. 18*

27   Bid them wash their faces,
And keep their teeth clean. *II, iii, l. 65*

28 I thank you for your voices, thank you,
Your most sweet voices. *II, iii, l. 179*

29 The mutable, rank-scented many. *III, i, l. 65*

30 Hear you this Triton of the minnows? mark you
His absolute "shall"? *III, i, l. 88*

31 What is the city but the people? *III, i, l. 198*

32 His nature is too noble for the world:
He would not flatter Neptune for his trident,
Or Jove for 's power to thunder. His heart's his
  mouth:
What his breast forges, that his tongue must vent.[2]
        III, i, l. 254

---

[1] One of the soldiers seeing her, angrily said unto her: is that well done Charmian? Very well said she again, and meet for a princess descended of so many noble kings. — PLUTARCH, *Lives,* translated [1579] by THOMAS NORTH

[2] See Marcus Manilius, 104:9, and Benjamin Franklin, 301:*n*3.

1   The beast
With many heads butts me away.

Coriolanus, IV, i, l. 1

2   O! a kiss
Long as my exile, sweet as my revenge!   *V, iii, l. 44*

3   Chaste as the icicle
That's curdied by the frost from purest snow,
And hangs on Dian's temple.   *V, iii, l. 65*

4   He wants nothing of a god but eternity and a
heaven to throne in.   *V, iv, l. 25*

5 They'll give him death by inches.   *V, iv, l. 43*

6 If you have writ your annals true, 'tis there,
That, like an eagle in a dovecote, I
Flutter'd your Volscians in Corioli:
Alone I did it.   *V, v, l. 114*

7 Thou hast done a deed whereat valor will weep.

V, v, l. 135

8 He shall have a noble memory.   *V, v, l. 155*

9 See, where she comes apparell'd like the spring.

Pericles [1608–1609], act I, sc. i, l. 12

10 Few love to hear the sins they love to act.   *I, i, l. 92*

11 The sad companion, dull-ey'd melancholy.   *I, ii, l. 2*

12   *Third Fisherman:* . . . Master, I marvel how the
fishes live in the sea.
First Fisherman: Why, as men do a-land; the great
ones eat up the little ones.[1]   *II, i, l. 29*

13   Lest the bargain should catch cold and starve.

Cymbeline [1609–1610], act I, sc. iv, l. 186

14   Hath his bellyful of fighting.   *II, i, l. 24*

15 Hark! hark! the lark at heaven's gate sings,
And Phoebus 'gins arise,
His steeds to water at those springs
On chalic'd flowers that lies;
And winking Mary-buds begin
To ope their golden eyes:
With everything that pretty is,
My lady sweet, arise.   *II, iii, l. 22*

16 As chaste as unsunn'd snow.   *II, v, l. 13*

17 Some griefs are med'cinable.   *III, ii, l. 33*

18 O! for a horse with wings!   *III, ii, l. 49*

19 The game is up.   *III, iii, l. 107*

20   Slander,
Whose edge is sharper than the sword, whose tongue
Outvenoms all the worms of Nile, whose breath
Rides on the posting winds and doth belie

All corners of the world.   *III, iv, l. 35*

21 I have not slept one wink.   *III, iv, l. 103*

22   Weariness
Can snore upon the flint when resty sloth
Finds the down pillow hard.   *III, vi, l. 33*

23   An angel! or, if not,
An earthly paragon!   *III, vi, l. 42*

24   Society is no comfort
To one not sociable.   *IV, ii, l. 12*

25   I wear not
My dagger in my mouth.   *IV, ii, l. 78*

26 Fear no more the heat o' the sun,
Nor the furious winter's rages;
Thou thy worldly task hast done,
Home art gone, and ta'en thy wages;
Golden lads and girls all must,
As chimney-sweepers, come to dust.   *IV, ii, l. 258*

27 Quiet consummation have;
And renowned be thy grave!   *IV, ii, l. 280*

28 Fortune brings in some boats that are not steer'd.

IV, iii, l. 46

29 Hang there like fruit, my soul,
Till the tree die!   *V, v, l. 264*

30 From fairest creatures we desire increase,
That thereby beauty's rose might never die.

Sonnets[2] [1609], 1, l. 1

31 When forty winters shall besiege thy brow,
And dig deep trenches in thy beauty's field.

Sonnet 2, l. 1

32 Thou art thy mother's glass, and she in thee
Calls back the lovely April of her prime.

Sonnet 3, l. 9

33 Music to hear, why hear'st thou music sadly?
Sweets with sweet war not, joy delights in joy.

Sonnet 8, l. 1

---

[2]Most of the sonnets were written before 1598, according to the
Palladis Tamia [1598] of Francis Meres [1565–1647]. They were
published [1609] by Thomas Thorpe [c. 1569–1635?], who may
have written the dedication:

TO THE ONLIE BEGETTER OF
THESE INSUING SONNETS
MR. W. H., ALL HAPPINESSE
AND THAT ETERNITIE
PROMISED
BY
OUR EVER-LIVING POET
WISHETH
THE WELL-WISHING
ADVENTURER IN
SETTING
FORTH
T.T.

---

[1]Men lived like fishes; the great ones devoured the small. —
Algernon Sidney, *Discourses on Government, ch. 2, sec. 18*

1   Everything that grows
Holds in perfection but a little moment.
Sonnet 15, l. 1

2 Shall I compare thee to a summer's day?
Thou art more lovely and more temperate:
Rough winds do shake the darling buds of May,
And summer's lease hath all too short a date.
Sonnet 18, l. 1

3 But thy eternal summer shall not fade.
Sonnet 18, l. 9

4 The painful warrior famoused for fight,
After a thousand victories, once foil'd,
Is from the books of honor razed quite,
And all the rest forgot for which he toil'd.
Sonnet 25, l. 9

5 When in disgrace with fortune and men's eyes
I all alone beweep my outcast state,
And trouble deaf heaven with my bootless cries.
Sonnet 29, l. 1

6 Desiring this man's art, and that man's scope,
With what I most enjoy contented least;
Yet in these thoughts myself almost despising,
Haply I think on thee.   *Sonnet 29, l. 7*

7 For thy sweet love remember'd such wealth brings
That then I scorn to change my state with kings.
Sonnet 29, l. 13

8 When to the sessions of sweet silent thought
I summon up remembrance of things past,
I sigh the lack of many a thing I sought,
And with old woes new wail my dear times' waste.
Sonnet 30, l. 1

9 But if the while I think on thee, dear friend,
All losses are restor'd and sorrows end.
Sonnet 30, l. 13

10 Full many a glorious morning have I seen.
Sonnet 33, l. 1

11 Roses have thorns, and silver fountains mud;
Clouds and eclipses stain both moon and sun,
And loathsome canker lives in sweetest bud.
All men make faults.   *Sonnet 35, l. 2*

12 Be thou the tenth Muse.   *Sonnet 38, l. 9*

13 For nimble thought can jump both sea and land.
Sonnet 44, l. 7

14 Against that time when thou shalt strangely pass,
And scarcely greet me with that sun, thine eye,
When love, converted from the thing it was,
Shall reasons find of settled gravity.   *Sonnet 49, l. 5*

15 Not marble, nor the gilded monuments
Of princes, shall outlive this powerful rime.
Sonnet 55, l. i.

16 Like as the waves make towards the pebbled shore,
So do our minutes hasten to their end.
Sonnet 60, l. 1

17 Time doth transfix the flourish set on youth
And delves the parallels in beauty's brow.
Sonnet 60, l. 9

18 When I have seen by Time's fell hand defaced
The rich proud cost of outworn buried age,
When sometime lofty towers I see down-rased
And brass eternal slave to mortal rage;
When I have seen the hungry ocean gain
Advantage on the kingdom of the shore,
And the firm soil win of the wat'ry main,
Increasing store with loss and loss with store.
Sonnet 64, l. 1

19 Ruin hath taught me thus to ruminate,
That Time will come and take my love away.
This thought is as a death, which cannot
    choose
But weep to have that which it fears to lose.
Sonnet 64, l. 11

20 Tir'd with all these, for restful death I cry.
Sonnet 66, l. 1

21 And art made tongue-tied by authority.
Sonnet 66, l. 9

22 And simple truth miscall'd simplicity,
And captive good attending captain ill.
Sonnet 66, l. 11

23 No longer mourn for me when I am dead
Than you shall hear the surly sullen bell
Give warning to the world that I am fled
From this vile world, with vilest worms to dwell.
Sonnet 71, l. 1

24 That time of year thou mayst in me behold
When yellow leaves, or none, or few, do hang
Upon those boughs which shake against
    the cold,
Bare ruin'd choirs, where late the sweet
    birds sang.   *Sonnet 73, l. 1*

25 Clean starved for a look.   *Sonnet 75, l. 10*

26 Who is it that says most? which can say more
Than this rich praise, — that you alone are you?
Sonnet 84, l. 1

27 Farewell! thou art too dear for my possessing,
And like enough thou know'st thy estimate.
Sonnet 87, l. 1

28 In sleep a king, but, waking, no such matter.
Sonnet 87, l. 14

29 Ah! do not, when my heart hath 'scap'd this sorrow,
Come in the rearward of a conquer'd woe;

Give not a windy night a rainy morrow,
To linger out a purpos'd overthrow.
Sonnet 90, l. 5

1 They that have power to hurt and will do none,
That do not do the thing they most do show,
Who, moving others, are themselves as stone,
Unmoved, cold, and to temptation slow.
Sonnet 94, l. 1

2 They are the lords and owners of their faces,
Others but stewards of their excellence.
The summer's flower is to the summer sweet,
Though to itself it only live and die.
Sonnet 94, l. 7

3 Lilies that fester smell far worse than weeds.[1]
Sonnet 94, l. 14

4 The hardest knife ill-used doth lose his edge.
Sonnet 95, l. 14

5 How like a winter hath my absence been.
Sonnet 97, l. 1

6 From you have I been absent in the spring,
When proud-pied April, dress'd in all his trim,
Hath put a spirit of youth in everything.
Sonnet 98, l. 1

7 Sweets grown common lose their dear delight.
Sonnet 102, l. 12

8 To me, fair friend, you never can be old,
For as you were when first your eye I ey'd,
Such seems your beauty still.   *Sonnet 104, l. 1*

9 When in the chronicle of wasted time
I see descriptions of the fairest wights,
And beauty making beautiful old rime,
In praise of ladies dead and lovely knights,
Then, in the blazon of sweet beauty's best,
Of hand, of foot, of lip, of eye, of brow,
I see their antique pen would have express'd
Even such a beauty as you master now.
Sonnet 106, l. 1

10 Not mine own fears, nor the prophetic soul
Of the wide world dreaming on things to come,
Can yet the lease of my true love control,
Suppos'd as forfeit to a confin'd doom.
The mortal moon hath her eclipse endur'd,
And the sad augurs mock their own presage;
Incertainties now crown themselves assur'd,
And peace proclaims olives of endless age.
Sonnet 107, l. 1

---

[1]As in the nature of things, those which most admirably flourish, most swiftly fester or putrefy, as roses, lilies, violets, while others last: so in the lives of men, those that are most blooming, are soonest turned into the opposite. — PLINY THE ELDER, *Natural History, bk. XVI, ch. 15*

11 O! never say that I was false of heart,
Though absence seem'd my flame to qualify.
Sonnet 109, l. 1

12 That is my home of love: if I have rang'd,
Like him that travels, I return again.   *Sonnet 109, l. 5*

13 Alas! 'tis true I have gone here and there,
And made myself a motley to the view,
Gor'd mine own thoughts, sold cheap what is most
dear,
Made old offenses of affections new.
Sonnet 110, l. 1

14   My nature is subdu'd
To what it works in, like the dyer's hand.
Sonnet 111, l. 6

15 Let me not to the marriage of true minds
Admit impediments. Love is not love
Which alters when it alteration finds,
Or bends with the remover to remove:
O, no! it is an ever-fixed mark,
That looks on tempests and is never shaken;
It is the star to every wandering bark,
Whose worth's unknown, although his height be
taken.
Love's not Time's fool, though rosy lips and cheeks
Within his bending sickle's compass come;
Love alters not with his brief hours and weeks,
But bears it out even to the edge of doom.
If this be error, and upon me prov'd,
I never writ, nor no man ever lov'd.
Sonnet 116

16 What potions have I drunk of Siren tears,
Distill'd from limbecks foul as hell within.
Sonnet 119, l. 1

17 O benefit of ill!   *Sonnet 119, l. 9*

18 And ruin'd love, when it is built anew,
Grows fairer than at first, more strong, far greater.
Sonnet 119, l. 11

19 'Tis better to be vile than vile esteem'd,
When not to be receives reproach of being.
Sonnet 121, l. 1

20 The expense of spirit in a waste of shame
Is lust in action; and till action, lust
Is perjur'd, murderous, bloody, full of blame,
Savage, extreme, rude, cruel, not to trust;
Enjoy'd no sooner but despised straight;
Past reason hunted; and no sooner had,
Past reason hated, as a swallow'd bait,
On purpose laid to make the taker mad:
Mad in pursuit, and in possession so;
Had, having, and in quest to have, extreme;
A bliss in proof, — and prov'd, a very woe;
Before, a joy propos'd; behind, a dream.

All this the world well knows; yet none knows well
To shun the heaven that leads men to this hell.
Sonnet 129

1 My mistress' eyes are nothing like the sun;
Coral is far more red than her lips' red:
If snow be white, why then her breasts are dun;
If hairs be wires, black wires grow on her head.
Sonnet 130, l. 1

2 When my love swears that she is made of truth,
I do believe her, though I know she lies.
Sonnet 138, l. 1

3 Two loves I have of comfort and despair,
Which like two spirits do suggest me still.
Sonnet 144, l. 1

4 Poor soul, the center of my sinful earth.
Sonnet 146, l. 1

5 So shalt thou feed on Death, that feeds on men,
And Death once dead, there's no more dying then.
Sonnet 146, l. 13

6 Past cure I am, now Reason is past care,
And frantic-mad with evermore unrest.
Sonnet 147, l. 9

7 For I have sworn thee fair, and thought thee bright,
Who art as black as hell, as dark as night.
Sonnet 147, l. 13

8 You pay a great deal too dear for what's given freely.
*The Winter's Tale [1610–1611],
act I, sc. i, l. 18*

9 Two lads that thought there was no more behind
But such a day tomorrow as today,
And to be boy eternal. *I, ii, l. 63*

10 We were as twinn'd lambs that did frisk i' the sun,
And bleat the one at the other: what we chang'd
Was innocence for innocence. *I, ii, l. 67*

11 Paddling palms and pinching fingers. *I, ii, l. 116*

12 Affection! thy intention stabs the center:
Thou dost make possible things not so held,
Communicat'st with dreams. *I, ii, l. 139*

13 He makes a July's day short as December.
I, ii, l. 169

14 A sad tale's best for winter.
I have one of sprites and goblins. *II, i, l. 24*

15 The silence often of pure innocence
Persuades when speaking fails. *II, ii, l. 41*

16 It is a heretic that makes the fire,
Not she which burns in 't. *II, iii, l. 115*

17 I am a feather for each wind that blows.
II, iii, l. 153

18 What's gone and what's past help
Should be past grief. *III, ii, l. 223*

19 Exit, pursued by a bear.[1] *III, iii, l. 57*

20 This is fairy gold, boy, and 'twill prove so.
III, iii, l. 127

21 Then comes in the sweet o' the year. *IV, ii, l. 3*

22 A snapper-up of unconsidered trifles. *IV, ii, l. 26*

23 For the life to come, I sleep out the thought
of it. *IV, ii, l. 30*

24 Jog on, jog on, the footpath way,
And merrily hent the stile-a:
A merry heart goes all the day,
Your sad tires in a mile-a. *IV, ii, l. 133*

25 For you there's rosemary and rue; these keep
Seeming and savor all the winter long. *IV, iii, l. 74*

26 Here's flowers for you:
Hot lavender, mints, savory, marjoram,
The marigold, that goes to bed wi' the sun,
And with him rises weeping: these are flowers
Of middle summer, and I think they are given
To men of middle age. *IV, iii, l. 103*

27 Daffodils,
That come before the swallow dares, and take
The winds of March with beauty. *IV, iii, l. 118*

28 What you do
Still betters what is done. *IV, iii, l. 135*

29 When you do dance, I wish you
A wave o' the sea, that you might ever do
Nothing but that. *IV, iii, l. 140*

30 Lawn as white as driven snow. *IV, iii, l. 220*

31 I love a ballad in print, a-life, for then we are sure
they are true. *IV, iii, l. 262*

32 The self-same sun that shines upon his court
Hides not his visage from our cottage, but
Looks on alike. *IV, iii, l. 457*

33 I'll queen it no inch further,
But milk my ewes and weep. *IV, iii, l. 462*

34 Prosperity's the very bond of love,
Whose fresh complexion and whose heart together
Affliction alters. *IV, iii, l. 586*

35 Let me have no lying; it becomes none but
tradesmen. *IV, iii, l. 747*

36 To purge melancholy. *IV, iii, l. 792*

37 There's time enough for that. *V, iii, l. 128*

---

[1]Perhaps the most famous stage direction in English.

1   He hath no drowning mark upon him; his complexion is perfect gallows.
      The Tempest [1611–1612],
      act I, sc. i, l. 33

2   Now would I give a thousand furlongs of sea for an acre of barren ground.   *I, i, l. 70*

3   I would fain die a dry death.   *I, i, l. 73*

4   What seest thou else
In the dark backward and abysm of time?   *I, ii, l. 49*

5   By telling of it,
Made such a sinner of his memory,
To credit his own lie.   *I, ii, l. 100*

6 Your tale, sir, would cure deafness.   *I, ii, l. 106*

7   My library
Was dukedom large enough.   *I, ii, l. 109*

8   The very rats
Instinctively have quit it.   *I, ii, l. 147*

9 Knowing I lov'd my books, he furnish'd me,
From mine own library with volumes that
I prize above my dukedom.   *I, ii, l. 166*

10 I [Ariel] will be correspondent to command,
And do my spiriting gently.   *I, ii, l. 297*

11 You taught me language; and my profit on 't
Is, I know how to curse: the red plague rid you,
For learning me your language!   *I, ii, l. 363*

12 Come unto these yellow sands,
And then take hands:
Curtsied when you have, and kiss'd —
The wild waves whist, —
Foot it featly here and there.   *I, ii, l. 375*

13 This music crept by me upon the waters,
Allaying both their fury, and my passion,
With its sweet air.   *I, ii, l. 389*

14 Full fathom five thy father lies;
Of his bones are coral made:
Those are pearls that were his eyes:
Nothing of him that doth fade,
But doth suffer a sea-change
Into something rich and strange.[1]   *I, ii, l. 394*

15 The fringed curtains of thine eye advance.
    I, ii, l. 405

16   Lest too light winning
Make the prize light.   *I, ii, l. 448*

17 There's nothing ill can dwell in such a temple:
If the ill spirit have so fair a house,
Good things will strive to dwell with 't.   *I, ii, l. 454*

18   He receives comfort like cold porridge.   *II, i, l. 10*

19 I' the commonwealth I would by contraries
Execute all things; for no kind of traffic
Would I admit; no name of magistrate;
Letters should not be known; riches, poverty,
And use of service, none; contract, succession,
Bourn, bound of land, tilth, vineyard, none;
No use of metal, corn, or wine, or oil;
No occupation; all men idle, all;
And women too, but innocent and pure.[2]
    II, i, l. 154

20 What's past is prologue.   *II, i, l. 261*

21 Open-ey'd Conspiracy
His time doth take.   *II, i, l. 309*

22   A very ancient and fish-like smell.   *II, ii, l. 27*

23   Misery acquaints a man with strange bedfellows.   *II, ii, l. 42*

24   How cam'st thou to be the siege of this mooncalf?   *II, ii, l. 115*

25   I shall laugh myself to death.   *II, ii, l. 167*

26 'Ban, 'Ban, Ca — Caliban,
Has a new master — Get a new man.   *II, ii, l. 197*

27   For several virtues
Have I lik'd several women.   *III, i, l. 42*

28 *Ferdinand:* ... Here's my hand.
Miranda: And mine, with my heart in't.
    III, i, l. 89

29   Thou deboshed fish thou.   *III, ii, l. 30*

30   Keep a good tongue in your head.   *III, ii, l. 41*

31 Flout 'em, and scout 'em; and scout 'em, and flout 'em;
Thought is free.[3]   *III, ii, l. 133*

32   He that dies pays all debts.   *III, ii, l. 143*

33   The isle is full of noises,
Sounds and sweet airs, that give delight, and hurt not.
Sometimes a thousand twangling instruments
Will hum about mine ears; and sometimes voices,
That, if I then had wak'd after long sleep,
Will make me sleep again.   *III, ii, l. 146*

34   A kind
Of excellent dumb discourse.   *III, iii, l. 38*

35   Do not give dalliance
Too much the rein.   *IV, i, l. 51*

---

[1] The last three lines are inscribed on P. B. Shelley's gravestone.

[2] It is a nation, would I answer Plato, that hath no kind of traffic, no knowledge of letters, no intelligence of numbers, no name of magistrate, nor of politic superiority; no use of service, of riches or poverty, no contracts, no successions, no partitions, no occupation but idle; no respect of kindred, but common, no apparel but natural, no manuring of lands, no use of wine, corn, or metal. — MONTAIGNE, *Essays, bk. I, ch. 30, Of the Cannibals*

[3] Thought is free. — *Twelfth-Night, act I, sc. iii, l. 73*

1 Our revels now are ended. These our actors,
  As I foretold you, were all spirits and
  Are melted into air, into thin air:
  And, like the baseless fabric of this vision,
  The cloud-capp'd towers, the gorgeous palaces,
  The solemn temples, the great globe itself,
  Yea, all which it inherit, shall dissolve
  And, like this insubstantial pageant faded,
  Leave not a rack behind. We are such stuff
  As dreams are made on, and our little life
  Is rounded with a sleep.   *IV, i, l. 148*

2 With foreheads villainous low.   *IV, i, l. 252*

3   But this rough magic
  I here abjure.   *V, i, l. 50*

4   I'll break my staff,
  Bury it certain fathoms in the earth,
  And, deeper than did ever plummet sound,
  I'll drown my book.   *V, i, l. 54*

5 Where the bee sucks, there suck I
  In a cowslip's bell I lie;
  There I couch when owls do cry.
  On the bat's back I do fly
  After summer merrily:
  Merrily, merrily shall I live now
  Under the blossom that hangs on the bough.
                      V, i, l. 88

6   O brave new world,
  That has such people in't!   *V, i, l. 183*

7 Let us not burden our remembrances
  With a heaviness that's gone.   *V, i, l. 199*

8   This thing of darkness I
  Acknowledge mine.   *V, i, l. 274*

9 And my ending is despair,
  Unless I be reliev'd by prayer,
  Which pierces so that it assaults
  Mercy itself and frees all faults.   *Epilogue, l. 15*

10   No man's pie is freed
  From his ambitious finger.
          King Henry the Eighth[1] *[1613],*
          act I, sc. i, l. 52

11 The force of his own merit makes his way.   *I, i, l. 64*

12 Heat not a furnace for your foe so hot
  That it do singe yourself.   *I, i, l. 140*

13 If I chance to talk a little wild, forgive me;
  I had it from my father.   *I, iv, l. 26*

14 The mirror of all courtesy.   *II, i, l. 53*

15 Go with me, like good angels, to my end;
  And, as the long divorce of steel falls on me,

Make of your prayers one sweet sacrifice,
And lift my soul to heaven.   *II, i, l. 75*

16 This bold bad man.   *II, ii, l. 44*

17   'Tis better to be lowly born,
  And range with humble livers in content,
  Than to be perk'd up in a glist'ring grief
  And wear a golden sorrow.   *II, iii, l. 19*

18   I would not be a queen
  For all the world.   *II, iii, l. 45*

19 Orpheus with his lute made trees,
  And the mountain-tops that freeze,
  Bow themselves, when he did sing.   *III, i, l. 3*

20 Heaven is above all yet; there sits a judge
  That no king can corrupt.   *III, i, l. 99*

21   'Tis well said again;
  And 'tis a kind of good deed to say well:
  And yet words are no deeds.   *III, ii, l. 153*

22   And then to breakfast with
  What appetite you have.   *III, ii, l. 203*

23 I have touch'd the highest point of all my greatness;
  And from that full meridian of my glory,
  I haste now to my setting: I shall fall
  Like a bright exhalation in the evening,
  And no man see me more.   *III, ii, l. 224*

24 Press not a falling man too far.[2]
                      III, ii, l. 334

25 Farewell! a long farewell, to all my greatness!
  This is the state of man: today he puts forth
  The tender leaves of hopes; tomorrow blossoms,
  And bears his blushing honors thick upon him;
  The third day comes a frost, a killing frost;
  And, when he thinks, good easy man, full surely
  His greatness is a-ripening, nips his root,
  And then he falls, as I do. I have ventur'd,
  Like little wanton boys that swim on bladders,
  This many summers in a sea of glory,
  But far beyond my depth: my high-blown pride
  At length broke under me, and now has left me,
  Weary and old with service, to the mercy
  Of a rude stream, that must forever hide me.
  Vain pomp and glory of this world, I hate ye:
  I feel my heart new open'd. O! how wretched
  Is that poor man that hangs on princes' favors!
  There is, betwixt that smile we would aspire to,
  That sweet aspect of princes, and their ruin,
  More pangs and fears than wars or women have;
  And when he falls, he falls like Lucifer,
  Never to hope again.
                      III, ii, l. 352

---

[1] Written by SHAKESPEARE and JOHN FLETCHER; see 236 and 238.

[2] 'Tis a cruelty / To load a falling man. — *King Henry VIII, act V, sc. iii, l. 76*

1 A peace above all earthly dignities,
A still and quiet conscience.
King Henry VIII, III, ii, l. 380

2 A load would sink a navy. *III, ii, l. 384*

3 And sleep in dull cold marble. *III, ii, l. 434*

4 Cromwell, I charge thee, fling away ambition:
By that sin fell the angels. *III, ii, l. 441*

5 Love thyself last: cherish those hearts that hate thee;
Corruption wins not more than honesty.
Still in thy right hand carry gentle peace,
To silence envious tongues: be just, and fear not.
Let all the ends thou aim'st at be thy country's,
Thy God's, and truth's; then if thou fall'st, O
Cromwell!
Thou fall'st a blessed martyr! *III, ii, l. 444*

6 Had I but serv'd my God with half the zeal[1]
I serv'd my king, he would not in mine age
Have left me naked to mine enemies. *III, ii, l. 456*

7 An old man, broken with the storms of state,
Is come to lay his weary bones among ye;
Give him a little earth for charity. *IV, ii, l. 21*

8 He gave his honors to the world again,
His blessed part to heaven, and slept in peace.
IV, ii, l. 29

9 So may he rest; his faults lie gently on him!
IV, ii, l. 31

10 He was a man
Of an unbounded stomach. *IV, ii, l. 33*

11 Men's evil manners live in brass; their virtues
We write in water. *IV, ii, l. 45*

12 He was a scholar, and a ripe and good one;
Exceeding wise, fair-spoken, and persuading;
Lofty and sour to them that lov'd him not;
But, to those men that sought him sweet as
summer. *IV, ii, l. 51*

13 To dance attendance on their lordships' pleasures.
V, ii, l. 30

14 Nor shall this peace sleep with her; but as when
The bird of wonder dies, the maiden phoenix,
Her ashes new-create another heir
As great in admiration as herself. *V, v, l. 40*

15 Wherever the bright sun of heaven shall shine,
His honor and the greatness of his name
Shall be, and make new nations. *V, v, l. 51*

16 Some come to take their ease
And sleep an act or two. *Epilogue, l. 2*

---

[1] Had I served God as well in every part / As I did serve my king and master still, / My scope had not this season been so short, / Nor would have had the power to do me ill. — THOMAS CHURCHYARD [c. 1520–1604], *Death of Morton* [1593]

17 Good friend, for Jesus' sake forbear
To dig the dust enclosed here;
Blest be the man that spares these stones,
And curst be he that moves my bones.
Shakespeare's epitaph

John Davies of Hereford
c. 1565–1618

18 Beauty's but skin deep.
A Select Second Husband for Sir Thomas Overburie's Wife [1616], st. 13

James I
1566–1625

19 A custom loathsome to the eye, hateful to the nose, harmful to the brain, dangerous to the lungs, and in the black, stinking fume thereof, nearest resembling the horrible Stygian smoke of the pit that is bottomless. *A Counterblast to Tobacco [1604]*

Thomas Campion
1567–1620

20 My sweetest Lesbia, let us live and love,
And though the sager sort our deeds reprove,
Let us not weigh them. Heaven's great lamps do dive
Into their west, and straight again revive,
But soon as once set is our little light,
Then must we sleep one ever-during night.
A Book of Airs [1601], pt. I, poem 1

21 Follow thy fair sun, unhappy shadow,
Though thou be black as night,
And she made all of light,
Yet follow thy fair sun, unhappy shadow.
A Book of Airs, pt. I, poem 4

22 Then wilt thou speak of banqueting delights,
Of masks and revels which sweet youth did make.
A Book of Airs, pt. I, poem 20

23 Rose-cheeked Laura, come;
Sing thou smoothly with thy beauty's
Silent music, either other
Sweetly gracing.
Observations on the Art of English Poesie [1602], ch. 8

24 Never weather-beaten sail more willing bent to shore,
Never tired pilgrim's limbs affected slumber more,
Than my weary sprite now longs to fly out of my
troubled breast!
O come quickly, sweetest Lord, and take my soul
to rest.
Two Books of Airs, First Book [c. 1612], poem 11

1 The summer hath his joys,
  And winter his delights;
  Though love and all his pleasures are but toys,
  They shorten tedious nights.
      Third Book of Airs [1617], poem 5

2 Thrice toss these oaken ashes in the air,
  Thrice sit thou mute in this enchanted chair;
  Then thrice three times tie up this true love's knot,
  And murmur soft: "She will, or she will not."
      Third Book of Airs, poem 9

3 There is a garden in her face
  Where roses and white lilies grow;
  A heavenly paradise is that place
  Wherein all pleasant fruits do flow.
  There cherries grow which none may buy,
  Till "cherry-ripe"[1] themselves do cry.
      Fourth Book of Airs [1617], poem 4

Thomas Nashe
1567–1601

4 Spring, the sweet spring, is the year's pleasant king;
  Then blooms each thing, then maids dance in a ring,
  Cold doth not sting, the pretty birds do sing.
  Cuckoo, jug-jug, pu-we, to-witta-woo!
      *Summer's Last Will and Testament
      [1600]. Spring, st. 1*

5 From winter, plague and pestilence, good Lord,
      deliver us!
      *Summer's Last Will and Testament.
      Autumn, refrain*

6 Brightness falls from the air;
  Queens have died young and fair;
  Dust hath closed Helen's eye.
  I am sick, I must die.
      Lord, have mercy on us!
      *Summer's Last Will and Testament.
      Adieu! Farewell Earth's Bliss!*

Tommaso Campanella
1568–1639

7   Now that they are called masters, [they] are
ashamed again to become disciples.
      The Defense of Galileo[2]

8   The new philosophy proceeds from the world, the
book of God.
      The Defense of Galileo

Sir Henry Wotton
1568–1639

9 How happy is he born and taught,
  That serveth not another's will;
  Whose armor is his honest thought,
  And simple truth his utmost skill!
      *The Character of a Happy Life [1614],
      st. 1*

10 Who God doth late and early pray,
   More of his grace than gifts to send,
   And entertains the harmless day
   With a well-chosen book or friend.
      The Character of a Happy Life, st. 5

11 Lord of himself, though not of lands;
   And having nothing, yet hath all.
      The Character of a Happy Life, st. 6

12 He first deceased; she for a little tried
   To live without him, liked it not, and died.
      *Upon the Death of Sir Albert Morton's
      Wife [1651]*

13 Hanging was the worst use a man could be put to.
      *The Disparity Between Buckingham and
      Essex [1651]*

14   An ambassador is an honest man sent to lie abroad
for the commonwealth.[3]
      Reliquiae Wottonianae [1651]

15   The itch of disputing will prove the scab of
churches.[4]   *A Panegyric to King Charles [1651]*

Sir John Davies
1569–1626

16 I know my soul hath power to know all things,
   Yet is she blind and ignorant in all:
   I know I'm one of Nature's little kings,
   Yet to the least and vilest things am thrall.
      *Nosce Teipsum [1599].
      Of Humane Knowledge, st. 44*

17 I know my life's a pain, and but a span;
   I know my sense is mocked in ev'ry thing:
   And to conclude, I know myself a man,
   Which is a proud, and yet a wretched thing.
      Nosce Teipsum. Of Humane Knowledge, st. 45

---

[1]"Cherry-ripe" was a familiar street cry of the time. See Robert Herrick, 240:12.

[2]Translated by GRANT MCCOLLEY.

[3]In a letter to Velserus [1612], Wotton says that this "merry definition of an ambassador...I had chanced to set down at my friend's, Mr. Christopher Fleckmore, in his Album."

[4]He directed that the stone over his grave be inscribed: Hic jacet hujus sententiae primus auctor: DISPUTANDI PRURITUS ECCLESIARUM SCABIES. Nomen alias quaere [Here lies the author of this phrase: "The itch for disputing is the sore of churches." Seek his name elsewhere]. — IZAAK WALTON, *Life of Wotton* [1651]

Johannes Kepler
1571–1630

1   I am much occupied with the investigation of physical causes. My aim in this is to show that the celestial machine is not similar to a divine animated being, but similar to a clock.
To Hewart von Hohenburg [February 10, 1605]

2   So long as the mother, Ignorance, lives, it is not safe for Science, the offspring, to divulge the hidden causes of things.   *Somnium (Dream)*[1] *[1634]*

Thomas Dekker
1572–1632

3 This age thinks better of a gilded fool
Than of a threadbare saint in wisdom's school.
Old Fortunatus [1600], act I, sc. i

4 Honest labor bears a lovely face.
Patient Grissell [1603], act II, sc. i

5 We are ne'er like angels till our passion dies.
The Honest Whore, pt. II [1630], act I, sc. ii

John Donne[2]
1572–1631

6 I wonder by my troth, what thou, and I
Did, till we lov'd? were we not wean'd till then
But suck'd on country pleasures, childishly?
Or snorted we in the seven sleepers' den?
The Good Morrow, st. 1

7 And now good morrow to our waking souls,
Which watch not one another out of fear;
For love, all love of other sights controls,
And makes one little room, an everywhere.
Let sea-discoverers to new worlds have gone,
Let maps to other, worlds on worlds have shown,
Let us possess one world, each hath one,
    and is one.   *The Good Morrow, st. 2*

8 My face in thine eye, thine in mine appears,
And true plain hearts do in the faces rest,
Where can we find two better hemispheres
Without sharp North, without declining West?
The Good Morrow, st. 3

---

[1]Translated by PATRICIA KIRKWOOD.

[2]John Donne, Anne Donne, Un-done. — *Letter to his wife* [1602], quoted in *The Life of Dr. John Donne* by IZAAK WALTON [1675 edition]
The poems we quote from were published, for the first time unless otherwise noted, in Donne's posthumous *Poems* [1633; further editions 1635–1669]. The general composition dates are: Songs and Sonnets (through *Farewell to Love*, 230:5) about 1593–1601, with some considerably later; Elegies about 1593–1598; and Holy Sonnets about 1609–1611, 1615–1617.

9 Go, and catch a falling star,
Get with child a mandrake root,
Tell me, where all past years are,
Or who cleft the Devil's foot.
Teach me to hear mermaids singing.
Song (Go and Catch a Falling Star), st. 1

10   And swear
    No where
Lives a woman true, and fair.
Song (Go and Catch a Falling Star), st. 2

11 Though she were true, when you met her,
And last, till you write your letter,
    Yet she
    Will be
False, ere I come, to two, or three.
Song (Go and Catch a Falling Star), st. 3

12 I have done one braver thing
Than all the Worthies did;
And yet a braver thence doth spring,
Which is, to keep that hid.   *The Undertaking, st. 1*

13 But he who loveliness within
Hath found, all outward loathes,
For he who color loves, and skin,
Loves but their oldest clothes.
The Undertaking, st. 4

14 And dare love that, and say so too,
And forget the He and She.
The Undertaking, st. 5

15   Busy old fool, unruly Sun,
    Why dost thou thus,
Through windows, and through curtains call on us?
Must to thy motions lovers' seasons run?
The Sun Rising, st. 1

16 Love, all alike, no season knows, nor clime,
Nor hours, days, months, which are the rags of
    time.   *The Sun Rising, st. 1*

17 She is all states, and all princes, I,
Nothing else is.   *The Sun Rising, st. 3*

18 For God sake hold your tongue, and let me love.
The Canonization, st. 1

19 The Phoenix riddle hath more wit
By us, we two being one, are it.
So to one neutral thing both sexes fit,
We die and rise the same, and prove
Mysterious by this love.   *The Canonization, st. 3*

20 As well a well-wrought urn becomes
The greatest ashes, as half-acre tombs.
The Canonization, st. 4

21 I am two fools, I know,
For loving, and for saying so
In whining poetry.   *The Triple Fool, st. 1*

1 Who are a little wise, the best fools be.
The Triple Fool, st. 2

2 Sweetest love, I do not go,
For weariness of thee,
Nor in hope the world can show
A fitter love for me;
But since that I
Must die at last, 'tis best,
To use my self in jest
Thus by feign'd deaths to die.
Song (Sweetest Love, I Do Not Go), st. 1

3 Yesternight the sun went hence,
And yet is here today.
Song (Sweetest Love, I Do Not Go), st. 2

4 But think that we
Are but turn'd aside to sleep.
Song (Sweetest Love, I Do Not Go), st. 5

5 When I died last, and dear, I die
As often as from thee I go. *The Legacy, st. 1*

6 Oh do not die, for I shall hate
All women so, when thou art gone. *A Fever, st. 1*

7 Twice or thrice had I loved thee,
Before I knew thy face or name.
Air and Angels, st. 1

8 'Tis true, 'tis day; what though it be?
O wilt thou therefore rise from me?
Why should we rise, because 'tis light?
Did we lie down, because 'twas night?
Love which in spite of darkness brought us hither
Should in despite of light keep us together.
Break of Day, st. 1

9 All Kings, and all their favorites,
All glory of honors, beauties, wits,
The sun itself, which makes times, as they pass,
Is elder by a year, now, than it was
When thou and I first one another saw:
All other things, to their destruction draw,
Only our love hath no decay;
This, no tomorrow hath, nor yesterday,
Running, it never runs from us away,
But truly keeps his first, last, everlasting day.
The Anniversary, st. 1

10 Send home my long strayed eyes to me,
Which (Oh) too long have dwelt on thee.
The Message, st. 1

11 'Tis the year's midnight, and it is the day's.
A Nocturnal upon St. Lucy's Day,
being the shortest day, st. 1

12 The world's whole sap is sunk:
The general balm th' hydroptic earth hath drunk,
Whither, as to the bed's-feet, life is shrunk,

Dead and interr'd; yet all these seem to laugh,
Compared with me, who am their epitaph.
A Nocturnal upon St. Lucy's Day, st. 1

13 For I am every dead thing,
In whom love wrought new alchemy.
For his art did express
A quintessence even from nothingness,
From dull privations, and lean emptiness
He ruin'd me, and I am re-begot
Of absence, darkness, death; things which are not.
A Nocturnal upon St. Lucy's Day, st. 2

14 Come live with me, and be my love,
And we will some new pleasures prove
Of golden sands, and crystal brooks,
With silken lines, and silver hooks.
The Bait,[1] st. 1

15 Dull sublunary lovers' love
(Whose soul is sense) cannot admit
Absence, because it doth remove
Those things which elemented it.
A Valediction Forbidding Mourning, st. 4

16 Our two souls therefore which are one,
Though I must go, endure not yet
A breach, but an expansion,
Like gold to airy thinness beat.
A Valediction Forbidding Mourning, st. 6

17 If they be two, they are two so
As stiff twin compasses are two,
Thy soul the fixt foot, makes no show
To move, but doth, if the other do.
A Valediction Forbidding Mourning, st. 7

18 Our eye-beams twisted, and did thread
Our eyes, upon one double string;
So to entergraft our hands, as yet
Was all the means to make us one,
And pictures in our eyes to get
Was all our propagation. *The Extasy, l. 7*

19 That subtle knot which makes us man:
So must pure lovers' souls descend
T' affections, and to faculties,
Which sense may reach and apprehend,
Else a great Prince in prison lies. *The Extasy, l. 64*

20 Love's mysteries in souls do grow,
But yet the body is his book. *The Extasy, l. 71*

21 I long to talk with some old lover's ghost,
Who died before the god of love was born.
Love's Deity, st. 1

---

[1]Included by Izaak Walton in *The Compleat Angler, ch. 12,* as "made by Dr. Donne, and made to shew the world that he could make soft and smooth verses, when he thought smoothness worth his labor."

1 Who ever comes to shroud me, do not harm
          Nor question much
   That subtle wreath of hair, which crowns my arm;
   The mystery, the sign you must not touch,
          For 'tis my outward soul,
   Viceroy to that, which then to heaven being gone,
          Will leave this to control,
   And keep these limbs, her provinces, from
          dissolution.   *The Funeral, st. 1*

2 A bracelet of bright hair about the bone.
                                The Relic, st. 1

3 Take heed of loving me.
                            The Prohibition, st. 1

4 So, so, break off this last lamenting kiss,
   Which sucks two souls, and vapors both away.
                            The Expiration, st. 1

5   Ah cannot we
   As well as cocks and lions jocund be,
   After such pleasures?   *Farewell to Love, st. 3*

6 Love built on beauty, soon as beauty, dies.
                    Elegies, no. 2, The Anagram, l. 27

7 Nature's lay idiot, I taught thee to love.
                    Elegies, 7, Nature's Lay Idiot, l. 1

8   The Alphabet
   Of flowers.   *Elegies, 7, Nature's Lay Idiot, l. 9*

9 No spring, nor summer beauty hath such grace,
   As I have seen in one autumnal face.
                        Elegies, 9, The Autumnal, l. 1

10 Who ever loves, if he do not propose
   The right true end of love, he's one that goes
   To sea for nothing but to make him sick.
                    Elegies, 18, Love's Progress, l. 1

11 Those set our hairs, but these our flesh upright.
   Elegies, 19, To His Mistress Going to Bed, l. 24

12 O my America! my new-found land.
   Elegies, 19, To His Mistress Going to Bed, l. 27

13 Full nakedness! All joys are due to thee,
   As souls unbodied, bodies unclothed must be,
   To taste whole joys.
   Elegies, 19, To His Mistress Going to Bed, l. 33

14 Sir, more than kisses, letters mingle souls;
   For, thus friends absent speak.
          Verse Letter to Sir Henry Wotton,
          written before April 1598, l. 1

15 And new philosophy calls all in doubt,
   The element of fire is quite put out;
   The sun is lost, and the earth, and no man's wit
   Can well direct him where to look for it.
   And freely men confess that this world's spent,
   When in the planets, and the firmament

They seek so many new; then see that this
Is crumbled out again to his atomies.
'Tis all in pieces, all coherence gone;
All just supply, and all relation:
Prince, subject, Father, Son, are things forgot.
          An Anatomy of the World.
          The First Anniversary
          [first published 1611],[1] *l. 205*

16   Her pure, and eloquent blood
   Spoke in her cheeks, and so distinctly wrought,
   That one might almost say, her body thought.
          Of the Progress of the Soul.
          The Second Anniversary
          [first published 1612], l. 244

17 Nature's great masterpiece, an Elephant,
   The only harmless great thing; the giant
   Of beasts.   *On the Progress of the Soul, st. 39*

18 I am a little world made cunningly
   Of elements, and an angelic sprite.
                        Holy Sonnets, no. 5, l. 1

19 At the round earth's imagin'd corners, blow
   Your trumpets, angels, and arise, arise
   From death, you numberless infinities
   Of souls.   *Holy Sonnets, 7, l. 1*

20 All whom war, dearth, age, agues, tyrannies,
   Despair, law, chance, hath slain.   *Holy Sonnets, 7, l. 6*

21 If poisonous minerals, and if that tree,
   Whose fruit threw death on else immortal us,
   If lecherous goats, if serpents envious
   Cannot be damn'd; alas; why should I be?
                        Holy Sonnets, 9, l. 1

22 Death be not proud, though some have called thee
   Mighty and dreadful, for thou art not so,
   For those whom thou think'st thou dost overthrow,
   Die not, poor death, nor yet canst thou kill me.
                        Holy Sonnets, 10, l. 1

23 Thou art slave to fate, chance, kings, and desperate
   men.   *Holy Sonnets, 10, l. 9*

24 One short sleep past, we wake eternally,
   And death shall be no more; death, thou shalt die.
                        Holy Sonnets, 10, l. 13

25 What if this present were the world's last night?
                        Holy Sonnets, 13, l. 1

26 Batter my heart, three-person'd God; for you
   As yet but knock, breathe, shine, and seek to mend.
                        Holy Sonnets, 14, l. 1

27 Show me, dear Christ, Thy spouse, so bright and
   clear.   *Holy Sonnets, 18,*[2] *l. 1*

---

[1]"Anniversary" of the death of Elizabeth Drury [c. 1595–1610].
[2]First published in 1899.

1 Since I am coming to that holy room,
Where, with thy choir of saints forevermore,
I shall be made thy music; as I come
I tune the instrument here at the door,
And what I must do then, think here before.
> *Hymn to God My God, in My Sickness*
> *[written c. 1623 or 1631], st. 1*

2 Whilst my physicians by their love are grown
Cosmographers, and I their map, who lie
Flat on this bed.   *Hymn to God My God, st. 2*

3 Wilt thou forgive that sin where I begun,
Which was my sin, though it were done before?
Wilt thou forgive that sin; through which I run,
And do run still: though still I do deplore?
When thou hast done, thou hast not done,
For, I have more.
> *A Hymn to God the Father [first published 1633]*

4 I observe the physician with the same diligence as
he the disease.
> *Devotions upon Emergent Occasions [1624], no. 6*

5 I do nothing upon myself, and yet am mine own
executioner.
> *Devotions upon Emergent Occasions, 12*

6 The flea, though he kill none, he does all the harm
he can.   *Devotions upon Emergent Occasions, 12*

7 All mankind is of one Author, and is one volume;
when one man dies, one chapter is not torn out of the
book, but translated into a better language; and every
chapter must be so translated.
> *Devotions upon Emergent Occasions, 17*

8 No man is an island, entire of itself; every man is a
piece of the continent, a part of the main; if a clod be
washed away by the sea, Europe is the less, as well as if
a promontory were, as well as if a manor of thy friends
or of thine own were; any man's death diminishes me,
because I am involved in mankind; and therefore
never send to know for whom the bell tolls; it tolls for
thee.   *Devotions upon Emergent Occasions, 17*

9 What gnashing is not a comfort, what gnawing of
the worm is not a tickling, what torment is not a marriage bed to this damnation, to be secluded eternally,
eternally, eternally from the sight of God?
> *LXXX Sermons [1640], no. 76,*
> *preached to the Earl of Carlisle*
> *[c. autumn 1622]*

10 Now God comes to thee, not as in the dawning of
the day, not as in the bud of the spring, but as the sun
at noon to illustrate all shadows, as the sheaves in harvest, to fill all penuries, all occasions invite his mercies, and all times are his seasons.
> *LXXX Sermons, 3,*
> *preached on Christmas Day [1625]*

11 I throw myself down in my chamber, and I call in
and invite God and his angels thither, and when they
are there, I neglect God and his angels, for the noise
of a fly, for the rattling of a coach, for the whining
of a door.
> *LXXX Sermons, 80, preached at the*
> *funeral of Sir William Cokayne*
> *[December 12, 1626]*

12 And what is so intricate, so entangling as death?
Who ever got out of a winding sheet?
> *LXXX Sermons, 54, preached to the*
> *King at Whitehall [April 5, 1628]*

13 Poor intricated soul! Riddling, perplexed, labyrinthical soul!
> *LXXX Sermons, 48, preached upon the*
> *Day of St. Paul's Conversion*
> *[January 25, 1629]*

14 When my mouth shall be filled with dust, and the
worm shall feed, and feed sweetly upon me, when the
ambitious man shall have no satisfaction if the poorest
alive tread upon him, nor the poorest receive any contentment in being made equal to princes, for they
shall be equal but in dust.
> *XXVI Sermons [1661], no. 26, Death's Duel,*
> *last sermon [February 15, 1631][1]*

Ben Jonson[2]
c. 1573–1637

15 As sure as death.
> *Every Man in His Humour [1598], act II, sc. i*

16 As he brews, so shall he drink.
> *Every Man in His Humour, II, i*

17 It must be done like lightning.
> *Every Man in His Humour, IV, 5*

18 Art hath an enemy called Ignorance.
> *Every Man out of His Humour [1599],*
> *act I, sc. i*

19 There shall be no love lost.
> *Every Man out of His Humour, II, i*

20 Oh, I could still
(Like melting snow upon some craggy hill)
Drop, drop, drop, drop,
Since nature's pride is, now, a wither'd daffodil.
> *Cynthia's Revels [1600], act I, sc. ii. Echo's Song*

---

[1] Called by His Majesty's household the Doctor's Own Funeral
Sermon. — *Preface to the first edition* [1632]

[2] O rare Ben Jonson! — *Epitaph*
  Which was done at the charge of Jack [Sir John] Young, who,
walking there when the grave was covering, gave the fellow 18
pence to cut it. — JOHN AUBREY, *Brief Lives* [1669–1696]
  See also William Drummond, 238:23.

1   True happiness
Consists not in the multitude of friends,
But in the worth and choice.
Cynthia's Revels, III, ii

2 Queen and huntress, chaste and fair,
Now the sun is laid to sleep,
Seated in thy silver chair,
State in wonted manner keep:
Hesperus entreats thy light,
Goddess, excellently bright.
Cynthia's Revels, V, iii

3   Of all wild beasts preserve me from a tyrant; and of
all tame, a flatterer.   *Sejanus [1603], act I*

4 Calumnies are answered best with silence.
Volpone [1606], act II, sc. ii

5 Come my Celia, let us prove,
While we can, the sports of love;
Time will not be ours forever,
He at length our good will sever.
Spend not then his gifts in vain;
Suns that set may rise again,
But if once we lose this light,
'Tis with us perpetual night.   *Song, To Celia [1607]*

6 Still to be neat, still to be drest,
As you were going to a feast.
Epicene; or, The Silent Woman [1609], act I, sc. i

7 Give me a look, give me a face,
That makes simplicity a grace;
Robes loosely flowing, hair as free,
Such sweet neglect more taketh me
Than all the adulteries of art:
They strike mine eyes, but not my heart.
Epicene; or, The Silent Woman, I, i

8 The dignity of truth is lost with much protesting.
Catiline's Conspiracy [1611], act III, sc. ii

9 Truth is the trial of itself
And needs no other touch,
And purer than the purest gold,
Refine it ne'er so much.   *On Truth [1616], st. 1*

10 Farewell, thou child of my right hand, and joy!
My sin was too much hope of thee, loved boy.
Epigrams [1616].
On My First Son [written c. 1603]

11 Rest in soft peace, and, asked, say here doth lie
Ben Jonson his best piece of poetry:
For whose sake, henceforth, all his vows be such,
As what he loves may never like too much.
Epigrams. On My First Son

12 Nor shall our cups make any guilty men:
But, at our parting, we will be, as when
We innocently met.
Epigrams. Inviting a Friend to Supper

13 Underneath this stone doth lie
As much beauty as could die;
Which in life did harbor give
To more virtue than doth live.
Epigrams. Epitaph on Elizabeth, Lady H ——

14 Follow a shadow, it still flies you;
Seem to fly it, it will pursue:
So court a mistress, she denies you;
Let her alone, she will court you.
The Forest [1616]. Follow a Shadow, st. 1

15 Whilst that for which all virtue now is sold,
And almost every vice — almighty gold.
The Forest. Epistle to Elizabeth,
Countess of Rutland

16 Drink to me only with thine eyes,
And I will pledge with mine;
Or leave a kiss but in the cup
And I'll not look for wine.[1]
The thirst that from the soul doth rise
Doth ask a drink divine;
But might I of Jove's nectar sup,
I would not change for thine.
The Forest. To Celia, st. 1

17 I sent thee late a rosy wreath,
Not so much honoring thee
As giving it a hope that there
It could not wither'd be.
But thou thereon didst only breathe,
And sent'st it back to me;
Since when it grows and smells, I swear,
Not of itself, but thee.
The Forest. To Celia, st. 2

18   Reader, look,
Not at his picture, but his book.
On the portrait of Shakespeare prefixed
to the First Folio [1623]

19   Soul of the age!
The applause, delight, the wonder of our stage!
My Shakespeare, rise; I will not lodge thee by
Chaucer or Spenser, or bid Beaumont lie
A little further, to make thee a room;
Thou art a monument, without a tomb,
And art alive still, while thy book doth live,
And we have wits to read, and praise to give.
To the Memory of My Beloved, the Author,
Mr. William Shakespeare [1623]

20 Marlowe's mighty line.
To the Memory of My Beloved, the Author,
Mr. William Shakespeare

---

[1]Drink to me with your eyes alone.... And if you will, take the cup
to your lips and fill it with kisses, and give it so to me. —
Philostratus [c. 181–250], *Letter 24*

1 And though thou hadst small Latin and less Greek.
> *To the Memory of My Beloved, the Author,*
> *Mr. William Shakespeare*

2 Call forth thundering Aeschylus.
> *To the Memory of My Beloved, the Author,*
> *Mr. William Shakespeare*

3 He was not of an age but for all time.
> *To the Memory of My Beloved, the Author,*
> *Mr. William Shakespeare*

4 Who casts to write a living line, must sweat.
> *To the Memory of My Beloved, the Author,*
> *Mr. William Shakespeare*

5 For a good poet's made, as well as born.
> *To the Memory of My Beloved, the Author,*
> *Mr. William Shakespeare*

6 Sweet Swan of Avon!
> *To the Memory of My Beloved, the Author,*
> *Mr. William Shakespeare*

7 Those that merely talk and never think,
That live in the wild anarchy of drink.[1]
> *Underwoods [1640]. An Epistle,*
> *Answering to One That Asked to*
> *Be Sealed of the Tribe of Ben*

8 In small proportions we just beauties see,
And in short measures life may perfect be.
> *Underwoods. To the Immortal Memory of*
> *Sir Lucius Cary and Sir Henry Morison*

9 What a deal of cold business doth a man misspend the better of life in! — in scattering compliments, tendering visits, gathering and venting news, following feasts and plays, making a little winter love in a dark corner.
> *Timber; or, Discoveries Made upon*
> *Men and Matter [1640], topic 11*

10 Greatness of name in the father . . . oft-times overwhelms the son; they stand too near one another. The shadow kills the growth: so much, that we see the grandchild come more and oftener to be heir of the first.
> *Timber; or, Discoveries Made upon*
> *Men and Matter, topic 50*

11 The players have often mentioned it as an honor to Shakespeare that in his writing (whatsoever he penned) he never blotted out a line. My answer hath been, "Would he had blotted a thousand." . . . I loved the man [Shakespeare] and do honor his memory, on this side idolatry, as much as any.
> *Timber; or, Discoveries Made upon*
> *Men and Matter, topic 64*

12 Though the most be players, some must be spectators.
> *Timber; or, Discoveries Made upon*
> *Men and Matter, topic 86*

Richard Barnfield
1574–1627

13 The waters were his winding sheet, the sea was made
for his tomb;
Yet for his fame the ocean sea, was not sufficient
room.   *Epitaph on Hawkins*[2] *[1595]*

14 As it fell upon a day
In the merry month of May,
Sitting in a pleasant shade
Which a grove of myrtles made.
> *Poems: In Divers Humours [1598]. Ode*

Joseph Hall
1574–1656

15 'Mongst all these stirs of discontented strife,
O, let me lead an academic life;
To know much, and to think for nothing, know
Nothing to have, yet think we have enow.
> *Discontent of Men with Their Condition*

Thomas Heywood
c. 1574–c. 1641

16 I will walk on eggs.
> *A Woman Killed with Kindness [1607],*
> *sc. xiii*

17 O God! O God! that it were possible
To undo things done; to call back yesterday!
That Time could turn up his swift sandy glass,
To untell the days, and to redeem these hours.
> *A Woman Killed with Kindness, xiii*

18 Pack clouds away, and welcome day,
With night we banish sorrow.
> *Pack Clouds Away [1630], st. 1*

19 Seven cities warr'd for Homer being dead,
Who living had no roof to shroud his head.[3]
> *Hierarchie of the Blessed Angels [1635]*

---

[1]They never taste who always drink; / They always talk who never think. — Matthew Prior, *Upon this Passage in the Scaligerana*

[2]Sir John Hawkins [1532–1595], second in command to Drake on the expedition to the West Indies, died at sea off Puerto Rico.

[3]Seven cities strive for the learned root of Homer: / Smyrna, Chios, Colophon, Ithaca, Pylos, Argos, Athens. — *Anonymous epigram,* translated by J. W. Mackail.

Seven wealthy towns contend for Homer dead, / Through which the living Homer begged his bread. — Thomas Seward [1708–1790], *On Homer* [1788]

John Marston
c. 1575–c. 1634

1 This earth is only the grave and Golgotha wherein all things that live must rot.
> *The Malcontent [1603], act IV, sc. v*

2 Oblivioni sacrum [Sacred to oblivion]. *Epitaph*

Cyril Tourneur
1575–1626

3 O, think upon the pleasure of the palace,
Securèd ease and state, the stirring meats
Ready to move out of the dishes,
That e'en now quicken when they're eaten!
Banquets abroad by torch light, music, sports,
Bare-headed vassals that had ne'er the fortune
To keep on their own hats, but let horns wear 'em!
Nine coaches waiting, hurry, hurry, hurry!
> *The Revenger's Tragedy*[1] *[1607], act II, sc. i*

4 Does the silkworm expend her yellow labors
For thee? For thee does she undo herself?
Are lordships sold to maintain ladyships,
For the poor benefit of a bewildering minute?
> *The Revenger's Tragedy, III, iv*

Robert Burton
1577–1640

5 All my joys to this are folly,
Naught so sweet as melancholy.
> *The Anatomy of Melancholy [1621–1651].*
> *The Author's Abstract*

6 I would help others, out of a fellow-feeling.[2]
> *The Anatomy of Melancholy.*
> *Democritus to the Reader*

7 They lard their lean books with the fat of others' works.
> *The Anatomy of Melancholy.*
> *Democritus to the Reader*

8 We can say nothing but what hath been said. Our poets steal from Homer.... Our story-dressers do as much; he that comes last is commonly best.
> *The Anatomy of Melancholy.*
> *Democritus to the Reader*

9 A dwarf standing on the shoulders of a giant may see farther than a giant himself.
> *The Anatomy of Melancholy.*
> *Democritus to the Reader*

10 Old friends become bitter enemies on a sudden for toys and small offenses.
> *The Anatomy of Melancholy.*
> *Democritus to the Reader*

11 Penny wise, pound foolish.
> *The Anatomy of Melancholy.*
> *Democritus to the Reader*

12 Women wear the breeches . . . in a word, the world turned upside downward.
> *The Anatomy of Melancholy.*
> *Democritus to the Reader*

13 All poets are mad.
> *The Anatomy of Melancholy.*
> *Democritus to the Reader*

14 Every man hath a good and a bad angel attending on him in particular, all his life long.
> *The Anatomy of Melancholy,*
> *pt. I, sec. 2, member 1, subsec. 2*

15 That which Pythagoras said to his scholars of old, may be forever applied to melancholy men, *A fabis abstinete,* eat no beans.
> *The Anatomy of Melancholy,*
> *pt. I, sec. 2, member 2, subsec. 1*

16 Cookery is become an art, a noble science; cooks are gentlemen.
> *The Anatomy of Melancholy,*
> *pt. I, sec. 2, member 2, subsec. 2*

17 No rule is so general, which admits not some exception.[3]
> *The Anatomy of Melancholy,*
> *pt. I, sec. 2, member 2, subsec. 3*

18 Idleness is an appendix to nobility.
> *The Anatomy of Melancholy,*
> *pt. I, sec. 2, member 2, subsec. 6*

19 Why doth one man's yawning make another yawn?
> *The Anatomy of Melancholy,*
> *pt. I, sec. 2, member 3, subsec. 2*

20 They do not live but linger.
> *The Anatomy of Melancholy,*
> *pt. I, sec. 2, member 3, subsec. 10*

21 [Desire is] a perpetual rack, or horsemill, according to Austin [Saint Augustine], still going round as in a ring.
> *The Anatomy of Melancholy,*
> *pt. I, sec. 2, member 3, subsec. 11*

22 A mere madness, to live like a wretch and die rich.
> *The Anatomy of Melancholy,*
> *pt. I, sec. 2, member 3, subsec. 12*

---

[1]Many scholars now attribute *The Revenger's Tragedy* to Thomas Middleton [1580–1627].

[2]A fellow-feeling makes one wondrous kind. — David Garrick, *Prologue on Quitting the Stage* [1776]

---

[3]The exception proves the rule. — *Proverb*

1   I may not here omit those two main plagues and common dotages of human kind, wine and women, which have infatuated and besotted myriads of people; they go commonly together.
> *The Anatomy of Melancholy,*
> *pt. I, sec. 2, member 3, subsec. 13*

2   All our geese are swans.[1]
> *The Anatomy of Melancholy,*
> *pt. I, sec. 2, member 3, subsec. 14*

3   They are proud in humility; proud in that they are not proud.
> *The Anatomy of Melancholy,*
> *pt. I, sec. 2, member 3, subsec. 14*

4   We can make mayors and officers every year, but not scholars.
> *The Anatomy of Melancholy, pt. I, sec. 2,*
> *member 3, subsec. 15*

5   *Hinc quam sic calamus saevior ense, patet.* The pen worse than the sword.
> *The Anatomy of Melancholy, pt. I, sec. 2,*
> *member 4, subsec. 4*

6   See one promontory (said Socrates of old), one mountain, one sea, one river, and see all.[2]
> *The Anatomy of Melancholy, pt. I, sec. 2,*
> *member 4, subsec. 7*

7   One was never married, and that's his hell; another is, and that's his plague.
> *The Anatomy of Melancholy, pt. I, sec. 2,*
> *member 4, subsec. 7*

8   Who cannot give good counsel? 'Tis cheap, it costs them nothing.
> *The Anatomy of Melancholy, pt. II, sec. 2,*
> *member 3*

9   Many things happen between the cup and the lip.[3]
> *The Anatomy of Melancholy, pt. II, sec. 2,*
> *member 3*

10   All places are distant from heaven alike.
> *The Anatomy of Melancholy, pt. II, sec. 2,*
> *member 4*

11   The commonwealth of Venice in their armory have this inscription: "Happy is that city which in time of peace thinks of war."
> *The Anatomy of Melancholy, pt. II, sec. 2,*
> *member 6*

12   Tobacco, divine, rare, superexcellent tobacco, which goes far beyond all the panaceas, potable gold, and philosopher's stones, a sovereign remedy to all diseases...but as it is commonly abused by most men, which take it as tinkers do ale, 'tis a plague, a mischief, a violent purger of goods, lands, health, hellish, devilish and damned tobacco, the ruin and overthrow of body and soul.
> *The Anatomy of Melancholy, pt. II, sec. 4,*
> *member 2, subsec. 2*

13   "Let me not live," said Aretine's Antonia, "if I had not rather hear thy discourse than see a play."
> *The Anatomy of Melancholy, pt. III, sec. 1,*
> *member 1, subsec. 1*

14   Birds of a feather will gather together.
> *The Anatomy of Melancholy, pt. III, sec. 1,*
> *member 1, subsec. 2*

15   No cord nor cable can so forcibly draw, or hold so fast, as love can do with a twined thread.[4]
> *The Anatomy of Melancholy, pt. III, sec. 2,*
> *member 1, subsec. 2*

16   To enlarge or illustrate this power and effect of love is to set a candle in the sun.[5]
> *The Anatomy of Melancholy, pt. III, sec. 2,*
> *member 1, subsec. 2*

17   One religion is as true as another.
> *The Anatomy of Melancholy, pt. III, sec. 4,*
> *member 2, subsec. 1*

18   A good conscience is a continual feast.
> *The Anatomy of Melancholy, pt. III, sec. 4,*
> *member 2, subsec. 3*

19   What physic, what chirurgery, what wealth, favor, authority can relieve, bear out, assuage, or expel a troubled conscience? A quiet mind cureth all.
> *The Anatomy of Melancholy, pt. III, sec. 4,*
> *member 2, subsec. 5*

20   Be not solitary, be not idle.
> *The Anatomy of Melancholy, pt. III, sec. 4,*
> *member 2, subsec. 6*

---

[1]Every man thinks his own geese swans. — CHARLES DICKENS, *The Cricket on the Hearth* [1845], *Chirp the Second*

[2]A blade of grass is always a blade of grass, whether in one country or another. — SAMUEL JOHNSON, in HESTER PIOZZI, *Anecdotes of Samuel Johnson* [1786]

[3]A very ancient proverb, sometimes attributed to Homer.
There is many a slip 'twixt the cup and the lip. — PALLADAS [fl. 400], *Epigram,* translated by J. W. MACKAIL
Though men determine, the gods do dispose; and ofttimes many things fall out between the cup and the lip. — ROBERT GREENE, *Perimedes the Blacksmith* [1588]

---

[4]One hair of a woman can draw more than a hundred pair of oxen. — JAMES HOWELL, *Letters* [1645–1655], *bk. II, no. 4*
She knows her man, and when you rant and swear, / Can draw you to her with a single hair. — JOHN DRYDEN, *Persius* [1693], *satire V, l. 246*

[5]And hold their farthing candle to the sun. — EDWARD YOUNG, *Love of Fame, satire VII, l. 99*
And hold their glimmering tapers to the sun. — GEORGE CRABBE, *The Parish Register* [1807], *pt. I, introduction*

William Harvey
1578–1657

1   The heart of animals is the foundation of their life, the sovereign of everything within them, the sun of their microcosm.

>   *De Motu Cordis et Sanguinis (On the Motion of the Heart and Blood)*[1] *[1628], dedication to King Charles*

2   All we know is still infinitely less than all that still remains unknown.

>   *De Motu Cordis et Sanguinis, dedication to Dr. Argent and Other Learned Physicians*

3   I profess both to learn and to teach anatomy, not from books but from dissections; not from positions of philosophers but from the fabric of nature.

>   *De Motu Cordis et Sanguinis, dedication to Dr. Argent and Other Learned Physicians*

4   I appeal to your own eyes as my witness and judge.

>   *De Generatione Animalium (On the Generation of Animals)*[1] *[1651], introduction*

John Fletcher
1579–1625

5 And he that will to bed go sober
Falls with the leaf in October.

>   *Rollo, Duke of Normandy [1639] (in collaboration with* Jonson *and others), act II, sc. ii*

6 Three merry boys, and three merry boys,
And three merry boys are we.[2]
As ever did sing in a hempen string
Under the gallows tree.

>   *Rollo, Duke of Normandy, III, ii*

7 Weep no more, nor sigh, nor groan,
Sorrow calls no time that's gone;
Violets plucked, the sweetest rain
Makes not fresh nor grow again.

>   *The Queen of Corinth [1647] (in collaboration with* Massinger *and a third author), act III, sc. ii*

8 Let's meet, and either do or die.[3]

>   *The Island Princess [1647], act II, sc. ii*

9 Hence, all you vain delights,
As short as are the nights
Wherein you spend your folly!
There's naught in this life sweet
But only melancholy;
O sweetest melancholy!

>   *The Nice Valor [1647]. Melancholy*[4]

Thomas Middleton
1580–1627

10   Better the day, better the deed.[5]

>   *Michaelmas Term [1607], act III, sc. i*

11   Since the worst comes to the worst.[6]

>   *Michaelmas Term, III, iv*

12   What is got over the Devil's back (that's by knavery), is spent under the belly (that's by lechery).[7]

>   *Michaelmas Term, IV, i*

13   Have you summoned your wits from wool-gathering?[8]

>   *The Family of Love [1608], act V, sc. iii*

14   By my faith the fool has feathered his nest well.[9]

>   *The Roaring Girl [1611], act I, sc. i*

15 I that am of your blood was taken from you
For your better health; look no more upon't,
But cast it to the ground regardlessly,
Let the common sewer take it from distinction.

>   *The Changeling [written 1622], act V, sc. iii*

16 As the case stands.

>   *The Old Law [1656], act II, sc. i*

17   On his last legs.   *The Old Law, V, i*

18   How many honest words have suffered corruption since Chaucer's days!

>   *No Wit, No Help, Like a Woman's [1657], act II, sc. i*

19   By many a happy accident.

>   *No Wit, No Help, Like a Woman's, IV, i*

---

[1]Translated by Robert Willis.

[2]Three merry men be we. — George Peele, *Old Wives' Tale* [1595]

[3]This expression is a kind of common property, being the motto, we believe, of a Scottish family. — Walter Scott, review of Thomas Campbell's *Gertrude of Wyoming* [1809], where it appears *(pt. III, l. 37)*: Tomorrow let us do or die!

[4]This poem is frequently and with some likelihood attributed to William Strode {1602–1645}.

[5]The better the day, the worse deed. — Matthew Henry, *Commentaries, Genesis 3*

[6]If the worst comes to the worst. — *Discovery of the Knights of the Poste* [1597]

[7]What is got over the Devil's back is spent under the belly. — François Rabelais, *Works, bk. V* [1552], *ch. 11*

Isocrates was in the right to insinuate that what is got over the Devil's back is spent under his belly. — Alain René Lesage, *Gil Blas, bk. VIII, ch. 9*

[8]My understanding has forsook me, and is gone a-woolgathering. — Cervantes, *Don Quixote, pt. II, bk. IV, ch. 38*

[9]We will feather our nests ere time may us espy. — Anonymous, *A Merry Interlude Entitled Respublica* [1553], *act III, sc. vi*

1   Anything for a Quiet Life.
    Title of play [1662]
    (in collaboration with JOHN WEBSTER)

John Webster
c. 1580–c. 1625

2   I saw him now going the way of all flesh.
    Westward Hoe [1607]
    (in collaboration with DEKKER), act II, sc. ii

3   Call for the robin redbreast and the wren,
    Since o'er shady groves they hover,
    And with leaves and flowers do cover
    The friendless bodies of unburied men.
    The White Devil [1612], act V, sc. iv

4   But keep the wolf far thence, that's foe to men,
    For with his nails he'll dig them up again.
    The White Devil, V, iv

5   Prosperity doth bewitch men, seeming clear;
    But seas do laugh, show white, when rocks are
        near.   *The White Devil, V, vi*

6   I am Duchess of Malfi still.
    The Duchess of Malfi [1623], act IV, sc. ii

7   I know death hath ten thousand several doors
    For men to take their exits.[1]
    The Duchess of Malfi, IV, ii

8   Heaven-gates are not so highly arch'd
    As princes' palaces; they that enter there
    Must go upon their knees.
    The Duchess of Malfi, IV, ii

9   *Ferdinand:* Cover her face; mine eyes dazzle; she died
        young.
    Bosola: I think not so; her infelicity
        Seemed to have years too many.
    The Duchess of Malfi, IV, ii

10 Other sins only speak; murder shrieks out.
    The Duchess of Malfi, IV, ii

11 Vain the ambition of kings
    Who seek by trophies and dead things
    To leave a living name behind,
    And weave but nets to catch the wind.[2]
    The Devil's Law Case [1623], song

---

[1]The thousand doors that lead to death. — THOMAS BROWNE, *Religio Medici, pt. I, sec. 44*

Death hath so many doors to let out life. — JOHN FLETCHER AND PHILIP MASSINGER, *The Custom of the Country* [1647], *act II, sc. ii*

Death hath a thousand doors to let out life. — PHILIP MASSINGER, *A Very Woman* [1665], *act V, sc. iv*

[2]Since in a net I seek to hold the wind. — THOMAS WYATT, *Sonnet, Whoso List to Hunt*

Sir Thomas Overbury
1581–1613

12 Give me, next good, an understanding wife,
    By nature wise, not learned much by art.
    A Wife [1614]

James Ussher
1581–1656

13 According to our chronology, [the creation of the world] fell upon the entrance of the night preceding the twenty third day of October in the year of the Julian Calendar, 710 [4004 B.C.E.].
    The Annals of the World [1658]

Richard Corbet
1582–1635

14 Farewell, rewards and fairies,
    Good housewives now may say.
    The Fairies Farewell, st. 1

15 Who of late for cleanliness,
    Finds sixpence in her shoe?
    The Fairies Farewell, st. 1

Philip Massinger
1583–1640

16 Be wise;
    Soar not too high to fall; but stoop to rise.
    Duke of Milan [1623], act I, sc. ii

17 He that would govern others, first should be
    The master of himself.
    The Bondman [1624], act I, sc. iii

18 To be nobly born
    Is now a crime.
    The Roman Actor [1629], act I, sc. i

19 A New Way to Pay Old Debts
    Title of play [1632]

Francis Beaumont
c. 1584–1616

20 What things have we seen
    Done at the Mermaid! heard words that have been
    So nimble, and so full of subtle flame,
    As if that everyone from whence they came,
    Had meant to put his whole wit in a jest,
    And resolv'd to live a fool, the rest
    Of his dull life.
    Letter to Ben Jonson [1640]

Beaumont and Fletcher[1]
[Francis Beaumont c. 1584–1616]
[John Fletcher 1579–1625]

1   It is always good
When a man has two irons in the fire.
The Faithful Friends [c. 1608], act I, sc. ii

2 As cold as cucumbers.
Cupid's Revenge [1615], act I, sc. i

3 Kiss till the cow comes home.[2]
The Scornful Lady [1616], act III, sc. i

4 There is a method in man's wickedness —
It grows up by degrees.
A King and No King [1619], act V, sc. iv

5 Upon my buried body lie lightly, gentle earth.
The Maid's Tragedy [1619], act II, sc. ii

6 The devil take the hindmost!
Philaster [1620], act V, sc. iii

7 Whistle, and she'll come to you.
Wit Without Money [1639], act IV, sc. iv

Miyamoto Musashi
c. 1584–1645

8 Surpass today what you were yesterday, go beyond those of poor skill tomorrow, and exceed those who are skillful later.[3]
A Book of Five Rings [c. 1643]. Direct Transmission

John Selden
1584–1654

9   *Scrutamini scripturas* [Let us look at the scriptures]. These two words have undone the world.
Table Talk [1689]. Bible, Scripture

10   Old friends are best. King James used to call for his old shoes; they were easiest for his feet.
Table Talk. Friends

11   Humility is a virtue all preach, none practice; and yet everybody is content to hear.
Table Talk. Humility

12   Ignorance of the law excuses no man; not that all men know the law, but because 'tis an excuse every man will plead, and no man can tell how to refute him.
Table Talk. Law

13   Wit and wisdom are born with a man.
Table Talk. Learning

14   Take a straw and throw it up into the air — you shall see by that which way the wind is.
Table Talk. Libels

15   Marriage is a desperate thing.
Table Talk. Marriage

16   Thou little thinkest what a little foolery governs the whole world.[4]   *Table Talk. Pope*

17   They that govern most make the least noise.
Table Talk. Power

18   Syllables govern the world.   *Table Talk. Power*

19   Wise men say nothing in dangerous times.
Table Talk. Wisdom

20   Preachers say, Do as I say, not as I do.
Table Talk. Preaching

21   A king is a thing men have made for their own sakes, for quietness' sake. Just as in a family one man is appointed to buy the meat.
Table Talk. Of a King

Tirso de Molina
[Gabriel Téllez]
c. 1584–1648

22   Through his honor I conquered him. For these peasants carry their honor in their hands so that they may constantly consult it; this same honor that once felt so much at home in the city but now has taken refuge in a more rural setting.
*El Burlador de Sevilla (The Rogue of Seville)[5]
[1630], act III, sc. iii*

William Drummond
1585–1649

23   He [Ben Jonson] is a great lover and praiser of himself, a contemner and scorner of others; given rather to lose a friend than a jest; jealous of every word and action of those about him (especially after drink, which is one of the elements in which he liveth); a dissembler of ill parts which reign in him, a bragger of some good that he wanteth; thinketh

---

[1]Of whose partnership John Aubrey said: "There was a wonderful consimility of fancy. They lived together not far from the playhouse, had one wench in the house between them, the same clothes and cloak, &c."

[2]Also familiar as: Till the cows come home.

[3]Translated by WILLIAM SCOTT WILSON.

[4]Behold, my son, with how little wisdom the world is governed. — AXEL OXENSTIERNA [1583–1654], in a letter [1648] to his son

[5]Translated by ROBERT O'BRIEN.
This is the original Don Juan play.

nothing well but what either he himself or some of his friends and countrymen hath said or done.

Informations and Manners of
Ben Jonson to W. D. when he came to
Scotland upon foot, 1619

John Ford
c. 1586–1639

1 Diamond cut diamond.

The Lover's Melancholy [1629], act I, sc. i

2   Remember
When we last gathered roses in the garden,
I found my wits; but truly you lost yours.

The Broken Heart [1629], act IV, sc. ii

3 'Tis Pity She's a Whore.   *Title of play [1633]*

Thomas Rainsborough
d. 1648

4   The poorest he that is in England hath a life to live as the greatest he.

In the army debates at Putney [October 29, 1647]

Thomas Hobbes
1588–1679

5   Words are wise men's counters, they do but reckon with them, but they are the money of fools.

Leviathan [1651], pt. I, ch. 4

6   The privilege of absurdity; to which no living creature is subject but man only.   *Leviathan, I, 5*

7   Sudden glory is the passion which maketh those grimaces called laughter.   *Leviathan, I, 6*

8   The secret thoughts of a man run over all things, holy, profane, clean, obscene, grave, and light, without shame or blame.   *Leviathan, I, 8*

9   During the time men live without a common power to keep them all in awe, they are in that condition which is called *war;* and such a war, as is of every man, against every man.   *Leviathan, I, 13*

10   [In a state of nature] No arts; no letters; no society; and which is worst of all, continual fear and danger of violent death; and the life of man, solitary, poor, nasty, brutish, and short.   *Leviathan, I, 13*

11   The passion to be reckoned upon, is fear.

Leviathan, I, 14

12   The Papacy is not other than the Ghost of the deceased Roman Empire, sitting crowned upon the grave thereof.   *Leviathan, IV, ch. 47*

13   Such truth as opposeth no man's profit nor pleasure is to all men welcome.

Leviathan, A Review and Conclusion

14   I am about to take my last voyage, a great leap in the dark.   *Last words*

15   Fear and I were born twins together.[1]

Autobiography [1680], l. 26

John Winthrop
1588–1649

16   For we must consider that we shall be as a city upon a hill. The eyes of all people are upon us, so that if we shall deal falsely with our God in this work we have undertaken, and so cause Him to withdraw His present help from us, we shall be made a story and a byword through the world.

A Model of Christian Charity [1630],
a sermon delivered on board the Arbella

George Wither
1588–1667

17 Shall I wasting in despair
Die because a woman's fair?
Or make pale my cheeks with care
'Cause another's rosy are?
Be she fairer than the day,
Or the flow'ry meads in May,
If she be not so to me,
What care I how fair she be?

Fair Virtue [1622]. Sonnet 4, st. 1

18 'Twas I that beat the bush,
The bird to others flew.

A Love Sonnet [1622], st. 11

19 Though I am young, I scorn to flit
On the wings of borrowed wit.

The Shepherd's Hunting [1622]. Eclogue 4

William Bradford
1590–1657

20   They knew they were pilgrims.[2]

Of Plymouth Plantation [1620–1647], ch. 7

---

[1]Ut pareret geminos, meque metumque simul.

Literally: She [my mother] gave birth to twins, myself and fear together.

Hobbes's mother, by his account, gave birth to him prematurely due to her anxiety over the impending invasion of the Spanish Armada.

[2]It was owing to this passage, first printed in 1669, that the *Mayflower's* company came eventually to be called the Pilgrim Fathers.

1 So they committed themselves to the will of God and resolved to proceed.

Of Plymouth Plantation, 9

2 Being thus arrived in a good harbor, and brought safe to land, they fell upon their knees and blessed the God of Heaven, who had brought them over the vast and furious ocean, and delivered them from all the perils and miseries thereof, again to set their feet on the firm and stable earth, their proper element.

Of Plymouth Plantation, 9

3 And for the season it was winter, and they that know the winters of that country know them to be sharp and violent, and subject to cruel and fierce storms, dangerous to travel to known places, much more to search an unknown coast.... For summer being done, all things stand upon them with a weather-beaten face, and the whole country, full of woods and thickets, represented a wild and savage hue.

Of Plymouth Plantation, 9

4 But it pleased God to visit us then with death daily, and with so general a disease that the living were scarce able to bury the dead.

Of Plymouth Plantation, 12

5 Thus out of small beginnings greater things have been produced by His hand that made all things of nothing, and gives being to all things that are; and, as one small candle may light a thousand, so the light here kindled hath shone unto many, yea in some sort to our whole nation.

Of Plymouth Plantation, 21

William Basse
d. c. 1653

6 Renowned Spenser, lie a thought more nigh
To learned Chaucer; and rare Beaumont, lie
A little nearer Spenser; to make room
For Shakespeare in your threefold fourfold tomb.

On Mr. Wm. Shakespeare [c. 1616]

William Browne
1591–c. 1645

7 Underneath this sable hearse
Lies the subject of all verse:
Sidney's sister, Pembroke's mother.
Death, ere thou hast slain another
Fair and learned and good as she,
Time shall throw a dart at thee.

*Epitaph on the Countess of
Pembroke [1621]*

8 There is no season such delight can bring,
As summer, autumn, winter, and the spring.   *Variety*

Robert Herrick
1591–1674

9 I sing of brooks, of blossoms, birds, and bowers:
Of April, May, of June, and July flowers.
I sing of Maypoles, Hock-carts, wassails, wakes,
Of bridegrooms, brides, and of their bridal cakes.

Hesperides [1648]. Argument of His Book

10 What is a kiss? Why this, as some approve:
The sure, sweet cement, glue, and lime of love.

Hesperides. A Kiss

11 Bid me to live, and I will live
Thy Protestant to be,
Or bid me love, and I will give
A loving heart to thee.

*Hesperides. To Anthea, Who May Command
Him Any Thing*

12 Cherry ripe, ripe, ripe, I cry,
Full and fair ones; come and buy!
If so be you ask me where
They do grow, I answer, there,
Where my Julia's lips do smile;
There's the land, or cherry-isle.

Hesperides. Cherry Ripe

13 It is the end that crowns us, not the fight.

Hesperides. The End

14 Some asked how pearls did grow, and where?
Then spoke I to my girl
To part her lips, and showed them there
The quarelets of pearl.

*Hesperides. The Rock of Rubies,
and the Quarrie of Pearls*

15 A sweet disorder in the dress
Kindles in clothes a wantonness.

Hesperides. Delight in Disorder

16 A winning wave, deserving note,
In the tempestuous petticoat,
A careless shoestring, in whose tie
I see a wild civility,
Do more bewitch me than when art
Is too precise in every part.

Hesperides. Delight in Disorder

17 When a daffodil I see,
Hanging down his head t'wards me,
Guess I may what I must be:
First, I shall decline my head;
Secondly, I shall be dead;
Lastly, safely buryed.

Hesperides. Divination by a Daffodil

1 You say to me-wards your affection's strong;
Pray love me little, so you love me long.
Hesperides. Love Me Little, Love Me Long

2 Night makes no difference 'twixt the Priest and Clerk;
Joan as my Lady is as good i' the dark.
Hesperides. No Difference i' th' Dark

3 Give me a kiss, and to that kiss a score;
Then to that twenty, add a hundred more:
A thousand to that hundred: so kiss on,
To make that thousand up a million.
Treble that million, and when that is done,
Let's kiss afresh, as when we first begun.
Hesperides. To Anthea: Ah, My Anthea!

4 Gather ye rosebuds while ye may,
Old Time is still a-flying,
And this same flower that smiles today
Tomorrow will be dying.[1]
Hesperides. To the Virgins to Make Much of Time

5 Fair daffodils, we weep to see
You haste away so soon.
Hesperides. To Daffodils

6 Her pretty feet, like snails, did creep
A little out, and then,
As if they played at bo-peep,
Did soon draw in again.
*Hesperides. To Mistress Susanna Southwell:
Upon Her Feet*

7 Her eyes the glowworm lend thee,
The shooting stars attend thee;
And the elves also,
Whose little eyes glow
Like the sparks of fire, befriend thee.
Hesperides. The Night Piece — To Julia

8 Made us nobly wild, not mad.
Hesperides. Ode for Ben Jonson

9 Outdid the meat, outdid the frolic wine.
Hesperides. Ode for Ben Jonson

10 Attempt the end, and never stand to doubt;
Nothing's so hard but search will find it out.
Hesperides. Seek and Find

11 Get up, sweet Slug-a-bed, and see
The dew bespangling herb and tree.
Hesperides. Corinna's Going A-Maying

12 'Tis sin,
Nay, profanation to keep in.
Hesperides. Corinna's Going A-Maying

13 So when or you or I are made
A fable, song, or fleeting shade,

All love, all liking, all delight
Lies drowned with us in endless night.
Hesperides. Corinna's Going A-Maying

14 Whenas in silks my Julia goes,
Then, then (methinks) how sweetly flows
That liquefaction of her clothes.
Next, when I cast mine eyes and see
That brave vibration each way free;
Oh how that glittering taketh me!
Hesperides. Upon Julia's Clothes

15 Here a little child I stand
Heaving up my either hand.
Cold as paddocks though they be,
Here I lift them up to Thee,
For a benison to fall
On our meat, and on us all.
*His Noble Numbers [1648].
Another Grace for a Child*

Henry King
1592–1669

16   Thou art the book,
The library whereon I look.   *The Exequy [1657]*

17   Then we shall rise
And view ourselves with clearer eyes
In that calm region where no night
Can hide us from each other's sight.   *The Exequy*

18 Sleep on, my Love, in thy cold bed,
Never to be disquieted!
My last good-night! Thou wilt not wake,
Till I thy fate shall overtake;
Till age, or grief, or sickness, must
Marry my body to that dust
It so much loves, and fill the room
My heart keeps empty in thy tomb.
Stay for me there; I will not fail
To meet thee in that hollow vale.   *The Exequy*

19 But hark! my pulse like a soft drum
Beats my approach, tells thee I come.   *The Exequy*

20 We that did nothing study but the way
To love each other, with which thoughts the day
Rose with delight to us, and with them set,
Must learn the hateful art, how to forget.
The Surrender

Francis Quarles
1592–1644

21 No man is born unto himself alone;
Who lives unto himself, he lives to none.
Esther [1621], sec. 1, Meditation 1

---

[1] See *The Wisdom of Solomon* 2:8, 29:32; Horace, 96:11; Ronsard, 150:8; and Spenser, 160:9.

1 The way to bliss lies not on beds of down,
And he that had no cross deserves no crown.
Esther, sec. 9, Meditation 9

2 Be wisely worldly, be not worldly wise.
Emblems [1635], bk. II, no. 2

3 The slender debt to Nature's quickly paid,[1]
Discharged, perchance, with greater ease than
made. *Emblems, II, 13*

4 The road to resolution lies by doubt:
The next way home's the farthest way about.[2]
Emblems, IV, 2, Epigram

5 My soul, sit thou a patient looker-on;
Judge not the play before the play is done:
Her plot hath many changes; every day
Speaks a new scene; the last act crowns the play.
Epigram. Respice Finem (Consider the End)

George Herbert
1593–1633

6 A verse may find him who a sermon flies.[3]
The Temple [1633]. The Church Porch, st. 1

7 Drink not the third glass, which thou canst not tame
When once it is within thee.
The Temple. The Church Porch, st. 5

8 Dare to be true: nothing can need a lie:
A fault, which needs it most, grows two thereby.[4]
The Temple. The Church Porch, st. 13

9 By all means use sometimes to be alone.
The Temple. The Church Porch, st. 25

10 By no means run in debt: take thine own measure.
Who cannot live on twenty pound a year,
Cannot on forty.
The Temple. The Church Porch, st. 30

11 Wit's an unruly engine, wildly striking
Sometimes a friend, sometimes the engineer.
The Temple. The Church Porch, st. 41

12 Be useful where thou livest.
The Temple. The Church Porch, st. 55

13 Man is God's image; but a poor man is
Christ's stamp to boot: both images regard.
The Temple. The Church Porch, st. 64

14 Was ever grief like mine?
The Temple. The Church. The Sacrifice, refrain

15 For thirty pence he did my death devise,
Who at three hundred did the ointment prize.
The Temple. The Church. The Sacrifice, st. 3

16 Man stole the fruit, but I must climb the tree.
The Temple. The Church. The Sacrifice, st. 49

17 I got me flowers to strew Thy way,
I got me boughs off many a tree:
But Thou wast up by break of day,
And brought'st Thy sweets along with Thee.
The Temple. The Church. Easter, st. 4

18 Who says that fictions only and false hair
Become a verse? Is there in truth no beauty?[5]
The Temple. The Church. Jordan, st. 1

19 Sweet day, so cool, so calm, so bright,
The bridal of the earth and sky.
The Temple. The Church. Virtue, st. 1

20 Sweet spring, full of sweet days and roses,
A box where sweets compacted lie.
The Temple. The Church. Virtue, st. 3

21 Only a sweet and virtuous soul,
Like season'd timber, never gives.
The Temple. The Church. Virtue, st. 4

22 Who goes to bed and does not pray,
Maketh two nights to every day.
The Temple. The Church. Charms and Knots, st. 4

23 Nothing wears clothes, but Man; nothing doth need
But he to wear them.
The Temple. The Church. Providence, st. 28

24 Most things move th' under-jaw, the crocodile not.[6]
Most things sleep lying, th' elephant leans or
stands.[7]
The Temple. The Church. Providence, st. 35

25 God's works are wide, and let in future times;
His ancient justice overflows our crimes.
*The Temple. The Church. The Bunch of
Grapes, st. 2*

26 I struck the board, and cried, No more:
I will abroad.
What? shall I ever sigh and pine?
My lines and life are free; free as the road,
Loose as the wind, as large as store.
Shall I be still in suit?

---

[1] To die is a debt we must all of us discharge. — EURIPIDES, *Alcestis, l. 418*

[2] The longest way round is the shortest way home. — *Proverb*

[3] That many people read a song / Who will not read a sermon. — WINTHROP MACKWORTH PRAED [1802–1839], *The Chant of the Brazen Head [1826], st. 1*

[4] And he that does one fault at first, / And lies to hide it, makes it two. — ISAAC WATTS, *Divine Songs, no. 15*

[5] See John Keats, 410:20 and note.

[6] The crocodile does not move the lower jaw, but is the only animal that brings down its upper jaw to the under one. — HERODOTUS, *Histories, bk. II, Customs of the Egyptians*

[7] Leans the huge elephant. — JAMES THOMSON, *The Seasons, Summer [1727], l. 725*

Have I no harvest but a thorn
To let me blood, and not restore
What I have lost with cordial fruit?
   Sure there was wine
Before my sighs did dry it; there was corn
Before my tears did drown it;
Is the year only lost to me?
Have I no bays to crown it?
The Temple. The Church. The Collar

1 Call in thy death's head there: tie up thy fears.
The Temple. The Church. The Collar

2 But as I rav'd and grew more fierce and wild
   At every word,
Methought I heard one calling, *Child!*
   And I replied, *My Lord.*
The Temple. The Church. The Collar

3 He would adore my gifts instead of me,
And rest in Nature, not the God of Nature:
So both should losers be.
The Temple. The Church. The Pulley, st. 3

4 Let him be rich and weary, that at least,
If goodness lead him not, yet weariness
May toss him to my breast.
The Temple. The Church. The Pulley, st. 4

5   Grief melts away
   Like snow in May,
As if there were no such cold thing.
The Temple. The Church. The Flower, st. 1

6 Who would have thought my shrivel'd heart
Could have recovered greenness?
The Temple. The Church. The Flower, st. 2

7 And now in age I bud again,
After so many deaths I live and write;
I once more smell the dew and rain,
And relish versing: O my only light,
   It cannot be
   That I am he
On whom thy tempests fell all night.
The Temple. The Church. The Flower, st. 6

8 The harbingers are come. See, see their mark;
White is their color, and behold my head.
The Temple. The Church. The Forerunners, st. 1

9 Teach me, my God and King,
In all things thee to see
And what I do in any thing,
To do it as for thee.
The Temple. The Church. The Elixir, st. 1

10 A servant with this clause
Makes drudgery divine:
Who sweeps a room, as for thy laws,
Makes that and th' action fine.
The Temple. The Church. The Elixir, st. 5

11 Love bade me welcome: yet my soul drew back,
   Guilty of dust and sin.
But quick-ey'd Love, observing me grow slack
   From my first entrance in,
Drew nearer to me, sweetly questioning,
   If I lack'd anything.
The Temple. The Church. Love, st. 1

12 You must sit down, says Love, and taste my meat:
So I did sit and eat.
The Temple. The Church. Love, st. 3

13 Religion stands on tiptoe in our land,
Ready to pass to the American strand.
The Church Militant [1633], l. 235

14   Love, and a cough, cannot be hid.
   *Jacula Prudentum (Outlandish Proverbs)
   [1651], no. 49*

15   When a dog is drowning, everyone offers him
drink.   *Jacula Prudentum, 77*

16   Deceive not thy physician, confessor, nor lawyer.
Jacula Prudentum, 105

17   Who would do ill ne'er wants occasion.
Jacula Prudentum, 116

18   Well may he smell fire, whose gown burns.
Jacula Prudentum, 138

19   Love your neighbor, yet pull not down your
hedge.   *Jacula Prudentum, 141*

20   Marry your son when you will; your daughter
when you can.   *Jacula Prudentum, 149*

21   The mill cannot grind with the water that's past.
Jacula Prudentum, 153

22   Good words are worth much, and cost little.
Jacula Prudentum, 155

23   Hell is full of good meanings and wishings.[1]
Jacula Prudentum, 170

24   Where the drink goes in, there the wit goes out.
Jacula Prudentum, 187

25   Whose house is of glass, must not throw stones at
another.[2]   *Jacula Prudentum, 196*

26   By suppers more have been killed than Galen ever
cured.   *Jacula Prudentum, 272*

27   The lion is not so fierce as they paint him.[3]
Jacula Prudentum, 289

---

[1]Sir, Hell is paved with good intentions. — SAMUEL JOHNSON [1775]; from BOSWELL, *Life of Johnson, vol. I, p. 555* (Everyman edition)

[2]People in glass houses shouldn't throw stones. — *Proverb*

[3]The lion is not so fierce as painted. — THOMAS FULLER [1608–1661], *Expecting Preferment* [1648]

1   Go not for every grief to the physician, nor for every quarrel to the lawyer, nor for every thirst to the pot.
Jacula Prudentum, 290

2   The best mirror is an old friend.
Jacula Prudentum, 296

3   When you are an anvil, hold you still; when you are a hammer, strike your fill.[1]
Jacula Prudentum, 338

4   He that lies with the dogs, riseth with fleas.
Jacula Prudentum, 343

5   He that is not handsome at twenty, nor strong at thirty, nor rich at forty, nor wise at fifty, will never be handsome, strong, rich, or wise.
Jacula Prudentum, 349

6   The buyer needs a hundred eyes, the seller not one.
Jacula Prudentum, 390

7   Trust not one night's ice.
Jacula Prudentum, 453

8   For want of a nail the shoe is lost, for want of a shoe the horse is lost, for want of a horse the rider is lost.
Jacula Prudentum, 499

9   Pension never enriched young man.
Jacula Prudentum, 515

10   One enemy is too much.
Jacula Prudentum, 523

11   Living well is the best revenge.
Jacula Prudentum, 524

12   Thursday come, and the week is gone.
Jacula Prudentum, 587

13   Time is the rider that breaks youth.
Jacula Prudentum, 615

14   Show me a liar, and I'll show thee a thief.
Jacula Prudentum, 652

15   One father is more than a hundred schoolmasters.
Jacula Prudentum, 686

16   Reason lies between the spur and the bridle.
Jacula Prudentum, 711

17   God's mill grinds slow, but sure.
Jacula Prudentum, 747

18   He that lends, gives.
Jacula Prudentum, 787

19   Words are women, deeds are men.[2]
Jacula Prudentum, 843

20   Poverty is no sin.
Jacula Prudentum, 844

21   None knows the weight of another's burthen.
Jacula Prudentum, 880

22   One hour's sleep before midnight is worth three after.
Jacula Prudentum, 882

23   He hath no leisure who useth it not.
Jacula Prudentum, 897

24   Half the world knows not how the other half lives.
Jacula Prudentum, 907

25   Life is half spent before we know what it is.
Jacula Prudentum, 917

26   The eye is bigger than the belly.
Jacula Prudentum, 1018

27   His bark is worse than his bite.
Jacula Prudentum, 1090

28   There is an hour wherein a man might be happy all his life, could he find it.
Jacula Prudentum, 1143

29   Woe be to him that reads but one book.
Jacula Prudentum, 1146

Izaak Walton
1593–1683

30   But God, who is able to prevail, wrestled with him, as the Angel did with Jacob, and marked him; marked him for his own.   *Life of Donne [1640]*

31   I have laid aside business, and gone a-fishing.
The Compleat Angler [1653–1655].
Epistle to the Reader

32   Angling may be said to be so like the mathematics that it can never be fully learnt.
The Compleat Angler. Epistle to the Reader

33   As no man is born an artist, so no man is born an angler.
The Compleat Angler. Epistle to the Reader

34   I shall stay him no longer than to wish him a rainy evening to read this following discourse; and that if he be an honest angler, the east wind may never blow when he goes a-fishing.
The Compleat Angler. Epistle to the Reader

35   I am, Sir, a brother of the Angle.
The Compleat Angler, pt. I, ch. 1

---

[1]Stand like an anvil when it is beaten upon. — SAINT IGNATIUS THEOPHORUS, bishop of Antioch [fl. c. 100]
When you are the anvil, bear — / When you are the hammer, strike. — EDWIN MARKHAM, *Preparedness* [1928]

[2]Fatti maschii parole femine [Manly deeds, womanly words]. — *Motto of Maryland*

1   Doubt not but angling will prove to be so pleasant that it will prove to be, like virtue, a reward to itself.[1]

Sir Henry Wotton . . . was a most dear lover, and a frequent practicer of the art of angling; of which he would say, "it was an employment for his idle time, which was then not idly spent . . . a rest to his mind, a cheerer of his spirits, a diverter of sadness, a calmer of unquiet thoughts, a moderator of passions, a procurer of contentedness; and that it begat habits of peace and patience in those that professed and practiced it."

The Compleat Angler, I, 1

2   You will find angling to be like the virtue of humility, which has a calmness of spirit and a world of other blessings attending upon it.[2]

The Compleat Angler, I, 1

3   I remember that a wise friend of mine did usually say, "That which is everybody's business is nobody's business."   *The Compleat Angler, I, 2*

4   An honest ale-house where we shall find a cleanly room, lavender in the windows, and twenty ballads stuck about the wall.

The Compleat Angler, I, 2

5   I love such mirth as does not make friends ashamed to look upon one another next morning.

The Compleat Angler, I, 5

6   No man can lose what he never had.

The Compleat Angler, I, 5

7   We may say of angling as Dr. Boteler[3] said of strawberries: "Doubtless God could have made a better berry, but doubtless God never did"; and so, if I might be judge, God never did make a more calm, quiet, innocent recreation than angling.

The Compleat Angler, I, 5

8   Thus use your frog. . . . Put your hook through his mouth, and out at his gills; . . . and then with a fine needle and silk sew the upper part of his leg, with only one stitch, to the arming-wire of your hook; or tie the frog's leg, above the upper joint, to the armed-wire; and in so doing use him as though you loved him.

The Compleat Angler, I, 8

9   Look to your health; and if you have it, praise God, and value it next to a good conscience; for health is the second blessing that we mortals are capable of; a blessing that money cannot buy.

The Compleat Angler, I, 21

10   Let the blessing of Saint Peter's Master be . . . upon all that are lovers of virtue, and dare trust in his Providence, and be quiet and go a-angling.

The Compleat Angler, I, 21

11   The great secretary of Nature and all learning, Sir Francis Bacon.   *Life of Herbert [1670]*

James Howell
c. 1594–1666

12   All work and no play makes Jack a dull boy.

Proverbs [1659]

Thomas Carew
c. 1595–c. 1639

13 Here lies a King that rul'd, as he thought fit
The universal monarchy of wit;
Here lies two flamens, and both those the best:
Apollo's first, at last the true God's priest.
An Elegy upon the Death of Dr. Donne [1633]

14 Ask me no more where Jove bestows,
When June is past, the fading rose;
For in your beauty's orient deep
These flowers, as in their causes, sleep.
Poems [1640]. To Celia, st. 1

15 Ask me no more whither doth haste
The nightingale when May is past;
For in your sweet dividing throat
She winters and keeps warm her note.
Poems. To Celia, st. 3

16 Ask me no more if east or west
The Phoenix builds her spicy nest;
For unto you at last she flies,
And in your fragrant bosom dies.
Poems. To Celia, st. 5

17 Give me more love or more disdain;
The torrid or the frozen zone:
Bring equal ease unto my pain;
The temperate affords me none.
Poems. Mediocrity in Love Rejected, st. 1

18 He that loves a rosy cheek,
Or a coral lip admires,

---

[1]Ipsa quidem virtus sibimet pulcherrima merces [Virtue herself is her own fairest reward]. — SILIUS ITALICUS [c. 25–99 C.E.], *Punica, bk. XIII, l. 663*

Virtue was sufficient of herself for happiness. — DIOGENES LAERTIUS, *Lives of Eminent Philosophers, bk. XLII, Plato*

That virtue is her own reward, is but a cold principle. — THOMAS BROWNE, *Religio Medici, pt. I, sec. 47*

Virtue is its own reward. — MATTHEW PRIOR, *Imitations of Horace, bk. III, ode 2* [1692]

I think mankind by thee would be less bored / If only thou wert not thine own reward. — JOHN KENDRICK BANGS [1862–1922], *A Hint to Virtue* [1897]

[2]There is certainly something in angling . . . that tends to produce a gentleness of spirit, and a pure serenity of mind. — WASHINGTON IRVING, *The Sketch-Book. The Angler*

[3]This praise of the strawberry first appeared in the second edition of *The Angler* [1655].

Or, from starlike eyes, doth seek
Fuel to maintain his fires;
As old Time makes these decay,
So his flames must waste away.
>   *Poems. Disdain Returned, st. 1*

1 The firstling of the infant year.   *Poems. The Primrose*

2 The magic of a face.
>   *Poems. Epitaph on the Lady S——*

René Descartes
1596–1650

3   I suppose the body to be just a statue or a machine made of earth.[1]
>   *Treatise on Man [1633], paragraph 2*

4   Good sense is of all things in the world the most equally distributed, for everybody thinks he is so well supplied with it, that even those most difficult to please in all other matters never desire more of it than they already possess.
>   *Discourse on the Method [1637], pt. I*

5   It is not enough to have a good mind. The main thing is to use it well.   *Discourse on the Method, I*

6   The greatest minds are capable of the greatest vices as well as of the greatest virtues.
>   *Discourse on the Method, I*

7   The first precept was never to accept a thing as true until I knew it as such without a single doubt.
>   *Discourse on the Method, I*

8   One cannot conceive anything so strange and so implausible that it has not already been said by one philosopher or another.   *Discourse on the Method, II*

9   I think, therefore I am.[2]
>   *Discourse on the Method, IV*

10   I will devote myself sincerely and without reservation to the general demolition of my opinions.[3]
>   *Meditations on First Philosophy [1641].*
>   *First Meditation*

James Shirley
1596–1666

11   How little room
Do we take up in death that, living, know
No bounds!
>   *The Wedding [1626], act IV, sc. iv*

---

[1]Translated by Robert Stoothoff.

[2]Cogito, ergo sum.
Je pense, donc je suis.

[3]Translated by John Cottingham.

12 Only the actions of the just
Smell sweet and blossom in their dust.
>   *The Lady of Pleasure [1635]*

13 The glories of our blood and state
Are shadows, not substantial things;
There is no armor against fate;
Death lays his icy hand on kings.
>   *Contention of Ajax and Ulysses [1659],*
>   *sc. iii*

Oliver Cromwell
1599–1658

14   A few honest men are better than numbers.
>   *Letter to Sir W. Spring*
>   *[September 1643]*

15   The State, in choosing men to serve it, takes no notice of their opinions. If they be willing faithfully to serve it, that satisfies.
>   *Before the battle of Marston Moor*
>   *[July 2, 1644]*

16   I beseech you, in the bowels of Christ, think it possible you may be mistaken.
>   *Letter to the General Assembly of the Church*
>   *of Scotland [August 3, 1650]*

17   You have sat too long here for any good you have been doing lately.... Depart, I say; and let us have done with you. In the name of God, go!
>   *To the Rump Parliament*
>   *[April 20, 1653]*

18   Necessity hath no law. Feigned necessities, imaginary necessities...are the greatest cozenage that men can put upon the Providence of God, and make pretenses to break known rules by.
>   *To Parliament [September 12, 1654]*

19   I would have been glad to have lived under my woodside, and to have kept a flock of sheep, rather than to have undertaken this government.
>   *To Parliament [1658]*

20   Mr. Lely, I desire you would use all your skill to paint my picture truly like me, and not flatter me at all; but remark all these roughnesses, pimples, warts, and everything as you see me, otherwise I will never pay a farthing for it.[4]
>   *From Horace Walpole, Anecdotes of*
>   *Painting in England [1762–1771]*

21   It is not my design to drink or to sleep, but my design is to make what haste I can to be gone.
>   *Dying words*

---

[4]Warts and all. — *Saying*

Pedro Calderón de la Barca
1600–1681

1   What is life? A madness. What is life? An illusion, a shadow, a story. And the greatest good is little enough: for all life is a dream, and dreams themselves are only dreams.[1]

Life Is a Dream, act II, l. 1195

2   But whether it be dream or truth, to do well is what matters. If it be truth, for truth's sake. If not, then to gain friends for the time when we awaken.

Life Is a Dream, III, l. 236

3   What surprises you, if a dream taught me this wisdom, and if I still fear I may wake up and find myself once more confined in prison? And even if this should not happen, merely to dream it is enough. For this I have come to know, that all human happiness finally ceases, like a dream.

Life Is a Dream, III, l. 1114

Martin Parker
c. 1600–c. 1656

4 Ye gentlemen of England
That live at home at ease,
Ah! little do you think upon
The dangers of the seas.   *Song*

Pierre de Fermat
1601–1665

5   I have discovered a truly marvellous demonstration [of this general theorem[2]] which this margin is too narrow to contain.

Note [c. 1637] in his copy of
CLAUDE BACHET [1581–1638],
Arithmetic of Diophantus [1621]

Baltasar Gracián y Morales
1601–1658

6   Life is a warfare against the malice of others.[3]

The Art of Worldly Wisdom [1647]

Jules Cardinal Mazarin
1602–1661

7   I must leave all that! Farewell, dear paintings that I have loved so much and which have cost me so much.[4]

Remark shortly before his death

Roger Williams
c. 1603–1683

8   There goes many a ship to sea, with many hundred souls in one ship, whose weal and woe is common, and is a true picture of a commonwealth or a human combination or society. It hath fallen out sometimes that both Papists and Protestants, Jews and Turks may be embarked in one ship; upon which supposal I affirm that all the liberty of conscience that ever I pleaded for turns upon these two hinges — that none of the Papists, Protestants, Jews or Turks be forced to come to the ship's prayers or worship, nor compelled from their own particular prayers or worship, if they practice any.

Letter to the Town of Providence
[January 1655]

Friedrich von Logau
1604–1655

9 Armed peace.

Poetic Aphorisms (Sinngedichten) [1654]

10 Though the mills of God grind slowly, yet they grind exceeding small.[5]

Poetic Aphorisms. Retribution

Sir Thomas Browne
1605–1682

11   I dare, without usurpation, assume the honorable style of a Christian.

Religio Medici (The Religion of a Doctor)
[1643], pt. I, sec. 1

12   I could never divide myself from any man upon the difference of an opinion, or be angry with his judgment for not agreeing with me in that from which perhaps within a few days I should dissent myself.   *Religio Medici, I, 6*

13   Many . . . have too rashly charged the troops of error, and remain as trophies unto the enemies of truth.   *Religio Medici, I, 6*

---

[1]Que es la pequeño: / Que toda la vida es sueño, / y los sueños sueños son.
Translated by EDWARD and ELIZABETH HUBERMAN.

[2]Fermat's last theorem. Restated in modern terms: The equation $x^n + y^n = z^n$, where $x, y,$ and z are nonzero integers, has no solution for n greater than 2. Mathematician Andrew Wiles (b. 1953) proved Fermat's theorem in 1994.

[3]Adapted from the translation of JOSEPH JACOBS.

[4]Il faut quitter tout cela! Adieu, chers tableaux que j'ai tant aimés et qui m'ont tant coûté.

[5]Translated by HENRY WADSWORTH LONGFELLOW.

1   A man may be in as just possession of truth as of a city, and yet be forced to surrender.
Religio Medici, I, 6

2   As for those wingy mysteries in divinity, and airy subtleties in religion, which have unhinged the brains of better heads, they never stretched the *pia mater* of mine.
Religio Medici, I, 9

3   I love to lose myself in a mystery, to pursue my Reason to an *O altitudo!*   *Religio Medici, I, 9*

4   Rich with the spoils of Nature.
Religio Medici, I, 13

5   We carry with us the wonders we seek without us: There is all Africa and her prodigies in us.
Religio Medici, I, 15

6   All things are artificial, for nature is the art of God.[1]   *Religio Medici, I, 16*

7   Obstinacy in a bad cause is but constancy in a good.   *Religio Medici, I, 25*

8   Persecution is a bad and indirect way to plant religion.   *Religio Medici, I, 25*

9   Not picked from the leaves of any author, but bred amongst the weeds and tares of mine own brain.
Religio Medici, I, 36

10   I am not so much afraid of death, as ashamed thereof. 'Tis the very disgrace and ignominy of our natures, that in a moment can so disfigure us, that our nearest friends, wife, and children, stand afraid and start at us.   *Religio Medici, I, 40*

11   How shall the dead arise, is no question of my faith; to believe only possibilities, is not faith, but mere philosophy.   *Religio Medici, I, 48*

12   The heart of man is the place the devil dwells in: I feel sometimes a hell within myself.
Religio Medici, I, 51

13   There is no road or ready way to virtue.
Religio Medici, I, 55

14   All places, all airs make unto me one country; I am in England, everywhere, and under any meridian.
Religio Medici, II, 1

15   But how shall we expect charity towards others, when we are uncharitable to ourselves? Charity begins at home, is the voice of the world; yet is every man his greatest enemy, and, as it were, his own executioner.   *Religio Medici, II, 4*

16   I could be content that we might procreate like trees, without conjunction, or that there were any way to perpetuate the World without this trivial and vulgar way of coition.   *Religio Medici, II, 9*

17   Sure there is music even in the beauty, and the silent note which Cupid strikes, far sweeter than the sound of an instrument. For there is a music wherever there is a harmony, order, or proportion; and thus far we may maintain the music of the spheres.
Religio Medici, II, 9

18   For the world, I count it not an inn, but a hospital; and a place not to live, but to die in.
Religio Medici, II, 11

19   There is surely a piece of divinity in us, something that was before the elements, and owes no homage unto the sun.   *Religio Medici, II, 11*

20   When we desire to confine our words, we commonly say they are spoken under the rose.[2]
Vulgar Errors [1645]

21   An old and gray-headed error.   *Vulgar Errors*

22   Times before you, when even living men were antiquities; when the living might exceed the dead, and to depart this world could not be properly said to go unto the greater number.
Urn-Burial; or, Hydriotaphia [1658].
Dedication

23   With rich flames, and hired tears, they solemnized their obsequies.   *Urn-Burial, ch. 3*

24   Were the happiness of the next world as closely apprehended as the felicities of this, it were a martyrdom to live.   *Urn-Burial, 4*

25   These dead bones have . . . quietly rested under the drums and tramplings of three conquests.
Urn-Burial, 5

26   Time which antiquates antiquities, and hath an art to make dust of all things.   *Urn-Burial, 5*

27   What song the Sirens sang, or what name Achilles assumed when he hid himself among women, though puzzling questions, are not beyond all conjecture.
Urn-Burial, 5

28   The long habit of living indisposeth us for dying.   *Urn-Burial, 5*

---

[1] The course of Nature is the art of God. — EDWARD YOUNG, *Night Thoughts, Night IX, l. 1267*

[2] Sub rosa.
    In strict confidence. The origin of the phrase is obscure but the story is that Cupid gave Harpocrates (the god of silence) a rose, to bribe him not to betray the amours of Venus. Hence the flower became the emblem of silence and was sculptured on the ceilings of banquet-rooms, to remind the guests that what was spoken *sub vino* was not to be repeated *sub divo*. In the sixteenth century it was placed over confessionals. — *Brewer's Dictionary of Phrase and Fable, 14th ed.* [1989]

1   The iniquity of oblivion blindly scattereth her poppy, and deals with the memory of men without distinction to merit of perpetuity.   *Urn-Burial, 5*

2   Oblivion is not to be hired: the greater part must be content to be as though they had not been, to be found in the register of God, not in the record of man.   *Urn-Burial, 5*

3   The night of time far surpasseth the day, and who knows when was the equinox?   *Urn-Burial, 5*

4   Man is a noble animal, splendid in ashes, and pompous in the grave.   *Urn-Burial, 5*

5   That unextinguishable laugh in heaven.   *The Garden of Cyrus [1658], ch. 2*

6   Life itself is but the shadow of death, and souls departed but the shadows of the living. All things fall under this name. The sun itself is but the dark simulacrum, and light but the shadow of God.   *The Garden of Cyrus, 4*

7   To keep our eyes open longer were but to act our Antipodes. The huntsmen are up in America, and they are already past their first sleep in Persia. But who can be drowsy at that hour which freed us from everlasting sleep? or have slumbering thoughts at that time, when sleep itself must end, and, as some conjecture, all shall awake again?   *The Garden of Cyrus, 5*

Anne Bigot Cornuel
1605–1694

8 No man is a hero to his valet.[1]   *Attributed*

Pierre Corneille
1606–1684

9   To conquer without risk is to triumph without glory.   *Le Cid [1636], act II, sc. ii*

10   And the combat ceased for want of combatants.   *Le Cid, IV, iii*

11   Do your duty, and leave the rest to heaven.   *Horace [1639], act II, sc. viii*

12   All evils are equal when they are extreme.   *Horace, III, iv*

13   The worst of all states is the people's state.   *Cinna [1640], act II, sc. i*

14   Who is all-powerful should fear everything.   *Cinna, IV, ii*

15   The manner of giving is worth more than the gift.   *Le Menteur (The Liar) [1642], act I, sc. i*

---

[1]Il n'y avoit point de héros pour les valets de chambre.

16   A liar is always lavish of oaths.   *Le Menteur, III, v*

17   Guess if you can, choose if you dare.   *Héraclius [1646], act IV, sc. iv*

18 A service beyond all recompense
Weighs so heavy that it almost gives offense.   *Suréna [1674], act III, sc. i*

Sir William Davenant
1606–1668

19 The lark now leaves his wat'ry nest
And, climbing, shakes his dewy wings.   *Song [1638], st. 1*

Edmund Waller
1606–1687

20 Illustrious acts high raptures do infuse,
And every conqueror creates a muse.   *Panegyric to My Lord Protector*

21 Guarded with ships, and all our sea our own.   *To My Lord of Falkland*

22 That which her slender waist confin'd
Shall now my joyful temples bind;
No monarch but would give his crown
His arms might do what this has done.   *On a Girdle [1664]*

23 My joy, my grief, my hope, my love,
Did all within this circle move!   *On a Girdle*

24   Go, lovely rose!
Tell her that wastes her time and me
    That now she knows,
When I resemble her to thee,
How sweet and fair she seems to be.   *Go, Lovely Rose [1664]*

25   So all we know
Of what they do above
Is that they happy are, and that they love.   *Upon the Death of My Lady Rich [1664]*

26 Poets that lasting marble seek
Must carve in Latin or in Greek.   *Of English Verse [1668]*

27 Poets lose half the praise they should have got,
Could it be known what they discreetly blot.   *Upon Roscommon's Translation of Horace, De Arte Poetica*

28 The soul's dark cottage, batter'd and decay'd,
Lets in new light through chinks that Time has made;
Stronger by weakness, wiser, men become
As they draw near to their eternal home.

Leaving the old, both worlds at once they view,
That stand upon the threshold of the new.
On the Divine Poems [1686]

Thomas Fuller

1608–1661

1   Drawing near her death, she sent most pious thoughts as harbingers to heaven; and her soul saw a glimpse of happiness through the chinks of her sickness-broken body.   *Life of Monica [1642]*

2   He knows little who will tell his wife all he knows.
The Holy State and the Profane State [1642].
The Good Husband

3   Light, God's eldest daughter, is a principal beauty in a building.
The Holy State and the Profane State.
Of Building

4   Learning hath gained most by those books by which the printers have lost.
The Holy State and the Profane State. Of Books

5   Deceive not thyself by overexpecting happiness in the married estate.... Remember the nightingales which sing only some months in the spring, but commonly are silent when they have hatched their eggs.
The Holy State and the Profane State. Of Marriage

6   Fame sometimes hath created something of nothing.
The Holy State and the Profane State. Of Fame

7   Anger is one of the sinews of the soul; he that wants it hath a maimed mind.
The Holy State and the Profane State. Of Anger

8   It is always darkest just before the day dawneth.
Pisgah Sight [1650], bk. II, ch. 2

John Milton

1608–1674

9 This is the month, and this the happy morn,
Wherein the Son of Heav'n's eternal King,
Of wedded maid and virgin mother born,
Our great redemption from above did bring;
For so the holy sages once did sing,
That He our deadly forfeit should release,
And with His Father work us a perpetual peace.
On the Morning of Christ's Nativity [1629],
st. 1, l. 1

10 It was the winter wild
While the Heav'n-born child
All meanly wrapt in the rude manger lies.
On the Morning of Christ's Nativity.
The Hymn, st. 1, l. 29

11 No war, or battle's sound
Was heard the world around.
The idle spear and shield were high up hung.
On the Morning of Christ's Nativity.
The Hymn, st. 4, l. 53

12 Time will run back and fetch the Age of Gold.
On the Morning of Christ's Nativity.
The Hymn, st. 14, l. 135

13 The Oracles are dumb.
On the Morning of Christ's Nativity.
The Hymn, st. 19, l. 173

14 Peor and Baalim
Forsake their temples dim.
On the Morning of Christ's Nativity.
The Hymn, st. 22, l. 197

15 What needs my Shakespeare for his honor'd bones,
The labor of an age in piled stones,
Or that his hallow'd relics should be hid
Under a star-y-pointing pyramid?
Dear son of memory, great heir of fame,
What need'st thou such weak witness of thy name?
On Shakespeare [1630]

16 How soon hath Time, the subtle thief of youth,
Stol'n on his wing my three-and-twentieth year.
On His Having Arrived at the
Age of Twenty-three [1631]

17 As ever in my great Taskmaster's eye.
On His Having Arrived at the Age of
Twenty-three

18 Such sweet compulsion doth in music lie.
Arcades [1630–1634], l. 68

19 Hence, loathed Melancholy,
Of Cerberus and blackest Midnight born,
In Stygian cave forlorn,
'Mongst horrid shapes, and shrieks, and sights
unholy.   *L'Allegro [1631], l. 1*

20 So buxom, blithe, and debonair.   *L'Allegro, l. 24*

21 Haste thee, Nymph, and bring with thee
Jest, and youthful jollity,
Quips and cranks and wanton wiles,
Nods and becks and wreathed smiles.
L'Allegro, l. 25

22 Sport, that wrinkled Care derides,
And Laughter, holding both his sides.
Come, and trip it, as you go,
On the light fantastic toe.   *L'Allegro, l. 31*

23 The mountain nymph, sweet liberty.   *L'Allegro, l. 36*

24 Mirth, admit me of thy crew,
To live with her, and live with thee,
In unreproved pleasures free.   *L'Allegro, l. 38*

1 While the cock with lively din
Scatters the rear of darkness thin,
And to the stack, or the barn door,
Stoutly struts his dames before,
Oft list'ning how the hounds and horn
Cheerly rouse the slumb'ring morn.   *L'Allegro, l. 49*

2 And every shepherd tells his tale
Under the hawthorn in the dale.   *L'Allegro, l. 67*

3 Meadows trim, with daisies pied,
Shallow brooks, and rivers wide;
Towers and battlements it sees
Bosom'd high in tufted trees,
Where perhaps some beauty lies,
The cynosure of neighboring eyes.

                       L'Allegro, l. 75

4 And the jocund rebecks sound
To many a youth, and many a maid,
Dancing in the checkered shade.
And young and old come forth to play
On a sunshine holiday.   *L'Allegro, l. 94*

5 Then to the spicy nut-brown ale.   *L'Allegro, l. 100*

6 Tower'd cities please us then,
And the busy hum of men.   *L'Allegro, l. 117*

7   Ladies, whose bright eyes
Rain influence, and judge the prize.

                       L'Allegro, l. 121

8 And pomp, and feast, and revelry,
With mask, and antique pageantry,
Such sights as youthful poets dream
On summer eves by haunted stream.
Then to the well-trod stage anon,
If Jonson's learned sock be on,
Or sweetest Shakespeare, Fancy's child,
Warble his native wood-notes wild,
And ever, against eating cares,
Lap me in soft Lydian airs,
Married to immortal verse
Such as the meeting soul may pierce,
In notes with many a winding bout
Of linked sweetness long drawn out.

                       L'Allegro, l. 127

9 Such strains as would have won the ear
Of Pluto, to have quite set free
His half-regain'd Eurydice.
These delights, if thou canst give,
Mirth, with thee, I mean to live.   *L'Allegro, l. 148*

10 Hence vain deluding Joys,
The brood of Folly without father bred!
                  Il Penseroso [1631], l. 1

11 Hail divinest Melancholy.   *Il Penseroso, l. 12*

12 Sober, steadfast, and demure.   *Il Penseroso, l. 32*

13 And looks commercing with the skies,
Thy rapt soul sitting in thine eyes.
                  Il Penseroso, l. 39

14 And add to these retired Leisure,
That in trim gardens takes his pleasure.
                  Il Penseroso, l. 49

15 Sweet bird, that shunn'st the noise of folly,
Most musical, most melancholy!
                  Il Penseroso, l. 61

16   I walk unseen
On the dry smooth-shaven green,
To behold the wandering moon,
Riding near her highest noon,
Like one that had been led astray
Through the heav'n's wide pathless way,
And oft, as if her head she bow'd,
Stooping through a fleecy cloud.   *Il Penseroso, l. 65*

17 Oft, on a plat of rising ground,
I hear the far-off curfew sound
Over some wide-watered shore,
Swinging low with sullen roar.   *Il Penseroso, l. 73*

18 Where glowing embers through the room
Teach light to counterfeit a gloom,
Far from all resort of mirth,
Save the cricket on the hearth.   *Il Penseroso, l. 79*

19 Sometime let gorgeous Tragedy
In sceptered pall come sweeping by,
Presenting Thebes, or Pelops' line,
Or the tale of Troy divine.   *Il Penseroso, l. 97*

20 Or bid the soul of Orpheus sing
Such notes as, warbled to the string,
Drew iron tears down Pluto's cheek.
                Il Penseroso, l. 105

21 Or call up him that left half told
The story of Cambuscan bold.   *Il Penseroso, l. 109*

22 Where more is meant than meets the ear.
                Il Penseroso, l. 120

23 And storied windows richly dight,
Casting a dim religious light.
There let the pealing organ blow,
To the full-voiced choir below,
In service high, and anthems clear
As may, with sweetness, through mine ear
Dissolve me into ecstasies,
And bring all Heaven before mine eyes.
                Il Penseroso, l. 159

24 Before the starry threshold of Jove's Court
My mansion is.   *Comus [1634], l. 1*

25 Above the smoke and stir of this dim spot
Which men call earth.   *Comus, l. 5*

1 Yet some there be that by due steps aspire
  To lay their just hands on that golden key
  That opes the palace of Eternity.

  Comus, l. 12

2 An old, and haughty nation proud in arms.

  Comus, l. 33

3 What never yet was heard in tale or song,
  From old or modern bard, in hall or bower.

  Comus, l. 44

4 Bacchus, that first from out the purple grape
  Crush'd the sweet poison of misused wine.

  Comus, l. 46

5 These my sky-robes, spun out of Iris' woof.

  Comus, l. 83

6 The star that bids the shepherd fold.   *Comus, l. 93*

7 And the gilded car of day,
  His glowing axle doth allay
  In the steep Atlantic stream.   *Comus, l. 95*

8 Midnight shout and revelry,
  Tipsy dance and jollity.   *Comus, l. 103*

9 What hath night to do with sleep?   *Comus, l. 122*

10 Ere the blabbing eastern scout,
   The nice morn on th' Indian steep,
   From her cabin'd loophole peep.   *Comus, l. 138*

11 Come, knit hands, and beat the ground,
   In a light fantastic round.   *Comus, l. 143*

12   A thousand fantasies
   Begin to throng into my memory,
   Of calling shapes, and beck'ning shadows dire,
   And airy tongues that syllable men's names
   On sands and shores and desert wildernesses.

   Comus, l. 205

13 Was I deceiv'd or did a sable cloud
   Turn forth her silver lining on the night?

   Comus, l. 221

14 Sweet Echo, sweetest nymph, that liv'st unseen
   Within thy airy shell
   By slow Meander's margent green,
   And in the violet-embroider'd vale.   *Comus, l. 230*

15 How sweetly did they float upon the wings
   Of silence, through the empty-vaulted night,
   At every fall smoothing the raven down
   Of darkness till it smil'd!   *Comus, l. 249*

16 Such sober certainty of waking bliss.

   Comus, l. 263

17 Virtue could see to do what Virtue would
   By her own radiant light, though sun and moon
   Were in the flat sea sunk. And Wisdom's self
   Oft seeks to sweet retired solitude,

Where, with her best nurse Contemplation,
She plumes her feathers, and lets grow her wings.

   Comus, l. 373

18 Tis Chastity, my brother, Chastity:
   She that has that, is clad in complete steel.

   Comus, l. 420

19 How charming is divine philosophy!
   Not harsh and crabbed, as dull fools suppose,
   But musical as is Apollo's lute,
   And a perpetual feast of nectar'd sweets
   Where no crude surfeit reigns.   *Comus, l. 476*

20 Fill'd the air with barbarous dissonance.

   Comus, l. 550

21   I was all ear,
   And took in strains that might create a soul
   Under the ribs of Death.   *Comus, l. 560*

22   That power
   Which erring men call Chance.   *Comus, l. 587*

23 Praising the lean and sallow abstinence.

   Comus, l. 709

24 Beauty is Nature's coin, must not be hoarded,
   But must be current, and the good thereof
   Consists in mutual and partaken bliss.   *Comus, l. 739*

25 Beauty is Nature's brag, and must be shown
   In courts, at feasts, and high solemnities,
   Where most may wonder at the workmanship;
   It is for homely features to keep home —
   They had their name thence; coarse complexions
   And cheeks of sorry grain will serve to ply
   The sampler, and to tease the huswife's wool.
   What need a vermeil-tinctur'd lip for that,
   Love-darting eyes, or tresses like the morn?

   Comus, l. 745

26 Sabrina fair,
   Listen where thou art sitting
   Under the glassy, cool, translucent wave,
   In twisted braids of lilies knitting
   The loose train of thy amber-dropping hair;
   Listen for dear honor's sake,
   Goddess of the silver lake,
        Listen and save.   *Comus, l. 859*

27 But now my task is smoothly done:
   I can fly, or I can run.   *Comus, l. 1012*

28 Love Virtue, she alone is free,
   She can teach ye how to climb
   Higher than the sphery chime;
   Or, if Virtue feeble were,
   Heav'n itself would stoop to her.   *Comus, l. 1019*

29 Yet once more, O ye laurels, and once more
   Ye myrtles brown, with ivy never sere,
   I come to pluck your berries harsh and crude,

And with forc'd fingers rude
Shatter your leaves before the mellowing year.
Lycidas [1637], l. 1

1   He knew
Himself to sing, and build the lofty rhyme.
Lycidas, l. 10

2 Hence with denial vain, and coy excuse.   *Lycidas, l. 18*

3 Under the opening eyelids of the morn,
We drove afield; and both together heard
What time the gray-fly winds her sultry horn,
Batt'ning our flocks with the fresh dews of night.
Lycidas, l. 26

4 But O the heavy change, now thou art gone,
Now thou art gone and never must return!
Lycidas, l. 37

5 As killing as the canker to the rose.   *Lycidas, l. 45*

6 Alas! what boots it with incessant care
To tend the homely slighted shepherd's trade,
And strictly meditate the thankless Muse?
Were it not better done as others use,
To sport with Amaryllis in the shade,
Or with the tangles of Neaera's hair?
Fame is the spur that the clear spirit doth raise
(That last infirmity of noble mind)[1]
To scorn delights, and live laborious days;
But the fair guerdon when we hope to find,
And think to burst out into sudden blaze,
Comes the blind Fury with th' abhorred shears,
And slits the thin-spun life.   *Lycidas, l. 64*

7 Fame is no plant that grows on mortal soil.
Lycidas, l. 78

8 It was that fatal and perfidious bark,
Built in th' eclipse, and rigg'd with curses dark,
That sunk so low that sacred head of thine.
Lycidas, l. 100

9 Last came, and last did go,
The Pilot of the Galilean lake;
Two massy keys he bore of metals twain,
(The golden opes, the iron shuts amain).
Lycidas, l. 108

10 Blind mouths! That scarce themselves know how to
    hold
A sheep-hook.   *Lycidas, l. 119*

11 The hungry sheep look up, and are not fed,
But swoln with wind and the rank mist they draw,
Rot inwardly, and foul contagion spread:

---

[1]That thirst [for applause], if the last infirmity of noble minds, is also the first infirmity of weak ones; and on the whole, the strongest impulsive influence of average humanity. — JOHN RUSKIN, *Sesame and Lilies* [1865], *Of Kings' Treasuries*, sec. 3.
See Tacitus, 110:10.

Besides what the grim wolf with privy paw
Daily devours apace, and nothing said;
But that two-handed engine at the door
Stands ready to smite once, and smite no more.
Lycidas, l. 123

12 Whether beyond the stormy Hebrides,
Where thou perhaps under the whelming tide
Visit'st the bottom of the monstrous world.
Lycidas, l. 156

13 Look homeward, Angel, now, and melt with ruth.
Lycidas, l. 163

14 For Lycidas your sorrow is not dead,
Sunk though he be beneath the watery floor;
So sinks the day-star in the ocean bed;
And yet anon repairs his drooping head,
And tricks his beams, and with new-spangled ore
Flames in the forehead of the morning sky.
So Lycidas sunk low, but mounted high,
Through the dear might of him that walk'd the
    waves.   *Lycidas, l. 166*

15 At last he rose, and twitch'd his mantle blue:
Tomorrow to fresh woods and pastures new.
Lycidas, l. 192

16 O nightingale, that on yon bloomy spray
Warbl'st at eve, when all the woods are still.
Sonnet. To the Nightingale [c. 1637], l. 1

17 Thy liquid notes that close the eye of day.
Sonnet. To the Nightingale, l. 5

18 Where the bright seraphim in burning row
Their loud uplifted angel trumpets blow.
At a Solemn Music [c. 1637], l. 10

19   A poet soaring in the high region of his fancies,
with his garland and singing robes about him.
*The Reason of Church Government [1641],
bk. II, introduction*

20   By labor and intent study (which I take to be my
portion in this life), joined with the strong propensity
of nature, I might perhaps leave something so written
to after-times, as they should not willingly let it die.
*The Reason of Church Government, II,
introduction*

21   Beholding the bright countenance of truth in the
quiet and still air of delightful studies.
*The Reason of Church Government, II,
introduction*

22   He who would not be frustrate of his hope to write
well hereafter in laudable things ought himself to be a
true poem.   *Apology for Smectymnuus [1642]*

23   His words ... like so many nimble and airy servitors trip about him at command.
Apology for Smectymnuus

1 Truth...never comes into the world but like a bastard, to the ignominy of him that brought her forth.[1]

> *The Doctrine and Discipline of Divorce [1643], introduction*

2 Let not England forget her precedence of teaching nations how to live.

> *The Doctrine and Discipline of Divorce, introduction*

3 Litigious terms, fat contentions, and flowing fees.

> *Tractate of Education [1644]*

4 Inflamed with the study of learning and the admiration of virtue; stirred up with high hopes of living to be brave men and worthy patriots, dear to God, and famous to all ages. *Tractate of Education*

5 Ornate rhetoric taught out of the rule of Plato.... To which poetry would be made subsequent, or indeed rather precedent, as being less subtle and fine, but more simple, sensuous, and passionate.

> *Tractate of Education*

6 In those vernal seasons of the year, when the air is calm and pleasant, it were an injury and sullenness against Nature not to go out, and see her riches, and partake in her rejoicing with heaven and earth.

> *Tractate of Education*

7 As good almost kill a man as kill a good book: who kills a man kills a reasonable creature, God's image; but he who destroys a good book kills reason itself.

> *Areopagitica [1644]*

8 A good book is the precious lifeblood of a master spirit, embalmed and treasured up on purpose to a life beyond life. *Areopagitica*

9 I cannot praise a fugitive and cloistered virtue, unexercised and unbreathed, that never sallies out and sees her adversary, but slinks out of the race, where that immortal garland is to be run for, not without dust and heat. *Areopagitica*

10 Where there is much desire to learn, there of necessity will be much arguing, much writing, many opinions; for opinion in good men is but knowledge in the making. *Areopagitica*

11 God is decreeing to begin some new and great period in His Church, even to the reforming of Reformation itself: what does He then but reveal Himself to His servants, and as His manner is, first to His Englishmen?

> *Areopagitica*

12 Methinks I see in my mind a noble and puissant nation rousing herself like a strong man after sleep, and shaking her invincible locks. Methinks I see her as an eagle mewing her mighty youth, and kindling her undazzled eyes at the full midday beam.

> *Areopagitica*

13 Give me the liberty to know, to utter, and to argue freely according to conscience, above all liberties.

> *Areopagitica*

14 Though all the winds of doctrine were let loose to play upon the earth, so Truth be in the field, we do injuriously, by licensing and prohibiting, to misdoubt her strength. Let her and Falsehood grapple; who ever knew Truth put to the worse, in a free and open encounter? *Areopagitica*

15 Men of most renowned virtue have sometimes by transgressing most truly kept the law.

> *Tetrachordon [1644–1645]*

16 For such kind of borrowing as this, if it be not bettered by the borrower, among good authors is accounted Plagiarè. *Eikonoklastes [1649], ch. 23*

17 None can love freedom heartily, but good men; the rest love not freedom, but license.

> *Tenure of Kings and Magistrates [1649]*

18 No man who knows aught, can be so stupid to deny that all men naturally were born free.

> *Tenure of Kings and Magistrates*

19 Peace hath her victories
No less renown'd than war.

> *To the Lord General Cromwell [1652]*

20 When I consider how my light is spent,
Ere half my days, in this dark world and wide,
And that one talent which is death to hide
Lodg'd with me useless.

> *On His Blindness [1652]*

21 Doth God exact day-labor, light denied?

> *On His Blindness*

22 Who best
Bear his mild yoke, they serve him best: his state
Is kingly; thousands at his bidding speed,
And post o'er land and ocean without rest;
They also serve who only stand and wait.

> *On His Blindness*

23 Avenge, O Lord, thy slaughter'd saints, whose bones
Lie scatter'd on the Alpine mountains cold;
Ev'n them who kept thy truth so pure of old
When all our fathers worshipp'd stocks and stones
Forget not.

> *On the Late Massacre in Piedmont [1655]*

24 Yet I argue not
Against Heav'n's hand or will, nor bate one jot

---

[1]Still rule those minds on earth / At whom sage Milton's wormwood words were hurled: / "Truth like a bastard comes into the world / Never without ill-fame to him who gives her birth"?— THOMAS HARDY, *Lausanne* [1897]

Of heart or hope; but still bear up, and steer
Right onward.
> *To Cyriack Skinner, upon His Blindness*
> *[c. 1655]*

1 Methought I saw my late espoused saint
Brought to me like Alcestis from the grave.
> *On His Deceased Wife [c. 1658]*

2 But oh! as to embrace me she inclin'd,
I wak'd, she fled, and day brought back my night.
> *On His Deceased Wife*

3 Of Man's first disobedience, and the fruit
Of that forbidden tree whose mortal taste
Brought death into the world, and all our woe,
With loss of Eden.
> *Paradise Lost [1667], bk. I, l. 1*

4 Things unattempted yet in prose or rhyme.
> *Paradise Lost, l. 16*

5　　　What in me is dark
Illumine, what is low raise and support;
That to the height of this great argument
I may assert eternal Providence,
And justify the ways of God to men.
> *Paradise Lost, I, l. 22*

6 The infernal serpent; he it was, whose guile,
Stirr'd up with envy and revenge, deceiv'd
The mother of mankind.
> *Paradise Lost, I, l. 34*

7　　　Him the Almighty Power
Hurl'd headlong flaming from th' ethereal sky
With hideous ruin and combustion down
To bottomless perdition, there to dwell
In adamantine chains and penal fire,
Who durst defy th' Omnipotent to arms.
> *Paradise Lost, I, l. 44*

8 No light, but rather darkness visible.
> *Paradise Lost, I, l. 63*

9 Regions of sorrow, doleful shades, where peace
And rest can never dwell, hope never comes
That comes to all.　　　*Paradise Lost, I, l. 65*

10　　　What though the field be lost?
All is not lost; th' unconquerable will,
And study of revenge, immortal hate,
And courage never to submit or yield.
> *Paradise Lost, I, l. 105*

11　　　To be weak is miserable,
Doing or suffering.　　*Paradise Lost, I, l. 157*

12 And out of good still to find means of evil.
> *Paradise Lost, I, l. 165*

13 The seat of desolation, void of light.
> *Paradise Lost, I, l. 181*

14 A mind not to be chang'd by place or time.
The mind is its own place, and in itself
Can make a heav'n of hell, a hell of heav'n.
> *Paradise Lost, I, l. 253*

15 To reign is worth ambition though in hell:
Better to reign in hell than serve in heav'n.
> *Paradise Lost, I, l. 262*

16 His spear, to equal which the tallest pine
Hewn on Norwegian hills, to be the mast
Of some great ammiral, were but a wand,
He walk'd with, to support uneasy steps
Over the burning marle.
> *Paradise Lost, I, l. 292*

17 Thick as autumnal leaves that strow the brooks
In Vallombrosa.
> *Paradise Lost, I, l. 302*

18 Awake, arise, or be forever fallen!
> *Paradise Lost, I, l. 330*

19　　　Spirits, when they please,
Can either sex assume, or both.
> *Paradise Lost, I, l. 423*

20　　　When night
Darkens the streets, then wander forth the sons
Of Belial, flown with insolence and wine.
> *Paradise Lost, I, l. 500*

21 Th' imperial ensign, which, full high advanc'd,
Shone like a meteor, streaming to the wind.[1]
> *Paradise Lost, I, l. 536*

22 Sonorous metal blowing martial sounds:
At which the universal host up sent
A shout that tore hell's concave, and beyond
Frighted the reign of Chaos and old Night.
> *Paradise Lost, I, l. 540*

23　　　Anon they move
In perfect phalanx, to the Dorian mood
Of flutes and soft recorders.
> *Paradise Lost, I, l. 549*

24　　　His form had yet not lost
All her original brightness, nor appear'd
Less than archangel ruin'd, and th' excess
Of glory obscur'd.　　*Paradise Lost, I, l. 591*

25　　　The sun ...
In dim eclipse, disastrous twilight sheds
On half the nations, and with fear of change
Perplexes monarchs.　*Paradise Lost, I, l. 594*

26　　　Care
Sat on his faded cheek, but under brows
Of dauntless courage.　*Paradise Lost, I, l. 601*

---

[1] Streamed like a meteor to the troubled air. — THOMAS GRAY, *The Bard*, sec. I, st. 2, l. 6

1 Thrice he assay'd, and thrice, in spite of scorn,
  Tears, such as angels weep, burst forth.
  Paradise Lost, I, l. 619

2   Who overcomes
  By force hath overcome but half his foe.
  Paradise Lost, I, l. 648

3 Mammon, the least erected spirit that fell
  From heaven; for ev'n in heaven his looks and
        thoughts
  Were always downward bent, admiring more
  The riches of heaven's pavement, trodden gold,
  Than aught divine or holy else enjoyed
  In vision beatific.   *Paradise Lost, I, l. 679*

4   Let none admire
  That riches grow in hell; that soil may best
  Deserve the precious bane.   *Paradise Lost, I, l. 690*

5   From morn
  To noon he fell, from noon to dewy eve,
  A summer's day; and with the setting sun
  Dropp'd from the zenith like a falling star.
  Paradise Lost, I, l. 742

6 High on a throne of royal state, which far
  Outshone the wealth of Ormus and of Ind,
  Or where the gorgeous East with richest hand
  Showers on her kings barbaric pearl and gold,
  Satan exalted sat, by merit rais'd
  To that bad eminence; and from despair
  Thus high uplifted beyond hope, aspires
  Beyond thus high, insatiate to pursue
  Vain war with heav'n.   *Paradise Lost, II, l. 1*

7   Moloch, scepter'd king,
  Stood up, the strongest and the fiercest spirit
  That fought in heav'n; now fiercer by despair.
  Paradise Lost, II, l. 44

8   Rather than be less
  Car'd not to be at all.   *Paradise Lost, II, l. 47*

9 My sentence is for open war.
  Paradise Lost, II, l. 51

10 Which if not victory is yet revenge.
  Paradise Lost, II, l. 105

11 But all was false and hollow; through his tongue
  Dropp'd manna, and could make the worse appear
  The better reason.   *Paradise Lost, II, l. 112*

12   For who would lose,
  Though full of pain, this intellectual being,
  Those thoughts that wander through eternity,
  To perish rather, swallow'd up and lost
  In the wide womb of uncreated night,
  Devoid of sense and motion?
  Paradise Lost, II, l. 146

13 Unrespited, unpitied, unrepriev'd.
  Paradise Lost, II, l. 185

14   The never-ending flight
  Of future days.   *Paradise Lost, II, l. 221*

15 Thus Belial with words cloth'd in reason's
        garb
  Counsel'd ignoble ease, and peaceful sloth,
  Not peace.   *Paradise Lost, II, l. 226*

16   With grave
  Aspect he rose, and in his rising seem'd
  A pillar of state; deep on his front engraven
  Deliberation sat and public care;
  And princely counsel in his face yet shone,
  Majestic though in ruin.
  Paradise Lost, II, l. 300

17   To sit in darkness here
  Hatching vain empires.
  Paradise Lost, II, l. 377

18 The palpable obscure.   *Paradise Lost, II, l. 406*

19   Long is the way
  And hard, that out of hell leads up to light.
  Paradise Lost, II, l. 432

20 Their rising all at once was as the sound
  Of thunder heard remote.
  Paradise Lost, II, l. 476

21 Others apart sat on a hill retir'd,
  In thoughts more elevate, and reason'd high
  Of Providence, foreknowledge, will, and fate,
  Fix'd fate, free will, foreknowledge absolute,
  And found no end, in wand'ring mazes lost.
  Paradise Lost, II, l. 557

22 Vain wisdom all, and false philosophy.
  Paradise Lost, II, l. 565

23   Arm th' obdur'd breast
  With stubborn patience as with triple steel.
  Paradise Lost, II, l. 568

24 Far off from these a slow and silent stream,
  Lethe the river of oblivion rolls.
  Paradise Lost, II, l. 582

25 At certain revolutions all the damn'd
  Are brought: and feel by turns the bitter change
  Of fierce extremes, extremes by change more
        fierce.
  Paradise Lost, II, l. 597

26 Whence and what art thou, execrable shape?
  Paradise Lost, II, l. 681

27 Before mine eyes in opposition sits
  Grim Death my son and foe.
  Paradise Lost, II, l. 803

1 Hot, cold, moist, and dry, four champions fierce,[1]
  Strive here for mast'ry.   *Paradise Lost, II, l. 898*

2   To compare
  Great things with small.   *Paradise Lost, II, l. 921*

3 With ruin upon ruin, rout on rout,
  Confusion worse confounded.
                  Paradise Lost, II, l. 995

4 And fast by hanging in a golden chain,
  This pendent world, in bigness as a star
  Of smallest magnitude close by the moon.
                  Paradise Lost, II, l. 1051

5 Hail, holy light! offspring of heav'n firstborn.[2]
                  Paradise Lost, III, l. 1

6   Thus with the year
  Seasons return; but not to me returns
  Day, or the sweet approach of ev'n or morn,
  Or sight of vernal bloom, or summer's rose,
  Or flocks, or herds, or human face divine;
  But cloud instead, and ever-during dark
  Surrounds me, from the cheerful ways of men
  Cut off, and for the book of knowledge fair
  Presented with a universal blank
  Of Nature's works to me expung'd and raz'd,
  And wisdom at one entrance quite shut out.
                  Paradise Lost, III, l. 40

7 See golden days, fruitful of golden deeds,
  With Joy and Love triumphing.
                  Paradise Lost, III, l. 337

8 Dark with excessive bright.   *Paradise Lost, III, l. 380*

9 Into a limbo large and broad, since called
  The Paradise of Fools, to few unknown.
                  Paradise Lost, III, l. 495

10 The hell within him.
                  Paradise Lost, IV, l. 20

11   At whose sight all the stars
   Hide their diminish'd heads.[3]
                  Paradise Lost, IV, l. 34

12 Me miserable! which way shall I fly
   Infinite wrath, and infinite despair?
   Which way I fly is hell; myself am hell;
   And in the lowest deep a lower deep,
   Still threat'ning to devour me, opens wide,
   To which the hell I suffer seems a heaven.
                  Paradise Lost, IV, l. 73

---

[1]Hot and cold, and moist and dry. — DU BARTAS, *Divine Weeks and Works. Second Day*

[2]God's first creature, which was light. — FRANCIS BACON, *The New Atlantis* [1626]

Light, the prime work of God. — MILTON, *Samson Agonistes, l. 70*

[3]Ye little stars! hide your diminished rays. — ALEXANDER POPE, *Moral Essays, epistle III, l. 282*

13 So farewell hope, and with hope farewell fear,
   Farewell remorse: all good to me is lost;
   Evil, be thou my good.   *Paradise Lost, IV, l. 108*

14   And on the Tree of Life,
   The middle tree and highest there that grew,
   Sat like a cormorant.   *Paradise Lost, IV, l. 194*

15 A heaven on earth.   *Paradise Lost, IV, l. 208*

16 Flowers of all hue, and without thorn the rose.
                  Paradise Lost, IV, l. 256

17   Not that fair field
   Of Enna, where Proserpin gathering flowers
   Herself a fairer flower by gloomy Dis
   Was gathered, which cost Ceres all that pain
   To seek her through the world.
                  Paradise Lost, IV, l. 268

18 Two of far nobler shape erect and tall,
   Godlike erect, with native honor clad
   In naked majesty seem'd lords of all.
                  Paradise Lost, IV, l. 288

19 For contemplation he and valor form'd,
   For softness she and sweet attractive grace;
   He for God only, she for God in him.
                  Paradise Lost, IV, l. 297

20   Implied
   Subjection, but requir'd with gentle sway,
   And by her yielded, by him best receiv'd,
   Yielded with coy submission, modest pride,
   And sweet reluctant amorous delay.
                  Paradise Lost, IV, l. 307

21 Adam the goodliest man of men since born
   His sons, the fairest of her daughters Eve.
                  Paradise Lost, IV, l. 323

22 Imparadis'd in one another's arms.
                  Paradise Lost, IV, l. 506

23   Live while ye may,
   Yet happy pair.   *Paradise Lost, IV, l. 533*

24 Now came still evening on, and twilight gray
   Had in her sober livery all things clad.
                  Paradise Lost, IV, l. 598

25   The wakeful nightingale,
   She all night long her amorous descant sung;
   Silence was pleas'd: now glow'd the firmament
   With living sapphires: Hesperus, that led
   The starry host, rode brightest, till the moon,
   Rising in clouded majesty, at length
   Apparent queen unveil'd her peerless light,
   And o'er the dark her silver mantle threw.
                  Paradise Lost, IV, l. 602

26 With thee conversing I forget all time,
   All seasons, and their change; all please alike.

Sweet is the breath of morn, her rising sweet,
With charm of earliest birds.

Paradise Lost, IV, l. 639

1   Sweet the coming on
Of grateful ev'ning mild, then silent night
With this her solemn bird, and this fair moon,
And these the gems of heaven, her starry train.

Paradise Lost, IV, l. 646

2 Millions of spiritual creatures walk the earth
Unseen, both when we wake, and when we sleep.

Paradise Lost, IV, l. 677

3   In naked beauty more adorn'd,
More lovely, than Pandora.

Paradise Lost, IV, l. 713

4   Eas'd the putting off
These troublesome disguises which we wear.

Paradise Lost, IV, l. 739

5 Hail wedded love, mysterious law, true source
Of human offspring.   *Paradise Lost, IV, l. 750*

6 Squat like a toad, close at the ear of Eve.

Paradise Lost, IV, l. 800

7 Not to know me argues yourselves unknown.

Paradise Lost, IV, l. 830

8   Abash'd the Devil stood,
And felt how awful goodness is, and saw
Virtue in her shape how lovely.

Paradise Lost, IV, l. 846

9 All hell broke loose.   *Paradise Lost, IV, l. 918*

10 Like Teneriff or Atlas unremoved.

Paradise Lost, IV, l. 987

11   The starry cope
Of heaven.   *Paradise Lost, IV, l. 992*

12   His sleep
Was airy light from pure digestion bred.

Paradise Lost, V, l. 3

13   My latest found,
Heaven's last, best gift, my ever new delight!

Paradise Lost, V, l. 18

14 These are thy glorious works, Parent of good.

Paradise Lost, V, l. 153

15 Him first, him last, him midst, and without end.

Paradise Lost, V, l. 165

16 A wilderness of sweets.   *Paradise Lost, V, l. 294*

17 So saying, with dispatchful looks in haste
She turns, on hospitable thoughts intent.

Paradise Lost, V, l. 331

18   Freely we serve,
Because we freely love, as in our will

To love or not; in this we stand or fall.

Paradise Lost, V, l. 538

19   What if earth
Be but the shadow of heaven, and things therein
Each to other like, more than on earth is thought?

Paradise Lost, V, l. 574

20 Hear all ye Angels, progeny of light,
Thrones, Dominations, Princedoms, Virtues,
    Powers.   *Paradise Lost, V, l. 600*

21 Among the faithless, faithful only he.

Paradise Lost, V, l. 897

22   Morn,
Wak'd by the circling hours, with rosy hand
Unbarr'd the gates of light.

Paradise Lost, VI, l. 2

23 Servant of God, well done, well hast thou fought
The better fight, who single hast maintained
Against revolted multitudes the cause
Of truth, in word mightier than they in arms.

Paradise Lost, VI, l. 29

24 He onward came; far off his coming shone.

Paradise Lost, VI, l. 768

25 More safe I sing with mortal voice, unchang'd
To hoarse or mute, though fall'n on evil days,
On evil days though fall'n, and evil tongues;
In darkness, and with dangers compass'd round,
And solitude.   *Paradise Lost, VII, l. 24*

26   Out of one man a race
Of men innumerable.   *Paradise Lost, VII, l. 155*

27   There Leviathan
Hugest of living creatures, on the deep
Stretch'd like a promontory sleeps or swims,
And seems a moving land, and at his gills
Draws in, and at his trunk spouts out a sea.

Paradise Lost, VII, l. 412

28 The planets in their stations list'ning stood,
While the bright pomp ascended jubilant.
Open, ye everlasting gates, they sung,
Open, ye heavens, your living doors; let in
The great Creator from his work return'd
Magnificent, his six days' work, a world.

Paradise Lost, VII, l. 563

29 The angel ended, and in Adam's ear
So charming left his voice that he awhile
Thought him still speaking, still stood fix'd to hear.

Paradise Lost, VIII, l. 1

30 Liquid lapse of murmuring streams.

Paradise Lost, VIII, l. 263

31 And feel that I am happier than I know.

Paradise Lost, VIII, l. 282

1 Her virtue and the conscience of her worth,
That would be woo'd, and not unsought be won.
Paradise Lost, VIII, l. 502

2 The sum of earthly bliss.   *Paradise Lost, VIII, l. 522*

3   So absolute she seems
And in herself complete, so well to know
Her own, that what she wills to do or say,
Seems wisest, virtuousest, discreetest, best.
Paradise Lost, VIII, l. 547

4 Accuse not Nature, she hath done her part;
Do thou but thine.   *Paradise Lost, VIII, l. 561*

5 My unpremeditated verse.
Paradise Lost, IX, l. 24

6   Unless an age too late, or cold
Climate, or years damp my intended wing.
Paradise Lost, IX, l. 44

7 The serpent subtlest beast of all the field.
Paradise Lost, IX, l. 86

8 For solitude sometimes is best society,
And short retirement urges sweet return.
Paradise Lost, IX, l. 249

9 As one who long in populous city pent.
Paradise Lost, IX, l. 445

10 God so commanded, and left that command
Sole daughter of his voice; the rest, we live
Law to ourselves, our reason is our law.
Paradise Lost, IX, l. 652

11   Her rash hand in evil hour
Forth reaching to the fruit, she pluck'd, she eat:
Earth felt the wound, and Nature from her seat,
Sighing through all her works, gave signs of woe
That all was lost.   *Paradise Lost, IX, l. 780*

12 So dear I love him, that with him all deaths
I could endure, without him live no life.
Paradise Lost, IX, l. 832

13   In her face excuse
Came prologue, and apology too prompt.
Paradise Lost, IX, l. 853

14 O fairest of creation! last and best
Of all God's works! creature in whom excell'd
Whatever can to sight or thought be form'd,
Holy, divine, good, amiable, or sweet!
How art thou lost, how on a sudden lost,
Defac'd, deflower'd, and now to Death devote?
Paradise Lost, IX, l. 896

15   I feel
The link of nature draw me: flesh of flesh,
Bone of my bone thou art, and from thy state
Mine never shall be parted, bliss or woe.
Paradise Lost, IX, l. 913

16 Our state cannot be sever'd; we are one,
One flesh; to lose thee were to lose myself.
Paradise Lost, IX, l. 958

17   I shall temper so
Justice with mercy.   *Paradise Lost, X, l. 77*

18 Pandemonium, city and proud seat
Of Lucifer.
Paradise Lost, X, l. 424

19 A dismal universal hiss, the sound
Of public scorn.   *Paradise Lost, X, l. 508*

20 Death . . . on his pale horse.
Paradise Lost, X, l. 588

21 Demoniac frenzy, moping melancholy,
And moon-struck madness.
Paradise Lost, XI, l. 485

22 Nor love thy life, nor hate; but what thou liv'st
Live well; how long or short permit to Heaven.
Paradise Lost, XI, l. 553

23 A bevy of fair women.   *Paradise Lost, XI, l. 582*

24   The evening star,
Love's harbinger.   *Paradise Lost, XI, l. 588*

25 The brazen throat of war.
Paradise Lost, XI, l. 713

26   For now I see
Peace to corrupt no less than war to waste.
Paradise Lost, XI, l. 783

27 An olive leaf he brings, pacific sign.
Paradise Lost, XI, l. 860

28 The world was all before them, where to choose
Their place of rest, and Providence their guide:
They hand in hand with wand'ring steps and slow
Through Eden took their solitary way.
Paradise Lost, XII, l. 646

29   Most men admire
Virtue who follow not her lore.
Paradise Regained [1671], bk. I, l. 482

30 Skill'd to retire, and in retiring draw
Hearts after them tangled in amorous nets.
Paradise Regained, II, l. 161

31   Beauty stands
In the admiration only of weak minds
Led captive.   *Paradise Regained, II, l. 220*

32 Of whom to be disprais'd were no small praise.
Paradise Regained, III, l. 56

33 Elephants endorsed with towers.
Paradise Regained, III, l. 329

34 Dusk faces with white silken turbans wreath'd.
Paradise Regained, IV, l. 76

1   The childhood shows the man,
As morning shows the day.
                    Paradise Regained, IV, l. 220

2 Athens, the eye of Greece, mother of arts
And eloquence.   *Paradise Regained, IV, l. 240*

3   The olive grove of Academe,
Plato's retirement, where the Attic bird
Trills her thick-warbled notes the summer long.
                    Paradise Regained, IV, l. 244

4   Socrates . . .
Whom well inspir'd the oracle pronounc'd
Wisest of men.   *Paradise Regained, IV, l. 274*

5 The first and wisest of them all professed
To know this only, that he nothing knew.[1]
                    Paradise Regained, IV, l. 293

6 Deep vers'd in books and shallow in himself.
                    Paradise Regained, IV, l. 327

7   Till morning fair
Came forth with pilgrim steps, in amice gray.
                    Paradise Regained, IV, l. 426

8 Eyeless in Gaza, at the mill with slaves.
                    Samson Agonistes [1671], l. 41

9 O dark, dark, dark, amid the blaze of noon,
Irrecoverably dark, total eclipse
Without all hope of day!   *Samson Agonistes, l. 80*

10 The sun to me is dark
And silent as the moon,
When she deserts the night,
Hid in her vacant interlunar cave.
                    Samson Agonistes, l. 86

11 To live a life half dead, a living death.
                    Samson Agonistes, l. 100

12   Apt words have power to suage
The tumors of a troubled mind.
                    Samson Agonistes, l. 184

13 Just are the ways of God,
And justifiable to men;
Unless there be who think not God at all.
                    Samson Agonistes, l. 293

14 What boots it at one gate to make defense,
And at another to let in the foe?
                    Samson Agonistes, l. 560

15 My race of glory run, and race of shame,
And I shall shortly be with them at rest.
                    Samson Agonistes, l. 597

16 But who is this, what thing of sea or land?
Female of sex it seems,

That so bedeck'd, ornate, and gay,
Comes this way sailing
Like a stately ship
Of Tarsus, bound for th' isles
Of Javan or Gadire,
With all her bravery on, and tackle trim,
Sails fill'd, and streamers waving,
Courted by all the winds that hold them play;
An amber scent of odorous perfume
Her harbinger?   *Samson Agonistes, l. 710*

17 *Dalila:* In argument with men a woman ever
Goes by the worse, whatever be her cause.
Samson: For want of words, no doubt, or lack of
    breath!   *Samson Agonistes, l. 903*

18 Fame, if not double-faced, is double-mouthed,
And with contrary blast proclaims most deeds;
On both his wings, one black, the other white,
Bears greatest names in his wild airy flight.
                    Samson Agonistes, l. 971

19 Yet beauty, though injurious, hath strange power,
After offense returning, to regain
Love once possess'd.   *Samson Agonistes, l. 1003*

20 Love-quarrels oft in pleasing concord end;
Not wedlock-treachery.
                    Samson Agonistes, l. 1008

21 Boast not of what thou would'st have done, but do
What then thou would'st.
                    Samson Agonistes, l. 1104

22 He's gone; and who knows how he may report
Thy words by adding fuel to the flame?
                    Samson Agonistes, l. 1350

23 For evil news rides post, while good news baits.
                    Samson Agonistes, l. 1538

24 Suspense in news is torture.
                    Samson Agonistes, l. 1569

25 Nothing is here for tears, nothing to wail
Or knock the breast, no weakness, no contempt,
Dispraise, or blame, nothing but well and fair,
And what may quiet us in a death so noble.
                    Samson Agonistes, l. 1721

26 All is best, though we oft doubt,
What the unsearchable dispose
Of highest Wisdom brings about.
                    Samson Agonistes, l. 1745

27 Calm of mind, all passion spent.
                    Samson Agonistes, l. 1758

28   Such bickerings to recount, met often in these our
writers, what more worth is it than to chronicle the
wars of kites or crows flocking and fighting in the air?
                    The History of England [1670], bk. IV

---

[1]See Socrates, 70:6.

Edward Hyde, Earl of Clarendon
1609–1674

1   He [Hampden] had a head to contrive, a tongue to persuade, and a hand to execute any mischief.
History of the Rebellion [1702–1704], vol. III, bk. VII, sec. 84

Sir John Suckling
1609–1642

2 Why so pale and wan, fond lover?
  Prithee, why so pale?
  Will, when looking well can't move her,
  Looking ill prevail?   *Aglaura [1638]. Song, st. 1*

3 Quit, quit, for shame, this will not move,
  This cannot take her.
  If of herself she will not love,
  Nothing can make her.
  The devil take her!   *Aglaura. Song, st. 3*

4 High characters (cries one), and he would see
  Things that ne'er were, nor are, nor ne'er will be.
  The Goblins [1639], epilogue

5 Her feet beneath her petticoat
  Like little mice, stole in and out,
  As if they feared the light;
  But oh, she dances such a way!
  No sun upon an Easter-day
  Is half so fine a sight.
  A Ballad upon a Wedding [1641], st. 8

6 I prithee send me back my heart,
  Since I cannot have thine;
  For if from yours you will not part,
  Why then shouldst thou have mine?
  Fragmenta Aurea [1646]. Song, st. 1

7 'Tis not the meat, but 'tis the appetite
  Makes eating a delight.
  Fragmenta Aurea. Of Thee, Kind Boy, st. 3

8 Out upon it, I have loved
  Three whole days together;
  And am like to love three more,
  If it prove fair weather.
  Fragmenta Aurea. A Poem with the Answer, st. 1

Asai Ryoi
c. 1612–1691

9   Living only for the moment, turning our full attention to the pleasures of the moon, the snow, the cherry blossoms and the maples, singing songs, drinking wine and diverting ourselves in just floating, floating; caring not a whit for the poverty staring us in the face, refusing to be disheartened, like a gourd floating along with the river current: this is what we call ukiyo.[1]
Tales of the Floating World [1661]

Anne Bradstreet
c. 1612–1672

10 I am obnoxious to each carping tongue
   Who says my hand a needle better fits,
   A poet's pen all scorn I should thus wrong,
   For such despite they cast on female wits:
   If what I do prove well, it won't advance,
   They'll say it's stol'n, or else it was by chance.
   The Prologue [1650], l. 25

11   Let Greeks be Greeks, and Women what they are.   *The Prologue, l. 37*

12   Youth is the time of getting, middle age of improving, and old age of spending.
Meditations Divine and Moral [1664], 3

13   Authority without wisdom is like a heavy axe without an edge, fitter to bruise than polish.
Meditations Divine and Moral, 12

14   Sore laborers have hard hands and old sinners have brawny consciences.
Meditations Divine and Moral, 36

15 If ever two were one, then surely we.
   If ever man were loved by wife, then thee;
   If ever wife was happy in a man,
   Compare with me ye women if you can.
   To My Dear and Loving Husband [1678]

16   After a short time I changed my condition and was married, and came into this country, where I found a new world and new manners, at which my heart rose. But after I was convinced it was the way of God, I submitted to it and joined the church at Boston.
To My Dear Children [1867]

Samuel Butler
1612–1680

17 When civil fury first grew high,
   And men fell out they knew not why.
   Hudibras, pt. I [1663], canto I, l. 1

18 And pulpit, drum ecclesiastic,[2]
   Was beat with fist, instead of a stick.
   Hudibras, pt. I, canto I, l. 11

---

[1]Translated by RICHARD LANE.

[2]This is the first we hear of the "drum ecclesiastic" beating up for recruits in worldly warfare in our country. — WASHINGTON IRVING, *Knickerbocker's History of New York, bk. V, ch. 7*

1 Beside, 'tis known he could speak Greek
　As naturally as pigs squeak:[1]
　That Latin was no more difficile
　Than to a blackbird 'tis to whistle.
　　　　　Hudibras, pt. I, canto I, l. 51

2 He could distinguish and divide
　A hair 'twixt south and southwest side,
　On either which he would dispute,
　Confute, change hands, and still confute.
　　　　　Hudibras, pt. I, canto I, l. 67

3 He'd run in debt by disputation,
　And pay with ratiocination.
　　　　　Hudibras, pt. I, canto I, l. 77

4 For rhetoric, he could not ope
　His mouth, but out there flew a trope.
　　　　　Hudibras, pt. I, canto I, l. 81

5 For all a rhetorician's rules
　Teach nothing but to name his tools.
　　　　　Hudibras, pt. I, canto I, l. 89

6 A Babylonish dialect
　Which learned pedants much affect.
　　　　　Hudibras, pt. I, canto I, l. 93

7 For he by geometric scale,
　Could take the size of pots of ale.
　　　　　Hudibras, pt. I, canto I, l. 121

8 And wisely tell what hour o' th' day
　The clock doth strike, by algebra.
　　　　　Hudibras, pt. I, canto I, l. 125

9 'Twas Presbyterian true blue.
　　　　　Hudibras, pt. I, canto I, l. 191

10 Such as do build their faith upon
　The holy text of pike and gun.
　　　　　Hudibras, pt. I, canto I, l. 195

11 And prove their doctrine orthodox,
　By apostolic blows and knocks.
　　　　　Hudibras, pt. I, canto I, l. 199

12 The trenchant blade, Toledo trusty,
　For want of fighting was grown rusty,
　And ate into itself, for lack
　Of somebody to hew and hack.
　　　　　Hudibras, pt. I, canto I, l. 357

13 　　　I'll make the fur
　Fly 'bout the ears of the old cur.
　　　　　Hudibras, pt. I, canto III, l. 277

14 I am not now in fortune's power:
　He that is down can fall no lower.
　　　　　Hudibras, pt. I, canto III, l. 877

15 Cleric before, and Lay behind;
　A lawless linsey-woolsey brother,
　Half of one order, half another.
　　　　　Hudibras, pt. I, canto III, l. 1226

16 For what is worth in anything
　But so much money as 'twill bring?
　　　　　*Hudibras, pt. II [1664], canto I,
　　　　　l. 465*

17 Love is a boy by poets styled;
　Then spare the rod, and spoil the child.
　　　　　Hudibras, pt. II, canto I, l. 843

18 Oaths are but words, and words but wind.
　　　　　Hudibras, pt. II, canto II, l. 107

19 He that imposes an oath makes it,
　Not he that for convenience takes it;
　Then how can any man be said
　To break an oath he never made?
　　　　　Hudibras, pt. II, canto II, l. 377

20 　　　As the ancients
　Say wisely, have a care o' th' main chance,
　And look before you ere you leap;
　For as you sow, ye are like to reap.
　　　　　Hudibras, pt. II, canto II, l. 501

21 What makes all doctrines plain and clear?
　About two hundred pounds a year.
　And that which was proved true before,
　Prove false again? Two hundred more.
　　　　　Hudibras, pt. III [1678], canto I, l. 1277

22 He that complies against his will
　Is of his own opinion still.
　　　　　Hudibras, pt. III, canto III, l. 547

23 Neither have the hearts to stay,
　Nor wit enough to run away.
　　　　　Hudibras, pt. III, canto III, l. 569

James Graham, Marquess of Montrose
1612–1650

24 I'll make thee glorious by my pen,
　And famous by my sword.[2]
　　　　　My Dear and Only Love, st. 5

---

[1]He Greek and Latin speaks with greater ease / Than hogs eat acorns, and tame pigeons peas. — LIONEL CRANFIELD, EARL OF MIDDLESEX [1575–1645], *Panegyric on Tom Coriate*, in *Coriate's Crudities* [1611]

[2]I'll make thee famous by my pen, / And glorious by my sword. — WALTER SCOTT, *The Legend of Montrose*, ch. 15

Richard Crashaw
c. 1613–1649

1 The conscious water saw its God, and blushed.[1]
  Epigrammata Sacra [1634].
  Aquae in Vinum Versae
  (Water Turned into Wine)

2 Two went to pray? Oh, rather say
  One went to brag, the other to pray.
  Steps to the Temple [1648].
  Two Went Up into the Temple to Pray

3 Whoe'er she be,
  That not impossible she
  That shall command my heart and me.
  Steps to the Temple.
  Wishes to His Supposed Mistress, l. 1

4 Where'er she lie,
  Locked up from mortal eye,
  In shady leaves of destiny.
  Steps to the Temple.
  Wishes to His Supposed Mistress, l. 4

5 Life that dares send
  A challenge to his end,
  And when it comes, say, Welcome, friend!
  Steps to the Temple.
  Wishes to His Supposed Mistress, l. 85

6 I would be married, but I'd have no wife,
  I would be married to a single life.
  Steps to the Temple. On Marriage

7 All those fair and flagrant things.
  The Flaming Heart upon the
  Book of Saint Teresa [1652], l. 34

8 Love's passives are his activ'st part.
  The wounded is the wounding heart.
  The Flaming Heart upon the
  Book of Saint Teresa, l. 73

9 O thou undaunted daughter of desires!
  The Flaming Heart upon the
  Book of Saint Teresa, l. 93

10 By all the eagle in thee, all the dove.
  The Flaming Heart upon the
  Book of Saint Teresa, l. 95

11 Poor world (said I) what wilt thou do
  To entertain this starry stranger?

Is this the best thou canst bestow?
A cold, and not too cleanly, manger?
Contend, ye powers of heav'n and earth,
To fit a bed for this huge birth.
  Hymn of the Nativity [1652], st. 6

12 Proud world, said I, cease your contest,
  And let the mighty babe alone.
  The phoenix builds the phoenix' nest.
  Love's architecture is his own.
  The babe whose birth embraves this morn,
  Made his own bed ere he was born.
  Hymn of the Nativity, st. 7

13 Welcome, all wonders in one sight!
  Eternity shut in a span.
  Hymn of the Nativity, Full Chorus

François, Duc de La Rochefoucauld
1613–1680

14 Self-love is the greatest of all flatterers.
  Reflections; or, Sentences and
  Moral Maxims [1678], maxim 2

15 We all have strength enough to endure the misfortunes of others.   *Reflections, maxim 19*

16 Philosophy triumphs easily over past evils and future evils; but present evils triumph over it.
  Reflections, maxim 22

17 We need greater virtues to sustain good fortune than bad.   *Reflections, maxim 25*

18 If we had no faults of our own, we would not take so much pleasure in noticing those of others.
  Reflections, maxim 31

19 Self-interest speaks all sorts of tongues, and plays all sorts of roles, even that of disinterestedness.
  Reflections, maxim 39

20 We are never so happy nor so unhappy as we imagine.   *Reflections, maxim 49*

21 To succeed in the world, we do everything we can to appear successful.   *Reflections, maxim 56*

22 There is no disguise which can for long conceal love where it exists or simulate it where it does not.
  Reflections, maxim 70

23 There are very few people who are not ashamed of having been in love when they no longer love each other.   *Reflections, maxim 71*

24 True love is like ghosts, which everybody talks about and few have seen.   *Reflections, maxim 76*

25 The love of justice in most men is simply the fear of suffering injustice.   *Reflections, maxim 78*

---

[1] Nympha pudica Deum vidit, et erubuit. — Quoted by SAMUEL JOHNSON [1778]; from BOSWELL, *Life of Johnson, vol. II, p. 218* (Everyman edition)
  The bashful stream hath seen its God and blushed. — AARON HILL [1685–1750], *The Miracle at Cana* [published 1753]
  The water hears thy faintest word, / And blushes into wine. — JOHN SAMUEL BEWLEY MONSELL [1811–1875], *Mysterious Is Thy Presence, Lord* [1866], st. 1

1   Silence is the best tactic for him who distrusts himself.   *Reflections, maxim 79*

2   It is more ignominious to mistrust our friends than to be deceived by them.   *Reflections, maxim 84*

3   Everyone complains of his memory, and no one complains of his judgment.   *Reflections, maxim 89*

4   Old people like to give good advice, as solace for no longer being able to provide bad examples.   *Reflections, maxim 93*

5   The mind is always the dupe of the heart.[1]   *Reflections, maxim 102*

6   Nothing is given so profusely as advice.   *Reflections, maxim 110*

7   The true way to be deceived is to think oneself more clever than others.   *Reflections, maxim 127*

8   We would rather speak ill of ourselves than not talk about ourselves at all.   *Reflections, maxim 138*

9   Usually we praise only to be praised.   *Reflections, maxim 146*

10   Our repentance is not so much regret for the ill we have done as fear of the ill that may happen to us in consequence.   *Reflections, maxim 180*

11   Who lives without folly is not so wise as he thinks.   *Reflections, maxim 209*

12   Hypocrisy is the homage that vice pays to virtue.   *Reflections, maxim 218*

13   There is great skill in knowing how to conceal one's skill.   *Reflections, maxim 245*

14   The pleasure of love is in loving. We are happier in the passion we feel than in that we arouse.   *Reflections, maxim 259*

15   Absence diminishes mediocre passions and increases great ones, as the wind blows out candles and fans fire.   *Reflections, maxim 276*

16   We always like those who admire us; we do not always like those whom we admire.   *Reflections, maxim 294*

17   The gratitude of most men is merely a secret desire to receive greater benefits.[2]   *Reflections, maxim 298*

18   We frequently forgive those who bore us, but cannot forgive those whom we bore.   *Reflections, maxim 304*

19   Lovers never get tired of each other, because they are always talking about themselves.   *Reflections, maxim 312*

20   In jealousy there is more self-love than love.   *Reflections, maxim 324*

21   We confess to little faults only to persuade ourselves that we have no great ones.   *Reflections, maxim 327*

22   We pardon to the extent that we love.   *Reflections, maxim 330*

23   We rarely find that people have good sense unless they agree with us.[3]   *Reflections, maxim 347*

24   Jealousy is always born together with love, but it does not always die when love dies.   *Reflections, maxim 361*

25   We may give advice, but we do not inspire conduct.   *Reflections, maxim 378*

26   The veracity which increases with old age is not far from folly.   *Reflections, maxim 416*

27   Few people know how to be old.   *Reflections, maxim 423*

28   Nothing prevents our being natural so much as the desire to appear so.   *Reflections, maxim 431*

29   In their first passion women love their lovers, in the others they love love.   *Reflections, maxim 471*

30   Quarrels would not last long if the fault were only on one side.   *Reflections, maxim 496*

31   In the misfortune of our best friends we often find something that is not displeasing.[4]   *Reflections, maxim 583*

Jeremy Taylor
1613–1667

32   Too quick a sense of constant infelicity.   *Holy Dying [1651]*

33   Every schoolboy knows it.   *On the Real Presence [1654], sec. V, subsec. 1*

---

[1]The Mind lives on the Heart / Like any Parasite. — EMILY DICKINSON, *The Mind lives on the Heart* [c. 1876]

[2]A lively sense of future favors. — ROBERT WALPOLE, *definition of the gratitude of place-expectants;* from WILLIAM HAZLITT, *English Comic Writers* [1819], *Wit and Humor*

[3]"That was excellently observed," say I when I read a passage in another where his opinion agrees with mine. When we differ, then I pronounce him to be mistaken. — JONATHAN SWIFT, *Thoughts on Various Subjects*

[4]*Maxim 583* is one of the "maximes supprimées" discarded before the 1678 edition.

In all distresses of our friends / We first consult our private ends; / While Nature, kindly bent to ease us, / Points out some circumstance to please us. — JONATHAN SWIFT, a paraphrase of Rochefoucauld's maxim in *On the Death of Dr. Swift* [1731]

1   The union of hands and hearts.
Sermons [1653], The Marriage Ring, pt. I

2   No man ever repented that he arose from the table sober, healthful, and with his wits about him.
Sermons, The Marriage Ring, I

Thomas Ady
fl. 1655

3 Matthew, Mark, Luke, and John,
The bed be blest that I lie on.
Four angels to my bed,
Four angels round my head,[1]
One to watch, and one to pray,
And two to bear my soul away.
A Candle in the Dark [1655]

Richard Baxter
1615–1691

4   In necessary things, unity; in doubtful things, liberty; in all things, charity.[2]   *Motto*

Roger de Bussy-Rabutin
1618–1693

5   God is usually on the side of the big squadrons and against the small ones.[3]
*Letter to the Comte de Limoges
[October 18, 1677]*

Abraham Cowley
1618–1667

6 This only grant me, that my means may lie
Too low for envy, for contempt too high.
A Vote [1636]

7 Well then; I now do plainly see
This busy world and I shall ne'er agree;
The very honey of all earthly joy
Does of all meats the soonest cloy,
And they (methinks) deserve my pity,
Who for it can endure the stings,
The crowd, and buzz and murmurings,
Of this great hive, the city.   *The Wish [1647]*

8 Ah yet, ere I descend to the grave
May I a small house and large garden have;
And a few friends, and many books, both true,
Both wise, and both delightful too!   *The Wish*

9 The thirsty earth soaks up the rain,
And drinks, and gapes for drink again.
The plants suck in the earth, and are
With constant drinking fresh and fair.
Anacreon [1656], no. II, Drinking

10 A mighty pain to love it is,
And 'tis a pain that pain to miss;
But of all pains, the greatest pain
It is to love, but love in vain.   *Anacreon, VII, Gold*

11 Nothing is there to come, and nothing past,
But an eternal now does always last.
Davideis [1656], bk. I, l. 361

12 What shall I do to be forever known,
And make the age to come my own?
The Motto [1656]

13 Life is an incurable disease.
To Dr. Scarborough [1656]

14 Ye fields of Cambridge, our dear Cambridge, say,
Have ye not seen us walking every day?
Was there a tree about which did not know
The love betwixt us two?
On the Death of Mr. William Harvey[4] [1657]

15 God the first garden made, and the first city.
The Garden [1664], essay 5

Richard Lovelace
1618–1658

16 Oh, could you view the melody
Of every grace
And music of her face,[5]
You'd drop a tear;
Seeing more harmony
In her bright eye
Than now you hear.
Lucasta [1649]. Orpheus to Beasts

17 Tell me not, sweet, I am unkind,
That from the nunnery
Of thy chaste breast and quiet mind,
To war and arms I fly.
Lucasta. To Lucasta: Going to the Wars, st. 1

18 I could not love thee, dear, so much,
Lov'd I not honor more.
Lucasta. To Lucasta: Going to the Wars, st. 3

---

[1]Usual version: Bless the bed that I lie on. / Four corners to my bed, / Four angels round my head.

[2]In necessariis unitas; in dubiis libertas; in omnibus caritas.

[3]It is said that God is always for the big battalions. — VOLTAIRE, *Letter to M. le Riche* [February 6, 1770]
Providence is always on the side of the last reserve. — *Attributed to* NAPOLEON

[4]See William Harvey, 236.

[5]The mind, the music breathing from her face. — LORD BYRON, *The Bride of Abydos, canto I, st. 6*

1 When I lie tangled in her hair,
And fettered to her eye,
The gods that wanton in the air
Know no such liberty.
Lucasta. To Althea: From Prison, st. 1

2 Stone walls do not a prison make,[1]
Nor iron bars a cage;
Minds innocent and quiet take
That for an hermitage;
If I have freedom in my love,
And in my soul am free,
Angels alone that soar above
Enjoy such liberty.
Lucasta. To Althea: From Prison, st. 4

3 If to be absent were to be
Away from thee;
Or that when I am gone,
You and I were alone;
Then, my Lucasta, might I crave
Pity from blust'ring wind, or swallowing wave.
Lucasta. To Lucasta:
Going Beyond the Seas, st. 1

Ninon de L'Enclos
1620–1705

4 Old age is woman's hell.[2] *Attributed*

Jean de La Fontaine
1621–1695

5 We believe no evil till the evil's done.
Fables, bk. I [1668], fable 8

6 We heed no instincts but our own. *Fables, I, 8*

7 The opinion of the strongest is always the best.
Fables, I, 10

8 Better to suffer than to die: that is mankind's
motto. *Fables, I, 16*

9 By the work one knows the workman.
Fables, I, 21

10 I bend but do not break. *Fables, I, 22*

11 It is a double pleasure to deceive the deceiver.
Fables, II [1668], 15

12 It is impossible to please all the world and one's
father. *Fables, III [1668], 1*

13 Beware, as long as you live, of judging people by
appearances. *Fables, VI [1668], 5*

14 People who make no noise are dangerous.
Fables, VIII [1678–1679], 23

15 He knows the universe, and himself he does not
know. *Fables, VIII, 26*

16 A hungry stomach cannot hear.[3]
Fables, IX [1678–1679], 17

Andrew Marvell
1621–1678

17 The inglorious arts of peace.
Upon Cromwell's Return from
Ireland [1650]

18 He[4] nothing common did or mean
Upon that memorable scene,
But with his keener eye
The axe's edge did try.
Upon Cromwell's Return from Ireland

19 So much one man can do,
That does both act and know.
Upon Cromwell's Return from Ireland

20 Had we but world enough, and time,
This coyness, lady, were no crime.
To His Coy Mistress [1650–1652]

21 I would
Love you ten years before the Flood,
And you should, if you please, refuse
Till the conversion of the Jews.
My vegetable love should grow
Vaster than empires, and more slow.
To His Coy Mistress

22 But at my back I always hear
Time's winged chariot hurrying near;
And yonder all before us lie
Deserts of vast eternity. *To His Coy Mistress*

23 Then worms shall try
That long preserved virginity,
And your quaint honor turn to dust,
And into ashes all my lust.
The grave's a fine and private place,
But none, I think, do there embrace.
To His Coy Mistress

24 Thus, though we cannot make our sun
Stand still, yet we will make him run.
To His Coy Mistress

---

[1]Stone walls a prisoner make, but not a slave. — WILLIAM WORDSWORTH, *Humanity* [1829]

[2]La vieillesse est l'enfer des femmes.

---

[3]Ventre affamé n'a point d'oreilles.

[4]King Charles I.

1 Annihilating all that's made
To a green thought in a green shade.
The Garden [1650–1652]

2 Casting the body's vest aside,
My soul into the boughs does glide. *The Garden*

3 My love is of a birth as rare
As 'tis for object strange and high;
It was begotten by despair
Upon impossibility.
The Definition of Love [1650–1652], st. 1

4 As lines, so loves oblique, may well
Themselves in every angle greet;
But ours, so truly parallel,
Though infinite, can never meet.

Therefore the love which us doth bind
But fate so enviously debars,
Is the conjunction of the mind,
And opposition of the stars.
The Definition of Love, st. 7, 8

5 Where the remote Bermudas ride,
In th' ocean's bosom unespied.
Bermudas [1657], l. 1

6 He hangs in shades the orange bright,
Like golden lamps in a green night. *Bermudas, l. 17*

7 And all the way, to guide their chime,
With falling oars they kept the time. *Bermudas, l. 39*

Molière [Jean-Baptiste Poquelin]
1622–1673

8 To pull the chestnuts out of the fire with the cat's paw.[1]
L'Étourdi (The Blunderer) [1655], act III, sc. vi

9 We die only once, and for such a long time!
Le Dépit Amoureux (The Amorous Quarrel) [1656], act V, sc. iii

10 The world, dear Agnes, is a strange affair.
L'École des Femmes (The School of Women) [1662], act II, sc. vi

11 There is no rampart that will hold out against malice. *Tartuffe [1664], act I, sc. i*

12 Those whose conduct gives room for talk are always the first to attack their neighbors.
Tartuffe, I, i

13 She is laughing up her sleeve at you.
Tartuffe, I, vi

14 A woman always has her revenge ready.
Tartuffe, II, ii

15 Cover that bosom that I must not see: souls are wounded by such things.[2]
Tartuffe, III, ii

16 Although I am a pious man, I am not the less a man. *Tartuffe, III, iii*

17 To create a public scandal is what's wicked; to sin in private is not a sin. *Tartuffe, IV, v*

18 We have changed all that.[3]
Le Médecin Malgré Lui (The Doctor in Spite of Himself) [1666], act II, sc. vi

19 On some preference esteem is based; to esteem everything is to esteem nothing.
Le Misanthrope [1666], act I, sc. i

20 He's a wonderful talker, who has the art of telling you nothing in a great harangue.
Le Misanthrope, II, v

21 He makes his cook his merit, and the world visits his dinners and not him. *Le Misanthrope, II, v*

22 You see him laboring to produce *bons mots*.
Le Misanthrope, II, v

23 The more we love our friends, the less we flatter them; it is by excusing nothing that pure love shows itself. *Le Misanthrope, II, v*

24 Doubts are more cruel than the worst of truths.
Le Misanthrope, III, vii

25 Anyone may be an honorable man, and yet write verse badly.
Le Misanthrope, IV, i

26 I prefer an accommodating vice to an obstinate virtue. *Amphitryon [1666], act I, sc. iv*

27 My Lord Jupiter knows how to sugarcoat the pill. *Amphitryon, III, x*

28 You've asked for it, Georges Dandin, you've asked for it.[4]
Georges Dandin [1668], act I, sc. ix

29 Good Heavens! For more than forty years I have been speaking prose without knowing it.
Le Bourgeois Gentilhomme [1670], act II, sc. iv

30 All that is not prose is verse; and all that is not verse is prose. *Le Bourgeois Gentilhomme, II, iv*

---

[1]Tirer les marrons du feu avec la patte du chat. — *Proverb, familiar in many languages*

[2]Couvrez ce sein que je ne saurais voir: / Par de pareils objets les âmes sont blessées.

[3]Nous avons changé tout cela.

[4]Vous l'avez voulu, Georges Dandin, vous l'avez voulu.

1   My fair one, let us swear an eternal friendship.[1]
        Le Bourgeois Gentilhomme, IV, i

2   What the devil was he doing in that galley?[2]
        Les Fourberies de Scapin (Scapin's Deceits)
        [1671], act II, sc. xi

3   Grammar, which knows how to control even kings.[3]
        Les Femmes Savantes (The Learned Ladies)
        [1672], act II, sc. vi

4   A learned fool is more foolish than an ignorant one.   *Les Femmes Savantes, IV, iii*

5   Ah, there are no longer any children!
        Le Malade Imaginaire
        (The Imaginary Invalid) [1673],
        act II, sc. xi

6   Nearly all men die of their remedies, and not of their illnesses.
        Le Malade Imaginaire, III, iii

Algernon Sidney
1622–1683

7 This hand, unfriendly to tyrants,
  Seeks with the sword placid repose under liberty.[4]
        Life and Memoirs of Algernon Sidney

8 It is not necessary to light a candle to the sun.
        Discourses on Government [1698],
        ch. 2, sec. 23

Henry Vaughan
1622–1695

9 Happy those early days, when I
  Shin'd in my angel-infancy!

---

[1]Madam, I have been looking for a person who disliked gravy all my life; let us swear eternal friendship. — SYDNEY SMITH [1771–1845], *Lady Holland's Memoir* [1855], *vol. I, ch. 9*

[2]Que diable allait-il faire dans cette galère?
Que diable aller faire aussi dans la galère d'un Turc? d'un Turc! [What the deuce did he want on board a Turk's galley? A Turk!] — CYRANO DE BERGERAC [1619–1655], *Le Pédant Joué* [1654], *act II, sc. iv*
  The saying of Molière came into his head: "But what the devil was he doing in that galley?" and he laughed at himself. — LEO TOLSTOY, *War and Peace, bk. IV, ch. 6*

[3]Sigismund [1368–1437], Holy Roman emperor, at the Council of Constance [1414] said to a prelate who had objected to His Majesty's grammar: Ego sum rex Romanus, et supra grammaticam [I am the Roman king, and am above grammar].

[4]Manus haec, inimica tyrannis, / Ense petit placidam sub libertate quietem.
  The second line is the motto of the Commonwealth of Massachusetts: By the sword we seek peace, but peace only under liberty.

Before I understood this place
Appointed for my second race.
        Silex Scintillans (The Fiery Flint),
        pt. I [1650]. The Retreat, l. 1

10 But felt through all this fleshly dress
  Bright shoots of everlastingness.
        Silex Scintillans, I. The Retreat, l. 19

11 Some men a forward motion love,
  But I by backward steps would move.
        Silex Scintillans, I. The Retreat, l. 29

12 O joys! Infinite sweetness! with what flowers
  And shoots of glory, my soul breaks, and buds!
        Silex Scintillans, I. The Morning-Watch, l. 1

13   Prayer is
    The world in tune,
    A spirit-voice,
    And vocal joys,
  Whose echo is heaven's bliss.
    O let me climb
  When I lie down!
        Silex Scintillans,
        I. The Morning-Watch, l. 18

14 I saw Eternity the other night
  Like a great ring of pure and endless light.
    All calm, as it was bright;
  And round beneath it, Time in hours, days, years,
    Driv'n by the spheres
  Like a vast shadow mov'd; in which the world
    And all her train were hurl'd.
        Silex Scintillans, I. The World

15 My soul, there is a country
  Far beyond the stars
  Where stands a winged sentry
  All skillful in the wars:
  There, above noise and danger,
  Sweet Peace is crown'd with smiles,
  And One born in a manger
  Commands the beauteous files.
        Silex Scintillans, I. Peace, st. 1

16 They are all gone into the world of light!
  And I alone sit lingering here;
  Their very memory is fair and bright,
  And my sad thoughts doth clear.
        Silex Scintillans, pt. II [1655].
        They Are All Gone, st. 1

17 I see them walking in an air of glory
  Whose light doth trample on my days,
  My days, which are at best but dull and hoary,
  Mere glimmering and decays.
        Silex Scintillans, II. They Are All Gone, st. 3

18 Dear, beauteous death, the jewel of the just!
  Shining nowhere but in the dark;

What mysteries do lie beyond thy dust,
Could man outlook that mark!
>> *Silex Scintillans, II. They Are All Gone, st. 5*

1 I cannot reach it, and my striving eye
Dazzles at it, as at eternity.
>> *Silex Scintillans, II. Childhood*

2   Dear Night! this world's defeat;
The stop to busy fools; care's check and curb;
The day of spirits; my soul's calm retreat
    Which none disturb!
Christ's progress, and His prayer-time;
The hours to which high Heaven doth chime.
>> *Silex Scintillans, II. The Night, l. 25*

3 There is in God, some say,
A deep but dazzling darkness.
>> *Silex Scintillans, II. The Night, l. 49*

Blaise Pascal
1623–1662

4   Things are always at their best in their beginning.   *Lettres Provinciales [1656–1657], no. 4*

5   I have made this letter longer than usual, because I lack the time to make it short.[1]
>> *Lettres Provinciales, 16*

6   True eloquence takes no heed of eloquence, true morality takes no heed of morality.
>> *Penséees (Thoughts) [1670], no. 4*

7   Do you wish people to think well of you? Don't speak well of yourself.   *Pensées, 44*

8   Physical science will not console me for the ignorance of morality in the time of affliction.   *Pensées, 67*

9   What is man in nature? Nothing in relation to the infinite, everything in relation to nothing, a mean between nothing and everything.[2]   *Pensées, 72*

10   I lay it down as a fact that if all men knew what others say of them, there would not be four friends in the world.   *Pensées, 101*

11   The state of man: inconstancy, boredom, anxiety.[3]
>> *Pensées, 127*

12   I have discovered that all human evil comes from this, man's being unable to sit still in a room.
>> *Pensées, 139*

13   Cleopatra's nose, had it been shorter, the whole face of the world would have been changed.   *Pensées, 162*

14   The eternal silence of these infinite spaces terrifies me.[4]   *Pensées, 206*

15   The last act is bloody, no matter how happy the rest of the play.   *Pensées, 210*

16   We shall die alone.[5]   *Pensées, 211*

17   "God is, or He is not." But to which side shall we incline? Reason can decide nothing here. There is an infinite chaos which separated us. A game is being played at the extremity of this infinite distance where heads or tails will turn up. What will you wager? . . . If you win, you win everything; if you lose, you lose nothing. Wager, then, without hesitation that He is.   *Pensées, 233*

18   The heart has its reasons which reason knows nothing of.[6]   *Pensées, 277*

19   We know the truth, not only by the reason, but by the heart.   *Pensées, 282*

20   Justice without strength is helpless, strength without justice is tyrannical. . . . Unable to make what is just strong, we have made what is strong just.
>> *Pensées, 298*

21   Man is but a reed, the weakest in nature, but he is a thinking reed.[7]   *Pensées, 347*

22   Man is neither angel nor beast; and the misfortune is that he who would act the angel acts the beast.[8]
>> *Pensées, 358*

23   Evil is easy, and has infinite forms.   *Pensées, 408*

24   To ridicule philosophy is really to philosophize.[9]
>> *Pensées, 430*

25   What a chimera then is man! What a novelty! What a monster, what a chaos, what a contradiction, what a prodigy! Judge of all things, feeble earthworm, depository of truth, a sink of uncertainty and error, the glory and the shame of the universe.
>> *Pensées, 434*

26   Self is hateful.[10]   *Pensées, 455*

27   Men blaspheme what they do not know.
>> *Pensées, 556*

---

[1]Je n'ai fait celle-ci plus longue parceque je n'ai pas eu le loisir de la faire plus courte.

Not that the story need be long, but it will take a long while to make it short. — HENRY DAVID THOREAU, *Letter to Mr. B* [November 16, 1857]

[2]Qu'est-ce que l'homme dans la nature? Un néant à l'égard de l'infini, un tout à l'égard du néant, un milieu entre rien et tout.

[3]Condition de l'homme: inconstance, ennui, inquiétude.

[4]Le silence éternel de ces espaces infinis m'effraie.

[5]On mourra seul.

[6]Le coeur a ses raisons que la raison ne connaît point.

[7]L'homme n'est qu'un roseau, le plus faible de la nature, mais c'est un roseau pensant.

[8]L'homme n'est ni ange ni bête; et le malheur veut que qui veut faire l'ange fait la bête.

[9]Se moquer de la philosophie, c'est vraiment philosopher.

[10]Le moi est haïssable.

1   Men never do evil so completely and cheerfully as when they do it from religious conviction.

Pensées, 894

2   "The God of Abraham, the God of Isaac, the God of Jacob," not of philosophers and scholars.

Writing found in Pascal's effects after
his death

George Fox[1]
1624–1691

3   Be patterns, be examples in all countries, places, islands, nations wherever you come; that your carriage and life may preach among all sorts of people, and to them; then you will come to walk cheerfully over the world, answering that of God in every one; whereby in them you may be a blessing, and make the witness of God in them to bless you.

To Friends in the Ministry [1656].
Statement from Jail

4   The Lord showed me, so that I did see clearly, that he did not dwell in these temples which men had commanded and set up, but in people's hearts . . . his people were his temple, and he dwelt in them.

Journal [1694]

5   When the Lord sent me forth into the world, He forbade me to put off my hat to any, high or low.

Journal

6   [It was] Justice Bennet of Derby, who was the first that called us Quakers, because we bid them tremble at the word of the Lord. This was in the year 1650.

Journal

7   He [Oliver Cromwell] said: "I see there is a people risen and come up that I cannot win either with gifts, honors, offices or places; but all other sects and people I can."   *Journal*

Thomas Sydenham
1624–1689

8   Fever itself is Nature's instrument.

Medical Observations[2] [1676], ch. 5

John Aubrey
1626–1697

9   I have heard him [William Harvey] say, that after his book of the circulation of the blood came out,

that he fell mightily in his practice, and that 'twas believed by the vulgar that he was crack-brained; and all the physicians were against his opinion.

Brief Lives [1690]. William Harvey

10   He [Thomas Hobbes] had read much, if one considers his long life; but his contemplation was more than his reading. He was wont to say that if he had read as much as other men, he should have known no more than other men.

Brief Lives. Thomas Hobbes

11   He [John Milton] was so fair that they called him *the Lady of Christ's College.*

Brief Lives. John Milton

12   Mr. William Shakespeare was born at Stratford upon Avon in the County of Warwick. His father was a butcher, and I have been told heretofore by some of the neighbors, that when he was a boy he exercised his father's trade, but when he killed a calf he would do it in a high style and make a speech.

Brief Lives. William Shakespeare

Marie de Rabutin-Chantal, Marquise de Sévigné
1626–1696

13   True friendship is never serene.

Letter to Madame de Grignan
[September 10, 1671]

14   Racine will go out of style like coffee.

Attributed

Jacques Bénigne Bossuet
1627–1704

15   The greatest weakness of all weaknesses is to fear too much to appear weak.

Politique Tirée de l'Écriture Sainte
(Politics Drawn from Holy Scripture)
[1679]

16   The inexorable boredom that is at the core of life.

From M. A. Couturier [1897–1954]
Se Garder Libre (Keeping Free) [1962]

Robert Boyle
1627–1691

17   I am not ambitious to appear a man of letters: I could be content the world should think I had scarce looked upon any other book than that of nature.

The Philosophical Works of Robert Boyle
[1738], vol. I, preliminary discourse

---

[1]Founder of the Society of Friends (Quakers).

[2]Translation from *Bulletin of The New York Academy of Medicine*, vol. IV [1928]. Original work in Latin: *Observationes Medicinae*.

John Ray
1627–1705

1   In a calm sea every man is a pilot.
English Proverbs [1670]

2   If wishes were horses, beggars might ride.
English Proverbs

3   Money begets money.   *English Proverbs*

4   Blood is thicker than water.   *English Proverbs*

5   Misery loves company.   *English Proverbs*

John Bunyan
1628–1688

6 Some said, "John, print it"; others said, "Not so."
Some said, "It might do good"; others said, "No."
The Pilgrim's Progress [1678].
Apology for His Book

7   As I walked through the wilderness of this world.   *The Pilgrim's Progress, pt. I*

8   I saw a man clothed with rags . . . a book in his hand, and a great burden upon his back.
The Pilgrim's Progress, I

9   The name of the one was Obstinate and the name of the other Pliable.   *The Pilgrim's Progress, I*

10   The name of the slough was Despond.
The Pilgrim's Progress, I

11   Every fat [vat] must stand upon his bottom.[1]
The Pilgrim's Progress, I

12   The gentleman's name was Mr. Worldly-Wise-Man.   *The Pilgrim's Progress, I*

13   A very stately palace before him, the name of which was Beautiful.   *The Pilgrim's Progress, I*

14   The valley of Humiliation.
The Pilgrim's Progress, I

15   A foul Fiend coming over the field to meet him; his name is Apollyon.   *The Pilgrim's Progress, I*

16   I will talk of things heavenly, or things earthly; things moral, or things evangelical; things sacred, or things profane; things past, or things to come; things foreign, or things at home; things more essential, or things circumstantial.   *The Pilgrim's Progress, I*

17   It beareth the name of Vanity Fair, because the town where 'tis kept is lighter than vanity.
The Pilgrim's Progress, I

18   Hanging is too good for him, said Mr. Cruelty.
The Pilgrim's Progress, I

19   My great-grandfather was but a water-man, looking one way, and rowing another.
The Pilgrim's Progress, I

20   A castle called Doubting Castle, the owner whereof was Giant Despair.
The Pilgrim's Progress, I

21   They came to the Delectable Mountains.
The Pilgrim's Progress, I

22   A great horror and darkness fell upon Christian.
The Pilgrim's Progress, I

23   So I awoke, and behold it was a dream.
The Pilgrim's Progress, I

24   A man that could look no way but downwards with a muckrake in his hand.[2]
The Pilgrim's Progress, pt. II

25 He that is down, needs fear no fall,
He that is low, no pride.
The Pilgrim's Progress. Shepherd Boy's Song

26 Who would true valor see,
Let him come hither;
One here will constant be,
Come wind, come weather.
There's no discouragement
Shall make him once relent
His first avow'd intent
    To be a pilgrim.
The Pilgrim's Progress. Shepherd Boy's Song

27   My sword I give to him that shall succeed me in my pilgrimage, and my courage and skill to him that can get it. My marks and scars I carry with me, to be a witness for me, that I have fought His battles who now will be my rewarder.
The Pilgrim's Progress. Shepherd Boy's Song

28   So he passed over, and all the trumpets sounded for him on the other side.
The Pilgrim's Progress. Shepherd Boy's Song

29   The captain of all these men of death that came against him to take him away, was the Consumption, for it was that that brought him down to the grave.
The Life and Death of Mr. Badman [1680]

Sir William Temple
1628–1699

30   When all is done, human life is, at the greatest and the best, but like a froward child, that must be played

---

[1]Every tub must stand upon its bottom. — CHARLES MACKLIN, *The Man of the World* [1781], *act I, sc. ii*

[2]See Theodore Roosevelt, 571:9.

with and humored a little to keep it quiet till it falls asleep, and then the care is over.

> *Miscellanea, pt. II [1690]. Of Poetry*

George Villiers, Duke of Buckingham
1628–1687

1   Ay, now the plot thickens very much upon us.

> *The Rehearsal [written 1663, performed 1671], act III, sc. ii*

Charles II
1630–1685

2   Let not poor Nelly starve.

> *On his deathbed. From* GILBERT BURNET *[1643–1715], The History of My Own Times [1724–1734], vol. I, bk. 2, ch. 17*

3   He had been, he said, an unconscionable time dying; he hoped that they would excuse it.

> *From* THOMAS BABINGTON MACAULAY, *History of England [1849], vol. I, ch. 4*

Richard Cumberland
1631–1718

4   It is better to wear out than to rust out.

> *From* BISHOP GEORGE HORNE *[1730–1792], Sermon on the Duty of Contending for the Truth [1786]*

John Dryden
1631–1700

5   By viewing Nature, Nature's handmaid Art,
Makes mighty things from small beginnings grow.

> *Annus Mirabilis [1667], st. 155*

6   He [Shakespeare] was the man who of all modern, and perhaps ancient poets, had the largest and most comprehensive soul.   *Essay of Dramatic Poesy [1668]*

7   He was naturally learned; he needed not the spectacles of books to read Nature; he looked inwards, and found her there.   *Essay of Dramatic Poesy*

8   Pains of love be sweeter far
Than all other pleasures are.

> *Tyrannic Love [1669], act IV, sc. i*

9   I am as free as Nature first made man,
Ere the base laws of servitude began,
When wild in woods the noble savage ran.

> *The Conquest of Granada [1669–1670], pt. I, act I, sc. i*

10   Death in itself is nothing; but we fear
To be we know not what, we know not where.

> *Aureng-Zebe [1676], act IV, sc. i*

11   When I consider life, 'tis all a cheat;
Yet, fool'd with hope, men favor the deceit;
Trust on, and think tomorrow will repay.
Tomorrow's falser than the former day.

> *Aureng-Zebe, IV, i*

12   The wretched have no friends.

> *All for Love [1678], act III, sc. i*

13   Your Cleopatra; Dolabella's Cleopatra; every man's Cleopatra.

> *All for Love, IV, i*

14   In pious times, ere priestcraft did begin,
Before polygamy was made a sin.

> *Absalom and Achitophel, pt. I [1680], l. 1*

15   Whate'er he did was done with so much ease,
In him alone, 'twas natural to please.

> *Absalom and Achitophel, I, l. 27*

16   Of these the false Achitophel was first,
A name to all succeeding ages curs'd.
For close designs and crooked counsels fit,
Sagacious, bold, and turbulent of wit,
Restless, unfix'd in principles and place,
In power unpleas'd, impatient of disgrace;
A fiery soul, which working out its way,
Fretted the pygmy-body to decay:
And o'er-inform'd the tenement of clay.
A daring pilot in extremity;
Pleased with the danger, when the waves went high
He sought the storms; but for a calm unfit,
Would steer too nigh the sands to boast his wit.
Great wits are sure to madness near allied,
And thin partitions do their bounds divide.[1]

> *Absalom and Achitophel, I, l. 150*

17   Bankrupt of life, yet prodigal of ease.

> *Absalom and Achitophel, I, l. 168*

18   And all to leave what with his toil he won
To that unfeather'd two-legg'd thing, a son.

> *Absalom and Achitophel, I, l. 169*

19   In friendship false, implacable in hate,
Resolved to ruin or to rule the state.

> *Absalom and Achitophel, I, l. 173*

20   All empire is no more than power in trust.

> *Absalom and Achitophel, I, l. 411*

21   Better one suffer, than a nation grieve.

> *Absalom and Achitophel, I, l. 416*

---

[1]Remembrance and reflection how allied! / What thin partitions sense from thought divide! — ALEXANDER POPE, *An Essay on Man, epistle I, l. 225*

1 Who think too little, and who talk too much.
Absalom and Achitophel, I, l. 534

2 A man so various that he seem'd to be
Not one, but all mankind's epitome:
Stiff in opinions, always in the wrong;
Was everything by starts, and nothing long:
But, in the course of one revolving moon,
Was chemist, fiddler, statesman, and buffoon.
Absalom and Achitophel, I, l. 545

3 So over violent, or over civil,
That every man with him was God or Devil.
Absalom and Achitophel, I, l. 557

4 His tribe were God Almighty's gentlemen.
Absalom and Achitophel, I, l. 645

5 Nor is the people's judgment always true:
The most may err as grossly as the few.
Absalom and Achitophel, I, l. 781

6 Of ancient race by birth, but nobler yet
In his own worth.
Absalom and Achitophel, I, l. 900

7 Made still a blund'ring kind of melody;
Spurr'd boldly on, and dash'd through thick and
thin,
Through sense and nonsense, never out nor in.
Free from all meaning, whether good or bad,
And in one word, heroically mad.
Absalom and Achitophel,[1] *pt. II [1682], l. 413*

8 For every inch that is not fool is rogue.
Absalom and Achitophel, pt. II, l. 463

9   There is a pleasure sure
In being mad which none but madmen know.[2]
The Spanish Friar [1681], act II, sc. i

10 And, dying, bless the hand that gave the blow.
The Spanish Friar, II, i

11   They say everything in the world is good for
something.
The Spanish Friar, III, ii

12   Dead men tell no tales.[3]
The Spanish Friar, IV, ii

13 All human things are subject to decay,
And, when fate summons, monarchs must obey.
Mac Flecknoe [1682], l. 1

14 The rest to some faint meaning make pretense,
But Shadwell[4] never deviates into sense.

Some beams of wit on other souls may fall,
Strike through and make a lucid interval;
But Shadwell's genuine night admits no ray,
His rising fogs prevail upon the day.
Mac Flecknoe, l. 19

15 And torture one poor word ten thousand ways.
Mac Flecknoe, l. 208

16   Wit will shine
Through the harsh cadence of a rugged line.
To the Memory of Mr. Oldham [1684], l. 15

17 Happy the man, and happy he alone,
He who can call today his own;
He who, secure within, can say,
Tomorrow, do thy worst, for I have liv'd today.
Imitation of Horace, bk. III, ode 29 [1685], l. 65

18 Not heaven itself upon the past has power;
But what has been, has been, and I have had my
hour.   *Imitation of Horace, III, 29, l. 71*

19 Since heaven's eternal year is thine.
*To the Pious Memory of Mrs. Anne Killegrew
[1686], l. 15*

20 O gracious God! how far have we
Profaned thy heavenly gift of poesy!
*To the Pious Memory of
Mrs. Anne Killegrew, l. 56*

21 Her wit was more than man, her innocence a child.
To the Pious Memory of Mrs. Anne Killegrew, l. 70

22 Then cold, and hot, and moist, and dry,
In order to their stations leap,
And Music's power obey.
From harmony, from heavenly harmony,
This universal frame began:
From harmony to harmony
Through all the compass of the notes it ran,
The diapason closing full in Man.
A Song for Saint Cecilia's Day, 1687, st. 1

23 What passion cannot Music raise and quell?
A Song for Saint Cecilia's Day, 1687, st. 2

24 The trumpet's loud clangor
Excites us to arms.
A Song for Saint Cecilia's Day, 1687, st. 3

25 The soft complaining flute,
In dying notes, discovers
The woes of hopeless lovers.
A Song for Saint Cecilia's Day, 1687, st. 4

26 The trumpet shall be heard on high
The dead shall live, the living die,
And Music shall untune the sky!
*A Song for Saint Cecilia's Day, 1687, Grand
Chorus*

---

[1] In collaboration with NAHUM TATE. See 281.

[2] There is a pleasure in poetic pains / Which only poets know. —
WILLIAM COWPER, *The Task, bk. II, The Timepiece, l. 285*

[3] Cited in the play text as a proverb.

[4] Thomas Shadwell [c. 1642–1692].

1 Of all the tyrannies on human kind
The worst is that which persecutes the mind.
*The Hind and the Panther [1687],
pt. I, l. 239*

2 And kind as kings upon their coronation day.
The Hind and the Panther, I, l. 271

3 Much malice mingled with a little wit.
The Hind and the Panther, III, l. 1

4 For present joys are more to flesh and blood
Than a dull prospect of a distant good.
The Hind and the Panther, III, l. 364

5 T' abhor the makers, and their laws approve,
Is to hate traitors and the treason love.
The Hind and the Panther, III, l. 706

6 Possess your soul with patience.
The Hind and the Panther, III, l. 839

7 Three poets, in three distant ages born,
Greece, Italy, and England did adorn.
The first in loftiness of thought surpass'd;
The next, in majesty; in both the last.
The force of Nature could no further go.
To make a third, she joined the former two.
Under Mr. Milton's Picture [1688]

8 This is the porcelain clay of humankind.[1]
Don Sebastian [1690], act I, sc. i

9   A knockdown argument: 'tis but a word and a
blow.   *Amphitryon [1690], act I, sc. i*

10   Whistling to keep myself from being afraid.[2]
Amphitryon, III, i

11 Theirs was the giant race, before the flood.
Epistle to Congreve [1693], l. 5

12 Genius must be born, and never can be taught.
Epistle to Congreve, l. 60

13 Arms, and the man I sing,[3] who, forced by fate,
And haughty Juno's unrelenting hate.
Virgil, Aeneid [1697], bk. I, l. 1

14 None but the brave deserves the fair.
Alexander's Feast [1697], l. 15

15   With ravish'd ears
The monarch hears;
Assumes the god,
Affects to nod,
And seems to shake the spheres.
Alexander's Feast, l. 37

16 Sound the trumpets; beat the drums . . .
Now give the hautboys breath; he comes, he
comes.   *Alexander's Feast, l. 50*

17   Rich the treasure,
Sweet the pleasure —
Sweet is pleasure after pain.
Alexander's Feast, l. 58

18 Fallen, fallen, fallen, fallen,
Fallen from his high estate,
And welt'ring in his blood;
Deserted, at his utmost need,
By those his former bounty fed,
On the bare earth expos'd he lies,
With not a friend to close his eyes.
Alexander's Feast, l. 77

19 Sigh'd and look'd, and sigh'd again.
Alexander's Feast, l. 120

20 And, like another Helen, fir'd another Troy.
Alexander's Feast, l. 154

21 Could swell the soul to rage, or kindle soft desire.
Alexander's Feast, l. 160

22 He rais'd a mortal to the skies,
She drew an angel down.   *Alexander's Feast, l. 169*

23 Lord of yourself, uncumber'd with a wife.
Epistle to John Driden of Chesterton [1700], l. 18

24 Better to hunt in fields, for health unbought,
Than fee the doctor for a nauseous draught.
The wise, for cure, on exercise depend;
God never made his work for man to mend.
Epistle to John Driden of Chesterton, l. 92

25 All, all of a piece throughout:
Thy chase had a beast in view;
Thy wars brought nothing about;
Thy lovers were all untrue.
'Tis well an old age is out,
And time to begin a new.
The Secular Masque [1700], l. 96

26   [Of Chaucer's *Canterbury Tales:*] Here is God's
plenty.
*Fables Ancient and Modern
[1700], preface*

27 For Art may err, but Nature cannot miss.
*Fables Ancient and Modern.
The Cock and the Fox, l. 452*

28 She hugg'd the offender, and forgave the offense:
Sex to the last.[4]
*Fables Ancient and Modern.
Cymon and Iphigenia, l. 367*

---

[1]The precious porcelain of human clay. — LORD BYRON, *Don Juan,
canto IV, st. 11*

[2]Whistling aloud to bear his courage up. — ROBERT BLAIR [1699–
1746], *The Grave* [1743], *l. 58*

[3]See Virgil, 93:28.

---

[4]And love the offender, yet detest the offense. — ALEXANDER POPE,
Eloisa to Abelard, l. 192

1 Here lies my wife: here let her lie!
Now she's at rest, and so am I.
Epitaph intended for his wife

William Stoughton
1631–1701

2 God hath sifted a nation that he might send choice grain into this wilderness.[1]
Election sermon at Boston [April 29, 1669]

Anton van Leeuwenhoek
1632–1723

3 We cannot in any better manner glorify the Lord and Creator of the universe than that in all things, how small soever they appear to our naked eyes, but which have yet received the gift of life and power of increase, we contemplate the display of his omnificence and perfections with the utmost admiration.
*The Select Works of
Anthony van Leeuwenhoek*[2] *[1798]*

John Locke
1632–1704

4 New opinions are always suspected, and usually opposed, without any other reason but because they are not already common.
*Essay Concerning Human Understanding
[1690], dedicatory epistle*

5 No man's knowledge here can go beyond his experience.
*Essay Concerning Human Understanding,
bk. II, ch. 1, sec. 19*

6 It is one thing to show a man that he is in an error, and another to put him in possession of truth.
*Essay Concerning Human Understanding,
IV, 7, 11*

7 All men are liable to error; and most men are, in many points, by passion or interest, under temptation to it.
*Essay Concerning Human Understanding,
IV, 20, 17*

8 In the beginning, all the world was America.
*Second Treatise of Civil Government [1690],
sec. 49*

9 Wherever Law ends, Tyranny begins.
Second Treatise of Civil Government, 202

10 A sound mind in a sound body, is a short but full description of a happy state in this world.
*Some Thoughts Concerning Education
[1693], sec. 1*

11 Good and evil, reward and punishment, are the only motives to a rational creature: these are the spur and reins whereby all mankind are set on work, and guided.[3]
Some Thoughts Concerning Education, 54

12 He that will have his son have a respect for him and his orders, must himself have a great reverence for his son.
Some Thoughts Concerning Education, 65

13 Virtue is harder to be got than a knowledge of the world; and, if lost in a young man, is seldom recovered.   *Some Thoughts Concerning Education, 70*

14 The only fence against the world is a thorough knowledge of it.
Some Thoughts Concerning Education, 88

Benedict [or Baruch] Spinoza[4]
1632–1677

15 Peace is not an absence of war, it is a virtue, a state of mind, a disposition for benevolence, confidence, justice.
Theological-Political Treatise [1670]

16 Nature abhors a vacuum.
Ethics[5] *[1677], pt. I, proposition 15: note*

17 God and all the attributes of God are eternal.
Ethics, I, proposition 19

18 Nothing exists from whose nature some effect does not follow.   *Ethics, I, proposition 36*

---

[3]By education, then, I mean goodness in the form in which it is first acquired by a child . . . the rightly disciplined state of pleasures and pains whereby a man from his first beginnings on will abhor what he should abhor and relish what he should relish. — PLATO, *Laws, bk. II*

In educating the young we use pleasure and pain as rudders to steer their course. — ARISTOTLE, *Nicomachean Ethics, bk. X*

[4]Ein Gottbetrunkener Mensch [A God-intoxicated man]. — NOVALIS (FRIEDRICH VON HARDENBERG), *Fragmente und Studien 1799–1800*

The Lord blot out his name under heaven. The Lord set him apart for destruction from all the tribes of Israel, with all the curses of the firmament which are written in the Book of the Law. . . . There shall no man speak to him, no man write to him, no man show him any kindness, no man stay under the same roof with him, no man come nigh him. — *Amsterdam synagogue's excommunication of Spinoza* [1656]

[5]Translated by ANDREW BOYLE.

---

[1]God had sifted three kingdoms to find the wheat for this planting. — HENRY WADSWORTH LONGFELLOW, *The Courtship of Miles Standish, pt. IV*

[2]Translated by SAMUEL HOOLE.

1   He who would distinguish the true from the false must have an adequate idea of what is true and false.   *Ethics, II, proposition 42: proof*

2   Will and Intellect are one and the same thing.
Ethics, II, proposition 49: corollary

3   He that can carp in the most eloquent or acute manner at the weakness of the human mind is held by his fellows as almost divine.   *Ethics, III: preface*

4   Surely human affairs would be far happier if the power in men to be silent were the same as that to speak. But experience more than sufficiently teaches that men govern nothing with more difficulty than their tongues.   *Ethics, III, proposition 2: note*

5   Pride is therefore pleasure arising from a man's thinking too highly of himself.
Ethics, III, proposition 26: note

6   It may easily come to pass that a vain man may become proud and imagine himself pleasing to all when he is in reality a universal nuisance.
Ethics, III, proposition 30: note

7   Self-complacency is pleasure accompanied by the idea of oneself as cause.
Ethics, III, proposition 51: note

8   It therefore comes to pass that everyone is fond of relating his own exploits and displaying the strength both of his body and his mind, and that men are on this account a nuisance one to the other.
Ethics, III, proposition 54: note

9   I refer those actions which work out the good of the agent to courage, and those which work out the good of others to nobility. Therefore temperance, sobriety, and presence of mind in danger, etc., are species of courage; but modesty, clemency, etc., are species of nobility.
Ethics, III, proposition 59: note

10   Fear cannot be without hope nor hope without fear.   *Ethics, III, definition 13: explanation*

11   Those who are believed to be most abject and humble are usually most ambitious and envious.
Ethics, III, definition 29: explanation

12   One and the same thing can at the same time be good, bad, and indifferent, e.g., music is good to the melancholy, bad to those who mourn, and neither good nor bad to the deaf.   *Ethics, IV: preface*

13   Man is a social animal.
Ethics, IV, proposition 35: note

14   Men will find that they can prepare with mutual aid far more easily what they need, and avoid far more easily the perils which beset them on all sides, by united forces.   *Ethics, IV, proposition 35: note*

15   Avarice, ambition, lust, etc., are nothing but species of madness.[1]   *Ethics, IV, proposition 44: note*

16   He whose honor depends on the opinion of the mob must day by day strive with the greatest anxiety, act and scheme in order to retain his reputation. For the mob is varied and inconstant, and therefore if a reputation is not carefully preserved it dies quickly.
Ethics, IV, proposition 58: note

17   To give aid to every poor man is far beyond the reach and power of every man. . . . Care of the poor is incumbent on society as a whole.
Ethics, IV, appendix, 17

18   We feel and know that we are eternal.
Ethics, V, proposition 23: note

19   All excellent things are as difficult as they are rare.
Ethics, V, proposition 42: note

20   The things which . . . are esteemed as the greatest good of all . . . can be reduced to these three headings: to wit, Riches, Fame, and Pleasure. With these three the mind is so engrossed that it cannot scarcely think of any other good.
*Tractatus de Intellectus Emendatione
(On the Improvement of Understanding)
[1677], ch. I, sec. 3*

Sir Christopher Wren[2]
1632–1723

21   Si monumentum requiris circumspice [If you would see the man's monument, look around].
Inscription in St. Paul's Cathedral, London. Written by Wren's son

Wentworth Dillon, Earl of Roscommon
c. 1633–1685

22   Choose an author as you choose a friend.
Essay on Translated Verse [1684], l. 96

23   Immodest words admit of no defense,
For want of decency is want of sense.
Essay on Translated Verse, l. 113

Samuel Pepys
1633–1703

24   I pray God to keep me from being proud.
Diary, March 22, 1660

---

[1] To me, avarice seems not so much a vice, as a deplorable piece of madness. — THOMAS BROWNE, *Religio Medici*, pt. 2, sec. 13

[2] See E. C. Bentley, 629:2.

1   This morning came home my fine camlet cloak, with gold buttons, and a silk suit, which cost me much money, and I pray God to make me able to pay for it.   *Diary, July 1, 1660*

2   And so to bed.   *Diary, July 22, 1660, passim*

3   I am unwilling to mix my fortune with him that is going down the wind.   *Diary, September 6, 1660*

4   I went out to Charing Cross, to see Major-General Harrison hanged, drawn, and quartered; which was done there, he looking as cheerful as any man could do in that condition.
                          Diary, October 13, 1660

5   A good honest and painful sermon.
                          Diary, March 17, 1661

6   One, by his own confession to me, that can put on two several faces, and look his enemies in the face with as much love as his friends. But, good God! what an age is this, and what a world is this! that a man cannot live without playing the knave and dissimulation.   *Diary, September 1, 1661*

7   Though he be a fool, yet he keeps much company, and will tell all he sees or hears, and so a man may understand what the common talk of the town is.
                          Diary, September 2, 1661

8   My wife, poor wretch.
                   Diary, September 18, 1661, passim

9   Thanks be to God, since my leaving drinking of wine, I do find myself much better, and do mind my business better, and do spend less money, and less time lost in idle company.
                          Diary, January 26, 1662

10   As happy a man as any in the world, for the whole world seems to smile upon me.
                          Diary, October 31, 1662

11   To the Trinity House, where a very good dinner among the old soakers.   *Diary, February 15, 1665*

12   But Lord! how everybody's looks, and discourse in the street, is of death, and nothing else; and few people going up and down, that the town is like a place distressed and forsaken.[1]
                          Diary, August 30, 1665

13   Strange to see how a good dinner and feasting reconciles everybody.   *Diary, November 9, 1665*

14   Saw a wedding in the church . . . and strange to see what delight we married people have to see these poor fools decoyed into our condition.
                          Diary, December 25, 1665

---

[1]The time of the Great Plague.

15   Musick and women I cannot but give way to, whatever my business is.   *Diary, March 9, 1666*

16   Home, and, being washing-day, dined upon cold meat.   *Diary, April 4, 1666*

17   Musick is the thing of the world that I love most.   *Diary, July 30, 1666*

18   This day I am, by the blessing of God, 34 years old, in very good health and mind's content, and in condition of estate much beyond whatever my friends could expect of a child of theirs, this day 34 years. The Lord's name be praised! and may I be ever thankful for it.   *Diary, February 23, 1667*

19   But it is pretty to see what money will do.
                          Diary, March 21, 1667

20   To church; and with my mourning, very handsome, and new periwig, make a great show.
                          Diary, March 31, 1667

21   But to think of the clatter they make with his coach, and his own fine clothes, and yet how meanly they live within doors, and nastily, and borrowing everything of neighbors.   *Diary, April 1, 1667*

22   Whose red nose makes me ashamed to be seen with him.   *Diary, May 3, 1667*

23   Gives me some kind of content to remember how painful it is sometimes to keep money, as well as to get it.   *Diary, October 11, 1667*

24   I find my wife hath something in her gizzard, that only waits an opportunity of being provoked to bring up; but I will not, for my content-sake, give it.
                          Diary, June 17, 1668

25   In appearance, at least, he being on all occasions glad to be at friendship with me, though we hate one another, and know it on both sides.
                          Diary, September 22, 1668

26   I do hate to be unquiet at home.
                          Diary, January 21, 1669

27   And so I betake myself to that course, which is almost as much as to see myself go into my grave; for which, and all the discomforts that will accompany my being blind, the good God prepare me!
                   Diary, May 31, 1669 (final entry)

Robert Hooke
1635–1703

28   The truth is, the science of Nature has been already too long made only a work of the brain and the fancy: It is now high time that it should return to the plainness and soundness of observations on material and obvious things.   *Micrographia [1665]*

Nicolas Boileau-Despréaux
1636–1711

1 Happy who in his verse can gently steer
From grave to light, from pleasant to severe.
The Art of Poetry[1] *[1674], canto I, l. 75*

2 At last comes Malherbe[2] and, the first to do so in
France, brings to his verse a smooth cadence.
The Art of Poetry, I, l. 131

3 Whate'er is well conceived is clearly said,
And the words to say it flow with ease.
The Art of Poetry, I, l. 153

4 He [Molière] pleases all the world, but cannot
please himself. *Satire 2, l. 94*[3]

5 In spite of every sage whom Greece can show,
Unerring wisdom never dwelt below;
Folly in all of every age we see,
The only difference lies in the degree. *Satire 4, l. 37*

6 Of all the creatures that creep, swim, or fly,
Peopling the earth, the waters, and the sky,
From Rome to Iceland, Paris to Japan,
I really think the greatest fool is man. *Satire 8, l. 1*

7 But satire, ever moral, ever new,
Delights the reader and instructs him, too.
She, if good sense refine her sterling page,
Oft shakes some rooted folly of the age.
Satire 8, l. 257

Thomas Ken
1637–1711

8 Praise God, from whom all blessings flow!
Praise Him, all creatures here below!
Praise Him above, ye heavenly host!
Praise Father, Son, and Holy Ghost!
Doxology [1709]

Mary Rowlandson
c. 1637–c. 1710/1711

9 The portion of some is to have their Affliction by
drops, now one drop and then another; but the dregs
of the Cup, the wine of astonishment, like a sweeping
rain that leaveth no food, did the Lord prepare to be
my portion.
*A Narrative of the Captivity and Restoration
of Mrs. Mary Rowlandson [1682]*

---

[1]Translated by JOHN DRYDEN.

[2]Enfin Malherbe vint.

[3]Dates of composition of Boileau's Satires are not definitely known
but likely fall between 1683 and 1694.

Thomas Traherne
c. 1637–1674

10 You never enjoy the world aright, till the sea itself
floweth in your veins, till you are clothed with the
heavens, and crowned with the stars: and perceive
yourself to be the sole heir of the whole world.
*Centuries of Meditations [1908],
century I, sec. 29*

11 The corn was orient and immortal wheat, which
never should be reaped, nor was ever sown. I thought
it had stood from everlasting to everlasting.
Centuries of Meditations, III, 3

12 How like an angel came I down!
Wonder [1910], st. 1

13 I within did flow
With seas of life like wine. *Wonder, st. 3*

Louis XIV
1638–1715

14 I am the state.[4]
*Attributed remark before the parliament
in 1651*

15 Has God forgotten all I have done for him?[5]
*Attributed remark upon hearing the news of
the French defeat at Malplaquet [1709]*

16 I almost had to wait.[6]
*Attributed remark when a coach he had
ordered arrived just in time*

Jean Racine
1639–1699

17 I loved him too much not to hate him at all!
Andromaque [1667], act II

18 You are Emperor, my lord, and yet you weep?
Bérénice [1670], act IV, sc. v

19 My only hope lies in my despair.
Bajazet [1672], act I, sc. iv

20 You have named him, not I.[7]
Phèdre [1677], act I, sc. iii

21 It is no longer a passion hidden in my heart: it is
Venus herself fastened to her prey.[8] *Phèdre, I, iii*

---

[4]L'état c'est moi.

[5]Dieu a donc oublié tout ce que j'ai fait pour lui?

[6]J'ai failli attendre.

[7]C'est toi qui l'a nommé.

[8]Ce n'est plus une ardeur dans mes veines cachée. / C'est Vénus
toute entière à sa proie attachée.

1   Innocence has nothing to dread.   *Phèdre, III, vi*

2   Crime like virtue has its degrees; and timid innocence was never known to blossom suddenly into extreme license.   *Phèdre, IV, ii*

3   To repair the irreparable ravages of time.
Athalie [1691], act II, sc. v

Aphra Behn
1640–1689

4   A brave world, sir, full of religion, knavery, and change: we shall shortly see better days.
The Roundheads [1677]

5   Variety is the soul of pleasure.
The Rover, pt. II [1680], act I

6   Money speaks sense in a language all nations understand.
The Rover, pt. II, act III, sc. i

7   Beauty unadorned.
The Rover, pt. II, act IV, sc. ii

8   Love ceases to be a pleasure, when it ceases to be a secret.
The Lover's Watch [1686]. Four O'Clock, General Conversation

9   Faith, sir, we are here today, and gone tomorrow.
The Lucky Chance [1686–1687], act IV

William Wycherley
1641–1715

10   A mistress should be like a little country retreat near the town, not to dwell in constantly, but only for a night and away.
The Country Wife [1675], act I, sc. i

Sir Isaac Newton
1642–1727

11   If I have seen further it is by standing on the shoulders of Giants.[1]
Letter to Robert Hooke [February 5, 1675 / 1676]

12   I frame no hypotheses; for whatever is not deduced from the phenomena is to be called an hypothesis; and hypotheses, whether metaphysical or physical, whether of occult qualities or mechanical, have no place in experimental philosophy.
*Letter to Robert Hooke
[February 5, 1675/1676]*

13   Errors are not in the art but in the artificers.
*Philosophiae Naturalis Principia
Mathematica (Mathematical Principles of
Natural Philosophy)[2] [1687], preface*

14   Every body continues in its state of rest, or of uniform motion in a right line, unless it is compelled to change that state by forces impressed upon it.
Principia Mathematica. Laws of Motion, I

15   The change of motion is proportional to the motive force impressed; and is made in the direction of the right line in which that force is impressed.[3]
Principia Mathematica. Laws of Motion, II

16   To every action there is always opposed an equal reaction: or, the mutual actions of two bodies upon each other are always equal, and directed to contrary parts.
Principia Mathematica. Laws of Motion, III

17   God in the beginning formed matter in solid, massy, hard, impenetrable, movable particles, of such sizes and figures, and with such other properties, and in such proportion to space, as most conduced to the end for which he formed them.   *Optics [1704]*

18   I do not know what I may appear to the world; but to myself I seem to have been only like a boy playing on the seashore, and diverting myself in now and then finding a smoother pebble or a prettier shell than ordinary, whilst the great ocean of truth lay all undiscovered before me.
*From DAVID BREWSTER [1781–1868],
Memoirs of Newton [1855], vol. II, ch. 27*

19   O Diamond! Diamond! thou little knowest the mischief done!
*Said to a pet dog who knocked over
a candle and set fire to his papers*

Bashō [Matsuo Bashō]
1644–1694

20   The months and days are the travelers of eternity. The years that come and go are also voyagers.... I too for years past have been stirred by the sight of a solitary cloud drifting with the wind to ceaseless thoughts of roaming.
The Narrow Road of Oku (Oku no Hosomichi)[4]

21 Such stillness —
The cries of the cicadas
Sink into the rocks.   *The Narrow Road of Oku*

---

[1]See Bernard of Chartres, 124:7.

[2]Translated by ANDREW MOTTE.

[3]In modern terms, acceleration is directly proportional to applied force.

[4]Translated by DONALD KEENE.

1 Clear cascades!
Into the waves scatter
Blue pine needles.[1]   *Conversations with Bashō*

2 An old pond —
A frog leaping in —
The sound of water.[2]   *Haiku*

3 A rough sea!
Stretched out over Sado
The Milky Way.[2]   *Haiku*

4 On a journey, ill,
And over fields all withered, dreams
Go wandering still.[3]   *Haiku*

William Penn
1644–1718

5   No Cross, No Crown.
                              Title of pamphlet [1669]

6   Any government is free to the people under it
where the laws rule and the people are a party to the
laws.   *Frame of Government [1682]*

7   Truth often suffers more by the heat of its defenders than from the arguments of its opposers.
                 Some Fruits of Solitude [1693]. Temper

8   It is a reproach to religion and government to
suffer so much poverty and excess.
                       Some Fruits of Solitude.
                       Frugality or Bounty

9   They that love beyond the world cannot be separated by it. Death is but crossing the world, as friends
do the seas; they live in one another still.
                       Some Fruits of Solitude.
                       Union of Friends

10   Men are generally more careful of the breed of
their horses and dogs than of their children.
                 Some Fruits of Solitude. Right Marriage

11   It were endless to dispute upon everything that is
disputable.   *Some Fruits of Solitude. Bearing*

12   Have a care therefore where there is more sail than
ballast.   *Some Fruits of Solitude. Respect*

13   The public must and will be served.
                    Some Fruits of Solitude. A Public Life

14   Let the people think they govern and they will be
governed.
                    Some Fruits of Solitude. Government

---

[1]Edited by WILLIAM THEODORE DE BARY.
[2]Translated by DANA B. YOUNG.
[3]Translated by HAROLD G. HENDERSON.

Edward Taylor
c. 1644–1729

15 Who spread its canopy? Or curtains spun?
Who in this bowling alley bowled the sun?
          Poetical Works [published 1939]. God's
          Determinations Touching His Elect, preface

16 For in Christ's coach saints sweetly sing
As they to glory ride therein.
          Poetical Works. The Joy of Church Fellowship
          Rightly Attended

17 Make me, O Lord, thy spinning-wheel complete.
                    Poetical Works. Housewifery

18 It's food too fine for angels; yet come, take
And eat thy fill! It's Heaven's sugar cake.
          Poetical Works. Sacramental Meditations, no. 8

19 Is Christ thy advocate to plead thy cause?
Art thou his client? Such shall never slide.
He never lost his case.
          Poetical Works. Sacramental Meditations, 38

20 My case is bad. Lord, be my advocate.
My sin is red: I'm under God's arrest.
          Poetical Works. Sacramental Meditations, 38

Jean de La Bruyère
1645–1696

21   We come too late to say anything which has not
been said already.
          Les Caractères [1688]. Des Ouvrages de
          l'Esprit (On Works of the Spirit)

22   Liberality consists less in giving a great deal than in
gifts well timed.
          Les Caractères. Du Coeur (On the Heart)

23   Time, which strengthens friendship, weakens love.
                    Les Caractères. Du Coeur

24   We must laugh before we are happy, for fear we
die before we laugh at all.   *Les Caractères. Du Coeur*

25   To laugh at men of sense is the privilege of fools.
          Les Caractères. De la Société (On Society)

26   There are but three events in a man's life: birth,
life and death. He is not conscious of being born,
he dies in pain, and he forgets to live.
          Les Caractères. De l'Homme (On Man)

John Wilmot, Earl of Rochester
1647–1680

27 Here lies our sovereign lord the King,
Whose promise none relies on;

He never said a foolish thing,
Nor ever did a wise one.   *Epitaph on Charles II*[1]

1 A merry monarch, scandalous and poor.
   A Satire on King Charles II [1697]

2 Reason, which fifty times for one does err,
Reason, an ignis fatuus of the mind.
   A Satire Against Mankind [1675], l. 11

3 Books bear him up a while, and make him try
To swim with bladders of philosophy.
   A Satire Against Mankind, l. 20

4 Then Old Age and Experience, hand in hand,
Lead him to death, and make him understand,
After a search so painful and so long,
That all his life he has been in the wrong.
   A Satire Against Mankind, l. 25

5 There's not a thing on earth that I can name,
So foolish, and so false, as common fame.
   Did E'er This Saucy World [c. 1680]

William III, Prince of Orange
1650–1702

6   There is one certain means by which I can be sure never to see my country's ruin: I will die in the last ditch.
   From DAVID HUME, *History of England [1754–1757], ch. 65*

Juana Inés de la Cruz
1651–1695

7 Foolish men who accuse
a woman mindlessly—
you cannot even see
you cause what you abuse.
   Las Redondillas (Quatrains),[2] *st. 1*

8   Since I first gained the use of reason my inclination towards learning has been so violent and strong that neither the scoldings of other people . . . nor my own reflections . . . have been able to stop me from following this natural impulse that God gave me. He alone must know why; and He knows too that I have begged Him to take away the light of my understanding, leaving only enough for me to keep His law, for anything else is excessive in a woman, according to some people, and others say it is even harmful.   *Reply to Sor Filotea de la Cruz*[3] *[1691]*

---

[1] By tradition, it is said this epitaph was written on the bedchamber door of Charles II. Upon seeing it, the king remarked, "This is very true, for my words are my own, and my actions are my ministers'."

[2] Translated by WILLIS and ALICKI BARNSTONE.

[3] Translated by RACHEL PHILLIPS.

François de Salignac de la Mothe Fénelon
1651–1715

9   Do not men die fast enough without being destroyed by each other? Can any man be insensible of the brevity of life? and can he who knows it, think life too long?   *Télémaque [1699], bk. VII*

10   To be always ready for war, said Mentor, is the surest way to avoid it.   *Télémaque, X*

Thomas Otway
1652–1685

11 What mighty ills have not been done by
      woman!
Who was 't betrayed the Capitol? — A woman!
Who lost Mark Antony the world? — A woman!
Who was the cause of a long ten years' war,
And laid at last old Troy in ashes? — Woman!
Destructive, damnable, deceitful woman!
   The Orphan [1680], act III, sc. i

12 O woman! lovely woman! Nature made thee
To temper man: we had been brutes without
      you;
Angels are painted fair, to look like you.
   Venice Preserved [1682], act I, sc. i

Nahum Tate
1652–1715

13 While shepherds watch'd their flocks by night,
All seated on the ground,
The angel of the Lord came down,
And glory shone around.
   Christmas Hymn [1700], st. 1

14 Glad tidings of great joy I bring
To you and all mankind.
   Christmas Hymn, st. 1

Nathaniel Lee
c. 1653–1692

15 Then he will talk — good gods! how he will talk!
   *The Rival Queens; or, The Death of
   Alexander the Great [1677],
   act I, sc. iii*

16 When Greeks joined Greeks, then was the tug
of war.
   *The Rival Queens; or, The Death of
   Alexander the Great, IV, ii*

Chikamatsu Monzaemon
1653–1725

1   Art is something which lies in the slender margin between the real and the unreal.[1]
Quoted by HOZUMI IKAN *[1692–1769] in Naniwa Miyage (The Puppet Stage) [1738]*

Andrew Fletcher of Saltoun
1655–1716

2   If a man were permitted to make all the ballads, he need not care who should make the laws of a nation.
Conversation Concerning a Right Regulation of Governments for the Common Good of Mankind [1704]

John Dennis
1657–1734

3   They will not let my play run, and yet they steal my thunder![2]
Remark

Daniel Defoe
1660–1731

4 Wherever God erects a house of prayer,
The Devil always builds a chapel there;
And 'twill be found, upon examination,
The latter has the largest congregation.
The True-Born Englishman [1701], pt. I, l. 1

5 From this amphibious ill-born mob began
That vain, ill-natur'd thing, an Englishman.
The True-Born Englishman, I, l. 132

6 In their religion they are so uneven,
That each man goes his own byway to heaven.
The True-Born Englishman, II, l. 104

7 And of all plagues with which mankind are curs'd,
Ecclesiastic tyranny's the worst.
The True-Born Englishman, II, l. 299

8 All men would be tyrants if they could.
The Kentish Petition [1712–1713]

---

[1] Translated by DONALD KEENE.

[2] For his play *Appius and Virginia* [1709], Dennis had invented a new species of thunder. "The tragedy however was coldly received, notwithstanding such assistance, and was acted but a short time. Some nights after, Mr. Dennis, being in the pit at the representation of *Macbeth,* heard his own thunder made use of; upon which he rose in a violent passion, and exclaimed, with an oath, that it was his thunder. 'See,' said he, 'how the rascals use me! They will not let my play run, and yet they steal my thunder!'" — *Biographia Britannica, vol. V, p. 103*

9 The best of men cannot suspend their fate:
The good die early, and the bad die late.
Character of the Late Dr. S. Annesley [1715]

10   He bid me [Robinson Crusoe] observe it, and I should always find that the calamities of life were shared among the upper and lower part of mankind; but that the middle station had the fewest disasters.
Robinson Crusoe[3] [1719]

11   One day, about noon, going towards my boat, I was exceedingly surprised with the print of a man's naked foot on the shore, which was very plain to be seen in the sand.   *Robinson Crusoe*

12   My man Friday.   *Robinson Crusoe*

Matthew Henry
1662–1714

13   He rolls it under his tongue as a sweet morsel.
Commentaries [1708–1710], Psalm 36

14   Our creature comforts.   *Commentaries, Psalm 37*

15   To fish in troubled waters.
Commentaries, Psalm 60

16   Here is bread, which strengthens man's heart, and therefore called the staff of life.[4]
Commentaries, Psalm 104

17   It was a common saying among the Puritans, "Brown bread and the Gospel is good fare."
Commentaries, Isaiah 30

18   None so blind as those that will not see.
Commentaries, Jeremiah 20

19   Judas had given them the slip.
Commentaries, Luke 22

20   After a storm comes a calm.
Commentaries, Acts 9

21   Men of polite learning and a liberal education.
Commentaries, Acts 10

22   All this and heaven too.
Life of Philip Henry [published 1809]

Thomas [Tom] Brown
1663–1704

23 I do not love thee, Doctor Fell.
The reason why I cannot tell;

---

[3] See Jean-Jacques Rousseau, 312:25.

[4] Bread is the staff of life. — JONATHAN SWIFT, *A Tale of a Tub*
Corn, which is the staff of life. — EDWARD WINSLOW [1595–1655], *Good News from New England* [1624]

But this alone I know full well,
I do not love thee, Doctor Fell.[1]
Written while a student at Christ Church, Oxford

Mary de la Rivière Manley
1663–1724

1   No time like the present.
The Lost Lover [1696], act IV, sc. i

Cotton Mather
1663–1728

2   I write the wonders of the Christian religion,
flying from the depravations of Europe, to the American strand: and, assisted by the Holy Author of that
religion, I do, with all conscience of truth, required
therein by Him, who is the Truth itself, report the
wonderful displays of His infinite power, wisdom,
goodness, and faithfulness, wherewith his Divine Providence hath irradiated an Indian wilderness.
*Magnalia Christi Americana (The Glorious Works
of Christ in America) [1702], introduction*

The New England Primer[2]

3 In Adam's fall
We sinned all.

4 My book and heart
Must never part.

5 Peter denied
His Lord, and cried.

6 Xerxes did die,
And so must I.

7 Zaccheus he
Did climb the tree
Our Lord to see.

8 Our days begin with trouble here,
Our life is but a span,
And cruel death is always near,
So frail a thing is man.

9 Now I lay me down to sleep,[3]
I pray the Lord my soul to keep;

If I should die before I wake,
I pray the Lord my soul to take.

Matthew Prior
1664–1721

10 All jargon of the schools.
I Am That I Am, An Ode [1688]

11 The end must justify the means.   *Hans Carvel [1700]*

12 Be to her virtues very kind;
Be to her faults a little blind;
Let all her ways be unconfin'd;
And clap your padlock — on her mind!
An English Padlock [1707]

13 He rang'd his tropes, and preach'd up patience;
Back'd his opinion with quotations.
Paulo Purganti and His Wife [1708]

14 Cured yesterday of my disease,
I died last night of my physician.
The Remedy Worse than the Disease [1714]

15 His noble negligences teach
What others' toils despair to reach.
Alma [1718], canto II, l. 7

Sir John Vanbrugh[4]
1664–1726

16   Once a woman has given you her heart you can
never get rid of the rest of her.
The Relapse [1697], act III, sc. i

17   No man worth having is true to his wife, or can be
true to his wife, or ever was, or ever will be so.
The Relapse, III, ii

18   He laughs best who laughs last.[5]
The Country House [1706], act II, sc. v

19   Much of a muchness.
*The Provok'd Husband [1728]
(completed by* Colley Cibber*), act I, sc. i*

John Pomfret
1667–1702

20 We live and learn, but not the wiser grow.[6]
Reason [1700], l. 112

---

[1] Je ne vous aime pas, Hylas; / Je n'en saurois dire la cause, / Je sais
seulement une chose; / C'est que je ne vous aime pas. — Roger de
Bussy-Rabutin [1618–1693], *Maximes d'Amours* [1666]
See Martial, 107:7.

[2] As early as 1691, Benjamin Harris of Boston advertised the
forthcoming second impression of the *New England Primer*. The
oldest known copy extant is dated 1727.

[3] The first record of this prayer is found in the *Enchiridion Leonis*
[1160]. The early editions of the *Primer* give the first line of the
prayer as: Now I lay me down to take my sleep. The familiar version
of the line appeared in the edition of 1784. In the edition of 1814
the second line reads: I pray thee, Lord, my soul to keep.

[4] Under this stone, Reader, survey / Dead Sir John Vanbrugh's
house of clay. / Lie heavy on him, Earth! for he / Laid many heavy
loads on thee! — Abel Evans [1679–1737]. Vanbrugh was the
architect of Blenheim Palace.

[5] Better the last smile than the first laughter. — John Ray [1627–
1705], *Proverbs* [1670]

[6] It is good to live and learn. — Cervantes, *Don Quixote, pt. II, ch. 32*
Live and learn, / Not first learn and then live. — Robert
Browning, *Parleyings with Certain People* [1887]. *With Christopher
Smart, sec. IX*

Jonathan Swift

1667–1745

1 Books, like men their authors, have no more than one way of coming into the world, but there are ten thousand to go out of it, and return no more.
A Tale of a Tub [1704], dedication

2 Books, the children of the brain.
A Tale of a Tub, sec. 1

3 As boys do sparrows, with flinging salt upon their tails. *A Tale of a Tub, 7*

4 Satire is a sort of glass, wherein beholders do generally discover everybody's face but their own.
The Battle of the Books [1704]

5 Instead of dirt and poison we have rather chosen to fill our hives with honey and wax; thus furnishing mankind with the two noblest of things, which are sweetness and light. *The Battle of the Books*

6 Laws are like cobwebs, which may catch small flies, but let wasps and hornets break through.
A Critical Essay upon the Faculties of the Mind [1707]

7 There is nothing in this world constant, but inconstancy.
A Critical Essay upon the Faculties of the Mind

8 'Tis very warm weather when one's in bed.
Journal to Stella [November 8, 1710]

9 With my own fair hands.
Journal to Stella [January 4, 1711]

10 We are so fond of one another, because our ailments are the same.
Journal to Stella [February 1, 1711]

11 I love good creditable acquaintance; I love to be the worst of the company.
Journal to Stella [May 17, 1711]

12 May my enemies live here [London] in summer!
Journal to Stella [August 27, 1711]

13 We were to do more business after dinner; but after dinner is after dinner — an old saying and a true, "much drinking, little thinking."
Journal to Stella [February 26, 1712]

14 We have just religion enough to make us hate, but not enough to make us love one another.
Thoughts on Various Subjects; from Miscellanies [1711]

15 When a true genius appears in the world, you may know him by this sign, that the dunces are all in confederacy against him.
Thoughts on Various Subjects; from Miscellanies

16 It is pleasant to observe, how free the present age is in laying taxes on the next. *Future ages shall talk of this; this shall be famous to all posterity.* Whereas their time and thoughts will be taken up about present things, as ours are now.
Thoughts on Various Subjects; from Miscellanies

17 Censure is the tax a man pays to the public for being eminent.
Thoughts on Various Subjects; from Miscellanies

18 Every man desires to live long, but no man would be old.
Thoughts on Various Subjects; from Miscellanies

19 A nice man is a man of nasty ideas.
Thoughts on Various Subjects; from Miscellanies

20 Vision is the art of seeing things invisible.
Thoughts on Various Subjects; from Miscellanies [1726]

21 'Tis an old maxim in the schools,
That flattery's[1] the food of fools;
Yet now and then your men of wit
Will condescend to take a bit.
Cadenus and Vanessa[2] [1713]

22 Proper words in proper places, make the true definition of a style.
Letter to a Young Clergyman [January 9, 1720]

23 If Heaven had looked upon riches to be a valuable thing, it would not have given them to such a scoundrel.
Letter to Miss Vanhomrigh [August 12, 1720]

24 He [the Emperor] is taller by almost the breadth of my nail, than any of his court, which alone is enough to strike an awe into the beholders.
*Gulliver's Travels [1726].
Voyage to Lilliput, ch. 2*

25 *All true believers shall break their eggs at the convenient end:* and which is the convenient end, seems, in my humble opinion, to be left to every man's conscience. *Gulliver's Travels. Voyage to Lilliput, 4*

26 I cannot but conclude the bulk of your natives to be the most pernicious race of little odious vermin that nature ever suffered to crawl upon the surface of the earth.
Gulliver's Travels. Voyage to Brobdingnag, ch. 6

---

[1]"Vanity's" in some texts.

[2]When the poem of "Cadenus and Vanessa" was the general topic of conversation, someone said, "Surely that Vanessa must be an extraordinary woman that could inspire the Dean to write so finely upon her." Mrs. Johnson smiled, and answered that "she thought that point not quite so clear; for it was well known the Dean could write finely upon a broomstick." — SAMUEL JOHNSON, *Lives of the Poets, Life of Swift*

1   And he gave it for his opinion, that whoever could make two ears of corn or two blades of grass to grow upon a spot of ground where only one grew before, would deserve better of mankind, and do more essential service to his country, than the whole race of politicians put together.[1]

> *Gulliver's Travels. Voyage to Brobdingnag, 7*

2   He had been eight years upon a project for extracting sunbeams out of cucumbers, which were to be put in vials hermetically sealed, and let out to warm the air in raw inclement summers.

> *Gulliver's Travels. Voyage to Laputa, ch. 5*

3   I said the thing which was not. (For they have no word in their language to express lying or falsehood.)

> *Gulliver's Travels. Voyage to the*
> *Houyhnhnms, ch. 3*

4   I told him...that we ate when we were not hungry, and drank without the provocation of thirst.

> *Gulliver's Travels. Voyage to the*
> *Houyhnhnms, 6*

5 Behold his funeral appears,
Nor widow's sighs, nor orphan's tears,
Wont at such times each heart to pierce,
Attend the progress of his hearse.
And what of that? his friends may say,
He had those honors in his day.
True to his profit and his pride,
He made them weep before he died.

> *A Satirical Elegy on the Death of a Late*
> *Famous General [1722], l. 17*

6 A set of phrases learnt by rote;
A passion for a scarlet coat;
When at a play to laugh, or cry,
Yet cannot tell the reason why:
Never to hold her tongue a minute;
While all she prates has nothing in it.

> *The Furniture of a Woman's Mind [1727]*

7 For conversation well endu'd;
She calls it witty to be rude;
And, placing raillery in railing,
Will tell aloud your greatest failing.

> *The Furniture of a Woman's Mind*

8   Not die here in a rage, like a poisoned rat in a hole.   *Letter to Bolingbroke [March 21, 1729]*

9 Yet malice never was his aim;
He lash'd the vice but spar'd the name.
No individual could resent,
Where thousands equally were meant.
His satire points at no defect
But what all mortals may correct;

For he abhorr'd that senseless tribe
Who call it humor when they gibe.

> *Verses on the Death of Dr. Swift [1731], l. 459*

10 Hobbes clearly proves that every creature
Lives in a state of war by nature.

> *On Poetry. A Rhapsody [1733]*

11 So, naturalists observe, a flea
Hath smaller fleas that on him prey;
And these have smaller still to bite 'em;
And so proceed *ad infinitum*.
Thus every poet, in his kind,
Is bit by him that comes behind.

> *On Poetry. A Rhapsody*

12 Conversation is but carving!
Give no more to every guest
Than he's able to digest.
Give him always of the prime,
And but little at a time.
Carve to all but just enough,
Let them neither starve nor stuff,
And that you may have your due,
Let your neighbor carve for you.   *Conversation*

13 Under an oak, in stormy weather,
I joined this rogue and whore together;
And none but he who rules the thunder
Can put this rogue and whore asunder.

> *Marriage certificate.[2]*

14   The sight of you is good for sore eyes.[3]

> *Polite Conversation [1738], dialogue 1*

15   'Tis as cheap sitting as standing.

> *Polite Conversation, 1*

16   I hate nobody: I am in charity with all the world.

> *Polite Conversation, 1*

17   You were half seas over.

> *Polite Conversation, 1*

18   I won't quarrel with my bread and butter.

> *Polite Conversation, 1*

19   She's no chicken; she's on the wrong side of thirty, if she be a day.

> *Polite Conversation, 1*

20   She wears her clothes, as if they were thrown on her with a pitchfork.

> *Polite Conversation, 1*

21   He was a bold man that first eat an oyster.

> *Polite Conversation, 2*

---

[1] He who makes two blades of grass grow in place of one renders a service to the state. — VOLTAIRE, *Letter to M. Moreau* [1765]

[2] By tradition, a mock certificate dashed off by Swift when he hastily married a couple under an oak tree during a rainstorm.

[3] What a sight for sore eyes that would be! — WILLIAM HAZLITT, *Of Persons One Would Wish to Have Seen* [1826]

1   That's as well said, as if I had said it myself.
Polite Conversation, 2

2   Fingers were made before forks, and hands before knives.   *Polite Conversation, 2*

3   She has more goodness in her little finger, than he has in his whole body.   *Polite Conversation, 2*

4   Lord, I wonder what fool it was that first invented kissing!   *Polite Conversation, 2*

5   The best doctors in the world are Doctor Diet, Doctor Quiet, and Doctor Merryman.
Polite Conversation, 2

6   May you live all the days of your life.
Polite Conversation, 2

7   I always love to begin a journey on Sundays, because I shall have the prayers of the church to preserve all that travel by land, or by water.
Polite Conversation, 2

8   I thought you and he had been hand-and-glove.   *Polite Conversation, 2*

9   She watches him, as a cat would watch a mouse.
Polite Conversation, 3

10   She pays him in his own coin.
Polite Conversation, 3

11   There was all the world and his wife.
Polite Conversation, 3

12   Hail, fellow, well met,
All dirty and wet:
Find out if you can,
Who's master, who's man.
My Lady's Lamentation [1765], l. 171

13   I shall be like that tree, I shall die at the top.
From SIR WALTER SCOTT, *Life of Swift [1814]*

14   Good God! What a genius I had when I wrote that book *[A Tale of a Tub].*
From SIR WALTER SCOTT, *Life of Swift*

15   Ubi saeva indignatio ulterius cor lacerare nequit [Where savage indignation can lacerate his heart no more].[1]
*Epitaph. Inscribed on Swift's grave,
Saint Patrick's, Dublin*

Alain René Lesage
1668–1747

16   It may be said that his wit shines at the expense of his memory.   *Gil Blas [1715–1735], bk. III, ch. 11*

17   The pleasure of talking is the inextinguishable passion of a woman, coeval with the act of breathing.
Gil Blas, VII, 7

18   Facts are stubborn things.   *Gil Blas, X, 1*

Giovanni Battista [Giambattista] Vico
1668–1744

19   The nature of things is nothing other than that they come into being at certain times and in certain ways. Wherever the same circumstances are present, the same phenomena arise and no others.
Scienza Nuova (New Science)[2] [1725]

20   In that dark night which shrouds from our eyes the most remote antiquity, a light appears which cannot lead us astray; I speak of this incontestable truth: the social world is certainly the work of man.
Scienza Nuova

21   Governments must be conformable to the nature of the governed; governments are even a result of that nature.   *Scienza Nuova*

William Congreve
1670–1729

22   Eternity was in that moment.
The Old Bachelor [1693], act IV, sc. vii

23   Married in haste, we may repent at leisure.
The Old Bachelor, V, viii

24   It is the business of a comic poet to paint the vices and follies of human kind.
*The Double Dealer [1694],
epistle dedicatory*

25   Retired to their tea and scandal, according to their ancient custom.   *The Double Dealer, act I, sc. i*

26   No mask like open truth to cover lies,
As to go naked is the best disguise.
The Double Dealer, V, iv

27   Thou liar of the first magnitude.
Love for Love [1695], act II, sc. ii

28   I warrant you, if he danced till doomsday, he thought I was to pay the piper.[3]   *Love for Love, II, v*

29   O fie, miss, you must not kiss and tell.
Love for Love, II, x

---

[1]See William Butler Yeats, 595:8.

[2]Translated by JULES MICHELET.

[3]Pay the piper: phrase for settling the score. He who pays the piper calls the tune. — *Proverb*

1 Music has charms to soothe a savage breast,
To soften rocks, or bend a knotted oak.
The Mourning Bride [1697], act I, sc. i

2 Heaven has no rage like love to hatred turned,
Nor hell a fury like a woman scorned.
The Mourning Bride, III, viii

3 Here she comes i' faith full sail, with her fan spread and streamers out, and a shoal of fools for tenders. — Ha, no, I cry her mercy!
The Way of the World [1700], act II, sc. iv

4 I nauseate walking; 'tis a country diversion, I loathe the country.   *The Way of the World, IV, iv*

5 Let us be very strange and well-bred: Let us be as strange as if we had been married a great while; and as well-bred as if we were not married at all.
The Way of the World, IV, iv

6 If I continue to endure you a little longer, I may by degrees dwindle into a wife.
The Way of the World, IV, iv

7 Thou art a retailer of phrases, and dost deal in remnants of remnants.   *The Way of the World, IV, ix*

8 O, she is the antidote to desire.
The Way of the World, IV, xiv

John Toland
1670–1722

9 All things are from the whole, and the whole is from all things.   *Pantheisticon [1720]*

Bernard Mandeville
1670–1733

10 Private Vices, Public Benefits.
The Fable of the Bees [1714]. Subtitle

11 The moral virtues are the political offspring which flattery begot upon pride.
The Fable of the Bees.
An Enquiry into the Origin of Moral Virtue

Colley Cibber
1671–1757

12 As good be out of the world as out of the fashion.
Love's Last Shift [1696], act II

13 Possession is eleven points in the law.
Woman's Wit [1697], act I

14 Off with his head — so much for Buckingham.
Richard III (altered) [1700], act IV, sc. iii

15 Perish the thought!   *Richard III (altered), V, v*

16 This business will never hold water.
She Wou'd and She Wou'd Not [1703], act IV

17 Old houses mended,
Cost little less than new before they're ended.
The Double Gallant [1707], prologue

18 Stolen sweets are best.[1]
The Rival Fools [1709], act I

Joseph Addison
1672–1719

19 Reading is to the mind what exercise is to the body.   *Tatler [1709–1711], no. 147*

20 The spacious firmament on high,
With all the blue ethereal sky,
And spangled heavens, a shining frame,
Their great Original proclaim.
Ode [in The Spectator, no. 465, August 23, 1712]

21 Soon as the evening shades prevail,
The moon takes up the wondrous tale,
And nightly to the listening earth
Repeats the story of her birth;
While all the stars that round her burn,
And all the planets in their turn,
Confirm the tidings as they roll,
And spread the truth from pole to pole.   *Ode*

22 'Tis not in mortals to command success,
But we'll do more, Sempronius; we'll deserve it.
Cato [1713], act I, sc. ii

23 Blesses his stars and thinks it luxury.   *Cato, I, iv*

24 My voice is still for war.
Gods! can a Roman senate long debate
Which of the two to choose, slavery or death?
Cato, II, i

25 The woman that deliberates is lost.[2]   *Cato, IV, i*

26 Curse on his virtues! they've undone his country.
Cato, IV, iv

27 What pity is it
That we can die but once to serve our country!
Cato, IV, iv

28 When vice prevails, and impious men bear sway,
The post of honor is a private station.[3]   *Cato, IV, iv*

---

[1]See *Proverbs 9:17*, 20:9, and Leigh Hunt, 392:14.

[2]Origin of the saying: He who hesitates is lost.

[3]Give me, kind Heaven, a private station, / A mind serene for contemplation! / Title and profit I resign; / The post of honor shall be mine. — JOHN GAY, *Fables, pt. II, The Vulture, the Sparrow, and Other Birds*

1 From hence, let fierce contending nations know
What dire effects from civil discord flow.   *Cato, V, iv*

2   Thus I live in the world rather as a spectator of mankind than as one of the species.
The Spectator, no. 1 [March 1, 1711]

3   If I can any way contribute to the diversion or improvement of the country in which I live, I shall leave it, when I am summoned out of it, with the secret satisfaction of thinking that I have not lived in vain.   *The Spectator, 1*

4   I shall endeavor to enliven morality with wit, and to temper wit with morality.
The Spectator, 10 [March 12, 1711]

5   True happiness is of a retired nature, and an enemy to pomp and noise; it arises, in the first place, from the enjoyment of one's self; and, in the next, from the friendship and conversation of a few select companions.   *The Spectator, 15 [March 17, 1711]*

6   There is not a more unhappy being than a superannuated idol.   *The Spectator, 73 [May 24, 1711]*

7   A man that has a taste of music, painting, or architecture, is like one that has another sense, when compared with such as have no relish of those arts.
The Spectator, 93 [June 16, 1711]

8   Much might be said on both sides.
The Spectator, 122 [July 20, 1711]

9   Authors have established it as a kind of rule, that a man ought to be dull sometimes; as the most severe reader makes allowances for many rests and nodding places in a voluminous writer.
The Spectator, 124 [July 23, 1711]

10   Books are the legacies that a great genius leaves to mankind, which are delivered down from generation to generation, as presents to the posterity of those who are yet unborn.
The Spectator, 166 [September 10, 1711]

11   Good nature is more agreeable in conversation than wit, and gives a certain air to the countenance which is more amiable than beauty.
The Spectator, 169 [September 13, 1711]

12   Were I to prescribe a rule for drinking, it should be formed upon a saying quoted by Sir William Temple: the first glass for myself, the second for my friends, the third for good humor, and the fourth for mine enemies.
The Spectator, 195 [October 13, 1711]

13   A true critic ought to dwell rather upon excellencies than imperfections, to discover the concealed beauties of a writer, and communicate to the world such things as are worth their observation.
The Spectator, 291 [February 2, 1712]

14   These widows, sir, are the most perverse creatures in the world.   *The Spectator, 335 [March 25, 1712]*

15   Mirth is like a flash of lightning, that breaks through a gloom of clouds, and glitters for a moment; cheerfulness keeps up a kind of daylight in the mind, and fills it with a steady and perpetual serenity.   *The Spectator, 381 [May 17, 1712]*

16   Our disputants put me in mind of the skuttle fish, that when he is unable to extricate himself, blackens all the water about him, till be becomes invisible.
The Spectator, 476 [September 5, 1712]

17   The fraternity of the henpecked.
The Spectator, 482 [September 12, 1712]

18   We are always doing, says he, something for Posterity, but I would fain see Posterity do something for us.   *The Spectator, 583 [August 20, 1714]*

19   See in what peace a Christian can die.
Dying words [1719]. From EDWARD YOUNG, Conjectures on Original Composition [1759]

Edmond Hoyle
1672–1769

20   When in doubt, win the trick.
Hoyle's Games Improved[1] *[1790], edited by CHARLES JONES*

Sir Richard Steele
1672–1729

21   I am come to a tavern alone to eat a steak, after which I shall return to the office.
Letters to His Wife [October 28, 1707]

22   A little in drink, but at all times yr faithful husband.   *Letters to His Wife [September 27, 1708]*

23   The finest woman in nature should not detain me an hour from you; but you must sometimes suffer the rivalship of the wisest men.
Letters to His Wife [September 17, 1712]

24   When you fall into a man's conversation, the first thing you should consider is, whether he has a greater inclination to hear you, or that you should hear him.
The Spectator, no. 49 [April 26, 1711]

25   Age in a virtuous person, of either sex, carries in it an authority which makes it preferable to all the pleasures of youth.
The Spectator, 153 [August 25, 1711]

[1]Hoyle published a *Short Treatise on Whist* [1742], which in subsequent editions added rules for playing piquet, backgammon, chess, and other games. His *Laws* [1760] for whist were not superseded until 1864; hence the saying, "according to Hoyle."

François Goyot de Pitavals
1673–1743

1 Causes Célèbres.
*Title of book recounting famous trials
and judgments*

Nicholas Rowe
1674–1718

2 As if Misfortune made the throne her seat,
And none could be unhappy but the great.[1]
The Fair Penitent [1703], prologue

3 Is this that haughty gallant, gay Lothario?
The Fair Penitent, act V, sc. i

Isaac Watts
1674–1748

4 Were I so tall to reach the pole,
Or grasp the ocean with my span,
I must be measured by my soul;
The mind's the standard of the man.
*Horae Lyricae (Lyrical Hours) [1706],
bk. II, False Greatness*

5 Let dogs delight to bark and bite,
For God hath made them so.
*Divine Songs [1715], no. 16,
Against Quarreling and Fighting*

6 But, children, you should never let
Such angry passions rise;
Your little hands were never made
To tear each other's eyes.
*Divine Songs, 16,
Against Quarreling and Fighting*

7 Birds in their little nests agree;
And 'tis a shameful sight,
When children of one family
Fall out, and chide, and fight.
*Divine Songs, 17,
Love Between Brothers and Sisters*

8 How doth the little busy bee
Improve each shining hour,[2]
And gather honey all the day
From every opening flower!
Divine Songs, 20, Against Idleness and Mischief

9 For Satan finds some mischief still
For idle hands to do.
Divine Songs, 20, Against Idleness and Mischief

10 Hush! my dear, lie still and slumber,
Holy angels guard thy bed!
Heavenly blessings without number
Gently falling on thy head.
Divine Songs, 35, A Cradle Hymn

11 'Tis the voice of the sluggard; I heard him complain,
"You have wak'd me too soon, I must slumber
again."[3]
Divine Songs, 39, The Sluggard

12 O God, our help in ages past,
Our hope for years to come,
Our shelter from the stormy blast,
And our eternal home.   *Psalm 90 [1719], st. 1*

13 A thousand ages in Thy sight
Are like an evening gone;
Short as the watch that ends the night
Before the rising sun.   *Psalm 90, st. 4*

14 Time, like an ever-rolling stream,
Bears all its sons away;
They fly forgotten, as a dream
Dies at the opening day.   *Psalm 90, st. 5*

15 Joy to the world! the Lord is come;
Let earth receive her King.
Let ev'ry heart prepare Him room,
And heav'n and nature sing.
Psalm 98 [1719], st. 1

16 When I can read my title clear
To mansions in the skies,
I'll bid farewell to every fear,
And wipe my weeping eyes.
*Hymns and Spiritual Songs,
bk. II, hymn 65*

17 There is a land of pure delight,
Where saints immortal reign;
Infinite day excludes the night,
And pleasures banish pain.
Hymns and Spiritual Songs, II, 66

William Somerville[4]
1675–1742

18 Let all the learned say what they can,
'Tis ready money makes the man.
Ready Money [1727]

19   The chase, the sport of kings;
Image of war, without its guilt.
The Chase [1735], bk. I, l. 13

---

[1]None think the great unhappy, but the great. — EDWARD YOUNG,
Love of Fame, satire I, l. 238
[2]See Lewis Carroll, 513:15.

[3]See Lewis Carroll, 515:5.

[4]Of whom Samuel Johnson, in *Lives of the Poets*, made the famous
remark, "He writes very well for a gentleman."
See Samuel Johnson, 311:5 and note.

Sir Robert Walpole
1676–1745

1   The balance of power.
Speech in the House of Commons
[February 13, 1741]

2   All those men have their price.
From WILLIAM COXE *[1747–1828],*
Memoirs of Walpole [1798], vol. IV

3   Anything but history, for history must be false.
Walpoliana, no. 141

Henry St. John, Viscount Bolingbroke
1678–1751

4   Truth lies within a little and certain compass, but error is immense.   *Reflections upon Exile [1716]*

5   Nations, like men, have their infancy.
On the Study and Use of History [1752], letter 4

George Farquhar
1678–1707

6   I have fed purely upon ale; I have eat my ale, and I always sleep upon ale.
The Beaux' Stratagem [1707], act I, sc. i

7   My Lady Bountiful.
The Beaux' Stratagem, I, i

8   'Twas for the good of my country that I should be abroad.[1] — Anything for the good of one's country — I'm a Roman for that.   *The Beaux' Stratagem, III, ii*

9   Spare all I have, and take my life.
The Beaux' Stratagem, V, ii

Thomas Parnell
1679–1718

10 My days have been so wondrous free,
The little birds that fly
With careless ease from tree to tree,
Were but as bless'd as I.   *Song[2] [1714], st. 1*

---

[1]Leaving his country for his country's sake. — CHARLES FITZGEFFREY [c. 1575–1638], *The Life and Death of Sir Francis Drake* [1596], *st. 213*

True patriots all; for, be it understood, / We left our country for our country's good. — *Prologue for opening of playhouse at New South Wales* [January 16, 1796]; attributed to the famous pickpocket known as GEORGE BARRINGTON [1755–c. 1840]

[2]Set to music by FRANCIS HOPKINSON [1737–1791]; one of the earliest American songs.

11 Let those love now who never loved before;
Let those who always loved, now love the more.
Translation of the Pervigilium Veneris

Edward Young
1683–1765

12 The love of praise, howe'er conceal'd by art,
Reigns more or less, and glows in ev'ry heart.
Love of Fame [1725–1728], satire I, l. 51

13 Some for renown, on scraps of learning dote,
And think they grow immortal as they quote.
Love of Fame, I, l. 89

14   Be wise with speed;
A fool at forty is a fool indeed.
Love of Fame, II, l. 282

15 One to destroy, is murder by the law;
And gibbets keep the lifted hand in awe;
To murder thousands takes a specious name,
War's glorious art, and gives immortal fame.
Love of Fame, VII, l. 55

16 The man that makes a character makes foes.
To Mr. Pope, epistle I, l. 28

17 In records that defy the tooth of time.
The Statesman's Creed

18 Tired nature's sweet restorer, balmy sleep!
Night Thoughts [1742–1745]. Night I, l. 1

19 Night, sable goddess! from her ebon throne,
In rayless majesty, now stretches forth
Her leaden scepter o'er a slumbering world.
Night Thoughts. Night I, l. 18

20 Creation sleeps! 'Tis as the general pulse
Of life stood still, and Nature made a pause;
An awful pause! prophetic of her end.
Night Thoughts. Night I, l. 23

21 Be wise today; 'tis madness to defer.
Night Thoughts. Night I, l. 390

22 Procrastination is the thief of time.
Night Thoughts. Night I, l. 393

23 At thirty, a man suspects himself a fool;
Knows it at forty, and reforms his plan;
At fifty chides his infamous delay,
Pushes his prudent purpose to resolve;
In all the magnanimity of thought
Resolves, and re-resolves; then dies the same.
Night Thoughts. Night I, l. 417

24 All men think all men mortal but themselves.
Night Thoughts. Night I, l. 424

25 Man wants but little, nor that little long.
Night Thoughts. Night IV, l. 118

1 A God all mercy is a God unjust.
Night Thoughts. Night IV, l. 233

2 By night an atheist half believes a God.
Night Thoughts. Night V, l. 177

3   Like our shadows,
Our wishes lengthen as our sun declines.
Night Thoughts. Night V, l. 661

4 Death loves a shining mark, a signal blow.
Night Thoughts. Night V, l. 1011

5 Too low they build, who build beneath the stars.
Night Thoughts. Night VIII, l. 215

Sir William Pulteney, Earl of Bath
1684–1764

6 Since twelve honest men have decided the cause,
And were judges of fact, though not judges of laws.
The Honest Jury [1729], st. 3

George Berkeley
1685–1753

7   And what are these fluxions? The velocities of evanescent increments. And what are these same evanescent increments? They are neither finite quantities,
nor quantities infinitely small, nor yet nothing. May
we not call them ghosts of departed quantities?
The Analyst [1734], sec. 35

8   He who says there is no such thing as an honest
man, you may be sure is himself a knave.
Maxims Concerning Patriotism [1750], no. 20

9 Westward the course of empire takes its way;[1]
The four first acts already past,
A fifth shall close the drama with the day:
Time's noblest offspring is the last.
*On the Prospect of Planting Arts and
Learning in America [1752], st. 6*

John Gay[2]
1685–1732

10 Whence is thy learning? Hath thy toil
O'er books consumed the midnight oil?
*Fables, pt. I [1727]. The Shepherd
and the Philosopher*

11 When we risk no contradiction,
It prompts the tongue to deal in fiction.
Fables, I. The Elephant and the Bookseller

12 In every age and clime we see
Two of a trade can never agree.
Fables, I. The Rat-catcher and Cats

13 Those who in quarrels interpose
Must often wipe a bloody nose.   *Fables, I. The Mastiffs*

14 I hate the man who builds his name
On ruins of another's fame.
Fables, I. The Poet and the Rose

15 And when a lady's in the case,
You know all other things give place.
Fables, I. The Hare and Many Friends

16 From wine what sudden friendship springs!
Fables, II [1738]. The Squire and His Cur

17 If with me you'd fondly stray.
Over the hills and far away.[3]
*The Beggar's Opera [1728], act I,
sc. xiii, air 16*

18 Youth's the season made for joys,
Love is then our duty.
The Beggar's Opera, II, iv, air 22

19 Man may escape from rope and gun;
Nay, some have outliv'd the doctor's pill:
Who takes a woman must be undone,
That basilisk is sure to kill.
The fly that sips treacle is lost in the sweets,
So he that tastes woman, woman, woman,
He that tastes woman, ruin meets.
The Beggar's Opera, II, viii, air 26

20 Life is a jest; and all things show it.
I thought so once; but now I know it.
My Own Epitaph

Aaron Hill
1685–1750

21 Tender-handed stroke a nettle,
And it stings you for your pains;
Grasp it like a man of mettle,
And it soft as silk remains.
*Verses Written on Windows.
In a Journey to Scotland*

Henry Carey
c. 1687–1743

22 Namby Pamby's little rhymes,
Little jingle, little chimes.   *Namby Pamby[4]*

---

[1] Westward the star of empire takes its way. — JOHN QUINCY ADAMS, *Oration at Plymouth* [1802]

[2] See Alexander Pope's *Epitaph on Gay*, 294:13.

[3] O'er the hills and far away. — THOMAS D'URFEY [1653–1723], *Pills to Purge Melancholy* [1719]

[4] Ambrose Phillips... who had the honor of bringing into fashion a species of composition which has been called, after his name, Namby Pamby. — THOMAS BABINGTON MACAULAY, *Review of Aikin's Life of Addison*

1 Of all the girls that are so smart,
There's none like pretty Sally.
She is the darling of my heart,
And she lives in our alley.
Sally in Our Alley [1729], st. 1

2 God save our gracious king!
Long live our noble king!
God save the king! *God Save the King [c. 1740]*

Pierre Carlet de Chamblain de Marivaux
1688–1763

3 In this world, you must be a bit too kind in order to be kind enough.
*Le Jeu de l'Amour et du Hasard
(The Game of Love and Chance) [1730],
act I, sc. ii*

Alexander Pope
1688–1744

4 Happy the man whose wish and care
A few paternal acres bound,
Content to breathe his native air
In his own ground. *Ode on Solitude [c. 1700], st. 1*

5 Thus let me live, unseen, unknown,
Thus unlamented let me die,
Steal from the world, and not a stone
Tell where I lie. *Ode on Solitude, st. 5*

6 Where'er you walk, cool gales shall fan the glade,
Trees, where you sit, shall crowd into a shade:
Where'er you tread, the blushing flow'rs shall rise,
And all things flourish where you turn your eyes.
Pastorals [1704]. Summer, l. 73

7 Nor Fame I slight, nor for her favors call;
She comes unlook'd for, if she comes at all.
The Temple of Fame [1711], l. 513

8 'Tis with our judgments as our watches, none
Go just alike, yet each believes his own.
An Essay on Criticism [1711], pt. I, l. 9

9 Let such teach others who themselves excel,
And censure freely who have written well.
An Essay on Criticism, I, l. 15

10 Some are bewilder'd in the maze of schools,
And some made coxcombs nature meant but fools.
An Essay on Criticism, I, l. 26

11 Those oft are stratagems which errors seem,
Nor is it Homer nods, but we that dream.
An Essay on Criticism, I, l. 179

12 A little learning is a dangerous thing;
Drink deep, or taste not the Pierian spring:
There shallow draughts intoxicate the brain,
And drinking largely sobers us again.
An Essay on Criticism, II, l. 15

13 True wit is nature to advantage dress'd,
What oft was thought, but ne'er so well express'd.
An Essay on Criticism, II, l. 97

14 Words are like leaves; and where they most abound,
Much fruit of sense beneath is rarely found.
An Essay on Criticism, II, l. 109

15 Such labored nothings, in so strange a style,
Amaze th' unlearn'd, and make the learned smile.
An Essay on Criticism, II, l. 126

16 Be not the first by whom the new are tried,
Nor yet the last to lay the old aside.
An Essay on Criticism, II, l. 135

17 As some to church repair,
Not for the doctrine, but the music there.
These equal syllables alone require,
Though oft the ear the open vowels tire;
While expletives their feeble aid do join,
And ten low words oft creep in one dull line.
An Essay on Criticism, II, l. 142

18 Then, at the last and only couplet fraught
With some unmeaning thing they call a thought,
A needless Alexandrine ends the song,
That, like a wounded snake, drags its slow length
along.
An Essay on Criticism, II, l. 154

19 True ease in writing comes from art, not chance,
As those move easiest who have learn'd to dance.
'Tis not enough no harshness gives offense;
The sound must seem an echo to the sense.
An Essay on Criticism, II, l. 162

20 At ev'ry trifle scorn to take offense.
An Essay on Criticism, II, l. 186

21 Some judge of authors' names, not works, and then
Nor praise nor blame the writings, but the men.
An Essay on Criticism, II, l. 212

22 Some praise at morning what they blame at night,
But always think the last opinion right.
An Essay on Criticism, II, l. 230

23 To err is human, to forgive divine.
An Essay on Criticism, II, l. 325

24 All seems infected that th' infected spy,
As all looks yellow to the jaundic'd eye.
An Essay on Criticism, II, l. 358

25 For fools rush in where angels fear to tread.
An Essay on Criticism, III, l. 65

1 But where's the man who counsel can bestow,
Still pleas'd to teach, and yet not proud to know?
An Essay on Criticism, III, l. 71

2 Vital spark of heav'nly flame!
Quit, oh quit, this mortal frame:
Trembling, hoping, ling'ring, flying,
Oh the pain, the bliss of dying!
The Dying Christian to His Soul [1712], st. 1

3 What dire offense from amorous causes springs,
What mighty contests rise from trivial things!
The Rape of the Lock [1712], canto I, l. 1

4 On her white breast a sparkling cross she wore,
Which Jews might kiss, and infidels adore.
The Rape of the Lock, II, l. 7

5 If to her share some female errors fall,
Look on her face, and you'll forget 'em all.
The Rape of the Lock, II, l. 17

6 Fair tresses man's imperial race ensnare,
And beauty draws us with a single hair.
The Rape of the Lock, II, l. 27

7 Here thou, great Anna![1] whom three realms obey,
Dost sometimes counsel take — and sometimes
tea.   *The Rape of the Lock, III, l. 7*

8 At every word a reputation dies.
The Rape of the Lock, III, l. 16

9 The hungry judges soon the sentence sign,
And wretches hang that jurymen may dine.
The Rape of the Lock, III, l. 21

10 Let spades be trumps! she said, and trumps they
were.   *The Rape of the Lock, III, l. 46*

11 But when to mischief mortals bend their will,
How soon they find fit instruments of ill!
The Rape of the Lock, III, l. 125

12 The meeting points the sacred hair dissever
From the fair head, forever, and forever!
Then flash'd the living lightning from her eyes,
And screams of horror rend th' affrighted skies.
The Rape of the Lock, III, l. 153

13 To wake the soul by tender strokes of art,
To raise the genius, and to mend the heart;
To make mankind, in conscious virtue bold,
Live o'er each scene, and be what they behold:
For this the Tragic Muse first trod the stage.
Prologue to Mr. Addison's Cato [1713], l. 1

14 Here hills and vales, the woodland and the plain,
Here earth and water seem to strive again,
Not chaos-like together crush'd and bruis'd,
But, as the world, harmoniously confus'd:

Where order in variety we see,
And where, though all things differ, all agree.
Windsor Forest [1713], l. 11

15 Party-spirit, which at best is but the madness of
many for the gain of a few.
Letter to E. Blount [August 27, 1714]

16 The wrath of Peleus' son, the direful spring
Of all the Grecian woes, O goddess sing!
*Translation of the Iliad [1715],
bk. I, l. 1*

17 She moves a goddess, and she looks a queen.
Translation of the Iliad, III, l. 208

18 Tell me, Muse, of the man of many wiles.
Translation of the Odyssey [1725–1756], bk. I, l. 1

19 True friendship's laws are by this rule express'd,
Welcome the coming, speed the parting guest.
Translation of the Odyssey, XV, l. 83

20 Dear, damn'd, distracting town, farewell!
Thy fools no more I'll tease:
This year in peace, ye critics, dwell,
Ye harlots, sleep at ease!
A Farewell to London [1715], st. 1

21 Luxurious lobster-nights, farewell,
For sober, studious days!
A Farewell to London, st. 12

22 Oh name forever sad! forever dear!
Still breath'd in sighs, still usher'd with a tear.
Eloisa to Abelard [1717], l. 31

23 Now warm in love, now with'ring in my bloom,
Lost in a convent's solitary gloom!
Eloisa to Abelard, l. 37

24 'Tis education forms the common mind:
Just as the twig is bent, the tree's inclin'd.
*Moral Essays [1731–1735]. Epistle I,
To Lord Cobham [1734], l. 149*

25 Most women have no characters at all.
*Moral Essays. Epistle II,
To Mrs. M. Blount [1735], l. 2*

26 Chaste to her husband, frank to all beside,
A teeming mistress, but a barren bride.
*Moral Essays. Epistle II,
To Mrs. M. Blount, l. 71*

27 Wise wretch! with pleasures too refin'd to please;
With too much spirit to be e'er at ease;
With too much quickness ever to be taught;
With too much thinking to have common thought.
You purchase pain with all that joy can give,
And die of nothing but a rage to live.
*Moral Essays. Epistle II,
To Mrs. M. Blount, l. 95*

---

[1]Queen Anne [1665–1714].

1 In men, we various ruling passions find;
In women, two almost divide the kind;
Those, only fix'd, they first or last obey,
The love of pleasure, and the love of sway.
Moral Essays. Epistle II,
To Mrs. M. Blount, l. 207

2 Men, some to business, some to pleasure take;
But ev'ry woman is at heart a rake.
Moral Essays. Epistle II,
To Mrs. M. Blount, l. 215

3 She who ne'er answers till a husband cools,
Or, if she rules him, never shows she rules;
Charms by accepting, by submitting, sways,
Yet has her humor most, when she obeys.
Moral Essays. Epistle II,
To Mrs. M. Blount, l. 261

4 And mistress of herself, though china fall.
Moral Essays. Epistle II,
To Mrs. M. Blount, l. 268

5 Woman's at best a contradiction still.
Moral Essays. Epistle II,
To Mrs. M. Blount, l. 270

6 Who shall decide when doctors disagree?[1]
Moral Essays. Epistle III,
To Lord Bathurst [1732], l. 1

7 But thousands die, without or this or that,
Die, and endow a college, or a cat.
Moral Essays. Epistle III,
To Lord Bathurst, l. 95

8 The ruling passion, be it what it will,
The ruling passion conquers reason still.
Moral Essays. Epistle III,
To Lord Bathurst, l. 153

9 Statesman, yet friend to truth! of soul sincere,
In action faithful, and in honor clear;
Who broke no promise, served no private end,
Who gain'd no title, and who lost no friend.
Moral Essays. Epistle V,
To Mr. Addison [written 1720], l. 67

10   "Blessed is the man who expects nothing, for he
shall never be disappointed" was the ninth
beatitude.
Letter to Fortescue
[September 23, 1725]

11 You beat your pate, and fancy wit will come:
Knock as you please, there's nobody at home.
Epigram: An Empty
House [1727]

12 Ye Gods! annihilate but space and time,
And make two lovers happy.
Martinus Scriblerus on the Art of Sinking in
Poetry [1728], ch. 11

13 In wit a man, simplicity a child.
Epitaph on Gay[2] [1732]

14 Awake, my St. John![3] leave all meaner things
To low ambition, and the pride of kings.
Let us, since life can little more supply
Than just to look about us, and to die,
Expatiate free o'er all this scene of man;
A mighty maze! but not without a plan.
An Essay on Man [1733–1734], epistle I, l. 1

15 Eye Nature's walks, shoot folly as it flies,
And catch the manners living as they rise:
Laugh where we must, be candid where we can;
But vindicate the ways of God to man.
An Essay on Man, I, l. 13

16 Say first, of God above or man below,
What can we reason but from what we know?
An Essay on Man, I, l. 17

17 Pleased to the last, he crops the flowery food,
And licks the hand just rais'd to shed his blood.
An Essay on Man, I, l. 83

18 Who sees with equal eye, as God of all,
A hero perish or a sparrow fall,
Atoms or systems into ruin hurl'd,
And now a bubble burst, and now a world.
An Essay on Man, I, l. 87

19 Hope springs eternal in the human breast:
Man never is, but always to be blest.
An Essay on Man, I, l. 95

20 Lo, the poor Indian! whose untutor'd mind
Sees God in clouds, or hears him in the wind;
His soul proud Science never taught to stray
Far as the solar walk or milky way;
Yet simple nature to his hope has giv'n,
Behind the cloud-topp'd hill, an humbler heav'n.
An Essay on Man, I, l. 99

21 Die of a rose in aromatic pain?
An Essay on Man, I, l. 200

22 All are but parts of one stupendous whole,
Whose body Nature is, and God the soul.
An Essay on Man, I, l. 267

23 All nature is but art, unknown to thee;
All chance, direction which thou canst not see;
All discord, harmony not understood;
All partial evil, universal good;

---

[1]When doctors differ who decides amid the milliard-headed throng? — RICHARD FRANCIS BURTON, *The Kasîdah of Hají Abdú El-Yazdi, pt. VIII, st. 29*

[2]See John Gay, 291.
[3]Bolingbroke.

And, spite of pride, in erring reason's spite,
One truth is clear, Whatever is, is right.
An Essay on Man, I, l. 289

1 Know then thyself, presume not God to scan;
The proper study of mankind is man.[1]
Placed on this isthmus of a middle state,
A being darkly wise and rudely great:
With too much knowledge for the skeptic side,
With too much weakness for the stoic's pride,
He hangs between; in doubt to act or rest;
In doubt to deem himself a god, or beast;
In doubt his mind or body to prefer;
Born but to die, and reas'ning but to err;
Alike in ignorance, his reason such,
Whether he thinks too little or too much;
Chaos of thought and passion, all confus'd;
Still by himself abus'd, or disabus'd;
Created half to rise, and half to fall;
Great lord of all things, yet a prey to all;
Sole judge of truth, in endless error hurl'd;
The glory, jest, and riddle of the world!
An Essay on Man, II, l. 1

2 Vice is a monster of so frightful mien,
As to be hated needs but to be seen;
Yet seen too oft, familiar with her face,
We first endure, then pity, then embrace.
An Essay on Man, II, l. 217

3 Behold the child, by Nature's kindly law,
Pleas'd with a rattle, tickled with a straw:
Some livelier plaything gives his youth delight,
A little louder, but as empty quite:
Scarfs, garters, gold, amuse his riper stage,
And beads and prayer books are the toys of age!
Pleas'd with this bauble still, as that before;
Till tir'd he sleeps, and life's poor play is o'er.
An Essay on Man, II, l. 275

4 Worth makes the man, and want of it the fellow;
The rest is all but leather or prunella.
An Essay on Man, IV, l. 203

5 A wit's a feather, and a chief a rod;
An honest man's the noblest work of God.
An Essay on Man, IV, l. 247

6 Slave to no sect, who takes no private road,
But looks through Nature up to Nature's God.
An Essay on Man, IV, l. 331

7 Thou wert my guide, philosopher, and friend.[2]
An Essay on Man, IV, l. 390

8 That true self-love and social are the same.
An Essay on Man, IV, l. 396

9 Shut, shut the door, good John! fatigu'd, I said;
Tie up the knocker! say I'm sick, I'm dead.
The Dog-star rages!
Epistle to Dr. Arbuthnot [1734].
Prologue to Imitations of Horace, l. 1

10 As yet a child, nor yet a fool to fame,
I lisp'd in numbers, for the numbers came.
Epistle to Dr. Arbuthnot.
Prologue to Imitations of Horace, l. 127

11 This long disease, my life.
Epistle to Dr. Arbuthnot.
Prologue to Imitations of Horace, l. 132

12 Means not, but blunders round about a meaning;
And he whose fustian's so sublimely bad,
It is not poetry, but prose run mad.
Epistle to Dr. Arbuthnot.
Prologue to Imitations of Horace, l. 186

13 Were there one whose fires
True Genius kindles, and fair Fame inspires,
Bless'd with each talent, and each art to please,
And born to write, converse, and live with ease;
Should such a man, too fond to rule alone,
Bear, like the Turk, no brother near the throne;
View him with scornful, yet with jealous eyes,
And hate for arts that caus'd himself to rise;
Damn with faint praise, assent with civil leer,
And, without sneering, teach the rest to sneer;
Willing to wound, and yet afraid to strike,
Just hint a fault, and hesitate dislike;
Alike reserv'd to blame or to commend,
A tim'rous foe, and a suspicious friend;
Dreading e'en fools, by flatterers besieged,
And so obliging that he ne'er oblig'd;
Like Cato, give his little Senate laws,
And sit attentive to his own applause.
Epistle to Dr. Arbuthnot.
Prologue to Imitations of Horace,
l. 193

14 Let Sporus tremble — "What? that thing of silk,
Sporus, that mere white curd of ass's milk?
Satire or sense, alas! can Sporus feel?
Who breaks a butterfly upon a wheel?"
Epistle to Dr. Arbuthnot.
Prologue to Imitations of Horace, l. 305

15 Yet let me flap this bug with gilded wings,
This painted child of dirt, that stinks and stings;

---

[1]Trees and fields tell me nothing: men are my teachers. — PLATO, *Phaedrus*

La vraie science et la vraie étude de l'homme, c'est l'homme [The true science and the true study of man is man]. — PIERRE CHARRON [1541–1603], *Traité de la Sagesse* [1601], bk. I, preface

Das eigentliche Studium der Menschheit ist der Mensch [The proper study of mankind is man]. — GOETHE, *Elective Affinities*, bk. II, ch. 7

---

[2]Is this my guide, philosopher, and friend? — POPE, *Imitations of Horace, epistle I, bk. I, l. 177*

Whose buzz the witty and the fair annoys,
Yet wit ne'er tastes, and beauty ne'er enjoys.
Epistle to Dr. Arbuthnot.
Prologue to Imitations of Horace, l. 309

1 And he himself one vile antithesis.
Epistle to Dr. Arbuthnot.
Prologue to Imitations of Horace, l. 325

2 Wit that can creep, and pride that licks the dust.
Epistle to Dr. Arbuthnot.
Prologue to Imitations of Horace, l. 333

3 Unlearn'd, he knew no schoolman's subtle art,
No language, but the language of the heart.
Epistle to Dr. Arbuthnot.
Prologue to Imitations of Horace, l. 398

4 I cannot sleep a wink.
Imitations of Horace [1733–1738],
satire I, bk. II, l. 12

5 Satire's my weapon, but I'm too discreet
To run amuck, and tilt at all I meet.
Imitations of Horace, I, II, l. 69

6 There St. John mingles with my friendly bowl
The feast of reason and the flow of soul.
Imitations of Horace, I, II, l. 127

7 I've often wish'd that I had clear,
For life, six hundred pounds a year;
A handsome house to lodge a friend,
A river at my garden's end,
A terrace walk, and half a rood
Of land set out to plant a wood.
Imitations of Horace, VI, II, l. 1

8 Give me again my hollow tree,
A crust of bread, and liberty.
Imitations of Horace, VI, II, l. 220

9 A patriot is a fool in ev'ry age.
Imitations of Horace,
Epilogue to the Satires, Dialogue I, l. 41

10 Not to go back is somewhat to advance,
And men must walk, at least, before they dance.
Imitations of Horace, epistle I, bk. I, l. 53

11 Get place and wealth, if possible with grace;
If not, by any means get wealth and place.
Imitations of Horace, I, I, l. 103

12   The people's voice is odd,
It is, and it is not, the voice of God.
Imitations of Horace, I, II, l. 89

13 In quibbles angel and archangel join,
And God the Father turns a school-divine.
Imitations of Horace, I, II, l. 101
(on Paradise Lost)

14 The mob of gentlemen who wrote with ease.
Imitations of Horace, I, II, l. 108

15 One simile that solitary shines
In the dry desert of a thousand lines.
Imitations of Horace, I, II, l. 111

16 Ev'n copious Dryden wanted, or forgot,
The last and greatest art — the art to blot.
Imitations of Horace, I, II, l. 280

17 There still remains, to mortify a wit,
The many-headed monster of the pit.
Imitations of Horace, I, II, l. 304

18 We poets are (upon a poet's word)
Of all mankind the creatures most absurd:
The season when to come, and when to go,
To sing, or cease to sing, we never know.
Imitations of Horace, I, II, l. 358

19 Vain was the chief's, the sage's pride!
They had no poet, and they died.[1]
Imitations of Horace, odes,
bk. IV, ode 9, st. 4

20 Father of all! in every age,
In every clime ador'd,
By saint, by savage, and by sage,
Jehovah, Jove, or Lord!
The Universal Prayer
[1738], st. 1

21 And binding Nature fast in fate,
Left free the human will.
The Universal Prayer, st. 3

22 I am his Highness'[2] dog at Kew;
Pray tell me, sir, whose dog are you?
On the collar of a dog

23 Nature and Nature's laws lay hid in night:
God said, Let Newton be! and all was light.
Epitaph intended for Sir Isaac Newton

24 Whether thou choose Cervantes' serious air,
Or laugh and shake in Rabelais' easy chair.
The Dunciad [1728–1743], bk. I, l. 21

25 Poetic Justice, with her lifted scale,
Where, in nice balance, truth with gold she weighs,
And solid pudding against empty praise.
The Dunciad, I, l. 52

26 Next o'er his books his eyes began to roll,
In pleasing memory of all he stole.
The Dunciad, I, l. 127

27 A brain of feathers, and a heart of lead.
The Dunciad, II, l. 44

---

[1] See Pindar, 64:8, and Horace, 97:14.
[2] Frederick, Prince of Wales.

1 Peel'd, patch'd, and piebald, linsey-woolsey brothers,
   Grave mummers! sleeveless some, and shirtless
       others.
   That once was Britain.

   The Dunciad, III, l. 115

2 And proud his mistress' orders to perform,
   Rides in the whirlwind and directs the storm.

   The Dunciad, III, l. 263

3 A wit with dunces, and a dunce with wits.

   The Dunciad, IV, l. 90

4 The Right Divine of Kings to govern wrong.

   The Dunciad, IV, l. 188

5   Stuff the head
   With all such reading as was never read:
   For thee explain a thing till all men doubt it,
   And write about it, Goddess, and about it.

   The Dunciad, IV, l. 249

6 Religion blushing veils her sacred fires,
   And unawares Morality expires.
   Nor public flame, nor private, dares to shine;
   Nor human spark is left, nor glimpse divine!
   Lo! thy dread empire Chaos! is restor'd:
   Light dies before thy uncreating word;
   Thy hand, great Anarch! lets the curtain fall,
   And universal darkness buries all.

   The Dunciad, IV, l. 649

Lady Mary Wortley Montagu
1689–1762

7 And we meet, with champagne and a chicken, at last.

   The Lover [1748]

8 Be plain in dress, and sober in your diet;
   In short, my deary, kiss me, and be quiet.

   *A Summary of Lord Lyttelton's
   Advice to a Lady [1731–1733]*

9 Satire should, like a polished razor keen,
   Wound with a touch that's scarcely felt or seen.

   *Verses to the Imitator of the First Satire
   of the Second Book of Horace*[1]

10   I wish you would moderate that fondness you
   have for your children. I do not mean you should
   abate any part of your care, or not do your duty to
   them in its utmost extent; but I would have you early
   prepare yourself for disappointments, which are heavy
   in proportion to their being surprising.

   *Letter to her daughter
   [February 19, 1753]*

Charles de Secondat, Baron de Montesquieu[2]
1689–1755

11   A man should be mourned at his birth, not at his
   death.

   *Lettres Persanes (Persian Letters) [1721],
   no. 40*

12   If triangles had a god, he would have three sides.

   Lettres Persanes, 59

13   Liberty is the right of doing whatever the laws
   permit.

   *De l'Esprit des Lois (On the Spirit of Laws)
   [1748], bk. XI, ch. 3*

14   Useless laws weaken the necessary laws.

   De l'Esprit des Lois, XXIX, 16

15   If I knew of something that could serve my nation
   but would ruin another, I would not propose it to my
   prince, for I am first a man and only then a
   Frenchman . . . because I am necessarily a man, and
   only accidentally am I French.

   *Pensées et Fragments Inédits
   de Montesquieu [1899], vol. I*

16   You have to study a great deal to know a little.

   Pensées et Fragments, I

17   The ancient books are for authors; the new ones,
   for readers.

   Pensées et Fragments, I

John Byrom
1692–1763

18 God bless the King, I mean the Faith's Defender;
   God bless — no harm in blessing — the Pretender;
   But who Pretender is, or who is King,
   God bless us all — that's quite another thing.

   *Miscellaneous Poems [1773].
   To an Officer in the Army, Extempore;
   Intended to Allay the Violence of
   Party Spirit*

19 Some say, that Signor Bononcini,
   Compared to Handel's a mere ninny;
   Others aver, to him, that Handel
   Is scarcely fit to hold a candle.
   Strange! that such high dispute should be
   'Twixt Tweedledum and Tweedledee.[3]

   *Miscellaneous Poems. On the Feuds
   Between Handel and Bononcini*

---

[1] Referring to Alexander Pope's imitation.

[2] See Thomas Carlyle, 408:9 and note.
[3] See Lewis Carroll, 515:19.

Philip Dormer Stanhope, Earl of Chesterfield
1694–1773

1   Measures not men.
  Letters to His Son [published 1774]
  [March 6, 1742]

2   Whatever is worth doing at all, is worth doing well.   *Letters to His Son [March 10, 1746]*

3   The knowledge of the world is only to be acquired in the world, and not in a closet.
  Letters to His Son [October 4, 1746]

4   An injury is much sooner forgotten than an insult.   *Letters to His Son [October 9, 1746]*

5   Do as you would be done by, is the surest method that I know of pleasing.[1]
  Letters to His Son [October 16, 1747]

6   Take the tone of the company that you are in.
  Letters to His Son [October 16, 1747]

7   I knew once a very covetous, sordid fellow,[2] who used frequently to say, "Take care of the pence, for the pounds will take care of themselves."
  Letters to His Son [November 6, 1747]

8   Advice is seldom welcome; and those who want it the most always like it the least.
  Letters to His Son [January 29, 1748]

9   Speak of the moderns without contempt, and of the ancients without idolatry.
  Letters to His Son [February 22, 1748]

10   Wear your learning, like your watch, in a private pocket: and do not pull it out and strike it, merely to show that you have one.
  Letters to His Son [February 22, 1748]

11   Manners must adorn knowledge, and smooth its way through the world. Like a great rough diamond, it may do very well in a closet by way of curiosity, and also for its intrinsic value.
  Letters to His Son [July 1, 1748]

12   Without some dissimulation no business can be carried on at all.   *Letters to His Son [May 22, 1749]*

13   Idleness is only the refuge of weak minds.
  Letters to His Son [July 20, 1749]

14   Style is the dress of thoughts.
  Letters to His Son [November 24, 1749]

15   Dispatch is the soul of business.
  Letters to His Son [February 5, 1750]

16   Let blockheads read what blockheads wrote.
  Letters to His Son [November 1, 1750]

17   The chapter of knowledge is a very short, but the chapter of accidents is a very long one.
  To Solomon Dayrolles
  [February 16, 1753]

18   I assisted at the birth of that most significant word "flirtation," which dropped from the most beautiful mouth in the world.
  The World [December 5, 1754], no. 101

19 Unlike my subject will I frame my song,
It shall be witty, and it shan't be long.
  Epigram on ("Long") Sir Thomas Robinson

Francis Hutcheson
1694–1746

20   That action is best which procures the greatest happiness for the greatest numbers.[3]
  Inquiry Concerning Moral Good and Evil [1720], sec. 3

François Quesnay
1694–1774

21   Laissez faire, laissez passer.[4]

  Attributed

Voltaire [François Marie Arouet]
1694–1778

22   We know many truths; we have discovered many useful inventions. Let us console ourselves for not knowing possible connections between a spider and the ring of Saturn, and continue examining what is within our reach.
  Letters Concerning the English Nation[5] [1734]. Letter 25: On the Pensées of Pascal

23   O what fine times, this age of iron!
  Le Mondain (The Worldling) [1736]

---

[1]See *Matthew 7:12*, 33:18; Confucius, 61:20; Aristotle, 77:12; and Hillel, 102:27.

[2]William Lowndes [1652–1724], Secretary of the Treasury in the reigns of William III, Queen Anne, and George I. See Lewis Carroll, 514:20.

[3]See Jeremy Bentham, 342:5.

[4]Let it be, let it pass.
The phrase is not readily translatable, and also appears as: Laissez faire, laissez aller. It has also been attributed to PIERRE LE PESANT BOISGUILLEBERT [1646–1714] and JEAN CLAUDE GOURNAY [1712–1759]. It was widely used by the Physiocrats in urging freedom from government interference, and was adopted by Adam Smith.

[5]Translated by LEONARD TANCOCK.

1   The superfluous, a very necessary thing.
Le Mondain

2   The only reward to be expected from literature is contempt if one fails and hatred if one succeeds.
Letter to Mlle. Quinault [August 16, 1738]

3   The secret of being a bore is to tell everything.
*Sept Discours en Vers sur l'Homme
(Seven Discourses on Man, in Verse) [1738]*

4   Love truth, but pardon error.
Sept Discours en Vers sur l'Homme

5   He who is merely just is severe.
Letter to Frederick the Great [1740]

6   It is better to risk saving a guilty person than to condemn an innocent one.   *Zadig [1747], ch. 6*

7   This agglomeration which was called and which still calls itself the Holy Roman Empire is neither holy, nor Roman, nor an Empire.
Essai sur les Moeurs (Essay on Manners) [1756]

8   In this best of all possible worlds...everything is for the best.[1]   *Candide*[2] *[1759], ch. 1*

9   If this is the best of all possible worlds, what are the others like?   *Candide, 6*

10   [Optimism] is a mania for saying things are well when one is in hell.   *Candide, 19*

11   In this country [England] it is useful from time to time to kill one admiral in order to encourage the others.[3]   *Candide, 23*

12   This is the happiest of all men, for he is superior to everything he possesses.   *Candide, 25*

13   Work keeps us from three great evils, boredom, vice, and poverty.[4]   *Candide, 30*

14   We must cultivate our garden.[5]   *Candide, 30*

15   There are truths which are not for all men, nor for all times.
*Letter to Cardinal de Bernis
[April 23, 1761]*

16   One feels like crawling on all fours after reading your work.   *Letter to Rousseau [August 31, 1761]*

17   Whatever you do, crush the infamous thing [superstition], and love those who love you.[6]
*Letter to d'Alembert
[November 28, 1762]*

18   Common sense is not so common.
*Dictionnaire Philosophique [1764].
Common Sense*

19   In general, the art of government consists in taking as much money as possible from one class of citizens to give to the other.
Dictionnaire Philosophique. Money

20   We have a natural right to make use of our pens as of our tongue, at our peril, risk and hazard.
*Dictionnaire Philosophique.
Liberty of the Press*

21   The best is the enemy of the good.[7]
*Dictionnaire Philosophique.
Dramatic Art*

22   Very learned women are to be found, in the same manner as female warriors; but they are seldom or never inventors.
Dictionnaire Philosophique. Women

23   Men use thought only to justify their wrong-doings, and speech only to conceal their thoughts.
*Dialogue 14. Le Chapon et la Poularde
(The Capon and the Hen) [1766]*

24   I have never made but one prayer to God, a very short one: "O Lord, make my enemies ridiculous." And God granted it.
*Letter to M. Damilaville
[May 16, 1767]*

25   History is no more than the portrayal of crimes and misfortunes.[8]   *L'Ingénu [1767], ch. 10*

26   Thought depends absolutely on the stomach, but in spite of that, those who have the best stomachs are not the best thinkers.
Letter to d'Alembert [August 20, 1770]

27   If God did not exist, it would be necessary to invent him.[9]
*Épître à l'Auteur du Livre des
Trois Imposteurs (To the Author of
"The Three Imposters") [November 10, 1770]*

28   Change everything, except your loves.
*Sur l'Usage de la Vie
(On the Use of Life) [1770]*

---

[1]Dans ce meilleur des mondes possibles...tout est au mieux.
The best of all possible worlds. — GOTTFRIED WILHELM VON LEIBNIZ [1646–1716], *Essays on the Goodness of God, the Freedom of Man, and the Origin of Evil* [1710]

[2]Translated by ROBERT M. ADAMS.

[3]Pour encourager les autres.
The reference is to Admiral John Byng, who was executed in 1757 for failing to relieve Minorca.

[4]Le travail éloigne de nous trois grands maux, l'ennui, le vice, et le besoin.

[5]Il faut cultiver notre jardin.

---

[6]Quoi que vous fassiez, écrasez l'infâme, et aimez qui vous aime.

[7]Le mieux est l'ennemi du bien.

[8]L'histoire n'est que le tableau des crimes et des malheurs.

[9]See Ovid, 102:4.

1   I am very fond of truth, but not at all of martyrdom.   *Letter to d'Alembert [February 1776]*

2   The embarrassment of riches.[1]
          Le Droit du Seigneur, act II, sc. vi

3 Who has not the spirit of his age,
   Of his age has all the unhappiness.[2]
               Letter to Madame du Châtelet

4   I advise you to go on living solely to enrage those who are paying your annuities. It is the only pleasure I have left.   *Letter to Madame du Deffand*

5   Liberty of thought is the life of the soul.
          Essay on Epic Poetry
          (written in English)

6 Whoever you are, behold your master,
   He is, or was, or has to be.[3]
          On a statuette of Cupid in the
          Cirey Gardens

7   I disapprove of what you say, but I will defend to the death your right to say it.   *Attributed*[4]

8   I die adoring God, loving my friends, not hating my enemies, and detesting superstition.
               Written February 28, 1778

William Oldys
1696–1761

9 Busy, curious, thirsty fly,
   Drink with me, and drink as I.
          On a Fly Drinking out of a Cup of Ale, st. 1

Marie de Vichy-Chamrond,
Marquise du Deffand
1697–1780

10   [Of Voltaire:] He has invented history.
          From ÉDOUARD FOURNIER [1819–1880],
          L'Esprit dans l'Histoire [1857]

---

[1]L'Embarras des Richesses. — ABBÉ D'ALLAINVAL [1700–1753], *title of play* [1726]

[2]Qui n'a pas l'esprit de son âge, / De son âge a tout le malheur.

[3]Qui que tu sois, voici ton maître; / Il l'est — le fut — ou le doit être.

[4]This sentence is not Voltaire's, but was first used in quoting a letter from Voltaire to Helvétius in *The Friends of Voltaire* [1906] by S. G. Tallentyre (E. Beatrice Hall). She claims it was a paraphrase of Voltaire's words in the *Essay on Tolerance:* Think for yourselves and let others enjoy the privilege to do so too.

   Norbert Guterman, in *A Book of French Quotations* [1963], suggests that the probable source for the quotation is a line in a letter to M. le Riche [February 6, 1770]: "Monsieur l'abbé, I detest what you write, but I would give my life to make it possible for you to continue to write."

11   The first step is the hardest.[5]
          Letter to d'Alembert [July 7, 1763]

Charles Macklin
c. 1697–1797

12   The law is a sort of hocus-pocus science.[6]
          Love à la Mode [1759], act II, sc. i

John Dyer
1699–1757

13 A little rule, a little sway,
   A sunbeam in a winter's day,
   Is all the proud and mighty have
   Between the cradle and the grave.
          Grongar Hill [1726], l. 89

James Thomson
1700–1748

14 See, Winter comes to rule the varied year,
   Sullen and sad.   *The Seasons. Winter [1726], l. 1*

15   Welcome, kindred glooms!
   Congenial horrors, hail!   *The Seasons. Winter, l. 5*

16 Cruel as death, and hungry as the grave.
          The Seasons. Winter, l. 393

17   There studious let me sit,
   And hold high converse with the mighty dead.
          The Seasons. Winter, l. 431

18 Come, gentle Spring! ethereal mildness, come.
          The Seasons. Spring [1728], l. 1

19 Delightful task! to rear the tender thought,
   To teach the young idea how to shoot.
          The Seasons. Spring, l. 1152

20 An elegant sufficiency, content,
   Retirement, rural quiet, friendship, books.
          The Seasons. Spring, l. 1161

21 Crown'd with the sickle, and the wheaten sheaf,
   While Autumn, nodding o'er the yellow plain,
   Comes jovial on.   *The Seasons. Autumn [1730], l. 1*

---

[5]This remark refers to the legend that Saint Denis, carrying his head in his hands, walked from Montmartre to St. Denis, a few miles north of Paris. Voltaire wrote to Madame du Deffand [January 1764] that one of her bons mots was quoted in the notes of *La Pucelle, canto 1:* Il n'y a que le premier pas qui coûte.

[6]Hocus was an old cunning attorney. — DR. JOHN ARBUTHNOT [1667–1735], *Law Is a Bottomless Pit; or, History of John Bull* [1712], *ch. 5*

   The words of consecration, "Hoc est corpus," were travestied into a nickname for jugglery, as "Hocus-pocus." — JOHN RICHARD GREEN [1837–1883], *A Short History of the English People* [1874], *ch. 7*

1 Or where the Northern ocean, in vast whirls,
Boils round the naked melancholy isles
Of farthest Thulè, and th' Atlantic surge
Pours in among the stormy Hebrides.
The Seasons. Autumn, l. 862

2 Come then, expressive silence, muse His praise.
A Hymn [1730], l. 118

3 When Britain first, at Heaven's command,
Arose from out the azure main,
This was the charter of the land,
And guardian angels sung this strain:
Rule, Britannia, rule the waves;
Britons never will be slaves.   *Alfred [1740], act II, sc. v*

4 A pleasing land of drowsyhead it was.
The Castle of Indolence [1748], canto I, st. 6

Jonathan Edwards
1703–1758

5 Resolved, never to do anything which I should be afraid to do if it were the last hour of my life.
Seventy Resolutions [1722–1723]

6 Intend to live in continual mortification, and never to expect or desire any worldly ease or pleasure.   *Diary [1723]*

7 There are beauties that are more palpable and explicable, and there are hidden and secret beauties . . . These hidden beauties are commonly by far the greatest, because the more complex a beauty is, the more hidden it is.   *Beauty of the World [1725]*

8 A little, wretched, despicable creature; a worm, a mere nothing, and less than nothing; a vile insect that has risen up in contempt against the majesty of Heaven and earth.
The Justice of God in the Damnation of Sinners [1734]

9 The heart is like a viper, hissing and spitting poison at God.
Men Naturally God's Enemies [1736], sec. 1, pt. 4

10 My wickedness, as I am in myself, has long appeared to me perfectly ineffable, and infinitely swallowing up all thought and imagination; like an infinite deluge or infinite mountains over my head.
Personal Narrative [1740]

11 The God that holds you over the pit of hell, much as one holds a spider,[1] or some loathsome insect over the fire, abhors you, and is dreadfully provoked: his wrath towards you burns like fire; he looks upon you as worthy of nothing else, but to be cast into the fire.   *Sinners in the Hands of an Angry God [1741]*

---

[1]See Robert Lowell, 787:3 and note.

12 This dictate of common sense.
Freedom of Will [1754], sec. 3

Thomas Morell
1703–1784

13 See, the conquering hero comes!
Sound the trumpet, beat the drums![2]
Joshua [1748], pt. III

John Wesley
1703–1791

14 I went to America to convert the Indians; but oh! who shall convert me?   *Journal [January 24, 1738]*

15 I look upon the world as my parish.
Journal [June 11, 1739]

16 That execrable sum of all villainies, commonly called the Slave Trade.   *Journal [February 12, 1772]*

17 Though I am always in haste, I am never in a hurry.   *Letters [December 10, 1777]*

18 Let it be observed, that slovenliness is no part of religion; that neither this nor any text of Scripture, condemns neatness of apparel. Certainly this is a duty, not a sin. "Cleanliness is, indeed, next to godliness."   *Sermon 93, On Dress*

19 Do all the good you can,
By all the means you can,
In all the ways you can,
In all the places you can,
At all the times you can,
To all the people you can,
As long as ever you can.   *John Wesley's Rule*

Benjamin Franklin[3]
1706–1790

20 The body of Benjamin Franklin, Printer (like the cover of an old book, its contents torn out and

---

[2]Handel used this in his oratorios *Judas Maccabaeus* [April 1, 1747] and *Joshua* [March 9, 1748], the libretti of which were written by Morell.

[3]Eripuit coelo fulmen mox sceptra tyrannis [He snatched the thunderbolt from heaven, then the scepter from tyrants]. — *Attributed to* Baron Turgot [1727–1781]

This line was inscribed on Houdon's bust of Franklin in 1778.

Antiquity would have raised altars to this mighty genius, who, to the advantage of mankind, compassing in his mind the heavens and the earth, was able to restrain alike thunderbolts and tyrants. — Mirabeau, *Address upon the Death of Franklin* [June 11, 1790]

See Marcus Manilius, 104:9, and Shakespeare, 219:32.

I succeed him; no one could replace him. — Thomas Jefferson (to Charles Gravier, Comte de Vergennes, who had remarked, "You replace Mr. Franklin" as envoy to France)

stripped of its lettering and gilding), lies here, food for worms; but the work shall not be lost, for it will (as he believed) appear once more in a new and more elegant edition, revised and corrected by the Author.
Epitaph on Himself [composed in 1728]

1   Eat to live, and not live to eat.[1]
Poor Richard's Almanac [1733]. May

2   After three days men grow weary, of a wench, a guest, and weather rainy.
Poor Richard's Almanac. June

3   There is no little enemy.
Poor Richard's Almanac. September

4   Without justice, courage is weak.
Poor Richard's Almanac [1734]. January

5   Blame-all and Praise-all are two blockheads.
Poor Richard's Almanac. February

6   Where there's marriage without love, there will be love without marriage.
Poor Richard's Almanac. May

7   Avarice and happiness never saw each other, how then should they become acquainted.
Poor Richard's Almanac. November

8   A little house well filled, a little field well tilled, and a little wife well willed, are great riches.
Poor Richard's Almanac [1735]. February

9   Necessity never made a good bargain.
Poor Richard's Almanac. April

10   Three may keep a secret, if two of them are dead.   *Poor Richard's Almanac. July*

11   Opportunity is the great bawd.
Poor Richard's Almanac. September

12   Early to bed and early to rise, makes a man healthy, wealthy, and wise.
Poor Richard's Almanac. October

13   Here comes the orator! with his flood of words, and his drop of reason.
Poor Richard's Almanac. October

14   Some are weatherwise, some are otherwise.
Poor Richard's Almanac. December

15   God helps them that help themselves.
Poor Richard's Almanac [1736]. June

16   Don't throw stones at your neighbors', if your own windows are glass.
Poor Richard's Almanac. August

17   There are three faithful friends — an old wife, an old dog, and ready money.
Poor Richard's Almanac [1738]. January

18   If you would not be forgotten,
As soon as you are dead and rotten,
Either write things worthy reading,
Or do things worth the writing.
Poor Richard's Almanac. May

19   Keep your eyes wide open before marriage, half shut afterwards.   *Poor Richard's Almanac. June*

20   None but the well-bred man knows how to confess a fault, or acknowledge himself in an error.
Poor Richard's Almanac. November

21   An empty bag cannot stand upright.
Poor Richard's Almanac [1740]. January

22   He that riseth late, must trot all day, and shall scarce overtake his business at night.
Poor Richard's Almanac [1742]. August

23   Experience keeps a dear school, but fools will learn in no other.
Poor Richard's Almanac [1743]. December

24   The used key is always bright.
Poor Richard's Almanac [1744]. July

25   When the well's dry, we know the worth of water.[2]   *Poor Richard's Almanac [1746]. January*

26   Dost thou love life? Then do not squander time; for that's the stuff life is made of.
Poor Richard's Almanac. June

27   Lost time is never found again.
Poor Richard's Almanac [1748]. January

28   He that's secure is not safe.
Poor Richard's Almanac. August

29   Little strokes,
Fell great oaks.
Poor Richard's Almanac [1750]. August

30   The cat in gloves catches no mice.
Poor Richard's Almanac [1754]. February

31   Work as if you were to live a hundred years,
Pray as if you were to die tomorrow.
Poor Richard's Almanac [1757]. May

32   A word to the wise is enough, and many words won't fill a bushel.
Poor Richard's Almanac [1758]. Preface: Courteous Reader

---

[1] See Socrates, 70:7 and note.

[2] Do not let your chances like sunbeams pass you by, / For you never miss the water till the well runs dry. — ROWLAND HOWARD [fl. 1876], *You Never Miss the Water* [1876]

1   He that lives upon hope will die fasting.
    Poor Richard's Almanac. Preface:
    Courteous Reader

2   Three removes is as bad as a fire.
    Poor Richard's Almanac. Preface:
    Courteous Reader

3   A little neglect may breed great mischief...for want of a nail the shoe was lost; for want of a shoe the horse was lost; and for want of a horse the rider was lost.
    Poor Richard's Almanac. Preface:
    Courteous Reader

4   Eighth and lastly. They are so grateful!!
    Reasons for Preferring an
    Elderly Mistress [1745]

5   Remember that time is money.[1]
    Advice to a Young Tradesman [1748]

6   Those who would give up essential liberty, to purchase a little temporary safety, deserve neither liberty nor safety.
    Address in the Pennsylvania Assembly
    [November 1755]

7   Idleness and pride tax with a heavier hand than kings and parliaments. If we can get rid of the former, we may easily bear the latter.
    Letter on the Stamp Act [July 11, 1765]

8   The grand leap of the whale up the Fall of Niagara is esteemed, by all who have seen it, as one of the finest spectacles in nature.
    To the editor of a London newspaper [1765], intended to chaff the English for their ignorance of America

9 Here Skugg lies snug
As a bug in a rug.
    Letter to Miss Georgiana Shipley
    [September 1772]

10   You and I were long friends: you are now my enemy, and I am   Yours,
                              B. Franklin
    Letter to William Strahan [July 5, 1775]

11   We must all hang together, or assuredly we shall all hang separately.
    At the signing of the Declaration of
    Independence [July 4, 1776]

12   Poor man, said I, you pay too much for your whistle.
    The Whistle [1779]

13   Here you would know and enjoy what posterity will say of Washington. For a thousand leagues have nearly the same effect with a thousand years.
    Letter to George Washington [March 5, 1780]

14   George Washington, Commander of the American armies, who, like Joshua of old, commanded the sun and the moon to stand still, and they obeyed him.   *A toast at a dinner in Versailles*[2]

15   No nation was ever ruined by trade.
    Thoughts on Commercial Subjects

16   There never was a good war or a bad peace.[3]
    Letter to Josiah Quincy [September 11, 1783]

17   I wish the bald eagle had not been chosen as the representative of our country; he is a bird of bad moral character...like those among men who live by sharping and robbing, he is generally poor, and often very lousy...
    The turkey...is a much more respectable bird, and withal a true original native of America.
    Letter to Sarah Bache [January 26, 1784]

18   He [the sun] gives light as soon as he rises.
    An Economical Project[4] *[1784]*

19   A republic, if you can keep it.[5]
    Response [September 18, 1787]

20   Our new Constitution is now established, and has an appearance that promises permanency; but in this world nothing can be said to be certain, except death and taxes.
    Letter to Jean-Baptiste Leroy [November 13, 1789]

21   The next thing most like living one's life over again seems to be a recollection of that life, and to make that recollection as durable as possible by putting it down in writing.
    Autobiography[6] *[1731–1759], ch. 1*

22   Eat not to dullness; drink not to elevation.
    Autobiography, 6

[2]The British minister had proposed a toast to George III, in which he likened him to the sun, and the French minister had toasted Louis XVI, comparing him with the moon.

[3]I cease not to advocate peace; even though unjust it is better than the most just war. — CICERO, *To Atticus, bk. VII, letter 14*
    It hath been said that an unjust peace is to be preferred before a just war. — SAMUEL BUTLER [1612–1680], *Butler's Remains* [1759], *Speeches in the Rump Parliament*

[4]Letter to the *Journal de Paris* advocating Daylight Saving Time.

[5]In Philadelphia, a Mrs. Powel "asked Dr. Franklin, Well, Doctor, what have we got a republic or a monarchy? A republic, replied the Doctor, if you can keep it." Recorded by James McHenry, one of Washington's aides, in his diary; published in the *American Historical Review, vol. XI* [1906], *p. 618.*

[6]The *Autobiography,* begun in 1771, was first published (unauthorized, mangled, and in French) in 1791, and in complete form in 1868.

[1]We reckon hours and minutes to be dollars and cents. — SAM SLICK [T. C. HALIBURTON, 1796–1865], *The Clockmaker* [1836]

1   I shall never ask, never refuse, nor ever resign an office. *Autobiography, 8*

2   Human felicity is produced not so much by great pieces of good fortune that seldom happen, as by little advantages that occur every day. *Autobiography, 9*

3   When men are employed, they are best contented; for on the days they worked they were good-natured and cheerful, and, with the consciousness of having done a good day's work, they spent the evening jollily; but on our idle days they were mutinous and quarrelsome. *Autobiography, 10*

Georges Louis Leclerc de Buffon
1707–1788

4   [Of the horse:] The noblest conquest man has ever made. *L'Histoire Naturelle [1749–1788]*

5   The style is the man himself.[1]
Discourse (on his admission to the French Academy) [1753]

6   Genius is nothing but a greater aptitude for patience. *Attributed*[2]

Henry Fielding
1707–1754

7 All Nature wears one universal grin.
Tom Thumb [1730], act I, sc. i

8 When I'm not thanked at all, I'm thanked enough; I've done my duty, and I've done no more.
Tom Thumb, I, iii

9 Oh, the roast beef of England, And old England's roast beef![3]
The Grub Street Opera [1731], act III, sc. iii

10 I am as sober as a judge.
Don Quixote in England [1734], act III, sc. xiv

11 The dusky night rides down the sky, And ushers in the morn; The hounds all join in glorious cry, The huntsman winds his horn, And a-hunting we will go.[4]
A-Hunting We Will Go [1734], st. 1

12   To whom nothing is given, of him can nothing be required. *Joseph Andrews [1742], bk. II, ch. 8*

13   I describe not men, but manners; not an individual, but a species. *Joseph Andrews, III, 1*

14   They are the affectation of affectation.
Joseph Andrews, III, 3

15   Public schools are the nurseries of all vice and immorality. *Joseph Andrews, III, 5*

16   Love and scandal are the best sweeteners of tea.
Love in Several Masques [1743]

17   This story will never go down.
Tumble-Down Dick [1744], air I

18   Thwackum was for doing justice, and leaving mercy to heaven.
Tom Jones [1749], bk. III, ch. 10

19   Can any man have a higher notion of the rule of right and the eternal fitness of things?
Tom Jones, IV, 4

20   Distinction without a difference.
Tom Jones, VI, 13

21   O! more than Gothic ignorance.
Tom Jones, VII, 3

22   An amiable weakness.[5]   *Tom Jones, X, 8*

23   His designs were strictly honorable, as the phrase is; that is, to rob a lady of her fortune by way of marriage. *Tom Jones, XI, 4*

24   Hairbreadth missings of happiness look like the insults of Fortune. *Tom Jones, XIII, 2*

25   The republic of letters.   *Tom Jones, XIV, 1*

26   It hath been often said, that it is not death, but dying which is terrible.
Amelia [1751], bk. III, ch. 4

---

[1]Le style c'est l'homme même.

[2]Le génie n'est qu'une plus grande aptitude à la patience.
Hérault de Séchelles, in *Voyage à Montbard*, first attributed this to Buffon. It is quoted by Matthew Arnold in "A French Coleridge" [*Essays in Criticism*, 1865]. There is also a popular proverb: Genius is patience.
Genius is an intuitive talent for labor. — JOHANNES WALAEUS [JAN VAN WALE, 1604–1699]
Patience is a necessary ingredient of genius. — BENJAMIN DISRAELI, *The Young Duke* [1831]
Genius involves . . . an infinite capacity for taking trouble. — LESLIE STEPHEN [1832–1904], *English Thought in the Eighteenth Century*, vol. II [1876]
See Thomas Carlyle, 408:8; and Jane Ellice Hopkins, 528:11.

[3]The Roast Beef of Old England. — RICHARD LEVERIDGE [c. 1670–1758], *title of poem*

[4]It's of three jovial huntsmen, and a-hunting they did go; / And they hunted, and they holloed, and they blew their horns also; / Look ye there! — *The Three Jovial Huntsmen* (old English ballad), st. 1

[5]Amiable weaknesses of human nature. — EDWARD GIBBON, *The History of the Decline and Fall of the Roman Empire*, bk. I, ch. 14
It was an amiable weakness. — RICHARD BRINSLEY SHERIDAN, *The School for Scandal* [1777], act V, sc. i

1 When widows exclaim loudly against second marriages, I would always lay a wager that the man, if not the wedding day, is absolutely fixed on.
Amelia, VI, 8

2 One of my illustrious predecessors.[1]
Covent Garden Journal [January 11, 1752]

Linnaeus [Carl von Linné]
1707–1778

3 Nature does not proceed by leaps.[2]
Philosophia Botanica [1750], sec. 77

4 A professor can never better distinguish himself in his work than by encouraging a clever pupil, for the true discoverers are among them, as comets amongst the stars.
From biography[3] by THEODOR MAGNUS FRIES [1832–1913], ch. 9

5 Live innocently; God is here.
From biography by THEODOR MAGNUS FRIES, 15 (inscribed over the door of Linnaeus's bedchamber)

6 If a tree dies, plant another in its place.
From biography by THEODOR MAGNUS FRIES, 15

Charles Wesley
1707–1788

7 "Christ, the Lord, is risen today,"
Sons of men and angels say,
Raise your joys and triumphs high,
Sing, ye heavens, and earth reply.
Hymns and Sacred Poems [1739]. Christ, the Lord, Is Risen Today

8 Jesus, lover of my soul,
Let me to Thy bosom fly,
While the waters nearer roll,
While the tempest still is high;
Hide me, O my Savior, hide,
Till the storm of life is past;
Safe into the haven glide,
O receive my soul at last.
Hymns and Sacred Poems [1740]. Jesus, Lover of My Soul

9 Gentle Jesus, meek and mild,
Look upon a little child;
Pity my simplicity,
Suffer me to come to thee.
Hymns and Sacred Poems [1742]. Gentle Jesus, Meek and Mild

10 Hark! the herald angels sing
Glory to the newborn King;
Peace on earth, and mercy mild,
God and sinners reconciled!
Joyful all ye nations rise,
Join the triumph of the skies;
With th' angelic host proclaim
Christ is born in Bethlehem.[4]
Hymns and Sacred Poems [1753]. Christmas Hymn: Hark! the Herald Angels Sing

William Pitt, Earl of Chatham
1708–1778

11 The atrocious crime of being a young man, which the honorable gentleman [Walpole] has with such spirit and decency charged upon me, I shall neither attempt to palliate nor deny; but content myself with wishing that I may be one of those whose follies may cease with their youth, and not of that number who are ignorant in spite of experience.
Speech in the House of Commons[5] [March 6, 1741]

12 The poorest man may in his cottage bid defiance to all the forces of the Crown. It may be frail — its roof may shake — the wind may blow through it — the storm may enter — the rain may enter — but the King of England cannot enter — all his force dares not cross the threshold of the ruined tenement!
Speech in the House of Commons [1763]

13 I rejoice that America has resisted. Three millions of people, so dead to all the feelings of liberty, as voluntarily to submit to be slaves, would have been fit instruments to make slaves of the rest.
Speech in the House of Commons [January 14, 1766]

14 Confidence is a plant of slow growth in an aged bosom; youth is the season of credulity.
Speech in the House of Commons [January 14, 1766]

---

[1] Illustrious predecessor.—EDMUND BURKE, *The Present Discontents* [1770]

I tread in the footsteps of illustrious men. . . . In receiving from the people the sacred trust twice confined to my illustrious predecessor [Andrew Jackson].—MARTIN VAN BUREN [1782–1862], *Inaugural Address* [March 4, 1837]

[2] Natura non facit saltus.

[3] Translated by BENJAMIN DAYDON JACKSON.

[4] GEORGE WHITEFIELD [1714–1770] altered lines 1 and 2, 7 and 8, from Wesley's original:

Hark, how all the welkin rings, / "Glory to the King of kings." . . . / Universal nature say, / "Christ the Lord is born today."

[5] By some accounts, Samuel Johnson claimed authorship of this speech: "That speech I wrote in a garret, in Exeter Street." — ARTHUR MURPHY [1727–1805], *An Essay on the Life and Genius of Samuel Johnson* [1792]

1 Unlimited power is apt to corrupt the minds of those who possess it; and this I know, my lords, that where laws end, tyranny begins.
Case of Wilkes. Speech [January 9, 1770]

2 There is something behind the throne greater than the King himself.
Speech in the House of Lords [March 2, 1770]

3 I love the Americans because they love liberty, and I love them for the noble efforts they made in the last war. *Speech in the House of Lords [March 2, 1770]*

4 Reparation for our rights at home, and security against the like future violations.[1]
Letter to the Earl of Shelburne [September 29, 1770]

5 If I were an American, as I am an Englishman, while a foreign troop was landed in my country, I never would lay down my arms — never — never — never! You cannot conquer America.
Speech [November 18, 1777]

6 I invoke the genius of the Constitution.
Speech [November 18, 1777]

Samuel Johnson
1709–1784

7 Of all the griefs that harass the distrest,
Sure the most bitter is a scornful jest.
*London [1738] (an imitation of the
Third Satire of Juvenal), l. 166*

8 This mournful truth is ev'rywhere confessed —
Slow rises worth, by poverty depress'd.[2]
London, l. 176

9 When learning's triumph o'er her barb'rous foes
First rear'd the stage, immortal Shakespeare rose;
Each change of many-color'd life he drew,
Exhausted worlds, and then imagin'd new:
Existence saw him spurn her bounded reign,
And panting Time toil'd after him in vain.
*Prologue at the Opening of
Drury Lane Theatre [1747]*

10 Cold approbation gave the ling'ring bays,
For those who durst not censure, scarce could praise.
Prologue at the Opening of Drury Lane Theatre

11 Declamation roar'd, while Passion slept.
Prologue at the Opening of Drury Lane Theatre

12 The wild vicissitudes of taste.
Prologue at the Opening of Drury Lane Theatre

13 For we that live to please must please to live.
Prologue at the Opening of Drury Lane Theatre

14 Studious to please, yet not ashamed to fail.
Prologue to the Tragedy of Irene [1749]

15 Let observation with extensive view
Survey mankind, from China to Peru.[3]
Vanity of Human Wishes [1749], l. 1

16 Deign on the passing world to turn thine eyes,
And pause a while from learning to be wise.
There mark what ills the scholar's life assail —
Toil, envy, want, the patron, and the jail.
Vanity of Human Wishes, l. 157

17 He left the name at which the world grew pale,
To point a moral, or adorn a tale.
Vanity of Human Wishes, l. 221

18 "Enlarge my life with multitude of days!"
In health, in sickness, thus the suppliant prays:
Hides from himself his state, and shuns to know
That life protracted is protracted woe.
Vanity of Human Wishes, l. 255

19 Must helpless man, in ignorance sedate,
Roll darkling down the torrent of his fate?
Vanity of Human Wishes, l. 345

20 With these [Love, Patience, Faith] celestial Wisdom calms the mind,
And makes the happiness she does not find.
Vanity of Human Wishes, l. 367

21 Curiosity is one of the permanent and certain characteristics of a vigorous mind.
The Rambler[4] [March 12, 1751]

22 No place affords a more striking conviction of the vanity of human hopes than a public library.
The Rambler [March 23, 1751]

23 I am not yet so lost in lexicography as to forget that words are the daughters of earth, and that things are the sons of heaven. *Dictionary [1755], preface*

24 CLUB — An assembly of good fellows, meeting under certain conditions. *Dictionary*

25 ESSAY — A loose sally of the mind; an irregular indigested piece; not a regular and orderly composition. *Dictionary*

---

[1]Indemnity for the past and security for the future. — JOHN RUSSELL, *Life and Times of Charles James Fox* [1859–1860], vol. III, p. 345, letter to the Honorable T. Maitland

[2]Three years later Johnson wrote, "Mere unassisted merit advances slowly, if — what is not very common — it advances at all."

[3]Thomas De Quincey quotes with approval, but without naming him, the criticism of a writer who contends that this couplet amounts in effect to this: "Let observation with extensive observation observe mankind extensively." — *Rhetoric* [1828]

[4]For the *Rambler* motto, see Johnson's translation of Boethius, 117:5 and note.

1 EXCISE — A hateful tax levied upon commodities, and adjudged not by the common judges of property, but wretches hired by those to whom excise is paid.
Dictionary

2 GRUBSTREET — The name of a street near Moorsfield, London, much inhabited by writers of small histories, dictionaries, and temporary poems.
Dictionary

3 LEXICOGRAPHER — A writer of dictionaries, a harmless drudge.
Dictionary

4 OATS — A grain which in England is generally given to horses, but in Scotland supports the people.[1]
Dictionary

5 Among the calamities of war, may be justly numbered the diminution of the love of truth, by the falsehoods which interest dictates, and credulity encourages.[2]
The Idler [1758–1760], no. 30

6 The joy of life is variety; the tenderest love requires to be rekindled by intervals of absence.   *The Idler, 39*

7 He is no wise man who will quit a certainty for an uncertainty.
The Idler, 57

8 Ye who listen with credulity to the whispers of fancy, and pursue with eagerness the phantoms of hope; who expect that age will perform the promises of youth, and that the deficiencies of the present day will be supplied by the morrow; attend to the history of Rasselas, Prince of Abyssinia.
Rasselas [1759], ch. 1

9 To a poet nothing can be useless.   *Rasselas, 10*

10 Human life is everywhere a state in which much is to be endured and little to be enjoyed.
Rasselas, 11

11 Marriage has many pains, but celibacy has no pleasures.
Rasselas, 26

12 Example is always more efficacious than precept.
Rasselas, 30

13 The endearing elegance of female friendship.
Rasselas, 46

14 How small, of all that human hearts endure,
That part which laws or kings can cause or cure!

---

[1]It was pleasant to me to find, that "oats," the "food of horses," were so much used as the food of the people in Dr. Johnson's own town. — JAMES BOSWELL, *Life of Johnson, vol. I, p. 628* (Everyman edition)

I own that by my definition of *oats* I meant to vex them [the Scots]. — JOHNSON, in BOSWELL, *Life of Johnson, vol. II, p. 434* (Everyman edition)

[2]The first casualty when war comes is truth — HIRAM WARREN JOHNSON [1866–1945], *remark in U.S. Senate* [1918]. *Attributed.*

Still to ourselves in every place consign'd,
Our own felicity we make or find.
Lines added to OLIVER GOLDSMITH,
The Traveller [1763–1764]

15 Whoever wishes to attain an English style, familiar but not coarse, and elegant but not ostentatious, must give his days and nights to the volumes of Addison.   *Lives of the Poets [1779–1781]. Addison*

16 To be of no church is dangerous. Religion, of which the rewards are distant, and which is animated only by faith and hope, will glide by degrees out of the mind unless it be invigorated and reimpressed by external ordinances, by stated calls to worship, and the salutary influence of example.
Lives of the Poets. Milton

17 The father of English criticism.
Lives of the Poets. Dryden

18 He delighted to tread upon the brink of meaning.   *Lives of the Poets. Dryden*

19 The *Churchyard* abounds with images which find a mirror in every mind, and with sentiments to which every bosom returns an echo.
Lives of the Poets. Gray

20 I am disappointed by that stroke of death [Garrick's], which has eclipsed the gaiety of nations, and impoverished the public stock of harmless pleasure.
Lives of the Poets. Edmund Smith

21 New things are made familiar, and familiar things are made new.   *Lives of the Poets. Pope*

22 To circumscribe poetry by a definition will only show the narrowness of the definer, though a definition which shall exclude Pope will not easily be made.   *Preface to the Works of Pope [1781]*

23 Tomorrow I purpose to regulate my room.
Prayers and Meditations [1785]. 1764

24 Preserve me from unseasonable and immoderate sleep.   *Prayers and Meditations. 1767*

25 Every man naturally persuades himself that he can keep his resolutions, nor is he convinced of his imbecility but by length of time and frequency of experiment.   *Prayers and Meditations. 1770*

26 This world, where much is to be done and little to be known.
Prayers and Meditations. 1770.
Against Inquisitive and Perplexing Thoughts

27 [Sunday] should be different from another day. People may walk, but not throw stones at birds. There may be relaxation, but there should be no levity.
From JAMES BOSWELL, Journal of a Tour to the
Hebrides [1785]. August 20, 1773

1   I have, all my life long, been lying till noon; yet I tell all young men, and tell them with great sincerity, that nobody who does not rise early will ever do any good.

> *From* Boswell, *Journal of a Tour to the Hebrides. September 14, 1773*

2   Gratitude is a fruit of great cultivation; you do not find it among gross people.

> *From* Boswell, *Journal of a Tour to the Hebrides. September 20, 1773*

3   Here closed in death th' attentive eyes
That saw the manners in the face.

> *Epitaph on Hogarth [1786]*

4   When the hoary Sage replied,
"Come, my lad, and drink some beer."

> *From* Mrs. Piozzi,[1] *Anecdotes of Samuel Johnson [1786]*

5   He was a very good hater.

> *From* Mrs. Piozzi, *Anecdotes of Samuel Johnson*

6   The law is the last result of human wisdom acting upon human experience for the benefit of the public.

> *From* Mrs. Piozzi, *Anecdotes of Samuel Johnson*

7   The use of traveling is to regulate imagination by reality, and instead of thinking how things may be, to see them as they are.

> *From* Mrs. Piozzi, *Anecdotes of Samuel Johnson*

8   Dictionaries are like watches; the worst is better than none, and the best cannot be expected to go quite true.

> *From* Mrs. Piozzi, *Anecdotes of Samuel Johnson*

9   Books that you may carry to the fire, and hold readily in your hand, are the most useful after all.

> *From* Sir John Hawkins *[1719–1789], Life of Johnson [1787]. Apothegms*

10   As with my hat[2] upon my head
I walk'd along the Strand,
I there did meet another man
With his hat in his hand.[3]

> *Anecdotes of Johnson by* George Steevens *[1736–1800]*

11   Abstinence is as easy to me as temperance would be difficult.   *Anecdotes of Johnson by* Hannah More

12   *Boswell:* That, sir, was great fortitude of mind.
Johnson: No, sir; stark insensibility.

> *From* James Boswell, *Life of Johnson*[4] *[1791], November 5, 1728*

13   [Of Pembroke College:] Sir, we are a nest of singing birds.   *From* Boswell, *Life of Johnson, 1730*

14   I'll come no more behind your scenes, David [Garrick]; for the silk stockings and white bosoms of your actresses excite my amorous propensities.

> *From* Boswell, *Life of Johnson, 1749*

15   A man may write at any time, if he will set himself doggedly to it.

> *From* Boswell, *Life of Johnson, March 1750*

16   Wretched un-idea'd girls.

> *From* Boswell, *Life of Johnson, 1753*

17   Is not a patron, my lord, one who looks with unconcern on a man struggling for life in the water, and when he has reached ground encumbers him with help? The notice which you have been pleased to take of my labors, had it been early, had been kind; but it has been delayed till I am indifferent, and cannot enjoy it; till I am solitary, and cannot impart it; till I am known, and do not want it.

> *From* Boswell, *Life of Johnson, February 7, 1754 (Letter to Lord Chesterfield)*

18   [Of Lord Chesterfield:] This man, I thought, had been a Lord among wits; but, I find, he is only a wit among Lords!

> *From* Boswell, *Life of Johnson, 1754*

19   Sir, he [Bolingbroke] was a scoundrel, and a coward: a scoundrel, for charging a blunderbuss against religion and morality; a coward, because he had not resolution to fire it off himself, but left half a crown to a beggarly Scotchman, to draw the trigger after his death.

> *From* Boswell, *Life of Johnson, March 6, 1754*

20   Ignorance, madame, pure ignorance.[5]

> *From* Boswell, *Life of Johnson, 1755*

21   If a man does not make new acquaintances as he advances through life, he will soon find himself left alone. A man, sir, should keep his friendship in a constant repair.[6]

> *From* Boswell, *Life of Johnson, 1755*

22   Towering in the confidence of twenty-one.

> *From* Boswell, *Life of Johnson, January 9, 1758*

---

[1] Hester Thrale Piozzi [1741–1821]. See 335:5.

[2] Elsewhere found: I put my hat.

[3] A parody on Thomas Percy's [1729–1811] ballad *The Hermit of Warkworth [1771]*.

[4] Edited by G. B. Hill and revised by L. F. Powell [1934].

[5] When asked by a lady why he defined "pastern" as the "knee" of a horse in his Dictionary.

[6] Keep your friendships in repair. — Ralph Waldo Emerson, *Uncollected Lectures: Table-Talk* [1864]

1   Being in a ship is being in a jail, with the chance of being drowned.
From BOSWELL, *Life of Johnson, March 1759*

2   Sir, I think all Christians, whether Papists or Protestants, agree in the essential articles, and that their differences are trivial, and rather political than religious.[1]   *From* BOSWELL, *Life of Johnson, 1763*

3   The noblest prospect which a Scotchman ever sees is the high road that leads him to England!
From BOSWELL, *Life of Johnson, July 6, 1763*

4   A man ought to read just as inclination leads him; for what he reads as a task will do him little good.
From BOSWELL, *Life of Johnson, July 14, 1763*

5   If he does really think that there is no distinction between virtue and vice, why, sir, when he leaves our houses let us count our spoons.
From BOSWELL, *Life of Johnson, July 14, 1763*

6   Sir, your levelers wish to level *down* as far as themselves; but they cannot bear leveling *up* to themselves.
From BOSWELL, *Life of Johnson, July 21, 1763*

7   Sherry[2] is dull, naturally dull; but it must have taken him a great deal of pains to become what we now see him. Such an excess of stupidity, sir, is not in Nature.
From BOSWELL, *Life of Johnson, July 28, 1763*

8   Sir, a woman preaching is like a dog's walking on his hinder legs. It is not done well; but you are surprised to find it done at all.
From BOSWELL, *Life of Johnson, July 31, 1763*

9   This was a good dinner enough, to be sure, but it was not a dinner to *ask* a man to.
From BOSWELL, *Life of Johnson, July 31, 1763*

10   A very unclubable man.[3]
From BOSWELL, *Life of Johnson, 1764*

11   It matters not how a man dies, but how he lives.
From BOSWELL, *Life of Johnson, October 26, 1769*

12   That fellow seems to me to possess but one idea, and that is a wrong one.
From BOSWELL, *Life of Johnson, 1770*

13   A gentleman who had been very unhappy in marriage, married immediately after his wife died: Johnson said, it was the triumph of hope over experience.   *From* BOSWELL, *Life of Johnson, 1770*

14   A decent provision for the poor is the true test of civilization.   *From* BOSWELL, *Life of Johnson, 1770*

15   All denominations of Christians have really little difference in point of doctrine, though they may differ widely in external forms.
From BOSWELL, *Life of Johnson, 1772*

16   Nobody can write the life of a man, but those who have eat and drunk and lived in social intercourse with him.
From BOSWELL, *Life of Johnson, March 31, 1772*

17   I am a great friend to public amusements; for they keep people from vice.
From BOSWELL, *Life of Johnson, March 31, 1772*

18   There is more knowledge of the heart in one letter of Richardson's than in all *Tom Jones*.
From BOSWELL, *Life of Johnson, April 6, 1772*

19   Why, sir, if you were to read Richardson for the story, your impatience would be so much fretted that you would hang yourself. But you must read him for the sentiment, and consider the story as only giving occasion to the sentiment.
From BOSWELL, *Life of Johnson, April 6, 1772*

20   A cow is a very good animal in the field; but we turn her out of a garden.
From BOSWELL, *Life of Johnson, April 15, 1772*

21   Much may be made of a Scotchman if he be *caught* young.[4]
From BOSWELL, *Life of Johnson, Spring 1772*

22   It is a foolish thing well done.[5]
From BOSWELL, *Life of Johnson, April 3, 1773*

23   No, sir, do *you* read books *through*?[6]
From BOSWELL, *Life of Johnson, April 19, 1773*

24   An old tutor of a college said to one of his pupils: Read over your compositions, and wherever you meet with a passage which you think is particularly fine, strike it out.
From BOSWELL, *Life of Johnson, April 30, 1773*

25   You are the most unscottified of your countrymen.   *From* BOSWELL, *Life of Johnson, May 1, 1773*

26   The woman's a whore, and there's an end on 't.[7]   *From* BOSWELL, *Life of Johnson, May 7, 1773*

---

[1] I do not find that the age or country makes the least difference; no, nor the language the actor spoke, nor the religion which they professed — whether Arab in the desert, or Frenchman in the Academy. I see that sensible men and conscientious men all over the world were of one religion of well-doing and daring. — RALPH WALDO EMERSON, *Lectures and Biographical Sketches* [1883], *The Preacher*

[2] Thomas Sheridan [1719–1788], actor, lecturer, and author.

[3] Sir John Hawkins [1719–1789], author.

[4] Of Lord Mansfield, educated in England.

[5] Of Oliver Goldsmith's apology in the *London Chronicle* for beating Evans the bookseller.

[6] Upon being asked by Lord Elphinstone if he had read a new book through.

[7] Of Lady Diana Beauclerk, divorced.

1   Attack is the reaction; I never think I have hit hard unless it rebounds.

From BOSWELL, *Life of Johnson, April 2, 1775*

2   Most vices may be committed very genteelly: a man may debauch his friend's wife genteelly: he may cheat at cards genteelly.

From BOSWELL, *Life of Johnson, April 6, 1775*

3   A man will turn over half a library to make one book.

From BOSWELL, *Life of Johnson, April 6, 1775*

4   Patriotism is the last refuge of a scoundrel.

From BOSWELL, *Life of Johnson, April 7, 1775*

5   Knowledge is of two kinds. We know a subject ourselves, or we know where we can find information upon it.

From BOSWELL, *Life of Johnson, April 18, 1775*

6   In lapidary inscriptions a man is not upon oath.

From BOSWELL, *Life of Johnson, 1775*

7   There is nothing which has yet been contrived by man by which so much happiness is produced as by a good tavern or inn.[1]

From BOSWELL, *Life of Johnson, March 21, 1776*

8   No man but a blockhead ever wrote except for money.

From BOSWELL, *Life of Johnson, April 5, 1776*

9   Life is a progress from want to want, not from enjoyment to enjoyment.

From BOSWELL, *Life of Johnson, May 1776*

10   Sir, you have but two topics, yourself and me. I am sick of both.

From BOSWELL, *Life of Johnson, May 1776*

11   Life admits not of delays; when pleasure can be had, it is fit to catch it. Every hour takes away part of the things that please us, and perhaps part of our disposition to be pleased.

From BOSWELL, *Life of Johnson, September 1, 1777*

12   Depend upon it, sir, when a man knows he is to be hanged in a fortnight, it concentrates his mind wonderfully.

From BOSWELL, *Life of Johnson, September 19, 1777*

13   When a man is tired of London, he is tired of life; for there is in London all that life can afford.

From BOSWELL, *Life of Johnson, September 20, 1777*

14   It is a man's own fault, it is from want of use, if his mind grows torpid in old age.

From BOSWELL, *Life of Johnson, April 9, 1778*

15   Johnson had said that he could repeat a complete chapter of *The Natural History of Iceland,* from the Danish of Horrebow, the whole of which was exactly thus: "Ch. LXXII. *Concerning snakes.* There are no snakes to be met with throughout the whole island."[2]

From BOSWELL, *Life of Johnson, April 13, 1778*

16   Every state of society is as luxurious as it can be. Men always take the best they can get.

From BOSWELL, *Life of Johnson, April 14, 1778*

17   A country governed by a despot is an inverted cone.

From BOSWELL, *Life of Johnson, April 14, 1778*

18   I am willing to love all mankind, except an American.

From BOSWELL, *Life of Johnson, April 15, 1778*

19   As the Spanish proverb says, "He, who would bring home the wealth of the Indies, must carry the wealth of the Indies with him." So it is in traveling, a man must carry knowledge with him if he would bring home knowledge.

From BOSWELL, *Life of Johnson, April 17, 1778*

20   It is better to live rich, than to die rich.

From BOSWELL, *Life of Johnson, April 17, 1778*

21   Were it not for imagination, sir, a man would be as happy in the arms of a chambermaid as of a duchess.

From BOSWELL, *Life of Johnson, May 9, 1778*

22   I would rather be attacked than unnoticed. For the worst thing you can do to an author is to be silent as to his works.

From BOSWELL, *Life of Johnson, March 26, 1779*

23   I remember a passage in Goldsmith's *Vicar of Wakefield,* which he was afterwards fool enough to expunge: "I do not love a man who is zealous for nothing."

From BOSWELL, *Life of Johnson, March 26, 1779*

24   Claret is the liquor for boys; port for men; but he who aspires to be a hero must drink brandy.

From BOSWELL, *Life of Johnson, April 7, 1779*

25   Worth seeing? yes; but not worth going to see.

From BOSWELL, *Life of Johnson, October 12, 1779*

26   If you are idle, be not solitary; if you are solitary, be not idle.

From BOSWELL, *Life of Johnson, October 27, 1779*

---

[1]Following this remark, Johnson quoted (not quite correctly):

Whoe'er has traveled life's dull round, / Whate'er his various tour has been, / May sigh to think how oft he found / His warmest welcome at an inn. — WILLIAM SHENSTONE [1714–1763]; *written on a window of an inn at Henley*

Robert Leighton [1611–1684], archbishop of Glasgow, often said that if he were to choose a place to die in, it should be an inn. — JOHNSON, *Works, vol. I, p. 76*

[2]Chapter XLII is still shorter: "There are no owls of any kind in the whole island."

1   A Frenchman must be always talking, whether he knows anything of the matter or not; an Englishman is content to say nothing, when he has nothing to say.   *From* Boswell, *Life of Johnson, 1780*

2   Greek, sir, is like lace; every man gets as much of it as he can.   *From* Boswell, *Life of Johnson, 1780*

3   [Of Oliver Goldsmith:] No man was more foolish when he had not a pen in his hand, or more wise when he had.   *From* Boswell, *Life of Johnson, 1780*

4   There are people whom one should like very well to drop, but would not wish to be dropped by.
    From Boswell, *Life of Johnson, March 1781*

5   My friend was of opinion that when a man of rank appeared in that character [as an author], he deserved to have his merit handsomely allowed.[1]
    From Boswell, *Life of Johnson, May 1781*

6   A jest breaks no bones.
    From Boswell, *Life of Johnson, June 4, 1781*

7   Officious, innocent, sincere,
Of every friendless name the friend.
    From Boswell, *Life of Johnson, January 20, 1782 (on the death of Robert Levett)*

8   To let friendship die away by negligence and silence, is certainly not wise. It is voluntarily to throw away one of the greatest comforts of this weary pilgrimage.
    From Boswell, *Life of Johnson, March 20, 1782*

9   Whatever you have, spend less.
    From Boswell, *Life of Johnson, December 7, 1782*

10   I never have sought the world; the world was not to seek me.
    From Boswell, *Life of Johnson, March 23, 1783*

11   Clear your mind of cant.
    From Boswell, *Life of Johnson, May 15, 1783*

12   Who drives fat oxen should himself be fat.[2]
    From Boswell, *Life of Johnson, June 1784*

13   I have found you an argument; but I am not obliged to find you an understanding.
    From Boswell, *Life of Johnson, June 1784*

14   Blown about by every wind of criticism.
    From Boswell, *Life of Johnson, June 1784*

15   Don't attitudenize.
    From Boswell, *Life of Johnson, June 1784*

16   I look upon every day to be lost, in which I do not make a new acquaintance.
    From Boswell, *Life of Johnson, November 1784*

17   God bless you, my dear!
    From Boswell, *Life of Johnson, December 13, 1784 (last words)*

Julien Offray de La Mettrie
1709–1751

18   Man is a machine and ... in the whole universe there is but a single substance variously modified.
    L'Homme Machine[3] *[1748], conclusion*

Theodore Tronchin
1709–1781

19   In medicine, sins of commission are mortal, sins of omission venial.
    Quoted in Bulletin of New York Academy of Medicine, V [1929], 151

David Hume
1711–1776

20   Generally speaking, the errors in religion are dangerous; those in philosophy only ridiculous.
    A Treatise of Human Nature [1739], bk. I, pt. iv, sec. vii

21   Reason is, and ought only to be the slave of the passions, and can never pretend to any other office than to serve and obey them.
    A Treatise of Human Nature, II, iii, iii

22   Avarice, the spur of industry.
    Essays [1741–1742]. Of Civil Liberty

23   Beauty in things exists in the mind which contemplates them.   *Essays. Of Tragedy*

24   No testimony is sufficient to establish a miracle, unless the testimony be of such a kind that its falsehood would be more miraculous than the fact which it endeavors to establish.
    An Enquiry Concerning Human Understanding [1748]. Of Miracles

25   The Christian religion not only was at first attended with miracles, but even at this day cannot be believed by any reasonable person without one.
    An Enquiry Concerning Human Understanding. Of Miracles

---

[1]Usually quoted as: When a nobleman writes a book, he ought to be encouraged.
    See William Somerville, 289:*n4.*

[2]Parody on: Who rules o'er freemen should himself be free. —
Henry Brooke [c. 1703–1783], *Gustavus Vasa* [1739]

[3]Translated by M. W. Calkins.

1   Opposing one species of superstition to another, set them a-quarreling; while we ourselves, during their fury and contention, happily make our escape into the calm, though obscure, regions of philosophy.   *The Natural History of Religion [1757]*

2   Never literary attempt was more unfortunate than my Treatise of Human Nature. It fell deadborn from the press.   *My Own Life [1777], ch. 1*

Frederick the Great
1712–1786

3   For every state, from the smallest to the largest, the principle of enlargement is the fundamental law of life.   *History of My Own Time [1743]*

4   Politics consists more in profiting from favorable circumstances than preparing them in advance.   *Political Testament [1752]*

5   By push of bayonets, no firing till you see the whites of their eyes.[1]   *At Prague [May 6, 1757]*

6   Rascals, would you live forever?[2]
*When the Guards hesitated at Kolin
[June 18, 1757]*

7   The prince is the first servant of his state.
Memoirs of the House of Brandenburg [1758]

8   God is always with the strongest battalions.
*Letter to the Duchess Luise Dorothea
von Gotha [May 8, 1760]*

9   I am tired of ruling over slaves.
Last words [April 1, 1786]

Edward Moore
1712–1757

10   This is adding insult to injury.
The Foundling [1748], act V, sc. ii

11   I am rich beyond the dreams of avarice.
The Gamester [1753], act II, sc. ii

Jean-Jacques Rousseau
1712–1778

12   The first man who, having fenced in a piece of land, said, "This is mine," and found people naïve

enough to believe him, that man was the true founder of civil society.
*Discourse upon the Origin and Foundation
of the Inequality Among Mankind [1754]*

13   Never exceed your rights, and they will soon become unlimited.
*Discourse upon the Origin and Foundation
of the Inequality Among Mankind*

14   Money is the seed of money, and the first guinea is sometimes more difficult to acquire than the second million.
*Discourse upon the Origin and Foundation
of the Inequality Among Mankind*

15   Man is born free, and everywhere he is in chains.[3]
The Social Contract [1762], I, ch. 1

16   The strongest is never strong enough to be always the master, unless he transforms his strength into right, and obedience into duty.
The Social Contract, I, 3

17   The right of conquest has no foundation other than the right of the strongest.
The Social Contract, I, 4

18   In the strict sense of the term, a true democracy has never existed, and never will exist.
The Social Contract, III, 4

19   The body politic, like the human body, begins to die from its birth, and bears in itself the causes of its destruction.   *The Social Contract, III, 11*

20   Good laws lead to the making of better ones; bad ones bring about worse.   *The Social Contract, III, 15*

21   Everything is good when it leaves the hands of the Creator; everything degenerates in the hands of man.   *Émile; or, On Education [1762], I*

22   I shall always maintain that whoso says in his heart, "There is no God," while he takes the name of God upon his lips, is either a liar or a madman.
Émile; or, On Education, I

23   People who know little are usually great talkers, while men who know much say little.
Émile; or, On Education, I

24   Nature never deceives us; it is always we who deceive ourselves.   *Émile; or, On Education, III*

25   There exists one book, which, to my taste, furnishes the happiest treatise of natural education. What then is this marvelous book? Is it Aristotle? Is it Pliny, is it Buffon? No — it is *Robinson Crusoe*.[4]
Émile; or, On Education, III

---

[1]See William Prescott, 321:7.

[2]Ihr Racker, wollt ihr ewig leben?
Come on, you sons of bitches! Do you want to live forever? — World War I American battle cry attributed to Marine Sergeant DANIEL DALY [1874–1937] at the battle of Belleau Wood, June 1918.

---

[3]L'homme est né libre, et partout il est dans les fers.
[4]See Daniel Defoe, 282:10.

1   Self-love makes more libertines than love.
Émile; or, On Education, IV

2   Provided a man is not mad, he can be cured of every folly but vanity.
Émile; or, On Education, IV

3   A man says what he knows, a woman says what will please.   *Émile; or, On Education, V*

4   I have entered on an enterprise which is without precedent, and will have no imitator. I propose to show my fellows a man as nature made him, and this man shall be myself.
Confessions [1781–1788], bk. I

5   Remorse sleeps during a prosperous period but wakes up in adversity.   *Confessions, II*

6   It is too difficult to think nobly when one only thinks to get a living.   *Confessions, II*

7   Hatred, as well as love, renders its votaries credulous.   *Confessions, V*

8   At length I recollected the thoughtless saying of a great princess, who, on being informed that the country people had no bread, replied, "Let them eat cake."[1]   *Confessions, VI*

9   The thirst after happiness is never extinguished in the heart of man.   *Confessions, IX*

10   He[2] thinks like a philosopher, but governs like a king.   *Confessions, XII*

Josiah Tucker
1712–1799

11   What is true of a shopkeeper is true of a shop-keeping nation.[3]
Tract Against Going to War for the Sake of Trade [1763]

Denis Diderot
1713–1784

12   My thoughts are my trollops.
Rameau's Nephew[4]

13   If your little savage were left to himself and to his native blindness, he would in time join the infant's reasoning to the grown man's passion — he would strangle his father and sleep with his mother.
Rameau's Nephew

14   I can be expected to look for truth but not to find it.   *Pensées Philosophiques [1746], no. 29*

15   L'esprit de l'escalier [staircase wit].[5]
Paradoxe sur le Comédien

16   From fanaticism to barbarism is only one step.
Essai sur le Mérite de la Vertu

Laurence Sterne
1713–1768

17   Only the brave know how to forgive.... A coward never forgave; it is not in his nature.
Sermons, vol. I [1760], no. 12

18   This sad vicissitude of things.   *Sermons, I, 15*

19   I wish either my father or my mother, or indeed both of them, as they were in duty both equally bound to it, had minded what they were about when they begot me.   *Tristram Shandy, bk. I [1760], ch. 1*

20   "Pray, my dear," quoth my mother, "have you not forgot to wind up the clock?" — "Good G—!" cried my father, making an exclamation, but taking care to moderate his voice at the same time — "Did ever woman, since the creation of the world, interrupt a man with such a silly question?"
Tristram Shandy, I, 1

21   So long as a man rides his hobbyhorse peaceably and quietly along the king's highway, and neither compels you or me to get up behind him — pray, sir, what have either you or I to do with it?
Tristram Shandy, I, 7

22   The very essence of gravity was design, and consequently deceit...it was no better, but often worse, than what a French wit had long ago defined it, — viz., *A mysterious carriage of the body to cover the defects of the mind.*   *Tristram Shandy, I, 11*

23   For every ten jokes, thou hast got an hundred enemies.   *Tristram Shandy, I, 12*

24   He was within a few hours of giving his enemies the slip forever.   *Tristram Shandy, I, 12*

25   Whistled up to London, upon a Tom Fool's errand.   *Tristram Shandy, I, 16*

26   'Tis known by the name of perseverance in a good cause — and of obstinacy in a bad one.
Tristram Shandy, I, 17

---

[1]Qu'ils mangent de la brioche.
This remark is usually attributed to Marie Antoinette after her arrival in France in 1770, but the sixth book of the *Confessions* was written two or three years earlier.

[2]Frederick the Great.

[3]See Adam Smith, 319:7.

[4]Translated by JACQUES BARZUN and RALPH H. BOWEN.

---

[5]The witty retort thought of only after the conversation is finished and one is on one's way downstairs.

1   There was a strange kind of magick bias, which good or bad names, as he called them, irresistibly impressed upon our characters and conduct.... How many Caesars and Pompeys, he would say, by mere inspiration of the names, have been rendered worthy of them?   *Tristram Shandy, I, 19*

2   Persuasion hung upon his lips.
          Tristram Shandy, I, 19

3   Digressions, incontestably, are the sunshine — they are the life, the soul of reading; take them out of this book for instance — you might as well take the book along with them.   *Tristram Shandy, I, 22*

4   The history of a soldier's wound beguiles the pain of it.   *Tristram Shandy, I, 25*

5   Writing, when properly managed (as you may be sure I think mine is), is but a different name for conversation.   *Tristram Shandy, II [1760], ch. 11*

6   Go, poor devil, get thee gone! Why should I hurt thee? This world surely is wide enough to hold both thee and me.
          Tristram Shandy, II, 12 (Uncle Toby to the fly)

7   That's another story,[1] replied my father.
          Tristram Shandy, II, 17

8   Trust that man in nothing who has not a conscience in everything.   *Tristram Shandy, II, 17*

9   It is in the nature of an hypothesis, when once a man has conceived it, that it assimilates every thing to itself, as proper nourishment; and, from the first moment of your begetting it, it generally grows the stronger by every thing you see, hear, read, or understand.   *Tristram Shandy, II, 19*

10   Good — bad — indifferent.
          Tristram Shandy, III [1761–1762], ch. 2

11   "Our armies swore terribly in Flanders," cried my uncle Toby — "but nothing to this."
          Tristram Shandy, III, 11

12   Of all the cants which are canted in this canting world, though the cant of hypocrites may be the worst, the cant of criticism is the most tormenting!
          Tristram Shandy, III, 12

13   'Twould be as much as my life was worth.
          Tristram Shandy, III, 20

14   One of the two horns of my dilemma.
          Tristram Shandy, IV [1761–1762], ch. 26

15   The feather put into his cap of having been abroad.   *Tristram Shandy, IV, 31*

16   Now or never was the time.
          Tristram Shandy, IV, 31

17   There is a Northwest Passage to the intellectual world.   *Tristram Shandy, V [1761–1762], ch. 42*

18   The Accusing Spirit, which flew up to heaven's chancery with the oath, blushed as he gave it in; and the Recording Angel, as he wrote it down, dropped a tear upon the word and blotted it out forever.[2]
          Tristram Shandy, VI [1761–1762], ch. 8

19   A man should know something of his own country, too, before he goes abroad.
          Tristram Shandy, VII [1765], ch. 2

20   Ho! 'tis the time of salads.
          Tristram Shandy, VII, 17

21   L—d! said my mother, what is all this story about? — A Cock and a Bull, said Yorick.
          Tristram Shandy, IX [1767], ch. 33

22   They order, said I, this matter better in France.
          A Sentimental Journey [1768], l. 1

23   I pity the man who can travel from Dan to Beersheba and cry, 'Tis all barren!
          A Sentimental Journey. In the Street, Calais

24   Hail, ye small, sweet courtesies of life! for smooth do ye make the road of it.
          A Sentimental Journey. The Pulse, Paris

25   I think there is a fatality in it — I seldom go to the place I set out for.
          A Sentimental Journey. The Address, Versailles

26   God tempers the wind, said Maria, to the shorn lamb.   *A Sentimental Journey. Maria*

Étienne Bonnot de Condillac [L'Abbé de Condillac]
1715–1780

27   We cannot recollect the ignorance in which we were born.
          Traité des Sensations (Treatise on Sensations) [1754], dedication

Claude Adrien Helvétius
1715–1771

28   Truth is a torch that gleams through the fog without dispelling it.   *De l'Esprit[3] [1758], preface*

---

[1]But that is another story. — RUDYARD KIPLING, *Plain Tales from the Hills. Three and — an Extra*

[2]But sad as angels for the good man's sin, / Weep to record, and blush to give it in. — THOMAS CAMPBELL, *Pleasures of Hope, pt. II, l. 357*

[3]Voltaire, when he read *De l'Esprit*, wrote the author: "Your book is dictated by the soundest reason. You had better get out of France as quickly as you can." The book was condemned by the *parlement* and burned.

1 What makes men happy is liking what they have to do. This is a principle on which society is not founded.

De l'Esprit, preface

2 We don't call a man mad who believes that he eats God, but we do the one who says he is Jesus Christ.

De l'Esprit, preface

3 Remorse is nothing more than a foresight of the bodily pain to which some crime has exposed us.[1]

Treatise on Man [1771], sec. II, ch. 4

Thomas Gray
1716–1771

4 Ye distant spires, ye antique towers,
That crown the wat'ry glade.

On a Distant Prospect of Eton College [1742], st. 1

5 Still as they run they look behind,
They hear a voice in every wind,
And snatch a fearful joy.

On a Distant Prospect of Eton College, st. 4

6 Alas, regardless of their doom,
The little victims play!
No sense have they of ills to come,
Nor care beyond today.

On a Distant Prospect of Eton College, st. 6

7 Grim-visag'd comfortless Despair.

On a Distant Prospect of Eton College, st. 7

8 To each his suff'rings: all are men,
Condemn'd alike to groan,
The tender for another's pain,
Th' unfeeling for his own.
Yet ah! why should they know their fate,
Since sorrow never comes too late,
And happiness too swiftly flies?
Thought would destroy their paradise.
No more; where ignorance is bliss,
'Tis folly to be wise.

On a Distant Prospect of Eton College, st. 10

9 What female heart can gold despise?
What cat's averse to fish?

On the Death of a Favorite Cat [1747], st. 4

10 A fav'rite has no friend!

On the Death of a Favorite Cat, st. 6

11 The curfew tolls the knell of parting day,
The lowing herd wind slowly o'er the lea,

------
[1]Translated by W. HOOPER.

The plowman homeward plods his weary way,
And leaves the world to darkness and to me.

Elegy Written in a Country Churchyard [1750], st. 1

12 Now fades the glimmering landscape on the sight,
And all the air a solemn stillness holds,
Save where the beetle wheels his droning flight,
And drowsy tinklings lull the distant folds.

Elegy Written in a Country Churchyard, st. 2

13 Save that from yonder ivy-mantled tow'r
The moping owl does to the moon complain.

Elegy Written in a Country Churchyard, st. 3

14 Each in his narrow cell forever laid,
The rude forefathers of the hamlet sleep.

Elegy Written in a Country Churchyard, st. 4

15 The breezy call of incense-breathing Morn.

Elegy Written in a Country Churchyard, st. 5

16 For them no more the blazing hearth shall burn,
Or busy housewife ply her evening care.

Elegy Written in a Country Churchyard, st. 6

17 Let not ambition mock their useful toil,
Their homely joys, and destiny obscure;
Nor grandeur hear with a disdainful smile,
The short and simple annals of the poor.

Elegy Written in a Country Churchyard, st. 8

18 The boast of heraldry, the pomp of pow'r,
And all that beauty, all that wealth e'er gave,
Awaits alike the inevitable hour:
The paths of glory lead but to the grave.

Elegy Written in a Country Churchyard, st. 9

19 Where through the long-drawn aisle and fretted vault
The pealing anthem swells the note of praise.

Elegy Written in a Country Churchyard, st. 10

20 Can storied urn, or animated bust
Back to its mansion call the fleeting breath?
Can honor's voice provoke the silent dust,
Or flatt'ry soothe the dull cold ear of death?

Elegy Written in a Country Churchyard, st. 11

21 Hands, that the rod of empire might have sway'd,
Or wak'd to ecstasy the living lyre.

Elegy Written in a Country Churchyard, st. 12

22 But knowledge to their eyes her ample page
Rich with the spoils of time did ne'er unroll;
Chill penury repress'd their noble rage,
And froze the genial current of the soul.

Elegy Written in a Country Churchyard, st. 13

23 Full many a gem of purest ray serene,
The dark unfathom'd caves of ocean bear:
Full many a flower is born to blush unseen,
And waste its sweetness on the desert air.

Elegy Written in a Country Churchyard, st. 14

1 Some village Hampden, that with dauntless breast
The little tyrant of his fields withstood;
Some mute inglorious Milton here may rest,
Some Cromwell guiltless of his country's blood.
Elegy Written in a Country Churchyard, st. 15

2 To scatter plenty o'er a smiling land,
And read their hist'ry in a nation's eyes.
Elegy Written in a Country Churchyard, st. 16

3 Far from the madding crowd's ignoble strife,
Their sober wishes never learn'd to stray;
Along the cool sequester'd vale of life
They kept the noiseless tenor of their way.
Elegy Written in a Country Churchyard, st. 19

4 For who to dumb forgetfulness a prey,
This pleasing anxious being e'er resign'd,
Left the warm precincts of the cheerful day,
Nor cast one longing ling'ring look behind?
Elegy Written in a Country Churchyard, st. 22

5 Mindful of th' unhonor'd dead.
Elegy Written in a Country Churchyard, st. 24

6 Here rests his head upon the lap of Earth
A youth to fortune and to fame unknown.
Fair Science frown'd not on his humble birth,
And Melancholy mark'd him for her own.
Elegy Written in a Country Churchyard. The Epitaph, st. 1

7 Large was his bounty, and his soul sincere,
Heav'n did a recompense as largely send:
He gave to mis'ry all he had, a tear,
He gain'd from Heav'n ('twas all he wish'd) a friend.
Elegy Written in a Country Churchyard. The Epitaph, st. 2

8 No farther seek his merits to disclose,
Or draw his frailties from their dread abode,
(There they alike in trembling hope repose,)
The bosom of his Father and his God.
Elegy Written in a Country Churchyard. The Epitaph, st. 3

9 The meanest floweret of the vale,
The simplest note that swells the gale,
The common sun, the air, the skies,
To him are opening paradise.
Ode on the Pleasure Arising from Vicissitude [1754], l. 49

10 O'er her warm cheek and rising bosom move
The bloom of young Desire and purple light of
Love.   *The Progress of Poesy [1754], I. 3, l. 16*

11 Far from the sun and summer-gale,
In thy green lap was Nature's Darling[1] laid.
The Progress of Poesy, III. 1, l. 1

12 Or ope the sacred source of sympathetic tears.
The Progress of Poesy, III. 1, l. 12

13 He[2] pass'd the flaming bounds of place and time:
The living throne, the sapphire-blaze,
Where angels tremble, while they gaze,
He saw; but blasted with excess of light,
Closed his eyes in endless night.
The Progress of Poesy, III. 2, l. 4

14 Ruin seize thee, ruthless King!
Confusion on thy banners wait,
Though fann'd by Conquest's crimson wing
They mock the air with idle state.
The Bard [1757], sec. I st. 1, l. 1

15 Fair laughs the morn, and soft the zephyr blows,
While proudly riding o'er the azure realm
In gallant trim the gilded vessel goes;
Youth on the prow, and Pleasure at the helm;
Regardless of the sweeping whirlwind's sway,
That, hush'd in grim repose, expects his evening
prey.   *The Bard, II, 2, l. 9*

16 Iron sleet of arrowy shower
Hurtles in the darken'd air.
The Fatal Sisters [1761], l. 3

17 Too poor for a bribe, and too proud to importune,
He had not the method of making a fortune.
On His Own Character [1761]

Yosa Buson
1716–1784

18 This piercing cold I feel:
my dead wife's comb, in our bedroom
under my heel...[3]   *Haiku*

David Garrick
1717–1779

19 Let others hail the rising sun:
I bow to that whose course is run.
An Ode on the Death of Mr. Pelham [1754]

20 Heart of oak are our ships,
Heart of oak are our men:
We always are ready;
Steady, boys, steady;
We'll fight, and we'll conquer again and again.
Heart of Oak [c. 1770]

21 Here lies Nolly Goldsmith, for shortness called Noll,
Who wrote like an angel, but talked like poor Poll.
Impromptu epitaph on Oliver Goldsmith

---

[1]Shakespeare.

[2]Milton.

[3]Translated by HAROLD G. HENDERSON.

Horace Walpole
1717–1797

1   Our supreme governors, the mob.
   Letters. To Sir Horace Mann
   [September 7, 1743]

2   *Serendipity* . . . you will understand it better by the derivation than by the definition. I once read a silly fairy tale, called *The Three Princes of Serendip:* as their highnesses traveled, they were always making discoveries, by accidents and sagacity, of things they were not in quest of. . . . Now do you understand *serendipity?*
   Letters. To Sir Horace Mann
   [January 28, 1754]

3   It is charming to totter into vogue.
   Letters. To G. A. Selwyn
   [December 2, 1765]

4   The next Augustan age will dawn on the other side of the Atlantic. There will, perhaps, be a Thucydides at Boston, a Xenophon at New York, and, in time, a Virgil at Mexico, and a Newton at Peru. At last, some curious traveler from Lima will visit England and give a description of the ruins of St. Paul's, like the editions of Balbec and Palmyra.[1]
   Letters. To Sir Horace Mann
   [November 24, 1774]

5   This world is a comedy to those that think, a tragedy to those that feel.
   Letters. To the Countess of Upper Ossory
   [August 16, 1776]

6   Prognostics do not always prove prophecies — at least the wisest prophets make sure of the event first.
   Letters. To Thomas Walpole
   [February 19, 1785]

Samuel Foote
1720–1777

7   He is not only dull himself, but the cause of dullness in others.
   From James Boswell, *Life of Johnson [1791], 1783*

Dennis O'Kelly
1720–1787

8   It will be Eclipse first, the rest nowhere.
   Prediction at Epsom [May 3, 1769],
   when the great racehorse
   Eclipse was to run his first race.

---

[1]See Thomas Macaulay, 419:17.

John Woolman
1720–1772

9   Though I felt uneasy at the thought of writing an instrument of slavery . . . through weakness I gave way and wrote it; but . . . said before my master and the Friend that I believed slavekeeping to be a practice inconsistent with the Christian religion. This, in some degree, abated my uneasiness; yet . . . I should have been clearer if I had desired to be excused from it, as a thing against my conscience.
   Journal [1774]

William Collins
1721–1759

10 How sleep the brave, who sink to rest,
   By all their country's wishes bless'd!
   Ode Written in the Beginning
   of the Year 1746, st. 1

11 By fairy hands their knell is rung,
   By forms unseen their dirge is sung;
   There Honor comes, a pilgrim gray,
   To bless the turf that wraps their clay,
   And Freedom shall awhile repair,
   To dwell a weeping hermit there!
   Ode Written in the Beginning
   of the Year 1746, st. 2

12 If aught of oaten stop or pastoral song
   May hope, O pensive Eve, to soothe thine ear.
   Ode to Evening [1747], l. 1

13 Now air is hush'd, save where the weak-ey'd bat,
   With short shrill shriek flits by on leathern wing,
   Or where the beetle winds
   His small but sullen horn.
   Ode to Evening, l. 9

14 'Twas sad by fits, by starts 'twas wild.
   The Passions [1747], l. 28

Jeanne Antoinette Poisson, Marquise de Pompadour
1721–1764

15 Après nous le déluge [After us the deluge].[2]
   Reputed reply to Louis XV [November 5,
   1757] after the defeat of the French and
   Austrian armies by Frederick the Great
   in the battle of Rossbach

---

[2]The attribution to Madame de Pompadour is made in *Mémoires de Madame de Hausset* [1824]; others attribute the saying to the king. It is actually an old French proverb.

Tobias Smollett
1721–1771

1   He was formed for the ruin of our sex.
*The Adventures of Roderick Random
[1748], ch. 22*

2   That great Cham of literature, Samuel Johnson.
Letter to John Wilkes [March 16, 1759]

3   8 June. At London. I am pent up in frowsy lodgings, where there is not room enough to swing a cat.
The Expedition of Humphry Clinker [1771], vol. II

Samuel Adams
1722–1803

4   Let us contemplate our forefathers, and posterity, and resolve to maintain the rights bequeathed to us from the former, for the sake of the latter. The necessity of the times, more than ever, calls for our utmost circumspection, deliberation, fortitude and perseverance. Let us remember that "if we suffer tamely a lawless attack upon our liberty, we encourage it, and involve others in our doom." It is a very serious consideration...that millions yet unborn may be the miserable sharers of the event.   *Speech [1771]*

5   What a glorious morning for America![1]
*Upon hearing the gunfire at Lexington,
Massachusetts [April 19, 1775]*

6   Driven from every other corner of the earth, freedom of thought and the right of private judgment in matters of conscience direct their course to this happy country as their last asylum.
Speech, Philadelphia [August 1, 1776]

Christopher Smart
1722–1771

7 Tell them I Am, Jehovah said
To Moses; while earth heard in dread,
And smitten to the heart,
At once above, beneath, around,
All nature, without voice or sound,
Replied, O Lord, Thou art.
A Song to David [1763], st. 40

8 For adoration all the ranks
Of angels yield eternal thanks,
And David in the midst.   *A Song to David, st. 51*

9 Where ask is have, where seek is find,
Where knock is open wide.   *A Song to David, st. 77*

10 And now the matchless deed's achiev'd,
Determin'd, dar'd, and done.
A Song to David, st. 86

11 For I bless God in the libraries of the learned and for all the booksellers in the world.
*Jubilate Agno (Rejoice in the Lamb)
[1758–1763], fragment B1, l. 79*

12 Let James rejoice with the Skuttle-Fish who foils his foe by the effusion of his ink.
Jubilate Agno, fragment B2, l. 125

13 For every word has its marrow in the English tongue for order and for delight.
Jubilate Agno, fragment B2, l. 595

14 For I will consider my Cat Jeoffrey,
For he is the servant of the Living God, duly and daily serving him.   *Jubilate Agno, fragment B2, l. 695*

15 For he counteracts the Devil, who is Death, by brisking about the life.
Jubilate Agno, fragment B2, l. 720

Sir William Blackstone
1723–1780

16   Man was formed for society.
*Commentaries on the Laws of England
[1765–1769], introduction*

17   The king, moreover, is not only incapable of doing wrong, but even of thinking wrong: he can never mean to do an improper thing: in him is no folly or weakness.   *Commentaries, bk. I, ch. 7*

18   The royal navy of England hath ever been its greatest defense and ornament; it is its ancient and natural strength; the floating bulwark of our island.
Commentaries, I, 13

19   Time whereof the memory of man runneth not to the contrary.[2]   *Commentaries, I, 18*

20   That the king can do no wrong is a necessary and fundamental principle of the English constitution.
Commentaries, III, 17

21   It is better that ten guilty persons escape than one innocent suffer.   *Commentaries, IV, 27*

Adam Smith
1723–1790

22   It is not from the benevolence of the butcher, the brewer, or the baker that we expect our dinner, but

---

[1] The phrase was adopted by the town of Lexington as a legend for the town seal.

[2] The favorite phrase of their law is "a custom whereof the memory of man runneth not back to the contrary." — RALPH WALDO EMERSON, *English Traits* [1856]

from their regard to their own interest. We address ourselves, not to their humanity but to their self-love.

> *An Inquiry into the Nature and Causes of the Wealth of Nations [1776], vol. I, bk. I, ch. 2*

1 A monopoly granted either to an individual or to a trading company has the same effect as a secret in trade or manufactures.

> *An Inquiry into the Nature and Causes of the Wealth of Nations, I, I, 7*

2 People of the same trade seldom meet together, even for merriment and diversion, but the conversation ends in a conspiracy against the public, or in some contrivance to raise prices.

> *An Inquiry into the Nature and Causes of the Wealth of Nations, I, I, 10, pt. 2*

3 With the greater part of rich people, the chief enjoyment of riches consists in the parade of riches, which in their eyes is never so complete as when they appear to possess those decisive marks of opulence which nobody can possess but themselves.

> *An Inquiry into the Nature and Causes of the Wealth of Nations, I, I, 11, pt. 2*

4 It is the highest impertinence and presumption, therefore, in kings and ministers to pretend to watch over the economy of private people, and to restrain their expense.... They are themselves always, and without any exception, the greatest spendthrifts in the society.

> *An Inquiry into the Nature and Causes of the Wealth of Nations, I, II, 3*

5 Every individual necessarily labors to render the annual revenue of the society as great as he can. He generally indeed neither intends to promote the public interest, nor knows how much he is promoting it.... He intends only his own gain, and he is in this, as in many other cases, led by an invisible hand to promote an end which was no part of his intention.... By pursuing his own interest he frequently promotes that of the society more effectually than when he really intends to promote it. I have never known much good done by those who affected to trade for the public good.

> *An Inquiry into the Nature and Causes of the Wealth of Nations, I, IV, 2*

6 The statesman who should attempt to direct private people in what manner they ought to employ their capitals would not only load himself with a most unnecessary attention, but assume an authority which could safely be trusted, not only to no single person, but to no council or senate whatever, and which would nowhere be so dangerous as in the hands of a man who had folly and presumption enough to fancy himself fit to exercise it.

> *An Inquiry into the Nature and Causes of the Wealth of Nations, II, IV, 2*

7 To found a great empire for the sole purpose of raising up a people of customers, may at first sight appear a project fit only for a nation of shopkeepers. It is, however, a project altogether unfit for a nation of shopkeepers; but extremely fit for a nation whose government is influenced by shopkeepers.[1]

> *An Inquiry into the Nature and Causes of the Wealth of Nations, II, IV, 7, pt. 3*

8 The discovery of America, and that of a passage to the East Indies by the Cape of Good Hope, are the two greatest and most important events recorded in the history of mankind.

> *An Inquiry into the Nature and Causes of the Wealth of Nations, II, IV, 7, pt. 3*

9 Consumption is the sole end and purpose of all production; and the interest of the producer ought to be attended to only so far as it may be necessary for promoting that of the consumer.

> *An Inquiry into the Nature and Causes of the Wealth of Nations, II, IV, 8*

10 All systems either of preference or of restraint, therefore, being thus completely taken away, the obvious and simple system of natural liberty establishes itself of its own accord. Every man, as long as he does not violate the laws of justice, is left perfectly free to pursue his own interest his own way, and to bring both his industry and capital into competition with those of any other man or order of men.

> *An Inquiry into the Nature and Causes of the Wealth of Nations, II, IV, 9*

Adam Ferguson
1723–1816

11 Every step and every movement of the multitude, even in what are termed enlightened ages, are made with equal blindness to the future; and nations stumble upon establishments, which are indeed the result of human action, but not the execution of any human design.

> *An Essay on the History of Civil Society [1767], pt. III, sec. 2*

---

[1]Let Pitt then boast of his victory to his nation of shopkeepers. — BERTRAND BARÈRE [1755–1841], *Speech* [June 11, 1794]

But it may be said as a rule, that every Englishman in the Duke of Wellington's army paid his way. The remembrance of such a fact surely becomes a nation of shopkeepers. — WILLIAM MAKEPEACE THACKERAY, *Vanity Fair*, vol. I, ch. 28

See Josiah Tucker, 313:11.

Immanuel Kant
1724–1804

1   Out of wood so crooked and perverse as that which man is made of, nothing absolutely straight can ever be wrought.
> *The Idea of a Universal History [1784].*
> *Proposition 6*[1]

2   Two things fill the mind with ever-increasing wonder and awe, the more often and the more intensely the mind of thought is drawn to them: the starry heavens above me and the moral law within me.
> *Critique of Practical Reason [1788]*

3   Morality is not properly the doctrine of how we may make ourselves happy, but how we may make ourselves worthy of happiness.
> *Critique of Practical Reason*

4   There is...only a single categorical imperative and it is this: Act only on that maxim through which you can at the same time will that it should become a universal law.
> *The Metaphysic of Morals*[2] *[1797], ch. 11*

Robert, Lord Clive
1725–1774

5   By God, Mr. Chairman, at this moment I stand astonished at my own moderation!
> *Reply During Parliamentary Inquiry [1773]*

Logan[3]
1725–1780

6   I appeal to any white man to say if he ever entered Logan's cabin hungry and he gave him not meat; if ever he came cold and naked and he clothed him not?
> *Message to Lord Dunmore, governor of*
> *Virginia [November 11, 1774]. From*
> THOMAS JEFFERSON, *Notes on Virginia*
> *[1784–1785]*

George Mason
1725–1792

7   That all men are by nature equally free and independent, and have certain inherent rights, of which, when they enter into a state of society, they cannot by any compact deprive or divest their posterity; namely, the enjoyment of life and liberty, with the means of acquiring and possessing property, and pursuing and obtaining happiness and safety.
> *Virginia Bill of Rights*[4] *[June 12, 1776],*
> *article 1*

8   Government is, or ought to be instituted for the common benefit, protection, and security of the people, nation, or community; of all the various modes and forms of government, that is best which is capable of producing the greatest degree of happiness and safety, and is most effectually secured against the danger of maladministration.   *Virginia Bill of Rights, 3*

9   The freedom of the press is one of the greatest bulwarks of liberty, and can never be restrained but by despotic governments.   *Virginia Bill of Rights, 12*

Giacomo Girolamo Casanova de Seingalt
1725–1798

10   You will laugh when you learn that I thought nothing of deceiving idiots, scoundrels and fools when I needed to do so. As for my deceptions of women, these are not of the sort to be tallied, since when love has a hand in things, each party usually dupes the other.[5]
> *Histoire de Ma Vie (The Story of My Life)*
> *[1791–1798]*

11   Cultivating whatever gave pleasure to my senses was always the chief business of my life; I have never found any occupation more important. Feeling that I was born for the sex opposite to mine, I have always loved it and done all I could to make myself loved by it.[6]   *Histoire de Ma Vie*

12   Whatever St. Augustine may say, human creatures would not perform the work of generation if they did not find pleasure in it, and if there was not in that great work an irresistible attraction for them.[7]
> *Histoire de Ma Vie*

John Newton[8]
1725–1807

13 Amazing grace! How sweet the sound
That saved a wretch like me!

---

[1]Translated by THOMAS DE QUINCEY.

[2]Translated by A. D. LINDSAY.

[3]Tah-gah-jute. Leader of the Mingo Indians.

[4]See Patrick Henry, 332:1. Henry drafted Article 16, on religious freedom.

[5]Translated by STEPHEN SARTARELLI and SOPHIE HAWKES.

[6]Translated by WILLARD TRASK.

[7]Translated by ARTHUR MACHEN et al.

[8]Newton wrote his own epitaph: John Newton, clerk, once an infidel and libertine, a servant of slaves in Africa, was by the rich mercy of our Lord and Savior Jesus Christ preserved, restored, pardoned, and appointed to preach the Faith he had long labored to destroy.

I once was lost, but now am found,
Was blind, but now I see.
Olney Hymns [1779]. Amazing Grace

1 Glorious things of thee are spoken,
Zion, city of our God.   *Olney Hymns. Glorious Things*

2   The real or supposed necessity of treating the
Negroes with rigor gradually brings a numbness upon
the heart and renders those who are engaged in it too
indifferent to the sufferings of their fellow creatures.[1]
Letters and Sermons [1780].
Thoughts upon the African Slave Trade

James Otis[2]
1725–1783

3   An act against the Constitution is void; an act
against natural equity is void.
Argument Against the Writs of
Assistance [1761]

4   Taxation without representation is tyranny.[3]
Attributed [1763]

James Hutton
1726–1797

5   If an organized body is not in the situation and circumstances best adapted to its sustenance and propagation, then, in conceiving an indefinite variety
among the individuals of that species, we must be
assured, that, on the one hand, those which depart
most from the best adapted constitution, will be most
liable to perish, while, on the other hand, those organized bodies, which most approach to the best constitution for the present circumstances, will be best
adapted to continue, in preserving themselves and
multiplying the individuals of their race.
An Investigation into the Principles
of Knowledge [1794]

6   The result, therefore, of this physical inquiry [into
the age of the earth] is, that we find no vestige of a
beginning — no prospect of an end.
The Theory of the Earth [1795]

William Prescott
1726–1795

7   Don't one of you fire until you see the whites of
their eyes.[4]   *At Bunker Hill [June 17, 1775]*

Jane Elliot
1727–1805

8 I've heard them lilting, at the ewe milking,
Lasses a' lilting, before dawn of day;
But now they are moaning, on ilka green loaning;
The flowers of the forest are a' wede away.
The Flowers of the Forest[5]

Anne Robert Jacques Turgot, Baron de l'Aulne
1727–1781

9   They [the Americans] are the hope of this world.
They may become its model.
Letter to Dr. Richard Price
[March 22, 1778]

Oliver Goldsmith[6]
c. 1728–1774

10   One writer excels at a plan or a title page, another
works away the body of the book, and a third is a dab
at an index.   *The Bee [1759], no. 1*

11 Remote, unfriended, melancholy, slow,
Or by the lazy Scheldt, or wandering Po.
The Traveller [1764], l. 1

12 Where'er I roam, whatever realms to see,
My heart untravel'd fondly turns to thee;
Still to my brother turns with ceaseless pain,
And drags at each remove a lengthening chain.
The Traveller, l. 7

13 Such is the patriot's boast, where'er we roam,
His first, best country ever is, at home.
The Traveller, l. 73

---

[1]This is a paraphrase of Newton's original words: Unlimited
power, instigated by revenge, and where the heart, by a long
familiarity with the sufferings of slaves, is become callous and
insensible to the pleadings of humanity, is terrible!

[2][Otis arguing] was a flame of fire…the seeds of patriots and
heroes were then and there sown. — JOHN ADAMS, *Works* [1850–
1856], *vol. II*

[3]This maxim was the guide and watchword of all the friends of
liberty. Otis actually said: No parts of His Majesty's dominions can
be taxed without their consent. — OTIS, *Rights of the Colonies*
[1764], *p. 64*

[4]Also attributed to ISRAEL PUTNAM [1718–1790].
See Frederick the Great, 312:5.

[5]Sir Walter Scott in *Minstrelsy of the Scottish Border* says that *The
Flowers of the Forest* was written to an ancient tune and that the last
line, the refrain, is indisputably ancient. The air was also used for
verses by Alison Cockburn [1713–1794].

[6]Olivarii Goldsmith, Poetae, Physici, Historici, qui nullum fere
scribendi genus non tetigit, Nullum quod tetigit non ornavit [To
Oliver Goldsmith, Poet, Naturalist, Historian, who left scarcely any
style of writing untouched, and touched nothing that he did not
adorn]. — SAMUEL JOHNSON, quoted in JAMES BOSWELL, *Life of
Johnson* [1791], *June 22, 1776*

1 They please, are pleas'd, they give to get esteem,
  Till, seeming blest, they grow to what they seem.[1]
                              The Traveller, l. 265

2 Pride in their port, defiance in their eye,
  I see the lords of humankind[2] pass by.
                              The Traveller, l. 327

3 The land of scholars, and the nurse of arms.[3]
                              The Traveller, l. 356

4 For just experience tells; in every soil,
  That those that think must govern those that toil.
                              The Traveller, l. 371

5 Laws grind the poor, and rich men rule the law.
                              The Traveller, l. 386

6 A book may be very amusing with numerous
  errors, or it may be very dull without a single
  absurdity.
                  The Vicar of Wakefield [1766], preface

7 I . . . chose my wife, as she did her wedding gown,
  not for a fine glossy surface, but such qualities as
  would wear well.   *The Vicar of Wakefield, ch. 1*

8 Handsome is that handsome does.
                        The Vicar of Wakefield, 1

9 I find you want me to furnish you with argument
  and intellects too.   *The Vicar of Wakefield, 7*

10 Man wants but little here below,
  Nor wants that little long.
          The Vicar of Wakefield, 8
          [The Hermit (Edwin and Angelina), st. 8]

11 She was all of a muck of sweat.
                        The Vicar of Wakefield, 9

12 The naked every day he clad
  When he put on his clothes.
          The Vicar of Wakefield, 17 [An Elegy
          on the Death of a Mad Dog, st. 3]

13 And in that town a dog was found,
  As many dogs there be,
  Both mongrel, puppy, whelp, and hound,
  And curs of low degree.
                  The Vicar of Wakefield, 17, st. 4

14 The dog, to gain some private ends,
  Went mad, and bit the man.
                  The Vicar of Wakefield, 17, st. 5

15 The man recover'd of the bite,
  The dog it was that died.
                  The Vicar of Wakefield, 17, st. 8

16 When lovely woman stoops to folly,[4]
  And finds too late that men betray,
  What charm can soothe her melancholy?
  What art can wash her guilt away?
              The Vicar of Wakefield, 24. Song, st. 1

17 The only art her guilt to cover,
  To hide her shame from every eye,
  To give repentance to her lover,
  And wring his bosom, is — to die.
              The Vicar of Wakefield, 24. Song, st. 2

18 This same philosophy is a good horse in the stable,
  but an arrant jade on a journey.
              The Good-Natur'd Man [1768], act I

19 He calls his extravagance, generosity; and his
  trusting everybody, universal benevolence.
                      The Good-Natur'd Man, I

20 Silence gives consent.   *The Good-Natur'd Man, II*

21 Sweet Auburn! loveliest village of the plain.
                      The Deserted Village [1770], l. 1

22 Ill fares the land, to hastening ills a prey,
  Where wealth accumulates, and men decay;
  Princes and lords may flourish, or may fade;
  A breath can make them, as a breath has made;
  But a bold peasantry, their country's pride,
  When once destroy'd, can never be supplied.
                      The Deserted Village, l. 51

23 His best companions, innocence and health;
  And his best riches, ignorance of wealth.
                      The Deserted Village, l. 61

24 How happy he who crowns in shades like these,
  A youth of labor with an age of ease.
                      The Deserted Village, l. 99

25 The watchdog's voice that bay'd the whispering
      wind,
  And the loud laugh that spoke the vacant mind.[5]
                      The Deserted Village, l. 121

26 Truth from his lips prevail'd with double sway,
  And fools, who came to scoff, remain'd to pray.
                      The Deserted Village, l. 179

27 To me more dear, congenial to my heart,
  One native charm, than all the gloss of art.
                      The Deserted Village, l. 253

28 Her modest looks the cottage might adorn,
  Sweet as the primrose peeps beneath the thorn.
                      The Deserted Village, l. 329

---

[1]The character of the French.

[2]The British.

[3]England.

[4]See T. S. Eliot, 676:13.

[5]Frequent and loud laughter is the characteristic of folly and ill manners: it is the manner in which the mob express their silly joy at silly things, and they call it being merry. In my mind there is nothing so illiberal and so ill-bred as audible laughter. — EARL OF CHESTERFIELD, *Letters* [March 9, 1748]

1 In my time, the follies of the town crept slowly among us, but now they travel faster than a stagecoach. *She Stoops to Conquer [1773], act I*

2 I love everything that's old: old friends, old times, old manners, old books, old wines.
She Stoops to Conquer, I

3 The very pink of perfection.
She Stoops to Conquer, I

4 The first blow is half the battle.
She Stoops to Conquer, II

5 They liked the book the better the more it made them cry. *She Stoops to Conquer, II*

6 Ask me no questions, and I'll tell you no fibs.[1]
She Stoops to Conquer, III

7 On the stage he was natural, simple, affecting;
'Twas only that when he was off he was acting.
Retaliation [1774], l. 101

8 There is no arguing with Johnson: for if his pistol misses fire, he knocks you down with the butt end of it.
From JAMES BOSWELL, *Life of Johnson [1791].*
October 26, 1769

9 [To Dr. Johnson:] If you were to make little fishes talk, they would talk like whales.
From BOSWELL, *Life of Johnson, April 27, 1773*

10 You may all go to pot.
Verses in reply to an invitation to dine at
Dr. Baker's

John Stark
1728–1822

11 My men, yonder are the Hessians. They were bought for seven pounds and ten pence a man. Are you worth more? Prove it. Tonight, the American flag floats from yonder hill or Molly Stark sleeps a widow!
Before the battle of Bennington [August 16, 1777]

Edmund Burke[2]
1729–1797

12 We have a degree of delight, and that no small one, in the real misfortunes and pains of others.
A Philosophical Inquiry into the Origin
of Our Ideas of the Sublime and the
Beautiful [1756], pt. I, sec. 14

13 Custom reconciles us to everything.
Of the Sublime and Beautiful,
sec. 18

14 There is, however, a limit at which forbearance ceases to be a virtue.
Observations on a Late Publication
on the Present State of the Nation [1769]

15 The wisdom of our ancestors.[3]
Observations on a Late Publication
on the Present State of the Nation

16 When bad men combine, the good must associate; else they will fall one by one, an unpitied sacrifice in a contemptible struggle.
Thoughts on the Cause of the Present
Discontents [April 23, 1770]

17 Of this stamp is the cant of, Not men, but measures; a sort of charm by which many people get loose from every honorable engagement.
Thoughts on the Cause of the Present Discontents

18 So to be patriots as not to forget we are gentlemen.
Thoughts on the Cause of the Present
Discontents

19 Public life is a situation of power and energy; he trespasses against his duty who sleeps upon his watch, as well as he that goes over to the enemy.
Thoughts on the Cause of the
Present Discontents

20 Reflect how you are to govern a people who think they ought to be free, and think they are not. Your scheme yields no revenue; it yields nothing but discontent, disorder, disobedience; and such is the state of America, that after wading up to your eyes in blood, you could only end just where you begun; that is, to tax where no revenue is to be found, to — my voice fails me; my inclination indeed carries me no farther — all is confusion beyond it.
First Speech on the Conciliation with
America. American Taxation
[April 19, 1774]

21 I have in general no very exalted opinion of the virtue of paper government.
Second Speech on Conciliation with America.
The Thirteen Resolutions [March 22, 1775]

22 Young man, there is America — which at this day serves for little more than to amuse you with stories of savage men and uncouth manners; yet shall, before you taste of death, show itself equal to the whole of

---

[1] Them that asks no questions isn't told a lie. — RUDYARD KIPLING, *A Smuggler's Song* [1906], *st. 6*

[2] You could not stand five minutes with that man [Burke] beneath a shed while it rained, but you must be convinced you had been standing with the greatest man you had ever seen. — SAMUEL JOHNSON, *Johnsonian Miscellanies* [1897], *vol. I, p. 290*

[3] *De Sapienta Veterum (The Wisdom of the Ancients)* — FRANCIS BACON, *title of work* [1609]
The phrase is also in Burke's *Discussion on the Traitorous Correspondence Bill* [1793].

that commerce which now attracts the envy of the world.

Second Speech on Conciliation with America. The Thirteen Resolutions

1 When we speak of the commerce with our colonies, fiction lags after truth; invention is unfruitful, and imagination cold and barren.

Second Speech on Conciliation with America. The Thirteen Resolutions

2 A people who are still, as it were, but in the gristle, and not yet hardened into the bone of manhood.

Second Speech on Conciliation with America. The Thirteen Resolutions

3 Through a wise and salutary neglect [of the colonies], a generous nature has been suffered to take her own way to perfection; when I reflect upon these effects, when I see how profitable they have been to us, I feel all the pride of power sink and all presumption in the wisdom of human contrivances melt and die away within me. My rigor relents. I pardon something to the spirit of liberty.

Second Speech on Conciliation with America. The Thirteen Resolutions

4 The use of force alone is but *temporary*. It may subdue for a moment; but it does not remove the necessity of subduing again: and a nation is not governed, which is perpetually to be conquered.

Second Speech on Conciliation with America. The Thirteen Resolutions

5 Nothing less will content me, than *whole America*.

Second Speech on Conciliation with America. The Thirteen Resolutions

6 Abstract liberty, like other mere abstractions, is not to be found.

Second Speech on Conciliation with America. The Thirteen Resolutions

7 In no country perhaps in the world is law so general a study [as in America].... This study renders men acute, inquisitive, dexterous, prompt in attack, ready in defense, full of resources.... They augur misgovernment at a distance, and snuff the approach of tyranny in every tainted breeze.

Second Speech on Conciliation with America. The Thirteen Resolutions

8 I do not know the method of drawing up an indictment against an whole people.

Second Speech on Conciliation with America. The Thirteen Resolutions

9 The march of the human mind is slow.

Second Speech on Conciliation with America. The Thirteen Resolutions

10 All government — indeed, every human benefit and enjoyment, every virtue and every prudent act — is founded on compromise and barter.

Second Speech on Conciliation with America. The Thirteen Resolutions

11 Slavery they can have anywhere. It is a weed that grows in every soil.

Second Speech on Conciliation with America. The Thirteen Resolutions

12 Deny them [the colonies] this participation of freedom, and you break that sole bond, which originally made, and must still preserve the unity of the empire.

Second Speech on Conciliation with America. The Thirteen Resolutions

13 It is the love of the [British] people; it is their attachment to their government, from the sense of the deep stake they have in such a glorious institution, which gives you both your army and your navy, and infuses into both that liberal obedience, without which your army would be a base rabble, and your navy nothing but rotten timber.

Second Speech on Conciliation with America. The Thirteen Resolutions

14 Magnanimity in politics is not seldom the truest wisdom; and a great empire and little minds go ill together.

Second Speech on Conciliation with America. The Thirteen Resolutions

15 Corrupt influence, which is itself the perennial spring of all prodigality, and of all disorder; which loads us, more than millions of debt; which takes away vigor from our arms, wisdom from our councils, and every shadow of authority and credit from the most venerable parts of our constitution.

Speech on the Economical Reform [1780]

16 He was not merely a chip of the old block, but the old block itself.

On Pitt's first speech [February 26, 1781]

17 A rapacious and licentious soldiery.

Speech on Fox's East India Bill [1783]

18 An event has happened, upon which it is difficult to speak, and impossible to be silent.

Impeachment of Warren Hastings [May 5, 1789]

19 Resolved to die in the last dike of prevarication.

Impeachment of Warren Hastings [May 7, 1789]

20 There is but one law for all, namely, that law which governs all law, the law of our Creator, the law of humanity, justice, equity — the law of nature, and of nations.

Impeachment of Warren Hastings [May 28, 1794]

1   They made and recorded a sort of institute and digest of anarchy, called the Rights of Man.
On the Army Estimates [1790]

2   People will not look forward to posterity who never look backward to their ancestors.
Reflections on the Revolution in France [1790]

3   Government is a contrivance of human wisdom to provide for human wants. Men have a right that these wants should be provided for by this wisdom.
Reflections on the Revolution in France

4   The age of chivalry has gone. That of sophisters, economists, and calculators has succeeded, and the glory of Europe is extinguished forever.
Reflections on the Revolution in France

5   Kings will be tyrants from policy, when subjects are rebels from principle.
Reflections on the Revolution in France

6   Learning will be cast into the mire, and trodden down under the hoofs of a swinish multitude.
Reflections on the Revolution in France

7   Because half a dozen grasshoppers under a fern make the field ring with their importunate chink, whilst thousands of great cattle, reposed beneath the shadow of the British oak, chew the cud and are silent, pray do not imagine that those who make the noise are the only inhabitants of the field; that, of course, they are many in number; or that, after all, they are other than the little shriveled, meager, hopping, though loud and troublesome *insects* of the hour.   *Reflections on the Revolution in France*

8   Superstition is the religion of feeble minds.
Reflections on the Revolution in France

9   Good order is the foundation of all good things.   *Reflections on the Revolution in France*

10   You can never plan the future by the past.
Letter to a member of the National Assembly [1791]

11   Old religious factions are volcanoes burnt out.
Speech on the Petition of the Unitarians [1792]

12   The cold neutrality of an impartial judge.
Preface to Brissot's Address [1794]

13   Mere parsimony is not economy. . . . Expense, and great expense, may be an essential part of true economy.   *Letter to a Noble Lord [1796]*

14   And having looked to Government for bread, on the very first scarcity they will turn and bite the hand that fed them.
Thoughts and Details on Scarcity [1800]

15   The only thing necessary for the triumph of evil is for good men to do nothing.
Attributed[1]

Gotthold Ephraim Lessing
1729–1781

16   No person must have to.
Nathan der Weise [1779], act I, sc. iii

17   People are not always what they seem.
Nathan der Weise, I, vi

18   The true beggar is the true king.
Nathan der Weise, II, end

John Parker
1729–1775

19   Stand your ground. Don't fire unless fired upon, but if they mean to have a war let it begin here!
To his Minute Men at Lexington, Massachusetts [April 19, 1775]

Speckled Snake[2]
c. 1729–1829

20   When the white man had warmed himself before the Indians' fire and filled himself with their hominy, he became very large. With a step he bestrode the mountains, and his feet covered the plains and the valleys. His hand grasped the eastern and the western sea, and his head rested on the moon.
Statement when President Andrew Jackson recommended that the Cherokees, Chickasaws, Choctaws, Creeks, and Seminoles move west beyond the Mississippi [1829]

21   Brothers, I have listened to a great many talks from our great father.[3] But they always began and ended in this: "Get a little further; you are too near me."
Statement when President Andrew Jackson recommended that the Cherokees, Chickasaws, Choctaws, Creeks, and Seminoles move west beyond the Mississippi

---

[1]Vigorous searches have failed to locate this quotation anywhere in Burke's writings. It may be a paraphrase of Burke, 323:16.

[2]A Creek.

[3]President Jackson.

Thomas Osbert Mordaunt
1730–1809

1 One crowded hour of glorious life
Is worth an age without a name.
　Verses Written During the War
　[1756–1763]. From the Bee
　[October 12, 1791]

Josiah Wedgwood
1730–1795

2 Am I not a man and a brother?
　On a medallion[1] *[1787]*

Charles Churchill
1731–1764

3 Genius is of no country.
　The Rosciad [1761], l. 207

4 Apt alliteration's artful aid.
　The Prophecy of Famine [1763], l. 86

5 Though by whim, envy, or resentment led,
They damn those authors whom they never read.
　The Candidate [1764], l. 57

6 　　Be England what she will,
With all her faults she is my country still.[2]
　The Farewell, l. 27

William Cowper
1731–1800

7 Oh! for a closer walk with God.
　Olney Hymns [1779], no. 1,
　Walking with God

8 What peaceful hours I once enjoy'd!
How sweet their memory still!
But they have left an aching void
The world can never fill.
　Olney Hymns, 1, Walking with God

9 God moves in a mysterious way
His wonders to perform;
He plants his footsteps in the sea
And rides upon the storm.
　Olney Hymns, 35, Light Shining out of
　Darkness

10 Behind a frowning providence
He hides a smiling face.
　Olney Hymns, 35, Light Shining out of Darkness

11 How much a dunce that has been sent to roam
Excels a dunce that has been kept at home!
　The Progress of Error [1782], l. 415

12 A fool must now and then be right, by chance.
　Conversation [1782], l. 96

13 His wit invites you by his looks to come,
But when you knock it never is at home.
　Conversation, l. 303

14 Absence of occupation is not rest,
A mind quite vacant is a mind distress'd.
　Retirement [1782], l. 623

15 I praise the Frenchman [La Bruyère], his remark was
　shrewd—
How sweet, how passing sweet, is solitude!
But grant me still a friend in my retreat
Whom I may whisper — solitude is sweet.
　Retirement, l. 739

16 I am monarch of all I survey,
My right there is none to dispute.
　Verses Supposed to Be Written by Alexander
　Selkirk [1782], st. 1

17 O Solitude! where are the charms
That sages have seen in thy face?
　Verses Supposed to Be Written by Alexander
　Selkirk

18 A hat not much the worse for wear.
　History of John Gilpin [1785], st. 46

19 God made the country, and man made the town.
　The Task [1785], bk. I, The Sofa, l. 749

20 Oh for a lodge in some vast wilderness,
Some boundless contiguity of shade,
Where rumor of oppression and deceit,
Of unsuccessful or successful war,
Might never reach me more.
　The Task, II, The Timepiece, l. 1

21 Slaves cannot breathe in England; if their lungs
Receive our air, that moment they are free!
They touch our country, and their shackles fall.
　The Task, II, The Timepiece, l. 40

22 Variety's the very spice of life.
　The Task, II, The Timepiece, l. 606

23 From reveries so airy, from the toil
Of dropping buckets into empty wells,
And growing old in drawing nothing up.
　The Task, III, The Garden, l. 188

24 Who loves a garden loves a greenhouse too.
　The Task, III, The Garden, l. 566

---

[1]Representing a black man in chains, with one knee on the ground and both hands lifted up to heaven. This was adopted as a seal by the Anti-Slavery Society of London.

[2]England, with all thy faults I love thee still, / My country! — WILLIAM COWPER, *The Task, bk. II, The Timepiece, l. 206*

1 Now stir the fire, and close the shutters fast,
  Let fall the curtains, wheel the sofa round,
  And, while the bubbling and loud-hissing urn
  Throws up a steamy column, and the cups,
  That cheer but not inebriate, wait on each,
  So let us welcome peaceful evening in.
        The Task, IV, The Winter Evening, l. 36

2 'Tis pleasant, through the loopholes of retreat,
  To peep at such a world; to see the stir
  Of the great Babel, and not feel the crowd.
        The Task, IV, The Winter Evening, l. 88

3 But war's a game, which, were their subjects wise,
  Kings would not play at.
        The Task, V, The Winter Morning Walk,
        l. 187

4 There is in souls a sympathy with sounds;
  And as the mind is pitch'd the ear is pleas'd
  With melting airs or martial, brisk, or grave:
  Some chord in unison with what we hear
  Is touch'd within us, and the heart replies.
        The Task, VI, Winter Walk at Noon, l. 1

5   Here the heart
  May give a useful lesson to the head,
  And Learning wiser grow without his books.
        The Task, VI, Winter Walk at Noon, l. 85

6 Knowledge is proud that he has learn'd so much;
  Wisdom is humble that he knows no more.
        The Task, VI, Winter Walk at Noon, l. 96

7 An honest man, close-button'd to the chin,
  Broadcloth without, and a warm heart within.
        Epistle to Joseph Hill [1785], l. 62

8 Shine by the side of every path we tread
  With such a luster, he that runs may read.
        Tirocinium [1785], l. 79

9 Toll for the brave —
  The brave! that are no more;
  All sunk beneath the wave,
  Fast by their native shore!
        On the Loss of the Royal George[1] *[1791], st. 1*

10 No voice divine the storm allayed,
    No light propitious shone;
  When, snatched from all effectual aid,
    We perished, each alone:
  But I beneath a rougher sea,
  And whelmed in deeper gulfs than he.
        The Castaway [1799], l. 61

---

[1] The *Royal George* was an English man-of-war of 108 guns, which suddenly heeled over, under the strain caused by the shifting of guns, while being refitted at Spithead, August 29, 1782. The commander, Admiral Kempenfeldt, and eight hundred of the sailors, marines, and visitors on board were drowned.

Erasmus Darwin
1731–1802

11 Soon shall thy arm, unconquer'd steam! afar
  Drag the slow barge, or drive the rapid car;
  Or on wide-waving wings expanded bear
  The flying-chariot through the fields of air.
        The Botanic Garden, pt. I [1789], l. 289

12   Would it be too bold to imagine, that in the great length of time, since the earth began to exist, perhaps millions of ages before the commencement of the history of mankind, would it be too bold to imagine, that all warm-blooded animals have arisen from one living filament which the Great First Cause endued with animality . . . and thus possessing the faculty of continuing to improve by its own inherent activity, and of delivering down those improvements by generation to its posterity, world without end![2]

        Zoonomia [1794]

Charles Lee
1731–1782

13   Beware that your Northern laurels do not change to Southern willows.[3]
        To General Horatio Gates after the surrender
        of Burgoyne at Saratoga [October 17, 1777]

Pierre de Beaumarchais
1732–1799

14   Judging by the virtues expected of a servant, does your Excellency know many masters who would be worthy valets?
        The Barber of Seville [1775], act I, sc. ii

15   I quickly laugh at everything, for fear of having to cry.[4]   *The Barber of Seville, I, ii*

16   You went to some trouble to be born, and that's all.[5]
        The Marriage of Figaro [1784], act V,
        sc. iii

17   If censorship reigns there cannot be sincere flattery, and only small men are afraid of small writings.   *The Marriage of Figaro, V, iii*

---

[2] Here the grandfather of Charles Darwin announces his own early theory of organic evolution.

[3] Gates was later defeated by Cornwallis at Camden, South Carolina [August 16, 1780], and was relieved of his command.

[4] Je me presse de rire de tout, de peur d'être obligé d'en pleurer.

[5] Vous vous êtes donné la peine de naître, et rien de plus.

John Dickinson
1732–1808

1 Then join hand in hand, brave Americans all! By uniting we stand, by dividing we fall.[1]

The Liberty Song [1768]

Richard Henry Lee
1732–1794

2   That these united colonies are, and of right ought to be, free and independent states; that they are absolved from all allegiance to the British crown; and that all political connection between them and the State of Great Britain is, and ought to be, totally dissolved.

Resolution moved at the Continental Congress[2] [June 7, 1776; adopted July 2]

George Washington[3]
1732–1799

3   I can with truth assure you, I heard Bulletts whistle and believe me there was something charming in the sound.

Letter to his brother John [May 31, 1754]

4   Discipline is the soul of an army. It makes small numbers formidable; procures success to the weak, and esteem to all.

Letter of Instructions to the Captains of the Virginia Regiments [July 29, 1759]

5   Let us therefore animate and encourage each other, and show the whole world that a Freeman, contending for liberty on his own ground, is superior to any slavish mercenary on earth.

General Orders, Headquarters, New York [July 2, 1776]

6   The time is now near at hand which must probably determine whether Americans are to be freemen or slaves; whether they are to have any property they can call their own; whether their houses and farms are to be pillaged and destroyed, and themselves consigned to a state of wretchedness from which no human efforts will deliver them. The fate of unborn millions will now depend, under God, on the courage and conduct of this army. Our cruel and unrelenting enemy leaves us only the choice of brave resistance, or the most abject submission. We have, therefore, to resolve to conquer or die.

Address to the Continental Army before the battle of Long Island [August 27, 1776]

7   There is nothing that gives a man consequence, and renders him fit for command, like a support that renders him independent of everybody but the State he serves.

Letter to the president of Congress, Heights of Harlem [September 24, 1776]

8   To place any dependence upon militia, is, assuredly, resting upon a broken staff.

Letter to the president of Congress, Heights of Harlem

9   Without a decisive naval force we can do nothing definitive. And with it, everything honorable and glorious.   *To Lafayette [November 15, 1781]*

10   If men are to be precluded from offering their sentiments on a matter which may involve the most serious and alarming consequences that can invite the consideration of mankind, reason is of no use to us; the freedom of speech may be taken away, and dumb and silent we may be led, like sheep to the slaughter.

Address to officers of the Army [March 15, 1783]

11   The preservation of the sacred fire of liberty, and the destiny of the republican model of government, are justly considered as deeply, perhaps as finally staked, on the experiment entrusted to the hands of the American people.

First Inaugural Address [April 30, 1789]

12   Happily the Government of the United States, which gives to bigotry no sanction, to persecution no assistance, requires only that they who live under its protection should demean themselves as good citizens in giving it on all occasions their effectual support.

Letter to the Jewish congregation of Newport, Rhode Island [1790]

13   To be prepared for war is one of the most effectual means of preserving peace.

First Annual Address [to both houses of Congress, January 8, 1790]

14   The basis of our political systems is the right of the people to make and to alter their constitutions of government.   *Farewell Address [September 17, 1796]*

15   Let me now...warn you in the most solemn manner against the baneful effects of the spirit of party.   *Farewell Address*

---

[1]United we stand, divided we fall. — *A watchword of the American Revolution*

[2]See John Adams, 329:18.

[3]The Father of your Country. — HENRY KNOX [1750–1806], *Letter to Washington* [March 19, 1787]

I can't tell a lie. I did cut it [the cherry tree] with my hatchet. — *Attributed to* WASHINGTON *as a child;* MASON LOCKE WEEMS [1759–1825], *The Life of George Washington* [1800]

1   Observe good faith and justice toward all nations. Cultivate peace and harmony with all.... The Nation which indulges toward another an habitual hatred or an habitual fondness is in some degree a slave. It is a slave to its animosity or to its affection, either of which is sufficient to lead it astray from its duty and its interest.
Farewell Address

2   The great rule of conduct for us in regard to foreign nations is, in extending our commercial relations to have with them as little political connection as possible.
Farewell Address

3   'Tis our true policy to steer clear of permanent alliances, with any portion of the foreign world.
Farewell Address

4   There can be no greater error than to expect or calculate upon real favors from nation to nation.
Farewell Address

5   It is well, I die hard, but I am not afraid to go.
Last words [December 14, 1799]

John Adams[1]
1735–1826

6   Now to what higher object, to what greater character, can any mortal aspire than to be possessed of all this knowledge, well digested and ready at command, to assist the feeble and friendless, to discountenance the haughty and lawless, to procure redress of wrongs, the advancement of right, to assert and maintain liberty and virtue, to discourage and abolish tyranny and vice?
Letter to Jonathan Sewall [October 1759]

7   A pen is certainly an excellent instrument to fix a man's attention and to inflame his ambition.
Diary [November 14, 1760]

8   I always consider the settlement of America with reverence and wonder, as the opening of a grand scene and design in providence, for the illumination of the ignorant and the emancipation of the slavish part of mankind all over the earth.
Notes for "A Dissertation on the Canon and Feudal Law" [1765]

9   Liberty cannot be preserved without a general knowledge among the people, who have a right ... and a desire to know; but besides this, they have a right, an indisputable, unalienable, indefeasible, divine right to that most dreaded and envied kind of knowledge, I mean of the characters and conduct of their rulers.
A Dissertation on the Canon and Feudal Law [1765]

10   Let every sluice of knowledge be opened and set a-flowing.
A Dissertation on the Canon and Feudal Law

11   Facts are stubborn things;[2] and whatever may be our wishes, our inclinations, or the dictates of our passions, they cannot alter the state of facts and evidence.
Argument in Defense of the [British] Soldiers in the Boston Massacre Trials [December 1770]

12   There is danger from all men. The only maxim of a free government ought to be to trust no man living with power to endanger the public liberty.
Notes for an Oration at Braintree, Massachusetts [Spring 1772]

13   This is the most magnificent movement of all! There is a dignity, a majesty, a sublimity, in this last effort of the patriots that I greatly admire. The people should never rise without doing something to be remembered — something notable and striking. This destruction of the tea is so bold, so daring, so firm, intrepid and inflexible, and it must have so important consequences, and so lasting, that I can't but consider it as an epocha in history!
Diary [on the Boston Tea Party, December 17, 1773]

14   A government of laws, and not of men.[3]
"Novanglus" papers, Boston Gazette [1774], no. 7. Incorporated [1780] in the Massachusetts Constitution

15   Metaphysicians and politicians may dispute forever, but they will never find any other moral principle or foundation of rule or obedience, than the consent of governors and governed.
"Novanglus" papers, Boston Gazette, no. 7

16   I agree with you that in politics the middle way is none at all.
Letter to Horatio Gates [March 23, 1776]

17   You bid me burn your letters. But I must forget you first.
Letter to Abigail Adams [April 28, 1776]

18   Yesterday, the greatest question was decided which ever was debated in America, and a greater perhaps never was nor will be decided among men. A

---

[1]He is as disinterested as the being who made him: he is profound in his view; and accurate in his judgment, except where knowledge of the world is necessary to form a judgment. — THOMAS JEFFERSON [January 30, 1787]

[2]Cf. Facts are stupid things. — RONALD REAGAN in a slip of the tongue at the 1988 Republican National Convention.

[3]Adams credits this formulation to JAMES HARRINGTON [1611–1677]. Adams's use of the phrase gave it wide circulation in America.

resolution was passed without one dissenting colony, "that these United Colonies are, and of right ought to be, free and independent States."[1]

Letter to Abigail Adams [July 3, 1776]

1   The second day of July, 1776,[2] will be the most memorable epoch in the history of America. I am apt to believe that it will be celebrated by succeeding generations as the great anniversary festival. It ought to be commemorated as the day of deliverance, by solemn acts of devotion to God Almighty. It ought to be solemnized with pomp and parade, with shows, games, sports, guns, bells, bonfires, and illuminations, from one end of this continent to the other, from this time forward forevermore.

Second Letter to Abigail Adams [July 3, 1776]

2   The happiness of society is the end of government.   *Thoughts on Government [1776]*

3   Fear is the foundation of most governments.

Thoughts on Government

4   The judicial power ought to be distinct from both the legislative and executive, and independent upon both, that so it may be a check upon both, as both should be checks upon that.

Thoughts on Government

5   Virtue is not always amiable.

Diary [February 9, 1779]

6   By my physical constitution I am but an ordinary man.... Yet some great events, some cutting expressions, some mean hypocrisies, have at times thrown this assemblage of sloth, sleep, and littleness into rage like a lion.   *Diary [April 26, 1779]*

7   I must study politics and war that my sons may have liberty to study mathematics and philosophy. My sons ought to study mathematics and philosophy, geography, natural history, naval architecture, navigation, commerce, and agriculture, in order to give their children a right to study painting, poetry, music, architecture, statuary, tapestry, and porcelain.

Letter to Abigail Adams [May 12, 1780]

8   You will never be alone with a poet in your pocket.

Letter to John Quincy Adams [May 14, 1781]

9   Every project has been found to be no better than committing the lamb to the custody of the wolf, except that one which is called a *balance of power*.

Letter to Roger Sherman [July 17, 1789]

10   My country has in its wisdom contrived for me the most insignificant office [the vice-presidency] that ever the invention of man contrived or his imagination conceived; and as I can do neither good nor evil, I must be borne away by others and meet the common fate.

Letter to Abigail Adams [December 19, 1793]

11   Great is the guilt of unnecessary war.

Letter to Abigail Adams [May 19, 1794]

12   I pray Heaven to bestow the best of blessings on this house and all that shall hereafter inhabit it. May none but honest and wise men ever rule under this roof.[3]

Letter to Abigail Adams [November 2, 1800]

13   I had heard my father say that he never knew a piece of land [to] run away or break.

Autobiography [1802–1807]

14   You and I ought not to die before we have explained ourselves to each other.

Letter to Thomas Jefferson [July 15, 1813]

15   Remember, democracy never lasts long. It soon wastes, exhausts, and murders itself. There never was a democracy yet that did not commit suicide.

Letter to John Taylor [April 15, 1814]

16   The fundamental article of my political creed is that despotism, or unlimited sovereignty, or absolute power, is the same in a majority of a popular assembly, an aristocratical council, an oligarchical junto, and a single emperor.

*Letter to Thomas Jefferson
[November 13, 1815]*

17   But what do we mean by the American Revolution? Do we mean the American war? The Revolution was effected before the war commenced. The Revolution was in the minds of the people; a change in their religious sentiments, of their duties and obligations.   *Letter to Hezekiah Niles [February 13, 1818]*

18   Thomas — Jefferson — still surv —[4]

Last words [July 4, 1826]

Isaac Bickerstaffe

c. 1735–c. 1812

19 There was a jolly miller once
Lived on the River Dee;
He worked and sang from morn till night

---

[1]See Richard Henry Lee, 328:2.

[2]On July 2, 1776, the resolution for independence, drafted by Richard Henry Lee of Virginia, was adopted by a committee including John Adams. On July 4 the Declaration of Independence was agreed to, engrossed, signed by John Hancock, and sent to the legislatures of the States.

[3]Written the day after Adams moved into the new Presidential Mansion. President Franklin D. Roosevelt had it inscribed on the mantelpiece of the State Dining Room.

[4]Jefferson at Monticello died the same day — the fiftieth anniversary of the adoption of the Declaration of Independence.

No lark more blithe than he.
Love in a Village [1762], act I, sc. ii

1 And this the burthen of his song
Forever used to be,
"I care for nobody, not I,
If no one cares for me."[1]
Love in a Village, I, ii

Michel Guillaume Jean de Crèvecoeur [J. Hector St. John]
1735–1813

2   What then is the American, this new man? He is either an European, or the descendant of an European, hence that strange mixture of blood, which you will find in no other country.... Here individuals of all nations are melted into a new race of men, whose labors and posterity will one day cause great changes in the world.
Letters from an American Farmer [1782], no. III

3   Men are like plants; the goodness and flavor of the fruit proceeds from the peculiar soil and exposition in which they grow.
Letters from an American Farmer, III

4   There is room for every body in America; has he any particular talent or industry? He exerts it in order to procure a livelihood, and it succeeds.
Letters from an American Farmer, III

Charles Joseph, Prince de Ligne
1735–1814

5   The Congress doesn't run — it waltzes.[2]
Comment to Comte Auguste de La Garde–Chambonas [1814]

Paul Revere
1735–1818

6   To the memory of the glorious Ninety-two: members of the Honorable House of Representatives of the Massachusetts Bay who, undaunted by the insolent menaces of villains in power, from a strict regard to conscience and the liberties of their constituents on the 30th of June 1768 voted NOT TO RESCIND.
Inscription on Revere's silver "Liberty" bowl [1768]

7   If the British went out by water, to show two lanterns in the North Church steeple; and if by land, one as a signal, for we were apprehensive it would be difficult to cross the Charles River or get over Boston Neck.[3]
Signal code arranged with Colonel Conant of the Charlestown Committee of Safety [April 16, 1775]. Letter to Dr. Jeremy Belknap

Patrick Henry
1736–1799

8   Caesar had his Brutus; Charles the First his Cromwell; and George the Third ["Treason!" cried the Speaker] — *may profit by their example.* If *this* be treason, make the most of it.
Speech on the Stamp Act, House of Burgesses, Williamsburg, Virginia [May 29, 1765]

9   I am not a Virginian, but an American.
Speech in the First Continental Congress, Philadelphia [October 14, 1774]

10   It is natural for man to indulge in the illusions of hope. We are apt to shut our eyes against a painful truth, and listen to the song of that siren till she transforms us into beasts. Is this the part of wise men, engaged in a great and arduous struggle for liberty? Are we disposed to be the number of those who, having eyes, see not, and having ears, hear not, the things which so nearly concern their temporal salvation? For my part, whatever anguish of spirit it may cost, I am willing to know the whole truth; to know the worst, and to provide for it.
Speech in Virginia Convention, Richmond [March 23, 1775]

11   I have but one lamp by which my feet are guided, and that is the lamp of experience. I know no way of judging of the future but by the past.
Speech in Virginia Convention, Richmond

12   We are not weak if we make a proper use of those means which the God of Nature has placed in our power.... The battle, sir, is not to the strong alone; it is to the vigilant, the active, the brave.
Speech in Virginia Convention, Richmond

13   It is vain, sir, to extenuate the matter. The gentlemen may cry, Peace, peace! but there is no peace. The war has actually begun! The next gale that sweeps from the north will bring to our ears the clash of resounding arms! Our brethren are already in the field! Why stand we here idle? What is it that the gentlemen wish? What would they have? Is life so dear or

---

[1]Naebody cares for me, / I care for naebody. — ROBERT BURNS, *I Hae a Wife o' My Ain* [1788], st. 4

[2]Le Congrès ne marche pas, il danse [said of the Congress of Vienna].

[3]See Henry Wadsworth Longfellow, 437:16.

peace so sweet as to be purchased at the price of chains and slavery? Forbid it, Almighty God. I know not what course others may take, but as for me, give me liberty or give me death!

Speech in Virginia Convention, Richmond

1   That religion, or the duty which we owe to our Creator, and the manner of discharging it, can be directed only by reason and conviction, not by force or violence; and therefore all men are equally entitled to the free exercise of religion, according to the dictates of conscience; and that it is the mutual duty of all to practice Christian forbearance, love, and charity towards each other.

Virginia Bill of Rights[1] *[June 12, 1776], article 16*

Edward Gibbon
1737–1794

2   The various modes of worship, which prevailed in the Roman world, were all considered by the people, as equally true; by the philosopher, as equally false; and by the magistrate, as equally useful.

The History of the Decline and Fall of the Roman Empire [1776–1788], ch. 2

3   The principles of a free constitution are irrevocably lost, when the legislative power is nominated by the executive.

The History of the Decline and Fall of the Roman Empire, 3

4   Their united reigns [the Antonines'] are possibly the only period of history in which the happiness of a great people was the sole object of government.[2]

The History of the Decline and Fall of the Roman Empire, 3

5   History . . . is indeed little more than the register of the crimes, follies, and misfortunes of mankind.

The History of the Decline and Fall of the Roman Empire, 3

6   Corruption, the most infallible symptom of constitutional liberty.

The History of the Decline and Fall of the Roman Empire, 21

7   Our sympathy is cold to the relation of distant misery.

The History of the Decline and Fall of the Roman Empire, 49

8   [On the possibility of an Arab victory at Poitiers:] Perhaps the interpretation of the Koran would now be taught in the schools of Oxford, and her pulpits might demonstrate to a circumcised people the sanctity and truth of the revelation of Mahomet.

The History of the Decline and Fall of the Roman Empire, 52

9   The winds and waves are always on the side of the ablest navigators.

The History of the Decline and Fall of the Roman Empire, 68

10   Vicissitudes of fortune, which spares neither man nor the proudest of his works, which buries empires and cities in a common grave.

The History of the Decline and Fall of the Roman Empire, 71

11   All that is human must retrograde if it do not advance.

The History of the Decline and Fall of the Roman Empire, 71

12   The successors of Charles the Fifth may disdain their brethren of England; but the romance of *Tom Jones,* that exquisite picture of human manners, will outlive the palace of the Escurial and the imperial eagle of the house of Austria.

Memoirs (Autobiography) [1796]

13   Decent easy men, who supinely enjoyed the gifts of the founder.   *Memoirs*

14   It was here [at the age of seventeen] that I suspended my religious inquiries.   *Memoirs*

15   I saw and loved.   *Memoirs*

16   I sighed as a lover, I obeyed as a son.   *Memoirs*

17   [Of London:] Crowds without company, and dissipation without pleasure.   *Memoirs*

18   The captain of the Hampshire grenadiers[3] . . . has not been useless to the historian of the Roman Empire.   *Memoirs*

19   It was at Rome, on the fifteenth of October 1764, as I sat musing amidst the ruins of the Capitol, while the barefoot friars were singing vespers in the Temple of Jupiter, that the idea of writing the decline and fall of the city first started to my mind.   *Memoirs*

Thomas Paine
1737–1809

20 From the east to the west blow the trumpet to arms! Through the land let the sound of it flee;

---

[1]See George Mason, 320:*n*4. Mason drafted Articles 1, 3, and 12.

[2]Ah, might we read in America's signs / The Age restored of the Antonines. — HERMAN MELVILLE, *Timoleon* [1891], *The Age of the Antonines, st. 3*

[3]Gibbon was a captain in the Hampshire militia from June 12, 1759, to December 23, 1762.

Let the far and the near all unite, with a cheer,
In defense of our Liberty Tree.
The Liberty Tree [July 1775], st. 4

1 Society in every state is a blessing, but Government, even in its best state, is but a necessary evil; in its worst state, an intolerable one.
Common Sense [January 9–10, 1776]

2 O! ye that love mankind! Ye that dare oppose not only the tyranny but the tyrant, stand forth! Every spot of the Old World is overrun with oppression. Freedom hath been hunted round the globe. Asia and Africa have long expelled her. Europe regards her like a stranger and England hath given her warning to depart. O! receive the fugitive and prepare in time an asylum for mankind.
Common Sense

3 We have it in our power to begin the world over again.
Common Sense

4 When we are planning for posterity, we ought to remember that virtue is not hereditary.
Common Sense

5 He who dares not offend cannot be honest.
The Forester's Letters [1776], no. 3 [April 22]

6 These are the times that try men's souls. The summer soldier and the sunshine patriot will, in this crisis, shrink from the service of their country; but he that stands it *now*, deserves the love and thanks of man and woman. Tyranny, like hell, is not easily conquered; yet we have this consolation with us, that the harder the conflict, the more glorious the triumph. What we obtain too cheap, we esteem too lightly; it is dearness only that gives everything its value. Heaven knows how to put a proper price upon its goods; and it would be strange indeed, if so celestial an article as *Freedom* should not be highly rated.
The American Crisis, no. 1
[December 23, 1776]

7 Panics, in some cases, have their uses; they produce as much good as hurt. Their duration is always short; the mind soon grows through them and acquires a firmer habit than before. But their peculiar advantage is, that they are the touchstones of sincerity and hypocrisy, and bring things and men to light, which might otherwise have lain forever undiscovered.
The American Crisis, 1

8 Not a place upon earth might be so happy as America. Her situation is remote from all the wrangling world, and she has nothing to do but to trade with them.
The American Crisis, 1

9 A bad cause will ever be supported by bad means and bad men.
The American Crisis, 2 [January 13, 1777]

10 Those who expect to reap the blessings of freedom must, like men, undergo the fatigue of supporting it.
The American Crisis, 4 [September 12, 1777]

11 It is not a field of a few acres of ground, but a cause, that we are defending, and whether we defeat the enemy in one battle, or by degrees, the consequences will be the same. *The American Crisis, 4*

12 We fight not to enslave, but to set a country free, and to make room upon the earth for honest men to live in. *The American Crisis, 4*

13 It is the object only of war that makes it honorable. And if there was ever a *just* war since the world began, it is this in which America is now engaged.
The American Crisis, 5 [March 21, 1778]

14 War involves in its progress such a train of unforeseen and unsupposed circumstances...that no human wisdom can calculate the end. It has but one thing certain, and that is to increase taxes.
Prospects on the Rubicon [1787]

15 [Burke] is not affected by the reality of distress touching his heart, but by the showy resemblance of it striking his imagination. He pities the plumage, but forgets the dying bird.
The Rights of Man, pt. I [1791]

16 My country is the world and my religion is to do good. *The Rights of Man, II [1792], ch. 5*

17 A thing moderately good is not so good as it ought to be. Moderation in temper is always a virtue; but moderation in principle is always a vice.[1]
The Rights of Man, II, 5

18 I believe in one God and no more, and I hope for happiness beyond this life. I believe in the equality of man; and I believe that religious duties consist in doing justice, loving mercy, and endeavoring to make our fellow creatures happy.
The Age of Reason [1793], pt. I

19 My own mind is my own church.
The Age of Reason, I

20 It is with a pious fraud as with a bad action; it begets a calamitous necessity of going on.
The Age of Reason, I

21 When authors and critics talk of the sublime, they see not how nearly it borders on the ridiculous.
The Age of Reason, II, note

---

[1]See Barry Goldwater, 758:10.

Ethan Allen
1738–1789

1 [Captain Delaplace[1]] gazed at Allen in bewildered astonishment. "By whose authority do you act?" exclaimed he. "In the name of the great Jehovah, and the Continental Congress!" replied Allen.
From Washington Irving, *Life of Washington [1855–1859], vol. I, ch. 38*

William Bartram
1739–1823

2 [On the alligator:] Behold him rushing forth from the flags and reeds. His enormous body swells. His plaited tail brandished high, floats upon the lake. The waters like a cataract descend from his opening jaws. Clouds of smoke issue from his dilated nostrils. The earth trembles with his thunder.
Travels Through North and South Carolina, Georgia, East and West Florida, the Cherokee Country, Etc. [1791]

James Boswell
1740–1795

3 That favorite subject, Myself.
Letter to Temple [July 26, 1763]

4 I am, I flatter myself, completely a citizen of the world. In my travels through Holland, Germany, Switzerland, Italy, Corsica, France, I never felt myself from home.
Journal of a Tour to the Hebrides [1773]

5 My definition of man is "a cooking animal." The beasts have memory, judgment, and all the faculties and passions of our mind, in a certain degree; but no beast is a cook. . . . Man alone can dress a good dish; and every man whatever is more or less a cook, in seasoning what he himself eats.
Journal of a Tour to the Hebrides

6 He who praises everybody, praises nobody.
Life of Johnson[2] [1791], footnote [March 30, 1778]

7 We cannot tell the precise moment when friendship is formed. As in filling a vessel drop by drop, there is at last a drop which makes it run over; so in a series of kindnesses there is at last one which makes the heart run over.
Life of Johnson [September 1777]

8 I think no innocent species of wit or pleasantry should be suppressed; and that a good pun may be admitted among the smaller excellencies of lively conversation.
Life of Johnson [June 1784]

Louis Sébastien Mercier
1740–1814

9 Extremes Meet.
Tableaux de Paris [1782], vol. IV, ch. 348, title

Donatien Alphonse François, Marquis de Sade
1740–1814

10 Yes, I am a libertine, I admit it freely. I have dreamed of doing everything that it is possible to dream of in that line. But I have certainly not done all the things I have dreamt of and never shall. Libertine I may be, but I am not a criminal, I am not a murderer.
Letter to his wife [1781]

11 Cruelty is simply the energy in a man civilization has not yet altogether corrupted: therefore it is a virtue, not a vice.
Philosophy in the Bedroom[3] [1795]

12 The debility to which Nature condemned woman incontestably proves that her design is for man, who then more than ever enjoys his strength, to exercise it in all the violent forms that suit him best, by means of tortures, if he be so inclined, or worse.
Philosophy in the Bedroom

Augustus Montague Toplady
1740–1778

13 Rock of Ages, cleft for me,
Let me hide myself in thee.
Rock of Ages[4] [1775], st.1

Sébastien Roch Nicolas Chamfort
1741–1794

14 The most wasted day of all is that on which we have not laughed.
Maxims and Thoughts, 1

---

[1]Commandant at Fort Ticonderoga, New York [May 10, 1775].
[2]See also excerpts from Boswell, *Life of Johnson*, 308:12–311:17.

[3]Translated by Richard Seaver and Austryn Wainhouse.
[4]Music by Thomas Hastings [1784–1872].

1   Love as it exists in society is merely the mingling of two fantasies and the contact of two skins.[1]
Maxims and Thoughts, 359

2   Be my brother, or I will kill you.[2]
From THOMAS CARLYLE,
The French Revolution, vol. II, pt. 1, ch. 12

Johann Kaspar Lavater
1741–1801

3   Say not you know another entirely, till you have divided an inheritance with him.
Aphorisms on Man [c. 1788], no. 157

4   The public seldom forgive twice.
Aphorisms on Man, 606

Hester Lynch Thrale Piozzi [Mrs. Thrale]
1741–1821

5   Johnson's conversation was by much too strong for a person accustomed to obsequiousness and flattery; it was *mustard in a young child's mouth!*
From JAMES BOSWELL, *Life of Johnson.*
May 1781

Gebhard Leberecht von Blücher
1742–1819

6   Ever forward, but slowly.
While leading the Russians at Leipzig [October 19, 1813]

7   May the pens of the diplomats not ruin again what the people have attained with such exertions.
After the battle of Waterloo [1815]

Georg Christoph Lichtenberg
1742–1799

8   Nothing contributes more to peace of soul than having no opinion at all.[3]   *Aphorisms*

9   To do just the opposite is also a form of imitation.   *Aphorisms*

10   I am always grieved when a man of real talent dies. The world needs such men more than Heaven does.   *Aphorisms*

11   Soothsayers make a better living in the world than truthsayers.   *Aphorisms*

12   There are people who think that everything one does with a serious face is sensible.   *Aphorisms*

13   I would often rather read what a famous author has cut from one of his works than what he has let stand.   *Aphorisms*

14   I am convinced that a person doesn't only love himself in others; he also hates himself in others.
Aphorisms

15   Every man also has his moral backside which he refrains from showing unless he has to and keeps covered as long as possible with the trousers of decorum.[4]   *Aphorisms*

16   How did you enjoy yourself with these people? Answer: very much, almost as much as I do when alone.[4]   *Aphorisms*

17   Nowadays we already have books about books and descriptions of descriptions.[4]   *Aphorisms*

18   It requires no especially great talent to write in such a way that another will be very hard put to it to understand what you have written.[4]   *Aphorisms*

19   A book is a mirror: if an ape looks into it an apostle is unlikely to look out.[4]   *Aphorisms*

William Henry, Duke of Gloucester
1743–1805

20   Another damned, thick, square book! Always scribble, scribble, scribble! Eh! Mr. Gibbon?
Upon receiving from EDWARD GIBBON
volume II of the History of the Decline and Fall of the Roman Empire [1781].
From Best's Literary Memorials [1829]

Thomas Jefferson
1743–1826

21   A lively and lasting sense of filial duty is more effectually impressed on the mind of a son or daughter by reading *King Lear*, than by all the dry volumes of ethics, and divinity, that ever were written.
Letter to Robert Skipwith [August 3, 1771]

22   The God who gave us life, gave us liberty at the same time.
Summary View of the Rights of British America [1774]

---

[1]L'amour, tel qu'il existe dans la société, est l'échange de deux fantaisies et le contacte de deux épidermes.
Translated by W. S. MERWIN.

[2]Sois mon frère ou je te tue.
A rephrasing of the revolutionary watchword: Fraternity or death.

[3]Translated by FRANZ MAUTNER and HENRY HATFIELD unless otherwise noted.

---

[4]Translated by R. J. HOLLINGDALE.

1   When, in the course of human events, it becomes necessary for one people to dissolve the political bands which have connected them with another, and to assume among the powers of the earth the separate and equal station to which the laws of nature and of nature's God entitle them, a decent respect to the opinions of mankind requires that they should declare the causes which impel them to the separation. We hold these truths to be self-evident; that all men are created equal; that they are endowed by their creator with certain unalienable[1] rights; that among these are life, liberty, and the pursuit of happiness; that to secure these rights, governments are instituted among men, deriving their just powers from the consent of the governed; that whenever any form of government becomes destructive of these ends, it is the right of the people to alter or to abolish it, and to institute new government, laying its foundation on such principles, and organizing its powers in such form, as to them shall seem most likely to effect their safety and happiness.
Declaration of Independence [July 4, 1776]

2   We must therefore...hold them [the British] as we hold the rest of mankind, enemies in war, in peace friends.   *Declaration of Independence*

3   And for the support of this declaration, with a firm reliance on the protection of divine providence, we mutually pledge to each other our lives, our fortunes, and our sacred honor.   *Declaration of Independence*

4   Ignorance is preferable to error; and he is less remote from the truth who believes nothing, than he who believes what is wrong.
Notes on the State of Virginia [1781–1785], query 6

5   The legitimate powers of government extend to such acts only as are injurious to others. But it does me no injury for my neighbor to say there are twenty gods, or no God. It neither picks my pocket nor breaks my leg.   *Notes on the State of Virginia, 17*

6   The Newtonian principle of gravitation is now more firmly established, on the basis of reason, than it would be were the government to step in, and to make it an article of necessary faith. Reason and experiment have been indulged, and error has fled before them.   *Notes on the State of Virginia, 17*

7   Subject opinion to coercion: whom will you make your inquisitors? Fallible men; men governed by bad passions, by private as well as public reasons.
Notes on the State of Virginia, 17

8   Is uniformity [of opinion] attainable? Millions of innocent men, women, and children, since the introduction of Christianity, have been burnt, tortured, fined, imprisoned; yet we have not advanced one inch towards uniformity. What has been the effect of coercion? To make one half the world fools, and the other half hypocrites.   *Notes on the State of Virginia, 17*

9   Indeed, I tremble for my country when I reflect that God is just.   *Notes on the State of Virginia, 18*

10   Those who labor in the earth are the chosen people of God, if ever He had a chosen people, whose breasts He has made His peculiar deposit for substantial and genuine virtue.
Notes on the State of Virginia, 19

11   He who permits himself to tell a lie once, finds it much easier to do it a second and third time, till at length it becomes habitual; he tells lies without attending to it, and truths without the world's believing him. This falsehood of the tongue leads to that of the heart, and in time depraves all its good dispositions.   *Letter to Peter Carr [August 19, 1785]*

12   The basis of our government being the opinion of the people, the very first object should be to keep that right; and were it left to me to decide whether we should have a government without newspapers, or newspapers without a government, I should not hesitate a moment to prefer the latter.
Letter to Colonel Edward Carrington [January 16, 1787]

13   Experience declares that man is the only animal which devours his own kind; for I can apply no milder term to the governments of Europe, and to the general prey of the rich on the poor.
Letter to Colonel Edward Carrington [January 16, 1787]

14   I hold it, that a little rebellion, now and then, is a good thing, and as necessary in the political world as storms in the physical.
Letter to James Madison [January 30, 1787]

15   What country before ever existed a century and a half without a rebellion?...The tree of liberty must be refreshed from time to time with the blood of patriots and tyrants. It is its natural manure.
Letter to William Stevens Smith [November 13, 1787]

16   No society can make a perpetual constitution, or even a perpetual law. The earth belongs always to the living generation.
Letter to James Madison [September 6, 1789]

17   The republican is the only form of government which is not eternally at open or secret war with the rights of mankind.
Letter to William Hunter [March 11, 1790]

---

[1]Frequently quoted as "inalienable."

All men are born free and equal, and have certain natural, essential and unalienable rights. — *Constitution of Massachusetts* [1780]

1   We are not to expect to be translated from despotism to liberty in a featherbed.
Letter to Lafayette [April 2, 1790]

2   Let what will be said or done, preserve your *sang-froid* immovably, and to every obstacle, oppose patience, perseverance, and soothing language.
Letter to William Short [March 18, 1792]

3   Delay is preferable to error.
Letter to George Washington [May 16, 1792]

4   We confide in our strength, without boasting of it; we respect that of others, without fearing it.
*Letter to William Carmichael and
William Short [June 30, 1793]*

5   The second office of the government is honorable and easy, the first is but a splendid misery.
Letter to Elbridge Gerry [May 13, 1797]

6   Offices are as acceptable here as elsewhere, and whenever a man has cast a longing eye on them, a rottenness begins in his conduct.
Letter to Tench Coxe [May 21, 1799]

7   I have sworn upon the altar of God, eternal hostility against every form of tyranny over the mind of man.
*Letter to Dr. Benjamin Rush
[September 23, 1800]*

8   We are all Republicans — we are all Federalists. If there be any among us who would wish to dissolve this Union or to change its republican form, let them stand undisturbed as monuments of the safety with which error of opinion may be tolerated where reason is left free to combat it.
First Inaugural Address [March 4, 1801]

9   But would the honest patriot, in the full tide of successful experiment, abandon a government which has so far kept us free and firm, on the theoretic and visionary fear that this government, the world's best hope, may by possibility want energy to preserve itself?   *First Inaugural Address*

10   Sometimes it is said that man cannot be trusted with the government of himself. Can he, then, be trusted with the government of others? Or have we found angels in the forms of kings to govern him? Let history answer this question.
First Inaugural Address

11   Still one thing more, fellow citizens — a wise and frugal government, which shall restrain men from injuring one another, which shall leave them otherwise free to regulate their own pursuits of industry and improvement, and shall not take from the mouth of labor the bread it has earned. This is the sum of good government, and this is necessary to close the circle of our felicities.   *First Inaugural Address*

12   Equal and exact justice to all men, of whatever state or persuasion, religious or political; peace, commerce, and honest friendship with all nations, entangling alliances with none....Freedom of religion; freedom of the press, and freedom of person under the protection of the *habeas corpus,* and trial by juries impartially selected. These principles form the bright constellation which has gone before us, and guided our steps through an age of revolution and reformation. The wisdom of our sages and the blood of our heroes have been devoted to their attainment. They should be the creed of our political faith, the text of civil instruction, the touchstone by which to try the services of those we trust; and should we wander from them in moments of error or alarm, let us hasten to retrace our steps and to regain the road which alone leads to peace, liberty, and safety.
First Inaugural Address

13   Believing with you that religion is a matter which lies solely between man and his God, that he owes account to none other for his faith or his worship, that the legitimate powers of government reach actions only, and not opinions, I contemplate with sovereign reverence that act of the whole American people which declared that their legislature should "make no law respecting an establishment of religion, or prohibiting the free exercise thereof," thus building a wall of separation between Church and State.
*Letter to the Danbury Baptists
[January 1, 1802]*

14   Whensoever hostile aggressions...require a resort to war, we must meet our duty and convince the world that we are just friends and brave enemies.
Letter to Andrew Jackson [December 3, 1806]

15   The care of human life and happiness, and not their destruction, is the first and only legitimate object of good government.
*To the Republican Citizens of Washington
County, Maryland [March 31, 1809]*

16   While in Europe, I often amused myself with contemplating the characters of the then reigning sovereigns of Europe. Louis XVI was a fool, of my own knowledge, and in despite of the answers made at his trial. The King of Spain was a fool, and of Naples the same. They passed their lives in hunting, and despatched two courtiers a week, one thousand miles, to let each other know what game they had killed the preceding days. The King of Sardinia was a fool. All these were Bourbons. The Queen of Portugal, a Braganza, was an idiot by nature. And so was the King of Denmark. Their sons, as regents, exercised the powers of government. The King of Prussia, successor to the great Frederick, was a mere hog in body as well as in mind. Gustavus of Sweden, and Joseph of

Austria, were really crazy, and George of England you know was in a straight waistcoat.
Letter to Governor John Langdon
[March 4, 1810]

1   Politics, like religion, hold up the torches of martyrdom to the reformers of error.
Letter to James Ogilvie [August 4, 1811]

2   But though an old man, I am but a young gardener.
Letter to Charles Willson Peale [August 20, 1811]

3   The earth belongs to the living, not to the dead.
Letter to John W. Eppes [June 24, 1813]

4   I agree with you that there is a natural aristocracy among men. The grounds of this are virtue and talents.   *Letter to John Adams [October 28, 1813]*

5   Merchants have no country. The mere spot they stand on does not constitute so strong an attachment as that from which they draw their gains.
Letter to Horatio G. Spafford [March 17, 1814]

6   I cannot live without books.
Letter to John Adams [June 10, 1815]

7   If a nation expects to be ignorant and free, in a state of civilization, it expects what never was and never will be.
Letter to Colonel Charles Yancey
[January 6, 1816]

8   Enlighten the people generally, and tyranny and oppressions of body and mind will vanish like evil spirits at the dawn of day.
Letter to Du Pont de Nemours [April 24, 1816]

9   I have the consolation to reflect that during the period of my administration not a drop of the blood of a single fellow citizen was shed by the sword of war or of the law.
Letter to papal nuncio Count Dugnani
[February 14, 1818]

10   But this momentous question [the Missouri Compromise], like a firebell in the night awakened and filled me with terror. I considered it the knell of the Union.   *Letter to John Holmes [April 22, 1820]*

11   [On slavery:] We have the wolf by the ear, and we can neither hold him, nor safely let him go. Justice is in one scale, and self-preservation in the other.
Letter to John Holmes [April 22, 1820]

12   I know no safe depository of the ultimate powers of the society but the people themselves; and if we think them not enlightened enough to exercise their control with a wholesome discretion, the remedy is not to take it from them, but to inform their discretion.
Letter to William Charles Jarvis
[September 28, 1820]

13   We are not afraid to follow truth wherever it may lead, nor to tolerate any error so long as reason is left free to combat it.
Letter to William Roscoe [December 27, 1820]

14   That one hundred and fifty lawyers should do business together ought not to be expected.
Autobiography [January 6, 1821],
on the United States Congress

15   And even should the cloud of barbarism and despotism again obscure the science and liberties of Europe, this country remains to preserve and restore light and liberty to them. In short, the flames kindled on the fourth of July, 1776, have spread over too much of the globe to be extinguished by the feeble engines of despotism; on the contrary, they will consume these engines and all who work them.
Letter to John Adams [September 12, 1821]

16   The generation which commences a revolution can rarely complete it.
Letter to John Adams [September 4, 1823]

17   Men by their constitutions are naturally divided into two parties: (1) Those who fear and distrust the people, and wish to draw all powers from them into the hands of the higher classes. (2) Those who identify themselves with the people, have confidence in them, cherish and consider them as the most honest and safe, although not the most wise depository of the public interests. In every country these two parties exist; and in every one where they are free to think, speak, and write, they will declare themselves.   *Letter to Henry Lee [August 10, 1824]*

18   Never buy what you do not want, because it is cheap; it will be dear to you.
A Decalogue of Canons for Observation in
Practical Life [February 21, 1825]

19   When angry, count ten before you speak; if very angry, an hundred.
A Decalogue of Canons for Observation
in Practical Life

20   The good old Dominion, the blessed mother of us all.   *Thoughts on Lotteries [1826]*

21   This is the Fourth?   *Last words [July 4, 1826]*[1]

Antoine Laurent Lavoisier
1743–1794

22   It is impossible to dissociate language from science or science from language, because every natural science always involves three things: the sequence of phenomena on which the science is based; the

---

[1]John Adams died the same day. See 330:18.

abstract concepts which call these phenomena to mind; and the words in which the concepts are expressed. To call forth a concept a word is needed; to portray a phenomenon, a concept is needed. All three mirror one and the same reality.[1]

Traité Elémentaire de Chimie
(Elementary Treatise on Chemistry) [1789]

1   If, by the term *elements,* we mean to express the simple and indivisible molecules that compose bodies, it is probable that we know nothing about them; but if, on the contrary, we express by the term *elements* or *principles of bodies* the idea of the last point reached by analysis, all substances that we have not yet been able to decompose by any means are elements to us.[2]   *Traité Elémentaire de Chimie*

William Paley
1743–1805

2   Who can refute a sneer?
Moral Philosophy [1785], vol. II, bk. V, ch. 9

The Letters of Junius[3]
1769–1771

3   One precedent creates another. They soon accumulate and constitute law. What yesterday was fact, today is doctrine.   *Dedication to the English Nation*

4   The liberty of the press is the palladium of all the civil, political, and religious rights of an Englishman.   *Dedication to the English Nation*

5   I believe there is yet a spirit of resistance in this country, which will not submit to be oppressed; but I am sure there is a fund of good sense in this country, which cannot be deceived.
No. 16, to the Printer of the Public Advertiser
(H. S. Woodfall) [July 19, 1769]

6   We owe it to our ancestors to preserve entire those rights, which they have delivered to our care: we owe it to our posterity, not to suffer their dearest inheritance to be destroyed.
No. 20, to the Printer of the
Public Advertiser [August 8, 1769]

7   When the constitution is openly invaded, when the first original right of the people, from which all laws derive their authority, is directly attacked,

inferior grievances naturally lose their force, and are suffered to pass by without punishment or observation.
No. 30, to the Printer of the
Public Advertiser [October 17, 1769]

8   There is a moment of difficulty and danger at which flattery and falsehood can no longer deceive, and simplicity itself can no longer be misled.
No. 35, to the Printer of the
Public Advertiser [December 19, 1769]

9   They [the Americans] equally detest the pageantry of a king, and the supercilious hypocrisy of a bishop.
No. 35, to the Printer of the
Public Advertiser [December 19, 1769]

10   The injustice done to an individual is sometimes of service to the public. Facts are apt to alarm us more than the most dangerous principles.
No. 41, to Lord Mansfield
[November 14, 1770]

Constitution of the United States
1787

11   We the people of the United States, in order to form a more perfect Union, establish justice, insure domestic tranquillity, provide for the common defense, promote the general welfare, and secure the blessings of liberty to ourselves and our posterity do ordain and establish this Constitution for the United States of America.

Preamble

12   The President, Vice-President, and all civil officers of the United States, shall be removed from office on impeachment for, and conviction of, treason, bribery, or other high crimes and misdemeanors.

Article II, sec. 4

13   Treason against the United States, shall consist only in levying war against them, or in adhering to their enemies, giving them aid and comfort. No person shall be convicted of treason unless on the testimony of two witnesses to the same overt act, or on confession in open court.

Article III, sec. 3

14   This Constitution, and the laws of the United States, which shall be made in pursuance thereof; and all treaties made, or which shall be made, under the authority of the United States, shall be the Supreme Law of the land; and the judges in every State shall be bound thereby, any thing in the Constitution or laws of any State to the contrary notwithstanding.

Article VI, sec. 2

---

[1]Translated by J. LIPETZ, D. E. GERSHENSON, and D. A. GREENBERG.

[2]Translated by D. McKIE.

[3]Pseudonym of the author of a series of letters [1769–1771] in the London *Public Advertiser* (published in book form, 1772). They have been attributed to, among others, Sir Philip Francis, Lord Shelburne, Lord George Sackville, and Lord Temple.

1   Congress shall make no law respecting an establishment of religion, or prohibiting the free exercise thereof; or abridging the freedom of speech, or of the press; or the right of the people peaceably to assemble, and to petition the government for a redress of grievances.

First Amendment [1791][1]

2   A well-regulated militia, being necessary to the security of a free State, the right of the people to keep and bear arms, shall not be infringed.

Second Amendment [1791]

3   The right of the people to be secure ... against unreasonable searches and seizures, shall not be violated, and no warrants shall issue, but upon probable cause.   *Fourth Amendment [1791]*

4   Nor shall any person be subject for the same offense to be twice put in jeopardy of life or limb; nor shall be compelled in any criminal case to be a witness against himself, nor be deprived of life, liberty, or property, without due process of law.

Fifth Amendment [1791]

5   In all criminal prosecutions, the accused shall enjoy the right to a speedy and public trial, by an impartial jury of the State and district wherein the crime shall have been committed.

Sixth Amendment [1791]

6   The right of trial by jury shall be preserved.

Seventh Amendment [1791]

7   Excessive bail shall not be required, nor excessive fines imposed, nor cruel and unusual punishment inflicted.

Eighth Amendment [1791]

8   All persons born or naturalized in the United States, and subject to the jurisdiction thereof, are citizens of the United States and of the State wherein they reside. No State shall ... abridge the privileges or immunities of citizens of the United States; nor shall any State deprive any person of life, liberty, or property, without due process of law; nor deny to any person within its jurisdiction the equal protection of the laws.

Fourteenth Amendment [1868], sec. 1

9   The right of citizens of the United States to vote shall not be denied or abridged ... on account of race, color, or previous condition of servitude.

Fifteenth Amendment [1870], sec. 1

10   The right of citizens of the United States to vote shall not be denied or abridged ... on account of sex.

Nineteenth Amendment [1920], sec. 1

---

[1]The first ten amendments are known as the Bill of Rights.

Abigail Adams[2]
1744–1818

11   In the new code of laws which I suppose it will be necessary for you to make I desire you would remember the ladies, and be more generous and favorable to them than your ancestors. Do not put such unlimited power into the hands of the husbands. Remember all men would be tyrants if they could. If particular care and attention is not paid to the ladies we are determined to foment a rebellion, and will not hold ourselves bound by any laws in which we have no voice, or representation.

Letter to John Adams [March 31, 1776]

12   Whilst you are proclaiming peace and good will to men, emancipating all nations, you insist upon retaining an absolute power over wives. But you must remember that arbitrary power is like most other things which are very hard, very liable to be broken — and notwithstanding all your wise laws and maxims we have it in our power not only to free ourselves but to subdue our masters, and without violence throw both your natural and legal authority at our feet.

Letter to John Adams [May 7, 1776]

13   Deliver me from your cold phlegmatic preachers, politicians, friends, lovers and husbands.

Letter to John Adams [August 5, 1776]

14   If we mean to have heroes, statesmen and philosophers, we should have learned women. ... If much depends as is allowed upon the early education of youth and the first principles which are instilled take the deepest root, great benefit must arise from literary accomplishments in women.

Letter to John Adams [August 14, 1776]

15   It is really mortifying, sir, when a woman possessed of a common share of understanding considers the difference of education between the male and female sex, even in those families where education is attended to. ... Nay why should your sex wish for such a disparity in those whom they one day intend for companions and associates. Pardon me, sir, if I cannot help sometimes suspecting that this neglect arises in some measure from an ungenerous jealousy of rivals near the throne.

Letter to John Thaxter [February 15, 1778]

16   I regret the trifling narrow contracted education of the females of my own country.

Letter to John Adams [June 30, 1778]

---

[2]Had she lived to the age of the Patriarchs ... every day of her life would have been filled with clouds of goodness and love. — JOHN QUINCY ADAMS, *Memoirs, vol. IV, 157–158, 202*

1   If we do not lay out ourselves in the service of mankind whom should we serve?
Letter to John Thaxter [September 29, 1778]

2   These are times in which a genius would wish to live. It is not in the still calm of life, or in the repose of a pacific station, that great characters are formed. . . . Great necessities call out great virtues.
Letter to John Quincy Adams
[January 19, 1780]

3   A little of what you call frippery is very necessary towards looking like the rest of the world.
Letter to John Adams [May 1, 1780]

4   Learning is not attained by chance, it must be sought for with ardor and attended to with diligence.
Letter to John Quincy Adams
[May 8, 1780]

5   Patriotism in the female sex is the most disinterested of all virtues. Excluded from honors and from offices, we cannot attach ourselves to the State or Government from having held a place of eminence. Even in the freest countries our property is subject to the control and disposal of our partners, to whom the laws have given a sovereign authority. Deprived of a voice in legislation, obliged to submit to those laws which are imposed upon us, is it not sufficient to make us indifferent to the public welfare? Yet all history and every age exhibit instances of patriotic virtue in the female sex; which considering our situation equals the most heroic of yours.
Letter to John Adams [June 17, 1782]

6   You know what is before you. The whips and scorpions, the thorns without roses, the dangers, anxieties, and weight of Empire.
Letter to John Adams [February 20, 1796]

Rowland Hill
1744–1833

7   He did not see any reason why the devil should have all the good tunes.
Sermons. From E. W. BROOME, The Reverend Rowland Hill, p. 93

Jean Baptiste Lamarck
1744–1829

8   FIRST LAW. In every animal . . . a more frequent and continuous use of any organ gradually strengthens, develops and enlarges that organ . . . while the permanent disuse of any organ imperceptibly weakens and deteriorates it, and progressively diminishes its functional capacity, until it finally disappears.

SECOND LAW. All the acquisitions or losses wrought by nature in individuals . . . are preserved by reproduction to the new individuals which arise.
Philosophie Zoologique[1] *[1809],*
pt. II, ch. 7

9   Habits form a second nature.[2]
Philosophie Zoologique, II, 7

Josiah Quincy
1744–1775

10   Blandishments will not fascinate us, nor will threats of a "halter" intimidate. For, under God, we are determined that wheresoever, whensoever, or howsoever we shall be called to make our exit, we will die free men.
Observations on the Boston
Port Bill [1774]

Hannah More
1745–1833

11   Is it not a fundamental error to consider children as innocent beings, whose little weaknesses may perhaps want some correction, rather than as beings who bring into the world a corrupt nature and evil dispositions, which it should be the great end of education to rectify?
Strictures on the Modern System of Female Education [1799]

Francisco José de Goya y Lucientes
1746–1828

12   The world is a masquerade. Face, dress, and voice are all false. All wish to appear as what they are not, all deceive and do not even know themselves.
Text accompanying plate 6 of
Los Caprichos (The Fantasies)[3] *[1799]*

13   The sleep of reason produces monsters.
Los Caprichos. Title of Plate 43[4]

---

[1]Translated by HUGH ELLIOT.

[2]Habit is a second nature and it destroys the first. — BLAISE PASCAL, *Pensées, no. 376*

[3]Translated by PHILIP HOFER.

[4]Translated by HILDA HARRIS.

In plate 43 the artist rests, his head in his arms, on a desk inscribed with the Spanish title of the plate: El sueño de la razón produce monstruos.

This text accompanied the plate: Imagination abandoned by Reason produces impossible monsters: united with her, she is the mother of the arts and the source of their wonders.

John Paul Jones
1747–1792

1   I wish to have no connection with any ship that does not sail *fast;* for I intend to go *in harm's way.*
Letter [November 16, 1778]

2   I have not yet begun to fight.
Attributed. Aboard the Bonhomme Richard
[September 23, 1779]

François Alexandre Frédéric, Duc de La Rochefoucauld–Liancourt
1747–1827

3   *Louis XVI:* Is it a revolt?
La Rochefoucauld–Liancourt: No, Sire, it is a revolution.
Upon learning at Versailles of the fall of the Bastille [1789]

John O'Keeffe
1747–1833

4   You should always except the present company.
The London Hermit; or, Rambles in Dorsetshire [1793]

Jeremy Bentham
1748–1832

5   It is the greatest happiness of the greatest number that is the measure of right and wrong.[1]
A Fragment on Government [1776]

6   A full-grown horse or dog is beyond comparison a more rational, as well as a more conversable animal, than an infant of a day, or a week, or even a month old. But suppose the case were otherwise, what would it avail? The question is not, Can they reason? nor, Can they talk? but, Can they suffer?
Introduction to the Principles of Morals and Legislation [1789]

Emmanuel Joseph Sieyès
1748–1836

7   I survived.[2]
Upon being asked what he had done during the Reign of Terror of the French Revolution

---

[1]See Francis Hutcheson, 298:20.

[2]J'ai vécu.

Charles James Fox
1749–1806

8   [On the fall of the Bastille:] How much the greatest event it is that ever happened in the world! and how much the best!
*Letter to Richard Fitzpatrick [July 30, 1789].
From* LORD JOHN RUSSELL, *Life and Times of C. J. Fox [1859–1866], vol. II, p. 361*

Johann Wolfgang von Goethe
1749–1832

9 There is strong shadow where there is much light.
Götz von Berlichingen [1773], act I

10 One lives but once in the world.
Clavigo [1774], act I, sc. i

11 If you inquire what the people are like here,
I must answer, "The same as everywhere!"
The Sorrows of Young Werther[3]
[1774–1787]. May 17

12 Noble be man,
Helpful and good!
For that alone
Sets him apart
From every other creature
On earth.
The Divine [1783]

13 I sing as the bird sings
That lives in the boughs.[4]
Wilhelm Meister's Apprenticeship [1786–1830], bk. II, ch. 11

14 Who ne'er his bread in sorrow ate,
Who ne'er the mournful midnight hours
Weeping upon his bed has sate,
He knows you not, ye Heavenly Powers.[5]
Wilhelm Meister's Apprenticeship, II, 13

15 Knowst thou the land where the lemon trees bloom,[6]
Where the gold orange glows in the deep thicket's gloom,
Where a wind ever soft from the blue heaven blows,
And the groves are of laurel and myrtle and rose?
Wilhelm Meister's Apprenticeship, III, 1

---

[3]See William Makepeace Thackeray, 459:14.

[4]Ich singe, wie der Vogel singt / Der in den Zweigen wohnet.

[5]Wer nie sein Brod mit Tränen ass, / Wer nie die kummervollen Nächte / Auf seinem Bette weinend sass, / Der kennt euch nicht, ihr himmlischen Mächte.
Translated by HENRY WADSWORTH LONGFELLOW as motto for book I of *Hyperion* [1839].

[6]Kennst du das Land, wo die Zitronen blühn?

1   One ought, every day at least, to hear a little song, read a good poem, see a fine picture, and, if it were possible, to speak a few reasonable words.
Wilhelm Meister's Apprenticeship, V, 1

2   To know of someone here and there whom we accord with, who is living on with us, even in silence — this makes our earthly ball a peopled garden.
Wilhelm Meister's Apprenticeship, VII, 5

3   Art is long, life short; judgment difficult, opportunity transient.
Wilhelm Meister's Apprenticeship, VII, 9

4 Seeking with the soul the land of the Greeks.
Iphigenia in Tauris [1787], act I, sc. i

5 A useless life is an early death.
Iphigenia in Tauris, I, ii

6   Life teaches us to be less harsh with ourselves and with others.   *Iphigenia in Tauris, IV, iv*

7   In art the best is good enough.[1]
Italian Journey. March 3, 1787

8   A talent is formed in stillness, a character in the world's torrent.   *Torquato Tasso, I, ii*

9 The spirits that I summoned up
I now can't rid myself of.
The Sorcerer's Apprentice [1797]

10   Three things are to be looked to in a building: that it stand on the right spot; that it be securely founded; that it be successfully executed.
Elective Affinities[2] [1808], bk. I, ch. 9

11   The sum which two married people owe to one another defies calculation. It is an infinite debt, which can only be discharged through all eternity.
Elective Affinities, I, 9

12   One is never satisfied with a portrait of a person that one knows.   *Elective Affinities, II, 2*

13   The fate of the architect is the strangest of all. How often he expends his whole soul, his whole heart and passion, to produce buildings into which he himself may never enter.   *Elective Affinities, II, 3*

14   Let us live in as small a circle as we will, we are either debtors or creditors before we have had time to look round.   *Elective Affinities, II, 4*

15   No one would talk much in society, if he knew how often he misunderstands others.
Elective Affinities, II, 4

16   A teacher who can arouse a feeling for one single good action, for one single good poem, accomplishes more than he who fills our memory with rows on rows of natural objects, classified with name and form.   *Elective Affinities, II, 7*

17   One never goes so far as when one doesn't know where one is going.
Letter to Karl Friedrich Zelter
[December 3, 1812]

18 Who wants to understand the poem
Must go to the land of poetry;
Who wishes to understand the poet
Must go to the poet's land.
Divan of East and West [1819], motto

19   For I have been a man, and that means to have been a fighter.
Divan of East and West. Book of Paradise

20   Literature is the fragment of fragments; only the least amount of what has happened and has been spoken was written down, the least of what has been recorded in writing has survived.[3]
Wilhelm Meister's Journeyman Years [1821], bk. II, Reflections in the Spirit of the Wanderers

21   We really only learn from books we cannot judge. The author of a book we could really judge ought surely to be learning from us.[3]
Art and Antiquity, vol. 5, no. 3 [1826]

22   One must *be* something to be able to *do* something.
Conversation with Johann Peter Eckermann
[October 20, 1828]

23   If I work incessantly to the last, nature owes me another form of existence when the present one collapses.   *Letter to Eckermann [February 4, 1829]*

24   I call architecture frozen music.[4]
Letter to Eckermann [March 23, 1829]

25   The artist may be well advised to keep his work to himself till it is completed, because no one can readily help him or advise him with it . . . but the scientist is wiser not to withhold a single finding or a single conjecture from publicity.   *Essay on Experimentation*

26 Age does not make us childish, as they say.
It only finds us true children still.
Faust [1808–1832]. The First Part. Prelude on the Stage

27 Man errs as long as he strives.[5]
Faust. The First Part. Prologue in Heaven

---

[1]In der Kunst ist das Beste gut genug.

[2]Translated by JAMES ANTHONY FROUDE.

[3]Translated by ELISABETH STOPP.

[4]Ich die Baukunst eine erstarrte Musik nenne.
Since it [architecture] is music in space, as it were a frozen music. — FRIEDRICH VON SCHELLING [1775–1854], *Philosophie der Kunst* [1802–1803], *p. 576*

[5]Es irrt der Mensch, so lang er strebt.

1 And here, poor fool! with all my lore
I stand! no wiser than before.[1]
Faust. The First Part. Night, Faust in His Study

2 Am I a god? I see so clearly!
Faust. The First Part. Night, Faust in His Study

3 Two souls alas! dwell in my breast.
*Faust. The First Part.
Outside the Gate of the Town*

4 I am the Spirit that always denies![2]
Faust. The First Part. Faust's Study

5 Dear friend, all theory is gray,
And green the golden tree of life.
*Faust. The First Part. Mephistopheles
and the Student*

6 Just trust yourself, then you will know how to live.
*Faust. The First Part. Mephistopheles and the
Student*

7 A true German can't stand the French,
Yet willingly he drinks their wines.
Faust. The First Part. Auerbach's Cellar

8 My peace is gone,
My heart is heavy.[3]
Faust. The First Part. Gretchen's Room

9 Law is mighty, mightier necessity.
Faust. The Second Part, act I, A Spacious Hall

10 Once a man's thirty, he's already old,
He is indeed as good as dead.
It's best to kill him right away.
Faust. The Second Part, II, The Gothic Chamber

11 I love those who yearn for the impossible.
*Faust. The Second Part, II,
Classical Walpurgis Night*

12 The deed is everything, the glory nothing.
*Faust. The Second Part, IV,
A High Mountain Range*

13 Of freedom and of life he only is deserving
Who every day must conquer them anew.[4]
Faust. The Second Part, V, Court of the Palace

14 Who strives always to the utmost,
For him there is salvation.[5]
Faust. The Second Part, V, Mountain Gorges

15 The Eternal Feminine draws us on.[6]
Faust. The Second Part, V, Heaven, last line

16 Do you wish to roam farther and farther?
See! The Good lies so near.
Only learn to seize good fortune,
For good fortune's always here.   *Remembrance*

17 In limitations he first shows himself the master,
And the law can only bring us freedom.
What We Bring [1802]

18 Create, artist! Do not talk!   *Saying*

19 O'er all the hilltops
Is quiet now,
In all the treetops
Hearest thou
Hardly a breath;
The birds are asleep in the trees:
Wait; soon like these
Thou too shalt rest.[7]   *Wanderer's Nightsong*

20 Individuality of expression is the beginning and
end of all art.   *Proverbs in Prose*

21 Nothing is more damaging to a new truth than an
old error.   *Proverbs in Prose*

22 Doubt grows with knowledge.   *Proverbs in Prose*

23 The greatest happiness for the thinking man is to
have fathomed the fathomable, and to quietly revere
the unfathomable.   *Proverbs in Prose*

24 First and last, what is demanded of genius is love
of truth.   *Proverbs in Prose*

25 A man's manners are a mirror in which he shows
his portrait.   *Proverbs in Prose*

26 All intelligent thoughts have already been
thought; what is necessary is only to try to think them
again.[8]   *Proverbs in Prose*

27 Nothing is more terrible than ignorance in
action.[8]   *Proverbs in Prose*

28 Of all peoples the Greeks have dreamt the dream
of life best.[9]   *Proverbs in Prose*

29 Everything that emancipates the spirit without
giving us control over ourselves is harmful.
Proverbs in Prose

30 America, you have it better than our continent,
the old one.[10]   *Almanac for the Muses [1831]*

31 Without haste, but without rest.   *Motto*

---

[1]Da stehe ich nun, ich armer Thor! / Und bin so klug als wie
zuvor.
Translated by BAYARD TAYLOR.

[2]Ich bin der Geist der stets verneint.

[3]Meine Ruh' ist hin, / Mein Herz ist schwer.

[4]Nur der verdient sich Freiheit wie das Leben der täglich sie
erobern muss.

[5]Wer immer strebend sich bemüht, / Den können wir erlösen.

---

[6]Das Ewig-Weibliche zieht uns hinan.

[7]Translated by HENRY WADSWORTH LONGFELLOW.

[8]Translated by NORBERT GUTERMAN.

[9]Translated by BAILEY SAUNDERS.

[10]Amerika, du hast es besser — als unser Kontinent, das alte.

1   More light![1]   *Last words*

2   He who doesn't see his lover's faults as virtues is not in love.[2]   *Posthumous Maxims*

Pierre Simon de Laplace
1749–1827

3   Given for one instant an intelligence which could comprehend all the forces by which nature is animated and the respective positions of the beings which compose it, if moreover this intelligence were vast enough to submit these data to analysis, it would embrace in the same formula both the movements of the largest bodies in the universe and those of the lightest atom; to it nothing would be uncertain, and the future as the past would be present to its eyes.
Oeuvres, vol. VII, Théorie Analytique des Probabilités [1812–1820], introduction

4   The theory of probabilities is at bottom nothing but common sense reduced to calculus.
Oeuvres, VII, Théorie Analytique des Probabilités, introduction

5   Sire, I have no need of that hypothesis.[3]
From Eric Temple Bell,
Men of Mathematics [1937]

Honoré Gabriel Riqueti, Comte de Mirabeau
1749–1791

6   Go and tell those who have sent you that we are here by the will of the nation and that we shall not leave save at the point of bayonets.
Speech in the States-General [June 23, 1789]

John Philpot Curran
1750–1817

7   The condition upon which God hath given liberty to man is eternal vigilance;[4] which condition if he

---

[1]Someday perhaps the inner light will shine forth from us, and then we shall need no other light. — Goethe, *Elective Affinities, pt. II, ch. 3*

[2]Translated by Elisabeth Stopp.

[3]Reply to Napoleon Bonaparte's remark upon receiving a copy of Laplace's *Mécanique Céleste:* You have written this huge book on the system of the world without once mentioning the author of the universe.

[4]Attributed also to Thomas Jefferson.
  Commonly quoted: Eternal vigilance is the price of liberty.
  There is one safeguard known generally to the wise, which is an advantage and security to all, but especially to democracies as against despots. What is it? Distrust. — Demosthenes, *Philippic 2, sec. 24*

break, servitude is at once the consequence of his crime and the punishment of his guilt.
Speech upon the Right of Election of the Lord Mayor of Dublin [July 10, 1790]

James Madison
1751–1836

8   By a faction, understand a number of citizens, whether amounting to a majority or minority of the whole, who are united and actuated by some common impulse of passion, or of interest, adverse to the rights of other citizens, or to the permanent and aggregate interests of the community.
The Federalist [1787], no. 10

9   A zeal for different opinions concerning religion, concerning government, and many other points, as well of speculation as of practice; an attachment of different leaders ambitiously contending for preeminence and power; or to persons of other descriptions whose fortunes have been interesting to the human passions, have, in turn, divided mankind into parties, inflamed them with mutual animosity, and rendered them much more disposed to vex and oppress each other than to cooperate for their common good. . . . But the most common and durable source of factions has been the various and unequal distribution of property.
The Federalist, no. 10

10   To secure the public good, and private rights, against the danger of . . . faction, and at the same time to preserve the spirit and form of popular government, is then the great object to which our inquiries are directed.   *The Federalist, no. 10*

11   The accumulation of all powers, legislative, executive, and judiciary, in the same hands, whether of one, a few, or many, and whether hereditary, self-appointed, or elective, may justly be pronounced the very definition of tyranny.
The Federalist, no. 47

12   If men were angels, no government would be necessary. If angels were to govern men, neither external nor internal controls on government would be necessary. In framing a government which is to be administered by men over men, the great difficulty lies in this: you must first enable the government to control the governed; and in the next place oblige it to control itself.   *The Federalist, no. 51*

13   I believe there are more instances of the abridgment of the freedom of the people by gradual and silent encroachments of those in power than by violent and sudden usurpations.
Speech in the Virginia Convention [June 16, 1788]

1 A popular Government, without popular information, or the means of acquiring it, is but a Prologue to a Farce or a Tragedy; or, perhaps both.
Letter to W. T. Barry [August 4, 1822]

Richard Brinsley Sheridan
1751–1816

2 'Tis safest in matrimony to begin with a little aversion. *The Rivals [1775], act I, sc. ii*

3 Never say more than is necessary.
The Rivals, II, i

4 I know you are laughing in your sleeve.
The Rivals, II, i

5 If I reprehend anything in this world, it is the use of my oracular tongue, and a nice derangement of epitaphs! *The Rivals, III, iii*

6 Too civil by half. *The Rivals, III, iv*

7 Our ancestors are very good kind of folks; but they are the last people I should choose to have a visiting acquaintance with. *The Rivals, IV, i*

8 The quarrel is a very pretty quarrel as it stands; we should only spoil it by trying to explain it.
The Rivals, IV, iii

9 Through all the drama — whether damned or not — Love gilds the scene, and women guide the plot.
The Rivals, epilogue

10 Tale-bearers are as bad as the tale-makers.
The School for Scandal [1777], act I, sc. i

11 Here's to the maiden of bashful fifteen;
Here's to the widow of fifty;
Here's to the flaunting, extravagant quean,
And here's to the housewife that's thrifty.
Let the toast pass —
Drink to the lass;
I'll warrant she'll prove an excuse for the glass.
The School for Scandal, III, iii

12 An unforgiving eye, and a damned disinheriting countenance. *The School for Scandal, IV, i*

13 Be just before you're generous.
The School for Scandal, IV, i

14 There is not a passion so strongly rooted in the human heart as envy. *The Critic [1779], act I, sc. i*

15 Egad, I think the interpreter is the hardest to be understood of the two! *The Critic, I, ii*

16 A practitioner in panegyric, or, to speak more plainly, a professor of the art of puffing.
The Critic, I, ii

17 The number of those who undergo the fatigue of judging for themselves is very small indeed.
The Critic, I, ii

18 Certainly nothing is unnatural that is not physically impossible. *The Critic, II, i*

19 You write with ease to show your breeding,
But easy writing's curst hard reading.
Clio's Protest [1819]

20 The right honorable gentleman is indebted to his memory for his jests, and to his imagination for his facts. *Sheridaniana. Speech in Reply to Mr. Dundas*

Johann Heinrich Voss
1751–1826

21 Who does not love wine, women, and song
Remains a fool his whole life long.[1] *Attributed*

Thomas Chatterton[2]
1752–1770

22 Mie love ys dedde,
Gon to hys death-bedde,
Al under the wyllowe-tree. *Mynstrelles Songe*[3]

Philip Freneau
1752–1832

23 Then rushed to meet the insulting foe;
They took the spear — but left the shield.[4]
*To the Memory of the Brave Americans
Who Fell at Eutaw Springs, S.C., September 8,
1781 [1786], st. 5*

24 O come the time, and haste the day,
When man shall man no longer crush,
When Reason shall enforce her sway,
Nor these fair regions raise our blush,
Where still the African complains,
And mourns his yet unbroken chains.
*On the Emigration to America and Peopling
the Western Country [1786]*

---

[1] Wer nicht liebt Wein, Weib und Gesang, / Der bleibt ein Narr sein Leben lang.

The couplet has also been attributed to Luther, apparently on no better authority than an eighteenth-century jingle in which "Luther" is needed to rhyme with "Futter."

[2] See William Wordsworth, 369:16.

[3] This is from the poems of "Thomas Rowley," an imaginary fifteenth-century Bristol poet invented by Chatterton. Editions of the poems appeared in 1778 and 1782, and were exposed [1777–1778] by Thomas Tyrwhitt.

[4] When Prussia hurried to the field, / And snatched the spear, but left the shield. — WALTER SCOTT, *Marmion, canto III, introduction*

Friedrich Maximilian von Klinger
1752–1831

1   Sturm und Drang [Storm and Stress]
Title of play [1776]

Leonard MacNally
1752–1820

2 On Richmond Hill there lives a lass
More bright than Mayday morn;
Whose charms all other maids' surpass —
A rose without a thorn.
The Lass of Richmond Hill,[1] st. 1

Gouverneur Morris
1752–1816

3   The mob begin to think and to reason. Poor reptiles! it is with them a vernal morning; they are struggling to cast off their winter's slough, they bask in the sunshine, and ere noon they will bite, depend upon it. The gentry begin to fear this.... I see, and I see it with fear and trembling, that if the disputes with *Great Britain* continue, we shall be under the worst of all possible dominions; we shall be under the domination of a riotous mob.
Letter to John Penn [May 20, 1774]

Joseph de Maistre
1753–1821

4   In my lifetime I have seen Frenchmen, Italians, Russians, etc.; thanks to Montesquieu, I even know that *one can be Persian*. But as for *man*, I declare that I have never in my life met him; if he exists, he exists unknown to me.[2]
Considerations on France [1796].
On Divine Influence in Constitutions

5   Every nation has the government it deserves.
Letter to X [1811]

6   The sword of justice has no scabbard.
Les Soirées de Saint-Pétersbourg [1821].
Premier Entretien (First Dialogue)

Antoine de Rivarol
1753–1801

7   What is not clear is not French.
Discours sur l'Universalité de la
Langue Française [1784]

Joel Barlow
1754–1812

8 My morning incense, and my evening meal —
The sweets of Hasty Pudding.
The Hasty Pudding [1792], canto I

George Crabbe
1754–1832

9 In idle wishes fools supinely stay;
Be there a will, and wisdom finds a way.
The Birth of Flattery [1807]

10 Habit with him was all the test of truth,
"It must be right: I've done it from my youth."
The Borough [1810]. Letter 3, The Vicar

11 Wild were his dreams, and oft he rose in fright,
Waked by his view of horrors in the night, —
Horrors that would the sternest minds amaze,
Horrors that demons might be proud to raise:
And though he felt forsaken, grieved at heart,
To think he lived from all mankind apart,
Yet, if a man approached, in terrors he would start.
The Borough. Letter 22,
The Poor of the Borough: Peter Grimes

12 At certain stations he would view the stream,
As if he stood bewildered in a dream,
Or that some power had chained him for a time,
To feel a curse or meditate on crime.
The Borough. Letter 22,
The Poor of the Borough: Peter Grimes

13 With friends and gay companions round them, then
Men boldly speak and have the hearts of men;
Who, with opponents seated, miss the aid
Of kind applauding looks, and grow afraid.
Tales [1810]. The Dumb Orators

William Drennan
1754–1820

14 Nor one feeling of vengeance presume to defile
The cause, or the men, of the Emerald Isle.[3]
Erin [1795], st. 3

Joseph Joubert
1754–1824

15   The soul paints itself in our machines.
Notebooks[4] [1794]

---

[1]Also attributed to JAMES UPTON [1670–1749] and W. HUDSON.
[2]Translated by RICHARD LEBRUN.

[3]The first known use of this term for Ireland.
[4]Translated by PAUL AUSTER.

1 God is the place where I do not remember the rest. *Notebooks [1796]*

2 The style is the thought itself. *Notebooks [1798]*

3 Everything is made through images. They enter us through all the other senses, as through the eye. An echo (they say) is an image of the voice. All our affections are produced by images of touching. Our whole body is a mirror. *Notebooks [1803]*

Jeanne Manon Phlipon Roland de la Platière [Madame Roland]
1754–1793

4 O liberty! O liberty! What crimes are committed in thy name!
Last words, before her death on the guillotine. From ALPHONSE DE LAMARTINE, Histoire des Girondins [1847]

Charles Maurice de Talleyrand-Périgord
1754–1838

5 Black as the devil,
Hot as hell,
Pure as an angel,
Sweet as love.[1] *Recipe for coffee*

6 [Of the Bourbons:] They have learned nothing, and forgotten nothing.[2]
Attributed. From CHEVALIER DE PANAT, letter to Mallet du Pan [January 1796]

7 [Of the battle of Borodino, 1812:] It is the beginning of the end.[3]
From ÉDOUARD FOURNIER [1819–1880], L'Esprit dans l'Histoire [1857]

8 The United States has thirty-two religions but only one dish. *Attributed*

9 Women sometimes forgive a man who forces the opportunity, but never a man who misses one.
Attributed

10 [To a young diplomat:] Don't be eager![4]
From CHARLES AUGUSTIN SAINTE-BEUVE, Portraits de Femmes [1858]. Madame de Staël

11 War is much too serious a matter to be entrusted to the military.[5] *Attributed.*

Bertrand Barère de Vieuzac
1755–1841

12 The tree of liberty only grows when watered by the blood of tyrants.
Speech in the National Convention [January 16, 1793]

13 It is only the dead who do not return.
Speech [1794]

Anthelme Brillat-Savarin
1755–1826

14 Animals feed themselves, men eat; but only wise men know the art of eating.
The Physiology of Taste[6] [1825]. Aphorisms

15 Tell me what you eat, and I shall tell you what you are.
The Physiology of Taste. Aphorisms

16 The discovery of a new dish does more for human happiness than the discovery of a star.
The Physiology of Taste. Aphorisms

17 Alcohol is the prince of liquids, and carries the palate to its highest pitch of exaltation.[7]
The Physiology of Taste. On Drinks

Jean-Pierre Claris de Florian
1755–1794

18 Pleasure of love lasts only a moment, sorrow of love lasts all life long.[8] *Célestine [1784]*

Samuel Hahnemann
1755–1843

19 Similia similibus curantur [Likes are cured by likes].
Organon of the Rational Art of Healing [1810]

---

[1]Noir comme le diable, / Chaud comme l'enfer, / Pur comme un ange, / Doux comme l'amour.
This appears as an inscription on many old coffeepots.

[2]Ils n'ont rien appris, ni rien oublié.

[3]Voilà le commencement de la fin.

[4]Pas de zèle!

---

[5]La guerre! C'est une chose trop grave pour la confier à des militaires. Sometimes quoted as: War is much too serious to leave to the generals.
Quoted by Aristide Briand to David Lloyd George during World War I; also attributed to GEORGES CLEMENCEAU.

[6]Translated by M. F. K. FISHER unless otherwise noted.

[7]Translated by FAYETTE ROBINSON.

[8]Plaisir d'amour ne dure qu'un moment, / Chagrin d'amour dure toute la vie.

Nathan Hale
1755–1776

1 I only regret that I have but one life to lose for my country.

Last words, before being hanged by the British as a spy [September 22, 1776]

Alexander Hamilton
1755–1804

2 A national debt, if it is not excessive, will be to us a national blessing.[1]

Letter to Robert Morris [April 30, 1781]

3 I believe the British government forms the best model the world ever produced.... This government has for its object public strength and individual security.

Debates of the Federal Convention[2] [June 18, 1787]

4 All communities divide themselves into the few and the many. The first are the rich and wellborn, the other the mass of the people.... The people are turbulent and changing; they seldom judge or determine right. Give therefore to the first class a distinct, permanent share in the government. They will check the unsteadiness of the second, and as they cannot receive any advantage by a change, they therefore will ever maintain good government.

Debates of the Federal Convention [June 18, 1787]

5 We are now forming a republican government. Real liberty is neither found in despotism or the extremes of democracy, but in moderate governments.

Debates of the Federal Convention [June 26, 1787]

6 Let Americans disdain to be the instruments of European greatness. Let the thirteen States, bound together in a strict and indissoluble Union, concur in erecting one great American system, superior to the control of all transatlantic force or influence, and able to dictate the terms of the connection between the old and the new world!

The Federalist [1787–1788], no. 11

7 Government implies the power of making laws. It is essential to the idea of a law, that it be attended with a sanction; or, in other words, a penalty or punishment for disobedience. *The Federalist, no. 15*

8 Why has government been instituted at all? Because the passions of men will not conform to the dictates of reason and justice, without constraint.

The Federalist, no. 15

9 In the general course of human nature, a power over a man's subsistence amounts to a power over his will. *The Federalist, no. 79*

10 Every power vested in a government is in its nature sovereign, and includes by force of the term a right to employ all the means requisite...to the attainment of the ends of such power.

Opinion on the Constitutionality of the Bank [February 23, 1791]

11 If the end be clearly comprehended within any of the specified powers, and if the measure have an obvious relation to that end, and is not forbidden by any particular provision of the Constitution, it may safely be deemed to come within the compass of the national authority.

Opinion on the Constitutionality of the Bank

Louis XVIII
1755–1824

12 Punctuality is the politeness of kings.[3]

A favorite saying

John Marshall
1755–1835

13 It is emphatically the province and duty of the judicial department to say what the law is.... If two laws conflict with each other, the courts must decide on the operation of each.... This is of the very essence of judicial duty.

Marbury v. Madison, 1 Cranch 1317 [1803]

14 We must never forget that it is a *constitution* we are expounding.

McCulloch v. Maryland, 4 Wheaton 316, 407 [1819]

15 This provision is made in a constitution, intended to endure for ages to come, and consequently, to be adapted to the various *crises* of human affairs.

McCulloch v. Maryland, 4 Wheaton 316, 415

16 Let the end be legitimate, let it be within the scope of the constitution, and all means which are appropriate, which are plainly adapted to that end, which are not prohibited, but consistent with the letter and spirit of the constitution, are constitutional.

McCulloch v. Maryland, 4 Wheaton 316, 421

---

[1]At the time we were funding our national debt, we heard much about "a public debt being a public blessing." — THOMAS JEFFERSON, *Letter to John W. Epps* [November 6, 1813]

[2]At which the Constitution was written. The convention took place May 14–September 17, 1787.

[3]L'exactitude est la politesse des rois.

1   The power to tax involves the power to destroy.
McCulloch v. Maryland, 4 Wheaton 316, 431

2   The people made the Constitution, and the people can unmake it. It is the creature of their own will, and lives only by their will.
Cohens v. Virginia, 6 Wheaton (19 U.S.) 264, 389 [1821]

3   The Cherokee Nation . . . is a distinct community, occupying its own territory . . . which the citizens of Georgia have no right to enter but with the assent of the Cherokees themselves or in conformity with treaties and with the acts of Congress.[1]
Worcester v. Georgia, 315 U.S. 515 [1832]

Martin Joseph Routh
1755–1854

4   You will find it a very good practice always to verify your references, sir.
From J. W. Burgon [1813–1888], Memoir of Dr. Routh, Quarterly Review [July 1878]

Aaron Burr
1756–1836

5   Law is whatever is boldly asserted and plausibly maintained.
Quoted in James Parton [1822–1891], The Life and Times of Aaron Burr [1864]

Henry [Light-Horse Harry] Lee
1756–1818

6   To the memory of the Man, first in war, first in peace, and first in the hearts of his countrymen.
Eulogy on the death of Washington[2] [December 1799]

William Blake
1757–1827

7   How sweet I roam'd from field to field,
And tasted all the summer's pride,
Till I the prince of love beheld,
Who in the sunny beams did glide!
Poetical Sketches [1783]. Song (How Sweet I Roamed), st. 1

8   He loves to sit and hear me sing,
Then, laughing, sports and plays with me;
Then stretches out my golden wing,
And mocks my loss of liberty.
Poetical Sketches. Song (How Sweet I Roamed), st. 4

9   Like a fiend in a cloud,
With howling woe,
After night I do crowd,
And with night will go.
Poetical Sketches. Mad Song, st. 3

10   Piping down the valleys wild,
Piping songs of pleasant glee,
On a cloud I saw a child,
And he laughing said to me:

"Pipe a song about a Lamb."
So I piped with merry cheer;
"Piper, pipe that song again."
So I piped; he wept to hear.
Songs of Innocence [1789–1790]. Introduction, st. 1, 2

11   And I made a rural pen,
And I stain'd the water clear,
And I wrote my happy songs
Every child may joy to hear.
Songs of Innocence. Introduction, st. 5

12   Little Lamb, who made thee?
Dost thou know who made thee?
Gave thee life and bid thee feed
By the stream and o'er the mead;
Gave thee clothing of delight,
Softest clothing, woolly, bright.
Songs of Innocence. The Lamb, st. 1

13   Little Lamb, I'll tell thee,
Little Lamb, I'll tell thee:
He is called by thy name,
For he calls himself a Lamb.
He is meek and he is mild;
He became a little child.
I a child, and thou a lamb,
We are called by his name.
Little Lamb, God bless thee!
Little Lamb, God bless thee!
Songs of Innocence. The Lamb, st. 2

14   My mother bore me in the southern wild,
And I am black, but O! my soul is white;
White as an angel is the English child,
But I am black as if bereav'd of light.
Songs of Innocence. The Little Black Boy, st. 1

15   And we are put on earth a little space,
That we may learn to bear the beams of love,

---

[1]In response to Marshall's decision, Andrew Jackson remarked, "John Marshall has made his decision: now let him enforce it."

[2]Based on resolutions presented to the House of Representatives a week earlier. In the resolutions, the statement ends with "fellow-citizens."

And these black bodies and this sunburnt face
Is but a cloud, and like a shady grove.
Songs of Innocence. The Little Black Boy, st. 4

1 I'll shade him from the heat till he can bear
To lean in joy upon our Father's knee;
And then I'll stand and stroke his silver hair,
And be like him and he will then love me.
Songs of Innocence. The Little Black Boy, st. 7

2 When my mother died I was very young,
And my father sold me while yet my tongue
Could scarcely cry 'weep! 'weep! 'weep! 'weep!
So your chimneys I sweep, and in soot I sleep.
Songs of Innocence.
The Chimney Sweeper, st. 1

3 To Mercy, Pity, Peace, and Love
All pray in their distress;
And to these virtues of delight
Return their thankfulness.
Songs of Innocence. The Divine Image, st. 1

4 For Mercy has a human heart,
Pity, a human face,
And Love, the human form divine,
And Peace, the human dress.
Songs of Innocence. The Divine Image, st. 3

5 And all must love the human form,
In heathen, turk, or jew;
Where Mercy, Love, & Pity dwell
There God is dwelling too.
Songs of Innocence. The Divine Image, st. 5

6 The moon like a flower
In heaven's high bower,
With silent delight,
Sits and smiles on the night.
Songs of Innocence. Night, st. 1

7 When the voices of children are heard on the green
And laughing is heard on the hill,
My heart is at rest within my breast
And everything else is still.
Songs of Innocence. Nurse's Song, st. 1

8 Can I see another's woe,
And not be in sorrow too?
Can I see another's grief,
And not seek for kind relief?
Songs of Innocence. On Another's Sorrow, st. 1

9 Does the Eagle know what is in the pit?
Or wilt thou go ask the Mole?
Can Wisdom be put in a silver rod?
Or Love in a golden bowl?
The Book of Thel [1789–1792].
Thel's Motto

10 The reason Milton wrote in fetters when he wrote
of Angels and God, and at liberty when of Devils and

Hell, is because he was a true poet and of the Devil's
party without knowing it.
The Marriage of Heaven and Hell
[1790–1793]. Note to The Voice of the Devil

11 The road of excess leads to the palace of wisdom.
The Marriage of Heaven and Hell. Proverbs
of Hell, l. 3.

12 Eternity is in love with the production of time.
The Marriage of Heaven and Hell. Proverbs
of Hell, l. 10

13 No bird soars too high, if he soars with his own
wings.
The Marriage of Heaven and Hell.
Proverbs of Hell, l. 15

14 The pride of the peacock is the glory of God.
The lust of the goat is the bounty of God.
The wrath of the lion is the wisdom of God.
The nakedness of woman is the work of God.
The Marriage of Heaven and Hell. Proverbs
of Hell, l. 22

15 The cistern contains: the fountain overflows.
The Marriage of Heaven and Hell. Proverbs
of Hell, l. 35

16 Think in the morning. Act in the noon. Eat in the
evening. Sleep in the night.
The Marriage of Heaven and Hell. Proverbs
of Hell, l. 41

17 The tygers of wrath are wiser than the horses of
instruction.
The Marriage of Heaven and Hell. Proverbs
of Hell, l. 44

18 You never know what is enough unless you know
what is more than enough.
The Marriage of Heaven and Hell. Proverbs
of Hell, l. 46

19 Improvement makes straight roads; but the crooked
roads without improvement are roads of genius.
The Marriage of Heaven and Hell. Proverbs
of Hell, l. 66

20 Sooner murder an infant in its cradle than nurse
unacted desires.
The Marriage of Heaven and Hell. Proverbs
of Hell, l. 67

21 Truth can never be told so as to be understood, and
not be believ'd.
The Marriage of Heaven and Hell. Proverbs
of Hell, l. 69

22 Enough! or too much.
The Marriage of Heaven and Hell. Proverbs
of Hell, l. 70

1 One Law for the Lion & Ox is Oppression.
  The Marriage of Heaven and Hell.
  A Memorable Fancy

2 For every thing that lives is Holy.
  The Marriage of Heaven and Hell.
  A Song of Liberty

3 Never seek to tell thy love
  Love that never told can be;
  For the gentle wind does move
  Silently, invisibly.

  I told my love, I told my love,
  I told her all my heart;
  Trembling, cold, in ghastly fears —
  Ah, she doth depart.

  Soon as she was gone from me
  A traveler came by
  Silently, invisibly —
  Oh, was no deny.
  Poems [written c. 1791–1792]
  from Blake's Notebook. Never Seek to Tell

4 I ask'd a thief to steal me a peach:
  He turned up his eyes.
  I ask'd a lithe lady to lie her down:
  Holy and meek, she cries.

  As soon as I went
  An angel came.
  He wink'd at the thief
  And smil'd at the dame —

  And without one word said
  Had a peach from the tree,
  And still as a maid
  Enjoy'd the lady.
  Poems from Blake's Notebook. I Asked a Thief

5 Love to faults is always blind,
  Always is to joy inclin'd,
  Lawless, wing'd, and unconfin'd,
  And breaks all chains from every mind.
  Poems from Blake's Notebook. Love to Faults

6 Abstinence sows sand all over
  The ruddy limbs and flaming hair,
  But Desire gratified
  Plants fruits of life and beauty there.
  Poems from Blake's Notebook.
  Abstinence Sows Sand

7 If you trap the moment before it's ripe,
  The tears of repentance you'll certainly wipe;
  But if once you let the ripe moment go
  You can never wipe off the tears of woe.
  Poems from Blake's Notebook.
  If You Trap the Moment

8 He who binds to himself a joy
  Does the winged life destroy;

But he who kisses the joy as it flies
Lives in eternity's sunrise.
  Poems from Blake's Notebook. Several
  Questions Answered, no. 1, He Who Binds

9 What is it men in women do require?
  The lineaments of Gratified Desire.
  What is it women do in men require?
  The lineaments of Gratified Desire.
  Poems from Blake's Notebook. Several
  Questions Answered, 4, What Is It

10 Hear the voice of the Bard!
  Who Present, Past, and Future sees,
  Whose ears have heard
  The Holy Word
  That walk'd among the ancient trees.
  Songs of Experience [1794].
  Introduction, st. 1

11 Turn away no more.
  Why wilt thou turn away?
  The starry floor,
  The wat'ry shore
  Is giv'n thee till the break of day.
  Songs of Experience. Introduction, st. 4

12 Love seeketh not itself to please,
  Nor for itself hath any care,
  But for another gives its ease,
  And builds a Heaven in Hell's despair.
  Songs of Experience.
  The Clod and the Pebble, st. 1

13 Love seeketh only self to please,
  To bind another to its delight,
  Joys in another's loss of ease,
  And builds a Hell in Heaven's despite.
  Songs of Experience. The Clod and the Pebble, st. 3

14 O Rose, thou art sick.
  The invisible worm
  That flies in the night,
  In the howling storm,

  Has found out thy bed
  Of crimson joy,
  And his dark secret love
  Does thy life destroy.
  Songs of Experience. The Sick Rose

15 Little Fly,
  Thy summer's play
  My thoughtless hand
  Has brushed away.

  Am not I
  A fly like thee?
  Or art not thou
  A man like me?

  For I dance

And drink and sing,
Till some blind hand
Shall brush my wing.
> *Songs of Experience. The Fly, st. 1–3*

1 Tyger! Tyger! burning bright
In the forests of the night,
What immortal hand or eye
Could frame thy fearful symmetry?

In what distant deeps or skies
Burnt the fire of thine eyes?
On what wings dare he aspire?
What the hand dare seize the fire?
> *Songs of Experience. The Tyger, st. 1, 2*

2 What the hammer? what the chain?
In what furnace was thy brain?
What the anvil? what dread grasp
Dare its deadly terrors clasp?

When the stars threw down their spears
And water'd heaven with their tears,
Did he smile his work to see?
Did he who made the Lamb make thee?
> *Songs of Experience. The Tyger, st. 4, 5*

3 In every cry of every man,
In every infant's cry of fear,
In every voice, in every ban,
The mind-forg'd manacles I hear.
> *Songs of Experience. London, st. 2*

4 But most through midnight streets I hear
How the youthful harlot's curse
Blasts the newborn infant's tear
And blights with plagues the marriage hearse.
> *Songs of Experience. London, st. 4*

5 Pity would be no more,
If we did not make somebody poor;
And Mercy no more could be,
If all were as happy as we.
> *Songs of Experience. The Human
> Abstract, st. 1*

6 My mother groan'd! my father wept.
Into the dangerous world I leapt:
Helpless, naked, piping loud,
Like a fiend hid in a cloud.
> *Songs of Experience. Infant Sorrow, st. 1*

7 I was angry with my friend;
I told my wrath, my wrath did end.
I was angry with my foe;
I told it not, my wrath did grow.
> *Songs of Experience. A Poison Tree, st. 1*

8 Cruelty has a human heart,
And Jealousy a human face;

Terror, the human form divine,
And Secrecy, the human dress.
> *A Divine Image,*[1] *st. 1*

9   To generalize is to be an idiot. To particularize is
the alone distinction of merit — general knowledges
are those knowledges that idiots possess.
> *Annotations to Sir Joshua Reynolds's
> Discourses, pp. xcvii–xcviii*

10 My specter around me night and day
Like a wild beast guards my way.
My emanation far within
Weeps incessantly for my sin.
> *Poems [written c. 1804] from Blake's
> Notebook. My Specter, st. 1*

11 And throughout all eternity
I forgive you, you forgive me.
> *Poems [c. 1804] from Blake's Notebook.
> My Specter, st. 14*

12 Mock on, mock on, Voltaire, Rousseau.
Mock on, mock on — 'tis all in vain!
You throw the sand against the wind,
And the wind blows it back again.
> *Poems [c. 1804] from Blake's Notebook. Mock
> On, st. 1*

13 There is a smile of love,
And there is a smile of deceit,
And there is a smile of smiles
In which these two smiles meet.
> *Poems from the Pickering Manuscript
> [c. 1805]. The Smile, st. 1*

14 To see a world in a grain of sand
And a heaven in a wild flower,
Hold infinity in the palm of your hand
And eternity in an hour.
> *Poems from the Pickering Manuscript.
> Auguries of Innocence, l. 1*

15 A robin redbreast in a cage
Puts all Heaven in a rage.
> *Poems from the Pickering Manuscript.
> Auguries of Innocence, l. 5*

16 A dog starv'd at his master's gate
Predicts the ruin of the state.
> *Poems from the Pickering Manuscript.
> Auguries of Innocence, l. 9*

17 He who shall hurt the little wren
Shall never be belov'd by men.
> *Poems from the Pickering Manuscript.
> Auguries of Innocence, l. 29*

---

[1]This poem was written and etched by Blake [1790–1791] as a
"Song of Experience" linked with *The Divine Image* in *Songs of
Innocence* (see 351:3, 351:4, and 351:5), but in the published *Songs
of Experience* it was replaced by *The Human Abstract* (353:5).

1 A truth that's told with bad intent
  Beats all the lies you can invent.
          Poems from the Pickering Manuscript.
          Auguries of Innocence, l. 53

2 Man was made for joy and woe,
  And when this we rightly know
  Through the world we safely go.
          Poems from the Pickering Manuscript.
          Auguries of Innocence, l. 56

3 He who shall teach the child to doubt
  The rotting grave shall ne'er get out.
          Poems from the Pickering Manuscript.
          Auguries of Innocence, l. 87

4 The strongest poison ever known
  Came from Caesar's laurel crown.
          Poems from the Pickering Manuscript.
          Auguries of Innocence, l. 97

5 He who doubts from what he sees
  Will ne'er believe, do what you please.
  If the sun and moon should doubt
  They'd immediately go out.
          Poems from the Pickering Manuscript.
          Auguries of Innocence, l. 107

6 The harlot's cry from street to street
  Shall weave old England's winding sheet.
          Poems from the Pickering Manuscript.
          Auguries of Innocence, l. 115

7 God Appears and God is Light
  To those poor Souls who dwell in Night,
  But does a Human Form Display
  To those who Dwell in Realms of day.
          Poems from the Pickering Manuscript.
          Auguries of Innocence, l. 129

8 And did those feet in ancient time
  Walk upon England's mountains green?
  And was the holy Lamb of God
  On England's pleasant pastures seen?

  And did the Countenance Divine
  Shine forth upon our clouded hills?
  And was Jerusalem builded here
  Among these dark Satanic mills?

  Bring me my bow of burning gold,
  Bring me my arrows of desire,
  Bring me my spear — O clouds, unfold!
  Bring me my chariot of fire!

  I will not cease from mental fight,
  Nor shall my sword sleep in my hand,
  Till we have built Jerusalem
  In England's green and pleasant land.
          Milton [c. 1809], prefatory poem

9 Great things are done when men and mountains
      meet;
  This is not done by jostling in the street.
          Poems [written c. 1807–1809] from Blake's
          Notebook. Great Things Are Done

10 The Angel that presided o'er my birth
   Said, "Little creature, formed of joy and mirth,
   Go love without the help of any thing on earth."
          Poems [c. 1807–1809] from Blake's Notebook.
          The Angel That Presided

11 Grown old in love from seven till seven times seven,
   I oft have wish'd for Hell for ease from Heaven.
          Poems [c. 1807–1809] from Blake's Notebook.
          Grown Old in Love

12   Poetry fettered fetters the human race. Nations are
   destroyed, or flourish, in proportion as their poetry,
   painting, and music are destroyed or flourish!
          Jerusalem [c. 1818–1820]. To the Public,
          plate 1

13 He who would do good to another must do it in
       minute particulars;
   General good is the plea of the scoundrel, hypocrite,
       and flatterer:
   For art and science cannot exist but in minutely
       organized particulars.
          Jerusalem, ch. 3, plate 55, l. 60

14 England! awake! awake! awake!
   Jerusalem thy sister calls!
   Why wilt thou sleep the sleep of death
   And close her from thy ancient walls?
          Jerusalem, 4, prefatory poem, plate 77,
          st. 1

15 The vision of Christ that thou dost see
   Is my vision's greatest enemy.
          The Everlasting Gospel [written c. 1818],
          sec. 4, l. 1

16 Both read the Bible day and night,
   But thou read'st black where I read white.
          The Everlasting Gospel, 4, l. 13

17 This life's dim windows of the soul
   Distorts the heavens from pole to pole
   And leads you to believe a lie
   When you see with, not through, the eye.[1]
          The Everlasting Gospel, 5, l. 101

18 I am sure this Jesus will not do
   Either for Englishman or Jew.
          The Everlasting Gospel, 8

---

[1]We are led to believe a lie / When we see not through the eye. —
BLAKE, *Auguries of Innocence, l. 125*

James Gillray
c. 1757–1815

1   The Old Lady of Threadneedle Street[1]
Title of cartoon [1797]

Fisher Ames
1758–1808

2   A monarchy is a merchantman which sails well, but will sometimes strike on a rock, and go to the bottom; a republic is a raft which will never sink, but then your feet are always in the water.
Speech in the House of Representatives [1795]

John Heath
1758–1810

3   Love of wisdom [philosophy] the guide of life.[2]
Greek phrase for Phi Beta Kappa, society founded at the College of William and Mary [December 5, 1776]

James Monroe
1758–1831

4   National honor is national property of the highest value.   *First Inaugural Address [March 4, 1817]*

5   The American continents . . . are henceforth not to be considered as subjects for future colonization by any European powers.
Annual Message to Congress [December 2, 1823]. The Monroe Doctrine

6   In the wars of the European powers in matters relating to themselves we have never taken any part, nor does it comport with our policy so to do.
Annual Message to Congress. The Monroe Doctrine

7   We owe it, therefore, to candor, and to the amicable relations existing between the United States and those powers to declare that we should consider any attempt on their part to extend their system to any portion of this hemisphere as dangerous to our peace and safety. With the existing colonies or dependencies of any European power we . . . shall not interfere. But with the governments . . . whose independence we have . . . acknowledged, we could not view any interposition for the purpose of oppressing them, or controlling, in any other manner, their destiny, by any

European power, in any other light than as a manifestation of an unfriendly disposition toward the United States.
Annual Message to Congress. The Monroe Doctrine

Horatio Nelson, Viscount Nelson
1758–1805

8   Westminster Abbey, or victory!
At the battle of Cape St. Vincent [February 14, 1797]. From ROBERT SOUTHEY, Life of Nelson [1813], ch. 4

9   I have only one eye, I have a right to be blind sometimes. . . . I really do not see the signal.
At the battle of Copenhagen [1801]. From ROBERT SOUTHEY, Life of Nelson, 9

10   Something must be left to chance; nothing is sure in a sea fight beyond all others.
Memorandum to the fleet, off Cadiz [October 9, 1805]

11   But, in case signals can neither be seen or perfectly understood, no captain can do very wrong if he places his ship alongside that of the enemy.
Memorandum to the fleet, off Cadiz

12   England expects every man will do his duty.[3]
At the battle of Trafalgar [October 21, 1805]. From ROBERT SOUTHEY, Life of Nelson [1813], ch. 9

13   Thank God, I have done my duty.
At the battle of Trafalgar. From ROBERT SOUTHEY, Life of Nelson, 9

14   Kiss me, Hardy.
At the battle of Trafalgar. From ROBERT SOUTHEY, Life of Nelson, 9

Red Jacket
[Sagoyewatha][4]
c. 1758–1830

15   We first knew you a feeble plant which wanted a little earth whereon to grow. We gave it to you; and afterward, when we could have trod you under our feet, we watered and protected you; and now you have grown to be a mighty tree, whose top reaches the clouds, and whose branches overspread the whole

---

[1]The Bank of England.

[2]Philosophia biou kybernetes. The name Phi Beta Kappa is from the Greek initial letters in the phrase.

[3]This famous sentence is thus first reported: Say to the fleet, England confides that every man will do his duty. Captain Pasco, Nelson's flag lieutenant, suggested substituting "expects" for "confides," which was adopted. Captain Blackwood, who commanded the *Euryalus*, says that the correction suggested was from "Nelson expects" to "England expects."

[4]Seneca chief.

land, whilst we, who were the tall pine of the forest, have become a feeble plant and need your protection.   *Statement [c. 1792]*

Maximilien Robespierre
1758–1794

1   Terror is nothing other than prompt, stern, inflexible justice; terror thus issues from virtue; it is less a particular maxim than a consequence of the general principle of democracy applied to the most pressing needs of the fatherland.[1]
> *Speech to the National Convention*
> *[February 5, 1794]*

2   The revolutionary government is the despotism of liberty against tyranny.
> *Speech to the National Convention*
> *[February 5, 1794]*

3   Death is the beginning of immortality.
> *Speech to the National Convention [July 26, 1794]*

Robert Burns
1759–1796

4 Wee, sleekit, cow'rin, tim'rous beastie,
  O, what a panic's in thy breastie!
  Thou need na start awa sae hasty,
      Wi' bickering brattle!   *To a Mouse [1785], st. 1*

5 I'm truly sorry man's dominion
  Has broken Nature's social union.   *To a Mouse, st. 2*

6 The best laid schemes o' mice and men
  Gang aft a-gley.   *To a Mouse, st. 7*

7   Nature's law,
  That man was made to mourn.
> *Man Was Made to Mourn [1786], st. 4*

8 Man's inhumanity to man.
  Makes countless thousands mourn!
> *Man Was Made to Mourn, st. 7*

9 He wales a portion with judicious care;
  And "Let us worship God" he says, with
        solemn air.
> *The Cotter's Saturday Night [1786], st. 12*

10 From scenes like these, old Scotia's grandeur springs,
   That makes her loved at home, revered abroad:
   Princes and lords are but the breath of kings,
   "An honest man's the noblest work of God."
> *The Cotter's Saturday Night, st. 19*

11 Gie me ae spark o' Nature's fire,
   That's a' the learning I desire.
> *First Epistle to J. Lapraik [1786], st. 13*

---
[1] Translated by Laura Mason.

12 The social, friendly, honest man,
   Whate'er he be,
   'Tis he fulfills great Nature's plan,
   And none but he!
> *Second Epistle to J. Lapraik [1786], st. 15*

13 On ev'ry hand it will allow'd be,
   He's just — nae better than he should be.
> *A Dedication to Gavin Hamilton [1786]*

14 His locked, lettered, braw brass collar
   Showed him the gentleman an' scholar.
> *The Twa Dogs [1786], st. 3*

15 An' there began a lang digression
   About the lords o' the creation.   *The Twa Dogs, st. 6*

16 Oh wad some power the giftie gie us
   To see oursels as ithers see us!
   It wad frae monie a blunder free us,
       An' foolish notion.   *To a Louse [1786], st. 8*

17 Wee, modest, crimson-tipped flow'r,
   Thou's met me in an evil hour;
   For I maun crush amang the stoure
   Thy slender stem:
   To spare thee now is past my pow'r,
   Thou bonie gem.
> *To a Mountain Daisy [1786], st. 1*

18 Perhaps it may turn out a sang,
   Perhaps turn out a sermon.
> *Epistle to a Young Friend [1786], st. 1*

19 I waive the quantum o' the sin,
   The hazard of concealing:
   But, och! it hardens a' within,
   And petrifies the feeling!
> *Epistle to a Young Friend, st. 6*

20 An atheist-laugh's a poor exchange
   For Deity offended.
> *Epistle to a Young Friend, st. 9*

21 There's nought but care on ev'ry han',
   In every hour that passes, O:
   What signifies the life o' man,
   An' 't were nae for the lasses, O.
> *Green Grow the Rashes, O [1787], st. 1*

22 Auld Nature swears, the lovely dears
   Her noblest work she classes, O:
   Her prentice han' she tried on man,
   An' then she made the lasses, O.
> *Green Grow the Rashes, O, st. 5*

23 Green grow the rashes, O;
   Green grow the rashes, O;
   The sweetest hours that e'er I spend
   Are spent among the lasses, O.
> *Green Grow the Rashes, O, chorus*

1 I wasna fou, but just had plenty.
Death and Dr. Hornbook [1787], st. 3

2 John Barleycorn got up again,
And sore surprised them all.
John Barleycorn [1787], st. 3

3 Then gently scan your brother man,
Still gentler sister woman;
Tho' they may gang a kennin wrang,
To step aside is human.
Address to the Unco Guid [1787], st. 7

4 O, my Luve is like a red, red rose,
That's newly sprung in June.
O, my Luve is like the melodie,
That's sweetly played in tune.
*Johnson's Musical Museum [1787–1796]. A
Red, Red Rose, st. 1*

5 Contented wi' little and cantie wi' mair.
*Johnson's Musical Museum.
Contented wi' Little, st. 1*

6 Ye banks and braes o' bonny Doon,
How can ye bloom sae fresh and fair?
How can ye chant, ye little birds,
And I sae weary fu' o' care!
Thou'll break my heart, thou warbling bird,
That wantons thro' the flowering thorn!
Thou minds me o' departed joys,
Departed never to return.
*Johnson's Musical Museum.
The Banks o' Doon, st. 1*

7 Chords that vibrate sweetest pleasure
Thrill the deepest notes of woe.
*Johnson's Musical Museum.
Sensibility How Charming, st. 4*

8 Ae fond kiss, and then we sever;
Ae farewell and then forever!
Johnson's Musical Museum. Ae Fond Kiss, st. 1

9 But to see her was to love her,
Love but her, and love forever.
Had we never lov'd sae kindly,
Had we never lov'd sae blindly,
Never met — or never parted —
We had ne'er been brokenhearted.
*Johnson's Musical Museum.
Ae Fond Kiss, st. 2*

10 It was a' for our rightfu' King
We left fair Scotland's strand.
*Johnson's Musical Museum.
It Was A' for Our Rightfu' King, st. 1*

11 Now a' is done that men can do,
And a' is done in vain.
*Johnson's Musical Museum.
It Was A' for Our Rightfu' King, st. 2*

12 He turn'd him right and round about
Upon the Irish shore;
And gae his bridle reins a shake,
With adieu forevermore,
   My dear —
And adieu forevermore!
*Johnson's Musical Museum.
It Was A' for Our Rightfu' King, st. 3*

13 John Anderson my jo, John,
When we were first acquent,
Your locks were like the raven,
Your bonie brow was brent;
But now your brow is beld, John,
Your locks are like the snaw,
But blessings on your frosty pow,
John Anderson my jo!
*Johnson's Musical Museum.
John Anderson My Jo, st. 1*

14 Farewell to the Highlands, farewell to the North,
The birthplace of valor, the country of worth!
Wherever I wander, wherever I rove,
The hills of the Highlands for ever I love.
*Johnson's Musical Museum.
My Heart's in the Highlands, st. 1*

15 My heart's in the Highlands, my heart is not here,
My heart's in the Highlands a-chasing the deer;
A-chasing the wild deer, and following the roe,
My heart's in the Highlands wherever I go.
*Johnson's Musical Museum.
My Heart's in the Highlands, chorus*

16 O whistle, and I'll come to you, my lad:
Tho' father and mither and a' should gae mad.
*Whistle, and I'll Come to You,
My Lad*

17 Should auld acquaintance be forgot,
And never brought to min'?
Should auld acquaintance be forgot,
And days o' auld lang syne?
Auld Lang Syne [1788], st. 1

18 For auld lang syne, my dear,
For auld lang syne,
We'll tak a cup o' kindness yet
For auld lang syne!

Auld Lang Syne, chorus

19 Flow gently, sweet Afton, among thy green braes,
Flow gently, I'll sing thee a song in thy praise.
My Mary's asleep by thy murmuring stream,
Flow gently, sweet Afton, disturb not her dream.
Afton Water [1789], st. 1

20 This day Time winds th' exhausted chain,
To run the twelvemonth's length again.
New Year's Day [1791], st. 1

1 The voice of Nature loudly cries,
  And many a message from the skies,
  That something in us never dies.
                    New Year's Day, st. 3

2 When Nature her great masterpiece design'd,
  And fram'd her last, best work, the human mind,
  Her eye intent on all the mazy plan,
  She form'd of various stuff the various Man.
                    To Robert Graham [1791], st. 1

3 Whare sits our sulky, sullen dame,
  Gathering her brows like gathering storm,
  Nursing her wrath to keep it warm.
                    Tam o' Shanter [1791], l. 10

4 Ah, gentle dames! it gars me greet
  To think how monie counsels sweet,
  How monie lengthened, sage advices,
  The husband frae the wife despises.
                    Tam o' Shanter, l. 33

5 His ancient, trusty, drouthy crony;
  Tam lo'ed him like a vera brither —
  They had been fou for weeks thegither.
                    Tam o' Shanter, l. 43

6 But pleasures are like poppies spread —
  You seize the flow'r, its bloom is shed;
  Or like the snow falls in the river —
  A moment white — then melts forever.
                    Tam o' Shanter, l. 59

7 Inspiring bold John Barleycorn!
  What dangers thou canst make us scorn!
  Wi' tippenny, we fear nae evil;
  Wi' usquebae, we'll face the devil!
                    Tam o' Shanter, l. 105

8 As Tammie glow'red, amazed, and curious,
  The mirth and fun grew fast and furious.
                    Tam o' Shanter, l. 143

9 Her cutty sark, o' Paisley harn,
  That while a lassie she had worn,
  In longitude tho' sorely scanty,
  It was her best, and she was vauntie.
                    Tam o' Shanter, l. 171

10 "Weel done, Cutty Sark!"[1]   *Tam o' Shanter, l. 189*

11 She is a winsome wee thing,
  She is a handsome wee thing,
  She is a lo'esome wee thing,
      This sweet wee wife o' mine.
                    My Wife's a Winsome Wee Thing [1792],
                    chorus

12 The golden hours on angel wings
  Flew o'er me and my dearie;
  For dear to me as light and life
  Was my sweet Highland Mary.
                    Highland Mary [1792], st. 2

13 But, oh! fell death's untimely frost,
  That nipt my flower sae early.   *Highland Mary, st. 3*

14 Some hae meat and canna eat,
  And some wad eat that want it;
  But we hae meat, and we can eat,
  And sae the Lord be thankit.
                    The Selkirk Grace [1793] (attributed)

15 O Mary, at thy window be!
  It is the wish'd, the trysted hour.
                    Mary Morison [1793], st. 1

16 Scots wha hae wi' Wallace bled,
  Scots wham Bruce has aften led,
  Welcome to your gory bed
      Or to victorie.

  Now's the day, and now's the hour;
  See the front o' battle lour!
  See approach proud Edward's power —
      Chains and slaverie!
                    Scots Wha Hae [1794], st. 1, 2

17 Lay the proud usurpers low!
  Tyrants fall in every foe!
  Liberty's in every blow!
  Let us do or die!   *Scots Wha Hae, st. 6*

18 The rank is but the guinea's stamp,
  The man's the gowd for a' that.
                    For A' That and A' That [1795], st. 1

19 A prince can mak a belted knight,
  A marquis, duke, and a' that;
  But an honest man's aboon his might,
  Guid faith, he mauna fa' that.
                    For A' That and A' That, st. 4

20 For a' that and a' that,
  It's coming yet, for a' that,
  That man to man the world o'er
  Shall brothers be for a' that.
                    For A' That and A' That, st. 5

21 For a' that, and a' that,
  An' twice as muckle 's a' that,
  I've lost but ane, I've twa behin',
  I've wife eneugh for a' that.
                    Posthumous Pieces [1799]. The Jolly Beggars,
                    chorus

22 God knows, I'm no the thing I should be,
  Nor am I even the thing I could be.
                    Posthumous Pieces. To the Reverend John
                    M'Math, st. 8

---

[1]The famous tea clipper *Cutty Sark*, built in 1869, had the story of Tam o' Shanter carved upon bow and counter. Nannie, with flying locks and scanty shift, was the figurehead.

1 If there's another world, he lives in bliss;
　If there is none, he made the best of this.
　　　　Posthumous Pieces. Epitaph on William Muir

2 In durance vile here must I wake and weep,
　And all my frowsy couch in sorrow steep.
　　　　Posthumous Pieces. Epistle from Esopus to Maria

3 It's guid to be merry and wise,
　It's guid to be honest and true,
　It's guid to support Caledonia's cause
　And bide by the buff and the blue.
　　　　*Posthumous Pieces. Here's a Health to Them
　　　　That's Awa', st. 1*

Georges Jacques Danton
1759–1794

4　Everything belongs to the fatherland when the fatherland is in danger.
　　　　*Speech to the Legislative Assembly
　　　　[August 28, 1792]*

5　Audacity, more audacity, always audacity.[1]
　　　　*Speech to the Legislative Assembly
　　　　[September 2, 1792]*

6　Show my head to the people, it is worth seeing.
　　　　Last words, addressed to the executioner

William Pitt
1759–1806

7　Necessity is the plea for every infringement of human freedom. It is the argument of tyrants; it is the creed of slaves.
　　　　*Speech in the House of Commons
　　　　[November 18, 1783]*

Johann [Christoph] Friedrich von Schiller
1759–1805

8 The joke loses everything when the joker laughs himself.
　　　　*The Conspiracy of Fiesco [1783],
　　　　act I, sc. vii*

9 Did you think the lion was sleeping because he didn't roar?　　*The Conspiracy of Fiesco, I, xviii*

10 Joy, thou spark from Heav'n immortal,
　Daughter of Elysium!
　Drunk with fire, toward Heaven advancing
　Goddess, to thy shrine we come.

Thy sweet magic brings together
What stern Custom spreads afar;
All men become brothers
Where thy happy wing-beats are.[2]
　　　　Ode to Joy [1785], st. 1

11 There are three lessons I would write,
　Three words as with a burning pen,
　In tracings of eternal light
　Upon the hearts of men.
　　　　Hope, Faith, and Love [c. 1786], st. 1

12 World history is the world's court.[3]
　　　　Resignation [1786]

13 What one refuses in a minute
　No eternity will return.　　*Resignation*

14 O who knows what slumbers in the background of
　the times?　　*Don Carlos [1787], act I, sc. i*

15 Great souls suffer in silence.　　*Don Carlos, I, iv*

16 The richest monarch in the Christian world;
　The sun in my own dominions never sets.[4]
　　　　Don Carlos, I, vi

17 If you want to know yourself,
　Just look how others do it;
　If you want to understand others,
　Look into your own heart.
　　　　Tabulae Votivae (Votive Tablets) [1797]

18　Posterity weaves no garlands for imitators.
　　　　Wallenstein's Camp [1798], prologue

19　He who has done his best for his own time has lived for all times.
　　　　Wallenstein's Camp, prologue

20　Life is earnest, art is gay.
　　　　Wallenstein's Camp, prologue

21　Whatever is not forbidden is permitted.
　　　　Wallenstein's Camp, sc. vi

---

[1] Il nous faut de l'audace, encore de l'audace, toujours de l'audace.

[2] Alle Menschen werden Brüder, / Wo dein sanfter Flügel weilt. Translated by THEODORE SPENCER (adapted). Music by LUDWIG VAN BEETHOVEN.

[3] Die Weltgeschichte ist das Weltgericht.

[4] Why should the brave Spanish soldier brag the sun never sets in the Spanish dominions, but ever shineth on one part or other we have conquered for our king? — JOHN SMITH [1580–1631], *Advertisements for the Unexperienced, etc.* [1631]
　It may be said of them [the Hollanders] as of the Spaniards, that the sun never sets on their dominions. — THOMAS GAGE [d. 1656], *New Survey of the West Indies* [1648], *Epistle Dedicatory*
　The sun never sets on the immense empire of Charles V. — WALTER SCOTT, *Life of Napoleon* [1827]
　His Majesty's dominions, on which the sun never sets. — JOHN WILSON [CHRISTOPHER NORTH, 1785–1854], *Noctes Ambrosianae, no. 20* [April 1829]

1 Many a crown shines spotless now
That yet was deeply sullied in the winning.
The Death of Wallenstein[1] *[1798]*,
act II, sc. ii

2 There's no such thing as chance;
And what to us seems merest accident
Springs from the deepest source of destiny.
The Death of Wallenstein, II, iii

3   What is the short meaning of the long speech?
The Piccolomini [1799], act I, sc. ii

4   War nourishes war.[2]   *The Piccolomini, I, ii*

5   In thy breast are the stars of thy fate.
The Piccolomini, II, vi

6   You say it as you understand it.
The Piccolomini, II, vi

7   When the wine goes in, strange things come
out.   *The Piccolomini, II, xii*

8 I am better than my reputation.
Mary Stuart [1801], act III, sc. iv

9 Against stupidity the very gods
Themselves contend in vain.[3]
The Maid of Orleans [1801], act III, sc. vi

10 Pain is short, and joy is eternal.
The Maid of Orleans, last lines

11 The mountain cannot frighten one who was born
on it.   *Wilhelm Tell [1804], act III, sc. i*

12 Who reflects too much will accomplish little.
Wilhelm Tell, III, i

13 You saw his weakness, and he will never forgive
you.   *Wilhelm Tell, III, i*

14 This feat of Tell, the archer, will be told
While yonder mountains stand upon their base.
By heaven! The apple's cleft right through the
core.   *Wilhelm Tell, III, iii*

Mary Wollstonecraft
[Godwin]
1759–1797

15   No man chooses evil because it is evil; he only mistakes it for happiness, the good he seeks.
A Vindication of the Rights of Men [1790]

16   Virtue can only flourish amongst equals.
A Vindication of the Rights of Men

17   Till women are more rationally educated, the progress in human virtue and improvement in knowledge
must receive continual checks.
A Vindication of the Rights of Woman
[1792], ch. 3

18   If women be educated for dependence; that is, to
act according to the will of another fallible being, and
submit, right or wrong, to power, where are we to
stop?   *A Vindication of the Rights of Woman, 3*

19   Women are systematically degraded by receiving
the trivial attentions which men think it manly to pay
to the sex, when, in fact, men are insultingly supporting their own superiority.
A Vindication of the Rights of Woman, 4

20   It would be an endless task to trace the variety of
meannesses, cares, and sorrows into which women
are plunged by the prevailing opinion that they were
created rather to feel than reason, and that all the
power they obtain must be obtained by their charms
and weakness.
A Vindication of the Rights of Woman, 4

21   It is justice, not charity, that is wanting in the
world.   *A Vindication of the Rights of Woman, 4*

22   Women ought to have representatives, instead of
being arbitrarily governed without any direct share
allowed them in the deliberations of government.
A Vindication of the Rights of Woman, 9

23   Till society is very differently constituted, parents,
I fear, will still insist on being obeyed because they
will be obeyed, and constantly endeavor to settle that
power on a divine right which will not bear the investigation of reason.
A Vindication of the Rights of Woman, 11

24   Every political good carried to the extreme must
be productive of evil.
The French Revolution [1794], bk. V, ch. 4

25   Executions, far from being useful examples to the
survivors, have, I am persuaded, a quite contrary
effect, by hardening the heart they ought to terrify.
Besides, the fear of an ignominious death, I believe,
never deterred anyone from the commission of a
crime, because in committing it the mind is roused
to activity about present circumstances.
Letters Written During a Short Residence
in Sweden, Norway, and Denmark [1796],
letter 19

26   It is the preservation of the species, not of individuals, which appears to be the design of Deity
throughout the whole of nature.
Letters Written During a Short Residence
in Sweden, Norway, and Denmark, 22

---

[1]Translated by Samuel Taylor Coleridge.

[2]Der Krieg ernährt den Krieg.

[3]Against boredom even the gods themselves struggle in vain. —
Friedrich Nietzsche, *The Antichrist*, aphorism 48

François Noël Babeuf
[Gracchus]
1760–1797

1 We aim at something more sublime and more equitable—the common good, or the community of goods.... We demand, we would have, the communal enjoyment of the fruits of the earth, fruits which are for everyone.
Manifesto of the Equals [c. 1795]

Camille Desmoulins
1760–1794

2 I am thirty-three—the age of the good sans-culotte Jesus; an age fatal to revolutionists.
Said before his execution

[Claude] Joseph Rouget de Lisle
1760–1836

3 Allons, enfants de la patrie,
Le jour de gloire est arrivé!...
Aux armes, citoyens!
Formez vos bataillons!
Marchons! Marchons! Qu'un sang impur
Abreuve nos sillons!
[Forward, sons of France,
The day of glory has come!...
To arms, citizens!
Line up in battalions!
Let us march on! Let the impure blood
of enemies drench our fields!]
The Marseillaise[1] [1792]

Antoine [Jacques Claude Joseph] Boulay de la Meurthe
1761–1840

4 It is worse than a crime, it is a blunder.[2]
On the execution of the Duc d'Enghien [1804], quoted in C.-A. Ste.-Beuve, Nouveaux Lundis [1870]

George Colman the Younger
1762–1836

5 Not to be sneezed at.
The Heir-at-Law [1797], act II, sc. i

6 John Bull;[3] or, The Englishman's Fireside
Title of play [1803]

7 His heart runs away with his head.
Who Wants a Guinea? [1805], act I, sc. i

8 O Miss Bailey!
Unfortunate Miss Bailey!
Love Laughs at Locksmiths [1806], act II, song

9 Says he, "I am a handsome man, but I'm a gay deceiver."
Love Laughs at Locksmiths, II, song

Johann Paul Friedrich Richter
[Jean Paul]
1763–1825

10 Weltschmerz.[4]
Selina; or, Above Immortality [1827]

Samuel Rogers
1763–1855

11 Never less alone than when alone.
Human Life [1819], l. 756

12 By many a temple half as old as Time.
Italy. A Farewell

13 It doesn't much signify whom one marries, for one is sure to find next morning that it was someone else.
Table Talk

Kobayashi Issa
1763–1828

14 In its eye
the far-off hills are mirrored—
dragonfly![5]
Haiku

15 The world of dew
Is the world of dew,
And yet...
And yet...[5]
Haiku

Gaston Pierre Marc, Duc de Lévis
1764–1830

16 Noblesse oblige [Rank has its obligations].
Maxims and Reflections [1808]

---

[1]Composed in the garrison at Strasbourg and originally called *Chant de Guerre de l'Armée du Rhin*, the *Marseillaise* took its name from the patriots of Marseille, who first made it known in Paris.

[2]C'est pire qu'un crime, c'est une faute.

---

[3]The origin of a certain personification of the British character.

[4]Literally, world pain.

[5]Translated by Harold G. Henderson.

Thomas Morton
1764–1838

1   What will Mrs. Grundy say? What will Mrs. Grundy think?
> *Speed the Plow [1798], act I, sc. i*

Ann Radcliffe
1764–1823

2 Fate sits on these dark battlements and frowns,
And as the portal opens to receive me,
A voice in hollow murmurs through the courts
Tells of a nameless deed.
> *The Mysteries of Udolpho [1794],*
> *motto*

Robert Goodloe Harper
1765–1825

3   Millions for defense, but not one cent for tribute.[1]
> *Toast at banquet for John Marshall*
> *[June 18, 1798]*

Sir James Mackintosh
1765–1832

4   The Commons, faithful to their system, remained in a wise and masterly inactivity.
> *Vindiciae Gallicae (A Defense of the French*
> *Revolution) [1791]*

5   Disciplined inaction.
> *History of the Revolution in England in*
> *1688 [1834], ch. 7*

James Smithson
1765–1829

6   To found at Washington, under the name of the Smithsonian Institution, an establishment for the increase and diffusion of knowledge among men.[2]
> *Bequest [1829] with which the Smithsonian*
> *Institution was established [1846]*

Thomas Robert Malthus
1766–1834

7   Population, when unchecked, increases in a geometrical ratio. Subsistence increases only in an arithmetical ratio. A slight acquaintance with numbers will show the immensity of the first power in comparison of the second.
> *An Essay on the Principle of*
> *Population [1798], ch. 1*

8   The histories of mankind that we possess are histories only of the higher class.
> *An Essay on the Principle of Population, ch. 2*

Ernst Friedrich Herbert von Münster
1766–1839

9   Absolutism tempered by assassination.
> *Description of the Russian Constitution*

Carolina Oliphant, Baroness Nairne
1766–1845

10 Charlie is my darling, the young Chevalier.
> *Life and Songs [1869]. Charlie Is My Darling*[3]

11 We'll up an' gie them a blaw, a blaw,
Wi' a hundred pipers an' a', an' a'.
> *Life and Songs. The Hundred Pipers*

12 I'm wearin' awa'
To the land o' the leal.
> *Life and Songs. The Land o' the Leal*

Germaine de Staël
[Anna Louise Germaine Necker, Baronne de Staël-Holstein]
1766–1817

13   Love is the whole history of a woman's life, it is but an episode in a man's.[4]
> *De l'Influence des Passions [1796]*

14   A man must know how to defy opinion; a woman how to submit to it.   *Delphine [1802]*

15   To understand everything makes one tolerant.[5]
> *Corinne [1807], bk. XVIII, ch. 5*

---

[1]In 1797 a secret agent from Talleyrand told Charles Cotesworth Pinckney, minister to the French republic, that the American commissioners who were in Paris to protest French attacks on U.S. shipping would be received only if they paid a $50,000 bribe and made a large loan to the French government. Pinckney's reply was: "Not a sixpence, sir." Later, Harper's remark was attributed to him.

[2]Quoted by John Quincy Adams in the *Committee Report on the Smithson Bequest* [March 5, 1840].

---

[3]Also attributed to JAMES HOGG.

[4]L'amour est l'histoire de la vie des femmes, c'est un episode dans celle des hommes.

[5]Tout comprendre rend très indulgent.

Attributed to GERMAINE DE STAËL are similar phrases: Comprendre c'est pardonner [To understand is to forgive]. Tout comprendre c'est tout pardonner [To know everything is to forgive everything].

John Quincy Adams
1767–1848

1   I can never join with my voice in the toast which I see in the papers attributed to one of our gallant naval heroes. I cannot ask of heaven success, even for my country, in a cause where she should be in the wrong. *Fiat justitia, pereat coelum* [Let justice be done though heaven may perish]. My toast would be, may our country be always successful, but whether successful or otherwise, always right.

Letter to John Adams [August 1, 1816]

2   [America] goes not abroad in search of monsters to destroy. She is the well-wisher to the freedom and independence of all. She is the champion and vindicator only of her own.

Address [July 4, 1821]

3   America, with the same voice which spoke herself into existence as a nation, proclaimed to mankind the inextinguishable rights of human nature, and the only lawful foundations of government.

Address [July 4, 1821]

4   America...well knows that by once enlisting under other banners than her own, were they even the banners of foreign independence, she would involve herself beyond the power of extraction, in all the wars of interest and intrigue, of individual avarice, envy, and ambition, which assume the colors and usurp the standard of freedom. The fundamental maxims of her policy would insensibly change from liberty to force....She might become dictatress of the world. She would be no longer the ruler of her own spirit.

Address [July 4, 1821]

5   Individual liberty is individual power, and as the power of a community is a mass compounded of individual powers, the nation which enjoys the most freedom must necessarily be in proportion to its numbers the most powerful nation.

Letter to James Lloyd [October 1, 1822]

6   The public history of all countries, and all ages, is but a sort of mask, richly colored. The interior working of the machinery must be foul.

Diary entry [November 9, 1822]

7   This house will bear witness to his piety; this town, his birthplace, to his munificence; history to his patriotism; posterity to the depth and compass of his mind. *From his epitaph for John Adams*[1] *[1829]*

8   In charity to all mankind, bearing no malice or ill will to any human being, and even compassionating those who hold in bondage their fellow men, not knowing what they do.

Letter to A. Bronson [July 30, 1838]

9   The great problem of legislation is, so to organize the civil government of a community...that in the operation of human institutions upon social action, self-love and social may be made the same.

Society and Civilization; in the American Review [July 1845]

10   To furnish the means of acquiring knowledge is...the greatest benefit that can be conferred upon mankind. It prolongs life itself and enlarges the sphere of existence.

Report on the establishment of the Smithsonian Institution [c. 1846]

11   This is the last of earth! I am content.

Last words [February 21, 1848]

Black Hawk[2]
1767–1838

12   I saw my evil day at hand. The sun rose dim on us in the morning, and at night it sank in a dark cloud, and looked like a ball of fire. That was the last sun that shone on Black Hawk. His heart is dead....He is now a prisoner to the white man.

Speech upon surrender, Prairie du Chien, Wisconsin [August 27, 1832]

13   [Black Hawk] has done nothing for which an Indian ought to be ashamed. He has fought for his countrymen, the squaws and papooses, against white men, who came year after year, to cheat them and take away their lands. You know the cause of our making war.[3] It is known to all white men. They ought to be ashamed of it.

Speech upon surrender, Prairie du Chien, Wisconsin [August 27, 1832]

Andrew Jackson
1767–1845

14   The individual who refuses to defend his rights when called by his Government, deserves to be a slave, and must be punished as an enemy of his country and friend to her foe.

Proclamation to the people of Louisiana from Mobile [September 21, 1814]

---

[1]Inscribed on one of the portals of the United First Parish Church Unitarian (Church of the Presidents), Quincy, Massachusetts.

[2]Ma-ke-tai-me-she-kia-kiak. Chief of the Sauk and Fox Indians.

[3]The Black Hawk War [1832].

1   The brave man inattentive to his duty, is worth little more to his country, than the coward who deserts her in the hour of danger.
> *To troops who had abandoned their lines during the battle of New Orleans [January 8, 1815]*

2   Our Federal Union! it must be preserved!
> *Toast at Jefferson Birthday Celebration [1830]*

3   Every man is equally entitled to protection by law; but when the laws undertake to add . . . artificial distinctions, to grant titles, gratuities, and exclusive privileges, to make the rich richer and the potent more powerful, the humble members of society — the farmers, mechanics, and laborers — who have neither the time nor the means of securing like favors to themselves, have a right to complain of the injustice of their government.   *Veto of the Bank Bill [July 10, 1832]*

4   There are no necessary evils in government. Its evils exist only in its abuses. If it would confine itself to equal protection, and, as Heaven does its rains, shower its favors alike on the high and the low, the rich and the poor, it would be an unqualified blessing.   *Veto of the Bank Bill*

5   One man with courage makes a majority.
> *Attributed*

Louis Antoine Léon de Saint-Just
1767–1794

6   Nobody can rule guiltlessly.[1]
> *Address to the Convention [November 13, 1792]*

7   No liberty for the enemies of liberty.[2]
> *Jacobin slogan, 1793. Attributed*

8   Happiness is a new idea in Europe.[3]
> *Report on the Means of Implementing the Decree Against the Enemies of the Revolution [1794]*

Jean-Baptiste Say
1767–1832

9   It is production which opens a demand for products. . . . A product is no sooner created, than it, from that instant, affords a market for other products to the full extent of its own value.[4]
> *A Treatise on Political Economy [1803]*

François René de Chateaubriand
1768–1848

10   [On his conversion to Christianity:] I wept and I believed.[5]   *Le Génie du Christianisme [1802]*

11   The original writer is not one who imitates nobody, but one whom nobody can imitate.[6]
> *Le Génie du Christianisme*

12   Aristocracy has three successive ages: the age of superiorities, the age of privileges, the age of vanities. Originating in the first, it degenerates in the second and becomes extinct in the third.
> *Mémoires d'Outre Tombe (Memoirs from Beyond the Grave) [1848–1850], bk. 1, ch. 1*

13   Murder will never be in my eyes an object of admiration and an argument for freedom; I know nothing more servile, more despicable, more cowardly, more narrow-minded than a terrorist.
> *Mémoires d'Outre Tombe, 4, 13*

14   Napoleon was all the weaknesses and all the greatnesses of man.[7]   *Mémoires d'Outre Tombe, 22, 20*

Charlotte Corday [Marie-Anne Charlotte de Corday d'Armont]
1768–1793

15   I killed one man to save one hundred thousand.
> *At her trial for the assassination of Jean-Paul Marat [1743–1793] [July 1793]*

Friedrich Schleiermacher
1768–1834

16   I lie on the bosom of the infinite world. At this moment I am its soul, for I feel all its powers and its infinite life as my own.
> *On Religion[8] [1799]. On the Essence of Religion*

Tecumseh[9]
1768–1813

17   These lands are ours. No one has a right to remove us, because we were the first owners. The

---

[1] On ne peut pas régner innocent.
The epigraph for Arthur Koestler's *Darkness at Noon* [1940].

[2] Pas de liberté pour les ennemis de la liberté.

[3] Le bonheur est une idée neuve en Europe.

[4] Say's so-called law of markets, popularly rephrased as "Supply creates its own demand."

[5] J'ai pleuré et j'ai cru.

[6] L'écrivain original n'est pas celui qui n'imite personne, mais celui que personne ne peut imiter.

[7] As cited by Jacques Barzun in *Romanticism and the Modern Ego* [1947].

[8] Edited by Richard Crouter.

[9] Chief of the Shawnees.

Great Spirit above has appointed this place for us, on which to light our fires, and here we will remain. As to boundaries, the Great Spirit knows no boundaries, nor will his red children acknowledge any.[1]

To Joseph Barron, messenger of President James Madison [1810]

1 My father! The Great Spirit is my father! The earth is my mother — and on her bosom I will recline.

Council at Vincennes, Indiana Territory [August 14, 1810]. Answer to request to sit at "his father's" (Governor William Henry Harrison's) side

2 Sell a country! Why not sell the air, the clouds and the great sea, as well as the earth? Did not the Great Spirit make them all for the use of his children?

Council at Vincennes, Indiana Territory [August 14, 1810]. Speech to Harrison

3 Our lives are in the hands of the Great Spirit. He gave to our ancestors the lands which we possess. We are determined to defend them, and if it is His will, our bones shall whiten on them, but we will never give them up.[2]

Speech to Major General Henry Procter, British commander, Fort Malden [September 1813]

Napoleon I
[Napoleon Bonaparte]
1769–1821

4 Soldiers, from the summit of yonder pyramids forty centuries look down upon you.

In Egypt [July 21, 1798]

5 Go, sir, gallop, and don't forget that the world was made in six days. You can ask me for anything you like, except time.

To an aide [1803]. From R. M. JOHNSTON [1867–1920], The Corsican [1910]

6 A form of government that is not the result of a long sequence of shared experiences, efforts, and endeavors can never take root.

[1803]. From J. CHRISTOPHER HEROLD [1919–1964], The Mind of Napoleon [1955]

7 From the sublime to the ridiculous is but a step.[3]

To the Abbé du Pradt, on the return from Russia [1812], referring to the retreat from Moscow

8 You write to me that it's impossible; the word is not French. *Letter to General Lemarois [July 9, 1813]*

9 What is the throne? — a bit of wood gilded and covered with velvet. I am the state — I alone am here the representative of the people. Even if I had done wrong you should not have reproached me in public — people wash their dirty linen at home.[4] France has more need of me than I of France.

To the Senate [1814]

10 France is invaded; I am leaving to take command of my troops, and, with God's help and their valor, I hope soon to drive the enemy beyond the frontier. *At Paris [January 23, 1814]*

11 The bullet that will kill me is not yet cast.

At Montereau [February 17, 1814]

12 The Allied Powers having proclaimed that the Emperor Napoleon is the sole obstacle to the reestablishment of peace in Europe, he, faithful to his oath, declares that he is ready to descend from the throne, to quit France, and even to relinquish life, for the good of his country.

Act of Abdication [April 4, 1814]

13 Unite for the public safety, if you would remain an independent nation.

Proclamation to the French People [June 22, 1815]

14 Wherever wood can swim, there I am sure to find this flag of England. *At Rochefort [July 1815]*

15 Whatever shall we do in that remote spot? Well, we will write our memoirs. Work is the scythe of time. *On board H.M.S. Bellerophon [August 1815]*

16 [Of his relations with the Empress Josephine:] I generally had to give in.

On St. Helena [May 19, 1816]

17 My maxim was, *la carrière est ouverte aux talents* [the road is open to the talented], without distinction of birth or fortune. *On St. Helena [March 3, 1817]*

18 Two o'clock in the morning courage: I mean unprepared courage.[5]

[December 4, 5, 1815].
From EMMANUEL DE LAS CASES [1766–1842], Mémorial de Ste-Hélène [1823]

---

[1]He remembered the belligerent ants, who claimed their boundaries, and the pacific geese, who did not. . . . All those puffins, razorbills, guillemots and kittiwakes had lived together peacefully, preserving their own kinds of civilization without war — because they claimed no boundaries. — T. H. WHITE [1906–1964], *The Once and Future King* [1939], *bk. IV, ch. 14*

[2]Tecumseh was killed in the battle of the Thames River [October 5, 1813].

[3]Du sublime au ridicule il n'y a qu'un pas.
The saying has been attributed also to TALLEYRAND.

[4]Il faut laver son linge sale en famille [One should wash one's dirty linen at home]. — *Saying current since about 1720*

[5]Le courage de l'improviste.

1   Madame Montholon having inquired what troops he considered the best, "Those which are victorious, Madame," replied the Emperor.
> *From* Louis de Bourrienne *[1769–1834], Memoirs [1829]*

2   A silk stocking filled with mud.
> *Description of Talleyrand*[1]

3   An army marches on its stomach.[2]   *Attributed*

4   Every French soldier carries a marshal's baton in his knapsack.[3]   *Attributed*

5   Perfidious Albion.[4]   *Attributed*

6   Chief of the Army.[5]   *Last words*

Arthur Wellesley, Duke of Wellington
1769–1852

7   Nothing except a battle lost can be half so melancholy as a battle won.
> *Dispatch from the field of Waterloo [June 1815]*

8   I used to say of him [Napoleon] that his presence on the field made the difference of forty thousand men.
> *[November 2, 1831]. From* Philip Henry, Earl of Stanhope *[1781–1855], Notes of Conversations with the Duke of Wellington [1888]*

9   The only thing I am afraid of is fear.
> *[November 3, 1831]. From* Philip Henry Stanhope, *Notes of Conversations with the Duke of Wellington*

10   Ours [our army] is composed of the scum of the earth — the mere scum of the earth.
> *[November 4, 1831]. From* Philip Henry Stanhope, *Notes of Conversations with the Duke of Wellington*

11   [Of troops sent to fight in the War of 1812:] They wanted this iron fist to command them.
> *[November 8, 1840]. From* Philip Henry Stanhope, *Notes of Conversations with the Duke of Wellington*

12   There is no mistake; there has been no mistake; and there shall be no mistake.
> *Wellingtoniana [1832], p. 78*

13   I don't care a twopenny damn what becomes of the ashes of Napoleon Bonaparte.   *Attributed*

14   The battle of Waterloo was won on the playing fields of Eton.
> *From* Sir William Fraser *[1826–1898], Words on Wellington [1889]*

15   Publish and be damned.
> *Attributed. His response when the courtesan Harriette Wilson threatened to publish her memoirs and his letters*

Ludwig van Beethoven
1770–1827

16   I want to seize fate by the throat.
> *Letter to Dr. Franz Wegeler [November 16, 1801]*

17   What humiliation when someone who stood next to me heard a flute in the distance and I heard nothing, or when someone heard the shepherd boy singing and again I heard nothing. Such misfortune brought me to the edge of despair, and I might have brought an end to my life — only my art held me back.
> *The Heiligenstadt Testament [1802]*

18   Art! Who comprehends her? With whom can one consult concerning this great goddess?
> *Letter to Bettina von Arnim [August 11, 1810]*

19   The world is a king, and, like a king, desires flattery in return for favor; but true art is selfish and perverse — it will not submit to the mold of flattery.
> *Conversations [March 1820]*

20   Es muss sein [It must be]!
> *String Quartet no. 16 in F Major, op. 135 [1826]. Notation at Allegro in final movement*

Pierre Jacques Étienne, Count Cambronne
1770–1842

21   The Guards die, but never surrender.[6]
> *Attributed. Reply to surrender demand at Waterloo [1815]*

---

[1] Attributed by C.-A. Sainte-Beuve.

[2] No man can be a patriot on an empty stomach. — William Cowper Brann [1855–1898], *The Iconoclast, Old Glory* [July 4, 1893]

[3] Tout soldat français porte dans sa giberne le bâton de maréchal de France.

[4] L'Angleterre, ah! la perfide Angleterre. — Jacques Bénigne Bossuet, *Premier Sermon sur la Fête de la Circoncision* [1654]

[5] Tête d'armée.

---

[6] La Garde meurt, mais ne se rend pas.

Probably the invention of a French journalist; Cambronne denied ever having said it. "Merde!," a more likely reply also attributed to him, has been euphemized as "Le mot de Cambronne."

The finest word, perhaps, that a Frenchman ever uttered....To speak that word, and then to die, what could be more grand! for to accept death is to die, and it is not the fault of this man, if, in the storm of grape, he survived. — Victor Hugo, *Les Misérables, Cosette, bk. I, ch. 15*

George Canning
1770–1827

1 I give thee sixpence! I will see thee damned first.
The Anti-Jacobin, no. 11 [1797].
The Friend of Humanity and the
Knife-Grinder, st. 9

2 A steady patriot of the world alone,
The friend of every country but his own.
The Anti-Jacobin, no. 36 [1798].
New Morality, l. 113

3 Give me th'avowed, th'erect, the manly foe,
Bold I can meet — perhaps may turn his blow;
But of all plagues, good Heav'n, thy wrath can send,
Save, save, oh! save me from the Candid Friend![1]
The Anti-Jacobin, no. 36. New Morality,
l. 207

4 When our perils are past, shall our gratitude sleep?
No — here's to the pilot that weathered the storm.
Song for the Inauguration of the Pitt Club
[May 25, 1802]

Georg Wilhelm Friedrich Hegel
1770–1831

5 The truth is concrete.
Encyclopedia of the Physical Sciences
[1817–1830], introduction

6 Philosophy is its own time comprehended in
thoughts.   *Philosophy of Right[2] [1821], preface*

7 What is reasonable is real; that which is real is reasonable.   *Philosophy of Right*

8 The owl of Minerva spreads its wings only with the
falling of dusk.   *Philosophy of Right*

9 What experience and history teach is this — that
people and governments never have learned anything
from history, or acted on principles deduced from it.
Philosophy of History[3] [1832], introduction

10 Amid the pressure of great events, a general principle gives no help.
Philosophy of History, introduction

11 To him who looks upon the world rationally, the
world in its turn presents a rational aspect. The relation is mutual.   *Philosophy of History, introduction*

12 The history of the world is none other than the
progress of the consciousness of freedom.
Philosophy of History, introduction

13 We may affirm absolutely that nothing great in the
world has been accomplished without passion.
Philosophy of History, introduction

14 It is a matter of perfect indifference where a thing
originated; the only question is: "Is it true in and for
itself?"
Philosophy of History, pt. III, sec. 3, ch. 2

James Hogg
1770–1835

15 We'll o'er the water, we'll o'er the sea,
We'll o'er the water to Charlie;
Come weal, come woe, we'll gather and go,
And live and die wi' Charlie.
O'er the Water to Charlie [1821]

16 Nothing in the world delights a truly religious
people so much, as consigning them to eternal damnation.
The Private Memoirs and Confessions of a
Justified Sinner [1824]

Friedrich Hölderlin
1770–1843

17 Ah, where will I find
Flowers, come winter,
And where the sunshine
And shade of the earth?
Walls stand cold
And speechless, in the wind
The weathervanes creak.[4]   *Half of Life [c. 1801]*

18 Near and
Hard to grasp, the god.
Yet where danger lies,
Grows that which saves.[4]   *Patmos [1802]*

Joseph Hopkinson
1770–1842

19 Hail, Columbia! happy land!
Hail, ye heroes! heaven-born band!
Who fought and bled in Freedom's cause.
Hail, Columbia[5] [1798], st. 1

---

[1]Defend me from my friends; I can defend myself from my enemies. — *Attributed to* Claude Louis Hector, Duc de Villars [1653–1734], *when taking leave of Louis XIV*

[2]Translated by T. M. Knox.

[3]Translated by J. Sibree.
Quoted by G. B. Shaw in *The Revolutionist's Handbook, an appendix to Man and Superman.*

---

[4]Translated by Richard Sieburth.

[5]The music, generally attributed to Philip Phile [c. 1734–1793], was Washington's inaugural march. Hopkinson supplied verses at a singer's request, and the song won instant acclaim.

William Wordsworth
1770–1850

1 And homeless near a thousand homes I stood,
And near a thousand tables pined and wanted food.
*Guilt and Sorrow [written 1791–1794,
published 1842], st. 41*

2 —— A simple child,[1]
That lightly draws its breath,
And feels its life in every limb,
What should it know of death?
We Are Seven [1798], st. 1

3 Have I not reason to lament
What man has made of man?
Lines Written in Early Spring [1798], st. 6

4 Nor less I deem that there are Powers
Which of themselves our minds impress;
That we can feed this mind of ours
In a wise passiveness.
Expostulation and Reply [1798], st. 6

5 Come forth into the light of things,
Let Nature be your teacher.
The Tables Turned [1798], st. 4

6 One impulse from a vernal wood
May teach you more of man,
Of moral evil and of good,
Than all the sages can.   *The Tables Turned, st. 6*

7   That best portion of a good man's life,
His little, nameless, unremembered acts
Of kindness and of love.
*Lines Composed a Few Miles Above Tintern
Abbey [1798], l. 33*

8   Blessed mood,
In which the burthen of the mystery,
In which the heavy and the weary weight
Of all this unintelligible world,
Is lightened.
*Lines Composed a Few Miles Above Tintern
Abbey, l. 37*

9 While with an eye made quiet by the power
Of harmony, and the deep power of joy,
We see into the life of things.
*Lines Composed a Few Miles Above Tintern
Abbey, l. 47*

10   The sounding cataract
Haunted me like a passion: the tall rock,
The mountain, and the deep and gloomy wood,
Their colors and their forms, were then to me

An appetite; a feeling and a love,
That had no need of a remoter charm,
By thought supplied, nor any interest
Unborrowed from the eye.
*Lines Composed a Few Miles Above Tintern
Abbey, l. 76*

11   I have learned
To look on nature, not as in the hour
Of thoughtless youth; but hearing oftentimes
The still, sad music of humanity,
Nor harsh nor grating, though of ample power
To chasten and subdue. And I have felt
A presence that disturbs me with the joy
Of elevated thoughts; a sense sublime
Of something far more deeply interfused,
Whose dwelling is the light of setting suns,
And the round ocean and the living air,
And the blue sky, and in the mind of man:
A motion and a spirit, that impels
All thinking things, all objects of all thought,
And rolls through all things.
*Lines Composed a Few Miles Above Tintern
Abbey, l. 88*

12 Knowing that Nature never did betray
The heart that loved her.
*Lines Composed a Few Miles Above Tintern
Abbey, l. 122*

13 Fair seedtime had my soul, and I grew up
Fostered alike by beauty and by fear.
*The Prelude [written 1799–1805,
published 1850], bk. I, l. 301*

14 Dust as we are, the immortal spirit grows
Like harmony in music; there is a dark
Inscrutable workmanship that reconciles
Discordant elements, makes them cling together
In one society.   *The Prelude, I, l. 340*

15   The grim shape
Towered up between me and the stars, and still,
For so it seemed, with purpose of its own
And measured motion like a living thing,
Strode after me.   *The Prelude, I, l. 381*

16   Where the statue stood
Of Newton with his prism and silent face,
The marble index of a mind forever
Voyaging through strange seas of thought, alone.
The Prelude, III, l. 60

17 But Europe at that time was thrilled with joy,
France standing on the top of golden hours,
And human nature seeming born again.
The Prelude, VI, l. 339

18 Bliss was it in that dawn to be alive,
But to be young was very heaven!
The Prelude, XI, l. 108

---

[1] In the first edition the line is: A simple child, dear brother Jim. It was reduced to the current text in the 1815 edition of Wordsworth's poems.

1   There is
One great society alone on earth:
The noble Living and the noble Dead.
                    The Prelude, XI, l. 393

2 Prophets of Nature, we to them will speak
A lasting inspiration, sanctified
By reason, blest by faith: what we have loved,
Others will love, and we will teach them how;
Instruct them how the mind of man becomes
A thousand times more beautiful than the earth
On which he dwells.   *The Prelude, XIV, l. 444*

3   Poetry is the breath and finer spirit of all knowledge; it is the impassioned expression which is in the
countenance of all Science.
          Lyrical Ballads [2nd ed., 1800]. Preface

4   In spite of difference of soil and climate, of language and manners, of laws and customs — in spite
of things silently gone out of mind, and things violently destroyed, the Poet binds together by passion
and knowledge the vast empire of human society, as
it is spread over the whole earth, and over all time.
                 Lyrical Ballads. Preface

5   I have said that poetry is the spontaneous overflow
of powerful feelings: it takes its origin from emotion
recollected in tranquillity.
                 Lyrical Ballads. Preface

6 What fond and wayward thoughts will slide
Into a lover's head!
"O mercy!" to myself I cried,
"If Lucy should be dead!"
       *Strange Fits of Passion Have I Known
       [1800], st. 7*

7 She dwelt among the untrodden ways
Beside the springs of Dove,
A maid whom there were none to praise
And very few to love:[1]

A violet by a mossy stone
Half hidden from the eye!
—Fair as a star, when only one
Is shining in the sky.

She lived unknown, and few could know
When Lucy ceased to be;
But she is in her grave, and, oh,
The difference to me!
    She Dwelt Among the Untrodden Ways [1800]

8 A slumber did my spirit seal;
I had no human fears:
She seemed a thing that could not feel

The touch of earthly years.
No motion has she now, no force;

She neither hears nor sees;
Rolled round in earth's diurnal course,
With rocks, and stones, and trees.
    A Slumber Did My Spirit Seal [1800]

9   A fingering slave,
One that would peep and botanize
Upon his mother's grave?
         A Poet's Epitaph [1800], st. 5

10 A reasoning, self-sufficing thing,
An intellectual All-in-all!   *A Poet's Epitaph, st. 8*

11 The harvest of a quiet eye.
          A Poet's Epitaph, st. 13

12 Something between a hindrance and a help.
          Michael [1800], l. 189

13 I traveled among unknown men,
In lands beyond the sea;
Nor, England! did I know till then
What love I bore to thee.
   I Traveled Among Unknown Men [1807], st. 1

14 My heart leaps up when I behold
   A rainbow in the sky:
So was it when my life began;
So is it now I am a man;
So be it when I shall grow old,
   Or let me die!
The child is father of the man;
And I could wish my days to be
Bound each to each by natural piety.[2]
         My Heart Leaps Up [1807]

15 Sweet childish days, that were as long
As twenty days are now.
     *To a Butterfly (I've Watched
     You Now a Full Half-Hour) [1807], st. 2*

16 I thought of Chatterton,[3] the marvelous boy,
The sleepless soul that perished in his pride;
Of him[4] who walked in glory and in joy
Following his plow, along the mountainside:
By our own spirits are we deified:
We Poets in our youth begin in gladness;
But thereof come in the end despondency and
    madness.
    Resolution and Independence [1807], st. 7

17 Choice word and measured phrase, above the reach
Of ordinary men.
       Resolution and Independence, st. 14

---

[1]He lived amidst th' untrodden ways / To Rydal Lake that lead; / A bard whom there were none to praise, / And very few to read. / Unread his works — his "Milk White Doe" / With dust is dark and dim; / It's still in Longmans' shop, and oh! / The difference to him! — *Parody by* HARTLEY COLERIDGE [1796–1849]

[2]The last three lines are the epigraph for *Intimations of Immortality*, 370:13–371:5.

[3]See Thomas Chatterton, 346:22.

[4]Robert Burns.

1 And mighty poets in their misery dead.
> *Resolution and Independence, st. 17*

2 Earth has not anything to show more fair:
Dull would he be of soul who could pass by
A sight so touching in its majesty.
> *Composed upon Westminster Bridge,*
> *September 3, 1802 [1807], l. 1*

3 Ne'er saw I, never felt, a calm so deep!
The river glideth at his own sweet will!
Dear God! the very houses seem asleep;
And all that mighty heart is lying still!
> *Composed upon Westminster Bridge,*
> *September 3, 1802, l. 11*

4 Plain living and high thinking are no more:
The homely beauty of the good old cause
Is gone; our peace, our fearful innocence,
And pure religion breathing household laws.
> *Written in London, September 1802 [1807]*

5 It is a beauteous evening, calm and free,
The holy time is quiet as a nun
Breathless with adoration.
> *It Is a Beauteous Evening [1807], l. 1*

6 Thou liest in Abraham's bosom all the year;
And worship'st at the Temple's inner shrine,
God being with thee when we know it not.
> *It Is a Beauteous Evening, l. 12*

7 Once did she hold the gorgeous east in fee:
And was the safeguard of the west.
> *On the Extinction of the Venetian Republic*
> *[1807], l. 1*

8 Thou hast great allies;
Thy friends are exultations, agonies,
And love, and man's unconquerable mind.
> *To Toussaint L'Ouverture [1807], l. 12*

9 Milton! thou shouldst be living at this hour:
England hath need of thee: she is a fen
Of stagnant waters. *London, 1802 [1807], l. 1*

10 Thy soul was like a star, and dwelt apart;
Thou hadst a voice whose sound was like the sea:
Pure as the naked heavens, majestic, free,
So didst thou travel on life's common way,
In cheerful godliness. *London, 1802, l. 9*

11 We must be free or die, who speak the tongue
That Shakespeare spake; the faith and morals hold
Which Milton held.
> *It Is Not to Be Thought Of [1807], l. 11*

12 The music in my heart I bore
Long after it was heard no more.
> *The Solitary Reaper [1807], st. 4*

13 There was a time when meadow, grove, and stream,
The earth, and every common sight,
To me did seem
Appareled in celestial light,
The glory and the freshness of a dream.
It is not now as it hath been of yore—
Turn wheresoe'er I may,
By night or day,
The things which I have seen I now can see no more.
> *Ode. Intimations of Immortality from*
> *Recollections of Early Childhood [1807],*
> *st. 1*

14 The Rainbow comes and goes,
And lovely is the Rose.
> *Ode. Intimations of Immortality from*
> *Recollections of Early Childhood, st. 2*

15 The sunshine is a glorious birth;
But yet I know, where'er I go,
That there hath passed away a glory from the earth.
> *Ode. Intimations of Immortality from*
> *Recollections of Early Childhood, st. 2*

16 Whither is fled the visionary gleam?
Where is it now, the glory and the dream?
> *Ode. Intimations of Immortality from*
> *Recollections of Early Childhood, st. 4*

17 Our birth is but a sleep and a forgetting:
The soul that rises with us, our life's star,
Hath had elsewhere its setting,
And cometh from afar:
Not in entire forgetfulness,
And not in utter nakedness,
But trailing clouds of glory do we come
From God, who is our home:
Heaven lies about us in our infancy!
Shades of the prison-house begin to close
Upon the growing boy.
> *Ode. Intimations of Immortality from*
> *Recollections of Early Childhood, st. 5*

18 The youth, who daily farther from the east
Must travel, still is Nature's priest,
And by the vision splendid
Is on his way attended;
At length the man perceives it die away,
And fade into the light of common day.
> *Ode. Intimations of Immortality from*
> *Recollections of Early Childhood, st. 5*

19 As if his whole vocation
Were endless imitation.
> *Ode. Intimations of Immortality from*
> *Recollections of Early Childhood, st. 7*

20 O joy! that in our embers
Is something that doth live,
That nature yet remembers
What was so fugitive!
> *Ode. Intimations of Immortality from*
> *Recollections of Early Childhood, st. 9*

1 High instincts before which our mortal nature
Did tremble like a guilty thing surprised.
Ode. Intimations of Immortality from
Recollections of Early Childhood, st. 9

2 Truths that wake,
To perish never.
Ode. Intimations of Immortality from
Recollections of Early Childhood, st. 9

3 Though inland far we be,
Our souls have sight of that immortal sea
Which brought us hither.
Ode. Intimations of Immortality from
Recollections of Early Childhood, st. 9

4 Though nothing can bring back the hour
Of splendor in the grass, of glory in the flower.
Ode. Intimations of Immortality from
Recollections of Early Childhood, st. 10

5 The clouds that gather round the setting sun
Do take a sober coloring from an eye
That hath kept watch o'er man's mortality;
Another race hath been, and other palms are won.
Thanks to the human heart by which we live,
Thanks to its tenderness, its joys, and fears,
To me the meanest flower that blows can give
Thoughts that do often lie too deep for tears.
Ode. Intimations of Immortality from
Recollections of Early Childhood, st. 11

6 She was a phantom of delight
When first she gleamed upon my sight;
A lovely apparition, sent
To be a moment's ornament.
She Was a Phantom of Delight [1807], st. 1

7 And now I see with eye serene
The very pulse of the machine.
She Was a Phantom of Delight, st. 3

8 A perfect woman, nobly planned,
To warn, to comfort, and command.
And yet a Spirit still, and bright
With something of angelic light.
She Was a Phantom of Delight, st. 3

9 I wandered lonely as a cloud
That floats on high o'er vales and hills,
When all at once I saw a crowd,
A host, of golden daffodils.
I Wandered Lonely as a Cloud [1807], st. 1

10 Continuous as the stars that shine
And twinkle on the milky way.
I Wandered Lonely as a Cloud, st. 2

11 Ten thousand saw I at a glance,
Tossing their heads in sprightly dance.
I Wandered Lonely as a Cloud, st. 2

12 A poet could not but be gay,
In such a jocund company.
I Wandered Lonely as a Cloud, st. 3

13 That inward eye
Which is the bliss of solitude.
I Wandered Lonely as a Cloud, st. 4

14 Stern daughter of the voice of God!
O Duty! *Ode to Duty [1807], st. 1*

15 A light to guide, a rod
To check the erring, and reprove. *Ode to Duty, st. 1*

16 Me this unchartered freedom tires;
I feel the weight of chance desires;
My hopes no more must change their name,
I long for a repose that ever is the same.
Ode to Duty, st. 5

17 Thou dost preserve the stars from wrong;
And the most ancient heavens, through Thee, are
fresh and strong. *Ode to Duty, st. 7*

18 The light that never was, on sea or land,
The consecration, and the poet's dream.
Elegiac Stanzas. Suggested by a Picture of
Peele Castle in a Storm [1807], st. 4

19 A deep distress hath humanized my Soul.
Elegiac Stanzas. Suggested by a Picture of
Peele Castle in a Storm, st. 9

20 Who is the happy Warrior? Who is he
That every man in arms should wish to be?
Character of the Happy Warrior [1807], l. 1

21 Who, doomed to go in company with pain,
And fear, and bloodshed, miserable train!
Turns his necessity to glorious gain.
Character of the Happy Warrior, l. 12

22 Nuns fret not at their convent's narrow room.
Nuns Fret Not [1807], l. 1

23 The world is too much with us; late and soon,
Getting and spending, we lay waste our powers:
Little we see in Nature that is ours;
We have given our hearts away, a sordid boon!
The World Is Too Much with Us [1807], l. 1

24 Great God! I'd rather be
A pagan suckled in a creed outworn;
So might I, standing on this pleasant lea,
Have glimpses that would make me less forlorn;
Have sight of Proteus rising from the sea;
Or hear old Triton blow his wreathèd horn.
The World Is Too Much with Us, l. 9

25 Where lies the land to which yon ship must go?
Fresh as a lark mounting at break of day,
Festively she puts forth in trim array.
Where Lies the Land [1807], l. 1

1 Dreams, books, are each a world; and books, we know,
Are a substantial world, both pure and good:
Round these, with tendrils strong as flesh and blood,
Our pastime and our happiness will grow.
　　　　　　　Personal Talk [1807], sonnet 3

2 A power is passing from the earth.
　　　　　　Lines on the Expected Dissolution of
　　　　　　Mr. Fox [1807], st. 5

3 Two voices are there: one is of the sea,[1]
One of the mountains; each a mighty voice.
　　　　　Thought of a Briton on the Subjugation
　　　　　of Switzerland [1807], l. 1

4 　　　Every great and original writer, in proportion as
he is great or original, must himself create the taste
by which he is to be relished.
　　　　　　Letter to Lady Beaumont [May 21, 1807]

5 　　　　Strongest minds
Are often those of whom the noisy world
Hears least.　　　　*The Excursion[2] [1814], bk. I, l. 91*

6 　　　The good die first,
And they whose hearts are dry as summer dust
Burn to the socket.　　　*The Excursion, I, l. 500*

7 　　　　I have seen
A curious child, who dwelt upon a tract
Of inland ground, applying to his ear
The convolutions of a smooth-lipped shell,
To which, in silence hushed, his very soul
Listened intensely; and his countenance soon
Brightened with joy, for from within were heard
Murmurings, whereby the monitor expressed
Mysterious union with its native sea.
Even such a shell the universe itself
Is to the ear of Faith; and there are times,
I doubt not, when to you it doth impart
Authentic tidings of invisible things;
Of ebb and flow, and ever-during power;
And central peace, subsisting at the heart
Of endless agitation.　　　*The Excursion, IV, l. 1132*

8 　　　　One in whom persuasion and belief
Had ripened into faith, and faith become
A passionate intuition.　　　*The Excursion, IV, l. 1293*

9 Surprised by joy — impatient as the wind.
　　　　　　Surprised by Joy [1815], l. 1

10 An ampler ether, a diviner air.
　　　　　　Laodamia [1815], st. 18

---

[1]Two voices are there: one is of the deep; . . . / And one is of an old half-witted sheep / Which bleats articulate monotony, / And indicates that two and one are three. . . . / And, Wordsworth, both art thine. — JAMES KENNETH STEPHEN [1859–1892], *Sonnet, Wordsworth* [1891]

[2]This will never do. — FRANCIS JEFFREY [1773–1850], *opening sentence, review of* WORDSWORTH, *Excursion, Edinburgh Review* [1814]

11 Enough, if something from our hands have power
To live, and act, and serve the future hour.
　　　　　　The River Duddon [1820], sonnet 34,
　　　　　　Afterthought, l. 10

12 We feel that we are greater than we know.
　　　　　The River Duddon, 34, Afterthought, l. 14

13 The unimaginable touch of Time.
　　　　　Ecclesiastical Sonnets [1822], pt. III, sonnet
　　　　　34. Mutability

14 Give all thou canst; high Heaven rejects the lore
Of nicely calculated less or more.
　　　　　Ecclesiastical Sonnets, III, 43. Inside of King's
　　　　　College Chapel, Cambridge, l. 6

15 But hushed be every thought that springs
From out the bitterness of things.
　　　　　Elegiac Stanzas. Addressed to Sir G. H. B.
　　　　　[1827], st. 7

16 Scorn not the sonnet; Critic, you have frowned,
Mindless of its just honors; with this key
Shakespeare unlocked his heart.
　　　　　　Scorn Not the Sonnet [1827], l. 1

17 Small service is true service while it lasts:
Of humblest friends, bright creature! scorn not one:
The daisy, by the shadow that it casts,
Protects the lingering dewdrop from the sun.
　　　　　To a Child. Written in Her Album [1835]

Thomas John Dibdin
1771–1841

18 Oh, it's a snug little island!
A right little, tight little island.
　　　　　　　The Snug Little Island

James Montgomery
1771–1854

19 Prayer is the soul's sincere desire,
Uttered or unexpressed;
The motion of a hidden fire
That trembles in the breast.
　　　　　　What Is Prayer? [1818], st. 1

Sir Walter Scott
1771–1832

20 The way was long, the wind was cold,
The Minstrel was infirm and old;
His withered cheek, and tresses gray,
Seem'd to have known a better day.
　　　The Lay of the Last Minstrel [1805], introduction

1 I cannot tell how the truth may be;
I say the tale as 'twas said to me.
The Lay of the Last Minstrel, canto II, st. 22

2 In peace, Love tunes the shepherd's reed;
In war, he mounts the warrior's steed;
In halls, in gay attire is seen;
In hamlets, dances on the green.
Love rules the court, the camp, the grove,
And men below, and saints above;
For love is heaven, and heaven is love.
The Lay of the Last Minstrel, III, st. 2

3 Breathes there the man, with soul so dead,
Who never to himself hath said,
This is my own, my native land!
Whose heart hath ne'er within him burn'd
As home his footsteps he hath turn'd
From wandering on a foreign strand!
If such there breathe, go, mark him well;
For him no Minstrel raptures swell;
High though his titles, proud his name,
Boundless his wealth as wish can claim;
Despite those titles, power, and pelf,
The wretch, concentered all in self,
Living, shall forfeit fair renown,
And, doubly dying, shall go down
To the vile dust, from whence he sprung,
Unwept, unhonor'd, and unsung.
The Lay of the Last Minstrel, VI, st. 1

4 O Caledonia! stern and wild,
Meet nurse for a poetic child!
Land of brown heath and shaggy wood;
Land of the mountain and the flood!
The Lay of the Last Minstrel, VI, st. 2

5 November's sky is chill and drear,
November's leaf is red and sear.
Marmion [1808], canto I, introduction, st. 1

6 Stood for his country's glory fast,
And nail'd her colors to the mast!
Marmion, I, introduction, st. 10

7 But search the land of living men,
Where wilt thou find their like again?
Marmion, I, introduction, st. 11

8 And come he slow, or come he fast,
It is but Death who comes at last.
Marmion, II, st. 30

9 Oh, young Lochinvar is come out of the West,
Through all the wide Border his steed was the best.
Marmion, V, st. 12 [Lochinvar, st. 1]

10 So faithful in love, and so dauntless in war,
There never was knight like the young Lochinvar.
Marmion, V, st. 12 [Lochinvar, st. 1]

11 For a laggard in love, and a dastard in war,
Was to wed the fair Ellen of brave Lochinvar.
Marmion, V, st. 12 [Lochinvar, st. 2]

12 With a smile on her lips, and a tear in her eye.
Marmion, V, st. 12 [Lochinvar, st. 5]

13 Heap on more wood! — the wind is chill;
But let it whistle as it will,
We'll keep our Christmas merry still.
Marmion, VI, introduction, st. 1

14   And dar'st thou, then,
To beard the lion in his den,
The Douglas in his hall?
Marmion, VI, introduction, st. 14

15 Oh, what a tangled web we weave,
When first we practice to deceive!
Marmion, VI, introduction, st. 17

16 O Woman! in our hours of ease,
Uncertain, coy, and hard to please,
And variable as the shade
By the light quivering aspen made;
When pain and anguish wring the brow,
A ministering angel thou!
Marmion, VI, st. 30

17 To all, to each, a fair goodnight,
And pleasing dreams, and slumbers light!
Marmion, L'Envoy

18 The stag at eve had drunk his fill,
Where danced the moon on Monan's rill,
And deep his midnight lair had made
In lone Glenartney's hazel shade.
*The Lady of the Lake [1810],
canto I, st. 1*

19 In listening mood she seemed to stand,
The guardian Naiad of the strand.
The Lady of the Lake, I, st. 17

20 The will to do, the soul to dare.
The Lady of the Lake, I, st. 21

21 Soldier, rest! thy warfare o'er,
Sleep the sleep that knows not breaking,
Dream of battled fields no more,
Days of danger, nights of waking.
The Lady of the Lake, I, st. 31

22 Hail to the Chief who in triumph advances![1]
The Lady of the Lake, II, st. 19

23 Like the dew on the mountain,
Like the foam on the river,
Like the bubble on the fountain,

---

[1]The verses beginning with this line were set to music by JAMES SANDERSON [1769–c.1841]. The march has become traditionally attached to the president of the United States.

Thou art gone, and forever!
The Lady of the Lake, III, st. 16
[Coronach, st. 3]

1 And, Saxon — I am Roderick Dhu!
The Lady of the Lake, V, st. 9

2 Come one, come all! this rock shall fly
From its firm base as soon as I.
The Lady of the Lake, V, st. 10

3 Respect was mingled with surprise,
And the stern joy which warriors feel
In foemen worthy of their steel.
The Lady of the Lake, V, st. 10

4 Where, where was Roderick then!
One blast upon his bugle horn
Were worth a thousand men!
The Lady of the Lake, VI, st. 18

5 A mother's pride, a father's joy.
Rokeby [1813], canto III, st. 15

6 Oh, Brignal banks are wild and fair,
And Greta woods are green,
And you may gather garlands there
Would grace a summer queen.   *Rokeby, III, st. 16*

7   It's no fish ye're buying, it's men's lives.
The Antiquary [1816], ch. 11

8 Time will rust the sharpest sword,
Time will consume the strongest cord;
That which molders hemp and steel,
Mortal arm and nerve must feel.
Harold the Dauntless [1817], canto I, st. 4

9   Sea of upturned faces.
Rob Roy [1817], ch. 20

10   My foot is on my native heath, and my name is
MacGregor.   *Rob Roy, 34*

11 Vacant heart, and hand, and eye,
Easy live and quiet die.
The Bride of Lammermoor [1819],
ch. 3. Lucy Ashton's Song

12   There is a southern proverb — fine words butter
no parsnips.
The Legend of Montrose [1819], ch. 3

13   The happy combination of fortuitous circum-
stances.
The Monastery [1820].
Answer of the Author of Waverley to the
Letter of Captain Clutterbuck

14   As old as the hills.   *The Monastery, ch. 9*

15 Oh, poverty parts good company.
The Abbot [1820], ch. 7

16   Tell that to the marines — the sailors won't
believe it.[1]
Redgauntlet [1824], vol. II, ch. 7

17   Recollect that the Almighty, who gave the dog to
be companion of our pleasures and our toils, hath
invested him with a nature noble and incapable of
deceit.   *The Talisman [1825], ch. 24*

18   A miss is as good as a mile.
Journal [December 3, 1825]

Sydney Smith
1771–1845

19   In the four quarters of the globe, who reads an
American book, or goes to an American play, or looks
at an American picture or statue? . . . Under which of
the old tyrannical governments of Europe is every
sixth man a slave, whom his fellow-creatures may buy,
and sell, and torture?
In Edinburgh Review [January–May 1820]

20   If you choose to represent the various parts in life
by holes upon a table, of different shapes — some cir-
cular, some triangular, some square, some oblong —
and the persons acting these parts by bits of wood of
similar shapes, we shall generally find that the triangular person has got into the square hole, the oblong
into the triangular, and a square person has squeezed
himself into the round hole.[2]
Sketches of Moral Philosophy [1850]

21   That knuckle-end of England — that land of
Calvin, oatcakes, and sulphur.
Lady Holland's Memoir [1855],
vol. I, ch. 2

22   Preaching has become a byword for long and dull
conversation of any kind; and whoever wishes to
imply, in any piece of writing, the absence of everything agreeable and inviting, calls it a sermon.
Lady Holland's Memoir, I, 3

23   Avoid shame, but do not seek glory — nothing so
expensive as glory.   *Lady Holland's Memoir, I, 4*

24   Take short views, hope for the best, and trust in
God.   *Lady Holland's Memoir, I, 6*

25   Not body enough to cover his mind decently
with; his intellect is improperly exposed.
Lady Holland's Memoir, I, 9

---

[1]"Right," quoth Ben, "that will do for the marines." — LORD
BYRON, *The Island, canto II, last line*
"That will do for the marines, but the sailors won't believe it" is an
old saying.

[2]Generally accepted as the origin of the phrase: A square peg in a
round hole.

1   He has spent all his life in letting down empty buckets into empty wells; and he is frittering away his age in trying to draw them up again.
Lady Holland's Memoir, I, 9

2   Ah, you flavor everything; you are the vanilla of society.   *Lady Holland's Memoir, I, 9*

3   As the French say, there are three sexes — men, women, and clergymen.
Lady Holland's Memoir, I, 9

4   Daniel Webster struck me much like a steam engine in trousers.   *Lady Holland's Memoir, I, 9*

5   Live always in the best company when you read.
Lady Holland's Memoir, I, 10

6   Never give way to melancholy; resist it steadily, for the habit will encroach.   *Lady Holland's Memoir, I, 10*

7   He was a one-book man. Some men have only one book in them; others, a library.
Lady Holland's Memoir, I, 11

8   Marriage resembles a pair of shears, so joined that they can not be separated; often moving in opposite directions, yet always punishing anyone who comes between them.[1]   *Lady Holland's Memoir, I, 11*

9 Serenely full, the epicure would say,
Fate cannot harm me, I have dined today.
Lady Holland's Memoir, I, 11

10   What you don't know would make a great book.   *Lady Holland's Memoir, I, 11*

11   In composing, as a general rule, run your pen through every other word you have written; you have no idea what vigor it will give your style.
Lady Holland's Memoir, I, 11

12   Thank God for tea! What would the world do without tea? — how did it exist? I am glad I was not born before tea.   *Lady Holland's Memoir, I, 11*

13   That sign of old age, extolling the past at the expense of the present.
Lady Holland's Memoir, I, 11

14   We know nothing of tomorrow; our business is to be good and happy today.
Lady Holland's Memoir, I, 12

Samuel Taylor Coleridge
1772–1834

15 O the one life within us and abroad,
Which meets all motion and becomes its soul,

---

[1]We are the two halves of a pair of scissors, when apart, Pecksniff, but together we are something. — CHARLES DICKENS, *Martin Chuzzlewit, ch. 11*

A light in sound, a sound-like power in light,
Rhythm in all thought, and joyance everywhere —
Methinks, it should have been impossible
Not to love all things in a world so filled.
The Eolian Harp [1795], l. 26

16   And what if all of animated nature
Be but organic harps diversely fram'd,
That tremble into thought, as o'er them sweeps
Plastic and vast, one intellectual breeze,
At once the Soul of each, and God of All?
The Eolian Harp, l. 44

17 It is an ancient Mariner,
And he stoppeth one of three.
"By thy long gray beard and glittering eye,
Now wherefore stopp'st thou me?"
*The Rime of the Ancient Mariner [1798],
pt. I, st. 1*

18 The guests are met, the feast is set:
May'st hear the merry din.
The Rime of the Ancient Mariner, I, st. 2

19 He holds him with his glittering eye —
The Wedding Guest stood still,
And listens like a three years' child:
The Mariner hath his will.
The Rime of the Ancient Mariner, I, st. 4

20 The ship was cheered, the harbor cleared,
Merrily did we drop
Below the kirk, below the hill,
Below the lighthouse top.
The Rime of the Ancient Mariner, I, st. 6

21 The Wedding Guest here beat his breast,
For he heard the loud bassoon.
The Rime of the Ancient Mariner, I, st. 8

22 The bride hath paced into the hall,
Red as a rose is she.
The Rime of the Ancient Mariner, I, st. 9

23 And now there came both mist and snow,
And it grew wondrous cold:
And ice, mast-high, came floating by,
As green as emerald.
The Rime of the Ancient Mariner, I, st. 13

24 The ice was here, the ice was there,
The ice was all around:
It cracked and growled, and roared and howled,
Like noises in a swound!
The Rime of the Ancient Mariner, I, st. 15

25 "God save thee, ancient Mariner!
From the fiends, that plague thee thus! —
Why look'st thou so?" — "With my crossbow
I shot the Albatross."
The Rime of the Ancient Mariner, I, st. 20

1 The fair breeze blew, the white foam flew,
The furrow followed free;
We were the first that ever burst
Into that silent sea.
The Rime of the Ancient Mariner, II, st. 5

2 As idle as a painted ship
Upon a painted ocean.
The Rime of the Ancient Mariner, II, st. 8

3 Water, water, everywhere,
Nor any drop to drink.
The Rime of the Ancient Mariner, II, st. 9

4 The very deep did rot: O Christ!
That ever this should be!
Yea, slimy things did crawl with legs
Upon the slimy sea.
The Rime of the Ancient Mariner, II, st. 10

5 About, about, in reel and rout
The death fires danced at night.
The Rime of the Ancient Mariner, II, st. 11

6 I bit my arm, I sucked the blood,
And cried, A sail! a sail!
The Rime of the Ancient Mariner, III, st. 4

7 Her lips were red, her looks were free,
Her locks were yellow as gold:
Her skin was white as leprosy,
The nightmare Life-in-Death was she,
Who thicks man's blood with cold.
The Rime of the Ancient Mariner, III, st. 11

8 "The game is done! I've won, I've won!"
Quoth she, and whistles thrice.
*The Rime of the Ancient Mariner,
III, st. 12*

9 The sun's rim dips, the stars rush out:
At one stride comes the dark;
With far-heard whisper o'er the sea
Off shot the specter bark.
*The Rime of the Ancient Mariner,
III, st. 13*

10 We listened and looked sideways up!
Fear at my heart, as at a cup,
My lifeblood seemed to sip.
*The Rime of the Ancient Mariner,
III, st. 14*

11 The hornèd Moon, with one bright star
Within the nether tip.
*The Rime of the Ancient Mariner,
III, st. 14*

12 Each turned his face with a ghastly pang,
And cursed me with his eye.
*The Rime of the Ancient Mariner,
III, st. 15*

13 I fear thee, ancient Mariner!
I fear thy skinny hand!
And thou art long, and lank, and brown,
As is the ribbed sea-sand.[1]
The Rime of the Ancient Mariner, IV, st. 1

14 Alone, alone, all, all alone;
Alone on a wide, wide sea.
The Rime of the Ancient Mariner, IV, st. 3

15 The moving moon went up the sky,
And nowhere did abide;
Softly she was going up,
And a star or two beside.
The Rime of the Ancient Mariner, IV, st. 10

16 Her beams bemocked the sultry main,
Like April hoarfrost spread;
But where the ship's huge shadow lay,
The charmed water burnt alway
A still and awful red.
The Rime of the Ancient Mariner, IV, st. 11

17 O happy living things! no tongue
Their beauty might declare:
A spring of love gushed from my heart,
And I blessed them unaware.
The Rime of the Ancient Mariner, IV, st. 14

18 Oh sleep! it is a gentle thing,
Beloved from pole to pole.
The Rime of the Ancient Mariner, V, st. 1

19 A noise like of a hidden brook
In the leafy month of June,
That to the sleeping woods all night
Singeth a quiet tune.
The Rime of the Ancient Mariner, V, st. 18

20   The man hath penance done,
And penance more will do.
The Rime of the Ancient Mariner, V, st. 26

21 Like one that on a lonesome road
Doth walk in fear and dread,
And having once turned round walks on,
And turns no more his head;
Because he knows a frightful fiend
Doth close behind him tread.
The Rime of the Ancient Mariner, VI, st. 10

22 Is this the hill? is this the kirk?
Is this mine own countree?
The Rime of the Ancient Mariner, VI, st. 14

23 No voice; but oh! the silence sank
Like music on my heart.
The Rime of the Ancient Mariner, VI, st. 22

---

[1]A note by Coleridge in *Sibylline Leaves* [1817] says: "For [these] lines I am indebted to Mr. Wordsworth."

1 And the owlet whoops to the wolf below,
   That eats the she-wolf's young.
   The Rime of the Ancient Mariner, VII, st. 5

2 "Ha! ha!" quoth he, "full plain I see,
   The Devil knows how to row."
   The Rime of the Ancient Mariner, VII, st. 12

3 I pass, like night, from land to land;
   I have strange power of speech;
   That moment that his face I see,
   I know the man that must hear me:
   To him my tale I teach.
   The Rime of the Ancient Mariner, VII, st. 17

4 O Wedding Guest! This soul hath been
   Alone on a wide wide sea:
   So lonely 'twas, that God himself
   Scarce seemèd there to be.
   The Rime of the Ancient Mariner, VII, st. 19

5 He prayeth well who loveth well
   Both man and bird and beast.
   The Rime of the Ancient Mariner, VII, st. 22

6 He prayeth best who loveth best
   All things both great and small;
   For the dear God who loveth us,
   He made and loveth all.
   The Rime of the Ancient Mariner, VII, st. 23

7 A sadder and a wiser man
   He rose the morrow morn.
   The Rime of the Ancient Mariner, VII, st. 25

8 'Tis a month before the month of May,
   And the Spring comes slowly up this way.
   Christabel [1797–1800], pt. I, l. 21

9 The one red leaf, the last of its clan,
   That dances as often as dance it can.
   Christabel, I, l. 49

10 Her gentle limbs did she undress,
   And lay down in her loveliness.   *Christabel, I, l. 237*

11 A sight to dream of, not to tell!   *Christabel, I, l. 252*

12 That saints will aid if men will call:
   For the blue sky bends over all!   *Christabel, I, l. 330*

13 Alas! they had been friends in youth;
   But whispering tongues can poison truth;
   And constancy lives in realms above;
   And life is thorny; and youth is vain;
   And to be wroth with one we love
   Doth work like madness in the brain.
   Christabel, II, l. 408

14 The frost performs its secret ministry,
   Unhelped by any wind.
   Frost at Midnight [1798], l. 1

15   Therefore all seasons shall be sweet to thee,
   Whether the summer clothe the general earth
   With greenness, or the redbreast sit and sing
   Betwixt the tufts of snow on the bare branch
   Of mossy apple-tree, while the nigh thatch
   Smokes in the sun-thaw; whether the eave-drops fall
   Heard only in the trances of the blast,
   Or if the secret ministry of frost
   Shall hang them up in silent icicles,
   Quietly shining to the quiet moon.
   Frost at Midnight, l. 65

16 Forth from his dark and lonely hiding place
   (Portentous sight!) the owlet Atheism,
   Sailing on obscene wings athwart the noon,
   Drops his blue-fringèd lids, and holds them close,
   And hooting at the glorious sun in Heaven,
   Cries out, "Where is it?"
   Fears in Solitude [1798], l. 81

17 In Xanadu did Kubla Khan
   A stately pleasure dome decree:
   Where Alph, the sacred river, ran
   Through caverns measureless to man
   Down to a sunless sea.
   So twice five miles of fertile ground
   With walls and towers were girdled round.
   Kubla Khan [1798], l. 1

18 A savage place! as holy and enchanted
   As e'er beneath a waning moon was haunted
   By woman wailing for her demon-lover!
   Kubla Khan, l. 14

19 Five miles meandering with a mazy motion.
   Kubla Khan, l. 25

20 Ancestral voices prophesying war!
   Kubla Khan, l. 30

21 It was a miracle of rare device,
   A sunny pleasure dome with caves of ice!
   Kubla Khan, l. 35

22 A damsel with a dulcimer
   In a vision once I saw:
   It was an Abyssinian maid,
   And on her dulcimer she played,
   Singing of Mount Abora.   *Kubla Khan, l. 37*

23 Could I revive within me
   Her symphony and song,
   To such a deep delight 'twould win me,
   That with music loud and long,
   I would build that dome in air,
   That sunny dome! those caves of ice!
   And all who heard should see them there,
   And all should cry, Beware! Beware!
   His flashing eyes, his floating hair!
   Weave a circle round him thrice,
   And close your eyes with holy dread,

For he on honeydew hath fed,
And drunk the milk of Paradise.   *Kubla Khan, l. 42*

1 Strongly it bears us along in swelling and limitless
    billows,
Nothing before and nothing behind but the sky and
    the ocean.
           The Homeric Hexameter (translated from
           SCHILLER*) [1799?]*

2 In the hexameter rises the fountain's silvery column;
In the pentameter aye falling in melody back.
           The Ovidian Elegiac Metre
           (translated from SCHILLER*) [1799]*

3 All thoughts, all passions, all delights,
Whatever stirs this mortal frame,
All are but ministers of Love,
And feed his sacred flame.   *Love [1799], st. 1*

4 Earth, with her thousand voices, praises God.
           Hymn Before Sunrise, in the Vale of
           Chamouni [1802], last line

5 What is an epigram? A dwarfish whole,
Its body brevity, and wit its soul.
                     An Epigram [1802]

6 I see, not feel, how beautiful they are!
                     Dejection: An Ode [1802], st. 2

7   It were a vain endeavor,
           Though I should gaze forever
On that green light that lingers in the west:
I may not hope from outward forms to win
The passion and the life, whose fountains are
           within.   *Dejection: An Ode, st. 3*

8 O lady! we receive but what we give
And in our life alone does Nature live.
                     Dejection: An Ode, st. 4

9 A light, a glory, a fair luminous cloud
Enveloping the earth.   *Dejection: An Ode, st. 4*

10 Joy is the sweet voice, joy the luminous cloud —
We in ourselves rejoice!
And thence flows all that charms or ear or sight,
All melodies the echoes of that voice,
All colors a suffusion from that light.
                     Dejection: An Ode, st. 5

11 Trochee trips from long to short;
From long to long in solemn sort
Slow Spondee stalks.   *Metrical Feet [1806]*

12 With Donne, whose muse on dromedary trots,
Wreathe iron pokers into true-love knots.
                     On Donne's Poetry [c. 1818]

13 Flowers are lovely; love is flower-like;
Friendship is a sheltering tree.
           Youth and Age [1823–1832], st. 2

14 All Nature seems at work. Slugs leave their lair —
The bees are stirring — birds are on the wing —
And Winter slumbering in the open air,
Wears on his smiling face a dream of Spring!
And I the while, the sole unbusy thing,
Nor honey make, nor pair, nor build, nor sing.
           Work Without Hope [February 21, 1825], l. 1

15 Work without Hope draws nectar in a sieve,
And Hope without an object cannot live.
                     Work Without Hope, l. 13

16 I counted two and seventy stenches,
All well defined, and several stinks.   *Cologne [1828]*

17   In looking at objects of Nature while I am
thinking, as at yonder moon dim-glimmering
through the dewy window-pane, I seem rather to be
seeking, as it were *asking* for, a symbolical language
for something within me that already and forever
exists, than observing anything new.
           Anima Poetae (Soul of the Poet) [1805], ch. 4

18   If a man could pass through Paradise in a dream,
and have a flower presented to him as a pledge that
his soul had really been there, and if he found that
flower in his hand when he awoke — Ay! — and what
then?   *Anima Poetae, 9*

19   Poetry is not the proper antithesis to prose, but to
science. Poetry is opposed to science, and prose to
metre. The proper and immediate object of science
is the acquirement, or communication, of truth; the
proper and immediate object of poetry is the communication of immediate pleasure.
                     Definitions of Poetry [1811]

20   Reviewers are usually people who would have
been poets, historians, biographers, etc., if they
could; they have tried their talents at one or at the
other, and have failed; therefore they turn critics.
           Lectures on Shakespeare and Milton [1811–1812]

21   The last speech [Iago's soliloquy], the motive-
hunting of a motiveless malignity — how awful!
                     Notes on Shakespeare [c. 1812]

22   The most general definition of beauty . . . Multeity
in Unity.
           On the Principles of Genial Criticism [1814]

23   The Good consists in the congruity of a thing with
the laws of the reason and the nature of the will, and
in its fitness to determine the latter to actualize the
former: and it is always discursive. The Beautiful arises
from the perceived harmony of an object, whether
sight or sound, with the inborn and constitutive rules
of the judgment and imagination: and it is always
intuitive.   *On the Principles of Genial Criticism*

24   The imagination . . . that reconciling and mediatory power, which incorporating the reason in images

of the sense and organizing (as it were) the flux of the senses by the permanence and self-circling energies of the reason, gives birth to a system of symbols, harmonious in themselves, and consubstantial with the truths of which they are the conductors.
The Statesman's Manual [1816]

1   Not the poem which we have *read,* but that to which we *return,* with the greatest pleasure, possesses the genuine power, and claims the name of *essential poetry.*   *Biographia Literaria [1817], ch. 1*

2   Every reform, however necessary, will by weak minds be carried to an excess, that itself will need reforming.   *Biographia Literaria, 1*

3   Until you understand a writer's ignorance, presume yourself ignorant of his understanding.
Biographia Literaria, 12

4   During the act of knowledge itself, the objective and subjective are so instantly united, that we cannot determine to which of the two the priority belongs.
Biographia Literaria, 12

5   The primary imagination I hold to be the living power and prime agent of all human perception, and as a repetition in the finite mind of the eternal act of creation in the infinite I Am.
Biographia Literaria, 13

6   The secondary [imagination]...dissolves, diffuses, dissipates, in order to re-create; or where this process is rendered impossible, yet still at all events it struggles to idealize and to unify. It is essentially vital, even as all objects (*as* objects) are essentially fixed and dead.   *Biographia Literaria, 13*

7   The fancy is indeed no other than a mode of memory emancipated from the order of time and space.   *Biographia Literaria, 13*

8   The two cardinal points of poetry, the power of exciting the sympathy of the reader by a faithful adherence to the truth of nature, and the power of giving the interest of novelty by the modifying colors of imagination.   *Biographia Literaria, 14*

9   That willing suspension of disbelief for the moment, which constitutes poetic faith.
Biographia Literaria, 14

10   A poem is that species of composition, which is opposed to works of science, by proposing for its immediate object pleasure, not truth; and from all other species (having this object in common with it) it is discriminated by proposing to itself such delight from the whole, as is compatible with a distinct gratification from each component part.
Biographia Literaria, 14

11   A poem of any length neither can be, or ought to be, all poetry.   *Biographia Literaria, 14*

12   The poet, described in *ideal* perfection, brings the whole soul of man into activity, with the subordination of its faculties to each other, according to their relative worth and dignity. He diffuses a tone and spirit of unity, that blends, and (as it were) *fuses,* each into each, by that synthetic and magical power... imagination.   *Biographia Literaria, 14*

13   [Imagination] reveals itself in the balance or reconciliation of opposite or discordant qualities: of sameness, with difference; of the general, with the concrete; the idea, with the image; the individual, with the representative; the sense of novelty and freshness, with old and familiar objects; a more than usual state of emotion, with more than usual order; judgment ever awake and steady self-possession, with enthusiasm and feeling profound or vehement; and while it blends and harmonizes the natural and the artificial, still subordinates art to nature; the manner to the matter; and our admiration of the poet to our sympathy with the poetry.
Biographia Literaria, 14

14   No man was ever yet a great poet, without being at the same time a profound philosopher.
Biographia Literaria, 15

15   While [Shakespeare] darts himself forth and passes into all the forms of human character and passion, the one Proteus of the fire and the flood, [Milton] attracts all forms and things to himself, into the unity of his own *Ideal.* All things and modes of action shape themselves anew in the being of Milton; while Shakespeare becomes all things, yet for ever remaining himself.   *Biographia Literaria, 15*

16   Our myriad-minded Shakespeare.[1]
Biographia Literaria, 15

17   The best part of human language, properly so called, is derived from reflection on the acts of the mind itself.[2]   *Biographia Literaria, 17*

18   Now Art, used collectively for painting, sculpture, architecture and music, is the mediatress between, and reconciler of, nature and man. It is, therefore, the power of humanizing nature, of infusing the thoughts and passions of man into everything which is the object of his contemplation.
On Poesy or Art [1818]

---

[1]A phrase which I have borrowed from a Greek monk, who applies it to a patriarch of Constantinople. — COLERIDGE's *footnote*

[2]The poem of the act of the mind. — WALLACE STEVENS, *Of Modern Poetry*

1   The artist must imitate that which is within the thing, that which is active through form and figure, and discourses to us by symbols.

On Poesy or Art

2   The heart should have fed upon the truth, as insects on a leaf, till it be tinged with the color, and show its food in every...minutest fiber.

On Poesy or Art

3   I wish our clever young poets would remember my homely definitions of prose and poetry; that is, prose = words in their best order; poetry = the best words in their best order.

Table Talk [July 12, 1827]

4   The man's desire is for the woman; but the woman's desire is rarely other than for the desire of the man.

Table Talk [July 23, 1827]

5   That passage is what I call the sublime dashed to pieces by cutting too close with the fiery four-in-hand round the corner of nonsense.

Table Talk [July 23, 1827]

6   The happiness of life is made up of minute fractions — the little soon forgotten charities of a kiss or smile, a kind look, a heartfelt compliment, and the countless infinitesimals of pleasurable and genial feeling.

The Friend. The Improvisatore [1828]

7   Every man is born an Aristotelian or a Platonist. I do not think it possible that anyone born an Aristotelian can become a Platonist; and I am sure that no born Platonist can ever change into an Aristotelian.... The one considers reason a quality, or attribute; the other considers it a power.

Table Talk [July 2,1830]

8   Beneath this sod
A poet lies, or that which once seemed he —
Oh, lift a thought in prayer for S.T.C.!
That he, who many a year, with toil of breath,
Found death in life, may here find life in death.

Epitaph written for himself [1833]

Novalis
[Baron Friedrich von Hardenberg]
1772–1801

9   We are near awakening when we dream that we dream.

Pollen [1798]

10   Novels arise out of the shortcomings of history.

Fragments and Studies [1799–1800]

11   I often feel, and ever more deeply I realize, that Fate and character are the same conception.[1]

Heinrich von Ofterdingen [1802], bk. 2

Josiah Quincy Jr.
1772–1864

12   If this bill [for the admission of Orleans Territory as a State] passes, I am compelled to declare it as my deliberate opinion that the bonds of this Union are virtually dissolved; that the States which compose it are free from their moral obligations; and that, as it will be the right of all, so it will be the duty of some, to prepare definitely for a separation — amicably if they can; violently if they must.[2]

*Speech in the House of Representatives
[January 14, 1811]*

David Ricardo
1772–1823

13   Labor, like all other things which are purchased and sold, and which may be increased or diminished in quantity, has its natural and its market price. The natural price of labor is that price which is necessary to enable the laborers, one with another, to subsist and perpetuate their race, without either increase or diminution.

*On the Principles of Political Economy and
Taxation [1817], ch. 5*

14   Nothing contributes so much to the prosperity and happiness of a country as high profits.

*On Protection to Agriculture
[1820], sec. 5*

15   There is no way of keeping profits up but by keeping wages down.

On Protection to Agriculture, sec. 6

Friedrich von Schlegel
1772–1829

16   The historian is a prophet in reverse.

Athenaeum [1798–1800]

---

[1]"Character," — says Novalis, in one of his questionable aphorisms — "character is destiny." — GEORGE ELIOT, *The Mill on the Floss, vol. 3, bk. 6*

[2]The gentleman [Quincy] cannot have forgotten his own sentiment, uttered even on the floor of this House, "Peaceably if we can, forcibly if we must." — HENRY CLAY, *Speech* [January 8, 1813]

William Henry Harrison[1]
1773–1841

1   We admit of no government by divine right . . . the only legitimate right to govern is an express grant of power from the governed.
Inaugural Address [March 4, 1841]

2   A decent and manly examination of the acts of government should be not only tolerated, but encouraged.   *Inaugural Address [March 4, 1841]*

Prince Klemens von Metternich
1773–1859

3   Revolutions begin in the best heads, and run steadily down to the populace.
Quoted by RALPH WALDO EMERSON *in*
Fortune of the Republic [1863]

John Randolph
1773–1833

4   The surest way to prevent war is not to fear it.
Speech in the House of Representatives
[March 5, 1806]

5   [Of Edward Livingston:] He is a man of splendid abilities, but utterly corrupt. He shines and stinks like rotten mackerel by moonlight.
From W. CABELL BRUCE *[1860–1946],*
John Randolph of Roanoke [1923], vol. II

Robert Southey
1774–1843

6 It was a summer evening;
Old Kaspar's work was done,
And he before his cottage door
Was sitting in the sun;
And by him sported on the green
His little grandchild Wilhelmine.
The Battle of Blenheim [1798], st. 1

7 "'Tis some poor fellow's skull," said he,
"Who fell in the great victory."
The Battle of Blenheim, st. 3

8 But what they fought each other for,
I could not well make out.
The Battle of Blenheim, st. 6

9 "And everybody praised the duke,
Who this great fight did win."
"But what good came of it at last?"
Quoth little Peterkin.
"Why, that I cannot tell," said he;
"But 'twas a famous victory."
The Battle of Blenheim, st. 11

10 "You are old, Father William," the young man cried,
"The few locks which are left you are gray;
You are hale, Father William — a hearty old man:
Now tell me the reason, I pray."
The Old Man's Comforts and
How He Gained Them[2] [1799], st. 1

11 "In the days of my youth, I remembered my God,
And he hath not forgotten my age."
The Old Man's Comforts and
How He Gained Them, st. 6

12 And then they knew the perilous rock,
And blessed the Abbot of Aberbrothok.
The Inchcape Rock[3] [1802], st. 4

13 Till the vessel strikes with a shivering shock —
"O Christ! It is the Inchcape Rock."
The Inchcape Rock, st. 15

14 Curses are like young chickens, they always come home to roost.
The Curse of Kehama [1810], motto

15 My days among the dead are past;
Around me I behold,
Where'er these casual eyes are cast,
The mighty minds of old.
My Days Among the Dead Are Past [1818], st. 1

16 Yet leaving here a name, I trust,
That will not perish in the dust.
My Days Among the Dead Are Past, st. 4

17   Agreed to differ.   *Life of Wesley [1820]*

18 From his brimstone bed, at break of day,
A-walking the Devil is gone,
To look at his little snug farm of the world,
And see how his stock went on.
The Devil's Walk [1830], st. 1

19 His coat was red, and his breeches were blue,
And there was a hole where his tail came through.
The Devil's Walk, st. 3

---

[1]Tippecanoe and Tyler, Too.—A. C. ROSS [fl. c. 1840], *Presidential campaign song* [1840]

The iron-armed soldier, the true-hearted soldier, / The gallant old soldier of Tippecanoe. — GEORGE POPE MORRIS [1802–1864], *campaign song for Harrison* [1840], *sung to the tune of The Old Oaken Bucket*

[2]Of several parodies of this poem, the one by Lewis Carroll is probably better known than the original. See 514:4–514:7.

[3]A rock in the North Sea, off the Firth of Tay, Scotland, dangerous to navigators because it is covered with every tide. There is a tradition that a warning bell was fixed on the rock by the Abbot of Aberbrothok, which was stolen by a sea pirate, who perished on the rock a year later.

Jane Austen[1]

1775–1817

1   An annuity is a very serious business; it comes over and over every year, and there is no getting rid of it.
Sense and Sensibility [1811], bk. I, ch. 2

2   It is not time or opportunity that is to determine intimacy; — it is disposition alone. Seven years would be insufficient to make some people acquainted with each other, and seven days are more than enough for others.   *Sense and Sensibility, I, 12*

3   It is a truth universally acknowledged, that a single man in possession of a good fortune, must be in want of a wife.   *Pride and Prejudice [1813], ch. 1*

4   She [Mrs. Bennet] was a woman of mean understanding, little information, and uncertain temper.
Pride and Prejudice, 1

5   A lady's imagination is very rapid; it jumps from admiration to love, from love to matrimony in a moment.   *Pride and Prejudice, 6*

6   May I ask whether these pleasing attentions proceed from the impulse of the moment, or are the result of previous study?
Pride and Prejudice, 14

7   Mr. Collins had only to change from Jane to Elizabeth — and it was soon done — done while Mrs. Bennet was stirring the fire.
Pride and Prejudice, 15

8   You have delighted us long enough.
Pride and Prejudice, 18

9   Without thinking highly either of men or of matrimony, marriage had always been her object; it was the only honorable provision for well-educated young women of small fortune, and however uncertain of giving happiness, must be their pleasantest preservative from want.
Pride and Prejudice, 22

10   Mrs. Bennet was restored to her usual querulous serenity.   *Pride and Prejudice, 42*

11   You ought certainly to forgive them, as a Christian, but never to admit them in your sight, or allow their names to be mentioned in your hearing.
Pride and Prejudice, 57

12   For what do we live, but to make sport for our neighbors, and laugh at them in our turn?
Pride and Prejudice, 57

13   I have been a selfish being all my life, in practice, though not in principle.
Pride and Prejudice, 58

14   A large income is the best recipe for happiness I ever heard of. It certainly may secure all the myrtle and turkey part of it.
Mansfield Park [1814], bk. II, ch. 4

15   One half of the world cannot understand the pleasures of the other.   *Emma [1815], ch. 9*

16   It was a delightful visit — perfect, in being much too short.   *Emma, 13*

17   With men he can be rational and unaffected, but when he has ladies to please every feature works.
Emma, 13

18   Nobody who has not been in the interior of a family can say what the difficulties of any individual of that family may be.   *Emma, 18*

19   The sooner every party breaks up, the better.
Emma, 25

20   Business, you know, may bring money, but friendship hardly ever does.   *Emma, 34*

21   "Only a novel" . . . in short, only some work in which the greatest powers of the mind are displayed, in which the most thorough knowledge of human nature, the happiest delineation of its varieties, the liveliest effusions of wit and humor are conveyed to the world in the best chosen language.
Northanger Abbey [1818], ch. 5

22   She had been forced into prudence in her youth, she learned romance as she grew older — the natural sequence of an unnatural beginning.
Persuasion [1818], ch. 4

23   I do not want people to be very agreeable, as it saves me the trouble of liking them a great deal.
Letters. To her sister Cassandra
[December 24, 1798]

24   We met a gentleman in a buggy, who, on minute examination, turned out to be Dr. Hall — and Dr. Hall in such very deep mourning that either his mother, his wife, or himself must be dead.
Letters. To her sister Cassandra
[May 17, 1799]

25   3 or 4 families in a Country Village is the very thing to work on.
Letter to her niece Anna Austen
[September 9, 1814]

---

[1][Miss Austen] had a talent for describing the involvements and feelings and characters of ordinary life which is to me the most wonderful I ever met with. The Big Bow-Wow strain I can do myself like any now going; but the exquisite touch, which renders ordinary commonplace things and characters interesting, from the truth of the description and the sentiment, is denied to me. — WALTER SCOTT, *Journal* [March 14, 1826]

1   The little bit (two inches wide) of ivory on which I work with so fine a brush as produces little effect after much labor.
*Letters. To J. Edward Austen
[December 16, 1816]*

Jacob Henry
1775–1847

2   The proud monuments of liberty knew that … governments were only concerned about the actions and conduct of man, and not his speculative notions. Who among us feels himself so exalted above his fellows, as to have a right to dictate to them their mode of belief?
*Speech on being refused his seat,
on religious grounds, in the
North Carolina legislature [1808]*

Charles Lamb
1775–1834

3 I have had playmates, I have had companions,
In my days of childhood, in my joyful school days —
All, all are gone, the old familiar faces.
Old Familiar Faces [1798]

4   Separate from the pleasure of your company, I don't much care if I never see a mountain in my life.   *Letter to William Wordsworth [1801]*

5   Anything awful makes me laugh. I misbehaved once at a funeral.   *Letter to Robert Southey [1815]*

6   [Of Coleridge:] An archangel a little damaged.
Letter to William Wordsworth [1816]

7   The red-letter days, now become, to all intents and purposes, dead-letter days.
Essays of Elia [1823]. Oxford in the Vacation

8   The human species, according to the best theory I can form of it, is composed of two distinct races, the men who borrow, and the men who lend.
Essays of Elia. The Two Races of Men

9   Your borrowers of books — those mutilators of collections, spoilers of the symmetry of shelves, and creators of odd volumes.
Essays of Elia. The Two Races of Men

10   A clear fire, a clean hearth, and the rigor of the game.
Essays of Elia. Mrs. Battle's Opinions on Whist

11   Sentimentally I am disposed to harmony; but organically I am incapable of a tune.
Essays of Elia. A Chapter on Ears

12   Credulity is the man's weakness, but the child's strength.
Essays of Elia. Witches, and Other Night Fears

13   Not many sounds in life, and I include all urban and all rural sounds, exceed in interest a knock at the door.   *Essays of Elia. Valentine's Day*

14   Presents, I often say, endear absents.
Essays of Elia. A Dissertation upon Roast Pig

15   I came home forever!
*Letter to Bernard Barton [1825], on leaving
his "33 years' desk" at the East India House*

16 Who first invented work, and bound the free
And holiday-rejoicing spirit down?   *Work*

17   A poor relation — is the most irrelevant thing in nature.
*Last Essays of Elia [1833].
Poor Relations*

18   I love to lose myself in other men's minds.
*Last Essays of Elia. Detached Thoughts
on Books and Reading*

19   Books think for me.
*Last Essays of Elia. Detached Thoughts
on Books and Reading*

20   How sickness enlarges the dimensions of a man's self to himself.   *Last Essays of Elia. The Convalescent*

21   Your absence of mind we have borne, till your presence of body came to be called in question by it.
Last Essays of Elia. Amicus Redivivus

22   A pun is a pistol let off at the ear; not a feather to tickle the intellect.
*Last Essays of Elia. Popular Fallacies: IX,
That the Worst Puns Are the Best*

23   The good things of life are not to be had singly, but come to us with a mixture.
*Last Essays of Elia. Popular Fallacies: XIII,
That You Must Love Me and Love My Dog*

24   The greatest pleasure I know is to do a good action by stealth, and to have it found out by accident.   *Table Talk. In the Athenaeum [1834]*

Walter Savage Landor
1775–1864

25 Ah what avails the sceptred race,
Ah what the form divine!   *Rose Aylmer [1806]*

26 Rose Aylmer, whom these wakeful eyes
May weep, but never see,
A night of memories and of sighs
I consecrate to thee.   *Rose Aylmer*

1   Of all failures, to fail in a witticism is the worst, and the mishap is the more calamitous in a drawn-out and detailed one.

> *Imaginary Conversations [1824–1829].*
> *Chesterfield and Chatham*

2 When we play the fool, how wide
The theatre expands! beside,
How long the audience sits before us!
How many prompters! what a chorus!

> *Plays [1846], st. 2*

3 There is delight in singing, though none hear
Beside the singer.

> *To Robert Browning [1846]*

4 I strove with none, for none was worth my strife;
Nature I loved; and next to Nature, Art.
I warm'd both hands before the fire of life;
It sinks, and I am ready to depart.

> *I Strove with None [1853]*

John Constable

1776–1837

5   There is nothing ugly; *I never saw an ugly thing in my life:* for let the form of an object be what it may, — light, shade, and perspective will always make it beautiful.

> *Quoted in C. R. Leslie [1794–1859],*
> *Memoirs of the Life of*
> *John Constable [1843]*

Thomas Campbell

1777–1844

6 'Tis distance lends enchantment to the view,
And robes the mountain in its azure hue.[1]

> *Pleasures of Hope [1799], pt. I, l. 7*

7 On the green banks of Shannon, when Sheelah was
    nigh,
No blithe Irish lad was so happy as I;
No harp like my own could so cheerily play,
And wherever I went was my poor dog Tray.[2]

> *The Harper [1799], st. 1*

8 Ye mariners of England,
That guard our native seas;
Whose flag has braved, a thousand years,
The battle and the breeze!

> *Ye Mariners of England [1800], st. 1*

9 Britannia needs no bulwarks,
No towers along the steep;
Her march is o'er the mountain waves,
Her home is on the deep.

> *Ye Mariners of England, st. 3*

10 'Tis the sunset of life gives me mystical lore,
And coming events cast their shadows before.[3]

> *Lochiel's Warning [1802]*

11 The combat deepens. On, ye brave,
Who rush to glory or the grave!
Wave, Munich! all thy banners wave,
And charge with all thy chivalry!

> *Hohenlinden [1802], st. 7*

12 There was silence deep as death,
And the boldest held his breath,
For a time.   *Battle of the Baltic [1805], st. 2*

13 Ye are brothers! ye are men!
And we conquer but to save.

> *Battle of the Baltic, st. 5*

14 Oh leave this barren spot to me!
Spare, woodman, spare the beechen tree!

> *The Beech Tree's Petition, st. 1*

15 Oh! once the harp of Innisfail
Was strung full high to notes of gladness;
But yet it often told a tale
Of more prevailing sadness.

> *O'Connor's Child [1810], st. 1*

Henry Clay

1777–1852

16   If you wish to avoid foreign collision, you had better abandon the ocean.

> *Speech in the House of Representatives*
> *[January 22, 1812]*

17   Government is a trust, and the officers of the government are trustees; and both the trust and the trustees are created for the benefit of the people.

> *Speech at Ashland, Kentucky*
> *[March 1829]*

18   I have heard something said about allegiance to the South. I know no South, no North, no East, no West, to which I owe any allegiance.... The Union, sir, is my country.

> *Speech in the Senate [1848]*

19   The Constitution of the United States was made not merely for the generation that then existed, but

---

[1]The mountains too, at a distance, appear airy masses and smooth, but seen near at hand they are rough. — Diogenes Laertius [fl. c. 200 c.e.], *Pyrrho, sec. 9*

[2]My Old Dog Tray — Stephen C. Foster, *title of song*

[3]Often do the spirits / Of great events stride on before the events, / And in today already walks tomorrow. — Johann Friedrich von Schiller, *Death of Wallenstein, act V, sc. iii* Translated by Samuel Taylor Coleridge.

for posterity — unlimited, undefined, endless, perpetual posterity.
Speech in the Senate [January 29, 1850]

1   I would rather be right than be President.[1]
Speech in the Senate [1850]

Lorenzo Dow
1777–1834

2   You will be damned if you do. — And you will be damned if you don't [definition of Calvinism].
Reflections on the Love of God

Carl Friedrich Gauss
1777–1855

3   Mathematics is the queen of the sciences.
From SARTORIUS VON WALTERSHAUSEN [1809–1876], Gauss zum Gedächtniss (Gauss: A Memorial) [1856]

Heinrich von Kleist
1777–1811

4   Grace appears most purely in that human form which either has no consciousness or an infinite consciousness. That is, in the puppet or in the god.[2]
On the Marionette Theater [1810]

Roger B. Taney
1777–1864

5   [On slaves and their descendants:] They are not included, and were not intended to be included, under the word "citizens" in the Constitution, and can therefore claim none of the rights and privileges which that instrument provides for and secures to citizens of the United States.
Dred Scott v. Sandford [1857]

Valentine Blacker
1778–1823

6   Put your trust in God, my boys, and keep your powder dry!
From EDWARD HAYES [b. 1800?], Ballads of Ireland [1856]. Oliver's Advice, An Orange Ballad

Henry Peter Brougham, Baron Brougham and Vaux
1778–1868

7   What is valuable is not new, and what is new is not valuable.
From The Edinburgh Review [c. 1802], The Work of Thomas Young

8   In my mind, he was guilty of no error — he was chargeable with no exaggeration — he was betrayed by his fancy into no metaphor, who once said that all we see about us, Kings, Lords, and Commons, the whole machinery of the State, all the apparatus of the system, and its varied workings, end in simply bringing twelve good men into a box.
Present State of the Law [February 7, 1828]

9   The great unwashed.   *Attributed*

Robert Emmet
1778–1803

10   Let no man write my epitaph. . . . When my country takes her place among the nations of the earth, *then and not till then,* let my epitaph be written.[3]
On being sentenced to death for Irish nationalist activity [September 19, 1803]

William Hazlitt
1778–1830

11   Hamlet is a name: his speeches and sayings but the idle coinage of the poet's brain. What then, are they not real? They are as real as our own thoughts. Their reality is in the reader's mind. It is *we* who are Hamlet.
Characters of Shakespeare's Plays [1817]

12   The love of liberty is the love of others; the love of power is the love of ourselves.
Political Essays [1819]. The Times Newspaper

13   One has no notion of him [William Cobbett] as making use of a fine pen, but a great mutton-fist; his style stuns readers. . . . He is too much for any single newspaper antagonist; "lays waste" a city orator or Member of Parliament, and bears hard upon the government itself. He is a kind of *fourth estate* in the politics of the country.[4]
Table Talk [1821–1822]. Character of Cobbett

---

[1]Said when told that his defense of the Compromise of 1850 would endanger his chances for the presidency.

[2]Translated by IDRIS PARRY.

[3]Emmet left no written version of his speech from the docket. Various versions exist.

[4]See Thomas Carlyle, 406:9 and note.

1   It is better to be able neither to read nor write than to be able to do nothing else.
Table Talk. On the Ignorance of the Learned

2   Danger is a good teacher, and makes apt scholars. So are disgrace, defeat, exposure to immediate scorn, and laughter.   *Table Talk. The Indian Jugglers*

3   What I mean by living to one's self is living in the world, as in it, not of it. . . . It is to be a silent spectator of the mighty scene of things; . . . to take a thoughtful, anxious interest in what is passing in the world, but not to feel the slightest inclination to make or meddle with it.
Table Talk. On Living to One's Self

4   There is not a more mean, stupid, dastardly, pitiful, selfish, spiteful, envious, ungrateful animal than the Public. It is the greatest of cowards, for it is afraid of itself.   *Table Talk. On Living to One's Self*

5   He who lives wisely to himself and to his own heart looks at the busy world through the loop-holes of retreat, and does not want to mingle in the fray.
Table Talk. On Living to One's Self

6   When a man is dead, they put money in his coffin, erect monuments to his memory, and celebrate the anniversary of his birthday in set speeches. Would they take any notice of him if he were living? No!
Table Talk. On Living to One's Self

7   One of the pleasantest things in the world is going a journey; but I like to go by myself.
Table Talk. On Going a Journey

8   When I am in the country I wish to vegetate like the country.   *Table Talk. On Going a Journey*

9   The soul of a journey is liberty, perfect liberty, to think, feel, do just as one pleases.
Table Talk. On Going a Journey

10   Give me the clear blue sky over my head, and the green turf beneath my feet, a winding road before me, and a three hours' march to dinner — and then to thinking! It is hard if I cannot start some game on these lone heaths.
Table Talk. On Going a Journey

11   No young man ever thinks he shall die.
Table Talk. On the Fear of Death

12   We never do anything well till we cease to think about the manner of doing it.
Sketches and Essays [1823]. On Prejudice

13   If I have not read a book before, it is, to all intents and purposes, new to me, whether it was printed yesterday or three hundred years ago.
Sketches and Essays. On Reading New Books

14   Men of genius do not excel in any profession because they labor in it, but they labor in it because they excel.   *Characteristics [1823], no. 416*

15   We are not hypocrites in our sleep.
On Dreams [1823]

16   I believe in the theoretical benevolence, and the practical malignity of man.
Aphorisms on Man [1830], no. 46

Stephen Decatur
1779–1820

17   Our country! In her intercourse with foreign nations may she always be in the right; but our country, right or wrong.[1]
Toast given at Norfolk [April 1816].
From Alexander Slidell Mackenzie *[1803–1849], Life of Stephen Decatur*[2] *[1848]*

Thomas, Lord Denman
1779–1854

18   Trial by jury, instead of being a security to persons who are accused, will be a delusion, a mockery, and a snare.
O'Connell v. The Queen [September 4, 1844]

Francis Scott Key
1779–1843

19 Oh, say, can you see by the dawn's early light,
What so proudly we hailed at the twilight's last gleaming?
Whose broad stripes and bright stars, through the perilous fight,
O'er the ramparts we watched were so gallantly streaming?
And the rockets' red glare, the bombs bursting in air,
Gave proof through the night that our flag was still there.
Oh, say, does that star-spangled banner yet wave
O'er the land of the free and the home of the brave?
The Star-Spangled Banner [September 14, 1814], st. 1

---

[1]I hope to find my country in the right: however, I will stand by her, right or wrong. — John Jordan Crittenden [1787–1863], *On the Mexican War*

[2]*Niles' Weekly Register* [Baltimore; April 20, 1816] gives a slightly different reading: *Our Country*— In her intercourse with foreign nations may she always be in the *right,* and always *successful, right* or *wrong.*

1 Blessed with victory and peace, may the Heaven-
   rescued land
Praise the Power that hath made and preserved us a
   nation.
Then conquer we must, when our cause it is just,
And this be our motto, "In God is our trust."

                 The Star-Spangled Banner, st. 4

Clement Clarke Moore
1779–1863

2 'Twas the night before Christmas, when all through
   the house
Not a creature was stirring — not even a mouse;
The stockings were hung by the chimney with care,
In hopes that St. Nicholas soon would be there.
         A Visit from St. Nicholas [December 1823]

3 "Happy Christmas to all, and to all a goodnight!"
                  A Visit from St. Nicholas

Thomas Moore
1779–1852

4 Faintly as tolls the evening chime,
  Our voices keep tune and our oars keep time.
        Poems Relating to America.
        A Canadian Boat Song, st. 1

5 Go where glory waits thee!
  But while fame elates thee,
  Oh, still remember me!
        Irish Melodies [1807–1834].
        Go Where Glory Waits Thee, st. 1

6 Oh, breathe not his name! let it sleep in the shade,
  Where cold and unhonor'd his relics are laid.
        Irish Melodies.
        Oh, Breathe Not His Name, st. 1

7 And the tear that we shed, though in secret it rolls,
  Shall long keep his memory green in our souls.
        Irish Melodies.
        Oh, Breathe Not His Name, st. 2

8 The harp that once through Tara's halls
  The soul of music shed,
  Now hangs as mute on Tara's walls
  As if that soul were fled.
       Irish Melodies. The Harp That Once Through
       Tara's Halls, st. 1

9 Believe me, if all those endearing young charms
  Which I gaze on so fondly today,
  Were to change by tomorrow and fleet in my arms,
  Like fairy gifts fading away,

Thou would'st still be ador'd as this moment thou
  art,
Let thy loveliness fade as it will,
And around the dear ruin each wish of my heart
Would entwine itself verdantly still.
        Irish Melodies. Believe Me, If All Those
        Endearing Young Charms, st. 1

10 But there's nothing half so sweet in life
  As love's young dream.
        Irish Melodies. Love's Young Dream, st. 1

11 'Tis the last rose of summer,
  Left blooming alone;
  All her lovely companions
  Are faded and gone.
        Irish Melodies.
        The Last Rose of Summer, st. 1

12 The Minstrel Boy to the war is gone,
  In the ranks of death you'll find him.
  His father's sword he has girded on,
  And his wild harp slung behind him.
        Irish Melodies. The Minstrel Boy, st. 1

13   And the best of all ways
     To lengthen our days
  Is to steal a few hours from the night, my dear.
        Irish Melodies.
        The Young May Moon, st. 1

14 You may break, you may shatter the vase, if you will,
  But the scent of the roses will hang round it still.[1]
        Irish Melodies. Farewell!
        But Whenever, st. 3

15 The light that lies
  In woman's eyes,
  Has been my heart's undoing.
        Irish Melodies. The Time I've Lost in Wooing,
        st. 1

16   My only books
     Were woman's looks,
  And folly's all they've taught me.
        Irish Melodies. The Time I've Lost in Wooing,
        st. 1

17 Oft in the stilly night,
  Ere Slumber's chain has bound me,
  Fond Memory brings the light
  Of other days around me;
    The smiles, the tears,
    Of boyhood's years,
  The words of love then spoken;
    The eyes that shone

---

[1] The jar will long keep the fragrance of what it was once steeped in
when new. — HORACE, *Epistles, bk. I, no. ii, l. 69*
  The image was frequently used in the classical period; unglazed
ware is more absorbent than glazed.

Now dimmed and gone,
The cheerful hearts now broken.
National Airs [1815]. Oft in the Stilly Night, st. 1

1   I feel like one,
       Who treads alone
Some banquet hall deserted,
       Whose lights are fled,
       Whose garlands dead,
And all but he departed.
National Airs. Oft in the Stilly Night, st. 2

2 What though youth gave love and roses,
Age still leaves us friends and wine.
National Airs. Spring and Autumn, st. 1

3 Oh! ever thus, from childhood's hour,
I've seen my fondest hope decay;
I never loved a tree or flower,
But 'twas the first to fade away.
I never nurs'd a dear gazelle
To glad me with its soft black eye,
But when it came to know me well,
And love me, it was sure to die.
Lalla Rookh [1817], pt. V

4 Like Dead Sea fruits, that tempt the eye,
But turn to ashes on the lips.   *Lalla Rookh, V*

5   Paradise itself were dim
And joyless, if not shared with him!   *Lalla Rookh, VI*

Joseph Story
1779–1845

6   [The law] is a jealous mistress, and requires a long
and constant courtship. It is not to be won by trifling
favors, but by lavish homage.
*The Value and Importance of Legal Studies
[August 5, 1829]*

William Ellery Channing
1780–1842

7   We do, then, with all earnestness, though without
reproaching our brethren, protest against the irrational and unscriptural doctrine of the Trinity. "To
us," as to the Apostle and the primitive Christians,
"there is one God, even the Father." With Jesus, we
worship the Father, as the only living and true God.
We are astonished, that any man can read the New
Testament, and avoid the conviction, that the Father
alone is God.
Unitarian Christianity [Baltimore, 1819]

8   I see the marks of God in the heavens and the
earth, but how much more in a liberal intellect, in

magnanimity, in unconquerable rectitude, in a philanthropy which forgives every wrong, and which
never despairs of the cause of Christ and human
virtue! I do and I must reverence human nature. . . . I
thank God that my own lot is bound up with that of
the human race.
*Likeness to God [Providence,
Rhode Island, 1828]*

9   There are seasons, in human affairs, of inward and
outward revolution, when new depths seem to be
broken up in the soul, when new wants are unfolded
in multitudes, and a new and undefined good is thirsted for. These are periods when . . . *to dare* is the
highest wisdom.
Complete Works [1879]. The Union [1829]

Karl von Clausewitz
1780–1831

10   War is not merely a political act, but also a real
political instrument, a continuation of political commerce, a carrying out of the same by other means.[1]
On War[2] [1833]

11   The great uncertainty of all data in war is a peculiar
difficulty, because all action must, to a certain extent,
be planned in a mere twilight, which in addition
not infrequently — like the effect of a fog or moonshine — gives to things exaggerated dimensions and
unnatural appearance.[3]   *On War*

Charles Caleb Colton
1780–1832

12   When you have nothing to say, say nothing.
Lacon [1820–1822], vol. I, no. 183

13   Imitation is the sincerest of flattery.
Lacon, I, 217

Philip Hone
1780–1851

14   By and by we shall have balloons and pass over to
Europe between sun and sun. Oh, for the good old
days of heavy post-coaches and speed at the rate of six
miles an hour!
Diary [November 28, 1844]

---

[1]Der Krieg ist nichts anderes als die Fortsetzung der Politik mit
anderen Mitteln.
[2]Translated by J. J. GRAHAM.
[3]Often cited as the source of the concept of "the fog of war."

Charles Miner
1780–1865

1   When I see a merchant overpolite to his customers, begging them to taste a little brandy and throwing half his goods on the counter — thinks I, that man has an ax to grind.

> *Essays from the Desk of Poor Robert the Scribe [1815]. Who'll Turn Grindstones*[1]

Frances [Milton] Trollope
1780–1863

2   Let no one who wishes to receive agreeable impressions of American manners, commence their travels in a Mississippi steamboat.

> *Domestic Manners of the Americans [1832]*

Ebenezer Elliott
1781–1849

3 Not kings and lords, but nations!
Not thrones and crowns, but men!

> *Corn Law Rhymes [1828].
> When Wilt Thou Save the People?, st. 1*

4 God save the people!

> *Corn Law Rhymes. When Wilt Thou Save the People?, st. 1*

5 What is a communist? One who hath yearnings
For equal division of unequal earnings.

> *Poetical Works [1846]. Epigram*

James Lawrence
1781–1813

6   Tell the men to fire faster and not to give up the ship; fight her till she sinks.[2]

> *On board the U.S. frigate Chesapeake
> [June 1, 1813]*

John C[aldwell] Calhoun
1782–1850

7   The very essence of a free government consists in considering offices as public trusts, bestowed for the good of the country, and not for the benefit of an individual or a party.   *Speech [February 13, 1835]*

8   A power has risen up in the government greater than the people themselves, consisting of many and various and powerful interests, combined into one mass, and held together by the cohesive power of the vast surplus in the banks.[3]   *Speech [May 27, 1836]*

9   The surrender of life is nothing to sinking down into acknowledgment of inferiority.

> *Speech in the Senate [February 19, 1847]*

Thomas H. Palmer
1782–1861

10 'Tis a lesson you should heed,
Try, try again.
If at first you don't succeed,
Try, try again.   *Teacher's Manual*[4] *[1840]*

Ann Taylor
1782–1866

Jane Taylor
1783–1824

11 Who ran to help me when I fell,
And would some pretty story tell,
Or kiss the place to make it well?
  My mother.

> *Original Poems for Infant Minds [1804]. My
> Mother [by* ANN TAYLOR*], st. 6*

12 Twinkle, twinkle, little star,
How I wonder what you are,
Up above the world so high,
Like a diamond in the sky![5]

> *Rhymes for the Nursery [1806]. The Star, st. 1*

13 I like little pussy, her coat is so warm;
And if I don't hurt her she'll do me no harm.

> *Rhymes for the Nursery. I Like Little Pussy [by*
> JANE TAYLOR*], st. 1*

Daniel Webster
1782–1852

14   It is, sir, as I have said, a small college, and yet there are those who love it.

> *Dartmouth College Case [1818]*

---

[1]First published in *Luzerne Federalist* [September 7, 1810]. Because of the similarity of the title to *Poor Richard*, the phrase "an ax to grind" has often been attributed to BENJAMIN FRANKLIN.

[2]Usually quoted as "Don't give up the ship"; Captain Lawrence's final order as he was carried below, fatally wounded, before the capture of his ship by the British frigate *Shannon*.

---

[3]From this speech comes the phrase: Cohesive power of public plunder.

[4]Later popularized by EDWARD HICKSON [1803–1870] in his *Moral Songs* [1857] and often attributed to him or cited as a proverb.

[5]See Lewis Carroll, 514:15.

1   Labor in this country is independent and proud. It has not to ask the patronage of capital, but capital solicits the aid of labor.   *Speech [April 2, 1824]*

2   We wish that this column, rising towards heaven among the pointed spires of so many temples dedicated to God, may contribute also to produce in all minds a pious feeling of dependence and gratitude. We wish, finally, that the last object to the sight of him who leaves his native shore, and the first to gladden his who revisits it, may be something which shall remind him of the liberty and the glory of his country.
Address on Laying the Cornerstone of the
Bunker Hill Monument [June 17, 1825]

3   Sink or swim, live or die, survive or perish, I give my hand and my heart to this vote.[1]
Discourse in Commemoration of Adams and
Jefferson, Faneuil Hall, Boston
[August 2, 1826]

4   It is my living sentiment, and by the blessing of God it shall be my dying sentiment — Independence now and Independence forever.[2]
Discourse in Commemoration of Adams
and Jefferson, Faneuil Hall, Boston
[August 2, 1826]

5   Washington is in the clear upper sky.
Discourse in Commemoration of
Adams and Jefferson, Faneuil Hall,
Boston [August 2, 1826]

6   The gentleman has not seen how to reply to this, otherwise than by supposing me to have advanced the doctrine that a national debt is a national blessing.
Second Speech on Foote's Resolution
[January 26, 1830]

7   I shall enter on no encomium upon Massachusetts; she needs none. There she is.[3] Behold her, and judge for yourselves. There is her history; the world knows it by heart. The past, at least, is secure. There is Boston and Concord and Lexington and Bunker Hill; and there they will remain forever.
Second Speech on Foote's Resolution
[January 26, 1830]

8   The people's government, made for the people, made by the people, and answerable to the people.[4]
Second Speech on Foote's Resolution
[January 26, 1830]

9   When my eyes shall be turned to behold for the last time the sun in heaven, may I not see him shining on the broken and dishonored fragments of a once glorious Union; on States dissevered, discordant, belligerent; on a land rent with civil feuds, or drenched, it may be, in fraternal blood.
Second Speech on Foote's Resolution
[January 26, 1830]

10   Liberty and Union, now and forever, one and inseparable.
Second Speech on Foote's Resolution
[January 26, 1830]

11   There is no refuge from confession but suicide; and suicide is confession.
Argument on the murder of Captain White
[April 6, 1830]

12   He smote the rock of the national resources, and abundant streams of revenue gushed forth. He touched the dead corpse of the Public Credit, and it sprung upon its feet.
Speech on Hamilton [March 10, 1831]

13   God grants liberty only to those who love it, and are always ready to guard and defend it.
Speech [June 3, 1834]

14   One country, one constitution, one destiny.
Speech [March 15, 1837]

15   When tillage begins, other arts follow. The farmers therefore are the founders of human civilization.
On Agriculture [January 13, 1840]

16   America has furnished to the world the character of Washington. And if our American institutions had done nothing else, that alone would have entitled them to the respect of mankind.
On the Completion of the Bunker Hill
Monument [June 17, 1843]

17   Justice, sir, is the great interest of man on earth.
On Mr. Justice Story [September 12, 1845]

18   Inconsistencies of opinion, arising from changes of circumstances, are often justifiable.
Speech [July 25 and 27, 1846]

19   Liberty exists in proportion to wholesome restraint.
Speech at the Charleston Bar Dinner
[May 10, 1847]

20   I was born an American; I will live an American; I shall die an American.   *Speech [July 17, 1850]*

21   Faneuil Hall, the cradle of American liberty.
Letter [April 1851]

22   Men hang out their signs indicative of their respective trades: shoemakers hang out a gigantic

---

[1] Live or die, sink or swim. — GEORGE PEELE, *Edward I* [c. 1584]

[2] On the day of his [John Adams's] death, hearing the noise of bells and cannon, he asked the occasion. On being reminded that it was "Independent Day," he replied, "Independence forever." — DANIEL WEBSTER, *Works* [1903], *vol. I*

[3] Generally misquoted as "Massachusetts, there she stands."

[4] Our sovereign, the people. — CHARLES JAMES FOX, *toast* [1798], *for which his name was erased from the Privy Council*
See Abraham Lincoln, 446:5, and Theodore Parker, 457:9.

shoe; jewelers, a monster watch; and the dentist hangs out a gold tooth; but up in the mountains of New Hampshire, God Almighty has hung out a sign to show that there He makes men.
On the Old Man of the Mountain;[1] *attributed*

1   I still live.
Last words [October 24, 1852]

Simón Bolívar
1783–1830

2   A state too extensive in itself, or by virtue of its dependencies, ultimately falls into decay; its free government is transformed into a tyranny; it disregards the principles which it should preserve, and finally degenerates into despotism. The distinguishing characteristic of small republics is stability: the character of large republics is mutability.
Letter from Jamaica
[Summer 1815]

3   Those who have served the cause of the revolution have plowed the sea.   *Attributed*

4   The three greatest dolts in the world: Jesus Christ, Don Quixote, and I.   *Attributed*

Reginald Heber
1783–1826

5 From Greenland's icy mountains,
From India's coral strand,
Where Afric's sunny fountains
Roll down their golden sand.
Hymns. Missionary Hymn
[1819], st. 1

6 Though every prospect pleases,
And only man is vile.
Hymns. Missionary Hymn, st. 2

7 The heathen in his blindness
Bows down to wood and stone.
Hymns. Missionary Hymn, st. 2

8 Holy, Holy, Holy! Lord God Almighty!
Early in the morning our song shall rise to Thee:
Holy, Holy, Holy! Merciful and Mighty!
God in Three Persons, Blessed Trinity.
Hymns. Holy, Holy, Holy! [1827]

Washington Irving
1783–1859

9   The renowned and antient city of Gotham.[2]
Salmagundi [November 11, 1807]

10   How convenient it would be to many of our great men and great families of doubtful origin, could they have the privilege of the heroes of yore, who, whenever their origin was involved in obscurity, modestly announced themselves descended from a god.
Knickerbocker's History of New York
[1809], bk. II, ch. 3

11   His wife "ruled the roast," and in governing the governor, governed the province, which might thus be said to be under petticoat government.
Knickerbocker's History of New York, IV, 4

12   They claim to be the first inventors of those recondite beverages, cocktail, stonefence, and sherry cobbler.   *Knickerbocker's History of New York, IV, 241*

13   Those men are most apt to be obsequious and conciliating abroad, who are under the discipline of shrews at home.
The Sketch-Book [1819–1820]. Rip Van Winkle

14   A sharp tongue is the only edged tool that grows keener with constant use.
The Sketch-Book. Rip Van Winkle

15   That happy age when a man can be idle with impunity.   *The Sketch-Book. Rip Van Winkle*

16   A woman's whole life is a history of the affections.   *The Sketch-Book. The Broken Heart*

17   His [the author's] renown . . . has been purchased, not by deeds of violence and blood, but by the diligent dispensation of pleasure.
The Sketch-Book. Westminster Abbey
[The Poets' Corner]

18   Whenever a man's friends begin to compliment him about looking young, he may be sure that they think he is growing old.
Bracebridge Hall [1822]. Bachelors

19   The almighty dollar, that great object of universal devotion throughout our land.
Wolfert's Roost [1855]. The Creole Village

Stendhal [Henri Beyle]
1783–1842

20   I call "crystallization" that action of the mind that discovers fresh perfections in its beloved at every turn of events.   *De l'Amour (On Love) [1822], ch. 1*

---

[1]Natural rock formation in the shape of a human profile, in the Presidential Range of the White Mountains; it collapsed in 2003. It gave Nathaniel Hawthorne the theme of his story *The Great Stone Face* [1850].

[2]The first use of Gotham as a moniker for New York City.

1   A wise woman never yields by appointment. It should always be an unforeseen happiness.
De l'Amour, 60

2   Prudery is a kind of avarice, the worst of all.
De l'Amour, fragments

3   In matters of sentiment, the public has very crude ideas; and the most shocking fault of women is that they make the public the supreme judge of their lives.
De l'Amour, fragments

4   Courtiers of all ages feel one great need: to speak in such a way that they do not say anything.
Racine and Shakespeare [1823]

5   A novel is a mirror that strolls along a highway. Now it reflects the blue of the skies, now the mud puddles underfoot.
Le Rouge et le Noir (The Red and the Black)[1]
[1830]

6   There is no such thing as "natural law": this expression is nothing but old nonsense. Prior to laws, what is natural is only the strength of the lion, or the need of the creature suffering from hunger or cold, in short, need.
Le Rouge et le Noir

7   The count had reached his *fifties:* a cruel word whose resonance can perhaps be fully appreciated only by a man desperately in love.
La Chartreuse de Parme (The Charterhouse of Parma) [1839], ch. 7

8   I see but one rule: to be clear. If I am not clear, all my world crumbles to nothing.
Reply to Balzac [October 30, 1840]

9   Wit lasts no more than two centuries.
Reply to Balzac

10   It is the nobility of their style which will make our writers of 1840 unreadable forty years from now.
Manuscript note [1840]

11   Love has always been the most important business in my life, I should say the only one.
La Vie d'Henri Brulard [1890]

[James Henry] Leigh Hunt
1784–1859

12   This Adonis in loveliness was a corpulent man of fifty.[2]
The Examiner [March 22, 1812]

13   Green little vaulter in the sunny grass.
To the Grasshopper and the Cricket [1817]

14   Stolen sweets are always sweeter,
Stolen kisses much completer,
Stolen looks are nice in chapels,
Stolen, stolen, be your apples.[3]
Song of Fairies Robbing an Orchard [1830], l. 5

15   There lived a knight, when knighthood was in flow'r,
Who charmed alike the tilt-yard and the bower.
The Gentle Armour [1832], canto I

16   Abou Ben Adhem (may his tribe increase!)
Awoke one night from a deep dream of peace.
Abou Ben Adhem [1838]

17   An angel writing in a book of gold.
Abou Ben Adhem

18   Write me as one that loves his fellow men.
Abou Ben Adhem

19   And showed the names whom love of God had bless'd,
And lo! Ben Adhem's name led all the rest.
Abou Ben Adhem

20   Jenny kissed me when we met,
Jumping from the chair she sat in;
Time, you thief, who love to get
Sweets into your list, put that in:
Say I'm weary, say I'm sad,
Say that health and wealth have missed me,
Say I'm growing old, but add,
Jenny kissed me.[4]
Rondeau [1838]

Henry John Temple, Viscount Palmerston
1784–1865

21   We have no eternal allies and we have no perpetual enemies. Our interests are eternal and perpetual, and these interests it is our duty to follow.
Speech in the House of Commons on foreign policy [March 1, 1848]

Zachary Taylor
1784–1850

22   Hurrah for Old Kentuck! That's the way to do it. Give 'em hell, damn 'em.
Shouted to the 2nd Kentucky Regiment on seeing them rally in battle [Buena Vista, Mexico, February 23, 1847]

---

[1] Translated by NORBERT GUTERMAN.

[2] For this reference to the Prince Regent, Hunt was imprisoned.

[3] See *Proverbs 9:17,* 20:9, and Colley Cibber, 287:18.

[4] Jenny was Jane Welsh Carlyle [1801–1866], who kissed Hunt when he brought Carlyle good news.

1   A little more grape, Captain Bragg.
*Attributed [Buena Vista, Mexico,
February 23, 1847]*

2   Tell him to go to hell.
*Reply to Santa Anna's demand for surrender
[Buena Vista, Mexico, February 23, 1847]*

Thomas De Quincey
1785–1859

3   If a man "whose talk is of oxen" should become
an opium-eater, the probability is, that (if he is not
too dull to dream at all) — he will dream about oxen.
*Confessions of an English Opium Eater
[1822–1856]. Preliminary Confessions*

4   The burden of the incommunicable.
Confessions of an English Opium Eater, pt. I

5   So, then, Oxford Street, stonyhearted stepmother,
thou that listenest to the sighs of orphans, and
drinkest the tears of children, at length I was dismissed from thee.
Confessions of an English Opium Eater, I

6   Thou only givest these gifts to man, and thou hast
the keys of Paradise, O just, subtle, and mighty
opium!   *Confessions of an English Opium Eater, II*

7   If once a man indulges himself in murder, very
soon he comes to think little of robbing; and from
robbing he comes next to drinking and Sabbath-
breaking, and from that to incivility and procrastination.
*Murder Considered as One of the
Fine Arts [1827]*

Lady Caroline Lamb
1785–1828

8   [Of Byron:] Mad, bad, and dangerous to know.
Journal [March 1812]

Thomas Love Peacock
1785–1866

9 Not drunk is he who from the floor
Can rise alone and still drink more;
But drunk is he who prostrate lies,
Without the power to drink or rise.
*The Misfortunes of Elphin [1829],
ch. 3, heading (translated from the Welsh)*

10   Ancient sculpture is the true school of modesty.
But where the Greeks had modesty, we have cant;
where they had poetry, we have cant; where they had
patriotism, we have cant; where they had anything
that exalts, delights, or adorns humanity, we have
nothing but cant, cant, cant.
Crotchet Castle [1831], ch. 7

Oliver Hazard Perry
1785–1819

11   We have met the enemy, and they are ours.[1]
*Dispatch from U.S. brig Niagara to
General William Henry Harrison,
announcing his victory at the battle of
Lake Erie [September 10, 1813]*

Samuel Woodworth
1785–1842

12 How dear to this heart are the scenes of my childhood,
When fond recollection presents them to view!
The Old Oaken Bucket

13 The old oaken bucket, the iron-bound bucket,
The moss-covered bucket which hung in the well.
The Old Oaken Bucket

David Crockett
1786–1836

14 I leave this rule for others when I'm dead,
Be always sure you're right — then go ahead.[2]
Narrative of the Life of Colonel Crockett [1834]

15   If I could rest anywhere it would be in Arkansaw
where the men are of the real half-horse, half-alligator
breed such as grows nowhere else on the face of the
earth.   *Narrative of the Life of Colonel Crockett*

16   Don't shoot, Colonel, I'll come down: I know
I'm a gone coon.[3]
Story told by Crockett of a treed raccoon

William Learned Marcy
1786–1857

17   They see nothing wrong in the rule that to the
victor belong the spoils of the enemy.
Speech in the Senate [January 1832]

---

[1]We have met the enemy and he is us. — WALT KELLY [1913–
1973], 1970 *Pogo* cartoon, used in 1971 Earth Day poster. In its
original form: We shall meet the enemy, and not only may he be
ours, he may be us. — *The Pogo Papers* [1953], *introduction*

[2]Crockett's motto in the War of 1812.

[3]A humorous Revolutionary War expression referring to a story
about a backwoods spy dressed in raccoon skins who said to the
British soldiers who discovered him, "I'm a gone coon." — STUART
BERG FLEXNER [1928–1990], *I Hear America Talking* [1976]

Winfield Scott
1786–1866

1   The enemy say that Americans are good at a long shot, but cannot stand the cold iron. I call upon you instantly to give a lie to the slander. Charge!
Address to the 11th Infantry Regiment
[Chippewa, Canada, June 5, 1814]

2   Say to the seceded States, "Wayward sisters, depart in peace."
Letter to W. H. Seward [March 3, 1861]

Seattle[1]
c. 1786–1866

3   When the last red man has vanished from this earth, and his memory is only a story among the whites, these shores will still swarm with the invisible dead of my people. And when your children's children think they are alone in the fields, the forests, the shops, the highways, or the quiet of the woods, they will not be alone. There is no place in this country where a man can be alone. At night when the streets of your town and cities are quiet, and you think they are empty, they will throng with the returning spirits that once thronged them, and that still love these places. The white man will never be alone. Let him be just and deal kindly with my people, for the dead are not powerless.
Speech to governor of Washington Territory
[c. 1855]

François Guizot
1787–1874

4   Enrich yourselves![2]
Speech [March 1, 1843]

Emma Willard
1787–1870

5   Rocked in the cradle of the deep.
The Cradle of the Deep [1831]

---

[1]Chief of the Suquamish and Dowamish tribes of Puget Sound. The city of Seattle was named after him.
  Translated and published by HENRY A. SMITH [1830–1915] more than thirty years [1887] after the speech, whose date and location are uncertain. Smith's version reflects the then-current idea that American Indians were destined to die out entirely and contains many anachronisms and other errors of fact. Later versions (such as a TV documentary and a popular picture book) are highly embellished. The speech's authenticity is disputed.

[2]Enrichissez-vous!

George Noel Gordon, Lord Byron
1788–1824

6   "Friendship is Love without his wings!"
L'Amitié Est l'Amour sans Ailes[3]
[written 1806]

7   For years fleet away with the wings of the dove.
The First Kiss of Love [1806], st. 7

8   I only know we loved in vain;
I only feel — farewell! farewell!
Farewell! If Ever Fondest Prayer
[1808], st. 2

9   Near this spot are deposited the remains of one who possessed beauty without vanity, strength without insolence, courage without ferocity, and all the virtues of Man, without his vices. This praise, which would be unmeaning flattery if inscribed over human ashes, is but a just tribute to the memory of Boatswain, a dog.
Inscription on the monument of a
Newfoundland dog [1808]

10 The poor dog, in life the firmest friend,
The first to welcome, foremost to defend.
Inscription on the monument of a
Newfoundland dog

11   I'll publish right or wrong:
Fools are my theme, let satire be my song.
English Bards and Scotch Reviewers
[1809], l. 5

12 'Tis pleasant, sure, to see one's name in print;
A book's a book, although there's nothing in 't.
English Bards and Scotch Reviewers, l. 51

13 A man must serve his time to every trade
Save censure — critics all are ready-made.
English Bards and Scotch Reviewers, l. 63

14 With just enough of learning to misquote.
English Bards and Scotch Reviewers, l. 66

15   As soon
Seek roses in December, ice in June;
Hope constancy in wind, or corn in chaff;
Believe a woman or an epitaph,
Or any other thing that's false, before
You trust in critics.
English Bards and Scotch Reviewers, l. 75

16 Better to err with Pope, than shine with Pye.
English Bards and Scotch Reviewers, l. 102

17 Maid of Athens, ere we part,
Give, oh give me back my heart!
Maid of Athens [1810], st. 1

---

[3]A French proverb.

1 Vex'd with mirth the drowsy ear of night.
  *Childe Harold's Pilgrimage, canto I
  [1812], st. 2*

2 Had sigh'd to many, though he loved but one.
  Childe Harold's Pilgrimage, I, st. 5

3 Might shake the saintship of an anchorite.[1]
  Childe Harold's Pilgrimage, I, st. 11

4 War, war is still the cry, "War even to the knife!"[2]
  Childe Harold's Pilgrimage, I, st. 86

5 Gone — glimmering through the dream of things
      that were.
  Childe Harold's Pilgrimage, II [1812], st. 2

6 A schoolboy's tale, the wonder of an hour!
  Childe Harold's Pilgrimage, II, st. 2

7 Who would be free themselves must strike the blow.
  Childe Harold's Pilgrimage, II, st. 76

8 Where'er we tread 'tis haunted, holy ground.
  Childe Harold's Pilgrimage, II, st. 88

9 What is the worst of woes that wait on age?
  What stamps the wrinkle deeper on the brow?
  To view each loved one blotted from life's page,
  And be alone on earth, as I am now.
  Childe Harold's Pilgrimage, II, st. 98

10 Once more upon the waters, yet once more!
  And the waves bound beneath me as a steed
  That knows his rider!
  Childe Harold's Pilgrimage, III [1816], st. 2

11   Years steal
  Fire from the mind as vigor from the limb;
  And life's enchanted cup but sparkles near the brim.
  Childe Harold's Pilgrimage, III, st. 8

12 And Harold stands upon this place of skulls.
  Childe Harold's Pilgrimage, III, st. 18

13 There was a sound of revelry by night,
  And Belgium's capital had gather'd then
  Her beauty and her chivalry, and bright
  The lamps shone o'er fair women and brave men.
  A thousand hearts beat happily; and when
  Music arose with its voluptuous swell,
  Soft eyes look'd love to eyes which spake again,
  And all went merry as a marriage bell.
  But hush! hark! a deep sound strikes like a rising
      knell!
  Childe Harold's Pilgrimage, III, st. 21

14 Did ye not hear it? — No! 'twas but the wind,
  Or the car rattling o'er the stony street.
  On with the dance! let joy be unconfined;
  No sleep till morn, when Youth and Pleasure meet
  To chase the glowing hours with flying feet.
  Childe Harold's Pilgrimage, III, st. 22

15 Like to the apples on the Dead Sea's shore,
  All ashes to the taste.
  Childe Harold's Pilgrimage, III, st. 34

16   Thou fatal Waterloo.
  Millions of tongues record thee, and anew
  Their children's lips shall echo them, and say —
  "Here, where the sword united nations drew,
  Our countrymen were warring on that day!"
  And this is much, and all which will not pass away.[3]
  Childe Harold's Pilgrimage, III, st. 35

17 He who ascends to mountaintops, shall find
  The loftiest peaks most wrapt in clouds and snow;
  He who surpasses or subdues mankind
  Must look down on the hate of those below.
  Childe Harold's Pilgrimage, III, st. 45

18 All tenantless, save to the crannying wind.
  Childe Harold's Pilgrimage, III, st. 47

19 History's purchased page to call them great.
  Childe Harold's Pilgrimage, III, st. 48

20 To fly from, need not be to hate, mankind.
  Childe Harold's Pilgrimage, III, st. 69

21 I live not in myself, but I become
  Portion of that around me: and to me
  High mountains are a feeling, but the hum
  Of human cities torture.
  Childe Harold's Pilgrimage, III, st. 72

22 Fame is the thirst of youth.
  Childe Harold's Pilgrimage, III, st. 112

23 I have not loved the world, nor the world me;
  I have not flatter'd its rank breath, nor bow'd
  To its idolatries a patient knee.
  Childe Harold's Pilgrimage, III, st. 113

24   I stood
  Among them, but not of them; in a shroud
  Of thoughts which were not their thoughts.
  Childe Harold's Pilgrimage, III, st. 113

25 I stood in Venice on the Bridge of Sighs,
  A palace and a prison on each hand.
  Childe Harold's Pilgrimage, IV [1818], st. 1

---

[1]Such lips would tempt a saint; such hands as those / Would make an anchorite lascivious. — JOHN FORD, *'Tis Pity She's a Whore, act I, sc. iii, l. 196*

[2]War even to the knife! — JOSÉ DE PALAFOX Y MELZI [1775–1847] Palafox, governor of Saragossa, had been summoned by the besieging French to surrender the city [1808].

[3]This was the passage Sir Winston Churchill quoted to President Franklin D. Roosevelt when both agreed to substitute the term United Nations for Associated Powers in the pact that the two leaders wished all the free nations to sign. [In a conference at the White House, January 1942]

1 Where Venice sate in state, throned on her hundred
   isles.   *Childe Harold's Pilgrimage, IV, st. 1*

2 She looks a sea Cybele, fresh from ocean,
   Rising with her tiara of proud towers
   At airy distance, with majestic motion,
   A ruler of the waters and their powers.
                   Childe Harold's Pilgrimage, IV, st. 2

3 The beings of the mind are not of clay;
   Essentially immortal, they create
   And multiply in us a brighter ray
   And more beloved existence.
                   Childe Harold's Pilgrimage, IV, st. 5

4 'Tis solitude should teach us how to die;
   It hath no flatterers; vanity can give
   No hollow aid; alone — man with his God must
      strive.   *Childe Harold's Pilgrimage, IV, st. 33*

5 Italia! O Italia! thou who hast
   The fatal gift of beauty.
                   Childe Harold's Pilgrimage, IV, st. 42

6 Let these describe the undescribable.
                   Childe Harold's Pilgrimage, IV, st. 53

7 The starry Galileo, with his woes.
                   Childe Harold's Pilgrimage, IV, st. 54

8 The poetry of speech.
                   Childe Harold's Pilgrimage, IV, st. 58

9 O Rome! my country! city of the soul!
                   Childe Harold's Pilgrimage, IV, st. 78

10 Yet, Freedom! yet thy banner, torn, but flying,
   Streams like the thunderstorm *against* the wind.
                   Childe Harold's Pilgrimage, IV, st. 98

11 Alas! our young affections run to waste,
   Or water but the desert.
                   Childe Harold's Pilgrimage, IV, st. 120

12 Of its own beauty is the mind diseased.
                   Childe Harold's Pilgrimage, IV, st. 122

13 Butcher'd to make a Roman holiday!
                   Childe Harold's Pilgrimage, IV, st. 141

14 "While stands the Coliseum, Rome shall stand;
   When falls the Coliseum, Rome shall fall;
   And when Rome falls — the world."[1]
                   Childe Harold's Pilgrimage, IV, st. 145

15 Oh! that the desert were my dwelling place.
                   Childe Harold's Pilgrimage, IV, st. 177

16 There is a pleasure in the pathless woods,
   There is a rapture on the lonely shore,
   There is society, where none intrudes,

---

[1] The saying of the ancient pilgrims, quoted from Bede by EDWARD
GIBBON in *History of the Decline and Fall of the Roman Empire, ch. 71.*

By the deep sea, and music in its roar:
I love not man the less, but Nature more.
                   Childe Harold's Pilgrimage, IV, st. 178

17 Roll on, thou deep and dark blue ocean — roll!
   Ten thousand fleets sweep over thee in vain;
   Man marks the earth with ruin — his control
   Stops with the shore.
                   Childe Harold's Pilgrimage, IV, st. 179

18 He sinks into thy depths with bubbling groan,
   Without a grave, unknell'd, uncoffin'd, and
      unknown.
                   Childe Harold's Pilgrimage, IV, st. 179

19 Time writes no wrinkle on thine azure brow —
   Such as creation's dawn beheld, thou rollest now.
                   Childe Harold's Pilgrimage, IV, st. 182

20 Thou glorious mirror, where the Almighty's form
   Glasses itself in tempests.
                   Childe Harold's Pilgrimage, IV, st. 183

21 Dark-heaving — boundless, endless, and sublime —
   The image of Eternity.
                   Childe Harold's Pilgrimage, IV, st. 183

22 And I have loved thee, Ocean! and my joy
   Of youthful sports was on thy breast to be
   Borne, like thy bubbles, onward: from a boy
   I wanton'd with thy breakers.
                   Childe Harold's Pilgrimage, IV, st. 184

23   I awoke one morning and found myself famous.
      *Entry in Memoranda after publication
      of first two cantos of Childe Harold's
      Pilgrimage. From* THOMAS MOORE, *Life of Byron
      [1830], ch. 14*

24 I die — but first I have possess'd,
   And come what may, I have been bless'd.
                   The Giaour [1813], l. 1114

25 Mark! where his carnage and his conquests cease!
   He makes a solitude, and calls it — peace!
                   The Bride of Abydos [1813], canto II, st. 20

26   The fatal facility of the octosyllabic verse.
                   The Corsair [1814]. Dedication

27 Such hath it been — shall be — beneath the sun
   The many still must labor for the one.
                   The Corsair, canto I, st. 8

28 The Cincinnatus of the West,
   Whom envy dared not hate,
   Bequeathed the name of Washington
   To make man blush there was but one!
                   *Ode to Napoleon Bonaparte [1814],
                   st. 19*

29 Lord of himself — that heritage of woe.
                   Lara [1814], canto I, st. 2

1 She walks in beauty, like the night
  Of cloudless climes and starry skies;
  And all that's best of dark and bright
  Meet in her aspect and her eyes:
  Thus mellow'd to that tender light
  Which heaven to gaudy day denies.
> *Hebrew Melodies [1815]. She Walks in*
> *Beauty, st. 1*

2 The Assyrian came down like the wolf on the fold,
  And his cohorts were gleaming in purple and gold;
  And the sheen of their spears was like stars on the sea,
  When the blue wave rolls nightly on deep Galilee.
> *Hebrew Melodies. The Destruction of*
> *Sennacherib, st. 1*

3 And the might of the Gentile, unsmote by the sword,
  Hath melted like snow in the glance of the Lord!
> *Hebrew Melodies. The Destruction of*
> *Sennacherib, st. 6*

4 There's not a joy the world can give like that it takes
    away,
  When the glow of early thought declines in feeling's
    dull decay.   *Stanzas for Music [1815], st. 1*

5 The glory and the nothing of a name.
> *Churchill's Grave [1816], l. 43*

6 Fare thee well! and if forever,
  Still forever, fare thee well.
> *Fare Thee Well [1816], st. 1*

7 Sighing that Nature form'd but one such man,
  And broke the die, in molding Sheridan.
> *Monody on the Death of Sheridan [1816],*
> *l. 117*

8 Eternal Spirit of the chainless Mind!
  Brightest in dungeons, Liberty! thou art.
> *The Prisoner of Chillon [1816].*
> *Sonnet on Chillon, l. 1*

9 A light broke in upon my brain —
  It was the carol of a bird;
  It ceased, and then it came again,
  The sweetest song ear ever heard.
> *The Prisoner of Chillon. Sonnet on Chillon,*
> *st. 10*

10 There be none of Beauty's daughters
   With a magic like thee;
   And like music on the waters
   Is thy sweet voice to me.
> *Stanzas for Music [1816], st. 1*

11 I had a dream which was not all a dream.
> *Darkness [1816]*

12 Though the day of my destiny's over,
   And the star of my fate hath declined.
> *Stanzas to Augusta [1816], st. 1*

13 My boat is on the shore,
   And my bark is on the sea;
   But, before I go, Tom Moore,
   Here's a double health to thee!
   Here's a sigh to those who love me,
   And a smile to those who hate;
   And, whatever sky's above me,
   Here's a heart for every fate.
> *To Thomas Moore [1817], st. 1, 2*

14 So we'll go no more a-roving
   So late into the night,
   Though the heart be still as loving,
   And the moon be still as bright.

   For the sword outwears its sheath,
   And the soul wears out the breast,
   And the heart must pause to breathe,
   And love itself have rest.

   Though the night was made for loving,
   And the day returns too soon,
   Yet we'll go no more a-roving
   By the light of the moon.
> *So We'll Go No More A-Roving [1817]*

15 Sorrow is knowledge: they who know the most
   Must mourn the deepest o'er the fatal truth,
   The Tree of Knowledge is not that of Life.
> *Manfred [1817], act I, sc. i*

16   The day before I left Rome I saw three robbers guillotined.... The first turned me quite hot and thirsty, and made me shake so that I could hardly hold the opera-glass (I was close, but determined to see, as one should see every thing, once, with attention); the second and third (which shows how dreadfully soon things grow indifferent), I am ashamed to say, had no effect on me as a horror, though I would have saved them if I could.
> *Letter to John Murray [May 30, 1817]*

17 I love the language, that soft bastard Latin,
   Which melts like kisses from a female mouth.
> *Beppo [1818], st. 44*

18 [Of Samuel Taylor Coleridge:] I wish he would explain his explanation.
> *Don Juan. Dedication [written 1818], st. 2*

19 But — Oh! ye lords of ladies intellectual,
   Inform us truly, have they not henpeck'd you all?
> *Don Juan, canto I [1818], st. 22*

20 Her stature tall — I hate a dumpy woman.
> *Don Juan, I, st. 61*

21 What men call gallantry, and gods adultery,
   Is much more common where the climate's sultry.
> *Don Juan, I, st. 63*

1 Christians have burnt each other, quite persuaded
   That all the Apostles would have done as they did.
   Don Juan, I, st. 83

2 A little still she strove, and much repented,
   And whispering "I will ne'er consent" —
         consented.   *Don Juan, I, st. 117*

3 'Tis sweet to hear the watchdog's honest bark
   Bay deep-mouth'd welcome as we draw near home;
   'Tis sweet to know there is an eye will mark
   Our coming, and look brighter when we come.
   Don Juan, I, st. 123

4 Sweet is revenge — especially to women.
   Don Juan, I, st. 124

5 Pleasure's a sin, and sometimes sin's a pleasure.
   Don Juan, I, st. 133

6 Man's love is of man's life a thing apart,
   'Tis woman's whole existence.
   Don Juan, I, st. 194

7 What is the end of fame? 'tis but to fill
   A certain portion of uncertain paper:
   Some liken it to climbing up a hill,
   Whose summit, like all hills, is lost in vapor.
   Don Juan, I, st. 218

8 There's nought, no doubt, so much the spirit calms
   As rum and true religion.
   Don Juan, II [1819], st. 34

9 A solitary shriek, the bubbling cry
   Of some strong swimmer in his agony.
   Don Juan, II, st. 53

10 Let us have wine and women, mirth and laughter,
    Sermons and soda water the day after.
    Don Juan, II, st. 178

11 Man, being reasonable, must get drunk;
    The best of life is but intoxication.
    Don Juan, II, st. 179

12   For man, to man so oft unjust,
    Is always so to women; one sole bond
    Awaits them, treachery is all their trust;
    Taught to conceal, their bursting hearts despond
    Over their idol, till some wealthier lust
    Buys them in marriage — and what rests beyond?
    A thankless husband, next a faithless lover,
    Then dressing, nursing, praying, and all's over.
    Don Juan, II, st. 200

13 In her first passion woman loves her lover,
    In all the others, all she loves is love.
    Don Juan, III [1821], st. 3

14 Think you, if Laura had been Petrarch's wife,
    He would have written sonnets all his life?
    Don Juan, III, st. 8

15 The isles of Greece, the isles of Greece![1]
    Where burning Sappho loved and sung.
    Don Juan, III, st. 86 [song, st. 1]

16 Eternal summer gilds them yet,
    But all, except their sun, is set.
    Don Juan, III, st. 86 [song, st. 1]

17 The mountains look on Marathon,
    And Marathon looks on the sea;
    And musing there an hour alone,
    I dreamed that Greece might still be free.
    Don Juan, III, st. 86 [song, st. 3]

18 Earth! render back from out thy breast
    A remnant of our Spartan dead!
    Of the three hundred grant but three,
    To make a new Thermopylae.
    Don Juan, III, st. 86 [song, st. 7]

19 What, silent still? and silent all?
    Ah! no; — the voices of the dead
    Sound like a distant torrent's fall.
    Don Juan, III, st. 86 [song, st. 8]

20 And if I laugh at any mortal thing,
    'Tis that I may not weep.
    Don Juan, IV [1821], st. 4

21   I've stood upon Achilles' tomb,
    And heard Troy doubted; time will doubt of Rome.
    Don Juan, IV, st. 101

22 There's not a sea the passenger e'er pukes in,
    Turns up more dangerous breakers than the Euxine.
    Don Juan, V [1821], st. 5

23 And put himself upon his good behavior.
    Don Juan, V, st. 47

24 The women pardon'd all except her face.
    Don Juan, V, st. 113

25 A lady of "a certain age," which means
    Certainly aged.
    Don Juan, VI [1823], st. 69

26 Not so Leonidas and Washington,
    Whose every battlefield is holy ground,
    Which breathes of nations saved, not worlds
         undone.   *Don Juan, VIII [1823], st. 5*

27 When Bishop Berkeley said "there was no matter,"
    And proved it — 'twas no matter what he said.
    Don Juan, XI [1823], st. 1

28 And, after all, what is a lie? 'Tis but
    The truth in masquerade.   *Don Juan, XI, st. 37*

29 'Tis strange the mind, that very fiery particle,

---

[1] From isles of Greece / The princes orgulous, their high blood chaf'd, / Have to the port of Athens sent their ships. — SHAKESPEARE, *Troilus and Cressida, prologue*

Should let itself be snuff'd out by an article.
Don Juan, XI, st. 60 (of John Keats)

1 The English winter — ending in July,
To recommence in August.
Don Juan, XIII [1823], st. 42

2 Society is now one polish'd horde,
Formed of two mighty tribes, the *Bores* and *Bored*.
Don Juan, XIII, st. 95

3   All human history attests
That happiness for man — the hungry sinner! —
Since Eve ate apples, much depends on dinner.
Don Juan, XIII, st. 99

4 Of all the horrid, hideous notes of woe,
Sadder than owl songs or the midnight blast,
Is that portentous phrase, "I told you so."
Don Juan, XIV [1823], st. 50

5 'Tis strange — but true; for truth is always strange;
Stranger than fiction.[1]   *Don Juan, XIV, st. 101*

6 The antique Persians taught three useful things —
To draw the bow, to ride, and speak the truth.
Don Juan, XVI [1824], st. 1

7 Oh, talk not to me of a name great in story;
The days of our youth are the days of our glory;
And the myrtle and ivy of sweet two-and-twenty
Are worth all your laurels, though ever so plenty.
*Stanzas Written on the Road Between
Florence and Pisa [1821], st. 1*

8 All farewells should be sudden.
Sardanapalus [1821], act V

9   The best of prophets of the future is the past.
Journal [January 28, 1821]

10   Because
He is all-powerful, must all-good, too, follow?
I judge but by the fruits — and they are bitter —
Which I must feed on for a fault not mine.
Cain [1821], act I, sc. i

11 Who killed John Keats?
"I," says the Quarterly,
So savage and Tartarly;
" 'Twas one of my feats."   *John Keats [c. 1821]*

12   He seems
To have seen better days, as who has not
Who has seen yesterday?   *Werner [1822], act I, sc. i*

13 The "good old times" — all times when old are
good —
Are gone.   *The Age of Bronze [1823], st. 1*

14 [Of Napoleon:] Whose game was empires and whose
stakes were thrones,
Whose table earth — whose dice were human bones.
The Age of Bronze, st. 3

15 Sublime tobacco! which from east to west
Cheers the tar's labor or the Turkman's rest.[2]
The Island [1823], canto II, st. 19

16 My days are in the yellow leaf;
The flowers and fruits of love are gone;
The worm, the canker, and the grief
Are mine alone!
On My Thirty-sixth Year [1824], st. 2

17 Seek out — less often sought than found —
A soldier's grave, for thee the best;
Then look around, and choose thy ground,
And take thy rest.   *On My Thirty-sixth Year, st. 10*

18   Now Barabbas was a publisher.
Alleged alteration in the Bible, John 18:40[3]

Sarah Josepha Hale
1788–1879

19 Mary had a little lamb,
Its fleece was white as snow,
And everywhere that Mary went,
The lamb was sure to go.
*Mary's Lamb,[4] st. 1. From The Juvenile
Miscellany [September 1830]*

Arthur Schopenhauer
1788–1860

20   To marry is to halve your rights and double your
duties.
*The World as Will and Idea [1819],
vol. II*

21   Hatred comes from the heart; contempt from the
head; and neither feeling is quite within our control.
*Studies in Pessimism[5] [1851]. Psychological
Observations*

---

[1]Le vrai peut quelquefois n'être pas vraisemblable [Truth may
sometimes be improbable]. — BOILEAU, *The Art of Poetry, canto III
l. 48*

Truth is stranger than fiction, but not so popular. — *Anonymous*

[2]Let Aristotle and all your philosophers say what they like, there is
nothing to be compared with tobacco. — MOLIÈRE, *Dom Juan; ou Le
Festin de Pierre* [1665], *act I, sc. i*
Translated by CURTIS HIDDEN PAGE.

[3]The publisher John Murray sent Byron a Bible in acknowledgment of a favor, and the poet returned it with the word "robber"
changed to "publisher."

[4]According to *The Story of Mary's Little Lamb* [1928], the first
three stanzas of the poem are by John Roulstone [1805–1822];
Sarah Josepha Hale's "genius completed the poem in its present
form" (six stanzas); "Mary" was Mary Elizabeth Sawyer [1806–
1889] of Sterling, Massachusetts; and the events of the poem are
true.

[5]Translated by T. BAILEY SAUNDERS.

1   Every man takes the limits of his own field of vision for the limits of the world.
Studies in Pessimism. Psychological Observations

2   Every parting gives a foretaste of death; every coming together again a foretaste of the resurrection.
Studies in Pessimism. Psychological Observations

3   Dissimulation is innate in woman, and almost as much a quality of the stupid as of the clever.
Studies in Pessimism. On Women

4   The two foes of human happiness are pain and boredom.   *Essays. Personality; or, What a Man Is*

5   A man who has no mental needs, because his intellect is of the narrow and normal amount, is, in the strict sense of the word, what is called a philistine.
Essays. Personality; or, What a Man Is

6   Do not shorten the morning by getting up late; look upon it as the quintessence of life, as to a certain extent sacred.   *Counsels and Maxims, ch. 2*

James Fenimore Cooper
1789–1851

7   Few men exhibit greater diversity, or, if we may so express it, greater antithesis of character than the native warrior of North America. In war, he is daring, boastful, cunning, ruthless, self-denying, and self-devoted; in peace, just, generous, hospitable, revengeful, superstitious, modest, and commonly chaste.   *The Last of the Mohicans [1826]*

8   [Coming upon a woodland lake:] This is grand! 'tis solemn! 'tis an education of itself to look upon!
The Deerslayer [1841], ch. 2

9   The American axe! It has made more real and lasting conquests than the sword of any warlike people that ever lived; but they have been conquests that have left civilization in their train instead of havoc and destruction....A brief quarter of a century has seen these wonderful changes wrought; and at the bottom of them all lies this beautiful, well-prized, ready, and efficient implement, the American axe!
The Chainbearer [1845], ch. 6

Astolphe Louis Léonard, Marquis de Custine
1790–1857

10   This empire [Russia], vast as it is, is only a prison to which the emperor holds the key.
La Russie en 1839.[1] *Peterhof, July 23, 1839*

11   Whoever has really seen Russia will find himself content to live anywhere else. It is always good to know that a society exists where no happiness is possible because, by a law of nature, man cannot be happy unless he is free.
La Russie en 1839. Conclusion

Fitz-Greene Halleck
1790–1867

12   Green be the turf above thee,
Friend of my better days!
None knew thee but to love thee,
Nor named thee but to praise.
On the Death of Joseph Rodman Drake [1820], st. 1

13   One of the few, the immortal names
That were not born to die.
Marco Bozzaris [1855], st. 7

Alphonse de Lamartine
1790–1869

14   O time, arrest your flight! and you, propitious hours, arrest your course! Let us savor the fleeting delights of our most beautiful days![2]
The Lake [1820], st. 6

15   The more I see of the representatives of the people, the more I admire my dogs.
From A. G. G. D'Orsay [1801–1852], Letter to John Forster [1850]

John Howard Payne
1791–1852

16   'Mid pleasures and palaces though we may roam,
Be it ever so humble, there's no place like home.[3]
Home, Sweet Home. From the opera Clari, the Maid of Milan [1823]

Victor Cousin
1792–1867

17   We need religion for religion's sake, morality for morality's sake, art for art's sake.
Cours de Philosophie [1818]

---

[1]Translated by PHYLLIS PENN KOHLER.

[2]O temps, suspends ton vol! et vous, heures propices, / Suspendez votre cours! / Laissez-nous savourer les rapides délices / Des plus beaux de nos jours!

[3]Home is home, be it never so homely. — *English proverb* [c. 1300]

Frederick Marryat
1792–1848

1   It's just six of one and half a dozen of the other.
The Pirate [1836], ch. 4

2 I haven't the gift of the gab, my sons — because I'm
bred to the sea.   *The Old Navy [1837], st. 1*

3   I am sure the Americans can fix nothing without a
drink. If you meet, you drink; if you part, you drink; if
you make acquaintance, you drink.... They commence it early in life, and they continue it, until they
drop into the grave.
A Diary in America [1839], series 2

4   Every man paddle his own canoe.
Settlers in Canada [1844], ch. 8

Joseph Mohr
1792–1848

5 Silent night! Holy night![1]
All is calm, all is bright.   *Holy Night [1818]*

Lord John Russell
1792–1878

6   If peace cannot be maintained with honor, it is no
longer peace.
Speech at Greenock [September 19, 1853]

7   Among the defects of the bill, which were
numerous, one provision was conspicuous by its presence and another by its absence.
*Speech to the electors of the City of London
[April 1859]*

Percy Bysshe Shelley
1792–1822

8 Power, like a desolating pestilence,
Pollutes whate'er it touches; and obedience,
Bane of all genius, virtue, freedom, truth,
Makes slaves of men, and, of the human frame,
A mechanized automaton.
Queen Mab [1813], pt. III

9 The awful shadow of some unseen Power
Floats though unseen among us — visiting
This various world with as inconstant wing
As summer winds that creep from flower to flower.
Hymn to Intellectual Beauty [1816], st. 1

10 Spirit of Beauty, that dost consecrate
With thine own hues all thou dost shine upon
Of human thought or form.
Hymn to Intellectual Beauty, st. 2

11 Some say that gleams of a remoter world
Visit the soul in sleep — that death is slumber,
And that its shapes the busy thoughts outnumber
Of those who wake and live.
Mont Blanc [1816], st. 3

12 Man's yesterday may ne'er be like his morrow;
Nought may endure but Mutability.
Mutability [1816], st. 4

13 I met a traveler from an antique land
Who said: Two vast and trunkless legs of stone
Stand in the desert. Near them, on the sand,
Half sunk, a shattered visage lies, whose frown,
And wrinkled lip, and sneer of cold command,
Tell that its sculptor well those passions read.
Which yet survive, stamped on these lifeless things,
The hand that mocked them and the heart that fed:
And on the pedestal these words appear:
"My name is Ozymandias, king of kings:
Look on my works, ye Mighty, and despair!"
Nothing beside remains. Round the decay
Of that colossal wreck, boundless and bare,
The lone and level sands stretch far away.
Ozymandias [1817]

14 I could lie down like a tired child,
And weep away the life of care
Which I have borne and yet must bear,
Till death like sleep might steal on me.
*Stanzas Written in Dejection near Naples
[1818], st. 4*

15   Ere Babylon was dust,
The Magus Zoroaster, my dead child,
Met his own image walking in the garden,
That apparition, sole of men, he saw.
Prometheus Unbound [1818–1819], act I, l. 191

16 The good want power, but to weep barren tears.
The powerful goodness want: worse need for them.
The wise want love; and those who love want wisdom;
And all best things are thus confused with ill.
Prometheus Unbound, I, l. 625

17 Peace is in the grave.
The grave hides all things beautiful and good:
I am a God and cannot find it there.
Prometheus Unbound, I, l. 638

18 From the dust of creeds outworn.
Prometheus Unbound, I, l. 697

19 Forms more real than living man,
Nurslings of immortality!
Prometheus Unbound, I, l. 748

---

[1]Stille Nacht! Heilige Nacht!
Music by Franz Grüber [1787–1863].

1 To know nor faith, nor love nor law; to be
Omnipotent but friendless is to reign.
Prometheus Unbound, II, sc. iv, l. 47

2 Death is the veil which those who live call life:
They sleep, and it is lifted.[1]
Prometheus Unbound, III, iii, l. 113

3 Familiar acts are beautiful through love.
Prometheus Unbound, IV, l. 403

4 Man, who wert once a despot and a slave;
A dupe and a deceiver; a decay;
A traveler from the cradle to the grave
Through the dim light of this immortal day.
Prometheus Unbound, IV, l. 549

5 To suffer woes which Hope thinks infinite;
To forgive wrongs darker than death or night;
To defy Power, which seems omnipotent;
To love, and bear; to hope till Hope creates
From its own wreck the thing it contemplates;
Neither to change, nor falter, nor repent;
This, like thy glory, Titan, is to be
Good, great and joyous, beautiful and free;
This is alone Life, Joy, Empire, and Victory.
Prometheus Unbound, IV, l. 570

6   I love all waste
And solitary places; where we taste
The pleasure of believing what we see
Is boundless, as we wish our souls to be.
Julian and Maddalo [1819], l. 14

7   It is our will
That thus enchains us to permitted ill —
We might be otherwise — we might be all
We dream of happy, high majestical.
Where is the love, beauty and truth we seek,
But in our mind?
Julian and Maddalo, l. 170

8 Chameleons feed on light and air:
Poets' food is love and fame.
An Exhortation [1819], st. 1

9 O wild West Wind, thou breath of Autumn's
being,
Thou, from whose unseen presence the leaves
dead
Are driven, like ghosts from an enchanter fleeing,
Yellow, and black, and pale, and hectic red,
Pestilence-stricken multitudes.
Ode to the West Wind [1819], l. 1

10 Wild Spirit, which art moving everywhere;
Destroyer and preserver; hear, oh, hear!
Ode to the West Wind, l. 13

11   Thou dirge
Of the dying year, to which this closing night
Will be the dome of a vast sepulcher.
Ode to the West Wind, l. 23

12 Oh, lift me as a wave, a leaf, a cloud!
I fall upon the thorns of life! I bleed!
Ode to the West Wind, l. 44

13 Make me thy lyre, even as the forest is:
What if my leaves are falling like its own!
The tumult of thy mighty harmonies
Will take from both a deep, autumnal tone,
Sweet though in sadness. Be thou, Spirit fierce,
My spirit! Be thou me, impetuous one!
Ode to the West Wind, l. 57

14 The trumpet of a prophecy! O Wind,
If winter comes, can spring be far behind?
Ode to the West Wind, l. 68

15 Men of England, wherefore plow
For the lords who lay ye low?
Song to the Men of England [1819], st. 1

16 Nothing in the world is single,
All things by a law divine
In one spirit meet and mingle.
Love's Philosophy [1819], st. 1

17 I arise from dreams of thee
In the first sweet sleep of night,
When the winds are breathing low,
And the stars are shining bright.
The Indian Serenade [1819], st. 1

18 Hell is a city much like London —
A populous and smoky city.
Peter Bell the Third [1819], pt. III, st. 1

19 An old, mad, blind, despised and dying king.[2]
England in 1819 [written 1819], l. 1

20 I met Murder on the way —
He had a mask like Castlereagh.[3]
The Mask of Anarchy [written 1819], st. 2

21   One by one, and two by two,
He tossed them human hearts to chew.
The Mask of Anarchy, st. 3

22 Rise like Lions after slumber
In unvanquishable number —
Shake your chains to earth like dew
Which in sleep had fallen on you —
Ye are many — they are few.
The Mask of Anarchy, st. 38, 91

---

[1]Lift not the painted veil which those who live / Call Life.
—SHELLEY, *Sonnet* [1818]

---

[2]George III [1738–1820].
[3]Robert Stewart, Viscount Castlereagh [1769–1822].

1 A lovely lady, garmented in light
  From her own beauty.
                    The Witch of Atlas [1820], st. 5

2 Hail to thee, blithe spirit!
  Bird thou never wert,
  That from Heaven, or near it,
  Pourest thy full heart
  In profuse strains of unpremeditated art.
                    To a Skylark [1821], st. 1

3 And singing still dost soar, and soaring ever singest.
                    To a Skylark, st. 2

4 Thou art unseen — but yet I hear thy shrill delight.
                    To a Skylark, st. 4

5 We look before and after,
  And pine for what is not;
  Our sincerest laughter
  With some pain is fraught;
  Our sweetest songs are those that tell of saddest
    thought.   *To a Skylark, st. 18*

6 Teach me half the gladness
  That thy brain must know,
  Such harmonious madness,
  From my lips would flow,
  The world should listen then, as I am listening
    now.   *To a Skylark, st. 21*

7 Kings are like stars — they rise and set, they have
  The worship of the world, but no repose.
                    Hellas [1821], l. 195

8 The world's great age begins anew,
  The golden years return,
  The earth doth like a snake renew
  Her winter weeds outworn.   *Hellas, l. 1060*

9 The world is weary of the past,
  Oh, might it die or rest at last!   *Hellas, final chorus*

10 What! alive, and so bold, O earth?
                    *Written on Hearing the News of the Death
                    of Napoleon [1821], st. 1*

11 I never was attached to that great sect,
  Whose doctrine is, that each one should select
  Out of the crowd a mistress or a friend,
  And all the rest, though fair and wise, commend
  To cold oblivion, though 'tis in the code
  Of modern morals, and the beaten road
  Which those poor slaves with weary footsteps tread
  Who travel to their home among the dead
  By the broad highway of the world, and so
  With one chained friend, perhaps a jealous foe,
  The dreariest and the longest journey go.
  True love in this differs from gold and clay,
  That to divide is not to take away.
                    Epipsychidion [1821], l. 149

12 I weep for Adonais [John Keats][1] — he is dead!
  Oh, weep for Adonais! though our tears
  Thaw not the frost which binds so dear a head!
                    Adonais [1821], st. 1

13   Till the Future dares
  Forget the Past, his fate and fame shall be
  An echo and a light unto eternity!   *Adonais, st. 1*

14 To that high capital, where kingly Death
  Keeps his pale court in beauty and decay,
  He came.   *Adonais, st. 7*

15 Lost Angel of a ruined Paradise!   *Adonais, st. 10*

16 Ah woe is me! Winter is come and gone,
  But grief returns with the revolving year.
                    Adonais, st. 18

17   The intense atom glows
  A moment, then is quenched in a most cold repose.
                    Adonais, st. 20

18 Alas! that all we loved of him should be,
  But for our grief, as if it had not been,
  And grief itself be mortal!   *Adonais, st. 21*

19 As long as skies are blue, and fields are green,
  Evening must usher night, night urge the morrow,
  Month follow month with woe, and year wake year to
    sorrow.   *Adonais, st. 21*

20 The Pilgrim of Eternity [Lord Byron], whose fame
  Over his living head like heaven is bent,
  An early but enduring monument,
  Came, veiling all the lightnings of his song
  In sorrow.   *Adonais, st. 30*

21 In mockery of monumental stone.   *Adonais, st. 35*

22 He hath awakened from the dream of life.
                    Adonais, st. 39

23 He has outsoared the shadow of our night;
  Envy and calumny and hate and pain,
  And that unrest which men miscall delight
  Can touch him not and torture not again;
  From the contagion of the world's slow stain
  He is secure, and now can never mourn
  A heart grown cold, a head grown gray in vain.
                    Adonais, st. 40

24 He lives, he wakes — 'tis Death is dead, not he.
                    Adonais, st. 41

25 He is made one with Nature: there is heard
  His voice in all her music, from the moan
  Of thunder to the song of night's sweet bird.
                    Adonais, st. 42

---

[1]Morning star, you shone among the living; and now in death you shine, evening star, on the dead. — PLATO, *Aster (Star)*, epigraph (in Greek) for Shelley's *Adonais*

1 He is a portion of the loveliness
  Which once he made more lovely.   *Adonais, st. 43*

2 The One remains, the many change and pass;
  Heaven's light forever shines, earth's shadows fly;
  Life, like a dome of many-colored glass,
  Stains the white radiance of eternity,
  Until Death tramples it to fragments — Die,
  If thou wouldst be with that which thou dost seek!
                                        Adonais, st. 52

3 The soul of Adonais, like a star,
  Beacons from the abode where the Eternal are.
                                        Adonais, st. 55

4 Music, when soft voices die,
  Vibrates in the memory;
  Odors, when sweet violets sicken,
  Live within the sense they quicken.

  Rose leaves, when the rose is dead,
  Are heaped for the beloved's bed;
  And so thy thoughts, when thou art gone,
  Love itself shall slumber on.
            To ——: Music, When Soft Voices Die
            [1821]

5 One word is too often profaned
  For me to profane it,
  One feeling too falsely disdained
  For thee to disdain it.
            To ——: One Word Is Too Often Profaned
            [1821], st. 1

6 The desire of the moth for the star,
  Of the night for the morrow,
  The devotion to something afar
  From the sphere of our sorrow.
            To ——: One Word Is Too Often Profaned,
            st. 2

7 Swiftly walk o'er the western wave, Spirit of Night!
                              To Night [1821], st. 1

8 Rarely, rarely, comest thou,
  Spirit of Delight!
            Song: Rarely, Rarely, Comest Thou [1821],
            st. 1

9 Let me set my mournful ditty
  To a merry measure;
  Thou wilt never come for pity,
  Thou wilt come for pleasure.
            Song: Rarely, Rarely, Comest Thou, st. 4

10 When the lamp is shattered
   The light in the dust lies dead —
   When the cloud is scattered
   The rainbow's glory is shed.
            When the Lamp Is Shattered [1822], st. 1

11 Best and brightest, come away!
            To Jane: The Invitation [1822], l. 1

12 Away, away, from men and towns,
   To the wild wood and the downs.
            To Jane: The Invitation, l. 21

13 The great secret of morals is love; or a going out of
   our own nature, and an identification of ourselves
   with the beautiful which exists in thought, action,
   or person not our own....The great instrument of
   moral good is the imagination; and poetry administers to the effect by acting upon the cause.
            A Defense of Poetry [1821]

14 Poetry is the record of the best and happiest
   moments of the happiest and best minds.
            A Defense of Poetry

15 Poets are the hierophants of an unapprehended
   inspiration; the mirrors of the gigantic shadows
   which futurity casts upon the present.
            A Defense of Poetry

16 Poets are the unacknowledged legislators of the
   world.   *A Defense of Poetry*

Thaddeus Stevens
1792–1868

17 Though the President is Commander-in-Chief,
   Congress is his commander; and, God willing,
   he shall obey. He and his minions shall learn that this
   is not a Government of kings and satraps, but a
   Government of the people, and that Congress is the
   people.
            Speech in House of Representatives
            [January 3, 1867]

John Clare
1793–1864

18 I am! yet what I am who cares, or knows?
   My friends forsake me like a memory lost.
            I Am [c. 1844], l. 1

19 Untroubling and untroubled where I lie —
   The grass below — above the vaulted sky.
            I Am, l. 17

20 Till kicked and torn and beaten out he lies
   And leaves his hold and cackles, groans, and dies.
            Badger [c. 1835–1837]

21 Lover of swamps
   The quagmire overgrown
   With hassock tufts of sedge — where fear encamps
   Around thy home alone

   The trembling grass
   Quakes from the human foot

Nor bears the weight of man to let him pass
Where he alone and mute

Sitteth at rest
To the Snipe [1821–1824], l. 1

1 Summer pleasures they are gone like to visions every
  one
And the cloudy days of autumn and of winter cometh
  on
I tried to call them back but unbidden they are gone
Far away from heart and eye and for ever far away
Remembrances [1832?], l. 1

2 Say maiden wilt thou go with me
In this strange death of life-to-be
To live in death and be the same
Without this life or home or name
At once to be and not to be
An Invite to Eternity [c. 1847], l. 17

3   There is nothing but poetry about the existence
of childhood real simple soul-moving poetry the
laughter and joy of poetry and not its philosophy and
there is nothing of poetry about manhood but
the reflection and the remembrance of what has
been — nothing more   *From the notebooks*

Felicia [Dorothea] Hemans
1793–1835

4 The breaking waves dashed high
  On a stern and rock-bound coast,
  And the woods, against a stormy sky,
  Their giant branches tossed.
The Landing of the Pilgrim Fathers [1826], st. 1

5 A band of exiles moored their bark
  On a wild New England shore.
The Landing of the Pilgrim Fathers, st. 2

6 The boy[1] stood on the burning deck,
  Whence all but he had fled.
Casabianca [1826], st. 1

7 The stately homes of England!
  How beautiful they stand,
  Amidst their tall ancestral trees,
  O'er all the pleasant land![2]
The Homes of England [1827], st. 1

----

[1]Giacomo Casabianca, whose father, Louis, at the battle of the Nile [1798], commanded the flagship *Orient*. It took fire and blew up, the commander was mortally wounded, and when most of the crew fled, Giacomo, according to tradition, remained aboard to help his father.

[2]The stately homes of England, / How beautiful they stood / Before their recent owners / Relinquished them for good. — E. V. KNOX [1881–1971], *The Stately Homes* [*Punch,* July 21, 1920]
  See Quentin Crisp, 752:3.
  See Virginia Woolf, 654:6.

Henry Francis Lyte
1793–1847

8 Abide with me: fast falls the eventide;
  The darkness deepens; Lord, with me abide:
  When other helpers fail, and comforts flee,
  Help of the helpless, O abide with me.
Eventide [1847], st. 1

Lucretia [Coffin] Mott
1793–1880

9   Let woman then go on — not asking favors, but
claiming as a right the removal of all hindrances to her
elevation in the scale of being — let her receive
encouragement for the proper cultivation of all her
powers, so that she may enter profitably into the
active business of life . . . Then in the marriage union,
the independence of the husband and wife will be
equal, their dependence mutual, and their obligations
reciprocal.
*Discourse on Woman [December 17, 1849],
last paragraph*

William Cullen Bryant
1794–1878

10 To him who in the love of Nature holds
  Communion with her visible forms, she speaks
  A various language.
Thanatopsis [1817–1821], l. 1

11 Go forth, under the open sky, and list
  To Nature's teachings.   *Thanatopsis, l. 14*

12   The hills,
  Rock-ribbed, and ancient as the sun.
Thanatopsis, l. 37

13 So live, that when thy summons comes to join
  The innumerable caravan which moves
  To that mysterious realm, where each shall take
  His chamber in the silent halls of death,
  Thou go not, like the quarry-slave at night,
  Scourged to his dungeon, but, sustained and soothed
  By an unfaltering trust, approach thy grave,
  Like one that wraps the drapery of his couch
  About him, and lies down to pleasant dreams.
Thanatopsis, l. 73

14 He who, from zone to zone,
  Guides through the boundless sky thy certain flight,
  In the long way that I must tread alone,
  Will lead my steps aright.
To a Waterfowl [1818], st. 8

15 The groves were God's first temples.
A Forest Hymn [1824]

1 Loveliest of lovely things are they,
On earth, that soonest pass away.
The rose that lives its little hour
Is prized beyond the sculptured flower.
A Scene on the Banks of the Hudson [1828], st. 3

2 The melancholy days are come, the saddest of the year,
Of wailing winds, and naked woods, and meadows
brown and sere.
The Death of the Flowers [1832], st. 1

3 These are the gardens of the desert, these
The unshorn fields, boundless and beautiful,
For which the speech of England has no name —
The prairies. *The Prairies [1833]*

4 Truth, crushed to earth, shall rise again.
The Battlefield [1839], st. 9

Cornelius Vanderbilt
1794–1877

5 You have undertaken to cheat me. I won't sue
you, for the law is too slow. I'll ruin you.
Letter to former business associates [1853]

William Whewell
1794–1866

6 It is a test of true theories not only to account for
but to predict phenomena.
Philosophy of the Inductive Sciences, aphorism 39

Thomas Carlyle
1795–1881

7 Were we to characterize this age of ours by any
single epithet, we should be tempted to call it . . .
above all others, the Mechanical Age. . . . The same
habit regulates not our modes of action alone, but
our modes of thought and feeling. Men are grown
mechanical in head and in heart, as well as in hand.
Signs of the Times [1829]

8 Whoso belongs only to his own age, and reverences only its gilt Popinjays or soot-smeared Mumbo-
jumbos, must needs die with it.
On Boswell's Life of Johnson [1832]

9 The stupendous Fourth Estate, whose wide
world-embracing influences what eye can take in?[1]
On Boswell's Life of Johnson

10 All work is as seed sown; it grows and spreads, and
sows itself anew.
On Boswell's Life of Johnson

11 The courage we desire and prize is not the courage
to die decently, but to live manfully.
On Boswell's Life of Johnson

12 No man who has once heartily and wholly laughed
can be altogether irreclaimably bad.
*Sartor Resartus (The Tailor Retailored)
[1833–1834], bk. I, ch. 4*

13 He who first shortened the labor of copyists by
device of movable types was disbanding hired armies,
and cashiering most kings and senates, and creating a
whole new democratic world: he had invented the art
of printing. *Sartor Resartus, I, 5*

14 Man is a tool-using animal. . . . Without tools he is
nothing, with tools he is all. *Sartor Resartus, I, 5*

15 Be not the slave of Words. *Sartor Resartus, I, 8*

16 What you see, yet can not see over, is as good as
infinite. *Sartor Resartus, II, 1*

17 Sarcasm I now see to be, in general, the language
of the Devil; for which reason I have long since as
good as renounced it.
Sartor Resartus, II, 4

18 The Everlasting No.
Sartor Resartus, II, 7 (chapter title)

19 With stupidity and sound digestion man may front
much. *Sartor Resartus, II, 7*

20 Great men are the inspired (speaking and acting)
texts of that divine Book of Revelations, whereof a
chapter is completed from epoch to epoch, and by
some named History.
Sartor Resartus, II, 8

21 The Everlasting Yea.
Sartor Resartus, II, 9 (chapter title)

22 Man's unhappiness, as I construe, comes of his
greatness; it is because there is an Infinite in him,
which with all his cunning he cannot quite bury
under the Finite.
Sartor Resartus, II, 9

23 As the Swiss inscription says: *Sprechen ist silbern,
Schweigen ist golden* — "Speech is silvern, Silence is
golden"; or, as I might rather express it, speech is of
time, silence is of eternity.[2]
Sartor Resartus, III, 3

---

[1] [Edmund] Burke said there were Three Estates in Parliament;
but, in the Reporters' Gallery yonder, there sat a Fourth Estate
more important far than they all. — CARLYLE, *On Heroes and Hero
Worship* [1841], *The Hero as Man of Letters*
See William Hazlitt, 385:13.

[2] Silence is deep as Eternity; speech is shallow as Time. — CARLYLE,
Critical and Miscellaneous Essays. Sir Walter Scott [1838]
[Carlyle] loves silence somewhat platonically. — GIUSEPPI MAZZINI
[1805–1872]; *from* JANE WELSH CARLYLE, *Letter to Mrs. Stirling*
[October 1843]

1 France was long a despotism tempered by epigrams.
History of the French Revolution [1837],
pt. I, bk. I, ch. 1

2 No lie you can speak or act but it will come, after longer or shorter circulation, like a bill drawn on Nature's Reality, and be presented there for payment — with the answer, No effects.
History of the French Revolution, I, III, 1

3 To a shower of gold most things are penetrable.
History of the French Revolution, I, III, 7

4 A whiff of grapeshot.
History of the French Revolution, I, V, 3

5 O poor mortals, how ye make this earth bitter for each other. *History of the French Revolution, I, V, 5*

6 Battles, in these ages, are transacted by mechanism; with the slightest possible development of human individuality or spontaneity; men now even die, and kill one another, in an artificial manner.
History of the French Revolution, I, VII, 4

7 History a distillation of rumor.
History of the French Revolution, I, VII, 5

8 The sea-green Incorruptible [Robespierre].
History of the French Revolution, II, VI, 7

9 Aristocracy of the Moneybag.
History of the French Revolution, II, VII, 7

10 Democracy is, by the nature of it, a self-canceling business; and gives in the long run a net result of zero. *Chartism [1839], ch. 6, Laissez-Faire*

11 A well-written Life is almost as rare as a well-spent one.
Critical and Miscellaneous Essays
[1839–1857]. Richter

12 The great law of culture is: Let each become all that he was created capable of being.
Critical and Miscellaneous Essays. Richter

13 The three great elements of modern civilization, gunpowder, printing, and the Protestant religion.
Critical and Miscellaneous Essays.
The State of German Literature

14 There is no heroic poem in the world but is at bottom a biography, the life of a man; also, it may be said, there is no life of a man, faithfully recorded, but is a heroic poem of its sort, rhymed or unrhymed.
Critical and Miscellaneous Essays.
Sir Walter Scott

15 No man lives without jostling and being jostled; in all ways he has to elbow himself through the world, giving and receiving offense.
Critical and Miscellaneous Essays.
Sir Walter Scott

16 The uttered part of a man's life, let us always repeat, bears to the unuttered, unconscious part a small unknown proportion. He himself never knows it, much less do others.
Critical and Miscellaneous Essays.
Sir Walter Scott

17 The history of the world is but the biography of great men.[1]
On Heroes and Hero Worship [1841].
The Hero as Divinity

18 A vein of poetry exists in the hearts of all men.
On Heroes and Hero Worship. The Hero as Poet

19 The Age of Miracles is forever here!
On Heroes and Hero Worship. The Hero as Priest

20 All that mankind has done, thought, gained or been: it is lying as in magic preservation in the pages of books.
On Heroes and Hero Worship.
The Hero as Man of Letters

21 The true university of these days is a collection of books.
On Heroes and Hero Worship.
The Hero as Man of Letters

22 The suffering man ought really to consume his own smoke; there is no good in emitting smoke till you have made it into fire.[2]
On Heroes and Hero Worship.
The Hero as Man of Letters

23 Adversity is sometimes hard upon a man; but for one man who can stand prosperity, there are a hundred that will stand adversity.
On Heroes and Hero Worship.
The Hero as Man of Letters

24 "A fair day's wages for a fair day's work": it is as just a demand as governed men ever made of governing. It is the everlasting right of man.
Past and Present [1843], bk. I, ch. 3

25 Fire is the best of servants; but what a master![3]
Past and Present, II, 9

26 All work, even cotton spinning, is noble; work is alone noble. . . . A life of ease is not for any man, nor for any god.
Past and Present, III, 4

---

[1]History is the essence of innumerable biographies. — CARLYLE, *On History* [1830]

[2]Would that he consumed his own smoke. — HERMAN MELVILLE, *Moby-Dick, ch. 96*

Consume your own smoke. — ROBERT BROWNING, *Of Pacchiarotto* [1876], *sec. 25*

[3]Mammon is like fire: the usefulest of all servants, if the frightfulest of all masters! — CARLYLE, *Past and Present, bk. IV, ch. 7*

1   Every noble crown is, and on earth will forever be, a crown of thorns.   *Past and Present, III, 8*

2   He who takes not counsel of the Unseen and Silent, from him will never come real visibility and speech.   *Past and Present, III, 12*

3   Captains of Industry.
      Past and Present, IV, 4 (chapter title)

4   There is endless merit in a man's knowing when to have done.   *Francia [1845]*

5   He that works and *does* some Poem, not he that merely *says* one, is worthy of the name of Poet.
      Introduction to Cromwell's Letters and Speeches [1845]

6   Respectable Professors of the Dismal Science.[1]
      Latter Day Pamphlets, no. 1 [1850]

7   A healthy hatred of scoundrels.
      Latter Day Pamphlets, 12

8   "Genius" (which means transcendent capacity of taking trouble, first of all).[2]
      Life of Frederick the Great [1858–1865], bk. IV, ch. 3

9   Happy the people whose annals are blank in history books![3]   *Life of Frederick the Great, XVI, 1*

10 So here hath been dawning
      Another blue Day:
      Think wilt thou let it
      Slip useless away.   *Today [1823–1833]*

11 Lord Bacon could as easily have created the planets as he could have written Hamlet.
      Remark in discussion

Joseph Rodman Drake
1795–1820

12 When Freedom from her mountain height,
      Unfurled her standard to the air,
      She tore the azure robe of night,
      And set the stars of glory there.
      The American Flag [1819], st. 1

John Woodcock Graves
1795–1886

13 D' ye ken John Peel with his coat so gay?
      D' ye ken John Peel at the break of day?

D' ye ken John Peel when he's far far away
With his hounds and his horn in the morning?

'Twas the sound of his horn brought me from my
      bed,
And the cry of his hounds, has me ofttimes led;
For Peel's view-hollo would waken the dead,
Or the fox from his lair in the morning.
      John Peel [1832]

John Keats
1795–1821

14 How many bards gild the lapses of time!
      Poems [1817]. Sonnet.
      How Many Bards Gild the Lapses of Time

15 To one who has been long in city pent,
      'Tis very sweet to look into the fair
      And open face of heaven.
      Poems. Sonnet.
      To One Who Has Been Long in City Pent

16 He mourns that day so soon has glided by:
      E'en like the passage of an angel's tear
      That falls through the clear ether silently.
      Poems. Sonnet.
      To One Who Has Been Long in City Pent

17 Much have I travel'd in the realms of gold,
      And many goodly states and kingdoms seen;
      Round many western islands have I been
      Which bards in fealty to Apollo hold.
      Oft of one wide expanse had I been told
      That deep-brow'd Homer ruled as his
            demesne;
      Yet did I never breathe its pure serene
      Till I heard Chapman speak out loud and bold:
      Then felt I like some watcher of the skies
      When a new planet swims into his ken;
      Or like stout Cortez when with eagle eyes
      He star'd at the Pacific — and all his men
      Look'd at each other with a wild surmise —
      Silent, upon a peak in Darien.
      Poems. Sonnet. On First Looking into
      Chapman's Homer

18 And other spirits there are standing apart
      Upon the forehead of the age to come;
      These, these will give the world another heart,
      And other pulses. Hear ye not the hum
      Of mighty workings——?
      Listen awhile, ye nations, and be dumb.
      Poems. Sonnet. Addressed to the Same
      (Benjamin Robert Haydon)

19 The poetry of earth is never dead.
      Poems. Sonnet.
      On the Grasshopper and the Cricket

---

[1]Referring to political economy and social science, Carlyle also in his *Occasional Discourse on the Negro Question* [1849] speaks of "What we might call, by way of eminence, the Dismal Science."

[2]See Georges Buffon, 304:6, and Jane Ellice Hopkins, 528:11.

[3]Carlyle identifies this as "Montesquieu's aphorism."

1 O for ten years, that I may overwhelm
　Myself in poesy; so I may do the deed
　That my own soul has to itself decreed.
　　　　Poems. Sleep and Poetry, l. 96

2 And can I ever bid these joys farewell?
　Yes, I must pass them for a nobler life,
　Where I may find the agonies, the strife
　Of human hearts.
　　　　Poems. Sleep and Poetry, l. 122

3　　　A drainless shower
　Of light is poesy; 'tis the supreme of power;
　'Tis might half slumb'ring on its own right arm.
　　　　Poems. Sleep and Poetry, l. 235

4 But strength alone though of the Muses born
　Is like a fallen angel: trees uptorn,
　Darkness, and worms, and shrouds, and sepulchers
　Delight it; for it feeds upon the burrs
　And thorns of life; forgetting the great end
　Of poesy, that it should be a friend
　To soothe the cares, and lift the thoughts of man.
　　　　Poems. Sleep and Poetry, l. 241

5　　There is not a fiercer hell than the failure in a great
object.
　　　　Endymion [1818], preface

6　　The imagination of a boy is healthy, and the
mature imagination of a man is healthy; but there is
a space of life between, in which the soul is in a ferment, the character undecided, the way of life uncertain, the ambition thicksighted: thence proceeds
mawkishness, and the thousand bitters which those
men I speak of must necessarily taste in going over
the following pages.
　　　　Endymion, preface

7 A thing of beauty is a joy forever:
　Its loveliness increases; it will never
　Pass into nothingness; but still will keep
　A bower quiet for us, and a sleep
　Full of sweet dreams, and health, and quiet
　　breathing.
　　　　Endymion, bk. I, l. 1

8　　　The grandeur of the dooms
　We have imagined for the mighty dead.
　　　　Endymion, I, l. 20

9 Wherein lies happiness? In that which becks
　Our ready minds to fellowship divine,
　A fellowship with essence; till we shine,
　Full alchemiz'd, and free of space. Behold
　The clear religion of heaven!　*Endymion, I, l. 777*

10　　　The crown of these
　Is made of love and friendship, and sits high
　Upon the forehead of humanity.
　　　　Endymion, I, l. 800

11 A hope beyond the shadow of a dream.
　　　　Endymion, I, l. 857

12 A virgin purest lipp'd, yet in the lore
　Of love deep learned to the red heart's core.
　　　　Poems [1820]. Lamia, pt. I, l. 189

13 Let the mad poets say whate'er they please
　Of the sweets of Fairies, Peris, Goddesses,
　Haunters of cavern, lake, and waterfall,
　As a real woman, lineal indeed
　From Pyrrha's pebbles or old Adam's seed.
　　　　Poems. Lamia, I, l. 328

14 Love in a hut, with water and a crust,
　Is — Love, forgive us! — cinders, ashes, dust.
　　　　Poems. Lamia, II, l. 1

15 Do not all charms fly
　At the mere touch of cold philosophy?
　　　　Poems. Lamia, II, l. 229

16 Philosophy will clip an angel's wings.
　　　　Poems. Lamia, II, l. 234

17 For them the Ceylon diver held his breath,
　And went all naked to the hungry shark;
　For them his ears gush'd blood; for them in death
　The seal on the cold ice with piteous bark
　Lay full of darts; for them alone did seethe
　A thousand men in troubles wide and dark:
　Half-ignorant, they turn'd an easy wheel,
　That set sharp racks at work, to pinch and peel.
　　　　Poems. Isabella; or, The Pot of Basil,
　　　　st. 15

18 St. Agnes' Eve — Ah, bitter chill it was!
　The owl, for all his feathers, was a-cold.
　The hare limp'd trembling through the
　　frozen grass,
　And silent was the flock in woolly fold.
　　　　Poems. The Eve of St. Agnes, st. 1

19 The music, yearning like a God in pain.
　　　　Poems. The Eve of St. Agnes, st. 7

20 Asleep in lap of legends old.
　　　　Poems. The Eve of St. Agnes, st. 15

21 Sudden a thought came like a full-blown rose,
　Flushing his brow, and in his pained heart
　Made purple riot.
　　　　Poems. The Eve of St. Agnes, st. 16

22 Unclasps her warmed jewels one by one;
　Loosens her fragrant bodice; by degrees
　Her rich attire creeps rustling to her knees.
　　　　Poems. The Eve of St. Agnes, st. 26

23 Beyond a mortal man impassion'd far
　At these voluptuous accents, he arose,
　Ethereal, flush'd, and like a throbbing star
　Seen mid the sapphire heaven's deep repose;

Into her dream he melted, as the rose,
Blendeth its odour with the violet, —
Solution sweet: meantime the frost-wind blows
Like Love's alarum pattering the sharp sleet
Against the window-panes; St. Agnes' moon
    hath set.
                Poems. The Eve of St. Agnes, st. 36

1 And they are gone: aye, ages long ago
  These lovers fled away into the storm.
                Poems. The Eve of St. Agnes, st. 42

2 My heart aches, and a drowsy numbness pains
  My sense, as though of hemlock I had drunk,
  Or emptied some dull opiate to the drains
  One minute past, and Lethe-wards had sunk.
                Poems. Ode to a Nightingale, st. 1

3 That thou, light-winged Dryad of the trees,
    In some melodious plot
  Of beechen green, and shadows numberless,
  Singest of summer in full-throated ease.
                Poems. Ode to a Nightingale, st. 1

4 O, for a draught of vintage! that hath been
  Cool'd a long age in the deep-delved earth,
  Tasting of Flora and the country green,
  Dance, and Provençal song, and sunburnt mirth!
  O, for a beaker full of the warm South,
  Full of the true, the blushful Hippocrene,
  With beaded bubbles winking at the brim,
    And purple-stained mouth.
                Poems. Ode to a Nightingale, st. 2

5 Fade far away, dissolve, and quite forget
  What thou among the leaves hast never known,
  The weariness, the fever, and the fret
  Here, where men sit and hear each other groan;
  Where palsy shakes a few, sad, last gray hairs,
  Where youth grows pale, and specter-thin,
    and dies;
  Where but to think is to be full of sorrow
    And leaden-eyed despairs.
                Poems. Ode to a Nightingale, st. 3

6 Already with thee! tender is the night.
                Poems. Ode to a Nightingale, st. 4

7 I cannot see what flowers are at my feet,
  Nor what soft incense hangs upon the boughs,
  But, in embalmed darkness, guess each sweet.
                Poems. Ode to a Nightingale, st. 5

8 The murmurous haunt of flies on summer eves.
                Poems. Ode to a Nightingale, st. 5

9 Darkling I listen; and, for many a time
  I have been half in love with easeful Death,
  Call'd him soft names in many a mused rhyme,
  To take into the air my quiet breath;
  Now more than ever seems it rich to die,
  To cease upon the midnight with no pain,

While thou art pouring forth thy soul abroad
    In such an ecstasy!
  Still wouldst thou sing, and I have ears in vain —
  To thy high requiem become a sod.
                Poems. Ode to a Nightingale, st. 6

10 Thou wast not born for death, immortal Bird!
  No hungry generations tread thee down;
  The voice I hear this passing night was heard
  In ancient days by emperor and clown:
  Perhaps the self-same song that found a path
  Through the sad heart of Ruth, when, sick
    for home,
  She stood in tears amid the alien corn;
  The same that oft-times hath
  Charm'd magic casements, opening on the foam
  Of perilous seas, in faery lands forlorn.
                Poems. Ode to a Nightingale, st. 7

11 Forlorn! the very word is like a bell
  To toll me back from thee to my sole self!
                Poems. Ode to a Nightingale, st. 8

12 Was it a vision, or a waking dream?
  Fled is that music: — Do I wake or sleep?
                Poems. Ode to a Nightingale, st. 8

13 Thou still unravish'd bride of quietness,
  Thou foster-child of silence and slow time,
  Sylvan historian, who canst thus express
  A flowery tale more sweetly than our rhyme:
  What leaf-fring'd legend haunts about
    thy shape?
                Poems. Ode on a Grecian Urn, st. 1

14 What men or gods are these? What maidens loth?
  What mad pursuit? What struggle to escape?
  What pipes and timbrels? What wild ecstasy?
                Poems. Ode on a Grecian Urn, st. 1

15 Heard melodies are sweet, but those unheard
  Are sweeter.
                Poems. Ode on a Grecian Urn, st. 2

16 Forever wilt thou love, and she be fair!
                Poems. Ode on a Grecian Urn, st. 2

17 Forever piping songs forever new.
                Poems. Ode on a Grecian Urn, st. 3

18 Who are these coming to the sacrifice?
  To what green altar, O mysterious priest,
  Lead'st thou that heifer lowing at the skies,
  And all her silken flanks with garlands drest?
                Poems. Ode on a Grecian Urn, st. 4

19 O Attic shape! Fair attitude!
                Poems. Ode on a Grecian Urn, st. 5

20 When old age shall this generation waste,
  Thou shalt remain, in midst of other woe
  Than ours, a friend to man, to whom thou say'st,

"Beauty is truth, truth beauty,"[1] — that is all
Ye know on earth, and all ye need to know.
> *Poems. Ode on a Grecian Urn, st. 5*

1   To make delicious moan
Upon the midnight hours.   *Poems. Ode to Psyche, st. 3*

2 A bright torch, and a casement ope at night,
To let the warm Love in!   *Poems. Ode to Psyche, st. 5*

3 Ever let the fancy roam,
Pleasure never is at home.   *Poems. Fancy, l. 1*

4 Bards of Passion and of Mirth,
Ye have left your souls on earth!
Have ye souls in heaven too,
Double-lived in regions new?
> *Poems. Ode written on the blank page
> before* BEAUMONT AND FLETCHER,
> *The Fair Maid of the Inn*

5 Souls of Poets dead and gone,
What Elysium have ye known,
Happy field or mossy cavern,
Choicer than the Mermaid Tavern?
Have ye tippled drink more fine
Than mine host's Canary wine?
> *Poems. Lines on the Mermaid Tavern*

6 Season of mists and mellow fruitfulness,
Close bosom-friend of the maturing sun.
> *Poems. To Autumn, st. 1*

7 Who hath not seen thee oft amid thy store?
Sometimes whoever seeks abroad may find
Thee sitting careless on a granary floor,
Thy hair soft-lifted by the winnowing wind;
Or on a half-reap'd furrow sound asleep,
Drows'd with the fume of poppies while thy hook
Spares the next swath and all its twined flowers.
> *Poems. To Autumn, st. 2*

8 Where are the songs of Spring? Ay, where are they?
Think not of them, thou hast thy music too, —
While barred clouds bloom the soft-dying day,
And touch the stubble-plains with rosy hue;
Then in a wailful choir the small gnats mourn
Among the river sallows, borne aloft
Or sinking as the light wind lives or dies;
And full-grown lambs loud bleat from hilly bourn;
Hedge-crickets sing; and now with treble soft

The red-breast whistles from a garden-croft;
And gathering swallows twitter in the skies.
> *Poems. To Autumn, st. 3*

9 No, no, go not to Lethe, neither twist
Wolf's-bane, tight-rooted, for its poisonous wine.
> *Poems. Ode on Melancholy, st. 1*

10 Then glut thy sorrow on a morning rose.
> *Poems. Ode on Melancholy, st. 2*

11 She dwells with Beauty — Beauty that must die;
And Joy, whose hand is ever at his lips
Bidding adieu; and aching Pleasure nigh,
Turning to poison while the bee-mouth sips:
Ay, in the very temple of Delight
Veil'd Melancholy has her sovran shrine,
Though seen of none save him whose strenuous
     tongue
Can burst Joy's grape against his palate fine;
His soul shall taste the sadness of her might,
And be among her cloudy trophies hung.
> *Poems. Ode on Melancholy, st. 3*

12 Deep in the shady sadness of a vale
Far sunken from the healthy breath of morn,
Far from the fiery noon, and eve's one star,
Sat gray-hair'd Saturn, quiet as a stone.
> *Poems. Hyperion: A Fragment, bk. I, l. 1*

13 How beautiful, if sorrow had not made
Sorrow more beautiful than Beauty's self.
> *Poems. Hyperion: A Fragment, I, l. 35*

14 For to bear all naked truths,
And to envisage circumstance, all calm,
That is the top of sovereignty.
> *Poems. Hyperion: A Fragment, II, l. 203*

15 Knowledge enormous makes a God of me.
Names, deeds, gray legends, dire events, rebellions,
Majesties, sovran voices, agonies,
Creations and destroyings, all at once
Pour into the wide hollows of my brain,
And deify me, as if some blithe wine
Or bright elixir peerless I had drunk,
And so become immortal.
> *Poems. Hyperion: A Fragment, III, l. 113*

16 My spirit is too weak — mortality
Weighs heavily on me like unwilling sleep,
And each imagin'd pinnacle and steep
Of godlike hardship, tells me I must die
Like a sick Eagle looking at the sky.[2]
> *Life, Letters, and Literary Remains
> of John Keats [1848], edited by* RICHARD
> MONCKTON MILNES [1809–1885].
> *On Seeing the Elgin Marbles*

---

[1] If asked who said "Beauty is truth, truth beauty!" a great many readers would answer "Keats." But Keats said nothing of the sort. It is what he said the Grecian Urn said, his description and criticism of a certain kind of work of art, the kind from which the evils and problems of this life, the "heart high sorrowful and cloyed," are deliberately excluded. The Urn, for example, depicts, among other beautiful sights, the citadel of a hill town; it does not depict warfare, the evil which makes the citadel necessary. — W. H. AUDEN, *The Dyer's Hand. Robert Frost*
See George Herbert, 242:18.

[2] Printed in the *Examiner* [February 23, 1817].

1 This living hand, now warm and capable
Of earnest grasping, would, if it were cold
And in the icy silence of the tomb,
So haunt thy days and chill thy dreaming nights
That thou would wish thine own heart dry of blood
So in my veins red life might stream again,
And thou be conscience-calm'd — see here it is —
I hold it towards you.
> *Life, Letters, and Literary Remains of John
> Keats. Fragment: This Living Hand*

2 O, what can ail thee, knight-at-arms,
Alone and palely loitering?
The sedge has withered from the lake,
And no birds sing!
> *Life, Letters, and Literary Remains of John
> Keats. La Belle Dame Sans Merci,*[1] *st. 1*

3 I met a lady in the meads
Full beautiful, a faery's child;
Her hair was long, her foot was light,
And her eyes were wild.
> *Life, Letters, and Literary Remains of John
> Keats. La Belle Dame Sans Merci, st. 4*

4 She looked at me as she did love,
And made sweet moan.
> *Life, Letters, and Literary Remains of John
> Keats. La Belle Dame Sans Merci, st. 5*

5 I saw pale kings and princes too,
Pale warriors, death-pale were they all;
They cried — "La Belle Dame sans Merci
Hath thee in thrall!"
> *Life, Letters, and Literary Remains of John
> Keats. La Belle Dame Sans Merci, st. 10*

6 It keeps eternal whisperings around
Desolate shores, and with its mighty swell
Gluts twice ten thousand caverns.
> *Life, Letters, and Literary Remains of John
> Keats. La Belle Dame Sans Merci,
> On the Sea*[2]

7 When I have fears that I may cease to be
Before my pen has glean'd my teeming brain.
> *Life, Letters, and Literary Remains of John
> Keats. Sonnet. When I Have Fears*

8 When I behold, upon the night's starr'd face,
Huge cloudy symbols of a high romance.
> *Life, Letters, and Literary Remains of John
> Keats. Sonnet. When I Have Fears*

9 Then on the shore
Of the wide world I stand alone, and think
Till love and fame to nothingness do sink.
> *Life, Letters, and Literary Remains of John
> Keats. Sonnet. When I Have Fears*

10 Bright star, would I were steadfast as thou art —
Not in lone splendor hung aloft the night
And watching, with eternal lids apart,
Like nature's patient, sleepless Eremite,
The moving waters at their priestlike task
Of pure ablution round earth's human shores.
> *Life, Letters, and Literary Remains of John
> Keats. Sonnet. Bright Star*[3]

11 I am certain of nothing but of the holiness of the Heart's affections and the truth of Imagination — What the imagination seizes as Beauty must be truth — whether it existed before or not.
> *Letter to Benjamin Bailey
> [November 22, 1817]*

12 The Imagination may be compared to Adam's dream — he awoke and found it truth.
> *Letter to Benjamin Bailey
> [November 22, 1817]*

13 O for a Life of Sensations rather than of Thoughts!
> *Letter to Benjamin Bailey
> [November 22, 1817]*

14 I scarcely remember counting upon any Happiness — I look not for it if it be not in the present hour — nothing startles me beyond the Moment. The setting sun will always set me to rights — or if a Sparrow come before my Window I take part in its existence and pick about the Gravel.
> *Letter to Benjamin Bailey
> [November 22, 1817]*

15 At once it struck me, what quality went to form a Man of Achievement especially in Literature & which Shakespeare possessed so enormously — I mean *Negative Capability,* that is, when man is capable of being in uncertainties, Mysteries, doubts, without any irritable reaching after fact & reason.
> *Letter to George and Thomas Keats
> [December 22, 1817]*

16 We hate poetry that has a palpable design upon us — and if we do not agree, seems to put its hand in its breeches pocket. Poetry should be great & unobtrusive, a thing which enters into one's soul, and does not startle it or amaze it with itself, but with its subject.
> *Letter to John Hamilton Reynolds
> [February 3, 1818]*

---

[1] Title of a French poem by ALAIN CHARTIER [c. 1385–c. 1433]. First printed by Leigh Hunt in the *Indicator* [May 10, 1820].

[2] From want of regular rests, I have been rather *narvus,* and the passage in *Lear* — "Do you not hear the sea?" — has haunted me intensely. — KEATS, *Letter to John Hamilton Reynolds* [April 17, 1817]
Edgar: . . . Hark! do you hear the sea? — SHAKESPEARE, *King Lear,* act IV, sc. vi, l. 4

[3] Written on a blank page in Keats's copy of Shakespeare's *Poems.*

1   Poetry should surprise by a fine excess and not by Singularity — it should strike the Reader as a wording of his own highest thoughts, and appear almost a Remembrance.

Letter to John Taylor [February 27, 1818]

2   If poetry comes not as naturally as the Leaves to a tree it had better not come at all.

Letter to John Taylor [February 27, 1818]

3   Scenery is fine — but human nature is finer.

Letter to Benjamin Bailey [March 13, 1818]

4   Axioms in philosophy are not axioms until they are proved upon our pulses: We read fine — things but never feel them to the full until we have gone the same steps as the Author.

*Letter to John Hamilton Reynolds
[May 3, 1818]*

5   I compare human life to a large Mansion of Many Apartments, two of which I can only describe, the doors of the rest being as yet shut upon me.

*Letter to John Hamilton Reynolds
[May 3, 1818]*

6   I begin to get a little acquainted with my own strength and weakness. — Praise or blame has but a momentary effect on the man whose love of beauty in the abstract makes him a severe critic on his own Works.   *Letter to James Hessey [October 8, 1818]*

7   The Genius of Poetry must work out its own salvation in a man: It cannot be matured by law & precept, but by sensation & watchfulness in itself — That which is creative must create itself — In Endymion, I leaped headlong into the Sea, and thereby have become better acquainted with the Soundings, the quicksands, & the rocks, than if I had stayed upon the green shore, and piped a silly pipe, and took tea & comfortable advice. — I was never afraid of failure; for I would sooner fail than not be among the greatest.

Letter to James Hessey [October 8, 1818]

8   I think I shall be among the English Poets after my death.

*Letter to George and Georgiana Keats
[October 14, 1818]*

9   As to the poetical character itself... it is not itself — it has no self — it is every thing and nothing... It has as much delight in conceiving an Iago as an Imogen.

*Letter to Richard Woodhouse
[October 27, 1818]*

10   A Poet is the most unpoetical of anything in existence; because he has no Identity — he is continually infor[ming] — and filling some other Body.

*Letter to Richard Woodhouse
[October 27, 1818]*

11   A Man's life of any worth is a continual allegory — and very few eyes can see the Mystery of his life — a life like the scriptures, figurative.... Lord Byron cuts a figure, but he is not figurative — Shakespeare led a life of Allegory: his works are the comments on it.

*Letter to George and Georgiana Keats
[February 14–May 3, 1819]*

12   I myself am pursuing the same instinctive course as the veriest human animal you can think of — I am however young writing at random — straining at particles of light in the midst of a great darkness — without knowing the bearing of any one assertion of any one opinion. Yet may I not in this be free from sin?

*Letter to George and Georgiana Keats
[March 19, 1819]*

13   Nothing ever becomes real till it is experienced — Even a proverb is no Proverb to you till your Life has illustrated it.

*Letter to George and Georgiana Keats
[March 19, 1819]*

14   Call the world if you Please "The vale of Soul-making."

*Letter to George and Georgiana Keats
[April 21, 1819]*

15   Do you not see how necessary a World of Pains and troubles is to School an Intelligence and make it a soul? A Place where the heart must feel and suffer in a thousand diverse ways!

*Letter to George and Georgiana Keats
[April 21, 1819]*

16   I have two luxuries to brood over in my walks, your Loveliness and the hour of my death. O that I could have possession of them both in the same minute.

To Fanny Brawne [July 25, 1819]

17   "If I should die," said I to myself, "I have left no immortal work behind me — nothing to make my friends proud of my memory — but I have lov'd the principle of beauty in all things, and if I had had time I would have made myself remember'd."

To Fanny Brawne [c. February 1820]

18   I have an habitual feeling of my real life having passed, and that I am leading a posthumous existence.

*Letter to Charles Armitage Brown;
Keats's last letter [November 30, 1820]*

19   I can scarcely bid you good bye even in a letter. I always made an awkward bow. God bless you!

*Letter to Charles Brown;
[November 30, 1820]*

1   Here lies one whose name was writ in water.[1]

Epitaph for himself [1821]

Leopold von Ranke
1795–1886

2   You have reckoned that history ought to judge the past and to instruct the contemporary world as to the future. The present attempt does not yield to that high office. It only wants to show what actually happened.[2]

*Geschichte der Romanischen und
Germanischen Volker von 1494 bis 1514
(History of the Romance and Germanic
Peoples, 1494–1514) [1824], preface*

Fanny [Frances] Wright
1795–1852

3   The press does not speak the voice of the nation. It does not even speak the voice of those who write for it.   *[1829]*

Alfred Bunn
1796–1860

4 I dreamt that I dwelt in marble halls,
With vassals and serfs at my side.

The Bohemian Girl [1843], act II, song

Horace Mann
1796–1859

5   Lost, yesterday, somewhere between sunrise and sunset, two golden hours, each set with sixty diamond minutes. No reward is offered, for they are gone forever.   *Aphorism*

William Hickling Prescott
1796–1859

6   What, then, must have been the emotions of the Spaniards, when, after working their toilsome way into the upper air, the cloudy tabernacle parted before their eyes, and they beheld these fair scenes in all their pristine magnificence and beauty![3] It was like the spectacle which greeted the eyes of Moses from the summit of Pisgah, and, in the warm glow of their feelings, they cried out, "It is the promised land!"

The Conquest of Mexico [1843], bk. III, ch. 8

7   Drawing his sword he [Pizarro] traced a line with it on the sand from East to West. Then, turning towards the South, "Friends and comrades!" he said, "on that side are toil, hunger, nakedness, the drenching storm, desertion, and death; on this side ease and pleasure. There lies Peru with its riches; here, Panama and its poverty. Choose, each man, what best becomes a brave Castilian. For my part, I go to the South." So saying, he stepped across the line.

The Conquest of Peru [1847], bk. II, ch. 4

Joseph Brackett
1797–1882

8 'Tis the gift to be simple, 'tis the gift to be free,
'Tis the gift to come down where we ought to be,
And when we find ourselves in the place just right,
'Twill be in the valley of love and delight.

Simple Gifts[4] [1848]

Paul Delaroche
1797–1856

9 [Upon first seeing a daguerreotype:] From today painting is dead.

Attributed [1839]

Heinrich Heine
1797–1856

10 On wings of song, my dearest,
I will carry you off.

Auf Flügeln des Gesanges[5]

11 I will not mourn, although my heart is torn,
Oh, love forever lost! I will not mourn.

Ich grolle nicht[6]

---

[1]Among the many things he has requested of me tonight, this is the principal—that on his gravestone shall be this inscription.— *Letter from* Joseph Severn [1793–1879], *in* Richard Monckton Milnes [1809–1885], *Life, Letters, and Literary Remains of John Keats* [1848]

[2]Wie es eigentlich gewesen ist.

[3]From this summit [Popocatépetl, 17,887 feet] could be seen the great city of Mexico, and the whole of the lake, and all the towns which were built in it.— Bernal Díaz del Castillo [c. 1492–c. 1581], *Historia Verdadera de la Conquista de la Nueva España, pt. IV, ch. 53*

[4]A Shaker song.

[5]Auf Flügeln des Gesanges, / Herzliebchen, trag ich dich fort.
Translated by Louis Untermeyer.

[6]Ich grolle nicht, und wenn das Herz auch bricht, / Ewig verlornes Lieb! Ich grolle nicht.
Translated by Louis Untermeyer.

1 I cannot tell why this imagined
Despair has fallen upon me;
The ghost of an ancient legend
That will not let me be.   *Lorelei*[1]

2 Child, you are like a flower,
So sweet and pure and fair.
I look at you, and sadness
Touches me with a prayer.

      Du bist wie eine Blume[2]

3   Wherever they burn books they will also, in the
end, burn human beings.

      Almansor: A Tragedy [1823]

4   Don't send a poet to London.

      English Fragments [1828], ch. 2, London

5   Christianity is an idea, and as such is indestructible
and immortal, like every idea.

      *History of Religion and Philosophy
in Germany [1834], vol. I*

6   People in those old times had convictions; we
moderns only have opinions. And it needs more than
a mere opinion to erect a Gothic cathedral.

      The French Stage [1837], ch. 9

7   Wild, dark times are rumbling toward us, and the
prophet who wishes to write a new apocalypse will
have to invent entirely new beasts, and beasts so terrible that the ancient animal symbols of Saint John
will seem like cooing doves and cupids in comparison.   *Lutezia; or, Paris*[3] *[1854]*

8   The future smells of Russian leather, of blood, of
godlessness and of much whipping. I advise our
grandchildren to come into the world with very thick
skin on their backs.   *Lutezia; or, Paris*

9 So we keep asking, over and over,
Until a handful of earth
Stops our mouths —
But is that an answer?

      Lazarus [1854], sec. 1, st. 4

10   Of course he [God] will forgive me; that's his
business.[4]   *Last words [1856]*

11 No author is a man of genius to his publisher.

      Attributed

---

[1]Ich weiss nicht, was soll es bedeuten, / Dass ich so traurig bin; /
Ein Märchen aus alten Zeiten, / Das kommt mir nicht aus dem Sinn.
Translated by LOUIS UNTERMEYER.

[2]Du bist wie eine Blume, / So hold und schön und rein; / Ich
schau dich an, und Wehmut / Schleicht mir ins Herz hinein.
Translated by LOUIS UNTERMEYER.

[3]A collection of newspaper articles Heine had published on French
culture and politics.

[4]Bien sûr, il me pardonnera; c'est son métier.

Samuel Lover
1797–1868

12 Reproof on her lip, but a smile in her eye.

      Rory O'More [1836], st. 1

13 "For there's luck in odd numbers," says Rory
O'More.   *Rory O'More, st. 3*

Sir Charles Lyell
1797–1875

14   Although we are mere sojourners on the surface of
the planet, chained to a mere point in space, enduring
but for a moment of time, the human mind is not
only enabled to number worlds beyond the unassisted ken of mortal eye, but to trace the events of
indefinite ages before the creation of our race, and is
not even withheld from penetrating into the dark
secrets of the ocean, or the interior of the solid globe;
free, like the spirit which the poet described as animating the universe.

      Principles of Geology, vol. I [1830], ch. 13

15   It may be said that, so far from having a materialistic tendency, the supposed introduction into the
earth at successive geological periods of life — sensation, instinct, the intelligence of the higher mammalia
bordering on reason, and lastly, the improvable
reason of Man himself — presents us with a picture
of the ever-increasing dominion of mind over matter.

      *The Geological Evidences of the Antiquity
of Man [1863]*

Mary [Wollstonecraft] Shelley
1797–1851

16   Nothing contributes so much to tranquilize the
mind as a steady purpose — a point on which the soul
may fix its intellectual eye.

      Frankenstein [1818], Letter I

17   I beheld the wretch — the miserable monster
whom I had created.   *Frankenstein, ch. 5*

18   All men hate the wretched; how, then, must I be
hated, who am miserable beyond all living things! Yet
you, my creator, detest and spurn me, thy creature, to
whom thou art bound by ties only dissoluble by the
annihilation of one of us.   *Frankenstein, 10*

Sojourner Truth
[Isabella Van Wagener]
c. 1797–1883

19   Frederick, is God dead?

      Question to speaker FREDERICK DOUGLASS
[c. 1850]

1   That man... says that women need to be helped into carriages, and lifted over ditches, and to have the best place everywhere. Nobody ever helps me into carriages, or over mud puddles, or gives me any best place, and aren't I a woman?... I have plowed, and planted, and gathered into barns, and no man could head me — and aren't I a woman? I could work as much and eat as much as a man (when I could get it), and bear the lash as well — and aren't I a woman? I have borne thirteen children and seen them most all sold off into slavery, and when I cried out with a mother's grief, none but Jesus heard — and aren't I a woman?
Speech at Woman's Rights Convention,
Akron, Ohio [1851]

2   That... man... says women can't have as much rights as man, cause Christ wasn't a woman. Where did your Christ come from?... From God and a woman. Man had nothing to do with him.
Speech at Woman's Rights Convention,
Akron, Ohio

3   The rich rob the poor and the poor rob one another.   *Saying*

Alfred de Vigny
1797–1863

4   I love the sound of the horn, at night, in the depth of the woods.[1]
Le Cor (The Horn) [1826]

5   God! how sad is the sound of the horn deep in the woods![2]   *Le Cor*

6   I [Nature] am called a mother, but I am a grave.
La Maison du Berger
(The House of the Shepherd) [1864]

Auguste Comte
1798–1857

7   Love our principle, order our foundation, progress our goal.
Système de Politique Positive
[1851–1854]

8   Nothing at bottom is real except humanity.[3]
Système de Politique Positive

9   The dead govern the living.
Catéchisme Positiviste [1852]

Eugène Delacroix
1798–1863

10   O young artist, you search for a subject — everything is a subject. Your subject is yourself, your impressions, your emotions in the presence of nature.
Oeuvres Littéraires [1829–1863],
pt. II, ch. 2, On Painting

11   Painting is only a bridge linking the painter's mind with that of the viewer.
Journal [July 18, 1850]

12   Mediocre people have an answer for everything and are astonished at nothing.[4]
Journal [February 25, 1852]

13   The first virtue of a painting is to be a feast for the eyes.
Journal [June 22, 1863]

August Heinrich Hoffmann
[Hoffmann von Fallersleben]
1798–1874

14   Deutschland, Deutschland über Alles [Germany above everything].
Title of poem [September 1, 1841]

Giacomo Leopardi
1798–1837

15   No one is so completely disenchanted with the world, nor knows it so thoroughly, nor is so much disgusted with it, but that when it begins to smile upon him he does not become partially reconciled to it.[5]
Pensieri [early 1830s]

16   The time will come when this universe and nature herself will be no more. And just as of very great human kingdoms and empires and of their marvelous exploits, which were so very famous in other ages, there remains no sign of fame whatsoever; so too of the entire world, and of the infinite vicissitudes and calamities of all created things, no single trace will remain; but a naked silence and a most profound quiet will fill the immensity of space. Thus, this stupendous and frightening mystery of universal existence, before it can be declared or understood, will vanish and be lost.[6]
Operette Morali [1835]. The Song of the
Great Wild Rooster

---

[1]J'aime le son du cor, le soir, au fond des bois.

[2]Dieu! que le son du cor est triste au fond des bois!

[3]Il n'y a, au fond, de réel que l'humanité.

[4]Translated by WALTER PACH.

[5]Translated by JAMES THOMSON.

[6]Translated by GIOVANNI CECCHETTI.

1   Every day we lose something; one of the illusions, which are our only riches, perishes or diminishes. Experience or truth divests us every day of part of our possessions. We do not live, except in losing.[1]

Zibaldone, I, 467 [1817–1832]

Jules Michelet
1798–1874

2   England is an empire, Germany is a nation, a race, France is a person.   *Histoire de France [1833–1867]*

3   The silences of history must be made to speak [Il faut faire parler les silences de l'histoire].[2]

Journal entry [January 30, 1842]

David Macbeth Moir
1798–1851

4 From the lone sheiling of the misty island
Mountains divide us, and the waste of seas —
Yet still the blood is strong, the heart is Highland,
And we in dreams behold the Hebrides.[3]

The Lone Sheiling [Canadian Boat Song, 1829]

Dionysios Solomos
1798–1857

5 We knew thee of old,
O divinely restored,
By the light of thine eyes
And the light of thy sword.

From the graves of our slain
Shall thy valor prevail
As we greet thee again —
Hail, Liberty! Hail!

Hymn to Liberty[4] *[1823], st. 1, 2*

[Amos] Bronson Alcott
1799–1888

6   The true teacher defends his pupils against his own personal influence. He inspires self-trust. He guides their eyes from himself to the spirit that quickens him. He will have no disciple.

*Orphic Sayings. From The Dial [July 1840].
The Teacher*

7 Who loves a garden still his Eden keeps,
Perennial pleasures plants, and wholesome harvests
   reaps.   *Tablets [1868]*

8   One must be a wise reader to quote wisely and well.   *Table Talk [1877]. Quotation*

9   To be ignorant of one's ignorance is the malady of the ignorant.   *Table Talk. Discourse*

Honoré de Balzac
1799–1850

10   It is easier to be a lover than a husband for the simple reason that it is more difficult to be witty every day than to say pretty things from time to time.

Physiologie du Mariage [1829]

11   Marriage must ceaselessly combat a monster that devours everything: habit.

Physiologie du Mariage

12   In the desert there is all — and yet nothing.... God is there and man is not.

A Passion in the Desert [1830]

13   I am a galley slave to pen and ink.

Lettres [1832]

14   Our heart is a treasury; if you spend all its wealth at once you are ruined. We find it as difficult to forgive a person for displaying his feeling in all its nakedness as we do to forgive a man for being penniless.

Le Père Goriot[5] *(Old Goriot) [1835]*

15   The secret of great fortunes with no apparent source is a forgotten crime.   *Le Père Goriot*

16   "Temptations can be got rid of." "How?" "By yielding to them."   *Le Père Goriot*

17   And thus Bureaucracy, the giant power wielded by pygmies, came into the world.[6]

*Les Employés (The Government Clerks)
[1836]*

18   Those sweetly smiling angels with pensive looks, innocent faces, and cash-boxes for hearts.

La Cousine Bette [1846], ch. 15

19   I shatter every obstacle.[7]

Inscribed on his walking stick

---

[1]Translated by IRIS ORIGO and JOHN HEATH-STUBBS.

[2]Translated by RICHARD HOWARD.

[3]This poem, titled *Canadian Boat Song*, appeared [September 1829] anonymously in the *Noctes Ambrosianae* series in *Blackwood's Edinburgh Magazine*. It has been attributed to (among others) John Wilson ("Christopher North"), John Galt, John Lockhart, Sir Walter Scott, and David Macbeth Moir, who is now generally accepted as the author.

[4]Translated by RUDYARD KIPLING.

The first four stanzas of this hymn (of 158 stanzas) were adopted as the Greek national anthem.

[5]Translated by MARION AYTON CRAWFORD.

[6]Translated by JAMES WARING.

[7]Je casse tout obstacle.

Rufus Choate
1799–1859

1   We join ourselves to no party that does not carry the flag and keep step to the music of the Union.
Letter to the Whig Convention, Worcester, Massachusetts [October 1, 1855]

Thomas Hood
1799–1845

2 I remember, I remember
The house where I was born,
The little window where the sun
Came peeping in at morn.
I Remember, I Remember [1827], st. 1

3   Now 'tis little joy
To know I'm farther off from heaven
Than when I was a boy.
I Remember, I Remember, st. 4

4 And there is even a happiness
That makes the heart afraid.
Ode to Melancholy [1827]

5 There's not a string attuned to mirth
But has its chord in melancholy.   *Ode to Melancholy*

6 I saw old Autumn in the misty morn
Stand shadowless like silence, listening
To silence.   *Ode: Autumn [1827], st. 1*

7 O bed! O bed! delicious bed!
That heaven upon earth to the weary head.
*Miss Kilmansegg and Her Precious Leg.
Her Dream, st. 8*

8 With fingers weary and worn,
With eyelids heavy and red,
A woman sat in unwomanly rags
Plying her needle and thread—
Stitch! stitch! stitch!
In poverty, hunger, and dirt.
The Song of the Shirt [1843], st. 1

9 She sang the Song of the Shirt.
The Song of the Shirt, st. 1

10 Work! work! work!
The Song of the Shirt, st. 2

11 O men, with sisters dear!
O men, with mothers and wives!
It is not linen you're wearing out,
But human creatures' lives!
The Song of the Shirt, st. 4

12 O God! that bread should be so dear,
And flesh and blood so cheap!
The Song of the Shirt, st. 5

13 One more unfortunate,
Weary of breath,
Rashly importunate,
Gone to her death!

Take her up tenderly,
Lift her with care;
Fashioned so slenderly,
Young, and so fair!
The Bridge of Sighs [1844], st. 1, 2

14 Alas for the rarity
Of Christian charity
Under the sun!   *The Bridge of Sighs, st. 9*

15 No warmth, no cheerfulness, no healthful ease,
No comfortable feel in any member—
No shade, no shine, no butterflies, no bees,
No fruits, no flowers, no leaves, no birds—
November!   *No! [1844]*

Mary Howitt
1799–1888

16 "Will you walk into my parlor?" said the Spider to the Fly;
" 'Tis the prettiest little parlor that ever you did spy."
The Spider and the Fly [1844]

Alexander Sergeyevich Pushkin
1799–1837

17   Reason's icy intimations,
and records of a heart in pain.
Eugene Onegin[1] [1823], dedication

18 Unforced, as conversation passed,
he had the talent of saluting
felicitously every theme,
of listening like a judge supreme
while serious topics were disputing,
or, with an epigram-surprise,
of kindling smiles in ladies' eyes.
Eugene Onegin, ch. 1, st. 5

19 Why fight what's known to be decisive?
Custom is despot of mankind.
Eugene Onegin, 1, st. 25

20 The illness with which he'd been smitten
should have been analyzed when caught,
something like *spleen*, that scourge of Britain,
or Russia's *chondria*, for short.
Eugene Onegin, 1, st. 38

21 Love passed, the muse appeared, the weather
of mind got clarity newfound;

[1]Translated by CHARLES JOHNSTON.

now free, I once more weave together
emotion, thought, and magic sound.
Eugene Onegin, 2, st. 59

1 And thus he[1] mused: "From here, indeed
Shall we strike terror in the Swede;
And here a city, by our labor
Founded, shall gall our haughty neighbor;
'Here cut' — so Nature gives command —
'Your window through on Europe: stand
Firm-footed by the sea, unchanging!' "
The Bronze Horseman[2] [written 1833]

John Brown
1800–1859

2   Had I so interfered in behalf of the rich, the
powerful, the intelligent, the so-called great, or in
behalf of any of their friends...every man in this
court would have deemed it an act worthy of reward
rather than punishment.
Last speech to the court [November 2, 1859]

3   I am yet too young to understand that God is any
respecter of persons. I believe that to have interfered
as I have done...in behalf of His despised poor, was
not wrong, but right. Now, if it is deemed necessary
that I should forfeit my life for the furtherance of the
ends of justice, and mingle my blood further with the
blood of my children, and with the blood of millions
in this slave country whose rights are disregarded by
wicked, cruel, and unjust enactments, I submit: so let
it be done!
Last speech to the court [November 2, 1859]

4   This *is* a beautiful country.
*Remark as he rode to the gallows,
seated on his coffin [December 2, 1859]*

Julia Crawford
1800–1885

5 Kathleen Mavourneen! the gray dawn is breaking,
The horn of the hunter is heard on the hill.
Kathleen Mavourneen [1835], st. 1

Thomas Babington, Lord Macaulay
1800–1859

6   Free trade, one of the greatest blessings which a
government can confer on a people, is in almost every
country unpopular.
Essay on Mitford's History of Greece [1824]

7   Nobles by the right of an earlier creation, and
priests by the imposition of a mightier hand.
On Milton [1825]

8   The dust and silence of the upper shelf.
On Milton

9   Perhaps no person can be a poet, or can even enjoy
poetry, without a certain unsoundness of mind.
On Milton

10   There is only one cure for the evils which newly
acquired freedom produces, and that cure is freedom.
On Milton

11   The English Bible — a book which if everything
else in our language should perish, would alone suffice to show the whole extent of its beauty and power.
On John Dryden [1828]

12   Men are never so likely to settle a question rightly
as when they discuss it freely.
Southey's Colloquies on Society [1830]

13   We know no spectacle so ridiculous as the British
public in one of its periodical fits of morality.
On Moore's Life of Lord Byron [1831]

14   Reform, that you may preserve.
Debate on the First Reform Bill [March 2, 1831]

15 Ye diners-out from whom we guard our spoons.[3]
Political Georgics

16 Such night in England ne'er had been, nor ne'er
again shall be.   *The Armada [1833], l. 34*

17   She [the Roman Catholic Church] may still exist
in undiminished vigor when some traveler from New
Zealand shall, in the midst of a vast solitude, take his
stand on a broken arch of London Bridge to sketch
the ruins of St. Paul's.[4]
*On Leopold von Ranke's History of the Popes
[1840]*

18   In order that he might rob a neighbor whom he
had promised to defend, black men fought on the
coast of Coromandel and red men scalped each other
by the great lakes of North America.
On Frederick the Great [1842]

19 To every man upon this earth
Death cometh soon or late;

---

[1]Peter I (the Great) [1672–1725].

[2]Translated by OLIVER ELTON.

[3]The louder he talked of his honor, the faster we counted our
spoons. — RALPH WALDO EMERSON, *The Conduct of Life, Worship*

[4]Who knows but that hereafter some traveler like myself will sit
down upon the banks of the Seine, the Thames, or the Zuyder Zee,
where now, in the tumult of enjoyment, the heart and the eyes are
too slow to take in the multitude of sensations? Who knows but he
will sit down solitary amid silent ruins, and weep a people inurned
and their greatness changed into an empty name? — CONSTANTIN DE
VOLNEY [1757–1820], *Ruins [1791], ch. 11*

See Horace Walpole, 317:4.

And how can man die better
Than facing fearful odds
For the ashes of his fathers,
And the temples of his gods?
Lays of Ancient Rome [1842]. Horatius, st. 27

1   He [Richard Steele] was a rake among scholars, and a scholar among rakes.
*Review of Lucy Aikin's Life and
Writings of Addison [1843]*

2   A man who has never looked on Niagara has but a faint idea of a cataract; and he who has not read Barère's *Memoirs* may be said not to know what it is to lie.   *On Mémoires de Bertrand Barère [1844]*

3   Those who compare the age in which their lot has fallen with a golden age which exists only in imagination, may talk of degeneracy and decay; but no man who is correctly informed as to the past will be disposed to take a morose or desponding view of the present.
*History of England [1849–1861],
vol. I, ch. 1*

4   The Puritan hated bear-baiting, not because it gave pain to the bear, but because it gave pleasure to the spectators.
History of England, I, 2

5   Your Constitution is all sail and no anchor.
*Letter to H. S. Randall, author of a Life of
Thomas Jefferson [May 23, 1857]*

Helmuth von Moltke
1800–1891

6   First ponder, then dare.[1]   *Attributed*

7   The fate of every nation rests in its own power.
*To the German Reichstag
[March 1, 1880]*

8   Perpetual peace is a dream, and it is not even a beautiful dream. War is an element in the order of the world ordained by God. In it the noblest virtues of mankind are developed; courage and the abnegation of self, faithfulness to duty, and a spirit of sacrifice: the soldier gives his life. Without war the world would stagnate, and lose itself in materialism.[2]
*Letter to Johann Kaspar Bluntschli
[December 11, 1880]*

9   No plan of operations reaches with any certainty beyond the first encounter with the enemy's main force.
Kriegsgeschichtliche Einzelschriften [1880]

---

[1] Erst wägen, dann wagen.
[2] Translated by T. E. HOLLAND.

Nat Turner
1800–1831

10   'Twas my object to carry terror and destruction wherever we went.[3]
The Confessions of Nat Turner [1832]

Jane [Baillie] Welsh Carlyle
1801–1866

11   A positive engagement to marry a certain person at a certain time, at all haps and hazards, I have always considered the most ridiculous thing on earth.
To Thomas Carlyle [January 1825]

12   In spite of the honestest efforts to annihilate my *I-ity*, or merge it in what the world doubtless considers my better half, I still find myself a self-subsisting and alas! self-seeking *me*.
To John Sterling [June 4, 1835]

13   Oh Lord! If you but knew what a brimstone of a creature I am behind all this beautiful amiability!
To Eliza Stodart [February 29, 1836]

14   Instead of boiling up individuals into the species, I would draw a chalk circle round every individuality, and preach to it to keep within that, and preserve and cultivate its identity.
To John Sterling [August 5, 1845]

15   I can see that the Lady has a genius for ruling, whilst I have a genius for *not being ruled*.
To Thomas Carlyle [September 28, 1845]

16   The surest way to get a thing in this life is to be prepared for doing without it, to the exclusion even of hope.
Journal, August 1849

17   The triumphal procession air which, in our manners and customs, is given to marriage at the outset — that singing of *Te Deum* before the battle has begun.
To Miss Barnes [August 24, 1859]

Thomas Cole
1801–1848

18   Over all, rocks, wood, and water, brooded the spirit of repose, and the silent energy of nature stirred the soul to its inmost depths.
Essay on American Scenery [1835]

---

[3] The white lawyer Thomas R. Gray wrote the pamphlet *The Confessions of Nat Turner*, reportedly assembling the text from Turner's oral jailhouse account of the 1831 slave rebellion.

David Glasgow Farragut
1801–1870

1   Damn the torpedoes — full speed ahead!
At the battle of Mobile Bay [August 5, 1864]

George Perkins Marsh
1801–1882

2   Man is everywhere a disturbing agent. Wherever he plants his foot, the harmonies of nature are turned to discords.   *Man and Nature [1864], ch. 1*

John Henry Cardinal Newman
1801–1890

3 Time hath a taming hand.
Persecution [1832], st. 3

4 Lead, kindly Light, amid the encircling gloom;
Lead thou me on!
The night is dark, and I am far from home;
Lead thou me on!
Keep thou my feet: I do not ask to see
The distant scene; one step enough for me.
The Pillar of Cloud [1833].
Lead Kindly Light, st. 1

5   May He support us all the day long, till the shades lengthen, and the evening comes, and the busy world is hushed, and the fever of life is over, and our work is done! Then in His mercy may He give us safe lodging, and a holy rest, and peace at the last!
Sermon [1834]. Wisdom and Innocence[1]

6   In a higher world it is otherwise, but here below to live is to change, and to be perfect is to have changed often.
Essay on the Development of Christian Doctrine [1845], ch. 1

7   Growth [is] the only evidence of life.
Apologia pro Vita Sua (Defense of One's Life) [1864], ch. 1

8   From the age of fifteen, dogma has been the fundamental principle of my religion: I know no other religion; I cannot enter into the idea of any other sort of religion; religion, as a mere sentiment, is to me a dream and a mockery.
Apologia pro Vita Sua, ch. 2

9 It is thy very energy of thought
Which keeps thee from thy God.
Dream of Gerontius [1866], pt. III

---

[1]An adapted version of this text appears in the Book of Common Prayer [1979].

10   There is a knowledge which is desirable, though nothing come of it, as being of itself a treasure, and a sufficient remuneration of years of labor.
The Idea of a University [1873].
Discourse V, pt. 6

11   Ex umbris et imaginibus in veritatem [From shadows and symbols into the truth]!
His own epitaph at Edgbaston

William Henry Seward
1801–1872

12   Shall I tell you what this collision [of free and slave labor] means? ... It is an irrepressible conflict between opposing and enduring forces, and it means that the United States must and will, sooner or later, become entirely a slave-holding nation or entirely a free-labor nation.
Speech at Rochester, New York [October 25, 1858]

13   I know, and all the world knows, that revolutions never go backward.
Speech at Rochester, New York [October 25, 1858]

Brigham Young
1801–1877

14   This is the place!
On first seeing the valley of the Great Salt Lake [July 24, 1847]

Lydia Maria Child
1802–1880

15   We first crush people to the earth, and then claim the right of trampling on them forever, because they are prostrate.
An Appeal on Behalf of That Class of Americans Called Africans [1833]

16   They [the slaves] have stabbed themselves for freedom — jumped into the waves for freedom — starved for freedom — fought like very tigers for freedom! But they have been hung, and burned, and shot — and their tyrants have been their historians!
An Appeal on Behalf of That Class of Americans Called Africans

17 Over the river and through the wood,
To grandfather's house we go;
The horse knows the way
To carry the sleigh,
Through the white and drifted snow.
Flowers for Children [1844–1846].
Thanksgiving Day, st. 1

1   Woman stock is rising in the market. I shall not live to see women vote, but I'll come and rap at the ballot box.
Letter to Sarah Shaw [August 3, 1856]

2   Yours for the unshackled exercise of every faculty by every human being.
Message to woman suffrage supporters [c. 1875]

David Christy
1802–c. 1868

3   Cotton Is King; or, The Economical Relations of Slavery.[1]   *Title of book [1855]*

Alexandre Dumas the Elder
1802–1870

4   All for one, one for all, that is our motto.
The Three Musketeers [1844], ch. 9

5   Nothing succeeds like success.[2]
Ange Pitou [1854], vol. I

6   Let us look for the woman.[3]
The Mohicans of Paris [1854–1855], vol. III, ch. 10, 11

Victor Hugo
1802–1885

7   These two halves of God, the Pope and the emperor.   *Hernani [1830], act IV, sc. ii*

8   An invasion of armies can be resisted, but not an idea whose time has come.[4]
Histoire d'un Crime [written 1852], conclusion

9   Waterloo! Waterloo! Waterloo! Dismal plain![5]
Les Châtiments (Castigations) [1853]. Expiation

10   You have created a new thrill.[6]
Letter to Baudelaire [October 6, 1859]

11   Great grief is a divine and terrible radiance which transfigures the wretched.
Les Misérables[7] [1862]. Fantine, bk. V, ch. 13

12   Napoleon . . . mighty somnambulist of a vanished dream.
Les Misérables. Cosette, bk. I, ch. 13

13   Waterloo is a battle of the first rank won by a captain of the second.
Les Misérables. Cosette, I, 16

14   Would you realize what Revolution is, call it Progress; and would you realize what Progress is, call it Tomorrow.
Les Misérables. Cosette, I, 17

15   Great blunders are often made, like large ropes, of a multitude of fibers.
Les Misérables. Cosette, V, 10

16   A man is not idle because he is absorbed in thought. There is a visible labor and there is an invisible labor.
Les Misérables. Cosette, VII, 8

17   No one ever keeps a secret so well as a child.
Les Misérables. Cosette, VIII, 8

18   To rise at six, to dine at ten,
To sup at six, to sleep at ten,
Makes a man live for ten times ten.
Inscription over the door of Hugo's study

19   I represent a party which does not yet exist: the party of revolution, civilization.
This party will make the twentieth century.
There will issue from it first the United States of Europe, then the United States of the World.
On the wall of the room in which Hugo died, Place des Vosges, Paris

Letitia Elizabeth Landon
1802–1838

20 Few, save the poor, feel for the poor.   *The Poor*

Harriet Martineau
1802–1876

21   Wealth and opinion were practically worshipped before Washington opened his eyes on the sun which was to light him to his deeds; and the worship of Opinion is, at this day, the established religion of the United States.
Society in America [1837], vol. II

---

[1]Take away *time is money*, and what is left of England? take away *cotton is king*, and what is left of America? — VICTOR HUGO, *Les Misérables* [1862], *Marius, bk. IV, ch. 4*

[2]Rien ne réussit comme le succès. — *French proverb*

[3]Cherchons la femme.
The phrase "Cherchez la femme" is attributed to JOSEPH FOUCHÉ [1759–1820].

[4]On résiste à l'invasion des armées; on ne résiste pas à l'invasion des idées. (Literally, one can resist the invasion of armies, but not the invasion of ideas.)

[5]Waterloo! Waterloo! Waterloo! Morne plaine!

[6]Vous créez un frisson nouveau.

---

[7]Translated by CHARLES E. WILBOUR.

George Pope Morris
1802–1864

1 Woodman, spare that tree!
  Touch not a single bough!
  In youth it sheltered me,
  And I'll protect it now.
  Woodman, Spare That Tree [1830], st. 1

2 The union of hearts — the union of hands —
  And the flag of our Union forever!
  The Flag of Our Union [1851]

William Allen
1803–1879

3 Fifty-four forty, or fight![1]
  Speech in the Senate [1844]

Thomas Lovell Beddoes
1803–1849

4 The anchor heaves, the ship swings free,
  The sails swell full. To sea, to sea!
  Death's Jest-Book [1850]. Song from the Ship, st. 2

5 If there were dreams to sell,
  What would you buy?
  Some cost a passing-bell;
  Some a light sigh.   *Dream-Pedlary [1851], st. 1*

George Borrow
1803–1881

6 There's night and day, brother, both sweet things;
  sun, moon, and stars, brother, all sweet things;
  there's likewise a wind on the heath. Life is very
  sweet, brother; who would wish to die?
  Lavengro [1851], ch. 25

7 I learned . . . to fear God, and to take my own
  part.   *Lavengro, 86*

8 Youth will be served, every dog has his day, and
  mine has been a fine one.   *Lavengro, 92*

9 Youth is the only season for enjoyment, and the
  first twenty-five years of one's life are worth all the
  rest of the longest life of man, even though those
  five-and-twenty be spent in penury and contempt,
  and the rest in the possession of wealth, honors,
  respectability.   *The Romany Rye [1857], ch. 30*

Orestes A. Brownson
1803–1876

10 What we object to is the division of society into
  two classes, of which one class owns the capital, and
  the other performs the labor.
  *Defense of the article The Laboring Classes
  [October 1840]*

Edward Bulwer-Lytton, Baron Lytton
1803–1873

11 In other countries poverty is a misfortune — with
  us it is a crime.
  England and the English [1833]

12 Rank is a great beautifier.
  The Lady of Lyons [1838], act II, sc. i

13 Beneath the rule of men entirely great,
  The pen is mightier than the sword.
  Richelieu [1839], act II, sc. ii

14 It was a dark and stormy night.[2]
  Paul Clifford [1840], opening words

William Driver
1803–1886

15 I name thee Old Glory.
  As the flag was hoisted to the masthead of his brig[3]

Ralph Waldo Emerson
1803–1882

16 To think is to act.
  Motto for Journal [1835]

17 It is one of the blessings of old friends that you can
  afford to be stupid with them.
  Journal [August 31, 1838]

18 What is the hardest task in the world? To think.
  Journal [November 14, 1838]

19 Do your thing & I shall know you.
  Journal [July 7, 1839]

20 We die of words. We are hanged, drawn and quar-
  tered by dictionaries. We walk in the vale of shadows.
  It is an age of hobgoblins.
  Journal [September 14–17, 1839]

---

[1]Slogan of expansionist Democrats in the 1844 presidential campaign, in which the Oregon boundary definition was a pressing issue. The new Democratic President, James K. Polk, compromised [1846] with Great Britain on the 49th parallel.

[2]See Charles Schulz, 800:9.

[3]On August 10, 1831, a large American flag was presented to Driver, captain of the *Charles Doggett,* by a band of women in recognition of his bringing the British mutineers of the ship *Bounty* from Tahiti back to their former home, Pitcairn Island.

1 Good-bye, proud world! I'm going home;
  Thou art not my friend and I'm not thine.
                Poems [1847]. Good-bye, st. 1

2 Nor knowest thou what argument
  Thy life to thy neighbor's creed has lent.
  All are needed by each one;
  Nothing is fair or good alone.
                Poems. Each and All, st. 1

3 I wiped away the weeds and foam,
  I fetched my sea-born treasures home;
  But the poor, unsightly, noisome things
  Had left their beauty on the shore,
  With the sun and the sand and the wild uproar.
                Poems. Each and All, st. 3

4 I like a church; I like a cowl;
  I love a prophet of the soul;
  And on my heart monastic aisles
  Fall like sweet strains or pensive smiles;
  Yet not for all his faith can see
  Would I that cowlèd churchman be.
                Poems. The Problem, st. 1

5 The hand that rounded Peter's dome,
  And groined the aisles of Christian Rome,
  Wrought in a sad sincerity;
  Himself from God he could not free;
  He builded better than he knew —
  The conscious stone to beauty grew.
                Poems. The Problem, st. 2

6 Line in nature is not found;
  Unit and universe are round;
  In vain produced, all rays return;
  Evil will bless, and ice will burn.   *Poems. Uriel, st. 2*

7 Announced by all the trumpets of the sky,
  Arrives the snow.
                Poems. The Snowstorm, l. 1

8   Enclosed
  In a tumultuous privacy of storm.
                Poems. The Snowstorm, l. 8

9 In May, when sea winds pierced our solitudes,
  I found the fresh Rhodora in the woods.
                Poems. The Rhodora, l. 1

10 Rhodora! if the sages ask thee why
  This charm is wasted on the earth and sky,
  Tell them, dear, that if eyes were made for seeing,
  Then Beauty is its own excuse for being.
                Poems. The Rhodora, l. 9

11 Things are of the snake.
        Poems. Ode Inscribed to W. H. Channing, st. 6

12 Things are in the saddle,
  And ride mankind.
        Poems. Ode Inscribed to W. H. Channing, st. 6

13 There are two laws discrete,
  Not reconciled —
  Law for man, and law for thing.
        Poems. Ode Inscribed to W. H. Channing, st. 7

14 Give all to love;
  Obey thy heart;
  Friends, kindred, days,
  Estate, good fame,
  Plans, credit and the Muse,
  Nothing refuse.
                Poems. Give All to Love, st. 1

15 Heartily know,
  When half-gods go,
  The gods arrive.
                Poems. Give All to Love, st. 6

16 Love not the flower they pluck, and know it not,
  And all their botany is Latin names.
                Poems. Blight

17 By the rude bridge that arched the flood,
  Their flag to April's breeze unfurled,
  Here once the embattled farmers stood,
  And fired the shot heard round the world.
        Poems. Hymn Sung at the Completion of the
        Battle Monument, Concord, Massachusetts
        [July 4, 1837], st. 1

18 "Pass in, pass in," the angels say,
  "In to the upper doors,
  Nor count compartments of the floors,
  But mount to paradise
  By the stairway of surprise."   *Poems. Merlin I*

19 God said, I am tired of kings,
  I suffer them no more;
  Up to my ear the morning brings
  The outrage of the poor.
        May-Day and Other Pieces [1867].
        Boston Hymn, st. 2

20 Today unbind the captive,
  So only are ye unbound;
  Lift up a people from the dust,
  Trump of their rescue, sound!
        May-Day and Other Pieces. Boston Hymn,
        st. 17

21 So nigh is grandeur to our dust,
  So near is God to man,
  When Duty whispers low, *Thou must,*
  The youth replies, *I can.*
        May-Day and Other Pieces. Voluntaries, III

22 Wilt thou seal up the avenues of ill?
  Pay every debt, as if God wrote the bill.
        May-Day and Other Pieces. "Suum Cuique"

23 Daughters of Time, the hypocritic Days,
  Muffled and dumb like barefoot dervishes,

And marching single in an endless file,
Bring diadems and fagots in their hands.
May-Day and Other Pieces. Days

1   I, too late,
Under her solemn fillet saw the scorn.
May-Day and Other Pieces. Days

2 It is time to be old,
To take in sail.
May-Day and Other Pieces. Terminus

3 Obey the voice at eve obeyed at prime.
May-Day and Other Pieces. Terminus

4 If the red slayer think he slays,
Or if the slain think he is slain,
They know not well the subtle ways
I keep, and pass, and turn again.[1]
May-Day and Other Pieces. Brahma

5 They reckon ill who leave me out;
When me they fly, I am the wings;
I am the doubter and the doubt,
And I the hymn the Brahmin sings.
May-Day and Other Pieces. Brahma

6 I am the owner of the sphere,
Of the seven stars and the solar year,
Of Caesar's hand, and Plato's brain,
Of Lord Christ's heart, and Shakespeare's strain.
May-Day and Other Pieces. History

7   To different minds, the same world is a hell, and a heaven.   *Journal [December 20, 1822]*

8   Four snakes gliding up and down a hollow for no purpose that I could see — not to eat, not for love, but only gliding.   *Journal [April 11, 1834]*

9   I wish to write such rhymes as shall not suggest a restraint, but contrariwise the wildest freedom.
Journal [June 27, 1839]

10   You shall have joy, or you shall have power, said God; you shall not have both.
Journal [October 1842]

11   The sky is the daily bread of the eyes.
Journal [May 25, 1843]

12   Poetry must be as new as foam, and as old as the rock.   *Journal [March 1845]*

13   Life consists in what a man is thinking of all day.
Journal [August 1847]

14   *Immortality.* I notice that as soon as writers broach this question they begin to quote. I hate quotation. Tell me what you know.
Journal [May 1849]

15   Blessed are those who have no talent!
Journal [February 1850]

16   The word *liberty* in the mouth of Mr. Webster sounds like the word *love* in the mouth of a courtesan.
Journal [February 12(?), 1851]

17   I trust a good deal to common fame, as we all must. If a man has good corn, or wood, or boards, or pigs, to sell, or can make better chairs or knives, crucibles or church organs, than anybody else, you will find a broad hard-beaten road to his house, though it be in the woods.[2]
Journal [February 1855]

18   The blazing evidence of immortality is our dissatisfaction with any other solution.
Journal [July 1855]

19   The foregoing generations beheld God and nature face to face; we, through their eyes. Why should not we also enjoy an original relation to the universe?
Nature [1836, 1849]. Introduction

20   Undoubtedly we have no questions to ask which are unanswerable. We must trust the perfection of the creation so far, as to believe that whatever curiosity the order of things has awakened in our minds, the order of things can satisfy.   *Nature. Introduction*

21   Crossing a bare common, in snow puddles, at twilight, under a clouded sky, without having in my thoughts any occurrence of special good fortune, I have enjoyed a perfect exhilaration. I am glad to the brink of fear.   *Nature, sec. 1*

22   Standing on the bare ground . . . all mean egotism vanishes. I become a transparent eyeball; I am nothing; I see all; the currents of the Universal Being circulate through me; I am part or particle of God.
Nature, 1

23   Give me health and a day, and I will make the pomp of emperors ridiculous.   *Nature, 3*

24   Every natural fact is a symbol of some spiritual fact.   *Nature, 4*

25   A man is a god in ruins.   *Nature, 4*

26   The scholar is the delegated intellect. In the right state he is *Man Thinking.*
The American Scholar [1837], introduction

---

[1] See *The Upanishads,* 50:5.

[2] If a man can write a better book, preach a better sermon, or make a better mousetrap than his neighbor, though he builds his house in the woods the world will make a beaten path to his door. — *Attributed to* EMERSON *(in a lecture) by* SARAH S. B. YULE *and* MARY S. KEENE, *Borrowings* [1889]. Often cited as: Build a better mousetrap and the world will beat a path to your door.

1   Meek young men grow up in libraries, believing it their duty to accept the views which Cicero, which Locke, which Bacon have given, forgetful that Cicero, Locke and Bacon were only young men in libraries when they wrote these books.
The American Scholar, sec. 2

2   There is then creative reading as well as creative writing.   *The American Scholar, 2*

3   Character is higher than intellect.
The American Scholar, 3

4   In self-trust all the virtues are comprehended.
The American Scholar, 3

5   Wherever Macdonald[1] sits, there is the head of the table.   *The American Scholar, 3*

6   This time, like all times, is a very good one, if we but know what to do with it.
The American Scholar, 3

7   I embrace the common, I explore and sit at the feet of the familiar, the low. Give me insight into to-day, and you may have the antique and future worlds. What would we really know the meaning of? The meal in the firkin; the milk in the pan; the ballad in the street; the news of the boat.
The American Scholar, 3

8   If the single man plant himself indomitably on his instincts, and there abide, the huge world will come round to him.[2]
The American Scholar, 3

9   If utterance is denied, the thought lies like a burden on the man. Always the seer is a sayer.
Divinity School Address [1838]

10   Men grind and grind in the mill of a truism, and nothing comes out but what was put in. But the moment they desert the tradition for a spontaneous thought, then poetry, wit, hope, virtue, learning, anecdote, all flock to their aid.
Literary Ethics [1838]

11   I have no expectation that any man will read history aright who thinks that what was done in a remote age, by men whose names have resounded far, has any deeper sense than what he is doing today.
Essays: First Series [1841]. History

12   We are always coming up with the emphatic facts of history in our private experience and verifying them here. All history becomes subjective; in other words, there is properly no history; only biography.
Essays: First Series. History

---

[1]Often quoted as "Macgregor."

[2]All things come round to him who will but wait. — HENRY WADSWORTH LONGFELLOW, *Tales of a Wayside Inn, The Student's Tale* [1863]

13   It is the fault of our rhetoric that we cannot strongly state one fact without seeming to belie some other.   *Essays: First Series. History*

14   To believe your own thought, to believe that what is true for you in your private heart is true for all men — that is genius.
Essays: First Series. Self-Reliance

15   Society everywhere is in conspiracy against the manhood of every one of its members. . . . The virtue in most request is conformity. Self-reliance is its aversion. It loves not realities and creators, but names and customs.
Essays: First Series. Self-Reliance

16   Whoso would be a man must be a nonconformist.   *Essays: First Series. Self-Reliance*

17   I am ashamed to think how easily we capitulate to badges and names, to large societies and dead institutions.
Essays: First Series. Self-Reliance

18   It is easy in the world to live after the world's opinion; it is easy in solitude to live after our own; but the great man is he who in the midst of the crowd keeps with perfect sweetness the independence of solitude.   *Essays: First Series. Self-Reliance*

19   A foolish consistency is the hobgoblin of little minds, adored by little statesmen and philosophers and divines. With consistency a great soul has simply nothing to do.
Essays: First Series. Self-Reliance

20   To be great is to be misunderstood.
Essays: First Series. Self-Reliance

21   An institution is the lengthened shadow of one man.   *Essays: First Series. Self-Reliance*

22   I like the silent church before the service begins, better than any preaching.
Essays: First Series. Self-Reliance

23   Discontent is the want of self-reliance: it is infirmity of will.
Essays: First Series. Self-Reliance

24   For every Stoic was a Stoic; but in Christendom where is the Christian?
Essays: First Series. Self-Reliance

25   Nothing can bring you peace but yourself.
Essays: First Series. Self-Reliance

26   Every sweet hath its sour; every evil its good.
Essays: First Series. Compensation

27   For everything you have missed, you have gained something else; and for everything you gain, you lose something.
Essays: First Series. Compensation

1   Everything in Nature contains all the powers of Nature. Everything is made of one hidden stuff.
Essays: First Series. Compensation

2   All mankind love a lover.
Essays: First Series. Love

3   Thou art to me a delicious torment.
Essays: First Series. Friendship

4   Almost all people descend to meet.
Essays: First Series. Friendship

5   Happy is the house that shelters a friend.
Essays: First Series. Friendship

6   A friend is a person with whom I may be sincere. Before him, I may think aloud.
Essays: First Series. Friendship

7   A friend may well be reckoned the masterpiece of Nature.   *Essays: First Series. Friendship*

8   Two may talk and one may hear, but three cannot take part in a conversation of the most sincere and searching sort.
Essays: First Series. Friendship

9   The only reward of virtue is virtue; the only way to have a friend is to be one.
Essays: First Series. Friendship

10   I do then with my friends as I do with my books. I would have them where I can find them, but I seldom use them.   *Essays: First Series. Friendship*

11   In skating over thin ice our safety is in our speed.   *Essays: First Series. Prudence*

12   Heroism feels and never reasons and therefore is always right.
Essays: First Series. Heroism

13   Beware when the great God lets loose a thinker on this planet.
Essays: First Series. Circles

14   Nature abhors the old, and old age seems the only disease;[1] all others run into this one.
Essays: First Series. Circles

15   Nothing great was ever achieved without enthusiasm.   *Essays: First Series. Circles*

16   Nothing astonishes men so much as common sense and plain dealing.
Essays: First Series. Art

17   A man may love a paradox without either losing his wit or his honesty.
Walter Savage Landor. From The Dial [1841], XII

18   There is always a certain meanness in the argument of conservatism, joined with a certain superiority in its fact.   *The Conservative [1842]*

19   For it is not meters, but a metermaking argument that makes a poem — a thought so passionate and alive that like the spirit of a plant or an animal it has an architecture of its own, and adorns nature with a new thing.
Essays: Second Series [1844]. The Poet

20   Language is the archives of history.... Language is fossil poetry.
Essays: Second Series. The Poet

21   Nature and books belong to the eyes that see them.   *Essays: Second Series. Experience*

22   The less government we have, the better — the fewer laws, and the less confided power.
Essays: Second Series. Politics

23   Money, which represents the prose of life, and which is hardly spoken of in parlors without an apology, is, in its effects and laws, as beautiful as roses.
Essays: Second Series. Nominalist and Realist

24   Every man is wanted, and no man is wanted much.
Essays: Second Series. Nominalist and Realist

25   The reward of a thing well done, is to have done it.
Essays: Second Series. Nominalist and Realist

26   As to what are called the masses, and common men — there are no common men. All men are at last of a size.
Representative Men [1850]. The Uses of Great Men

27   Every hero becomes a bore at last.
Representative Men. The Uses of Great Men

28   Great geniuses have the shortest biographies.
Representative Men. Plato; or, The Philosopher

29   Things added to things, as statistics, civil history, are inventories. Things used as language are inexhaustibly attractive.
Representative Men. Plato; or, The Philosopher

30   Keep cool: it will be all one a hundred years hence.[2]
Representative Men. Montaigne; or, The Skeptic

---

[1] Old age is an incurable disease (senectus enim insanabilis morbus est). — SENECA, *Epistles, no. 108, sec. 28*

[2] What matters what anybody thinks? "It will be all the same a hundred years hence." That is the most sensible proverb ever invented. — GEORGE DU MAURIER, *Peter Ibbetson* [1891]

1 Is not marriage an open question, when it is alleged, from the beginning of the world, that such as are in the institution wish to get out, and such as are out wish to get in?
Representative Men. Montaigne; or, The Skeptic

2 Self-reliance, the height and perfection of man, is reliance on God.
The Fugitive Slave Law [1854]

3 Great men, great nations, have not been boasters and buffoons, but perceivers of the terror of life, and have manned themselves to face it.
The Conduct of Life [1860]. Fate

4 Men are what their mothers made them.
The Conduct of Life. Fate

5 Coal is a portable climate.
The Conduct of Life. Wealth

6 The world is his, who has money to go over it.
The Conduct of Life. Wealth

7 Art is a jealous mistress.
The Conduct of Life. Wealth

8 Solitude, the safeguard of mediocrity, is to genius the stern friend.
The Conduct of Life. Culture

9 There is always a best way of doing everything, if it be to boil an egg. Manners are the happy ways of doing things. *The Conduct of Life. Behavior*

10 I wish that life should not be cheap, but sacred. I wish the days to be as centuries, loaded, fragrant.
The Conduct of Life. Considerations by the Way

11 Our chief want in life is somebody who shall make us do what we can.
The Conduct of Life. Considerations by the Way

12 Make yourself necessary to somebody.
The Conduct of Life. Considerations by the Way

13 Beauty without grace is the hook without the bait. *The Conduct of Life. Beauty*

14 Never read any book that is not a year old.
The Conduct of Life. In Praise of Books

15 Instead of engineering for all America, he was the captain of a huckleberry party. Pounding beans[1] is good to the end of pounding empires one of these days; but if, at the end of years, it is still only beans!
Eulogy for Henry David Thoreau [1862]

16 There are always two parties, the party of the Past and the party of the Future; the Establishment and the Movement.
Historic Notes of Life and Letters in New England [1867]

17 The key to the period appeared to be that the mind had become aware of itself. . . . The young men were born with knives in their brain, a tendency to introversion, self-dissection, anatomizing of motives.
Historic Notes of Life and Letters in New England

18 Hitch your wagon to a star.
Society and Solitude [1870]. Civilization

19 The true test of civilization is, not the census, nor the size of cities, nor the crops — no, but the kind of man the country turns out.
Society and Solitude. Civilization

20 Every genuine work of art has as much reason for being as the earth and the sun.
Society and Solitude. Art

21 A masterpiece of art has in the mind a fixed place in the chain of being, as much as a plant or a crystal.
Society and Solitude. Art

22 We boil at different degrees.
Society and Solitude. Eloquence

23 Can anybody remember when the times were not hard and money not scarce?
Society and Solitude. Works and Days

24 'Tis the good reader that makes the good book; . . . in every book he finds passages which seem confidences or asides hidden from all else and unmistakably meant for his ear.
Society and Solitude. Success

25 We do not count a man's years until he has nothing else to count. *Society and Solitude. Old Age*

26 A mollusk is a cheap edition [of man] with a suppression of the costlier illustrations, designed for dingy circulation, for shelving in an oyster-bank or among the seaweed.
Power and Laws of Thought [c. 1870]

27 I have heard with admiring submission the experience of the lady who declared that the sense of being perfectly well-dressed gives a feeling of inward tranquillity which religion is powerless to bestow.
Letters and Social Aims. Social Aims

28 Great men are they who see that spiritual is stronger than any material force, that thoughts rule the world.
Letters and Social Aims. Progress and Culture, Phi Beta Kappa Address [July 18, 1876]

---

[1]See Henry David Thoreau, 475:11.

1 Next to the originator of a good sentence is the first quoter of it.[1]
Letters and Social Aims. Quotation and Originality

2 By necessity, by proclivity, and by delight, we all quote.
Letters and Social Aims. Quotation and Originality

3 Wit makes its own welcome, and levels all distinctions.
Letters and Social Aims. The Comic

4 What is a weed? A plant whose virtues have not yet been discovered.
Fortune of the Republic [1878]

5 To live without duties is obscene.
Lectures and Biographical Sketches [1883]. Aristocracy

6 Speak the affirmative; emphasize your choice by utter ignoring of all that you reject.
Lectures and Biographical Sketches. The Preacher

7 Genius has no taste for weaving sand.
Lectures and Biographical Sketches. The Scholar

8 This world we live in is but thickened light.
Lectures and Biographical Sketches. The Scholar

9 All the thoughts of a turtle are turtles, and of a rabbit, rabbits.
The Natural History of Intellect [1893]

10 When you strike at a king, you must kill him.
Recollected by OLIVER WENDELL HOLMES JR. *From* MAX LERNER *[1902–1992], The Mind and Faith of Justice Holmes [1943]*

Robert Stephen Hawker
1803–1875

11 And shall Trelawny die?[2]
Here's twenty thousand Cornish men
Will know the reason why.
The Song of the Western Men [1825], st. 1

---

[1]There is not less wit nor less invention in applying rightly a thought one finds in a book, than in being the first author of that thought. — PIERRE BAYLE [1647–1706], *Dictionnaire Historique et Critique* [1697–1702]

[2]A popular phrase throughout Cornwall since the imprisonment in the Tower of London [1688] of Sir Jonathan Trelawny [1650–1721] with six other prelates for refusing to recognize the Declaration of Indulgence issued by James II.

Robert Smith Surtees
1803–1864

12 Jorrocks' Jaunts and Jollities.
Title of novel [1838]

13 Three things I never lends — my 'oss, my wife, and my name. *Hillingdon Hall [1845], ch. 33*

14 More people are flattered into virtue than bullied out of vice.
The Analysis of the Hunting Field [1846], ch. 1

Fyodor Tyutchev
1803–1873

15 Like first love, the heart of Russia will not forget you. *Tribute to Pushkin [January 29, 1837]*

16 Homeland of patience, land of the Russian people. *These Poor Villages [1855]*

Benjamin Disraeli, Earl of Beaconsfield
1804–1881

17 I hate definitions.
Vivian Grey [1826], bk. II, ch. 6

18 Variety is the mother of Enjoyment.
Vivian Grey, V, 4

19 I repeat . . . that all power is a trust; that we are accountable for its exercise; that, from the people, and for the people, all springs, and all must exist.
Vivian Grey, VI, 7

20 A *dark* horse, which had never been thought of, and which the careless St. James had never even observed in the list, rushed past the grandstand in sweeping triumph.
The Young Duke [1831], bk. II, ch. 5

21 Yes, I am a Jew, and when the ancestors of the right honorable gentleman were brutal savages in an unknown island, mine were priests in the temple of Solomon.[3] *Reply to a taunt by Daniel O'Connell*

22 What we anticipate seldom occurs; what we least expected generally happens.
Henrietta Temple [1837], bk. II, ch. 4

23 Though I sit down now, the time will come when you will hear me.
Maiden speech in the House of Commons [1837]

---

[3]The gentleman will please remember that when his half-civilized ancestors were hunting the wild boar in the forests of Silesia, mine were the princes of the earth. — JUDAH P. BENJAMIN [1811–1884], *reply to a senator; from* BEN PERLEY POORE [1820–1887], *Reminiscences of Sixty Years in the National Metropolis* [1886]

1   A government of statesmen or of clerks? Of Humbug or Humdrum?
Coningsby [1844], bk. II, ch. 4

2   I rather like bad wine... one gets so bored with good wine.
Sybil; or, The Two Nations [1845], bk. I, ch. 1

3   Two nations, between whom there is no intercourse and no sympathy; who are as ignorant of each other's habits, thoughts, and feelings as if they were dwellers in different zones, or inhabitants of different planets; who are formed by a different breeding, are fed by a different food, are ordered by different manners, and are not governed by the same laws... *the rich and the poor.*
Sybil; or, The Two Nations, II, 5

4   Property has its duties as well as its rights.[1]
Sybil; or, The Two Nations, 11

5   Little things affect little minds.
Sybil; or, The Two Nations, III, 2

6   The right honorable gentleman [Sir Robert Peel] caught the Whigs bathing and walked away with their clothes.
Speech in the House of Commons [February 28, 1845]

7   A precedent embalms a principle.
Speech on the expenditures of the country [February 22, 1848]

8   How much easier it is to be critical than to be correct.   *Speech [January 24, 1860]*

9   Is man an ape or an angel? I, my lord, I am on the side of the angels. I repudiate with indignation and abhorrence those newfangled theories.
Speech at Oxford Diocesan Conference [November 25, 1864]

10   I have climbed to the top of the greasy pole.
To friends, on being made prime minister [1868]

11   When a man fell into his anecdotage, it was a sign for him to retire.
Lothair [1870], ch. 28

12   You know who the critics are? The men who have failed in literature and art.
Lothair, 35

13   "My idea of an agreeable person," said Hugo Bohun, "is a person who agrees with me."
Lothair, 41

---

[1] Property has its duties as well as its rights. — THOMAS DRUMMOND [1797–1840; inventor of the Drummond light], *Letter to the Landlords of Tipperary* [May 22, 1838]

14   Increased means and increased leisure are the two civilizers of man.
Speech to the Conservatives of Manchester [April 3, 1872]

15   The secret of success is constancy to purpose.
Speech [June 24, 1872]

16   The health of the people is really the foundation upon which all their happiness and all their powers as a state depend.   *Speech [July 24, 1877]*

17   Lord Salisbury and myself have brought you back peace — but a peace I hope with honor.
Speech in the House of Commons [July 16, 1878]

18   A series of congratulatory regrets.
Speech at Knightsbridge [July 27, 1878]

19   A sophistical rhetorician [Gladstone], inebriated with the exuberance of his own verbosity, and gifted with an egotistical imagination that can at all times command an interminable and inconsistent series of arguments to malign an opponent and to glorify himself.   *Speech at Knightsbridge [July 27, 1878]*

20   The harebrained chatter of irresponsible frivolity.
Speech at the Guildhall, London [November 9, 1878]

21   No, it is better not. She would only ask me to take a message to Albert.
On his deathbed, declining a visit from Queen Victoria

Gavarni
[Sulpice Guillaume Chevalier]
1804–1866

22   Les Enfants Terribles [The Terrible Children].
Title of series of prints [1865]

Nathaniel Hawthorne
1804–1864

23   Unfathomable to mere mortals is the lore of fiends.   *Young Goodman Brown [1835]*

24   By the sympathy of your human hearts for sin ye shall scent out all the places — whether in church, bedchamber, street, field, or forest — where crime has been committed, and shall exult to behold the whole earth one stain of guilt, one mighty blood spot.   *Young Goodman Brown*

25   As the moral gloom of the world overpowers all systematic gaiety, even so was their home of wild mirth made desolate amid the sad forest.
The Maypole of Merrymount [1836]

1   Soon, likewise, my old native town will loom upon me through the haze of memory, a mist brooding over and around it; as if it were no portion of the real earth, but an overgrown village in a cloud-land, with only imaginary inhabitants to people its wooden houses, and walk its homely lanes, and the unpicturesque prolixity of its main street. Henceforth, it ceases to be a reality of my life; I am a citizen of somewhere else.

The Scarlet Letter [1850].
The Custom-House

2   If a man, sitting all alone, cannot dream strange things, and make them look like truth, he need never try to write romances.

The Scarlet Letter. The Custom-House

3   On the breast of her gown, in fine red cloth, surrounded with an elaborate embroidery and fantastic flourishes of gold thread, appeared the letter A.

The Scarlet Letter, ch. 2

4   My heart was a habitation large enough for many guests, but lonely and chill, and without a household fire. I longed to kindle one! It seemed not so wild a dream.   *The Scarlet Letter, 4*

5   There is a fatality, a feeling so irresistible and inevitable that it has the force of doom, which almost invariably compels human beings to linger around and haunt, ghostlike, the spot where some great and marked event has given the color to their lifetime; and still the more irresistibly, the darker the tinge that saddens it.   *The Scarlet Letter, 5*

6   Let the black flower blossom as it may!

The Scarlet Letter, 14

7   "Never, never!" whispered she. "What we did had a consecration of its own."

The Scarlet Letter, 17

8   The scarlet letter was her passport into regions where other women dared not tread. Shame, Despair, Solitude! These had been her teachers — stern and wild ones — and they had made her strong, but taught her much amiss.

The Scarlet Letter, 18

9   No man, for any considerable period, can wear one face to himself, and another to the multitude, without finally getting bewildered as to which may be the true.   *The Scarlet Letter, 20*

10   The book, if you would see anything in it, requires to be read in the clear, brown, twilight atmosphere in which it was written; if opened in the sunshine, it is apt to look exceedingly like a volume of blank pages.

Twice-Told Tales [1851], preface

11   Not to be deficient in this particular, the author has provided himself with a moral — the truth,

namely, that the wrongdoing of one generation lives into the successive ones.

The House of the Seven Gables [1851],
preface

12   God will give him blood to drink!

The House of the Seven Gables, ch. 1

13   It is often instructive to take the woman's, the private and domestic view, of a public man; nor can anything be more curious than the vast discrepancy between portraits intended for engraving, and the pencil-sketches that pass from hand to hand, behind the original's back.

The House of the Seven Gables, 8

14   All his life long, he had been learning how to be wretched, as one learns a foreign tongue; and now, with the lesson thoroughly at heart, he could with difficulty comprehend his little airy happiness.

The House of the Seven Gables, 10

15   What other dungeon is so dark as one's own heart! What jailer so inexorable as one's self!

The House of the Seven Gables, 11

16   What we call real estate — the solid ground to build a house on — is the broad foundation on which nearly all the guilt of this world rests.

The House of the Seven Gables, 17

17   Of all the events which constitute a person's biography, there is scarcely one . . . to which the world so easily reconciles itself as to his death.

The House of the Seven Gables, 21

18   No author, without a trial, can conceive of the difficulty of writing a romance about a country where there is no shadow, no antiquity, no mystery, no picturesque and gloomy wrong, nor anything but a commonplace prosperity, in broad and simple daylight, as is happily the case with my dear native land.

The Marble Faun [1860], preface

19   The hand of one person may express more than the face of another.

American Notebooks [1841–1852]

20   Some man of powerful character to command a person, morally subjected to him, to perform some act. The commanding person suddenly to die; and, for all the rest of his life, the subjected one continues to perform that act.   *American Notebooks*

21   The situation of a man in the midst of a crowd, yet as completely in the power of another, life and all, as if they two were in the deepest solitude.

American Notebooks

22   America is now wholly given over to a damned mob of scribbling women.

Letter to William Ticknor [1855]

1   Mountains are earth's undecaying monuments.
Sketches from Memory [1868].
The Notch of the White Mountains

Osceola
1804–1838

2   When I make up my mind, I act. If I speak, what I say, I will do. If the hail rattles, let the flowers be crushed. The oak of the forest will lift up its head to the sky and the storm, towering and unscathed.
Statement during treaty negotiation,
Second Seminole War [1836]

Charles-Augustin Sainte-Beuve
1804–1869

3   Vigny, more secret,
As if in his tower of ivory, retired before noon.[1]
Pensées d'Août (Thoughts of August),
to M. Villemain [1837], st. 3

4   Silence is the sovereign contempt.[2]
Mes Poisons (My Poisons) [published 1926]

George Sand [Amandine Aurore Lucile Dupin, Baronne Dudevant]
1804–1876

5   Love, bumping his head blindly against all the obstacles of civilization.   *Indiana [1832], preface*

6   No human creature can give orders to love.
Jacques [1834]

7   Deliberately, women are given a deplorable education.... While man frees himself from constraining civil and religious bonds, he is only too glad to have woman hold tightly to the Christian principle of suffering and keeping her silence.
Letters to Marcie [1837]

8   We cannot tear out a single page of our life, but we can throw the whole book in the fire.
Mauprat [1837]

9   Charity degrades those who receive it and hardens those who dispense it.   *Consuelo [1842]*

---

[1]Vigny, plus secret, / Comme en sa tour d'ivoire, avant midi, rentrait.
—Alfred [Victor] de Vigny [1797–1863]
Origin of the term "ivory tower."
The poet, retired in his Tower of Ivory, isolated, according to his desire, from the world of man, resembles, whether he so wishes or not, another solitary figure, the watcher enclosed for months at a time in a lighthouse at the head of a cliff. — JULES DE GAULTIER [1858–1942], *La Guerre et les Destinées de l'Art*

[2]Le silence seul est le souverain mépris.

---

10   They [the peasants] were born kings of the earth far more truly than those who possess it only from having bought it.
The Haunted Pool [1851]

11   In our wholly factitious society, to have no cash at all means frightful want or absolute powerlessness.
Histoire de Ma Vie (Story of My Life)
[1856]

12   Revolutions...have put one half of France in mourning for the other.   *Histoire de Ma Vie*

13   There is only one happiness in life, to love and be loved.
Letter to Lina Calamatta [March 31, 1862]

14   The whole secret of the study of nature lies in learning how to use one's eyes.
Nouvelles Lettres d'un Voyageur [1869]

15   I would rather believe that God did not exist than believe that He was indifferent.
Impressions et Souvenirs [1896]

Sarah Flower Adams
1805–1848

16 E'en though it be a cross
That raiseth me;
Still all my song would be,
Nearer, My God, to Thee,
Nearer, My God, to Thee,
  Nearer to Thee.
Nearer, My God, to Thee, st. 1

Hans Christian Andersen
1805–1875

17   They could see she was a real princess and no question about it, now that she had felt one pea all the way through twenty mattresses and twenty more feather beds. Nobody but a princess could be so delicate.
Fairy Tales[3] [1835]. The Princess and the Pea

18   We [sea folk] can live to be three hundred years old, but when we perish we turn into mere foam on the sea.
Fairy Tales. The Little Mermaid

19   "But he hasn't got anything on," a little child said.   *Fairy Tales. The Emperor's New Clothes*

20   The little live nightingale...had come to sing of comfort and hope. As he sang, the phantoms grew pale, and still more pale, and the blood flowed

---

[3]Translated by JEAN HERSHOLT.

quicker and quicker through the Emperor's feeble body. Even Death listened, and said, "Go on, little nightingale, go on!" *Fairy Tales. The Nightingale*

1   His own image . . . was no longer the reflection of a clumsy, dirty, gray bird, ugly and offensive. He himself was a swan! Being born in a duck yard does not matter, if only you are hatched from a swan's egg.
Fairy Tales. The Ugly Duckling

William Lloyd Garrison
1805–1879

2   Our country is the world — our countrymen are all mankind.   *Motto of The Liberator [1831]*

3   Let Southern oppressors tremble — let their secret abettors tremble — let their Northern apologists tremble — let all the enemies of the persecuted blacks tremble.   *The Liberator, no. 1 [January 1, 1831]*

4   I will be as harsh as truth and as uncompromising as justice. On this subject I do not wish to think, or speak, or write, with moderation. No! No! Tell a man whose house is on fire to give a moderate alarm; tell him to moderately rescue his wife from the hands of the ravisher; tell the mother to gradually extricate her babe from the fire into which it has fallen; but urge me not to use moderation.   *The Liberator, 1*

5   I am in earnest — I will not equivocate — I will not excuse — I will not retreat a single inch; and I will be heard!   *The Liberator, 1*

6   The compact which exists between the North and the South is a covenant with death and an agreement with hell.
Resolution adopted by the Anti-Slavery Society [January 27, 1843]

7   Wherever there is a human being, I see God-given rights inherent in that being, whatever may be the sex or complexion.
Speech at the Woman's Rights Convention [1853]

Sidney Sherman
1805–1873

8   Remember the Alamo![1]
Battle cry, San Jacinto [April 21, 1836]; attributed

---

[1]On March 6, 1836, five days after Texas declared independence from Mexico, President Antonio López de Santa Anna attacked the Alamo, the fortified mission at San Antonio; captured it after every Texan had been killed or wounded; and put the wounded to death. He was defeated at San Jacinto [April 21, 1836] by the Texas army, commanded by Samuel Houston. Sidney Sherman was a colonel in the army.

Alexis de Tocqueville
1805–1859

9   I know of no country, indeed, where the love of money has taken stronger hold on the affections of men and where a profounder contempt is expressed for the theory of the permanent equality of property.
Democracy in America,[2] *vol. I, pt. I [1835], ch. 3*

10   Within these limits the power vested in the American courts of justice of pronouncing a statute to be unconstitutional forms one of the most powerful barriers that have ever been devised against the tyranny of political assemblies.
Democracy in America, I, I, 6

11   I have never been more struck by the good sense and the practical judgment of the Americans than in the manner in which they elude the numberless difficulties resulting from their Federal Constitution.
Democracy in America, I, I, 8

12   The English or American lawyer investigates what was done, the French lawyer what was most likely intended. One wants decisions; the other, reasons.[3]
Democracy in America, I, II, 8

13   In America, there are no noblemen or men of letters, and the people distrust the wealthy. Lawyers therefore constitute the superior political class and the most intellectual segment of society.[3]
Democracy in America, I, II, 8

14   The American's principal means of action is liberty; the Russian's, servitude.
Their points of departure are different, their ways diverse. Yet each seems called by a secret design of Providence some day to sway the destinies of half the globe.[3]
Democracy in America, I, II, 10

15   They [the Americans] have all a lively faith in the perfectibility of man, they judge that the diffusion of knowledge must necessarily be advantageous, and the consequences of ignorance fatal; they all consider society as a body in a state of improvement, humanity as a changing scene, in which nothing is, or ought to be, permanent; and they admit that what appears to them today to be good, may be superseded by something better tomorrow.
Democracy in America, I, II, 18

16   America is a land of wonders, in which everything is in constant motion and every change seems an

---

[2]The Henry Reeve text, as revised by Francis Bowen, corrected and edited by Phillips Bradley [1945], unless otherwise noted.

[3]Translated by ARTHUR GOLDHAMMER.

improvement. The idea of novelty is there indissolubly connected with the idea of amelioration.
Democracy in America, I, II, 18

1 There are at the present time two great nations in the world....I allude to the Russians and the Americans....Their starting-point is different and their courses are not the same; yet each of them seems marked out by the will of Heaven to sway the destinies of half the globe.
Democracy in America, I, II, 18

2 Democratic nations care but little for what has been, but they are haunted by visions of what will be; in this direction their unbounded imagination grows and dilates beyond all measure....Democracy, which shuts the past against the poet, opens the future before him.
Democracy in America, II, I, 17

3 Thus not only does democracy make every man forget his ancestors, but it hides his descendants and separates his contemporaries from him; it throws him back forever upon himself alone and threatens in the end to confine him entirely within the solitude of his own heart.
Democracy in America, II, II, 2

4 Various forms of religious madness are quite common in the United States.[1]
Democracy in America, II, II, 12

5 If I were asked...to what the singular prosperity and growing strength of that people [the Americans] ought mainly to be attributed, I should reply: To the superiority of their women.
Democracy in America, II, III, 12

6 The love of wealth is therefore to be traced, as either a principal or accessory motive, at the bottom of all that the Americans do; this gives to all their passions a sort of family likeness.
Democracy in America, II, III, 17

7 Never was any such event [the French Revolution], stemming from factors so far back in the past, so inevitable yet so completely unforeseen.
The Old Regime and the French Revolution[2] *[1856], pt. I, ch. 1*

8 When a people which has put up with an oppressive rule over a long period without protest suddenly finds the government relaxing its pressure, it takes up arms against it.
The Old Regime and the French Revolution, III, 4

9 Experience teaches that the most dangerous moment for a bad government is usually when it begins to reform itself.[3]
The Old Regime and the French Revolution, III, 4

Elizabeth Barrett Browning
1806–1861

10 Thou large-brained woman and large-hearted man.   *To George Sand, A Desire [1844]*

11 Knowledge by suffering entereth,
And life is perfected by death.
A Vision of Poets [1844], last lines

12 Do ye hear the children weeping, O my brothers,
Ere the sorrow comes with years?
The Cry of the Children [1844], st. 1

13 I tell you hopeless grief is passionless.
Grief [1844], l. 1

14 Therefore to this dog will I,
Tenderly not scornfully,
Render praise and favor.
To Flush, My Dog [1844], st. 14

15 "Guess now who holds thee?" — "Death," I said.
But there
The silver answer rang — "Not Death, but Love."
Sonnets from the Portuguese [1850], no. 1

16 Because God's gifts put man's best dreams to shame.   *Sonnets from the Portuguese, 26*

17 How do I love thee? Let me count the ways.
I love thee to the depth and breadth and height
My soul can reach, when feeling out of sight
For the ends of Being and ideal Grace.
Sonnets from the Portuguese, 43

18 I love thee with the breath,
Smiles, tears, of all my life! — and, if God choose,
I shall but love thee better after death.
Sonnets from the Portuguese, 43

19 Life, struck sharp on death,
Makes awful lightning.
Aurora Leigh[4] *[1857], bk. I, l. 210*

20 I should not dare to call my soul my own.
Aurora Leigh, II, l. 786

21 A little sunburnt by the glare of life.
Aurora Leigh, IV, l. 1140

22 Since when was genius found respectable?
Aurora Leigh, VI, l. 275

---

[1]Translated by ARTHUR GOLDHAMMER.
[2]Translated by STUART GILBERT unless otherwise noted.

[3]Translated by ALAN KAHAN.
[4]See Edward FitzGerald, 442:11.

John Stuart Mill
1806–1873

1 The sole end for which mankind are warranted, individually or collectively, in interfering with the liberty of action of any of their number is self-protection. *On Liberty [1859], introduction*

2 If all mankind minus one were of one opinion, and only one person were of the contrary opinion, mankind would be no more justified in silencing that one person than he, if he had the power, would be justified in silencing mankind. *On Liberty, ch. 2*

3 We can never be sure that the opinion we are endeavoring to stifle is a false opinion; and if we were sure, stifling it would be an evil still. *On Liberty, 2*

4 There is no such thing as absolute certainty, but there is assurance sufficient for the purposes of human life. *On Liberty, 2*

5 It is a piece of idle sentimentality that truth, merely as truth, has any inherent power denied to error, of prevailing against the dungeon and the stake. *On Liberty, 2*

6 He who knows only his own side of the case, knows little of that. *On Liberty, 2*

7 The fatal tendency of mankind to leave off thinking about a thing when it is no longer doubtful is the cause of half their errors. *On Liberty, 2*

8 The liberty of the individual must be thus far limited; he must not make himself a nuisance to other people. *On Liberty, 3*

9 Whatever crushes individuality is despotism, by whatever name it may be called. *On Liberty, 3*

10 Everyone who receives the protection of society owes a return for the benefit. *On Liberty, 4*

11 The individual is not accountable to society for his actions, insofar as these concern the interests of no person but himself. *On Liberty, 5*

12 Liberty consists in doing what one desires. *On Liberty, 5*

13 Unearned increment. *Dissertations and Discussions [1859]*

14 Instead of the function of governing, for which it is radically unfit, the proper office of a representative assembly is to watch and control the government. *Dissertations and Discussions*

15 The creed which accepts as the foundation of morals Utility, or the Greatest Happiness Principle, holds that actions are right in proportion as they tend to promote happiness, wrong as they tend to produce the reverse of happiness. *Utilitarianism [1863], ch. 2*

16 The social state is at once so natural, so necessary, and so habitual to man, that...he never conceives himself otherwise than as a member of a body. *Utilitarianism, 3*

17 It is only a man here and there who has any tolerable knowledge of the character even of the women of his own family. *The Subjection of Women [1869], ch. 1*

18 The generality of the male sex cannot yet tolerate the idea of living with an equal. *The Subjection of Women, 2*

19 Marriage is the only actual bondage known to our law. There remain no legal slaves, except the mistress of every house. *The Subjection of Women, 4*

20 The moral regeneration of mankind will only really commence, when the most fundamental of the social relations [marriage] is placed under the rule of equal justice, and when human beings learn to cultivate their strongest sympathy with an equal in rights and in cultivation. *The Subjection of Women, 4*

21 Ask yourself whether you are happy, and you cease to be so. *Autobiography [1873], ch. 5*

Charles Francis Adams
1807–1886

22 It would be superfluous in me to point out to your Lordship that this is war. *Dispatch to Earl Russell [September 5, 1863]*

Jean Louis Rodolphe Agassiz
1807–1873

23 The eye of the trilobite tells us that the sun shone on the old beach where he lived; for there is nothing in nature without a purpose, and when so complicated an organ was made to receive the light, there must have been light to enter it. *Geological Sketches [1870], ch. 2*

24 Study nature, not books. *Motto*

Giuseppe Garibaldi
1807–1882

25 I offer neither pay, nor quarters, nor provisions; I offer hunger, thirst, forced marches, battles and death. Let him who loves his country in his heart, and not with his lips only, follow me. *From G. M. Trevelyan [1876–1962], Garibaldi's Defense of the Roman Republic [1907–1911]*

Robert E[dward] Lee
1807–1870

1 It is well that war is so terrible, or we should grow too fond of it.
> *On seeing a Federal charge repulsed at Fredericksburg [December 1862]*

2 Strike the tent.   *Last words [October 12, 1870]*

Henry Wadsworth Longfellow
1807–1882

3 I heard the trailing garments of the Night
Sweep through her marble halls.
> *Hymn to Night [1839], st. 1*

4 Tell me not, in mournful numbers,
Life is but an empty dream!
For the soul is dead that slumbers,
And things are not what they seem.

Life is real! Life is earnest!
And the grave is not its goal;
Dust thou art, to dust returnest,
Was not spoken of the soul.
> *A Psalm of Life [1839], st. 1, 2*

5 Art is long, and Time is fleeting,
And our hearts, though stout and brave,
Still, like muffled drums, are beating
Funeral marches to the grave.
> *A Psalm of Life, st. 4*

6 Lives of great men all remind us
We can make our lives sublime.
And, departing, leave behind us
Footprints on the sands of time.
> *A Psalm of Life, st. 7*

7 Let us, then, be up and doing,
With a heart for any fate;
Still achieving, still pursuing,
Learn to labor and to wait.   *A Psalm of Life, st. 9*

8 It was the schooner Hesperus,
That sailed the wintry sea;
And the skipper had taken his little daughter,
To bear him company.
> *The Wreck of the Hesperus [1842], st. 1*

9 But the father answered never a word,
A frozen corpse was he.
> *The Wreck of the Hesperus, st. 12*

10 Christ save us all from a death like this,
On the reef of Norman's Woe!
> *The Wreck of the Hesperus, st. 22*

11 Under the spreading chestnut tree
The village smithy stands;

The smith a mighty man is he
With large and sinewy hands.
And the muscles of his brawny arms
Are strong as iron bands.
> *The Village Blacksmith [1842], st. 1*

12 His brow is wet with honest sweat,
He earns whate'er he can,
And looks the whole world in the face,
For he owes not any man.
> *The Village Blacksmith, st. 2*

13 Something attempted, something done,
Has earned a night's repose.
> *The Village Blacksmith, st. 7*

14 Into each life some rain must fall,
Some days must be dark and dreary.
> *The Rainy Day [1842], st. 3*

15 A banner with the strange device,
Excelsior!   *Excelsior [1842], st. 1*

16 The day is done, and the darkness
Falls from the wings of Night,
As a feather is wafted downward
From an eagle in his flight.
> *The Day Is Done [1845], st. 1*

17 The bards sublime,
Whose distant footsteps echo
Through the corridors of Time.
> *The Day Is Done, st. 5*

18 And the night shall be filled with music,
And the cares, that infest the day,
Shall fold their tents, like the Arabs,
And as silently steal away.
> *The Day Is Done, st. 11*

19 I shot an arrow into the air,
It fell to earth, I knew not where.
> *The Arrow and the Song [1845], st. 1*

20 This is the forest primeval. The murmuring pines and the hemlocks . . .
Stand like Druids of old.   *Evangeline [1847], l. 1*

21 Build me straight, O worthy Master!
Staunch and strong, a goodly vessel.
> *The Building of the Ship [1849], l. 1*

22 And see! she stirs!
She starts — she moves — she seems to feel
The thrill of life along her keel.
> *The Building of the Ship, l. 349*

23 Sail on, O Ship of State!
Sail on, O Union, strong and great!
Humanity with all its fears,
With all the hopes of future years,
Is hanging breathless on thy fate!
> *The Building of the Ship, l. 378*

1 All your strength is in your union.
All your danger is in discord;
Therefore be at peace henceforward,
And as brothers live together.
The Song of Hiawatha [1855], pt. I

2 By the shores of Gitche Gumee,
By the shining Big-Sea-Water,
Stood the wigwam of Nokomis,
Daughter of the Moon, Nokomis.
The Song of Hiawatha, III

3 From the waterfall he named her,
Minnehaha, Laughing Water.
The Song of Hiawatha, IV

4 As unto the bow the cord is,
So unto the man is woman,
Though she bends him, she obeys him,
Though she draws him, yet she follows,
Useless each without the other!
The Song of Hiawatha, X

5 If we could read the secret history of our enemies,
we should find in each man's life sorrow and suffering
enough to disarm all hostility.
Driftwood [1857]

6 If I am not worth the wooing, I surely am not worth
the winning.
*The Courtship of Miles Standish [1858],
pt. III*

7 "Why don't you speak for yourself, John?"
The Courtship of Miles Standish, III

8 The long mysterious Exodus of death.
The Jewish Cemetery at Newport [1858], st. 1

9 A boy's will is the wind's will,
And the thoughts of youth are long, long
thoughts. *My Lost Youth [1858], refrain*

10 I remember the black wharves and the slips,
And the sea-tides tossing free;
And Spanish sailors with bearded lips,
And the beauty and majesty of the ships,
And the magic of the sea.
My Lost Youth, st. 3

11 A Lady with a Lamp [Florence Nightingale] shall
stand
In the great history of the land,
A noble type of good,
Heroic womanhood.
Santa Filomena [1858], st. 10

12 Between the dark and the daylight,
When the night is beginning to lower,
Comes a pause in the day's occupations,
That is known as the Children's Hour.
The Children's Hour [1860], st. 1

13 I hear in the chamber above me
The patter of little feet. *The Children's Hour, st. 2*

14 Grave Alice, and laughing Allegra,
And Edith with golden hair.
The Children's Hour, st. 3

15 Listen, my children, and you shall hear,
Of the midnight ride of Paul Revere,
On the eighteenth of April, in Seventy-five;
Hardly a man is now alive
Who remembers that famous day and year.
*Tales of a Wayside Inn [1863–1874], pt. I,
The Landlord's Tale: Paul Revere's Ride, st. 1*

16 One if by land, and two if by sea;[1]
And I on the opposite shore will be,
Ready to ride and spread the alarm
Through every Middlesex village and farm.
*Tales of a Wayside Inn, I, The Landlord's
Tale: Paul Revere's Ride, st. 2*

17 The fate of a nation was riding that night.
*Tales of a Wayside Inn, I, The Landlord's
Tale: Paul Revere's Ride, st. 8*

18 He seemed the incarnate "Well, I told you so!"
*Tales of a Wayside Inn, I, The Poet's Tale:
The Birds of Killingworth, st. 9*

19 Ships that pass in the night, and speak each other in
passing,
Only a signal shown and a distant voice in the
darkness;
So on the ocean of life we pass and speak one
another,[2]
Only a look and a voice; then darkness again and a
silence.
*Tales of a Wayside Inn, III,
The Theologian's Tale: Elizabeth, pt. IV*

20 The love of learning, the sequestered nooks,
And all the sweet serenity of books.
Morituri Salutamus[3] [1874], st. 21

21 Three silences there are: the first of speech,
The second of desire, the third of thought.
The Three Silences of Molinos [1877]

22 The holiest of all holidays are those
Kept by ourselves in silence and apart;
The secret anniversaries of the heart.
Holidays [1878]

---

[1]See Paul Revere, 331:7.

[2]Two lives that once part are as ships that divide. — EDWARD
ROBERT BULWER-LYTTON, *A Lament* [1853]

As vessels starting from ports thousands of miles apart pass close to
each other in the naked breadths of the ocean, nay, sometimes even
touch in the dark. — OLIVER WENDELL HOLMES, *Professor at the
Breakfast-Table* [1860]

[3]See Suetonius, 111:n1.

1 In the long, sleepless watches of the night.
The Cross of Snow [1879]

2 There was a little girl
Who had a little curl
Right in the middle of her forehead;
And when she was good
She was very, very good,
But when she was bad she was horrid.
There Was a Little Girl[1]

John Greenleaf Whittier
1807–1892

3 No fetters in the Bay State — no slave upon our
land!
Massachusetts to Virginia [1843], st. 24

4 The Night is mother of the Day,
The Winter of the Spring,
And ever upon old Decay
The greenest mosses cling.
A Dream of Summer [1847], st. 4

5 So fallen! so lost! the light withdrawn
Which once he wore!
The glory from his gray hairs gone
Forevermore!
Ichabod[2] *[1850], st. 1*

6   From those great eyes
The soul has fled:
When faith is lost, when honor dies,
The man is dead!   *Ichabod, st. 8*

7 Blessings on thee, little man,
Barefoot boy, with cheek of tan!
The Barefoot Boy [1856], st. 1

8 Health that mocks the doctor's rules,
Knowledge never learned of schools.
The Barefoot Boy, st. 2

9 The age is dull and mean. Men creep,
Not walk.
*Lines Inscribed to Friends Under Arrest
for Treason Against the Slave
Power [1856], st. 1*

10 For of all sad words of tongue or pen,
The saddest are these: "It might have been!"[3]
Maud Muller [1856], st. 53

---

[1]By tradition attributed to Longfellow.

[2]This poem was the outcome of the surprise and grief and forecast of evil consequences which I felt on reading the seventh of March speech of Daniel Webster in support of the "compromise," and the Fugitive Slave Law. No partisan or personal enmity dictated it. — WHITTIER's *Note*

[3]See Arthur Guiterman, 609:12.

11 Up from the meadows rich with corn,
Clear in the cool September morn.
Barbara Frietchie [1864], st. 1

12 The clustered spires of Frederick stand
Green-walled by the hills of Maryland.
Barbara Frietchie, st. 2

13 "Shoot, if you must, this old gray head,
But spare your country's flag," she said.
Barbara Frietchie, st. 18

14 "Who touches a hair of yon gray head
Dies like a dog! March on!" he said.
Barbara Frietchie, st. 21

15 The sun that brief December day
Rose cheerless over hills of gray,
And, darkly circled, gave at noon
A sadder light than waning moon.
Snowbound [1866], l. 1

16 Shut in from all the world without,
We sat the clean-winged hearth about.
Snowbound, l. 155

17 Angel of the backward look.   *Snowbound, l. 714*

18 Dear Lord and Father of mankind,
Forgive our foolish ways!
Reclothe us in our rightful mind,
In purer lives Thy service find,
In deeper reverence, praise.
The Brewing of Soma [1872]

Salmon P[ortland] Chase
1808–1873

19   The Constitution, in all its provisions, looks to an indestructible Union composed of indestructible States.
*Decision in Texas v. White,
7 Wallace 725 [1868]*

Jefferson Davis
1808–1889

20   All we ask is to be left alone.
*Address at inauguration as president
of the Confederacy [1861]*

Andrew Johnson
1808–1875

21   If I have played the Judas, who has been my Christ that I have played the Judas with? Was it Thad Stevens? Was it Wendell Phillips? Was it Charles Sumner? These are the men that stop and compare themselves

with the Savior; and everybody that differs with them in opinion, and to try to stay and arrest their diabolical and nefarious policy, is to be denounced as a Judas.

> *Speech, St. Louis [September 8, 1866];
> cited in articles of impeachment against
> Johnson, 1868*

Alphonse Karr
1808–1890

1 The more things change, the more they remain the same.[1]

> *Les Guêpes (The Wasps) [January 1849]*

Marie Edme Patrice Maurice, Comte de Mac-Mahon
1808–1893

2 Here I am, and here I stay.[2]

> *At Sevastopol [September 1855]*

Gérard de Nerval [Gérard Labrunie]
1808–1855

3 The jailer is another kind of captive — is the jailer envious of his prisoner's dreams?

> *Fragments de Faust [1828]*

4 Dream is a second life. I have never been able to cross through those gates of ivory or horn which separate us from the invisible world without a sense of dread.   *Aurélia[3] [1854], pt. I*

5 For those who have no faith in immortality, its joys and sorrows, certain fatal situations can result in despair and suicide.   *Aurélia, pt. II*

6 I am the somber one, the unconsoled widower,
The Prince of Aquitaine whose tower was destroyed.[4]
My only star is dead, and my star-studded lute
Wears the black sun of Melancholy.

> *Les Chimères [1854]. El Desdichado*

7 In what way is a lobster more ridiculous than a dog, a cat, a gazelle, a lion, or any other animal you take for a walk? I'm fond of lobsters. They're

peaceful, serious, know the secrets of the deep, don't bark, and don't invade our privacy like dogs.

> *On walking with a leashed lobster in the
> Palais-Royal gardens. From* THÉOPHILE
> GAUTIER, *Portraits et Souvenirs
> Littéraires [1875]*

George Washington Patten
c. 1808–1882

8 If we must perish in the fight,
Oh! let us die like men.

> *Oh! Let Us Die like Men, st. 4*

Samuel Francis Smith
1808–1895

9 My country, 'tis of thee,
Sweet land of liberty,
Of thee I sing:
Land where my fathers died,
Land of the pilgrims' pride,
From every mountainside
Let freedom ring.   *America [1831], st. 1*

10 Long may our land be bright
With freedom's holy light;
Protect us by thy might,
Great God, our King!   *America, st. 4*

Charles Robert Darwin
1809–1882

11 Both in space and time, we seem to be brought somewhat near to that great fact — the mystery of mysteries — the first appearance of new beings on this earth.

> *The Voyage of the Beagle [1845], ch. 17.
> Galapagos Archipelago*

12 I never dreamed that islands, about fifty or sixty miles apart, and most of them in sight of each other, formed of precisely the same rocks, placed under a quite similar climate, would have been differently tenanted.

> *The Voyage of the Beagle, 18.
> Galapagos Archipelago*

13 I have called this principle, by which each slight variation, if useful, is preserved, by the term Natural Selection.   *On the Origin of Species [1859], ch. 3*

14 The expression often used by Mr. Herbert Spencer, of the Survival of the Fittest, is more accurate, and is sometimes equally convenient.[5]

> *On the Origin of Species, 3*

---

[1]Plus ça change, plus c'est la même chose.

[2]J'y suis, j'y reste.

[3]Translated by RICHARD SIEBURTH.

[4]Je suis le ténébreux, le veuf, l'inconsolé, / Le Prince d'Aquitaine à la tour abolie.
T. S. Eliot quotes the second line in *The Waste Land, l. 429.*

---

[5]See Herbert Spencer, 490:7.

1   We will now discuss in a little more detail the Struggle for Existence.[1]

On the Origin of Species, 3

2   All we can do, is to keep steadily in mind that each organic being is striving to increase in a geometrical ratio; that each at some period of its life, during some season of the year, during each generation or at intervals, has to struggle for life and to suffer great destruction. When we reflect on this struggle, we may console ourselves with the full belief, that the war of nature is not incessant, that no fear is felt, that death is generally prompt, and that the vigorous, the healthy, and the happy survive and multiply.

On the Origin of Species, 3

3   When the views advanced by me in this volume, and by Mr. Wallace, and when analogous views on the origin of species are generally admitted, we can dimly foresee that there will be a considerable revolution in natural history.

On the Origin of Species, 3

4   It is interesting to contemplate an entangled bank, clothed with many plants of many kinds, with birds singing on the bushes, with various insects flitting about, and with worms crawling through the damp earth, and to reflect that these elaborately constructed forms, so different from each other, and dependent on each other in so complex a manner, have all been produced by laws acting around us.

On the Origin of Species, 3

5   From the war of nature, from famine and death, the most exalted object which we are capable of conceiving, namely, the production of the higher animals, directly follows. There is grandeur in this view of life, with its several powers, having been originally breathed by the Creator into a few forms or into one, and that whilst this planet has gone cycling on according to the fixed law of gravity, from so simple a beginning endless forms most beautiful and most wonderful have been and are being evolved.

On the Origin of Species, 15

6   I had no intention to write atheistically. But I own that I cannot see as plainly as others do, and as I should wish to do, evidence of design and beneficence on all sides of us. There seems to me too much misery in the world.

Letter to Asa Gray [May 22, 1860]

7   I am inclined to look at everything as resulting from designed laws, with the details, whether good or bad, left to the working out of what we may call chance. Not that this notion at *all* satisfies me. I feel most deeply that the whole subject is too profound for the human intellect. A dog might as well speculate on the mind of Newton. Let each man hope and believe what he can.

Letter to Asa Gray [May 22, 1860]

8   I cannot look at the universe as the result of blind chance, yet I can see no evidence of beneficent design, or indeed of design of any kind, in the details.

Letter to J. D. Hooker [July 12, 1870]

9   Ignorance more frequently begets confidence than does knowledge: it is those who know little, not those who know much, who so positively assert that this or that problem will never be solved by science.

The Descent of Man [1871], introduction

10   The Simiadae then branched off into two great stems, the New World and Old World monkeys; and from the latter at a remote period, Man, the wonder and the glory of the universe, proceeded.[2]

The Descent of Man, ch. 6

11   A hairy quadruped, furnished with a tail and pointed ears, probably arboreal in its habits.

The Descent of Man, 21

12   For my own part I would as soon be descended from that heroic little monkey, who braved his dreaded enemy in order to save the life of his keeper; or from that old baboon, who, descending from the mountains, carried away in triumph his young comrade from a crowd of astonished dogs — as from a savage who delights to torture his enemies, offers up bloody sacrifices, practices infanticide without remorse, treats his wives like slaves, knows no decency, and is haunted by the grossest superstitions.

The Descent of Man, 21

13   Man with all his noble qualities . . . with his godlike intellect which has penetrated into the movements and constitution of the solar system . . . still bears in his bodily frame the indelible stamp of his lowly origin.

The Descent of Man, 21

14   The plow is one of the most ancient and most valuable of man's inventions; but long before he existed the land was in fact regularly plowed, and still continues to be thus plowed by earthworms. It may be doubted whether there are many other animals which have played so important a part in the history of the world, as have these lowly organized creatures.

The Formation of Vegetable Mold Through the Action of Worms [1881], ch. 7

---

[1] The perpetual struggle for room and food. — THOMAS MALTHUS, *Essay on the Principle of Population, ch. 3*

[2] I confess freely to you, I could never look long upon a monkey, without very mortifying reflections. — WILLIAM CONGREVE, *Letter to Dennis* [1695]

1 As for a future life, every man must judge for himself between conflicting vague probabilities.
*From Life and Letters of Charles Darwin
[1887], edited by* FRANCIS DARWIN
[1848–1925]

2 I love fools' experiments. I am always making them.
*From Life and Letters of Charles Darwin,
edited by* FRANCIS DARWIN

3 My mind seems to have become a kind of machine for grinding general laws out of large collections of facts. *Autobiography [1892], ch. 2*

Edward FitzGerald
1809–1883

4 Wake! For the Sun who scatter'd into flight
The Stars before him from the Field of night,
Drives Night along with them from Heav'n and strikes
The Sultan's Turret with a Shaft of Light.
The Rubáiyát of Omar Khayyám,[1] *st. 1*

5 Awake! for Morning in the Bowl of Night
Has flung the Stone that puts the Stars to flight:
And Lo! the Hunter of the East has caught
The Sultan's Turret in a Noose of Light.
*The Rubáiyát of Omar Khayyám,
st. 1 [first edition]*

6 Now the New Year reviving old Desires,
The thoughtful Soul to Solitude retires.
The Rubáiyát of Omar Khayyám, st. 4

7 Come, fill the Cup, and in the fire of Spring
The Winter garment of Repentance fling:
The Bird of Time has but a little way
To fly — and Lo! the Bird is on the Wing.
*The Rubáiyát of Omar Khayyám,
st. 7 [first edition]*

8 The Leaves of Life keep falling one by one.
The Rubáiyát of Omar Khayyám, st. 8

9 Each Morn a thousand Roses brings, you say:
Yes, but where leaves the Rose of Yesterday?
The Rubáiyát of Omar Khayyám, st. 9

10 A Book of Verses underneath the Bough,
A Jug of Wine, a Loaf of Bread — and Thou
Beside me singing in the Wilderness —
Oh, Wilderness were Paradise enow!
The Rubáiyát of Omar Khayyám, st. 12

11 Ah, take the Cash, and let the Credit go,
Nor heed the rumble of a distant Drum!
The Rubáiyát of Omar Khayyám, st. 13

12 Think, in this batter'd Caravanserai
Whose Portals are alternate Night and Day,
How Sultan after Sultan with his Pomp
Abode his destin'd Hour, and went his way.
The Rubáiyát of Omar Khayyám, st. 17

13 They say the Lion and the Lizard keep
The Courts where Jamshyd gloried and drank deep:
And Bahram, that great Hunter — the Wild Ass
Stamps o'er his Head, but cannot break his sleep.
The Rubáiyát of Omar Khayyám, st. 18

14 I sometimes think that never blows so red
The Rose as where some buried Caesar bled;
That every Hyacinth the Garden wears
Dropt in her Lap from some once lovely Head.
The Rubáiyát of Omar Khayyám, st. 19

15 Ah, my Belovèd, fill the Cup that clears
Today of past Regrets and future Fears:
Tomorrow! — Why, Tomorrow I may be
Myself with Yesterday's Sev'n thousand Years.
The Rubáiyát of Omar Khayyám, st. 21

16 For some we loved, the loveliest and the best
That from his Vintage rolling Time hath prest.
The Rubáiyát of Omar Khayyám, st. 22

17 Ah, make the most of what we yet may spend,
Before we too into the Dust descend;
Dust into Dust, and under Dust, to lie,
Sans Wine, sans Song, sans Singer, and — sans End!
The Rubáiyát of Omar Khayyám, st. 24

18 Myself when young did eagerly frequent
Doctor and Saint, and heard great argument
About it and about: but evermore
Came out by the same door wherein I went.
The Rubáiyát of Omar Khayyám, st. 27

19 And this was all the Harvest that I reap'd —
"I came like Water, and like Wind I go."
The Rubáiyát of Omar Khayyám, st. 28

20 There was the Door to which I found no Key;
There was the Veil through which I might not see.
Some little talk awhile of Me and Thee
There was — and then no more of Thee and Me.
The Rubáiyát of Omar Khayyám, st. 32

21 "While you live,
Drink! — for, once dead, you never shall return."
The Rubáiyát of Omar Khayyám, st. 35

22 'Tis all a Checkerboard of Nights and Days
Where Destiny with Men for Pieces plays:

---

[1]Translated from the Persian of OMAR KHAYYÁM [died c. 1133] in four editions, 1859, 1868, 1872, and 1879. The fourth edition is used here, unless otherwise stated.

Hither and thither moves, and mates, and slays,
And one by one back in the Closet lays.
> *The Rubáiyát of Omar Khayyám,*
> *st. 49 [first edition]*

1   Striking from the Calendar
Unborn Tomorrow and dead Yesterday.
> *The Rubáiyát of Omar Khayyám, st. 57*

2 The Moving Finger writes; and, having writ,
Moves on: nor all your Piety nor Wit
Shall lure it back to cancel half a Line,
Nor all your Tears wash out a Word of it.
> *The Rubáiyát of Omar Khayyám, st. 71*

3   That inverted Bowl we call The Sky,
Whereunder crawling coop'd we live and die.
> *The Rubáiyát of Omar Khayyám,*
> *st. 72 [first edition]*

4 Ah, Moon of my Delight who know'st no wane.
> *The Rubáiyát of Omar Khayyám,*
> *st. 74 [first edition]*

5 After a momentary silence spake
Some Vessel of a more ungainly Make;
"They sneer at me for leaning all awry:
What! did the Hand then of the Potter shake?"
> *The Rubáiyát of Omar Khayyám, st. 86*

6 Who *is* the Potter, pray, and who the Pot?
> *The Rubáiyát of Omar Khayyám,*
> *st. 87*

7 Indeed the Idols I have loved so long
Have done my credit in this World much wrong:
Have drown'd my Glory in a shallow Cup,
And sold my Reputation for a Song.
> *The Rubáiyát of Omar Khayyám, st. 93*

8 I wonder often what the Vintners buy
One half so precious as the stuff they sell.
> *The Rubáiyát of Omar Khayyám, st. 95*

9 Ah Love! could you and I with Him conspire
To grasp this Sorry Scheme of Things entire,
Would not we shatter it to bits—and then
Remold it nearer to the Heart's Desire!
> *The Rubáiyát of Omar Khayyám, st. 99*

10 And when like her, O Saki, you shall pass
Among the Guests Star-scatter'd on the Grass,
And in your joyous errand reach the spot
Where I made One—turn down an empty Glass!
> *The Rubáiyát of Omar Khayyám, st. 101*

11   Mrs. Browning's death was rather a relief to me, I
must say; no more Aurora Leighs, thank God![1]
> *Letter [July 15, 1861]*

---

[1]See Elizabeth Barrett Browning, 434:19.

William Ewart Gladstone
1809–1898

12   Decision by majorities is as much an expedient as
lighting by gas.
> *Speech in the House of Commons [1858]*

13   You cannot fight against the future. Time is on
our side.
> *Speech on the Reform Bill [1866]*

14   Out of the range of practical politics.
> *Speech at Dalkeith [November 26, 1879]*

15   The resources of civilization are not yet exhausted.
> *Speech at Leeds [October 7, 1881]*

16   All the world over, I will back the masses against
the classes.
> *Speech at Liverpool [June 28, 1886]*

17   I have always regarded that Constitution as the
most remarkable work known to me in modern times
to have been produced by the human intellect, at a
single stroke (so to speak), in its application to political affairs.
> *Letter to the committee in charge of the*
> *celebration of the centennial of the American*
> *Constitution [July 20, 1887]*

18   Justice delayed is justice denied.   *Attributed*

Nikolai Vasilievich Gogol
1809–1852

19   It is no use to blame the looking glass if your face
is awry.
> *The Inspector-General [1836], epigraph*

20   Of course, Alexander the Great was a hero, but
why smash the chairs?
> *The Inspector-General, epigraph*

21   I tell everyone very plainly that I take bribes, but
what kind of bribes? Why, greyhound puppies. That's
a totally different matter.
> *The Inspector-General, act I, sc. i*

22   What are you laughing at? You are laughing at
yourselves!
> *The Inspector-General, V, viii*

23   And for a long time yet, led by some wondrous
power, I am fated to journey hand in hand with my
strange heroes and to survey the surging immensity
of life, to survey it through the laughter that all can
see and through the tears unseen and unknown by
anyone.   *Dead Souls [1842], vol. I, ch. 7*

24   Rus! Rus! I see you, from my lovely enchanted
remoteness I see you: a country of dinginess, and

bleakness and dispersal; no arrogant wonders of nature crowned by the arrogant wonders of art appear within you to delight or terrify the eyes.... So what is the incomprehensible secret force driving me towards you? Why do I constantly hear the echo of your mournful song as it is carried from sea to sea through your entire expanse?...And since you are without end yourself, is it not within you that a boundless thought will be born?[1]

Dead Souls, II, 11

1 Oh troika, winged troika, tell me who invented you? Surely, nowhere but among a nimble nation could you have been born: in a country which has taken itself in earnest and has evenly spread far and wide over half of the globe, so that once you start counting the milestones you may count on till a speckled haze dances before your eyes....

Rus, are you not similar in your headlong motion to one of those nimble troikas that none can overtake? The flying road turns into smoke under you, bridges thunder and pass, all falls back and is left behind!...And what does this awesome motion mean? What is the passing strange force contained in these passing strange steeds? Steeds, steeds, what steeds! Has the whirlwind a home in your manes?...Rus, whither are you speeding so? Answer me. No answer. The middle bell trills out in a dream its liquid soliloquy; the roaring air is torn to pieces and becomes wind; all things on earth fly by and other nations and states gaze askance as they step aside and give her the right of way.[1]

Dead Souls, II, concluding paragraphs

2 I shall laugh my bitter laugh.

Epitaph on Gogol's tombstone

Oliver Wendell Holmes
1809–1894

3 Ay, tear her tattered ensign down!
Long has it waved on high,
And many an eye has danced to see
That banner in the sky;
Beneath it rung the battle shout,
And burst the cannon's roar —
The meteor of the ocean air
Shall sweep the clouds no more.

Old Ironsides[2] [1830], st. 1

4 There is no time like the old time, when you and I
were young.

No Time like the Old Time, st. 1

---

[1]Translated by VLADIMIR NABOKOV.

[2]This poem roused such popular feeling that it is generally credited with saving the frigate *Constitution*, now preserved in Boston Harbor, from being dismantled as unfit for service.

5 A thought is often original, though you have uttered it a hundred times.

The Autocrat of the Breakfast-Table [1858], ch. 1

6 Insanity is often the logic of an accurate mind overtasked.

The Autocrat of the Breakfast-Table, 2

7 Man has his will — but woman has her way!

The Autocrat of the Breakfast-Table, 2

8 Put not your trust in money, but put your money in trust.

The Autocrat of the Breakfast-Table, 2

9 I find the great thing in this world is not so much where we stand, as in what direction we are moving: To reach the port of heaven, we must sail sometimes with the wind and sometimes against it — but we must sail, and not drift, nor lie at anchor.

The Autocrat of the Breakfast-Table, 4

10 Build thee more stately mansions, O my soul,
As the swift seasons roll!
Leave thy low-vaulted past!

The Autocrat of the Breakfast-Table, 4
[The Chambered Nautilus, st. 5]

11 Sin has many tools, but a lie is the handle which fits them all.

The Autocrat of the Breakfast-Table, 6

12 Have you heard of the wonderful one-hoss shay,
That was built in such a logical way
It ran a hundred years to a day?

The Autocrat of the Breakfast-Table, 11
[The Deacon's Masterpiece, st. 1]

13 End of the wonderful one-hoss shay.
Logic is logic. That's all I say.

The Autocrat of the Breakfast-Table, 11
[The Deacon's Masterpiece, st. 12]

14 He comes of the Brahmin caste of New England. This is the harmless, inoffensive, untitled aristocracy.

The Brahmin Caste of New England [1860]

15 And if I should live to be
The last leaf upon the tree
In the spring,
Let them smile, as I do now,
At the old forsaken bough
Where I cling.

The Last Leaf [1831], st. 8

Abraham Lincoln
1809–1865

16 If the good people, in their wisdom, shall see fit to keep me in the background, I have been too familiar with disappointments to be very much chagrined.

Address at New Salem, Illinois
[March 9, 1832]

1   Politicians [are] a set of men who have interests aside from the interests of the people, and who, to say the most of them, are, taken as a mass, at least one long step removed from honest men. I say this with the greater freedom because, being a politician myself, none can regard it as personal.
Speech in the Illinois Legislature
[January 11, 1837]

2   If destruction be our lot we must ourselves be its author and finisher. As a nation of freemen we must live through all time, or die by suicide.
Address at the Young Men's Lyceum,
Springfield, Illinois [January 27, 1838]

3   There is no grievance that is a fit object of redress by mob law.
Address at the Young Men's Lyceum,
Springfield, Illinois [January 27, 1838]

4   Any people anywhere, being inclined and having the power, have the *right* to rise up, and shake off the existing government, and form a new one that suits them better.
Speech in the House of Representatives
[January 12, 1848]

5   No man is good enough to govern another man without that other's consent.
Speech at Peoria, Illinois [October 16, 1854]

6   I hate [slavery] because it deprives the republican example of its just influence in the world — enables the enemies of free institutions, with plausibility, to taunt us as hypocrites — causes the real friends of freedom to doubt our sincerity.
Speech at Peoria, Illinois [October 16, 1854]

7   The ballot is stronger than the bullet.
Speech at Bloomington, Illinois [May 19, 1856]

8   "A house divided against itself cannot stand." I believe this government cannot endure permanently half slave and half free. I do not expect the Union to be dissolved — I do not expect the house to fall — but I do expect it will cease to be divided. It will become all one thing, or all the other.
Speech at the Republican State Convention,
Springfield, Illinois [June 16, 1858]

9   Nobody has ever expected me to be President. In my poor, lean, lank face nobody has ever seen that any cabbages were sprouting out.[1]
Second campaign speech against Stephen
Douglas, Springfield, Illinois [July 17, 1858]

---

[1]They have seen in his [Douglas's] round, jolly, fruitful face, post offices, land offices, marshalships and cabinet appointments, chargeships and foreign missions, bursting and sprouting out in wonderful exuberance, ready to be laid hold of by their greedy hands. — LINCOLN, *Second campaign speech against Douglas, Springfield, Illinois* [July 17, 1858]

10   As I would not be a *slave,* so I would not be a *master.* This expresses my idea of democracy. Whatever differs from this, to the extent of the difference, is no democracy.
Fragment [August 1, 1858?].
From ROY P. BASLER *[1906–1989],*
The Collected Works of Abraham Lincoln
[1953], vol. II, p. 532

11   When . . . you have succeeded in dehumanizing the Negro; when you have put him down and made it forever impossible for him to be but as the beasts of the field; when you have extinguished his soul and placed him where the ray of hope is blown out in darkness like that which broods over the spirits of the damned, are you quite sure that the demon you have roused will not turn and rend you?
Speech at Edwardsville, Illinois
[September 11, 1858]

12   That is the issue that will continue in this country when these poor tongues of Judge Douglas and myself shall be silent. It is the eternal struggle between these two principles — right and wrong — throughout the world. They are the two principles that have stood face to face from the beginning of time; and will ever continue to struggle. The one is the common right of humanity, and the other the divine right of kings. It is the same principle in whatever shape it develops itself.
Reply, seventh and last joint debate,
Alton, Illinois [October 15, 1858]

13   This is a world of compensations; and he who would be no slave must consent to have no slave. Those who deny freedom to others deserve it not for themselves, and, under a just God, cannot long retain it.
Letter to H. L. Pierce and others
[April 6, 1859]

14   Public opinion in this country is everything.
Speech at Columbus, Ohio [September 16, 1859]

15   It is said an Eastern monarch once charged his wise men to invent him a sentence, to be ever in view, and which should be true and appropriate in all times and situations. They presented him the words: "And this, too, shall pass away." How much it expresses! How chastening in the hour of pride! How consoling in the depths of affliction!
Address to the Wisconsin State Agricultural
Society, Milwaukee [September 30, 1859]

16   Let us have faith that right makes might, and in that faith let us to the end dare to do our duty as we understand it.
Address at Cooper Union, New York
[February 27, 1860]

1 No one, not in my situation, can appreciate my feeling of sadness at this parting. To this place, and the kindness of these people, I owe everything. Here I have lived a quarter of a century, and have passed from a young to an old man. Here my children have been born, and one is buried. I now leave, not knowing when or whether ever I may return, with a task before me greater than that which rested upon Washington. Without the assistance of that Divine Being who ever attended him, I cannot succeed. With that assistance I cannot fail. Trusting in Him who can go with me, and remain with you, and be everywhere for good, let us confidently hope that all will yet be well.

Farewell Address, Springfield, Illinois
[February 11, 1861]

2 If we do not make common cause to save the good old ship of the Union on this voyage, nobody will have a chance to pilot her on another voyage.

Address at Cleveland, Ohio
[February 15, 1861]

3 It is safe to assert that no government proper ever had a provision in its organic law for its own termination.

First Inaugural Address [March 4, 1861]

4 If by the mere force of numbers a majority should deprive a minority of any clearly written constitutional right, it might, in a moral point of view, justify revolution — certainly would if such a right were a vital one.

First Inaugural Address

5 This country, with its institutions, belongs to the people who inhabit it. Whenever they shall grow weary of the existing government, they can exercise their constitutional right of amending it, or their revolutionary right to dismember or overthrow it.

First Inaugural Address

6 Why should there not be a patient confidence in the ultimate justice of the people? Is there any better or equal hope in the world?

First Inaugural Address

7 While the people retain their virtue and vigilance, no administration, by any extreme of wickedness or folly, can very seriously injure the government in the short space of four years.

First Inaugural Address

8 I think the necessity of being *ready* increases. Look to it.

Letter (this is the whole message) to Governor
Andrew G. Curtin of Pennsylvania
[April 8, 1861]

9 This is essentially a people's contest.... It is a struggle for maintaining in the world that form and substance of government whose leading object is to elevate the condition of men — to lift artificial weights from all shoulders — to clear the paths of laudable pursuit for all — to afford all an unfettered start, and a fair chance, in the race of life.

Message to Congress in Special Session
[July 4, 1861]

10 Labor is prior to, and independent of, capital. Capital is only the fruit of labor, and could never have existed if labor had not first existed. Labor is the superior of capital, and deserves much the higher consideration. Capital has its rights, which are as worthy of protection as any other rights.

First Annual Message to Congress
[December 3, 1861]

11 My paramount object in this struggle is to save the Union, and is not either to save or to destroy slavery. If I could save the Union without freeing any slave, I would do it; and if I could save it by freeing all the slaves, I would do it; and if I could do it by freeing some and leaving others alone, I would also do that.

Letter to Horace Greeley [August 22, 1862]

12 I shall try to correct errors when shown to be errors; and I shall adopt new views so fast as they shall appear to be true views.... I intend no modification of my oft-expressed personal wish that all men, everywhere, could be free.

Letter to Horace Greeley [August 22, 1862]

13 On the first day of January in the year of our Lord, one thousand eight hundred and sixty-three, all persons held as slaves within any state, or designated part of a state, the people whereof shall then be in rebellion against the United States shall be then, thenceforward, and forever free.

Preliminary Emancipation Proclamation
[September 22, 1862][1]

14 [I feel] somewhat like the boy in Kentucky who stubbed his toe while running to see his sweetheart. The boy said he was too big to cry, and far too badly hurt to laugh.

Reply as to how he felt about the New York
elections. From Frank Leslie's Illustrated
Weekly [November 22, 1862]

15 If there ever could be a proper time for mere catch arguments, that time surely is not now. In times like the present, men should utter nothing for which they would not willingly be responsible through time and in eternity.

Second Annual Message to Congress
[December 1, 1862]

---

[1]The Emancipation Proclamation was issued one hundred days later [January 1, 1863].

1   Fellow citizens, we cannot escape history. We of this Congress and this administration will be remembered in spite of ourselves. No personal significance or insignificance can spare one or another of us. The fiery trial through which we pass will light us down in honor or dishonor to the last generation. We say we are for the Union. The world will not forget that we say this. We know how to save the Union. The world knows we do know how to save it. We, even we here, hold the power and bear the responsibility. In giving freedom to the slave, we assure freedom to the free — honorable alike in what we give and what we preserve. We shall nobly save or meanly lose the last, best hope of earth. Other means may succeed; this could not fail. The way is plain, peaceful, generous, just — a way which if followed the world will forever applaud and God must forever bless.

Second Annual Message to Congress
[December 1, 1862]

2   Beware of rashness, but with energy and sleepless vigilance go forward and give us victories.

Letter to Major General Joseph Hooker
[January 26, 1863]

3   The Father of Waters again goes unvexed to the sea.

Letter to James C. Conkling
[August 26, 1863]

4   I have endured a great deal of ridicule without much malice; and have received a great deal of kindness, not quite free from ridicule. I am used to it.

Letter to James H. Hackett [November 2, 1863]

5   Fourscore and seven years ago our fathers brought forth on this continent, a new nation, conceived in Liberty, and dedicated to the proposition that all men are created equal.

Now we are engaged in a great civil war, testing whether that nation or any nation so conceived and so dedicated can long endure. We are met on a great battlefield of that war. We have come to dedicate a portion of that field, as a final resting place for those who here gave their lives that that nation might live. It is altogether fitting and proper that we should do this.

But, in a larger sense, we cannot dedicate — we cannot consecrate — we cannot hallow — this ground. The brave men, living and dead, who struggled here, have consecrated it far above our poor power to add or detract. The world will little note nor long remember what we say here, but it can never forget what they did here. It is for us, the living, rather to be dedicated here to the unfinished work which they who fought here have thus far so nobly advanced. It is rather for us to be here dedicated to the great task remaining before us — that from these honored dead we take increased devotion to that cause for which they gave the last full measure of devotion; that we here highly resolve that these dead shall not have died in vain; that this nation, under God, shall have a new birth of freedom; and that government of the people, by the people, for the people,[1] shall not perish from the earth.

Address at Gettysburg
[November 19, 1863]

6   The President last night had a dream. He was in a party of plain people and as it became known who he was they began to comment on his appearance. One of them said, "He is a common-looking man." The President replied, "Common-looking people are the best in the world: that is the reason the Lord makes so many of them."

Diary entry written by John Hay[2]
[December 23, 1863]

7   I claim not to have controlled events, but confess plainly that events have controlled me.

Letter to A. G. Hodges [April 4, 1864]

8   I do not allow myself to suppose that either the convention or the League have concluded to decide that I am either the greatest or best man in America, but rather they have concluded that it is not best to swap horses while crossing the river, and have further concluded that I am not so poor a horse that they might not make a botch of it in trying to swap.

Reply to the National Union League
[June 9, 1864]

9   Truth is generally the best vindication against slander.

Letter to Secretary of War Edwin Stanton,
refusing to dismiss Postmaster-General
Montgomery Blair [July 18, 1864]

10   It has long been a grave question whether any government, not too strong for the liberties of its people, can be strong enough to maintain its existence in great emergencies.

Response to a serenade [November 10, 1864]

11   I desire so to conduct the affairs of this administration that if at the end, when I come to lay down the reins of power, I have lost every other friend on earth, I shall at least have one friend left, and that friend shall be down inside me.

Reply to the Missouri Committee of
Seventy [1864]

12   Dear Madam, I have been shown in the files of the War Department a statement of the Adjutant-General

---

[1] See Daniel Webster, 390:8 and note, and Theodore Parker, 457:9.

[2] From *Letters of John Hay and Extracts from His Diary* [published 1939]. John Hay [1838–1905] served as an assistant private secretary to President Lincoln.

of Massachusetts that you are the mother of five sons who have died gloriously on the field of battle. I feel how weak and fruitless must be any words of mine which should attempt to beguile you from the grief of a loss so overwhelming. But I cannot refrain from tendering to you the consolation that may be found in the thanks of the Republic they died to save. I pray that our heavenly Father may assuage the anguish of your bereavement, and leave you only the cherished memory of the loved and lost, and the solemn pride that must be yours to have laid so costly a sacrifice upon the altar of freedom.

> *Letter to Mrs. Bixby*[1] *[November 21, 1864]*

1   It may seem strange that any men should dare to ask a just God's assistance in wringing their bread from the sweat of other men's faces, but let us judge not, that we be not judged.

> *Second Inaugural Address [March 4, 1865]*

2   Fondly do we hope, fervently do we pray, that this mighty scourge of war may speedily pass away. Yet, if God wills that it continue until all the wealth piled by the bondsman's two hundred and fifty years of unrequited toil shall be sunk, and until every drop of blood drawn with the lash shall be paid by another drawn with the sword, as was said three thousand years ago, so still it must be said, "The judgments of the Lord are true and righteous altogether."

With malice toward none, with charity for all, with firmness in the right as God gives us to see the right, let us strive on to finish the work we are in, to bind up the nation's wounds, to care for him who shall have borne the battle and for his widow and his orphan, to do all which may achieve and cherish a just and lasting peace among ourselves and with all nations.

> *Second Inaugural Address*

3   I have always thought that all men should be free; but if any should be slaves, it should be first those who desire it for themselves, and secondly those who desire it for others. Whenever I hear anyone arguing for slavery, I feel a strong impulse to see it tried on him personally.

> *Address to an Indiana Regiment*
> *[March 17, 1865]*

4   Important principles may and must be inflexible.

> *Last public address, Washington, D.C.*
> *[April 11, 1865]*

5   If you once forfeit the confidence of your fellow citizens, you can never regain their respect and esteem. It is true that you may fool all the people some of the time; you can even fool some of the people all the time; but you can't fool all of the people all the time.

> *To a caller at the White House. From*
> ALEXANDER K. MCCLURE *[1828–1909],*
> *Lincoln's Yarns and Stories [1904]*

6   If I were to try to read, much less answer, all the attacks made on me, this shop might as well be closed for any other business. I do the very best I know how — the very best I can; and I mean to keep doing so until the end. If the end brings me out all right, what is said against me won't amount to anything. If the end brings me out wrong, ten angels swearing I was right would make no difference.

> *Conversation at the White House. From*
> FRANCIS B. CARPENTER *[1830–1900],*
> *Six Months at the White House with*
> *Abraham Lincoln [1866]*

Benjamin Peirce
1809–1880

7   Mathematics is the science which draws necessary conclusions.

> *Linear Associative Algebra [1870], first sentence*

Edgar Allan Poe
1809–1849

8 All that we see or seem
Is but a dream within a dream.

> *A Dream Within a Dream*
> *[1827, revised 1849], l. 10*

9 The happiest day — the happiest hour
My sear'd and blighted heart hath known,
The highest hope of pride and power,
I feel hath flown.

> *The Happiest Day [1827], st. 1*

10 From childhood's hour I have not been
As others were — I have not seen
As others saw.

> *Alone [written 1829, published 1875], l. 1*

11 Hast thou not torn the Naiad from her flood,
The Elfin from the green grass, and from me
The summer dream beneath the tamarind tree?

> *Sonnet. To Science [1829], l. 12*

12 Helen, thy beauty is to me
Like those Nicean barks of yore,
That gently, o'er a perfumed sea,
The weary, wayworn wanderer bore
To his own native shore.

On desperate seas long wont to roam,
Thy hyacinth hair, thy classic face,

---

[1] The five sons of Lydia Bixby did serve in the Union army, but it was later discovered that only two died in the war.

Thy Naiad airs have brought me home
To the glory that was Greece,
And the grandeur that was Rome.

To Helen [1831], st. 1, 2

1 If I could dwell
Where Israfel[1]
Hath dwelt, and he where I,
He might not sing so wildly well
A mortal melody,
While a bolder note than this might swell
From my lyre within the sky.   *Israfel [1831], st. 8*

2 Lo! Death has reared himself a throne
In a strange city, lying alone
Far down within the dim West,
Where the good and the bad and the worst and the
    best
Have gone to their eternal rest.

The City in the Sea [1831], st. 1

3 The viol, the violet, and the vine.

The City in the Sea, st. 2

4 While from a proud tower in the town
Death looks gigantically down.

The City in the Sea, st. 3

5 And when, amid no earthly moans,
Down, down that town shall settle hence,
Hell, rising from a thousand thrones,
Shall do it reverence.

The City in the Sea, st. 5

6 Thou wast that all to me, love,
For which my soul did pine —
A green isle in the sea, love,
A fountain and a shrine,
All wreathed with fairy fruits and flowers,
And all the flowers were mine.

To One in Paradise [1834], st. 1

7 And all my days are trances,
And all my nightly dreams
Are where thy gray eye glances,
And where thy footstep gleams —
In what ethereal dances,
By what eternal streams.   *To One in Paradise, st. 4*

8   During the whole of a dull, dark, and soundless day in the autumn of the year, when the clouds hung oppressively low in the heavens, I had been passing alone, on horseback, through a singularly dreary tract of country, and at length found myself, as the shades of the evening drew on, within view of the melancholy House of Usher.

The Fall of the House of Usher [1839]

---

[1]Poe's epigraph for the poem: And the angel Israfel, whose heartstrings are a lute, and who has the sweetest voice of all God's creatures. — *Koran*

9 In the greenest of our valleys
By good angels tenanted,
Once a fair and stately palace —
Radiant palace — reared its head.

The Haunted Palace [1839], st. 1

10   [In response to charges that he had been influenced by the Germans:] If in many of my productions terror has been the thesis, I maintain that terror is not of Germany, but of the soul — that I have deduced this terror only from its legitimate sources, and urged it only to its legitimate results.

Tales of the Grotesque and Arabesque [1840]

11   There are some secrets which do not permit themselves to be told. Men die nightly in their beds, wringing the hands of ghostly confessors and looking them piteously in the eyes — die with despair of heart and convulsion of throat, on account of the hideousness of mysteries which will not *suffer themselves* to be revealed.   *The Man of the Crowd [1840]*

12   They who dream by day are cognizant of many things which escape those who dream only by night.

Eleonora [1841]

13   And now was acknowledged the presence of the Red Death. He had come like a thief in the night. And one by one dropped the revellers in the blood-bedewed halls of their revel, and died each in the despairing posture of his fall. And the life of the ebony clock went out with that of the last of the gay. And the flames of the tripods expired. And Darkness and Decay and the Red Death held illimitable dominion over all.

The Masque of the Red Death [1842]

14 And much of Madness, and more of Sin,
And Horror the soul of the plot.

The Conqueror Worm [1843], st. 3

15 While the angels, all pallid and wan,
Uprising, unveiling, affirm
That the play is the tragedy, "Man,"
And its hero the Conqueror Worm.

The Conqueror Worm, st. 5

16   There is something in the unselfish and self-sacrificing love of a brute, which goes directly to the heart of him who has had frequent occasion to test the paltry friendship and gossamer fidelity of mere Man.   *The Black Cat [1843]*

17   True! — nervous — very, very dreadfully nervous I had been and am; but why *will* you say that I am mad?   *The Tell-Tale Heart [1843]*

18   The boundaries which divide Life from Death are at best shadowy and vague. Who shall say where the one ends, and where the other begins?

The Premature Burial [1844]

1 From a wild weird clime that lieth, sublime,
Out of Space — out of Time.
Dreamland [1845], st. 1

2 With me poetry has been not a purpose, but a passion; and the passions should be held in reverence: they must not — they cannot at will be excited, with an eye to the paltry compensations, or the more paltry commendations, of mankind.
The Raven and Other Poems [1845], preface

3 Once upon a midnight dreary, while I pondered, weak and weary,
Over many a quaint and curious volume of forgotten lore —
While I nodded, nearly napping, suddenly there came a tapping,
As of someone gently rapping, rapping at my chamber door.
The Raven [1845], st. 1

4 Ah, distinctly I remember it was in the bleak December;
And each separate dying ember wrought its ghost upon the floor.
The Raven, st. 2

5 Sorrow for the lost Lenore —
For the rare and radiant maiden whom the angels name Lenore —
Nameless *here* for evermore.
The Raven, st. 2

6 The silken, sad, uncertain rustling of each purple curtain.
The Raven, st. 3

7 Deep into that darkness peering, long I stood there wondering, fearing,
Doubting, dreaming dreams no mortal ever dared to dream before.
The Raven, st. 5

8 "Ghastly grim and ancient Raven wandering from the Nightly shore —
Tell me what thy lordly name is on the Night's Plutonian shore!"
Quoth the Raven, "Nevermore."
The Raven, st. 8

9 "Prophet!" said I, "thing of evil! — prophet still, if bird or devil!"
The Raven, st. 15

10 "Take thy beak from out my heart, and take thy form from off my door!"
Quoth the Raven, "Nevermore." *The Raven, st. 17*

11 And the Raven, never flitting, still is sitting, *still* is sitting
On the pallid bust of Pallas just above my chamber door.
The Raven, st. 18

12 And my soul from out that shadow that lies floating on the floor
Shall be lifted — nevermore!
The Raven, st. 18

13 The Imp of the Perverse.[1] *Title of story [1845]*

14 The skies they were ashen and sober;
The leaves they were crispèd and sere —
The leaves they were withering and sere:
It was night in the lonesome October
Of my most immemorial year.
Ulalume [1847], st. 1

15 It was down by the dank tarn of Auber,
In the ghoul-haunted woodland of Weir.
Ulalume, st. 1

16 Here once, through an alley Titanic,
Of cypress, I roamed with my Soul —
Of cypress, with Psyche, my Soul. *Ulalume, st. 2*

17 Thus I pacified Psyche and kissed her,
And tempted her out of her gloom. *Ulalume, st. 8*

18 The plots of God are perfect. The Universe is a plot of God. *Eureka: A Prose Poem [1848]*

19 "Over the Mountains
Of the Moon,
Down the Valley of the Shadow,
Ride, boldly ride,"
The shade replied —
"If you seek for Eldorado!"
Eldorado [1849], st. 4

20 And the fever called "Living"
Is conquered at last.
For Annie [1849], st. 1

21 And this maiden she lived with no other thought
Than to love and be loved by me.
Annabel Lee [1849], st. 1

22 *I* was a child and *she* was a child,
In this kingdom by the sea,
But we loved with a love that was more than love —
I and my Annabel Lee —
With a love that the wingèd seraphs of Heaven
Coveted her and me. *Annabel Lee, st. 2*

23 And neither the angels in Heaven above
Nor the demons down under the sea,
Can ever dissever my soul from the soul
Of the beautiful Annabel Lee. *Annabel Lee, st. 5*

24 In her sepulcher there by the sea —
In her tomb by the sounding sea. *Annabel Lee, st. 6*

25 Keeping time, time, time,
In a sort of Runic rhyme,
To the tintinnabulation that so musically wells
From the bells, bells, bells, bells,
Bells, bells, bells. *The Bells [1849], st. 1*

---

[1]Perverseness is one of the primitive impulses of the human heart. — POE, *The Black Cat*

1   I hold that a long poem does not exist. I maintain that the phrase "a long poem" is simply a flat contradiction in terms.   *The Poetic Principle [1850]*

2   There neither exists nor can exist any work more thoroughly dignified — more supremely noble than this very poem — this poem *per se* — this poem which is a poem and nothing more — this poem written solely for the poem's sake.   *The Poetic Principle*

3   I would define, in brief, the poetry of words as the rhythmical creation of Beauty. Its sole arbiter is taste. With the intellect or with the conscience, it has only collateral relations. Unless incidentally, it has no concern whatever either with duty or with truth.
   The Poetic Principle

Pierre Joseph Proudhon
1809–1865

4   Property is theft![1]
   What Is Property? [1840], ch. 1

5   God is stupidity and cowardice; God is hypocrisy and falsehood; God is tyranny and poverty; God is evil. For as long as men bow before altars, mankind will remain damned, the slaves of kings and priests.
   Economic Contradictions [1846]

Alfred, Lord Tennyson
1809–1892

6 There hath he lain for ages and will lie
Battening upon huge seaworms in his sleep,
Until the latter fire shall heat the deep;
Then once by man and angels to be seen,
In roaring he shall rise and on the surface die.
   The Kraken [1830], l. 11

7 Weeded and worn the ancient thatch
Upon the lonely moated grange.[2]
   Mariana [1830], st. 1

8 She said, "I am aweary, aweary,
I would that I were dead!"   *Mariana, refrain*

9 A still small voice spake unto me,
"Thou art so full of misery,
Were it not better not to be?"
   The Two Voices [1832], st. 1

10 I know that age to age succeeds,
Blowing a noise of tongues and deeds,
A dust of systems and of creeds.
   The Two Voices, st. 69

11 Like glimpses of forgotten dreams.
   The Two Voices, st. 127

12 No life that breathes with human breath
Has ever truly longed for death.
   The Two Voices, st. 132

13   In after-dinner talk,
Across the walnuts and the wine.
   The Miller's Daughter [1832], st. 4

14 Self-reverence, self-knowledge, self-control,
These three alone lead life to sovereign power.
   Oenone [1832], l. 142

15 You must wake and call me early, call me early,
   mother dear;
Tomorrow 'ill be the happiest time of all the glad
   New Year;
Of all the glad New Year, mother, the maddest,
   merriest day;
For I'm to be Queen o' the May, mother, I'm to be
   Queen o' the May.
   The May Queen [1832], st. 1

16 In the afternoon they came unto a land
In which it seemed always afternoon.
   The Lotos-Eaters [1832], st. 1

17 Music that gentlier on the spirit lies,
Than tir'd eyelids upon tir'd eyes.
   The Lotos-Eaters. Choric Song, st. 1

18   Ah, why
Should life all labor be?
   The Lotos-Eaters. Choric Song, st. 4

19 Let us alone. Time driveth onward fast,
And in a little while our lips are dumb.
Let us alone. What is it that will last?
All things are taken from us, and become
Portions and parcels of the dreadful Past.
   The Lotos-Eaters. Choric Song, st. 4

20 Give us long rest or death, dark death or dreamful
   ease.   *The Lotos-Eaters. Choric Song, st. 4*

21 Surely, surely, slumber is more sweet than toil, the
   shore
Than labor in the deep mid-ocean, wind and wave
   and oar;
Oh rest ye, brother mariners, we will not wander
   more.   *The Lotos-Eaters. Choric Song, last lines*

22 Dan Chaucer, the first warbler, whose sweet breath
Preluded those melodious bursts that fill
The spacious times of great Elizabeth
With sounds that echo still.
   A Dream of Fair Women [1832], st. 2

23 A daughter of the gods, divinely tall,
And most divinely fair.
   A Dream of Fair Women, st. 22

---

[1] La propriété c'est le vol!
[2] See Shakespeare, 207:4.

1 The lion on your old stone gates
Is not more cold to you than I.
Lady Clara Vere de Vere [1833], st. 3

2 The gardener Adam and his wife
Smile at the claims of long descent.
Lady Clara Vere de Vere, st. 7

3 'Tis only noble to be good.
Kind hearts are more than coronets,
And simple faith than Norman blood.
Lady Clara Vere de Vere, st. 7

4 Many-tower'd Camelot.
The Lady of Shalott [1842], pt. I, st. 1

5 "Tirra lirra," by the river
Sang Sir Lancelot. *The Lady of Shalott, III, st. 4*

6 She left the web, she left the loom,
She made three paces thro' the room,
She saw the water-lily bloom,
She saw the helmet and the plume,
   She look'd down to Camelot.
Out flew the web and floated wide;
The mirror crack'd from side to side.
"The curse is come upon me," cried
   The Lady of Shalott.
The Lady of Shalott, III, st. 5

7   The great brand
Made lightnings in the splendor of the moon,
And flashing round and round, and whirled in an
   arch,
Shot like a streamer of the northern morn,
Seen where the moving isles of winter shock
By night, with noises of the northern sea,
So flashed and fell the brand Excalibur.
Morte d'Arthur [1842], l. 136

8   Half light, half shade,
She stood, a sight to make an old man young.
The Gardener's Daughter [1842], l. 139

9 The long mechanic pacings to and fro,
The set gray life, and apathetic end.
Love and Duty [1842], l. 17

10   Ah! when shall all men's good
Be each man's rule, and universal peace
Lie like a shaft of light across the land,
And like a lane of beams athwart the sea,
Through all the circle of the golden year?
The Golden Year [1842], l. 47

11 It little profits that an idle king,
By this still hearth, among these barren crags,
Match'd with an aged wife, I mete and dole
Unequal laws unto a savage race. *Ulysses [1842], l. 1*

12   I will drink
Life to the lees. *Ulysses, l. 6*

13 Much have I seen and known; cities of men
And manners, climates, councils, governments,
Myself not least, but honor'd of them all;
And drunk delight of battle with my peers,
Far on the ringing plains of windy Troy.
I am a part of all that I have met;
Yet all experience is an arch wherethrough
Gleams that untravel'd world. *Ulysses, l. 13*

14 How dull it is to pause, to make an end,
To rust unburnished, not to shine in use,
As though to breathe were life! *Ulysses, l. 22*

15 And this gray spirit yearning in desire
To follow knowledge like a sinking star,
Beyond the utmost bound of human thought.
Ulysses, l. 30

16 This is my son, mine own Telemachus. *Ulysses, l. 33*

17 Death closes all: but something ere the end,
Some work of noble note, may yet be done,
Not unbecoming men that strove with gods.
Ulysses, l. 51

18   The deep
Moans round with many voices. Come, my friends,
'Tis not too late to seek a newer world.
Push off, and sitting well in order smite
The sounding furrows, for my purpose holds
To sail beyond the sunset, and the baths
Of all the western stars, until I die.
It may be that the gulfs will wash us down;
It may be we shall touch the Happy Isles,
And see the great Achilles, whom we knew.
Ulysses, l. 55

19 To strive, to seek, to find, and not to yield.
Ulysses, l. 70

20 Comrades, leave me here a little, while as yet 'tis early
   morn:
Leave me here, and when you want me, sound upon
   the bugle horn. *Locksley Hall [1842], l. 1*

21 In the spring a young man's fancy lightly turns to
   thoughts of love. *Locksley Hall, l. 20*

22 He will hold thee, when his passion shall have spent
   its novel force,
Something better than his dog, a little dearer than his
   horse. *Locksley Hall, l. 49*

23   This is the truth the poet sings,
That a sorrow's crown of sorrow is remembering
   happier things. *Locksley Hall, l. 75*

24 Like a dog, he hunts in dreams. *Locksley Hall, l. 79*

25 With a little hoard of maxims preaching down a
   daughter's heart. *Locksley Hall, l. 94*

1 But the jingling of the guinea helps the hurt that
     Honor feels.   *Locksley Hall, l. 105*

2 For I dipp'd into the future, far as human eye could
     see,
  Saw the Vision of the world, and all the wonder that
     would be;
  Saw the heavens fill with commerce, argosies of magic
     sails,
  Pilots of the purple twilight, dropping down with
     costly bales;
  Heard the heavens fill with shouting, and there rain'd
     a ghastly dew
  From the nations' airy navies grappling in the central
     blue.   *Locksley Hall, l. 119*

3 Till the war drum throbbed no longer and the battle
     flags were furled
  In the Parliament of man, the Federation of the
     world.   *Locksley Hall, l. 127*

4 And the kindly earth shall slumber, lapp'd in universal
     law.   *Locksley Hall, l. 130*

5 Yet I doubt not through the ages one increasing
     purpose runs,
  And the thoughts of men are widened with the
     process of the suns.   *Locksley Hall, l. 137*

6 Knowledge comes, but wisdom lingers.
       Locksley Hall, l. 141

7 Woman is the lesser man, and all thy passions,
     match'd with mine,
  Are as moonlight unto sunlight, and as water unto
     wine.   *Locksley Hall, l. 151*

8 I will take some savage woman, she shall rear my
     dusky race.   *Locksley Hall, l. 168*

9 I the heir of all the ages, in the foremost files of
     time.   *Locksley Hall, l. 178*

10 Let the great world spin forever down the ringing
     grooves of change.   *Locksley Hall, l. 182*

11 Better fifty years of Europe than a cycle of Cathay.
       Locksley Hall, l. 184

12 And o'er the hills and far away
  Beyond their utmost purple rim,
  Beyond the night, across the day,
  Through all the world she followed him.
     The Day Dream [1842]. The Departure, st. 4

13 My strength is as the strength of ten,
  Because my heart is pure.
       Sir Galahad [1842], st. 1

14 Cophetua sware a royal oath;
  "This beggar maid shall be my queen!"
     The Beggar Maid [1842], st. 2

15 Break, break, break,
  On thy cold gray stones, O Sea!
  And I would that my tongue could utter
  The thoughts that arise in me.

  O, well for the fisherman's boy,
  That he shouts with his sister at play!
  O, well for the sailor lad,
  That he sings in his boat on the bay!

  And the stately ships go on
  To their haven under the hill;
  But O, for the touch of a vanish'd hand,
  And the sound of a voice that is still!
     Break, Break, Break [1842], st. 1–3

16 But the tender grace of a day that is dead
  Will never come back to me.
     Break, Break, Break, st. 4

17 And quoted odes, and jewels five-words-long
  That on the stretched forefinger of all Time
  Sparkle forever.   *The Princess [1847], pt. II, l. 355*

18 Sweet and low, sweet and low,
  Wind of the western sea,
  Low, low, breathe and blow,
  Wind of the western sea!
  Over the rolling waters go,
  Come from the dying moon, and blow,
  Blow him again to me;
  While my little one, while my pretty one, sleeps.
     The Princess, III [song, Sweet and Low, st. 1]

19 The splendor falls on castle walls
  And snowy summits old in story:
  The long light shakes across the lakes,
  And the wild cataract leaps in glory.
  Blow, bugle, blow, set the wild echoes flying,
  Blow, bugle; answer, echoes, dying, dying, dying.
     The Princess, IV [song,
     The Splendor Falls, st. 1]

20 The horns of Elfland faintly blowing.
     The Princess, IV [song,
     The Splendor Falls, st. 2]

21 Tears, idle tears, I know not what they mean,
  Tears from the depth of some divine despair
  Rise in the heart, and gather to the eyes,
  In looking on the happy autumn fields,
  And thinking of the days that are no more.
     The Princess, IV [song, Tears,
     Idle Tears, st. 1]

22 Dear as remember'd kisses after death,
  And sweet as those by hopeless fancy feign'd
  On lips that are for others; deep as love,
  Deep as first love, and wild with all regret;
  O Death in Life, the days that are no more.
     The Princess, IV [song, Tears, Idle Tears, st. 4]

1 O Swallow, Swallow, flying, flying South,
  Fly to her, and fall upon her gilded eaves,
  And tell her, tell her, what I tell to thee.
     The Princess, IV [song, O Swallow, Swallow, st. 1]

2 Man is the hunter; woman is his game.
     The Princess, V, l. 147

3 Man for the field and woman for the hearth:
  Man for the sword and for the needle she:
  Man with the head and woman with the heart:
  Man to command and woman to obey;
  All else confusion.
     The Princess, V, l. 437

4 Ask me no more: thy fate and mine are seal'd:
  I strove against the stream and all in vain:
  Let the great river take me to the main:
  No more, dear love, for at a touch I yield;
  Ask me no more.
     The Princess, VII [song, Ask Me No More,
     st. 3]

5 Now sleeps the crimson petal, now the white;
  Nor waves the cypress in the palace walk;
  Nor winks the gold fin in the porphyry font:
  The firefly wakens: waken thou with me.
     The Princess, VII [song, Now Sleeps the
     Crimson Petal, st. 1]

6 Now lies the Earth all Danaë to the stars,
  And all thy heart lies open unto me.
     The Princess, VII [song, Now Sleeps the
     Crimson Petal, st. 3]

7   Sweet is every sound,
  Sweeter thy voice, but every sound is sweet;
  Myriads of rivulets hurrying through the lawn,
  The moan of doves in immemorial elms,
  And murmuring of innumerable bees.
     The Princess, VII, l. 203

8 Believing where we cannot prove.
     In Memoriam[1] [1850]. Prologue, st. 1

9 Our little systems have their day.
     In Memoriam. Prologue, st. 5

10 Let knowledge grow from more to more,
  But more of reverence in us dwell;
  That mind and soul, according well,
  May make one music as before.
     In Memoriam. Prologue, st. 7

11 I sometimes hold it half a sin
  To put in words the grief I feel;
  For words, like Nature, half reveal
  And half conceal the Soul within.
     In Memoriam, pt. 5, st. 1

12 But, for the unquiet heart and brain
  A use in measured language lies;
  The sad mechanic exercise,
  Like dull narcotics numbing pain.
     In Memoriam, 5, st. 2

13 And from his ashes may be made
  The violet of his native land.
     In Memoriam, 18, st. 1

14 I do but sing because I must,
  And pipe but as the linnets sing.
     In Memoriam, 21, st. 6

15 'Tis better to have loved and lost
  Than never to have loved at all.[2]
     In Memoriam, 27, st. 4

16 How fares it with the happy dead?
     In Memoriam, 44, st. 1

17 Be near me when my light is low.
     In Memoriam, 50, st. 1

18 And Time, a maniac scattering dust,
  And Life, a Fury slinging flame.
     In Memoriam, 50, st. 2

19 Do we indeed desire the dead
  Should still be near us at our side?
     In Memoriam, 51, st. 1

20 Hold thou the good; define it well;
  For fear divine Philosophy
  Should push beyond her mark, and be
  Procuress to the Lords of Hell.
     In Memoriam, 53, st. 4

21 Oh yet we trust that somehow good
  Will be the final goal of ill.
     In Memoriam, 54, st. 1

22   But what am I?
  An infant crying in the night:
  An infant crying for the light:
  And with no language but a cry.
     In Memoriam, 54, st. 5

23 So careful of the type she seems,
  So careless of the single life.
     In Memoriam, 55, st. 2

24   The great world's altar-stairs,
  That slope through darkness up to God.
     In Memoriam, 55, st. 4

---

[1] In memory of Arthur Henry Hallam [1811–1833].

[2] Say what you will, 'tis better to be left than never to have been loved. — WILLIAM CONGREVE, *The Way of the World, act II, sc. vi*
Better to love amiss than nothing to have loved. — GEORGE CRABBE, *Tales. The Struggles of Conscience*
'Tis better to have fought and lost / Than never to have fought at all. — ARTHUR HUGH CLOUGH, *Peschiera* [1849]

1 Nature, red in tooth and claw.
In Memoriam, 56, st. 4

2 O Sorrow, wilt Thou live with me
No casual mistress, but a wife.
In Memoriam, 59, st. 1

3 So many worlds, so much to do,
So little done, such things to be.
In Memoriam, 73, st. 1

4   Fresh from brawling courts
And dusty purlieus of the law.
In Memoriam, 89, st. 3

5 There lives more faith in honest doubt,
Believe me, than in half the creeds.
In Memoriam, 96, st. 3

6 He seems so near, and yet so far.
In Memoriam, 97, st. 6

7 Ring out, wild bells, to the wild sky!
In Memoriam, 106, st. 1

8 Ring out the old, ring in the new,
Ring, happy bells, across the snow:
The year is going, let him go;
Ring out the false, ring in the true.
In Memoriam, 106, st. 2

9 Ring out old shapes of foul disease,
Ring out the narrowing lust of gold;
Ring out the thousand wars of old,
Ring in the thousand years of peace.
In Memoriam, 106, st. 7

10 Love is and was my lord and king.
In Memoriam, 126, st. 1

11   Wearing all that weight
Of learning lightly like a flower.
In Memoriam, epilogue, st. 10

12 One God, one law, one element,
And one far-off divine event,
To which the whole creation moves.
In Memoriam, epilogue, st. 36

13 He clasps the crag with crooked hands;
Close to the sun in lonely lands,
Ring'd with the azure world he stands.

The wrinkled sea beneath him crawls;
He watches from his mountain walls,
And like a thunderbolt he falls.   *The Eagle [1851]*

14 Bury the Great Duke
With an empire's lamentation.
Ode on the Death of the Duke of Wellington [1852], st. 1

15 The last great Englishman is low.
Ode on the Death of the Duke of Wellington, st. 3

16 O iron nerve to true occasion true,
O fall'n at length, that tower of strength
Which stood four-square to all the winds that blew.
Ode on the Death of the Duke of Wellington, st. 4

17 Speak no more of his renown.
Lay your earthly fancies down,
And in the vast cathedral leave him.
God accept him, Christ receive him.
Ode on the Death of the Duke of Wellington, st. 9

18 Half a league, half a league,
Half a league onward,
All in the valley of death
Rode the six hundred.
The Charge of the Light Brigade[1] *[1854], st. 1*

19 "Forward, the Light Brigade!"
Was there a man dismay'd?
The Charge of the Light Brigade, st. 2

20 Someone had blundered.
The Charge of the Light Brigade, st. 2

21 Theirs not to make reply,
Theirs not to reason why,
Theirs but to do and die.
The Charge of the Light Brigade, st. 2

22 Cannon to right of them,
Cannon to left of them,
Cannon in front of them
Volley'd and thunder'd.
The Charge of the Light Brigade, st. 3

23 Into the jaws of death,
Into the mouth of hell
Rode the six hundred.
The Charge of the Light Brigade, st. 3

24 I come from haunts of coot and hern,
I make a sudden sally
And sparkle out among the fern,
To bicker down a valley.
The Brook [1855], song, st. 1

25 For men may come and men may go,
But I go on forever.
The Brook, song, st. 6

26 Faultily faultless, icily regular, splendidly null,
Dead perfection, no more.
Maud [1855], pt. I, sec. ii, l. 6

27 And ah for a man to arise in me,
That the man I am may cease to be!   *Maud, I, x, st. 6*

28 Gorgonized me from head to foot,
With a stony British stare.   *Maud, I, xiii, st. 2*

---

[1]See Pierre Bosquet, 456:11.

1 Come into the garden, Maud,
  For the black bat, night, has flown,
  Come into the garden, Maud,
  I am here at the gate alone.   *Maud, I, xxii, st. 1*

2 All night have the roses heard
  The flute, violin, bassoon;
  All night has the casement jessamine stirr'd
  To the dancers dancing in tune;
  Till a silence fell with the waking bird,
  And a hush with the setting moon.
                                        Maud, I, xxii, st. 3

3 She is coming, my own, my sweet;
  Were it ever so airy a tread,
  My heart would hear her and beat,
  Were it earth in an earthy bed;
  My dust would hear her and beat,
  Had I lain for a century dead;
  Would start and tremble under her feet,
  And blossom in purple and red.
                                        Maud, I, xxii, st. 11

4 Ah Christ, that it were possible
  For one short hour to see
  The souls we loved, that they might tell us
  What and where they be.   *Maud, II, iv, st. 3*

5 The woods decay, the woods decay and fall,
  The vapors weep their burthen to the ground,
  Man comes and tills the field and lies beneath,
  And after many a summer dies the swan.
                                        Tithonus [1860], l. 1

6 Here at the quiet limit of the world.   *Tithonus, l. 7*

7 Man's word is God in man.
              *Idylls of the King [1859–1885].
              The Coming of Arthur, l. 132*

8 Clothed in white samite, mystic, wonderful.
              *Idylls of the King. The Coming of Arthur,
              l. 284*

9 Live pure, speak true, right wrong, follow the
      King —
  Else, wherefore born?
              Idylls of the King. Gareth and Lynette, l. 117

10 Our hoard is little, but our hearts are great.
              *Idylls of the King. The Marriage of Geraint,
              l. 352*

11 For man is man and master of his fate.
              *Idylls of the King. The Marriage of Geraint,
              l. 355*

12 It is the little rift within the lute,
  That by and by will make the music mute,
  And ever widening slowly silence all.
              *Idylls of the King. Merlin and Vivien,
              l. 388*

13 Elaine the fair, Elaine the lovable,
  Elaine, the lily maid of Astolat.
              Idylls of the King. Lancelot and Elaine, l. 1

14   But, friend, to me
  He is all fault who hath no fault at all.
  For who loves me must have a touch of earth.
              Idylls of the King. Lancelot and Elaine, l. 131

15 He makes no friend who never made a foe.
              Idylls of the King. Lancelot and Elaine, l. 1082

16 The days will grow to weeks, the weeks to months,
  The months will add themselves and make the years,
  The years will roll into the centuries,
  And mine will ever be a name of scorn.
              Idylls of the King. Guinevere, l. 619

17 I found Him in the shining of the stars,
  I mark'd Him in the flowering of His fields,
  But in His ways with men I find Him not.
              Idylls of the King. The Passing of Arthur, l. 9

18 So all day long the noise of battle roll'd
  Among the mountains by the winter sea.
              Idylls of the King. The Passing of Arthur, l. 170

19 And slowly answer'd Arthur from the barge:
  The old order changeth, yielding place to new;
  And God fulfills himself in many ways,
  Lest one good custom should corrupt the world.
              Idylls of the King. The Passing of Arthur, l. 407

20   More things are wrought by prayer
  Than this world dreams of. Wherefore, let thy voice
  Rise like a fountain for me night and day.
              Idylls of the King. The Passing of Arthur, l. 415

21 From the great deep to the great deep he goes.
              Idylls of the King. The Passing of Arthur, l. 445

22 Cast all your cares on God; that anchor holds.
              Enoch Arden [1864], l. 222

23 The worst is yet to come.   *Sea Dreams [1864], l. 301*

24   He said likewise
  That a lie which is half a truth is ever the blackest of
      lies,
  That a lie which is all a lie may be met and fought with
      outright,
  But a lie which is part a truth is a harder matter to
      fight.   *The Grandmother [1864], st. 8*

25 Dosn't thou 'ear my 'erse's legs, as they canters awaäy?
  Proputty, proputty, proputty — that's what I 'ears
      'em saäy.
              Northern Farmer: New Style [1869], st. 1

26 Doänt thou marry for munny, but goä wheer
      munny is!   *Northern Farmer: New Style, st. 5*

27 Flower in the crannied wall,
  I pluck you out of the crannies,

I hold you here, root and all, in my hand,
Little flower — but *if* I could understand
What you are, root and all, and all in all,
I should know what God and man is.
Flower in the Crannied Wall [1869]

1 All the charm of all the Muses often flowering in a
       lonely word.   *To Virgil [1882], st. 3*

2 Cleave ever to the sunnier side of doubt.
The Ancient Sage [1885], l. 68

3 I am Merlin
Who follow the Gleam.
Merlin and the Gleam [1889], st. 1

4 Sunset and evening star,
And one clear call for me!
And may there be no moaning of the bar,
When I put out to sea,

But such a tide as moving seems asleep,
Too full for sound and foam,
When that which drew from out the boundless deep
Turns again home.
Crossing the Bar [1889], st. 1, 2

5 Twilight and evening bell,
And after that the dark.   *Crossing the Bar, st. 3*

6 I hope to see my Pilot face to face
When I have crossed the bar.   *Crossing the Bar, st. 4*

Robert Charles Winthrop
1809–1894

7   Our Country — whether bounded by the St.
John's and the Sabine, or however otherwise
bounded[1] or described, and be the measurements
more or less — still our Country, to be cherished in all
our hearts, to be defended by all our hands.
Toast at Faneuil Hall [Fourth of July, 1845]

8   A star for every State, and a State for every star.
Address on Boston Common [1862]

Henry Alford
1810–1871

9 Come, ye thankful people, come,
Raise the song of harvest-home;
All is safely gathered in,
Ere the winter storms begin.
Come, Ye Thankful People, Come [1844]

P[hineas] T[aylor] Barnum
1810–1891

10   The public appears disposed to be amused even
when they are conscious of being deceived.
*The Life of P. T. Barnum:
Written by Himself [1855]*

Pierre [Jean François Joseph] Bosquet
1810–1861

11   It is magnificent, but it is not war.[2]
*On the charge of the Light Brigade at
Balaklava [October 25, 1854]*

Margaret Fuller
1810–1850

12   Who would be a goody that could be a genius?
On women[3]

13   I myself am more divine than any I see.
Letter to Emerson [March 1, 1838]

14   The especial genius of women I believe to be electrical in movement, intuitive in function, spiritual in
tendency.   *The Dial [July 1843], The Great Lawsuit*

15   It does not follow because many books are written
by persons born in America that there exists an American literature. Books which imitate or represent the
thoughts and life of Europe do not constitute an
American literature. Before such can exist, an original
idea must animate this nation and fresh currents of
life must call into life fresh thoughts along its shores.
Papers on Literature and Art [1846]

16   I now know all the people worth knowing in
America, and I find no intellect comparable to
my own.
*Memoirs of Margaret Fuller Ossoli [1852],
vol. I, pt. 4*

17   Genius will live and thrive without training, but
it does not the less reward the watering pot and
pruning knife.
Diary. From THOMAS WENTWORTH
HIGGINSON, *Life of Margaret Fuller Ossoli
[1884], ch. 18*

18   I accept the universe.[4]   *Attributed*

---

[1]The United States — bounded on the north by the Aurora
Borealis, on the south by the precession of the equinoxes, on the
east by the primeval chaos, and on the west by the Day of
Judgment. — JOHN FISKE [1842–1901], *Manifest Destiny* [1880]

[2]C'est magnifique, mais ce n'est pas la guerre.
See Tennyson, 454:18.

[3]As recorded in the journal of RALPH WALDO EMERSON [October
20, 1837].

[4]By God! she'd better. — *Thomas Carlyle's reported comment*

Elizabeth Cleghorn Gaskell
1810–1865

1   A man is *so* in the way in the house.
Cranford [1851–1853], ch. 1

2   I'll not listen to reason.... Reason always means what someone else has got to say.
Cranford, 14

James Sloan Gibbons
1810–1892

3 We are coming, Father Abraham, three hundred thousand more.
Three Hundred Thousand More[1]
[1862], st. 1

William Miller
1810–1872

4 Wee Willie Winkie rins through the town,
Upstairs and downstairs, in his nichtgown,
Tirlin' at the window, cryin' at the lock,
"Are the weans in their bed? for it's now ten o'clock."
Willie Winkie [1863]

Alfred de Musset
1810–1857

5 I have come too late into a world too old.[2]
Rolla [1833]

6   Do Not Trifle with Love.[3]
Title of a comedy [1834]

7 The most despairing songs are the loveliest of all,
I know immortal ones composed only of tears.
Les Nuits. La Nuit de Mai
(A Night in May) [1835]

Theodore Parker
1810–1860

8   Truth never yet fell dead in the streets; it has such affinity with the soul of man, the seed however broadcast will catch somewhere and produce its hundredfold.
A Discourse of Matters Pertaining to Religion [1842]

9   A democracy — that is a government of all the people, by all the people, for all the people;[4] of course, a government of the principles of eternal justice, the unchanging law of God; for shortness' sake I will call it the idea of Freedom.
The American Idea[5] *[May 29, 1850]*

Robert [Alexander] Schumann
1810–1856

10   Hats off, gentlemen — a genius!
On first hearing Frédéric Chopin's music [1831]

Edmund Hamilton Sears
1810–1876

11 It came upon the midnight clear,
That glorious song of old,
From angels bending near the earth
To touch their harps of gold:
"Peace on the earth, good will to men
From heav'n's all-gracious King."
The world in solemn stillness lay
To hear the angels sing.
The Angel's Song [1850], st. 1

Martin Farquhar Tupper
1810–1889

12 Error is a hardy plant: it flourisheth in every soil.
Proverbial Philosophy [1838–1842].
Of Truth in Things False

13 Nature's own Nobleman, friendly and frank,
Is a man with his heart in his hand!
Nature's Nobleman [1844], st. 1

John Bright
1811–1889

14   Force is not a remedy.
Speech at Birmingham
[November 16, 1880]

---

[1]Song to help raise volunteers for the Union Army.

[2]Je suis venu trop tard dans un monde trop vieux.

[3]On Ne Badine Pas avec l'Amour.

[4]Parker used the same phrase in a speech delivered in Boston [May 31, 1854] and in a sermon in the Music Hall, Boston [July 4, 1858]. William H. Herndon visited Boston and on his return to Springfield, Illinois, took with him some of Parker's sermons and addresses. In his *Abraham Lincoln, vol. II, p. 65,* Herndon says that Lincoln marked with pencil this portion of the Music Hall address: "Democracy is direct self-government, over all the people, by all the people, for all the people."
  See Abraham Lincoln, 446:5, and Daniel Webster, 390:8.

[5]Speech at the New England Anti-Slavery Convention, Boston.

1   My opinion is that the Northern States will manage somehow to muddle through.
Said during the American Civil War.
From Justin McCarthy [1830–1912],
Reminiscences, vol. 1 [1899]

Fanny Fern
[Sara Payson Parton]
1811–1872

2   The way to a man's heart is through his stomach.
Fern Leaves [1853]

Théophile Gautier
1811–1872

3   Everything passes — Robust art
Alone is eternal.
The bust
Survives the city.[1]

L'Art [1832]

Horace Greeley
1811–1872

4   The best business you can go into you will find on your father's farm or in his workshop. If you have no family or friends to aid you, and no prospect opened to you there, turn your face to the great West,[2] and there build up a home and fortune.
From James Parton [1822–1891],
Life of Horace Greeley [1855].
To Aspiring Young Men

5   I never said all Democrats were saloon keepers. What I said was that all saloon keepers were Democrats.

Attributed

Wendell Phillips
1811–1884

6   When I look upon these crowded thousands, and see them trample on their consciences and the rights of their fellow-men at the bidding of a piece of parchment, I say my *curse* be on the Constitution of these United States.
Speech against the Fugitive Slave Law
[October 30, 1842]

7   Revolutions are not made; they come. A revolution is as natural a growth as an oak. It comes out of the past. Its foundations are laid far back.
Speech [January 8, 1852]

8   We live under a government of men — and morning newspapers.
Speech to the Massachusetts Anti-Slavery
Society [January 28, 1852]

9   More than all other people, we are afraid of each other.
Speech given to celebrate the Irish patriot
Daniel O'Connell [August 6, 1870]

10   The best use of laws is to teach men to trample bad laws under their feet.   *Speech [April 12, 1852]*

11   One on God's side is a majority.[3]
Speech [November 1, 1859]

12   Every man meets his Waterloo at last.
Speech [November 1, 1859]

Harriet Beecher Stowe[4]
1811–1896

13   Eliza made her desperate retreat across the river just in the dusk of twilight. The gray mist of evening, rising slowly from the river, enveloped her as she disappeared up the bank, and the swollen current and floundering masses of ice presented a hopeless barrier between her and her pursuer.
Uncle Tom's Cabin [1852], ch. 8

14   I [Topsy] 'spect I grow'd. Don't think nobody never made me.   *Uncle Tom's Cabin, 20*

15   Whipping and abuse are like laudanum; you have to double the dose as the sensibilities decline.
Uncle Tom's Cabin, 20

16   My soul an't yours, Mas'r! You haven't bought it, — ye can't buy it! It's been bought and paid for, by one that is able to keep it.   *Uncle Tom's Cabin, 33*

17   All places where women are excluded tend downward to barbarism; but the moment she is introduced, there come in with her courtesy, cleanliness, sobriety, and order.
The Chimney-Corner, pt. 2,
Woman's Sphere [1868]

18   I did not write it. God wrote it. I merely did His dictation.
Uncle Tom's Cabin [1879], Introduction

---

[1]Tout passe — L'art robuste / Seul a l'éternité; / Le buste / Survit à la cité.

[2]See John Babsone Lane Soule, 471:2.

[3]See John Knox, 150:2.

[4]So you're the little woman who wrote the book that made this great war! —Abraham Lincoln, *on meeting the author of Uncle Tom's Cabin* [November 25, 1862]. *Attributed*

Charles Sumner
1811–1874

1　Where Slavery is, there Liberty cannot be; and where Liberty is, there Slavery cannot be.
> *Slavery and the Rebellion; speech at Cooper Institute [November 5, 1864]*

2　There is the National flag. He must be cold, indeed, who can look upon its folds rippling in the breeze without pride of country. If in a foreign land, the flag is companionship, and country itself, with all its endearments.
> *Are We a Nation? [November 19, 1867]*

William Makepeace Thackeray
1811–1863

3　This I set down as a positive truth. A woman with fair opportunities, and without a positive hump, may marry whom she likes.[1]
> *Vanity Fair [1847–1848], vol. I, ch. 4*

4　Them's my sentiments.　*Vanity Fair, I, 21*

5　Everybody in Vanity Fair must have remarked how well those live who are comfortably and thoroughly in debt; how they deny themselves nothing; how jolly and easy they are in their minds.
> *Vanity Fair, I, 22*

6　How to Live Well on Nothing a Year.
> *Vanity Fair, I, 36 (title)*

7　I think I could be a good woman if I had five thousand a year.　*Vanity Fair, II, 1*

8　Ah! *Vanitas vanitatum!* Which of us is happy in this world? Which of us has his desire? or, having it, is satisfied? — Come, children, let us shut up the box and the puppets, for our play is played out.
> *Vanity Fair, II, 27*

9　He who meanly admires mean things is a Snob.
> *The Book of Snobs [1848], ch. 2*

10　Rake's Progress.[2]
> *Pendennis [1848–1850], ch. 19 (title)*

11　Remember, it's as easy to marry a rich woman as a poor woman.　*Pendennis, 28*

12　'Tis not the dying for a faith that's so hard, Master Harry — every man of every nation has done that — 'tis the living up to it that's difficult.
> *Henry Esmond [1852], bk. I, ch. 6*

13　The wicked are wicked, no doubt, and they go astray and they fall, and they come by their deserts; but who can tell the mischief which the very virtuous do?　*The Newcomes [1853–1855], ch. 20*

14　Charlotte, having seen his body
Borne before her on a shutter,
Like a well-conducted person,
Went on cutting bread and butter.
> *Ballads [1855]. Sorrows of Werther*[3]

15　Women like not only to conquer, but to be conquered.
> *The Virginians [1857–1859], ch. 4*

16　Next to the very young, I suppose the very old are the most selfish.　*The Virginians, 61*

17　It is to the middle class we must look for the safety of England.
> *The Four Georges [1860]. George III*

18　George, be a King!
> *The Four Georges. Princess Augusta to her son George III*

Robert Browning
1812–1889

19　The year's at the spring
And day's at the morn;
Morning's at seven;
The hillside's dew-pearled;
The lark's on the wing;
The snail's on the thorn:
God's in his heaven —
All's right with the world.
> *Pippa Passes [1841], pt. I*

20　Some unsuspected isle in far-off seas.
> *Pippa Passes, II*

21　In the morning of the world,
When earth was nigher heaven than now.
> *Pippa Passes, III*

22　You know, we French stormed Ratisbon.
> *Incident of the French Camp [1842], st. 1*

23　"You're wounded!" "Nay," the soldier's pride
Touched to the quick, he said:
"I'm killed, Sire!" And his chief beside,
Smiling the boy fell dead.
> *Incident of the French Camp, st. 5*

---

[1]I should like to see any kind of a man, distinguishable from a gorilla, that some good and even pretty woman could not shape a husband out of. — OLIVER WENDELL HOLMES, *The Professor at the Breakfast-Table* [1860]

The whole world is strewn with snares, traps, gins and pitfalls for the capture of men by women. — GEORGE BERNARD SHAW, *Man and Superman, epistle dedicatory*

[2]The Rake's Progress. — WILLIAM HOGARTH [1697–1764], *title of series of paintings and engravings* [1735]

[3]See Goethe, 342:11.

1 That's my last Duchess painted on the wall,
  Looking as if she were alive.
  My Last Duchess [1842], l. 1

2   She had
  A heart — how shall I say? — too soon made glad.
  My Last Duchess, l. 21

3   I gave commands;
  Then all smiles stopped together.
  My Last Duchess, l. 45

4 Marching along, fifty-score strong,
  Great-hearted gentlemen, singing this song.
  Cavalier Tunes [1842]. Marching Along, st. 1

5 Boot, saddle, to horse, and away!
  Cavalier Tunes. Boot and Saddle, refrain

6 Hamelin Town's in Brunswick,
  By famous Hanover city.
  The Pied Piper of Hamelin [1845], st. 1

7   Rats!
  They fought the dogs and killed the cats,
  And bit the babies in the cradles,
  And ate the cheeses out of the vats,
  And licked the soup from the cooks' own
    ladles.
  The Pied Piper of Hamelin, st. 2

8 And out of the houses the rats came tumbling.
  Great rats, small rats, lean rats, brawny rats,
  Brown rats, black rats, gray rats, tawny rats.
  Grave old plodders, gay young friskers,
  Fathers, mothers, uncles, cousins,
  Cocking tails and pricking whiskers,
  Families by tens and dozens,
  Brothers, sisters, husbands, wives —
  Followed the Piper for their lives.
  The Pied Piper of Hamelin, st. 7

9 When the liquor's out, why clink the cannikin?
  The Flight of the Duchess [1845], st. 16

10 It's a long lane that knows no turnings.
  The Flight of the Duchess, st. 17

11 Just for a handful of silver he left us,
  Just for a riband to stick in his coat.
  The Lost Leader[1] *[1845], st. 1*

12 We that had loved him so, followed him, honored
    him,
  Lived in his mild and magnificent eye,
  Learned his great language, caught his clear accents,
  Made him our pattern to live and to die!
  The Lost Leader, st. 1

13 Shakespeare was of us, Milton was for us,
  Burns, Shelley, were with us — they watch from their
    graves!
  The Lost Leader, st. 1

14 One more devils'-triumph and sorrow for angels,
  One more wrong to man, one more insult to God!
  The Lost Leader, st. 2

15 It was roses, roses all the way.
  The Patriot [1845], st. 1

16 I sprang to the stirrup, and Joris, and he;
  I galloped, Dirck galloped, we galloped all three.
  How They Brought the Good News from
  Ghent to Aix [1845], st. 1

17 Round the cape of a sudden came the sea,
  And the sun looked over the mountain's rim:
  And straight was a path of gold for him,
  And the need of a world of men for me.
  Parting at Morning [1845]

18 Oh, to be in England now that April's there,
  And whoever wakes in England sees, some morning,
    unaware,
  That the lowest boughs and the brushwood sheaf
  Round the elm tree bole are in tiny leaf,
  While the chaffinch sings on the orchard bough
  In England — now!
  Home Thoughts, from Abroad [1845], l. 1

19 That's the wise thrush; he sings each song twice over,
  Lest you should think he never could recapture
  The first fine careless rapture!
  Home Thoughts, from Abroad, l. 14

20 Nobly, nobly Cape Saint Vincent to the northwest
    died away;
  Sunset ran, one glorious blood-red, reeking into
    Cadiz Bay.
  Home Thoughts, from the Sea [1845], l. 1

21 The Savior at his sermon on the mount,
  Saint Praxed in a glory, and one Pan
  Ready to twitch the Nymph's last garment off.
  The Bishop Orders His Tomb at Saint
  Praxed's Church [1845], l. 59

22 And then how I shall lie through centuries,
  And hear the blessed mutter of the mass,
  And see God made and eaten all day long,
  And feel the steady candle flame, and taste
  Good strong thick stupefying incense smoke!
  The Bishop Orders His Tomb at Saint
  Praxed's Church, l. 80

23 Let's contend no more, Love,
  Strive nor weep:
  All be as before, Love,
  — Only sleep!
  A Woman's Last Word [1855], st. 1

---

[1]Often assumed to refer to William Wordsworth.

1 Where the quiet-colored end of evening smiles.
Love Among the Ruins [1855], st. 1

2 Oh heart! oh blood that freezes, blood that burns!
Earth's returns
For whole centuries of folly, noise and sin!
Shut them in,
With their triumphs and their glories and the rest!
Love is best!
Love Among the Ruins, st. 7

3 Your ghost will walk, you lover of trees,
(If our loves remain)
In an English lane.
De Gustibus [1855], st. 1

4 Open my heart, and you will see
Graved inside of it, "Italy."   *De Gustibus, st. 2*

5   Only I discern
Infinite passion, and the pain
Of finite hearts that yearn.
Two in the Campagna [1855], st. 12

6 Escape me?
Never —
Beloved!
While I am I, and you are you.
Life in a Love [1855], l. 1

7 To dry one's eyes and laugh at a fall,
And baffled, get up and begin again.
Life in a Love, l. 13

8 Ah, did you once see Shelley plain,
And did he stop and speak to you,
And did you speak to him again?
How strange it seems, and new![1]
Memorabilia [1855], st. 1

9 What's become of Waring
Since he gave us all the slip?
Waring [1855], pt. I, st. 1

10 In Vishnu-land what Avatar?
Waring, I, st. 6

11 Who knows but the world may end tonight?
The Last Ride Together [1855], st. 2

12 The instant made eternity —
And heaven just prove that I and she
Ride, ride together, forever ride?
The Last Ride Together, st. 10

13 He said, "What's time? Leave Now for dogs and apes!
Man has Forever."
A Grammarian's Funeral [1855], l. 81

14 He ventured neck or nothing — heaven's success
Found, or earth's failure.
A Grammarian's Funeral, l. 109

15 That low man seeks a little thing to do,
Sees it and does it;
This high man, with a great thing to pursue,
Dies ere he knows it.
That low man goes on adding one to one,
His hundred's soon hit;
This high man, aiming at a million,
Misses an unit.
That, has the world here — should he need the next,
Let the world mind him!
This, throws himself on God, and unperplexed
Seeking shall find Him.
A Grammarian's Funeral, l. 113

16   Days decrease,
And autumn grows, autumn in everything.
Andrea del Sarto [1855], l. 44

17 Less is more.[2]
Andrea del Sarto, l. 78

18 Ah, but a man's reach should exceed his grasp,
Or what's a heaven for?
Andrea del Sarto, l. 97

19 I am grown peaceful as old age tonight.
Andrea del Sarto, l. 244

20   Truth that peeps
Over the glasses' edge when dinner's done.
Bishop Blougram's Apology [1855], l. 17

21 The common problem, yours, mine, everyone's,
Is — not to fancy what were fair in life
Provided it could be — but, finding first
What may be, then find how to make it fair
Up to our means.
Bishop Blougram's Apology, l. 87

22 Just when we are safest, there's a sunset touch,
A fancy from a flower bell, someone's death,
A chorus ending from Euripides.
Bishop Blougram's Apology, l. 183

23 Our interest's on the dangerous edge of things.
The honest thief, the tender murderer,
The superstitious atheist, demirep
That loves and saves her soul in new French books.
Bishop Blougram's Apology, l. 396

24   You call for faith:
I show you doubt, to prove that faith exists.
The more of doubt, the stronger faith, I say,
If faith o'ercomes doubt.
Bishop Blougram's Apology, l. 601

---

[1]And did you once find Browning plain? / And did he really seem quite clear? / And did you read the book again? / How strange it seems, and queer. — CHARLES WILLIAM STUBBS [1845–1912], *Memorabile!* [1899]

[2]A favorite aphorism of the architect Ludwig Mies van der Rohe [1886–1969].

1 No, when the fight begins within himself,
 A man's worth something.
            Bishop Blougram's Apology, l. 693

2 While you sat and played toccatas, stately at the
 clavichord.
            A Toccata of Galuppi's [1855], st. 6

3 What of soul was left, I wonder, when the kissing had
 to stop?
            A Toccata of Galuppi's, st. 14

4 Dear dead women, with such hair, too — what's
 become of all the gold
 Used to hang and brush their bosoms? I feel chilly
 and grown old.
            A Toccata of Galuppi's, st. 15

5   God is seen God
 In the star, in the stone, in the flesh, in the soul and
 the clod.   *Saul [1855], st. 17*

6 Do I find love so full in my nature, God's ultimate
 gift,
 That I doubt his own love can compete with it?
 Here, the parts shift?   *Saul, st. 17*

7 'Tis not what man does which exalts him, but what
 man would do!   *Saul, st. 18*

8   We're made so that we love
 First when we see them painted, things we have
 passed
 Perhaps a hundred times nor cared to see;
 And so they are better, painted — better to us,
 Which is the same thing. Art was given for that.
            Fra Lippo Lippi [1855], l. 300

9 Rafael made a century of sonnets.
            One Word More [1855], pt. 2

10 On the earth the broken arcs; in the heaven, a perfect
 round.
            Abt Vogler [1864], st. 9

11 The high that proved too high, the heroic for earth
 too hard,
 The passion that left the ground to lose itself in the
 sky,
 Are music sent up to God by the lover and the
 bard.   *Abt Vogler, st. 10*

12 The C Major of this life.   *Abt Vogler, st. 12*

13 Grow old along with me!
 The best is yet to be,
 The last of life, for which the first was made.
 Our times are in his hand.
            Rabbi Ben Ezra [1864], st. 1

14 Irks care the crop-full bird? Frets doubt the maw-
 crammed beast?
            Rabbi Ben Ezra, st. 4

15 Then welcome each rebuff
 That turns earth's smoothness rough,
 Each sting that bids nor sit nor stand, but go!
 Be our joys three parts pain!
 Strive, and hold cheap the strain;
 Learn, nor account the pang; dare, never grudge the
 throe!   *Rabbi Ben Ezra, st. 6*

16 What I aspired to be,
 And was not, comforts me.   *Rabbi Ben Ezra, st. 7*

17 Therefore I summon age
 To grant youth's heritage.
            Rabbi Ben Ezra, st. 13

18 Look not thou down but up!
            Rabbi Ben Ezra, st. 30

19 Such ever was love's way: to rise, it stoops.
            A Death in the Desert [1864], l. 134

20 Progress, man's distinctive mark alone,
 Not God's, and not the beasts': God is, they are;
 Man partly is, and wholly hopes to be.
            A Death in the Desert, l. 586

21 Setebos, Setebos, and Setebos!
 'Thinketh, He dwelleth i' the cold o' the moon.
            Caliban upon Setebos [1864], l. 24

22 The best way to escape His ire
 Is, not to seem too happy.
            Caliban upon Setebos, l. 256

23 How sad and bad and mad it was —
 But then, how it was sweet!
            Confessions [1864], st. 9

24 Fear death? — to feel the fog in my throat,
 The mist in my face.   *Prospice [1864], l. 1*

25 No! let me taste the whole of it, fare like my peers,
 The heroes of old,
 Bear the brunt, in a minute pay glad life's arrears
 Of pain, darkness, and cold.   *Prospice, l. 17*

26 We find great things are made of little things,
 And little things go lessening till at last
 Comes God behind them.
            Mr. Sludge, "The Medium" [1864], l. 1112

27 'Tis because stiffish cock-tail, taken in time,
 Is better for a bruise than arnica.
            Mr. Sludge, "The Medium," l. 1478

28 O Lyric Love, half angel and half bird,
 And all a wonder and a wild desire.
            The Ring and the Book [1868–1869],
            bk. I, l. 1391

29 That's all we may expect of man, this side
 The grave: his good is — knowing he is bad.
            The Ring and the Book, VI,
            Giuseppe Caponsacchi, l. 142

1 'Twas a thief said the last kind word to Christ:
Christ took the kindness and forgave the theft.
> *The Ring and the Book, VI,*
> *Giuseppe Caponsacchi, l. 869*

2 All poetry is difficult to read,
— The sense of it is, anyhow.
> *The Ring and the Book, VII,*
> *Pompilia, l. 1154*

3   Through such souls alone
God stooping shows sufficient of His light
For us i' the dark to rise by. And I rise.
> *The Ring and the Book, VII,*
> *Pompilia, l. 1843*

4 Faultless to a fault.
> *The Ring and the Book, IX, Juris Doctor*
> *Johannes-Baptista Bottinius, l. 1175*

5   The curious crime, the fine
Felicity and flower of wickedness.
> *The Ring and the Book, X, The Pope, l. 589*

6 White shall not neutralize the black, nor good
Compensate bad in man, absolve him so:
Life's business being just the terrible choice.
> *The Ring and the Book, X, The Pope, l. 1235*

7 You never know what life means till you die:
Even throughout life, 'tis death that makes life live,
Gives it whatever the significance.
> *The Ring and the Book, XI, Guido, l. 2373*

8 A man in armor is his armor's slave.
> *Herakles [1871]*

9   That far land we dream about,
Where every man is his own architect.
> *Red Cotton Nightcap Country [1873], pt. II*

10   A secret's safe
'Twixt you, me, and the gatepost!
> *The Inn Album [1875], II*

11 Ignorance is not innocence but sin.
> *The Inn Album, V*

12 Have you found your life distasteful?
My life did and does smack sweet.
Was your youth of pleasure wasteful?
Mine I saved and hold complete.
Do your joys with age diminish?
When mine fail me, I'll complain.
Must in death your daylight finish?
My sun sets to rise again.
> *At the "Mermaid" [1876], st. 10*

13 Out of the wreck I rise.
> *Ixion [1883], l. 121*

14 Never the time and the place
And the loved one all together!
> *Never the Time and the Place [1883]*

15 But little do or can the best of us:
That little is achieved through Liberty.
> *Why I Am a Liberal [1885], l. 9*

16 A minute's success pays the failure of years.
> *Apollo and the Fates [1886], st. 42*

Samuel Dickinson Burchard
1812–1891

17   We are Republicans, and don't propose to leave our party and identify ourselves with the party whose antecedents have been Rum, Romanism, and Rebellion.
> *Speaking for a deputation of clergymen*
> *calling upon James G. Blaine, the Republican*
> *presidential candidate, in New York*
> *[October 29, 1884]*

Charles Dickens
1812–1870

18   A smattering of everything, and a knowledge of nothing.
> *Sketches by Boz [1836–1837]. Tales, ch. 3*

19   He had used the word [humbug] in its Pickwickian sense.
> *Pickwick Papers [1836–1837], ch. 1*

20   "An observer of human nature, sir," said Mr. Pickwick.   *Pickwick Papers, 2*

21   "It wasn't the wine," murmured Mr. Snodgrass, in a broken voice. "It was the salmon."
> *Pickwick Papers, 8*

22   I wants to make your flesh creep.
> *Pickwick Papers, 8*

23   Tongue; well that's a wery good thing when it an't a woman's.   *Pickwick Papers, 19*

24   Be wery careful o' widders all your life.
> *Pickwick Papers, 20*

25   I took a good deal o' pains with his eddication, sir; let him run in the streets when he was very young, and shift for hisself. It's the only way to make a boy sharp, sir.   *Pickwick Papers, 20*

26   Eccentricities of genius.   *Pickwick Papers, 30*

27   Keep yourself *to* yourself.   *Pickwick Papers, 32*

28   Poetry's unnat'ral; no man ever talked poetry 'cept a beadle on Boxin' Day.
> *Pickwick Papers, 33*

29   She'll wish there was more, and that's the great art o' letter-writin'.   *Pickwick Papers, 33*

1 Never mind the character, and stick to the alleybi. *Pickwick Papers, 33*

2 She knows wot's wot, she does. *Pickwick Papers, 37*

3 *They* don't mind it; it's a regular holiday to them — all porter and skittles.[1] *Pickwick Papers, 41*

4 Anythin' for a quiet life, as the man said wen he took the sitivation at the lighthouse. *Pickwick Papers, 43*

5 Right as a trivet. *Pickwick Papers, 50*

6 Oliver Twist has asked for more! *Oliver Twist [1837–1838], ch. 2*

7 "The artful Dodger." *Oliver Twist, 8*

8 "Hard," replied the Dodger. "As nails," added Charley Bates. *Oliver Twist, 9*

9 There is a passion for hunting something deeply implanted in the human breast. *Oliver Twist, 10*

10 I'll eat my head. *Oliver Twist, 10*

11 I only know two sorts of boys. Mealy boys, and beef-faced boys. *Oliver Twist, 10*

12 There's light enough for wot I've got to do. *Oliver Twist, 47*

13 "If the law supposes that," said Mr. Bumble... "the law is a ass, a idiot." *Oliver Twist, 51*

14 He had but one eye, and the popular prejudice runs in favor of two. *Nicholas Nickleby [1838–1839], ch. 4*

15 Subdue your appetites, my dears, and you've conquered human natur. *Nicholas Nickleby, 5*

16 There are only two styles of portrait painting; the serious and the smirk. *Nicholas Nickleby, 10*

17 Oh! they're too beautiful to live, much too beautiful! *Nicholas Nickleby, 14*

18 I pity his ignorance and despise him. *Nicholas Nickleby, 15*

19 The infant phenomenon. *Nicholas Nickleby, 23*

20 The unities, sir...are a completeness — a kind of universal dove-tailedness with regard to place and time. *Nicholas Nickleby, 24*

---

[1]Life is with such all beer and skittles; / They are not difficult to please / About their victuals. — CHARLES STUART CALVERLEY [1831–1884], *Contentment* [1872]

Life ain't all beer and skittles, and more's the pity. — GEORGE DU MAURIER, *Trilby, pt. I*

See Thomas Hughes, 498:11.

21 A demd, damp, moist, unpleasant body! *Nicholas Nickleby, 34*

22 Bring in the bottled lightning, a clean tumbler, and a corkscrew. *Nicholas Nickleby, 49*

23 All is gas and gaiters. *Nicholas Nickleby, 49*

24 My life is one demd horrid grind. *Nicholas Nickleby, 64*

25 He has gone to the demnition bowwows. *Nicholas Nickleby, 64*

26 What is the odds so long as the fire of soul is kindled at the taper of conwiviality, and the wing of friendship never moults a feather! *The Old Curiosity Shop [1841], ch. 2*

27 She's the ornament of her sex. *The Old Curiosity Shop, 5*

28 That vague kind of penitence which holidays awaken next morning. *The Old Curiosity Shop, 40*

29 "Did you ever taste beer?" "I had a sip of it once," said the small servant. "Here's a state of things!" cried Mr. Swiveller.... "She *never* tasted it — it can't be tasted in a sip!" *The Old Curiosity Shop, 57*

30 It was a maxim with Foxey — our revered father, gentlemen — "Always suspect everybody." *The Old Curiosity Shop, 66*

31 Rather a tough customer in argyment. *Barnaby Rudge [1841], ch. 1*

32 Oh gracious, why wasn't I born old and ugly? *Barnaby Rudge, 70*

33 Any man may be in good spirits and good temper when he's well dressed. There ain't much credit in that. *Martin Chuzzlewit [1843–1844], ch. 5*

34 With affection beaming in one eye, and calculation shining out of the other. *Martin Chuzzlewit, 8*

35 "Do not repine, my friends," said Mr. Pecksniff, tenderly. "Do not weep for me. It is chronic." *Martin Chuzzlewit, 9*

36 Keep up appearances whatever you do. *Martin Chuzzlewit, 11*

37 "Do other men for they would do you." That's the true business precept. *Martin Chuzzlewit, 11*

38 Buy an annuity cheap, and make your life interesting to yourself and everybody else that watches the speculation. *Martin Chuzzlewit, 18*

39 Leave the bottle on the chimleypiece, and don't ask me to take none, but let me put my lips to it when I am so dispoged. *Martin Chuzzlewit, 19*

1   "She's the sort of woman now," said Mould...
"one would almost feel disposed to bury for nothing:
and do it neatly, too!"   *Martin Chuzzlewit, 25*

2   He'd make a lovely corpse.
                                Martin Chuzzlewit, 25

3   Oh Sairey, Sairey, little do we know wot lays afore
us!   *Martin Chuzzlewit, 40*

4   I don't believe there's no sich a person!
                                Martin Chuzzlewit, 49

5   Oh, but he was a tightfisted hand at the grindstone. Scrooge! a squeezing, wrenching, grasping,
scraping, clutching, covetous old sinner! Hard and
sharp as flint, from which no steel had ever struck out
generous fire; secret, and self-contained, and solitary
as an oyster.
                        A Christmas Carol [1843], stave 1

6   "Bah," said Scrooge. "Humbug!"
                                A Christmas Carol, 1

7   I [Marley's Ghost] wear the chain I forged in
life.   *A Christmas Carol, 1*

8   "I am the Ghost of Christmas Past." "Long past?"
inquired Scrooge.... "No. Your past."
                                A Christmas Carol, 2

9   In came a fiddler... and tuned like fifty stomachaches. In came Mrs. Fezziwig, one vast substantial
smile.   *A Christmas Carol, 2*

10   I am the Ghost of Christmas Present.
                                A Christmas Carol, 3

11   As good as gold [Tiny Tim].
                                A Christmas Carol, 3

12   "God bless us every one!" said Tiny Tim, the last
of all.   *A Christmas Carol, 3*

13   "I am in the presence of the Ghost of Christmas
Yet to Come?" said Scrooge.   *A Christmas Carol, 4*

14   I will honor Christmas in my heart, and try to keep
it all the year.   *A Christmas Carol, 4*

15   It *was* a turkey! He could never have stood upon
his legs, that bird! He would have snapped 'em off
short in a minute, like sticks of sealing wax.
                                A Christmas Carol, 5

16 Oh let us love our occupations,
Bless the squire and his relations,
Live upon our daily rations,
And always know our proper stations.
                        The Chimes [1844], second quarter

17   "Wal'r, my boy," replied the Captain, "in the Proverbs of Solomon you will find the following words,
'May we never want a friend in need, nor a bottle to
give him!' When found, make a note of."
                        Dombey and Son [1848], ch. 15

18   The bearings of this observation lays in the application on it.   *Dombey and Son, 23*

19   You'll find us rough, sir, but you'll find us ready.
                    David Copperfield [1849–1850], ch. 3

20   I am a lone lorn creetur... and everythink goes
contrary with me.   *David Copperfield, 3*

21   Barkis is willin'.   *David Copperfield, 5*

22   "In case anything turned up," which was his [Mr.
Micawber's] favorite expression.
                                David Copperfield, 11

23   I never will desert Mr. Micawber.
                                David Copperfield, 12

24   Annual income twenty pounds, annual expenditure nineteen nineteen six, result happiness. Annual
income twenty pounds, annual expenditure twenty
pounds ought and six, result misery.
                                David Copperfield, 12

25   It's a mad world. Mad as Bedlam.
                                David Copperfield, 14

26   Never... be mean in anything; never be false;
never be cruel.   *David Copperfield, 15*

27   I'm a very umble person.[1]
                                David Copperfield, 16

28   The mistake was made of putting some of the
trouble out of King Charles's head into my head.[2]
                                David Copperfield, 17

29   It was as true... as turnips is. It was as true... as
taxes is. And nothing's truer than them.
                                David Copperfield, 21

30   What a world of gammon and spinnage it is,
though, ain't it!   *David Copperfield, 22*

31   Nobody's enemy but his own.
                                David Copperfield, 25

32   Accidents will occur in the best-regulated
families.   *David Copperfield, 28*

33   Ride on! Rough-shod if need be, smooth-shod if
that will do, but ride on! Ride on over all obstacles,
and win the race!   *David Copperfield, 28*

34   A long pull, and a strong pull, and a pull all
together.   *David Copperfield, 30*

35   He's a-going out with the tide.
                                David Copperfield, 30

---

[1]Not only humble but umble, which I look upon to be the
comparative, or, indeed, superlative degree. — ANTHONY TROLLOPE,
Doctor Thorne [1858], *ch. 4*

[2]"King Charles's head" has passed into common use in the English
language as a phrase meaning some whimsical obsession. —
G. B. STERN [1890–1973], *Monogram* [1936]

1   I ate umble pie with an appetite.
David Copperfield, 39

2   Let sleeping dogs lie — who wants to rouse 'em?
David Copperfield, 39

3   Skewered through and through with office pens, and bound hand and foot with red tape.
David Copperfield, 43

4   It's only my child-wife.   *David Copperfield, 44*

5   There can be no disparity in marriage like unsuitability of mind and purpose.
David Copperfield, 45

6   A man must take the fat with the lean.
David Copperfield, 51

7   Trifles make the sum of life.
David Copperfield, 53

8   The seamen said it blew great guns.
David Copperfield, 55

9   He is an honorable, obstinate, truthful, high-spirited, intensely prejudiced, perfectly unreasonable man.
Bleak House [1852–1858], ch. 2

10   This is a London particular....A fog, miss.
Bleak House, 3

11   The Lawyers have twisted it into such a state of bedevilment that the original merits of the case have long disappeared from the face of the earth....It's about nothing but Costs, now. We are always appearing, and disappearing, and swearing, and interrogating, and filing, and cross-filing, and arguing, and sealing, and motioning, and referring, and reporting, and revolving about the Lord Chancellor and all his satellites, and equitably waltzing ourselves off to dusty death, about Costs. That's the great question. All the rest, by some extraordinary means, has melted away.   *Bleak House, 8*

12   Not to put too fine a point upon it.
Bleak House, 11

13   [Old Mr. Turveydrop] was not like anything in the world but a model of Deportment.
Bleak House, 14

14   Now, what I want is Facts. Teach these boys and girls nothing but Facts. Facts alone are wanted in life. Plant nothing else, and root out everything else.
Hard Times [1854], bk. I, ch. 1

15   "Are you in pain, dear mother?" "I think there's a pain somewhere in the room," said Mrs. Gradgrind, "but I couldn't positively say that I have got it."
Hard Times, II, 9

16   There is a wisdom of the head, and . . . a wisdom of the heart.   *Hard Times, III, 1*

17   I am the only child of parents who weighed, measured, and priced everything; for whom what could not be weighed, measured, and priced had no existence.   *Little Dorrit [1857–1858], bk. I, ch. 2*

18   Whatever was required to be done, the Circumlocution Office was beforehand with all the public departments in the art of perceiving — HOW NOT TO DO IT.   *Little Dorrit, I, 10*

19   Papa, potatoes, poultry, prunes, and prism, are all very good words for the lips: especially prunes and prism.   *Little Dorrit, II, 5*

20   Once a gentleman, and always a gentleman.
Little Dorrit, II, 28

21   It was the best of times, it was the worst of times.   *A Tale of Two Cities [1859], bk. I, ch. 1*

22   A wonderful fact to reflect upon, that every human creature is constituted to be that profound secret and mystery to every other.
A Tale of Two Cities, I, 3

23   It is a far, far better thing that I do, than I have ever done; it is a far, far better rest that I go to, than I have ever known.   *A Tale of Two Cities, III, 15*

24   In the little world in which children have their existence, whosoever brings them up, there is nothing so finely perceived and so finely felt, as injustice.
Great Expectations [1860–1861], ch. 8

25   Ever been the best of friends!
Great Expectations, 18

26   My guiding star always is, Get hold of portable property.   *Great Expectations, 24*

27   Take nothing on its looks; take everything on evidence. There's no better rule.
Great Expectations, 40

28   Money and goods are certainly the best of references.
Our Mutual Friend [1864–1865], bk. I, ch. 4

29   I want to be something so much worthier than the doll in the doll's house.   *Our Mutual Friend, I, 55*

30   That's the state to live and die in! . . . R-r-rich!
Our Mutual Friend, III, 5

31   We must scrunch or be scrunched.
Our Mutual Friend, III, 5

Ivan Aleksandrovich Goncharov
1812–1891

32   "And he was as intelligent as other people, his soul was pure and clear as crystal; he was noble and affectionate — and yet he did nothing!"

"But why? What was the reason?"

"The reason . . . what reason was there? Oblomovism!" *Oblomov [1859], pt. IV, ch. 12*

Alexander Ivanovich Herzen
1812–1870

1 Communism is a Russian autocracy turned upside down.

The Development of Revolutionary Ideas in Russia [1851]

2 Russia's future will be a great danger for Europe and a great misfortune for Russia if there is no emancipation of the individual. One more century of present despotism will destroy all the good qualities of the Russian people.

The Development of Revolutionary Ideas in Russia

Edward Lear
1812–1888

3 There was an Old Man with a beard,
Who said: "It is just as I feared!
    Two owls and a hen,
    Four larks and a wren
Have all built their nests in my beard."

Book of Nonsense [1846]. Limerick

4 How pleasant to know Mr. Lear!
Who has written such volumes of stuff!
Some think him ill-tempered and queer,
But a few think him pleasant enough.

Nonsense Songs [1871]. Preface, st. 1

5 He has ears, and two eyes, and ten fingers,
Leastways if you reckon two thumbs;
Long ago he was one of the singers,
But now he is one of the dumbs.

Nonsense Songs. Preface, st. 3

6 His body is perfectly spherical,
He weareth a runcible hat.

Nonsense Songs. Preface, st. 5

7 The Owl and the Pussycat went to sea
In a beautiful pea-green boat,
They took some honey, and plenty of money,
Wrapped up in a five-pound note.
The Owl looked up to the stars above,
And sang to a small guitar,
"O lovely Pussy! O Pussy, my love,
What a beautiful Pussy you are."

The Owl and the Pussycat [1871], st. 1

8 Pussy said to the Owl, "You elegant fowl!
How charmingly sweet you sing!

O let us be married! too long we have tarried:
But what shall we do for a ring?"
They sailed away, for a year and a day,
To the land where the Bong-tree grows
And there in a wood a Piggy-wig stood
With a ring at the end of his nose.

The Owl and the Pussycat, st. 2

9 "Dear Pig, are you willing to sell for one shilling
Your ring?" Said the Piggy, "I will."

The Owl and the Pussycat, st. 3

10 They dined on mince, and slices of quince,
Which they ate with a runcible spoon;
And hand in hand, on the edge of the sand,
They danced by the light of the moon.

The Owl and the Pussycat, st. 3

11 Far and few, far and few,
Are the lands where the Jumblies live;
Their heads are green, and their hands are blue,
And they went to sea in a sieve.

The Jumblies [1871], st. 1

12 Calico Pie,
    The little Birds fly
Down to the calico tree,
    Their wings were blue,
    And they sang "Tilly-loo!"
    Till away they flew —
And they never came back to me!

Calico Pie [1871], st. 1

13 Calico Jam,
    The little Fish swam,
Over the syllabub sea.

Calico Pie, st. 2

14 Who, or why, or which, or what,
Is the Akond of Swat?

The Akond of Swat[1] [1877], l. 1

15 On the coast of Coromandel
    Where the early pumpkins blow,
    In the middle of the woods
    Lived the Yonghy-Bonghy-Bò.
Two old chairs, and half a candle,
One old jug without a handle —
    These were all his worldly goods.

The Courtship of the Yonghy-Bonghy-Bò [1877], st. 1

16 There he heard a Lady talking,
To some milk-white Hens of Dorking —
    " 'Tis the Lady Jingly Jones!"

The Courtship of the Yonghy-Bonghy-Bò, st. 2

---

[1]Pray tell me, good reader, if tell me you can, / What's the Ahkoond of Swat to you folks or to me? — EUGENE FIELD, *The Ahkoond of Swat* [1884]

1 "I would be your wife most gladly!"
(Here she twirled her fingers madly),
  "But in England I've a mate!"
    The Courtship of the Yonghy-Bonghy-Bò,
    st. 5

2 When awful darkness and silence reign
Over the great Gromboolian plain,
  Through the long, long wintry nights.
    The Dong with the Luminous Nose [1877],
    st. 1

3 When storm-clouds brood on the towering heights
Of the hills of the Chankly Bore.
    The Dong with the Luminous Nose, st. 1

4 The Pobble who has no toes
Had once as many as we;
When they said, "Some day you may lose them all" —
He replied, "Fish fiddle-de-dee!"
    The Pobble Who Has No Toes [1877], st. 1

5 It's a fact the whole world knows,
That Pobbles are happier without their toes.
    The Pobble Who Has No Toes, st. 6

Samuel Smiles
1812–1904

6   The spirit of self-help is the root of all genuine growth in the individual; and, exhibited in the lives of many, it constitutes the true source of national vigor and strength.

    Self-Help [1859]

Henry Ward Beecher
1813–1887

7   Where is human nature so weak as in the bookstore!
    Star Papers [1855]. Subtleties of Book
    Buyers

8   A thoughtful mind, when it sees a nation's flag, sees not the flag only, but the nation itself; and whatever may be its symbols, its insignia, he reads chiefly in the flag the government, the principles, the truths, the history which belongs to the nation that sets it forth.   *The National Flag [1861]*

9   What the mother sings to the cradle goes all the way down to the coffin.
    Quoted in Proverbs from Plymouth Pulpit
    [1887], selected by WILLIAM DRYSDALE
    [1852–1901]

10   Now comes the mystery.
    Last words [March 8, 1887]

Claude Bernard
1813–1878

11   Observation is a passive science, experimentation an active science.
    Introduction à l'Étude de la Médecine
    Expérimentale (Introduction to the Study
    of Experimental Medicine) [1865][1]

12   The science of life...is a superb and dazzlingly lighted hall which may be reached only by passing through a long and ghastly kitchen.
    Introduction à l'Étude

13   Our ideas are only intellectual instruments which we use to break into phenomena; we must change them when they have served their purpose, as we change a blunt lancet that we have used long enough.   *Introduction à l'Étude*

14   All the vital mechanisms, varied as they are, have only one object, that of preserving constant the conditions of life in the internal environment.
    Leçons sur les Phénomènes de la Vie Communs
    aux Animaux et aux Végétaux (Lessons
    on Reactions Common to Animals and
    Plants) [1878–1879][2]

Georg Büchner
1813–1837

15   The revolution is like Saturn — it eats its children.[3]   *Danton's Death [1835]*

16   Some part of me, I don't know which, contradicts the rest.   *Danton's Death*

17   Woyzeck, I shudder when I think that the earth takes a whole day to rotate. What a waste of time! And where's it going to end? Woyzeck, the very sight of a millwheel depresses me.[3]   *Woyzeck [1837], sc. i*

John William Burgon
1813–1888

18 A rose-red city half as old as time.
    Petra [1845]

Harriet Ann Jacobs
1813–1897

19   Notwithstanding my grandmother's long and faithful service to her owners, not one of her children

---

[1]Translated by HENRY COPLEY GREENE.
[2]Translated by J. M. D. OLMSTEAD.
[3]Translated by VICTOR PRICE.

escaped the auction block. These God-breathing machines are no more, in the sight of their masters, than the cotton they plant, or the horses they tend.
Incidents in the Life of a Slave-Girl [1861], ch. 1

1   Reader, my story ends with freedom; not in the usual way, with marriage. I and my children are now free.
Incidents in the Life of a Slave-Girl, 4

Søren Kierkegaard
1813–1855

2   Philosophy is perfectly right in saying that life must be understood backward. But then one forgets the other clause — that it must be lived forward.
Journals and Papers[1] *[1843], vol. I*

3   I see it all perfectly; there are two possible situations — one can do either this or that. My honest opinion and my friendly advice is this: do it or do not do it — you will regret both.
Either / Or[1] *[1843], pt. 2*

4   The absurd . . . the fact that with God everything is possible. The absurd does not belong to the distinctions that lie within the proper compass of the understanding. It is not identical with the improbable, the unexpected, the unforeseen.
Fear and Trembling [1843].
Preliminary Outpouring

5   The relief in speaking is that it translates me into the universal.
Fear and Trembling.[2] *Epilogue*

6   All essential knowledge relates to existence, or only such knowledge as has an essential relationship to existence is essential knowledge.
Concluding Unscientific Postscript[3]
[1846]

7   For without risk there is no faith, and the greater the risk, the greater the faith.
Concluding Unscientific Postscript

8   Many people think . . . that the Christian commandments (for instance, loving your neighbor as yourself) are purposely made too strict — rather like the clock being put half an hour fast to prevent them getting up much too late in the morning.
Journal entry[4] *[1848]*

9   Take away the paradox from a thinker and you have a professor.
Journal entry [1849]

John Louis O'Sullivan
1813–1895

10   That government is best which governs least.[5]
Motto of United States Magazine and Democratic Review [inaugural issue, 1837]

11   Our manifest destiny is to overspread the continent allotted by Providence for the free development of our yearly multiplying millions.
United States Magazine and Democratic Review [July–August 1845]

Richard Wagner
1813–1883

12 O thou, my gracious evening star.
Tannhäuser [1845]

Mikhail Bakunin
1814–1876

13   The urge for destruction is also a creative urge.
Reaction in Germany [1842]

14   From each according to his faculties, to each according to his needs; that is what we wish, sincerely and energetically.[6]
Anarchist manifesto [1870]

Frederick William Faber
1814–1863

15 Faith of our fathers! holy faith!
We will be true to thee till death.
A Pledge of Faithfulness [1849]

Mikhail Yurievich Lermontov
1814–1841

16   *A Hero of Our Time,* gentlemen, is indeed a portrait, but not of a single individual; it is a portrait composed of all the vices of our generation in the fullness of their development.
A Hero of Our Time [1840].
Author's introduction

---

[1]Translated by HOWARD V. HONG and EDNA H. HONG.

[2]Translated by SYLVIA WALSH.

[3]Translated by WALTER LOWRIE.

[4]Translated by ALISTAIR HANNAY.

[5]Henry David Thoreau cites this motto in the opening of *Civil Disobedience.*

[6]See Karl Marx, 478:5 and note.

1 A solitary sail that rises
White in the blue mist on the foam —
What is it in far lands it prizes?
What does it leave behind at home?
A Sail[1] *[1841], st. 1*

Charles Mackay
1814–1889

2   Men, it has been well said, think in herds; it will
be seen that they go mad in herds, while they only
recover their senses slowly, and one by one.
*Extraordinary Popular Delusions
and the Madness of Crowds [1841]*

John Lothrop Motley
1814–1877

3   As long as he [William of Orange] lived, he was
the guiding-star of a whole brave nation, and when
he died the little children cried in the streets.
*The Rise of the Dutch Republic [1856],
pt. VI, ch. 7*

Edwin McMasters Stanton
1814–1869

4   Now he [Lincoln] belongs to the ages.
*On the death of Lincoln
[April 15, 1865]*

Otto von Bismarck
1815–1898

5   Woe to the statesman who does not seek in these
times a case for war that still holds up after the war
is over.
*Speech to Prussian parliament
[December 3, 1850]*

6   The great questions of the time are not decided by
speeches and majority decisions — that was the error
of 1848 and 1849 — but by iron and blood.[2]
*Speech to Prussian parliament
[September 30, 1862]*

7   Politics is not an exact science.[3]
*Speech to Prussian parliament
[December 18, 1863]*

8   Only a completely ready state can permit the
luxury of a liberal government.
Speech [1866]

9   Let us put Germany in the saddle, so to speak — it
already knows how to ride.
*Speech to the North German Reichstag
[March 11, 1867]*

10   Politics is the art of the possible.[4]
Remark [August 11, 1867]

11   A conquering army on the border will not be
halted by the power of eloquence.
*Speech to the North German Reichstag
[September 24, 1867]*

12   We Germans fear God, but nothing else in the
world.
Speech to the Reichstag [February 6, 1888]

Richard Henry Dana
1815–1882

13 Six days shalt thou labor and do all thou art able,
And on the seventh — holystone the decks and scrape
the cable.
Two Years Before the Mast [1840], ch. 3

14   If California ever becomes a prosperous country,
this bay [San Francisco] will be the center of its prosperity.
Two Years Before the Mast, 26

David Davis
1815–1886

15   The Constitution of the United States is a law for
rulers and people, equally in war and in peace, and
covers with the shield of its protection all classes of
men, at all times, and under all circumstances. No
doctrine, involving more pernicious consequences,
was ever invented by the wit of man than that any of
its provisions can be suspended during any of the
great exigencies of government.
*Ex Parte Milligan, 4 Wallace 2,
120–121 [1866]*

Daniel Decatur Emmett
1815–1904

16 I wish I was in de land ob cotton,
Old times dar am not forgotten.

---

[1]Translated by C. M. BOWRA.
[2]Eisen und Blut.
[3]Die Politik ist Keine exacte Wissenschaft.

[4]Die Politik ist die Lehre von Möglichen.

Look away, look away,
Look away, Dixie[1] Land.
Dixie's Land [1859], st. 1

1 In Dixie's land, we'll took our stand,
To lib an' die in Dixie!
Dixie's Land, chorus

John Babsone Lane Soule
1815–1891

2 Go west, young man.[2]
Article in the Terre Haute (Indiana) Express [1851]

Elizabeth Cady Stanton
1815–1902

3 We hold these truths to be self-evident, that all men and women are created equal.[3]
First Woman's Rights Convention, Seneca Falls, New York [July 19–20, 1848]. Declaration of Sentiments

4 The history of mankind is a history of repeated injuries and usurpations on the part of man toward woman, having in direct object the establishment of an absolute tyranny over her.
First Woman's Rights Convention, Seneca Falls, New York. Declaration of Sentiments

5 Resolved, That it is the duty of the women of this country to secure to themselves their sacred right to the elective franchise.
First Woman's Rights Convention, Seneca Falls, New York. Resolution IX

6 The prejudice against color, of which we hear so much, is no stronger than that against sex. It is produced by the same cause, and manifested very much in the same way. The Negro's skin and the woman's sex are both prima facie evidence that they were intended to be in subjection to the white Saxon man.
Speech before the New York Legislature [February 18, 1860]

7 Woman's degradation is in man's idea of his sexual rights. Our religion, laws, customs, are all founded on the belief that woman was made for man. Come what will, my whole soul rejoices in the truth that I have uttered.[4]
Letter to Susan B. Anthony [June 14, 1860]

8 Our "pathway" is straight to the ballot box, with no variableness nor shadow of turning. . . . We demand in the Reconstruction suffrage for all the citizens of the Republic. I would not talk of Negroes or women, but of citizens.
Letter to Thomas Wentworth Higginson [January 13, 1868]

9 You may go over the world and you will find that every form of religion that has breathed upon this earth, has degraded women. There is not one that has not always made her subject to man.
Speech to the Seventeenth Annual Convention of the National Woman Suffrage Association [January 1885]

Anthony Trollope
1815–1882

10 The tenth Muse who now governs the periodical press. *The Warden [1855], ch. 14*

11 One of her instructors in fashion had given her to understand that curls were not the thing. "They'll always pass muster," Miss Dunstable had replied, "when they are done up with bank notes."
Doctor Thorne [1858], ch. 16

12 There is no road to wealth so easy and respectable as that of matrimony. *Doctor Thorne, 18*

13 I cannot hold with those who wish to put down the insignificant chatter of the world.
Framley Parsonage [1861], vol. I, ch. 10

14 I have never walked down Fifth Avenue alone without thinking of money. I have never walked there with a companion without talking of it.
North America [1862], ch. 14

15 Always remember . . . that when you go into an attorney's office door, you will have to pay for it, first or last.
The Last Chronicle of Barset [1867], vol. I, ch. 20

16 It's dogged as does it. It ain't thinking about it.
The Last Chronicle of Barset, I, 61

---

[1] *Dixie* comes from the ten-dollar notes issued by the Citizens' Bank in bilingual Louisiana before the Civil War and bearing the French word *dix*, ten, on the reverse side. Soon New Orleans, then Louisiana and the entire South were called "the land of Dixie." — STUART BERG FLEXNER [1928–1990], *I Hear America Talking* [1976]

There are other stories of this term's origin as well.

[2] Horace Greeley used the expression in an editorial in the *New York Tribune*. As the saying "Go west, young man, and grow up with the country" gained popularity, Greeley printed Soule's article, to show the source of his inspiration.

See Horace Greeley, 458:4.

[3] See Thomas Jefferson, 336:1.

[4] Referring to resolutions she had introduced at the tenth National Woman's Rights Convention [May 10, 1860], declaring that under certain circumstances divorce was justifiable.

1 It has been the great fault of our politicians that they have all wanted to do something.
Phineas Finn [1869], ch. 13

2 Who is there that abstains from reading that which is printed in abuse of himself?
Phineas Finn, 47

3 He must have known me had he seen me as he was wont to see me, for he was in the habit of flogging me constantly. Perhaps he did not recognize me by my face.
An Autobiography [1883], ch. 1

4 Three hours a day will produce as much as a man ought to write.
An Autobiography, 15

5 It had at this time become my custom . . . to write with my watch before me, and to require from myself 250 words every quarter of an hour. I have found that the 250 words have been forthcoming as regularly as my watch went.
An Autobiography, 15

6 Of all the needs a book has, the chief need is that it be readable.
An Autobiography, 19

Charlotte Brontë
1816–1855

7 We wove a web in childhood,
A web of sunny air.
Retrospection [1846], st. 1

8 The human heart has hidden treasures,
In secret kept, in silence sealed.
Evening Solace [1846], st. 1

9 Conventionality is not morality. Self-righteousness is not religion. To attack the first is not to assail the last.
Jane Eyre [1847], preface

10 It is in vain to say human beings ought to be satisfied with tranquility: they must have action; and they will make it if they cannot find it.
Jane Eyre, ch. 12

11 Reader, I married him.
Jane Eyre, 38

12 An abundant shower of curates has fallen upon the north of England. *Shirley [1849], ch. 1*

13 Unromantic as Monday morning.
Shirley, 1

14 I am neither a man nor a woman but an author.
*Letter to William Smith Williams
[August 16, 1849]*

Ellen Sturgis Hooper
1816–1848

15 I slept and dreamed that life was beauty.
I woke — and found that life was duty.
Beauty and Duty [1840]

Eugène Pottier
1816–1887

16 Arise, ye prisoners of starvation,
Arise, ye wretched of the earth,
For justice thunders condemnation —
A better world's in birth.
The Internationale[1] [1871]

General Julius von Hartmann
1817–1878

17 Absolute liberty of military action in time of war is an indispensable condition of military success. . . . It is a gratuitous illusion to suppose that modern war does not demand far more brutality, far more violence, and an action far more general than was formerly the case.
Military Necessities and Humanity [1877]

Henry David Thoreau
1817–1862

18 I am a parcel of vain strivings tied
By a chance bond together.
Sic Vita [1841], st. 1

19 We are as much as we see. Faith is sight and knowledge. The hands only serve the eyes.
Journal [1906]. April 10, 1841

20 The Indian . . . stands free and unconstrained in Nature, is her inhabitant and not her guest, and wears her easily and gracefully. But the civilized man has the habits of the house. His house is a prison.
Journal. April 26, 1841

21 It is a great art to saunter.[2]
Journal. April 26, 1841

22 A slight sound at evening lifts me up by the ears, and makes life seem inexpressibly serene and grand. It may be in Uranus, or it may be in the shutter.
Journal. July 10–12, 1841

---

[1] Music by PIERRE DEGEYTER [1848–1932].

[2] *Sauntering* . . . derived "from idle people who roved about the country, in the Middle Ages, and asked charity, under pretense of going *à la Sainte Terre*," to the Holy Land, till the children exclaimed, "There goes a Sainte-Terrer." — THOREAU, *Walking* [1862]

1 For many years I was self-appointed inspector of snowstorms and rainstorms, and did my duty faithfully, though I never received one cent for it.
Journal. February 22 [1845–1847][1]

2 Some circumstantial evidence is very strong, as when you find a trout in the milk.
Journal. November 11, 1850

3 Nothing is so much to be feared as fear.
Journal. September 7, 1851

4 The bluebird carries the sky on his back.
Journal. April 3, 1852

5 The perception of beauty is a moral test.
Journal. June 21, 1852

6 The youth gets together his materials to build a bridge to the moon, or, perchance, a palace or temple on the earth, and, at length, the middle-aged man concludes to build a woodshed with them.
Journal. July 14, 1852

7 Fire is the most tolerable third party.
Journal. January 2, 1853

8 Nature is full of genius, full of the divinity; so that not a snowflake escapes its fashioning hand.
Journal. January 5, 1856

9 The same law that shapes the earth-star shapes the snow-star. As surely as the petals of a flower are fixed, each of these countless snow-stars comes whirling to earth. *Journal. January 5, 1856*

10 That man is the richest whose pleasures are the cheapest.
Journal. March 11, 1856

11 The savage in man is never quite eradicated.
Journal. September 26, 1859

12 Talk of mysteries! Think of our life in nature — daily to be shown matter, to come in contact with it — rocks, trees, wind on our cheeks! the *solid* earth! the *actual* world! the *common sense! Contact! Contact! Who* are we? *where* are we?
The Maine Woods, Ktaadn [1848]

13 I think that we should be men first, and subjects afterward. It is not desirable to cultivate a respect for the law, so much as for the right.
Civil Disobedience[2] *[1849]*

14 How does it become a man to behave toward this American government today? I answer that he cannot without disgrace be associated with it.
Civil Disobedience

15 A wise man will not leave the right to the mercy of chance, nor wish it to prevail through the power of the majority. There is but little virtue in the action of masses of men. *Civil Disobedience*

16 I came into this world, not chiefly to make this a good place to live in, but to live in it, be it good or bad. *Civil Disobedience*

17 Any man more right than his neighbors constitutes a majority of one. *Civil Disobedience*

18 Under a government which imprisons any unjustly, the true place for a just man is also a prison . . . the only house in a slave State in which a free man can abide with honor. *Civil Disobedience*

19 I saw that the State was half-witted, that it was timid as a lone woman with her silver spoons, and that it did not know its friends from its foes, and I lost all my remaining respect for it, and pitied it.
Civil Disobedience

20 The vessel, though her masts be firm,
Beneath her copper bears a worm.
A Week on the Concord and Merrimack Rivers [1849]. Monday [Though All the Fates Should Prove Unkind, st. 2]

21 Methinks my own soul must be a bright invisible green.
A Week on the Concord and Merrimack Rivers. Wednesday

22 It takes two to speak the truth — one to speak, and another to hear.
A Week on the Concord and Merrimack Rivers. Wednesday

23 Even the death of friends will inspire us as much as their lives. . . . Their memories will be encrusted over with sublime and pleasing thoughts, as monuments of other men are overgrown with moss; for our friends have no place in the graveyard.
A Week on the Concord and Merrimack Rivers. Wednesday

24 Go where we will on the *surface* of things, men have been there before us.
A Week on the Concord and Merrimack Rivers. Thursday

25 The frontiers are not east or west, north or south, but wherever a man *fronts* a fact.
A Week on the Concord and Merrimack Rivers. Thursday

26 A true account of the actual is the rarest poetry, for common sense always takes a hasty and superficial view.
A Week on the Concord and Merrimack Rivers. Thursday

---

[1]No year in Thoreau's dateline.

[2]Originally published under the title *Resistance to Civil Government.*

1 My life has been the poem I would have writ,
But I could not both live and utter it.
> *A Week on the Concord and Merrimack*
> *Rivers. My Life Has Been the Poem*
> *I Would Have Writ*

2 As if our birth had at first sundered things, and we had been thrust up through into nature like a wedge, and not till the wound heals and the scar disappears, do we begin to discover where we are, and that nature is one and continuous everywhere.
> *A Week on the Concord and Merrimack*
> *Rivers. Friday*

3 What are the earth and all its interests beside the deep surmise which pierces and scatters them?
> *A Week on the Concord and Merrimack*
> *Rivers. Friday*

4 It is so rare to meet with a man outdoors who cherishes a worthy thought in his mind, which is independent of the labor of his hands.
> *A Week on the Concord and Merrimack*
> *Rivers. Friday*

5 The eye may see for the hand, but not for the mind.
> *A Week on the Concord and Merrimack*
> *Rivers. Friday*

6 The fate of the country...does not depend on what kind of paper you drop into the ballot box once a year, but on what kind of man you drop from your chamber into the street every morning.
> *Slavery in Massachusetts [1854]*

7 I should not talk so much about myself if there were anybody else whom I knew as well.
> *Walden [1854], ch. 1, Economy*

8 I have traveled a good deal in Concord.
> *Walden, 1, Economy*

9 Public opinion is a weak tyrant compared with our own private opinion. What a man thinks of himself, that it is which determines, or rather, indicates, his fate.
> *Walden, 1, Economy*

10 As if you could kill time without injuring eternity.
> *Walden, 1, Economy*

11 The mass of men lead lives of quiet desperation. What is called resignation is confirmed desperation.
> *Walden, 1, Economy*

12 It is a characteristic of wisdom not to do desperate things.
> *Walden, 1, Economy*

13 It is never too late to give up our prejudices.
> *Walden, 1, Economy*

14 Age is no better, hardly so well, qualified for an instructor as youth, for it has not profited so much as it has lost.
> *Walden, 1, Economy*

15 Most of the luxuries, and many of the so-called comforts, of life are not only not indispensable, but positive hindrances to the elevation of mankind.
> *Walden, 1, Economy*

16 To be a philosopher is not merely to have subtle thoughts, nor even to found a school, but so to love wisdom as to live accordingly to its dictates, a life of simplicity, independence, magnanimity, and trust.
> *Walden, 1, Economy*

17 Beware of all enterprises that require new clothes.
> *Walden, 1, Economy*

18 In the long run men hit only what they aim at.
> *Walden, 1, Economy*

19 The swiftest traveler is he that goes afoot.
> *Walden, 1, Economy*

20 It is not necessary that a man should earn his living by the sweat of his brow unless he sweats easier than I do.
> *Walden, 1, Economy*

21 When a man dies he kicks the dust.
> *Walden, 1, Economy*

22 As for doing good, that is one of the professions which are full.
> *Walden, 1, Economy*

23 There is no odor so bad as that which arises from goodness tainted.
> *Walden, 1, Economy*

24 If I knew for a certainty that a man was coming to my house with the conscious design of doing me good, I should run for my life.
> *Walden, 1, Economy*

25 There are a thousand hacking at the branches of evil to one who is striking at the root.
> *Walden, 1, Economy*

26 Philanthropy is almost the only virtue which is sufficiently appreciated by mankind.
> *Walden, 1, Economy*

27 A man is rich in proportion to the number of things which he can afford to let alone.
> *Walden, 2, Where I Lived, and*
> *What I Lived For*

28 I know of no more encouraging fact than the unquestionable ability of man to elevate his life by a conscious endeavor.
> *Walden, 2, Where I Lived, and*
> *What I Lived For*

29 I went to the woods because I wished to live deliberately, to front only the essential facts of life, and see if I could not learn what it had to teach, and not, when I came to die, discover that I had not lived.
> *Walden, 2, Where I Lived, and*
> *What I Lived For*

1 Our life is frittered away by detail.... Simplify, simplify.
Walden, 2, Where I Lived, and What I Lived For

2 We do not ride on the railroad; it rides upon us.
Walden, 2, Where I Lived, and What I Lived For

3 Be it life or death, we crave only reality.
Walden, 2, Where I Lived, and What I Lived For

4 Time is but the stream I go a-fishing in.
Walden, 2, Where I Lived, and What I Lived For

5 Books must be read as deliberately and reservedly as they were written.   *Walden, 3, Reading*

6 How many a man has dated a new era in his life from the reading of a book.
Walden, 3, Reading

7 I love a broad margin to my life.
Walden, 4, Sounds

8 Our horizon is never quite at our elbows.
Walden, 5, Solitude

9 I never found the companion that was so companionable as solitude. We are for the most part more lonely when we go abroad among men than when we stay in our chambers. A man thinking or working is always alone, let him be where he will.
Walden, 5, Solitude

10 I had three chairs in my house: one for solitude, two for friendship, three for society.
Walden, 6, Visitors

11 I was determined to know beans.
Walden, 7, The Beanfield

12 Through want of enterprise and faith men are where they are, buying and selling, and spending their lives like serfs.   *Walden, 10, Baker Farm*

13 They [wood stumps] warmed me twice — once while I was splitting them, and again when they were on the fire.[1]   *Walden, 13, Housewarming*

14 Heaven is under our feet as well as over our heads.   *Walden, 16, The Pond in Winter*

15 While men believe in the infinite, some ponds will be thought to be bottomless.
Walden, 16, The Pond in Winter

16 Through our own recovered innocence we discern the innocence of our neighbors.
Walden, 17, Spring

17 It is not worth while to go round the world to count the cats in Zanzibar.
Walden, 18, Conclusion

18 As if there were safety in stupidity alone.
Walden, 18, Conclusion

19 If one advances confidently in the direction of his dreams, and endeavors to live the life which he has imagined, he will meet with a success unexpected in common hours.   *Walden, 18, Conclusion*

20 If a man does not keep pace with his companions, perhaps it is because he hears a different drummer. Let him step to the music which he hears, however measured or far away.   *Walden, 18, Conclusion*

21 It is life near the bone where it is sweetest.
Walden, 18, Conclusion

22 Rather than love, than money, than fame, give me truth.   *Walden, 18, Conclusion*

23 Only that day dawns to which we are awake. There is more day to dawn. The sun is but a morning star.
Walden, 18, Conclusion

24 I hear many condemn these men because they were so few. When were the good and the brave ever in a majority?
A Plea for Captain John Brown [1859]

25 I speak for the slave when I say that I prefer the philanthropy of Captain Brown to that philanthropy which neither shoots me nor liberates me.
A Plea for Captain John Brown

26 So we defend ourselves and our henroosts, and maintain slavery.
A Plea for Captain John Brown

27 He is not Old Brown any longer; he is an angel of light.
A Plea for Captain John Brown

28 Eastward I go only by force; but westward I go free.   *Walking [1862]*

29 In wildness is the preservation of the world.[2]
Walking

30 I believe in the forest, and in the meadow, and in the night in which the corn grows.   *Walking*

31 Life consists with wildness. The most alive is the wildest. Not yet subdued to man, its presence refreshes him.   *Walking*

32 Men will lie on their backs, talking about the fall of man, and never make an effort to get up.
Life Without Principle [1863]

---

[1]Who splits his own wood warms himself twice. — *Saying*

[2]Motto of the Wilderness Society.
See John Muir, 533:6.

1   A man may stand there [Cape Cod] and put all America behind him.   *Cape Cod [1865], ch. 10*

2   [When asked about life after death:] One world at a time.   *Said a few days before his death*

Alexander II
1818–1881

3   Better to abolish serfdom from above than to wait till it begins to abolish itself from below.
          Speech in Moscow [March 30, 1856]

Cecil Frances Alexander
1818–1895

4 All things bright and beautiful,
All creatures great and small,
All things wise and wonderful,
The Lord God made them all.
          All Things Bright and Beautiful [1848], st. 1

5 Once in royal David's city
Stood a lowly cattle shed,
Where a mother laid her baby
In a manger for his bed:
Mary was that mother mild,
Jesus Christ her little child.
          Once in Royal David's City[1] [1848], st. 1

Josh Billings [Henry Wheeler Shaw]
1818–1885

6   Love iz like the meazles; we kant have it bad but onst, and the later in life we have it the tuffer it goes with us.
          Josh Billings: His Sayings [1865]. Affurisms

7   Poverty iz the stepmother ov genius.
          Josh Billings: His Sayings. Affurisms

8 The wheel that squeaks the loudest
Is the one that gets the grease.   *The Kicker*

9   It is better to know nothing than to know what ain't so.[2]   *Proverb [1874]*

Emily Brontë
1818–1848

10 Sleep not, dream not; this bright day
Will not, cannot last for aye;

---

[1] Music by HENRY J. GAUNTLETT [1805–1876].

[2] Better know nothing than half-know many things — FRIEDRICH NIETZSCHE, *Thus Spake Zarathustra*, pt. IV, ch. 64

Bliss like thine is bought by years
Dark with torment and with tears.
          Sleep Not [1846], st. 1

11 Cold in the earth — and fifteen wild Decembers
From those brown hills have melted into spring.
          Remembrance [1846], st. 3

12 Once drinking deep of that divinest anguish,
How could I seek the empty world again?
          Remembrance, st. 8

13 Yes, as my swift days near their goal,
'Tis all that I implore:
In life and death a chainless soul,
With courage to endure.
          The Old Stoic [1846], st. 3

14 No coward soul is mine,
No trembler in the world's storm-troubled sphere:
I see Heaven's glories shine,
And faith shines equal, arming me from fear.
          Last Lines [1846], st. 1

15 There is not room for Death.   *Last Lines, st. 7*

16 So hopeless is the world without,
The world within I doubly prize;
Thy world, where guile and hate and doubt
And cold suspicion never rise;
Where thou and I and Liberty
Have undisputed sovereignty.
          To Imagination [1846], st. 2

17   [Said by Catherine:] I *am* Heathcliff.
          Wuthering Heights [1847], ch. 9

18   I lingered round them, under that benign sky: watched the moths fluttering among the heath and harebells; listened to the soft wind breathing through the grass; and wondered how anyone could ever imagine unquiet slumbers for the sleepers in that quiet earth.   *Wuthering Heights, last words*

Frederick Douglass
c. 1818–1895

19   Every tone [of the songs of the slaves] was a testimony against slavery, and a prayer to God for deliverance from chains.
          Narrative of the Life of Frederick Douglass [1845], ch. 2

20   You have seen how a man was made a slave; you shall see how a slave was made a man.
          Narrative of the Life of Frederick Douglass, 10

21   What, to the American slave, is your Fourth of July? I answer: A day that reveals to him, more than all other days in the year, the gross injustice and

cruelty to which he is the constant victim. To him your celebration is a sham.
Speech at Rochester, New York
[July 4, 1852]

1   You profess to believe that "of one blood God made all nations of men to dwell on the face of all the earth" — and hath commanded all men, everywhere, to love one another — yet you notoriously hate (and glory in your hatred!) all men whose skins are not colored like your own!
Speech at Rochester, New York
[July 4, 1852]

2   The ground which a colored man occupies in this country is, every inch of it, sternly disputed.
Speech at the American and Foreign
Anti-Slavery Society annual meeting,
New York City [May 1853]

3   The whole history of the progress of human liberty shows that all concessions yet made to her august claims have been born of earnest struggle.... If there is no struggle, there is no progress. Those who profess to favor freedom, and yet deprecate agitation, are men who want crops without plowing up the ground, they want rain without thunder and lightning. They want the ocean without the awful roar of its many waters.
Speech at Canandaigua, New York
[August 3, 1857]

4   The destiny of the colored American ... is the destiny of America.
Speech at the Emancipation League,
Boston [February 12, 1862]

5   The relation subsisting between the white and colored people of this country is the great, paramount, imperative, and all-commanding question for this age and nation to solve.
Speech at the Church of the Puritans,
New York City [May 1863]

6   Despite of it all, the Negro remains ... cool, strong, imperturbable, and cheerful.
Speech on the twenty-first anniversary of
Emancipation in the District of Columbia,
Washington, D.C. [April 1883]

7   In all the relations of life and death, we are met by the color line.
Speech at the Convention of Colored Men,
Louisville, Kentucky [September 24, 1883]

8   No man can put a chain about the ankle of his fellow man without at last finding the other end fastened about his own neck.
Speech at Civil Rights Mass Meeting,
Washington, D.C. [October 22, 1883]

9   Where justice is denied, where poverty is enforced, where ignorance prevails, and where any one class is made to feel that society is in an organized conspiracy to oppress, rob, and degrade them, neither persons nor property will be safe.
Speech on the twenty-fourth anniversary of
Emancipation in the District of Columbia,
Washington, D.C. [April 1886]

10   We Negroes love our country. We fought for it. We ask only that we be treated as well as those who fought against it.
Speech at the World's Columbian Exposition
[August 25, 1892]

George Duffield
1818–1888

11 Stand up! — stand up for Jesus!   *Hymn [1858]*

Karl Marx
1818–1883

12   Religion ... is the opium of the people.
Critique of the Hegelian Philosophy of
Right [1844], introduction

13   The philosophers have only interpreted the world in various ways. The point is to *change* it.[1]
Theses on Feuerbach [1845], no. 11

14   Hegel remarks somewhere[2] that all great world-historic facts and personages appear, so to speak, twice. He forgot to add: the first time as tragedy, the second time as farce.
The Eighteenth Brumaire of Louis Napoleon[3]
[1852], pt. 1

15   Men make their own history, but they do not make it just as they please; they do not make it under circumstances chosen by themselves, but under circumstances directly encountered, given and transmitted from the past. The tradition of all the dead generations weighs like a nightmare on the brain of the living.
The Eighteenth Brumaire of Louis
Bonaparte, 1

16   What was new in what I did was: (1) to demonstrate that the *existence of classes* is tied only to *definite*

---

[1] Inscribed on Marx's tomb in Highgate Cemetery, London. Translated by LOYD D. EASTON and KURT H. GUDDAT.

[2] Napoleon was twice defeated, and the Bourbons twice expelled. By repetition that which at first appeared merely a matter of chance and contingency, becomes a real and ratified existence. — G. W. F. HEGEL, *Lectures on the Philosophy of History* [1837], *pt. III, sec. 2*

[3] Translated by SAUL K. PADOVER.

historical phases of development of production; (2) that the class struggle necessarily leads to the *dictatorship of the proletariat;* (3) that this dictatorship is only a transition to the *dissolution of all classes* and leads to the formation of a *classless society.*

> *Letter to Joseph Weydemeyer*[1]
> *[March 5, 1852]*

1   There is only one antidote to mental suffering, and that is physical pain.   *Herr Vogt [1860]*

2   Nothing can have value without being an object of utility. If it be useless, the labor contained in it is useless, cannot be reckoned as labor, and cannot therefore create value.

> *Capital*[1] *[1867–1883], pt. II, ch. 3*

3   The intellectual desolation, artificially produced by converting immature human beings into mere machines.   *Capital, II, 10*

4   When commercial capital occupies a position of unquestioned ascendancy, it everywhere constitutes a system of plunder.   *Capital, II, 21*

5   From each according to his abilities, to each according to his needs.[2]

> *Critique of the Gotha Program [1875]*

6   All I know is that I am not a Marxist.[3]

> *Quoted in* Friedrich Engels, *Letter to Conrad Schmidt [August 3, 1890]*

Karl Marx
1818–1883
and
Friedrich Engels
1820–1895

7   A specter is haunting Europe — the specter of Communism. All the powers of old Europe have entered into a holy alliance to exorcise this specter: Pope and Czar, Metternich and Guizot, French Radicals and German police spies.

> *The Communist Manifesto*[4] *[1848], opening lines*

8   The history of all hitherto existing society is the history of class struggles. Freeman and slave, patrician and plebeian, lord and serf, guild master and journeyman, in a word, oppressor and oppressed, stood in constant opposition to each other, carried on an uninterrupted, now hidden, now open fight, a fight that each time ended, either in a revolutionary reconstitution of society at large, or in the common ruin of the contending classes.

> *The Communist Manifesto, sec. 1*

9   The executive of the modern state is but a committee for managing the common affairs of the whole bourgeoisie.[5] The bourgeoisie has, historically, played a most revolutionary role.

> *The Communist Manifesto, 1*

10   The bourgeoisie, by the rapid improvement of all instruments of production, by the immensely facilitated means of communication, draws all, even the most barbarian, nations into civilization.

> *The Communist Manifesto, 1*

11   Of all the classes that stand face to face with the bourgeoisie today, the proletariat alone is a really revolutionary class. The other classes decay and finally disappear in the race of modern industry; the proletariat is its special and essential product.[6]

> *The Communist Manifesto, 1*

12   In this sense, the theory of the Communists may be summed up in the single sentence: Abolition of private property.

> *The Communist Manifesto, 2*

13   In proportion as the antagonism between classes within the nation vanishes, the hostility of one nation to another will come to an end.

> *The Communist Manifesto, 2*

14   The ruling ideas of each age have ever been the ideas of its ruling class.

> *The Communist Manifesto, 2*

15   The communists disdain to conceal their views and aims. They openly declare that their ends can be

---

[1]Abridged edition prepared by Julian Borchardt, translated by Stephen L. Trask.

[2]This phrase is in quotation marks, and it is believed that Marx is quoting or paraphrasing either Louis Blanc [1811–1882] or Morelly [fl. 1773]:

> Let each produce according to his aptitudes and his force; let each consume according to his need. — Louis Blanc, *Organisation du Travail* [1840]

> Nothing in society will belong to anyone, either as a personal possession or as capital goods, except the things for which the person has immediate use, for either his needs, his pleasures, or his daily work. Every citizen will make his particular contribution to the activities of the community according to his capacity, his talent and his age; it is on this basis that his duties will be determined, in conformity with the distributive laws. — Morelly, *Le Code de la Nature* [1755]

> See Mikhail Bakunin, 469:14.

[3]Translated by Donna Torr.

[4]Translated by Samuel Moore.

[5]By bourgeoisie is meant the class of modern capitalists, owners of the means of social production and employers of wage labor. — Engels, *notes to The Communist Manifesto* [1888 edition]

[6]By proletariat [is meant] the class of modern wage laborers who, having no means of production of their own, are reduced to selling their labor power in order to live. — Engels, *notes to The Communist Manifesto* [1888 edition]

obtained only by forcible overthrow of all existing social conditions. Let the ruling classes tremble at a communist revolution. The proletarians have nothing to lose but their chains. They have a world to win. Working men of all countries, unite![1]

The Communist Manifesto, 4

John Mason Neale
1818–1866

1 Good King Wenceslas looked out
On the feast of Stephen,
When the snow lay round about,
Deep and crisp and even.

Good King Wenceslas, st. 1

2 Jerusalem the golden, with milk and honey blest,
Beneath thy contemplation sink heart and voice
oppressed.

Hymn from the Latin of SAINT BERNARD OF CLUNY, *De Contemptu Mundi, pt. V, Urbs Syon Aurea [c. 1145; translated 1858], st. 1*

3 O come, O come, Emmanuel,
And ransom captive Israel.

Hymn from the Latin, Veni, Veni, Emmanuel [twelfth century; translated 1861], st. 1

Francis Edward Smedley
1818–1864

4 All's fair in love and war.[2]

Frank Fairlegh [1850], ch. 50

Ivan Sergeyevich Turgenev
1818–1883

5 A nihilist is a man who does not bow to any authorities, who does not take any principle on trust, no matter with what respect that principle is surrounded.

Fathers and Sons[3] *[1862], ch. 5*

6 That vague, crepuscular time, the time of regrets that resemble hopes, of hopes that resemble regrets, when youth has passed, but old age has not yet arrived.

Fathers and Sons, 7

7 The courage not to believe in anything.

Fathers and Sons, 14

8 In days of doubt, in days of sad brooding on my country's fate, thou alone art my rod and my staff— mighty, true, free Russian speech! But for thee, how not to fall into despair, seeing all that happens at home? Yet who can think that such a tongue is not given to a great people?

Senilia [1882]

Arthur Hugh Clough
1819–1861

9 Grace is given of God, but knowledge is bought in the market.

The Bothie of Tober-na-Vuolich [1848], pt. IV

10 A world where nothing is had for nothing.

The Bothie of Tober-na-Vuolich, VIII

11 And almost everyone when age,
Disease, or sorrows strike him,
Inclines to think there is a God,
Or something very like Him.

Dipsychus [1862], pt. I, sc. v

12 Say not the struggle nought availeth,
The labour and the wounds are vain,
The enemy faints not, nor faileth,
And as things have been, things remain.

If hopes were dupes, fears may be liars;
It may be, in yon smoke concealed,
Your comrades chase e'en now the fliers,
And, but for you, possess the field.

For while the tired waves, vainly breaking,
Seem here no painful inch to gain,
Far back through creeks and inlets making
Came, silent, flooding in, the main,

And not by eastern windows only,
When daylight comes, comes in the light,
In front the sun climbs slow, how slowly,
But westward, look, the land is bright.

Say Not the Struggle Nought Availeth [1862]

13 No graven images may be
Worshipped, except the currency.

The Latest Decalogue [1862], l. 3

14 Thou shalt not covet, but tradition
Approves all forms of competition.

The Latest Decalogue, l. 19

Gustave Courbet
1819–1877

15 It is hard to please everyone. It is impossible to tell you all the insults my painting of this year has won

---

[1]More familiar as: Workers of the world, unite!

[2]All policy's allowed in war and love. — SUSANNAH CENTLIVRE [c. 1667–1723], *Love at a Venture* [1706], *act I*

[3]Translated by HARRY STEVENS.

me, but I don't care, for when I am no longer controversial I will no longer be important.[1]

Letter to his family [June 15, 1852]

George Eliot
[Marian Evans Cross]
1819–1880

1   Worldly faces never look so worldly as at a funeral.

Scenes of Clerical Life [1858], bk. 3, ch. 25

2   These fellow mortals, every one, must be accepted
as they are.   *Adam Bede [1859], ch. 17*

3   There's no real making amends in this world, any
more nor you can mend a wrong subtraction by
doing your addition right.   *Adam Bede, 18*

4   It's but little good you'll do a-watering the last
year's crops.   *Adam Bede, 18*

5   A patronizing disposition always has its meaner
side.   *Adam Bede, 27*

6   It's them that take advantage that get advantage i'
this world.   *Adam Bede, 32*

7   Deep, unspeakable suffering may well be called a
baptism, a regeneration, the initiation into a new
state.   *Adam Bede, 42*

8   We hand folks over to God's mercy, and show
none ourselves.   *Adam Bede, 42*

9   The law's made to take care o' raskills.

The Mill on the Floss [1860], bk. III, ch. 4

10   There is no hopelessness so sad as that of early
youth, when the soul is made up of wants, and has
no long memories, no superadded life in the life of
others.   *The Mill on the Floss, III, 5*

11   I've never any pity for conceited people, because I
think they carry their comfort about with them.[2]

The Mill on the Floss, V, 4

12   The happiest women, like the happiest nations,
have no history.   *The Mill on the Floss, VI, 3*

13   Nothing is so good as it seems beforehand.

Silas Marner [1861], ch. 18

14   In our springtime every day has its hidden growths
in the mind, as it has in the earth when the little
folded blades are getting ready to pierce the ground.

Felix Holt, the Radical [1866], ch. 18

15   One way of getting an idea of our fellow-country-
men's miseries is to go and look at their pleasures.

Felix Holt, the Radical, 28

16   O may I join the choir invisible
Of those immortal dead who live again
In minds made better by their presence.

O May I Join the Choir Invisible [1867]

17   Prophecy is the most gratuitous form of error.

Middlemarch [1871–1872], ch. 10

18   If we had a keen vision of all that is ordinary in
human life, it would be like hearing the grass grow
or the squirrel's heart beat, and we should die of that
roar which is the other side of silence.

Middlemarch, 22

19   If youth is the season of hope, it is often so only in
the sense that our elders are hopeful about us.

Middlemarch, 55

20   People glorify all sorts of bravery except the
bravery they might show on behalf of their nearest
neighbors.

Middlemarch, 72

21   There is no creature whose inward being is so
strong that it is not greatly determined by what lies
outside it.

Middlemarch, finale

22   The growing good of the world is partly dependent on unhistoric acts; and that things are not so ill
with you and me as they might have been, is half
owing to the number who lived faithfully a hidden
life, and rest in unvisited tombs.

Middlemarch, finale

23   'Tis God gives skill,
But not without men's hands: He could not make
Antonio Stradivari's violins
Without Antonio.

Stradivarius [1873]

24   Hostesses who entertain much must make up
their parties as ministers make up their cabinets, on
grounds other than personal liking.

Daniel Deronda [1876], bk. I, ch. 5

25   A difference of taste in jokes is a great strain on the
affections.

Daniel Deronda, II, 15

Thomas Dunn English
1819–1902

26 Oh! don't you remember sweet Alice, Ben Bolt?
Sweet Alice, whose hair was so brown.

Ben Bolt [1843]

---

[1]Translated by PETRA TEN-DOESSCHATE CHU.

[2]There is not enough of love and goodness in the world to throw
any of it away on conceited people. — FRIEDRICH NIETZSCHE,
Human, All Too Human, sec. 129

Julia Ward Howe
1819–1910

1 Mine eyes have seen the glory of the coming of the
  Lord;
  He is trampling out the vintage where the grapes of
  wrath are stored;
  He hath loosed the fateful lightning of His terrible,
  swift sword;
  His truth is marching on.
  Battle Hymn of the Republic [1862], st. 1

2 In the beauty of the lilies Christ was born across
  the sea,
  With a glory in His bosom that transfigures you
  and me;
  As He died to make men holy, let us die to make
  men free. *Battle Hymn of the Republic, st. 5*

Charles Kingsley
1819–1875

3 Give me the political economist, the sanitary
reformer, the engineer; and take your saints and virgins, relics and miracles. The spinning-jenny and the
railroad, Cunard's liners and the electric telegraph, are
to me ... signs that we are, on some points at least, in
harmony with the universe. *Yeast [1848], ch. 5*

4 Oh Mary, go and call the cattle home ...
  Across the sands of Dee.
  The Sands of Dee [1849], st. 1

5 For men must work, and women must weep,
  And there's little to earn and many to keep,
  Though the harbor bar be moaning.
  The Three Fishers [1851], st. 1

6 And the sooner it's over, the sooner to sleep;
  And good-bye to the bar and its moaning.
  The Three Fishers, st. 3

7 When all the world is young, lad,
  And all the trees are green;
  And every goose a swan, lad,
  And every lass a queen;
  Then hey for boot and horse, lad,
  And round the world away:
  Young blood must have its course, lad,
  And every dog his day.
  Water Babies [1863]. Song II, st. 1

James Russell Lowell
1819–1891

8 Blessed are the horny hands of toil!
  A Glance Behind the Curtain [1843]

9 They are slaves who fear to speak
  For the fallen and the weak.
  Stanzas on Freedom [1843], st. 4

10 They are slaves who dare not be
  In the right with two or three.
  Stanzas on Freedom, st. 4

11 The nurse of full-grown souls is solitude.
  Columbus [1844]

12 Once to every man and nation comes the moment to
  decide,
  In the strife of Truth with Falsehood, for the good or
  evil side.
  The Present Crisis [1844], st. 5

13 Truth forever on the scaffold, Wrong forever on the
  throne —
  Yet that scaffold sways the future, and, behind the
  dim unknown,
  Standeth God within the shadow, keeping watch
  above his own. *The Present Crisis, st. 8*

14 Not only around our infancy
  Doth heaven with all its splendors lie;
  Daily, with souls that cringe and plot,
  We Sinais climb and know it not.
  *The Vision of Sir Launfal [1848],
  prelude to pt. I, st. 2*

15 For a cap and bells our lives we pay,
  Bubbles we buy with a whole soul's tasking;
  'Tis heaven alone that is given away,
  'Tis only God may be had for the asking.
  The Vision of Sir Launfal, st. 4

16 And what is so rare as a day in June?
  Then, if ever, come perfect days.
  The Vision of Sir Launfal, st. 5

17 In creating, the only hard thing's to begin;
  A grass-blade's no easier to make than an oak.
  A Fable for Critics [1848]

18 And I honor the man who is willing to sink
  Half his present repute for the freedom to think,
  And, when he has thought, be his cause strong or
  weak,
  Will risk t' other half for the freedom to speak.
  A Fable for Critics

19 There comes Poe, with his raven, like Barnaby
  Rudge,
  Three fifths of him genius and two fifths sheer
  fudge. *A Fable for Critics*

20 Nature fits all her children with something to do,
  He who would write and can't write, can surely
  review. *A Fable for Critics*

21 Ez fer war, I call it murder —
  There you hev it plain an' flat;

I don't want to go no furder
Than my Testament fer that.
> *The Biglow Papers. Series I [1848], no. 1, st. 5*

1   You've gut to git up airly
Ef you want to take in God.
> *The Biglow Papers. I, 1, st. 5*

2 I *don't* believe in princerple,
But oh I *du* in interest.
> *The Biglow Papers. I, 6, st. 9*

3 My gran'ther's rule was safer 'n 'tis to crow:
Don't never prophesy — onless ye know.
> *The Biglow Papers. Series II [1866], no. 2*

4 It's 'most enough to make a deacon swear.
> *The Biglow Papers. II, 2*

5 Ef you want peace, the thing you've gut tu du
Is jes' to show you're up to fightin', tu.
> *The Biglow Papers. II, 2*

6 No, never say nothin' without you're compelled tu,
An' then don't say nothin' thet you can be held tu.
> *The Biglow Papers. II, 5*

7 When I was a beggarly boy,
And lived in a cellar damp,
I had not a friend nor a toy,
But I had Aladdin's lamp.   *Aladdin [1868], st. 1*

8   There is no good in arguing with the inevitable.
The only argument available with an east wind is to
put on your overcoat.
> *Democracy [October 6, 1884]*

9   Things always seem fairer when we look back at
them, and it is out of that inaccessible tower of the
past that Longing leans and beckons.
> *Literary Essays, vol. I [1864–1890].*
> *A Few Bits of Roman Mosaic*

10   It was in making education not only common to
all, but in some sense compulsory on all, that the destiny of the free republics of America was practically
settled.
> *Literary Essays, vol. II [1870–1890].*
> *New England Two Centuries Ago*

11   Every man feels instinctively that all the beautiful
sentiments in the world weigh less than a single lovely
action.
> *Literary Essays, II. New England Two*
> *Centuries Ago*

Herman Melville
1819–1891

12   When the inhabitants of some sequestered island
first descry the "big canoe" of the European rolling
through the blue waters towards their shores, they
rush down to the beach in crowds, and with open
arms stand ready to embrace the strangers. Fatal
embrace! They fold to their bosoms the viper whose
sting is destined to poison all their joys.
> *Typee [1846], ch. 4*

13   You cannot spill a drop of American blood without
spilling the blood of the whole world. . . . We are not a
nation, so much as a world.
> *Redburn [1849], ch. 33*

14   Genius all over the world stands hand in hand,
and one shock of recognition runs the whole circle
round.   *Hawthorne and His Mosses [1850]*

15   And we Americans are the peculiar, chosen
people — the Israel of our time; we bear the ark of the
liberties of the world.
> *White-Jacket [1850], ch. 36*

16   Are there no Moravians in the Moon, that not a
missionary has yet visited this poor pagan planet of
ours, to civilize civilization and christianize Christendom?
> *White Jacket, 64*

17   The grand truth about Nathaniel Hawthorne. He
says NO! in thunder; but the Devil himself cannot
make him say *yes*.
> *Letter to Nathaniel Hawthorne*
> *[April 16, 1851]*

18   Call me Ishmael.   *Moby-Dick [1851], ch. 1*

19   Let the most absent-minded of men be plunged in
his deepest reveries — stand that man upon his legs,
set his feet a-going, and he will infallibly lead you
to water, if water there be in all that region. . . . Meditation and water are wedded forever.
> *Moby-Dick, 1*

20   There floated into my inmost soul, endless processions of the whale, and, mid most of them all, one
grand hooded phantom, like a snow hill in the air.
> *Moby-Dick, 1*

21   Better sleep with a sober cannibal than a drunken
Christian.   *Moby-Dick, 3*

22   Woe to him who seeks to pour oil upon the waters
when God has brewed them into a gale! Woe to him
who seeks to please rather than to appall!
> *Moby-Dick, 9*

23   A whale-ship was my Yale College and my
Harvard.   *Moby-Dick, 24*

24   Thou great democratic God! . . . who didst pick up
Andrew Jackson from the pebbles; who didst hurl
him upon a war-horse; who didst thunder him higher
than a throne!
> *Moby-Dick, 26*

1 And this is what ye have shipped for, men! to chase that white whale on both sides of land, and over all sides of earth, till he spouts black blood and rolls fin out. *Moby-Dick, 36*

2 All visible objects, man, are but as pasteboard masks . . . strike, strike through the mask! *Moby-Dick, 36*

3 All that most maddens and torments; all that stirs up the lees of things; all truth with malice in it; all that cracks the sinews and cakes the brain; all the subtle demonisms of life and thought; all evil, to crazy Ahab, were visibly personified, and made practically assailable in Moby Dick. He piled upon the whale's white hump the sum of all the general rage and hate felt by his whole race from Adam down; and then, as if his chest had been a mortar, he burst his hot heart's shell upon it. *Moby-Dick, 41*

4 Though in many of its aspects this visible world seems formed in love, the invisible spheres were formed in fright. *Moby-Dick, 42*

5 For as this appalling ocean surrounds the verdant land, so in the soul of man there lies one insular Tahiti, full of peace and joy, but encompassed by all the horrors of the half known life. *Moby-Dick, 58*

6 There are some enterprises in which a careful disorderliness is the true method. *Moby-Dick, 82*

7 To produce a mighty book, you must choose a mighty theme. No great and enduring volume can ever be written on the flea, though many there be who have tried it. *Moby-Dick, 104*

8 By heaven, man, we are turned round and round in this world, like yonder windlass, and Fate is the handspike. *Moby-Dick, 132*

9 All collapsed, and the great shroud of the sea rolled on as it rolled five thousand years ago. *Moby-Dick, 135*

10 Dollars damn me. *Letter to Nathaniel Hawthorne [June 1851]*

11 What we take to be our strongest tower of delight, only stands at the caprice of the minutest event — the falling of a leaf, the hearing of a voice, or the receipt of one little bit of paper scratched over with a few small characters by a sharpened feather. *Pierre [1852], bk. IV*

12 One trembles to think of that mysterious thing in the soul, which seems to acknowledge no human jurisdiction, but in spite of the individual's own innocent self, will still dream horrid dreams, and mutter unmentionable thoughts. *Pierre, IV*

13 A smile is the chosen vehicle for all ambiguities. *Pierre, IV*

14 Of all the preposterous assumptions of humanity over humanity, nothing exceeds most of the criticisms made on the habits of the poor by the well-housed, well-warmed, and well-fed. *Poor Man's Pudding and Rich Man's Crumbs [1854]*

15 I would prefer not to. *Bartleby the Scrivener [1856]*

16 A man with some evil design, would he not be likely to speak well of that stupidity which was blind to his depravity, and malign that intelligence from which it might not be hidden? *The Piazza Tales [1856]. Benito Cereno*

17 No voice, no low, no howl is heard; the chief sound of life here is a hiss. *The Piazza Tales. The Encantadas, or Enchanted Isles*

18 The poor old Past,
The Future's slave. *Battle-Pieces and Aspects of the War [1866]. The Conflict of Convictions, st. 6*

19 All wars are boyish, and are fought by boys. *Battle-Pieces. The March into Virginia*

20 What troops
Of generous boys in happiness thus bred —
Saturnians through life's Tempe led,
Went from the North and came from the South,
With golden mottoes in the mouth,
To lie down midway on a bloody bed. *Battle-Pieces. On the Slain Collegians, st. 2*

21 Foemen at morn, but friends at eve —
Fame or country least their care:
(What like a bullet can undeceive!) *Battle-Pieces. Shiloh, l. 14*

22 All civil charms
And priestly spells which late held hearts in awe —
Fear-bound, subjected to a better sway
Than sway of self; these like a dream dissolve,
And man rebounds whole aeons back in nature. *Battle-Pieces. The House-top, l. 12*

23 If Luther's day expand to Darwin's year,
Shall that exclude the hope — foreclose the fear? *Clarel [1876]. Epilogue*

24 Dies, all dies!
The grass it dies, but in vernal rain
Up it springs and it lives again;
Over and over, again and again
It lives, it dies and it lives again. *Pontoosuce [1924], l. 71*

1 Ah, why should tears the pale cheek fret
For aught that waneth here below.
Let go, let go! *Pontoosuce, l. 88*

2 An uncommon prudence is habitual with the subtler depravity, for it has everything to hide.
Billy Budd [1924], ch. 13

3 God bless Captain Vere! *Billy Budd, 25*

4 But me they'll lash in hammock, drop me deep.
Fathoms down, fathoms down, how I'll dream fast
asleep.
I feel it stealing now. Sentry, are you there?
Just ease these darbies [manacles] at the wrist,
And roll me over fair!
I am sleepy, and the oozy weeds about me twist.
Billy Budd, 25

John Ruskin
1819–1900

5 He is the greatest artist who has embodied, in the sum of his works, the greatest number of the greatest ideas.
Modern Painters, vol. I [1843], pt. I, ch. 2

6 To know anything well involves a profound sensation of ignorance. *Modern Painters, I, I, 3*

7 The foam is not cruel.[1] ... The state of mind which attributes to it these characters of a living creature is one in which the reason is unhinged by grief. All violent feelings ... produce in us a falseness in all our impressions of external things, which I would generally characterize as the "Pathetic Fallacy."
Modern Painters, III [1856], IV, 12

8 The essence of lying is in deception, not in words. *Modern Painters, V [1860], IX, 7*

9 Remember that the most beautiful things in the world are the most useless; peacocks and lilies for instance.
The Stones of Venice [1851–1853], vol. I, ch. 2

10 All great art is the work of the whole living creature, body and soul, and chiefly of the soul.
The Stones of Venice, I, 4

11 Blue color is everlastingly appointed by the Deity to be a source of delight.
Lectures on Architecture and Painting [1853], no. I

12 There is no wealth but life.
Unto This Last [1862], sec. 77

13 Let us reform our schools, and we shall find little reform needed in our prisons.
Unto This Last, essay 2

14 There is no law of history any more than of a kaleidoscope.
Letter to James Anthony Froude [February 1864]

15 Life being very short, and the quiet hours of it few, we ought to waste none of them in reading valueless books.
Sesame and Lilies [1865], preface

16 All books are divisible into two classes: the books of the hour, and the books of all time.
Sesame and Lilies. Of Kings' Treasuries, sec. 8

17 Borrowers are nearly always ill-spenders, and it is with lent money that all evil is mainly done and all unjust war protracted.
The Crown of Wild Olive [1866], lecture 1

18 Give a little love to a child, and you get a great deal back. *The Crown of Wild Olive, 1*

19 Taste ... is the *only* morality. ... Tell me what you like, and I'll tell you what you are.
The Crown of Wild Olive, 2

20 Life without industry is guilt, industry without art is brutality.
Lectures on Art [1870]. III, The Relation of Art to Morals

21 Every increased possession loads us with a new weariness. *The Eagle's Nest [1872], ch. 5*

22 Architecture ... the adaptation of form to resist force. *Val d'Arno [1874], ch. 6*

23 The first duty of government is to see that people have food, fuel, and clothes. The second, that they have means of moral and intellectual education.
Fors Clavigera [1876], letter 67

24 Great nations write their autobiographies in three manuscripts — the book of their deeds, the book of their words, and the book of their art.
St. Mark's Rest [1877], preface

Max Schneckenburger
1819–1849

25 Dear Fatherland, no danger thine:
Firm stands thy watch along the Rhine.[2]
The Watch on the Rhine (Die Wacht am Rhein) [1840], chorus

---

[1] The cruel crawling foam. — CHARLES KINGSLEY, *The Sands of Dee, st. 4*

[2] Lieb Vaterland, magst ruhig sein, / Fest steht und treu die Wacht am Rhein.

Victoria
1819–1901

1 I will be good.
> *On first seeing a chart of the line of*
> *succession to the throne [March 11, 1830]*

2 *Great* events make me quiet and calm; it is only trifles that irritate my nerves.
> *Letter to King Leopold of Belgium*
> *[April 4, 1848]*

3 I don't dislike babies, though I think very young ones rather disgusting.
> *Letter to her daughter Victoria (Vicky)*
> *[May 8, 1872]*

4 We are not interested in the possibilities of defeat.
> *To A. J. Balfour [December 1899]*

5 We are not amused.
> *Attributed. Upon seeing an imitation of*
> *herself by Alexander Grantham Yorke,*
> *groom-in-waiting to the Queen [January 2,*
> *1900]. From* CAROLINE HOLLAND,
> *Notebooks of a Spinster Lady [1919]*

6 He [William Gladstone] speaks to me as if I was a public meeting.
> *From* GEORGE W. E. RUSSELL *[1853–1919],*
> *Collections and Recollections [1898], ch. 14*

William Ross Wallace
1819–1881

7 The hand that rocks the cradle
Is the hand that rules the world.
> *The Hand That Rules the World, st. 1*

Walt Whitman
1819–1892

8 The United States themselves are essentially the greatest poem.
> *Preface to the first edition of Leaves of*
> *Grass[1] [1855]*

9 All beauty comes from beautiful blood and a beautiful brain.
> *Preface to the first edition of Leaves of Grass*

10 This is what you shall do: Love the earth and sun and the animals, despise riches, give alms to every one that asks, stand up for the stupid and crazy, devote your income and labor to others, hate tyrants, argue not concerning God.
> *Preface to the first edition of Leaves of Grass*

11 The proof of a poet is that his country absorbs him as affectionately as he has absorbed it.
> *Preface to the first edition of Leaves of Grass*

12 One's-Self I sing, a simple separate person,
Yet utter the word Democratic, the word En-Masse.
> *One's-Self I Sing*

13 O to be self-balanced for contingencies,
To confront night, storms, hunger, ridicule,
accidents, rebuffs, as the trees and animals do.
> *Me Imperturbe*

14 I hear America singing, the varied carols I hear.
> *I Hear America Singing*

15 I celebrate myself, and sing myself,
And what I assume you shall assume,
For every atom belonging to me as good belongs to you.

I loafe and invite my soul,
I lean and loafe at my ease observing a spear of
summer grass.   *Song of Myself, pt. 1*

16 Stop this day and night with me and you shall possess
the origin of all poems.   *Song of Myself, 2*

17 Swiftly arose and spread around me the peace and
knowledge that pass all the argument of the
earth,
And I know that the hand of God is the promise of
my own,
And I know that the spirit of God is the brother of my
own,
And that all the men ever born are also my brothers,
and the women my sisters and lovers,
And that a kelson of the creation is love.
> *Song of Myself, 5*

18 A child said *What is the grass?* fetching it to me with
full hands;
How could I answer the child? I do not know what it
is any more than he.

I guess it must be the flag of my disposition, out of
hopeful green stuff woven.   *Song of Myself, 6*

19 And now it seems to me the beautiful uncut hair of
graves.   *Song of Myself, 6*

20 Has any one supposed it lucky to be born?
I hasten to inform him or her it is just as lucky to die,
and I know it.   *Song of Myself, 7*

21 And the look of the bay mare shames silliness out
of me.   *Song of Myself, 13*

---

[1]The first edition of *Leaves of Grass,* published anonymously by its author in July 1855, contained a long preface and twelve untitled poems. Over the next four decades Whitman revised and enlarged his book. The texts and sequence of the verse quotations here are those of the so-called Deathbed Edition [Philadelphia, 1891–1892].

1 This is the grass that grows wherever the land is and
   the water is,
This is the common air that bathes the globe.
Song of Myself, 17

2 Have you heard that it was good to gain the day?
I also say it is good to fall, battles are lost in the same
   spirit in which they are won.
Song of Myself, 18

3 I find no sweeter fat than sticks to my own bones.
Song of Myself, 20

4 My foothold is tenon'd and mortis'd in granite,
I laugh at what you call dissolution,
And I know the amplitude of time.
Song of Myself, 20

5 I am the poet of the Body and I am the poet of the
   Soul.
Song of Myself, 21

6 I am he that walks with the tender and growing night,
I call to the earth and sea half-held by the night.

Press close bare-bosom'd night — press close
   magnetic nourishing night!
Night of south winds — night of the large few stars!
Still nodding night — mad naked summer night.
Song of Myself, 21

7 Walt Whitman, a kosmos, of Manhattan the son,
Turbulent, fleshy, sensual, eating, drinking and
   breeding,
No sentimentalist, no stander above men and women
   or apart from them,
No more modest than immodest.

Unscrew the locks from the doors!
Unscrew the doors themselves from their jambs!
Song of Myself, 24

8 The scent of these arm-pits aroma finer than prayer,
This head more than churches, bibles, and all the
   creeds.
Song of Myself, 24

9 I dote on myself, there is that lot of me and all so
   luscious.
Song of Myself, 24

10 Steep'd amid honey'd morphine, my windpipe
   throttled in fakes of death.
Song of Myself, 26

11 I merely stir, press, feel with my fingers, and am happy,
To touch my person to someone else's is about as
   much as I can stand.
Song of Myself, 27

12 Logic and sermons never convince,
The damp of the night drives deeper into my soul.
Song of Myself, 30

13 I believe a leaf of grass is no less than the journey-
   work of the stars.
Song of Myself, 31

14 I think I could turn and live with animals, they are so
   placid and self-contain'd,

I stand and look at them long and long.

They do not sweat and whine about their condition,
They do not lie awake in the dark and weep for their
   sins,
They do not make me sick discussing their duty to
   God,
Not one is dissatisfied, not one is demented with the
   mania of owning things,
Not one kneels to another, nor to his kind that lived
   thousands of years ago,
Not one is respectable or unhappy over the whole
   earth.
Song of Myself, 32

15 I am the man, I suffer'd, I was there.
Song of Myself, 33

16 Agonies are one of my changes of garments.
Song of Myself, 33

17 I have said that the soul is not more than the body,
And I have said that the body is not more than the
   soul,
And nothing, not God, is greater to one than one's
   self is,
And whoever walks a furlong without sympathy walks
   to his own funeral drest in his shroud.
Song of Myself, 48

18 Do I contradict myself?
Very well then I contradict myself,
(I am large, I contain multitudes.)   *Song of Myself, 51*

19 I sound my barbaric yawp over the roofs of the
   world.
Song of Myself, 52

20 I bequeath myself to the dirt to grow from the grass I
   love,
If you want me again look for me under your
   boot-soles.
Song of Myself, 52

21 If anything is sacred the human body is sacred.
I Sing the Body Electric, 8

22 Through you I drain the pent-up rivers of myself,
In you I wrap a thousand onward years.
A Woman Waits for Me

23 As Adam early in the morning,
Walking forth from the bower refresh'd with sleep,
Behold me where I pass, hear my voice, approach,
Touch me, touch the palm of your hand to my body
   as I pass,
Be not afraid of my body.
As Adam Early in the Morning

24 Afoot and light-hearted I take to the open road,
Healthy, free, the world before me,
The long brown path before me leading wherever I
   choose.

Henceforth I ask not good-fortune, I myself am
   good-fortune.   *Song of the Open Road, 1*

1 The glories strung like beads on my smallest sights
and hearings, on the walk in the street and the
passage over the river.
Crossing Brooklyn Ferry, 2

2 A great city is that which has the greatest men and
women,
If it be a few ragged huts it is still the greatest city in
the whole world.
Song of the Broad-Axe, 4

3 Come Muse migrate from Greece and Ionia,
Cross out please those immensely overpaid accounts,
That matter of Troy and Achilles' wrath, and Aeneas',
Odysseus' wanderings,
Placard "Removed" and "To Let" on the rocks of
your snowy Parnassus.
Song of the Exposition, 2

4 We must march my darlings, we must bear the brunt
of danger,
We the youthful sinewy races, all the rest on us
depend,
Pioneers! O pioneers!
Pioneers! O Pioneers![1]

5 Out of the cradle endlessly rocking,
Out of the mocking-bird's throat, the musical
shuttle,
Out of the Ninth-month midnight.
Out of the Cradle Endlessly Rocking

6 When I heard the learn'd astronomer,
When the proofs, the figures, were ranged in columns
before me,
When I was shown the charts and diagrams, to add,
divide, and measure them,
When I sitting heard the astronomer where he
lectured with much applause in the lecture-
room,
How soon unaccountable I became tired and sick,
Till rising and gliding out I wander'd off by myself,
In the mystical moist night-air, and from time to
time,
Look'd up in perfect silence at the stars.
When I Heard the Learn'd Astronomer

7 Words! book-words! what are you?
Song of the Banner at Daybreak

8 Young man I think I know you — I think this face is
the face of the Christ himself,
Dead and divine and brother of all, and here again he
lies.
*A Sight in Camp in the Daybreak Gray
and Grim*

9 Many a soldier's loving arms about this neck have
cross'd and rested,

Many a soldier's kiss dwells on these bearded lips.
The Wound-Dresser

10 Give me the splendid silent sun with all his beams
full-dazzling.
Give Me the Splendid Silent Sun, 1

11 Word over all, beautiful as the sky,
Beautiful that war and all its deeds of carnage must in
time be utterly lost,
That the hands of the sisters Death and Night
incessantly softly wash again, and ever again, this
soil'd world;
For my enemy is dead, a man divine as myself is
dead.
Reconciliation

12 When lilacs last in the dooryard bloom'd,
And the great star early droop'd in the western sky in
the night,
I mourn'd, and yet shall mourn with ever-returning
spring.
When Lilacs Last in the Dooryard Bloom'd, 1

13 Nor for you, for one alone,
Blossoms and branches green to coffins all I bring,
For fresh as the morning, thus would I chant a song
for you O sane and sacred death.
When Lilacs Last in the Dooryard Bloom'd, 7

14 Come lovely and soothing death,
Undulate round the world, serenely arriving, arriving,
In the day, in the night, to all, to each,
Sooner or later delicate death.
When Lilacs Last in the Dooryard Bloom'd, 14

15 Dark mother always gliding near with soft feet,
Have none chanted for thee a chant of fullest
welcome?
When Lilacs Last in the Dooryard Bloom'd, 14

16 O Captain! my Captain! our fearful trip is done,
The ship has weather'd every rack, the prize we
sought is won,
The port is near, the bells I hear, the people all
exulting.
O Captain! My Captain!, st. 1

17 Exult O shores, and ring O bells!
But I with mournful tread,
Walk the deck my Captain lies,
Fallen cold and dead.
O Captain! My Captain!, st. 3

18 There was a child went forth every day,
And the first object he look'd upon, that object he
became. *There Was a Child Went Forth*

19 The horizon's edge, the flying sea-crow, the
fragrance of salt marsh and shore mud,
These became part of that child who went forth every
day, and who now goes, and will always go forth
every day. *There Was a Child Went Forth*

---

[1]Willa Cather's 1913 novel *O Pioneers!* alludes to this poem. See
Cather, 615:7–9.

1 To me every hour of the light and dark is a miracle,
Every cubic inch of space is a miracle.
                                        Miracles

2 A batter'd, wreck'd old man,
Thrown on this savage shore, far from home,
Pent by the sea and dark rebellious brows, twelve
    dreary months,
Sore, stiff with many toils, sicken'd and nigh to death,
I take my way along the island's edge,
Venting a heavy heart.   *Prayer of Columbus*

3 I dream in my dream all the dreams of the other
    dreamers,
And I become the other dreamers.
                                      The Sleepers, 1

4 I am she who adorn'd herself and folded her hair
    expectantly,
My truant lover has come, and it is dark.
                                      The Sleepers, 1

5 A noiseless patient spider,
I mark'd where on a little promontory it stood
    isolated,
Mark'd how to explore the vacant vast surrounding,
It launch'd forth filament, filament, filament out of
    itself,
Ever unreeling them, ever tirelessly speeding them.
                          A Noiseless Patient Spider

6 Camerado, this is no book,
Who touches this touches a man.   *So Long!*

7   I depart from materials,
I am as one disembodied, triumphant, dead.
                                        So Long!

8   Those things most listened for, certainly those are
the things least said.
            Open Letter to Ralph Waldo Emerson
            [1856]

9   As for me, I love screaming, wrestling, boiling-hot
days.
            Open Letter to Ralph Waldo Emerson

10   He [President Abraham Lincoln] has a face like a
hoosier Michael Angelo, so awful ugly it becomes
beautiful, with its strange mouth, its deep-cut, criss-
cross lines, and its doughnut complexion.
                          Letter [March 19, 1863]

11   Never was there, perhaps, more hollowness of
heart than at present, and here in the United States.
Genuine belief seems to have left us.
                          Democratic Vistas [1871]

12   It [Democracy] is a great word, whose history, I
suppose, remains unwritten, because that history has
yet to be enacted.
                                Democratic Vistas

13   I say of all this tremendous and dominant play of
solely materialistic bearings upon current life in the
United States, with the results as already seen, accu-
mulating, and reaching far in the future, that they
must either be confronted and met by at least an
equally subtle and tremendous force-infusion for purposes of spiritualization, for the pure conscience, for
genuine esthetics, and for absolute and primal manli-
ness and womanliness — or else our modern civilization, with all its improvements, is in vain, and we are
on the road to a destiny, a status, equivalent, in its real
world, to that of the fabled damned.
                                Democratic Vistas

14   *The Real War Will Never Get in the Books.* And so
good-bye to the war.
            Specimen Days [1882]. The Real War Will
            Never Get in the Books

15   Such was the war. It was not a quadrille in a ballroom. Its interior history will not only never be
written — its practicality, minutiae of deeds and passions, will never even be suggested.
            Specimen Days. The Real War Will Never
            Get in the Books

16   To have great poets, there must be great audiences, too.
                    Collect [1882]. Notes Left Over

17   So here I sit in the early candle-light of old age — I
and my book — casting backward glances over our
travel'd road.
            November Boughs [1888]. A Backward
            Glance O'er Travel'd Roads

18   The strongest and sweetest songs yet remain to be
sung.
            November Boughs. A Backward Glance
            O'er Travel'd Roads

19   Books are not men —   *Notebook entry*

Susan B[rownell] Anthony
1820–1906

20   The men and women of the North are slave-
holders, those of the South slaveowners. The guilt
rests on the North equally with the South.
            Speech on No Union with Slaveholders [1857]

21   Make [your employers] understand that you are in
their service as workers, not as women.
            The Revolution (woman suffrage newspaper)
            [October 8, 1868]

22   Join the union, girls, and together say *Equal Pay*
for Equal Work.
            The Revolution (woman suffrage newspaper)
            [March 18, 1869]

1   Woman must not depend upon the protection of man, but must be taught to protect herself.
Speech in San Francisco [July 1871]

2   Here, in the first paragraph of the Declaration [of Independence], is the assertion of the natural right of all to the ballot; for how can "the consent of the governed" be given, if the right to vote be denied?
*Is It a Crime for a Citizen of the United States to Vote? Speech [1873]
before her trial for voting*

3   Marriage, to women as to men, must be a luxury, not a necessity; an incident of life, not all of it. And the only possible way to accomplish this great change is to accord to women equal power in the making, shaping and controlling of the circumstances of life.
Speech on Social Purity [spring 1875]

Émile Augier
1820–1889

4   Nostalgia for the mud.[1]
Le Mariage d'Olympe [1855]

Dion Boucicault
1820–1890

5   Yes, quit the house and never darken the threshold of its doors again.   *Flying Scud [1866], act I*

Florence Nightingale
1820–1910

6   It may seem a strange principle to enunciate as the very first requirement in a Hospital that it should do the sick no harm.[2]   *Notes on Hospitals [1859], preface*

Theodore O'Hara
1820–1867

7 Sons of the dark and bloody ground.[3]
The Bivouac of the Dead [1847], st. 9

George Frederick Root
1820–1895

8 Tramp! Tramp! Tramp! the boys are marching,
Cheer up, comrades, they will come,

---

[1]La nostalgie de la boue.

[2]See Hippocrates, 70:15.

[3]Kentucky, from its history as a hunting and burial territory for warring Indian tribes.

And beneath the starry flag
We shall breathe the air again
Of the free land in our own beloved home.
Tramp! Tramp! Tramp! [1862]

9 Yes, we'll rally round the flag, boys, we'll rally once again,
Shouting the battle cry of Freedom.
The Battle Cry of Freedom [1863]

Sir William Howard Russell
1820–1907

10   The Russians dashed on towards that thin redline streak tipped with a line of steel.[4]
To The Times of London from the Crimea, describing the British infantry at Balaklava [October 25, 1854]

William Tecumseh Sherman
1820–1891

11   You cannot qualify war in harsher terms than I will. War is cruelty, and you cannot refine it.
Letter to James M. Calhoun, mayor of Atlanta, and others [September 12, 1864]

12   Hold the fort! I am coming![5]
Attributed signal from Kennesaw Mountain to General John Murray Corse at Allatoona Pass [October 5, 1864]

13   We are not only fighting hostile armies, but a hostile people, and must make old and young, rich and poor, feel the hard hand of war.
Letter to Henry W. Halleck [December 24, 1864]

14   The legitimate object of war is a more perfect peace.   *Speech at St. Louis [July 20, 1865]*

15   War is at best barbarism. . . . Its glory is all moonshine. It is only those who have neither fired a shot nor heard the shrieks and groans of the wounded who cry aloud for blood, more vengeance, more desolation. War is hell.
Attributed to a graduation address at Michigan Military Academy [June 19, 1879]

---

[4]Soon the men of the column began to see that though the scarlet line was slender, it was very rigid and exact. — A. W. KINGLAKE [1809–1891], *Invasion of the Crimea* [1863–1887], *vol. III, p. 455*
    It's "Thin red line of 'eroes" when the drums begin to roll. — RUDYARD KIPLING, *Tommy, st. 3*

[5]He actually said: "Hold out. Relief is coming." General Corse replied: "I am short a cheekbone and an ear, but am able to whip all hell yet."
    Hold the fort, for I am coming! — PHILIP PAUL BLISS [1838–1876], *Hold the Fort, refrain of a hymn dedicated to Sherman* [1875]

1   I will not accept if nominated and will not serve if elected.[1]

> *Message to Republican National Convention*
> *[June 5, 1884]*

Herbert Spencer
1820–1903

2   The poverty of the incapable, the distresses that come upon the imprudent, the starvation of the idle, and those shoulderings aside of the weak by the strong, which leave so many "in shallows and in miseries," are the decrees of a large, farseeing benevolence.   *Social Statics [1851], pt. III, ch. 25*

3   Every cause produces more than one effect.
> *Essays on Education [1861]. On Progress:*
> *Its Law and Cause*

4   Old forms of government finally grow so oppressive that they must be thrown off even at the risk of reigns of terror.
> *Essays on Education. On Manners and Fashion*

5   The fact disclosed by a survey of the past that majorities have been wrong must not blind us to the complementary fact that majorities have usually not been entirely wrong.
> *First Principles [1861]*

6   We have unmistakable proof that throughout all past time, there has been a ceaseless devouring of the weak by the strong.   *First Principles*

7   This survival of the fittest which I have here sought to express in mechanical terms, is that which Mr. Darwin has called "natural selection, or the preservation of favored races in the struggle for life."[2]
> *Principles of Biology [1864–1867],*
> *pt. III, ch. 12*

8   The ultimate result of shielding men from the effects of folly is to fill the world with fools.
> *Essays [1891]. State Tamperings with*
> *Money Banks*

Harriet Tubman
c. 1820–1913

9   When I found I had crossed that line,[3] I looked at my hands to see if I was the same person. There was such a glory over everything.
> *To her biographer Sarah H. Bradford [c. 1868]*

10   I started with this idea in my head, "There's two things I've got a right to . . . death or liberty."
> *To her biographer Sarah H. Bradford*

11   'Twant me, 'twas the Lord. I always told him, "I trust to you. I don't know where to go or what to do, but I expect you to lead me," and he always did.
> *To her biographer Sarah H. Bradford*

John Tyndall
1820–1893

12   Heat Considered as a Mode of Motion.
> *Title of treatise [1863]*

13   The brightest flashes in the world of thought are incomplete until they have been proved to have their counterparts in the world of fact.
> *Fragments of Science, vol. II. Scientific*
> *Materialism [1868]*

14   Superstition may be defined as constructive religion which has grown incongruous with intelligence.
> *Fragments of Science, II.*
> *Science and Man [1877]*

15   Religious feeling is as much a verity as any other part of human consciousness; and against it, on the subjective side, the waves of science beat in vain.
> *Fragments of Science, II. Professor Virchow*
> *and Evolution [1879]*

Henri-Frédéric Amiel
1821–1881

16   To be misunderstood even by those whom one loves is the cross and bitterness of life. It is the secret of that sad and melancholy smile on the lips of great men which so few understand; it is the cruelest trial reserved for self-devotion; it is what must have oftenest wrung the heart of the Son of man; and if God could suffer, it would be the wound we should be forever inflicting upon Him. He also — He above all — is the great misunderstood, the least comprehended.[4]

> *Journal Intime [May 27, 1849]*

17   Charm: the quality in others that makes us more satisfied with ourselves.[4]

> *Journal Intime [1866]*

18   To know how to grow old is the masterwork of wisdom, and one of the most difficult chapters in the great art of living.[4]

> *Journal Intime [September 21, 1874]*

---

[1] The familiar version is: If nominated I will not run; if elected I will not serve.

[2] See Charles Darwin, 439:14.

[3] On her first escape from slavery [1845].

[4] Translated by MARY A. WARD.

Charles Baudelaire
1821–1867

1 Hypocrite lecteur — mon semblable — mon frère
[Hypocrite reader — my double — my brother]!
Les Fleurs du Mal (Flowers of Evil) [1861].
Au Lecteur (To the Reader), st. 10

2 The poet is like the prince of the clouds
Who haunts the tempest and laughs at the archer;
Exiled on the ground in the midst of jeers,
His giant wings prevent him from walking.[1]
Les Fleurs du Mal. L'Albatros, st. 4

3 Perfumes, colors and sounds echo one another.[2]
Les Fleurs du Mal. Correspondances

4 Mother of memories, mistress of mistresses.[3]
Les Fleurs du Mal. Le Balcon, st. 1

5 There, there is nothing else but grace and measure,
Richness, quietness and pleasure.[4]
Les Fleurs du Mal. L'Invitation au Voyage,
refrain

6 I have more memories than if I were a thousand
years old.[5]
Les Fleurs du Mal. Spleen, l. 1

7 I am the wound and the knife!
I am the blow and the cheek!
I am the limbs and the wheel —
The victim and the executioner![6]
Les Fleurs du Mal. L'Héautontimorouménos
(The Self-Tormentor)

8 Here is the charming evening, the criminal's friend;
It comes like an accomplice, with stealthy tread.[7]
Les Fleurs du Mal. Le Crépuscule du Soir
(Twilight)

9 What is that sad, dark island? — It is Cythera,
They tell us, a country famous in song,
Banal Eldorado of all the old bachelors.
Look! after all, it is a poor land![8]
Les Fleurs du Mal. Un Voyage à Cythère

10 O Death, old captain, it is time! raise the anchor![9]
Les Fleurs du Mal. Le Voyage, pt. VIII

11 Be charming, and shut up![10]
Les Fleurs du Mal. Sonnet d'Automne, st. 1

12 What do I care that you are good?
Be beautiful! and be sad![11]
Nouvelles Fleurs du Mal [1866–1868].
Madrigal Triste, st. 1

13　Dandyism is the last spark of heroism amid decadence.　*The Painter of Modern Life [1863]*

14　This life is a hospital, where each patient is possessed by a desire to change beds.[12]
Petits Poèmes en Prose [1869], no. 48

15　There can be no progress (real, that is, moral) except in the individual and by the individual himself.
Mon Coeur mis à nu (My Heart Laid Bare)
[1887], no. XV

16　There are in every man, at every hour, two simultaneous postulations, one towards God, the other towards Satan.　*Mon Coeur mis à nu, XIX*

17　There exist only three beings worthy of respect: the priest, the soldier, the poet. To know, to kill, to create.[13]　*Mon Coeur mis à nu, XXII*

18　Theory of the true civilization. It is not to be found in gas or steam or table turning. It consists in the diminution of the traces of original sin.
Mon Coeur mis à nu, LIX

19　One must work, if not from taste then at least from despair. For, to reduce everything to a single truth: work is less boring than pleasure.
Mon Coeur mis à nu

20　You must shock the bourgeois.[14]　*Attributed*

Sir Richard Francis Burton
1821–1890

21 Do what thy manhood bids thee do, from none but
self expect applause;
He noblest lives and noblest dies who makes and
keeps his self-made laws.
The Kasîdah of Hájî Abdû El-Yezdî [1880],
pt. VIII, st. 37

---

[1]Le Poète est semblable au prince des nuées / Qui hante la tempête et se rit de l'archer; / Exilé sur le sol au milieu des huées, / Ses ailes de géant l'empêchent de marcher.

[2]Les parfums, les couleurs, et les sons se répondent.

[3]Mère des souvenirs, maîtresse des maîtresses.

[4]Là, tout n'est qu'ordre et beauté, / Luxe, calme et volupté.
Translated by Richard Wilbur.

[5]J'ai plus de souvenirs que si j'avais mille ans.

[6]Je suis la plaie et le couteau! / Je suis le soufflet et la joue! / Je suis les membres et la roue, / Et la victime et le bourreau!

[7]Voici le soir charmant, ami du criminel; / Il vient comme un complice, à pas de loup.

[8]Quelle est cette île triste et noire? — C'est Cythère, / Nous dit-on, un pays fameux dans les chansons, / Eldorado banal de tous les vieux garçons. / Regardez! après tout, c'est une pauvre terre.

[9]Ô Mort, vieux capitaine, il est temps! levons l'ancre!

[10]Sois charmante et tais-toi!

[11]Que m'importe que tu sois sage? / Sois belle! et sois triste!

[12]Cette vie est un hôpital où chaque malade est possédé du désir de changer de lit.
Translated by Keith Waldrop.

[13]Il n'existe que trois êtres respectables: le prêtre, le guerrier, le poète. Savoir, tuer, et créer.

[14]Il faut épater le bourgeois.

Crowfoot[1]
1821–1890

1   What is life? It is the flash of a firefly in the night. It is the breath of a buffalo in the wintertime. It is the little shadow which runs across the grass and loses itself in the sunset.

Last words [1890]

Fyodor Mikhaylovich Dostoyevsky
1821–1881

2   Man is a creature that can get used to anything, and I think that is the best definition of him.[2]

The House of the Dead [1860],
pt. 1, ch. 1

3   I swear, gentlemen, that to be too conscious is an illness — a real thoroughgoing illness.

Notes from the Underground[3] [1864],
ch. 2

4   Petersburg, the most theoretical and intentional town on the whole terrestrial globe.

Notes from the Underground, 2

5   Man is sometimes extraordinarily, passionately, in love with suffering.

Notes from the Underground, 9

6   Man grows used to everything, the scoundrel!

Crime and Punishment[3] [1866],
book I, ch. 2

7   If you were to destroy in mankind the belief in immortality, not only love but every living force maintaining the life of the world would at once be dried up.

The Brothers Karamazov[3] [1879–1880],
bk. II, ch. 6

8   I want to tell you now about the insects to whom God gave "sensual lust." . . . I am that insect, brother, and it is said of me especially. All we Karamazovs are such insects, and, angel as you are, that insect lives in you too, and will stir a tempest in your blood. Tempests, because sensual lust is a tempest — worse than a tempest! Beauty is a terrible and awful thing! It is terrible because it has not been fathomed, for God sets us nothing but riddles. Here the boundaries meet and all contradictions exist side by side.

The Brothers Karamazov, III, 3

9   What to the mind is shameful is beauty and nothing else to the heart. Is there beauty in Sodom?

Believe me, that for the immense mass of mankind beauty is found in Sodom. Did you know that secret? The awful thing is that beauty is mysterious as well as terrible. God and devil are fighting there, and the battlefield is the heart of man.

The Brothers Karamazov, III, 3

10   If the devil doesn't exist, but man has created him, he has created him in his own image and likeness.

The Brothers Karamazov, V, 4

11   Is there in the whole world a being who would have the right to forgive and could forgive? I don't want harmony. From love of humanity I don't want it. . . . I would rather remain with my unavenged suffering and unsatisfied indignation, *even if I were wrong*. Besides, too high a price is asked for harmony; it's beyond our means to pay so much to enter on it. And so I hasten to give back my entrance ticket. . . . It's not God that I don't accept, Alyosha, only I most respectfully return Him the ticket.

The Brothers Karamazov, V, 4

12   Imagine that you are creating a fabric of human destiny with the object of making men happy in the end, giving them peace and rest at last, but that it was essential and inevitable to torture to death only one tiny creature . . . and to found that edifice on its unavenged tears, would you consent to be the architect on those conditions? Tell me, and tell the truth.[4]

The Brothers Karamazov, V, 4

13   So long as man remains free he strives for nothing so incessantly and so painfully as to find someone to worship.

The Brothers Karamazov, V, 5

14   We have corrected Thy work and have founded it upon *miracle, mystery* and *authority*. And men rejoiced that they were again led like sheep, and that the terrible gift that brought them such suffering, was, at last, lifted from their hearts.

The Brothers Karamazov, V, 5

15   Men reject their prophets and slay them, but they love their martyrs and honor those whom they have slain.

The Brothers Karamazov, VI, 3

16   Who doesn't desire his father's death?

The Brothers Karamazov, XII, 5

---

[1] Blackfoot warrior and orator.

[2] Translated by DAVID MCDUFF.

[3] Translated by CONSTANCE GARNETT.

[4] "Do you remember the passage where he [Rousseau] asks the reader what he would do if he could make a fortune by killing an old mandarin in China by simply exerting his will, without stirring from Paris?" "Yes." "Well?" "Bah! I'm at my thirty-third mandarin." "Don't play the fool. Look here, if it were proved to you that the thing was possible and you only needed to nod your head, would you do it?" "Is your mandarin well stricken in years? But, bless you, young or old, paralytic or healthy, upon my word — The devil take it! Well, no." — HONORÉ DE BALZAC, *Le Père Goriot*

1   They have their Hamlets, but we still have our Karamazovs!

The Brothers Karamazov, XII, 9

2   But profound as psychology is, it's a knife that cuts both ways.

The Brothers Karamazov, XII, 10

3   We have all come out of Gogol's *Overcoat*.[1]

Attributed

Mary Baker Eddy
1821–1910

4   Our Father-Mother God, all-harmonious.

Science and Health with Key to the Scriptures [1875], ch. 1

5   Jesus of Nazareth was the most scientific man that ever trod the globe. He plunged beneath the material surface of things, and found the spiritual cause.

Science and Health with Key to the Scriptures, 10

6   Spirit is the real and eternal; matter is the unreal and temporal.

Science and Health with Key to the Scriptures, 14

Gustave Flaubert
1821–1880

7   One must not always think that feeling is everything. Art is nothing without form.

Letter to Madame Louise Colet [August 12, 1846]

8   One becomes a critic when one cannot be an artist, just as a man becomes a stool pigeon when he cannot be a soldier.

Letter to Madame Louise Colet [October 22, 1846]

9   But since everything has its reason, and the fantasy of an individual seems to me just as legitimate as the appetite of a million men and capable of holding just as important a place in the world, we must . . . live for our vocation, climb up into our ivory tower, and there, like a dancer amid her perfumes, remain alone with our dreams.[2]

Letter to Louise Colet [April 24, 1852]

10   The author in his work should be like God in the universe: everywhere present and nowhere visible.

Letter to Louise Colet [December 9, 1852]

11   There was an air of indifference about them [the male guests], a calm produced by the gratification of every passion . . . that special brutality which comes from the habit of breaking down half-hearted resistances that keep one fit and tickle one's vanity — the handling of blooded horses, the pursuit of loose women.

Madame Bovary[3] [1857], pt. I, ch. 8

12   It never occurred to her that if the drainpipes of a house are clogged, the rain may collect in pools on the roof; and she suspected no danger until suddenly she discovered a crack in the wall.

Madame Bovary, II, 5

13   Human speech is like a cracked kettle on which we tap crude rhythms for bears to dance to, while we long to make music that will melt the stars.[4]

Madame Bovary, II, 12

14   She [Madame Bovary] had that indefinable beauty that comes from happiness, enthusiasm, success — a beauty that is nothing more or less than a harmony of temperament and circumstances.

Madame Bovary, II, 12

15   We shouldn't maltreat our idols: the gilt comes off on our hands.[5]   *Madame Bovary, III, 6*

16   Of all the icy blasts that blow on love, a request for money is the most chilling and havoc-wreaking.

Madame Bovary, III, 8

17   Anyone's death always releases something like an aura of stupefaction, so difficult is it to grasp this irruption of nothingness and to believe that it has actually taken place.   *Madame Bovary, III, 9*

18   The writer in his work must be like God in his creation — invisible and all-powerful: he must be everywhere felt, but never seen.

Letter to Mademoiselle Leroyer de Chantepie [March 18, 1857]

19   The one way of tolerating existence is to lose oneself in literature as in a perpetual orgy.

Letter to Mademoiselle Leroyer de Chantepie [September 4, 1858]

20   Axiom: hatred of the bourgeois is the beginning of wisdom.

Letter to George Sand [May 10, 1867]

---

[1]This statement, traditionally attributed to Dostoyevsky, appears in Eugène-Melchior de Vogüé [1848–1910], *Le Roman Russe* [1886], *ch. 3:* "The more I read the Russians, the more I understand the observation one of them made to me: 'We have all come out of Gogol's *Overcoat*.' "

[2]Translated by Geoffrey O'Brien.

[3]Translated by Francis Steegmuller.

[4]La parole humaine est comme un chaudron fêlé où nous battons des melodies à faire danser les ours, quand on voudrait attendrir les étoiles.

[5]Il ne faut pas toucher aux idoles: la dorure en reste aux mains.

1   Be regular and orderly in your life like a bourgeois,
so that you may be violent and original in your work.
Letter to Gertrude Tennant
[December 25, 1876]

2   What is beautiful is moral, that is all there is to it.
Letter to Maupassant [October 26, 1880]

3   *I* am Madame Bovary.[1]
From Francis Steegmuller
[1906–1994], Flaubert and
Madame Bovary [1939], pt. 3

Nathan Bedford Forrest
1821–1877

4 Get there first with the most men.[2]
Reported by General Basil Duke and
General Richard Taylor

Hermann Ludwig Ferdinand von Helmholtz
1821–1894

5   Nature as a whole possesses a store of force
which cannot in any way be either increased or diminished . . . therefore, the quantity of force in Nature is
just as eternal and unalterable as the quantity of
matter. . . . I have named [this] general law "The Principle of the Conservation of Force."[3]
Über die Erhaltung der Kraft
(On the Conservation of Force) [1847]

6   Whoever, in the pursuit of science, seeks after
immediate practical utility, may generally rest assured
that he will seek in vain. All that science can achieve is
a perfect knowledge and a perfect understanding of
the action of natural and moral forces.
Academic discourse, Heidelberg [1862]

Frederick Goddard Tuckerman
1821–1873

7 His heart was in his garden; but his brain
Wandered at will among the fiery stars.
Poems [1860]. Sonnets: Second Series,
no. 7, l. 1

---

[1]Madame Bovary, c'est moi!

[2]There are different versions of this statement. The most familiar
one is catchy yet unverifiable: Git thar fustest with the mostest.

[3]Translated by E. Atkinson.
Helmholtz's "force" is equivalent to the modern physicist's
"energy."

William H[enry] Vanderbilt
1821–1885

8   The public be damned.
Reply to a newspaper reporter
[October 2, 1882]

Matthew Arnold
1822–1888

9   Be his [Sophocles']
My special thanks, whose even-balanced soul,
From first youth tested up to extreme old age,
Business could not make dull, nor passion wild:
Who saw life steadily and saw it whole.
To a Friend [1849], l. 8

10 Others abide our question. Thou art free.
We ask and ask: Thou smilest and art still,
Out-topping knowledge.
Shakespeare [1849], l. 1

11 Strong is the soul, and wise, and beautiful:
The seeds of godlike power are in us still:
Gods are we, bards, saints, heroes, if we will.
Written in Emerson's Essays [1849], l. 11

12 Come, dear children, let us away;
Down and away below!
Now my brothers call from the bay,
Now the great winds shoreward blow,
Now the salt tides seaward flow;
Now the wild white horses play,
Champ and chafe and toss in the spray.
The Forsaken Merman [1849], st. 1

13 Where great whales come sailing by,
Sail and sail, with unshut eye,
Round the world forever and aye.
The Forsaken Merman, st. 4

14 Fate gave, what Chance shall not control,
His sad lucidity of soul.
Resignation [1849], l. 197

15 The world in which we live and move
Outlasts aversion, outlasts love:
Outlasts each effort, interest, hope,
Remorse, grief, joy.
Resignation, l. 215

16 Yet they, believe me, who await
No gifts from Chance, have conquered Fate.
Resignation, l. 247

17 We cannot kindle when we will
The fire that in the heart resides,
The spirit bloweth and is still,
In mystery our soul abides.
Morality [1852], st. 1

1 Calm Soul of all things! make it mine
  To feel, amid the city's jar,
  That there abides a peace of thine,
  Man did not make, and can not mar.
            Lines Written in Kensington Gardens
            [1852], st. 10

2 Hither and thither spins
  The windborne, mirroring soul;
  A thousand glimpses wins,
  And never sees a whole.
            Empedocles on Etna [1852], act I, sc. ii, l. 82

3 Be neither saint- nor sophist-led, but be a man!
            Empedocles on Etna, I, ii, l. 136

4 Thou hast no *right* to bliss.
            Empedocles on Etna, I, ii, l. 160

5 We do not what we ought;
  What we ought not, we do;
  And lean upon the thought
  That chance will bring us through.
            Empedocles on Etna, I, ii, l. 237

6 Nature, with equal mind,
  Sees all her sons at play;
  Sees man control the wind,
  The wind sweep man away.
            Empedocles on Etna, I, ii, l. 257

7 So, loath to suffer mute,
  We, peopling the void air,
  Make Gods to whom to impute
  The ills we ought to bear.
            Empedocles on Etna, I, ii, l. 277

8 Is it so small a thing
  To have enjoyed the sun,
  To have lived light in the spring,
  To have loved, to have thought, to have done;
  To have advanced true friends, and beat down
        baffling foes?
            Empedocles on Etna, II, l. 397

9 The day in its hotness,
  The strife with the palm;
  The night in her silence,
  The stars in their calm.
            Empedocles on Etna, II, l. 465

10 Yes, in the sea of life enisled,
  With echoing straits between us thrown,
  Dotting the shoreless watery wild,
  We mortal millions live *alone*.
            To Marguerite. Continued [1852], l. 1

11 But often in the world's most crowded streets,
  But often, in the din of strife,
  There rises an unspeakable desire
  After the knowledge of our buried life.
            The Buried Life [1852], l. 45

12 And long we try in vain to speak and act
  Our hidden self, and what we say and do
  Is eloquent, is well — but 'tis not true!
            The Buried Life, l. 64

13   What actions are the most excellent? Those, certainly, which most powerfully appeal to the great primary human affections: to those elementary feelings which subsist permanently in the race, and which are independent of time. These feelings are permanent and the same; that which interests them is permanent and the same also.   *Preface to Poems [1853]*

14 Go, for they call you, Shepherd, from the hill.
            The Scholar Gypsy [1853], st. 1

15 Thou waitest for the spark from heaven: and we,
  Light half-believers of our casual creeds,
  Who never deeply felt, nor clearly willed . . .
  Who hesitate and falter life away,
  And lose tomorrow the ground won today —
  Ah! do not we, wanderer! await it too?
            The Scholar Gypsy, st. 18

16   And amongst us one,
  Who most has suffered, takes dejectedly
  His seat upon the intellectual throne.
            The Scholar Gypsy, st. 19

17 Oh, born in days when wits were fresh and clear,
  And life ran gaily as the sparkling Thames;
  Before this strange disease of modern life,
  With its sick hurry, its divided aims,
  Its heads o'ertaxed, its palsied hearts, was rife.
            The Scholar Gypsy, st. 21

18 Still nursing the unconquerable hope,
  Still clutching the inviolable shade.
            The Scholar Gypsy, st. 22

19 Strew on her roses, roses,
  And never a spray of yew!
  In quiet she reposes;
  Ah, would that I did too!
            Requiescat [1853], st. 1

20 Her cabined, ample spirit
  It fluttered and failed for breath.
  Tonight it doth inherit
  The vasty hall of death.   *Requiescat, st. 4*

21 Truth sits upon the lips of dying men.
            Sohrab and Rustum, l. 656

22   Sanity — that is the great virtue of the ancient literature; the want of that is the great defect of the modern, in spite of its variety and power.
            Preface to Poems [1854]

23 Wandering between two worlds, one dead,
  The other powerless to be born.
            Stanzas from the Grande Chartreuse
            [1855], st. 15

1 The translator of Homer should above all be penetrated by a sense of four qualities of his author: that he is eminently rapid; that he is eminently plain and direct, both in the evolution of his thought and in the expression of it, that is, both in his syntax and in his words; that he is eminently plain and direct in the substance of his thought, that is, in his matter and ideas; and, finally, that he is eminently noble.

On Translating Homer [1861]

2 The grand style arises in poetry, when a noble nature, poetically gifted, treats with simplicity or with severity a serious subject.

On Translating Homer

3 Nations are not truly great solely because the individuals composing them are numerous, free, and active; but they are great when these numbers, this freedom, and this activity are employed in the service of an ideal higher than that of an ordinary man, taken by himself.

Democracy [1861]

4 For the creation of a masterwork of literature two powers must concur, the power of the man and the power of the moment, and the man is not enough without the moment.

The Function of Criticism at the Present Time [1864]

5 The critical power . . . tends, at last, to make an intellectual situation of which the creative power can profitably avail itself . . . to make the best ideas prevail.

The Function of Criticism at the Present Time

6 There is the world of ideas and there is the world of practice; the French are often for suppressing the one and the English the other; but neither is to be suppressed.

The Function of Criticism at the Present Time

7 I am bound by my own definition of criticism: *a disinterested endeavor to learn and propagate the best that is known and thought in the world.*

The Function of Criticism at the Present Time

8 Whispering from her towers [Oxford] the last enchantments of the Middle Age. . . . Home of lost causes, and forsaken beliefs, and unpopular names, and impossible loyalties!

Essays in Criticism, first series [1865], preface

9 Poetry is simply the most beautiful, impressive and wisely effective mode of saying things, and hence its importance.

Essays in Criticism, first series. Heinrich Heine

10 *Philistine* must have originally meant, in the mind of those who invented the nickname, a strong, dogged, unenlightened opponent of the chosen people, of the children of the light.

Essays in Criticism, first series. Heinrich Heine

11 On the breast of that huge Mississippi of falsehood called *History,* a foam-bell more or less is no consequence.[1]

Essays in Criticism, first series. Literary Influence of Academies [1864]

12 Are ye too changed, ye hills?
See, 'tis no foot of unfamiliar men
Tonight from Oxford up your pathway strays!
Here came I often, often, in old days —
Thyrsis [Arthur Hugh Clough] and I; we still had
   Thyrsis then. *Thyrsis [1866], st. 1*

13 That sweet city [Oxford] with her dreaming spires.

Thyrsis, st. 2

14 The bloom is gone, and with the bloom go I.

Thyrsis, st. 6

15 Yes, thou art gone! and round me too the night
In ever-nearing circle weaves her shade.

Thyrsis, st. 14

16 The sea is calm tonight.
The tide is full, the moon lies fair
Upon the straits; on the French coast, the light
Gleams, and is gone; the cliffs of England stand,
Glimmering and vast, out in the tranquil bay.

Dover Beach [1867], st. 1

17 Listen! you hear the grating roar
Of pebbles which the waves draw back, and fling,
At their return, up the high strand,
Begin, and cease, and then again begin,
With tremulous cadence slow, and bring
The eternal note of sadness in. *Dover Beach, st. 1*

18 Sophocles long ago
Heard it on the Aegean. *Dover Beach, st. 2*

19 The sea of faith
Was once, too, at the full, and round earth's shore
Lay like the folds of a bright girdle furled.
But now I only hear
Its melancholy, long, withdrawing roar,
Retreating, to the breath
Of the night-wind, down the vast edges drear
And naked shingles of the world.

Ah, love, let us be true
To one another! for the world, which seems
To lie before us like a land of dreams,
So various, so beautiful, so new,
Hath really neither joy, nor love, nor light,

---

[1]This passage appeared only in the first appearance of the essay, in *Cornhill Magazine* [August 1864].

History is nothing more than the belief in the senses, the belief in falsehood. — FRIEDRICH NIETZSCHE, *The Twilight of the Idols,* "Reason" in Philosophy, sec. I

History is more or less bunk. — HENRY FORD [1863–1947], interview with Charles N. Wheeler, *Chicago Tribune* [May 25, 1916]

Nor certitude, nor peace, nor help for pain;
And we are here as on a darkling plain
Swept with confused alarms of struggle and flight,
Where ignorant armies clash by night.
Dover Beach, st. 3, 4

1 Creep into thy narrow bed,
Creep, and let no more be said!
The Last Word [1867], st. 1

2 Let the long contention cease!
Geese are swans, and swans are geese.
The Last Word, st. 2

3 Charge once more, then, and be dumb!
Let the victors, when they come,
When the forts of folly fall,
Find thy body by the wall.   *The Last Word, st. 4*

4 Cruel, but composed and bland,
Dumb, inscrutable and grand,
So Tiberius might have sat,
Had Tiberius been a cat.   *Poor Matthias [1867]*

5 Style . . . is a peculiar recasting and heightening, under a certain condition of spiritual excitement, of what a man has to say, in such a manner as to add dignity and distinction to it.
On the Study of Celtic Literature [1867], sec. 6

6 The power of the Latin classic is in *character,* that of the Greek is in *beauty.* Now character is capable of being taught, learnt, and assimilated: beauty hardly.
Schools and Universities on the Continent [1868]

7 The whole scope of the essay is to recommend culture as the great help out of our present difficulties; culture being a pursuit of our total perfection by means of getting to know, on all the matters which most concern us, the best which has been thought and said in the world.
Culture and Anarchy [1869], preface

8 Our society distributes itself into Barbarians, Philistines, and Populace; and America is just ourselves, with the Barbarians quite left out, and the Populace nearly.   *Culture and Anarchy, preface*

9 I am a Liberal, yet I am a Liberal tempered by experience, reflection, and renouncement, and I am, above all, a believer in culture.
Culture and Anarchy, introduction

10 Culture is then properly described not as having its origin in curiosity, but as having its origin in the love of perfection; it is *a study of perfection.*
Culture and Anarchy. Sweetness and Light

11 Greatness is a spiritual condition worthy to excite love, interest, and admiration.
Culture and Anarchy. Sweetness and Light

12 Not a having and a resting, but a growing and a becoming is the character of perfection as culture conceives it.
Culture and Anarchy. Sweetness and Light

13 He who works for sweetness and light united, works to make reason and the will of God prevail.
Culture and Anarchy. Sweetness and Light

14 The men of culture are the true apostles of equality.
Culture and Anarchy. Sweetness and Light

15 Everything in our political life tends to hide from us that there is anything wiser than our ordinary selves.
Culture and Anarchy. Barbarians, Philistines, Populace

16 Conduct is three-fourths of our life and its largest concern.   *Literature and Dogma [1873], ch. 1*

17 The freethinking of one age is the common sense of the next.   *God and the Bible [1875]*

18 Choose equality.
Mixed Essays [1879]. Equality

19 Inequality . . . has the natural and necessary effect, under the present circumstances, of materializing our upper class, vulgarizing our middle class, and brutalizing our lower class.
Mixed Essays. Equality

20 For poetry the idea is everything; the rest is a world of illusion, of divine illusion. Poetry attaches its emotion to the idea; the idea *is* the fact. The strongest part of our religion today is its unconscious poetry.
Introduction to T. H. WARD [1845–1926], English Poets [1880]

21 That which in England we call the middle class is in America virtually the nation.
A Word About America [1882]

22 [A] beautiful and ineffectual angel [Shelley], beating in the void his luminous wings in vain.
Essays in Criticism, second series [1888]. Byron

Rudolf [Julius Emanuel] Clausius
1822–1888

23 Heat cannot of itself pass from a colder to a hotter body.
The Second Law of Thermodynamics[1] [1850]

---

[1]Translated by WALTER D. BROWN.

Heat will of its own accord flow only from a hot object to a cold object. — JOSIAH WILLARD GIBBS [1839–1903], *Scientific Papers* [1906], *The Second Law of Thermodynamics*

Ulysses S[impson] Grant
1822–1885

1   No terms except an unconditional and immediate surrender can be accepted. I propose to move immediately upon your works.
> *To General S. B. Buckner,*
> *Fort Donelson [February 16, 1862]*

2   I propose to fight it out on this line, if it takes all summer.
> *Dispatch to Washington, before Spotsylvania*
> *Court House [May 11, 1864]*

3   Wherever the enemy goes let our troops go also.
> *Dispatch to General Henry W. Halleck*
> *from City Point, Virginia*
> *[August 1, 1864]*

4   The war is over — the rebels are our countrymen again.
> *Upon stopping his men from cheering after*
> *Lee's surrender at Appomattox Court House*
> *[April 9, 1865]*

5   Let us have peace.
> *Accepting nomination for the presidency*
> *[May 29, 1868]*

6   Let no guilty man escape, if it can be avoided. No personal considerations should stand in the way of performing a public duty.
> *Endorsement of a letter relating to the*
> *Whiskey Ring [July 29, 1875]*

7   Leave the matter of religion to the family altar, the church, and the private school, supported entirely by private contributions. Keep the church and the State forever separate.
> *Speech at Des Moines, Iowa [1875]*

8   I think I am a verb instead of a personal pronoun. A verb is anything that signifies to be; to do; or to suffer. I signify all three.
> *Undated note to Dr. John Douglas*
> *[July 1885]*

Edward Everett Hale
1822–1909

9   Behind all these men you have to do with, behind officers, and government, and people even, there is the country herself, your country, and . . . you belong to her as you belong to your own mother. Stand by her, boy, as you would stand by your mother.
> *The Man Without a Country [1863]*

10   He loved his country as no other man has loved her, but no man deserved less at her hands.
> *The Man Without a Country.*
> *Epitaph of Philip Nolan*

Thomas Hughes
1822–1896

11   Life isn't all beer and skittles; but beer and skittles, or something better of the same sort, must form a good part of every Englishman's education.[1]
> *Tom Brown's Schooldays [1857], pt. I, ch. 2*

William Porcher Miles
1822–1899

12   "Vote early and vote often," the advice openly displayed on the election banners in one of our northern cities.
> *Speech in the House of Representatives*
> *[March 31, 1858]*

Frederick Law Olmsted
1822–1903
and
Calvert Vaux
1824–1895

13   The Park [Central Park, New York City] throughout is a single work of art, and as such subject to the primary law of every work of art, namely, that it shall be framed upon a single, noble motive, to which the design of all its parts, in some more or less subtle way, shall be confluent and helpful.
> *Report submitted with "Greensward"[2]*
> *Plan, awarded first prize by the Board of*
> *Commissioners of the Central Park*
> *[April 28, 1858]*

14   It is one great purpose of the Park to supply to the hundreds of thousands of tired workers, who have no opportunity to spend their summers in the country, a specimen of God's handiwork that shall be to them, inexpensively, what a month or two in the White Mountains or the Adirondacks is, at great cost, to those in easier circumstances.
> *Report submitted with "Greensward"*
> *Plan, awarded first prize by the Board*
> *of Commissioners of the Central Park*

---

[1]See Charles Dickens, 464:3 and note.

[2]Pseudonym of Olmsted and Vaux in submitting their plan.

Louis Pasteur
1822–1895

1   In the fields of observation chance favors only the prepared mind.[1]
> *Inaugural lecture, University of Lille [December 7, 1854]*

2   No, a thousand times no; there does not exist a category of science to which one can give the name applied science. There are science and the applications of science, bound together as the fruit to the tree which bears it.[2]
> *Pourquoi la France n'a pas trouvé des hommes supérieurs au moment du péril.[3] From Revue Scientifique [1871]*

Red Cloud[4]
1822–1909

3   We were told that they [federal troops] wished merely to pass through our country...to seek for gold in the Far West....Yet before the ashes of the council fire are cold, the Great Father is building his forts among us. You have heard the sound of the white soldier's axe upon the Little Piney. His presence here is...an insult to the spirits of our ancestors. Are we then to give up their sacred graves to be plowed for corn? Dakotas, I am for war.
> *Speech at council at Fort Laramie, Wyoming [1866]*

Heinrich Schliemann
1822–1890

4   I have gazed on the face of Agamemnon.
> *Telegram to the king of Greece, upon excavating the fifth and last grave at Mycenae [August 1876]*

Théodore de Banville
1823–1891

5 We'll to the woods no more,
The laurels all are cut.[5]
> *Nous N'Irons Plus aux Bois [1846]*

---

[1] Dans les champs de l'observation le hasard ne favorise que les esprits préparés.

[2] Translated by I. BERNARD COHEN.

[3] Why France has not found superior men at the moment of peril.

[4] Mahpiua Luta, Oglala Sioux chief.

[5] Nous n'irons plus aux bois, / Les lauriers sont coupés. Adapted by A. E. HOUSMAN. From an old nursery rhyme.

Mary Chesnut
1823–1886

6   I think this journal will be disadvantageous for me, for I spend the time now like a spider spinning my own entrails.
> *Diary entry [March 11, 1861]*

7   This *only* I see. Like the patriarchs of old our men live all in one house with their wives and their concubines, and the mulattoes one sees in every family exactly resemble the white children — and every lady tells you who is the father of all the mulatto children in everybody's household, but those in her own she seems to think drop from the clouds, or pretends so to think.
> *Diary entry [March 18, 1861]*

8   Does anybody wonder so many women die? Grief and constant anxiety kill nearly as many women as men die on the battlefield.
> *Diary entry [June 9, 1862]*

William Johnson Cory
1823–1892

9 They told me, Heraclitus, they told me you were dead;
They brought me bitter news to hear and bitter tears to shed.
I wept as I remembered how often you and I
Had tired the sun with talking and sent him down the sky.
And now that thou art lying, my dear old Carian guest,
A handful of gray ashes, long, long ago at rest,
Still are thy pleasant voices, thy *Nightingales*, awake,
For Death, he taketh all away, but them he cannot take.
> *Heraclitus [1858]. Translated from Callimachus[6]*

Richard Genée
1823–1895

and

Carl Haffner
1804–1874

10   Happy is he who can forget what cannot be changed.[7]
> *Die Fledermaus (The Bat) [1874], act I*

---

[6] See Callimachus, 83:1.

[7] Glücklich ist, wer vergisst, / Was doch nicht zu ändern ist.

Thomas Wentworth Higginson
1823–1911

1   When a thought takes one's breath away, a lesson on grammar seems an impertinence.
Preface to EMILY DICKINSON'S *Poems, first series [1890]*

Leopold Kronecker
1823–1891

2   God made integers, all else is the work of man.
From a speech made in 1886, as quoted in HEINRICH WEBER'S *obituary of Kronecker [1893]*

George Martin Lane
1823–1897

3 The waiter roars it through the hall:
"We don't give bread with one fish ball!"
Lay of the Lone Fish Ball [1855], st. 10

Francis Parkman
1823–1893

4   The growth of New England was a result of the aggregate efforts of a busy multitude, each in his narrow circle toiling for himself, to gather competence or wealth. The expansion of New France was the achievement of a gigantic ambition striving to grasp a continent. It was a vain attempt.
Pioneers of France in the New World [1865], introduction

5   A boundless vision grows upon us; an untamed continent; vast wastes of forest verdure; mountains silent in primeval sleep; river, lake, and glimmering pool; wilderness oceans mingling with the sky. Such was the domain which France conquered for civilization. Plumed helmets gleamed in the shade of its forests, priestly vestments in its dens and fastnesses of ancient barbarism. Men steeped in antique learning, pale with the close breath of the cloister, here spent the noon and evening of their lives, ruled savage hordes with a mild, parental sway, and stood serene before the direst shapes of death. Men of courtly nurture, heirs to the polish of a far-reaching ancestry, here, with their dauntless hardihood, put to shame the boldest sons of toil.
Pioneers of France in the New World, introduction

6   The most momentous and far-reaching question ever brought to issue on this continent was: Shall France remain here or shall she not?
Montcalm and Wolfe [1884], introduction

Coventry Patmore
1823–1896

7 Love wakes men, once a lifetime each;
They lift their heavy lids, and look;
And, lo, what one sweet page can teach,
They read with joy, then shut the book.
The Angel in the House [1854–1856], bk. 1, canto 8. Prelude 2: The Revelation

8 A Woman is a foreign land,
Of which, though there he settle young,
A man will ne'er quite understand
The customs, politics, and tongue.
The Angel in the House, bk. II, canto 9. Prelude 2: The Foreign Land

9 For want of me the world's course will not fail;
When all its work is done, the lie shall rot;
The truth is great, and shall prevail,
When none cares whether it prevail or not.
The Unknown Eros [1877]. Magna Est Veritas

10   Those who know God know that it is quite a mistake to suppose that there are only five senses.
The Rod, the Root, and the Flower [1896]. Aurea Dicta, no. 142

William Brighty Rands
[Matthew Browne]
1823–1882

11 Never do today what you can
Put off till tomorrow.[1]   *Lilliput Levee*

[Joseph] Ernest Renan
1823–1892

12   The whole of history is incomprehensible without him [Jesus].   *Life of Jesus [1863], introduction*

13   O Lord, if there is a Lord, save my soul, if I have a soul.   *Prayer of a Skeptic*

14   Religion is not a popular error; it is a great instinctive truth, sensed by the people, expressed by the people.   *Les Apôtres (The Apostles) [1866]*

15   To have common glories in the past, a common will in the present; to have done great things together, to will to do the like again — these are the essential conditions for the making of a people.
What Is a Nation?[2] [1882]

---

[1]No idleness, no laziness, no procrastination; never put off till tomorrow what you can do today. — EARL OF CHESTERFIELD, *Letters* [December 26, 1749]

[2]Translated by WILLIAM G. HUTCHISON.

John Sherman
1823–1900

1   I have come home to look after my fences.
Speech to his neighbors, Mansfield, Ohio

William Marcy Tweed [Boss Tweed]
1823–1878

2   As long as I count the votes, what are you going to do about it?
Statement by the "Boss" of Tammany Hall on the ballot in New York City [November 1871]

Alfred Russel Wallace
1823–1913

3   Every species has come into existence coincident both in space and time with a preexisting closely allied species.
On the Law Which Has Regulated the Introduction of New Species [1855]

William Allingham
1824–1889

4 Up the airy mountain,
Down the rushy glen,
We daren't go a-hunting
For fear of little men.   *The Fairies, st. 1*

Barnard Elliott Bee
1824–1861

5   There is Jackson, standing like a stone wall!
Of General T. J. Jackson at the battle of Bull Run [July 21, 1861]

Phoebe Cary
1824–1871

6 And though hard be the task,
"Keep a stiff upper lip."
Keep a Stiff Upper Lip

[William] Wilkie Collins
1824–1889

7   "I haven't much time to be fond of anything," says Sergeant Cuff. "But when I *have* a moment's fondness to bestow, most times . . . the roses get it."
The Moonstone [1868]. First Period, ch. 12

Alexandre Dumas the Younger
1824–1895

8   Business? It's quite simple. It's other people's money.[1]
La Question d'Argent (The Question of Money) [1857], act II, sc. vii

Thomas Jonathan [Stonewall] Jackson
1824–1863

9   My duty is to obey orders.   *A favorite aphorism*

10   Let us cross over the river, and rest under the trees.
Last words [May 10, 1863]

William Thomson, Lord Kelvin
1824–1907

11   When you can measure what you are speaking about, and express it in numbers, you know something about it; but when you cannot measure it, when you cannot express it in numbers, your knowledge is of a meager and unsatisfactory kind: it may be the beginning of knowledge, but you have scarcely, in your thoughts, advanced to the stage of *science*.
Popular Lectures and Addresses [1891–1894]

George Macdonald
1824–1905

12 Said the Wind to the Moon, "I will blow you out!"
The Wind and the Moon, st. 1

13   You will be dead so long as you refuse to die.
What's Mine's Mine [1886], ch. 31

14   The world and my being, its life and mine, were one. The microcosm and macrocosm were at length atoned, at length in harmony. I lived in everything; everything entered and lived in me.
Lilith [1895], ch. 45

T[homas] H[enry] Huxley
1825–1895

15   I cannot but think that he who finds a certain proportion of pain and evil inseparably woven up in the life of the very worms, will bear his own share with more courage and submission.
On the Educational Value of the Natural History Sciences [1854]

---

[1]Les affaires, c'est bien simple, c'est l'argent des autres.

1   To a person uninstructed in natural history, his country or seaside stroll is a walk through a gallery filled with wonderful works of art, nine-tenths of which have their faces turned to the wall.
*On the Educational Value of the
Natural History Sciences*

2   Extinguished theologians lie about the cradle of every science as the strangled snakes beside that of Hercules.
Darwiniana. The Origin of Species [1860]

3   The method of scientific investigation is nothing but the expression of the necessary mode of working of the human mind.
*Our Knowledge of the Causes of the
Phenomena of Organic Nature [1863]*

4   The improver of natural knowledge absolutely refuses to acknowledge authority, as such. For him, skepticism is the highest of duties, blind faith the one unpardonable sin.
*On the Advisableness of Improving
Natural Knowledge [1866]*

5   The chess board is the world, the pieces are the phenomena of the universe, the rules of the game are what we call the laws of Nature. The player on the other side is hidden from us. We know that his play is always fair, just, and patient. But also we know, to our cost, that he never overlooks a mistake, or makes the smallest allowance for ignorance.
A Liberal Education [1868]

6   For every man the world is as fresh as it was at the first day, and as full of untold novelties for him who has the eyes to see them.   *A Liberal Education*

7   M. Comte's philosophy in practice might be compendiously described as Catholicism *minus* Christianity.   *On the Physical Basis of Life [1868]*

8   The great tragedy of Science — the slaying of a beautiful hypothesis by an ugly fact.
Biogenesis and Abiogenesis [1870]

9   There is the greatest practical benefit in making a few failures early in life.
On Medical Education [1870]

10   Size is not grandeur, and territory does not make a nation.
On University Education [1876]

11   If a little knowledge is dangerous, where is the man who has so much as to be out of danger?
On Elemental Instruction in Physiology [1877]

12   Irrationally held truths may be more harmful than reasoned errors.
*The Coming of Age of The Origin of
Species [1880]*

13   It is the customary fate of new truths to begin as heresies and to end as superstitions.
*The Coming of Age of The Origin
of Species*

14   I asserted — and I repeat — that a man has no reason to be ashamed of having an ape for his grandfather. If there were an ancestor whom I should feel shame in recalling it would rather be a man — a man of restless and versatile intellect — who, not content with an equivocal success in his own sphere of activity, plunges into scientific questions with which he has no real acquaintance, only to obscure them by an aimless rhetoric, and distract the attention of his hearers from the real point at issue by eloquent digressions and skilled appeals to religious prejudice.
*Reply to Wilberforce's question.[1] From
Leonard Huxley [1860–1933], Life and
Letters of Thomas Henry Huxley [1900], vol. I*

George Edward Pickett
1825–1875

15   Up, men, and to your posts! Don't forget today that you are from Old Virginia.
*Command at the beginning of his division's
charge at Gettysburg [July 3, 1863]*

Adelaide Anne Procter
1825–1864

16 Seated one day at the organ,
  I was weary and ill at ease,
  And my fingers wandered idly
  Over the noisy keys.
A Lost Chord[2] [1858], st. 1

17 But I struck one chord of music
  Like the sound of a great Amen.
A Lost Chord, st. 2

Bayard Taylor
1825–1878

18 From the desert I come to thee
  On a stallion shod with fire,
  And the winds are left behind
  In the speed of my desire.
Bedouin Song [1853], st. 1

---

[1] If anyone were to be willing to trace his descent through an ape as his *grandfather,* would he be willing to trace his descent similarly on the side of his *grandmother?* — Samuel Wilberforce [1805–1873], *at the British Association for the Advancement of Science* [1860]

[2] The poem was used as lyrics for the song *The Lost Chord* [1877]. Music by Sir Arthur Sullivan [1842–1900].

William Whiting
1825–1878

1 Eternal Father, strong to save,
Whose arm doth bind the restless wave,
Who bidd'st the mighty ocean deep
Its own appointed limits keep,
O, hear us when we cry to Thee
For those in peril on the sea!
The Hymn of the U.S. Navy[1] *[1860].*
Eternal Father, Strong to Save, st. 1

Walter Bagehot
1826–1877

2   Writers, like teeth, are divided into incisors and
molars. Sydney Smith[2] was a "molar."
Estimates of Some Englishmen and Scotchmen
[1858]. The First Edinburgh Reviewers

3   So long as the human heart is strong and the
human reason weak, Royalty will be strong because
it appeals to diffused feeling, and Republics weak
because they appeal to understanding.
The English Constitution [1867], ch. 2

4   The sovereign has, under a constitutional monarchy such as ours, three rights — the right to be consulted, the right to encourage, the right to warn.
The English Constitution, 3

5   [The British monarchy:] Its mystery is its life. We
must not let in daylight upon magic. We must not
bring the Queen into the combat of politics, or she
will cease to be reverenced by all combatants.
The English Constitution, 4

6   One of the greatest pains to human nature is the
pain of a new idea.
Physics and Politics [1869], ch. 5

Dinah Maria Mulock Craik
1826–1887

7 Oh, my son's my son till he gets him a wife,
But my daughter's my daughter all her life.
Magnus and Morna [1876], sc. 2, song

J[ohn] W[illiam] De Forest
1826–1906

8   The Great American Novel.
Title of essay, The Nation [January 9, 1868]

Stephen Collins Foster
1826–1864

9 Oh! Susanna, oh, don't you cry for me,
I've come from Alabama, with my banjo on my
knee.   *Oh! Susanna*[3] *[1848], chorus*

10 Gwine to run all night!
Gwine to run all day!
I'll bet my money on de bobtail nag —
Somebody bet on de bay.
Camptown Races [1850], chorus

11 Way down upon the Swanee River,
Far, far away,
There's where my heart is turning ever;
There's where the old folks stay.
The Old Folks at Home [1851], st. 1

12 All the world is sad and dreary
Ev'rywhere I roam,
Oh! darkies, how my heart grows weary,
Far from the old folks at home.
The Old Folks at Home, chorus

13 Weep no more, my lady,
Oh! weep no more today!
We will sing one song for the old Kentucky home,
For the old Kentucky home far away.
My Old Kentucky Home [1853], chorus

14 I dream of Jeanie with the light brown hair,
Floating, like a vapor, on the soft summer air.
Jeanie with the Light Brown Hair [1854], st. 1

15 I'm coming, I'm coming, for my head is bending
low;
I hear those gentle voices calling, "Old Black Joe."
Old Black Joe [1860], st. 3

16 Beautiful dreamer, wake unto me,
Starlight and dewdrop are waiting for thee.
Beautiful Dreamer [1864], st. 1

G[eorge] W[illiam] Hunt
c. 1829–1904

17 We don't want to fight, but, by jingo, if we do,
We've got the ships, we've got the men, we've got the
money, too.
Song[4] *[1878]*

---

[1]Music by JOHN BACCHUS DYKES [1823–1876].
[2]See Sydney Smith, 374:19 and following.

[3]Sung for the first time by Nelson Kneass in Andrews' Eagle Ice
Cream Saloon, Pittsburgh, Pennsylvania [September 11, 1847]. It
quickly became a worldwide hit.
[4]Sung by Gilbert Hastings Macdermott (Farrell) [1845–1901],
"the Great Macdermott." The song gave the terms "jingo" and
"jingoism" to the political vocabulary, though the phrase "by
jingo" had been used earlier by Oliver Goldsmith and Thomas
Hood.

George B[rinton] McClellan
1826–1885

1 All quiet along the Potomac.
Frequent report from his
Union headquarters [1861]

[Samuel] Ward McAllister
1827–1895

2   There are only about 400 people in fashionable New York Society. If you go outside that number you strike people who are either not at ease in a ballroom or else make other people not at ease.
Quoted in The New York Tribune
[March 25, 1888]

Charles Eliot Norton
1827–1908

3   A knowledge of Greek thought and life, and of the arts in which the Greeks expressed their thought and sentiment, is essential to high culture. A man may know everything else, but without this knowledge he remains ignorant of the best intellectual and moral achievements of his own race.
Letter to F. A. Tupper [1885]

Anna Bartlett Warner
1827–1915

4 Jesus loves me — this I know,
For the Bible tells me so.
The Love of Jesus [1858]

Henrik Ibsen
1828–1906

5   Look into any man's heart you please, and you will always find, in every one, at least one black spot which he has to keep concealed.
Pillars of Society[1] *[1877], act III*

6   The spirit of truth and the spirit of freedom — they are the pillars of society.
Pillars of Society, IV

7   Our house has never been anything but a playroom. I have been your doll wife, just as at home I was Daddy's doll child. And the children in turn have been my dolls. I thought it was fun when you came and played with me, just as they thought it was fun

when I went and played with them. That's been our marriage, Torvald.
A Doll's House[1] *[1879], act III*

8   If I'm ever to reach any understanding of myself and the things around me, I must learn to stand alone. That's why I can't stay here with you any longer.
A Doll's House, III

9   I have another duty equally sacred . . . My duty to myself.
A Doll's House, III

10   *Helmer:* First and foremost, you are a wife and mother.
Nora: That I don't believe any more. I believe that first and foremost I am an individual, just as much as you are.   *A Doll's House, III*

11   To crave for happiness in this world is simply to be possessed by a spirit of revolt. What right have we to happiness?
Ghosts[1] *[1881], act I*

12   I am half inclined to think we are all ghosts, Mr. Manders. It is not only what we have inherited from our fathers that exists again in us, but all sorts of old dead ideas and all kinds of old dead beliefs and things of that kind. They are not actually alive in us; but there they are dormant, all the same, and we can never be rid of them. Whenever I take up a newspaper and read it, I fancy I see ghosts creeping between the lines. There must be ghosts all over the world. They must be as countless as grains of the sands, it seems to me. And we are so miserably afraid of the light, all of us.   *Ghosts, II*

13   Mother, give me the sun.
Ghosts, III

14   I hold that man is in the right who is most closely in league with the future.
Letter to Georg Brandes [January 3, 1882]

15   A community is like a ship; everyone ought to be prepared to take the helm.
An Enemy of the People[1] *[1882], act I*

16   The minority is always right.
An Enemy of the People, IV

17   You should never wear your best trousers when you go out to fight for freedom and truth.
An Enemy of the People, V

18   The strongest man in the world is he who stands most alone.
An Enemy of the People, V

19   Always do that, wild ducks do. Go plunging right to the bottom . . . as deep as they can get . . . hold on

---

[1]Translated by WILLIAM ARCHER.

with their beaks to the weeds and stuff — and all the other mess you find down there. Then they never come up again.

> *The Wild Duck*[1] *[1884], act II*

1   Take the life-lie away from the average man and straightaway you take away his happiness.

> *The Wild Duck, V*

2   Oh courage...oh yes! If only one had that... Then life might be livable, in spite of everything.

> *Hedda Gabler*[1] *[1890], act II*

3   Everything I touch seems destined to turn into something mean and farcical.   *Hedda Gabler, IV*

4   The younger generation will come knocking at my door.

> *The Master Builder*[2] *[1892], act I*

5   And when I stood there, high over everything, and was hanging the wreath over the vane, I said to him: Hear me now, thou Mighty One! From this day forward, I will be a free builder — I too, in my sphere — just as thou in thine. I will never more build churches for thee — only homes for human beings.

> *The Master Builder, III*

George Meredith
1828–1909

6   I expect that Woman will be the last thing civilized by Man.

> *The Ordeal of Richard Feverel [1859], ch. 1*

7 Not till the fire is dying in the grate,
Look we for any kinship with the stars.
Oh, wisdom never comes when it is gold,
And the great price we pay for it full worth;
We have it only when we are half earth.

> *Modern Love [1862], st. 4*

8 And if I drink oblivion of a day,
So shorten I the stature of my soul.

> *Modern Love, st. 12*

9 What are we first? First, animals; and next
Intelligences at a leap; on whom
Pale lies the distant shadow of the tomb.

> *Modern Love, st. 30*

10   In tragic life, God wot,
No villain need be! Passions spin the plot:
We are betrayed by what is false within.

> *Modern Love, st. 43*

11 Ah, what a dusty answer gets the soul
When hot for certainties in this our life!

> *Modern Love, st. 50*

12   [Comedy] it is who proposes the correcting of pretentiousness, of inflation, of dullness, and of the vestiges of rawness and grossness yet to be found among us. She is the ultimate civilizer, the polisher.

> *The Egoist [1879]. Prelude*

13 Cynicism is intellectual dandyism.

> *The Egoist, ch. 7*

14   In...the book of Egoism, it is written, possession without obligation to the object possessed approaches felicity.

> *The Egoist, 14*

15 For singing till his heaven fills,
'Tis love of earth that he instills,
And ever winging up and up,
Our valley is his golden cup,
And he the wine which over flows
To lift us with him as he goes.

> *The Lark Ascending [1881], l. 65*

16 The song seraphically free
Of taint of personality.

> *The Lark Ascending, l. 95*

17   A witty woman is a treasure; a witty beauty is a power.

> *Diana of the Crossways [1885], ch. 1*

18   What a woman thinks of women is the test of her nature.

> *Diana of the Crossways, 1*

19   Ireland gives England her soldiers, her generals too.   *Diana of the Crossways, 2*

20 With patient inattention hear him prate.

> *Bellerophon [1887], st. 4*

21 Full lasting is the song, though he,
The singer, passes.

> *The Thrush in February [1888], st. 17*

22 Behold the life at ease; it drifts,
The sharpened life commands its course.

> *Hard Weather [1888], l. 71*

Dante Gabriel Rossetti
1828–1882

23 The blessed damozel leaned out
From the gold bar of Heaven;
Her eyes were deeper than the depth
Of waters stilled at even;
She had three lilies in her hand,
And the stars in her hair were seven.

> *The Blessed Damozel [1850], st. 1*

---

[1]Translated by A. G. CHATER.
[2]Translated by EDMUND GOSSE and WILLIAM ARCHER.

1 And the souls mounting up to God
  Went by her like thin flames.
                    The Blessed Damozel, st. 7

2 One thing then learned remains to me —
  The woodspurge has a cup of three.
                    The Woodspurge [1870], st. 4

3 Tell me now in what hidden way is
  Lady Flora the lovely Roman?
  Where's Hipparchia, and where is Thaïs,
  Neither of them the fairer woman.
  Where is Echo, beheld of no man
  Only heard on river and mere —
  She whose beauty was more than human? . . .
  But where are the snows of yesteryear?
                    The Ballad of Dead Ladies
                    (After François Villon) [1870], st. 1

4 A sonnet is a moment's monument —
  Memorial from the soul's eternity
  To one dead deathless hour.
                    Sonnets from the House of Life [1870–1881].
                    Poem

5 Beauty like hers is genius.
                    Sonnets from the House of Life, no. 18,
                    Genius in Beauty

6   My name is Might-have-been;
  I am also called No-more, Too-late, Farewell.
                    Sonnets from the House of Life, 97,
                    A Superscription

7 When vain desire at last, and vain regret
  Go hand in hand to death, and all is vain,
  What shall assuage the unforgotten pain
  And teach the unforgetful to forget?
                    Sonnets from the House of Life, 101,
                    The One Hope

8 I have been here before,
  But when or how I cannot tell;
  I know the grass beyond the door,
  The sweet keen smell,
  The sighing sound, the lights around the shore.
                    Sudden Light [1881], st. 1

Henry Timrod
1828–1867

9 Sleep sweetly in your humble graves,
   Sleep martyrs of a fallen cause! —
  Though yet no marble column craves
   The pilgrim here to pause.[1]
                    Lines; Charleston Daily Courier [1866]

Leo Nikolayevich Tolstoy
1828–1910

10   The hero of my tale, whom I love with all the power of my soul, whom I have tried to portray in all his beauty, who has been, is, and will be beautiful, is Truth.   *Sevastopol in May 1855 [1855]*

11   One can live splendidly in the world, if one can work and love, work for that which one loves, and love that at which one works.[2]
                    Letter to Valeria Arsenyev
                    [November 9, 1856]

12   The old man . . . used to say that a nap "after dinner was silver — before dinner, golden."[3]
                    War and Peace [1865–1869],
                    bk. I, ch. 15

13   "What's this? am I falling? my legs are giving way under me," he thought, and fell on his back. He opened his eyes, hoping to see how the struggle of the French soldiers with the artilleryman was ending, and eager to know whether the red-haired artilleryman was killed or not, whether the cannons had been taken or saved. But he saw nothing of all that. Above him there was nothing but the sky — the lofty sky, not clear, but still immeasurably lofty, with gray clouds creeping quietly over it.
                    War and Peace,[4] *III, 16*

14   Three days afterwards the little princess was buried, and Prince Andrey went to the steps of the tomb to take his last farewell of her. Even in the coffin the face was the same, though the eyes were closed. "Ah, what have you done to me?" it still seemed to say.   *War and Peace, IV, 9*

15   In historical events great men — so called — are but the labels that serve to give a name to an event, and like labels, they have the least possible connection with the event itself. Every action of theirs, that seems to them an act of their own free will, is in an historical sense not free at all, but in bondage to the whole course of previous history, and predestined from all eternity.   *War and Peace, IX, 1*

16   The strongest of all warriors are these two — Time and Patience.   *War and Peace, X, 16*

17   He [Platon Karataev] did not understand, and could not grasp the significance of words taken apart from the sentence. Every word and every action of his was the expression of a force uncomprehended by him, which was his life.

                    War and Peace, XII, 13

---

[1]Sung on the occasion of decorating the graves of Confederate dead in Magnolia Cemetery, Charleston, S. C., 1866.

[2]Translated by S. S. Koteliansky and Virginia Woolf.
[3]Translated by Louise and Aylmer Maude.
[4]Translated by Constance Garnett.

1   Pure and complete sorrow is as impossible as pure and complete joy.

      War and Peace, XV, 1

2   The subject of history is the life of peoples and of humanity. To catch and pin down in words — that is, to describe directly the life, not only of humanity, but even of a single people, appears to be impossible.

      War and Peace, epilogue, pt. II, ch. 1

3   Happy families are all alike; every unhappy family is unhappy in its own way.[1]

      Anna Karenina [1875–1877],
      pt. I, ch. 1

4   She [Anna] was doing what she always did when she saw him [Vronsky] — comparing the image of him in her imagination (incomparably superior, and impossible in reality) with him as he was.[2]

      Anna Karenina, IV, 2

5   Ivan Ilych's life had been most simple and most ordinary and therefore most terrible.

      The Death of Ivan Ilych[3] *[1886]*

6   Ivan Ilych saw that he was dying, and he was in continuous despair.

    In the depth of his heart he knew he was dying, but not only was he not accustomed to the thought, he simply did not and could not grasp it.

    The syllogism he had learned from Kiezewetter's Logic: "Caius is a man, men are mortal, therefore Caius is mortal," had always seemed to him correct as applied to Caius, but certainly not as applied to himself. That Caius — man in the abstract — was mortal, was perfectly correct, but he was not Caius, not an abstract man, but a creature quite, quite separate from all others.

      The Death of Ivan Ilych

7   Six feet of land was all that he needed.

      How Much Land Does a Man Need? [1886]

8   Art is a human activity having for its purpose the transmission to others of the highest and best feelings to which men have risen.

      What Is Art? [1898], ch. 8

9   Man survives earthquakes, epidemics, the horrors of disease, and all the agonies of the soul, but for all time his most tormenting tragedy has been, is, and will be — the tragedy of the bedroom.

      From Maksim Gorky. Reminiscences of
      Leo Nikolayevich Tolstoy [1920]

---

[1]Translated by Louise and Aylmer Maude.
[2]Translated by Joel Carmichael.
[3]Translated by Aylmer Maude.

Jules Verne
1828–1905

10   Nothing can astound an American.

      From the Earth to the Moon [1865],
      ch. 3

Roscoe Conkling
1829–1888

11   Parties are not built up by deportment, or by ladies' magazines, or gush.

      Speech at the New York State Republican
      Party Convention [September 27, 1877]

Geronimo
1829–1909

12   It [Arizona] is my land, my home, my father's land, to which I now ask to be allowed to return. I want to spend my last days there, and be buried among those mountains. If this could be I might die in peace, feeling that my people, placed in their native homes, would increase in numbers, rather than diminish as at present, and that our name would not become extinct.

      To President Grant from the reservation at
      Fort Sill, Oklahoma, after surrender [1877]

Carl Schurz
1829–1906

13   My country, right or wrong; if right, to be kept right; and if wrong, to be set right.

      Remarks in the U.S. Senate
      [February 29, 1872]

Charles Dudley Warner
1829–1900

14   To own a bit of ground, to scratch it with a hoe, to plant seeds, and watch the renewal of life — this is the commonest delight of the race, the most satisfactory thing a man can do.

      My Summer in a Garden [1870].
      Preliminary

15   What a man needs in gardening is a cast-iron back, with a hinge in it.

      My Summer in a Garden.
      Third Week

16   Politics makes strange bedfellows.

      My Summer in a Garden.
      Fifteenth Week

Thomas Edward Brown
1830–1897

1 A Garden is a lovesome thing, God wot!
My Garden [1875]

Porfirio Díaz
1830–1915

2   Poor Mexico, so far from God and so close to the
United States.   *Attributed*

Emily Dickinson
1830–1886

3 Surgeons must be very careful
When they take the knife!
Underneath their fine incisions
Stirs the Culprit — *Life!*
No. 108 [c. 1859][1]

4 For each ecstatic instant
We must an anguish pay
In keen and quivering ratio
To the ecstasy.
No. 125 [c. 1859], st. 1

5 To fight aloud, is very brave —
But *gallanter,* I know
Who charge within the bosom
The Cavalry of Woe —
No. 126 [c. 1859], st. 1

6 These are the days when Birds come back —
A very few — a Bird or two —
To take a backward look.

These are the days when skies resume
The old — old sophistries of June —
A blue and gold mistake.
No. 130 [c. 1859], st. 1, 2

7 The thought beneath so slight a film —
Is more distinctly seen —
As laces just reveal the surge —
Or Mists — the Apennine —   *No. 210 [c. 1860]*

8 I taste a liquor never brewed,
From Tankards scooped in Pearl —
No. 214 [c. 1860], st. 1

9 Inebriate of Air — am I —
And Debauchee of Dew —
Reeling — through endless summer days —
From inns of Molten Blue —   *No. 214, st. 2*

10 Till Seraphs swing their snowy Hats —
And Saints — to windows run —
To see the little Tippler
Leaning against the — Sun —   *No. 214, st. 4*

11 Blazing in Gold and quenching in Purple
Leaping like Leopards to the Sky . . .
And the Juggler of Day is gone.
No. 228 [c. 1861]

12 "Hope" is the thing with feathers —
That perches in the soul —
And sings the tune without the words —
And never stops — at all —
No. 254 [c. 1861], st. 1

13 There's a certain Slant of light,
Winter Afternoons —
That oppresses, like the Heft
Of Cathedral Tunes —
No. 258 [c. 1861], st. 1

14 I'm Nobody! Who are you?
Are you — Nobody — too?
Then there's a pair of us!
Don't tell! they'd advertise — you know!

How dreary — to be — Somebody!
How public — like a Frog —
To tell one's name — the livelong June —
To an admiring Bog!   *No. 288 [c. 1861]*

15 I tasted — careless — then —
I did not know the Wine
Came once a World — Did you?
Oh, had you told me so —
This Thirst would blister — easier — now
No. 296 [c. 1861], st. 3

16 The Soul selects her own Society —
Then — shuts the Door —
To her divine Majority —
Present no more —
No. 303 [c. 1862], st. 1

17 I'll tell you how the Sun rose —
A Ribbon at a time —   *No. 318 [1862], l. 1*

18 Some keep the Sabbath going to Church —
I keep it, staying at Home —
With a bobolink for a Chorister —
And an Orchard, for a Dome —
No. 324 [1862], st. 1

19 So instead of getting to Heaven, at last —
I'm going, all along.   *No. 324, st. 3*

20 After great pain, a formal feeling comes.
No. 341 [c. 1862], st. 1

21 Of Course — I prayed —
And did God Care?

---

[1]All quotations are from *The Complete Poems of Emily Dickinson*
[1960], edited by Thomas H. Johnson. Dates are of composition,
not publication.

He cared as much as on the Air
A Bird — had stamped her foot —
And cried "Give Me" —   *No. 376 [c. 1862], l. 1*

1 No Rack can torture me —
My Soul — at Liberty —
Behind this mortal Bone
There knits a bolder One —
                    No. 384 [c. 1862], st. 1

2 Except Thyself may be
Thine Enemy —
Captivity is Consciousness —
So's Liberty.   *No. 384, st. 4*

3 Good Morning — Midnight —
I'm coming Home —
Day — got tired of Me —
How could I — of Him?
                    No. 425 [c. 1862], st. 1

4 Much Madness is divinest Sense —
To a discerning Eye —
Much Sense — the starkest Madness —
'Tis the Majority

In this, as All, prevail —
Assent — and you are sane —
Demur — you're straightway dangerous —
And handled with a Chain.   *No. 435 [c. 1862]*

5 This is my letter to the World
That never wrote to Me —
The simple News that Nature told —
With tender Majesty.
                    No. 441 [c. 1862], st. 1

6 I died for Beauty — but was scarce
Adjusted in the Tomb
When One who died for Truth, was lain
In an adjoining Room —
                    No. 449 [c. 1862], st. 1

7 And so, as Kinsmen, met a Night —
We talked between the Rooms —
Until the Moss had reached our lips —
And covered up — our names —   *No. 449, st. 3*

8 It was not Death, for I stood up,
And all the Dead, lie down —
                    No. 510 [c. 1862], st. 1

9 I reckon — when I count at all —
First — Poets — Then the Sun —
Then Summer — Then the Heaven of God —
And then — the List is done —

But, looking back — the First so seems
To Comprehend the Whole —
The Others look a needless Show —
So I write — Poets — All —
                    No. 569 [c. 1862], st. 1, 2

10 I like to see it lap the Miles —
And lick the Valleys up —
                    No. 585 [c. 1862], st. 1

11 And neigh like Boanerges —
Then punctual as a Star
Stop — docile and omnipotent
At its own stable door —
                    No. 585, st. 4

12 I asked no other thing —
No other — was denied —
I offered Being — for it —
The Mighty Merchant sneered —

Brazil? He twirled a Button —
Without a glance my way —
"But — Madam — is there nothing else —
That We can show — Today?"   *No. 621 [c. 1862]*

13 The Brain — is wider than the Sky —
For — put them side by side —
The one the other will contain
With ease — and You — beside.
                    No. 632 [1862], st. 1

14 I cannot live with You —
It would be Life —
And Life is over there —
Behind the Shelf.
                    No. 640 [c. 1862], st. 1

15 And that White Sustenance —
Despair —   *No. 640, st. 12*

16 Pain — has an Element of Blank —
It cannot recollect
When it begun — or if there were
A time when it was not —
                    No. 650 [c. 1862], st. 1

17 Because I could not stop for Death,
He kindly stopped for me —
The Carriage held but just Ourselves
And Immortality.
                    No. 712 [c. 1863], st. 1

18 Alter! When the Hills do —
Falter! When the Sun
Question if His Glory
Be the Perfect One —

Surfeit! When the Daffodil
Doth of the Dew —
Even as Herself — Sir —
I will — of You —   *No. 729 [c. 1863]*

19 God gave a Loaf to every Bird —
But just a Crumb — to Me —
                    No. 791 [c. 1863], st. 1

20 This quiet Dust was Gentlemen and Ladies
And Lads and Girls —

Was laughter and ability and Sighing,
And Frocks and Curls.

No. 813 [c. 1864], st. 1

1 Adventure most unto itself
   The Soul condemned to be —
   Attended by a single Hound
   Its own identity.

No. 822 [c. 1864], st. 4

2 Dying! To be afraid of thee
   One must to thine Artillery
   Have left exposed a Friend —
   Than thine old Arrow is a Shot
   Delivered straighter to the Heart
   The leaving Love behind.

No. 831 [c. 1864], st. 1

3 Love — is anterior to Life —
   Posterior — to Death —
   Initial of Creation, and
   The Exponent of Earth.

No. 917 [c. 1864]

4 If I can stop one Heart from breaking
   I shall not live in vain
   If I can ease one Life the Aching
   Or cool one Pain
   Or help one fainting Robin
   Unto his Nest again
   I shall not live in Vain.

No. 919 [c. 1864]

5 A narrow Fellow in the Grass
   Occasionally rides —

No. 986 [c. 1865], st. 1

6 But never met this Fellow
   Attended or alone
   Without a tighter breathing
   And Zero at the Bone —

No. 986, last stanza

7 The Dying, is a trifle, past
   But living, this include
   The dying multifold — without
   The Respite to be dead.

No. 1013 [c. 1865]

8 'Twas my one Glory —
   Let it be
   Remembered
   I was owned of Thee —

No. 1028 [c. 1865]

9 I never saw a Moor —
   I never saw the Sea —
   Yet know I how the Heather looks
   And what a Billow be.

   I never spoke with God
   Nor visited in Heaven —
   Yet certain am I of the spot
   As if the Checks were given —

No. 1052 [c. 1865]

10 Experiment to me
   Is every one I meet

If it contain a Kernel?
The Figure of a Nut

Presents upon a Tree
Equally plausibly,
But Meat within, is requisite
To Squirrels, and to Me.

No. 1073 [c. 1865]

11 The Bustle in a House
   The Morning after Death
   Is solemnest of industries
   Enacted upon Earth —

   The Sweeping up the Heart,
   And putting Love away
   We shall not want to use again
   Until Eternity.

No. 1078 [c. 1866]

12 We never know how high we are
   Till we are called to rise
   And then, if we are true to plan
   Our statures touch the skies.

No. 1176 [c. 1870], st. 1

13 A word is dead
   When it is said,
   Some say.
   I say it just
   Begins to live
   That day.

No. 1212 [c. 1872]

14 There is no Frigate like a Book
   To take us Lands away
   Nor any Coursers like a Page
   Of prancing Poetry —
   This Traverse may the poorest take
   Without oppress of Toll —
   How frugal is the Chariot
   That bears the Human Soul!

No. 1263 [c. 1873]

15 I thought that nature was enough
   Till Human nature came
   But that the other did absorb
   As Parallax a Flame —

No. 1286 [c. 1873], st. 1

16 Until the Desert knows
   That Water grows
   His Sands suffice
   But let him once suspect
   That Caspian Fact
   Sahara dies.

No. 1291 [c. 1873], st. 1

17 Not with a Club, the Heart is broken
   Nor with a Stone —
   A Whip so small you could not see it
   I've known
   To lash the Magic Creature
   Till it fell.

No. 1304 [c. 1874], st. 1

1 A little Madness in the Spring
  Is wholesome even for the King.   *No. 1333 [c. 1875]*

2 Love's stricken "why"
  Is all that love can speak —
  Built of but just a syllable
  The hugest hearts that break.   *No. 1368 [c. 1876]*

3   I am glad you love the Blossoms so well. I hope
you love Birds too. It is economical. It saves going
to Heaven.
                       Letter to Eugenia Hall [1876]

4 Bees are Black, with Gilt Surcingles —
  Buccaneers of Buzz.
                   No. 1405 [c. 1877], st. 1

5 The Pedigree of Honey
  Does not concern the Bee —
  A Clover, any time, to him,
  Is Aristocracy.
            No. 1627 [c. 1884], version II

6 A Drunkard cannot meet a Cork
  Without a Revery —
  And so encountering a Fly
  This January Day
  Jamaicas of Remembrance stir
  That send me reeling in.   *No. 1628 [c. 1884]*

7 Eden is that old-fashioned House
  We dwell in every day
  Without suspecting our abode
  Until we drive away.
               No. 1657 [n.d.], st. 1

8 I took one Draught of Life —
  I'll tell you what I paid —
  Precisely an existence —
  The market price, they said.

  They weighed me, Dust by Dust —
  They balanced Film with Film,
  Then handed me my Being's worth —
  A single Dram of Heaven!   *No. 1725 [n.d.]*

9 My life closed twice before its close —
  It yet remains to see
  If Immortality unveil
  A third event to me

  So huge, so hopeless to conceive
  As these that twice befell.
  Parting is all we know of heaven,
  And all we need of hell.   *No. 1732 [n.d.]*

10 That it will never come again
  Is what makes life so sweet.
              No. 1741 [n.d.], st. 1

11 The only secret people keep
  Is Immortality.   *No. 1748 [n.d.]*

12 To make a prairie it takes a clover and one bee,
  One clover, and a bee,
  And revery.
  The revery alone will do,
  If bees are few.   *No. 1755 [n.d.]*

13 Elysium is as far as to
  The very nearest Room
  If in that Room a Friend await
  Felicity or Doom —

  What Fortitude the Soul contains,
  That it can so endure
  The accent of a coming Foot —
  The opening of a Door —   *No. 1760 [n.d.]*

14 That Love is all there is,
  Is all we know of Love;
  It is enough, the freight should be
  Proportioned to the groove.
                No. 1765 [n.d.]

15   If I read a book and it makes my whole body so
cold no fire can ever warm me, I know that is poetry.
If I feel physically as if the top of my head were taken
off, I know that is poetry. These are the only ways I
know it. Is there any other way?
       From Martha Gilbert Dickinson Bianchi
       *[1866–1943], Life and Letters of Emily
       Dickinson [1924]*

16   Little Cousins, Called back.[1]
                     Last letter [May 1886]

Mother Jones [Mary Harris Jones]
1830–1930

17   Pray for the dead and fight like hell for the living!
       *The Autobiography of Mother Jones
       [1925], ch. 6*

18   I have never had a vote, and I have raised hell all
over this country. You don't need a vote to raise hell!
You need convictions and a voice!
       *Speech [1915], quoted in The Autobiography
       of Mother Jones, 22*

Alexander Muir
1830–1906

19   And joined in love together,
  The Thistle, Shamrock, Rose entwine
  The Maple Leaf forever!
           The Maple Leaf Forever [1867]

---

[1] Called Back. — Hugh Conway [Frederick John Fargus, 1847–1885], *title of book* [1883]

Christina Georgina Rossetti
1830–1894

1 My heart is like a singing bird.
A Birthday [1861], st. 1

2   The birthday of my life
Is come, my love is come to me.
A Birthday, st. 2

3 When I am dead, my dearest,
Sing no sad songs for me;
Plant thou no roses at my head,
Nor shady cypress tree.
Be the green grass above me
With showers and dewdrops wet;
And if thou wilt, remember
And if thou wilt, forget.
Song [1862], st. 1

4 Remember me when I am gone away,
Gone far away into the silent land.
Remember [1862], l. 1

5 Better by far you should forget and smile
Than that you should remember and be sad.
Remember, l. 13

6 In the bleak midwinter
Frosty wind made moan,
Earth stood hard as iron,
Water like a stone;
Snow had fallen, snow on snow,
Snow on snow,
In the bleak midwinter,
Long ago.
A Christmas Carol

7 Oh roses for the flush of youth,
And laurel for the perfect prime;
But pluck an ivy branch for me
Grown old before my time.
Song [1862]

8 Who has seen the wind?
Neither you nor I:
But when the trees bow down their heads,
The wind is passing by.
Who Has Seen the Wind? [1872], st. 2

9 God strengthen me to bear myself;
That heaviest weight of all to bear,
Inalienable weight of care.
Who Shall Deliver Me? [1875], st. 1

10 Sleeping at last, the trouble and turmoil over,
Sleeping at last, the struggle and horror past,
Cold and white, out of sight of friend and of
lover,
Sleeping at last.
Sleeping at Last [1893], st. 1

Alexander Smith
1830–1867

11   Death is the ugly fact which Nature has to hide,
and she hides it well.
*Dreamthorp [1863]. Of Death and the Fear
of Dying*

George Graham Vest
1830–1904

12   The one absolutely unselfish friend that man can
have in this selfish world, the one that never deserts
him, the one that never proves ungrateful or treacherous, is his dog.... When all other friends desert,
he remains.[1]   *Speech in the Senate [1884]*

Ignatius Donnelly
1831–1901

13   The Democratic Party is like a mule — without
pride of ancestry or hope of posterity.
Attributed

James A[bram] Garfield
1831–1881

14   Fellow citizens! God reigns, and the Government
at Washington still lives!
*Attributed speech on the assassination
of Lincoln [April 15, 1865]*

15   I am not willing that this discussion should close
without mention of the value of a true teacher. Give
me a log hut, with only a simple bench, Mark
Hopkins[2] on one end and I on the other, and you
may have all the buildings, apparatus and libraries
without him.
*Address to Williams College Alumni,
New York [December 28, 1871]*

Edward Robert Bulwer-Lytton, Earl of Lytton [Owen Meredith]
1831–1891

16 Genius does what it must, and talent does what it can.
Last Words of a Sensitive Second-Rate Poet

---

[1]If you want a friend in Washington, go buy a dog. — *Saying*

[2]Mark Hopkins [1802–1887], president of Williams College
[1836–1872] and president of the American Board of Commissioners for Foreign Missions [1857–1881].

For Education is Making Men; / So is it now, so was it when / Mark
Hopkins sat on one end of a log / And James Garfield sat on the
other. — ARTHUR GUITERMAN [1871–1943], *Education* [1935]

James Clerk Maxwell
1831–1879

1   All the mathematical sciences are founded on relations between physical laws and laws of numbers, so that the aim of exact science is to reduce the problems of nature to the determination of quantities by operations with numbers.

On Faraday's Lines of Force [1856]

2   The opinion seems to have got abroad, that in a few years all the great physical constants will have been approximately estimated, and that the only occupation which will be left to men of science will be to carry on these measurements to another place of decimals.

Address at Cambridge University
[October 1871]

Philip Henry Sheridan
1831–1888

3   The only good Indians I ever saw were dead.[1]
Attributed remark at Fort Cobb,
Indian Territory [January 1869]

Sitting Bull[2]
c. 1831–1890

4   What treaty that the white man ever made with us have they kept? Not one. When I was a boy the Sioux owned the world; the sun rose and set on their land; they sent ten thousand men to battle. Where are the warriors today? Who slew them? Where are our lands? Who owns them? . . . What law have I broken? Is it wrong for me to love my own? Is it wicked for me because my skin is red? Because I am a Sioux; because I was born where my father lived; because I would die for my people and my country?   *Statement*

Louisa May Alcott
1832–1888

5   Christmas won't be Christmas without any presents.

Little Women [1868–1869], pt. I, ch. 1

6   Housekeeping ain't no joke.

Little Women, I, 11

7   The spring sunshine streamed in like a benediction over the placid face upon the pillow — a face so full of painless peace, that those who loved it best smiled through their tears, and thanked God that Beth was well at last.

Little Women, II, 17

8   Women have been called queens a long time, but the kingdom given them isn't worth ruling.

An Old-Fashioned Girl [1870], ch. 13

9   Resolved to take Fate by the throat and shake a living out of her.

From EDNAH D. CHENEY [1824–1904],
Louisa May Alcott, Her Life, Letters,
and Journals [1889], ch. 5

Lewis Carroll
[Charles Lutwidge Dodgson]
1832–1898

10 All in the golden afternoon
Full leisurely we glide,
For both our oars with little skill
By little arms are plied
While little hands make vain pretense
Our wanderings to guide.

Alice's Adventures in Wonderland [1865],
introduction, st. 1

11   Down the Rabbit-Hole.
Alice's Adventures in Wonderland,
title of ch. 1

12   "What is the use of a book," thought Alice, "without pictures or conversations?"
Alice's Adventures in Wonderland,
ch. 1

13   Do cats eat bats? . . . Do bats eat cats?
Alice's Adventures in Wonderland, 1

14   Curiouser and curiouser!
Alice's Adventures in Wonderland, 2

15 How doth the little crocodile
Improve his shining tail,
And pour the waters of the Nile
On every golden scale![3]

How cheerfully he seems to grin,
How neatly spreads his claws,
And welcomes little fishes in
With gently smiling jaws!
Alice's Adventures in Wonderland, 2

---

[1]Edward Sylvester Ellis [1840–1916] reported that after Custer's fight with Black Kettle's band of Cheyenne Indians, the Comanche Chief Toch-a-way (Turtle Dove) was presented to General Sheridan. The Indian said: "Me Toch-a-way, me good Indian." The reply, as reported by Ellis but vehemently denied by Sheridan, is given in the text; the phrase is more often heard in the version: The only good Indian is a dead Indian.

[2]Tatanka Yotanka, Sioux warrior.

[3]See Isaac Watts, 289:8.

1 "I'll be judge, I'll be jury," said cunning old Fury;
"I'll try the whole cause, and condemn you to
     death."
> *Alice's Adventures in Wonderland, 3*

2 Oh my fur and whiskers!
> *Alice's Adventures in Wonderland, 4*

3 "I can't explain *myself*, I'm afraid, sir," said Alice,
"because I'm not myself, you see."
"I don't see," said the Caterpillar.
> *Alice's Adventures in Wonderland, 5*

4 "You are old, Father William," the young man said,
"And your hair has become very white;
And yet you incessantly stand on your head —
Do you think, at your age, it is right?"[1]
> *Alice's Adventures in Wonderland.*
> *You Are Old, Father William, st. 1*

5 "In my youth," said his father, "I took to the law,
And argued each case with my wife;
And the muscular strength which it gave to my jaw,
Has lasted the rest of my life."
> *Alice's Adventures in Wonderland.*
> *You Are Old, Father William, st. 6*

6 "I have answered three questions, and that is
     enough,"
Said his father. "Don't give yourself airs!
Do you think I can listen all day to such stuff?
Be off, or I'll kick you downstairs!"
> *Alice's Adventures in Wonderland.*
> *You Are Old, Father William, st. 8*

7 Those serpents! There's no pleasing them!
> *Alice's Adventures in Wonderland.*
> *You Are Old, Father William, st. 8*

8 "If everybody minded their own business," said
the Duchess in a hoarse growl, "the world would go
round a deal faster than it does."
> *Alice's Adventures in Wonderland, 6*

9 "Talking of axes," said the Duchess, "chop off her
head!"   *Alice's Adventures in Wonderland, 6*

10 Speak roughly to your little boy,
And beat him when he sneezes:
He only does it to annoy,
Because he knows it teases.
> *Alice's Adventures in Wonderland, 6*

11 "If it had grown up," she said to herself, "it would
have made a dreadfully ugly child; but it makes rather
a handsome pig, I think."
> *Alice's Adventures in Wonderland, 6*

12 "All right," said the [Cheshire] Cat; and this time
it vanished quite slowly, beginning with the end of
the tail, and ending with the grin, which remained
some time after the rest of it had gone.
> *Alice's Adventures in Wonderland, 6*

13 "Then you should say what you mean," the March
Hare went on.
"I do," Alice hastily replied; "at least — at least I
mean what I say — that's the same thing, you know."
"Not the same thing a bit!" said the Hatter.
"Why, you might just as well say that 'I see what I eat'
is the same thing as 'I eat what I see'!"
> *Alice's Adventures in Wonderland, 7*

14 "It was the *best* butter," the March Hare meekly
replied.   *Alice's Adventures in Wonderland, 7*

15 Twinkle, twinkle, little bat!
How I wonder what you're at!
Up above the world you fly,
Like a teatray in the sky.[2]
> *Alice's Adventures in Wonderland, 7*

16 "Take some more tea," the March Hare said to
Alice, very earnestly.
"I've had nothing yet," Alice replied in an
offended tone: "so I can't take more."
"You mean you can't take *less*," said the Hatter:
"it's very easy to take *more* than nothing."
> *Alice's Adventures in Wonderland, 7*

17 They drew all manner of things — everything that
begins with an M...such as mousetraps, and the
moon, and memory, and muchness — you know you
say things are "much of a muchness."
> *Alice's Adventures in Wonderland, 7*

18 The Queen turned crimson with fury, and after
glaring at her for a moment like a wild beast, began
screaming, "Off with her head! Off with — "
> *Alice's Adventures in Wonderland, 8*

19 "Tut, tut, child," said the Duchess. "Everything's
got a moral if only you can find it."
> *Alice's Adventures in Wonderland, 9*

20 Take care of the sense and the sounds will take
care of themselves.[3]
> *Alice's Adventures in Wonderland, 9*

21 "We called him Tortoise because he taught us,"
said the Mock Turtle angrily. "Really you are very
dull!"
> *Alice's Adventures in Wonderland, 9*

22 "Reeling and Writhing, of course, to begin with,"
the Mock Turtle replied, "and the different branches
of Arithmetic — Ambition, Distraction, Uglification,
and Derision."
> *Alice's Adventures in Wonderland, 9*

---

[1]See Robert Southey, 381:10.

[2]See Ann and Jane Taylor, 389:12.

[3]See the Earl of Chesterfield, 298:7.

1   Advance twice, set to partners . . . change lobsters, and retire in same order.
Alice's Adventures in Wonderland, 10

2   "Will you walk a little faster?" said a whiting to a snail, "There's a porpoise close behind us, and he's treading on my tail."
Alice's Adventures in Wonderland.
The Lobster-Quadrille, st. 1

3   Will you, won't you, will you, won't you, will you join the dance?
Alice's Adventures in Wonderland.
The Lobster-Quadrille, st. 1

4   The further off from England the nearer is to France —
Then turn not pale, beloved snail, but come and join the dance.
Alice's Adventures in Wonderland.
The Lobster-Quadrille, st. 3

5   'Tis the voice of the Lobster: I heard him declare "You have baked me too brown, I must sugar my hair."[1]
Alice's Adventures in Wonderland.
'Tis the Voice of the Lobster

6   Soup of the evening, beautiful soup!
Alice's Adventures in Wonderland.
Turtle Soup

7   Begin at the beginning . . . and go on till you come to the end: then stop.
Alice's Adventures in Wonderland, 12

8   Sentence first — verdict afterwards.
Alice's Adventures in Wonderland, 12

9   You're nothing but a pack of cards!
Alice's Adventures in Wonderland, 12

10   Child of the pure, unclouded brow
And dreaming eyes of wonder!
Though time be fleet and I and thou
Are half a life asunder,
Thy loving smile will surely hail
The love-gift of a fairy tale.
Through the Looking-Glass [1872],
introduction, st. 1

11   "The horror of that moment," the King went on, "I shall never, *never* forget!"
"You will, though," the Queen said, "if you don't make a memorandum of it."
Through the Looking-Glass, ch. 1

12   'Twas brillig, and the slithy toves
Did gyre and gimble in the wabe;
All mimsy were the borogoves,
And the mome raths outgrabe.

Beware the Jabberwock, my son!
The jaws that bite, the claws that catch!
Beware the Jubjub bird, and shun
The frumious Bandersnatch!
Through the Looking-Glass.
Jabberwocky, st. 1, 2

13   And, as in uffish thought he stood,
The Jabberwock, with eyes of flame,
Came whiffling through the tulgey wood,
And burbled as it came!

One, two! One, two! And through and through
The vorpal blade went snicker-snack!
He left it dead, and with its head
He went galumphing back.

"And hast thou slain the Jabberwock?
Come to my arms, my beamish boy!
O frabjous day! Callooh! Callay!"
He chortled in his joy.
Through the Looking-Glass.
Jabberwocky, st. 4–6

14   Curtsy while you're thinking what to say. It saves time.
Through the Looking-Glass, 2

15   "Now! Now!" cried the Queen. "Faster! Faster!"
Through the Looking-Glass, 2

16   "A slow sort of country!" said the Queen. "Now, *here,* you see, it takes all the running you can do, to keep in the same place. If you want to get somewhere else, you must run at least twice as fast as that!"
Through the Looking-Glass, 2

17   Speak in French when you can't think of the English for a thing — turn out your toes when you walk — and remember who you are!
Through the Looking-Glass, 2

18   "If you think we're waxworks," he said, "you ought to pay, you know. Waxworks weren't made to be looked at for nothing. Nohow!"
Through the Looking-Glass, 4

19   "Contrariwise," continued Tweedledee, "if it was so, it might be; and if it were so, it would be; but as it isn't, it ain't. That's logic."
Through the Looking-Glass, 4

20   The sun was shining on the sea,
Shining with all his might:
He did his very best to make
The billows smooth and bright —
And this was odd, because it was
The middle of the night.
Through the Looking-Glass.
The Walrus and the Carpenter, st. 1

[1]See Isaac Watts, 289:11.

1 The Walrus and the Carpenter
Were walking close at hand:
They wept like anything to see
Such quantities of sand:
"If this were only cleared away,"
They said, "it would be grand!"

"If seven maids with seven mops
Swept it for half a year,
Do you suppose," the Walrus said,
"That they could get it clear?"
"I doubt it," said the Carpenter,
And shed a bitter tear.
> *Through the Looking-Glass.*
> *The Walrus and the Carpenter, st. 4, 5*

2 "O Oysters, come and walk with us!"
The Walrus did beseech.
"A pleasant walk, a pleasant talk,
Along the briny beach."
> *Through the Looking-Glass.*
> *The Walrus and the Carpenter, st. 6*

3 And thick and fast they came at last,
And more, and more, and more —
All hopping through the frothy waves,
And scrambling to the shore.
> *Through the Looking-Glass.*
> *The Walrus and the Carpenter, st. 9*

4 "The time has come," the Walrus said,
"To talk of many things:
Of shoes — and ships — and sealing wax —
Of cabbages — and kings —
And why the sea is boiling hot —
And whether pigs have wings."
> *Through the Looking-Glass.*
> *The Walrus and the Carpenter, st. 11*

5 "But wait a bit," the Oysters cried,
"Before we have our chat;
For some of us are out of breath,
And all of us are fat!"
> *Through the Looking-Glass.*
> *The Walrus and the Carpenter, st. 12*

6 The Carpenter said nothing but
"The butter's spread too thick!"
> *Through the Looking-Glass.*
> *The Walrus and the Carpenter, st. 16*

7 "I weep for you," the Walrus said:
"I deeply sympathize."
With sobs and tears he sorted out
Those of the largest size,
Holding his pocket-handkerchief
Before his streaming eyes.
> *Through the Looking-Glass.*
> *The Walrus and the Carpenter, st. 17*

8 But answer came there none[1] —
And this was scarcely odd, because
They'd eaten every one.
> *Through the Looking-Glass.*
> *The Walrus and the Carpenter, st. 18*

9 Twopence a week, and jam every other day.
> *Through the Looking-Glass, st. 5*

10 "The rule is, jam tomorrow, and jam yesterday —
but never jam today."
"It must come sometimes to 'jam today,'" Alice
objected.
"No, it can't," said the Queen. "It's jam every
other day: today isn't any other day, you know."
> *Through the Looking-Glass, st. 5*

11 "It's a poor sort of memory that only works backwards," the Queen remarked.
> *Through the Looking-Glass, st. 5*

12 Consider anything, only don't cry!
> *Through the Looking-Glass, st. 5*

13 "There's no use trying," she said: "one *can't*
believe impossible things."
"I daresay you haven't had much practice," said
the Queen. "When I was your age, I always did it for
half-an-hour a day. Why, sometimes I've believed as
many as six impossible things before breakfast."
> *Through the Looking-Glass, st. 5*

14 They gave it me — for an unbirthday present.
> *Through the Looking-Glass, st. 6*

15 "But 'glory' doesn't mean 'a nice knockdown
argument,'" Alice objected.
"When *I* use a word," Humpty Dumpty said, in
rather a scornful tone, "it means just what I choose
it to mean — neither more nor less."
"The question is," said Alice, "whether you *can*
make words mean so many different things."
"The question is," said Humpty Dumpty, "which
is to be master — that's all."
> *Through the Looking-Glass, st. 6*

16 It's as large as life and twice as natural.
> *Through the Looking-Glass, st. 7*

17 His answer trickled through my head,
Like water through a sieve.
> *Through the Looking-Glass, st. 8*

18 What's the French for fiddle-de-dee?
> *Through the Looking-Glass, st. 9*

19 It isn't etiquette to cut anyone you've been introduced to. Remove the joint!
> *Through the Looking-Glass, st. 9*

---

[1]But answer came there none. — Sir Walter Scott, *The Bridal of Triermain* [1813], *canto III, st. 10*

1 He would answer to "Hi!" or to any loud cry
Such as "Fry me!" or "Fritter my wig!"
To "What-you-may-call-um!" or
"What-was-his-name!"
But especially "Thing-um-a-jig!"
*The Hunting of the Snark [1876].
Fit I, st. 9*

2 "What's the good of Mercator's North Poles and
Equators,
Tropics, Zones and Meridian Lines?"
So the Bellman would cry: and the crew would
reply,
"They are merely conventional signs!"
The Hunting of the Snark, II, st. 3

3 It frequently breakfasts at five-o'clock tea,
And dines on the following day.
The Hunting of the Snark, II, st. 17

4 There was silence supreme! Not a shriek, not a
scream,
Scarcely even a howl or a groan,
As the man they called "Ho!" told his story of woe
In an antediluvian tone.
The Hunting of the Snark, III, st. 3

5 It is this, it is this that oppresses my soul.
The Hunting of the Snark, III, st. 11

6 They sought it with thimbles, they sought it with
care;
They pursued it with forks and hope;
They threatened its life with a railway share;
They charmed it with smiles and soap.
The Hunting of the Snark, V, st. 1

7 For the Snark *was* a Boojum, you see.
The Hunting of the Snark, VIII, st. 9

8 He thought he saw an Elephant,
That practiced on a fife:
He looked again, and found it was
A letter from his wife.
"At length I realize," he said,
"The bitterness of Life!"
Sylvie and Bruno [1889], ch. 5

9 He thought he saw a Buffalo
Upon the chimneypiece:
He looked again, and found it was
His sister's husband's niece.
Sylvie and Bruno, 6

10 He thought he saw an Albatross
That fluttered round the lamp:
He looked again, and found it was
A penny postage stamp.
"You'd best be getting home," he said,
"The nights are very damp."
Sylvie and Bruno, 12

William Croswell Doane
1832–1913

11 Ancient of Days, who sittest throned in glory,
To thee all knees are bent, all voices pray.
Hymn [1886], st. 1

H[enry] C[lay] Work
1832–1884

12 Father, dear father, come home with me now,
The clock in the belfry strikes one;
You said you were coming right home from
the shop
As soon as your day's work was done.
Come Home, Father [1864], st. 1

13 "Hurrah! hurrah! we bring the Jubilee!
Hurrah! Hurrah! the flag that makes you free!"
So we sang the chorus from Atlanta to the sea,
While we were marching through Georgia.
Marching Through Georgia [1865], chorus

Johannes Brahms
1833–1897

14 If there is anybody here I have not offended, I
apologize.
Upon leaving a party; attributed

Adam Lindsay Gordon
1833–1870

15 A little season of love and laughter,
Of light and life, and pleasure and pain,
And a horror of outer darkness after,
And dust returneth to dust again.[1]
The Swimmer [1870]

Major-General Charles C. Gordon
1833–1885

16 Now mark this, if the Expeditionary Force, and I
ask no more than two hundred men, does not come
in ten days, the town may fall; and I have done my
best for the honor of our country. Goodbye.
*Khartoum journal, final entry
[December 14, 1885]*

---

[1]A little time for laughter, / A little time to sing, / A little time
to kiss and cling, / And no more kissing after. — PHILIP BOURKE
MARSTON [1850–1887], *After [1875], st. 1*

John Marshall Harlan
1833–1911

1   Our Constitution is color-blind, and neither knows nor tolerates classes among citizens. In respect of civil rights, all citizens are equal before the law. The humblest is the peer of the most powerful.

Dissenting opinion, Plessy v. Ferguson 163
U.S. 537, 559 [1896]

Robert [Green] Ingersoll
1833–1899

2   Like an armed warrior, like a plumed knight, James G. Blaine marched down the halls of the American Congress and threw his shining lance full and fair against the brazen foreheads of the defamers of his country and the maligners of his honor.

Speech nominating Blaine for President,
National Republican Convention
[June 15, 1876]

3   An honest God is the noblest work of man.

The Gods [1876]

4   Every cradle asks us "Whence?" and every coffin "Whither?" The poor barbarian, weeping above his dead, can answer these questions as well as the robed priest of the most authentic creed.

Address at a child's grave
[January 8, 1882]

5   We, too, have our religion, and it is this: Help for the living, hope for the dead.

Address at a child's grave

6 Justice is the only worship.
Love is the only priest.
Ignorance is the only slavery.
Happiness is the only good.
The time to be happy is now,
The place to be happy is here,
The way to be happy is to make others so.

Creed[1]

Petroleum V. Nasby
[David Ross Locke]
1833–1888

7 The contract 'twixt Hannah, God and me,
Was not for one or twenty years, but for eternity.

Hannah Jane [1871], st. 29

Alfred Nobel
1833–1896

8   My factories may make an end of war sooner than your congresses. The day when two army corps can annihilate each other in one second, all civilized nations, it is to be hoped, will recoil from war and discharge their troops.

From Bertha von Suttner, Memoiren
[Stuttgart, 1909]

John Emerich Edward Dalberg-Acton, Lord Acton
1834–1902

9   There is no error so monstrous that it fails to find defenders among the ablest men. Imagine a congress of eminent celebrities such as More, Bacon, Grotius, Pascal, Cromwell, Bossuet, Montesquieu, Jefferson, Napoleon, Pitt, etc. The result would be an Encyclopedia of Error.

Letter to Mary Gladstone [April 24, 1881]

10   Power tends to corrupt and absolute power corrupts absolutely.

Letter to Bishop Mandell Creighton
[April 5, 1887]

11   Advice to Persons About to Write History — Don't.

Letter to Bishop Mandell Creighton,
postscript

12   Liberty is not a means to a higher political end. It is itself the highest political end.

The History of Freedom and Other Essays
[1907], ch. 1

13   Writers the most learned, the most accurate in details, and the soundest in tendency, frequently fall into a habit which can neither be cured nor pardoned — the habit of making history into the proof of their theories.

The History of Freedom and Other Essays, 8

Sabine Baring-Gould
1834–1924

14 Onward, Christian soldiers,
Marching as to war,
With the Cross of Jesus
Going on before!

Onward, Christian Soldiers[2] *[1864],*
st. 1

---

[1]This collection of Ingersoll's sayings — some from his writings, some attributed — have come to be known as his creed. There are other versions.

---

[2]Music by Sir Arthur Sullivan [1842–1900].

1 Now the day is over,
Night is drawing nigh;
Shadows of the evening
Steal across the sky.
Now the Day Is Over [1865], st. 1

Charles Farrar Browne
[Artemus Ward]
1834–1867

2 My pollertics, like my religion, bein of a exceedin accommodatin character.
Artemus Ward: His Book [1862]. The Crisis

3 I'm not a politician and my other habits air good.
Artemus Ward: His Book.
Fourth of July Oration

4 The prevailin weakness of most public men is to SLOP OVER! Washington never slopt over.
Artemus Ward: His Book.
Fourth of July Oration

5 The Puritans nobly fled from a land of despotism to a land of freedim, where they could not only enjoy their own religion, but could prevent everybody else from enjoyin *his*.[1]
London Punch Letters, no. 5 [1866]

Edgar Degas
1834–1917

6 Some forms of success are indistinguishable from panic.[2]   *Notebooks*

7 A picture is something which requires as much knavery, trickery, and deceit as the perpetration of a crime. Paint falsely, and then add the accent of nature.   *Attributed*

George [Louis Palmella Busson]
du Maurier
1834–1896

8 A little work, a little play,
To keep us going — and so, good day!

A little warmth, a little light,
Of love's bestowing — and so, good night![3]

A little fun, to match the sorrow
Of each day's growing — and so, good morrow!

A little trust that when we die
We reap our sowing! and so — good-bye!
Trilby [1894], pt. VIII

Charles William Eliot
1834–1926

9 Enter to grow in wisdom.
Depart to serve better thy country and thy kind.
Inscriptions on the 1890 Gate to Harvard Yard

10 To the Fifty-fourth Regiment of Massachusetts Infantry:
The white officers, taking life and honor in their hands, cast in their lot with men of a despised race unproved in war, and risked death as inciters of servile insurrection if taken prisoners, besides encountering all the common perils of camp march and battle.
The black rank and file volunteered when disaster clouded the Union cause, served without pay for eighteen months till given that of white troops, faced threatened enslavement if captured, were brave in action, patient under heavy and dangerous labors, and cheerful amid hardships and privations.
Together they gave to the nation and the world undying proof that Americans of African descent possess the pride, courage, and devotion of the patriot soldier. One hundred and eighty thousand such Americans enlisted under the Union flag in 1863–1865.
Inscription on the Robert Gould Shaw Monument by Augustus Saint-Gaudens, Boston Common [1897][4]

Marshall Field
1834–1906

11 Give the lady what she wants!
Instruction to manager of his Chicago department store

Ernst Heinrich Haeckel
1834–1919

12 Ontogenesis, or the development of the individual, is a short and quick recapitulation of phylogenesis,[5] or the development of the tribe to which it

---

[1]The Puritan's idea of Hell is a place where everybody has to mind his own business. — *Attributed to* WENDELL PHILLIPS [1811–1884]

[2]Translated by THEODORE REFF.

[3]La vie est vaine: / Un peu d'amour, / Un peu de haine... / Et puis — bonjour! / La vie est brève: / Un peu d'espoir, / Un peu de rêve / Et puis — bonsoir! — LÉON MONTENAKEN [b. 1859], *Peu de Chose* [1894]

[4]See Paul Laurence Dunbar, 613:14, and Robert Lowell, 787:19.

[5]Frequently quoted: Ontogeny recapitulates phylogeny. See Sigmund Freud, 563:6.

belongs, determined by the laws of inheritance and adaptation.

The History of Creation[1] *[1868]*

Walter Kittredge
1834–1905

1 We're tenting tonight on the old campground,
  Give us a song to cheer
  Our weary hearts, a song of home
  And friends we love so dear.

Tenting on the Old Campground [1864], st. 1

William Morris
1834–1896

2   Well, if this is poetry, it is very easy to write.

*Remark [1854]. From J. W. MACKAIL
[1859–1945], Life of William Morris [1899]*

3 I was half mad with beauty on that day.

The Defense of Guenevere [1858], l. 109

4 Had she come all the way for this,
  To part at last without a kiss?
  Yea, had she borne the dirt and rain
  That her own eyes might see him slain
  Beside the haystack in the floods?

The Haystack in the Floods [1858], l. 1

5 Dreamer of dreams, born out of my due time,
  Why should I strive to set the crooked straight?

*The Earthly Paradise [1868–1870].
An Apology, st. 4*

6 Love is enough, though the world be awaning.

Love Is Enough [1872]

7   If you want a golden rule that will fit everybody,
this is it: Have nothing in your houses that you do not
know to be useful, or believe to be beautiful.

The Beauty of Life [1880]

8   What I mean by Socialism is a condition of society
in which there should be neither rich nor poor,
neither master nor master's man, neither idle nor
overworked, neither brain-sick brain workers nor
heart-sick hand workers, in a word, in which all men
would be living in equality of condition, and would
manage their affairs unwastefully, and with the full
consciousness that harm to one would mean harm
to all — the realization at last of the meaning of the
word *commonwealth*.

How I Became a Socialist [1894]

Frank [Richard] Stockton
1834–1902

9   Which came out of the opened door — the lady or
the tiger?

The Lady or the Tiger? [1884]

James Thomson
1834–1882

10 Statues and pictures and verse may be grand,
  But they are not the Life for which they stand.

Art [1865], st. 3, l. 19

11 The City is of Night; perchance of Death,
  But certainly of Night.

The City of Dreadful Night [1874], st. 1

12 I find no hint throughout the Universe
  Of good or ill, of blessing or of curse;
  I find alone Necessity Supreme.

The City of Dreadful Night, st. 14

James McNeill Whistler
1834–1903

13   The rare few, who, early in life, have rid themselves of the friendship of the many.

The Gentle Art of Making Enemies [1890]

14   To say of a picture, as is often said in its praise, that
it shows great and earnest labor, is to say that it is
incomplete and unfit for view.

The Gentle Art of Making Enemies

15   The masterpiece should appear as the flower to
the painter — perfect in its bud as in its bloom —
with no reason to explain its presence — no mission
to fulfill — a joy to the artist, a delusion to the philanthropist — a puzzle to the botanist — an accident of
sentiment and alliteration to the literary man.

The Gentle Art of Making Enemies

16   Art should be independent of all claptrap —
should stand alone, and appeal to the artistic sense
of eye or ear, without confounding this with emotions entirely foreign to it, as devotion, pity, love,
patriotism, and the like. All these have no kind of
concern with it.

The Gentle Art of Making Enemies

17   I am not arguing with you — I am telling you.

The Gentle Art of Making Enemies

18   *Wilde:* I wish I'd said that.
  Whistler: You will, Oscar, you will.

*From L. C. INGLEBY [1876–1923],
Oscar Wilde [1907]*

---

[1]Translated by E. R. LANKESTER.

Thomas Brigham Bishop
1835–1905

1 John Brown's body lies a-moldering in the grave,
His soul is marching on.

John Brown's Body, st. 1

Phillips Brooks
1835–1893

2 O little town of Bethlehem!
How still we see thee lie;
Above thy deep and dreamless sleep
The silent stars go by;
Yet in thy dark streets shineth
The everlasting Light;
The hopes and fears of all the years
Are met in thee tonight.

O Little Town of Bethlehem [1867], st. 1

Samuel Butler
1835–1902

3 The man who lets himself be bored is even more contemptible than the bore.

The Fair Haven [1873]. Memoir, ch. 3

4 A hen is only an egg's way of making another egg.

Life and Habit [1877], ch. 8

5 It was very good of God to let Carlyle and Mrs. Carlyle marry one another and so make only two people miserable instead of four.

*Letter to Miss E. M. A. Savage
[November 21, 1884]*

6 It is far safer to know too little than too much. People will condemn the one, though they will resent being called upon to exert themselves to follow the other.   *The Way of All Flesh [1903], ch. 5*

7 Young people have a marvelous faculty of either dying or adapting themselves to circumstances. Even if they are unhappy — very unhappy — it is astonishing how easily they can be prevented from finding it out, or at any rate from attributing it to any other cause than their own sinfulness.

The Way of All Flesh, 6

8 Every man's work, whether it be literature or music or pictures or architecture or anything else, is always a portrait of himself.

The Way of All Flesh, 14

9 One great reason why clergymen's households are generally unhappy is because the clergyman is so much at home or close about the house.

The Way of All Flesh, 24

10 The advantage of doing one's praising for oneself is that one can lay it on so thick and exactly in the right places.

The Way of All Flesh, 34

11 Life is the art of drawing sufficient conclusions from insufficient premises.

Notebooks [1912]. Life

12 All progress is based upon a universal innate desire on the part of every organism to live beyond its income.   *Notebooks. Life*

13 An apology for the Devil: It must be remembered that we have only heard one side of the case. God has written all the books.

*Notebooks. Higgledy-Piggledy: An Apology
for the Devil*

14 God is Love — I dare say. But what a mischievous devil Love is!   *Notebooks. God Is Love*

15 I do not mind lying, but I hate inaccuracy.

Notebooks. Truth and Convenience: Falsehood

Andrew Carnegie
1835–1919

16 Upon the sacredness of property civilization itself depends — the right of the laborer to his hundred dollars in the savings bank, and equally the legal right of the millionaire to his millions.

*Wealth. From the North American Review
[June 1889]*

17 Surplus wealth is a sacred trust which its possessor is bound to administer in his lifetime for the good of the community.

Wealth. From the North American Review

18 The man who dies...rich dies disgraced.

Wealth. From the North American Review

19 Three generations from shirtsleeves to shirt-sleeves.[1]   *Triumphant Democracy [1886]*

Mark Twain[2]
[Samuel Langhorne Clemens]
1835–1910

20 The serene confidence which a Christian feels in four aces.

*Letter to The Golden Era (San Francisco)
[May 22, 1864]*

---

[1] There's nobbut three generations atween clog and clog. — *Lancashire proverb, which Carnegie liked to quote*

[2] A pseudonym apparently derived from the Mississippi steamboating term signifying two fathoms (12 feet) of depth.

1   I *have* had a "call" to literature, of a low order —
i.e. humorous. It is nothing to be proud of, but it is
my strongest suit ... seriously scribbling to excite the
laughter of God's creatures.

> *Letter to Orion and Mary Clemens*
> *[October 19, 1865]*

2   I don't see no p'ints about that frog that's any
better'n any other frog.

> *The Notorious Jumping Frog of Calaveras*
> *County*[1] *[1865]*

3   I'll resk forty dollars that he can outjump any frog
in Calaveras county.

> *The Notorious Jumping Frog of*
> *Calaveras County*

4   They spell it Vinci and pronounce it Vinchy; foreigners always spell better than they pronounce.

> *The Innocents Abroad [1869], ch. 19*

5   There's millions in it!

> *The Gilded Age (stage version) [1874]*

6   Barring that natural expression of villainy which
we all have, the man looked honest enough.

> *Sketches [1875]. A Mysterious Visit*

7   Tom appeared on the sidewalk with a bucket of
whitewash and a long-handled brush. He surveyed
the fence, and all gladness left him and a deep melancholy settled down upon his spirit. Thirty yards of
board fence nine feet high. Life to him seemed
hollow, and existence but a burden.

> *The Adventures of Tom Sawyer [1876],*
> *ch. 2*

8   Work consists of whatever a body is *obliged* to
do. . . . Play consists of whatever a body is not obliged
to do.

> *The Adventures of Tom Sawyer, 2*

9   She makes me wash, they comb me all to thunder;
she won't let me sleep in the woodshed. . . . The
widder eats by a bell; she goes to bed by a bell; she
gits up by a bell — everything's so awful reg'lar a
body can't stand it.

> *The Adventures of Tom Sawyer, 35*

10   There is a sumptuous variety about the New
England weather that compels the stranger's admiration — and regret. The weather is always doing something there; always attending strictly to business;
always getting up new designs and trying them on
the people to see how they will go. . . . Yes, one of the
brightest gems in the New England weather is the
dazzling uncertainty of it.

> *Speech. The Weather [1876]*

---

[1] Frequently cited as "The Celebrated Jumping Frog of Calaveras
County."

11   I am a great & sublime fool. But then I am God's
fool, & all His works must be contemplated with
respect.

> *Letter to William Dean Howells*
> *[December 28(?), 1877]*

12   I'm the man they call Sudden Death and General
Desolation! Sired by a hurricane, dam'd by an earthquake. . . . When I'm playful I use the meridians of
longitude and parallels of latitude for a seine, and
drag the Atlantic Ocean for whales! I scratch my head
with the lightning and purr myself to sleep with the
thunder!

> *Life on the Mississippi [1883], ch. 3*

13   I can picture that old time to myself now, just as
it was then: the white town drowsing in the sunshine
of a summer's morning ... the great Mississippi,
the majestic, the magnificent Mississippi, rolling its
mile-wide tide along, shining in the sun.

> *Life on the Mississippi, 4*

14   I was gratified to be able to answer promptly, and
I did. I said I didn't know.

> *Life on the Mississippi, 6*

15   Your true pilot cares nothing about anything on
earth but the river, and his pride in his occupation
surpasses the pride of kings.

> *Life on the Mississippi, 7*

16   By the Shadow of Death, but he's a lightning
pilot!

> *Life on the Mississippi, 7*

17   I'll learn him or kill him.

> *Life on the Mississippi, 8*

18   When I find a well-drawn character in fiction
or biography, I generally take a warm personal
interest in him, for the reason that I have known him
before — met him on the river.

> *Life on the Mississippi, 18*

19   The first time I ever saw St. Louis, I could have
bought it for six million dollars, and it was the mistake of my life that I did not do it.

> *Life on the Mississippi, 22*

20   There is no architecture in New Orleans, except in
the cemeteries.

> *Life on the Mississippi, 41*

21   All the modern inconveniences.

> *Life on the Mississippi, 43*

22   Persons attempting to find a motive in this narrative will be prosecuted; persons attempting to find a
moral in it will be banished; persons attempting to
find a plot in it will be shot.

> *Adventures of Huckleberry Finn [1885].*
> *Notice*

1   You don't know about me, without you have read a book by the name of "The Adventures of Tom Sawyer," but that ain't no matter. That book was made by Mr. Mark Twain, and he told the truth, mainly. There was things which he stretched, but mainly he told the truth. That is nothing. I never seen anybody but lied, one time or another.
Adventures of Huckleberry Finn, ch. 1

2   It was kind of solemn, drifting down the big still river, laying on our backs looking up at the stars, and we didn't ever feel like talking loud, and it warn't often that we laughed, only a little kind of a low chuckle. We had mighty good weather, as a general thing, and nothing ever happened to us at all, that night, nor the next, nor the next.
Adventures of Huckleberry Finn, 12

3   "Pilgrim's Progress," about a man that left his family it didn't say why. I read considerable in it now and then. The statements was interesting, but tough.   *Adventures of Huckleberry Finn, 17*

4   We said there warn't no home like a raft, after all. Other places do seem so cramped up and smothery, but a raft don't. You feel mighty free and easy and comfortable on a raft.
Adventures of Huckleberry Finn, 18

5   It was a monstrous big river down there.
Adventures of Huckleberry Finn, 19

6   All kings is mostly rapscallions.
Adventures of Huckleberry Finn, 23

7   Hain't we got all the fools in town on our side? and ain't that a big enough majority in any town?
Adventures of Huckleberry Finn, 26

8   You can't pray a lie.
Adventures of Huckleberry Finn, 31

9   I studied a minute, sort of holding my breath, and then says to myself: "All right, then, I'll *go* to hell."
Adventures of Huckleberry Finn, 31

10   I reckon I got to light out for the Territory ahead of the rest, because Aunt Sally she's going to adopt me and sivilize me and I can't stand it. I been there before.
Adventures of Huckleberry Finn, 43

11   He [George Washington Cable] has taught me to abhor and detest the Sabbath-day and hunt up new and troublesome ways to dishonor it.
Letter to William Dean Howells [February 27, 1885]

12   The difference between the *almost*-right word & the *right* word is really a large matter — it's the difference between the lightning bug and the lightning.
Letter to George Bainton [October 15, 1888]

13   We saw a faraway town sleeping in a valley by a winding river; and beyond it, on a hill, a vast gray fortress, with towers and turrets, the first I had ever seen, out of a picture.
"Bridgeport?" said I, pointing.
"Camelot," said he.
A Connecticut Yankee in King Arthur's Court [1889]. A Word of Explanation

14   Whenever the literary German dives into a sentence, that is the last you are going to see of him till he emerges on the other side of his Atlantic with his verb in his mouth.
A Connecticut Yankee in King Arthur's Court, ch. 22

15   Tell the truth or trump — but get the trick.
Pudd'nhead Wilson [1894]. Pudd'nhead Wilson's Calendar, ch. 1

16   Adam was but human — this explains it all. He did not want the apple for the apple's sake, he wanted it only because it was forbidden.
Pudd'nhead Wilson. Pudd'nhead Wilson's Calendar, 2

17   Training is everything. The peach was once a bitter almond; cauliflower is nothing but cabbage with a college education.
Pudd'nhead Wilson. Pudd'nhead Wilson's Calendar, 5

18   One of the most striking differences between a cat and a lie is that a cat has only nine lives.
Pudd'nhead Wilson. Pudd'nhead Wilson's Calendar, 7

19   The holy passion of Friendship is of so sweet and steady and loyal and enduring a nature that it will last through a whole lifetime, if not asked to lend money.
Pudd'nhead Wilson. Pudd'nhead Wilson's Calendar, 8

20   Why is it that we rejoice at a birth and grieve at a funeral? It is because we are not the person involved.
Pudd'nhead Wilson. Pudd'nhead Wilson's Calendar, 9

21   When angry, count four; when very angry, swear.
Pudd'nhead Wilson. Pudd'nhead Wilson's Calendar, 10

22   As to the Adjective: when in doubt, strike it out.
Pudd'nhead Wilson. Pudd'nhead Wilson's Calendar, 11

23   Nothing so needs reforming as other people's habits.
Pudd'nhead Wilson. Pudd'nhead Wilson's Calendar, 15

1   Put all your eggs in the one basket and — WATCH THAT BASKET.
> *Pudd'nhead Wilson. Pudd'nhead Wilson's Calendar, 15*

2   If you pick up a starving dog and make him prosperous, he will not bite you. This is the principal difference between a dog and a man.
> *Pudd'nhead Wilson. Pudd'nhead Wilson's Calendar, 16*

3   Few things are harder to put up with than the annoyance of a good example.
> *Pudd'nhead Wilson. Pudd'nhead Wilson's Calendar, 19*

4   It were not best that we should all think alike; it is difference of opinion that makes horse-races.
> *Pudd'nhead Wilson. Pudd'nhead Wilson's Calendar, 19*

5   [Citing a familiar "American joke":] In Boston they ask, How much does he know? in New York, How much is he worth? in Philadelphia, Who were his parents?   *What Paul Bourget Thinks of Us [1895]*

6   He saw nearly all things as through a glass eye, darkly.   *Fenimore Cooper's Literary Offenses [1895]*

7   When a person has a poor ear for music he will flat and sharp right along without knowing it. He keeps near the tune, but it is *not* the tune. When a person has a poor ear for words, the result is a literary flatting and sharping; you perceive what he is intending to say, but you also perceive that he doesn't *say* it. This is Cooper.   *Fenimore Cooper's Literary Offenses*

8   Be good and you will be lonesome.
> *Following the Equator [1897]. Pudd'nhead Wilson's New Calendar, frontispiece caption*

9   Noise proves nothing. Often a hen who has merely laid an egg cackles as if she had laid an asteroid.
> *Following the Equator. Pudd'nhead Wilson's New Calendar, 5*

10   Truth is the most valuable thing we have. Let us economize it.
> *Following the Equator. Pudd'nhead Wilson's New Calendar, 7*

11   It could probably be shown by facts and figures that there is no distinctly native American criminal class except Congress.
> *Following the Equator. Pudd'nhead Wilson's New Calendar, 8*

12   Everything human is pathetic. The secret source of Humor itself is not joy but sorrow. There is no humor in heaven.
> *Following the Equator. Pudd'nhead Wilson's New Calendar, 10*

13   Pity is for the living, envy is for the dead.
> *Following the Equator. Pudd'nhead Wilson's New Calendar, 19*

14   It is by the goodness of God that in our country we have those three unspeakably precious things: freedom of speech, freedom of conscience, and the prudence never to practice either of them.
> *Following the Equator. Pudd'nhead Wilson's New Calendar, 20*

15   "Classic." A book which people praise and don't read.
> *Following the Equator. Pudd'nhead Wilson's New Calendar, 25*

16   Man is the only animal that blushes. Or needs to.
> *Following the Equator. Pudd'nhead Wilson's New Calendar, 27*

17   Each person is born to one possession which outvalues all his others — his last breath.
> *Following the Equator. Pudd'nhead Wilson's New Calendar, 42*

18   It takes your enemy and your friend, working together, to hurt you to the heart; the one to slander you and the other to get the news to you.
> *Following the Equator. Pudd'nhead Wilson's New Calendar, 45*

19   In statesmanship get the formalities right, never mind about the moralities.
> *Following the Equator. Pudd'nhead Wilson's New Calendar, 65*

20   Everyone is a moon, and has a dark side which he never shows to anybody.
> *Following the Equator. Pudd'nhead Wilson's New Calendar, 66*

21   The report of my death was an exaggeration.
> *Note to London correspondent of the New York Journal [June 1, 1897]*

22   Always do right. This will gratify some people, and astonish the rest.
> *Card sent to the Young People's Society, Greenpoint Presbyterian Church, Brooklyn [February 16, 1901]*

23   The modern patriotism, the true patriotism, the only rational patriotism, is *loyalty to the Nation* ALL *the time, loyalty to the Government when it deserves it.*[1]
> *The Czar's Soliloquy [1905]*

24   I believe that our Heavenly Father invented man because he was disappointed in the monkey.
> *Autobiographical Dictation [November 24, 1906]*

---

[1]Often cited as: Patriotism is supporting your country all the time and your government when it deserves it.

1   Laws are sand, customs are rock. Laws can be evaded and punishment escaped, but an openly transgressed custom brings sure punishment.
The Gorky Incident [1906]

2   Thunder is good, thunder is impressive; but it is the lightning that does the work.
Letter to an Unidentified Person
[August 28, 1908]

3   Power, money, persuasion, supplication, persecution — these can lift at a colossal humbug — push it a little — weaken it a little, century by century, but only laughter can blow it to rags and atoms at a blast. Against the assault of laughter nothing can stand.
The Mysterious Stranger [1922], ch. 10

4   O kind missionary, O compassionate missionary, leave China! come home and convert these Christians!
Europe and Elsewhere [1923].
The United States of Lyncherdom

5   You tell me whar a man gits his corn pone, en I'll tell you what his 'pinions is.
Europe and Elsewhere. Corn-Pone Opinions

6   Biographies are but the clothes and buttons of the man — the biography of the man himself cannot be written.   *Autobiography [1924], vol. I*

7   [Man] has imagined a heaven, and has left entirely out of it the supremest of all his delights ... sexual intercourse! ... His heaven is like himself: strange, interesting, astonishing, grotesque. I give you my word, it has not a single feature in it that he *actually values.*
Letters from the Earth [1962], II

8   [The Bible] has noble poetry in it; and some clever fables; and some blood-drenched history; and a wealth of obscenity; and upwards of a thousand lies.
Letters from the Earth, III

9   When I was younger I could remember anything, whether it happened or not; but I am getting old, and soon I shall remember only the latter.
From ALBERT BIGELOW PAINE *[1861–1937],*
Mark Twain, A Biography [1912]

10   Clothes make the man. Naked people have little or no influence in society.   *Attributed*

11   Everybody talks about the weather, but nobody does anything about it.[1]   *Attributed*

12   Golf is a good walk spoiled.   *Attributed*

---

[1]Considerable contemporary evidence associates this quotation with Charles Dudley Warner (see 507). A variant version — "We all grumble about the weather but nothing is *done* about it" — appears in Robert Underwood Johnson's recollections of Mark Twain (*Remembered Yesterdays* [1923]).

Isabella Mary Beeton
1836–1865

13   A place for everything and everything in its place.[2]
The Book of Household Management [1861]

14   Clear as you go.
The Book of Household Management

Joseph Chamberlain
1836–1914

15   The day of small nations has long passed away. The day of Empires has come.
Speech. Birmingham [May 12, 1904]

Sir W[illiam] S[chwenck] Gilbert
1836–1911

16 Oh, I am a cook and a captain bold
And the mate of the *Nancy* brig,
And a bo'sun tight, and a midshipmite,
And the crew of the captain's gig.
The "Bab" Ballads [1866–1871].
The Yarn of the "Nancy Bell," st. 3

17 As innocent as a new-laid egg.
Engaged [1877], act I

18 I'm called Little Buttercup — dear little Buttercup,
Though I could never tell why.
H.M.S. Pinafore [1878], act I

19 I am the Captain of the *Pinafore;*
And a right good captain too!   *H.M.S. Pinafore, I*

20 And I'm never, never sick at sea!
What, never?
No, never!
What, *never?*
Hardly ever!
He's hardly ever sick at sea!
Then give three cheers, and one cheer more
For the hardy Captain of the *Pinafore!*
H.M.S. Pinafore, I

21 And so do his sisters, and his cousins, and his aunts!
His sisters and his cousins,
Whom he reckons up by dozens,
And his aunts!   *H.M.S. Pinafore, I*

22 When I was a lad I served a term
As office boy to an Attorney's firm.
I cleaned the windows and I swept the floor

---

[2]In a well-conducted man-of-war ... everything is in its place, and there is a place for everything. — FREDERICK MARRYAT, *Masterman Ready* [1842]

And I polished up the handle of the big front door.
I polished up that handle so carefullee
That now I am the Ruler of the Queen's Navee!
H.M.S. Pinafore, I

1 Stick close to your desks and *never go to sea,*
And you all may be Rulers of the Queen's Navee!
H.M.S. Pinafore, I

2 Things are seldom what they seem,
Skim milk masquerades as cream.
H.M.S. Pinafore, II

3 He is an Englishman!
For he himself has said it,
And it's greatly to his credit,
That he is an Englishman!　*H.M.S. Pinafore, II*

4 For he might have been a Roosian,
A French or Turk or Proosian,
Or perhaps Itali-an.
But in spite of all temptations
To belong to other nations,
He remains an Englishman.　*H.M.S. Pinafore, II*

5 It is, it is a glorious thing
To be a Pirate King.
Pirates of Penzance [1879], act I

6 I am the very model of a modern Major-General.
I've information vegetable, animal, and mineral,
I know the Kings of England, and I quote the fights historical,
From Marathon to Waterloo, in order categorical.
Pirates of Penzance, I

7 When the foeman bares his steel,
Tarantara, tarantara!
We uncomfortable feel,
Tarantara.　*Pirates of Penzance, II*

8 When constabulary duty's to be done,
The policeman's lot is not a happy one.
Pirates of Penzance, II

9 Come, friends, who plow the sea,
Truce to navigation,
Take another station;
Let's vary piracee
With a little burglaree.[1]
Pirates of Penzance, II

10 You must lie upon the daisies and discourse in novel phrases of your complicated state of mind,
The meaning doesn't matter if it's only idle chatter of a transcendental kind.
And everyone will say,
As you walk your mystic way,

---

[1]Sir Arthur Sullivan's music for these lines is familiar as the tune of the chorus "Hail, hail, the gang's all here," from the song "Alabama Jubilee" [1915].

"If this young man expresses himself in terms too deep for *me,*
Why, what a very singularly deep young man this deep young man must be!"
Patience [1881], act I

11 Though the Philistines may jostle, you will rank as an apostle in the high aesthetic band,
If you walk down Piccadilly with a poppy or a lily in your medieval hand.
And everyone will say,
As you walk your flowery way,
"If he's content with a vegetable love, which would certainly not suit *me,*
Why, what a most particularly pure young man this pure young man must be!"　*Patience, I*

12 Prithee, pretty maiden, will you marry me?
(Hey, but I'm hopeful, willow, willow, waly!)
Patience, I

13 Francesca da Rimini, miminy, piminy,
Je-ne-sais-quoi young man!　*Patience, II*

14 A greenery-yallery, Grosvenor Gallery,
Foot-in-the-grave young man!　*Patience, II*

15 I see no objection to stoutness, in moderation.
Iolanthe [1882], act I

16 None shall part us from each other,
One in life and death are we:
All in all to one another —
I to thee and thou to me!
Thou the tree and I the flower —
Thou the idol; I the throng —
Thou the day and I the hour —
Thou the singer; I the song!　*Iolanthe, I*

17 Bow, bow, ye lower middle classes!
Bow, bow, ye tradesmen, bow, ye masses.
Iolanthe, I

18 The Law is the true embodiment
Of everything that's excellent.
It has no kind of fault or flaw,
And I, my Lords, embody the Law.　*Iolanthe, I*

19 Pretty young wards in Chancery.　*Iolanthe, I*

20 For I'm not so old, and not so plain,
And I'm quite prepared to marry again.　*Iolanthe, I*

21 When I went to the Bar as a very young man
(Said I to myself, said I).　*Iolanthe, I*

22 I often think it's comical
How nature always does contrive
That every boy and every gal,
That's born into the world alive,
Is either a little Liberal,
Or else a little Conservative!　*Iolanthe, II*

1 Here's a pretty kettle of fish!   *Iolanthe, II*

2 The House of Peers, throughout the war,
Did nothing in particular,
And did it very well.   *Iolanthe, II*

3 When you're lying awake with a dismal headache, and
repose is taboo'd by anxiety,
I conceive you may use any language you choose to
indulge in, without impropriety.   *Iolanthe, II*

4 For you dream you are crossing the Channel, and
tossing about in a steamer from Harwich —
Which is something between a large bathing machine
and a very small second-class carriage.
    Iolanthe, II

5 Faint heart never won fair lady!
Nothing venture, nothing win —
Blood is thick, but water's thin —
In for a penny, in for a pound[1] —
It's Love that makes the world go round!
    Iolanthe, II

6 I love my fellow creatures — I do all the good I can —
Yet everybody says I'm such a disagreeable man!
And I can't think why!
    Princess Ida [1884], act I

7 A wandering minstrel I —
A thing of shreds and patches,
Of ballads, songs and snatches,
And dreamy lullaby!
    The Mikado [1885], act I

8 To sit in solemn silence in a dull dark dock,
In a pestilential prison, with a life-long lock,
Awaiting the sensation of a short, sharp shock,
From a cheap and chippy chopper on a big black
block.   *The Mikado, I*

9 I can't help it. I was born sneering.   *The Mikado, I*

10 As some day it may happen that a victim must be
found,
I've got a little list — I've got a little list.
Of society offenders who might well be
underground,
And who never would be missed — who never would
be missed.   *The Mikado, I*

11 Then the idiot who praises, with enthusiastic tone,
All centuries but this, and every country but his
own.   *The Mikado, I*

12 Three little maids from school are we,
Pert as a schoolgirl well can be,
Filled to the brim with girlish glee.   *The Mikado, I*

13 Ah, pray make no mistake,
We are not shy;
We're very wide awake,
The moon and I!   *The Mikado, II*

14 Here's a pretty state of things!
Here's a pretty how-de-do!   *The Mikado, II*

15 My object all sublime
I shall achieve in time —
To let the punishment fit the crime.[2]
    The Mikado, II

16 A source of innocent merriment!   *The Mikado, II*

17 On a cloth untrue
With a twisted cue
And elliptical billiard balls.   *The Mikado, II*

18 I seized him by his little pig-tail,
And on his knees fell he,
As he squirmed and struggled,
And gurgled and guggled,
I drew my snickersnee!   *The Mikado, II*

19 Merely corroborative detail, intended to give
artistic verisimilitude to an otherwise bald and unconvincing narrative.   *The Mikado, II*

20 The flowers that bloom in the spring, tra la,
Have nothing to do with the case.   *The Mikado, II*

21 On a tree by a river a little tomtit
Sang "Willow, titwillow, titwillow!"
And I said to him, "Dicky-bird, why do you sit
Singing 'Willow, titwillow, titwillow!'
"Is it weakness of intellect, birdie?" I cried,
"Or a rather tough worm in your little inside?"
With a shake of his poor little head he replied,
"Oh, willow, titwillow, titwillow!"
    The Mikado, II

22 He uses language that would make your hair curl.
    Ruddigore [1887], act I

23 When the footpads quail at the night-bird's wail, and
black dogs bay at the moon,
Then is the specters' holiday — then is the ghosts'
high noon!
    Ruddigore, II

24 I have a song to sing, O!
Sing me your song, O!
    The Yeomen of the Guard [1888], act I

25 It's a song of a merryman, moping mum,
Whose soul was sad, and whose glance was glum,
Who sipped no sup, and who craved no crumb,
As he sighed for the love of a lady.
    The Yeomen of the Guard, I

---

[1]Well, then o'er shoes, o'er boots. And in for a penny, in for a
Pound. — EDWARD RAVENSCROFT [fl. 1671–1697], *The Canterbury
Guests; Or, A Bargain Broken* [1695], *act V, sc. i*

---

[2]See Cicero, 88:12.

1 He led his regiment from behind —
He found it less exciting.

The Gondoliers [1889], act I

2   That celebrated,
Cultivated,
Underrated
Nobleman,
The Duke of Plaza Toro!   *The Gondoliers, I*

3 No soldier in that gallant band
Hid half as well as he did.
He lay concealed throughout the war,
And so preserved his gore, O!   *The Gondoliers, I*

4 Of *that* there is no manner of doubt —
No probable, possible shadow of doubt —
No possible doubt whatever.   *The Gondoliers, I*

5 The gratifying feeling that our duty has been done.

The Gondoliers, II

6 When everyone is somebodee,
Then no one's anybody!   *The Gondoliers, II*

7 The world has joked incessantly for over fifty
centuries.
And every joke that's possible has long ago been
made.

His Excellency: The Played-Out Humorist [1894]

Bret Harte
[Francis Brett Harte]
1836–1902

8   Tell the boys I've got the Luck with me now.

The Luck of Roaring Camp [1868]

9   Beneath this tree lies the body of JOHN OAKHURST,
who struck a streak of bad luck on the 23rd of
November, 1850, and handed in his checks on the
7th of December, 1850.

The Outcasts of Poker Flat [1869]

10 Which I wish to remark,
And my language is plain,
That for ways that are dark
And for tricks that are vain,
The heathen Chinee is peculiar,
Which the same I would rise to explain.

Plain Language from Truthful James [1870]

Jane Ellice Hopkins
1836–1904

11   Genius is an infinite capacity for taking pains.[1]

Work Amongst Working Men [1870]

---

[1]See Georges Buffon, 304:6, and Thomas Carlyle, 408:8.

Leopold von Sacher-Masoch
1836–1895

12   Through his passion nature has given man into
woman's hands, and the woman who does not
know how to make him her subject, her slave, her toy,
and how to betray him with a smile in the end is
not wise.[2]

Venus in Furs [1870]

John Burroughs
1837–1921

13 Serene, I fold my hands and wait,
Nor care for wind, nor tide, nor sea;
I rave no more 'gainst time or fate,
For lo! my own shall come to me.

Waiting [1876], st. 1

14   I was born with a chronic anxiety about the
weather.

Is It Going to Rain? [1877]

15   One goes to Nature only for hints and half-truths.
Her facts are crude until you have absorbed them or
translated them. . . . It is not so much what we see as
what the thing seen suggests.

*Signs and Seasons [1886].
A Sharp Lookout*

16   It is always easier to believe than to deny. Our
minds are naturally affirmative.

*The Light of Day [1900].
The Modern Skeptic*

17   We are rooted to the air through our lungs and to
the soil through our stomachs. We are walking trees
and floating plants.

*Leaf and Tendril [1908].
The Grist of the Gods*

18   Nature teaches more than she preaches. There are
no sermons in stones. It is easier to get a spark out of
a stone than a moral.

*Time and Change [1912].
The Gospel of Nature*

Grover Cleveland
1837–1908

19   Your every voter, as surely as your chief magistrate, exercises a public trust.[3]

Inaugural Address [March 4, 1885]

---

[2]Translated by FERNANDA SAVAGE.

[3]"Public office is a public trust" was used by the Cleveland
administration as its motto.

George Dewey
1837–1917

1   You may fire when you are ready, Gridley.
> *To the captain of Admiral Dewey's flagship
> at the battle of Manila Bay [May 1, 1898]*

William Dean Howells
1837–1920

2   Our novelists, therefore, concern themselves with the more smiling aspects of life, which are the more American, and seek the universal in the individual rather than the social interests.
> *The Editor's Study [Harper's,
> September 1886]*

3   Clemens was sole, incomparable, the Lincoln of our literature.   *My Mark Twain [1910]*

4   What the American public wants is *a tragedy with a happy ending.*
> *To Edith Wharton; quoted in her French
> Ways and Their Meaning [1919]*

5   Some people can stay longer in an hour than others can in a week.   *Attributed*

J[ohn] P[ierpont] Morgan
1837–1913

6   A man always has two reasons for what he does — a good one, and the real one.
> *From Owen Wister [1860–1938],
> Roosevelt: The Story of a Friendship [1930]*

7   Any man who has to ask about the annual upkeep of a yacht can't afford one.   *Attributed*

8   Never be on the bear side but on the bull side when the United States is in question.[1]   *Attributed*

Horace Porter
1837–1921

9   A mugwump is a person educated beyond his intellect.
> *A slogan of the Cleveland-Blaine campaign [1884]*

Innes Randolph
1837–1887

10 Oh, I'm a good old rebel, that's what I am.
> *A Good Old Rebel [c. 1870], st. 1*

---

[1]Also attributed to Junius S. Morgan [1813–1890].

11 I won't be reconstructed, and I don't give a damn.
> *A Good Old Rebel, st. 4*

Algernon Charles Swinburne
1837–1909

12 When the hounds of spring are on winter's traces,
The mother of months in meadow or plain
Fills the shadows and windy places
With lisp of leaves and ripple of rain;
And the brown bright nightingale amorous
Is half assuaged for Itylus,
For the Thracian ships and the foreign faces,
The tongueless vigil, and all the pain.
> *Atalanta in Calydon [1865], chorus, st. 1*

13 For winter's rains and ruins are over,
And all the season of snows and sins;
The days dividing lover and lover,
The light that loses, the night that wins;
And time remembered is grief forgotten,
And frosts are slain and flowers begotten,
And in green underwood and cover
Blossom by blossom the spring begins.
> *Atalanta in Calydon, st. 4*

14 Before the beginning of years
There came to the making of man
Time, with a gift of tears;
Grief, with a glass that ran;
Pleasure, with pain for leaven;
Summer, with flowers that fell;
Remembrance fallen from heaven,
And madness risen from hell;
Strength without hands to smite;
Love that endures for a breath;
Night, the shadow of light,
And life, the shadow of death.
> *Atalanta in Calydon, chorus, st. 1*

15 For words divide and rend;
But silence is most noble till the end.
> *Atalanta in Calydon, chorus, st. 1*

16   Change in a trice
The lilies and languors of virtue
For the raptures and roses of vice.
> *Dolores [1866], st. 9*

17 O splendid and sterile Dolores,
Our Lady of Pain.   *Dolores, st. 9*

18 The delight that consumes the desire,
The desire that outruns the delight.   *Dolores, st. 14*

19 For the crown of our life as it closes
Is darkness, the fruit there of dust.   *Dolores, st. 20*

20 What ailed us, O gods, to desert you
For creeds that refuse and restrain?

Come down and redeem us from virtue,
Our Lady of Pain.   *Dolores, st. 35*

1 Lo, this is she that was the world's delight.
                         Laus Veneris [1866], st. 3

2 Ah, yet would God this flesh of mine might be
Where air might wash and long leaves cover me;
Where tides of grass break into foam of flowers,
Or where the wind's feet shine along the sea.
                              Laus Veneris, st. 14

3 O sad kissed mouth, how sorrowful it is!
                              Laus Veneris, st. 79

4 To have known love, how bitter a thing it is.
                             Laus Veneris, st. 103

5 There will no man do for your sake, I think,
What I would have done for the least word said.
I had wrung life dry for your lips to drink,
Broken it up for your daily bread.
                  The Triumph of Time [1866], st. 12

6 At the door of life, by the gate of breath,
There are worse things waiting for men than death.
                        The Triumph of Time, st. 20

7 I will go back to the great sweet mother,
Mother and lover of men, the sea.
                        The Triumph of Time, st. 33

8 I have lived long enough, having seen one thing, that
love hath an end.
                     Hymn to Proserpine [1866], l. 1

9 Thou hast conquered, O pale Galilean;[1] the world has
    grown gray from thy breath;
We have drunken of things Lethean, and fed on the
    fullness of death.
Laurel is green for a season, and love is sweet for a
    day;
But love grows bitter with treason, and laurel outlives
    not May.
Sleep, shall we sleep after all? for the world is not
    sweet in the end;
For the old faiths loosen and fall, the new years ruin
    and rend.   *Hymn to Proserpine, l. 35*

10 For there is no God found stronger than death; and
    death is a sleep.
                        Hymn to Proserpine, l. 110

11 If love were what the rose is,
And I were like the leaf,
Our lives would grow together
In sad or singing weather.   *A Match [1866], st. 1*

12 If you were April's lady,
And I were lord in May.   *A Match, st. 5*

---
[1]See Julian, 114:9.

13 If you were queen of pleasure,
And I were king of pain,
We'd hunt down love together,
Pluck out his flying feather,
And teach his feet a measure,
And find his mouth a rein.   *A Match, st. 6*

14 For life is sweet, but after life is death.
This is the end of every man's desire.
            A Ballad of Burdens [1866]. L'Envoy

15 Here, where the world is quiet;
Here, where all trouble seems
Dead winds' and spent waves' riot
In doubtful dreams of dreams.
          The Garden of Proserpine [1866], st. 1

16 I am tired of tears and laughter,
And men that laugh and weep;
Of what may come hereafter
For men that sow and reap:
I am weary of days and hours,
Blown buds of barren flowers,
Desires and dreams and powers
And everything but sleep.
              The Garden of Proserpine, st. 2

17 We are not sure of sorrow,
And joy was never sure.
             The Garden of Proserpine, st. 10

18 Ah that such sweet things should be fleet,
Such fleet things sweet!   *Félise [1866], st. 22*

19 And the best and the worst of this is
That neither is most to blame,
If you have forgotten my kisses
And I have forgotten your name.
                      An Interlude [1866], st. 14

20 I am that which began;
Out of me the years roll;
Out of me God and man;
I am equal and whole;
God changes, and man, and the form of them bodily;
I am the soul.   *Hertha [1871], st. 1*

21 In the gray beginning of years, in the twilight of
    things that began,
The word of the earth in the ears of the world, was it
    God? was it man?   *Hymn of Man [1871]*

22 Glory to Man in the highest! for Man is the master of
    things.   *Hymn of Man*

23 Poor splendid wings so frayed and soiled and torn!
            A Ballad of François Villon [1878], st. 3

24 Villon, our sad bad glad mad brother's name.
              A Ballad of François Villon, refrain

25 In a coign of the cliff between lowland and highland,
At the sea-down's edge between windward and lee,

Walled round with rocks as an inland island,
The ghost of a garden fronts the sea.
> *A Forsaken Garden [1878], st. 1*

1 Sleep; and if life was bitter to thee, pardon,
If sweet, give thanks; thou hast no more to live;
And to give thanks is good, and to forgive.
> *Ave Atque Vale: In Memory of Charles
> Baudelaire [1878], st. 17*

2 Body and spirit are twins: God only knows which is
which.
> *The Higher Pantheism in a Nutshell
> [1880], st. 7*

3 God, whom we see not, is: and God, who is not,
we see:
Fiddle, we know, is diddle: and diddle, we take it,
is dee.
> *The Higher Pantheism in a Nutshell, st. 12*

Henry [Brooks] Adams
1838–1918

4 Politics, as a practice, whatever its professions, has
always been the systematic organization of hatreds.
> *The Education of Henry Adams [1907],
> ch. 1*

5 Accident counts for much in companionship as in
marriage.
> *The Education of Henry Adams, 4*

6 Women have, commonly, a very positive moral
sense; that which they will, is right; that which they
reject, is wrong; and their will, in most cases, ends
by settling the moral.
> *The Education of Henry Adams, 6*

7 All experience is an arch, to build upon.
> *The Education of Henry Adams, 6*

8 Only on the edge of the grave can man conclude
anything.
> *The Education of Henry Adams, 6*

9 No man, however strong, can serve ten years as
schoolmaster, priest, or senator, and remain fit for
anything else. *The Education of Henry Adams, 7*

10 Although the Senate is much given to admiring in
its members a superiority less obvious or quite invisible to outsiders, one Senator seldom proclaims his
own inferiority to another, and still more seldom likes
to be told of it. *The Education of Henry Adams, 7*

11 Friends are born, not made.
> *The Education of Henry Adams, 7*

12 A friend in power is a friend lost.
> *The Education of Henry Adams, 7*

13 The effect of power and publicity on all men is the
aggravation of self, a sort of tumor that ends by killing
the victim's sympathies.
> *The Education of Henry Adams, 10*

14 Young men have a passion for regarding their
elders as senile.
> *The Education of Henry Adams, 11*

15 Knowledge of human nature is the beginning and
end of political education.
> *The Education of Henry Adams, 12*

16 The American mind exasperated the European as
a buzz-saw might exasperate a pine forest.
> *The Education of Henry Adams, 12*

17 Intimates are predestined.
> *The Education of Henry Adams, 13*

18 Chaos often breeds life, when order breeds
habit. *The Education of Henry Adams, 13*

19 At best, the renewal of broken relations is a nervous matter.
> *The Education of Henry Adams, 16*

20 [Charles] Sumner's mind had reached the calm of
water which receives and reflects images without
absorbing them; it contained nothing but itself.
> *The Education of Henry Adams, 16*

21 The difference is slight, to the influence of an
author, whether he is read by five hundred readers,
or by five hundred thousand; if he can select the five
hundred, he reaches the five hundred thousand.
> *The Education of Henry Adams, 17*

22 The progress of Evolution from President Washington to President Grant was alone evidence enough
to upset Darwin.
> *The Education of Henry Adams, 17*

23 A teacher affects eternity; he can never tell where
his influence stops.
> *The Education of Henry Adams, 20*

24 One friend in a lifetime is much; two are many;
three are hardly possible. Friendship needs a certain
parallelism of life, a community of thought, a rivalry
of aim. *The Education of Henry Adams, 20*

25 What one knows is, in youth, of little moment;
they know enough who know how to learn.
> *The Education of Henry Adams, 21*

26 He had often noticed that six months' oblivion
amounts to newspaper death, and that resurrection
is rare. Nothing is easier, if a man wants it, than rest,
profound as the grave.
> *The Education of Henry Adams, 22*

27 Morality is a private and costly luxury.
> *The Education of Henry Adams, 22*

1 Practical politics consists in ignoring facts.
The Education of Henry Adams, 24

2 Nothing in education is so astonishing as the amount of ignorance it accumulates in the form of inert facts. *The Education of Henry Adams, 25*

3 Power when wielded by abnormal energy is the most serious of facts.
The Education of Henry Adams, 28

4 Modern politics is, at bottom, a struggle not of men but of forces.
The Education of Henry Adams, 28

5 We combat obstacles in order to get repose, and, when got, the repose is insupportable.
The Education of Henry Adams, 29

6 No one means all he says, and yet very few say all they mean, for words are slippery and thought is viscous. *The Education of Henry Adams, 31*

7 Even in America, the Indian summer of life should be a little sunny and a little sad, like the season, and infinite in wealth and depth of tone — but never hustled.

The Education of Henry Adams, 35

John Wilkes Booth
1838–1865

8 Sic semper tyrannis! The South is avenged!
After shooting President Lincoln
[April 14, 1865]

James Bryce
1838–1922

9 Europeans often ask, and Americans do not always explain, how it happens that this great office [the presidency], the greatest in the world, unless we except the Papacy, to which any man can rise by his own merits, is not more frequently filled by great and striking men.
The American Commonwealth [1888],
vol. I, ch. 8

10 The government of cities is the one conspicuous failure of the United States.
The American Commonwealth, I, 51

John Milton Hay
1838–1905

11 I'll hold her nozzle agin the bank
Till the last galoot's ashore.
Pike County Ballads [1871]. Jim Bludso, st. 5

12 And Christ ain't a-going to be too hard
On a man that died for men.
Pike County Ballads. Jim Bludso,
st. 7

13 It [the Spanish-American War] has been a splendid little war, begun with the highest motives, carried on with magnificent intelligence and spirit, favored by that fortune which loves the brave.
Letter to Theodore Roosevelt
[July 27, 1898]

14 The open door.
To the Cabinet regarding completion of the trade policy he had negotiated with China [January 2, 1900]

William Edward Hartpole Lecky
1838–1903

15 The Augustinian doctrine of the damnation of unbaptized infants and the Calvinistic doctrine of reprobation . . . surpass in atrocity any tenets that have ever been admitted into any pagan creed.
History of European Morals [1869],
vol. I, ch. 1

George Leybourne
1842–1886

16 He flies through the air with the greatest
of ease,
This daring young man on the flying trapeze;
His figure is handsome, all girls he can please,
And my love he purloined her away!
The Man on the Flying Trapeze[1] [1860]

Lydia Kamekeha Liliuokalani
1838–1917

17 Farewell to thee, farewell to thee . . .
Until we meet again.
Aloha Oe (Farewell to Thee) [1878]

Ernst Mach
1838–1916

18 Physics is experience, arranged in economical order.
The Economical Nature of Physical Inquiry [1882]

---

[1]Music by ALFRED LEE.

John, Viscount Morley
of Blackburn
1838–1923

1 Where it is a duty to worship the sun it is pretty sure to be a crime to examine the laws of heat.
Voltaire [1872]

2 You have not converted a man because you have silenced him.
Rousseau [1876]

3 The great business of life is to be, to do, to do without, and to depart.
Address on Aphorisms [1887]

4 No man can climb out beyond the limitations of his own character.
Critical Miscellanies [1908]. Robespierre

5 Success depends on three things: who says it, what he says, how he says it; and of these three things, what he says is the least important.
Recollections [1917], vol. II, bk. 5, ch. 4

John Muir
1838–1914

6 In God's wildness lies the hope of the world — the great fresh unblighted, unredeemed wilderness.[1]
Alaska Fragment [1890]

7 When we try to pick out anything by itself, we find it hitched to everything else in the universe.
My First Summer in the Sierra [1911]

8 All the wilderness seems to be full of tricks and plans to drive and draw us up into God's light.
My First Summer in the Sierra

9 The clearest way into the Universe is through a forest wilderness.
John of the Mountains [1938]

10 The mountains are fountains of men as well as of rivers, of glaciers, of fertile soil. The great poets, philosophers, prophets, able men whose thought and deeds have moved the world, have come down from the mountains — mountain-dwellers who have grown strong there with the forest trees in Nature's workshops.
John of the Mountains

11 Most people are *on* the world, not in it — have no conscious sympathy or relationship to anything about them — undiffused, separate, and rigidly alone like marbles of polished stone, touching but separate.
John of the Mountains

12 How hard to realize that every camp of men or beast has this glorious starry firmament for a roof!

In such places standing alone on the mountaintop it is easy to realize that whatever special nests we make — leaves and moss like the marmots and birds, or tents or piled stone — we all dwell in a house of one room — the world with the firmament for its roof — and are sailing the celestial spaces without leaving any track.
John of the Mountains

Philippe Auguste Villiers
de L'Isle-Adam
1838–1889

13 I have thought too much to stoop to action![2]
Axel [1890]

Paul Cézanne
1839–1906

14 Taste is the best judge, but it is rare. Art is accessible only to a very small number of individuals.[3]
Letter to Émile Bernard [May 12, 1904]

15 Right now a moment of time is fleeting by! Capture its reality in paint! To do that we must put all else out of our minds. We must become that moment, make ourselves a sensitive recording plate . . . give the image of what we actually see, forgetting everything that has been seen before our time.
From JOACHIM GASQUET [1873–1921], Paul Cézanne[4] [1921]

16 The day is coming when a single carrot, freshly observed [in a painting], will set off a revolution.
From JOACHIM GASQUET, Paul Cézanne

17 Treat nature in terms of the cylinder, the sphere, the cone, all in perspective.
From ÉMILE BERNARD [1868–1941], Paul Cézanne [1925]

18 Monet is only an eye — but what an eye![5]
From AMBROISE VOLLARD [1866–1939], Cézanne [1937], ch. 7

Francis Pharcellus Church
1839–1906

19 Yes, Virginia, there is a Santa Claus. . . . Thank God! he lives, and he lives forever. A thousand years from now, Virginia, nay ten times ten thousand years

---

[1]See Henry David Thoreau, 475:29.

[2]J'ai trop pensé pour daigner agir!
[3]Translated by JULIE LAWRENCE COCHRAN.
[4]Translated by NORBERT GUTERMAN.
[5]Monet n'est qu'un oeil — mais quel oeil!
Translated by HAROLD L. VAN DOREN.

from now, he will continue to make glad the heart of childhood.[1]

Editorial in the New York Sun
[September 21, 1897]

Henry George
1839–1897

1 So long as all the increased wealth which modern progress brings goes but to build up great fortunes, to increase luxury and make sharper the contrast between the House of Have and the House of Want, progress is not real and cannot be permanent.

Progress and Poverty [1879].
Introductory: The Problem

Joaquim Machado de Assis
1839–1908

2 There is only one genuine misfortune: not to be born.[2]

Epitaph of a Small Winner [1881]

Walter Pater
1839–1894

3 Every intellectual product must be judged from the point of view of the age and the people in which it was produced.

Studies in the History of the Renaissance
[1873]. Mirandola

4 Hers is the head upon which all "the ends of the world are come," and the eyelids are a little weary. It is a beauty wrought out from within upon the flesh, the deposit, little cell by cell, of strange thoughts and fantastic reveries and exquisite passions. Set it for a moment beside one of those white Greek goddesses or beautiful women of antiquity, and how would they be troubled by this beauty, into which the soul with all its maladies has passed?

Studies in the History of the Renaissance.
Leonardo da Vinci [Mona Lisa]

5 She is older than the rocks among which she sits; like the vampire, she has been dead many times, and learned the secrets of the grave; and has been a diver in deep seas, and keeps their fallen day about her; and trafficked for strange webs with Eastern merchants: and as Leda, was the mother of Helen of Troy, and, as Saint Anne, the mother of Mary; and all this has

been to her but as the sound of lyres and flutes, and lives only in the delicacy with which it has molded the changing lineaments, and tinged the eyelids and the hands.

Studies in the History of the Renaissance.
Leonardo da Vinci [Mona Lisa]

6 All art constantly aspires towards the condition of music.

Studies in the History of the Renaissance.
The School of Giorgione

7 Not the fruit of experience, but experience itself, is the end.

Studies in the History of the Renaissance.
Conclusion

8 To burn always with this hard, gemlike flame, to maintain this ecstasy, is success in life.

Studies in the History of the Renaissance.
Conclusion

9 Art comes to you proposing frankly to give nothing but the highest quality to your moments as they pass.

Studies in the History of the Renaissance.
Conclusion

10 To know when one's self is interested, is the first condition of interesting other people.

Marius the Epicurean [1885], ch. 6

11 It is the addition of strangeness to beauty that constitutes the romantic character in art.

Appreciation [1889]. Postscript

Charles Sanders Peirce
1839–1914

12 Do not block the way of inquiry.

Collected Papers [1931–1958],
vol. I, par. 135

13 The idea does not belong to the soul; it is the soul that belongs to the idea.

Collected Papers, I, 216

14 Every man is fully satisfied that there is such a thing as truth, or he would not ask any question.

Collected Papers, V, 211

15 Let us not pretend to doubt in philosophy what we do not doubt in our hearts.

Collected Papers, V, 265

16 All the evolution we know of proceeds from the vague to the definite.

Collected Papers, VI, 191

17 Our whole past experience is continually in our consciousness, though most of it sunk to a great

---

[1]Responding to a letter from eight-year-old Virginia O'Hanlon: "Please tell me the truth; is there a Santa Claus?"

[2]Translated by WILLIAM L. GROSSMAN.

depth of dimness. I think of consciousness as a bottomless lake, whose waters seem transparent, yet into which we can clearly see but a little way.

Collected Papers, VII, 547

1   When I communicate my thought and my sentiments to a friend with whom I am in full sympathy, so that my feelings pass into him and I am conscious of what he feels, do I not live in his brain as well as in my own — most literally?

Collected Papers, VII, 591

2   Unless man have a natural bent in accordance with nature's, he has no chance of understanding nature at all.

A Neglected Argument for the Reality of God [1908]

James Ryder Randall
1839–1908

3 Avenge the patriotic gore
That flecked the streets of Baltimore,
And be the battle queen of yore,
Maryland! My Maryland!

Maryland! My Maryland! [1861], st. 1

John Davison Rockefeller
1839–1937

4   God gave me my money. I believe the power to make money is a gift from God....I believe it is my duty to make money and still more money and to use the money I make for the good of my fellow man according to the dictates of my conscience.[1]

In an interview [1905]

Alexander [Clubber] Williams
1839–1917

5   There is more law in a policeman's nightstick than in a decision of the Supreme Court.

Attributed

6   I've been having chuck steak ever since I've been on the force, and now I'm going to have a bit of tenderloin.[2]

Attributed

Wilfrid Scawen Blunt
1840–1922

7 Ay, this is the famed rock, which Hercules
And Goth and Moor bequeathed us. At this door
England stands sentry.

Gibraltar

[Henry] Austin Dobson
1840–1921

8 Time goes, you say? Ah no!
Alas, Time stays, *we* go.

The Paradox of Time [1875], st. 1

9 Fame is a food that dead men eat —
I have no stomach for such meat.

Fame Is a Food That Dead Men Eat [1906], l. 1

Thomas Hardy
1840–1928

10 These purblind Doomsters had as readily strown
Blisses about my pilgrimage as pain.

Hap [1866]

11 When I set out for Lyonnesse,
A hundred miles away,
The rime was on the spray,
And starlight lit my lonesomeness.

When I Set Out for Lyonnesse [1870], st. 1

12   Good, but not religious-good.

Under the Greenwood Tree [1872], ch. 2

13   A lover without indiscretion is no lover at all.

The Hand of Ethelberta [1876]

14   In fact, precisely at this transitional point of its nightly roll into darkness the great and particular glory of the Egdon waste began, and nobody could be said to understand the heath who had not been there at such a time. It could best be felt when it could not clearly be seen.

The Return of the Native [1878], ch. 1

15   The place became full of a watchful intentness now; for when other things sank brooding to sleep the heath appeared slowly to awake and listen.

The Return of the Native, 1

16   The great inviolate place had an ancient permanence which the sea cannot claim. Who can say of a particular sea that it is old? Distilled by the sun, kneaded by the moon, it is renewed in a year, in a day, or in an hour. The sea changed, the fields changed, the rivers, the villages, and the people changed, yet Egdon remained.

The Return of the Native, 1

---

[1]He's kind iv a society f'r the previntion of croolty to money. If he finds a man misusing his money he takes it away fr'm him an' adopts it. — FINLEY PETER DUNNE [1867–1936], *Mr. Dooley Says* [1910]

[2]On being assigned [1876] as a police inspector to New York City's district most notorious for vice, which thus acquired its name.

1   The hard, half-apathetic expression of one who deems anything possible at the hands of Time and Chance, except, perhaps, fair play.

The Mayor of Casterbridge [1886], ch. 1

2   And all her shining keys will be took from her, and her cupboards opened, and little things 'a didn't wish seen, anybody will see; and her wishes and ways will be as nothing!   *The Mayor of Casterbridge, 18*

3   That Elizabeth-Jane Farfrae be not told of my death, or be made to grieve on account of me. And that I be not buried in consecrated ground. And that no sexton be asked to toll the bell. And that nobody is wished to see my dead body. And that no murners walk behind me at my funeral. And that no flours be planted on my grave. And that no man remember me.

The Mayor of Casterbridge, 45
[Henchard's will]

4   That cold accretion called the world, which, so terrible in the mass, is so unformidable, even pitiable, in its units.   *Tess of the D'Urbervilles [1891], ch. 13*

5   "Justice" was done, and the President of the Immortals (in Aeschylean phrase) had ended his sport with Tess.   *Tess of the D'Urbervilles, 59*

6   But nobody did come, because nobody does.

Jude the Obscure [1895], pt. I, ch. 4

7   The fundamental error of their matrimonial union; that of having based a permanent contract on a temporary feeling.   *Jude the Obscure, I, 11*

8   But sometimes a woman's love of being loved gets the better of her conscience.

Jude the Obscure, IV, 5

9   Done because we are too menny.

Jude the Obscure, VI, 2

10 I leant upon a coppice gate
When Frost was specter-gray,
And Winter's dregs made desolate
The weakening eye of day.

The Darkling Thrush [1900], st. 1

11 An aged thrush, frail, gaunt, and small,
In blast-beruffled plume.

The Darkling Thrush, st. 3

12 So little cause for carolings
Of such ecstatic sound
Was written on terrestrial things
Afar or nigh around,
That I could think there trembled through
His happy good-night air
Some blessed hope, whereof he knew
And I was unaware.   *The Darkling Thrush, st. 4*

13 Yes; quaint and curious war is!
You shoot a fellow down
You'd treat if met where any bar is,
Or help to half-a-crown.

The Man He Killed [1902], st. 5

14 What of the Immanent Will and its designs?
It works unconsciously as heretofore,
External artistries in circumstance.

The Dynasts [1904–1908], pt. I, forescene

15 A local cult called Christianity.

The Dynasts, I, Spirit of the Years, sc. vi

16   My argument is that War makes rattling good history; but Peace is poor reading.

The Dynasts, II, Spirit Sinister

17 And as the smart ship grew
In stature, grace, and hue,
In shadowy silent distance grew the Iceberg too.

The Convergence of the Twain
(Lines on the Loss of the Titanic) [1914], st. 8

18 Woman much missed, how you call to me, call to me,
Saying that now you are not as you were
When you had changed from the one who was all
    to me,
But as at first, when our day was fair.

The Voice [1914], st. 1

19 What of the faith and fire within us
Men who march away
Ere the barn cocks say
Night is growing gray,
Leaving all that here can win us.

Men Who March Away [1914], st. 1

20 That night your great guns, unawares,
Shook all our coffins as we lay,
And broke the chancel window-squares,
We thought it was the Judgment Day.

Channel Firing [1914], st. 1

21 We two kept house, the Past and I,
    The Past and I;
Through all my tasks it hovered nigh,
Leaving me never alone.

The Ghost of the Past [1914], st. 1

22 Only a man harrowing clods
In a slow silent walk
With an old horse that stumbles and nods
Half asleep as they stalk.

Only thin smoke without flame
From the heaps of couch grass:
Yet this will go onward the same
Though dynasties pass.

Yonder a maid and her wight
Come whispering by;
War's annals will cloud into night
Ere their story die.

In Time of "The Breaking of Nations" [1915]

1 Ah, no; the years, the years;
Down their chiseled names the raindrop plows.
During Wind and Rain [1917], st. 4

2 This is the weather the shepherd shuns,
And so do I. *Weathers [1922], st. 2*

3 And meadow rivulets overflow,
And drops on gate bars hang in a row,
And rooks in families homeward go,
And so do I. *Weathers, st. 2*

Chief Joseph[1]
c. 1840–1904

4 Our chiefs are killed....The old men are all dead....The little children are freezing to death. My people, some of them have run away to the hills and have no blankets, no food. No one knows where they are, perhaps freezing to death. I want to have time to look for my children and see how many of them I can find. Maybe I can find them among the dead. Hear me, my chiefs. My heart is sick and sad. From where the sun now stands I will fight no more forever.
To the Nez Percé tribe after surrender to General Nelson A. Miles [battle of Bear Paw Mountains, Montana, September 30–October 5, 1877]

Alfred Thayer Mahan
1840–1914

5 The world has never seen a more impressive demonstration of the influence of sea power upon its history. Those far distant, storm-beaten ships, upon which the Grand Army never looked, stood between it and the dominion of the world.
The Influence of Sea Power upon the French Revolution and Empire, 1793–1812 [1892], vol. II, p. 118

6 Whether they will or no, Americans must begin to look outward.
The Interest of America in Sea Power [1897]

William Graham Sumner
1840–1910

7 The Forgotten Man...delving away in patient industry, supporting his family, paying his taxes, casting his vote, supporting the church and the school...but he is the only one for whom there is no provision in the great scramble and the big divide. Such is the Forgotten Man. He works, he votes,

generally he prays—but his chief business in life is to pay....Who and where is the Forgotten Man in this case, who will have to pay for it all?
Speech. The Forgotten Man [1883]

8 Where torture has been long applied we find that it is developed to grades of incredible horror.
Folkways [1907], ch. 5

John Addington Symonds
1840–1893

9 These things shall be — a loftier race
Than e'er the world hath known shall rise
With flame of freedom in their souls,
And light of knowledge in their eyes.
The Days That Are to Be, st. 1

10 They shall be gentle, brave and strong
To spill no drop of blood, but dare
All that may plant man's lordship firm
On earth and fire and sea and air.
The Days That Are to Be, st. 2

Émile Zola
1840–1902

11 I am little concerned with beauty or perfection. I don't care for the great centuries. All I care about is life, struggle, intensity. I am at ease in my generation.
My Hates [1866]

12 A work of art is a corner of creation seen through a temperament. *My Hates*

13 My own art is a negation of society, an affirmation of the individual, outside all rules and demands of society. *My Hates*

14 Metaphysical man is dead; our whole field of enquiry is transformed by physiological man.
The Experimental Novel [1880]

15 Truth is on the march and nothing can stop it.
Article in Le Figaro [November 25, 1897]

16 J'accuse.
Title of open letter to the president of the French Republic, L'Aurore [January 13, 1898]

Georges Clemenceau
1841–1929

17 It is easier to make war than peace.[2]
Speech [1919]

---

[1]Hinmaton-Yalaktit: Thunder Rolling in the Mountains.

[2]Il est plus facile de faire la guerre que la paix.

1 America is the only nation in history which miraculously has gone directly from barbarism to degeneration without the usual interval of civilization.
Attributed

2 Military justice is to justice as military music is to music. *Attributed*

Oliver Wendell Holmes, Jr.
1841–1935

3 The life of the law has not been logic: it has been experience. *The Common Law [1881], Lecture I*

4 The law embodies the story of a nation's development through many centuries, and it cannot be dealt with as if it contained only the axioms and corollaries of a book of mathematics. *The Common Law, I*

5 I think that, as life is action and passion, it is required of a man that he should share the passion and action of his time at peril of being judged not to have lived. *Memorial Day Address [1884]*

6 Through our great good fortune, in our youth our hearts were touched with fire.
Memorial Day Address

7 I say to you in all sadness of conviction, that to think great thoughts you must be heroes as well as idealists. *The Profession of the Law [1886]*

8 Certainty generally is illusion, and repose is not the destiny of man. *The Path of the Law [1897]*

9 The remoter and more general aspects of the law are those which give it universal interest. It is through them that you not only become a great master in your calling, but connect your subject with the universe and catch an echo of the infinite, a glimpse of its unfathomable process, a hint of the universal law.
The Path of the Law

10 Life is an end in itself, and the only question as to whether it is worth living is whether you have enough of it.
Speech at Bar Association Dinner, Boston [1900]

11 A great man represents a great ganglion in the nerves of society, or, to vary the figure, a strategic point in the campaign of history, and part of his greatness consists in his being *there*.
John Marshall [1901]

12 Taxes are what we pay for civilized society.
Compañía de Tabacos v. Collector, 275 U.S. 87, 100 [1904]

13 Great cases like hard cases make bad law.
Northern Securities Co. v. United States, 193 U.S. 197, 400 [1904]

14 The Fourteenth Amendment does not enact Mr. Herbert Spencer's *Social Statics*.
Lochner v. New York, 198 U.S. 45, 75 [1905]

15 General propositions do not decide concrete cases. The decision will depend on a judgment or intuition more subtle than any articulate major premise.
Lochner v. New York, 198 U.S. 45, 78

16 Life is painting a picture, not doing a sum.
The Class of '61. From Speeches [1913]

17 The only prize much cared for by the powerful is power. The prize of the general is not a bigger tent, but command.
Law and the Court [1913]

18 I recognize without hesitation that judges do and must legislate, but they can do so only interstitially; they are confined from molar to molecular motions.
Southern Pacific Co. v. Jensen, 244 U.S. 205, 221 [1917]

19 The common law is not a brooding omnipresence in the sky but the articulate voice of some sovereign or quasi sovereign that can be identified.
Southern Pacific Co. v. Jensen, 244 U.S. 205, 222 [1917]

20 Certitude is not the test of certainty. We have been cocksure of many things that were not so.
Natural Law [1918]

21 The most stringent protection of free speech would not protect a man in falsely shouting fire in a theater and causing a panic.... The question in every case is whether the words used are used in such circumstances and are of such a nature as to create a clear and present danger that they will bring about the substantive evils that Congress has a right to prevent.
Schenck v. United States, 249 U.S. 47 [1919]

22 When men have realized that time has upset many fighting faiths, they may come to believe even more than they believe the very foundations of their own conduct that the ultimate good desired is better reached by free trade in ideas — that the best test of truth is the power of the thought to get itself accepted in the competition of the market, and that truth is the only ground upon which their wishes safely can be carried out. That at any rate is the theory of our Constitution. It is an experiment, as all life is an experiment.
Abrams v. United States, 250 U.S. 616, 630 [1919]

23 I dare say that I have worked off my fundamental formula on you that the chief end of man is to frame general propositions and that no general proposition is worth a damn.
Letter to Sir Frederick Pollock [1920]

1   Have faith and pursue the unknown end.
> *Letter to John C. H. Wu [1924]*

2   Upon this point a page of history is worth a volume of logic.
> *New York Trust Co. v. Eisner, 256 U.S. 345, 349 [1921]*

3   It is said that this manifesto is more than a theory, that it was an incitement. Every idea is an incitement.
> *Gitlow v. New York, 268 U.S. 652, 673 [1925]*

4   Three generations of imbeciles are enough.
> *Buck v. Bell, 274 U.S. 200, 207 [1927]*

5   The power to tax is not the power to destroy while this Court sits.
> *Panhandle Oil Co. v. Knox, 277 U.S. 223 [1928]*

6   For my part I think it a less evil that some criminals should escape than that the government should play an ignoble part. . . . If the existing code does not permit district attorneys to have a hand in such dirty business [wiretapping], it does not permit the judge to allow such iniquities to succeed.
> *Olmstead v. United States, 277 U.S. 438, 470 [1928]*

7   If there is any principle of the Constitution that more imperatively calls for attachment than any other it is the principle of free thought — not free thought for those who agree with us but freedom for the thought that we hate.
> *United States v. Schwimmer, 279 U.S. 644, 653 [1928]*

8   The riders in a race do not stop short when they reach the goal. There is a little finishing canter before coming to a standstill. There is time to hear the kind voice of friends and to say to one's self: "The work is done." But just as one says that, the answer comes: "The race is over, but the work never is done while the power to work remains." The canter that brings you to a standstill need not be only coming to rest. It cannot be, while you still live. For to live is to function. That is all there is in living.
> *Radio address on his ninetieth birthday [March 8, 1931]*

9   Young man, the secret of my success is that at an early age I discovered I was not God.
> *Reply to a reporter's question on his ninetieth birthday [March 8, 1931]*

10   Oh, to be seventy again![1]
> *At ninety, upon seeing a beautiful young woman. Attributed*

---

[1]If only one were eighty! — COUNT FRIEDRICH VON WRANGEL [1784–1877], *attributed*

11   [On Franklin D. Roosevelt:] Second-class intellect, first-class temperament.   *Attributed*

12   I like to pay taxes. With them I buy civilization.
> *Quoted in* FELIX FRANKFURTER *[1882–1965], Mr. Justice Holmes and the Supreme Court [1939]*

W[illiam] H[enry] Hudson
1841–1922

13   I . . . thanked the Author of my being for the gift of that wild forest, those green mansions where I had found so great a happiness!
> *Green Mansions [1904], ch. 5*

Joaquin [Cincinnatus Hiner or Heine] Miller
c. 1841–1913

14 Behind him lay the gray Azores,
Behind the Gates of Hercules;
Before him not the ghost of shores,
Before him only shoreless seas.   *Columbus, st. 1*

15 He gained a world; he gave that world
Its grandest lesson: "On! sail on!"   *Columbus, st. 5*

Pierre Auguste Renoir
1841–1919

16   I have a predilection for painting that lends joyousness to a wall.
> *From* AMBROISE VOLLARD *[1866–1939], Renoir [1919]*

Edward Rowland Sill
1841–1887

17   But Lord,
Be merciful to me, a fool!   *The Fool's Prayer*

Sir Henry Morton Stanley
1841–1904

18   Doctor Livingstone, I presume?
> *On meeting David Livingstone in Ujiji, Central Africa [November 10, 1871]*

Ambrose Bierce
1842–c. 1914

19 Mark how my fame rings out from zone to zone:
A thousand critics shouting: "He's unknown!"
> *Couplet*

1 Peyton Farquhar was dead; his body, with a broken neck, swung gently from side to side beneath the timbers of the Owl Creek bridge.
In the Midst of Life[1] *[1891].*
An Occurrence at Owl Creek Bridge

2 To men a man is but a mind. Who cares
What face he carries or what form he wears?
But woman's body is the woman. O
Stay thou, my sweetheart, and do never go.
The Devil's Dictionary[2] *[1906]*

3 *Achievement, n.* the death of endeavor and the birth of disgust.
The Devil's Dictionary

4 *Advice, n.* the smallest current coin.
The Devil's Dictionary

5 *Bore, n.* a person who talks when you wish him to listen.
The Devil's Dictionary

6 *Cynic, n.* a blackguard whose faulty vision sees things as they are, not as they ought to be.
The Devil's Dictionary

7 *Edible, adj.* good to eat, and wholesome to digest, as a worm to a toad, a toad to a snake, a snake to a pig, a pig to a man, and a man to a worm.
The Devil's Dictionary

8 *Habit, n.* a shackle for the free.
The Devil's Dictionary

9 *Labor, n.* one of the processes by which A acquires property for B.
The Devil's Dictionary

10 *Lawsuit, n.* a machine which you go into as a pig and come out as a sausage.
The Devil's Dictionary

11 *Marriage, n.* a community consisting of a master, a mistress, and two slaves, making in all, two.
The Devil's Dictionary

12 *Prejudice, n.* a vagrant opinion without visible means of support.
The Devil's Dictionary

13 *Saint, n.* a dead sinner revised and edited.
The Devil's Dictionary

14 You are not permitted to kill a woman who has wronged you, but nothing forbids you to reflect that she is growing older every minute. You are avenged 1440 times a day.
Epigrams

15 The covers of this book are too far apart.
Capsule book review. Attributed

---

[1] First published as *Tales of Soldiers and Civilians*, retitled in 1892.
[2] First published as *The Cynic's Word Book*, retitled in 1911.

William James
1842–1910

16 I have often thought that the best way to define a man's character would be to seek out the particular mental or moral attitude in which, when it came upon him, he felt himself most deeply and intensely active and alive. At such moments there is a voice inside which speaks and says: "This is the real me!"
Letter to his wife, Alice Gibbons James [1878]

17 The concrete man has but one interest — to be right. That to him is the art of all arts, and all means are fair which help him to it.
The Sentiment of Rationality [1882]

18 All our scientific and philosophic ideals are altars to unknown gods.
The Dilemma of Determinism [1884]

19 Habit is ... the enormous flywheel of society, its most precious conservative agent. It alone is what keeps us all within the bounds of ordinance.
The Principles of Psychology [1890], ch. 4

20 There is no more miserable human being than one in whom nothing is habitual but indecision.
The Principles of Psychology, 4

21 Keep the faculty of effort alive in you by a little gratuitous exercise every day. That is, be systematically ascetic or heroic in little unnecessary points, do every day or two something for no other reason than that you would rather not do it, so that when the hour of dire need draws nigh, it may find you not unnerved and untrained to stand the test.
The Principles of Psychology, 4

22 The hell to be endured hereafter, of which theology tells, is no worse than the hell we make for ourselves in this world by habitually fashioning our characters in the wrong way.
The Principles of Psychology, 4

23 We are spinning our own fates, good or evil, and never to be undone. Every smallest stroke of virtue or of vice leaves its never so little scar.... Nothing we ever do is, in strict scientific literalness, wiped out.
The Principles of Psychology, 4

24 Consciousness ... does not appear to itself chopped up in bits.... A "river" or a "stream" are the metaphors by which it is most naturally described. In talking of it hereafter, let us call it the stream of thought, of consciousness, or of subjective life.
The Principles of Psychology, 9

25 As we take, in fact, a general view of the wonderful stream of our consciousness, what strikes us first is this different pace of its parts. Like a bird's life, it

seems to be made of an alternation of flights and perchings. *The Principles of Psychology, 9*

1 As the brain changes are continuous, so do all these consciousnesses melt into each other like dissolving views. Properly they are but one protracted consciousness, one unbroken stream. *The Principles of Psychology, 9*

2 The last peculiarity of consciousness to which attention is to be drawn in this first rough description of its stream is that . . . it is always interested more in one part of its object [thought] than in another, and welcomes and rejects, or chooses, all the while it thinks. *The Principles of Psychology, 9*

3 An act has no ethical quality whatever unless it be chosen out of several all equally possible. *The Principles of Psychology, 9*

4 In its widest possible sense, however, a man's Self is the sum total of all that he *can* call his, not only his body and his psychic powers, but his clothes and his house, his wife and children, his ancestors and friends, his reputation and works, his lands and horses, and yacht and bank account. All these things give him the same emotions. If they wax and prosper, he feels triumphant; if they dwindle and die away, he feels cast down. *The Principles of Psychology, 10*

5 The baby, assailed by eyes, ears, nose, skin, and entrails at once, feels it all as one great blooming, buzzing confusion. *The Principles of Psychology, 13*

6 Let anyone try, I will not say to arrest, but to notice or attend to, the *present* moment of time. One of the most baffling experiences occurs. Where is it, this present? It has melted in our grasp, fled ere we could touch it, gone in the instant of becoming. *The Principles of Psychology, 15*

7 Genius . . . means little more than the faculty of perceiving in an unhabitual way. *The Principles of Psychology, 19*

8 The art of being wise is the art of knowing what to overlook. *The Principles of Psychology, 22*

9 The more rational statement is that we feel sorry because we cry, angry because we strike, afraid because we tremble, and not that we cry, strike, or tremble because we are sorry, angry, or fearful, as the case may be. Without the bodily states following on the perception, the latter would be purely cognitive in form, pale, colorless, destitute of emotional warmth. *The Principles of Psychology, 25*

10 I wished, by treating Psychology *like* a natural science, to help her to become one. *A Plea for Psychology as a Natural Science [1892]*

11 In the deepest heart of all of us there is a corner in which the ultimate mystery of things works sadly. *The Will to Believe [1897]. Is Life Worth Living?*

12 It is only by risking our persons from one hour to another that we live at all. And often enough our faith beforehand in an uncertified result is the only thing that makes the result come true. *The Will to Believe. Is Life Worth Living?*

13 This life is worth living, we can say, since it is what we make it, from the moral point of view. *The Will to Believe. Is Life Worth Living?*

14 Be not afraid of life. Believe that life *is* worth living, and your belief will help create the fact. *The Will to Believe. Is Life Worth Living?*

15 All the higher, more penetrating ideals are revolutionary. They present themselves far less in the guise of effects of past experience than in that of probable causes of future experience. *The Will to Believe. The Moral Philosopher and the Moral Life*

16 There is but one unconditional commandment, which is that we should seek incessantly, with fear and trembling, so to vote and to act as to bring about the very largest total universe of good which we can see. *The Will to Believe. The Moral Philosopher and the Moral Life*

17 An unlearned carpenter of my acquaintance once said in my hearing: "There is very little difference between one man and another; but what little there is, is very important." This distinction seems to me to go to the root of the matter. *The Will to Believe. The Importance of Individuals*

18 Religion . . . shall mean for us the feelings, acts, and experiences of individual men in their solitude. *The Varieties of Religious Experience [1902], lecture 2*

19 Religion . . . is a man's total reaction upon life. *The Varieties of Religious Experience, 2*

20 We can act *as if* there were a God; feel *as if* we were free; consider Nature *as if* she were full of special designs; lay plans *as if* we were to be immortal; and we find then that these words do make a genuine difference in our moral life. *The Varieties of Religious Experience, 3*

21 There is no doubt that healthy-mindedness is inadequate as a philosophical doctrine, because the evil facts which it refuses positively to account for are a genuine portion of reality; and they may after all be the best key to life's significance, and possibly the only openers of our eyes to the deepest levels of truth. *The Varieties of Religious Experience, 7*

1   Our normal waking consciousness, rational consciousness as we call it, is but one special type of consciousness, whilst all about it, parted from it by the filmiest of screens, there lie potential forms of consciousness entirely different. We may go through life without suspecting their existence; but apply the requisite stimulus, and at a touch they are there in all their completeness, definite types of mentality which probably somewhere have their field of application and adaptation.
The Varieties of Religious Experience, 16

2   The God whom science recognizes must be a God of universal laws exclusively, a God who does a wholesale, not a retail business. He cannot accommodate his processes to the convenience of individuals.
The Varieties of Religious Experience, 20

3   Most people live, whether physically, intellectually or morally, in a very restricted circle of their potential being. They *make use* of a very small portion of their possible consciousness, and of their soul's resources in general, much like a man who, out of his whole bodily organism, should get into a habit of using and moving only his little finger. Great emergencies and crises show us how much greater our vital resources are than we had supposed.
Letter to W. Lutoslawski [May 6, 1906]

4   The moral flabbiness born of the exclusive worship of the bitch-goddess SUCCESS. That — with the squalid cash interpretation put on the word success — is our national disease.
Letter to H. G. Wells [September 11, 1906]

5   The philosophy which is so important in each of us is not a technical matter; it is our more or less dumb sense of what life honestly and deeply means. It is only partly got from books; it is our individual way of just seeing and feeling the total push and pressure of the cosmos.
Pragmatism [1907], lecture 1

6   No particular results then, so far, but only an attitude of orientation, is what the pragmatic method means. The attitude of looking away from first things, principles, "categories," supposed necessities; and of looking toward last things, fruits, consequences, facts.
Pragmatism, 2

7   I myself believe that the evidence for God lies primarily in inner personal experiences.
Pragmatism, 3

8   Our minds thus grow in spots; and like grease spots, the spots spread. But we let them spread as little as possible: we keep unaltered as much of our old knowledge, as many of our old prejudices and beliefs, as we can. We patch and tinker more than we renew. The novelty soaks in; it stains the ancient mass; but it is also tinged by what absorbs it.
Pragmatism, 5

9   Truth *happens* to an idea. It *becomes* true, is *made* true by events. Its verity *is* in fact an event, a process: the process namely of its verifying itself, its veri-*fication*. Its validity is the process of its valid-*ation*.
Pragmatism, 6

10   Pluralism lets things really exist in the each-form or distributively. Monism thinks that the all-form or collective-unit form is the only form that is rational.
A Pluralistic Universe [1909], lecture 8

11   History is a bath of blood.
Memories and Studies [1910].
The Moral Equivalent of War

12   So long as antimilitarists propose no substitute for war's disciplinary function, no *moral equivalent* of war, analogous, as one might say, to the mechanical equivalent of heat, so long they fail to realize the full inwardness of the situation.
Memories and Studies.
The Moral Equivalent of War

13   One need only shut oneself in a closet and begin to think of the fact of one's being there, of one's queer bodily shape in the darkness (a thing to make children scream at, as Stevenson says), of one's fantastic character and all, to have the wonder steal over the detail as much as over the general fact of being, and to see that it is only familiarity that blunts it. Not only that *anything* should be, but that *this* very thing should be, is mysterious! Philosophy stares, but brings no reasoned solution, for from nothing to being there is no logical bridge.
Some Problems of Philosophy [1911], ch. 3

14   The "through-and-through" universe seems to suffocate me with its infallible impeccable all-pervasiveness....It seems too buttoned-up and white-chokered and clean-shaven a thing to speak in the name of the vast slow-breathing unconscious Kosmos with its dread abysses and its unknown tides.
Essays in Radical Empiricism [1912], ch. 12,
Absolutism and Empiricism

Prince Pyotr Alekseyevich Kropotkin
1842–1921

15   Sociability is as much a law of nature as mutual struggle...mutual aid is as much a law of animal life as mutual struggle.

Mutual Aid [1902]

Sidney Lanier
1842–1881

1 Ye marshes, how candid and simple and nothing-
   withholding and free
Ye publish yourselves to the sky and offer yourselves
   to the sea!
        The Marshes of Glynn [1877], l. 65

2 As the marsh hen secretly builds on the watery sod,
Behold I will build me a nest on the greatness of God:
I will fly in the greatness of God as the marsh hen flies
In the freedom that fills all the space 'twixt the marsh
   and the skies:
By so many roots as the marsh grass sends in the sod
I will heartily lay me a-hold on the greatness of God:
Oh, like to the greatness of God is the greatness
   within
The range of the marshes, the liberal marshes of
   Glynn.
        The Marshes of Glynn, l. 71

3 Out of the hills of Habersham,
Down the valleys of Hall.
        Song of the Chattahoochee [1877], st. 1

4 Into the woods my Master went,
Clean forspent, forspent.
Into the woods my Master came,
Forspent with love and shame.
        A Ballad of Trees and the Master [1877], st. 1

Stéphane Mallarmé
1842–1898

5   Poetry is the expression, in human language
restored to its essential rhythm, of the mysterious
meaning of the aspects of existence: in this way it con-
fers authenticity on our time on earth and constitutes
the only spiritual task there is.[1]
        Letter to Leo d'Orfer [June 27, 1884]

6   The flesh is sad, alas, and I have read all the
books.[2]
        Poésies [1887]. Brise Marine (Sea Breeze)

7   Such as into himself at last Eternity has changed
him.[3]   *Poésies. Le Tombeau d'Edgar Poe*

8   A Throw of the Dice Will Never Abolish
Chance.[4]   *Poésies. Title of poem*

9   To *name* an object is to take away three-fourths of
the pleasure given by a poem. This pleasure consists

in guessing little by little: to *suggest* it, that is the
ideal.[5]
        *Sur l'Évolution Littéraire [Enquête de Jules
        Huret, 1891]*

10   The whole world is made to end up in a beautiful
book.[6]   *Sur l'Évolution Littéraire*

11   You don't make a poem with ideas, but with
words.[7]
        From Paul Valéry, Degas, Danse, Dessin [1936]

Alfred Marshall
1842–1924

12   We might as reasonably dispute whether it is the
upper or the under blade of a pair of scissors that cuts
a piece of paper, as whether value is governed by utility or cost of production.
        Principles of Economics [1890]

George Washington Plunkitt
1842–1924

13   [Definition of "honest graft":] I seen my opportunities and I took 'em.
        *From William L. Riordon [1861–1909],
        Plunkitt of Tammany Hall [1905]*

14   The politician who steals is worse than a thief. He
is a fool. With all the grand opportunities around for
the man with a political pull, there's no excuse for
stealin' a cent.
        *From William L. Riordon, Plunkitt of
        Tammany Hall*

Russell H. Conwell
1843–1925

15   I say you ought to get rich, and it is your duty to
get rich. . . . Money is power, and you ought to be reasonably ambitious to have it! You ought because you
can do more good with it than you could without it.
        Acres of Diamonds [1890]

Henry James
1843–1916

16   The face of nature and civilization in this our
country is to a certain point a very sufficient literary

---

[1]Translated by Rosemary Lloyd.

[2]La chair est triste, hélas! et j'ai lu tous les livres.

[3]Tel qu'en Lui-Même enfin l'éternité le change.

[4]Un coup de dés n'abolira jamais le hasard.

---

[5]*Nommer* un objet, c'est supprimer les trois-quarts de la jouissance
du poème qui est fait peu à peu: le *suggérer*.

[6]Tout au monde est fait pour aboutir dans un beau livre.

[7]Ce n'est point avec des idées que l'on fait des vers, c'est avec des
mots.

field. But it will yield its secrets only to a really *grasping* imagination.... To write well and worthily of American things one need even more than elsewhere to be a *master*.

> *Letter to Charles Eliot Norton*
> *[January 16, 1871]*

1   It's a complex fate, being an American, and one of the responsibilities it entails is fighting against a superstitious valuation of Europe.

> *Letter [1872] quoted in* PERCY LUBBOCK *[1879–1965], Letters of Henry James [1920], vol. I, biographical note*

2   It takes a great deal of history to produce a little literature.   *Hawthorne [1879], ch. 1*

3   Whatever question there may be of his [Thoreau's] talent, there can be none, I think, of his genius. It was a slim and crooked one, but it was eminently personal. He was unperfect, unfinished, inartistic; he was worse than provincial — he was parochial.

> *Hawthorne, 4*

4   Cats and monkeys, monkeys and cats — all human life is there.

> *The Madonna of the Future [1879]*

5   Under certain circumstances there are few hours in life more agreeable than the hour dedicated to the ceremony known as afternoon tea.

> *The Portrait of a Lady [1881], ch. 1*

6   The real offense, as she ultimately perceived, was her having a mind of her own at all. Her mind was to be his — attached to his own like a small garden plot to a deer park.   *The Portrait of a Lady, 42*

7   Sorrow comes in great waves — no one can know that better than you — but it rolls over us, and though it may almost smother us it leaves us on the spot, and we know that if it is strong we are stronger, inasmuch as it passes and we remain. It wears us, uses us, but we wear it and use it in return; and it is blind, whereas we after a manner see.

> *Letter to Grace Norton [July 28, 1883]*

8   The only reason for the existence of a novel is that it does attempt to represent life.

> *The Art of Fiction [1888]*

9   If I should certainly say to a novice, "Write from experience and experience only," I should feel that this was rather a tantalizing monition if I were not careful immediately to add, "Try to be one of the people on whom nothing is lost."

> *The Art of Fiction*

10   We must grant the artist his subject, his idea, his *donnée:* our criticism is applied only to what he makes of it.... If we pretend to respect the artist at all, we must allow him his freedom of choice, in the face, in particular cases, of innumerable presumptions that the choice will not fructify. Art derives a considerable part of its beneficial exercise from flying in the face of presumptions.   *The Art of Fiction*

11   There are few things more exciting to me...than a psychological reason.   *The Art of Fiction*

12   We work in the dark — we do what we can — we give what we have. Our doubt is our passion, and our passion is our task. The rest is the madness of art.

> *The Middle Years [1893]*

13   Vereker's secret...the general intention of his books: the string the pearls were strung on, the buried treasure, the figure in the carpet.

> *The Figure in the Carpet [1896]*

14   I caught him, yes, I held him — it may be imagined with what passion; but at the end of a minute I began to feel what it truly was that I held. We were alone with the quiet day, and his little heart, dispossessed, had stopped.

> *The Turn of the Screw [1898], ending*

15   Live all you can; it's a mistake not to. It doesn't so much matter what you do in particular, so long as you have your life. If you haven't had that what *have* you had?...What one loses one loses; make no mistake about that.... The right time is *any* time that one is still so lucky as to have.... Live!

> *The Ambassadors [1903], bk. V, ch. 2*

16   There is, I think, no more nutritive or suggestive truth...than that of the perfect dependence of the "moral" sense of a work of art on the amount of felt life concerned in producing it. The question comes back thus, obviously, to the kind and the degree of the artist's prime sensibility, which is the soil out of which his subject springs.

> *Prefaces [1907–1909].*
> *The Portrait of a Lady*

17   The house of fiction has in short not one window, but a million — a number of possible windows not to be reckoned rather; every one of which has been pierced, or is still pierceable, in its vast front, by the need of the individual vision and by the pressure of the individual will.

> *Prefaces. The Portrait of a Lady*

18   The fatal futility of Fact.

> *Prefaces. The Spoils of Poynton*

19   The effort really to see and really to represent is no idle business in face of the *constant* force that makes for muddlement. The great thing is indeed that the muddled state too is one of the very sharpest of the realities, that it also has color and form and character, has often in fact a broad and rich comicality.

> *Prefaces. What Maisie Knew*

1   To criticize is to appreciate, to appropriate, to take intellectual possession, to establish in fine a relation with the criticized thing and to make it one's own.
Prefaces. What Maisie Knew

2   The historian, essentially, wants more documents than he can really use; the dramatist only wants more liberties than he can really take.
Prefaces. The Aspern Papers

3   In art economy is always beauty.
Prefaces. The Altar of the Dead

4   The terrible *fluidity* of self-revelation.
Prefaces. The Ambassadors

5   I'm glad you like adverbs — I adore them; they are the only qualifications I really much respect.
Letter to Miss M. Betham Edwards
[January 5, 1912]

6   We must know, as much as possible, in our beautiful art . . . what we are talking about — and the only way to know is to have lived and loved and cursed and floundered and enjoyed and suffered. I think I don't regret a single "excess" of my responsive youth — I only regret, in my chilled age, certain occasions and possibilities I didn't embrace.
Letter to Hugh Walpole [August 21, 1913]

7   I still, in presence of life . . . have reactions — as many as possible. . . . It's, I suppose, because I am that queer monster, the artist, an obstinate finality, an inexhaustible sensibility. Hence the reactions — appearances, memories, many things, go on playing upon it with consequences that I note and "enjoy" (grim word!) noting. It all takes doing — and I *do*. I believe I shall do yet again — it is still an act of life.
Letter to Henry Adams [March 21, 1914]

8   It is art that *makes* life, makes interest, makes importance, for our consideration and application of these things, and I know of no substitute whatever for the force and beauty of its process.
Letter to H. G. Wells [July 10, 1915]

9   So it has come at last — the Distinguished Thing.
Of his final illness [December 2, 1915]

10   Summer afternoon — summer afternoon; to me those have always been the two most beautiful words in the English language.
Quoted by EDITH WHARTON *[1862–1937],*
A Backward Glance [1934], ch. 10

William McKinley
1843–1901

11   There was nothing left for us to do but to take them all, and to educate the Filipinos, and uplift and civilize and Christianize them, and by Go[d]
do the very best we could for them, as our fel[low]
for whom Christ also died.
On his decision to claim the Philippine
Islands for the United States [1899]

Robert Bridges
1844–1930

12   Whither, O splendid ship, thy white sails crowding,
Leaning across the bosom of the urgent West,
That fearest nor sea rising, nor sky clouding,
Whither away, fair rover, and what thy quest?
Shorter Poems, bk. II [1880],
no. 2 (A Passer-By), st. 1

13   When men were all asleep, the snow came flying,
In large white flakes falling on the city brown,
Stealthily and perpetually settling and loosely lying,
Hushing the latest traffic of the drowsy town.
Shorter Poems, III, 2 (London Snow), l. 1

14   I love all beauteous things,
I seek and adore them;
God hath no better praise,
And man in his hasty days
Is honored for them.   *Shorter Poems, IV, 1, st. 1*

Robert Jones Burdette
1844–1914

15   There are two days in the week about which and upon which I never worry. Two carefree days, kept sacredly free from fear and apprehension. One of these days is Yesterday. . . . And the other day I do not worry about is Tomorrow.
The Golden Day [1910]

Anatole France [Jacques Anatole François Thibault]
1844–1924

16   I do not know any reading more easy, more fascinating, more delightful than a catalogue.
The Crime of Sylvestre Bonnard[1] *[1881].*
The Log, December 24, 1849

17   To know is nothing at all; to imagine is everything.   *The Crime of Sylvestre Bonnard, pt. II, ch. 2*

18   Those who have given themselves the most concern about the happiness of peoples have made their neighbors very miserable.
The Crime of Sylvestre Bonnard, II, 4

---

[1]Translated by LAFCADIO HEARN.

1   The whole art of teaching is only the art of awakening the natural curiosity of young minds for the purpose of satisfying it afterwards.
The Crime of Sylvestre Bonnard, II, 4

2   The law, in its majestic equality, forbids the rich as well as the poor to sleep under bridges, to beg in the streets, and to steal bread.
The Red Lily [1894], ch. 7

Gerard Manley Hopkins
1844–1889

3 And I have asked to be
  Where no storms come,
Where the green swell is in the havens dumb,
  And out of the swing of the sea.
Poems[1] *[1918]. No. 20, Heaven-Haven, st. 2*

4 Elected Silence, sing to me
And beat upon my whorlèd ear,
Pipe me to pastures still and be
The music that I care to hear.
Poems. No. 24, The Habit of Perfection, st. 1

5   Thou mastering me
      God! giver of breath and bread;
    World's strand, sway of the sea;
  Lord of living and dead;
Thou hast bound bones and veins in me, fastened me flesh,
And after it almost unmade, what with dread,
      Thy doing: and dost thou touch me afresh?
Over again I feel thy finger and find thee.
Poems. No. 28, The Wreck of the Deutschland, st. 1

6 The world is charged with the grandeur of God.
Poems. No. 31, God's Grandeur, l. 1

7 Look at the stars! look, look up at the skies!
O look at all the fire-folk sitting in the air!
Poems. No. 32, The Starlight Night, l. 1

8 Nothing is so beautiful as Spring —
When weeds, in wheels, shoot long and lovely and lush.   *Poems. No. 33, Spring, l. 1*

9 I caught this morning morning's minion, kingdom of daylight's dauphin, dapple-dawn-drawn
    Falcon, in his riding
  Of the rolling level underneath him steady air, and striding
High there, how he rung upon the rein of a wimpling wing
In his ecstasy!   *Poems. No. 36, The Windhover, l. 1*

10 The achieve of, the mastery of the thing!
Poems. No. 36, The Windhover, l. 8

11 Brute beauty and valor and act, oh, air, pride, plume, here
Buckle!   *Poems. No. 36, The Windhover, l. 9*

12 Glory be to God for dappled things.
Poems. No. 37, Pied Beauty, l. 1

13 All things counter, original, spare, strange;
  Whatever is fickle, freckled (who knows how?)
  With swift, slow; sweet, sour; adazzle, dim;
He fathers-forth whose beauty is past change: Praise him.   *Poems. No. 37, Pied Beauty, l. 7*

14 Summer ends now; now, barbarous in beauty, the stooks arise
  Around; up above, what wind-walks! what lovely behavior
Of silk-sack clouds! Has wilder, willful-wavier
Meal-drift molded ever and melted across skies?
Poems. No. 38, Hurrahing in Harvest, st. 1

15 Felix Randal the farrier, O he is dead then? My duty all ended,
  Who have watched his mold of man, big-boned and hardy-handsome,
Pining, pining.   *Poems. No. 53, Felix Randal, st. 1*

16 When thou at the random grim forge, powerful amidst peers,
  Didst fettle for the great gray drayhorse his bright and battering sandal!
Poems. No. 53, Felix Randal, st. 4

17 Margaret, are you grieving
  Over Goldengrove unleaving?
*Poems. No. 55, Spring and Fall:
To A Young Child, l. 1*

18 It is the blight man was born for,
  It is Margaret you mourn for.
*Poems. No. 55, Spring and Fall:
To A Young Child, l. 12*

19 What would the world be, once bereft
Of wet and of wildness? Let them be left,
O let them be left, wildness and wet;
Long live the weeds and the wilderness yet.
Poems. No. 56, Inversnaid, l. 13

20 As kingfishers catch fire, dragonflies draw flame.
Poems. No. 57, l. 1

21 How to keep — is there any any, is there none such, nowhere known some, bow or brooch or braid or brace, lace, latch or catch or key to keep
Back beauty, keep it, beauty, beauty, beauty . . . from vanishing away?
*Poems. No. 59, The Leaden Echo and
the Golden Echo, l. 1*

---

[1]First published in 1918, edited by Robert Bridges. Poem numbers are from the third edition [1948], edited by W. H. Gardner.

1 I say that we are wound
With mercy round and round
As if with air.
> *Poems. No. 60, The Blessed Virgin Compared to the Air We Breathe, l. 34*

2 World-mothering air, air wild,
Wound with thee, in thee isled,
Fold home, fast fold thy child.
> *Poems. No. 60, The Blessed Virgin Compared to the Air We Breathe, l. 124*

3 Not, I'll not, carrion comfort, Despair, not feast on thee;
Not untwist — slack they may be — these last strands of man
In me or, most weary, cry *I can no more.* I can;
Can something, hope, wish day come, not choose not to be.
> *Poems. No. 64, Carrion Comfort, l. 1*

4 That night, that year
Of now done darkness I wretch lay wrestling with (my God!) my God.
> *Poems. No. 64, Carrion Comfort, l. 13*

5 No worst, there is none. Pitched past pitch of grief,
More pangs will, schooled at forepangs, wilder wring.
> *Poems. No. 65, No Worst, l. 1*

6 O the mind, mind has mountains; cliffs of fall
Frightful, sheer, no-man-fathomed.
> *Poems. No. 65, No Worst, l. 9*

7 I wake and feel the fell of dark, not day.
What hours, O what black hours we have spent
This night.
> *Poems. No. 69, I Wake and Feel, l. 1*

8 I am gall, I am heartburn.
> *Poems. No. 69, I Wake and Feel, l. 9*

9 I am all at once what Christ is, since he was what I am, and
This Jack, joke, poor potsherd, patch, matchwood, immortal diamond,
Is immortal diamond.
> *Poems. No. 72, That Nature Is a Heraclitean Fire and of the Comfort of the Resurrection, l. 22*

10 No doubt my poetry errs on the side of oddness. I hope in time to have a more balanced and Miltonic style. But as air, melody, is what strikes me most of all in music, and design in painting, so design, pattern, or what I am in the habit of calling *inscape* is what I above all aim at in poetry. Now it is the virtue of design, pattern, or inscape to be distinctive, and it is the vice of distinctiveness to become queer. This vice I cannot have escaped.
> *Letter to Robert Bridges [February 15, 1879]*

Friedrich Wilhelm Nietzsche
1844–1900

11 Only as an aesthetic phenomenon is existence and the world eternally justified.
> *The Birth of Tragedy*[1] *[1872]*

12 Our destiny exercises its influence over us even when, as yet, we have not learned its nature: it is our future that lays down the law of our today.
> *Human, All Too Human*[2] *[1878], sec. 7*

13 Every tradition grows ever more venerable — the more remote is its origin, the more confused that origin is. The reverence due to it increases from generation to generation. The tradition finally becomes holy and inspires awe.
> *Human, All Too Human, 96*

14 Oh, those Greeks! They knew how to live. What is required for that is to stop courageously at the surface, the fold, the skin, to adore appearance, to believe in forms, tones, words, in the whole Olympus of appearance. Those Greeks were superficial — out of profundity.
> *The Gay Science*[3] *[1882], sec. 4*

15 Masters of the first rank are revealed by the fact that in great as well as small matters they know how to end perfectly, whether it is a matter of ending a melody or a thought, or the fifth act of a tragedy or an action of state. The best of the second rank always become restless as the end approaches and do not manage to slope into the sea in such proud and calm harmony as, for example, the mountains at Portofino — where the Bay of Genoa ends its melody.
> *The Gay Science, 281*

16 When Zarathustra was alone...he said to his heart: "Could it be possible! This old saint in the forest hath not yet heard of it, that God *is dead!*"[4]
> *Thus Spake Zarathustra*[5] *[1883–1891], prologue, ch. 2*

17 Man is a rope stretched between the animal and the Superman — a rope over an abyss.
> *Thus Spake Zarathustra, prologue, 3*

18 I want to teach men the sense of their existence, which is the Superman, the lightning out of the dark cloud man.
> *Thus Spake Zarathustra, prologue, 7*

---

[1]Translated by RONALD SPEIRS.

[2]Translated by ALEXANDER HARVEY.

[3]Translated by WALTER KAUFMAN.

[4]God is dead. God remains dead. And we have killed him. — NIETZSCHE, *The Gay Science, sec. 125*

Dieu est mort! le ciel est vide — Pleurez! enfants, vous n'avez plus de père. — GÉRARD DE NERVAL, *Les Chimères* [1854], *Le Christ aux Oliviers*.

[5]Translated by THOMAS COMMON.

1   This is the hardest of all: to close the open hand out of love, and keep modest as a giver.
Thus Spake Zarathustra, pt. II, ch. 23

2   Distrust all in whom the impulse to punish is powerful.   *Thus Spake Zarathustra, II, 29*

3   We ought to learn from the kine one thing: ruminating.
Thus Spake Zarathustra, IV, 68

4   If ye would go up high, then use your own legs! Do not get yourselves *carried* aloft; do not seat yourselves on other people's backs and heads!
Thus Spake Zarathustra, IV, 73

5   It is certainly not the least charm of a theory that it is refutable.
Beyond Good and Evil[1] *[1885–1886], pt. I, sec. 18*

6   It is not the strength but the duration of great sentiments that makes great men.
Beyond Good and Evil, IV, 72

7   In revenge and in love woman is more barbarous than man.   *Beyond Good and Evil, IV, 139*

8   Whoever fights monsters should see to it that in the process he does not become a monster. And when you look long into an abyss, the abyss also looks into you.   *Beyond Good and Evil, IV, 146*

9   The thought of suicide is a great consolation: by means of it one gets successfully through many a bad night.
Beyond Good and Evil, IV, 157

10   Blessed are the forgetful: for they get the better even of their blunders.
Beyond Good and Evil, IV, 217

11   Is not life a hundred times too short for us to bore ourselves?   *Beyond Good and Evil, IV, 227*

12   Mozart, the last chord of a centuries-old great European taste.
Beyond Good and Evil, IV, 245

13   The melancholia of everything completed!
Beyond Good and Evil, IX, 277

14   The masters have been done away with; the morality of the common man has triumphed.
Genealogy of Morals [1887], essay 1, aphorism 9

15   At the core of all these aristocratic races the beast of prey is not to be mistaken, the magnificent *blond beast*, avidly rampant for spoil and victory.
Genealogy of Morals, 1, 11

16   The broad effects which can be obtained by punishment in man and beast are the increase of fear, the sharpening of the sense of cunning, the mastery of the desires; so it is that punishment tames man, but does not make him "better."
Genealogy of Morals, 2, 15

17   The sick are the greatest danger for the healthy; it is not from the strongest that harm comes to the strong, but from the weakest.
Genealogy of Morals, 3, 14

18   A strong and well-constituted man digests his experiences (deeds and misdeeds all included) just as he digests his meats, even when he has some tough morsels to swallow.
Genealogy of Morals, 3, 16

19   There was really only one Christian, and he died on the cross.
The Antichrist[2] *[1888], aphorism 39*

20   Only sick music makes money these days.
The Case of Wagner[2] *[1888]*

21   *Amor fati*: that is my innermost nature. And as regards my long sickness, do I not owe to it unutterably more than I owe to my health?
Nietzsche contra Wagner[3] *[1888]*

22   What is it: is man only a blunder of God, or God only a blunder of man?
The Twilight of the Idols [1888]. Things the Germans Lack, sec. 2

23   If a man have a strong faith he can indulge in the luxury of skepticism.
The Twilight of the Idols. Things the Germans Lack, 12

24   Liberal institutions straightway cease from being liberal the moment they are soundly established: once this is attained no more grievous and more thorough enemies of freedom exist than liberal institutions.
The Twilight of the Idols. Things the Germans Lack, 38

25   It is my ambition to say in ten sentences what everyone else says in a whole book — what everyone else does *not* say in a whole book.
The Twilight of the Idols. Things the Germans Lack, 51

26   Love is the state in which man sees things most widely different from what they are. The force of illusion reaches its zenith here, as likewise the sweetening and transfiguring power. When a man is in love he

---

[1]Translated by HELEN ZIMMERN.

[2]Translated by JUDITH NORMAN.

[3]Translated by THOMAS COMMON.

endures more than at other times; he submits to everything.

The Antichrist[1] *[1888], aphorism 23*

1   God created woman. And boredom did indeed cease from that moment — but many other things ceased as well! Woman was God's *second* mistake.

The Antichrist, 48

2   Life always gets harder toward the summit — the cold increases, responsibility increases.

The Antichrist, 57

3   I call Christianity the one great curse, the one enormous and innermost perversion, the one great instinct of revenge, for which no means are too venomous, too underhand, too underground and too petty — I call it the one immortal blemish of mankind.   *The Antichrist, 62*

4   My doctrine is: Live that thou mayest desire to live again — that is thy duty — for in any case thou wilt live again!

Eternal Recurrence,[1] *sec. 27*

5   Nothing on earth consumes a man more quickly than the passion of resentment.

Ecce Homo[1] *[1888]*

6   I believe only in French culture, and regard everything else in Europe which calls itself "culture" as a misunderstanding. I do not even take the German kind into consideration.

Ecce Homo

7   Wherever Germany extends her sway, she ruins culture.   *Ecce Homo*

8   As an artist, a man has no home in Europe save in Paris.   *Ecce Homo*

9   My time has not yet come either; some are born posthumously.

Ecce Homo

10   No one can draw more out of things, books included, than he already knows. A man has no ears for that to which experience has given him no access.

Ecce Homo

11   The Germans are like women, you can scarcely ever fathom their depths — they haven't any.[2]

Ecce Homo

12   One must separate from anything that forces one to repeat No again and again.

Ecce Homo

Arthur William Edgar O'Shaughnessy
1844–1881

13 We are the music-makers,
  And we are the dreamers of dreams,
  Wandering by lone sea breakers,
  And sitting by desolate streams;
  World-losers and world-forsakers,
  On whom the pale moon gleams:
  Yet we are the movers and shakers
  Of the world forever, it seems.   *Ode, st. 1*

William Archibald Spooner[3]
1844–1930

14   Kinquering Congs their titles take.

Announcing the hymn in college chapel

15   You have deliberately tasted two worms and you can leave Oxford by the next town drain.

Dismissing a student. Attributed

16   I remember your name perfectly, but I just can't think of your face.   *Attributed*

Paul Verlaine
1844–1896

17 The long sobs
  Of the violins
  Of autumn
  Pierce my heart
  With monotonous languor.[4]

Poèmes Saturniens (Poems Under Saturn)
[1866]. Chanson d'Automne (Autumn Song)

18 There is weeping in my heart
  Like the rain falling on the city.[5]

Romances sans Paroles
(Songs Without Words) [1874], poem III

19 What have you done, you there
  Weeping without cease,
  Tell me, yes you, what have you done
  With all your youth?[6]

Sagesse (Wisdom) [1881], poem III, st. 6

20 Take eloquence and wring its neck![7]

Jadis et Naguère (Recently and Formerly)
[1884]. L'Art Poétique

---

[3]Canon Spooner, for many years warden of New College, Oxford, was famous for unintentional transposition of (usually initial) word sounds, giving rise to the term "spoonerism."

[4]Les sanglots longs / Des violons / De l'automne / Blessent mon coeur / D'une langueur / Monotone.

[5]Il pleure dans mon coeur / Comme il pleut sur la ville.

[6]Qu'as-tu fait, O toi que voilà / Pleurant sans cesse, / Dis, qu'as-tu fait, toi que voilà / De ta jeunesse?

[7]Prends l'éloquence et tords-lui son cou!

---

[1]Translated by ANTHONY M. LUDOVICI.

[2]Man thinks woman profound — why? Because he can never fathom her depths. Woman is not even shallow. — NIETZSCHE, *The Twilight of the Idols, Maxims and Missiles, sec. 27*

1 And all else is literature.[1]
Jadis et Naguère. L'Art Poetique

John B. Bogart
1845–1921

2   When a dog bites a man, that is not news, because it happens so often. But if a man bites a dog, that is news.
From FRANK M. O'BRIEN [1875–1943],
The Story of The (New York) Sun [1918]

John Banister Tabb
1845–1909

3 Out of the dusk a shadow,
    Then a spark;
Out of the clouds a silence,
    Then a lark;
Out of the heart a rapture,
    Then a pain;
Out of the dead, cold ashes,
    Life again.   *Evolution [1894]*

Punch

4   You pays your money and you takes your choice.
vol. X, pt. 16 [1846]

5   What is Matter? — Never mind.
What is Mind? — No matter.
XXIX, 19 [1855]

6   I'm afraid you've got a bad egg, Mr. Jones.
Oh no, my Lord, I assure you! Parts of it are excellent!   *CIX, 222 [1895]*

Charles Dupee Blake
1846–1903

7 Rock-a-bye-baby on the tree top,
When the wind blows the cradle will rock,
When the bough breaks the cradle will fall,
And down will come baby, cradle and all.
Attributed

Léon Bloy
1846–1917

8   There is no human being on earth who is capable of declaring who he is, with certainty. No one knows what he has come to this world to do, to what his

acts, feelings, ideas correspond, or what his real *name* is, his imperishable Name in the registry of Light.[2]
The Soul of Napoleon [1912]

Comte de Lautréamont [Isidore Ducasse]
1846–1870

9   Beautiful...as the fortuitous encounter of a sewing machine and an umbrella on a dissecting table.[3]   *Les Chants de Maldoror [1868–1869]*

Charles Prestwich Scott
1846–1932

10   The primary office of a newspaper is the gathering of news...comment is free, but facts are sacred.
In the Manchester Guardian [May 6, 1926]

Alexander Graham Bell
1847–1922

11   Mr. Watson, come here, I want you.[4]
To his assistant [March 10, 1876]

Thomas A[lva] Edison
1847–1931

12   There is no substitute for hard work.
Life [1932], ch. 24

13   Genius is one percent inspiration and ninety-nine percent perspiration.   *Life, 24*

Giuseppe Giacosa
1847–1906
and
Luigi Illica
1857–1919

14   Your tiny hand is frozen, let me warm it in mine.[5]
La Bohème[6] [1896], act I

---

[1]Et tout le reste est littérature.

[2]As quoted by JORGE LUIS BORGES in *The Nightingale of Keats*, translated by RUTH L. C. SIMMS in *Other Inquisitions* [1975].

[3]Beau...comme la rencontre fortuite sur une table de dissection d'une machine à coudre et d'un parapluie.
Frequently quoted by the surrealists.

[4]The first intelligible words transmitted by telephone.

[5]Che gelida manina, se la lasci riscaldar.

[6]Music by GIACOMO PUCCINI [1858–1924].

1   I lived for art, I lived for love; never did I harm a living soul.[1]
Tosca[2] *[1900], act II*

Henry Demarest Lloyd
1847–1903

2   Corporations have no souls, but they can love each other.
Wealth Against Commonwealth [1894]

John Locke
1847–1889

3 O Ireland, isn't it grand you look —
Like a bride in her rich adornin'?
And with all the pent-up love of my heart
I bid you the top o' the mornin'!
The Exile's Return (Th' an'am an Dhia: My Soul to God), st. 1

Milton Nobles
1847–1924

4 The villain still pursued her.
The Phoenix [1875], act I, sc. iii

Albert Pinkham Ryder
1847–1917

5   The artist needs but a roof, a crust of bread, and his easel, and all the rest God gives him in abundance. He must live to paint and not paint to live.
Attributed

Bram [Abraham] Stoker
1847–1912

6   Listen to them — the children of the night. What music they make!
Dracula [1897], ch. 2

Arthur James Balfour
1848–1930

7   His Majesty's Government view with favor the establishment in Palestine of a national home for the Jewish people, and will use their best endeavors to facilitate the achievement of this object, it being clearly understood that nothing shall be done which may prejudice the civil and religious rights of existing non-Jewish communities in Palestine, or the rights and political status enjoyed by Jews in any other country.
The Balfour Declaration. Letter to Lionel Walter, Lord Rothschild [November 2, 1917]

Paul Gauguin
1848–1903

8   Where Do We Come From? What Are We? Where Are We Going?[3]
Title of painting [1897–1898]

9   Life being what it is, one dreams of revenge — and has to content oneself with dreaming.[4]
Avant et Après (Before and After) [1903]

Joel Chandler Harris
1848–1908

10   Hit look lak sparrer-grass, hit feel lak sparrer-grass, hit tas'e lak sparrer-grass, en I bless ef 'taint sparrer-grass.
Nights with Uncle Remus [1883], ch. 27

11   Jaybird don't rob his own nes'.
Uncle Remus Songs and Sayings [1886]. Plantation Proverbs

12   Youk'n hide de fier, but w'at you gwine do wid de smoke?
Uncle Remus: Plantation Proverbs

13   Tar-baby ain't sayin' nuthin', en Brer Fox, he lay low.   *Uncle Remus and His Friends [1892]*

14   Bred en bawn in a brier-patch, Brer Fox.
Uncle Remus and His Friends

15   You do de pullin', Sis Cow, en I'll do de gruntin'.
Uncle Remus and His Friends

Joris Karl Huysmans
1848–1907

16   The loveliest tune imaginable becomes vulgar and insupportable as soon as the public begins to hum it and the hurdy-gurdies make it their own.
À Rebours (Against the Grain)[5] *[1884], ch. 9*

---

[1]Vissi d'arte, vissi d'amore, non feci male ad anima viva.
[2]Music by GIACOMO PUCCINI [1858–1924].

[3]D'où venons-nous? Que sommes-nous? Où allons-nous?
[4]Translated by VAN WYCK BROOKS.
[5]Translated by JOHN HOWARD.

Alice James
1848–1892

1   Ah! Those strange people who have the courage to be unhappy! *Are* they unhappy, by-the-way?
Diary [July 12, 1889]

2   When will women begin to have the first glimmer that above all other loyalties is the loyalty to Truth, *i.e.*, to yourself, that husband, children, friends and country are as nothing to that?
Diary [November 19, 1889]

3   I suppose one has a greater sense of intellectual degradation after an interview with a doctor than from any human experience.
Letter to her brother William
[September 27, 1890]

Richard Jefferies
1848–1887

4   It is eternity now. I am in the midst of it. It is about me in the sunshine; I am in it, as the butterfly in the light-laden air. Nothing has to come; it is now. Now is eternity; now is the immortal life.
The Story of My Heart [1883]

Sir Edmund [William] Gosse
1849–1928

5   My father's theory[1] . . . was defined by a hasty press as being this — that God hid the fossils in the rocks in order to tempt geologists into infidelity.
Father and Son [1907], ch. 5

William Ernest Henley
1849–1903

6 As dust that drives, as straws that blow,
Into the night go one and all.
Ballade of Dead Actors [1888], l. 27

7 Out of the night that covers me,
Black as the Pit from pole to pole,
I thank whatever gods may be
For my unconquerable soul.

In the fell clutch of circumstance,
I have not winced nor cried aloud;
Under the bludgeonings of chance
My head is bloody, but unbowed.
Echoes [1888], no. 4, In Memoriam
R. T. Hamilton Bruce ("Invictus"), st. 1, 2

---

[1]British naturalist Philip Henry Gosse [1810–1888], who opposed the uniformitarian geological theory of Charles Lyell [1797–1875].

8 I am the master of my fate;
I am the captain of my soul.
Echoes, 4, In Memoriam R. T. Hamilton
Bruce ("Invictus"), st. 4

9 Or ever the knightly years were gone
With the old world to the grave,
I was a King in Babylon
And you were a Christian Slave.
Echoes, 37, To W. A., st. 1

Sarah Orne Jewett
1849–1909

10   Wrecked on the lee shore of age.
The Country of the Pointed Firs [1896],
ch. 7

11   We were standing where there was a fine view of the harbor and its long stretches of shore all covered by the great army of the pointed firs, darkly cloaked and standing as if they waited to embark. As we looked far seaward among the outer islands, the trees seemed to march seaward still, going steadily over the heights and down to the water's edge.
The Country of the Pointed Firs, 7

12   In the life of each of us, I said to myself, there is a place remote and islanded, and given to endless regret or secret happiness.
The Country of the Pointed Firs, 15

13   So we die before our own eyes; so we see some chapters of our lives come to their natural end.
The Country of the Pointed Firs, 21

14   To work in silence and with all one's heart, that is the writer's lot; he is the only artist who must be solitary and yet needs the widest outlook on the world.
Letter to Willa Cather [December 1908]

15   The thing that teases the mind over and over for years, and at last gets itself put down rightly on paper — whether little or great, it belongs to Literature.
Letter to Willa Cather. Quoted in preface
to The Country of the Pointed Firs and
Other Stories [1925]

Emma Lazarus
1849–1887

16   Give me your tired, your poor,
Your huddled masses yearning to breathe free,
The wretched refuse of your teeming shore,

Send these, the homeless, tempest-tost to me:
I lift my lamp beside the golden door.[1]

*The New Colossus: Inscription for the Statue
of Liberty, New York Harbor [1883]*

Sir William Osler
1849–1919

1   The greater the ignorance the greater the dogmatism.   *Montreal Medical Journal [1902]*

2   The natural man has only two primal passions, to
get and to beget.

Science and Immortality [1904], ch. 2

3   Take the sum of human achievement in action, in
science, in art, in literature — subtract the work of the
men above forty, and while we should miss great
treasures, even priceless treasures, we would practically be where we are today. . . . The effective, moving,
vitalizing work of the world is done between the ages
of twenty-five and forty.[2]

*From HARVEY CUSHING [1869–1939],
The Life of Sir William Osler [1925],
vol. I, ch. 24 [The Fixed Period]*

4   My second fixed idea is the uselessness of men
above sixty years of age, and the incalculable benefit
it would be in commercial, political, and in professional life, if as a matter of course, men stopped work
at this age.[2]

*From HARVEY CUSHING, The Life of
Sir William Osler, I, 24 [The Fixed Period]*

James Whitcomb Riley
1849–1916

5 The ripest peach is highest on the tree.
The Ripest Peach, st. 1

6 That old sweetheart of mine.
An Old Sweetheart of Mine, st. 12

7 An' all us other children, when the supper things is
        done,
We set around the kitchen fire an' has the mostest fun
A-list'nin' to the witch-tales 'at Annie tells about,
An' the Gobble-uns 'at gits you
Ef you
    Don't
        Watch
            Out!

Little Orphant Annie [1883], st. 1

8 'Long about knee-deep in June,
  'Bout the time strawberries melts
On the vine.

Knee-Deep in June [1883], st. 1

9 Oh! the old swimmin' hole! When I last saw the
    place,
The scenes was all changed, like the change in
    my face.

The Old Swimmin' Hole [1883], st. 5

10 O, it sets my heart a-clickin' like the tickin' of a clock,
When the frost is on the punkin and the fodder's in
    the shock.

When the Frost Is on the Punkin [1883], st. 3

August Strindberg
1849–1912

11   I loathe people who keep dogs. They are cowards
who haven't got the guts to bite people themselves.
A Madman's Diary [1895], pt. 3

Edward Bellamy
1850–1898

12   We hold the period of youth sacred to education,
and the period of maturity, when the physical forces
begin to flag, equally sacred to ease and agreeable
relaxation.
Looking Backward, 2000–1887 [1888], ch. 6

13   The nation guarantees the nurture, education,
and comfortable maintenance of every citizen from
the cradle to the grave.   *Looking Backward, 9*

14   An American credit card . . . is just as good in
Europe as American gold used to be.
Looking Backward, 13

15   *Looking Backward* was written in the belief that
the Golden Age lies before us and not behind us.
Looking Backward, author's postscript

Hermann Ebbinghaus
1850–1909

16   Psychology has a long past, but only a short history.
*Abriss der Psychologie (Summary of
Psychology) [1908], opening sentence*

Eugene Field
1850–1895

17 It always was the biggest fish I caught that got
    away.   *Our Biggest Fish [1889], st. 2*

---

[1]Set to music by IRVING BERLIN for *Miss Liberty* [1949].

[2]Address at Johns Hopkins University, Baltimore [February 22,
1905]. This address caused much discussion and misquotation. It
was headlined in the press: OSLER RECOMMENDS CHLOROFORM AT SIXTY.

1 Wynken, Blynken, and Nod one night
Sailed off in a wooden shoe —
Sailed on a river of crystal light
Into a sea of dew.
Wynken, Blynken, and Nod (Dutch Lullaby)
[1889], st. 1

2 The little toy dog is covered with dust,
But sturdy and staunch he stands;
And the little toy soldier is red with rust,
And his musket molds in his hands;
Time was when the little toy dog was new,
And the soldier was passing fair;
And that was the time when our Little Boy Blue
Kissed them and put them there.
Little Boy Blue [1889], st. 1

3 The gingham dog went "Bow-wow-wow!"
And the calico cat replied "Mee-ow!"
The air was littered, an hour or so,
With bits of gingham and calico.
The Duel [1894], st. 2

4 'Most all the time, the whole year round, there ain't
no flies on me,
But jest 'fore Christmas I'm as good as I kin be!
Jest 'Fore Christmas [1894], st. 1

Samuel Gompers
1850–1924

5 To protect the workers in their inalienable rights
to a higher and better life; to protect them, not only
as equals before the law, but also in their health, their
homes, their firesides, their liberties as men, as
workers, and as citizens; to overcome and conquer
prejudices and antagonism; to secure to them the
right to life, and the opportunity to maintain that life;
the right to be full sharers in the abundance which is
the result of their brain and brawn, and the civilization of which they are the founders and the mainstay.... The attainment of these is the glorious
mission of the trade unions.
Speech [1898]

Mary Ellen [Mary Elizabeth] Lease
1850–1933

6 Raise less corn and more hell!
Advice to Kansas farmers [1890]. Attributed

Henry Cabot Lodge
1850–1924

7 Let us have done with British-Americans and
Irish-Americans and German-Americans, and so on,
and all be Americans.... If a man is going to be an
American at all let him be so without any qualifying
adjectives; and if he is going to be something else, let
him drop the word American from his personal
description.
The Day We Celebrate (Forefathers' Day).
Address, New England Society of Brooklyn
[December 21, 1888]

Guy de Maupassant
1850–1893

8 Conversation...is the art of never appearing a
bore, of knowing how to say everything interestingly,
to entertain with no matter what, to be charming with
nothing at all.
Sur l'Eau (On the Water) [1888]

Bill [Edgar Wilson] Nye
1850–1896

9 Wagner's music is better than it sounds.
From Mark Twain's Autobiography [1924]

Robert Louis Stevenson
1850–1894

10 Every man is his own doctor of divinity, in the last
resort.
An Inland Voyage [1878]. Noyon Cathedral

11 For my part, I travel not to go anywhere, but to go.
I travel for travel's sake. The great affair is to move.
Travels with a Donkey [1878]

12 Marriage is like life in this — that it is a field of
battle, and not a bed of roses.
Virginibus Puerisque [1881], pt. I, ch. 1

13 The cruelest lies are often told in silence.
Virginibus Puerisque, I, 4,
Truth of Intercourse

14 Old and young, we are all on our last cruise.
Virginibus Puerisque, II, Crabbed Age
and Youth

15 Books are good enough in their own way, but
they are a mighty bloodless substitute for life.
Virginibus Puerisque, III, An Apology
for Idlers

16 Perpetual devotion to what a man calls his business, is only to be sustained by perpetual neglect of
many other things.
Virginibus Puerisque, III, An Apology
for Idlers

1   There is no duty we so much underrate as the duty of being happy.
> *Virginibus Puerisque, III,*
> *An Apology for Idlers*

2   To travel hopefully is a better thing than to arrive.
> *Virginibus Puerisque, VI, El Dorado*

3   Now, we know that life is only a stage to play the fool upon as long as the part amuses us. There was one more convenience lacking to modern comfort; a decent easy way to quit that stage; the back stairs to liberty; or, as I said this moment, Death's private door. This . . . is supplied by the Suicide Club.
> *New Arabian Nights [1882].*
> *The Suicide Club*

4 Fifteen men on the Dead Man's Chest — [1]
Yo-ho-ho, and a bottle of rum!
Drink and the devil had done for the rest —
Yo-ho-ho, and a bottle of rum!
> *Treasure Island [1883], ch. 1*

5   "What is the Black Spot, Captain?" . . . "That's a summons, mate."
> *Treasure Island, 3*

6   Pieces of eight, pieces of eight, pieces of eight!
> *Treasure Island, 10*

7   Them that die'll be the lucky ones.
> *Treasure Island, 20*

8 In winter I get up at night
And dress by yellow candlelight.
In summer, quite the other way,
I have to go to bed by day.
> *A Child's Garden of Verses [1885].*
> *Bed in Summer, st. 1*

9 A child should always say what's true
And speak when he is spoken to,
And behave mannerly at table;
At least as far as he is able.
> *A Child's Garden of Verses. Whole Duty*
> *of Children*

10 Whenever the moon and stars are set,
Whenever the wind is high,
All night long in the dark and wet,
A man goes riding by.

---

[1] Treasure Island came out of Kingsley's *At Last,* where I got the Dead Man's Chest — and that was the seed. — R. L. STEVENSON, *Letter to Sidney Colvin* [May 1884]
    We were crawling slowly along, looking out for Virgin Gorda; the first of those numberless isles which Columbus, so goes the tale, discovered on St. Ursula's day, and named them after the saint and her eleven thousand mythical virgins. Unfortunately, English buccaneers have since given to most of them less poetic names. The Dutchman's Cap, Broken Jerusalem, The Dead Man's Chest, Rum Island, and so forth, mark a time and race more prosaic. — CHARLES KINGSLEY, *At Last* [1870], *ch. 1*

Late in the night when the fires are out,
Why does he gallop and gallop about?
> *A Child's Garden of Verses. Windy Nights,*
> *st. 1*

11 The strangest things are there for me,
Both things to eat and things to see,
And many frightening sights abroad
Till morning in the land of Nod.
> *A Child's Garden of Verses.*
> *The Land of Nod, st. 3*

12 I have a little shadow that goes in and out with me,
And what can be the use of him is more than I can see.
He is very, very like me from the heels up to the head;
And I see him jump before me, when I jump into my bed.
> *A Child's Garden of Verses. My Shadow, st. 1*

13 The world is so full of a number of things,
I'm sure we should all be as happy as kings.
> *A Child's Garden of Verses. Happy Thought*

14   All human beings, as we meet them, are commingled out of good and evil.
> *Strange Case of Dr. Jekyll and Mr. Hyde*
> *[1886], ch. 10*

15   They were a rough lot indeed, as sailors mostly are; being men rooted out of all the kindly parts of life, and condemned to toss together on the rough seas, with masters no less cruel.
> *Kidnapped [1886], ch. 7*

16 Under the wide and starry sky,
Dig the grave and let me lie.
Glad did I live and gladly die,
And I laid me down with a will.

This be the verse you grave for me:
Here he lies where he longed to be;
Home is the sailor, home from sea,
And the hunter home from the hill.
> *Underwoods [1887], bk. I, In English.*
> *Requiem*

17 My body which my dungeon is,
And yet my parks and palaces.
> *Underwoods, I, In English. My Body*
> *Which My Dungeon Is*

18   Not every man is so great a coward as he thinks he is — nor yet so good a Christian.
> *The Master of Ballantrae [1889].*
> *Mr. Mackellar's Journey*

19   Nothing like a little judicious levity.
> *The Wrong Box [1889], ch. 7*

20   Do you know what the Governor of South Carolina said to the Governor of North Carolina? It's a

long time between drinks, observed that powerful thinker.

The Wrong Box, 8

1   So long as we love we serve; so long as we are loved by others, I would almost say that we are indispensable; and no man is useless while he has a friend.

Across the Plains [1892]. Lay Morals

2   If your morals make you dreary, depend upon it, they are wrong. I do not say give them up, for they may be all you have, but conceal them like a vice lest they should spoil the lives of better and simpler people.

Across the Plains. Lay Morals

3   Here lies one who meant well, tried a little, failed much: — surely that may be his epitaph of which he need not be ashamed.

Across the Plains. Lay Morals

4 Wealth I ask not, hope nor love,
Nor a friend to know me;
All I ask, the heaven above
And the road below me.

Songs of Travel [1896]. The Vagabond, st. 4

5 The untented Kosmos my abode,
I pass, a willful stranger;
My mistress still the open road
And the bright eyes of danger.

Songs of Travel. Youth and Love, st. 3

6 I will make you brooches and toys for your delight
Of birdsong at morning and starshine at night.

Songs of Travel. Romance, st. 1

7 Bright is the ring of words
When the right man rings them.

Songs of Travel. No. 14, st. 1

8 Trusty, dusky, vivid, true,
With eyes of gold and bramble dew,
Steel-true and blade-straight
The great artificer
Made my mate.

Songs of Travel. My Wife, st. 1

9 Be it granted me to behold you again in dying,
Hills of home!

Songs of Travel. To S. R. Crockett, st. 3

10   Ice and iron cannot be welded.

Weir of Hermiston [1896]

11   Our mission in life is not to succeed, but to continue to fail, in the best of spirits.

Letters and Miscellanies of Robert Louis Stevenson [1898]. Reflection and Remarks on Human Life

12   Give us grace and strength to forbear and to persevere. . . . Give us courage and gaiety and the quiet mind, spare to us our friends, soften to us our enemies.

Prayer[1]

13   Youth is wholly experimental.

Letter to a Young Gentleman

Rose Hartwick Thorpe
1850–1939

14 She breathed the husky whisper —
"Curfew must not ring tonight."

Curfew Must Not Ring Tonight [1882], st. 2

Ella Wheeler Wilcox
1850–1919

15 No! the two kinds of people on earth that I mean
Are the people who lift and the people who lean.

To Lift or to Lean

16 Laugh, and the world laughs with you;
Weep, and you weep alone.

Solitude,[2] *st. 1*

Kate Chopin
[Katherine O'Flaherty]
1851–1904

17   Mrs. Pontellier was beginning to realize her position in the universe as a human being, and to recognize her relations as an individual to the world within and about her.

The Awakening [1899], ch. VI

18   The voice of the sea is seductive; never ceasing, whispering, clamoring, murmuring, inviting the soul to wander for a spell in abysses of solitude; to lose itself in mazes of inward contemplation.

The Awakening, VI

19   Perhaps it is better to wake up after all, even to suffer, rather than to remain a dupe to illusions all one's life.

The Awakening, XXXVIII

20   For the first time in her life she stood naked in the open air, at the mercy of the sun, the breeze that beat upon her, and the waves that invited her.

The Awakening, XXXIX

---

[1] On the bronze memorial to Stevenson in St. Giles Cathedral, Edinburgh, Scotland.

[2] Music by Louis Moreau Gottschalk [1829–1869].

Ferdinand Foch
1851–1929

1   My center is giving way, my right is pushed back, situation excellent, I am attacking.[1]
*At the second battle of the Marne [1918].
From B. H. LIDDELL HART, Reputations
Ten Years After [1928]*

Robert Bontine Cunninghame-Graham
1852–1936

2   God forbid that I should go to any heaven in which there are no horses.
Letter to Theodore Roosevelt [1917]

Edwin Markham
1852–1940

3 Bowed by the weight of centuries he leans
Upon his hoe and gazes on the ground,
The emptiness of ages in his face,
And on his back the burden of the world.
The Man with the Hoe[2] [1899], st. 1

4 O masters, lords and rulers in all lands,
Is this the handiwork you give to God?
The Man with the Hoe, st. 3

5 A man to match the mountains[3] and the sea.
Lincoln, The Man of the People [1901], st. 1

6 The color of the ground was in him, the red earth,
The smack and tang of elemental things.
Lincoln, The Man of the People, st. 2

7   He went down
As when a lordly cedar, green with boughs,
Goes down with a great shout upon the hills,
And leaves a lonesome place against the sky.
Lincoln, The Man of the People, st. 4

George Moore
1852–1933

8   All reformers are bachelors — all extreme reformers have been bachelors.
The Bending of the Bough [1900], act I

---

[1]Mon centre cède, ma droite recule, situation excellente, j'attaque.

[2]Inspired by Jean-François Millet's painting.

[3]A man to match his mountains, not to creep / Dwarfed and abased below them. — JOHN GREENLEAF WHITTIER, *Among the Hills* [1869], *prelude*
Bring me men to match my mountains. — SAM WALTER FOSS [1858–1911], *The Coming American* [1894]

Edgar Watson Howe
1853–1937

9   There is nothing so well known as that we should not expect something for nothing — but we all do and call it Hope.
Country Town Sayings [1911]

José [Julian] Martí [y Perez]
1853–1895

10   A knowledge of different literatures is the best way to free one's self from the tyranny of any of them.
On Oscar Wilde [1882]

11   A grain of poetry suffices to season a century.
Dedication of the Statue of Liberty [1887]

12   Others go to bed with their mistresses; I with my ideas.
Letter [1890]

13   Mankind is composed of two sorts of men — those who love and create, and those who hate and destroy.
Letter to a Cuban farmer [1893]

14 I wish to leave the world
By its natural door;
In my tomb of green leaves
They are to carry me to die.
Do not put me in the dark
To die like a traitor;
I am good, and like a good thing
I will die with my face to the sun.
A Morir (To Die) [1894]

15   Only those who hate the Negro see hatred in the Negro.
Manifesto of Montecristi [1895]

16   I have lived in the monster [the United States] and I know its insides; and my sling is the sling of David.
Letter to Manuel Mercado [1895]

Cecil [John] Rhodes
1853–1902

17   I desire to encourage and foster an appreciation of the advantages which will result from the union of the English-speaking peoples throughout the world, and to encourage in the students from the United States of America an attachment to the country from which they have sprung without I hope withdrawing them or their sympathies from the land of their adoption or birth.
His will, establishing the Rhodes Scholarships

James A. Bland
1854–1911

1 Carry me back to old Virginny,
There's where the cotton and the corn and taters
grow;
There's where the birds warble sweet in the
springtime,
There's where this old darky's heart am longed to go.
Carry Me Back to Old Virginny [1875], st. 1

Sir James George Frazer
1854–1941

2   By religion, then, I understand a propitiation or
conciliation of powers superior to man which are
believed to direct and control the course of nature
and of human life.
The Golden Bough[1] *[1922], ch. 4*

3   It is a common rule with primitive people not to
waken a sleeper, because his soul is away and might
not have time to get back.   *The Golden Bough, 18*

4   The awe and dread with which the untutored
savage contemplates his mother-in-law are amongst
the most familiar facts of anthropology.
The Golden Bough, 18

5   When all is said and done our resemblances to the
savage are still far more numerous than our differences from him.   *The Golden Bough, 23*

Thomas Riley Marshall
1854–1925

6   What this country needs is a really good five-
cent cigar.[2]   *Remark while presiding over the Senate*

Jules Henri Poincaré
1854–1912

7   To doubt everything and to believe everything are
two equally convenient solutions; each saves us from
thinking.   *Science and Hypothesis*[3] *[1902]*

8   Science is built up with facts, as a house is with
stones. But a collection of facts is no more a science
than a heap of stones is a house.
Science and Hypothesis

9   Principles are conventions and definitions in
disguise.
Science and Hypothesis

10   Thought is only a gleam in the midst of a long
night. But it is this gleam which is everything.
The Value of Science[3] *[1904]*

11   Discovery is discernment, selection.
Science and Method[4] *[1908].*
The Scientist and Science

12   The scientist does not study nature because it
is useful to do so. He studies it because he takes
pleasure in it, and he takes pleasure in it because it
is beautiful. If nature were not beautiful, it would
not be worth knowing, and life would not be worth
living.
Science and Method. The Selection of Facts

Arthur Rimbaud
1854–1891

13   I went out under the sky, Muse! and I was your
vassal.[5]
Ma Bohème (My Bohemian Existence)
[1870]. Fantaisie

14   I say one must be a *seer*, make oneself a *seer*. The
poet makes himself a *seer* by an immense, long, deliberate *derangement* of all the senses.[6]
Letter to Paul Demeny
[May 15, 1871]

15   *I* is an other.[7]
Letters to Georges Izambard
[May 13, 1871] and Paul Demeny
[May 15, 1871]

16 My sad heart foams at the stern.[8]
Le Coeur Volé (Stolen Heart) [1871]

17 Lighter than a cork I danced on the waves.[9]
Le Bateau Ivre (The Drunken Boat)
[1871]

18   I have bathed in the Poem
Of the Sea . . .
Devouring the green azures.[10]
Le Bateau Ivre

---

[1]Abridged one-volume edition. The original appeared in twelve
volumes [1890–1915].

[2]What this country needs is a good five-cent nickel. — FRANKLIN P.
ADAMS [1881–1960]

[3]Translated by G. B. HALSTED.

[4]Translated by FRANCIS MAITLAND.

[5]J'allais sous le ciel, Muse! et j'étais ton féal.

[6]Je dis qu'il faut être *voyant*, se faire *voyant*. Le poète se fait *voyant*
par un long, immense et raisonné *dérèglement* de tous les sens.

[7]*Je* est un autre.

[8]Mon triste coeur bave à la poupe.

[9]Plus léger qu'un bouchon j'ai dansé sur les flots.

[10]Je me suis baigné dans le Poème / De la Mer . . . / Dévorant les
azurs verts.

1 I have seen the sunset, stained with mystic horrors,
Illumine the rolling waves with long purple forms,
Like actors in ancient plays.[1]   *Le Bateau Ivre*

2 I long for Europe of the ancient parapets.[2]
Le Bateau Ivre

3 I have seen starry archipelagoes! and islands
Whose raving skies are opened to the voyager:
Is it in these bottomless nights that you sleep, in exile,
A million golden birds, O future Vigor?[3]
Le Bateau Ivre

4 Black A, white E, red I, green U, blue O: vowels,
Someday I shall recount your latent births.[4]
Voyelles (Vowels) [1871]

5 It is found again.
What? Eternity.
It is the sea
Gone with the sun.[5]   *L'Éternité [1872]*

6 O seasons, O châteaux,
What soul is without flaws?[6]
O Saisons, O Châteaux [1872]

7 One evening, I sat Beauty in my lap. — And I
found her bitter. — And I cursed her.
Une Saison en Enfer (A Season in Hell)
[1873]

8 I found I could extinguish all human hope from
my soul.   *Une Saison en Enfer*

9 Baptism enslaved me.
Une Saison en Enfer. Nuit de l'Enfer
(Night in Hell)

10 I am the master of fantasy.
Une Saison en Enfer. Nuit de l'Enfer

11 Old poetics played a large part in my alchemy of
the word.
Une Saison en Enfer. Délires II (Deliria II)

12 I! I who fashioned myself a sorcerer or an angel,
who dispensed with all morality, I have come back
to the earth.   *Une Saison en Enfer. Adieu*

13 One must be absolutely modern.
Une Saison en Enfer. Adieu

---

[1]J'ai vu le soleil bas, taché d'horreurs mystiques, / Illuminant de
longs figements violets, / Pareils à des acteurs des drames très
antiques.

[2]Je regrette l'Europe aux anciens parapets!

[3]J'ai vu des archipels sidéraux! et des îles / Dont les cieux délirants
sont ouverts au voyageur: / Est-ce en ces nuits sans fonds que tu dors
et t'exiles, / Million d'oiseaux d'or, ô future Vigueur?

[4]A noir, E blanc, I rouge, U vert, O bleu: voyelles, / Je dirai
quelque jour vos naissances latentes!

[5]Elle est retrouvée, / Quoi? — L'Éternité. / C'est la mer allée /
Avec le soleil.

[6]O saisons, O châteaux / Quelle âme est sans défauts?

Willard Duncan Vandiver
1854–1932

14 I come from a state that raises corn and cotton and
cockleburs and Democrats, and frothy eloquence
neither convinces nor satisfies me. I am from Missouri. You have got to show me.
Speech at a naval banquet in Philadelphia [1899]

Oscar [Fingal O'Flahertie Wills] Wilde
1854–1900

15 Tread lightly, she is near
Under the snow,
Speak gently, she can hear
The daisies grow.   *Requiescat [1874], st. 1*

16 [On Leadville:] Over the piano was printed a
notice: Please do not shoot the pianist. He is doing
his best.   *Impressions of America [1883]*

17 I was disappointed with Niagara — most people
must be disappointed with Niagara. Every American
bride is taken there, and the sight of the stupendous
waterfall must be one of the earliest, if not the
keenest, disappointments in American married life.
Impressions of America

18 And down the long and silent street,
The dawn, with silver-sandaled feet,
Crept like a frightened girl.
The Harlot's House [1885], st. 6

19 A poet can survive everything but a misprint.
Review of The Children of the Poets [1886]

20 Thinking is the most unhealthy thing in the
world, and people die of it just as they die of any other
disease. Fortunately, in England at any rate, thought
is not catching.   *The Decay of Lying [1889]*

21 Paradox though it may seem — and paradoxes are
always dangerous things — it is none the less true that
Life imitates art far more than Art imitates life.
The Decay of Lying

22 As long as war is regarded as wicked, it will always
have its fascination. When it is looked upon as vulgar,
it will cease to be popular.
The Critic as Artist [1891], pt. II

23 There is no such thing as a moral or an immoral
book. Books are well written, or badly written. That
is all.   *The Picture of Dorian Gray [1891], preface*

24 All art is quite useless.
The Picture of Dorian Gray, preface

25 There is only one thing in the world worse than
being talked about, and that is not being talked
about.   *The Picture of Dorian Gray, ch. 1*

1 A man cannot be too careful in the choice of his enemies. *The Picture of Dorian Gray, 1*

2 The only way to get rid of a temptation is to yield to it. *The Picture of Dorian Gray, 2*

3 He knew the precise psychological moment[1] when to say nothing. *The Picture of Dorian Gray, 2*

4 The only difference between a caprice and a lifelong passion is that the caprice lasts a little longer. *The Picture of Dorian Gray, 2*

5 Children begin by loving their parents; as they grow older they judge them; sometimes they forgive them. *The Picture of Dorian Gray, 5*

6 Nowadays we are all of us so hard up that the only pleasant things to pay are compliments. They're the only things we can pay. *Lady Windermere's Fan [1892], act I*

7 I can resist everything except temptation. *Lady Windermere's Fan, I*

8 We are all in the gutter, but some of us are looking at the stars. *Lady Windermere's Fan, III*

9 In this world there are only two tragedies. One is not getting what one wants, and the other is getting it. *Lady Windermere's Fan, III*

10 What is a cynic? A man who knows the price of everything, and the value of nothing. *Lady Windermere's Fan, III*

11 Experience is the name everyone gives to their mistakes. *Lady Windermere's Fan, III*

12 I have never admitted that I am more than twentynine, or thirty at the most. Twenty-nine when there are pink shades, thirty when there are not.[2] *Lady Windermere's Fan, IV*

13 *Mrs. Allonby:* They say, Lady Hunstanton, that when good Americans die they go to Paris.[3]
Lady Hunstanton: Indeed? And when bad Americans die, where do they go to?
Lord Illingworth: Oh, they go to America. *A Woman of No Importance [1893], act I*

14 The youth of America is their oldest tradition. It has been going on now for three hundred years. *A Woman of No Importance, I*

15 *Lord Illingworth:* The Book of Life begins with a man and a woman in a garden.
Mrs. Allonby: It ends with Revelations. *A Woman of No Importance, I*

16 I suppose society is wonderfully delightful. To be in it is merely a bore. But to be out of it simply a tragedy. *A Woman of No Importance, III*

17 One should either be a work of art or wear a work of art. *Phrases and Philosophies [1894]*

18 Really, if the lower orders don't set us a good example, what on earth is the use of them? *The Importance of Being Earnest [1895], act I*

19 Her hair has turned quite gold from grief. *The Importance of Being Earnest, I*

20 I have invented an invaluable permanent invalid called Bunbury, in order that I may be able to go down into the country whenever I choose. *The Importance of Being Earnest, I*

21 Of course the music is a great difficulty. You see, if one plays good music, people don't listen, and if one plays bad music people don't talk. *The Importance of Being Earnest, I*

22 To lose one parent, Mr. Worthing, may be regarded as a misfortune; to lose both looks like carelessness. *The Importance of Being Earnest, I*

23 Relations are simply a tedious pack of people, who haven't got the remotest knowledge of how to live, nor the smallest instinct about when to die. *The Importance of Being Earnest, I*

24 I never travel without my diary. One should always have something sensational to read in the train. *The Importance of Being Earnest, II*

25 Thirty-five is a very attractive age. London society is full of women of the very highest birth who have, of their own free choice, remained thirty-five for years. *The Importance of Being Earnest, III*

26 The fact is, that civilization requires slaves. The Greeks were quite right there. Unless there are slaves to do the ugly, horrible, uninteresting work, culture and contemplation become almost impossible. Human slavery is wrong, insecure, and demoralizing. On mechanical slavery, on the slavery of the machine, the future of the world depends. *The Soul of Man Under Socialism [1895]*

27 Charity creates a multitude of sins. *The Soul of Man Under Socialism*

---

[1]In all considerations the psychological momentum or factor must be allowed to play a prominent part, for without its cooperation there is little to be hoped from the work of the artillery. — *Neue Preussische Kreuzzeitung* [December 16, 1870], *commenting upon the siege of Paris*

An error in translation gave us the phrase "psychological moment" (i.e., the critical moment).

[2]When you come to write my epitaph, Charles, let it be in these delicious words, "She had a long twenty-nine." — SIR JAMES BARRIE, *Rosalind [1912]*

[3]Good Americans, when they die, go to Paris. — THOMAS GOLD APPLETON [1812–1884]; *from* OLIVER WENDELL HOLMES, *The Autocrat of the Breakfast-Table, ch. 6*

1 I never saw a man who looked
With such a wistful eye
Upon that little tent of blue
Which prisoners call the sky.
> *The Ballad of Reading Gaol [1898],*
> *pt. I, st. 3*

2 When a voice behind me whispered low,
"That fellow's got to swing."
> *The Ballad of Reading Gaol, I, st. 4*

3 Yet each man kills the thing he loves,
By each let this be heard,
Some do it with a bitter look,
Some with a flattering word.
The coward does it with a kiss,
The brave man with a sword!
> *The Ballad of Reading Gaol, I, st. 7*

4 It is sweet to dance to violins
When Love and Life are fair:
To dance to flutes, to dance to lutes
Is delicate and rare:
But it is not sweet with nimble feet
To dance upon the air!
> *The Ballad of Reading Gaol, II, st. 9*

5 Something was dead in each of us,
And what was dead was Hope.
> *The Ballad of Reading Gaol, III, st. 31*

6 Where there is sorrow there is holy ground.
> *De Profundis [1905]*

7 The English country gentleman galloping after a fox — the unspeakable in full pursuit of the uneatable. *De Profundis*

8 One must have a heart of stone to read the death of Little Nell without laughing.
> *From* RICHARD ELLMANN *[1918–1987],*
> *Oscar Wilde [1988]*

9 I am dying beyond my means.
> *Attributed*

Henry Cuyler Bunner
1855–1896

10 Off with your hat as the flag goes by!
> *Airs from Arcady [1888]. The Old Flag, st. 1*

Eugene V[ictor] Debs
1855–1926

11 While there is a lower class I am in it, while there is a criminal element I am of it; while there is a soul in prison, I am not free.
> *Speech at trial for sedition [September 14, 1918]*

Margaret Wolfe Hungerford
1855–1897

12 Beauty is in the eye of the beholder.
> *Molly Bawn [1878]*

Robert M. La Follette Sr.
1855–1925

13 I think all men recognize that in time of war the citizen must surrender some rights for the common good which he is entitled to enjoy in time of peace. But, sir, the right to control their own government according to constitutional forms is not one of the rights that the citizens of this country are called upon to surrender in time of war.
> *Speech in the Senate [October 6, 1917]*

Andrew Mellon
1855–1937

14 Liquidate labor, liquidate stocks, liquidate the farmers, liquidate real estate.... It will purge the rottenness out of the system.[1]
> *Herbert Hoover, Memoirs [1952]*

Sir Arthur Wing Pinero
1855–1934

15 From forty till fifty a man is at heart either a stoic or a satyr.
> *The Second Mrs. Tanqueray [1893], act I*

Olive Schreiner
[Ralph Iron]
1855–1920

16 There never was a man who said one word for woman but he said two for man and three for the whole human race.
> *The Story of an African Farm [1883],*
> *pt. 2, ch. 4*

17 Men are like the earth and we are the moon; we turn always one side to them, and they think there is no other, because they don't see it — but there is.
> *The Story of an African Farm, 2, 4*

18 You can't love a man till you've had a baby with him.
> *The Story of an African Farm, 2, 14*

---

[1]Mellon's advice to Secretary of the Treasury Herbert Hoover, following the stock market crash of 1929.

William Sharp [Fiona Macleod]
1855–1905

1 My heart is a lonely hunter[1] that hunts on a lonely
hill.   *The Lonely Hunter, st. 6*

L[yman] Frank Baum
1856–1919

2   The wicked Witch of the East.
         The Wonderful Wizard of Oz[2] *[1900], ch. 2*

3   The road to the City of Emeralds is paved with
yellow brick.   *The Wonderful Wizard of Oz, 2*

4   There is no place like home.
                   The Wonderful Wizard of Oz, 4

5   I'm really a very good man; but I'm a very bad
Wizard.   *The Wonderful Wizard of Oz, 15*

Francis Bellamy
1856–1931

6   I pledge allegiance to my flag and to the republic
for which it stands: one nation indivisible, with liberty
and justice for all.
         The Pledge of Allegiance to the Flag[3] *[1888]*

Louis D[embitz] Brandeis
1856–1941

7   Sunlight is said to be the best of disinfectants; electric light the most efficient policeman.[4]
                     Other People's Money [1914], ch. 5

8   Those who won our independence believed that
the final end of the State was to make men free to
develop their faculties; and that in its government the
deliberative forces should prevail over the arbitrary.
They valued liberty both as an end and as a means.
They believed liberty to be the secret of happiness and
courage to be the secret of liberty.
                    Whitney v. California, 274 U.S. 357,
                    375 [1927]

---

[1]Carson McCullers's 1940 novel *The Heart is a Lonely Hunter*
takes its title from this poem.

[2]See E. Y. Harburg, 711:12, and Noel Langley, Florence Ryerson,
and Edgar Allan Woolf, 764.

[3]In 1888 JAMES B. UPHAM [1845–1905] wrote a draft that
Bellamy, chairman of a national celebration of the 400th anniversary
of America's discovery, helped put in this form.
    More than thirty years later, "my flag" was changed to "the flag of
the United States of America"; in 1954 an act of Congress added
"under God."

[4]Often quoted as "Sunlight is the best disinfectant"; similar sayings
are used in advertisements as early as 1903.

9   Fear of serious injury cannot alone justify suppression of free speech and assembly. Men feared witches
and burned women. It is the function of speech to
free men from the bondage of irrational fears.
              Whitney v. California, 274 U.S. 357, 376

10   They [the makers of the Constitution] conferred,
as against the Government, the right to be let
alone — the most comprehensive of rights and the
right most valued by civilized men.
              Olmstead v. United States, 277 U.S. 438,
              478 [1928]

11   To take risks is the very essence of Jewish life,
that is, to take necessary risks. The wise man seeks
not to avoid but to minimize risks. He minimizes
them by using judgment and by knowledge and by
thinking. These are, fortunately, preeminently Jewish
attributes.   *Speech [November 24, 1929]*

12   Denial of the right to experiment may be fraught
with serious consequences to the Nation. It is one of
the happy incidents of the federal system that a single
courageous State may, if its citizens choose, serve as a
laboratory; and try novel social and economic experiments without risk to the rest of the country.
              New State Ice Company v. Liebmann,
              285 U.S. 262, 311 [1932]

13   If we would guide by the light of reason, we must
let our minds be bold.
              New State Ice Co. v. Liebmann,
              285 U.S. 262, 311

14   The Court bows to the lessons of experience and
the force of better reasoning, recognizing that the
process of trial and error, so fruitful in the physical
sciences, is appropriate also in the judicial function.
              Burnet v. Coronado Oil and Gas Co.,
              285 U.S. 393, 406 [1932]

15   There is in most Americans some spark of idealism, which can be fanned into a flame. It takes
sometimes a divining rod to find what it is; but when
found, and that means often, when disclosed to the
owners, the results are often most extraordinary.
              The Words of Justice Brandeis [1953]

Sigmund Freud
1856–1939

16   The new psychoanalytic method [is] . . . somewhat
subtle but irreplaceable, so fruitful has it proved
to be in explaining obscure unconscious mental
processes.[5]
       Heredity and the Etiology of the Neuroses [1896]

---

[5]Translated by M. MEYER.
    Apparently Freud's first published use of the root term
"psychoanalytic."

1   The interpretation of dreams is the royal road to a knowledge of the unconscious activities of the mind.

> *The Interpretation of Dreams*[1] *[1900],*
> *ch. 7*

2   When a member of my family complains to me of having bitten his tongue, pinched a finger, or the like, he does not get the sympathy he hopes for but instead the question: "Why did you do that?"

> *The Psychopathology of Everyday Life*[1] *[1901],*
> *ch. 8*

3   The creative writer acts no differently from the child at play: he creates a fantasy world, which he takes very seriously; that is to say, he invests large amounts of emotion in it, while marking it off sharply from reality.

> *The Creative Writer and Daydreaming*[1]
> *[1907]*

4   Happiness is the deferred fulfillment of a prehistoric wish. That is why wealth brings so little happiness; money is not an infantile wish.

> *Letter to Wilhelm Fliess*[2] *[January 16, 1898]*

5   Our hysterical patients suffer from reminiscences.

> *Five Lectures on Psychoanalysis [1910],*
> *no. I*[1]

6   The psychic development of the individual is a short repetition of the course of development of the race.[3]

> *Leonardo da Vinci*[1] *[1910]*

7   The excremental is all too intimately and inseparably bound up with the sexual; the position of the genitals — *inter urinas et faeces* — remains the decisive and unchangeable factor. One might say here, varying a well-known saying of the great Napoleon: "Anatomy is destiny."

> *On the Universal Tendency to Debasement*
> *in the Sphere of Love*[1] *[1912]*

8   At bottom God is nothing other than an exalted father.   *Totem and Taboo*[1] *[1913], pt. 4*

9   We believe that civilization has been created under the pressure of the exigencies of life at the cost of satisfaction of the instincts.

> *Introductory Lectures on Psychoanalysis*[1]
> *[1916–1917], no. I*

10   No one believes in his own death.

> *Thoughts for the Times on War and*
> *Death [1915], pt. 2*

11   If a man has been his mother's undisputed darling he retains throughout life the triumphant feeling, the confidence in success, which not seldom brings actual success with it.

> *A Childhood Memory of Goethe's*[1] *[1917]*

12   The poets and philosophers before me discovered the unconscious; what I discovered was the scientific method by which the unconscious can be studied.

> *On his seventieth birthday [1926].*
> *From* LIONEL TRILLING, *The Liberal*
> *Imagination [1957]*

13   The sexual life of adult women is a "dark continent" for psychology.[4]

> *The Question of Lay Analysis*[1] *[1926], pt. 4*

14   No, our science is no illusion. But an illusion it would be to suppose that what science cannot give us we can get elsewhere.

> *The Future of an Illusion*[1] *[1927]*

15   A culture which leaves unsatisfied and drives to rebelliousness so large a number of its members neither has a prospect of continued existence nor deserves it.   *The Future of an Illusion*

16   Before the problem of the creative writer, analysis must lay down its arms.

> *Dostoevsky and Parricide*[1] *[1928]*

17   Men have gained control over the forces of nature to such an extent that with their help they could have no difficulty in exterminating one another to the last man. They know this, and hence comes a large part of their current unrest, their unhappiness and their mood of anxiety.

> *Civilization and Its Discontents*[1] *[1930],*
> *pt. VIII*

18   The ego's relation to the id might be compared with that of a rider to his horse. The horse supplies the locomotive energy, while the rider has the privilege of deciding on the goal and of guiding the powerful animal's movement. But only too often there arises between the ego and the id the not precisely ideal situation of the rider being obliged to guide the horse along the path by which it itself wants to go.

> *New Introductory Lectures on*
> *Psycho-analysis*[1] *[1933], no. 31*

19   The poor ego . . . serves three severe masters and does what it can to bring their claims and demands into harmony with one another. No wonder that the ego so often fails in its task. Its three tyrannical masters are the external world, the super-ego and the id.

> *New Introductory Lectures on*
> *Psycho-analysis, 31*

20   Where id was, there ego shall be.

> *New Introductory Lectures on*
> *Psycho-analysis, 31*

---

[1]Translated by JAMES STRACHEY.

[2]Translated by ERIC MOSBACHER and JAMES STRACHEY.

[3]See Ernst Heinrich Haeckel, 519:12.

[4]The phrase "dark continent" appears in English in the original German text.

1   Religion is an illusion and it derives its strength from its readiness to fit in with our instinctual wishful impulses.
New Introductory Lectures on Psycho-analysis, 35

2   It almost looks as if analysis were the third of those "impossible" professions in which one can be quite sure of unsatisfying results. The other two, much older-established, are the bringing-up of children and the government of nations.
Analysis Terminable and Interminable[1] *[1937]*

3   Intolerance of groups is often, strangely enough, exhibited more strongly against small differences than against fundamental ones.
Moses and Monotheism[2] *[1938], ch. III, pt. 1*

4   Judaism had been a religion of the father; Christianity became a religion of the son. The old God the Father fell back behind Christ; Christ, the Son, took his place, just as every son had hoped to do in primeval times. *Moses and Monotheism, III, 1*

5   The great question . . . which I have not been able to answer, despite my thirty years of research into the feminine soul, is "What does a woman want?"[3]
From ERNEST JONES [1879–1958], Life and Work of Sigmund Freud, vol. II [1955], ch. 16

6   Yes, America is gigantic, but a giant mistake.
From ERNEST JONES, Free Associations [1962]

7   [Regarding what a normal person should be able to do:] To love and to work.[4]
From ERIK ERIKSON, Childhood and Society [1963]

8   Sometimes a cigar is just a cigar.   *Attributed*

H[enry] Rider Haggard
1856–1925

9   She-who-must-be-obeyed.   *She [1887]*

Elbert Hubbard
1856–1915

10   It is not book learning young men need, nor instruction about this and that, but a stiffening of the vertebrae which will cause them to be loyal to a trust, to act promptly, concentrate their energies, do a thing — "carry a message to Garcia."[5]
A Message to Garcia [March 1899]

Robert E[dwin] Peary
1856–1920

11   The Eskimo, Ootah, had his own explanation. Said he: "The devil is asleep or having trouble with his wife, or we should never have come back so easily."
The North Pole [1910]

Henri Philippe Pétain
1856–1951

12   They shall not pass.[6]
Attributed. Verdun [February 26, 1916]

George Bernard Shaw
1856–1950

13   It's well to be off with the Old Woman before you're on with the New.
The Philanderer [1893], act II

14   The test of a man or woman's breeding is how they behave in a quarrel.   *The Philanderer, IV*

15   People are always blaming their circumstances for what they are. I don't believe in circumstances. The people who get on in this world are the people who get up and look for the circumstances they want, and, if they can't find them, make them.
Mrs. Warren's Profession [1893], act II

16   There are no secrets better kept than the secrets that everybody guesses.
Mrs. Warren's Profession, III

17   A great devotee of the Gospel of Getting On.
Mrs. Warren's Profession, IV

18   My method is to take the utmost trouble to find the right thing to say, and then to say it with the utmost levity.   *Answers to Nine Questions [1896]*

19   We have no more right to consume happiness without producing it than to consume wealth without producing it.   *Candida [1898], act I*

---

[1]Translated by JOAN RIVIERE.
[2]Translated by JAMES STRACHEY.
[3]Was will das Weib?
[4]Lieben und arbeiten.

[5]At the outbreak of the Spanish-American War, Andrew S. Rowan was sent to communicate with General Calixto Garcia. He landed in an open boat near Turquino Peak in Cuba [April 24, 1898], executed the mission, and brought back information regarding the insurgent army.

[6]Ils ne passeront pas.
The inscription on the Verdun medal is: On ne passe pas.

1   The great advantage of a hotel is that it's a refuge from home life.
You Never Can Tell [1898], act II

2   The worst sin towards our fellow creatures is not to hate them, but to be indifferent to them: that's the essence of inhumanity.
The Devil's Disciple [1901], act II

3   This is the true joy in life, the being used for a purpose recognized by yourself as a mighty one; the being thoroughly worn out before you are thrown on the scrap heap; the being a force of nature instead of a feverish selfish little clod of ailments and grievances complaining that the world will not devote itself to making you happy.
Man and Superman [1903], epistle dedicatory

4   A lifetime of happiness! No man alive could bear it: it would be hell on earth.
Man and Superman, act I

5   The more things a man is ashamed of, the more respectable he is.   *Man and Superman, I*

6   Hell is full of musical amateurs: music is the brandy of the damned.   *Man and Superman, III*

7   An Englishman thinks he is moral when he is only uncomfortable.   *Man and Superman, III*

8   There are two tragedies in life. One is to lose your heart's desire. The other is to gain it.[1]
Man and Superman, IV

9   He who can, does. He who cannot, teaches.
Man and Superman. Maxims for Revolutionists

10   Marriage is popular because it combines the maximum of temptation with the maximum of opportunity.
Man and Superman. Maxims for Revolutionists

11   If you strike a child, take care that you strike it in anger, even at the risk of maiming it for life. A blow in cold blood neither can nor should be forgiven.
Man and Superman. Maxims for Revolutionists

12   My way of joking is to tell the truth. It's the funniest joke in the world.
John Bull's Other Island [1904], act II

13   The greatest of our evils and the worst of our crimes is poverty.
Major Barbara [1905], preface

14   I am a Millionaire. That is my religion.
Major Barbara, act II

15   With the single exception of Homer, there is no eminent writer, not even Sir Walter Scott, whom I can despise so entirely as I despise Shakespeare when I measure my mind against his. . . . It would positively be a relief to me to dig him up and throw stones at him.
Dramatic Opinions and Essays [1907]. Blaming the Bard

16   When two people are under the influence of the most violent, most insane, most delusive, and most transient of passions, they are required to swear that they will remain in that excited, abnormal, and exhausting condition continuously until death do them part.   *Getting Married [1908], preface*

17   Assassination is the extreme form of censorship.
The Shewing-up of Blanco Posnet [1909]. The Rejected Statement, pt. I

18   If parents would only realize how they bore their children!   *Misalliance [1910], episode I*

19   It is impossible for an Englishman to open his mouth, without making some other Englishman hate or despise him; English is not accessible even to Englishmen.   *Pygmalion*[2] *[1913], preface*

20   Women upset everything. When you let them into your life, you find that the woman is driving at one thing and you're driving at another.
Pygmalion, act II

21   *Pickering:* Have you no morals, man?
Doolittle: Can't afford them, Governor.
Pygmalion, II

22   I'm one of the undeserving poor.
Pygmalion, II

23   Gin was mother's milk to her.   *Pygmalion, III*

24   All great truths begin as blasphemies.
Annajanska [1919]

25   You see things; and you say, "Why?" But I dream things that never were; and I say, "Why not?"
Back to Methuselah [1921], pt. I, act I

26   Everything happens to everybody sooner or later if there is time enough.   *Back to Methuselah, V*

Louis Henri Sullivan
1856–1924

27   Form ever follows function.
The Tall Office Building Artistically Considered. From Lippincott's Magazine [March 1896]

---

[1]See Oscar Wilde, 560:9.

[2]The play upon which the musical *My Fair Lady* is based. See Alan Jay Lerner, 790:7–12.

Frederick Winslow Taylor
1856–1915

1   In the past the man has been first. In the future the System must be first.
The Principles of Scientific Management [1911], ch. 1

Brandon Thomas
1856–1914

2   I am Charley's aunt from Brazil, where the nuts come from.   *Charley's Aunt [1892], act I*

Booker T[aliaferro] Washington
1856–1915

3   In all things that are purely social we [black and white] can be as separate as the fingers, yet one as the hand in all things essential to mutual progress.
Speech at the Cotton States and International Exposition, Atlanta [September 18, 1895]

4   No race can prosper till it learns that there is as much dignity in tilling a field as in writing a poem.
Up from Slavery [1901]

5   You can't hold a man down without staying down with him.   *Attributed*

Woodrow Wilson
1856–1924

6   The United States must be neutral in fact as well as in name.... We must be impartial in thought as well as in action.
Message to the Senate [August 19, 1914]

7   You deal in the raw material of opinion, and, if my convictions have any validity, opinion ultimately governs the world.
Address to the Associated Press [April 20, 1915]

8   There is such a thing as a man being too proud to fight.
Address to Foreign-Born Citizens [May 10, 1915]

9   [The Civil War] created in this country what had never existed before — a national consciousness. It was not the salvation of the Union; it was the rebirth of the Union.
Memorial Day Address [1915]

10   We have stood apart, studiously neutral.
Message to Congress [December 7, 1915]

11   America cannot be an ostrich with its head in the sand.
Speech at Des Moines [February 1, 1916]

12   It must be a peace without victory.... Only a peace between equals can last.
Address to the Senate [January 22, 1917]

13   Armed neutrality is ineffectual enough at best.
Address to Congress, asking for a declaration of war [April 2, 1917]

14   The world must be made safe for democracy.
Address to Congress, asking for a declaration of war

15   The day has come when America is privileged to spend her blood and her might for the principles that gave her birth and happiness and the peace which she has treasured.
Address to Congress, asking for a declaration of war

16   1. Open covenants of peace, openly arrived at.
2. Absolute freedom of navigation upon the seas....
5. A free, open-minded, and absolutely impartial adjustment of all colonial claims.
Address to Congress (The Fourteen Points) [January 8, 1918]

17   14. A general association of nations must be formed ... for the purpose of affording mutual guarantees of political independence and territorial integrity to great and small states alike.
Address to Congress (The Fourteen Points)

18   It is like writing history with lightning. And my only regret is that it is all so terribly true.
Attributed. On seeing D. W. GRIFFITH's movie The Birth of a Nation, at the White House [February 18, 1915]

Edward F[rancis] Albee
1857–1930

19   Never give a sucker an even break.
Attributed[1]

Robert Baden-Powell
1857–1941

20   The scouts' motto is founded on my initials. It is: Be Prepared, which means, you are always to be in a state of readiness in mind and body to do your duty.
Scouting for Boys [1908], pt. 1

---

[1]Often attributed to W. C. Fields, who uttered it in the Broadway musical *Poppy* [1923]. He made the quote famous.

1 Your forefathers worked hard, fought hard, and died hard to make this Empire for you. Don't let them look down from heaven, and see you loafing about with hands in your pockets doing nothing to keep it up. *Scouting for Boys, 5*

Joseph Conrad
1857–1924

2 A work that aspires, however humbly, to the condition of art should carry its justification in every line.
The Nigger of the Narcissus
[1898], preface

3 But the artist appeals to that part of our being which is not dependent on wisdom; to that in us which is a gift and not an acquisition — and, therefore, more permanently enduring. He speaks to our capacity for delight and wonder, to the sense of mystery surrounding our lives: to our sense of pity, and beauty, and pain.
The Nigger of the Narcissus, preface

4 My task . . . to make you hear, to make you feel — it is, before all, to make you see. That — and no more, and it is everything.
The Nigger of the Narcissus, preface

5 The ship, a fragment detached from the earth, went on lonely and swift like a small planet.
The Nigger of the Narcissus, ch. 2

6 Goodbye, brothers! You were a good crowd. As good a crowd as ever fisted with wild cries the beating canvas of a heavy foresail; or tossing aloft, invisible in the night, gave back yell for yell to a westerly gale.
The Nigger of the Narcissus, 5

7 There is a weird power in a spoken word. . . . And a word carries far — very far — deals destruction through time as the bullets go flying through space.
Lord Jim [1900], ch. 15

8 That faculty of beholding at a hint the face of his desire and the shape of his dream, without which the earth would know no lover and no adventurer.
Lord Jim, 16

9 To the destructive element submit yourself.
Lord Jim, 20

10 Only a moment; a moment of strength, of romance, of glamour — of youth! . . . A flick of sunshine upon a strange shore, the time to remember, the time for a sigh, and — goodbye! — Night — Goodbye . . . !
Youth: A Narrative [1902]

11 She strode like a grenadier, was strong and upright like an obelisk, had a beautiful face, a candid brow, pure eyes, and not a thought of her own in her head.
Tales of Unrest [1902]. The Return

12 Running . . . all over the sea trying to get behind the weather. *Typhoon [1902], ch. 2*

13 We live, as we dream — alone.
Heart of Darkness[1] [1902], pt. I

14 I don't like work — no man does — but I like what is in work — the chance to find yourself. Your own reality — for yourself, not for others — what no other man can ever know. *Heart of Darkness, I*

15 No fear can stand up to hunger, no patience can wear it out, disgust simply does not exist where hunger is; and as to superstition, beliefs, and what you may call principles, they are less than chaff in a breeze. *Heart of Darkness, II*

16 Exterminate all the brutes![2]
Heart of Darkness, II

17 The horror! The horror!
Heart of Darkness, III

18 Mistah Kurtz — he dead.
Heart of Darkness, III

19 The terrorist and the policeman both come from the same basket. Revolution, legality — countermoves in the same game; forms of idleness at bottom identical. *The Secret Agent [1907], ch. 4*

20 A man's real life is that accorded to him in the thoughts of other men by reason of respect or natural love. *Under Western Eyes [1911], pt. I, ch. 1*

21 Who knows what true loneliness is — not the conventional word, but the naked terror? To the lonely themselves it wears a mask. The most miserable outcast hugs some memory or some illusion. Now and then a fatal conjunction of events may lift the veil for an instant. For an instant only. No human being could bear a steady view of moral solitude without going mad.
Under Western Eyes, I, 2

---

[1]"Heart of Darkness" is experience . . . but it is experience pushed a little (and only very little) beyond the actual facts of the case for the perfectly legitimate, I believe, purpose of bringing it home to the minds and bosoms of the readers. . . . That somber theme had to be given a sinister resonance, a tonality of its own, a continued vibration that, I hoped, would hang in the air and dwell on the ear after the last note had been struck. — CONRAD, *Youth: A Narrative, author's preface*

[2]For two hundred years, the Judges of England sat on the Bench, condemning to the penalty of death every man, woman, and child who stole property to the value of five shillings; and, during all that time, not one Judge ever remonstrated against the law. We English are a nation of brutes, and ought to be exterminated to the last man. — JOHN BRIGHT [1880]; in HENRY ADAMS, *The Education of Henry Adams, ch. 12*

1   Let a fool be made serviceable according to his folly.   *Under Western Eyes, I, 3*

2   The scrupulous and the just, the noble, humane, and devoted natures; the unselfish and the intelligent may begin a movement — but it passes away from them. They are not the leaders of a revolution. They are its victims.   *Under Western Eyes, II, 3*

3   The belief in a supernatural source of evil is not necessary; men alone are quite capable of every wickedness.   *Under Western Eyes, II, 4*

4   Only in men's imagination does every truth find an effective and undeniable existence. Imagination, not invention, is the supreme master of art as of life.   *A Personal Record [1912], ch. 1*

5   But what I felt most was my being a stranger to the ship; and if all the truth must be told, I was somewhat of a stranger to myself.
                   The Secret Sharer [1912], ch. 1

6   The world of finance is a mysterious world in which, incredible as the fact may appear, evaporation precedes liquidation. First the capital evaporates, and then the company goes into liquidation.
                   Victory [1915], ch. 1

7   The very young have, properly speaking, no moments. It is the privilege of early youth to live in advance of its days in all the beautiful continuity of hope which knows no pauses and no introspection.
                   The Shadow Line [1916], ch. 1

Émile Coué
1857–1926

8   Every day, in every way, I'm getting better and better.[1]
       *Formula of his faith cures, inscribed
       in his sanitarium, Nancy, France*

Clarence [Seward] Darrow
1857–1938

9   You may hang these boys; you may hang them by the neck until they are dead. But in doing it you will turn your face toward the past.... I am pleading for the future. I am pleading for a time when hatred and cruelty will not control the hearts of men, when we can learn by reason and judgment and understanding and faith that all life is worth saving, and that mercy is the highest attribute of man.
       *Plea in defense of Richard Loeb and
       Nathan Leopold, Jr. [August 22, 1924]*

10   I do not consider it an insult, but rather a compliment to be called an agnostic. I do not pretend to know where many ignorant men are sure — that is all that agnosticism means.
       *Scopes trial, Dayton, Tennessee
       [July 13, 1925]*

11   I don't believe in God because I don't believe in Mother Goose.
                   Speech at Toronto [1930]

12   There is no such thing as justice — in or out of court.
                   Interview at Chicago [April 1936]

John Davidson
1857–1909

13 In anguish we uplift
A new unhallowed song:
The race is to the swift;
The battle to the strong.
                   War Song, st. 1

14 And blood in torrents pour
In vain — always in vain,
For war breeds war again.
                   War Song, st. 7

[Johann] Paul Dresser [Jr.]
1857–1906

15 Oh the moonlight's fair tonight along the Wabash.
From the fields there comes the breath of new-mown hay;
Through the sycamores the candle lights are gleaming,
On the banks of the Wabash, far away.
       *On the Banks of the Wabash,
       Far Away [1897]*

George Gissing
1857–1903

16   Keep apart, keep apart, and preserve one's soul alive — that is the teaching for the day. It is ill to have been born in these times, but one can make a world within the world.
       Letter to his brother [September 22, 1885]

17   When I think of all the sorrow and the barrenness that has been wrought in my life by want of a few more pounds per annum than I was able to earn, I stand aghast at money's significance.
       *The Private Papers of Henry Rycroft
       [1903]. Spring, sec. 5*

---

[1]Tous les jours, à tous les points de vue, je vais de mieux en mieux.

Ferdinand de Saussure
1857–1913

1   Psychologically, setting aside its expression in words, our thought is simply a vague, shapeless mass.[1]
Course in General Linguistics [1916], ch. 4

Edgar Smith
1857–1938

2 You may tempt the upper classes
With your villainous demitasses,
But Heaven will protect the working girl.
Heaven Will Protect the Working Girl [1909]

Frank Lebby Stanton
1857–1927

3 Sweetes' li'l' feller —
Everybody knows;
Dunno what ter call 'im,
But he's mighty lak' a rose!
Mighty Lak' a Rose[2] [1901], st. 1

Thorstein Veblen
1857–1929

4   Conspicuous consumption of valuable goods is a means of reputability to the gentleman of leisure.
The Theory of the Leisure Class [1899], ch. 4

5   With the exception of the instinct of self-preservation, the propensity for emulation is probably the strongest and most alert and persistent of the economic motives proper.
The Theory of the Leisure Class, 5

6   The dog . . . commends himself to our favor by affording play to our propensity for mastery, and as he is also an item of expense, and commonly serves no industrial purpose, he holds a well-assured place in men's regard as a thing of good repute.
The Theory of the Leisure Class, 6

7   The office of the leisure class in social evolution is to retard the movement and to conserve what is obsolescent.
The Theory of the Leisure Class, 7

8   The walking-stick serves the purpose of an advertisement that the bearer's hands are employed otherwise than in useful effort, and it therefore has utility as

an evidence of leisure. But it is also a weapon and it meets a felt need of barbarian man on that ground.
The Theory of the Leisure Class, 10

Liberty Hyde Bailey
1858–1954

9   If it were possible for every person to own a tree and to care for it, the good results would be beyond estimation.
The Holy Earth [1915]. The Subdividing of the Land

Franz Boas
1858–1942

10   There is no fundamental difference in the ways of thinking of primitive and civilized man. A close connection between race and personality has never been established.
The Mind of Primitive Man [1938 edition]

11   The behavior of an individual is therefore determined not by his racial affiliation, but by the character of his ancestry and his cultural environment.
Race and Democratic Society [1945], ch. 4

Sam Walter Foss
1858–1911

12 The woods were made for the hunters of dreams,
The brooks for the fishers of song;
To the hunters who hunt for the gunless game
The streams and the woods belong.
The Bloodless Sportsman [1897], st. 3

13 Let me live in a house by the side of the road
And be a friend to man.[3]
The House by the Side of the Road [1897], st. 2

H[enry] W[atson] Fowler
1858–1933
and
F[rancis] G[eorge] Fowler
1870–1918

14   Prefer geniality to grammar.
The King's English [1906], ch. 2

15   HACKNEYED PHRASES. . . . The purpose with which these phrases are introduced is for the most part that

---

[1]Translated by ROY HARRIS.
[2]Music by ETHELBERT NEVIN [1862–1901].

[3]See Homer, 51:10 and note.

of giving a fillip to a passage that might be humdrum without them . . . but their true use when they come into the writer's mind is as danger signals; he should take warning that when they suggest themselves it is because what he is writing is bad stuff, or it would not need such help; let him see to the substance of his cake instead of decorating with sugarplums.

A Dictionary of Modern English Usage[1]
[1926]

1   QUOTATION. . . . A writer expresses himself in words that have been used before because they give his meaning better than he can give it himself, or because they are beautiful or witty, or because he expects them to touch a chord of association in his reader, or because he wishes to show that he is learned and well read. Quotations due to the last motive are invariably ill-advised; the discerning reader detects it and is contemptuous; the undiscerning is perhaps impressed, but even then is at the same time repelled, pretentious quotations being the surest road to tedium.

A Dictionary of Modern English Usage

2   THAT, *relative pronoun* . . . The two kinds of relative clause, to one of which *that* and to the other of which *which* is appropriate, are the defining and the nondefining;[2] and if writers would agree to regard *that* as the defining relative pronoun, and *which* as the nondefining, there would be much gain both in lucidity and in ease. Some there are who follow this principle now, but it would be idle to pretend that it is the practice either of the most or of the best writers.

A Dictionary of Modern English Usage

Remy de Gourmont
1858–1915

3   Aesthetic emotion puts man in a state favorable to the reception of erotic emotion. Art is the accomplice of love. Take love away and there is no longer art.

Le Chemin de Velours (The Velvet Road)[3]
[1902]

4   Of all sexual aberrations perhaps the most curious is chastity.[4]

The Natural Philosophy of Love [1904]

5   Man is a successful animal, that's all.

Promenades Philosophiques [1905]

---

[1]To the memory of my brother Francis George Fowler . . . who shared with me the planning of this book, but did not live to share the writing. — H. W. FOWLER, *preface to the first edition*

[2]In American English, restrictive and nonrestrictive.

[3]Translated by W. A. BRADLEY.

[4]Translated by EZRA POUND.

Ruggiero Leoncavallo
1858–1919

6   The comedy is finished.[5]

I Pagliacci (The Clowns) [1892],
last words

Adolph S[imon] Ochs
1858–1935

7   All the news that's fit to print.

Motto of the New York Times [1896]

Ohiyesa
[Charles Alexander Eastman][6]
1858–1939

8   [The Indian] sees no need for setting apart one day in seven as a holy day, since to him all days are God's.

The Soul of the Indian [1911]

Max Planck
1858–1947

9   We have no right to assume that any physical laws exist, or if they have existed up to now, that they will continue to exist in a similar manner in the future.

The Universe in the Light of Modern
Physics [1931]

10   An important scientific innovation rarely makes its way by gradually winning over and converting its opponents: it rarely happens that Saul becomes Paul. What does happen is that its opponents gradually die out and that the growing generation is familiarized with the idea from the beginning.

The Philosophy of Physics [1936]

Theodore Roosevelt
1858–1919

11   No triumph of peace is quite so great as the supreme triumphs of war.

Speech at the Naval War College
[June 2, 1897]

12   I wish to preach, not the doctrine of ignoble ease, but the doctrine of the strenuous life.

Speech before the Hamilton Club,
Chicago [April 10, 1899]

---

[5]La commedia è finita.

[6]Santee Dakota.

1 Far better it is to dare mighty things, to win glorious triumphs, even though checkered by failure, than to take rank with those poor spirits who neither enjoy much nor suffer much, because they live in the gray twilight that knows not victory nor defeat.

Speech before the Hamilton Club,
Chicago

2 I am as strong as a bull moose and you can use me to the limit.

Letter to Marcus Alonzo Hanna
[June 17, 1900]

3 No man is justified in doing evil on the ground of expediency.

The Strenuous Life: Essays and Addresses
[1900]. The Strenuous Life

4 In life, as in a football game, the principle to follow is: Hit the line hard.

The Strenuous Life: Essays and Addresses.
The American Boy

5 There is a homely adage which runs, "Speak softly and carry a big stick; you will go far." If the American nation will speak softly and yet build and keep at a pitch of the highest training a thoroughly efficient navy, the Monroe Doctrine will go far.

Speech at Minnesota State Fair
[September 2, 1901]

6 The first requisite of a good citizen in this Republic of ours is that he shall be able and willing to pull his weight.

Speech at New York City
[November 11, 1902]

7 I hope you will not have a building of any kind, not a summer cottage, a hotel, or anything else, to mar the wonderful grandeur, the sublimity, the loneliness and beauty of the canyon. Leave it as it is.

Speech at the Grand Canyon [May 6, 1903]

8 A man who is good enough to shed his blood for his country is good enough to be given a square deal afterwards. More than that no man is entitled to, and less than that no man shall have.

Speech at Springfield, Illinois [July 4, 1903]

9 The men with the muckrakes are often indispensable to the well-being of society, but only if they know when to stop raking the muck, and to look upward to the celestial crown above them.... If they gradually grow to feel that the whole world is nothing but muck their power of usefulness is gone.[1]

Address on the laying of the cornerstone
of the House Office Building,
Washington, D.C. [April 14, 1906]

10 Malefactors of great wealth.

Speech at Provincetown, Massachusetts
[August 20, 1907]

11 Nature-faker.

Everybody's Magazine [September 1907]

12 To waste, to destroy, our natural resources, to skin and exhaust the land instead of using it so as to increase its usefulness, will result in undermining in the days of our children the very prosperity which we ought by right to hand down to them amplified and developed.

Message to Congress [December 3, 1907]

13 It is not the critic who counts; not the man who points out how the strong man stumbles, or where the doer of deeds could have done them better. The credit belongs to the man who is actually in the arena, whose face is marred by dust and sweat and blood; who strives valiantly; who errs and comes up short again and again, because there is no effort without error or shortcoming.

Speech at the Sorbonne, Paris
[April 23, 1910]

14 The nation behaves well if it treats the natural resources as assets which it must turn over to the next generation increased, and not impaired, in value.

Speech to the Colorado Live Stock Association
[August 29, 1910]

15 Every man holds his property subject to the general right of the community to regulate its use to whatever degree the public welfare may require it.

Speech at Osawatomie, Kansas
[August 31, 1910]

16 I took the Isthmus, started the Canal, and then left Congress — not to debate the Canal, but to debate me.... While the debate goes on the Canal does too.

Speech at University of California,
Berkeley [March 23, 1911]

17 We stand at Armageddon and we battle for the Lord.

Speech at Progressive Party Convention,
Chicago [June 17, 1912]

18 The lunatic fringe in all reform movements.

Autobiography [1913]

19 There is no room in this country for hyphenated Americanism.... The one absolutely certain way of bringing this nation to ruin, of preventing all possibility of its continuing to be a nation at all, would be to permit it to become a tangle of squabbling nationalities.

Speech before the Knights of Columbus,
New York City [October 12, 1915]

---

[1]See John Bunyan, 271:24.

1   One of our defects as a nation is a tendency to use what have been called "weasel words." When a weasel sucks eggs the meat is sucked out of the egg. If you use a "weasel word" after another there is nothing left of the other.   *Speech at St. Louis [May 31, 1916]*

2   Put out the light.
Last words [January 6, 1919]

Georg Simmel
1858–1918

3   Under certain circumstances, one nowhere feels as lonely and lost as in the metropolitan crowd.
The Metropolis and Mental Life[1] *[1903]*

Graham Wallas
1858–1932

4   The little girl had the making of a poet in her who, being told to be sure of her meaning before she spoke, said, "How can I know what I think till I see what I say?"   *The Art of Thought [1926], ch. 4*

Katharine Lee Bates
1859–1929

5 O beautiful for spacious skies,
For amber waves of grain,
For purple mountain majesties
Above the fruited plain!
America! America!
God shed his grace on thee
And crown thy good with brotherhood
From sea to shining sea!
America the Beautiful[2] *[1893], st. 1*

Henri Bergson
1859–1941

6   Laughter has no greater foe than emotion. . . . To produce the whole of its effect, then, the comic demands something like a momentary anesthesia of the heart.
Laughter[3] *[1900], ch. 1, sec. i*

7   The major task of the twentieth century will be to explore the unconscious, to investigate the subsoil of the mind.
Le Rêve (The Dream) [1901]

8   The present contains nothing more than the past, and what is found in the effect was already in the cause.
L'Evolution Créatrice (Creative Evolution) [1907], ch. 1

9   Intelligence . . . is the faculty of making artificial objects, especially tools to make tools.
L'Evolution Créatrice, 2

10   L'élan vital [the vital spirit].
L'Evolution Créatrice, 2

11   . . . the essential function of the universe, which is a machine for the making of gods.
The Two Sources of Religion and Morality[4] *[1932]*

12   Act like a man of thought and think like a man of action.
Message to the Descartes Congress [1937]

Carrie Chapman [Lane] Catt
1859–1947

13   No written law has ever been more binding than unwritten custom supported by popular opinion.
Speech, Why We Ask for the Submission of an Amendment, at Senate hearing on woman's suffrage [February 13, 1900]

14   When a just cause reaches its flood tide . . . whatever stands in the way must fall before its overwhelming power.
Speech, Is Woman Suffrage Progressing? [Stockholm, 1911]

John Dewey
1859–1952

15   We naturally associate democracy . . . with freedom of action, but freedom of action without freed capacity of thought behind it is only chaos.
Democracy in Education, in The Elementary School Teacher [December 1903]

16   The connections of the ear with vital and outgoing thought and emotion are immensely closer and more varied than those of the eye. Vision is a spectator; hearing is a participator.
The Public and Its Problems [1927], sec. 6

17   Every great advance in science has issued from a new audacity of imagination.
The Quest for Certainty [1929], ch. 11

---

[1]Translated by KURT H. WOLFF.
[2]Music by SAMUEL A. WARD [1848–1903].
[3]Translated by CLOUDESLEY BRERETON and FRED ROTHWELL.

---

[4]Translated by R. ASHLEY AUDRA and CLOUDESLEY BRERETON.

1   An educated person is the person who has the power to go on and get more education.
The Need for a Philosophy of Education [1934]

2   Education is not preparation for life; education is life itself.   *Attributed*

Sir Arthur Conan Doyle
1859–1930

3   London, that great cesspool into which all the loungers of the Empire are irresistibly drained.
A Study in Scarlet [1887]

4   I cannot live without brainwork. What else is there to live for? Stand at the window here. Was there ever such a dreary, dismal, unprofitable world? See how the yellow fog swirls down the streets and drifts across the dun-colored houses. . . . What is the use of having powers, Doctor, when one has no field upon which to exert them?
The Sign of Four [1890], ch. 1

5   When you have eliminated the impossible, whatever remains, *however improbable,* must be the truth.
The Sign of Four, 6

6   The unofficial force — the Baker Street irregulars.
The Sign of Four, 8

7   You see, but you do not observe. The distinction is clear.
The Adventures of Sherlock Holmes [1891]. A Scandal in Bohemia

8   To Sherlock Holmes she [Irene Adler] is always *the* woman.
The Adventures of Sherlock Holmes. A Scandal in Bohemia

9   It is quite a three-pipe problem.
The Adventures of Sherlock Holmes. The Red-Headed League

10   It has long been an axiom of mine that the little things are infinitely the most important.
The Adventures of Sherlock Holmes. A Case of Identity

11   Singularity is almost invariably a clue. The more featureless and commonplace a crime is, the more difficult is it to bring it home.
The Adventures of Sherlock Holmes. The Boscombe Valley Mystery

12   My name is Sherlock Holmes. It is my business to know what other people don't know.
The Adventures of Sherlock Holmes. The Adventure of the Blue Carbuncle

13   The lowest and vilest alleys of London do not present a more dreadful record of sin than does the smiling and beautiful countryside.
The Adventures of Sherlock Holmes. The Adventure of the Copper Beeches

14   ". . . the curious incident of the dog in the nighttime."
"The dog did nothing in the nighttime."
"That was the curious incident," remarked Sherlock Holmes.
The Memoirs of Sherlock Holmes [1894]. Silver Blaze

15   Like all Holmes's reasoning the thing seemed simplicity itself when it was once explained.
The Memoirs of Sherlock Holmes. The Stock-Broker's Clerk

16   You know my methods, Watson.
The Memoirs of Sherlock Holmes. The Crooked Man

17   "Excellent!" I [Watson] cried.
"Elementary," said he [Holmes].
The Memoirs of Sherlock Holmes. The Crooked Man

18   [Professor Moriarty] is the Napoleon of crime, Watson. He is the organizer of half that is evil and of nearly all that is undetected in this great city.
The Memoirs of Sherlock Holmes. The Final Problem

19   They were the footprints of a gigantic hound!
The Hound of the Baskervilles [1902], ch. 2

20   Come, Watson, come! The game is afoot.
The Return of Sherlock Holmes [1904]. The Adventure of the Abbey Grange

21   The fair sex is your department.
The Return of Sherlock Holmes. The Second Stain

22   We are dealing with an exceptionally astute and dangerous man . . . one of the most unscrupulous rascals that Australia has ever evolved — and for a young country it has turned out some very finished types.
His Last Bow [1917]. The Disappearance of Lady Frances Carfax

Havelock Ellis
1859–1939

23   The omnipresent process of sex, as it is woven into the whole texture of our man's or woman's body, is the pattern of all the process of our life.
The New Spirit [1890]

1   The text of the Bible is but a feeble symbol of the Revelation held in the text of Men and Women.
Impressions and Comments [entry for September 12, 1913]

2   All civilization has from time to time become a thin crust over a volcano of revolution.
Little Essays of Love and Virtue [1922], ch. 7

3   The greatest task before civilization at present is to make machines what they ought to be, the slaves, instead of the masters of men.
Little Essays of Love and Virtue, 7

4   Dancing is the loftiest, the most moving, the most beautiful of the arts, because it is no mere translation or abstraction from life; it is life itself.
The Dance of Life [1923], ch. 2

5   The place where optimism most flourishes is the lunatic asylum.   *The Dance of Life, 3*

6   The sun and the moon and the stars would have disappeared long ago . . . had they happened to be within the reach of predatory human hands.
The Dance of Life, 7

Kenneth Grahame
1859–1932

7   There is *nothing* — absolutely nothing — half so much worth doing as simply messing about in boats . . . or with boats. . . . In or out of 'em, it doesn't matter.
The Wind in the Willows [1908], ch. 1

8   The Piper at the Gates of Dawn.
The Wind in the Willows, 7, chapter title

9 The clever men at Oxford
Know all that there is to be knowed.
But they none of them know one half as much
As intelligent Mr. Toad!
The Wind in the Willows, 10

A[lfred] E[dward] Housman[1]
1859–1936

10 Loveliest of trees, the cherry now
Is hung with bloom along the bough.
A Shropshire Lad [1896], no. 2, st. 1

11 Now, of my threescore years and ten,
Twenty will not come again,
And take from seventy springs a score,
It only leaves me fifty more.

And since to look at things in bloom
Fifty springs are little room,
About the woodlands I will go
To see the cherry hung with snow.
A Shropshire Lad, 2, st. 2, 3

12 Clay lies still, but blood's a rover;
Breath's a ware that will not keep.
Up, lad: when the journey's over
There'll be time enough to sleep.
A Shropshire Lad, 4 (Reveille), st. 6

13 Lovers lying two and two
Ask not whom they sleep beside,
And the bridegroom all night through
Never turns him to the bride.
A Shropshire Lad, 12, st. 4

14 When I was one-and-twenty
I heard a wise man say,
"Give crowns and pounds and guineas
But not your heart away."
A Shropshire Lad, 13, st. 1

15 When I was one-and-twenty
I heard him say again,
"The heart out of the bosom
Was never given in vain;
'Tis paid with sighs aplenty
And sold for endless rue."
And I am two-and-twenty,
And Oh, 'tis true, 'tis true.
A Shropshire Lad, 13, st. 2

16 His folly has not fellow
Beneath the blue of day
That gives to man or woman
His heart and soul away.
A Shropshire Lad, 14, st. 3

17 Oh, when I was in love with you,
Then I was clean and brave,
And miles around the wonder grew
How well I did behave.

And now the fancy passes by,
And nothing will remain,
And miles around they'll say that I
Am quite myself again.
A Shropshire Lad, 18, st. 1, 2

18 And silence sounds no worse than cheers
After earth has stopped the ears.
A Shropshire Lad, 19 (To an Athlete Dying Young), st. 4

---

[1] I am not a pessimist but a pejorist (as George Eliot said she was not an optimist but a meliorist); and that philosophy is founded on my observation of the world, not on anything so trivial and irrelevant as personal history. — HOUSMAN, *autobiographical note written for a French translation of his poems*

1 The bells they sound on Bredon,
  And still the steeples hum.
  "Come all to church, good people" —
  Oh, noisy bells, be dumb;
  I hear you, I will come.

  A Shropshire Lad, 21, st. 7

2 The lads that will die in their glory and never be
    old.

  A Shropshire Lad, 23, st. 4

3 And fire and ice within me fight
  Beneath the suffocating night.

  A Shropshire Lad, 30, st. 4

4 There, like the wind through woods in riot,
  Through him the gale of life blew high;
  The tree of man was never quiet:
  Then 'twas the Roman, now 'tis I.

  A Shropshire Lad, 31, st. 4

5 Oh tarnish late on Wenlock Edge,
  Gold that I never see.

  A Shropshire Lad, 39, st. 3

6 Into my heart an air that kills
  From yon far country blows:
  What are those blue remembered hills,
  What spires, what farms are those?

  That is the land of lost content,
  I see it shining plain,
  The happy highways where I went
  And cannot come again.

  A Shropshire Lad, 40, st. 1, 2

7 Earth and high heaven are fixed of old and founded
    strong.

  A Shropshire Lad, 48, st. 1

8 Far in a western brookland
  That bred me long ago
  The poplars stand and tremble
  By pools I used to know.

  A Shropshire Lad, 52, st. 1

9 With rue my heart is laden
  For golden friends I had,
  For many a rose-lipped maiden
  And many a lightfoot lad.

  A Shropshire Lad, 54, st. 1

10 By brooks too broad for leaping
   The lightfoot boys are laid.

  A Shropshire Lad, 54, st. 2

11 In all the endless road you tread
   There's nothing but the night.

  A Shropshire Lad, 60, st. 2

12 Oh many a peer of England brews
   Livelier liquor than the Muse,
   And malt does more than Milton can

To justify God's ways to man.[1]
  Ale, man, ale's the stuff to drink
  For fellows whom it hurts to think.

  A Shropshire Lad, 62, st. 2

13 Mithridates, he died old.[2]

  A Shropshire Lad, 62, st. 4

14 Pass me the can, lad; there's an end of May.

  Last Poems [1922], 9, st. 1

15 The troubles of our proud and angry dust
   Are from eternity, and shall not fail.
   Bear them we can, and if we can we must.
   Shoulder the sky, my lad, and drink your ale.

  Last Poems, 9, st. 7

16 The laws of God, the laws of man,
   He may keep that will and can;
   Not I: let God and man decree
   Laws for themselves and not for me.

  Last Poems, 12, l. 1

17 And how am I to face the odds
   Of man's bedevilment and God's?
   I, a stranger and afraid
   In a world I never made.   *Last Poems, 12, l. 15*

18 Strapped, noosed, nighing his hour,
   He stood and counted them and cursed his luck;
   And then the clock collected in the tower
   Its strength, and struck.

  Last Poems, 15 (Eight O'Clock), st. 2

19 Happy bridegroom, Hesper brings
   All desired and timely things.
   All whom morning sends to roam,
   Hesper loves to lead them home.
   Home return who him behold,
   Child to mother, sheep to fold,
   Bird to nest from wandering wide:
   Happy bridegroom, seek your bride.

  Last Poems, 24 (Epithalamium), st. 3

20 These, in the day when heaven was falling,
   The hour when earth's foundations fled,
   Followed their mercenary calling
   And took their wages and are dead.

  *Last Poems, 37 (Epitaph on an Army
  of Mercenaries),[3] st. 1*

21 Hope lies to mortals
   And most believe her,

---

[1]See Milton, 255:5 and 260:13.

[2]Housman's passage is based on the belief of the ancients that Mithridates the Great [c. 135–63 B.C.E.] had so saturated his body with poisons that none could injure him. When captured by the Romans he tried in vain to poison himself, then ordered a Gallic mercenary to kill him.

[3]The British regulars who made the retreat from Mons, beginning on August 24, 1914.

But man's deceiver
Was never mine.
More Poems [1936], 6, st. 1

1 The rainy Pleiads wester,
Orion plunges prone,
And midnight strikes and hastens,
And I lie down alone.[1]   *More Poems, 11, st. 1*

2 Life, to be sure, is nothing much to lose,
But young men think it is, and we were young.
More Poems, 36, l. 3

3 We now to peace and darkness
And earth and thee restore
Thy creature that thou madest
And wilt cast forth no more.
More Poems, 47 (For My Funeral), st. 3

4 Good night; ensured release,
Imperishable peace,
Have these for yours.[2]
While sky and sea and land
And earth's foundations stand
And heaven endures.
More Poems, 48 (Alta Quies), st. 1

5   Experience has taught me, when I am shaving of a
morning, to keep watch over my thoughts, because, if
a line of poetry strays into my memory, my skin bristles so that the razor ceases to act. . . . The seat of this
sensation is the pit of the stomach.
The Name and Nature of Poetry [1933]

Jerome K[lapka] Jerome
1859–1927

6   Let your boat of life be light, packed with only
what you need — a homely home and simple pleasures, one or two friends, worth the name, someone
to love and someone to love you, a cat, a dog, and a
pipe or two, enough to eat and enough to wear, and
a little more than enough to drink; for thirst is a dangerous thing.
Three Men in a Boat [1889], ch. 3

7   I like work: it fascinates me. I can sit and look at it
for hours. I love to keep it by me; the idea of getting
rid of it nearly breaks my heart.
Three Men in a Boat, 15

8   "Nothing, so it seems to me," said the stranger,
"is more beautiful than the love that has weathered
the storms of life. . . . The love of the young for the
young, that is the beginning of life. But the love of

the old for the old, that is the beginning of — of
things longer."
The Passing of the Third Floor Back [1908]

William James Lampton
1859–1917

9 Same old slippers,
Same old rice,
Same old glimpse of
Paradise.   *June Weddings, st. 10*

Charles E. Stanton
1859–1933

10 [As U.S. forces joined the Allies:] Lafayette, we
are here.[3]
*Address at the tomb of Lafayette,
Picpus Cemetery, Paris [July 4, 1917]*

Francis Thompson
1859–1907

11 Look for me in the nurseries of Heaven.[4]
To My Godchild [1891]

12 Nothing begins, and nothing ends,
That is not paid with moan;
For we are born in other's pain,
And perish in our own.   *Daisy [1893], st. 15*

13 I fled Him, down the nights and down the days;
I fled Him, down the arches of the years;
I fled Him, down the labyrinthine ways
Of my own mind; and in the mist of tears
I hid from Him, and under running laughter.
The Hound of Heaven [1893], l. 1

14 But with unhurrying chase,
And unperturbèd pace,
Deliberate speed, majestic instancy,
They beat — and a Voice beat
More instant than the Feet —
"All things betray thee, who betrayest Me."
The Hound of Heaven, l. 10

15 Across the margent of the world I fled,
And troubled the gold gateways of the stars.
The Hound of Heaven, l. 25

16 I said to dawn, Be sudden; to eve, Be soon.
The Hound of Heaven, l. 30

---

[1]See Sappho, 56:8.

[2]These three lines are on the tablet over Housman's grave in the
parish church at Ludlow, Shropshire, England.

[3]Lafayette, nous voilà!

[4]Inscribed on Thompson's tombstone in Kensal Green Cemetery,
London.

1 My days have crackled and gone up in smoke.
The Hound of Heaven, l. 122

2 All which I took from thee I did but take,
   Not for thy harms,
   But just that thou might'st seek it in My arms.
The Hound of Heaven, l. 171

3 O world invisible, we view thee,
   O world intangible, we touch thee,
   O world unknowable, we know thee.
The Kingdom of God ("In No Strange
Land") [1913], st. 1

4 The angels keep their ancient places;
   Turn but a stone, and start a wing!
   'Tis ye, 'tis your estrangèd faces,
   That miss the many-splendored thing.
The Kingdom of God, st. 4

Jane Addams
1860–1935

5 The cure for the ills of Democracy is more Democracy.[1]
Democracy and Social Ethics [1902]

6 Private beneficence is totally inadequate to deal with the vast numbers of the city's disinherited.
Twenty Years at Hull House [1910]

7 The common stock of intellectual enjoyment should not be difficult of access because of the economic position of him who would approach it.
Twenty Years at Hull House

Sir James M[atthew] Barrie
1860–1937

8 Shall we make a new rule of life from tonight: always to try to be a little kinder than is necessary?
The Little White Bird [1902], ch. 4

9 His lordship may compel us to be equal upstairs, but there will never be equality in the servants' hall.
The Admirable Crichton [1903], act I

10 Every time a child says, "I don't believe in fairies," there is a fairy somewhere that falls down dead.
Peter Pan [1904], act I

11 Do you believe in fairies?...If you believe, clap your hands!
Peter Pan, IV

12 It's a sort of bloom on a woman. If you have it [charm], you don't need to have anything else, and if you don't have it, it doesn't much matter what else you have. Some women, the few, have charm for all; and most have charm for one. But some have charm for none.
What Every Woman Knows [1908], act I

13 The tragedy of a man who has found himself out.
What Every Woman Knows, IV

14 Every man who is high up loves to think that he has done it all himself; and his wife smiles, and lets it go at that. It's our only joke. Every woman knows that.
What Every Woman Knows, IV

John Collins Bossidy
1860–1928

15 And this is good old Boston,
   The home of the bean and the cod,
   Where the Lowells talk to the Cabots
   And the Cabots talk only to God.[2]
Toast, Holy Cross Alumni Dinner [1910]

William Jennings Bryan
1860–1925

16 The humblest citizen of all the land, when clad in the armor of a righteous cause, is stronger than all the hosts of Error.
Speech at the National Democratic
Convention, Chicago [1896]

17 Destroy our farms and the grass will grow in the streets of every city in the country.
Speech at the National Democratic
Convention, Chicago [1896]

18 You shall not press down upon the brow of labor this crown of thorns. You shall not crucify mankind upon a cross of gold.[3]
Speech at the National Democratic
Convention, Chicago [1896]

Haddon Chambers
1860–1921

19 The long arm of coincidence.
Captain Swift [1888], act II

---

[1] This saying, popular among progressives, did not originate with Addams. It appears, for example, in *The Encyclopedia of Social Reform* of 1897.

[2] Patterned on the toast given at the twenty-fifth anniversary dinner of the Harvard Class of 1880, by a Westerner:

Here's to old Massachusetts, / The home of the sacred cod, / Where the Adamses vote for Douglas, / And the Cabots walk with God.

[3] I shall not help crucify mankind upon a cross of gold. I shall not aid in pressing down upon the bleeding brow of labor this crown of thorns. — BRYAN, *speech in the House of Representatives* [December 22, 1894]

Anton Pavlovich Chekhov
1860–1904

1   I feel more confident and more satisfied when I reflect that I have two professions and not one. Medicine is my lawful wife and literature is my mistress. When I get tired of one I spend the night with the other. Though it's disorderly it's not so dull, and besides, neither really loses anything through my infidelity.
> *Letter to A. S. Suvorin*[1]
> *[September 11, 1888]*

2   I would like to be a free artist and nothing else, and I regret God has not given me the strength to be one.
> *Letter to Alexei Pleshcheev*[1]
> *[October 4, 1888]*

3   My holy of holies is the human body, health, intelligence, talent, inspiration, love, and the most absolute freedom imaginable, freedom from violence and lies, no matter what form the latter two take. Such is the program I would adhere to if I were a major artist.
> *Letter to Alexei Pleshcheev [October 4, 1888]*

4   An artist must pass judgment only on what he understands; his range is limited as that of any other specialist — that's what I keep repeating and insisting upon. Anyone who says that the artist's field is all answers and no questions has never done any writing or had any dealings with imagery. An artist observes, selects, guesses and synthesizes.
> *Letter to A. S. Suvorin*[1]
> *[October 27, 1888]*

5   One must not put a loaded rifle on the stage if no one is thinking of firing it.[2]
> *Letter to A. S. Lazarev-Gruzinsky*
> *[November 1, 1889]*

6   I am in mourning for my life. I am unhappy.
> *The Seagull*[3] *[1896], act I*

7   I try to catch every sentence, every word you and I say, and quickly lock all these sentences and words away in my literary storehouse because they might come in handy.
> *The Seagull, II*

8   People should be beautiful in every way — in their faces, in the way they dress, in their thoughts and in their innermost selves.
> *Uncle Vanya*[3] *[1897], act I*

9   We shall find peace. We shall hear the angels, we shall see the sky sparkling with diamonds.
> *Uncle Vanya, IV*

10   When a man spends the least possible number of movements over one definite action, that is grace.
> *Letter to Maxim Gorky*[4] *[January 3, 1899]*

11   To Moscow, to Moscow, to Moscow!
> *Three Sisters [1901], act II*

12   All Russia is our orchard.
> *The Cherry Orchard*[3] *[1904], act II*

13   Everyone has something to hide. *The Notebooks*

14   But perhaps the universe is suspended on the tooth of some monster.
> *The Notebooks*

Baron Corvo
[Frederick William Rolfe]
1860–1913

15   He took one long slow breath: crossed right hand over left upon his breast: became like a piece of a pageant; and responded "I will."
> *Hadrian the Seventh [1904], ch. 3*

16   Pray for the repose of his soul. He was so tired.
> *Hadrian the Seventh, closing lines*

Harry M[icajah] Daugherty
1860–1941

17   Fifteen or twenty tired men sitting around a table in a smoke-filled room behind locked doors.[5]
> *Attributed by Leonard Wood*

Charlotte Perkins Gilman
1860–1935

18   There are things in that wallpaper that nobody knows about but me, or ever will.

Behind that outside pattern the dim shapes get clearer every day.

It is always the same shape, only very numerous.

And it is like a woman stooping down and creeping about behind that pattern.
> *The Yellow Wallpaper [1892]*

19 There's a whining at the threshold —
There's a scratching at the floor —

---

[1]Translated by SIMON KARLINSKY.

[2]A fuller version: If you say in the first chapter that there is a rifle hanging on a wall, in the second or third chapter it absolutely must go off. If it's not going to be fired, it shouldn't be hanging there. — FATHER SERGIUS SHCHUKIN, memoir of Chekhov published in *Russian Thought* [1911]

[3]Translated by RONALD HINGLY.

[4]Translated by CONSTANCE GARNETT.

[5]The phrase, in variant forms, is commonly attributed to Daugherty, presidential campaign manager for Senator Warren G. Harding.

To work! To work! In Heaven's name!
The wolf is at the door!
In This Our World [1893].
The Wolf at the Door, st. 6

1 The labor of women in the house, certainly, enables men to produce more wealth than they otherwise could; and in this way women are economic factors in society. But so are horses.
Women and Economics [1898],
ch. 1

2 There is no female mind. The brain is not an organ of sex. As well speak of a female liver.
Women and Economics, 8

3 The people people choose for friends
Your common sense appall,
But the people people marry
Are the queerest folk of all.
Queer People [1899]

Theodor Herzl
1860–1904

4 We are one people — our enemies have made us one whether we will or not, as has repeatedly happened in history. Affliction binds us together, and thus united, we suddenly discover our strength. Yes, we are strong enough to form a State, and, indeed, a model State.
The Jewish State [1896]

5 If you will it, it is not a fable.
Altneuland [1902]

William Ralph Inge
1860–1954

6 A man may build himself a throne of bayonets, but he cannot sit on it.
From Wit and Wisdom of Dean Inge [1927],
edited by JAMES MARCHANT *[1867–1956],*
no. 108

Sir D'Arcy Wentworth Thompson
1860–1948

7 Numerical precision is the very soul of science.
On Growth and Form [1917],
ch. 1

8 The harmony of the world is made manifest in Form and Number, and the heart and soul and all the poetry of Natural Philosophy are embodied in the concept of mathematical beauty.
On Growth and Form, epilogue

Owen Wister
1860–1938

9 When you call me that, *smile!*
The Virginian [1902], ch. 2

[William] Bliss Carman
1861–1929

10 The scarlet of the maples can shake me like a cry
Of bugles going by.
A Vagabond Song [1896], st. 2

11 There is something in October sets the gypsy blood astir.
A Vagabond Song, st. 3

Louise Imogen Guiney
1861–1920

12 He has done with roofs and men,
Open, Time, and let him pass.
Open, Time [1893], st. 7

13 A short life in the saddle, Lord!
Not long life by the fire.
The Knight Errant [1893], st. 2

Albert Bigelow Paine
1861–1937

14 The Great White Way. *Title of book [1901]*

Sir Walter Raleigh
1861–1922

15 I wish I loved the human race;
I wish I loved its silly face;
I wish I liked the way it walks;
I wish I liked the way it talks;
And when I'm introduced to one
I wish I thought, *What jolly fun!*
Wishes of an Elderly Man; wished at a
garden party [June 1914]

Italo Svevo [Aron Ettore Schmitz]
1861–1928

16 One need only remind oneself of all that we expect from life to see how very strange it is, and to arrive at the conclusion that man has found his way into it by mistake and does not really belong there.
Confessions of Zeno[1] *[1923]*

---

[1]Translated by BERYL DE ZOETE.

1 Life is neither good nor bad; it is original.
Confessions of Zeno

Rabindranath Tagore
1861–1941

2 When one knows thee, then alien there is none,
then no door is shut. Oh, grant me my prayer that I
may never lose the touch of the one in the play of the
many. *Gitanjali [1913]*

3 At my dying hour, and over my long life,
A clock strikes somewhere at the city's edge.
Poem [1941]

Frederick Jackson Turner
1861–1932

4 The frontier is the outer edge of the wave — the
meeting-point between savagery and civilization...
the line of most rapid and effective Americanization.
The wilderness masters the colonist.
*The Significance of the Frontier in
American History [1893]*

5 And now, four centuries from the discovery of
America, at the end of a hundred years of life under
the Constitution, the frontier has gone, and with its
going has closed the first period of American history.
*The Significance of the Frontier in
American History*

Alfred North Whitehead
1861–1947

6 Civilization advances by extending the number of
important operations which we can perform without
thinking about them.
*An Introduction to Mathematics [1911],
ch. 5*

7 The science of pure mathematics, in its modern
developments, may claim to be the most original
creation of the human spirit.
*Science and the Modern World [1925],
ch. 2*

8 The greatest invention of the nineteenth century
was the invention of the method of invention.
Science and the Modern World, 6

9 The religious vision, and its history of persistent
expansion, is our one ground for optimism. Apart
from it, human life is a flash of occasional enjoyments
lighting up a mass of pain and misery, a bagatelle of
transient experience.
Science and the Modern World, 12

10 Rationalism is an adventure in the clarification of
thought.
Process and Reality [1929], pt. I, ch. 1, sec. 3

11 The safest general characterization of the European philosophical tradition is that it consists of a
series of footnotes to Plato.
Process and Reality, II, 1, 1

12 In the real world, it is more important that a proposition be interesting than that it be true.
Adventures of Ideas [1933], 16

13 A general definition of civilization: a civilized
society is exhibiting the five qualities of truth, beauty,
adventure, art, peace.
Adventures of Ideas, 19

14 The deliberate aim at Peace very easily passes into
its bastard substitute, Anesthesia.
Adventures of Ideas, 20

15 There are no whole truths; all truths are half-
truths. It is trying to treat them as whole truths that
plays the devil.
*Dialogues of Alfred North Whitehead
[1953], as recorded by LUCIEN PRICE
[1883–1964], prologue*

16 The vitality of thought is in adventure. *Ideas won't
keep.* Something must be done about them. When the
idea is new, its custodians have fervor, live for it, and,
if need be, die for it.
*Dialogues of Alfred North Whitehead,
ch. 12 [April 28, 1938]*

17 A culture is in its finest flower before it begins to
analyze itself.
*Dialogues of Alfred North Whitehead,
22 [August 17, 1941]*

18 Intellect is to emotion as our clothes are to our
bodies; we could not very well have civilized life
without clothes, but we would be in a poor way if
we had only clothes without bodies.
*Dialogues of Alfred North Whitehead,
29 [June 10, 1943]*

A[rthur] C[hristopher] Benson
1862–1925

19 Land of hope and glory, mother of the free,
How shall we extol thee, who are born of thee?
Wider still and wider shall thy bounds be set;
God, who made thee mighty, make thee
mightier yet.
Land of Hope and Glory[1] [1902], chorus

---

[1]First *Pomp and Circumstance* march by SIR EDWARD ELGAR
[1857–1934].

Albert [Jeremiah] Beveridge
1862–1927

1 This party comes from the grass roots. It has grown from the soil of the people's hard necessities.
Address at the Bull Moose Convention,
Chicago [August 5, 1912]

James W. Blake
1862–1935

2 East Side, West Side, all around the town,
The tots sang "Ring-a-rosie," "London Bridge is
    falling down";
Boys and girls together, me and Mamie O'Rorke,
Tripped the light fantastic on the sidewalks of
    New York.   *The Sidewalks of New York[1] [1894]*

Nicholas Murray Butler
1862–1947

3 An expert is one who knows more and more about less and less.
Commencement address,
Columbia University

John Jay Chapman
1862–1933

4 If an inhabitant of another planet should visit the earth, he would receive, on the whole, a truer notion of human life by attending an Italian opera than he would by reading Emerson's volumes. He would learn from the Italian opera that there were two sexes; and this, after all, is probably the fact with which the education of such a stranger ought to begin.
Emerson and Other Essays [1898]

5 The New Testament, and to a very large extent the Old, *is* the soul of man. You cannot criticize it. It criticizes you.   *Letter [March 26, 1898]*

6 Everybody in America is soft, and hates conflict. The cure for this, both in politics and social life, is the same — hardihood. Give them raw truth.
Practical Agitation [1898]

7 The present in New York is so powerful that the past is lost.   *Letter [1909]*

8 As I read the newspaper accounts of the scene enacted here in Coatesville a year ago, I seemed to get a glimpse into the unconscious soul of this country. I saw a seldom revealed picture of the American heart and of the American nature. I seemed to be looking into the heart of the criminal — a cold thing, an awful thing. I said to myself, "I shall forget this, we shall all forget it; but it will be there. What I have seen is not an illusion. It is the truth. I have seen death in the heart of this people." For to look at the agony of a fellow-being and remain aloof means death in the heart of the onlooker.
Speech at prayer meeting,[2] Coatesville,
Pennsylvania [August 18, 1912]

Claude [Achille] Debussy
1862–1918

9 Art is of absolutely no use to the masses.
Monsieur Croche, the Dilettante Hater [1927]

Edward, Viscount Grey of Fallodon
1862–1933

10 The lamps are going out all over Europe; we shall not see them lit again in our lifetime.
Comment [August 3, 1914],
on the eve of World War I

O. Henry [William Sydney Porter]
1862–1910

11 If men knew how women pass the time when they are alone, they'd never marry.
The Four Million [1906].
Memoirs of a Yellow Dog

12 It was beautiful and simple as all truly great swindles are.
The Gentle Grafter [1908].
The Octopus Marooned

13 Life is made up of sobs, sniffles, and smiles, with sniffles predominating.
The Gentle Grafter. The Octopus Marooned

14 Bagdad-on-the-Subway.[3]
Roads of Destiny [1909]. The Discounters of Money

15 History is bright and fiction dull with homely men who have charmed women.
Roads of Destiny. Next to Reading Matter

---

[1]Music by CHARLES B. LAWLOR [1852–1925].

[2]On the anniversary of a lynching [August 12, 1911] in Coatesville.

[3]Also in *A Madison Square Arabian Night, A Night in New Arabia,* and *What You Want.*

1   East is East, and West is San Francisco, according to Californians. Californians are a race of people; they are not merely inhabitants of a State.
Strictly Business [1910]. A Municipal Report

2   It couldn't have happened anywhere but in little old New York.[1]
Whirligigs [1910]. A Little Local Color

3   Take it from me — he's got the goods.
The Unprofitable Servant

4   Turn up the lights — I don't want to go home in the dark.[2]   *Last words [June 5, 1910]*

Charles Evans Hughes
1862–1948

5   We are under a Constitution, but the Constitution is what the judges say it is, and the judiciary is the safeguard of our liberty and of our property under the Constitution.
Speech at Elmira, New York [May 3, 1907]

Maurice Maeterlinck
1862–1949

6   It is always a mistake not to close one's eyes, whether to forgive or to look better into oneself.
Pelléas et Mélisande [1892]

7   There are no dead.
The Blue Bird [1909], act IV, sc. ii

Sir Henry Newbolt
1862–1938

8 To set the cause above renown,
  To love the game beyond the prize,
  To honor, while you strike him down,
  The foe that comes with fearless eyes;
  To count the life of battle good
  And dear the land that gave you birth,
  And dearer yet the brotherhood
  That binds the brave of all the earth.
The Island Race [1898]. Clifton Chapel, st. 2

9 *Qui procul hinc*, the legend's writ,
  The frontier grave is far away —
  Qui ante diem periit:
  Sed miles, sed pro patria.[3]
The Island Race. Clifton Chapel, st. 4

---

[1]Also in *A Midsummer Knight's Dream, Past One at Rooney's,* and *The Rubber Plant's Story.*

[2]I'm Afraid to Go Home in the Dark. — HARRY H. WILLIAMS [1879–1922], *title of song* [1907]

[3]Who died far away, before his time: but as a soldier, for his country.

10 Now the sunset breezes shiver,
   And she's fading down the river,
   But in England's song forever
   She's the Fighting Téméraire.
The Island Race. The Fighting Téméraire, st. 6

11 Play up! play up! and play the game!
The Island Race. Vitaï Lampada, refrain

Edith [Newbold Jones] Wharton
1862–1937

12   Everything about her was at once vigorous and exquisite, at once strong and fine. He had a confused sense that she must have cost a great deal to make, that a great many dull and ugly people must, in some mysterious way, have been sacrificed to produce her.
The House of Mirth [1905], bk. I, ch. 1

13   The civilized instinct finds a subtler pleasure in making use of its antagonist than in confounding him.   *The House of Mirth, I, 12*

14   He seemed a part of the mute melancholy landscape, an incarnation of its frozen woe, with all that was warm and sentient in him fast bound below the surface.   *Ethan Frome [1911]*

15   Almost everybody in the neighborhood had "troubles," frankly localized and specified; but only the chosen had "complications." To have them was in itself a distinction, though it was also, in most cases, a death warrant. People struggled on for years with "troubles," but they almost always succumbed to "complications."   *Ethan Frome*

16   Mrs. Ballinger is one of the ladies who pursue Culture in bands, as though it were dangerous to meet it alone.   *Xingu [1916]*

17   The essence of taste is suitability. Divest the word of its prim and priggish implications, and see how it expresses the mysterious demand of eye and mind for symmetry, harmony, and order.
French Ways and Their Meaning [1919], ch. 3

18   An unalterable and unquestioned law of the musical world required that the German text of French operas sung by Swedish artists should be translated into Italian for the clearer understanding of English-speaking audiences.
The Age of Innocence [1920], ch. 1

19   In the rotation of crops there was a recognized season for wild oats; but they were not sown more than once.   *The Age of Innocence, 31*

20   It was the old New York way of taking life "without effusion of blood": the way of people who dreaded scandal more than disease, who placed decency above courage, and who considered that

nothing was more ill-bred than "scenes," except the behavior of those who gave rise to them.
The Age of Innocence, 33

1   The worst of doing one's duty was that it apparently unfitted one for doing anything else.
The Age of Innocence, 34

2   I often wonder whether a frumpy old woman can ever be quite fair in her estimate of a young and lovely one.
Letter to Bernard Berenson [March 20, 1922]

3   There's no such thing as old age; there is only sorrow.
A Backward Glance [1934]. A First Word

4   In spite of illness, in spite even of the archenemy sorrow, one *can* remain alive long past the usual date of disintegration if one is unafraid of change, insatiable in intellectual curiosity, interested in big things, and happy in small ways.
A Backward Glance. A First Word

Black Elk [Hehaka Sapa]
1863–1950

5   Everything an Indian does is in a circle, and that is because the power of the world always works in circles, and everything tries to be round. In the old days when we were a strong and happy people, all our power came to us from the sacred hoop of the nation, and so long as the hoop was unbroken the people flourished.
Black Elk Speaks, Being the Life Story of a Holy Man of the Oglala Sioux [1961], as told through JOHN G. NEIHARDT *[1881–1973]*

C[onstantine] P[eter] Cavafy
1863–1933

6 But Argos can do without the sons of Atreus.
Ancient houses are not eternal.
When the Watchman Saw the Light[1] *[1900]*

7   We won't be deceived
by titles such as Indispensable and Unique and Great.
Someone else indispensable and unique and great
can always be found at a moment's notice.
When the Watchman Saw the Light

8 Pleasure will have much to teach him.
He will not be afraid of the destructive act;
one half of the house must be pulled down.
This way he will grow virtuously into knowledge.
Strengthening the Spirit [1903]

9 What are we all waiting for
gathered together like this on the public square?
The Barbarians are coming today.
Waiting for the Barbarians[2] *[1904], l. 1*

10 You'll not find another place, you'll not find another sea.
This city is going to follow you.
The City[3] *[1910], l. 9*

11 Setting out on the voyage to Ithaca
you must pray that the way be long,
full of adventures and experiences.
Ithaca[4] *[1911], l. 11*

12 Body, remember not only how much you were loved,
not only the beds you lay on,
but also those desires glowing openly
in eyes that looked at you,
trembling for you in voices.
Body, Remember[5] *[1918]*

13 I created you while I was happy, while I was sad,
with so many incidents, so many details.

And, for me, the whole of you has been transformed into feeling.
In the Same Space[4] *[1929]*

William Randolph Hearst
1863–1951

14   You furnish the pictures and I'll furnish the war.
Attributed instructions to artist FREDERIC REMINGTON *[1861–1909] in Havana, Cuba*[6] *[March 1898]*

Edvard Munch
1863–1944

15   Nature is not only what is visible to the eye — it also shows the inner images of the soul — the images on the reverse side of the eyes.
Letter by JOHAN H. LANGAARD *[b. 1899] and* REIDAR REVOLD *[b. 1918] [1907–1908] quoted in Edvard Munch [1963]*

---

[2]Translated by W. H. AUDEN and MARGUERITE YOURCENAR.

[3]Translated by ROBERT LIDDELL.

[4]Translated by JOHN MAVROGORDATO.

[5]Translated by EDMUND KEELEY and PHILLIP SHERRARD.

[6]Hearst always denied sending such a telegram, and there is no proof that he ever did, even though it accurately reflects his views at the time. — JOYCE MILTON, *The Yellow Kids: Foreign Correspondents in the Heyday of Yellow Journalism* [1989]
See Mankiewicz and Welles, 714:3.

---

[1]Translated by EDMUND KEELEY and GEORGE SAVIDIS.

Sir Arthur Thomas Quiller-Couch
1863–1944

1   Whenever you feel an impulse to perpetuate a piece of exceptionally fine writing, obey it — whole-heartedly — and delete it before sending your manuscript to press. Murder your darlings.
On the Art of Writing [1916]. On Style

George Santayana
1863–1952

2   Happiness is the only sanction of life; where happiness fails, existence remains a mad and lamentable experiment.
The Life of Reason [1905–1906], vol. I, Reason in Common Sense

3   That life is worth living is the most necessary of assumptions, and, were it not assumed, the most impossible of conclusions.
The Life of Reason, I, Reason in Common Sense

4   Fanaticism consists in redoubling your efforts when you have forgotten your aim.
The Life of Reason, I, Reason in Common Sense

5   Those who cannot remember the past are condemned to repeat it.[1]
The Life of Reason, I, Reason in Common Sense

6   When Socrates and his two great disciples composed a system of rational ethics they were hardly proposing practical legislation for mankind. . . . They were merely writing an eloquent epitaph for their country.
The Life of Reason, V, Reason in Science

7   Let a man once overcome his selfish terror at his own finitude, and his finitude is, in one sense, overcome.
The Ethics of Spinoza [1910], introduction

8   Perhaps the only true dignity of man is his capacity to despise himself.
The Ethics of Spinoza, introduction

9   The Bible is literature, not dogma.
The Ethics of Spinoza, introduction

10   American life is a powerful solvent. It seems to neutralize every intellectual element, however tough and alien it may be, and to fuse it in the native good will, complacency, thoughtlessness, and optimism.
Character and Opinion in the United States [1920]

11   There is no cure for birth and death save to enjoy the interval.
Soliloquies in England and Later Soliloquies [1922]. War Shrines

12   My atheism, like that of Spinoza, is true piety towards the universe and denies only gods fashioned by men in their own image, to be servants of their human interests.
Soliloquies in England and Later Soliloquies. On My Friendly Critics

13   Scepticism is the chastity of the intellect, and it is shameful to surrender it too soon or to the first comer.
Scepticism and Animal Faith [1923], ch. 9

14   The young man who has not wept is a savage, and the old man who will not laugh is a fool.
Dialogues in Limbo [1926], ch. 3

15   Religion in its humility restores man to his only dignity, the courage to live by grace.
Dialogues in Limbo, 4

Konstantin Sergeyevich Alekseyev Stanislavski
1863–1938

16   There are no small parts, there are only small actors.   *My Life in Art[2] [1924]*

17   Our type of creativeness is the conception and birth of a new being — the person in the part. It is a natural act similar to the birth of a human being.
An Actor Prepares[3] [1936], ch. 16

18   In the creative process there is the father, the author of the play; the mother, the actor pregnant with the part; and the child, the role to be born.
An Actor Prepares, 16

Ernest L[awrence] Thayer
1863–1940

19   There was ease in Casey's manner as he stepped into his place,
There was pride in Casey's bearing, and a smile on Casey's face,
And when, responding to the cheers, he lightly doffed his hat,

---

[1]Santayana's aphorism must be reversed: too often it is those who *can* remember the past who are condemned to repeat it. — ARTHUR M. SCHLESINGER, JR., *The Inscrutability of History* [1968]

[2]Translated by J. J. ROBBINS.
[3]Translated by ELIZABETH REYNOLDS HAPGOOD.

No stranger in the crowd could doubt 'twas Casey at the bat. *Casey at the Bat [1888], st. 6*

1 Oh! somewhere in this favored land the sun is shining bright;
The band is playing somewhere, and somewhere hearts are light;
And somewhere men are laughing and somewhere children shout,
But there is no joy in Mudville — mighty Casey has struck out. *Casey at the Bat, st. 13*

Sir Roger Casement
1864–1916

2   Where all your rights become only an accumulated wrong; where men must beg with bated breath for leave to subsist in their own land, to think their own thoughts, to sing their own songs, to garner the fruits of their own labors . . . then surely it is braver, a saner and truer thing, to be a rebel in act and deed against such circumstances as these than tamely to accept it as the natural lot of men.
Statement from prison [June 29, 1916]

Richard Harding Davis
1864–1916

3   The marines have landed and the situation is well in hand. *Attributed [1885]*

Elinor Glyn
1864–1943

4   He had that nameless charm, with a strong magnetism which can only be called "it."
"It" [1927]

Joseph Hayden
fl. 1896

5 There'll be a hot time in the old town tonight.
A Hot Time in the Old Town[1] *[1896]*

Richard Hovey
1864–1900

6 For it's always fair weather
When good fellows get together

With a stein on the table and a good song ringing clear. *A Stein Song [1898], st. 1*

Hermann Minkowski
1864–1909

7   The views of space and time which I wish to lay before you have sprung from the soil of experimental physics, and therein lies their strength. They are radical. Henceforth space by itself, and time by itself, are doomed to fade away into mere shadows, and only a kind of union of the two will preserve an independent reality. *Space and Time [1908]*

Andrew Barton [Banjo] Paterson
1864–1941

8 Once a jolly swagman camped by a billabong,
Under the shade of a coolibah tree,
And he sang as he sat and waited for his billy-boil,
"Who'll come a-waltzing Matilda with me?"[2]
Waltzing Matilda [1903]

Jules Renard
1864–1910

9   To have a horror of the bourgeois is bourgeois.[3]
Journal, April 10, 1889

10   Failure is not our only punishment for laziness: there is also the success of others.[4]
Journal, January 2, 1898

11   I am not sincere even when I am saying that I am not sincere. *Journal, November 21, 1906*

12   We don't understand life any better at forty than at twenty, but we know it and admit it.
Journal, February 12, 1907

13   There are moments when everything goes well; don't be frightened, it won't last.
Journal, October 30, 1908

Miguel de Unamuno
1864–1936

14   Consciousness is a disease.
The Tragic Sense of Life [1913], ch. 1

---

[1]Hayden's text for a march, *A Hot Time in the Old Town Tonight* [1886], by THEODORE AUGUST METZ [1848–1936], later a favorite of Theodore Roosevelt's Rough Riders in Cuba, and still later Roosevelt's campaign song.

[2]Swagman: tramp. Billabong: waterhole. Coolibah: eucalyptus. Billy: container used for brewing tea. Matilda: a bundle containing personal belongings.
  Music by MARIE COWAN [d. 1919].
  [3]L'horreur des bourgeois est bourgeoise.
  [4]Pour nous punir le notre paresse, il y a, outre nos insuccès, les succès des autres.

1 True science teaches, above all, to doubt and be ignorant.
The Tragic Sense of Life, 5

2 To believe in God is to yearn for His existence and, furthermore, it is to act as if He did exist.
The Tragic Sense of Life, 8

3 Martyrs create faith, faith does not create martyrs.
The Tragic Sense of Life, 9

4 The devil is an angel too.   *Two Mothers [1920]*

5 Faith which does not doubt is dead faith.
The Agony of Christianity [1925]

6 And killing time is perhaps the essence of comedy, just as the essence of tragedy is killing eternity.
San Manuel Bueno, Martír [1930], prologue

7 I would say that teleology is theology, and that God is not a "because," but rather an "in order to."
San Manuel Bueno, prologue

Max Weber
1864–1920

8 Charisma knows only inner determination and inner restraint.... The charismatic leader gains and maintains authority solely by proving his strength in life.[1]
Wirtschaft und Gesellschaft (Economy and Society) [1922], pt. III, ch. 9

Israel Zangwill
1864–1926

9 America is God's crucible, the great melting pot where all the races of Europe are melting and reforming![2]
The Melting Pot [1908], act I

Mrs. Patrick Campbell
[Beatrice Stella Tanner Campbell]
1865–1940

10 It doesn't matter what you do in the bedroom as long as you don't do it in the street and frighten the horses.
Quoted in DAPHNE FIELDING [1904–1997], The Duchess of Jermyn Street [1964]

Edith [Louisa] Cavell
1865–1915

11 I realize that patriotism is not enough. I must have no hatred or bitterness towards anyone.
Last words [October 12, 1915], before her execution by the Germans

Elsie De Wolfe [Lady Mendl]
1865–1950

12 I believe in plenty of optimism and white paint, comfortable chairs with lights beside them, open fires on the hearth and flowers wherever they "belong," mirrors and sunshine in all rooms.
The House in Good Taste[3] [1913], ch. 4

George V
1865–1936

13 How is the Empire?
Attributed last words[4] [January 21, 1936]

Laurence Hope
[Adela Florence Cory Nicolson]
1865–1904

14 To have — to hold — and — in time — let go!
India's Love Lyrics [1901]. The Teak Forest, st. 10

15 Pale hands I loved beside the Shalimar.
India's Love Lyrics. Kashmiri Song, st. 1

Rudyard Kipling
1865–1936

16 I have eaten your bread and salt.
I have drunk your water and wine.
The deaths ye died I have watched beside
And the lives ye led were mine.
Departmental Ditties [1886]. Prelude, st. 1

17 Little Tin Gods on Wheels.
Departmental Ditties. Public Waste, st. 4

18 The toad beneath the harrow knows
Exactly where each tooth point goes;

---

[1]Translated by H. H. GERTH and C. WRIGHT MILLS.

[2]The point about the melting pot . . . is that it did not happen. — NATHAN GLAZER [b. 1925] and DANIEL PATRICK MOYNIHAN, *Beyond the Melting Pot* [1963]
See Michel de Crèvecoeur, 331:2.

[3]Ghostwritten by RUBY ROSS WOOD [1881–1950].

[4]As reported by Buckingham Palace. As reported in the diary of LORD DAWSON, the king's physician, however, George's last words were "God damn you."

The butterfly upon the road
Preaches contentment to that toad.
>*Departmental Ditties. Pagett, M.P., prelude*

1 And a woman is only a woman, but a good cigar is a smoke.
>*Departmental Ditties. The Betrothed, st. 25*

2   It takes a great deal of Christianity to wipe out uncivilized Eastern instincts, such as falling in love at first sight.
>*Plain Tales from the Hills [1888]. Lispeth*

3   Never praise a sister to a sister, in the hope of your compliments reaching the proper ears.
>*Plain Tales from the Hills. False Dawn*

4   Many religious people are deeply suspicious. They seem — for purely religious purposes, of course — to know more about iniquity than the unregenerate.
>*Plain Tales from the Hills. Watches of the Night*

5   Lalun is a member of the most ancient profession in the world.
>*In Black and White [1888]. On the City Wall*

6 Down to Gehenna or up to the Throne,
He travels the fastest who travels alone.[1]
>*Soldiers Three [1888]. The Winners (L' Envoi: What Is the Moral?), st. 1*

7   More men are killed by overwork than the importance of the world justifies.
>*The Phantom 'Rickshaw [1888]*

8 Oh, East is East, and West is West, and never the twain shall meet,
Till Earth and Sky stand presently at God's great Judgment Seat;
But there is neither East nor West, border, nor breed, nor birth,
When two strong men stand face to face, though they come from the ends of the earth!
>*The Ballad of East and West [1889]*

9   Bite on the bullet, old man, and don't let them think you're afraid.
>*The Light That Failed [1890–1891]*

10 If I were damned of body and soul,
I know whose prayers would make me whole,
Mother o' mine, O mother o' mine.
>*Mother o' Mine [1891]*

11 And the end of the fight is a tombstone white with the name of the late deceased,
And the epitaph drear: "A Fool lies here who tried to hustle the East."   *The Naulahka [1892], ch. 5*

12 When Earth's last picture is painted, and the tubes are twisted and dried,
When the oldest colors have faded, and the youngest critic has died,
We shall rest, and, faith, we shall need it — lie down for an eon or two,
Till the Master of All Good Workmen shall put us to work anew.
>*When Earth's Last Picture Is Painted [1892]*

13 They rise to their feet as He passes by, gentlemen unafraid.
>*Ballads and Barrack Room Ballads [1892, 1893]. Dedication, st. 5*

14 "What are the bugles blowin' for?" said Files-on-Parade.
"To turn you out, to turn you out," the Color-Sergeant said.
>*Ballads and Barrack Room Ballads. Danny Deever,[2] st. 1*

15 They've taken of his buttons off an' cut his stripes away,
An' they're hangin' Danny Deever in the mornin'.
>*Ballads and Barrack Room Ballads. Danny Deever, st. 1*

16 We aren't no thin red 'eroes.
>*Ballads and Barrack Room Ballads. Tommy, st. 4*

17 For it's Tommy this, an' Tommy that, an' "Chuck 'im out, the brute!"
But it's "Savior of 'is country" when the guns begin to shoot.
>*Ballads and Barrack Room Ballads. Tommy, st. 5*

18 So 'ere's *to* you, Fuzzy-Wuzzy, at your 'ome in the Soudan;
You're a pore benighted 'eathen but a first-class fightin' man.
>*Ballads and Barrack Room Ballads. Fuzzy-Wuzzy, st. 1*

19 Though I've belted you an' flayed you,
By the livin' Gawd that made you,
You're a better man than I am, Gunga Din!
>*Ballads and Barrack Room Ballads. Gunga Din, st. 5*

20 'Ave you 'eard o' the Widow at Windsor
With a hairy gold crown on 'er 'ead?
>*Ballads and Barrack Room Ballads. The Widow at Windsor, st. 1*

---

[1]He may well win the race that runs by himself. — BENJAMIN FRANKLIN, *Poor Richard's Almanac* [1757]

[2]Music by WALTER DAMROSCH [1862–1950].

1 By the old Moulmein Pagoda, lookin' eastward to
   the sea,
   There's a Burma girl a-settin', and I know she thinks
   o' me;
   For the wind is in the palm trees, and the temple bells
   they say:
   "Come you back, you British soldier; come you back
   to Mandalay!"
   > *Ballads and Barrack Room Ballads.*
   > *Mandalay,[1] st. 1*

2 On the road to Mandalay,
   Where the flyin' fishes play,
   An' the dawn comes up like thunder outer China
   'crost the Bay!
   > *Ballads and Barrack Room Ballads.*
   > *Mandalay, st. 1*

3 Ship me somewheres east of Suez, where the best is
   like the worst,
   Where there aren't no Ten Commandments, an' a
   man can raise a thirst.
   > *Ballads and Barrack Room Ballads.*
   > *Mandalay, st. 6*

4 The Devil whispered behind the leaves, "It's pretty,
   but is it Art?"
   > *Ballads and Barrack Room Ballads.*
   > *The Conundrum of the Workshops, st. 1*

5 To the legion of the lost ones, to the cohort of the
   damned.
   > *Ballads and Barrack Room Ballads.*
   > *Gentlemen Rankers, st. 1*

6 We're poor little lambs who've lost our way,
        Baa! Baa! Baa!
   We're little black sheep who've gone astray,
        Baa — aa — aa!
   Gentlemen rankers out on the spree,
   Damned from here to Eternity,
   God ha' mercy on such as we,
        Baa! Yah! Baa!
   > *Ballads and Barrack Room Ballads.*
   > *Gentlemen Rankers, refrain*

7 We have done with Hope and Honor, we are lost to
   Love and Truth,
   We are dropping down the ladder rung by rung;
   And the measure of our torment is the measure of our
   youth.
   God help us, for we knew the worst too young!
   > *Ballads and Barrack Room Ballads.*
   > *Gentlemen Rankers, st. 4*

8 And what should they know of England who only
   England know?
   > *Ballads and Barrack Room Ballads.*
   > *The English Flag, st. 1*

---

[1]Music by OLEY SPEAKS [1874–1948].

9 The sin ye do by two and two ye must pay for one
   by one.
   > *Ballads and Barrack Room Ballads.*
   > *Tomlinson, l. 60*

10 There's a legion that never was 'listed,
   That carries no colors or crest.
   > *Ballads and Barrack Room Ballads.*
   > *The Lost Legion, st. 1*

11 There are nine and sixty ways of constructing tribal
   lays,
   And every single one of them is right.
   > *Ballads and Barrack Room Ballads.*
   > *In the Neolithic Age, st. 5*

12 There be triple ways to take, of the eagle or the snake,
   Or the way of a man with a maid;
   But the sweetest way to me is a ship's upon the sea
   In the heel of the Northeast Trade.
   > *Ballads and Barrack Room Ballads.*
   > *The Long Trail, st. 5*

13 When you're wounded and left on Afghanistan's
   plains,
   And the women come out to cut up what remains,
   Jest roll to your rifle and blow out your brains
   An' go to your Gawd like a soldier.
   > *The Young British Soldier [1892]*

14 Back to the Army again, sergeant,
   Back to the Army again.
   Out o' the cold an' the rain.
   > *Back to the Army Again [1894], refrain*

15   We be of one blood, ye and I.
   > *The Jungle Book [1894]. Kaa's Hunting*

16   Is there anything in the jungle too little to be
   killed?
   > *The Jungle Book. Kaa's Hunting*

17 Brother, thy tail hangs down behind.
   > *The Jungle Book. Road Song of the*
   > *Bandar-Log, refrain*

18 Now this is the Law of the Jungle — as old and as true
   as the sky;
   And the Wolf that shall keep it may prosper, but the
   Wolf that shall break it must die.
   > *The Second Jungle Book [1895].*
   > *The Law of the Jungle, st. 1*

19 When Pack meets with Pack in the Jungle, and
   neither will go from the trail,
   Lie down till the leaders have spoken — it may be fair
   words shall prevail.
   > *The Second Jungle Book.*
   > *The Law of the Jungle, st. 6*

20 Now these are the Laws of the Jungle, and many and
   mighty are they;

But the head and the hoof of the Law and the haunch
and the hump is — Obey!
*The Second Jungle Book. The Law of the
Jungle, st. 19*

1 They change their skies above them,
But not their hearts that roam.
The Nativeborn [1895], st. 2

2 The Liner she's a lady, an' she never looks nor
'eeds —
The Man-o'-War's 'er 'usband, an' 'e gives 'er all she
needs,
But, oh, the little cargo boats that sail the wet seas
roun',
They're just the same as you an' me a-plyin' up and
down!
The Liner She's a Lady [1895], st. 1

3 I've taken my fun where I've found it.
The Ladies [1895], st. 1

4 For the Colonel's Lady an' Judy O'Grady
Are sisters under their skins! *The Ladies, st. 8*

5 A fool there was and he made his prayer
(Even as you and I!)
To a rag and a bone and a hank of hair
(We called her the woman who did not care)
But the fool he called her his lady fair —
(Even as you and I!)
The Vampire [1897], st. 1

6 Daughter am I in my mother's house;
But mistress in my own.
Our Lady of the Snows [1898], st. 1

7 God of our fathers, known of old,
Lord of our far-flung battle line,
Beneath whose awful Hand we hold
Dominion over palm and pine —
Lord God of Hosts, be with us yet,
Lest we forget — lest we forget!
Recessional [1899], st. 1

8 The tumult and the shouting dies;
The captains and the kings depart. *Recessional, st. 2*

9 Lo, all our pomp of yesterday
Is one with Nineveh and Tyre! *Recessional, st. 3*

10 Lesser breeds without the Law. *Recessional, st. 4*

11 For frantic boast and foolish word —
Thy mercy on Thy People, Lord! *Recessional, st. 5*

12 Take up the White Man's burden,[1]
Send forth the best ye breed —

Go, bind your sons to exile
To serve your captives' need.
The White Man's Burden [1899], st. 1

13 Little Friend of All the World.
Kim [1901], ch. 1

14 This is a great and terrible world. I never knew
there were so many men alive in it. *Kim, 3*

15 The flanneled fools at the wicket or the muddied oafs
at the goals.
The Islanders [1902], l. 31

16 I keep six honest serving men
(They taught me all I knew);
Their names are What and Why and When
And How and Where and Who.
*The Just-So Stories [1902].
The Elephant's Child*

17 The great gray-green, greasy Limpopo River, all
set about with fever-trees.
The Just-So Stories. The Elephant's Child

18 The Cat. He walked by himself, and all places were
alike to him.
*The Just-So Stories. The Cat That Walked
by Himself*

19 He went back through the wet wild woods, waving his wild tail, and walking by his wild lone. But
he never told anybody.
*The Just-So Stories. The Cat That Walked
by Himself*

20 Who hath desired the sea? — the sight of salt water
unbounded.
The Sea and the Hills [1903], st. 1

21 Something hidden. Go and find it. Go and look
behind the Ranges —
Something lost behind the Ranges. Lost and waiting
for you. Go! *The Explorer [1903], st. 2*

22 Boots — boots — boots — boots — movin' up and
down again!
There's no discharge in the war! *Boots [1903], st. 1*

23 'Tisn't beauty, so to speak, nor good talk necessarily. It's just It. Some women'll stay in a man's
memory if they once walked down a street.
Traffics and Discoveries [1904]. Mrs. Bathurst

24 Of all the trees that grow so fair,
Old England to adorn,
Greater are none beneath the Sun,
Than oak, and ash, and thorn.
Puck of Pook's Hill [1906]. A Tree Song, st. 1

25 Brothers and Sisters, I bid you beware
Of giving your heart to a dog to tear.
The Power of the Dog [1909]

---

[1]Pile on the brown man's burden / To gratify your greed. —
*Response to Kipling's poem published in London Truth [1899] and
much reprinted;* variously attributed to HENRY LABOUCHÈRE [1831–
1912] and JOHN HOLLINGSHEAD [1827–1904].

1 If you can meet with Triumph and Disaster
And treat those two impostors just the same.
Rewards and Fairies [1910]. If, st. 2

2 If you can talk with crowds and keep your virtue,
Or walk with Kings — nor lose the common touch.
Rewards and Fairies. If, st. 4

3 Yours is the Earth and everything that's in it,
And — which is more — you'll be a Man, my son!
Rewards and Fairies. If, st. 4

4 The female of the species is more deadly than the
male.   *The Female of the Species [1911], st. 1*

5 Oh, Adam was a gardener, and God who made him
sees
That half a proper gardener's work is done upon his
knees.   *The Glory of the Garden, st. 8*

6 What stands if Freedom fall?
Who dies if England live?
For All We Have and Are [1914], st. 4

7 I could not look on Death, which being known,
Men led me to him, blindfold and alone.
*Epitaphs of the War, 1914–1918 [1919].
The Coward*

8   Hot and bothered.
*Independence. Rectorial Address at
St. Andrews [October 10, 1923]*

9   When your Daemon is in charge, do not try to
think consciously. Drift, wait, and obey.
*Something of Myself for My Friends Known
and Unknown [1937], ch. 8*

Baroness Emmuska Orczy
1865–1947

10 We seek him here, we seek him there,
Those Frenchies seek him everywhere.
Is he in heaven? — Is he in hell?
That demmed, elusive Pimpernel?
The Scarlet Pimpernel [1905], ch. 12

Logan Pearsall Smith
1865–1946

11   There are two things to aim at in life: first, to get
what you want; and, after that, to enjoy it. Only the
wisest of mankind achieve the second.
Afterthoughts [1931]

12   Solvency is entirely a matter of temperament and
not of income.   *Afterthoughts*

13   There are few sorrows, however poignant, in
which a good income is of no avail.   *Afterthoughts*

14   What I like in a good author is not what he says,
but what he whispers.   *Afterthoughts*

15   People say that life is the thing, but I prefer
reading.   *Afterthoughts*

16   There is more felicity on the far side of baldness
than young men can possibly imagine.
Afterthoughts

Arthur Symons
1865–1945

17 And I would have, now love is over,
An end to all, an end:
I cannot, having been your lover,
Stoop to become your friend!
After Love [1892], st. 3

18   Without charm there can be no fine literature, as
there can be no perfect flower without fragrance.
*The Symbolist Movement in Literature
[1899]. Stéphane Mallarmé*

19   The mystic too full of God to speak intelligibly to
the world.
*The Symbolist Movement in Literature.
Arthur Rimbaud*

William Butler Yeats[1]
1865–1939

20 The woods of Arcady are dead,
And over is their antique joy;
Of old the world on dreaming fed;
Gray Truth is now her painted toy.
*Crossways [1889]. The Song of the
Happy Shepherd, st. 1*

21 Down by the salley gardens my love and I did meet;
She passed the salley gardens with little snow-white
feet.
She bid me take love easy, as the leaves grow on the
tree;
But I, being young and foolish, with her would not
agree.   *Crossways. Down by the Salley Gardens*

22 She bid me take life easy, as the grass grows on the
weirs;
But I was young and foolish, and now am full
of tears.   *Crossways. Down by the Salley Gardens*

23 The years like great black oxen tread the world,
And God the herdsman goads them on behind,
And I am broken by their passing feet.
The Countess Cathleen [1892], last lines

---

[1] See W. H. Auden, 749:2.

1 Red Rose, proud Rose, sad Rose of all my days!
  Come near me, while I sing the ancient ways.
  The Rose [1893]. To the Rose Upon the
  Rood of Time, st. 1

2 I will arise and go now, and go to Innisfree,
  And a small cabin build there, of clay and wattles
    made:
  Nine bean-rows will I have there, a hive for the
    honeybee,
  And live alone in the bee-loud glade.
  The Rose. The Lake Isle of Innisfree,[1] *st. 1*

3 A pity beyond all telling
  Is hid in the heart of love.   *The Rose. The Pity of Love*

4 The brawling of a sparrow in the eaves,
  The brilliant moon and all the milky sky,
  And all that famous harmony of leaves,
  Had blotted out man's image and his cry.
  The Rose. The Sorrow of Love, st. 1

5 When you are old and gray and full of sleep,
  And nodding by the fire, take down this book.[2]
  The Rose. When You Are Old, st. 1

6 How many loved your moments of glad grace,
  And loved your beauty with love false or true,
  But one man loved the pilgrim soul in you,
  And loved the sorrows of your changing face.
  The Rose. When You Are Old, st. 2

7   The Land of Faery,
  Where nobody gets old and godly and grave,
  Where nobody gets old and crafty and wise,
  Where nobody gets old and bitter of tongue.
  The Land of Heart's Desire [1894], l. 48

8   Land of Heart's Desire,
  Where beauty has no ebb, decay no flood,
  But joy is wisdom, time an endless song.
  The Land of Heart's Desire, l. 373

9 All things uncomely and broken, all things worn out
    and old,
  The cry of a child by the roadway, the creak of a
    lumbering cart,
  The heavy steps of the plowman, splashing the wintry
    mold,
  Are wronging your image that blossoms a rose in the
    deeps of my heart.
  The Wind Among the Reeds [1899].
  The Lover Tells of the Rose in His Heart, st. 1

10 And God stands winding His lonely horn,
  And time and the world are ever in flight.
  The Wind Among the Reeds. Into the Twilight

11 And pluck till time and times are done
  The silver apples of the moon,
  The golden apples of the sun.
  The Wind Among the Reeds. The Song
  of Wandering Aengus, st. 3

12 Had I the heavens' embroidered cloths,
  Enwrought with gold and silver light.
  The Wind Among the Reeds. He Wishes
  for the Cloths of Heaven

13 But I, being poor, have only my dreams;
  I have spread my dreams under your feet;
  Tread softly because you tread on my dreams.
  The Wind Among the Reeds. He Wishes
  for the Cloths of Heaven

14 When I play on my fiddle in Dooney,
  Folk dance like a wave of the sea.
  The Wind Among the Reeds.
  The Fiddler of Dooney, st. 1

15 One sinks in on God; we do not see the truth; God
  sees the truth in us. . . . Tell them, Fool, that
  when the life and the mind are broken, the truth
  comes through them like peas through a broken
  peascod.
  The Hour-Glass [1903]

16 O heart! O heart! if she'd but turn her head,
  You'd know the folly of being comforted.
  In the Seven Woods [1904].
  The Folly of Being Comforted

17 Never give all the heart, for love
  Will hardly seem worth thinking of
  To passionate women if it seem
  Certain, and they never dream
  That it fades out from kiss to kiss;
  For everything that's lovely is
  But a brief, dreamy kind delight.
  In the Seven Woods. Never Give
  All the Heart

18 I said, "A line will take us hours maybe;
  Yet if it does not seem a moment's thought,
  Our stitching and unstitching has been naught.
  Better go down upon your marrow-bones
  And scrub a kitchen pavement, or break stones."
  In the Seven Woods. Adam's Curse, st. 1

19 For to articulate sweet sounds together
  Is to work harder than all these, and yet
  Be thought an idler by the noisy set
  Of bankers, schoolmasters, and clergymen
  The martyrs call the world.
  In the Seven Woods. Adam's Curse, st. 1

---

[1] I had still the ambition, formed in Sligo in my teens, of living in imitation of Thoreau on Innisfree, a little island in Lough Gill, and when walking through Fleet Street very homesick I heard a little tinkle of water and saw a fountain in a shop window which balanced a little ball upon its jet, and began to remember lake water. From the sudden remembrance came my poem Innisfree. — YEATS, *The Trembling of the Veil* [1926]

[2] See Pierre de Ronsard, 150:7.

1   It's certain there is no fine thing
Since Adam's fall but needs much laboring.
> *In the Seven Woods. Adam's Curse,*
> *st. 3*

2 I heard the old, old men say,
"All that's beautiful drifts away
Like the waters."
> *In the Seven Woods. The Old Men*
> *Admiring Themselves in the Water*

3 The friends that have it I do wrong
When ever I remake a song
Should know what issue is at stake,
It is myself that I remake.
> *The Collected Works in Verse and Prose of*
> *William Butler Yeats [1908], vol. II,*
> *untitled preliminary poem*

4 Why, what could she have done, being what she is?
Was there another Troy for her to burn?
> *The Green Helmet and Other Poems [1910].*
> *No Second Troy*

5 The fascination of what's difficult
Has dried the sap out of my veins, and rent
Spontaneous joy and natural content
Out of my heart.
> *The Green Helmet and Other Poems.*
> *The Fascination of What's Difficult*

6 Wine comes in at the mouth
And love comes in at the eye;
That's all we shall know for truth
Before we grow old and die.
> *The Green Helmet and Other Poems.*
> *A Drinking Song*

7 Though leaves are many, the root is one;
Through all the lying days of my youth
I swayed my leaves and flowers in the sun;
Now I may wither into the truth.
> *The Green Helmet and Other Poems.*
> *The Coming of Wisdom with Time*

8 In dreams begins responsibility.[1]
> *Responsibilities [1914], epigraph*
> *(from an old play)*

9 Pardon, old fathers.
> *Responsibilities, preliminary poem*

10 Was it for this the wild geese spread
The gray wing upon every tide;
For this that all that blood was shed,
For this Edward Fitzgerald died,
And Robert Emmet and Wolfe Tone,
All that delirium of the brave?

---

[1]Source of *In Dreams Begin Responsibilities,* the title of a short
story and a book by Delmore Schwartz.

Romantic Ireland's dead and gone,
It's with O'Leary in the grave.
> *Responsibilities. September 1913, st. 3*

11 Be secret and exult,
Because of all things known
That is most difficult.
> *Responsibilities. To a Friend Whose Work*
> *Has Come to Nothing*

12 The uncontrollable mystery on the bestial floor.
> *Responsibilities. The Magi, last line*

13 I made my song a coat
Covered with embroideries
Out of old mythologies
From heel to throat;
But the fools caught it,
Wore it in the world's eyes
As though they'd wrought it.
Song, let them take it,
For there's more enterprise
In walking naked.   *Responsibilities. A Coat*

14 We make out of the quarrel with others, rhetoric, but
of the quarrel with ourselves, poetry.
> *Per Amica Silentia Lunae [1917]*

15 Upon the brimming water among the stones
Are nine-and-fifty swans.
> *The Wild Swans at Coole [1919].*
> *The Wild Swans at Coole, st. 1*

16 Unwearied still, lover by lover,
They paddle in the cold
Companionable streams or climb the air;
Their hearts have not grown old.
> *The Wild Swans at Coole.*
> *The Wild Swans at Coole, st. 4*

17 Some burn damp faggots, others may consume
The entire combustible world in one small room.
> *The Wild Swans at Coole. In Memory of*
> *Major Robert Gregory, st. 11*

18 What made us dream that he could comb gray hair?
> *The Wild Swans at Coole. In Memory of*
> *Major Robert Gregory, st. 11*

19   A thought
Of that late death took all my heart for speech.
> *The Wild Swans at Coole. In Memory of*
> *Major Robert Gregory, st. 12*

20 I know that I shall meet my fate
Somewhere among the clouds above;
Those that I fight I do not hate,
Those that I guard I do not love;
My country is Kiltartan Cross,
My countrymen Kiltartan's poor.
> *The Wild Swans at Coole. An Irish*
> *Airman Foresees His Death, l. 1*

1 Nor law, nor duty bade me fight,
  Nor public men, nor cheering crowds,
  A lonely impulse of delight
  Drove to this tumult in the clouds.
  The Wild Swans at Coole. An Irish Airman
  Foresees His Death, l. 9

2 And I may dine at journey's end
  With Landor and with Donne.
  The Wild Swans at Coole. To a Young Beauty,
  st. 3

3 All the wild witches, those most noble ladies,
  For all their broomsticks and their tears,
  Their angry tears, are gone.
  The Wild Swans at Coole. Lines Written in
  Dejection, l. 4

4 I knew a phoenix in my youth, so let them have
      their day.
  The Wild Swans at Coole. His Phoenix,
  refrain

5 Hands, do what you're bid:
  Bring the balloon of the mind
  That bellies and drags in the wind
  Into its narrow shed.
  The Wild Swans at Coole. The Balloon
  of the Mind

6 We have lit upon the gentle, sensitive mind
  And lost the old nonchalance of the hand;
  Whether we have chosen chisel, pen or brush,
  We are but critics, or but half create.
  The Wild Swans at Coole. Ego Dominus
  Tuus, l. 12

7 All changed, changed utterly:
  A terrible beauty is born.
  Michael Robartes and the Dancer [1921].
  Easter 1916, st. 1

8 Too long a sacrifice
  Can make a stone of the heart.
  O when may it suffice?
  Michael Robartes and the Dancer. Easter
  1916, st. 4

9 Turning and turning in the widening gyre
  The falcon cannot hear the falconer;
  Things fall apart[1]; the center cannot hold;
  Mere anarchy is loosed upon the world,
  The blood-dimmed tide is loosed, and
      everywhere
  The ceremony of innocence is drowned;
  The best lack all conviction, while the worst
  Are full of passionate intensity.
  Michael Robartes and the Dancer.
  The Second Coming, st. 1

---

[1] Title of book [1958] by Chinua Achebe [b. 1930].

10   Now I know
  That twenty centuries of stony sleep
  Were vexed to nightmare by a rocking cradle,
  And what rough beast, its hour come round
      at last,
  Slouches towards Bethlehem to be born?
  Michael Robartes and the Dancer.
  The Second Coming, st. 2

11 Imagining in excited reverie
  That the future years had come,
  Dancing to a frenzied drum,
  Out of the murderous innocence of the sea.
  Michael Robartes and the Dancer.
  A Prayer for My Daughter, st. 2

12   For such,
  Being made beautiful overmuch,
  Consider beauty a sufficient end,
  Lose natural kindness and maybe
  The heart-revealing intimacy
  That chooses right, and never find a friend.
  Michael Robartes and the Dancer.
  A Prayer for My Daughter, st. 3

13 It's certain that fine women eat
  A crazy salad with their meat.
  Michael Robartes and the Dancer.
  A Prayer for My Daughter, st. 4

14 In courtesy I'd have her chiefly learned;
  Hearts are not had as a gift but hearts are earned.
  Michael Robartes and the Dancer.
  A Prayer for My Daughter, st. 5

15 And many a poor man that has roved,
  Loved and thought himself beloved,
  From a glad kindness cannot take his eyes.
  Michael Robartes and the Dancer.
  A Prayer for My Daughter, st. 5

16 If there's no hatred in a mind
  Assault and battery of the wind
  Can never tear the linnet from the leaf.
  Michael Robartes and the Dancer.
  A Prayer for My Daughter, st. 7

17 An intellectual hatred is the worst,
  So let her think opinions are accursed.
  Have I not seen the loveliest woman born
  Out of the mouth of Plenty's horn,
  Because of her opinionated mind
  Barter that horn and every good
  By quiet natures understood
  For an old bellows full of angry wind?
  Michael Robartes and the Dancer.
  A Prayer for My Daughter, st. 8

18   All hatred driven hence,
  The soul recovers radical innocence
  And learns at last that it is self-delighting,

Self-appeasing, self-affrighting,
And that its own sweet will is Heaven's will.
    Michael Robartes and the Dancer.
    A Prayer for My Daughter, st. 9

1 That is no country for old men. The young
In one another's arms, birds in the trees
— Those dying generations — at their song,
The salmon-falls, the mackerel-crowded seas,
Fish, flesh, or fowl, commend all summer long
Whatever is begotten, born, and dies.
Caught in that sensual music all neglect
Monuments of unaging intellect.
    The Tower [1928]. Sailing to Byzantium,
    st. 1

2 An aged man is but a paltry thing,
A tattered coat upon a stick, unless
Soul clap its hands and sing, and louder sing
For every tatter in its mortal dress.
    The Tower. Sailing to Byzantium,
    st. 2

3 Consume my heart away; sick with desire
And fastened to a dying animal
It knows not what it is; and gather me
Into the artifice of eternity.
    The Tower. Sailing to Byzantium,
    st. 3

4 Once out of nature I shall never take
My bodily form from any natural thing,
But such a form as Grecian goldsmiths make
Of hammered gold and gold enameling
To keep a drowsy Emperor awake;
Or set upon a golden bough to sing
To lords and ladies of Byzantium
Of what is past, or passing, or to come.[1]
    The Tower. Sailing to Byzantium,
    st. 4

5 What shall I do with this absurdity —
O heart, O troubled heart — this caricature,
Decrepit age that has been tied to me
As to a dog's tail?   *The Tower. The Tower, I*

6 Does the imagination dwell the most
Upon a woman won or a woman lost?
    The Tower. The Tower, II, st. 13

7 The night can sweat with terror as before
We pieced our thoughts into philosophy,
And planned to bring the world under a rule,
Who are but weasels fighting in a hole.
    The Tower. Nineteen Hundred and
    Nineteen, I, st. 4

---

[1]I have read somewhere that in the Emperor's palace at Byzantium was a tree made of gold and silver, and artificial birds that sang. — YEATS's *note*

8 But is there any comfort to be found?
Man is in love and loves what vanishes,
What more is there to say?
    The Tower. Nineteen Hundred and
    Nineteen, I, st. 6

9 O but we dreamed to mend
Whatever mischief seemed
To afflict mankind, but now
That winds of winter blow
Learn that we were crack-pated when we dreamed.
    The Tower. Nineteen Hundred and
    Nineteen, III, st. 3

10 Come let us mock at the great
That had such burdens on the mind
And toiled so hard and late
To leave some monument behind,
Nor thought of the leveling wind.
    The Tower. Nineteen Hundred and
    Nineteen, V, st. 1

11 Much did I rage when young,
Being by the world oppressed,
But now with flattering tongue
It speeds the parting guest.
    The Tower. Youth and Age

12 Odor of blood when Christ was slain
Made all Platonic tolerance vain
And vain all Doric discipline.
    The Tower. Two Songs from a Play, II,
    st. 1

13 Everything that man esteems
Endures a moment or a day.
Love's pleasure drives his love away,
The painter's brush consumes his dreams.
    The Tower. Two Songs from a Play, II, st. 2

14 Whatever flames upon the night
Man's own resinous heart has fed.
    The Tower. Two Songs from a Play, II, st. 2

15 Locke sank into a swoon;
The Garden died;
God took the spinning-jenny
Out of his side.
    The Tower. Fragments, I

16 A shudder in the loins engenders there
The broken wall, the burning roof and tower
And Agamemnon dead.
    The Tower. Leda and the Swan, st. 3

17 Labor is blossoming or dancing where
The body is not bruised to pleasure soul,
Nor beauty born out of its own despair,
Nor blear-eyed wisdom out of midnight oil.
O chestnut tree, great-rooted blossomer,
Are you the leaf, the blossom or the bole?

O body swayed to music, O brightening glance,
How can we know the dancer from the dance?
> *The Tower. Among School Children, st. 8*

1 Never to have lived is best, ancient writers say;
Never to have drawn the breath of life, never to have
looked into the eye of day;
The second best's a gay goodnight and quickly turn
away.   *From "Oedipus at Colonus," st. 3*

2 What they undertook to do
They brought to pass;
All things hang like a drop of dew
Upon a blade of grass.
> *Words for Music Perhaps [1932].*
> *Gratitude to the Unknown Instructors*

3   That toil of growing up;
The ignominy of boyhood; the distress
Of boyhood changing into man;
The unfinished man and his pain.
> *The Winding Stair and Other Poems [1933].*
> *A Dialogue of Self and Soul, II, st. 1*

4 I am content to live it all again
And yet again, if it be life to pitch
Into the frog-spawn of a blind man's ditch.
> *The Winding Stair and Other Poems.*
> *A Dialogue of Self and Soul, II, st. 3*

5 When such as I cast out remorse
So great a sweetness flows into the breast
We must laugh and we must sing,
We are blest by everything,
Everything we look upon is blest.
> *The Winding Stair and Other Poems.*
> *A Dialogue of Self and Soul, II, st. 4*

6   But what is Whiggery?
A leveling, rancorous, rational sort of mind
That never looked out of the eye of a saint
Or out of drunkard's eye.
> *The Winding Stair and Other Poems.*
> *The Seven Sages*

7   Only God, my dear,
Could love you for yourself alone
And not your yellow hair.
> *The Winding Stair and Other Poems.*
> *For Anne Gregory, st. 3*

8 Swift has sailed into his rest;
Savage indignation there
Cannot lacerate his breast,
Imitate him if you dare,
World-besotted traveler; he
Served human liberty.
> *The Winding Stair and Other Poems.*
> *Swift's Epitaph*[1]

---
[1] See Jonathan Swift, 286:15.

9 The intellect of man is forced to choose
Perfection of the life, or of the work,
And if it take the second must refuse
A heavenly mansion, raging in the dark.
> *The Winding Stair and Other Poems.*
> *The Choice, st. 1*

10 The unpurged images of day recede;
The Emperor's drunken soldiery are abed;
Night resonance recedes, night-walkers' song
After great cathedral gong.
> *The Winding Stair and Other Poems.*
> *Byzantium, st. 1*

11 At midnight on the Emperor's pavement flit
Flames that no faggot feeds, nor steel has lit.
> *The Winding Stair and Other Poems.*
> *Byzantium, st. 4*

12 An agony of flame that cannot singe a sleeve.
> *The Winding Stair and Other Poems.*
> *Byzantium, st. 4*

13 That dolphin-torn, that gong-tormented sea.
> *The Winding Stair and Other Poems.*
> *Byzantium, st. 5*

14 No man has ever lived that had enough
Of children's gratitude or woman's love.
> *The Winding Stair and Other Poems.*
> *Vacillation, III, st. 1*

15 Things said or done long years ago,
Or things I did not do or say
But thought that I might say or do,
Weigh me down, and not a day
But something is recalled,
My conscience or my vanity appalled.
> *The Winding Stair and Other Poems.*
> *Vacillation, V, st. 2*

16 Homer is my example and his unchristened
heart.
> *The Winding Stair and Other Poems.*
> *Vacillation, VIII*

17 Somewhere beyond the curtain
Of distorting days
Lives that lonely thing
That shone before these eyes
Targeted, trod like Spring.
> *The Winding Stair and Other Poems.*
> *Quarrel in Old Age, st. 2*

18 I had wild Jack for a lover.
> *The Winding Stair and Other Poems.*
> *Words for Music Perhaps, V, Crazy Jane*
> *on God, st. 4*

19 "Fair and foul are near of kin,
And fair needs foul," I cried.

"My friends are gone, but that's a truth
Nor grave nor bed denied."
> *The Winding Stair and Other Poems.*
> *Words for Music Perhaps, VI,*
> *Crazy Jane Talks with the Bishop, st. 2*

1 But Love has pitched his mansion in
The place of excrement
For nothing can be sole or whole
That has not been rent.
> *The Winding Stair and Other Poems.*
> *Words for Music Perhaps, VI,*
> *Crazy Jane Talks with the Bishop, st. 3*

2 What were all the world's alarms
To mighty Paris when he found
Sleep upon a golden bed
That first dawn in Helen's arms?
> *The Winding Stair and Other Poems.*
> *Words for Music Perhaps, XVI,*
> *Lullaby, st. 1*

3 Speech after long silence; it is right,
All other lovers being estranged or dead . . .
That we descant and yet again descant
Upon the supreme theme of Art and Song:
Bodily decrepitude is wisdom; young
We loved each other and were ignorant.
> *The Winding Stair and Other Poems.*
> *Words for Music Perhaps, XVII,*
> *After Long Silence*

4 I carry the sun in a golden cup,
The moon in a silver bag.[1]
> *The Winding Stair and Other Poems.*
> *Words for Music Perhaps, XIX,*
> *Those Dancing Days Are Gone*

5 I gave what other women gave
That stepped out of their clothes,
But when this soul, its body off,
Naked to naked goes,
He it has found shall find therein
What none other knows.
> *The Winding Stair and Other Poems.*
> *A Woman Young and Old, IX,*
> *A Last Confession, st. 3*

6 He that sings a lasting song
Thinks in a marrowbone.
> *A Full Moon in March [1935].*
> *A Prayer for Old Age, st. 1*

7 I pray — for fashion's word is out
And prayer comes round again —

---

[1]"The sun in a golden cup" . . . though not "the moon in a silver bag," is a quotation from the last of Mr. Ezra Pound's *Cantos.* — YEATS's *note*

That I may seem, though I die old,
A foolish, passionate man.
> *A Full Moon in March. A Prayer for*
> *Old Age, st. 3*

8   Whence had they come,
The hand and lash that beat down frigid Rome?
What sacred drama through her body heaved
When world-transforming Charlemagne was
    conceived?
> *A Full Moon in March. Supernatural Songs,*
> *VIII, Whence Had They Come?*

9 All perform their tragic play,
There struts Hamlet, there is Lear.
> *Last Poems [1936–1939]. Lapis Lazuli,*
> *st. 2*

10   Heaven blazing into the head:
Tragedy wrought to its uttermost.
Though Hamlet rambles and Lear rages,
And all the drop-scenes drop at once
Upon a hundred thousand stages,
It cannot grow by an inch or an ounce.
> *Last Poems. Lapis Lazuli, st. 2*

11 Their eyes mid many wrinkles, their eyes,
Their ancient, glittering eyes, are gay.
> *Last Poems. Lapis Lazuli, st. 5*

12 If soul may look and body touch,
Which is the more blest?
> *Last Poems. The Lady's Second Song, st. 3*

13 My temptation is quiet.
Here at life's end
Neither loose imagination,
Nor the mill of the mind
Consuming its rag and bone,
Can make the truth known.
> *Last Poems. An Acre of Grass, st. 2*

14 Grant me an old man's frenzy,
Myself must I remake
Till I am Timon and Lear
Or that William Blake
Who beat upon the wall
Till Truth obeyed his call.
> *Last Poems. An Acre of Grass, st. 3*

15 An old man's eagle mind.
> *Last Poems. An Acre of Grass, st. 4*

16 Hurrah for revolution and more cannon-shot!
A beggar upon horseback lashes a beggar on foot.
Hurrah for revolution and cannon come again!
The beggars have changed places, but the lash
    goes on.
> *Last Poems. The Great Day*

17 You think it horrible that lust and rage
Should dance attention upon my old age;

They were not such a plague when I was young;
What else have I to spur me into song?
> *Last Poems. The Spur*

1 John Synge, I and Augusta Gregory, thought
All that we did, all that we said or sang
Must come from contact with the soil, from that
Contact everything Antaeus-like grew strong.
> *Last Poems. The Municipal Gallery Revisited, st. 6*

2 Think where man's glory most begins and ends,
And say my glory was I had such friends.
> *Last Poems. The Municipal Gallery Revisited, st. 7*

3 Down the mountain walls
From where Pan's cavern is
Intolerable music falls.
Foul goat-head, brutal arm appear,
Belly, shoulder, bum,
Flash fishlike; nymphs and satyrs
Copulate in the foam.
> *Last Poems. News for the Delphic Oracle, st. 3*

4 Like a long-legged fly upon the stream
His mind moves upon silence.
> *Last Poems. Long-Legged Fly, refrain*

5 What shall I do for pretty girls
Now my old bawd is dead?
> *Last Poems. John Kinsella's Lament for Mrs. Mary Moore, refrain*

6 Fifteen apparitions have I seen;
The worst a coat upon a coat-hanger.
> *Last Poems. The Apparitions, refrain*

7 Players and painted stage took all my love,
And not those things that they were emblems of.
> *Last Poems. The Circus Animals' Desertion, II, st. 3*

8 Now that my ladder's gone,
I must lie down where all the ladders start,
In the foul rag-and-bone shop of the heart.
> *Last Poems. The Circus Animals' Desertion, III*

9 Irish poets, learn your trade,
Sing whatever is well made.
> *Last Poems. Under Ben Bulben, V*

10 Under bare Ben Bulben's head
In Drumcliff churchyard Yeats is laid.
> *Last Poems. Under Ben Bulben, VI*

11 On limestone quarried near the spot
By his command these words are cut:
Cast a cold eye

On life, on death.
Horseman, pass by![1]
> *Last Poems. Under Ben Bulben, VI*

12 I am still of opinion that only two topics can be of the least interest to a serious and studious mood — sex and the dead.
> *The Letters of W. B. Yeats*

13 We poets would die of loneliness but for women, and we choose our men friends that we may have somebody to talk about women with.
> *The Letters of W. B. Yeats. Letter to Olivia Shakespeare [1936]*

14 Even when the poet seems most himself…he is never the bundle of accident and incoherence that sits down to breakfast; he has been reborn as an idea, something intended, complete.
> *A General Introduction for My Work [1937]*

George W. Young
fl. 1900

15 The lips that touch liquor must never touch mine!
> *The Lips That Touch Liquor, st. 5*

George Ade
1866–1944

16 In uplifting, get underneath.
> *Fables in Slang [1899]. The Good Fairy*

17 Stay with the procession or you will never catch up.
> *Forty Modern Fables [1901]. The Old-Time Pedagogue*

18 But, R - e - m - o - r - s - e!
The water-wagon is the place for me; …
It is no time for mirth and laughter,
The cold, gray dawn of the morning after!
> *The Sultan of Sulu [1902]. Remorse*

Gelett Burgess
1866–1951

19 I never saw a purple cow,
I never hope to see one;
But I can tell you, anyhow,
I'd rather see than be one.
> *The Purple Cow [1895]*

20 The Goops they lick their fingers,
And the Goops they lick their knives;
They spill their broth on the tablecloth —

---

[1]The last three lines are inscribed on Yeats's gravestone.

Oh, they lead disgusting lives!
The Goops they talk while eating,
    And loud and fast they chew;
And that is why I'm glad that I
    Am not a Goop — are you?
        Goops and How to Be Them.
        Table Manners, I [1900]

1   Ah, yes, I wrote the "Purple Cow" —
    I'm sorry, now, I wrote it!
    But I can tell you, anyhow,
    I'll kill you if you quote it.
        Cinq Ans Après (Five Years Later) [1914]

Benedetto Croce
1866–1952

2   Every true history is contemporary history.[1]
        History: Its Theory and Practice [1917]

Harry Dacre
d. 1922

3   Daisy, Daisy, give me your answer, do!
    I'm half crazy, all for the love of you!
    It won't be a stylish marriage,
    I can't afford a carriage,
    But you'll look sweet upon the seat
    Of a bicycle built for two!

        Daisy Bell [1892]

Civilla Durfee Martin
1866–1948

4   His eye is on the sparrow
    And I know He watches me.
        His Eye Is on the Sparrow [1904]

Beatrix Potter
1866–1943

5   Once upon a time there were four little Rabbits,
    and their names were — Flopsy, Mopsy, Cottontail,
    and Peter.   *The Tale of Peter Rabbit [1902]*

6   But don't go into Mr. McGregor's garden.
        The Tale of Peter Rabbit

7   The water was all slippy-sloppy in the larder and
    the back passage. But Mr. Jeremy liked getting his
    feet wet; nobody ever scolded him, and he never
    caught a cold.
        The Tale of Mr. Jeremy Fisher [1906]

Lincoln Steffens
1866–1936

8   [On Chicago:] First in violence, deepest in dirt;
lawless, unlovely, ill-smelling, irreverent, new; an
overgrown gawk of a village, the "tough" among
cities, a spectacle for the nation.
        The Shame of the Cities [1904]

9   "So you've been over into Russia?" said Bernard
Baruch, and I answered very literally, "I have been
over into the future, and it works."[2]
        Autobiography [1931], ch. 18

Sun Yat-sen
1866–1925

10   The Chinese people have only family and clan solidarity; they do not have national spirit . . . they are just
a heap of loose sand. . . . Other men are the carving
knife and serving dish; we are the fish and the meat.
        China as a Heap of Loose Sand[3] *[1924]*

H[erbert] G[eorge] Wells
1866–1946

11   Are we not Men?
        The Island of Dr. Moreau [1896], ch. 12

12   Yet across the gulf of space, minds that are to our
minds as ours are to those of the beasts that perish,
intellects vast and cool and unsympathetic, regarded
this earth with envious eyes, and slowly and surely
drew their plans against us.
        The War of the Worlds [1898], ch. 1

13   At times I suffer from the strangest sense of
detachment from myself and the world about me; I
seem to watch it all from the outside, from somewhere inconceivably remote, out of time, out of
space, out of the stress and tragedy of it all.
        The War of the Worlds, ch. 7

14   The Social Contract is nothing more or less than
a vast conspiracy of human beings to lie to and
humbug themselves and one another for the general
Good. Lies are the mortar that bind the savage individual man into the social masonry.
        Love and Mr. Lewisham [1899], ch. 23

15   Moral indignation is jealousy with a halo.
        The Wife of Sir Isaac Harman [1914], ch. 9

---

[1]Translated by DOUGLAS AINSLIE.

[2]On Steffens's return from revolutionary Russia in 1919. Its more
familiar form is: I have seen the future, and it works. — STEFFENS,
letter to Marie Howe [April 3, 1919].

[3]From *Sources of Chinese Tradition* [1960], edited by WILLIAM
THEODORE DE BARY.

1 Nothing could have been more obvious to the people of the early twentieth century than the rapidity with which war was becoming impossible. And as certainly they did not see it. They did not see it until the atomic bombs burst in their fumbling hands.
The World Set Free [1914]

2 The catastrophe of the atomic bombs which shook men out of cities and businesses and economic relations, shook them also out of their old-established habits of thought, and out of the lightly held beliefs and prejudices that came down to them from the past.
The World Set Free

3 The professional military mind is by necessity an inferior and unimaginative mind; no man of high intellectual quality would willingly imprison his gifts in such a calling.
The Outline of History [1920], ch. 40

4 Human history becomes more and more a race between education and catastrophe.
The Outline of History, 41

5 Life begins perpetually. Gathered together at last under the leadership of man . . . unified, disciplined, armed with the secret powers of the atom and with knowledge as yet beyond dreaming, Life, forever dying to be born afresh, forever young and eager, will presently stand upon this earth as upon a footstool, and stretch out its realm amidst the stars.
The Outline of History, 41

6 The Shape of Things to Come.
Title of book [1933]

7 The New World Order.
Title of book [1940]

Stanley Baldwin
1867–1947

8 When you think about the defense of England you no longer think of the chalk cliffs of Dover. You think of the Rhine. That is where our frontier lies today.
Speech in the House of Commons [July 30, 1934]

Julien Benda
1867–1956

9 The Treachery of the Intellectuals.[1]
Title of book [1927]

[Enoch] Arnold Bennett
1867–1931

10 Being a husband is a whole-time job.
The Title [1918], act I

11 Pessimism, when you get used to it, is just as agreeable as optimism.
Things That Have Interested Me [1918]

Vicente Blasco-Ibáñez
1867–1928

12 [On the crowd in an arena:] It was the roar of the real, the only beast.
Sangre y Arena (Blood and Sand) [1908]

Pierre Bonnard
1867–1947

13 It's not a matter of painting life. It's a matter of giving life to painting. *Notes [1946]*

Ernest Dowson
1867–1900

14 Last night, ah, yesternight, betwixt her lips and mine
There fell thy shadow, Cynara! thy breath was shed
Upon my soul between the kisses and the wine;
And I was desolate and sick of an old passion,
Yea, I was desolate and bowed my head:
I have been faithful to thee, Cynara! in my fashion.[2]
Non Sum Qualis Eram Bonae sub Regno Cynarae (I Am Not What I Was Under Good Cynara's Reign) [1896], st. 1

15 I have forgot much, Cynara! gone with the wind,
Flung roses, roses riotously with the throng.
Non Sum Qualis Eram Bonae sub Regno Cynarae, st. 3

16 I cried for madder music and for stronger wine,
But when the feast is finished and the lamps expire,
Then falls thy shadow, Cynara! the night is thine.
Non Sum Qualis Eram Bonae sub Regno Cynarae, st. 4

17 They are not long, the weeping and the laughter,
Love and desire and hate:
I think they have no portion in us after
We pass the gate.

They are not long, the days of wine and roses;
Out of a misty dream

---

[1]La trahison des clercs.

[2]See Cole Porter, 692:5, and Horace, 97:11.

Our path emerges for a while, then closes
Within a dream.
>   *Vitae Summa Brevis Spem Nos Vetat*
>   *Incohare Longam (Life's Brief Span*
>   *Forbids Long-Reaching Hopes)*[1] *[1896]*

Finley Peter Dunne [Mr. Dooley]
1867–1936

1   Life'd not be worth livin' if we didn't keep our inimies.
>   *Mr. Dooley in Peace and in War [1898].*
>   *On New Year's Resolutions*

2   Th' dead ar-re always pop'lar. I knowed a society wanst to vote a monyment to a man an' refuse to help his fam'ly, all in wan night.
>   *Mr. Dooley in Peace and in War.*
>   *On Charity*

3   No matther whether th' constitution follows th' flag or not, th' supreme coort follows th' iliction returns.
>   *Mr. Dooley's Opinions [1900]. The Supreme*
>   *Court's Decisions*

4   I think a lie with a purpose is wan iv th' worst kind an' th' mos' profitable.
>   *Mr. Dooley's Opinions. On Lying*

5   Th' dimmycratic party ain't on speakin' terms with itsilf.
>   *Mr. Dooley's Opinions. Mr. Dooley Discusses*
>   *Party Politics*

6   Hogan's r-right whin he says: "Justice is blind." Blind she is, an' deef an' dumb an' has a wooden leg.
>   *Mr. Dooley's Opinions. Cross-Examinations*

7   No wan cares to hear what Hogan calls "Th' short an' simple scandals iv th' poor."
>   *Mr. Dooley's Opinions. Cross-Examinations*

8   'Twas founded be th' Puritans to give thanks f'r bein' presarved fr'm th' Indyans, an'...we keep it to give thanks we are presarved fr'm th' Puritans.
>   *Mr. Dooley's Opinions. Thanksgiving*

9   Vice...is a creature of such heejous mien...that th' more ye see it th' betther ye like it.
>   *Mr. Dooley's Opinions. The Crusade Against Vice*

10   If ye live enough befure thirty ye won't care to live at all afther fifty.
>   *Mr. Dooley's Opinions. Casual Observations*

11   Among men, Hinnissy, wet eye manes dhry heart.
>   *Mr. Dooley's Opinions. Casual Observations*

12   A fanatic is a man that does what he thinks th' Lord wud do if He knew th' facts iv th' case.
>   *Mr. Dooley's Opinions. Casual Observations*

13   Thrust ivrybody, but cut th' ca-ards.
>   *Mr. Dooley's Opinions. Casual Observations*

14   If a man is wise, he gets rich, an' if he gets rich, he gets foolish, or his wife does. That's what keeps the money movin' around.
>   *Observations by Mr. Dooley [1902].*
>   *Newport*

15   But th' best thing about a little judicyous swearin' is that it keeps th' temper. 'Twas intinded as a compromise between runnin' away an' fightin'. Befure it was invinted they was on'y th' two ways out iv an argymint.
>   *Observations by Mr. Dooley. Swearing*

16   Th' newspaper does ivrything f'r us. It runs th' polis foorce an' th' banks, commands th' milishy, conthrols th' ligislachure, baptizes th' young, marries th' foolish, comforts th' afflicted, afflicts th' comfortable, buries th' dead an' roasts thim afterward.
>   *Observations by Mr. Dooley. Newspaper*
>   *Publicity*

17   Th' prisidincy is th' highest office in th' gift iv th' people. Th' vice-prisidincy is th' next highest an' th' lowest. It isn't a crime exactly. Ye can't be sint to jail f'r it, but it's a kind iv a disgrace. It's like writin' anonymous letters.
>   *Dissertations by Mr. Dooley [1906].*
>   *The Vice-President*

18   "Ye ra-aly do think dhrink is a nicissry evil?" said Mr. Hennessy.
      "Well," said Mr. Dooley, "if it's an evil to a man, it's not nicissry, an' if it's nicissry it's an evil."
>   *Dissertations by Mr. Dooley. The Bar*

John Galsworthy
1867–1933

19   Nobody tells me anything.
>   *Repeatedly spoken by James Forsyte*
>   *in The Man of Property [1906]*
>   *and In Chancery [1920]*

20   Justice is a machine that, when someone has once given it the starting push, rolls on of itself.
>   *Justice [1910], act II*

21   Public opinion's always in advance of the law.
>   *Windows [1922], act I*

22   A man of action forced into a state of thought is unhappy until he can get out of it.
>   *Maid in Waiting [1931], ch. 3*

---

[1]See Horace, 96:5.

Kaethe [Schmidt] Kollwitz
1867–1945

1 I am gradually approaching the period in my life when work comes first.... No longer diverted by other emotions, I work the way a cow grazes.
Diary[1] *[April 1910]*

Luigi Pirandello
1867–1936

2 Six Characters in Search of an Author.
Title of play

3 Each of us — on the outside, in front of others — dresses in dignity, but inside himself he is well aware of these unconfessable things that pass through the secrecy of his heart.
Six Characters in Search of an Author[2] *[1921], act I*

4 Life is a very sad piece of buffoonery, because we have ... the need to fool ourselves continuously by the spontaneous creation of a reality (one for each and never the same for everyone) which, from time to time, reveals itself to be vain and illusory.
Autobiographical Sketch in Le Lettere, Rome[3] *[October 15, 1924]*

Henry L[ewis] Stimson
1867–1950

5 Gentlemen do not read each other's mail.[4]
On Active Service in Peace and War [1948]

Joseph Weber
1867–1942
and
Lew Fields
1867–1941

6 Who was that lady I saw you with last night? She ain't no lady; she's my wife.
Vaudeville routine [1887]

---

[1] Translated by RICHARD and CLARA WINSTON.

[2] Translated by MARK MUSA.

[3] Translated by WILLIAM MURRAY.

[4] Explaining his 1929 decision, as Secretary of State, to close down the department's codebreaking agency (the American "black chamber").

Wilbur Wright
1867–1912
and
Orville Wright
1871–1948

7 Success. Four flights Thursday morning. All against twenty-one-mile wind. Started from level with engine power alone. Average speed through air thirty-one miles. Longest fifty-nine seconds. Inform press. Home Christmas.
Telegram to the Reverend Milton Wright, from Kitty Hawk, N.C. [December 17, 1903]

Émile Auguste Chartier [Alain]
1868–1951

8 To think is to say *no*.
Le Citoyen Contre les Pouvoirs (The Citizen Against the Powers) [1926]

9 Nothing is more dangerous than an idea, when you have only one idea.
Propos sur la Religion (Comments on Religion) [1938]

Paul Claudel
1868–1955

10 You explain nothing, O poet, but thanks to you all things become explicable.   *La Ville [1897], act I*

11 When man tries to imagine Paradise on earth, the immediate result is a very respectable Hell.
Conversations dans le Loir-et-Cher [1929]

Norman Douglas
1868–1952

12 You can tell the ideals of a nation by its advertisements.   *South Wind [1917], ch. 7*

13 Many a man who thinks to found a home discovers that he has merely opened a tavern for his friends.   *South Wind, 24*

W[illiam] E[dward] B[urghardt] Du Bois
1868–1963

14 The problem of the twentieth century is the problem of the color line.
To the Nations of the World; address to Pan-African conference, London [1900]

1 Why did God make me an outcast and a stranger in mine own house?
The Souls of Black Folk [1903]

2 Herein lies the tragedy of the age: not that men are poor — all men know something of poverty; not that men are wicked — who is good? Not that men are ignorant — what is truth? Nay, but that men know so little of men. *The Souls of Black Folk*

3 It is a peculiar sensation, this double-consciousness, this sense of always looking at one's self through the eyes of others. . . . One feels his twoness — an American, a Negro; two Souls, two thoughts, two unreconciled strivings; two warring ideals in one dark body, whose dogged strength alone keeps it from being torn asunder.
The Souls of Black Folk

4 The Negro folk-song — the rhythmic cry of the slave — stands today not simply as the sole American music, but as the most beautiful expression of human experience born this side the seas. It has been neglected, it has been, and is, half despised, and above all it has been persistently mistaken and misunderstood; but notwithstanding, it still remains as the singular spiritual heritage of the nation and the greatest gift of the Negro people.
The Souls of Black Folk

5 The Talented Tenth of the Negro race must be made leaders of thought and missionaries of culture among their people. No others can do this work and Negro colleges must train men for it. The Negro race, like all other races, is going to be saved by its exceptional men.
The Talented Tenth [1903]

6 The cost of liberty is less than the price of repression.
John Brown [1909]. The Legacy of John Brown

7 The cause of war is preparation for war.
Of the Children of Peace [1914]

8 The discovery of personal whiteness among the world's peoples is a very modern thing — a nineteenth and twentieth century matter, indeed. The ancient world would have laughed at such a distinction. The Middle Age regarded skin color with mild curiosity; and even up into the eighteenth century we were hammering our national manikins into one, great, Universal Man, with fine frenzy which ignored color and race even more than birth. Today we have changed all that, and the world in a sudden, emotional conversion has discovered that it is white and by that token, wonderful!
*Darkwater [1920].
The Souls of White Folk*

9 The dark world is going to submit to its present treatment just as long as it must and not one moment longer. *Darkwater. The Souls of White Folk*

10 The return from your work must be the satisfaction which that work brings you and the world's need of that work. With this, life is heaven, or as near heaven as you can get. Without this — with work which you despise, which bores you, and which the world does not need — this life is hell.
*To His Newborn Great-Grandson;
address on his ninetieth birthday [1958]*

11 Believe in life! Always human beings will live and progress to greater, broader, and fuller life.
*Last message to the world [written 1957].
Read at his funeral [1963]*

John Nance Garner
1868–1967

12 The vice-presidency isn't worth a pitcher of warm piss. *Attributed*

Maxim Gorki[1]
[Aleksei Maksimovich Peshkov]
1868–1936

13 Let the storm rage ever stronger![2]
Song of a Stormy Petrel [1901]

14 Lies — there you have the religion of slaves and taskmasters.[3]
The Lower Depths [1903]

15 How marvelous is Man! How proud the word rings — Man! *The Lower Depths*

16 In time I came to understand that out of the misery and murk of their lives the Russian people had learned to make sorrow a diversion, to play with it like a child's toy; seldom are they diffident about showing their happiness. And so, through their tedious weekdays, they made a carnival of grief; a fire is entertainment; and on a vacant face a bruise becomes an adornment.
Autobiography [1913]. Childhood

17 The proletarian state must bring up thousands of excellent "mechanics of culture," "engineers of the soul."[4] *Speech at the Writers' Congress [1934]*

---

[1]Gorki, "the bitter one," was the writer's pseudonym for his first sketch in a Tiflis newspaper [1892].

[2]This became a rallying cry of the revolutionaries.

[3]The censor forbade this line to be spoken on the stage.

[4]Attributed to Joseph Stalin in conversation with Gorki [October 26, 1934].

1   The basic hero of our books should be labor; that is, man organized by the processes of labor.
Speech at the Writers' Congress

E[dward] V[errall] Lucas
1868–1938

2   The French never allow a distinguished son of France to lack a statue.
Wanderings and Diversions [1926].
Zigzags in France

3   Americans are people who prefer the Continent to their own country, but refuse to learn its languages.
Wanderings and Diversions.
The Continental Dictionary

Edmond Rostand
1868–1918

4 A great nose indicates a great man —
Genial, courteous, intellectual,
Virile, courageous.
Cyrano de Bergerac[1] *[1897], act I*

Robert Falcon Scott
1868–1912

5   Had we lived, I should have had a tale to tell of the hardihood, endurance, and courage of my companions which would have stirred the heart of every Englishman. These rough notes and our dead bodies must tell the tale.[2]
Diary of the Terra Nova Expedition to the Antarctic.[3] *Message to the Public*

6   [Concerning the South Pole:] Great God! this is an awful place.
Scott's Last Expedition: Journals
[January 17, 1912]

7   It was blowing a blizzard. He [Capt. Lawrence E. G. Oates] said, "I am just going outside and may be some time." He went out into the blizzard and we have not seen him since.
Scott's Last Expedition: Journals
[March 12, 1912]

8   Every day we have been ready to start for our depot *eleven miles* away, but outside the door of the tent it remains a scene of whirling drift. I do not think

we can hope for any better things now. We shall stick it out to the end, but we are getting weaker, of course, and the end cannot be far.

It seems a pity, but I do not think I can write more.
R. SCOTT
For God's sake look after our people.
Scott's Last Expedition: Journals
[Thursday, March 29, 1912 (last entry)]

Luther Standing Bear[4]
1868–1939

9   Only to the white man was nature a "wilderness" and only to him was the land "infested" with "wild" animals and "savage" people. To us it was tame. Earth was bountiful and we were surrounded with the blessings of the Great Mystery. Not until the hairy man from the east came and with brutal frenzy heaped injustices upon us and the families that we loved was it "wild" for us. When the very animals of the forest began fleeing from his approach, then it was that for us the "Wild West" began.
Land of the Spotted Eagle [1933]

William Allen White
1868–1944

10   What's the matter with Kansas?[5]
Emporia Gazette, Kansas [August 15, 1896]

11   Tinhorn politicians.
Emporia Gazette [October 25, 1901]

12   All dressed up, with nowhere to go.
Of the Progressive Party in 1916, after
Theodore Roosevelt retired from presidential
competition

13   The talent of a meat-packer, the morals of a moneychanger and the manners of an undertaker.
Obituary of Frank A. Munsey
[December 23, 1925]

Laurence Binyon
1869–1943

14 They shall grow not old, as we that are left grow old:
Age shall not weary them, nor the years condemn.
At the going down of the sun and in the morning
We will remember them.
For the Fallen [1914], st. 4

---

[1]Translated by BRIAN HOOKER.

[2]Inscribed on the memorial to Captain Scott and his companions, Waterloo Place, London.

[3]Found by search party [November 1912]. First published [1913] as *Scott's Last Expedition: Journals.*

[4]Chief of the Oglala Tribe of the Sioux Nation.

[5]Title of book [2004] by THOMAS FRANK [b. 1965].

Neville Chamberlain
1869–1940

1 For the second time in our history, a British Prime Minister has returned from Germany bringing peace with honor. I believe it is peace for our time.... Go home and get a nice quiet sleep.
Address from 10 Downing Street, London [September 30, 1938], after returning from the Munich Conference

2 Hitler has missed the bus.
Speech in the House of Commons [April 4, 1940]

Mohandas Karamchand [Mahatma] Gandhi[1]
1869–1948

3 Nonviolence is the first article of my faith. It is also the last article of my creed.
Defense against charge of sedition [March 23, 1922]

4 The term *Satyagraha* was coined by me...in order to distinguish it from the movement then going on...under the name of Passive Resistance.

Its root meaning is "holding on to truth," hence "force of righteousness." I have also called it love force or soul force. In the application of *Satyagraha,* I discovered in the earliest stages that pursuit of truth did not permit violence being inflicted on one's opponent, but that he must be weaned from error by patience and sympathy. For what appears truth to the one may appear to be error to the other. And patience means self-suffering. So the doctrine came to mean vindication of truth, not by the infliction of suffering on the opponent, but on one's self.[2]
Defense against charge of sedition [March 23, 1922]

5 Nonviolence and truth *(Satya)* are inseparable and presuppose one another. There is no god higher than truth.
True Patriotism: Some Sayings of Mahatma Gandhi [1939]

6 What difference does it make to the dead, the orphans, and the homeless, whether the mad destruction is wrought under the name of totalitarianism or the holy name of liberty or democracy?
Non-Violence in Peace and War, vol. I [1942]

André Gide
1869–1951

7 Families, I hate you! Shut-in homes, closed doors, jealous possessions of happiness.[3]
Les Nourritures Terrestres (Fruits of the Earth) [1897], bk. IV

8 What another would have done as well as you, do not do it. What another would have said as well as you, do not say it; written as well, do not write it. Be faithful to that which exists nowhere but in yourself— and thus make yourself indispensable.
Les Nourritures Terrestres. Envoi

9 The most decisive actions of our life...are most often unconsidered actions.
Les Faux Monnayeurs (The Counterfeiters) [1926]

10 It is with noble sentiments that bad literature gets written.[4]　*Letter to François Mauriac [1928]*

Strickland Gillilan
1869–1954

11 Adam
Had 'em.
Lines on the Antiquity of Microbes[5] [1904]

Emma Goldman
1869–1940

12 Crime is naught but misdirected energy.
Anarchism and Other Essays [1910]. Anarchism

13 The keynote of government is injustice.
Anarchism and Other Essays. Anarchism

14 Anarchism, then, really stands for the liberation of the human mind from the dominion of religion; the liberation of the human body from the shackles and restraints of government. Anarchism stands for a social order based on the free grouping of individuals for the purpose of producing real social wealth.
Anarchism and Other Essays. Anarchism

15 If I can't dance I don't want to be in your revolution.　*Attributed[6]*

---

[3]Familles, je vous hais! foyers clos; portes refermées; possessions jalouses du bonheur.

[4]C'est avec de beaux sentiments qu'on fait de la mauvaise littérature.

[5]Said to be the shortest poem in the language. Alternative title: *Fleas.*

[6]A T-shirt slogan [1973] compatible with Goldman's ideas but with no supporting source in her speeches or writings. See ALIX KATES SHULMAN, "Dances with Feminists," *The Women's Review of Books* [December 1991].

---

[1]Mahatma: Great Soul.

[2]See Martin Luther King, Jr., 823:10.

1   The greatest bulwark of capitalism is militarism.
Anarchism and Other Essays. Patriotism

Stephen [Butler] Leacock
1869–1944

2   He flung himself from the room, flung himself upon his horse and rode madly off in all directions.
Nonsense Novels [1911]. Gertrude the Governess

Edgar Lee Masters
1869–1950

3 All, all, are sleeping on the hill.
Spoon River Anthology [1915]. The Hill, refrain

4 Hear me, ambitious souls,
Sex is the curse of life!
Spoon River Anthology. Margaret Fuller Slack

5 Seeds in a dry pod, tick, tick, tick,
Tick, tick, tick, what little iambics,
While Homer and Whitman roared in the pines!
Spoon River Anthology. Petit, the Poet

6 Degenerate sons and daughters,
Life is too strong for you —
It takes life to love life.
Spoon River Anthology. Lucinda Matlock

7 Out of me unworthy and unknown
The vibrations of deathless music.
Spoon River Anthology. Anne Rutledge

8 I am Anne Rutledge who sleep beneath these weeds,
Beloved in life of Abraham Lincoln.
Spoon River Anthology. Anne Rutledge

Henri Matisse
1869–1954

9   I want to reach that state of condensation of sensations which constitutes a picture.
Notes d'un Peintre[1] *(Notes of a Painter) [1908]*

10   What interests me most is neither still life nor landscape, but the human figure. It is through it that I best succeed in expressing the almost religious feeling I have towards life.   *Notes d'un Peintre*

11   What I dream of is an art that is equilibrated, pure and calm, free of disturbing subject matter, an art that

can be for any intellectual worker, for the business man or the writer, a means of soothing the soul, something like a comfortable armchair in which one can rest from physical fatigue.
Notes d'un Peintre[2]

12   Exactitude Is Not Truth.
Title of essay [1947]

William Vaughn Moody
1869–1910

13   Gigantic, willful, young,
Chicago sitteth at the northwest gates.
An Ode in Time of Hesitation [1901], st. 3

14   O ye who lead,
Take heed!
Blindness we may forgive, but baseness we will
    smite.   *An Ode in Time of Hesitation, st. 9*

Edwin Arlington Robinson
1869–1935

15 I would have rid the earth of him
Once, in my pride.
I never knew the worth of him
Until he died.   *An Old Story [1897], st. 3*

16 Life is the game that must be played.
Ballade by the Fire [1897]. Envoy

17 There is ruin and decay
In the House on the Hill:
They are all gone away,
There is nothing more to say.
The House on the Hill [1897], last stanza

18 He glittered when he walked.
Richard Cory [1897], st. 2

19 So on we worked, and waited for the light,
And went without the meat, and cursed the bread;
And Richard Cory, one calm summer night,
Went home and put a bullet through his head.
Richard Cory, st. 4

20 Miniver Cheevy, child of scorn,
Grew lean while he assailed the seasons;
He wept that he was ever born,
And he had reasons.
Miniver Cheevy [1910], st. 1

21 Miniver Cheevy, born too late,
Scratched his head and kept on thinking;
Miniver coughed and called it fate,
And kept on drinking.   *Miniver Cheevy, st. 8*

---

[1]Translated by JACK D. FLAM.

[2]Translated by ALEXANDER ROMM.

1 I shall have more to say when I am dead.
John Brown [1920], last line

2 Here where the wind is always north-northeast
And children learn to walk on frozen toes.
New England [1923], st. 1

William Strunk, Jr.
1869–1946

3   Omit needless words.
   Vigorous writing is concise. A sentence should contain no unnecessary words, a paragraph no unnecessary sentences, for the same reason that a drawing should have no unnecessary lines and a machine no unnecessary parts. This requires not that the writer make all his sentences short, or that he avoid all detail and treat his subjects only in outline, but that every word tell.
The Elements of Style [1918], ch. 2, sec. 13

Booth Tarkington
1869–1946

4   There are two things that will be believed of any man whatsoever, and one of them is that he has taken to drink.   *Penrod [1914], ch. 10*

Frank Lloyd Wright
1869–1959

5   No house should ever be *on* any hill or on anything. It should be *of* the hill, belonging to it, so hill and house could live together each the happier for the other.   *An Autobiography [1932]*

6   The physician can bury his mistakes, but the architect can only advise his client to plant vines.
New York Times Magazine [October 4, 1953]

Bernard M[annes] Baruch
1870–1965

7   Behind the black portent of the new atomic age lies a hope which, seized upon with faith, can work out salvation.... Let us not deceive ourselves: we must elect world peace or world destruction.
Address to the United Nations Atomic Energy Commission [June 14, 1946]

8   We are in the midst of a cold war[1] which is getting warmer.
Speech before the Senate Committee [1948]

---

[1]The phrase was first used by Baruch in 1947.

Hilaire Belloc
1870–1953

9 Child! do not throw this book about;
Refrain from the unholy pleasure
Of cutting all the pictures out!
Preserve it as your chiefest treasure.
A Bad Child's Book of Beasts [1896], dedication

10 When people call this beast to mind,
They marvel more and more
At such a little tail behind,
So large a trunk before.
A Bad Child's Book of Beasts. The Elephant

11 The chief defect of Henry King
Was chewing little bits of string.
Cautionary Tales [1907]. Henry King

12 Matilda told such dreadful lies,
It made one gasp and stretch one's eyes;
Her aunt, who, from her earliest youth,
Had kept a strict regard for truth,
Attempted to believe Matilda:
The effort very nearly killed her.
Cautionary Tales. Matilda

13 For every time she shouted "Fire!"
They only answered "Little liar!"
And therefore when her aunt returned,
Matilda, and the house, were burned.
Cautionary Tales. Matilda

14 Here richly, with ridiculous display,
The Politician's corpse was laid away.
While all of his acquaintance sneered and slanged
I wept: for I had longed to see him hanged.
Epitaph on the Politician Himself [1923]

15 I'm tired of Love: I'm still more tired of Rhyme.
But Money gives me pleasure all the time.
Fatigue [1923]

16 Of this bad world the loveliest and the best
Has smiled and said "Good Night," and gone to
rest.   *On a Dead Hostess [1923]*

17 When I am dead, I hope it may be said:
"His sins were scarlet, but his books were read."
On His Books [1923]

18 How slow the shadow creeps: but when 'tis past
How fast the shadows fall. How fast! How fast!
On a Sundial [1938]

Benjamin Nathan Cardozo
1870–1938

19   Justice is not to be taken by storm. She is to be wooed by slow advances.
The Growth of the Law [1924]

1   What has once been settled by a precedent will not be unsettled overnight, for certainty and uniformity are gains not lightly to be sacrificed.
The Paradoxes of Legal Science [1928]

2   As I search the archives of my memory, I seem to discern six types or methods [of judicial writing] which divide themselves from one another with measurable distinctness. There is the type magisterial or imperative; the type laconic or sententious; the type conversational or homely; the type refined or artificial, smelling of the lamp, verging at times upon preciosity or euphuism; the type demonstrative or persuasive; and finally the type tonsorial or agglutinative, so called from the shears and the pastepot which are its implements and emblem.
Law and Literature [1931]

3   [The Constitution] was framed upon the theory that the peoples of the several states must sink or swim together, and that in the long run prosperity and salvation are in union and not division.
Baldwin v. Seelig, 294 U.S. 511, 523 [1935]

4   Freedom of expression is the matrix, the indispensable condition, of nearly every other form of freedom.
Palko v. Connecticut, 302 U.S. 319, 327 [1937]

Lord Alfred Bruce Douglas
1870–1945

5   I am the Love that dare not speak its name.
Two Loves [1894]

Arthur J. Lamb
1870–1928

6 Her beauty was sold for an old man's gold,
She's a bird in a gilded cage.
A Bird in a Gilded Cage [1900]

Sir Harry Lauder
1870–1950

7   I Love a Lassie.   *Title of song [1905]*

8   Roamin' in the Gloamin'.
Title of song [1910]

9 Oh, it's nice to get up in the mornin',
But it's nicer to lie in bed.
It's Nice to Get Up in the Mornin'
[1913]

Vladimir Ilyich Lenin
[Vladimir Ilyich Ulyanov]
1870–1924

10   "The revolution's decisive victory over tsarism" means the establishment of the *revolutionary-democratic dictatorship of the proletariat and the peasantry.*
Two Tactics of Social-Democracy [1905], ch. 6

11   We shall now proceed to construct the socialist order.
Speech at the Congress of Soviets[1]
[October 26, 1917]

12   Every cook has to learn how to govern the state.
Will the Bolsheviks Retain Government Power? [1917]

13   The war is relentless: it puts the alternative in a ruthless relief: either to perish, or to catch up with the advanced countries and outdistance them, too, in economic matters.
The Impending Catastrophe and How to Fight It [1917]

14   The suppression of the bourgeois state by the proletarian state is impossible without a violent revolution.   *The State and Revolution [1918], ch. 1*

15   So long as the state exists there is no freedom. When there is freedom, there will be no state.
The State and Revolution, 5

16   Communism is Soviet government plus the electrification of the whole country.
New External and Internal Position and the Problems of the Party [1920]

17   It is true that liberty is precious — so precious that it must be rationed.
Attributed. Quoted by SIDNEY *[1859–1947]* AND BEATRICE *[1858–1943]* WEBB, *Soviet Communism: A New Civilization? [1936]*

Adolf Loos
1870–1933

18   Cultural evolution is synonymous with the removal of ornament from articles in daily use.
Ornament and Crime [1908]

Rosa Luxemburg
1870–1919

19   I hope to die at my post: in the streets or in prison.   *Letter from prison [c. 1917]*

---

[1]Translated by MAX EASTMAN.

1   Freedom is always freedom for the one who thinks differently.

The Russian Revolution [1922]

Watty Piper
[Mabel Caroline Bragg]
1870–1945

2   I think I can. I think I can. I think I can.

The Little Engine That Could [1930]

Roscoe Pound
1870–1964

3   The law must be stable, but it must not stand still.

Introduction to the Philosophy of Law [1922]

Saki
[Hector Hugh Munro]
1870–1916

4   The cook was a good cook, as cooks go; and as cooks go she went.

Reginald [1904]. Reginald on Besetting Sins

5   Women and elephants never forget an injury.

Reginald. Reginald on Besetting Sins

6   I might have been a goldfish in a glass bowl for all the privacy I got.

Reginald. The Innocence of Reginald

7 Sredni Vashtar went forth,
His thoughts were red thoughts and his teeth were white.
His enemies called for peace, but he brought them death.
Sredni Vashtar the Beautiful.

The Chronicles of Clovis. Sredni Vashtar

8   The sacrifices of friendship were beautiful in her eyes as long as she was not asked to make them.

Beasts and Super-Beasts [1914]. Fur

9   A little inaccuracy sometimes saves tons of explanation.

The Square Egg [1924]. Clovis on the Alleged Romance of Business

10   I hate babies. They're so human — they remind one of monkeys.

The Watered Pot [1924]

T. Laurence Seibert
1877–1917

11 Casey Jones! Orders in his hand.
Casey Jones! Mounted to the cabin,
Took his farewell journey to that promised land.

Casey Jones [1902][1]

Stephen Crane
1871–1900

12   The cold passed reluctantly from the earth, and the retiring fogs revealed an army stretched out on the hills, resting. As the landscape changed from brown to green, the army awakened, and began to tremble with eagerness at the noise of rumors.

The Red Badge of Courage [1895], opening sentences

13   They were going to look at war, the red animal — war, the blood-swollen god.

The Red Badge of Courage, ch. 3

14   At times he regarded the wounded soldiers in an envious way. He conceived persons with torn bodies to be peculiarly happy. He wished that he, too, had a wound, a red badge of courage.

The Red Badge of Courage, 9

15   The red sun was pasted in the sky like a wafer.

The Red Badge of Courage, 9

16   He had fought like a pagan who defends his religion.

The Red Badge of Courage, 17

17   He had been to touch the great death, and found that, after all, it was but the great death. He was a man.   *The Red Badge of Courage, 24*

18   None of them knew the color of the sky.

The Open Boat [1897], first line

19 In the desert
I saw a creature, naked, bestial,
Who, squatting upon the ground,
Held his heart in his hands,
And ate of it.
I said, "Is it good, friend?"

---

[1]Adapted from verses by WALLACE SAUNDERS. Music by EDDIE NEWTON [1869–1915].

Of the many versions of this traditional ballad, the most familiar is printed in CARL SANDBURG, *The American Songbag* [1927]. It begins: Come all you rounders, for I want you to hear / The story of a brave engineer. / Casey Jones was the rounder's name, / On a big eight-wheeler of a mighty fame.

"For I'm going to run till she leaves the rail — or make it on time with the southbound mail." — *Inscription on monument to* JOHN LUTHER "CASEY" JONES [1864–1900], *in Calvary Cemetery, Jackson, Tennessee*

"It is bitter — bitter," he answered;
"But I like it
"Because it is bitter,
"And because it is my heart."[1]
The Black Riders [1895], III

1 Should the wide world roll away
  Leaving black terror
  Limitless night,
  Nor God, nor man, nor place to stand
  Would be to me essential
  If thou and thy white arms were there
  And the fall to doom a long way.
  The Black Riders, X

2 Do not weep, maiden, for war is kind.
  Because your lover threw wild hands toward the sky
  And the affrighted steed ran on alone,
  Do not weep.
  War is kind.
  War Is Kind [1899]. War Is Kind, st. 1

3 A man said to the universe:
  "Sir, I exist!"
  "However," replied the universe,
  "The fact has not created in me
  A sense of obligation."
  War Is Kind. War Is Kind, fragment

W[illiam] H[enry] Davies
1871–1940

4 What is this life if, full of care,
  We have no time to stand and stare?
  Leisure [1911]

Theodore Dreiser
1871–1945

5   When a girl leaves her home at eighteen, she does one of two things. Either she falls into saving hands and becomes better, or she rapidly assumes the cosmopolitan standard of virtue and becomes worse.
Sister Carrie [1900], ch. 1

6   The city has its cunning wiles, no less than the infinitely smaller and more human tempter. There are large forces which allure with all the soulfulness of expression possible in the most cultured human. The gleam of a thousand lights is often as effective as the persuasive light in a wooing and fascinating eye.
Sister Carrie, 1

7   Our civilization is still in a middle stage, scarcely beast, in that it is no longer wholly guided by instinct; scarcely human, in that it is not yet wholly guided by reason.
Sister Carrie, 8

8   In your rocking chair by your window shall you dream such happiness as you may never feel.
Sister Carrie, 50

9   An American Tragedy.   *Title of novel [1925]*

10 Oh, the moonlight's fair tonight along the Wabash,
   From the fields there comes the breath of new-mown hay;
   Through the sycamores the candle lights are gleaming
   On the banks of the Wabash, far away.
   On the Banks of the Wabash[2] [1897], chorus

Arthur Guiterman
1871–1943

11 Amoebas at the start
   Were not complex;
   They tore themselves apart
   And started Sex.   *Sex [1923], st. 1*

12 Of all cold words of tongue or pen
   The worst are these: "I knew him when — "[3]
   Prophets in Their Own Country [1927]

Ralph Hodgson
1871–1962

13 I saw in vision
   The worm in the wheat,
   And in the shops nothing
   For people to eat;
   Nothing for sale in
   Stupidity Street.
   Stupidity Street [1913], st. 2

14 Time, you old gypsy man,
   Will you not stay,
   Put up your caravan
   Just for one day?
   Time, You Old Gypsy Man [1916], st. 1

James Weldon Johnson
1871–1938

15 We have come over a way that with tears has been watered,

---

[1]*Because It Is Bitter, and Because It Is My Heart* [1990] is a novel by JOYCE CAROL OATES [b. 1938].

[2]Likely written by Dreiser but credited to his songwriter brother, PAUL DRESSER. See 568:15.

[3]See John Greenleaf Whittier, 438:10.

We have come, treading our path through the blood
of the slaughtered.
Lift Every Voice and Sing [1900], st. 2

1   The colored people of this country know and
understand the white people better than the white
people know and understand them.
*The Autobiography of an Ex-Colored Man
[1912], ch. 2*

2   Every race and every nation should be judged by
the best it has been able to produce, not by the worst.
*The Autobiography of an Ex-Colored
Man, 10*

3   Your arm's too short to box with God.
*The Autobiography of an
Ex-Colored Man, 10*

4 O black and unknown bards of long ago,
How came your lips to touch the sacred fire?
How, in your darkness, did you come to know
The power and beauty of the minstrels' lyre?
O Black and Unknown Bards [1917], st. 1

5 And God stepped out on space,
And He looked around and said,
"I'm lonely —
I'll make me a world."
God's Trombones [1927]. The Creation, st. 1

6 With His head in His hands,
God thought and thought,
Till He thought: I'll make me a man!
God's Trombones. The Creation, st. 10

7   Find Sister Caroline . . .
And she's tired —
She's weary —
Go down, Death, and bring her to me.
God's Trombones. Go Down, Death, st. 5

8   It is from the blues that all that may be called
American music derives its most distinctive characteristic.   *Black Manhattan [1930], ch. 11*

Herbert George Ponting
1871–1935

9 On the outside grows the furside, on the inside grows
the skinside;
So the furside is the outside, and the skinside is the
inside.[1]   *The Sleeping Bag[2] [1911]*

---

[1]He, to get the cold side outside, / Put the warm side fur side
inside. / That's why he put the fur side inside, / Why he put the
skin side outside, / Why he turned them inside outside. — GEORGE
A. STRONG [1832–1922], *The Modern Hiawatha* [1856]

[2]For the *South Polar Times*, Midwinter Day [June 22, 1911],
prepared by the men of Captain Robert Falcon Scott's last Antarctic
expedition. Ponting was the photographer for the Scott expedition.

Marcel Proust
1871–1922

10   On no days of our childhood did we live so fully
perhaps as those we thought we had left behind
without living them, those that we spent with a
favorite book.   *On Reading [1905]*

11   For a long time I used to go to bed early.[3]
*Remembrance of Things Past[4] [1913–1927].
Swann's Way, opening line*

12   The facts of life do not penetrate to the sphere in
which our beliefs are cherished; as it was not they that
engendered those beliefs, so they are powerless to
destroy them.
*Remembrance of Things Past.
Swann's Way*

13   Once I had recognized the taste of the crumb of
madeleine soaked in her decoction of lime flowers
which my aunt used to give me . . . immediately the
old gray house upon the street, where her room was,
rose up like the scenery of a theater.
*Remembrance of Things Past.
Swann's Way*

14   In his younger days a man dreams of possessing
the heart of the woman whom he loves; later, the
feeling that he possesses the heart of a woman may
be enough to make him fall in love with her.
*Remembrance of Things Past.
Swann's Way*

15   What artists call posterity is the posterity of the
work of art.
*Remembrance of Things Past.
Within a Budding Grove, pt. I*

16   Not only does one not retain all at once the truly
rare works, but even within such works it is the least
precious parts that one perceives first. Less deceptive
than life, these great masterpieces do not give us their
best at the beginning.
*Remembrance of Things Past.
Within a Budding Grove, I*

17   The time which we have at our disposal every day
is elastic; the passions that we feel expand it, those that
we inspire contract it; and habit fills up what remains.
*Remembrance of Things Past.
Within a Budding Grove, I*

18   All the great things we know have come to us
from neurotics. It is they and only they who have
founded religions and created great works of art.
*Remembrance of Things Past. The
Guermantes Way. My Grandmother's Illness*

---

[3]*Longtemps je me suis couché de bonne heure.*

[4]*À la Recherche du Temps Perdu*, translated by C. K. SCOTT
MONCRIEFF unless otherwise noted.

1   Like everybody who is not in love, he imagined that one chose the person whom one loved after endless deliberations and on the strength of various qualities and advantages.

> *Remembrance of Things Past.*
> *Cities of the Plain, pt. I*

2   They buried him, but all through the night of mourning, in the lighted windows, his books arranged three by three kept watch like angels with outspread wings and seemed, for him who was no more, the symbol of his resurrection.

> *Remembrance of Things Past.*
> *The Captive, pt. I*

3   The bonds that unite another person to ourself exist only in our mind. Memory as it grows fainter relaxes them, and notwithstanding the illusion by which we would fain be cheated and with which, out of love, friendship, politeness, deference, duty, we cheat other people, we exist alone. Man is the creature that cannot emerge from himself, that knows his fellows only in himself; when he asserts the contrary, he is lying.

> *Remembrance of Things Past.*
> *The Sweet Cheat Gone*

4   There is not a woman in the world the possession of whom is as precious as that of the truths which she reveals to us by causing us to suffer.

> *Remembrance of Things Past.*
> *The Sweet Cheat Gone*

5   We are healed of a suffering only by experiencing it to the full.

> *Remembrance of Things Past.*
> *The Sweet Cheat Gone*

6   Happiness is beneficial for the body but it is grief that develops the powers of the mind.

> *Remembrance of Things Past.*
> *The Past Recaptured*[1]

7   In reality every reader is, while he is reading, the reader of his own self. The writer's work is merely a kind of optical instrument which he offers to the reader to enable him to discern what, without this book, he would perhaps never have perceived in himself.

> *Remembrance of Things Past.*
> *Time Regained*[2]

8   Only through art can we get outside of ourselves and know another's view of the universe which is not the same as ours and see landscapes which would otherwise have remained unknown to us like the landscapes of the moon. Thanks to art, instead of seeing a single world, our own, we see it multiply until we have before us as many worlds as there are original artists.

> *The Maxims of Marcel Proust*[3] *[1948]*

9   A book is the product of a different *self* from the self we manifest in our habits, in our social life, in our vices.

> *Contre Sainte-Beuve [1954]. The Method*
> *of Sainte-Beuve*[4]

Ernest Rutherford
1871–1937

10   We cannot control atomic energy to an extent which would be of any value commercially, and I believe we are not likely ever to be able to do so.

> *Speech to the British Association for the*
> *Advancement of Science [1933]*

John Millington Synge
1871–1909

11   What is the price of a thousand horses against a son where there is one son only?

> *Riders to the Sea [1904]*

12   They're all gone now, and there isn't anything more the sea can do to me.

> *Riders to the Sea*

13   When I was writing *The Shadow of the Glen* . . . I got more aid than any learning could have given me from a chink in the floor of the old Wicklow house where I was staying, that let me hear what was being said by the servant girls in the kitchen.

> *The Playboy of the Western World [1907],*
> *preface*

14   May I meet him with one tooth and it aching, and one eye to be seeing seven and seventy divils in the twists of the road, and one old timber leg on him to limp into the scalding grave. There he is now crossing the strands, and that the Lord God would send a high wave to wash him from the world.[5]

> *The Playboy of the Western World,*
> *act II*

---

[1]Translated by Frederick A. Blossom.

[2]Translated by C. K. Scott Moncrieff and Terence Kilmartin.

[3]Edited and translated by Justin O'Brien.

[4]Translated by Sylvia Townsend Warner.

[5]May the grass grow at your door and the fox build his nest on your hearthstone. May the light fade from your eyes, so you never see what you love. May your own blood rise against you, and the sweetest drink you take be the bitterest cup of sorrow. May you die without benefit of clergy; may there be none to shed a tear at your grave, and may the hearthstone of hell be your best bed forever. — *Traditional Wexford curse*

1 Oh my grief, I've lost him surely. I've lost the only Playboy of the Western World.
> *The Playboy of the Western World, III, curtain line*

2 A man who is not afraid of the sea will soon be drowned, he said, for he will be going out on a day he shouldn't. But we do be afraid of the sea, and we do only be drownded now and again.
> *The Aran Islands [1907]*

3 There is no language like the Irish for soothing and quieting.
> *The Aran Islands*

Paul Valéry
1871–1945

4 The folly of mistaking a paradox for a discovery, a metaphor for a proof, a torrent of verbiage for a spring of capital truths, and oneself for an oracle, is inborn in us.
> *Introduction to the Method of Leonardo da Vinci*[1] *[1895]*

5 Collect all the facts that can be collected about the life of Racine and you will never learn from them the art of his verse. All criticism is dominated by the outworn theory that the man is the cause of the work as in the eyes of the law the criminal is the cause of the crime. Far rather are they both the effects.
> *Introduction to the Method of Leonardo da Vinci*

6 The sea, the ever renewing sea![2]
> *Charmes [1922]. Le Cimetière Marin (Graveyard by the Sea)*

7 The wind is rising . . . we must attempt to live.[3]
> *Charmes. Le Cimetière Marin*

8 Poetry is simply literature reduced to the essence of its active principle. It is purged of idols of every kind, of realistic illusions, of any conceivable equivocation between the language of "truth" and the language of "creation."
> *Littérature [1930]*

9 Just as water, gas, and electricity are brought into our houses from far off to satisfy our needs in response to a minimal effort, so we shall be supplied with visual or auditory images, which will appear and disappear at a simple movement of the hand, hardly more than a sign.
> *Pieces on Art*[4] *[1934]. The Conquest of Ubiquity*

10 An intelligent woman is a woman with whom one can be as stupid as one wants.
> *Mauvaises Pensées et Autres (Wicked Thoughts and Others) [1941]*

11 That which has always been accepted by everyone, everywhere, is almost certain to be false.
> *Tel Quel*[5] *[1941–1943]*

12 Politeness is organized indifference.
> *Tel Quel*

13 Politics is the art of preventing people from minding their own business.
> *Tel Quel*

14 A poem is never finished, only abandoned.
> *From W. H.* AUDEN, *A Certain World [1970]*

Sir Max Beerbohm
1872–1956

15 Most women are not so young as they are painted.
> *A Defense of Cosmetics [1894]*

16 To give an accurate and exhaustive account of that period would need a far less brilliant pen than mine.
> *Eighteen Eighty [1895]*

17 She was one of the people who say: "I don't know anything about music really, but I know what I like."
> *Zuleika Dobson [1911], ch. 9*

18 Of all the objects of hatred, a woman once loved is the most hateful. *Zuleika Dobson, 13*

19 I have known no man of genius who had not to pay, in some affliction or defect either physical or spiritual, for what the gods had given him.
> *No. 2. The Pines [1914]*

20 To say that a man is vain means merely that he is pleased with the effect he produces on other people. A conceited man is satisfied with the effect he produces on himself.
> *Quia Imperfectum [1918]*

21 Anywhere but in England it would be impossible for two solitary men, howsoever much reduced by influenza, to spend five or six days in the same hostel and not exchange a single word. This is one of the charms of England.
> *Seven Men [1919]. A. V. Laider*

---

[1] Translated by THOMAS MCGREEVY.

[2] La mer, la mer toujours recommencée!

[3] Le vent se lève . . . il faut tenter de vivre.

[4] Translated by RALPH MANHEIM.

---

[5] Translated by STUART GILBERT.

1   Strange, when you come to think of it, that of all the countless folk who have lived before our time on this planet not one is known in history or in legend as having died of laughter.

Laughter [1920]

2   Good sense about trivialities is better than nonsense about things that matter.

An Inquiry into a Convention
[Saturday Review, December 19, 1903]

Patrick Reginald Chalmers
1872–1942

3   What's lost upon the roundabouts we pulls up on the swings![1]

Roundabouts and Swings [1912],
st. 2

Calvin Coolidge
1872–1933

4   There is no right to strike against the public safety by anybody, anywhere, any time.

Telegram to Samuel Gompers, president
of the American Federation of Labor,
on the Boston police strike
[September 14, 1919]

5   Civilization and profits go hand in hand.

Speech in New York City
[November 27, 1920]

6   The chief business of the American people is business.

Speech to the American Society of Newspaper
Editors [January 17, 1925]

7   I do not choose to run for President in 1928.

Statement to reporters
[August 2, 1927]

8   He said he was against it.

On being asked what a clergyman preaching
on sin had said

9   They hired the money, didn't they?

Attributed. Comment on European war
debts [1925]

10   When a great many people are unable to find work, unemployment results.

Attributed

[Edward] Gordon Craig
1872–1966

11   That is what the title of artist means: one who perceives more than his fellows, and who records more than he has seen.

On the Art of the Theatre [1911]

Sergei Pavlovich Diaghilev
1872–1929

12   Astound me! I'll wait for you to astound me.
To Jean Cocteau [1912].
From Jean Cocteau, *Journals [1956], ch. 1*

Paul Laurence Dunbar
1872–1906

13   It is not a carol of joy or glee,
But a prayer that he sends from his heart's deep core . . .
I know why the caged bird sings![2]

Sympathy [1899], st. 3

14   Since thou[3] and those who died with thee for right
Have died, the Present teaches, but in vain!
Robert Gould Shaw [1900], st. 2

15   It's easy 'nough to titter w'en de stew is smokin' hot,
But hit's mighty ha'd to giggle w'en dey's nuffin' in de pot.

Philosophy [1903], st. 4

Learned Hand
1872–1961

16   Our procedure has always been haunted by the ghost of the innocent man convicted. It is an unreal dream. What we need to fear is the archaic formalism and the watery sentiment that obstructs, delays, and defeats the prosecution of crime.

United States v. Garsson [1923]

17   Any one may so arrange his affairs that his taxes shall be as low as possible; he is not bound to choose that pattern which will best pay the Treasury; there is not even a patriotic duty to increase one's taxes.

Helvering v. Gregory [1934]

---

[1]A fairground saying.
What you lose on the swings, you make up on the roundabouts.
—P. G. Wodehouse, *Psmith in the City* [1910], *ch. 26.*

[2]Title of autobiography [1969] by Maya Angelou [b. 1928].

[3]Colonel Robert Gould Shaw, white commander of the 54th Massachusetts regiment (first enlisted black regiment in the Civil War), died with many others of the regiment at Fort Wagner [July 18, 1863].
See Charles W. Eliot, 519:10, and Robert Lowell, 787:19.

1   This much I think I do know — that a society so riven that the spirit of moderation is gone, no court *can* save; that a society where that spirit flourishes, no court *need* save; that in a society which evades its responsibility by thrusting upon the courts the nurture of that spirit, that spirit in the end will perish.
The Contribution of an Independent Judiciary to Civilization [1942]

2   "I beseech ye in the bowels of Christ, think that ye may be mistaken."[1] I should like to have that written over the portals of every church, every school, and every courthouse, and, may I say, of every legislative body in the United States. I should like to have every court begin, "I beseech ye in the bowels of Christ, think that we may be mistaken."
Morals in Public Life [1951]

3   I had rather take my chance that some traitors will escape detection than spread abroad a spirit of general suspicion and distrust, which accepts rumor and gossip in place of undismayed and unintimidated inquiry.
Speech to the Board of Regents, University of the State of New York [October 24, 1952]

4   That community is already in the process of dissolution where each man begins to eye his neighbor as a possible enemy, where nonconformity with the accepted creed, political as well as religious, is a mark of disaffection; where denunciation, without specification or backing, takes the place of evidence; where orthodoxy chokes freedom of dissent; where faith in the eventual supremacy of reason has become so timid that we dare not enter our convictions in the open lists, to win or lose.
Speech to the Board of Regents, University of the State of New York [October 24, 1952]

Wee Willie Keeler
[William Henry O'Kelleher]
1872–1923

5   Hit 'em where they ain't.
Attributed in The Brooklyn Eagle [July 29, 1901]

John McCrae
1872–1918

6 In Flanders fields the poppies blow
Between the crosses, row on row.
In Flanders Fields [1915], st. 1

7 Take up our quarrel with the foe;
To you from failing hands we throw
The Torch: be yours to hold it high!
If ye break faith with us who die
We shall not sleep, though poppies grow
In Flanders fields.   *In Flanders Fields, st. 3*

Bertrand Russell, Earl Russell
1872–1970

8   Mathematics may be defined as the subject in which we never know what we are talking about, nor whether what we are saying is true.
Recent Work on the Principles of Mathematics [1901]. In International Monthly, vol. 4

9   Mathematics, rightly viewed, possesses not only truth, but supreme beauty — a beauty cold and austere, like that of sculpture, without appeal to any part of our weaker nature, without the gorgeous trappings of painting or music, yet sublimely pure, and capable of a stern perfection such as only the greatest art can show.   *The Study of Mathematics [1902]*

10   Mathematics takes us still further from what is human, into the region of absolute necessity, to which not only the actual world, but every possible world, must conform.   *The Study of Mathematics*

11   I shall rot and nothing of my ego will survive.
What I Believe [1925]

12   I say quite deliberately that the Christian religion, as organized in its churches, has been and still is the principal enemy of moral progress in the world.
Why I Am Not a Christian [1927]

13   It is undesirable to believe a proposition when there is no ground whatever for supposing it to be true.   *Skeptical Essays [1928], ch. 1*

14   It seems to be the fate of idealists to obtain what they have struggled for in a form which destroys their ideals.   *Marriage and Morals [1929], ch. 7*

15   Very few men and women who have had a conventional upbringing have learnt to feel decently about sex and marriage. Their education has taught them that deceitfulness and lying are considered virtues by parents and teachers; that sexual relations, even within marriage, are more or less disgusting, and that in propagating the species men are yielding to their animal nature while women are submitting to a painful duty.   *Marriage and Morals, 8*

16   To fear love is to fear life, and those who fear are already three parts dead.   *Marriage and Morals, 19*

17   The psychology of adultery has been falsified by conventional morals, which assume, in monogamous

---

[1]See Oliver Cromwell, 246:16.

countries, that attraction to one person cannot coexist with a serious affection for another. Everybody knows that this is untrue.

Marriage and Morals, 16

1   Fear is the main source of superstition, and one of the main sources of cruelty. To conquer fear is the beginning of wisdom.

Unpopular Essays [1950].
An Outline of Intellectual Rubbish

2   The most savage controversies are those about matters as to which there is no good evidence either way. Persecution is used in theology, not in arithmetic, because in arithmetic there is knowledge, but in theology only opinion.

Unpopular Essays.
An Outline of Intellectual Rubbish

Harlan Fiske Stone
1872–1946

3   While unconstitutional exercise of power by the executive and legislative branches of the government is subject to judicial restraint, the only check upon our own exercise of power is our own sense of self-restraint. For the removal of unwise laws from the statute books appeal lies not to the courts but to the ballot and to the processes of democratic government.

Dissent in United States v. Butler,
297 U.S. 1 [1936]

Carl [Lotus] Becker
1873–1945

4   Economic distress will teach men, if anything can, that realities are less dangerous than fancies, that fact-finding is more effective than fault-finding.

Progress and Power [1935]

George Bennard
1873–1958

5 I will cling to the old rugged cross,
And exchange it some day for a crown.

The Old Rugged Cross [1913], refrain

Willa [Sibert] Cather
1873–1947

6   One cannot divine nor forecast the conditions that will make happiness; one only stumbles upon them by chance, in a lucky hour, at the world's end somewhere, and holds fast to the days, as to fortune or fame.

Le Lavandou [1902]

7   There are only two or three human stories, and they go on repeating themselves as fiercely as if they had never happened before.

O Pioneers![1] [1913], pt. II, ch. 4

8   The history of every country begins in the heart of a man or a woman.

O Pioneers!, II, 4

9   I like trees because they seem more resigned to the way they have to live than other things do.

O Pioneers!, II, 8

10   I tell you there is such a thing as creative hate!

The Song of the Lark [1915], pt. I

11   If there was a road I could not make it out in the faint starlight. There was nothing but land: not a country at all, but the material out of which countries are made.

My Ántonia [1918], bk. I, ch. 1

12   That is happiness; to be dissolved into something complete and great.[2]

My Ántonia, I, 2

13   Winter lies too long in country towns; hangs on until it is stale and shabby, old and sullen.

My Ántonia, II, 7

14   Whatever we had missed, we possessed together the precious, the incommunicable past.

My Ántonia, final line

15   Only solitary men know the full joys of friendship. Others have their family; but to a solitary and an exile his friends are everything.

Shadows on the Rock [1931], bk. III, ch. 5

Arthur Chapman
1873–1935

16 Out where the handclasp's a little stronger,
Out where the smile dwells a little longer,
That's where the West begins.

Out Where the West Begins [1917], st. 1

Colette [Sidonie Gabrielle Colette]
1873–1954

17   The eyes of women followed his progress with silent homage, the more candid among them bestowing that passing stupefaction which can be neither feigned nor hidden.

Chéri[3] [1920]

18   Whether you are dealing with an animal or a child, to convince is to weaken.

Le Pur et l'Impur [1932]

---

[1]See Walt Whitman, 487:4.

[2]Inscribed on Willa Cather's gravestone in Jaffrey Center, New Hampshire.

[3]Translated by ROGER SENHOUSE.

1 It was towards the end of June that incompatibility became established between them like a new season of the year. *The Cat [1933], ch. 7*

2 Those pleasures so lightly called physical. *Mélanges [1939]*

3 One of the best things about love is just recognizing a man's step when he climbs the stairs. *Occupation[1] [1941]*

4 The three great stumbling blocks in a girl's education...*homard a l'Américaine,*[2] a boiled egg, and asparagus. *Gigi [1944]*

5 The day after that wedding night I found that a distance of a thousand miles, abyss and discovery and irremediable metamorphosis, separated me from the day before. *Noces [1944]*

Walter de la Mare
1873–1956

6 "Is there anybody there?" said the Traveler,
Knocking on the moonlit door;
And his horse in the silence champed the grasses
Of the forest's ferny floor. *The Listeners [1912]*

7 "Tell them that I came, and no one answered,
That I kept my word," he said. *The Listeners*

8 Nought but vast sorrow was there —
The sweet cheat gone. *The Ghost [1912]*

9 Who said "Peacock Pie"?
The old king to the sparrow:
Who said "Crops are ripe"?
Rust to the harrow. *The Song of the Mad Prince [1913]*

10 Poor Jim Jay
Got stuck fast
In Yesterday. *Jim Jay [1913]*

11 It's a very odd thing —
As odd as can be —
That whatever Miss T. eats
Turns into Miss T. *Miss T. [1913]*

12 Slowly, silently, now the moon
Walks the night in her silver shoon. *Silver [1913]*

Ford Madox [Hueffer] Ford
1873–1939

13 A fervent young admirer exclaimed: "By Jove, the Good Soldier is the finest novel in the English language!" whereupon my friend John Rodker, who has always had a properly tempered admiration for my work, remarked in his clear, slow drawl: "Ah, yes. It is, but you have left out a word. It is the finest French novel in the English language!" *The Good Soldier [1915]. Dedicatory letter*

14 This is the saddest story I have ever heard. *The Good Soldier, first line*

15 Only two classes of books are of universal appeal: the very best and the very worst. *Joseph Conrad [1924]*

16 No more Hope, no more Glory, no more parades for you and me.... Na poo, finny![3] *No More Parades [1925]*

Lena Guilbert Ford
d. 1918

17 Keep the home fires burning,[4]
While your hearts are yearning;
Though your lads are far away
They dream of home.
There's a silver lining
Through the dark cloud shining;
Turn the dark cloud inside out,
Till the boys come home. *Keep the Home Fires Burning [1915]*

Ellen Glasgow
1873–1945

18 No idea is so antiquated that it was not once modern. No idea is so modern that it will not someday be antiquated. *Address to the Modern Language Association [1936]*

19 Preserve, within a wild sanctuary, an inaccessible valley of reveries. *A Certain Measure [1943]*

W[illiam] C[hristopher] Handy
1873–1958

20 I hate to see the evenin' sun go down. *The St. Louis Blues [1914]*

---

[1]Translated by DAVID LE VAY.

[2]Lobster cooked in the American style.

[3]World War I slang version of Il n'y a plus, fini.

[4]First line attributed to IVOR NOVELLO [1893–1951], who composed the music.

Otto Harbach
1873–1963

1 When a lovely flame dies,
Smoke gets in your eyes.
Roberta[1] [1933]. Smoke Gets in Your Eyes

Alfred Jarry
1873–1907

2 Hey! Not so fast, or we might arrive on time. Freedom means never arriving on time—never, never!
*Ubu Roi (Ubu the King)[2] [1896],
act I, sc. ii*

G[eorge] E[dward] Moore
1873–1958

3 It appears to me that in Ethics, as in all other philosophical studies, the difficulties and disagreements, of which history is full, are mainly due to a very simple cause: namely to the attempt to answer questions, without first discovering precisely *what* question it is which you desire to answer.
Principia Ethica [1903], preface

Charles Péguy
1873–1914

4 Surrender is essentially an operation by means of which we set about explaining instead of acting.
Les Cahiers de la Quinzaine [1905]

5 Everything begins in mysticism and ends in politics.[3] *Notre Jeunesse (Our Youth) [1910]*

6 Freedom is a system based on courage.
*From Daniel Halévy [1872–1962],
Life of Charles Péguy [1918]*

Emily Post
1873–1960

7 Ideal conversation must be an exchange of thought, and not, as many of those who worry most about their shortcomings believe, an eloquent exhibition of wit or oratory. *Etiquette [1922]*

8 To do exactly as your neighbors do is the only sensible rule. *Etiquette*

Sime Silverman
1873–1933

9 Wall St. Lays an Egg.
*Headline announcing stock market crash,
Variety [October 30, 1929]*

Alfred [Emanuel] Smith[4]
1873–1944

10 The kiss of death.
*Alluding to William Randolph Hearst's
support of Ogden Mills, Smith's unsuccessful
opponent for governor of New York State
[1926]*

11 Let's look at the record.
Campaign speeches [1927]

12 The Governor of New York State does not have to be an acrobat.
*Speech in behalf of Franklin
D. Roosevelt [1928]*

13 No matter how thin you slice it, it's still baloney.
Campaign speeches [1936]

H[enry] M[ajor] Tomlinson
1873–1958

14 The sea is at its best at London, near midnight, when you are within the arms of a capacious chair, before a glowing fire, selecting phases of the voyages you will never make.
The Sea and the Jungle [1912]

15 As to the sea itself, love it you cannot. Why should you? I will never believe again the sea was ever loved by anyone whose life was married to it. It is the creation of Omnipotence, which is not of humankind and understandable, and so the springs of its behavior are hidden.
The Sea and the Jungle

Maurice Baring
1874–1945

16 [On Pushkin's drama *Mozart and Salieri*:] We see the contrast between the genius which does what it must and the talent which does what it can.
*An Outline of Russian Literature [1914].
The New Age: Pushkin*

---

[1]Music by Jerome Kern [1885–1945].

[2]Translated by Cyril Connelly and Simon Watson Taylor.

[3]Tout commence en mystique et finit en politique.

[4]He is the Happy Warrior of the political battlefield. — Franklin D. Roosevelt, *nominating speech, Democratic National Convention* [June 26, 1924]. See William Wordsworth, 371:20.

Arthur Henry Reginald Buller
1874–1944

1 There was a young lady named Bright,
Whose speed was far faster than light;
    She set out one day
    In a relative way,
And returned home the previous night.
        Limerick. In Punch [December 19, 1923]

G[ilbert] K[eith] Chesterton
1874–1936

2   The human race, to which so many of my readers
belong, has been playing at children's games from the
beginning, and will probably do it till the end, which
is a nuisance for the few people who grow up.
        The Napoleon of Notting Hill [1904],
        bk. 1, ch. 1

3   Truth must of necessity be stranger than fiction....
For fiction is the creation of the human mind, and
therefore is congenial to it.
        The Club of Queer Trades [1905]

4 Burn from my brain and from my breast
Sloth, and the cowardice that clings,
And stiffness and the soul's arrest:
And feed my brain with better things.
        A Ballade of a Book Reviewer [1908], st. 3

5   He was one of those who are driven early in life
into too conservative an attitude by the bewildering
folly of most revolutionists...His respectability was
spontaneous and sudden, a rebellion against rebellion.   *The Man Who Was Thursday [1908], ch. 4*

6   The poor have sometimes objected to being
governed badly; the rich have always objected to
being governed at all.
        The Man Who Was Thursday, 11

7   The madman is not the man who has lost his
reason. The madman is the man who has lost everything except his reason.   *Orthodoxy [1909]*

8   The Christian ideal has not been tried and found
wanting. It has been found difficult; and left untried.
        What's Wrong with the World [1910],
        pt. I, ch. 5

9   Nothing sublimely artistic has ever arisen out of
mere art, any more than anything essentially reasonable has ever arisen out of pure reason. There must
always be a rich moral soil for any great aesthetic
growth.
        A Defense of Nonsense [1911]

10 For the great Gaels of Ireland
Are the men that God made mad,

For all their wars are merry,
And all their songs are sad.
        The Ballad of the White Horse [1911],
        bk. II

11   The whole difference between construction and
creation is exactly this: that a thing constructed can
only be loved after it is constructed; but a thing created is loved before it exists.
        Preface to DICKENS, Pickwick Papers [1911]

12   A good joke is the one ultimate and sacred thing
which cannot be criticized. Our relations with a good
joke are direct and even divine relations.
        Preface to DICKENS, Pickwick Papers

13 Step softly, under snow or rain,
To find the place where men can pray;
The way is all so very plain
That we may lose the way.   *The Wise Men [1913]*

14 To an open house in the evening
Home shall men come,
To an older place than Eden
And a taller town than Rome.
        The House of Christmas [1915]

15 And Noah he often said to his wife when he sat down
    to dine,
"I don't care where the water goes if it doesn't get
    into the wine."   *Wine and Water [1915]*

Sir Winston Spencer Churchill[1]
1874–1965

16   I pass with relief from the tossing sea of Cause and
Theory to the firm ground of Result and Fact.
        The Malakand Field Force [1898]

17   It is better to be making the news than taking it; to
be an actor rather than a critic.
        The Malakand Field Force

18   Nothing in life is so exhilarating as to be shot at
without result.
        The Malakand Field Force

19   There are men in the world who derive as stern an
exaltation from the proximity of disaster and ruin, as
others from success.
        The Malakand Field Force

20   Terminological inexactitude.
        Speech in the House of Commons
        [February 22, 1906]

21   The maxim of the British people is "Business as
usual."
        Speech at the Guildhall [November 9, 1914]

---

[1]See Roosevelt and Churchill, 653:14 and following.

1   Politics are almost as exciting as war, and quite as dangerous. In war you can only be killed once, but in politics many times.   *Remark [1920]*

2   By being so long in the lowest form [at Harrow] I gained an immense advantage over the cleverer boys.... I got into my bones the essential structure of the ordinary British sentence — which is a noble thing.... Naturally I am biased in favor of boys learning English; I would make them all learn English: and then I would let the clever ones learn Latin as an honor, and Greek as a treat.
Roving Commission: My Early Life [1930]

3   It is a good thing for an uneducated man to read books of quotations. Bartlett's *Familiar Quotations* is an admirable work, and I studied it intently. The quotations when engraved upon the memory give you good thoughts. They also make you anxious to read the authors and look for more.
Roving Commission: My Early Life

4   You will make all kinds of mistakes; but as long as you are generous and true, and also fierce, you cannot hurt the world or even seriously distress her. She was made to be wooed and won by youth.
Roving Commission: My Early Life

5   Decided only to be undecided, resolved to be irresolute, adamant for drift, solid for fluidity, all-powerful to be impotent.[1]
While England Slept [1936]

6   Dictators ride to and fro upon tigers which they dare not dismount. And the tigers are getting hungry.[2]   *While England Slept*

7   I have watched this famous island descending incontinently, fecklessly, the stairway which leads to a dark gulf.   *While England Slept*

8   The German dictator, instead of snatching the victuals from the table, has been content to have them served to him course by course.
Speech on the Munich agreement,
House of Commons [October 5, 1938]

9   That long [Canadian] frontier from the Atlantic to the Pacific Oceans, guarded only by neighborly respect and honorable obligations, is an example to every country and a pattern for the future of the world.
Speech in honor of R. B. Bennett,
Canada Club, London [April 20, 1939]

10   I cannot forecast to you the action of Russia. It is a riddle wrapped in a mystery inside an enigma.
Radio broadcast [October 1, 1939]

11   For each and for all, as for the Royal Navy, the watchword should be, "Carry on, and dread nought."
Speech on traffic at sea,
House of Commons [December 6, 1939]

12   I have nothing to offer but blood, toil, tears and sweat.[3]
First Statement as Prime Minister,
House of Commons [May 13, 1940]

13   Victory at all costs, victory in spite of all terror, victory however long and hard the road may be; for without victory there is no survival.
First Statement as Prime Minister,
House of Commons

14   We shall not flag or fail. We shall go on to the end. We shall fight in France, we shall fight on the seas and oceans, we shall fight with growing confidence and growing strength in the air, we shall defend our island, whatever the cost may be, we shall fight on the beaches, we shall fight on the landing grounds, we shall fight in the fields and in the streets, we shall fight in the hills; we shall never surrender.
Speech on Dunkirk, House of Commons
[June 4, 1940]

15   Let us... brace ourselves to our duties, and so bear ourselves that if the British Empire and its Commonwealth last for a thousand years, men will still say: "This was their finest hour."
Speech in the House of Commons
[June 18, 1940]

16   We shall defend every village, every town and every city. The vast mass of London itself, fought street by street, could easily devour an entire hostile army; and we would rather see London laid in ruins and ashes than that it should be tamely and abjectly enslaved.
Radio broadcast [July 14, 1940]

17   Never in the field of human conflict was so much owed by so many to so few.
Tribute to the Royal Air Force,
House of Commons [August 20, 1940]

18   The British Empire and the United States will have to be somewhat mixed up together in some of their affairs for mutual and general advantage. For

---

[1]Of Stanley Baldwin's policies.

[2]He who rides a tiger is afraid to dismount. — WILLIAM SCARBOROUGH [fl. c. 1875], *Chinese Proverbs* [1875], *no. 2082*

[3]Mollify it with thy tears, or sweat, or blood. — JOHN DONNE, *An Anatomy of the World, I, 430–431*

Year after year they voted cent per cent, / Blood, sweat, and tear-wrung millions — why? for rent! — LORD BYRON, *The Age of Bronze, st. 14*

Their sweat, their tears, their blood bedewed the endless plain. — CHURCHILL, *The Unknown War* [1931], referring to the armies of the czar before the Russian Revolution.

Churchill alluded to his promise of blood, toil, tears, and sweat in subsequent speeches on October 8, 1940; May 7 and December 2, 1941; and January 27 and November 10, 1942.

my own part, looking out upon the future, I do not view the process with any misgivings.

Tribute to the Royal Air Force,
House of Commons [August 20, 1940]

1   Death and sorrow will be the companions of our journey; hardship our garment; constancy and valor our only shield. We must be united, we must be undaunted, we must be inflexible.

Report on the war, House of Commons
[October 8, 1940]

2   We are waiting for the long-promised invasion. So are the fishes.

Radio broadcast to the French people
[October 21, 1940]

3   Here is the answer which I will give to President Roosevelt.... Give us the tools, and we will finish the job.

Radio broadcast [February 9, 1941]

4   This is one of those cases in which the imagination is baffled by the facts.

Remark in the House of Commons following
the parachute descent in Scotland of
Rudolf Hess [May 13, 1941]

5   The British nation is unique in this respect. They are the only people who like to be told how bad things are, who like to be told the worst.

Report on the war, House of Commons
[June 10, 1941]

6   A vile race of quislings[1] — to use the new word which will carry the scorn of mankind down the centuries.

Speech at St. James's Palace, London
[June 12, 1941]

7   The destiny of mankind is not decided by material computation. When great causes are on the move in the world ... we learn that we are spirits, not animals, and that something is going on in space and time, and beyond space and time, which, whether we like it or not, spells duty.

Radio broadcast to America on receiving
the honorary degree of Doctor of Laws
from the University of Rochester, New York
[June 16, 1941]

8   Hitler is a monster of wickedness, insatiable in his lust for blood and plunder. Not content with having all Europe under his heel, or else terrorized into various forms of abject submission, he must now carry his work of butchery and desolation among the vast multitudes of Russia and of Asia.... So now this bloodthirsty guttersnipe must launch his mechanized armies upon new fields of slaughter, pillage and devastation.

Radio broadcast on the German invasion
of Russia [June 22, 1941]

9   We will have no truce or parley with you [Hitler], or the grisly gang who work your wicked will. You do your worst — and we will do our best.

Speech to the London County Council
[July 14, 1941]

10   The V sign is the symbol of the unconquerable will of the occupied territories, and a portent of the fate awaiting the Nazi tyranny.

Message to the people of Europe on launching
the V for Victory propaganda campaign
[July 20, 1941]

11   Nothing is more dangerous in wartime than to live in the temperamental atmosphere of a Gallup Poll,[2] always feeling one's pulse and taking one's temperature.

Report on the war, House of Commons
[September 30, 1941]

12   Never give in, never give in, never, never, never — in nothing, great or small, large or petty — never give in except to convictions of honor and good sense.

Address at Harrow School
[October 29, 1941]

13   Do not let us speak of darker days; let us speak rather of sterner days. These are not dark days: these are great days — the greatest days our country has ever lived; and we must all thank God that we have been allowed, each of us according to our stations, to play a part in making these days memorable in the history of our race.

Address at Harrow School
[October 29, 1941]

14   In the past we have had a light which flickered, in the present we have a light which flames, and in the future there will be a light which shines over all the land and sea.

Speech on war with Japan, House of Commons
[December 8, 1941]

15   What kind of people do they [the Japanese] think we are?

Speech to the U.S. Congress
[December 26, 1941]

16   We have not journeyed all this way across the centuries, across the oceans, across the mountains,

---

[1]Vidkun Quisling, head of the Nasjonal Samling party in Norway, who cooperated and collaborated with the Nazis when Germany invaded Norway [April 9, 1940]. Quisling was executed [October 23, 1945].

[2]Dr. George H. Gallup [1901–1984] founded the American Institute of Public Opinion in 1935.

across the prairies, because we are made of sugar candy.
>*Speech to the Canadian Senate and House of Commons, Ottawa [December 30, 1941]*

1   When I warned [the French] that Britain would fight on alone whatever they did, their generals told their prime minister and his divided cabinet, "In three weeks England will have her neck wrung like a chicken." Some chicken; some neck.
>*Speech to the Canadian Senate and House of Commons, Ottawa [December 30, 1941]*

2   The late M. Venizelos[1] observed that in all her wars England — he should have said Britain, of course — always wins one battle — the last.
>*Speech at the Lord Mayor's Day Luncheon, London [November 10, 1942]*

3   Now this is not the end. It is not even the beginning of the end. But it is, perhaps, the end of the beginning.
>*Speech at the Lord Mayor's Day Luncheon, London*

4   I have not become the King's First Minister in order to preside over the liquidation of the British Empire.
>*Speech at the Lord Mayor's Day Luncheon, London*

5   The soft underbelly of the Axis.
>*Report on the war, House of Commons [November 11, 1942]*

6   In war-time, truth is so precious that she should always be attended by a bodyguard of lies.
>*Remark at Teheran Conference [December 1943]*

7   "Not in vain" may be the pride of those who have survived and the epitaph of those who fell.[2]
>*Speech in the House of Commons [September 28, 1944]*

8   The United States is a land of free speech. Nowhere is speech freer — not even here where we sedulously cultivate it even in its most repulsive form.
>*Speech in the House of Commons [September 28, 1944]*

9   He [President Franklin D. Roosevelt] died in harness, and we may well say in battle harness, like his soldiers, sailors, and airmen, who side by side with ours are carrying on their task to the end all over the world. What an enviable death was his.
>*Speech in the House of Commons [April 17, 1945]*

10   I think "No comment" is a splendid expression. I am using it again and again. I got it from Sumner Welles.
>*To reporters at the Washington, D.C., airport, after conferring with President Truman at the White House [February 12, 1946]*

11   From Stettin in the Baltic to Trieste in the Adriatic an iron curtain[3] has descended across the Continent.
>*Address at Westminster College, Fulton, Missouri [March 5, 1946]*

12   In War: Resolution. In Defeat: Defiance. In Victory: Magnanimity. In Peace: Good Will.
>*The Second World War: Moral of the Work, vol. I, The Gathering Storm [1948]*

13   No one can guarantee success in war, but only deserve it.
>*The Second World War: Moral of the Work, II, Their Finest Hour [1949]*

14   When you have to kill a man it costs nothing to be polite.
>*The Second World War: Moral of the Work, III, The Grand Alliance [1950]*

15   Everyone has his day and some days last longer than others.
>*Speech in the House of Commons [January 1952]*

16   To jaw-jaw is always better than to war-war.
>*At a White House luncheon [June 26, 1954]*

17   A fanatic is one who can't change his mind and won't change the subject.   *Saying*

18   The inherent vice of capitalism is the unequal sharing of blessings; the inherent virtue of socialism is the equal sharing of miseries.   *Saying*

---

[1]Eleutherios Venizelos [1864–1936], Greek statesman.

[2]The eight thousand paratroopers of the First British Airborne Division who landed in Arnhem, Holland, behind the German lines and held the area for nine days and nights, with a loss of six thousand [September 1944].

[3]An iron curtain had dropped between him and the outer world — H. G. WELLS, *The Food of the Gods* [1904]

France . . . a nation of forty millions with a deep-rooted grievance and an iron curtain at its frontier. — GEORGE WASHINGTON CRILE [1864–1943], *A Mechanistic View of War and Peace* [1915]

With a rumble and a roar, an iron curtain is descending on Russian history. — VASILI ROZANOV [1856–1919], *Apocalypse of Our Time* [1918]

We were behind the "iron curtain" at last. — ETHEL ANNAKIN SNOWDEN [1881–1951], *Through Bolshevik Russia* [1920]

The Nazi minister of enlightenment and propaganda, Paul Joseph Goebbels, used the phrase "iron curtain" in reference to the USSR in *Das Reich* [February 23, 1945].

Churchill used it in a top-secret telegram to President Truman [May 12, 1945].

1   Short words are best and the old words when short are best of all.   *Saying*

2   It is hard, if not impossible, to snub a beautiful woman — they remain beautiful and the rebuke recoils.   *Saying*

3   This is the sort of English up with which I will not put.   *Attributed*

Francis Macdonald Cornford
1874–1973

4   Every public action which is not customary, either is wrong, or, if it is right, is a dangerous precedent. It follows that nothing should ever be done for the first time.

> *Microcosmographia Academica: Being a Guide for the Young Academic Politician [1908], ch. 7*

Clarence Day
1874–1935

5   Aside from a few odd words in Hebrew, I took it completely for granted that God had never spoken anything but the most dignified English.

> *Life with Father [1935]. Father Interferes with the Twenty-third Psalm*

6   "If you don't go to other men's funerals," he told Father stiffly, "they won't go to yours."

> *Life with Father. Father Plans to Get Out*

Robert Frost
1874–1963

7 They would not find me changed from him they
    knew —
Only more sure of all I thought was true.
                              Into My Own [1913], st. 4

8 Ah, when to the heart of man
Was it ever less than a treason
To go with the drift of things,
To yield with a grace to reason,
And bow and accept the end
Of a love or a season?
                              Reluctance [1913], st. 4

9 I'm going out to clean the pasture spring;
I'll only stop to rake the leaves away
(And wait to watch the water clear, I may):
I shan't be gone long. — You come too.
                              The Pasture [1914], st. 1

10 Something there is that doesn't love a wall.
                              Mending Wall [1914]

11 My apple trees will never get across
And eat the cones under his pines, I tell him.
He only says, "Good fences make good neighbors."[1]
                              Mending Wall

12 Before I built a wall I'd ask to know
What I was walling in or walling out.
                              Mending Wall

13 And nothing to look backward to with pride,
And nothing to look forward to with hope.
                              The Death of the Hired Man [1914]

14 Home is the place where, when you have to go there,
They have to take you in.
                              The Death of the Hired Man

15   The nearest friends can go
With anyone to death, comes so far short
They might as well not try to go at all.
                              Home Burial [1914]

16 Most of the change we think we see in life
Is due to truths being in and out of favor.
                              The Black Cottage [1914]

17 Pressed into service means pressed out of shape.
                              The Self-Seeker [1914]

18 I shall be telling this with a sigh
Somewhere ages and ages hence:
Two roads diverged in a wood, and I —
I took the one less traveled by,
And that has made all the difference.
                              The Road Not Taken [1916], st. 4

19 I'd like to get away from earth awhile
And then come back to it and begin over.
May no fate willfully misunderstand me
And half grant what I wish and snatch me away
Not to return. Earth's the right place for love:
I don't know where it's likely to go better.
                              Birches [1916]

20 One could do worse than be a swinger of birches.
                              Birches

21 I shall set forth for somewhere,
I shall make the reckless choice
Some say when they are in voice
And tossing so as to scare
The white clouds over them on,
I shall have less to say,
But I shall be gone.   *The Sound of the Trees [1916]*

22   A poem . . . begins as a lump in the throat, a sense of wrong, a homesickness, a lovesickness. It is never a thought to begin with. It is at its best when it is a tantalizing vagueness.

> *Letter to Louis Untermeyer [January 1, 1916]*

---

[1]See George Herbert, 243:19.

1   Do you know,
Considering the market, there are more
Poems produced than any other thing?
No wonder poets sometimes have to *seem*
So much more businesslike than businessmen.
Their wares are so much harder to get rid of.
New Hampshire [1923]

2 The snake stood up for evil in the Garden.
The Ax-Helve [1923]

3 Why make so much of fragmentary blue
In here and there a bird, or butterfly,
Or flower, or wearing-stone, or open eye,
When heaven presents in sheets the solid hue?
Fragmentary Blue [1923], st. 1

4 Some say the world will end in fire,
Some say in ice.
From what I've tasted of desire
I hold with those who favor fire.
But if it had to perish twice,
I think I know enough of hate
To say that for destruction ice
Is also great
And would suffice.   *Fire and Ice [1923]*

5 The way a crow
Shook down on me
The dust of snow
From a hemlock tree

Has given my heart
A change of mood
And saved some part
Of a day I had rued.   *Dust of Snow [1923]*

6 Whose woods these are I think I know.
His house is in the village though;
He will not see me stopping here
To watch his woods fill up with snow.
*Stopping by Woods on a Snowy Evening
[1923], st. 1*

7 My little horse must think it queer
To stop without a farmhouse near.
Stopping by Woods on a Snowy Evening, st. 2

8 The woods are lovely, dark and deep.
But I have promises to keep,
And miles to go before I sleep,
And miles to go before I sleep.
Stopping by Woods on a Snowy Evening, st. 4

9 Love at the lips was touch
As sweet as I could bear;
And once that seemed too much;
I lived on air.
To Earthward [1923], st. 1

10 Now no joy but lacks salt
That is not dashed with pain

And weariness and fault;
I crave the stain

Of tears, the aftermark
Of almost too much love,
The sweet of bitter bark
And burning clove.   *To Earthward, st. 5, 6*

11 Keep cold, young orchard. Goodbye and keep cold.
Dread fifty above more than fifty below.
Goodbye and Keep Cold [1923]

12   It is absurd to think that the only way to tell if a
poem is lasting is to wait and see if it lasts. The right
reader of a good poem can tell the moment it strikes
him that he has taken an immortal wound — that he
will never get over it.
*The Poetry of Amy Lowell. From the
Christian Science Monitor [May 16, 1925]*

13 It looked as if a night of dark intent
Was coming, and not only a night, an age.
Someone had better be prepared for rage.
There would be more than ocean-water broken
Before God's last *Put out the Light* was spoken.
Once by the Pacific [1928]

14 Tree at my window, window tree,
My sash is lowered when night comes on;
But let there never be curtain drawn
Between you and me.
Tree at My Window [1928], st. 1

15 That day she put our heads together,
Fate had her imagination about her,
Your head so much concerned with outer,
Mine with inner, weather.   *Tree at My Window, st. 4*

16 I have been one acquainted with the night.
Acquainted with the Night [1928]

17 If, as they say, some dust thrown in my eyes
Will keep my talk from getting overwise,
I'm not the one for putting off the proof.
Let it be overwhelming.   *Dust in the Eyes [1928]*

18 Don't join too many gangs. Join few if any.
Join the United States and join the family —
But not much in between unless a college.
Build Soil [1932]

19 The sun was warm but the wind was chill.
You know how it is with an April day
When the sun is out and the wind is still,
You're one month on in the middle of May.
But if you so much as dare to speak,
A cloud comes over the sunlit arch,
A wind comes off a frozen peak,
And you're two months back in the middle of
March.
Two Tramps in Mud Time [1936], st. 3

1 But yield who will to their separation,
My object in living is to unite
My avocation and my vocation
As my two eyes make one in sight.
Only where love and need are one,
And the work is play for mortal stakes,
Is the deed ever really done
For Heaven and the future's sakes.
Two Tramps in Mud Time, st. 9

2 No memory of having starred
Atones for later disregard,
Or keeps the end from being hard.

Better to go down dignified
With boughten friendship by your side
Than none at all. Provide, provide!
Provide, Provide [1936], st. 6, 7

3 The old dog barks backward without getting up.
I can remember when he was a pup.
The Span of Life [1936]

4 I never dared to be radical when young
For fear it would make me conservative when old.
Precaution [1936]

5 The land was ours before we were the land's.
She was our land more than a hundred years
Before we were her people.
The Gift Outright[1] *[1941]*

6 She is as in a field a silken tent
At midday when a sunny summer breeze
Has dried the dew and all its ropes relent,
So that in guys it gently sways at ease.
The Silken Tent [1942]

7 But strictly held by none, is loosely bound
By countless silken ties of love and thought
To everything on earth the compass round,
And only by one's going slightly taut
In the capriciousness of summer air
Is of the slightest bondage made aware.
The Silken Tent

8   Happiness Makes Up in Height for What It Lacks
in Length.   *Title of poem [1942]*

9 Far in the pillared dark
Thrush music went —
Almost like a call to come in
To the dark and lament.

But no, I was out for stars:
I would not come in.
I meant not even if asked,
And I hadn't been.   *Come In [1942], st. 4, 5*

10 And were an epitaph to be my story
I'd have a short one ready for my own.
I would have written of me on my stone:
I had a lover's quarrel with the world.
The Lesson for Today [1942]

11 We dance round in a ring and suppose,
But the Secret sits in the middle and knows.
The Secret Sits [1942]

12 Back out of all this now too much for us,
Back in a time made simple by the loss
Of detail, burned, dissolved, and broken off
Like graveyard marble sculpture in the weather,
There is a house that is no more a house
Upon a farm that is no more a farm
And in a town that is no more a town.
Directive [1947]

13 First there's the children's house of make believe,
Some shattered dishes underneath a pine,
The playthings in the playhouse of the children.
Weep for what little things could make them glad.
Directive

14 Here are your waters and your watering place.
Drink and be whole again beyond confusion.
Directive

15 Have I not walked without an upward look
Of caution under stars that very well
Might not have missed me when they shot and fell?
It was a risk I had to take — and took.
Bravado [1947]

16   Any eye is an evil eye
That looks in on to a mood apart.
A Mood Apart [1947]

17 All those who try to go it sole alone,
Too proud to be beholden for relief,
Are absolutely sure to come to grief.
Haec Fabula Docet [1947]

18 It asks a little of us here.
It asks of us a certain height,
So when at times the mob is swayed
To carry praise or blame too far,
We may take something like a star
To stay our minds on and be staid.
Take Something Like a Star [1949]

19 Forgive, O Lord, my little jokes on Thee
And I'll forgive Thy great big one on me.
From In the Clearing [1962]

20 I am assured at any rate
Man's practically inexterminate.
Someday I must go into that.
There's always been an Ararat
Where someone someone else begat
To start the world all over at.
A-Wishing Well [1962]

---

[1]Read first before the Phi Beta Kappa Society at William and Mary College [December 5, 1941], later at the inauguration of President John F. Kennedy [January 20, 1961].

1 It takes all sorts of in and outdoor schooling
To get adapted to my kind of fooling.
It Takes All Sorts [1962]

2 Unless I'm wrong
I but obey
The urge of a song:
I'm — bound — away!

And I may return
If dissatisfied
With what I learn
From having died.
Away! [1962], st. 5, 6

3 The figure a poem makes. It begins in delight and ends in wisdom...in a clarification of life — not necessarily a great clarification, such as sects and cults are founded on, but in a momentary stay against confusion.
Collected Poems [1939]. Preface

4 No tears in the writer, no tears in the reader.
Collected Poems. Preface

5 Like a piece of ice on a hot stove the poem must ride on its own melting.... Read it a hundred times; it will forever keep its freshness as a metal keeps its fragrance. It can never lose its sense of a meaning that once unfolded by surprise as it went.
Collected Poems. Preface

6 It is only a moment here and a moment there that the greatest writer has.
Letter to Sidney Cox [January 2, 1925]

7 Poetry is a way of taking life by the throat.
Comment[1]

8 Talking is a hydrant in the yard and writing is a faucet upstairs in the house. Opening the first takes all the pressure off the second.
Letter to Sidney Cox [January 3, 1937]

9 Families break up when people take hints you don't intend and miss hints you do intend.
*Paris Review interview
[Summer-Fall 1960]*

10 Always fall in with what you're asked to accept. Take what is given, and make it over your way. My aim in life has always been to hold my own with whatever's going. Not against: with.
Comment

11 I've given offense by saying I'd as soon write free verse as play tennis with the net down.
Interview [1959]

12 Education is...hanging around until you've caught on.
Comment

13 Poetry is what is lost in translation. It is also what is lost in interpretation. That little poem means just what it says it means, nothing less but nothing more.
Quoted in LOUIS UNTERMEYER *[1885–1977],
Robert Frost: A Backward Look [1964]*

Lewis Hine
1874–1940

14 While photographs may not lie, liars may photograph.
*Social Photography: How the Camera May
Help in the Social Uplift [1909]*

Hugo von Hofmannsthal
1874–1929

15 It's all a mystery, so much is mysterious.
And we are here to endure it.
And in the How, there lies the whole
    difference —[2]
Der Rosenkavalier[3] *[1911], act I*

16 Depth must be hidden. Where? On the surface.
The Book of Friends [1922]

Herbert [Clark] Hoover
1874–1964

17 The American system of rugged individualism.[4]
*Campaign speech, New York City
[October 22, 1928]*

18 The grass will grow in the streets of a hundred cities.
Speech [October 31, 1932]

19 Older men declare war. But it is youth that must fight and die. And it is youth who must inherit the tribulation, the sorrow, and the triumphs that are the aftermath of war.
*Speech at the Republican National
Convention, Chicago [June 27, 1944]*

20 The only trouble with capitalism is capitalists; they're too damn greedy. *Attributed*

---

[1]Cited in ELIZABETH S. SERGEANT, *Robert Frost: The Trial by Existence* [1960], ch. 18.

[2]Das alles ist geheim, so viel geheim. / Und man ist dazu da, dass man's ertragt. / Und in dem "Wie" da liegt der ganze Unterschied.

[3]Music by RICHARD STRAUSS [1864–1949].

[4]Hoover popularized but did not coin this phrase:
While I can make no claim for having introduced the term "rugged individualism," I should be proud to have invented it. It has been used by American leaders for over a half-century in eulogy of those God-fearing men and women of honesty whose stamina and character and fearless assertion of rights led them to make their own way in life. — HOOVER, *The Challenge to Liberty* [1934], *ch. 5*

Harold L[eClair] Ickes
1874–1952

1   I am against government by crony.
On resigning as secretary of the interior
[February 1946]

Charles [Edward] Ives
1874–1954

2   Music may be yet unborn. Perhaps no music has ever been written or heard. Perhaps the birth of art will take place at the moment in which the last man who is willing to make a living out of art is gone and gone forever.
Essays Before a Sonata [1920], epilogue

3   It will probably be centuries, at least generations, before man will discover all or even most of the value in a quarter-tone extension. And when he does, nature has plenty of other things up her sleeve.
Some "Quarter-Tone" Impressions
[1924–1925], sec. 1

Karl Kraus
1874–1936

4   I and my public understand each other very well: it does not hear what I say, and I don't say what it wants to hear.   *Aphorism*[1]

5   When the end of the world comes, I want to be living in retirement.   *Aphorism*

6   Heinrich Heine so loosened the corsets of the German language that today every little salesman can fondle her breasts.   *Aphorism*

7   An aphorism never coincides with the truth: it is either a half-truth or one-and-a-half truths.
Aphorism

8   Psychoanalysis is that mental illness for which it regards itself as therapy.   *Aphorism*

9   A woman is, occasionally, quite a serviceable substitute for masturbation. It takes an abundance of imagination, to be sure.   *Aphorism*

10   There are two kinds of writers, those who are and those who aren't. With the first, content and form belong together like soul and body; with the second, they match each other like body and clothes.
Aphorism

11   A historian is often only a journalist facing backwards.   *Aphorism*

---

[1]Aphorisms translated by HARRY ZOHN.

12   How is the world ruled and led to war? Diplomats lie to journalists and believe the lies when they see them in print.
Aphorism

Amy Lowell
1874–1925

13   A pattern called a war.
Christ! What are patterns for?   *Patterns [1916]*

14   Sappho would speak, I think, quite openly,
And Mrs. Browning guard a careful silence,
But Emily would set doors ajar and slam them
And love you for your speed of observation.
The Sisters [1922]

15   Heart-leaves of lilac all over New England,
Roots of lilac under all the soil of New England,
Lilac in me because I am New England.
Lilacs [1922]

W[illiam] Somerset Maugham
1874–1965

16   Like all weak men he laid an exaggerated stress on not changing one's mind.
Of Human Bondage [1915], ch. 39

17   People ask you for criticism, but they only want praise.   *Of Human Bondage, 50*

18   There is nothing so degrading as the constant anxiety about one's means of livelihood. . . . Money is like a sixth sense without which you cannot make a complete use of the other five.
Of Human Bondage, 51

19   I forget who it was that recommended men for their soul's good to do each day two things they disliked . . . it is a precept that I have followed scrupulously; for every day I have got up and I have gone to bed.
The Moon and Sixpence [1919], ch. 2

20   Do you know that conversation is one of the greatest pleasures in life? But it wants leisure.
The Trembling of a Leaf [1921], ch. 3

21   The tragedy of love is indifference.
The Trembling of a Leaf, 4

22   No one can be a humbug for five-and-twenty years. Hypocrisy is the most difficult and nerve-racking vice that any man can pursue; it needs an unceasing vigilance and a rare detachment of spirit. It cannot, like adultery or gluttony, be practiced at spare moments; it is a whole-time job.
Cakes and Ale [1930], ch. 1

1   I [Death] was astonished to see him in Baghdad, for I had an appointment with him tonight in Samarra.   *Sheppy [1933], act III*

2   She [Sadie Thompson] gathered herself together. No one could describe the scorn of her expression or the contemptuous hatred she put into her answer. "You men! You filthy dirty pigs! You're all the same, all of you. Pigs! Pigs!"   *Altogether [1934]. Rain*

3   I would sooner read a timetable or a catalogue than nothing at all. They are much more entertaining than half the novels that are written.   *The Summing Up [1938]*

Alice Duer Miller
1874–1942

4 The white cliffs of Dover, I saw rising steeply
  Out of the sea that once made her [England]
    secure.   *The White Cliffs [1940], I*

5 But in a world where England is finished and dead,
  I do not wish to live.   *The White Cliffs, LII*

L[ucy] M[aud] Montgomery
1874–1908

6   A graveyard of buried hopes is about as romantic a thing as one can imagine.   *Anne of Green Gables [1908], ch. 5*

Arnold Schoenberg
1874–1951

7   Art is the desperate cry of those who experience in themselves the fate of humanity.   *Aphorisms [1909]*

8   The expression "atonal music" is most unfortunate — it is on a par with calling flying "the art of not falling," or swimming "the art of not drowning."   *Twelve-Tone Composition [1923]*

9   If it is art, it is not for all, and if it is for all, it is not art.   *New Music, Outmoded Music, Style and Idea [1946]*

Arthur A. Schomburg
1874–1938

10   The American Negro must remake his past in order to make his future.   *The Negro Digs Up His Past [The Survey Graphic, March 1925]*

Robert William Service
1874–1958

11 This is the Law of the Yukon, that only the strong
    shall thrive;
  That surely the weak shall perish, and only the fit
    survive.
  Dissolute, damned and despairful, crippled and
    palsied and slain,
  This is the Will of the Yukon — Lo, how she makes it
    plain!   *The Law of the Yukon [1907], st. 6*

12 Back of the bar, in a solo game, sat Dangerous Dan
    McGrew,
  And watching his luck was his light-o'-love, the lady
    that's known as Lou.   *The Shooting of Dan McGrew [1907], st. 1*

13 The Northern Lights have seen queer sights,
  But the queerest they ever did see
  Was that night on the marge of Lake Lebarge
  I cremated Sam McGee.   *The Cremation of Sam McGee [1907], st. 1*

Gertrude Stein
1874–1946

14   Rose is a rose is a rose is a rose.   *Sacred Emily [1913]*

15   I am writing for myself and strangers.   *The Making of Americans [1925]. Martha Hersland*

16   The creator of the new composition in the arts is an outlaw until he is a classic.   *Composition as Explanation [1926]*

17   You are all a lost generation.[1]   *Used by ERNEST HEMINGWAY as an epigraph for The Sun Also Rises*

18 To know to know to love her so.
  Four saints prepare for saints.   *Four Saints in Three Acts[2] [1927]*

19 Pigeons on the grass alas.   *Four Saints in Three Acts*

20   Before the Flowers of Friendship Faded Friendship Faded.   *Title [1930]*

---

[1]Ernest Hemingway stated that the remark was originally made by a garage owner in the Midi to Gertrude Stein in reference to his young mechanics, who were "une génération perdue."

[2]Music by VIRGIL THOMSON [1896–1989].

1   I murmured to Picasso that I liked his portrait of Gertrude Stein. Yes, he said, everybody says that she does not look like it but that does not make any difference, she will.
The Autobiography of Alice B. Toklas [1933]

2   Remarks are not literature [said to Hemingway].
The Autobiography of Alice B. Toklas

3   [Ezra Pound] was a village explainer, excellent if you were a village, but if you were not, not.
The Autobiography of Alice B. Toklas

4   I talk a lot I like to talk and I talk even more than that I may say I talk most of the time and I listen a fair amount too and as I have said the essence of being a genius is to be able to talk and listen to listen while talking and talk while listening but and this is very important very important indeed talking has nothing to do with creation.
What Are Master-pieces and Why Are There So Few of Them [1935]

5   Nothing could bother me more than the way a thing goes dead once it has been said.
What Are Master-pieces and Why Are There So Few of Them

6   America is my country and Paris is my home town.
An American and France [1936]

7   If nobody had to die how would there be room enough for any of us who now live to have lived.
The Geographical History of America [1936]

8   In the United States there is more space where nobody is than where anybody is.
This is what makes America what it is.
The Geographical History of America

9   I am I because my little dog knows me.
The Geographical History of America

10   Think of the Bible and Homer think of Shakespeare and think of me.
The Geographical History of America

11   It takes a lot of time to be a genius, you have to sit around so much doing nothing really doing nothing.
Everybody's Autobiography [1937], ch. 2

12   [Of Oakland, California:] There is no there there.
Everybody's Autobiography, 4

13   I am Rose my eyes are blue
I am Rose and who are you
I am Rose and when I sing
I am Rose like anything.
The World Is Round [1939]

14   I just tell you, and though I don't sound like it I've got plenty of sense, there ain't any answer, there ain't going to be any answer, there never has been any answer, that's the answer.
Brewsie and Willie [1946]

15   What is the answer? [*I was silent.*] In that case, what is the question?
Last words. From Alice B. Toklas *[1877–1967],* What Is Remembered *[1963]*

Trumbull Stickney
1874–1904

16 Live blindly and upon the hour. The Lord,
Who was the Future, died full long ago.
Knowledge which is the Past is folly.
Dramatic Verses [1902].
Untitled sonnet

17 Be still. The Hanging Gardens were a dream
That over Persian roses flew to kiss
The curlèd lashes of Semiramis.
Troy never was, nor green Skamander stream.
Dramatic Verses. Untitled sonnet

18 Sir, say no more.
Within me 't is as if
The green and climbing eyesight of a cat
Crawled near my mind's poor birds.
Dramatic Fragments [1904], no. 5

Bert Williams[1]
1874–1922

19   I have never been able to discover that there was anything disgraceful in being a colored man. But I have often found it inconvenient — in America.[2]
The Comic Side of Trouble [American Magazine, 1918]

Harry Williams
1874–1924

20 It's a long way to Tipperary, it's a long way to go;
It's a long way to Tipperary, to the sweetest girl I know!
Goodbye, Piccadilly, farewell, Leicester Square,
It's a long, long way to Tipperary, but my heart's right there!   *Tipperary [1908]*

---

[1]The funniest man I ever saw, and the saddest man I ever knew. — W. C. Fields *on Bert Williams*

[2]Often quoted as: It's no disgrace to be colored, but it's awfully inconvenient.

It's no disgrace to be black, but it's very often inconvenient. — James Weldon Johnson, *Autobiography of an Ex-Colored Man* [1912]

E[dmund] C[lerihew][1] Bentley
1875–1956

1 The Art of Biography
Is different from Geography.
Geography is about Maps,
But Biography is about Chaps.
> *Biography for Beginners [1905].*
> *Introduction*

2 Sir Christopher Wren
Said "I am going to dine with some men.
If anybody calls
Say I am designing St. Paul's."
> *Biography for Beginners.*
> *Sir Christopher Wren*[2]

3 John Stuart Mill
By a mighty effort of will
Overcame his natural bonhomie
And wrote *Principles of Political Economy*.
> *Biography for Beginners.*
> *John Stuart Mill*

4 George the Third
Ought never to have occurred.
One can only wonder
At so grotesque a blunder.[3]
> *Biography for Beginners. George III*

Mary McLeod Bethune
1875–1955

5   What does the Negro want? His answer is very simple. He wants only what all other Americans want. He wants opportunity to make real what the Declaration of Independence and the Constitution and the Bill of Rights say, what the Four Freedoms establish. While he knows these ideals are open to no man completely, he wants only his equal chance to obtain them.
> *"Certain Unalienable Rights."*
> *From What the Negro Wants [1944],*
> *edited by RAYFORD W. LOGAN*
> *[1897–1982]*

6   If we accept and acquiesce in the face of discrimination, we accept the responsibility ourselves and allow those responsible to salve their conscience by believing that they have our acceptance and concurrence. We should, therefore, protest openly everything . . . that smacks of discrimination or slander.
> *"Certain Unalienable Rights."*
> *From What the Negro Wants,*
> *edited by RAYFORD W. LOGAN*

John Buchan,
Lord Tweedsmuir
1875–1940

7   It's a great life if you don't weaken.
> *Mr. Standfast [1919]*

Edgar Rice Burroughs
1875–1950

8   As the body rolled to the ground Tarzan of the Apes placed his foot upon the neck of his lifelong enemy, and raising his eyes to the full moon threw back his fierce young head and voiced the wild and terrible cry of his people.
> *Tarzan of the Apes [1914], ch. 7*

9   I am Tarzan of the Apes. I want you. I am yours. You are mine.[4]
> *Tarzan of the Apes, 18*

Aleister Crowley
1875–1947

10   Do what thou wilt shall be the whole of the Law.[5]
> *Book of the Law [1909]*

Hasegawa Nyozekan
1875–1969

11   The war was started as the result of a mistaken intuitive "calculation" which transcended mathematics. We believed with a blind fervor that we could triumph over scientific weapons and tactics by means of our mystic will. . . . The characteristic reliance on intuition by Japanese had blocked the objective cognition of the modern world.
> *The Lost Japan [1952]*

---

[1] A humorous quatrain in the form Bentley popularized is known as a clerihew.

[2] See Christopher Wren, 276:21.

[3] George the First was always reckoned / Vile, but viler George the Second; / And what mortal ever heard / Any good of George the Third? / When from earth the Fourth descended / God be praised, the Georges ended! — WALTER SAVAGE LANDOR, *epigram after hearing Thackeray's lectures, The Four Georges* [1855]

[4] Me Tarzan, you Jane. — Johnny Weissmuller [1904–1984] did not utter these words in the movie *Tarzan the Ape Man* [1932]. The actor jokingly said them in an interview: I didn't have to act in *Tarzan the Ape Man* — just said "Me Tarzan, you Jane." — *Photoplay magazine* [June 1932]

[5] See François Rabelais, 145:9 and note.

Carl Gustav Jung
1875–1961

1   Without this playing with fantasy no creative work has ever yet come to birth. The debt we owe to the play of imagination is incalculable.
Psychological Types [1923], ch. 1

2   The great problems of life — sexuality, of course, among others — are always related to the primordial images of the collective unconscious. These images are really balancing or compensating factors which correspond with the problems life presents in actuality. This is not to be marveled at, since these images are deposits representing the accumulated experience of thousands of years of struggle for adaptation and existence.   *Psychological Types, 5*

3   The meeting of two personalities is like the contact of two chemical substances: if there is any reaction, both are transformed.
Modern Man in Search of a Soul [1933]

4   Aging people should know that their lives are not mounting and unfolding but that an inexorable inner process forces the contraction of life. For a young person it is almost a sin — and certainly a danger — to be too much occupied with himself; but for the aging person it is a duty and a necessity to give serious attention to himself.
Modern Man in Search of a Soul

5   All ages before ours believed in gods in some form or other. Only an unparalleled impoverishment in symbolism could enable us to rediscover the gods as psychic factors, which is to say, as archetypes of the unconscious. No doubt this discovery is hardly credible as yet.
The Integration of the Personality [1939]

6   If there is anything that we wish to change in the child, we should first examine it and see whether it is not something that could better be changed in ourselves.
The Integration of the Personality

7   The conscious mind allows itself to be trained like a parrot, but the unconscious does not — which is why St. Augustine thanked God for not making him responsible for his dreams.
Psychology and Alchemy [1953]

8   The little world of childhood with its familiar surroundings is a model of the greater world. The more intensively the family has stamped its character upon the child, the more it will tend to feel and see its earlier miniature world again in the bigger world of adult life.
Collected Works, vol. 4,
The Theory of Psychoanalysis [1913]

9   This whole creation is essentially subjective, and the dream is the theater where the dreamer is at once scene, actor, prompter, stage manager, author, audience, and critic.
Collected Works, vol. 8, General Aspects of
Dream Psychology [1916]

10   Where love rules, there is no will to power; and where power predominates, there love is lacking. The one is the shadow of the other.
Collected Works, vol. 7, On Psychology
of the Unconscious [1943]

Antonio Machado
1875–1939

11   Wayfarer, there is no way,
you make the way as you go.
As you go, you make the way
and stopping to look behind,
you see the path that your feet
will never travel again.
Wayfarer, there is no way —
only foam trails in the sea.
The Castilian Country[1] [1912].
Proverbs and Song-Verse

12   It's not the basic I
that the poet is after
but the essential you.
New Songs[1] [1924]. Proverbs
and Song-Verse

Thomas Mann
1875–1955

13   We are most likely to get angry and excited in our opposition to some idea when we ourselves are not quite certain of our own position, and are inwardly tempted to take the other side.
Buddenbrooks [1903], pt. VIII, ch. 2

14   Beauty can pierce one like a pain.
Buddenbrooks, XI, 2

15   Space, like time, engenders forgetfulness; but it does so by setting us bodily free from our surroundings and giving us back our primitive, unattached state.... Time, we say, is Lethe; but change of air is a similar draught, and, if it works less thoroughly, does so more quickly.
The Magic Mountain[2] [1924],
ch. 1

---

[1]Translated by ALAN S. TRUEBLOOD.
[2]Translated by H. T. LOWE-PORTER.

1 A man lives not only his personal life, as an individual, but also, consciously or unconsciously, the life of his epoch and his contemporaries.

The Magic Mountain, 2

2 What we call tedium is rather an abnormal shortening of the time consequent upon monotony. Great spaces of time passed in unbroken uniformity tend to shrink together in a way to make the heart stop beating for fear; when one day is like all the others, then they are all like one; complete uniformity would make the longest life seem short, and as though it had stolen away from us unawares. Habituation is a falling asleep or fatiguing of the sense of time; which explains why young years pass slowly, while later life flings itself faster and faster upon its course.

The Magic Mountain, 4

3 The only religious way to think of death is as part and parcel of life; to regard it, with the understanding and the emotions, as the inviolable condition of life.

The Magic Mountain, 5

4 Time has no divisions to mark its passage, there is never a thunderstorm or blare of trumpets to announce the beginning of a new month or year. Even when a new century begins it is only we mortals who ring bells and fire off pistols.

The Magic Mountain, 5

5 Opinions cannot survive if one has no chance to fight for them. *The Magic Mountain, 6*

6 All interest in disease and death is only another expression of interest in life. *The Magic Mountain, 6*

7 Speech is civilization itself. The word, even the most contradictory word, preserves contact — it is silence which isolates. *The Magic Mountain, 6*

8 A man's dying is more the survivors' affair than his own. *The Magic Mountain, 6*

9 What we call mourning for our dead is perhaps not so much grief at not being able to call them back as it is grief at not being able to want to do so.

The Magic Mountain, 7

10 In almost every artist nature is inborn a wanton and treacherous proneness to side with the beauty that breaks hearts, to single out aristocratic pretensions and pay them homage.

Stories of Three Decades [1936].
Death in Venice

11 Hold fast the time! Guard it, watch over it, every hour, every minute! Unregarded it slips away, like a lizard, smooth, slippery, faithless, a pixy wife. Hold every moment sacred. Give each clarity and meaning, each the weight of thine awareness, each its true and due fulfillment.

The Beloved Returns [1939]

Hughes Mearns
1875–1965

12 As I was going up the stair
I met a man who wasn't there.
He wasn't there again today.
I wish, I wish he'd stay away.

The Psycho-ed [1910]. Antigonish[1]

Rainer Maria Rilke
1875–1926

13 Yes, everything that is truly seen *must* become a poem.

Journal entry [1900]

14 A good marriage is that in which each appoints the other guardian of his solitude.

Letter to Emanuel von Bodman
[August 17, 1901][2]

15 Once the realization is accepted that even between the *closest* human beings infinite distances continue to exist, a wonderful living side by side can grow up, if they succeed in loving the distance between them which makes it possible for each to see the other whole against the sky.

Letter to Emanuel Von Bodman
[August 17, 1901]

16 Fame is, after all, only the sum of all the misunderstandings that gather around a new name.

Auguste Rodin [1902]

17 Who has no house now will not build him one.[3]

The Book of Pictures [1902]. Autumn Day

18 Works of art are indeed always products of having been in danger, of having gone to the very end in an experience, to where man can go no further.

Letter to Clara Rilke [June 24, 1907]

19 He was a poet and hated the approximate.

The Journal of My Other Self[4] *[1910]*

20 Beauty's nothing
but beginning of Terror we're still just able to bear,
and why we adore it so is because it serenely
disdains to destroy us. Each single angel is terrible.

Duino Elegies[5] *[1923], no. 1*

21 We're never single-minded, unperplexed, like migratory birds. *Duino Elegies, 4*

---

[1]Later adapted in the song *The Little Man Who Wasn't There* [1939].

[2]Translated by JANE BARNARD GREENE and M. D. HERTER NORTON.

[3]Wer jetzt kein Haus hat, baut sich keines mehr. Translated by C. F. MACINTYRE.

[4]Translated by JOHN LINTON.

[5]Translated by J. B. LEISHMAN and STEPHEN SPENDER.

1   The most visible joy can only reveal itself to us when we've transformed it, within.   *Duino Elegies, 7*

2 Us the most fleeting of all. Just once,
everything, only for once. Once and no more. And we, too,
once. And never again. But this
having been once, though only once,
having been once on earth — can it ever be
canceled?   *Duino Elegies, 9*

3   Are we, perhaps, *here* just for saying: House. Bridge, Fountain, Gate, Jug, Fruit tree, Window, — possibly: Pillar, Tower?   *Duino Elegies, 9*

4   Death is the side of life which is turned away from us.
Letter to W. von Hulewicz
[November 13, 1925]

5   Love consists in this, that two solitudes protect and touch and greet each other.
Letters to a Young Poet[1] *[1929]*

6   The future enters into us, in order to transform itself in us, long before it happens.
Letters to a Young Poet

7   Love your solitude and bear with sweet-sounding lamentation the suffering it causes you.
Letters to a Young Poet

8   Live the questions now. Perhaps you will then gradually, without noticing it, live along some distant day into the answer.   *Letters to a Young Poet*

9   In the difficult are the friendly forces, the hands that work on us.   *Selected Letters*

10   You must change your life.
New Poems. Archaic Torso of Apollo

Rafael Sabatini
1875–1950

11   He was born with a gift of laughter and a sense that the world was mad. And that was all his patrimony.   *Scaramouche [1921], ch. 1*

Albert Schweitzer
1875–1965

12   Late on the third day, at the very moment when, at sunset, we were making our way through a herd of hippopotamuses, there flashed upon my mind, unforeseen and unsought, the phrase, "Reverence for Life."   *Out of My Life and Thought [1949]*

13   Affirmation of life is the spiritual act by which man ceases to live unreflectively and begins to devote himself to his life with reverence in order to raise it to its true value. To affirm life is to deepen, to make more inward, and to exalt the will to live.
Out of My Life and Thought

Sherwood Anderson
1876–1941

14   All of the men and women the writer had ever known had become grotesques.
Winesburg, Ohio [1919].
The Book of the Grotesque

15   Everyone in the world is Christ and they are all crucified.
Winesburg, Ohio. The Philosopher

16   I am a lover and have not found my thing to love.
Winesburg, Ohio. Tandy

Constantin Brancusi
1876–1957

17   It is not hard to work; it is hard to begin to work.
Attributed

Sarah N[orcliffe] Cleghorn
1876–1959

18 The golf links lie so near the mill
That almost every day
The laboring children can look out
And watch the men at play.
The Golf Links Lie So Near the Mill [1915]

Frank Hague
1876–1956

19   Listen, here is the law! I am the law![2]
Speech at Emory Methodist Episcopal Church,
Jersey City [November 10, 1937]

Ian Hay [John Hay Beith]
1876–1952

20   What do you mean, funny? Funny peculiar or funny ha-ha?
Housemaster/Bachelor Born [1938]

---

[1]Translated by M. D. Herter Norton.

[2]In reference to his role as mayor of Jersey City [1917–1947].

Max Jacob
1876–1944

1 The poet's expression of joy conceals his despair at not having found the reality of joy.
La Défense de Tartufe [1919]

2 When you get to the point where you cheat for the sake of beauty, you're an artist.[1]
Art Poétique [1922]

Charles F[ranklin] Kettering
1876–1958

3 We should all be concerned about the future because we will have to spend the rest of our lives there.
Seed for Thought [1949]

Maxim Maximovich Litvinov
1876–1951

4 Peace is indivisible.[2]
Speech to the League of Nations, Geneva, condemning Italian aggression in Ethiopia [July 1, 1936]

Jack [John Griffith] London
1876–1916

5 There is an ecstasy that marks the summit of life, and beyond which life cannot rise. And such is the paradox of living, this ecstasy comes when one is most alive, and it comes as a complete forgetfulness that one is alive. *The Call of the Wild [1903], ch. 3*

6 A good idea, he thought, to sleep off to death. It was like taking an anaesthetic. Freezing was not so bad as people thought. There were lots worse ways to die.... Then the man drowsed off into what seemed to him the most comfortable and satisfying sleep he had ever known. *To Build a Fire [1908]*

F. T. Marinetti
1876–1944

7 We wish to glorify war–the sole cleanser of the world—.... We wish to destroy the museums, libraries, academies of any sort, and fight against moralism, feminism, and every kind of materialist, self-serving cowardice.
Futurist Manifesto[3] [1909]

Wilson Mizner
1876–1933

8 Life's a tough proposition, and the first hundred years are the hardest. *Saying*

9 Be nice to people on your way up because you'll meet them on your way down. *Saying*

10 When you steal from one author, it's plagiarism; if you steal from many, it's research. *Saying*

Pope Pius XII [Eugenio Pacelli]
1876–1958

11 Private property is a natural fruit of labor, a product of intense activity of man, acquired through his energetic determination to ensure and develop with his own strength his own existence and that of his family, and to create for himself and his own an existence of just freedom, not only economic, but also political, cultural and religious.
Radio broadcast [September 1, 1944]

Tell Taylor
1876–1937
and
Ole Olsen
1892–1963

12 We're in the army now,
We're not behind a plow;
We'll never get rich
A-diggin' a ditch,
We're in the army now.
We're in the Army Now[4] [1917]

G[eorge] M[acaulay] Trevelyan
1876–1962

13 The year 1848 was the turning point at which modern history failed to turn.
British History in the Nineteenth Century [1922], ch. 19

---

[1] C'est au moment où l'on triche pour le beau que l'on est artiste.

[2] In an earlier speech at the League [September 5, 1935] during the Italian preparations for the invasion, Litvinov used a similar phrase: "The thesis of the indivisibility of peace ... It has now become clear to the whole world that each war is the creation of a preceding war and the generator of new present or future wars."

[3] Translated by DOUG THOMSON.

[4] Music by ISHAM JONES [1894–1956]. Often cited as "You're in the Army Now."

Isadora Duncan
1877–1927

1   Oh, she is coming, the dancer of the future ... more glorious than any woman who has yet been: more beautiful than the Egyptian, than the early Italian, than all women of past centuries — the highest intelligence in the freest body!

The Dancer of the Future[1] *[1903]*

2   I see only the ideal. But no ideals have ever been fully successful on this earth.[2]

My Life [1927]

Rose Fyleman
1877–1957

3 There are fairies at the bottom of our garden!

The Fairies [1920], st. 1

Hermann Hesse
1877–1962

4   Knowledge can be communicated but not wisdom.

Siddhartha[3] *[1922]*

Sir James Hopwood Jeans
1877–1946

5   Taking a very gloomy view of the future of the human race, let us suppose that it can only expect to survive for two thousand million years longer, a period about equal to the past age of the earth. Then, regarded as a being destined to live for three-score years and ten, humanity, although it has been born in a house seventy years old, is itself only three days old.

The Wilder Aspects of Cosmogony [1928]

6   From the intrinsic evidence of his creation, the Great Architect of the Universe now begins to appear as a pure mathematician.

The Mysterious Universe [1930]

John M[unro] Woolsey
1877–1945

7   I am quite aware that owing to some of its scenes [James Joyce's] *Ulysses* is a rather strong draught to ask some sensitive, though normal, persons to take. But my considered opinion, after long reflection, is that whilst in many places the effect of *Ulysses* on the reader is somewhat emetic, nowhere does it tend to be an aphrodisiac.

Ulysses may, therefore, be admitted into the United States.

U.S. v. One Book Called "Ulysses,"
5 Federal Supplement 182, 184 [1933], III

Martin Buber
1878–1965

8   How would man exist if God did not need him, and how would you exist? You need God in order to be, and God needs you — for that is the meaning of your life.[4]

I and Thou [1923]

9   The world is not divine sport; it is divine destiny. There is divine meaning in the life of the world, of man, of human persons, of you and of me.[5]

I and Thou

George M[ichael] Cohan
1878–1942

10   Always Leave Them Laughing When You Say Goodbye

Mother Goose [1903], title of song

11 Give my regards to Broadway,
Remember me to Herald Square,
Tell all the gang at Forty-second Street
That I will soon be there.

Little Johnny Jones [1904].
Give My Regards to Broadway

12 I'm a Yankee Doodle dandy,
A Yankee Doodle do or die;
A real live nephew of my Uncle Sam's
Born on the Fourth of July.

Little Johnny Jones. Yankee
Doodle Dandy

---

[1]Constructed from notes in a copy book.

[2]Hart Crane uses this sentence as an epigraph in his 1930 poem *The Bridge*. See 720:4–9.

[3]Translated by HILDA ROSNER.

---

[4]Translated by WALTER KAUFMANN.

[5]Translated by RONALD GREGOR SMITH.

1   The Yanks are coming,
The drums rum-tumming everywhere.
Over There [1917]

2 And we won't come back till it's over over there.
Over There

Adelaide Crapsey
1878–1914

3 These be
Three silent things:
The falling snow . . . the hour
Before the dawn . . . the mouth of one
Just dead.   *Cinquain: Triad [1915]*

Don[ald Robert Perry] Marquis
1878–1937

4 I love you as New Englanders love pie!
Sonnets to a Red-Haired Lady [1922], no. XII

5 dedicated to babs
with babs knows what
and babs knows why
archy and mehitabel[1] *[1927]*

6 oh i should worry and fret
death and i will coquette
there s a dance in the old dame yet
toujours gai toujours gai
archy and mehitabel. the song of mehitabel

7 procrastination is the
art of keeping
up with yesterday
archy and mehitabel. certain maxims of archy

8 an optimist is a guy
that has never had
much experience
archy and mehitabel. certain maxims of archy

9   what in hell
have i done to deserve
all these kittens
archy and mehitabel. mehitabel and her kittens

10 dance mehitabel dance
caper and shake a leg
what little blood is left
will fizz like wine in a keg
*archy and mehitabel. mehitabel dances
with boreas*

11 coarse
jocosity

---

[1]Archy, a cockroach, is unable to use the shift key on the typewriter for capitals and punctuation.
    Published later with other works by archy as *the lives and times of archy and mehitabel* [1943].

catches the crowd
shakespeare
and i
are often
low browed
archy and mehitabel. archy confesses

12 it wont be long now it wont be long
man is making deserts of the earth
it wont be long now
before man will have it used up
so that nothing but ants
and centipedes and scorpions
can find a living on it
*archy does his part [1935]. what the
ants are saying*

13 what man calls civilization
always results in deserts
archy does his part. what the ants are saying

14 it wont be long now it wont be long
till earth is barren as the moon
and sapless as a mumbled bone
archy does his part. what the ants are saying

John Masefield
1878–1967

15 I must down to the seas again, to the lonely sea and
the sky,
And all I ask is a tall ship and a star to steer her by,
And the wheel's kick and the wind's song and the
white sail's shaking,
And a gray mist on the sea's face and a gray dawn
breaking.   *Sea Fever [1902], st. 1*

16 I must down to the seas again, for the call of the
running tide
Is a wild call and a clear call that may not be denied.
Sea Fever, st. 2

17 I must down to the seas again, to the vagrant
gypsy life,
To the gull's way and the whale's way where the
wind's like a whetted knife;
And all I ask is a merry yarn from a laughing
fellow rover,
And quiet sleep and a sweet dream when the long
trick's over.   *Sea Fever, st. 3*

18 It's a warm wind, the west wind, full of birds' cries.
The West Wind [1902], st. 1

William Pitkin
1878–1953

19   Life Begins at Forty.   *Title of book [1932]*

Carl Sandburg
1878–1967

1 I am the people — the mob — the crowd — the mass.
Do you know that all the great work of the world is
   done through me?
I Am the People, the Mob [1916]

2 Hog butcher for the world,
Tool maker, stacker of wheat,
Player with railroads and the nation's freight handler;
Stormy, husky, brawling,
City of the big shoulders. *Chicago [1916]*

3 The fog comes
on little cat feet.
It sits looking
over harbor and city
on silent haunches
and then moves on. *Fog [1916]*

4 Pile the bodies high at Austerlitz and Waterloo.
Shovel them under and let me work —
I am the grass; I cover all. *Grass [1918]*

5 I tell you the past is a bucket of ashes.
Prairie [1918]

6 When Abraham Lincoln was shoveled into the tombs,
he forgot the copperheads and the assassin . . . in
the dust, in the cool tombs.
Cool Tombs [1918]

7 Why is there always a secret singing
When a lawyer cashes in?
Why does a hearse horse snicker
Hauling a lawyer away?
The Lawyers Know Too Much [1920]

8 Lay me on an anvil, O God.
Beat me and hammer me into a crowbar.
Let me pry loose old walls.
Let me lift and loosen old foundations.
Prayers of Steel [1920]

9 Sometime they'll give a war and nobody will
   come.[1]
The People, Yes [1936]

10   The people will live on.
The learning and blundering people will live on.
They will be tricked and sold and again sold
And go back to the nourishing earth for rootholds.
The People, Yes

11 The people know the salt of the sea
and the strength of the winds
lashing the corners of the earth.
The people take the earth

as a tomb of rest and a cradle of hope.
Who else speaks for the Family of Man?
The People, Yes

Upton [Beall] Sinclair
1878–1968

12   Now and then a visitor wept, to be sure; but this
slaughtering machine went on, visitors or no visitors.
It was like some horrible crime committed in a dungeon, all unseen and unheeded, buried out of sight
and of memory. *The Jungle [1906], ch. 3*

13   It is difficult to get a man to understand something, when his salary depends upon his not understanding it!
I, Candidate for Governor:
And How I Got Licked [1935]

Joseph Stalin
[Iosif Vissarionovich Dzhugashvili]
1878–1953

14   Print is the sharpest and the strongest weapon of
our party. *Speech [April 19, 1923]*

15   You are engineers of human souls.
Speech to writers [October 26, 1932]

16   The Hitlerite blackguards . . . have turned Europe
into a prison of nations,[2] and this they call the new
order in Europe.
Address to the Moscow Soviet
[November 6, 1942]

17   The Pope! How many divisions has *he* got?
From WINSTON CHURCHILL,
The Gathering Storm [1948]

18   You cannot make a revolution with silk gloves.
Attributed

19   A single death is a tragedy, a million deaths is a
statistic. *Attributed*

Edward Thomas
1878–1917

20 How weak and little is the light,
All the universe of sight,
Love and delight,
Before the might,
If you love it not, of night.

Out in the Dark [1917]

---

[1]Suppose They Gave a War, and No One Came. — CHARLOTTE
KEYES [1914–1980], *article in McCall's* [October 1966]

[2]The saying that Russia is a prison of nations. — VLADIMIR ILYICH
LENIN, *On the Question of a National Policy* [1914] (and elsewhere)

Robert Walser

1878–1956

1   Now, the wearing of uniforms simultaneously humiliates and exalts us. We look like unfree people, and that is possibly a disgrace, but we also look nice in our uniforms, and that sets us apart from the deep disgrace of those people who walk around in their very own clothes but in torn and dirty ones. To me, for instance, wearing a uniform is very pleasant because I never did know, before, what clothes to put on.[1]

Jakob von Gunten [1909]

Nancy [Witcher Langhorne] Astor

1879–1964

2   I married beneath me. All women do.

Attributed

Ethel Barrymore

1879–1959

3   That's all there is, there isn't any more.

Signature curtain line added by her to the play Sunday [1904] by THOMAS RACEWARD[2]

Louis Brownlow

1879–1963

4   They [the President's aides] should be possessed of high competence, great physical vigor, and a passion for anonymity.[3]

Administrative Management in the Government of the United States: Report of the President's Committee on Administrative Management [January 1937]

James Branch Cabell

1879–1958

5   I am willing to taste any drink once.

Jurgen [1919], ch. 16

6   The optimist proclaims that we live in the best of all possible worlds; and the pessimist fears this is true.

The Silver Stallion [1926], ch. 26

Albert Einstein

1879–1955

7   $E = mc^2$.

Statement of the mass-energy equivalence relationship[4] *[1905]*

8   The most beautiful thing we can experience is the mysterious. It is the source of all true art and science.

What I Believe [1930]

9   To know that what is impenetrable to us really exists, manifesting itself as the highest wisdom and the most radiant beauty which our dull faculties can comprehend only in their most primitive forms — this knowledge, this feeling, is at the center of all true religiousness. In this sense, and in this sense only, I belong in the ranks of devoutly religious men.

What I Believe

10   Concern for man himself and his fate must always form the chief interest of all technical endeavors, concern for the great unsolved problems of the organization of labor and the distribution of goods — in order that the creations of our mind shall be a blessing and not a curse to mankind. Never forget this in the midst of your diagrams and equations.

Address, California Institute of Technology [1931]

11   The eternal mystery of the world is its comprehensibility.... The fact that it is comprehensible is a miracle.[5]

Physics and Reality [1936]

12   The whole of science is nothing more than a refinement of everyday thinking.

Physics and Reality

13   Physical concepts are free creations of the human mind, and are not, however it may seem, uniquely determined by the external world.

Evolution of Physics [1938]

14   Some recent work by E. Fermi and L. Szilard, which has been communicated to me in manuscript, leads me to expect that the element uranium may be turned into a new and important source of energy in the immediate future. Certain aspects of the situation

---

[1]Translated by CHRISTOPHER MIDDLETON.

[2]Pseudonym of the actors T. Wigney Percyval, Horace Hodges, and Edward Irwin.

[3]Tell the President that the way to solve his problem is to find that one man who would turn out to be . . . possessed of high competence, great physical vigor, and a passion for anonymity. — TOM JONES [1870–1955] *(private secretary to Prime Minister Stanley Baldwin) to Brownlow* [1936]

[4]Energy equals mass times the speed of light squared.

The original statement is: If a body gives off the energy L in the form of radiation, its mass diminishes by L/c^2. — EINSTEIN, *Ist die Tragheit eines Korpers von Seinem Energieghalt Abhangig?* [1905]

[5]Often quoted as: The most incomprehensible thing about the universe is that it is comprehensible.

which has arisen seem to call for watchfulness and, if necessary, quick action on the part of the Administration.

> *Letter to President Franklin D. Roosevelt [August 2, 1939] (It resulted in the provision of government funds to develop the atom bomb.)*

1   This new phenomena [atomic energy] would also lead to the construction of bombs.... A single bomb of this type, carried by boat and exploded in a port, might very well destroy the whole port, together with some of the surrounding territory. However, such bombs might very well prove to be too heavy for transportation by air.

> *Letter to President Franklin D. Roosevelt [August 2, 1939]*

2   As long as there are sovereign nations possessing great power, war is inevitable.

> *Einstein on the atomic bomb. From the Atlantic Monthly [November 1945]*

3   I do not believe that civilization will be wiped out in a war fought with the atomic bomb. Perhaps two thirds of the people of the earth might be killed, but enough men capable of thinking, and enough books, would be left to start again, and civilization could be restored.

> *Einstein on the atomic bomb. From the Atlantic Monthly*

4   Since I do not foresee that atomic energy is to be a great boon for a long time, I have to say that for the present it is a menace. Perhaps it is well that it should be. It may intimidate the human race into bringing order into its international affairs, which, without the pressure of fear, it would not do.

> *Einstein on the atomic bomb. From the Atlantic Monthly*

5   I shall never believe that God plays dice with the world.

> *From PHILIPP FRANK [1884–1966], Einstein, His Life and Times [1947]*

6   The Lord God is subtle, but malicious he is not.[1]

> *Inscription in Jones Hall, Princeton University*

7   Every intellectual who is called before one of the committees ought to refuse to testify, i.e., he must be prepared ... for the sacrifice of his personal welfare in the interest of the cultural welfare of his country.... This kind of inquisition violates the spirit of the Constitution.

  If enough people are ready to take this grave step they will be successful. If not, then the intellectuals

of this country deserve nothing better than the slavery which is intended for them.

> *Letter to William Frauenglass[2] [May 16, 1953]*

8   The unleashed power of the atom has changed everything save our modes of thinking, and we thus drift toward unparalleled catastrophes.

> *From RALPH E. LAPP [1917–2004], The Einstein Letter That Started It All. In the New York Times Magazine [August 2, 1964]*

9   Something deeply hidden had to be behind things.

> *From RALPH E. LAPP, The Einstein Letter That Started It All. [August 2, 1964] [autobiographical handwritten note]*

E[dward] M[organ] Forster
1879–1970

10   Only connect! That was the whole of her sermon. Only connect the prose and the passion, and both will be exalted, and human love will be seen at its height. Live in fragments no longer. Only connect, and the beast and the monk, robbed of the isolation that is life to either, will die.

> *Howards End [1910], ch. 22*

11   Death destroys a man: the idea of Death saves him.

> *Howards End, 27*

12   The echo began in some indescribable way to undermine her hold on life. Coming at a moment when she chanced to be fatigued, it had managed to murmur, "Pathos, piety, courage — they exist, but are identical, and so is filth. Everything exists, nothing has value." If one had spoken vileness in that place, or quoted lofty poetry, the [echo's] comment would have been the same — "Ou-boum."

> *A Passage to India [1924]*

13   If I had to choose between betraying my country and betraying my friend, I hope I should have the guts to betray my country.

> *Two Cheers for Democracy [1951]. What I Believe*

14   Two cheers for Democracy: one because it admits variety and two because it permits criticism. Two cheers are quite enough: there is no occasion to give three.

> *Two Cheers for Democracy. What I Believe*

---

[1] Raffiniert ist der Herr Gott, aber Boshaft ist er nicht.

[2] Einstein's letter was published in the *New York Times* [June 12, 1953]. Frauenglass had been subpoenaed to testify before the Senate Internal Security Subcommittee.

[Stella Maria] Miles Franklin
1879–1954

1   Weariness! Weariness! This was life — my life — my career, my brilliant career! I was fifteen — fifteen! A few fleeting hours and I would be as old as those around me.

My Brilliant Career [1901], ch. 5

Edmund L. Gruber
1879–1941

2 Over hill, over dale, we have hit the dusty trail
And those caissons go rolling along.

The Caisson Song[1] [1908]

3 Oh, it's hi-hi-yee! for the field artilleree,
Shout out your numbers loud and strong,
And where'er we go, you will always know
That those caissons are rolling along.

The Caisson Song

Joe Hill [Joseph Hillstrom]
1879–1915

4 Work and pray, live on hay,
You'll get pie in the sky when you die.

The Preacher and the Slave [1911]

5   Don't waste any time mourning — organize!

*Letter to William D. Haywood
[November 18, 1915,
the day before Hill's execution]*

Paul Klee
1879–1940

6   When looking at any significant work of art, remember that a more significant one probably has had to be sacrificed.

Diary entry[2] [December 1904]

7   Color possesses me — I don't have to pursue it.... That is the meaning of this happy hour: Color and I are one. I am a painter.

Diary entry [April 1914]

8   Art does not reproduce the visible; rather, it makes visible.[3]

Creative Credo [1920]

9   [On drawing:] An active line on a walk, moving freely without a goal. A walk for a walk's sake.

Pedagogical Sketchbook [1925]

Vachel Lindsay
1879–1931

10 Booth died blind and still by faith he trod,
Eyes still dazzled by the ways of God.

*General William Booth Enters into
Heaven [1913], sec. II*

11 Sleep softly . . . eagle[4] forgotten . . . under the stone.

*The Eagle That Is Forgotten [1913],
st. 5*

12 Factory windows are always broken.
Somebody's always throwing bricks,
Somebody's always heaving cinders,
Playing ugly Yahoo tricks.

Factory Windows [1914], st. 1

13 Fat black bucks in a wine-barrel room,
Barrel-house kings; with feet unstable,
Sagged and reeled and pounded on the table,
Pounded on the table,
Beat an empty barrel with the handle of a broom.

The Congo [1914], pt. I

14 Then I saw the Congo, creeping through the black,
Cutting through the forest with a golden track.

The Congo, I

15 Be careful what you do,
Or Mumbo-Jumbo, God of the Congo,
And all of the other
Gods of the Congo,
Mumbo-Jumbo will hoo-doo you.

The Congo, I

16 A bronzed, lank man! His suit of ancient black,
A famous high top-hat and plain worn shawl
Make him the quaint great figure that men love,
The prairie-lawyer, master of us all.

*Abraham Lincoln Walks at Midnight
[1914], st. 3*

17 Planting the trees that would march and train
On, in his name to the great Pacific,

---

[1]The 1st Battalion of the 5th Field Artillery relieved the 2nd Battalion in the Philippines [April 1908]. Gruber, then a lieutenant in the 5th, was asked to write a song to symbolize the spirit of the reunited regiment. There are many variant wordings.

[2]Translated by Pierre B. Schneider, R. Y. Zachary, and Max Knight.

[3]Translated by Norbert Guterman.

[4]John Peter Altgeld [1847–1902; governor of Illinois, 1893–1897], widely criticized for pardoning, in June 1893, the anarchists who had been in prison since the Haymarket riot in Chicago on May 4, 1886. Altgeld believed their trial had been grossly mishandled.

Like Birnam Wood to Dunsinane,
Johnny Appleseed[1] swept on.
In Praise of Johnny Appleseed [1921]

Jack Norworth
1879–1959

1 Take me out to the ball game,
Take me out with the crowd.
Buy me some peanuts and cracker-jack—
I don't care if I never get back.
Take Me Out to the Ball Game[2] *[1908]*

2 For it's one, two, three strikes you're out
At the old ball game.
Take Me Out to the Ball Game

Will[iam Penn Adair] Rogers
1879–1935

3   All I know is just what I read in the papers.
Prefatory remark

4   I tell you folks, all politics is applesauce.
The Illiterate Digest [1924], p. 30

5   Everything is funny as long as it is happening to
somebody else.   *The Illiterate Digest, p. 131*

6   More men have been elected between sundown
and sunup than ever were elected between sunup and
sundown.   *The Illiterate Digest, p. 152*

7   A comedian can only last till he either takes himself
serious or his audience takes him serious.
Syndicated newspaper article [June 28, 1931]

8   Politics has got so expensive that it takes lots of
money to even get beat with.
Syndicated newspaper article [June 28, 1931]

9   My forefathers didn't come over on the *Mayflower*, but they met the boat.[3]   *Remark*

10   I joked about every prominent man in my lifetime,
but I never met one I didn't like.   *Epitaph*

Wallace Stevens
1879–1955

11 Twenty men crossing a bridge,
Into a village,

Are twenty men crossing twenty bridges,
Into twenty villages,
Or one man
Crossing a single bridge into a village.
Metaphors of a Magnifico [1923]

12 The book of moonlight is not written yet.
The Comedian as the Letter C [1923], pt. III, st. 1

13 And as he came he saw that it was spring,
A time abhorrent to the nihilist
Or searcher for the fecund minimum.
The Comedian as the Letter C, III, st. 4

14 The natives of the rain are rainy men.
The Comedian as the Letter C, IV, st. 1

15 The plum survives its poems.
The Comedian as the Letter C, V, st. 1

16 Green crammers of the green fruits of the world.
The Comedian as the Letter C, VI, st. 2

17 Poetry is the supreme fiction, madame.
A High-Toned Old Christian Woman [1923]

18 Let be be finale of seem.
The only emperor is the emperor of ice-cream.
The Emperor of Ice-Cream [1923]

19 Only, here and there, an old sailor,
Drunk and asleep in his boots,
Catches tigers
In red weather.
Disillusionment of Ten O'Clock [1923]

20 Complacencies of the peignoir, and late
Coffee and oranges in a sunny chair.
Sunday Morning [1923], st. 1

21 She says, "But in contentment I still feel
The need of some imperishable bliss."
Death is the mother of beauty; hence from her,
Alone, shall come fulfillment to our dreams
And our desires.
Sunday Morning, st. 5

22 We live in an old chaos of the sun,
Or old dependency of day and night,
Or island solitude, unsponsored, free,
Of that wide water, inescapable.
Deer walk upon our mountains, and the quail
Whistle about us their spontaneous cries;
Sweet berries ripen in the wilderness;
And, in the isolation of the sky,
At evening, casual flocks of pigeons make
Ambiguous undulations as they sink,
Downward to darkness, on extended wings.
Sunday Morning, st. 8

23 Chieftain Iffucan of Azcan in caftan
Of tan with henna hackles, halt!
Bantams in Pine Woods [1923], st. 1

---

[1]John Chapman [1774–1845].
   Remember Johnny Appleseed, / All ye who love the apple; / He
served his kind by word and deed, / in God's grand greenwood
chapel. —WILLIAM HENRY VENABLE [1836–1920], *Johnny
Appleseed, st. 25*
   [2]Music by ALBERT VON TILZER [1878–1956].
   [3]Rogers was part Cherokee.

1 Damned universal cock, as if the sun
  Was blackamoor to bear your blazing tail.
  Bantams in Pine Woods, st. 2

2 I placed a jar in Tennessee,
  And round it was, upon a hill.
  It made the slovenly wilderness
  Surround that hill.
  Anecdote of the Jar [1923], st. 1

3   Frogs Eat Butterflies. Snakes Eat Frogs. Hogs Eat
  Snakes. Men Eat Hogs.   *Title of poem [1923]*

4 Just as my fingers on these keys
  Make music, so the self-same sounds
  On my spirit make a music, too.
  Peter Quince at the Clavier [1923], pt. I

5 Beauty is momentary in the mind —
  The fitful tracing of a portal;
  But in the flesh it is immortal.

  The body dies; the body's beauty lives.
  Peter Quince at the Clavier, IV

6 Susanna's music touched the bawdy strings
  Of those white elders; but, escaping,
  Left only Death's ironic scraping.
  Now, in its immortality, it plays
  On the clear viol of her memory,
  And makes a constant sacrament of praise.
  Peter Quince at the Clavier, IV

7 I do not know which to prefer,
  The beauty of inflections
  Or the beauty of innuendoes,
  The blackbird whistling
  Or just after.
  *Thirteen Ways of Looking at a Blackbird
  [1923], st. 5*

8 She sang beyond the genius of the sea.
  The water never formed to mind or voice,
  Like a body wholly body, fluttering
  Its empty sleeves; and yet its mimic motion
  Made constant cry, caused constantly a cry,
  That was not ours although we understood,
  Inhuman, of the veritable ocean.
  *The Idea of Order at Key West [1936],
  st. 1*

9 Poetry is the subject of the poem.
  *The Man with the Blue Guitar [1937],
  pt. XXII*

10 I am a native in this world
  And think in it as a native thinks.
  The Man with the Blue Guitar, XXVIII

11   Light
  Is the lion that comes down to drink.
  The Glass of Water [1942], st. 2

12 A. A violent order is disorder; and
  B. A great disorder is an order. These
  Two things are one.
  Connoisseur of Chaos [1942], st. 1

13 He is like a man
  In the body of a violent beast.
  Its muscles are his own . . .

  The lion sleeps in the sun.
  Its nose is on its paws.
  It can kill a man.
  Poetry Is a Destructive Force [1942], st. 4, 5

14 One's grand flights, one's Sunday baths,
  One's tootings at the weddings of the soul
  Occur as they occur.
  *The Sense of the Sleight-of-Hand Man [1942],
  st. 1*

15 And, capable, created in his mind,
  Eventual victor, out of the martyrs' bones
  The ultimate elegance: the imagined land.
  Mrs. Alfred Uruguay [1942], st. 4

16 It was the last nostalgia: that he
  Should understand.
  Esthétique du Mal [1944], pt. X

17 The greatest poverty is not to live
  In a physical world, to feel that one's desire
  Is too difficult to tell from despair.
  Esthétique du Mal, XV

18 Thus the theory of description matters most.
  It is the theory of the word for those

  For whom the word is the making of the world,
  The buzzing world and lisping firmament.

  It is a world of words to the end of it,
  In which nothing solid is its solid self.
  Description Without Place [1947], pt. VII

19   Torn by dreams,

  By the terrible incantations of defeats
  And by the fear that defeats and dreams
    are one.

  The whole race is a poet that writes down
  The eccentric propositions of its fate.
  Men Made out of Words [1947]

20 The inconceivable idea of the sun.

  You must become an ignorant man again
  And see the sun again with an ignorant eye
  And see it clearly in the idea of it.
  *Notes Toward a Supreme Fiction [1947].
  It Must Be Abstract, pt. I*

21 The death of one god is the death of all.
  *Notes Toward a Supreme Fiction.
  It Must Be Abstract, I*

1 It is the celestial ennui of apartments
That sends us back to the first idea.
> *Notes Toward a Supreme Fiction.*
> *It Must Be Abstract, II*

2 And still the grossest iridescence of ocean
Howls hoo and rises and howls hoo and falls.
> *Notes Toward a Supreme Fiction.*
> *It Must Be Abstract, III*

3 We are the mimics. Clouds are pedagogues.
> *Notes Toward a Supreme Fiction.*
> *It Must Be Abstract, IV*

4 The President ordains the bee to be
Immortal.
> *Notes Toward a Supreme Fiction.*
> *It Must Change, II*

5 Booming and booming of the new-come bee.
> *Notes Toward a Supreme Fiction.*
> *It Must Change, II*

6   He chose to include the things
That in each other are included, the whole,
The complicate, the amassing harmony.
> *Notes Toward a Supreme Fiction.*
> *It Must Give Pleasure, VI*

7 These external regions, what do we fill them with
Except reflections, the escapades of death,
Cinderella fulfilling herself beneath the roof.
> *Notes Toward a Supreme Fiction.*
> *It Must Give Pleasure, VIII*

8   Perhaps
The man-hero is not the exceptional monster,
But he that of repetition is most master.
> *Notes Toward a Supreme Fiction.*
> *It Must Give Pleasure, IX*

9 They will get it straight one day at the Sorbonne.
> *Notes Toward a Supreme Fiction.*
> *It Must Give Pleasure, X*

10 And one trembles to be so understood and, at last,
To understand, as if to know became
The fatality of seeing things too well.
> *The Novel [1950], st. 16*

11 We keep coming back and coming back
To the real: to the hotel instead of the hymns
That fall upon it out of the wind.
> *An Ordinary Evening in New Haven*
> *[1950], pt. IX*

12 Total grandeur of a total edifice,
Chosen by an inquisitor of structures
For himself. He stops upon this threshold
As if the design of all his words takes form
And frame from thinking and is realized.
> *To an Old Philosopher in Rome [1950], st. 16*

13 Light the first light of evening, as in a room
In which we rest and, for small reason, think
The world imagined is the ultimate good.
> *Final Soliloquy of the Interior Paramour*
> *[1950], st. 1*

14 We say God and the imagination are one . . .
How high that highest candle lights the dark.[1]
> *Final Soliloquy of the Interior Paramour, st. 5*

15 There it was, word for word,
The poem that took the place of a mountain.
> *The Poem That Took the Place of a*
> *Mountain [1952], st. 1*

16 His self and the sun were one
And his poems, although makings of his self,
Were no less makings of the sun.
> *The Planet on the Table [1954],*
> *st. 3*

17 That scrawny cry — It was
A chorister whose *c* preceded the choir.
It was part of the colossal sun.
> *Not Ideas About the Thing but the*
> *Thing Itself [1954], st. 5*

18 The palm at the end of the mind,
Beyond the last thought, rises . . .

A gold-feathered bird
Sings in the palm.
> *Of Mere Being [1957], st. 1, 2*

19   The essential gaudiness of poetry.
> *Stevens's note to The Emperor of Ice-Cream*

20   The essential thing in form is to be free in whatever form is used. A free form does not assure freedom. As a form, it is just one more form. So that it comes to this, I suppose, that I believe in freedom regardless of form.
> *A Note on Poetry [1937]*

21   What makes the poet the potent figure that he is, or was, or ought to be, is that he creates the world to which we turn incessantly and without knowing it and that he gives to life the supreme fictions without which we are unable to conceive of it.
> *The Noble Rider and the Sound of*
> *Words [1942]*

22   The subject matter of poetry is not that "collection of solid, static objects extended in space" but the life that is lived in the scene that it composes; and so reality is not that external scene but the life that is lived in it. Reality is things as they are.
> *The Necessary Angel [1951]*

---

[1]Ellipses are in the original text.

1 The humble are they that move about the world with the lure of the real in their hearts.
The Necessary Angel. About One of Marianne Moore's Poems

2 A poet looks at the world as a man looks at a woman.   *Opus Posthumous [1957]. Adagia*

3 All history is modern history.
Opus Posthumous. Adagia

4 All poetry is experimental poetry.
Opus Posthumous. Adagia

5 The poet is priest of the invisible.
Opus Posthumous. Adagia

6 In the world of words, the imagination is one of the forces of nature.   *Opus Posthumous. Adagia*

7 God is in me or else is not at all (does not exist).
Opus Posthumous. Adagia

8 The world is a force, not a presence.
Opus Posthumous. Adagia

9 Poetry is a search for the inexplicable.
Opus Posthumous. Adagia

Emiliano Zapata
1879–1919

10 Men of the South! It is better to die on your feet than to live on your knees![1]   *Attributed*

Leon Trotsky
[Lev Davidovich Bronstein]
1879–1940

11 The literary "fellow travelers" of the Revolution.   *Literature and Revolution [1923], ch. 2*

12 The dictatorship of the Communist Party is maintained by recourse to every form of violence.
Terrorism and Communism [1924]

13 Revolutions are always verbose.
History of the Russian Revolution[2] [1930], vol. 2

14 [To the Mensheviks:] You are bankrupts; your role is played out. Go where you belong from now on — into the dustbin of history![3]
Speech to the Soviet Congress [1917]

15 It was the supreme expression of the mediocrity of the apparatus that Stalin himself rose to his position.
My Life [1930], ch. 40

16 The vengeance of history is more terrible than the vengeance of the most powerful General Secretary.
Stalin [1946], ch. 12

Guillaume Apollinaire
[Wilhelm Apollinaris de Kostrowitsky]
1880–1918

17 Shepherdess, O Eiffel Tower, your flock of bridges is bleating this morning.[4]
Alcools[5] (Spirits) [1913]. Zone

18 Under Pont Mirabeau flows the Seine.[6]
Alcools. Le Pont Mirabeau (Mirabeau Bridge)

19 Come night, strike hour.
Days go, I endure.[7]
Alcools. Le Pont Mirabeau, refrain

20 I hibernated in my past.[8]
Alcools. La Chanson du Mal-Aimé (Song of the Poorly Loved), st. 10

21 O Milky Way, sister in whiteness
To Canaan's rivers and the bright
Bodies of lovers drowned,
Can we follow toilsomely
Your path to other nebulae?[9]
Alcools. La Chanson du Mal-Aimé, st. 13 (also st. 27)

George Asaf [George H. Powell]
1880–1951

22 What's the use of worrying?
It never was worthwhile,
So, pack up your troubles in your old kit-bag,
And smile, smile, smile.
Pack Up Your Troubles in Your Old Kit-Bag[10] [1915]

Alexander Blok
1880–1921

23 With your whole body, with your whole heart, with your whole conscience, listen to the Revolu-

---

[1]Mejor morir a pie que vivir en rodillas.
Later a Republican watchword in the Spanish Civil War [1936–1939], especially identified with a speech at Madrid [July 18, 1936] by La Pasionaria [Dolores Ibarruri]. See 707:9.
See Franklin D. Roosevelt, 653:5.

[2]Translated by MAX EASTMAN.

[3]That great dust-heap called "history." — AUGUSTINE BIRRELL [1850–1933], *essay on Thomas Carlyle* [1884]

[4]Bergère ô tour Eiffel le troupeau des ponts bêle ce matin.

[5]Translated by WILLIAM MEREDITH.

[6]Sous le pont Mirabeau coule la Seine.

[7]Vienne la nuit sonne l'heure / Les jours s'en vont je demeure.

[8]J'ai hiverné dans mon passé.
Translated by ROGER SHATTUCK.

[9]Voie lactée ô soeur lumineuse / Des blancs ruisseaux de Chanaan / Et des corps blancs des amoureuses / Nageurs morts suivrons-nous d'ahan / Ton cours vers d'autres nébuleuses.

[10]Music by FELIX POWELL [1878–1942].

tion.... This is the music everyone who has ears should hear.

> *The Intelligentsia and the Revolution*
> *[1918]*

W[illiam] C[laude] Fields
1880–1946

1   It ain't a fit night out for man or beast.
> *The Fatal Glass of Beer [1933]*

2   Anyone who hates children and dogs can't be all bad.[1]
> *Attributed*

3   Here lies W. C. Fields. I would rather be living in Philadelphia.
> *Attributed epitaph*

George [Joseph] Herriman
1880–1944

4   I ain't a Kat...and I ain't Krazy...it's what's behind me that I am...it's the idea behind me, Ignatz, and that's wot I am.
> *Krazy Kat (comic strip) [1913 and after]*

Helen Keller
1880–1968

5   The mystery of language was revealed to me. I knew then that "w-a-t-e-r" meant the wonderful cool something that was flowing over my hand. That living word awakened my soul, gave it light, joy, set it free!
> *The Story of My Life [1902], ch. 4*

Douglas MacArthur
1880–1964

6   The history of failure in war can almost be summed up in two words: too late.
> *Statement on aid to Great Britain [1940]*

7   I shall return.
> *On arriving in Australia from the*
> *Philippines [March 30, 1942]*

8   I have returned. By the grace of Almighty God, our forces stand again on Philippine soil.
> *On landing on Leyte [October 17, 1944]*

9   I see that the old flagpole still stands. Have your troops hoist the colors to its peak, and let no enemy ever haul them down.
> *To Colonel George M. Jones and 503rd*
> *Regimental Combat Team, who recaptured*
> *Corregidor [March 2, 1945]*

10   In war there is no substitute for victory.
> *Address to a Joint Meeting of Congress*
> *[April 19, 1951]*

11   I still remember the refrain of one of the most popular barracks ballads of that day, which proclaimed most proudly that old soldiers never die; they just fade away. I now close my military career and just fade away.[2]
> *Address to a Joint Meeting of Congress*
> *[April 19, 1951]*

George C[atlett] Marshall
1880–1959

12   If man does find the solution for world peace it will be the most revolutionary reversal of his record we have ever known.
> *Biennial Report of the Chief of Staff,*
> *United States Army [September 1, 1945]*

13   Our policy is directed not against any country or doctrine but against hunger, poverty, desperation and chaos. Its purpose should be the revival of a working economy in the world so as to permit the emergence of political and social conditions in which free institutions can exist.
> *Address at Harvard University [June 5,*
> *1947], announcing the European Recovery*
> *Plan (Marshall Plan)*

14   It is not enough to fight. It is the spirit which we bring to the fight that decides the issue. It is morale that wins the victory.
> *Military Review [October 1948]*

15   [On World War II:] We could not indulge in a Seven Years War. A king can perhaps do that, but you cannot have such a protracted struggle in a democracy in the face of mounting casualties.[3]
> *The Papers of George Catlett Marshall [1981]*

H[enry] L[ouis] Mencken
1880–1956

16   The virulence of the national appetite for bogus revelation.
> *A Book of Prefaces [1917], ch. 1*

---

[1]Anyone who hates babies and dogs can't be all bad. — LEO C. ROSTEN [1908–1997], *in tribute to Fields at a banquet* [1939]
  The quip has become more familiar in the form attributed to Fields.

---

[2]See Anonymous, 887:4.

[3]Often cited as: A democracy cannot fight a Seven Years War.

1   Time is a great legalizer, even in the field of morals.
A Book of Prefaces, 4

2   The public ... demands certainties. ... But there *are* no certainties.
Prejudices, First Series [1919], ch. 3

3   All successful newspapers are ceaselessly querulous and bellicose. They never defend anyone or anything if they can help it; if the job is forced upon them, they tackle it by denouncing someone or something else.
Prejudices, First Series, 13

4   The great artists of the world are never Puritans, and seldom even ordinarily respectable.
Prejudices, First Series, 16

5   There is always an easy solution to every human problem — neat, plausible, and wrong.
The Divine Afflatus [1920]

6   [On Warren G. Harding:] He writes the worst English I have ever encountered. It reminds me of a string of wet sponges; it reminds me of tattered washing on the line; it reminds me of stale bean soup, of college yells, of dogs barking idiotically through endless nights. It is so bad that a sort of grandeur creeps into it.
Baltimore Evening Sun [March 7, 1921]

7   If, after I depart this vale, you ever remember me and have thought to please my ghost, forgive some sinner and wink your eye at some homely girl.
Epitaph. From Smart Set [December 1921]

8   There are no mute, inglorious Miltons, save in the hallucinations of poets. The one sound test of a Milton is that he functions as a Milton.
Prejudices, Third Series [1922], ch. 3

9   Nine times out of ten, in the arts as in life, there is actually no truth to be discovered; there is only error to be exposed.
Prejudices, Third Series, 3

10   Faith may be defined briefly as an illogical belief in the occurrence of the improbable.
Prejudices, Third Series, 14

11   To be happy one must be (*a*) well fed, unhounded by sordid cares, at ease in Zion, (*b*) full of a comfortable feeling of superiority to the masses of one's fellow men, and (*c*) delicately and unceasingly amused according to one's taste. It is my contention that, if this definition be accepted, there is no country in the world wherein a man constituted as I am — a man of my peculiar weakness, vanities, appetites, and aversions — can be so happy as he can be in the United States.
On Being An American [1922]

12   The whole aim of practical politics is to keep the populace alarmed (and hence clamorous to be led to safety) by an endless series of hobgoblins, most of them imaginary.
In Defense of Women [1922]

13   The difference between a moral man and a man of honor is that the latter regrets a discreditable act, even when it has worked and he has not been caught.
Prejudices, Fourth Series [1924], ch. 11

14   Out where the grass grows high, and the horned cattle dream away the lazy afternoons, and men still fear the powers and principalities of the air — out there between the corn-rows he held his old puissance to the end.
In Memoriam: W[illiam] J[ennings] B[ryan] [1925]

15   No one in this world, so far as I know ... has ever lost money by underestimating the intelligence of the great masses of the plain people.[1]
Notes on journalism, Chicago Tribune [September 19, 1926]

16   Of all escape mechanisms, death is the most efficient.   *A Book of Burlesques [1928]*

17   When A annoys or injures B on the pretense of saving or improving X, A is a scoundrel.
Newspaper Days: 1899–1906 [1941]

18   Conscience is the inner voice which warns us somebody may be looking.
A Mencken Chrestomathy [1949]. Sententiae

19   Puritanism — The haunting fear that someone, somewhere, may be happy.
A Mencken Chrestomathy. Sententiae

20   There are some people who read too much: the bibliobibuli. I know some who are constantly drunk on books, as other men are drunk on whiskey or religion. They wander through this most diverting and stimulating of worlds in a haze, seeing nothing and hearing nothing.
Minority Report: H. L. Mencken's Notebooks [1956]

21   The booboisie.   *Passim*

Robert [von Edler] Musil
1880–1942

22   There is nothing in this world as invisible as a monument.   *Monuments [1927]*

23   The number of portraits one saw of [Emperor Franz Joseph] was almost as great as the number of inhabitants of his realms. ... Believing in his existence was rather like seeing certain stars although they ceased to exist thousands of years ago.
The Man Without Qualities[2] [1930], bk. I, ch. 20

---

[1]Often misquoted as: No one ever went broke underestimating the intelligence of the American People.

[2]Translated by EITHNE WILKINS and ERNST KAISER.

Alfred Noyes
1880–1958

1 The wind was a torrent of darkness among the gusty
    trees,
The moon was a ghostly galleon tossed upon cloudy
    seas,
The road was a ribbon of moonlight over the purple
    moor,
And the highwayman came riding—
    Riding—riding—
The highwayman came riding, up to the old
    inn-door.
The Highwayman [1906]

2 I'll come to thee by moonlight, though hell should
    bar the way.   *The Highwayman*

Jeannette Rankin
1880–1973

3   I want to stand by my country, but I cannot vote
for war.
Upon casting her vote in the U.S. House of
Representatives against U.S. entry into World
War I [1917]

Grantland Rice
1880–1954

4 When the One Great Scorer comes to write against
    your name—
He marks—not that you won or lost—but how you
    played the game.
Alumnus Football [1908]

5   Outlined against a blue-gray October sky, the
Four Horsemen rode again. In dramatic lore they
were known as Famine, Pestilence, Destruction, and
Death. These are only aliases. Their real names are
Stuhldreher, Miller, Crowley, and Layden.[1]
Story on Notre Dame football victory over
Army, New York Tribune
[October 19, 1924]

Oswald Spengler
1880–1936

6   The decline of the West, which at first sight may
appear, like the corresponding decline of the Classical

Culture, a phenomenon limited in time and space,
we now perceive to be a philosophical problem that,
when comprehended in all its gravity, includes within
itself every great question of Being.
The Decline of the West[2] [1918–1923].
Introduction

7   Optimism is cowardice. We are born into this time
and must bravely follow the path to the destined
end.   *Man and Technics[2] [1931]*

Josiah Stamp
1880–1941

8   A pessimist looks at his glass and says it is half
empty; an optimist looks at it and says it is half full.
Attributed

Marie Stopes
1880–1958

9   An impersonal and scientific knowledge of the
structure of our bodies is the surest safeguard against
prurient curiosity and lascivious gloating.
Married Love [1918], ch. 5

[Giles] Lytton Strachey
1880–1932

10   The art of biography seems to have fallen on evil
times in England. . . . With us, the most delicate and
humane of all the branches of the art of writing has
been relegated to the journeymen of letters; we do
not reflect that it is perhaps as difficult to write a good
life as to live one.
Eminent Victorians [1918]. Preface

11   If this is dying, then I don't think much of it.
Last words. From MICHAEL HOLROYD
[b. 1935], Lytton Strachey [1968], vol. II

Franklin P[ierce]
Adams [F.P.A.]
1881–1960

12 Ruthlessly pricking our gonfalon bubble,
Making a Giant hit into a double,
Words that are weighty with nothing but trouble:
"Tinker to Evers to Chance."[3]
Baseball's Sad Lexicon [New York Evening
Mail, July 10, 1910]

---

[1] *The Four Horsemen* refers to the four allegorical horses in
Revelation 6:1–8. The football players are Harry Stuhldreher, Don
Miller, Jim Crowley, and Elmer Layden. Their coach was Knute
Rockne; see 682.

[2] Translated by CHARLES FRANCIS ATKINSON.

[3] Joe Tinker (shortstop), Johnny Evers (second baseman), and
Frank Chance (first baseman) of the Chicago Cubs.

1 The best you get is an even break.
    Weights and Measures [1917].
    Ballade of Schopenhauer's Philosophy

2 Of making many books there is no end —
So Sancho Panza said, and so say I.
Thou wert my guide, philosopher and friend
When only one is shining in the sky.
    Something Else Again [1920]. Lines on and
    from Bartlett's Familiar Quotations

Daisy Ashford [Margaret Mary Norman]
1881–1972

3 Bernard always had a few prayers in the hall and
some whiskey afterwards as he was rarther pious.
    The Young Visiters [1919], ch. 3

4 Here on a golden chair was seated the prince of
Wales in a lovely ermine cloak and a small but costly
crown.   *The Young Visiters, 6*

Joseph Campbell [Seosamh MacCathmhaoil]
1881–1944

5 As a white candle
In a holy place,
So is the beauty
Of an aged face.   *The Old Woman [1905], st. 1*

Padraic Colum
1881–1972

6 A little house — a house of my own —
Out of the wind's and the rain's way.
    An Old Woman of the Roads [1907], st. 6

Sir Alexander Fleming
1881–1955

7 It is the lone worker who makes the first advance
in a subject: the details may be worked out by a team,
but the prime idea is due to the enterprise, thought
and perception of an individual.
    Address at Edinburgh University [1951]

Edgar A[lbert] Guest
1881–1959

8 It takes a heap o' livin' in a house t' make it home,
A heap o' sun an' shadder, an' ye sometimes have

t' roam
Afore ye really 'preciate the things ye lef' behind,
An' hunger fer 'em somehow, with 'em allus on
    yer mind.   *Home [1916]*

Pope John XXIII [Angelo Giuseppe Roncalli]
1881–1963

9 The social progress, order, security and peace
of each country are necessarily connected with the
social progress, order, security and peace of all other
countries.
    Pacem in Terris. Encyclical letter
    [April 11, 1963]

10 The representative of the highest spiritual
authority of the earth is glad, indeed boasts, of being
the son of a humble but robust and honest laborer.
    Remark to the mayor of Fleury-sur-Loire.
    From Wit and Wisdom of Good Pope John[1]
    [1963] collected by Henri Fesquet
    [b. 1916]

11 Learn how to be a policeman, because that cannot
be improvised. As regards being pope, you will see
later. Anybody can be pope; the proof of this is that
I have become one.
    Letter to a young boy. From Wit and
    Wisdom of Good Pope John,
    collected by Henri Fesquet

Pablo Picasso
1881–1973

12 The quality of a painter depends on the amount of
the past he carries with him.   *Attributed*

13 To me there is no past or future in art. If a work
cannot always live in the present, it must not be considered art at all.
    The Art [May 25, 1923]

14 Painting is not done to decorate apartments. It is
an instrument of war for attack and defense against
the enemy.
    Statement About the Artist as a Political
    Being [1945]

15 God is really only another artist. He invented the
giraffe, the elephant, and the cat. He has no real style.
He just keeps on trying other things.
    From Françoise Gilot *[b. 1921] and*
    Carlton Lake *[1915–2006],*
    Life with Picasso [1964], ch. 1

---

[1] Translated by Salvator Attanasio.

1   Painting isn't an aesthetic operation; it's a form of magic designed as a mediator between this strange hostile world and us, a way of seizing the power by giving form to our terrors as well as our desires.
*From FRANÇOISE GILOT and CARLTON LAKE,
Life with Picasso, 6*

Pierre Teilhard de Chardin
1881–1955

2   Everything that rises must converge.[1]
Faith in Man [1947]

3   If there were no internal propensity to unite, even at a prodigiously rudimentary level — indeed in the molecule itself — it would be physically impossible for love to appear higher up.
*The Phenomenon of Man[2] [1955],
bk. IV, ch. 2, sec. 2*

4   In one manner or the other, it still remains true that, even in the view of a mere biologist, the human epic resembles nothing so much as a way of the Cross.   *The Phenomenon of Man. Appendix*

5   We have only to believe. And the more threatening and irreducible reality appears, the more firmly and desperately must we believe. Then, little by little, we shall see the universal horror unbend, and then smile upon us, and then take us in its more than human arms.
*The Divine Milieu[2] [1957], pt. III,
ch. 3, sec. B*

William Temple
1881–1944

6   There is no structural organization of society which can bring about the coming of the Kingdom of God on earth, since all systems can be perverted by the selfishness of man.
The Malvern Manifesto [1941]

Ludwig Edler von Mises
1881–1973

7   The market economy as such does not respect political frontiers. Its field is the world.
Human Action [1949]

8   Everybody thinks of economics whether he is aware of it or not. In joining a political party and in casting his ballot, the citizen implicitly takes a stand upon essential economic theories.   *Human Action*

James J. Walker
1881–1946

9   [On censorship:] No girl was ever ruined by a book.[3]   *Attributed*

10   A reformer is a guy who rides through a sewer in a glass-bottomed boat.   *Attributed*

[Sir] P[elham] G[renville] Wodehouse
1881–1975

11 So always look for the silver lining
And try to find the sunny side of life.
Sally[4] [1920]. Look for the Silver Lining

12   "Sir Jasper Finch-Farrowmere?" said Wilfred.
"ffinch-ffarrowmere," corrected the visitor, his sensitive ear detecting the capital letters.
*Meet Mr. Mulliner [1927].
A Slice of Life*

13   There is no time, sir, at which ties do not matter.
*Very Good, Jeeves! [1930].
Jeeves and the Impending Doom*

14   No good can come of association with anything labelled Gwladys or Ysobel or Ethyl or Mabelle or Kathryn. But particularly Gwladys.
Very Good, Jeeves. The Spot of Art

15   Into the face of the young man who sat on the terrace of the Hotel Magnifique at Cannes there had crept a look of furtive shame, the shifty, hangdog look which announces that an Englishman is about to talk French.
*The Luck of the Bodkins [1936].
The Luck of the Bodkins*

16   I could see that if not actually disgruntled, he was far from being gruntled.
*The Code of the Woosters [1938].
The Code of the Woosters*

Stefan Zweig
1881–1942

17   It is a law of life that human beings, even the geniuses among them, do not pride themselves on their

---

[1]Translated by NORMAN DENNY.
See Flannery O'Connor, 809:12.
[2]Translated by BERNARD WALL.

---

[3]Sometimes cited as: No woman was ever ruined by a book.
[4]Music by JEROME KERN [1885–1945]. BUDDY DE SYLVA may have contributed lyrics.

actual achievements but that they want to impress others, want to be admired and respected because of things of much lower import and value.

Balzac [1959]

Max Born
1882–1970

1   The human race has today the means for annihilating itself—either in a fit of complete lunacy, i.e., in a big war, by a brief fit of destruction, or by careless handling of atomic technology, through a slow process of poisoning and of deterioration in its genetic structure.

Bulletin of the Atomic Scientists
[June 1957]

Georges Braque
1882–1963

2   Truth exists, only lies are invented.

Pensées sur l'Art[1] (Thoughts on Art)

3   In art there is only one thing that counts; the thing you can't explain.

Pensées sur l'Art

Father Divine [George Baker]
c. 1882–1965

4   Peace, it's wonderful.

Motto of the Peace Mission Movement

Sir Arthur Stanley Eddington
1882–1944

5   I shall use the phrase "time's arrow" to express this one-way property of time which has no analogue in space.

The Nature of the Physical World
[1928], ch. 4

6   If an army of monkeys were strumming on typewriters they *might* write all the books in the British Museum.

The Nature of the Physical World, 4

7   The road to a knowledge of the stars leads through the atom; and important knowledge of the atom has been reached through the stars.

Stars and Atoms [1928], lecture 1

---

[1]Translated by STANLEY APPLEBAUM.

Felix Frankfurter
1882–1965

8   The [Fifteenth] Amendment nullifies sophisticated as well as simple-minded modes of discrimination.

Lane v. Wilson, 307 U.S. 268, 275 [1939]

9   The history of liberty has largely been the history of the observance of procedural safeguards.

McNabb v. United States,
318 U.S. 332, 347 [1943]

10   One who belongs to the most vilified and persecuted minority in history is not likely to be insensible to the freedoms guaranteed by our Constitution. . . . But as judges we are neither Jew nor Gentile, neither Catholic nor agnostic.

Flag Salute Cases, 319 U.S. 624, 646 [1943]

11   It is a fair summary of history to say that the safeguards of liberty have been forged in controversies involving not very nice people.

Dissenting opinion, United States v.
Rabinowitz [1950]

12   In a democratic society like ours, relief must come through an aroused popular conscience that sears the conscience of the people's representatives.

Baker v. Carr, 369 U.S. 186, 270 [1962]

13   I know of no title that I deem more honorable than that of Professor of the Harvard Law School.

Of Law and Life and Other Things [1965]

Jean Giraudoux
1882–1944

14   Faithful women are all alike, they think only of their fidelity, never of their husbands.

Amphitryon 38 [1929]

Samuel Goldwyn[2]
1882–1974

15   Include me out.   *Attributed*

16   In two words: im-possible.

Attributed

17   I read part of it all the way through.

Attributed

---

[2]Goldwynisms—as his colorful misuses of English were popularly referred to—abounded. With so many gag writers working for him, hardly a lunch in Hollywood went by without somebody's concocting a malapropism and passing it off as something Sam Goldwyn had just said to him.—A. SCOTT BERG [b. 1949], *Goldwyn: A Biography* [1989]

1   Anybody who goes to see a psychiatrist ought to have his head examined.   *Attributed*

2   A verbal agreement isn't worth the paper it's written on.   *Attributed*

William Frederick Halsey Jr.
1882–1959

3   Attack — Repeat — Attack.
> *Dispatch to the South Pacific Force before the battle of Santa Cruz Islands [October 26, 1942]*

4   Hit hard, hit fast, hit often.
> *Formula for waging war*

5   Our ships have been salvaged and are retiring at high speed toward the Japanese fleet.
> *Radio message after Japanese claims that most of the U.S. Third Fleet had either been sunk or had retired [October 1944]*

James Joyce
1882–1941

6   There is no heresy or no philosophy which is so abhorrent to my church as a human being.
> *Letter to Lady Gregory [November 1902]*

7   I think people might be willing to pay for the special odor of corruption which, I hope, floats over my stories.
> *Letter to publisher Grant Richards [October 15, 1905]*

8   He was outcast from life's feast.
> *Dubliners [1916]. A Painful Case*

9   Snow was general all over Ireland. It was falling on every part of the dark central plain, on the treeless hills, falling softly upon the Bog of Allen and, farther westward, softly falling into the dark mutinous Shannon waves. It was falling, too, upon every part of the lonely churchyard on the hill where Michael Furey lay buried. It lay thickly drifted on the crooked crosses and headstones, on the spears of the little gate, on the barren thorns. His soul swooned slowly as he heard the snow falling faintly through the universe and faintly falling, like the descent of their last end, upon all the living and the dead.
> *Dubliners. The Dead*

10 Ireland is the old sow that eats her farrow.
> *A Portrait of the Artist as a Young Man [1916], ch. 5*

11 The artist, like the God of the creation, remains within or behind or beyond or above his handiwork, invisible, refined out of existence, indifferent, paring his fingernails.
> *A Portrait of the Artist as a Young Man, 5*

12 I desire to press in my arms the loveliness which has not yet come into the world.
> *A Portrait of the Artist as a Young Man, 5*

13 Welcome, O life! I go to encounter for the millionth time the reality of experience and to forge in the smithy of my soul the uncreated conscience of my race.
>   April 27. Old father, old artificer, stand me now and ever in good stead.
> *A Portrait of the Artist as a Young Man, 5, concluding words of Stephen Dedalus*

14 Agenbite of inwit.[1] Conscience.
> *Ulysses [1922]*

15 History, Stephen said, is a nightmare from which I am trying to awake.
> *Ulysses*

16 A man of genius makes no mistakes. His errors are volitional and are the portals of discovery.
> *Ulysses*

17 Shakespeare is the happy hunting ground of all minds that have lost their balance.
> *Ulysses*

18 I thought well as well him as another and then I asked him with my eyes to ask again yes and then he asked me would I yes to say yes my mountain flower and first I put my arms around him yes and drew him down to me so he could feel my breasts all perfume yes and his heart was going like mad and yes I said yes I will Yes.   *Ulysses, last words*

19 riverrun, past Eve and Adam's, from swerve of shore to bend of bay, brings us by a commodius vicus of recirculation back to Howth Castle and Environs.
> *Finnegans Wake [1939], bk. I (opening)*

20 Here Comes Everybody.   *Finnegans Wake, I*

21   O
>   tell me all about
>   Anna Livia! I want to hear all
> about Anna Livia. Well, you know Anna Livia? Yes, of course, we all know Anna Livia. Tell me all. Tell me now.
> *Finnegans Wake, I*

22 Can't hear with bawk of bats, all thim liffeying waters of. Ho, talk save us! My foos won't moos. I

---

[1] *Ayenbite of Inwyt* [remorse of conscience]. — Title of treatise on the seven deadly sins by DAN MICHEL OF NORTHGATE [fourteenth century]

feel as old as yonder elm. A tale told of Shaun or Shem? All Livia's daughtersons. Dark hawks hear us. Night! Night! My ho head halls. I feel as heavy as yonder stone. Tell me of John or Shaun? Who were Shem and Shaun the living sons or daughters of? Night now! Tell me, tell me, tell me, elm! Night night! Telmetale of stem or stone. Beside the rivering waters of, hitherandthithering waters of. Night!

Finnegans Wake, I

1 Three quarks[1] for Muster Mark!

Finnegans Wake, II

2 First we feel. Then we fall.

Finnegans Wake, IV

3 I am passing out. O bitter ending! I'll slip away before they're up. They'll never see. Nor know. Nor miss me. And it's old and old it's sad and old it's sad and weary I go back to you, my cold father, my cold mad father, my cold mad feary father, till the near sight of the mere size of him, the moyles and moyles of it, moananoaning, makes me seasilt saltsick and I rush, my only, into your arms, I see them rising! Save me from those therrble prongs!

Finnegans Wake, IV

Fiorello H[enry] La Guardia
1882–1947

4 Ticker tape ain't spaghetti.
Speech to the United Nations Relief and Rehabilitation Administration [March 29, 1946]

5 When I make a mistake it's a beaut!
On an indefensible appointment

A[lan] A[lexander] Milne
1882–1956

6 James James
Morrison Morrison
Weatherby George Dupree
Took great care of his Mother
Though he was only three.
James James
Said to his Mother,
"Mother," he said, said he,
"You must never go down to the end of the town if
you don't go down with me."
When We Were Very Young [1924]. Disobedience

7 I do like a little bit of butter to my bread!
When We Were Very Young. The King's Breakfast

8 I am a Bear of Very Little Brain, and long words Bother me.
Winnie-the-Pooh [1926], ch. 4

9 Time for a little something.   *Winnie-the-Pooh, 6*

10 Wherever they go, and whatever happens to them on the way, in that enchanted place on the top of the Forest, a little boy and his Bear will always be playing.
The House at Pooh Corner [1928]

Sam [Taliaferro] Rayburn
1882–1961

11 A jackass can kick a barn down, but it takes a carpenter to build one.
Remark [c. 1953]

12 To get along, go along.   *Attributed*

Franklin Delano Roosevelt[2]
1882–1945

13 There is nothing I love as much as a good fight.
Interview in the New York Times [January 22, 1911]

14 These unhappy times call for the building of plans...that build from the bottom up and not from the top down, that put their faith once more in the forgotten man[3] at the bottom of the economic pyramid.
Radio address [April 7, 1932]

15 The country needs and, unless I mistake its temper, the country demands bold, persistent experimentation. It is common sense to take a method and try it. If it fails, admit it frankly and try another. But above all, try something.
Address at Oglethorpe University, Atlanta, Georgia [May 22, 1932]

16 I pledge you, I pledge myself, to a new deal for the American people.[4]
Speech accepting the Democratic nomination for the presidency, Chicago [July 2, 1932]

---

[1]The origin of the physicist Murray Gell-Mann's name [1964] for one of the elementary particles of matter.

[2]See Walter Lippmann, 685:4.

[3]All honor to the one that in this hour / Cries to the world as from a lighted tower— / Cries for the Man Forgotten. — EDWIN MARKHAM, *The Forgotten Man [1932]*

[4]It seemed to me that what the nine hundred and ninety-four dupes needed was a new deal. — MARK TWAIN, *A Connecticut Yankee in King Arthur's Court, ch. 13*

1   There is no indispensable man.[1]
    Campaign speech, New York City
    [November 3, 1932]

2   The only thing we have to fear is fear itself.
    First Inaugural Address [March 4, 1933]

3   In the field of world policy I would dedicate this nation to the policy of the good neighbor.[2]
    First Inaugural Address
    [March 4, 1933]

4   If I were asked to state the great objective which Church and State are both demanding for the sake of every man and woman and child in this country, I would say that that great objective is "a more abundant life."
    Address to the Federal Council of Churches of Christ [December 6, 1933]

5   We are moving forward to greater freedom, to greater security for the average man than he has ever known before in the history of America.
    Fireside Chat [September 30, 1934]

6   Out of this modern civilization economic royalists carved new dynasties. . . . The royalists of the economic order have conceded that political freedom was the business of the Government, but they have maintained that economic slavery was nobody's business.
    Speech accepting the presidential renomination [June 27, 1936]

7   This generation of Americans has a rendezvous with destiny.
    Speech accepting the presidential renomination

8   Better the occasional faults of a government that lives in a spirit of charity than the consistent omissions of a government frozen in the ice of its own indifference.
    Speech accepting the presidential renomination

9   I have seen war. . . . I hate war.
    Address at Chautauqua, New York
    [August 14, 1936]

10   I should like to have it said of my first Administration that in it the forces of selfishness and of lust for power met their match. I should like to have it said of my second Administration that in it these forces met their master.
    Speech at Madison Square Garden
    [October 31, 1936]

11   [On certain political opponents:] They are unanimous in their hatred for me — and I welcome their hatred.
    Reelection campaign speech
    [October 31, 1936]

12   I see one-third of a nation ill-housed, ill-clad, ill-nourished.
    Second Inaugural Address
    [January 20, 1937]

13   The test of our progress is not whether we add more to the abundance of those who have much; it is whether we provide enough for those who have too little.
    Second Inaugural Address
    [January 20, 1937]

14   Instinctively we recognized a deeper need — the need to find through government the instrument of our united purpose to solve for the individual the ever-rising problems of a complex civilization. Repeated attempts at their solution without the aid of government had left us baffled and bewildered.
    Second Inaugural Address
    [January 20, 1937]

15   We have always known that heedless self-interest was bad morals; we know now that it is bad economics.
    Second Inaugural Address
    [January 20, 1937]

16   The nation that destroys its soil destroys itself.
    Letter to governors on soil conservation
    [February 26, 1937]

17   The epidemic of world lawlessness is spreading. When an epidemic of physical disease starts to spread, the community approves and joins in a quarantine of the patients in order to protect the health of the community against the spread of the disease.
    Speech at Chicago[3]
    [October 5, 1937]

18   The only sure bulwark of continuing liberty is a government strong enough to protect the interests of the people, and a people strong enough and well enough informed to maintain its sovereign control over its government.
    Fireside Chat [April 14, 1938]

19   A program whose basic thesis is not that the system of free private enterprise for profit has failed in this generation, but that it has not yet been tried.
    Message on Concentration of Economic Power
    [April 29, 1938]

---

[1]Il n'y a point d'homme nécessaire. — *French proverb*

[2]I am as desirous of being a good neighbor as I am of being a bad subject. — HENRY DAVID THOREAU, *Civil Disobedience*

[3]The "Quarantine the Aggressors" speech.

1   On this tenth day of June 1940 the hand that held the dagger has struck it into the back of its neighbor.[1]
   Address at the University of Virginia,
   Charlottesville [June 10, 1940]

2   I have said this before, but I shall say it again and again and again: Your boys are not going to be sent into any foreign wars.
   Campaign speech in Boston
   [October 30, 1940]

3   We must be the great arsenal of democracy.
   Fireside Chat [December 29, 1940]

4   We look forward to a world founded upon four essential human freedoms. The first is freedom of speech and expression — everywhere in the world. The second is freedom of every person to worship God in his own way — everywhere in the world. The third is freedom from want . . . everywhere in the world. The fourth is freedom from fear . . . anywhere in the world.[2]
   Message to Congress [January 6, 1941]

5   We, too, born to freedom, and believing in freedom, are willing to fight to maintain freedom. We, and all others who believe as deeply as we do, would rather die on our feet than live on our knees.[3]
   On receiving the degree of Doctor of Civil Law
   from Oxford University [June 19, 1941]

6   Yesterday, December 7, 1941 — a date which will live in infamy — the United States of America was suddenly and deliberately attacked by naval and air forces of the Empire of Japan.
   War Message to Congress [December 8, 1941]

7   Books cannot be killed by fire. People die, but books never die. No man and no force can abolish memory. . . . In this war, we know, books are weapons.
   Message to the American Booksellers
   Association [April 23, 1942]

8   It is not a tax bill but a tax relief bill providing relief not for the needy but for the greedy.
   Tax bill veto message [February 22, 1944]

9   I think I have a right to resent, to object to libelous statements about my dog.[4]
   Speech at the Teamsters' Dinner,
   Washington, D.C. [September 23, 1944]

10   All of our people all over the country — except the pure-blooded Indians — are immigrants or descendants of immigrants, including even those who came over here on the *Mayflower.*
   Campaign speech in Boston
   [November 4, 1944]

11   The American people are quite competent to judge a political party that works both sides of a street.
   Campaign speech in Boston
   [November 4, 1944]

12   We have learned that we cannot live alone, at peace; that our own well-being is dependent on the well-being of other nations, far away. We have learned that we must live as men, and not as ostriches, nor as dogs in the manger. We have learned to be citizens of the world, members of the human community.
   Fourth Inaugural Address
   [January 20, 1945]

13   More than an end to war, we want an end to the beginnings of all wars.
   Address written for Jefferson Day broadcast
   [April 13, 1945][5]

Franklin Delano Roosevelt
1882–1945

and

Winston Churchill
1874–1965

14   First, their countries seek no aggrandizement, territorial or other.
   Second, they desire to see no territorial changes that do not accord with the freely expressed wishes of the peoples concerned.
   Atlantic Charter, drawn up aboard the
   U.S.S. Augusta in Argentia Harbor,
   Newfoundland [issued August 14, 1941]

15   Sixth, after the final destruction of the Nazi tyranny, they hope to see established a peace which will afford to all nations the means of dwelling in safety within their own boundaries, and which will afford assurance that all the men in all the lands may live out their lives in freedom from fear and want.
   Atlantic Charter, drawn up aboard the
   U.S.S. Augusta in Argentia Harbor,
   Newfoundland [issued August 14, 1941]

16   Eighth, they believe that all of the nations of the world, for realistic as well as spiritual reasons, must

---

[1]Italian Foreign Minister Count Galeazzo Ciano had just notified the French ambassador that Italy considered herself at war with France beginning June 11.

[2]See Roosevelt and Churchill, 653:15.

[3]See Emiliano Zapata, 634:8.

[4]It had been charged that the President's Scottie, Fala, allegedly stranded in the Aleutian Islands, had been brought home by a destroyer at a cost of millions.

[5]President Roosevelt died on April 12, at Warm Springs, Georgia.

come to the abandonment of the use of force. Since no future peace can be maintained if land, sea or air armaments continue to be employed by nations which threaten, or may threaten, aggression outside of their frontiers, they believe, pending the establishment of a wider and permanent system of general security, that the disarmament of such nations is essential.

> *Atlantic Charter, drawn up aboard the*
> *U.S.S. Augusta in Argentia Harbor,*
> *Newfoundland [issued August 14, 1941]*

James Stephens
1882–1950

1   Women are wiser than men because they know less and understand more.

> *The Crock of Gold [1912], ch. 2*

2 I hear a sudden cry of pain!
There is a rabbit in a snare.   *The Snare [1915]*

3 Forgive us all our trespasses,
Little creatures, everywhere!

> *Little Things [1924], st. 5*

Virginia Woolf
1882–1941

4   On or about December, 1910, human character changed. I am not saying that one went out, as one might into a garden, and there saw that a rose had flowered, or that a hen had laid an egg. The change was not sudden and definite like that.

> *Mr. Bennett and Mrs. Brown [1924]*

5   In people's eyes, in the swing, tramp, and trudge; in the bellow and uproar; the carriages, motor cars, omnibuses, vans, sandwich men shuffling and swinging; brass bands; barrel organs; in the triumph and the jingle and the strange high singing of some aeroplane overhead was what she loved; life; London; this moment in June.   *Mrs. Dalloway [1925]*

6   Those comfortably padded lunatic asylums which are known, euphemistically, as the stately homes of England.[1]

> *The Common Reader [1925].*
> *Lady Dorothy Nevill*

7   Trivial personalities decomposing in the eternity of print.   *The Common Reader. The Modern Essay*

8   There is no room for the impurities of literature in an essay.

> *The Common Reader. The Modern Essay*

9   That complete statement which is literature.

> *The Common Reader.*
> *How It Strikes a Contemporary*

10   The word-coining genius, as if thought plunged into a sea of words and came up dripping.

> *The Common Reader.*
> *An Elizabethan Play*

11   I have had my vision.

> *To the Lighthouse [1927], last line*

12   In every human being a vacillation from one sex to the other takes place, and often it is only the clothes that keep the male or female likeness, while underneath the sex is the very opposite of what is above.

> *Orlando [1928]*

13   A biography is considered complete if it merely accounts for six or seven selves, whereas a person may well have as many thousand.

> *Orlando, ch. 6*

14   A woman must have money and a room of her own if she is to write fiction.

> *A Room of One's Own [1929], ch. 1*

15   One cannot think well, love well, sleep well, if one has not dined well.

> *A Room of One's Own, 1*

16   The beauty of the world which is so soon to perish, has two edges, one of laughter, one of anguish, cutting the heart asunder.

> *A Room of One's Own, 2*

17   Women have served all these centuries as looking-glasses possessing the magic and delicious power of reflecting the figure of man at twice its natural size.

> *A Room of One's Own, 2*

18   It is the masculine values that prevail . . . This is an important book, the critic assumes, because it deals with war. This is an insignificant book because it deals with the feelings of women in a drawing-room.

> *A Room of One's Own, 4*

19   Death is the enemy. . . . Against you I will fling myself, unvanquished and unyielding, O Death.

> *The Waves [1931]*

20   Surely it was time someone invented a new plot, or that the author came out from the bushes.

> *Between the Acts [1941]*

Eubie [James Herbert] Blake
1883–1983

21   If I'd known I was going to live this long, I'd have taken better care of myself.

> *Attributed [1983]*

---

[1]See Felicia Hemans, 405:7 and note.

Coco [Gabrielle] Chanel
1883–1971

1   Fashion is made to become unfashionable.
Quoted in Life magazine [August 19, 1957]

2   Fashion does not exist unless it goes down into the streets.
Quoted in EDMONDE CHARLES-ROUX [b. 1920], Chanel and Her World [1979]

3   Fashion is architecture: it is a matter of proportions.   *Remark*

4   I wanted to give a woman comfortable clothes that would flow with her body. A woman is closest to being naked when she is well dressed.
Remark

Kahlil Gibran
1883–1931

5   Let there be spaces in your togetherness.
The Prophet [1923]. On Marriage

6   Work is love made visible. And if you cannot work with love but only with distaste, it is better that you should leave your work and sit at the gate of the temple and take alms of those who work with joy.
The Prophet. On Work

7   You pray in your distress and in your need; would that you might pray also in the fullness of your joy and in your days of abundance.
The Prophet. On Prayer

Walter Gropius
1883–1969

8   Let us create a new guild of craftsmen, without the class distinctions which raise an arrogant barrier between craftsman and artist. Let us together desire, conceive, and create the new building of the future, which will embrace architecture and sculpture and painting in one unity and which will rise one day toward heaven from the hands of a million workers like the crystal symbol of a new faith.
Proclamation of the Weimar Bauhaus [1919]

Willie Howard
1883–1949

9   Comes de revolution, we'll eat strawberries and cream!
Ballyhoo of 1932 (vaudeville) [1932]

Franz Kafka
1883–1924

10   I think we ought to read only the kind of books that wound and stab us.... We need the books that affect us like a disaster, that grieve us deeply, like the death of someone we loved more than ourselves, like being banished into forests far from everyone, like a suicide. A book must be the axe for the frozen sea inside us.
Letter to Oskar Pollak [January 27, 1904]

11   Don't despair, not even over the fact that you don't despair.[1]
Diary entry [July 21, 1913]

12   What have I in common with Jews? I have almost nothing in common with myself and should stand very quietly in a corner, content that I can breathe.[2]
Diary entry [January 8, 1914]

13   No one else could ever be admitted here, since this gate was made only for you. I am now going to shut it.
Parables.[1] Before the Law [1914]

14   As Gregor Samsa awoke one morning from uneasy dreams he found himself transformed in his bed into a gigantic insect.[3]
The Metamorphosis[4] [1915], opening line

15   The Messiah will come only when he is no longer necessary; he will come only on the day after his arrival; he will come, not on the last day, but on the very last.
Parables.[4] The Coming of the Messiah [1917]

16   The true way goes over a rope which is not stretched at any great height but just above the ground. It seems more designed to make people stumble than to be walked upon.
The Great Wall of China [1917]. Reflections

17   You do not need to leave your room. Remain sitting at your table and listen. Do not even listen, simply wait. Do not even wait, be quite still and solitary. The world will freely offer itself to you to be unmasked, it has no choice, it will roll in ecstasy at your feet.
The Great Wall of China. Reflections

---

[1]Translated by MIKE MITCHELL.

[2]Translated by MARTIN GREENBERG with HANNAH ARENDT.

[3]When I read the line I thought to myself I didn't know anyone was allowed to write things like that. If I had known, I would have started writing a long time ago. So I immediately started writing short stories. — GABRIEL GARCÍA MÁRQUEZ, *Paris Review interview* [1981]

[4]Translated by WILLA and EDWIN MUIR.

1   Only our concept of time makes it possible for us to speak of the Day of Judgment by that name; in reality it is a summary court in perpetual session.
The Great Wall of China. Reflections

2   "Like a dog!" he said. It seemed as if his shame would live on after him.
The Trial[1] *[1925], final lines*

3   This village belongs to the Castle, and whoever lives here or passes the night here does so in a manner of speaking in the Castle itself. Nobody may do that without the Count's permission.
The Castle[2] *[1926]*

4   A first sign of the beginning of knowledge is the wish to die.   *Aphorism*

Nikos Kazantzakis
1883–1957

5   How simple and frugal a thing is happiness: a glass of wine, a roast chestnut, a wretched little brazier, the sound of the sea.... All that is required to feel that here and now is happiness is a simple, frugal heart.
Zorba the Greek[3] *[1946], ch. 7*

6   "Life is trouble," Zorba continued. "Death, no. To live — do you know what that means? To undo your belt and look for trouble!"
Zorba the Greek, 8

7   The highest point a man can attain is not Knowledge, or Virtue, or Goodness, or Victory, but something even greater, more heroic and more despairing: Sacred Awe!   *Zorba the Greek, 24*

8   The doors of heaven are adjacent and identical: both green, both beautiful. Take care, Adam!
The Last Temptation of Christ[4]
[1960], ch. 18

John Maynard Keynes
1883–1946

9   He [Clemenceau] had one illusion — France; and one disillusion — mankind, including Frenchmen.
Economic Consequences of the Peace [1919],
ch. 3

10   He [Woodrow Wilson] could write Notes from Sinai or Olympus; he could remain unapproachable in the White House or even in the Council of Ten and be safe. But if he once stepped down to the intimate equality of the Four, the game was evidently up.
Economic Consequences of the Peace, 3

11   *Long run* is a misleading guide to current affairs. *In the long run* we are all dead.
A Tract on Monetary Reform [1923], ch. 3

12   Marxian Socialism must always remain a portent to the historians of opinion — how a doctrine so illogical and so dull can have exercised so powerful and enduring an influence over the minds of men, and, through them, the events of history.
The End of Laissez-Faire [1925], ch. 3

13   The engine which drives Enterprise is not Thrift, but Profit.   *A Treatise on Money [1930]*

14   If enterprise is afoot, wealth accumulates, whatever may be happening to thrift; and if enterprise is asleep, wealth decays, whatever thrift may be doing.
A Treatise on Money

15   The love of money as a possession — as distinguished from the love of money as a means to the enjoyments and realities of life — will be recognized for what it is, a somewhat disgusting morbidity, one of those semi-criminal, semi-pathological propensities which one hands over with a shudder to the specialists in mental disease.
Essay in Persuasion [1931], pt. V

16   If economists could manage to get themselves thought of as humble, competent people, on a level with dentists, that would be splendid!
Essays in Persuasion, V

17   Words ought to be a little wild for they are the assault of thoughts on the unthinking.
In the New Statesman and Nation
[July 15, 1933]

18   Of the maxims of orthodox finance, none, surely, is more antisocial than the fetish of liquidity.... It forgets that there is no such thing as liquidity of investment for the community as a whole.
The General Theory of Employment,
Interest and Money [1936], ch. 12

Alfred Hart Miles
1883–1956

19 Anchors aweigh, my boys,
Anchors aweigh!
Farewell to college joys,
We sail at break of day.
Anchors Aweigh[5] *[1907]*

---

[1]Translated by MIKE MITCHELL.
[2]Translated by WILLA and EDWIN MUIR.
[3]Translated by CARL WILDMAN.
[4]Translated by P. A. BIEN.

[5]Music by CHARLES A. ZIMMERMAN [1861–1916].

Benito Mussolini
1883–1945

1   The Italian proletariat needs a blood bath for its force to be renewed.
Editorial, Popolo d'Italia [1920]

2   War is to man as motherhood is to woman.
Speech [May 1934]

3   We have buried the putrid corpse of liberty.
Speech. From MAURICE PARMELEE [1882–1969], Bolshevism, Fascism, and the Liberal-Democratic State [1934]

4   War alone brings up to its highest tension all human energy and puts the stamp of nobility upon the peoples who have the courage to face it.
Written for The Italian Encyclopedia. From GEORGE SELDES [1890–1995], Sawdust Caesar [1935]

José Ortega y Gasset
1883–1955

5   Rancor is an outpouring of a feeling of inferiority.
Meditations on Quixote [1911]

6   I am myself and what is around me, and if I do not save it, it shall not save me.
Meditations on Quixote

7   The Mediterraneans, who do not think clearly, do see clearly.
Meditations on Quixote

8   Culture is not life in its entirety, but just the moment of security, strength, and clarity.
Meditations on Quixote

9   A society without an aristocracy, without an elite minority, is not a society.
Invertebrate Spain [1922], ch. 4

10   Conversation is the socializing instrument par excellence, and in its style one can see reflected the capacities of a race.
Invertebrate Spain, 7

11   Europe is really a swarm: many bees on a single course.
The Revolt of the Masses [1930], prologue

12   Minorities are individuals or groups of individuals especially qualified. The masses are the collection of people not specially qualified.
The Revolt of the Masses, ch. 1

13   A revolution only lasts fifteen years, a period which coincides with the effectiveness of a generation.
The Revolt of the Masses, 10

14   The metaphor is probably the most fertile power possessed by man.
The Dehumanization of Art [1948]

15   I am a Spaniard, that is to say, a man without imagination.
Esthetic Essays [1956]

Margaret Sanger
1883–1966

16   No woman can call herself free who does not own and control her body. No woman can call herself free until she can choose consciously whether she will or will not be a mother.
Woman and the New Race [1920], ch. 8

17   The truth was out. It illuminated the world. Motherhood no longer cringed before the relentless laws of fecundity.
My Fight for Birth Control [1931]

Joseph Alois Schumpeter
1883–1950

18   Entrepreneurial profit...is the expression of the value of what the entrepreneur contributes to production in exactly the same sense that wages are the value expression of what the worker "produces." It is not a profit of exploitation any more than are wages.
The Theory of Economic Development [1934], ch. 4

19   Marxism is essentially a product of the bourgeois mind.
Capitalism, Socialism, and Democracy [1942], ch. 1

20   Economic progress, in capitalist society, means turmoil.
Capitalism, Socialism, and Democracy, 3

21   Every piece of business strategy...must be seen in its role in the perennial gale of creative destruction.
Capitalism, Socialism, and Democracy, 7

22   Capitalism inevitably and by virtue of the very logic of its civilization creates, educates and subsidizes a vested interest in social unrest.
Capitalism, Socialism, and Democracy, 13

23   Bureaucracy is not an obstacle to democracy but an inevitable complement to it.
Capitalism, Socialism, and Democracy, 18

24   The great political questions take their place in the psychic economy of the typical citizen with those leisure-hour interests that have not yet attained the rank of hobbies, and with the subjects of irresponsible conversation.
Capitalism, Socialism, and Democracy, 21

1   As a matter of practical necessity, socialist democracy may eventually turn out to be more of a sham than capitalist democracy ever was.
Capitalism, Socialism, and Democracy, 23

Joseph Warren Stilwell
1883–1946

2   I claim we got a hell of a beating. We got run out of Burma and it is humiliating as all hell. I think we ought to find out what caused it, go back and retake it.
*Statement [New Delhi, May 24, 1942]
on the American retreat from Burma*

Edgard Varèse
1883–1965

3   To stubbornly conditioned ears, anything new in music has always been called noise. But after all what is music but organized noises?
The Electronic Medium [1962]

William Carlos Williams
1883–1963

4   No wreaths please —
especially no hothouse flowers.
Some common memento is better,
something he prized and is known by:
his old clothes — a few books perhaps.
Tract [1917]

5 Who shall say I am not
the happy genius of my household?
Danse Russe [1917]

6 I walk back streets
admiring the houses
of the very poor.
Pastoral [1917]

7 I have discovered that most of
the beauties of travel are due to
the strange hours we keep to see them.
January Morning [1917], sec. 1

8 Old age is
a flight of small
cheeping birds
skimming
bare trees
above a snow glaze.
To Waken an Old Lady [1921]

9 By the road to the contagious hospital
under the surge of the blue

mottled clouds driven from the
northeast — a cold wind.
Spring and All [1923], no. I

10 They enter the new world naked,
cold, uncertain of all
save that they enter.
Spring and All, I

11 From the petal's edge a line starts
that being of steel
infinitely fine, infinitely
rigid penetrates
the Milky Way
without contact —
Spring and All, VII

12 The pure products of America
go crazy —
Spring and All, XVIII

13 as if the earth under our feet
were
an excrement of some sky

and we degraded prisoners
destined
to hunger until we eat filth
Spring and All, XVIII

14 so much depends
upon

a red wheel
barrow

glazed with rain
water

beside the white
chickens
Spring and All, XXI

15 The crowd at the ball game
is moved uniformly

by a spirit of uselessness
which delights them —
Spring and All, XXVI

16 Say it, no ideas but in things.
Paterson [1927], bk. 1

17 As the rain falls
so does
your love

bathe every
open
object of the world —
Rain [1930]

18 In summer the song
sings itself

above the muffled words —
The Botticellian Trees [1930]

19 I have eaten
the plums

that were in
the icebox

and which
you were probably
saving
for breakfast

Forgive me
they were delicious
so sweet
and so cold   *This Is Just to Say [1934]*

1 Mothlike in mists, scintillant in the minute

brilliance of cloudless days, with broad bellying sails
they glide to the wind tossing green water
from their sharp prows while over them the crew
      crawls.
                                     The Yachts [1935], st. 2, 3

2 It's the anarchy of poverty
delights me.   *The Poor [1938], st. 1*

3   THESE
are the desolate, dark weeks
when nature in its barrenness
equals the stupidity of man.

The year plunges into night
and the heart plunges
lower than night.
                                     These [1938], st. 1, 2

4   A poem is a small (or large) machine made of
words.   *The Wedge [1944]. Preface*

5   What common language to unravel?
                                     The Wedge. Paterson: The Falls

6 Then back to the party!
      and they maled
and femaled you jealously
      Beautiful Thing
as if to discover whence and
      by what miracle
there should escape, what?
                                     Paterson [1949], bk. 3

7 The descent beckons
as the ascent beckoned.
                                     The Desert Music [1954]. The Descent

8 It is difficult
to get the news from poems,
yet men die miserably every day
for lack
of what is found there.
                                     Asphodel, That Greeny Flower [1955]

9 All men by their nature give praise.
      It is all
         they can do.
                                     Pictures from Breughel [1962]. The Gift

Gaston Bachelard
1884–1962

10   If I were asked to name the chief benefit of the
house, I should say: the house shelters daydreaming,
the house protects the dreamer, the house allows one
to dream in peace.
                                     The Poetics of Space[1] *[1958], ch. 1*

Will[iam Jacob] Cuppy
1884–1949

11   The Dodo never had a chance. He seems to have
been invented for the sole purpose of becoming
extinct and that was all he was good for.
                                     How to Become Extinct [1941].
                                     The Dodo

Texas [Mary Louise Cecilia] Guinan
1884–1933

12   Hello, sucker!
                                     Greeting to nightclub patrons

Bert Kalmar
1884–1947
Harry Ruby
1895–1974
and
S[idney] J[oseph] Perelman
1904–1979

13   I'd horsewhip you if I had a horse.
                                     Horse Feathers (screenplay) [1932],
                                     spoken by Groucho Marx

Alice [Lee] Roosevelt Longworth
1884–1980

14   I do wish [Calvin Coolidge] did not look as if he
had been weaned on a pickle.
                                     Crowded Hours [1933]. Attributing the
                                     remark to a fellow-patient of her doctor's

15   If you can't say anything good about someone, sit
right here by me.
                                     Embroidered on a pillow in her
                                     sitting room

---

[1]Translated by MARIA JOLAS.

Bronislaw Malinowski
1884–1942

1   The emotional attitude of man has a greater sway over custom than has reason. The main attitude of a native to other, alien groups is that of hostility and mistrust. The fact that to a native every stranger is an enemy is an ethnographic feature reported from all parts of the world.
Argonauts of the Western Pacific [1922], ch. 13

Lily Morris
1884–1952

Fred W. Leigh
1871–1924

and

Charles Collins
1874–1923

2 Why am I always the bridesmaid,
Never the blushing bride?
Why Am I Always the Bridesmaid?
[1917]

Sean O'Casey
1884–1964

3   The whole worl's in a state o' chassis.
Juno and the Paycock [1924], act I and passim

4   One minute with him is all I ask; one minute alone with him, while you're runnin' for th' priest an' th' doctor.   *The Plough and the Stars [1926], act II*

5   A few hundhred scrawls o' chaps with a couple o' guns and Rosary beads, again' a hundhred thousand thrained men with horse, fut an' artillery...an' he wants us to fight fair!   *The Plough and the Stars, IV*

[Anna] Eleanor Roosevelt[1]
1884–1962

6   No one can make you feel inferior without your consent.   *This Is My Story [1937]*

7   You gain strength, courage and confidence by every experience in which you really stop to look fear in the face. You are able to say to yourself, "I lived

through this horror. I can take the next thing that comes along."...You must do the thing you think you cannot do.   *You Learn by Living [1960]*

[Alfred] Damon Runyon
1884–1946

8   Always try to rub up against money, for if you rub up against money long enough, some of it may rub off on you.
Guys and Dolls[2] [1931].
A Very Honorable Guy

9   I long ago come to the conclusion that all life is 6 to 5 against.
Money from Home [1935]. A Nice Price

10   A freeloader is a confirmed guest. He is the man who is always willing to come to dinner.
Short Takes [1946]. Freeloading Ethics

Edward Sapir
1884–1939

11   All grammars leak.
Language: An Introduction to the Study of Speech [1921], ch. 2

12   Language and our thought-grooves are inextricably interwoven, are, in a sense, one and the same.
Language: An Introduction to the Study of Speech, 10

Sara Teasdale
1884–1933

13 When I am dead and over me bright April
Shakes out her rain-drenched hair,
Though you should lean above me broken-hearted,
I shall not care.   *I Shall Not Care, st. 1*

Norman [Mattoon] Thomas
1884–1968

14   I'd rather see America save her soul than her face.
Speech before antiwar protest,
Washington, D.C. [November 27, 1965]

---

[1]She would rather light candles than curse the darkness and her glow has warmed the world. — ADLAI E. STEVENSON [November 7, 1962]

It is better to light one candle than curse the darkness. — *Motto of the Christopher Society*

---

[2]One of these days in your travels a guy is going to come to you and show you a nice brand-new deck of cards on which the seal is not yet broken, and that guy is going to offer to bet you that he can make the Jack of Spades jump out of the deck and squirt cider in your ear. But, son, do not bet that man, for as sure as you stand there you are going to wind up with an earful of cider. — FRANK LOESSER, JO SWERLING, and ABE BURROWS. *Guys and Dolls: A Musical Fable of Broadway* [1951], *act I, sc. i*

Harry S. Truman
1884–1972

1 When they told me yesterday what had happened [the death of F. D. Roosevelt], I felt like the moon, the stars and all the planets had fallen on me.
To reporters the day after his accession to the presidency [April 13, 1945]

2 When Kansas and Colorado have a quarrel over the water in the Arkansas River they don't call out the National Guard in each state and go to war over it. They bring a suit in the Supreme Court of the United States and abide by the decision. There isn't a reason in the world why we cannot do that internationally.
Speech in Kansas City [April 1945]

3 Sixteen hours ago an American airplane dropped one bomb on Hiroshima. . . . The force from which the sun draws its power has been loosed against those who brought war to the Far East.
First announcement of the atomic bomb [August 6, 1945]

4 The release of atomic energy constitutes a new force too revolutionary to consider in the framework of old ideas.
Message to Congress on atomic energy [October 3, 1945]

5 Means of destruction hitherto unknown, against which there can be no adequate military defense, and in the employment of which no single nation can in fact have a monopoly.
Declaration on Atomic Energy by President Truman and Prime Ministers Clement Attlee (Britain) and W. L. Mackenzie King (Canada) [November 15, 1945]

6 I wonder how far Moses would have gone if he had taken a poll in Egypt? What would Jesus Christ have preached if He had taken a poll in the land of Israel?
Memo to himself [1954?]

7 If you can't stand the heat, get out of the kitchen.
Saying

8 Once a decision was made, I did not worry about it afterward.
Memoirs [1955], vol. II, Years of Trial and Hope, ch. 1

9 The Marshall Plan will go down in history as one of America's greatest contributions to the peace of the world.
Memoirs, II, Years of Trial and Hope, 8

10 To me, party platforms are contracts with the people.
Memoirs, II, Years of Trial and Hope, 13

11 If there is one basic element in our Constitution, it is civilian control of the military.
Memoirs, II, Years of Trial and Hope, 19

12 There is a right kind and wrong kind of victory, just as there are wars for the right thing and wars that are wrong from every standpoint. . . . The kind of victory MacArthur had in mind — victory by the bombing of Chinese cities, victory by expanding the conflict to all of China — would have been the wrong kind of victory.
Memoirs, II, Years of Trial and Hope, 19

13 The buck stops here.
Sign on Truman's desk during his presidency. From ALFRED STEINBERG [1917–1995], The Man from Missouri [1962]

14 The only thing new in the world is the history you don't know.
From MERLE MILLER [1919–1986], Plain Speaking: An Oral Biography of Harry S. Truman [1974], ch. 23

15 Secrecy and a free, democratic government don't mix.
From MERLE MILLER, Plain Speaking: An Oral Biography of Harry S. Truman, 35

Charter of the United Nations

16 We, the peoples of the United Nations
Determined to save succeeding generations from the scourge of war, which twice in our lifetime has brought untold sorrow to mankind, and
To reaffirm faith in fundamental human rights, in the dignity and worth of the human person, in the equal right of men and women and of nations large and small, and . . . for these ends
To practice tolerance and live together in peace with one another as good neighbors, and
To unite our strength to maintain international peace and security . . .
Have resolved to combine our efforts to accomplish these aims.
Charter of the United Nations [June 1945], preamble[1]

Sophie Tucker[2]
c. 1884–1966

17 From birth to age eighteen, a girl needs good parents. From eighteen to thirty-five, she needs good

---

[1]Based on a draft by JAN CHRISTIAN SMUTS [1870–1950].

[2]Known as "The Last of the Red-Hot Mamas" from the title of a song by JACK YELLEN [1892–1991], which she introduced in 1928.

looks. From thirty-five to fifty-five, she needs a good personality. From fifty-five on, she needs good cash. *Said at sixty-nine*

1 I have been poor and I have been rich. Rich is better. *Attributed*

Niels Bohr
1885–1962

2 In our description of nature the purpose is not to disclose the real essence of the phenomena but only to track down, so far as it is possible, relations between the manifold aspects of our experience.
Atomic Theory and the Description of Nature [1934]

Isak Dinesen [Karen Blixen]
1885–1962

3 What is man, when you come to think upon him, but a minutely set, ingenious machine for turning with infinite artfulness, the red wine of Shiraz into urine?
Seven Gothic Tales [1934]. The Dreamers

4 That old saying which the peasants call the bachelors' prayer: "I pray thee, good Lord, that I may not be married. But if I am to be married, that I may not be a cuckold. But if I am to be a cuckold, that I may not know. But if I am to know, that I may not mind."
Seven Gothic Tales. The Poet

5 I had seen a herd of elephant traveling through dense native forest . . . pacing along as if they had an appointment at the end of the world.
Out of Africa [1937], pt. I, ch. 1

6 If I know a song of Africa—I thought—of the giraffe, and the African new moon lying on her back, of the plows in the fields, and the sweaty faces of the coffee-pickers, does Africa know a song of me? Would the air over the plain quiver with a color that I had had on, or the children invent a game in which my name was, or the full moon throw a shadow over the gravel of the drive that was like me, or would the eagles of Ngong look out for me?
Out of Africa, I, 4

7 I have before seen other countries, in the same manner, give themselves to you when you are about to leave them. *Out of Africa, V, 1*

DuBose Heyward
1885–1940

8 Summertime
And the livin' is easy,

Fish are jumpin',
And the cotton is high.
Oh, your daddy's rich,
And your ma is good lookin';
So hush, little baby,
Don' yo' cry.[1]
Porgy and Bess [1935]. Summertime

Ring Lardner
1885–1933

9 "Are you lost, daddy?" I arsked tenderly.
"Shut up," he explained.
The Young Immigrunts [1920]

10 A good many young writers make the mistake of enclosing a stamped, self-addressed envelope, big enough for the manuscript to come back in. This is too much of a temptation to the editor.
How to Write Short Stories [1924]

D[avid] H[erbert] Lawrence
1885–1930

11 I love Frieda so much I don't like to talk about it. I never knew what love was before. . . . The world is wonderful and beautiful and good beyond one's wildest imagination. Never, never, never could one conceive what love is, beforehand, never. Life *can* be great—quite god-like. It *can* be so. God be thanked I have proved it.
Letter to Sallie Hopkin [June 2, 1912]

12 You love me so much, you want to put me in your pocket. And I should die there smothered.
Sons and Lovers [1913], ch. 15

13 Not I, not I, but the wind that blows through me!
A fine wind is blowing the new direction of Time.
Song of a Man Who Has Come Through [1920]

14 If only I am keen and hard like the sheer tip of a wedge
Driven by invisible blows,
The rock will split, we shall come at the wonder, we shall find the Hesperides.
Song of a Man Who Has Come Through

15   The glamor
Of childish days is upon me, my manhood is cast
Down in the flood of remembrance, I weep like a child for the past.
Piano [1920]

---

[1]Music by GEORGE [1898–1937] and IRA GERSHWIN [1896–1983].

1   How can there be any secrets, we are all the same organisms? How can there be any secrecy, when everything is known to all of us?
                    Women in Love [1921], ch. 19

2   Never trust the artist. Trust the tale.
        Studies in Classic American Literature [1922], ch. 1

3   The essential American soul is hard, isolate, stoic, and a killer.
                    Studies in Classic American Literature, 5

4   He was a little model, was Benjamin. Doctor Franklin. Snuff-colored little man! Immortal soul and all!
                    Studies in Classic American Literature, 2

5 I never saw a wild thing
Sorry for itself.
                    Self-Pity [1923]

6 A snake came to my water trough
On a hot, hot day, and I in pajamas for the heat,
To drink there.   *Snake [1923]*

7 For he seemed to me again like a king,
Like a king in exile, uncrowned in the underworld,
Now due to be crowned again.   *Snake*

8   "Sometimes," said she, "I think that is my *permanent* feeling towards people. I like the world, the sky and the earth and the greater mystery beyond. But people — yes, they are all monkeys to me."
                    The Plumed Serpent [1926], ch. 17

9   Living, I want to depart to where *I am.*
                    The Plumed Serpent, 17

10   Ours is essentially a tragic age, so we refuse to take it tragically. The cataclysm has happened, we are among the ruins, we start to build up new little habitats, to have new little hopes. It is rather hard work; there is now no smooth road into the future: but we go round, or scramble over the obstacles. We've got to live, no matter how many skies have fallen.
                    Lady Chatterley's Lover [1928], ch. 1

11   I believe especially in being warm-hearted in love, in fucking with a warm heart. I believe if men could fuck with warm hearts, and the women take it warm-heartedly, everything would come all right. It's all this cold-hearted fucking that is death and idiocy.
                    Lady Chatterley's Lover, 14

12   This is John Thomas marryin' Lady Jane.
                    Lady Chatterley's Lover, 15

13   Necessary, forever necessary, to burn out false shames and smelt the heaviest ore of the body into purity.
                    Lady Chatterley's Lover, 16

14 How beastly the bourgeois is
especially the male of the species.
                    How Beastly the Bourgeois Is [1929]

15   Beauty is a mystery. You can neither eat it nor make flannel out of it.
                    Sex Versus Loveliness [1930]

16   Sex and beauty are inseparable, like life and consciousness. And the intelligence which goes with sex and beauty, and arises out of sex and beauty, is intuition.   *Sex Versus Loveliness*

17   Brilliant glorious eternal heaven above: and brilliant sulphureous torture-lake away below. This is the vision of eternity of all Patmossers. They could not be happy in heaven unless they *knew* their enemies were unhappy in hell.   *Apocalypse [1931]*

18   If it were a question of brute force, not a single human baby would survive for a fortnight.
                    Sketches of Etruscan Places [1932], ch. 2

19   Every great discovery or decision comes by an act of divination. Facts are fitted round afterwards.
                    Sketches of Etruscan Places, 3

20   It must have been a wonderful old world, that old world where everything appeared alive and shining in the dusk of contact with all things, not merely as an isolated individual thing played upon by daylight; where each thing had a clear outline, visually, but in its very clarity was related emotionally or vitally to strange other things, one thing springing from another, things mentally contradictory fusing together emotionally, so that a lion could be at the same moment also a goat, and not a goat.   *Sketches of Etruscan Places, 4*

21   Whales in mid-ocean, suspended in the waves of the sea
great heaven of whales in the waters, old
    hierarchies.
And enormous mother whales lie dreaming suckling
    their whale-tender young
and dreaming with strange whale eyes wide open
    in the waters of the beginning and the end.
                    Whales Weep Not! [1932]

22 Reach me a gentian, give me a torch!
Let me guide myself with the blue, forked torch of a
    flower
down the darker and darker stairs, where blue is
    darkened on blueness
even where Persephone goes, just now, from the
    frosted September
to the sightless realm where darkness is awake upon
    the dark.   *Bavarian Gentians [1932]*

23 Build then the ship of death, for you must take the
longest journey, to oblivion.
                    The Ship of Death [1932], sec. V

Sam M. Lewis
1885–1959

and

Joe Young
1889–1939

1   How You Gonna Keep 'Em Down on the Farm
After They've Seen Paree?
Title and refrain of song[1] *[1919]*

Sinclair Lewis
1885–1951

2   His name was George F. Babbitt [and]...he was
nimble in the calling of selling houses for more than
people could afford to pay.   *Babbitt [1922], ch. 1*

3   A sensational event was changing from the brown
suit to the gray the contents of his pockets. He was
earnest about these objects. They were of eternal
importance, like baseball or the Republican Party.
Babbitt, 1

4   I've never done a single thing I've wanted to in my
whole life! I don't know 's I've accomplished anything except just get along.   *Babbitt, 34*

5   Every compulsion is put upon writers to become
safe, polite, obedient, and sterile. In protest, I
declined election to the National Institute of Arts and
Letters some years ago, and now I must decline the
Pulitzer Prize.[2]
*Letter declining the Pulitzer Prize for his
novel Arrowsmith [1926]*

6   What is love?...It is the morning and the evening
star.   *Elmer Gantry [1927], ch. 20*

7   Our American professors like their literature clear
and cold and pure and very dead.
*The American Fear of Literature.
Address in Stockholm on receiving the Nobel
Prize for Literature [December 12, 1930]*

8   It Can't Happen Here.   *Title of book [1935]*

[Ferdinand] Jelly Roll Morton
c. 1885–1941

9   Now in one of my earliest tunes, "New Orleans
Blues," you can notice the Spanish tinge. In fact, if
you can't manage to put tinges of Spanish in your
tunes, you will never be able to get the right seasoning, I call it, for jazz.
Interview with Alan Lomax [1938]

Chester William Nimitz
1885–1966

10   Uncommon valor was a common virtue.
*Of the Marines at Iwo Jima
[February–May 1945]*

George S[mith] Patton
1885–1945

11   Wars may be fought with weapons, but they are
won by men. It is the spirit of the men who follow
and of the man who leads that gains the victory.
In the Cavalry Journal [September 1933]

12   Battle is the most magnificent competition in
which a human being can indulge. It brings out all
that is best; it removes all that is base.
Message to his troops [1943]

13   A pint of sweat will save a gallon of blood.[3]
*War As I Knew It, Appendix D, letter
[April 3, 1944]*

14   A good plan violently executed now is better than
a perfect plan next week.
War As I Knew It [1947], pt. 3

Ezra Pound
1885–1972

15   All great art is born of the metropolis.
Letter to Harriet Monroe [November 7, 1913]

16   Poetry must be as well written as prose.
Letter to Harriet Monroe [January 1915]

17   Objectivity and again objectivity, and expression:
no hindside-before-ness, no straddled adjectives (as
"addled mosses dank"), no Tennysonianness of
speech; nothing — nothing that you couldn't, in
some circumstance, in the stress of some emotion,
actually say.
Letter to Harriet Monroe [January 1915]

18 The leaves fall early this autumn, in wind.
The paired butterflies are already yellow with August
Over the grass in the West garden;
They hurt me. I grow older.
*The River Merchant's Wife: A Letter
(After Rihaku) [1915]*

19 Your mind and you are our Sargasso Sea.
Portrait d'une Femme [1916]

---

[1]Music by WALTER DONALDSON [1893–1947].

[2]Lewis became a member of the Institute in 1935.

---

[3]A drop of sweat on the drill ground will save many drops of blood
on the battlefield. — AUGUST WILLICH [1810–1878], *The Army:
Standing Army or National Army?* [1866]

¹ The apparition of these faces in the crowd;
   Petals on a wet, black bough.
                            In a Station of the Metro [1916]

² Winter is icumen in,
   Lhude sing Goddamm,
   Raineth drop and staineth slop,
   And how the wind doth ramm!
   Sing: Goddamm.¹
                            Ancient Music [1916]

³   Go in fear of abstractions.
               Pavannes and Divagations [1918].
               A Retrospect

⁴ For three years, out of key with his time,
   He strove to resuscitate the dead art
   Of poetry; to maintain "the sublime"
   In the old sense. Wrong from the start—
   No, hardly, but seeing he had been born
   In a half savage country, out of date.
               Hugh Selwyn Mauberley. E.P. Ode pour
               l'élection de son sepulchre [1920], sec. I

⁵ His true Penelope was Flaubert,
   He fished by obstinate isles.
               Hugh Selwyn Mauberley. E.P. Ode pour
               l'élection de son sepulchre, I

⁶ The age demanded an image
   Of its accelerated grimace,
   Something for the modern stage,
   Not, at any rate, an Attic grace.
               Hugh Selwyn Mauberley. E.P. Ode pour
               l'élection de son sepulchre, II

⁷ Better mendacities
   Than the classics in paraphrase!
               Hugh Selwyn Mauberley. E.P. Ode pour
               l'élection de son sepulchre, II

⁸ Some quick to arm,
   some for adventure,
   some from fear of weakness,
   some from fear of censure,
   some for love of slaughter, in imagination,
   learning later . . .
   some in fear, learning love of slaughter;
   Died some, pro patria,
         non "dulce" non "et decor" . . .
   walked eye-deep in hell
   believing in old men's lies, the unbelieving
   came home, home to a lie.
               Hugh Selwyn Mauberley. E.P. Ode pour
               l'élection de son sepulchre, IV ²

⁹ There died a myriad,
   And of the best, among them,

For an old bitch gone in the teeth,
For a botched civilization.

Charm, smiling at the good mouth,
Quick eyes gone under earth's lid,

For two gross of broken statues,
For a few thousand battered books.
               Hugh Selwyn Mauberley. E.P. Ode pour
               l'élection de son sepulchre, V

10   As for literature
   It gives no man a sinecure.
   And no one knows, at sight, a masterpiece.
   "And give up verse, my boy,
   There's nothing in it."
               Hugh Selwyn Mauberley. E.P. Ode pour
               l'élection de son sepulchre, IX. Mr. Nixon

11 With *Usura*
   With usura hath no man a house of good stone
   each block cut smooth and well fitting.
               Cantos [1925–1959], XLV

12 No picture is made to endure nor to live with
   but it is made to sell and sell quickly
   with usura, sin against nature,
   is thy bread ever more of stale rags
   is thy bread dry as paper.   *Cantos, XLV*

13 What thou lovest well remains, the rest is dross
   What thou lov'st well shall not be reft from thee
   What thou lov'st well is thy true heritage
   Whose world, or mine or theirs or is it of none?
   First came the seen, then thus the palpable
         Elysium, though it were in the halls of hell.
   What thou lovest well is thy true heritage.
               Cantos, LXXXI

14 The ant's a centaur in his dragon world.
   Pull down thy vanity, it is not man
   Made courage, or made order, or made grace,
         Pull down thy vanity, I say pull down.
   Learn of the green world what can be thy place
   In scaled invention or true artistry,
   Pull down thy vanity,
         Paquin pull down!
   The green casque has outdone your elegance.
               Cantos, LXXXI

15   Artists are the antennae of the race.
               ABC of Reading [1934]

16   An epic is a poem including history.
               ABC of Reading

17   Great literature is simply language charged with
   meaning to the utmost possible degree.
               ABC of Reading

18   Poetry atrophies when it gets too far from
   music.   *ABC of Reading*

19   Literature is news that *stays* news.
               ABC of Reading

---

¹See Anonymous, 880:5.

²Ellipses are in the original text.

1   Properly, we should read for power. Man reading should be man intensely alive. The book should be a ball of light in one's hand.
> *Guide to Kulchur [1938]. Zweck, or the Aim*

Humbert Wolfe
1885–1940

2 Listen! the wind is rising,
  and the air is wild with leaves,
  We have had our summer evenings,
  now for October eves!
> *Autumn (Resignation) [1926], st. 2*

Elinor [Hoyt] Wylie
1885–1928

3 We shall walk in velvet shoes:
  Wherever we go
  Silence will fall like dews
  On white silence below.
> *Velvet Shoes [1921], st. 4*

4 Avoid the reeking herd,
  Shun the polluted flock,
  Live like that stoic bird
  The eagle of the rock.
> *The Eagle and the Mole [1921], st. 1*

5 If you would keep your soul
  From spotted sight or sound,
  Live like the velvet mole;
  Go burrow underground.

  And there hold intercourse
  With roots of trees and stones,
  With rivers at their source,
  And disembodied bones.
> *The Eagle and the Mole, st. 5, 6*

6   Honeyed words like bees,
  Gilded and sticky, with a little sting.
> *Pretty Words [1921]*

7 I was, being human, born alone;
  I am, being woman, hard beset;
  I live by squeezing from a stone
  The little nourishment I get.
> *Let No Charitable Hope [1923], st. 2*

8 If any have a stone to throw
  It is not I, ever or now.   *The Pebble [1929]*

9 The worst and best are both inclined
  To snap like vixens at the truth;
  But, O, beware the middle mind
  That purrs and never shows a tooth!
> *Nonsense Rhyme [1929], st. 2*

Karl Barth
1886–1968

10   It may be that when the angels go about their task of praising God, they play only Bach. I am sure, however, that when they are together *en famille* they play Mozart and that then too our dear Lord listens with special pleasure.
> *Wolfgang Amadeus Mozart [1956]*

11   Conscience is the perfect interpreter of life.
> *The Word of God and the Word of Man [1957]*

12   We have before us the fiendishness of business competition and the world war, passion and wrongdoing, antagonism between classes and moral depravity within them, economic tyranny above and the slave spirit below.
> *The Word of God and the Word of Man*

David Ben-Gurion
1886–1973

13   In Israel, in order to be a realist you must believe in miracles.   *Interview [October 5, 1956]*

Gottfried Benn
1886–1956

14 Crises of expression and spasms of eros:
  that's the man of today,
  the inside a vacuum,
  the continuity of personality
  provided by his suit,
  which with stout cloth might be good for ten years.
> *Fragments*[1] *[1953]*

Hugo La Fayette Black
1886–1971

15   No higher duty, or more solemn responsibility, rests upon this Court than that of translating into living law and maintaining this constitutional shield deliberately planned and inscribed for the benefit of every human being subject to our Constitution — of whatever race, creed or persuasion.
> *Chambers v. Florida, 309 U.S. 227 [1938]*

16   The First Amendment has erected a wall between church and state. That wall must be kept high and impregnable. We could not approve the slightest breach.
> *Everson v. Board of Education, 330 U.S. 1 [1947]*

---

[1]Translated by MICHAEL HOFMANN.

1 It is my belief that there *are* "absolutes" in our Bill of Rights, and that they were put there on purpose by men who knew what words meant and meant their prohibitions to be "absolutes."
Interview Before the American
Jewish Congress [April 14, 1962]

2 An unconditional right to say what one pleases about public affairs is what I consider to be the minimum guarantee of the First Amendment.
New York Times Company v. Sullivan,
376 U.S. 254 [1964]

3 In revealing the workings of government that led to the Vietnam War, the newspapers nobly did precisely that which the Founders hoped and trusted they would do.
Concurring opinion on the publication
of the Pentagon Papers [1971]

Randolph Silliman Bourne
1886–1918

4 The magical good fortune of attractive personal appearance makes its way almost without effort in the world, breaking down all sorts of walls of disapproval and lack of interest. Even the homely person can attract by personal charm. But deformity cannot even be charming.
The Handicapped — by One of Them [1911]

5 War is the health of the state. It automatically sets in motion throughout society those irresistible forces for uniformity, for passionate cooperation with the Government in coercing into obedience the minority groups and individuals which lack the larger herd sense.
The State [1918]

Frances Cornford
1886–1960

6 Magnificently unprepared
For the long littleness of life.
Rupert Brooke[1] [1915]

H.D. [Hilda Doolittle]
1886–1961

7 Nor skin nor hide nor fleece
　　Shall cover you,
Nor curtain of crimson nor fine
Shelter of cedar-wood be over you,
　　Nor the fir-tree
　　Nor the pine.
Lethe [1924], st. 1

8 so you may say,
"Greek flower; Greek ecstasy
reclaims for ever

one who died
following
intricate songs' lost measure."
Epitaph. Red Roses for Bronze [1931]

9 O, give me burning blue

and brittle burnt sea-weed
above the tide-line,

as I stand, still unsatisfied,
under the long shadow-on-snow of the pine.
The Flowering of the Rod [1946], pt. 4

Al Jolson
1886–1950

10 You ain't heard nothin' yet, folks.
Ad lib remark in the first talking motion
picture, The Jazz Singer [July 1927]

Gus Kahn
1886–1941

11 He's washin' dishes and baby clothes,
He's so ambitious he even sews.
But don't forget, folks,
That's what you get, folks,
For makin' whoopee!
Whoopee [1928]. Makin' Whoopee

Gus Kahn
1886–1941

and

Raymond B. Egan
1890–1952

12 There's nothing surer,
The rich get rich and the poor get poorer,
In the meantime, in between time,
Ain't we got fun.　*Ain't We Got Fun [1921]*

Joyce Kilmer
1886–1918

13 I think that I shall never see
A poem lovely as a tree.[2]
Trees [1913], l. 1

---

[1]See Rupert Brooke, 669.

[2]See Ogden Nash, 732:9.

1 Poems are made by fools like me,
But only God can make a tree.

Trees, l. 11

Aldo Leopold
1886–1948

2   We abuse land because we regard it as a commodity belonging to us. When we see land as a community to which we belong, we may begin to use it with love and respect.

A Sand County Almanac [1949], foreword

3   There are two spiritual dangers in not owning a farm. One is the danger of supposing that breakfast comes from the grocery, and the other that heat comes from the furnace.

A Sand County Almanac. February

4   A thing is right when it tends to preserve the integrity, stability, and beauty of the biotic community.

A Sand County Almanac.
The Land Ethic

5   The cowman who cleans his range of wolves does not realize that he is taking over the wolf's job of trimming the herd to fit the range. He has not learned to think like a mountain. Hence we have dustbowls, and rivers washing the future into the sea.

A Sand County Almanac.
The Quality of Landscape

6   Conservation is a state of harmony between men and land.

A Sand County Almanac. The Land Ethic

George Leigh Mallory
1886–1924

7   [When asked why he wanted to climb Mount Everest:] Because it is there.

Antonio Porchia
1886–1968

8   What we pay for with our lives never costs too much.   *Voices[1] [1943]*

9   The fear of separation is all that unites.   *Voices*

Siegfried Sassoon
1886–1967

10   I believe that the war, upon which I entered as a war of defense and liberation, has now become a war

of aggression and conquest....I have seen and endured the sufferings of the troops, and I can no longer be a party to prolong these sufferings for ends which I believe to be evil and unjust.

Finished with the War: A Soldier's
Declaration [July 1917]

11 Soldiers are citizens of death's gray land.

Dreamers [1918]

12 Soldiers are dreamers; when the guns begin
They think of firelit homes, clean beds, and wives.

Dreamers

13 And when the war is done and youth stone dead
I'd toddle safely home and die — in bed.

Base Details [1918]

14 Who will remember, passing through this gate,
The unheroic dead who fed the guns?
Who shall absolve the foulness of their fate —
Those doomed, conscripted, unvictorious ones?

On Passing the New Menin Gate [1918]

15   In war-time the word *patriotism* means suppression of truth.

Memoirs of an Infantry Officer [1930]

Jun'ichirō Tanizaki
1886–1965

16   The parlor may have its charms, but the Japanese toilet truly is a place of spiritual repose. It always stands apart from the main building, at the end of a corridor, in a grove fragrant with leaves and moss. No words can describe that sensation as one sits in the dim light, basking in the faint glow reflected from the shoji, lost in meditation or gazing out at the garden.

In Praise of Shadows[2] [1933]

Paul [Johannes] Tillich
1886–1965

17   The name of this infinite and inexhaustible depth and ground of all being is *God*.

The Shaking of the Foundations [1948], ch. 7

18   Grace strikes us when we are in great pain and restlessness....Sometimes at that moment a wave of light breaks into our darkness, and it is as though a voice were saying: "You are accepted."

The Shaking of the Foundations, 19

19   The basic anxiety, the anxiety of a finite being about the threat of non-being, cannot be eliminated. It belongs to existence itself.

The Courage to Be [1952], ch. 2

---

[1]Translated by W. S. MERWIN.

[2]Translated by THOMAS J. HARPER and EDWARD G. SEIDENSTICKER.

Edward Weston
1886–1958

1   The camera sees more than the eye, so why not make use of it?[1]

Daybook [April 20, 1923 entry] [1926]

2   Photography suits the temper of this age — of active bodies and minds. It is a perfect medium for one whose mind is teeming with ideas, imagery, for a prolific worker who would be slowed down by painting or sculpting, for one who sees quickly and acts decisively, accurately.

Daybook [June 19, 1930 entry]

Ruth [Fulton] Benedict
1887–1948

3   From the moment of his birth the customs into which [an individual] is born shape his experience and behavior. By the time he can talk, he is the little creature of his culture.

Patterns of Culture [1934], ch. 1

4   In world history, those who have helped to build the same culture are not necessarily of one race, and those of the same race have not all participated in one culture. In scientific language, culture is not a function of race.

*Race: Science and Politics [1940],
ch. 2*

Rupert Brooke[2]
1887–1915

5 Breathless, we flung us on the windy hill,
Laughed in the sun, and kissed the lovely grass.

The Hill [1910]

6 And then you suddenly cried, and turned away.

The Hill

7   Oh! yet
Stands the church clock at ten to three?
And is there honey still for tea?

The Old Vicarage, Grantchester [1912]

8 Fish say, they have their stream and pond;
But is there anything beyond?

Heaven [1913]

9 Then, the cool kindliness of sheets, that soon
Smooth away trouble; and the rough male kiss
Of blankets; grainy wood; live hair that is
Shining and free; blue-massing clouds; the keen
Unpassioned beauty of a great machine;
The benison of hot water; furs to touch;
The good smell of old clothes.

The Great Lover [1914]

10 If I should die, think only this of me:
That there's some corner of a foreign field
That is forever England.

The Soldier [1914]

11 Now, God be thanked, Who has matched us with His hour,
And caught our youth, and wakened us from sleeping.

Peace [1914]

12 Blow out, you bugles, over the rich dead!
There's none of these so lonely and poor of old,
But, dying, has made us rarer gifts than gold.

The Dead [1914]

Blaise Cendrars
1887–1961

13   Such music is not only a new art form but a new reason for living.

On hearing Duke Ellington in Paris [1939]

Ralph Chaplin
1887–1961

14 Solidarity forever!
For the union makes us strong.

Solidarity Forever[3] [1915]

Marcel Duchamp
1887–1965

15   The only works of art America has given are her plumbing and her bridges.

The Richard Mutt Case [1917]

16   I have come to the personal conclusion that while all artists are not chess players, all chess players are artists.

Address to the New York State Chess Association [August 30, 1952]

17   Besides, it's always other people who die.

Epitaph

---

[1]This version of the quotation is often attributed to Weston; however, the original text is this: Photography has certain inherent qualities which are only possible with photography — one being the delineation of detail — So why not take advantage of this attribute? Why limit yourself to what your eyes see when you have such an opportunity to extend your vision?

[2]See Frances Cornford, 667:6.

[3]Sung to the tune of *John Brown's Body*.

Marcus Garvey
1887–1940

1   We are not engaged in domestic politics, in church building or in social uplift work, but we are engaged in nation building.

> *Speech, The Principles of the Universal Negro Improvement Association, at New York City [November 25, 1922]*

2   To see your enemy and know him is part of the complete education of man.

> *Philosophy and Opinions of Marcus Garvey [1923], ch. 2*

3   Black men, you were once great; you will be great again. Lose not courage, lose not faith, go forward.

> *Philosophy and Opinions of Marcus Garvey, 4*

Robinson Jeffers
1887–1962

4 Lend me the stone strength of the past and I will
   lend you
The wings of the future, for I have them.

> *To the Rock That Will Be a Cornerstone [1924]*

5   The deep dark-shining
Pacific leans on the land,
Feeling his cold strength
To the outmost margins.

> *Night [1925]*

6 I'd sooner, except the penalties, kill a man than a
   hawk.

> *Hurt Hawks [1928]*

7   I have grown to believe
A stone is a better pillow than many visions.

> *Clouds of Evening [1930]*

8 The strong lean upon death as on a rock.

> *Gale in April [1930]*

9 "Keep clear of the dupes that talk democracy
And the dogs that talk revolution,
Drunk with talk, liars and believers.
I believe in my tusks.
Long live freedom and damn the ideologies,"
Said the gamey black-maned wild boar
Tusking the turf on Mal Paso Mountain.

> *The Stars Go over the Lonely Ocean [1940], st. 4*

10   As for me, I would rather
Be a worm in a wild apple than a son of man.

> *Original Sin [1948]*

Le Corbusier
[Charles Édouard Jeanneret]
1887–1965

11   Architecture is the masterly, correct, and magnificent play of masses brought together in light.

> *Toward a New Architecture [1923]*

12   A house is a machine for living in.[1]

> *Toward a New Architecture*

Emilio Mola
1887–1937

13   Fifth column.[2]

> *Phrase, Spanish Civil War [1936–1939]*

[Arthur R.] Pop Momand
1887–1987

14   Keeping Up with the Joneses.

> *Title of comic strip [1913]*

Sir Bernard Law Montgomery,
Viscount Montgomery of Alamein
1887–1976

15   To us is given the honor of striking a blow for freedom which will live in history, and in the better days that lie ahead men will speak with pride of our doings.

> *Message to his troops, on the eve of the Allied invasion of Europe [June 5, 1944]*

Marianne Moore
1887–1972

16 Dürer would have seen a reason for living in a town
   like this.   *The Steeple-Jack [1935], st. 1*

17   The sweet air coming into your house on a
fine day, from water etched
   with waves as formal as the scales on a fish.

> *The Steeple-Jack, st. 1*

18 Of the crow-blue mussel shells, one keeps
adjusting the ash heaps;
       opening and shutting itself like

an
injured fan.   *The Fish [1935], st. 1, 2*

---

[1] Une maison est une machine-à-habiter.

[2] Mola, one of Franco's generals, boasted that he had four columns of troops to lead against Madrid and a fifth column of sympathizers inside Madrid.

1 I, too, dislike it.
    Reading it, however, with a perfect contempt
        for it, one discovers in
    it, after all, a place for the genuine.
                Poetry [1935; revised 1967]

2 Nor till the poets among us can be
    "literalists of
    the imagination" — above
        insolence and triviality and can present

for inspection, "imaginary gardens with real
    toads in them," shall we have
    it.
        Poetry, st. 4, 5 (excluded in 1967 revision)[1]

3 I wonder what Adam and Eve
    think of it by this time.   *Marriage [1935]*

4   Ecstasy affords
the occasion and expediency determines the form.
        The Past Is the Present [1935]

5 My father used to say,
    "Superior people never make long visits,
    have to be shown Longfellow's grave
    or the glass flowers at Harvard."   *Silence [1935]*

6 "The deepest feeling always shows itself in silence;
    not in silence, but restraint."
Nor was he insincere in saying, "Make my house your
        inn."[2]
Inns are not residences.   *Silence*

7   There is a great amount of poetry in unconscious
fastidiousness.   *Critics and Connoisseurs [1935]*

8   What is our innocence,
what is our guilt? All are
    naked, none is safe.   *What Are Years? [1941]*

9 The power of the visible
is the invisible.
    He "Digesteth Harde Yron" [1941], st. 8

10 I am troubled, I'm dissatisfied, I'm Irish.
    Spenser's Ireland [1941], last line

11 Another armored animal — scale
    lapping scale with spruce cone regularity until they
form the uninterrupted central
    tail row!   *The Pangolin [1941], st. 1*

12   Bedizened or stark
    naked, man, the self, the being we call human,
        writing
master to this world.   *The Pangolin, st. 8*

13 Among animals, *one* has a sense of humor.
    Humor saves a few steps, it saves years.
        The Pangolin, st. 8

14   The prey of fear, he, always
    curtailed, extinguished, thwarted by the dusk,
        work partly done,
says to the alternating blaze,
        "Again the sun!
anew each day; and new and new and new,
that comes into and steadies my soul."
        The Pangolin, st. 9

15   The world's an orphans' home. Shall
    we never have peace without sorrow?
without pleas of the dying for
    help that won't come. O
quiet form upon the dust, I cannot
look and yet I must.
        In Distrust of Merits [1941], st. 7

16 I inwardly did nothing.
O Iscariot-like crime!   *In Distrust of Merits, st. 8*

17   What sap
went through that little thread
to make the cherry red!   *Nevertheless [1944], st. 11*

18 They say there is a sweeter air
    where it was made, than we have here.
        A Carriage from Sweden [1944]

19   THE MIND IS AN ENCHANTING THING
is an enchanted thing,
    like the glaze on a
katydid-wing
    subdivided by sun
    till the nettings are legion.
        The Mind Is an Enchanting Thing [1944], st. 1

20 We don't like flowers that do
    not wilt; they must die, and nine
    she-camel hairs aid memory.
        The Sycamore [1956], st. 2

21   O to be a dragon,
a symbol of the power of Heaven — of silkworm
size or immense; at times invisible.
    Felicitous phenomenon!
        O to Be a Dragon [1959]

22 To wear the arctic fox
you have to kill it.
    The Arctic Ox (or Goat) [1959], st. 1

23 Camels are snobbish
and sheep, unintelligent;
    water buffaloes, neurasthenic —
even murderous.
Reindeer seem over-serious.
    The Arctic Ox (or Goat), st. 9

---

[1] Omissions are not accidents. — MARIANNE MOORE, *Complete Poems* [1967], *author's note*

[2] MOORE's *note:* Edmund Burke, in *Burke's Life*, by James Prior: "Throw yourself into a coach," said he. "Come down and make my house your inn."

1 Why an inordinate interest in animals and athletes? They are subjects for art and exemplars of it, are they not? minding their own business. Pangolins, hornbills, pitchers, catchers, do not pry or prey — or prolong the conversation; do not make us self-conscious; look their best when caring least.

A Marianne Moore Reader [1961], foreword

Samuel Eliot Morison
1887–1976

2 A tough but nervous, tenacious but restless race [the Yankees]; materially ambitious, yet prone to introspection, and subject to waves of religious emotion.... A race whose typical member is eternally torn between a passion for righteousness and a desire to get on in the world.

Maritime History of Massachusetts [1921], ch. 2

3 America was discovered accidentally by a great seaman who was looking for something else; when discovered it was not wanted; and most of the exploration for the next fifty years was done in the hope of getting through or around it. America was named after a man who discovered no part of the New World. History is like that, very chancy.

The Oxford History of the American People [1965], ch. 2

Edwin Muir
1887–1959

4 I take my journey back to seek my kindred,
Old founts dried up whose rivers run far on
Through you and me.

The Labyrinth [1949]. The Journey Back

5 The killing beast that cannot kill
Swells and swells in his fury till
You'd almost think it was despair.

Collected Poems [1952]. The Combat

6 Since then they have pulled our ploughs and borne
our loads,
But that free servitude still can pierce our hearts.
Our life is changed; their coming our beginning.

Collected Poems. The Horses.

Georgia O'Keeffe
1887–1986

7 I find that I have painted my life — things happening in my life — without knowing.

Georgia O'Keeffe [1976]

8 I had to create an equivalent for what I felt about what I was looking at — not copy it.

Georgia O'Keeffe

Erwin Schrödinger
1887–1961

9 If you cannot — in the long run — tell everyone what you have been doing, your doing has been worthless.

Science and Humanism [1951]

10 We do not belong to this material world that science constructs for us. We are not in it; we are outside. We are only spectators.

Nature and the Greeks [1954]

Edith Sitwell
1887–1964

11 Lily O'Grady,
Silly and shady,
Longing to be
A lazy lady.

Facade[1] [1923]. Popular Song

12 Still falls the Rain —
Dark as the world of man, black as our loss —
Blind as the nineteen hundred and forty nails
Upon the Cross.

Still Falls the Rain [1940]

Alexander Woollcott
1887–1943

13 The two oldest professions in the world — ruined by amateurs.

Shouts and Murmurs. The Knock at the Stage Door [1922]

14 All the things I really like to do are either immoral, illegal, or fattening. *Remark*

Maxwell Anderson
1888–1959

15 Oh, it's a long, long while
From May to December,
But the days grow short,
When you reach September.

Knickerbocker Holiday[2] [1938]. September Song

---

[1] Music by WILLIAM WALTON [1902–1983].
[2] Music by KURT WEILL [1900–1950].

1 Oh, the days dwindle down
  To a precious few ...
  And these few precious days
  I'll spend with you.
  Knickerbocker Holiday. September Song

2 But I've been walking through the night and the day
  Till my eyes get weary and my head turns grey,
  And sometimes it seems maybe God's gone away,
  Forgetting the promise that we heard him say —
  And we're lost out here in the stars —
  Lost in the Stars[1] [1949]

Irving Berlin
1888–1989

3 And if you care to hear
  The "Swanee River"
  Played in ragtime,
  Come on and hear,
  Come on and hear
  Alexander's Ragtime Band.
  Alexander's Ragtime Band [1911]

4 You've got to get up, you've got to get up,
  You've got to get up this morning!
  *Oh! How I Hate to Get Up in the Morning
  [1918]*

5 A Pretty Girl Is Like a Melody.
  Ziegfeld Follies [1919], title of song

6 The song is ended,
  But the melody lingers on.
  *The Song Is Ended (but the Melody
  Lingers On) [1927]*

7 If you're blue and you
  Don't know where to go to,
  Why don't you go where Harlem sits,
  Puttin' on the Ritz? *Puttin' on the Ritz [1928]*

8 Heaven,
  I'm in heaven,
  And my heart beats so that I can hardly speak;
  And I seem to find the happiness I seek
  When we're out together dancing
  Cheek to cheek.
  Top Hat [1935]. Cheek to Cheek

9 There may be trouble ahead,
  But while there's moonlight and music
  And love and romance,
  Let's face the music and dance.
  *Follow the Fleet [1935]. Let's Face the Music
  and Dance*

10 God bless America,
  Land that I love.
  God Bless America [1938]

11 From the mountains to the prairies,
  To the oceans white with foam,
  God bless America,
  My home sweet home! *God Bless America*

12 I'm dreaming of a white Christmas.
  Holiday Inn [1942]. White Christmas

13 This is the army, Mr. Jones,
  No private baths or telephones.
  This Is the Army [1942], title song

14 There's No Business Like Show Business.
  Annie Get Your Gun [1946], title of song

15 Anything You Can Do, I Can Do Better.
  Annie Get Your Gun, title of song

Georges Bernanos
1888–1948

16 Hell, Madame, is to love no longer.
  *Le Journal d'un Curé de Campagne
  (The Diary of a Country Priest) [1936]*

17 No one discovers the depths of his own loneliness.
  Le Journal d'un Curé de Campagne

18 Democracies cannot dispense with hypocrisy any
  more than dictatorships can with cynicism.
  Nous Autres Français (We French) [1939]

19 The most dangerous of our calculations are those
  we call illusions.
  Dialogue des Carmélites [1949]

Henry Beston
1888–1968

20 The world today is sick to its thin blood for lack of
  elemental things, for fire before the hands, for water
  welling from the earth, for air, for the dear earth itself
  underfoot.
  The Outermost House [1928], ch. 1

21 The three great elemental sounds in nature are the
  sound of rain, the sound of wind in a primeval wood,
  and the sound of outer ocean on a beach.
  The Outermost House, 3

22 For a moment of night we have a glimpse of
  ourselves and of our world islanded in its stream of
  stars — pilgrims of mortality, voyaging between hori-
  zons across the eternal seas of space and time.
  The Outermost House, 3

---

[1]Musical based on the novel *Cry, the Beloved Country* [1948] by
ALAN PATON [1903–1988]. Music by KURT WEILL [1900–1950].

Dale Carnegie
1888–1955

1   How to Win Friends and Influence People
Title of book [1938]

Joyce Cary [Arthur Joyce Lunel]
1888–1957

2   Sara could commit adultery at one end and weep for her sins at the other, and enjoy both operations at once.
The Horse's Mouth [1944], ch. 8

Raymond Chandler
1888–1959

3   There was a desert wind blowing that night. It was one of those hot dry Santa Anas that come down through the mountain passes and curl your hair and make your nerves jump and your skin itch. On nights like that every booze party ends in a fight. Meek little wives feel the edge of the carving knife and study their husbands' necks.
Red Wind [1938]

4   "A nice state of affairs when a man has to indulge his vices by proxy," he said dryly.
The Big Sleep [1939], ch. 2

5   What did it matter where you lay once you were dead? In a dirty sump or in a marble tower on top of a high hill? You were dead, you were sleeping the big sleep, you were not bothered by things like that.
The Big Sleep, 32

6   Even on Central Avenue, not the quietest dressed street in the world, he looked about as inconspicuous as a tarantula on a slice of angel food.
Farewell, My Lovely [1940], ch. 1

7   A blonde to make a bishop kick a hole in a stained glass window.
Farewell, My Lovely 13

8   I stepped out into the night air that nobody had yet found out how to option. But a lot of people were probably trying. They'd get around to it.
The Little Sister [1949]

9   When in doubt, have a man come through the door with a gun in his hand.
Trouble Is My Business [1950].
Introduction

10   Down these mean streets a man must go who is not himself mean.
The Simple Art of Murder [1950]

11   The actual writing is what you live for. The rest is something you have to get through in order to arrive at the point.
Letter to Hamish Hamilton
[September 19, 1951]

12   "Alcohol is like love," he said. "The first kiss is magic, the second is intimate, the third is routine. After that you take the girl's clothes off."
The Long Goodbye [1953], ch. 4

13   There is no trap so deadly as the trap you set for yourself.
The Long Goodbye, 12

14   Organized crime is just the dirty side of the sharp dollar.
The Long Goodbye, 48

Giorgio de Chirico
1888–1978

15   Architecture completes nature.
The Sense of Architecture [1920]

John Foster Dulles
1888–1959

16   You have to take chances for peace, just as you must take chances in war.... The ability to get to the verge without getting into the war is the necessary art. If you try to run away from it, if you are scared to go to the brink,[1] you are lost.
Life magazine [January 16, 1956]

T[homas] S[tearns] Eliot
1888–1965

17 Let us go then, you and I,
When the evening is spread out against the sky
Like a patient etherized upon a table.
The Love Song of J. Alfred Prufrock [1917]

18 In the room the women come and go
Talking of Michelangelo.
The Love Song of J. Alfred Prufrock

19 There will be time to murder and create.
The Love Song of J. Alfred Prufrock

20 And indeed there will be time
To wonder, "Do I dare?" and, "Do I dare?"
The Love Song of J. Alfred Prufrock

21 I have measured out my life with coffee spoons.
The Love Song of J. Alfred Prufrock

---

[1]From the phrase "to the brink" developed "brinkmanship."

1 I should have been a pair of ragged claws
   Scuttling across the floors of silent seas.
                    The Love Song of J. Alfred Prufrock

2 Should I, after tea and cakes and ices,
   Have the strength to force the moment to its crisis?
                    The Love Song of J. Alfred Prufrock

3 I have seen the moment of my greatness flicker,
   And I have seen the eternal Footman hold my coat,
       and snicker,
   And in short, I was afraid.
                    The Love Song of J. Alfred Prufrock

4 No! I am not Prince Hamlet, nor was meant to be;
   Am an attendant lord, one that will do
   To swell a progress, start a scene or two,
   Advise the prince; no doubt, an easy tool,
   Deferential, glad to be of use,
   Politic, cautious, and meticulous;
   Full of high sentence, but a bit obtuse;
   At times, indeed, almost ridiculous —
   Almost, at times, the Fool.
                    The Love Song of J. Alfred Prufrock

5 I grow old ... I grow old. ...
   I shall wear the bottoms of my trousers rolled.
                    The Love Song of J. Alfred Prufrock

6 Shall I part my hair behind? Do I dare to eat a peach?
   I shall wear white flannel trousers, and walk upon the
       beach.
   I have heard the mermaids singing, each to each.

   I do not think that they will sing to me.
                    The Love Song of J. Alfred Prufrock

7 Till human voices wake us, and we drown.
                    The Love Song of J. Alfred Prufrock

8 And I must borrow every changing shape
   To find expression.
                    Portrait of a Lady [1917], sec. III

9 I am aware of the damp souls of housemaids
   Sprouting despondently at area gates.
                    Morning at the Window [1917]

10 The readers of the *Boston Evening Transcript*
    Sway in the wind like a field of ripe corn.
                    The Boston Evening Transcript [1917]

11 Upon the glazen shelves kept watch
    Matthew and Waldo, guardians of the faith,
    The army of unalterable law.
                    Cousin Nancy [1917]

12 His laughter tinkled among the teacups.
                    Mr. Apollinax [1917]

13 Stand on the highest pavement of the stair —
    Lean on a garden urn —
    Weave, weave the sunlight in your hair.
                    La Figlia Che Piange [1917], st. 1

14 Simple and faithless as a smile and shake of the
    hand.   *La Figlia Che Piange, st. 2*

15 Sometimes these cogitations still amaze
    The troubled midnight and the noon's repose.
                    La Figlia Che Piange, st. 3

16   He had a mind so fine that no idea could
    violate it.   *In Memory of Henry James [1918]*

17   It [tradition] cannot be inherited, and if you want
    it you must obtain it by great labor.
                    Tradition and the Individual Talent [1919]

18   The progress of an artist is a continual self-
    sacrifice, a continual extinction of personality.
                    Tradition and the Individual Talent

19   Poetry is not a turning loose of emotion, but an
    escape from emotion; it is not the expression of per-
    sonality, but an escape from personality. But, of
    course, only those who have personality and emo-
    tions know what it means to want to escape from
    these things.   *Tradition and the Individual Talent*

20   The only way of expressing emotion in the form
    of art is by finding an "objective correlative"; in
    other words, a set of objects, a situation, a chain of
    events which shall be the formula of that *particular*
    emotion.
                    Hamlet and His Problems [1919]

21 Here I am, an old man in a dry month,
    Being read to by a boy, waiting for rain.
                    Gerontion [1920]

22 After such knowledge, what forgiveness? Think now
    History has many cunning passages, contrived
        corridors
    And issues, deceives with whispering ambitions,
    Guides us by vanities.   *Gerontion*

23 Neither fear nor courage saves us. Unnatural vices
    Are fathered by our heroism. Virtues
    Are forced upon us by our impudent crimes.
    These tears are shaken from the wrath-bearing tree.
                    Gerontion

24 The hippopotamus's day
    Is passed in sleep; at night he hunts;
    God works in a mysterious way —
    The Church can sleep and feed at once.
                    The Hippopotamus [1920], st. 6

25 Webster was much possessed by death
    And saw the skull beneath the skin.
                    Whispers of Immortality [1920], st. 1

26 He knew the anguish of the marrow
    The ague of the skeleton;
    No contact possible to flesh
    Allayed the fever of the bone.
                    Whispers of Immortality, st. 4 [of Donne]

1 Uncorseted, her friendly bust
Gives promise of pneumatic bliss.
> *Whispers of Immortality, st. 5*

2 The nightingales are singing near
The Convent of the Sacred Heart,

And sang within the bloody wood
When Agamemnon cried aloud,
And let their liquid siftings fall
To stain the stiff dishonored shroud.
> *Sweeney Among the Nightingales [1920],*
> *st. 9, 10*

3 Immature poets imitate; mature poets steal.
> *Philip Massinger [1920]*

4 In the seventeenth century a dissociation of sensibility set in, from which we have never recovered; and this dissociation, as is natural, was aggravated by the influence of the two most powerful poets of the century, Milton and Dryden.
> *The Metaphysical Poets [1921]*

5 April is the cruellest month, breeding
Lilacs out of the dead land, mixing
Memory and desire, stirring
Dull roots with spring rain.
> *The Waste Land [1922]. pt. I,*
> *The Burial of the Dead*

6 You know only
A heap of broken images, where the sun beats,
And the dead tree gives no shelter, the cricket no relief,
And the dry stone no sound of water. Only
There is shadow under this red rock,
(Come in under the shadow of this red rock),
And I will show you something different from either
Your shadow at morning striding behind you
Or your shadow at evening rising to meet you;
I will show you fear in a handful of dust.
> *The Waste Land. I, The Burial of the Dead*

7 I had not thought death had undone so many.[1]
Sighs, short and infrequent, were exhaled.[2]
> *The Waste Land. I, The Burial of the Dead*

8 I think we are in rats' alley
Where the dead men lost their bones.
> *The Waste Land. II, A Game of Chess*

9 O O O O that Shakespeherian Rag —
It's so elegant
So intelligent. *The Waste Land. II, A Game of Chess*

10 Hurry up please its time.
> *The Waste Land. II, A Game of Chess*

11 But at my back from time to time I hear[3]
The sound of horns and motors, which shall bring
Sweeney to Mrs. Porter in the spring.
O the moon shone bright on Mrs. Porter
And on her daughter
They wash their feet in soda water.
> *The Waste Land. III, The Fire Sermon*

12 At the violet hour, when the eyes and back
Turn upward from the desk, when the human engine waits
Like a taxi throbbing waiting,
I Tiresias, though blind, throbbing between two lives.
> *The Waste Land. III, The Fire Sermon*

13 When lovely woman stoops to folly[4] and
Paces about her room again, alone,
She smooths her hair with automatic hand,
And puts a record on the gramophone.
> *The Waste Land. III, The Fire Sermon*

14 Phlebas the Phoenician, a fortnight dead,
Forgot the cry of gulls, and the deep sea swell
And the profit and loss.
> *The Waste Land. IV, Death by Water*

15 Here is no water but only rock.
> *The Waste Land. V, What the Thunder Said*

16 Who is the third who walks always beside you?
> *The Waste Land. V, What the Thunder Said*

17 *Dayadhvam:* I have heard the key
Turn in the door once and turn once only
We think of the key, each in his prison
Thinking of the key, each confirms a prison.
> *The Waste Land. V, What the Thunder Said*

18 These fragments I have shored against my ruins.
> *The Waste Land. V, What the Thunder Said*

19 We are the hollow men
We are the stuffed men
Leaning together
Headpiece filled with straw. Alas!
> *The Hollow Men [1925], sec. I*

20 Shape without form, shade without color,
Paralyzed force, gesture without motion;

Those who have crossed
With direct eyes, to death's other Kingdom
Remember us — if at all — not as lost
Violent souls, but only
As the hollow men
The stuffed men.
> *The Hollow Men, I*

---

[1] Dante, *Inferno, canto III, ll. 55–57.*
[2] Dante, *Inferno, canto IV, ll. 25–27.*
[3] See Andrew Marvell, 266:22.
[4] See Oliver Goldsmith, 322:16.

1 Between the idea
And the reality
Between the motion
And the act
Falls the Shadow.　　　　　*The Hollow Men, V*

2 This is the way the world ends
Not with a bang but a whimper.　　*The Hollow Men, V*

3　　　I'll convert *you!*
Into a stew.
A nice little, white little, missionary stew!
　　　　　　　　Sweeney Agonistes [1926]

4 Birth, and copulation, and death.
That's all the facts when you come to brass tacks.
　　　　　　　　　　Sweeney Agonistes

5 Two live as one
One live as two
Two live as three
Under the bam
Under the boo
Under the bamboo tree.　　　*Sweeney Agonistes*

6 A cold coming we had of it,
Just the worst time of the year.
　　　　　　　　Journey of the Magi [1927]

7　　　Poets in our civilization, as it exists at present, must be *difficult*.... The poet must become more and more comprehensive, more allusive, more indirect, in order to force, to dislocate if necessary, language into its meaning.
　　　　　　　　The Metaphysical Poets

8　　　The great poet, in writing himself, writes his time.
　　　　Shakespeare and the Stoicism of Seneca [1927]

9　　　The general point of view may be described as classicist in literature, royalist in politics, and Anglo-Catholic in religion.
　　　　For Lancelot Andrews [1928], preface

10　　Genuine poetry can communicate before it is understood.　　　　　　*Dante [1929]*

11　　More can be learned about how to write poetry from Dante than from any English poet.... The language of each great English poet is his own language; the language of Dante is the perfection of a common language.　　　　　　　　　　*Dante*

12 Because I do not hope to turn again[1]
Because I do not hope
Because I do not hope to turn.
　　　　　　　Ash-Wednesday [1930], I

13 Because these wings are no longer wings to fly
But merely vans to beat the air

---
[1]GUIDO CAVALCANTI [c. 1255–1300], *Perch'io Non Spero.*

The air which is now thoroughly small and dry
Smaller and dryer than the will
Teach us to care and not to care
Teach us to sit still.　　　　*Ash-Wednesday, I*

14 Terminate torment
Of love unsatisfied
The greater torment
Of love satisfied.　　　　*Ash-Wednesday, II*

15 Blown hair is sweet, brown hair over the mouth
　　blown,
Lilac and brown hair;
Distraction, music of the flute, stops and steps of the
　　mind over the third stair,
Fading, fading; strength beyond hope and despair
Climbing the third stair.　　*Ash-Wednesday, III*

16　　　Redeem
The time. Redeem
The unread vision in the higher dream
While jeweled unicorns draw by the gilded hearse.
　　　　　　　　　　Ash-Wednesday, IV

17 Against the Word the unstilled world still whirled
About the center of the silent Word.
　　　　　　　　　　Ash-Wednesday, V

18 Wavering between the profit and the loss
In this brief transit where the dreams cross
The dreamcrossed twilight between birth and
　　dying.　　　　　　*Ash-Wednesday, VI*

19 The white sails still fly seaward, seaward flying
Unbroken wings.

And the lost heart stiffens and rejoices
In the lost lilac and the lost sea voices
And the weak spirit quickens to rebel
For the bent goldenrod and the lost sea smell.
　　　　　　　　　　Ash-Wednesday, VI

20 What seas what shores what gray rocks and what
　　islands
What water lapping the bow
And scent of pine and the woodthrush singing
　　through the fog
What images return
O my daughter.　　　　　*Marina [1930]*

21 Stone, bronze, stone, steel, stone, oakleaves, horses'
　　heels
Over the paving.
　　　　Coriolan [1931]. pt. I, Triumphal March

22　　As things are, and as fundamentally they must always be, poetry is not a career, but a mug's game. No honest poet can ever feel quite sure of the permanent value of what he has written: he may have wasted his time and messed up his life for nothing.
　　　　The Use of Poetry and the Use of Criticism [1933], conclusion

1 Yet we have gone on living,
Living and partly living.
Murder in the Cathedral [1935], pt. I

2 They know and do not know, what it is to act or
suffer.
They know and do not know, that acting is suffering.
Murder in the Cathedral, I

3 Saint and Martyr rule from the tomb.
Murder in the Cathedral, I

4 The last temptation is the greatest treason:
To do the right deed for the wrong reason.
Murder in the Cathedral, I

5 Human kind cannot bear very much reality.[1]
Murder in the Cathedral, II

6 Time present and time past
Are both perhaps present in time future,
And time future contained in time past.
Four Quartets. Burnt Norton [1935], pt. I

7 Footfalls echo in the memory
Down the passage which we did not take
Towards the door we never opened
Into the rose garden.
Four Quartets. Burnt Norton, I

8 Garlic and sapphires in the mud
Clot the bedded axle-tree.
The trilling wire in the blood
Sings below inveterate scars
And reconciles forgotten wars.
Four Quartets. Burnt Norton, II

9 At the still point of the turning world.
Neither flesh nor fleshless.
Four Quartets. Burnt Norton, II

10   Except for the point, the still point,
There would be no dance, and there is only the
dance.
Four Quartets. Burnt Norton, II

11 Sudden in a shaft of sunlight
Even while the dust moves
There rises the hidden laughter
Of children in the foliage
Quick now, here, now, always —
Ridiculous the waste sad time
Stretching before and after.
Four Quartets. Burnt Norton, V

12 Macavity, Macavity, there's no one like Macavity,
He's broken every human law, he breaks the law of
gravity.
His powers of levitation would make a fakir stare,

And when you reach the scene of the crime —
Macavity's not there!
Old Possum's Book of Practical Cats [1939].
Macavity: The Mystery Cat

13 In my beginning is my end.
Four Quartets. East Coker [1940], pt. I

14   Keeping time,
Keeping the rhythm in their dancing
As in their living in the living seasons
The time of the seasons and the constellations
The time of milking and the time of harvest
The time of the coupling of man and woman
And that of beasts. Feet rising and falling.
Eating and drinking. Dung and death.
Four Quartets. East Coker, I

15 What is the late November doing
With the disturbance of the spring.
Four Quartets. East Coker, II

16 A periphrastic study in a worn-out poetical fashion,
Leaving one still with the intolerable wrestle
With words and meanings. The poetry does not
matter.
Four Quartets. East Coker, II

17 The houses are all gone under the sea.
Four Quartets. East Coker, II

18 The dancers are all gone under the hill.
Four Quartets. East Coker, II

19 O dark dark dark.[2] They all go into the dark,
The vacant interstellar spaces, the vacant into the
vacant.
Four Quartets. East Coker, III

20 And we all go with them, into the silent funeral,
Nobody's funeral, for there is no one to bury.
I said to my soul, be still,[3] and let the dark come upon
you
Which shall be the darkness of God.
Four Quartets. East Coker, III

21 To arrive where you are, to get from where you are
not,
You must go by a way wherein there is no ecstasy.
In order to arrive at what you do not know
You must go by the way which is the way of
ignorance.   *Four Quartets. East Coker, III*

22   And so each venture
Is a new beginning, a raid on the inarticulate
With shabby equipment always deteriorating
In the general mess of imprecision of feeling,
Undisciplined squads of emotion.
Four Quartets. East Coker, V

---

[1]Also in ELIOT's *Four Quartets. Burnt Norton, pt. I.*

[2]See Milton, 260:9.
[3]See *Psalm 46:10,* 16:28.

1 Home is where one starts from. As we grow older
  The world becomes stranger, the pattern more
      complicated
  Of dead and living. Not the intense moment
  Isolated, with no before and after,
  But a lifetime burning in every moment
  And not the lifetime of one man only
  But of old stones that cannot be deciphered.
                    Four Quartets. East Coker, V

2 Love is most nearly itself
  When here and now cease to matter.
  Old men ought to be explorers
  Here and there does not matter
  We must be still and still moving
  Into another intensity
  For a further union, a deeper communion
  Through the dark cold and the empty desolation,
  The wave cry, the wind cry, the vast waters
  Of the petrel and the porpoise. In my end is my
      beginning.
                    Four Quartets. East Coker, V

3 I do not know much about gods; but I think that the
      river
  Is a strong brown god — sullen, untamed and
      intractable.
                    *Four Quartets. The Dry Salvages [1941],
                    pt. I*

4 The sea is the land's edge also, the granite
  Into which it reaches, the beaches where it tosses
  Its hints of earlier and other creation:
  The starfish, the hermit crab, the whale's
      backbone;
  The pools where it offers to our curiosity
  The more delicate algae and the sea anemone.
  It tosses up our losses, the torn seine,
  The shattered lobsterpot, the broken oar
  And the gear of foreign dead men. The sea has many
      voices.
                    Four Quartets. The Dry Salvages, I

5 Time the destroyer is time the preserver.
                    Four Quartets. The Dry Salvages, II

6   Not fare well,
  But fare forward, voyagers.
                    Four Quartets. The Dry Salvages, III

7   Music heard so deeply
  That it is not heard at all, but you are the music
  While the music lasts.
                    Four Quartets. The Dry Salvages, V

8 What the dead had no speech for, when living,
  They can tell you, being dead: the communication
  Of the dead is tongued with fire beyond the language
      of the living.
                    Four Quartets. Little Gidding [1942], pt. I

9 In the uncertain hour before the morning
  Near the ending of interminable night
  At the recurrent end of the unending
  After the dark dove with the flickering tongue
  Had passed below the horizon of his homing.
                    Four Quartets. Little Gidding, II

10 Since our concern was speech, and speech impelled us
  To purify the dialect of the tribe.[1]
                    Four Quartets. Little Gidding, II

11 Who then devised the torment? Love.
  Love is the unfamiliar Name
  Behind the hands that wove
  The intolerable shirt of flame
  Which human power cannot remove.
      We only live, only suspire
      Consumed by either fire or fire.
                    Four Quartets. Little Gidding, IV

12 We shall not cease from exploration
  And the end of all our exploring
  Will be to arrive where we started
  And know the place for the first time.
                    Four Quartets. Little Gidding, V

13 A condition of complete simplicity
  (Costing not less than everything)
  And all shall be well and
  All manner of thing shall be well[2]
  When the tongues of flame are infolded
  Into the crowned knot of fire
  And the fire and the rose are one.
                    Four Quartets. Little Gidding, V

14 Where is the wisdom we have lost in knowledge?
  Where is the knowledge we have lost in
      information?   *Chorus from "The Rock" [1934]*

15 Just when you think you're on the point of release
  From loneliness, then loneliness swoops down upon
      you.   *The Confidential Clerk [1954]*

16   Most editors are failed writers — but so are most
  writers.
                    *From ROBERT GIROUX [1914–2008],
                    The Education of an Editor [1982]*

Jules Furthman
1888–1966

17   It took more than one man to change my name to
  Shanghai Lily.
                    *Shanghai Express (screenplay) [1932],
                    spoken by Marlene Dietrich*

---

[1]Donner un sens plus pur aux mots de la tribu. — STÉPHANE
MALLARMÉ, *Le Tombeau d'Edgar Poe*
[2]See Julian of Norwich, 131:14.

Jules Furthman
1888–1966

and

William Faulkner
1897–1962

1   Maybe just whistle. You know how to whistle, don't you, Steve? You just put your lips together and blow.

To Have and Have Not (screenplay) [1944],
spoken by Lauren Bacall

Haven Gillespie
1888–1975

2   He's making a list
And checking it twice,
Gonna find out
Who's naughty and nice,
Santa Claus is comin' to town.

Santa Claus Is Comin' to Town[1] [1934]

Joseph [Patrick] Kennedy
1888–1969

3   Don't get mad, get even.   *Attributed*

Ronald Arbuthnott Knox
1888–1957

4   There once was a man who said, "God
Must think it exceedingly odd
If he finds that this tree
Continues to be
When there's no one about in the Quad."

Limerick on idealism[2]

William L[eonard] Laurence
1888–1977

5   A great ball of fire about a mile in diameter, changing colors as it kept shooting upward, from deep purple to orange, expanding, growing bigger, rising as it was expanding, an elemental force freed from its bonds after being chained for billions of years.

On the first atom bomb explosion.[3] In the
New York Times [September 26, 1945]

---

[1]Music by J. Fᴀᴇᴅ Cᴏᴏᴛs [1897–1985].

[2]Dear Sir, Your astonishment's odd: / *I* am always about in the Quad; / And that's why the tree / Will continue to be, / Since observed by Yours Faithfully, God. — *Anonymous rejoinder*

[3]At Alamogordo, New Mexico [July 16, 1945]. See J. Robert Oppenheimer, 739:8.

---

6   At first it was a giant column that soon took the shape of a supramundane mushroom.

On the first atom bomb explosion.
In the New York Times
[September 26, 1945]

T[homas] E[dward]
Lawrence[4]
1888–1935

7   I loved you, so I drew these tides of men into my
       hands and wrote my will across the sky in stars.
To earn you Freedom, the seven-pillared worthy
       house, that your eyes might be shining for me
When we came.

Seven Pillars of Wisdom[5] [1926],
dedication

8   War upon rebellion was messy and slow, like eating soup with a knife.

Seven Pillars of Wisdom, bk. 3

9   There could be no honor in a sure success, but much might be wrested from a sure defeat.

Revolt in the Desert [1927],
ch. 19

Leadbelly [Huddie Ledbetter]
1888–1949

10 Good mornin', blues, blues how do you do?
Good mornin', blues, blues how do you do?
I'm doin' all right, good mornin', how are you?

Good Morning Blues [1940]

Katherine Mansfield
1888–1923

11 If there was one thing that he hated more than another it was the way she had of waking him in the morning. She did it on purpose, of course. It was her way of establishing her grievance for the day.

Bliss [1920].
Mr. Reginald Peacock's Day

12 I want, by understanding myself, to understand others. I want to be all that I am capable of becoming. . . . This all sounds very strenuous and serious. But now that I have wrestled with it, it's no longer so. I feel happy — deep down. *All is well.*

Journal [1922], last entry

---

[4]Lawrence changed his name to T. E. Shaw in 1927.

[5]See *Proverbs 9:1, 20:7.*

Eugene O'Neill
1888–1953

1   Dat ole davil, sea.   *Anna Christie [1922], act I*

2   Gimme a whiskey — ginger ale on the side. And don't be stingy, baby.[1]   *Anna Christie, I*

3   We's all poor nuts and things happen, and we yust get mixed in wrong, that's all.   *Anna Christie, IV*

4   For de little stealin' dey gits you in jail soon or late. For de big stealin' dey makes you emperor and puts you in de Hall o' Fame when you croaks. If dey's one thing I learns in ten years on de Pullman cars listenin' to de white quality talk, it's dat same fact.
The Emperor Jones [1920], sc. i

5   *Yank:* Sure! Lock me up! Put me in a cage! Dat's de on'y answer yuh know. G'wan, lock me up!
Policeman: What you been doin'?
Yank: Enough to gimme life for! I was born, see? Sure, dat's de charge. Write it in de blotter. I was born, get me!   *The Hairy Ape [1922], sc. vii*

6   Desire Under the Elms   *Title of play [1924]*

7   Strange interlude! Yes, our lives are merely strange dark interludes in the electrical display of God the Father!   *Strange Interlude [1928], pt. II, act IX*

8   Mourning Becomes Electra
Title of dramatic trilogy [1931]

9   The damned don't cry.
*Mourning Becomes Electra [1931].
The Haunted, act III*

10   The dead! Why can't the dead die!
*Mourning Becomes Electra.
The Haunted, IV*

11   A Long Day's Journey into Night
Title of play [1956]

12   Born in a goddam hotel room and dying in a hotel room!
Last words. From LOUIS SHEAFFER [1912–1993], O'Neill: Son and Artist [1973]

Fernando Pessoa
1888–1935

13   Nature is parts without a whole.
This is perhaps the mystery they speak of.[2]
The Keeper of Sheep, poem 47 (writing as Albert Caeiro) [c. 1914]

14   How should I know what I'll be, I who don't know what I am?
Be what I think? But I think of being so many things!
And there are so many who think of being the same thing that we can't all be it!
Genius? At this moment
A hundred thousand brains are dreaming they're geniuses like me,
And it may be that history won't remember even one,
All their imagined conquests amounting to so much dung.
The Tobacco Shop[2] (writing as Álvaro de Campos) [1928]

15   The only freedom the gods grant us
Is this: to submit
Of our own free will to their sovereignty.
We should do just that,
Since only in the illusion of freedom
Does freedom exist.[2]
The only freedom the gods grant us (writing as Ricardo Reis) [1914]

16   Out of a few misunderstandings with reality we construct beliefs and hopes, and we live on these crusts, which we call bread, just like poor children who play at being happy.[3]
The Book of Disquiet (writing as Bernardo Soares) [1982]

John Crowe Ransom
1888–1974

17   Captain Carpenter rose up in his prime
Put on his pistols and went riding out.
Captain Carpenter [1924], st. 1

18   Two evils, monstrous either one apart,
Possessed me, and were long and loath at going:
A cry of Absence, Absence, in the heart,
And in the wood the furious winter blowing.
Winter Remembered [1924]

19   The lazy geese, like a snow cloud
Dripping their snow on the green grass,
Tricking and stopping, sleepy and proud,
Who cried in goose, Alas.
Bells for John Whiteside's Daughter [1924]

20   Here lies a lady of beauty and high degree.
Of chills and fever she died, of fever and chills,
The delight of her husband, her aunts, an infant of three,
And of medicos marveling sweetly on her ills.
Here Lies a Lady [1924]

---

[1]Made famous in the movie version [1930] as the silent-film star Greta Garbo's first speech in a talkie.

[2]Translated by RICHARD ZENITH.

[3]Translated by ALFRED MACADAM.

1 God have mercy on the sinner
Who must write with no dinner,
No gravy and no grub,
No pewter and no pub,
No belly and no bowels,
Only consonants and vowels.
Survey of Literature [1927]

Knute [Kenneth] Rockne
1888–1931

2   Show me a good and gracious loser and I'll show you a failure.[1]
Remark to Wisconsin basketball coach Walter Meanwell [1920s]

3   Win just one for the Gipper.[2]
Attributed

Carl Schmitt
1888–1985

4   The specific political distinction to which political actions and motives can be reduced is that between friend and enemy.... The political enemy need not be morally evil or aesthetically ugly; he need not appear as an economic competitor, and it may even be advantageous to engage with him in business transactions. But he is, nevertheless, the other, the stranger; and it is sufficient for his nature that he is, in a specifically intense way, existentially something different and alien, so that in the extreme case conflicts with him are possible.
The Concept of the Political[3] *[1927]*

5   All genuine political theories presuppose man to be evil, i.e., by no means an unproblematic but a dangerous and dynamic being.
The Concept of the Political

Alan Seeger
1888–1916

6 I have a rendezvous with Death
At some disputed barricade,

When spring comes back with rustling shade
And apple blossoms fill the air.
I Have a Rendezvous with Death [1916]

7 And I to my pledged word am true,
I shall not fail that rendezvous.
I Have a Rendezvous with Death

Frances Steloff
1888–1989

8 Wise men fish here.
Sign of The Gotham Book Mart,[4]
New York City

Giuseppe Ungaretti
1888–1970

9 To joyously savor one single
instant of initial
life I seek an innocent
country[5]

Wanderer [1918]

Bartolomeo Vanzetti
1888–1927

10   If it had not been for this thing, I might have lived out my life talking at street corners to scorning men. I might have died unmarked, unknown, a failure. Now we are not a failure. This is our career and our triumph. Never in our full life could we hope to do such work for tolerance, for justice, for man's understanding of man, as now we do by accident.
Letter to his son [April 1927]

11   Our words — our lives — our pains: nothing! The taking of our lives — lives of a good shoemaker and a poor fish peddler — all! That last moment belongs to us — that agony is our triumph.
Letter to his son [April 1927]

12   I found myself compelled to fight back from my eyes the tears, and quanch my heart trobling to my throat to not weep before him. But Sacco's name will live in the hearts of the people when your name, your laws, institutions and your false god are but a dim rememoring of a cursed past in which man was wolf to the man.
Last speech to the court[6]

---

[1]More familiar version: Show me a good loser and I'll show you a loser.

[2]According to tradition, the football player George Gipp [1895–1920] made a deathbed request that Rockne spur Notre Dame to victory, on one occasion, especially for him.

[3]Translated by GEORGE SCHWAB.

---

[4]Founded by Steloff in 1920.

[5]Translated by JOSEPH CARY.

[6]Vanzetti and Nicola Sacco, Italian anarchists, were executed August 23, 1927, by the Commonwealth of Massachusetts on charges, never conclusively proved, of murder and robbery.

Henry A[gard] Wallace
1888–1965

1   Some have spoken of the "American Century." I say that the century on which we are entering — the century which will come out of this war — can be and must be the century of the common man.
Speech to Free World Association
[May 8, 1942]

2   The people's revolution is on the march, and the devil and all his angels cannot prevail against it.
Speech to Free World Association
[May 8, 1942]

Conrad Aiken
1889–1973

3 Music I heard with you was more than music,
And bread I broke with you was more than bread.
Now that I am without you, all is desolate;
All that was once so beautiful is dead.
Bread and Music [1914]

4 All lovely things will have an ending,
All lovely things will fade and die,
And youth, that's now so bravely spending,
Will beg a penny by and by.
Disenchantment [1916], pt. 4

5   The hiss was now becoming a roar — the whole world was a vast moving screen of snow — but even now it said peace, it said remoteness, it said cold, it said sleep.   *Silent Snow, Secret Snow [1932]*

Anna Akhmatova [Anna Andreyevna Gorenko]
1889–1966

6 If you can't give me love and peace,
Then give me bitter fame.
Rosary [composed 1913,
published 1914]

7 No foreign sky protected me,
no stranger's wing shielded my face.
I stand as witness to the common lot,
survivor of that time, that place.
Requiem[1] [composed mainly 1935–1940].
Epigraph [composed 1961]

8   In the terrible years of the Yezhov terror I spent seventeen months waiting in line outside the prison in Leningrad. One day somebody in the crowd

identified me . . . and asked me in a whisper . . . "Can you describe this?" And I said: "I can."
Requiem. Instead of a Preface [composed 1957]

9 That was a time when only the dead
could smile.
Requiem. Prologue [composed 1935–1940]

10 I should be proud to have my memory graced,
but only if the monument be placed . . .
here, where I endured three hundred hours
in line before the implacable iron bars.
Requiem. Epilogue [composed 1940], pt. II

Robert [Charles] Benchley
1889–1945

11   Why don't you get out of that wet coat and into a dry martini?
Attributed[2]

12   There may be said to be two classes of people in the world; those who constantly divide the people of the world into two classes, and those who do not.
Of All Things [1921], ch. 20

13   In America there are two classes of travel — first-class, and with children.
Kiddie-Kar Travel [1923]

14   Streets full of water. Please advise.
Telegram from Venice (attributed)

Charlie [Sir Charles Spencer] Chaplin
1889–1977

15   Wars, conflict, it's all business. One murder makes a villain; millions a hero. Numbers sanctify.
Monsieur Verdoux[3] (screenplay) [1947]

16   [The tramp character:] A tramp, a gentleman, a poet, a dreamer, a lonely fellow, always hopeful of romance and adventure.
My Autobiography [1964], ch. 10

17   All I need to make a comedy is a park, a police-man, and a pretty girl.   *My Autobiography, 10*

18   I am known in parts of the world by people who have never heard of Jesus Christ.[4]
From LITA GREY CHAPLIN [1908–1995],
My Life with Chaplin [1966]

---

[2]Spoken by him in the movie *The Major and the Minor* [1942] but, according to his account, borrowed from a similar line spoken by his friend Charles Butterworth in the Mae West movie *Every Day's a Holiday* [1937].

[3]Orson Welles is credited with developing the idea for the film.

[4]See John Lennon, 847:12.

---

[1]Translated by STANLEY KUNITZ with MAX HAYWARD.

Jean Cocteau
1889–1963

1   Mirrors are the doors through which Death comes and goes.
> *Orpheus [1926], sc. vii [Also, screenplay, 1950]*

2   Mirrors should reflect a little before throwing back images.[1]
> *Des Beaux-Arts Considérés Comme un Assassinat (The Fine Arts as an Assassination) [1932]*

3   First find, then search.[2]
> *Journal d'un Inconnu (Journal of an Unknown) [1953]*

4 The matters I relate
Are true lies.[3]
> *The Journals of Jean Cocteau [1956]. Quoted by* WALLACE FOWLIE *[1908–1998] in the introduction*

Martin Heidegger
1889–1976

5   Language is the house of Being.
> *What Are Poets For?[4] [1947]*

6   Man acts as though *he* were the shaper and master of language, while in fact *language* remains the master of man.
> *Building Dwelling Thinking[4] [1951]*

7   Questioning is the piety of thought.
> *The Question Concerning Technology[5] [1953], pt. 1*

Adolf Hitler
1889–1945

8   My adversaries . . . applied the one means that wins the easiest victory over reason: terror and force.
> *Mein Kampf (My Battle) [1933], vol. I, ch. 2*

9   A majority can never replace the man. . . . Just as a hundred fools do not make one wise man, an heroic decision is not likely to come from a hundred cowards.
> *Mein Kampf, I, 3*

10   Strength lies not in defense but in attack.
> *Mein Kampf, I, 3*

11   All propaganda has to be popular and has to adapt its spiritual level to the perception of the least intelligent of those towards whom it intends to direct itself.
> *Mein Kampf, I, 6*

12   The great masses of the people . . . will more easily fall victims to a big lie than to a small one.
> *Mein Kampf, I, 10*

13   I go the way that Providence dictates with the assurance of a sleepwalker.
> *Speech [March 15, 1936]*

14   I want today once again to make a prophecy: if the international Jewish financiers within and without Europe succeed once more in plunging the nations into another world war, the result will be not the Bolshevization of the world and with it a victory for Judaism. The result will be the extermination of the Jewish race in Europe.
> *Speech to the Reichstag [January 30, 1939]*

15   After all, who remembers the Armenians?
> *Attributed remark, prior to the invasion of Poland [1939]*

16   After fifteen years of work I have achieved, as a common German soldier and merely with my fanatical will power, the unity of the German nation, and have freed it from the death sentence of Versailles.[6]
> *Proclamation to the troops on taking over the leadership of the German armed forces [December 21, 1941]*

17   This war no longer bears the characteristics of former inter-European conflicts. It is one of those elemental conflicts which usher in a new millennium and which shake the world once in a thousand years.
> *Speech to the Reichstag [April 26, 1942]*

18   Is Paris burning?[7]
> *Asked at the Oberkommando der Wehrmacht, Rastenburg, Germany [August 25, 1944]*

George S. Kaufman
1889–1961

19   Satire is what closes Saturday night.
> *Saying*

---

[1]Les miroirs feraient bien de réfléchir un peu avant de renvoyer les images.

[2]Trouver d'abord, chercher après.

I don't seek, I find. — PABLO PICASSO, as quoted in ALFRED H. BARR, *Picasso* [1946]

[3]Les choses que je conte / Sont des mensonges vrais.

[4]Translated by ALBERT HOFSTADTER.

[5]Translated by WILLIAM LOVITT.

[6]The Allied and Associated Governments affirm and Germany accepts the responsibility of Germany and her Allies for causing all the loss and damage to which the Allied and Associated Governments and their nationals have been subjected as a consequence of the war imposed upon them by the aggression of Germany and her Allies. — *Article 231 (the "war guilt clause"), Treaty of Versailles* [June 28, 1919]

[7]Brennt Paris?

George S. Kaufman
1889–1961

and

Edna Ferber
1885–1968

1   You're through in pictures, and plays, and vaudeville, and radio, and everything! You're a corpse, and you don't know it. Go get yourself buried.
Dinner at Eight [1932], act III, sc. ii

Walter Lippmann
1889–1974

2   There can be no higher law in journalism than to tell the truth and shame the devil.
Liberty and the News [1920].
Journalism and the Higher Law

3   What each man does is based not on direct and certain knowledge, but on pictures made by himself or given to him. . . . The way in which the world is imagined determines at any particular moment what men will do.
Public Opinion [1922], ch. 1,
The World Outside and the Pictures
in Our Heads

4   Franklin D. Roosevelt is no crusader. He is no tribune of the people. He is no enemy of entrenched privilege. He is a pleasant man who, without any important qualifications for the office, would very much like to be President.
Today and Tomorrow [January 8, 1932]

5   A free press is not a privilege but an organic necessity in a great society. . . . A great society is simply a big and complicated urban society.
Address at the International Press Institute
Assembly, London [May 27, 1965]

Jawaharlal Nehru
1889–1964

6   I want nothing to do with any religion concerned with keeping the masses satisfied to live in hunger, filth, and ignorance. I want nothing to do with any order, religious or otherwise, which does not teach people that they are capable of becoming happier and more civilized, on this earth, capable of becoming true *man*, master of his fate and captain of his soul.
From EDGAR SNOW,
Journey to the Beginning [1958]

Carl O[rtwin] Sauer
1889–1975

7   We have not yet learned the difference between yield and loot.
Theme of Plant and Animal Destruction
in Economic History [1938]

Arnold Joseph Toynbee
1889–1975

8   Civilizations, I believe, come to birth and proceed to grow by successfully responding to successive challenges. They break down and go to pieces if and when a challenge confronts them which they fail to meet.
Civilization on Trial [1948], ch. 4

Ludwig [Josef Johann] Wittgenstein
1889–1951

9   The world is all that is the case.[1]
Tractatus Logico-Philosophicus[2] *[1922], 1*

10   The *limits of my language* mean the limits of my world.
Tractatus-Logico-Philosophicus, 5.6

11   What we cannot speak about we must pass over in silence.[3]
Tractatus Logico-Philosophicus, 7

12   The human body is the best picture of the human soul.   *Philosophical Investigations [1953]*

13   Philosophy may in no way interfere with the actual use of language; it can in the end only describe it. . . . It leaves everything as it is.
Philosophical Investigations

14   What is your aim in philosophy? — To show the fly the way out of the fly-bottle.
Philosophical Investigations

15   Philosophy, as we use the word, is a fight against the fascination which forms of expression exert on us.
The Blue and Brown Books [1958]

Karel Čapek
1890–1938

16   Rossum's Universal Robots[4]
R.U.R. [1920]

---

[1]Die Welt ist alles, was der Fall ist.
[2]Translated by D. F. PEARS and B. F. McGUINNESS.
[3]Wovon man nicht sprechen kann, darüber muss man schweigen.
[4]The term "robot" came into English through Čapek's play.

Agatha Christie
1890–1976

1   "This affair must all be unraveled from within."
He [Hercule Poirot] tapped his forehead. "These
little gray cells. It is 'up to them'—as you say
over here."
> *The Mysterious Affair at Styles [1920],*
> *ch. 10*

2   It is completely unimportant. That is why it is so
interesting.
> *The Murder of Roger Ackroyd [1926]*

Marc[us Cook] Connelly
1890–1980

3   Gangway for de Lawd God Jehovah!
> *The Green Pastures*[1] *[1930]*

Elmer Davis
1890–1958

4   The first and great commandment is: Don't let
them scare you.
> *But We Were Born Free [1954]*

Charles [André Joseph Marie] de Gaulle
1890–1970

5   France has lost a battle. But France has not lost
the war.
> *BBC broadcast from London to the*
> *French people after the fall of France*
> *[June 18, 1940]*

6   Whatever happens, the flame of the French resistance must not and shall not die.
> *BBC broadcast [June 18, 1940]*

7   Since those whose duty it was to hold the sword
of France have let it fall, I have picked up its broken
point.
> *Radio address [July 13, 1940]*

8   If I live, I will fight, wherever I must, as long as I
must, until the enemy is defeated and the national
stain washed clean.
> *Les Mémoires de Guerre, vol. I [1954]*

9   France cannot be France without greatness.
> *Les Mémoires de Guerre, I*

---

[1]Suggested by Roark Bradford's stories, *Ol' Man Adam an' His Chillun* [1928].

10   I always thought I was Jeanne d'Arc and Bonaparte. How little one knows oneself.
> *Reply to speaker who compared him to*
> *Robespierre. From Figaro Littéraire [1958]*

11   Only peril can bring the French together. One
can't impose unity out of the blue on a country that
has 265 different kinds of cheese.   *Attributed*

Marjory Stoneman Douglas
1890–1998

12   There are no other Everglades in the world....
The miracle of the light pours over the green and
brown expanse of saw grass and of water, shining and
slow-moving below, the grass and water that is the
meaning of the central fact of the Everglades of
Florida. It is a river of grass.
> *The Everglades: River of Grass [1947], ch. 1*

Dwight D[avid] Eisenhower
1890–1969

13   People of Western Europe: A landing was made
this morning on the coast of France by troops of the
Allied Expeditionary Force. This landing is part of the
concerted United Nations plan for the liberation of
Europe, made in conjunction with our great Russian
allies.... I call upon all who love freedom to stand
with us now. Together we shall achieve victory.
> *Broadcast on D-Day [June 6, 1944]*

14   I shall go to Korea.
> *Campaign speech, Detroit, Michigan*
> *[October 25, 1952]*

15   Every gun that is made, every warship launched,
every rocket fired signifies, in the final sense, a theft
from those who hunger and are not fed, those who
are cold and are not clothed.
> *Speech [April 16, 1953]*

16   This conjunction of an immense military establishment and a large arms industry is new in the American
experience. We must guard against the acquisition of
unwarranted influence, whether sought or unsought,
by the military-industrial complex. The potential for
the disastrous rise of misplaced power exists and will
persist.
> *Farewell Radio and Television*
> *Address to the American People*
> *[January 17, 1961]*

17   Biggest damfool mistake I ever made.
> *Recalling his appointment [1953]*
> *of Earl Warren as Chief Justice of the*
> *United States*

Gene Fowler
1890–1960

1 Writing is easy. All you do is stare at a blank sheet of paper until drops of blood form on your forehead.

Attributed[1]

Frances Goodrich
1890–1984

Albert Hackett
1900–1995

and

Frank Capra
1897–1991

2 Strange, isn't it? Each man's life touches so many other lives. When he isn't around he leaves an awful hole, doesn't he?

It's a Wonderful Life [1947]

3 Look, Daddy. Teacher says, "Every time a bell rings an angel gets his wings."

It's a Wonderful Life

Samuel Hoffenstein
1890–1947

4 Babies haven't any hair;
Old men's heads are just as bare;
Between the cradle and the grave
Lies a haircut and a shave.

Songs of Faith in the Year After Next, VIII

Hanns Johst
1890–1978

5 When I hear the word "culture" . . . I reach for my pistol.[2]

Schlageter [1933]

Robert Ley
1890–1945

6 Strength through joy.[3]

Instruction for the German Labor Front [December 2, 1933]

H[oward] P[hillips] Lovecraft
1890–1937

7 The most merciful thing in the world, I think, is the inability of the human mind to correlate all its contents.

The Call of Cthulhu [1928], ch. 1

8 In his house at R'lyeh dead Cthulhu waits dreaming.

The Call of Cthulhu, 2

9 From even the greatest of horrors irony is seldom absent.

The Shunned House [1937]

William A. Maguire
1890–1953

10 Praise the Lord and pass the ammunition.[4]

Attributed

Claude McKay
1890–1948

11 Upon the clothes behind the tenement,
That hang like ghosts suspended from the lines,
Linking each flat, but to each indifferent,
Incongruous and strange the moonlight shines.

A Song of the Moon

12 Although she feeds me bread of bitterness,
And sinks into my throat her tiger's tooth,
Stealing my breath of life, I must confess
I love this cultured hell that tests my youth!
Her vigor flows like tides into my blood,
Giving me strength erect against her hate.
Her bigness sweeps my being like a flood.

America

13 If we must die, let it not be like hogs
Hunted and penned in an inglorious spot.

If We Must Die

14 Like men we'll face the murderous, cowardly pack,
Pressed to the wall, dying, but fighting back!

If We Must Die

Giorgio Morandi
1890–1964

15 I believe that nothing can be more abstract, more unreal, than what we actually see.

Interview with Edouard Roditi [1960]

---

[1]Also attributed (in a variant form) to sports columnist RED [WALTER WELLESLEY] SMITH [1905–1982].

[2]Wenn ich Kultur höre . . . entsichere ich meinen Browning. Often attributed to HERMANN GOERING.

[3]Kraft durch Freude.

---

[4]Basis of the popular World War II song [1942] of that title by FRANK LOESSER [1910–1969].

Christopher Morley
1890–1957

1   There is only one success — to be able to spend your life in your own way.
Where the Blue Begins [1922]

2   Life is a foreign language; all men mispronounce it.   *Thunder on the Left [1925], ch. 14*

Boris Pasternak
1890–1960

3 I am alone; all drowns in the Pharisees' hypocrisy.
To live your life is not as simple as to cross a field.[1]
Hamlet[2] [1946]

4 You are eternity's hostage
A captive of time.   *Night[2] [1957]*

5 But what are pity, conscience, or fear
To the brazen pair, compared
With the living sorcery
Of their hot embraces?   *Bacchanalia[2] [1957], st. 4*

6 It snowed and snowed, the whole world over,
Snow swept the world from end to end.
A candle burned on the table;
A candle burned.
*Doctor Zhivago[3] [1958].
The Poems of Yurii Zhivago[4] (ch. 17),
Winter Night, st. 1*

7 A corner draft fluttered the flame
And the white fever of temptation
Upswept its angel wings that cast
A cruciform shadow.
*Doctor Zhivago.
The Poems of Yurii Zhivago[4] (ch. 17),
Winter Night, st. 7*

8   And when the war broke out, its real horrors, its real dangers, its menace of real death were a blessing compared with the inhuman reign of the lie, and they brought relief because they broke the spell of the dead letter.   *Doctor Zhivago, epilogue*

9   Departure beyond the borders of my country is for me equivalent to death.
Letter to Nikita Khrushchev[5] [1958]

10 I am caught like a beast at bay.
Somewhere are people, freedom, light,

But all I hear is the baying of the pack,
There is no way out for me.   *The Nobel Prize[2] [1959]*

Katherine Anne Porter
1890–1980

11   Miracles are instantaneous, they cannot be summoned, but come of themselves, usually at unlikely moments and to those who least expect them.
Ship of Fools [1962]

Jean Rhys
1890–1979

12   I often want to cry. That is the only advantage women have over men — at least they can cry.
Good Morning, Midnight [1939], ch. 2

"Red" Rowley
fl. 1915

13 Mademoiselle from Armenteers,
Hasn't been kissed in forty years,
Hinky dinky, parley-voo.
Mademoiselle from Armentières[6]

Elsa Schiaparelli
1890–1973

14   Fashion is born by small facts, trends, or even politics, never by trying to make little pleats and furbelows, by trinkets, by clothes easy to copy, or by the shortening or lengthening of a skirt.
Shocking Life [1954]

15   Remember — twenty per cent of women have inferiority complexes. Seventy per cent have illusions. . . . Ninety per cent are afraid of being conspicuous and of what people will say. So they buy a gray suit. They should dare to be different.
Shocking Life. The Twelve Commandments for Women

Casey [Charles Dillon] Stengel
c. 1890–1975

16   I had many years that I was not so successful as a ballplayer, as it is a game of skill.
Testimony before U.S. Senate Subcommittee on Antitrust and Monopoly [July 9, 1958]

---

[1]See Anonymous: Russian, 897:11.

[2]Translated by MAX HAYWARD.

[3]Translated by MAX HAYWARD and MANYA HARARI.

[4]*The Poems of Yurii Zhivago* translated by BERNARD GUILBERT GUERNEY.

[5]Translated by ELENA LEVIN.

---

[6]Soldiers' song of World War I, with innumerable versions. The tune and verse structure were based on a British Army song composed by ALFRED JAMES WALDEN ["HARRY WINCOTT," 1867–1947].

1 Can't anybody here play this game?
On the Mets' 1962 season; attributed

2 There comes a time in every man's life and I've had many of them. *Remark[1]*

3 Most people my age are dead. *Remark*

B. Traven
1890–1969

4 Badges, to god-damned hell with badges! We have no badges. In fact, we don't need badges. I don't have to show you any stinking badges.[2]
The Treasure of the Sierra Madre (novel) [1927]

Joseph N[ye] Welch
1890–1960

5 Until this moment, Senator, I think I never really gauged your cruelty or your recklessness.... Have you no sense of decency, sir, at long last? Have you left no sense of decency?
Response to Senator Joseph R. McCarthy during Senate hearings on alleged subversive activities in the U.S. Army [June 9, 1954]

Charles E[rwin] Wilson
1890–1961

6 For years I thought what was good for our country was good for General Motors, and vice versa. The difference did not exist.
To the Senate Committee on Armed Services [1953]

Mikhail Bulgakov
1891–1940

7 Manuscripts don't burn.[3]
The Master and Margarita [written 1929–1940, published 1966–1967], ch. 24

A. P. Carter
1891–1960

8 Can the circle be unbroken
Bye and bye, Lord, bye and bye

There's a better home a-waiting
In the sky, Lord, in the sky.
Can the Circle Be Unbroken[4] [1935]

Al Dubin
1891–1945

9 Come and meet
Those dancing feet
On the avenue
I'm taking you to,
Forty-second Street.
42nd Street [1932]. Forty-second Street[5]

10 We're in the money,
We're in the money,
We've got a lot of what it takes to get along!
*Gold Diggers of 1933 [1933].
The Gold Diggers' Song (We're in the Money)[5]*

11 Tip-Toe Thru' the Tulips with Me
Title of song [1939][6]

Antonio Gramsci
1891–1937

12 All men are intellectuals . . . but not all men have in society the function of intellectuals.
Prison Notebooks [1933–1934]

13 History is at once freedom and necessity.
Prison Notebooks

14 State = political society + civil society, in other words hegemony protected by the armor of coercion.
Prison Notebooks

Sidney Howard
1891–1939

15 Fiddle-dee-dee. War, war, war. This war talk's spoiling all the fun at every party this spring. I get so bored I could scream.[7]
Gone with the Wind (screenplay) [1939], spoken by Vivien Leigh

Zora Neale Hurston
1891–1960

16 I am not tragically colored. There is no great sorrow dammed up in my soul, nor lurking behind

---

[1]Stengel said this often, and it is inscribed on his grave marker.

[2]See John Huston, 746:2.

[3]When Bulgakov's novel, left unfinished at his death, was published in Moscow in the late 1960s, this line achieved proverbial status among Russian intellectuals.

[4]This song is by ADA HABERSHON and CHARLES GABRIEL. Carter's arrangement made it famous.

[5]Music by HARRY WARREN.

[6]Music by JOE BURKE.

[7]Other, uncredited screenwriters contributed to the screenplay: Oliver H. P. Garrett, Ben Hecht, Jo Swerling, John Van Druten. The lines do not appear in Margaret Mitchell's novel.

my eyes.... I do not weep at the world—I am too busy sharpening my oyster knife.
How It Feels to Be Colored Me [1928]

1   Someone is always at my elbow reminding me that I am the granddaughter of slaves. It fails to register depression with me. Slavery is sixty years in the past. The operation was successful and the patient is doing well, thank you.
How It Feels to Be Colored Me

2   Ships at a distance have every man's wish on board. For some they come in with the tide. For others they sail forever on the horizon, never out of sight, never landing until the Watcher turns his eyes away in resignation, his dreams mocked to death by Time. That is the life of men.
Their Eyes Were Watching God [1937], ch. 1

3   Women forget all those things they don't want to remember, and remember everything they don't want to forget. The dream is the truth. Then they act and do things accordingly.
Their Eyes Were Watching God, 1

4   De nigger woman is de mule uh de world so fur as Ah can see. Ah been prayin' fuh it tuh be different wid you.
Their Eyes Were Watching God, 2

5   "It's uh known fact, Pheoby, you got tuh *go* there tuh *know* there."
Their Eyes Were Watching God, 20

6   Gods always behave like the people who make them.
Tell My Horse [1938], ch. 15

7   I was a Southerner and had the map of Dixie on my tongue.
Dust Tracks on a Road [1942], ch. 8

8   I have been in Sorrow's kitchen and licked out all the pots.
Dust Tracks on a Road, 16

Jomo Kenyatta [Kamau Wa Ngengi]
1891–1978

9   The African is conditioned, by the cultural and social institutions of centuries, to a freedom of which Europe has little conception, and it is not in his nature to accept serfdom forever. He realizes that he must fight unceasingly for his own complete emancipation; for without this he is doomed to remain the prey of rival imperialisms.
Facing Mount Kenya: The Tribal Life of the Gikuyu (Kikuyu) [1938], conclusion

10   We must try to trust one another. Stay and cooperate.[1]
Statement, as first president of the Republic of Kenya, to the white settlers [1964]

Nella Larsen
1891–1964

11   I'm homesick, not for America, but for Negroes.
Quicksand [1928], ch. 16

Osip Emilevich Mandelstam
1891–1938

12   Petersburg! I still possess a list of addresses,
Which will help me to hear the voices of the dead.
Leningrad [1930]

13   We live, deaf to the land beneath us,
Ten steps away no one hears our speeches,

But where there's so much as half a conversation
The Kremlin's mountaineer will get his mention.
Stalin [1934], st. 1, 2

14   One by one forging his laws, to be flung
Like horseshoes at the head, the eye, or the groin.

And every killing is a treat
For the broad-chested Ossete.   *Stalin, st. 7, 8*

Jack McGowan
1891–1977
and
Kay Van Riper
d. 1948

15   Come on, kids, let's put on a show!
Babes in Arms (screenplay) [1939], spoken by Mickey Rooney

Henry Miller
1891–1980

16   Every man with a bellyful of the classics is an enemy to the human race.   *Tropic of Cancer [1934]*

17   I have no money, no resources, no hopes. I am the happiest man alive.   *Tropic of Cancer*

18   I made up my mind that I would hold on to nothing, that I would expect nothing, that

---

[1]Harambee [Swahili for "Let's pull together"]. — *National motto of Kenya*

henceforth I would live as an animal, a beast of prey, a rover, a plunderer. *Tropic of Cancer*

1 I am a patriot — of the 14th Ward Brooklyn, where I was raised. The rest of the United States doesn't exist for me, except as idea, or history, or literature. *Black Spring [1936]*

2 It's good to be just plain happy; it's a little better to know that you're happy; but to understand that you're happy and to know why and how...and still be happy, be happy in the being and the knowing, well that is beyond happiness, that is bliss. *The Colossus of Maroussi [1941], pt. I*

3 The aim of life is to live, and to live means to be aware, joyously, drunkenly, serenely, divinely aware. *The Wisdom of the Heart [1941]*

4 [On America:] Of nothing are you allowed to get the real odor or the real savor. Everything is sterilized and wrapped in cellophane.
Max and the White Phagocytes [1938].
Glittering Pie

Elliot Paul
1891–1958

5 The last time I see Paris will be on the day I die. The city was inexhaustible, and so is its memory. *The Last Time I Saw Paris [1942], pt. II, 23*

Cole [Albert] Porter
1891–1964

6 We're all alone
No chaperon
Can get our number,
The world's in slumber,
Let's misbehave. *Paris [1928]. Let's Misbehave*

7 You do something to me,
Something that simply mystifies me.
Fifty Million Frenchmen [1929].
You Do Something to Me

8 Love for sale,
Appetizing young love for sale.
Love that's fresh and still unspoiled,
Love that's only slightly soiled,
Love for sale.
The New Yorkers [1930]. Love for Sale

9 Night and day you are the one,
Only you beneath the moon and under the sun.
Gay Divorce [1932]. Night and Day

10 I get no kick from champagne.
Mere alcohol doesn't thrill me at all,

So tell me why should it be true
That I get a kick out of you.
Anything Goes [1934]. I Get a Kick Out of You

11 In olden days, a glimpse of stocking
Was looked on as something shocking,
But now, God knows,
Anything goes. *Anything Goes. Anything Goes*

12 You're the Nile,
You're the Tower of Pisa,
You're the smile
On the Mona Lisa....
But if, Baby, I'm the bottom you're the top!
Anything Goes. You're the Top!

13 It was great fun,
But it was just one of those things.
Jubilee [1935]. Just One of Those Things

14 I've got you under my skin,
I've got you deep in the heart of me,
So deep in my heart, you're really a part of me,
I've got you under my skin.
Born to Dance [1936].
I've Got You Under My Skin

15 It's delightful, it's delicious, it's de-lovely.
Red, Hot and Blue [1936]. It's De-Lovely

16 But I'm always true to you, darlin', in my fashion,
Yes, I'm always true to you, darlin', in my way.
Kiss Me, Kate [1948]. Always True to
You in My Fashion

Nelly Sachs
1891–1970

17 O the chimneys
On the ingeniously devised habitations of death
When Israel's body drifted as smoke
Through the air —
Was welcomed by a star, a chimney sweep,
A star that turned black
Or was it a ray of sun?[1] *O the Chimneys [1947]*

18 A stranger always has
his homeland in his arms
like an orphan
for which he may be seeking
nothing but a grave.[1] *Someone Comes [1958]*

19 We, the rescued,
Beg you:
Show us your sun, but gradually.
Lead us from star to star, step by step.
Be gentle when you teach us to live again.[2]
Chorus of the Rescued

---

[1] Translated by MICHAEL HAMBURGER.
[2] Translated by MICHAEL ROLOFF.

David Sarnoff
1891–1971

1   I regard radio broadcasting as a sort of cleansing instrument for the mind, just as the bathtub is for the body.

Quoted in EVAN SCHWARTZ,
The Last Lone Inventor [2002]

Haile Selassie
1891–1975

2   Outside the kingdom of the Lord there is no nation which is greater than any other. God and history will remember your judgment.

Speech, the League of Nations[1] *[1936]*

Hu Shih[2]
1891–1962

3   Only when we realize that there is no eternal, unchanging truth or absolute truth can we arouse in ourselves a sense of intellectual responsibility.

La Jeunesse Nouvelle [April 1919]

Earl Warren
1891–1974

4   To separate [black children] from others of similar age and qualifications solely because of their race generates a feeling of inferiority as to their status in the community that may affect their hearts and minds in a way unlikely ever to be undone....We conclude that in the field of public education the doctrine of "separate but equal"[3] has no place. Separate educational facilities are inherently unequal.

*Brown v. Board of Education of Topeka,
347 U.S. 483 [1954]*[4]

5   Legislators represent people, not trees or acres.

Reynolds v. Sims [1964]

6   When an individual is taken into custody or otherwise deprived of his freedom by the authorities and is subjected to questioning...he must be warned prior to any questioning that he has the right to remain silent, that anything he says can be used against him in a court of law, that he has the right to the presence of an attorney, and that if he cannot afford an attorney one will be appointed for him prior to any questioning if he so desires.

Miranda v. Arizona, 384 U.S. 436 [1965]

George Aiken
1892–1984

7   The United States could well declare unilaterally that this stage of the Vietnam war is over — that we have "won" in the sense that our Armed Forces are in control of most of the field and no potential enemy is in a position to establish its authority over South Vietnam.

Speech in the U.S. Senate [October 19, 1966]

Erich Auerbach
1892–1957

8   Abraham, Jacob, or even Moses produces a more concrete, direct, and historical impression than the figures of the Homeric world — not because they are better described in terms of sense (the contrary is the case) but because the confused, contradictory multiplicity of events, the psychological and factual cross-purposes, which true history reveals, have not disappeared in the representation but still remain clearly perceptible.   *Mimesis [1946]*

Djuna Barnes
1892–1982

9 Life, the permission to know death.

Nightwood [1936]

Walter Benjamin
1892–1940

10   To be happy is to be able to become aware of oneself without fright.   *One-Way Street [1928]*

11   Books and harlots have their quarrels in public.

One-Way Street

12   Of all the ways of acquiring books, writing them oneself is regarded as the most praiseworthy method....Writers are really people who write books not because they are poor, but because they are dissatisfied with the books which they could buy but do not like.   *Unpacking My Library*[5] *[1931]*

13   Collectors are people with a tactical instinct; their experience teaches them that when they capture a

---

[1]He sought sanctions against Italy, which had invaded Ethiopia.

[2]From *Sources of Chinese Tradition* [1960], edited by WILLIAM THEODORE DE BARY.

[3]All railway companies carrying passengers in their coaches in the state shall provide equal but separate accommodations for the white and colored races. — *Louisiana Acts of 1890, no. III, p. 152;* quoted by Mr. Justice HENRY B. BROWN in *Plessy v. Ferguson, 163 U.S. 537* [1896]

[4]In a later implementation of the same case (*349 U.S. 294* [1955]), the Supreme Court asked that desegregation proceed "with all deliberate speed."

[5]Translated by HARRY ZOHN.

strange city, the smallest antique shop can be a fortress, the most remote stationery store a key position. How many cities have revealed themselves to me in the marches I undertook in the pursuit of books!

Unpacking My Library

1 Even the most perfect reproduction of a work of art is lacking in one element: its presence in time and space, its unique existence at the place where it happens to be.... The presence of the original is the prerequisite to the concept of authenticity.

The Work of Art in the Age of Mechanical Reproduction [1936]

2 Technical reproduction can put the copy of the original into situations which would be out of reach for the original itself. Above all, it enables the original to meet the beholder halfway, be it in the form of a photograph or a phonograph record. The cathedral leaves its locale to be received in the studio of a lover of art; the choral production, performed in an auditorium or in the open air, resounds in the drawing room.

The Work of Art in the Age of Mechanical Reproduction

3 One might generalize by saying: the technique of reproduction detaches the reproduced object from the domain of tradition. By making many reproductions it substitutes a plurality of copies for a unique existence. And in permitting the reproduction to meet the beholder or the listener in his own particular situation, it reactivates the object reproduced. These two processes lead to a tremendous shattering of tradition.

The Work of Art in the Age of Mechanical Reproduction

4 The products of art and science owe their existence not merely to the effort of the great geniuses that created them, but also to the unnamed drudgery of their contemporaries. There is no document of culture which is not at the same time a document of barbarism.

Edward Fuchs: Collector and Historian [1937]

Charles Brackett
1892–1969
and
Billy [Samuel] Wilder
1906–2002

5 [Joe Gillis]: You used to be in silent pictures. You used to be big.

[Norma Desmond]: I *am* big. It's the *pictures* that got small.

Sunset Boulevard (screenplay) [1950], spoken by William Holden and Gloria Swanson

James M. Cain
1892–1977

6 The Postman Always Rings Twice

Title of book [1934]

7 They threw me off the hay truck about noon.

The Postman Always Rings Twice [1934], opening line

Mort Dixon
1892–1956

8 I'm looking over a four-leaf clover
That I overlooked before.

I'm Looking Over a Four-Leaf Clover [1927]

Francisco Franco
[Francisco Paulino Hermenegildo Teódulo Franco y Bahamonde, Salgado y Pardo de Andrade]
1892–1975

9 Our regime is based on bayonets and blood, not on hypocritical elections.

Quoted in HERBERT L. MATTHEWS, *Half of Spain Died [1973]*

Walter C. Hagen
1892–1969

10 You're only here for a short visit. Don't hurry. Don't worry. And be sure to smell the flowers along the way.

The Walter Hagen Story [1956]

John Burdon Sanderson Haldane
1892–1964

11 Now, my suspicion is that the universe is not only queerer than we suppose, but queerer than we *can* suppose.... I suspect that there are more things in heaven and earth than are dreamed of, in any philosophy. That is the reason why I have no philosophy myself, and must be my excuse for dreaming.

Possible Worlds [1927]

12 The Creator, if He exists, has a special preference[1] for beetles.

Quoted in Journal of the British Interplanetary Society [July 1951]

---

[1]Often quoted as: ... an inordinate fondness for beetles.

Robert H[oughwout] Jackson
1892–1954

1 Chaos serves no social end.
> *State Tax Commission of Utah v. Aldrich,*
> *316 U.S. 174, 196 [1942]*

2   If there is any fixed star in our constitutional constellation, it is that no official, high or petty, can prescribe what shall be orthodox in politics, nationalism, religion, or other matters of opinion or force citizens to confess by word or act their faith therein.
> *West Virginia State Board of Education v.*
> *Barnett, 319 U.S. 642 [1943]*

3   The first trial in history for crimes against the peace of the world imposes a grave responsibility. The wrongs which we seek to condemn and punish have been so calculated, so malignant and so devastating that civilization cannot tolerate their being ignored because it cannot survive their being repeated.
> *Opening address before the International*
> *Military Tribunal, Nuremberg [1945]*

4   The common sense of mankind demands that law shall not stop with the punishment of petty crimes by little people. It must also reach men who possess themselves of great power and make deliberate and concerted use of it to set in motion evils which leave no home in the world untouched.
> *Opening address before the International*
> *Military Tribunal, Nuremberg*

5   There is danger that, if the Court does not temper its doctrinaire logic with a little practical wisdom, it will convert the constitutional Bill of Rights into a suicide pact.
> *Terminiello v. Chicago, 337 U.S. 1, 37*
> *[1949]*

6   It is not the function of our Government to keep the citizen from falling into error; it is the function of the citizen to keep the Government from falling into error.
> *American Communications Association v.*
> *Douds, 339 U.S. 382 [1950]*

7   Men are more often bribed by their loyalties and ambitions than by money.
> *Dissenting opinion, United States v.*
> *Wunderlich, 342 U.S. 98 [1951]*

8   There are indications that the Constitution did not contemplate that the title Commander-in-Chief *of the Army and Navy* will constitute him also Commander-in-Chief of the country, its industries and its inhabitants. He has no monopoly of "war powers," whatever they are.
> *Youngstown Sheet & Tube Company v.*
> *Sawyer, 343 U.S. 579, 643–644 [1952]*

9   The day that this country ceases to be free for irreligion, it will cease to be free for religion.
> *Dissenting opinion, Zorach v. Clausor,*
> *343 U.S. 306, 325 [1952]*

Robert S[taughton] Lynd
1892–1970
and
Helen Merrell Lynd
1896–1982

10   It is characteristic of mankind to make as little adjustment as possible in customary ways in the face of new conditions; the process of social change is epitomized in the fact that the first Packard car body delivered to the manufacturer had a whipstock on the dashboard.
> *Middletown [1929], pt. VI, ch. 29*

Hugh MacDiarmid
[Christopher Murray Grieve]
1892–1978

11 The inward gates of a bird are always open.
It does not know how to shut them.
That is the secret of its song,
But whether any man's are ajar is doubtful.
> *Stony Limits [1934]. On a Raised Beach*

12 The cornet solo of our Gaelic islands
Will sound out every now and again
Through all eternity.

I have heard it and am content for ever.
> *The Islands of Scotland [1939].*
> *Island Funeral*

13 But now I know it is the earth
And not the water that is unstable,
For at every rise and fall of the pellucid tide
It seems as though it were the shingle
And the waving forest of sea-growth
That moves — and not the water!
> *A Lap of Honour [1967]. Diamond Body*

Archibald MacLeish
1892–1982

14 There with vast wings across the canceled skies,
There in the sudden blackness the black pall
Of nothing, nothing, nothing — nothing at all.
> *The End of the World [1926]*

15 A poem should not mean
But be.
> *Ars Poetica [1926]*

1 And here face downward in the sun
  To feel how swift how secretly
  The shadow of the night comes on.
          You, Andrew Marvell [1930]

2 We were the first that found that famous country:
  We marched by a king's name: we crossed the sierras:
  Unknown hardships we suffered: hunger.
          Conquistador [1932]. Bernál Díaz' Preface

3 America was promises . . .
  It was Man who had been promised.
          America Was Promises [1939]

4   Races didn't bother the Americans. They were
something a lot better than any race. They were a
People. They were the first self-constituted, self-
created People in the history of the world.
          The American Cause [1940]

Edna St. Vincent Millay
1892–1950

5 All I could see from where I stood
  Was three long mountains and a wood.
          Renascence [1912], l. 1

6 The world stands out on either side
  No wider than the heart is wide;
  Above the world is stretched the sky, —
  No higher than the soul is high.
  The heart can push the sea and land
  Farther away on either hand;
  The soul can split the sky in two,
  And let the face of God shine through.
  But East and West will pinch the heart
  That can not keep them pushed apart;
  And he whose soul is flat — the sky
  Will cave in on him by and by.
          Renascence, last lines

7 O world, I cannot hold thee close enough!
          God's World [1917], st. 1

8 My candle burns at both ends;
  It will not last the night;
  But, ah, my foes, and, oh, my friends —
  It gives a lovely light.[1]
          A Few Figs from Thistles [1920].
          First Fig

9 We were very tired, we were very merry —
  We had gone back and forth all night on the ferry.
          A Few Figs from Thistles. Recuerdo

10 Death devours all lovely things;
  Lesbia with her sparrow

---

[1] I burned my candle at both ends, / And now have neither foes nor friends. — SAMUEL HOFFENSTEIN, *Songs of Fairly Utter Despair, 8*

Shares the darkness — presently
  Every bed is narrow.
          Passer Mortuus Est [1921], st. 1

11 I know I am but summer to your heart,
  And not the full four seasons of the year.
          I Know I Am But Summer [1923], l. 1

12 What lips my lips have kissed, and where, and why,
  I have forgotten, and what arms have lain
  Under my head till morning;
          What Lips My Lips Have Kissed [1923], l. 1

13 I only know that summer sang in me
  A little while, that in me sings no more.
          What Lips My Lips Have Kissed, l. 13

14   Euclid alone
  Has looked on Beauty bare. Fortunate they
  Who, though once only and then but far away,
  Have heard her massive sandal set on stone.
          Euclid Alone Has Looked on Beauty Bare
          [1923], l. 11

15 If ever I said, in grief or pride,
  I tired of honest things, I lied.
          The Goose Girl [1923], l. 5

16 How strange a thing is death, bringing to his knees,
      bringing to his antlers
  The buck in the snow . . .
  Life, looking out attentive from the eyes of the doe.
          The Buck in the Snow [1928]

17 I am not resigned to the shutting away of loving
      hearts in the hard ground.
  So it is, and so it will be, for so it has been, time out of
      mind:
  Into the darkness they go, the wise and the lovely.
      Crowned
  With lilies and with laurel they go; but I am not
      resigned.
          Dirge Without Music [1928], st. 1

18 Love is not all: it is not meat nor drink
  Nor slumber nor a roof against the rain;
  Nor yet a floating spar to men that sink.
          Love Is Not All [1931], l. 1

19 Childhood Is the Kingdom Where Nobody Dies
          Title of poem [1934]

Reinhold Niebuhr
1892–1971

20   God, give us grace to accept with serenity the
things that cannot be changed, courage to change the
things which should be changed, and the wisdom to
distinguish the one from the other.
          The Serenity Prayer [1943]

1   Goodness, armed with power, is corrupted; and pure love without power is destroyed.
Beyond Tragedy [1938]

2   The prophet himself stands under the judgment which he preaches. If he does not know that, he is a false prophet.
Beyond Tragedy

3   Man's capacity for justice makes democracy possible; but man's inclination to injustice makes democracy necessary.
The Children of Light and the Children of Darkness [1944]

4   Democracy is a method of finding proximate solutions for insoluble problems.
The Children of Light and the Children of Darkness

5 Humor is a prelude to faith and
Laughter is the beginning of prayer.
Discerning the Signs of the Times [1949]

6   Nothing worth doing is completed in our lifetime; therefore, we must be saved by hope. Nothing true or beautiful or good makes complete sense in any immediate context of history; therefore, we must be saved by faith. Nothing we do, however virtuous, can be accomplished alone; therefore, we are saved by love.
The Irony of American History [1952]

Martin Niemoeller
1892–1984

7   In Germany they came first for the Communists, and I didn't speak up because I wasn't a Communist. Then they came for the Jews, and I didn't speak up because I wasn't a Jew. Then they came for the trade unionists, and I didn't speak up because I wasn't a trade unionist. Then they came for the Catholics, and I didn't speak up because I was a Protestant. Then they came for me, and by that time no one was left to speak up.
Attributed

Harold [Wallace] Ross
1892–1951

8   *The New Yorker* will not be edited for the old lady from Dubuque.[1]
Upon founding The New Yorker [1925]

9   Is Moby Dick the whale or the man?
From JAMES THURBER,
The Years with Ross [1958]

Bruno Schulz
1892–1942

10   Everyone knows that in a run of normal uneventful years that great eccentric, Time, begets sometimes other years, different, prodigal years which — like a sixth, smallest toe — grow a thirteenth freak month.
The Street of Crocodiles [1934].
The Night of the Great Season

J[ohn] R[onald] R[euel] Tolkien
1892–1973

11   In a hole in the ground there lived a hobbit. Not a nasty, dirty, wet hole, filled with the ends of worms and an oozy smell, nor yet a dry, bare, sandy hole with nothing in it to sit down on or to eat: it was a hobbit-hole, and that means comfort.
The Hobbit, or There and Back Again [1937], ch. 1

12   We are plain quiet folk and have no use for adventures. Nasty disturbing uncomfortable things! Make you late for dinner! I can't think what anybody sees in them.
The Hobbit, or There and Back Again, 1

13   [Spoken by Gollum:] Where iss it, where iss it: my Precious, my Precious? It's ours, it is, and we wants it.
The Two Towers [1955], ch. 1

14 One Ring to rule them all, One Ring to find them,
One Ring to bring them all and in the darkness bind them.
The Fellowship of the Ring [1965], bk. I, ch. 2

15   I cordially dislike allegory in all its manifestations, and always have done so since I grew old and wary enough to detect its presence. I much prefer history, true or feigned, with its varied applicability to the thought and experience of readers.
Foreword to The Lord of the Rings, second edition [1966]

César Vallejo
1892–1938

16 I shall die in Paris, in a rainstorm,
On a day I already remember.
I shall die in Paris — it does not bother me —
Doubtless on a Thursday, like today, in autumn.[2]
Poemas Humanos [1939].
Black Stone on Top of a White Stone

---

[1] Later this became "the little old lady from Dubuque."

[2] Translated by THOMAS MERTON.

Rebecca West
[Cicely Isabel Fairfield]
1892–1983

1 I myself have never been able to find out precisely what Feminism is: I only know that people call me a Feminist whenever I express sentiments that differentiate me from a doormat or a prostitute.
The Clarion [November 14, 1913]

Wendell L[ewis] Willkie
1892–1944

2 Freedom is an indivisible word. If we want to enjoy it, and fight for it, we must be prepared to extend it to everyone, whether they are rich or poor, whether they agree with us or not, no matter what their race or the color of their skin.
One World, ch. 13

3 The Constitution does not provide for first and second class citizens.
An American Program [1944], ch. 2

Jack Yellen
1892–1991

4 Happy days are here again,
The skies above are clear again:
Let us sing a song of cheer again,
Happy days are here again!
Happy Days Are Here Again [1929][1]

Omar Bradley
1893–1981

5 The world has achieved brilliance without conscience. Ours is a world of nuclear giants and ethical infants.
Address on Armistice Day [1948]

6 In war there is no second prize for the runner-up.
In the Military Review [February 1950]

7 Red China is not the powerful nation seeking to dominate the world. Frankly, in the opinion of the Joint Chiefs of Staff, this strategy would involve us in the wrong war, at the wrong place, at the wrong time, and with the wrong enemy.
Testimony to the Committee on Armed Services and Committee on Foreign Affairs, U.S. Senate [May 15, 1951]

Lew Brown
1893–1958

8 Life is just a bowl of cherries,
Don't take it serious; it's too mysterious.
George White's Scandals of 1931.
Life Is Just a Bowl of Cherries

Lew Brown
1893–1958

and

Buddy [George Gard]
De Sylva
1895–1950

9 And love can come to everyone,
The best things in life are free.
Good News[2] *[1927].*
The Best Things in Life Are Free

10 Keep your sunny side up.
Sunny Side Up[2] *[1929], title song*

James Bryant Conant
1893–1978

11 He who enters a university walks on hallowed ground.
Notes on the Harvard Tercentenary [1936]

Jimmy [James Francis]
Durante
1893–1980

12 Goodnight, Mrs. Calabash, wherever you are.
Radio series sign-off [1942]

13 Everybody wants ta get inta the act!
Catchphrase

Hermann Goering
1893–1946

14 Submit to me as soon as possible a draft showing . . . measures already taken for the execution of the intended final solution of the Jewish question.
Directive (drafted by Adolf Eichmann)[3]
to Reinhard Heydrich [July 31, 1941]

---

[1] With music by MILTON AGER [1893–1979], this song was played at the 1932 Democratic presidential convention and became a campaign song for Franklin D. Roosevelt.

[2] Music by RAY HENDERSON.
[3] See Eichmann, 744:*n*1.

Vicente Huidobro
1893–1948

1   The poet is a little god.   *Ars Poetica [1916]*

Alexander Korda
1893–1956

2   It's not enough to be Hungarian, you must have talent too.[1]   *Attributed*

Joseph Wood Krutch
1893–1970

3   When a man wantonly destroys one of the works of man we call him Vandal. When he wantonly destroys one of the works of God we call him Sportsman.
Reverence for Life: The Vandal and the Sportsman [1956]

Harold [Joseph] Laski
1893–1950

4   We live under a system by which the many are exploited by the few, and war is the ultimate sanction of that exploitation.

Plan or Perish [1945]

5   It would be madness to let the purposes or the methods of private enterprise set the habits of the age of atomic energy.   *Plan or Perish*

Huey Long
1893–1935

6   "Every Man a King." Every man to eat when there is something to eat; all to wear something when there is something to wear. That makes us all a sovereign.
Radio speech [February 23, 1934]

Anita Loos
1893–1981

7   Gentlemen always seem to remember blondes.
Gentlemen Prefer Blondes [1925], ch. 1

8   She always believed in the old adage, "Leave them while you're looking good."
Gentlemen Prefer Blondes, 1

9   Kissing your hand may make you feel very, very good, but a diamond and sapphire bracelet lasts forever.
Gentlemen Prefer Blondes, 4

Mao Tse-tung
1893–1976

10   A revolution is not the same as inviting people to dinner, or writing an essay, or painting a picture.... A revolution is an insurrection, an act of violence by which one class overthrows another.
Selected Works of Mao Tse-tung [1965], vol. I, p. 28

11   Every Communist must grasp the truth: "Political power grows out of the barrel of a gun."
Selected Works of Mao Tse-tung, II, 224

12   The people are like water and the army is like fish.
Aspects of China's Anti-Japanese Struggle [1948]

13   The policy of letting a hundred flowers blossom and a hundred schools of thought contend is designed to promote the flourishing of the arts and the progress of science; it is designed to enable a socialist culture to thrive in our land.
Speech at Peking [February 27, 1957]

John P[hillips] Marquand
1893–1960

14   Marriage ... is a damnably serious business, particularly around Boston.
The Late George Apley [1937], ch. 11

William Moulton Marston
1893–1947

15   As lovely as Aphrodite — as wise as Athena — with the speed of Mercury and the strength of Hercules — she is known only as Wonder Woman, but who she is, or whence she came, nobody knows!
All Star Comics #8 [1941]

Vladimir Vladimirovich Mayakovski
1893–1930

16 If you wish,
I shall grow irreproachably tender:
Not a man, but a cloud in trousers!
Cloud in Trousers[2] [1915]

---

[1]Orson Welles is said to have responded to this: "It's not enough to have talent, you must also be Hungarian."

[2]Translated by GEORGE REAVEY.

1 Citizen!
 Consider my traveling expenses:
 Poetry—
  all of it—
   is a journey to the unknown.
      Conversation with a Tax Collector
      About Poetry[1] *[1926]*

2 But I subdued myself,
  setting my heel
 On the throat
  of my own song.
        At the Top of My Voice[2]

Joan Miró
1893–1983

3   I want to assassinate painting.   *Attributed*

Wilfred Owen
1893–1918

4 Above all, this book is not concerned with Poetry,
 The subject of it is War, and the pity of War.
 The Poetry is in the pity.
 All a poet can do is warn.[3]
        Poems [1920], preface

5 If you could hear, at every jolt, the blood
 Come gargling from the froth-corrupted lungs,
 Obscene as cancer, bitter as the cud
 Of vile, incurable sores on innocent tongues,—
 My friend, you would not tell with such high zest
 To children ardent for some desperate glory,
 The old Lie: *Dulce et decorum est*
 Pro patria mori.
        Poems. Dulce et Decorum Est

6 What passing bells for these who die as cattle?
 Only the monstrous anger of the guns.
 Only the stuttering rifles' rapid rattle
 Can patter out their hasty orisons.
        The Anthem for Doomed Youth, st. 1

7 And each slow dusk a drawing-down of blinds.
        The Anthem for Doomed Youth, st. 1

8 Red lips are not so red
 As the stained stones kissed by the English dead.
        Greater Love

9 Courage was mine, and I had mystery,

Wisdom was mine, and I had mastery:
 To miss the march of this retreating world
 Into vain citadels that are not walled.
        Strange Meeting

Dorothy Parker
1893–1967

10 Four be the things I am wiser to know:
 Idleness, sorrow, a friend, and a foe.
        Enough Rope [1927]. Inventory, st. 1

11 Four be the things I'd been better without:
 Love, curiosity, freckles, and doubt.
        Enough Rope. Inventory, st. 2

12 Scratch a lover, and find a foe.
        Enough Rope. Ballade of a Great Weariness,
        st. 1

13 Men seldom make passes
 At girls who wear glasses.
        Enough Rope. News Item

14 Guns aren't lawful;
 Nooses give;
 Gas smells awful;
 You might as well live.
        Enough Rope. Résumé

15 Why is it no one ever sent me yet
 One perfect limousine, do you suppose?
 Ah no, it's always just my luck to get
  One perfect rose.
        Enough Rope. One Perfect Rose, st. 3

16   Brevity is the soul of lingerie.
      Caption for Vogue; cited by ALEXANDER
      WOOLLCOTT *in While Rome Burns [1934]*

17 Oh, life is a glorious cycle of song,
 A medley of extemporanea;
 And love is a thing that can never go wrong;
 And I am Marie of Roumania.
        Comment [1937]

18   Runs the gamut of emotions from A to B.
      Attributed theater review, comment on a player

19   Excuse my dust.
        Epitaph, suggested by herself

Dorothy L[eigh] Sayers
1893–1957

20   Death in particular seems to provide the minds of
 the Anglo-Saxon race with a greater fund of innocent
 amusement than any other single subject.
      Introduction to The Third Omnibus
      of Crime [1935]

---

[1]Translated by MAX HAYWARD.

[2]Translated by GEORGE REAVEY.

[3]The last three lines serve as the motto for Benjamin Britten's *War Requiem (Op. 66)*, which uses the Latin text of the Mass for the Dead and some of the poems of Wilfred Owen.

Maj. Gen. Oliver P. Smith, USMC
1893–1977

1   We're not retreating, we're just advancing in a different direction.[1]

Korea, December 1950; attributed

Freya Stark
1893–1993

2   The true call of the desert, of the mountains, or the sea, is their silence — free of the networks of dead speech.   *Perseus in the Wind [1948]*

Albert Szent-Györgyi von Nagyrapolt
1893–1986

3   Discovery consists of seeing what everybody has seen and thinking what nobody has thought.

From I. J. GOOD (ed.), The Scientist Speculates [1962]

Max Weinreich
1893–1969

4   A language is a dialect with an army and navy.

Yivo Bleter [1945]

Mae West
1893–1980

5   Goodness had nothing to do with it.[2]

Night After Night (screenplay) [1932]

6   When women go wrong, men go right after them.

She Done Him Wrong (screenplay) [1933]

7   Why don't you come up sometime and see me?[3] . . . Come on up, I'll tell your fortune.

She Done Him Wrong

8   Beulah, peel me a grape.

I'm No Angel (screenplay) [1933]

9   I used to be Snow White, but I drifted.

I'm No Angel

10   When I'm good, I'm very good, but when I'm bad I'm better.   *I'm No Angel*

---

[1]Often quoted as: Retreat, hell! We're just attacking in another direction.

[2]In reply to "Goodness, what beautiful diamonds!"
Also the title of her autobiography [1959].

[3]Frequently misquoted as "Come up and see me sometime."

11   You ought to get out of those wet clothes and into a dry martini.[4]   *Every Day's a Holiday [1937]*

Fred Allen [John Florence Sullivan]
1894–1956

12   I have just returned from Boston. It is the only sane thing to do if you find yourself up there.

Letter to Groucho Marx [June 12, 1953]

13   Imitation is the sincerest form of television.

Attributed

Meher Baba
1894–1969

14 Don't worry, be happy.   *Attributed*

Isaac [Emmanuelovich] Babel
1894–1941

15   A phrase is born into the world both good and bad at the same time. The secret lies in a slight, an almost invisible twist. The lever should rest in your hand, getting warm, and you can only turn it once, not twice.   *Guy de Maupassant[5] [1924]*

16   No steel can pierce the human heart so chillingly as a period at the right moment.[6]

Guy de Maupassant

17   Forget for a while that you have glasses on your nose and autumn in your heart.

Odessa Stories [1926].
How Things Were Done in Odessa

18   Speaking of silence, we can't help talking about me, the past master of this genre.

Speech at First Writers' Congress [1934]

Louis Ferdinand Céline [Louis Ferdinand Destouches]
1894–1961

19   Those who talk about the future are scoundrels. It is the present that matters. To evoke one's posterity is to make a speech to maggots.

Voyage au Bout de la Nuit
(Journey to the End of the Night) [1932]

20   Almost every desire a poor man has is a punishable offense.   *Journey to the End of the Night*

---

[4]Often attributed to Robert Benchley, who spoke a similar line in *The Major and the Minor* [1942]. See Benchley, 683:11.

[5]Translated by WALTER MORISON.

[6]Translated by MAX HAYWARD.

James Ashmore Creelman
1894–1941

and

Ruth Rose
1896–1978

1   He was a king and a god in the world he knew, but now he comes to civilization merely a captive — a show to gratify your curiosity. Ladies and gentlemen, look at Kong, the Eighth Wonder of the World!
King Kong (screenplay) [1933]

2   It was beauty killed the beast.
King Kong, final line

E[dward] E[stlin] Cummings
1894–1962

3   Take me up into your mind once or twice before I die (you know why: just because the eyes of you and me will be full of dirt some day). Quickly take me up into the bright child of your mind.
The Enormous Room [1922].
Jean Le Nègre

4 All in green went my love riding
on a great horse of gold
into the silver dawn.
All in green went my love riding [1923]

5 in Just-
spring when the world is mud-
luscious the little
lame balloonman
whistles far and wee
Chansons Innocentes [1923], 1

6 when the world is puddle-wonderful
Chansons Innocentes, 1

7 Buffalo Bill's
defunct
       who used to
       ride a watersmooth-silver
                    stallion
and break onetwothreefourfive pigeons-
       justlikethat
            Jesus
he was a handsome man
       and what i want to know is
how do you like your blueeyed boy
Mister Death
Portraits [1923], 8

8 the Cambridge ladies who live in furnished souls
are unbeautiful and have comfortable minds.
Sonnets — Realities [1923], I

9 take it from me kiddo
believe me
my country, 'tis of

you, land of the Cluett
Shirt Boston Garter and Spearmint
Girl With The Wrigley Eyes (of you
land of the Arrow Ide
and Earl &
Wilson
Collars) of you i
sing: land of Abraham Lincoln and Lydia
    E. Pinkham,
land above all of Just Add Hot Water And
    Serve —
from every B.V.D.

let freedom ring

amen.
POEM, OR BEAUTY HURTS
MR. VINAL [1926]

10 next to of course god america i
love you land of the pilgrims' and so forth
next to of course god america i [1926]

11 i sing of Olaf glad and big
whose warmest heart recoiled at war
i sing of Olaf glad and big [1931]

12 "I will not kiss your f.ing flag"
i sing of Olaf glad and big

13 "there is some s. I will not eat"
i sing of Olaf glad and big

14 unless statistics lie he was
more brave than me:more blond than you.
i sing of Olaf glad and big

15 somewhere i have never traveled, gladly beyond
any experience, your eyes have their silence.
somewhere I have never traveled [1931]

16 nobody, not even the rain, has such small hands
somewhere I have never traveled

17 anyone lived in a pretty how town
(with up so floating many bells down)
spring summer autumn winter
he sang his didn't he danced his did.
anyone lived in a pretty how town [1940]

18 my father moved through dooms of love
through sames of am through haves of give,
singing each morning out of each night
my father moved through depths of height
my father moved through dooms of love [1940]

19 and nothing quite so least as truth
— i say though hate were why men breathe —
because my father lived his soul
love is the whole and more than all
my father moved through dooms of love

1 pity this busy monster, manunkind,
not. Progress is a comfortable disease.
One Times One [1944], 14

2   We doctors know
a hopeless case if — listen: there's a hell
of a good universe next door; let's go
One Times One, 14

John Ford
[John Martin Feeney]
1894–1973

3   I have never thought about what I was doing in terms of art, or "this is great," or "world-shaking," or anything like that. To me, it was always a job of work — which I enjoyed immensely — and that's it.
Interview with *Peter Bogdanovich [1966]*

Arthur Freed
1894–1973

4 Singin' in the rain, just singin' in the rain.
What a glorious feeling, I'm happy again.
Singin' in the Rain[1] *[1929]*

Dashiell Hammett
1894–1961

5   There are four rules for shadowing: Keep behind your subject as much as possible; never try to hide from him; act in a natural manner no matter what happens; and never meet his eye.
Zigzags of Treachery [1924]

6   He felt like somebody had taken the lid off life and let him look at the works.
The Maltese Falcon [1930], ch. 7

7   That's the part of it I [Sam Spade] always liked. He [Flitcraft] adjusted himself to beams falling, and then no more of them fell, and he adjusted himself to their not falling. *The Maltese Falcon, 7*

8   The cheaper the crook, the gaudier the patter.
The Maltese Falcon, 12

9   When a man's partner is killed he's supposed to do something about it. It doesn't make any difference what you thought of him. He was your partner and you're supposed to do something about it.
The Maltese Falcon, 20

10   The Thin Man   *Title of novel [1934]*

Herman Hupfeld
1894–1951

11 You must remember this, a kiss is still a kiss,
A sigh is just a sigh;
The fundamental things apply,
As time goes by.
Everybody's Welcome [1931]. As Time Goes By[2]

12 It's still the same old story,
A fight for love and glory,
A case of do or die!
The world will always welcome lovers,
As time goes by.
Everybody's Welcome. As Time Goes By[2]

Aldous [Leonard] Huxley
1894–1963

13   A bad book is as much of a labor to write as a good one; it comes as sincerely from the author's soul.
Point Counter Point [1928], ch. 13

14   Chastity — the most unnatural of all the sexual perversions.
Eyeless in Gaza [1936], ch. 27

15   What the rest of us see only under the influence of mescalin, the artist is congenitally equipped to see all the time.
The Doors of Perception [1954]

16   That humanity at large will ever be able to dispense with Artificial Paradises seems very unlikely. Most men and women lead lives at the worst so painful, at the best so monotonous, poor and limited that the urge to escape, the longing to transcend themselves if only for a few moments, is and has always been one of the principal appetites of the soul.
The Doors of Perception

17   Armaments, universal debt, and planned obsolescence — those are the three pillars of Western prosperity.
Island [1962]

Nikita Sergeyevich Khrushchev
1894–1971

18   Cult of personality.
Special Report to Twentieth Party Congress [February 1956]

19   About the capitalist states, it doesn't depend on you whether or not we exist. If you don't like us,

---

[1]Music by NACIO HERB BROWN.

[2]Also in the film *Casablanca [1943]*.

don't accept our invitations, and don't invite us to come and see you. Whether you like it or not, history is on our side. We will bury you.[1]

> *Reported statement at reception for*
> *Wladyslaw Gomulka at the Polish Embassy,*
> *Moscow [November 18, 1956]*

1   Politicians are the same all over: they promise to build a bridge even where there is no river.

> *Press conference in Glen Cove, New York,*
> *during U.S. visit [October 1960]*

Ted Koehler
1894–1973

2 I gotta right to sing the blues,
I gotta right to feel low down,
I gotta right to hang around
Down around the river.

> *Earl Carroll's Vanities [1932].*
> *I Gotta Right to Sing the Blues*

3 Don't know why
There's no sun up in the sky,
Stormy weather,
Since my man and I ain't together,
Keeps rainin' all the time.

> *The Cotton Club Parade [1933]. Stormy*
> *Weather (Keeps Rainin' All the Time)*

Harold MacMillan
1894–1986

4   We have not overthrown the divine right of kings to fall down for the divine right of experts.

> *Speech [August 16, 1950]*

5   Most of our people have never had it so good.[2]

> *Speech at Bedford, England*
> *[July 20, 1957]*

6   The wind of change is blowing through this continent and whether we like it or not, the growth of national consciousness is a political fact.

> *Speech to South African Parliament*
> *[February 3, 1960]*

7   [When asked to identify the greatest challenge for a statesman:] Events, my dear boy, events.

> *Attributed*

---

[1]Neither the original nor the translation of the last two sentences appeared in either *Pravda* or the *New York Times*, which carried the rest of the text. Another possible translation of the last sentence is: We shall be present at your funeral; i.e., we shall outlive you; but the above is the familiar version.

[2]Adapted for the campaign slogan "You Never Had It So Good."

J. B. Priestley
1894–1984

8   At this moment, or any moment, we're only a cross-section of our real selves. What we *really* are is the whole stretch of ourselves, all our time, and when we come to the end of this life, all those selves, all our time, will be us — the real you, the real me. And then perhaps we'll find ourselves in another time, which is only a kind of dream.

> *Time and the Conways [1937], act 2*

9   We don't live alone. We are members of one body. We are responsible for each other. And I tell you that the time will soon come when, if men will not learn that lesson, then they will be taught it in fire and blood and anguish.

> *An Inspector Calls [1945], act 3*

Samson Raphaelson
1894–1983

10   In every living soul, a spirit cries for expression — perhaps this plaintive, wailing song of Jazz is, after all, the misunderstood utterance of a prayer.

> *The Jazz Singer [1927], opening title*

Jean Renoir
1894–1979

11   Everybody has his reasons.[3]

> *La Règle du Jeu (The Rules of the Game)*
> *[1939], screenplay*

Charles Reznikoff
1894–1976

12 How shall we mourn you who are killed and
        wasted,
sure that you would not die with your work unended,
as if the iron scythe in the grass stops for a flower?

> *Rhythms [1918], poem 14*

13 I have learnt the Hebrew blessing before eating
        bread;
is there no blessing before reading Hebrew?

> *Five Groups of Verse [1927],*
> *Building Boom*

14 I like the streets of New York City, where I was born,
better than these streets of palms.
No doubt, my father liked his village in Ukrainia
better than the streets of New York City;
and my grandfather the city and its synagogue,

---

[3]Tout le monde a ses raisons.

where he once read aloud the holy books,
better than the village
in which he dickered in the market-place.
*Going To and Fro and Walking Up and
Down [1941]. Autobiography: Hollywood*

Elzie Crisler Segar
1894–1938

1   I yam what I yam, an' that's all I yam!
*Thimble Theatre (comic strip) [c. 1932],
Popeye speaking*

Genevieve Taggard
1894–1948

2 Try tropic for your balm,
Try storm,
And after storm, calm.
Try snow of heaven, heavy, soft, and slow,
Brilliant and warm.
Nothing will help, and nothing do much harm.
*Of the Properties of Nature for Healing
an Illness, st. 1*

James Thurber
1894–1961

3   Well, if I called the wrong number, why did you answer the phone?
Caption for cartoon in The New Yorker

4   I love the idea of there being two sexes, don't you?   *Caption for cartoon in The New Yorker*

5   He knows all about art, but he doesn't know what he likes.   *Caption for cartoon in The New Yorker*

6   It's a naive domestic Burgundy without any breeding, but I think you'll be amused by its presumption.   *Caption for cartoon in The New Yorker*

7   I suppose that the high-water mark of my youth in Columbus, Ohio, was the night the bed fell on my father.   *My Life and Hard Times [1933], ch.1*

8   In Martinique, when the whistle blew for the tourists to get back on the ship, I had a quick, wild, and lovely moment when I decided I wouldn't get back on the ship. I did, though. And I found that somebody had stolen the pants to my dinner jacket.
My Life and Hard Times. A Note at the End

9   Early to rise and early to bed makes a male healthy and wealthy and dead.
*Fables for Our Time [1940].
The Shrike and the Chipmunks*

10   You might as well fall flat on your face as lean over too far backward.
*Fables for Our Time.
The Bear Who Let It Alone*

11   The world is so full of a number of things, I am sure we should all be as happy as kings, and you know how happy kings are.[1]
Fables for Our Time. The Green Isle in the Sea

12   You Could Look It Up[2]
Title of story [1941]

13   Red Barber announces the Dodger games and he uses those expressions—picked them up down South.... "Tearing up the pea patch" means going on a rampage; "sitting in the catbird seat" means sitting pretty, like a batter with three balls and no strikes on him.
*The Thurber Carnival [1945].
The Catbird Seat*

Jean Toomer
1894–1967

14 O can't you see it, O can't you see it,
Her skin is like dusk on the eastern horizon
...When the sun goes down.
Cane [1923]. Karintha

15 Wind is in the cane. Come along.
Cane leaves swaying, rusty with talk,
Scratching choruses above the guinea's squawk,
Wind is in the cane. Come along.
Cane. Carma

16 A feast of moon and men and barking hounds,
An orgy for some genius of the South
With blood-hot eyes and cane-lipped scented mouth,
Surprised in making folk songs from soul sounds.
Cane. Georgia Dusk, st. 2

Mark Van Doren
1894–1972

17 Wit is the only wall
Between us and the dark.   *Wit, st. 1*

Norbert Wiener
1894–1964

18   We have decided to call the entire field of control and communication theory, whether in the machine

---

[1]See Robert Louis Stevenson, 555:13.

[2]Subsequently popularized by and associated with Casey Stengel, 688, who used it as a conversation clincher.

or in the animal, by the name of Cybernetics, which we form from the Greek [for] steersman.

Cybernetics [1948]

1 The independent scientist who is worth the slightest consideration as a scientist has a consecration which comes entirely from within himself: a vocation which demands the possibility of supreme self-sacrifice.

The Human Use of Human Beings [1950]

Edward, Duke of Windsor [Edward VIII]
1894–1972

2 I have found it impossible to carry the heavy burden of responsibility and to discharge my duties as King as I would wish to do without the help and support of the woman I love.[1]

Farewell broadcast after abdication [December 11, 1936]

Bud [William] Abbott
1895–1974
and
Lou Costello [Louis Francis Cristillo]
1906–1959

3 Who's on first, What's on second, I Don't Know's on third — *The Naughty Nineties [1945]*

Mikhail Bakhtin
1895–1975

4 Carnival is not a spectacle seen by the people; they live in it, and everyone participates because its very idea embraces all the people. While carnival lasts, there is no other life outside it. During carnival time life is subject only to its laws, that is, the laws of its own freedom.[2] *Rabelais and His World [1965]*

Jack [William Harrison] Dempsey
1895–1983

5 Honey, I just forgot to duck.

To his wife, after losing the heavyweight title to Gene Tunney [September 23, 1926]

Buddy [George Gard] DeSylva
1895–1950

6 Look for the silver lining
Whene'er a cloud
Appears in the blue.

Sally [1920]. Look for the Silver Lining

Paul Éluard [Eugène Grindel]
1895–1952

7 I was born to know you
To give you your name
Freedom.[3] *Poésie et Vérité [1942]. Liberté*

8 Farewell sadness
Good morning sadness.[4]

Poésie et Vérité. La Vie Immédiate

R[ichard] Buckminster Fuller
1895–1983

9 Don't fight forces; use them.

Shelter [1932]

10 God is a verb.

No More Secondhand God [1963]

11 For at least two million years men have been reproducing and multiplying on a little automated Spaceship Earth.

Prospect for Humanity [1964]

12 Synergy means behavior of whole systems unpredicted by the behavior of their parts.

What I Have Learned [1966]. How Little I Know

13 Now there is one outstandingly important fact regarding Spaceship Earth, and that is that no instruction book came with it.

Operating Manual for Spaceship Earth [1969]

14 Thinking is a momentary dismissal of irrelevancies.

Utopia or Oblivion [1969]

15 I am the only guinea pig I have.

Address to Engineering Society at Tel Aviv [June 16, 1972]

16 Nature is trying very hard to make us succeed, but nature does not depend on us. We are not the only experiment.

Interview in the Minneapolis Tribune [April 30, 1978]

---

[1]Apparently written for Edward by Winston Churchill. See SARAH BRADFORD, *George VI* [1989], *p. 202.*

[2]Translated by HÉLÈNE ISWOLSKY.

[3]Je suis né pour te connaître / Pour te nommer / Liberté.
[4]Adieu tristesse / Bonjour tristesse.

Robert [Ranke] Graves
1895–1985

1 As you are woman, so be lovely:
  As you are lovely, so be various,
  Merciful as constant, constant as various,
  So be mine, as I yours for ever.
                    Pygmalion to Galatea

2 Take your delight in momentariness,
  Walk between dark and dark — a shining space
  With the grave's narrowness, though not its peace.
                                  Sick Love

3 Impossible men: idle, illiterate,
    Self-pitying, dirty, sly,
  For whose appearance even in City Parks
    Excuses must be made to casual passers-by.

  Has God's supply of tolerable husbands
    Fallen, in fact, so low
  Or do I always over-value woman
    At the expense of man?
        Do I?
          It might be so.
        A Slice of Wedding Cake

4   A well-chosen anthology is a complete dispensary
  of medicine for the more common mental disorders,
  and may be used as much for prevention as cure.
                    On English Poetry, 29

5   The reason why the hairs stand on end, the eyes
  water, the throat is constricted, the skin crawls and a
  shiver runs down the spine when one writes or reads
  a true poem is that a true poem is necessarily an invocation of the White Goddess, or Muse, the Mother of
  All Living, the ancient power of fright and lust — the
  female spider or the queen bee whose embrace is
  death.[1]   *The White Goddess [1948], ch. 1*

Oscar Hammerstein II
1895–1960

6 Tote dat barge!
  Lif' dat bale!
  Git a little drunk,
  An' you land in jail.
  Ah gits weary
  An' sick of tryin'
  Ah'm tired of livin'
  An' skeered of dyin',
  But Ol' Man River,
  He jes' keeps rollin' along.
            Show Boat[2] [1927]. Ol' Man River

7 The last time I saw Paris, her heart was warm
      and gay.
  I heard the laughter of her heart in every street café.
          The Last Time I Saw Paris[3] [1940]

8 Oh, what a beautiful mornin'
  Oh, what a beautiful day.
  I got a beautiful feelin'
  Everything's going my way.
          *Oklahoma![4] [1943]. Oh, What a Beautiful
          Mornin'*

9 The corn is as high as an elephant's eye,
  An' it looks like it's climbin' clear up to the sky.
          Oklahoma! Oh, What a Beautiful Mornin'

10 Ev'rythin's up to date in Kansas City.
  They've gone about as fur as they c'n go!
                    Oklahoma! Kansas City

11 When you walk through a storm
  Keep your head up high
  And don't be afraid of the dark.
  At the end of the storm
  Is a golden sky
  And the sweet, silver song of a lark.
      Carousel[4] [1945]. You'll Never Walk Alone

12 Some enchanted evening...
  You may see a stranger
  Across a crowded room.
      *South Pacific[5] [1949].
      Some Enchanted Evening*

13   There Is Nothing Like a Dame.
                  South Pacific. Title of song

14 You've got to be taught
  Before it's too late
  Before you are six, or seven, or eight
  To hate all the people your relatives hate
  You've got to be carefully taught.
          *South Pacific. You've Got to Be
          Carefully Taught*

15 Happy talk,
  Keep talkin' happy talk,
  Talk about t'ings you like to do.
  You gotta have a dream;
  If you don't have a dream
  How you gonna have a dream come true?
                  South Pacific. Happy Talk

16 Raindrops on roses and whiskers on kittens,
  Bright copper kettles and warm woolen mittens,

---

[1]See Emily Dickinson, 511:15, and A. E. Housman, 576:5.
[2]Based on the novel *Show Boat* [1926], by Edna Ferber. Music by
Jerome Kern.

[3]Music by Jerome Kern.
See Elliot Paul, 691:5.
[4]Music by Richard Rodgers.
[5]Based on *Tales of the South Pacific* [1947], by James A.
Michener. Music by Richard Rodgers.

Brown paper packages tied up with strings —
These are a few of my favorite things.
The Sound of Music[1] *[1959].*
My Favorite Things

Lorenz [Milton] Hart
1895–1943

1 We'll have Manhattan,
The Bronx and Staten
Island too.   *Manhattan*[1] *[1925]*

2 Ten cents a dance —
That's what they pay me;
Gosh, how they weigh me down!
Ten cents a dance —
Pansies and rough guys,
Tough guys who tear my gown!
Simple Simon [1930]. Ten Cents a Dance

3 I get too hungry for dinner at eight.
I like the theater, but never come late.
I never bother with people I hate.
That's why the lady is a tramp.
Babes in Arms[1] *[1937]. The Lady Is a Tramp*

4 My funny valentine,
Sweet comic valentine,
You make me smile with my heart.
Your looks are laughable,
Unphotographable,
Yet you're my fav'rite work of art.
Babes in Arms. My Funny Valentine

5 The sleepless nights,
The daily fights,
The quick toboggan when you reach the heights —
I miss the kisses and I miss the bites.
I wish I were in love again!
Babes in Arms. I Wish I Were in Love Again

6 I'm wild again,
Beguiled again,
A simpering, whimpering child again —
Bewitched, bothered and bewildered am I.
Pal Joey[1] *[1940]. Bewitched,*
Bothered and Bewildered

L[esley] P[oles] Hartley
1895–1972

7 The past is a foreign country; they do things differently there.
The Go-Between [1953], prologue

Max Horkheimer
1895–1973
and
Theodor W. Adorno
1903–1969

8 In the most general sense of progressive thought, the Enlightenment has always aimed at liberating men from fear and establishing their sovereignty. Yet the fully enlightened earth radiates disaster triumphant.
Dialectic of Enlightenment [1944]

Dolores Ibarruri [La Pasionaria][2]
1895–1989

9 No pasarán [They shall not pass]![3]
Republican watchword in the Spanish Civil War [1936–1939]

Dorothea Lange
1895–1965

10 The camera is an instrument that teaches people to see without a camera.
Quoted in Photographs of a Lifetime [1982]

Basil Henry Liddell Hart
1895–1970

11 Keep strong, if possible. In any case, keep cool. Have unlimited patience. Never corner an opponent, and always assist him to save his face. Put yourself in his shoes — so as to see things through his eyes. Avoid self-righteousness like the devil — nothing so self-blinding.
Deterrent or Defense [1960].
Advice to Statesmen

Groucho [Julius Henry] Marx
1895–1977

12 I never forget a face, but in your case I'll make an exception.   *Saying*

13 Please accept my resignation. I don't care to belong to any club that will accept me as a member.
The Groucho Letters [1967]

---

[1]Music by RICHARD RODGERS.

[2]See Emiliano Zapata, 634:8 and note.

[3]End of radio speech [July 18, 1936] calling on the women of Spain to help defend the Republic.

John McNulty
1895–1956

1　They were talking about a certain hangout and Johnny said, "Nobody goes there anymore. It's too crowded."[1]

Some Nights When Nothing Happens
Are the Best Nights in This Place [1943]

Lewis Mumford
1895–1990

2　Every generation revolts against its fathers and makes friends with its grandfathers.

The Brown Decades [1931]

3　For over against the convenience of instantaneous communication is the fact that the great economical abstractions of writing, reading, and drawing, the media of reflective thought and deliberate action, will be weakened.　*Technics and Civilization [1934]*

4　The clock, not the steam-engine, is the key-machine of the modern industrial age.

Technics and Civilization

5　Layer upon layer, past times preserve themselves in the city until life itself is finally threatened with suffocation; then, in sheer defense, modern man invents the museum.　*The Culture of Cities [1938]*

Edward E. Paramore, Jr.
1895–1956

6 Oh, the North Countree is a hard countree
That mothers a bloody brood;
And its icy arms hold hidden charms
For the greedy, the sinful and lewd.
And strong men rust, from the gold and the lust
That sears the Northland soul.

The Ballad of Yukon Jake [1921]

Andy Razaf
1895–1973

7 Ain't misbehavin',
I'm savin' my love for you.

Ain't Misbehavin'[2] [1929]

8 Just 'cause you're black folks think you lack,
They laugh at you and scorn you too,
What did I do to be so black and blue?

Black and Blue[2] [1929]

Morrie Ryskind
1895–1985

9　One morning I shot an elephant in my pajamas. How he got into my pajamas I'll never know.

Animal Crackers (screenplay) [1930],
spoken by Groucho Marx

Bill Wilson
1895–1971

10　We admitted we were powerless over alcohol — that our lives had become unmanageable. Came to believe that a Power greater than ourselves could restore us to sanity.

Alcoholics Anonymous [1939]

Edmund Wilson
1895–1972

11　It may be that there is nothing more demoralizing than a small but adequate income.

Memoirs of Hecate County [1946]

12　In the arts as in the sciences a certain freedom for experimentation is necessary: one must allow a good deal of apparently gratuitous, and even empty or ridiculous work, if one wants to get masterpieces.

The Shores of Light [1952]

13　I have had a good many more uplifting thoughts, creative and expansive visions — while soaking in comfortable baths or drying myself after bracing showers — in well-equipped American bathrooms than I have ever had in any cathedral.

A Piece of My Mind [1956], ch. 4

14　The wars fought by human beings are stimulated as a rule primarily by the same instincts as the voracity of a sea slug.　*Patriotic Gore [1962]. Introduction*

15　Whenever we engage in a war or move in on some other country, it is always to liberate somebody.

Patriotic Gore. Introduction

16　The cruellest thing that has happened to Lincoln since he was shot by Booth has been to fall into the hands of Carl Sandburg.[3]

Patriotic Gore, ch. 3

17　We tended to imagine Canada as a kind of vast hunting preserve convenient to the United States.

O Canada [1965]

18　We have earned the slogan, "Yanks, go home!"

Europe without Baedeker, 1967 edition

---

[1]Often attributed to Yogi Berra, 806.
[2]Music by THOMAS [FATS] WALLER and HARRY BROOKS.

---

[3]Referring to Sandburg's six-volume biography, *Abraham Lincoln* [1926–1939].

J[oseph] R[andolph] Ackerley
1896–1967

1   What strained and anxious lives dogs must lead, so emotionally involved in the world of men, whose affections they strive endlessly to secure, whose authority they are expected unquestioningly to obey, and whose minds they can never do more than imperfectly reach and comprehend.

My Dog Tulip [1965]. Appendix

Antonin Artaud
1896–1948

2   Without an element of cruelty at the root of every spectacle, the theater is not possible.

The Theater and Its Double [1938]

3   Where there is a stink of shit there is a smell of being.

To Have Done with the Judgment of God [1947]

Philip Barry
1896–1949

4   The time to make your mind up about people, is never.

The Philadelphia Story (play) [1939], act ii, sc. 2

Edmund Blunden
1896–1974

5 I am for the woods against the world,
But are the woods for me?   *The Kiss*

6 Then is not Death at watch
Within those secret waters?
What wants he but to catch
Earth's heedless sons and daughters?

The Midnight Skaters

André Breton
1896–1966

7   Surrealism is based on the belief in the superior reality of certain forms of previously neglected associations, in the omnipotence of dream, in the disinterested play of thought.

Manifesto of Surrealism [1924]

8   Subjectivity and objectivity commit a series of assaults on each other during a human life out of which the first one suffers the worse beating.[1]

Nadja [1928], preface

---

[1]Translated by CESAR ALBINI.

9   Beauty will be CONVULSIVE or will not be at all.   *Nadja, last line*

10   It is at the movies that the only absolutely modern mystery is celebrated.

From J. H. MATHEWS, Surrealism and Film

George Burns
[Nathan Birnbaum]
1896–1996

11   It's nice to be here. When you're 99 years old, it's nice to be anywhere.

People Magazine [January 1995]

Howard Dietz
1896–1983

12 A show
That is really a show
Sends you out
With a kind of a glow
And you say
As you go on your way
"That's entertainment."

The Band Wagon [1953]. That's Entertainment

Everett McKinley Dirksen
1896–1969

13   A billion here, a billion there, and pretty soon you're talking about real money.

Attributed

John [Roderigo]
Dos Passos
1896–1970

14   Make sure he ain't a dinge, boys.
Make sure he ain't a guinea or a kike,
how can you tell a guy's a hunredpercent when all you've got's a gunnysack full of bones, bronze buttons stamped with the screaming eagle and a pair of roll puttees?

1919 [1932]. The Body of an American

15   America our nation has been beaten by strangers who have bought the laws and fenced off the meadows and cut down the woods for pulp and turned our pleasant cities into slums and sweated the wealth out of our people and when they want to they hire the executioner to throw the switch.

The Big Money [1936].
They have clubbed us off the streets

F[rancis] Scott [Key] Fitzgerald
1896–1940

1   The victor belongs to the spoils.
The Beautiful and Damned [1922]

2   Everyone suspects himself of at least one of the cardinal virtues, and this is mine: I am one of the few honest people that I have ever known.
The Great Gatsby [1925], ch. 3

3   The city seen from the Queensboro Bridge is always the city seen for the first time, in its first wild promise of all the mystery and the beauty in the world.   *The Great Gatsby, 4*

4   Jay Gatsby of West Egg, Long Island, sprang from his Platonic conception of himself. He was a son of God — a phrase which, if it means anything, means just that — and he must be about His Father's business, the service of a vast, vulgar, and meretricious beauty.   *The Great Gatsby, 6*

5   Her voice is full of money.
The Great Gatsby, 7

6   They were careless people, Tom and Daisy — they smashed up things and creatures and then retreated back into their money or their vast carelessness, or whatever it was that kept them together, and let other people clean up the mess they had made.
The Great Gatsby, 9

7   Gatsby believed in the green light, the orgiastic future that year by year recedes before us.
The Great Gatsby, 9

8   So we beat on, boats against the current, borne back ceaselessly into the past.
The Great Gatsby, last line

9   Let me tell you about the very rich.[1] They are different from you and me. They possess and enjoy early, and it does something to them, makes them soft where we are hard, and cynical where we are trustful.   *The Rich Boy [1926]*

10   I remember riding in a taxi one afternoon between very tall buildings under a mauve and rosy sky; I began to bawl because I had everything I wanted and knew I would never be so happy again.
My Lost City [1932]

11   The change came a long way back, but at first it didn't show. The manner remains intact for some time after the morale cracks.
Tender Is the Night [1934]

12   Before I go on with this short history, let me make a general observation — the test of a first-rate intelligence is the ability to hold two opposed ideas in the mind at the same time, and still retain the ability to function.   *The Crack-Up [1936]*

13   But at three o'clock in the morning, a forgotten package has the same tragic importance as a death sentence, and the cure doesn't work — and in a real dark night of the soul it is always three o'clock in the morning.   *The Crack-Up*

14   It was about then [1920] that I wrote a line which certain people will not let me forget: "She was a faded but still lovely woman of twenty-seven."
Early Success [1937]

15   Oh, Joe, can't producers ever be wrong? I'm a good writer — honest. I thought you were going to play fair.
Letter to Joseph L. Mankiewicz[2]
[January 20, 1938]

16   There never was a good biography of a good novelist. There couldn't be. He is too many people, if he's any good.   *Notebooks [1978]*

17   If you're strong enough, there *are* no precedents.   *Notebooks*

18   Show me a hero and I will write you a tragedy.
Notebooks

19   There are no second acts in American lives.
Notebooks

20   It is in the thirties that we want friends. In the forties we know they won't save us any more than love did.   *Notebooks*

Ira Gershwin[3]
1896–1983

21 Oh, lady be good
To me.
Lady Be Good [1924]. Oh, Lady Be Good

22 'S wonderful! 'S marvelous —
You should care for me!
Funny Face [1927]. 'S Wonderful

23 I got rhythm,
I got music,
I got my man —
Who could ask for anything more?
Girl Crazy [1930]. I Got Rhythm

24 Of thee I sing, baby,
You have got that certain thing, baby,

---

[1]See Ernest Hemingway, 721:15 and note 4.

[2]Mankiewicz had overseen the drastic rewriting of Fitzgerald's screenplay for *Three Comrades*.

[3]Music for all the lyrics is by GEORGE GERSHWIN.

Shining star and inspiration
Worthy of a mighty nation,
Of thee I sing!   *Of Thee I Sing [1931], title song*

1   A Woman Is a Sometime Thing
            Porgy and Bess[1] *[1935], title of song*

2 I got plenty of nothin',
   And nothin's plenty for me.
            Porgy and Bess. I Got Plenty of Nothin'

3 It ain't necessarily so —
   The things that you're liable
   To read in the Bible —
   It ain't necessarily so.
            Porgy and Bess. It Ain't Necessarily So

4 You say eether and I say eyether,
   You say neether and I say nyther;
   Eether, eyether, neether, nyther —
   Let's call the whole thing off!
            Shall We Dance [1937].
            Let's Call the Whole Thing Off

5 The way you wear your hat,
   The way you sip your tea,
   The mem'ry of all that —
   No, no! They can't take that away from me!
            Shall We Dance. They Can't Take
            That Away from Me

6 Nice work if you can get it,
   And you can get it if you try.
            A Damsel in Distress [1937]. Nice Work

7 A foggy day in London Town
   Had me low and had me down.
   I viewed the morning with alarm.
   The British Museum had lost its charm.
            A Damsel in Distress. A Foggy Day

8 In time the Rockies may crumble,
   Gibraltar may tumble
   (They're only made of clay),
   But our love is here to stay.
            The Goldwyn Follies [1937].
            Love Is Here to Stay

E. Y. Harburg [Isidore Hochberg]
1896–1981

9 Once I built a railroad, now it's done.
   Brother, can you spare a dime?
            Americana[2] *[third edition, 1932].*
            Brother, Can You Spare a Dime?

10 It's only a paper moon,
    Sailing over a cardboard sea,
    But it wouldn't be make-believe
    If you believed in me.[3]
            It's Only a Paper Moon [1933]

11 Last night
    When we were young
    Love was a star,
    A song unsung,
    Life was so new,
    So real, so right,
    Ages ago,
    Last night.
            Last Night When We Were Young[4] *[1936]*

12 Somewhere over the rainbow
    Bluebirds fly.
    Birds fly over the rainbow —
    Why then, oh why can't I?
            The Wizard of Oz[5] *[1939]. Over the Rainbow*

13 When I'm not near the girl I love,
    I love the girl I'm near.
            Finian's Rainbow[6] *[1947].*
            When I'm Not Near the Girl I Love

14 When I'm not facing the face that I fancy,
    I fancy the face I face.
            Finian's Rainbow.
            When I'm Not Near the Girl I Love

15 How are things in Glocca Morra this fine day?
            Finian's Rainbow.
            How Are Things in Glocca Morra?

Howard Hawks
1896–1977

16   Hell, the first thing you've got to do if you're going to make a picture is to get a story. The next thing is to get a good script, the next thing is to figure out who the hell is going to play in it, your characters, and then after that to make it.
            Quoted in GERALD MAST, *Howard Hawks, Storyteller [1982]*

Joe Jacobs
1896–1940

17   We wuz robbed!
            After the heavyweight title fight between Max Schmeling and Jack Sharkey [June 21, 1932]

---

[1]*Porgy and Bess. — Title of play [1927] by* DUBOSE HEYWARD *[1885–1940] and* DOROTHY HEYWARD *[1890–1961], and of opera [1935] by* GEORGE GERSHWIN

[2]*Music by* JAY GORNEY.

[3]*Music by* HAROLD ARLEN. *Lyrics co-written with* BILLY ROSE.
[4]*Music by* HAROLD ARLEN.
See L. Frank Baum, 562:2–5.
[5]*Music by* HAROLD ARLEN.
[6]*Music by* BURTON LANE.

1   I should of stood in bed.

> *After leaving a sickbed to attend the World*
> *Series in Detroit [October 1935]*
> *and betting on the loser*

Giuseppe di Lampedusa
1896–1957

2   If we want things to stay as they are, things will have to change.

> *The Leopard*[1] *[1957]*

3   Love. Of course, love. Flames for a year, ashes for thirty.

> *The Leopard*

4   The Sicilians never want to improve for the simple reason that they think themselves perfect.

> *The Leopard*

Eugenio Montale
1896–1981

5   Too many lives are needed to make just one.

> *Summer [1939]*

Liam O'Flaherty
1896–1984

6   He [the informer] was a poor weak human being like themselves, a human soul, weak and helpless in suffering, shivering in the toils of the eternal struggle of the human soul with pain.

> *The Informer [1925]*

Jean Piaget
1896–1980

7   If only we could know what was going on in a baby's mind while observing him in action we could certainly understand everything there is to psychology.

> *La Première Année de l'Enfant [1927]*

Dawn Powell
1896–1965

8   True gaiety is based on a foundation of realism. All right, we know we're dying, we know we're poor, that is off our minds — we eat, sleep, make merry but we are not kidding ourselves that we are rich and beautiful or that Santa Claus and two blondes will soon come down the chimney.... Gaiety should be brave, it should have stout legs of truth, not a gelatine base of dreams and wishes.

> *Diary entry [May 22, 1939]*

9   There is really one city for everyone just as there is one major love.

> *Diary entry [July 6, 1953]*

Robert E[mmet] Sherwood
1896–1955

10   The trouble with me is, I belong to a vanishing race. I'm one of the intellectuals.

> *The Petrified Forest [1934]*

Wallis, Duchess of Windsor
[Wallis Simpson]
1896–1986

11   You can't be too rich or too thin.[2]

> *Los Angeles Times [June 17, 1970]*

Dodie [Dorothy Gladys] Smith
1896–1990

12   "Why, that's Cruella de Vil," said Mrs. Dearly. "We were at school together. She was expelled for drinking ink."

> *The Hundred and One Dalmatians [1956]*

Tristan Tzara
1896–1963

13   DADA DADA DADA; — the roar of contorted pains, the interweaving of contraries and all contradictions, freaks and irrelevancies: LIFE.

> *Dada Manifesto [1918]*

Arthur [Bugs] Baer
1897–1969

14   You can take a boy out of the country but you can't take the country out of a boy.

> *Hollywood with "Bugs" Baer and Henry*
> *Major [1938]*

---

[1]Translated by Archibald Colquhoun.

---

[2]This quip is widely attributed to Wallis, Duchess of Windsor, but may have originated with the socialite Babe Paley in 1969 or with an even earlier source.

Georges Bataille
1897–1962

1   Eroticism is assenting to life even in death.
Eroticism [1957]

2   Beauty is desired in order that it may be befouled; not for its own sake, but for the joy brought by the certainty of profaning it.   *Eroticism*

Louise Bogan
1897–1970

3 Women have no wilderness in them,
They are provident instead,
Content in the tight hot cell of their hearts
To eat dusty bread.   *Women [1922], st. 1*

4 I burned my life, that I might find
A passion wholly of the mind,
Thought divorced from eye and bone,
Ecstasy come to breath alone.
The Alchemist [1923], st. 1

5 Up from the bronze, I saw
Water without a flaw
Rush to its rest in air,
Reach to its rest, and fall.
Roman Fountain [1937], st. 1

6 There was so much to love I could not love it all;
I could not love it enough.
After the Persian [1951]

Frank Capra
1897–1991

7   One man, one film.   *Personal motto*

Bernard De Voto
1897–1955

8   The West begins where the average annual rainfall drops below twenty inches. When you reach the line which marks that drop — for convenience, the one hundredth meridian — you have reached the West.
The Plundered Province.
In Harper's Magazine [August 1934]

9   The achieved West had given the United States something that no people had ever had before, an internal, domestic empire.
The Year of Decision [1943]

10   You can no more keep a martini in the refrigerator than you can keep a kiss there. The proper union of gin and vermouth is a great and sudden glory; it is one of the happiest marriages on earth and one of the shortest-lived.
The Hour [1951]

William Faulkner
1897–1962

11   Time is dead as long as it is being clicked off by little wheels; only when the clock stops does time come to life.
The Sound and the Fury [1929].
June Second 1910

12   I've seed de first en de last. . . . I seed de beginnin, en now I sees de endin.
The Sound and the Fury. April Eighth 1928

13   Because no battle is ever won he said. They are not even fought. The field only reveals to man his own folly and despair, and victory is an illusion of philosophers and fools.
The Sound and the Fury. April Eighth 1928

14   They [the Negroes] will endure. They are better than we are. Stronger than we are. Their vices are vices aped from white men or that white men and bondage have taught them: improvidence and intemperance and evasion — not laziness: evasion: of what white men had set them to, not for their aggrandizement or even comfort but his own.
The Bear [1932], pt. IV

15   Poor man. Poor mankind.
Light in August [1932], ch. 4

16   Memory believes before knowing remembers. Believes longer than recollects, longer than knowing even wonders.   *Light in August, 6*

17   Too much happens. . . . Man performs, engenders, so much more than he can or should have to bear. That's how he finds that he can bear anything. . . . That's what's so terrible.   *Light in August, 13*

18   Tell about the South. What's it like there. What do they do there. Why do they live there. Why do they live at all.
Absalom, Absalom! [1936], ch. 6

19   Gettysburg.[1] . . . You cant understand it. You would have to be born there.
Absalom, Absalom!, 9

20   Why do you hate the South?
I dont hate it. . . . I dont hate it. . . . *I dont hate it* he thought, panting in the cold air, the iron New England dark; *I dont. I dont! I dont hate it! I dont hate it!*
Absalom, Absalom!, 9

---

[1]Representing, in context, the South.

1   JEFFERSON, YOKNAPATAWPHA CO., Mississippi. Area, 2400 Square Miles. Population, Whites, 6298; Negroes, 9313. WILLIAM FAULKNER, Sole Owner & Proprietor.

Absalom, Absalom!, inscription on endpaper map drawn by author

2   Between grief and nothing I will take grief.

The Wild Palms [If I Forget Thee, Jerusalem] [1939]

3   He [the writer] must teach himself that the basest of all things is to be afraid; and, teaching himself that, forget it forever, leaving no room in his workshop for anything but the old verities and truths of the heart, the old universal truths lacking which any story is ephemeral and doomed — love and honor and pity and pride and compassion and sacrifice.

Speech upon receiving the Nobel Prize [December 10, 1950]

4   I decline to accept the end of man.

Speech upon receiving the Nobel Prize

5   I believe that man will not merely endure: he will prevail.

Speech upon receiving the Nobel Prize

6   He is immortal, not because he alone among creatures has an inexhaustible voice, but because he has a soul, a spirit capable of compassion and sacrifice and endurance.

Speech upon receiving the Nobel Prize

7   The past is never dead. It's not even past.

Requiem for a Nun [1951], act 1

8   The writer's only responsibility is to his art. He will be completely ruthless if he is a good one. . . . If a writer has to rob his mother, he will not hesitate; the "Ode on a Grecian Urn" is worth any number of old ladies.

From Writers at Work:
The Paris Review Interviews [1959]

Paul Joseph Goebbels
1897–1945

9   Once we have power, we shall never again give it up, unless we are carried out as corpses from our offices.

Diary entry [August 6, 1932]

10   We can do without butter, but, despite all our love of peace, not without arms. One cannot shoot with butter but with guns.[1]

Address in Berlin [January 17, 1936]

---

[1]Probably the origin of the slogan: Guns or butter.

Herman J[acob] Mankiewicz
1897–1953

11   [On Hollywood:] There are millions to be grabbed out here, and your only competition is idiots. Don't let this get around.

Cable to Ben Hecht [1926]

Herman J[acob] Mankiewicz
1897–1953
and
Orson Welles
1915–1985

12   You provide the prose poems, I'll provide the war.

Citizen Kane (screenplay) [1941],
spoken by Orson Welles

13   Old age . . . it's the only disease you don't look forward to being cured of.

Citizen Kane, spoken by Everett Sloane

14   You're right, Mr. Thatcher. I did lose a million dollars last year. I expect to lose a million dollars this year. I expect to lose a million dollars next year. You know, Mr. Thatcher, at the rate of a million dollars a year, I'll have to close this place in sixty years.

Citizen Kane, spoken by Orson Welles

15   It's no trick to make a lot of money, if all you want is to make a lot of money.

Citizen Kane, spoken by Everett Sloane

16   Mr. Kane was a man who got everything he wanted, and then lost it. Maybe Rosebud was something he couldn't get or something he lost. Anyway, it wouldn't have explained anything. I don't think any word can explain a man's life. No, I guess Rosebud is just a piece in a jigsaw puzzle, a missing piece.

Citizen Kane

David McCord
1897–1997

17 By and by
God caught his eye.

Epitaphs: The Waiter

18 The decent docent doesn't doze;
He teaches standing on his toes.
His student dassn't doze and does,
And that's what teaching is and was.

What Cheer [1945]

Horace McCoy
1897–1955

1   "Why did you kill her?" the policeman in the rear seat asked.... "They shoot horses, don't they?" I said.   *They Shoot Horses, Don't They? [1935]*

Thornton [Niven] Wilder
1897–1975

2   Even memory is not necessary for love. There is a land of the living and a land of the dead and the bridge is love, the only survival, the only meaning.
     The Bridge of San Luis Rey [1927], last lines

3   George Brush is my name
     America's my nation
     Luddington's my dwelling place
     And Heaven's my destination.
          Heaven's My Destination [1934],
          title page poem[1]

4   The morning star always gets wonderful bright the minute before it has to go, — doesn't it?
     Our Town [1938], act I

5   But listen, it's not finished: the United States of America; Continent of North America; Western Hemisphere; the Earth; the Solar System; the Universe; the Mind of God, — that's what it said on the envelope.   *Our Town, I*

6   Most everybody in the world climbs into their graves married.
     Our Town, II

7   The dead don't stay interested in us living people for very long. Gradually, gradually, they let go hold of the earth . . . and the ambitions they had . . . and the pleasures they had . . . and the things they suffered . . . and the people they loved. They get weaned away from earth — that's the way I put it — weaned away.[2]   *Our Town, III*

8   Oh, earth, you're too wonderful for anybody to realize you.... Do any human beings ever realize life while they live it? — every, every minute?
     Our Town, III

9   On the stage it is always now.
     Some Thoughts on Playwriting [1941]

10   The whole world's at sixes and sevens, and why the house hasn't fallen down about our ears long ago is a miracle to me.
     The Skin of Our Teeth [1942], act I

11   My advice to you is not to inquire why or whither, but just enjoy your ice cream while it's on your plate — that's my philosophy.
     The Skin of Our Teeth, I

12   Ninety-nine percent of the people in the world are fools and the rest of us are in great danger of contagion.   *The Matchmaker [1954], act I*

13   There is nothing like eavesdropping to show you that the world outside your head is different from the world inside your head.   *The Matchmaker, III*

14   The test of an adventure is that when you're in the middle of it, you say to yourself, "Oh, now I've got myself into an awful mess; I wish I were sitting quietly at home." And the sign that something's wrong with you is when you sit quietly at home wishing you were out having lots of adventure.
     The Matchmaker, IV

Walter Winchell
1897–1972

15   Good evening, Mr. and Mrs. America and all the ships at sea! This is Walter Winchell in New York. Let's go to press.
     Signature opening lines for his weekly
     radio broadcasts

Ludwig Bemelmans
1898–1962

16   In an old house in Paris
     that was covered with vines
     lived twelve little girls in two straight lines.
          Madeline [1939]

Stephen Vincent Benét
1898–1943

17   Oh, Georgia booze is mighty fine booze,
     The best yuh ever poured yuh,
     But it eats the soles right offen yore shoes,
     For Hell's broke loose in Georgia.
          The Mountain Whippoorwill [1923], st. 48

18   I have fallen in love with American names,
     The sharp names that never get fat,
     The snakeskin titles of mining claims,
     The plumed war bonnet of Medicine Hat,
     Tucson and Deadwood and Lost Mule Flat.
          American Names [1927], st. 1

19   Bury my heart at Wounded Knee.
          American Names, st. 7

---

[1]Labeled by Wilder: Doggerel verse which children of the Middle West were accustomed to write in their schoolbooks.

[2]Ellipses are in the original text.

1 American Muse, whose strong and diverse heart
　So many men have tried to understand
　But only made it smaller with their art,
　Because you are as various as your land.
　　　　John Brown's Body [1928]. Invocation, st. 1

2 You can weigh John Brown's body well enough,
　But how and in what balance weigh John Brown?
　　　　John Brown's Body, bk. I

3 Stonewall Jackson, wrapped in his beard and his
　　silence.
　　　　John Brown's Body, IV

4 　If two New Hampshiremen aren't a match for the
　devil, we might as well give the country back to the
　Indians.
　　　　The Devil and Daniel Webster [1936]

5 When Daniel Boone goes by at night
　The phantom deer arise
　And all lost, wild America
　Is burning in their eyes.　　*Daniel Boone [1942]*

Bertolt Brecht
1898–1956

6 　Of those cities will remain what passed through
　them, the wind!
　　　　Of Poor B.B.[1] [1927]

7 Oh, the shark has pretty teeth, dear —
　And he shows them pearly white —
　Just a jackknife has Macheath, dear —
　And he keeps it out of sight.
　　　　The Threepenny Opera[2] (Die
　　　　Dreigroschenoper) [1928]. Prelude,
　　　　The Ballad of Mack the Knife (Moritat)

8 　Till you feed us, right and wrong can wait.
　　　　The Threepenny Opera, act II, sc. 3

9 　What's breaking into a bank compared with
　founding a bank?
　　　　The Threepenny Opera, III, 9

10 Oh! Moon of Alabama
　We now must say good-bye
　We've lost our good old mama
　And must have whiskey
　Oh, you know why!
　　　　Rise and Fall of the City of Mahagonny[3]
　　　　(Aufstieg und Fall der Stadt Mahagonny)
　　　　[1931]. Alabama Song

11 O Germany, pale mother!
　　　　Germany [1933]

12 Unhappy is the land that needs a hero.
　　　　Galileo [1937–1939]

13 Truly, I live in dark times!
　The guileless word is folly. A smooth forehead
　Suggests insensitivity. The man who laughs
　Has simply not yet had
　The terrible news.
　　　　To Those Born Later[4] (An die
　　　　Nachgeborenen) [1938], opening lines

14 　Alas, we
　Who wished to lay the foundations of kindness,
　Could not ourselves be kind.
　But you, when at last it comes to pass
　That man can help his fellow man,
　Do not judge us
　Too harshly.
　　　　To Those Born Later[5]

15 　What they could do with round here is a good
　war. What else can you expect with peace running
　wild all over the place? You know what the trouble
　with peace is? No organization.
　　　　Mother Courage and Her Children
　　　　[1941], sc. 1

16 War is like love, it always finds a way.
　　　　Mother Courage and Her Children,
　　　　sc. 6

Big Bill Broonzy
[William Lee Conley Bradley]
1898–1958

17 If you was white, should be all right,
　If you was brown, could stick around,
　But as you's black, whoa brother,
　Get back, get back, get back.
　　　　Black, Brown and White [1951]

William O[rville] Douglas
1898–1980

18 　The Fifth Amendment is an old friend and a good
　friend. It is one of the great landmarks in man's
　struggle to be free of tyranny, to be decent and civi-
　lized.

　　　　An Almanac of Liberty [1954]

---

[1]Translated by MICHAEL HOFMANN.

[2]Music by KURT WEILL. Translated by MARC BLITZSTEIN. Based on the libretto of *The Beggar's Opera* by JOHN GAY.

[3]Music by KURT WEILL.

---

[4]Translated by JOHN WILLETT.

[5]Translated by H. R. HAYS.

Federico García Lorca
1898–1936

1 In the parched path
   I have seen the good lizard
   (one drop of crocodile)
   meditating.
   The Old Lizard (El Lagarto Viejo) [1921][1]

2 Green, how much I want you green.
   Green wind. Green branches.
   The ship upon the sea
   and the horse in the mountain.
   Somnambule Ballad (Romance Sonámbulo)
   [1928][2]

3 I touched her sleeping breasts,
   and they opened to me suddenly
   like spikes of hyacinth.
   The Faithless Wife (La Casada Infiel) [1928][2]

4 Black are the horses.
   The horseshoes are black.
   On the dark capes glisten
   stains of ink and of wax.
   Their skulls are leaden,
   which is why they don't weep.
   With their patent leather souls
   they come down the street.
   Ballad of the Spanish Civil Guard
   (Romance de la Guardia Civil Española)
   [1928][3]

5 At five in the afternoon.
   Ah, that fatal five in the afternoon!
   It was five by all the clocks!
   It was five in the shade of the afternoon!
   Lament for Ignacio Sanchez Mejias
   (Llanto por Ignacio Sanchez Mejias)
   [1935],[2] *I*

6 I will not see it!

   Tell the moon to come
   for I do not want to see the blood
   of Ignacio on the sand.
   Lament for Ignacio Sanchez Mejias, II

7 The New York dawn has
   four columns of mud
   and a hurricane of black doves
   that paddle in putrescent waters.
   The Poet in New York (Poeta en Nueva York)
   [1940]. The Dawn[2] *(La Aurora), st. 1*

8 The light is buried under chains and noises
   in impudent challenge of rootless science.
   Through the suburbs sleepless people stagger,
   as though just delivered from a shipwreck of
      blood.
   The Poet in New York. The Dawn, st. 5

George Gershwin
1898–1937

9 True music...must repeat the thought and
   inspirations of the people and the time. My people are
   Americans. My time is today.
   From Edward Jablonski *and* Lawrence
   D. Stewart, *The Gershwin Years [1926]*

10 The rhythms of American popular music are more
   or less brittle; they should be made to snap, and at
   times to crackle. The more sharply the music is
   played, the more effective it sounds.
   George Gershwin's Songbook [1932],
   introduction

Willis Goldbeck
1898–1979
and
James Warner Bellah
1899–1976

11 This is the West, sir. When the legend becomes
   fact, print the legend.[4]
   The Man Who Shot Liberty Valence
   (screenplay) [1962], spoken by
   Carleton Young

C[live] S[taples] Lewis
1898–1963

12 The safest road to Hell is the gradual one — the
   gentle slope, soft underfoot, without sudden turnings, without milestones, without signposts.
   The Screwtape Letters [1941], letter 12

13 The Future . . . something which everyone reaches
   at the rate of sixty minutes an hour, whatever he does,
   whoever he is.   *The Screwtape Letters, 25*

14 God whispers to us in our pleasures, speaks in our
   conscience, but shouts in our pains: it is His megaphone to rouse a deaf world.
   The Problem of Pain [1962]

---

[1] Translated by Lysander Kemp.
[2] Translated by Stephen Spender and Joan Gili.
[3] Translated by A. L. Lloyd.

---

[4] If the myth gets bigger than the man, print the myth. — Dorothy Johnson, "The Man Who Shot Liberty Valance" (short story) [1949].

Henry Luce
1898–1967

1   The world of the 20th century, if it is to come to life in any nobility of health and vigor, must be to a significant degree an American century.
The American Century [1941]

Gen. A[nthony] C[lement] McAuliffe
1898–1975

2   Nuts!
In response to German request to surrender, Bastogne [December 22, 1944]

Golda Meir
1898–1978

3   We only want that which is given naturally to all peoples of the world, to be masters of our own fate, only of our fate, not of others, and in cooperation and friendship with others.
Address to Anglo-American Committee of Inquiry [March 25, 1946]

4   There was no such thing as Palestinians. . . . It was not as though there was a Palestinian people . . . and we came and threw them out and took their country away from them. They did not exist.
Interview in the Sunday Times (London) [June 15, 1969]

Gunnar Myrdal
1898–1987

5   The treatment of the Negro is America's greatest and most conspicuous scandal.
An American Dilemma [1944]

Amelia Earhart [Putnam]
1898–1937

6 Courage is the price that life exacts for granting peace.
The soul that knows it not, knows no release
From little things;
Knows not the livid loneliness of fear,
Nor mountain heights where bitter joy can hear
The sound of wings.   *Courage [1927]*

7   I want to do it because I want to do it. Women must try to do things as men have tried. When they fail, their failure must be but a challenge to others.
Last letter to her husband, George Putnam [1937]

Paul Robeson
1898–1976

8   My father was a slave, and my people died to build this country, and I'm going to stay right here and have a part of it, just like you. And no fascist-minded people like you will drive me from it. Is that clear?
Testimony before House Un-American Activities Committee [June 12, 1956]

W[alter] C[arruthers] Sellar
1898–1951

and

R[obert] J[ulian] Yeatman
1897–1968

9   The Norman Conquest was a Good Thing, as from this time onwards England stopped being conquered and thus was able to become top nation.
1066 and All That [1930]

Preston Sturges
[Edmund Preston Biden]
1898–1959

10   You're certainly a funny girl for anybody to meet who's just been up the Amazon for a year.
The Lady Eve [1941], spoken by Henry Fonda to Barbara Stanwyck

11   Oh, do I know them? I positively swill in their ale.
The Lady Eve, screenplay [1941], spoken by Eric Blore

12   To the memory of those who made us laugh: the motley mountebanks, the clowns, the buffoons, in all times and in all nations, whose efforts have lightened our burden a little, this picture is affectionately dedicated.
Sullivan's Travels (movie) [1941], opening title

13   There's a lot to be said for making people laugh . . . did you know that's all some people have? It isn't much . . . but it's better than nothing in this cockeyed caravan.
Sullivan's Travels, spoken by Joel McCrea

Jorge Luis Borges
1899–1986

14 Patio, heaven's watercourse.
The patio is the slope

down which the sky flows into the house.
Serenely
eternity waits at the crossway of the stars.

Fervor of Buenos Aires (Fervor de Buenos Aires) [1923]. Un Patio[1]

1   On some shelf in some hexagon, it was argued, there must exist a book that is the cipher and perfect compendium *of all other books*, and some librarian must have examined that book; this librarian is analogous to a god.

The Library of Babel [1941]

2   Any life, no matter how long or complex it may be, is made up essentially *of a single moment*—the moment in which a man finds out, once and for all, who he is.

The Aleph [1949]. The Biography of Tadeo Isidoro Cruz (Biografía de Tadeo Isidoro Cruz) (1829–1874)

3   A man gradually identifies himself with the form of his fate; a man is, in the long run, his own circumstances.

The Aleph. The Writing of the God (La Escritura de Dios)

4   In all the world, one man has been born, one man has died.   *You*[2]

5   Every writer creates his own precursors.

Kafka and His Precursors [1951]

6   It would be exaggerating to say that our relationship is hostile; I live, I let myself live, so that Borges can weave his literature and that literature justifies me.... I don't know which of us is writing this page.[3]

Personal Anthology (Antologia Personal) [1961]. Borges and Myself (Borges y Yo)

7   I have known what the Greeks did not: uncertainty.

Ficciones [1962]. The Babylon Lottery[4]

8   Little by little I came to realize the strange irony of events. I had always imagined Paradise as a kind of library. Others think of a garden or of a palace. There I was, the center, in a way, of nine hundred thousand books in various languages, but I found I could barely make out the title pages and the spines.

Seven Nights[5] *[1980]. Blindness*

9   The Falklands thing was a fight between two bald men over a comb.

On the 1982 Britain-Argentina conflict

---

[1]Translated by ROBERT FITZGERALD.
[2]Translated by ALASTAIR REID.
[3]Translated by RACHEL PHILLIPS.
[4]Translated by ANTHONY KERRIGAN.
[5]Translated by ELIOT WEINBERGER.

Elizabeth Bowen
1899–1973

10   The innocent are so few that two of them seldom meet—when they do meet, their victims lie strewn all round.

The Death of the Heart [1938]

Hoagy Carmichael
1899–1981

11 I need someone to love me,
Need somebody to carry me home to San Francisco
And bury my body there.

To Have and Have Not [1944]. Hong Kong Blues

Noël Coward
1899–1973

12 Mad dogs and Englishmen go out in the midday sun.

Mad Dogs and Englishmen

13 I'll see you again,
Whenever spring breaks through again.

Bittersweet [1929], act I, sc. ii

14 But I believe that since my life began
The most I've had is just
A talent to amuse.

If Love Were All [1929]

15   Strange how potent cheap music is.

Private Lives [1930], act I

16   Don't Let's Be Beastly to the Germans

Title of song

17   Learn the lines and don't bump into the furniture.

Attributed. Advice on acting

Hart Crane
1899–1932

18 We make our meek adjustments,
Contented with such random consolations
As the wind deposits
In slithered and too ample pockets.

Chaplinesque [1926]

19   High in the azure steeps
Monody shall not wake the mariner.
This fabulous shadow only the sea keeps.

At Melville's Tomb [1926]

20 O, I have known metallic paradises
Where cuckoos clucked to finches
Above the deft catastrophes of drums.

While titters hailed the groans of death
Beneath gyrating awnings I have seen
The incunabula of the divine grotesque.
>> *For the Marriage of Faustus and Helen*
>> *[1926]*

1 The bottom of the sea is cruel.
>> *Voyages [1926], I, st. 3*

2 And yet this great wink of eternity,
Of rimless floods, unfettered leewardings.
>> *Voyages, II, st. 1*

3 Slagged of the hurricane — I, cast within its flow,
Congeal by afternoons here, satin and vacant.
You have given me the shell, Satan, — carbonic
>> amulet
Sere of the sun exploded in the sea.
>> *O Carib Isle! [1926–1928]*

4 Down Wall, from girder into street noon leaks,
A rip-tooth of the sky's acetylene.
>> *The Bridge [1930]. To Brooklyn Bridge*

5 And biased by full sails, meridians reel
Thy purpose — still one shore beyond desire!
The sea's green crying towers a-sway, Beyond.
>> *The Bridge. Ave Maria*

6 Damp tonnage and alluvial march of days . . .
Tortured with history, its one will — flow!
>> *The Bridge. The River (Mississippi)*

7 The swift red flesh, a winter king —
Who squired the glacier woman down the sky?
She ran the neighing canyons all the spring;
She spouted arms; she rose with maize — to die.
>> *The Bridge. The Dance*

8 The phonographs of hades in the brain
Are tunnels that re-wind themselves, and love
A burnt match skating in a urinal —
>> *The Bridge. The Tunnel*

9 And why do I often meet your visage here,
Your eyes like agate lanterns — on and on
Below the toothpaste and the dandruff ads?
And did their riding eyes right through your side,
And did their eyes like unwashed platters ride?
And Death, aloft — gigantically down[1]
Probing through you — toward me, O evermore!
>> *The Bridge. The Tunnel*

10 And so it was I entered the broken world
To trace the visionary company of love, its voice
An instant in the wind (I know not whither
>> hurled)
But not for long to hold each desperate choice.
>> *The Broken Tower [1932]*

---

[1] See Edgar Allan Poe, 448:4.

Robert Crawford
1899–1961

11 Off we go into the wild blue yonder,
Climbing high into the sun.
>> *The Air Force Song[2] [1939]*

Thomas A. Dorsey
1899–1993

12 Precious Lord, take my hand,
Lead me on, let me stand,
I am tired, I am weak, I am worn.
Through the storm, through the night
Lead me on to the light,
Take my hand, precious Lord,
Lead me home.
>> *Take My Hand, Precious Lord [1932]*

Duke [Edward Kennedy] Ellington
1899–1974

13 It Don't Mean a Thing If It Ain't Got That Swing
>> *Title of song[3] [1932]*

14 Fate is being kind to me; fate doesn't want me to
be too famous too young.
>> *On being denied the Pulitzer Prize*
>> *at the age of 66 [1965]*

15 Poor little Sweet Pea, Billy Strayhorn, William
Thomas Strayhorn, the biggest human being who
ever lived, a man with the greatest courage, the most
majestic artistic stature, a highly skilled musician
whose impeccable taste commanded the respect of all
musicians and the admiration of all listeners.
>> *Eulogy for Billy Strayhorn [1967]. Liner*
>> *notes: . . . And His Mother Called Him Bill*

16 Music is my mistress, and she plays second fiddle
to no one. >> *Music Is My Mistress [1973]*

Friedrich August von Hayek
1899–1992

17 The system of private property is the most important guaranty of freedom, not only for those who
own property, but scarcely less for those who do not.
>> *The Road to Serfdom [1944], ch. 8*

---

[2] Originally titled "What Do You Think of the Air Corps Now?", the song was soon retitled "The Army Air Corps." In 1947, "U.S. Air Force" replaced "Army Air Corps" in the title and lyrics.

[3] Music by DUKE ELLINGTON, lyrics by IRVING MILLS. "Bubber [Miley] was the first man I heard use the expression, 'it don't mean a thing if it ain't got that swing.'" — Duke Ellington in *Jazz Journal*, December 1965

1 I am certain that nothing has done so much to destroy the juridical safeguards of individual freedom as the striving after this mirage of social justice.
Economic Freedom and Representative Government [1973]

Ernest Hemingway
1899–1961

2 You and me, we've made a separate peace.
In Our Time [1924], ch. 6

3 It is awfully easy to be hard-boiled about everything in the daytime, but at night it is another thing.
The Sun Also Rises[1] *[1926], ch. 4*

4 It makes one feel rather good deciding not to be a bitch.... It's sort of what we have instead of God.
The Sun Also Rises, 19

5 "Oh, Jake," Brett said, "we could have had such a damned good time together."...
"Yes," I said. "Isn't it pretty to think so?"
The Sun Also Rises, last lines

6 I had seen nothing sacred, and the things that were glorious had no glory and the sacrifices were like the stockyards at Chicago if nothing was done with the meat except to bury it...Abstract words such as glory, honor, courage, or hallow were obscene.
A Farewell to Arms [1929], ch. 27

7 The world breaks everyone and afterward many are strong at the broken places. But those that will not break it kills. It kills the very good and the very gentle and the very brave impartially. If you are none of these you can be sure that it will kill you too but there will be no special hurry.
A Farewell to Arms, 34

8 You never had time to learn. They threw you in and told you the rules and the first time they caught you off base they killed you.
A Farewell to Arms, 41

9 It was like saying good-bye to a statue. After a while I went out and left the hospital and walked back to the hotel in the rain. *A Farewell to Arms, 41*

10 Grace under pressure.[2]
Definition of "guts." From DOROTHY PARKER, *The Artist's Reward, in The New Yorker [November 30, 1929]*

11 I know only that what is moral is what you feel good after and what is immoral is what you feel bad after. *Death in the Afternoon [1932], ch. 1*

12 I was trying to write then and I found the greatest difficulty, aside from knowing truly what you really felt, rather than what you were supposed to feel, had been taught to feel, was to put down what really happened in action; what the actual things were which produced the emotion that you experienced...the real thing, the sequence of motion and fact which made the emotion and which would be as valid in a year or in ten years or, with luck and if you stated it purely enough, always.
Death in the Afternoon, 1

13 If he wrote it he could get rid of it. He had gotten rid of many things by writing them.
Winner Take Nothing [1933]. Fathers and Sons

14 All modern American literature comes from one book by Mark Twain called *Huckleberry Finn.*
Green Hills of Africa [1935], ch. 1

15 The rich were dull and they drank too much.... He remembered poor Julian[3] and his romantic awe of them and how he had started a story once that began, "The very rich are different from you and me." And how someone had said to Julian, Yes, they have more money.[4]
The Fifth Column and The First Forty-Nine Stories [1938]. The Snows of Kilimanjaro

16 Kilimanjaro is a snow-covered mountain 19,710 feet high, and is said to be the highest mountain in Africa. Its western summit is called the Masai "Ngàje Ngài," the House of God. Close to the western summit there is the dried and frozen carcass of a leopard. No one has explained what the leopard was seeking at that altitude.
The Fifth Column and The First Forty-Nine Stories. The Snows of Kilimanjaro, epigraph

17 But did thee feel the earth move?
For Whom the Bell Tolls [1940], ch. 13

18 If we win here we will win everywhere. The world is a fine place and worth the fighting for and I hate very much to leave it.
For Whom the Bell Tolls, 43

---

[1]See *Ecclesiastes 1:5, 22:21.*

[2]After skiing with the Hemingways in 1926, Gerald Murphy was "absolutely elated" when Hemingway praised his courage in venturing down the slopes for the first time as "grace under pressure." See HONORIA MURPHY DONNELLY with RICHARD N. BILLINGS, *Sara & Gerald* [1982].

[3]In original publication, "poor Scott Fitzgerald" [*Esquire*, August 1936].

[4]In 1936 Maxwell Perkins, the legendary editor of Fitzgerald and Hemingway at Charles Scribner's Sons, lunched with Hemingway and the critic Mary Colum. When Hemingway announced, "I am getting to know the rich," Mary Colum replied, "The only difference between the rich and other people is that the rich have more money." — MATTHEW J. BRUCCOLI [1931–], *Scott and Ernest* [1978]

See F. Scott Fitzgerald, 710:9.

1   Cowardice, as distinguished from panic, is almost always simply a lack of ability to suspend the functioning of the imagination.
Men at War [1942], introduction

2   Time is the least thing we have of.
From The New Yorker profile by LILLIAN ROSS[1] *[May 13, 1950]*

3   I must be worthy of the great DiMaggio who does all things perfectly even with the pain of the bone spur in his heel.
The Old Man and the Sea [1952]

4   A man can be destroyed but not defeated.
The Old Man and the Sea

5   The most essential gift for a good writer is a built-in, shock-proof, shit detector. This is the writer's radar and all great writers have had it.
Interview in Paris Review [Spring 1958]

6   You write until you come to a place where you still have your juice and know what will happen next and you stop and try to live through until the next day when you hit it again.
Interview in Paris Review

7   If I started to write elaborately, or like someone introducing or presenting something, I found that I could cut that scrollwork or ornament out and throw it away and start with the first true simple declarative sentence I had written.
A Moveable Feast [1964]

8   If you are lucky enough to have lived in Paris as a young man, then wherever you go for the rest of your life, it stays with you, for Paris is a moveable feast.
A Moveable Feast, epigraph

Alfred Hitchcock
1899–1980

9   What is drama, after all, but life with the dull bits cut out.
To FRANÇOIS TRUFFAUT
in Hitchcock/Truffaut [1967]

10   The more successful the villain, the more successful the picture.   *Hitchcock/Truffaut*

11   [On *Rear Window:*] I'll bet you that nine out of ten people, if they see a woman across the courtyard undressing for bed, or even a man puttering around in his room, will stay and look; no one turns away and says, "It's none of my business." They could pull down their blinds, but they never do; they stand there and look out.   *Hitchcock/Truffaut*

12   Some films are slices of life. Mine are slices of cake.   *Hitchcock/Truffaut*

13   The "MacGuffin" is the term we use to cover all that sort of thing: to steal plans or documents, or discover a secret, it doesn't matter what it is. And the logicians are wrong in trying to figure out the truth of a MacGuffin, since it's beside the point. The only thing that really matters is that in the picture the plans, documents, or secrets must seem to be of vital importance to the characters.
Hitchcock/Truffaut

Robert Maynard Hutchins
1899–1977

14   The death of democracy is not likely to be an assassination from ambush. It will be a slow extinction from apathy, indifference, and undernourishment.   *Great Books [1954]*

Nadezhda Mandelstam
1899–1980

15   I decided it is better to scream. This pitiful sound, which sometimes, goodness knows how, reaches into the remotest prison cell, is a concentrated expression of the last vestige of human dignity. It is a man's way of leaving a trace, of telling people how he lived and died. By his screams he asserts his right to live, sends a message to the outside world demanding help and calling for resistance. If nothing else is left, one must scream. Silence is the real crime against humanity.
Hope Against Hope[2] [1970]

16   The fear that goes with the writing of verse has nothing in common with the fear one experiences in the presence of the secret police. Our mysterious awe in the face of existence itself is always overridden by the more primitive fear of violence and destruction.
Hope Against Hope

17   The astonishing thing is not that so many of us went to concentration camps or died there, but that some of us survived. Caution did not help. Only chance could save you.
Hope Abandoned

Joseph Moncure March
1899–1977

18 A rogue —
But her manner was gay and delicious.

---

[1]Reprinted in book form: *Portrait of Hemingway* [1961].

[2]Translated by MAX HAYWARD.

She could make a Baptist preacher choke
With laughter over a dirty joke.
　　　　　　　　　　　The Wild Party [1928]

1　Would you be shocked if I put on something more comfortable?[1]
　　　Hell's Angels (screenplay) [1930],
　　　spoken by Jean Harlow

Max Miller
1899–1967

2　I Cover the Waterfront　　*Title of book [1932]*

Vladimir Nabokov
1899–1977

3　The cradle rocks above an abyss, and common sense tells us that our existence is but a brief crack of light between two eternities of darkness.
　　　　　　　Speak, Memory [1947], ch. 1

4　I reject completely the vulgar, shabby, fundamentally medieval world of Freud, with its crankish quest for sexual symbols (something like searching for Baconian acrostics in Shakespeare's work) and its bitter little embryos spying, from their natural nooks, upon the love life of their parents.
　　　　　　　　　　Speak, Memory, 1

5　Lolita, light of my life, fire of my loins. My sin, my soul.　　*Lolita [1955], pt. I, ch. 1*

6　You can always count on a murderer for a fancy prose style.　　　　　　*Lolita, I, 1*

7　Between the age limits of nine and fourteen there occur maidens who, to certain bewitched travelers, twice or many times older than they, reveal their nature, which is not human, but nymphic (that is, demoniac); and these chosen creatures I propose to designate as "nymphets."　　*Lolita, I, 5*

8　I am thinking of aurochs and angels, the secret of durable pigments, prophetic sonnets, the refuge of art. And this is the only immortality you and I may share, my Lolita.
　　　　　　　　Lolita, last paragraph

9　For me a work of fiction exists only insofar as it affords me what I shall bluntly call aesthetic bliss.
　　　　　　　On a Book Entitled Lolita

10　Like so many aging college people, Pnin had long since ceased to notice the existence of students on the campus.　　*Pnin [1957], ch. 3, sec. 6*

11　Life is a great surprise. I do not see why death should not be an even greater one.
　　　　　　　　　　Pale Fire [1962]

12　In high art and pure science detail is everything.
　　　　　　　　Strong Opinions [1973]

13　Play! Invent the world! Invent reality!
　　　　　　Look at the Harlequins! [1974]

14　[On adultery:] A most conventional way to rise above the conventional.
　　　　　Lectures on Literature [1980].
　　　　　Gustave Flaubert

Leo Strauss
1899–1973

15　We are now brought face to face with a tyranny which holds out the threat of becoming, thanks to "the conquest of nature" and in particular of human nature, what no other tyranny ever became: perpetual and universal.　　*On Tyranny [1948]*

16　In what then does philosophic politics consist? In satisfying the city that the philosophers are not atheists, that they do not desecrate everything sacred to the city, that they reverence what the city reverences, that they are not subversives, in short that they are not irresponsible adventurers but good citizens and even the best of citizens. This is the defense of philosophy which was required always and everywhere, whatever the regime might have been.
　　　　　　　　　　　　On Tyranny

E[lwyn] B[rooks] White
1899–1985

17　"It's broccoli, dear."
"I say it's spinach, and I say the hell with it."
　　　Caption for cartoon by Carl Rose
　　　in The New Yorker [December 8, 1928]

18　I don't know which is more discouraging, literature or chickens.
　　　Letter to James Thurber [November 18, 1938]

19　I have since become a salt-water man, but sometimes in summer there are days when the restlessness of the tides and the fearful cold of the sea water and the incessant wind that blows across the afternoon and into the evening make me wish for the placidity of a lake in the woods.
　　　　　Once More to the Lake [1941]

20　Humor can be dissected, as a frog can, but the thing dies in the process and the innards are discouraging to any but the pure scientific mind.
　　　　　Some Remarks on Humor [1941]

---

[1]Harry Behn [1898–1973] and Howard Estabrook [1884–1978] were the principal writers on the film, but March is generally credited with this line of dialogue.

1   When Mrs. Frederick C. Little's second son was born, everybody noticed that he was not much bigger than a mouse. The truth of the matter was, the baby looked very much like a mouse in every way. He was only two inches high; and he had a mouse's sharp nose, a mouse's tail, a mouse's whiskers, and the pleasant, shy manner of a mouse. Before he was many days old he was not only looking like a mouse but acting like one, too — wearing a gray hat and carrying a small cane.

Stuart Little [1945], ch. 1

2   "My name is Margalo," said the bird, softly, in a musical voice. "I come from fields once tall with wheat, from pastures deep in fern and thistle; I come from vales of meadowsweet, and I love to whistle."

Stuart Little, 8

3   Democracy is the recurrent suspicion that more than half of the people are right more than half of the time.

The Wild Flag [1946]

4   I am a member of a party of one, and I live in an age of fear. Nothing lately has unsettled my party and raised my fears so much as your editorial, on Thanksgiving Day, suggesting that employees should be required to state their beliefs in order to hold their jobs. The idea is inconsistent with our constitutional theory and has been stubbornly opposed by watchful men since the early days of the Republic.

Letter to the New York Herald Tribune [November 29, 1947]

5   Commuters give the city its tidal restlessness; natives give it solidity and continuity; but the settlers give it passion.

Here Is New York [1949]

6   The city, for the first time in its long history, is destructible. A single flight of planes no bigger than a wedge of geese can quickly end this island fantasy, burn the towers, crumble the bridges, turn the underground passages into lethal chambers, cremate the millions. The intimation of mortality is part of New York now: in the sound of jets overhead, in the black headlines of the latest edition.

Here Is New York

7   It was the best place to be, thought Wilbur, this warm delicious cellar, with the garrulous geese, the changing seasons, the heat of the sun, the passage of swallows, the nearness of rats, the sameness of sheep, the love of spiders, the smell of manure, and the glory of everything.   *Charlotte's Web [1952], ch. 22*

8   None of the new spiders ever quite took her place in his heart. She was in a class by herself. It is not often that someone comes along who is a true friend and a good writer. Charlotte was both.

Charlotte's Web, 22

9   Writing is one way to go about thinking, and the practice and habit of writing not only drain the mind but supply it, too.

The Elements of Style [1959 edition]

[Pearl] Polly Adler
1900–1962

10   A House Is Not a Home   *Title of book [1953]*

Louis [Satchmo] Armstrong
1900–1971

11   Man, if you gotta ask you'll never know.[1]

Reply when asked what jazz is

Basil Bunting
1900–1985

12 I am shifting rivermist, not to be trusted.
   I do not ask anything extraordinary of myself.
   I like a nap after dinner
   and to see the seasons come round in good order.

Chomei at Toyama [1933]

13 Brag, sweet tenor bull,
   descant on Rawthey's madrigal,
   each pebble its part
   for the fells' late spring.

Briggflatts [1966]

14 It is easier to die than to remember.

Briggflatts

15 Sycamore seed twirling,
   O, writhe to its measure!
   Dust swirling trims pleasure.
   Thorns prance in a gale.
   In air snow flickers,
   twigs tap,
   elms drip.

   Swaggering, shimmering fall,
   drench and towel us all!   *Briggflatts*

16 Pens are too light.
   Take a chisel to write.   *Briggflatts*

17 A strong song tows
   us, long earsick.
   Blind, we follow
   rain slant, spray flick
   to fields we do not know.

Briggflatts

---

[1]Lady, if you got to ask you ain't got it. — THOMAS [FATS] WALLER [1904–1943], *when asked to explain rhythm*

1 Then is Now. The star you steer by is gone,
its tremulous thread spun in the hurricane
spider floss on my cheek; light from the zenith
spun when the slowworm lay in her lap
fifty years ago.   *Briggflatts*

Luis Buñuel
1900–1983

2   The Discreet Charm of the Bourgeoisie
                 Title of motion picture [1972]

3   In the end, belief and the lack of it amount to the
same thing. If someone were to prove to me — right
this minute — that God, in all his luminousness,
exists, it wouldn't change a single aspect of my
behavior.
                          My Last Sigh[1] *[1982]*

Lenore Coffee
1900–1984

4   What a dump!
                 Beyond the Forest (screenplay) [1949],
                 spoken by Bette Davis

Robert Desnos
1900–1945

5 I have so fiercely dreamed of you
And walked so far and spoken of you so,
Loved a shade of you so hard
That now I've no more left of you.
                          Last Poem[2]

Theodosius Dobzhansky
1900–1975

6   Nothing in Biology Makes Sense Except in the
Light of Evolution.
                          Title of essay [1973]

Elizabeth, Queen Mother of England
1900–2002

7   I am almost glad we have been bombed. Now I
feel I can look the East End in the face.
                 Comment on the German bombing of
                 Buckingham Palace [September 1940]

Erich Fromm
1900–1980

8   Freedom, although it has brought [modern man]
independence and rationality, has made him isolated
and, thereby, anxious and powerless.
                 Escape from Freedom [1941]. Foreword

9   Man's nature, his passions and anxieties, are a cultural product; as a matter of fact, man himself is the
most important creation and achievement of the
continuous human effort, the record of what we call
history.
                          Escape from Freedom, ch. 1

Abel Green
1900–1973

10   Sticks Nix Hick Pix.
                 Headline about rural audiences' rejection
                 of movies with rural themes, Variety
                 [July 17, 1935]

James Hilton
1900–1954

11   The austere serenity of Shangri-La. Its forsaken
courts and pale pavilions shimmered in repose from
which all the fret of existence had ebbed away, leaving
a hush as if moments hardly dared to pass.
                          Lost Horizon [1933], ch. 5

12   Anno domini — that's the most fatal complaint of
all in the end.   *Goodbye, Mr. Chips [1934], ch. 1*

Cyril Hume
1900–1966

13   Monsters from the Id!
                 Forbidden Planet (screenplay) [1956],
                 spoken by Walter Pidgeon

[Ayatolla] Ruholla Khomeini
1900–1989

14   The author of the Satanic Verses book [Salman
Rushdie[3]], which is against Islam, the Prophet, and
the Koran, and all those involved in its publication
who were aware of its content, are sentenced to
death. I ask all Moslems to execute them wherever
they find them.
                          Statement [February 14, 1989]

---

[1] Mi último suspiro.
[2] Translated by X. J. KENNEDY.

[3] See Salman Rushdie, 865:12.

Raphael Lemkin
1900–1959

1   By genocide[1] we mean the destruction of a nation or of an ethnic group.
Axis Rule in Occupied Europe [1944]

Margaret Mitchell
1900–1949

2   Until you've lost your reputation, you never realize what a burden it was or what freedom really is [spoken by Rhett Butler].
Gone with the Wind [1936], pt. II, ch. 9

3   The usual masculine disillusionment in discovering that a woman has a brain.
Gone with the Wind, IV, 36

4   Death and taxes and childbirth! There's never any convenient time for any of them.
Gone with the Wind, IV, 38

5   My dear, I don't give a damn [Rhett Butler to Scarlett O'Hara].[2]   *Gone with the Wind, V, 63*

6   I'll think of some way to get him back. After all, tomorrow is another day.
Gone with the Wind, last line

Mitchell Parish
1900–1993

7 We lived our little drama,
We kissed in a field of white,
And stars fell on Alabama last night.
Stars Fell on Alabama[3] [1934]

Stephen Potter
1900–1969

8   What is gamesmanship? Most difficult of questions to answer briefly. "The Art of Winning Games Without Actually Cheating" — that is my personal "working definition."
The Theory and Practice of Gamesmanship [1947]

9   *How to be one up* — how to make the other man feel that something has gone wrong, however slightly.   *Some Notes on Lifemanship [1950]*

---

[1]Lemkin coined the word (by combining a Greek and a Latin root) and introduced it in this passage.

[2]Frankly, my dear, I don't give a damn. — SIDNEY HOWARD [1891–1939], *screenplay for Gone with the Wind* [1939]

[3]Music by FRANK PERKINS.

V[ictor] S[awdon] Pritchett
1900–1997

10   Our laughter is only a note or two short of a scream of fear.
The Living Novel and Later Appreciations [1964]

11   I come from a set of storytellers and moralists.... The storytellers were forever changing the tale and the moralists tampering with it in order to put it in an edifying light.
A Cab at the Door [1967], ch. 1

12   How extraordinary it is that one feels most guilt about the sins one is unable to commit.
Midnight Oil [1971]

Ernie Pyle
1900–1945

13   I write from the worm's-eye point of view.
Here Is Your War [1943]

Leo Robin
1900–1984

14   Diamonds Are a Girl's Best Friend
Gentlemen Prefer Blondes[4] [1949], title of song

Antoine de Saint-Exupéry
1900–1944

15   Although human life is priceless, we always act as if something had an even greater price than life.... But what is that something?
Night Flight [1931], ch. 14

16   Love does not consist in gazing at each other but in looking outward together in the same direction.
Wind, Sand and Stars [1939]

17   Grown-ups never understand anything for themselves, and it is tiresome for children to be always and forever explaining things to them.
The Little Prince[5] [1943], ch. 1

18   It is only with the heart that one can see rightly; what is essential is invisible to the eye.
The Little Prince, 21

---

[4]See Anita Loos, 698:7.
Music by JULE STYNE.

[5]Translated by KATHERINE WOODS.

George Seferis
[Giorgios Sefiriades]
1900–1971

1 Three years
we waited intently for the herald
closely watching
the pines the shore and the stars.
Mythistorema[1] *[1935], I*

2 We were searching to rediscover the first seed
so that the ancient drama could begin again.
Mythistorema, I

3 Wherever I travel Greece wounds me.
In the Manner of G.S. [1936]

4   Each of us earns his death, his own death,
which belongs to no one else
and this game is life.   *The Last Day [1939]*

5 Sometimes it crosses my mind that the things I
write here are nothing
other than images that prisoners or sailors tattoo
on their skin.   *Logbook II [1944], epigraph*

6 As pines
keep the shape of the wind
even when the wind has fled and is no longer
there,
so words
guard the shape of man
even when man has fled and is no longer there.
On Stage[2] *[1966], 6*

Douglas Sirk
1900–1987

7   The angles are the director's thoughts. The lighting is his philosophy.
From JON HALLIDAY, *Sirk on Sirk [1972]*

Adlai E[wing] Stevenson
1900–1965

8   The problem of cat versus bird is as old as time. If
we attempt to resolve it by legislation who knows but
what we may be called upon to take sides as well in the
age old problems of dog versus cat, bird versus bird,
and even bird versus worm.... The State of Illinois
and its local governing bodies already have enough
to do without trying to control feline delinquency.
*As governor of Illinois, vetoing a
bird-protection bill [April 23, 1949]*

9   Let's talk sense to the American people.
*Speech accepting the Democratic presidential
nomination [July 26, 1952]*

Thomas Wolfe
1900–1938

10   A stone, a leaf, an unfound door.
Look Homeward, Angel [1929], foreword

11   Which of us has known his brother? Which of us
has looked into his father's heart? Which of us has not
remained forever prison-pent? Which of us is not forever a stranger and alone?
Look Homeward, Angel, foreword

12   O lost, and by the wind grieved, ghost, come back
again.   *Look Homeward, Angel, foreword*

13   It'd take a guy a lifetime to know Brooklyn t'roo
and t'roo. An' even den, yuh wouldn't know it all.
Only the dead know Brooklyn t'roo an' t'roo.
Only the Dead Know Brooklyn [1935]

14   If a man has a talent and cannot use it, he has
failed. If he has a talent and uses only half of it, he
has partly failed. If he has a talent and learns somehow
to use the whole of it, he has gloriously succeeded,
and won a satisfaction and a triumph few men ever
know.
The Web and the Rock [1939], ch. 30

15   I believe that we are lost here in America, but I
believe we shall be found.
You Can't Go Home Again [1940], ch. 48

Robert Bresson
1901–1999

16   The point is not to direct someone, but to direct
oneself.   *Notes on the Cinematographer [1975]*

John Collier
1901–1980

17   Young people who need a love potion very seldom
have five thousand dollars. If they had they would not
need a love potion.   *The Chaser [1940]*

René Jules Dubos
1901–1982

18   The general formula of [ecological] management
for the future might be, think globally and act locally.
*The Wooing of Earth [1980]. Humankind
and the Earth*

---

[1]Translated by EDMUND KEELEY and PHILIP SHERRARD.
[2]Translated by WALTER KAISER.

Robert Francis
1901–1987

1 His art is eccentricity, his aim
How not to hit the mark he seems to aim at,

His passion how to avoid the obvious,
His technique how to vary the avoidance.

The others throw to be comprehended. He
Throws to be a moment misunderstood.
The Orb Weaver [1960]. Pitcher

Stuart Gorrell
1901–1963

2 Georgia, Georgia
The whole day through;
Just an old sweet song
Keeps Georgia on my mind.
Georgia on My Mind[1] [1930]

Werner Karl Heisenberg
1901–1976

3 The more precisely we determine the position [of an electron], the more imprecise is the determination of velocity at this instant, and vice versa.[2]
On the Perceptual Content of Quantum Theoretical Kinematics and Mechanics [1927]

4 Every tool carries with it the spirit by which it has been created. *Physics and Philosophy [1958]*

5 Since the measuring device has been constructed by the observer...we have to remember that what we observe is not nature in itself but nature exposed to our method of questioning.
Physics and Philosophy

Emperor Hirohito
1901–1989

6 The war situation has developed not necessarily to Japan's advantage.
Broadcast to the Japanese people announcing surrender [August 14, 1945]

7 The enemy has begun to employ a new and most cruel bomb, the power of which to do damage is, indeed, incalculable, taking the toll of many innocent lives. Should we continue to fight, it would not only result in an ultimate collapse and obliteration of the Japanese nation, but also it would lead to the total extinction of human civilization. Such being the case, how are we to save the millions of our subjects, or to atone ourselves before the hallowed spirits of our imperial ancestors?... It is according to the dictates of time and fate that we have resolved to pave the way for a grand peace for all the generations to come by enduring the unavoidable and suffering what is insufferable.
Broadcast to the Japanese people announcing surrender

C[yril] L[ionel] R[obert] James
1901–1989

8 In politics all abstract terms conceal treachery.
The Black Jacobins [1938]

9 Eminence engenders enemies.
The Black Jacobins

Jacques Lacan
1901–1981

10 The unconscious is structured like a language.
Écrits [1966]

André Malraux
1901–1976

11 The sons of torture-victims make good terrorists.
Man's Fate (La Condition Humaine) [1933]

12 One cannot create an art that speaks to men when one has nothing to say.
Man's Hope (L'Espoir) [1938]

13 The great mystery is not that we should have been thrown down here at random between the profusion of matter and that of the stars; it is that from our very prison we should draw, from our own selves, images powerful enough to deny our nothingness.
Les Noyers de l'Altenburg (The Walnut Trees of Altenburg) [1943]

14 All art is a revolt against man's fate.
The Voices of Silence (Les Voix du Silence) [1951]

15 The extermination camps, in endeavoring to turn man into a beast, intimated that it is not life alone which makes him man.
Anti-Memoirs [1967]. La Condition Humaine, sec. 2

---

[1]Music by HOAGY CARMICHAEL.

[2]Heisenberg's "uncertainty principle."

Eric Maschwitz[1]
1901–1969

1 The sigh of midnight trains in empty stations,
  Silk stockings thrown aside, dance invitations:
  Oh how the ghost of you clings!
  These foolish things
  Remind me of you.
  Spread It Around [1936]. These Foolish Things[2]

Margaret Mead
1901–1978

2   As the traveler who has once been from home is
wiser than he who has never left his own doorstep,
so a knowledge of one other culture should sharpen
our ability to scrutinize more steadily, to appreciate
more lovingly, our own.
  *Coming of Age in Samoa [1928],
  introduction*

3   We know of no culture that has said, articulately,
that there is no difference between men and women
except in the way they contribute to the creation of
the next generation.
  Male and Female [1948]

4   The mind is not sex-typed.
  Blackberry Winter [1972], ch. 5

Michael Oakeshott
1901–1990

5   Neither the truth nor the character of history
depend, in any way, upon its having some lesson to
teach us. And if ever we persuade ourselves that the
past has taught us something, we may be certain
that it is not the historical past which has been our
teacher.
  Experience and Its Modes [1933]

6   To be conservative, then, is to prefer the familiar
to the unknown, to prefer the tried to the untried,
fact to mystery, the actual to the possible, the limited
to the unbounded, the near to the distant, the sufficient to the superabundant, the convenient to the
perfect, present laughter to utopian bliss.
  On Being Conservative [1956]

7   In political activity, then, men sail a boundless and
bottomless sea; there is neither harbor for shelter
nor floor for anchorage, neither starting-place nor
appointed destination. The enterprise is to keep afloat

on an even keel; the sea is both friend and enemy; and
the seamanship consists in using the resources of a
traditional manner of behavior in order to make a
friend of every hostile occasion.
  Rationalism in Politics [1962]

8   A plan to resist all planning may be better than
its opposite, but it belongs to the same style of
politics.   *Rationalism in Politics*

Kalervo Oberg
1901–1973

9   Culture shock
  *Culture Shock and the Problem of
  Adjustment to New Cultural Environments
  [1954]*

Laura Riding
1901–1991

10   That lost literature which only death reads.
  *Collected Poems [1938]. When Love Becomes
  Words*

11 O vocables of love,
  The end of an end is an echo,
  A last cry follows a last cry.
  Finality of finality
  Is perfection's touch of folly.
  Collected Poems [1938]. O Vocables of Love

Jimmy Rushing
1901–1972

Eddie Durham
1906–1987

and

Count [William] Basie
1904–1984

12   Sent for you yesterday, and here you come today.
  Sent for You Yesterday [1938]

Ned Washington
1901–1976

13 When you wish upon a star,
  Makes no diff'rence who you are,
  Anything your heart desires will come to you.
  *Pinocchio [1940]. When You Wish Upon
  a Star*[3]

---

[1]Eric Maschwitz is often credited as Holt Marvell.
[2]Music by JACK STRACHEY and HARRY LINK.

[3]Music by LEIGH HARLINE.

Arna Bontemps
1902–1973

1 Yet what I sowed and what the orchard yields
My brother's sons are gathering stalk and root,
Small wonder then my children glean in fields
They have not sown, and feed on bitter fruit.
A Black Man Talks of Reaping [1963],
st. 3

2 Yet would we die as some have done:
Beating a way for the rising sun.
The Daybreakers [1963]

Fernand Braudel
1902–1985

3 Can there be any study of humanity, in 1946, without historians who are ambitious, conscious of their duties and of their immense powers?
The Mediterranean [1946]. Preface to the
first edition

Thomas E[dmund] Dewey
1902–1971

4 That's why it's time for a change.[1]
Campaign speech at San Francisco
[September 21, 1944]

Carlos Drummond de Andrade
1902–1987

5 In the middle of the road there was a stone
there was a stone in the middle of the road
there was a stone
in the middle of the road there was a stone.
Some Poetry [1930]. In the Middle of the
Road [2]

Erik [Homburger] Erikson
1902–1994

6 The identity crisis ... occurs in that period of the life cycle when each youth must forge for himself some central perspective and direction, some working unity, out of the effective remnants of his childhood and the hopes of his anticipated adulthood.
Young Man Luther [1958], ch. 1

---

[1]The phrase was used extensively in the campaigns of 1944, 1948, and 1952.

[2]Translated by ELIZABETH BISHOP.

Stella Gibbons
1902–1989

7 Something nasty in the woodshed.
Cold Comfort Farm [1932], ch. 8

Eric Hoffer
1902–1983

8 We can be absolutely certain only about things we do not understand. A doctrine that is understood is shorn of its strength. *The True Believer [1951]*

9 Facts are counterrevolutionary.
The Passionate State of Mind [1955]

Langston Hughes
1902–1967

10 This is the mountain standing in the way of any true Negro art in America — this urge within the race toward whiteness, the desire to pour racial individuality into the mold of American standardization, and to be as little Negro and as much American as possible.
The Negro Artist and the Racial Mountain,
in The Nation [June 23, 1926]

11 It is the duty of the younger Negro artist ... to change through the force of his art that old whispering "I want to be white," hidden in the aspirations of his people, to "Why should I want to be white? I am a Negro — and beautiful!"
The Negro Artist and the Racial Mountain

12 We build our temples for tomorrow, strong as we know how, and we stand on top of the mountain, free within ourselves.
The Negro Artist and the Racial Mountain

13 I've known rivers:
I've known rivers ancient as the world and older
than the flow of human blood in human
veins.
My soul has grown deep like the rivers.
The Negro Speaks of Rivers [1926]

14 I am a Negro:
Black as the night is black,
Black like the depths of my Africa.
Negro [1926]

15 Rest at pale evening ...
A tall slim tree ...
Night coming tenderly
Black like me. *Dream Variations [1926]*

16 Droning a drowsy syncopated tune,
Rocking back and forth to a mellow croon,

I heard a Negro play.
Down on Lenox Avenue the other night
By the pale dull pallor of an old gas light
  He did a lazy sway . . .
  He did a lazy sway . . .
To the tune o' those Weary Blues.
The Weary Blues [1926]

1 I got the Weary Blues
  And I can't be satisfied.   *The Weary Blues*

2 Life for me ain't been no crystal stair.
Mother to Son [1926]

3 I, too, sing America.
  I am the darker brother.
I, Too [1926]

4 Listen, Christ,
  You did alright in your day, I reckon —
  But that day's gone now.
  They ghosted you up a swell story, too,
  Called it Bible —
  But it's dead now.   *Goodbye Christ [1932]*

5 O, let America be America again —
  The land that never has been yet —
Let America Be America Again [1938]

6 Ordinary Negroes hadn't heard of the Negro Renaissance. And if they had, it hadn't raised their wages any.   *The Big Sea [1940]*

7 Wear it
  Like a banner
  For the proud —
  Not like a shroud.   *Color [1943]*

8 Good morning, daddy!
  Ain't you heard
  The boogie-woogie rumble
  Of a dream deferred?   *Dream Boogie [1951]*

9 What happens to a dream deferred?
    Does it dry up
    like a raisin in the sun?
    Or fester like a sore —
    And then run?
    Does it stink like rotten meat?
    Or crust and sugar over —
    like a syrupy sweet?

    Maybe it just sags
    like a heavy load.

    Or does it explode?   *Harlem [1951]*

10 As I learn from you,
   I guess you learn from me —
   although you're older — and white —
   and somewhat more free.
Theme for English B [1951]

11 Negro blood is sure powerful — because just *one* drop of black blood makes a colored man. *One* drop — you are a Negro! . . . Black is powerful.[1]
Simple Takes a Wife [1953]

12 Murmuring gently
   Over *fraises du bois,*
   "I'm so ashamed of being white."
Dinner Guest: Me [1965]

Charles A[ugustus] Lindbergh[2]
1902–1974

13 We (that's my ship and I) took off rather suddenly. We had a report somewhere around 4 o'clock in the afternoon before that the weather would be fine, so we thought we would try it.
Lindbergh's Own Story. In the New York Times [May 23, 1927]

14 I saw a fleet of fishing boats. . . . I flew down almost touching the craft and yelled at them, asking if I was on the right road to Ireland.
   They just stared. Maybe they didn't hear me. Maybe I didn't hear them. Or maybe they thought I was just a crazy fool. An hour later I saw land.
Lindbergh's Own Story. In the New York Times

15 I live only in the moment in this strange, unmortal space, crowded with beauty, pierced with danger.
The Spirit of St. Louis [1953]

Norman Maclean
1902–1990

16 In our family, there was no clear line between religion and fly fishing.
A River Runs Through It [1976]

17 Eventually, all things merge into one, and a river runs through it.   *A River Runs Through It*

18 I am haunted by waters.
A River Runs Through It

Karl Popper
1902–1994

19 The Open Society and Its Enemies
Title of book [1945]

---

[1] See Stokely Carmichael and Charles Hamilton, 850:3.

[2] In the spring of '27, something bright and alien flashed across the sky. A young Minnesotan [Lindbergh] who seemed to have had nothing to do with his generation did a heroic thing, and for a moment people set down their glasses in country clubs and speakeasies and thought of their old best dreams. — F. SCOTT FITZGERALD

1   The history of power politics is nothing but the history of international crime and mass murder.
The Open Society and Its Enemies [1945]

2   There is no history of mankind, there is only an indefinite number of histories of all kinds of aspects of human life. And one of these is the history of political power. This is elevated into the history of the world.
The Open Society and Its Enemies

3   In so far as a scientific statement speaks about reality, it must be falsifiable: and in so far as it is not falsifiable, it does not speak about reality.[1]
The Logic of Scientific Discovery, appendix to 1959 edition

4   The more we learn about the world, and the deeper our learning, the more conscious, specific, and articulate will be our knowledge of what we do not know, our knowledge of our ignorance. For this, indeed, is the main source of our ignorance — the fact that our knowledge can be only finite, while our ignorance must necessarily be infinite.
Conjectures and Refutations [1968]

Ogden Nash
1902–1971

5   Candy
Is dandy
But liquor
Is quicker.
Hard Lines [1931]. Reflections on Ice-Breaking

6   The turtle lives 'twixt plated decks
Which practically conceal its sex.
I think it clever of the turtle
In such a fix to be so fertile.
Hard Lines. The Turtle

7   The Bronx?
No, thonx!
Hard Lines. Geographical Reflection

8   I think that I shall never see
A billboard lovely as a tree.
Indeed, unless the billboards fall
I'll never see a tree at all.[2]
Happy Days [1933]. Song of the Open Road

9   There is something about a Martini,
Ere the dining and dancing begin,
And to tell you the truth,
It is not the vermouth —
I think that perhaps it's the gin.
The Primrose Path [1935]. A Drink with Something in It

10   The trouble with a kitten is
THAT
Eventually it becomes a
CAT.
The Face Is Familiar [1941]. The Kitten

11   I believe a little incompatibility is the spice of life, particularly if he has income and she is pattable.
Versus [1949]. I Do, I Will, I Have

12   How confusing the beams from memory's lamp are;
One day a bachelor, the next a grampa.
What is the secret of the trick?
How did I get so old so quick?
You Can't Get There from Here [1957]. Preface to the Past

13   Here lies my past. Good-bye I have kissed it;
Thank you, kids. I wouldn't have missed it.
You Can't Get There from Here. Preface to the Past

George Gaylord Simpson
1902–1984

14   Man is the result of a purposeless and natural process that did not have him in mind.
The Meaning of Evolution [1949]

Curt Siodmak
1902–2000

15   Even a man who's pure in heart
And says his prayers at night
May become a wolf when the wolfbane blooms
And the autumn moon is bright.
The Wolf Man [1941], film script

Stevie [Margaret Florence] Smith
1902–1971

16   I was much too far out all my life
And not waving but drowning.
Not Waving but Drowning [1957]

17   Why does my Muse only speak when she is unhappy?
She does not, I only listen when I am unhappy.
My Muse [1962]

---

[1] Popper is "varying and generalizing" Einstein's statement "In so far as the statements of mathematics speak about reality, they are not certain, and in so far as they are certain, they do not speak about reality."

[2] See Joyce Kilmer, 667:13.

John [Ernst] Steinbeck
1902–1968

1   They's movement now. People moving. We know why, an' we know how. Movin' 'cause they got to. That's why folks always move. Movin' 'cause they want somepin better'n what they got. An' that's the on'y way they'll ever git it.
The Grapes of Wrath [1939], ch. 13

2   Man, unlike any other thing organic or inorganic in the universe, grows beyond his work, walks up the stairs of his concepts, emerges ahead of his accomplishments.   *The Grapes of Wrath, 14*

3   Okie use' ta mean you was from Oklahoma. Now it means you're scum. Don't mean nothing itself, it's the way they say it.   *The Grapes of Wrath, 18*

4   Why, Tom, we're the people that live. They ain't gonna wipe us out. Why, we're the people — we go on.
The Grapes of Wrath, 20

5   A strange species we are. We can stand anything God and nature can throw at us save only plenty. If I wanted to destroy a nation, I would give it too much, and I would have it on its knees, miserable, greedy, and sick.
Letter to Adlai Stevenson
[November 5, 1959]

Meredith Willson
1902–1984

6 Ya got trouble, folks,
Right here in River City.
Trouble with a capital "T"
And that rhymes with "P"
And that stands for Pool!
The Music Man [1957]. Ya Got Trouble

Darryl F. Zanuck
1902–1979

7   Don't say yes until I finish talking.
Cited in Mel Gussow, *Don't Say Yes Until I Finish Talking [1971]*

Cesare Zavattini
1902–1989

8   [On the principles of Italian neorealism:] I believe in imagination, but I have more faith in reality, in people. I am not interested in prearranged encounters, in the drama of things that happen to come together.   *Umberto D. [1953]*

Roy Acuff
1903–1992

9 I was born in Dixie in a boomer's shack,
Just a little shanty by the railroad track,
The humming of the drivers was my lullaby
And a freight train whistle taught me how to cry.
Freight Train Blues[1] [1936]

Theodor Adorno
1903–1969

10   To write poetry after Auschwitz is barbaric.
Cultural Criticism and Society [1949]

11   For a man who no longer has a homeland, writing becomes a place to live.
Minima Moralia [1974]

Lewis Allan [Abel Meeropol]
1903–1986

12 Southern trees bear a strange fruit,
Blood on the leaves and blood at the root,
Black body swinging in the Southern breeze,
Strange fruit hanging from the poplar trees.[2]
Strange Fruit [1937]

Tallulah [Brockman] Bankhead
1903–1968

13   There is less in this than meets the eye.
Remark to Alexander Woollcott at Aglavaine and Selysette by Maurice Maeterlinck *[January 3, 1922]*

14   I'm as pure as the driven slush.   *Attributed*

15   Cocaine habit-forming? Of course not. I ought to know. I've been using it for years.
Tallulah [1952]

Bruno Bettelheim
1903–1990

16   Punishment may make us obey the orders we are given, but at best it will only teach an obedience to authority, not a self-control which enhances our self-respect.
A Good Enough Parent [1987]

---

[1]Song by John Lair.

[2]The poem was made into a song, most famously performed by Billie Holiday.

Count Galeazzo Ciano
1903–1944

1   As always, victory finds a hundred fathers but defeat is an orphan.[1]
*The Ciano Diaries, 1939–1943 [1946].
September 9, 1942*

Cyril [Vernon] Connolly
1903–1974

2   There are about forty-nine masochists to one sadist.   *The Rock Pool [1936]*

3   There is no more somber enemy of good art than the pram in the hall.
Enemies of Promise [1938]

4   Every admirer is a potential enemy.
Enemies of Promise

5   All charming people have something to conceal, usually their total dependence on the appreciation of others.   *Enemies of Promise*

6   Obesity is a mental state, a disease brought on by boredom and disappointment.
The Unquiet Grave [1945], pt. I

7   Imprisoned in every fat man a thin one is wildly signaling to be let out.[2]
The Unquiet Grave, II

8   It is closing time in the gardens of the West and from now on an artist will be judged only by the resonance of his solitude or the quality of his despair.
Editorial in Horizon [Dec. 1949–Jan. 1950]

Countee Cullen
1903–1946

9 Yet do I marvel at this curious thing:
To make a poet black, and bid him sing!
Yet Do I Marvel [1925]

10 One three centuries removed
From the scenes his fathers loved,
Spicy grove, cinnamon tree,
What is Africa to me?   *Heritage [1925]*

11 Not yet has my heart or head
In the least way realized
They and I are civilized.   *Heritage*

---

[1] There's an old saying that victory has a hundred fathers and defeat is an orphan. — JOHN F. KENNEDY, *after the debacle at the Bay of Pigs, Cuba* [April 21, 1961]

[2] Outside every fat man there was an even fatter man trying to close in. — KINGSLEY AMIS [1922–1995], *One Fat Englishman* [1963]

William Thomas Cummings
1903–1944

12   There are no atheists in the foxholes.
*Field sermon, Bataan [1942].
From CARLOS P. ROMULO, I Saw the Fall of the Philippines [1942]*

Vernon Duke [Vladimir Dukelsky]
1903–1969

13 Autumn in New York
Is often mingled with pain.
Dreamers with empty hands
May sigh for exotic lands;
It's Autumn in New York,
It's good to live it again.
Autumn in New York [1935]

Lou Gehrig
1903–1941

14   For the past two weeks, you've been reading about a bad break. Today I consider myself the luckiest man on the face of the earth.
At Yankee Stadium, July 4, 1939

Malcolm Muggeridge
1903–1990

15   As Man alone, Jesus could not have saved us; as God alone, he would not; Incarnate, he could and did.   *Jesus [1975], pt. I*

Lorine Niedecker
1903–1970

16 O my floating life
Do not save love
        for things
            Throw *things*
    to the flood
        North Central [1968]. Paean to Place

17 Nobody, nothing
        ever gave me
            greater thing

than time
        unless light
            and silence

which if intense
        makes sound
            North Central. Wintergreen Ridge

Anaïs Nin
1903–1977

1   It's all right for a woman to be, above all, human. I am a woman first of all.
The Diary of Anaïs Nin, vol. I [1966], June 1933

2   Dreams are necessary to life.
The Diary of Anaïs Nin, II [1967], June 1936 (letter to her mother)

3   Sex loses all its power and magic when it becomes explicit, mechanical, overdone, when it becomes a mechanistic obsession. It becomes a bore.
Delta of Venus [1978]

George Orwell [Eric Blair]
1903–1950

4   Clothes are powerful things. Dressed in a tramp's clothes it is very difficult, at any rate for the first day, not to feel that you are genuinely degraded.
Down and Out in Paris and London [1933]

5   I shall never again think that all tramps are drunken scoundrels, nor expect a beggar to be grateful when I give him a penny, nor be surprised if men out of work lack energy, nor subscribe to the Salvation Army, nor pawn my clothes, nor refuse a handbill, nor enjoy a meal at a smart restaurant.
Down and Out in Paris and London

6   I was born into what you might describe as the lower-upper-middle class.
The Road to Wigan Pier [1937]

7   A joke worth laughing at always has an idea behind it, and usually a subversive idea.
Charles Dickens [1940]

8   As I write, highly civilized human beings are flying overhead, trying to kill me.
The Lion and the Unicorn [1941]

9   A dirty joke is not...a serious attack upon morality, but it is a sort of mental rebellion, a momentary wish that things were otherwise.
The Art of Donald McGill [1941]

10   If liberty means anything at all it means the right to tell people what they do not want to hear.
The Freedom of the Press [1945]

11   All animals are equal, but some animals are more equal than others.
Animal Farm [1945], ch. 10

12   The great enemy of clear language is insincerity. When there is a gap between one's real and one's declared aims, one turns, as it were instinctively to long words and exhausted idioms, like a cuttlefish squirting out ink.
Politics and the English Language [1946]

13   Political language...is designed to make lies sound truthful and murder respectable, and to give an appearance of solidity to pure wind.
Politics and the English Language

14   All writers are vain, selfish, and lazy, and at the very bottom of their motives lies a mystery. Writing a book is a horrible, exhausting struggle, like a long bout of some painful illness. One would never undertake such a thing if one were not driven by some demon whom one can neither resist nor understand.
Why I Write [1948]

15   It was a bright cold day in April and the clocks were striking thirteen.
1984 [1949], opening line

16   Big Brother is watching you.
1984, pt. I, ch. 1

17   War is peace. Freedom is slavery. Ignorance is strength.
1984, I, 1

18   "Who controls the past," ran the Party slogan, "controls the future: who controls the present controls the past."
1984, I, 3

19   In the end we shall make thoughtcrime literally impossible, because there will be no words in which to express it.
1984, I, 5

20   *Doublethink* means the power of holding two contradictory beliefs in one's mind simultaneously, and accepting both of them.
1984, II, 9

21   Power is not a means; it is an end. One does not establish a dictatorship in order to safeguard a revolution; one makes the revolution in order to establish the dictatorship. The object of persecution is persecution. The object of torture is torture. The object of power is power.
1984, III, 3

22   If you want a picture of the future, imagine a boot stamping on a human face — forever.   *1984, III, 3*

23   At 50, everyone has the face he deserves.
Notebook entry, April 17, 1949

24   Saints should always be judged guilty until they are proved innocent.
Reflections on Gandhi [1949]

Raymond Queneau
1903–1976

25   The classical author who writes his tragedy observing a certain number of known rules is freer than the poet who writes down whatever comes into his head

and is slave to other rules of which he knows nothing.

Bâtons, Chiffres et Lettres [1950]

Casey [Kenneth C.] Robinson
1903–1979

1   Where's the rest of me?

Kings Row (screenplay) [1942], spoken by Ronald Reagan[1]

2   Oh, Jerry, don't ask for the moon. We have the stars.

Now Voyager (screenplay) [1942], spoken by Bette Davis

Georges Simenon
1903–1989

3   Writing is not a profession but a vocation of unhappiness.

Interview in Paris Review [1955]

Benjamin [McLane] Spock
1903–1998

4   Trust yourself. You know more than you think you do.

The Common Sense Book of Baby and Child Care [1946], ch. 1

Evelyn Waugh
1903–1966

5   I expect you'll be becoming a schoolmaster, sir. That's what most of the gentlemen does, sir, that gets sent down for indecent behavior.

Decline and Fall [1928], Prelude

6   Anyone who has been to an English public school will always feel comparatively at home in prison. It is the people brought up in the gay intimacy of the slums ... who find prison so soul destroying.

Decline and Fall, pt. III, ch. 4

7   "*What war?*" said the Prime Minister sharply. "No one has said anything to me about a war. I really think I should have been told. I'll be damned," he said defiantly, "if they shall have a war without consulting me. What's a cabinet for, if there's not more mutual confidence than that? What do they want a war for, anyway?"

Vile Bodies [1930], ch. 8

---

[1]Also the title of Reagan's autobiography [1965].

8   We will not have any Dickens today ... but tomorrow, and the day after that, and the day after that. Let us read *Little Dorrit* again.

A Handful of Dust [1934], ch. 6

9   Feather-footed through the plashy fen passes the questing vole.   *Scoop [1938], bk. I, ch. 2, sec. 1*

10   Randolph Churchill went into hospital ... to have a lung removed. It was announced that the trouble was not "malignant." ... It was a typical triumph of modern science to find the only part of Randolph that was not malignant and remove it.

Diaries [March 1964]

Nathanael West
1903–1940

11   Are you in trouble? — Do-you-need-advice? — Write-to-Miss-Lonelyhearts-and-she-will-help-you.

Miss Lonelyhearts [1933]

12   The Miss Lonelyhearts are the priests of twentieth-century America.   *Miss Lonelyhearts*

13   [On the Hollywood studio system:] A sargasso of the imagination!

The Day of the Locust [1939]

14   It is hard to laugh at the need for beauty and romance, no matter how tasteless, even horrible, the results of that are. But it is easy to sigh. Few things are sadder than the truly monstrous.

The Day of the Locust

Peter Arno
1904–1968

15   Hey, Jack, which way to Mecca?

Caption for cartoon of American tourists driving past praying Arab [1938]

16   Well, back to the old drawing board.

Caption for cartoon showing designer walking away from crashed plane [1941]

George Balanchine
1904–1983

17   Ballet is the one place where art flourishes because of a woman; woman is the goddess, the poetess, the muse. That is why I have a company with beautiful girl dancers.   *Quoted in Life [June 11, 1965]*

18   Publicity overrates everything. Picasso's overrated. I'm overrated. Even Jack Benny's overrated.

Interview, cited in BERNARD TAPER, Balanchine: A Biography [1996]

Joseph Campbell
1904–1987

1   Myth is the secret opening through which the inexhaustible energies of the cosmos pour into human cultural manifestation. Religions, philosophies, arts, the social forms of primitive and historic man, prime discoveries in science and technology, the very dreams that blister sleep, boil up from the basic, magic ring of myth.
The Hero with a Thousand Faces [1949].
Prologue

2   Follow your bliss.[1]
The Power of Myth [1988]

Salvador Dalí
1904–1989

3   The only difference between a madman and myself is that I am not mad.
Entry in Diary of a Genius [1966]

4   In order to acquire a growing and lasting respect in society, it is a good thing, if you possess great talent, to give, early in your youth, a very hard kick to the right shin of the society that you love. After that, be a snob.
Entry in Diary of a Genius

5   Take me, I am the drug; take me, I am hallucinogenic.   *Dalí by Dalí [1970]*

6   Those who do not want to imitate anything, produce nothing.   *Dalí by Dalí*

Deng Xiaoping
1904–1997

7   Yellow cat, black cat, as long as it catches mice, it is a good cat.[2]
Speech [1962]

Richard Eberhart
1904–2005

8 I stood there in the whirling summer,
My hand capped a withered heart,
And thought of China and of Greece,
Of Alexander in his tent;

Of Montaigne in his tower,
Of Saint Theresa in her wild lament.
Collected Poems, 1930–1960 [1960].
The Groundhog

9 It is what man does not know of God
Composes the visible poem of the world.
Collected Poems, 1930–1960. On a Squirrel
Crossing the Road in Autumn in New
England

Witold Gombrowicz
1904–1969

10   Spirit is born of the imitation of spirit and a writer must pretend to be a writer in order finally to become a writer.
Diary, Vol. 1 [entry from 1953]

11   An idea abstracted from man does not fully exist. . . . There is no word that is not also flesh.
Diary [entry from 1954]

12   Do you want to know who you are? Don't ask. Act.   *Diary, Vol. 2 [entry from 1959]*

Cary Grant
[Archibald Alexander Leach]
1904–1986

13   Everybody wants to be Cary Grant. Even *I* want to be Cary Grant.   *Attributed*

Graham Greene
1904–1991

14   There is always one moment in childhood when the door opens and lets the future in.
The Power and the Glory [1940], pt. I, ch. 1

15   It was for this world that Christ had died: the more evil you saw and heard about you, the greater glory lay around the death; it was too easy to die for what was good or beautiful, for home or children or a civilization — it needed a God to die for the half-hearted and the corrupt.
The Power and the Glory, II, 1

16   When you visualized a man or a woman carefully, you could always begin to feel pity. . . . Hate was just a failure of imagination.
The Power and the Glory, II, 3

17   One can't love humanity. One can only love people.
The Ministry of Fear [1943], bk. II, ch. 2

---

[1]This quotation comes from a longer sentence of CAMPBELL's: If you do follow your bliss, you put yourself on a kind of track that has been there all the while, waiting for you, and the life that you ought to be living is the one you are living.

[2]Translated by ROSS TERRILL.
Deng identified this as "a saying from Sichuan Province."

1   In human relations kindness and lies are worth a thousand truths.
        The Heart of the Matter [1948], bk. I, pt. I, ch. 2, sec. iv

2   No human being can really understand another, and no one can arrange another's happiness.
        The Heart of the Matter, II, III, 1, i

3   He entered the territory of lies without a passport for return.
        The Heart of the Matter, II, III, 2, i

4   In childhood all books are books of divination, telling us about the future, and like the fortune-teller who sees a long journey in the cards or death by water they influence the future. I suppose that is why books excited us so much. What do we ever get nowadays from reading to equal the excitement and the revelation in those first fourteen years?
        The Lost Childhood and Other Essays [1951]

5   Our worst enemies here are not the ignorant and the simple, however cruel; our worst enemies are the intelligent and corrupt.
        The Human Factor [1978], pt. III, ch. 3

Moss Hart
1904–1961

6   The only credential the city [New York] asked was the boldness to dream. For those who did, it unlocked its gates and its treasures, not caring who they were or where they came from.
        Act One [1959], pt. II

Christopher [William Bradshaw] Isherwood
1904–1986

7   I am a camera with its shutter open, quite passive, recording, not thinking. Recording the man shaving at the window opposite and the woman in the kimono washing her hair. Some day, all this will have to be developed, carefully printed, fixed.
        Goodbye to Berlin [1939], A Berlin Diary

George F[rost] Kennan
1904–2005

8   The main element of any United States policy toward the Soviet Union must be that of a long-term, patient but firm and vigilant containment of Russian expansive tendencies.
        The Sources of Soviet Conduct, in Foreign Affairs [July 1947]

9   A war regarded as inevitable or even probable, and therefore much prepared for, has a very good chance of eventually being fought.
        The Cloud of Danger [1977], ch. 13

A[bbott] J[oseph] Liebling
1904–1963

10   A boxer, like a writer, must stand alone.
        The Sweet Science [1956]. Introduction

11   When I watch a fight, I like to study one boxer's problem, solve it, and then communicate my solution vocally.
        The Sweet Science. Boxing with the Naked Eye

12   Freedom of the press is guaranteed only to those who own one.
        Do You Belong in Journalism? in The New Yorker [May 14, 1960]

13   Louisiana politics is of an intensity and complexity that are matched, in my experience, only in the republic of Lebanon.
        The Earl of Louisiana [1961]

14   No sane man can afford to dispense with debilitating pleasures; no ascetic can be considered reliably sane. Hitler was the archetype of the abstemious man.
        Between Meals [1962]. La Nautique

15   I can write faster than anybody who can write better, and I can write better than anybody who can write faster.   *Attributed*

Pablo Neruda
[Neftalí Ricardo Reyes y Basualto]
1904–1973

16   there are so many people dead
        and so many sea-walls that the red sun used to split,
        and so many heads that the boats hit,
        and so many hands that have closed around kisses,
        and so many things I would like to forget.
        Residencia en la Tierra (Residence on Earth) [1925–1935]. No Hay Olvido (Sonata) [There Is No Forgetfulness (Sonata)][1]

17   Treacherous
        generals:
        look at my dead house,
        look at broken Spain.
        Residencia en la Tierra (Residence on Earth), series III [1947]. Explico Algunas Cosas (I Explain a Few Things)[2]

---

[1]Translated by ROBERT BLY.
[2]Translated by DONALD D. WALSH.

1 But from each hollow of Spain
Spain comes forth.
> *Residencia en la Tierra, III. Explico*
> *Algunas Cosas*

2 But from each crime are born bullets
that will one day seek out in you
where the heart lies.
> *Residencia en la Tierra, III. Explico*
> *Algunas Cosas*

3 Come up with me, American love.

Kiss these secret stones with me.
The torrential silver of the Urubamba
makes the pollen fly to its golden cup.
The hollow of the bindweed's maze,
the petrified plant, the inflexible garland,
soar above the silence of these mountain coffers.
> *Canto General (General Song) [1950].*
> *Alturas de Macchu Picchu*[1]
> *(The Heights of Macchu Picchu)*

4 What a great language I have, it's a fine language
we inherited from the fierce Conquistadors. . . . They
carried everything off and left us everything. . . .
They left us the words.
> *Confieso Que He Vivido: Memorias*
> *(Memoirs)*[2] *[1974], ch. 2*

5 I continue to work with the materials I have, the
materials I am made of. With feelings, beings, books,
events, and battles, I am omnivorous. I would like to
swallow the whole earth. I would like to drink the
whole sea. *Confieso Que He Vivido: Memorias, 11*

J[ulius] Robert Oppenheimer
1904–1967

6 It did not take atomic weapons to make man want
peace, a peace that would last. But the atomic bomb
was the turn of the screw. It has made the prospect
of future war unendurable.
> *The Atomic Bomb and College Education*
> *[1946]*

7 In some sort of crude sense which no vulgarity, no
humor, no overstatement can quite extinguish, the
physicists have known sin; and this is a knowledge
which they cannot lose.
> *Physics in the Contemporary World, lecture at*
> *Massachusetts Institute of Technology*
> *[November 25, 1947]*

8 We knew the world would not be the same. A few
people laughed, a few people cried. Most people were

silent. I remembered the line from the Hindu scripture, the *Bhagavad Gita*. . . . "I am become Death,
the destroyer of worlds." I suppose we all thought
that, one way or another.
> *Recalling the explosion of the first atomic*
> *bomb near Alamogordo, New Mexico [July*
> *16, 1945].*[3] *From* Len Giovanitti *and* Fred
> Freed, *The Decision to Drop the Bomb [1965]*

S[idney] J[oseph] Perelman
1904–1979

9 Outside of a spring lamb trotting into a slaughter-
house, there is nothing in the animal kingdom as
innocent and foredoomed as the new purchaser of a
country place. The moment he scratches his signature
on the deed, it is open season and no limit to the bag.
> *Acres and Pains [1947], ch. 2*

10 There are nineteen words in Yiddish that convey
gradations of disparagement from a mild, fluttery
helplessness to a state of downright, irreconcilable
brutishness. All of them can be usefully employed to
pinpoint the kind of individuals I write about.
> *Interview in Paris Review [1964]*

Dr. Seuss [Theodor Seuss Geisel]
1904–1991

11 I meant what I said
And I said what I meant . . .[4]
An elephant's faithful
One hundred per cent!
> *Horton Hatches the Egg [1940]*

12 You will see something new.
Two things. And I call them
Thing One and Thing Two.
> *The Cat in the Hat [1957]*

Isaac Bashevis Singer
1904–1991

13 Where was He, the jealous and vengeful God, now
that America and England and Russia were rebuilding
Germany? And what was He doing, "He who settest
free the captives," for those millions whom Stalin had
imprisoned in slave-labor camps? No, even if there
was a God, Jacob Anfang would not serve Him.

---

[1]Translated by Nathaniel Tarn.

[2]Translated by Hardie St. Martin.

---

[3]Oppenheimer also recalled another line from the *Bhagavad Gita*,
"If the radiance of a thousand suns. . . ." See 84:13.

Now we are all sons of bitches. — Kenneth Tompkins Bainbridge
[1904–1996]. Oppenheimer later remarked that this was "the best
thing anyone said after the test."

[4]Ellipses are in the original text.

If there was a God, He was probably a cosmic Hitler who for His honor and His greatness was prepared to torture whole generations, entire peoples.

Shadows on the Hudson [1957–1958]

1   Buildings will collapse, power plants will stop generating electricity. Generals will drop atomic bombs on their own populations. Mad revolutionaries will run in the streets, crying fantastic slogans. I have often thought it would begin in New York. This metropolis has all the symptoms of a mind gone berserk.

The Cafeteria[1] [1986]

2   It seems that the analysis of character is the highest human entertainment. And literature does it, unlike gossip, without mentioning real names.

Isaac Bashevis Singer Talks … About Everything, interview with Richard Burgin in the New York Times Magazine [November 26, 1978]

3   There is a quiet humor in Yiddish and a gratitude for every day of life, every crumb of success, each encounter of love.…In a figurative way, Yiddish is the wise and humble language of us all, the idiom of a frightened and hopeful humanity.

Nobel lecture, Stockholm [December 8, 1978]

4   Children don't read to find their identity. They don't read to free themselves of guilt, to quench the thirst for rebellion, or to get rid of alienation. They have no use for psychology. They detest sociology.…They still believe in good, the family, angels, devils, witches, goblins, logic, clarity, punctuation and other such obsolete stuff.

Address at Nobel Prize banquet, Stockholm [December 10, 1978]

Betty [Wehner] Smith
1904–1972

5   There's a tree that grows in Brooklyn. Some people call it the Tree of Heaven. No matter where its seed falls, it makes a tree which struggles to reach the sky.

A Tree Grows in Brooklyn [1943]

Raymond Aron
1905–1983

6   [On the Cold War:] Peace impossible, war improbable.[2]

Le Grand Schisme (The Great Schism) [1948]

7   Communist interpretation is never wrong. Logicians will object in vain that a theory which exempts itself from all refutations escapes from the order of truth.

L'Opium des Intellectuels (The Opium of the Intellectuals) [1955]

Marc Blitzstein
1905–1964

8 That's a storm that's going to last until
The final wind blows … and when the wind blows,
The Cradle Will Rock.

The Cradle Will Rock (libretto) [1937]

Elias Canetti
1905–1994

9   Some sentences release their poison only after years.

Notebook entry [1942] in The Human Province [1973]

10   People who cannot find their way out of history are lost, and so are their nations.

Notebook entry [1943] in The Human Province

11   The unity of a nation consists mainly in its being able to act, when necessary, like a single paranoiac.

Notebook entry [1945] in The Human Province

Christian Dior
1905–1957

12   In a century which attempts to tear the heart out of every mystery, fashion guards its secret well, and is the best possible proof that there is still magic abroad.

Dior by Dior [1957]

Dorothy Fields
1905–1974

13 I can't give you anything but love, baby,
That's the only thing I've plenty of, baby.

Blackbirds of 1928 [1928]. I Can't Give You Anything but Love

14 Grab your coat and get your hat,
Leave your worry on the doorstep,
Just direct your feet
To the sunny side of the street.

On the Sunny Side of the Street [1930]

---

[1]Translated by ISAAC BASHEVIS SINGER and DOROTHEA STRAUS.

[2]Paix impossible, guerre improbable.

1 A fine romance, with no kisses!
  A fine romance, my friend, this is!
  We should be like a couple of hot tomatoes,
  But you're as cold as yesterday's mashed potatoes.
  Swing Time [1936]. A Fine Romance

2 Pick yourself up,
  Dust yourself off,
  Start all over again.
  Swing Time. Pick Yourself Up

J[ames] William Fulbright
1905–1995

3   When public men indulge themselves in abuse, when they deny others a fair trial, when they resort to innuendo and insinuation, to libel, scandal, and suspicion, then our democratic society is outraged, and democracy is baffled. It has no apparatus to deal with the boor, the liar, the lout, and the antidemocrat in general.
  Address to the U.S. Senate [February 2, 1954]

4   A policy that can be accurately, though perhaps not prudently, defined as one of "peaceful coexistence."
  Speech in the Senate [March 27, 1964]

5   The citizen who criticizes his country is paying it an implied tribute.
  Speech to the American Newspaper Publishers Association [April 28, 1966]

6   The attitude above all others which I feel sure is no longer valid is the arrogance of power, the tendency of great nations to equate power with virtue and major responsibilities with a universal mission.
  The Arrogance of Power [1967]

Greta Garbo
[Greta Gustafson]
1905–1990

7   I want to be alone.[1]   *Attributed*

Dag Hammarskjöld
1905–1961

8 The longest journey
  Is the journey inwards
  Of him who has chosen his destiny.
  Markings [1964]

---

[1]Garbo maintained that her most famous remark was always misquoted.... "I only said, 'I want to be *let* alone!'" — JOHN BAINBRIDGE, *in Life* [January 24, 1955]

Lillian Hellman
1905–1984

9   There are people who eat the earth and eat all the people on it like in the Bible with the locusts. And other people who stand around and watch them eat it.
  The Little Foxes[2] [1939], act III

10   For every man who lives without freedom, the rest of us must face the guilt.
  Watch on the Rhine [1941], act II

11   I am most willing to answer all questions about myself...But...I am not willing, now or in the future, to bring bad trouble to people who, in my past association with them, were completely innocent of any talk or any action that was disloyal or subversive.
  Letter to the House Committee on Un-American Activities [May 19, 1952]

12   I cannot and will not cut my conscience to fit this year's fashions.
  Letter to the House Committee on Un-American Activities

13   People change and forget to tell each other.
  Toys in the Attic [1960]

Patrick Kavanagh
1905–1967

14 Patrick Maguire, the old peasant, can neither be
      damned nor glorified:
  The graveyard in which he will lie will be just a deep-
      drilled potato-field
  Where the seed gets no chance to come through
  To the fun of the sun.
  The tongue in his mouth is the root of a yew.
  The Great Hunger [1942]

Arthur Koestler
1905–1983

15   One may not regard the world as a sort of metaphysical brothel for emotions.
  Darkness at Noon[3] [1941]. The Second Hearing

16   The definition of the individual was: a multitude of one million divided by one million.
  Darkness at Noon. The Grammatical Fiction

17   The Yogi and the Commissar
  Title of book [1945]

---

[2]See *Song of Solomon 2:15*, 24:10.
[3]Translated by DAPHNE HARDY.

Stanley Kunitz
1905–2006

1 I recognize the gods' capricious hand
And write this poem for money, rage, and love.
The Thief [1958]

2 The thing that eats the heart is mostly heart.
*The Thing That Eats the Heart [1958],
last line*

3 *Liebchen,*
with whom should I quarrel
except in the hiss of love,
that harsh, irregular flame? *The Quarrel [1979]*

4 In every house of marriage
there's room for an interpreter. *Route Six [1979]*

5 After all,
we are partners in this land,
co-signers of a covenant.
At my touch the wild
braid of creation
trembles.
*Next-to-Last Things [1985]. The Snakes of
September*

6 You have become like us,
disgraced and mortal.
Next-to-Last Things. The Wellfleet Whale

Phyllis McGinley
1905–1977

7 Meek-eyed parents hasten down the ramps
To greet their offspring, terrible from camps.
Ode to the End of Summer

8 Prince, I warn you, under the rose,
Time is the thief you cannot banish.
These are my daughters, I suppose.
But where in the world did the children vanish?
Ballade of Lost Objects [1954]

Barnett Newman
1905–1970

9 Instead of making *cathedrals* out of Christ, man,
or "life," we are making it out of ourselves, out of our
own feelings. *The Sublime Is Now [1948]*

John O'Hara
1905–1970

10 An artist is his own fault.
*The Portable F. Scott Fitzgerald [1945],
introduction*

Anthony Powell
1905–2000

11 Parents — especially step-parents — are sometimes
a bit of a disappointment to their children. They don't
fulfill the promise of their early years.
A Buyer's Market [1952]

12 Self-love seems so often unrequited.
The Acceptance World [1955]

13 Books Do Furnish a Room *Title of book [1971]*

Ayn Rand
1905–1982

14 Civilization is the progress toward a society of
privacy. The savage's whole existence is public, ruled
by the laws of his tribe. Civilization is the process of
setting man free from men.
The Fountainhead [1943]

15 Great men can't be ruled. *The Fountainhead*

16 Kill reverence and you've killed the hero in man.
The Fountainhead

17 I would give the greatest sunset in the world for
one sight of New York's skyline.
The Fountainhead

18 If you ask me to name the proudest distinction of
Americans — I would choose — because it contains
all the others — the fact that they were the people
who created the phrase "to *make* money." No
other language or nation had ever used these words
before. . . . Americans were the first to understand that
wealth has to be created. *Atlas Shrugged [1957]*

Jean Paul Sartre
1905–1980

19 Everything is gratuitous, this garden, this city and
myself. When you suddenly realize it, it makes you
feel sick and everything begins to drift . . . that's
nausea. *La Nausée (Nausea) [1938]*

20 Man is not the sum of what he has but the totality
of what he does not yet have, of what he might have.
Situations [1939], I

21 We do not do what we want and yet we are
responsible for what we are — that is the fact.
Situations, II

22 Man can will nothing unless he has first understood that he must count on no one but himself; that
he is alone, abandoned on earth in the midst of his
infinite responsibilities, without help, with no other

aim than the one he sets himself, with no other destiny than the one he forges for himself on this earth.

> *L'Être et le Néant (Being and Nothingness) [1943]*

1   Man is a useless passion.   *L'Être et le Néant*

2   I am condemned to be free.   *L'Être et le Néant*

3   Hell is — other people![1]

> *Huis-Clos (No Exit) [1944], sc. v*

4   Existence precedes essence.

> *Existentialism Is a Humanism [1946]*

5   Words are loaded pistols.

> *Literature and Existentialism [1949]*

6   I was escaping from Nature and at last becoming myself, that Other whom I was aspiring to be in the eyes of others.   *Les Mots[2] (The Words) [1964]*

7   If I relegate impossible Salvation to the prop-room, what remains? A whole man, composed of all men and as good as all of them and no better than any.   *Les Mots*

8   A writer must refuse to allow himself to be transformed into an institution.

> *Declaration refusing the Nobel Prize [October 22, 1964]*

9   I don't need God in order to love my neighbor.

> *Quoted in* SIMONE DE BEAUVOIR, *La Cérémonie des Adieux [1981] (English translation, Adieux: A Farewell to Sartre [1984])*

Wallace Stanley Sayre
1905–1972

10   In any dispute, the intensity of feeling is inversely proportional to the value of the stakes at issue. That is why academic politics are so bitter.   *Saying[3]*

Sir C[harles] P[ercy] Snow
1905–1980

11   Literary intellectuals at one pole — at the other scientists.... Between the two a gulf of mutual incomprehension.

> *The Two Cultures and the Scientific Revolution [1959]*

---

[1] L'enfer, c'est les Autres.

[2] Translated by BERNARD FRECHTMAN.

[3] "Sayre's Law" is sometimes cited as: "The politics of the university are so intense because the stakes are so low." Often but mistakenly attributed to HENRY A. KISSINGER.

12   A good many times I have been present at gatherings of people who, by the standards of the traditional culture, are thought highly educated and who have with considerable gusto been expressing their incredulity at the illiteracy of scientists. Once or twice I have been provoked and have asked the company how many of them could describe the Second Law of Thermodynamics. The response was cold: it was also negative. Yet I was asking something which is about the scientific equivalent of: *Have you read a work of Shakespeare's?*

> *The Two Cultures and the Scientific Revolution*

Diana Trilling
1905–1996

13   We are all of us, men and women both, the creatures of culture: we do and feel what our societies ask us to, and the demands put upon us are not always consistent or precisely correlated with biology.

> *Female Biology in a Male Culture [1970]*

Lionel Trilling
1905–1976

14   In the United States at this time liberalism is not only the dominant but even the sole intellectual tradition.

> *The Liberal Imagination [1950]. Preface*

15   The poet is in command of his fantasy, while it is exactly the mark of the neurotic that he is possessed by his fantasy.

> *The Liberal Imagination. Freud and Literature*

16   There is no connection between the political ideas of our educated class and the deep places of the imagination.

> *The Liberal Imagination. The Function of the Little Magazine*

17   Occasions are rare when the best literature becomes, as it were, the folk literature, and generally speaking literature has always been carried on within small limits and under great difficulties.

> *The Liberal Imagination. The Function of the Little Magazine*

Dalton Trumbo
1905–1976

18   You plan the wars you masters of men plan the wars and point the way and we will point the gun.

> *Johnny Got His Gun [1939]*

Robert Penn Warren
1905–1989

1   The end of man is knowledge, but there's one thing he can't know. He can't know whether knowledge will save him or kill him. He will be killed, all right, but he can't know whether he is killed because of the knowledge which he has got or because of the knowledge which he hasn't got and which if he had it, would save him.   *All the King's Men [1946]*

2 Long ago, in Kentucky, I, a boy, stood
By a dirt road, in first dark, and heard
The great geese hoot northward.

I could not see them, there being no moon
And the stars sparse. I heard them.

I did not know what was happening in my heart.
    Audubon: A Vision [1969]

Hannah Arendt
1906–1975

3   Hell in the most literal sense was embodied by those types of camps perfected by the Nazis, in which the whole of life was thoroughly and systematically organized with a view to the greatest possible torment.
    The Origins of Totalitarianism [1951], ch. 12

4   Totalitarianism strives not toward despotic rule over men, but toward a system in which men are superfluous.   *The Origins of Totalitarianism, 12*

5   Bureaucracy, the rule of nobody.
    The Human Condition [1958], ch. 6

6   It was as though in those last minutes he [Eichmann][1] was summing up the lessons that this long course in human wickedness had taught us — the lesson of the fearsome, word-and-thought-defying *banality of evil.*
    Eichmann in Jerusalem: A Report on the Banality of Evil [1963], ch. 15

7   No punishment has ever possessed enough power of deterrence to prevent the commission of crimes. On the contrary, whatever the punishment, once a specific crime has appeared for the first time, its reappearance is more likely than its initial emergence could have been.
    Eichmann in Jerusalem: A Report on the Banality of Evil, epilogue

8   Where all, or almost all, are guilty, nobody is.
    Eichmann in Jerusalem: A Report on the Banality of Evil, epilogue

---

[1]To sum it all up, I must say I regret nothing. — [Karl] Adolf Eichmann [1906–1962], *while awaiting trial in Israel*

9   The hypocrite's crime is that he bears false witness against himself. What makes it so plausible to assume that hypocrisy is the vice of vices is that integrity can indeed exist under the cover of all other vices except this one. Only crime and the criminal, it is true, confront us with the perplexity of radical evil; but only the hypocrite is really rotten to the core.
    On Revolution [1963], ch. 2

10   The climax of terror is reached when the police state begins to devour its own children, when yesterday's executioner becomes today's victim.
    On Violence [1970]

Richard Armour
1906–1989

11 Shake and shake
The catsup bottle.
None will come,
And then a lot'll.   *Going to Extremes [1949]*

Samuel Beckett
1906–1989

12   Language is best used where it is most efficiently abused.   *Letter to Axel Kaun [July 9, 1937]*

13   The sun shone, having no alternative, on the nothing new.   *Murphy [1938]*

14   That's how it is on this bitch of an earth.
    Waiting for Godot [1952], act I

15   Nothing happens, nobody comes, nobody goes, it's awful!   *Waiting for Godot, I*

16   He can't think without his hat.
    Waiting for Godot, I

17   We are all born mad. Some remain so.
    Waiting for Godot, II

18   *Estragon:* I can't go on like this.
Vladimir: That's what you think.
    Waiting for Godot, II

19   What I'd like now is to speak of the things that are left, say my goodbyes, finish dying.   *Molloy [1955]*

20   Then I went back into the house and wrote, It is midnight. The rain is beating on the windows. It was not midnight. It was not raining.
    Molloy, closing words

21   *Clov:* Do you believe in the life to come?
Hamm: Mine was always like that.
    Endgame [1957]

22   Nothing is funnier than unhappiness.
    Endgame

1 Where I am, I don't know, I'll never know, in the silence you don't know, you must go on, I can't go on, I'll go on.
The Unnamable [1959], closing words

2 I'm not unhappy enough. [*Pause.*] That was always my unhap, unhappy, but not unhappy enough.
Rough for Theatre I [1979]

3 Ever tried. Ever failed. No matter. Try again. Fail again. Fail better.
Worstward Ho [1983]

John Betjeman
1906–1984

4 He rose, and he put down The Yellow Book.
He staggered — and, terrible-eyed,
He brushed past the palms on the staircase
And was helped to a hansom outside.
The Arrest of Oscar Wilde at the Cadogan Hotel [1937], st. 9

5 Gracious Lord, oh bomb the Germans.
Spare their women for Thy Sake,
And if that is not too easy
We will pardon Thy Mistake.
But, gracious Lord, whate'er shall be,
Don't let anyone bomb me.
In Westminster Abbey [1940]

Dietrich Bonhoeffer
1906–1945

6 When Christ calls a man, he bids him come and die.
The Cost of Discipleship [1937]

7 Cheap grace is the deadly enemy of our Church.
The Cost of Discipleship

William J[oseph] Brennan, Jr.
1906–1997

8 All ideas having even the slightest redeeming social importance — unorthodox ideas, controversial ideas, even ideas hateful to the prevailing climate of opinion — have the full protection of the guaranties.... But implicit in the history of the First Amendment is the rejection of obscenity as utterly without redeeming social importance.
Roth v. United States [1957]

9 Debate on public issues should be uninhibited, robust, and wide open, and that ... may well include vehement, caustic, and sometimes unpleasantly sharp attacks on government and public officials.
New York Times Co. v. Sullivan [1964]

10 The chilling effect upon the exercise of First Amendment rights may derive from the fact of the prosecution, unaffected by prospects of its success or failure.
Dombrowski v. Pfister [1965]

11 If the right of privacy means anything, it is the right of the individual, married or single, to be free from unwarranted governmental intrusion into matters so fundamentally affecting a person as the decision whether to bear or beget a child.
Eisenstadt v. Baird [1972]

12 Our nation has had a long and unfortunate history of sex discrimination . . . rationalized by an attitude of "romantic paternalism" which, in practical effect, put women not on a pedestal, but in a cage.
Frontiero v. Richardson [1973]

13 We current Justices read the Constitution in the only way that we can: as Twentieth Century Americans.... For the genius of the Constitution rests not in any static meaning it might have had in a world that is dead and gone, but in the adaptability of its great principles to cope with current problems and current needs.
Speech, Washington, D.C. [October 12, 1985]

Lord Buckley [Richard Myrle Buckley]
1906–1960

14 But I'm gonna put a cat on you was the coolest, grooviest, swingin'est, wailin'est, strongest, swingin'est cat that ever stomped on this jumpin' green sphere. And they called this here cat The Nazz.
The Parabolic Revelations of the Late Lord Buckley, LP [1952]. The Nazz

15 Hipsters, flipsters, and finger-poppin' daddies,
Knock me your lobes,
I came to lay Caesar out,
Not to hip you to him.
The bad jazz that a cat blows
Wails long after he's cut out,
The groovy is often stashed with their frames.
Hipsters, Flipsters, and Finger Poppin' Daddies, Knock Me Your Lobes, LP [1955]. Marc Antony's Funeral Oration

William Empson
1906–1984

16 Slowly the poison the whole blood stream fills.
It is not the effort nor the failure tires.
The waste remains, the waste remains and kills.
Poems [1935]. Missing Dates

17 Imagine then, by miracle, with me,
(Ambiguous gifts, as what gods give must be)

What could not possibly be there,
And learn a style from a despair.
                              Poems. This Last Pain

1   Life involves maintaining oneself between contradictions that can't be solved by analysis.
                              Note to the poem Bacchus [1940]

John Huston
1906–1987

2   Badges? We ain't got no badges. We don't need no badges. I don't have to show you any stinking badges!
The Treasure of the Sierra Madre (screenplay) [1948], spoken by Alfonso Bedoya[1]

John Huston
1906–1987
and
Ben Maddow
1909–1992

3   Crime is only a left-handed form of human endeavor.
The Asphalt Jungle (screenplay) [1950], spoken by Louis Calhern

Philip Johnson
1906–2005

4   You cannot not know history.   *Maxim*

Charles Lederer
1906–1976

5   I bring you a warning — every one of you listening to my voice. Tell the world, tell this to everybody wherever they are: *watch the skies*, everywhere, keep looking — *keep watching the skies!*
The Thing (screenplay) [1951]

6   I always say a kiss on the hand might feel very good, but a diamond tiara lasts forever.
Gentlemen Prefer Blondes (screenplay) [1953], spoken by Marilyn Monroe

Curtis [Emerson] LeMay
1906–1990

7   My solution to the problem [of North Vietnam] would be to tell them frankly that they've got

to draw in their horns and stop their aggression, or we're going to bomb them back into the Stone Age.
Mission with LeMay [1965]

Oscar Levant
1906–1972

8   Strip away the phoney tinsel of Hollywood and you find the real tinsel underneath.
Quoted in Alvah Cecil Bessie's Inquisition in Eden [1965]

9   Marriage is a triumph of habit over hate.
Memoirs of an Amnesiac [1965]

Anne Morrow Lindbergh
1906–2001

10   The wave of the future is coming and there is no fighting it.
The Wave of the Future [1940]

11   I . . . understand why the saints were rarely married women. I am convinced it has nothing inherently to do, as I once supposed, with chastity or children. It has to do primarily with distractions. . . . Woman's normal occupations in general run counter to creative life, or contemplative life or saintly life.
Gift from the Sea [1955], ch. 2

12   By and large, mothers and housewives are the only workers who do not have regular time off. They are the great vacationless class.
Gift from the Sea, 3

Clifford Odets
1906–1963

13   This is your life and mine! It's skull and bones every incha the road! Christ, we're dyin' by inches!
Waiting for Lefty [1935]

14   Go out and fight so life shouldn't be printed on dollar bills.
Awake and Sing! [1935]

15   I'm no spring chicken. The clock goes and Bessie goes. Only my machinery can't be fixed.
Awake and Sing!

16   We could have made beautiful music together.
The General Died at Dawn (screenplay) [1936]

---

[1]See B. Traven, 689:4.

1 A job is a home to a homeless man.
The Country Girl [1950]

Clifford Odets
1906–1963
and
Ernest Lehman
1915–2005

2 I'd hate to take a bite out of you; you're a cookie full of arsenic.
Sweet Smell of Success (screenplay) [1957], spoken by Burt Lancaster

3 I don't want tips from the kitty. I'm in the big game with the big players. My experience I can give you in a nutshell, and I didn't dream it in a dream either. Dog eat dog. In brief: from now on the best of everything is good enough for me.
Sweet Smell of Success (screenplay), spoken by Tony Curtis

4 My right hand hasn't seen my left hand in thirty years.
Sweet Smell of Success (screenplay), spoken by Burt Lancaster

5 You're dead, son. Get yourself buried.[1]
Sweet Smell of Success (screenplay), spoken by Burt Lancaster

Satchel [Leroy] Paige
c. 1906–1982

6 Avoid fried meats which angry up the blood. If your stomach disputes you, lie down and pacify it with cool thoughts. Keep the juices flowing by jangling around gently as you move. Go very light on the vices, such as carrying on in society. The social ramble ain't restful. Avoid running at all times. Don't look back. Something might be gaining on you.
How to Stay Young [1953]

Harold Rosenberg
1906–1978

7 The canvas began to appear to one American painter after another as an arena in which to act — rather than as a space in which to reproduce, redesign, analyze, or "express" an object, actual or imagined. What was to go on the canvas was not a picture but an event.
Art News [1952]

8 Action Painting has to do with self-creation or self-definition or self-transcendence; but this

---

[1]See George S. Kaufman and Edna Ferber, 685:1.

dissociates it from self-expression, which assumes the acceptance of the ego as it is, with its wound and its magic.
Jackson Pollock exhibition catalogue [1958]

George Sanders
1906–1972

9 Dear World, I am leaving you because I am bored. I feel I have lived long enough. I am leaving you with your worries in this sweet cesspool. Good luck.
Suicide note, April 25, 1972

Jim Thompson
1906–1977

10 The darkness and myself. Everything else was gone. And the little that was left of me was going, faster and faster.
Savage Night [1953]

Laurens Van der Post
1906–1996

11 Life is its own journey, presupposes its own change and movement, and one tries to arrest them at one's eternal peril.
Venture to the Interior [1951], pt. III, ch. 12

Elmer Wheeler
1906–1968

12 Don't sell the steak; sell the sizzle. It is the sizzle that sells the steak and not the cow, although the cow is, of course, mighty important.
Principle number 1 of salesmanship [c. 1936]

Billy Wilder
1906–2002
and
Charles Brackett
1892–1969

13 We didn't need dialogue. We had faces.
Sunset Boulevard (screenplay) [1950], spoken by Gloria Swanson

14 All right, Mr. DeMille, I'm ready for my close-up.
Sunset Boulevard (screenplay), spoken by Gloria Swanson

Billy Wilder
1906–2002

and

Raymond Chandler
1888–1959

1   How could I have known that murder can sometimes smell like honeysuckle?
*Double Indemnity (screenplay) [1944],
spoken by Fred MacMurray*

Billy Wilder
1906–2002

and

I. A. L. Diamond
[Itzek Domnici]
1920–1988

2   Look how she moves! It's like Jell-O on springs.
*Some Like It Hot (screenplay) [1959],
spoken by Jack Lemmon about Marilyn
Monroe*

Henny Youngman
1906–1998

3   Take my wife . . . please!   *Comedy line*

W[ystan] H[ugh] Auden[1]
1907–1973

4 Let us honor if we can
The vertical man
Though we value none
But the horizontal one.

      Epigraph for Poems [1930]

5 Sir, no man's enemy, forgiving all
But will his negative inversion, be prodigal.

      Sir, No Man's Enemy [1930]

6 Harrow the house of the dead; look shining at
New styles of architecture, a change of heart.

      Sir, No Man's Enemy

7 The greater the love, the more false to its object,
Not to be born is the best for man;
After the kiss comes the impulse to throttle,
Break the embraces, dance while you can.

      O Who Can Ever Gaze His Fill [1936]

---

[1]Dates of composition follow *Collected Poems, ed.* Edward
Mendelsohn [London, 1991].

8 The stars are dead. The animals will not look.
We are left alone with our day, and the time is short,
    and History to the defeated
May say Alas but cannot help or pardon.

      Spain [1937]

9 O plunge your hands in water,
Plunge them in up to the wrist;
Stare, stare in the basin
And wonder what you've missed.

The glacier knocks in the cupboard,
The desert sighs in the bed,
And the crack in the tea cup opens
A lane to the land of the dead.

      *As I Walked Out One Evening [1937],
st. 10, 11*

10 Lay your sleeping head, my love,
Human on my faithless arm.   *Lullaby [1937], st. 1*

11 Every farthing of the cost,
All the dreaded cards foretell,
Shall be paid, but from this night
Not a whisper, not a thought,
Not a kiss nor look be lost.   *Lullaby, st. 3*

12 About suffering they were never wrong,
The Old Masters: how well they understood
Its human position; how it takes place
While someone else is eating or opening a window
Or just walking dully along.

      Musée des Beaux Arts [1938]

13 Stop all the clocks, cut off the telephone,
Prevent the dog from barking with a juicy bone,
Silence the pianos and with muffled drum
Bring out the coffin, let the mourners come.

      Funeral Blues [1938]

14 He was my North, my South, my East and West,
My working week and my Sunday rest,
My noon, my midnight, my talk, my song;
I thought that love would last forever: I was wrong.

      Funeral Blues

15 Evil is unspectacular and always human,
And shares our bed and eats at our own table.

      Herman Melville [1939]

16 I sit in one of the dives
On Fifty-second Street
Uncertain and afraid
As the clever hopes expire
Of a low dishonest decade:
Waves of anger and fear
Circulate over the bright
And darkened lands of the earth,
Obsessing our private lives;
The unmentionable odor of death
Offends the September night.

      September 1, 1939 [1939], st. 1

1 We must love one another or die.
September 1, 1939, st. 8

2 For poetry makes nothing happen: it survives
In the valley of its saying where executives
Would never want to tamper
In Memory of W. B. Yeats, 2 [1939]

3 Earth, receive an honored guest;
William Yeats is laid to rest.
Let the Irish vessel lie
Emptied of its poetry.
In Memory of W. B. Yeats, 3, st. 1

4 In the nightmare of the dark
All the dogs of Europe bark.
In Memory of W. B. Yeats, 3, st. 2

5 Intellectual disgrace
Stares from every human face,
And the seas of pity lie
Locked and frozen in each eye.
In Memory of W. B. Yeats, 3, st. 3

6 To us he is no more a person
Now but a whole climate of opinion.
In Memory of Sigmund Freud [1939], st. 17

7 One rational voice is dumb: over a grave
The household of Impulse mourns one dearly loved.
Sad is Eros, builder of cities,
And weeping anarchic Aphrodite.
In Memory of Sigmund Freud, st. 28

8 Law, says the judge as he looks down his nose,
Speaking clearly and most severely,
Law is as I've told you before,
Law is as you know I suppose,
Law is but let me explain it once more,
Law is The Law.   *Law Like Love [1939], st. 4*

9 Like love we don't know where or why
Like love we can't compel or fly
Like love we often weep
Like love we seldom keep.
Law Like Love, last stanza

10 Our researchers into Public Opinion are content
That he held the proper opinions for the time of year;
When there was peace, he was for peace; when there
was war, he went.
The Unknown Citizen (To JS/07/M/378
This Marble Monument Is Erected by the
State) [1939]

11 Was he free? Was he happy? The question is absurd:
Had anything been wrong, we should certainly have
heard.
The Unknown Citizen (To JS/07/M/378
This Marble Monument Is Erected by the State)

12 When he laughed, respectable senators burst with
laughter,

And when he cried the little children died in the
streets.   *Epitaph on a Tyrant [1940]*

13 At Dirty Dick's and Sloppy Joe's
We drank our liquor straight,
Some went upstairs with Margery,
And some, alas, with Kate.
The Sea and the Mirror [1944]. Master and
Boatswain

14 And children swarmed to him like settlers. He
became a land.   *Edward Lear [1945]*

15 Thou shalt not sit
With statisticians nor commit
A social science.
Under Which Lyre [1946], st. 27

16 If thou must choose
Between the chances, choose the odd;
Read the *New Yorker;* trust in God;
And take short views.
Under Which Lyre, last stanza

17 Thousands have lived without love, not one
without water.
Homage to Clio [1957]. First Things First

18 Some books are undeservedly forgotten; none are
undeservedly remembered.
The Dyer's Hand [1962]. Pt. I, Reading

19 It takes little talent to see clearly what lies under
one's nose, a good deal of it to know in which direction to point that organ.
The Dyer's Hand, I, Writing

20 Whatever its actual content and overt interest,
every poem is rooted in imaginative awe. Poetry can
do a hundred and one things, delight, sadden, disturb, amuse, instruct — it may express every possible
shade of emotion, and describe every conceivable
kind of event, but there is only one thing that all
poetry must do; it must praise all it can for being and
for happening.
The Dyer's Hand, II, Making, Knowing and
Judging

21 Though the great artists of the past could not
change the course of history, it is only through their
work that we are able to break bread with the dead,
and without communion with the dead a fully human
life is impossible.
Secondary Worlds [1968]. Words and the
Word

Jacques Barzun
1907–

22 Whoever wants to know the heart and mind
of America had better learn baseball, the rules and

realities of the game—and do it by watching first some high school or small-town teams.

God's Country and Mine [1954], ch. 8

Rachel [Louise] Carson
1907–1964

1   The sea lies all about us. The commerce of all lands must cross it. The very winds that move over the lands have been cradled on its broad expanse and seek ever to return to it. The continents themselves dissolve and pass to the sea, in grain after grain of eroded land. So the rains that rose from it return again in rivers. In its mysterious past it encompasses all the dim origins of life and receives in the end, after, it may be, many transmutations, the dead husks of that same life. For all at last returns to the sea—to Oceanus, the ocean river, like the everflowing stream of time, the beginning and the end.

The Sea Around Us [1951], ch. 14, ending

2   The edge of the sea is a strange and beautiful place. All through the long history of Earth it has been an area of unrest where waves have broken heavily against the land, where the tides have pressed forward over the continents, receded, and then returned. For no two successive days is the shore line precisely the same.

The Edge of the Sea [1955]

3   In an age when man has forgotten his origins and is blind even to his most essential needs for survival, water along with other resources has become the victim of his indifference.   *Silent Spring [1962]*

4   Over increasingly large areas of the United States, spring now comes unheralded by the return of the birds, and the early mornings are strangely silent where once they were filled with the beauty of bird song.   *Silent Spring*

5   As crude a weapon as the cave man's club, the chemical barrage has been hurled against the fabric of life.   *Silent Spring*

Daphne du Maurier
1907–1989

6   Last night I dreamt I went to Manderley again.
Rebecca [1938], first line

Loren Eiseley
1907–1977

7   We are all potential fossils still carrying within our bodies the crudities of former existences, the marks of

a world in which living creatures flow with little more consistency than clouds from age to age.

The Immense Journey [1957]

Mircea Eliade
1907–1986

8   Healer and psychopomp, the shaman is these because he commands the techniques of ecstasy—that is, because his soul can safely abandon his body and roam at vast distances, can penetrate the underworld and rise to the sky. Through his own ecstatic experience he knows the roads of the extraterrestrial regions. He can go below and above because he has already been there.

Shamanism: Archaic Techniques of Ecstasy[1] *[1951]*

9   There are...privileged places, qualitatively different from all others—a man's birthplace, or the scenes of his first love, or certain places in the first foreign city he visited in youth. Even for the most frankly nonreligious man, all these places still retain an exceptional, a unique quality: they are the "holy places" of his private universe, as if it were in such spots that he had received the revelation of a reality *other* than that in which he participates through his ordinary daily life.

The Sacred and the Profane[1] *[1957]*

Christopher Fry
1907–2005

10 I travel light; as light,
That is, as a man can travel who will
Still carry his body around because
Of its sentimental value.

The Lady's Not for Burning [1950],
act I

11 Religion
Has made an honest woman of the supernatural.
The Lady's Not for Burning, II

Robert A. Heinlein
1907–1988

12   An armed society is a polite society.
Beyond This Horizon [1948]

13   I am all that I grok.
Stranger in a Strange Land [1961]

---

[1]Translated by WILLARD R. TRASK.

A. D. [Alec Derwent] Hope
1907–2000

1 And her five cities, like five teeming sores,
Each drains her: a vast parasite robber-state
Where second-hand Europeans pullulate
Timidly on the edge of alien shores.

Australia [1939]

Louis MacNeice
1907–1963

2 It's no go my honey love, it's no go my poppet;
Work your hands from day to day, the winds will
blow the profit.
The glass is falling hour by hour, the glass will fall
forever,
But if you break the bloody glass you won't hold up
the weather.

Bagpipe Music, last stanza

John Wayne
1907–1979

3 Talk low, talk slow, and don't say too much.

Advice on acting

Simone de Beauvoir
1908–1986

4 I wish that every human life might be pure transparent freedom.

The Blood of Others [1946]

5 This has always been a man's world, and none of
the reasons hitherto brought forward in explanation
of this fact has seemed adequate.

The Second Sex [1949–1950], pt. II, ch. 4

6 It is not in giving life but in risking life that man is
raised above the animal; that is why superiority has
been accorded in humanity not to the sex that brings
forth but to that which kills.

The Second Sex, II, 4

7 One is not born a woman, one becomes one.[1]

The Second Sex, IV, 12

8 When we abolish the slavery of half of humanity,
together with the whole system of hypocrisy that it
implies, then the "division" of humanity will reveal its
genuine significance and the human couple will find
its true form.

The Second Sex, VII, conclusion

9 It is for man to establish the reign of liberty in the
midst of the world of the given. To gain the supreme
victory, it is necessary, for one thing, that by and
through their natural differentiation men and women
unequivocally affirm their brotherhood.

The Second Sex, VII, conclusion

Harry A[ndrew] Blackmun
1908–1999

10 The right of privacy . . . is broad enough to encompass a woman's decision whether or not to terminate
her pregnancy.

Roe v. Wade, 410 U.S. 153 [1973]

11 In order to get beyond racism, we must first take
account of race. There is no other way.

*Regents of the University of California v.
Bakke, 438 U.S. 265 [1978]*

12 For today, at least, the law of abortion stands
undisturbed. For today, the women of this Nation
still retain the liberty to control their destinies. But
the signs are evident and very ominous, and a chill
wind blows.

*Webster v. Reproductive Health Services,
492 U.S. 490 [1989]*

13 From this day forward, I no longer shall tinker
with the machinery of death.

*Dissenting opinion in Callins v. Collins,
510 U.S. 1141 [1994]*

Sydney Boehm
1908–1990

14 We're sisters under the mink.

*The Big Heat (screenplay) [1953],
spoken by Gloria Grahame*

Johnny Burke
1908–1964

15 Ev'ry time it rains it rains pennies from Heaven.
Don't you know each cloud contains pennies from
Heaven?

Pennies from Heaven[2] [1936]

16 Love is tearful or it's gay,
It's a problem or it's play,
It's a heartache either way
But beautiful!

But Beautiful[3] [1947]

---

[1]On ne naît pas femme, on le devient.

[2]Music by ARTHUR JOHNSTON.
[3]Music by JIMMY VAN HEUSEN.

Henri Cartier-Bresson
1908–2004

1 The Decisive Moment[1]
Title of book [1952]

2 We photographers deal in things which are continually vanishing, and when they have vanished, there is no contrivance on earth which can make them come back again.
The Decisive Moment [1952]

Quentin Crisp [Denis Charles Pratt]
1908–1999

3 I became one of the stately homos[2] of England.
The Naked Civil Servant [1968]

4 I now know that if you describe things as better than they are, you are considered to be romantic; if you describe things as worse than they are, you will be called a realist; and if you describe things exactly as they are, you will be thought of as a satirist.
The Naked Civil Servant

5 There was no need to do any housework at all. After the first four years the dirt doesn't get any worse.
The Naked Civil Servant

Bette Davis [Ruth Elizabeth Davis]
1908–1989

6 [Of a starlet:] There goes the famous good time that was had by all.
Attributed

M[ary] F[rances] K[ennedy] Fisher
1908–1992

7 In America we eat, collectively, with a glum urge for food to fill us. We are ignorant of flavor. We are as a nation taste-blind.
Serve It Forth [1937]

8 There is a communion of more than our bodies when bread is broken and wine drunk.
The Gastronomical Me [1943]. Foreword

9 When I write of hunger, I am really writing about love and the hunger for it, and warmth and the love of it and the hunger for it ... and then the warmth and richness and fine reality of hunger satisfied ... and it is all one.[3]
The Gastronomical Me. Foreword

10 Sharing food with another human being is an intimate act that should not be indulged in lightly.
An Alphabet for Gourmets [1949].
A is for Dining Alone

11 It is said that a few connoisseurs, such as old George Saintsbury, can recall *physically* the bouquet of certain great vintages a half century after tasting them. I am a mouse among elephants now, but I can say just as surely that this minute, in a northern California valley, I can taste-smell-hear-see and then feel between my teeth the potato chips I ate slowly one November afternoon in 1936, in the bar of the Lausanne Palace.
With Bold Knife and Fork [1969].
Once a Tramp, Always ...

Ian [Lancaster] Fleming
1908–1964

12 I would like a medium Vodka dry Martini — with a slice of lemon peel. Shaken and not stirred, please.
Dr. No [1958], ch. 14

John Kenneth Galbraith
1908–2006

13 One can relish the varied idiocy of human action during a panic to the full, for, while it is a time of great tragedy, nothing is being lost but money.
The Great Crash, 1929 [1955], ch. 1

14 Wealth is not without its advantages and the case to the contrary, although it has often been made, has never proved widely persuasive.
The Affluent Society [1958], ch. 1

15 The hallmark of the conventional wisdom is acceptability. It has the approval of those to whom it is addressed.
The Affluent Society, 2

16 It is far, far better and much safer to have a firm anchor in nonsense than to put out on the troubled seas of thought.
The Affluent Society, 11

17 The leisure class has been replaced by another and much larger class to which work has none of the older connotation of pain, fatigue, or other mental or physical discomfort. We have failed to observe the

---

[1]This was the American title; the French title was *Images à la Sauvette* [Images on the Run]. In his introduction, Cartier-Bresson cites CARDINAL DE RETZ [1614–1679]: "There is nothing in this life that does not have a decisive moment."

[2]See Felicia Hemans, 405:7.

[3]Ellipses are in the original text.

emergence of this New Class, as it may be simply called.

The Affluent Society, 24

1 The superior confidence which people repose in the tall man is well merited. Being tall, he is more visible than other men and being more visible, he is much more closely watched. In consequence, his behavior is far better than that of smaller men.

The Scotch [1964]

2 We are becoming the servants in thought, as in action, of the machine we have created to serve us.

The New Industrial State [1967], ch. 1

3 The individual serves the industrial system not by supplying it with savings and the resulting capital; he serves it by consuming its products.

The New Industrial State, 4

4 What is called a high standard of living consists, in considerable measure, in arrangements for avoiding muscular energy, increasing sensual pleasure and for enhancing caloric intake above any nutritional requirement. Nonetheless, the belief that increased production is a worthy social goal is very nearly absolute.

The New Industrial State, 14

5 All of the great leaders have had one characteristic in common: it was the willingness to confront unequivocally the major anxiety of people in their time. This, and not much else, is the essence of leadership.

The Age of Uncertainty [1977], ch. 12

6 The enemy of the conventional wisdom is not ideas but the march of events.

The Affluent Society [1977 edition],
The Concept of the Conventional Wisdom

7 Trickle-down theory — the less than elegant metaphor that if one feeds the horse enough oats, some will pass through to the road for the sparrows.

The Culture of Contentment [1992], ch. 8

Lyndon B[aines] Johnson
1908–1973

8 I will do my best. That is all I can do. I ask for your help — and God's.

Statement after assassination of
John F. Kennedy [November 22, 1963]

9 Come now, let us reason together.

Saying

10 All I have I would have given gladly not to be standing here today.

First address to Congress as President
[November 27, 1963]

11 We have talked long enough in this country about equal rights. We have talked for a hundred years or more. It is time now to write the next chapter — and to write in the books of law.

First address to Congress as President

12 Unfortunately, many Americans live on the outskirts of hope — some because of their poverty, and some because of their color, and all too many because of both. Our task is to help replace their despair with opportunity. This administration today, here and now, declares unconditional war on poverty in America.

State of the Union Address
[January 8, 1964]

13 There is no Negro problem. There is no Southern problem. There is no Northern problem. There is only an American problem.

Address to Congress [March 15, 1964]

14 We still seek no wider war.

Radio / television speech [August 4, 1964]
on the Gulf of Tonkin resolution

15 This nation, this generation, in this hour has man's first chance to build a Great Society, a place where the meaning of man's life matches the marvels of man's labor.

Address, accepting the presidential
nomination [August 1964]

16 We are not about to send American boys nine or ten thousand miles away from home to do what Asian boys ought to be doing for themselves.

Remark at Akron University, Akron,
Ohio [October 21, 1964]

17 With America's sons in the fields far away, with America's future under challenge right here at home, with our hopes and the world's hopes for peace in the balance every day, I do not believe that I should devote an hour or a day of my time to any personal partisan causes or to any duties other than the awesome duties of this office — the Presidency of your country. Accordingly, I shall not seek, and I will not accept, the nomination of my party for another term as your President.

Television address [March 31, 1968]

Otto Kerner, Jr.
1908–1976

18 Our nation is moving toward two societies, one black, one white — separate and unequal.

Report of the National Advisory
Commission on Civil Disorders [1968], p. 1

Claude Lévi-Strauss
1908–2009

1   The world began without the human race and it will end without it.... Man has never — save only when he reproduces himself — done other than cheerfully dismantle million upon million of structures and reduce their elements to a state in which they can no longer be reintegrated.
Tristes Tropiques[1] *[1955]. Conclusion*

2   I therefore claim to show, not how men think in myths, but how myths operate in men's minds without their being aware of the fact.
The Raw and the Cooked[2] *[1964].*
Overture

3   The scientific mind does not so much provide the right answers as ask the right questions.
The Raw and the Cooked. Overture

Albert Maltz
1908–1985
and
Malvin Wald
1917–2008

4   There are eight million stories in the naked city. This has been one of them.
The Naked City (screenplay) [1948]

Thurgood Marshall
1908–1993

5   While the Union survived the Civil War, the Constitution did not.
Speech to San Francisco Patent and
Trademark Law Association, Maui, Hawaii
[May 6, 1987]

Joseph R[aymond] McCarthy
1908–1957

6   I have here in my hand a list of two hundred and five [people] that were known to the Secretary of State as being members of the Communist Party and who nevertheless are still working and shaping the policy of the State Department.
Speech, Wheeling, West Virginia
[February 9, 1950]

Olivier Messaien
1908–1992

7   The birds are the opposite of time. They represent our longing for light, for stars, for rainbows, and for jubilant song.
Program note for Quartet for the
End of Time [1941]

8   Certain people are annoyed that I believe in God. But I want people to know that God is present in everything, in the concert hall, in the ocean, on a mountain, even on the underground.
Interview with Jean-Christophe Marti
[January 1992]

Edward R[oscoe] Murrow
1908–1965

9   This — is London.
Opening phrase for broadcasts from London
during World War II [1939–1945]

10   I pray you to believe what I have said about Buchenwald. I have reported what I saw and heard, but only part of it. For most of it I have no words.
Broadcast report from London on
Buchenwald concentration camp
[April 15, 1945]

11   We must not confuse dissent with disloyalty.
See It Now (broadcast). Report on Senator
Joseph R. McCarthy [March 7, 1954]

12   We will not be driven by fear into an age of unreason if we... remember that we are not descended from fearful men, not from men who feared to write, to speak, to associate and to defend causes which were, for the moment unpopular.
See It Now [March 7, 1954]

13   No one can terrorize a whole nation, unless we are all his accomplices.
See It Now [March 7, 1954]

14   Unless we get off our fat surpluses and recognize that television in the main is being used to distract, delude, amuse and insulate us, then television and those who finance it, those who look at it and those who work at it, may see a totally different picture too late.
Speech at the Radio and Television News
Directors Convention, Chicago
[October 15, 1958]

15   Good night, and good luck.
Broadcast sign-off

---

[1]Translated by JOHN RUSSELL.
[2]Translated by JOHN and DOREEN WEIGHTMAN.

Frank S. Nugent
1908–1965
and

Laurence Stallings
1894–1968

1 Never apologize, mister. It's a sign of weakness.[1]
She Wore a Yellow Ribbon (screenplay)
[1949], spoken by John Wayne

George Oppen
1908–1984

2 I know that no one would live out
Thirty years, fifty years if the world were ending
With his life.
The Materials [1962]. Image of the Engine

3 Possible
To use
Words provided one treat them
As enemies.
This in Which [1965].
A Language of New York

4 For the people of that flow
Are new, the old

New to age as the young
To youth
Of Being Numerous [1968].
Of Being Numerous

5 We are pressed, pressed on each other,
We will be told at once
Of anything that happens
Of Being Numerous. Of Being Numerous

6 Imagine a man in the ditch,
The wheels of the overturned wreck
Still spinning —

I don't mean he despairs, I mean if he does not
He sees in the manner of poetry
Of Being Numerous. Route

Cesare Pavese
1908–1950

7 The girls are all giggling, then one girl suddenly
remembers
the wild goat. Up there, on the hilltop, in the woods

and rocky ravines, the peasants saw him butting his
head
against the trees, looking for the nannies. He's gone
wild,
and the reason why is this: if you don't make an
animal work,
if you keep him only for stud, he likes to hurt, he
kills.
Hard Labor[2] [1936]. The Goat God

8 One stops being a child when one realizes that
telling one's trouble does not make it better.
This Business of Living: Diaries 1935–1950,
31st October 1937

9 Perfect behavior is born of complete indifference.
This Business of Living: Diaries 1935–1950,
21st February 1940

Theodore Roethke
1908–1963

10 My secrets cry aloud.
I have no need for tongue.
My heart keeps open house,
My doors are widely flung.
Open House [1941], st. 1

11 This urge, wrestle, resurrection of dry sticks,
Cut stems struggling to put down feet,
What saint strained so much,
Rose on such lopped limbs to a new life?
Cuttings (later) [1948]

12 Nothing would sleep in that cellar.
Root Cellar [1948]

13 Nothing would give up life:
Even the dirt kept breathing a small breath.
Root Cellar

14 Tugging all day at perverse life:
The indignity of it!   *Weed Puller [1948]*

15 The whiskey on your breath
Could make a small boy dizzy;
But I hung on like death:
Such waltzing was not easy.
My Papa's Waltz [1948], st. 1

16 I study the lives on a leaf: the little
Sleepers, numb nudgers in cold dimensions,
Beetles in caves, newts, stone-deaf fishes,
Lice tethered to long limp subterranean weeds,
Squirmers in bogs,
And bacterial creepers.
The Minimal [1948]

---

[1] Never contradict. Never explain. Never apologize. (Those are the secrets of a happy life!) — JOHN ARBUTHNOT FISHER [1841–1920], *Letter to The Times of London* [September 5, 1919]

[2] Translated by WILLIAM ARROWSMITH.

1 Fear was my father, Father Fear.
His look drained the stones.
The Lost Son [1948], 3. The Gibber

2 A lively understandable spirit
Once entertained you.
It will come again.
Be still.
Wait.
The Lost Son, 5. "It was beginning winter"

3 And the new plants, still awkward in their soil,
The lovely diminutives.
I could watch! I could watch!
I saw the separateness of all things!
A Field of Light [1948], III

4 I remember the neckcurls, limp and damp as tendrils,
And her quick look, a sidelong pickerel smile.
Elegy for Jane [1953]

5 I wake to sleep, and take my waking slow.
I feel my fate in what I cannot fear.
I learn by going where I have to go.
The Waking [1953]

6 I knew a woman, lovely in her bones,
When small birds sighed, she would sigh back at
them;
Ah, when she moved, she moved more ways than
one:
The shapes a bright container can contain!
I Knew a Woman [1958]

7 When I was a lark, I sang;
When I was a worm, I devoured.
What Can I Tell My Bones? [1958]

8 I see, in evening air,
How slowly dark comes down on what we do.
In Evening Air [1964]

9 I long for the imperishable quiet at the heart of
form.
The Longing [1964]

10 What I love is near at hand,
Always, in earth and air.   *The Far Field [1964], III*

11 In a dark time, the eye begins to see.
In a Dark Time [1964], st. 1

12 The soul has many motions, body one.
The Motion [1964], I

13 Brooding on God, I may become a man.
Pain wanders through my bones like a lost fire;
What burns me now? Desire, desire, desire.
The Marrow [1964], II

14 Lord, hear me out, and hear me out this day:
From me to Thee's a long and terrible way.
The Marrow, III

15 Now I adore my life
With the Bird, the abiding Leaf,

With the Fish, the questing Snail,
And the Eye altering all;
And I dance with William Blake
For love, for Love's sake.
Once More, the Round [1964]

William Saroyan
1908–1981

16   In the time of your life, live — so that in that good time there shall be no ugliness or death for yourself or for any life your life touches.
The Time of Your Life [1939]

17   Everybody's behind the eight-ball!
The Time of Your Life

18   No foundation. All the way down the line.
The Time of Your Life

19   If you give to a thief he cannot steal from you, and he is then no longer a thief.
The Human Comedy [1943], ch. 4

C[omer] Vann Woodward
1908–1999

20   The twilight zone that lies between living memory and written history is one of the favorite breeding places of mythology.
The Strange Career of Jim Crow [1955]

Richard Wright
1908–1960

21   He knew that the moment he allowed what his life meant to enter fully into his consciousness, he would either kill himself or someone else. So he denied himself and acted tough.
Native Son [1940], bk. I

22   Goddammit, look! We live here and they live there. We black and they white. They got things and we ain't. They do things and we can't. It's just like living in jail.
Native Son, I

23   Who knows when some slight shock, disturbing the delicate balance between social order and thirsty aspiration, shall send the skyscrapers in our cities toppling?
Native Son, I

24   If we had been allowed to participate in the vital processes of America's national growth, what would have been the textures of our lives, the pattern of our traditions, the routine of our customs, the state of our arts, the code of our laws, the function of our

government!...We black folk say that America would have been stronger and greater.
12 Million Black Voices [1941]

James Agee
1909–1955

1 We are talking now of summer evenings in Knoxville, Tennessee, in the time that I lived there so successfully disguised to myself as a child.
Knoxville: Summer of 1915 [1938]

2 If I could do it, I'd do no writing at all here. It would be photographs; the rest would be fragments of cloth, bits of cotton, lumps of earth, records of speech, pieces of wood and iron, phials of odors, plates of food and of excrement....A piece of the body torn out by the root might be more to the point.
Let Us Now Praise Famous Men [1941]. Preamble

3 All over Alabama the lamps are out. Every leaf drenches the touch; the spider's net is heavy. The roads lie there with nothing to use them. The fields lie there, with nothing at work in them, neither man nor beast.
Let Us Now Praise Famous Men. On the Porch: 1

4 Words cannot embody; they can only describe.
Let Us Now Praise Famous Men. On the Porch: 2

5 Several tons of dynamite are set off in this picture; none of it under the right people.
Review of the film Tycoon, in The Nation [February 14, 1948]

6 Most movies are like predigested food because they are mere reenactments of something that happened (if ever) back in the scripting stage.
Undirectable Director, in Life [September 18, 1950]

7 Nature, Mr. Allnut, is what we are put into this world to rise above.
The African Queen (screenplay) [1951], spoken by Katharine Hepburn

Nelson Algren
1909–1981

8 He had met him before, that certain down-at-heel vet growing stooped from carrying a thirty-five-pound monkey on his back.
The Man with the Golden Arm [1949]

9 [On Chicago:] Yet once you've come to be part of this particular patch, you'll never love another. Like loving a woman with a broken nose, you may well find lovelier lovelies. But never a lovely so real.
Chicago, City on the Make [1951]

10 A Walk on the Wild Side *Title of book [1956]*

11 Never play cards with a man called Doc. Never eat at a place called Mom's. Never sleep with a woman whose troubles are greater than your own.[1]
A Walk on the Wild Side [1956]

Eric Ambler
1909–1998

12 The important thing to know about an assassination or an attempted assassination is not who fired the shot, but who paid for the bullet.
A Coffin for Dimitrios [1939], ch. 2

13 International big business may conduct its operations with scraps of paper, but the ink it uses is human blood!
A Coffin for Dimitrios, 5

Sir Isaiah Berlin
1909–1997

14 There exists a great chasm between those, on one side, who relate everything to a single, central vision, one system more or less coherent or articulate, in terms of which they understand, think and feel...and, on the other side, those who pursue many ends, often unrelated and even contradictory....The first kind of intellectual and artistic personality belongs to the hedgehogs, the second to the foxes....Dante belongs to the first category, Shakespeare to the second.
The Hedgehog and the Fox[2] [1953], pt. 1

15 One belief, more than any other, is responsible for the slaughter of individuals on the altars of the great historical ideals....This is the belief that somewhere, in the past or in the future, in divine revelation or in the mind of an individual thinker, in the pronouncements of history or science, or in the simple heart of an uncorrupted good man, there is a final solution.
Two Concepts of Liberty [1958]

Peter Drucker
1909–2005

16 Leave enough time unscheduled; anyone in a decision-making position should, as a rule, schedule no more than half his time.
How to Be an Effective Executive [1961], in Nation's Business

---

[1]Although Algren made these "rules" famous, they are adapted from advice in a letter to Algren from his friend Dave Peltz.

[2]See Archilochus, 55:2.

1 No More Salvation by Society
Chapter title in The New Realities [1989]

2 Every organization of today has to build into its very structure *the management of change.*
Post-capitalist Society [1993]

Julius J. Epstein
1909–2000

Philip G. Epstein
1909–1952

and

Howard Koch
1916–1995

3 Of all the gin joints in all the towns in all the world, she walks into mine!
Casablanca (screenplay) [1942], spoken by Humphrey Bogart

4 Play it, Sam.[1]
Casablanca (screenplay), spoken by Ingrid Bergman

5 Here's looking at you, kid.
Casablanca (screenplay), spoken by Humphrey Bogart

6 We'll always have Paris.
Casablanca (screenplay), spoken by Humphrey Bogart

7 I'm *shocked, shocked* to find that gambling is going on here!
Casablanca (screenplay), spoken by Claude Rains

8 Round up the usual suspects.
Casablanca (screenplay), spoken by Claude Rains

9 Louis, I think this is the beginning of a beautiful friendship.
Casablanca (screenplay), closing line, spoken by Humphrey Bogart

Barry Goldwater
1909–1998

10 Extremism in the defense of liberty is no vice. And . . . moderation in the pursuit of justice is no virtue.
Speech accepting the Republican presidential nomination [July 16, 1964]

11 A government that is big enough to give you all you want is big enough to take it all away.
Campaign speech [October 21, 1964]

12 You don't need to be "straight" to fight and die for your country; you just need to shoot straight.
Quoted in Pure Goldwater [1993]

Clement Greenberg
1909–1994

13 Kitsch is mechanical and operates by formulas. Kitsch is vicarious experience and faked sensations. . . . Kitsch is the epitome of all that is spurious in the life of our times.
Avant-Garde and Kitsch [1939]

14 All profoundly original art looks ugly at first.
Review in The Nation [April 7, 1945]

Chester Himes
1909–1984

15 My feelings are too intense. I hate too bitterly, I love too exaltingly, I pity too extravagantly, I hurt too painfully. We American blacks call that "soul."
The Quality of Hurt [1972]

Edwin [Herbert] Land
1909–1991

16 The bottom line is in heaven.
Reply [1977] rejecting view that only the bottom line of the balance sheet shows the worth of a product

Stanislaw J[erzy] Lec
1909–1966

17 One has to multiply thoughts to the point where there aren't enough policemen to control them.
Unkempt Thoughts[2] [1962]

18 No snowflake in an avalanche ever feels responsible.
More Unkempt Thoughts[2] [1968]

19 Get out of the way of justice. She is blind.
More Unkempt Thoughts

20 Most of the sighs we hear have been edited.
More Unkempt Thoughts

---

[1]Play it! — *Casablanca*, spoken by Humphrey Bogart.

[2]Translated by JACEK GALAZKA.

Malcolm Lowry
1909–1957

1 And this is how I sometimes think of myself, as a great explorer who has discovered some extraordinary land from which he can never return to give his knowledge to the world: but the name of this land is hell.

It is not Mexico of course but in the heart.
Under the Volcano [1947], ch. 1

2 How alike are the groans of love, to those of the dying.
Under the Volcano, 12

3 Somebody threw a dead dog after him down the ravine.
Under the Volcano, last line

Joseph L[eo] Mankiewicz
1909–1993

4 Fasten your seatbelts. It's going to be a bumpy night.
All About Eve (screenplay) [1950],
spoken by Bette Davis

Johnny Mercer
1909–1976

5 Skylark,
Have you seen a valley green with spring
Where my heart can go a-journeying,
Over the shadows and the rain
To a blossom-covered lane?
Skylark[1] [1941]

6 That old black magic has me in its spell,
That old black magic that you weave so well.
Those icy fingers up and down my spine,
The same old witchcraft when your eyes
   meet mine.
Star Spangled Rhythm [1942].
That Old Black Magic[2]

7 So, set 'em up, Joe,
I've got a little story you oughta know.
We're drinking, my friend,
To the end of a brief episode,
Make it one for my baby
And one more for the road.
The Sky's the Limit [1943]. One for My Baby
(And One More for the Road)[2]

8 You've got to
Ac-cent-tchu-ate the positive,

E-lim-my-nate the negative,
Latch on to the affirmative,
Don't mess with Mister In-between.
Here Come the Waves [1944].
Ac-cent-tchu-ate the Positive[2]

9 Days may be cloudy or sunny,
We're in or we're out of the money,
But I'm with you always,
I'm with you rain or shine!
St. Louis Woman [1946].
Come Rain or Come Shine[2]

10 Your lips were like a red and ruby chalice,
Warmer than a summer night.
The clouds were like an alabaster palace,
Rising to a snowy height.
Each star its own aurora borealis,
Suddenly you held me tight.
I could see the midnight sun.
Midnight Sun[3] [1949]

11 We're after the same
Rainbow's end,
Waitin' round the bend,
My huckleberry friend,
Moon River
And me.
Breakfast at Tiffany's [1961].
Moon River[4]

12 The days of wine and roses
Laugh and run away
Like a child at play
Through a meadow land
Toward a closing door
A door marked "Nevermore"
That wasn't there before
Days of Wine and Roses[4] [1962]

Elting E[lmore] Morison
1909–1995

13 The computer is no better than its program.
Men, Machines and Modern Times
[1966]

Kwame Nkrumah
1909–1972

14 We prefer self-government with danger to servitude in tranquility.
Axioms of Kwame Nkrumah [1967]

---

[1]Music by HOAGY CARMICHAEL.

[2]Music by HAROLD ARLEN.

[3]Music by SONNY BURKE and LIONEL HAMPTON.

[4]Music by HENRY MANCINI.

C[yril] Northcote Parkinson
1909–1993

1   Work expands so as to fill the time available for its completion.

Parkinson's Law [1957], ch. 1

2   Perfection of planned layout is achieved only by institutions on the point of collapse.

Parkinson's Law

3   Expenditure rises to meet income.

Parkinson's Law

David Riesman
1909–2002

4   While all people want and need to be liked by some of the people some of the time, it is only the modern other-directed types who make this their chief source of direction and chief area of sensitivity.

The Lonely Crowd [1950], ch. 1

5   Today the future occupation of all moppets is to be skilled consumers.

The Lonely Crowd, 3

Stephen Spender
1909–1995

6 I think continually of those who were truly great . . .
The names of those who in their lives fought for life,
Who wore at their hearts the fire's center.
Born of the sun they traveled a short while towards the sun,
And left the vivid air signed with their honor.

I Think Continually of Those

7   He's still half with us
Conniving slyly, yet he knows he's gone
Into that cellar where they'll never find him,
Happy to be alone, his last work done,
Word freed from world, into a different wood.

Collected Poems [1986]. Auden's Funeral, sec. 1

Wallace Stegner
1909–1993

8   We simply need that wild country available to us, even if we never do more than drive to its edge and look in. For it can be a means of reassuring ourselves of our sanity as creatures, a part of the geography of hope.

Letter to David Pesonen [1960]

Tommy Trinder
1909–1989

9   [On American troops stationed in Britain during World War II:] Overpaid, overfed, oversexed, and over here.

Attributed

Simone Weil
1909–1943

10   What a country calls its vital economic interests are not the things which enable its citizens to live, but the things which enable it to make war. Petrol is more likely than wheat to be a cause of international conflict.

The Power of Words [1937]

11   Force is as pitiless to the man who possesses it, or thinks he does, as it is to its victims; the second it crushes, the first it intoxicates. The truth is, nobody really possesses it.

The Iliad, or The Poem of Force [1940]

12   Attachment is the great fabricator of illusions; reality can be attained only by someone who is detached.

Gravity and Grace (La Pesanteur et la Grâce) [1947]

13   All sins are attempts to fill voids.

Gravity and Grace

14   Imaginary evil is romantic and varied; real evil is gloomy, monotonous, barren, boring. Imaginary good is boring, real good is always new, marvelous, intoxicating. "Imaginative literature," therefore, is either boring or immoral or a mixture of both.

Gravity and Grace

15   Purity is the ability to contemplate defilement.

Gravity and Grace

16   Man alone can enslave man.

Oppression and Liberty [1958]. Reflections Concerning the Causes of Liberty and Social Oppression

Eudora Welty
1909–2001

17   The storm had rolled away to faintness like a wagon crossing a bridge.

A Curtain of Green [1941].
A Piece of News

1 The excursion is the same when you go looking for your sorrow as when you go looking for your joy.
The Wide Net [1943]. The Wide Net

2 All they could see was sky, water, birds, light, and confluence. It was the whole morning world.
The Optimist's Daughter [1978]

3 Writing fiction has developed in me an abiding respect for the unknown in a human lifetime and a sense of where to look for the threads, how to follow, how to connect, find in the thick of the tangle what clear line persists. The strands are all there: to the memory nothing is ever really lost.
One Writer's Beginnings [1984]. Finding a Voice

4 I am a writer who came of a sheltered life. A sheltered life can be a daring life as well. For all serious daring starts from within.
One Writer's Beginnings. Finding a Voice

Jean Anouilh
1910–1987

5 This horror and all these useless gestures, this grotesque adventure is ours. We must live it. Death is absurd also. *Romeo and Jeannette [1946]*

6 And under this carnival disguise the heart of an old youngster who is still waiting to give his all. But how to be recognized under this mask? This is what they call a fine career.
The Waltz of the Toreadors [1952]. English version

Margaret Wise Brown
1910–1952

7 Goodnight stars
Goodnight air
Goodnight noises everywhere
Goodnight Moon [1947]

Jacques-Yves Cousteau
1910–1997

8 Sometimes we are lucky enough to know that our lives have been changed, to discard the old, embrace the new, and run headlong down an immutable course. It happened to me at Le Mourillon on that summer's day, when my eyes were opened to the sea. *The Silent World [1953], ch. 1*

9 We must go and see for ourselves.[1]
Motto of his ship Calypso

[1] Il faut aller voir.

Tony [Two-Ton] Galento
1910–1979

10 I'll moider de bum.
Before his unsuccessful fight with Joe Louis for the heavyweight championship [June 28, 1939]

Jean Genet
1910–1986

11 Our domestic life and the law of our Homes do not resemble your Homes. We love each other without love. Our homes do not have the sacramental character. Fags are the great immoralists.
Our Lady of the Flowers [1943]

12 Though it was at my heart's bidding that I chose the universe wherein I delight, I have at least the power of finding in it the many meanings I wish to find: *there is a close relationship between flowers and convicts.*
The Thief's Journal[2] *(Le Journal du Voleur) [1949]*

13 To achieve harmony in bad taste is the height of elegance. *The Thief's Journal*

14 I was already refusing to have taste. I forbade myself to have it. I knew that the cultivation of it would have not refined me but softened me.
The Thief's Journal

15 I call saintliness not a state but the moral procedure leading to it.
Quoted by JEAN PAUL SARTRE in Saint Genet [1952]

Frank Loesser
1910–1969

16 Here we are,
Out of cigarettes,
Holding hands and yawning,
Look how late it gets.

Two sleepy people, by dawn's early light,
And too much in love to say "Good night."
Thanks for the Memory [1938]. Two Sleepy People[3]

17 See what the boys in the back room will have
And tell them I'm having the same.
Destry Rides Again [1939]. See What the Boys in the Back Room Will Have[4]

[2] Translated by BERNARD FRECHTMAN.
[3] Music by HOAGY CARMICHAEL.
[4] Music by FREDERICK HOLLANDER.

1 I'd love to get you
 On a slow boat to China.
 All to myself alone.
   On a Slow Boat to China [1948]

2 When you meet a gent
 Paying all kinds of rent
 For a flat
 That would flatten the Taj Mahal
 Call it sad, call it funny,
 But it's better than even money
 That the guy's only doin' it for some doll.
   Guys and Dolls [1950]. Guys and Dolls

3 Ask me how do I feel,
 Ask me now that we're cozy and clinging.
 Well, sir, all I can say is,
 If I were a bell I'd be ringing.
   Guys and Dolls. If I Were a Bell

Charles Olson
1910–1970

4   I take SPACE to be the central fact to man born in America, from Folsom cave to now. I spell it large because it comes large here. Large, and without mercy.   *Call Me Ishmael [1947]*

5   What does not change / is the will to change.
   The Kingfishers [1949]

6 I have had to learn the simplest things
 last. Which made for difficulties.
   The Maximus Poems [1953].
   Maximus, to himself

7 As the dead prey upon us,
 they are the dead in ourselves,
 awake, my sleeping ones, I cry out to you,
 disentangle the nets of being!
   The Distances [1960]. As the Dead Prey
   upon Us

Abraham Polonsky
1910–1999

8   What are you gonna do? Kill me? Everybody dies.
   Body and Soul (screenplay) [1947],
   spoken by John Garfield

Mother Teresa
[Agnes Gonxha Bojaxhiu]
1910–1997

9   Let us do something beautiful for God.   *Motto*

10   Today the greatest means, the greatest destroyer of peace, is abortion. . . . Because if a mother can kill her own child, what is left for me to kill you and you kill me?
   Speech on accepting the Nobel Peace Prize
   [1979]

J. L. Austin
1911–1960

11   I am not sure importance is important: truth is.
   Philosophical Papers [1961]

Elizabeth Bishop
1911–1979

12 This iceberg cuts its facets from within.
 Like jewelry from a grave
 it saves itself perpetually and adorns
 Only itself.   *The Imaginary Iceberg [1946], st. 3*

13 Icebergs behoove the soul
 (both being self-made from elements least visible)
 to see them so: fleshed, fair, erected, indivisible.
   The Imaginary Iceberg, st. 3

14   Until everything
 was rainbow, rainbow, rainbow!
 And I let the fish go.   *The Fish [1946]*

15   Everything only connected by "and" and "and."
   Over 2,000 Illustrations and a Complete
   Concordance [1948]

16 Cold dark deep and absolutely clear,
 element bearable to no mortal,
 to fish and to seals . . .   *At the Fishhouses [1955]*

17 It is like what we imagine knowledge to be:
 dark, salt, clear, moving, utterly free,
 drawn from the cold hard mouth
 of the world, derived from the rocky breasts
 forever, flowing and drawn, and since
 our knowledge is historical, flowing, and flown.
   At the Fishhouses

18   Should we have stayed at home,
 wherever that may be?   *Questions of Travel [1965]*

19 His beak is focussed; he is preoccupied,

 looking for something, something, something.
 Poor bird, he is obsessed!
 The millions of grains are black, white, tan, and gray,
 mixed with quartz grains, rose and amethyst.
   Sandpiper [1965]

20 *Time to plant tears,* says the almanac.
 The grandmother sings to the marvelous stove
 and the child draws another inscrutable house.
   Sestina [1965]

21   The staring sailor
 that shakes his watch

that tells the time
of the poet, the man
that lies in the house of Bedlam.
Visits to St. Elizabeths [1965], st. 11

1 — Yesterday brought to today so lightly!
(A yesterday I find almost impossible to lift.)
Five Flights Up [1976]

2 I knew that nothing stranger
had ever happened.
In the Waiting Room [1976]

3 How had I come to be here
like them, and overhear
a cry of pain that could have
got loud and worse but hadn't?
In the Waiting Room

4 Home-made, home-made! But aren't we all?
Crusoe in England [1976]

5 I'd have
nightmares of other islands
stretching away from mine, infinities
of islands, islands spawning islands
like frogs' eggs turning into polliwogs
of islands, knowing that I had to live
on each and every one, eventually,
for ages, registering their flora,
their fauna, their geography.
Crusoe in England

6 — And Friday, my dear Friday, died of measles
seventeen years ago come March.
Crusoe in England

7 The art of losing isn't hard to master;
so many things seem filled with the intent
to be lost that their loss is no disaster.

Lose something every day. Accept the fluster
of lost door keys, the hour badly spent.
The art of losing isn't hard to master.
Geography III [1976]. One Art

8 Life and the memory of it cramped,
dim, on a piece of Bristol board.   *Poem [1976]*

9 "Fun" — it always seemed to leave you at a loss.
North Haven [1978]

E. M. Cioran
1911–1995

10 All our thoughts are a function of our ailments. If
we understand certain things, the credit for it goes to
the gaps in our health — and to them alone.
The New Gods[1] [1969]. Strangled Thoughts

11 We are all deep in a hell each moment of which is a
miracle.
The New Gods. Strangled Thoughts

12 A book is a postponed suicide.
The Trouble with Being Born[1] [1973]

Jay Dratler
1911–1968

Samuel Hoffenstein
1890–1947

and

Betty Reinhardt
1909–1954

13 I don't use a pen. I write with a goose quill dipped
in venom.[2]
Laura (screenplay) [1944],
spoken by Clifton Webb

Max Frisch
1911–1991

14 If anyone has a conscience it's generally a guilty
one.
The Fire Raisers[3] [1953]

15 When you love someone you leave every possibility open to them, and in spite of all the memories
of the past you are ready to be surprised, again and
again surprised, at how different they are, how various, not a finished image.
I'm Not Stiller [1954]

16 Technology…the knack of so arranging the
world that we don't have to experience it.
Homo Faber [1957]

17 We wanted a labor force, but humans came.
On immigrant workers in Europe;
Foreword [1965] to ALEXANDER J. SEILER,
Siamo Italiani

Samuel Fuller
1911–1997

18 For moviegoers to get the idea of real combat,
you'd have to shoot at them every so often from
either side of the screen.   *A Third Face [2002]*

---

[1] Translated by RICHARD HOWARD.

[2] The line may have originated with RING LARDNER, JR. [1915–
2000], who worked on the screenplay but is not listed in the movie
credits.

[3] Published first in German as *Biedermann und die Brandstifter*.

William Golding
1911–1993

1   Ralph wept for the end of innocence, the darkness of man's heart, and the fall through the air of the true, wise friend called Piggy.

The Lord of the Flies [1954], ch. 12

Paul Goodman
1911–1972

2   Where there is official censorship it is a sign that speech is serious. Where there is none, it is pretty certain that the official spokesmen have all the loudspeakers.

Growing Up Absurd [1960]

3   American society has tried so hard and so ably to defend the practice and theory of production for profit and not primarily for use that now it has succeeded in making its jobs and products profitable and useless.   *Growing Up Absurd*

Clark Kerr
1911–2003

4   The university has become the multiversity and the nature of the presidency has followed this change.... The president of the multiversity is leader, educator, wielder of power, pump; he is also officeholder, caretaker, inheritor, consensus seeker, persuader, bottleneck. But he is mostly a mediator.

The Uses of the University. The Godkin Lectures at Harvard University [1963]

Noel Langley
1911–1981

Florence Ryerson
1892–1965

and

Edgar Allan Woolf
1881–1948

5   Toto, I've a feeling we're not in Kansas anymore.

The Wizard of Oz (screenplay)[1] *[1939], spoken by Judy Garland*

6   I'll get you, my pretty, and your little dog, too.

The Wizard of Oz (screenplay), spoken by Margaret Hamilton

7   Pay no attention to that man behind the curtain!

The Wizard of Oz (screenplay), spoken by Frank Morgan

8   Lions, and tigers, and bears! Oh, my!

The Wizard of Oz (screenplay), spoken by Judy Garland

9   Who would have thought a good little girl like you could destroy my beautiful wickedness?

The Wizard of Oz (screenplay), spoken by Margaret Hamilton

Marshall [Herbert] McLuhan
1911–1980

10   The medium is the message.

Understanding Media [1964], title of first chapter

11   There is a basic principle that distinguishes a hot medium like radio from a cool one like the telephone, or a hot medium like the movie from a cool one like TV.... Hot media are...low in participation, and cool media are high in participation or completion by the audience.   *Understanding Media, ch. 2*

12   The new electronic interdependence recreates the world in the image of a global village.

The Medium Is the Massage [1967]

13   Vietnam was lost in the living rooms of America — not on the battlefields of Vietnam.

Montreal Gazette [May 16, 1975]

Czeslaw Milosz
1911–2004

14 The purpose of poetry is to remind us
how difficult it is to remain just one person,
for our house is open, there are no keys in the doors,
and invisible guests come in and out at will.

Ars Poetica? [1968]

15 May the gentle mountains and the bells of the flocks
Remind us of everything we have lost,
For we have seen on our way and fallen in love
With the world that will pass in a twinkling.

Collected Poems 1931–1987.[2] *On Pilgrimage.*

16 Human reason is beautiful and invincible.
No bars, no barbed wire, no pulping of books,
No sentence of banishment can prevail against it.

Collected Poems 1931–1987.[2] *Incantation.*

---

[1] See L. Frank Baum, 562:2–5.

[2] Translated from the Polish by CZESLAW MILOSZ and ROBERT HASS.

Flann O'Brien [Brian O'Nolan]
1911–1966

1   A pint of plain is your only man.
At Swim-Two-Birds [1939]

2   Strictly speaking, this story should not be written or told at all. To write it or to tell it is to spoil it. This is because the man who had the strange experience we are going to talk about never mentioned it to anybody, and the fact that he kept his secret and sealed it up completely in his memory is the whole point of the story. Thus we must admit that handicap at the beginning — that it is absurd for us to tell the story, absurd for anybody to listen to it and unthinkable that anybody should believe it.
John Duffy's Brother [1941]

Kenneth Patchen
1911–1972

3 Let us have madness openly, O men
Of my generation. Let us follow
The footsteps of this slaughtered age.
Let Us Have Madness Openly [1936]

4 I'd like to die like this . . .
with the dark fingers of the water
closing and unclosing over these sleepy lights
and a sad bell somewhere murmuring good night.
Crossing on Staten Island Ferry [1939]

5 Do I not deal with angels
When her lips I touch.   *For Miriam [1942]*

6 I take the word Europe
Or the word death
And tear them into tiny pieces;
I scatter them at your feet.
Cloth of the Tempest [1943]. The Dimensions of the Morning

7 I am the magical mouse
I don't eat cheese
I eat sunsets
And the tops of trees.
The Magical Mouse [1952], st. 1

8 Oh lonesome's a bad place
To get crowded into.   *Lonesome Boy Blues [1952]*

Nicholas Ray
[Raymond Nicholas Kienzle]
1911–1979

9   It was never all in the script. If it were, why make the movie?
I Was Interrupted [1993]. I Hate a Script

Ronald [Wilson] Reagan
1911–2004

10   No government ever voluntarily reduces itself in size. Government programs, once launched, never disappear. Actually, a government bureau is the nearest thing to eternal life we'll ever see on this earth.
TV broadcast [October 27, 1964]

11   Government is like a big baby — an alimentary canal with a big appetite at one end and no responsibility at the other.
Remark while campaigning for governor of California [1965]

12   We're the party that wants to see an America in which people can still get rich.
Remark at Republican congressional dinner, Washington, D.C. [May 4, 1982]

13   [It is] the march of freedom and democracy which will leave Marxism-Leninism on the ash heap of history as it has left other tyrannies which stifle the freedom and muzzle the self-expression of the people.
Address to British Parliament [June 8, 1982]

14   Let us beware that while [Soviet rulers] preach the supremacy of the state, declare its omnipotence over individual man, and predict its eventual domination over all the peoples of the earth, they are the focus of evil in the modern world. . . . I urge you to beware the temptation . . . to ignore the facts of history and the aggressive impulses of all evil empires, to simply call the arms race a giant misunderstanding and thereby remove yourself from the struggle between right and wrong, good and evil.
Speech to the National Association of Evangelicals [March 8, 1983]

15   I will not make age an issue. . . . I am not going to exploit for political purposes my opponent's youth and inexperience.
Television debate with Walter Mondale [October 21, 1984]

16   It's difficult to believe that people are starving in this country because food isn't available.
Press conference [June 11, 1986]

17   The nine most terrifying words in the English language are, "I'm from the government and I'm here to help."
Press conference [August 12, 1986]

18   Come here to this gate! Mr. Gorbachev, open this gate! Mr. Gorbachev, tear down this wall!
Remarks at the Brandenburg Gate, West Berlin [June 12, 1987]

1 We must always deal from strength and insist on verification of every agreement. In my meetings with the General Secretary I repeated several times a Russian proverb — "doveryai no proveryai" — "trust but verify."
Letter to Gerald B. Broussard [February 15, 1988]

E[rnst] F[riedrich] Schumacher
1911–1977

2 Small Is Beautiful: Economics As If People Mattered
Title of book [1973]

John Archibald Wheeler
1911–2008

3 There is nothing in the world except empty curved space. Matter, charge, electromagnetism and other fields are only manifestations of the curvature of space.
Quoted in New Scientist [September 26, 1974]

Tennessee [Thomas Lanier] Williams
1911–1983

4 Knowledge — Zzzzzp!   Money — Zzzzzp! — Power! That's the cycle democracy is built on!
The Glass Menagerie [1945], sc. vii

5 Time is the longest distance between two places.   *The Glass Menagerie, sc. vii*

6 I don't want realism....I'll tell you what I want. Magic! Yes, yes, magic!...I don't tell the truth, I tell what *ought* to be the truth.
A Streetcar Named Desire [1947], sc. ix

7 Whoever you are — I have always depended on the kindness of strangers.
A Streetcar Named Desire, sc. xi

8 Time rushes toward us with its hospital tray of infinitely varied narcotics, even while it is preparing us for its inevitably fatal operation.
The Rose Tattoo [1950]. Foreword, The Timeless World of a Play

9 Mendacity is a system that we live in. Liquor is one way out an' death's the other.
Cat on a Hot Tin Roof [1955], act II

10 Nothing's more determined than a cat on a tin roof — is there? Is there, baby?
Cat on a Hot Tin Roof, III, last line

11 We're all of us sentenced to solitary confinement inside our own skins, for life.
Orpheus Descending [1955]

12 For love I make characters in plays.
Collected Stories [1980]. Preface: The Man in the Overstuffed Chair [c. 1960]

Charles Addams
1912–1988

13 May I borrow a cup of cyanide?   *Cartoon caption*

14 Wait a minute, can't you? I've only got three hands.   *Cartoon caption*

Jorge Amado
1912–2001

15 Color of cinnamon
Clove's sweet smell,
I've come a long way
To see Gabrielle.
Gabriela, Clove and Cinnamon (Gabriela, Cravo e Canela) [1958], epigraph

Jean Améry [Hans Mayer]
1912–1978

16 Torture has an indelible character. Whoever was tortured, stays tortured.
At the Mind's Limits [1966]

Michelangelo Antonioni
1912–2007

17 Eros is sick.
Statement for the premiere of L'Avventura at the Cannes film festival, 1960

18 The first quality of a director is to see. This quality is also valuable in dealing with actors. The actor is one of the elements of the image.
Reflections on the Film Actor [1961]

John Cage
1912–1992

19 I believe that the use of noise to make music will continue and increase until we reach a music produced through the aid of electrical instruments which will make available for musical purposes any and all sounds that can be heard.
The Future of Music: Credo [1937]

1 Wherever we are, what we hear is mostly noise. When we ignore it, it disturbs us. When we listen to it, we find it fascinating.

The Future of Music: Credo

John Cheever
1912–1982

2 When the beginnings of self-destruction enter the heart it seems no bigger than a grain of sand.

Journal entry [1952]

3 Fear tastes like a rusty knife and do not let her into your house. Courage tastes of blood. Stand up straight. Admire the world. Relish the love of a gentle woman. Trust in the Lord.

The Wapshot Chronicle [1957], ch. 36, end

4 I will never come back, and if I do there will be nothing left, there will be nothing left but the head-stones to record what has happened; there will really be nothing at all.

The Wapshot Scandal [1963], final line

5 Fifty percent of the people in the world are home-sick all the time.

The Brigadier and the Golf Widow [1964].
The Bella Lingua

6 The sea that morning was iridescent and dark. My wife and my sister were swimming — Diana and Helen — and I saw their uncovered heads, black and gold in the dark water. I saw them come out and I saw that they were naked, unshy, beautiful, and full of grace, and I watched the naked women walk out of the sea.   *Stories [1978]. Goodbye, My Brother*

7 Then it is dark; it is a night where kings in golden suits ride elephants over the mountains.

Stories. The Country Husband

8 It was at the highest point in the arc of a bridge that I became aware suddenly of the depth and bitter-ness of my feelings about modern life, and of the pro-foundness of my yearning for a more vivid, simple, and peaceable world.

Stories. The Angel of the Bridge

Julia Child
1912–2004

9 This is a book for the servantless American cook who can be unconcerned on occasion with budgets, waistlines, time schedules, children's meals, the parent-chauffeur-den mother syndrome, or anything else which might interfere with the enjoyment of pro-ducing something wonderful to eat.

Mastering the Art of French Cooking [1961]

Karl Deutsch
1912–1992

10 To have power means not to have to give in, and to force the environment or the other person to do so. Power in this narrow sense is the priority of output over intake, the ability to talk instead of listen. In a sense, it is the ability to afford not to learn.

The Nerves of Government [1966]

Lawrence [George] Durrell
1912–1990

11 There are only three things to be done with a woman. . . . You can love her, suffer for her, or turn her into literature.   *Justine [1957], pt. I*

12 I felt once more the strange equivocal power of the city — its flat alluvial landscape and exhausted airs . . . Alexandria; which is neither Greek, Syrian nor Egyptian, but a hybrid: a joint.   *Justine, I*

13 We are the children of our landscape; it dictates behavior and even thought in the measure to which we are responsive to it.   *Justine, I*

Milton Friedman
1912–2006

14 Freedom in economic arrangements is itself a component of freedom broadly understood, so eco-nomic freedom is an end in itself. . . . Economic freedom is also an indispensable means toward the achievement of political freedom.

Capitalism and Freedom [1962], ch. 1

15 Underlying most arguments against the free market is a lack of belief in freedom itself.

Capitalism and Freedom, 1

16 There's no such thing as a free lunch.[1]

Attributed

Northrop Frye
1912–1991

17 Imagination creates reality, and as desire is a part of imagination, the world we desire is more real than the world we passively accept.

Fearful Symmetry [1947]

18 Criticism . . . is to art what history is to action and philosophy to wisdom.

Anatomy of Criticism [1957]

---

[1]Also attributed to economist ALVIN H. HANSEN [1887–1975].

1   The primary function of education is to make one maladjusted to ordinary society.
Elementary Teaching and Elemental Scholarship [1964]

Woody [Woodrow Wilson] Guthrie
1912–1967

2 California is a garden of Eden
A paradise to live in or see
But believe it or not
You won't find it so hot
If you ain't got the do-re-mi

Do-Re-Mi [1937]

3 Some will rob you with a six-gun
And some with a fountain pen.

Pretty Boy Floyd [1939]

4 Well, it's always we ramble, that river and I,
All along your green valley I'll work till I die,
My land I'll defend with my life, if it be,
'Cause my pastures of plenty must always be free.

Pastures of Plenty [1941]

5 This land is your land, this land is my land,
From California to the New York island,
From the redwood forest to the Gulf Stream waters,
This land was made for you and me.

This Land Is Your Land [1956]

6   This Machine Kills Fascists.

Inscribed on his guitar

Eugène Ionesco
1912–1994

7   Take a perfect circle, caress it and you'll have a vicious circle.
The Bald Soprano (La Cantatrice Chauve) [1950]

8   There are more dead people than living. And their numbers are increasing. The living are getting rarer.

Rhinoceros[1] [1960], act I

9   We haven't the time to take our time.
Exit the King (Le Roi Se Meurt) [1963]

Edmond Jabès
1912–1991

10   I talked to you about the difficulty of being Jewish, which is the same as the difficulty of writing.

For Judaism and writing are but the same waiting, the same hope, the same wearing out.
The Book of Questions[2] [1965]. The Book of the Absent: Third Part

William Lederer
1912–2009
and
Eugene Burdick
1918–1965

11   The Ugly American
Title of book [1958]

Pope John Paul I [Albino Luciani]
1912–1978

12   He is Father. Even more, God is Mother, who does not want to harm us.
At Sunday Angelus blessing, St. Peter's Square [September 17, 1978]

13   I am only a poor man, accustomed to small things and silence.
Illustrissimi [1978], epilogue

Mary [Therese] McCarthy
1912–1989

14   Every word she [Lillian Hellman] writes is a lie, including "and" and "the."
Television interview [1980]

Thomas P. [Tip] O'Neill, Jr.
1912–1994

15   All politics is local.   *Saying*

Jackson Pollock
1912–1956

16   Today painters do not have to go to a subject matter outside of themselves. Most modern painters work from a different source. They work from within.
Radio interview with William Wright, 1950

17   I *am* nature.
Response to the idea that he wasn't painting from nature

---

[1]Translated by DEREK PROUSE.

[2]Translated by ROSMARIE WALDROP.

May Sarton [Eleanore Marie Sarton]
1912–1995

1 There is no end to the work of salvage
  In the drowning high seas of Christmas
  When loneliness, in the name of Christ
  (That longing!), attacks the world.
    Christmas Letter to a Psychiatrist [1970]

Studs [Louis] Terkel
1912–2008

2   Perhaps it is this specter that most haunts working
men and women: the planned obsolescence of people
that is of a piece with the planned obsolescence of the
things they make. Or sell.
    Working [1972], introduction

3   Hope has never trickled down. It has always
sprung up.   *Hope Dies Last [2003]*

Barbara W. Tuchman
1912–1989

4   Dead battles, like dead generals, hold the military
mind in their dead grip and Germans, no less than
other peoples, prepare for the last war.
    The Guns of August [1962], ch. 2

Alan Mathison Turing
1912–1954

5   I propose to consider the question, "Can
machines think?"
    *Computing Machinery and Intelligence
    [October 1950]*

6   I believe that at the end of the century the use of
words and general educated opinion will have altered
so much that one will be able to speak of machines
thinking without expecting to be contradicted.
    Computing Machinery and Intelligence

Patrick White
1912–1990

7   There's many benefits from a good read, just as
some must sing a lungful of psalm, or take the bottle
down from the shelf.
    The Tree of Man [1955], ch. 1

8   Inspiration descends only in flashes, to clothe circumstances; it is not stored up in a barrel, like salt herrings, to be doled out.
    Voss [1957], ch. 2

Tom Adair
1913–1988

9 Let's go again to Niag'ra,
  This time we'll look at the Fall.
  Let's leave our hut, Dear,
  Get out of our rut, Dear,
  Let's get away from it all.
    Let's Get Away from It All[1] *[1940]*

Menachem Begin
1913–1992

10   A great day in the annals of two ancient nations,
Egypt and Israel, whose sons met in battle five times,
fighting and falling. . . . It is thanks to our fallen
heroes that we could have reached this day.
    *On signing the Egyptian-Israeli peace treaty,
    Washington, D.C.*[2] *[March 26, 1979]*

Sammy Cahn
1913–1993

11 Love and marriage, love and marriage,
  Go together like a horse and carriage.
    Our Town[3] *(television musical) [1955].
    Love and Marriage*

12 Love is lovelier
  The second time around.
  Just as wonderful with both feet on the ground.
  It's that second time you hear your love song sung
  Makes you think perhaps that love, like youth, is
    wasted on the young.
    High Time [1960]. The Second Time Around[3]

Albert Camus
1913–1960

13   Mother died today, or maybe it was yesterday.
    The Stranger (L'Étranger) [1942], pt. I

14   For the first time, the first, I laid my heart open to
the benign indifference of the universe. To feel it so
like myself, indeed, so brotherly, made me realize that
I'd been happy, and that I was happy still.
    The Stranger, IV

15   There is but one truly serious philosophical problem, and that is suicide. Judging whether life is or

---

[1] Music by MATT DENNIS.
[2] See Anwar al-Sadat, 791:5.
[3] Music by JIMMY VAN HEUSEN.

is not worth living amounts to answering the fundamental question of philosophy.
The Myth of Sisyphus (Le Mythe de Sisyphe)
[1942]

1   The absurd is the essential concept and the first truth.   *The Myth of Sisyphus*

2   The struggle to reach the top is itself enough to fulfill the heart of man. One must believe that Sisyphus is happy.   *The Myth of Sisyphus*

3   It is not rebellion itself which is noble but the demands it makes upon us.
The Plague (La Peste) [1947]

4   Can one be a saint if God does not exist? That is the only concrete problem I know of today.
The Plague

5   Thus, too, they came to know the incorrigible sorrow of all prisoners and exiles, which is to live in company with a memory that serves no purpose.
The Plague

6   He knew what those jubilant crowds did not know but could have learned from books: that the plague bacillus never dies or disappears for good; that it can lie dormant for years and years in furniture and linen-chests; that it bides its time in bedrooms, cellars, trunks, and bookshelves; and that perhaps the day would come when, for the bane and the enlightening of men, it would rouse up its rats again and send them forth to die in a happy city.   *The Plague*

7   In the depth of winter, I finally learned that within me there lay an invincible summer.
Summer (L'Été) [1954]. Return to Tipasa

8   I shall tell you a great secret, my friend. Do not wait for the last judgment. It takes place every day.
The Fall (La Chute) [1956]

9   A single sentence will suffice for modern man: he fornicated and read the papers.   *The Fall*

10   For there to be equivalence [between a premeditated crime and a crime of "pure violence"], the death penalty would have to punish a criminal who had warned his victim of the date at which he would inflict a horrible death on him and who, from that moment onward, had confined him at his mercy for months. Such a monster is not encountered in private life.
Reflections on the Guillotine [1957]

Robert Capa
[Endre Ernö Friedmann]
1913–1954

11   If your pictures aren't good enough, you aren't close enough.   *Maxim*

Aimé Césaire
1913–2008

12   And above all, my body as well as my soul, beware of assuming the sterile attitude of a spectator, for life is not a spectacle, a sea of miseries is not a proscenium, a man screaming is not a dancing bear....
Notebook of a Return to the Native Land[1] [1939]

13 my negritude riddles with holes
the dense affliction of its worthy patience.
Notebook of a Return to the Native Land
[1947]

Robertson Davies
1913–1995

14   Vaudeville audiences...could give the loudest sighs I have ever heard. Prisoners in the Bastille couldn't have touched them.
World of Wonders [1976]. A Bottle in the Smoke, pt. VIII

15   The magician Merlin had a strange laugh, and it was heard when nobody else was laughing....He laughed because he knew what was coming next.
World of Wonders. A Bottle in the Smoke, VIII

16   She was worse than a blabber; she was a hinter. It gave her pleasure to rouse curiosity and speculation about dangerous things.
What's Bred in the Bone [1985].
What Would Not Out of the Flesh?

Gerald R[udolph] Ford
1913–2006

17   I'm a Ford, not a Lincoln.
Comment after his nomination for the
vice-presidency [October 12, 1973]

18   Our long national nightmare is over.
On being sworn in as President
[August 9, 1974]

19   A government big enough to give you everything you want is a government big enough to take from you everything you have.[2]
Address to joint session of Congress
[August 12, 1974]

Philip Guston
1913–1980

20   The visible world, I think, is abstract and mysterious enough.   *Lecture [1978]*

---

[1]Translated by CLAYTON ESHLEMAN and ANNETTE SMITH.
[2]See Barry Goldwater, 758:11.

Donald Francis Mason
1913–1990

1 Sighted sub, sank same.
*Radio message to U.S. Navy Base
[January 28, 1942]*

Richard M[ilhous] Nixon
1913–1994

2 The kids, like all kids, loved the dog [Checkers], and I just want to say this, right now, that regardless of what they say about it, we are going to keep it.
Radio and TV speech responding to allegations of a political slush fund [September 23, 1952]

3 Isn't it better to talk about the relative merits of washing machines than the relative strength of rockets?
To Nikita Khrushchev in Moscow "kitchen debate" [1959]

4 You won't have Nixon to kick around anymore, because, gentlemen, this is my last press conference.
To the press [November 7, 1962]

5 The great silent majority.
Speech [November 3, 1969]

6 The Chinese are a great and vital people who should not remain isolated from the international community.... It is certainly in our interest, and in the interest of peace and stability in Asia and the world, that we take what steps we can toward improved practical relations with Peking.
First Foreign Policy Report to Congress [February 1970]

7 If when the chips are down, the world's most powerful nation ... acts like a pitiful, helpless giant, the forces of totalitarianism and anarchy will threaten free nations and free institutions throughout the world.
Televised speech [April 30, 1970] announcing major United States offensive into Cambodia

8 I want you all to stonewall it.
Presidential transcript [March 22, 1973]

9 People have got to know whether or not their President is a crook. Well, I'm not a crook.
Press conference [November 11, 1973]

10 Always give your best, never get discouraged, never be petty; always remember, others may hate you. Those who hate you don't win unless you hate them. And then you destroy yourself.
Address to members of the administration on leaving office [August 9, 1974]

11 I brought myself down. I gave them a sword, and they stuck it in. And they twisted it with relish. And, I guess, if I had been in their position, I'd have done the same thing.
Interview with David Frost [May 4, 1977]

12 When the President does it, that means that it is not illegal.
Interview with David Frost [May 19, 1977]

Tillie Olsen
1913–2007

13 She would not exchange her solitude for anything. Never again to be forced to move to the rhythms of others.
Tell Me a Riddle [1961], title story, sec. 1

14 Only help her to know — help make it so there is cause for her to know — that she is more than this dress on the ironing board, helpless before the iron.
Tell Me a Riddle. I Stand Here Ironing

15 Women are traditionally trained to place others' needs first ... their satisfaction to be in making it possible for others to use their abilities.
Silences [1978], pt. I

Rosa Parks
1913–2005

16 I had felt for a long time, that if I was ever told to get up so a white person could sit, that I would refuse to do so.
Recalling her refusal to give up her seat on a Montgomery, Alabama, bus [December 1, 1955]

Ad[olph Frederick] Reinhardt
1913–1967

17 Fine art can only be defined as exclusive, negative, absolute and timeless. It is not practical, useful, related, applicable, or subservient to anything else.
Twelve Rules for a New Academy [1953]

Muriel Rukeyser
1913–1980

18 Fly down, Death: Call me:
I have become a lost name. *Madboy's Song, refrain*

19 What would happen if one woman told the truth about her life?
The world would split open. *Käthe Kollwitz, sec. III*

Delmore Schwartz
1913–1966

1 Time is the school in which we learn,
  Time is the fire in which we burn.
  > *For Rhoda [1938]*

2 That inescapable animal walks with me.
  Has followed me since the black womb held,
  Moves where I move, distorting my gesture,
  A caricature, a swollen shadow,
  A stupid clown of the spirit's motive,
  Perplexes and affronts with his own darkness,
  The secret life of belly and bone.
  > *The Heavy Bear Who Goes with Me [1959],
  > st. 3*

3 The mind is a city like London,
  Smoky and populous: it is a capital
  Like Rome, ruined and eternal,
  Marked by the monument which no one
  Now remembers.
  > *The Mind Is an Ancient and Famous Capital
  > [1959]*

4   Even paranoids have real enemies.
  > *Attributed*

Karl Shapiro
1913–2000

5 One day beside some flowers near his nose
  He will be thinking, *When will I look at it?*
  And pain, still in the middle distance, will reply
  At what? and he will know it's gone,
  O where! and begin to tremble and cry.
  He will begin to cry as a child cries
  Whose puppy is mangled under a screaming wheel.
  > *V-Letter [1944]. The Leg*

6 To hurt the Negro and avoid the Jew
  Is the curriculum.
  > *Poems of a Jew [1958]. University*

7   I am an atheist who says his prayers.
  > *The Bourgeois Poet [1964]. I Am an Atheist
  > Who Says His Prayers*

8   I didn't go to the funeral of poetry. I stayed home
  and watched it on television.
  > *The Bourgeois Poet. The Funeral of Poetry*

Irwin Shaw
1913–1984

9   God Was Here but He Left Early
  > *Title of story [1968] and book [1973]*

May Swenson
1913–1989

10 Body my house
  my horse my hound
  what will I do
  when you are fallen
  > *Question [1954], st. 1*

11 Where can I go
  without my mount
  all eager and quick
  How will I know
  in thicket ahead
  is danger or treasure
  when Body my good
  bright dog is dead
  > *Question, st. 3*

12 The summer that I was ten–
  Can it be there was only one
  summer that I was ten?
  > *The Centaur [1958]*

13 Youth is given. One must put it away
  like a doll in a closet,
  take it out and play with it only
  on holidays.
  > *How to Be Old [1963]*

14 It's done
  on a diamond,
  and for fun.
  It's about
  home, and it's
  about run.
  > *Analysis of Baseball [1963]*

15 My face
  a negative in the slate
  window,
  I sit
  in a lit
  corridor that races
  through a dark
  one.
  > *Riding the "A" [1963]*

Lewis Thomas
1913–1993

16   What is [the earth] *most* like? . . . It is *most* like a
  single cell.
  > *The Lives of a Cell [1974]. The Lives of a Cell*

17   There is really no such creature as a single individual; he has no more life of his own than a cast-off cell
  marooned from the surface of your skin.
  > *The Lives of a Cell. Antaeus in Manhattan*

18   Viewed from the distance of the moon, the astonishing thing about the earth . . . is that it is alive. . . .
  Aloft, floating free beneath the moist, gleaming mem-
  brane of bright blue sky, is the rising earth, the only
  exuberant thing in this part of the cosmos. . . . It has

the organized, self-contained look of a live creature, full of information, marvelously skilled in handling the sun.

> *The Lives of a Cell. The World's Biggest Membrane*

1 We are, perhaps, uniquely among the earth's creatures, the worrying animal. We worry away our lives, fearing the future, discontent with the present, unable to take in the idea of dying, unable to sit still.

> *The Medusa and the Snail [1979]. The Youngest and Brightest Thing Around*

2 I am a member of a fragile species, still new to the earth, the youngest creatures of any scale, here only a few moments as evolutionary time is measured, a juvenile species, a child of a species ... in real danger at the moment of leaving behind only a thin layer of our fossils, radioactive at that. *The Fragile Species [1992]*

John Berryman
1914–1972

3 We must travel in the direction of our fear.
> *A Point of Age [1942]*

4 Mountainous, woman not breaks and will bend:
sways God nearby: anguish comes to an end.
Blossomed Sarah, and I
blossom. Is that thing alive? I hear a famisht howl.
> *Homage to Mistress Bradstreet [1953], st. 21*

5 Huffy Henry hid   the day,
Unappeasable Henry sulked.
> *77 Dream Songs [1964], poem no. 1*

6 I don't see how Henry, pried
open for all the world to see, survived.
> *77 Dream Songs, 1*

7 Life, friends, is boring. We must not say so.
> *77 Dream Songs, 14*

8   Two daiquiris
withdrew into a corner of the gorgeous room
and one told the other a lie.   *77 Dream Songs, 16*

9 But never did Henry, as he thought he did,
end anyone and hacks her body up
and hide the pieces, where they may be found.
He knows: he went over everyone, & nobody's
    missing.
Often he reckons, in the dawn, them up.
Nobody is ever missing.   *77 Dream Songs, 29*

10 He stared at ruin. Ruin stared straight back.
He thought they were old friends.
> *77 Dream Songs, 45*

11 I myself walked at the funeral of tenderness.
> *77 Dream Songs, 46*

12   Something can (has) been said for sobriety but
very little.   *77 Dream Songs, 57*

13 But I do guess mos peoples gonna *lose*.
> *77 Dream Songs, 60*

14 The world is gradually becoming a place
where I do not care to be any more.
> *His Toy, His Dream, His Rest [1968], poem no. 149*

15 It is a true error to marry with poets
or to be by them.
> *His Toy, His Dream, His Rest, 187*

16   Decent fall the cloths
over a high income.
> *His Toy, His Dream, His Rest, 196*

17 What was it missing, then, at the man's heart
so that he does not wound?
> *His Toy, His Dream, His Rest, 219 (So Long? Stevens)*

18 I haven't lost a battle yet but I am tense
for the first losing.
> *His Toy, His Dream, His Rest, 315*

19 Offering dragons quarter is no good,
they regrow all their parts & come on again,
they have to be killed.
> *His Toy, His Dream, His Rest, 316*

20 When will indifference come.
> *His Toy, His Dream, His Rest, 384*

Daniel J[oseph] Boorstin
1914–2004

21   A pseudo-event ... comes about because someone has planned, planted, or incited it. Typically, it is not a train wreck or an earthquake, but an interview.
> *The Image [1962], ch. 1*

22   The celebrity is a person who is known for his well-knownness.   *The Image, 1*

Julia de Burgos
1914–1953

23 We come from not being and march toward not
    being:
nothing between two nothings, zero between two
    zeros,
and since between two nothings nothing can be,
let's drink to the splendor of not being our bodies.
> *Poema en Veinte Surcos [1938]. Nothing*[1]

---

[1] Translated by ALIKI BARNSTONE and WILLIS BARNSTONE.

William Seward Burroughs
1914–1997

1   Junk is not a kick. It is a way of life.
Junky[1] *[1953]*

2   The title means exactly what the words say: NAKED Lunch — a frozen moment when everyone sees what is on the end of every fork.
Naked Lunch [1959]. Introduction

3   There is only one thing a writer can write about: *what is in front of his senses at the moment of writing.*
Naked Lunch

4   Our national drug is alcohol. We tend to regard the use of any other drug with special horror.
Naked Lunch

5   The face of "evil" is always the face of total need.
Deposition: Testimony Concerning a Sickness [1960]; reprinted in Naked Lunch [1962 edition]

Julio Cortázar
1914–1984

6   There was a time when I thought a great deal about the axolotls. I went to see them in the aquarium at the Jardin des Plantes and stayed for hours watching them, observing their immobility, their faint movements. Now I am an axolotl.
Final del juego[2] *(End of the Game) [1956]. Axolotl*

7   As if the species in every individual were on guard against letting himself go too far along the road of tolerance, intelligent doubt, sentimental vacillation. At some given point the callus, the sclerosis, the definition is born: black or white, radical or conservative, homo- or heterosexual, the San Lorenzo team or the Boca Juniors, meat or vegetables, business or poetry.
Rayuela[3] *(Hopscotch) [1963]*

Ralph [Waldo] Ellison
1914–1994

8   I am an invisible man.... I am a man of substance, of flesh and bone, fiber and liquids — and I might even be said to possess a mind. I am invisible, understand, simply because people refuse to see me.
Invisible Man [1952], prologue

9   Live with your head in the lion's mouth. I want you to overcome 'em with yeses, undermine 'em with grins, agree 'em to death and destruction, let 'em swoller you till they vomit or bust wide open.
Invisible Man, ch. 1

10   While one can do nothing about choosing one's relatives one can, as artist, choose one's "ancestors."
Shadow and Act [1964]. The World and the Jug

11   When American life is most American it is apt to be most theatrical.
Shadow and Act. Change the Joke and Slip the Yoke

John Hersey
1914–1993

12   There was no sound of planes. The morning was still; the place was cool and pleasant.

Then a tremendous flash of light cut across the sky. Mr. Tanimoto has a distinct recollection that it traveled from east to west, from the city toward the hills. It seemed a sheet of sun. Both he and Mr. Matsuo reacted in terror.... Under what seemed to be a local dust cloud, the day grew darker and darker.
Hiroshima [1946], ch. 1

13   There, in the tin factory, in the first moment of the atomic age, a human being was crushed by books.
Hiroshima, 1

Randall Jarrell
1914–1965

14 From my mother's sleep I fell into the State,
And I hunched in its belly till my wet fur froze.
Six miles from earth, loosed from its dream of life,
I woke to black flak and the nightmare fighters.
When I died they washed me out of the turret with a hose.
The Death of the Ball Turret Gunner [1944]

15   You know what I was,
You see what I am: change me, change me!
The Woman at the Washington Zoo [1960]

16 But I identify myself, as always,
With something that there's something wrong with,
With something human.
The One Who Was Different [1965]

17   A novel is a prose narrative of some length that has something wrong with it.
An Unread Book [1965]

---

[1]Originally published as *Junkie* under the pseudonym William Lee.
[2]Translated by PAUL BLACKBURN.
[3]Translated by GREGORY RABASSA.

Weldon Kees
1914–1955

1 Robinson in Glen plaid jacket, Scotch-grain shoes,
Black four-in-hand and oxford button-down,
The jeweled and silent watch that winds itself,
   the brief-
Case, covert topcoat, clothes for spring, all covering
His sad and usual heart, dry as a winter leaf.
Poems 1947–1954 [1954]. Aspects of
Robinson

Robert Lindner
1914–1956

2   The psychopath...is a rebel, a religious dis-
obeyer of prevailing codes and standards. Moreover,
clinical experience with such individuals makes it
appear that the psychopath is a rebel without a cause,
an agitator without a slogan, a revolutionary without
a program.
Rebel Without a Cause: The Story of a
Criminal Psychopath [1944]

Joe Louis [Joseph Louis Borrow]
1914–1981

3   [On his military service:] I have only done what
any red-blooded American would do. We gonna do
our part, and we will win, because we are on God's
side.
Speech at Madison Square Garden [March
10, 1942]

4   He can run, but he can't hide.
Remark before his heavyweight title fight with
Billy Conn [June 19, 1946]

Bernard Malamud
1914–1986

5   There comes a time in a man's life when to get
where he has to go — if there are no doors or windows — he walks through a wall.
Rembrandt's Hat [1972]. Man in the
Drawer

6   There is no life that can be recaptured wholly; as it
was. Which is to say that all biography is ultimately
fiction. What does that tell you about the nature of
life, and does one really want to know?
Dubin's Lives [1979], ch. 1

7   One's fantasy goes for a walk and returns with a
bride.
Long Work, Short Life [1985]

Hugh Martin
1914–2011

and

Ralph Blane
1914–1995

8 Through the years we all will be together,
If the Fates allow.
Hang a shining star upon the highest bough,
And have yourself a merry little Christmas now.
Meet Me in St. Louis [1944].
Have Yourself a Merry Little Christmas

Vance Packard
1914–1996

9   The Hidden Persuaders   *Title of book [1957]*

Norman Panama
1914–2003

and

Melvin Frank
1913–1983

10   The pellet with the poison is in the vessel with the
pestle, the chalice from the palace has the brew that is
true.
The Court Jester (screenplay) [1956],
spoken by Danny Kaye

Ross Parker
1914–1974

and

Hughie Charles
1907–1995

11 There'll always be an England
While there's a country lane,
Wherever there's a cottage small
Beside a field of grain.
There'll Always Be an England [1939]

Nicanor Parra
1914–

12 I wish to make a noise with my feet.
I want my soul to find its proper body.
Poems and Anti-Poems [1958]. Piano Solo[1]

---

[1]Translated by WILLIAM CARLOS WILLIAMS.

Octavio Paz
1914–1998

1   Would it not be true to say that North Americans prefer to use reality rather than to know it?

The Labyrinth of Solitude[1] *(El Labrinto de la Soledad) [1950], ch. 1*

2   Solitude lies at the lowest depth of the human condition. Man is the only being who feels himself to be alone and the only one who is searching for the Other.

The Labyrinth of Solitude, appendix

3 a crystal willow, a poplar of water,
a tall fountain the wind arches over,
a tree deep-rooted yet dancing still,
a course of a river that turns, moves on,
doubles back, and comes full circle,
forever arriving:

Sunstone[2] *[1957]*

4   the world changes
if two, dizzy and entwined, fall
on the grass   *Sunstone*

5   To read a poem is to hear it with our eyes; to hear it is to see it with our ears.

Alternating Current [1967]. Recapitulations

6   Touched by poetry, language is more fully language and at the same time is no longer language: it is a poem.

Claude Lévi-Strauss[1] *[1967], ch. 3*

7 We are condemned
to kill time:
Thus we die
bit by bit

*Tale of Two Gardens
(Cuento de dos jardines) [1968]*

8 My steps along this street
Resound
          in another street
In which
          I hear my steps
Passing along this street
In which
Only the mist is real.

Configurations. Here (Aquí)[3]

9 The absolutes the eternities
Their outlying districts

Are not my theme
I am hungry for life and for death also
I know what I know and I write it.

Configurations. Vrindaban,[4] *l. 152*

10   There can be a "boom" in petroleum or wheat, but there can't be a boom in the novel and less still in poetry.

Seven Voices [1972], interview

Sun Ra
[Herman Poole Blount]
1914–1993

11   It's after the end of the world. Don't you know that yet?

Space Is the Place [1974]

Henry Reed
1914–1986

12 To-day we have naming of parts. Yesterday,
We had daily cleaning. And to-morrow morning,
We shall have what to do after firing. But to-day,
To-day we have naming of parts.

*Lessons of the War [1946]. I,
Naming of Parts*

13 And the various holds and rolls and throws and
     breakfalls
Somehow or other I always seemed to put
In the wrong place. And as for war, my wars
Were global from the start.

Lessons of the War. III, Unarmed Combat

Budd Schulberg
1914–2009

14   What Makes Sammy Run?

Title of book [1941]

15   Going through life with a conscience is like driving your car with the brakes on.

What Makes Sammy Run? [1941]

16   A one-way ticket to Palookaville.

*On the Waterfront (screenplay) [1954],
spoken by Marlon Brando*

17   I could've been a contender. I could've had class and been somebody. Real class. Instead of a bum, let's face it, which is what I am.

*On the Waterfront (screenplay), spoken by
Marlon Brando*

---

[1]Translated by RACHEL PHILLIPS.
[2]Translated by ELIOT WEINBERGER.
[3]Translated by CHARLES TOMLINSON.

[4]Translated by LYSANDER KEMP.

Jerry Siegel
1914–1996
and
Joe Shuster
1914–1992

1   Faster than a speeding bullet, more powerful than a locomotive, able to leap tall buildings at a single bound — look, up there in the sky, it's a bird, it's a plane, it's Superman!

                    Superman (comic strip) [June 1938]

Dylan Thomas
1914–1953

2 The force that through the green fuse drives the
    flower
Drives my green age; that blasts the roots of trees
Is my destroyer.
And I am dumb to tell the crooked rose
My youth is bent by the same wintry fever.
        The Force That Through the Green Fuse
        Drives the Flower [1934]

3 Light breaks where no sun shines;
  Where no sea runs, the waters of the heart
  Push in their tides.
      Light Breaks Where No Sun Shines [1934]

4 They dance between their arclamps and our skull,
  Impose their shots, throwing the nights away.
  We watch the show of shadows kiss or kill,
  Flavoured of celluloid give love the lie.
             Our Eunuch Dreams [1934]

5 The hand that signed the paper felled a city;
  Five sovereign fingers taxed the breath,
  Doubled the globe of dead and halved a country;
  These five kings did a king to death.
       The Hand That Signed the Paper [1936]

6 And death shall have no dominion.
         Refrain and title of poem [1943]

7 After the first death there is no other.
    A Refusal to Mourn the Death, by Fire,
    of a Child in London [1946]

8 Forgotten mornings when he walked with his mother
    Through the parables
      Of sunlight
And the legend of the green chapels.
            Poem in October [1946]

9 Now as I was young and easy under the apple boughs
  About the lilting house and happy as the grass was
    green.
             Fern Hill [1946], st. 1

10 And honored among wagons I was prince of the
    apple towns.   *Fern Hill, st. 1*

11 In the sun that is young once only,
    Time let me play and be
  Golden in the mercy of his means.
             Fern Hill, st. 1

12   And the sabbath rang slowly
In the pebbles of the holy streams. *Fern Hill, st. 2*

13 And honored among foxes and pheasants by the gay
    house
Under the new-made clouds and happy as the heart
    was long,
    In the sun born over and over,
        I ran my heedless ways.   *Fern Hill, st. 5*

14   Time held me green and dying
Though I sang in my chains like the sea.
             Fern Hill, st. 6

15 Do not go gentle into that good night,
  Old age should burn and rave at close of day;
  Rage, rage against the dying of the light.
    Do Not Go Gentle into That Good Night
    [1952]

16   One Christmas was so much like another, in those years around the seatown corner now and out of all sound except the distant speaking of the voices I sometimes hear a moment before sleep, that I can never remember whether it snowed for six days and six nights when I was twelve or whether it snowed for twelve days and twelve nights when I was six.
    Quite Early One Morning [1954].
    A Child's Christmas in Wales

17   It is spring, moonless night in the small town, starless and bible-black.
           Under Milk Wood [1954]

Rudy [Rudolph] Toombs
c. 1914–1962

18 I looked down the bar at the bartender
He said, "Now what do you want, Johnny?"
"One bourbon, one scotch, and one beer"
    One Bourbon, One Scotch, One Beer[1] *[1953]*

E[dward] Digby Baltzell
1915–1996

19   There is a crisis in American leadership in the middle of the twentieth century that is partly due, I think, to the declining authority of an

---

[1]This song was later recorded and popularized by JOHN LEE HOOKER [1917–2001].

establishment which is now based on an increasingly castelike White-Anglo Saxon-Protestant (WASP) upper class.

The Protestant Establishment [1964], ch. 1

Roland Barthes
1915–1980

1   I think that cars today are almost the exact equivalent of the great Gothic cathedrals: I mean the supreme creation of an era, conceived with passion by unknown artists, and consumed in image if not in usage by a whole population which appropriates them as a purely magical object.

Mythologies[1] [1957]. The New Citroën

2   What the public wants is the image of passion, not passion itself.   *Mythologies. The World of Wrestling*

3   The birth of the reader must be at the cost of the death of the Author.

The Death of the Author[2] [1968]

4   The goal of literary work (of literature as work) is to make the reader no longer a consumer but a producer of the text.   *S/Z[3] [1970]*

5   The text you write must prove to me *that it desires me.*   *The Pleasure of the Text[3] [1973]*

6   Language is a skin: I rub my language against the other. It is as if I had words instead of fingers, or fingers at the tip of my words. My language trembles with desire.

A Lover's Discourse: Fragments,[4] "Talking" [1977]

Saul Bellow
1915–2005

7   I am an American, Chicago born — Chicago, that somber city — and go at things as I have taught myself, free-style, and will make the record in my own way: first to knock, first admitted; sometimes an innocent knock, sometimes a not so innocent.

The Adventures of Augie March [1953], opening line

8   There was a disturbance in my heart, a voice that spoke there and said, *I want, I want, I want!* It happened every afternoon, and when I tried to suppress it it got even stronger. . . . It never said a thing except *I want, I want, I want!*

Henderson the Rain King [1959]

9   I am simply a human being, more or less.

Herzog [1964]

10   As though to be Jewish weren't trouble enough, the poor woman was German, too.

Mr. Sammler's Planet [1970], pt. I

11   The idea of making the century's great crime look dull is not banal. Politically, psychologically, the Germans had an idea of genius. The banality was only camouflage. What better way to get the curse out of murder than to make it look ordinary, boring, or trite? . . . Banality is the adopted disguise of a very powerful will to abolish conscience.

Mr. Sammler's Planet, I

12   New York makes one think of the collapse of civilization, about Sodom and Gomorrah, the end of the world. The end wouldn't come as a surprise here. Many people already bank on it.

Mr. Sammler's Planet, VI

13   There's almost nothing personal in success. Success is always money's own success.

Humboldt's Gift [1975]

14   Boredom is an instrument of social control. Power is the power to impose boredom, to command stasis, to combine this stasis with anguish. The real tedium, deep tedium, is seasoned with terror and with death.   *Humboldt's Gift*

15   The body, she says, is subject to the forces of gravity. But the soul is ruled by levity, pure.

Him with His Foot in His Mouth [1984], title story

16   Who is the Tolstoy of the Zulus? The Proust of the Papuans? I'd be glad to read him.

Remark [1988], telephone interview

Caroline Bird
1915–1995

17   Sexism is judging people by their sex where sex doesn't matter.

"On Being Born Female," Vital Speeches of the Day [November 15, 1968]

Leigh Brackett
1915–1978
and
Lawrence Kasdan
1949–

18   If once you start down the dark path, forever will it dominate your destiny. Consume you it will.

The Empire Strikes Back [1980], spoken by Frank Oz as Yoda

---

[1]Translated by ANNETTE LAVERS.
[2]Translated by STEPHEN HEATH.
[3]Translated by RICHARD MILLER.
[4]Translated by RICHARD HOWARD.

Jerome S[eymour] Bruner
1915–

1 The shrewd guess, the fertile hypothesis, the courageous leap to a tentative conclusion — these are the most valuable coin of the thinker at work.
The Process of Education [1960]

2 Any subject can be taught effectively in some intellectually honest form to any child at any stage of development.
The Process of Education

Willie [William James] Dixon
1915–1992

3 On the seventh hour
On the seventh day
On the seventh month
The seventh doctor say
He was born for good luck
And that you'll see
I got seven hundred dollars
Don't you mess with me
Hoochie Coochie Man [1954].
Recorded by Muddy Waters

4 Men lies about that,
Some of 'em cries about that,
Some of 'em dies about that,
Everybody fightin' about a spoonful,
That spoon, that spoon, that.
Spoonful [1960]. Recorded by Howlin' Wolf

Garrett Hardin
1915–2003

5 We can never do merely one thing.
Hardin's First Law of Ecology

6 The Tragedy of the Commons
Title of essay published in Science
[December 13, 1968]

7 Ruin is the destination toward which all men rush, each pursuing his own best interest in a society that believes in the freedom of the commons. Freedom in a commons brings ruin to all.
The Tragedy of the Commons [1968]

Billie Holiday
[Eleanora Fagan]
1915–1959

8 Love is just like a faucet,
It turns off and on,
And sometimes when you think it's on, baby,
It has turned off and gone.
Fine and Mellow [recorded 1944]

Billie Holiday
[Eleanora Fagan]
1915–1959
and
Arthur Herzog, Jr.
1927–1983

9 Them that's got shall get,
Them that's not shall lose,
So the Bible said, and it still is news.
Mama may have,
Papa may have,
But God bless the child that's got his own!
God Bless the Child [1941]

Bart Howard
1915–2004

10 Fly me to the moon, and let me play among the stars;
Let me see what spring is like on Jupiter and Mars.
In other words, hold my hand!
In other words, darling, kiss me!
Fly Me to the Moon [1954]

Alfred Kazin
1915–1998

11 A classic is a book that survives the circumstances that made it possible yet alone keeps those circumstances alive.
Review in The New Republic
[August 29, 1988]

Jerome Lawrence
1915–2004
and
Robert E. Lee
1918–1994

12 Life is a banquet, and most poor sons-of-bitches[1] are starving to death.
Auntie Mame, stage play [1956] based on the
novel [1955] by Patrick Dennis

---

[1]In the 1958 screen version, "sons-of-bitches" was changed to "suckers."

Ernest Lehman
1915–2005

1   I allowed the soothing music and the muted sounds of the city and the rich, sweet smell of success that permeated the room to lull my senses.
Tell Me About It Tomorrow (novella) [1950],
retitled The Sweet Smell of Success[1] *[1957]*

2   Seems to me you fellows could stand a little less training from the FBI and a little more from the Actors Studio.
North by Northwest (screenplay) [1959],
spoken by James Mason to Cary Grant

3   That plane's dustin' crops where there ain't no crops.
North by Northwest (screenplay)

Sir Peter Brian Medawar
1915–1987

4   Among scientists are collectors, classifiers, and compulsive tidiers-up; many are detectives by temperament and many are explorers; some are artists and others artisans. There are poet-scientists and philosopher-scientists and even a few mystics.
The Art of the Soluble [1967]

Arthur Miller
1915–2005

5   I don't say he's a great man. Willy Loman never made a lot of money. His name was never in the paper. He's not the finest character that ever lived. But he's a human being, and a terrible thing is happening to him. So attention must be paid. He's not to be allowed to fall into his grave like an old dog. Attention, attention must be finally paid to such a person.   *Death of a Salesman [1949], act I*

6   Never fight fair with a stranger, boy. You'll never get out of the jungle that way.
Death of a Salesman, I

7   You can't eat the orange and throw the peel away — a man is not a piece of fruit.
Death of a Salesman, II

8   For a salesman, there is no rock bottom to the life. He don't put a bolt to a nut, he don't tell you the law or give you medicine. He's a man way out there in the blue, riding on a smile and a shoeshine. And when they start not smiling back — that's an earthquake.
Death of a Salesman, Requiem

9   A salesman is got to dream, boy. It comes with the territory.   *Death of a Salesman, Requiem*

10   I have not moved from there to here without I think to please you, and still an everlasting funeral marches round your heart.
The Crucible [1953], act II

11   I am inclined to notice the ruin in things, perhaps because I was born in Italy.
A View from the Bridge [1955], act I

Paul A. Samuelson
1915–2009

12   Man does not live by GNP alone.
Economics [1973], ch. 40

Frank Sinatra
1915–1998

13   I'm not unmindful of man's seeming need for faith; I'm for *anything* that gets you through the night, be it prayer, tranquilizers, or a bottle of Jack Daniels.   *Interview in Playboy [February 1963]*

Jean Stafford
1915–1979

14   To her own heart, which was shaped exactly like a valentine, there came a winglike palpitation, a delicate exigency, and all the fragrance of all the flowery springtime love affairs that ever were seemed waiting for them in the whiskey bottle.
Children Are Bored on Sundays [1953],
title story

Potter Stewart
1915–1985

15   I shall not today attempt further to define [pornography]...But I know it when I see it; and the motion picture[2] involved in this case is not that.
Concurring opinion in U.S. Supreme Court,
Jacobellis v. Ohio [1964]

Billy Strayhorn
1915–1967

16 A week in Paris will ease the bite of it.
All I care is to smile in spite of it.   *Lush Life [1936]*

---

[1] *Sweet Smell of Success (screenplay)* [1957], *(musical)* [2002].

[2] The film in question was LOUIS MALLE's *Les Amants (The Lovers).*

1 Romance is mush, stifling those who strive.
I'll live a lush life in some small dive,
And there I'll be, while I rot with the rest
Of those whose lives are lonely, too.

Lush Life

Alan Watts
1915–1973

2   If you really want to spend some years in a Japanese monastery, there is no earthly reason why you shouldn't. Or if you want to spend your time hopping freight cars and digging Charlie Parker, it's a free country.

*Chicago Review [1958]. Beat Zen,
Square Zen, and Zen*

Orson Welles
1915–1985

3   The only way to stay out of trouble is to grow old, so I guess I'll concentrate on that. Maybe I'll live so long that I'll forget her — maybe I'll die trying.

The Lady from Shanghai (screenplay) [1948]

4   In Italy for thirty years under the Borgias they had warfare, terror, murder, bloodshed, but they produced Michelangelo, Leonardo da Vinci, and the Renaissance. In Switzerland they had brotherly love, they had five hundred years of democracy and peace. And what did that produce? The cuckoo-clock.

*Speech written into The Third Man
(screenplay by Graham Greene and
Carol Reed) [1949]*

5   A certain great and powerful king once asked a poet: "What can I give you of all that I have?" He wisely replied, "Anything sir . . . except your secret."

*Mister Arkadin (screenplay) [1955],
opening title*

6   A policeman's job is only easy in a police state.

*Touch of Evil [1958], spoken by Charlton
Heston*

7   [On the RKO studio:] This is the biggest electric train set any boy ever had.   *Attributed*

8   I like the old masters, by which I mean John Ford, John Ford, and John Ford.   *Attributed*

John Malcolm Brinnin
1916–1998

9 I seek a father who most need a son.

Oedipus: His Cradle Song [1963]

10 Another hill town;
another dry Cinzano in the sun.

Hotel Paradiso è Commerciale [1963]

11 We have all done this before; we're bored and terrified.   *Flight 539 [1963]*

Francis [Harry Compton] Crick
1916–2004

12   "You," your joys and your sorrows, your memories and your ambitions, your sense of personal identity and free will, are in fact no more than the behavior of a vast assembly of nerve cells and their associated molecules.

The Astonishing Hypothesis [1994]

Walter Cronkite
1916–2009

13   To say that we are closer to victory today is to believe, in the face of the evidence, the optimists who have been wrong in the past. To suggest that we are on the edge of defeat is to yield to unreasonable pessimism. To say that we are mired in stalemate seems the only realistic, yet unsatisfactory, conclusion.

*Who? What? When? Where? Why? A Report
from Vietnam [February 27, 1968]*

14   And that's the way it is.

Sign-off sentence, CBS Evening News

Elizabeth Hardwick
1916–2007

15   Collaborating in the very private way of love or the highest kind of friendship . . . is the way for gifted, energetic wives of writers to a sort of composition of their own, this peculiar illusion of collaboration.

*Seduction and Betrayal: Women in
Literature [1974]. Amateurs*

16   This is the unspoken contract of a wife and her works. In the long run wives are to be paid in a peculiar coin — consideration for their feelings. And it usually turns out this is an enormous, unthinkable inflation few men will remit, or if they will, only with a sense of being overcharged.

*Seduction and Betrayal: Women in
Literature. Amateurs*

17   I think all writing is profoundly unmarried.

*Interview with Richard Locke, The New York
Times [April 29, 1979]*

Richard Hofstadter
1916–1970

1   The Emancipation Proclamation of January 1, 1863, had all the moral grandeur of a bill of lading.
The American Political Tradition and the Men Who Made It [1948]

2   The distinguishing thing about the paranoid style is not that its exponents see conspiracies or plots here and there in history, but that they regard a "vast" or "gigantic" conspiracy as *the motive force* in historical events. History is a conspiracy, set in motion by demonic forces of almost transcendent power, and what is felt to be needed to defeat it is not the usual methods of political give-and-take, but an all-out crusade.
The Paranoid Style in American Politics and Other Essays [1965]

Shirley Jackson
1916–1965

3   "It isn't fair, it isn't right," Mrs. Hutchinson screamed, and then they were upon her.
The Lottery [1948], last line

Jane Jacobs
1916–2006

4   Lowly, unpurposeful and random as they may appear, sidewalk contacts are the small change from which a city's wealth of public life may grow.
The Death and Life of Great American Cities [1961]

5   Old ideas can sometimes use new buildings. New ideas must use old buildings.
The Death and Life of Great American Cities

6   The point of cities is multiplicity of choice.
The Death and Life of Great American Cities

Florynce Rae Kennedy
1916–2000

7   If men could get pregnant, abortion would be a sacrament.
From GLORIA STEINEM, The Verbal Karate of Florynce R. Kennedy, Esq. [1973]

Bernard Lewis
1916–

8   We are a facing a mood and a movement far transcending the level of issues and policies and the governments that pursue them. This is no less than a clash of civilizations[1] — the perhaps irrational but surely historic reaction of an ancient rival against our Judeo-Christian heritage, our secular present, and the worldwide expansion of both.
The Roots of Muslim Rage [1990]

Robert S[trange] McNamara
1916–2009

9   We of the Kennedy and Johnson administrations who participated in the decisions on Vietnam acted according to what we thought were the principles and traditions of this nation. We made our decisions in the light of those values. Yet we were wrong, terribly wrong. We owe it to future generations to explain why.
In Retrospect [1995], preface

10   We all make mistakes. We know we make mistakes. I don't know any military commander, who is honest, who would say he has not made a mistake. There's a wonderful phrase: "the fog of war." What "the fog of war" means is: war is so complex it's beyond the ability of the human mind to comprehend all the variables. Our judgment, our understanding, are not adequate. And we kill people unnecessarily.
Comment in The Fog of War [2003], documentary film by Errol Morris

11   Rationality will not save us.   *The Fog of War*

C[harles] Wright Mills
1916–1962

12   By the power elite, we refer to those political, economic, and military circles which as an intricate set of overlapping cliques share decisions having at least national consequences. In so far as national events are decided, the power elite are those who decide them.
The Power Elite [1956], ch. 1, The Higher Circles

Albert Murray
1916–

13   *American culture, even in its most rigidly segregated precincts, is patently and irrevocably composite. It is, regardless of all the hysterical protestations of those who would have it otherwise, incontestably mulatto.*

---

[1]The phrase "clash of civilizations" was popularized by Samuel Huntington in his essay "A Clash of Civilizations?" [1993], published in *Foreign Affairs* and in the book *The Clash of Civilizations and the Remaking of the World Order* [1996].

Indeed, for all their traditional antagonisms and obvious differences, the so-called black and so-called white people of the United States resemble nobody else in the world so much as they resemble each other.

The Omni-Americans [1970]

Walker Percy
1916–1990

1   The fact is I am quite happy in a movie, even a bad movie. Other people, so I have read, treasure memorable moments in their lives.   *The Moviegoer [1961]*

Herbert Simon
1916–2001

2   A wealth of information creates a poverty of attention.
Designing Organizations for an Information-Rich World [1971]

Harold Wilson
1916–1995

3   A week is a long time in politics.
Attributed

Robert Anderson
1917–2009

4   Years from now — when you talk about this — and you will — be kind.
Tea and Sympathy (play) [1953]

Gwendolyn Brooks
1917–2000

5 Maud went to college.
Sadie stayed at home.
Sadie scraped life
With a fine-tooth comb.
A Street in Bronzeville [1945]. Sadie and Maud, st. 1

6 Abortions will not let you forget.
You remember the children you got that you did not get.
A Street in Bronzeville. The Mother, st. 1

7 What shall I give my children? who are poor,
Who are adjudged the leastwise of the land.
Annie Allen [1949]. The Womanhood. The Children of the Poor, sonnet 2

8 Exhaust the little moment. Soon it dies.
And be it gash or gold it will not come
Again in this identical disguise.
Annie Allen. Exhaust the Little Moment

9 And remembering . . .
Remembering, with twinklings and twinges,
As they lean over the beans in their rented back room
that is full of beads and receipts and dolls and
cloths, tobacco crumbs, vases and fringes.
The Bean Eaters [1960]. The Bean Eaters, st. 3

10 We real cool. We
Left school. We
Lurk late. We
Strike straight. We
Sing sin. We
Thin gin. We
Jazz June. We
Die soon.   *The Bean Eaters. We Real Cool*

11 He opened us —
who was a key,
who was a man.
In the Mecca [1968]. After Mecca. Malcolm X

12 The time
cracks into furious flower. Lifts its face
all unashamed. And sways in wicked grace.
In the Mecca. The Second Sermon on the Warpland, st. 4

13 Big Bessie's feet hurt like nobody's business,
but she stands — bigly — under the unruly scrutiny,
stands in the wild weed.
In the wild weed
she is a citizen.
In the Mecca. The Second Sermon on the Warpland, st. 4

Anthony Burgess
[John Anthony Burgess Wilson]
1917–1993

14   What's it going to be then, eh?
A Clockwork Orange [1962]

15   That shut her up real horrorshow and lovely.
A Clockwork Orange

Robert C. Byrd
1917–2010

16   On this February day, as this nation stands at the brink of battle, every American on some level must be contemplating the horrors of war.

Yet this Chamber is, for the most part, silent — ominously, dreadfully silent. There is no debate, no discussion, no attempt to lay out for the nation the pros and cons of this particular war. There is nothing.

We stand passively mute in the United States Senate, paralyzed by our own uncertainty, seemingly stunned by the sheer turmoil of events.

Speech on the impending invasion of Iraq [February 12, 2003]

Arthur C[harles] Clarke
1917–2008

1   I can never look now at the Milky Way without wondering from which of those banked clouds of stars the emissaries are coming.   *The Sentinel [1951]*

2 1. When a distinguished but elderly scientist states that something is possible, he is almost certainly right. When he states that something is impossible, he is very probably wrong. 2. The only way of discovering the limits of the possible is to venture a little way past them into the impossible. 3. Any sufficiently advanced technology is indistinguishable from magic.

Clarke's Three Laws, in Profiles of the Future [1962]

Arthur C[harles] Clarke
1917–2008
and
Stanley Kubrick
1928–1999

3   Open the pod bay doors, Hal.
2001: A Space Odyssey (screenplay) [1968]

4   Dave. Stop. Stop. Will you. Stop, Dave. Will you stop, Dave. Stop, Dave. I'm afraid. I'm afraid, Dave. Dave. My mind is going. I can feel it. I can feel it. My mind is going. There is no question about it. I can feel it. I can feel it. I can feel it. I'm afraid.

2001: A Space Odyssey (screenplay), spoken by Douglas Rain as the HAL computer

5   The thing's hollow — it goes on forever — and — oh my God! — *it's full of stars!*
2001: A Space Odyssey (screenplay)

Betty Comden
1917–2006
and
Adolph Green
1914–2002

6 New York, New York,
A helluva town.
The Bronx is up and the Battery's down,

And people ride in a hole in the ground.
New York, New York,
It's a helluva town!
On the Town [1944]. New York, New York

7 Now you must wake up,
All dreams must end.
Take off your makeup,
The party's over,
It's all over,
My friend.
Bells Are Ringing [1956]. The Party's Over

Joe Darion
1917–2001

8 To dream the impossible dream,
To reach the unreachable star!
Man of La Mancha [1965]. The Impossible Dream[1]

Manny Farber
1917–2008

9   A peculiar fact about termite-tapeworm-fungus-moss art is that it goes always forward eating its own boundaries, and, likely as not, leaves nothing in its path other than the signs of eager, industrious, unkempt activity.
White Elephant Art vs. Termite Art [1962]

Leslie Fiedler
1917–2003

10   The existence of overt homosexuality threatens to compromise an essential aspect of American sentimental life: the camaraderie of the locker room and ball park, the good fellowship of the poker game and fishing trip, a kind of passionless passion, at once gross and delicate, homoerotic in the boy's sense, possessing an innocence above suspicion.
Come Back to the Raft Ag'in, Huck Honey, Partisan Review [1948]

David Goodis
1917–1967

11   It was a tough break. Parry was innocent. On top of that he was a decent sort of guy who never bothered people and wanted to lead a quiet life. But there was too much on the other side and on his side of it there was practically nothing. The judge handed him a life sentence and he was taken to San Quentin.
Dark Passage [1946]

---

[1]Music by MITCH LEIGH.

Katharine [Meyer] Graham
1917–2001

1   If one is rich and one's a woman, one can be quite misunderstood.
The Power That Didn't Corrupt [1974]

2   What I essentially did was to put one foot in front of the other, shut my eyes, and step off the ledge. The surprise was that I landed on my feet.
Personal History [1997], ch. 18 (on becoming president of the Washington Post Co. in September 1963)

Fannie Lou Hamer
1917–1977

3   I'm sick and tired of being sick and tired.[1]
Speech delivered with Malcolm X at the Williams Institutional CME Church, Harlem [1964]

John Fitzgerald Kennedy
1917–1963

4   It was involuntary. They sank my boat.
Remark when asked how he became a hero. Quoted in ARTHUR M. SCHLESINGER, JR., *A Thousand Days [1965], ch. 4*

5   The New Frontier of which I speak is not a set of promises — it is a set of challenges. It sums up not what I intend to offer the American people, but what I intend to ask of them.
Speech accepting the Democratic presidential nomination [July 15, 1960]

6   I am not the Catholic candidate for President. I am the Democratic Party's candidate for President, who happens also to be a Catholic.
Speech to Greater Houston Ministerial Association [September 12, 1960]

7   I believe in an America where the separation of Church and State is absolute — where no Catholic prelate would tell the President (should he be a Catholic) how to act, and no Protestant minister would tell his parishioners for whom to vote — where no church or church school is granted any public funds or political preference.
Speech to Greater Houston Ministerial Association

8   Sometimes party loyalty asks too much.
Accepting Arthur M. Schlesinger's support for a Republican candidate [1960]

9   For of those to whom much is given, much is required. And when at some future date the high court of history sits in judgment on each of us, recording whether in our brief span of service we fulfilled our responsibilities to the state, our success or failure, in whatever office we hold, will be measured by the answers to four questions: First, were we truly men of courage . . . Second, were we truly men of judgment . . . Third, were we truly men of integrity . . . Finally, were we truly men of dedication?
Speech to the Massachusetts State Legislature [January 9, 1961]

10   Let the word go forth from this time and place, to friend and foe alike, that the torch has been passed to a new generation of Americans, born in this century, tempered by war, disciplined by a hard and bitter peace, proud of our ancient heritage, and unwilling to witness or permit the slow undoing of those human rights to which this nation has always been committed, and to which we are committed today at home and around the world.

Let every nation know, whether it wishes us well or ill, that we shall pay any price, bear any burden, meet any hardship, support any friend, oppose any foe to assure the survival and the success of liberty.
Inaugural address [January 20, 1961]

11   Let us never negotiate out of fear, but let us never fear to negotiate.
Inaugural address

12   All this will not be finished in the first one hundred days. Nor will it be finished in the first one thousand days, nor in the life of this Administration, nor even perhaps in our lifetime on this planet. But let us begin.
Inaugural address

13   And so, my fellow Americans, ask not what your country can do for you; ask what you can do for your country.[2]
Inaugural address

---

[1] Inscribed on her gravestone as "I am sick and tired of being sick and tired."

[2] For, stripped of the temporary associations which gave rise to it, it is now the moment when by common consent we pause to become conscious of our national life and to rejoice in it, to recall what our country has done for each of us, and to ask ourselves what we can do for our country in return. — OLIVER WENDELL HOLMES, JR., *Address Before John Sedgwick Post No. 4, Grand Army of the Republic* [May 30, 1884]

As has often been said, the youth who loves his Alma Mater will always ask, not "What can she do for me?" but "What can I do for her?" — LE BARON RUSSELL BRIGGS [1855–1934], *Routine and Ideals* [1904], *College Life*

In the great fulfillment we must have a citizenship less concerned about what the government can do for it and more anxious about what it can do for the nation. — WARREN G[AMALIEL] HARDING [1865–1923], *Republican National Convention, Chicago* [June 7, 1916]

This thought had lain in Kennedy's mind for a long time. As far back as 1945 he had noted down in a looseleaf notebook a quotation from Rousseau: "As soon as any man says of the affairs of the state, What does it matter to me? the state may be given up as lost." — ARTHUR M. SCHLESINGER, JR., *A Thousand Days* [1965], *prologue, footnote*

1 I believe this nation should commit itself to achieving the goal, before this decade is out, of landing a man on the moon and returning him safely to earth.
Address to joint session of Congress [May 25, 1961]

2 Mankind must put an end to war — or war will put an end to mankind.
Address to the United Nations [September 25, 1961]

3 Somebody once said that Washington was a city of Northern charm and Southern efficiency.
Remarks to the trustees and advisory committee of the National Cultural Center [November 14, 1961]

4 There is always inequity in life. Some men are killed in a war and some men are wounded, and some men never leave the country... Life is unfair.
Press conference [March 21, 1962]

5 I think this is the most extraordinary collection of talent, of human knowledge, that has ever been gathered together at the White House, with the possible exception of when Thomas Jefferson dined alone.
Address at a White House dinner and reception honoring Nobel Prize winners [April 1962]

6 My father always told me that all businessmen were sons of bitches, but I never believed it till now.
Comment on price increases proposed by U.S. Steel [April 1962]

7 We choose to go to the moon.
Speech at Rice University [September 12, 1962]

8 We will not prematurely or unnecessarily risk the costs of world-wide nuclear war in which even the fruits of victory would be ashes in our mouth — but neither will we shrink from that risk at any time it must be faced.... I call upon Chairman Khrushchev to halt and eliminate this clandestine, reckless, and provocative threat to world peace and to stable relations between our two nations.... He has an opportunity now to move the world back from the abyss of destruction.
Television address on Soviet missiles in Cuba [October 22, 1962]

9 We don't see the end of the tunnel, but I must say I don't think it is darker than it was a year ago, and in some ways lighter.
Press conference [December 12, 1962]

10 If we cannot end now our differences, at least we can help make the world safe for diversity.
Address at American University, Washington, D.C. [June 10, 1963]

11 What kind of a peace do we seek? Not a Pax Americana enforced on the world by American weapons of war.
Address at American University

12 No one has been barred on account of his race from fighting or dying for America — there are no "white" or "colored" signs on the foxholes or graveyards of battle.
Message to Congress on proposed civil rights bill [June 19, 1963]

13 All free men, wherever they may live, are citizens of Berlin. And therefore, as a free man, I take pride in the words "Ich bin ein Berliner."
Address at City Hall, West Berlin [June 26, 1963]

14 Yesterday, a shaft of light cut into the darkness.... For the first time, an agreement has been reached on bringing the forces of nuclear destruction under international control.
Television address in Washington [July 26, 1963][1]

15 When power leads man toward arrogance, poetry reminds him of his limitations. When power narrows the areas of man's concern, poetry reminds him of the richness and diversity of his existence. When power corrupts, poetry cleanses, for art establishes the basic human truths which must serve as the touchstone of our judgment.
Address at Amherst College [October 26, 1963]

16 We're heading into nut country today.[2]
To Jacqueline Kennedy [November 22, 1963]

John Latouche
1917–1956

17 A fat pink cloud hangs over the hill
Unfolding like a rose.
If you hold my hand and sit real still
You can hear the grass as it grows.
The Golden Apple [1954]. Lazy Afternoon[3]

Gershon Legman
1917–1999

18 Murder is a crime. Describing murder is not. Sex is not a crime. Describing sex *is*.
Love and Death: A Study in Censorship [1949]

---

[1]In Moscow on July 25, Averell Harriman, Lord Hailsham, and Andrei Gromyko initialed the nuclear test ban treaty.

[2]Cited in WILLIAM MANCHESTER, *The Death of a President* [1967].

[3]Music by JEROME MOROSS.

Edward N. Lorenz
1917–2008

1   Predictability: Does the Flap of a Butterfly's Wings in Brazil Set Off a Tornado in Texas?
Title of paper[1] *[1972]*

Robert [Traill Spence] Lowell
1917–1977

2 I will catch Christ with a greased worm.
The Drunken Fisherman [1946], st. 5

3 I saw the spiders marching through air,
Swimming from tree to tree that mildewed day
In latter August when the hay
Came creaking to the barn.[2]
Mr. Edwards and the Spider [1946], st. 1

4 This is the Black Widow, death.
Mr. Edwards and the Spider, st. 5

5 Who asks for me, the Shelley of my age,
must lay his heart out for my bed and board.
Words for Hart Crane [1959]

6 I doodle handlebar
moustaches on the last Russian Czar.
Grandparents [1959]

7 We are old-timers,
each of us holds a locked razor.
Waking in the Blue [1959]

8 I keep no rank nor station.
Cured, I am frizzled, stale and small.
Home After Three Months Away [1959]

9 Only teaching on Tuesdays, bookworming
in pajamas fresh from the washer each morning,
I hog a whole house on Boston's
"hardly passionate Marlborough Street."[3]
Memories of West Street and Lepke [1959]

10 These are the tranquillized *Fifties,*
and I am forty. Ought I to regret my seedtime?
I was a fire-breathing Catholic C.O.,
and made my manic statement,
telling off the state and president, and then
sat waiting sentence in the bull pen
beside a Negro boy with curlicues
of marijuana in his hair.
Memories of West Street and Lepke

11 Flabby, bald, lobotomized,
he drifted in a sheepish calm,
where no agonizing reappraisal
jarred his concentration on the electric chair —
hanging like an oasis in his air
of lost connections.
Memories of West Street and Lepke

12 Tamed by *Miltown,* we lie on Mother's bed.
Man and Wife [1959]

13   Oh my *Petite,*
clearest of all God's creatures, still all air and nerve.
Man and Wife

14 your old-fashioned tirade —
loving, rapid, merciless —
breaks like the Atlantic Ocean on my head.
Man and Wife

15 Gored by the climacteric of his want,
he stalls above me like an elephant.
"To Speak of Woe That Is in Marriage" [1959]

16 My mind's not right.

A car radio bleats,
"Love, O careless Love. . . ." I hear
my ill-spirit sob in each blood cell,
as if my hand were at its throat. . . .
I myself am hell;
nobody's here.[4]   *Skunk Hour [1959], st. 5, 6*

17 Father, forgive me
my injuries,
as I forgive
those I
have injured!

You never climbed
Mount Sion, yet left
dinosaur
death-steps on the crust,
where I must walk.

Middle Age [1964], st. 3, 4

18 I am tired. Everyone's tired of my turmoil.
Eye and Tooth [1964], st. 9

19 Two months after marching through Boston,
half the regiment was dead;
at the dedication,
William James could almost hear the bronze
Negroes[5] breathe.

---

[1] Delivered at American Association for the Advancement of Science.

[2] Jonathan Edwards, the Calvinist theologian, wrote at the age of twelve a series of scientific observations on the spider. See Edwards, 301:11.

[3] The quotation is from Henry James.

[4] Ellipses are in the original text.

[5] On the Saint-Gaudens monument to Colonel Robert Gould Shaw and the 54th Massachusetts Regiment.
    There on foot go the dark outcasts, so true to nature that one can almost hear them breathing as they march. —WILLIAM JAMES, *Oration at Dedication of the Monument* [May 31, 1897]
    See Charles W. Eliot, 519:10, and Paul L. Dunbar, 613:14.

Their monument sticks like a fishbone
in the city's throat.
Its Colonel is as lean
as a compass-needle.

He has an angry wrenlike vigilance,
a greyhound's gentle tautness;
he seems to wince at pleasure,
and suffocate for privacy.

For the Union Dead [1964], st. 7–9

1 on Boylston Street, a commercial photograph
shows Hiroshima boiling.

For the Union Dead, st. 14

2 When I crouch to my television set,
the drained faces of Negro school-children rise like
balloons.

For the Union Dead, st. 15

3 The Aquarium is gone. Everywhere,
giant finned cars nose forward like fish;
a savage servility
slides by on grease.

For the Union Dead, st. 17

4 We beg delinquents for our life.

*Central Park. In the New York Review
[October 1965]*

5 O to break loose, like the chinook
salmon jumping and falling back,
nosing up to the impossible
stone and bone-crushing waterfall.

Waking Early Sunday Morning [1967], st. 1

6 Pity the planet, all joy gone
from this sweet volcanic cone;
peace to our children when they fall
in small war on the heels of small
war.

*Waking Early Sunday Morning,
last stanza*

7 Rome, if built at all, must be built in a day.

Marcus Cato 234–149 B.C.E. [1973]

8 No one like one's mother and father ever lived.

Returning [1973]

9 After loving you so much, can I forget
you for eternity, and have no other choice?

Obit [1973]

10 The line must terminate.
Yet my heart rises, I know I've gladdened a lifetime
knotting, undoing a fishnet of tarred rope;
the net will hang on the wall when the fish are eaten,
nailed like illegible bronze on the futureless future.

Fishnet [1973]

11 If I could go through it all again,
the slender iron rungs of growing up,

I would be as young as any,
a child lost
in unreality and loud music.

Realities [1977]

12 It has taken me the time since you died
to discover you are as human as I am...
if I am.

To Mother [1977]

13 We feel the machine slipping from our hands
as if someone else were steering;
if we see the light at the end of the tunnel,
it's the light of the oncoming train.

Since 1939 [1977]

14 We are poor passing facts,
warned by that to give
each figure in the photograph
his living name.

Epilogue [1977]

Carson [Smith] McCullers
1917–1967

15   This was the summer when for a long time she had not been a member. She belonged to no club and was a member of nothing in the world. Frankie had become an unjoined person who hung around in the doorways, and she was afraid.

The Member of the Wedding [1946], ch. 1

16   If you walk along the main street on an August afternoon there is nothing whatsoever to do.

The Ballad of the Sad Café [1951]

Arthur M[eier] Schlesinger, Jr.
1917–2007

17   Above all he [John F. Kennedy] gave the world for an imperishable moment the vision of a leader who greatly understood the terror and the hope, the diversity and the possibility, of life on this planet and who made people look beyond nation and race to the future of humanity.

A Thousand Days [1965], ch. 37

18   The answer to the runaway Presidency is not the messenger-boy Presidency. The American democracy must discover a middle ground between making the President a czar and making him a puppet.

The Imperial Presidency [1973], preface

19   The constitutional Presidency — as events so apparently disparate as the Indochina War and the

Watergate affair showed — has become the imperial Presidency.

The Imperial Presidency, preface

Merle Travis
1917–1983

1 You load sixteen tons, what do you get?
Another day older and deeper in debt.
Saint Peter, don't you call me 'cause I can't go[1]
I owe my soul to the company store.

Sixteen Tons [1947]

Robert Warshow
1917–1955

2   No convention of the gangster film is more strongly established than this: it is dangerous to be alone. And yet the very conditions of success make it impossible not to be alone.... The successful man is an outlaw.

The Gangster as Tragic Hero [1948]

William H[ollingsworth] Whyte, Jr.
1917–1999

3   This book is about the organization man. If the term is vague, it is because I can think of no other way to describe the people I am talking about.... They are the ones of our middle class who have left home, spiritually as well as physically, to take the vows of organization life, and it is they who are the mind and soul of our great self-perpetuating institutions.

The Organization Man [1956], pt. I, ch. 1

4   Sprawl is bad aesthetics; it is bad economics. Five acres are being made to do the work of one, and do it very poorly. *Urban Sprawl [1958]*

Spiro T[heodore] Agnew
1918–1996

5   To some extent, if you've seen one city slum you've seen them all.

Election campaign speech at Detroit [October 18, 1968]

6   A spirit of national masochism prevails, encouraged by an effete corps of impudent snobs who characterize themselves as intellectuals.

Speech in New Orleans [October 19, 1969]

---

[1]The third line is often sung as "Say, brother, don't you call me 'cause I can't go."

7   In the United States today, we have more than our share of the nattering nabobs of negativism.

Speech at California Republican state convention [September 11, 1970]

André Bazin
1918–1958

8   I imagine the supreme cinematic perversion to consist of an execution projected in reverse, like those comical newsreels where one sees the diver bursting up out of the water toward his diving board.

What Is Cinema? [1958]. Death Every Afternoon

Leonard Bernstein
1918–1990

9   Music, of all the arts, stands in a special region, unlit by any star but its own, and utterly without meaning...except its own, a meaning in musical terms, not in terms of words.

The Joy of Music [1959]

10   The key to the mystery of a great artist: that for reasons unknown to him or to anyone else, he will give away his energies and his life just to make sure that one note follows another inevitably.... The composer, by doing this, leaves us at the finish with the feeling that something is right in the world, that something checks throughout, something that follows its own laws consistently, something we can trust, that will never let us down.

The Joy of Music. Beethoven's Fifth Symphony

William Bronk
1918–1999

11   Here it was always the light
that mattered, and only the light. Once, it had seemed
the objects mattered: the light was to see
    them by.
Examined, they yielded nothing, nothing real.
They were for seeing the light in various ways.
They gathered it, released it, held it in.
In them, the light revealed itself, took shape.
Objects are nothing. There is only the light, the light!

*The World, the Worldless [1964].
The Annihilation of Matter*

12 I lie along the body of this life,
all night stilling my breath to listen to breath,
feeling its weight heavy against my weight.

That Tantalus [1971]. The Body of This Life

Howard Cosell
[Howard William Cohen]
1918–1995

1   There it is, ladies and gentlemen, the Bronx is burning.

> *Reporting a fire during the World Series,*
> *from Yankee Stadium [October 12, 1977]*

Richard P[hillips] Feynman
1918–1988

2   If, in some cataclysm, all of scientific knowledge were to be destroyed, and only one sentence passed on to the next generations of creatures, what statement would contain the most information in the fewest words? I believe it is the *atomic hypothesis* (or the atomic fact, or whatever you wish to call it) that *all things are made of atoms — little particles that move around in perpetual motion, attracting each other when they are a little distance apart, but repelling upon being squeezed into one another.*

> *The Feynman Lectures on Physics [1963]*

3   I think I can safely say that nobody understands quantum mechanics.

> *The Character of Physical Law [1965]*

4   You know how it always is, every new idea, it takes a generation or two until it becomes obvious that there's no real problem. I cannot define the real problem, but I'm not sure there's no real problem.

> *Simulating Physics with Computers [1982]*

5   For a successful technology, reality must take precedence over public relations, for nature cannot be fooled.

> *Report on space shuttle Challenger disaster [1986]*

Ann Landers [Esther P. Lederer]
1918–2002

6   Women complain about sex more often than men. Their gripes fall into two major categories: (1) Not enough. (2) Too much.

> *Truth Is Stranger . . . [1968], ch. 2*

Alan Jay Lerner
1918–1986

7 Oh, wouldn't it be loverly?

> *My Fair Lady*[1] *[1956], act I, Wouldn't It Be*
> *Loverly?*

8 The rain in Spain stays mainly in the plain.

> *My Fair Lady, I, The Rain in Spain*

9 I could have danced all night!

> *My Fair Lady, I, I Could Have Danced All*
> *Night!*

10 Get me to the church on time!

> *My Fair Lady, II, Get Me to the Church on*
> *Time*

11 Why can't a woman be more like a man?

> *My Fair Lady, II, A Hymn to Him*

12 I've grown accustomed . . . to her face.[2]

> *My Fair Lady, II, I've Grown Accustomed to*
> *Her Face*

13 Thank heaven for little girls!
For little girls get bigger every day.

> *Gigi*[1] *[1958], Thank Heaven for Little Girls*

14 Don't let it be forgot
That once there was a spot
For one brief shining moment that was known
As Camelot.

> *Camelot*[1] *[1960], end*

15   On a Clear Day You Can See Forever[3]

> *Title song of musical comedy [1965]*

16   The answers make us wise, but the questions make us human.

> *On a Clear Day You Can See Forever [1965]*

Nelson [Rolihlahla] Mandela
1918–

17   The struggle is my life.

> *Statement to the press [June 26, 1961]*

18   I have fought against white domination, and I have fought against black domination. I have cherished the ideal of a democratic and free society in which all persons will live together in harmony and with equal opportunities. It is an ideal which I hope to live for and achieve. But, if needs be, it is an ideal for which I am prepared to die.

> *Statement in the dock*[4] *[April 20, 1964]*

19   Only free men can negotiate; prisoners cannot enter into contracts.

> *Statement from prison [February 10, 1985]*

20   I am not truly free if I am taking away someone else's freedom, just as surely as I am not free when

---

[1]Music by Frederick Loewe.
Musical based on George Bernard Shaw's *Pygmalion*. See Shaw, 565:19–23.

[2]Ellipses are in the original text.

[3]Music by Burton Lane.

[4]Also quoted by him on his release from prison [February 11, 1990].

my freedom is taken away from me. The oppressed and the oppressor alike are robbed of their humanity.

Long Walk to Freedom [1994]

Edwin O'Connor
1918–1968

1   "God be good to the man," she said. "He was mean as a panther, but good luck to him."

The Last Hurrah [1956], ch. 8

2   I'm not just an elected official of the city; I'm a tribal chieftain as well.   *The Last Hurrah, 8*

Dean Riesner
1918–2002

and

John Milius
1944–

3   You've got to ask yourself one question. Do I feel lucky? Well, do you, punk?

Dirty Harry (screenplay) [1971], spoken by Clint Eastwood

Anwar al-Sadat
1918–1981

4   Peace is much more precious than a piece of land.   *Speech in Cairo [March 8, 1978]*

5   Let there be no more war or bloodshed between Arabs and Israelis. Let there be no more suffering or denial of rights. Let there be no more despair or loss of faith.

On signing the Egyptian–Israeli peace treaty, Washington, D.C. [March 26, 1979][1]

Alexander Isayevich Solzhenitsyn
1918–2008

6   A great writer is, so to speak, a second government in his country. And for that reason no regime has ever loved great writers, only minor ones.

The First Circle[2] [1964]

7   There was peace in their hearts. They were filled with the fearlessness of those who have lost *everything*, the fearlessness which is not easy to come by but which endures.   *The First Circle*

---

[1] See Menachem Begin, 769:10.
[2] Translated by THOMAS P. WHITNEY.

8   The sole substitute for an experience which we have not ourselves lived through is art and literature.   *Nobel Lecture [1972]*

9   Literature transmits incontrovertible condensed experience … from generation to generation. In this way literature becomes the living memory of a nation.   *Nobel Lecture*

10   Violence does not and cannot exist by itself; it is invariably intertwined with *the lie*.

Nobel Lecture

11   The Kolyma was the greatest and most famous island, the pole of ferocity of that amazing country of Gulag, which, though scattered in an archipelago geographically, was, in the psychological sense, fused into a continent — an almost invisible, almost imperceptible country inhabited by the Zek people.

The Gulag Archipelago 1918–1956[2] [1974, in translation], I, preface

12   If only there were evil people somewhere insidiously committing evil deeds, and it were necessary only to separate them from the rest of us and destroy them. But the line dividing good and evil cuts through the heart of every human being. And who is willing to destroy a piece of his own heart?

The Gulag Archipelago 1918–1956, I, ch. 4

13   The Western world has lost its civil courage, both as a whole and separately, in each country, each government, each political party, and of course in the United Nations.

The Exhausted West. Commencement address at Harvard University [June 8, 1978]

14   I have spent all my life under a Communist regime, and I will tell you that a society without any objective legal scale is a terrible one indeed. But a society with no other scale but the legal one is not quite worthy of man either.

The Exhausted West. Commencement address at Harvard University

Muriel Spark
1918–2006

15   The one certain way for a woman to hold a man is to leave him for religion.

The Comforters [1957], ch. 1

16   Give me a girl at an impressionable age, and she is mine for life.

The Prime of Miss Jean Brodie [1962], ch. 1

17   One's prime is elusive. You little girls, when you grow up, must be on the alert to recognize your prime at whatever time of your life it may occur.   *The Prime of Miss Jean Brodie, 1*

1   It is impossible to persuade a man who does not disagree, but smiles.
The Prime of Miss Jean Brodie, 4

Bobby Troup
1918–1999

2 If you ever plan to motor west,
Travel my way, take the highway that's the best,
Get your kicks on Route Sixty-six!
(Get Your Kicks on) Route 66! [1946]

Daniel Bell
1919–2011

3   Capitalism, it is said, is a system wherein man exploits man. And communism — is vice versa.
The End of Ideology [1960]

Ervin Drake
[Ervin Maurice Druckman]
1919–

4 But now the days are short,
I'm in the Autumn of the year,
And now I think of my life
As vintage wine from the old kegs.
From the brim to the dregs
It poured sweet and clear;
It was a very good year!
It Was a Very Good Year [1966]

Robert Duncan
1919–1988

5 Often I am permitted to return to a meadow
as if it were a given property of the mind
that certain bounds hold against chaos,

that is a place of first permission,
everlasting omen of what is.
*The Opening of the Field [1960]. Often I Am
Permitted to Return to a Meadow*

Lawrence Ferlinghetti
1919–

6 Constantly risking absurdity
                              and death
      whenever he performs
                        above the heads
                              of his audience
the poet like an acrobat

climbs on rime
      to a high wire of his own making
A Coney Island of the Mind [1958]

Robert L. Heilbroner
1919–2005

7   [The great economists] can be called the worldly philosophers, for they sought to embrace in a scheme of philosophy the most worldly of all of man's activities — his drive for wealth.
The Worldly Philosophers [1953]. Introduction

Pauline Kael
1919–2001

8   Irresponsibility is part of the pleasure of all art; it is the part the schools cannot recognize.
*Going Steady [1968]. Trash, Art,
and the Movies*

9   The words "Kiss Kiss Bang Bang," which I saw on an Italian movie poster, are perhaps the briefest statement imaginable of the basic appeal of movies.
*Kiss Kiss Bang Bang [1968].
A Note on the Title*

10   For some moviegoers, movies probably contribute to that self-defeating romanticizing of expectations which makes life a series of disappointments. They watch the same movies over and over on television, as if they were constantly returning to the scene of the crime — the life they were so busy dreaming about that they never lived it.
Kiss Kiss Bang Bang. Movies on Television

Doris Lessing
1919–

11   It isn't only the terror everywhere, and the fear of being conscious of it, that freezes people. It's more than that. People know they are in a society dead or dying. They are refusing emotion because at the end of every emotion are property, money, power. They work and despise their work, and so freeze themselves.
The Golden Notebook [1962]. Free Women, 4

12   A woman without a man cannot meet a man, any man, of any age, without thinking, even if it's for a half-second, Perhaps this is *the* man.
The Golden Notebook. Free Women, 5

13   None of you [men] ask for anything — except everything, but just for so long as you need it.
The Golden Notebook. Free Women, 5

Primo Levi
1919–1987

1   The dark echoed with outlandish orders in that curt, barbaric barking of Germans in command which seems to give vent to a millennial anger.
Survival in Auschwitz[1] *[1960], ch. 2*

2   I am not even alive enough to know how to kill myself.   *Survival in Auschwitz, 15*

3   Today I think that if for no other reason than that an Auschwitz existed, no one in our age should speak of Providence.
Survival in Auschwitz, 17

4   Up to the moment of this writing…the Nazi concentration camp system still remains a *unicum*, both in its extent and its quality. At no other place or time has one seen a phenomenon so unexpected and so complex: never have so many human lives been extinguished in so short a time, and with so lucid a combination of technological ingenuity, fanaticism, and cruelty.
The Drowned and the Saved [1986]

Wladziu Valentino [Lee] Liberace
1919–1987

5   I cried all the way to the bank.
Liberace: An Autobiography [1973], ch. 2

Iris Murdoch
1919–1999

6   All theorizing is flight. We must be ruled by the situation itself and this is unutterably particular. Indeed it is something to which we can never get close enough, however hard we may try as it were to crawl under the net.
Under the Net [1954]

Laurence J[ohnston] Peter
1919–1990

7   In a hierarchy, every employee tends to rise to his level of incompetence.
The Peter Principle [1969]

8   If you don't know where you're going, you will probably end up somewhere else.
The Peter Principle

9   Work is done by those [employees] who have not yet reached their level of incompetence.
The Peter Principle

J[erome] D[avid] Salinger
1919–2010

10   What really knocks me out is a book that, when you're all done reading it, you wish the author that wrote it was a terrific friend of yours and you could call him up on the phone whenever you felt like it.
The Catcher in the Rye [1951], ch. 3

11   I keep picturing all these little kids playing some game in this big field of rye…. If they're running and they don't look where they're going I have to come out from somewhere and *catch* them. That's all I'd do all day. I'd just be the catcher in the rye and all. I know it's crazy.[2]
The Catcher in the Rye, 22

12   There isn't anyone *any*where that isn't Seymour's Fat Lady. Don't you know that? Don't you know that goddam secret yet? And don't you know — *listen to me, now* — *don't you know who that Fat Lady really is?*…Ah, buddy. Ah, buddy. It's Christ Himself. Christ Himself, buddy.[3]
Franny and Zooey [1961]

Pete [Peter] Seeger
1919–

13 Where have all the flowers gone?
The girls have picked them every one.
Oh, when will they ever learn?
Where Have All the Flowers Gone? [1961]

14 We're waist deep in the Big Muddy
And the big fool says to push on.
Waist Deep in the Big Muddy [1967]

Pete [Peter] Seeger
1919–

and

Lee Hays
1914–1981

15 If I had a hammer,
I'd hammer in the morning,

---

[1]Translated by STUART WOOLF.

[2]See Anonymous, 883:3.
[3]Ellipses are in the original text.

I'd hammer in the evening,
All over this land.
I'd hammer out danger,
I'd hammer out a warning,
I'd hammer out love between my brothers and my
    sisters,
All over this land.

If I Had a Hammer [1949]

Pierre Trudeau
1919–2000

1   [On U.S.-Canadian relations:] Living next to you is in some ways like sleeping with an elephant. No matter how friendly and even-tempered the beast, one is affected by every twitch and groan.

*Speech at National Press Club
[March 25, 1969]*

George [Corley] Wallace
1919–1998

2   I draw the line in the dust and toss the gauntlet before the feet of tyranny. And I say, Segregation now! Segregation tomorrow! Segregation forever!

*Inaugural address as governor of Alabama
[January 14, 1963]*

Bella [Savitzky] Abzug
1920–1998

3   There are those who say I'm impatient, impetuous, uppity, rude, profane, brash and overbearing. . . . But whatever I am — and this ought to be made very clear at the outset — I am a very serious woman.

Bella! [1972]

Ray Bradbury
1920–2012

4   There was always a minority afraid of something, and a great majority afraid of the dark, afraid of the future, afraid of the past, afraid of the present, afraid of themselves and shadows of themselves.

The Martian Chronicles [1950]

Charles Bukowski
1920–1994

5   There is nothing more boring than the truth.

Notes of a Dirty Old Man [1969]

Paul Celan [Antschel]
1920–1970

6 Black milk of daybreak we drink you at night
we drink you at noon death is a master from Germany
we drink you at sundown and in the morning we
    drink
    and we drink you
death is a master from Germany his eyes are blue . . .
he sets his pack on to us he grants us a grave in the air
he plays with the serpents and daydreams death is a
    master
    from Germany   *Death Fugue [1952]*[1]

7 It is time the stone made an effort to flower,
time unrest had a beating heart.
It is time it were time.

Corona[2] *[1952]*

Leona Helmsley
1920–2007

8   We don't pay taxes. Only the little people pay taxes.

Quoted in New York Times[3] *[July 12, 1989]*

Frank Herbert
1920–1986

9   Fear is the mind-killer. . . . I will face my fear.

Dune [1965]

Pope John Paul II [Karol Wojtyla]
1920–2005

10   The greatness of work is inside man.

*Easter Vigil and Other Poems [1979].
The Quarry, I, Material*

11   We must ask ourselves whether there will continue to accumulate over the heads of this new generation of children the threat of common extermination. . . . Are the children to receive the arms race from us as a necessary inheritance?

Speech at the United Nations [October 2, 1979]

12   You are our dearly beloved brothers, and in a certain way, it could be said that you are our elder brothers.

*On visit to the Synagogue of Rome
[April 13, 1986]*

---

[1]Translated from the German, *Todesfuge,* by Michael Hamburger.

[2]Translated by Michael Hamburger.

[3]In testimony by housekeeper Elizabeth Baum at Helmsley's trial for tax evasion.

1   The culture of life means respect for nature and protection of God's work of creation. In a special way it means respect for human life from the first moment of conception until its natural end.

Speech, Denver, Colorado [August 15, 1993]

Irving Kristol
1920–2009

2   A liberal who has been mugged by reality.[1]

Definition of a neoconservative;
New York Times [December 6, 1981]

Timothy Leary
1920–1996

3   Turn On, Tune In, Drop Out.

Slogan (title of lecture) [1967]

Howard Nemerov
1920–1991

4 His lordly darkness decked in filth
Bearded with weed like a lady's favor,
He is a black planet.

The Blue Swallows [1967]. The Mud Turtle

5 There is in space a small black hole
Through which, say our astronomers,
The whole damn thing, the universe,
Must one day fall. That will be all.

Cosmic Comics [1975]

6 The world is full of mostly invisible things,
And there is no way but putting the mind's eye,
Or its nose, in a book, to find them out,
Things like the square root of Everest
Or how many times Byron goes into Texas,
Or whether the law of the excluded middle
Applies west of the Rockies.

To David, about His Education [1977]

Mario Puzo
1920–1999

7   I'll make him an offer he can't refuse.

The Godfather (novel) [1969]

8   Lawyers can steal more money with a briefcase than a thousand men with guns and masks.

The Godfather [1969]

---

[1] A variation on the earlier catchphrase, "A conservative is a liberal who's just been mugged."

Mario Puzo
1920–1999

and

Francis Ford Coppola
1939–

9   Leave the gun. Take the cannoli.

The Godfather (screenplay) [1972],
spoken by Peter Clemenza

10   Keep your friends close, but your enemies closer.

The Godfather Part II (screenplay) [1974],
spoken by Al Pacino

11   If anything in this life is certain, if history has taught us anything, it's that you can kill anyone.

The Godfather Part II, spoken by Al Pacino

John Paul Stevens
1920–

12   Although we may never know with complete certainty the identity of the winner of this year's presidential election, the identity of the loser is perfectly clear. It is the nation's confidence in the judge as an impartial guardian of the rule of law.

Dissenting opinion in U.S. Supreme Court,
Bush v. Gore [December 12, 2000]

13   While American democracy is imperfect, few outside the majority of this court would have thought its flaws included a dearth of corporate money in politics.

Dissenting opinion, Citizens United v.
Federal Election Commission,
January 21, 2010

Robert Townsend
1920–1998

14   Twenty percent of any given group of salesmen will always produce 80 percent of the sales.

Further Up the Organization [1984]

Stewart [Lee] Udall
1920–2010

15   A land ethic for tomorrow should be as honest as Thoreau's *Walden,* and as comprehensive as the sensitive science of ecology. It should stress the oneness of our resources and the live-and-help-live logic of the great chain of life. If, in our haste to "progress," the economics of ecology are disregarded by citizens and policy makers alike, the result will be an ugly America.   *The Quiet Crisis [1963], ch. 14*

Jack [John Randolph] Webb
1920–1982
et al.[1]

1   The story you have just heard is true. Only the names have been changed to protect the innocent.
Dragnet (radio and television)

Sloan Wilson
1920–2003

2   The Man in the Gray Flannel Suit
Title of novel [1955]

Lloyd Bentsen
1921–2006

3   [To Dan Quayle:] Senator, I served with Jack Kennedy. I knew Jack Kennedy, Jack Kennedy was a friend of mine. Senator, you are no Jack Kennedy.
Vice-Presidential Debate [October 5, 1988]

Rodney Dangerfield [Jacob Cohen]
1921–2004

4   I can't get no respect.   *Comedy signature line*

Alexander Dubček
1921–1992

5   Socialism with a human face.
Slogan of the Prague Spring [1968]

Friedrich Dürrenmatt
1921–1990

6   What was once thought can never be unthought.
The Physicists [1962]

Betty [Naomi] Friedan
1921–2006

7   The problem lay buried, unspoken, for many years in the minds of American women. It was a strange stirring, a sense of dissatisfaction, a yearning that women suffered in the middle of the twentieth century in the United States. Each suburban wife struggled with it alone. As she made the beds, shopped for groceries, matched slipcover material, ate peanut butter sandwiches with her children, chauffeured Cub Scouts and Brownies, lay beside her husband at night — she was afraid to ask even of herself the silent question — "Is this all?"
The Feminine Mystique [1963], ch. 1

8   The problem that has no name — which is simply the fact that American women are kept from growing to their full human capacities — is taking a far greater toll on the physical and mental health of our country than any known disease.
The Feminine Mystique, 14

9   This uneasy sense of battles won, only to be fought over again, of battles that should have been won, according to all the rules, and yet are not, of battles that suddenly one does not really want to win, and the weariness of battle altogether — how many women feel it?
The Second Stage [1981]

Alex Haley
1921–1992

10   [On West African oral historians:] It is rightly said that when a griot dies, it is as if a library has burned to the ground.
Roots [1976]

Bill [William Henry] Mauldin
1921–2003

11   I feel like a fugitive from th' law of averages.
*Up Front [1945].
Caption for cartoon*

12   Look at an infantryman's eyes and you can tell how much war he has seen.
Up Front. Caption for cartoon

13   Beautiful view. Is there one for the enlisted men?
Up Front. Caption for cartoon

Julius K[ambarage] Nyerere
1921–1999

14   The survival of our wildlife is a matter of grave concern to all of us in Africa. These wild creatures amid the wild places they inhabit are not only important as a source of wonder and inspiration but are an integral part of our natural resources and of our future livelihood and well-being.
*The Arusha Declaration, Tanganyika
[September 1961]*

[1] Exact attribution of this line is difficult; many writers worked on the *Dragnet* series.

John Rawls
1921–2002

1   Justice is the first virtue of social institutions, as truth is of systems of thought. A theory however elegant and economical must be rejected or revised if it is untrue; likewise laws and institutions no matter how efficient and well-arranged must be reformed or abolished if they are unjust.   *A Theory of Justice [1971]*

2   Each person possesses an inviolability founded on justice that even the welfare of society as a whole cannot override.   *A Theory of Justice*

Gene [Eugene Wesley] Roddenberry
1921–1991

3   Space — the final frontier... These are the voyages of the starship *Enterprise*. Its five-year mission: to explore strange new worlds, to seek out new life and new civilizations, to boldly go where no man has gone before.
   Star Trek (television series) [1966–1969]

Andrei Dmitrievich Sakharov
1921–1989

4   A thermonuclear war cannot be considered a continuation of politics by other means. It would be a means to universal suicide.
   Progress, Coexistence, and Intellectual Freedom [1968]

5   Intellectual freedom is the only guarantee of a scientific-democratic approach to politics, economic development, and culture.
   Progress, Coexistence, and Intellectual Freedom

Sophie Scholl
1921–1943

6   Finally, someone has to make a start. We only said and wrote what many people think. They just don't dare to express it.
   At the White Rose trial in Munich [1942]

Leonardo Sciascia
1921–1989

7   The truth is at the bottom of a well: look into it and you see the sun or the moon; but if you throw yourself in, there's no more sun or moon: just truth.   *The Day of the Owl [1961]*

George David Weiss
1921–2010

and

Bob Thiele
1922–1996

8 I see skies of blue, and clouds of white,
   The bright blessed day, the dark sacred night.
   And I think to myself... what a wonderful world.
   What a Wonderful World [1968]

Richard [Purdy] Wilbur
1921–

9 But up in his room by artificial light
   My father paints the summer.
   My Father Paints the Summer [1947]

10 The beautiful changes as a forest is changed
   By a chameleon's tuning his skin to it.
   The Beautiful Changes [1947], st. 2

11 I dreamt the past was never past redeeming:
   But whether this was false or honest dreaming
   I beg death's pardon now. And mourn the dead.
   The Pardon [1950], last stanza

12   The eyes open to a cry of pulleys,
   And spirited from sleep, the astounded soul
   Hangs for a moment bodiless and simple
   as false dawn.
              Outside the open window
   The morning air is all awash with angels.
   Love Calls Us to the Things of This World [1956]

13   The soul shrinks
   From all that it is about to remember,
   From the punctual rape of every blessèd day,
   And cries,
        "Oh, let there be nothing on earth but laundry,
   Nothing but rosy hands in the rising steam
   And clear dances done in the sight of heaven."
   Love Calls Us to the Things of This World

14 Mind in its purest play is like some bat
   That beats about in caverns all alone,
   Contriving by a kind of senseless wit
   Not to conclude against a wall of stone.

   It has no need to falter or explore;
   Darkly it knows what obstacles are there,
   And so may weave and flitter, dip and soar
   In perfect courses through the blackest air.

   And has this simile a like perfection?
   The mind is like a bat. Precisely. Save

That in the very happiest intellection
A graceful error may correct the cave.
                                    Mind [1956]

1 The werewolf's painful change. Turning his head
      away
  On the sweaty bolster, he tries to remember
  The mood of manhood,

  But lies at last, as always,
  Letting it happen, the fierce fur soft to his face,
  Hearing with sharper ears.
                                    Beasts [1956], st. 3, 4

2 Ask us, prophet, how we shall call
  Our natures forth when that live tongue is all
  Dispelled, that glass obscured or broken

  In which we have said the rose of our love and the
      clean
  Horse of our courage, in which beheld
  The singing locust of the soul unshelled,
  And all we mean or wish to mean.
                                Advice to a Prophet [1961], st. 7, 8

3 All bitter things conduce to sweet,
      As this example shows;
  Without the little spirochete
  We'd have no chocolate to eat,
  Nor would tobacco's fragrance greet
      The European nose.
                        Pangloss's Song: A Comic Opera Lyric [1961]

4   What you hope for
  Is that at some point of the pointless journey,
  Indoors or out, and when you least expect it,
  Right in the middle of your stride, like that,
  So neatly that you never feel a thing,
  The kind assassin Sleep will draw a bead
  And blow your brains out.
                                    Walking to Sleep [1969]

5 In her room at the prow of the house
  Where light breaks, and the windows are tossed with
      linden,
  My daughter is writing a story.
                                    The Writer [1976]

Whitney M[oore] Young, Jr.
1921–1971

6   Black is beautiful when it is a slum kid studying to
enter college, when it is a man learning new skills for a
new job, or a slum mother battling to give her kids a
chance for a better life. But white is beautiful, too,
when it helps change society to make our system
work for black people also. White is ugly when it
oppresses blacks — and so is black ugly when black
people exploit other blacks. No race has a monopoly

on vice or virtue, and the worth of an individual is not
related to the color of his skin.
                        *Beyond Racism: Building an Open Society
                        [1969], ch. 4*

Sir Kingsley Amis
1922–1995

7   A dusty thudding in his head made the scene
before him beat like a pulse. His mouth had been
used as a latrine by some small creature of the night,
and then as its mausoleum. During the night,
too, he'd somehow been on a cross-country run
and then been expertly beaten up by secret police.
He felt bad.   *Lucky Jim [1954], ch. 6*

8 Death has got something to be said for it:
  There's no need to get out of bed for it;
  Wherever you may be,
  They bring it to you, free.
                                Delivery Guaranteed [1979]

George Axelrod
1922–2003

9   The Seven Year Itch   *Title of play [1952]*

Al Dvorin
1922–2004

10   Elvis has left the building.
              *Attributed. Signature catchphrase at Elvis
              Presley concerts*

Michael Flanders
1922–1975
and
Donald Swann
1923–1994

11 I don't eat people,
   I won't eat people,
   I don't eat people,
   Eating people is wrong!
                        The Reluctant Cannibal [1956]

William Gaddis
1922–1998

12   What is it they want from a man that they didn't
get from the work? What do they expect? What is
there left of him when he's done his work? What's any

artist but the dregs of his work? the human shambles that follows it around.   *The Recognitions [1955]*

Erving Goffman
1922–1982

1   There seems to be no agent more effective than another person in bringing a world for oneself alive.
    Encounters: Two Studies in the Sociology of Interaction [1961]

Jack Kerouac
1922–1969

2   We're a *beat* generation.[1]
    Remark [November 1948]. From JOHN CLELLON HOLMES, *Nothing More to Declare [1967]*

3   But then they danced down the street like dingle-dodies, and I shambled after as I've been doing all my life after people who interest me, because the only people for me are the mad ones, the ones who are mad to live, mad to talk, mad to be saved, desirous of everything at the same time, the ones who never yawn or say a commonplace thing, but burn, burn, burn like fabulous yellow roman candles exploding like spiders across the stars and in the middle you see the blue centerlight pop and everybody goes "Awww!"   *On the Road [1957]*

Seymour Krim
1922–1989

4   *You've got it made.* How the words sing a swift jazz poem of success, hi-fi, the best chicks (or guys), your name in lights, pot to burn, jets to L.A. and London, bread in the bank, baby, a fortress built around your ego like a magic suit of armor!
    Views of a Near-Sighted Cannoneer [1961]. Making It!

Thomas Kuhn
1922–1996

5   Examining the record of past research from the vantage of contemporary historiography, the historian of science may be tempted to exclaim that when paradigms change, the world itself changes with them. Led by a new paradigm, scientists adopt new

instruments and look in new places. Even more important, during revolutions scientists see new and different things when looking with familiar instruments in places they have looked before.
    The Structure of Scientific Revolutions [1962]

Philip Larkin
1922–1985

6 Why should I let the toad *work*
Squat on my life?
Can't I use my wit as a pitchfork
And drive the brute off?   *Toads [1955]*

7 Marrying left your maiden name disused.
    Maiden Name [1955]

8 Home is so sad. It stays as it was left,
Shaped to the comfort of the last to go
As if to win them back.
    Home Is So Sad [1964]

9 Never such innocence again.   *MCMXIV [1964]*

10 Where can we live but days?   *Days [1964]*

11 If I were called in
To construct a religion
I should make use of water.
    Water [1964]

12 Give me your arm, old toad;
Help me down Cemetery Road.
    Toads Revisited [1964]

13 Sexual intercourse began
In nineteen sixty-three
(Which was rather late for me) —
Between the end of the *Chatterley* ban
And the Beatles' first LP.
    Annus Mirabilis [1974]

14 One of those old-type *natural* fouled-up guys.
    Posterity [1974]

15 They fuck you up, your mum and dad.
They may not mean to, but they do.
They fill you with the faults they had
And add some extra, just for you.
    This Be The Verse [1974]

16 Perhaps being old is having lighted rooms
Inside your head, and people in them, acting.
People you know, yet can't quite name.
    The Old Fools [1974]

17   Deprivation is for me what daffodils were for Wordsworth.
    Interview with London Observer [1979], collected in Required Writing [1983]

---

[1]A man is beat whenever he goes for broke and wagers the sum of his resources on a single number; and the young generation has done that continually from early youth. — JOHN CLELLON HOLMES [1906–1988], *"This Is the Beat Generation," New York Times Magazine* [November 16, 1952].

John G[illespie] Magee, Jr.
1922–1941

1 Oh! I have slipped the surly bonds of Earth
And danced the skies on laughter-silvered wings;
Sunward I've climbed, and joined the tumbling
    mirth
Of sun-split clouds, — and done a hundred things
You have not dreamed of — wheeled and soared and
    swung
High in the sunlit silence. Hov'ring there,
I've chased the shouting wind along, and flung
My eager craft through footless halls of air . . .

Up, up the long, delirious, burning blue
I've topped the wind-swept heights with easy
    grace
Where never lark nor ever eagle flew —
And, while with silent lifting mind I've trod
The high untrespassed sanctity of space,
Put out my hand, and touched the face of God.

High Flight[1] *[1941]*

George McGovern
1922–

2   The Great Society lost its greatness in the jungles
of Indochina.

Lecture, Oxford University [January 21, 1973]

Bob Merrill
1922–1998

3 People, people who need people
Are the luckiest people in the world.

People[2] *[1963]*

John A. Powers
1922–1980

4   All systems go. Everything is A-OK.

*Statement as public information officer for
U.S. space program [1959–1964]*

Yitzhak Rabin
1922–1995

5   One does not make peace with one's friends. One
makes peace with one's enemies.

Quoted in Jerusalem Post [November 26, 1993]

Philip Rieff
1922–2006

6   The most complex analyses grow beautifully
simple as they become public objects.

Fellow Teachers [1973]

Alain Robbe-Grillet
1922–2008

7   The true writer has nothing to say. What counts is
the way he says it.[3]

For a New Novel [1963]

Alice S[chaerr] Rossi
1922–2009

8   The single most impressive fact about the attempt
by American women to obtain the right to vote is
how long it took.

*The Feminist Papers [1973]. Along the
Suffrage Trail*

Charles M[onroe] Schulz
1922–2000

9   *It was a dark and stormy night.*[4] *Suddenly a scream
pierced the air. . . .* Good writing takes enormous concentration.

Peanuts (comic strip)

10   Big sisters are the crab grass in the lawn of life.

Peanuts

11   [*Linus:*] After you've died, do you get to come
back?
[*Charlie Brown:*] If they stamp your hand.

Peanuts

12   I love mankind — it's PEOPLE I can't stand!

You're a Winner, Charlie Brown [1960]

Joseph Stefano
1922–2006

13   A boy's best friend is his mother.

*Psycho (screenplay) [1960], spoken by Anthony
Perkins*

14   We all go a little mad sometimes. Haven't you?

Psycho (screenplay), spoken by Anthony Perkins

---

[1]Ellipses are in the original text.
[2]Music by JULE STYNE.

[3]Le véritable écrivain n'a rien à dire, il a seulement une manière de
le dire.
[4]See Edward Bulwer-Lytton, 423:14.

Jesse Marvin Unruh
1922–1987

1 Money is the mother's milk of politics. *Remark*

Kurt Vonnegut, Jr.
1922–2007

2 Hello babies. Welcome to earth. It's hot in the summer and cold in the winter. It's round and wet and crowded. At the outside, babies, you've got about a hundred years here. There's only one rule that I know of, babies — :
"God damn it, you've got to be kind."
God Bless You, Mr. Rosewater [1965]

3 So it goes.
Slaughterhouse-Five [1969],
ch. 1 and passim

4 Billy Pilgrim has come unstuck in time.
Slaughterhouse-Five, 2

5 You know — we've had to imagine the war here, and we have imagined that it was being fought by aging men like ourselves. We had forgotten that wars were fought by babies. When I saw those freshly shaved faces, it was a shock. "My God, my God — " I said to myself, "it's the Children's Crusade."
Slaughterhouse-Five, 5

Diane Arbus
1923–1971

6 A photograph is a secret about a secret. The more it tells you, the less you know.
From the monograph Diane Arbus [1972]

7 You see someone on the street and essentially what you notice about them is the flaw.
From the monograph Diane Arbus

8 Most people go through life dreading they'll have a traumatic experience. Freaks were born with their trauma.
From the monograph Diane Arbus

Italo Calvino
1923–1985

9 Cities, like dreams, are made of desires and fears.
Invisible Cities [1972]

10 A classic is a book that has never finished saying what it has to say. *Why Read the Classics? [1981]*

11 I have tried to remove weight, sometimes from people, sometimes from heavenly bodies, sometimes from cities; above all I have tried to remove weight from the structure of stories and from language.
Six Memos for the Next Millennium [1988].
Lightness

12 In the even more congested times that await us, literature must aim at the maximum concentration of poetry and of thought.
Six Memos for the Next Millennium.
Quickness

13 Overambitious projects may be objectionable in many fields, but not in literature. . . . Only if poets and writers set themselves tasks that no one else dares imagine will literature continue to have a function.
Six Memos for the Next Millennium.
Multiplicity

Paddy Chayevsky
1923–1981

14 I'm mad as hell, and I'm not going to take this anymore. *Network (screenplay) [1976]*

James Dickey
1923–1997

15 A shudder of joy runs up
The trunk: the needles tingle;
One bird uncontrollably cries.
The wind changes round, and I stir
Within another's life. Whose life?
In the Tree House at Night [1962]

16 And I to my motorcycle
Parked like the soul of the junkyard
Restored, a bicycle fleshed
With power, and tore off
Up Highway 106, continually
Drunk on the wind in my mouth,
Wringing the handlebar for speed,
Wild to be wreckage forever.
Cherrylog Road [1963]

17 All families lie together, though some are burned alive.
The others try to feel
For them. Some can, it is often said.
The Firebombing [1965]

18 We have all been in rooms
We cannot die in. *Adultery [1967]*

19 Nothing can come
of this nothing can come

Of us: of me with my grim techniques
Or you who have sealed your womb

With a ring of convulsive rubber:

Although we come together,
Nothing will come of us.   *Adultery*

Freeman Dyson
1923–

1   A good cause can become bad if we fight for it
with means that are indiscriminately murderous. A
bad cause can become good if enough people fight
for it in a spirit of comradeship and self-sacrifice. In
the end it is how you fight, as much as why you fight,
that makes your cause good or bad.
Disturbing the Universe [1979]

2   Between matter as we observe it in the laboratory
and mind as we observe it in our own consciousness,
there seems to be only a difference in degree but not
in kind. If God exists and is accessible to us, then his
mind and ours may likewise differ from each other
only in degree and not in kind. We stand, in a manner
of speaking, midway between the unpredictability of
matter and the unpredictability of God.
Infinite in All Directions [1988]

Bob [Robert B.] Elliott
1923–

and

Ray [Raymond H.] Goulding
1922–1990

3   Hang by your thumbs, everybody! Write if you
get work!
Bob and Ray radio show [1946],
signature closing lines

Paula Fox
1923–

4   There was a siege going on: it had been going on
for a long time, but the besieged themselves were the
last to take it seriously.
Desperate Characters [1970]

Nadine Gordimer
1923–

5   The truth isn't always beauty, but the hunger for
it is.
A Bolter and the Invincible Summer [1963]

6   That was one of the things she held against missionaries: how they stressed Christ's submission to

humiliation, and so had conditioned the people of
Africa to humiliation by the white man.
Not for Publication [1965], title story

7   She filled her house with blacks, and white parsons
who went around preaching Jesus was a revolutionary, and then when the police walked in she was
surprised.   *The Conservationist [1974]*

Joseph Heller
1923–1999

8   He had decided to live forever or die in the
attempt, and his only mission each time he went up
was to come down alive.   *Catch-22 [1961], ch. 3*

9   There was only one catch and that was Catch-22,
which specified that a concern for one's own safety
in the face of dangers that were real and immediate
was the process of a rational mind. Orr was crazy and
could be grounded. All he had to do was ask; and as
soon as he did, he would no longer be crazy and
would have to fly more missions. . . . If he flew them
he was crazy and didn't have to; but if he didn't want
to he was sane and had to. . . . "That's some catch,
that Catch-22," he [Yossarian] observed. "It's the
best there is," Doc Daneeka agreed.   *Catch-22, 5*

Henry [Alfred] Kissinger
1923–

10   Power is the great aphrodisiac.[1]
In the New York Times [January 19, 1971]

11   Covert action should not be confused with missionary work.
Testimony before the Pike Commission [1975]

12   High office teaches decision-making, not substance. . . . A period in high office consumes intellectual capital; it does not create it.
The White House Years [1979], pt. II

13   History knows no resting places and no plateaus.
White House Years [1979], III

14   A conventional army loses if it does not win. The
guerrilla army wins if it does not lose.
The Vietnam Negotiation, in Foreign Affairs
[January 1969]

15   [Richard Nixon] would have been a great, great
man had somebody loved him.
Quoted in Stephen Ambrose, *Nixon:*
Ruin and Recovery 1973–1990 [1991]

---

[1] Also quoted as: Power is the ultimate aphrodisiac.

Denise Levertov
1923–1999

1 I like to find
what's not found
at once, but lies
within something of another nature
in repose, distinct.
　　　　　　Pleasures [1959]

2 Marvelous Truth, confront us
at every turn,
in every guise.
　　　　　　Matins [1962], VII

3 Two by two in the ark of
the ache of it.
　　　　　The Ache of Marriage [1964]

Györgi Ligeti
1923–2006

4　I am in a prison: one wall is the avant-garde, the other wall is the past, and I want to escape.
　　Lecture on modern music [March 10, 1993]

Norman Mailer
1923–2007

5　So there was a new breed of adventurers, urban adventurers who drifted out at night looking for action with a black man's code to fit their facts. The hipster had absorbed the existentialist synapses of the Negro, and for practical purpose could be considered a white Negro.
　　Advertisements for Myself [1959].
　　The White Negro

6　Chicago was a town where nobody could forget how the money was made. It was picked up from floors still slippery with blood.
　　Miami and the Siege of Chicago [1968]

7　In the air the Pentagon would then, went the presumption, turn orange and vibrate until all evil emissions had fled this levitation. At that point the war in Vietnam would end.
　　The Armies of the Night [1968], pt. III, ch. 5

8　A night journey on a bus was one of the few times when everything ambitious, wild, overconceived, hopeless, garish, and suffocatingly technical in American life nonetheless came together long enough to give the citizens a little peace, for it was only when they were on the move that Americans could feel anchored in their memories.
　　The Armies of the Night, IV, 5

9　The horror of the Twentieth Century was the size of each new event, and the paucity of its reverberation.
　　Of a Fire on the Moon [1970]

10　We are a Faustian age determined to meet the Lord or the Devil before we are done, and the ineluctable ore of the authentic is our only key to the lock.
　　Existential Errands [1972]. A Course in Film-Making

11　Then the Warden said, "Do you have anything you'd like to say?" and Gary looked up at the ceiling and hesitated, then said, "Let's do it." That was it.
　　The Executioner's Song [1979], ch. 38

Jaroslav Pelikan
1923–2006

12　Tradition is the living faith of the dead, traditionalism is the dead faith of the living.
　　The Vindication of Tradition [1984]

James Schuyler
1923–1991

13　　　Is it for miracles
We live? I like it when the morning sun lights up my
　　room
Like a yellow jelly bean, an inner glow. May mutters:
　　"Why
ask questions?" or, "What are the questions you wish
　　to ask?"　　　*Hymn to Life [1974]*

Eugene B. Sledge, Jr.
1923–2001

14　Slowly the reality of it all formed in my mind: we were expendable! It was difficult to accept. We come from a nation and a culture that values life and the individual. To find oneself in a situation where your life seems of little value is the ultimate in loneliness. It is a humbling experience.
　　With the Old Breed at Peleliu and Okinawa [1981], ch. 4

Philip Whalen
1923–2002

15 Old and ruined, all rotted and broken up
These plum trees function gorgeously
A few days every year
In a way nobody else does.
　　Scenes of Life at the Capital [1970]

Hank Williams
1923–1953

1 Hear that lonesome whippoorwill?
  He sounds too blue to fly.
  The midnight train is whining low,
  I'm so lonesome I could cry.
  I'm So Lonesome I Could Cry [1942]

2 I can settle down and be doing just fine
  Till I hear an old train rolling down the line,
  Then I hurry straight home and pack
  And if I didn't go, I believe I'd blow my stack
  I love you baby, but you gotta understand
  When the Lord made me he made a
       ramblin' man
  Ramblin' Man [1951]

3 Say hey, good lookin',
  What you got cookin',
  How's about cookin' something up with me?
  Hey, Good Lookin' [1951]

Hank Williams
1923–1953
and
Fred Rose
1898–1954

4 No matter how I struggle and strive,
  I'll never get out of this world alive.
  *I'll Never Get Out of This World Alive
  [1952]*

Yehuda Amichai
1924–2000

5 God has pity on kindergarten children.
  He has less pity on school children.
  And on grownups he has no pity at all,
  he leaves them alone,
  and sometimes they must crawl on all fours
  in the burning sand
  to reach the first-aid station
  covered with blood.
  God Has Pity on Kindergarten Children [1955]

James Baldwin
1924–1987

6   My life, my *real* life, was in danger, and not from
anything other people might do but from the hatred
I carried in my own heart.
  Notes of a Native Son [1955], title essay

7   Harlem had needed something to smash. To
smash something is the ghetto's chronic need.
  Notes of a Native Son, title essay

8   It is only in his music, which Americans are able to
admire because a protective sentimentality limits their
understanding of it, that the Negro in America has
been able to tell his story. It is a story which otherwise
has yet to be told and which no American is prepared
to hear.
  *Notes of a Native Son. Many
  Thousands Gone*

9   There exists among the intolerably degraded the
perverse and powerful desire to force into the arena
of the actual the fantastic crimes of which they have
been accused, achieving their vengeance and their
own destruction through making the nightmare real.
  *Notes of a Native Son. Many
  Thousands Gone*

10   People are trapped in history and history is
trapped in them.
  *Notes of a Native Son. Stranger
  in the Village*

11   Perhaps home is not a place but simply an irrevo-
cable condition. *Giovanni's Room [1956]*

12   Children have never been very good at listening to
their elders, but they have never failed to imitate
them.
  *Nobody Knows My Name [1961].
  Fifth Avenue, Uptown*

13   Money, it turned out, was exactly like sex, you
thought of nothing else if you didn't have it and
thought of other things if you did.
  *Nobody Knows My Name.
  The Black Boy Looks at the White Boy*

14   If we do not now dare everything, the fulfillment
of that prophecy, re-created from the Bible in song
by a slave, is upon us: *God gave Noah the rainbow sign,
No more water, the fire next time!*
  The Fire Next Time [1963], end

15   If they take you in the morning, they will be
coming for us that night.
  *Open Letter to My Sister Angela Y. Davis
  [1970]*

Robert Bolt
1924–1995

16   The law is not a "light" for you or any man to see
by; the law is not an instrument of any kind. The law
is a causeway upon which, so long as he keeps to it, a
citizen may walk safely.
  A Man for All Seasons [1960], act II

George [Herbert Walker] Bush
1924–

1   Voodoo economics.
> *Remark, presidential primary campaign*
> *[1980]*

2   We are a nation of communities, of tens and tens of thousands of ethnic, religious, social, business, labor union, neighborhood, regional and other organizations, all of them varied, voluntary, and unique . . . a brilliant diversity spread like stars, like a thousand points of light in a broad and peaceful sky.[1]
> *Acceptance speech, Republican National*
> *Convention, New Orleans [August 18, 1988]*

3   The Congress will push me to raise taxes, and I'll say no, and they'll push, and I'll say no, and they'll push again. And all I can say to them is read my lips: No New Taxes.
> *Acceptance speech, Republican National*
> *Convention, New Orleans*

4   I want a kinder, gentler nation.
> *Acceptance speech, Republican National*
> *Convention, New Orleans*

5   A line has been drawn in the sand.
> *On U.S. policy toward Iraq [August 8, 1990]*

6   We have before us the opportunity to forge for ourselves and for future generations a new world order — a world where the rule of law, not the law of the jungle, governs the conduct of nations.
> *On allied military attacks in the Gulf War*
> *[January 16, 1991]*

Truman Capote
1924–1984

7   Now Second Avenue is a dismal street, made from scraps and ends; part cobblestone, part asphalt, part cement; and its atmosphere of desertion is permanent.   *A Tree of Night [1949]. Miriam*

8   It was a terrible, strange-looking hotel. But Little Sunshine stayed on: it was his rightful home, he said, for if he went away, as he had once upon a time, other voices, other rooms, voices lost and clouded, strummed his dreams.
> *Other Voices, Other Rooms [1948], ch. 5*

9   It was a face beyond childhood, yet this side of belonging to a woman. I thought her anywhere

---

[1] Instantly he could see the town below now, coiling in a thousand fumes of homely smoke, now winking into a thousand points of friendly light its glorious small design, its aching passionate assurances of walls, warmth, comfort, food, and love. — THOMAS WOLFE, *The Web and the Rock* [1939]

between sixteen and thirty; as it turned out, she was shy two months of her nineteenth birthday.
> *Breakfast at Tiffany's [1958]*

10   [It] isn't writing at all — it's typing.
> *Comment [1959] on Beat Generation*
> *writers. From GERALD CLARKE, Capote*
> *[1988]*

11   I didn't want to harm the man. I thought he was a very nice gentleman. Soft-spoken. I thought so right up to the moment I cut his throat.
> *In Cold Blood [1966]*

Jimmy [James Earl, Jr.] Carter
1924–

12   We believe that the first time we're born, as children, it's human life given to us; and when we accept Jesus as our Savior, it's a new life. That's what "born again" means.
> *In an interview with Robert L. Turner*
> *[March 16, 1976]*

13   A simple and a proper function of government is just to make it easy for us to do good and difficult for us to do wrong.
> *Speech at Democratic National*
> *Convention [July 15, 1976]*

14   I've looked on a lot of women with lust. I've committed adultery in my heart many times. This is something that God recognizes I will do — and I have done it — and God forgives me for it.
> *Interview in Playboy magazine*
> *[October 1976]*

15   Two problems of our country — energy and malaise.
> *Remark at town meeting, Bardstown,*
> *Kentucky [July 31, 1979]*

Shirley Chisholm
1924–2005

16   Health is a human right, not a privilege to be purchased.
> *Speech in U.S. House of Representatives [1970]*

Arthur Charles Erickson
1924–2009

17   North American civilization is one of the ugliest to have emerged in human history, and it has engulfed the world. Asphalt and exhaust fumes clog the villages. . . . This great, though disastrous, culture can only change as we begin to stand off and see . . . the

inveterate materialism which has become the model for cultures around the globe.

Speech at Simon Fraser University [1973]

Henry Fairlie
1924–1990

1 By the "Establishment," I do not mean only the centers of official power — though they are certainly part of it — but rather the whole matrix of official and social relations within which power is exercised.

The Spectator [September 1955]

2 Love wants to enjoy in other ways the human beings whom it has enjoyed in bed; it looks forward to having breakfast. But in the morning Lust is always furtive. *Lust [1978]*

Alexander Haig
1924–2010

3 As of now, I am in control here, in the White House, pending the return of the vice president and in close touch with him. If something came up, I would check with him, of course.

After the attempted assassination of Ronald Reagan [March 30, 1981]

Zbigniew Herbert
1924–1998

4 The pebble
is a perfect creature

equal to itself
mindful of its limits

filled exactly
with a pebbly meaning   *Pebble*[1] *[1966]*

Joseph Kraft
1924–1986

5 Exit strategy

Washington Post [February 2, 1984]. Seeking an Exit Strategy

Rod Serling
1924–1975

6 You're traveling through another dimension, a dimension not only of sight and sound but of mind;

---

[1]Translated from the Polish by CZESLAW MILOSZ and PETER DALE SCOTT.

a journey into a wondrous land whose boundaries are that of imagination. That's the signpost up ahead — your next stop, the Twilight Zone.

The Twilight Zone (television series), opening narration [1959]

Wislawa Szymborska
1924–2012

7 Time has passed like a courier with urgent news.
But that's just our simile.
The character's invented, his haste is make-believe,
his news inhuman.

View with a Grain of Sand: Selected Poems[2] *[1993]. Title poem*

8 You were saved because you were the first.
You were saved because you were the last.
Alone. With others.
On the right. On the left.
Because it was raining. Because of the shade.
Because the day was sunny.

View with a Grain of Sand: Selected Poems. Could Have

Howard H. Baker, Jr.
1925–

9 What did the president know and when did he know it?

Senate Watergate Committee hearings [June 25, 1973]

Russell Baker
1925–

10 The only thing I was fit for was to be a writer, and this notion rested solely on my suspicion that I would never be fit for real work, and that writing didn't require any.

Growing Up [1982], ch. 9

Yogi [Lawrence Peter] Berra
1925–

11 It gets late early out there.
Quoted in Sporting News [August 7, 1971]

12 It ain't over till it's over.
Comment on National League pennant race [1973]

---

[2]Translated by STANISLAW BARAŃCZAK and CLARE CAVANAGH.

1   I really didn't say everything I said.
     Quoted in Sports Illustrated
     [March 17, 1986]

2   How can you think and hit at the same time?
     Remark

3   In baseball, you don't know nothing.
     Remark

4   Slump? I ain't in no slump. I just ain't hitting.
     Remark

5   You can observe a lot by watching.
     Remark

6   If people don't want to come out to the ball park, nobody's going to stop them.
     Attributed

7   It was déjà vu all over again.
     Attributed

8   When you come to a fork in the road, take it.
     Attributed

Lenny Bruce [Leonard Alfred Schneider]
1925–1966

9   Liberals can understand everything but people who don't understand them.
     The Essential Lenny Bruce [1967]

10   People should be taught what is, not what should be. All my humor is based on destruction and despair. If the whole world were tranquil, without disease and violence, I'd be standing in the breadline.
     The Essential Lenny Bruce,
     Epigraph

11   I'll die young, but it's like kissing God.
     On his drug addiction

William F[rank] Buckley, Jr.
1925–2008

12   *National Review* . . . stands athwart history, yelling Stop, at a time when no one is inclined to do so, or to have much patience with those who so urge it.
     Publisher's Statement, National Review,
     inaugural issue [November 19, 1955]

13   I should sooner live in a society governed by the first two thousand names in the Boston telephone directory than in a society governed by the two thousand faculty members of Harvard University.
     Rumbles Left and Right [1963]

Barbara Pierce Bush
1925–

14   Somewhere out in this audience may even be someone who will one day follow in my footsteps, and preside over the White House as the President's spouse. I wish him well!
     Remarks at Wellesley College Commencement
     [June 1, 1990]

John [Daniel] Ehrlichman
1925–1999

15   It'll play in Peoria.[1]   *Phrase [1970]*

16   I think we ought to let him [Patrick Gray] hang there. Let him twist slowly, slowly in the wind.
     Telephone conversation with John Dean
     [March 7/8, 1973]

Frantz Fanon
1925–1961

17   When I search for man in the technique and the style of Europe, I see only a succession of negations of man, and an avalanche of murders.
     The Wretched of the Earth[2] [1961]. Conclusion

18   I am black: I am the incarnation of a complete fusion with the world, an intuitive understanding of the earth, an abandonment of my ego in the heart of the cosmos.
     Black Skin, White Masks [1967]

Russell Hoban
1925–2011

19   If the past cannot teach the present and the father cannot teach the son, then history need not have bothered to go on, and the world has wasted a great deal of time.
     The Lion of Boaz-Jachin and Jachin-Boaz

20   A story is what remains when you leave out most of the action.   *Pilgermann*

Donald Justice
1925–2004

21   Men at forty
     Learn to close softly

---

[1]Meaning politically acceptable to "Middle America."
[2]Translated by CONSTANCE FARRINGTON.
See Eugène Pottier, 472:16.

The doors to rooms they will not be
Coming back to.   *Men at Forty [1967]*

Robert F[rancis] Kennedy
1925–1968

1   This world demands the qualities of youth: not a time of life but a state of mind, a temper of the will, a quality of the imagination, a predominance of courage over timidity, of the appetite for adventure over the love of ease.
Speech, University of Cape Town, South Africa [June 6, 1966]

2   These are not ordinary times and this is not an ordinary election. At stake is not simply the leadership of our party and even our country. It is our right to the moral leadership of this planet.
Announcing his candidacy for president [March 16, 1968]

3   We will have difficult times. We've had difficult times in the past. And we will have difficult times in the future. It is not the end of violence; it is not the end of lawlessness; and it's not the end of disorder. But the vast majority of white people and the vast majority of black people in this country want to live together, want to improve the quality of our life, and want justice for all human beings that abide in our land.
Remarks on the assassination of Martin Luther King, Jr., Indianapolis [April 4, 1968]

Kenneth Koch
1925–2002

4 Total absorption in poetry is one of the finest things in existence —
It should not make you feel guilty. Everyone is absorbed in something.
The sailor is absorbed in the sea. Poetry is the mediation of life.
The Art of Love [1975]. The Art of Poetry

Maxine [Winokur] Kumin
1925–

5 I took the lake between my legs.
Morning Swim [1965]

6 Something went crabwise
across the snow this morning.
The Presence [1970]

7 Our daughters and sons have burst
from the marionette show

leaving a tangle of strings
and gone into the unlit audience.
The Absent Ones [1972]

8 Can it be
I am the only Jew residing in Danville, Kentucky,
looking for matzoh in the Safeway and the A & P?
Living Alone with Jesus [1972]

9 When Sleeping Beauty wakes up
she is almost fifty years old.
Time to start planning her retirement cottage.
The Archaeology of a Marriage [1978]

Elmore Leonard
1925–

10   Try to leave out the parts that readers tend to skip.
Easy on the Adverbs, Exclamation Points, and Especially Hooptedoodle [2001]

Malcolm X
[El-Hajj Malik El-Shabazz]
1925–1965

11   If you're born in America with a black skin, you're born in prison.   *Interview [June 1963]*

12   The Negro "revolution" is controlled by these foxy white liberals, by the government itself. But the Black revolution is controlled only by God.
Speech [December 1, 1963]

13   Whether you're educated or illiterate, whether you live on the boulevard or in the alley, you're going to catch hell just like I am. We're all in the same boat and we all are going to catch the same hell from the same man. He just happens to be a white man.
The Ballot or the Bullet [April 3, 1964]

14   It'll be the ballot or the bullet. It'll be liberty or it'll be death.
The Ballot or the Bullet

15   I don't see any American dream; I see an American nightmare.
The Ballot or the Bullet

16   We didn't land on Plymouth Rock; the rock was landed on us.
The Ballot or the Bullet

17   We are not fighting for integration, nor are we fighting for separation. We are fighting for recognition as human beings. We are fighting for . . . human rights.
Speech, Black Revolution, New York [1964]

18   The day that the black man takes an uncompromising step and realizes that he's within his rights,

when his own freedom is being jeopardized, to use any means necessary to bring about his freedom or put a halt to that injustice, I don't think he'll be by himself.

> *Oxford Union Society debate*
> *[December 3, 1964]*

1   [On the assassination of President John F. Kennedy:] It was, as I saw it, a case of "the chickens coming home to roost." I said that the hate in white men had not stopped with the killing of defenseless black people, but that hate, allowed to spread unchecked, had finally struck down this country's Chief Magistrate.

> *Autobiography (as told to* ALEX HALEY*)*
> *[1964]*

2   New York was heaven to me. And Harlem was Seventh Heaven.

> *Autobiography*

Zhores Aleksandrovich Medvedev
1925–

3   Science and technology, and the various forms of art, all unite humanity in a single and interconnected system. As science progresses, the worldwide cooperation of scientists and technologists becomes more and more of a special and distinct intellectual community of friendship, in which, in place of antagonism, there is growing up a mutually advantageous sharing of work, a coordination of efforts, a common language for the exchange of information, and a solidarity, which are in many cases independent of the social and political differences of individual states.

> *The Medvedev Papers [1970], preface*

Yukio Mishima
1925–1970

4   Is there not a sort of remorse that precedes sin? Was it remorse at the very fact that I existed?

> *Confessions of a Mask [1949]*

Flannery O'Connor
1925–1964

5   I preach that there are all kinds of truth, your truth and somebody else's, but behind all of them there is only one truth and that is that there's no truth.

> *Wise Blood [1952], spoken by*
> *Hazel Motes*

6   "She would of been a good woman," The Misfit said, "if it had been somebody there to shoot her every minute of her life."

> *A Good Man Is Hard to Find [1953]*

7   Besides the neutral expression she wore when she was alone, Mrs. Freeman had two others, forward and reverse, that she used for all her human dealings. Her forward expression was steady and driving like the advance of a heavy truck.

> *Good Country People [1955]*

8   The novel is an art form and when you use it for anything other than art, you pervert it. . . . If you manage to use it successfully for social, religious, or other purposes, it is because you make it art first.

> *Letter to Father John McCown [May 9, 1956]*

9   I doubt if the texture of Southern life is any more grotesque than that of the rest of the nation, but it does seem evident that the Southern writer is particularly adept at recognizing the grotesque; and to recognize the grotesque, you have to have some notion of what is not grotesque and why.

> *Talk at Notre Dame University [spring 1957]*

10   Whenever I'm asked why Southern writers particularly have a penchant for writing about freaks, I say it is because we are still able to recognize one.

> *Some Aspects of the Grotesque in Southern*
> *Fiction [1960]*

11   Does one's integrity ever lie in what he is not able to do? I think that usually it does, for free will does not mean one will, but many wills conflicting in one man. Freedom cannot be conceived simply.

> *Author's Note to the second edition [1962]*
> *of Wise Blood*

12   Knowing who you are is good for one generation only.

> *Everything That Rises Must Converge*
> *[1965], title story*

13   I have settled, in short, from reading my own writings, that my subject in fiction is the action of grace in territory held largely by the devil.

> *Mystery and Manners [1969].*
> *On Her Own Work*

14   The main concern of the fiction writer is with mystery as it is incarnated in human life.

> *Mystery and Manners. Catholic Novelists and*
> *Their Readers*

Frank R. Pierson
1925–2012

15   What we've got here is failure to communicate.

> *Cool Hand Luke (screenplay) [1967]*

Robert Rauschenberg
1925–2008

1   I really feel sorry for people who think things like soap dishes or mirrors or Coke bottles are ugly, because they're surrounded by things like that all day long, and it must make them miserable.
Quoted in CALVIN TOMPKINS,
The Bride and the Bachelors [1965]

Jack Spicer
1925–1965

2   A really perfect poem has an infinitely small vocabulary.   *After Lorca [1957]*

3   The English department of the spirit — that great quagmire that lurks at the bottom of all of us.
Admonitions [1958]

4   Aimlessly
It pounds the shore. White and aimless signals. No One listens to poetry.   *Language [1965]*

William Styron
1925–2006

5   In depression this faith in deliverance, in ultimate restoration, is absent. The pain is unrelenting, and what makes the condition intolerable is the foreknowledge that no remedy will come — not in a day, an hour, a month, or a minute. . . . And this results in a striking experience — one which I have called, borrowing military terminology, the situation of the walking wounded.
Darkness Visible: A Memoir of Madness [1990]

Margaret [Hilda Roberts] Thatcher
1925–

6   You turn if you want to. The lady's not for turning.
Speech at Conservative Party conference, Brighton, England [October 10, 1980]

7   If you lead a country like Britain . . . you have to have a touch of iron about you.
On her reputation as The Iron Lady [March 21, 1986]

8   There's no such thing as society. There are individual men and women, and there are families. And no government can do anything except through people, and people must look to themselves first.
Interview [September 23, 1987]

9   In politics, if you want anything said, ask a man. If you want anything done, ask a woman.
Saying

Gore Vidal
1925–

10   The theater needs continual reminders that there is nothing more debasing than the work of those who do well what is not worth doing at all.
Quoted in Newsweek [March 25, 1968]

11   He turned being a Big Loser into a perfect triumph by managing to lose the presidency in a way bigger and more original than anyone else had ever lost it before.
Richard Nixon, in Esquire [December 1983]

12   Apparently, a democracy is a place where numerous elections are held at great cost without issues and with interchangeable candidates.
A View from the Diner's Club [1991]

A[rchie] R[andolph] Ammons
1926–2001

13   the sunlight has never
heard of trees
Gravelly Run [1960]

14 Though I have looked everywhere
I can find nothing lowly
in the universe.
Still [1972]

15 In nature there are few sharp lines.
Corson's Inlet [1972], l. 31

16   No humbling of reality to precept.
Corson's Inlet, l. 116

17 Not so much looking for the shape
as being available
to any shape that may be
summoning itself
through me
from the self not mine but ours.
Poetics [1972]

18 I attended the burial of all my rosy feelings:
I performed the rites, simple and decisive.
Transaction [1972]

19   I don't know about you,
but I'm sick of good poems, all those little
rondures
splendidly brought off, painted gourds on a shelf.
Sphere [1974]

John Berger
1926–

1   Men act and women appear. Men look at women. Women watch themselves being looked at.
> *Ways of Seeing [1972], ch. 3*

2   The nude is condemned to never being naked. Nudity is a form of dress.
> *Ways of Seeing, 3*

Chuck Berry
[Charles Edward Anderson]
1926–

3 Roll over Beethoven
And tell Tchaikovsky the news.
> *Roll Over Beethoven [1956]*

4 He never learned to read or write so well
But he could play a guitar just like ringing a bell.
> *Johnny B. Goode [1958]*

Robert Bly
1926–

5 I have wandered in a face, for hours,
Passing through dark fires.
I have risen to a body
Not yet born,
Existing like a light around the body,
Through which the body moves like a sliding moon.
> *The Light Around the Body [1967].*
> *Looking into a Face*

6 The sound of the rampaging Missouri,
Bending the reeds again and again — something
   inside us
Like a ghost train in the Rockies
About to be buried in snow!
Its long hoot
Making the owl in the Douglas fir turn his head.
> *The Light Around the Body. Asian Peace*
> *Offers Rejected Without Publication*

Mel Brooks
[Melvin Kaminsky]
1926–

7   It's simply a matter of creative accounting.
> *The Producers (screenplay) [1968]*

8   That's it, baby, if you've got it, flaunt it.
> *The Producers (screenplay)*

9 Springtime for Hitler and Germany,
Deutschland is happy and gay.

We're moving to a faster pace,
Look out, here comes the Master Race!
> *The Producers (screenplay)*

10   Where did we go right?
> *The Producers (screenplay)*

11   It's good to be the king.
> *History of the World, Part I (screenplay)*
> *[1981], spoken by Mel Brooks as Louis XVI*

Fidel Castro
1926–

12   History will absolve me.[1]
> *At his trial for raid on Moncada barracks*
> *[October 16, 1953]*

13   We are not only a Latin-American nation; we are an Afro-American nation also.
> *Speech in Havana [1977]*

14   I am not saying goodbye to you. I only wish to fight as a soldier of ideas.
> *Statement resigning as Cuba's president*
> *[February 19, 2008]*

John Coltrane
1926–1967

15   That's what music is to me — it's just another way of saying this is a big, beautiful universe we live in, that's been given to us, and here's an example of just how magnificent and encompassing it is.
> *Interview in Downbeat [April 12, 1962]*

16   It all has to do with it.   *A Love Supreme [1965]*

Robert Creeley
1926–2005

17 drive, he sd, for
christ's sake, look
out where yr going.
> *For Love [1962]. I Know a Man*

18 Into the company of love
it all returns.
> *For Love. For Love*

19 How can I die alone.
Where will I be then who am now alone,
what groans so pathetically
in this room where I am alone?
> *For Love. The Door*

---

[1] La Historia me absolvera.

Miles Davis
[Miles Dewey Davis III]
1926–1991

1 If you're not nervous, you're not paying attention.
Attributed

J. P. Donleavy
1926–

2 When I die I want to decompose in a barrel of porter and have it served in all the pubs in Dublin.
The Ginger Man [1955]

Morton Feldman
1926–1987

3 Art is a crucial, dangerous operation we perform on ourselves. Unless we take a chance, we die in art.
Give My Regards to Eighth Street: Collected Writings [2000]

Michel Foucault
1926–1984

4 As the archaeology of our thought easily shows, man is an invention of recent date. And one perhaps nearing its end.
The Order of Things [1966]

5 Discipline "makes" individuals; it is the specific technique of a power that regards individuals both as objects and as instruments of its exercise.
Discipline and Punish [1975]

6 The lyricism of marginality may find inspiration in the image of the "outlaw," the great social nomad, who prowls on the confines of a docile, frightened order.
Discipline and Punish

7 The individual is the product of power.
Preface to GILLES DELEUZE and FÉLIX GUATTARI, Anti-Oedipus [1978]

8 There are times in life when the question of knowing if one can think differently than one thinks, and perceive differently than one sees, is absolutely necessary if one is to go on looking and reflecting at all.
History of Sexuality, vol. 2 [1984]

Allen Ginsberg
1926–1997

9 I saw you, Walt Whitman, childless, lonely old grubber, poking among the meats in the refrigerator and eyeing the grocery boys.

I heard you asking questions of each: Who killed the pork chops? What price bananas? Are you my Angel?
A Supermarket in California [1955]

10 America free Tom Mooney
America save the Spanish Loyalists
America Sacco & Vanzetti must not die
America I am the Scottsboro boys.
America [1956]

11 America I've given you all and now I'm nothing.
America

12 America I'm putting my queer shoulder to the wheel.
America

13 I saw the best minds of my generation destroyed by madness, starving hysterical naked,
dragging themselves through the negro streets at dawn looking for an angry fix
angelheaded hipsters burning for the ancient heavenly connection to the starry dynamo in the machinery of night.
Howl [1956]

14 This is the end, the redemption from Wilderness, way for the Wonderer, House sought for All, black handkerchief washed clean by weeping.
Kaddish [1959], pt. I

15 O mother
what have I left out
O mother
what have I forgotten
Kaddish, IV

16 Candor ends paranoia.
Cosmopolitan Greetings [1986]

Alan Greenspan
1926–

17 Irrational exuberance
Speech [December 5, 1996]

18 An infectious greed seemed to grip much of our business community.... It is not that humans have become any more greedy than in generations past. It is that the avenues to express greed have grown so enormously.
Testimony before the Senate Banking Committee [July 16, 2002]

19 This modern risk-management paradigm held sway for decades. The whole intellectual edifice, however, collapsed in the summer of last year.
Congressional hearing [October 23, 2008]

Elizabeth Jennings
1926–2001

20 Since clarity suggests simplicity
And since the simple thing is here inapt,

I choose obscurities of tongue and touch,
The shadow side of language and the dark
　　Hinted in conversations close to quarrel,
Conceived within the mind in aftermaths.
　　　Song for a Birth or a Death [1961].
　　　The Counterpart

1 It is the dark, the dark that draws me back
　　Into a chaos where
Vocations, visions fail, the will grows slack
And I am stunned by silence everywhere.
　　　Song for a Birth or a Death. To a Friend
　　　with a Religious Vocation

2 Insects move and men like insects. Why
Are we set here, frightened of our reflections,
Living in fear yet desperate not to die?
　　　Collected Poems [1986]. Nothing

Elisabeth Kübler-Ross
1926–2004

3　Guilt is perhaps the most painful companion of
death.　　　*On Death and Dying [1969]*

Harper Lee
1926–

4　Shoot all the bluejays you want, if you can hit 'em,
but remember it's a sin to kill a mockingbird.
　　　To Kill a Mockingbird [1960], ch. 10

5　The one thing that doesn't abide by majority rule
is a person's conscience.
　　　To Kill a Mockingbird, 11

Carolyn Leigh
1926–1983

6 'Cause it's witchcraft,
Wicked witchcraft.
And although I know it's strictly taboo,
When you arouse the need in me,
My heart says, "Yes, indeed" in me,
"Proceed with what you're leadin' me to!"
　　　Witchcraft[1] *[1957]*

Richard Matheson
1926–

7　So close — the Infinitesimal and the Infinite. But
suddenly I knew they were really the two ends of
the same concept. The unbelievably small and the

---
[1]Music by CY COLEMAN.

unbelievably vast eventually meet, like the closing of
a gigantic circle.
　　　The Incredible Shrinking Man (screenplay)
　　　[1957]

James [Ingram] Merrill
1926–1995

8 Always that same old story —
Father Time and Mother Earth,
A marriage on the rocks.
　　　The Broken Home [1966]

9 Again last night I dreamed the dream called
　　Laundry.　　　*The Mad Scene [1966]*

10　　　　　　I knew
That life was fiction in disguise.
　　　Days of 1935 [1969]

11 Proust's Law (are you listening?) is twofold:
(a) What least thing our self-love longs for most
Others instinctively withhold;

(b) Only when time has slain desire
Is his wish granted to a smiling ghost
Neither harmed nor warmed, now, by the
　　fire.
　　　Days of 1971 [1969]

12 I yearned for the kind of unseasoned telling found
In legends, fairy tales, a tone licked clean
Over the centuries by mild old tongues,
Grandam to cub, serene, anonymous.
　　　The Book of Ephraim [1976], sec. A

13 What we dream up must be lived down, I think.
　　　The Book of Ephraim, I

14　　　　HE PREFERS
LIVE MUSIC TO A PATRON'S HUMDRUM SPHERES
Is this permitted? WHEN U ARE MOZART YES
He's living *now*? As what? A BLACK ROCK STAR
WHATEVER THAT IS.
　　　The Book of Ephraim, P

Newton N[orman] Minow
1926–

15　When television is bad, nothing is worse. I invite
you to sit down in front of your television set
when your station goes on the air . . . and keep
your eyes glued to that set until the station signs off.
I can assure you that you will observe a vast wasteland.

　　Speech as chairman of the Federal
　　Communications Commission to National
　　Association of Broadcasters, Washington,
　　D.C. [May 9, 1961]

Frank O'Hara
1926–1966

1   One need never leave the confines of New York to get all the greenery one wishes — I can't even enjoy a blade of grass unless I know there's a subway handy, or a record store or some other sign that people do not totally *regret* life.
> *Meditations in an Emergency [1957].*
> *Title poem*

2   It is easy to be beautiful; it is difficult to appear so.
> *Meditations in an Emergency. Title poem*

3 I wanted to be sure to reach you;
though my ship was on the way it got caught
in some moorings. I am always tying up
and then deciding to depart.
> *Meditations in an Emergency.*
> *To the Harbormaster*

4   You just go on your nerve. If someone's chasing you down the street with a knife you just run, you don't turn around and shout, "Give it up! I was a track star for Mineola Prep."
> *Personism: A Manifesto [1959]*

5 It is 12:20 in New York a Friday
three days after Bastille Day, yes
it is 1959 and I go get a shoeshine
because I will get off the 4:19 in Easthampton
at 7:15 and then go straight to dinner
and I don't know the people who will feed me
> *Lunch Poems [1964]. The Day Lady Died*

6 oh god it's wonderful
to get out of bed
and drink too much coffee
and smoke too many cigarettes
and love you so much
> *Lunch Poems. Steps*

7 LANA TURNER HAS COLLAPSED!
there is no snow in Hollywood
there is no rain in California
I have been to lots of parties
and acted perfectly disgraceful
but I never actually collapsed
oh Lana Turner we love you get up
> *Lunch Poems. Poem*

8 My quietness has a man in it, he is transparent
and he carries me quietly, like a gondola, through the
    streets.
> *Collected Poems [1967]. In Memory*
> *of My Feelings*

9 If anyone was looking
for me I hid behind a
tree and cried out "I am
an orphan."

And here I am, the
center of all beauty!
writing these poems!
Imagine!
> *Collected Poems. Autobiographia*
> *Literaria*

10 "Sun, don't go!" I was awake
at last. "No, go I must, they're calling
me."
"Who are they?"
             Rising he said, "Some
day you'll know. They're calling to you
too." Darkly he rose, and then I slept.
> *Collected Poems. A True Account of*
> *Talking to the Sun at Fire Island*

Peter Shaffer
1926–

11   We keep saying old people are square. Then when they suddenly aren't — we don't like it!
> *Equus [1973], act II, sc. 31*

12   [On a Mozart opera:] There are simply too many notes.
> *Amadeus (screenplay) [1984], spoken by*
> *Jeffrey Jones as Emperor Joseph II*

William D[eWitt] Snodgrass
1926–2009

13 It was the nature of the thing:
No moon outlives its leaving night,
No sun its day. And I went on
Rich in the loss of all I sing
To the threshold of waking light,
To larksong and the live, gray dawn.
So night by night, my life has gone.
> *Orpheus [1959]*

14 The sleek, expensive girls I teach,
Younger and pinker every year,
Bloom gradually out of reach.
> *April Inventory [1959]*

Charles Van Doren
1926–

15   I would give almost anything I have to reverse the course of my life in the last three years. . . . I have deceived my friends, and I had millions of them.
> *Statement to congressional committee*
> *investigating quiz show scandal [1959]*

Lew [Lewis Barrett] Welch
1926–1971

1 You can't fix it. You can't make it go away.
   I don't know what you're going to do about it,
But I know what I'm going to do about it. I'm just
   going to walk away from it.
   Ring of Bone: Collected Poems 1950–1971.
   Chicago Poem [1965]

Edward Abbey
1927–1989

2   Most of my wandering in the desert I've done
alone. Not so much from choice as from necessity—
I generally prefer to go into places where no one else
wants to go.   *Desert Solitaire [1968]*

John Ashbery
1927–

3 As I sit looking out of a window of the building
I wish I did not have to write the instruction manual
   on the uses of a new metal.
          Some Trees [1956]. The Instruction Manual

4   You and I
Are suddenly what the trees try
To tell us we are:
That their merely being there
Means something; that soon
We may touch, love, explain.

          Some Trees. Title poem

5 For this is action, this not being sure, this careless
Preparing, sowing the seeds crooked in the furrow,
Making ready to forget, and always coming back
To the mooring of starting out, that day so long ago.
          The Double Dream of Spring [1966].
          Soonest Mended

6   We were surprised once, long ago; and now we
can never be surprised again.
          Three Poems [1972]. The Recital

7   I thought that if I could put it all down, that
would be one way. And next the thought came
to me that to leave all out would be another, and
truer, way.

          Three Poems. The New Spirit

8 As Parmigianino did it, the right hand
Bigger than the head, thrust at the viewer
And swerving easily away, as though to protect
What it advertises.
          Self-Portrait in a Convex Mirror [1975].
          Title poem

9 Something like living occurs, a movement
Out of the dream into its codification.
          Self-Portrait in a Convex Mirror.
          Title poem

10 The seasons are no longer what they once were,
   But it is the nature of things to be seen only once,
   As they happen along, bumping into other things,
      getting along
   Somehow. That's where Orpheus made his
      mistake.
          Houseboat Days [1975]. Syringa

Cesar [Estrada] Chavez
1927–1993

11   Viva la huelga [Long live the strike]!
          Slogan of the United Farm Workers
          [the 1960s]

Edwin Edwards
1927–

12   The only way I can lose this election is if I'm
caught in bed with either a dead girl or a live boy.
          While campaigning for governor of Louisiana
          [1983]

Günter [Wilhelm] Grass
1927–

13   You can declare at the very start that it's impossible to write a novel nowadays, but then, behind
your back, so to speak, give birth to a whopper, a
novel to end all novels.
          The Tin Drum[1] [1959], bk. I,
          The Wide Skirt

14   Even bad books are books and therefore sacred.
          The Tin Drum. Rasputin and the Alphabet

Galway Kinnell
1927–

15 the rest of my days I spend
wandering, wondering
what, anyway,
was that sticky infusion, that rank flavor of blood, that
      poetry by which I lived?
          Body Rags [1968]. The Bear

16 In the half darkness we look at each other
and smile

---

[1]Translated by Ralph Manheim.

and touch arms across his little, startlingly muscled
    body—
this one whom habit of memory propels to the
    ground of his making,
sleeper only the mortal sounds can awake,
this blessing love gives again into our arms.
Mortal Acts, Mortal Words [1980].
After Making Love We Hear Footsteps

R[onald] D[avid] Laing
1927–1989

1   Madness need not be all breakdown. It may also
be breakthrough. It is potentially liberation and
renewal as well as enslavement and existential death.
The Politics of Experience [1967], ch. 6

Fran Landesman
1927–2011

2 Love seemed sure around the New Year,
Now it's April, love is just a ghost.
Spring arrived on time,
Only what became of you, Dear?
Spring can really hang you up the most!
Spring Can Really Hang You Up the Most
[1955]

3 All the sad young men,
Drifting through the town,
Drinking up the night,
Trying not to drown.
The Nervous Set [1959]. The Ballad of the Sad
Young Men

W[illiam] S[tanley] Merwin
1927–

4 You came back to us in a dream and we were not
    here.   *Come Back [1967]*

5 The dead will think the living are worth it we will
    know
Who we are
And we will all enlist again.
When the War Is Over [1967]

6 Every year without knowing it I have passed the
    day.
For the Anniversary of My Death [1967]

7 Of course there is nothing the matter with the stars
It is my emptiness among them
While they drift farther away in the invisible morning.
In the Winter of My Thirty-Eighth Year
[1967]

8 I think I was cold in the womb.
The Forebears [1971]

9 I am the son of the first fish who climbed ashore
    but the news has not yet reached my bowels.
Psalm: Our Fathers [1971]

10   Like shadows
of the plumbing
that is all that is left
of the great city.
The Plumbing [1971]

11 Some alien blessing
is on its way to us.
Midnight in Early Spring [1971]

Daniel Patrick Moynihan
1927–2003

12   The time may have come when the issue of race
could benefit from a period of "benign neglect."
Memo to President Nixon [1970]

13   To be Irish is to know that in the end the world
will break your heart.
Attributed

14   The central conservative truth is that it is culture,
not politics, that determines the success of a society.
The central liberal truth is that politics can change a
culture and save it from itself.
Lecture at Harvard University [1986]

Pope Benedict XVI
[Joseph Ratzinger]
1927–

15   We are moving toward a dictatorship of relativism
which does not recognize anything as for certain and
which has as its highest goal one's own ego and one's
own desires.
Homily at Pre-Conclave Mass
[April 18, 2005]

Kenneth Tynan
1927–1980

16   Show me a congenital eavesdropper with the
instincts of a peeping Tom and I will show you the
makings of a dramatist.
Pausing on the Stairs [1957]

17   What, when drunk, one sees in other women, one
sees in Garbo sober.
Curtains [1961]

Andy Warhol
1927–1987

1 In the future everyone will be world-famous for fifteen minutes.
> *Catalogue of his photo exhibition in Stockholm [1968]*

2 I want to be a machine.
> *Catalogue of his photo exhibition in Stockholm*

3 My instinct about painting says, "If you don't think about it, it's right."
> *The Philosophy of Andy Warhol: From A to B and Back Again [1975]*

4 A Coke is a Coke and no amount of money can get you a better Coke than the one the bum on the corner is drinking. All the Cokes are the same and all the Cokes are good.
> *The Philosophy of Andy Warhol: From A to B and Back Again*

5 People sometimes say that the way things happen in the movies is unreal, but actually it's the way things happen to you in life that's unreal. The movies make emotions look so strong and real, whereas when things really do happen to you, it's like watching television — you don't feel anything.
> *The Philosophy of Andy Warhol: From A to B and Back Again*

James Wright
1927–1980

6 Shake out the ruffle, turn and go,
Over the trellis blow the kiss.
Some of the guests will never know
Another night to shadow this.
Some of the birds awake in vines
Will never see another face
So frail, so lovely anyplace
Between the birdbath and the bines.
> *To a Hostess Saying Good Night*

7 I will putter as though I had not heard,
And lift him into my arms and sing
Whether he hears my song or not.
> *Mutterings over the Crib of a Deaf Child*

8 I lean back, as the evening darkens and comes on.
A chicken hawk floats over, looking for home.
I have wasted my life.
> *Lying in a Hammock at William Duffy's Farm in Pine Island, Minnesota*

9 Suddenly I realize
That if I stepped out of my body I would break
Into blossom.
> *The Branch Will Not Break [1963]. A Blessing*

Edward [Franklin] Albee
1928–

10 *George:* Who's afraid of Virginia Woolf...
Martha: I ... am ... George ... I am.
> *Who's Afraid of Virginia Woolf?*[1] *[1962]. The Exorcism*

11 You gotta have a swine to show you where the truffles are.
> *Who's Afraid of Virginia Woolf?, act II, Walpurgisnacht*

Maya Angelou [Marguerite Johnson]
1928–

12 The fact that the adult American Negro female emerges a formidable character is often met with amazement, distaste and even belligerence. It is seldom accepted as an inevitable outcome of the struggle won by survivors and deserves respect if not enthusiastic acceptance.
> *I Know Why the Caged Bird Sings [1969]*

13 You may trod me in the very dirt
But still, like dust, I'll rise.
> *Still I Rise [1978]. And Still I Rise*

14 History, despite its wrenching pain,
Cannot be unlived, but if faced
With courage, need not be lived again.
> *On the Pulse of Morning [1993]*[2]

[Avram] Noam Chomsky
1928–

15 Colorless green ideas sleep furiously.[3]
> *Syntactic Structures [1957], ch. 2*

16 I think it only makes sense to seek out and identify structures of authority, hierarchy, and domination in every aspect of life, and to challenge them; unless a

---

[1]Who's Afraid of the Big Bad Wolf? — *Title of song,* WALT DISNEY *film cartoon Three Little Pigs* [1933]. Ellipses are in the original text.

[2]Read at the inauguration of President Bill Clinton [January 20, 1993].

[3]Illustrating how meaning and syntax are independent of each other.

justification for them can be given, they are illegitimate, and should be dismantled, to increase the scope of human freedom.   *Interview [1995]*

Mary Daly
1928–2010

1   If God is male, then the male is God. The divine patriarch castrates women as long as he is allowed to live on in the human imagination.
Beyond God the Father [1973], ch. 1

Phillip K[indred] Dick
1928–1982

2   It's all the same, it's all him, the creator. That's who and what he is, he realized. The owners of these worlds. The rest of us just inhabit them and when he wants to he can inhabit them, too. Can kick over the scenery, manifest himself, push things in any direction he chooses. Even be any of us he cares to. All of us, in fact, if he desires. Eternal, outside of time and spliced-together segments of all other dimensions . . . *he can even enter a world in which he's dead.*
The Three Stigmata of Palmer Eldritch [1964]

3   We are not individuals. We are stations in a single Mind.   *Valis [1981]*

4   Reality is that which, when you stop believing in it, doesn't go away.
How to Build a Universe That Doesn't Fall Apart Two Days Later [1978]

Fred Ebb
1928–2004

5 What good is sitting alone in your room?
Come hear the music play;
Life is a cabaret, old chum,
Come to the cabaret.   *Cabaret[1] [1966], title song*

6 If I can make it there, I'm gonna make it anywhere,
It's up to you, New York, New York.
New York, New York [1977]

Carlos Fuentes
1928–2012

7   The U.S.–Mexico border, some of those who cross it say, is not really a border but a scar. Will it

heal? Will it bleed once more? When a Hispanic worker crosses this border, he sometimes asks, "Hasn't this always been our land? Am I not coming back to it? Is it not in some way ours?" He can taste it, hear its language, sing its songs and pray to its saints. Will this not always be in its bones a Hispanic land?
The Buried Mirror: Reflections on Spain and the New World [1992]

Gabriel García Márquez
1928–

8   The secret of a good old age is simply an honorable pact with solitude.
One Hundred Years of Solitude (Cien Años de Soledad)[2] [1967]

9   It was foreseen that the city of mirrors (or mirages) would be wiped out by the wind and exiled from the memory of men at the precise moment when Aureliano Babilonia would finish deciphering the parchments, and that everything written on them was unrepeatable since time immemorial and forevermore, because races condemned to one hundred years of solitude did not have a second opportunity on earth.

One Hundred Years of Solitude

Hannah Green
[Joanne Greenberg]
1928–1996

10   I Never Promised You a Rose Garden
Title of novel [1964]

[Ernesto] Che Guevara
1928–1967

11   Let me say, with the risk of appearing ridiculous, that the true revolutionary is guided by strong feelings of love. It is impossible to think of an authentic revolutionary without this quality.
Quoted in JON LEE ANDERSON, *Che Guevara: A Revolutionary Life [1997]*

12   Wherever death may surprise us, let it be welcome, provided that this, our battle cry, may have reached some receptive ears, and another hand may be extended to wield our weapon, and other men may be ready to intone the funeral dirge with the staccato singing of the machine-guns and new battle cries of war and victory.

Message to Tricontinental [1967]

---

[1]Based on the book by CHRISTOPHER ISHERWOOD. Music by JOHN KANDER.

[2]Translated by GREGORY RABASSA.

Michael Harrington
1928–1989

1   The other America, the America of poverty, is hidden today in a way that it never was before. Its millions are socially invisible to the rest of us. . . . The very development of American society is creating a new kind of blindness about poverty. The poor are increasingly slipping out of the very experience and consciousness of the nation.

> *The Other America: Poverty in the United States [1962], ch. 1*

Stanley Kubrick
1928–1999

2   The most terrifying fact about the universe is not that it is hostile but that it is indifferent.

> *Interview in Playboy [September 1968]*

3   The very meaninglessness of life forces man to create his own meaning. If it can be written or thought it can be filmed.

> *Cited in The Making of Kubrick's 2001, edited by* JEROME AGEL *[1970]*

4   Truth is too multi-faceted to be contained in a five-line summary.

> *Interview in Rolling Stone [August 27, 1987]*

Stanley Kubrick
1928–1999

Peter George
1924–1966

and

Terry Southern
1924–1995

5   I can no longer sit back and allow Communist infiltration, Communist indoctrination, Communist subversion, and the international Communist conspiracy to sap and impurify all of our precious bodily fluids.

> *Dr. Strangelove (screenplay) [1964], spoken by Sterling Hayden*

6   Gentlemen, you can't fight in here. This is the War Room!

> *Dr. Strangelove, spoken by Peter Sellers*

7   I think you're some kind of deviated prevert, and I think General Ripper found out about your preversion and that you were organizing some kind of mutiny of preverts.

> *Dr. Strangelove, spoken by Keenan Wynn*

Tom [Thomas Andrew] Lehrer
1928–

8 We will all go together when we go,
All suffused with an incandescent glow.

> *We Will All Go Together When We Go [1959]*

9 Remember the war against Franco?
That's the kind where each of us belongs.
Though he may have won all the battles,
We had all the good songs.

> *The Folk Song Army [1965]*

10 "Once the rockets are up, who cares where they come down?
That's not my department," says Wernher von Braun.

> *Wernher von Braun [1965]*

11   It is a sobering thought that when Mozart was my age, he had been dead for two years.

> *That Was the Year That Was [1965]*

Philip Levine
1928–

12 Give me back my young brother, hard
and furious, with wide shoulders and a curse
for God and burning eyes that look upon
all creation and say, You can have it.

> *7 Years from Somewhere [1979].*
> *You Can Have It*

Jim [James] A. Lovell, Jr.
1928–

13   Houston, we've had a problem here. Houston, we've had a problem.[1]

> *Message from Apollo 13, April 1970*

Cynthia Ozick
1928–

14   If we blow into the narrow end of the shofar, we will be heard far. But if we choose to be Mankind rather than Jewish and blow into the wider part, we will not be heard at all; for us America will have been in vain.   *Art and Ardor [1983]*

15   The whole peninsula of Florida was weighted down with regret. Everyone had left behind a real life.   *Rosa [1984]*

16   I wanted to use what I was, to be what I was born to be — not to have a "career," but to be that

---

[1]Often quoted as: Houston, we have a problem.

straightforward obvious unmistakable animal, a writer.   *Metaphor and Memory [1989]*

Robert M[aynard] Pirsig
1928–

1   The Buddha, the Godhead, resides quite as comfortably in the circuits of a digital computer or the gears of a cycle transmission as he does at the top of a mountain or in the petals of a flower.
Zen and the Art of Motorcycle Maintenance [1974]

2   Other people can talk about how to expand the destiny of mankind. I just want to talk about how to fix a motorcycle. I think that what I have to say has more lasting value.
Zen and the Art of Motorcycle Maintenance

3   An insane delusion can't be held by a group at all. A person isn't considered insane if there are a number of people who believe the same way.... If one other person starts to believe him, or maybe two or three, then it's a religion.[1]
Lila: An Inquiry into Morals [1991]

Jacques Rivette
1928–

4   When I talk about ideas, I really mean ideas of *mise en scène* or — if I were to be shocking about it — of framing, or the way shots are put together, which these days are the only ideas whose profundity I wish to recognize.
On Imagination. Cahiers du Cinéma [October 1953]

Andrew Sarris
1928–2012

5   To the extent that the cinema is a creature of the scientific spirit, it has inherited expectations of infinite development and improvement. It is as if this machine art were designed to transcend the vagaries of human inspiration. A Shakespeare may appear once in a millennium, but the express train of twentieth-century history cannot wait a century or even a decade for the world to be remade from the moonbeams of a movie projector.   *The American Cinema [1968]*

---

[1]Often misattributed to Pirsig's *Zen and the Art of Motorcycle Maintenance* in this form: When one person suffers from a delusion, it is called insanity. When many people suffer from a delusion, it is called Religion.

Richard Selzer
1928–

6   And if the surgeon is like a poet, then the scars you have made on countless bodies are like verses into the fashioning of which you have poured your soul. I think that if years later I were to see the trace from an old incision of mine, I should know it at once, as one recognizes his pet expressions.
Mortal Lessons: Notes on the Art of Surgery [1976]. The Knife

Maurice Sendak
1928–2012

7   Let the wild rumpus start!
Where the Wild Things Are [1963]

Anne Sexton
1928–1974

8   You, Doctor Martin, walk
from breakfast to madness. Late August,
I speed through the antiseptic tunnel where the
        moving dead still talk
of pushing their bones against the thrust
of cure. And I am queen of this summer hotel
        or the laughing bee on a stalk
        of death.
You, Doctor Martin [1960], st. 1

9 I have gone out, a possessed witch,
haunting the black air, braver at night.
Her Kind [1960]

10 A woman like that is not a woman, quite.
I have been her kind.
Her Kind

11 Leaving the page of the book carelessly open,
something unsaid, the phone off the hook
and the love, whatever it was, an infection.
Wanting to Die [1966], last stanza

12   Little Girl, My Stringbean, My Lovely Woman
Title of poem [1966]

13 Beauty is a simple passion,
but, oh my friends, in the end
you will dance the fire dance in iron shoes.
Snow White and the Seven Dwarfs [1971]

14 Though they washed her with wine
and rubbed her with butter
it was to no avail.
She lay as still as a gold piece.
Snow White and the Seven Dwarfs

L[ouis] E[dward] Sissman
1928–1976

1 Struck dumb by love among the walruses
And whales, the off-white polar bear with stuffing
Missing, the mastodons like muddy buses,
I sniff the mothproof air and lack for nothing.
*Dying: An Introduction [1967]. The
Museum of Comparative Zoology*

2   Through my
Invisible new veil
Of finity, I see
November's world —
Low scud, slick street, three giggling girls —
As, oddly, not as sombre
As December,
But as green
As anything:
As spring.   *Dying: An Introduction. Outbound*

Alvin Toffler
1928–

3   Future shock...the shattering stress and disorien-
tation that we induce in individuals by subjecting
them to too much change in too short a time.
Future Shock [1970], Introduction

James Dewey Watson
1928–
and
Francis [Harry Compton] Crick
1916–2004

4   This [double helix] structure has novel features
which are of considerable biological interest....It has
not escaped our notice that the specific pairing we
have postulated immediately suggests a possible
copying mechanism for the genetic material.
*Molecular Structure of Nucleic Acids, in
Nature[1] [April 25, 1953]*

Elie Wiesel
1928–

5   I was the accuser, God the accused. My eyes were
open and I was alone — terribly alone in a world
without God and without man.   *Night[2] [1958]*

---

[1]We told her [the typist of their article] that she was participating in
perhaps the most famous event in biology since Darwin's book.
— WATSON, *The Double Helix* [1968].

[2]Translated by STELLA RODWAY.

6   You'll try to reveal what should remain
hidden, you'll try to incite people to learn from
the past and rebel, but they will refuse to believe
you. They will not listen to you....You'll possess
the truth, you already do; but it's the truth of a
madman.
A Beggar in Jerusalem[3] [1970], ch. 5

7   Rejected by mankind, the condemned do not go
so far as to reject it in turn. Their faith in history
remains unshaken, and one may well wonder why.
They do not despair. The proof: they persist in sur-
viving not only to survive, but to testify.
The victims elect to become witnesses.
*One Generation After[3] [1970].
Readings*

A[l] Alvarez
1929–

8   No one is promiscuous in his way of dying. A man
who has decided to hang himself will never jump in
front of a train.
The Savage God [1971]

Roger Bannister
1929–

9   The earth seemed almost to move with me....I
had found a new source of power and beauty, a
source I never dreamt existed.
*Sports Illustrated [June 20, 1955].
The Joy of Running*

Jean Baudrillard
1929–2007

10   We are already more or less disconnected from our
history and thus also from its destination. That
means, then, that time can slow as it nears its end and
that the year 2000, in a certain way, will not take
place.
The Anorexic Ruins [1989]

11   We are becoming like cats, slyly parasitic, enjoying
an indifferent domesticity. Nice and smug in "the
social," our historic passions have withdrawn into the
glow of an artificial coziness, and our half-closed eyes
now seek little other than the peaceful parade of television pictures.
Cool Memories [1987]

---

[3]Translated by LILY EDELMAN and ELIE WIESEL.

Bert [Bertrand Russell] Berns
1929–1967
and
Jerry Ragovoy
1930–2011

1 Have another little piece of my heart now baby,

. . .

You know you got it if it makes you feel good.

Piece of My Heart [1967]

Hans Magnus Enzensberger
1929–

2 i speak for none of you now,
all you plotters of perfect crimes,
nor for me, nor for anyone.
i speak for those who can't speak,
for the deaf and dumb witnesses,
for otters and seals,
for the ancient owls of the earth.

poems for people who don't read poems [1968].
the end of the owls[1]

Oriana Fallaci
1929–2006

3   I have always looked on disobedience toward the oppressive as the only way to use the miracle of having been born. I have always looked on the silence of those who do not react or who indeed applaud as the real death of a woman or man.

Interview with History [1976]

Anne Frank
1929–1945

4   Whoever is happy will make others happy too. He who has courage and faith will never perish in misery!

Anne Frank: The Diary of a Young Girl[2]
[1952]. March 7, 1944

5   What *one* Christian does is his own responsibility, what *one* Jew does is thrown back at all Jews.

Anne Frank: The Diary of a Young Girl.
May 22, 1944

6   [Daddy] said: "All children must look after their own upbringing." Parents can only give good advice

---

[1]Translated by Jerome Rothenberg.
[2]Translated by B. M. Mooyart.

or put them on the right paths, but the final forming of a person's character lies in their own hands.

Anne Frank: The Diary of a Young Girl.
July 15, 1944

7   It's really a wonder that I haven't dropped all my ideals, because they seem so absurd and impossible to carry out. Yet I keep them, because in spite of everything I still believe that people are really good at heart. I simply can't build up my hopes on a foundation consisting of confusion, misery, and death. I see the world gradually being turned into a wilderness, I hear the ever approaching thunder, which will destroy us too, I can feel the sufferings of millions.

Anne Frank: The Diary of a Young Girl.
July 15, 1944

Brian Friel
1929–

8   To remember everything is a form of madness.

Translations [1980]

Thom Gunn
1929–2004

9 He turns revolt into a style, prolongs
The impulse to a habit of the time.

The Sense of Movement [1957]. Elvis Presley

10 True, they are not at rest yet,
but now that they are indeed
apart, winnowed from failures,
they withdraw to an orbit
and turn with disinterested
hard energy, like the stars.

My Sad Captains [1961], title poem

11 Direct me, gods, whose changes are all holy,
To where it flickers deep in grass, the moly:

Cool flesh of magic in each leaf and shoot,
From milky flower to the black forked root.

Moly [1971]

Jürgen Habermas
1929–

12   Philosophy remains true to its classic tradition by renouncing it.

Knowledge and Human Interests [1972]

Richard Howard
1929–

13   Save it all; you do not know
the value things will come to have until

the world grows dim around you, and your things
— however doubtful in the changing light,
       things are what you have
       left. And all you have.
               Untitled Subjects [1969]. 1915

X. J[oseph] Kennedy
1929–

1 One-woman waterfall, she wears
  Her slow descent like a long cape
  And pausing, on the final stair
  Collects her motions into shape.
           Nude Descending a Staircase, last stanza

2 I rang them up while touring Timbucktoo,
  Those bosom chums to whom you're known as
                       "Who?"
     To Someone Who Insisted I Look Up Someone

Martin Luther King, Jr.
1929–1968

3 The Negro's great stumbling block is not the White Citizen's Counciler or the Ku Klux Klanner, but the white moderate who is more devoted to "order" than to justice, ... who paternalistically believes he can set the timetable for another man's freedom.
     Letter from Birmingham Jail [April 16, 1963]

4 For years now I have heard the word "Wait!" It rings in the ears of every Negro with a piercing familiarity. This "Wait" has almost always meant "Never."
            Letter from Birmingham Jail

5 The question is not whether we will be extremists but what kind of extremist will we be.
            Letter from Birmingham Jail

6 If a man hasn't discovered something that he will die for, he isn't fit to live.
        Speech in Detroit [June 23, 1963]

7 I have a dream that one day on the red hills of Georgia the sons of former slaves and the sons of former slaveowners will be able to sit down together at the table of brotherhood.
     Speech at Civil Rights March on Washington
     [August 28, 1963]

8 I have a dream that my four little children will one day live in a nation where they will not be judged by the color of their skin, but by the content of their character.
     Speech at Civil Rights March on Washington
     [August 28, 1963]

9 When we let freedom ring, when we let it ring from every village and every hamlet, from every state and every city, we will be able to speed up that day when all of God's children, black men and white men, Jews and Gentiles, Protestants and Catholics, will be able to join hands and sing in the words of the old Negro spiritual, "Free at last! Free at last! Thank God Almighty, we are free at last!"[1]
     Speech at Civil Rights March on Washington
     [August 28, 1963]

10 Nonviolence is the answer to the crucial political and moral questions of our time; the need for man to overcome oppression and violence without resorting to oppression and violence.

  Man must evolve for all human conflict a method which rejects revenge, aggression and retaliation. The foundation of such a method is love.[2]
     Speech accepting the Nobel Peace Prize
     [December 11, 1964]

11 The tortuous road which has led from Montgomery to Oslo is a road over which millions of Negroes are traveling to find a new sense of dignity. It will, I am convinced, be widened into a superhighway of justice.
     Speech accepting the Nobel Peace Prize

12 I refuse to accept the idea that the "isness" of man's present nature makes him morally incapable of reaching up for the "oughtness" that forever confronts him.
     Speech accepting the Nobel Peace Prize

13 I refuse to accept the cynical notion that nation after nation must spiral down a militaristic stairway into the hell of nuclear destruction. I believe that unarmed truth and unconditional love will have the final word in reality.
     Speech accepting the Nobel Peace Prize

14 The Negro was willing to risk martyrdom in order to move and stir the social conscience of his community and the nation ... he would force his oppressor to commit his brutality openly, with the rest of the world looking on. ... Nonviolent resistance paralyzed and confused the power structures against which it was directed.
     Why We Can't Wait [1964]

15 A riot is at bottom the language of the unheard.
     Where Do We Go from Here? [1968]

16 Like anybody, I would like to live a long life. Longevity has its place. But I'm not concerned about

---

[1]King's epitaph, South View Cemetery, Atlanta, Georgia. See Anonymous: Spirituals, 898:19.

[2]See Mohandas Gandhi, 604:4.

that now. I just want to do God's will. And He's allowed me to go up to the mountain. And I've looked over, and I've seen the promised land. I may not get there with you, but I want you to know tonight that we as a people will get to the promised land....

So I'm happy tonight. I'm not worried about anything. I'm not fearing any man.

> *Address to sanitation workers, Memphis, Tennessee [April 3, 1968], the night before his assassination*

Milan Kundera
1929–

1   The struggle against power is the struggle of memory against forgetting.
> *The Book of Laughter and Forgetting*[1] *[1980]*

2   All man's life among men is nothing more than a battle for the ears of others.
> *The Book of Laughter and Forgetting*

3   The wisdom of the novel comes from having a question for everything. When Don Quixote went out into the world, that world turned into a mystery before his eyes. That is the legacy of the first European novel.
> *A Talk with the Author by* PHILIP ROTH[2] *[1980]*

4   Her drama was a drama not of heaviness but of lightness. What fell to her lot was not the burden but the unbearable lightness of being.
> *The Unbearable Lightness of Being*[1] *[1984], pt. III*

5   Kitsch excludes everything from its purview which is essentially unacceptable in human existence.
> *The Unbearable Lightness of Being, VI*

6   Kitsch causes two tears to flow in quick succession. The first tear says: How nice to see children running on the grass!

The second tear says: How nice to be moved, together with all mankind, by children running on the grass! It is the second tear that makes kitsch kitsch.
> *The Unbearable Lightness of Being, VIII*

7   Like parodies of themselves, theological notions are reflected in the triviality of our lives.
> *Slowness*[3] *[1995]*

---

[1]Translated by MICHAEL HENRY HEIM.
[2]Translated by VERA KUNDERA and PETER KUSSI.
[3]Translated by LINDA ASHER.

Ursula K[roeber] Le Guin
1929–

8   The king was pregnant.
> *The Left Hand of Darkness [1969], ch. 8*

9 Light is the left hand of darkness,
and darkness the right hand of light.
> *The Left Hand of Darkness, 16*

10   He had grown up in a country run by politicians who sent the pilots to man the bombers to kill the babies to make the world safer for children to grow up in.
> *The Lathe of Heaven [1971], ch. 6*

George Markstein
1929–1987

11   I am not a number, I am a free man!
> *The Prisoner (television series) [1968], spoken by Patrick McGoohan*

Claes Oldenburg
1929–

12   I am for an art that tells you the time of day, or where such and such a street is. I am for an art that helps old ladies across the street.
> *Statement for exhibition catalogue [1961]*

John [James] Osborne
1929–1994

13   I must say it's pretty dreary living in the American Age — unless you're an American, of course.
> *Look Back in Anger [1956], act I*

14   It's no good trying to fool yourself about love. You can't fall into it like a soft job, without dirtying up your hands. It takes muscle and guts. And if you can't bear the thought of messing up your nice, clean soul, you'd better give up the whole idea of life and become a saint.
> *Look Back in Anger, III, sc. ii*

Adrienne Rich
1929–2012

15 Your mind now, moldering like wedding-cake,
heavy with useless experience, rich
with suspicion, rumor, fantasy,
crumbling to pieces under the knife-edge
of mere fact.
> *Snapshots of a Daughter-in-Law [1963], st. 1*

1 A thinking woman sleeps with monsters.
The beak that grips her, she becomes.
Snapshots of a Daughter-in-Law, st. 3

2 Piece by piece I seem
to re-enter the world.
Necessities of Life [1966]

3   I am an instrument in the shape
of a woman trying to translate pulsations
into images   for the relief of the body
and the reconstruction of the mind.
Leaflets [1969]. Planetarium

4 The moment of change is the only poem.
Images for Godard [1971]

5 My visionary anger cleansing my sight.
The Stranger [1973]

6 I am the androgyne.
The Stranger

7 There is a ladder.
The ladder is always there
hanging innocently
close to the side of the schooner.
Diving into the Wreck [1973]

8 I came to explore the wreck.   *Diving into the Wreck*

9 I came to see the damage that was done
and the treasures that prevail.
I stroke the beam of my lamp
slowly along the flank
of something more permanent
than fish or weed.   *Diving into the Wreck*

10   When someone tells me a piece of the truth which
has been withheld from me, and which I needed in
order to see my life more clearly, it may bring acute
pain, but it can flood me with a cold, sea-sharp wash
of relief.
*Women and Honor: Some Notes on Lying
[1977]*

11   Re-vision — the act of looking back, of seeing
with fresh eyes, of entering an old text from a new
critical direction — is for women more than a chapter
in cultural history: it is an act of survival.
*On Lies, Secrets, and Silence [1979].
When We Dead Awaken*

George Steiner
1929–

12   We know now that a man can read Goethe or
Rilke in the evening, that he can play Bach and Schu-
bert, and go to his day's work at Auschwitz in the
morning.
Language and Silence [1967]

E[dward] O[sborne] Wilson
1929–

13   The evolutionary epic is probably the best myth
we will ever have.
On Human Nature [1978]

14   The truth is that we need invertebrates but
they don't need us. If human beings were to disappear tomorrow, the world would go on with little
change.... But if invertebrates were to disappear, I
doubt that the human species could last more than a
few months.
The Little Things That Run the World [1987]

15   Few will doubt that humankind has created a
planet-sized problem for itself. No one wished it so,
but we are the first species to become a geophysical
force, altering Earth's climate, a role previously
reserved for tectonics, sun flares, and glacial cycles.
Consilience: The Unity of Knowledge [1998]

16   The most dangerous of devotions, in my opinion,
is the one endemic to Christianity: *I was not born to be
of this world*. With a second life waiting, suffering can
be endured — especially in other people. The natural
environment can be used up. Enemies of the faith can
be savaged and suicidal martyrdom praised.
Consilience: The Unity of Knowledge

Chinua Achebe
1930–

17   In such a regime, I say, you died a good death if
your life had inspired someone to come forward and
shoot your murderer in the chest — without asking
to be paid.
A Man of the People [1966], closing sentence

Buzz Aldrin
[Edwin Eugene Aldrin, Jr.]
1930–

18   Beautiful! Beautiful! Magnificent desolation.
On setting foot on the moon [July 20, 1969]

Neil [Alden] Armstrong
1930–2012

19   Houston, Tranquility Base here. The Eagle has
landed.
On reaching the moon [July 20, 1969]

20   That's one small step for [a] man, one giant leap
for mankind.
On first stepping on the moon [July 20, 1969]

J[ames] G[raham] Ballard
1930–2009

1   However selective the conscious mind may be, most biological memories are unpleasant ones, echoes of danger and terror. Nothing endures for so long as fear.

The Drowned World [1962]

2   Science fiction is the apocalyptic literature of the twentieth century, the authentic language of Auschwitz, Eniwetok and Aldermaston.

The Drowned World, biographical note

3   Science and technology multiply around us. To an increasing extent they dictate the languages in which we speak and think. Either we use these languages, or we remain mute.   *Crash [1974]*

Allan Bloom
1930–1992

4   The most successful tyranny is not the one that uses force to assure uniformity but the one that removes the awareness of other possibilities.

The Closing of the American Mind [1987]

Harold Bloom
1930–

5   The Anxiety of Influence   *Title of book [1973]*

6   Strong students, like strong writers, will find the sustenance they must have. And strong students, like strong writers, will rise in the most unexpected places and times, to wrestle with the internalized violence pressed upon them by their teachers and precursors.

A Map of Misreading [1975]

7   [Poems] are necessarily about *other poems;* a poem is a response to a poem, as a poet is a response to a poet, or a person to his parent.

A Map of Misreading

Jimmy Breslin
1930–

8   The Gang That Couldn't Shoot Straight

Title of book [1970]

Harold Brodkey [Aaron Roy Weintraub]
1930–1996

9   This is something one must bear, beyond the claims of religion, not the idea of one's dying but the reality of one's death. One schools oneself in an acceptance of the terror. It is the shape that life takes toward its end. It is a form of life.

Dying: An Update [1994]

Warren Buffett
1930–

10   Buy stocks like you buy your groceries, not like you buy your perfume.

Quoted in Fortune [March 9, 1992]

11   You only find out who is swimming naked when the tide goes out.

Letter to Berkshire Hathaway shareholders [2001]

12   In our view, . . . derivatives are financial weapons of mass destruction, carrying dangers that, while now latent, are potentially lethal.

Berkshire Hathaway annual report [2002]

13   Be fearful when others are greedy, and be greedy when others are fearful.

Buy American. I Am. In the New York Times [October 16, 2008]

Ornette Coleman
1930–

14   Many people apparently don't trust their reactions to art or to music unless there is a verbal *explanation* for it. In music the only thing that matters is whether you *feel* it or not.

Change of the Century [1959], liner notes

Gregory Corso
1930–2001

15 When she introduces me to her parents
back straightened, hair finally combed, strangled
    by a tie,
should I sit knees together on their 3rd degree sofa
and not ask Where's the bathroom?
    *The Happy Birthday of Death [1960].
    Marriage*

Jacques Derrida
1930–2004

16   There is nothing outside of the text.[1]

Of Grammatology [1967]

---

[1] Il n'y a pas de hors-texte.

Clint Eastwood
[Clinton Eastwood, Jr.]
1930–

1 I do make an attempt to always get that first take.... You're not stepping up to *bunt*. You're stepping up to hit the damn thing.
From DAVID BRESKIN, Inner Views: Filmmakers in Conversation [1992]

Jean-Luc Godard
1930–

2 At the cinema we do not think, we are thought.[1]
Review of Works of Calder, Gazette du Cinéma [October 1950]

3 Photography is truth. The cinema is truth twenty-four times per second.
Le Petit Soldat [1960]

4 Film is like a battleground: There's love, hate, action, violence, death. In one word, emotions.
Pierrot le Fou (screenplay) [1965], spoken by Samuel Fuller

5 Give us this day our television, and an automobile, but deliver us from freedom.
Masculin-Féminin (screenplay) [1966], spoken by Chantal Goya

6 All you need for a movie is a gun and a girl.
Journal entry, quoted in Projections, ed. BOORMAN AND DONOHUE [1992]

A. R. Gurney
[Albert Ramsdell Gurney, Jr.]
1930–

7 There is nothing more dangerous than a lengthy cocktail hour.
The Cocktail Hour [1988]

Lorraine Hansberry
1930–1965

8 Eventually it comes to you: the thing that makes you exceptional, if you are at all, is inevitably that which must also make you lonely.
Journal entry [May 1, 1962]

Buck Henry
[Henry Zuckerman]
1930–

and

Calder Willingham
1922–1995

9 I want to say one word to you — just one word.... Plastics.
The Graduate (screenplay)[2] [1967]

Ted [Edward J.] Hughes
1930–1998

10 I imagine this midnight moment's forest:
Something else is alive
Beside the clock's loneliness
And this blank page where my fingers move.
*The Hawk in the Rain [1957].
The Thought-Fox*

11 ...with a sudden sharp hot stink of fox,
It enters the dark hole of the head.
The window is starless still; the clock ticks,
The page is printed.
*The Hawk in the Rain.
The Thought-Fox*

12 My feet are locked upon the rough bark.
It took the whole of Creation
To produce my foot, my each feather:
Now I hold Creation in my foot
Or fly up, and revolve it all slowly —
I kill where I please because it is all mine.
Hawk Roosting [1960]

13 Daylong this tomcat lies stretched flat
As an old rough mat, no mouth and no eyes,
Continual wars and wives are what
Have tattered his ears and battered his head.
Esther's Tomcat [1960]

14 The rat is in the trap, it is in the trap,
And attacking heaven and earth with a mouthful of screeches like torn tin.
The Rat's Dance [1967]

Jasper Johns
1930–

15 Take an object. Do something to it. Do something else to it.
Sketchbook Notes [1965]

---

[1] Au cinéma, nous ne pensons pas, nous sommes pensés.

[2] From the novel [1962] by CHARLES WEBB [1939–].

Frank [Francis] McCourt
1930–2009

1 Worse than the ordinary miserable childhood is the miserable Irish childhood, and worse yet is the miserable Irish Catholic childhood.

Angela's Ashes [1996], ch. 1

Sandra Day O'Connor
1930–

2 We have long since made clear that a state of war is not a blank check for the President when it comes to the rights of the Nation's citizens.

Hamdi v. Rumsfeld, 542 U.S. 507 [2004]

Harold Pinter
1930–2008

3 I said to this monk . . . I heard you got a stock of shoes here. Piss off, he said to me.

The Caretaker [1960], act I

4 If only I could get down to Sidcup! I've been waiting for the weather to break. He's got my papers, this man I left them with, it's got it all down there, I could prove everything. *The Caretaker, I*

5 The earth's about five million years old, at least. Who can afford to live in the past?

The Homecoming [1965], act III

6 I don't think we don't love each other.

Betrayal [1978], sc. 3

Wilfrid Sheed
1930–2011

7 If God had died in the blare of the twentieth century and in houses too new and cheap to be haunted, one must seek him in the old quiet places, where he might still live on in retirement.

The Good Word [1978], pt. I, ch. 12

8 Suicide . . . is about life, being in fact the sincerest form of criticism life gets. *The Good Word, I, 15*

Gary Snyder
1930–

9 Lay down these words
Before your mind like rocks.

Riprap [1959]. Title poem

10 "I'm sixty-eight" he said,
"I first bucked hay when I was seventeen.
I thought, that day I started,

I sure would hate to do this all my life.
And dammit, that's just what
I've gone and done."

Riprap. Hay for the Horses

11 this dream pops. it was real:
and it lasted forever.

The Back Country [1967]. For a Stone Girl at Sanchi

12 Wrathful but Calm, Austere but Comic, Smokey the Bear will
Illuminate those who would help him; but for those who would
hinder or slander him,

HE WILL PUT THEM OUT.

A Place in Space [1969]. Smokey the Bear Sutra

Stephen Sondheim
1930–

13 Tonight, tonight, won't be just any night.
Tonight there will be no morning star.

West Side Story[1] [1957]. Tonight

14 I like to be in America!
O.K. by me in America!
Ev'rything free in America
For a small fee in America! *West Side Story. America*

15 Dear kindly Sergeant Krupke,
You gotta understand,
It's just our bringin' upke
That gets us out of hand.
Our mothers all are junkies,
Our fathers all are drunks,
Golly Moses,
Natcherly we're punks!

West Side Story. Gee, Officer Krupke

16 Everything's Coming Up Roses

Gypsy[2] [1959]. Title of song

17 The concerts you enjoy together,
Neighbors you annoy together,
Children you destroy together,
That keep marriage intact.

Company[3] [1970]. The Little Things You Do Together

18 Here's to the ladies who lunch —
Everybody laugh —
Lounging in their caftans and planning a brunch
On their own behalf.

Company. The Ladies Who Lunch

---

[1]Music by LEONARD BERNSTEIN.
[2]Music by JULE STYNE.
[3]Music by STEPHEN SONDHEIM.

1 Every day a little death,
In the parlor, in the bed,
In the curtains, in the silver,
In the buttons, in the bread.
Every day a little sting,
In the heart and in the head.
A Little Night Music[1] *[1973].*
Every Day a Little Death

2 Isn't it rich?
Are we a pair?
Me here at last on the ground,
You in mid-air.
Send in the clowns.
A Little Night Music. Send in the Clowns

George Soros
1930–

3   As an anonymous participant in financial markets, I never had to weigh the social consequences of my actions.... I felt justified in ignoring them on the grounds that I was playing by the rules.
The Crisis of Global Capitalism [1998]

Derek Walcott
1930–

4 I who am poisoned with the blood of both,
Where shall I turn, divided to the vein?
I who have cursed
The drunken officer of British rule, how choose
Between this Africa and the English tongue I love?
A Far Cry from Africa [1962]

5 These palms are greater than Versailles,
for no man made them.   *Names [1976], II*

6 Then after Eden,
was there no surprise?
O yes, the awe of Adam
at the first bead of sweat.
Sea Grapes [1976]. The New World

7 The tourist archipelagoes of my South
are prisons too, corruptible, and though
there is no harder prison than writing verse,
what's poetry, if it is worth its salt,
but a phrase men can pass from hand to mouth?
Forest of Europe [1979]

8 The Caribbean was borne like an elliptical basin
in the hands of acolytes, and a people were absolved
of a history which they did not commit.
The Star-Apple Kingdom [1979]

---

[1]Music by STEPHEN SONDHEIM.

Donald Barthelme
1931–1989

9   Endings are elusive, middles are nowhere to be found, but worst of all is to begin, to begin, to begin.
Unspeakable Practices, Unnatural Acts [1968]. The Dolt

Sam Cooke
1931–1964

10 I was born by the river
In a little tent
And just like the river
I've been running ever since
It's been a long, a long time coming
But I know a change gonna come.
A Change Is Gonna Come [1963]

Sam Cooke
1931–1964

Lou Adler
1933–

and

Herb Alpert
1935–

11 Don't know much about history
Don't know much biology
Don't know much about a science book
Don't know much about the French I took
(What a) Wonderful World [1960]

Guy Debord
1931–1994

12   In societies dominated by modern conditions of production, life is presented as an immense accumulation of *spectacles*. Everything that was directly lived has receded into a representation.
The Society of the Spectacle [1967]

William Goldman
1931–

13   Follow the money.
All the President's Men (screenplay) [1976]

14   The single most important fact, perhaps, of the entire movie industry: NOBODY KNOWS ANYTHING.   *Adventures in the Screen Trade [1983]*

1 Whoever invented the meeting must have had Hollywood in mind. I think they should consider giving Oscars for meetings: Best Meeting of the Year, Best Supporting Meeting, Best Meeting Based on Material from Another Meeting.

Adventures in the Screen Trade

Mikhail Sergeyevich Gorbachev
1931–

2 The guilt of Stalin and his immediate entourage before the Party and the people for the mass repressions and lawlessness they committed is enormous and unforgivable.

Speech on the seventieth anniversary of the
Russian Revolution [November 2, 1987]

3 The idea of restructuring [*perestroika*]...combines continuity and innovation, the historical experience of Bolshevism and the contemporaneity of socialism.

Speech on the seventieth anniversary of the
Russian Revolution

Bert [Thomas Bertram] Lance
1931–

4 If it ain't broke, don't fix it.

Nation's Business [May 1977]

John Le Carré
[David John Moore Cornwell]
1931–

5 What do you think spies are: priests, saints, and martyrs? They're a squalid procession of vain fools, traitors too, yes; pansies, sadists and drunkards, people who play cowboys and Indians to brighten their rotten lives. Do you think they sit like monks in London balancing rights and wrongs?

The Spy Who Came In from the Cold [1963],
ch. 25

6 A mole is a deep penetration agent so called because he burrows deep into the fabric of Western imperialism.   *Tinker, Tailor, Soldier, Spy [1974]*

7 A committee is an animal with four back legs.

Tinker, Tailor, Soldier, Spy

John McPhee
1931–

8 Neon looks good in Nevada.

Basin and Range [1981]

9 On the geologic time scale, a human lifetime is reduced to a brevity that is too inhibiting to think about. The mind blocks the information.

Basin and Range

Toni Morrison
[Chloe Anthony Wofford]
1931–

10 I know what every colored woman in this country is doing....Dying. Just like me. But the difference is they dying like a stump. Me, I'm going down like one of those redwoods. I sure did live in this world.

Sula [1973]

11 Like any artist with no art form, she became dangerous.   *Sula*

12 When am I happy and when am I sad and what is the difference? What do I need to know to stay alive? What is true in the world? Her mind traveled crooked streets and aimless goat paths, arriving sometimes at profundity, other times at the revelations of a three-year-old.

Song of Solomon [1977], ch. 5

13 When you know your name, you should hang on to it, for unless it is noted down and remembered, it will die when you do.

Song of Solomon, 15

14 At no point in my life have I ever felt as though I were an American.

In the New York Times [January 5, 1986]

15 If a Negro got legs he ought to use them. Sit down too long, somebody will figure out a way to tie them up.

Beloved [1987]

16 Language alone protects us from the scariness of things with no names.

Nobel Prize acceptance speech [1993]

Mordecai Richler
1931–2001

17 "I'm world-famous," Dr. Parks said, "all over Canada."

The Incomparable Atuk [1963], ch. 4

Desmond Tutu
1931–

18 Having looked the beast of the past in the eye, having asked and received forgiveness and having made amends, let us shut the door on the past — not

in order to forget it but in order not to allow it to imprison us.

> *Report of South Africa's Truth and*
> *Reconciliation Commission [1998]. Foreword*

Tom [Thomas Kennerly, Jr.] Wolfe
1931–

1   At some point they painted the mud color over everything, even over the doorbell-buzzer box. They didn't bother to pull the wiring out. They just cut the wires and painted over the stubs. And there they have it, the color called Landlord's Brown, immune to time, flood, tropic heat, arctic chill, punk rumbles, slops, blood, leprotic bugs, cockroaches the size of mice, mice the size of rats, rats the size of Airedales, and lumpenprole tenants.

> *The Kandy-Kolored Tangerine-Flake*
> *Streamline Baby [1965]. Putting Daddy On*

2   The Life — that *feeling* — The Life — the late 1940s early 1950s American Teenage Drive-In Life.

> *The Electric Kool-Aid Acid Test*[1] *[1968], ch. 4*

3   A glorious place, a glorious age, I tell you! A very Neon Renaissance — And the myths that actually touched you at that time — not Hercules, Orpheus, Ulysses and Aeneas — but Superman, Captain Marvel, Batman.

> *The Electric Kool-Aid Acid Test, 4*

4   Radical Chic, after all, is only radical in style; in its heart it is part of Society and its traditions.

> *Radical Chic & Mau-Mauing the Flak*
> *Catchers [1970]*

5   The Me Decade and the Third Great Awakening

> *Title of essay [1976]*

6   The idea was to prove at every foot of the way up that you were one of the elected and anointed ones who had *the right stuff* and could move higher and higher and even — ultimately, God willing, one day — that you might be able to join that special few at the very top, that elite who had the capacity to bring tears to men's eyes, the very Brotherhood of the Right Stuff itself.

> *The Right Stuff [1979], ch. 2*

7   A cult is a religion with no political power.

> *In Our Time [1980]*

8   On Wall Street he and a few others — how many? — three hundred, four hundred, five hundred? — had become precisely that . . . Masters of the Universe.

> *The Bonfire of the Vanities [1987], ch. 1,*
> *The Master of the Universe*

---

[1]See Ken Kesey, 840:4.

Aharon Appelfeld
1932–

9   The Holocaust is a central event in many people's lives, but it has also become a metaphor for our century. There cannot be an end to speaking and writing about it.

> *In the New York Times [November 15, 1986]*

Johnny Cash
1932–2003

10   I shot a man in Reno just to watch him die.

> *Folsom Prison Blues [1955]*

11   I keep my eyes wide open all the time,
I keep the ends out for the tie that binds,
Because you're mine,
I walk the line.   *I Walk the Line [1956]*

Mario Cuomo
1932–

12   We campaign in poetry. But when we're elected we're forced to govern in prose.

> *Chubb Fellowship Lecture, Yale University*
> *[February 1, 1985]*

Umberto Eco
1932–

13   A dream is a scripture, and many scriptures are nothing but dreams.

> *The Name of the Rose [1980]*

Glenn Gould
1932–1982

14   The justification of art is the internal combustion it ignites in the hearts of men and not its shallow, externalized, public manifestations. The purpose of art is not the release of a momentary ejection of adrenaline but is, rather, the gradual, lifelong construction of a state of wonder and serenity.

> *Let's Ban Applause! [1962]*

[Richard Claxton] Dick Gregory
1932–

15   Last time I was down South, I walked into this restaurant. This White waitress came up to me and said, "We don't serve colored people here." I said, "That's

all right, I don't eat colored people, no way! Bring me a whole fried chicken."

> *Comedy routine [1961], quoted in Callus on My Soul: A Memoir [2000, with SHEILA P. MOSES]*

1   If a man calls me a nigger, he is calling me something I am not. The nigger exists only in his own mind; therefore his mind is the nigger. I must feel sorry for such a man.

> *The Shadow That Scares Me [1968]*

Geoffrey Hill
1932–

2 By blood we live, the hot, the cold,
To ravage and redeem the world:
There is no bloodless myth will hold.

> *For the Unfallen [1959]. Genesis*

Edward Hoagland
1932–

3   In order to really enjoy a dog, one doesn't merely try to train him to be semihuman. The point of it is to open oneself to the possibility of becoming partly a dog.   *Dogs, and the Tug of Life [1975]*

Jenny Joseph
1932–

4 When I am an old woman I shall wear purple
With a red hat which doesn't go, and doesn't
    suit me.   *Warning [1965]*

Ryszard Kapuściński
1932–2007

5   It's so very difficult to establish where the borderline runs between true power that subdues everything, power that creates the world or destroys it — where the borderline is between living power, great, even terrifying, and the appearance of power, the empty pantomime of ruling, being one's own dummy, only playing the role, not seeing the world, not hearing it, merely looking into oneself.   *The Emperor [1978]*

6   When is a crisis reached? When questions arise that can't be answered.   *A Warsaw Diary [1985]*

Edward Kennedy
1932–2009

7   For me, a few hours ago, this campaign came to an end. For all those whose cares have been our concern, the work goes on, the cause endures, the hope still lives, and the dream shall never die.

> *Speech at Democratic National Convention [August 12, 1980]*

Christopher Lasch
1932–1994

8   In a dying culture, narcissism appears to embody — in the guise of personal "growth" and "awareness" — the highest attainment of spiritual enlightenment. The custodians of culture hope, at bottom, merely to survive its collapse.

> *The Culture of Narcissism [1979]*

Little Richard
[Richard Penniman]
1932–

9   Awop-bop-a-loo-mop alop-bam-boom!

> *Tutti-Frutti [1955]*

V[idiadhar] S[urajprasad] Naipaul
1932–

10   The world is what it is.

> *A Bend in the River [1979]*

Carl Perkins
1932–1998

11 You can do anything,
But don't step on my blue suede shoes.

> *Blue Suede Shoes [1956]*

Sylvia Plath
1932–1963

12 This is the light of the mind, cold and planetary.

> *The Moon and the Yew Tree [1961]*

13 I took a deep breath and listened to the old brag of
    my heart.
I am, I am, I am.   *The Bell Jar [1963]*

14   To the person in the bell jar, blank and stopped as a dead baby, the world itself is the bad dream.

> *The Bell Jar*

15   The silence drew off, baring the pebbles and shells and all the tatty wreckage of my life. Then, at the rim of vision, it gathered itself, and in one sweeping tide, rushed me to sleep.

> *The Bell Jar*

1 A living doll, everywhere you look.
  It can sew, it can cook,
  It can talk, talk, talk....
  My boy, it's your last resort.
  Will you marry it, marry it, marry it.
                    The Applicant [1963]

2 I have done it again.
                    Lady Lazarus [1963], st. 1

3 Dying
  Is an art, like everything else.
  I do it exceptionally well.

  I do it so it feels like hell.
  I do it so it feels real.
  I guess you could say I've a call.
                    Lady Lazarus, st. 15, 16

4 Out of the ash
  I rise with my red hair
  And I eat men like air.
                    Lady Lazarus, last stanza

5 The woman is perfected.
  Her dead

  Body wears the smile of accomplishment,
  The illusion of a Greek necessity

  Flows in the scrolls of her toga,
  Her bare

  Feet seem to be saying:
  We have come so far, it is over.
                    Edge [1963]

6 What a thrill—
  My thumb instead of an onion.   *Cut [1963]*

7 You do not do, you do not do
  Any more, black shoe
  In which I have lived like a foot
  For thirty years, poor and white,
  Barely daring to breathe or Achoo.
                    Daddy [1963], st. 1

8 I have always been scared of *you,*
  With your Luftwaffe, your gobbledygoo.
  And your neat mustache
  And your Aryan eye, bright blue.
  Panzer-man, panzer-man, O You—   *Daddy, st. 9*

9 Every woman adores a Fascist,
  The boot in the face, the brute
  Brute heart of a brute like you.   *Daddy, st. 10*

10 White
   Godiva, I unpeel—
   Dead hands dead stringencies.   *Ariel [1965]*

11 And now I
   Foam to wheat, a glitter of seas.   *Ariel*

Donald Rumsfeld
1932–

12   Go massive. Sweep it all up. Things related and not.
                    Aide's notes on remarks at meeting
                    [September 11, 2001]

13   There are known knowns; there are things we know we know. We also know there are known unknowns. That is to say, we know there are some things we do not know. But there are also unknown unknowns—the ones we don't know we don't know.
                    Defense Department news briefing
                    [February 12, 2002]

14   You're thinking of Europe as Germany and France. I don't. I think that's old Europe.
                    Remark [January 22, 2003]

15   As you know, you go to war with the army you have. They're not the army you might want or wish to have at a later time.
                    Remark [December 8, 2004]

Shel[by] Silverstein
1932–1999

16 Well, my daddy left home when I was three,
   And didn't leave much to Ma and me,
   Just this old guitar and an empty bottle of booze.
   Now I don't blame him because he run and hid,
   But the meanest thing he ever did was
   Before he left, he went and named me Sue.
                    A Boy Named Sue [1969]

John Updike
1932–2009

17   Our noise for some seconds passed beyond excitement into a kind of immense open anguish, a cry to be saved. But immortality is nontransferable. The papers said that the other players, and even the umpires on the field, begged him to come out and acknowledge us in some way, but he never had and did not now. Gods do not answer letters.
                    Hub Fans Bid Kid[1] Adieu, in The New
                    Yorker [October 22, 1960]

18   Sex is like money; only too much is enough.
                    Couples [1968]

---

[1]Ted Williams of the Boston Red Sox, who played his last Fenway Park game on September 28, 1960.

1   That's one of my Goddam precious American rights, not to think about politics.

Rabbit Redux [1971]

2   We are cruel enough without meaning to be.

Rabbit Is Rich [1981]

3   Is not the decisive difference between comedy and tragedy that tragedy denies us another chance?

Self-Consciousness: Memoirs [1989]

Vine [Victor] Deloria, Jr.[1]
1933–2005

4   Tribalism is the strongest force at work in the world today.

Custer Died for Your Sins [1969], ch. 11

5   This country was a lot better off when the Indians were running it.

In the New York Times Magazine [March 3, 1970]

Jerry Leiber
1933–2011

and

Mike Stoller
1933–

6 You ain't nothin' but a hound dog cryin' all the time. Well, you ain't never caught a rabbit and you ain't no friend of mine.   *Hound Dog [1956]*

7 Take out the papers and the trash
Or you don't get no spending cash;
If you don't scrub that kitchen floor,
You ain't gonna rock 'n' roll no more.
Yakety yak, don't talk back.

Yakety Yak [1958]

Cormac McCarthy
1933–

8   All progressions from a higher to a lower order are marked by ruins and mystery and a residue of nameless rage.

Blood Meridian [1985], spoken by the judge

9   The man who believes that the secrets of the world are forever hidden lives in mystery and fear. Superstition will drag him down. The rain will erode the deeds of his life. But that man who sets himself the task of singling out the thread of order from the tapestry will by the decision alone have taken charge

of the world and it is only by such taking charge that he will effect a way to dictate the terms of his own fate.

Blood Meridian, spoken by the judge

10   It takes very little to govern good people. Very little. And bad people cant be governed at all. Or if they could I never heard of it.

No Country for Old Men [2005],
spoken by Sheriff Bell

11   He knew only that the child was his warrant. He said: If he is not the word of God God never spoke.

The Road [2006]

Joe Orton [John Kingsley]
1933–1967

12   I'd the upbringing a nun would envy and that's the truth. Until I was fifteen I was more familiar with Africa than my own body.

Entertaining Mr. Sloane [1964], act I

13   You were born with your legs apart. They'll send you to the grave in a Y-shaped coffin.

What the Butler Saw [1969], act I

14   Two young people — one mad and one sexually insatiable — both naked — are roaming this house. At all costs we must prevent a collision.

What the Butler Saw, II

Ann Willis Richards
1933–2006

15   Poor George, he can't help it — he was born with a silver foot in his mouth.

On Republican candidate George W. Bush
[July 18, 1988]

16   After all, Ginger Rogers did everything that Fred Astaire did. She just did it backwards and in high heels.[2]

Speech at Democratic National Convention,
Atlanta [1988]

17   [In response to a question about her legacy:] How about, "She changed the economic future of Texas." And that really beats what I feared my tombstone was going to say, and that was, "She kept a really clean house."

Quoted in the Houston Chronicle
[May 1, 1994]

---

[1]A Standing Rock Sioux.

[2]An earlier version of this appeared in the comic strip *Frank and Ernest* by Bob Thaves [1982]: Sure he [Fred Astaire] was great, but don't forget that Ginger Rogers did everything he did . . . backwards and in high heels.

Joan Rivers
[Joan Alexandra Molinsky]
1933–

1   Can we talk?   *Catchphrase*

2   Who knew?   *Catchphrase*

Philip Roth
1933–

3   The American writer in the middle of the twentieth century has his hands full in trying to understand, and then describe, and then make *credible* much of American reality. It stupefies, it sickens, it infuriates, and finally it is even a kind of embarrassment to one's own meager imagination. The actuality is continually outdoing our talents.
Writing American Fiction [1961]

4   Doctor Spielvogel, this is my life, my only life, and I'm living it in the middle of a Jewish joke! I am the son in the Jewish joke — *only it ain't no joke!*
Portnoy's Complaint [1969]. Whacking Off

5   A Jewish man with parents alive is a fifteen-year-old boy, and will remain a fifteen-year-old boy *till they die!*   *Portnoy's Complaint. Cunt Crazy*

6   So [said the doctor]. Now vee may perhaps to begin Yes?
Portnoy's Complaint. Punch Line

7   Here where the literary culture is held hostage, the art of narration flourishes by mouth. In Prague, stories aren't simply stories; it's what they have instead of life.
The Prague Orgy [1985]

8   The closest we can come to the truth about reality is in the fictions that we create about it.
The Counterlife [1986]. Introduction

9   The radio was playing "Easter Parade" and I thought, But this is Jewish genius on a par with the Ten Commandments. God gave Moses the Ten Commandments and then He gave to Irving Berlin "Easter Parade" and "White Christmas."... Easter he turns into a fashion show and Christmas into a holiday about snow.
Operation Shylock [1993]

10   He could not fucking die. How could he leave? How could he go? Everything he hated was here.
Sabbath's Theater [1995], final lines

11   But who is set up for the impossible that is going to happen? Who is set up for tragedy and the incomprehensibility of suffering? Nobody. The tragedy of the man not set up for tragedy — that is every man's tragedy.   *American Pastoral [1997]*

Oliver Sacks
1933–

12   Health is infinite and expansive in mode, and reaches out to be filled with the fullness of the world; whereas disease is finite and reductive in mode, and endeavors to reduce the world to itself.
Awakenings [1973]

Susan Sontag
1933–2004

13   Real art has the capacity to make us nervous.
Against Interpretation [1966]. Against Interpretation

14   In a culture whose already classical dilemma is the hypertrophy of the intellect at the expense of energy and sensual capability, interpretation is the revenge of the intellect upon art.
Against Interpretation. Against Interpretation

15   In place of a hermeneutics we need an erotics of art.
Against Interpretation. Against Interpretation

16   The man who insists on high and serious pleasures is depriving himself of pleasure; he continually restricts what he can enjoy; in the constant exercise of his good taste he will eventually price himself out of the market, so to speak.
Against Interpretation. Notes on Camp

17   Camp is a vision of the world in terms of style — but a particular kind of style. It is the love of the exaggerated, the "off," of things-being-what-they-are-not.... The ultimate Camp statement: "it's good because it's awful."
Against Interpretation. Notes on Camp

18   So successful has been the camera's role in beautifying the world that photographs, rather than the world, have become the standard of the beautiful.
On Photography [1977]

19   Illness is the night-side of life, a more onerous citizenship. Everyone who is born holds dual citizenship, in the kingdom of the well and in the kingdom of the sick.   *Illness as Metaphor [1978]*

20   TB [tuberculosis] was a disease in the service of a romantic view of the world. Cancer is now in the service of a simplistic view of the world that can turn paranoid.   *Illness as Metaphor*

21   The AIDS crisis is evidence of a world in which nothing important is regional, local, limited; in which everything that can circulate does, and every problem is, or is destined to become, worldwide.
AIDS and Its Metaphors [1989]

1   Narratives can make us understand. Photographs do something else: they haunt us.
Regarding the Pain of Others [2003]

Andrei Andreyevich Voznesenski
1933–2010

2 I am Goya
of the bare field, by the enemy's beak gouged
till the craters of my eyes gape
I am grief

I am the tongue
of war, the embers of cities
on the snows of the year 1941
I am hunger
I Am Goya[1] *[1960], st. 1, 2*

3 They carried him[2] not to bury him:
They carried him down to crown him. . . .
The poet flourished here, disheveled,
Who would not bow before votive lamps
But to the common spade.
Leaves and Roots[1] *[1960]*

Steven Weinberg
1933–

4   It is very hard to realize that this present universe has evolved from an unspeakably unfamiliar early condition, and faces a future extinction of endless cold or intolerable heat. The more the universe seems comprehensible, the more it also seems pointless.
The First Three Minutes [1977]. Epilogue

5   One of the great achievements of science has been, if not to make it impossible for intelligent people to be religious, then at least to make it possible for them not to be religious. We should not retreat from this accomplishment.
Talk at the American Association for the Advancement of Science [1999]

Donald Westlake
[writing as Richard Stark]
1933–2008

6   His face was a chipped chunk of concrete, with eyes of flawed onyx. His mouth was a quick stroke, bloodless. His suit coat fluttered behind him, and his arms swung easy as he walked.
The Hunter [1962]

Flip Wilson
[Clerow Wilson, Jr.]
1933–1998

7   The devil made me do it.
Comic catchphrase [early 1970s]

Yevgeny Alexandrovich Yevtushenko
1933–

8 There is no Jewish blood in my veins,
But I am hated with a scabby hatred
By all the anti-Semites,
like a Jew.
And therefore
I am a true Russian.   *Babi Yar [1961]*

Amiri Baraka [LeRoi Jones]
1934–

9 Lately, I've become accustomed to the way
The ground opens up and envelops me
Each time I go out to walk the dog.
Preface to a Twenty Volume Suicide Note [1961]

10 Saturday mornings we listened to *Red Lantern* & his undersea folk.
At 11, *Let's Pretend* / & we did / & I, the poet, still do, Thank God!
In Memory of Radio [1961]

11 Walk it slow
where you go
walk it slow . . .
We in the world
Poor as dirt
   Don't get some rhythm
Somebody'll get hurt
the world is black
the world is green
the world is red, yellow, brown
the world is mean   *3rd World Blues [1979]*

Alan Bennett
1934–

12   To be heir to the throne is not a position; it is a predicament.
The Madness of George III (play)[3] *[1992]*

---

[1]Translated by STANLEY KUNITZ.
[2]Boris Pasternak.

---

[3]The screenplay for the 1994 movie *The Madness of King George* renders the line thus: To be Prince of Wales is not a position. It is a predicament.

Alan Bennett
1934–

Peter Cook
1937–1995

Sir Jonathan [Wolfe] Miller
1934–

and

Dudley Moore
1935–2002

1   I want you to lay down your life, Perkins. We need a futile gesture at this stage. It will raise the whole tone of the war.
Beyond the Fringe [1963]. Aftermyth of War

Wendell Berry
1934–

2 I come into the peace of wild things
who do not tax their lives with forethought
of grief.
Openings [1968]. The Peace of Wild Things

3 Denounce the government and embrace
the flag. Hope to live in that free
republic for which it stands.
*The Country of Marriage [1973]. Manifesto:
The Mad Farmer Liberation Front*

4   The wildness of the soil that we call fertility begins to diminish, and the soil itself begins to flee from us in water and wind.
*Home Economics [1987]. Getting Along with
Nature*

5   Eating is an agricultural act.
*What Are People For? [1990]. The Pleasures
of Eating*

James Brown
1934–2006

6 Say It Loud: "I'm Black and I'm Proud."
Some people say we've got a lot of malice,
Some say it's a lot of nerve.
But I say we won't quit moving
Until we get what we deserve.
*Say It Loud: "I'm Black and I'm Proud"
[1968] (song)*

7 Stay on the scene
Like a sex machine
*Get Up (I Feel Like Being Like a Sex
Machine) [1970]*

Donald Cammell
1934–1996

8   The only performance that makes it, that really makes it, that makes it all the way is the one that achieves madness.
*Performance (screenplay) [1970], spoken by
Mick Jagger*

Leonard Cohen
1934–

9 And you want to travel with her
And you want to travel blind
And you know that she will trust you
For you've touched her perfect body with your
mind.
Suzanne [1966]

10 Even damnation is poisoned with rainbows.
The Old Revolution [1969]

11 It goes like this
The fourth, the fifth
The minor fall, the major lift
The baffled king composing Hallelujah.
Hallelujah [1984]

Joan Didion
1934–

12   Writers are always selling somebody out.
*Slouching Towards Bethlehem [1968],
preface*

13   We tell ourselves stories in order to live.
The White Album [1979]

14   We look for the sermon in the suicide, for the social or moral lesson in the murder of five.
The White Album

Harlan Ellison
1934–

15   Love Ain't Nothing but Sex Misspelled
Title of book [1968]

David Halberstam
1934–2007

16   The Best and the Brightest
Title of book [1972]

Frederic Jameson
1934–

1   The Prison-House of Language
Title of book [1972]

Audre Lorde
1934–1992

2   The woman's place of power within each of us is neither white nor surface; it is dark, it is ancient, and it is deep.
Poetry Is Not a Luxury [1977]

3   The Master's Tools Will Never Dismantle the Master's House   *Title of essay [1979]*

Janet Malcolm
1934–

4   Human nature is such that when we are suddenly taken up by someone whom we consider superior and admirable, we accept his attentions calmly, whereas when we are dropped we cannot rest until we feel we have got to the bottom of the person's profound irrationality.   *In the Freud Archives [1983]*

5   Every journalist who is not too stupid or too full of himself to notice what is going on knows that what he does is morally indefensible. He is a kind of confidence man, preying on people's vanity, ignorance, or loneliness, gaining their trust and betraying them without remorse.
The Journalist and the Murderer [1990], pt. I

Charles Manson
1934–

6   They are your children. You taught them. I didn't teach them.
Statement at trial [November 20, 1970]

Sir Jonathan [Wolfe] Miller
1934–

7   I'm not a Jew. I'm Jew-*ish*. I don't go the whole hog.   *Beyond the Fringe [1960]*

N[avarre] Scott Momaday
1934–

8   Words were medicine; they were magic and invisible. They came from nothing into sound and meaning.

They were beyond price; they could neither be bought nor sold.
House Made of Dawn [1968], January 26

9   Loneliness is an aspect of the land. All things in the plain are isolate; there is no confusion of objects in the eye, but *one* hill or *one* tree or *one* man. To look upon that landscape in the early morning, with the sun at your back, is to lose the sense of proportion. Your imagination comes to life, and this, you think, is where Creation was begun.
The Way to Rainy Mountain [1969]

Mary Quant
1934–

10   I didn't think of the mini as sexual but as an instrument of liberation. I wanted to make clothes that you could move in, skirts you could run and dance in, but, of course, wearing clothes like that made you feel and look sexy.
The Daily Telegraph [1967].
The Meaning of the Mini

Wole [Akinwande Oluwole] Soyinka
1934–

11   The man dies in all who keep silent in the face of tyranny.   *The Man Died [1972]*

Gloria Steinem
1934–

12   Any woman who chooses to behave like a full human being should be warned that the armies of the status quo will treat her as something of a dirty joke; that's their natural and first weapon.
Sisterhood in Ms. [spring 1972]

13   I can sometimes deal with men as equals and therefore can afford to like them.   *Sisterhood in Ms.*

14   Some of us are becoming the men we wanted to marry.
Speech at Yale University [September 1981]

Mark Strand
1934–

15   Ink runs from the corners of my mouth.
There is no happiness like mine.
I have been eating poetry.
Eating Poetry [1968]

1 Wherever I am
I am what is missing.   *Keeping Things Whole [1969]*

2 Nothing could stop you.
Not the best day. Not the quiet. Not the ocean
  rocking.
You went on with your dying.
    Elegy for My Father [1970]. 3. Your Dying

3 Nobody knows you. You are the neighbor of nothing.
    Elegy for My Father. 6. The New Year

4 Now you invent the boat of your flesh and set it upon
  the waters
and drift in the gradual swell, in the laboring salt.
Now you look down. The waters of childhood are
  there.
    Where Are the Waters of Childhood? [1978]

5 If a man publicly denounces poetry,
  His shoes will fill with urine.
    The New Poetry Handbook, st. 10

6 If a man finishes a poem,
    he shall bathe in the blank wake of his passion
    and be kissed by white paper.
    The New Poetry Handbook, st. 21

Robert Towne
[Robert Bertram Schwartz]
1934–

7   Politicians, ugly buildings, and whores all get
respectable if they last long enough.
    Chinatown (screenplay) [1974]

8   Most people never have to face the fact that at
the right time and the right place, they're capable of
anything.   *Chinatown (screenplay)*

Woody Allen
[Allen Stuart Konigsberg]
1935–

9   This trial is a travesty. It's a travesty of a mockery
of a sham of a mockery of a travesty of two mockeries
of a sham.   *Bananas*[1] *[1971]*

10   Is sex dirty? Only if it's done right.[2]
    *Everything You Always Wanted to Know
    About Sex [1972]*

11   Not only is there no God, but try getting a
plumber on weekends.
    Getting Even [1972]. My Philosophy

12   How wrong Emily Dickinson was! Hope is not
"the thing with feathers."[3] The thing with feathers
has turned out to be my nephew. I must take him
to a specialist in Zurich.
    *Without Feathers [1975]. From the Allen
    Notebooks*

13   It's not that I'm afraid to die. I just don't want to
be there when it happens.
    Without Feathers. Death (A Play)

14   On the plus side, death is one of the few things
that can be done as easily lying down.
    Without Feathers. The Early Essays

15   [Sex:] The most fun I've ever had without
laughing.[4]   *Annie Hall (screenplay)*[5] *[1977]*

16   Don't knock masturbation. It's sex with someone
I love.   *Annie Hall (screenplay)*

17   A relationship, I think, is like a shark, you know? It
has to constantly move forward or it dies, and I think
what we got on our hands is a dead shark.
    Annie Hall (screenplay)

18   Early in life I was visited by the bluebird of
anxiety.
    New York Times Magazine [April 22, 1979]

19   Life doesn't imitate art, it imitates bad television.
    Husbands and Wives (screenplay) [1992]

20   Eighty percent of success is showing up.
    Interview

Susan Brownmiller
1935–

21   Man's discovery that his genitalia could serve as a
weapon to generate fear must rank as one of the most
important discoveries of prehistoric times, along with
the use of fire and the first crude stone axe.
    *Against Our Will: Men, Women, and Rape
    [1975], ch. 1*

[Leroy] Eldridge Cleaver
1935–1998

22   Rape was an insurrectionary act.... I wanted
to send waves of consternation throughout the
white race.   *Soul on Ice [1968]. On Becoming*

23   You're either part of the solution or part of the
problem.   *Speech, San Francisco [1968]*

---

[1] Written with MICKEY ROSE.

[2] Cf. ALLEN's *Take the Money and Run:* One of the prison
psychiatrists asked me if I thought sex was dirty, and I said it is if
you're doing it right.

[3] See Emily Dickinson, 508:12.

[4] Giving canonical form to a quip already familiar on American
college campuses for several decades.

[5] Written with MARSHALL BRICKMAN [1941–].

the Dalai Lama [Tenzin Gyatso, born Lhamo Dhondup]
1935–

1   Because violence can only breed more violence and suffering, our struggle must remain nonviolent and free of hatred. We are trying to end the suffering of our people, not to inflict suffering on others.
Nobel Peace Prize acceptance speech [December 10, 1989]

Preston Foster
1935–

2 I got my mojo working
But it just don't work on you.
Got My Mojo Working[1] *[1956]*

Ken Kesey
1935–2001

3   A sound of cornered-animal fear and hate and surrender and defiance...like the last sound the treed and shot and falling animal makes as the dogs get him, when he finally doesn't care any more about anything but himself and his dying.
One Flew over the Cuckoo's Nest [1962], pt. IV

4   There are going to be times when we can't wait for somebody. Now, you're either on the bus or off the bus. If you're on the bus, and you get left behind, then you'll find it again. If you're off the bus in the first place — then it won't make a damn.
Quoted by TOM WOLFE *in The Electric Kool-Aid Acid Test*[2] *[1968], ch. 6*

W[illiam] P. Kinsella
1935–

5   If you build it, he will come.
Shoeless Joe[3] *[1982]*

Larry Kramer
1935–

6   [On AIDS:] We're all going to go crazy, living this epidemic every minute, while the rest of the world goes on out there, all around us, as if nothing is happening, going on with their own lives and not knowing what it's like, what we're going through. We're living through war, but where they're living it's peacetime, and we're all in the same country.
The Normal Heart [1985]

David Lodge
1935–

7   Literature is mostly about having sex and not much about having children. Life is the other way round.
The British Museum Is Falling Down [1965]

Mary Oliver
1935–

8   There is only one question:

how to love this world.
House of Light [1990]. Spring

9 I don't want to end up simply having visited this world.
New and Selected Poems [1992]. When Death Comes

10 When it's over, I want to say: all my life
I was a bride married to amazement.
I was the bridegroom taking the world into my arms.
New and Selected Poems. When Death Comes

11   The world where the owl is endlessly hungry and endlessly on the hunt is the world in which I live too.
Blue Pastures [1995]. Owls

Elvis Presley
1935–1977

12 Well since my baby left me
Well I found a new place to dwell
Well it's down at the end of lonely street
At Heartbreak Hotel.
Heartbreak Hotel[4] *[1956]*

13 Love me tender, love me sweet,
Never let me go.
Love Me Tender[5] *[1956]*

[Edna] Annie Proulx
1935–

14   I wish I knew how to quit you.
Brokeback Mountain [1997]

---

[1]The song was first recorded for Dare Records by ANN COLE; MUDDY WATERS recorded and popularized a slightly different version in 1957.

[2]See Tom Wolfe, 831:2–3.

[3]Basis for the movie *Field of Dreams* [1989].

---

[4]Written with MAE BOREN AXTON [1907–1997] and TOMMY DURDEN [1920–1999].

[5]Written with VERA MATSON.

Edward Said
1935–2003

1   Orientalism...a Western style for dominating, restructuring, and having authority over the Orient.
Orientalism [1978]

2   Exile is predicated on the existence of, love for, and a real bond with one's native place; the universal truth of exile is not that one has lost that love or home, but that inherent in each is an unexpected, unwelcome loss. Regard experiences then as if they were about to disappear.
Culture and Imperialism [1993]

Don DeLillo
1936–

3   A conspiracy is everything that ordinary life is not. It's the inside game, cold, sure, undistracted, forever closed off to us. We are the flawed ones, the innocents, trying to make some rough sense of the daily jostle. Conspirators have a logic and a daring beyond our reach.
Libra [1988]

4   The future belongs to crowds.   *Mao II [1991]*

5   Longing on a large scale is what makes history.
Underworld [1997]

Walon Green
1936–
and
Sam Peckinpah
1925–1984

6   If they move, kill 'em.
The Wild Bunch (screenplay) [1969]

7   We all dream of being a child again, even the worst of us. Perhaps the worst most of all.
The Wild Bunch (screenplay)

Václav Havel
1936–2011

8   God—I don't know why—wanted me to be a Czech. It was not my choice. But I accept it, and I try to do something for my country because I live here.   *Interview [1988]*

9   The tragedy of modern man is not that he knows less and less about the meaning of his own life, but that it bothers him less and less.
Letters to Olga [1988]

Abbie [Abbott] Hoffman
1936–1989

10   Steal This Book   *Title of book [1971]*

11   Sacred cows make the tastiest hamburger.
Remark. Recalled at his death

Barbara C. Jordan
1936–1996

12   "We, the people." It is a very eloquent beginning. But when that document[1] was completed on the seventeenth of September in 1787 I was not included in that "We, the people." I felt somehow for many years that George Washington and Alexander Hamilton just left me out by mistake. But through the process of amendment, interpretation and court decision, I have finally been included in "We, the people."
Statement at Debate on Articles of Impeachment, House of Representatives, Ninety-third Congress [July 25, 1974]

Anthony Kennedy
1936–

13   The hard fact is that sometimes we must make decisions we do not like. We make them because they are right, right in the sense that the law and the Constitution, as we see them, compel the result. And so great is our commitment to the process that, except in the rare case, we do not pause to express distaste for the result, perhaps for fear of undermining a valued principle that dictates the decision.
Texas v. Johnson 491 U.S. 397 [1989]

Florence King
1936–

14   Democracy is the fig leaf of elitism.
Reflections in a Jaundiced Eye [1989]

Kris Kristofferson
1936–
and
Fred Foster
1931–

15 Freedom's just another word for nothin' left to lose, And nothin' ain't worth nothin' but it's free.
Me and Bobby McGee [1969]

---

[1]Preamble to the Constitution of the United States.

John McCain
1936–

1   Yet those who claim their liberty but not their duty to the civilization that ensures it, live a half-life, having indulged their self-interest at the cost of their self-respect.... Sacrifice for a cause greater than your self-interest, and you invest your lives with the eminence of that cause, your self-respect assured.
Speech at Boston College convocation
[September 18, 2006]

2   I'd much rather lose a campaign than lose a war.
Interview with Larry King
[January 10, 2007]

3   The fundamentals of America's economy are strong.
Interview on Bloomberg TV
[April 17, 2008]

Georges Perec
1936–1982

4   Despite appearances, puzzling is not a solitary game: every move the puzzler makes, the puzzlemaker has made before; every piece the puzzler picks up, and picks up again, and studies and strokes, every combination he tries, and tries a second time, every blunder and every insight, each hope and each discouragement have all been designed, calculated, and decided by the other.
Life: A User's Manual [1978]. Preamble

Antonin Scalia
1936–

5   The Imperial Judiciary lives. It is instructive to compare this Nietzschean vision of us unelected, life-tenured judges — leading a Volk who will be "tested by following," and whose very "belief in themselves" is mystically bound up in their "understanding" of a Court that "speak[s] before all others for their constitutional ideals" — with the somewhat more modest role envisioned for these lawyers by the Founders.
Dissent in Planned Parenthood v. Casey,
505 U.S. 833 [1992]

Frank Stella
1936–

6   What you see is what you see.
Quoted in Bruce Glaser,
Questions to Stella and Judd [1964]

Claude Brown
1937–2002

7   The children of these disillusioned colored pioneers inherited the total lot of their parents — the disappointments, the anger. To add to their misery, they had little hope of deliverance. For where does one run to when he's already in the promised land?
Manchild in the Promised Land [1965]

Johnnie Cochran, Jr.
1937–2005

8   If it doesn't fit, then you must acquit.[1]
Closing argument, murder trial of
O. J. Simpson [September 27, 1995]

Sonny Curtis
1937–

9   I fought the law, and the law won.
I Fought the Law [1958]. Hit 1964 single by
The Bobby Fuller Four

Richard Farina
1937–1966

10   Been Down So Long It Looks Like Up to Me
Title of book [1966]

Susan Howe
1937–

11   Poetry is the great stimulation of life. Poetry leads past possession of self to transfiguration beyond gender. Poetry is redemption from pessimism.
My Emily Dickinson [1985]

Saddam Hussein [Saddam Hussein Abd al-Majid al-Tikriti]
1937–2006

12   Everybody must realize that this battle will be the mother of all battles, and that God wanted us to wage the battle of liberating the nation and humanity, the

---

[1]The reference is to a glove found at the scene of the crime. In *A Lawyer's Life*, Cochran writes, "Not only was this the most memorable line in the entire trial, it's the line that eventually will be cited by *Bartlett's Familiar Quotations*, the line endlessly quoted to me by people, the line by which I'll be remembered, and I suspect it will probably be my epitaph."

battle of liberating Jerusalem and the holy shrines on the land of Iraq.   *Speech [September 20, 1990]*

Thomas Nagel
1937–

1   It isn't just that I don't believe in God.... It's that I hope there is no God! I don't want there to be a God; I don't want the universe to be like that.
    The Last Word [1997]

Colin Powell
1937–

2   [On invading Iraq:] You break it, you own it.
    Remark [2003] cited in Bob Woodward, *Plan of Attack [2004]*

Thomas Pynchon
1937–

3   Yet who can presume to say *what* the war wants, so vast and aloof it is ... so *absentee.*
    Gravity's Rainbow [1973]

4   Proverbs for Paranoids, 3: If they can get you asking the wrong questions, they don't have to worry about answers.   *Gravity's Rainbow*

Erich Segal
1937–2010

5   Love means not ever having to say you're sorry.[1]   *Love Story [1970]*

Tom Stoppard
1937–

6   You're familiar with the tragedies of antiquity, are you? The great homicidal classics?
    Rosencrantz and Guildenstern Are Dead [1967], act I

7   The bad end unhappily, the good unluckily. That is what tragedy means.[2]
    Rosencrantz and Guildenstern Are Dead, II

---

[1]Love means never having to say you're sorry. — *Love Story (screenplay)* [1970], spoken by Ali MacGraw.

[2]Cf. Oscar Wilde, *The Importance of Being Earnest*, act II: "The good ended happily, and the bad unhappily. That is what Fiction means." Spoken by Miss Prism.

8   If rationality were the criterion for things being allowed to exist, the world would be one gigantic field of soya beans!   *Jumpers [1972], act I*

9   War is capitalism with the gloves off.
    Travesties [1974], act I

10   I learned three things in Zurich during the war. I wrote them down. Firstly, you're either a revolutionary or you're not, and if you're not you might as well be an artist as anything else. Secondly, if you can't be an artist, you might as well be a revolutionary ... I forget the third thing.
    Travesties, last lines

11   You can persuade a man to believe almost anything provided he is clever enough, but it is much more difficult to persuade someone less clever.
    Professional Foul [1978], sc. 14

Hunter S. Thompson
1937–2005

12   Fear and Loathing in Las Vegas
    Title of book [1971]

13   We were somewhere around Barstow on the edge of the desert when the drugs began to take hold.
    Fear and Loathing in Las Vegas [1971]

14   [On America:] Just a nation of 220 million used car salesmen with all the money we need to buy guns, and no qualms at all about killing anybody else in the world who tries to make us uncomfortable.
    Fear and Loathing on the Campaign Trail '72 [1973]

15   Gonzo journalism ... is a style of "reporting" based on William Faulkner's idea that the best fiction is far more *true* than any kind of journalism — and the best journalists have always known this.
    The Great Shark Hunt [1979]

16   When the going gets weird, the weird turn pro.
    The Great Shark Hunt

Eleanor Bergstein
1938–

17   Nobody puts Baby in a corner.
    Dirty Dancing (screenplay) [1987], spoken by Patrick Swayze

Stewart Brand
1938–

18   Information wants to be free.
    The Media Lab: Inventing the Future at M.I.T. [1987]

Raymond Carver
1938–1988

1   Maxine said it was another tragedy in a long line of low-rent tragedies.
> *What We Talk About When We Talk About Love [1981]. One More Thing*

2   You have to eat and keep going. Eating is a small, good thing in a time like this.
> *Cathedral [1983]. A Small, Good Thing*

3   　　　Father, I love you,
yet how can I say thank you, I who can't hold my
　　　liquor either
and don't even know the places to fish.
> *Photograph of My Father in His Twenty-Second Year [1984]*

4   Autobiography is the poor man's history.
> *Where I'm Calling From [1988]. Blackbird Pie*

John Dean
1938–

5   We have a cancer within, close to the Presidency, that is growing.
> *From The [Nixon] Presidential Transcripts [March 21, 1973]*

6   It's a limited hang-out.[1]
> *To Richard Nixon, The Presidential Transcripts [March 22, 1973]*

Curt Flood
1938–1997

7   After twelve years in the major leagues, I do not feel I am a piece of property to be bought and sold irrespective of my wishes.
> *Letter to Bowie Kuhn, Commissioner of Major League Baseball [December 24, 1969]*

A. Bartlett Giamatti
1938–1989

8   [Baseball] breaks your heart. It is designed to break your heart. The game begins in the spring, when everything else begins again, and it blossoms in the summer, filling the afternoons and evenings, and then as soon as the chill rains come, it stops, and leaves you to face the fall alone.
> *The Green Fields of the Mind [1977]*

John Guare
1938–

9   Everybody on this planet is separated by only six other people. Six degrees of separation. Between us and everybody else on this planet.
> *Six Degrees of Separation [1990]*

Joyce Carol Oates
1938–

10   This is a work of history in fictional form — that is, in personal perspective, which is the only kind of history that exists.
> *Them [1969]. Author's Note*

11   The use of language is all we have to pit against death and silence.
> *At the National Book Awards [1970]*

12   Love commingled with hate is more powerful than love. Or hate.
> *On Boxing [1987]*

Laurel Thatcher Ulrich
1938–

13   Well-behaved women seldom make history.
> *Virtuous Women Found, American Quarterly [Spring 1976]*

Margaret Atwood
1939–

14   A divorce is like an amputation, you survive but there's less of you.
> *Surfacing [1972]*

15 A word after a word
after a word is power.
> *True Stories [1981]. Spelling*

16 I would like to be the air
that inhabits you for a moment
only. I would like to be that unnoticed
& that necessary.
> *True Stories. Variation on the Word "Sleep"*

17   Nobody dies from lack of sex. It's lack of love we die from.
> *The Handmaid's Tale [1985]*

Alan Ayckbourn
1939–

18   The only thing for old age is a brave face, a good tailor and comfortable shoes.
> *The Norman Conquests: Table Manners [1975], act 2, sc.1*

---

[1]John Ehrlichman added, "It's a modified limited hang-out."

Jim [James Alan] Bouton
1939–

1   You spend a good piece of your life gripping a baseball and in the end it turns out that it was the other way around all the time.
Ball Four [1970]

John Cleese
1939–

2   Pretentious? *Moi?*
Fawlty Towers [1979]. The Psychiatrist

Francis Ford Coppola
1939–
and
John Milius
1944–

3   I love the smell of napalm in the morning. You know, one time we had a hill bombed for twelve hours. . . . The smell, you know that gasoline smell. Smelled like victory.
Apocalypse Now (screenplay) [1979],
spoken by Robert Duvall

Marvin Gaye [Marvin Pentz Gay, Jr.]
1939–1984

4 Father, father
We don't need to escalate
War is not the answer
For only love can conquer hate
What's Going On [1971]. Title song

5 Make me wanna holler
The way they do my life
What's Going On. Inner City Blues

Gerry Goffin
1939–
and
Carole King
1942–

6 Tonight you're mine completely
You give your love so sweetly
Tonight the light of love is in your eyes
But will you love me tomorrow?
Will You Love Me Tomorrow [1960]

Germaine Greer
1939–

7   Women have very little idea of how much men hate them.
The Female Eunuch [1970].
Loathing and Disgust

8   Is it too much to ask that women be spared the daily struggle for superhuman beauty in order to offer it to the caresses of a subhumanly ugly mate?
The Female Eunuch. Loathing and Disgust

Seamus [Justin] Heaney
1939–

9 Between my finger and my thumb
The squat pen rests.
I'll dig with it.
Death of a Naturalist [1966].
Digging

10 I shouldered a kind of manhood
stepping in to lift the coffins
of dead relations.
North [1975]. Funeral Rites, I

11 It all came back to me last night, stirred
By the sootfall of your things at bedtime,
Your head-down, tail-up hunt in a bottom
    drawer
For the black plunge-line nightdress.
Field Work [1979]. The Skunk

12 And that moment when the bird sings very close
To the music of what happens.
Field Work. Song

13 You lose more of yourself than you redeem
Doing the decent thing.
Station Island [1984], XII

14 History says, *Don't hope*
On this side of the grave.
But then, once in a lifetime
The longed-for tidal wave
Of justice can rise up
And hope and history rhyme.
The Cure at Troy [1990]

Dave Hickey
1939–

15   People despise critics because people despise weakness, and criticism is the weakest thing you can do in

writing. It is the written equivalent of air guitar — flurries of silent, sympathetic gestures with nothing at their heart but the memory of the music.

Air Guitar [1997]

William Least Heat-Moon [William Lewis Trogdon]
1939–

1   On the old highway maps of America, the main routes were red and the back roads blue. Now even the colors are changing. But in those brevities just before dawn and a little after dark — times neither day nor night — the old roads return to the sky some of its color. Then, in truth, they cast a mysterious shadow of blue, and it's that time when the pull of the blue highway is strongest, when the open road is a beckoning, a strangeness, a place where a man can lose himself.

Blue Highways [1982]. Preface

Richard Klein
1939–

2   Perhaps one stops smoking only when one starts to love cigarettes, becoming so enamored of their charms and so grateful for their benefits that one at last begins to grasp how much is lost by giving them up, how urgent it is to find substitutes for some of the seductions and powers that cigarettes so magnificently combine.

Cigarettes Are Sublime [1993]

Richard Posner
1939–

3   When urgent considerations of the public safety require compromise with the normal principles constraining law enforcement, the normal principles may have to bend. The Constitution is not a suicide pact.[1]

Decision in Edmond v. Goldsmith,
U.S. 7th Circuit Court of Appeals [1999]

---

[1]Cf. Judge ROBERT H. JACKSON, in a dissenting opinion in *Terminiello v. Chicago* [1949]: The choice is not between order and liberty. It is between liberty with order and anarchy without either. There is danger that, if the Court does not temper its doctrinaire logic with a little practical wisdom, it will convert the constitutional Bill of Rights into a suicide pact.
    Cf. also Justice ARTHUR GOLDBERG in *Kennedy v. Mendoza-Martinez, U.S. Supreme Court* [1963]: The powers of Congress to require military service for the common defense are broad and far-reaching, for while the Constitution protects against invasions of individual rights, it is not a suicide pact.

James Rado [James Radomski]
1939–
and
Gerome Ragni
1942–1991

4 When the moon is in the seventh house
And Jupiter aligns with Mars,
Then peace will guide the planets,
And love will steer the stars;
This is the dawning of the age of Aquarius,
The age of Aquarius.

Hair[2] *[1966]. Aquarius*

Grace Slick [Grace Barnett Wing]
1939–

5 One pill makes you larger
And one pill makes you small
And the ones that mother gives you
Don't do anything at all.
Go ask Alice
When she's ten feet tall.

White Rabbit [1967]

Ronald L. Ziegler
1939–2003

6   This is the operative statement. The others are inoperative.

Statement as Richard Nixon's press secretary
[April 17, 1973]

Marshall Berman
1940–

7   To be modern is to find ourselves in an environment that promises us adventure, power, joy, growth, transformation of ourselves and the world — and, at the same time, that threatens to destroy everything we have, everything we know, everything we are.

All That Is Solid Melts into Air [1982]

Joseph Brodsky
1940–1996

8   Had we been choosing our leaders on the basis of their reading experience and not their political programs, there would be much less grief on earth. . . . I

---

[2]Music by GALT MACDERMOT.

believe...that for someone who has read a lot of Dickens, to shoot his like in the name of some idea is more problematic than for someone who has read no Dickens.

Nobel Prize acceptance speech [1987]

Tom Brokaw
1940–

1 This is the greatest generation any society has ever produced.

On the 50th anniversary of D-Day, to World War II veterans [1994]

Angela Carter
1940–1992

2 It is far easier for a woman to lead a blameless life than it is for a man; all she has to do is to avoid sexual intercourse like the plague.

Wayward Girls and Wicked Women [1986]

Bruce Chatwin
1940–1989

3 "Music," said Arkady, "is a memory bank for finding one's way about the world."

The Songlines [1987]

J[ohn] M[axwell] Coetzee
1940–

4 Belief may be no more, in the end, than a source of energy, like a battery which one clips into an idea to make it run. As happens when one writes: believing whatever has to be believed in order to get the job done.

Elizabeth Costello [2003]

Gao Xingjian
1940–

5 Once literature is contrived as the hymn of the nation, the flag of the race, the mouthpiece of a political party or the voice of a class or a group it can be employed as a mighty and all-engulfing tool of propaganda. However, such literature loses what is inherent in literature, ceases to be literature, and becomes a substitute for power and profit.

The Case for Literature (Nobel Lecture) [2000]

Michael Herr
1940–

6 There was a famous story, some reporters asked a door gunner, "How can you shoot women and children?" and he'd answered, "It's easy, you just don't lead 'em so much."

Dispatches [1977]. Breathing In

7 I think Vietnam was what we had instead of happy childhoods.

Dispatches. Colleagues

8 Out on the street I couldn't tell the Vietnam veterans from the rock and roll veterans. The sixties had made so many casualties, its war and its music had run power off the same circuit for so long they didn't even have to fuse.

Dispatches. Breathing Out

9 As one American major said, in a successful attempt at attaining history, "We had to destroy Ben Tre in order to save it."[1]

Dispatches. Hell Sucks

Maxine Hong Kingston
1940–

10 Chinese-Americans, when you try to understand what things in you are Chinese, how do you separate what is peculiar to childhood, to poverty, insanities, one family, your mother who marked your growing with stories, from what is Chinese? What is Chinese tradition and what is the movies?

The Woman Warrior [1976]. No Name Woman

John [Ono] Lennon
1940–1980

11 Will the people in the cheaper seats clap your hands? All the rest of you, if you'll just rattle your jewelry.

At Royal Variety Performance by the Beatles, London [November 4, 1963]

12 We're more popular than Jesus now.[2] I don't know which will go first — rock 'n' roll or Christianity.

Interview in London Evening Standard [March 4, 1966]

13 God is a concept
By which we measure our pain.   *God [1970]*

---

[1] Often quoted as: We had to destroy the village in order to save it.
[2] See Charlie Chaplin, 683:18.

1 The dream is over...
I was the Dreamweaver
But now I'm reborn
I was the Walrus
But now I'm John. *God*

2 They hurt you at home and they hit you at school
They hate you if you're clever and they despise a fool
Till you're so fucking crazy you can't follow their
    rules
A working class hero is something to be
  Working Class Hero [1970]

3 Keep you doped with religion and sex and TV
And you think you're so clever and classless and free
But you're still fucking peasants as far as I can see.
  Working Class Hero

John Lennon
1940–1980
and
Sir Paul McCartney
1942–

4   I'll tell you something
I think you'll understand,
Then I'll say that something,
I want to hold your hand.
  I Want to Hold Your Hand [1963]

5 She told me she worked in the morning
And started to laugh,
I told her I didn't
And crawled off to sleep in the bath.
And when I awoke
I was alone,
This bird had flown.
So I lit a fire,
Isn't it good
Norwegian wood. *Norwegian Wood [1965]*

6 There's a shadow hanging over me,
Oh yesterday came suddenly. *Yesterday [1965]*

7 All the lonely people, where do they all belong?
  Eleanor Rigby [1966]

8 It's a thousand pages give or take a few,
I'll be writing more in a week or two.
I can make it longer if you like the style,
I can change it round
And I want to be a paperback writer.
  Paperback Writer [1966]

9 So we sailed on to the sun
Till we found a sea of green,
And we lived beneath the waves
In our yellow submarine.
  Yellow Submarine [1966]

10 Everybody seems to think I'm lazy,
I don't mind, I think they're crazy
Running everywhere at such a speed
Till they find there's no need.
Please don't spoil my day, I'm miles away
And after all I'm only sleeping.
  I'm Only Sleeping [1966]

11 When I get older losing my hair
Many years from now
Will you still be sending me a Valentine
Birthday greetings, bottle of wine.
If I'd been out till quarter to three
Would you lock the door,
Will you still need me, will you still feed me
When I'm sixty-four.
  When I'm Sixty-Four [1967]

12 I saw a film today, oh boy.
The English army had just won the war.
A crowd of people turned away.
But I just had to look,
Having read the book.
I'd love to turn you on. *A Day in the Life [1967]*

13 Oh I get by with a little help from my friends
Mmm get high with a little help from my friends.
  With a Little Help from My Friends [1967]

14 You say you want a revolution
Well you know
we all want to change the world...
But when you talk about destruction
Don't you know that you can count me out
Don't you know it's gonna be alright.
  Revolution [1968]

15 Now Rocky Raccoon he fell back in his room
Only to find Gideon's Bible.
Gideon checked out and he left it no doubt
To help with good Rocky's revival.
  Rocky Raccoon [1968]

16 Words are flowing out
Like endless rain into a paper cup
They slither while they pass, they slip away
Across the universe
  Across the Universe [1968]

17 And so I quit the police department
And got myself a steady job
And though she tried her best to help me
She could steal but she could not rob.
  *She Came in Through the Bathroom
  Window [1969]*

18 You never give me your money
You only give me your funny paper
And in the middle of negotiations
You break down.
  You Never Give Me Your Money [1969]

1 And in the end the love you take is equal to the love
  you make.   *The End [1969]*

Phil Ochs
1940–1976

2 It's always the old to lead us to the wars,
  Always the young to fall.
                    I Ain't Marching Anymore [1965]

3 I'm sure it wouldn't interest anybody
  Outside of a small circle of friends.
                    A Small Circle of Friends [1967]

Smokey Robinson
[William Robinson, Jr.]
1940–

4 So take a good look at my face
  You'll see my smile looks out of place
  If you look closer it's easy to trace
  The tracks of my tears
            *The Tracks of My Tears [1965]. Recorded
            by Smokey Robinson and the Miracles*

Pharoah [Ferrell] Sanders
1940–

and

Leon Thomas
1937–1999

5 The creator has a master plan,
  Peace and happiness for every man.
            *Karma [1968]. The Creator Has a
            Master Plan*

Jack Weinberg
1940–

6   We have a saying in the movement that we don't
  trust anybody over thirty.
            *Interview on Free Speech movement
            at University of California, Berkeley
            [1964]*

Edmund White
1940–

7   San Francisco is where gay fantasies come true,
  and the problem the city presents is whether, after all,
  we wanted these particular dreams to be fulfilled — or
  would we have preferred others? Did we know what
  price these dreams would exact? Did we anticipate the
  ways in which, vivid and continuous, they would
  unsuit us for the business of daily life? Or should our
  notion of daily life itself be transformed?
                        States of Desire [1980]

Norman Whitfield
1940–2008

and

Barrett Strong
1941–

8 War —
  What is it good for?
  Absolutely nothing.
            War [1970], sung by Edwin Starr

Frank Zappa
1940–1993

9   Rock journalism is people who can't write inter-
  viewing people who can't talk in order to provide articles for people who can't read.
            Quoted in Kelly Fisher Lowe's *The Words
            and Music of Frank Zappa [2006]*

10 Who are the brain police?
            Freak Out! [1966]. Who Are the Brain Police?

Paul Anka
1941–

11 I've lived a life that's full, I traveled each and ev'ry
  highway,
  And more, much more than this, I did it my way.
                        My Way[1] [1969]

Roberto Calasso
1941–

12   A life in which the gods are not invited is not
  worth living. It will be quieter, but there won't be any
  stories.
            *The Marriage of Cadmus and Harmony
            [1988]*

---

[1]Music by Claude François, Jacques Revaux, and Giles Thibaut.
Signature song of Frank Sinatra [1915–1998]. In November
1989 Soviet leader Mikhail Gorbachev announced (through a
Foreign Ministry spokesman) that "the Sinatra Doctrine" had
replaced the "Brezhnev Doctrine" for the east bloc nations:
"Hungary and Poland are doing it their way."

Philip [Joseph] Caputo
1941–

1 Stack 'em like cordwood. Victory was a high body-count, defeat a low kill-ratio, war a matter of arithmetic. *A Rumor of War [1977]*

2 You're going to learn that one of the most brutal things in the world is your average nineteen-year-old American boy. *A Rumor of War*

Stokely Carmichael [Kwame Toure]
1941–1998

and

Charles [Vernon] Hamilton
1929–

3 Black power[1] . . . is a call for black people in this country to unite, to recognize their heritage, to build a sense of community. It is a call for black people to begin to define their own goals, to lead their own organizations and to support those organizations. It is a call to reject the racist institutions and values of this society. *Black Power! [1967], ch. 2*

Dick [Richard Bruce] Cheney
1941–

4 If there's a one percent chance that Pakistani scientists are helping al-Qaeda build or develop a nuclear weapon, we have to treat it as a certainty in terms of our response.
> *At a meeting with CIA director George Tenet and National Security Advisor Condoleezza Rice [November 2001]*

George Clinton
1941–

5 Free your mind and your ass will follow
The kingdom of heaven is within
> *Free Your Mind . . . and Your Ass Will Follow [1970]. Recorded by Funkadelic*

6 God bless . . . Chocolate City . . . and its vanilla suburbs.
> *Chocolate City [1975]. Recorded by Parliament*

---

[1] Carmichael had used the phrase "Black power" in a speech in Greenwood, Mississippi [June 17, 1966].

To demand these God-given rights is to seek black power — what I call audacious power — the power to build black institutions of splendid achievement. — ADAM CLAYTON POWELL, JR. [1908–1972], *Baccalaureate address at Howard University* [May 29, 1966]
See Langston Hughes, 731:11.

Billy Collins
1941–

7 Of all the questions you might want to ask
about angels, the only one you ever hear
is how many can dance on the head of a pin.

No curiosity about how they pass the eternal time
besides circling the Throne chanting in Latin
or delivering a crust of bread to a hermit on earth
or guiding a boy and a girl across a rickety wooden
bridge.
> *Questions About Angels [1991]. Questions About Angels*

8 I love the sound of the bone against the plate
and the fortress-like look of it
lying before me in a moat of risotto,
the meat soft as the leg of an angel
who has lived a purely airborne existence.
> *The Art of Drowning [1995]. Osso Buco*

Richard Dawkins
1941–

9 We are survival machines — robot vehicles blindly programmed to preserve the selfish molecules known as genes. This is a truth which still fills me with astonishment.
> *The Selfish Gene [1976]. Preface*

10 Intelligent life on a planet comes of age when it first works out the reason for its own existence. If superior creatures from space ever visit earth, the first question they will ask, in order to assess the level of our civilization, is: "Have they discovered evolution yet?"
> *The Selfish Gene, ch. 1*

11 Natural selection, the blind, unconscious, automatic process which Darwin discovered, and which we now know is the explanation for the existence and apparently purposeful form of all life, has no purpose in mind. It has no mind and no mind's eye. It does not plan for the future. It has no vision, no foresight, no sight at all. If it can be said to play the role of watchmaker in nature, it is the *blind* watchmaker.
> *The Blind Watchmaker [1986], ch. 1*

Desmond Dekker
1941–2006

12 Dem a loot, dem a shoot, dem a wail
A Shanty Town
Dem rude boys out on probation
A Shanty Town

Dem a rude when dem come up to town
A Shanty Town
007 (Shanty Town) [1967]

Bob Dylan
[Robert Zimmerman]
1941–

1 How many roads must a man walk down
Before you call him a man? ...
The answer, my friend, is blowin' in the wind,
The answer is blowin' in the wind.
Blowin' in the Wind [1962]

2 Where black is the color, where none is the number,
And I'll tell it and think it and speak it and breathe it,
And reflect from the mountain so all souls can see it,
Then I'll stand on the ocean until I start sinkin',
But I'll know my song well before I start singin',
And it's a hard, it's a hard, it's a hard, it's a hard,
It's a hard rain's a-gonna fall.
A Hard Rain's A-Gonna Fall [1962]

3 Come you masters of war
You that build all the guns
You that build the death planes
You that build the big bombs
You that hide behind walls
You that hide behind desks
I just want you to know
I can see through your masks
Masters of War [1963]

4 When your rooster crows at the break of dawn
Look out your window and I'll be gone
You're the reason I'm trav'lin' on
Don't think twice, it's all right
Don't Think Twice, It's All Right [1963]

5 The order is
Rapidly fadin'.
And the first one now
Will later be last
For the times they are a-changin'.
The Times They Are A-Changin' [1963]

6 But I was so much older then
I'm younger than that now.
My Back Pages [1964]

7 Yonder stands your orphan with his gun
Crying like a fire in the sun
Look out, the saints are comin' through
And it's all over now, Baby Blue.
It's All Over Now, Baby Blue [1965]

8 From the fool's gold mouthpiece
The hollow horn plays wasted words
Proves to warn

That he not busy being born
Is busy dying.
It's Alright, Ma (I'm Only Bleeding)
[1965]

9 But even the president of the United States
Sometimes must have to stand naked.
It's Alright, Ma (I'm Only Bleeding)

10 While money doesn't talk, it swears.
It's Alright, Ma (I'm Only Bleeding)

11 And if my thought-dreams could be seen
They'd probably put my head in a guillotine
But it's alright, Ma, it's life and life only
It's Alright, Ma (I'm Only Bleeding)

12 Hey! Mr. Tambourine Man, play a song for me,
I'm not sleepy and there is no place I'm going to.
Mr. Tambourine Man [1965]

13 Take me for a trip upon your magic swirlin' ship,
My senses have been stripped,
My hands can't feel to grip,
My toes too numb to step
Wait only for my boot heels to be wanderin'.
Mr. Tambourine Man

14 How does it feel
To be on your own
With no direction home
Like a complete unknown
Like a rolling stone?
Like a Rolling Stone [1965]

15 You don't need a weather man
To know which way the wind blows
Subterranean Homesick Blues [1965]

16 The pump don't work
'Cause the vandals took the handles.
Subterranean Homesick Blues

17 You got a lot of nerve
To say you are my friend
When I was down
You just stood there grinning.
Positively 4th Street [1965]

18 And here I sit so patiently
Waiting to find out what price
You have to pay to get out of
Going through all these things twice.
*Stuck Inside of Mobile with the Memphis Blues
Again* [1966]

19 To live outside the law, you must be honest.
Absolutely Sweet Marie [1966]

20 I see my light come shining
From the west unto the east

Any day now, any day now
I shall be released.
I Shall Be Released [1967]

1 There are many here among us
Who feel that life is but a joke
All Along the Watchtower [1968]

Barbara Ehrenreich
1941–

2 Exercise is the yuppie version of bulimia.
The Worst Years of Our Lives [1990]

3 No matter that patriotism is too often the refuge of scoundrels. Dissent, rebellion, and all-around hell-raising remain the true duty of patriots.
The Worst Years of Our Lives

Nora Ephron
1941–2012

4 There is no reason to confuse television news with journalism. *Scribble Scrabble [1978]*

5 I'll have what she's having.
When Harry Met Sally (screenplay) [1989], spoken by Estelle Reiner

Stephen Jay Gould
1941–2002

6 Wind back the tape of life to the early days of the Burgess Shale; let it play again from an identical starting point, and the chance becomes vanishingly small that anything like human intelligence would grace the replay.
Wonderful Life: The Burgess Shale and the Nature of History [1989]

Robert Hass
1941–

7 All the new thinking is about loss.
In this it resembles the old thinking.
The idea, for example, that each particular erases
the luminous clarity of a general idea.
Praise [1979]. Meditation at Lagunitas

Robert Hunter
1941–

8 What a long, strange trip it's been.
Truckin' [1970]. Recorded by The Grateful Dead

Jesse Jackson
1941–

9 My constituency is the desperate, the damned, the disinherited, the disrespected, and the despised.
Speech at Democratic National Convention, San Francisco [July 17, 1984]

10 My right and my privilege to stand here before you has been won — won in my lifetime — by the blood and the sweat of the innocent.
Speech at Democratic National Convention, Atlanta [July 19, 1988]

11 When I look out at this convention, I see the face of America, red, yellow, brown, black and white. We are all precious in God's sight — the real rainbow coalition.
Speech at Democratic National Convention, Atlanta

Trent Lott
1941–

12 I want to say this about my state. When Strom Thurmond ran for president, we voted for him. We're proud of it. And if the rest of the country had followed our lead, we wouldn't have had all these problems over all these years, either.
At Strom Thurmond's 100th birthday party [December 5, 2002]

Derek Mahon
1941–

13 I lived there as a boy and know the coal
Glittering in its shed, late-afternoon
Lambency informing the deal table,
The ceiling cradled in a radiant spoon.
I must be lying low in a room there,
A strange child with a taste for verse,
While my hard-nosed companions dream of fire
And sword upon parched veldt and fields of rain-swept gorse.
The Hunt by Night [1982]. Courtyards in Delft

Robin Morgan
1941–

14 Let it all hang out. Let it seem bitchy, catty, dykey, frustrated, crazy, Solanesque,[1] nutty, frigid, ridiculous,

_____

[1] *Solanesque* refers to VALERIE SOLANAS, who wrote the *SCUM* [Society for Cutting Up Men] *Manifesto* and who gained notoriety for shooting Andy Warhol.

bitter, embarrassing, man-hating, libelous, pure, unfair, envious, intuitive, low-down, stupid, petty, liberating. *We are the women that men have warned us about.*

Goodbye to All That [1970]

1   Pornography is the theory, and rape the practice.   *Going Too Far [1977]*

Laura Mulvey
1941–

2   In a world ordered by sexual imbalance, pleasure in looking has been split between active/male and passive/female. The determining male gaze projects its fantasy onto the female figure, which is styled accordingly.

Visual Pleasure and Narrative Cinema [1975]

Otis Redding
1941–1967

3 All I'm asking for
Is a little respect when I come home.

Respect [1965]

Otis Redding
1941–1967
and
Steve Cropper
1941–

4 I'm sittin' on the dock of the bay,
Watchin' the tide roll away.
I'm just sittin' on the dock of the bay,
Wastin' time.

Sittin' on the Dock of the Bay [1967]

Helen Reddy
1941–

5 If I have to, I can do anything.
I am strong, I am invincible, I am woman.

I Am Woman [1972]

David Thomson
1941–

6   How could anyone *be* "Cary Grant"? But how can anyone, ever after, not consider the attempt?

A Biographical Dictionary of Film [1975]

Harlan Ullman
1941–
and
James Wade, Jr.
1930–

7   Shock and Awe   *Title of paper [1996]*

George F[rederick] Will
1941–

8   Football combines the two worst features of American life. It's violence punctuated by committee meetings.

FOX News broadcast [1998]

Muhammad Ali[1]
1942–

9   I am the greatest.
Slogan, inspired by wrestler Gorgeous George

10   Float like a butterfly, sting like a bee.
Boxing credo, devised by aide Drew "Bundini" Brown

11   Not only do I knock 'em out, I pick the round.
Statement [December 1962]

12   I ain't got no quarrel with them Viet Cong.
On the draft [February 1966]

Michael Bloomberg
1942–

13   On September 11, 2001, thousands of first responders heroically rushed to the scene and saved tens of thousands of lives. More than 400 of those first responders did not make it out alive. In rushing into those burning buildings, not one of them asked "What God do you pray to?" "What beliefs do you hold?"

Statement defending the right to build a mosque in lower Manhattan [August 3, 2010]

Daniel Dennett
1942–

14   Philosophers' Syndrome: mistaking a failure of imagination for an insight into necessity.

Consciousness Explained [1991]

---

[1]Formerly Cassius Clay.

Ian Dury
1942–2000

1 Sex and drugs and rock and roll
Is all my brain and body need
Sex and drugs and rock and roll
Is very good indeed.
Sex & Drugs & Rock & Roll [1977]

Stephen [William] Hawking
1942–

2   What is it that breathes fire into the equations and makes a universe for them to describe?
A Brief History of Time [1988], ch. 12

3   If we do discover a complete [unified] theory [of the universe], it should in time be understandable in broad principle by everyone, not just a few scientists. Then we shall all, philosophers, scientists, and just ordinary people, be able to take part in the discussion of the question of why it is that we and the universe exist. If we find the answer to that, it would be the ultimate triumph of human reason — for then we should know the mind of God.
A Brief History of Time. Conclusion

4   We have only to look at ourselves to see how intelligent life might develop into something we wouldn't want to meet.
Into the Universe with Stephen Hawking (television series) [2010]

Jimi [James Marshall] Hendrix
1942–1970

5 'Scuse me while I kiss the sky.
Are You Experienced [1967]. Purple Haze

6 I'm gonna wave my freak flag high.
Axis: Bold as Love [1967]. If 6 Was 9

Werner Herzog [Werner H. Stipetić]
1942–

7   You should look straight at a film; that's the only way to see one. Film is not the art of scholars but of illiterates.
Quoted in the New York Times [September 11, 1977]

John Irving
1942–

8   In the world according to Garp, we are all terminal cases.
The World According to Garp [1978]

Erica Jong
1942–

9   The zipless fuck is absolutely pure. It is free of ulterior motives. There is no power game. The man is not "taking" and the woman is not "giving." No one is attempting to cuckold a husband or humiliate a wife. No one is trying to prove anything or get anything out of anyone. The zipless fuck is the purest thing there is. And it is rarer than the unicorn.
Fear of Flying [1973], ch. 1

Garrison Keillor
1942–

10   That's the news from Lake Wobegon, where all the women are strong, the men are good-looking, and all the children are above average.
A Prairie Home Companion [1974–   ], signature line

11   The little town that time forgot, that the decades cannot improve.
A Prairie Home Companion

12   A good newspaper is never quite good enough but a lousy newspaper is a joy forever.
That Old "Picayune-Moon" [1990]

Carole King
1942–

13 You just call out my name
And you know wherever I am
I'll come running to see you again.
Winter, spring, summer, or fall
All you have to do is call
And I'll be there, hey, hey, yeah.
You've got a friend.
Tapestry [1971]. You've Got a Friend

Curtis Mayfield
1942–1999

14 Some people think we don't have the right
To say it's my country
Before they give in they'd rather fuss and fight
Than say it's my country
I've paid three hundred years or more

Of slave-driving sweat and welts on my back
This is my country   *This Is My Country [1968]*

Lou [Lewis Allan] Reed
1942–

1 And what costume shall the poor girl wear
To all tomorrow's parties
A hand-me-down dress from who knows where
To all tomorrow's parties
      All Tomorrow's Parties [1966]. Recorded by
      The Velvet Underground, sung by Nico

2 When I'm rushing on my run
And I feel just like Jesus's son
      Heroin [1967]. Recorded by The Velvet
      Underground

Martin Rees
1942–

3   [On extraterrestrial life:] Absence of evidence is
not evidence of absence.
      Quoted in Project Cyclops, edited by B. M.
      OLIVER and J. BILLINGHAM [1973]

Mario Savio
1942–1996

4   There is a time when the operation of the machine
becomes so odious, makes you so sick at heart, that
you can't take part; you can't even passively take part.
And you've got to put your bodies upon the gears
and upon the wheels, upon the levers, upon all the
apparatus, and you've got to make it stop.
      Speech in Sproul Plaza [December 2, 1964]

Martin Scorsese
1942–
and
Mardik Martin
1937–

5   You don't make up for your sins in church, you do
it in the streets. You do it at home. The rest is bullshit
and you know it.   *Mean Streets (screenplay) [1973]*

Paul Simon
1942–

6 Hello darkness my old friend
I've come to talk with you again.
      The Sounds of Silence [1964]

7 The words of the prophets
Are written on the subway walls
And tenement halls
And whispered in the sounds of silence.
      The Sounds of Silence

8 Where have you gone, Joe DiMaggio?
A nation turns its lonely eyes to you.
      Mrs. Robinson [1966]

9 A man hears what he wants to hear and disregards
the rest.
      The Boxer [1968]

10 Like a bridge over troubled water
I will lay me down.
      Bridge over Troubled Water [1969]

11 When I look back on all the crap I learned in high
      school
It's a wonder I can think at all.
      Kodachrome [1973]

12 You know the nearer your destination, the more
you're slip slidin' away.
      Slip Slidin' Away [1977]

13 If you'll be my bodyguard
I can be your long lost pal,
I can call you Betty
and, Betty, when you call me
You can call me Al.
      You Can Call Me Al [1985]

14 The Mississippi Delta was shining
like a National guitar.
      Graceland [1986]

Brendan V. Sullivan, Jr.
1942–

15   I'm not a potted plant. I'm here as the lawyer.
That's my job.
      Response to Senator Daniel Inouye
      during Senate hearings on Irangate
      [July 9, 1987]

Brian Wilson
1942–

16 Where did your long hair go?
Where is the girl I used to know?
How could you lose that happy glow?
Oh Caroline, no.
      Pet Sounds [1966]. Caroline, No. Recorded
      by The Beach Boys

Brian Wilson
1942–
and
Mike Love
1941–

1 Well, she got her daddy's car
And she cruised through the hamburger stand now
Seems she forgot all about the library
Like she told her old man now
And with the radio blasting goes cruising
Just as fast as she can now
And she'll have fun, fun, fun
Till her daddy takes the T-Bird away
Fun, Fun, Fun [1964]. Recorded by the Beach Boys

Tammy Wynette
[Virginia Wynette Pugh]
1942–1998
and
Billy Sherrill
1936–

2 Stand by your man
And tell the world you love him,
Keep giving all the love you can.
Stand by Your Man[1] *[1968]*

3 But if you love him you'll forgive him
Even though he's hard to understand.
And if you love him, oh be proud of him
'Cause after all he's just a man.
Stand by Your Man

Mars Bonfire [Dennis Edmonton]
1943–

4 Like a true nature's child
We were born, born to be wild
We can climb so high
I never wanna die
Born to Be Wild [1968]. Recorded by Steppenwolf

H. Rap [Hubert Gerold] Brown
1943–

5   Violence is as American as cherry pie.
Press conference [July 27, 1967]

---

[1]In 1992 her [Wynette's] name and best-known song entered the
Presidential campaign when Hillary Rodham Clinton, stressing that
her defense of her husband against charges of adultery was more
than routine, said in a "60 Minutes" interview: "I'm not sitting
here like some little woman standing by my man like Tammy
Wynette." — *New York Times* [April 8, 1998]

David Cronenberg
1943–
and
Charles Edward Pogue
1950–

6   Be afraid. Be very afraid.
The Fly (screenplay)[2] *[1986]*

R[obert] Crumb
1943–

7   Keep on truckin'.
Slogan of cartoon character

Nikki Giovanni
1943–

8 show me someone not full of herself and i'll show you
   a hungry person
Poem for a Lady Whose Voice I Like [1970],
last line

9   I really hope no white person ever has cause
to write about me
because they never understand
Black love is Black wealth and they'll
probably talk about my hard childhood
and never understand that
all the while I was quite happy.
Nikki-Rosa [1970]

Louise Glück
1943–

10 Fish bones walked the waves off Hatteras
And there were other signs
That Death wooed us, by water, wooed us
By land:
Firstborn [1968]. Cottonmouth Country

George Harrison
1943–2001

11 If you drive a car, I will the tax the street,
If you try to sit, I will tax your seat,
If you get too cold, I will tax the heat,
If you take a walk, I will tax your feet.
Taxman [1966]

---

[2]Based on a short story by GEORGE LANGELAAN.

Mick [Michael Philip] Jagger
1943–

and

Keith Richards
1943–

1 I can't get no satisfaction . . .
I can't get no girl reaction.
(I Can't Get No) Satisfaction [1965].
Recorded by The Rolling Stones

2 Well I'm sitting here thinkin' just how sharp I am
I'm an under assistant West Coast promo man
The Under Assistant West Coast Promotion
Man [1965]

3 And though she's not really ill
There's a little yellow pill
She goes running for the shelter
Of a mother's little helper
And it helps her on her way, gets her through her
busy day.
Mother's Little Helper [1966]

4 All of my friends from school grew up and settled
down
And they mortgaged off their lives
One thing's not said too much, but I think it's true
They just get married 'cause there's nothing else
to do
Sitting on a Fence [1967]

5 Please allow me to introduce myself,
I'm a man of wealth and taste.
I've been around for long, long years,
Stolen many a man's soul and faith.
Sympathy for the Devil [1968]

6 Just as every cop is a criminal and all the sinners
saints.
Sympathy for the Devil

7 Well, we all need someone we can lean on,
And if you want it, well, you can lean on me.
Let It Bleed [1969]

8 You can't always get what you want
But if you try sometimes
You just might find
You get what you need.
You Can't Always Get What You Want
[1969]

Janis Joplin
1943–1970

9 Down on me, down on me,
Looks like everybody in this whole round world
Is down on me.   *Down on Me [1967]*

10 Lord, won't you buy me a Mercedes-Benz,
My friends all drive Porsches,
I must make amends.
Mercedes-Benz [1970]

John [Forbes] Kerry
1943–

11   How do you ask a man to be the last man to die in
Vietnam? How do you ask a man to be the last man to
die for a mistake?
Statement to Senate Foreign Relations
Committee [April 22, 1971]

12   [On a vote to fund the Iraq war:] I actually did
vote for the $87 billion, before I voted against it.
Remark [March 16, 2004]

Phillip Lopate
1943–

13   Over the years I have developed a distaste for the
spectacle of *joie de vivre*, the knack of knowing how
to live. Not that I disapprove of all hearty enjoyment
of life. A flushed sense of happiness can overtake a
person anywhere, and one is no more to blame for
it than the Asiatic flu or a sudden benevolent change
in the weather (which is often joy's immediate cause).
No, what rankles me is the stylization of this private
condition into a bullying social ritual.
Against Joie de Vivre [1987]

Leonard Matlovich
1943–1988

14   When I was in the military, they gave me a
medal for killing two men and a discharge for loving
one.

Inscription on tombstone

Christine McVie
[Christine Anne Perfect]
1943–

15 Don't stop thinking about tomorrow,
Don't stop, it'll soon be here.
It'll be better than before,
Yesterday's gone, yesterday's gone.
Rumours [1976]. Don't Stop.[1] Recorded by
Fleetwood Mac

---

[1]Theme song of Bill Clinton's 1992 presidential campaign.

Joni Mitchell
1943–

1 They paved paradise
And put up a parking lot.   *Big Yellow Taxi [1969]*

2 We are stardust,
We are golden,
And we've got to get ourselves
Back to the garden.   *Woodstock [1969]*

3 By the time we got to Woodstock we were half a
million strong
And everywhere there was song and celebration
And I dreamed I saw the bombers riding shotgun in
the sky
And they were turning into butterflies above our
nation   *Woodstock*

Jim Morrison
1943–1971

4 Come on, baby, light my fire
Try to set the night on fire.
Light My Fire [1967]. Recorded by The Doors

5 Desperately in need of some stranger's hand
In a desperate land
The End [1967]. Recorded by The Doors

6 Lost in a Roman wilderness of pain
And all the children are insane   *The End*

7 Cancel my subscription to the resurrection,
Send my credentials to the house of detention.
When the Music's Over [1967].
Recorded by The Doors

8 I am the Lizard King
I can do anything.
The Celebration of the Lizard [1968].
Recorded by The Doors

Robbie Robertson
[Jaime Royal Klegerman]
1943–

9 I pulled into Nazareth, was feelin' 'bout half-past
dead
I just need some place where I can lay my head.
"Hey, mister, can you tell where a man might find a
bed?"
He just grinned and shook my hand; "No" was all he
said.
Music from Big Pink [1968].
The Weight. Recorded by The Band

10 Up on Cripple Creek she sends me
If I spring a leak she mends me

I don't have to speak, she defends me
A drunkard's dream if I ever did see one
The Band [1969]. Up on Cripple Creek.
Recorded by The Band

Marilynne Robinson
1943–

11   Love is holy because it is like grace — the worthiness of its object is never really what matters.
Gilead [2004]

Wallace Shawn
1943–

12   It's the same with any kind of *prophecy* or sign or an
omen, because if you believe in omens, then that
means the universe — I mean, I don't even know how
to begin to describe this. That means that the future is
somehow sending messages backwards to the present!
Which means that the future must *exist* in some sense
already in order to be able to send these messages.
And it also means that things in the universe are there
for a purpose: to give us messages. Whereas I think
that things in the universe are just *there*. I mean, they
don't *mean* anything. I mean, you know, if the turtle's
egg falls out of the tree and splashes on the paving
stones, it's just because that turtle was clumsy, by accident. And to decide whether to send my ships off to
war on the basis of that seems a big mistake to me.
My Dinner with André (screenplay) [1981]

Roger Waters
1943–

13 We don't need no education
We don't need no thought control
No dark sarcasm in the classroom
Teacher leave them kids alone
Hey! Teacher! Leave them kids alone
All in all it's just another brick in the wall.
All in all you're just another brick in the wall.
The Wall [1979]. Another Brick in the Wall
(Part 2). Recorded by Pink Floyd

William Broyles, Jr.
1944–
and
Al Reinert

14   Failure is not an option.
Apollo 13 (screenplay) [1995]

James Carville
1944–

1 It's the economy, stupid.
Political campaign motto [1992]

Ray Davies
1944–

2 The tax man's taken all my dough
And left me in my stately home,
Lazing on a sunny afternoon.
Sunny Afternoon [1966]. Recorded by The Kinks

3 Girls will be boys and boys will be girls
It's a mixed up, muddled up, shook up world except for Lola.
Lola [1970]. Recorded by The Kinks

Buchi Emecheta
1944–

4 If you don't have children the longing for them will kill you, and if you do, the worrying over them will kill you. *The Joys of Motherhood [1979]*

Rudolph W[illiam] Giuliani
1944–

5 The number of casualties will be more than any of us can bear ultimately.
Press conference [September 11, 2001]

6 Show your confidence. Show you're not afraid. Go to restaurants. Go shopping.
Press conference [September 12, 2001]

Bill Griffith
1944–

7 Are we having fun yet?
Zippy the Pinhead (comic strip) [1979]

Rem Koolhaas
1944–

8 New York is a city that will be replaced by another city. *Delirious New York [1978]*

George [W.] Lucas [Jr.]
1944–

9 Evil empire *Star Wars (screenplay) [1977]*

10 May the Force be with you!
Star Wars (screenplay), spoken by Alec Guinness

11 Rebel spaceships, striking from a hidden base, have won their first victory against the evil Galactic Empire. *Star Wars (title crawl)*

12 The Empire Strikes Back *Title of movie [1980]*

Daniel Pennac [Daniel Pennacchioni]
1944–

13 The Reader's Bill of Rights: The right to not read...to skip pages...to not finish...to reread... to read anything...to escapism...to read anywhere...to browse...to read out loud...to not defend your tastes. *The Rights of the Reader[1] [2006]*

Tim Rice
1944–

14 Don't cry for me, Argentina.
Evita[2] [1976]

Richard Rodriguez
1944–

15 The child reminds the adult: to seek intimate sounds is to seek the company of intimates. I do not expect to hear those sounds in public. I would dishonor those I have loved, and those I love now, to claim anything else. I would dishonor our intimacy by holding on to a particular language and calling it my family language. Intimacy cannot be trapped within words; it passes through words. It passes.
Aria: A Memoir of a Bilingual Childhood [1980]

W[infried] G[eorg] Sebald
1944–2001

16 From the earliest times, human civilization has been no more than a strange luminescence growing more intense by the hour, of which no one can say when it will begin to wane and when it will fade away. For the time being, our cities still shine through the night, and the fires still spread.
The Rings of Saturn[3] [1998]

---

[1]Originally published in French as *Comme un Roman* [1992]. Translated by SARAH ADAMS.

[2]Music by ANDREW LLOYD WEBBER.

[3]Originally published in German as *Die Ringe des Saturn* [1995]. Translated by MICHAEL HULSE.

1   Perhaps we all lose our sense of reality to the precise degree to which we are engrossed in our own work, and perhaps that is why we see in the increasing complexity of our mental constructs a means for greater understanding, even while intuitively we know that we shall never be able to fathom the imponderables that govern our course through life.
The Rings of Saturn [1998]

2   Whenever one is imagining a bright future, the next disaster is just around the corner.
The Rings of Saturn

3   We take almost all the decisive steps in our lives as a result of slight inner adjustments of which we are barely conscious.
Austerlitz [2001]

4   If you look at a dog following the advice of his nose, he traverses a patch of land in a completely unplottable manner. And he invariably finds what he's looking for.
Interview with Joseph Cuomo, Queens College, New York [March 13, 2001]

Vernor Vinge
1944–

5   We are on the edge of change comparable to the rise of human life on Earth. The precise cause of this change is the imminent creation by technology of entities with greater than human intelligence.
The Coming Technological Singularity: How to Survive in the Post-Human Era [1993]

Alice Walker
1944–

6   Nobody's as powerful as we make them out to be.
The Third Life of Grange Copeland [1970]

7   Our mothers and grandmothers have, more often than not anonymously, handed on the creative spark, the seed of the flower they themselves never hoped to see.
In Search of Our Mothers' Gardens [1974]

8   Any God I ever felt in church I brought in with me.
The Color Purple [1982]

9   I think it pisses God off if you walk by the color purple in a field somewhere and don't notice it.
The Color Purple

10   I'm pore, I'm black, I may be ugly and can't cook, a voice say to everything listening. But I'm here.
The Color Purple

David Chase
1945–

11   Cunnilingus and psychiatry brought us to this.
The Sopranos [1999], season 1, ep. 13

Annie Dillard
1945–

12   I had been my whole life a bell, and never knew it until at that moment I was lifted and struck.
Pilgrim at Tinker Creek [1974], ch. 2

John Fogerty
1945–

13 Some folks are born made to wave the flag;
Ooh, they're red, white, and blue.
And when the band plays "Hail to the Chief,"
They point the cannon at you.

It ain't me, it ain't me — I ain't no senator's son.
It ain't me, it ain't me — I ain't no fortunate one.
Fortunate Son [1969]. Recorded by Creedence Clearwater Revival

14 Hope you got your things together,
Hope you are quite prepared to die.
Looks like we're in for nasty weather.
One eye is taken for an eye.

Don't go around tonight,
Well it's bound to take your life.
There's a bad moon on the rise.
Bad Moon Rising [1969]. Recorded by Creedence Clearwater Revival

15 Still the rain kept pouring, falling on my ears,
And I wonder, still I wonder, who'll stop the rain.
Who'll Stop the Rain [1970]. Recorded by Creedence Clearwater Revival

Barbara Kruger
1945–

16   I shop therefore I am.
Text on artwork

Greil Marcus
1945–

1   We make the oldest stories new when we succeed, and we are trapped by the old stories when we fail.
Mystery Train [1976]

2   No failure in America, whether of love or money, is ever simple; it is always a kind of betrayal, of a mass of shadowy, shared hopes.
Mystery Train

Bob Marley
1945–1981

3 One good thing about music
When it hits you
You feel no pain.
Trench Town Rock [1971]

4 Slave driver, the table is turn.
Catch a fire so you can get burn.
Catch a Fire [1973]. Slave Driver

5 Every day the bucket a go a well
One day the bottom a go drop out.
Burnin' [1973]. I Shot the Sheriff

6 A hungry mob is an angry mob.
*Natty Dread [1974]. Them Belly Full
(But We Hungry)*

7 And hey Mr. Cop
Ain't got no birth certificate on me now
Natty Dread. Rebel Music (3 O'Clock Roadblock)

8 We're leaving Babylon
We're going to our Father's land.
Movement of Jah People [1977]

Steve Martin
1945–

9   Comedy Is Not Pretty!
Title of album [1979]

J. D. McClatchy
1945–

10 Decades now of looking back at it —
in some old satellite's rearview mirror, say —
has something to show beyond the folds and
    feeders,
the volumes of magma risen into native rock
or the buried flow of old fires cooling
in ocean beds. The damage has been memorized.
Lines on My Face [1997]

Don[ald] McLean
1945–

11 Bye, Bye, Miss American Pie
Drove my Chevy to the levee but the levee was dry
Them good old boys were drinkin'
Whiskey and Rye
Singin' this'll be the day that I die
This'll be the day that I die
American Pie [1971]

Van [George Ivan] Morrison
1945–

12 All the girls walk by dressed up for each other
And the boys do the boogie woogie
On the corner of the street
And the people passing by just stare in wild wonder
And the inside jukebox roars just like thunder
Tupelo Honey [1971]. Wild Night

Carly Simon
1945–

13 You're so vain, you probably think this song is about you.   *You're So Vain [1972]*

Stephen Stills
1945–

14 Paranoia strikes deep,
Into your life it will creep.
It starts when you're always afraid.
Step out of line, the men come and take you away.
*For What It's Worth [1966].
Recorded by Buffalo Springfield*

Pete [Peter] Townshend
1945–

15 Hope I die before I get old.
This is my generation.   *My Generation [1965]*

16 See me, feel me
Touch me, heal me.
Tommy [1969]. Go to the Mirror

17 It's only teenage wasteland.
Who's Next [1971]. Baba O'Riley

18 I'll tip my hat to the new constitution
Take a bow for the new revolution . . .
And I'll get on my knees and pray
We don't get fooled again.
Who's Next. Won't Get Fooled Again

1 Meet the new boss
Same as the old boss.
Who's Next. Won't Get Fooled Again

Wim [Ernst Wilhelm] Wenders
1945–

2 The Yanks have colonized our subconscious.
Kings of the Road (screenplay) [1976]

August Wilson, Jr.
1945–2005

3 As long as the colored man look to white folks to put the crown on what he say...as long as he looks to white folks for approval...then he ain't never gonna find out who he is and what he's about.[1]
Ma Rainey's Black Bottom [1984], act 1

4 It got so I used all of myself up in the making of that song. Then I was the song in search of itself. That song rattling in my throat and I'm looking for it.
Joe Turner's Come and Gone [1988], act II, sc. 2

Neil Young
1945–

5 Tin soldiers and Nixon coming,
We're finally on our own.
This summer I hear the drumming,
Four dead in Ohio.   *Ohio [1970]*

6 Every junkie's like a setting sun.
The Needle and the Damage Done [1972]

7 It's better to burn out than to fade away.
My My, Hey Hey (Out of the Blue) [1979]

Adam Zagajewski
1945–

8 Try to praise the mutilated world.
Without End: New and Selected Poems [2002].Try To Praise the Mutilated World[2]

Julian Barnes
1946–

9 Why does the writing make us chase the writer? Why can't we leave well enough alone? Why aren't the books enough?   *Flaubert's Parrot [1984], ch. 1*

---

[1] Ellipses are in the original text.
[2] Translated by CLARE CAVANAGH.

Steve [Stephen Bantu] Biko
1946–1977

10 The most potent weapon in the hands of the oppressor is the mind of the oppressed.
Statement as witness [May 3, 1976][3]

11 The basic tenet of black consciousness is that the black man must reject all value systems that seek to make him a foreigner in the country of his birth and reduce his basic human dignity.
Statement as witness [May 3, 1976][3]

George W[alker] Bush
1946–

12 This is an impressive crowd — the haves and the have-mores. Some people call you the elite; I call you my base.
Alfred E. Smith Memorial Dinner [October 19, 2000]

13 Our nation is chosen by God and commissioned by history to be a model to the world of justice.
Address to joint session of Congress [September 20, 2001]

14 States like these[4]...constitute an axis of evil, arming to threaten the peace of the world.
State of the Union address [2002]

15 There are some who feel like — that if they attack us — that we may decide to leave prematurely.... My answer is, bring 'em on.
Press conference [July 2, 2003]

16 The best way to get the news is from objective sources, and the most objective sources I have are people on my staff who tell me what's happening in the world.
Interview with Brit Hume, FOX News [September 22, 2003]

17 I'm the decider, and I decide what is best.
To reporters, defending Secretary of Defense Donald Rumsfeld [April 18, 2006]

Bill [William Jefferson] Clinton
1946–

18 I'll be with you until the last dog dies.
Primary campaign speech, Dover, New Hampshire [February 12, 1992]

---

[3] From *Black Consciousness in South Africa* [1979], edited by MILLARD ARNOLD [1946–   ].
[4] Iraq, Iran, and North Korea.

1 I feel your pain.
Remark at a primary campaign rally
[March 26, 1992]

2 I experimented with marijuana a time or two. And I didn't like it, and didn't inhale, and never tried it again. *Television interview [March 29, 1992]*

3 I do not believe that the politics of personal destruction is what the American people are interested in. *News conference [March 8, 1994]*

4 The era of big government is over.
State of the Union address [January 23, 1996]

5 I am going to say this again: I did not have sexual relations with that woman, Miss Lewinsky.
News conference [January 26, 1998]

6 It depends on what the meaning of the word "is" is. If the — if he — if "is" means is and never has been, that is not — that is one thing. If it means there is none, that was a completely true statement.
Grand jury testimony [August 17, 1998]

Andrea [Rita] Dworkin
1946–2005

7 Women do not believe that men believe what pornography says about women. But they do. From the worst to the best of them, they do.
Pornography [1981]

Gretel Ehrlich
1946–

8 We Americans are great on fillers, as if what we have, what we are, is not enough. . . . We have only to look at the houses we build to see how we build *against* space, the way we drink against pain and loneliness. We fill up space as if it were a pie shell, with things whose opacity further obstructs our ability to see what is already there.
The Solace of Open Spaces [1985]

Sally Field
1946–

9 You like me, right now, you like me!
Accepting the Academy Award for Best
Actress for Places in the Heart [1985]

Adam Michnik
1946–

10 Impotence in the face of armed evil is probably the worst of human humiliations. When six hulks pin you to the ground, you are helpless. But you do not want to give up your natural right to dignity: you are not going to reach any agreements with the ruffians, you are not going to make any commitments. . . . Your ordinary instinct for self-preservation and your basic sense of human dignity will make you say NO.
Letters from Prison [1985]. Why You Are
Not Signing . . . : A Letter from Białołęka
Internment Camp 1982

Tim O'Brien
1946–

11 A true war story is never moral. It does not instruct, nor encourage virtue, nor suggest models of proper human behavior, nor restrain men from doing the things men have always done. If a story seems moral, do not believe it. If at the end of a war story you feel uplifted, or if you feel that some small bit of rectitude has been salvaged from the larger waste, then you have been made the victim of a very old and terrible lie.
The Things They Carried [1990]

Paul Schrader
1946–

12 Someday a real rain will come and wash all this scum off the streets.
Taxi Driver (screenplay) [1976],
spoken by Robert DeNiro

13 You talkin' to me? You talkin' to me? You talkin' to *me?* Then who the hell else are you talkin' to? You talkin' to me? Well I'm the only one here.
Taxi Driver (screenplay), spoken by Robert DeNiro

Patti [Patricia Lee] Smith
1946–

14 Jesus died for somebody's sins but not mine.
Horses [1975]. Gloria[1]

David Allen Stockman
1946–

15 [On reducing the federal government:] Starve the beast.
Catchphrase [early 1980s]

---

[1]Patti Smith's "Gloria" is based on the 1964 song by VAN MORRISON.

Oliver Stone
1946–

1   Greed is good! Greed is right! Greed works!
Greed will save the U.S.A.![1]
> *Wall Street (screenplay) [1987], spoken by*
> *Michael Douglas*

Laurie Anderson
1947–

2 Paradise
Is exactly like
Where you are right now
Only much much
Better.   *Language Is a Virus [1986]*

Paul Auster
1947–

3   No one calls at eight o'clock on a Sunday morning
unless it is to give news that cannot wait. And news
that cannot wait is always bad news.
> *The Invention of Solitude [1982].*
> *Portrait of an Invisible Man*

Hillary Rodham Clinton
1947–

4   I suppose I could have stayed home and baked
cookies and had teas.
> *Press interview on conflict of interest*
> *[March 17, 1992]*

5   Human rights are women's rights and women's
rights are human rights.
> *Speech at UN Fourth World Conference on*
> *Women, Beijing [September 5, 1995]*

6   It Takes a Village   *Title of book [1996]*

7   We've been married for twenty-two years. And I
have learned a long time ago that the only two people
who count in any marriage are the two who are in it.
> *The Today show (television interview)*
> *[January 27, 1998]*

8   The great story . . . is this vast right-wing conspiracy that has been conspiring against my husband
since the day he announced for President.
> *The Today show (television interview)*
> *[January 27, 1998]*

---

[1]Greed is all right. . . . Greed is healthy. You can be greedy and still
feel good about yourself. — IVAN FREDERICK BOESKY [1937–],
commencement address at University of California, Berkeley [May
18, 1986].

Larry David
1947–

9   It's about nothing, everything else is about something; this, it's about nothing.
> *Seinfeld (television series). The Pitch*
> *[September 16, 1992]*

Arlo Guthrie
1947–

10 You can get anything you want at Alice's Restaurant.
> *Alice's Restaurant [1966]*

Don Henley
1947–

Don Felder
1947–

and

Glenn Frey
1948–

11 You can check out anytime you like,
But you can never leave.
> *Hotel California [1976]. Recorded by the Eagles*

Sir Elton John
[Reginald Kenneth Dwight]
1947–

and

Bernie Taupin
1950–

12 They crawled out of the woodwork
And they whispered into your brain.
They set you on a treadmill
And they made you change your name.
And it seems to me you lived your life
Like a candle in the wind.
> *Candle in the Wind (Goodbye Norma Jean)*
> *[1973]*

Jane Kenyon
1947–1995

13 Let it come, as it will, and don't
be afraid. God does not leave us
comfortless, so let evening come.
> *Let Evening Come [1990]*

1 I slept in a bed
in a room with paintings
on the walls, and
planned another day
just like this day.
But one day, I know,
it will be otherwise.   *Otherwise [1993]*

Stephen King
1947–

2 I recognize terror as the finest emotion . . . and so I will try to terrorize the reader. But if I find I cannot terrify him/her, I will try to horrify; and if I find I cannot horrify, I'll go for the gross-out.

Danse Macabre [1981]

David Mamet
1947–

3 Aaronow: Yes. I mean are you actually *talking* about this, or are we just . . .
Moss: No, we're just . . .
Aaronow: We're just "*talking*" about it.
Moss: We're just *speaking* about it. (*Pause.*) As an idea.
Aaronow: As an idea.
Moss: Yes.
Aaronow: We're not actually *talking* about it.

Glengarry Glen Ross (play) [1984]

4 Who ever told you that you could work with *men*?   *Glengarry Glen Ross*

5 Life in the movie business is like the . . . beginning of a new love affair: it's full of surprises, and you're constantly getting fucked.   *Speed-the-Plow [1988]*

6 It's called a confidence game. Why? Because you give me your confidence? No. Because I give you mine.

House of Games (screenplay) [1987],
spoken by Joe Mantegna

7 Always be closing.
Glengarry Glen Ross (screenplay) [1992],
spoken by Alec Baldwin

8 First prize is a Cadillac Eldorado. . . . Second prize is a set of steak knives. Third prize is you're fired.
Glengarry Glen Ross (screenplay),
spoken by Alec Baldwin

Herbert Muschamp
1947–2007

9 [On an architectural design by Santiago Cala-trava:] A city is never more fully human than when

expertise — our own or someone else's — allows us access to ebullience, lightness and delight.
New York Times [March 3, 2004]

P[atrick] J[ake] O'Rourke
1947–

10 Every government is a parliament of whores. The trouble is, in a democracy the whores are us.
Parliament of Whores [1991]

[Ahmed] Salman Rushdie[1]
1947–

11 Most of what matters in our lives takes place in our absence.

Midnight's Children [1981]

12 Where there is no belief, there is no blasphemy.
The Satanic Verses [1988]

13 Literature is the one place in any society where, within the secrecy of our own heads, we can hear voices talking about everything in every possible way.

Is Nothing Sacred? [1990]

Joe Walsh
1947–

Glenn Frey
1948–

and

Don Henley
1947–

14 Life in the fast lane
Surely make you lose your mind.
Life in the Fast Lane [1976].
Recorded by the Eagles

Lester [Leslie Conway] Bangs
1948–1982

15 The first mistake of Art is to assume that it's serious.

James Taylor Marked for Death [1971]

---

[1]See Ruholla Khomeini, 725:14.

Charles Philip Arthur George, Prince of Wales
1948–

1   Give this much to the Luftwaffe. When it knocked down our buildings, it didn't replace them with anything more offensive than rubble. *We did that.*

Speech in London [December 1987]

Jimmy Cliff
1948–

2 As sure as the sun will shine
I'm going to get it, what's mine
And then the harder they come
The harder they fall,
One and all.

The Harder They Come [1972]

Jean-Marie Colombani
1948–

3   We are all Americans[1]

Editorial headline [September 13, 2001]

Nick Drake
1948–1974

4 I saw it written and I saw it say
Pink moon is on its way
And none of you stand so tall
Pink moon's gonna get you all.   *Pink Moon [1972]*

William Gibson
1948–

5   Cyberspace. A consensual hallucination experienced daily by billions of legitimate operators, in every nation, by children being taught mathematical concepts....A graphic representation of data abstracted from the banks of every computer in the human system. Unthinkable complexity.

Neuromancer [1984]

Al [Albert Arnold] Gore, Jr.
1948–

6   The global environmental crisis is, as we say in Tennessee, real as rain, and I cannot stand the

thought of leaving my children with a degraded earth and a diminished future.

Earth in the Balance [1992]

7   During my service in the United States Congress, I took the initiative in creating the Internet. I took the initiative in moving forward a whole range of initiatives that have proven to be important to our country's economic growth and environmental protection, improvements in our educational system.[2]

Interview on CNN [March 9, 1999]

8   I am Al Gore; I used to be the next president of the United States of America.

An Inconvenient Truth [2006]

9   Making mistakes in centuries and generations past would have consequences that we could overcome. We don't have that luxury anymore.

An Inconvenient Truth

S[usan] E[loise] Hinton
1948–

10   That Was Then, This Is Now

Title of book [1971]

Leslie Marmon Silko
1948–

11 It's only a matter of time, Indian
you can't sleep with the river forever.

Storyteller [1981]. Indian Song: Survival

James Taylor
1948–

12 I've seen fire and I've seen rain
I've seen sunny days that I thought would never end
I've seen lonely times when I could not find a friend
But I always thought that I'd see you again.

Sweet Baby James [1970]. Fire and Rain

Clarence Thomas
1948–

13   This is a circus. It's a national disgrace. And from my standpoint, as a black American, as far as I am concerned, it is a high-tech lynching for uppity blacks who in any way deign to think for themselves, to do for themselves, to have different ideas, and it is a message that unless you kowtow to an older order, this is

---

[1] *Nous sommes tous Américains.* This was the headline in *Le Monde* two days after the September 11, 2001, terrorist attacks on the World Trade Center in New York.

[2] Often mischaracterized as a claim to have "invented the Internet."

what will happen to you, you will be lynched, destroyed, caricatured by a committee of the U.S. Senate, rather than hung from a tree.

Supreme Court confirmation hearings [1991]

Martin Amis
1949–

1   My head is a city, and various pains have taken up residence in various parts of my face. A gum-and-bone ache has launched a cooperative on my upper west side. Across the park, neuralgia has rented a duplex in my fashionable east seventies. Downtown, my chin throbs with lofts of jaw-loss. As for my brain, my hundreds, it's Harlem up there, expanding in the summer fires. *Money [1985]*

2   Never trust a poet who can drive. Never trust a poet at the wheel. If he *can* drive, distrust the poems. *The Information [1995]*

Richard Hell [Richard Meyers]
1949–

3 I belong to the blank generation
I can take it or leave it each time
Blank Generation [1977]

Christopher Hitchens
1949–2011

4   The secular state is the guarantee of religious pluralism. This apparent paradox, again, is the simplest and most elegant of political truths.   *Ireland [1998]*

5   Beware the irrational, however seductive. Shun the 'transcendent' and all who invite you to subordinate or annihilate yourself. Distrust compassion; prefer dignity for yourself and others. Don't be afraid to be thought arrogant or selfish. Picture all experts as if they were mammals. Never be a spectator of unfairness or stupidity. Seek out argument and disputation for their own sake; the grave will supply plenty of time for silence. Suspect your own motives, and all excuses. Do not live for others any more than you would expect others to live for you.
Letters to a Young Contrarian [2001]

6   Human decency is not derived from religion. It precedes it. *God Is Not Great [2007]*

7   What can be asserted without evidence can also be dismissed without evidence.[1]   *God Is Not Great*

---

[1]This quotation, often taken as original, is actually a translation of the Latin phrase *Quod gratis asseritur, gratis negatur.*

Trevor Horn
1949–

8   Video Killed the Radio Star[2]
Title of song [1979]. Recorded by The Buggles

Lawrence Kasdan
1949–

and

George Lucas
1944–

9   You weak-minded fool! He's using an old Jedi mind-trick.
Return of the Jedi [1983], spoken by Larry Ward as Jabba the Hutt

Ed King
1949–

Ronnie Van Zant
1948–1977

and

Gary Rossington
1951–

10 Sweet home Alabama
Where skies are so blue
Sweet home Alabama
Lord, I'm coming home to you.
Second Helping [1974]. Sweet Home Alabama. Recorded by Lynyrd Skynyrd

August Kleinzahler
1949–

11 But when Johnny goes out

on Johnny's own Time
he's out there doing the only one thing:
he's burning off all the stillborn Johnnys
that hatched in his head in the night.
And that John, he won't ever come home,
not until he's right.
Earthquake Weather [1989]. On Johnny's Time

12 Cities each have a kind of light,
a color even,
or set of undertones
determined by the river or hills
as well as by the stone

---

[2]Music by BRUCE WOOLLEY, GEOFF DOWNES, and TREVOR HORN.

of their countless buildings.
I cannot yet recall what city this is I'm in.
It must be close to dawn.
> *The Strange Hours Travelers Keep [2003].*
> *On Waking in a Room and Not Knowing*
> *Where One Is*

Gil Scott-Heron
1949–2011

1 You will not be able to stay home, brother.
You will not be able to plug in, turn on, and
    cop out.
You will not be able to lose yourself on scag
and skip out for beer during commercial breaks.
The revolution will not be televised.
> *The Revolution Will Not Be Televised [1970]*

Bruce Springsteen
1949–

2 We gotta get out while we're young
'Cause tramps like us, baby, we were born
    to run.
> *Born to Run [1975]*

3 Is a dream a lie if it don't come true
Or is it something worse?
> *The River [1980]*

4 We made a promise we swore we'd always remember
No retreat, baby, no surrender.
> *No Surrender [1984]*

5 Down in the shadow of the penitentiary,
Out by the gas fires of the refinery;
I'm ten years burning down the road,
Nowhere to run, ain't got nowhere to go.
> *Born in the U.S.A. [1984]*

Tom Waits
1949–

6 And the things you can't remember
Tell the things you can't forget
That history puts a saint in every dream.
> *Rain Dogs [1985]. Time*

Eliot Weinberger
1949–

7   Poetry is that which is worth translating. The
poem dies when it has no place to go.
> *Notes on Poetry [1988]. Translating*

Walter Becker
1950–
and
Donald Fagen
1948–

8 I'll learn to work the saxophone
I'll play just what I feel
Drink Scotch whiskey all night long
And die behind the wheel
> *Aja [1977]. Deacon Blues. Recorded*
> *by Steely Dan*

Anne Carson
1950–

9   Infants begin to see by noticing the edges of
things. How do they know an edge is an edge? By
passionately wanting it not to be. The experience of
eros as lack alerts a person to the boundaries of himself, of other people, of things in general. It is the
edge separating my tongue from the taste for which
it longs that teaches me what an edge is.
> *Eros the Bittersweet [1986]*

10   As lover you reach forward to a point in time
called "then" when you will bite into the long-
desired apple. Meanwhile you are aware that as soon
as "then" supervenes upon "now," the bittersweet
moment, which is your desire, will be gone. You
cannot want that, and yet you do.
> *Eros the Bittersweet*

11 SPIRIT RULES SECRETLY ALONE THE BODY
    ACHIEVES NOTHING
is something you know
instinctively at fourteen and can still remember even
    with hell in your head
at sixteen.   *Autobiography of Red [1998]*

Paul Goldberger
1950–

12   [On the World Trade Center buildings in New
York:] So utterly banal as to be unworthy of the headquarters of a bank in Omaha.
> *The City Observed [1979]*

Jenny Holzer
1950–

13   Protect Me from What I Want
> *Title of installation, Times Square*
> *[1985–1986]*

1   Abuse of power comes as no surprise.
Text on artwork

Fran Lebowitz
1950–

2   Remember that as a teenager you are at the last stage in your life when you will be happy to hear that the phone is for you.
Social Studies [1981]

3   If you're going to America, bring your own food.
Social Studies

Melissa Mathison
1950–

4   E.T. phone home.
E.T.: The Extra Terrestrial (screenplay) [1982]

Peggy [Margaret Ellen] Noonan
1950–

5   Beware the politically obsessed. They are often bright and interesting, but they have something missing in their natures; there is a hole, an empty place, and they use politics to fill it up. It leaves them somehow misshapen.
What I Saw at the Revolution [1990]

Wendy Wasserstein
1950–2006

6   No matter how lonely you get or how many birth announcements you receive, the trick is not to get frightened. There's nothing wrong with being alone.
Isn't It Romantic [1983]

Stevie Wonder [Stevland Hardaway Judkins, later Morris]
1950–

7 You've killed all our leaders,
  I don't even have to do nothing to you,
  You'll cause your own country to fall.
Talking Book [1972]. Big Brother

8 Thirteen month old baby broke the lookin' glass,
  Seven years of bad luck, good things in
     your past.

When you believe in things that you don't
  understand
Then you suffer,
Superstition ain't the way.
Talking Book. Superstition

Sven Birkerts
1951–

9   This "domination by the author" has been, at least until now, the *point* of writing and reading. The author masters the resources of language to create a vision that will engage and in some way overpower the reader; the reader goes to the work to be subjected to the creative will of another.
The Gutenberg Elegies: The Fate of Reading in an Electronic Age [1994]

Eric Holder
1951–

10   Though this nation has proudly thought of itself as an ethnic melting pot, in things racial we have always been and continue to be, in too many ways, essentially a nation of cowards. Though race related issues continue to occupy a significant portion of our political discussion, and though there remain many unresolved racial issues in this nation, we, average Americans, simply do not talk enough with each other about race.
Remarks at the Department of Justice African American History Month Program [February 18, 2009]

Michael Kinsley
1951–

11   A gaffe is when a politician tells the truth.
The Guardian [January 14, 1992]

Joey Ramone [Jeffry Ross Hyman]
1951–2001

12 Twenty-twenty-twenty-four hours to go
  I wanna be sedated
  Nothing to do, nowhere to go
  I wanna be sedated
Road to Ruin [1978]. I Wanna Be Sedated. Recorded by The Ramones

Jonathan Richman
1951–

1 I'm in love with the modern world
Massachusetts when it's late at night
And the neon when it's cold outside
I've got the radio on
*Roadrunner [1972]. Recorded by
The Modern Lovers*

Fred[erick] Schneider
1951–

[Julian] Keith Strickland
1953–

Ricky Wilson
1953–1985

Cindy [Cynthia Leigh] Wilson
1957–

and

Kate [Catherine Elizabeth] Pierson
1948–

2 You're living in your own private Idaho.
*Wild Planet [1980]. Private Idaho.
Recorded by The B-52s*

Sting [Gordon Matthew Sumner]
1951–

3 We are spirits in the material world.
*Ghost in the Machine [1981]. Spirits in the
Material World. Recorded by The Police*

Robert Zemeckis
1951–

and

[Michael Robert] Bob Gale
1951–

4   You've got a real attitude problem, McFly. You're a slacker!

Back to the Future [1985]

Douglas Adams
1952–2001

5   In the beginning the Universe was created. This has made a lot of people very angry and been widely regarded as a bad move.
The Hitchhiker's Guide to the Galaxy, radio serial [1978]

Jean-Dominique Bauby
1952–1997

6   My diving bell becomes less oppressive, and my mind takes flight like a butterfly. There is so much to do. You can wander off in space or in time, set out for Tierra del Fuego or for King Midas's court. You can visit the woman you love, slide down beside her and stroke her still-sleeping face.
The Diving Bell and the Butterfly[1] [1997]

David Byrne
1952–

7 Judy's in the bedroom, inventing situations.
Bob is on the street today, scouting up locations.
They've enlisted all their family.
They've enlisted all their friends.
It helped save their relationship,
And made it work again.
More Songs About Buildings and Food [1978]. Found a Job

8 The band in heaven, they play my favorite song
Play it once again
Play it all night long
Fear of Music [1979]. Heaven

9 This ain't no party. This ain't no disco. This ain't no fooling around.
Fear of Music. Life During Wartime

10 And you may find yourself living in a shotgun shack
And you may find yourself in another part of the world
And you may find yourself behind the wheel of a large automobile
And you may find yourself in a beautiful house . . . with a beautiful wife
And you may ask yourself, "Well . . . how did I get here?"
*Remain in Light [1980].
Once in a Lifetime*

[1]Translated by JEREMY LEGGATT.

Rita Dove
1952–

1 You start out with one thing, end
up with another, and nothing's
like it used to be, not even the future.
The Yellow House on the Corner
[1980]. O

2 Every day a wilderness — no
shade in sight. Beulah
patient among knickknacks,
the solarium a rage
of light, a grainstorm
as her gray cloth brings
dark wood to life.   *Museum [1983]. Dusting*

3 If you can't be free, be a mystery.
Grace Notes [1989]. Canary

[Yoshihiro] Francis Fukuyama
1952–

4   What we may be witnessing is not just the end of
the Cold War, or the passing of a particular period
of postwar history, but the end of history as such: that
is, the end point of man's ideological evolution and
the universalization of Western liberal democracy as
the final form of human government.
The End of History? [1989]

Anne Herbert
1952–

5   Practice random kindness and senseless acts of
beauty.
Random Kindness and Senseless Acts of
Beauty [1985]

Orhan Pamuk
1952–

6   There are moments in all our lives when we realize, even as we experience them, that we are living
through events we will never forget, even long afterward.
My Name Is Red[1] *[2001]*

7   The writer who shuts himself up in a room
and first goes on a journey inside himself will, over
the years, discover literature's eternal rule: he must
have the artistry to tell his own stories as if they
were other people's stories, and to tell other

people's stories as if they were his own, for this is
what literature is.
Nobel Lecture [2006]

Vladimir Putin
1952–

8   The collapse of the Soviet Union was the greatest
geopolitical catastrophe of the century.
Address to the Russian Parliament
[April 25, 2005]

Joe Strummer
[John Graham Mellor]
1952–2002
and
Mick [Michael Lewis] Jones
1955–

9 The ice age is coming, the sun's zooming in
Meltdown expected, the wheat is growing thin
Engines stop running, but I have no fear
'Cause London is drowning and I live by the river
London Calling [1979]. Title song.
Recorded by The Clash

Tony [Anthony Charles Lynton] Blair
1953–

10   She was the People's Princess, and that's how
she will stay...in our hearts and in our memories
forever.
Statement on the death of Diana, Princess of
Wales [August 31, 1997]

Paul Krugman
1953–

11   Supply-side economics...is like one of those
African viruses that, however often it may be eradicated from the settled areas, is always out there in the
bush, waiting for new victims.
Slate [August 16, 1996]

Mary [Theresa] Schmich
1953–

12   Ladies and gentlemen of the class of 'ninety-seven:
Wear sunscreen.
     If I could offer you only one tip for the future,
sunscreen would be it. The long-term benefits of
sunscreen have been proved by scientists, whereas the

[1]Originally published in Turkish, as *Benim Adım Kırmızı* [1998].
English translation by ERDAĞ M. GÖKNAR.

est of my advice has no basis more reliable than my own meandering experience.
> *Mock commencement address.*[1] *Chicago Tribune [June 1, 1997]*

K[wame] Anthony Appiah
1954–

1　There are no races: there is nothing in the world that can do all we ask race to do for us.
> *In My Father's House: Africa in the Philosophy of Culture [1992]*

James Cameron
1954–

2　I'm the king of the world!
> *Titanic (screenplay) [1997], spoken by Leonardo DiCaprio*

Joel Coen
1954–
and
Ethan Coen
1957–

3　Now in Russia they got it mapped out, so that everyone pulls for everyone else: that's the theory, anyway. But what I know about is Texas. And, down here, you're on your own.
> *Blood Simple (screenplay) [1984]*

[Karen] Louise Erdrich
1954–

4　I was in love with the whole world and all that lived in its rainy arms.
> *Love Medicine [1984]. The Good Tears*

James Gleick
1954–

5　Tiny differences in input could quickly become overwhelming differences in output.... In weather, for example, this translates into what is only half-jokingly known as the Butterfly Effect — the notion that a butterfly stirring the air today in Peking can transform storm systems next month in New York.
> *Chaos [1987], Prologue*

---

[1]Erroneously attributed to KURT VONNEGUT, JR.

Patricia Campbell Hearst [Shaw]
1954–

6　Stockholm Syndrome is what it is called when you begin to identify with your captors.... They get nicer every day that they don't kill you.
> *Television interview [2001]*

Annie Lennox
1954–
and
Dave Stewart
1952–

7　Some of them want to use you
Some of them want to get used by you
Some of them want to abuse you
Some of them want to be abused
Sweet dreams are made of this
Who am I to disagree?
> *Sweet Dreams (Are Made of This) [1983]. Recorded by the Eurythmics*

Michael Moore
1954–

8　We live in a time when we have fictitious election results that elect a fictitious president . . . a time where we have a man sending us to war for fictitious reasons.... We are against this war, Mr. Bush. Shame on you, Mr. Bush.
> *Academy Award acceptance speech [2003]*

Adam Phillips
1954–

9　At its best monogamy may be the wish to find someone to die with; at its worst it is a cure for the terrors of aliveness. They are easily confused.
> *Monogamy [1996]*

10　A couple is a conspiracy in search of a crime. Sex is often the closest they can get.　*Monogamy*

Condoleezza Rice
1954–

11　The problem here is that there will always be some uncertainty about how quickly [Saddam Hussein] can acquire nuclear weapons. But we don't want the smoking gun to be a mushroom cloud.
> *Interview with CNN [September 8, 2002]*

Luc Sante
1954–

1 New York's ghosts are the unresting souls of the poor, the marginal, the dispossessed, the depraved, the defective, the recalcitrant. They are the guardian spirits of the urban wilderness in which they lived and died.

Low Life: Lures and Snares of Old New York [1991]. Preface

2 Every human being is an archeological site.

The Factory of Facts [1998]

3 Not very long ago, the whole world smoked, no room was truly furnished unless it contained an ashtray, and all of waking life was measured out in cigarettes.

Our Friend the Cigarette [2004]

Jerry [Jerome] Seinfeld
1954–

4 Everybody lies about sex. People lie during sex. If it weren't for lies, there'd be no sex.

New York Times [December 18, 1998]

Sonia Sotomayor
1954–

5 Justice O'Connor has often been cited as saying that a wise old man and wise old woman will reach the same conclusion in deciding cases.... I would hope that a wise Latina woman with the richness of her experiences would more often than not reach a better conclusion than a white male who hasn't lived that life.

Speech at University of California, Berkeley, School of Law [October 26, 2001]

Rick Warren
1954–

6 The Purpose Driven Life

Title of book [2002]

7 It's not about you.

The Purpose Driven Life, opening sentence

Bill Gates [William Henry Gates III]
1955–

8 Success is a lousy teacher. It seduces smart people into thinking they can't lose.

The Road Ahead [1995]

John Gilmore
1955–

9 The Net interprets censorship as damage and routes around it.

Quoted in TIME [December 6, 1993]

Steve Jobs
1955–2011

10 It's more fun to be a pirate than to join the navy.

Quoted in JOHN SCULLEY and JOHN A. BYRNE, Odyssey: Pepsi to Apple [1987]

11 That's been one of my mantras — focus and simplicity. Simple can be harder than complex: You have to work hard to get your thinking clean to make it simple. But it's worth it in the end because once you get there, you can move mountains.

Interview in Businessweek [May 1998]

12 Your time is limited, so don't waste it living someone else's life.

Commencement speech at Stanford University [2005]

13 Oh wow. Oh wow. Oh wow.   *Last words [2011]*

John E. Jones III
1955–

14 To be sure, Darwin's theory of evolution is imperfect. However, the fact that a scientific theory cannot yet render an explanation on every point should not be used as a pretext to thrust an untestable alternative hypothesis grounded in religion into the science classroom or to misrepresent well-established scientific propositions.... The breathtaking inanity of the Board's decision is evident when considered against the factual backdrop which has now been fully revealed through this trial.

Ruling against the teaching of intelligent design in Kitzmiller v. Dover [December 20, 2005]

Michael Pollan
1955–

15 "Industrial organic" might sound like an oxymoron, but it is a reality.

Gourmet [September 2002]. Sustaining Vision

16 Eat food. Not too much. Mostly plants.

In Defense of Food [2008]

Eric Schmidt[1]
1955–

1   The Internet is the first thing that humanity has built that humanity doesn't understand, the largest experiment in anarchy that we have ever had.
Speech at Netscape Communications Developers' conference [1996]

Chris Carter
1956–

2   The Truth Is Out There.
The X-Files [1993–2002], tagline

Larry Charles
1956–

3   We're not gay!
Not that there's anything wrong with that.
Seinfeld [1993], The Outing. Spoken by Jason Alexander and Jerry Seinfeld

Mike Godwin
1956–

4   As an online discussion grows longer, the probability of a comparison involving Nazis or Hitler approaches one.   *Godwin's Law [1990]*

Chris Hedges
1956–

5   The rush of battle is often a potent and lethal addiction, for war is a drug.
War Is a Force That Gives Us Meaning [2002]

Tony Kushner
1956–

6   People in a boat, waiting, terrified, while implacable, unsmiling men, irresistibly strong, seize . . . maybe the person next to you, maybe you, and with no warning at all, with time only for a quick intake of air you are pitched into freezing, turbulent water and salt and darkness to drown.
Angels in America, pt. I: Millennium Approaches [1992]

7   There are no angels in America.
Angels in America: Millennium Approaches

8   Lawyers are . . . the High Priests of America.[2]
Angels in America: Perestroika

Peter Mehlman
1956–
and
Jill Franklyn

9   I gotta tell you, I am loving this yada yada thing. I can gloss over my whole life story.
Seinfeld [1997], The Yada Yada.
Spoken by Jason Alexander

Grover Norquist
1956–

10   My goal is to cut government in half in twenty-five years, to get it down to the size where we can drown it in the bathtub.   *The Nation [April 26, 2001]*

11   Bipartisanship is another name for date rape.[3]
Denver Post [May 26, 2003]

Johnny Rotten [John Lydon]
1956–

12 There's no future in England's dreaming
No future, no future, no future for you
No future, no future, no future for me
Never Mind the Bollocks, Here's the Sex Pistols [1977]. God Save the Queen

13   Ever get the feeling you've been cheated?
Parting words at last pre-breakup Sex Pistols concert [January 14, 1978]

Osama [bin Mohammed bin Awad] bin Laden
1957–2011

14   To kill Americans and their allies, both civil and military, is an individual duty of every Muslim who can, in any country where this is possible, until the Aqsa mosque [in Jerusalem] and the Haram mosque [in Mecca] are freed from their grip, and until their armies, shattered and broken-winged, depart from all the lands of Islam, incapable of threatening any Muslim.   *Declaration of jihad [February 1998]*

15   We calculated in advance the number of casualties from the enemy, who would be killed based on the position of the tower. We calculated that the floors

---

[1]Schmidt, later the CEO of Google, was at the time a Sun Microsystems executive.

[2]Ellipses in original.
[3]Sometimes attributed to DICK ARMEY.

that would be hit would be three or four floors. I was the most optimistic of them all. . . . Due to my experience in this field, I was thinking that the fire from the gas in the plane would melt the iron structure of the building and collapse the area where the plane hit and all the floors above it only. This is all that we had hoped for.

> *Transcript of videotape [released by the U.S. government December 2001]*

Cameron Crowe
1957–

1 Show me the money!
> *Jerry Maguire (screenplay) [1996], spoken by Cuba Gooding, Jr.*

2 You had me at hello.
> *Jerry Maguire (screenplay), spoken by Renée Zellweger*

Richard Powers
1957–

3 Each thing is what it is only through everything else.   *The Gold Bug Variations [1991]*

Grandmaster Flash [Joseph Saddler]
1958–

4 Don't push me 'cause I'm close to the edge
I'm tryin' not to lose my head
It's like a jungle sometimes
It makes me wonder how I keep from going under.
> *The Message [1982]*

Michael Jackson
1958–2009
and
Lionel Richie
1950–

5 We are the world,
We are the children,
We are the ones
To make a better day.   *We Are the World [1985]*

Madonna [Louise Ciccone]
1958–

6 I have the same goal I've had since I was a girl. I want to rule the world.
> *Quoted in People [July 27, 1992]*

Rahm Emanuel
1959–

7 You never want a serious crisis to go to waste.
> *Quoted in Wall Street Journal [November 21, 2008]*

Eric Schlosser
1959–

8 The United States now has more prison inmates than full-time farmers.   *Fast Food Nation [2002]*

Ron Suskind
1959–

9 "What you've got is everything — and I mean everything — being run by the political arm. It's the reign of the Mayberry Machiavellis."
> *Quoting John J. Dilulio, Jr., on the administration of President George W. Bush; Esquire [January 1, 2003]. Why Are These Men Laughing?*

10 The aide said that guys like me were "in what we call the reality-based community," which he defined as people who "believe that solutions emerge from your judicious study of discernible reality. . . . That's not the way the world really works anymore. . . . We're an empire now, and when we act, we create our own reality."
> *Interview with an unnamed aide to President George W. Bush (later identified as Karl Rove); New York Times Magazine [October 17, 2004]. Without a Doubt*

Chuck D [Carlton Douglas Ridenhour]
1960–

11 Don't Believe the Hype
> *Title of song [1988]. Recorded by Public Enemy*

12 Rap music is the invisible TV station that black people never had.[1]
> *At Black Expo Seminar on Rap [July 22, 1989]*

Jonathan Larson
1960–1996

13 No Day But Today
> *Rent [1996]. Title of song*

---

[1]Sometimes quoted as: Rap is black America's CNN.

Randy Pausch
1960–2008

1   You get people to help you by telling the truth. Being earnest. I'll take an earnest person over a hip person every day, because hip is short term. Earnest is long term.

The Last Lecture [September 18, 2007]

Michael Stipe
1960–

Peter Buck
1956–

Mike Mills
1958–

Bill Berry
1958–

2   It's the End of the World as We Know It (And I Feel Fine)

Document [1987]. Title of song. Recorded by R.E.M.

3 That's me in the corner
That's me in the spotlight
Losing my religion

Out of Time [1991]. Losing My Religion. Recorded by R.E.M.

Nassim Nicholas Taleb
1960–

4   The more data we have, the more likely we are to drown in it.

Fooled by Randomness [2001]

5   Economic, financial, and political predictors... are quite ashamed to say anything outlandish to their clients — and yet *events, it turns out, are almost always outlandish.*   *The Black Swan [2007]*

Chris Anderson
1961–

6   The Long Tail   *Title of essay [2004]*

Douglas Coupland
1961–

7   Generation X

Title of book [1991]

Diana [Frances Spencer], Princess of Wales
1961–1997

8   There were three of us in this marriage, so it was a bit crowded.

BBC television interview [November 20, 1995]

9   I'd like to be a queen in people's hearts... someone's got to go out there and love people and show it.

BBC television interview [November 20, 1995]

Barack [Hussein] Obama
1961–

10   I don't oppose all wars. And I know that in this crowd today, there is no shortage of patriots, or of patriotism. What I am opposed to is a dumb war. What I am opposed to is a rash war.

Speech to anti-war rally in Chicago [October 2, 2002]

11   Yes, we can![1]

Slogan [2004 Illinois senate campaign and 2008 presidential campaign]

12   The pundits like to slice-and-dice our country into Red States and Blue States; Red States for Republicans, Blue States for Democrats. But I've got news for them, too. We worship an awesome God in the Blue States, and we don't like federal agents poking around our libraries in the Red States. We coach Little League in the Blue States and have gay friends in the Red States. There are patriots who opposed the war in Iraq and patriots who supported it. We are one people, all of us pledging allegiance to the stars and stripes, all of us defending the United States of America.

Keynote address at Democratic National Convention [2004]

13   I stand here today, grateful for the diversity of my heritage, aware that my parents' dreams live on in my precious daughters. I stand here knowing that my story is part of the larger American story, that I owe a debt to all of those who came before me, and that, in no other country on earth, is my story even possible.

Keynote address at Democratic National Convention

14   Hope in the face of difficulty. Hope in the face of uncertainty. The audacity of hope! In the end, that is God's greatest gift to us.

Keynote address at Democratic National Convention

---

[1]Cf. the slogan of United Farm Workers: Sí, se puede (Yes, it can be done).

1   Today, together, we can finish the work that needs to be done, and usher in a new birth of freedom on this Earth.[1]

Speech announcing presidential candidacy, Springfield, Illinois [February 10, 2007]

2   It was a creed written into the founding documents that declared the destiny of a nation. Yes we can. It was whispered by slaves and abolitionists as they blazed a trail towards freedom through the darkest of nights. Yes we can. It was sung by immigrants as they struck out from distant shores and pioneers who pushed westward against an unforgiving wilderness. Yes we can. It was the call of workers who organized; women who reached for the ballot; a President who chose the moon as our new frontier; and a King who took us to the mountaintop and pointed the way to the Promised Land.

Speech after the New Hampshire primary [January 8, 2008]

3   You go into some of these small towns in Pennsylvania, a lot like a lot of small towns in the Midwest, the jobs have been gone now for 25 years and nothing's replaced them. And they fell through the Clinton administration, and the Bush administration, and each successive administration has said that somehow these communities are gonna regenerate and they have not. So it's not surprising then that they get bitter, they cling to guns or religion or antipathy towards people who aren't like them or anti-immigrant sentiment or anti-trade sentiment as a way to explain their frustrations.

At a San Francisco fundraiser [April 6, 2008]

4   We know that our patchwork heritage is a strength, not a weakness. We are a nation of Christians and Muslims, Jews and Hindus — and non-believers. We are shaped by every language and culture, drawn from every end of this Earth; and because we have tasted the bitter swill of civil war and segregation, and emerged from that dark chapter stronger and more united, we cannot help but believe that the old hatreds shall someday pass; that the lines of tribe shall soon dissolve; that as the world grows smaller, our common humanity shall reveal itself; and that America must play its role in ushering in a new era of peace.

Inaugural address [January 20, 2009]

5   Our troops come from every corner of this country — they are black, white, Latino, Asian, and Native American. They are Christian and Hindu, Jewish and Muslim. And, yes, we know that some of them are gay. Starting this year, no American will be forbidden from serving the country they love because of who they love.

State of the Union address [January 25, 2011]

6   Today, at my direction, the United States launched a targeted operation against that compound in Abbottabad, Pakistan. A small team of Americans carried out the operation with extraordinary courage and capability. No Americans were harmed. They took care to avoid civilian casualties. After a firefight, they killed Osama bin Laden and took custody of his body.

Speech [May 2, 2011]

7   The American people did not choose this fight. It came to our shores, and started with the senseless slaughter of our citizens.

Speech [May 2, 2011]

Alexander Payne
1961–

8   I like to think about the life of wine, how it's a living thing. I like to think about what was going on the year the grapes were growing, how the sun was shining, if it rained. I like to think about all the people who tended and picked the grapes. And, if it's an old wine, how many of them must be dead by now.

Sideways (screenplay) [2004], spoken by Virginia Madsen

Chuck [Charles Michael] Palahniuk
1962–

9   The first rule of fight club is you don't talk about fight club. . . . The second rule of fight club is you don't talk about fight club.

Fight Club (novel) [1996]

Jon Stewart [Jonathan Stuart Leibowitz]
1962–

10   Here it is . . . your moment of Zen.

Nightly signoff, The Daily Show

David Foster Wallace
1962–2008

11   Make no mistake: irony tyrannizes us.

E Unibus Pluram: Television and U.S. Fiction [1993]

12   The truth will set you free. But not until it is finished with you.

Infinite Jest [1996]

---

[1] Cf. "birth of freedom" in the Gettysburg Address (Lincoln 446:5).

1 Both destiny's kisses and its dope-slaps illustrate an individual person's basic personal powerlessness over the really meaningful events in his life: i.e., almost nothing important that ever happens to you happens because you engineer it. Destiny has no beeper; destiny always leans trenchcoated out of an alley with some sort of *Psst* that you usually can't even hear because you're in such a rush to or from something important you've tried to engineer.

Infinite Jest

2 You burn with hunger for food that does not exist.

Infinite Jest

3 Is it all right to boil a sentient creature alive just for our gustatory pleasure?

Gourmet [August 2004]. Consider the Lobster

4 Still, after all the abstract intellection, there remain the facts of the frantically clanking lid, the pathetic clinging to the edge of the pot. Standing at the stove, it is hard to deny in any meaningful way that this is a living creature experiencing pain and wishing to avoid/escape the painful experience. To my lay mind, the lobster's behavior in the kettle appears to be the expression of a *preference:* and it may well be that an ability to form preferences is the decisive criterion for real suffering.

Consider the Lobster

5 The capital-T Truth is about life *before* death. It is about making it to 30, or maybe 50, without wanting to shoot yourself in the head. It is about simple awareness — awareness of what is so real and essential, so hidden in plain sight all around us, that we have to keep reminding ourselves, over and over: "This is water, this is water."

Commencement address, Kenyon College [May 21, 2005]

Kool Moe Dee
[Mohandas Dewese]
1963–

6 Guns, we don't like to use 'em
Unless our enemies choose 'em
We prefer to fight you on like a man and
Beat you down with our hands, and bodyslam you
At the wild, wild west.

How Ya Like Me Now [1987]. Wild Wild West

Stephen Colbert
1964–

7 Here's how it works. The President makes decisions. He's the decider. The press secretary announces those decisions, and you people of the press type those decisions down. Make, announce, type. Just put 'em through a spell check and go home. Get to know your family again. Make love to your wife. Write that novel you got kicking around in your head. You know, the one about the intrepid Washington reporter with the courage to stand up to the administration? You know — fiction!

White House Correspondents' Dinner [April 29, 2006]

Niall Ferguson
1964–

8 [The United States] is an empire . . . that dare not speak its name. It is an empire in denial.

Empire: The Rise and Demise of the British World Order and the Lessons for Global Power [2002]

Sarah Palin
1964–

9 I love those hockey moms. You know, they say the difference between a hockey mom and a pit bull? Lipstick.

Speech at Republican National Convention [September 3, 2008]

10 They're our next-door neighbors, and you can actually see Russia from land here in Alaska, from an island in Alaska.[1]

Interview with Charles Gibson [September 11, 2008]

11 The America I know and love is not one in which my parents or my baby with Down Syndrome will have to stand in front of Obama's "death panel."

Facebook posting [August 7, 2009]

KRS-One
[Lawrence Parker]
1965–

12 We gotta put our heads together, and stop the violence
Cause real bad boys move in silence
When you're in a club, you come to chill out
Not watch someone's blood just spill out
That's what these other people want to see
Another race fight endlessly

Stop the Violence [1988]. Recorded by Boogie Down Productions

---

[1]Parodied by TINA FEY on *Saturday Night Live* as: I can see Russia from my house.

Rodney King
1965–2012

1 People, I just want to say, you know, can we all get along?

Statement following Los Angeles riots [May 1, 1992]

J[oanne] K[athleen] Rowling
1965–

2 Before we begin our banquet, I would like to say a few words. And here they are: Nitwit! Oddment! Tweak!

Harry Potter and the Sorcerer's Stone [1998], ch. 7

3 I hope you're pleased with yourselves. We could all have been killed — or worse, expelled.

Harry Potter and the Sorcerer's Stone, 9

4 It is our choices, Harry, that show what we truly are, far more than our abilities.

Harry Potter and the Chamber of Secrets [1998], ch. 18

Kurt Cobain
1967–1994

5 I'd rather be dead than cool.

Stay Away [1991]. Recorded by Nirvana

6 Teenage angst has paid off well
Now I'm bored and old.

Serve the Servants [1993]. Recorded by Nirvana

Todd Beamer
1968–2001

7 Let's roll.[1]

Before storming the cockpit of United Airlines Flight 93 [September 11, 2001]

Monty Python's Flying Circus
1969–1974[2]

8 This parrot is no more. It has ceased to be. It's expired and gone to meet its maker. This is a late parrot. It's a stiff. Bereft of life, it rests in peace. If you hadn't nailed it to the perch, it would be pushing up the daisies. It's rung down the curtain and joined the choir invisible. This is an ex-parrot.

Series 1, episode 8 [1969]

9 I cut down trees, I skip and jump,
I like to press wild flowers.
I put on women's clothing
And hang around in bars.

Series 1, episode 9 [1969]

10 *Nobody* expects the Spanish Inquisition!

Series 2, episode 2 [1970]

11 I'd like to welcome the pommy bastard to God's own earth, and I'd like to remind him that we don't like stuck-up sticky-beaks here.

Series 2, episode 9 [1970]

12 Mr. Bun: What have you got, then?
Waitress: Well there's egg and bacon; egg, sausage and bacon; egg and spam; egg, bacon and spam; egg, bacon, sausage and spam; spam, bacon, sausage and spam; spam, egg, spam, spam, bacon and spam; spam, spam, spam, egg and spam; spam, spam, spam, spam, spam, baked beans, spam, spam, spam and spam; or lobster thermidor aux crevettes with a mornay sauce garnished with truffle pâté, brandy and a fried egg on top and spam.

Series 2, episode 12 [1970]

Trey Parker
1969–

and

Matt Stone
1971–

13 Oh my God, they killed Kenny!

Catchphrase, South Park (television series) [1997–]

Sesame Street
1969–

14 Me want cookie!   *Spoken by Cookie Monster*[3]

15 It's not that easy bein' green.

Bein' Green.[4] *Sung by Kermit the Frog*

Colson Whitehead
1969–

16 No matter how long you have been here, you are a New Yorker the first time you say, That used to be

---

[1] The 9/11 Commission Report indicates that "a passenger" yelled, "Roll it!" The passenger is not specifically identified as Beamer.

[2] Series first shown on BBC television between 1969 and 1974. Written and conceived by GRAHAM CHAPMAN, JOHN CLEESE, TERRY GILLIAM, ERIC IDLE, TERRY JONES, and MICHAEL PALIN.

[3] Character created by JEFFREY A. MOSS [1942–1998].

[4] Words and music by JOE RAPOSO [1937–1989].

Munsey's, or That used to be the Tic Toc Lounge....
You are a New Yorker when what was there before is
more real and solid than what is here now.
                          The Colossus of New York [2004]

M. Night Shyamalan
1970–

1   I see dead people.
                   *The Sixth Sense (screenplay) [1999],
                   spoken by Haley Joel Osment*

Natalie Maines
1974–

2   Just so you know, we're ashamed the President of
the United States is from Texas.
                   *From the stage at The Dixie Chicks concert in
                   London [March 10, 2003]*

Robert Lopez
1975–
and
Jeff Marx
1970–

3   The Internet Is for Porn
                   Avenue Q [2002]. Title of song

Justin Timberlake
1981–

4   I am sorry if anyone was offended by the wardrobe
malfunction during the halftime performance at the
Super Bowl. It was not intentional and is regrettable.
                   *Apologizing for brief exposure of Janet
                   Jackson's breast [February 2, 2004]*

Anonymous

5 Sumer is icumen in,
  Lhude sing cuccu!
Groweth sed, and bloweth med,
And springth the wude nu —
  Sing cuccu![1]   *Cuckoo Song [c. 1250]*

6   A new broom sweeps clean.
                              Saying [13th century]

7 Ich am of Irlonde
  Ant of the holy lande

Of Irlonde.
Gode sire, pray ich the,
For of saynte charite,
Come ant dance wyth me
  In Irlonde.
                   Ich Am of Irlonde[2] [14th century]

8 When Adam delved and Eve span
  Who was then a gentleman?
                   Text used by JOHN BALL *for his speech at
                   Blackheath to the men in Wat Tyler's
                   Rebellion [1381]*

9   Hew not too high lest the chips fall in thine eye.
                              Proverb [14th century]

10 I must go walk so the wood so wild,
     And wander here and there
     In dread and deadly fear;
   For where I trusted I am beguiled,
     And all for one.
                        English verse [15th century]

11 I sing of a maiden
   That is makeless;
   King of all kings
   To her son she ches.
                   Carol. I Sing of a Maiden [15th century]

12 For in my mind, of all mankind
   I love but you alone.
                   The Nut-Brown Maid [15th century], refrain

13 For I must to the greenwood go,
   Alone, a banished man.
                        The Nut-Brown Maid, refrain

14 No burial this pretty pair
   Of any man receives,
   Till Robin Redbreast piously
   Did cover them with leaves.
                        The Children in the Wood, st. 16

15   Before you trust a man, eat a peck of salt with
him.   *Proverb[3]*

16   A fool's paradise.
                        Paston Letters [1462], no. 457

17   O Death, thou comest when I had thee least in
mind.
                        Everyman [before 1500], l. 119

18 Everyman, I will go with thee, and be thy guide,
   In thy most need to go by thy side.
                              Everyman, l. 522

---

[1]See Ezra Pound, 665:2.

[2]"I am of Ireland, / And the Holy Land of Ireland, / And time
runs on," cried she. / "Come out of charity, / Come dance with me
in Ireland." — YEATS, *The Winding Stair and Other Poems* [1933],
Words for Music Perhaps, no. 20, "I Am of Ireland," refrain

[3]An adage originating before Cicero, who quotes a version of it in
De Amicitia 19, 67.

1 O Western wind, when wilt thou blow,
   That the small rain down can rain?
   Christ, that my love were in my arms
   And I in my bed again!
                        O Western Wind [c. 1530]

2 Love me little, love me long,
   Is the burden of my song.
                Love Me Little [1569–1570], refrain

3 Multiplication is vexation,
   Division is as bad;
   The rule of three doth puzzle me,
   And practice drives me mad.
                        Elizabethan MS [1570]

4 Alas, my Love! ye do me wrong
   To cast me off discourteously:
   And I have loved you so long,
   Delighting in your company.
        *From A Handful of Pleasant Delights
        [1584], st. 1*

5 Greensleeves was all my joy,
   Greensleeves was my delight;
   Greensleeves was my heart of gold,
   And who but Lady Greensleeves.
        *From A Handful of Pleasant Delights,
        refrain*

6 Where griping griefs the heart would wound
   And doleful dumps the mind oppress,
   There music with her silver sound
   With speed is wont to send redress.[1]
                A Song to the Lute in Musicke, st. 1

7 It was a friar of orders gray
   Walked forth to tell his beads.
                The Friar of Orders Gray,[2] st. 1

8 Our joys as winged dreams do fly;
   Why then should sorrow last?
   Since grief but aggravates thy loss,
   Grieve not for what is past.
                The Friar of Orders Gray, st. 13

9 It's pride that puts this country down;
   Man, take thine old cloak about thee.
                Take Thy Old Cloak About Thee, st. 7

10   A fool and his money are soon parted.
                        English proverb

11 April is in my mistress' face,
   And July in her eyes hath place,

Within her bosom is September,
But in her heart a cold December.
        *From THOMAS MORLEY, Madrigals to Four
        Voices [1594]*

12   Hobson's choice[3]
                Phrase meaning no choice

13 Lo here a new Aurora!
        *From THOMAS MORLEY, The First Book of
        Canzonets to Two Voices [1595]*

14 Kill then, and bliss me,
   But first come kiss me.
        *From THOMAS MORLEY, The First Book of
        Ballets to Five Voices [1595]*

15 Shoot, false Love, I care not.
   Spend thy shafts and spare not.
        *From THOMAS MORLEY, The First Book of
        Ballets to Five Voices*

16 I was more true to Love than Love to me.
        *From JOHN DOWLAND, The First Book of Songs
        or Airs [1597]*

17 Crabbed age and youth cannot live together.
   Youth is full of pleasance, age is full of care.
                        The Passionate Pilgrim [1599]

18 Jerusalem, my happy home,
   When shall I come to thee?
   When shall my sorrows have an end?
   Thy joys when shall I see?
                        The Song of Mary [1601]

19 And let all women strive to be
   As constant as Penelope.
                        Constant Penelope, st. 18

20 Turn again, Whittington,
   Lord Mayor of London.[4]
                *Refrain of Bow Bells heard by Dick
                Whittington [c. 1605]*

21 If you will not when you may
   You shall not when you will, sir.
                *Blow Away the Morning Dew (Child Ballad
                no. 112) [1609]*

22 From the hag and hungry goblin
   That into rags would rend ye,
   And the spirit that stands by the naked man
   In the book of Moons defend ye!
                Tom o' Bedlam [17th century], st. 1

23 The law locks up both man and woman
   Who steals the goose from off the common,

---

[1]Another version is used by Shakespeare in *Romeo and Juliet, act IV, sc. v.*

[2]Composed by THOMAS PERCY [1728–1811] from fragments of ancient ballads in Shakespeare; published in his *Reliques of Ancient English Poetry* [1765].

[3]Liveryman Thomas Hobson [1544–1631] obliged customers "to take the horse which stood near the stable door," according to RICHARD STEELE, *The Spectator, no. 509* [October 14, 1712].

[4]Richard Whittington, son of a London mercer, rose to be mayor of London three times [1423].

But lets the greater felon loose
Who steals the common from the goose.
> From EDWARD POTTS CHEYNEY, *Social and
> Industrial History of England [1901],
> introduction*

1 Love not me for comely grace,
For my pleasing eye or face,
Nor for any outward part,
No, nor for a constant heart.
> From JOHN WILBYE, *Second Set of Madrigals
> [1609]*

2 The silver swan, who living had no note,
When death approached unlocked her silent throat;
Leaning her breast against the reedy shore,
Thus sung her first and last, and sung no more:
Farewell, all joys; O death, come close mine eyes;
More geese than swans now live, more fools than
    wise.
> From ORLANDO GIBBONS, *The First Set of
> Madrigals and Motets of Five Parts [1612], I*

3 Stay, O sweet, and do not rise!
The light that shines comes from thine eyes;
The day breaks not: it is my heart,
Because that you and I must part.
Stay, or else my joys will die,
And perish in their infancy.[1]
> From JOHN DOWLAND, *A Pilgrim's Solace [1612]*

4 We gather together to ask the Lord's blessing;
He chastens and hastens his will to make known;
The wicked oppressing now cease from distressing:
Sing praises to his Name; he forgets not his own.
> *Hymn*[2] *[1625]*

5 A zealous locksmith died of late,
And did arrive at heaven gate,
He stood without and would not knock,
Because he meant to pick the lock.
> *Epitaph upon a Puritanical Locksmith; from*
> WILLIAM CAMDEN, *Remains Concerning
> Britain [1637]*

6 If there is a paradise on the face of the earth,
It is this, oh! it is this, oh! it is this.
> *Mogul Inscription in the Red Fort at Delhi
> [1640]*

7   Hear no evil, see no evil, speak no evil.
> *Legend related to the "Three Wise Monkeys"
> carved over door of Sacred Stable, Nikko,
> Japan [17th century]*

---

[1] Attributed also to JOHN DONNE, and included in a variant form in the seventh edition of his poems [1669].

[2] Translated by THEODORE BAKER.
  Written by an unknown author in celebration of Dutch freedom from Spanish sovereignty at the end of the sixteenth century. — *The Hymnal 1940 Companion*

8 Over the mountains and over the waves,
Under the fountains and under the graves;
Under floods that are deepest, which Neptune obey,
Over rocks that are steepest, Love will find out the
    way.
> *Love Will Find Out the Way, st. 1*

9   All the brothers were valiant, and all the sisters
virtuous.
> *From the inscription on the tomb of the
> Duchess of Newcastle in Westminster Abbey
> [1673]*

10 Begone, dull Care! I prithee begone from me!
Begone, dull Care! Thou and I shall never agree.
> From JOHN PLAYFORD, *Musical Companion
> [1687]*

11 Though little, I'll work as hard as a Turk,
If you'll give me employ,
To plow and sow, and reap and mow,
And be a farmer's boy.
> *The Farmer's Boy [before 1689], st. 2*

12 Carriages without horses shall go,
And accidents fill the world with woe.
> *Attributed to Mother Shipton*[3]

13 Around the world thoughts shall fly
In the twinkling of an eye.
> *Attributed to Mother Shipton*

14 Under water men shall walk,
Shall ride, shall sleep, and talk;
In the air men shall be seen
In white, in black, and in green.
> *Attributed to Mother Shipton*

15 Iron in the water shall float
As easy as a wooden boat.
> *Attributed to Mother Shipton*

16 A swarm of bees in May
Is worth a load of hay;
A swarm of bees in June
Is worth a silver spoon;
A swarm of bees in July
Is not worth a fly.
> *Old English proverb*

17   When poverty comes in at the door, love flies out
the window.
> *Saying [17th century]*

18 Please to remember the fifth of November,
Gunpowder treason and plot.
> *Guy Fawkes rhyme [17th century]*

---

[3] Prophecies ascribed to the fictitious Mother Shipton first appeared in 1641.

1 It is so soon that I am done for,
  I wonder what I was begun for.
      For a child aged three weeks, Cheltenham
      Churchyard

2   Live and let live.   *Scottish proverb*

3   Coming through the rye.[1]
         The Bob-tailed Lass, refrain

4 God rest you merry, gentlemen,
  Let nothing you dismay;
  Remember Christ our Savior,
  Was born on Christmas Day.   *Carol*

5 The holly and the ivy,
  When they are both full grown,
  Of all the trees that are in the wood,
  The holly bears the crown:
  The rising of the sun
  And the running of the deer,
  The playing of the merry organ,
  Sweet singing in the choir.   *Carol*

6   Sister Anne, do you see anyone coming?
        Bluebeard; the cry of Fatima

7   Who will change old lamps for new?
      The Arabian Nights (A Thousand and One
      Nights).[2] The History of Aladdin

8   Open sesame!
      The Arabian Nights (A Thousand and One
      Nights). The History of Ali Baba

9   Drive a coach and six through an Act of Parliament.
      Credited to Sir Stephen Rice [1637–1715],
      Chief Baron of the Exchequer, by MACAULAY
      in History of England [1849–1861], ch. 12

10 The Campbells are comin', oho, oho.
         Song [c. 1715]

11 Fools' names, like fools' faces,
  Are often seen in public places.[3]   *Saying*

12 And this is law, I will maintain,
  Unto my dying day, sir,
  That whatsoever king shall reign,
  I'll still be the Vicar of Bray, sir!
      The Vicar of Bray [1734], chorus

13 Some talk of Alexander, and some of Hercules;
  Of Hector, and Lysander, and such great names as
    these;

But of all the world's brave heroes, there's none that
  can compare
With a tow, row, row, row, row, row for the British
  Grenadier.
      The British Grenadiers [c. 1750]

14   The united voice of all His Majesty's free and loyal
subjects in America — liberty and property, and no
stamps.
      Motto of various American colonial
      newspapers [1765–1766]

15 Yankee Doodle came to town
  Riding on a pony,
  He stuck a feather in his hat
  And called it macaroni.

  Yankee Doodle, keep it up,
  Yankee Doodle dandy,
  Mind the music and the step,
  And with the girls be handy.
      Yankee Doodle,[4] st. 1 and chorus

16   It's all in the day's work.
      Current since the 18th century

17 Man may work from sun to sun,
  But woman's work is never done.   *Saying*

18 Count that day lost whose low descending sun
  Views from thy hand no worthy action done.[5]
         Saying

19   Don't tread on me.
      Motto of the first official American flag; first
      raised by Lieutenant John Paul Jones in
      Commodore Esek Hopkins's flagship Alfred
      [December 3, 1775]

20 Our cargoes of meat, drink, and clothes beat the
  Dutch.   *Siege of Boston [1775]*

21   Rebellion to tyrants is obedience to God.[6]
      Motto on Thomas Jefferson's seal [c. 1776]

22 There were three gypsies a-come to my door,
  And downstairs ran this lady, O!
  One sang high and another sang low,
  And the other sang bonny, bonny Biscay, O!
      The Wraggle-Taggle Gypsies, O!, st. 1

---

[1]Gin a body meet a body / Coming through the rye; / Gin a body
kiss a body, / Need a body cry? — ROBERT BURNS, *Coming Through
the Rye, st. 1*
  See J. D. Salinger, 793:11.

[2]First European translation (ANTOINE GALLAND), 1704–1717.

[3]Collected by THOMAS FULLER [1654–1734], in *Gnomologia*
[1732].

---

[4]This version was sufficiently popular in America in 1767 to be
used in the ballad opera *The Disappointment; or, The Force of
Credulity* by ANDREW BARTON.
  Father and I went up to camp, / Along with Captain Goodwin; /
And there we saw the men and boys, / As thick as hasty pudding. /
Yankee doodle do. — *Version used by* ROYALL TYLER [1757–1826],
in The Contrast [1790]

[5]An earlier version, signed by JAMES BOBART [December 8, 1697],
begins "Think" rather than "Count."

[6]The motto of one, I believe, of the regicides of Charles I. — *Letter
from Thomas Jefferson to Edward Everett* [February 24, 1823]
  Jefferson's reference probably is to John Bradshaw [1602–1659].

1 She's gone with the wraggle-taggle gypsies, O!
The Wraggle-Taggle Gypsies, O!, st. 2

2 Down in the valley, the valley so low,
Hang your head over, hear the wind blow.
Down in the Valley

3 The goose hangs high.[1]
Saying

4 O Paddy dear, an' did ye hear the news that's goin'
round?
The shamrock is by law forbid to grow on Irish
ground!
No more St. Patrick's Day we'll keep, his color can't
be seen,
For there's a cruel law agin the wearin' o' the
Green!
The Wearing o' the Green [c. 1795]

5 For they're hangin' men an' women there for wearin'
o' the Green.
The Wearing o' the Green

6 With drums and guns, and guns and drums
The enemy nearly slew ye.
My darling dear, you look so queer,
Oh, Johnny, I hardly knew ye.
Irish folk song, st. 1

7 Christmas is coming, the geese are getting fat,
Please to put a penny in the old man's hat;
If you haven't got a penny, a ha'penny will do,
If you haven't got a ha'penny, God bless you!
Beggar's rhyme

8 From ghoulies and ghosties and long-leggety beasties
And things that go bump in the night, Good Lord,
deliver us!
Cornish prayer

9 O God, thy sea is so great, and my boat is so
small.
Breton fishermen's prayer

10 Rest and be thankful.
*Inscription on stone seat in the Scottish
Highlands, and title of one of William
Wordsworth's poems*

11 Don't cross the bridge until you come to it.
Proverb

12 It's gude to be merry and wise,
It's gude to be honest and true;
It's gude to be off with the old love,
Before you are on with the new.[2]
Rhyme

13 Oh, ye'll tak' the high road an' I'll tak' the low road,
An' I'll be in Scotland before ye;
But me and my true love will never meet again,
On the bonnie, bonnie banks o' Loch Lomond.
Loch Lomond, refrain

14 The woods are full of them.
Quoted by ALEXANDER WILSON, *American
Ornithology [1808], preface*

15 I wooed her in the wintertime
And in the summer too;
And the only, only thing I did that was wrong
Was to keep her from the foggy, foggy dew.
The Foggy, Foggy Dew, st. 1

16 Turkey in the straw, turkey in the hay,
Roll 'em up and twist 'em up a high tuckahaw,
And hit 'em up a tune called Turkey in the Straw.
Turkey in the Straw,[3] st. 1 and refrain

17 Sugar in the gourd and honey in the horn,
I never was so happy since the hour I was born.
Turkey in the Straw, st. 6

18 Jimmie crack corn and I don't care,
Old Massa's gone away.
The Blue-tail Fly, chorus

19 Give me that old-time religion,
It's good enough for me.
Hymn

20 It was good for Paul and Silas
And it's good enough for me.
Hymn

21 I expect to pass through this world but once; any
good thing therefore that I can do, or any kindness
that I can show to any fellow creature, let me do it
now; let me not defer or neglect it, for I shall not pass
this way again.[4]
Proverbial saying

22 I've been working on the railroad
All the livelong day,
I've been working on the railroad
To pass the time away.
Don't you hear the whistle blowing?
Rise up so early in the morn.
Don't you hear the captain shouting,
"Dinah blow your horn."
I've Been Working on the Railroad

---

[1] [Meaning:] All is wonderful, 1866. Sometimes said to be from "The goose honks high," referring to the fact that geese fly higher in good weather, but there is no evidence this is the origin of the term. — STUART BERG FLEXNER [1928–1990], *Listening to America* [1982]

[2] Quoted as an old song by ANTHONY TROLLOPE in *Barchester Towers* [1857], *ch. 46.*

[3] The classical American rural tune . . . steps around like an apple-faced farmhand . . . as American as Andrew Jackson, Johnny Appleseed, and Corn on the Cob. — CARL SANDBURG, *The American Songbag* [1927]

[4] This saying has been attributed to many authors, most especially to STEPHEN GRELLET [Étienne de Grellet du Mabillier, 1773–1855], although it has not been found in any of Grellet's writings.

1   OK

Abbreviation for humorous misspelling,
"oll korrect" [1838][1]

2 From the halls of Montezuma,
To the shores of Tripoli,
We fight our country's battles
On the land as on the sea.
The Marines' Hymn[2] *[1847], st. 1*

3 'Tis the gift to be simple,
'Tis the gift to be free,
'Tis the gift to come down
Where we ought to be.
Simple Gifts. Shaker song [c. 1848], st. 1

4 Buffalo gals, won't you come out tonight,
And dance by the light of the moon?   *Buffalo Gals*

5   Women and children first.
The Birkenhead Drill[3] *[February 26, 1852]*

6 Up and down the City Road,
In and out the Eagle,
That's the way the money goes—
Pop goes the weasel!
Pop Goes the Weasel[4] *[c. 1853]*

7   Free soil, free men, free speech, Frémont[5]
Republican party rallying cry [1856]

8   Muscular Christianity[6]
Popular term in the 19th century for
Christian social reform in England

9   It is a newspaper's duty to print the news and raise
hell.   *The Chicago Times [1861]*

10   Dirty work at the crossroads
Attributed to WALTER MELVILLE'S *melodrama*
The Girl Who Took the Wrong Turning; or,
No Wedding Bells for Him

11   The man on horseback
Popular term for General Georges Ernest
Boulanger [1837–1891]

---

[1]For the history of this "most popular typical American
expression," see STUART BERG FLEXNER [1928–1990], *I Hear
America Talking* [1976], *pp. 261–262.*

[2]See Anonymous, 888:1.

[3]The women and children were the first to be removed from the
sinking ship *Birkenhead.*

[4]The weasel was a hatter's tool, and "pop" was a term meaning to
pawn or "hock." The Eagle was a music hall in the City Road. The
song is attributed to W. R. MANDALE.

[5]John Charles Frémont [1813–1890] was the party's candidate
for President.

[6]A term applied (from about 1857) to the ideal of religious
character exhibited in the writings of Charles Kingsley. — *Oxford
English Dictionary*

His Christianity was muscular. — BENJAMIN DISRAELI, *Endymion*
[1880], *ch. 14*

12 John Henry told his captain,
Says, "A man ain't nothin' but a man,
And before I'd let your steam drill beat me down,
Lord,
I'd die with this hammer in my hand."
John Henry [1873]

13 You-all means a race or section,
Family, party, tribe, or clan;
You-all means the whole connection
Of the individual man.
You-All; from the Richmond Times-Dispatch

14 There is a tavern in the town,
And there my true love sits him down,
And drinks his wine with laughter and with glee,
And never, never thinks of me.
There Is a Tavern in the Town, st. 1

15 Adieu, adieu, kind friends, adieu, adieu, adieu,
I can no longer stay with you.
I'll hang my harp on a weeping willow-tree,
And may the world go well with thee.
There Is a Tavern in the Town, refrain

16 I belong to that highly respectable tribe
Which is known as the Shabby Genteel . . .
Too proud to beg, too honest to steal.
The Shabby Genteel; sung by Sol Smith Russell
[1848–1901] in A Poor Relation

17 Sow a thought, and you reap an act;
Sow an act, and you reap a habit;
Sow a habit, and you reap a character;
Sow a character, and you reap a destiny.
Quoted by SAMUEL SMILES *[1812–1904],*
in Life and Labor [1887]

18   Now is the time for all good men to come to the
aid of the party.
Practice sentence used in typing[7]

19   The quick brown fox jumps over the lazy dog.
Practice sentence used in typing (using
whole alphabet)

20   As Maine goes, so goes the nation.[8]
American political maxim [c. 1888]

21   Slide, Kelly, Slide
Title of song by J. W. KELLY *[1889]*

22 Lizzie Borden took an ax
And gave her mother forty whacks;

---

[7]Charles Weller, a court reporter, originated this expression in . . .
1867 to test the efficiency of the first practical typewriter which his
friend Christopher Sholes had constructed. — *Life* [April 11, 1955]

[8]As Maine goes, so goes Vermont. — JAMES A. FARLEY *[1888–
1976], statement to press [November 4, 1936], after predicting
correctly that Franklin D. Roosevelt would carry all but two states in
the presidential election*

When she saw what she had done
She gave her father forty-one!
> *Rhyme popular after the murder trial of*
> *Lizzie Borden, Fall River, Massachusetts*
> *[June 1893]*

1 Oh, why don't you work like other men do?
How the hell can I work when there's no work
  to do?
> *Hallelujah, I'm a Bum*[1] *[c. 1897]*

2 Remember the Maine![2]
> *Slogan in the Spanish-American War [1898]*

3 Frankie and Johnny were lovers, my gawd, how they
  could love,
Swore to be true to each other, true as the stars above;
He was her man, but he done her wrong.
> *Frankie and Johnny,*[3] *st. 1*

4 The codfish lays ten thousand eggs,
The homely hen lays one.
The codfish never cackles
To tell you what she's done.
And so we scorn the codfish,
While the humble hen we prize,
Which only goes to show you
That it pays to advertise.   *It Pays to Advertise*

5 One white foot — try him,
Two white feet — buy him,
Three white feet — look well about him;
Four white feet — go without him.[4]
> *Rhyme for a horse-buyer*

6 Time is of the essence.   *Saying*

7 All the world is queer save me and thee; and sometimes I think thee is a little queer.
> *Attributed to a Quaker, speaking to his wife*

8 You can always tell a Harvard man, but you can't
tell him much.
> *Attributed to* James Barnes *[1866–1936]*

9 There's a sucker born every minute.
> *Saying*[5]

10 Keeping up with the Joneses   *Popular saying*

11 Doesn't amount to Hannah Cook[6]
> *Saying common in Maine and on Cape Cod*

12 Hit's a lot worse to be soul-hungry than to be
body-hungry.
> *A Kentucky mountain woman asking for her*
> *granddaughter to be admitted to Berea*
> *College high school [c. 1900]. Quoted by* Carl
> R. Woodward *in The Wonderful World of*
> *Books, edited by Alfred Stefferud [1953]*

13 There ain't no such animal.
> *Caption for cartoon of a farmer at the circus*
> *looking at a dromedary. From Life*
> *[November 7, 1907], credited to Everybody's*
> *Magazine*

14 The Pyramids first, which in Egypt were laid;
Next Babylon's Gardens, for Amytis made;
Then Mausolos' Tomb of affection and guilt;
Fourth, the Temple of Dian in Ephesus built;
The Colossus of Rhodes, cast in brass, to the Sun;
Sixth, Jupiter's Statue, by Phidias done;
The Pharos of Egypt comes last, we are told,
Or the Palace of Cyrus, cemented with gold.
> *Seven Wonders of the Ancient World*

15 Use it up, wear it out;
Make it do, or do without.
> *New England maxim*

16 Something old, something new,
Something borrowed, something blue,
And a lucky sixpence in her shoe.[7]
> *Wedding rhyme*

17 Church ain't out till the fat lady sings.[8]
> *From* Fabia Rue Smith *and* Charles
> Rayford Smith, *Southern Words and Sayings*
> *[1976]*

18 Would you like to sin
With Elinor Glyn
On a tiger skin?

Or would you prefer
To err with her
On some other fur?
> *On Elinor Glyn's romantic novel,*
> *Three Weeks (1907), and its episode of illicit*
> *sex on a tiger skin*

---

[1]Also attributed to Harry McClintock.

[2]Derived from cartoon caption by Clifford K. Berryman [1869–1949] in *The Washington Post* [April 3, 1898]: If the row comes, Remember the Maine, and show the world how American sailors can fight.

[3]Traditional ballad; there are innumerable versions and verses.

[4]Three white feet and a white nose, / Rip off his skin and throw him to the crows. — *New Hampshire version of last two lines*

[5]Often attributed, but without substantiation, to P. T. Barnum [1810–1891]; possibly derived from the line in a popular nineteenth-century song, "There's a new jay [meaning, rube or mark] born every day." — Ralph Keyes, *Nice Guys Finish Seventh* [1992]

---

[6]Variously explained as a character who once lived on Campobello Island; a corruption of a phrase in Indian dialect; and a comparison with the worthlessness (for navigation) of a cook on board ship.

[7]There are variants for the less familiar last line, such as: And a silver sixpence in each shoe.

[8]Proverbial lore current in several variant forms, the most familiar and recent of which is: The opera ain't over till the fat lady sings. — Daniel John Cook [1926–], *television newscast, San Antonio, Texas* [April 1978]

1 We want bread and roses too.
   Slogan of women strikers, Lawrence,
   Massachusetts [1912]

2 "Shine, Shine, save poor me!
   I'll give you all the pussy a Shine can see."
   Shine says, "Now pussy's good, but pussy don't
      last —
   Shine's going to save his own black ass."
   And Shine swam on.   *Shine and the Titanic*[1]

3 Monkey in the tree,
   Lion on the ground.
   Monkey kept on signifying
   But he didn't come down.   *The Signifying Monkey*

4 Old soldiers never die;
   They only fade away![2]
                  British Army song [c. 1915]

5 I didn't raise my boy to be a soldier.
                  A Mother's Plea for Peace [1915]

6 She was poor but she was honest,
   And her parents was the same,
   Till she met a city feller,
   And she lost her honest name.   *Song [c. 1915]*

7 It's the same the whole world over,
   It's the poor wot gets the blame,
   It's the rich wot gets the pleasure,
   Ain't it all a bloomin' shame?   *Song, chorus*

8 Fifty million Frenchmen can't be wrong.[3]
   Saying popular with American soldiers
   during World War I [1917–1918]

9 Say it ain't so, Joe.
   Small boy to "Shoeless Joe" Jackson of the
   Chicago White Sox, as he emerged from a
   grand jury session [1920] on corruption
   in the 1919 World Series

10 One picture is worth a thousand words.
                  Misattributed "Chinese proverb"[4]

11 Don't sell America short.   *Saying [c. 1925]*

12 Don't lose
    Your head
    To gain a minute
    You need your head
    Your brains are in it.
       Burma-Shave, roadside advertisement
       [1925–1963]

13 No woman can be too rich or too thin.
                          Saying[5]

14 God is in the details.
                          Saying[6]

15 Lord, through this hour
    Be Thou our Guide,
    So by Thy power
    No foot shall slide.   *Westminster Chimes*

16 Climb high
    Climb far
    Your goal the sky
    Your aim the star.
       Inscription on Hopkins Memorial Steps,
       Williams College, Williamstown,
       Massachusetts

17 Mother, may I go out to swim?
    Yes, my darling daughter:
    Hang your clothes on a hickory limb
    And don't go near the water.   *Rhyme*

18 The difficult we do immediately. The impossible
    takes a little longer.
             Slogan of United States Army Service Forces

19 Loose lips sink ships.
                  Government slogan, World War II

20 Kilroy was here.
                  Army saying, World War II

21 SNAFU (Situation Normal All Fucked Up).
                  Army saying, World War II

22 G.I. Joe
             World War II term for infantryman[7]

---

[1]"Undoubtedly the most popular poem in the black vernacular. In this version of events, the sole survivor of the *Titanic* is a black menial referred to as Shine, who turns out to be a champion swimmer." — HENRY LOUIS GATES, JR., *"Sudden Def," The New Yorker* [June 19, 1995]

[2]See Douglas MacArthur, 644:11.

[3]Sometimes "forty" or "thirty" is heard instead of "fifty." When Texas Guinan and her troupe were refused entry into France [1931], she was quoted as saying: "It goes to show that fifty million Frenchmen *can* be wrong." She promptly renamed her show *Too Hot for Paris,* and toured the United States with it.

[4]"One look is worth a thousand words." Fred R. Barnard, in *Printers' Ink,* 8 Dec., 1921, p. 96. He changed it to "One picture is worth a thousand words" in *Printers' Ink,* 10 March, 1927, p. 114, and called it "a Chinese proverb, so that people would take it seriously." — BURTON STEVENSON, ed., *The Home Book of Proverbs, Maxims, and Familiar Phrases* [1948]

[5]Frequently attributed to the DUCHESS OF WINDSOR and others. Tell a female she's thin and she's yours for life. — ANNE BERNAYS [1930–], *Professor Romeo* [1989]

[6]A popular aphorism with the architect Ludwig Mies van der Rohe and the art historian Aby Warburg; attributed *[Le bon Dieu est dans le détail]* to GUSTAVE FLAUBERT but without verification; possibly derived from seventeenth-century humanist CASPAR BARLAEUS [1584–1648] [God hides in the smallest pieces].

[7]This name, chosen for the soldier in LIEUTENANT DAVE BREGER's comic strip for *Yank,* the Army weekly, first appeared in the issue of June 17, 1942. Writing in *Time* [February 26, 1945], Lieutenant Breger said: "I decided on 'G.I. Joe,' the 'G.I.' [Government Issue] because of its prevalence in Army talk, and the 'Joe' for the alliterative effect."

1 And when he goes to heaven
To Saint Peter he will tell:
Another Marine reporting, sir;
I've served my time in hell![1]
*Epitaph on grave of Pfc. Cameron of the
Marine Corps, Guadalcanal [1942]*

2 Stay with me, God. The night is dark,
The night is cold: my little spark
Of courage dies. The night is long;
Be with me, God, and make me strong.
A Soldier — His Prayer,[2] st. 1

3 We sure liberated the hell out of this place.
*American soldier in the ruins of a French
village [1944]; quoted by* MAX MILLER,
The Far Shore [1945]

4 Spartan simplicity must be observed. Nothing will
be done merely because it contributes to beauty, convenience, comfort, or prestige.
*From the Office of the Chief Signal Officer,
U.S. Army [May 29, 1945]*

5 In brightest day, in blackest night,[3]
No evil shall escape my sight.
Let those who worship evil's might
Beware my power, Green Lantern's light!
*Green Lantern's oath in Green Lantern
comics [mid-1940s onward]*

6 Time is a river without banks. *Saying*

7 Till Hell freezes over. *Saying*

8 One man, one vote. *Civil rights slogan*

9 Do not fold, spindle, or mutilate.
*Instructions on punch cards and computer
cards [c. 1950s]*

10 That's the way the cookie crumbles.
Saying [1950s]

11 "Murphy's Law": If something can go wrong, it
will. *Saying[4] [1950s]*

12 Winning isn't everything, it's the only thing.
*Saying [1953], often attributed to U.C.L.A.
football coach Henry ("Red") Sanders
[1905–1958][5]*

13 What, Me Worry?
*Mad magazine ("Alfred E. Neuman") motto
[1955], adapted from a turn-of-the-century
advertising slogan*

14 Black is beautiful.
Slogan [1960s]

15 We shall overcome, we shall overcome,
We shall overcome some day
Oh, deep in my heart I do believe
We shall overcome some day.
*Adapted [1960s] for the civil rights movement
from an old religious song[6]*

16 We are the people of this generation, bred in at
least modest comfort, housed now in universities,
looking uncomfortably to the world we inherit.
*Students for a Democratic Society, Port
Huron Statement [1962], Preamble*

17 Eyeball to eyeball.[7]
Common expression

18 Here men from the planet Earth first set foot on
the moon, July 1969 A.D. We came in peace for all
mankind.
*Plaque on moon marking the U.S. landing
there [July 1969]*

19 Beam me up, Scotty. There's no intelligent life
down here.
*Invented [early 1970s] by fans of Star Trek
television series[8]*

20 A woman needs a man like a fish needs a bicycle.
Feminist slogan coined by Irina Dunn [1970]

21 A mind is a terrible thing to waste.
*United Negro College Fund advertising
slogan[9] [1972]*

Anonymous: African

22 In the time when Dendid created all things,
He created the sun,
And the sun is born, and dies, and comes again.
Old Song (Dinka)

---

[1]From *The Marines' Hymn;* see Anonymous, 885:2.

[2]This poem, found on a scrap of paper in a slit trench in Tunisia during the battle of El Agheila, was printed in *Poems from the Desert,* by members of the British Eighth Army [1944].

[3]Some of the published comics use "darkest night" rather than "blackest night."

[4]Included in Arthur Bloch's collection of popular sayings, *Murphy's Law* [1977]. In its original form [1949] by EDWARD ALOYSIUS MURPHY, JR. [1917–1990]: "If there is more than one way to do a job, and one of those ways will end in disaster, then someone will do it that way." — BRIAN BURRELL, *The Words We Live By* [1997], *pp. 146–149*

[5]Compare: Winning isn't everything, but wanting to win is. — VINCE [VINCENT THOMAS] LOMBARDI [1913–1970], *interview* [1962]

[6]Originating in pre–Civil War days, this song was adapted [c. 1900] by C. ALBERT TINDLEY as a Baptist hymn called "I'll Overcome Some Day." It became famous as a protest theme when sung by black workers on picket lines in Charleston, S.C. [1946].

[7]We're eyeball to eyeball, and I think the other fellow just blinked. — DEAN RUSK [1909–1994], *Conversation* [October 24, 1962] *during the Cuban missile crisis*

[8]Catchphrase based on a line from *Star Trek* scripts: Beam us up, Mr. Scott.

[9]What a waste it is to lose one's mind or not to have a mind is very wasteful. — DAN [J. DANFORTH] QUAYLE [1947–], *address to United Negro College Fund* [May 1989]

1 He created man,
And man is born, and dies, and does not come
    again.   *Old Song (Dinka)*

2   Somewhere the Sky touches the Earth, and the
name of that place is the End.   *Saying (Wakamba)*

3   All animals of the forest are alike, though we eat
some and not others, because we the Dorobo and the
animals all live side by side in the forest.
                              From a Dorobo

4   Everything has an end.   *Saying (Masai)*

5   When elephants fight it is the grass that suffers.
                              Proverb (Kikuyu)

6   To the person who seizes two things, one always
slips from his grasp!   *Proverb (Swahili)*

7   The lie has seven endings.   *Proverb (Swahili)*

8   Goodness sold itself, badness flaunted itself
about.   *Proverb (Swahili)*

9   Speak silver, reply gold.   *Proverb (Swahili)*

10   Wisdom is not bought.   *Proverb (Akan)*

11   Not even God is wise enough. *Proverb (Yoruba)*

12   Leave a log in the water as long as you like: it will
never be a crocodile.
                              Proverb (Guinea-Bissau)

Anonymous: Ballads

13 The king sits in Dunfermline town
Drinking the blude-red wine.
                              Sir Patrick Spens, st. 1

14 To Noroway, to Noroway,
To Noroway o'er the faem;
The king's daughter o' Noroway,
'Tis thou must bring her hame.
                              Sir Patrick Spens, st. 4

15 I saw the new moon late yestreen
Wi' the auld moon in her arm;
And if we gang to sea, master,
I fear we'll come to harm.
                              Sir Patrick Spens, st. 10

16 O laith, laith were our gude Scots lords
To wet their cork-heel'd shoon;
But lang or a' the play was play'd
They wat their hats aboon.
                              Sir Patrick Spens, st. 15

17 Half owre, half owre to Aberdour,
'Tis fifty fathoms deep;
And there lies gude Sir Patrick Spens,
Wi' the Scots lords at his feet!
                              Sir Patrick Spens, st. 19

18 "And what will ye leave to your ain mither dear,
Edward, Edward?"   *Edward, Edward, st. 7*

19 "The curse of hell frae me sall ye bear,
Sic counsels ye give to me, O!"
                              Edward, Edward, st. 7

20 Fight on, my merry men all;
For why, my life is at an end.[1]   *Chevy Chase*

21 A fairer lady there never was seen
Than the blind beggar's daughter of Bethnal Green.
            *The Beggar's Daughter of Bethnal Green,[2]
            st. 33*

22 When captains courageous, whom death could not
        daunt,
Did march to the siege of the city of Gaunt,
They mustered their soldiers by two and by three,
And the foremost in battle was Mary Ambree.
                              Mary Ambree,[3] st. 1

23 "I'll rest," said he, "but thou shalt walk";
So doth this wandering Jew
From place to place, but cannot rest
For seeing countries new.
                              The Wandering Jew, st. 9

24 Glasgerion swore a full great oath,
By oak, and ash and thorn.   *Glasgerion, st. 19*

25 In Scarlet town, where I was born,
There was a fair maid dwellin',
Made every youth cry Well-a-day!
Her name was Barbara Allen.

All in the merry month of May,
When green buds they were swellin',
Young Jemmy Grove on his deathbed lay,
For love of Barbara Allen.
                              Barbara Allen's Cruelty, st. 1, 2

26 So slowly, slowly rase she up,
And slowly she came nigh him,
And when she drew the curtain by —
"Young man, I think you're dyin'."
                              Barbara Allen's Cruelty, st. 4

27 True Thomas lay on Huntlie Bank;
A ferlie he spied wi' his e'e;
And there he saw a lady bright
Come riding down by the Eildon Tree.
                              Thomas the Rhymer, st. 1

---

[1]Says Johnnie, "Fight on, my merry men all, / I'm a little wounded, but I am not slain; / I will lay me down for to bleed a while, / Then I'll rise and fight with you again." — *Johnnie Armstrong's Last Goodnight, st. 18; from* DRYDEN's *Miscellanies* [1702]

[2]This very house was built by the blind beggar of Bednall Green, so much talked of and sung in ballads. — SAMUEL PEPYS, *Diary* [June 26, 1663]

[3]BEN JONSON calls any virago Mary Ambree, and JOHN FLETCHER alludes to Mary Ambree in *The Scornful Lady* [1616].

1 "A bed, a bed," Clerk Saunders said,
"A bed for you and me!"
"Fye na, fye na," said may Margaret,
"Till anes we married be!"   *Clerk Saunders, st. 2*

2 There were twa sisters sat in a bour;
Binnorie, O Binnorie!
There came a knight to be their wooer,
By the bonnie milldams o' Binnorie.   *Binnorie, st. 1*

3 There were three ravens sat on a tree,
They were as black as they might be.

The one of them said to his mate,
"Where shall we our breakfast take?"
The Three Ravens, st. 1, 2

4 Down there came a fallow doe
As great with young as she might go.
The Three Ravens, st. 6

5 She buried him before the prime,
She was dead herself ere evensong time.

God send every gentleman
Such hounds, such hawks, and such leman.
The Three Ravens, st. 9, 10

6 Mony a one for him maks mane,
But nane sall ken where he is gane:
O'er his white banes, when they are bare,
The wind sall blaw for evermair.
The Twa Corbies, st. 5

7 Ye Highlands and ye Lawlands,
O where hae ye been?
They hae slain the Earl of Murray,
And laid him on the green.
The Bonny Earl of Murray, st. 1

8 O waly, waly, up the bank,
And waly, waly, doun the brae,
And waly, waly, yon burnside,
Where I and my Love wont to gae!
Waly, Waly, st. 1

9 "What gat ye to your dinner, Lord Randal, my son?
What gat ye to your dinner, my handsome young
man?"
"I gat eels boil'd in broo'; mother, make my bed
soon,
For I'm weary wi' hunting, and fain wald lie
down."   *Lord Randal*

Anonymous: Cowboy Songs

10 As I was a-walking one morning for pleasure,
I spied a cowpuncher a-riding along.
Whoopee Ti Yi Yo, Git Along, Little Dogies

11 Whoopee ti yi yo, git along, little dogies,
It's your misfortune and none of my own,

Whoopee ti yi yo, git along, little dogies,
For you know Wyoming will be your new home.
Whoopee Ti Yi Yo, Git Along, Little Dogies

12 My foot in the stirrup, my pony won't stand,
Good-bye, Old Paint, I'm a-leavin' Cheyenne.
Good-bye, Old Paint

13 Foot in the stirrup and hand on the horn,
Best damned cowboy ever was born.
Come-a ti yi youpy, youpy yea, youpy yea,
Come-a ti yi youpy, youpy yea.
The Old Chisholm Trail

14 Last night as I lay on the prairie,
And looked at the stars in the sky,
I wondered if ever a cowboy
Would drift to that sweet bye-and-bye.
The Cowboy's Dream

15 As I walked out in the streets of Laredo,
As I walked out in Laredo one day,
I spied a poor cowboy wrapped up in white linen,
Wrapped up in white linen as cold as the clay.
The Cowboy's Lament, st. 1

16 Oh, beat the drum slowly[1] and play the fife lowly,
Play the Dead March as you carry me along;
Take me to the green valley, there lay the sod o'er me,
For I'm a young cowboy and I know I've done
wrong.   *The Cowboy's Lament, refrain*

17 Oh bury me not on the lone prairie
Where the wild coyotes will howl o'er me.
The Dying Cowboy

18 Oh, bury me out on the prairie,
Where the coyotes may howl o'er my grave.
Bury Me out on the Prairie

19   Remember the Red River Valley
And the cowboy that loves you so true.
Red River Valley

20 Oh, give me a home where the buffalo roam,
Where the deer and the antelope play,
Where seldom is heard a discouraging word
And the skies are not cloudy all day.
Home on the Range[2] *[1873]*

Anonymous: French

21   Revenons à nos moutons [Let us return to our
sheep (i.e., subject)].
Maître Pathelin (15th-century farce)

22   Il ne faut pas être plus royaliste que le roi [One
must not be more royalist than the king].
Saying from the time of Louis XVI

---

[1]Also familiar as: Oh, bang the drum slowly.
[2]Possibly written by BREWSTER HIGLEY.

1 Ça ira, ça tiendra [That will be, that will last].
Revolutionary song, based on a phrase of Benjamin Franklin's

2 Liberté! Égalité! Fraternité! [Liberty! Equality! Fraternity!]
Phrase from before the French Revolution, officially adopted in 1793

3 Tout passe, tout casse, tout lasse [Everything passes, everything perishes, everything palls].
Proverb

4 L'amour, l'amour fait tourner le monde [It's love, it's love that makes the world go round].
Song

5 On ne saurait faire une omelette sans casser des oeufs [You can't make an omelet without breaking eggs].
Proverb

6 Ami, entends-tu
Le vol noir — des corbeaux — sur nos plaines...

Ami, entends-tu
Les cris sourds — du pays — qu'on enchaine.[1]
Song of the Partisans [1940s]

7 Au clair de la lune,
Mon ami Pierrot,
Prête-moi ta plume
Pour écrire un mot.
Au Clair de la Lune[2]

Anonymous: North American Indian

8 Screaming the night away
With his great wing feathers
Swooping the darkness up;
I hear the Eagle bird
Pulling the blanket back
Off from the eastern sky.
Invitation Song (Iroquois)

9 Holy Mother Earth, the trees and all nature are witnesses of your thoughts and deeds.
Saying (Winnebago)

10 A people without history is like the wind on the buffalo grass.
Saying (Sioux)

11 Out of the earth
I sing for them
a Horse nation...

I sing for them
the animals.
I Sing for the Animals (Teton Sioux)

12 O our Mother the Earth, O our Father the Sky,
Your children are we, and with tired backs
We bring you gifts.
Song of the Sky Loom (Tewa)

13 May the warp be the white light of morning,
May the weft be the red light of evening,
May the fringes be the falling rain,
May the border be the standing rainbow.
Thus weave for us a garment of brightness.
Song of the Sky Loom (Tewa)

14 Lovely! See the cloud, the cloud appear!
Lovely! See the rain, the rain draw near!
Who spoke?
It was the little corn ear
High on the tip of the stalk.
Corn-grinding Song (Zuñi)

15 Big Blue Mountain Spirit,
The home made of blue clouds...
I am grateful for that mode of goodness there.
Chant (Apache)[3]

16 The black turkey gobbler, the tips of his beautiful tail;
above us the dawn becomes yellow.
The sunbeams stream forward.
Black Turkey Gobbler Chant (Apache)[4]

17 House made of dawn,
House made of evening light,
House made of the dark cloud....
Dark cloud is at the house's door,
The trail out of it is dark cloud,
The zigzag lightning stands high upon it.
Night Chant (Navajo)[5]

18 Happily may I walk.
May it be beautiful before me.
May it be beautiful behind me.
May it be beautiful below me.
May it be beautiful above me.
May it be beautiful all around me.
In beauty it is finished.
Night Chant (Navajo)

19 Hi! ni! ya! Behold the man of flint, that's me!
Four lightnings zigzag from me, strike and return.
War Chant (Navajo)

20 The ancient folk with evil spells, dashed to earth,
plowed under!
War Chant (Navajo)

---

[1]Friend, do you hear / The black flight — of our crows — on our plains... / Friend, do you hear / The faint cries — of the country — in chains.

[2]By the light of the moon, / My friend Pierrot, / Lend me your pen / To write a word.
This song, with music by JEAN-BAPTISTE LULLY [1632–1687], has been popular since the time of Louis XIV [1638–1715].

---

[3]Translated by HARRY HOIJER.

[4]Translated by PLINY E. GODDARD.

[5]Translated by WASHINGTON MATTHEWS.

1 Quarry mine, blessed am I
In the luck of the chase.
Comes the deer to my singing.
                              Hunting Song (Navajo)

2 Idlers and cowards are here at home now,
But the youth I love is gone to war, far hence.
Weary, lonely, for me he longs.   *Wind Song (Kiowa)*

3   In the beginning God gave to every people a cup
of clay, and from this cup they drank their life.
                              Proverb (Northern Paiute)

4 As long as the moon shall rise,
As long as the rivers shall flow,
As long as the sun shall shine,
As long as the grass shall grow.
                              Expression for term of a treaty

5 It ended . . .
With his body changed to light,
A star that burns forever in that sky.
                              The Flight of Quetzalcoatl (Aztec)[1]

6 I was out in my kayak . . .
and the seal came gently toward me.
Why didn't I harpoon him?
Was I sorry for him?
Was it the day, the spring day, the seal
playing in the sun
like me?   *Spring Fjord (Inuit)*[2]

Anonymous: Nursery Rhymes

7 A man of words and not of deeds
Is like a garden full of weeds.
                              A Man of Words and Not of Deeds

8 It's like a lion at the door;
And when the door begins to crack,
It's like a stick across your back;
And when your back begins to smart,
It's like a penknife in your heart;
And when your heart begins to bleed,
You're dead, and dead, and dead, indeed.
                              A Man of Words and Not of Deeds

9 Cock a doodle doo!
My dame has lost her shoe;
My master's lost his fiddle stick,
And knows not what to do.   *Cock a Doodle Doo*

10 Three blind mice, see how they run!
They all ran after the farmer's wife,
She cut off their tails with a carving knife,
Did you ever see such a sight in your life,
As three blind mice?   *Three Blind Mice*

11 A frog he would a-wooing go.
Sing heigh-ho says Rowley.
                              A Frog He Would A-Wooing Go

12 With a rowley powley gammon and spinach,
Heigh-ho says Anthony Rowley.
                              A Frog He Would A-Wooing Go, chorus

13 Old King Cole
Was a merry old soul,
And a merry old soul was he,
He called for his pipe,
And he called for his bowl,
And he called for his fiddlers three.   *Old King Cole*

14 The King of France went up the hill
With forty thousand men;
The King of France came down the hill
And ne'er went up again.   *The King of France*

15 Jack Sprat could eat no fat,
His wife could eat no lean;
And so betwixt them both,
They licked the platter clean.   *Jack Sprat*

16 Rain, rain, go away,
Come again another day.   *Rain, Rain*

17 Pat-a-cake, pat-a-cake, baker's man,
Bake me a cake as fast as you can;
Pat it and prick it, and mark it with B,
Put it in the oven for baby and me.   *Pat-a-Cake*

18 The lion and the unicorn
Were fighting for the crown;
The lion beat the unicorn
All round about the town.
Some gave them white bread,
And some gave them brown;
Some gave them plum cake,
And sent them out of town.
                              The Lion and the Unicorn

19 Little Jack Horner sat in the corner,
Eating a Christmas pie.
He put in his thumb, and pulled out a plum,
And said, "What a good boy am I!"
                              Little Jack Horner

20 London Bridge is falling down,
My fair lady.   *London Bridge*

21 Tell tale tit,
Your tongue shall be slit,
And all the dogs in our town
Shall have a bit.   *Tell Tale Tit*

22 As I was going to St. Ives,
I met a man with seven wives,
Each wife had seven sacks,
Each sack had seven cats,
Each cat had seven kits:

---

[1]Translated by JEROME ROTHENBERG.
[2]Translated by ARMAND SCHWERNER.

Kits, cats, sacks, and wives,
How many were there going to St. Ives?
                    As I Was Going to St. Ives

1 The man in the wilderness asked of me
How many strawberries grew in the sea.
I answered him as I thought good,
"As many as red herrings grow in the wood."
                    The Man in the Wilderness

2 Ladybug, ladybug, fly away home,
Your house is on fire, and your children will burn.
                    Ladybug, Ladybug

3 Hickory dickory dock,
The mouse ran up the clock,
The clock struck one,
The mouse ran down;
Hickory dickory dock.   *Hickory Dickory Dock*

4 Baa, baa, black sheep,
Have you any wool?
Yes, sir, yes, sir,
Three bags full:
One for my master,
And one for my dame,
And one for the little boy
Who lives down the lane.   *Baa, Baa, Black Sheep*

5 Mary, Mary, quite contrary,
How does your garden grow?
With silver bells, and cockleshells,
And pretty maids all in a row.
                    Mary, Mary, Quite Contrary

6 Oranges and lemons,
Say the bells of St. Clement's.
You owe me five farthings,
Say the bells of St. Martin's.
When will you pay me?
Say the bells of Old Bailey.
When I grow rich,
Say the bells of Shoreditch.   *Oranges and Lemons*

7 Here comes a candle to light you to bed,
Here comes a chopper to chop off your head.
                    Oranges and Lemons

8 "Who killed Cock Robin?"
"I," said the sparrow,
"With my bow and arrow,
I killed Cock Robin."
                    Who Killed Cock Robin?

9 "Who saw him die?"
"I," said the fly,
"With my little eye,
I saw him die."
                    Who Killed Cock Robin?

10 This little pig went to market;
This little pig stayed home;

This little pig had roast beef;
This little pig had none;
And this little pig cried, Wee, wee, wee!
All the way home.   *This Little Pig*

11 Little boy blue, come blow your horn,
The sheep's in the meadow, the cow's in the corn;
But where is the boy who looks after the sheep?
He's under the haystack fast asleep.
Will you wake him? No, not I,
For if I do, he'll be sure to cry.   *Little Boy Blue*

12 Simple Simon met a pieman
Going to the fair:
Says Simple Simon to the pieman,
"Let me taste your ware."   *Simple Simon*

13 Ding dong bell,
Pussy's in the well.
Who put her in?
Little Johnny Green.   *Ding Dong Bell*

14 Little Tom Tucker
Sings for his supper;
What shall he eat?
White bread and butter.
How will he cut it
Without e'er a knife?
How will he be married
Without e'er a wife?
                    Little Tom Tucker

15 Crosspatch, draw the latch,
Set by the fire and spin:
Take a cup and drink it up,
Then call your neighbors in.   *Crosspatch*

16 High diddle diddle
The cat and the fiddle,
The cow jumped over the moon;
The little dog laughed
To see such craft
And the dish ran away with the spoon.
                    High Diddle Diddle

17 Three wise men of Gotham
Went to sea in a bowl:
And if the bowl had been stronger,
My song had been longer.
                    Three Wise Men of Gotham

18 Jack and Jill went up the hill
To fetch a pail of water;
Jack fell down and broke his crown,
And Jill came tumbling after.   *Jack and Jill*

19 Seesaw, Margery Daw,
Jacky shall have a new master;
Jacky must have but a penny a day,
Because he can work no faster.
                    Seesaw, Margery Daw

1 Taffy was a Welshman, Taffy was a thief;
  Taffy came to my house and stole a piece of beef.
  I went to Taffy's house, Taffy wasn't in;
  Taffy came to my house and stole a silver pin.
  I went to Taffy's house; Taffy wasn't home.
  Taffy came to my house and stole a marrow bone.
  I went to Taffy's house and Taffy was in bed;
  So I picked up the poker and hit him in the head.
  Taffy Was a Welshman

2 The Queen of Hearts
  She made some tarts,
  All on a summer's day;
  The Knave of Hearts
  He stole the tarts,
  And took them clean away.   *The Queen of Hearts*

3 Bye baby bunting,
  Daddy's gone a-hunting.
  Gone to get a rabbit skin
  To wrap the baby bunting in.   *Bye Baby Bunting*

4 Come, let's to bed,
  Says Sleepyhead;
  Tarry awhile, says Slow;
  Put on the pot,
  Says Greedy-gut,
  We'll sup before we go.   *Let's to Bed*

5 Four and twenty tailors went to kill a snail,
  The best man among them durst not touch
      her tail.
  She put out her horns like a little Kyloe cow,
  Run, tailors, run, or she'll kill you all e'en now.
  Four and Twenty Tailors

6 Goosey goosey gander,
  Whither shall I wander?
  Upstairs and downstairs,
  And in my lady's chamber;
  There I met an old man who wouldn't say
      his prayers;
  I took him by the left leg
  And threw him down the stairs.
  Goosey Goosey Gander

7 Sing a song of sixpence,
  A pocket full of rye,
  Four and twenty blackbirds,
  Baked in a pie;
  When the pie was opened,
  The birds began to sing;
  Wasn't that a dainty dish
  To set before a king?

  The king was in his countinghouse
  Counting out his money;
  The queen was in the parlor
  Eating bread and honey;
  The maid was in the garden

Hanging out the clothes,
  Along came a blackbird,
  And snipped off her nose.
  Sing a Song of Sixpence

8 There was an old woman who lived in a shoe,
  She had so many children she didn't know what
      to do;
  She gave them some broth without any bread,
  She whipped them all soundly and put them to bed.
  There Was an Old Woman

9 Ride a cockhorse to Banbury Cross,
  To see a fine lady upon a white horse;
  Rings on her fingers and bells on her toes,
  She shall have music wherever she goes.
  Ride a Cockhorse

10 Tom, Tom, the piper's son,
  He learned to play when he was young.
  But all the tune that he could play
  Was "Over the hills and far away."
  Tom, Tom, the Piper's Son

11 Tom, Tom, the piper's son,
  Stole a pig, and away he run;
  The pig was eat, and Tom was beat,
  And Tom went howling down the street.
  Tom, Tom, the Piper's Son

12 "Where are you going to, my pretty maid?"
  "I'm going a-milking, sir," she said.
  Where Are You Going To, My Pretty Maid?

13 "My face is my fortune, sir," she said.
  Where Are You Going To, My Pretty Maid?

14 "Nobody asked you, sir," she said.
  Where Are You Going To, My Pretty Maid?

15 One a penny, two a penny, hot cross buns;
  If you have no daughters, give them to your sons.
  Hot Cross Buns

16 Pease-porridge hot, pease-porridge cold,
  Pease-porridge in the pot, nine days old.
  Pease-Porridge Hot

17 Curlylocks, Curlylocks,
  Wilt thou be mine?
  Thou shalt not wash dishes
  Nor yet feed the swine,
  But sit on a cushion
  And sew a fine seam,
  And feed upon strawberries,
  Sugar and cream.   *Curlylocks*

18 I had a little nut tree, nothing would it bear
  But a silver nutmeg and a golden pear;
  The king of Spain's daughter came to visit me,
  And all for the sake of my little nut tree.
  I Had a Little Nut Tree

1 Humpty Dumpty sat on a wall,
  Humpty Dumpty had a great fall;
  All the king's horses
  And all the king's men
  Couldn't put Humpty Dumpty together again.
                  Humpty Dumpty

2 Little Bo-peep has lost her sheep,
  And cannot tell where to find them;
  Leave them alone, and they'll come home,
  And bring their tails behind them.　*Little Bo-peep*

3 Little Polly Flinders
  Sat among the cinders,
  Warming her pretty little toes.
  Her mother came and caught her,
  And whipped her little daughter
  For spoiling her nice new clothes.
                 Little Polly Flinders

4 There was an old woman tossed in a blanket,
  Seventeen times as high as the moon;
  But where she was going no mortal could tell,
  For under her arm she carried a broom.
  Old woman, old woman, old woman, said I,
  Whither, ah whither, ah whither so high?
  To sweep the cobwebs from the sky,
  And I'll be with you by and by.
              There Was an Old Woman

5 The north wind doth blow,
  And we shall have snow,
  And what will poor robin do then,
  Poor thing? He'll sit in a barn,
  To keep himself warm,
  And hide his head under his wing,
  Poor thing!
             The North Wind Doth Blow

6 Old mother Hubbard
  Went to the cupboard,
  To fetch her poor dog a bone;
  But when she came there
  The cupboard was bare,
  And so the poor dog had none.
              Old Mother Hubbard

7 Pussy cat, pussy cat, where have you been?
  I've been to London to look at the queen.
  Pussy cat, pussy cat, what did you there?
  I frightened a little mouse under the chair.
                 Pussy Cat

8 Peter Piper picked a peck of pickled peppers;
  A peck of pickled peppers Peter Piper picked.
  If Peter Piper picked a peck of pickled peppers,
  Where's the peck of pickled peppers Peter Piper
     picked?　　　　　　　　*Peter Piper*

9 Monday's child is fair of face,
  Tuesday's child is full of grace,

Wednesday's child is full of woe,
Thursday's child has far to go,
Friday's child is loving and giving,
Saturday's child has to work for its living,
But a child that's born on the Sabbath day
Is fair and wise and good and gay.
        Monday's Child Is Fair of Face

10 Solomon Grundy,
  Born on a Monday,
  Christened on Tuesday,
  Married on Wednesday,
  Took ill on Thursday,
  Worse on Friday,
  Died on Saturday,
  Buried on Sunday:
  This is the end
  Of Solomon Grundy.　　　*Solomon Grundy*

11 What are little boys made of?
  Snips and snails, and puppy dogs' tails;
  That's what little boys are made of.
        What Are Little Boys Made Of?

12 What are little girls made of?
  Sugar and spice, and everything nice;
  That's what little girls are made of.
        What Are Little Girls Made Of?

13 Hickety pickety, my black hen,
  She lays eggs for gentlemen.
  Gentlemen come every day
  To see what my black hen doth lay.
           Hickety Pickety[1]

14 Little Miss Muffet
  Sat on a tuffet,
  Eating some curds and whey.
  Along came a spider,
  And sat down beside her,
  And frightened Miss Muffet away.
            Little Miss Muffet

15 Peter, Peter Pumpkin-Eater,
  Had a wife and couldn't keep her.
  He put her in a pumpkin shell,
  And there he kept her very well.
      Peter, Peter Pumpkin-Eater

16 Jack, be nimble,
  Jack, be quick,
  Jack, jump over the candlestick.　*Jack Be Nimble*

17 There was a crooked man, and he went a crooked
     mile,
  He found a crooked sixpence against a crooked stile;

---

[1]Higgledy-piggledy my white hen, / She lays eggs for gentlemen; / She cannot be persuaded by gun or lariat / To come across for the proletariat. — DOROTHY PARKER

He bought a crooked cat, which caught a crooked
    mouse,
And they all lived together in a little crooked
    house.
                             There Was a Crooked Man

1 Diddle diddle dumpling, my son John,
  He went to bed with his stockings on;
  One shoe off, one shoe on;
  Diddle diddle dumpling, my son John.
                        Diddle Diddle Dumpling

2 Rub-a-dub-dub,
  Three men in a tub,
  And who do you think they be?
  The butcher, the baker,
  The candlestick-maker;
  And all of them went to sea!   *Rub-a-Dub-Dub*

3 I saw three ships come sailing by,
  Come sailing by, come sailing by,
  I saw three ships come sailing by,
  On New Year's Day in the morning.
                          I Saw Three Ships

4 In fir tar is,
  In oak none is.
  In mud eel is,
  In clay none is.
  Goats eat ivy.
  Mares eat oats.   *In Fir Tar Is*

5 Lucy Locket lost her pocket,
  Kitty Fisher found it;
  There was not a penny in it,
  But a ribbon round it.   *Lucy Locket*

6 There were three jolly huntsmen,
  As I have heard them say,
  And they would go a-hunting
  Upon St. David's Day.
             There Were Three Jolly Huntsmen

7 All day they hunted,
  And nothing did they find,
  But a ship a-sailing,
  A-sailing with the wind.
             There Were Three Jolly Huntsmen

8 O do you know the muffin man,
  The muffin man, the muffin man,
  O do you know the muffin man,
  That lives in Drury Lane?   *The Muffin Man*

9 To market, to market, to buy a fat pig,
  Home again, home again, jiggety-jig.
                    To Market, To Market

10 Doctor Foster went to Gloucester
  In a shower of rain;
  He stepped in a puddle, up to his middle,
  And never went there again.   *Doctor Foster*

11 There was an old woman
  Lived under a hill;
  And if she's not gone,
  She lives there still.
                There Was an Old Woman

12 There was a little man, and he had a little gun,
  And his bullets were made of lead, lead, lead;
  He went to the brook, and saw a little duck,
  And shot it through the head, head, head.
                  There Was a Little Man

13 Lavender's blue, dilly dilly, lavender's green;
  When I am king, dilly dilly, you shall be queen.
                    Lavender's Blue

14 A dillar, a dollar,
  A ten o'clock scholar,
  What makes you come so soon?
  You used to come at ten o'clock,
  And now you come at noon.   *A Dillar, a Dollar*

15 One flew east, one flew west,
  One flew over the cuckoo's nest.   *One Flew East*

16 I had a little pony,
  His name was Dapple Gray;
  I lent him to a lady
  To ride a mile away.
  She whipped him, she slashed him,
  She rode him through the mire;
  I would not lend my pony now
  For all the lady's hire.   *I Had a Little Pony*

17 Polly, put the kettle on,
  We'll all have tea.
             Polly, Put the Kettle On, st. 1

18 Sukey, take it off again,
  They've all gone away.
             Polly, Put the Kettle On, st. 1

19 Little Tommy Tittlemouse
  Lived in a little house;
  He caught fishes
  In other men's ditches.
                Little Tommy Tittlemouse

20 The farmer in the dell, the farmer in the dell,
  Heigho! the derry oh, the farmer in the dell.
                The Farmer in the Dell

21 Hark! Hark! The dogs do bark,
  The beggars are coming to town;
  Some in rags, some in tags,
  And some in velvet gowns.   *Hark! Hark!*

22 Ten little Indians standing in a line —
  One went home, and then there were nine.
                Ten Little Indians

23 When good King Arthur ruled this land,
  He was a goodly king,

He bought three pecks of barley meal,
To make a bag pudding.   *Good King Arthur*

1 One misty, moisty morning,
When cloudy was the weather,
I chanced to meet an old man
Clothed all in leather;
He began to compliment,
And I began to grin —
"How do you do?" and "How do you do?"
And "How do you do?" again!
        One Misty, Moisty Morning

2 Bobby Shaftoe's gone to sea,
Silver buckles on his knee;
He'll come back and marry me,
Pretty Bobby Shaftoe.   *Bobby Shaftoe*

3 Fe fi fo fum!
I smell the blood of an Englishman;
Be he alive or be he dead,
I'll grind his bones to make my bread.   *Fe Fi Fo Fum*

4 Sing, sing! What shall I sing?
The cat's run away with the pudding-bag string.
        Sing, Sing! What Shall I Sing?

5 Shoe the horse, shoe the mare,
But let the little colt go bare.   *Shoe the Horse*

6 There was a man in our town,
And he was wondrous wise;
He jumped into a bramble bush
And scratched out both his eyes.
        There Was a Man in Our Town

7 There were two blackbirds,
Sitting on a hill,
The one named Jack,
The other named Jill;
Fly away, Jack! Fly away, Jill!
Come again, Jack! Come again, Jill!   *Two Blackbirds*

8 This is the farmer sowing the corn,
That kept the cock that crowed in the morn,
That waked the priest all shaven and shorn,
That married the man all tattered and torn,
That kissed the maiden all forlorn,
That milked the cow with the crumpled horn,
That tossed the dog
That worried the cat
That killed the rat
That ate the malt
That lay in the house that Jack built.
        The House That Jack Built

Anonymous: Russian

9   Let the woman into Paradise, she'll bring her cow
along.   *Proverb*

10   An egg is dear on Easter Day.   *Proverb*

11   To live a life through is not like crossing a field.[1]
        Proverb

12   The eggs do not teach the hen.   *Proverb*

13   Live with wolves, howl like a wolf.   *Proverb*

14   Don't hang noodles on my ears.   *Saying*

Anonymous: Shanties

15 Whiskey is the life of man,
Whiskey, Johnny!
Oh, I'll drink whiskey while I can,
Whiskey for my Johnny!
        Whiskey Johnny

16 Oh, blow the man down, bullies, blow the man down!
To me way-aye, blow the man down.
Oh, blow the man down, bullies, blow him right down!
Give me some time to blow the man down!
        Blow the Man Down

17 What shall we do with the drunken sailor,
Early in the morning?   *The Drunken Sailor*

18 Hooray and up she rises
Early in the morning.
        The Drunken Sailor, chorus

19 Oh, Shenandoah, I long to hear you,
Way-hay, you rolling river!
Oh, Shenandoah, I long to hear you,
Ha-ha, we're bound away,
'Cross the wide Missouri!   *Shenandoah*

20 A-roving, a-roving,
Since roving's been my ru-i-in,
I'll go no more a-roving
With you, fair maid!   *A-Roving*

21 Glos'ter girls they have no combs,
Heave away, heave away!
They comb their hair with codfish bones.
        The Codfish Shanty

22   Good-bye, fare you well!
We're homeward bound for New York town,
Hurrah, my boys, we're homeward bound!
        Good-bye, Fare You Well

23 Oh, the times are hard and the wages low;
Leave her, Johnny, leave her!
I'll pack my bag and go below.
It's time for us to leave her!   *Leave Her, Johnny*

---
[1]See Boris Pasternak, 688:3.

1 There were two lofty ships, from old England they
set sail,
Blow high, blow low, and so sailed we! . . .
Cruising down along the shores of High Barbaree!
High Barbaree

2 There was a ship came from the north country,
And the name of the ship was the Golden Vanity.
And they feared she might be taken by the Turkish
enemy,
That sails upon the Lowland, Lowland, Lowland,
That sails upon the Lowland sea. *The Golden Vanity*

3 Then blow ye winds, heigh-ho!
A-roving I will go,
I'll stay no more on England's shore,
To hear the music play.
I'm off on the morning train
To cross the raging main,
I'm taking a trip on a Government ship,
Ten thousand miles away!
Ten Thousand Miles Away

Anonymous: Spanish

4   A enemigo que huye puente de plata [If your
enemy turns to flee, give him a silver bridge].
Proverb

5   Al que madruga Dios le ayuda [God helps those
who get up early].
Proverb

6   Con pan y vino se anda el camino [With bread and
wine you can walk your road].
Proverb

7   El pez muere por la boca [The fish dies because he
opens his mouth]. *Proverb*

8   El que se sienta en la puerta de su casa verá pasar el
cadáver de su enemigo [He who sits at the door of his
house will watch his enemy's corpse go by].
Proverb

9   En boca cerrada no entran moscas [The closed
mouth swallows no flies]. *Proverb*

10   No por mucho madrugar amanece más temprano
[Dawn comes no sooner for the early riser].
Proverb

11   Quien bien te quiere te hará llorar [Whoever really
loves you will make you cry]. *Proverb*

12   El oro y amores eran malos de encubrir [Gold and
love affairs are difficult to hide].
Proverb

13   Dios te tenga en su santa mano [God keep you in
his holy hand]. *A farewell*

Anonymous: Spirituals

14 Nobody knows the trouble I've seen,
Nobody knows but Jesus.
Nobody Knows the Trouble I've Seen

15 Joshua fit the battle of Jericho,
And the walls come tumbling down.
Joshua Fit the Battle of Jericho

16 Sometimes I feel like a motherless child,
A long ways from home,
A long ways from home. *Motherless Child*

17 Go tell it on the mountain,
Over the hills and everywhere;
Go tell it on the mountain,
That Jesus Christ is born.
Go Tell It on the Mountain

18 Go down, Moses,
Way down in Egypt land,
Tell old Pharaoh,
Let my people go. *Go Down, Moses*

19 Free at last, free at last,
Thank God Almighty, we're free at last.[1]
Free at Last

20 I looked over Jordan, and what did I see? . . .
A band of angels coming after me,
Coming for to carry me home.
Swing Low, Sweet Chariot, st. 1

21 Swing low, sweet chariot,
Coming for to carry me home.
Swing Low, Sweet Chariot, refrain

22 Michael row the boat ashore,
Hallelujah! *Michael Row the Boat Ashore*

23 Rise and shine and give God the glory
For the year of Jubilee.
Rise and Shine

24 My Lord, what a morning,
When the stars begin to fall.
My Lord, What a Morning

25 You'll hear the trumpet sound,
To wake the nations underground,
Look in my God's right hand,
When the stars begin to fall.
My Lord, What a Morning

26 One more river,
And that's the river of Jordan,
One more river,
There's one more river to cross.
One More River

---

[1]See Martin Luther King, Jr., 823:9.

1 Oh, freedom! Oh, freedom!
  Oh, freedom over me!
  And before I'd be a slave, I'll be buried in my grave,
  And go home to my Lord and be free.
  Oh, Freedom!

2 Get on board, little children,
  There's room for many a more.
  Get on Board, Little Children

3 The Gospel train's a-coming.
  Get on Board, Little Children

4 Just like a tree that's standing by the water,
  We shall not be moved.   *We Shall Not Be Moved*

5 O Lord, I want to be in that number
  When the saints go marching in.
  When the Saints Go Marching In

INDEX

INDEX

INDEX

Please see the Index section of the Guide to the Use of Bartlett's Familiar Quotations, *page xi.*

A

A, black A white E, 559:4
  emotions from A to B, 699:18
  first write a crowned A, 133:16
  injures B or improving X, 645:17
  on gown letter A, 431:3
A', for a. that and a. that, 358:20
A-angling, be quiet and go a., 245:10
Aaron's rod, 7:34
Ab Iove principium, 92:n14
  ovo, 98:n10
  urbe condita, 119:28
Abandon, all hope a. who enter here, 128:6
  government which kept us free, 337:9
  learning and no sorrow, 57:9
  to cries and lamentations, 105:1
Abandoned, man a. on earth, 742:22
  poem never finished only a., 612:14
Abandonment of force, 653:16
Abased, whoso exalt himself be a., 35:14
Abashed the Devil stood, 258:8
Abatement and low price, 204:11
Abbot of Aberbrothok, 381:12
Abbottabad, against that compound in A., 877:6
Abednego, Shadrach Meshach and A., 28:22
A-begging, truth goes a., 144:4
Abel was keeper of sheep, 6:3
Aberbrothok, Abbot of A., 381:12
Aberdour, half owre to A., 889:17
Aberrations, of sexual a. curious chastity, 570:4
Abhor detest Sabbath-day, 523:11
  makers and laws approve, 274:5
Abhorred in my imagination, 202:12
  shears, 253:6
  that senseless tribe, 285:9
Abhors, God a. you, 301:11
  nature a. a vacuum, 275:16
Abide, fates impose that men a., 170:32
  nowhere did a., 376:15
  others a. our question, 494:10
  tyme nyl no man a., 135:18
  under the shadow of the Almighty, 17:28
  who shall a. in thy tabernacle, 15:10
  with me, 405:8
Abides, in mystery soul a., 494:17
  there a. peace of thine, 495:1

Abideth, earth a. forever, 22:21
  faith hope charity, 42:29
Abiding Leaf, 756:15
  shepherds a. in field, 37:17
Abiezer, vintage of A., 10:16
Abiit ad plures, 105:n9
  excessit evasit erupit, 87:n4
Abilities, far more than our a., 879:4
  from each according to a., 478:5
  possible for others to use a., 771:15
  splendid a. but utterly corrupt, 381:5
Ability, charge not soul save to a., 118:22
  laughter a. and Sighing, 509:20
  lean and low a., 205:24
  they never perform, 203:18
  to afford not to learn, 767:10
  to get to verge, 674:16
Abject are usually ambitious, 276:11
  submission, 328:6
Abjure, rough magic I a., 225:3
Able and willing to pull weight, 571:6
  at least as far as a., 555:9
  be a. for thine enemy, 205:30
  rather a. than learned, 152:7
Ablest navigators, 332:9
Ablution round earth's shores, 412:10
Abner a prince and a great man, 11:12
  smote him under the fifth rib, 11:11
Abode destined Hour, 441:12
  dread a., 316:8
  Last A. is Life, 119:3
  Olympus a. of the gods, 53:2
  refuge and a. of evil and vice, 136:22
  untented Kosmos my a., 556:5
Abodes, peaceful a. of the gods, 53:n1
Abolish, right to alter or a. it, 336:1
  serfdom from above, 476:3
  slavery of half of humanity, 751:8
  tyranny and vice, 329:6
Abolition of private property, 478:12
Abominably, imitated humanity so a., 200:9
Abomination, Mass an a., 144:6
  of desolation, 35:20
Abora, singing of Mount A., 377:22
Abortion, greatest destroyer of peace, 762:10
  men pregnant a. a sacrament, 782:7
  today law of a. undisturbed, 751:12
  will not give pessary to cause a., 70:14

Abortions will not let you forget, 783:6
Abou Ben Adhem, 392:16
Abound, grace a., 41:13
  joys a. as seasons fleet, 170:4
Abounded, where sin a., 41:13
About about in reel and rout, 376:5
  it and about but evermore, 441:18
  it's not a. you, 873:7
Above, at once a. beneath around, 318:7
  economic tyranny a., 666:12
  every good gift is from a., 45:22
  insolence and triviality, 671:2
  may it be beautiful a. me, 891:18
  whatever is below is like a., 113:3
  world stretched the sky, 695:6
Abraham, God of A. not of philosophers, 270:2
  Jacob Moses, 692:8
  that which has been sent down on A., 117:13
  thy name shall be A., 6:32
  we are coming Father A., 457:3
Abraham's, beggar in A. bosom, 38:17
  liest in A. bosom, 370:6
  sleep in A. bosom, 171:36
Abram dwelled in Canaan, 6:29
  O father A., 184:31
Abreast, one but goes a., 203:23
Abreuve nos sillons, 361:3
Abridging freedom of speech, 340:1
Abridgment of freedom, 345:13
Abroad for good of my country, 290:8
  know own country before goes a., 314:19
  lie a. for commonwealth, 227:14
  obsequious a., 391:13
  purchase great alliance, 170:29
  what should be not published a., 70:14
Absalom my son my son, 11:22
Absence, conspicuous by a., 401:7
  cry of A. A. in heart, 681:18
  cure of love, 156:22
  darkness death, 229:13
  diminishes mediocre passions, 264:15
  dote on his very a., 184:20
  doth breed continual remembrance, 137:n5
  like a winter my a., 222:5
  love cannot admit a., 229:15
  love rekindled by a., 307:6
  makes heart fonder, 101:17

Absence *(continued)*
    of evidence is not, 855:3
    of mind we have borne, 383:21
    of occupation not rest, 326:14
    of romance in my history, 71:12
    peace not a. of war, 275:15
    seemed my flame to qualify, 222:11
    takes place in our a., 865:11
    Ulysses' a., 219:22
Absent, friends a. speak, 230:14
    if to be a. were to be away, 266:3
    in body present in spirit, 42:12
    in the spring, 222:6
    let no one speak ill of a., 101:16
    one from another, 7:1
    room of a. child, 175:19
    thee from felicity, 202:31
Absentee, war vast aloof a., 843:3
Absentes, in a. felicior aestus amantes, 101:n5
Absenti nemo non nocuisse velit, 101:n4
Absent-minded, most a. of men
        plunged in reveries, 482:19
Absents, presents endear a., 383:14
Absit omen, 120:1
Absolute and in herself complete, 259:3
    atoms preserved by a. solidity, 89:17
    be a. for death, 206:32
    built a. trust, 214:15
    foreknowledge a., 256:21
    freedom of navigation, 566:16
    how a. the knave is, 202:10
    idea of knowledge, 76:1
    Johannes fac totum, 164:3
    mark you his a. shall, 219:30
    natures or kinds, 76:1
    notion of a. beauty, 74:5
    power corrupts absolutely, 518:10
    power in majority, 330:16
    power over wives, 340:12
Absolutely, corrupts a., 518:10
    nothing a. straight can be wrought, 320:1
Absolutes in Bill of Rights, 667:1
    meant prohibitions to be a., 667:1
    the a. the eternities, 776:9
Absolutism tempered by assassination, 362:9
Absolve, compensate bad in man a. him so,
        463:6
    foulness of their fate, 668:14
    history will a. me, 811:12
    pray God a. us all, 139:3
Absolved from allegiance, 328:2
    judge condemned when criminal a., 100:10
    people a. of history, 829:8
Absorb as Parallax a Flame, 510:15
Absorbed, everybody is a. in something, 808:4
Absorbing, reflects images without a., 531:20
Absorbs, country a. him affectionately, 485:11
    tinged by what a. it, 542:8
Abstain from fleshly lusts, 45:38
    from intentional wrongdoing, 70:14
Abstinence easy to me, 308:11
    lean and sallow a., 252:23
    lend easiness to next a., 201:13
    sows sand all over, 352:6
Abstinete, a fabis a., 234:15
Abstract concepts, 338:22
    love of beauty in a., 413:6
    man in the a., 507:6

Abstract *(continued)*
    nothing more a. than we see, 687:15
    words obscene, 721:6
Abstractions, go in fear of a., 665:3
Abstracts and brief chronicles, 199:13
Absurd, death a. also, 761:5
    is essential concept, 770:1
    lick a. pomp, 200:10
    poets creatures most a., 296:18
    question is a., 749:11
    the a. not the improbable, 469:4
    to be believed because a., 113:12
Absurdity, dull without a single a., 322:6
    man only subject to a., 239:6
    privilege of a., 239:6
    what to do with this a., 594:5
Abundance, add more to a., 652:13
    full sharers in a., 554:5
    if thou hast a., 29:28
    out of a. mouth speaketh, 34:12
    possesses virtue in a., 57:17
    pray in days of a., 655:7
    will not suffer him to sleep, 23:6
Abundant, more a. life, 652:4
    shower of curates, 472:12
Abundantly, have life more a., 39:30
Abuse, how long Catiline a. our patience, 87:5
    land as commodity, 668:2
    of greatness, 191:35
    of power comes as no surprise, 869:1
    reading that which is printed in a., 472:2
    whipping and a. like laudanum, 458:15
    wicked dreams a., 215:14
    you cause what you a., 281:7
Abused, by himself a. or disabused, 295:1
Abuses, evils exist only in a., 364:4
Abusing, abstain from a. bodies, 70:14
    of God's patience, 187:4
    stop a. my verses or publish, 107:8
Abysm of time, 224:4
Abyss, cradle rocks above a., 723:3
    discovery metamorphosis, 616:5
    look long into a., 548:8
    looks into you, 548:8
    man is rope over a., 547:17
Abysses, dread a. unknown tides, 542:14
    wander in a. of solitude, 556:18
Abyssinia, Rasselas Prince of A., 307:8
Abyssinian maid, 377:22
Academe, groves of A., 98:12
    olive grove of A., 260:3
Academes, they are the books the a., 174:24
Academi, inter silvas A., 98:n4
Academic life, 233:15
    politics are so bitter, 743:10
Academy, Frenchman in A., 309:n1
Accelerated grimace, 665:6
Acceleration proportional to applied force,
        279:n3
Accents, aged a. untimely words, 167:4
    caught his clear a., 460:12
    yet unknown, 192:18
Accept, bow and a. end, 622:8
    decline to a. end of man, 714:4
    fall in with what asked to a., 625:10
    God a. him, 454:17
    I will not a. if nominated, 490:1
    never a. thing as true, 246:7

Accept *(continued)*
    not God I don't a., 492:11
    tamely a., 585:2
    things that cannot be changed, 695:20
    universe, 456:18
    will for deed a., 145:n11
Acceptability, hallmark of conventional wisdom
        a., 752:15
Acceptable, be a. in thy sight, 15:19
    offices a. here, 337:6
Accepted, fellow mortals a. as they are, 480:2
    now is a. time, 43:16
    that which a. false, 612:11
    you are a., 668:18
Accepting, charms by a., 294:3
    not by a. favors, 72:2
    two contradictory beliefs, 735:20
Access and passage to remorse, 214:17
Accessible, English not a. to Englishmen,
        565:19
Accident, bundle of a. and incoherence,
        597:14
    by a. got its liberty, 142:8
    counts for much, 531:5
    found out by a., 383:24
    happy a., 236:19
    of sentiment, 520:15
    shot of a., 209:28
    what seems a. springs from destiny, 360:2
Accidentally, America discovered a., 672:3
    only a. am I French, 297:15
Accidents, chapter of a. very long, 298:17
    confront ridicule a. rebuffs, 485:13
    fill world, 882:12
    in best-regulated families, 465:32
    moving a. by flood, 207:37
    omissions are not a., 671:n1
    shackles a., 219:7
Accommodating vice, 267:26
Accommodations, equal but separate a.,
        692:n3
Accompany old age, 217:18
Accomplice, art a. of love, 570:3
    evening comes like a., 491:8
Accomplish little, 360:12
Accomplished anything except get along, 664:4
    desire a. is sweet, 20:22
    her warfare is a., 26:24
    nothing a. alone, 696:6
    nothing great a. without passion, 367:13
    plan of Zeus was being a., 50:10
Accomplisher, Zeus a., 63:28
Accomplishes without any action, 57:16
Accomplishing, armorers a. the knights, 189:18
    their appointed courses, 69:21
Accomplishment, smile of a., 833:5
Accomplishments, emerges ahead of a., 733:2
Accord, someone whom we a. with, 343:2
Accordance, activity in a. with excellence, 78:13
According, acted a. to what we thought, 782:9
    to every man a. to his work, 17:5
    to the fixed law of gravity, 440:5
Account, give accurate exhaustive a., 612:16
    of her life to clod, 190:23
    sent to my a., 198:12
Accounting, death the final a., 120:33
    matter of creative a., 811:7
    no a. for tastes, 120:14

Accounts, cross out overpaid a., 487:5
Accumulate, horrors a., 209:16
Accumulated experience, 630:2
    wrong, 585:2
Accumulates, where wealth a., 322:22
Accuracy tried by severe tests, 71:12
Accurate, give a. exhaustive account, 612:16
    in his judgment, 329:*n*1
Accursed craving for gold, 94:19
    fear most a. of base passions, 169:20
    he that first invented war, 167:19
    night she bore me, 67:13
    opinions are a., 593:17
Accuse, j'a., 537:16
    not a. me before the God, 3:10
    not Nature, 259:4
    not servant to his master, 22:13
Accused, I accuser God a., 821:5
Accuser, I a. God accused, 821:5
    no a. so terrible, 85:12
Accuses, excuses himself a. himself, 151:3
Accusing Spirit, 314:18
Accustomed to deliberate when drunk, 69:8
    to her face, 790:12
    to way ground opens up, 836:9
Aces, confidence in four a., 521:20
Acetylene, rip-tooth of sky's a., 720:4
Achaeans, brought upon the A. myriad woes,
    50:9
    well-greaved A., 51:2
Achates, faithful A., 94:28
    fidus A., 94:*n*13
Ache, age a. penury, 207:1
    ark of the a. of it, 803:3
    charm a. with air, 191:12
    gum-and-bone a., 867:1
Acheron, fear of A. be sent packing, 90:8
Aches, my heart a., 410:2
    sense a. at thee, 210:5
    when the head a., 157:4
Achieve and cherish peace, 447:2
    some a. greatness, 205:8
    the a. of the thing, 546:10
Achieved by others' death, 175:27
    matchless deed's a., 318:10
    nothing a. without enthusiasm, 427:15
    the a. West, 713:9
Achievement, bring it to a., 67:22
    death of endeavor, 540:3
    of continuous human effort, 725:9
    quality form Man of A., 412:15
    sum of human a., 553:3
    talent in every branch of a., 71:15
    wealth opportunity for a., 71:15
Achievements, not pride selves on a., 648:17
    of intellect everlasting, 92:10
Achieveth, naught n' assaieth naught n' a.,
    132:24
Achieving, still a. still pursuing, 436:7
Achilles, not even A. bring to fulfillment, 52:11
    O fortunate youth A., 80:21
    see the great A., 451:18
    what name A. assumed, 248:27
    wrath of A., 50:9
Achilles', Troy and A. wrath, 487:3
    stood upon A. tomb, 398:21
Aching, bring my a. heart to rest, 86:18
    ease one Life the A., 510:4

Aching *(continued)*
    one tooth and it a., 611:14
    they have left a. void, 326:8
Achitophel, false A. was first, 272:16
Achoo, barely daring to A., 833:7
Acknowledge and bewail our sins, 49:5
    and confess our sins, 48:1
    restraint of reverence, 71:14
    thing of darkness I a. mine, 225:8
    us in some way, 833:17
Acknowledged, governments whose
    independence a., 355:7
Acknowledgment, transcribed without a.,
    104:13
A-clickin' like tickin' of a clock, 553:10
A-cold, owl a., 409:18
    poor Tom's a., 212:8
Acolytes, basin in hands of a., 829:8
A-coming, Gospel train's a., 899:3
Acorns, hogs eat a., 262:*n*1
    oaks from little a., 121:4
Acquaintance, creditable a., 284:11
    in which no new a., 311:16
    should auld a., 357:17
    sneered and slanged, 606:14
    visiting a., 346:7
Acquaintances, make new a., 308:21
Acquainted with grief, 27:5
    with the night, 623:16
Acquaints, misery a. with strange bedfellows,
    224:23
Acquent, when we were first a., 357:13
Acquiesce, if we a. in discrimination, 629:6
Acquire and beget a temperance, 200:6
Acquired, knowledge a. under compulsion,
    75:15
Acquiring and possessing property, 320:7
    ways of a. books, 692:12
Acquisitions or losses by nature, 341:8
Acquit, doesn't fit you must a., 842:8
Acre of barren ground, 224:2
Acres, a few paternal a. bound, 292:4
    five a. made to do the work, 789:4
    happy man works ancestral a., 95:27
    over whose a. blessed feet, 181:19
Acrobat, Governor of New York not an a.,
    617:12
    poet like an a., 792:6
Across, slip away a. the universe, 848:16
Acrostics, Baconian a., 723:4
Act against Constitution, 321:3
    against natural equity, 321:3
    an a. of survival, 825:11
    and do things accordingly, 690:3
    as if God did exist, 586:2
    as if there were God, 541:20
    beauty and valor and a., 546:11
    between motion and a., 677:1
    both a. and know, 266:19
    but not rely on own ability, 57:4
    everybody wants ta get inta a., 697:13
    has no ethical quality unless chosen, 541:3
    heaven helps not men who will not a.,
    59:*n*3
    in doubt to a. or rest, 295:1
    in the noon, 351:16
    last a. crowns play, 242:5
    last a. is bloody, 269:15

Act *(continued)*
    like a man of thought, 572:12
    locally, 727:18
    no a. of kindness ever wasted, 58:17
    not afraid of destructive a., 583:8
    not criminal unless intent criminal, 120:3
    of fear, 197:13
    of life, 545:7
    old age play's last a., 88:17
    only on that maxim, 320:4
    our Antipodes, 249:7
    perform every a. as though your last, 111:9
    poem of a. of mind, 379:*n*2
    power to live and a., 372:11
    prologues to swelling a., 214:10
    promptly, 564:10
    reap an a., 885:17
    sins they love to a., 220:10
    sleep an a. or two, 226:16
    to think is to a., 423:16
    two witnesses to overt a., 339:13
    virtue and prudent a., 324:10
    vote and a. to bring good, 541:16
    what it is to a. or suffer, 678:2
Acta est fabula, 120:2
Actaeon ego sum dominum cognoscite,
    102:*n*8
    I am A., 102:12
Acted according to what we thought, 782:9
    lofty scene be a. o'er, 192:18
Acting is suffering, 678:2
    of dreadful thing, 192:2
    only when off stage he was a., 323:7
    people inside your head a., 799:16
    surrender explaining not a., 617:4
Action, accomplishes without any a., 57:16
    advantage of taking no a., 57:14
    all a. planned in twilight, 388:11
    American's principal means of a., 433:14
    brave in a. patient under labors, 519:10
    faithful honor clear, 294:9
    feeling for single good a., 343:16
    fruit of a. not be motive, 84:9
    give a. its character, 73:23
    humans must have a., 472:10
    imitate a. of the tiger, 189:7
    imitation of a. that is serious, 79:3
    impartial in thought and a., 566:6
    in a. how like an angel, 199:5
    in bondage to history, 506:15
    in thought as in a., 753:2
    knowledge must come through a., 66:11
    leave out most of the a., 807:20
    life a. and passion, 538:5
    lose the name of a., 199:21
    lust in a., 222:20
    makes the a. fine, 243:10
    man is origin of his a., 78:9
    man of a. forced into thought, 600:22
    moment not of a. or inaction, 84:*n*8
    moments of a. and no a. linked, 136:23
    no worthy a. done, 883:18
    nor utterance nor speech, 193:4
    nothing more terrible than ignorance in a.,
    344:27
    of masses of men, 473:15
    on a. alone be thy interest, 84:9
    pious a. sugar o'er, 199:20

Action (*continued*)
pious fraud as with bad a., 333:20
predestined from eternity, 506:15
result of human a., 319:11
sense of honor in a., 72:4
sentiments weigh less than a., 482:11
suit a. to the word, 200:7
Tao takes no a., 57:13
test lies in a., 63:26
think like a man of a., 572:12
this is a. this not being sure, 815:5
thought too much for a., 533:13
to every a. equal reaction, 279:16
vice by a. dignified, 180:17
Actions, decisive a. unconsidered, 604:9
must be his spirit, 79:10
mutual a. of two bodies, 279:16
my a. are my ministers, 281:*n*1
powers of government reach a. not
opinions, 337:13
society exists for noble a., 78:24
speech is image of a., 55:15
think beforehand that a. be resolute, 79:24
thousand a. once afoot, 188:36
what a. most excellent, 495:13
when our a. do not, 217:3
work good of agent, 276:9
Active, deeply and intensely a., 540:16
experimentation a. science, 468:11
free a. individuals, 496:3
through form and figure, 380:1
to the vigilant a. brave, 331:12
Activest, his a. part, 263:8
Activities, knowledge of unconscious a. of
mind, 563:1
Activity in accordance with excellence, 78:13
property product of a., 633:11
Actor, better be a. than critic, 618:17
conceals state of mindlessness, 136:23
condemn fault and not a., 206:24
dreamer is a., 630:9
is one of elements of image, 766:18
pregnant with part, 584:18
well-graced a. leaves, 177:21
Actors, like a. in ancient plays, 559:1
more from the A. Studio, 780:2
no small parts only small a., 584:16
these our a. were spirits, 225:1
Acts, four a. already past, 291:9
his a. being seven ages, 194:25
let a play have five a., 98:27
nameless unremembered a., 368:7
no second a. in American lives, 710:19
only as are injurious to others, 336:5
our lives in a. exemplary, 163:18
with such a. fill a pen, 167:10
Actual, solid earth a. world, 473:12
true account of a. is poetry, 473:26
Actuality of thought is life, 78:1
Actus non facit reum, 120:3
Acute inquisitive dexterous, 324:7
Ad astra per aspera, 120:4
maiorem Dei gloriam, 149:*n*1
unguem factus homo, 95:*n*10
Ad infinitum, so proceed a., 285:11
Adage, poor cat i' the a., 215:2
Adam and his wife, 451:2
as A. early in morning, 486:23

Adam (*continued*)
awe of A., 829:6
called his wife's name Eve, 6:1
deep sleep upon A., 5:15
had 'em, 604:11
in A. all die, 43:1
offending A., 188:31
old A., 49:23
take care A., 656:8
the goodliest man, 257:21
was a gardener, 170:16, 590:5
was but human, 523:16
when A. delved, 880:8
wonder what A. and Eve think, 671:3
young A. Cupid, 179:30
Adamant for drift, 619:5
Adamantine chains, 255:7
Adam's dream, 412:12
from Pyrrha's pebbles or A. seed, 409:13
hold up A. profession, 202:3
in A. ear left voice, 258:29
in A. fall sinned, 283:3
riverrun past Eve and A., 650:19
since A. fall, 592:1
Adamses vote for Douglas, 577:*n*2
Adaptation, struggle for a., 630:2
Adapted, means plainly a. to end, 349:16
to my kind of fooling, 625:1
Adazzle dim, 546:13
Add hue to rainbow, 175:24
more to abundance, 652:13
one cubit to stature, 33:7
power to a. or detract, 446:5
some extra just for you, 799:15
to these retired Leisure, 251:14
to those with too much, 652:13
Added, all these things a. unto you, 33:10
Adder, like the deaf a., 16:39
stingeth like an a., 21:30
tread upon the lion and a., 17:29
Addiction, potent and lethal a., 874:5
Adding insult to injury, 312:10
Addison, volumes of A., 307:15
Addled mosses dank, 664:17
Address, prefer to a. myself to one man, 124:13
is must a word to be a. to princes, 151:15
Addressed her winged words, 50:14
Addressing popular audiences, 79:2
Adds precious seeing to the eye, 174:22
Adequate, no a. military defense, 661:5
strength not a. to resist, 79:14
Adeste fideles, 120:5
Adhere, time nor place did then a., 215:4
Adieu chers tableaux, 247:*n*4
fair day a., 175:15
forevermore my dear, 357:12
hand at lips bidding a., 411:11
kind friends, 885:15
tristesse, 705:*n*4
Adjacent, doors of heaven a. identical, 656:8
Adjective when in doubt strike out, 523:22
Adjectives, American without qualifying a.,
554:7
no straddled a., 664:17
Adjoining, lain in a. Room, 509:6
Adjunct, learning an a. to ourself, 174:20
Adjusted in the Tomb, 509:6
Adjustment of colonial claims, 566:16

Adjustments, slight inner a., 860:3
we make our meek a., 719:18
Adler, Irene A. always the woman, 573:8
Administer wealth for good, 521:17
Administration, conduct affairs of a., 446:11
during my a. no blood shed, 338:9
life of this A., 785:12
said of first A., 652:10
said of second A., 652:10
Administrations, Kennedy and Johnson a.,
782:9
Admirable, express and a., 199:5
something howsoever strange and a., 179:7
Admirably, those which most a. flourish,
222:*n*1
Admiral cheered them holding out hope, 139:7
from time to time kill one a., 299:11
Admiration, as great in a. as herself, 226:14
greatness worthy to excite a., 497:11
jumps from a. to love, 382:5
murder never be object of a., 364:13
of the poet, 379:13
only of weak minds, 259:31
season your a., 197:10
Admire, many a. few know, 71:8
most men a. virtue, 259:29
that riches grow in hell, 256:4
the world, 767:3
we like those who a. us, 264:16
Admired, celerity never more a., 218:29
few a. by own households, 153:10
that she might a. be, 173:34
Admirer, every a. potential enemy, 734:4
Admires, coral lip a., 245:18
meanly a. mean things, 459:9
Admiring Bog, 508:14
houses of the very poor, 658:6
Senate a. its members, 531:10
Admit impediments, 222:15
never a. them in sight, 382:11
no kind of traffic would I a., 224:19
Admitted, good pun may be a., 334:8
no one else a. here, 655:13
Adonais, soul of A. like star, 404:3
weep for A., 403:12
Adonis, my A. hath a sweet tooth, 162:6
this A. in loveliness, 392:12
Adopt, Aunt Sally to a. me, 523:10
character of octopus, 59:22
Adopted, banality is a. disguise, 778:11
Adoption, their a. tried, 197:22
Adopts, finds man misusing money a. it,
535:*n*1
Adoration, breathless with a., 370:5
down in a. falling, 127:1
for a. all the ranks, 318:8
Adore appearance believe in forms, 547:14
beauty because disdains to destroy,
631:20
command where I a., 205:7
I a. thee implore thee, 154:8
Jews kiss and infidels a., 293:4
my gifts instead of me, 243:3
now I a. my life, 756:15
seek and a. them, 545:14
Adored, in every clime a., 296:20
still be a., 387:9
Adoring, I die a. God, 300:8

Adorn, Greece Italy and England did a., 274:7
    manners must a. knowledge, 298:11
    modest looks cottage a., 322:28
    old England to a., 589:24
    point moral or a. tale, 306:17
Adorned, holy city a. for husband, 47:11
    I am she who a. herself, 488:4
    in naked beauty more a., 258:3
Adornin', bride in rich a., 551:3
Adornment, some women handsome without
    a., 87:17
Adorns only itself, 762:12
Adult, world of a. life, 630:8
Adulterers, drunkards liars and a., 211:3
Adulteries of art, 232:7
Adultery, committed a. in his heart, 32:18
    committed a. in my heart, 805:14
    gods call a., 397:21
    psychology of a., 614:17
    Sara could commit a. at one end, 674:2
    thou shalt not commit a., 8:14
    way to rise above conventional, 723:14
Adulthood, remnants of childhood hopes of a.,
    730:6
Advance in science from audacity of
    imagination, 572:17
    like a. of a heavy truck, 809:7
    not to go back to a., 296:10
    retrograde if not a., 332:11
    twice set to partners, 515:1
Advanced, death's pale flag not a., 181:13
    outdistance a. countries, 607:13
    true friends, 495:8
    views a. by me in this volume, 440:3
    work they who fought a., 446:5
Advances, Chief who in triumph a., 373:22
    in direction of dreams, 475:19
Advancing in different direction, 700:1
Advantage in the past judged, 79:8
    mixed up for mutual a., 619:18
    nailed for our a., 181:19
    nature to a. dressed, 292:13
    of taking no action, 57:14
    over cleverer boys, 619:2
    seen hungry ocean gain a., 221:18
    them that take a. get a., 480:6
    to whose a., 87:10
    women have over men, 688:12
Advantages, in hope of fair a., 185:3
    little a. every day, 304:2
    various qualities and a., 611:1
    wealth not without a., 752:14
Adventure, appetite for a., 808:1
    art peace, 580:13
    fair a. of tomorrow, 176:2
    most unto itself, 510:1
    some for a., 665:8
    test of an a., 715:14
    this grotesque a. ours, 761:5
    vitality of thought in a., 580:16
Adventurer, no lover and no a., 567:8
    well-wishing a., 220:n2
Adventures of Tom Sawyer, 523:1
    way full of a. and experiences, 583:11
    we have no use for a., 696:12
Adventuring, by a. both, 184:11
Adverbs only qualifications I respect, 545:5
Adversaries, do as a. do in law, 173:11

Adversary, sallies out and sees a., 254:9
    that mine a. had written a book, 14:10
    your a. the devil, 46:3
Adverse to rights of other citizens, 345:8
Adversity best discover virtue, 165:17
    blessing of New Testament, 165:15
    bread of a., 26:12
    enemy not hidden in a., 30:39
    faint in the day of a., 21:32
    in a. difficult to find friend, 79:n1
    in a. keep even mind, 96:20
    in a. mask is off, 90:9
    in day of a. consider, 23:13
    not without comforts, 165:16
    of sharpe a. worste kynde, 132:19
    remorse wakes up in a., 313:5
    sometimes hard, 407:23
    studies a refuge in a., 87:11
    sweet are uses of a., 193:37
    test of strong men, 103:25
    tries friends, 101:4
Adversity's sweet milk philosophy, 180:34
Advertise, don't tell they'd a., 508:14
    it pays to a., 886:4
Advertisement, walking-stick serves purpose of
    a., 569:8
Advertisements, tell ideals by a., 601:12
Advertises, protect what it a., 815:8
Advice, few profit by a., 99:20
    given as profusely as a., 264:6
    honest opinion and friendly a., 469:3
    is seldom welcome, 298:8
    old like to give good a., 264:4
    smallest current coin, 540:4
    tea and comfortable a., 413:7
    to Persons About to Write History, 518:11
    we may give a., 264:25
Advices, lengthened sage a., 358:4
Advise, Death whom none could a., 159:15
    please a., 683:14
    the prince, 675:4
Advisedly, entered into a., 49:13
Advisement, take wyf withouten a., 135:24
Advocate, good have no need of a., 76:16
    is Christ thy a., 280:19
    we have a. with the Father, 46:8
Aegean, booming surge of A., 74:2
    heard it on A., 496:18
Aeneas, mother of A. and his race, 89:9
Aeneas', matter of A. wanderings, 487:3
Aequam memento rebus in arduis, 96:n14
Aeschylus, thundering A., 233:2
Aeson, herbs that did renew A., 186:14
Aesthetic, moral soil for a. growth, 618:9
    painting not a. operation, 648:1
    rank as apostle in high a. band, 526:11
    work of fiction affords a. bliss, 723:9
Afeard, a soldier and a., 217:11
Affability, man of lowliness and a., 143:11
Affair, world is a strange a., 267:10
Affaires, les a. l'argent des autres, 501:n1
Affairs, arrange a. so taxes be low, 613:17
    crises of human a., 349:15
    debate of commonwealth a., 188:32
    long run misleading guide to a., 656:11
    nice state of a., 674:4
    office and a. of love, 190:26
    political a., 442:17

Affairs *(continued)*
    tide in a. of men, 193:13
    wealth the sinews of a., 82:7
Affamé, ventre a., 266:n3
Affect, learned pedants much a., 262:6
    study what you most a., 173:6
Affectation of affectation, 304:14
    spruce a., 174:28
Affected, zealously a. in good, 43:28
Affecting, natural simple a., 323:7
Affection and guilt, 886:14
    attraction and a., 614:17
    beaming in one eye, 464:34
    cannot hold bent, 205:1
    hath unknown bottom, 195:30
    let falling out be renewing of a., 85:n10
    neither heat a. limb, 206:34
    on things above, 44:11
    slave to animosity or a., 329:1
    thy intention stabs, 223:12
    two qualities inspire a., 78:19
Affectionately, country absorbs him a., 485:11
Affectioned ass, 204:30
    be kindly a., 41:31
Affection's, to me-wards your a. strong, 241:1
Affections dark as Erebus, 186:17
    great primary human a., 495:13
    great strain on a., 480:23
    hath not a Jew a., 185:11
    holiness of Heart's a., 412:11
    old offenses of a. new, 222:13
    produced by images of touching, 348:3
    run to waste, 396:11
    t' a. and to faculties, 229:19
    they strive to secure, 709:1
Affects to nod, 274:15
Affirm life, 632:13
    uprising unveiling a., 448:15
    what seems to be truth, 76:4
Affirmation of life, 632:13
Affirmative, minds naturally a., 528:16
    speak the a., 429:6
Affixed, thou deemest mountains a., 119:1
Afflict, coward conscience a. me, 172:8
Afflicted, commend those who are a., 48:15
    neither oppress the a., 21:21
    newspaper comforts a., 600:16
Affliction alters, 223:34
    binds us together, 579:4
    bread of a., 12:10
    consoling in depths of a., 444:15
    day of a., 30:37
    dense a. of worthy patience, 770:13
    forgetfulness of a., 30:37
    furnace of a., 26:36
    have their A. by drops, 278:9
    one day smile again, 174:6
    pay in a. or defect, 612:19
    remembering mine a. and misery, 28:12
    saveth in time of a., 30:10
    water of a., 12:10, 26:12
Afflicts the comfortable, 600:16
Afford, ask upkeep of yacht can't a. one, 529:7
    can a. to like them, 838:13
    can't a. them Governor, 565:21
    purest treasure mortal times a., 176:8
    selling houses for more than people could
    a., 664:2

Affords market for other products, 364:9
Affright air at Agincourt, 188:30
Affrighted, rend the a. skies, 293:12
    steed ran on alone, 609:2
Affronts with his own darkness, 772:2
Afghanistan's, wounded and left on A. plains, 588:13
A-fishing, east wind never blow when he goes a., 244:34
    gone a., 244:31
    time is stream I go a. in, 475:4
A-flowing, every sluice of knowledge set a., 329:10
A-flying, old Time is still a., 241:4
Afoot and light-hearted, 486:24
    game is a., 573:20
    game's a., 189:9
    swiftest traveler goes a., 474:19
    thousand actions once a., 188:36
Afraid, basest of things to be a., 714:3
    be a. be very a., 856:6
    be not a. neither dismayed, 9:35
    be not a. of greatness, 205:8
    be not a. of life, 541:14
    be not a. of sudden fear, 19:27
    be not a. to give that little, 29:28
    because we tremble, 541:9
    contempt for governor who is a., 65:12
    death is a. of him, 119:25
    don't be a., 864:13
    don't be a. of dark, 706:11
    don't let them think you're a., 587:9
    dying to be a. of thee, 510:2
    for the terror by night, 17:28
    Frankie was a., 788:15
    happiness makes heart a., 418:4
    in short I was a., 675:3
    it is I be not a., 34:28
    man not a. of sea, 612:2
    more a. than hurt, 147:3
    neither let it be a., 39:44
    not a. to die for friends, 97:15
    not a. to follow truth, 338:13
    not a. to go, 329:5
    not so much a. of death as ashamed, 248:10
    not that I'm a. to die, 839:13
    of fear, 366:9
    of the light, 504:12
    of themselves and shadows, 794:4
    of whom shall I be a., 15:27
    Public a. of itself, 386:4
    she was a. to ask, 796:7
    show you're not a., 859:6
    small men a. of writings, 327:17
    sore a., 37:17
    starts when you're always a., 861:14
    stranger and a., 575:17
    to do if last hour, 301:5
    to go home in dark, 582:*n*2
    to look upon God, 7:27
    to strike, 295:13
    uncertain and a., 748:16
    we are a. of each other, 458:9
    whistling to keep from being a., 274:10
    who's a. of Virginia Woolf, 817:10
    wife and children stand a., 248:10
Afresh, kiss a., 241:3

Africa, all A. and her prodigies, 248:5
    always something new out of A., 105:7
    Asia and A. expelled freedom, 333:2
    black like depths of my A., 730:14
    choose between A. and English tongue, 829:4
    conditioned people of A. to humiliation, 802:6
    does A. know song of me, 662:6
    ex A. semper aliquid novi, 105:*n*3
    Kilimanjaro highest in A., 721:16
    more familiar with A., 834:12
    song of A., 662:6
    survival of wildlife in A., 796:14
    what is A. to me, 734:10
African, Americans of A. descent, 519:10
    conditioned to freedom, 690:9
    new moon lying on back, 662:6
    where still A. complains, 346:24
Afric's sunny fountains, 391:5
Afro-American, not only Latin-American nation but A., 811:13
After, blackbird whistling or just a., 641:7
    first death, 777:7
    man a. his own heart, 10:40
    old man looks before and a., 50:28
    that out of all whooping, 195:10
    this therefore because of this, 121:8
    us the deluge, 317:15
After-dinner talk, 450:13
After-dinner's sleep, 206:34
Aftermark of too much love, 623:10
Aftermath of war, 625:19
Afternoon, all in golden a., 513:10
    fatal five in a., 717:5
    land in which always a., 450:16
    lazing on a sunny a., 859:2
    rude multitude call a., 174:27
    summer a. most beautiful words, 545:10
Afternoons, Jove send more a. as this, 168:13
    satin and vacant, 720:3
    Winter a., 508:13
Afterthoughts, stronger than all a., 67:21
After-times, leave something to a., 253:20
Afton, flow gently sweet A., 357:19
Again, it was déjà vu all over a., 807:7
Against, all life 6 to 5 a., 660:9
    every sword a. his fellow, 10:41
    he not with me a. me, 34:10
    hope believed in hope, 41:12
    in confederacy a. him, 284:15
    kick a. the pricks, 63:9
    not a. with, 625:10
    we build a. space, 863:8
    who can be a. us, 41:23
Agamemnon, brave men before A., 97:14
    cried aloud, 676:2
    dead, 594:16
    gazed on face of A., 499:4
Agate, eyes like a. lanterns, 720:9
    no bigger than a.-stone, 179:25
Age, accompany old a., 217:18
    ache penury, 207:1
    and body of the time, 200:8
    at your a. heyday in blood, 201:6
    atomic a., 606:7, 774:13
    Augustan a., 317:4
    beats off louring Old A., 141:11

Age *(continued)*
    belongs only to own a., 406:8
    best in four things, 165:8
    cannot wither her, 218:21
    carefulness bringeth a., 31:17
    cast me not off in the time of old a., 17:11
    centuries roll back to a. of gold, 97:12
    come to thy grave in full a., 13:14
    comfort to my a., 194:3
    contribution according to a., 478:*n*2
    crabbed a. and youth, 881:17
    dance attention on old a., 596:17
    decrepit a. tied to me, 594:5
    demanded an image, 665:6
    disease or sorrows strike, 479:11
    does not make us childish, 343:26
    drives my green a., 777:2
    early candle-light of old a., 488:17
    education best provision for old a., 77:13
    enchantments of the Middle A., 496:8
    fatal to revolutionists, 361:2
    father of all in every a., 296:20
    first moment of atomic a., 774:13
    folly in all of every a., 278:5
    fool in every a., 296:9
    forehead of the a. to come, 408:18
    foreign nations and the next a., 166:21
    fortify thy name against old a., 167:5
    freethinking of one a. common sense of next, 497:17
    full of care, 881:17
    given to men of middle a., 223:26
    gods have neither a. nor death, 66:17
    Golden A., 92:22
    golden a. in imagination, 420:3
    good God what an a., 277:6
    hardly feel pressure of a., 74:18
    he hath not forgotten my a., 381:11
    how free the present a. is, 284:16
    how tasteless and ill-bred, 91:13
    I will not make a. an issue, 765:15
    if youth but knew if old a. but could, 151:5
    ill layer-up of beauty, 190:9
    in a good old a., 6:30
    in a. I bud again, 243:7
    in the flower of their a., 10:33
    in year of his a., 120:6
    infirmity of his a., 210:32
    is grown so picked, 202:11
    key-machine of modern industrial a., 708:4
    labor of an a., 250:15
    lady of certain a., 398:25
    leaves friends and wine, 388:2
    lee shore of a., 552:10
    living in the American A., 824:13
    make a. to come my own, 265:12
    master spirits of this a., 192:20
    Mechanical A., 406:7
    middle a. time of improving, 261:12
    mind torpid in old a., 310:14
    most people my a. are dead, 689:3
    my a. lusty winter, 194:5
    no falsehood lingers to old a., 66:25
    no old a. only sorrow, 583:3
    nor sword nor a. destroy, 102:18
    not by a. is wisdom acquired, 83:9
    not of an a. but for all time, 233:3

Age *(continued)*

not one continued faithful until old a., 76:13

not only a night an a., 623:13

not profited so much as lost, 474:14

not so well qualified as youth, 474:14

not weary them, 603:14

of antiquity youth of world, 164:*n*4

of Aquarius, 846:4

of chivalry gone, 325:4

of discord and strife, 169:22

of ease, 322:24

of fear, 724:4

of gold, 97:12

of Gold, 250:12

of hobgoblins, 423:20

of iron, 298:23

of Miracles, 407:19

of revolution and reformation, 337:12

of superiorities privileges vanities, 364:12

of unreason, 754:12

Old A. and Experience, 281:4

Old A. coming bolt door, 119:27

old a. crown of life, 88:17

old a. in universal man, 164:*n*5

old a. is flight of birds, 658:8

old a. is woman's hell, 266:4

old a. lacking neither honor nor lyre, 96:15

old a. only disease, 427:14

old a. play's last act, 88:17

old a. should burn, 777:15

old a. time of spending, 261:12

olives of endless a., 222:10

only thing for old a. is, 844:18

or grief or sickness, 241:18

ours is essentially tragic a., 663:10

pays us with a. and dust, 159:16

peaceful as old a., 461:19

perform promises of youth, 307:8

prayers which are a. his alms, 163:4

preferable to youth, 288:25

regret in chilled a., 545:6

restored of the Antonines, 332:*n*2

returns the Golden A., 92:22

secret of a good old a., 818:8

shakes rooted folly of a., 278:7

shall be clearer than noonday, 13:22

Shelley of my a., 787:5

sign of old a., 375:13

smack of a. in you, 187:27

soon comes a., 160:9

soul of the a., 232:19

spirit of a., 300:3

tested to extreme old a., 494:9

the a. is dull and mean, 438:9

the harbor of all ills, 82:6

therefore summon a., 462:17

think at your a. it is right, 514:4

thinks better of gilded fool, 228:3

thirty-five attractive a., 560:25

this slaughtered a., 765:3

thou hast nor youth nor a., 206:34

'tis well an old a. is out, 274:25

to age succeeds, 450:10

too late or cold climate, 259:6

toys of a., 295:3

tragedy of the a., 602:2

veracity with old a., 264:26

Age *(continued)*

very staff of my a., 184:36

view a. of poverty, 186:7

war dearth a. agues, 230:20

weak evils a. and hunger, 194:24

what was done in remote a., 426:11

when a. in wit out, 191:3

when Mozart was my a., 819:11

when old a. shall generation waste, 410:20

when Thule no more ultimate, 104:7

will fade beauty's flower, 150:10

with stealing steps, 149:10

without a name, 326:1

wives companions for middle a., 165:20

world's great a. begins, 403:8

worst of woes wait on a., 395:9

youth and a. equally a burden, 74:18

youth passed old a. not arrived, 479:6

Aged, beauty of a. face, 647:5

certain age means a., 398:25

man paltry thing, 594:2

matched with a. wife, 451:11

thrush frail gaunt, 536:11

youth becomes as a., 206:34

Agenbite of inwit, 650:14

Agent, actions work good of a., 276:9

free a. you were before, 112:17

imagination a. of perception, 379:5

man is everywhere disturbing a., 421:2

Nature a. and patient at once, 77:14

thus the poor a. despised, 204:9

trust no a., 190:26

Age's, poison for a. tooth, 175:4

Ages, all a. believed in gods, 630:5

and ages hence, 622:18

aristocracy has three successive a., 364:12

before history, 327:12

cycle of the a. renewed, 92:22

emptiness of a. in face, 557:3

famous to all a., 254:4

God our help in a. past, 289:12

gone a. long ago, 410:1

heir of all a., 452:9

how many a. hence, 192:18

now he belongs to the a., 470:4

Rock of A., 334:13

seven a., 194:25

there hath he lain for a., 450:6

thousand a. in Thy sight, 289:13

three poets in three a., 274:7

through a. one purpose, 452:5

trace events of a., 415:14

what termed enlightened a., 319:11

Agglomeration called Holy Roman Empire, 299:7

Agglutinative, tonsorial or a. type, 607:2

Aggrandizement, no a. territorial or other, 653:14

Aggravate, I will a. my voice, 178:8

Aggravation of self, 531:13

Aggregate efforts of busy multitude, 500:4

interests of community, 345:8

Aggression of Germany, 684:*n*6

stop their a., 746:7

threaten a., 653:16

war of a. and conquest, 668:7

Aggressions, when a. require war, 337:14

Aggressors, quarantine the a., 652:*n*3

Aghast at money's significance, 568:17

Agincourt, affright air at A., 188:30

Aging people in contraction of life, 630:4

person give attention to self, 630:4

Agir, j'ai trop pensé pour a., 533:*n*2

Agitation, peace at heart of endless a., 372:7

those who deprecate a., 477:3

A-gley, gang aft a., 356:6

Aglow, all a. is the work, 93:24

Agnes, world dear A. is strange, 267:10

Agnes', St. A. Eve, 409:18

Agnosco veteris vestigia flammae, 94:*n*9

Agnostic, compliment to be called a., 568:10

judges neither Catholic nor a., 649:10

Agnosticism, that's all a. means, 568:10

Agnus Dei, 47:23

A-going out with tide, 465:35

Agonies, all the a. of the soul, 507:9

exultations a., 370:8

find a. strife of human hearts, 409:2

one of my changes of garments, 486:16

voices a. creations and destroyings, 411:15

Agonizing reappraisal, 787:11

Agony, charm a. with words, 191:12

of flame that cannot singe, 595:12

strong swimmer in a., 398:9

that a. our triumph, 682:11

Agree, all things differ all a., 293:14

birds in little nests a., 289:7

'em to death, 774:9

how a. kettle and pot, 30:41

not free thought for those who a., 539:7

people have good sense a. with us, 264:23

two of a trade never a., 291:12

whether they a. or not, 697:2

with her would not a., 590:21

Agreeable, do not want people a., 382:23

impressions of American manners, 389:2

in conversation, 288:11

person agrees with me, 430:13

what is more a. than home, 87:23

Agreed, except they be a., 29:2

to differ, 381:17

Agreement, living in a. with nature, 82:1

love is a., 167:7

on nuclear control, 786:14

verbal a. isn't worth paper written on, 650:2

with hell, 433:6

with hell are we at a., 26:8

Agrees, agreeable person a. with me, 430:13

what a. disagrees, 62:8

Agriculture, eating is an a. act, 837:5

navigation commerce a., 330:7

Ague of skeleton, 675:26

Agues, praise doth nourish a., 183:15

war dearth age a., 230:20

Ahab, all evil to crazy A., 483:3

he ran before A., 12:3

Ahead of the world, 57:22

sure you're right go a., 393:14

Ahkoond of Swat, 467:*n*1

A-hunting, daddy's gone a., 894:3

daren't go a., 501:4

upon St. David's Day, 896:6

we will go, 304:11

Aid, alliteration's artful a., 326:4

come to a. of party, 885:18

Aid *(continued)*
expletives feeble a. join, 292:17
giving enemies a. and comfort, 339:13
mutual a. law of animal life, 542:15
of kind applauding looks, 347:13
saints a. if men call, 377:12
small a. is wealth, 68:6
snatched from all effectual a., 327:10
thine a. supply strength bestow, 127:3
to interpretation of future, 71:12
to worker God lends a., 59:*n*3
vanity give no hollow a., 396:4
wit hope flock to a., 426:10
AIDS crisis, 835:21
Ail, what can a. thee, 412:2
Ailed, what a. us O gods, 529:20
Ailes de géant l'empêchent, 491:*n*1
Ailments, our a. are the same, 284:10
selfish clod of a., 565:3
Aim, fixed as an a. or butt, 188:34
forgotten a., 584:4
hit only what a. at, 474:18
malice never was his a., 285:9
man sets himself, 742:22
prince have no a. but war, 141:16
rivalry of a., 531:24
thought to a. at some good, 78:3
two things a. at in life, 590:11
who a. at great deeds must suffer, 87:3
your a. the star, 887:16
Aime, je ne vous a. pas Hylas, 283:*n*1
qui m'a. me suive, 130:*n*8
Aimest, all the ends thou a. at, 226:5
Aiming, slight not what's near by a. far, 67:17
Aimless rhetoric, 502:14
white and a. signals, 810:4
Ain't heard nothing yet, 667:10
hit 'em where they a., 614:5
if it a. broke, 830:4
necessarily so, 711:3
no such animal, 886:11
nothin' but hound dog, 834:6
she a. no lady, 601:6
we got fun, 667:12
Air, affright a. at Agincourt, 188:30
all a. and nerve, 787:13
allaying both with its sweet a., 224:13
always in earth and a., 756:10
awash with angels, 797:12
babbling gossip of the a., 204:22
bites shrewdly, 197:30
blackest a., 797:14
breathe his native a., 292:4
breathe the a. again, 489:8
brightness falls from the a., 227:6
Cervantes' serious a., 296:24
change of a., 630:15
charm ache with a., 191:12
chartered libertine, 188:33
common a. bathes globe, 486:1
common sun a. skies, 316:9
crows that wing midway a., 212:24
dance upon the a., 561:4
drinks water her keel plows a., 163:20
earth fire sea a., 537:10
earth or a., 196:18
eat men like a., 833:4
eating a. on promise of supply, 187:37

Air *(continued)*
emptier ever dancing in a., 177:17
fairer than evening a., 169:1
false as a. as water, 203:20
fields of a., 327:11
fight with strength in a., 619:14
flies through a. with ease, 532:16
fog and filthy a., 213:31
fowls of the a. shall tell, 13:25
fowls of the a. sow not, 33:6
happy good-night a., 536:12
haunting the black a., 820:9
he says with solemn a., 356:9
honor is a., 183:25
hurtles in darkened a., 316:16
I drew in the common a., 30:5
I eat the a., 200:14
I lived on a., 623:9
I sniff mothproof a., 821:1
I would like to be the a., 844:16
if lungs receive our a., 326:21
in a. men seen, 882:14
in a. Pentagon turn orange, 803:7
inebriate of A., 508:9
is delicate, 214:21
let out to warm a., 285:2
melted into thin a., 225:1
meteor of ocean a., 443:3
might wash leaves cover me, 530:2
mock a. with idle state, 316:14
most excellent canopy a., 199:5
nimbly and sweetly recommends itself, 214:21
now a. is hushed, 317:13
now thoroughly small, 677:13
of delightful studies, 253:21
on A. Bird stamped, 508:21
other passions fleet to a., 185:21
over the plain quiver, 662:6
retrace steps to upper a., 94:27
rooted to a. through our lungs, 528:17
round ocean and living a., 368:11
saw the a. with hand, 200:6
sightless couriers of a., 214:24
signed with their honor, 760:6
soft summer a., 503:14
solemn stillness holds, 315:12
speche in substaunce ys but a., 132:2
speed through a. thirty-one, 601:7
spiders marching through a., 787:3
stood naked in open a., 556:20
sweet a. coming into house, 670:17
sweeter a. where it was made, 671:18
take into a. my breath, 410:9
that kills, 575:6
thin a., 225:1
thrice toss oaken ashes in a., 227:2
trifles light as a., 209:10
troubled a., 255:*n*1
underneath him steady a., 546:9
vans to beat a., 677:13
walking in a. of glory, 268:17
wanton in the a., 266:1
waste sweetness on desert a., 315:23
water rush to rest in a., 713:5
way of eagle in a., 22:14
web of sunny a., 472:7
whether in earth or a., 196:18

Air *(continued)*
wild, 547:2
wild with leaves, 666:2
word honor is a., 183:25
world sick for a., 673:20
world-mothering a., 547:2
wound with mercy as if a., 547:1
written equivalent of a. guitar, 845:15
Air-drawn dagger, 216:18
Airly, git up a. to take in God, 482:1
Airmen, soldiers sailors a., 621:9
Airplane, strange high singing of a., 654:5
Airs, all a. make one country, 248:14
don't give yourself a., 514:6
melting a., 327:4
Naiad a., 447:12
soft Lydian a., 251:8
sounds and sweet a., 224:33
Airy distance with majestic motion, 396:2
ever so a. tread, 455:3
gold to a. thinness beat, 229:16
navies, 452:2
nothing, 179:6
reveries so a., 326:23
servitors, 253:23
subtleties in religion, 248:2
tongues that syllable, 252:12
unseen within thy a. shell, 252:14
Aisle, long-drawn a., 315:19
Aisles, monastic a., 424:4
of Christian Rome, 424:5
Ajalon, valley of A., 10:3
Ajar, doubtful if man's gates are a., 694:11
Akond of Swat, 467:14
Al, you can call me A., 855:13
Alabama, all over A. lamps are out, 757:3
come from A., 503:9
moon of A., 716:10
stars fell on A. last night, 726:7
sweet home A., 867:10
Alabaster box of ointment, 35:32
grandsire cut in a., 184:5
smooth as monumental a., 210:13
Alamo, remember the A., 433:8
Alarm, give moderate a., 433:4
ride and spread a., 437:16
Alarmed, keep the populace a., 645:12
Alarming, serious and a. consequences, 328:10
Alarms, confused a. of struggle, 496:19
world's a. to Paris, 596:2
Alarums, wars and a. unto nations, 160:23
Alas, cried in goose A., 681:19
how love can trifle, 173:35
my Love, 881:4
our young affections, 396:11
poor Yorick, 202:12
say A. but cannot help, 748:8
Alaska, see Russia from A., 878:10
Albatross, shot the A., 375:25
thought he saw A., 517:10
Albert, ask me to take message to A., 430:21
Albion, perfidious A., 366:5
Alcestis, like A. from the grave, 255:1
Alchemized, shine full a., 409:9
Alchemy, love wrought new a., 229:13
of the word, 559:11
richest a., 191:34
Alcides, none equal A. except himself, 104:5

Alcohol, admitted powerless over a., 708:10
   is like love, 674:12
   is prince of liquids, 348:17
   our national drug is a., 774:4
Alcoran, rather believe fables in A., 165:26
Alcuin my name learning I loved, 122:7
Alderman, agate on forefinger of a., 179:25
Ale, belly God send thee good a., 151:4
   cakes and a., 204:29
   fame for pot of a., 189:10
   fed purely upon a., 290:6
   ginger a. on the side, 681:2
   I swill in their a., 718:11
   man ale's the stuff, 575:12
   nut-brown a., 251:5
   of myghty a. a large quart, 134:26
   shoulder sky and drink a., 575:15
   sleep upon a., 290:6
   take size of pots of a., 262:7
Alea, iacta a. est, 89:*n*1
Ale-house, an honest a., 245:4
Aleppo, in A. once, 210:21
Alexander, Diogenes asked by A., 76:17
   if I were not A., 81:1
   in his tent, 737:8
   of course A. the Great was hero, 442:20
   some talk of A., 883:13
   trace noble dust of A., 202:13
Alexandria, strange power of A., 767:12
Alexandrian, present our A. revels, 219:10
Alexandrine, needless A. ends song, 292:18
Algae, delicate a. and sea anemone, 679:4
Algebra, clock doth strike by a., 262:8
Ali cibus aliis venenum, 90:*n*6
Alibi, stick to the a., 464:1
Alice, can't explain myself said A., 514:3
   go ask A., 846:5
   grave A., 437:14
   replied offended, 514:16
   what use of book thought A., 513:12
Alice's, at A. Restaurant, 864:10
Alien blessing on its way, 816:11
   corn, 410:10
   nothing human is a., 85:17
   something bright and a., 731:*n*2
   there is none, 580:2
Alieni appetens sui profusus, 92:*n*3
Alienum, humani nil a me a. puto, 85:*n*12
Alike, all animals of forest a., 889:3
   all places distant from heaven a., 235:10
   darkness and light a. to thee, 19:14
   destiny waits a., 63:12
   equals and unequals a., 75:18
   glory and danger a., 72:1
   looks on a., 223:32
   to suffer all a., 218:32
Alimentary canal with big appetite, 765:11
Alive and so bold O earth, 403:10
   astonishing thing earth is a., 772:18
   attitude in which most a., 540:16
   deeply and intensely a., 540:16
   divine force makes dead seem a., 137:17
   ecstasy comes when one is most a., 633:5
   get out of this world a., 804:4
   hardly a man now a., 437:15
   I am a. forevermore, 46:19
   in Christ all made a., 43:1
   in that dawn to be a., 368:18

Alive *(continued)*
   is that thing a., 773:4
   looking as if a., 460:1
   mission to come down a., 802:8
   more come through a., 52:1
   not a. enough to know how to kill self, 793:2
   remain a. past usual date, 583:4
   since none returned a. I answer, 129:7
   some burned a., 801:17
   something else is a., 827:10
   still while thy book live, 232:19
   the most a. is wildest, 475:31
   was dead and is a., 38:12
   when dead be brought forth a., 118:19
Aliveness, terrors of a., 872:9
All a green willow, 146:8
   aglow is the work, 93:24
   all alone, 376:14
   all are gone, 383:3
   all of a piece throughout, 274:25
   all sleeping on hill, 605:3
   and a. that tribe, 95:19
   are but ministers of Love, 378:3
   be as before Love, 460:23
   bed-time Hal and a. well, 183:24
   best of dark and bright, 397:1
   blind and ignorant in a., 227:16
   can we a. get along, 879:1
   changed changed utterly, 593:7
   charity for a., 447:2
   Christ is a. and in a., 44:12
   come out of Gogol's Overcoat, 493:3
   comes from the mind, 64:12
   cry and no wool, 137:*n*9
   death closes a., 451:17
   deliberate speed, 692:*n*4
   did you say a., 217:8
   down come baby and a., 550:7
   driven into same fold, 96:21
   eggs in one basket, 156:18
   else confusion, 453:3
   end crowns a., 204:6
   except sun is set, 398:16
   fish that cometh to net, 147:31
   flesh is grass, 26:26
   for a. that and a. that, 358:20
   for best in best of all possible worlds, 299:*n*1
   for love, 160:8
   for one, 422:4
   for our rightfu' King, 357:10
   from a. things one and from one a. things, 62:8
   gas and gaiters, 464:23
   Gaul divided into three parts, 88:21
   give a. to love, 424:14
   God for us a., 148:24
   God's above a., 208:24
   harm to one harm to a., 520:8
   having nothing yet hath a., 227:11
   hell broke loose, 258:9
   his faults observed, 193:12
   home-made but aren't we a., 763:4
   honorable men, 192:29
   hope abandon who enter here, 128:6
   I and you and a. of us, 193:1
   I could see from where I stood, 695:5

All *(continued)*
   I dare do a., 215:3
   I have is thine, 38:13
   I know you a., 181:33
   I write Poets A., 509:9
   in all, 197:9, 455:27
   in a. things charity, 265:4
   in all to one another, 526:16
   in confederacy against him, 284:15
   in day's work, 883:16
   in desert a. and nothing, 417:12
   in green went my love, 701:4
   in valley of death, 454:18
   is best though we doubt, 260:26
   is but toys, 215:30
   is done that men can do, 357:11
   is ephemeral, 112:3
   is flux, 61:26
   is mended, 179:18
   is not lost, 255:10
   is not well, 197:17
   is this a., 796:7
   is vanity, 22:21
   is well, 680:12
   it a. has to do with it, 811:16
   know a. except myself, 139:4
   lord of a. yet prey to a., 295:1
   lost save honor, 145:3
   mankind love lover, 427:2
   men created equal, 336:1, 446:5
   men have need of gods, 52:28
   men my compatriots, 153:16
   moderation in a. things, 85:13
   my days are trances, 448:7
   my pretty ones, 217:8
   news fit to print, 570:7
   noblest Roman of them a., 193:21
   not a. capable of everything, 92:24
   ocean the source of a., 51:31
   on our meat and on us a., 241:15
   once so beautiful is dead, 683:3
   one for a. a. for one, 172:31
   one from a., 114:5
   one law for a., 324:20
   our yesterdays have lighted fools, 217:23
   our youth our joys our a., 159:16
   passion spent, 260:27
   perform tragic play, 596:9
   persons share in government, 78:25
   quiet along Potomac, 504:1
   readiness is a., 202:26
   ripeness is a., 213:7
   root and a., 455:27
   round the town, 892:18
   safely gathered in, 456:9
   sees Me in a., 84:12
   shall be well, 131:14, 679:13
   shall die, 188:14
   should cry Beware, 377:23
   take him for a. in a., 197:9
   that is and shall be, 65:20
   that live must die, 196:25
   that we see or seem, 447:8
   that's beautiful drifts, 592:2
   the brothers too, 205:5
   the brothers valiant, 882:9
   the lonely people, 848:7
   the perfumes of Arabia, 217:14

All *(continued)*

the way home, 893:10
the winds of doctrine, 254:14
the world and his wife, 286:11
the world's a stage, 194:25
things are one, 62:1
things bright and beautiful, 476:4
things come of you Nature, 111:19
things come to who wait, 426:*n*2
things full of signs, 114:4
things how small soever, 275:3
things to all men, 42:18
things work together, 41:21
this above a., 197:24
this and heaven too, 282:22
this now too much for us, 624:12
this the world well knows, 222:20
time takes a. gives a., 158:16
to leave a. out would be, 815:7
tomorrow's parties, 855:1
unkindest cut of a., 192:35
waiting to give his a., 761:6
warts and a., 246:*n*4
was light, 296:23
was lost, 259:11
we are a. Americans, 866:3
we are sinners a., 170:9
we can do, 440:2
we know for truth, 592:6
we know of Love, 511:14
we need of hell, 511:9
well that ends well, 147:16
which will not pass away, 395:16
who love freedom, 686:13
with one voice, 40:39
work and no play, 245:12
world queer, 886:7
ye know on earth, 410:20
ye that pass by, 28:11
Allay, glowing axle doth a., 252:7
Allayed fever of bone, 675:26
no voice divine storm a., 327:10
Allaying fury and my passion, 224:13
not a drop of a. Tiber, 219:24
Allegiance, not bound to swear a., 97:17
to British, 328:2
to the South, 384:18
Allegory, I cordially dislike a., 696:15
life continual a., 413:11
Allegra, laughing A., 437:14
Allemand, je parle a. a mon cheval, 148:*n*16
Allen, name was Barbara A., 889:25
snow on Bog of A., 650:9
Alleviates, legacy a. sorrow, 158:13
Alley, in bowling a. bowled sun, 280:15
rats' a., 676:8
Sally in our a., 292:1
Titanic of cypress, 449:16
Alleys, lowest and vilest a. of London, 573:13
All-form only form rational, 542:10
All-good, must a. too follow, 399:10
All-harmonious, Father-Mother God a., 493:4
Alliance, holy a. to exorcise specter, 478:7
unless abroad purchase a., 170:29
Alliances, entangling a., 337:12
permanent a., 329:3

Allied Expeditionary Force, 686:13
great wits to madness a., 272:16
remembrance and reflection how a., 272:*n*1
Allies, great Russian a., 686:13
no eternal a., 392:21
thou hast great a., 370:8
All-in-all, intellectual A., 369:10
Alliteration, sentiment and a., 520:15
Alliteration's artful aid, 326:4
All-night vigil in soft face of girl, 65:25
Allnut, Nature Mr. A. we rise above, 757:7
Allons enfants de la patrie, 361:3
Allow not nature more than needs, 211:21
Allowance, no a. for ignorance, 502:5
Allowed, anyone a. to write like that, 655:*n*3
have merit handsomely a., 311:5
on every hand a. be, 356:13
the soothing music, 780:1
All-pervasiveness, infallible impeccable a., 542:14
All-powerful must all-good follow, 399:10
should fear everything, 249:14
to be impotent, 619:5
All's fair in love and war, 479:4
right with world, 459:19
well that ends well, 206:7
All-shaking, thou a. thunder, 211:24
Allure, large forces which a., 609:6
si vagabonde, 152:*n*9
Alluring, sea shows false a. smile, 90:6
Allusive, poet become more a., 677:7
Alluvial march of days, 720:6
Alma Mater, youth who loves A., 785:*n*2
Almanac, look in a. find out moonshine, 178:26
plant tears says a., 762:20
Almighty dollar, 391:19
gave dog, 374:17
gold, 232:15
shadow of the A., 17:28
thank God A. free at last, 823:9
that the A. would answer me, 14:10
Almighty's form glasses itself, 396:20
God A. gentlemen, 273:4
Almond, peach once bitter a., 523:17
tree shall flourish, 23:31
Almost everybody had troubles, 582:15
glad we have been bombed, 725:7
right word and right word, 523:12
thou persuadest me, 41:7
Alms, beg a. of palsied eld, 206:34
for oblivion, 203:21
give a. accordingly, 29:28
give a. to every one that asks, 485:10
of those who work with joy, 655:6
when thou doest a., 32:24
Alms-basket of words, 174:26
Almsman's gown, 177:12
Aloft, Death a., 720:9
invisible in night, 567:6
Aloha oe, 532:17
Alone a banished man, 880:13
alone all all alone, 376:14
and palely loitering, 412:2
art should stand a., 520:16
as sparrow a. upon house top, 18:5
be a. on earth, 395:9

Alone *(continued)*

being human born a., 666:7
better to live a., 64:14
beweep my outcast state, 221:5
born unto himself a., 241:21
Britain fight on a., 621:1
cannot live a. at peace, 653:12
clouded you will be a., 102:22
dangerous to be a., 789:2
go it sole a., 624:17
grief mine a., 399:16
heaven a. given away, 481:15
here at gate a., 455:1
how said I am a., 178:18
I a. sit lingering here, 268:16
I am a., 688:3
I did it, 220:6
I lie down a., 576:1
I only am escaped a., 12:38
I sleep a., 56:8
I want to be a., 741:7
in bee-loud glade, 591:2
in the midst of the earth, 25:4
in world without God, 821:5
Jacob was left a., 7:2
learn to stand a., 504:8
leaving me never a., 536:21
let her a. she will court you, 232:14
let me a., 13:18
let us a., 450:19
long way I tread a., 405:14
love but you a., 880:12
love lives not a. in brain, 174:21
man a. at moment of birth, 105:1
man is a., 742:22
man only feels a., 776:2
man thinking or working is a., 475:9
man with God strive, 396:4
never a. with poet in pocket, 330:8
never less a. than when a., 361:11
never less a. than wholly a., 88:8
nor for you for one a., 487:13
not a. God is within, 108:17
not good that man be a., 5:14
not live by bread a., 9:*n*3
nothing accomplished a., 696:6
nothing wrong with being a., 869:6
on wide wide sea, 376:14, 377:4
one minute a. with him, 660:4
paces about room a., 676:13
right to be let a., 562:10
sometimes be a., 242:9
soon find himself a., 308:21
strange city lying a., 448:2
stranger and a., 727:11
strongest stands a., 504:18
this room where I am a., 811:19
though in wilderness never a., 108:*n*8
through seas of thought a., 368:16
travels fastest a., 587:6
trodden the winepress a., 27:17
wandering in the desert I've done a., 815:2
we ask to be left a., 438:20
we exist a., 611:3
we live as we dream a., 567:13
we millions live a., 495:10
we perished each a., 327:10

Alone *(continued)*
we shall die a., 269:16
weep and you weep a., 556:16
we're a. no chaperon, 691:6
white man will never be a., 394:3
withouten compaignye, 134:23
you a. are you, 221:26
Along came a spider, 895:14
can we all get a., 879:1
to get a. go a., 651:12
Aloof in order to gain reputation, 76:6
Aloud, all a. wind doth blow, 175:1
not winced nor cried a., 552:7
secrets cry a., 755:10
think a., 427:6
to fight a. very brave, 508:5
Alpes, au-delà des A. l'Italie, 99:*n8*
in conspectu A. alterum latus Italiae,
99:*n8*
Alph the sacred river, 377:17
Alpha, I am A. and Omega, 47:15
Alphabet of flowers, 230:8
Alpine mountains cold, 254:23
Alps, beyond A. lies Italy, 99:12
Al-Qaeda, helping a. build nuclear weapon,
850:4
Already with thee, 410:6
Alright, it's a. Ma it's life, 851:11
it's gonna be a., 848:14
listen Christ you did a., 731:4
Altar, family a., 498:7
great world's a. stairs, 453:24
of freedom, 446:12
what green a., 410:18
with this inscription, 40:32
Altars, men bow before a., 450:5
of great historical ideals, 757:15
their a. their hearths, 92:8
to unknown gods, 540:18
Alter ego, 81:*n11*
make and a. constitutions, 328:14
right to a. or abolish it, 336:1
when Hills do, 509:18
Alteration, alters when it a. finds, 222:15
Altereth, law of the Medes and Persians which
a. not, 28:26
Alteri seculo, 85:*n5*
Altering, Eye a. all, 756:15
Alters, affliction a., 223:34
love a. not, 222:15
when it alteration finds, 222:15
Altitude, what leopard seeking at a., 721:16
Altitudo O a., 248:3
Alway, I would not live a., 13:18
Lo I am with you a., 36:24
Always be an England, 775:11
be closing, 865:7
believed a. everywhere by all, 116:23
count on a murderer, 723:6
fair weather, 585:6
I am with you a., 36:24
in earth and air, 756:10
poor a. with you, 35:34
suspect everybody, 464:30
that same old story, 813:8
they were a. making discoveries, 317:2
you know how it a. is, 790:4
Alyosha, not God I don't accept A., 492:11

Am, I a. I a. I a., 832:13
I a. that I a., 7:29
I a. what I a., 42:32
I a. what I yam that's all I yam, 704:1
I shop therefore I a., 860:16
not I a fly, 352:15
sames of a., 701:18
tell them I A., 318:7
what I a. so shall thou be, 122:6
Amanece no más temprano, 898:10
Amantium irae amoris integratio est, 85:*n10*
Amaryllis, anger of A. a sad thing, 92:19
sport with A., 253:6
Amassing harmony, 642:6
Amateurs, hell full of musical a., 565:6
ruined by a., 672:13
Amaze the unlearned, 292:15
Amazed and curious, 358:8
I am a. methinks, 175:32
wise a. temperate furious, 216:1
Amazement, married to a., 840:10
Amazing grace how sweet the sound, 320:13
Ambassador is an honest man, 227:14
Amber, bee preserved in a., 107:10
flies preserved in a., 107:*n4*
scent of odorous perfume, 260:16
waves of grain, 572:5
Amber-dropping hair, 252:26
Ambiguities, smile vehicle for a., 483:13
Ambiguous undulations, 640:22
Ambition a species of madness, 276:15
all the pride cruelty and a., 159:15
choked with a. of meaner sort, 169:18
Distraction Uglification, 514:22
drove men to become false, 92:5
fling away a., 226:4
let not a. mock, 315:17
low a. and pride of kings, 294:14
made of sterner stuff, 192:30
of living like Thoreau, 591:*n1*
pen instrument to inflame a., 329:7
soldier's virtue, 218:28
thicksighted, 409:6
to grasp continent, 500:4
to reign is worth a., 255:15
vain the a. of kings, 237:11
vaulting a., 214:24
wars that make a. virtue, 209:13
who doth a. shun, 194:13
Ambition's, young a. ladder, 191:36
Ambitions, let go hold of a., 715:7
men bribed by loyalties and a., 694:7
weakens their a., 56:14
whispering a., 675:22
Ambitious, abject usually a., 276:11
as a. I slew him, 192:26
be a. to have money, 543:15
finger, 225:10
man have no satisfaction, 231:14
materially a., 672:2
not a. to appear man of letters, 270:17
so a. he even sews, 667:11
we live in a. poverty, 109:17
Ambitiously, leaders a. contending, 345:9
Ambles, who Time a. withal, 195:15
Ambree, foremost in battle Mary A., 889:22
Ambrosia, streams flow with a., 68:3
Âme, quelle â. est sans défauts, 559:*n6*

Amelette Ronsardelette, 111:*n2*
Amelioration, novelty connected to a., 433:16
Amemus, vivamus atque a., 91:*n4*
Amen, sound of great A., 502:17
stuck in my throat, 215:20
will no man say a., 177:16
Amend, your ways, 27:29
Amended, little said soon a., 156:24
Amending, admitting fact and a. ways, 60:17
constitutional right of a., 445:5
Amendment, Fifth A. old friend, 716:18
First A. has erected wall, 666:16
First A. rights, 745:10
Fourteenth A. not enact Spencer, 538:14
implicit in history of First A., 745:8
guarantee of First A., 667:2
Amends, I must make a., 857:10
no making a. in world, 480:3
America, all lost wild A., 716:5
America, 572:5
bad Americans die go to A., 560:13
beaten by strangers, 709:15
born in A. black, 808:11
cannot be ostrich, 566:11
destiny of A., 477:4
destiny of republics of A., 482:10
discovered accidentally, 672:3
discovery of A., 319:8
don't sell A. short, 887:11
England and Russia rebuilding Germany,
739:13
everybody in A. soft, 581:6
four centuries from discovery of A., 580:5
free Tom Mooney, 812:10
furnished Washington, 390:16
gigantic but giant mistake, 564:6
given over to mob of scribbling women,
431:22
glorious morning for A., 318:5
God bless A., 673:10, 673:11
God's crucible, 586:9
goes not abroad in search of monsters,
363:2
gone to degeneration, 538:1
good evening Mr. Mrs. A., 715:15
greatest question debated in A., 329:18
heart and mind of A., 749:22
High Priests of A., 874:8
homesick not for A. but Negroes, 690:11
huntsmen are up in A., 249:7
I believe in an A. where, 785:7
I hear A. singing, 485:14
I know and love, 878:11
I like to be in A., 828:14
i love you, 701:10
I see the face of A., 852:11
I too sing A., 731:3
I went to A. to convert Indians, 301:14
if you're going to A., 869:3
I'm putting queer shoulder to wheel,
812:12
in A. no noblemen or men of letters,
433:13
in A. two classes of travel, 683:13
in beginning all the world was A., 275:8
in which people still get rich, 765:12
instead of engineering for all A., 428:15
is just ourselves, 497:8

America *(continued)*
  I've given you all, 812:11
  know all people worth knowing in A., 456:16
  land of wonders, 433:16
  let A. be A. again, 731:5
  lost in A. shall be found, 727:15
  melting pot, 586:9
  middle class in A. the nation, 497:21
  must play its role in, 877:4
  my country Paris home town, 628:6
  my new-found land, 230:12
  named after man, 672:3
  Negro in A. has been able, 804:8
  new regions A. we call New World, 140:16
  no angels in A., 874:7
  no failure in A., 861:2
  nothing less than whole A., 324:5
  of poverty, 819:1
  only art A. has given, 669:15
  proclaimed rights of human nature, 363:3
  pure products of A. go crazy, 658:12
  put all A. behind him, 476:1
  rejoice that A. resisted, 305:13
  remote from wrangling world, 333:8
  room for every body in A., 331:4
  save soul rather than face, 660:14
  settlement of A. a grand scene, 329:8
  so happy as A., 333:8
  spend blood and might, 566:15
  such is state of A., 323:20
  the other A., 819:1
  true original native of A., 303:17
  ugly A., 795:15
  war in which A. engaged, 333:13
  was promises, 695:3
  what is left of A., 422:*n*1
  will have been in vain, 819:14
  works of art A. has given, 669:15
  would be no longer ruler of own spirit, 363:4
  you cannot conquer A., 306:5
  you have it better, 344:30
  young man there is A., 323:22
  youth of A. tradition, 560:14
American, adult A. Negro female, 817:12
  any red-blooded A. would do, 775:3
  axe, 400:9
  bathrooms, 708:13
  blacks call that soul, 758:15
  born live and die an A., 390:20
  century, 683:1, 718:1
  chief business of A. people, 613:6
  come up with me A. love, 739:3
  complex fate being A., 544:1
  continents not for colonization, 355:5
  cradle of A. liberty, 390:21
  credit card good in Europe, 553:14
  crisis in A. leadership, 777:19
  culture, 782:13
  democracy is imperfect, 795:13
  destiny of colored A., 477:4
  don't see any A. dream, 808:15
  English or A. lawyer, 433:12
  essential A. soul is hard, 663:3
  every A. bride taken to Niagara, 559:17
  experiment of A. people, 328:11
  flag floats from hill, 323:11

American *(continued)*
  from blues A. music, 610:8
  Goddam precious A. rights, 834:1
  Great A. Novel, 503:8
  how behave toward A. government, 473:14
  I am an A., 778:7
  if I were A., 306:5
  imitate Europe not A. literature, 456:15
  impressions of A. manners, 389:2
  impressive fact about A. women, 800:8
  life powerful solvent, 584:10
  literature from one book, 721:14
  living in the A. Age, 824:13
  love mankind except A., 310:18
  make credible much of A. reality, 835:3
  mind exasperated European, 531:16
  minds of A. women, 796:7
  Miss A. Pie, 861:11
  Muse, 716:1
  names, 715:18
  never felt I were an A., 830:14
  new deal for A. people, 651:16
  nineteen-year-old A. boy, 850:2
  no A. criminal class except Congress, 524:11
  no A. will be forbidden, 877:5
  no second acts in A. lives, 710:19
  North A. civilization engulfed world, 805:17
  not about to send A. boys, 753:16
  not Virginian but A., 331:9
  nothing can astound A., 507:10
  part of the larger A. story, 876:13
  pass to A. strand, 243:13
  people did not choose, 877:7
  professors like literature dead, 664:7
  popular music, 717:10
  public wants tragedy with happy ending, 529:4
  seldom revealed picture of A. heart, 581:8
  sense to A. people, 727:9
  show world how A. sailors fight, 886:*n*2
  smiling aspects of life more A., 529:2
  society, 764:3
  sole A. music, 602:4
  system rugged individualism, 625:17
  Teenage Drive-In Life, 831:2
  tragedy, 609:9
  underestimating intelligence of A. people, 645:*n*1
  violence is as A. as cherry pie, 856:5
  what A. people are interested in, 863:3
  what do we mean by A. Revolution, 330:17
  what then is the A., 331:2
  when A. life is most A., 774:11
  who reads A. book goes to A. play, 374:19
  without qualifying adjectives, 554:7
  women kept from growing, 796:8
  write well of A. things, 543:16
  you cannot spill a drop of A. blood, 482:13
Americanism, hyphenated A., 571:19
Americanization, line of rapid effective A., 580:4
American's principal means of action, 433:14
Americans are peculiar chosen people, 482:15
  average A. do not talk, 869:10
  brave A. all, 328:1

Americans *(continued)*
  can fix nothing without drink, 401:3
  disdain to be instruments, 349:6
  do not always explain, 532:9
  first self-constituted People, 695:4
  freemen or slaves, 328:6
  good A. die go to Paris, 560:13
  good at long shot, 394:1
  hope of world, 321:9
  I love the A., 306:3
  in A. spark of idealism, 562:15
  kill A. and their allies, 874:14
  let us all be A., 554:7
  live on outskirts of hope, 753:12
  love of wealth in all A. do, 434:6
  must look outward, 537:6
  my people are A., 717:9
  new generation of A., 785:10
  no A. were harmed, 877:6
  North A. use reality, 776:1
  of African descent, 519:10
  prefer Continent, 603:3
  proudest distinction of A., 742:18
  races didn't bother A., 695:4
  refuse to learn languages, 603:3
  Russians and A., 434:1
  strength of A., 434:5
  this generation of A., 652:7
  we are all A., 866:3
  were the first to understand, 742:18
America's, fundamentals of A. economy, 842:3
  future under challenge, 753:17
  my nation, 715:3
  participate in A. growth, 756:24
  read in A. signs, 332:*n*2
  treatment of Negro A. greatest scandal, 718:5
Amerika du hast es besser, 344:*n*10
Âmes, par de pareils objets les â. blessées, 267:*n*2
Ami entends-tu, 891:6
Amiability, brimstone behind beautiful a., 420:13
Amiable, good a. or sweet, 259:14
  good nature more a. than beauty, 288:11
  how a. are thy tabernacles, 17:18
  lovely death, 175:18
  virtue not always a., 330:5
  weakness, 304:22
Amicable, candor and a. relations, 355:7
Amicably if they can, 380:12
Amice gray, 260:7
Amici diem perdidi, 107:*n*9
Amicus Plato sed magis amica veritas, 78:*n*1
A-milking sir she said, 894:12
Amiss, better to love a., 453:*n*2
  nothing comes a. so money comes, 173:10
  thou shalt never do a., 30:28
Amittuntur, non a. sed praemittuntur, 103:*n*7
Ammiral, mast of some great a., 255:16
Ammunition, praise Lord pass a., 687:10
Amo, odi et a., 91:*n*9
Amoebas at start not complex, 609:11
Among them but not of them, 395:24
Amor, and after A. vincit omnia, 133:16
  batallas de a. campo de pluma, 101:*n*10
  fati, 548:21

Angel *(continued)*
 to radiant a. linked, 198:10
 white as a. English child, 350:14
 wings cast shadow, 688:7
 would act a. acts beast, 269:22
 wrestled as A. with Jacob, 244:30
 writing in book, 392:17
 wrote like an a., 316:21
Angelheaded hipsters, 812:13
Angelic, Angles have a. faces, 121:28
 host proclaim, 305:10
 something of a. light, 371:8
 sprite, 230:18
Angelo, face like hoosier Michael A., 488:10
Angel's, her a. face, 160:5
 passage of a. tear, 408:16
 philosophy clip a. wings, 409:16
 wit and singular learning, 143:11
Angels, air awash with a., 797:12
 all pallid and wan, 448:15
 alone that soar above, 266:2
 and ministers of grace, 197:32
 are bright still, 217:5
 are painted fair, 281:12
 ascending and descending, 6:41, 39:2
 aurochs and a., 723:8
 band of a. coming after me, 898:20
 beggar carried by a., 38:17
 bending near earth, 457:11
 blow your trumpets a., 230:19
 books like a. with outspread wings, 611:2
 by good a. tenanted, 448:9
 by that sin fell the a., 226:4
 death nor life nor a., 41:26
 desire of power caused a. to fall, 165:24
 do I not deal with a., 765:5
 entertained a. unawares, 45:15
 fear to tread, 292:25
 food too fine for a., 280:18
 four a. on corners of earth, 46:33
 four a. to my bed, 265:3
 give his a. charge over thee, 17:29, 37:24
 go with me like good a., 225:15
 God and a. as surety, 118:16
 guardian a. sung this strain, 301:3
 hark the herald a. sing, 305:10
 hear a. sing, 457:11
 holy a. guard thy bed, 289:10
 in forms of kings, 337:10
 in heaven above, 449:23
 invite God and his a., 231:11
 keep ancient places, 577:4
 made him a little lower than the a., 15:5
 made spectacle to a., 42:11
 maiden a. name Lenore, 449:5
 make the a. weep, 206:28
 maketh his a. spirits, 45:6
 men a. no government necessary, 345:12
 men would be a., 165:*n*4
 Michael and a. fought, 47:1
 ne'er like a. till passion dies, 228:5
 no a. in America, 874:7
 on side of a., 430:9
 only God and a. lookers on, 164:16
 pass in a. say, 424:18
 progeny of light, 258:20
 questions to ask about a., 850:7
 sad as a., 314:*n*2

Angels *(continued)*
 send his a. with trumpet, 35:22
 sing thee to thy rest, 202:33
 sons of men and a. say, 305:7
 sorrow for a., 460:14
 swearing I was right, 447:6
 tears such as a. weep, 256:1
 they have the faces of a., 117:7
 tongues of a., 42:26
 trumpet-tongued, 214:24
 walking at peace, 118:16
 we shall hear a., 578:9
 when a. go praising God, 666:10
 where a. fear to tread, 292:25
 where a. tremble, 316:13
 with a. and archangels, 49:6
 with cash-boxes for hearts, 417:18
 women are a. wooing, 203:2
 wrote of A. and God, 351:10
 yield eternal thanks, 318:8
Angels' Bread made Bread of man, 127:2
 man did eat a. food, 17:16
Anger, a God slow to a., 12:30
 contempt and a. of lip, 205:15
 furious a., 30:34
 give vent to millennial a., 793:1
 he that is slow to a., 20:33
 is a short madness, 97:23
 is a weed, 116:13
 monstrous a. of guns, 699:6
 more in sorrow than a., 197:14
 of Amaryllis, 92:19
 of Lord kindled, 11:14
 of lovers renews love, 85:*n*10
 one of sinews of soul, 250:7
 provoke not children to a., 44:13
 slow to a., 20:38
 take care you strike in a., 565:11
 tread them in mine a., 27:17
 visionary a. cleansing sight, 825:5
 waves of a. and fear, 748:16
 words of pain tones of a., 128:8
Angle, brother of the A., 244:35
 in every a. greet, 267:4
Angler, honest a., 244:34
 no man born an a., 244:33
Angles are director's thoughts, 727:7
 race called A., 121:28
 that they were called A., 117:7
Angleterre, l'A. la perfide A., 366:*n*4
Angli, non A. sed Angeli, 117:*n*3
Angling, be quiet and go a-a., 245:10
 frequent practicer of a., 245:1
 like mathematics, 244:32
 like virtue of humility, 245:2
 never fully learnt, 244:32
 of a. as of strawberries, 245:7
 produce gentleness, 245:*n*2
 reward to itself, 245:1
Anglo-Catholic in religion, 677:9
Anglo-Saxon, death provides minds of A., 699:20
Angry, be ye a., 43:37
 bellows full of a. wind, 593:17
 feel a. because we strike, 541:9
 hungry mob is a. mob, 861:6
 I was a. with my foe, 353:7
 I was a. with my friend, 353:7

Angry *(continued)*
 like an a. ape, 206:28
 looking for a fix, 812:13
 opposition to idea, 630:13
 passions rise, 289:6
 proud and a. dust, 575:15
 tears gone, 593:3
 up the blood, 747:6
 when a. count four very a. swear, 523:21
 when a. count ten, 338:19
 wrenlike vigilance, 787:19
Angst, teenage a. has paid off well, 879:6
Anguis, latet a. in herba, 92:*n*15
Anguish comes to end, 773:4
 divinest a., 476:12
 edges of laughter and a., 654:16
 immense open a., 833:17
 in a. uplift new song, 568:13
 lessened by another's a., 179:21
 must an a. pay, 508:4
 of bereavement, 446:12
 of the marrow, 675:26
 pain and a. wring brow, 373:16
 whatever a. of spirit, 331:10
Anima, dum a. est spes est, 87:*n*11
Animae dimidium meae, 96:*n*1
Animal, aid law of a. life, 542:15
 ancient a. symbols of St. John, 415:7
 another armored a., 671:11
 any other a. you take for a walk, 439:7
 cow a good a. in field, 309:20
 fastened to dying a., 594:3
 inescapable a. walks with me, 772:2
 information vegetable a. mineral, 526:6
 man a noble a., 249:4
 man a political a., 78:16
 man a poor bare forked a., 212:3
 man a reasoning a., 103:14
 man a social a., 276:13
 man a successful a., 570:5
 man a tool-using a., 406:14
 man is raised above a., 751:6
 man only a. devours own kind, 336:13
 no a. more invincible than woman, 73:9
 no such a., 886:13
 poor bare forked a., 212:3
 post coitum omne a. triste, 121:7
 Public a mean a., 386:4
 red a. war, 608:13
 rope between a. and Superman, 547:17
 unmistakable a. a writer, 819:16
 we are worrying a., 773:1
 with four back legs, 830:7
 women as untamed a., 99:13
Animality, endued with a., 327:12
Animals, all a. equal, 735:11
 all a. of forest alike, 889:3
 among a., 671:13
 boy most unmanageable of a., 76:10
 could turn and live with a., 486:14
 feed themselves men eat, 348:14
 first a. then intelligences, 505:9
 heart of a., 236:1
 I sing for them the a., 891:11
 infuse themselves, 185:31
 interest in a. and athletes, 672:1
 love earth sun a., 485:10

Anyone *(continued)*
  who hates children, 644:2
Anythin' for quiet life, 464:4
Anything, as green as a., 821:2
  courage not to believe in a., 479:7
  for a quiet life, 237:1, 464:4
  for good of country, 290:8
  goes, 691:11
  he hasn't got a. on, 432:19
  I am Rose like a., 628:13
  is there a. beyond, 669:8
  labeled Gwladys, 648:14
  not a. to show more fair, 370:2
  nothing done while a. remained, 106:12
  possible except fair play, 536:1
  when younger could remember a., 525:9
  who could ask for a. more, 710:23
  wrong with that, 874:3
  you can do I can do better, 673:15
  you can get a. you want, 864:10
A-OK, everything is A., 800:4
Apart, born with legs a., 834:13
  covers of book too far a., 540:15
  keep a. keep a., 568:16
  man's love a thing a., 398:6
  mood a., 624:16
  through hatred borne a., 67:1
Apartments, celestial ennui of a., 642:1
  painting not done to decorate a., 647:14
Apathetic end, 451:9
Apathy, extinction from a., 722:14
Ape, Devil is ever God's a., 144:5
  for his grandfather, 502:14
  how like to us, 84:18
  if a. looks into mirror, 335:19
  like an angry a., 206:28
  or angel, 430:9
Aped, vices a. from white men, 713:14
Apennine, Mists the A., 508:7
Apes, I am Tarzan of the A., 629:9
  lead a. in hell, 173:12
  leave Now for dogs and a., 461:13
  Tarzan of the A., 629:8
Aphorism never coincides with truth, 626:7
Aphrodisiac, power the great a., 802:10
  Ulysses nowhere a., 634:7
Aphrodite, lovely as A., 698:15
  on your rich-wrought throne, 56:4
  sleep with golden A., 53:9
  spoke and loosened girdle, 51:29
  stronger bolts than A., 67:25
  weeping anarchic A., 749:7
  what delight without A., 55:3
  with intricate charms, 56:*n*4
  work of soft A., 56:9
Apish, tardy a. nation, 176:22
A-plyin' up and down, 589:2
Apocalypse, new a., 415:7
Apocalyptic literature of the twentieth century, 826:2
Apollo, bards in fealty to A., 408:17
  harsh after songs of A., 175:2
  I swear by A. Physician, 70:14
  nor does A. always stretch bow, 96:24
Apollo's, burned is A. laurel bough, 169:7
  first, 245:13
  musical as A. lute, 174:23, 252:19
Apollos watered, 42:7

Apollyon, foul Fiend A., 271:15
Apologists, Northern a. tremble, 433:3
Apologize, anybody not offended, I a., 517:14
  never a. mister, 755:1
Apology for Devil, 521:13
  too prompt, 259:13
Apostle is unlikely to look out, 335:19
  rank as a. in aesthetic band, 526:11
Apostles, I am least of a., 42:32
  true a. of equality, 497:14
  would have done as they, 398:1
Apostolic blows and knocks, 262:11
Apothecary, ounce of civet good a., 212:28
  true a. thy drugs quick, 181:15
Appall, common sense a., 579:3
  rather than to a., 482:22
Appalled, conscience and vanity a., 595:15
  property was thus a., 202:35
Appalling ocean surrounds land, 483:5
Apparatus, mediocrity of a., 643:15
Apparel, every true man's a., 207:10
  fashion wears out more a., 191:2
  gay a., 177:12
  oft proclaims the man, 197:23
Appareled in celestial light, 370:13
  like the spring, 220:9
Apparent queen unveiled her light, 257:25
Apparition, lovely a. sent, 371:6
  of these faces, 665:1
  that a. sole of men he saw, 401:15
Apparitions, fifteen a. seen, 597:6
Appeal, basic a. of movies, 792:9
  books of universal a., 616:15
  I a. to any white man, 320:6
  I a. unto Caesar, 41:3
  lies not to courts but to ballot, 615:3
Appeals to religious prejudice, 502:14
Appear, fishermen a. like mice, 212:24
  small vices do a., 212:30
  things not what a. to be, 108:21
  to be and appear not to be, 76:4
  while these visions did a., 179:18
  wish to a. as what they are, 341:12
Appearance, in a. at friendship, 277:25
  judge not according to a., 39:20
  looketh on the outward a., 10:43
  magical good fortune of attractive a., 667:4
  of new beings, 439:11
  takes on a. of nearby rock, 59:22
Appearances, judging people by a., 266:13
  keep up a., 464:36
  of power, 832:5
  often are deceiving, 58:14
  to mind are four kinds, 108:21
Appeared, there a. a chariot of fire, 12:11
Appears, God A. and God is Light, 354:7
  thine in mine a., 228:8
  when true Genius a., 284:15
Appeaseth strife, 20:33
Appendix, idleness an a. to nobility, 234:18
Appetite a feeling and a love, 368:10
  a universal wolf, 203:8
  alimentary canal with big a., 765:11
  breakfast with a., 225:22
  cloy hungry edge of a., 176:18
  comes with eating, 145:6
  for bogus revelation, 644:16
  good digestion wait on a., 216:16

Appetite *(continued)*
  increase of a., 197:1
  makes eating a delight, 261:7
  man given to a., 21:24
  may sicken, 204:10
  not meat but a., 261:7
  quench a. keep reason under control, 112:20
  sharpen with cloyless sauce his a., 218:18
  umble pie with a., 466:1
  will into a., 203:8
  with keen a. he sits down, 184:39
Appetites, cloy a. they feed, 218:21
  man of my a., 645:11
  not their a., 209:9
  one of principal a. of soul, 702:16
  subdue a. my dears, 464:15
Appius, that which A. says, 92:13
Applaud, old people a. it, 157:5
  thee to the very echo, 217:20
  world forever a., 446:1
Applause delight wonder of our stage, 232:19
  from none but self a., 491:21
  joy pleasance revel and a., 208:31
  lectured with much a., 487:6
  not least in honor or a., 161:*n*1
  sit attentive to own a., 295:13
Apple, as an a. reddens, 56:10
  blossoms fill air, 682:6
  cleft through core, 360:14
  did not want a. for a.'s sake, 523:16
  easy under the a. boughs, 777:9
  my a. trees never eat cones, 622:11
  of the eye, 15:13
  pickers passed it by, 56:10
  prince of a. towns, 777:10
  rotten at the heart, 184:27
  round as a. was his face, 132:6
  tree among the trees, 24:7
  worm in wild a., 670:10
  ye who love a., 640:*n*1
Apple-bearing Hesperian coast, 68:3
Apple-faced farmhand, 884:*n*3
Apple's cleft through core, 360:14
Apples, comfort me with a., 24:8
  golden a. of sun, 591:11
  of gold in pictures of silver, 21:33
  on Dead Sea's shore, 395:15
  silver a. of moon, 591:11
  since Eve ate a., 399:3
  small choice in rotten a., 173:7
Applesauce, politics is a., 640:4
Appleseed, Johnny A., 639:17
Apple-tree, bare branch of mossy a., 377:15
Appliance, by desperate a. relieved, 201:16
Appliances, with all a. to boot, 188:10
Application, lays in a. on it, 465:18
Applied, acceleration proportional to a. force, 279:*n*3
  science not exist, 499:2
Applies west of Rockies, 795:6
Apply our hearts unto wisdom, 17:26
  thine heart unto my knowledge, 21:19
Applying thought one finds, 429:*n*1
Appointed for my second race, 268:9
  house a. for all living, 14:8
  limits keep, 503:1
  their a. courses, 69:21
Appointeth the moon for seasons, 18:11

Ariseth (*continued*)
 sun a. they gather themselves, 18:11
Aristocracy, Clover any time A., 511:5
 has three successive ages, 364:12
 natural a. among men, 338:4
 not society without a., 657:9
 of Moneybag, 407:9
 untitled a., 443:14
Aristocratic, beast of prey in a. races, 548:15
 single out a. pretensions, 631:10
Aristotelian, every man born A. or Platonist, 380:7
Aristotle and all you philosophers, 399:*n*2
 bookes of A. and his philosophie, 133:23
 is it A. Pliny Buffon, 312:25
Aristotle's, live and die in A. works, 168:16
Arithmetic, branches of A., 514:22
Arithmetical, subsistence increases in a. ratio, 362:7
Arizona is my land, 507:12
Ark, make thee an a., 6:17
 of bulrushes, 7:23
 of God is taken, 10:37
 of the ache of it, 803:3
 Uzzah put hand to a., 11:14
 we bear a. of liberties of world, 482:15
Arkady, music said A., 847:3
Arkansaw, rest anywhere it would be in A., 393:15
Arks, these are the a., 167:5
Arm and burgonet of men, 218:12
 brutal a. appear, 597:3
 can honor set to a., 183:25
 clothed in white samite, 138:4
 doth bind restless wave, 503:1
 faithless a., 748:10
 give me your a. old toad, 799:12
 I bit my a., 376:6
 is very long, 69:22
 it in rags, 212:30
 long a. of coincidence, 577:19
 maketh flesh his a., 27:39
 mortal a. and nerve feel, 374:8
 on bended a. doglike, 62:27
 reared a. crested world, 219:8
 seal upon thine a., 24:25
 slumbering on own right a., 409:3
 some quick to a., 665:8
 soon shall thy a., 327:11
 the obdured breast, 256:23
 under a. carried broom, 895:4
 wreath of hair which crowns my a., 230:1
Arma, cedant a. togae, 88:*n*3
 virumque cano, 93:*n*12
Armageddon, place called A., 47:7
 we stand at A., 571:17
Armaments universal debt, planned obsolescence, 702:17
Armchair, like a comfortable a., 605:11
Armed at points exactly, 197:12
 Forces in control, 692:7
 goeth on to meet the a. men, 14:27
 goodness a. with power, 696:1
 neutrality, 566:13
 peace, 247:9
 rhinoceros, 216:20
 so strong in honesty, 193:10
 thrice a. that hath quarrel just, 170:7

Armed (*continued*)
 thy want as an a. man, 20:1
Armenians, who remembers A., 684:15
Armentières, mademoiselle from A., 688:13
Armes, aux a. citoyens, 361:3
Armies, anarchy scatters a., 65:22
 disbanding hired a., 406:13
 ignorant a. clash by night, 496:19
 mechanized a., 620:8
 not only fighting hostile a., 489:13
 resisted but not an idea, 422:8
 swore in Flanders, 314:11
 when a. are mobilized, 58:1
Arming me from fear, 476:14
Armor is his honest thought, 227:9
 man in a. slave, 463:8
 no a. against fate, 246:13
 of coercion, 689:14
 of light, 41:40
 of righteous cause, 577:16
 whole a. of God, 43:39
Armored, another a. animal, 671:11
Armorers accomplishing knights, 189:18
Armpits, scent of a. finer than prayer, 486:8
Arm's, your a. short to box with God., 610:3
Arms, a people takes up a., 434:8
 against a sea of troubles, 199:21
 analysis must lay down its a., 563:16
 and the man I sing, 93:28, 274:13
 blow trumpet to a., 332:20
 bring to our cars clash of a., 331:13
 by little a. plied, 513:10
 children receive a. race from us, 794:11
 come to my a., 515:13
 defy Omnipotent to a., 255:7
 everlasting a., 9:33
 excites us to a., 273:24
 foes will provide with a., 94:16
 fury provides a., 93:33
 haughty nation proud in a., 252:2
 Helen's a., 596:2
 hold hidden charms, 708:6
 hug it in my a., 206:36
 I never would lay down a., 306:5
 imparadised in one another's a., 257:22
 industry, 686:16
 Infinite Goodness has wide a., 129:13
 law stands mute in midst of a., 87:9
 laws and a. foundations of states, 141:15
 let a. yield to toga, 88:7
 lift him into my a., 817:7
 lord of folded a., 174:14
 love world and all in its rainy a., 872:4
 man in a. wish to be, 371:20
 many a soldier's loving a., 487:9
 mewling in nurse's a., 194:25
 might do what this has done, 249:22
 mightier than they in a., 258:23
 more than human a., 648:5
 muscles of brawny a., 436:11
 nurse of a., 322:3
 of chambermaid, 310:21
 press in a. the loveliness, 650:12
 race, 765:14
 right to keep and bear a., 340:2
 rush my only into your a., 651:3
 seek it in My a., 577:2
 spouted a., 720:7

Arms (*continued*)
 take your last embrace, 181:14
 takes vigor from a., 324:15
 that my love were in my a., 881:1
 three corners of world in a., 176:7
 thrice thrown a. about her neck, 94:18
 thy white a. were there, 609:1
 to a. citizens, 361:3
 to war and a. I fly, 265:17
 tries everything before a., 86:10
 we touch a., 815:16
 what a. have lain under head., 695:12
 with his a. outstretched, 203:24
 with open a. stand ready, 482:12
 young in one another's a., 594:1
Army awakened, 608:12
 back to the A. again, 588:14
 Chief of the A., 366:6
 composed of scum, 366:10
 conventional a., 802:14
 courage and conduct of a., 328:6
 language dialect with a., 700:4
 discipline soul of a., 328:4
 each a. hath a hand, 175:15
 fogs revealed an a., 608:12
 gives you a. and navy, 324:13
 go to war with the a., 833:15
 hum of either a., 189:18
 is like fish, 698:12
 language dialect with a., 700:4
 London devour entire a., 619:16
 marches on stomach, 366:3
 noble a. of Martyrs, 48:10
 not halted by eloquence, 470:11
 of pointed firs, 552:11
 of six hundred syllogisms, 141:12
 terrible as an a. with banners, 24:19
 this is the a., 673:13
 Wellington's a., 319:*n*1
 would be base rabble, 324:13
 you're in a. now, 633:12
Arnica, better for bruise than a., 462:27
Aroint thee witch, 213:33
Aromatic, as a. plants bestow, 165:*n*3
 die of rose in a. pain, 294:21
Arose a mother in Israel, 10:8
 from out azure main, 301:3
 people a. as one man, 10:28
 up a new king over Egypt, 7:22
Around, at once above beneath a., 318:7
 how they do get a. us, 73:10
 ice was all a., 375:24
 may it be beautiful a. me, 891:18
Arouse, happier in passion we feel than a., 264:14
Aroused popular conscience, 649:12
A-roving, go no more a., 397:14
 I will go, 898:3
 I'll go no more a., 897:20
Arrant jade on a journey, 322:18
 knave, 198:18
 knaves all, 199:25
 thankless a., 159:9
Array, trim a., 371:25
Arrayed, not a. like one of these, 33:9
Arrears, pay glad life's a., 462:25
Arrest, death strict in his a., 202:28
 I'm under God's a., 280:20

Arrêter tant de menus de ses agitations, 152:*n*9

Arrival, Messiah will come day after a., 655:15

Arrive at what you do not know, 678:21
    gods a., 424:15
    to a. where you are, 678:21
    travel better than to a., 555:2
    where we started, 679:12

Arrivé, le jour de gloire est a., 361:3

Arrived at island called Guanahaní, 139:8
    hour of departure has a., 74:11
    in good harbor, 240:2
    openly a. at, 566:16

Arrives the snow, 424:7
    too swift a. as tardy, 180:25

Arriving, forever a., 776:3
    serenely a., 487:14
    sometimes at profundity, 830:12

Arrogance, of power, 741:6
    power leads toward a., 786:15

Arrogancy of the proud, 25:21

Arrogant, not a. because of knowledge, 3:4

Arrow feathered with eagle's plumes, 59:18
    land of the A. Ide, 701:9
    my bow and a., 893:8
    phrase time's a., 649:5
    shot a. into air, 436:19
    sped a. comes not back, 98:*n*3
    that flieth by day, 17:28
    thine old A., 510:2

Arrows, as a. in the hand, 19:6
    bowe he bar and a. brighte, 134:18
    envy slays itself by own a., 119:22
    loosed several ways, 188:36
    love's keen a., 195:19
    of desire, 354:8
    of outrageous fortune, 199:21
    thine a. stick fast in me, 16:14
    which speak to the wise, 63:25

Arrowy shower, 316:16

Ars humana aedificavit urbes, 87:*n*1
    vita brevis a. longa, 71:*n*2

Arsenal of democracy, 653:3

Arsenic, you're a cookie full of a., 747:2

Arsked, are you lost daddy I a., 662:9

Art accessible only to small number, 533:14
    accomplice of love, 570:3
    adulteries of a., 232:7
    adventure a. peace, 580:13
    all a. quite useless, 559:24
    all the gloss of a., 322:27
    alone eternal, 458:3
    and science in particulars, 354:13
    artist with no a. form, 830:11
    aspires towards condition of music, 534:6
    be or wear work of a., 560:17
    birth of a., 626:2
    book of deeds words and a., 484:24
    Central Park single work of a., 498:13
    comes from a. not chance, 292:19
    comes proposing frankly, 534:9
    cookery become an a., 234:16
    dead a. of poetry, 665:4
    desiring this man's a., 221:6
    desperate cry, 627:7
    does not reproduce visible, 639:8
    dying is an a., 833:3
    each a. to please, 295:13
    erotics of a., 835:15

Art *(continued)*
    errors not in a., 279:13
    establishes human truths, 786:15
    expressing emotion in a., 675:20
    film is not the a. of scholars, 854:7
    first mistake of A., 865:15
    flying in face of presumptions, 544:10
    for art's sake, 400:17
    given for that, 462:8
    gives quality to moments, 534:9
    glib and oily a., 210:29
    great a. born of metropolis, 664:15
    great a. to saunter, 472:21
    has reason for being, 428:20
    hateful a. how to forget, 241:20
    hath an enemy Ignorance, 231:18
    high a. and pure science, 723:12
    I dream of a. equilibrated, 605:11
    if it is a. not for all, 627:9
    imagination master of a., 568:4
    imitates Nature, 105:*n*7
    imitation of nature, 103:18
    in a. best is good enough, 343:7
    in a. economy is beauty, 545:3
    in a. one thing that counts, 649:3
    independent of claptrap, 520:16
    individuality beginning and end of a., 344:20
    industry without a. brutality, 484:20
    is a crucial dangerous operation, 812:3
    jealous mistress, 428:7
    justification of a. is, 831:14
    keep pure both life and a., 70:14
    knows all about a., 704:5
    last and greatest a., 296:16
    lies in the slender margin, 282:1
    life doesn't imitate a., 839:19
    life earnest a. gay, 359:20
    life imitates a. more than A. imitates life, 559:21
    life is short a. long, 71:6
    lived for a. lived for love, 551:1
    long life short, 343:3
    long Time fleeting, 436:5
    made tongue-tied by authority, 221:21
    madness of a., 544:12
    makes life, 545:8
    may err, 274:27
    mediatress, 379:18
    moral sense of work of a., 544:16
    more matter with less a., 198:27
    music not only new a. form, 669:13
    my trade and a. is living, 152:14
    mysterious is source of a. and science, 637:8
    nature is but a. unknown, 294:23
    nature is the a. of God, 248:6
    nature's above a., 212:25
    Nature's handmaid A., 272:5
    neurotics created great works of a., 610:18
    never thought in terms of a., 702:3
    next to Nature A., 384:4
    no use for masses, 581:9
    not learned much by a., 237:12
    not thou man, 352:15
    nothing without form, 493:7
    novel is an a. form, 809:8
    o' letter-writing, 463:29

Art *(continued)*
    of angling, 245:1
    of being wise, 541:8
    of Biography different from Geography, 629:1
    of knowing what to overlook, 541:8
    of losing not hard, 763:7
    of necessities strange, 211:30
    of Racine's verse, 612:5
    of seeing things invisible, 284:20
    of teaching is awakening, 546:1
    of telling you nothing, 267:20
    only through a. get outside selves, 611:8
    only works of a. America has given, 669:15
    perfect reproduction of a., 693:1
    pleasure of all a., 792:8
    posterity of work of a., 610:15
    practice and thought forge a., 93:12
    pretty but is it A., 588:4
    products of a. and science, 693:4
    professor of a. of puffing, 346:16
    purpose inherent in a. so in nature, 77:14
    reactions to a. or to music, 826:14
    real a. has the capacity, 835:13
    refuge of a., 723:8
    revenge of the intellect upon a., 835:14
    revolt against fate, 728:14
    romantic character in a., 534:11
    schoolman's subtle a., 296:3
    science and a. unite humanity, 809:3
    selfish and perverse, 366:19
    should stand alone, 520:16
    smaller with their a., 716:1
    somber enemy of good a., 734:3
    subjects for a. and exemplars, 672:1
    subordinates a. to nature, 379:13
    substitute for experience, 791:8
    such music not only new a. form, 669:13
    take love away no a., 570:3
    tell thee what thou a., 157:29
    tender strokes of a., 293:13
    termite-tapeworm-fungus-moss a., 784:9
    thanks to a. see world multiply, 611:8
    that speaks, 728:12
    that tells time of day, 824:12
    theme of A. and Song, 596:3
    to blot, 296:16
    to find mind's construction, 214:15
    to make dust of all things, 248:26
    too precise in every part, 240:16
    transmission of highest feelings, 507:8
    unpremeditated a., 403:2
    war only a. necessary, 141:16
    war's glorious a., 290:15
    what a. wash guilt away, 322:16
    when looking at significant work of a., 639:6
    where love of man love of a., 70:18
    who comprehends a., 366:18
    wise men know a. of eating, 348:14
    work of a. corner of creation, 537:12
    work of body and soul, 484:10
    work that aspires to a., 567:2
    works of a. products of danger, 631:18
    works of a. turned to wall, 502:1
    writer's responsibility to a., 714:8
    you're my favorite work of a., 707:4

Artery, makes each petty a., 198:2

Artful, alliteration's a. aid, 326:4
    Dodger, 464:7
Arthur, good King A., 896:23
    King A. not dead, 138:16
    knightly endured pain, 138:5
    most renowned Christian king, 138:1
    slowly answered A., 455:19
Arthur's bosom, 189:4
Article, fundamental a. of political creed,
    330:16
    snuffed out by a., 398:29
Articles, Christians agree in a., 309:2
Articulate, bleats a. monotony, 372:n1
    coherent or a. system, 757:14
    sweet sounds together, 591:19
Articulations, splendid a., 149:11
Artifice of eternity, 594:3
Artificer, great a. made my mate, 556:8
    in brass and iron, 6:12
    lean unwashed a., 175:29
    old father old a., 650:13
Artificers, errors not in art but in a., 279:13
Artificial, all things are a., 248:6
    kill in a. manner, 407:6
    natural and a., 379:13
    objects especially tools, 572:9
    refined or a. type, 607:2
    speech lacking in a. graces, 87:17
Artillery, hi-hi-yee for field a., 639:3
    to thine A. left a Friend, 510:2
Artilleryman, red-haired a. killed or not, 506:13
Artisan, worthy a. of abominable work, 136:22
Artist, allow a. freedom of choice, 544:10
    almost every a. nature, 631:10
    barrier between craftsman and a., 655:8
    be free a. and nothing else, 578:2
    cheat for sake of beauty, 633:2
    create a. do not talk, 344:18
    critic when cannot be a., 493:8
    equipped to see, 702:15
    God only another a., 647:15
    grant a. his subject, 544:10
    greatest a. greatest ideas, 484:5
    if not a. be revolutionary, 843:10
    imitate that within, 380:1
    is his own fault, 742:10
    keep work to himself, 343:25
    key to mystery of great a., 789:10
    masterpiece joy to a., 520:15
    must be solitary, 552:14
    needs but a roof, 551:5
    never trust the a., 663:2
    no home save Paris, 549:8
    no man born an a., 244:33
    one can as a. choose, 774:10
    perceives more than fellows, 613:11
    progress of a. self-sacrifice, 675:18
    range limited as specialist, 578:4
    records more than has seen, 613:11
    remains within behind handiwork, 650:11
    search for subject, 416:10
    selects guesses synthesizes, 578:4
    speaks to our capacity, 567:3
    that queer monster the a., 545:7
    what an a. dies with me, 106:8
    what's any a. but the dregs, 798:12
    with no art form, 830:11
Artiste triche pour le beau, 633:n1

Artistic, intellectual a. personality, 757:14
    nothing a. from mere art, 618:9
    verisimilitude, 527:19
Artistries in circumstance, 536:14
Artistry, scaled invention or true a., 665:14
Artists, all a. not chess players, 669:16
    are antennae of the race, 665:15
    as many worlds as a., 611:8
    could not change history, 749:21
    great a. never Puritans, 645:4
    scientists a. and artisans, 780:4
    what a. call posterity, 610:15
Artless, full of a. jealousy, 201:22
Arts, Athens mother of a. eloquence, 260:2
    flourishing of the a., 698:13
    Imagination with Reason mother of a.,
        341:n4
    inglorious a. of peace, 266:17
    liberal a. study humanizes, 102:26
    medicine most distinguished of a., 71:2
    no a. no letters no society, 239:10
    no relish of those a., 288:7
    nurse of a. plenties, 190:6
    state of our a., 756:24
    stomach teacher of a., 105:12
    that caused to rise, 295:13
    they are the books the a., 174:24
    three a. with all things, 75:23
Aryan, neat mustache and A. eye, 833:8
As if, 541:20
A-sailing with the wind, 896:7
Ascend, base degrees by which a., 191:36
    if I a. up into heaven, 19:13
    into the hill of the Lord, 15:24
    Muse of fire a., 188:29
Ascendancy, capital in a. system of plunder,
    478:4
Ascended, bright pomp a. jubilant, 258:28
    into heaven, 48:11
Ascending, angels a. and descending, 6:41,
    39:2
Ascendit, quanto plus a., 126:n3
Ascends to mountaintops, 395:17
Ascent, no a. too steep for mortals, 96:3
Ascetic in unnecessary points, 540:21
    no a. reliably sane, 738:14
    systematically a., 540:21
Asclepius cured the body, 74:n1
    I swear by A., 70:14
    owe a cock to A., 70:9
Ash heap of history, 765:13
    oak a. and thorn, 589:24, 889:24
    one adjusting a. heaps, 670:18
    out of a. I rise, 833:4
Ashamed, epitaph of which not a., 556:3
    more a. more respectable, 565:5
    naked and were not a., 5:17
    no reason to be a. of ape, 502:14
    not a. to defend a friend, 31:10
    not a. to fail, 306:14
    of being white, 731:12
    of death, 248:10
    of having been in love, 263:23
    shame is a. to sit, 180:33
    to be seen with him, 277:22
    to look upon one another, 245:5
    to think how we capitulate, 426:17
    white men ought to be a., 363:13

Ashamed *(continued)*
    workman that needeth not to be a., 44:40
Ashen, skies a. and sober, 449:14
Ashes, all a. to taste, 395:15
    am I and dust, 122:6
    beauty for a., 27:16
    cinders a. dust, 409:14
    earth will dissolve in a., 47:20
    flames for year a. for thirty, 712:3
    from his a. made, 453:13
    fruits of victory would be a., 786:8
    handful of gray a. at rest, 499:9
    in a. olde is fyr yreke, 134:28
    in a. rather than enslaved, 619:16
    into a. all my lust, 266:23
    new-create another heir, 226:14
    of his fathers, 419:19
    of Napoleon Bonaparte, 366:13
    out of a. life again, 550:3
    past a bucket of a., 636:5
    put on sackcloth with a., 12:31
    speak to your silent a., 91:29
    splendid in a., 249:4
    to ashes, 49:20
    turn to a. on lips, 388:4
    well-wrought urn becomes greatest a.,
        228:20
    yesterday embryo tomorrow a., 112:7
Ashore, till last galoot's a., 532:11
Ashtray, unless it contained an a., 873:3
Asia and Africa expelled freedom, 333:2
    peace and stability in A., 771:6
    seven churches in A., 46:15
    vast multitudes of A., 620:8
Asian, do what A. boys ought to be doing,
    753:16
Aside, not idly stand a., 72:4
    to step a. is human, 357:3
Asinorum, pons a., 82:n1
Ask, all I a. is merry yarn, 635:17
    all I a. is tall ship, 635:15
    all we a. is to be left alone, 438:20
    and it shall be given, 33:16
    and ye shall receive, 40:4
    cease to a. what morrow will bring, 96:10
    don't a. act, 737:12
    don't a. me to take none, 464:39
    drink divine, 232:16
    for anything except time, 365:5
    for me tomorrow, 180:28
    for the old paths, 27:28
    I do not a. you much, 176:5
    if you got to a. you ain't got it, 724:n1
    me blessing, 213:8
    me no more, 453:4
    me no more where Jove bestows, 245:14
    me no questions, 323:6
    never a. refuse resign office, 304:1
    not a dinner to a. a man to, 309:9
    not a. extraordinary of myself, 724:12
    not offer people but a. of, 785:5
    not what country can do for you, 785:13
    not whom sleep beside, 574:13
    of him will they a. more, 38:6
    of thee forgiveness, 213:8
    she was afraid to a., 796:7
    the beasts, 13:25
    the Lord's blessing, 882:4

Ask *(continued)*
    us prophet, 798:2
    we a. and a., 494:10
    wealth I a. not, 556:4
    what you can do for country, 785:13
    where a. is have, 318:9
    who could a. for more, 710:23
    why I have no statue, 85:5
    wilt thou go a. the Mole, 351:9
    you might want to a., 850:7
Asked a lithe lady, 352:4
    for it Georges Dandin, 267:28
    how pearls did grow, 240:14
    no other thing, 509:12
    not come even if a., 624:9
    Oliver a. for more, 464:6
    one another the reason, 195:35
    thief to steal me peach, 352:4
    to be where no storms, 546:3
Askelon, publish it not in the streets of A.,
    11:7
Asking, keep a. over and over, 415:9
    only God had for a., 481:15
    shoot murderer without a. to be paid,
    825:17
Asks a little of us here, 624:18
    of us certain height, 624:18
Asleep, athwart noses as they lie a., 179:25
    awake and a. the same, 62:11
    birds are a. in trees, 344:19
    devil is a., 564:11
    drunk and a. in boots, 640:19
    half a. as they stalk, 536:22
    in lap of legends, 409:20
    is in world of his own, 108:8
    keep it quiet till it falls a., 271:30
    lips of those that are a. to speak, 24:23
    my Mary's a., 357:19
    on furrow sound a., 411:7
    sucks the nurse a., 219:16
    tide moving seems a., 456:4
    under haystack a., 893:11
    very houses seem a., 370:3
    when men were all a., 545:13
Asparagus stumbling block in girl's education,
    616:4
Aspect, lend the eye terrible a., 189:7
    meet in her a. and eyes, 397:1
    sweet a. of princes, 225:25
Aspects, relations between a. of experience,
    662:2
Aspen, as a. leef gan to quake, 132:18
    light quivering a., 373:16
Asphalt and exhaust fumes, 805:17
Aspics' tongues, 209:19
Aspiration, social order and thirsty a., 756:23
Aspirations, right a., 64:18
Aspire, by due steps a., 252:1
    light and will a., 171:8
    mind a. to higher things, 162:16
    on what wings date he a., 353:1
    smile we would a. to, 225:25
    to what greater character can mortal a.,
    329:6
Aspired to be and was not, 462:16
Aspires, art a. towards condition of music,
    534:6
Aspiring, all to have a. minds, 168:2

Ass, affectioned a., 204:30
    egregiously an a., 208:21
    enamored of an a., 179:1
    idle to play lyre not, 115:5
    jawbone of an a., 10:22
    knoweth his master's crib, 24:28
    law is a., 464:13
    not covet neighbor's a., 8:14
    opened the mouth of the a., 9:7
    recover and prove an a., 179:15
    riding upon an a., 29:14
    sinned against my brother the a., 126:1
    Wild A. Stamps o'er Head, 441:13
    will carry load, 158:9
    write me down an a., 191:10
    your a. will follow, 850:5
Assail, ills scholar's life a., 306:16
Assailed, everything hard to attain easily a.,
    111:5
    seasons, 605:20
Assassin, forgot copperheads and a., 636:6
    kind a. Sleep, 798:4
Assassinate, I want to a. painting, 699:3
Assassination, absolutism tempered by a.,
    362:9
    extreme censorship, 565:17
    trammel up consequence, 214:22
Assault, against a. of laughter nothing stand,
    525:3
    and battery of wind, 593:16
    of thoughts on unthinking, 656:17
Assaults, defend in a. of our enemies, 48:13
    mercy itself, 225:9
Assay so hard, 132:7
Assayed, thrice he a., 256:1
Assayeth, naught n' a. naught n' acheveth,
    132:24
Assays of bias, 198:23
Assemblage of sloth sleep and littleness, 330:6
Assemble, peaceably to a., 340:1
Assemblies, nails fastened by masters of a., 24:1
Assembling, slow in a., 71:13
Assembly, club a. of good fellows, 306:24
    power in majority of popular a., 330:16
    proper office of representative a., 435:14
    suppression of free a., 562:9
Assent and you are sane, 509:4
    with civil leer, 295:13
Assert eternal Providence, 255:5
Asserted, boldly a. plausibly maintained, 350:5
Assertions, convince hearers of own a., 74:15
Asses made to bear and you, 173:13
Asses' bridge, 82:n1
Assets to turn over to next generation,
    571:14
Assimilates every thing to itself, 314:9
Assist him to save face, 707:11
Assistance, gives persecution no a., 328:12
Assistant West Coast promo man, 857:2
Associate, the good must a., 323:16
Associated, cannot be a. with government,
    473:14
Association, no good can come of a., 648:14
    quotations touch chord of a., 570:1
Ass's, white curd of a. milk, 295:14
Assuage anguish of bereavement, 446:12
    words have power to a., 260:12
Assuaged, half a. for Itylus, 529:12

Assume a virtue, 201:12
    honorable style of Christian, 247:11
    spirits either sex a., 255:19
    what I a. you a., 485:15
Assumes, no vice but a. some virtue, 185:19
    the god affects to nod, 274:15
Assuming, start a. that men are bad, 142:7
Assumptions, most necessary of a., 584:3
Assurance given by looks, 169:9
    make a. double sure, 216:33
    of a man, 201:5
    sufficient for life, 435:4
Assurances of walls warmth comfort love,
    805:n1
Assure survival of liberty, 785:10
    you I heard Bulletts, 328:3
Assured, crown themselves a., 222:10
    ignorant of what he's most a., 206:28
Assyria, Sennacherib king of A., 12:19
Assyrian came down like wolf, 397:2
Astaire, did everything that Fred A. did, 834:16
Astern, look a. row ahead, 108:12
Asteroid, hen cackles as if laid a., 524:9
Astolat, lily maid of A., 455:13
Astonish, gratify some a. rest, 524:22
Astonished at my own moderation, 320:5
    mediocre people a. at nothing, 416:12
Astonishing thing about earth, 772:18
Astonishment, curse a. hissing and reproach,
    28:5
    fills me with a., 850:9
    thou shalt become an a., 9:26
    wine of a., 17:1, 278:9
Astonishment's, your a. odd, 680:n2
Astound me wait for you to astound me,
    613:12
    nothing can a. American, 507:10
Astra, ad a. per aspera, 120:4
    sic itur ad a., 95:n2
Astray, all likely to go a., 65:24
    black sheep gone a., 588:6
    if world go a., 129:22
    light which cannot lead a., 286:20
    one that had been led a., 251:16
    we like sheep have gone a., 27:7
Astrology disease not science, 124:12
Astronomer, when I heard learn'd a., 487:6
Astronomers, say a. universe must fall,
    795:5
Astronomy compels soul to look upwards,
    75:12
Astrophil, who knew not A., 169:8
Astute and dangerous man, 573:22
Asunder, half a life a., 515:10
    let no man put a., 49:18
    let not man put a., 35:2
    put this rogue and whore a., 285:13
    whirl a. and dismember me, 175:15
Asylum, optimism in lunatic a., 574:5
    prepare a. for mankind, 333:2
    their last a., 318:6
Asylums, comfortably padded a., 654:6
Ate cheeses out of vats, 460:7
    held heart in hands a. of it, 608:19
    peanut butter sandwiches, 796:7
    the malt, 897:8
    when we were not hungry, 285:4
    with runcible spoon, 467:10

Aten, O living A., 4:4
  shine as A. of daytime, 4:6
Atheism like that of Spinoza, 584:12
  little philosophy inclineth to a., 165:27
  owlet A., 377:16
Atheist half believes God, 291:2
  I am a. who says prayers, 772:7
  superstitious a., 461:23
Atheist-laugh's a poor exchange, 356:20
Atheistically, no intention to write a., 440:6
Atheists, no a. in foxholes, 734:12
Athena, gray-eyed A., 52:26
  wise as A., 698:15
Athenian, Thucydides an A., 71:11
Athenians commanded by myself, 62:18
  crushed gold-bearing Medes, 60:10
  war between Peloponnesians and A., 71:11
Athens, bringing owls to A., 73:2
  divine city, 64:7
  Euripides' land, 67:n1
  fix eyes on greatness of A., 72:4
  maid of A., 394:17
  nigh to Euboea, 74:2
  nurse of men, 66:18
  the eye of Greece, 260:2
  to A. sent ships, 398:n1
  weeds of A. he doth wear, 178:23
  what has A. to do with Jerusalem, 113:18
  ye men of A., 40:32
Athirst, man a. supposes mirage to be water,
  118:24
Athis, loved you once long ago A., 56:7
Athlete crowned in sweat of brow, 115:2
Athletes, interest in animals and a., 672:1
Athwart men's noses as asleep, 179:25
A-tiptoe, stand a. when day named, 189:26
Atlanta to the sea, 517:13
Atlantic, dawn on other side of A., 317:4
  drag A. for whales, 522:12
  frontier from A. to Pacific, 619:9
  Ocean on my head, 787:14
  steep A. stream, 252:7
  Thulè and A. surge, 301:1
Atlas, Teneriff or A. unremoved, 258:10
Atman dwells within our heart, 50:8
Atmosphere, clear brown twilight a., 431:10
  of Gallup Poll, 620:11
Atom belonging to me belongs to you, 485:15
  changed everything save thinking, 638:8
  intense a. glows, 403:17
  knowledge of stars through a., 649:7
  movements of lightest a., 345:3
  secret powers of a., 599:5
Atomic age, 606:7
  bomb turn of screw, 739:6
  bombs burst in hands, 599:1
  cannot control a. energy, 611:10
  careless handling of a. technology, 649:1
  energy a menace, 638:4
  energy lead to bombs, 638:1
  first moment of a. age, 774:13
  hypothesis, 790:2
  not take a. weapons to want peace, 739:6
  release of a. energy, 661:4
  war fought with a. bomb, 638:3
Atomies, crumbled out again to his a., 230:15
  team of little a., 179:25
Atom's weight of good, 119:19

Atoms, all things made of a., 790:2
  and compounds of atoms, 89:17
  cannot be swamped by force, 89:17
  in reality a. and space, 70:12
  or systems, 294:18
Atonal, expression a. music, 627:8
Atoned, microcosm and macrocosm a.,
  501:14
Atones for later disregard, 624:2
Atreus, Argos do without sons of A., 583:6
  son of A., 51:5
Atrocious crime of being young man, 305:11
Atrocity, doctrines surpass in a., 532:15
Attach golden chain from heaven, 51:16
Attachée, à sa proie a., 278:n8
Attachment fabricator of illusions, 760:12
  to government, 324:13
Attack all the more boldly, 94:26
  first to a. neighbors, 267:12
  if they a. us, 862:15
  is the reaction, 310:1
  lawless a. upon liberty, 318:4
  prompt in a., 324:7
  repeat attack, 650:3
  strength in a., 684:10
Attacked, rather a. than unnoticed, 310:22
  United States a., 653:6
Attacking, situation excellent I am a., 557:1
Attacks, sharp a. on government, 745:9
  try to answer a., 447:6
Attain, everything hard to a. easily assailed,
  111:5
Attainable, is uniformity of opinion a., 336:8
Attainment, Zeus grant a. of sweet delight,
  63:28
Attains upmost round, 191:36
Attempt and not the deed, 215:18
  fearing to a., 206:17
  literary a. unfortunate, 312:2
  the end, 241:10
  to define pornography, 780:15
  wind rising a. to live, 612:7
Attempted, something a. done, 436:13
Attend men and not women, 76:5
  shooting stars a. thee, 241:7
  to history of Rasselas, 307:8
Attendance, dance a., 226:13
Attendant, am an a. lord, 675:4
Attended by bodyguard of lies, 621:6
  is on his way a., 370:18
Attending, captive good a. captain ill, 221:22
  softest music to a. ears, 180:14
Attendre, j'ai failli a., 278:n6
Attention, dance a. on old age, 596:17
  like deep harmony, 176:20
  load himself with unnecessary a., 319:6
  must be paid, 780:5
  pay no a. to man behind curtain, 764:7
  pen instrument to fix a., 329:7
  poverty of a., 783:2
  you're not paying a., 812:1
Attentions, pleasing a., 382:6
  trivial a. men think manly, 360:19
Attentive eyes, 308:3
  sit a. to own applause, 295:13
Attic bird, 260:3
  not an A. grace, 665:6
  shape, 410:19

Attire comely not costly, 161:19
  in halls in gay a., 373:2
  man's a., 31:8
  rich a. creeps rustling, 409:22
Attitude, Fair a., 410:19
  in which most alive, 540:16
  of native to other, 660:1
Attitudenize, don't a., 311:15
Attorney, Hocus an old cunning a., 300:n6
  right to a., 692:6
Attorney's, go to a. office pay for it, 471:15
  office boy to A. firm, 525:22
Attraction and affection, 614:17
Attractive, sweet a. grace, 169:9, 257:19
  thirty-five a. age, 560:25
Attracts envy of world, 323:22
Attribute, no a. of superior man greater, 79:15
  to awe and majesty, 186:1
Attributes characters of living creature, 484:7
  God and a. of God eternal, 275:17
  preeminently Jewish a., 562:11
Attunement, from things that differ comes a.,
  62:7
Auber, dank tarn of A., 449:15
Auburn, sweet A., 322:21
Auction, escaped the a. block, 468:19
Audace, de l'a. encore de l'a., 359:n1
Audacia certe laus erit, 101:n3
Audacibus annue coeptis, 93:n4
Audacious power, 850:n1
Audacity more audacity always audacity, 359:5
  of hope, 876:14
  of imagination, 572:17
Audentes fortuna iuvat, 95:n3
Audi partem alteram, 116:n2
Audible, ill-bred as a. laughter, 322:n2
Audience, dreamer a. of dream, 630:9
  gone into unlit a., 808:7
  how long a. sits, 384:2
  never fail to laugh, 73:13
  participation by a., 764:11
  somewhere out in this a., 807:14
  takes him serious, 640:7
Audiences, addressing popular a., 79:2
  great poets great a., 488:16
  vaudeville a. give loudest sighs, 770:14
Auf Flügeln des Gesanges, 414:n5
Aught that I could ever read, 177:27
Augur misgovernment, 324:7
Augurs mock their own presage, 222:10
Augury, defy a., 202:26
  his powers of a., 50:26
  single best a. is to fight, 51:24
August, day in latter A., 787:3
  winter recommence in A., 399:1
  yellow with A., 664:18
Augustan, next A. age will dawn, 317:4
Augustine, whatever St. A. might say, 320:12
  why St. A. thanked God, 630:7
Augustinian doctrine of damnation, 532:15
Auld lang syne, 357:17, 357:18
  moon in her arm, 889:15
  should a. acquaintance, 357:17
Aunt, I am Charley's a. from Brazil, 566:2
  kept regard for truth, 606:12
Aunts, delight of husband a. infant, 681:20
  sisters cousins and a., 525:21
Aureám quisquis mediocritatem diliget, 96:n16

Aureliano Babilonia finish deciphering, 818:9
Aurochs and angels, 723:8
Aurora, new A., 881:13
Aurora Borealis, bounded on north by A., 456:*n*1
    each star its own a., 759:10
Aurora Leighs, no more A. thank God, 442:11
Auschwitz, authentic language of A., 826:2
    day's work at A., 825:12
    no other reason than an A. existed, 793:3
    to write poem after A. is barbaric, 733:10
Auspicious, one a. eye, 196:22
Austere beauty of mathematics, 614:9
Austerlitz, pile bodies at A., 636:4
Australia, unscrupulous rascals A. has evolved, 573:22
Austria, Tom Jones will outlive eagle of A., 332:12
Authentic, ineluctable ore of the a., 803:10
Authenticity, original prerequisite to a., 693:1
Author, all mankind one A. one volume, 231:7
    and finisher of our faith, 45:12
    choose a. as choose friend, 276:22
    classical a. who writes tragedy, 735:25
    death of the A., 778:3
    domination by the a., 869:9
    dreamer a. of dream, 630:9
    Holy A. of that religion, 283:2
    leaves of any a., 248:9
    neither man nor woman but a., 472:14
    no a. genius to publisher, 415:11
    of peace, 48:13
    of Satanic Verses book, 725:14
    ourselves a. and finisher, 444:2
    out from bushes, 654:20
    rather read what famous a. has cut, 335:13
    read by five hundred, 531:21
    revised and corrected by A., 301:20
    same steps as A., 413:4
    select five hundred readers, 531:21
    should be like God, 493:10
    Six Characters in Search of an A., 601:2
    steal from one a. plagiarism, 633:10
    thou Virgil art my master and a., 128:5
    time the a. of authors, 164:10
    what good a. whispers, 590:14
    what I like in good a., 590:14
    when man of rank an a., 311:5
    where any a. teaches such beauty, 174:20
    worst thing do to a., 310:22
    you wish a. that wrote it, 793:10
Authorities, nihilist not bow to a., 479:5
Authority, adduces a. uses not intellect, 140:6
    age in virtuous carries a., 288:25
    and show of truth, 191:5
    assume a. which could be trusted, 319:6
    base a. from others' books, 174:1
    by proving strength in life, 586:8
    by whose a. do you act, 334:1
    compass of national a., 349:11
    declining a. of establishment, 777:19
    every shadow of a., 324:15
    expected unquestioningly to obey, 709:1
    fit for public a., 65:21
    highest spiritual a., 647:10
    little brief a., 206:28
    miracle mystery a., 492:14
    no potential enemy to establish a., 692:7

Authority *(continued)*
    obedience to a., 733:16
    obedient to whomsoever in a., 71:14
    of Church moved me, 116:10
    sovereign a. of our partners, 341:5
    structures of a., 817:16
    throw your a. at our feet, 340:12
    tongue-tied by a., 221:21
    what's that a., 211:5
    without wisdom, 261:13
Author's, sincerely from a. soul, 702:13
Authors, among good a. accounted Plagiarè, 254:16
    ancient books are for a., 297:17
    books like men their a., 284:1
    damn a. they never read, 326:5
    established it as rule, 288:9
    old a. to read, 165:8
    steal from many a. research, 633:10
    time the author of a., 164:10
    when a. talk of sublime, 333:21
Authors', judge of a. names, 292:21
Autobiographies, nations write a., 484:24
Autobiography is the poor man's history, 844:4
Autocracy, communism a. upside down, 467:1
Automatic hand, 676:13
Automaton, mechanized a., 401:8
Automne, violons de l'a., 549:*n*4
Automobile, television and an a., 827:5
Autres, l'enfer c'est les A., 743:*n*1
    pour encourager les a., 299:*n*3
Autumn, cloudy days of a. cometh, 405:1
    dull dark day in a., 448:8
    glasses on nose a. in heart, 700:17
    happy a. fields, 452:21
    I saw old A., 418:6
    in everything, 461:16
    in misty morn, 418:6
    in New York, 734:13
    leaves fall early this a., 664:18
    moon is bright, 732:15
    no season such delight as a., 240:8
    nodding o'er yellow plain, 300:21
    of the year, 792:4
    that grew by reaping, 219:8
    violins of a., 549:17
Autumnal, deep a. tone, 402:13
    face, 230:9
    thick as a. leaves, 255:17
Autumn's, breath of A. being, 402:9
Available, starving because food isn't a., 765:16
    to any shape, 810:17
Availeth, say not struggle nought a., 479:12
Avalanche of murders, 807:17
    snowflake in a., 758:13
Avant-garde, one wall is the a., 803:4
Avarice a species of madness, 276:15
    and happiness, 302:7
    Pride Envy A. three sparks, 128:21
    prudery a kind of a., 392:2
    rich beyond dreams of a., 312:11
    seems not so much a vice, 276:*n*1
    spur of industry, 311:22
Avatar, in Vishnu-land what A., 461:10
Ave atque vale, 91:*n*10
    Caesar morituri te salutamus, 111:*n*1
Avenge O Lord thy slaughtered saints, 254:23
    patriotic gore, 535:3

Avenge *(continued)*
    wish of some is to a., 71:13
Avenged of Philistines, 10:25
    South is a., 532:8
    1440 times a day, 540:14
Avenger, mightest still the enemy and a., 15:5
Avenue, dancing feet on the a., 689:9
Avenues of ill, 424:22
Average man, 652:5
    where the children are above a., 854:10
Averages, fugitive from law of a., 796:11
Averni, facilis descensus A., 94:*n*12
Averse, what cat's a. to fish, 315:9
Aversion, in matrimony begin with a., 346:2
    world outlasts a., 494:15
Aversions, man of my a., 645:11
Aviary, mind is an a., 76:8
Avocation, my a. and my vocation, 624:1
Avoid evil do good, 64:13
    fall into Scylla to a. Charybdis, 185:*n*1
    not a. but minimize risks, 562:11
    perils by united forces, 276:14
    ready for war to a. it, 281:10
    reeking herd, 666:4
    self-righteousness, 707:11
    what is to come, 201:10
Avon, swan of A., 233:6
Avowed erect the manly foe, 367:3
Await, wanderer a. it too, 495:15
Awaits alike inevitable hour, 315:18
Awake, all shall a. again, 249:7
    and asleep the same, 62:11
    and sing, 26:4
    arise, 255:18
    birds a. in vines, 817:6
    Deborah and utter a song, 10:9
    England a., 354:14
    for Morning, 441:5
    for night is flying, 162:26
    I was a. at last, 814:10
    keep drowsy Emperor a., 594:4
    let mind a. and revive, 139:5
    lying a. with headache, 527:3
    mortal sounds can a., 815:16
    my lute a., 149:3
    my sleeping ones, 762:7
    my St. John, 294:14
    O north wind, 24:16
    only day dawns to which we are a., 475:23
    thy Nightingales a., 499:9
    wide a. the moon and I, 527:13
Awaken, friends for when we a., 247:2
Awakened, army a., 608:12
    living word a. my soul, 644:5
    the A. One (Buddha), 64:13
Awakening, near a. when dream that we dream, 380:9
    third great a., 831:5
A-walking, as I was a., 890:10
    Devil is gone, 381:18
A-waltzing Matilda, 585:8
Aware, mind a. of own rectitude, 94:6
    myths operate without being a. of fact, 754:2
    of damp souls, 675:9
    of oneself without fright, 692:10
    of slightest bondage made a., 624:7
    valet not a. of this, 79:13

Awareness, give each moment a., 631:11
　　of what is so real, 878:5
A-watering last year's crops, 480:4
Away and mock the time, 215:8
　　bound a., 897:19
　　from men and towns, 404:12
　　let's get a. from it all, 769:9
　　look a., 470:16
　　o'er hills and far a., 452:12
　　only for a night and a., 279:10
　　over hills and far a., 291:17, 894:10
　　pass not a., 6:33
　　should the wide world roll a., 609:1
　　slip slidin' a., 855:12
　　Time will take my love a., 221:19
　　you scullion, 188:2
Awe, attribute to a. and majesty, 186:1
　　devised to keep strong in a., 172:10
　　ever-increasing wonder and a., 320:2
　　imaginative a., 749:20
　　in face of existence, 722:16
　　lifted hand in a., 290:15
　　man from career of humor, 190:36
　　of Adam, 829:6
　　of such thing as myself, 191:24
　　romantic a. of rich, 721:15
　　Sacred A., 656:7
　　Shock and A., 853:7
　　strike a. into beholders, 284:24
　　tradition inspires a., 547:13
　　without common power to keep them in a.,
　　　239:9
Aweary of the sun, 217:24
　　she said I am a., 450:8
Awful, anything a. makes me laugh, 383:5
　　beneath a. Hand we hold, 589:7
　　felt how a. goodness is, 258:8
　　good because it's a., 835:17
　　nobody goes it's a., 744:15
　　pause prophetic of end, 290:20
　　shadow of unseen Power, 401:9
　　still and a. red, 376:16
Awfulness, got myself into an a., 715:14
A-whining, born naked and falls a., 105:n1
Awkward, always made a. bow, 413:19
　　in their soil, 756:3
Awoke and behold it was dream, 271:23
　　and found it truth, 412:12
　　and found myself famous, 396:23
　　one night from dream, 392:16
A-wooing, frog a. go, 892:11
Awry, currents turn a., 199:21
　　leaning all a., 442:5
Awww, everybody goes A., 799:3
Ax, Lizzie Borden took a., 885:22
　　to grind, 389:1
Axe, American a., 400:9
　　book a. for frozen sea inside us, 655:10
　　fitter to bruise, 261:13
　　laid unto the root, 32:8
　　neither hammer nor a., 11:31
Axe's edge did try, 266:18
Axes, talking of a., 514:9
Axiom hatred of bourgeois, 493:20
　　that little things most important, 573:10
Axioms, derives a. from particulars, 164:18
　　flies from particulars to a., 164:18
　　of mathematics, 538:4

Axioms *(continued)*
　　proved upon our pulses, 413:4
Axis of evil, 862:14
　　soft underbelly of A., 621:5
Axle, glowing a. doth allay, 252:7
Axolotl, now I am an a., 774:6
Axletree, clot bedded a., 678:8
Ayenbite of inwyt, 650:n1
Aylmer, Rose A. whom these eyes, 383:26
Ayuda, al que madruga Dios a., 898:5
Azcan, Chieftain Iffucan of A., 640:23
Azores, behind lay gray A., 539:14
　　devouring green a., 558:18
Aztecs by no means would give up, 144:12
Azure, arose from out a. main, 301:3
　　high in a. steeps, 719:19
　　riding o'er a. realm, 316:15
　　ringed with a. world, 454:13
　　robe of night, 408:12
Azurs, dévorant les a. verts, 558:n10

B

B, emotions from A to B, 699:18
　　mark it with B, 892:17
Baa baa baa, 588:6
　　baa black sheep, 893:4
Baalim, Peor and B., 250:14
Babbitt, his name was B., 664:2
Babbled of green fields, 189:4
Babbling drunkenness, 205:25
　　gossip of the air, 204:22
Babblings, profane and vain b., 44:38
Babe, birth-strangled b., 216:28
　　let mighty b. alone, 263:12
　　love b. that milks me, 215:5
　　pity like new-born b., 214:24
　　pretty B. all burning bright, 167:1
　　whose birth embraves morn, 263:12
Babel, name of it called B., 6:27
　　stir of the great B., 327:2
Babes, out of the mouth of b., 15:5
Babies, anyone who hates b., 644:n1
　　bit b. in cradles, 460:7
　　haven't hair, 687:4
　　hello b., 801:2
　　I don't dislike b., 485:3
　　I hate b., 608:10
　　kill b. make world safer, 824:10
　　wars fought by b., 801:5
Baboon who saved comrade, 440:12
Babs knows what and babs knows why,
　　635:5
Baby, all over now B. Blue, 851:7
　　and me, 892:17
　　assailed by eyes, ears, nose, skin, 541:5
　　blank and stopped as dead b., 832:14
　　bunting, 894:3
　　can't love man till b. with him, 561:18
　　down come b. and all, 550:7
　　figure of giant mass, 203:10
　　government like big b., 765:11
　　looked like mouse, 724:1
　　mother laid her b., 476:5
　　my b. at my breast, 219:16
　　nobody puts B. in a corner, 843:17
　　not single human b. survive, 663:18

Baby *(continued)*
　　of thee I sing b., 710:24
　　one for my b. and one for road, 759:7
　　rock-a-bye-b., 550:7
　　since my b. left me, 840:12
　　Tar-b. ain't sayin' nuthin', 551:13
Babylon, ere B. was dust, 401:15
　　I was King in B., 552:9
　　is fallen, 25:27, 47:5
　　king of B. stood at the parting, 28:16
　　we're leaving B., 861:8
Babylonish dialect, 262:6
Babylon's Gardens, 886:14
Baby's, know what going on in b. mind, 712:7
Bacchus that first, 252:4
　　with pink eyne, 218:27
Bach, angels play only B., 666:10
Bachelor, die a b., 190:36
　　one day b. next grampa, 732:12
　　see b. of threescore, 190:18
Bachelors, reformers are b., 557:8
Bachelors' prayer, 662:4
Back, African moon lying on b., 662:6
　　and side go bare, 151:4
　　at b. from time to time hear, 676:11
　　at my b. I always hear, 266:22
　　begins to smart, 892:8
　　borne me on his b., 202:12
　　care not who sees your b., 182:20
　　carries sky on b., 473:4
　　cast-iron b. with hinge, 507:15
　　dagger into b. of neighbor, 653:1
　　die with harness on our b., 217:25
　　Empire Strikes B., 859:12
　　eyes and b. turn upward, 676:12
　　follow and not see its b., 57:7
　　get b. get b. get b., 716:17
　　got over Devil's b., 236:12
　　I lean b., 817:8
　　in a time made simple, 624:12
　　mermaid on dolphin's b., 178:15
　　never came b. to me, 467:12
　　on b. burden of world, 557:3
　　on bat's b. I do fly, 225:5
　　see what boys in b. room will have, 761:17
　　shop entirely free, 152:11
　　showed his b. above element, 219:8
　　speed today put b. tomorrow, 160:26
　　think of some way to get him b., 726:6
　　to Army again, 588:14
　　to the old drawing board, 736:16
　　to you cold father, 651:3
　　unto ladder turns his b., 191:36
　　wallet at his b., 203:21
Backbone, whale's b., 679:4
Backed like a weasel, 200:26
Back-friend a shoulder-clapper, 172:25
Background, if people keep me in b., 443:16
　　slumbers in b. of the times, 359:14
Backing, plague upon such b., 182:20
Backs, birthrights proudly on b., 175:5
　　making beast with two b., 207:29
　　not seat on others' b., 548:4
Backside, every man has moral b., 335:15
Backslidings, our b. are many, 27:35
Backward, angel of b. look, 438:17
　　casting b. glances, 488:17
　　dark b. and abysm of time, 224:4

Backward *(continued)*
  goes who toils most, 129:19
  I by b. steps move, 268:11
  lean over too far b., 704:10
  life must be understood b., 469:2
  look b. to ancestors, 325:2
  look b. to with pride, 622:13
  old dog barks b., 624:3
  revolutions never go b., 421:13
Backwards, memory that only works b., 516:11
Bacon, accept views Cicero Locke B. have
    given, 426:1
  celebrities such as B., 518:9
  egg spam spam b. and spam, 879:12
  not written Hamlet, 408:11
  secretary of Nature and learning, 245:11
Baconian acrostics, 723:4
Bacterial creepers, 755:16
Bad Americans die go to America, 560:13
  and the b. unhappily, 843:*n2*
  as for b. all theirs dies, 68:20
  beginning makes bad ending, 68:16
  better b. epitaph, 199:13
  better for being a little b., 207:18
  bold b. man, 160:4, 225:16
  book as much labor, 702:13
  breeding, 72:12
  cannot wait is always b. news, 864:3
  can't be all b., 644:*n1*
  cause can become good, 802:1
  cause supported by bad means, 333:9
  charm to make b. good, 207:9
  circumstance makes action good or b.,
    73:23
  details whether good or b., 440:7
  end unhappily, 843:7
  even b. books are books, 815:14
  fustian's so sublimely b., 295:12
  good and b. angel, 234:14
  good b. indifferent, 276:12, 314:10
  good b. worst best, 448:2
  good die early b. late, 282:9
  great cases make b. law, 538:13
  grow into likeness of b. men, 76:9
  hates children can't be all b., 644:2
  he felt b., 798:7
  he is writing b. stuff, 569:15
  herdsmen ruin flocks, 53:25
  I have b. dreams, 199:3
  immoral what you feel b. after, 721:11
  laws bring about worse, 312:20
  life neither good nor b., 580:1
  mad b. and dangerous, 393:8
  man who brings b. news, 65:13
  man's good knowing he is b., 462:29
  man's refuge, 57:20
  meaning good or b., 273:7
  means and bad men, 333:9
  men live that they may eat, 70:7
  moon on the rise, 860:14
  moral character, 303:17
  neighbor is misfortune, 54:22
  never good to bring b. news, 218:25
  never good war or b. peace, 303:16
  no benefit in gifts of b. man, 67:18
  no man who laughed b., 406:12
  nothing either good or b., 199:2
  obstinacy in b. cause, 248:7, 313:26

Bad *(continued)*
  of this b. world, 606:16
  people cant be governed, 834:10
  persecution b. way to plant religion, 248:8
  phrase good and b. at same time, 700:15
  pious fraud as with b. action, 333:20
  prosperity comes to a b. man, 59:21
  provide b. examples, 264:4
  sad and b. and mad, 462:23
  sad b. brother's name, 530:24
  so b. grandeur creeps in, 645:6
  start assuming that men are b., 142:7
  streak of b. luck, 528:9
  things ill got had b. success, 170:22
  truth told with b. intent, 354:1
  very b. Wizard, 562:5
  war never slays b. man, 66:14
  when b. men combine, 323:16
  when b. she was horrid, 438:2
  when good very good when b. better,
    700:10
  when television is bad, 813:15
  world is grown so b., 171:23
Badge, mercy nobility's true b., 172:40
  of all our tribe, 184:28
  red b. of courage, 608:14
Badges, to god-damned hell with b., 689:4
  we ain't got no b., 746:2
Badine, on ne b. pas avec l'amour, 457:*n3*
Badness flaunted itself, 889:8
  you can get easily, 54:21
Baffled get up begin again, 461:7
  imagination b. by facts, 620:4
Baffling, beat down b. foes, 495:8
Bag and baggage, 195:9
  empty b. cannot stand, 302:21
  moon in silver b., 596:4
  pack b. and go below, 897:23
  sealed b. of ducats, 185:5
  to make b. pudding, 896:23
  your old kit-b., 643:22
Bagatelle of transient experience, 580:9
Bagdad-on-the-Subway, 581:14
Baggage, bag and b., 195:9
Bags, three b. full, 893:4
  two sealed b. of ducats, 185:5
Bah humbug, 465:6
Bahamas, arrived at island of B., 139:8
Bahram that great Hunter, 441:13
Bail, excessive b. nor excessive fines, 340:7
Bailey, bells of Old B., 893:6
  unfortunate Miss B., 361:8
Bait, as a swallowed b., 222:20
  hook well, 190:35
  hook without b., 428:13
  melancholy b., 184:9
  your b. of falsehood, 198:23
Baited like eagles, 183:12
Baits, good news b., 260:23
Bake me a cake, 892:17
Baked, funeral b. meats, 197:7
  in a pie, 894:7
  me too brown, 515:5
  stayed home and b. cookies, 864:4
Baker, butcher b. candlestick-maker, 896:2
  not from benevolence of b., 318:22
  Street irregulars, 573:6
Baker's man, 892:17

Balaam, ass said unto B., 9:7
Balance between order and aspiration, 756:23
  of power, 330:9
  or reconciliation of opposite, 379:13
  small dust of the b., 26:30
  uncertain b. of proud time, 164:4
Balanced and Miltonic style, 547:10
  Film with Film, 511:8
Balances, weighed in the b., 28:25
Balbec, editions of B. and Palmyra, 317:4
Bald, fight between two b. men, 719:9
  now your brow is b. John, 357:13
  otherwise b. unconvincing narrative,
    527:19
  wish b. eagle not chosen, 303:17
Baldness, felicity on far side of b., 590:16
Bale, lif dat b., 706:6
Bales, down with costly b., 452:2
Balfour Declaration, 551:7
Ball, balm scepter and b., 189:23
  crowd at b. game, 658:15
  earthly b. a peopled garden, 343:2
  great b. of fire, 680:5
  one fish b., 500:3
  take me out to b. game, 640:1
Ballad, I love a b. in print, 223:31
  in the street, 426:7
  to mistress' eyebrow, 194:25
Ballad-mongers, meter b., 182:35
Ballads, permitted to make all b., 282:2
  songs and snatches, 527:7
  stuck about wall, 245:4
Ballast, more sail than b., 280:12
Ballet flourishes because of woman, 736:17
Balloon of the mind, 593:5
Balloonman, little lame b., 701:5
Balloons, faces rise like b., 788:2
  have b. pass over to Europe, 388:14
Ballot, appeal lies not to court but b., 615:3
  joining political party casting b., 648:8
  natural right to b., 489:2
  or the bullet, 808:14
  paper you drop in b. box, 474:6
  pathway to b. box, 471:8
  rap at b. box, 422:1
  stronger than bullet, 444:7
Ballplayer, many years not successful as b.,
    688:16
Ballroom, not at ease in a b., 504:2
  war not quadrille in b., 488:15
Balls, elliptical billiard b., 527:17
Balm in Gilead, 27:31
  not the b. the scepter, 189:23
  of hurt minds, 215:21
  the hydroptic earth hath drunk, 229:12
  tropic for your b., 704:2
  wash b. from anointed king, 177:4
Balmy sleep, 290:18
  spring brings back b. warmth, 91:14
Baloney, it's still b., 617:13
Baltimore, gore that flecked streets of B.,
    535:3
Bam, under the b., 677:5
Bamboo, under the b. tree, 677:5
'Ban 'Ban Ca-Caliban, 224:26
Ban, in every voice every b., 353:3
Banal Eldorado of old bachelors, 491:9
  so b. as to be unworthy, 868:12

Banality of evil, 744:6
  was only camouflage, 778:11
Bananas, what price b., 812:9
Banbury Cross, 894:9
Band, Alexander's Ragtime B., 673:3
  heaven-born b., 367:19
  in heaven they play, 870:8
  no soldier in gallant b., 528:3
  of angels, 898:20
  of brothers, 190:1
  playing somewhere, 585:1
Bandersnatch, frumious B., 515:12
Bands, brass b. barrel organs, 654:5
  dissolve political b., 336:1
  drew them with b. of love, 28:38
  end of life cancels b., 183:6
  her hands as b., 23:16
  iron b., 436:11
  loose the b. of Orion, 14:23
  pursue Culture in b., 582:16
Bandusian, O fount B., 97:5
Bane of all genius, 401:8
  precious b., 256:4
Baneful spirit of party, 328:15
Banes, o'er his white b., 890:6
Bang, Kiss Kiss B. B., 792:9
  not with b. but whimper, 677:2
  the drum slowly, 890:*n*1
Banish all the world, 182:29
  pleasures b. pain, 289:17
  plump Jack, 182:29
  thief you cannot b., 742:8
  think not king did b. thee, 176:16
  understanding from his mind, 69:*n*3
  with night we b. sorrow, 233:18
Banished, alone a b. man, 880:13
  find moral in narrative be b., 522:22
  yet true-born Englishman, 176:19
Banishment, bitter bread of b., 177:3
  no sentence of b., 764:16
Banjo on my knee, 503:9
Bank and shoal of time, 214:22
  breathes upon b. of violets, 204:10
  contemplate entangled b., 440:4
  cried all the way to b., 793:5
  curls done up with b. notes, 471:11
  headquarters of b. in Omaha, 868:12
  many people already b. on it, 778:12
  moonlight sleeps upon this b., 186:15
  waly up the b., 890:8
  what's breaking into b., 716:9
  whereon wild thyme blows, 178:19
Bankers schoolmasters clergymen, 591:19
Bankrupt of life, 272:17
Banks and braes o' bonny Doon, 357:6
  Brignal b., 374:6
  newspaper runs b., 600:16
  o' Loch Lomond, 884:13
  of Wabash far away, 609:10
  Tiber trembled underneath b., 191:21
  time river without b., 888:6
  vast surplus in b., 389:8
Banner over me was love, 24:8
  royal b. and all quality, 209:13
  that b. in sky, 443:3
  torn but flying, 396:10
  wear it like b. for proud, 731:7
  with strange device, 436:15

Banner *(continued)*
  yet Freedom yet thy b., 396:10
Banners, all thy b. wave, 384:11
  confusion on thy b. wait, 316:14
  flout the sky, 213:32
  hang b. on outward walls, 217:21
  terrible as an army with b., 24:19
Banquet, before we begin our b., 879:2
  behave in life as at b., 109:6
  hall deserted, 388:1
  life is a b., 779:12
  partaken in anxiety, 59:1
  sated with b. of life, 90:14
Banqueting, speak of b. delights, 226:22
  upon borrowing, 31:5
Banquets abroad by torch light, 234:3
Baptism enslaved me, 559:9
  suffering may be b., 480:7
Baptist, make B. preacher choke, 722:18
Baptist's, John B. head in a charger, 34:24
Baptizing in name of Father, 36:23
Bar, back of b. in solo game, 627:12
  crossed the b., 456:6
  gold b. of Heaven, 505:23
  harbor b. moaning, 481:5
  no moaning of b., 456:4
  to B. as very young man, 526:21
Barabbas a publisher, 399:18
  stock of B., 186:8
  was a robber, 40:7
Barak, arise B. and lead captivity captive, 10:9
Barbara, name was B. Allen, 889:25
Barbarian, meets need of b. man, 569:8
  Scythian bond nor free, 44:12
  weeping above dead, 518:4
Barbarians Philistines Populace, 497:8
  the B. are coming, 583:9
Barbaric pearl and gold, 256:6
  sound my b. yawp, 486:19
Barbarism and despotism, 338:15
  document of b., 693:4
  fanaticism to b. one step, 313:16
  fastnesses of ancient b., 500:5
  from b. to degeneration, 538:1
  my native land prey to b., 114:14
  war is at best b., 489:15
Barbarous dissonance, 252:20
  in beauty stooks arise, 546:14
  multitude, 185:7
  triumph o'er her b. foes, 306:9
  woman more b. than man, 548:7
Bard, hear voice of the B., 352:10
  is envious of bard, 54:17
  music sent up by lover and b., 462:11
  old or modern b., 252:3
  whom none to praise, 369:*n*1
Bards, black and unknown b., 610:4
  gild lapses of time, 408:14
  have a share of honor, 53:10
  in fealty to Apollo, 408:17
  name me among lyric b., 96:1
  of Passion, 411:4
  saints heroes, 494:11
  sublime, 436:17
Bare, back and side go b., 151:4
  Ben Bulben's head, 597:10
  bodkin, 199:21
  cupboard was b., 895:6

Bare *(continued)*
  Goya of the b. field, 836:2
  imagination of feast, 176:18
  let little colt go b., 897:5
  looked on Beauty b., 695:14
  old men's heads b., 687:4
  on b. earth he lies, 274:18
  poor b. forked animal, 212:3
  ruined choirs, 221:24
Bare-bosomed, press close b. night, 486:6
Barefaced poverty drove me to verses, 98:13
Barefoot boy, 438:7
  dance b. on wedding day, 173:12
  dervishes, 424:23
  him that makes shoes go b., 147:*n*13
Barère's, not read B. Memoirs, 420:2
Bares, foeman b. steel tarantara, 526:7
Bargain catch cold and starve, 220:13
  in the way of b., 182:37
  necessity never good b., 302:9
  never better b. driven, 162:14
Barge, Arthur from the b., 455:19
  drag the slow b., 327:11
  like burnished throne, 218:20
Bark, all dogs of Europe b., 749:4
  and bite, 289:5
  band of exiles moored b., 405:5
  bitter b. burning clove, 623:10
  fatal and perfidious b., 253:8
  feet locked upon rough b., 827:12
  hark dogs do b., 896:21
  is on the sea, 397:13
  let no dog b., 184:7
  off shot the specter b., 376:9
  seal on cold ice with piteous b., 409:17
  see they b. at me, 212:11
  star to every wandering b., 222:15
  watchdog's honest b., 398:3
  worse than bite, 244:27
  yond tall anchoring b., 212:24
Barking, crowing of cocks and b. of dogs, 58:6
Barkis is willin', 465:21
Barks, Hylax b. in doorway, 93:2
  Nicean b. of yore, 447:12
  old dog b. backward, 624:3
Barley, land of wheat and b., 9:20
Barleycorn, inspiring bold John B., 358:7
  John B. got up again, 357:2
Barn, hay creaking to b., 787:3
  jackass can kick b. down, 651:11
  sit in a b., 895:5
  stack or the b. door, 251:1
Barnaby, like B. Rudge, 481:19
Barns, neither reap nor gather into b., 33:6
Barrage, chemical b. against life, 750:5
Barred on account of race, 786:12
  recognize good but be b., 63:30
Barrel, beat an empty b., 639:13
  inspiration not stored up in b., 769:8
  of meal wasted not, 11:42
  organs, 654:5
Barrel-house kings, 639:13
Barren, acre of b. ground, 224:2
  after summer b. winter, 170:4
  among b. crags, 451:11
  bride, 293:26
  buds of b. flowers, 530:16
  earth b. as moon, 635:14

Bay *(continued)*
    like b. of Portugal, 195:30
    look of b. mare shames silliness, 485:21
    no fetters in B. State, 438:3
    rather be dog and b. moon, 193:8
    reeking into Cadiz B., 460:20
    San Francisco b. center of prosperity, 470:14
    sings in boat on b., 452:15
    sittin' on the dock of the b., 853:4
    somebody bet on b., 503:10
    spreading himself like a green b. tree, 16:12
    where B. of Genoa ends melody, 547:15
Bayed the whispering wind, 322:25
Baying, hear b. of pack, 688:10
Bayonets, by push of b., 312:5
    leave at point of b., 345:6
    regime based on b. and blood, 693:9
    throne of b., 579:6
Bays, lingering b., 306:10
    no b. to crown it, 242:26
Be, afraid b. very a., 856:6
    appear to b. and appear not to b., 76:4
    at once b. and not b., 405:2
    better not to b., 450:9
    bold, 160:14
    business of life is to b., 533:3
    cheerful while you are alive, 3:7
    first say what you would b., 109:5
    he is or was or has to b., 300:6
    how could anyone b. Cary Grant, 853:6
    it must b., 366:20
    let b. b. finale of seem, 640:18
    merciful to me a fool, 539:17
    near me when light low, 453:17
    not the first, 292:16
    not to seem but b. best, 62:26
    not too bold, 160:15
    off depart, 87:*n*4
    off or I'll kick you, 514:6
    one must b. to do, 343:22
    poem should not mean but b., 694:15
    powers that b., 41:37
    say B. and it is, 118:12
    shalt b. what thou art promised, 214:16
    still and know that I am God, 16:28
    strong, 43:10
    such things to b., 454:3
    tell what and where b., 455:4
    that will b. that will last, 891:1
    the serpent under 't, 214:20
    there ye may b. also, 39:41
    thing that hath been is that which shall b., 22:24
    to b. or not to b., 199:21
    to her virtues very kind, 283:12
    tree continues to b., 680:4
    we say b. and it is, 118:12
    what I was born to b., 819:16
    with us yet, 589:7
    world place not care to b., 773:14
Beach, along briny b., 516:2
    fishermen that walk b., 212:24
    sound of outer ocean on b., 673:21
    they rush down to the b., 482:12
    walk upon the b., 675:6
Beaches, fight on b., 619:14
    where it tosses, 679:4
Beacon of the wise, 203:12

Beacons from where Eternal are, 404:3
Bead, first b. of sweat, 829:6
Beaded bubbles winking, 410:4
Beadle on Boxin' Day, 463:28
    very b. to humorous sigh, 174:13
Beadroll, Fame's eternal b., 160:16
Beads and prayer books, 295:3
    couple o' guns and Rosary b., 660:5
    give jewels for set of b., 177:12
    glories strung like b., 487:1
    receipts dolls vases, 783:9
    tell his b., 881:7
Beak, by enemy's b. gouged, 836:2
    from out my heart, 449:10
    grips her she becomes, 825:1
    is focused, 762:19
Beaker, bring me b. of wine, 72:11
    O for a b., 410:4
Beaks, hold on with b. to the weeds, 504:19
Be-all and end-all, 214:22
Beam, cast b. out of own eye, 33:14
    in thine own eye, 33:13
    me up Scotty, 888:19
    midday b., 254:12
    on starboard b. Charybdis, 185:*n*1
    us up Mr. Scott, 888:*n*8
Beamish boy, 515:13
Beams, adjusted to b. failing, 702:7
    all b. full-dazzling, 487:10
    athwart the sea, 451:10
    bemocked sultry main, 376:16
    best not to see b. of sun, 59:23
    how far far b. throws, 186:18
    in sunny b. did glide, 350:7
    layeth the b. of his chambers, 18:8
    learn to bear b. of love, 350:15
    of wit on other souls, 273:14
Bean, home of b. and cod, 577:15
    nine b.-rows have, 591:2
    stale b. soup, 645:6
Bean-fed horse beguile, 178:12
Beans, determined to know b., 475:11
    eat no b., 234:15
    gigantic field of soya b., 843:8
    over b. in their back room, 783:9
Bear all naked truths, 411:14
    any burden, 785:10
    asses made to b. and you, 173:13
    beams of love, 350:15
    blazing tail, 641:1
    brunt pay arrears, 462:25
    bush supposed a b., 179:6
    cannot b. mother's tears, 95:8
    care borne and yet must b., 401:14
    caves of ocean b., 315:23
    charmed life, 217:27
    cow and b. shall feed, 25:19
    decision to b. or beget child, 745:11
    exit pursued by a b., 223:19
    false witness, 8:14
    finds he can b. anything, 713:17
    flying-chariot, 327:11
    his friend's infirmities, 193:11
    his mild yoke, 254:22
    his own burden, 43:32
    ills we ought to b., 495:7
    infirmities of weak, 42:4
    it that the opposed beware thee, 197:23

Bear *(continued)*
    like the Turk, 295:13
    little boy and his Bear, 651:10
    man screaming is not dancing b., 770:12
    melancholy as lugged b., 181:26
    more than he can b., 713:17
    never be on b. side, 529:8
    not b. much reality, 678:5
    not every soil can b. all, 93:15
    nothing he not fitted to b., 112:10
    nothing would it b., 894:18
    of Very Little Brain, 651:8
    off-white polar b., 821:1
    pain to the b., 420:4
    pleasing punishment women b., 172:13
    punishment greater than I can b., 6:7
    right to keep and b. arms, 340:2
    rugged Russian b., 216:20
    shade him till he can b., 351:1
    sing savageness out of b., 209:26
    strengthen me to b. myself, 512:9
    sweet as I could b., 623:9
    sword of heaven will b., 207:6
    them we can, 575:15
    they shall b. thee up, 17:29, 37:24
    those ills we have, 199:21
    up and steer right onward, 254:24
    vapor like b. or lion, 218:39
    virgin shall b. a son, 25:13
    when you are anvil b., 244:*n*1
    whips and scorns of time, 199:21
    who would fardels b., 199:21
    wounded spirit who can b., 21:2
    yoke in his youth, 28:13
Bear-baiting, Puritan hated b., 420:4
Beard, built nests in b., 467:3
    hath not offended king, 143:10
    his b. was grizzled, 197:15
    husband with b., 190:21
    icicle on Dutchman's b., 205:17
    lion in his den, 373:14
    long gray b., 375:17
    of formal cut, 194:25
    Old Man with b., 467:3
    plucks dead lions by b., 175:7
    plucks off my b., 199:17
    white b. decreasing leg, 187:31
    wrapped in b. and silence, 716:3
Bearded like the pard, 194:25
    soldier's kiss on b. lips, 487:9
    with weed, 795:4
Beards, tarry until b. be grown, 11:16
Bearing birthrights proudly, 175:5
    on excellence of character, 78:12
    precious seed, 19:3
Bearings lays in application, 465:18
Bears all its sons away, 289:14
    each b. his own Hell, 94:34
    greatest names, 260:18
    his blushing honors, 225:25
    in itself causes of destruction, 312:19
    it out to edge of doom, 222:15
    rhythms for b. to dance to, 493:13
    sorrows with steadfast spirit, 54:4
    stamp of human condition, 153:11
    strongly it b. us, 378:1
    time b. away all things, 93:4

Beast, a very gentle b., 179:11
  beauty killed b., 701:2
  blond b., 548:15
  call this b. to mind, 606:10
  caught like b. at bay, 688:10
  civilization scarcely b., 609:7
  cursed above every b., 5:22
  deem himself god or b., 295:1
  either a b. or god, 78:18
  endeavoring to turn man into b., 728:15
  every b. of the forest is mine, 16:29
  first b. like a lion, 46:28
  fourth b. like a flying eagle, 46:28
  great strong b., 97:*n*13
  in view, 274:25
  killing b. that cannot kill, 672:5
  like man in body of b., 641:13
  like wild b. guards way, 353:10
  little better than b., 184:19
  making b. with two backs, 207:29
  man and bird and b., 377:5
  man neither angel nor b., 269:22
  mark or name of the b., 47:3
  maw-crammed b., 462:14
  more subtile than any b., 5:18
  multitude b. of many heads, 97:*n*13
  no b. is a cook, 334:5
  no b. so fierce but knows pity, 171:20
  no more, 201:19
  of prey in aristocratic races, 548:15
  only b. in arena the crowd, 599:12
  only connect b. and monk, 638:10
  owest b. no hide, 212:3
  Pellinore followed questing b., 138:3
  people a many-headed b., 97:20
  people resemble wild b., 142:8
  righteous man regardeth the life of his b.,
    20:18
  second b. like a calf, 46:28
  serpent subtlest b., 259:7
  starve the b., 863:15
  strangest b. ever he saw, 138:3
  that wants discourse of reason, 197:4
  third b. had a face as a man, 46:28
  what rough b., 593:10
  with many heads butts me, 220:1
  would act angel acts b., 269:22
Beastie, tim'rous b., 356:4
Beasties, long-leggety b., 884:8
Beastly, how b. bourgeois is, 663:14
  to the Germans, 719:16
Beast's, man's life cheap as b., 211:21
Beasts, ape vilest of b., 84:18
  ask the b., 13:25
  browse on their herbs, 4:7
  coupling of b., 678:14
  fly to wilderness, 79:18
  four b. had six wings, 46:28
  giant of b., 230:17
  invent new b. so terrible, 415:7
  judgment fled to b., 192:31
  nature teaches b. to know friends, 219:23
  of all wild b. preserve me from tyrant,
    232:3
  of the forest creep forth, 18:11
  pair of very strange b., 196:3
  shall be at peace with thee, 13:13
  small and great b., 18:11

Beasts *(continued)*
  transform ourselves into b., 208:31
  upon earth draw us to kingdom, 114:1
Beasts', not God's not b., 462:20
Beat a path to your door, 425:*n*2
  an empty barrel, 639:13
  Blake b. upon wall, 596:14
  down baffling foes, 495:8
  downward b. thy wings, 90:*n*1
  earth with unfettered foot, 96:17
  generation, 799:2
  gold to airy thinness b., 229:16
  heart hear her and b., 455:3
  him when he sneezes, 514:10
  his breast, 375:21
  man is b. when goes for broke, 799:*n*1
  me and hammer me, 636:8
  my people to pieces, 24:37
  so we b. on, 710:8
  sound trumpet b. drums, 301:13
  sound trumpets b. drums, 274:16
  swords into plowshares, 24:33
  the bush, 146:18, 239:18
  the drum slowly, 890:16
  the Dutch, 883:20
  the ground, 252:11
  they b. and Voice b., 576:14
  Turk b. a Venetian, 210:21
  upon whorled ear, 546:4
  water they b., 218:20
  waves of science b. in vain, 490:15
  with fist instead of stick, 261:18
  you b. your pate, 294:11
Beaten at all points, 72:9
  poop was b. gold, 218:20
  up by secret police, 798:7
Beatific, enjoyed in vision b., 256:3
  vision, 127:*n*5
Beating, got a hell of a b., 658:2
  in void luminous wings, 497:22
  way for rising sun, 730:2
Beatitude, ninth b., 294:10
Beatles', between Chatterley ban and B. first
    LP, 799:13
Beatrice a light between truth and intellect,
    129:17
Beats about in caverns, 797:14
  all lies you can invent, 354:1
  back envious siege, 176:25
  drum b. my approach tells thee I come,
    241:19
  upon high shore of world, 189:23
Beaumont, not bid B. lie, 232:19
  rare B., 240:6
Beaut, when I make mistake it's a b.,
    651:5
Beauteous, commands the b. files, 268:15
  dear b. death, 268:18
  evening calm and free, 370:5
  eye of heaven to garnish, 175:24
  kindness not b. looks, 173:21
  love all b. things, 545:14
  pearls in b. ladies' eyes, 173:36
  prove a b. flower, 180:11
Beauties, glory of honors b. wits, 229:9
  in small proportions b. see, 233:8
  more palpable and explicable, 301:7
Beautifier, rank great b., 423:12

Beautiful, a b. house with a b. wife, 870:10
  a faery's child, 412:3
  all b. drifts away, 592:2
  all b. sentiments in world, 482:11
  all once so b. is dead, 683:3
  all things bright and b., 476:4
  and ineffectual angel, 497:22
  and therefore to be wooed, 169:21
  as encounter of sewing machine, 550:9
  as the sky, 487:11
  be b. and be sad, 491:12
  beauty comes from b. blood b. brain, 485:9
  beauty making b. old rime, 222:9
  black is b., 888:14
  changes as forest, 797:10
  contours of legs b., 149:11
  dancing most b. art, 574:4
  dreamer, 503:16
  easy to be b. difficult to appear, 814:2
  face candid brow, 567:11
  for spacious skies, 572:5
  friendship, 758:9
  from perceived harmony, 378:23
  how b. they are, 378:6
  how b. they stand, 405:7
  how b. they stood, 405:*n*2
  human reason is b., 764:16
  I am Negro and b., 730:11
  identification with b., 404:13
  in faces dress thoughts, 578:8
  magnificent desolation, 825:18
  may it be b. before me, 891:18
  mind more b. than earth, 369:2
  most b. among gods, 54:14
  most b. most useless, 484:9
  most b. mouth in world, 298:18
  most b. thing is mysterious, 637:8
  nothing b. makes complete sense, 696:6
  nothing in houses not b., 520:7
  oh what a b. mornin', 706:8
  overmuch, 593:12
  palace B., 271:13
  pea-green boat, 467:7
  pleasure in nature because b., 558:12
  poetry most b. mode, 496:9
  Pussy you are, 467:7
  sacrifices of friendship b., 608:8
  scorn looks b., 205:15
  small is b., 766:2
  so awful ugly becomes b., 488:10
  so various so b. so new, 496:19
  something b. for God, 762:9
  sorrow more b., 411:13
  soup, 515:6
  Sredni Vashtar the B., 608:7
  standard of the b., 835:18
  swindles b. and simple, 581:12
  Thing, 659:6
  thing raises man, 142:16
  this is b. country, 419:4
  too b. to live, 464:17
  uncut hair of graves, 485:19
  upon the mountains, 27:3
  what is b. is moral, 494:2
  when I was b., 150:7
  wise and b., 494:11
Beauty, addition of strangeness to b., 534:11
  adventure art, 580:13

Beauty *(continued)*

all b. comes from blood and brain, 485:9
all that b. all that wealth, 315:18
and high degree, 681:20
and majesty of ships, 437:10
and virtue rarely together, 130:20
and wisdom rarely conjoined, 105:23
as much b. as could die, 232:13
barbarous in b. stooks, 546:14
beholding b. with eye of mind, 74:6
bereft of b., 173:25
body's b. lives, 641:5
born of own despair, 594:17
bought by judgment of eye, 174:8
brute b. and valor, 546:11
by b. and by fear, 368:13
center of all b., 814:9
cheat for sake of b., 633:2
clad in b. of thousand stars, 169:1
come near your b. with nails, 169:24
concept of mathematical b., 579:8
convenience comfort, 888:4
creation of B., 450:3
daily b. in his life, 210:11
dead black chaos, 171:14
Death mother of b., 640:21
definition of b., 378:22
desired so it be befouled, 713:2
doth of itself persuade, 172:29
draws with single hair, 293:6
dreamed life b., 472:15
ever ancient and ever new, 116:7
exists in mind, 311:23
extent of b. and power, 419:11
facts in naked simple b., 167:17
fatal gift of b., 396:5
for ashes, 27:16
fruits of life and b., 352:6
gift of God, 77:8
give b. in the inward soul, 74:3
good nature more amiable than b., 288:11
half mad with b., 520:3
has not been fathomed, 492:8
Helen's b. in brow of Egypt, 179:6
her b. and her chivalry, 395:13
I died for B., 509:6
ill layer-up of b., 190:9
images of b., 74:6
in all things, 413:17
in art economy is b., 545:3
in b. it is finished, 891:18
in eye of beholder, 561:12
in naked b. more adorned, 258:3
is a mystery, 663:15
is a simple passion, 820:13
is there b. in Sodom, 492:9
is there in truth no b., 242:18
is truth, 410:20
is vain, 22:20
keep back b., 546:21
killed beast, 701:2
know b. as b., 56:13
left b. on shore, 424:3
light from her own b., 403:1
like hers is genius, 506:5
little concerned with b., 537:11
looked on B. bare, 695:14
love b. truth we seek, 402:7

Beauty *(continued)*

love built on b., 230:6
loved your b., 591:6
lust not after her b., 20:2
making beautiful old rime, 222:9
mar wonderful b. of canyon, 571:7
mathematics supreme b., 614:9
momentary in mind, 641:5
must be truth, 412:11
Nature's brag, 252:25
Nature's coin, 252:24
ne'er enjoys, 295:15
neither heat limb nor b., 206:34
new source of power and b., 821:9
no excellent b., 166:14
no spring nor summer b., 230:9
notion of absolute b., 74:5
of aged face, 647:5
of good old cause, 370:4
of great machine, 669:9
of holiness, 15:30
of inflections, 641:7
of innuendoes, 641:7
of minstrels' lyre, 610:4
of own b. mind diseased, 396:12
of the lilies, 481:2
of world has edges, 654:16
orators dumb when b. pleadeth, 172:34
own excuse for being, 424:10
perception of b. moral test, 473:5
pierce like pain, 630:14
power of Greek in b., 497:6
principal b. in a building, 250:3
provoketh thieves, 193:34
renown which riches or b. confer, 92:3
sat B. in my lap, 559:7
sense of pity b. pain, 567:3
senseless acts of b., 871:5
sex and b. inseparable, 663:16
she walks in, 397:1
Sleeping B. wakes up, 808:9
smother up his b., 181:33
so long as b. shall be, 114:6
sold for old man's gold, 607:6
source of b. is in itself, 111:18
stands in admiration only, 259:31
stone to b. grew, 424:5
struggle for superhuman b., 845:8
sublimely pure, 614:9
such b. as you master, 222:9
such seems your b. still, 222:8
sufficient end, 593:12
take winds of March with b., 223:27
teaches such b. as woman's eye, 174:20
terrible and awful, 492:8
terrible b. is born, 593:7
that breaks hearts, 631:10
that comes from happiness, 493:14
that dost consecrate, 401:10
that must die, 411:11
their b. might declare, 376:17
thing of b. joy, 409:7
though injurious, 260:19
thy b. is to me, 447:12
'tisn't b. nor good talk, 589:23
to mind shameful to heart b., 492:9
too rich for use, 179:28
troubled by this b., 534:4

Beauty *(continued)*

truly blent, 204:20
truth isn't always b., 802:5
unadorned, 279:7
unmask her b. to moon, 197:19
vast vulgar meretricious b., 710:4
where b. has no ebb, 591:8
where perhaps some b. lies, 251:3
whose b. past change, 546:13
will be convulsive, 709:9
wit high birth, 203:25
with him b. slain, 171:14
without extravagance, 71:15
without grace, 428:13
without vanity, 394:9
witty b. a power, 505:17
worship in b. of holiness, 15:30
wrought out from within, 534:4
Beauty's, age will fade b. flower, 150:10
blazon of sweet b. best, 222:9
but skin deep, 226:18
ensign yet is crimson, 181:13
none of B. daughters, 397:10
nothing but beginning of Terror, 631:20
orient deep, 245:14
parallels in b. brow, 221:17
rose might never die, 220:30
sing smoothly with thy b. silent music,
    226:23
sorrow more beautiful than B. self, 411:13
thy b. field, 220:31
Beaver, young Harry with b. on, 183:13
Became, first object looked upon b., 487:18
nothing b. him like leaving, 214:14
Because, God not a b., 586:7
I do not hope, 677:12
it is bitter because it is my heart, 608:19
it is there, 668:7
Beckoning, open road is b., 846:1
shadows dire, 252:12
Beckons, descent b. as ascent, 659:7
Longing leans and b., 482:9
Becks, nods and b., 250:21
our minds to fellowship, 409:9
Become a kind of machine, 441:3
a saint, 824:14
all that may b. a man, 215:3
I have b. lost name, 771:18
ignorant man again, 641:20
let each b. all capable of, 407:12
man to behave toward government,
    473:14
not b. King's First Minister, 621:4
other dreamers, 488:3
them with half so good grace, 206:25
vilest things b. themselves, 218:21
you have b. like us, 742:6
Becomes, beak grips her she b., 825:1
blessed youth b. as aged, 206:34
that which is not b., 112:25
throned monarch better, 186:1
Becoming, growing and a b., 497:12
limit of b. mirth, 174:9
present gone instant of b., 541:6
some b. men we wanted to marry, 838:14
Bed, a b. Clerk Saunders said, 890:1
be blest that I lie on, 265:3
brimstone b., 381:18

Bed (*continued*)

by night on my b. I sought him, 24:12
candle to light to b., 893:7
celestial b., 198:10
creep into narrow b., 497:1
desert sighs in b., 748:9
die in b., 668:13
dull stale tired b., 210:33
early to b. early to rise, 302:12
early to rise early to b., 704:9
earth in earthy b., 455:3
every b. is narrow, 695:10
every day got up and gone to b., 626:19
fell on my father, 704:7
for this huge birth, 263:11
four angels to my b., 265:3
go to b. by day, 555:8
go to b. with lamb, 162:3
goes to b. and does not pray, 242:22
gravity out of his b., 182:24
has found out thy b., 352:14
heaped for beloved's b., 404:4
heart for my b. and board, 787:5
holy angels guard thy b., 289:10
horn brought me from b., 408:13
I go to b. with ideas, 557:12
I in my b. again, 881:1
I slept in a b., 865:1
I their map lie flat on this b., 231:2
in thy cold b., 241:18
laid in b. majestical, 189:23
let's to b. says Sleepyhead, 894:4
lie down on bloody b., 483:20
lie on Mother's b., 787:12
lies in his b. walks with me, 175:19
lovers to b., 179:17
made his own b. ere born, 263:12
made his pendent b., 214:21
make my b. in hell, 19:13
make my b. soon, 890:9
manger for his b., 476:5
marriage not b. of roses, 554:12
nicer to lie in b., 607:9
no need to get out of b., 798:8
nor grave nor b. denied, 595:19
O b. O delicious b., 418:7
outcries call me from naked b., 163:6
put them to b., 894:8
run into it as to lover's b., 219:2
should of stood in b., 712:1
sleep upon golden b., 596:2
Taffy was in b., 894:1
take up thy b., 36:26
to b. go sober, 236:5
used to go to b. early, 610:11
warm weather in b., 284:8
welcome to your gory b., 358:16
went to b. with stockings on, 896:1
what torment not a marriage b., 231:9
when I jump into my b., 555:12
where a man might find a b., 858:9
Zeus's b. of love, 68:3
Bedecked, so b. ornate and gay, 260:16
Bedeuten, ich weiss nicht was soll es b., 415:*n*1
Bedevilment, Lawyers twisted into state of b., 466:11
man's b. and God's, 575:17
Bedewed with liquid odors, 96:6

Bedfellows, strange b., 224:23, 507:16
Bedizened or stark naked, 671:12
Bedlam, lies in house of B., 762:21
mad as B., 465:25
Tom o' B., 211:4
Bedouins say We believe, 119:11
Bedroom, our b. under my heel, 316:18
Beds, as she made the b., 796:7
bliss not b. of down, 242:1
housewives in your b., 208:13
make thee b. of roses, 168:6
not only b. you lay on, 583:12
patient possessed by desire to change b., 491:14
think of clean b., 668:12
Bed's-feet, as to b. life is shrunk, 229:12
Bedtime, sootfall of your things at b., 845:11
would it were b. Hal, 183:24
Bee, booming of new-come b., 642:5
busy as a b., 162:4
busy b. improve each hour, 289:8
clover and one b., 511:12
how doth the busy b., 289:8
laughing b. on stalk, 820:8
love in my bosom like a b., 163:9
making money like b., 64:19
not good for swarm not good for b., 112:13
ordains b. to be immortal, 642:4
Pedigree not concern B., 511:5
preserved in amber, 107:10
sting like a b., 853:10
where the b. sucks, 225:5
Beech, sang beneath spreading b., 93:27
Beechen green and shadows, 410:3
spare the b. tree, 384:14
Beef, great eater of b., 204:15
meals of b. iron steel, 189:17
old England's roast b., 304:9
pig had roast b., 893:10
roast b. of old England, 304:*n*3
stole piece of b., 894:1
Beef-faced boys, 464:11
Bee-loud glade, 591:2
Bee-mouth, turning to poison while b. sips, 411:11
Been, It might have b., 438:10
what has b. has b., 273:18
Beer and skittles, 464:*n*1, 498:11
bourbon scotch and b., 777:18
chronicle small b., 208:17
come my lad and drink b., 308:4
did you ever taste b., 464:29
felony to drink small b., 170:13
Beersheba, Dan to B., 10:27, 314:23
Bees Black with Gilt Surcingles, 511:4
excel the b. for government, 154:11
for flies and hornets for bees, 143:15
helmet now hive for b., 163:4
honeyed words like b., 666:6
if b. are few, 511:12
innumerable b., 453:7
many b. on single course, 657:11
rob the Hybla b., 193:16
stirring birds on wing, 378:14
swarm of b. and honey in the carcass, 10:18
swarm of b. in May, 882:16
Beethoven, roll over B., 811:3

Beetle, Creator has preference for b., 693:12
poor b. we tread upon, 206:35
shard-borne b., 216:12
wheels droning flight, 315:12
winds sullen horn, 317:13
Beetles in caves, 755:16
o'er his base, 198:1
scarce so gross as b., 212:24
Befall, whatever b. you preordained, 112:21
Befallen, that which hath b. thee, 29:26
Befell, these that twice b., 511:9
Befits proud birth, 65:3
Before a joy proposed, 222:20
all be as b. Love, 460:23
clearest vision of what is b., 72:1
he is b. all things, 44:9
I been there b., 523:10
may it be beautiful b. me, 891:18
not lost but gone b., 103:17
old man looks b. and after, 50:28
reaching forth unto things b., 44:4
though it were done b., 231:3
to boldly go where no man gone b., 797:3
we begin our banquet, 879:2
what was there b., 879:16
you can call him a man, 851:1
Beforehand, not think b. of his words, 79:24
Befriend, good b. themselves, 66:16
like sparks of fire b. thee, 241:7
Beg alms of palsied eld, 206:34
cold comfort, 176:5
death's pardon now, 797:11
delinquents for our life, 788:4
leave to subsist, 585:2
often our own harms, 218:17
penny by and by, 683:4
sleep under bridges b. and steal, 546:2
to b. I am ashamed, 38:14
too proud to b., 885:16
virtue of vice pardon b., 201:11
you show us your sun, 691:19
Began, I am that which b., 530:20
this universal frame b., 273:22
to tremble with eagerness, 608:12
twilight of things that b., 530:21
violence and injury return on him who b., 90:20
Begat, fathers that b. us, 31:26
someone someone else b., 624:20
Beget, acquire and b. temperance, 200:6
decision to bear or b. child, 745:11
get and b., 553:2
Begets, kindness b. kindness, 65:5
money b. money, 271:3
Begetter, onlie b. of insuing sonnets, 220:*n*2
Begetting, moment of your b. it, 314:9
Beggar, be not made a b., 31:5
carried by angels, 38:17
is envious of beggar, 54:17
maid be queen, 452:14
on foot, 596:16
set a b. on horseback, 170:*n*1
that I am, 199:4
that is dumb, 159:8
true b. true king, 325:18
upon horseback, 596:16
Beggared all description, 218:20

Bettered, better b. expectation, 190:11
Betters, man who treats b. as b., 60:16
    what is done, 223:28
Betty, I can call you B., 855:13
Between acting of dreadful thing, 192:2
    dark and daylight, 437:12
    equals in power, 72:7
    how long halt ye b. two opinions, 11:43
    idea and reality, 677:1
    Lord watch b. me and thee, 7:1
    motion and act, 677:1
    no strife b. me and thee, 6:28
    us and everybody else, 844:9
Beulah patient among knickknacks, 871:2
    peel me a grape, 700:8
Beverages, recondite b., 391:12
Bevy of fair women, 259:23
Bewail, acknowledge and b. our sins, 49:5
Beware, all should cry B., 377:23
    Brothers and Sisters b., 589:25
    ides of March, 191:22
    Jabberwock, 515:12
    Jubjub bird, 515:12
    let buyer b., 120:10
    let us b., 765:14
    man of one book, 120:8
    my fangs, 185:24
    my lord of jealousy, 209:3
    of dog, 120:9
    of enterprises that require new clothes,
        474:17
    of entrance to quarrel, 197:23
    of false prophets, 33:20
    of judging by appearances, 266:13
    of punishing wrongfully, 3:8
    of rashness, 446:2
    politically obsessed, 869:5
    the middle mind, 666:9
    when thinker loose, 427:13
Beweep my outcast state, 221:5
Bewildered as to which face true, 431:9
    in maze of schools, 292:10
Bewildering, poor benefit of b. minute, 234:4
Bewitch, more b. me than when art, 240:16
    prosperity doth b. men, 237:5
Bewitched bothered and bewildered, 707:6
Bewitching, love brings b. grace, 67:25
    wine, 53:21
Bewrayed by his manners, 160:20
Bewrayeth, thy speech b. thee, 36:10
Beyond Alps lies Italy, 99:12
    far b. my depth, 225:25
    is there anything b., 669:8
    sea's towers a-sway B., 720:5
    this nothing but sandy deserts, 107:22
    utmost bound of thought, 451:15
Bhagavad Gita, remembered line from B.,
    739:8
Bharata, son of B., 84:8
Bias, assays of b., 198:23
    Commodity b. of the world, 175:12
    strange kind of magick b., 314:1
Bibendum, nunc est b., 96:*n*11
Bible, both read the B., 354:16
    English B., 419:11
    for the B. tells me so, 504:4
    has poetry fables history lies, 525:8
    like in B. with locusts, 741:9

Bible *(continued)*
    literature not dogma, 584:9
    only to find Gideon's B., 848:15
    so the B. said, 779:9
    studie but litel on B., 133:29
    swell story called it B., 731:4
    text of B. symbol, 574:1
    things you're liable to read in B., 711:3
    think of B. and Homer, 628:10
Bible-black, starless and b., 777:17
Bibles, head more than churches b. creeds,
    486:8
Bibliobibuli read too much, 645:20
Bicker down a valley, 454:24
    reason we b. creates war, 152:17
Bickering brattle, 356:4
Bickerings, such b. to recount, 260:28
Bicycle built for two, 598:3
    fish needs a b., 888:20
    fleshed with power, 801:16
Bid farewell to every fear, 289:16
    gave thee life b. thee feed, 350:12
    joys farewell, 409:2
    me discourse, 171:7
    me to live, 240:11
    not serve God if devil b., 207:28
    soul of Orpheus sing, 251:20
    them wash their faces, 219:27
    time return, 177:5
    you top o' the mornin', 551:3
Bidding, thousands at his b. speed, 254:22
Bide by the buff and the blue, 359:3
Bids, do what manhood b., 491:21
    it break, 217:7
Bien, sûr il me pardonnera, 415:10
Big Bessie's feet hurt, 783:13
    Blue Mountain Spirit, 891:15
    Brother watching you, 735:16
    canoe of the European, 482:12
    carry b. stick, 571:5
    city of b. shoulders, 636:2
    era of b. government, 898:21
    I'm in b. game with b. players, 747:3
    lie, 684:12
    sisters are crab grass, 800:10
    sleep, 674:5
    stealin' makes you emperor, 681:4
    this too would become b., 54:24
    turned B. Loser into triumph, 810:11
    waist deep in B. Muddy, 793:14
    words always punished, 66:1
    you used to be b., 693:5
Big-boned and hardy-handsome, 546:15
Bigger, eye b. than belly, 244:26
    lose presidency in a way b., 810:11
    no b. than agate-stone, 179:25
    planes no b. than wedge of geese, 724:6
    seems no b. than his head, 212:24
    they come harder fall, 69:*n*7
Biggest fish got away, 553:17
Bigness, her b. sweeps my being, 687:12
    world in b. as star, 257:4
Bigotry, gives b. no sanction, 328:12
Big-Sea-Water, shining B., 437:2
Bill, as if God wrote b., 424:22
    tax relief b., 653:8
Bill of Rights, absolutes in B., 667:1
    into suicide pact, 694:5, 846:*n*1

Bill *(continued)*
    make real the B., 629:5
    Reader's B. of Rights, 859:13
Billabong, camped by b., 585:8
Billboard lovely as tree, 732:8
Billboards, unless b. fall, 732:8
Billiard, elliptical b. balls, 527:17
Billion here billion there real money, 709:13
    vote for the $87 b., 857:12
Billions, chained to b. of years, 680:5
Billow above which is a billow, 118:24
    what a B. be, 510:9
Billows smooth and bright, 515:20
    swelling and limitless b., 378:1
Bill's, Buffalo B. defunct, 701:7
Billy-boil, waited for b., 585:8
Billy Pilgrim has come unstuck, 801:4
bin Laden, they killed Osama b., 877:6
Bind another to its delight, 352:13
    arm b. restless wave, 503:1
    love which us doth b., 267:4
    one Ring to b. them, 696:14
    shall my joyful temples b., 249:22
    the sweet influences of Pleiades, 14:23
    up my wounds, 172:7
    up nation's wounds, 447:2
Binding Nature fast in fate, 296:21
Binds brave of all earth, 582:8
    he who b. to himself a joy, 352:8
    so dear a head, 403:12
    tie that b., 831:11
Bines, between birdbath and b., 817:6
Binnorie, milldams o' B., 890:2
Biographers, reviewers would have been b.,
    378:20
Biographies clothes and buttons of man, 525:6
    geniuses shortest b., 427:28
    history innumerable b., 407:*n*1
Biography accounts for six or seven selves,
    654:13
    Art of B. different from Geography, 629:1
    art of b. fallen on evil times, 646:10
    heroic poem a b., 407:14
    history of world b., 407:17
    is about Chaps, 629:1
    is ultimately fiction, 775:6
    no history only b., 426:12
    of man cannot be written, 525:6
Biological, features of b. interest, 821:4
    memories are unpleasant, 826:1
Biologist, even in view of mere b., 648:4
Biology, demands not correlated with b.,
    743:13
    don't know much about b., 829:11
    most famous event in b., 821:*n*1
    nothing makes sense except evolution,
        725:6
Biotic, preserve b. community, 668:4
Bipartisanship is another name for, 874:11
Biped, divide b. class, 77:*n*1
Birches, swinger of b., 622:20
Bird, a very few a B. or two, 508:6
    Attic b., 260:3
    beat bush another take b., 146:*n*13
    cat versus b. old as time, 727:8
    change me to winged b., 68:2
    clumsy dirty gray b., 433:1
    crop-full b., 462:14

Bird *(continued)*
    divine b. of Zeus, 63:25
    flee as a b., 15:7
    forgets dying b., 333:15
    gates of b. always open, 694:11
    gold-feathered b. sings in palm, 642:18
    half angel half b., 462:28
    heart like singing b., 512:1
    here and there b. or butterfly, 623:3
    I sing as b. sings, 342:13
    immortal B., 410:10
    in gilded cage, 607:6
    in hand worth two in bush, 108:*n*3
    is on the Wing, 441:7
    it was carol of b., 397:9
    it's a b. plane Superman, 777:1
    Jubjub b., 515:12
    know why caged b. sings, 613:13
    live like stoic b., 666:4
    Loaf to every B., 509:19
    man and b. and beast, 377:5
    night's sweet b., 403:25
    no b. soars too high, 351:13
    no further than wanton's b., 180:15
    of bad moral character, 303:17
    of dawning, 196:19
    of night did sit, 191:32
    of Time, 441:7
    of wonder dies, 226:14
    or devil, 449:9
    poor b. he is obsessed, 762:19
    rare b. on earth, 109:18
    rise up at the voice of the b., 23:30
    said b. in musical voice, 724:2
    shall carry the voice, 23:25
    silence with waking b., 455:2
    soul of grandam inhabit b., 185:*n*2
    stamped foot, 508:21
    swift as b. or thought, 53:5
    that filleth own nest, 140:21
    that shunnest noise of folly, 251:15
    this her solemn b., 258:1
    thou never wert, 403:2
    thou warbling b., 357:6
    to nest from wandering, 575:19
    to others flew, 239:18
    turkey a more respectable b., 303:17
    uncontrollably cries, 801:15
    when the b. sings, 845:12
    with B. the abiding Leaf, 756:15
Birdbath, between b. and bines, 817:6
Birdcage, like summer b. in garden, 153:*n*3
Bird's, consciousness like b. life, 540:25
    night-b. wail, 527:23
    sweet b. throat, 194:11
Birds, all could see was sky water b., 761:2
    all the tribes of b. sang, 125:6
    are asleep in trees, 344:19
    are opposite of time, 754:7
    as b. caught in snare, 23:23
    awake in vines, 817:6
    bees stirring b. on wing, 378:14
    began to sing, 894:7
    blossoms b. and bowers, 240:9
    chant ye little b., 357:6
    charm of earliest b., 257:26
    days when B. come back, 508:6
    do sing, 227:4

Birds *(continued)*
    eagle suffers little b. to sing, 173:2
    fear b. of prey, 206:18
    fly from their nests, 4:7
    fly over the rainbow, 711:12
    fly to calico tree, 467:12
    I hope you love B. too, 511:3
    in little nests agree, 289:7
    in the trees, 594:1
    kinds of knowledge, 76:8
    little b. that fly, 290:10
    melodious b. sing madrigals, 168:5
    million golden b., 559:3
    mind an aviary of b., 76:8
    my mind's poor b., 628:18
    no b. in last year's nest, 158:12
    no b. sing, 412:2
    not only fine feathers make fine b., 59:3
    not throw stones at b., 307:27
    of a feather, 235:14
    of air have nests, 33:27
    old age flight of small chirping b., 658:8
    other men catch b., 146:18
    sing like b. i' the cage, 213:8
    sit brooding in snow, 175:1
    time of the singing of b., 24:9
    unperplexed like migratory b., 631:21
    warble sweet in springtime, 558:1
    we are nest of singing b., 308:13
    when b. do sing, 196:2
    when small b. sighed, 756:6
    where late sweet b. sang, 221:24
    without despair to get in, 153:12
    words like peeps of baby b., 80:12
Birds', wind full of b. cries, 635:18
Birdsong at morning, 556:6
Birnam wood to Dunsinane, 216:34, 639:17
Birth, ain't got no b. certificate, 861:7
    and copulation and death, 677:4
    Angel that presided o'er b., 354:10
    as if b. sundered, 474:2
    bed for this huge b., 263:11
    befits proud b., 65:3
    begins to die from b., 312:19
    better world's in b., 472:16
    between b. and dying, 677:18
    border nor breed nor b., 587:8
    certain is b. for the dead, 84:7
    creativeness is conception and b., 584:17
    day of one's b., 23:8
    dew of thy b., 160:*n*5
    distinction of b. or fortune, 365:17
    embraves this morn, 263:12
    false idol or noble true b., 76:5
    famous by their b., 176:24
    foreigner in country of b., 862:11
    from b. to age eighteen, 661:17
    frowned not on humble b., 316:6
    give b. to whopper, 815:13
    grievous burden was thy b., 171:37
    high b. vigor of bone, 203:25
    how many b. announcements, 869:6
    inquiries about events following b., 111:6
    land that gave you b., 582:8
    life and death, 280:26
    mourned at b. not death, 297:11
    my love of b. as rare, 267:3
    new b. of freedom, 446:5, 877:1

Birth *(continued)*
    no cure for b., 584:11
    of ancient race by b., 273:6
    of morning dew, 160:10
    rejoice at b. grieve at funeral, 523:20
    repeats story of her b., 287:21
    Savior's b. celebrated, 196:19
    sleep and a forgetting, 370:17
    sunshine a glorious b., 370:15
Birthday of my life, 512:2
Birthplace of valor, 357:14
Birthright, Esau sold his b., 6:38
Birthrights, bearing b. proudly, 175:5
Births, joyful b., 190:6
    vowels latent b., 559:4
Birth-strangled babe, 216:28
Bis dat qui cito dat, 120:7
Biscay, bonny bonny B. O, 883:22
Bishop, blonde to make b. kick hole in window,
        674:7
    hypocrisy of b., 339:9
Bit, a b. crowded marriage, 876:8
    babies in cradles, 460:7
    by him that comes behind, 285:11
    dogs have a b., 892:21
    hair of dog that b. us, 147:35
    I b. my arm sucked blood, 376:6
    though he had b. me, 213:3
    went mad and b. the man, 322:14
Bitch, deciding not to be a b., 721:4
    gone in the teeth, 665:9
    how it is on b. of earth, 744:14
    son of mongrel b., 211:13
Bitches, businessmen sons of b., 786:6
    now we are all sons of b., 739:*n*3
    sons of b. want to live forever, 312:*n*2
Bitch-goddess Success, 542:4
Bite, bark and b., 289:5
    bark worse than b., 244:27
    bullet, 587:9
    dead man cannot b., 88:20
    dog prosperous will not b., 524:2
    hand that fed them, 325:14
    hate to take a b. out of you, 747:2
    haven't guts to b. people themselves, 553:11
    jaws that b., 515:12
    man recovered of the b., 322:15
    smaller still to b. 'em, 285:11
    sorrow hath less power to b., 176:17
    this fish will b., 190:35
Bites, air b. shrewdly, 197:30
Biteth like a serpent, 21:30
Bitten, complains of having b. tongue, 563:2
Bitter, academic politics are so b., 743:10
    as coloquintida, 208:9
    as wormwood, 19:31
    bark and burning clove, 623:10
    because it is b. because is my heart, 608:19
    bread of banishment, 177:3
    chill it was, 409:18
    do it with b. look, 561:3
    every b. thing is sweet, 22:2
    feed on b. fruit, 730:1
    feel by turns b. change, 256:25
    found Beauty b., 559:7
    from fountain wells up b. taste, 90:17
    give me b. fame, 683:6
    herbs, 7:39

Blankets, people have no b., 537:4
 rough male kiss of b., 669:9
Blaspheme what they do not know, 269:27
Blasphemies, great truths begin as b., 565:24
Blasphemy, in soldier is flat b., 206:29
 Mass the greatest b., 144:6
 no belief there is no b., 865:12
Blast, contrary b. proclaims, 260:18
 drives wicked spirits, 128:15
 heard in the trances of b., 377:15
 midnight b., 399:4
 of war blows in our ears, 189:7
 one b. upon bugle horn, 374:4
 stormy b., 289:12
 striding the b., 214:24
Blast-beruffled plume, 536:11
Blasted with antiquity, 187:32
 with excess of light, 316:13
 with the east wind, 7:9
Blastments, contagious b. imminent, 197:19
Blasts, icy b. blow on love, 493:16
 newborn infant's tear, 353:4
 roots of trees, 777:2
Blaw, up an' gie them a b., 362:11
Blaze, burst out into sudden b., 253:6
 dark amid b. of noon, 260:9
 heavens b. forth, 192:10
 the sapphire b., 316:13
Blazing evidence of immortality, 425:18
 heaven b. into head, 596:10
 in Gold quenching in Purple, 508:11
 no more b. hearth, 315:16
 potentates b. in the heavens, 62:27
 tail, 641:1
Blazon of sweet beauty's best, 222:9
Blazoning, quirks of b. pens, 208:12
Bleak December, 449:4
 in b. midwinter frosty wind, 512:6
Bleakness, country of b., 442:24
Blear-eyed wisdom, 594:17
Bleat the one at the other, 223:10
Bleats articulate monotony, 372:n1
Bled, buried Caesar b., 441:14
 in Freedom's cause, 367:19
 Scots wha hae wi' Wallace b., 358:16
Bleed a while, 889:n1
 carcasses b. at sight of murderer, 136:n2
 heart begins to b., 892:8
 I fall upon thorns I b., 402:12
 if you prick us do we not b., 185:12
Bleeding brow of labor, 577:n3
 piece of earth, 192:22
 purple testament of b. war, 177:10
Blemish, Christianity immortal b., 549:3
 formed without b., 60:8
 lamb shall be without b., 7:38
Blent, beauty truly b., 204:20
Bless bed I lie on, 265:n1
 except thou b. me, 7:3
 God b. Captain Vere, 484:3
 God b. the Pretender, 297:18
 God b. us every one, 465:12
 God b. you, 884:7
 God b. you my dear, 311:17
 hand that gave blow, 273:10
 her when she is riggish, 218:21
 his name, 18:3
 hous from wikked wight, 134:25

Bless *(continued)*
 I b. God in libraries, 318:11
 Lord b. and keep thee, 9:2
 squire and relations, 465:16
 thee Bottom, 178:27
 them that curse you, 32:21
 turf that wraps clay, 317:11
 ye the Lord, 31:30
Blessed Abbot of Aberbrothok, 381:12
 all generations call me b., 37:10
 always to be b., 294:19
 are the dead, 47:6
 are the forgetful, 548:10
 are the meek, 32:14
 are the merciful, 32:14
 are the peacemakers, 32:14, 170:1
 are the poor in spirit, 32:14
 are the pure in heart, 32:14
 are they that mourn, 32:14
 are they that put their trust in him, 15:2
 are they which are persecuted, 32:14
 are they which hunger and thirst, 32:14
 are ye when men revile you, 32:14
 art thou among women, 37:6
 be he that cometh, 18:27
 be Lord God of Israel, 37:13
 be man that spares these stones, 226:17
 be the name of the Lord, 12:39
 bed be b. that I lie on, 265:3
 by country's wishes b., 317:10
 by everything, 595:5
 by yonder b. moon, 180:8
 candles of night, 186:22
 children call her b., 22:19
 come what may been b., 396:24
 damozel, 505:23
 endless sabbaths b. ones see, 123:9
 fell upon knees and b. God, 240:2
 green groves of the b., 94:32
 half part of b. man, 175:9
 hope whereof he knew, 536:12
 horny hands of toil, 481:8
 I had lived a b. time, 215:30
 is man who expects nothing, 294:10
 is the fruit of thy womb, 37:8
 is the man that trusteth, 27:39
 is the man that walketh not in counsel of
  ungodly, 14:40
 judge none b., 30:38
 little b. with soft phrase, 207:33
 Lord b. the latter end of Job, 14:39
 love of God had b., 392:19
 memory of the just is b., 20:11
 mood, 368:8
 more b. to give, 40:40
 mother of us all, 338:20
 mutter of Mass, 460:22
 over whose acres b. feet, 181:19
 part to heaven, 226:8
 plot this earth, 176:24
 quarry mine b. am I, 892:1
 sanctified by reason b. by faith, 369:2
 seeming b. they grow, 322:1
 soul or body more b., 596:12
 them unaware, 376:17
 they that have not seen, 40:13
 thou fallest a b. martyr, 226:5
 thrice and four times b., 93:32

Blessed *(continued)*
 to put cares away, 91:10
 twice b., 186:1
 were but as b. as I, 290:10
 who have no talent, 425:15
 whom thou blessest is b., 9:6
 with milk and honey b., 479:2
 youth becomes as aged, 206:34
Blessedness, perfect b. vision of God, 127:7
Blesses stars and thinks it luxury, 287:23
Blessest, whom thou b. is blessed, 9:6
Blesseth him that gives and him that takes,
 186:1
Blessing, alien b. on its way, 816:11
 and cursing, 9:29
 ask me b., 213:8
 brother hath taken away thy b., 6:40
 creations of mind b. not curse, 637:10
 good neighbor is great b., 54:22
 Hebrew b. before eating bread, 703:13
 I had most need of b., 215:20
 in them you may be b., 270:3
 love gives, 815:16
 money cannot buy, 245:9
 national debt b., 349:2, 390:6
 no harm in b., 297:18
 of Saint Peter's Master, 245:10
 out of God's b. into sun, 148:11
 public debt a public b., 349:n1
 society is a b., 333:1
 unqualified b., 364:4
 war b. compared with reign of lie, 688:8
Blessings, free trade one of b., 419:6
 God from whom all b. flow, 278:8
 health greatest of b., 71:5
 of old friends, 423:17
 on him who invented sleep, 158:8
 on thee little man, 438:7
 on this house, 330:12
 on your frosty pow, 357:13
 one of evils and another of b., 52:19
 reap b. of freedom, 333:10
 secure b. of liberty, 339:11
 two supreme b., 68:9
 unequal sharing of b., 621:18
 upon head of the just, 20:11
 use b. of gods with wisdom, 97:15
 without number, 289:10
Blew, fair breeze b., 376:1
 great guns, 466:8
 slug-horn to lips set and b., 212:n2
Blight man was born for, 546:18
Blighted, seared and b. heart, 447:9
Blights with plagues, 353:4
Blind and ignorant in all, 227:16
 as nails upon Cross, 672:12
 beggar's daughter, 889:21
 Booth died b., 639:10
 eyes of the b. shall be opened, 26:18
 eyes to the b., 14:7
 for being b. God prepare me, 277:27
 Fortune painted b. with muffler, 166:n1
 Fortune though b. not invisible, 166:12
 Fury with abhorred shears, 253:6
 guides, 35:16
 halt and b., 38:7
 he was as often seene, 134:18
 hearts, 90:1

Blind *(continued)*

I was b., 39:28
in country of b. one-eyed man king, 141:10
justice b. deef an' dumb, 600:6
justice is b., 758:19
leaders of the blind, 34:32
leading blind to pit, 115:1
love is b., 135:25, 185:1
love needs be b., 178:*n*1
love to faults always b., 352:5
man's ditch, 595:4
mouths, 253:10
none so b., 282:18
oblivion swallowed cities, 203:20
old mad b. despised king, 402:19
right to be b. sometimes, 355:9
sorrow b. whereas we see, 544:7
three b. mice, 892:10
till some b. hand, 352:15
Tiresias though b., 676:12
to faults a little b., 283:12
was b. but now I see, 320:13
watchmaker, 850:11
we follow, 724:17
winged Cupid painted b., 178:1
Blindly, had we never loved sae b., 357:9
Blindness about poverty, 819:1
heathen in his b., 391:7
left to native b., 313:13
we may forgive, 605:14
with equal b. to future, 319:11
Blinds, drawing-down of b., 699:7
Blindworms, newts and b. do no wrong, 178:22
Blinked, other fellow b., 888:*n*7
Bliss, beyond happiness is b., 691:2
bought by years, 476:10
contrary bringeth b., 169:22
cuckold lives in b., 209:3
deprived of everlasting b., 168:18
follow your b., 737:2, 737:*n*1
happy be and have immortal b., 160:12
he lives in b., 359:1
in our brows bent, 218:7
in proof, 222:20
kill and b. me, 881:14
mutual and partaken b., 252:24
need of imperishable b., 640:21
never parted b. or woe, 259:15
no right to b., 495:4
not beds of down, 242:1
of dying, 293:2
of solitude, 371:13
perfect b. and sole felicity, 168:2
pneumatic b., 676:1
shadow's b., 185:9
soul in b., 213:4
sum of earthly b., 259:2
waking b., 252:16
was it in that dawn, 368:18
where ignorance is b., 315:8
work of fiction affords aesthetic b., 723:9
Blisses about my pilgrimage, 535:10
Blister, never had b. in hand, 72:16
thirst b. easier, 508:15
Blithe, buxom b. and debonair, 250:20
Irish lad, 384:7
no lark more b. than he, 330:19

Blithe *(continued)*

spirit, 403:2
Blizzard, it was blowing a b., 603:7
Block, chip of old b., 324:16
do not b. way of inquiry, 534:12
each b. cut smooth, 665:11
escaped the auction b., 468:19
mind a b. of wax, 76:7
Blockhead, no man but a b., 310:8
Blockheads, Blame-all Praise-all b., 302:5
read what blockheads wrote, 298:16
Blocks, stumbling b. in girl's education, 616:4
Blond beast, 548:15
more b. than you, 701:14
Blonde to make bishop kick hole in window, 674:7
Blondes, gentlemen prefer b., 698:7
Blood, after book of circulation of b., 270:9
all nations one b., 40:33
at the root, 733:12
bath, 657:1
be on your own heads, 40:35
beauty comes from beautiful b., 485:9
bit arm sucked in b., 376:6
blow in cold b., 565:11
by b. we live, 832:2
by man shall his b. be shed, 6:24
can't spill drop of American b., 482:13
chalice of My B., 47:25
Christ's b. streams, 169:4
courage tastes of b., 767:3
created Man of b. clot, 119:18
created you of b. clot, 118:21
cry aloud for b., 489:15
delivered from shipwreck of b., 717:8
devise laws for b., 184:15
drenched in fraternal b., 390:9
drops of b. form on forehead, 687:1
ears gushed b., 409:17
earth one mighty b. spot, 430:24
effusion of b., 582:20
every drop of b. drawn, 447:2
fizz like wine, 635:10
flesh and b. so cheap, 418:12
floors still slippery with b., 803:6
for this all that b. shed, 592:10
freeze thy young b., 198:5
fried meats angry up b., 747:6
future smells of b., 415:8
glories of our b. and state, 246:13
good enough to shed b., 571:8
guiltless of country's b., 316:1
hand raised to shed b., 294:17
heart dry of b., 412:1
her young suck up b., 14:29
heyday in the b. is tame, 201:6
his b. be on us, 36:16
history is bath of b., 542:11
I that am of your b. taken from you, 236:15
impure b. drench field, 361:3
in b. stepped in so far, 216:25
in torrents pour, 568:14
inhabits our frail b., 205:25
iron and b., 470:6
is nipped and ways be foul, 174:33
is their thinking, 67:2
it will have b. they say, 216:23

Blood *(continued)*

liquors in my b., 194:4
lust for b. and plunder, 620:8
make thick my b., 214:17
man whose b. is snow-broth, 206:16
man whose b. is warm, 184:5
meditate on b., 190:7
mingle b. with b. of children, 419:3
more stirs to rouse lion, 182:5
Negro b. sure powerful, 731:11
new testament in my b., 42:25
no Jewish b. in my veins, 836:8
no sure foundation on b., 175:27
nor can b. be in sticks, 90:11
Norman b., 451:3
not a drop of b. shed, 338:9
not against flesh and b., 43:40
not see b. of Ignacio, 717:6
odor of b. when Christ slain, 594:12
of an Englishman, 897:3
of Christians is seed, 113:7
of martyrs seed of Church, 113:*n*4
of our heroes, 337:12
of patriots and tyrants, 336:15
of the lamb, 46:36
of the new testament, 36:3
of the slaughtered, 609:15
of this just person, 36:15
oh b. that freezes b. that burns, 461:2
old man had so much b., 217:12
one b. ye and I, 588:15
own b. rise against you, 611:*n*5
pint of sweat save gallon of b., 664:13
poisoned with b. of both, 829:4
present joys more to flesh and b., 274:4
pure and eloquent b., 230:16
rank flavor of b., 815:15
regime based on bayonets and b., 693:9
rivers older than flow of b., 730:13
sets gypsy b. astir, 579:11
shed by immortal King, 126:12
shed for you and for many, 47:25
sheds his b. with me, 190:1
sign to know gentle b., 161:8
smell b. of British man, 212:9
spend her b. and might, 566:15
spill no drop of b., 537:10
sprinkled upon garments, 27:17
still b. is strong, 417:4
stir men's b., 193:4
strong as flesh and b., 372:1
strong wyn reed as b., 134:8
summon up the b., 189:7
sun's o'ercast with b., 175:15
sweat and tear-wrung millions, 619:*n*3
sweat on drill ground save b. on battlefield, 664:*n*3
tears sweat or b., 619:*n*3
that strange mixture of b., 331:2
thick water's thin, 527:5
thicker than water, 271:4
thicks man's b. with cold, 376:7
till he spouts black b., 483:1
to drink, 431:12
toil tears sweat, 619:12
tree of liberty refreshed with b., 336:15
trilling wire in b., 678:8

Blood (*continued*)
  up to eyes in b., 323:20
  vigor flows into my b., 687:12
  voice of thy brother's b., 6:5
  wash this b. from hand, 215:24
  watered by b. of tyrants, 348:12
  weltering in his b., 274:18
  what little b. is left, 635:10
  when the b. burns, 197:28
  whoso sheddeth man's b., 6:24
  will have blood, 216:23
  without shedding of b., 45:10
  won by b. and sweat of innocent, 852:10
  young b. have its course, 481:7
Blood-dimmed tide loosed, 593:9
Blood-hot eyes, 704:16
Bloodless, no b. myth will hold, 832:2
  substitute for life, 554:15
  week of repose, 73:*n*2
Blood-red, sunset glorious b., 460:20
  wine, 889:13
Blood's a rover, 574:12
Bloodshed, fear and b., 371:21
Blood-swollen, war b. god, 608:13
Bloodthirsty guttersnipe, 620:8
Bloody and invisible hand, 216:13
  be b. bold and resolute, 216:32
  book of law, 207:32
  but unbowed, 552:7
  dark and b. ground, 489:7
  even so my b. thoughts, 209:20
  full of blame, 222:20
  last act is b., 269:15
  mothers a b. brood, 708:6
  often wipe b. nose, 291:13
  sang within the b. wood, 676:2
  treason flourished, 193:1
Bloom along the bough, 574:10
  barred clouds b. soft-dying day, 411:8
  flowers that b. in spring, 527:20
  gradually out of reach, 814:14
  how can ye b., 357:6
  is gone, 496:14
  its b. is shed, 358:6
  lemon trees b., 342:15
  look at things in b., 574:11
  now withering in my b., 293:23
  of young Desire, 316:10
  perfect in bud as in b., 520:15
  sight of vernal b., 257:6
  sort of b. on woman, 577:12
  water lily b., 451:6
  with the b. go I, 496:14
Bloomed, when lilacs in dooryard b., 487:12
Bloomin' shame, 887:7
Blooming, left b. alone, 387:11
Blooms each thing, 227:4
  when the wolfbane b., 732:15
Bloomy, nightingale on b. spray, 253:16
Blossom, blossomed Sarah and I b., 773:4
  by blossom spring begins, 529:13
  desert b. as the rose, 26:17
  in purple and red, 455:3
  in their dust, 246:12
  leaf b. or bole, 594:17
  letting hundred flowers b., 698:13
  May when lusty heart b., 138:9
  that hangs on bough, 225:5

Blossomed Sarah and I blossom, 773:4
Blossomer, great-rooted b., 594:17
Blossoming, labor b. or dancing, 594:17
Blossoms a rose in my heart, 591:9
  and branches to coffins I bring, 487:13
  apple b. fill air, 682:6
  birds and bowers, 240:9
  break into b., 817:9
  glad you love B. so well, 511:3
  of my sin, 198:12
  tomorrow b., 225:25
Blot, art to b., 296:16
  discreetly b., 249:27
  in thy scutcheon, 158:2
  Lord b. out his name, 275:*n*4
  out his name, 46:25
Blotted from life's page, 395:9
  out man's image, 591:4
  Shakespeare never b. line, 233:11
  unpleasantest words that b. paper, 185:23
  word out forever, 314:18
  would he had b. a thousand, 233:11
Blotter, write in b. I was born, 681:5
Blow, all aloud wind doth b., 175:1
  and swallow at same moment, 84:4
  as straws that b., 552:6
  bless hand that gave b., 273:10
  breathe and b., 452:18
  bugle blow, 452:19
  but a word and a b., 274:9
  come from moon and b., 452:18
  death loves signal b., 291:4
  east wind never b., 244:34
  first b. half battle, 323:4
  for freedom, 670:15
  great winds shoreward b., 494:12
  high blow low and so sailed we, 898:1
  him again to me, 452:18
  horrid deed in every eye, 214:24
  hot and cold, 59:11
  I the b. and cheek, 491:7
  I will b. you out, 501:12
  in cold blood not forgiven, 565:11
  liberty's in every b., 358:17
  might be the be-all, 214:22
  north wind doth b., 895:5
  on whom I please, 194:20
  out you bugles, 669:12
  out your brains, 588:13
  pay with a deadly b., 63:13
  pealing organ b., 251:23
  perhaps may turn his b., 367:3
  put your lips together and b., 680:1
  struck a deep mortal b., 63:6
  the kiss, 817:6
  the man down, 897:16
  thou winter wind, 195:1
  trumpet to arms, 332:20
  up an' gie them a b., 362:11
  upon my garden, 24:16
  when wilt thou b., 881:1
  who would be free strike b., 395:7
  wind come wrack, 217:25
  wind sail b., 890:6
  winds crack your cheeks, 211:24
  word and a b., 180:27
  wreathed horn, 371:24
  ye winds heigh-ho, 898:3

Blow (*continued*)
  your trumpets angels, 230:19
Bloweth, ill wind b. no man good, 148:21
  med, 880:5
  spirit b. and is still, 494:17
  wind b. where it listeth, 39:9
Blowin' in the wind, 851:1
  what bugles b. for, 587:14
Blowing, Elfland faintly b., 452:20
  furious winter b., 681:18
  it was b. a blizzard, 603:7
  new direction of Time, 662:13
  noise of tongues, 450:10
  what bugles b. for, 587:14
Blown buds of barren flowers, 530:16
  by wind of criticism, 311:14
  crimes broad b., 200:33
  dust that is b. away, 30:3
  hair is sweet, 677:15
  pipe b. by surmises, 187:21
  what though mast b. overboard, 171:1
  with restless violence, 206:38
Blows, apostolic b. and knocks, 262:11
  blast of war b. in ears, 189:7
  Dick the shepherd b. his nail, 174:33
  driven by invisible b., 662:14
  dust b. in your face, 212:18
  feather for each wind that b., 223:17
  from yon far country b., 575:6
  it in my face, 199:17
  man up like a bladder, 182:25
  meanest flower that b., 371:5
  never b. so red, 441:14
  soft zephyr b., 316:15
  taught by rod and b., 144:1
  vile b. and buffets, 216:7
  which way the wind b., 851:15
  wild thyme b., 178:19
  wind b. cradle rock, 550:7
  wind b. it back again, 353:12
  wind from blue heaven b., 342:15
  wind that b. through me, 662:13
Blude-red wine, 889:13
Bludgeonings of chance, 552:7
Blue, all over now Baby B., 851:7
  and don't know where to go, 673:7
  and gold mistake, 508:6
  Aryan eye bright b., 833:8
  beneath b. of day, 574:16
  Big B. Mountain Spirit, 891:15
  breeches b., 381:19
  buff and the b., 359:3
  color source of delight, 484:11
  daisies pied and violets b., 174:32
  darkened on blueness, 663:22
  ethereal sky, 287:20
  forked torch of flower, 663:22
  fragmentary b., 623:3
  grappling in central b., 452:2
  hands b., 467:11
  home made of b. clouds, 891:15
  I am Rose my eyes are b., 628:13
  inns of Molten B., 508:9
  lavender's b., 896:13
  little boy b. blow horn, 893:11
  Little Boy B. kissed them, 554:2
  little tent of b., 561:1
  living air and b. sky, 368:11

Blue *(continued)*
    O, 559:4
    pine needles, 280:1
    Presbyterian true b., 262:9
    promontory with trees, 218:39
    pull of the b. highway, 846:1
    Red States and B. States, 876:12
    remembered hills, 575:6
    roses red violets b., 160:11
    sky bends over all, 377:12
    so black and b., 708:8
    something b., 886:16
    suede shoes, 832:11
    true b., 262:9
    twitched his mantle b., 253:15
    wave rolls nightly, 397:2
    wings were b., 467:12
Bluebird carries sky, 473:4
    of anxiety, 839:18
Bluebirds, over rainbow b. fly, 711:12
Blueeyed boy, 701:7
Blue-fringed lids, 377:16
Bluejays, shoot all the b. you want, 813:4
Blue-massing clouds, 669:9
Blueness, blue darkened on b., 663:22
Blues, from b. American music, 610:8
    good mornin' b., 680:10
    I got the Weary B., 731:1
    to tune o' those Weary B., 730:16
Blume, du bist wie eine B., 415:n2
Blunder, frae monie a b. free us, 356:16
    man b. of God or God of man, 548:22
    so grotesque a b., 629:4
    worse than crime it is b., 361:4
Blunderbuss against religion, 308:19
Blundered, someone had b., 454:20
Blundering kind of melody, 273:7
    learning b. people live on, 636:10
Blunders, forgetful get better of b., 548:10
    like ropes, 422:15
    round meaning, 295:12
Blunt monster with uncounted heads, 187:21
    plain b. man, 193:3
Blush, born to b. unseen, 315:23
    fair regions raise our b., 346:24
    shame where is thy b., 201:7
    to give it in, 314:n2
    to make man b., 396:28
    truth does not b., 113:11
Blushed at herself, 207:35
    saw its God and b., 263:1
Blushes into wine, 263:n1
    man only animal that b., 524:16
Blushful Hippocrene, 410:4
Blushing, bears his b. honors, 225:25
    flowers shall rise, 292:6
    Religion b. veils fires, 297:6
Blustering, pity from b. wind, 266:3
Blut, Eisen und B., 470:n2
Blynken, Wynken B. and Nod, 554:1
Boanerges, neigh like B., 509:11
Board, back to the old drawing b., 736:16
    dim on Bristol b., 763:8
    get on b. little children, 899:2
    heart for bed and b., 787:5
    struck the b., 242:26
    well-benched ships, 55:18
Boards, ships are but b., 184:21

Boast, frantic b., 589:11
    having my freedom b. of nothing, 176:15
    let not him that girdeth on his harness b.,
        12:5
    not of what thou wouldst have done,
        260:21
    not thyself of tomorrow, 21:40
    now b. thee death, 219:17
    of heraldry, 315:18
    of this I can, 176:19
    such is the patriot's b., 321:13
Boasters, great nations not b., 428:3
Boasteth, when he is gone his way then he b.,
    21:12
Boastful, high and b. neighs, 189:18
    in war daring b., 400:7
Boasting, strength without b., 337:4
Boat, carry Caesar in your b., 89:3
    forefathers met the b., 640:9
    is on the shore, 397:13
    Michael row b. ashore, 898:22
    news of the b., 426:7
    of life be light, 576:6
    of your flesh, 839:4
    pea-green b., 467:7
    people in a b., 874:6
    rides through sewer, 648:10
    sea so great b. so small, 884:9
    sings in b. on bay, 452:15
    slow b. to China, 762:1
    they sank my b., 785:4
Boats against the current, 710:8
    messing about in b., 574:7
    oh the little cargo b., 589:2
    shallow bauble b., 203:4
    that are not steered, 220:28
Boatswain, memory of B. a dog, 394:9
    tight and midshipmite, 525:16
Bob is on the street today, 870:7
Bobolink for Chorister, 508:18
Bobtail nag, 503:10
Boca, el pez muere por la b., 898:7
    en b. cerrada no entran moscas, 898:9
Bodes some strange eruption, 196:12
Bodice, loosens fragrant b., 409:22
Bodies a living sacrifice, 41:29
    abstain from abusing b., 70:14
    are buried in peace, 31:28
    as clothes to b., 580:18
    as imagination b. forth, 179:6
    clothes without b., 580:18
    elements or principles of b., 339:1
    gave b. to commonwealth, 72:4
    molecules that compose b., 339:1
    movements of largest b., 345:3
    mutual actions of two b., 279:16
    nature works by b. unseen, 89:16
    of unburied men, 237:3
    our b. are our gardens, 208:7
    our selves our souls and b., 49:7
    persons with torn b. happy, 608:14
    pile b. at Austerlitz, 636:4
    princes like to heavenly b., 166:1
    remove weight from heavenly b., 801:11
    rough notes and dead b., 603:5
    single soul in two b., 77:10
    soldiers bore dead b. by, 181:36
    these black b., 350:15

Bodies *(continued)*
    unclothed, 230:13
Bodiless and simple, 797:12
Bodily decrepitude wisdom, 596:3
    exercise when compulsory, 75:15
    form from natural thing, 594:4
    form of them b., 530:20
    states following perception, 541:9
Bodkin, bare b., 199:21
Body, absent in b. present in spirit, 42:12
    achieves nothing, 868:11
    age and b. of the time, 200:8
    along b. of this life, 789:12
    and spirit twins, 531:2
    art work of b. and soul, 484:10
    Asclepius cured the b., 74:n1
    be not afraid of my b., 486:23
    book makes b. cold, 511:15
    carry b. for sentimental value, 750:10
    changed to light, 892:5
    continues in state of rest, 279:14
    damned for b., 587:10
    demd damp b., 464:21
    dies body's beauty lives, 641:5
    distressed in mind b. or estate, 48:15
    does not own and control b., 657:16
    each petty artery in b., 198:2
    employ b. to serve, 92:2
    filled and vacant mind, 189:23
    find thy b. by wall, 497:3
    for this is My B., 47:24
    gave b. to country's earth, 177:14
    gin a b. meet a b., 883:n1
    give b. to be burned, 42:27
    happiness beneficial for b., 611:6
    having seen his b. borne before her, 459:14
    health intelligence talent, 578:3
    her b. thought, 230:16
    her dead b. wears smile, 833:5
    highest intelligence in freest b., 634:1
    human b. best picture of soul, 685:12
    human b. sacred, 486:21
    I have risen to a b., 811:5
    ideals in one dark b., 602:3
    infirm and exhausted, 140:1
    is his book, 229:20
    is Nature God is soul, 294:22
    is not b. more than raiment, 33:6
    its b. brevity, 378:5
    John Brown's b., 521:1
    joint and motive of b., 204:4
    liberation of the human b., 604:14
    light around the b., 811:5
    light of the b., 33:3
    like b. wholly b., 641:8
    little b. mighty heart, 189:2
    loves world as his b., 57:5
    man member of b., 435:16
    marry my b. to that dust, 241:18
    material fortune associated with b., 111:7
    mind or b. to prefer, 295:1
    more familiar with Africa than own b.,
        834:12
    my b. my dungeon is, 555:17
    my good bright dog, 772:11
    my house, 772:10
    mysterious carriage of b., 313:22
    no riches above sound b., 31:15

Body *(continued)*
   not b. enough to cover mind, 374:25
   not bruised to pleasure soul, 594:17
   not more than soul, 486:17
   of Benjamin Franklin Printer, 301:20
   of each creature different, 71:9
   of this death, 41:18
   old in b. but never mind, 88:15
   one motion, 756:12
   oppressions of b. and mind, 338:8
   part of man's Self, 541:4
   pass from colder to hotter b., 497:23
   perfectly spherical, 467:6
   piece of b. torn out by root, 757:2
   Poet filling other B., 413:10
   poet of B. poet of Soul, 486:5
   politic like human body, 312:19
   power lies in mind and b., 92:2
   presence of b. in question, 383:21
   pygmy-b., 272:16
   reading to mind as exercise to b., 287:19
   remember, 583:12
   Resurrection of the b., 48:11
   ruler having human b. as subject, 74:19
   sex woven into whole b., 573:23
   sickness-broken b., 250:1
   so young b. with so old head, 185:32
   soul gentle companion of b., 111:2
   soul is form and doth b. make, 161:7
   soul its b. off, 596:5
   soul look b. touch, 596:12
   soul to find its proper b., 775:12
   sound mind in sound b., 109:26
   sound of b. and mind, 96:15
   startlingly muscled b., 815:16
   statue or machine of earth, 246:3
   stepped out of my b., 817:9
   subject to forces of gravity, 778:15
   swayed to music, 594:17
   swung gently, 540:1
   this is my b., 36:3, 42:24
   'tis mind makes b. rich, 173:22
   to be buried obscurely, 166:21
   touch palm of hand to my b., 486:23
   touched her perfect b., 837:9
   whole b. is mirror, 348:3
   whole b. not be cast into hell, 32:18
   with whole b. listen, 643:23
   without spirit dead, 45:26
   woman's b. the woman, 540:2
   worms destroy this b., 13:39
Bodyguard, if you'll be my b., 855:13
   of lies, 621:6
Body-hungry, soul-hungry worse than b., 886:12
Body's beauty lives, 641:5
   casting b. vest aside, 267:2
   go Soul the b. quest, 159:9
Bog, snow falling on B. of Allen, 650:9
   to an admiring B., 508:14
Bogus revelation, 644:16
Boil, dreams b. up from ring of myth, 737:1
   maketh the deep b. like a pot, 14:35
   sentient creature alive, 878:3
   we b. at different degrees, 428:22
Boiling, Hiroshima b., 788:1
   I love b-hot days, 488:9
   why sea b. hot, 516:4

Boils round naked isles, 301:1
Bois, cor au fond des b., 416:*n*1
   n'irons plus aux b., 499:*n*5
Boisterously, as b. maintained as gained, 175:22
Bold, alive and so b. O earth, 403:10
   and turbulent of wit, 272:16
   bad man, 160:4, 225:16
   be bloody b. and resolute, 216:32
   be b., 160:14
   be not too b., 160:15
   cook and captain b., 525:16
   in conscious virtue b., 293:13
   inspiring b. John Barleycorn, 358:7
   jockey of Norfolk not too b., 160:*n*6
   let our minds be b., 562:13
   look with favor on b. beginning, 93:10
   maiden never b., 207:35
   man first eat oyster, 285:21
   peasantry, 322:22
   persistent experimentation, 651:15
   righteous are b. as a lion, 22:5
   story of Cambuscan b., 251:21
   too b. to imagine, 327:12
   virtue is b., 207:3
   what makes robbers b. but lenity, 170:24
Bolder, knits a b. One, 509:1
   note than this swell, 448:1
Boldest held his breath, 384:12
   sons of toil, 500:5
Boldly, attack all the more b., 94:26
   ride, 449:19
   to b. go, 797:3
Boldness certain to win praise, 101:15
   to dream, 738:6
Bole, elm tree b., 460:18
   leaf blossom or b., 594:17
Bolingbroke, this canker B., 182:3
Bolshevism, combines B. socialism, 830:3
Bolster, head on sweaty b., 798:1
Bolt, Ben B., 480:26
   of Cupid fell, 178:16
   Old Age coming b. door, 119:27
Bolts, stronger b. than Aphrodite, 67:25
   up change, 219:7
   wresting from Jupiter his b., 104:9
Bomb, atomic b. turn of screw, 739:6
   don't let anyone b. me, 745:5
   Lord b. Germans, 745:5
   might destroy whole port, 638:1
   new and most cruel b., 728:7
   on Hiroshima, 661:3
   them into Stone Age, 746:7
   war fought with atomic b., 638:3
Bombast out blank verse, 164:3
   second sublime third b., 107:1
Bombastiloquent, 73:15
Bombed, almost glad we have been b., 725:7
Bombers, pilots man b. to kill babies, 824:10
   riding shotgun in the sky, 858:3
Bombing of Chinese cities, 661:12
Bombs, atomic b. burst in hands, 599:1
   atomic energy lead to b., 638:1
   bursting in air, 386:19
   drop atomic b. on own populations, 740:1
Bonaparte, ashes of Napoleon B., 366:13
   Jeanne d'Arc and B., 686:10

Bond, break that sole b., 324:12
   happy whom unbroken b. unites, 96:12
   I'll seal to such a b., 184:30
   let him look to his b., 185:10
   neither b. nor free, 44:12
   of iniquity, 40:20
   prosperity's very b. of love, 223:34
   so nominated in the b., 186:5
   take a b. of fate, 216:33
   tied by chance b., 472:18
   'tis not in the b., 186:6
   trust man on oath or b., 213:21
   universal and common b., 153:16
   which keeps me pale, 216:13
   word as good as b., 158:1
Bondage, hold fellow men in b., 363:8
   marriage only actual b., 435:19
   of irrational fears, 562:9
   out of the house of b., 8:1
   slightest b. made aware, 624:7
   to previous history, 506:15
Bondman in hand bears power, 191:33
Bondman's, in a b. key, 184:29
Bonds, man frees himself from b., 432:7
   of Union dissolved, 380:12
   surly b. of Earth, 800:1
   that unite only in mind, 611:3
Bondsman's unrequited toil, 447:2
Bone against the plate, 850:8
   behind mortal B., 509:1
   break b. suck out marrow, 145:4
   bright hair about the b., 230:2
   consuming rag and b., 596:13
   divorced from eye and b., 713:4
   every part of b. Nature makes b., 112:24
   fetch poor dog a b., 895:6
   fever of the b., 675:26
   flesh of flesh b. of b., 259:15
   life near b. sweetest, 475:21
   of manhood, 324:2
   of my bones, 5:16
   of thy bone, 155:5
   pain of b. spur in heel, 722:3
   rag and b. and hair, 589:5
   secret life of b., 772:2
   Taffy stole marrow b., 894:1
   vigor of b., 203:25
   Zero at the B., 510:6
Bone-crushing, nosing up to b. waterfall, 788:5
Boneless gums, 215:5
Bones, bone of my b., 5:16
   bound b. and veins in me, 546:5
   can these b. live, 28:18
   curst be he that moves my b., 226:17
   dead men lost b., 676:8
   dice human b., 399:14
   disembodied b., 666:5
   dry b., 28:19
   England keep my b., 175:31
   exercises b. with toil, 80:6
   full of dead men's b., 35:17
   good oft interred with b., 192:28
   grind b. to make bread, 897:3
   have quietly rested, 248:25
   honored b., 250:15
   jest breaks no b., 311:6
   lay his weary b. among ye, 226:7
   let us have tongs and b., 178:31

Books *(continued)*

marches undertook in pursuit of b., 692:13
monkeys write b. in British Museum, 649:6
more in woods than in b., 123:11
never die, 653:7
new French b., 461:23
next o'er his b., 296:26
no b. but score and tally, 170:17
no pulping of b., 764:16
not in your b., 190:16
not killed by fire, 653:7
of all time, 484:16
of making many b., 24:2, 647:2
of quotations, 619:3
of the hour, 484:16
old clothes a few b., 658:4
old manners b. wines, 323:2
only b. woman's looks, 387:16
out of olde b. newe science, 132:8
read deliberately as written, 475:5
read only b. that wound us, 655:10
reading valueless b., 484:15
rural quiet friendship b., 300:20
sins scarlet b. read, 606:17
some b. to be tasted, 166:17
spectacles of b., 272:7
study nature, not b., 435:24
sweet serenity of b., 437:20
they are the b. the arts, 174:24
think for me, 383:19
trees shall be my b., 195:2
twenty b. at his beddes heed, 133:23
two classes of b., 484:16
undeservedly forgotten, 749:18
university a collection of b., 407:21
ways of acquiring b., 692:12
we have b. about it, 335:17
we learn from b. can't judge, 343:21
well or badly written, 559:23
why aren't the b. enough, 862:9
worst b. universal appeal, 616:15
you may carry to fire, 308:9
Booksellers, for all b. in world, 318:11
Bookstore, human nature weak in b., 468:7
Book-words what are you, 487:7
Bookworming in pajamas, 787:9
Boom alop-bam-b., 832:9
in petroleum but not in poetry, 776:10
Booming of new-come bee, 642:5
surge of Aegean, 74:2
Boon, sordid b., 371:23
Boone, when Daniel B. goes by, 716:5
Boot, hey for b. and horse, 481:7
saddle to horse, 460:5
stamping on human face forever, 735:22
Booth died blind, 639:10
since Lincoln shot by B., 708:16
Bootless cries, 221:5
Boots boots boots, 589:22
drunk and asleep in b., 640:19
not to resist wind and tide, 170:32
well then o'er shoes o'er b., 527:*n*1
what b. it at one gate to make defense,
260:14
what b. with incessant care, 253:6
Boot-soles, look for me under b., 486:20
Booze, empty bottle of b., 833:16
Georgia b., 715:17

Booze *(continued)*

party ends in fight, 674:3
Bop, Awop-b.-a-loo-mop, 832:9
Bo-peep, as if they played at b., 241:6
little B., 895:2
Borden, Lizzie B. took ax, 885:22
Border nor breed nor birth, 587:8
not really a b. but a scar, 818:7
through all wide B., 373:9
Borders, departure beyond b. death, 688:9
invade b. of my realm, 151:7
Bore, accursed the night she b. me, 67:13
art of never appearing a b., 554:8
big book big b., 82:17
bored more contemptible than b., 521:3
Chankly B., 468:3
every hero becomes b., 427:27
forgive those who b. us, 264:18
life too short to b. ourselves, 548:11
me in southern wild, 350:14
secret of being a b., 299:3
sex becomes b., 735:3
soldiers b. dead bodies by, 181:36
talks wish him to listen, 540:5
to be in society a b., 560:16
Bored and terrified, 781:11
Bores and B., 399:2
I'm b. and old, 879:6
leaving World because I'm b., 747:9
mankind by thee less b., 245:*n*1
more contemptible than bore, 521:3
so b. I could scream, 689:15
with good wine, 430:2
Boredom, against b. gods struggle, 360:*n*3
at core of life, 270:16
foe of happiness, 400:4
God created woman b. ceased, 549:1
is instrument of social control, 778:14
obesity brought on by b., 734:6
state of man b., 269:11
vice and poverty, 299:13
Bores and Bored, 399:2
through his castle wall, 177:9
Borges, I live so B. can weave literature, 719:6
Borgias, Italy for thirty years under B., 781:4
Boring, life is b., 773:7
nothing more b. than the truth, 794:5
ordinary b. or trite, 778:11
Born, a man be b. again, 39:8
again, 805:12
all men b. free, 254:18
as one b. out of time, 42:32
as soon as we were b., 30:2
begotten b. and dies, 594:1
being b. to die, 166:24
being human b. alone, 666:7
best not to be b., 59:23
better to be lowly b., 225:17
blight man b. for, 546:18
bred en b. in brier-patch, 551:14
but I was free b., 40:43
but to die, 295:1
certain is death for the b., 84:7
Christ b. across sea, 481:2
Christ b. in Bethlehem, 305:10
cry for being b., 166:24
day perish wherein I was b., 13:3
died before god of love was b., 229:21

Born *(continued)*

else wherefore b., 455:9
envy b. from the start, 69:13
first b. as children, 805:12
for the sex opposite, 320:11
free, 254:18, 312:15
free and equal, 336:*n*1
friends b. not made, 531:11
genius must be b., 274:12
glad not b. before tea, 375:12
good if he had not been b., 36:2
happy is he b. and taught, 227:9
have to be b. there, 713:19
he not busy being b., 851:8
he was not b. to shame, 180:33
hour I was b., 884:17
house where I was b., 418:2
human race b. to fly upward, 129:21
I was b. dat's de charge, 681:5
I was b. to know you, 705:7
ignorance in which b., 314:27
in America black, 808:11
in days when wits were fresh, 495:17
in goddam hotel room, 681:12
in half savage country, 665:4
in my b. days, 155:16
in other's pain, 576:12
in soft regions b. soft men, 69:24
in this century, 785:10
into lower-upper-middle class, 735:6
jealousy b. with love, 264:24
Jesus Christ is b., 898:17
live die an American, 390:20
loveliest woman b., 593:17
lucky to be b., 485:20
made his own bed ere b., 263:12
man b. and dies, 889:1
man is b. free, 312:15
man is b. unto trouble, 13:11
man that is b. of a woman, 13:29
Miniver Cheevy b. too late, 605:21
misfortune: not to be b., 534:2
monster b. on itself, 209:22
naked and falls a-whining, 105:*n*1
no man b. an angler, 244:33
no man is b. unto himself, 241:21
nobly b. must nobly meet fate, 68:18
none of woman b., 216:32
not b. for death, 410:10
not b. under riming planet, 191:16
not b. woman becomes one, 751:7
not conscious of being b., 280:26
not to be b. best, 748:7
not to be b. surpasses thought, 66:19
of blackest Midnight b., 250:19
of the Spirit, 39:9
of the sun, 760:6
of Virgin Mary, 48:11
of virgin mother b., 250:9
old and ugly, 464:32
on a Monday, 895:10
on Christmas Day, 883:4
on Fourth of July, 634:12
One b. in a manger, 268:15
one man b. one man died, 719:4
out of my due time, 520:5
poet's made as well as b., 233:5
posthumously, 549:9

Born *(continued)*
 powerless to be b., 495:23
 risen to body not yet b., 811:5
 some are b. great, 205:8
 strength though of Muses b., 409:4
 sun b. and dies, 888:22
 sun b. over and over, 777:13
 terrible beauty b., 593:7
 they had never been b., 31:27
 thing I was b. to do, 167:6
 time to be b., 22:31
 to be nobly b. now crime, 237:18
 to be wild, 856:4
 to blush unseen, 315:23
 to set it right, 198:22
 to the manner b., 197:31
 to write, 295:13
 towards Bethlehem to be b., 593:10
 tramps like us were b. to run, 868:2
 under one law to another bound, 161:15
 under that was I b., 190:30
 unto us a child is b., 25:16
 unto you is b., 37:17
 we were not b. to sue, 176:10
 went to trouble to be b., 327:16
 wept that he was b., 605:20
 when we are b. we cry, 213:1
 with anxiety about weather, 528:14
 with gift of laughter, 632:11
 with legs apart, 834:13
 with silver foot, 834:15
 with silver spoon, 158:11
 would thou hadst ne'er been b., 210:5
Borne and yet must bear, 401:14
 back into past, 710:8
 his faculties so meek, 214:24
 like thy bubbles, 396:22
 me on his back, 202:12
 not b. this in my hot youth, 97:6
 oldest hath b. most, 213:16
 our loads, 672:6
 the burden, 35:6
 through hatred b. apart, 67:1
 well b. without defeat, 188:36
Borogoves, mimsy were b., 515:12
Borrow, every changing shape, 675:8
 men who b. men who lend, 383:8
Borrowed plumes, 59:2
 something b., 886:16
 wit, 239:19
Borrower is servant to the lender, 21:18
 neither b. nor lender be, 197:24
 of the night, 216:4
Borrowers always ill-spenders, 484:17
 of books, 383:9
Borrowing accounted Plagiarè, 254:16
 banqueting upon b., 31:5
 dulls edge of husbandry, 197:24
 everything of neighbors, 277:21
 only lingers it out, 187:36
Boshaft ist er nicht, 638:*n1*
Bosom, Abraham's b., 38:17, 171:36, 370:6
 Arthur's b., 189:4
 beggar in Abraham's b., 38:17
 can a man take fire in his b., 20:3
 carry them in his b., 26:29
 chums, 823:2
 crept into b. of the sea, 170:10

Bosom *(continued)*
 friend of sun, 411:6
 glory in His b., 481:2
 heart out of b., 574:15
 her hand on her b., 210:8
 I must not see, 267:15
 in ocean's b. unespied, 267:5
 in your fragrant b. dies, 245:16
 let me to Thy b. fly, 305:8
 liest in Abraham's b., 370:6
 loosened from her b. the girdle, 51:29
 of his Father and his God, 316:8
 of infinite world, 364:16
 of urgent West, 545:12
 sleep in Abraham's b., 171:36
 stuffed b. of perilous stuff, 217:19
 swell b. with thy fraught, 209:19
 third in your b., 180:20
 thorns that in b. lodge, 198:13
 warm cheek and rising b., 316:10
 which thy frozen b. bears, 207:*n2*
 wife of thy b., 9:22
 within b. is September, 881:11
 wring his b., 322:17
 write sorrow on b. of earth, 177:7
Bosomed high in tufted trees, 251:3
Bosoms, fold to their b. the viper, 482:12
 hair hang and brush b., 462:4
 men's business and b., 165:10
 waters lift their b., 203:7
 white b. of actresses, 308:14
Boss, meet the new b., 862:1
Bossuet, celebrities such as B., 518:9
Boston, a Thucydides at B., 317:4
 Cluett Shirt B. Garter, 701:9
 Concord Lexington, 390:7
 Evening Transcript, 675:10
 good old B., 577:15
 in B. ask how much does he know, 524:5
 joined the church at B., 261:16
 just returned from B., 700:12
 marching through B., 787:19
 marriage serious around B., 698:14
Boston's Marlborough Street, 787:9
Bo'sun tight and midshipmite, 525:16
Botanist, puzzle to b., 520:15
Botanize, peep and b., 369:9
Botany, all their b. Latin, 424:16
Botch of it trying to swap, 446:8
Botched civilization, 665:9
Boteler, Dr. B. said of strawberries, 245:7
Both, by adventuring b., 184:11
 I am with b., 175:15
 plague o' b. houses, 180:29
 wear b. for b. are thine, 171:21
Bother, long words B. me, 651:8
Bothered, hot and b., 590:8
Bottle, fragrance in whiskey b., 780:14
 friend in need nor b., 465:17
 leave b. on chimleypiece, 464:39
 my b. of salvation, 159:10
 of hay, 178:32
 shake and shake catsup b., 744:11
 take b. down from shelf, 769:7
Bottled lightning, 464:22
Bottleneck, president is b., 764:4
Bottles, new wine in old b., 33:34
 stay the b. of heaven, 14:25

Bottom, bless thee B., 178:27
 build from b. up, 651:14
 dive into b. of deep, 182:6
 every vat stand upon b., 271:11
 from shore sees sea s., 130:8
 I see not the b. of it, 203:27
 line is in heaven, 758:16
 not in one b. trusted, 184:1
 of sea is cruel, 720:1
 of the monstrous world, 253:12
 of the worst, 203:12
 sees into b. of my grief, 181:4
 sit on our own b., 153:22
 strike rock and go to b., 355:2
 unknown b. like bay of Portugal, 195:30
Bottomless, consciousness as b. lake, 534:17
 in b. nights you sleep, 559:3
 perdition, 255:7
 some ponds thought b., 475:15
Bouchon, plus léger qu'un b., 558:*n9*
Bough, apple reddens on high b., 56:10
 bloom along b., 574:10
 blossom that hangs on b., 225:5
 Book of Verses underneath B., 441:10
 breaks cradle fall, 550:7
 golden b., 594:4
 old forsaken b., 443:15
 sings on orchard b., 460:18
 touch not single b., 423:1
 wet black b., 665:1
Boughs, bird that lives in the b., 342:13
 cedar green with b., 557:7
 easy under the apple b., 777:9
 incense hangs upon b., 410:7
 lowest b. brushwood sheaf, 460:18
 off many a tree, 242:17
 shade of melancholy b., 194:22
 soul into b. does glide, 267:2
 which shake against cold, 221:24
Bought, beauty b. by judgment of eye, 174:8
 bliss b. by years, 476:10
 crooked cat, 895:17
 Dickon thy master b., 160:*n6*
 golden opinions, 215:1
 good names to be b., 181:27
 knowledge b. in market, 479:9
 neither b. nor sold, 838:8
 soul b. and paid for, 458:16
 strangers who b. laws, 709:15
 three pecks of meal, 896:23
 wisdom is not b., 889:10
Boughten friendship by side, 624:2
Bound bones and veins in me, 546:5
 born under one law to another b., 161:15
 bourn b. of land, 224:19
 by countless ties, 624:7
 by own definition of criticism, 496:7
 each to each, 369:14
 I'm b. away, 625:2
 in icy chains by thee, 207:*n2*
 in shallows and miseries, 193:13
 in saucy doubts, 216:15
 in with triumphant sea, 176:25
 leap tall buildings at single b., 777:1
 nothing but hath his b., 172:15
 of the everlasting hills, 7:21
 upon wheel of fire, 213:4
 utmost b. of thought, 451:15

Bound *(continued)*
    we're b. away, 897:19
    with red tape, 466:3
Boundaries, Great Spirit knows no b., 364:17
    here b. meet, 492:8
    in safety within b., 653:15
    which divide Life, 448:18
    without war because no b., 365:*n*1
Bounded in a nutshell, 199:3
    our Country however b., 456:7
    waters lift bosoms, 203:7
Boundless as we wish our souls, 402:6
    contiguity of shade, 326:20
    drew from b. deep, 456:4
    endless sublime, 396:21
    his wealth, 373:3
    vision grows, 500:5
Bounds, living know no b., 246:11
    of place and time, 316:13
    wider b. be set, 580:19
Bountiful, Lady B., 290:7
Bounty, for his b. no winter, 219:8
    large was his b., 316:7
    lust of goat b. of God, 351:14
    those his former b. fed, 274:18
Bourgeois, épater le b., 491:*n*14
    hatred of b. beginning of wisdom, 493:20
    how beastly b. is, 663:14
    horror of b. is b., 585:9
    Marxism product of b. mind, 657:19
    regularly and orderly like b., 494:1
    suppression of b. state, 607:14
    you must shock b., 491:20
Bourgeoisie class of modern capitalists, 478:*n*5
    discreet charm of b., 725:2
    draws nations into civilization, 478:10
    face to face with b., 478:11
    played revolutionary role, 478:9
Bourn bound of land, 224:19
    country from whose b., 199:21
    lambs bleat from hilly b., 411:8
Bourreau, la victime et le b., 491:*n*6
Bout, notes with many a winding b., 251:8
    with love, 60:1
Bovary, I am Madame B., 494:3
    Madame B. had beauty, 493:14
Bow, always made awkward b., 413:19
    and accept end, 622:8
    as unto b. cord is, 437:4
    better to b. than break, 147:10
    bow lower middle classes, 526:17
    cannot stand bent, 157:2
    down thine ear, 21:19
    draw b. ride and speak truth, 399:6
    he bar and arwes brighte, 134:18
    many strings to b., 147:26
    nor does Apollo always stretch b., 96:24
    of burning gold, 354:8
    or brooch or braid, 546:21
    set my b. in the cloud, 6:25
    strong men shall b. themselves, 23:30
    tensely strung easily broken, 100:7
    themselves when he did sing, 225:19
    what water lapping b., 677:20
    when trees b. heads, 512:8
    with my b. and arrow, 893:8
Bowed, at her feet he b., 10:12
    by weight of centuries, 557:3

Bowed *(continued)*
    he fell where he b., 10:12
    to idolatries patient knee, 395:23
Bowels, fatal b. of deep, 171:34
    news not yet reached my b., 816:9
    no belly no b., 682:1
    of Christ, 246:16, 614:2
    of compassion, 46:10
    were moved for him, 24:17
Bower, as Adam walking forth from b., 486:23
    charmed alike tilt-yard and b., 392:15
    in hall or b., 252:3
    in heaven's high b., 351:6
    keep b. quiet for us, 409:7
Bowers, blossoms birds and b., 240:9
Bowl, called for his b., 892:13
    golden b. be broken, 23:31
    goldfish in glass b., 608:6
    inverted B. we call Sky, 442:3
    life is b. of cherries, 697:8
    Love in a golden b., 351:9
    lurk I in gossip's b., 178:12
    of Night, 441:5
    roasted crabs hiss in b., 175:1
    went to sea in b., 893:17
Bowled, in bowling alley b. sun, 280:15
Bows down to wood and stone, 391:7
Bowwow, big B. strain, 382:*n*1
Bowwows, demnition b., 464:25
Box, alabaster b. of ointment, 35:32
    arm's too short to b. with God, 610:3
    paper you drop in ballot b., 474:6
    pathway to ballot b., 471:8
    twelve good men into b., 385:8
    where sweets compacted lie, 242:20
Boxer's, study one b. problem, 738:11
Boxin' Day, beadle on B., 463:28
Boy, barefoot b. 438:7
    be a farmer's b., 882:11
    beamish b., 515:13
    beggarly b., 482:7
    blueeyed b., 701:7
    Chatterton marvelous b., 369:16
    close upon the growing b., 370:17
    dead girl or a live b., 815:12
    didn't raise b. to be soldier, 887:5
    eternal, 223:9
    every b. and every gal, 526:22
    guiding a b. and a girl, 850:7
    if b. have not woman's gift, 173:5
    imagination of b. healthy, 409:6
    is most powerful of Hellenes, 62:18
    Jewish man remain fifteen-year-old b.,
      835:5
    lad of mettle a good b., 182:16
    let b. win his spurs, 131:2
    like b. playing on seashore, 279:18
    lily-livered b., 217:17
    little b. blue, 893:10
    Little B. Blue kissed them, 554:2
    little tiny b., 205:29
    love is a b., 262:17
    make a small b. dizzy, 755:15
    Minstrel B., 387:12
    most unmanageable of all animals, 76:10
    my greatness, 219:10
    my lovely living b., 155:3

Boy *(continued)*
    nineteen-year-old American b., 850:2
    office b. to Attorney's firm, 525:22
    only way to make b. sharp, 463:25
    parlous b., 171:31
    purblind wayward b., 174:14
    read to by a b., 675:21
    smiling b. fell dead, 459:23
    speak roughly to little b., 514:10
    stood on burning deck, 405:6
    too much hope of thee loved b., 232:10
    well for fisherman's b., 452:15
    what a good b. am I, 892:19
    who lives down lane, 893:4
    who looks after sheep, 893:11
    will you marry it, 833:1
    wine dear b. and truth, 55:19
    you can take b. out of country, 712:14
Boyhood changing into man, 595:3
    ignominy of b., 595:3
Boyhood's years, 387:17
Boyish, all wars b., 483:19
Boylston Street, on B. photograph, 788:1
Boy's best friend is mother, 800:13
    love, 212:10
    will wind's will, 437:9
Boys, all wars fought by b., 483:19
    and girls level with men, 219:5
    and girls together, 581:2
    are marching, 489:8
    as b. do sparrows, 284:3
    as flies to wanton b., 212:17
    claret the liquor for b., 310:24
    do the boogie woogie, 861:12
    do what Asian b. ought to be doing,
      753:16
    exposed for sale, 121:28
    generous b. in happiness bred, 483:20
    girls will be b., 859:3
    lightfoot b., 575:10
    little b. made of, 895:11
    mealy b. beef-faced b., 464:11
    not about to send American b., 753:16
    not sent into foreign wars, 653:2
    rally round flag b., 489:9
    see what b. in back room will have, 761:17
    steady b. steady, 316:20
    that swim on bladders, 225:25
    them good old b., 861:11
    there we saw men and b., 883:*n*4
    three merry b. are we, 236:6
    throw stones at frogs, 82:9
    till b. come home, 616:17
    you may hang these b., 568:9
Brace lace latch or catch, 546:21
    ourselves to duties, 619:15
Bracelet of bright hair, 230:2
Brach, Lady the b., 211:7
    rather hear Lady my b., 183:1
Bracing, drying after b. showers, 708:13
Bradford, there goes John B., 149:8
Brae, waly doun the b., 890:8
Braes, banks and b. o' bonny Doon, 357:6
    green b., 357:19
Brag, beauty is Nature's b., 252:25
    left this vault to b. of, 215:30
    old b. of my heart, 832:13
    one went to b., 263:2

Bread *(continued)*

living Homer begged b., 233:*n3*
Loaf of B. and Thou, 441:10
looked to Government for b., 325:14
neither yet b. to wise, 23:23
nor his seed begging b., 16:11
not live by b. only, 9:18
of adversity, 26:12
of affliction, 12:10
of deceit is sweet, 21:13
of heaven, 18:12
of idleness, 22:19
of life, 39:18
on which side b. buttered, 148:20
quarrel with b. and butter, 285:18
ravens brought him b., 11:40
seven days shall ye eat unleavened b., 7:42
shows b. in other hand, 83:10
sky daily b. of eyes, 425:11
some gave white b., 892:18
staff of life, 282:16
strengthens man's heart, 282:16
took b. and blessed it, 36:3
took b. and brake it, 151:14
unleavened b. and bitter herbs, 7:39
we want b. and roses too, 886:18
went on cutting b. and butter, 459:14
white b. and butter, 893:14
who ne'er his b. in sorrow ate, 342:14
whole stay of b., 24:36
with b. and wine walk road, 898:6
with one fish ball, 500:3
with you more than bread, 683:3
wringing b. from sweat, 447:1
Breadline, if world tranquil I'd be in b., 807:10
Breadth, taller by b. of nail, 284:24
Break, bend but do not b., 266:10
best you get is even b., 647:1
better to bow than b., 147:10
bids it b., 217:7
bloody glass, 751:2
break break, 452:15
bruised reed shall he not b., 26:34
civilizations b. fail to meet challenge, 685:8
embraces, 748:7
faith with us who die, 614:7
given thee till b. of day, 352:11
hugest hearts that b., 511:2
I'll b. my staff, 225:4
into blossoms, 817:9
into hundred thousand flaws, 211:23
it to our hope, 217:29
mounting at b. of day, 371:25
never give sucker even b., 566:19
never knew land to run away or b., 330:13
O to b. loose like chinook, 788:5
oath he never made, 262:19
off last lamenting kiss, 230:4
onetwothreefourfive pigeons, 701:7
rooster crows at b. of dawn, 851:4
shins against wit, 194:10
that sole bond, 324:12
those eyes the b. of day, 207:8
thou'll b. my heart, 357:6
time to b. down, 22:31
true believers b. eggs at convenient end, 284:25

Break *(continued)*

until the day b., 24:11
up by b. of day, 242:17
you b. it you own it, 843:2
you may b. you may shatter, 387:14
Breakdown, madness need not be all b., 816:1
Breakers, more dangerous b., 398:22
wandering by lone sea b., 549:13
wantoned with b., 396:22
Breakfalls, holds rolls throws b., 776:13
Breakfast, from b. to madness, 820:8
hope is good b. bad supper, 165:6
kills seven dozen Scots at b., 182:17
six impossible things before b., 516:13
where our b. take, 890:3
with appetite, 225:22
Breakfasts at five-o'clock tea, 517:3
Breaking, gray dawn b., 419:5, 635:15
sleep that knows not b., 373:21
stop Heart from b., 510:4
through foul and ugly mists, 181:33
tired waves vainly b., 479:12
waves dashed high, 405:4
wrestled until b. of day, 7:2
Breaks, beauty that b. hearts, 631:10
bough b. cradle fall, 550:7
butterfly upon wheel, 295:14
chains from every mind, 352:5
jest b. no bones, 311:6
lance of justice b., 212:30
law of gravity, 678:12
light through yonder window b., 179:31
like Atlantic Ocean, 787:14
my pate across, 199:17
rider that b. youth, 244:13
sooner every party b. up, 382:19
sorrow b. seasons, 171:30
sun b. through darkest clouds, 173:22
world b. everyone, 721:7
Breakthrough, madness may be b., 816:1
Breast, arm the obdured b., 256:23
deep in her b. lives silent wound, 94:22
Hampden with dauntless b., 316:1
heart at rest within b., 351:7
hope springs in human b., 294:19
lacerate his b., 595:8
my baby at my b., 219:16
Nature's learned b., 155:4
nunnery of thy chaste b., 265:17
of huge Mississippi, 496:11
one thought in b. another on tongue, 92:5
sail upon her patient b., 203:4
soothe a savage b., 287:1
soul wears out b., 397:14
sweetness flows into b., 595:5
thy b. encloseth my heart, 171:21
trembles in the b., 372:19
truth hath a quiet b., 176:12
two souls dwell in my b., 344:3
wail or knock the b., 260:25
weariness toss him to my b., 243:4
weary sprite longs fly from b., 226:24
Wedding Guest beat b., 375:21
what his b. forges, 219:32
Breastie, panic's in thy b., 356:4
Breastplate of faith, 44:20
what stronger b. than heart, 170:7

Breasts, come to my woman's b., 214:17
every salesman can fondle her b., 626:6
feel my b. all perfume, 650:18
from rocky b. forever flowing, 762:17
her b. are dun, 223:1
like two young roes, 24:13
touched her sleeping b., 717:3
Breath, a b. thou art, 206:33
a little flesh a little b., 111:8
bated b. and whispering humbleness, 184:29
boldest held his b., 384:12
breathes with human b., 450:12
by the gate of b., 530:6
call the fleeting b., 315:20
Chaucer whose sweet b., 450:22
dirt breathing a small b., 755:13
draw thy b. in pain, 202:31
dulcet and harmonious b., 178:15
ecstasy come to b., 713:4
every thing that hath b., 19:21
flattered its rank b., 395:23
fluttered failed for b., 495:20
fly away b., 205:3
from one mother both draw b., 64:4
give hautboys b. he comes, 274:16
giver of b. and bread, 546:5
he giveth b., 40:33
healthy b. of morn, 411:12
hearest hardly a b., 344:19
heaven's b. smells wooingly, 214:21
hot and cold with same b., 59:11
if b. terrible as terminations, 190:27
is in his nostrils, 24:35
kept b. to cool his pottage, 55:5
lightly draws its b., 368:2
love endures for b., 529:14
make them as breath made, 322:22
mouth-honor b., 217:18
my quiet b., 410:9
never drawn b. of life, 595:1
no b. at all, 213:14
of Autumn's being, 402:9
of life, 5:10, 595:1
of new-mown hay, 609:10
of the night-wind, 496:19
poetry b. of knowledge, 369:3
possession outvalues others last b., 524:17
princes but b. of kings, 356:10
rides on posting winds, 220:20
smiles tears of life, 434:18
some of us out of b., 516:5
stealing my b. of life, 687:12
stilling my b., 789:12
summer's ripening b., 180:11
sweet is the b. of morn, 257:26
thought takes b. away, 500:1
thy b. was shed, 599:14
toil of b., 380:8
took one long slow b., 578:15
utter sweet b., 179:5
want of words lack of b., 260:17
weary of b., 418:13
whiskey on your b., 755:15
world gray from thy b., 530:9
Breathe air again, 489:8
and blow, 452:18
as though to b. life, 451:14

Breathe *(continued)*
daring to b. or Achoo, 833:7
hate were why men b., 701:19
hear bronze Negroes b., 787:19
heart pause to b., 397:14
his native air, 292:4
if such there b., 373:3
not his name, 387:6
slaves cannot b. in England, 326:21
thou thereon didst only b., 232:17
yearning to b. free, 552:16
you but knock b. shine, 230:26
Breathed, still b. in sighs, 293:22
Breathes, hell itself b. out, 200:29
of nations saved, 398:26
there the man, 373:3
upon bank of violets, 204:10
with human breath, 450:12
Breathing, almost hear them b. as they march,
787:*n*5
health and quiet b., 409:7
household laws, 370:4
music b. from her face, 265:*n*5
talking coeval with b., 286:17
whether b. is eating, 73:17
without a tighter b., 510:6
Breathless, hanging b. on fate, 436:23
we flung us on hill, 669:5
with adoration, 370:5
Breath's a ware that will not keep, 574:12
Bred, dainties b. of a book, 174:15
en bawn in brier-patch, 551:14
me long ago, 575:8
where is fancy b., 185:17
Bredon, bells sound on B., 575:1
Breeches, coat red b. blue, 381:19
hand in b. pocket, 412:16
women wear the b., 234:12
Breed and haunt, 214:21
border nor b. nor birth, 587:8
feared by their b., 176:24
happy b. of men, 176:24
if sun b. maggots, 198:33
more careful of horses, 280:10
or England b. again, 167:10
use doth b. habit, 173:37
Breeding, bad b. and vulgar manner, 72:12
Burgundy without b., 704:6
eating drinking and b., 486:7
lilacs out of dead land, 676:5
test of man or woman's b., 564:14
who misleads not man of b., 80:14
write with ease to show b., 346:19
Breeds, familiarity b. contempt, 58:19
lesser b. without Law, 589:10
Breeze, Athena sent favorable b., 52:26
battle and the b., 384:8
fair b. blew, 376:1
flag to April's b., 424:17
folds rippling in b., 459:2
ghost fled like fluttering b., 94:18
plastic and vast one intellectual b., 375:16
that beat upon her, 556:20
tyranny in tainted b., 324:7
Breezes, sunset b. shiver, 582:10
Breezy call of Morn, 315:15
Brekekekex, 73:14
Brennt Paris, 684:*n*7

Brent, bonie brow was b., 357:13
Brer Fox he lay low, 551:13
Brethren, firstborn among many b., 41:22
for b. to dwell together, 19:10
forget love to friends and b., 29:23
least of these my b., 35:31
our b. already in field, 331:13
we be b., 6:28
Brève, la vie est b., 519:*n*3
Brevis, vita b. est, 71:*n*2
Brevity, its body b., 378:5
soul of lingerie, 699:16
soul of wit, 198:26
Brew that is true, 775:10
Brewed, taste liquor never b., 508:8
Brewer, not from benevolence of b., 318:22
Brewer's, I am a b. horse, 183:7
Brews, as he b. so shall he drink, 231:16
livelier liquor than Muse, 575:12
Bribe, too poor for b., 316:17
Bribed by loyalties and ambitions, 694:7
Bribery, treason b. or other high crimes,
339:12
Bribes, tell everyone I take b., 442:21
Brick, just another b. in the wall, 858:13
no more straw to make b., 7:32
road paved with yellow b., 562:3
Bricks, Rome a city of b., 99:6
somebody's always throwing b., 639:12
Bridal, bridegrooms brides and b. cakes, 240:9
of earth and sky, 242:19
Bride, always bridesmaid never b., 660:2
American b. taken to Niagara, 559:17
barren b., 293:26
bridegroom seek your b., 575:19
encounter darkness as a b., 206:36
goes to walk returns with b., 775:7
holy city as a b., 47:11
I was a b., 840:10
in her rich adornin', 551:3
never turns to b., 574:13
of quietness, 410:13
paced into the hall, 375:22
Bride-bed, thought b. to have decked, 202:18
Bridechamber, can children of b. mourn, 33:33
Bridegroom all night through, 574:13
coming out of his chamber, 15:16
fresh as a b., 181:35
happy b. Hesper brings, 575:19
I was the b., 840:10
in my death, 219:2
mourn as b. with them, 33:33
went forth to meet b., 35:25
Bridegrooms brides and bridal cakes, 240:9
Bridesmaid, always b. never bride, 660:2
Brides, bridegrooms b. and bridal cakes, 240:9
Bridge, and the b. is love, 715:2
asses' b., 82:*n*1
at highest point in arc of b., 767:8
body swung beneath b., 540:1
broken arch of London B., 419:17
build b. where no river, 703:1
don't cross b. until come to it, 884:11
from nothing to being no b., 542:13
give him silver b., 898:4
London B. falling down, 581:2, 892:20
of Sighs, 395:25
over troubled water, 855:10

Bridge *(continued)*
rickety wooden b., 850:7
rude b. that arched the flood, 424:17
twenty men crossing b., 640:11
youth build b. to moon, 473:6
Bridgeport said I pointing, 523:13
Bridges, crossing twenty b., 640:11
crumble the b., 724:6
flock of b. bleating, 643:17
forbids to sleep under b., 546:2
Bridle, between spur and b., 244:16
gae his b. reins a shake, 357:12
Brief as lightning in collied night, 177:28
as woman's love, 200:18
chronicles of the time, 199:13
December day, 438:15
dreamy kind delight, 591:17
hours and weeks, 222:15
little b. authority, 206:28
out out b. candle, 217:23
transit where dreams cross, 677:18
when b. I become obscure, 98:18
when our b. light has set, 91:5
Briefcase, steal more money with b., 795:8
Brier, bred en bawn in b.-patch, 551:14
thorough bush thorough b., 178:10
Briers, full of b. is working-day world, 193:33
Brig, mate of Nancy b., 525:16
Brigade, Light B., 454:19
Bright, all calm all b., 401:5
all calm as it was b., 268:14
all things b. beautiful, 476:4
and battering sandal, 546:16
and violet-crowned, 64:7
angels are b. still, 217:5
Apollo's lute, 174:23
April shakes out her hair, 660:13
autumn moon is b., 732:15
best of dark and b., 397:1
billows smooth and b., 515:20
bodies of lovers drowned, 643:21
bracelet of b. hair, 230:2
container can contain, 756:6
countenance of truth, 253:21
creature scorn not one, 372:17
dark with excessive b., 257:8
day is done, 219:9
day so cool so calm so b., 242:19
exhalation in the evening, 225:23
eye of heaven shined b., 160:5
eyes of danger, 556:5
girdle furled, 496:19
gleam of noble deeds, 64:5
goddess excellently b., 232:2
harmony in her b. eye, 265:16
he saw lady b., 889:27
honor b., 203:22
is the ring of words, 556:7
keep up your b. swords, 207:30
ladies whose b. eyes, 251:7
lamps shone o'er, 395:13
moon shines b., 186:14
moon still as b., 397:14
morning star gets wonderful b., 715:4
musical as b. Apollo's lute, 174:23
not gold that showeth b., 125:*n*2
orange b., 267:6
particular star, 205:31

Bronze, hear b. Negroes breathe, 787:19
   heart of b., 50:25
   mangled by the b. spear, 52:13
   monument more lasting than b., 97:9
   nailed like illegible b., 788:10
   stone b. stone steel, 677:21
   up from b. I saw, 713:5
   work with breathing b., 94:35
Bronzed lank man, 639:16
Brooch, bow or b. or braid, 546:21
   of gold ful sheene, 133:16
Brooches, make you b. and toys, 556:6
Brood, mothers a bloody b., 708:6
   of Folly, 251:10
Brooding, birds sit b. in snow, 175:1
   on God, 756:13
   sad b. on country's fate, 479:8
Brook, dwelt by the b. Cherith, 11:39
   many can b. the weather, 174:16
   noise like hidden b., 376:19
   smooth water where b. deep, 159:*n4*
   went to the b., 896:12
Brookland, far in western b., 575:8
Brooklyn, I am patriot of B., 691:1
   lifetime to know B., 727:13
   tree grows in B., 740:5
Brooks, as hart panteth after water b., 16:21
   books in running b., 193:37
   for fishers of song, 569:12
   golden sands crystal b., 229:14
   I sing of b., 240:9
   shallow b. and rivers wide, 251:3
   strow b. in Vallombrosa, 255:17
   too broad for leaping, 575:10
Broom, beat barrel with b., 639:13
   new b. sweeps clean, 880:6
   under arm carried b., 895:4
Broomstick, write finely upon b., 284:*n2*
Broomsticks, all their b. and tears, 593:3
Broth without any bread, 894:8
Brother, am I not man and b., 326:2
   and companion in tribulation, 46:14
   be my b. or I kill you, 335:2
   Big B. watching, 735:16
   came with subtilty, 6:40
   can you spare dime, 711:9
   dead divine b. of all, 487:8
   Death's b. Sleep, 94:29
   every one said to his b., 26:33
   every sword against his b., 28:20
   far off, 22:3
   fight against his b., 25:25
   gently scan b. man, 357:3
   give back my young b., 819:12
   hypocrite reader my b., 491:1
   I am darker b., 731:3
   I am that insect b., 492:8
   lawless linsey-woolsey b., 262:15
   life sweet b., 423:6
   lo'ed him like a b., 358:5
   man and b., 326:2
   my double my b., 491:1
   no b. near the throne, 295:13
   of the Angle, 244:35
   offended is harder to be won, 21:3
   Remus and his b. knew this life, 93:20
   shall be my b., 190:1
   sinned against my b. the ass, 126:1

Brother *(continued)*
   sleep Death's twin b., 51:*n2*
   sleep the b. of death, 51:30
   Sleep the B. to Death, 167:3
   sticketh closer than a b., 21:5
   still to my b. turns, 321:12
   Sun who brings us day, 125:9
   thy tail hangs down, 588:17
   to dragons, 14:9
   which of us known b., 727:11
   would brother cheat, 125:7
Brotherhood, crown good with b., 572:5
   love the b., 45:39
   men and women affirm b., 751:9
   of the Right Stuff, 831:6
   sit down at table of b., 823:7
   that binds brave, 582:8
Brotherly, feel it so b., 769:14
   love, 41:31, 45:15
Brother's, called b. father dad, 175:10
   keeper, 6:4
   mote in b. eye, 33:13
   murder, 200:31
   sad mad b. name, 530:24
   voice of thy b. blood, 6:5
   what I sowed b. sons gathering, 730:1
Brothers, all men born are my b., 485:17
   all the b. too, 205:5
   and Sisters beware, 589:25
   as b. live together, 437:1
   band of b., 190:1
   call from bay, 494:12
   forty thousand b., 202:20
   goodbye b., 567:6
   linsey-woolsey b., 297:1
   men become b., 359:10
   our dearly beloved b., 794:12
   shall b. be for a' that, 358:20
   valiant sisters virtuous, 882:9
   ye are b. ye are men, 384:13
Brought, Antony b. drunken forth, 219:10
   before the mountains were b. forth, 17:23
   daughters of music b. low, 23:30
   death into this world, 255:3
   forth on this continent, 446:5
   I b. myself down, 771:11
   me home to glory, 447:12
   mouse will be b. forth, 98:23
   never b. to min', 357:17
   nothing into this world, 44:34
   over vast and furious ocean, 240:2
   up in this city, 40:42
   which b. us hither, 371:3
Brow, athlete crowned in sweat of b., 115:2
   bonie b. was brent, 357:13
   candid b., 567:11
   dangerous b. by night, 192:3
   flushing his b., 409:21
   forty winters besiege thy b., 220:31
   grace seated on this b., 201:5
   Helen's beauty in b. of Egypt, 179:6
   no wrinkle on azure b., 396:19
   now your b. is beld John, 357:13
   of labor, 577:18
   of lip of eye of b., 222:9
   pain and anguish wring b., 373:16
   parallels in beauty's b., 221:17
   pure unclouded b., 515:10

Brow *(continued)*
   sweat of b., 474:20
   upon his b. shame ashamed, 180:33
   view with wrinkled b., 186:7
   wet with honest sweat, 436:12
   where he got that high b., 109:7
   wrinkle deeper on b., 395:9
Brown, baked me too b., 515:5
   bread and the Gospel, 282:17
   bright nightingale, 529:12
   changing from b. suit to gray, 664:3
   color called Landlord's B., 831:1
   hair and speaks small, 186:24
   green and b. expanse, 686:12
   hair over mouth, 677:15
   heath and shaggy wood, 373:4
   hills melted into spring, 476:11
   in b. study, 161:21
   Jeanie with light b. hair, 503:14
   long and lank and b., 376:13
   man's burden, 589:*n1*
   meadows b. and sere, 406:2
   myrtles b., 252:29
   not Old B. any longer, 475:27
   prefer philanthropy of Captain B., 475:25
   quick b. fox, 885:19
   some gave them b., 892:18
   strong b. god, 679:3
   world black red yellow b., 836:11
Brownies, Cub Scouts and B., 796:7
Browning, entsichere meinen B., 687:*n2*
   find B. plain, 461:*n1*
   Mrs. B. guard silence, 626:14
Browning's, Mrs. B. death relief, 442:11
Brown's, John B. body, 521:1
Brows, bliss in our b. bent, 218:7
   dark rebellious b., 488:2
   earned with sweat of b., 155:12
   like gathering storm, 358:3
   nodded with his darkish b., 50:18
   not seen in either of our b., 167:11
   of dauntless courage, 255:26
Bruce has aften led, 358:16
Brüder, alle Menschen werden B., 359:*n2*
Bruise, axe fitter to b., 261:13
   better for b. than arnica, 462:27
   it shall b. thy head, 5:23
   thou shalt b. his heel, 5:23
Bruised, body not b. to pleasure soul, 594:17
   reed shall he not break, 26:34
   together crushed and b., 293:14
Brunswick, Hamelin town's in B., 460:6
Brunt, bear b. pay arrears, 462:25
   stands b. of life, 67:23
Brush, blind hand b. my wing, 352:15
   essential in painting, 122:11
   George B. is my name, 715:3
   painter's b. consumes dreams, 594:13
   whether chisel pen b., 593:6
   whitewash and long-handled b., 522:7
   work with so fine a b., 383:1
Brushed past palms on staircase, 745:4
Brushwood sheaf, 460:18
Brutal arm appear, 597:3
   most b. thing nineteen-year-old boy, 850:2
Brutality, industry without art b., 484:20
   oppressor commit b. openly, 823:14
   that special b., 493:11

Brutalizing lower class, 497:19
Brute beauty and valor, 546:11
    chuck 'im out the b., 587:17
    heart of brute like you, 833:9
    love of a b., 448:16
    use wit drive b. off, 799:6
Brute, et tu B., 89:*n3*, 192:16
Brutes, exterminate b., 567:16
    nation of b., 567:*n2*
    not born to live like b., 129:6
    without you, 281:12
Brutish, nasty b. and short, 239:10
Brutus and Cassius not displayed, 110:3
    Caesar had his B., 331:8
    dear B., 191:26
    is an honorable man, 192:29
    makes mine greater, 193:11
    no orator as B. is, 193:3
    not kill B. not kill sons of B., 142:9
    you also B., 89:7
Bubble, fire burn cauldron b., 216:26
    gonfalon b., 646:12
    in stream, 112:26
    like b. on fountain, 373:23
    now a b. burst, 294:18
    reputation, 194:25
    world's a b., 166:22
Bubbles, borne like thy b. onward, 396:22
    earth hath b., 214:7
    man and his dwellings as b., 125:5
    we buy, 481:15
    winking at brim, 410:4
Bubbling and loud-hissing urn, 327:1
    cry of swimmer, 398:9
    sinks with b. groan, 396:18
Buccaneers of Buzz, 511:4
Buchenwald, believe what I said about B.,
    754:10
Buck in the snow, 695:16
    stops here, 661:13
Bucket down and full of tears am I, 177:17
    drop of a b., 26:30
    every day the b. go a well, 861:5
    old oaken b., 393:13
    past a b. of ashes, 636:5
    up doun as b. in a welle, 134:16
Buckets into empty wells, 326:23, 375:1
    two b. filling one another, 177:17
Buckingham, so much for B., 287:14
Buckle, pride plume here b., 546:11
Buckler, his truth thy shield and b., 17:28
Buckles, silver b. on knee, 897:2
Bucks, fat black b., 639:13
Bud, canker lives in sweetest b., 221:11
    in age I b. again, 243:7
    not as in b. of spring, 231:10
    rose is sweeter in b., 162:7
    this b. of love, 180:11
    worm i' the b., 205:4
Buddha, go for refuge to B., 64:20
    the Awakened One, 64:13
    the Godhead resides, 820:1
Buddy, Christ Himself b., 793:12
Budge, I'll not b. an inch, 173:4
Buds, cankers in musk-rose b., 178:20
    darling b. of May, 221:2
    green b. they were swellin', 889:25
    of barren flowers, 530:16

Buds *(continued)*
    soul breaks and b., 268:12
Buff and the blue, 359:3
Buffalo Bill's defunct, 701:7
    gals come out tonight, 885:4
    home where b. roam, 890:20
    life breath of b. in wintertime, 492:1
    thought he saw B., 517:9
    wind on b. grass, 891:10
Buffaloes, water b. neurasthenic, 671:23
Buffet, not wise who b. against love, 66:10
Buffets, blows and b. of world, 216:7
    fortune's b. and rewards, 200:11
Buffon, is it Aristotle Pliny B., 312:25
Buffoon, chemist fiddler and b., 273:2
Buffoonery, life piece of b., 601:4
Buffoons, great men not b., 428:3
Bug, flap b. with gilded wings, 295:15
    snug as a b. in rug, 303:9
Buggy, we met a gentleman in a b., 382:24
Bugle, blow b. blow, 452:19
    one blast upon b. horn, 374:4
    sound upon b. horn, 451:20
Bugles, blow out you b., 669:12
    cry of b. going by, 579:10
    what are b. blowin' for, 587:14
Build beneath stars, 291:5
    better mousetrap, 425:*n2*
    except the Lord b. the house, 19:4
    experience arch to b. upon, 531:7
    from bottom up, 651:14
    Great Society, 753:15
    houses and inhabit them, 27:22
    I can't b. up my hopes, 822:7
    if you b. it he will come, 840:5
    intending to b. tower, 38:8
    lofty rhyme, 253:1
    me nest on greatness of God, 543:2
    me straight, 436:21
    middle-aged b. woodshed, 473:6
    pair nor b. nor sing, 378:14
    ship of death, 663:23
    small cabin b. there, 591:2
    takes carpenter to b. barn, 651:11
    that dome in air, 377:23
    thee more stately mansions, 443:10
    they labor in vain that b. it, 19:4
    throne of bayonets, 579:6
    time to b. up, 22:31
    upon this rock b. my church, 34:37
    youth b. bridge to moon, 473:6
Builded better than knew, 424:5
    was Jerusalem b. here, 354:8
    wisdom hath b. her house, 20:7
Builder, I will be a free b., 505:5
Builders, stone which the b. refused, 18:25
Buildeth on vulgar heart, 187:38
Building castles in Spain, 137:14
    Elvis has left the b., 798:10
    I hope you won't have b., 571:7
    principal beauty in a b., 250:3
    roofs of gold, 188:35
    stole life o' the b., 215:28
    three things in b., 343:10
    we are nation b., 670:1
Buildings he may never enter, 343:13
    leap tall b. at single bound, 777:1
    new ideas must use old b., 782:5

Buildings *(continued)*
    riding in taxi between tall b., 710:10
    when Luftwaffe knocked down b., 866:1
    will collapse, 740:1
    you may have all the b., 512:15
Builds, Devil b. chapel there, 282:4
    Heaven in Hell's despair, 352:12
    Hell in Heaven's despite, 352:13
    marsh hen secretly b., 543:2
    phoenix b. phoenix' nest, 263:12
    phoenix b. spicy nest, 245:16
Built absolute trust, 214:15
    against will of gods, 51:23
    before I b. wall, 622:12
    bicycle b. for two, 598:3
    fortress b. by Nature for herself, 176:24
    house that Jack b., 897:8
    in such logical way, 443:12
    in the eclipse, 253:8
    love b. on beauty, 230:6
    nests in beard, 467:3
    of just a syllable, 511:2
    Rome not b. in one day, 147:25
    ruined love when b. anew, 222:18
    science b. with facts, 558:8
    till we have b. Jerusalem, 354:8
    what might've been b. anywhere, 148:29
    which b. desolate places, 13:4
Bulben's, bare Ben B. head, 597:10
Bulimia, yuppie version of b., 852:2
Bull, a Cock and a B., 314:21
    be on b. side, 529:8
    cloud that looked like b., 72:14
    handsome as b. that kidnapped Europa,
      87:24
    John B. or Englishman's Fireside, 361:6
    moose, 571:2
    savage b. bear yoke, 190:19
Bullet, ballot or the b., 808:14
    ballot stronger than b., 444:7
    bite b., 587:9
    faster than speeding b., 777:1
    like b. can undeceive, 483:21
    that will kill me not cast, 365:11
    through his head, 605:19
    who paid for the b., 757:12
Bullets, assure you I heard B., 328:3
    made of lead, 896:12
    paper b. of the brain, 190:36
    seek out where heart lies, 739:2
    word as b. flying, 567:7
Bullied out of vice, 429:14
Bullocks, whose talk is of b., 31:25
Bullpen, waiting sentence in b., 787:10
Bulls, plowman's story of b., 101:13
Bullshit, rest is b., 855:5
Bullying social ritual, 857:13
Bulrushes, ark of b., 7:23
Bulwark, floating b. of our island, 318:18
    never failing, 143:16
    greatest b. of capitalism, 605:1
    of continuing liberty, 652:18
    of Greece famous Athens, 64:7
Bulwarks, Britannia needs no b., 384:9
    greatest b. of liberty, 320:9
Bum, belly shoulder b., 597:3
    I'll moider de b., 761:10
    let's face it I am, 776:17

Bumbast out blank verse, 164:3
Bumble, the law is a ass said Mr. B., 464:13
Bump, don't b. into furniture, 719:17
   go b. in the night, 884:8
Bumping, love b. against obstacles of
   civilization, 432:5
Bumpy, fasten seatbelts b. night, 759:4
Bunbury, invaluable invalid B., 560:20
Bunch-backed, curse this pois'nous b. toad,
   171:24
Bunghole, stopping a b., 202:13
Bunk, history more or less b., 496:*n*1
Bunker Hill, there is Boston and B., 390:7
Buns, hot cross b., 894:15
Bunt, not stepping up to b., 827:1
Bunting, baby b., 894:3
Buoy too small for sight, 212:24
Burbled as it came, 515:13
Burden, bear any b., 785:10
   bear his own b., 43:32
   borne the b., 35:6
   brown man's b., 589:*n*1
   grasshopper shall be a b., 23:31
   great b. upon his back, 271:8
   grievous b. was thy birth, 171:37
   her lot not b., 824:4
   my b. is light, 34:9
   not b. our remembrances, 225:7
   of his song, 331:1
   of incommunicable, 393:4
   of my song, 881:2
   of the desert of the sea, 25:26
   of the mystery, 368:8
   of them is intolerable, 49:5
   on back b. of world, 557:3
   reputation was, 726:2
   vapors weep their b., 455:5
   weight of another's b., 244:21
   White Man's b., 589:12
   years are still a b., 67:8
   youth and age equally a b., 74:18
Burdens, had such b. on mind, 594:10
   they that bare b., 12:28
Burdensome, school in which nothing b.,
   117:1
   when life is b., 69:18
Bureaucracy, power wielded by pygmies,
   417:17
   not obstacle to democracy, 657:23
   the rule of nobody, 744:5
Burgeoning wood brings forth, 51:11
Burgess, early days of the B. Shale, 852:6
Burglaree, with a little b., 526:9
Burglary, flat b. as ever committed, 191:8
   vary piracee with b., 526:9
Burgonet, arm and b. of men, 218:12
Burgundy, naive domestic B., 704:6
Burial, no b. this pretty pair, 880:14
   of my rosy feelings, 810:18
Buried, bodies are b. in peace, 31:28
   body to be b. obscurely, 166:21
   Caesar bled, 441:14
   dies and is b. with them, 68:20
   get yourself b., 747:5
   go get yourself b., 685:1
   graveyard of b. hopes, 627:6
   here children born one b., 445:1
   him before prime, 890:5

Buried *(continued)*
   lie deep b., 59:23
   life, 495:11
   not b. in consecrated ground, 536:3
   old Adam b., 49:23
   on Sunday, 895:10
   problem lay b., 796:7
   putrid corpse of liberty, 657:3
   they b. him, 611:2
   want to be b. among mountains, 507:12
   was crucified dead and b., 48:11
   where Michael Furey b., 650:9
Buries empires in common grave, 332:10
   universal darkness b. all, 297:6
Burke said Reporters' Gallery Fourth Estate,
   406:*n*1
Burma girl a-settin', 588:1
   got run out of B., 658:2
Burn and rave, 777:15
   another Troy to b., 592:4
   better to b. out, 862:7
   better to marry than b., 42:15
   books burn human beings, 415:3
   catch a fire so you can get b., 861:4
   children will b., 893:2
   everything or throw into water, 144:12
   fire b. cauldron bubble, 216:26
   frost itself doth b., 201:7
   great sphere thou movest in, 219:3
   heart b. within us, 38:42
   I'll b. my books, 169:6
   like fabulous roman candles, 799:3
   manuscripts don't b., 689:7
   no blazing hearth b., 315:16
   old wood to b., 165:8
   out false shames, 663:13
   some b. damp faggots, 592:17
   stars that round her b., 287:21
   the towers, 724:6
   time the fire in which we b., 772:1
   to the socket, 372:6
   violent fires soon b. out, 176:23
   we b. daylight, 179:24
   what thou hast worshipped, 116:24
   with hard gemlike flame, 534:8
   you bid me b. letters, 329:17
Burned, and his feet not be b., 20:3
   bush b. with fire, 7:25
   candle b. on the table, 688:6
   feared witches and b. women, 562:9
   feet as if b. in a furnace, 46:17
   give my body to be b., 42:27
   half his Troy was b., 187:22
   heart ne'er within b., 373:3
   is Apollo's laurel bough, 169:7
   Matilda and house b., 606:13
   money b. out his purse, 143:6
   my life, 713:4
   on the water, 218:20
   some b. alive, 801:17
   take fire and his clothes not be b., 20:3
   topless towers of Ilium, 168:21
   while I was musing the fire b., 16:16
   word b. like a lamp, 31:29
   worship what thou hast b., 116:24
Burning and shining light, 39:14
   bow of b. gold, 354:8
   boy stood on b. deck, 405:6

Burning *(continued)*
   Bronx is b., 790:1
   burns out another's b., 179:21
   clove, 623:10
   eyes, 819:12
   fire in mind ever b., 159:4
   for ancient connection, 812:13
   I'm ten years b. down the road, 868:5
   is Paris b., 684:18
   keep home fires b., 616:17
   lifetime b. in moment, 679:1
   marle, 255:16
   pretty Babe all b. bright, 167:1
   roof and tower, 594:16
   Sappho, 398:15
   seraphim in b. row, 253:18
   three words as with b. pen, 359:11
   Tyger Tyger b. bright, 353:1
   your lights b., 38:5
Burnished, barge like b. throne, 218:20
   livery of b. sun, 184:33
Burns, blood that freezes blood that b., 461:2
   candle b. at both ends, 695:8
   not she which b. in 't, 223:16
   one fire b. out another's, 179:21
   Shelley with us, 460:13
   smell fire whose gown b., 243:18
   what b. me now, 756:13
   when the blood b., 197:28
Burnside, waly yon b., 890:8
Burnt, charmed water b. alway, 376:16
   child fire dreadeth, 148:1
   Christians b. each other, 398:1
   fire of thine eyes, 353:1
   millions of innocent b., 336:8
   night's candles are b. out, 181:2
   offering, 6:35
   offerings, 28:35
Burr, I am a kind of b., 207:12
Burrow, go b. underground, 666:5
Burrs and thorns of life, 409:4
Burst cannon's roar, 443:3
   first that ever b., 376:1
   hot heart's shell, 483:3
   now a bubble b., 294:18
Bursts, melodious b., 450:22
Burthen of the mystery, 368:8
   vapors weep their b., 455:5
   weight of another's b., 244:21
Bury body in San Francisco, 719:11
   for nothing, 465:1
   Great Duke, 454:14
   I come to b. Caesar, 192:28
   it fathoms in earth, 225:4
   let dead b. their dead, 33:28
   living scarce able to b. dead, 240:4
   me in their buryingplace, 7:18
   me not on lone prairie, 890:17
   me out on prairie, 890:18
   my heart at Wounded Knee, 715:19
   no one to b., 678:20
   physician can b. mistakes, 606:6
   we will b. you, 702:19
Buryingplace, bury me in their b., 7:18
Bus, either on b. or off b., 840:4
   Hitler missed b., 604:2
   night journey on b., 803:8
Buses, mastodons like muddy b., 821:1

C

Cabots talk only to God, 577:15
Cackles, codfish never c., 886:4
    groans and dies, 404:20
Cadence, harsh c. of rugged line, 273:16
    to his verse a smooth c., 278:2
    tremulous c. slow, 496:17
Cadillac, first prize is a C. Eldorado, 865:8
Cadiz, reeking into C. Bay, 460:20
Cadmean victory, 69:9
Caecorum, in regione c. rex est luscus, 141:n6
Caelum, quid si nunc c. ruat, 86:n2
Caesar, appeal unto C., 41:3
    buried C. bled, 441:14
    carry C. in your boat, 89:3
    every wound of C., 193:5
    great C. fell, 193:1
    had his Brutus, 331:8
    I come to bury C., 192:28
    I came to lay C. out, 745:15
    imperious C. dead, 202:14
    not that I loved C. less, 192:25
    O mighty C., 192:19
    poor cried C. wept, 192:30
    render unto C., 35:12
    thou art mighty yet, 193:19
    upon what meat C. feed, 191:27
    word of C. stood, 192:32
Caesar's, dead C. trencher, 218:33
    hand Plato's brain, 425:6
    I am, 149:5
    poison from C. crown, 354:4
    wife must be above suspicion, 88:n14
Caesars, how many C. and Pompeys, 314:1
Café, every street c., 706:7
Caftan of tan with henna, 640:23
Caftans, lounging in their c., 828:18
Cage, gilded c., 607:6
    nor iron bars a c., 266:2
    put me in a c., 681:5
    robin redbreast in c., 353:15
    sing like birds i' the c., 213:8
    women put not on pedestal but in c.,
      745:12
Caged, know why c. bird sings, 613:13
Cages, marriage as with c., 153:12
Cain, land God gave to C., 144:15
    set a mark upon C., 6:8
    terre Dieu donna à C., 144:n3
    was tiller of the ground, 6:3
    went out from presence of the Lord, 6:9
Caissons go rolling along, 639:2
Caius is a man, 507:6
Cake, bake c. fast as can, 892:17
    eat c. and have it, 148:23
    Heaven's sugar c., 280:18
    let them eat c., 313:8
    my films slices of c., 722:12
    see to substance of c., 569:15
    some gave plum c., 892:18
Cakes and ale, 204:29
    bridegrooms brides and bridal c., 240:9
Calabash, goodnight Mrs. C., 697:12
Calais, find C. lying in my heart, 150:5
Calamities of life, 282:10
    of war, 307:5
Calamitous in drawn-out witticism, 384:1
    necessity of going on, 333:20
    to the conquered, 72:9

Calamity, fortune not satisfied with one c.,
    99:25
    makes c. of so long life, 199:21
    no c. greater than lavish desires, 57:15
Calamus, hinc quam sic c. saevior ense patet,
    235:5
Calaveras, celebrated jumping frog of C.
    county, 522:n1
    outjump any frog in C. county, 522:3
Calcaria, de c. in carbonarium, 113:n9
Calculate, no wisdom can c. end, 333:14
Calculated, nicely c. less or more, 372:14
    so c. so malignant, 694:3
Calculation shining out of other, 464:34
    sum defies c., 343:11
Calculations, most dangerous c. we call
    illusions, 673:19
Calculators, age of c., 325:4
Calculus, common sense reduced to c., 345:4
Caldron of dissolute loves, 116:1
Caledonia stern and wild, 373:4
Caledonia's, support C. cause, 359:3
Calendar, a c. look in almanack, 178:26
    striking from C., 442:1
    year of Julian C. 710, 237:13
Calf and young lion together, 25:19
    bring fatted c., 38:11
    false as wolf to c., 203:20
    killed c. in high style, 270:12
    second beast like a c., 46:28
Calf's-skin on recreant limbs, 175:14
Caliban, 'Ban 'Ban Ca-C., 224:26
Calico cat replied Mee-ow, 554:3
    Jam, 467:13
    Pie, 467:12
    tree, 467:12
California, from C. to New York island, 768:5
    if C. becomes prosperous country, 470:14
    is garden of Eden, 768:2
Californians race of people, 582:1
Calix sanguinis mei, 47:25
Call, almost like c. to come, 624:9
    back yesterday, 177:5, 233:17
    bawd a bawd, 81:n7
    brothers c. from bay, 494:12
    cattle home, 481:4
    delicate creatures ours, 209:9
    don't c. out National Guard, 661:2
    dunno what to c. 'im, 569:3
    fig a fig, 81:10
    for robin redbreast, 237:3
    forth thundering Aeschylus, 233:2
    gods to witness, 213:18
    grief at not wanting to c. dead back,
      631:9
    had c. to literature, 522:1
    heaven and earth to witness, 9:13
    her blessed, 22:19
    him a man, 851:1
    how you c. no me c. to me, 536:18
    in and invite God, 231:11
    in thy death's head, 243:1
    let us c. thee devil, 208:30
    let's c. whole thing off, 711:4
    me early mother dear, 450:15
    me horse, 182:21
    me Ishmael, 482:18
    neighbors in, 893:15

Call (*continued*)
    nigh unto them that c., 19:18
    none dare c. it treason, 166:26
    nothing c. our own but death, 177:8
    of running tide, 635:16
    one clear c. for me, 456:4
    philosophy down from heavens, 88:5
    please to c. it rush-candle, 173:23
    saints aid if men c., 377:12
    spade a spade, 81:10
    spirits from vasty deep, 182:34
    that backing your friends, 182:20
    that which we c. a rose, 180:3
    the fleeting breath, 315:20
    through curtains c. on us, 228:15
    today his own, 273:17
    Truth obeyed c., 596:14
    try first thyself and after c. God, 59:n3
    upon all who love freedom, 686:13
    upon my soul, 204:21
    when you c. me that smile, 579:9
    wild c. and clear c., 635:16
    will they come when you c., 182:34
    you back dear love, 67:6
    you c. for faith, 461:24
    you c. me misbeliever, 184:28
    you can c. me Al, 855:13
    you could say I've a c., 833:3
    you just c. out my name, 854:13
    you Shepherd from hill, 495:14
Called brother's father dad, 175:10
    fool c. her lady fair, 589:5
    for his pipe, 892:13
    him soft names, 410:9
    it macaroni, 883:15
    Little Cousins C. back, 511:16
    many are c., 35:11
    neither two nor one c., 202:35
    out of Egypt c. my son, 32:1
    them untaught knaves, 181:36
    till we are c. to rise, 510:12
    whom he did predestinate he c., 41:22
Calleth, deep c. unto deep, 16:23
    them all by their names, 19:20
Callimachus, tomb of C., 82:18
Calling, followed mercenary c., 575:20
    they're c. me, 814:10
Callooh callay, 515:13
Calls back lovely April, 220:32
    fool c. you foolish, 68:10
    if anybody c., 629:2
    Jerusalem thy sister c., 354:14
    stated c. to worship, 307:16
    who c. me villain, 199:17
Calm, after storm c., 704:2
    after storm comes c., 282:20
    all c. all bright, 401:5
    all c. as it was bright, 268:14
    cankers of c. world, 183:17
    contending kings, 172:35
    day so cool so c., 242:19
    drifted in sheepish c., 787:11
    envisage circumstance c., 411:14
    escape into c. regions, 312:1
    evening c. and free, 370:5
    for a c. unfit, 272:16
    great events make me c., 485:2
    he of c. and happy nature, 74:18

Calm (continued)
  in c. sea every man pilot, 271:1
  quiet innocent recreation, 245:7
  my soul's c. retreat, 269:2
  region where no night, 241:17
  sea is c. tonight, 496:16
  so deep, 370:3
  Soul of all things, 495:1
  stars in their c., 495:9
Calme, luxe c. et volupté, 491:n4
Calmer of thoughts, 245:1
Calumniating, envious and c. time, 203:25
Calumnies answered best with silence, 232:4
Calumnious strokes, 197:19
Calumny, envy c. hate pain, 403:23
  thou shalt not escape c., 199:26
Calvary, place called C., 38:33
Calvin oatcakes and sulphur, 374:21
Calvinistic doctrine of reprobation, 532:15
Camaraderie of locker room and ball park,
    784:10
Cambridge ladies, 701:8
  ye fields of C., 265:14
Cambuscan, story of C. bold, 251:21
Cambyses', King C. vein, 182:26
Came back in dream, 816:4
  fear c. upon me, 13:7
  forth to see again stars, 129:8
  gave a war no one c., 636:n1
  I c. I saw I conquered, 89:6
  I c. like Water, 441:19
  I c. saw and overcame, 188:19
  it all c. back to me, 845:11
  naked c. I out, 12:39
  once a World, 508:15
  out from Egypt, 8:1
  Satan c. also, 12:35
  tell them I c., 616:7
  to dark tower c., 212:9
  to making of man, 529:14
  to scoff, 322:26
  upon midnight clear, 457:11
Camel, cloud in shape of a c., 200:26
  easier for c. to go, 35:4
  nine she-c. hairs aid memory, 671:20
  swallow a c., 35:35
Camelot, brief shining moment C., 790:14
  looked down to C., 451:6
  many-towered C., 451:4
  said he, 523:13
Camels are snobbish, 671:23
Camera, I am a c., 738:7
  sees more than the eye, 669:1
  teaches to see without c., 707:10
Camerado this is no book, 488:6
Camera's role in beautifying the world, 835:18
Camino, con pan y vino se anda c., 898:6
Camlet, my fine c. cloak, 277:1
Camouflage, banality was only c., 778:11
Camp, court the c. the grove, 373:2
  every c. has firmament for roof, 533:12
  father and I to c., 883:n4
  vision of style, 835:17
Campaign, rather lose a c., 842:2
  this c. came to an end, 832:7
  we c. in poetry, 831:12
Campaspe, Cupid and my C., 162:8
Campbells are comin', 883:10

Camped by billabong, 585:8
Campground, tenting on old c., 520:1
Camps, concentration c., 722:17
  terrible from c., 742:7
Campus, ceased to notice students on c., 723:10
  habet lumen auris acumen, 134:n2
Cam'st, how c. to be siege of this moon-calf,
    224:24
Can, cry I c. no more, 547:3
  guess if you c., 249:17
  he who c. does, 565:9
  I think I c., 608:2
  if poor whenever you c., 77:1
  if we c. we must, 575:15
  live as we c., 81:4
  live we how we c., 170:37
  make us do what we c., 428:11
  pass me the c. lad, 575:14
  something hope wish, 547:3
  we all get along, 879:1
  yes we c., 876:11, 877:2
  youth replies I c., 424:21
Cana, miracles in C., 39:5
Canaan, Abram dwelled in C., 6:29
Canada, imagine C. as vast hunting preserve,
    708:17
  world-famous all over C., 830:17
Canadian frontier pattern for world, 619:9
Canal, alimentary c. with big appetite, 765:11
  took the Isthmus started the C., 571:16
Canary wine, 411:5
Cancel all our vows, 167:11
  and tear to pieces, 216:13
  half a Line, 442:2
  power to c. captivity, 191:33
Canceled, across c. skies, 694:14
Cancels, end of life c. bands, 183:6
  time c. young pain, 183:6
Cancer is now in the service, 835:20
  we have a c. within, 844:5
Candid, be c. where we can, 294:15
  brow, 567:11
  save me from C. Friend, 367:3
  ye marshes how c., 543:1
Candidate, not Catholic c. for President, 785:6
Candidates, interchangeable c., 810:12
Candied, let c. tongue lick pomp, 200:10
Candle, bell book and c., 175:16
  better to light one c., 660:n1
  book bell and c., 138:12
  burned c. at both ends, 695:n1
  burned on table, 688:6
  burns at both ends, 695:8
  feel steady c. flame, 460:22
  highest c. lights dark, 642:14
  hold c. to my shames, 185:2
  hold farthing c. to sun, 235:n5
  how far c. throws beams, 186:18
  light c. to the sun, 268:8
  lights gleaming, 609:10
  lived like c. in wind, 864:12
  of understanding, 29:27
  one small c. light a thousand, 240:5
  out out brief c., 217:23
  put c. under a bushel, 32:16
  scarcely fit to hold c., 297:19
  set a c. in the sun, 235:16
  this day light such a c., 144:13

Candle (continued)
  to light you to bed, 893:7
  two chairs half c., 467:15
  white c. in holy place, 647:5
Candlelight, dress by yellow c., 555:8
  sit in early c. of old age, 488:17
Candlelit, old at evening c., 150:7
Candles are all out, 215:10
  blessed c. of night, 186:22
  burn like fabulous roman c., 799:3
  night's c. burnt out, 181:2
  rather light c., 660:n1
  when c. out all women fair, 108:11
Candlestick, jump over c., 895:16
  put candle on a c., 32:16
Candlestick-maker, butcher baker c., 896:2
Candor and amicable relations, 355:7
  ends paranoia, 812:16
Candy deal of courtesy, 182:7
  is dandy, 732:5
  not made of sugar c., 620:16
Cane, carrying a small c., 724:1
  wind is in the c., 704:15
Canem, cave c., 120:9
Canker, as killing as c. to rose, 253:5
  galls infants of spring, 197:19
  loathesome c., 221:11
  this c. Bolingbroke, 182:3
  worm c. and grief, 399:16
Cankers in musk-rose buds, 178:20
  of calm world, 183:17
Cannes, Hotel Magnifique at C., 648:15
Cannibal, better sleep with sober c., 482:21
Cannibals that each other eat, 208:2
Cannikin, why clink c., 460:9
Cannoli, take the c., 795:9
Cannon come again, 596:16
  to right of them, 454:22
Cannon's, burst c. roar, 443:3
  mouth, 194:25
Cannons taken or saved, 506:13
Cannon-shot, revolution more c., 596:16
Cannot define the real problem, 790:4
  he who c. teaches, 565:9
  history c. be unlived, 817:14
  it c. like adultery or gluttony, 626:22
  killing beast that c. kill, 672:5
  nature c. be fooled, 790:5
Canoe of the European, 482:12
  paddle own c., 401:4
Canon 'gainst self-slaughter, 196:29
Canopy, most excellent c. the air, 199:5
  who spread its c., 280:15
Canst, give all thou c., 372:14
Can't, I c. go on, 745:1
  if you c. be free, 871:3
Cant, clear your mind of c., 311:11
  nothing but c., 393:10
  of criticism, 314:12
  of hypocrites the worst, 314:12
  of Not men but measures, 323:17
Canted in this canting world, 314:12
Canter, little finishing c., 539:8
Canters, as they c. awaäy, 455:25
Cantie wi' mair, 357:5
Canting, canted in this c. world, 314:12
Cants which are canted, 314:12

Canvas of heavy foresail, 567:6
  on c. not a picture but an event, 747:7
  sail even with c. rent, 103:13
  set your full c. flying, 83:3
Canyon, mar beauty of c., 571:7
Canyons, neighing c., 720:7
Cap, feather in his c., 314:15
  for c. and bells lives pay, 481:15
  riband in c. of youth, 202:1
Capability and godlike reason, 201:19
  Negative C., 412:15
Capable, all I am c. of becoming, 680:12
  and wide revenge, 209:20
  become all c. of, 407:12
  created in his mind, 641:15
  hand now warm and c., 412:1
  mathematician c. of reasoning, 75:13
  not all c. of everything, 92:24
  of being in uncertainties, 412:15
  of every wickedness, 568:3
  of greatest vices, 246:6
  of nothing but dumbshows, 200:6
  they're c. of anything, 839:8
Capacities, growing to full human c., 796:8
Capacity, by c. is wisdom acquired, 83:9
  contribution according to c., 478:n2
  for delight and wonder, 567:3
  for taking pains, 528:11
  freed c. of thought, 572:15
  functional c., 341:8
  of taking trouble, 408:8
  receiveth as the sea, 204:11
  to despise himself, 584:8
Cap-a-pe, 197:12
Cape, nobly C. Saint Vincent, 460:20
  round c. of a sudden, 460:17
  wears descent like long c., 823:1
Cape Cod, man may stand there [C.], 476:1
Caper and shake a leg, 635:10
Capers, he c. he dances, 187:12
  nimbly in lady's chamber, 171:18
  strange c., 194:9
Capes, on dark c. glisten ink wax, 717:4
Capitaine, Ô Mort vieux c., 491:n9
Capital, Belgium's c. gathered, 395:13
  bring c. into competition, 319:10
  fruit of labor, 445:10
  has its rights, 445:10
  in ascendancy system of plunder, 478:4
  labor not ask patronage of c., 390:1
  labor prior to c., 445:10
  not by savings and c., 753:3
  one class owns c., 423:10
  sensitive ear detecting c. letters, 648:12
  where kingly Death, 403:14
Capitalism creates social unrest, 657:22
  greatest bulwark of c., 605:1
  inherent vice of c., 621:18
  system where man exploits man, 792:3
  trouble with c. capitalists, 625:20
  war is c. with gloves off, 843:9
Capitalist, more sham than c. democracy, 658:1
Capitalists owners of means of production, 478:n5
Capitol, musing amidst ruins of C., 332:19
  woman betrayed the C., 281:11
Capitulate to badges and names, 426:17
Capon, belly with good c. lined, 194:25

Capons, unless minutes c., 181:20
  you cannot feed c. so, 200:14
Caprice and lifelong passion, 560:4
  lasts a little longer, 560:4
  of minutest event, 483:11
Capricious, gods' c. hand, 742:1
Capriciousness of summer air, 624:7
Caps, threw their c., 219:21
Captain, captive good attending c. ill, 221:22
  Carpenter rose up, 681:17
  chief c. answered, 40:43
  cook and c. bold, 525:16
  Death old c., 491:10
  don't you hear c. shouting, 884:22
  his c. Christ, 177:14
  no c. do very wrong, 355:11
  O C. my C., 487:16
  of all these men of death, 271:29
  of Hampshire grenadiers, 332:18
  of his soul, 685:6
  of huckleberry party, 428:15
  of my soul, 552:8
  of second rank, 422:13
  of the Pinafore, 525:19
  right good c. too, 525:19
  should be judged as a c., 139:13
  soul the c. of life, 92:9
  walk deck my C. lies, 487:17
Captain's choleric word, 206:29
  crew of c. gig, 525:16
Captains and kings depart, 589:8
  courageous, 889:22
  of industry, 408:3
  thunder of the c., 14:28
Captive, carried us away c., 19:11
  good attending captain ill, 221:22
  he comes to civilization a c., 701:1
  Israel, 479:3
  jailer another kind of c., 439:3
  lead captivity c., 10:9
  of time, 688:4
  today unbind c., 424:20
  weak minds led c., 259:31
Captivity is Consciousness, 509:2
  lead c. captive, 10:9
  power to cancel his c., 191:33
Captors, identify with your c., 872:6
Capture of men by women, 459:n1
Captured, faced enslavement if c., 519:10
Capulet, I'll no longer be a C., 180:2
Car, drive the rapid c., 327:11
  gilded c. of day, 252:7
  got her daddy's c., 856:1
  radio bleats, 787:16
  rattling o'er stony street, 395:14
Caravan, innumerable c. which moves, 405:13
  put up your c., 609:14
Caravanserai, battered C., 441:12
Carcass fit for hounds, 192:4
  honey in the c. of the lion, 10:18
  of leopard, 721:16
  where c. is eagles gather, 35:21
Carcasses bleed at sight of murderer, 136:n2
Card, speak by the c., 202:10
Cards, cheat at c. genteelly, 310:2
  deck of c., 660:n2
  dreaded c. foretell, 748:11
  never play c. with man named Doc, 757:11

Cards *(continued)*
  nothing but pack of c., 515:9
  patience and shuffle c., 157:28
  played c. for kisses, 162:8
  thrust ivrybody but cut c., 600:13
Care, age full of c., 881:17
  and not to care, 677:13
  begone dull C., 882:10
  deliberation and public c., 256:16
  driveth away sleep, 31:18
  feeling c. of law, 161:17
  fig for c. fig for woe, 146:10
  for who shall have borne battle, 447:2
  full of c. no time, 609:4
  golden c., 188:20
  happy whose wish and c., 292:4
  housewife ply evening c., 315:16
  I c. for nobody, 331:1
  I don't c. one straw, 86:9
  I don't c. what they do, 586:10
  I prayed and did God C., 508:21
  I sae weary fu' o' c., 357:6
  I shall not c., 660:13
  inalienable weight of c., 512:9
  insensate c. of mortals, 90:n1
  irks c. the crop-full bird, 462:14
  Jimmie crack corn I don't c., 884:18
  keeps his watch, 180:18
  killed a cat, 191:15
  lose it that buy it with much c., 184:3
  nor c. beyond today, 315:6
  nor for itself hath c., 352:12
  not abate any part of c., 297:10
  not who sees your back, 182:20
  nought but c. on ev'ry han', 356:21
  of discipline is love, 30:4
  of life and happiness, 337:15
  of the poor, 276:17
  of this world, 34:17
  raveled sleave of c., 215:21
  Reason is past c., 223:6
  rest that knows no c., 90:14
  sat on his faded cheek, 255:26
  so wan with c., 181:18
  sought it with c., 517:6
  sounds take c. of themselves, 514:20
  taken better c. of myself, 654:21
  things past redress past c., 177:1
  weep away life of c., 401:14
  what boots it with incessant c., 253:6
  what c. I how fair she be, 239:17
  what is life if full of c., 609:4
  where c. lodges sleep never lie, 180:18
  windy side of c., 190:29
  woman who did not c., 589:5
  wrinkled C. derides, 250:22
Care-charmer Sleep, 167:3
Cared as much as Bird, 508:21
  not to be at all, 256:8
Career, awe man from c. of his humor, 190:36
  close military c. fade away, 644:11
  my c. my brilliant c., 639:1
  poetry not c., 677:22
  this is our c., 682:10
  what they call fine c., 761:6
Careful, be c. what you do, 639:15
  not c. what they mean, 173:2
  o' widders, 463:24

Century *(continued)*
   seventeenth c. dissociation, 676:4
Cerberus and blackest Midnight, 250:19
   give sop to C., 119:23
Ceremony, idol c., 189:22
   love useth enforced c., 193:6
   of innocence drowned, 593:9
   save c. save general c., 189:22
   that to great ones 'longs, 206:25
   thrice gorgeous c., 189:23
Ceres, which cost C. all that pain, 257:17
Certain about things we don't understand,
   730:8
   am I of the spot, 510:9
   because impossible, 113:13
   fill c. portion of uncertain paper, 398:7
   is birth for the dead, 84:7
   is death for the born, 84:7
   no c. life achieved, 175:27
   nothing c. except death and taxes, 303:20
   of his fate, 209:3
   of nothing but affection, 412:11
   permanent and c. characteristics, 306:21
   signs should prefigure events, 88:1
   there is no fine thing, 592:1
   way for woman to hold a man, 791:15
Certainties, begin with c. end in doubts,
   164:11
   begin with doubts end in c., 164:11
   hot for c., 505:11
   public demands c., 645:2
   there are no c., 645:2
Certainty, certitude not test of c., 538:20
   generally illusion, 538:8
   no such thing as absolute c., 435:4
   not lightly sacrificed, 607:1
   of the words of truth, 21:20
   quit c. for uncertainty, 307:7
   sober c. of waking bliss, 252:16
   without doubt, 126:7
Certificate, ain't got no birth c., 861:7
Certitude nor peace nor help, 496:19
   not test of certainty, 538:20
Certum est quia impossibile est, 113:*n*8
Cervantes' serious air, 296:24
Cervicem, utinam populus Romanus unam c.,
   104:*n*8
Cesspool, London great c., 573:3
C'est, Madame Bovary c. moi, 494:*n*1
Cetera quis nescit, 101:*n*9
Ceylon diver held breath, 409:17
Chafe, champ and c. and toss, 494:12
Chafed, high blood c., 398:*n*1
Chafes, on unnumbered pebbles c., 212:24
Chaff, hope corn in c., 394:15
   principles less than c., 567:15
   wheat hid in bushels of c., 184:10
   which the wind driveth away, 14:40
Chaffinch sings on bough, 460:18
Chagrined, not be very much c., 443:16
Chain about ankle of fellow man, 477:8
   drags lengthening c., 321:12
   fastened about own neck, 477:8
   free that anchor and c., 83:3
   golden c. from heaven, 51:16
   handled with a C., 509:4
   hanging in a golden c., 257:4
   of life, 795:15

Chain *(continued)*
   wear c. I forged, 465:7
   what the c., 353:2
   winds th' exhausted c., 357:20
Chained for billions of years, 680:5
Chainless soul, 476:13
   Spirit of c. Mind, 397:8
Chains, adamantine c. and fire, 255:7
   and slaverie, 358:16
   and slavery, 331:13
   bound in icy c., 207:*n*2
   breaks c. from every mind, 352:5
   cries of country in c., 891:*n*1
   everywhere he is in c., 312:15
   light buried under c., 717:8
   mourns his yet unbroken c., 346:24
   nothing to lose but c., 478:15
   Ocean loose c. of things, 104:7
   prayer for deliverance from c., 476:19
   sang in my c., 777:14
   shake your c. to earth like dew, 402:22
Chair, electric c. like oasis, 787:11
   in your rocking c. by window, 609:8
   is the c. empty, 172:4
   on golden c. seated prince of Wales, 647:4
   one c. for solitude, 475:10
   oranges in sunny c., 640:20
   Rabelais' easy c., 296:24
   sea best in c. before fire, 617:14
   seated in thy silver c., 232:2
   sit mute in enchanted c., 227:2
Chair, la c. triste hélas, 543:*n*2
Chairman, by God Mr. C., 320:5
Chairs, comfortable c. lights by them, 586:12
   three c. for society, 475:10
   two c. for friendship, 475:10
   two old c. half candle, 467:15
   why smash the c., 442:20
Chalice from the palace, 775:10
   this is c. of My Blood, 47:25
Chaliced, on c. flowers that lies, 220:15
Chalk cliffs of Dover, 599:8
Challenge of rootless science, 717:8
   send c. to his end, 263:5
Challenges, New Frontier is c., 785:5
   successfully responding to c., 685:8
Cham of literature, 318:2
Chamber, bridegroom coming out of his c.,
   15:16
   get you to my lady's c., 202:12
   he capers nimbly in lady's c., 171:18
   hear in c. above me, 437:13
   I throw myself down in my c., 231:11
   in my lady's c., 894:6
   in silent halls, 405:13
   rapping at c. door, 449:3
   Star C. matter, 186:23
   with naked foot stalking my c., 149:4
Chambering and wantonness, 41:40
Chambermaid, as happy in arms of c.,
   310:21
Chambers, layeth the beams of his c., 18:8
   turn underground passages into lethal c.,
   724:6
Chameleon's dish, 200:14
   tuning skin to it, 797:10
Chameleons feed on light, 402:8
Champ and chafe and toss, 494:12

Champagne and chicken at last, 297:7
   no kick from c., 691:10
Champed grasses, 616:6
Champion, people have always some c., 75:20
Champions, four c. fierce strive, 257:1
Chance, afford all fair c., 445:9
   all whom c. hath slain, 230:20
   and contingency, 477:*n*2
   at hands of Time and C., 536:1
   bludgeonings of c., 552:7
   comes from art not c., 292:19
   dart of c., 209:28
   dice never abolish c., 543:8
   direction thou canst not see, 294:23
   favors prepared mind, 499:1
   fool right by c., 326:12
   hour before this c., 215:30
   if c. will have me king, 214:12
   learning not attained by c., 341:4
   main c., 262:20
   may crown me, 214:12
   nativity c. or death, 187:19
   no gifts from C., 494:16
   no such thing as c., 360:2
   not leave right to c., 473:15
   of war, 202:37
   only c. could save you, 722:17
   power erring men call C., 252:22
   set my life on any c., 216:8
   shall not control, 494:14
   slave to fate c. kings, 230:23
   something left to c., 355:10
   stand to the main c., 162:1
   take c. that traitors escape, 614:3
   time and c. happeneth to all, 23:23
   Tinker to Evers to C., 646:12
   to find yourself, 567:14
   to talk a little wild, 225:13
   universe as result of blind c., 440:8
   unless we take a c., 812:3
   weight of c. desires, 371:16
   what we may call c., 440:7
   will bring us through, 495:5
   wisdom and deliberation follow c., 153:15
Chanced to meet old man, 897:1
Chancel, broke c. window-squares, 536:20
Chancellor, revolving about Lord C., 466:11
Chancery, wards in C., 526:19
Chances change by course, 166:27
   like sunbeams pass, 302:*n*2
   spake of disastrous c., 207:37
   take c. for peace, 674:16
Chancy, history very c., 672:3
Change and migration of the soul, 74:9
   anything we c. in child, 630:6
   bolts up c., 219:7
   by tomorrow and fleet, 387:9
   came a long way back, 710:11
   can't c. mind won't c. subject, 621:17
   chances c. by course, 166:27
   clime not disposition, 98:3
   edge of c., 860:5
   ever-whirling wheel of C., 160:22
   everything except loves, 299:28
   extremes by c. more fierce, 256:25
   fear of c., 255:25
   feel by turns bitter c., 256:25
   given heart c. of mood, 623:5

Change *(continued)*
gonna come, 829:10
hands and still confute, 262:2
heavy c. now thou art gone, 253:4
hopes no more c. name, 371:16
I would not c. for thine, 232:16
is the only poem, 825:4
life presupposes its c. and movement,
  747:11
lobsters and retire, 515:1
made you c. your name, 864:12
management of c., 758:2
me change me, 774:15
me to winged bird, 68:2
must c. ideas when served purpose, 468:13
my state with kings, 221:7
neither to c. nor falter nor repent, 402:5
never c. when love has found home,
  101:12
not sudden definite like that, 654:4
nothing endures but c., 61:27
of air, 630:15
of heart, 748:6
of motion proportional, 279:15
old lamps for new, 883:7
people c. what is in themselves, 118:9
places and which is thief, 212:29
plus ça change, 439:*n*1
point is to c. world, 477:13
process of social c., 694:10
religion knavery and c., 279:4
ringing grooves of c., 452:10
skies above them, 589:1
stamp of nature, 201:13
the many c. and pass, 404:2
the more things c., 439:1
time for a c., 730:4
time will c. your opinions, 76:11
times c. and move continually, 160:24
times c. and we c. with them, 121:19
to live is to c., 421:6
to virtue and worthiness, 191:34
too much c. too short time, 821:3
unafraid of c., 583:4
universe is c., 111:16
we all want to c. the world, 848:14
we think we see, 622:16
werewolf's painful c., 798:1
what doesn't c. is will to c., 762:5
what should be changed, 695:20
when worse it must c., 143:15
wind of c. is blowing, 703:6
you must c. your life, 632:10
Changé, nous avons c. tout cela, 267:*n*3
Changeable, young men's minds are c., 50:28
Changed, accept things that cannot be c.,
  695:20
Eternity has c. him, 543:7
forget what cannot be c., 499:10
from the one all to me, 536:18
I c. my condition, 261:16
innocence for innocence, 223:10
like change in my face, 553:9
mind not to be c., 255:14
minds of gods not c. suddenly, 52:29
not c. from him they knew, 622:7
our life is c., 672:6
our lives have been c., 761:8

Changed *(continued)*
sea c. Egdon remained, 535:16
something better c. in ourselves, 630:6
utterly, 593:7
we have c. all that, 267:18
we shall be c., 43:8
whole world have been c., 269:13
ye too c. ye hills, 496:12
Changeful mind of mortals, 64:10
presuming on c. potency, 204:2
Changes, agonies one of my c. of garments,
  486:16
cause great c. in the world, 331:2
follow c. of the moon, 209:5
God c. and man and form, 530:20
God c. not people until they change, 118:9
monthly c. in circled orb, 180:8
sky c. when wives, 195:29
woman often c., 94:*n*10
wonderful c. wrought, 400:9
Changeth, old order c., 455:19
sweareth to his own hurt and c. not, 15:11
Changing, borrow every c. shape, 675:8
shallow c. woman, 172:3
stress on not c. mind, 626:16
Chankly Bore, 468:3
Channel, crossing C. and tossing, 527:4
man merely c. for food, 140:2
Chant, do use to c. it, 205:2
how can ye c., 357:6
none chanted c. of welcome, 487:15
Chanted, none c. chant of welcome, 487:15
Chanticleer, lungs crow like c., 194:17
Chanting, exaltation in c. of Muses, 67:15
faint hymns to moon, 177:26
in Latin, 850:7
Chants doleful hymn, 176:3
Chaos and old Night, 255:22
beauty dead black c., 171:14
bounded by primeval c., 456:*n*1
breeds life, 531:18
freedom of action without freed thought c.,
  572:15
infinite c. which separated us, 269:17
is come again, 208:35
of the sun, 640:22
of thought and passion, 295:1
our policy against c., 644:13
rough unordered mass, 102:9
serves no social end, 694:1
this is why there is c., 80:9
thy dread empire C., 297:6
what a c. is man, 269:25
Chaos-like together crushed, 293:14
Chapel, Devil builds c. there, 282:4
Devil would build c., 144:5
God's greenwood c., 640:*n*1
Chapels had been churches, 184:14
legend of green c., 777:8
Chaperon, we're all alone no c., 691:6
Chapfallen, quite c., 202:12
Chapman, heard C. speak out loud and bold,
  408:17
Chapmen, you do as c. do, 203:28
Chapmen's, not uttered by c. tongues,
  174:8
Chaps, Biography is about C., 629:1
with couple o' guns, 660:5

Chapter of accidents very long, 298:17
of knowledge very short, 298:17
man dies c. not torn from book, 231:7
said he could repeat c., 310:15
say in first c. rifle hanging on wall, 578:*n*2
write the next c., 753:11
Chapters in art of living, 490:18
of lives to natural end, 552:13
Character, accommodation c., 519:2
adopt c. of octopus, 59:22
analysis of c. highest entertainment, 740:2
bearing on excellence of c., 78:12
best way to define c., 540:16
bird of bad moral c., 303:17
December 1910 human c. changed, 654:4
family stamped c. on child, 630:8
fate and c. same conception, 380:11
find well-drawn c., 522:18
formed in world's torrent, 343:8
give action its c., 73:23
good c. remembered, 3:9
higher than intellect, 426:3
his c. arbiter of everyone's fortune, 92:*n*11
liberal arts humanizes c., 102:26
lies in own hands, 822:6
limitations of own c., 533:4
man of powerful c., 431:20
man that makes c., 290:16
man's c. is his fate, 62:14
never mind the c., 464:1
of perfection, 497:12
poetical c., 413:9
power of Latin in c., 497:6
reap a c., 885:17
Characteristics of popular politician, 72:12
of vigorous mind, 306:21
Characterize this age of ours, 406:7
Characterless, mighty states c., 203:20
Characters, attributes c. of living creature,
  484:7
fashioning our c. wrong, 540:22
for love I make c. in plays, 766:12
high c. cries one, 261:4
impressed on our c. and conduct, 314:1
knowledge of c. of rulers, 329:9
most women have no c., 293:25
not in calm that great c. are formed, 341:2
Six C. in Search of Author, 601:2
Charge, compulsive ardor gives c., 201:7
Cromwell I c. thee, 226:4
give his angels c. over thee, 17:29
give lie to slander c., 394:1
not soul save to its ability, 118:22
once more be dumb, 497:3
such is the c., 74:7
with all thy chivalry, 384:11
within the bosom, 508:5
Charged troops of error, 247:13
Charger, John Baptist's head in c., 34:24
Chariest maid prodigal enough, 197:19
Charing Cross, went out to C. to see Harrison
  hanged, 277:4
Chariot, appeared a c. of fire, 12:11
flying-c. through air, 327:11
maketh clouds his c., 18:8
of fire, 354:8
of Israel, 12:12
swing low sweet c., 898:21

Chariot (*continued*)
that bears Human Soul, 510:14
Time's winged c., 266:22
why is his c. so long in coming, 10:13
Chariots, why tarry the wheels of his c., 10:13
Charisma inner determination inner restraint, 586:8
Charismatic leader gains authority, 586:8
Charitable, intents wicked or c., 197:33
men's c. speeches, 166:21
Charite, of saynte c., 880:7
Charities of kiss or smile, 380:6
Charity, and have not c., 42:26
anticipate c. by preventing poverty, 124:11
beareth all things, 42:28
begins at home, 85:16, 248:15
believeth all things, 42:28
come out of c., 880:n2
creates multitude of sins, 560:27
degrades, 432:9
edifieth, 42:17
endureth all things, 42:28
envieth not, 42:27
for all, 447:2
greatest is c., 42:29
hopeth all things, 42:28
I am in c. with world, 285:16
in all things c., 265:4
in c. no excess, 165:22
in c. to all mankind, 363:8
in love and c. with neighbors, 49:4
is kind, 42:27
justice not c. wanting in world, 360:21
little earth for c., 226:7
love friendship c., 203:25
never faileth, 42:28
not puffed up, 42:27
now abideth c., 42:29
of saynte c., 880:7
rarity of Christian c., 418:14
shall cover multitude of sins, 46:1
suffereth long, 42:27
towards each other, 332:1
towards others, 248:15
vaunteth not, 42:27
where c. neither fear nor ignorance, 125:11
Charity's golden ladder, 124:11
Charlemagne, world-transforming C., 596:8
Charles, immense empire of C. the Fifth, 359:n4
successors of C. the Fifth, 332:12
the First his Cromwell, 331:8
Charles's, King C. head, 465:28
Charley's, I am C. aunt from Brazil, 566:2
Charlie is my darling, 362:10
live and die wi' C., 367:15
o'er the water to C., 367:15
Charlotte true friend good writer, 724:8
went on cutting bread and butter, 459:14
Charm ache with air, 191:12
by thought supplied, 368:10
he had that nameless c., 585:4
homely person attract by c., 667:4
music oft hath such a c., 207:9
object in possession seldom retains c., 110:18
of all the Muses, 456:1
of earliest birds, 257:26

Charm (*continued*)
one native c., 322:27
quality in others, 490:17
simplicity and c., 95:23
smiling at good mouth, 665:9
some have c. for none, 577:12
some women c. all, 577:12
touching all the muses' c., 89:18
wasted on sky, 424:10
what c. soothe melancholy, 322:16
witch hath power to c., 196:19
without c. no literature, 590:18
Charmed alike tilt-yard and bower, 392:15
bear a c. life, 217:27
it with smiles and soap, 517:6
magic casements, 410:10
water burnt alway, 376:16
Charmers, will not hearken to voice of c., 16:39
Charmian is this well done, 219:18
Charming, be c. and shut up, 491:11
be c. with nothing, 554:8
evening criminal's friend, 491:8
form of government, 75:18
friendly and c. relationship, 144:7
how c. divine philosophy, 252:19
left his voice, 258:29
never so wisely, 16:39
people have something to conceal, 734:5
something c. in the sound, 328:3
to totter into vogue, 317:3
Charm's, peace the c. wound up, 214:3
Charms, Aphrodite with intricate c., 56:n3
by accepting, 294:3
do not all c. fly, 409:15
endearing young c., 387:9
icy arms hold c., 708:6
music has c. to soothe, 287:1
O Solitude where are c., 326:17
or ear or sight, 378:10
power obtained by c., 360:20
Charon could not prevent me, 67:6
Charter, large a c. as wind, 194:20
this was c. of land, 301:3
Chartered libertine, 188:33
Charybdis, I fall into C., 185:25
implacable C. guards left, 185:n1
on starboard beam C., 185:n1
Chase, blessed in luck of c., 892:1
glowing hours, 395:14
had a beast in view, 274:25
lead a wild-goose c., 156:11
piteous c., 194:1
the sport of kings, 289:19
to c. white whale, 483:1
unhurrying c., 576:14
writing make us c. the writer, 862:9
Chased shouting wind along, 800:1
Chasm, there exists a great c., 757:14
Chassis, state o' c., 660:3
Chaste and fair, 232:2
as ice, 199:26
as the icicle, 220:3
as unsunned snow, 220:16
fair c. unexpressive she, 195:3
modest and commonly c., 400:7
nunnery of thy c. breast, 265:17
to her husband, 293:26
was she not c., 107:23

Chasten, power to c. and subdue, 368:11
Chasteneth, he that loveth c. him, 20:23
whom the Lord loveth c., 45:13
Chastening in hour of pride, 444:15
Chastise, I will c. with scorpions, 11:37
Chastised, father hath c. you, 11:37
having been a little c., 29:34
Chastity, give me c. but not now, 116:4
most curious of sexual aberrations, 570:4
most unnatural sexual perversion, 702:14
my brother Chastity, 252:18
scepticism c. of intellect, 584:13
Chat, before we have our c., 516:5
Chat, la patte du c., 267:n1
Châteaux, O seasons O c., 559:6
Chatter against bird of Zeus, 63:25
harebrained c., 430:20
insignificant c. of world, 471:13
of transcendental kind, 526:10
those who have learned art c., 63:25
Chatterley, between C. ban and Beatles' LP, 799:13
Chatterton marvelous boy, 369:16
Chaucer, Dan C. first warbler, 450:22
nigh to learned C., 240:6
not lodge thee by C., 232:19
well of English, 160:16
whose sweet breath, 450:22
Chaucere, O reverend C., 141:8
Chaucer's, corruption since C. days, 236:18
Chaud comme l'enfer, 348:n1
Chaudron, parole humaine comme un c. fêlé, 493:n4
Chauffered Cub Scouts, 796:7
Cheap, flesh and blood so c., 418:12
good counsel c., 235:8
greet c. holde at litel prys, 135:11
hold c. the strain, 462:15
how potent c. music is, 719:15
life not c. but sacred, 428:10
man's life c. as beast's, 211:21
never buy because c., 338:18
sitting as standing, 285:15
sleep a c. pleasure, 158:8
sold c. what is most dear, 222:13
what we obtain too c., 333:6
Cheaper crook, gaudier patter, 702:8
seats clap your hands, 847:11
Cheapest, man richest whose pleasures c., 473:10
Cheat at cards genteelly, 310:2
came to c. them, 363:13
for sake of beauty, 633:2
life 'tis all a c., 272:11
out of love c. others, 611:3
sweet c. gone, 616:8
undertaken to c. me, 406:5
Cheated, feeling you've been c., 874:13
illusion by which c., 611:3
Cheating, art of winning games without c., 726:8
Check, care's c. and curb, 269:2
judicial power a c., 330:4
out anytime you like, 864:11
rod to c. the erring, 371:15
upon our exercise of power, 615:3
Checked, be c. for silence, 205:30
Checkerboard of Nights and Days, 441:22
Checkered shade, 251:4

Checkers, kids loved the dog C., 771:2
Checks, as if C. given, 510:9
    handed in his c., 528:9
Cheek, care sat on his faded c., 255:26
    feed on her damask c., 205:4
    he that loves a rosy c., 245:18
    I the blow and c., 491:7
    iron tears down Pluto's c., 251:20
    language in her eye her c., 204:4
    leans her c. upon her hand, 180:1
    of tan, 438:7
    she hangs on c. of night, 179:28
    that I might touch that c., 180:1
    turn the other c., 32:20
    warm c. and rising bosom, 316:10
    why should tears pale c. fret, 484:1
    withered c. tresses gray, 372:20
    yellow c. white beard, 187:31
Cheekbone, short a c. and ear, 489:*n*5
Cheeks, blood spoke in her c., 230:16
    blow winds and crack c., 211:24
    crimson in lips and c., 181:13
    make pale my c. with care, 239:17
    of sorry grain, 252:25
    rosy lips and c., 222:15
    stain my man's c., 211:22
    tears are on her c., 28:10
    wind on our c., 473:12
Cheer, al his c. as in his herte, 134:22
    at Christmas make good c., 150:11
    be of good c., 34:28, 40:5
    is best physician, 64:1
    our weary hearts, 520:1
    piped with merry c., 350:10
    sing song of c, again, 697:4
    small c. and great welcome, 172:19
    three cheers one c. more, 525:20
    unite with a c., 332:20
    up comrades they come, 489:8
Cheered, Admiral c. them holding out hope, 139:7
    ship was c., 375:20
Cheerer of spirits, 245:1
Cheerful, be c. while you are alive, 3:7
    giver, 43:19
    godliness, 370:10
    looking as c. as any man could do, 277:4
    merry heart maketh a c. countenance, 20:31
    warm precincts of c. day, 316:4
    ways of men cut off, 257:6
Cheerfully, do evil so c., 270:1
    he seems to grin, 513:15
    part with life c., 112:7
Cheerfulness keeps daylight in mind, 288:15
Cheering, public men nor c. crowds, 593:1
Cheerless over hills of gray, 438:15
Cheerly rouse the slumbering morn, 251:1
Cheers, responding to the c., 584:19
    silence no worse than c., 574:18
    tar's labor, 399:15
    three c. one cheer more, 525:20
    two c. for Democracy, 638:14
Cheese, country with 265 different kinds of c., 686:11
    moon made of green c., 148:19
Cheeses, ate c. out of vats, 460:7
Cheevy, Miniver C., 605:20

Chemical barrage against life, 750:5
    personalities like c. contact, 630:3
Chemist fiddler and buffoon, 273:2
Cherchez la femme, 422:*n*3
Cherish, achieve and c. peace, 447:2
    those hearts that hate thee, 226:5
    to love and to c., 49:16
    to love c. and obey, 49:24
Cherished, Country c. in hearts, 456:7
    memory of loved and lost, 446:12
Cherith, dwelt by the brook C., 11:39
Cherokee Nation is distinct community, 350:3
Cherries grow which none may buy, 227:3
    life is bowl of c., 697:8
Cherry, grew like a double c., 178:29
    hung with snow, 574:11
    I did cut c. tree, 328:*n*3
    now hung with bloom, 574:10
    ripe I cry, 240:12
    sap make c. red, 671:17
    violence is as American as c. pie, 856:5
Cherry-isle, there's land or c., 240:12
Cherry-ripe themselves do cry, 227:3
Cherub, he rode upon a c., 15:14
Cherubims east of the garden, 6:2
Cherubin, heaven's c. horsed, 214:24
    young and rose-lipped c., 210:4
Cherubin's, fyr-reed c. face, 134:7
Cherubins, young-eyed c., 186:15
Ches, to her son she c., 880:11
Cheshire Cat vanished slowly, 514:12
Chess, all c. players are artists, 669:16
    board is the world, 502:5
    pieces phenomena of universe, 502:5
Chest, as if c. a mortar, 483:3
    Dead Man's C., 555:4
    if it is well with your c., 98:4
    voice of iron c. of brass, 94:31
Chestnut, O c. tree, 594:17
    roast c. happiness, 656:5
    spreading c. tree, 436:11
Chestnuts, pull c. out of fire, 267:8
    sailor's wife had c., 213:33
Chevalier, the young C., 362:10
Chevy, drove my C. to the levee, 861:11
Chew cud and are silent, 325:7
Chewed, few books to be c., 166:17
Cheweth, whatsoever c. the cud, 8:23
Chewing food of fancy, 195:32
    little bits of string, 606:11
Cheyenne, I'm a-leavin' C., 890:12
Chic, radical C. only radical in style, 831:4
Chicago at northwest gates, 605:13
    first in violence deepest in dirt, 598:8
    once you're part of this patch, 757:9
    that somber city, 778:7
    was a town where nobody, 803:6
Chicken, champagne and c. at last, 297:7
    hawk floats over, 817:8
    I'm no spring c., 746:15
    in pot every Sunday, 161:12
    she's no c., 285:19
    some c. some neck, 621:1
Chickens, all my pretty c., 217:8
    as hen gathereth c., 35:18
    beside white c., 658:14
    coming home to roost, 809:1

Chickens *(continued)*
    count c. before hatched, 58:15
    literature or c., 723:18
Chide, fall out and c. and fight, 289:7
    God for countenance, 195:25
Chides, at fifty c. delay, 290:23
Chiding, better a little c., 187:20
Chief, a c. a rod, 295:5
    defect of Henry King, 606:11
    good and market, 201:19
    hail to the C., 373:22
    his c. beside, 459:23
    Magistrate hate struck down C., 809:1
    nourisher in life's feast, 215:21
    of the Army, 366:6
    sinners of whom I am c., 44:24
Chiefest treasure, 606:9
Chief's, vain the c. pride, 296:19
Chiefs, our c. are killed, 537:4
Chieftain Iffucan of Azcan, 640:23
    I'm a tribal c., 791:2
Child, a simple c., 368:2
    always say what's true, 555:9
    any c. at any stage, 779:2
    anything we change in c., 630:6
    as yet a c., 295:10
    beautiful a faery's c., 412:3
    became part of c. who went forth, 487:19
    behold the c., 295:3
    better is a poor and wise c., 23:3
    burnt c. fire dreadeth, 148:1
    creative writer like c. at play, 563:3
    christom c., 189:4
    cry as a c. cries, 772:5
    cry of c. by roadway, 591:9
    decision to bear or beget c., 745:11
    do not throw book, 606:9
    draws inscrutable house, 762:20
    dream of being a c. again, 841:7
    Eros Zeus's c., 67:25
    every c. may joy to hear, 350:11
    family stamped character on c., 630:8
    fast fold thy c., 547:2
    foster-c. of silence, 410:13
    get with c. mandrake root, 228:9
    give a little love to c., 484:18
    God bless the c., 779:9
    great with c. longing for prunes, 206:21
    hasn't got anything on c. said, 432:19
    he became a little c., 350:13
    heard one calling C., 243:2
    Heaven-born c., 250:10
    her innocence a c., 273:21
    here a little c. I stand, 241:15
    I spake as a c., 42:29
    I was a c., 449:22
    I weep like a c., 662:15
    if you strike a c., 565:11
    in simplicity a c., 294:13
    in the name of this C., 49:11
    is father of the man, 369:14
    is known by his doings, 21:11
    Jesus Christ her little c., 476:5
    keeps secret well, 422:17
    lie down like tired c., 401:14
    life like froward c., 271:30
    like three years' c., 375:19
    little c. shall lead them, 25:19

Child's, credulity c. strength, 383:12
  no c. pley to take wyf, 135:24
Child's-heart, not lose his c., 79:25
Chill and drear, 373:5
  bitter c. it was, 409:18
  mantle of wind and c. and rain, 137:13
  penury, 315:22
  sun was warm wind c., 623:19
  thy dreaming nights, 412:1
  wind is c., 373:13
Chilling, on love request for money c., 493:16
Chills, of c. and fever died, 681:20
Chilly, I feel c. and old, 462:4
Chime, faintly as tolls evening c., 387:4
  higher than the sphery c., 252:28
  hours to which Heaven c., 269:2
  to guide their c., 267:7
Chimera, what a c. is man, 269:25
Chimeras, how many vain c. have you created, 140:13
Chimes at midnight, 188:15
  little jingle little c., 291:22
Chimleypiece, bottle on c., 464:39
Chimney, as c-sweepers come to dust, 220:26
  hung by c. with care, 387:2
  old men from c. corner, 162:18
  on habitations of death, 691:17
Chimneypiece, Buffalo upon c., 517:9
Chimneys, your c. I sweep, 351:2
Chin, close-buttoned to the c., 327:7
  dogs shame the gray c., 52:13
  my c. throbs, 867:1
  new-reaped, 181:35
China 'crost the Bay, 588:2
  leave C. convert Christians, 525:4
  mankind from C. to Peru, 306:15
  not seeking to dominate world, 697:7
  slow boat to C., 762:1
  though c. fall, 294:4
  thought of C. and Greece, 737:8
Chinee, heathen C. is peculiar, 528:10
Chinese, bombing of C. cities, 661:12
  great and vital people, 771:6
  people have solidarity, 598:10
  what things in you are C., 847:10
Chinese-Americans when you try to understand, 847:10
Chink, importunate c., 325:7
  in floor of Wicklow house, 611:13
Chinks of her sickness-broken body, 250:1
  that Time has made, 249:28
Chinook, break loose like c. salmon, 788:5
Chip of old block, 324:16
Chips down nation acts helpless, 771:7
  lest c. fall in eye, 880:9
Chirurgery, what c. relieve conscience, 235:19
Chisel, take a c. to write, 724:16
  whether c. pen or brush, 593:6
Chiseled, down their c. names, 537:1
Chivalrous, proud and c. spirit, 79:10
Chivalry, age of c. gone, 325:4
  charge with all thy c., 384:11
  her beauty and her c., 395:13
Chocolate, God bless…C. City, 850:6
  no c. to eat, 798:3
Choice and master spirits, 192:20
  brave man's c. is danger, 68:7
  can I have no other c., 788:9

Choice (continued)
  careful in c. of enemies, 560:1
  grain into this wilderness, 275:2
  Hobson's c., 881:12
  in the worth and c., 232:1
  it was not my c., 841:8
  life's business c., 463:6
  multiplicity of c., 782:6
  pays money takes c., 550:4
  reckless c., 622:21
  small c. in rotten apples, 173:7
  with freedom of c. and honor, 141:3
  word measured phrase, 369:17
Choices Harry that show what we are, 879:4
Choir, chorister whose *c* preceded c., 642:17
  full-voiced c. below, 251:23
  invisible, 480:16
  of saints, 231:1
  singing in the c., 883:5
  wailful c., 411:8
Choirs, bare ruined c., 221:24
Choke them amid flowers, 90:17
Choked with ambition of meaner sort, 169:18
Choleric, captain's c. word, 206:29
Chondria, Russia's c. for short, 418:20
Choose, any language you c., 527:3
  author as you c. friend, 276:22
  between Africa and English tongue, 829:4
  between betraying country and friend, 638:13
  do not c. to run, 613:7
  equality, 497:18
  fool multitude c. by show, 185:6
  ground and take thy rest, 399:17
  if thou must c. c. the odd, 749:16
  if you dare, 249:17
  intellect forced to c., 595:9
  let's c. executors, 177:7
  likely man in preference to rich, 62:19
  not c. not to be, 547:3
  path leading wherever I c., 486:24
  people did not c. this fight, 877:7
  slavery or death, 287:24
  therefore c. life, 9:29
  to live without friends, 78:10
  we c. to go to the moon, 786:7
  what becomes Castilian, 414:7
  whether she will be a mother, 657:16
Choosers, beggars should be no c., 147:21
Chooses, consciousness c. object, 541:2
  intimacy that c. right, 593:12
  no man c. evil, 360:15
Chop off her head, 514:9
  off your head, 893:7
Chopper, cheap and chippy c., 527:8
  to chop off your head, 893:7
Choral production resounds, 693:2
Chord in melancholy, 418:5
  in unison is touched, 327:4
  struck c. of music, 502:17
Chords that vibrate pleasure, 357:7
Chorister, bobolink for C., 508:18
  whose *c* preceded choir, 642:17
Chortled in his joy, 515:13
Chorus ending from Euripides, 461:22
  from Atlanta to sea, 517:13
  what a c., 384:2
Choruses above guinea's squawk, 704:15
Chose, David c. him five smooth stones, 11:1

Chosen, few are c., 35:11
  I have c. you, 40:2
  Lord hath c. thee, 9:17
  only c. had complications, 582:15
  people children of light, 496:10
  people of God, 336:10
  vessel, 40:24
Choses que je conte, 684:*n3*
Choughs that wing air, 212:24
Choux, que la mort me trouve plantant mes c., 152:*n2*
Christ ain't a-going to be too hard, 532:12
  all at once what C. is, 547:9
  blood when C. slain, 594:12
  born across the sea, 481:2
  born in Bethlehem, 305:10
  bowels of C., 246:16, 614:2
  came from God and a woman, 416:2
  came to save sinners, 44:24
  catch C. with worm, 787:2
  deep did rot O C., 376:4
  Don Quixote and I, 391:4
  everyone in world is C., 632:15
  face is face of C. himself, 487:8
  for this world C. died, 737:15
  half a drop ah my C., 169:4
  Himself buddy, 793:12
  his captain C., 177:14
  I believe in Jesus C., 48:11
  in C. all made alive, 43:1
  is all and in all, 44:12
  is C. thy advocate, 280:19
  it is the Inchcape Rock, 381:13
  Jesus C. her little child, 476:5
  Jesus C. is born, 898:17
  Jesus C. the righteous, 46:8
  Jesus C. the same yesterday, 45:17
  joint heirs with C., 41:19
  keep your hearts through C. Jesus, 44:6
  kingdom and patience of Jesus C., 46:14
  kingdoms of his C., 46:39
  listen C. you did alright, 731:4
  our Lord, 49:8
  our Passover sacrificed, 42:14
  our Savior, 883:4
  people who never heard of Jesus C., 683:18
  receive him, 454:17
  redemption by Jesus C., 48:16
  risen from dead, 43:1
  save us all, 436:10
  Savior which is C., 37:17
  show me dear C. Thy spouse, 230:27
  so Judas did to C., 177:16
  testimony of Jesus C., 46:14
  that it were possible, 455:4
  that my love in my arms, 881:1
  the Lord risen today, 305:7
  the Son took Father's place, 564:4
  thief said last word to C., 463:1
  thou art the C., 34:36
  to live is C., 44:1
  took the kindness, 463:1
  vision of C. thou see, 354:15
  what are patterns for, 626:13
  when C. calls a man, 745:6
  who has been my C., 438:21
Christendom, christianize C., 482:16
  in C. where Christian, 426:24

Civil *(continued)*
  in respect of c. rights, 518:1
  over violent or over c., 273:3
  rights of Englishman, 339:4
  sea grew c. at her song, 178:15
  state = political society + c. society, 689:14
  text of c. instruction, 337:12
  too c. by half, 346:6
Civil War rebirth of Union, 566:9
Civilian control of military, 661:11
Civility, wild c., 240:16
Civilization advances by operations perform
    without thinking, 580:6
  and profits go hand in hand, 613:5
  botched c., 665:9
  bourgeoisie draws nations into c., 478:10
  cannot tolerate wrongs, 694:3
  civilize c., 482:16
  could be restored, 638:3
  created under pressure of exigencies, 563:9
  cruelty is energy c. not corrupted, 334:11
  definition of c., 580:13
  elements of modern c., 407:13
  ever-rising problems of complex c., 652:14
  farmers founders of c., 390:15
  France conquered for c., 500:5
  has been no more than, 859:16
  ignorant free in state of c., 338:7
  in middle stage, 609:7
  meeting-point between savagery and c.,
    580:4
  nature and c. literary field, 543:16
  New York the collapse of c., 778:12
  not wiped out by atomic war, 638:3
  obstacles of c., 432:5
  or else modern c. in vain, 488:13
  poets in our c. difficult, 677:7
  progress toward privacy, 742:14
  provision for poor is test of c., 309:14
  requires slaves, 560:26
  resources of c. not exhausted, 442:15
  results in deserts, 635:13
  speech is c., 631:7
  theory of true c., 491:18
  thin crust over revolution, 574:2
  total extinction of human c., 728:7
  true test of c. is man, 428:19
  usual interval of c., 538:1
  with taxes I buy c., 539:12
  workers mainstay of c., 554:5
Civilizations break down fail to meet, 658:8
  challenge, 685:8
  clash of c., 782:8
  grow by responding to challenges, 685:8
Civilize civilization, 482:16
  educate Filipinos uplift c. them, 545:11
Civilized instinct finds subtler pleasure, 582:13
  man has habits of house, 472:20
  no c. life without clothes, 580:18
  society five qualities, 580:13
  they and I are c., 734:11
  valued by c. men, 562:10
  Woman last thing c., 505:6
Civilizer, comedy the ultimate c., 505:12
Civilizers, two c. of man, 430:14
Civis Romanus sum, 87:*n*5
Clad in beauty of thousand stars, 169:1
  in complete steel, 252:18

Clad *(continued)*
  in sober livery c., 257:24
  morn in russet mantle c., 196:20
  naked every day he c., 322:12
  with native honor c., 257:18
Claim that our city is education, 72:3
  woman takes off c. to respect, 69:6
Claims, adjustment of colonial c., 566:16
  of long descent, 451:2
  snakeskin titles of mining c., 715:18
Clamoring, citizens c. for what is wrong, 96:27
Clamorous owl that nightly hoots, 178:21
Clamors, immortal Jove's dread c., 209:13
  venom c. of jealous woman, 172:26
Clan, family party tribe c., 885:13
  leaf last of its c., 377:9
Clangor, trumpet's loud c., 273:24
Clap, cheaper seats c. your hands, 847:11
  if you believe c. hands, 577:11
  padlock on her mind, 283:12
  soul c. hands and sing, 594:2
Clapper, his tongue the c., 190:38
Claps, at heaven's gates c. wings, 162:9
Claptrap, art independent of c., 520:16
Claret liquor for boys, 310:24
Clarification, adventure in c. of thought, 580:10
  poem ends in c. of life, 625:3
Clarity, culture moment of c., 657:8
  give each moment c., 631:11
  of a general idea, 852:7
  suggests simplicity, 812:20
Clarum et venerabile nomen, 106:*n*12
Clash, bring to our ears c. of arms, 331:13
  ignorant armies c., 496:19
  of civilizations, 782:8
Clasp, dare deadly terrors c., 353:2
  thrice tried to c. her image, 53:11
Clasps crag with crooked hands, 454:13
Class, born into lower-upper-middle c., 735:6
  brutalizing lower c., 497:19
  could've had c. been somebody, 776:17
  distinctions which raise barrier, 655:8
  ideas of ruling c., 478:14
  leisure c. replaced by New C., 752:17
  materializing upper c., 497:19
  middle c. best political community, 78:26
  middle c. in America the nation, 497:21
  middle c. safety of England, 459:17
  no criminal c. except Congress, 524:11
  of 'ninety-seven, 871:12
  office of leisure c., 569:7
  one c. overthrows another, 698:10
  ones of middle c. who left home, 789:3
  proletariat revolutionary c., 478:11
  second c. citizens, 697:3
  second-c. intellect first-c. temperament,
    539:11
  she was in c. by herself, 724:8
  struggle, 477:16
  struggles, 478:8
  taking from one c., 299:19
  vulgarizing middle c., 497:19
  while lower c. I am in it, 561:11
  White-Anglo Saxon-Protestant upper c.,
    777:19
  working c. hero, 848:2
Classes, all c. times circumstances, 470:15
  antagonism between c., 478:13, 666:12

Classes *(continued)*
  back masses against c., 442:16
  bow lower middle c., 526:17
  dissolution of all c., 477:16
  division of society into two c., 423:10
  draw powers into higher c., 338:17
  four c. of Idols, 164:19
  let ruling c. tremble, 478:15
  no c. among citizens, 518:1
  noblest work she c. O, 356:22
  of travel first-class and with children,
    683:13
  other c. decay disappear, 478:11
  ruin of contending c., 478:8
  tempt upper c., 569:2
  tied to historical phases, 477:16
  two c. of people in world, 683:12
Classic book people praise don't read,
    524:15
  face, 447:12
  is book that has never, 801:10
  is book that survives, 779:11
  survives circumstances, 779:11
Classicist in literature, 677:9
  royalist Anglo-Catholic, 677:9
Classics, great homicidal c., 843:6
  in paraphrase, 665:7
  man with bellyful of c. enemy, 690:16
Classified, objects c., 343:16
Classless, formation of c. society, 477:16
Clatter they make with his coach, 277:21
Clause, servant with this c., 243:10
  two kinds of relative c., 570:2
Clavichord, stately at the c., 462:2
Claw, from c. can tell a lion, 120:21
  red in tooth and c., 454:1
Clawed, age c. me in his clutch, 149:10
Claws, neatly spreads c., 513:15
  pair of ragged c., 675:1
  that catch, 515:12
Clay, beings of mind are not of c., 396:3
  bless turf that wraps c., 317:11
  dead and turned to c., 202:14
  feet of c., 28:21
  in c. none is, 896:4
  kingdoms are c., 218:3
  lies still, 574:12
  of c. and wattles made, 591:2
  porcelain c. of humankind, 274:8
  power over the c., 41:27
  say to him that fashioneth it, 26:35
  tenement of c., 272:16
  to every people cup of c., 892:3
  weak creatures of c., 73:5
  white linen cold as c., 890:15
Clean, bid them keep teeth c., 219:27
  create in me a c. heart, 16:32
  he that hath c. hands, 15:24
  hearth, 383:10
  horse of courage, 798:2
  let other people c. up mess, 710:6
  passed c. over Jordan, 9:36
  pasture spring, 622:9
  purge me and I shall be c., 16:31
  she kept a really c. house, 834:17
  starved for a look, 221:25
  then c. and brave, 574:17
  things holy profane c. obscene, 239:8

Clean (*continued*)
think of c. beds, 668:12
tumbler and corkscrew, 464:22
wash blood c. from hand, 215:24
Cleaned windows swept floor, 525:22
Cleaning, yesterday had daily c., 776:12
Cleanliness next to godliness, 301:18
who of late for c., 237:15
Cleanly, leave sack and live c., 183:37
not too c. manger, 263:11
room lavender in windows, 245:4
thus so c. I myself can free, 167:11
Cleanse stuffed bosom of perilous stuff, 217:19
thou me from secret faults, 15:18
thoughts of our hearts, 49:3
Cleansed, what God hath c., 40:26
Cleanser, war the sole c. of the world, 633:7
Cleanses, poetry c., 786:15
Clean-shaven, buttoned-up and c., 542:14
Clean-winged hearth, 438:16
Clear, action faithful honor c., 294:9
and present danger, 538:21
as crystal, 466:32
as nose in face, 146:n2
as the sun, 24:19
as you go, 525:14
brown twilight atmosphere, 431:10
but one rule to be c., 392:8
coast was c., 167:12
deep and absolutely c., 762:16
distinction is c., 573:7
doctrines plain and c., 262:21
fire clean hearth, 383:10
honor purchased by merit, 185:8
in cool September morn, 438:11
in his great office, 214:24
literature c. and cold, 664:7
loser is perfectly c., 795:12
my sad thoughts doth c., 268:16
no c. line, 731:16
one c. call for me, 456:4
read my title c., 289:16
religion of heaven, 409:9
spouse so bright and c., 230:27
summers wet and winters c., 93:11
they could get it c., 516:1
viol of her memory, 641:6
what is not c. is not French, 347:7
wild call and c. call, 635:16
your mind of cant, 311:11
Cleared, if this were only c., 516:1
ship cheered harbor c., 375:20
Clearer, age c. than noonday, 13:22
view ourselves with c. eyes, 241:17
Clearest of God's creatures, 787:13
way into Universe through forest, 533:9
who have c. vision, 72:1
Clearly, I see so c., 344:2
well conceived c. said, 278:3
Clearness, chief merit of language c., 112:22
Clears today of past Regrets, 441:15
Cleave, man c. to his like, 31:1
thou canst not c. the earth, 118:14
to sunnier side of doubt, 456:2
tongue c. to the roof of my mouth, 19:11
unto his wife, 5:17
wood there am I, 113:19

Cleft, apple's c. through core, 360:14
Rock of Ages c. for me, 334:13
who c. Devil's foot, 228:9
Clemenceau had one illusion, 656:9
Clemency a species of nobility, 276:9
Clemens Lincoln of literature, 529:3
Clement's, bells of St. C., 893:6
Cleopatra, every man's C., 272:13
squeaking C., 219:10
Cleopatra's nose, 269:13
Clergy, without benefit of c., 611:n5
Clergyman, avoid c. who is man of business, 115:8
so much at home, 521:9
who never refuses dinner, 115:10
Clergymen, bankers schoolmasters c., 591:19
men women and c., 375:3
Clergymen's households unhappy, 521:9
Cleric before and Lay behind, 262:15
Clerk, a bed C. Saunders said, 890:1
no difference 'twixt Priest and C., 241:2
ther was of Oxenford, 133:21
Clerks, gretteste c. noght wisest men, 135:1
Clever, encouraging c. pupil, 305:4
hopes expire, 748:16
men at Oxford, 574:9
of the turtle, 732:6
persuade someone less c., 843:11
think oneself more c., 264:7
wet mind and say something c., 72:11
young poets, 380:3
Cleverer, advantage over c. boys, 619:2
Cleverness that gets out of hand, 72:6
Clicked, off by little wheels, 713:11
Clickin' like tickin' of clock, 553:10
Client, art thou his c., 280:19
Clients, good counselors lack no c., 206:13
Cliff between lowland and highland, 530:25
dreadful summit of the c., 198:1
Cliffs of Dover, 599:8
of England stand, 496:16
of fall frightful sheer, 547:6
white c. of Dover, 627:4
would I were under the c., 68:2
Climacteric of his want, 787:15
Climate, age too late or cold c., 259:6
altering Earth's c., 825:15
coal portable c., 428:5
difference of soil and c., 369:4
whole c. of opinion, 749:6
Climate's sultry, 397:21
Climates councils governments, 451:13
Climax of terror, 744:10
Climb back to upper air, 94:27
but I must c. the tree, 242:16
fain c. yet fear to fall, 159:6
high climb far, 887:16
if heart fails c. not, 159:n3
let me c. when I lie down, 268:13
no man c. beyond limitations, 533:4
Sinais c. and know it not, 481:14
teach ye how to c., 252:28
Climbed, never c. Mount Sion, 787:17
to top of greasy pole, 430:10
Climber-upward turns face, 191:36
Climbest, moon c. skies, 162:21
Climbing, down thou c. sorrow, 211:17
high into the sun, 720:11

Climbing (*continued*)
liken fame to c. up a hill, 398:7
shakes his dewy wings, 249:19
still c. after knowledge infinite, 168:2
third stair, 677:15
Climbs, everybody c. into graves married, 715:6
higher monkey c. more see of behind, 126:6
in front sun c. slow, 479:12
Clime, change c. not disposition, 98:3
love no season knows nor c., 228:16
that lieth sublime, 449:1
Climes, cloudless c. starry skies, 397:1
Cling, bough where I c., 443:15
kiss and c., 517:n1
to old rugged cross, 615:5
together in one society, 368:14
Clings, desire for glory c., 110:10
Clink, why c. cannikin, 460:9
Clip, philosophy c. wings, 409:16
Cloak, covers man like c., 158:8
my fine camlet c., 277:1
not alone my inky c., 196:26
old c. about thee, 881:9
prince of Wales in lovely ermine c., 647:4
smylere with knyf under c., 134:19
sold even to c. I wore, 140:1
Cloaked, firs darkly c., 552:11
Clock, a-clickin' like tickin' of c., 553:10
celestial machine similar to c., 228:1
collected in tower, 575:18
doth strike by algebra, 262:8
forgot to wind c., 313:20
in belfry strikes one, 517:12
key-machine of modern industrial age, 708:4
like c. being put half hour fast, 469:8
stands c. at ten to three, 669:7
stops time come to life, 713:11
strikes at city's edge, 580:3
struck one, 893:3
ticks, 827:11
time made me numbering c., 177:23
will strike Devil will come, 169:4
Clock's loneliness, 827:10
Clocks, stop all the c., 748:13
tongues of bawds, 181:20
were striking thirteen, 735:15
Clod, a kneaded c., 206:38
feverish selfish little c., 565:3
if c. washed away, 231:8
in the soul in the c., 462:5
of wayward marl, 190:23
Clods, only a man harrowing c., 536:22
Clog, three generations atween c. and c., 521:n1
Clogged, if drainpipes of house c., 493:12
Cloister, pale with breath of c., 500:5
Cloistered, flown his c. flight, 216:12
virtue, 254:9
Close behind him tread, 376:21
cannot hold thee c. enough, 695:7
decay grossly c. it in, 186:15
designs crooked counsels, 272:16
draw the curtain c., 170:9
eyes with holy dread, 377:23
her from ancient walls, 354:14

Close *(continued)*
  life closed before its c., 511:9
  mistake not to c. eyes, 582:6
  not a friend to c. eyes, 274:18
  rave at c. of day, 777:15
  setting sun and music at c., 176:21
  shutters fast, 327:1
  the circle of felicities, 337:11
  up his eyes and draw curtain, 170:9
  upon the growing boy, 370:17
  wall up with English dead, 189:7
  you aren't c. enough, 770:11
Close-buttoned to the chin, 327:7
Close-up, I'm ready for my c., 747:14
Closed, dust hath c. Helen's eye, 227:6
  eyes in endless night, 316:13
  in death attentive eyes, 308:3
  mouth swallows no flies, 898:9
  twice before its close, 511:9
Closer, sticketh c. than a brother, 21:5
  walk with God, 326:7
Closes, life as it c., 529:19
  path emerges then c., 599:17
Closet, back in C. lays, 441:22
  do very well in a c., 298:11
  knowledge not in c., 298:3
  one need only shut oneself in c., 542:13
Closing, always be c., 865:7
  busy hammers c. rivets, 189:18
  diapason c. full in Man, 273:22
  time in gardens of West, 734:8
Clot bedded axle-tree, 678:8
  created Man of blood c., 119:18
  created you of blood c., 118:21
Cloth, cut my coat after my c., 147:7
  gray c. brings wood to life, 871:2
  meat drink and c. to us, 146:6
  untrue with twisted cue, 527:17
Clothe my naked villainy, 171:25
  summer c. general earth, 377:15
  with rags, 21:28
Clothed all in leather, 897:1
  and in right mind, 36:33
  his neck with thunder, 14:26
  in white samite held sword, 138:4
  in white samite mystic, 455:8
  man c. with rags, 271:8
  naked and he c. him, 320:6
  naked and ye c. me, 35:30
  with heavens, 278:10
Clothes, after that take the girl's c. off,
    674:12
  are powerful things, 735:4
  as c. to bodies, 580:18
  biographies but c. and buttons, 525:6
  enterprises that require new c., 474:17
  food fuel and c., 484:23
  for spring, 775:1
  give woman comfortable c., 655:4
  good smell of old c., 669:9
  hanging out c., 894:7
  his old c. a few books, 658:4
  keep male and female likeness, 654:12
  kindles in c. a wantonness, 240:15
  liquefaction of her c., 241:14
  loves but their oldest c., 228:13
  make the man, 525:10
  Mordecai rent his c., 12:31

Clothes *(continued)*
  never did know what c. to put on, 637:1
  nothing wears c. but Man, 242:23
  on hickory limb, 887:17
  part of man's Self, 541:4
  spoiling nice new c., 895:3
  stepped out of c., 596:5
  swaddling c., 37:16
  take fire and his c. not be burned, 20:3
  that you could move in, 838:10
  through tattered c., 212:30
  thrown on with pitchfork, 285:20
  upon c. behind tenement, 687:11
  walked away with c., 430:6
  when he put on his c., 322:12
Clothing, come in sheep's c., 33:20
  I put on women's c., 879:9
  of delight, 350:12
  softest c. woolly bright, 350:12
  strength and honor are her c., 22:18
  wolf in sheep's c., 58:13
Cloths, heavens' embroidered c., 591:12
Clotilda, God of C. grant victory, 116:25
Cloud, brightest day hath c., 170:4
  but c. and like shady grove, 350:15
  comes over sunlit arch, 623:19
  fair luminous c., 378:9
  fat pink c., 786:17
  flash of lightning in summer c., 112:26
  geese like snow c., 681:19
  house made of dark c., 891:17
  in shape of a camel, 200:26
  in trousers, 698:16
  joy the luminous c., 378:10
  lift me as wave leaf c., 402:12
  lightning out of dark c., 547:18
  like a fiend in a c., 350:9, 353:6
  like a man's hand, 12:2
  lovely see c. appear, 891:14
  of barbarism and despotism, 338:15
  of witnesses, 45:12
  on a c. I saw a child, 350:10
  pillar of c., 8:2
  sable c., 252:13
  seemed to be local dust c., 774:12
  set my bow in the c., 6:25
  silver lining when c. appears, 705:6
  Son of man coming in c., 38:29
  stirred by solitary c., 279:20
  stooping through a fleecy c., 251:16
  that looked like centaur, 72:14
  that's dragonish, 218:39
  through dark c. shining, 616:17
  wandered lonely as c., 371:9
  when c. is scattered, 404:10
Cloud-capped towers, 225:1
Cloud-Cuckoo-Land, 73:6
Clouded, moon rising in c. majesty, 257:25
Cloud-kissing Ilion, 172:38
Cloudless climes starry skies, 397:1
  fill sky with c. sunshine, 97:8
  scintillant in c. days, 659:1
Clouds and eclipses stain, 221:11
  are pedagogues, 642:3
  ascribing to c. the flame, 104:9
  barred c. bloom soft-dying day, 411:8
  base contagious c., 181:33
  blue-massing c., 669:9

Clouds *(continued)*
  cannot be in deep sea, 90:11
  color that paints morning evening c.,
    130:12
  creeping quietly over it, 506:13
  fill sky with black c., 97:8
  he that regardeth the c., 23:27
  her life filled with c. of goodness, 340:*n*2
  home made of blue c., 891:15
  hung oppressively, 448:8
  looks in the c., 191:36
  maketh the c. his chariot, 18:8
  mountains fleeting as c., 119:1
  new-made c., 777:13
  no pity sitting in c., 181:4
  nor c. soak with showers, 53:*n*1
  number the c. in wisdom, 14:25
  O c. unfold, 354:8
  out of c. silence, 550:3
  pack c. away, 233:18
  prince of c., 491:2
  return after the rain, 23:30
  round setting sun, 371:5
  scare white c. on, 622:21
  sees God in c., 294:20
  she seems to think hers drop from c., 499:7
  silk-sack c., 546:14
  somewhere among c. above, 592:20
  spirits of wise sit in c., 188:5
  storm-c. brood on heights, 468:3
  sun breaks through darkest c., 173:22
  sweep c. no more, 443:3
  trailing c. of glory, 370:17
  tumult in the c., 593:1
  under surge of blue mottled c., 658:9
  what with all these c., 73:6
  wrapt in c. and snow, 395:17
Cloud-topped hill, 294:20
Cloudy, among c. trophies hung, 411:11
  huge c. symbols, 412:8
  skies not c. all day, 890:20
  tabernacle parted, 414:6
  was the weather, 897:1
Clove, burning c., 623:10
Cloven tongues as of fire, 40:15
Clovenfooted, whatsoever is c., 8:23
Clover and one bee, 511:12
  any time Aristocracy, 511:5
  looking over four-leaf c., 693:8
Clove's sweet smell, 766:15
Clown, emperor and c., 410:10
  of spirit's motive, 772:2
Clowns, send in the c., 829:2
Cloy appetites they feed, 218:21
  hungry edge of appetite, 176:18
  of all meats soonest c., 265:7
Cloyless sauce, 218:18
Club, any c. that will accept me, 707:13
  assembly of good fellows, 306:24
  first rule of fight c., 877:9
  not with C. Heart broken, 510:17
  spear to thrust c. to strike, 145:2
Clue, singularity almost invariably a c., 573:11
Cluett, land of the C. Shirt, 701:9
Cluster, woes c., 201:*n*2
Clustered spires of Frederick, 438:12
Clutch, age clawed me in his c., 149:10
  come let me c. thee, 215:13

Come *(continued)*

    hither, 194:11
    home to roost, 381:14
    home with me now, 517:12
    hour is not yet c., 39:3
    Husband I c., 219:14
    I c. quickly, 47:14
    I c. to bury Caesar, 192:28
    I hear you I will c., 575:1
    I will c. again, 39:41
    I will never c. back, 767:4
    I would not c. in, 624:9
    idea whose time c., 422:8
    if c. to my house I will c. to yours, 102:28
    if not to c. will be now, 202:26
    if now 'tis not to c., 202:26
    if you build it he will c., 840:5
    in the rearward of woe, 221:29
    in under shadow, 676:6
    into the garden Maud, 455:1
    it shall not c. nigh thee, 17:28
    I've c. to talk with you again, 855:6
    jump the life to c., 214:22
    King of glory shall c. in, 15:25
    kiss me sweet and twenty, 204:26
    knit hands, 252:11
    know end ere it c., 193:18
    knowledge must c. through action, 66:11
    let it c., 864:13
    let me clutch thee, 215:13
    let us kiss and part, 167:11
    let us mock at great, 594:10
    let us sing unto Lord, 17:32
    let's away to prison, 213:8
    like shadows so depart, 217:1
    live with me and be my love, 168:4, 229:14
    Lord is c., 289:15
    lovely soothing death, 487:14
    men may c. and go, 454:25
    Messiah will c. day after arrival, 655:15
    Mr. Watson c. here, 550:11
    Muse migrate from Greece, 487:3
    my Celia let us prove, 232:5
    my coach, 201:26
    my lad and drink beer, 308:4
    my own c. to me, 528:13
    near me while I sing, 591:1
    never c. back to me, 452:16
    night strike hour, 643:19
    not between dragon and wrath, 210:27
    not near our fairy queen, 178:22
    not to steal away hearts, 193:3
    nothing can c. of this, 801:19
    nothing will c. of nothing, 210:24
    now and let us reason, 24:32
    O come Emmanuel, 479:3
    on kids, 690:15
    one come all, 374:2
    over into Macedonia, 40:30
    over way with tears watered, 609:15
    past and to c. seem best, 187:39
    past passing or to c., 594:4
    season to c. and go, 296:18
    seeling night, 216:13
    shan't be gone long you c. too, 622:9
    so far it is over, 833:5
    that it should c. to this, 196:30
    that it will never c. again, 511:10

Come *(continued)*

    that they might have life, 39:30
    things past or things to c., 271:16
    things to c., 203:10
    thou monarch of the vine, 218:27
    thou'lt c. no more, 213:14
    three corners of world, 176:7
    thy kingdom c., 32:25
    till boys c. home, 616:17
    Time will c., 221:19
    'tis the gift to c. down, 885:3
    to aid of party, 885:18
    to lay weary bones among ye, 226:7
    to my arms, 515:13
    to my woman's breasts, 214:17
    to pluck your berries, 252:29
    to see and be seen, 102:3
    to take their ease, 226:16
    to thee by moonlight, 646:2
    to this favor she must c., 202:12
    to this stage of fools, 213:1
    treading path through blood, 609:15
    unbutton here, 212:3
    until I c. in peace, 12:10
    unto me ye that labor, 34:9
    unto my love, 161:6
    unto these yellow sands, 224:12
    up and see me sometime, 700:*n*3
    up sometime and see me, 700:7
    weal come woe, 367:15
    what come may, 214:13
    what dreams may c., 199:21
    what is to c. I know not, 29:25
    what may I have been blessed, 396:24
    what may Sinon said, 103:4
    wheel is c. full circle, 213:11
    when shall I c. to thee, 881:18
    when will indifference c., 773:20
    whence had they c., 596:8
    whistle and I'll c. to you, 357:16
    whistle and she'll c. to you, 238:7
    will they c. when you call, 182:34
    with singing unto Zion, 26:39
    within bending sickle's compass c., 222:15
    women c. and go, 674:18
    won't c. back till it's over, 635:2
    worst is yet to c., 455:23
    ye thankful people, 456:9
    ye to the waters, 27:9
    you back to Mandalay, 588:1
    you spirits that tend, 214:17

Come-a ti yi youpy youpy yea, 890:13
Comedian can last till he takes himself serious,
    640:7
Comedians extemporally will stage us, 219:10
Comedy, all I need to make c., 683:17
    catastrophe of the old c., 211:4
    difference between c. and tragedy, 834:3
    Is Not Pretty, 861:9
    killing time essence of c., 586:6
    most lamentable c., 178:2
    the c. is finished, 570:6
    the ultimate civilizer, 505:12
    world is a c., 317:5
Comely, attire c. not costly, 161:19
    black but c., 24:4
    grace, 882:1
Comer, grasps in the c., 203:24

Comers, entertain all c., 51:10
Comes apparelled like spring, 220:9
    at one stride c. the dark, 376:9
    at the last, 177:9
    Autumn c. jovial on, 300:21
    conquering hero c., 301:13
    Death who c. at last, 373:8
    effect defective c. by cause, 198:29
    evening darkens and c. on, 817:8
    ever 'gainst that season c., 196:19
    fog c. on cat feet, 636:3
    God behind them, 462:26
    God c. as sun at noon, 231:10
    he c. he c., 274:16
    Here C. Everybody, 650:20
    hope never c., 255:9
    in the sweet o' the year, 223:21
    knowledge c. wisdom lingers, 452:6
    look who c. here, 175:17
    love that c. too late, 206:11
    moment to decide, 481:12
    pat he c., 211:4
    Rainbow c. and goes, 370:14
    something wicked this way c., 216:29
    unlooked for if c. at all, 292:7
    wine c. in at mouth, 592:6
Comest in such questionable shape, 197:33
    O Death thou c., 880:17
    whence c. thou, 12:36
Cometh, another generation c., 22:21
    behold the day c. that shall burn, 29:20
    forth like a flower, 13:29
    from afar, 370:17
    from whence c. my help, 18:30
    hour c. and now is, 39:13
    in the name of the Lord, 18:27
    joy c. in the morning, 16:1
    my help c. from the Lord, 18:30
    the night c., 39:27
    this dreamer c., 7:5
    whence it c., 39:9
Comets, discoverers as c., 305:4
    when beggars die no c., 192:10
Comfort and despair, 223:3
    bred in modest c., 888:16
    carrion c., 547:3
    conceited carry c., 480:11
    continual c. in a face, 169:9
    convenience lacking to modern c., 555:3
    gives c. in despair, 170:2
    giving enemies aid and c., 339:13
    hobbit-hole and that means c., 696:11
    I beg cold c., 176:5
    is any c. to be found, 594:8
    like cold porridge, 224:18
    me with apples, 24:8
    nightingale sing of c., 432:20
    of c. no man speak, 177:7
    she hath none to c. her, 28:10
    so will I c. you, 27:23
    society no c. to one not sociable, 220:24
    thy rod and thy staff c. me, 15:23
    to my age, 194:3
    warn to c. and command, 371:8
    what gnashing is not a c., 231:9
    ye my people, 26:23
Comfortable advice, 413:7
    and satisfying sleep, 633:6

Comfortable (continued)

feel free easy c. on a raft, 523:4
feeling of superiority, 645:11
give woman c. clothes, 655:4
minds, 701:8
newspaper afflicts c., 600:16
no c. feel, 418:15
progress a c. disease, 702:1

Comfortably in debt, 459:5
padded lunatic asylums, 654:6
speak c. to Jerusalem, 26:24

Comforted, be c. for him, 31:24
folly of being c., 591:16
they shall be c., 32:14
would not be c., 32:2

Comforters, miserable c. are ye all, 13:33

Comforteth, love c. like sunshine, 171:13
one whom his mother c., 27:23

Comfortless, God does not leave us c., 864:13
grim-visaged c. Despair, 315:7
not leave you c., 39:43

Comforts, adversity not without c., 165:16
creature c., 282:14
flee, 405:8
of life not indispensable, 474:15
of weary pilgrimage, 311:8
what I aspired c. me, 462:16

Comic demands anesthesia of heart, 572:6
poet paint follies, 286:24

Comical how nature contrive, 526:22

Comin', Campbells are c., 883:10

Coming back and coming back, 642:11
cold c. we had of it, 677:6
events cast shadows, 384:10
everything's c. up roses, 828:16
far off his c. shone, 258:24
for to carry me home, 898:21
Gospel train's a-c., 899:3
hither, 213:7
hold fort I am c., 489:12
I am c. says Death, 95:14
I'm c., 503:15
it's c. yet for a' that, 358:20
my own my sweet, 455:3
night of dark intent c., 623:13
of the Lord, 45:32, 481:1
oh she is c., 634:1
patient unto c. of Lord, 45:32
preserve thy going out and c. in, 18:30
see anyone c., 883:6
their c. our beginning, 672:6
through the rye, 883:3
to the sacrifice, 410:18
together foretaste of resurrection, 400:2
way of c. into world, 284:1
we are c. Father Abraham, 457:3
Yanks are c., 635:1

Comings-in, what are thy c., 189:22

Command, barking of Germans in c., 793:1
by his c. words cut, 597:11
correspondent to c., 224:10
eagle mount at thy c., 14:29
fit for c., 328:7
give what you c., 116:8
Heaven's c., 301:3
iron fist to c. them, 366:11
man to c., 453:3

Command (continued)

move only in c., 217:15
my heart and me, 263:3
not born to sue but to c., 176:10
not full c. of myself, 145:8
prize of general is c., 538:17
she might c. him tasks, 209:25
sneer of cold c., 401:13
success, 287:22
take c. of troops, 365:10
threaten and c., 201:5
warn to comfort and c., 371:8
where I adore, 205:7
who commands sea has c., 62:22

Commanded, do without being c., 77:11
God so c., 259:10
Hellenes c. by Athenians, 62:18
nature to be c. must be obeyed, 165:1
rain shower of c. tears, 173:5

Commander, Congress is his c., 404:17
to the people, 27:10

Commander-in-Chief not of country, 694:8
President is C., 404:17

Commandment, a new c., 39:39
first and great c., 35:13, 686:4
one unconditional c., 541:16

Commandments, aren't no Ten C., 588:3
Christian c. too strict, 469:8
fear God and keep his c., 24:2
hearkened to my c., 26:37
love me and keep my c., 8:12
on these two c. hang law and prophets, 35:13
set my ten c. in your face, 169:24
ten c., 8:22

Commands, he that c. sea is at liberty, 166:16
I gave c., 460:3
the beauteous files, 268:15
those he c. move in command, 217:15
war necessary to one who c., 141:16
who c. the sea has command, 62:22

Commedia è finita, 570:*n*5

Commemorated as day of deliverance, 330:1

Commencement of history, 327:12

Commend, all our swains c. her, 173:34
all summer long, 594:1
blame or to c., 295:13
my spirit, 38:37
those who are afflicted, 48:15
to cold oblivion, 403:11

Commendable, humility a thing c., 147:*n*2

Commendations, paltry c. of mankind, 449:2

Commended yellow stockings, 205:9

Comment, no c. splendid expression, 621:10

Commentary, that is whole Torah rest is c., 102:27

Commerce and honest friendship, 337:12
equal to whole of that c., 323:22
heavens fill with c., 452:2
navigation c. agriculture, 330:7
with our colonies, 324:1

Commercing, looks c. with the skies, 251:13

Commission, sins of c. mortal, 311:19

Commit, follies that themselves c., 185:1
history they did not c., 829:8
oldest sins newest ways, 188:24
shalt not c. a social science, 749:15
thou shalt not c. adultery, 8:14

Committed, crimes c. in thy name, 348:4

flat burglary as ever c., 191:8
sins most grievously c., 49:5
themselves to God, 240:1
to whom men have c. much, 38:6
vices c. genteelly, 310:2

Committee for affairs of bourgeoisie, 478:9
inquisition, 638:7
is an animal, 830:7
violence punctuated by c. meetings, 853:8

Committees, intellectual before c., 638:7

Commodities, hateful tax on c., 307:1

Commodity bias of the world, 175:12
of good names, 181:27
regard land as c., 668:2
smooth-faced gentleman C., 175:12
tickling C., 175:12

Commodius vicus of recirculation, 650:19

Common air bathes globe, 486:1
buries empires in c. grave, 332:10
call not thou c., 40:26
cause decays, 71:13
cause to save Union, 445:2
crossing bare c., 425:21
dictate of c. sense, 301:12
earth and every c. sight, 370:13
education forms c. mind, 293:24
faction united by c. impulse, 345:8
fade into light of c. day, 370:18
friends have all in c., 74:4
government for c. benefit, 320:8
hate the c. herd, 96:25
I drew in the c. air, 30:5
I embrace the c., 426:7
law not omnipresence, 538:19
law nothing but reason, 158:21
life's c. way, 370:10
make good thing too c., 187:34
man, 548:14
no c. men, 427:26
not jump with c. spirits, 185:7
nothing c. did or mean, 266:18
old c. arbitrator Time, 204:6
provide for c. defense, 339:11
right of humanity, 444:12
roll of c. men, 182:33
sense and plain dealing, 427:16
sense appall, 579:3
sense hasty superficial, 473:26
sense not so common, 299:18
sense of next age, 497:17
sense reduced to calculus, 345:4
steals c. from goose, 881:23
sun air skies, 316:9
sweets grown c., 222:7
talk of the town, 277:7
the actual world the c. sense, 473:12
thou knowest 'tis c., 196:25
touch, 590:2
uncommon valor c. virtue, 664:10
universal and c. bond, 153:16
weal and woe is c., 247:8
where climate's sultry, 397:21
witness to c. lot, 683:7

Common-looking people best, 446:6

Commonplace, more featureless c. a crime, 573:11
never yawn or say c., 799:3

Constitution (*continued*)
    letter and spirit of c., 349:16
    looks to indestructible Union, 438:19
    make real the C., 629:5
    most remarkable work, 442:17
    named a democracy, 71:14
    no society can make perpetual c., 336:16
    not merely for generation, 384:19
    not provide for second class, 697:3
    of United States the shield, 470:15
    one country one c., 390:14
    openly invaded, 339:7
    ordain and establish C., 339:11
    our C. is now established, 303:20
    people made the C., 350:2
    principle of English c., 318:20
    principles of free c. lost, 332:3
    venerable parts of c., 324:15
    what judges say it is, 582:5
Constitutional constellation, 694:2
    exercise c. right, 445:5
    inconsistent with c. theory, 724:4
    means which are c., 349:16
    shield, 666:15
    symptom of c. liberty, 332:6
Constitutions, make and alter c., 328:14
Constrained, worship God not c. by force,
    106:5
Constraineth, spirit within me c. me, 14:12
Construct beliefs and hopes, 681:16
    proceed to c. socialist order, 607:11
Constructed, thing c. loved after c., 618:11
Constructing tribal lays, 588:11
Construction and creation, 618:11
    find the mind's c., 214:15
Constructive, superstition c. religion, 490:14
Consul, my youth when Plancus was c., 97:6
Consule, fortunatam natam me c. Romam,
    88:*n*4
Consuls, each year new c., 111:4
Consulship, Rome natal neath my c., 88:9
Consult concerning great goddess, 366:18
    first c. our private ends, 264:*n*4
Consume according to need, 478:*n*2
    engines of despotism, 338:15
    entire combustible world, 592:17
    my heart away, 594:3
    own smoke, 407:22
    time c. strongest cord, 374:8
    without producing, 564:19
Consumed, bush was not c., 7:25
    by either fire or fire, 679:11
    days are c. like smoke, 18:4
    in image if not in usage, 778:1
    them as stubble, 8:7
Consumer, promoting interest of c., 319:9
Consumes, delight that c. desire, 529:18
    painter's brush c. dreams, 594:13
Consumeth, watching for riches c. flesh, 31:18
Consuming rag and bone, 596:13
    serves industrial system by c., 753:3
Consummated, marriages c. on earth, 162:11
Consummation devoutly to be wished, 199:21
    quiet c. have, 220:27
Consumption, captain of men of death was C.,
    271:29
    conspicuous c., 569:4
    of the purse, 187:36

Consumption (*continued*)
    purpose of all production, 319:9
Contact contact, 473:12
    of two skins, 335:1
    possible to flesh, 675:26
    with the soil, 597:1
    word preserves c., 631:7
Contagion, foul c. spread, 253:11
    of world's slow stain, 403:23
    rest of us in danger of c., 715:12
    to this world, 200:29
Contagious, base c. clouds, 181:33
    blastments imminent, 197:19
    by road to c. hospital, 658:9
Contain, I c. multitudes, 486:18
    margin too narrow to c., 247:5
    one the other will c., 509:13
    show c. and nourish all world, 174:24
Contained nothing but itself, 531:20
Container, bright c. can contain, 756:6
Containment of Russian expansive tendencies,
    738:8
Contains, the cistern c., 351:15
    what Fortitude Soul c., 511:13
Contemneth small things, 31:6
Contemplate entangled bank, 440:4
    our forefathers, 318:4
Contemplating characters of reigning
    sovereigns, 337:16
    how life goes swiftly, 139:5
Contemplation, beneath thy c., 479:2
    everything object of c., 379:18
    he for c. formed, 257:19
    her best nurse C., 252:17
    lose itself in mazes of inward c., 556:18
    mind serene for c., 287:*n*3
    more than reading, 270:10
    right c., 64:18
    sundry c. of my travels, 195:23
Contemplative or saintly life, 746:11
Contemporaries, drudgery of their c., 693:4
    man lives life of c., 631:1
Contempt against majesty of Heaven, 301:8
    and anger of lip, 205:15
    comes from head, 399:21
    familiarity breeds c., 58:19
    for c. too high, 265:6
    for governor who is afraid, 65:12
    if one fails, 299:2
    no weakness no c., 260:25
    of God contempt of self, 116:19
    reading it with perfect c., 671:1
    silence is c., 432:4
    speak of moderns without c., 298:9
    treating with c. all from God, 144:9
Contemptible, bored more c. than bore,
    521:3
    struggle, 323:16
Contemptuous, discerning reader c., 570:1
Contend, gods c. in vain, 360:9
    no more Love, 460:23
    seven towns c. for Homer, 233:*n*3
    ye powers of heaven, 263:11
Contender, could've been a c., 776:17
Contending, calm c. kings, 172:35
    fierce c. nations, 288:1
    for liberty, 328:5
    leaders ambitiously c., 345:9

Content, be c. with your lot, 59:6
    farewell c., 209:13
    humble livers in c., 225:17
    I am c., 363:11
    I am c. forever, 694:12
    in evening die c., 61:1
    in health and mind's c., 277:18
    in tight hot cell, 713:3
    in whatsoever state to be c., 44:8
    land of lost c., 575:6
    majority of men c., 142:3
    make c. with fortunes fit, 211:31
    money means and c., 195:5
    my crown is called c., 170:25
    natural c., 592:5
    nothing less will c. me, 324:5
    poor and c. is rich, 209:4
    shut up in measureless c., 215:12
    that we might procreate like trees, 248:16
    thoughts that savor of c., 164:2
    to breathe his native air, 292:4
    to entertain lag-end of my life, 183:21
    to live it all again, 595:4
    travelers must be c., 194:7
    with life retire from world, 95:18
    with my harm, 195:6
    with vegetable love, 526:11
    with your lot, 59:6
Contented, live on little with c. mind, 90:18
    men employed best c., 304:3
    most enjoy c. least, 221:6
    wi' little, 357:5
    with random consolations, 719:18
Contentedness, procurer of c., 245:1
Contention, let long c. cease, 497:2
    man of strife and c., 27:37
Contentions are like bars of a castle, 21:3
    fat c., 254:3
    of a wife, 21:7
Contentment, in c. still feel need, 640:21
    nor poorest receive c., 231:14
    preaches c. to toad, 586:18
    recover through c. with physician, 70:18
Contents, inability of mind to correlate all c.,
    687:7
    torn out and stripped, 301:20
Contest, this is a people's c., 445:9
Contests, what mighty c. rise, 293:3
Context, immediate c. of history, 696:6
Contiguity, boundless c. of shade, 326:20
Continence, give me c. but not now, 116:4
Continent allotted by Providence, 469:11
    Americans prefer C., 603:3
    brought forth on c., 446:5
    heart no island but c., 165:23
    iron curtain across C., 621:11
    man is a piece of the c., 231:8
    most momentous question on c., 500:6
    our c. the old one, 344:30
    sexual life of women dark c., 563:13
    striving to grasp c., 500:4
    untamed c., 500:5
Continental, Jehovah and C. Congress, 334:1
Continents, American c. not subjects for
    colonization, 355:5
    dissolve into sea, 750:1
Contingencies, O to be self-balanced for c.,
    485:13

Continual comfort in a face, 169:9
  contentions of wife are c. dropping, 21:7
  endeavor in c. motion, 188:34
  feast, 20:32
  live in c. mortification, 301:6
  small have c. plodders won, 174:1
Continually, think c. of truly great, 760:6
  times change and move c., 160:24
Continuation, thermonuclear war not c. of
    politics, 797:4
Continued, not one c. faithful until old age,
    76:13
Continues, tree c. to be, 680:4
Continueth, he fleeth and c. not, 13:29
Continuing, faculty of c. to improve, 327:12
  no c. city, 45:18
Continuity, restructuring combines c.
    innovation, 830:3
Continuous and seems always existing, 57:2
  as stars that shine, 371:10
  brain changes c., 541:1
  nature one and c., 474:2
  use of any organ, 341:8
Contract, passions we inspire c. time, 610:17
  permanent c. on temporary feeling, 536:7
  Social C. vast conspiracy, 598:14
  succession bourn none, 224:19
  'twixt Hannah God and me, 518:7
  unspoken c. of wife and her works,
    781:16
Contraction of life, 630:4
Contracts, prisoners cannot enter into c.,
    790:19
  with the people, 661:10
Contradict, do I c. myself, 486:18
  never c., 755:n1
Contradiction, phrase long poem c., 450:1
  what a c. is man, 269:25
  when we risk no c., 291:11
  woman's a c. still, 294:5
Contradictions exist side by side, 492:8
  that can't be solved by analysis, 746:1
Contradicts, some part of me c. the rest, 468:16
Contraries, by c. execute all things, 224:19
Contrariously, work c., 188:36
Contrariwise, 515:19
Contrary blast proclaims, 260:18
  bringeth bliss, 169:22
  everythink c. with me, 465:20
  Mary quite c., 893:5
  runneth not to the c., 318:19
  Spirit and flesh c., 43:30
  to the c. notwithstanding, 339:14
Contrast between genius and talent, 617:16
Contribute to diversion or improvement of
    country, 288:3
Contribution according to capacity, 478:n2
Contributions to peace of world, 661:9
Contrite, broken and c. heart, 16:35
Contrivance of human wisdom, 325:3
  to raise prices, 319:2
Contrivances, wisdom of human c., 324:3
Contrive, head to c., 261:1
  our fees to pilfer, 72:16
Contrived corridors, 675:22
Control and communication theory, 704:18
  cannot c. atomic energy, 611:10
  Chance shall not c., 494:14

Control (*continued*)
  civilian c. of military, 661:11
  enable government to c. governed, 345:12
  grammar c. even kings, 268:3
  I am in c. here, 806:3
  lease of my true love c., 222:10
  man c. the wind, 495:6
  men gained c. over nature, 563:17
  nuclear c., 786:14
  stops at the shore, 396:17
  without c. over ourselves, 344:29
Controlled, events c. me, 446:7
Controlling intelligence understands, 112:12
Controls, love of other sights c., 228:7
Controversial, when I am no longer c., 479:15
Controversies, most savage c., 615:2
Controversy, hearts of c., 191:25
Contumely, proud man's c., 199:21
Conturbat, Timor Mortis c. me, 141:6
Convenience comfort prestige, 888:4
  he that for c. takes oath, 262:19
  lacking to modern comfort, 555:3
Convenient, a c. season, 41:2
  break eggs at c. end, 284:25
  never c. time for any, 726:4
  that there be gods, 102:4
Convent of the Sacred Heart, 676:2
Convention, by c. there is color, 70:12
  when I look out at c., 852:11
Conventional army, 802:14
  hallmark of c. wisdom acceptability, 752:15
  merely c. signs, 517:2
Conventionality not morality, 472:9
Conventions, principles are c. and definitions,
    558:9
Convent's narrow room, 371:22
  solitary gloom, 293:23
Converge, everything that rises must c., 648:2
Conversation art of never appearing a bore,
    554:8
  for c. well endued, 285:7
  good nature agreeable in c., 288:11
  is but carving, 285:12
  Johnson's c. was mustard, 335:5
  must be exchange of thought, 617:7
  of most searching sort, 427:8
  of select companions, 288:5
  one of greatest pleasures, 626:20
  preaching word for dull c., 374:22
  smaller excellencies of c., 334:8
  socializing instrument, 657:10
  three cannot take part in c., 427:8
  unforced as c. passed, 418:18
  wants leisure, 626:20
  when you fall into a man's c., 288:24
  where there's half a c., 690:13
  writing name for c., 314:5
Conversational or homely type, 607:2
Conversations, without pictures or c.,
    513:12
Converse and live with ease, 295:13
  high c. with mighty dead, 300:17
Conversing I forget all time, 257:26
Conversion, refuse till c. of Jews, 266:21
Convert Bill of Rights, 694:5
  I went to America to c. Indians, 301:14
  who shall c. me, 301:14
  you into stew, 677:3

Converted and become as children, 34:40
  love c. from thing it was, 221:14
  silenced man not c., 533:2
Converting human beings to machines, 478:3
Convey the wise it call, 187:1
Convicted, Daniel had c. them, 31:31
Conviction, do evil from religious c., 270:1
  faithful to c. to old age, 76:13
  impeachment for and c. of high crimes,
    339:12
  sadness of c., 538:7
  the best lack all c., 593:9
Convictions, enter c. in open lists, 614:4
  people in old times had c., 415:6
Convince hearers of own assertions, 74:15
  logic and sermons never c., 486:12
  to c. is to weaken, 615:18
Convinced it was the way of God, 261:16
Conviviality, taper of c., 464:26
Convolutions of smooth-lipped shell, 372:7
Convulsive, beauty will be c., 709:9
Conwiviality, taper of c., 464:26
Cook, amount to Hannah C., 886:11
  and captain bold, 525:16
  every c. learn to govern, 607:12
  good c. as cooks go, 608:4
  ill c. that cannot lick fingers, 181:6
  makes his c. his merit, 267:21
  no beast is a c., 334:5
Cookery is an art a noble science, 234:16
Cookie, me want c., 879:14
  you're a c. full of arsenic, 747:2
Cookies, stayed home and baked c., 864:4
Cookin', what you got c., 804:3
Cooks are gentlemen, 234:16
  as c. go she went, 608:4
  Epicurean c., 218:18
  God sends meat Devil sends c., 146:n16
Cooks' own ladles, 460:7
Cool, day so c. so calm, 242:19
  glassy c. translucent wave, 252:26
  in any case keep c., 707:11
  in dust in c. tombs, 636:6
  keep c. it will be all one, 427:30
  kept breath to c. pottage, 55:5
  kindliness of sheets, 669:9
  Negro c. strong imperturbable, 477:6
  of the day, 5:20
  one Pain, 510:4
  place was c. and pleasant, 774:12
  rather be dead than c., 879:5
  sequestered vale of life, 316:3
  we real c., 783:10
Cooled a long age, 410:4
Coolest grooviest swingin'est wailin'est cat,
    745:1
Coolibah tree, 585:8
Coolidge look as if weaned on pickle, 659:14
Coolness, wind to bring c. to men, 53:1
Cools, till husband c., 294:3
Coon, gone c., 393:16
Cooped we live and die, 442:3
Cooper, this is C., 524:7
Cooperate, stay and c., 690:10
Cooperation with Government, 667:5
Cooperative on my upper west side, 867:1
Coort, supreme c. follows iliction, 600:3
Coot, haunts of c., 454:24

Costs, about nothing but C. now, 466:11
    good counsel c. nothing, 235:8
    nothing to be polite, 621:14
Cottage, hides not visage from our c., 223:32
    modest looks c. adorn, 322:28
    planning retirement c., 808:9
    poor man in mean c., 31:14
    poorest man in his c., 305:12
    soul's dark c., 249:28
    small, 775:11
Cottages, poor men's c. palaces, 184:14
Cotton, corn and c. and cockleburs, 559:14
    is king, 422:3
    land of c., 470:16
    spinning noble, 407:26
    where c. and taters grow, 558:1
Cottontail and Peter, 598:5
Couch, frowsy c. in sorrow steep, 359:2
    when owls do cry, 225:5
    wraps drapery of c., 405:13
Couché, longtemps je me suis c. de bonne
    heure, 610:*n*3
Cough, love and a c., 243:14
Coughed and called it fate, 605:21
Coughing drowns parson's saw, 175:1
Could all have been killed, 879:3
    if youth but knew if old age but c.,
      151:5
    nor even thing I c. be, 358:22
    have stayed home, 864:4
Couleurs, les parfums les c., 491:*n*2
Council, before ashes of c. fire cold, 499:3
    outcome of words is in the c., 52:2
    power in aristocratical c., 330:16
    unapproachable in C. of Ten, 656:10
    Zeus god of c., 50:22
Counciler, White Citizen's C., 823:3
Councilor ought not to sleep, 50:21
Councils, takes wisdom from c., 324:15
Counsel, good c. cheap, 235:8
    how hard for women to keep c., 192:13
    if this c. be of men, 40:18
    love overwhelms wise c., 54:14
    man who c. can bestow, 293:1
    of thine own heart, 31:22
    princely c. in his face, 256:16
    sometimes c. take, 293:7
    spirit of c. and might, 25:18
    three keep c. if two away, 148:8
    took sweet c. together, 16:37
    two may keep c., 148:*n*4
    walketh not in c. of ungodly, 14:40
    who darkeneth c. by words, 14:17
Counseled ignoble ease, 256:15
Counselor, name shall be called C., 25:16
Counselors, good c. lack no clients, 206:13
    kings and c. of the earth, 13:4
    multitude of c., 20:13
    wisest of c. Time, 64:23
Counsels, close designs crooked c., 272:16
    excellent things in c., 21:20
    hate c. not in such quality, 185:15
    how monie c. sweet, 358:4
    sic c. ye give, 889:19
Count, as long as I c. votes, 501:2
    cats in Zanzibar, 475:17
    chickens before hatched, 58:15
    had reached his fifties, 392:7

Count *(continued)*
    let me c. the ways, 434:17
    let us c. our spoons, 309:5
    milestones till haze dances, 443:1
    myself in nothing else so happy, 176:29
    myself king of space, 199:3
    on a murderer, 723:6
    that day lost, 883:18
    until nothing else to c., 428:25
    when angry c. ten, 338:19
    you can c. me out, 848:14
Counted as the small dust, 26:30
    them and cursed luck, 575:18
    two and seventy stenches, 378:16
Countenance, bright c. of truth, 253:21
    cannot lie, 169:9
    chide God for c., 195:25
    damned disinheriting c., 346:12
    did the C. Divine, 354:8
    heart changeth his c., 31:3
    his c. like richest alchemy, 191:34
    human c. composed of ten parts, 105:6
    Knight of the Sorrowful C., 156:4
    lift up his c. upon thee, 9:2
    lift up the light of thy c., 15:3
    like lightning, 36:22
    merry heart maketh a cheerful c., 20:31
    more in sorrow than anger, 197:14
    of all Science, 369:3
    soon brightened, 372:7
    that in your c. would call master, 211:5
    tyrant's threatening c., 96:27
Counter original spare strange, 546:13
Counteracts Devil who is Death, 318:15
Countercheck quarrelsome, 196:6
Counterfeit a gloom, 251:18
    Jove's dread clamors c., 209:13
    sleep death's c., 215:29
Countermoves, revolution legality c. in same
    game, 567:19
Counterparts in world of fact, 490:13
Counterrevolutionary, facts are c., 730:9
Counters, wise men's c., 239:5
Counteth, sitteth and c. cost, 38:8
Countinghouse, king in c., 894:7
Countless infinitesimals of feeling, 380:6
    thousands mourn, 356:8
Countree, is this mine own c., 376:22
    North C. hard c., 708:6
Countries give themselves to you, 662:7
    material out of which c. made, 615:11
    outdistance advanced c., 607:13
    peace of all c. connected, 647:9
    public history of all c., 363:6
    seek no aggrandizement, 653:14
    wandering through many c., 91:29
Country, abroad for good of c., 290:8
    absorbs poet, 485:11
    all places all airs one c., 248:14
    anything for good of c., 290:8
    as soldier for c., 582:*n*3
    ask not what c. do for you, 785:13
    behind people your c., 498:9
    belongs to people, 445:5
    best c. is at home, 321:13
    betraying c. betraying friend, 638:13
    better off when Indians running it, 834:5
    cannot ask success even for c., 363:1

Country *(continued)*
    can't take c. out of a boy, 712:14
    cause your own c. to fall, 869:7
    ceases to be free for irreligion, 694:9
    century of the c. man, 683:1
    cherished in hearts, 456:7
    citizen who criticizes c., 741:5
    cries of c. in chains, 891:*n*1
    defamers of his c., 518:2
    defended by our hands, 456:7
    departed into their own c., 31:37
    die but once to serve c., 287:27
    die in defense of his c., 51:33
    disable benefits of your c., 195:25
    diversion, 287:4
    divine nature gave us c., 87:2
    done my best for honor of c., 517:16
    dreary tract of c., 448:8
    epitaph for their c., 584:6
    essential service to c., 285:1
    every c. but his own, 527:11
    every C. hath its Machiavel, 141:*n*7
    fame noised throughout c., 10:1
    fate of c. not in ballot, 474:6
    father of your c., 328:*n*3
    fight for one's c., 51:24
    fight to set c. free, 333:12
    find my c. in the right, 386:*n*1
    Flora and c. green, 410:4
    foreign troop in my c., 306:5
    fornication but in another c., 168:11
    found that famous c., 695:2
    friend of every c. but own, 367:2
    from yon far c. blows, 575:6
    genius is of no c., 326:3
    gentleman galloping, 561:7
    give c. back to Indians, 716:4
    God made the c., 326:19
    good for c. good for General Motors,
      689:6
    good news from a far c., 21:35
    governed by despot, 310:17
    grow up with c., 471:*n*2
    half savage c., 665:4
    has 265 different kinds of cheese, 686:11
    history of c. begins in heart, 615:8
    honorable to die for one's c., 96:26
    I loathe the c., 287:4
    I seek an innocent c., 682:9
    I tremble for my c., 336:9
    in c. of blind one-eyed man king, 141:10
    in c. you praise city, 95:26
    in town, 107:19
    is this mine own c., 376:22
    it's a free c., 781:2
    know something of own c., 314:19
    lead c. like Britain, 810:7
    leaving c. for country's sake, 290:*n*1
    let who loves c. follow, 435:25
    little c. retreat, 279:10
    loved c. as no other man, 498:10
    master of sea Master of every c., 166:*n*3
    merchants have no c., 338:5
    move in on some other c., 708:15
    my c. is Kiltartan Cross, 592:20
    my c. is the world, 333:16
    my c. 'tis of thee, 439:9
    my c. 'tis of you, 701:9

Courtesy *(continued)*
in c. have her learned, 593:14
mirour of alle c., 135:4
mirror of all c., 225:14
pink of c., 180:22
Courthouse, portals of every c., 614:2
Courtier, heel of c., 202:11
Courtier's soldier's scholar's, 200:2
Courtiers of all ages feel one need, 392:4
Courtly nurture, 500:5
Courts, brawling c., 454:4
case still before c., 98:19
day in thy c., 17:20
forsaken c. pale pavilions, 725:11
hollow murmurs through c., 362:2
into his c. with praise, 18:3
laws conflict c. decide, 349:13
shown in c. at feasts, 252:25
thee on roses, 96:6
thrusting on c. nurture of spirit, 614:1
where Jamshyd gloried, 441:13
Cousins, Little C. Called back, 511:16
sisters c. and aunts, 525:21
Coûte, il n'y a que le premier pas qui c., 300:*n*5
Couvrez ce sein que je ne saurais voir, 267:*n*2
Covenant, co-signers of a c., 742:5
new and eternal c., 47:25
token of a c., 6:25
with death, 26:8, 433:6
words of the c., 8:22
Covenanted with him for silver, 35:35
Covenants, open c. of peace, 566:16
Cover, cunning sin c. itself, 191:5
her face, 237:9
I c. all, 636:4
like c. of old book, 301:20
only art guilt to c., 322:17
paste and c. to our bones, 177:8
that bosom I must not see, 267:15
thee with his feathers, 17:28
them with leaves, 880:14
Covered up our names, 509:7
Covers of book too far apart, 540:15
out of night that c., 552:7
who c. faults, 210:31
Covert action should not be confused, 802:11
from the tempest, 26:15
Covet, sin to c. honor, 189:25
thou shalt not c., 8:14, 479:14
Coveted her and me, 449:22
Covetous desires of the world, 49:11
man ever in want, 97:22
of others' possessions, 92:4
sordid fellow, 298:7
Covetousness, wealth cause of c., 168:9
Cow and bear shall feed, 25:19
good animal in field, 309:20
jumped over moon, 893:16
little Kyloe c., 894:5
purple c., 597:19
she'll bring her c. along, 897:9
sizzle sells steak not c., 747:12
till the c. comes home, 238:3
with crumpled horn, 897:8
work way c. grazes, 601:1
you do de pullin' Sis C., 551:15
Coward and brave held in same honor, 51:19
conscience dost afflict, 172:8

Coward *(continued)*
does it with kiss, 561:3
had not resolution to fire it, 308:19
never forgave, 313:17
no c. soul mine, 476:14
not so great a c. as thinks, 555:18
turns away, 68:7
worth little more than c., 364:1
Cowardice distinguished from panic, 722:1
God is stupidity and c., 450:5
here all c. be ended, 128:7
optimism is c., 646:7
that clings, 618:4
Cowardly, nothing more c. than terrorist,
364:13
war spares the c., 60:3
Cowards, conscience but word c. use,
172:10
conscience does make c., 199:21
die many times, 192:11
essentially a nation of c., 869:10
hundred c., 684:9
idlers and c. at home, 892:2
mannish c., 193:35
plague of all c., 182:18
Public greatest of c., 386:4
Cowboy, best damned c., 890:13
I wondered if ever a c., 890:14
I'm a young c., 890:16
that loves you so true, 890:19
wrapped in white linen, 890:15
Cowl does not make monk, 120:12
I like a c., 424:4
take wife or c., 155:*n*10
Cowled, I that c. churchman be, 424:4
Cowman who cleans range of wolves, 668:5
Cowpuncher a-riding along, 890:10
Cow'rin', wee sleekit c., 356:4
Cow's in the corn, 893:11
Cows, sacred c. make tastiest hamburger,
841:11
till the c. come home, 238:*n*2
Cowslip's, hang pearl in c. ear, 178:11
in c. bell I lie, 225:5
Coxcombs, some made c. nature meant fools,
292:10
Coy and hard to please, 373:16
denial vain and c. excuse, 253:2
yielded with c. submission, 257:20
Coyness, this c. were no crime, 266:20
Coyotes howl o'er grave, 890:18
wild c. howl o'er me, 890:17
Crab, hermit c. whale's backbone, 679:4
teach c. to walk straight, 72:17
very likeness of roasted c., 178:12
Crabbed age and youth, 881:17
philosophy not harsh and c., 252:19
talk of c. old men, 91:5
Crab-grass, big sisters are c., 800:10
Crabs, roasted c. hiss in bowl, 175:1
Crabwise, something c. across snow, 808:6
Crack any of those old jokes, 73:13
blow winds c. cheeks, 211:24
door begins to c., 892:8
heaven's vaults should c., 213:12
in tea cup opens, 748:9
nature's molds, 211:24
sail-yards tremble masts c., 163:20

Crack *(continued)*
she discovered c. in wall, 493:12
stretch out to c. of doom, 217:2
Crack-brained, believed by vulgar that he was
c., 270:9
Cracked growled roared howled, 375:24
the mirror c., 451:6
Cracker-jack, buy peanuts and c., 640:1
Crackled and gone up in smoke, 577:1
Crackling of thorns under a pot, 23:11
Crack-pated when we dreamed, 594:9
Cracks, now c. a noble heart, 202:33
sinews cakes brain, 483:3
Cradle asks whence, 518:4
between c. and grave, 300:13, 687:4
bough breaks c. fall, 550:7
earth c. of hope, 636:11
endlessly rocking, 487:5
from c. to grave, 402:4, 553:13
hand that rocks c., 485:7
murder infant in c., 351:20
of every science, 502:2
of liberty, 390:21
of the deep, 394:5
mother sings to c. goes to coffin, 468:9
procreant c., 214:21
rocks above abyss, 723:3
vexed to nightmare by c., 593:10
when wind blows C. Will Rock, 740:8
will rock, 550:7
Cradles, bit babies in c., 460:7
Craft, flung eager craft, 800:1
lyf so short c. so long, 132:7
Craftiness, taketh wise in their c., 13:12
Craftsman against craftsman, 54:17
barrier between c. and artist, 655:8
Craftsmanship, criticism easier than c., 74:1
Crafty afraid to act, 56:14
old and wise, 591:7
Crag, clasps c. with crooked hands, 454:13
of rock and strong place, 14:29
Crags, among these barren c., 451:11
Cram within this wooden O, 188:30
Crammed with distressful bread, 189:23
Crammers, green c. of green fruits, 640:16
Cramped, life and memory c., 763:8
Cranes of Ibycus, 58:*n*2
Crankish quest for sexual symbols, 723:4
Cranks, quips and c., 250:21
Crannied wall, 455:27
Crannies, pluck you out of c., 455:27
Crannying wind, 395:18
Crap, all the c. I learned in high school, 855:11
Cras amet qui nunquam amavit, 120:11
ingens iterabimus aequor, 96:*n*5
Craters of my eyes gape, 836:2
Crave, my mind forbids to c., 154:10
no pelf, 213:21
stain of tears, 623:10
then Lucasta might I c., 266:3
thyng we may nat have, 135:10
we crie alday and c., 135:10
Craved no crumb, 527:25
Craven, some c. scruple, 201:20
Craves a kind of wit, 205:11
Craving, accurst c. for gold, 94:19
Crawl upon earth, 284:26
with legs, 376:4

Crowns *(continued)*
last act c. play, 242:5
not c. but men, 389:3
walked c. and crownets, 219:8
Crows and choughs that wing air, 212:24
at the break of dawn, 851:4
black flight of c., 891:*n*1
throw him to c., 886:*n*4
wars of kites or c., 260:28
Crow's-feet, til c. be growen, 132:15
Cru, j'ai pleuré et j'ai c., 364:*n*5
Crucible, God's c., 586:9
Crucified dead and buried, 48:11
everyone Christ and all c., 632:15
let him be c., 36:14
Cruciform shadow, 688:7
Crucify mankind on cross of gold, 577:18
Son of God afresh, 45:9
Crude, berries harsh and c., 252:29
no c. surfeit reigns, 252:19
Crudities of former existence, 750:7
Cruel and unrelenting enemy, 328:6
and unusual punishment, 340:7
as death, 300:16
but composed and bland, 497:4
death of Pyramus, 178:2
doubts more c. than truths, 267:24
enough without meaning to, 834:2
foam is not c., 484:7
I must be c. to be kind, 201:14
jealousy is c. as the grave, 24:25
mother of sweet loves, 97:11
never be c., 465:26
savage extreme rude c., 222:20
slain by fair c. maid, 205:3
tender mercies of the wicked are c., 20:18
Cruelest lies told in silence, 554:13
she alive, 204:20
Cruella, that's C. de Vil, 712:12
Cruellest, April c. month, 676:5
thing happened to Lincoln, 708:16
Cruelly, Fortune c. scratched, 206:8
Cruelty, all the pride c. and ambition, 159:15
at root of every spectacle, 709:2
energy civilization not corrupted, 334:11
farewell fair c., 204:23
fear source of c., 615:1
full of direst c., 214:17
has human heart, 353:8
ingenuity, fanaticism, and c., 793:4
Mr. C., 271:18
never gauged your c., 689:5
to load falling man, 225:*n*2
war is c., 489:11
Cruise, all on our last c., 554:14
Cruising down shores of High Barbaree, 898:1
goes c. just as fast as she can, 856:1
Crumb, craved no c., 527:25
just a C. to Me, 509:19
of madeleine, 610:13
Crumble the bridges, 724:6
Crumbled out again to his atomies, 230:15
Crumbles, Time c. things, 77:15
Crumbling, mind c. to pieces, 824:15
Crumbs, dogs eat of c., 34:33
Crumpled, cow with c. horn, 897:8
Crusade, my God the Children's C., 801:5
Crusader, Franklin Roosevelt no c., 685:4

Cruse, little oil in a c., 11:41
Crush amang the stoure, 356:17
man shall man no longer c., 346:24
the infamous thing, 299:17
Crushed, human being c. by books, 774:13
most fragrant when c., 165:18
the sweet poison, 252:4
to ground diffuse sweets, 165:*n*3
together c. and bruised, 293:14
truth c. to earth, 406:4
Crushes, friend supports whom Fortune c.,
106:14
Crusoe, Robinson C., 282:10, 312:25
Crust and sugar over, 731:9
dinosaur death-steps on c., 787:17
eaten in peace, 59:1
of bread and liberty, 296:8
over volcano of revolution, 574:2
water and c., 409:14
Cry, all should c. Beware, 377:23
art is desperate c., 627:7
at a play to laugh or c., 285:6
battle c. of Freedom, 489:9
Bellman c. crew reply, 517:2
bubbling c. of swimmer, 398:9
but behold a c., 25:4
caused constantly a c., 641:8
cherry-ripe themselves do c., 227:3
consider anything don't c., 516:12
couch when owls do c., 225:5
damned don't c., 681:9
don't c. for me Argentina, 859:14
don't you c. for me, 503:9
every infant's c. of fear, 353:3
feel sorry because c., 541:9
for being born, 166:24
for restful death I c., 221:20
forgot c. of gulls, 676:14
God for Harry, 189:9
great c. in Egypt, 7:43
harlot's c. from street, 354:6
Havoc, 192:23
hear us when we c., 503:1
he'll be sure to c., 893:11
Hi or any loud c., 517:1
Hold hold, 214:18
hounds join in glorious c., 304:11
hush little baby don't yo' c., 662:8
I can no more, 547:3
I often want to c., 688:12
is still They come, 217:21
kitten and c. mew, 182:35
last c. follows a last c., 729:11
laugh for fear of having to c., 327:15
man's image and his c., 591:4
much c. no wool, 137:15
mum, 158:*n*2
my eyes out, 156:30
need a body c., 883:*n*1
of Absence Absence in heart, 681:18
of bugles going by, 579:10
of child by roadway, 591:9
of pulleys, 797:12
out liberty freedom, 192:17
out Olivia, 204:22
scarcely c. 'weep, 351:2
scrawny c. was a chorister, 642:17
secrets c. aloud, 755:10

Cry *(continued)*
shake me like a c., 579:10
so lonesome I could c., 804:1
stone shall c. out of wall, 29:8
stones c. out, 38:26
sudden c. of pain, 654:2
that was not ours, 641:8
the more it made them c., 323:5
this our battle c., 818:12
too big to c., 445:14
voice c. Sleep no more, 215:21
voiced c. of his people, 629:8
war war still the c., 395:4
wave c. wind c., 679:2
we c. that we are come, 213:1
we still should c., 166:24
what shall I c., 26:26
whoever loves you make you c., 898:11
Cryin' all the time, 834:6
at the lock, 457:4
Crying, first voice was c., 30:5
in the wilderness, 32:5
infant c. in night, 453:22
no more c., 47:12
watchmen on the heights are c., 162:26
with sighing and c., 154:8
Crystal, golden sands c. brooks, 229:14
river of c. light, 554:1
soul pure as c., 466:32
Crystallization action of mind, 391:20
Cthulhu, dead C. waits dreaming, 687:8
Cub, grandam to c., 813:12
Cubic inch of space a miracle, 488:1
Cubit, add one c. to stature, 33:7
Cuccu, lhude sing c., 880:5
Cuckold lives in bliss, 209:3
not be c., 662:4
Cuckoo, as c. is in June, 183:4
Cloud-C.-Land, 73:6
jug-jug pu-we, 227:4
lhude sing c., 880:5
thus sings he C., 174:32
Cuckoo-buds of yellow hue, 174:32
Cuckoo-clock, Switzerland produced c., 781:4
Cuckoo's, one flew over c. nest, 896:15
Cuckoos clucked to finches, 719:20
Cucullus non facit monachum, 120:12
Cucumbers, cold as c., 238:2
lodge in garden of c., 24:30
sunbeams out of c., 285:2
Cud, chew c. and are silent, 325:7
whatsoever cheweth the c., 8:23
Cudgel thy brains no more, 202:4
Cue is villainous melancholy, 211:4
twisted c., 527:17
Cueillez les roses de la vie, 150:*n*7
votre jeunesse, 150:*n*9
Cui bono fuerit, 87:*n*7
Culled, nosegay of c. flowers, 153:19
Culpa, mea c. mea c., 47:17
O felix c., 47:26
Culprit, stirs C. Life, 508:3
Cult called Christianity, 536:15
is a religion, 831:7
of personality, 702:18
Cultivate peace and harmony, 329:1
sedulously c. free speech, 621:8
we must c. our garden, 299:14

Cultivated, celebrated c. Duke, 528:2
Cultivates the golden mean, 96:22
Cultivation, equal in rights and in c., 435:20
Cultiver, il faut c. notre jardin, 299:*n*5
Cults, clarification c. founded on, 625:3
Cultural, character of c. environment, 569:11
　　freedom, 633:11
　　man's nature c. product, 725:9
Culture, above all believer in c., 497:9
　　believe only in French c., 549:6
　　custodians of c., 832:8
　　European c. a misunderstanding, 549:6
　　Germany ruins c., 549:7
　　great law of c., 407:12
　　great though disastrous c., 805:17
　　Greek essential to c., 504:3
　　hear word c. reach for pistol, 687:5
　　in finest flower, 580:17
　　individual creature of his c., 669:3
　　it is c. not politics, 816:14
　　knowledge of other c., 729:2
　　leaves unsatisfied drives to rebelliousness,
　　　563:15
　　mechanics of c., 602:17
　　men of c. true apostles, 497:14
　　moment of clarity, 657:8
　　no prospect of continued existence, 563:15
　　not function of race, 669:4
　　politics economic development c., 797:5
　　pursue C. in bands, 582:16
　　pursuit of perfection, 497:7
　　shock, 729:9
　　socialist c. thrive, 698:13
　　soul takes nothing but education and c.,
　　　74:17
　　study of perfection, 497:10
Cultures, materialism model for c., 805:17
Cum grano salis, 105:*n*5
Cumbered with much serving, 37:39
Cumin, tithe of anise and c., 35:15
Cunard's liners and telegraph, 481:3
Cunnilingus and psychiatry, 860:11
Cunning, Esau was a c. hunter, 6:37
　　history has c. passages, 675:22
　　Hocus old c. attorney, 300:*n*6
　　in war boastful c., 400:7
　　livery of hell, 206:37
　　men pass for wise, 166:3
　　more c. to be strange, 180:7
　　nature's sweet c. hand, 204:20
　　old Fury, 514:1
　　punishment sharpens c., 548:16
　　right hand forget her c., 19:11
　　sin cover itself, 191:5
　　truth which c. times put on, 185:20
　　what plighted c. hides, 210:31
Cunningest pattern, 210:14
Cunningly, little world made c., 230:18
Cup, between c. and lip, 235:9
　　come fill the C., 441:7
　　drained c. of Lethe, 95:28
　　dregs of the C., 278:9
　　drowned Glory in C., 442:7
　　fear at heart as at c., 376:10
　　giveth his color in the c., 21:30
　　he took the c., 36:3
　　is new testament in my blood, 42:25
　　leave a kiss but in the c., 232:16

Cup *(continued)*
　　let this c. pass, 36:5
　　life's enchanted c., 395:11
　　man in whose hand the c. is found, 7:14
　　my c. runneth over, 15:23
　　o' kindness yet, 357:18
　　of hot wine, 219:24
　　of trembling, 27:1
　　sun in golden c., 596:4
　　take c. drink it up, 893:15
　　that clears today, 441:15
　　to every people c. of clay, 892:3
　　valley his golden c., 505:15
　　woodspurge has c. of three, 506:2
Cupboard, glacier knocks in c., 748:9
　　was bare, 895:6
Cupboards, keys took and c. opened, 536:2
Cupid and my Campaspe, 162:8
　　bolt of C. fell, 178:16
　　has his camps, 101:23
　　paid, 162:8
　　senior-junior Dan C., 174:14
　　silent note C. strikes, 248:17
　　winged C. painted blind, 178:1
　　young Adam C., 179:30
Cupiditas, radix malorum est c., 44:*n*1
Cupido upon his shuldres wynges, 134:18
Cupid's, concludes with C. curse, 163:2
Cups, nor shall c. make guilty men, 232:12
　　that cheer, 327:1
　　when they are in their c., 29:23
Cur, ears of the old c., 262:13
Cur ergo haec ipse non facis, 115:*n*3
Curates, shower of c., 472:12
Curb, care's check and c., 269:2
Curd, white c. of ass's milk, 295:14
Curdied by frost from snow, 220:3
Curds and whey, 895:14
Cure, absence of c. of love, 156:22
　　disease kill patient, 166:8
　　for ills of Democracy, 577:5
　　laws or kings cause or c., 307:14
　　no c. for birth and death, 584:11
　　not worth the pain, 100:*n*1
　　on exercise depend, 274:24
　　past c. I am, 223:6
　　past hope past c. past help, 181:5
　　tale would c. deafness, 224:6
　　the c. is freedom, 419:10
　　thrust of c., 820:8
Cured, Asclepius c. the body, 74:*n*1
　　I am frizzled stale, 787:8
　　more than Galen c., 243:26
　　of every folly but vanity, 313:2
Cures, endure neither evils nor c., 99:9
　　opposites c. for opposites, 71:1
　　to fear worst c. worse, 203:17
Cureth, quiet mind c. all, 235:19
Curfew, far-off c. sound, 251:17
　　must not ring tonight, 556:14
　　tolls knell, 315:11
Curiosity, culture origin not in c., 497:10
　　do well in closet by way of c., 298:11
　　insatiable intellectual c., 583:4
　　love c. freckles doubt, 699:11
　　natural c. of young, 546:1
　　offers to our c., 679:4
　　order awakened c., 425:20

Curiosity *(continued)*
　　permanent and certain, 306:21
　　pleasure to rouse c., 770:16
　　show to gratify c., 701:1
Curious, amazed and c., 358:8
　　busy c. thirsty fly, 300:9
　　crime, 463:5
　　in unnecessary matters, 30:14
　　incident of dog, 573:14
　　quaint and c. war is, 536:13
　　seen a c. child, 372:7
　　volume of forgotten lore, 449:3
Curiouser and curiouser, 513:14
Curl, had a little c., 438:2
　　make your hair c., 527:22
Curled, wealthy c. darlings, 207:31
Curlicues of marijuana, 787:10
Curls done up with bank notes, 471:11
　　Frocks and C., 509:20
　　Hyperion's c., 201:5
Curlylocks wilt be mine, 894:17
Currency, no graven images except c., 479:13
Current, boats against the c., 710:8
　　genial c. of soul, 315:22
　　icy c. compulsive course, 209:20
　　misleading guide to c. affairs, 656:11
　　swollen c. masses of ice, 458:13
　　take c. when it serves, 193:14
　　time a river of strong c., 112:5
Currents, fresh c. of life, 456:15
　　turn awry, 199:21
Curriculum, hurt Negro avoid Jew is c., 772:6
Currite, lente c. noctis equi, 101:*n*11, 169:4
Curs of low degree, 322:13
Curse astonishment hissing and reproach, 28:5
　　began to c., 36:11
　　bless them that c. you, 32:21
　　Christianity one great c., 549:3
　　creations of mind blessing not c., 637:10
　　feel c. or meditate on crime, 347:12
　　for God, 819:12
　　get the c. out of murder, 778:11
　　God and die, 13:2
　　has come upon me, 451:6
　　his better angel, 210:17
　　I know how to c., 224:11
　　my c. be on the Constitution, 458:6
　　O c. of marriage, 209:9
　　of hell frae me, 889:19
　　on his virtues, 287:26
　　primal eldest c., 200:31
　　sex is c. of life, 605:4
　　the darkness, 660:*n*1
　　this pois'nous bunch-backed toad, 171:24
　　with book bell and candle, 138:12
　　youthful harlot's c., 353:4
Cursed above all cattle, 5:22
　　be he that moves my bones, 226:17
　　be man that trusteth in man, 27:39
　　be my tribe, 184:25
　　counted and c. luck, 575:18
　　drunken officer, 829:4
　　Fate has c. you, 67:14
　　floundered enjoyed, 545:6
　　hard reading, 346:19
　　me with his eye, 376:12
　　name to all ages c., 272:16
　　O c. spite, 198:22

Cursed *(continued)*
    past, 682:12
    plagues with which mankind c., 282:7
    sat Beauty in lap c. her, 559:7
    the bread, 605:19
    thoughts, 215:11
Curses all Eve's daughters, 187:17
    like young chickens, 381:14
    not loud but deep, 217:18
    of the firmament, 275:*n*4
    rigged with c. dark, 253:8
Cursing, blessing and c., 9:29
Cursores vitae lampada tradunt, 90:*n*2
Curtailed, always c. thwarted, 671:14
Curtain, Anarch lets c. fall, 297:6
    close his eyes and draw c., 170:9
    iron c., 621:11
    never c. between you and me, 623:14
    nor c. of crimson be over you, 667:7
    Priam's c., 187:22
    purple c., 449:6
    somewhere beyond c., 595:17
    when she drew c. by, 889:26
Curtained, dreams abuse c. sleep, 215:14
Curtains, fringed c. of thine eye, 224:15
    let fall the c., 327:1
    of Solomon, 24:4
    spread canopy or c. spun, 280:15
    through c. call on us, 228:15
Curtius Rufus seems descended from himself,
    76:*n*1
Curtsied when you have, 224:12
Curtsy, nice customs c. to great kings, 190:10
    while you're thinking, 515:14
Curved, empty c. space, 766:3
Cushion, sit on a c., 894:17
Custodians of new ideas have fervor, 580:16
Custody, committing lamb to c. of wolf, 330:9
    individual taken into c., 692:6
Custom, age cannot wither nor c. stale, 218:21
    despot of mankind, 418:19
    follow c. of church where you are, 114:*n*7
    Fortune more kind than her c., 186:7
    gods' c. to bring low greatness, 69:16
    greater sway over c., 660:1
    in all line of order, 203:5
    made property of easiness, 202:6
    make it their perch, 206:18
    more honored in breach, 197:31
    nature her c. holds, 202:2
    no law more binding than c., 572:13
    old c. made life sweet, 193:36
    one good c. corrupt, 455:19
    reconciles to everything, 323:13
    sitting at receipt of c., 33:30
    stern C. spreads afar, 359:10
    to whom c. due, 41:38
    tobacco a c. loathsome, 226:19
    whereof memory of man, 318:*n*2
Customary fate of new truths, 502:13
    suits of solemn black, 196:26
Customer, tough c., 464:31
Customers, empire for raising c., 319:7
Customs, language manners laws c., 369:4
    laws are sand c. rock, 525:1
    man is child of c. used to, 131:10
    nice c. curtsy to great kings, 190:10
    oh the times the c., 87:6

Customs *(continued)*
    politics and tongue, 500:8
    shape experience and behavior, 669:3
Cut anyone introduced to, 516:19
    diamond c. diamond, 239:1
    him out in little stars, 180:32
    I c. down trees skip and jump, 879:9
    if thy hand offend thee c. it off, 32:18
    in the evening it is c. down, 17:23
    is branch that might have grown, 169:7
    it is soon c. off and we fly away, 17:25
    it without e'er knife, 893:14
    laurels all c., 499:5
    like a flower and is c. down, 13:29
    moment I c. his throat, 805:11
    my coat after my cloth, 147:7
    not c. conscience to fit fashions, 741:12
    off in blossoms of sin, 198:12
    off tails, 892:10
    stems struggling, 755:11
    strangers who c. down woods, 709:15
    stripes away, 587:15
    unkindest c. of all, 192:35
    up what remains, 588:13
    ways of men c. off, 257:6
    where were the righteous c. off, 13:6
    with beard of formal c., 194:25
Cuts, psychology c. both ways, 493:2
Cutthroat dog, 184:28
Cutting all pictures out, 606:9
    corner of nonsense, 380:5
    through the forest, 639:14
Cutty sark o' Paisley harn, 358:9
    weel done C. Sark, 358:10
Cyanide, may I borrow a cup of c., 766:13
Cybele, sea C. fresh from ocean, 396:2
Cybernetics from Greek steersman, 704:18
Cyberspace, a consensual hallucination,
    866:5
Cycle, gears of a c. transmission, 820:1
    of Cathay, 452:11
    of the ages renewed, 92:22
Cycling, this planet has gone c. on, 440:5
Cygnet to this pale swan, 176:3
Cylinder, nature in terms of c., 533:17
Cymbal, tinkling c., 42:26
Cymbals, high sounding c., 19:21
    played before Lord on c., 11:13
Cynara, faithful to thee C., 599:14
    falls thy shadow C., 599:16
Cynic knows price of everything, 560:10
    sees things as they are, 540:6
Cynical, makes them c. where we are trustful,
    710:9
Cynicism, dictatorships cannot dispense with c.,
    673:18
    intellectual dandyism, 505:13
Cynosure of neighboring eyes, 251:3
Cypress, alley of c., 449:16
    in palace walk, 453:5
    sad c., 205:3
    shady c. tree, 512:3
Cyrus, Palace of C., 886:14
Cythera famous in song, 491:9
Czar, last Russian C., 787:6
    making President c. making him puppet,
    788:18
Czech, God wanted me to be a C., 841:8

D

Da da da iti, 50:*n*4
    mi basia mille, 91:*n*4
Dab at an index, 321:10
Dad, called brother's father d., 175:10
    they fuck you up your mum and d., 799:15
Dada the roar of contorted pains, 712:13
Daddy, are you lost d., 662:9
    left home, 833:16
    look d. Teacher says, 687:3
Daddy's gone a-hunting, 894:3
    your d. rich, 662:8
Daemon, when your D. in charge, 590:9
Daffodil, nature's pride withered d., 231:20
    surfeit when D. doth, 509:18
    when a d. I see, 240:17
Daffodils, fair d. we weep to see, 241:5
    host of golden d., 371:9
    that come before swallow, 223:27
    what d. were for Wordsworth, 799:17
Dagger, air-drawn d., 216:18
    into back of neighbor, 653:1
    is this a d. which I see, 215:13
    of the mind, 215:13
    wear not my d. in my mouth, 220:25
Daggers, give me the d., 215:23
    speak d. to her, 200:30
Daily beauty in his life, 210:11
    duly and d. serving him, 318:14
    give us our d. bread, 32:25
    wealth small aid for d. gladness, 68:6
    with souls that cringe, 481:14
Dainties bred of a book, 174:15
Daintiest last to make end sweet, 176:11
Dainty dish, 894:7
Daiquiris, two d. withdrew, 773:8
Daisies, lie upon the d., 526:10
    meadows trim with d. pied, 251:3
    pied and violets blue, 174:32
    she can hear d. grow, 559:15
    swich as men callen d., 133:7
Daisy by shadow it casts, 372:17
    give me answer do, 598:3
    there's a d., 201:31
Dakotas I am for war, 499:3
Dale, hawthorn in the d., 251:2
    over hill over d., 178:10
Dales, hills and valleys d. and fields, 168:*n*1
Dalliance, not give d. rein, 224:35
    primrose path of d., 197:20
    silken d., 189:1
Dallies with innocence of love, 205:2
Dam, all my chickens and their d., 217:8
Damage, came to see d. done, 825:9
    has been memorized, 861:10
Damaged, archangel a little d., 383:6
Damaging, nothing more d. than old error,
    344:21
Damask, feed on her d. cheek, 205:4
Dame, dance in old d. yet, 635:6
    has lost shoe, 892:9
    La Belle D. sans Merci, 412:5
    nothing like a d., 706:13
    one for my d., 893:4
    our sulky sullen d., 358:3
    smiled at the d., 352:4

Dangerous (*continued*)
 rouse speculation about d. things, 770:16
 say nothing in d. times, 238:19
 show thy d. brow by night, 192:3
 such men are d., 191:28
 thirst d. thing, 576:6
 to be of no church d., 307:16
 to meet Culture alone, 582:16
 to our peace and safety, 355:7
 who make no noise are d., 266:14
Dangers, concern for safety in face of d., 802:9
 defend us from d. of night, 48:18
 delays breed d., 161:20
 in what great d. ye spend little span, 90:1
 of the seas, 247:4
 she loved me for the d., 208:3
 thorns and d. of world, 175:32
 what d. thou make us scorn, 358:7
 with d. compassed round, 258:25
Daniel, cast D. into the den of lions, 28:27
 come to judgment, 186:3
 had convicted them, 31:31
 second D., 186:11
Dank, addled mosses d., 664:17
 tarn of Auber, 449:15
Danny, hangin' D. Deever, 587:15
Dante belongs to the first category, 757:14
 language of D. common language, 677:11
 more learned from D., 677:11
Daphnis, my songs draw D. home, 93:1
Dapple, name was D. Gray, 896:16
Dappled things, 546:12
Dapple-dawn-drawn Falcon, 546:9
Darbies, ease d. at wrist, 484:4
Dare all that may plant man's lordship, 537:10
 ask just God's assistance, 447:1
 call soul my own, 434:20
 choose if you d., 249:17
 deadly terrors clasp, 353:2
 do duty as understand it, 444:16
 don't d. to express it, 797:6
 first ponder then d., 420:6
 heart would deny and d. not, 217:18
 I d. do all, 215:3
 imitate him if you d., 595:8
 is highest wisdom, 388:9
 letting I d. not, 215:2
 love that and say so too, 228:14
 Love that d. not speak its name, 607:5
 mighty things, 571:1
 never d. utter untruth, 87:14
 never grudge throe, 462:15
 none d. call it treason, 166:26
 O what men d. do, 191:4
 slaves who d. not be, 481:10
 soul to d., 373:20
 speak truth as much as I d., 153:9
 to be ahead of the world, 57:22
 to be true, 242:8
 to be wise, 97:21
 to eat a peach, 675:6
 what hand d. seize fire, 353:1
 what man d. I d., 216:20
 women should d. be different, 688:15
 wonder Do I d., 674:20
Dared, determined d. and done, 318:10
 never d. be radical when young, 624:4
 none d. thou hast, 159:15

Daren't go a-hunting, 501:4
Dares, come before swallow d., 223:27
 he who d. not offend, 333:5
 life d. send challenge, 263:5
 who d. do more is none, 215:3
Darest thou then, 373:14
Darien, peak in D., 408:17
Daring, in war d. boastful, 400:7
 pilot in extremity, 272:16
 serious d. starts from within, 761:4
 well-doing and d., 309:*n*1
 young man on trapeze, 532:16
Dark, afraid to go home in d., 582:*n*2
 after that the d., 456:5
 all night in d. and wet, 555:10
 and bloody ground, 489:7
 and his d. secret love, 352:14
 and lonely hiding place, 377:16
 and stormy night, 423:14, 800:9
 as Erebus, 186:17
 as good in the d., 241:2
 as world of man, 672:12
 at one stride comes the d., 376:9
 backward and abysm of time, 224:4
 best of d. and bright, 397:1
 between d. and daylight, 437:12
 blanket of the d., 214:18
 blue ocean roll, 396:17
 Chromis did not save himself from d.
  death, 50:26
 clear moving utterly free, 762:17
 cloud at house's door, 891:17
 cold and empty desolation, 679:2
 come to d. and lament, 624:9
 comes down on what we do, 756:8
 dark dark amid blaze, 260:9
 dark dark spaces, 678:19
 dove with flickering tongue, 679:9
 dull d. soundless day, 448:8
 echoed with outlandish orders, 793:1
 ever-during d., 257:6
 everyone is a moon has d. side, 524:20
 fate sits on d. battlements, 362:2
 fear death as children fear d., 165:13
 fell of d. not day, 547:7
 go home in d., 582:4
 great leap in the d., 239:14
 hawks hear us, 650:22
 highest candle lights d., 642:14
 hole of the head, 827:11
 horse, 429:20
 hour or twain, 216:4
 in d. time eye begins to see, 756:11
 in nightmare of the d., 749:4
 in the d. and silent grave, 159:16
 inscrutable workmanship, 368:14
 iron New England d., 713:20
 irrecoverably d., 260:9
 it is d. d. that draws me, 813:1
 it is d. it is ancient, 838:2
 let d. come upon you, 678:20
 lie in d. weep for sins, 486:14
 life one long struggle in d., 90:2
 Maid and her Lord, 67:6
 mother always gliding near, 487:15
 mutinous Shannon waves, 650:9
 night is d., 421:4, 888:2
 night of d. intent, 623:13

Dark (*continued*)
 not d. days great days, 620:13
 not put me in d. to die, 557:14
 o'er d. silver mantle threw, 257:25
 old fantastical duke of d. corners, 207:11
 on d. theme trace verses of light, 89:18
 pillared d., 624:9
 raging in the d., 595:9
 rebellious brows, 488:2
 road whence no one returns, 91:3
 Satanic mills, 354:8
 sea iridescent and d., 767:6
 some days d. and dreary, 436:14
 soul's d. cottage, 249:28
 start down the d. path, 778:18
 sun to me is d., 260:10
 then it is d., 767:7
 they all go into d., 678:19
 to d. tower came, 212:9
 unfathomed caves, 315:23
 violets are d. too, 93:7
 walk between d. and d., 706:2
 wall between us and d., 704:17
 wandering in d. labyrinth, 167:15
 ways that are d., 528:10
 we are for the d., 219:9
 we work in d., 544:12
 what if Amyntas is d., 93:7
 what in me is d. illumine, 255:5
 who art d. as night, 223:7
 with excessive bright, 257:8
 with torment and tears, 476:10
 wood where straight way lost, 128:3
 woods lovely d. deep, 623:8
 world and wide, 254:20
 world present treatment, 602:9
Darken, never d. threshold of doors, 489:5
Darkened, blue d. on blueness, 663:22
 hurtles in d. air, 316:16
 sun or light be not d., 23:30
 windows be d., 23:30
Darkeneth, who d. counsel by words, 14:17
Darkens, evening d., 817:8
Darker and darker stairs, 663:22
 the tinge that saddens, 431:5
Darkest before day dawneth, 250:8
 sun breaks through d. clouds, 173:22
Dark-heaving boundless, 396:21
Darkies how heart grows weary, 503:12
Darkling I listen, 410:9
 plain, 496:19
 roll d. down torrent, 306:19
 stand varying shore, 219:3
Darkly he rose, 814:10
 it knows obstacles, 797:14
 saw through glass eye d., 524:6
 see through glass d., 42:29
 wise and rudely great, 295:1
Darkness, absence d. death, 229:13
 affronts with his own d., 772:2
 again and silence, 437:19
 and Decay and Red Death, 448:13
 and light alike to thee, 19:14
 and myself, 747:10
 and shadow of death, 13:20, 18:13, 37:15
 as children fear in d., 90:10
 awake upon dark, 663:22
 awful d. silence reign, 468:2

Darkness *(continued)*
blackness of d., 46:13
cast into outer d., 33:26
comprehended it not, 38:45
crown of our life is d., 529:19
curse the d., 660:*n*1
deep but dazzling d., 269:3
deep things out of d., 13:27
deepens, 405:8
distant voice in d., 437:19
downward to d. on wings, 640:22
embalmed d., 410:7
encounter d. as a bride, 206:36
falls from wings, 436:16
fell upon Christian, 271:22
gives light in d., 170:2
hello d. my old friend, 855:6
horror of outer d., 517:15
hovers earth is silent, 4:6
how great that d., 33:4
how in your d. know, 610:4
if light in thee be d., 33:4
in d. and with dangers, 258:25
in d. bind them, 696:14
in him is no d., 46:6
in what d. of life spend little span, 90:1
instruments of d., 214:9
into d. peering, 449:7
into d. they go, 695:17
into eternal d. fire and ice, 128:12
jaws of d. do devour it, 177:28
land of d. and shadow, 13:20
lead me from d. to light, 50:1
leaves world to d. to me, 315:11
lest d. come, 39:37
light excelleth d., 22:28
light is left hand of d., 824:9
light shineth in d., 38:45
lighten our d., 48:18
lordly d. decked in filth, 795:4
love in spite of d., 229:8
man ever in d., 119:6
no d. but ignorance, 205:27
no light but d. visible, 255:8
not walk in d., 39:24
of God, 678:20
of man's heart, 764:1
outer d., 33:26, 35:28, 517:15
over spirits of damned, 444:11
pain d. and cold, 462:25
peace and d., 576:3
people that walked in d., 25:15
people which sat in d., 32:12
pestilence that walketh in d., 17:28
prince of d. a gentleman, 212:7
raven down of d., 252:15
rulers of the d., 43:40
scatters rear of d. thin, 251:1
shaft of light in d., 786:14
shares the d., 695:10
sit in d. here, 256:17
such as sit in d., 18:13
swooping d. up, 891:8
them that sit in d., 37:15
this thing of d., 225:8
thou makest d., 18:11
through d. up to God, 453:24
two eternities of d., 723:3

Darkness *(continued)*
universal d. buries all, 297:6
upon face of the deep, 5:3
wave of light breaks into d., 668:18
we are not of d., 44:19
where d. let me sow light, 125:12
which may be felt, 7:36
wind torrent of d., 646:1
works of d., 41:40
worms and shrouds, 409:4
year of now done d., 547:4
Dark-shining Pacific, 670:5
Darky's heart longed to go, 558:1
Darling buds of May, 221:2
Charlie is my d., 362:10
daughter, 887:17
man been mother's undisputed d., 563:11
my d. dear, 884:6
my d. from the lions, 16:8
Nature's D., 316:11
of men and gods, 89:9
of my heart, 292:1
Darlings, murder your d., 584:1
we must march my d., 487:4
wealthy curled d., 207:31
Dart, time throw a d. at thee, 240:7
Darts, lay full of d., 409:17
Darwin, Evolution from Washington to Grant
upset D., 531:22
process which D. discovered, 850:11
Darwin's, Luther's day expand to D. year,
483:23
most famous event since D. book, 821:*n*1
theory of evolution, 873:14
Dash thy foot against a stone, 17:29, 37:24
Dashed, breaking waves d. high, 405:4
in pieces the enemy, 8:6
the brains out, 215:5
through thick and thin, 273:7
Dastard in war, 373:11
Dastardly pitiful Public, 386:4
Dat veniam corvis vexat censura columbas,
109:*n*5
Data, graphic representation of d., 866:5
more d. we have, 876:4
submit d. to analysis, 345:3
Date, out of d., 665:4
will live in infamy, 653:6
Datta (give), 50:*n*4
Daubed with slime and pitch, 7:23
Daughter all her life, 503:7
am I in mother's house, 589:6
as mother so her d., 28:15
at point of death, 36:34
beggar's d. of Bethnal Green, 889:21
fairer d. of fair mother, 96:13
harping on my d., 198:34
have you a d., 198:33
I have a d., 186:8
images return O my d., 677:20
king of Spain's d., 894:18
light God's eldest d., 250:3
marry d. when you can, 243:20
Mrs. Porter and d., 676:11
my d. is writing, 798:5
my d. O my ducats, 185:5
of debate, 151:10
of Elysium, 359:10

Daughter *(continued)*
of Herodias Salome danced, 34:23
of Moon Nokomis, 437:2
of the gods, 450:23
one fair d., 199:10
sole d. of his voice, 259:10
stern d. of voice of God, 371:14
taken his little d., 436:8
undaunted d. of desires, 263:9
whipped her little d., 895:3
yes my darling d., 887:17
your d. and the Moor, 207:29
Daughter's daughter all her life, 503:7
preaching down d. heart, 451:25
Daughters and sons gone, 808:7
curses all Eve's d., 187:17
degenerate sons and d., 605:6
earth's heedless sons and d., 709:6
fairest of her d. Eve, 257:21
have done virtuously, 22:20
if you have no d., 894:15
my d. I suppose, 742:8
none of Beauty's d., 397:10
O d. of Jerusalem, 24:4, 24:18
of music brought low, 23:30
of my father's house, 205:5
of Time, 424:23
prayers are d. of Zeus, 51:21
sage d. of Muses, 64:1
tigers not d., 212:21
who Shem and Shaun d. of, 650:22
words are d. of earth, 306:23
Daughtersons, all Livia's d., 650:22
Daunt, death could not d., 889:22
Dauntless, brows of d. courage, 255:26
Hampden with d. breast, 316:1
in war, 373:10
slug-horn to my lips, 212:*n*2
Dauphin, daylight's d., 546:9
Dave, will you stop D., 784:4
David, and D. his ten thousands, 11:3
as D. and the Sibyl say, 47:20
danced before the Lord, 11:15
died full of days, 12:27
in the city of D., 37:17
in the midst, 318:8
my sling the sling of D., 557:16
no more behind your scenes D., 308:14
played before the Lord, 11:13
prevailed over the Philistine, 11:2
the son of Jesse, 11:24
David's, once in royal D. city, 476:5
upon St. D. Day, 896:6
Davil, ole d. sea, 681:1
Daw, Margery D., 893:19
no wiser than a d., 169:15
Dawn becomes yellow, 891:16
before d. of day, 321:8
bodiless as false d., 797:12
comes no sooner for early riser, 898:10
comes up like thunder, 588:2
creation's d. beheld, 396:19
crows at the break of d., 851:4
gray d. breaking, 419:5, 635:15
house made of d., 891:17
in Helen's arms, 596:2
in that d. to be alive, 368:18
into silver d., 701:4

Dawn *(continued)*

it must be close to d., 867:12
live gray d., 814:13
Morning Star herald of d., 87:4
of morning after, 597:18
on other side of Atlantic, 317:4
Piper at the Gates of D., 574:8
rosy-fingered d., 50:17
said to d. Be sudden, 576:16
speeds a man, 54:26
star at d., 112:26
with silver-sandaled feet, 559:18

Dawneth, darkest before day d., 250:8

Dawning, bird of d., 196:19
here hath been d., 408:10
not as d. of day, 231:10

Dawn's early light, 386:19
light dispersed, 56:11

Dawns, day d. to which we are awake, 475:23

Daws, for d. to peck at, 207:26

Day, a little work and good d., 519:8
a summer's d. and with setting sun, 256:5
after wedding night, 616:5
all on summer's d., 894:2
all the livelong d., 884:22
alternation of night and d., 118:6
and night replacing each other, 80:11
and night shall not cease, 6:23
another blue d., 408:10
as it fell upon a d., 233:14
as morning shows the d., 260:1
be d. never so long, 148:18
be she fairer than the d., 239:17
beneath blue of d., 574:16
best d. first to flee, 93:21
better d. better deed, 236:10
beyond night across d., 452:12
bounded by D. of Judgment, 456:n1
breaks not it is heart, 882:3
brief December d., 438:15
bright cold d. in April, 735:15
bright d. is done, 219:9
bright d. not for aye, 476:10
brought back my night, 255:2
burden and heat of d., 35:6
by d. in a pillar of cloud, 8:2
called feast of Crispian, 189:26
cares that infest d., 436:18
children of the d., 44:19
close eye of d., 253:17
come another d., 892:16
come not on last d. but very last, 655:15
cometh that shall burn as oven, 29:20
compare thee to summer's d., 221:2
cool of the d., 5:20
count that d. lost, 883:18
creatures of a d., 63:31
dance barefoot on wedding d., 173:12
darkest before d. dawneth, 250:8
dawns to which we are awake, 475:23
death will have his d., 177:6
dependency of d. and night, 640:22
dies at the opening d., 289:14
dim light of immortal d., 402:4
dines on following d., 517:3
do each d. two things disliked, 626:19
dog hath a d., 147:34
dog will have his d., 202:22

Day *(continued)*

drink oblivion of d., 505:8
dying d. sir, 883:12
endures moment or d., 594:13
enter into night, 119:7
entertains the harmless d., 227:10
ere I had seen that d., 197:7
evening and morning were first d., 5:4
every d. a wilderness, 871:2
every d. got up and gone to bed, 626:19
every d. hidden growths, 480:14
every d. in every way, 568:8
every d. passed as if our last, 100:27
every dog has his d., 423:8
every dog his d., 481:7
every year passed d., 816:6
everyone has his d., 621:15
exact d.-labor light denied, 254:21
faint in the d. of adversity, 21:32
fair d. adieu, 175:15
famous d. and year, 437:15
fate put heads together, 623:15
fell of dark not d., 547:7
first last everlasting d., 229:9
fogs prevail upon the d., 273:14
follow as night the d., 197:24
forever and a d., 195:28
frabjous d., 515:13
friends I have lost a d., 107:21
from this d. forward, 49:16
gaudy blabbing remorseful d., 170:10
gilded car of d., 252:7
given thee till break of d., 352:11
go to bed by d., 555:8
God is d. night winter summer, 62:5
good to gain d., 486:2
got tired of Me, 509:3
great and dreadful d. of the Lord, 29:22
guest that tarrieth but a d., 30:3
gwine to run all d., 503:10
happiest d. happiest hour, 447:9
hath brightest d. a cloud, 170:4
he announced for President, 864:8
he that outlives this d., 189:26
health and a d., 425:23
hippopotamus's d., 675:24
home being washing-d., 277:16
how it is with April d., 623:19
I had rued, 623:5
I hate the d., 161:1
if she be a d., 285:19
in d. of adversity consider, 23:13
in d. of prosperity be joyful, 23:13
in its hotness, 495:9
in the d. of vengeance, 20:4
in the posteriors of this d., 174:27
in thy courts, 17:20
in which ye came out, 8:1
is at hand, 41:40
is done and darkness falls, 436:16
is for honest men, 68:8
is short labor long, 117:8
it is his d., 138:8
it was Christmas D., 167:2
jocund d. stands tiptoe, 181:2
joint-laborer with d., 196:14
July's d. short as December, 223:13

Day *(continued)*

just for one d., 609:14
kings upon coronation d., 274:2
knell of parting d., 315:11
known a better d., 372:20
left alone with our d., 748:8
let every man consider last d., 66:8
let the d. perish, 13:3
let them have their d., 593:4
light of common d., 370:18
little systems have d., 453:9
long weary d. have end, 161:6
looked into eye of d., 595:1
love resembleth April d., 173:29
maddest merriest d., 450:15
meditate d. and night, 14:40
men die miserably every d., 659:8
merry as d. is long, 190:22
merry heart goes all d., 223:24
mildewed d. in August, 787:3
most wasted d. of all, 334:14
mounting at break of d., 371:25
night and d. you are the one, 691:9
Night mother of D., 438:4
night of time surpasseth d., 249:3
No D. But Today, 875:13
not a d. without a line, 81:2
not as dawning of d., 231:10
not the best d., 839:2
not to me returns d., 257:6
not up soon as I, 176:2
now d. over, 519:1
now's the d., 358:16
of adversity, 23:13
of affliction, 30:37
of death better than birth, 23:8
of deliverance, 330:1
of Empires come, 525:15
of glory has come, 361:3
of Judgment, 656:1
of one's birth, 23:8
of prosperity, 30:37
of small things, 29:13
of spirits, 269:2
of the great reckoning, 3:10
of the Lord, 44:18
of vengeance, 20:4
of wrath, 47:20
On Clear D. You Can See Forever, 790:15
on seventh d. God ended his work, 5:9
one d. beside some flowers, 772:5
one d. is like all others, 631:2
pack clouds away and welcome d., 233:18
past and yet I saw no sun, 163:11
petty pace from d. to d., 217:23
planned another d., 865:1
precincts of cheerful d., 316:4
proper man as see in summer's d., 178:9
rain it raineth every d., 205:29, 211:31
rape of every blessed d., 797:13
rare as d. in June, 481:16
remember the sabbath d., 8:13
returns too soon, 397:14
Rome not built in one d., 147:25
rose with delight to us, 241:20
runs through roughest d., 214:13
saw my evil d., 363:12
seize the d., 96:11

Day *(continued)*

set down as gain each d., 96:10
seventh d. thou shalt not work, 8:13
shall declare it, 42:9
shall stand at the latter d., 13:39
she set out one d., 618:1
shineth unto perfect d., 19:29
sleep neither night nor d., 214:1
so cool so calm, 242:19
so foul and fair a d., 214:4
some d. you'll know, 814:10
soundless d. in autumn, 448:8
specter night and d., 353:10
spent but one d. thoroughly well, 137:9
St. Patrick's D., 884:4
sufficient unto d. is evil, 33:11
sun anew each d., 671:14
sun gone down while it was d., 27:36
sun shall not smite thee by d., 18:30
sunbeam in winter's d., 300:13
superfluous to demand time of d., 181:20
support us all d. long, 421:5
tender eye of pitiful d., 216:13
thanks to heroes reached this d., 769:10
that I die, 861:11
that is dead, 452:16
that shall burn as oven, 29:20
think every d. your last, 98:1
third d. comes a frost, 225:25
third d. he rose again, 48:11
third d. he will raise us up, 28:33
this d. for a memorial, 7:41
this January D., 511:6
those eyes the break of d., 207:8
those who dream by d., 448:12
thou d. I hour, 526:16
thought it Judgment D., 536:20
three days after Bastille D., 814:5
'tis true 'tis d., 229:8
today isn't any other d., 516:10
tomorrow a new d., 157:30
tomorrow as today, 223:9
tomorrow is another d., 726:6
turn by night or d., 370:13
two nights to every d., 242:22
unpurged images of d., 595:10
until the d. break, 24:11
unto day uttereth speech, 15:15
up by break of d., 242:17
was it the spring d., 892:6
we the ones to make better d., 875:5
weakening eye of d., 536:10
wedding d. fixed, 305:1
what a d. may bring, 21:40
when heaven was falling, 575:20
which the Lord hath made, 18:26
while it is d., 39:27
will come thou shalt wish for me, 171:24
without all hope of d., 260:9
withstand in the evil d., 43:40
wrestled until breaking of d., 7:2
year and a d., 467:8
yield d. to night, 169:10
Dayadhvam, 676:17
(sympathize), 50:*n*4
Daybreak, black milk of d., 794:6
Daydreaming, house shelters d., 659:10
Day-labor, exact d. light denied, 254:21

Daylight, between dark and d., 437:12
in death d. finish, 463:12
in the mind, 288:15
must not let d. in upon magic, 503:5
night but d. sick, 186:20
see a church by d., 190:24
we burn d., 179:24
when d. comes comes in light, 479:12
you love the d., 67:9
Daylight's dauphin, 546:9
Daylong tomcat lies stretched, 827:13
Day's, all in d. work, 883:16
at the morn, 459:19
death of each d. life, 215:21
end of this d. business, 193:18
every d. news, 207:5
good d. work, 304:3
long d. journey, 681:11
long d. task is done, 219:1
wages for day's work, 407:24
year's midnight and the d., 229:11
Days about which I never worry, 545:15
after three d. weary of guest, 302:2
all my d. are trances, 448:7
alluvial march of d., 720:6
among dead are past, 381:15
Ancient of d., 28:29
Ancient of D., 517:11
and nights to Addison, 307:15
are consumed like smoke, 18:4
are swifter than shuttle, 13:16
as thy d. so thy strength, 9:32
at best dull and hoary, 268:17
begin with trouble, 283:8
Checkerboard of Nights and D., 441:22
curtain of distorting d., 595:17
David died full of d., 12:27
dead-letter d., 383:7
decrease autumn grows, 461:16
dividing lover and lover, 529:13
dwindle down, 673:1
evil d. come not, 23:30
expect halcyon d., 169:12
fallen on evil d., 258:25
fasted forty d. and nights, 32:11
first thousand d., 785:12
fled Him down d., 576:13
flight of future d., 256:14
flowers withered while I spent my d., 122:9
forty d. and forty nights, 6:19
glamor of childish d., 662:15
go I endure, 643:19
golden d. of golden deeds, 257:7
good old d. of post-coaches, 388:14
greatest d. country lived, 620:13
halcyon d., 73:7, 169:12
happy d. here again, 697:4
happy those early d., 268:9
have been wondrous free, 290:10
his d. are as grass, 18:7
humanity only three d. old, 634:5
hypocritic D., 424:23
in joyful school d., 383:3
in length of d. understanding, 13:26
in my born d., 155:16
in my school-d., 184:11
in the d. of my youth, 381:11
in yellow leaf, 399:16

Days *(continued)*

joyfulness prolongeth his d., 31:16
leave them in midst of his d., 28:2
length of d. in her right hand, 19:25
light of other d., 387:17
live all d. of your life, 286:6
live laborious d., 253:6
long as twenty d. now, 369:15
looked on better d., 194:22
lying d. of my youth, 592:7
man born of a woman is of few d., 13:29
may be cloudy or sunny, 759:9
measure of my d., 16:17
melancholy d. are come, 406:2
Moses was there forty d., 8:22
multitude of d., 306:18
my dancing d. are done, 179:*n*2
my d. are past, 13:34
my d. are vanity, 13:18
my d. have crackled, 577:1
my d. of endless doubt, 159:2
nine d. old, 894:16
no guest welcome after three d., 83:12
nor hours d. months, 228:16
not dark d. great d., 620:13
number the d. of eternity, 30:8
o' auld lang syne, 357:17
of danger, 373:21
of Herod the king, 31:36
of Methuselah, 6:14
of our years, 17:25
of wine and roses, 599:17
of youth are d. of glory, 399:7
often often in old d., 496:12
on no days of childhood, 610:10
on the earth are as a shadow, 12:26
once in my d. be a madcap, 181:32
one of these d, 660:*n*2
our d. are scored against us, 107:13
past our dancing d., 179:27
precious d. spend with you, 673:1
red-letter d., 383:7
remember thy Creator in d. of thy youth,
  23:30
sad Rose of all my d., 591:1
salad d., 218:16
seemed but a few d., 6:44
seen better d., 194:23, 213:26, 399:12
seven d. are more than enough, 382:2
short when you reach September, 672:15
shortly see better d., 279:4
shuts up story of our d., 159:16
six d. shalt labor, 8:13, 470:13
slow drag of d., 67:8
so haunt thy d., 412:1
sober studious d., 293:21
some d. dark and dreary, 436:14
some d. longer than others, 621:15
spring full of sweet d., 242:20
sterner d. not darker d., 620:13
stink in three d., 83:*n*9
sweet childish d., 369:15
swift d. near their goal, 476:13
teach us to number our d., 17:26
that are no more, 452:21
that might be better spent, 160:26
that thy d. may be long, 8:14
then if ever perfect d., 481:16

Days *(continued)*

three whole d. together, 261:8
Time in hours d. years, 268:14
to come are wisest witnesses, 63:22
to Indian all d. are God's, 570:8
travelers of eternity, 279:20
untell the d., 233:17
virtue extends our d., 107:16
ways to lengthen our d., 387:13
weary of d. and hours, 530:16
when Birds come back, 508:6
where can we live but d., 799:10
will grow to weeks, 455:16
wish d. to be as centuries, 428:10
wish my d. to be, 369:14
world of happy d., 171:27
Days', his six d. work a world, 258:28
Dayspring from on high, 37:15
Day-star arise in your hearts, 46:4
in ocean bed, 253:14
Dazzle, mine eyes d., 237:9
Dazzled by ways of God, 639:10
Dazzles at it as at eternity, 269:1
Dazzling, all beams full-d., 487:10
deep but d. darkness, 269:3
uncertainty of New England weather,
522:10
De gustibus non disputandum, 120:14
te fabula, 95:*n6*
Deacon, enough to make d. swear, 482:4
Dead, Adonais is d., 403:12
Agamemnon d., 594:16
all once so beautiful d., 683:3
all the D. lie down, 509:8
always pop'lar, 600:2
and gone lady, 201:24
and rotten, 302:18
and turned to clay, 202:14
are but as pictures, 215:23
are not powerless, 394:3
art of poetry, 665:4
as one disembodied triumphant d., 488:7
barbarian weeping above d., 518:4
be brought forth alive, 118:19
beauty d. chaos comes, 171:14
being d. with him beauty slain, 171:14
besides the wench is d., 168:11
blow bugles over rich d., 669:12
Body my good dog d., 772:11
body without spirit is d., 45:26
brave men living and d., 446:5
breed maggots in d. dog, 198:33
broke spell of d. letter, 688:8
by ships lies a d. man, 52:16
Caesar's trencher, 218:33
called it Bible d. now, 731:4
certain is birth for the d., 84:7
Christ risen from d., 43:1
close wall with English d., 189:7
communication of d., 679:8
corpse of Public Credit, 390:12
corse in complete steel, 197:34
crucified d. buried, 48:11
day that is d., 452:16
days among d. past, 381:15
dead and dead indeed, 892:8
dear d. women, 462:4
Death once d., 223:5

Dead *(continued)*

deathless hour, 506:4
descent of last end on d., 650:9
desire d. be near us, 453:19
dishonor not trouble once I am d., 67:10
divine brother of all, 487:8
divine makes d. seem alive, 137:17
dooms imagined for d., 409:8
doubled globe of d., 777:5
earth that bears thee d., 183:31
earth to living not d., 338:3
England finished and d., 627:5
envy for the d., 524:13
envy of the d., 67:13
faith d. which does not doubt, 586:5
faith without works is d., 45:26
fallen cold and d., 487:17
fell at his feet as d., 46:18
for a ducat dead, 201:2
for Love is d., 162:15
for Lycidas sorrow not d., 253:14
forgotten as a d. man out of mind, 16:2
full of d. men's bones, 35:17
gear of foreign d. men, 679:4
God is d., 547:16
govern living, 416:9
great god Pan is d., 108:13
greatest service or injury to d. man, 74:17
half d. a living death, 260:11
half regiment d., 787:19
hands dead stringencies, 833:10
harrow house of d., 748:6
healthy wealthy and d., 704:9
hear voices of d., 690:12
Hector is d., 204:8
help for living hope for d., 518:5
her d. body wears smile, 833:5
herself ere evensong, 890:5
high converse with mighty d., 300:17
himself must be d., 382:24
honor dies man d., 438:6
how fares it with happy d., 453:16
how shall the d. arise, 248:11
how you to know about d., 61:7
I am every d. thing, 229:13
I see d. people, 880:1
ideas and dead beliefs, 504:12
if Lucy should be d., 369:6
immortal d. who live again, 480:16
in long run all d., 656:11
in praise of ladies d., 222:9
is at rest, 31:24
is God d., 415:19
is the king d., 172:4
kissed by English d., 699:8
know not any thing, 23:21
lain for century d., 455:3
land of d., 715:2, 748:9
law hath not been d., 206:26
left it d. and with head, 515:13
let d. bury their d., 33:28
life is shrunk d. and interred, 229:12
lift coffins of d. relations, 845:10
light in dust lies d., 404:10
like vampire d. many times, 534:5
lilacs out of d. land, 676:5
living and d. are same, 62:11
living dog better than d. lion, 23:21

Dead *(continued)*

living scarce able to bury d., 240:4
look at my d. house, 738:17
Lord of living and d., 546:5
love never sick old d., 159:4
Magus Zoroaster my d. child, 401:15
maid not d. but sleepeth, 33:35
man cannot bite, 88:20
Man's Chest, 555:4
men tell no tales, 273:12
mic love ys d., 346:22
mighty d., 300:17
mindful of unhonored d., 316:5
Mistah Kurtz he d., 567:18
more d. people than living, 768:8
more to say when d., 606:1
most people my age are d., 689:3
mourn the d., 797:11
mouth of one just d., 635:3
moving d. still talk of pushing bones, 820:8
Mozart had been d. two years, 819:11
my d. wife's comb, 316:18
my enemy is d. man divine d., 487:11
my lady's sparrow is d., 91:2
nature seems d., 215:14
newspaper buries d., 600:16
no longer mourn when I am d., 221:23
noble Living and noble D., 369:1
not a house where not one d., 7:43
not d. but gone before, 103:*n7*
not God of d., 38:27
not interested in living, 715:7
not make war on d., 148:30
now he is d. should I fast, 11:20
O he is d. then, 546:15
objects essentially d., 379:6
of d. nothing but good, 55:*n7*
old bawd is d., 597:5
old men are all d., 537:4
once d. never return, 441:21
one d. other powerless, 495:23
only d. know Brooklyn, 727:13
only d. who do not return, 348:13
only good Indians d., 513:3
out of d. cold ashes life, 550:3
outrage brave man d., 65:9
painting is d., 414:9
pattern of d. and living, 679:1
people so d. to liberty, 305:13
perfection, 454:26
Phlebas a fortnight d., 676:14
plucks d. lions by beard, 175:7
poetry of earth never d., 408:19
Poets d. and gone, 411:5
poets in misery d., 370:1
praised the d. already d., 22:32
pray for d. fight like hell for living, 511:17
prey on us, 762:7
professors like literature d., 664:7
quick and the d., 48:11
rather be d. than cool, 879:5
renown and grace is d., 215:30
Respite to be d., 510:7
rest her soul she's d., 202:9
resurrection of the d., 43:1
revisit in dreams the dear d., 67:5
romantic Ireland's d., 592:10
rough notes and d. bodies, 603:5

Dead *(continued)*
rule over the departed d., 53:18
say I'm sick I'm d., 295:9
Sea fruits, 388:4
Sea's shore, 395:15
seek living among d., 38:40
shall be raised, 43:8
shall live living die, 273:26
sheeted d., 196:15
shores will swarm with invisible d., 394:3
sleeping and the d. are alike, 4:9
smiling the boy fell d., 459:23
so dull so d. in look, 187:22
so long as refuse to die, 501:13
soldiers bore d. bodies by, 181:36
somebody threw d. dog down ravine, 759:3
something d. in each of us, 561:5
soul so d., 373:3
Spartan d., 398:18
speak ill of the d., 55:8
stars are d., 748:8
there are no d., 582:7
there are so many people d., 738:16
there he fell down d., 10:12
these d. not died in vain, 446:5
these honored d., 446:5
thing goes d. once said, 628:5
think living worth it, 816:5
thirty is as good as d., 344:10
though d. shall he live, 39:33
three keep secret if two d., 302:10
thy greatest enemy is d., 30:29
time is d., 713:11
time you have to spend d., 152:4
told me Heraclitus d., 499:9
took wages and are d., 575:20
topics of sex and the d., 597:12
travel to home among d., 403:11
tree gives no shelter, 676:6
trophies and d. things, 237:11
truth never fell d., 457:8
unhonored d., 316:5
until he is d. do not call man happy, 55:17
vast and middle of night, 197:11
voices of d. like torrent's fall, 398:19
warred for Homer being d., 233:19
was d. and is alive, 38:12
what d. had no speech for living, 679:8
what difference make to d., 604:6
what matter where lay when d., 674:5
when d. put money in coffin, 386:6
when I am d., 660:13
when I am d. my dearest, 512:3
when living might exceed d., 248:22
when only d. could smile, 683:9
where d. men lost bones, 676:8
which die in the Lord, 47:6
which he slew at his death, 10:26
who fed the guns, 668:14
why can't d. die, 681:10
winds' riot, 530:15
word d. when said, 510:13
would that I were d., 450:8
you're d. son, 747:5
youth stone d., 668:13
Dead March, play D. as you carry me, 890:16
Dead-born, fell d. from the press, 312:2

Dead-letter days, 383:7
Deadly, dare d. terrors clasp, 353:2
forfeit should release, 250:9
imminent d. breach, 207:37
more d. than mad dog's tooth, 172:26
more d. than male, 590:4
pay with a d. blow, 63:13
wither and come to d. use, 212:19
Deadwood and Lost Mule Flat, 715:18
Deaf, ears of the d. shall be unstopped, 26:18
God's megaphone to rouse d., 717:14
justice blind d. an' dumb, 600:6
like the d. adder, 16:39
live d. to land beneath us, 690:13
music good nor bad to d., 276:12
trouble d. heaven, 221:5
Deafness, tale would cure d., 224:6
Deal, candy d. of courtesy, 182:7
cost a great d. to make, 582:12
falsely with God, 239:16
in remnants of remnants, 287:7
infinite d. of nothing, 184:10
intolerable d. of sack, 182:31
kindly with my people, 394:3
new d., 651:16
of scorn looks beautiful, 205:15
square d., 571:8
to d. plainly, 213:5
with men as equals, 838:13
Dealing, common sense plain d., 427:16
hard d. teaches them suspect, 184:31
Deals with the feelings of women, 654:18
with war, 654:18
Dean could write finely upon broomstick, 284:*n*2
Dear as light and life, 358:12
as remembered kisses, 452:22
beauty for earth too d., 179:28
Brutus, 191:26
damned distracting town, 293:20
dead women, 462:4
experience keeps d. school, 302:23
Fatherland, 484:25
friends we love so d., 520:1
God bless you my d., 311:17
how d. to this heart, 393:12
I die, 229:5
is life so d., 331:13
jesses my d. heart-strings, 209:7
land that gave you birth, 582:8
Lord and Father, 438:18
lose their d. delight, 222:7
makes remembrance d., 206:9
my d. times' waste, 221:8
name forever sad forever d., 293:22
nurse of arts, 190:6
pay too d. for what's given freely, 223:8
Plato and truth are d., 78:4
Sir your astonishment's odd, 680:*n*2
so d. I love him, 259:12
sold cheap what is most d., 222:13
son of memory, 250:15
think on thee d. friend, 221:9
to God famous to all ages, 254:4
to me as ruddy drops, 192:8
to me more d., 322:27
too d. for my possessing, 221:27
Wotton a most d. lover, 245:1

Dearer, honor d. than life, 156:32
yet the brotherhood, 582:8
Dearest, met my d. foe in heaven, 197:7
nearest and d. enemy, 183:5
throw away d. thing owed, 214:14
when I am dead my d., 512:3
Dearness only gives value, 333:6
Dears, Nature swears the lovely d., 356:22
Dearth, war d. age agues, 230:20
Deary, flew o'er me and my d., 358:12
in short my d. kiss me, 297:8
Death, a little d., 829:1
a necessary end, 192:11
absence darkness d., 229:13
absurd also, 761:5
after d. better bad epitaph, 199:13
after first d. no other, 777:7
after life does please, 160:7
after life is d., 530:14
agree 'em to death, 774:9
aloft gigantically down, 720:9
amiable lovely d., 175:18
and i coquette, 635:6
and Night wash world, 487:11
and sorrow our companions, 620:1
and taxes, 303:20
any man's d. diminishes me, 231:8
anyone's d. releases stupefaction, 493:17
arise arise from d., 230:19
ashamed of d., 248:10
be absolute for d., 206:32
be not proud, 230:22
become sought-after refuge, 69:18
beggars mounted run horse to d., 170:18
better than day of birth, 23:8
birth copulation and d., 677:4
birth life and d., 280:26
Black Widow, 787:4
blackness of d., 90:8
blaze forth d. of princes, 192:10
body of this d., 41:18
bridegroom in my d., 219:2
bring d. to a friend, 65:17
bringeth to light the shadow of d., 13:27
brought d. into world, 255:3
Bustle in House Morning after D., 510:11
by inches, 220:5
by man came d., 43:1
came d. into the world, 29:33
captain of men of d., 271:29
certain is d. for the born, 84:7
certain to all, 188:14
chants doleful hymn to d., 176:3
Chromis did not save himself from dark d., 50:26
City of Night perchance D., 520:11
closed in d. attentive eyes, 308:3
closes all, 451:17
cold hand of d., 183:30
come away d., 205:3
come close eyes, 882:2
come lovely soothing d., 487:14
comes near so silently, 139:5
cometh soon or late, 419:19
could not daunt, 889:22
counteracts Devil who is D., 318:15
covenant with d., 26:8, 433:6
crossing the world, 280:9

Death (*continued*)

of each day's life, 215:21
of endeavor birth of disgust, 540:3
of friends inspire us, 473:23
of one god death of all, 641:21
of the most noblest knights, 138:13
old captain, 491:10
on else immortal us, 230:21
on his pale horse, 259:20
on life on d., 597:11
once dead, 223:5
one in life and d. are we, 526:16
one of few things done easily, 839:14
one of things Nature wills, 112:18
one studied in his d., 214:14
one talent d. to hide, 254:20
or dreamful ease, 450:20
our souls survive d., 101:*n6*
out of jaws of d., 155:*n2*
owe God a d., 188:16
painted d., 4:9
pale horse and on him was D., 46:32
part and parcel of life, 631:3
parting foretaste of d., 400:2
people given over to d., 90:22
pit against d. and silence, 844:11
posterior to D., 510:3
precious is the d. of his saints, 18:24
preferred d. before slavery, 106:7
presence of Red D., 448:13
protracting life not deduct from d., 90:15
proud d., 202:34
proud to take us, 219:6
provides fun of amusement, 699:20
quick even in d., 158:17
quiet us in d. so noble, 260:25
read d. of Little Nell, 561:8
reality of one's d., 826:9
reared himself throne, 448:2
redeem them from d., 28:40
remain until d. do part, 565:16
remembered kisses after d., 452:22
rendezvous with D., 682:6
report of my d. an exaggeration, 524:21
ribs of D., 252:21
ride not free horse to d., 158:9
right to d. or liberty, 490:10
sad stories of d. of kings, 177:8
seen d. in heart of people, 581:8
seized Argus, 54:2
sense of d. in apprehension, 206:35
sentence of Versailles, 684:16
set before you life and d., 9:29
set d. i' the other, 191:23
setter up and plucker down of kings,
    170:23
shall be no more, 230:24
shall be surely put to d., 8:16
shall have no dominion, 777:6
ship of d., 663:23
sickened and nigh to d., 488:2
side of life away from us, 632:4
silent halls of d., 405:13
single d. tragedy, 636:19
sit in shadow of d., 18:13, 37:15
slavery or d., 287:24
sleep brother of d., 51:30
Sleep Brother to D., 167:3

Death (*continued*)

sleep of d., 199:21
sleep the sleep of d., 354:14
slew at d. more than in life, 10:26
slew not him, 161:2
someone's d., 461:22
soul sorrowful unto d., 36:4
stalk of d., 820:8
state of nothingness, 74:9
storm desertion d., 414:7
strange d. of life-to-be, 405:2
strange that d. should sing, 176:3
strict in his arrest, 202:28
stroke of d. eclipsed gaiety, 307:20
struck sharp on d., 434:19
sudden d. best, 89:5
Sudden D. General Desolation, 522:12
suffuses all with blackness of d., 90:8
sure as d., 231:15
swallow up d. in victory, 26:2
swallowed up in d., 74:13
taxes childbirth, 726:4
think not disdainfully of d., 112:18
this thought is as a d., 221:19
those who died so cruel a d., 145:1
thou shalt die, 230:24
thou wilt bring me to d., 14:8
thought of that late d., 592:19
till d. us do part, 49:16
time of d. every moment, 84:*n8*
time race to d., 116:18
to accept d. is to die, 366:*n6*
to sleep off to d., 633:6
touch the great d., 608:17
tramples it to fragments, 404:2
true to thee till d., 469:15
truly longed for d., 450:12
try cause condemn to d., 514:1
twitches my ear, 95:14
two fates of dread d., 52:14
ugly fact Nature hides, 512:11
useless life is early d., 343:5
valley of d., 454:18
valley of shadow of d., 15:23
vasty hall of d., 495:20
veil called life, 402:2
visit us with d., 240:4
wages of sin is d., 41:16
warrant, 582:15
way to dusty d., 217:23
Webster possessed by d., 675:25
what should it know of d., 368:2
what sights of ugly d., 171:28
what we fear of d., 207:1
when is d. not within ourselves, 62:11
where is thy sting, 43:9
wherever d. may surprise us, 818:12
who comes at last, 373:8
will have his day, 177:6
will overtake you, 118:3
windpipe throttled in fakes of d., 486:10
with impartial tread, 96:4
wooed us by water, 856:10
world easily reconciles to d., 431:17
worse things than d., 530:6
worst is d., 177:6
your d. Heraclitus, 83:1
your Loveliness and my d., 413:16

Deathbed, Jemmy Grove on d. lay, 889:25
Death-bedde, gon to hys d., 346:22
Death-fires danced at night, 376:5
Deathless Aphrodite on your throne, 56:4
    dead d. hour, 506:4
    his mansions are d., 52:31
    music, 605:7
Death's, beg d. pardon now, 797:11
    brother Sleep, 94:29
    call in thy d. head, 243:1
    fell d. untimely frost, 358:13
    gray land, 668:11
    ironic scraping, 641:6
    other Kingdom, 676:20
    pale flag not advanced, 181:13
    private door, 555:3
    sleep d. counterfeit, 215:29
    sleep D. twin brother, 51:*n2*
Deaths, after so many d., 243:7
    all d. could endure, 259:12
    by feigned d. to die, 229:2
    die many times before d., 192:11
    million d. statistic, 636:19
    ye died watched beside, 586:16
Death-steps, dinosaur d., 787:17
Death-world claws at everything, 83:1
Debasing work to do well what not worth
    doing, 810:10
Debate, Congress not to d. Canal d. me,
    571:16
    daughter of d., 151:10
    of commonwealth affairs, 188:32
    on public issues uninhibited, 745:9
    Roman senate long d., 287:24
Debated, greatest question ever d., 329:18
Debauch friend's wife genteelly, 310:2
Debauchee of Dew, 508:9
Debility, Nature condemned woman to,
    334:12
Debonair, buxom blithe and d., 250:20
Deborah arose, 10:8
    awake D. and utter a song, 10:9
Deboshed, thou d. fish thou, 224:29
Debt, by no means run in d., 242:10
    comfortably in d., 459:5
    discharged through eternity, 343:11
    how well live in d., 459:5
    millions of d., 324:15
    national d. blessing, 349:2, 390:6
    pay every d., 424:22
    public d. public blessing, 349:*n1*
    remember to pay the d., 70:9
    run in d. by disputation, 262:3
    to die a d. we must discharge, 242:*n1*
    to imagination, 630:1
    to Nature's quickly paid, 242:3
Debtors, as we forgive our d., 32:25
    we are d. or creditors, 343:14
Debts, forgive us our d., 32:25
    he that dies pays all d., 224:32
    new way to pay old d., 237:19
    words pay no d., 203:16
Decade, before d. out landing man on moon,
    786:1
    low dishonest d., 748:16
    me d., 831:5
Decadence, last spark of heroism amid d.,
    491:13

Define, hold good d. it well, 453:20
Definite, change not sudden d., 654:4
    evolution from vague to d., 534:16
Definition, better by derivation than by d., 317:2
    circumscribe poetry by d., 307:22
    is born, 774:7
    of criticism, 496:7
    of individual, 741:16
    of man is cooking animal, 334:5
    of oats meant to vex, 307:n1
    of style, 284:22
    very d. of tyranny, 345:11
Definitions, I hate d., 429:17
    principles conventions and d., 558:9
Deflower, age that will pride d., 160:9
Deflowered and now to Death devote, 259:14
Deformity cannot be charming, 667:4
Defraud not the poor, 30:16
Defunct, Buffalo Bill's d., 701:7
Defy augury, 202:26
    man know how to d. opinion, 362:14
    Power which seems omnipotent, 402:5
    the Omnipotent to arms, 255:7
    tooth of time, 290:17
Degeneracy and decay, 420:3
Degenerate, power to d. into lower forms, 141:3
    sons and daughters, 605:6
Degenerates, extensive state d., 391:2
    in hands of man, 312:21
Degeneration, from barbarism to d., 538:1
Degradation not to overcome poverty, 71:15
    sense of intellectual d., 552:3
Degraded, among the intolerably d., 804:9
    religion has d. women, 471:9
    women d. by trivial attentions, 360:19
Degrades, charity d., 432:9
Degrading anxiety about livelihood, 626:18
Degree, beauty and high d., 681:20
    curs of low d., 322:13
    exalted them of low d., 37:11
    only difference lies in d., 278:5
    priority and place, 203:5
    take but d. away, 203:7
    unless d. preserved place not safe, 101:8
    when d. is shaked, 203:6
Degrees, boil at different d., 428:22
    by d. dwindle into a wife, 287:6
    crime like virtue has d., 279:2
    estates d. and offices, 185:8
    grows up by d., 238:4
    one battle or by d., 333:11
    scorning the base d., 191:36
    six d. of separation, 844:9
    what wound heal but by d., 208:34
Dehumanizing the Negro, 444:11
Dei, Agnus D., 47:23
Deified, by our own spirits d., 369:16
Deify me as if blithe wine I had drunk, 411:15
Deign on passing world, 306:16
Deity, design of D. preservation of species, 360:26
    everlastingly appointed by D., 484:11
    offended, 356:20
Déjà vu, it was d. all over again, 807:7
Dejected Mariana, 207:4
    most d. thing of fortune, 212:15

Dejectedly, takes d. his seat, 495:16
Delay, in d. no plenty, 204:26
    infamous d., 290:23
    law's d., 199:21
    preferable to error, 337:3
    sweet reluctant amorous d., 257:20
Delayed, justice d. justice denied, 442:18
    till I am indifferent, 308:17
Delays breed dangers, 161:20
    dangerous in war, 161:n6
    disease gained strength by d., 102:19
    have dangerous ends, 169:19
    life admits not of d., 310:11
Delectable Mountains, 271:21
    not because troubles are d. joy, 89:20
Delegated, scholar is d. intellect, 425:26
Delenda est Carthago, 85:n3
Delete before sending manuscript, 584:1
Deliberate, accustomed to d. when drunk, 69:8
    derangement of senses, 558:14
    speed, 576:14, 692:n4
Deliberately, live d., 474:29
    read as d. as written, 475:5
    shield d. planned, 666:15
Deliberates, woman that d. is lost, 287:25
Deliberation fortitude perseverance, 318:4
    sat and public care, 256:16
Deliberations, chose after endless d., 611:1
Deliberative forces over arbitrary, 562:8
Delicate, air is d., 214:21
    algae and sea anemone, 679:4
    and rare, 561:4
    creatures ours, 209:9
    fare in another's house, 31:14
    sooner or later d. death, 487:14
Delicious moan, 411:1
    they were d., 658:19
    torment, 427:3
Delight, aim of oratory to d., 87:20
    all love all liking all d., 241:13
    and wonder of our stage, 232:19
    appetite makes eating d., 261:7
    bind another to its d., 352:13
    blue color d., 484:11
    brief dreamy d., 591:17
    capacity for d. and wonder, 567:3
    clothing of d., 350:12
    commonest d. of race, 507:14
    desire that outruns d., 529:18
    dogs d. to bark and bite, 289:5
    ebullience lightness and d., 865:9
    enjoy d. with liberty, 160:27
    followed d. with heart unsatisfied, 122:6
    from the whole, 379:10
    give d. and hurt not, 224:33
    go to it with d., 218:36
    Greensleeves my d., 881:5
    hear thy shrill d., 403:4
    impulse of d., 593:1
    in conceiving Iago, 413:9
    in misfortunes, 323:12
    in singing, 384:3
    is in law of the Lord, 14:40
    labor we d. in physics pain, 215:27
    land of pure d., 289:17
    lo she that was world's d., 530:1
    love with d. discourses, 128:2
    lulled with dances and d., 178:19

Delight *(continued)*
    Moon of my D., 442:4
    my ever new d., 258:13
    never d. in another's misfortune, 100:13
    no season such d. can bring, 240:8
    of battle, 451:13
    of husband aunts infant, 681:20
    paint the meadows with d., 174:32
    phantom of d., 371:6
    plaything gives youth d., 295:3
    poem begins in d., 625:3
    spirit of D., 404:8
    strongest tower of d., 483:11
    studies a d. to the old, 87:11
    such deep d. 'twould win me, 377:23
    sweets grown common lose d., 222:7
    take your d. in momentariness, 706:2
    temple of D., 411:11
    that consumes desire, 529:18
    these virtues of d., 351:3
    toys for your d., 556:6
    unrest men miscall d., 403:23
    weighing d. and dole, 196:22
    what d. without Aphrodite, 55:3
    with silent d., 351:6
    Zeus grant sweet d., 63:28
Delighted spirit, 206:38
    us long enough, 382:8
Delighteth, speech finely framed d., 31:34
    whom the king d. to honor, 12:32
Delightful, both wise both d., 265:8
    delicious de-lovely, 691:15
    in this d. garden grows, 160:12
    still air of d. studies, 253:21
    task rear tender thought, 300:19
Delighting and instructing at the same time, 98:29
    in your company, 881:4
Delights, all d. are vain, 173:40
    all thoughts passions d., 378:3
    anarchy of poverty d. me, 659:2
    fleeting d. of days, 400:14
    from heart of fountain of d., 90:17
    hence all you vain d., 236:9
    joy d. in joy, 220:33
    man d. not me, 199:6
    reader and instructs too, 278:7
    scorn d., 253:6
    speak of banqueting d., 226:22
    supremest of d. sexual intercourse, 525:7
    these d. if thou canst give, 251:9
    uselessness which d. them, 658:15
    violent d. have violent ends, 180:24
    were dolphin-like, 219:8
    winter his d., 227:1
Delineation, happiest d., 382:21
Delinquency, trying to control feline d., 727:8
Delinquents, beg d. for life, 788:4
Delirium, all that d. of brave, 592:10
Deliver, from winter plague Lord d. us, 227:5
    good Lord d. us, 48:19, 884:8
    I will d. him to you, 35:35
    me from body of death, 41:18
    me from phlegmatic preachers, 340:13
    no human efforts d. them, 328:6
    round unvarnished tale d., 207:34
    thee from the snare, 17:28
    us from evil, 32:25

Deliverance, day of d., 330:1
  little hope of d., 842:7
  this faith in d., 810:5
Delivered from perils and miseries, 240:2
  upon mellowing of occasion, 174:18
Deliverer, Lord is my d., 11:23
Delivering a crust of bread, 850:7
  improvements by generation, 327:12
Dell, farmer in the d., 896:20
De-lovely, delightful delicious d., 691:15
Delta, Mississippi D., 855:14
Delude, television used to distract d., 754:14
Deluding, vain d. Joys, 251:10
Deluge, after us the d., 317:15
Déluge, après nous le d., 317:15
Delusion, insane d. can't be held, 820:3
  one person suffers from a d., 820:n1
  Solon was under a d., 75:14
  to the philanthropist, 520:15
  trial by jury a d., 386:18
Delusive, most d. of passions, 565:16
Delved, Adam d., 880:8
Delves parallels in beauty's brow, 221:17
Delving in patient industry, 537:7
Dem, a loot d. a shoot d. a wail, 850:12
Demand for products, 364:9
  superfluous to d. time of day, 181:20
Demanded an image, 665:6
Demands rebellion makes upon us, 770:3
Demd damp moist unpleasant body, 464:21
  horrid grind, 464:24
Demean themselves as good citizens, 328:12
Demented, not one is d., 486:14
Demesne, deep-browed Homer ruled as d., 408:17
Demeter, goddess D. or Earth, 68:9
Demi-Atlas of this earth, 218:12
Demi-paradise, this other Eden d., 176:24
DeMille, I'm ready for my close-up, 747:14
Demirep that loves, 461:23
Demitasses, villainous d., 569:2
Demmed elusive Pimpernel, 590:10
Demnition bowwows, 464:25
Democracies cannot dispense with hypocrisy, 673:18
  security to d. against despots, 345:n4
Democracy, American d. discover middle ground, 788:18
  applied to needs, 356:1
  arises out of notion, 78:27
  arsenal of d., 653:3
  as final form of government, 871:4
  associate d. with freedom of action, 572:15
  bureaucracy not obstacle to d., 657:23
  capacity for justice makes d. possible, 696:3
  charming form of government, 75:18
  clear of dupes that talk d., 670:9
  constitution named a d., 71:14
  cure for ills of D. more D., 577:5
  cycle d. built on, 766:4
  death of d., 722:14
  direct self-government, 457:n4
  freedom and d., 765:13
  government of people, 457:9
  if liberty and equality found in d., 78:25
  in d. whores are us, 865:10
  is a great word, 488:12
  is baffled, 741:3

Democracy *(continued)*
  is the fig leaf of elitism, 841:14
  is place where numerous elections, 810:12
  method of finding solutions, 696:4
  my idea of d., 444:10
  neither despotism nor d., 349:5
  never d. not commit suicide, 330:15
  never lasts long, 330:15
  passes into despotism, 75:19
  recurrent suspicion, 724:3
  self-canceling business, 407:10
  shuts past opens future, 434:2
  socialist d. may be sham, 658:1
  Switzerland years of d. and peace, 781:4
  true d. never existed, 312:18
  two cheers for D., 638:14
  whatever differs from this no d., 444:10
  world safe for d., 566:14
Democratic, basis of d. state, 78:31
  cherished ideal of d. society, 790:18
  created new d. world, 406:13
  establishes d. regime kill sons of Brutus, 142:9
  nations not care for past, 434:2
  party ain't on speakin' terms, 600:5
  Party like mule, 512:13
  Party's candidate for President, 785:6
  secrecy and d. government, 661:15
  society is outraged, 741:3
  society like ours, 649:12
  thou great d. God, 482:24
  utter word D., 485:12
Democrats, all saloon keepers D., 458:5
  Blue States for D., 876:12
  raises corn and D., 559:14
Demolition, general d. of opinions, 246:10
Demon, when your D. in charge, 590:9
  you have roused, 444:11
Demoniac frenzy, 259:21
Demonisms, subtle d. of life, 483:3
Demon-lover, wailing for her d., 377:18
Demons down under sea, 449:23
  horrors d. proud to raise, 347:11
Demonstrandum, quod erat d., 82:4
Demonstrating careless desolation, 195:17
Demonstration, truly marvellous d., 247:5
Demonstrative or persuasive type, 607:2
Demoralizing, human slavery d., 560:26
  nothing so d. as money, 65:14
Demur you're dangerous, 509:4
Demure, sober steadfast and d., 251:12
Den, beard lion in his d., 373:14
  cast Daniel into the d. of lions, 28:27
  cockatrice' d., 25:19
  living in underground d., 75:11
  made it a d. of thieves, 35:9
  seven sleepers' d., 228:6
Dendid, when D. created all things, 888:22
Denial, empire in d., 878:8
  of right to experiment, 562:12
  vain and coy excuse, 253:2
Denied, call may not be d., 635:16
  exact day-labor light d., 254:21
  himself and acted tough, 756:21
  justice delayed justice d., 442:18
  no other was d., 509:12
  Peter d. Lord, 283:5
  the faith, 44:31

Denied *(continued)*
  this only d. to God, 73:21
Denies, court a mistress she d. you, 232:14
  heaven to gaudy day d., 397:1
  Spirit that always d., 344:4
  voyager further sailing, 68:3
Denieth, antichrist d. the Father, 46:9
Denmark, ne'er villain in D., 198:18
  something rotten in D., 198:4
  sure it may be so in D., 198:17
Denoted foregone conclusion, 209:18
Denounces, if man publicly d. poetry, 839:5
Denouncing someone or something else, 645:3
Dens and fastnesses of barbarism, 500:5
  lay them down in their d., 18:11
Dentists, economists on level with d., 656:16
Denunciation in place of evidence, 614:4
Deny, easier to believe than d., 528:16
  me thrice, 36:11
  oh was no d., 352:3
  participation of freedom, 324:12
  poor heart would fain d., 217:18
  themselves nothing, 459:5
  thy father, 180:2
  us for our good, 218:17
Deo, gloria in excelsis D., 47:22
Deos fortioribus adesse, 110:n6
Depart, ah she doth d., 352:3
  be off, 87:n4
  captains and kings d., 589:8
  come like shadows so d., 217:1
  from evil, 16:7
  I d. from materials, 488:7
  I say let us have done, 246:17
  ready to d., 384:4
  servant d. in peace, 37:19
  then deciding to d., 814:3
  this vale, 645:7
  to be to do to d., 533:3
  to d. from evil is understanding, 14:5
  to serve better, 519:9
  when old he will not d. from it, 21:17
  when ye d. shake off dust, 33:39
Departed, all but he d., 388:1
  ghosts of d. quantities, 291:7
  glory is d. from Israel, 10:37
  he has d. withdrawn gone away, 87:7
  his spirit is d., 31:24
  into their own country, 31:37
  minds me o' d. joys, 357:6
  never to return, 357:6
  rule over the d. dead, 53:18
  sacred to d. spirit, 120:17
  souls d. shadows of living, 249:6
Departeth, heart d. from the Lord, 27:39
Departing, knolling d. friend, 187:23
  leave behind us, 436:6
Department, duty of judicial d., 349:13
  fair sex your d., 573:21
  that's not my d., 819:10
Departure beyond borders death, 688:9
  hour of d. has arrived, 74:11
  is taken for misery, 29:34
Depend, all rest on us d., 487:4
Depended, always d. on kindness of strangers, 766:7
Dependence, in marriage d. mutual, 405:9
  of art on felt life, 544:16

Desire *(continued)*
  no more d. rose, 174:2
  not mortal what you d., 102:10
  of discipline, 30:4
  of moth for star, 404:6
  of power in excess, 165:24
  one shore beyond d., 720:5
  outlive performance, 188:8
  perpetual rack, 234:21
  prayer soul's sincere d., 372:19
  pure and just d. of man, 142:16
  remold it nearer to D., 442:9
  satisfiest the d. of every living thing, 19:17
  second silence of d., 437:21
  shall fail, 23:31
  sick with d., 594:3
  speed of my d., 502:18
  that outruns delight, 529:18
  those who d. slavery, 447:3
  time has slain d., 813:11
  to a bottle of hay, 178:32
  to appear natural, 264:28
  to get on in world, 672:2
  to live again, 549:4
  to live beyond income, 521:12
  train noble natures not to d. more, 78:20
  under the elms, 681:6
  unspeakable d., 495:11
  vain d. vain regret, 506:7
  vanquished by d., 56:9
  we may be better strangers, 195:13
  what I've tasted of d., 623:4
  what we ought not to have, 100:21
  which of us has his d., 459:8
  without hope we live in d., 128:13
  without knowledge or d., 56:14
  wonder and wild d., 462:28
  yearning in d., 451:15
Desired and timely things, 575:19
  more to be d. than gold, 15:17
  pinch which hurts and is d., 219:15
  who hath d. sea, 589:20
Desires and dreams and powers, 530:16
  and petitions of thy servants, 48:17
  covetous d. of the world, 49:11
  dreams are made of d. and fears, 801:9
  from Death fulfillment to d., 640:21
  grant all things your heart d., 53:3
  have few d., 57:8
  heart's d. be with you, 193:28
  liberty doing what one d., 435:12
  mastery of d., 548:16
  no calamity greater than lavish d., 57:15
  nurse unacted d., 351:20
  painting gives form to d., 648:1
  reviving old D., 441:6
  sinful d. of the flesh, 49:11
  submitting things to d. of mind, 164:14
  those d. glowing openly, 583:12
  undaunted daughter of d., 263:9
  unto whom all d. known, 49:3
  weaned heart from low d., 143:1
  weight of chance d., 371:16
Desireth not death of sinner, 48:5
Desiring this man's art, 221:6
Desk, turn upward from d., 676:12
Desolate and sick of old passion, 599:14
  dark weeks, 659:3

Desolate *(continued)*
  home of mirth made d., 430:25
  shores, 412:6
  which built d. places, 13:4
  Winter's dregs made d., 536:10
  without you all is d., 683:3
Desolation, abomination of d., 35:20
  blood vengeance d., 489:15
  butchery and d., 620:8
  careless d., 195:17
  dark cold and empty d., 679:2
  intellectual d., 478:3
  magnificent d., 825:18
  seat of d. void of light, 255:13
  Sudden Death General D., 522:12
Despair, almost think it was d., 672:5
  at not having found joy, 633:1
  beauty born of own d., 594:17
  begotten by d., 267:3
  beyond hope and d., 677:15
  carrion comfort D., 547:3
  comfort and d., 223:3
  comfortless D., 315:7
  desire difficult to tell from d., 641:17
  divine d., 452:21
  don't d., 655:11
  dying and in d., 507:6
  edge of d., 366:17
  ending is d., 225:9
  fiercer by d., 256:7
  from d. high uplifted, 256:6
  Giant D., 271:20
  gives comfort in d., 170:2
  Hell's d., 352:12
  humor based on destruction d., 807:10
  imagined d. fallen upon me, 415:1
  in d. comes wisdom, 63:2
  infinite wrath and d., 257:12
  law chance hath slain, 230:20
  learn a style from a d., 745:17
  my only hope lies in d., 278:19
  never d., 96:7
  no more d. or loss of faith, 791:5
  of heart, 448:11
  rash-embraced d., 185:21
  replace d. with opportunity, 753:12
  result of fatal situations, 439:5
  reveals own folly and d., 713:13
  shall I wasting in d., 239:17
  Shame D. her teachers, 431:8
  toils d. to reach, 283:15
  where d. let me sow hope, 125:12
  White Sustenance D., 509:15
  ye Mighty and d., 401:13
Despairful, dissolute damned d., 627:11
Despairing songs loveliest, 457:7
Despairs, leaden-eyed d., 410:5
Desperandum, nil d., 96:*n*4
Desperate, by d. appliance relieved, 201:16
  diseases d. grown, 201:16
  in a d. land, 858:5
  marriage a d. thing, 238:15
  my constituency is the d., 852:9
  seas long wont to roam, 447:12
  slave to d. men, 230:23
  tempt not d. man, 181:10
  wisdom not to do d. things, 474:12
Desperately, deceitful and d. wicked, 28:1

Desperation, our policy against d., 644:13
  quiet d. confirmed d., 474:11
Despicable, wretched d. creature, 301:8
Despise, a contrite heart thou wilt not d., 16:35
  capacity to d. himself, 584:8
  hold to one d. other, 33:5
  ignorant d. education, 100:22
  not thy mother, 21:29
  pity ignorance d. him, 464:18
  riches, 485:10
  Shakespeare when I measure my mind, 565:15
  things of this life, 150:3
  what female heart gold d., 315:9
  with work you d., 602:10
Despised and dying king, 402:19
  and rejected of men, 27:5
  being unarmed be d., 141:17
  day of small things, 29:13
  disrespected and the d., 852:9
  poor infirm d. old man, 211:26
  race, 519:10
  straight, 222:20
  thus the poor agent d., 204:9
Despises, husband frae wife d., 358:4
Despising, myself almost d., 221:6
Despite, Heaven's d., 352:13
  its wrenching pain, 817:14
Despitefully, them which d. use you, 32:21
Despond, slough was D., 271:10
Despondently, sprouting d. at gates, 675:9
Desponding view of present, 420:3
Despot, country governed by d., 310:17
  custom d. of mankind, 418:19
  man once d. and slave, 402:4
Despotism, cloud of barbarism and d., 338:15
  degenerates into d., 391:2
  democracy passes into d., 75:19
  feeble engines of d., 338:15
  France d. tempered by epigrams, 407:1
  in majority of popular assembly, 330:16
  neither d. nor democracy, 349:5
  of liberty against tyranny, 356:2
  to liberty in featherbed, 337:1
  whatever crushes individuality is d., 435:9
  will destroy all good, 467:2
Despots, security against d., 345:*n*4
Destination, Heaven's my d., 715:3
Destined, his d. Hour, 441:12
  to poison all their joys, 482:12
Destinies, sway d. of half the globe, 434:1
Destiny, anatomy is d., 563:7
  chosen his d., 741:8
  exercises influence, 547:12
  expand the d. of mankind, 820:2
  hanging and wiving go by d., 146:*n*14
  has no beeper, 878:1
  man forges for himself, 742:22
  manifest d., 469:11
  not by material computation, 620:7
  obscure, 315:17
  of colored American, 477:4
  one country one d., 390:14
  reap a d., 885:17
  rendezvous with d., 652:7
  repose not d. of man, 538:8
  shady leaves of d., 263:4
  waits alike, 63:12

Destiny *(continued)*
　wedding is d., 146:19
　what seems accident springs from d., 360:2
　with Men for Pieces plays, 441:22
Destitute of emotional warmth, 541:9
Destroy, beauty disdains to d. us, 631:20
　Ben Tre in order to save it, 847:9
　does thy life d., 352:14
　farms grass will grow in streets, 577:17
　for one grape vine d., 172:32
　museums libraries, 633:7
　natural resources, 571:12
　nor sword nor age d., 102:18
　not come to d. law, 32:16
　not to d. but fulfill, 32:16
　one to d. is murder, 290:15
　power of reasoning, 76:2
　power to tax involves power to d., 350:1
　power to tax not power to d., 539:5
　they shall not hurt nor d., 25:19
　those who hate and d., 557:13
　thought would d. paradise, 315:8
　threatens to d. everything, 846:7
　village in order to save, 847:n1
　whom God wishes to d., 69:3, 121:11
　winged life d., 352:8
　worms d. this body, 13:39
Destroyed but not defeated, 722:4
　by each other, 281:9
　by madness, 812:13
　Carthage must be d., 85:6
　flower of kings and knights d., 138:14
　if men are d., 65:1
　last enemy d. is death, 43:2
　love without power d., 696:1
　Medici created and d. me, 140:15
　nations are d. or flourish, 354:12
　poetry painting music d., 354:12
　the very ruins d., 106:17
　things violently d., 369:4
　unique in world, 148:29
　when once d., 322:22
Destroyer and preserver hear, 402:10
　become Death d. of worlds, 739:8
　force that blasts trees is my d., 777:2
　time d. time preserver, 679:5
Destroying, prison soul d., 736:6
Destroyings, creations and d., 411:15
Destroys good book kills reason, 254:7
　habit d. first nature, 341:n2
　nation that d. soil, 652:16
　whoever d. single life is guilty, 117:9
Destructible, city is d. for first time, 724:6
Destruction, agree 'em to death and d., 774:9
　all other to d. draw, 229:9
　brought her dowry d., 63:3
　carry terror and d., 420:10
　causes of d., 312:19
　Famine Pestilence D. Death, 646:5
　fool's mouth is his d., 21:1
　for d. ice suffice, 623:4
　forces of nuclear d., 786:14
　gale of creative d., 657:21
　genocide d. of nation ethnic group, 726:1
　give enemies means of our d., 59:18
　hell of nuclear d., 823:13
　humor based on d. despair, 807:10
　I will be thy d., 28:40

Destruction *(continued)*
　if d. be our lot, 444:2
　means of d. hitherto unknown, 661:5
　of life and happiness, 337:15
　of Nazi tyranny, 653:15
　of tea so bold, 329:13
　politics of personal d., 863:3
　pride goeth before d., 20:37
　set him apart for d., 275:n4
　that wasteth at noonday, 17:28
　their going seemed utter d., 29:34
　thou turnest man to d., 17:23
　urge for d. creative urge, 469:13
　way that leadeth to d., 33:19
　when you talk about d., 848:14
　whose end is d., 44:5
　word deals d., 567:7
　world peace or world d., 606:7
Destructions, rescue my soul from their d., 16:8
Destructive damnable woman, 281:11
　element submit yourself, 567:9
　not afraid of d. act, 583:8
Detached, reality attained only by d., 760:12
Detachment, rare d. of spirit, 626:22
Detail, frittered away by d., 475:1
　is everything, 723:12
　merely corroborative d., 527:19
Details, God is in the d., 887:14
　left to chance, 440:7
　so many incidents so many d., 583:13
Detection, traitors escape d., 614:3
Detectives, scientists d. and explorers, 780:4
Detector, built-in shock-proof shit d., 722:5
Detention, house of d., 858:7
Deteriorating, shabby equipment d., 678:22
Determinate, every thing has d. idea, 76:2
Determination, charisma inner d., 586:8
　enough in mighty enterprises, 101:15
　of velocity, 728:3
Determine, disposition d. intimacy, 382:2
　education will d. future life, 75:7
　men d. gods dispose, 235:n3
　people seldom d. right, 349:4
Determined by what lies outside it, 480:21
　dared and done, 318:10
　to know beans, 475:11
Determines, way world imagined d. what men do, 685:3
Detest, abhor d. Sabbath-Day, 523:11
　creator d. and spurn me, 415:18
　I d. what you write, 300:n4
　love offender d. offense, 274:n4
　pageantry of king, 339:9
Detesting, die d. superstition, 300:8
Detract, power to add or d., 446:5
Detraction will not suffer it, 183:25
Deus, Domine D. Agnus Dei, 47:23
　ex machina, 81:9
　homo proponet D. disponit, 137:n4
　vult, 120:16
Deutschland is happy and gay, 811:9
　über Alles, 416:14
Devastation, slaughter pillage d., 620:8
Develop, men free to d. faculties, 562:8
Development, psychic d. of individual, 563:6
Develops and enlarges organ, 341:8
Deviates, Shadwell never d. into sense, 273:14

Deviation from truth is multiplied, 77:16
Device, banner with strange d., 436:15
　miracle of rare d., 377:21
　no work nor d. nor knowledge, 23:22
Devil, abashed the D. stood, 258:8
　an angel too, 586:4
　apology for D., 521:13
　a-walking the D. is gone, 381:18
　beggar will outride the D., 170:n1
　bird or d., 449:9
　black as the d., 348:5
　builds a chapel there, 282:4
　can cite Scripture, 184:26
　cannot make Hawthorne say yes, 482:17
　come and Faustus damned, 169:4
　counteracts D. who is Death, 318:15
　created in man's image, 492:10
　damn thee black, 217:16
　drink and d. had done, 555:4
　eat with d. have long spoon, 136:n1
　envy of the d., 29:33
　every man God or D., 273:3
　fears a painted d., 215:23
　from deceits of the d., 48:20
　give d. his due, 156:1
　go poor d., 314:6
　God and d. fighting, 492:9
　God sends meat D. sends cooks, 146:n16
　having trouble with wife, 564:11
　heart place d. dwells in, 248:12
　he's a very d., 205:23
　if d. doesn't exist, 492:10
　if the d. dress her not, 219:11
　is a gentleman, 212:n1
　is asleep, 564:11
　is ever God's ape, 144:5
　knows how to row, 377:2
　let the d. wear black, 200:15
　let us call thee d., 208:30
　Love a mischievous d., 521:14
　made me do it, 836:7
　man for himself D. for all, 148:n14
　match for d., 716:4
　Nazarite conjured the d., 184:22
　needs go whom d. drive, 148:15
　not serve God if d. bid, 207:28
　old serpent called the D., 47:2
　ole d. sea, 681:1
　puritan that he is, 204:30
　renounce the d., 49:11
　resist the d., 45:30
　sarcasm language of D., 406:17
　seem saint when most play d., 171:25
　showed him kingdoms, 37:23
　speak truth and shame D., 146:1
　sugar o'er d. himself, 199:20
　take her, 261:3
　take the hindmost, 238:6
　tell truth and shame d., 685:2
　territory held by the d., 809:13
　to pay, 156:36
　walketh about as roaring lion, 46:3
　what the d. was he doing in that galley, 268:2
　whispered behind leaves, 588:4
　why d. have all good tunes, 341:7
　wi' usquebae face the d., 358:7
　would build chapel, 144:5

Die *(continued)*

dead which d. in the Lord, 47:6
dear I d., 229:5
death thou shalt d., 230:24
deeds d. however nobly done, 160:25
desperate not to d., 813:2
do or d., 236:8, 358:17, 702:12
dry death, 224:3
easier to d. than remember, 724:14
easy live quiet d., 374:11
ere their story d., 536:22
fifteen-year-old till parents d., 835:5
fighting in defense of his country, 51:33
flowers must d., 671:20
for friends or fatherland, 97:15
for love, 205:32
for my people my country, 513:4
for such a long time, 267:9
for the people, 39:35
frogs do not d. in sport, 82:9
gladly d., 555:16
go since I needs must d., 159:9
good d. early bad late, 282:9
good d. first, 372:6
gross flesh sinks here to d., 177:25
Guards d. but never surrender, 366:21
hang there till tree d., 220:29
haven't instinct about when to d., 560:23
hazard of the d., 172:12
he could not fucking d., 835:10
here in rage, 285:8
honorable to d. for one's country, 96:26
hope I d. before I get old, 861:15
hope to d. at my post, 607:19
how can I d. alone, 811:19
how can man d. better, 419:19
how to d. harder lesson, 152:n3
I am sick I must d., 227:6
I d. but have possessed, 396:24
I d. hard, 329:5
I shall d. in Paris, 696:16
I shall not wholly d., 97:10
I to d. and you to live, 74:11
I will show you how to d., 152:n3
I'd like to d. like this, 765:4
if be with that which seek, 404:2
if I must d., 206:36
if I should d., 669:10
if it were now to d., 208:19
if man d. shall he live, 13:31
if nobody had to d., 628:7
if we must d., 687:13
if you poison us do we not d., 185:12
I'll d. young, 807:11
in Adam all d., 43:1
in bed, 668:13
in evening d. content, 61:1
in last dike, 324:19
in music, 74:n4
in the last ditch, 281:6
in this faith I will live and d., 139:1
in what peace a Christian can d., 288:19
is cast, 89:2
it will d. when you do, 830:13
jealousy not d. with love, 264:24
joys will d., 882:3
just to watch him d., 831:10
king tomorrow shall d., 30:33

Die *(continued)*

lack of love we d. from, 844:17
lads that d. in glory, 575:2
last man to d. for a mistake, 857:11
lest we d., 8:15
let friendship d., 311:8
let us d. like men, 439:8
lib and d. in Dixie, 471:1
live and d. for idea, 580:16
live and d. in Aristotle's works, 168:16
live and d. r-r-rich, 466:30
live and d. wi' Charlie, 367:15
live forever or d. in attempt, 802:8
live like a wretch and d. rich, 234:22
live through time or d. by suicide, 444:2
lives on hope d. fasting, 303:1
living know they shall d., 23:21
look about us and to d., 294:14
love me sure to d., 388:3
lovely things fade and d., 683:4
lucky to d. and I know it, 485:20
man can d. but once, 188:16
maybe I'll d. trying, 781:3
men d. fast enough, 281:9
men d. miserably every day, 659:8
men d. nightly in beds, 448:11
music when soft voices d., 404:4
must d. at last, 229:2
names not born to d., 400:13
never know life till d., 463:7
no young man ever thinks he shall d., 386:11
nobly d., 65:3
not d. before we have explained ourselves,
    330:14
not poor death, 230:22
not quickened except it d., 43:4
not that I'm afraid to d., 839:13
not willingly let it d., 253:20
of nothing but rage to live, 293:27
of remedies, 268:6
of rose in aromatic pain, 294:21
of that roar, 480:18
of words, 423:20
oh do not d., 229:6
old soldiers never d., 644:11, 887:4
on feet not live on knees, 653:5
on feet than live on knees, 643:10
on mine own sword, 217:26
only art is to d., 322:17
or let me d., 369:14
or rest at last, 403:9
pattern to live and d., 460:12
perceives it d. away, 370:18
pie in sky when you d., 639:4
poets d. of loneliness, 597:13
praise that will never d., 72:4
pray as if to d. tomorrow, 302:31
remember that we d. all, 30:29
reptiles carried thither d., 121:27
resolve to conquer or d., 328:6
reverences age d. with it, 406:8
rich, 310:20
rose with maize to d., 720:7
sail until I d., 451:18
seem though I d. old, 596:7
seems rich to d., 410:9
shall never d., 39:33
shall Trelawny d., 429:11

Die *(continued)*

sink or swim live or d., 390:3
someone to d. with, 872:9
something he will d. for, 823:6
Tamburlaine must d., 168:3
teach men to d., 152:3
teach us how to d., 396:4
tells me I must d., 411:16
the death of the righteous, 9:8
theirs but to do and d., 454:21
there smothered, 662:12
they seemed to d., 29:34
this'll be day that I d., 861:11
thou shalt surely d., 5:13
time to d., 22:31
to d. a debt we must discharge, 242:n1
to d. honorably greatest virtue, 60:12
to d. is gain, 44:1, 74:9
to d. to sleep, 199:21
too easy to d. for good or beautiful, 737:15
to itself it live and d., 222:2
to make men free, 481:2
toddle home d. in bed, 668:13
trust that when we d., 519:8
unlamented let me d., 292:5
unsung noblest deed will d., 64:8
unto the Lord, 42:2
we about to d. salute you, 111:1
we d. and we live, 119:9
we d. only once, 267:9
we d. soon, 783:10
we must, 170:37
we must be free or d., 370:11
we must needs d., 11:21
we shall d. alone, 269:16
we will d. free men, 341:10
when beggars d., 192:10
when good men d., 68:20
when he shall d. cut him in stars, 180:32
when I came to d., 474:29
when I d., 812:2
who saw him d., 893:9
who would wish to d., 423:6
why can't dead d., 681:10
wisdom shall d. with you, 13:23
with face to sun, 557:14
with hammer in hand, 885:12
with harness on our back, 217:25
with work unended, 703:12
with you be ready to d., 97:3
without benefit of clergy, 611:n5
without visiting one another, 58:6
Wolf that break it d., 588:18
world a place to d. in, 248:18
worse ways to d., 633:6
Xerxes did d., 283:6
ye shall d. like men, 17:17
youth fight and d., 625:19

Died, after you've d., 800:11
as one studied in death, 214:14
as soldier for his country, 582:n3
before god of love born, 229:21
Booth d. blind, 639:10
David d. full of days, 12:27
deaths ye d., 586:16
dog it was that d., 322:15
far away before his time, 582:n3
following songs' lost measure, 667:8

Discern infinite passion, 461:5
  innocence of neighbors, 475:16
Discerner of the thoughts, 45:7
Discerning, to a d. Eye, 509:4
Discernment, discovery is d., 558:11
Discharge, no d. in war, 23:19, 589:22
  to die a debt we must d., 242:*n*1
Discharged, debt d. through eternity, 343:11
  with greater ease, 242:3
Discharging less than tenth, 203:18
Disciple not above master, 34:3
  true teacher has no d., 417:6
Disciples, gave bread to d., 36:3
  masters ashamed to become d., 227:7
  threatening against d., 40:21
Discipline, care of d. is love, 30:4
  desire of d., 30:4
  Doric d. vain, 594:12
  makes individuals, 812:5
  organization and d. of war, 141:16
  soul of army, 328:4
  that I have established, 64:17
Disciplined by peace, 785:10
Disciplines, I know d. of wars, 189:13
Disclose, merits to d., 316:8
  not d. essence of phenomena, 662:2
Disclosed, before buttons be d., 197:19
Disco, this ain't no d., 870:9
Discomforts accompany my being blind,
  277:27
Disconnected from our history, 821:10
Discontent want of self-reliance, 426:23
  waste nights in d., 160:26
  wealth and poverty parents of d., 75:6
  winter of our d., 171:16
  yields nothing but d., 323:20
Discontented, stirs of d. strife, 233:15
Discontentment, no greater guilt than d.,
  57:15
Discord, age of d. and strife, 169:22
  civil d., 288:1
  danger in d., 437:1
  eke d. doth sow, 151:10
  harmony in d., 98:5
  harmony not understood, 294:23
  music must investigate d., 108:3
  so musical a d., 179:2
  what d. follows, 203:7
Discordant, concordant is d., 62:8
  reconciles d. elements, 368:14
  reconciliation of d. qualities, 379:13
  wavering multitude, 187:21
Discourage and abolish tyranny and vice, 329:6
Discouraged, lest they be d., 44:13
  never get d., 771:10
Discouragement, there's no d., 271:26
Discouraging, which more d. literature or
  chickens, 723:18
Discourse, bid me d., 171:7
  everybody's d. of death, 277:12
  excellent dumb d., 224:34
  in novel phrases, 526:10
  made us with large d., 201:19
  of fools is irksome, 31:12
  of reason, 197:4
  of the elders, 30:30
  rather thy d. than play, 235:13
Discourteously, cast me off d., 881:4

Discover everybody's face but own, 284:4
  I had not lived, 474:29
  who could d. God, 104:10
  you are human as I, 788:12
Discovered a truly marvellous demonstration,
  247:5
  America d. accidentally, 672:3
  I was not God, 539:9
  plant whose virtues not d., 429:4
  poets philosophers d. unconscious, 563:12
  when d. not wanted, 672:3
Discoverers among them as comets, 305:4
  ill d. think there is no land, 164:15
  sea-d. to new worlds, 228:7
Discovereth, he d. deep things, 13:27
Discoveries, they were always making d., 317:2
Discovering, only two ways of d. truth, 164:18
Discovers, depths of his own loneliness, 673:17
  flute in dying notes d., 273:25
  fresh perfection, 391:20
Discovery, abyss d. metamorphosis, 616:5
  comes by act of divination, 663:19
  errors portals of d., 650:16
  of America, 319:8, 580:5
  of personal whiteness, 602:8
  man's d. genitalia a weapon, 839:21
  mistaking paradox for d., 612:4
  new dish does more than d. of star, 348:16
  seeing what everybody seen nobody
    thought, 700:3
Discredit what they do not excel in, 80:9
Discreditable, regrets d. act, 645:13
Discreet charm of bourgeoisie, 725:2
  too d. to run amuck, 296:5
Discreetest, virtuousest d. best, 259:3
Discreetly blot, 249:27
  entered into reverently d. advisedly, 49:13
Discretion, better part of valor d., 183:34
  dronkenesse sepulture of his d., 136:10
  fair woman without d., 20:14
  inform their d., 338:12
  to the young man knowledge and d., 19:22
Discrimination, nation has history of sex d.,
  745:12
  protest d. and slander, 629:6
Discuss freely settle question, 419:12
Discussing duty to God, 486:14
Disdain, for thee to d. it, 404:5
  give me more love or more d., 245:17
  Lady D., 190:17
  to be instruments, 349:6
Disdained, one feeling d., 404:5
Disdainful smile, 315:17
Disdainfully, think not of d. of death, 112:18
Disdaining littlenesses, 76:6
Disdains, beauty d. to destroy us, 631:20
Disease, as physician observes d., 231:4
  astrology d. not science, 124:12
  brought on by boredom, 734:6
  called lack of money, 145:11
  consciousness d., 585:14
  cure d. kill patient, 166:8
  cured yesterday of my d., 283:14
  dreaded scandal more than d., 582:20
  fee bestow upon foul d., 210:28
  gained strength by delays, 102:19
  greater toll on health than any d., 796:8
  interest in d. interest in life, 631:6

Disease (*continued*)
  is finite and reductive, 835:12
  life is an incurable d., 265:13
  long d. my life, 295:11
  man survives horrors of d., 507:9
  medicine has to examine d., 108:3
  meet d. at first stage, 105:15
  of modern life, 495:17
  of not listening, 187:28
  old age only d., 427:14
  or sorrows strike him, 479:11
  people given over to d., 90:22
  remedies worse than d., 100:4
  remedy too strong for d., 66:22
  shapes of foul d., 454:9
  specialists in mental d., 656:15
  success our national d., 542:4
  TB was a d., 835:20
  the d. is incurable, 187:36
  to pretend to know is a d., 58:2
  tyranny's d., 63:16
  writing a contagious d., 123:10
Diseased, minister to mind d., 217:19
  nature breaks forth, 182:32
  of own beauty mind d., 396:12
  words are physicians of mind d., 63:17
Dis-eased, thou shalt not be d., 132:1
Diseases, as to d. make habit of two things,
  70:15
  desperate grown, 201:16
  for extreme d. extreme strictness, 71:7
Disembodied, as one d. triumphant dead,
  488:7
  bones, 666:5
Disenchanted with the world, 416:15
Disfigure, in a moment so d. us, 248:10
Disgrace and ignominy of natures, 248:10
  impatient of d., 272:16
  in d. with fortune and men's eyes,
    221:5
  intellectual d., 749:5
  lived without d. without praise, 128:9
  not without d. associated, 473:14
  vice-prisidincy a d., 600:17
Disgraced and mortal, 742:6
  dies rich dies d., 521:18
Disgruntled, if not actually d., 648:16
Disguise, again in this identical d., 783:8
  fair nature with rage, 189:7
  fiction in d., 813:10
  no d. can conceal love, 263:22
  profession is to d., 143:4
  to go naked best d., 286:26
Disguised to myself as a child, 757:1
Disguises, gods go in various d., 54:3
  troublesome d. we wear, 258:4
Disgust, achievement birth of d., 540:3
  not exist where hunger is, 567:15
Disgusting, Goops live d. lives, 597:20
  I think young ones d., 485:3
  sexual relations d., 614:15
Dish, as a man wipeth a d., 12:21
  butter in a lordly d., 10:11
  chameleon's d., 200:14
  dainty d., 894:7
  discovery of new d., 348:16
  feast of joy a d. of pain, 163:11
  fit for gods, 192:4

Distant *(continued)*
 religion of which rewards d., 307:16
 speaking of voices, 777:16
 ye d. spires, 315:4
Distasteful, found life d., 463:12
Distastes, prosperity not without d., 165:16
Distill, would men d. goodness out, 189:20
Distillation, history d. of rumor, 407:7
Distilled almost to jelly, 197:13
 from limbecks foul, 222:16
Distills, love d. desire, 67:25
Distinct, in repose d., 803:1
Distinction between virtue and vice, 309:5
 common sewer take it from d., 236:15
 is clear, 573:7
 make no d. between Trojan and Tyrian, 94:5
 without difference, 304:20
Distinctive, man's d. mark, 462:20
Distinctiveness, vice of d. become queer, 547:10
Distinctly I remember, 449:4
Distinguish, he could d. and divide, 262:2
 true from false, 276:1
 wisdom to d., 695:20
Distinguished, beginnings of things not d. by eye, 89:14
 come at last the D. Thing, 545:9
 no two men who cannot be d., 105:6
Distorting, curtain of d. days, 595:17
 my gesture, 772:2
Distorts, human understanding d., 164:20
 the heavens, 354:17
Distract, television used to d. delude amuse, 754:14
Distracted, seat in this d. globe, 198:15
Distracting, dear damned d. town, 293:20
Distraction music of flute, 677:15
 Uglification, 514:22
Distress, all pray in their d., 351:3
 deep d. hath humanized my Soul, 371:19
 economic d. will teach, 615:4
 needy in d., 25:33
 of boyhood into man, 595:3
 pray in your d. and need, 655:7
 reality of d., 333:15
Distressed, town like place d., 277:12
 vacant mind d., 326:14
 we commend those who are d., 48:15
Distresses of our friends, 264:n4
Distressful bread, 189:23
Distributed, good sense equally d., 246:4
Distribution according to need, 40:17
 unequal d. of property, 345:9
Distributively, pluralism lets exist d., 542:10
Distrust all in whom impulse to punish, 548:2
 fear and d. the people, 338:17
 here all d. left behind, 128:7
 is safeguard, 345:n4
 spirit of suspicion and d., 614:3
Distrusts, him who d. self, 264:1
Disturb not her dream, 357:19
Disturbance of the spring, 678:15
Disturbing delicate balance, 756:23
Disturbs, presence that d. me, 368:11
Disuse, iron rusts from d., 140:7
 of any organ, 341:8

Disused, marrying left maiden name d., 799:7
Ditch, a-diggin' a d., 633:12
 blind man's d., 595:4
 both fall into d., 34:32
 die in the last d., 281:6
Ditch-delivered by a drab, 216:28
Ditchers, gardeners d. and gravemakers, 202:3
Ditches, other men's d., 896:19
 women lifted over d., 416:1
Ditty, mournful d., 404:9
Diurnal, earth's d. course, 369:8
Dive, heaven's great lamps d., 226:20
 into bottom of deep, 182:6
Diver, Ceylon d. held breath, 409:17
 in deep seas, 534:5
Diverged, two roads d., 622:18
Divers, state of man in d. functions, 188:34
 why d. send out oil, 104:14
Diverse, man vain d. undulating, 151:17
 strong and d. heart, 716:1
Diversion or improvement of country, 288:3
 present life a d., 119:3
 walking 'tis a country d., 287:4
Diversions to sit under lamp, 130:14
Diversity, brilliant d. spread like stars, 805:2
 of my heritage, 876:13
 universal quality is d., 153:7
 world safe for d., 786:10
Diverter of sadness, 245:1
Diverting ourselves just floating, 261:9
Dives, I sit in one of the d., 748:16
Divest, deprive or d. posterity, 320:7
Divide and rule, 120:18
 biped class, 77:n1
 distinguish and d., 262:2
 et impera, 120:18
 great scramble and big d., 537:7
 Life from Death, 448:18
 mountains d. us, 417:4
 never d. upon opinion, 247:12
 not d. Sunday from week, 196:13
 sense from thought d., 272:n1
 therefore doth heaven d., 188:34
 thin partitions their bounds d., 272:16
 to d. is not to take away, 403:11
 two almost d. the kind, 294:1
 words d. and rend, 529:15
Divided an inheritance with him, 335:3
 duty, 208:4
 fair d. excellence, 175:9
 Gaul d. into three parts, 88:21
 have they not d. the prey, 10:14
 house d. against itself, 36:28, 444:8
 in death they were not d., 11:8
 mankind into parties, 345:9
 thy kingdom is d., 28:25
 we fall, 328:n1
Dividing asunder of soul and spirit, 45:7
 by d. we fall, 328:1
 lover and lover, 529:13
 your sweet d. throat, 245:15
Divine, against thy D. Majesty, 49:5
 all things by law d., 402:16
 and terrible radiance, 422:11
 ask a drink d., 232:16
 Athens d. city, 64:7
 bird of Zeus, 63:25

Divine *(continued)*
 Countenance D. shine forth, 354:8
 dead d. brother of all, 487:8
 despair, 452:21
 drink d., 232:16
 event, 454:12
 fellowship d., 409:9
 God the Father a school-d., 296:13
 good amiable or sweet, 259:14
 human face d., 257:6
 I myself more d., 456:13
 illusion, 497:20
 Love the human form d., 351:4
 love which greybeards call d., 171:6
 Majority, 508:16
 makes drudgery d., 243:10
 man d. as myself is dead, 487:11
 nature gave us country, 87:2
 no government by d. right, 381:1
 no voice d. the storm allayed, 327:10
 nor glimpse d., 297:6
 one who shares in the d., 104:10
 painting contains d. force, 137:17
 philosophy, 252:19
 Philosophy, 453:20
 reborn into highest forms which are d., 141:3
 relations with good joke, 618:12
 reliance on d. providence, 336:3
 revelation, 757:15
 Right D. of Kings, 297:4
 right of kings, 444:12
 sign indicates future, 70:5
 tale of Troy d., 251:19
 Terror the human form d., 353:8
 thought thinks of itself, 78:2
 to forgive d., 292:23
 tobacco d. rare, 235:12
 what the form d., 383:25
 whatever poet writes with d. inspiration, 70:10
 world is not d. sport, 634:9
Divinely, tall, 450:23
Divineness, Poesy participation of d., 164:14
Divinest anguish, 476:12
 Madness d. Sense, 509:4
 Melancholy, 251:11
Diving bell, 870:6
Divining, takes d. rod to find, 562:15
Divinities, new d. of his own, 74:7
Divinity, all the d. I understand, 157:23
 doth hedge a king, 201:29
 dry volumes of d., 335:21
 gives wealth even to wicked man, 59:20
 gossip a kind of d., 54:28
 in odd numbers, 187:19
 man own doctor of d., 554:10
 nature full of d., 473:8
 piece of d. in us, 248:19
 that shapes our ends, 202:23
 wingy mysteries in d., 248:2
Divisa, Gallia est omnis d. in partes tres, 88:n10
Division, equal d. of unequal earnings, 389:5
 is as bad, 881:3
 salvation not in d., 607:3
 saw d. grow together, 202:36
Divisions, how many d. has Pope got, 636:17

Divorce is like an amputation, 844:14
    long d. of steel, 225:15
Divorced from eye and bone, 713:4
Divulge, I will never d. such things, 70:14
Dix, French word d. on reverse, 471:*n*1
Dixie born in D. in boomer's shack, 733:9
    comes from ten-dollar notes, 471:*n*1
    Land, 470:16
    lib and die in D., 471:1
Dixit, ipse d., 120:30
Dizzy, how fearful and d., 212:24
    make a small boy d., 755:15
    two, d. and entwined, 776:4
Do, a' is done that men can d., 357:11
    all the good you can, 301:19
    all we can d., 440:2
    anything you can d. I can d., 673:15
    as chapmen do, 203:28
    as I say not as I do, 238:20
    as you would be done by, 298:5
    damned if you d., 385:2
    decided on what they will not d., 79:23
    devil made me d. it, 836:7
    don't d. it in street, 586:10
    each day two things disliked, 626:19
    go and d. likewise, 37:38
    great right do little wrong, 186:2
    hate to d. this all my life, 828:10
    his arms might d. what this has done,
        249:22
    how not to d. it, 466:18
    I dare d. all, 215:3
    I d. it more natural, 204:27
    if to d. as easy as to know, 184:14
    it after high Roman fashion, 219:6
    it as for thee, 243:9
    it or d. not it, 469:3
    it with thy might, 23:22
    just as one pleases, 386:9
    justice, 3:8
    justly and love mercy, 29:5
    know not what they d., 38:34
    know what he ought to d., 127:5
    let's d. it, 803:11
    make it d. or d. without, 886:15
    never d. today what can put off, 500:11
    no one knows what he can d., 100:33
    not as some pastors, 197:20
    not choose to run, 613:7
    not do thing they most do show, 222:1
    not do what we want, 742:21
    not go gentle, 777:15
    not kill, 3:8
    not we wanderer await, 495:15
    not what we ought, 495:5
    nothing we d. wiped out, 540:23
    now I'll d. 't, 200:32
    O what men dare d., 191:4
    one must be to d., 343:22
    or die, 236:8, 358:17, 702:12
    other men for they do you, 464:37
    reckless what I d., 216:7
    seeks little thing to d., 461:15
    something else to it, 827:15
    strong d. what they can, 72:7
    that thou doest d. quickly, 39:38
    the evil I d., 41:17
    the very best I can, 447:6

Do *(continued)*
    theirs but to d. and die, 454:21
    they d. things we can't, 756:22
    they know not what they d., 38:34
    thing I was born to d., 167:6
    thing that ends other deeds, 219:7
    thing think you cannot, 660:7
    things I did not d., 595:15
    things worth the writing, 302:18
    this in remembrance, 38:30
    this one thing I d., 44:4
    this will never d., 372:*n*2
    thou but thine, 259:4
    to be to d. to d. without, 533:3
    to will and to d. his pleasure, 44:3
    two things is to do neither, 99:16
    unto others as would have others do, 33:*n*1
    we d. what we can, 544:12
    well what not worth doing, 810:10
    what country d. for you, 785:13
    what d. about it, 501:2
    what have you or I to d. with it, 313:21
    what he may, 202:22
    what I will with mine, 35:7
    what man would d. exalts, 462:7
    what manhood bids, 491:21
    what then thou would'st, 260:21
    what d. they d. there, 713:18
    what thou wilt, 145:9
    what will I d. when you fallen, 772:10
    what you can d. for country, 785:13
    what you still betters what is done,
        223:28
    what you have to do, 109:5
    whatsoever thy hand findeth to d., 23:22
    will to d., 373:20
    without being commanded, 77:11
    write what men d., 164:17
    ye even so unto them, 33:18
    you d. not d., 833:7
    your thing, 423:19
Doc, never play cards with man called, 757:11
Docent, decent d., 714:18
Docile and omnipotent, 509:11
Dock, sittin' on the d. of the bay, 853:4
Doctor, after interview with d., 552:3
    and Saint, 441:18
    Diet Quiet Merryman, 286:5
    every man own d. of divinity, 554:10
    fee d. for nauseous draught, 274:24
    Foster went to Gloucester, 896:10
    Livingstone I presume, 539:18
    while runnin' for d., 660:4
Doctor's, outlived the d. pill, 291:19
Doctors, best d. in the world, 286:5
    we d. know hopeless case, 702:2
    when d. disagree, 294:6
Doctrinaire logic, 694:5
Doctrine, all the winds of d., 254:14
    Augustinian d. Calvinistic d., 532:15
    every wind of d., 43:36
    from women's eyes this d., 174:24
    go for refuge to D., 64:20
    hidden under strange verses, 128:23
    involving pernicious consequences, 470:15
    little difference in d., 309:15
    not for d. but music, 292:17
    of separate but equal, 692:4

Doctrine *(continued)*
    of strenuous life, 570:12
    prove their d. orthodox, 262:11
    so illogical and dull, 656:12
    that each one select, 403:11
    we don't understand, 730:8
    yesterday fact today d., 339:3
Doctrines, makes d. plain and clear, 262:21
Document of barbarism, 693:4
Documents, historian wants d., 545:2
Dodger, artful D., 464:7
Dodo never had a chance, 659:11
Doe, came a fallow d., 890:4
    life looking out from eyes of d., 695:16
Doer, speaker of words and d. of deeds, 51:20
Doers of the word, 45:24
    talkers no good d., 171:26
Does, dogged as d. it, 471:16
    following advice of his nose, 860:4
    he who can d., 565:9
    sees it and d. it, 461:15
    two reasons for what man d., 529:6
    what man d. based not on knowledge,
        685:3
Doeth, what thy right hand d., 32:24
    whatsoever he d. shall prosper, 14:40
    with youre owene thyng, 135:19
Doff it for shame, 175:14
Doffed, lightly d. hat, 584:19
Dog, absolutely unselfish friend is d., 512:12
    Almighty gave d., 374:17
    and your little d. too, 764:6
    better than his d., 451:22
    beware of d., 120:9
    bites man not news, 550:2
    Boatswain a d., 394:9
    Body my good bright d., 772:11
    breed maggots in dead d., 198:33
    cat d. pipe or two, 576:6
    circumcised d., 210:21
    commends himself to our favor, 569:6
    cut-throat d., 184:28
    did nothing in nighttime, 573:14
    dies like a d., 438:14
    each time I walk the d., 836:9
    eat d., 747:3
    every d. his day, 481:7
    fall in grave like old d., 780:5
    fetch poor d. a bone, 895:6
    gingham d. went Bow-wow, 554:3
    go buy a d., 512:*n*1
    grim king's d., 67:6
    hair of d. that bit us, 147:35
    has his day, 423:9
    hath a day, 147:34
    heart to d. to tear, 589:25
    hold-fast the only d., 189:6
    hound d. cryin' all the time, 834:6
    I am his Highness' d., 296:22
    in life firmest friend, 394:10
    in the manger, 59:4
    is thy servant a d., 12:15
    it was that died, 322:15
    jumps over lazy d., 885:19
    kids loved the d., 771:2
    let no d. bark, 184:7
    libelous statements about d., 653:9
    like a d. he said, 656:2

Dog *(continued)*

like d. hunts in dreams, 451:24
little d. laughed, 893:16
living d. better than dead lion, 23:21
man bites d., 550:2
might as well speculate, 440:7
mine enemy's d., 213:3
more ridiculous than a d., 439:7
my little d. knows me, 628:9
offers drowning d. drink, 243:15
old d. barks backward, 624:3
old d. Tray, 384:*n*2
old wife old d. ready money, 302:17
pick up starving d., 524:2
poor d. Tray, 384:7
rather be d. and bay the moon, 193:8
returneth to his vomit, 21:38
since I am a d. beware, 185:24
so poor he could not keep a d., 114:7
somebody threw dead d. down ravine,
     759:3
starved at master's gate, 353:16
this d. my d., 179:12
thou calledst me d., 185:24
to gain private ends, 322:14
to really enjoy a d., 832:3
to this d. praise, 434:14
tossed d. that worried cat, 897:8
toy d. covered with dust, 554:2
truth's a d. must to kennel, 211:7
turned to his own vomit, 46:5
until the last d. dies, 862:18
whose d. are you, 296:22
why should a d. have life, 213:14
will have his day, 202:22
wool of bat tongue of d., 216:27
Dogged as does it, 471:16
     strength, 602:3
     strong d. unenlightened, 496:10
Doggedly, set himself d. to it, 308:15
Doggerel, rym d., 136:12
Dogies, git along little d., 890:11
Doglike, on bended arm d., 62:27
Dogma, Bible literature not d., 584:9
     fundamental principle of religion, 421:8
Dogmatism, greater ignorance greater d., 553:1
Dog's, more deadly than mad d. tooth, 172:26
     walking on hinder legs, 309:8
Dogs, all d. of Europe bark, 749:4
     all the d. in town, 892:21
     as many d. there be, 322:13
     black d. bay at moon, 527:23
     crowing of cocks and barking of d., 58:6
     delight to bark and bite, 289:5
     drink running at the Nile, 103:3
     eat of crumbs, 34:33
     fought d. killed cats, 460:7
     hark d. do bark, 896:21
     hates babies and d., 644:*n*1
     hates children and d., 644:2
     leave Now for d. and apes, 461:13
     let slip d. of war, 192:23
     lies with d. riseth with fleas, 244:4
     little d. and all, 212:11
     loathe people who keep d., 553:11
     mad d. and Englishmen, 719:12
     more careful of breed of d., 280:10
     more I admire my d., 400:15

Dogs *(continued)*

not live as d. in manger, 653:12
shall eat Jezebel, 12:7
shame the gray head, 52:13
sleeping d. lie, 466:2
strained anxious lives d. lead, 709:1
straw d., 57:1
that talk revolution, 670:9
throw physic to the d., 217:19
which hath deeper mouth, 169:15
Dogs', puppy d. tails, 895:11
Dog-star rages, 295:9
Doing, cease to think about d., 386:12
     do well what not worth d., 810:10
     good one of professions which are full,
          474:22
     is another thing, 153:6
     it all takes d. and I do, 545:7
     joy's soul lies in d., 203:2
     learn by d., 78:6
     manners happy ways of d., 428:9
     miserable d. or suffering, 255:11
     secure friends by d. favors, 72:2
     tell what you've been d., 672:9
     the decent thing, 845:13
     up and d., 436:7
     worth d. is worth d. well, 298:2
Doings, amend ways and d., 27:29
     child known by his d., 21:11
     of mankind subject of my book, 109:11
Dolabella's Cleopatra, 272:13
Dolce far niente, 110:*n*13
     vita, 130:*n*4
Dole, happy man be his d., 146:*n*15
     happy man happy d., 146:20
     unequal laws, 451:11
     weighing delight and d., 196:22
Doleful, chants d. hymn, 176:3
     dumps, 173:*n*1, 881:6
     shades, 255:9
Doll, guy's doin' it for some d., 762:2
     in the doll's house, 466:29
     living d. can sew cook, 833:1
     put youth away like d., 772:13
     your d. wife, 504:7
Dollar, a dillar a d., 896:14
     almighty d., 391:19
     dirty side of sharp d., 674:14
     life shouldn't be printed on d. bills, 746:14
Dollars, bought St. Louis for six million d.,
          522:19
     damn me, 483:10
     hours and minutes d. and cents, 303:*n*1
Dolls cloths tobacco crumbs, 783:9
     the children my d., 504:7
Dolore, nessun maggior d., 128:*n*8
Dolores, splendid and sterile D., 529:17
Dolphin-like, his delights were d., 219:8
Dolphin's, mermaid on d. back, 178:15
Dolphin-torn gong-tormented sea, 595:13
Dolts, three greatest d., 391:4
Domain France conquered, 500:5
Dome, build that d. in air, 377:23
     of many-colored glass, 404:2
     of vast sepulcher, 402:11
     Orchard for a D., 508:18
     rounded Peter's d., 424:5
     stately pleasure d., 377:17

Dome *(continued)*

sunny d., 377:23
sunny pleasure d., 377:21
Domestic, insure d. tranquillity, 339:11
     internal d. empire, 713:9
     life and law of Homes, 761:11
     malice d. foreign levy, 216:11
     naive d. Burgundy, 704:6
Domestica, quae est d. sede iucundior, 87:*n*12
Domesticity, enjoying an indifferent d., 821:11
Domina mater ecclesia, 113:*n*5
Dominate, China not seeking to d. world,
          697:7
Domination, authority hierarchy and d., 817:16
     fought against white d. black d., 790:18
     over all the peoples, 765:14
Dominations, Thrones D. Princedoms, 258:20
Domine Deus speravi in te, 154:*n*6
Dominion, between Grand Army and d. of
          world, 537:5
     death hath no more d., 41:14
     death shall have no d., 777:6
     good old D., 338:20
     liberation from d. of religion, 604:14
     over every living thing, 5:8
     over palm and pine, 589:7
     truly sorry man's d., 356:5
Dominions, sun in d. never sets, 359:16
Dominus illuminatio mea, 15:*n*2
     vobiscum, 47:18
Domus tutissimum refugium, 158:23
Don Quixote and I, 391:4
     when D. Quixote went out into world,
          824:3
Done, a' is d. that men can do, 357:11
     because we are too menny, 536:9
     bright day is d., 219:9
     by the rule, 218:22
     Charmian is this well d., 219:18
     dared and d., 318:10
     do as you would be d. by, 298:5
     foolish thing well d., 309:22
     game is d. I've won, 376:8
     great things together, 500:15
     her wrong, 886:2
     him who has d. deed to suffer, 63:13
     his best for his time, 359:19
     I have d. it again, 833:2
     I have d. the state service, 210:20
     if d. when 'tis d., 214:22
     it unto the least, 35:31
     I've d. it from my youth, 347:10
     knowing when to have d., 408:4
     let justice be d., 120:22
     let what will be d., 337:2
     long day's task is d., 219:1
     much to be d., 307:26
     my dancing days are d., 179:*n*2
     my story being d., 208:3
     my task is smoothly d., 252:27
     nay I have d., 167:11
     no sooner said than d., 84:15
     no worthy action d., 883:18
     not my will be d., 38:31
     nothing should be d. for first time, 622:4
     one braver thing, 228:12
     reward of thing well d., 427:25
     servant of God well d., 258:23

Done *(continued)*
    sight of means makes ill deeds d., 175:30
    some villain hath d. me wrong, 172:*n*2
    still betters what is d., 223:28
    surprised to find it at all, 309:8
    take honor and my life is d., 176:9
    that which is d. is that which shall be d.,
        22:24
    there shall be d. a deed, 216:12
    things we ought not to, 48:3
    things won are d., 203:2
    thou hast d. thou hast not d., 231:3
    to deserve kittens, 635:9
    to have loved thought d., 495:8
    treason has d. his worst, 216:11
    'twere well d. quickly, 214:22
    want anything d. ask woman, 810:9
    we have d. this before, 781:11
    well begun is half d., 78:30
    well d. is quickly d., 99:5
    what another would have d. as well, 604:8
    what have I d. unto thee, 9:7
    what have you d. to me, 506:14
    what have you d. with your youth, 549:19
    what is over and d. with, 60:20
    what without Zeus is d., 63:8
    what's d. is d., 216:9
    when all is said and d., 558:5
    when the hurlyburly's d., 213:30
    who has begun has half d., 97:21
    work may yet be d., 451:17
    worldly task hast d., 220:26
Donna è mobile, 94:*n*10
Donne, John D. Anne D. Un-done, 228:*n*2
    whose muse on dromedary trots, 378:12
    with Landor and with D., 593:2
Donnée, subject idea d., 544:10
Donner un sens plus pur, 679:*n*1
Don't, Advice to Persons About to Write
        History D., 518:11
    be afraid, 864:13
    be gentle to your wife, 53:16
    Believe the Hype, 875:11
    cry for me Argentina, 859:14
    damned if you d., 385:2
    fire until you see whites of eyes, 321:7
    give up the ship, 389:*n*2
    go near water, 887:17
    I d. think we d. love each other, 828:6
    know much about history, 829:11
    look back, 747:6
    sell America short, 887:11
    sell steak sell sizzle, 747:12
    stop thinking about tomorrow, 857:15
    tell her everything, 53:16
    tread on me, 883:19
Doodle handlebar moustaches, 787:6
Doom, edge of d., 222:15
    fall to d. a long way, 609:1
    feeling has force of d., 431:5
    Felicity or D., 511:13
    forfeit to a confined d., 222:10
    involve others in our d., 318:4
    Master of Day of D., 117:11
    regardless of their d., 315:6
    stretch out to crack of d., 217:2
Doomed conscripted ones, 668:14
    story ephemeral and d., 714:3

Doomed *(continued)*
    to company with pain, 371:21
Dooms imagined for mighty dead, 409:8
    of love, 701:18
Doomsday, danced till d., 286:28
    is near, 183:16
Doomsters, purblind D., 535:10
Doon, banks and braes o' bonny D., 357:6
Dooney, play on fiddle in D., 591:14
Door, at its own stable d., 509:11
    at the d. of life, 530:6
    at this d. England stands sentry, 535:7
    before his cottage d., 381:6
    begins to crack, 892:8
    came out by same, 441:18
    dark cloud at house's d., 891:17
    death's private d., 555:3
    ever-open d., 51:*n*1
    foot wear steps of his d., 30:27
    form from off d., 449:10
    golden d., 552:16
    handle of big front d., 525:22
    he who sits at d. of house, 898:8
    hell of good universe next d., 702:2
    I am the d., 39:29
    know grass beyond d., 506:8
    leave world by natural d., 557:14
    lion at the d., 892:8
    moonlit d., 616:6
    no d. is shut, 580:2
    no right to open d., 74:12
    nor so wide as church d., 180:28
    of all subtleties, 56:12
    Old Age coming bolt d., 119:27
    open d., 532:14
    open to remedy, 155:21
    opening of a D., 511:13
    opens and lets future in, 737:14
    over that same d. was writ, 160:14
    put in his hand by the hole of the d., 24:17
    rapping at chamber d., 449:3
    shut the d. on the past, 830:18
    shut shut the d., 295:9
    sits on horse at hostess' d., 175:8
    stack or the barn d., 251:1
    stand at the d. and knock, 46:27
    steed stolen shut stable d., 147:18
    stone leaf unfound d., 727:10
    then shuts the D., 508:16
    three gypsies a-come to d., 883:22
    to which no Key, 441:20
    turn in d. once only, 676:17
    up to old inn-d., 646:1
    we never opened, 678:7
    what is wind in that d., 138:6
    whining of a d., 231:11
    wide as a church d., 180:28
    wolf from d., 140:20
    wolf is at the d., 578:19
    world make path to d., 425:*n*2
    younger generation knocking at d., 505:4
Doorkeeper in the house of my God, 17:20
Doormat or prostitute, 697:1
Doors are widely flung, 755:10
    as yet shut upon me, 413:5
    be ye lift up ye everlasting d., 15:25
    close softly d. to rooms, 807:21
    for men to take their exits, 237:7

Doors *(continued)*
    if no d. or windows, 775:5
    in to the upper d., 424:18
    never darken threshold of d., 489:5
    of heaven adjacent identical, 656:8
    open d. of his face, 14:33
    open your living d., 258:28
    pictures out of d., 208:13
    shut d. against setting sun, 213:22
    shut in the streets, 23:30
    shut-in homes closed d., 604:7
    ten thousand several d., 237:7
    to let out life, 237:*n*1
    unscrew d. themselves from jambs, 486:7
    unscrew locks from d., 486:7
Doorway, Hylax barks in d., 93:2
Doorways, unjoined person who hung in d.,
        788:15
Dooryard, lilacs last in d. bloomed, 487:12
Doped, keep you d. with religion and sex,
        848:3
Do-re-mi, if you ain't got the d., 768:2
Dorian mood of flutes, 255:23
Doric discipline, 594:12
Dorking, Hens of D., 467:16
Dormons, veillons dormants et veillants d.,
        153:*n*1
Dorobo and animals live side by side, 889:3
Dorure en reste aux mains, 493:*n*5
Dotages, plagues and d. of human kind, 235:1
Dote, I d. on myself, 486:9
    on his very absence, 184:20
    on scraps of learning, 290:13
Dotes yet doubts, 209:3
Double double toil and trouble, 216:26
    ducats stolen by daughter, 185:5
    eyes upon d. string, 229:18
    for all her sins, 26:24
    Giant hit into d., 646:12
    grew like a d. cherry, 178:29
    halve rights d. duties, 399:20
    health to thee, 397:13
    helix structure, 821:4
    hypocrite reader my d., 491:1
    make assurance d. sure, 216:33
    palter with us in d. sense, 217:29
    pleasure to deceive deceiver, 266:11
    single nature's d. name, 202:35
    snakes with d. tongue, 178:22
    we are d. in ourselves, 153:3
Double-consciousness peculiar sensation,
        602:3
Doubled globe of dead, 777:5
Double-faced, fame if not d., 260:18
Double-lived in regions new, 411:4
Double-mouthed, fame is d., 260:18
Doublethink means holding contradictory
        beliefs, 735:20
Doubly benefits who gives quickly, 99:15
    dying, 373:3
    seconded with will and power, 203:8
Doubt, all best though oft d., 260:26
    doubter and d., 425:5
    explain till all men d., 297:5
    faith dead which does not d., 586:5
    faith in honest d., 454:5
    frets d. maw-crammed beast, 462:14
    grows with knowledge, 344:22

Doubt *(continued)*
  I d. it said Carpenter, 516:1
  I d. some foul play, 197:17
  I show you d., 461:24
  in d. to act or rest, 295:1
  let us not pretend to d., 534:15
  loop to hang d. on, 209:15
  love curiosity freckles d., 699:11
  modest d. called beacon, 203:12
  more d. stronger faith, 461:24
  my days of endless d., 159:2
  never d. I love, 198:30
  never stand to d., 241:10
  new philosophy calls all in d., 230:15
  no manner of d., 528:4
  our d. is our passion, 544:12
  road to resolution lies by d., 242:4
  sun and moon should d., 354:5
  sunnier side of d., 456:2
  teach child to d., 354:3
  that sun doth move, 198:30
  thou stars are fire, 198:30
  time d. of Rome, 398:21
  to be once in d., 209:5
  to d. everything or believe, 558:7
  true science teaches d., 586:1
  truth to be liar, 198:30
  when in d. win trick, 288:20
  where d. let me sow faith, 125:12
  wherefore didst thou d., 34:29
Doubter and the doubt, 425:5
Doubtful disputations, 41:41
  dreams of dreams, 530:15
  in d. things liberty, 265:4
  nice hazard of d. hour, 183:11
  thinking about thing no longer d., 435:7
  thoughts, 185:21
Doubting Castle, 271:20
  dreaming dreams, 449:7
Doubtless come again with rejoicing, 19:3
  God never did, 245:7
Doubts are traitors, 206:17
  begin with certainties end in d., 164:11
  begin with d. end in certainties, 164:11
  dotes yet d., 209:3
  from what he sees, 354:5
  littlest d. are fear, 200:19
  more cruel than truths, 267:24
  saucy d. and fears, 216:15
Doughnut, face with d. complexion, 488:10
Douglas, Adamses vote for D., 577:*n*2
  in his hall, 373:14
  old song of Percy and D., 162:19
  owl in D. fir turn head, 811:6
  tongues of D. and myself, 444:12
Doux comme l'amour, 348:*n*1
Dove, all eagle in thee all d., 263:10
  beside the springs of D., 369:7
  descending like a d., 32:9
  found no rest, 6:20
  loves when it quarrels, 116:14
  more serpent than d., 168:10
  roar you gently as sucking d., 178:8
  that I had wings like a d., 16:36
  visited upon d., 109:12
  wings of the d., 394:7
  with flickering tongue, 679:9
Dovecote, like eagle in a d., 220:6

Dover, chalk cliffs of D., 599:8
  white cliffs of D., 627:4
Doves, be harmless as d., 34:1
  hurricane of black d., 717:7
  in immemorial elms, 453:7
Dovetailedness, universal d., 464:20
Down and away below, 494:12
  baby with D. Syndrome, 878:11
  been d. so long, 842:10
  bliss not beds of d., 242:1
  blow the man d., 897:16
  by salley gardens, 590:21
  can't hold man d. without staying d., 566:5
  come baby cradle and all, 550:7
  coming d. let me shift, 143:9
  from rising of the sun unto going d., 18:20
  gigantically d., 448:4, 720:9
  go d. again to the depths, 18:15
  go d. to the sea in ships, 18:14
  go up and d. as a talebearer, 8:27
  gone d. drain of eternity, 67:11
  he that is d., 271:25
  in the valley, 884:2
  keep 'em d. on farm, 664:1
  lay me d. in peace, 15:4
  lay them d. in their dens, 18:11
  levelers wish to level d., 309:6
  look not d. but up, 462:18
  maketh me to lie d., 15:23
  moon is d., 215:9
  on me down on me, 857:9
  on your knees, 195:20
  play tennis with the net d., 625:11
  road up and road d. one and same, 62:9
  Satan walking up and d., 12:36
  sloth finds d. pillow hard, 220:22
  smoothing the raven d., 252:15
  that town settle hence, 448:5
  the darker stairs, 663:22
  thou climbing sorrow, 211:17
  to Gehenna up to Throne, 587:6
  to seas again, 635:15
  unseen full of water, 177:17
  vast edges drear, 496:19
  who cares where they come d., 819:10
  who pulls me d., 169:4
  why art thou cast d., 16:22
  you'll meet them on way d., 633:9
Down-gyved to his ankle, 198:24
Down-rased, sometime lofty towers I see d., 221:18
Down's, sea-d. edge, 530:25
Downsitting, thou knowest my d., 19:12
Downstairs, kick you d., 514:6
Downtown my chin throbs, 867:1
Downward beat thy wings, 90:*n*1
  face d. in sun, 695:1
  thoughts always d. bent, 256:3
  to darkness, 640:22
  world turned upside d., 234:12
Downwards, look no way but d., 271:24
Downy, shake off this d. sleep, 215:29
Dowry, brought her d. destruction, 63:3
Doze, docent doesn't d., 714:18
  student dassn't d., 714:18
Dozen, kills seven d. Scots, 182:17
Dozens, reckons up by d., 525:21
Drab, ditch-delivered by a d., 216:28

Drachmas, buy repentance at ten thousand d., 79:11
Draft, corner d. fluttered flame, 688:7
Drag, slow d. of days, 67:8
  the slow barge, 327:11
  Zeus from heaven to earth, 51:16
Dragged, idleness d. toward evil, 71:4
Dragging themselves through negro streets, 812:13
Dragon, between d. and wrath, 210:27
  great d. was cast out, 47:2
  Michael fought against d., 47:1
  O to be a d., 671:21
  Saint George that swinged d., 175:8
  that is in the sea, 26:6
  world, 665:14
  young lion and the d., 17:29
Dragonflies draw flame, 546:20
Dragonfly, in eye hills mirrored d., 361:14
Dragonish, cloud that's d., 218:39
Dragons, brother to d., 14:9
  habitation of d., 26:16
  offering d. quarter no good, 773:19
Drags at each remove, 321:12
  bellies and d. in wind, 593:5
  its slow length along, 292:18
Drain of eternity, 67:11
  pent-up rivers of myself, 486:22
Drained cup of Lethe, 95:28
  faces of Negro school-children, 788:2
  loungers of Empire d., 573:3
Drainless shower of light, 409:3
Drainpipes, if d. of house clogged, 493:12
Drains, opiate to d., 410:2
Dram, single D. of Heaven, 511:8
Drama, ancient d. begin again, 727:2
  close d. with the day, 291:9
  life with dull bits cut out, 722:9
  not of heaviness but of lightness, 824:4
  of things that happen to come together, 733:8
  through her body heaved, 596:8
  we lived our little d., 726:7
  whether damned or not, 346:9
Dramatist, makings of a d., 816:16
  wants more liberties, 545:2
Drang, Sturm und D., 347:1
Drank our liquor straight, 749:13
  rich d. too much, 721:15
  without thirst, 285:4
Drapery, one that wraps d. of couch, 405:13
Draught, fee doctor for nauseous d., 274:24
  of Life, 511:8
  of vintage, 410:4
  one d. above heat, 204:19
Draughts, shallow d., 292:12
Draw able to d. with their feet, 60:5
  all other things to destruction d., 229:9
  as love with thread, 235:15
  began to d. to our end, 30:2
  bow ride and speak truth, 399:6
  close his eyes and d. curtain, 170:9
  evils d. men together, 79:1
  from one mother both d. breath, 64:4
  from others lesson, 85:18
  inward quality after, 218:32
  living faces from marble, 94:35
  my songs d. Daphnis home, 93:1

Dreams *(continued)*
 forgotten d., 450:11
 from Death fulfillment to d., 640:21
 gate of ivory for false d., 95:2
 go wandering still, 280:4
 have two gates, 54:6
 hunters of d., 569:12
 hunts in d., 451:24
 I have bad d., 199:3
 in d. begins responsibility, 592:8
 in d. behold Hebrides, 417:4
 interpretation of d. road to knowledge,
  563:1
 jailer envious of prisoner's d., 439:3
 joys as d. do fly, 881:8
 lies down to pleasant d., 405:13
 man's best d. to shame, 434:16
 men in exile feed on d., 63:10
 necessary to life, 735:2
 night full of ghastly d., 171:27
 no mortal dared before, 449:7
 not responsible for d., 630:7
 old men shall dream d., 28:41
 one d. of revenge, 551:9
 painter's brush consumes d., 594:13
 pleasing d. slumbers light, 373:17
 remain alone with d., 493:9
 revisit in d. the dear dead, 67:5
 rich beyond d. of avarice, 312:11
 sleep full of sweet d., 409:7
 spread d. under your feet, 591:13
 stuff as d. are made on, 225:1
 surely are difficult, 54:6
 sweet d. are made of this, 872:7
 than this world d. of, 455:20
 that blister sleep, 737:1
 themselves are only dreams, 247:1
 thought of old best d., 731:*n*2
 to sell, 423:5
 torn by d., 641:19
 transit where d. cross, 677:18
 tread softly on d., 591:13
 true I talk of d., 179:26
 voices strummed his d., 805:8
 we are dreamers of d., 549:13
 what d. may come, 199:21
 wild were his d., 347:11
Dreamt I went to Manderley again, 750:6
 of in your philosophy, 198:19
 past never past redeeming, 797:11
Dreamweaver, I was the D., 848:1
Dreamy, brief d. delight, 591:17
 lullaby, 527:4
Drear, chill and d., 373:5
 epitaph d., 587:11
 vast edges d., 496:19
Dreariest and longest journey, 403:11
Dreary, all world sad d., 503:12
 if your morals make you d., 556:2
 living in the American, 824:13
 midnight d., 449:3
 some days dark and d., 436:14
 these d. dumps, 173:1
 to be Somebody, 508:14
 tract of country, 448:8
Dregs, drunken the d., 27:1
 of Romulus, 87:21
 of the Cup, 278:9

Drenched in fraternal blood, 390:9
 our steeples, 211:24
Dress, all this fleshly d., 268:10
 by yellow candlelight, 555:8
 if the devil d. her not, 219:11
 Peace the human d., 351:4
 plain in d. sober in diet, 297:8
 Secrecy the human d., 353:8
 she is more than d. on ironing board,
  771:14
 style the d. of thoughts, 298:14
 sweet disorder in the d., 240:15
 tatter in mortal d., 594:2
Dressed, all d. up nowhere to go, 603:12
 April d. in all his trim, 222:6
 closest to naked when well d., 655:4
 good spirits when well d., 464:33
 in brief authority, 206:28
 lord neat trimly d., 181:35
 nature to advantage d., 292:13
 still to be d., 232:6
 walks to funeral d. in shroud, 486:17
Dresses in dignity, 601:3
Dressing nursing praying and all's over, 398:12
Drew everything that begins with M, 514:17
 from out boundless deep, 456:4
 many-colored life he d., 306:9
 men as they ought to be, 65:*n*1
 she d. an angel down, 274:22
 them with bands of love, 28:38
Dried frozen carcass of leopard, 721:16
 sap out of veins, 592:5
 tubes twisted and d., 587:12
Drift, adamant for d., 619:5
 everything begins to d., 742:19
 go with d. of things, 622:8
 in gradual swell, 839:4
 not d. or lie at anchor, 443:9
 outside tent whirling d., 603:8
 tell you my d., 190:31
 toward unparalleled catastrophes, 638:8
 wait and obey, 590:9
 we know your d., 190:*n*2
Drifted in sheepish calm, 787:11
 on crooked crosses, 650:9
Drifts, all beautiful d. away, 592:2
Drill, before steam d. beat me down, 885:12
 drop of sweat on d. ground, 664:*n*3
Drink, a little in d., 288:22
 ale's stuff to d., 575:12
 Americans fix nothing without d., 401:3
 and be whole again, 624:14
 and devil done for rest, 555:4
 and forget poverty, 22:15
 as he brews so shall he d., 231:16
 as oft as ye d. it, 42:25
 ask a d. divine, 232:16
 blood to d., 431:12
 cannot make horse d., 147:24
 come my lad and d. beer, 308:4
 dance and d. and sing, 352:15
 deep or taste not, 292:12
 divine, 232:16
 eat d. be merry, 23:20, 38:3
 felony to d. small beer, 170:13
 follow strong d., 25:5
 for tomorrow we die, 25:29
 for your lips to d., 530:5

Drink *(continued)*
 give me to d. mandragora, 218:10
 goes in wit goes out, 243:24
 good men eat and d. to live, 70:7
 herbs to d. smoke thereof, 139:9
 is nicissry evil, 600:18
 it up, 893:15
 it with pleasure, 30:31
 Jesus saith give me to d., 39:12
 life to the lees, 451:12
 light is lion comes to d., 641:11
 many companions for food and d., 59:19
 meat d. and cloth to us, 146:6
 more than enough to d., 576:6
 never taste who always d., 233:*n*1
 no longer water, 44:33
 nor any drop to d., 376:3
 not d. fruit of the vine, 36:3
 not meat nor d., 695:18
 not my design to d., 246:21
 not the third glass, 242:7
 not to elevation, 303:22
 oblivion of a day, 505:8
 offers drowning dog d., 243:15
 old wine to d., 165:8
 provokes desire, 215:26
 Russians' joy to d., 123:5
 shoulder sky d. ale, 575:15
 sleep is d. for the thirsty, 158:8
 snake came to d. there, 663:6
 snewed of mete and d., 133:27
 stagger but not with strong d., 26:10
 strive mightily d. as friends, 173:11
 strong d. is raging, 21:9
 sweetest d. be sorrow, 611:*n*5
 taken to d., 606:4
 thirsty and ye gave d., 35:30
 tippled d. more fine, 411:5
 to general joy of table, 216:19
 to me only with thine eyes, 232:16
 to the lass, 346:11
 unto him that is ready to perish, 22:15
 we d. you at night, 794:6
 when men d. they are rich, 72:11
 while you live d., 441:21
 wild anarchy of d., 233:7
 will not d. with you, 184:22
 willing to taste any d. once, 637:5
 wine of astonishment, 17:1
 with me and drink as I, 300:9
 with you in my Father's kingdom, 36:3
 ye all of it, 36:3
Drinker, God be merciful to this d., 125:3
Drinkest tears of children, 393:5
Drinking, and kept on d., 605:21
 and Sabbath-breaking, 393:7
 blude-red wine, 889:13
 deep of divinest anguish, 476:12
 eating d. and breeding, 486:7
 eating d. dung death, 678:14
 largely sobers us again, 292:12
 laws which ran like d. songs, 72:10
 much d. little thinking, 284:13
 my griefs, 177:17
 now is time for d., 96:17
 poor brains for d., 208:22
 prescribe rule for d., 288:12
 since leaving d. of wine, 277:9

Drinking *(continued)*
　Son of man came d., 34:8
　up the night, 816:3
　Whiskey and Rye, 861:11
　with d. fresh and fair, 265:9
Drinks and gapes for drink again, 265:9
　long time between d., 555:20
　she d. water her keel plows air, 163:20
　willingly d. their wines, 344:7
　wine with laughter, 885:14
Dripped, from eyelids d. love, 54:15
Dripping snow on green grass, 681:19
　thought came up d., 654:10
　water hollows stone, 89:15
Drive for wealth, 792:7
　he sd, 811:17
　needs go whom devil d., 148:15
　never trust poet who can d., 867:2
　one heat d. out another, 163:16
　out Nature with a pitchfork, 98:2
　Purpose D. Life, 873:6
　the rapid car, 327:11
　use wit d. brute off, 799:6
Drive-In, American Teenage D. Life, 831:2
Driven, all d. into same fold, 96:21
　by the spheres, 268:14
　from every other corner, 318:6
　leaves dead d. like ghosts, 402:9
　white as d. snow, 223:30
Drives my green age, 777:2
　Night from Heaven, 441:4
　through green fuse d. flower, 777:2
　where storm d. me I take shelter, 97:17
　who d. fat oxen, 311:12
Driveth, care d. away sleep, 31:18
　chaff which wind d. away, 14:40
　Jehu d. furiously, 12:17
　time d. onward, 450:19
Driving, is like the d. of Jehu, 12:17
　women d. at one thing you d. at another,
　　565:20
Dromedary, muse on d. trots, 378:12
Drone, frogs d. their lament, 93:14
Droning, beetle wheels d. flight, 315:12
Drooped, great star d. in western sky, 487:12
Drop but not be dropped by, 311:4
　created you of sperm d., 118:21
　d., d., d., d., 231:20
　drop-scenes d. at once, 596:10
　every d. drawn by lash, 447:2
　flood of words d. of reason, 302:13
　lips of a strange woman d. as honeycomb,
　　19:31
　makes it run over, 334:7
　me deep fathoms down, 484:4
　merrily did we d., 375:20
　nor any d. to drink, 376:3
　not a d. of blood shed, 338:9
　of a bucket, 26:30
　of allaying Tiber, 219:24
　of black blood, 731:11
　of sweat on drill ground, 664:*n*3
　one d. would save my soul, 169:4
　raineth d. staineth slop, 665:2
　tears as fast, 210:20
　turn on tune in d. out, 795:3
Dropped from zenith like star, 256:5
　his tongue d. manna, 256:11

Dropped *(continued)*
　iron curtain had d., 621:*n*3
　my love d. like a flower, 91:8
　not wish to be d. by, 311:4
　plates d. from his pocket, 219:8
　Recording Angel d. tear, 314:18
Droppeth as gentle rain, 186:1
Dropping buckets into empty wells, 326:23
　contentions of a wife are continual d., 21:7
　down ladder rung by rung, 588:7
　down with bales, 452:2
　one d. eye, 196:22
Drops, begotten d. of dew, 14:22
　blue-fringed lids, 377:16
　earliest to ground, 185:30
　to have their Affliction by d., 278:9
　number the d. of rain, 30:8
　of water hollow out stone, 89:*n*9
　on gate bars hang in row, 537:3
　that visit heart, 192:8
Drop-scenes, all d. drop at once, 596:10
Dross, rest is d., 665:13
　stoops not to shows of d., 185:3
Drought, careful in the year of d., 27:39
　of March perced to roote, 133:8
Drouthy, ancient trusty d. crony, 358:5
Drove my Chevy to the levee, 861:11
　out the man, 6:2
　them out of temple, 39:6
　to tumult in clouds, 593:1
Drown, before my tears did d. it, 242:26
　I'll d. my book, 225:4
　more likely to d. in it, 876:4
　neither can floods d. it, 24:26
　size where we can d. it, 874:10
　tears shall d. the wind, 214:24
　wake us and we d., 675:7
　what pain it was to d., 171:28
Drownded now and again, 612:2
Drowned, bodies of lovers d., 643:21
　ceremony of innocence d., 593:9
　Glory in shallow Cup, 442:7
　jail with chance of being d., 309:1
　not afraid of sea will be d., 612:2
　now and again, 612:2
　pluck up d. honor, 182:6
　the cocks, 211:24
　with us in endless night, 241:13
Drowning, London is d., 871:9
　no d. mark upon him, 224:1
　not waving but d., 732:16
　offers d. dog drink, 243:15
Drowns, coughing d. parson's saw, 175:1
　in Pharisees' hypocrisy, 688:3
　third d. him, 204:19
Drowsed, the man d. off into sleep, 633:6
　with fume of poppies, 411:7
Drowsiness shall clothe a man with rags, 21:28
Drowsing, white town d. in sunshine, 522:13
Drowsy, beetle with his d. hums, 216:12
　dull ear of d. man, 175:20
　ear of night, 395:1
　hushing traffic of d. town, 545:13
　keep d. Emperor awake, 594:4
　makes heaven d. with harmony, 174:23
　numbness pains, 410:2
　syrups of world, 209:11
　tinklings lull, 315:12

Drowsy *(continued)*
　who d. at that hour, 249:7
Drowsyhead, land of d., 301:4
Drudge, harmless d., 307:3
Drudgery, makes d. divine, 243:10
　of their contemporaries, 693:4
Drug, take me I am the d., 737:5
　which takes away grief, passion, 52:32
Drugs began to take hold, 843:13
　sex and d. and rock and roll, 854:1
　true apothecary thy d. quick, 181:15
Druids, stand like D. of old, 436:20
Drum, bang the d. slowly, 890:*n*1
　beat d. slowly, 890:16
　frenzied d., 593:11
　my pulse like soft d., 241:19
　pulpit d. ecclesiastic, 261:18
　rumble of distant D., 441:11
　spirit-stirring d., 209:13
　war d. throbbed no longer, 452:3
Drumcliff churchyard, 597:10
Drummer, different d., 475:20
Drums and tramplings of three conquests,
　　248:25
　hearts like muffled d., 436:5
　rum-tumming everywhere, 635:1
　sound trumpet beat d., 301:13
　sound trumpets beat d., 274:16
　with d. and guns, 884:6
Drunk, accustomed to deliberate when d.,
　　69:8
　and asleep in boots, 640:19
　delight of battle, 451:13
　git a little d. land in jail, 706:6
　hath not d. ink, 174:15
　hemlock I had d., 410:2
　hydroptic earth hath d., 229:12
　is he who prostrate lies, 393:9
　man being reasonable must get d., 398:11
　milk of Paradise, 377:23
　not d. who can rise, 393:9
　on wind in my mouth, 801:16
　stag d. his fill, 373:18
　we lie down in empty hills, 122:3
　what potions have I d., 222:16
　what when d. one sees, 816:17
　with fire, 359:10
　with talk, 670:9
　your water and wine, 586:16
Drunkard and glutton shall come to poverty,
　　21:28
　cannot meet Cork, 511:6
Drunkard's dream if I ever did see, 858:10
　eye, 595:6
Drunkards liars and adulterers, 211:3
Drunken, Antony brought d. forth, 219:10
　but not with wine, 26:10
　of things Lethean, 530:9
　sailor on a mast, 171:34
　sleep with d. Christian, 482:21
　stagger like a d. man, 18:16
　the dregs, 27:1
　what shall we do with d. sailor, 897:17
Drunkenness, babbling d., 205:25
　is sepulture of wit, 136:10
　not in rioting and d., 41:40
Drunks, our fathers are all d., 828:15
Drury, lives in D. Lane, 896:8

Dying *(continued)*
 bliss of d., 293:2
 born by d. and being damned, 144:8
 come from d. moon, 452:18
 day sir, 883:12
 despised and d. king, 402:19
 dirge of d. year, 402:11
 doubly d., 373:3
 echoes d. d. d., 452:19
 every colored woman d., 830:10
 fall, 204:10
 fastened to d. animal, 594:3
 flute in d. notes, 273:25
 forgets d. bird, 333:15
 generations, 594:1
 green and d., 777:14
 groans of love like those of d., 759:2
 has made us rarer gifts, 669:12
 himself and his d., 840:3
 I am d. Egypt d., 219:4
 idea of one's d., 826:9
 if d. don't think much of it, 646:11
 in d. we are born, 125:12
 in hotel room, 681:12
 is a trifle, 510:7
 is an art, 833:3
 living indisposeth for d., 248:28
 men enforce attention, 176:20
 more survivors' affair, 631:8
 multifold, 510:7
 no more d. then, 223:5
 not busy being born is busy d., 851:8
 not death but d. is terrible, 304:26
 not d. for faith hard, 459:12
 not grasp thought of d., 507:6
 of thirst by the fountain, 137:12
 promiscuous in his way of d., 821:8
 rage against d. of light, 777:15
 say my goodbyes finish d., 744:19
 separate d. ember, 449:4
 strike so he may feel is d., 104:11
 to be afraid of thee, 510:2
 tomorrow will be d., 241:4
 truth on lips of d., 495:21
 unconscionable time d., 272:3
 we know we're d., 712:8
 whether living is d., 73:17
 yet fancy ourselves eternal, 115:18
 you went on with d., 839:2
 young man you're d., 889:26
Dynamite, several tons of d., 757:5
Dynamo, starry d., 812:13
Dynasties, carved new d., 652:6
 go onward though d. pass, 536:22
Dynasty, taxation at beginning of d., 131:11

E

E equals mc^2, 637:7
 pur si muove, 167:*n*3
 white E red I, 559:4
Each, afraid of e. other, 458:9
 bears his own Hell, 94:34
 from e. according to abilities, 478:5
 gazing at e. other, 726:16
 hath one and is one, 228:7
 in sight of e. other, 439:12

Each *(continued)*
 man for hymself, 134:12
 singing e. to e., 675:6
 slow dusk, 699:7
 to e. according to needs, 478:5
 we look at e. other, 815:16
Each-form, pluralism lets exist in e., 542:10
Eager, don't be e., 348:10
 keep guest back who is e., 53:22
 mount e. and quick, 772:11
Eagle, bald e. not chosen, 303:17
 buttons stamped with screaming e., 709:14
 by all the e. in thee, 263:10
 does the E. know, 351:9
 fly as e. toward heaven, 21:26
 forgotten, 639:11
 fourth beast like flying e., 46:28
 from e. in his flight, 436:16
 has landed, 825:19
 I hear E. bird, 891:8
 in a dovecote, 220:6
 in and out the E., 885:6
 like sick E. looking at sky, 411:16
 mewing her mighty youth, 254:12
 mount up at thy command, 14:29
 never lark nor e. flew, 800:1
 of house of Austria, 332:12
 of the rock, 666:4
 old man's e. mind, 596:15
 or the snake, 588:12
 suffers little birds to sing, 173:2
 Tom Jones outlive imperial e., 332:12
 way of an e. in the air, 22:14
 with e. eyes, 408:17
Eagle's fate and mine are one, 59:*n*5
 feathered with e. plumes, 59:18
Eagles, baited like e., 183:12
 mount up with wings as e., 26:32
 of Ngong look out, 662:6
 prey where e. dare not perch, 171:23
 swifter than e., 11:8
 where carcass is e. gather, 35:21
Ear, as mind pitched e. pleased, 327:4
 bow down thine e., 21:19
 came o'er my e. like sweet sound, 204:10
 connections of e. closer than eye, 572:16
 deaf adder that stoppeth her e., 16:39
 Death twitches my e., 95:14
 drowsy e. of night, 395:1
 dull cold e. of death, 315:20
 dull e. of drowsy man, 175:20
 first blade then e., 36:29
 flea in mine e., 145:13
 give every man thy e., 197:23
 hang pearl in cowslip's e., 178:11
 heard of thee by hearing of the e., 14:38
 hearing e. seeing eye, 21:11
 I was all e., 252:21
 I will enchant thine e., 171:7
 in Adam's e. left voice, 258:29
 in one e. out other, 132:*n*3
 incline thine e., 26:21
 jest's prosperity lies in e., 174:31
 keep word of promise to our e., 217:29
 more meant than meets e., 251:22
 nor e. heard, 42:6
 nor the e. filled with hearing, 22:23
 of Faith, 372:7

Ear *(continued)*
 of jealousy heareth all, 29:30
 of man hath not seen, 179:4
 oon e. herde at tothir out, 132:20
 open vowels tire, 292:17
 piercing night's dull e., 189:18
 poor e. for music, 524:7
 reasonable good e. in music, 178:31
 rich jewel in Ethiop's e., 179:28
 short a cheekbone and e., 489:*n*5
 soothe thine e., 317:12
 squirt cider in your e., 660:*n*2
 sweetness through mine e., 251:23
 to my e. morning brings, 424:19
 toad at e. of Eve, 258:6
 unpleasing to a married e., 174:32
 we have wolf by e., 338:11
 whorled e., 546:4
 won the e. of Pluto, 251:9
 wood has a sharp e., 134:*n*2
 'Ear my 'erse's legs, 455:25
Earl, slain E. of Murray, 890:7
Earlier and other creation, 679:4
Earliest, charm of e. birds, 257:26
 drops e. to ground, 185:30
Early and latter rain, 45:32
 call me e. mother, 450:15
 git up e. to take in God, 482:1
 God helps those who get up e., 898:5
 good die e. bad late, 282:9
 had it been e. had been kind, 308:17
 happy those e. days, 268:9
 in the morning, 897:17
 it gets late e. out there, 806:11
 late and e. pray, 227:10
 leaves fall e., 664:18
 let e. education be amusement, 75:16
 nipt my flower sae e., 358:13
 not rise e. never do good, 308:1
 those that seek me e., 20:6
 to bed early to rise, 302:12
 to rise early to bed, 704:9
 too e. seen unknown, 179:29
 used to go to bed e., 610:11
 vote e. and often, 498:12
Early-born, dawn the e., 50:17
Earn, I e. that I eat, 195:6
 little to e., 481:5
 living by sweat of brow, 474:20
Earned, hearts are e., 593:14
 night's repose, 436:13
 with sweat of brows, 155:12
Earnest about these objects, 664:3
 between jest and e., 156:26
 frogs die in e., 82:9
 I am in e., 433:5
 life e. art gay, 359:20
 life real life e., 436:4
 person over hip person, 876:1
Earnings, division of unequal e., 389:5
Earns, each e. his death, 727:4
 whate'er he can, 436:12
Ear-piercing fife, 209:13
Ears, battle for the e. of others, 824:2
 belly has no e., 85:3
 blast of war in e., 189:7
 bring to our e. clash of arms, 331:13
 compliments reaching proper e., 587:3

Ears *(continued)*

earth has stopped e., 574:18
gushed blood, 409:17
have e. and hear not, 27:25
have e. but hear not, 18:22
have heard Holy Word, 352:10
having e. hear not, 331:10
he has e. and two eyes, 467:5
he that hath e., 34:7
hearing with sharper e., 798:1
hum about mine e., 224:33
I have e. in vain, 410:9
lend me your e., 192:28
let music creep in our e., 186:15
look with thine e., 212:29
my e. hum, 56:5
noise of water in mine e., 171:28
of people attentive unto law, 12:29
of the deaf shall be unstopped, 26:18
of the old cur, 262:13
only for what experience gives access,
  549:10
porches of mine e., 198:11
seven empty e., 7:9
seven good e., 7:9
small pitchers have wide e., 148:9
softest music to attending e., 180:14
sound lifts me by e., 472:22
speech delighteth the e., 31:34
split e. of groundlings, 200:6
tail and pointed e., 440:11
to hear, 34:7
trust e. less than eyes, 69:5
walls have e., 134:n2
with ravished e., 274:15
wode hath e., 134:15
woods have e., 134:n2
word of earth in e. of world, 530:21

Earth, a little e. whereon to grow, 355:15
abideth forever, 22:21
after e. stopped ears, 574:18
all Danaë to stars, 453:6
all e. o'erwhelm them, 197:18
all peoples of the e., 765:14
all the corners of e., 48:7
all things in e., 44:9
all ye know on e., 410:20
alone on e. as I am now, 395:9
always in e. and air, 756:10
and every common sight, 370:13
and grave and dust, 159:16
and high heaven, 575:7
and water strive again, 293:14
Angels bending near e., 457:11
argument of e., 485:17
as if e. were excrement, 658:13
as showers that water the e., 17:12
astonishing thing about e., 772:18
attacking heaven and e., 827:14
barren as moon, 635:14
beat e. with unfettered foot, 96:17
beauty for e. too dear, 179:28
belongs to living, 338:3
belongs to living generation, 336:16
bleeding piece of e., 192:22
body made of e., 246:3
brave of all the e., 582:8

Earth *(continued)*

bridal of e. and sky, 242:19
brightens when you dawn, 4:6
bringeth forth fruit, 36:29
call heaven and e. to witness, 9:13
call to e. and sea, 486:6
center of my sinful e., 223:4
cloud enveloping the e., 378:9
cold in the e., 476:11
combined essences of heaven and e., 86:16
confines of heaven and e., 119:13
confound all unity on e., 217:6
confound the language of all e., 6:27
covenant between me and the e., 6:25
cradle of hope, 636:11
crawling between heaven and e., 199:25
dashed to e. plowed under, 891:20
days on the e. are as a shadow, 12:26
deep places of the e., 17:32
deep-delved e., 410:4
degraded e. diminished future, 866:6
demi-Atlas of this e., 218:12
did quake, 36:21
did thee feel e. move, 721:17
dim spot men call e., 251:25
dust shall return to e., 23:31
ends of the e., 587:8
enslaved by love of e., 149:6
every living thing that moveth upon e., 5:8
every other creature on e., 342:12
Exponent of E., 510:3
fall to the base e., 177:2
false as sandy e., 203:20
Father Time and Mother E., 813:8
fell to e. knew not where, 436:19
fell upon the e., 30:5
felt the wound, 259:11
fire sea air, 537:10
get away from e. awhile, 622:19
giants in the e., 6:16
girdle round about e., 178:17
glance from heaven to e., 179:6
glory from the e., 370:15
God created heaven and e., 5:3
God light of heavens and e., 118:23
goddess Demeter or E., 68:9
going the way of all the e., 10:5
going to and fro in the e., 12:36
great society on e., 369:1
handful of e. stops mouths, 415:9
has not anything to show, 370:2
hath bubbles, 214:7
hear word of the Lord, 28:4
heard in dread, 318:7
heaven and e. pass away, 35:23
heaven and e. quilt and pillow, 122:3
heaven and e. to witness, 9:13
heaven like egg e. like yolk, 111:3
heaven on e., 257:15
heavens and e. mass sewn up, 118:20
hell on e., 565:4
help of any thing on e., 354:10
here men from planet E., 888:18
holy E. giver of life, 68:3
holy Mother E., 63:20
Holy Mother E., 891:9
how it is on bitch of e., 744:14
hurt not the e., 46:34

Earth *(continued)*

hydroptic e. hath drunk, 229:12
I have come back to e., 559:12
I will move the e., 83:5
if e. be shadow of heaven, 258:19
in darkness as if in death, 4:5
in e. I was his purgatorie, 135:9
in earthy bed, 455:3
indifferent children of e., 198:39
introduction into e. of life, 415:15
is full of his glory, 25:9
is full of thy riches, 18:11
is my mother, 365:1
is only grave, 234:1
is the Lord's, 15:24, 42:22
kindly e. slumber, 452:4
kindly fruits of the e., 49:2
kings and counselors of e., 13:4
ladder set up on the e., 6:41
lap of E., 316:6
lapped in universal law, 452:4
lards the lean e., 182:12
last best hope of e., 446:1
lay her in the e., 202:15
left souls on e., 411:4
let all the e. keep silence, 29:9
let loose to play upon e., 254:14
let the e. rejoice, 18:2
lie heavy on him E., 283:n4
lie lightly gentle e., 238:5
light be the e., 67:7
like snake renew, 403:8
like to swallow whole e., 739:5
little e. for charity, 226:7
Lord of heaven and e., 40:33
love e. sun animals, 485:10
love of e. he instills, 505:15
made the e. to tremble, 25:23
made thee neither of heaven nor e., 141:3
Maker of Heaven and e., 48:11
man making deserts of e., 635:12
man marks e. with ruin, 396:17
man on moon returning safely to e., 786:6
marriages consummated on e., 162:11
measuring e. and heaven, 76:6
meek shall inherit the e., 16:10
men like e. we are moon, 561:17
mind more beautiful than e., 369:2
more near e. than wont, 210:15
more things in heaven and e., 198:19,
  693:11
mortals make e. bitter, 407:5
most like single cell, 772:16
mountain rests on e., 4:10
new beings on this e., 439:11
new heaven and new e., 47:11
new heavens and a new e., 27:21
nigher heaven than now, 459:21
nightly to listening e., 287:21
no more a mother, 104:n10
not water is unstable, 694:13
nothing but hath bound in e., 172:15
nothing on e. but laundry, 797:13
of the e. earthy, 43:7
offered this trust to e., 119:6
on bare e. he lies, 274:18
on e. broken arcs, 462:10
on e. no sure happiness, 160:21

Endanger, power to e. public liberty, 329:12

Endearing elegance of female friendship, 307:13
    young charms, 387:9

Endeavor, achievement death of e., 540:3
    disinterested e. to learn, 496:7
    elevate life by conscious e., 474:28
    in continual motion, 188:34
    it were a vain e., 378:7

Endeavors to live life imagined, 475:19

Ended, God be praised Georges e., 629:*n*3
    his cares now all e., 188:25
    our revels now are e., 225:1
    so e. Sicilian expedition, 72:9
    with his body changed to light, 892:5

Endin, now sees de e., 713:12

Ending, all lovely things have e., 683:4
    bad beginning makes bad e., 68:16
    hard beginning good e., 147:1
    is despair, 225:9
    O bitter e., 651:3
    of interminable night, 679:9

Endings are elusive, 829:9
    lie has seven e., 889:7

Endless, in e. error hurled, 295:1
    my days of e. doubt, 159:2
    night, 241:13, 316:13
    olives of e. age, 222:10
    perpetual posterity, 384:19
    pure and e. light, 268:14
    regret or happiness, 552:12
    road you tread, 575:11
    summer days, 508:9
    time an e. song, 591:8
    whole vocation e. imitation, 370:19

Endlessly, cradle e. rocking, 487:5
    owl is e. hungry, 840:11

Endorsed, elephants e. with towers, 259:33

Endow college or cat, 294:7
    with all my goods I thee e., 49:25

Endowed by their creator, 336:1

Ends, all well that e. well, 147:16
    all's well that e. well, 206:7
    candle burns at both e., 695:8
    come from e. of earth, 587:8
    consult our private e., 264:*n*4
    delays have dangerous e., 169:19
    dog to gain private e., 322:14
    filled with e. of worms, 696:11
    his circuit unto the e. of it, 15:16
    Law e. Tyranny begins, 275:9
    man's glory most begins and e., 597:2
    means requisite to e., 349:10
    my story e. with freedom, 469:1
    needless Alexandrine e. song, 292:18
    of Being and ideal Grace, 434:17
    of world come, 534:4
    one e. other begins, 448:18
    smile upon fingers' e., 189:4
    strange eventful history, 194:25
    thing that e. other deeds, 219:7
    those who pursue many e., 757:14
    thou aimest at, 226:5
    violent delights have violent e., 180:24
    watch that e. night, 289:13
    way the world e., 677:2
    which I believe to be evil, 668:7

Ends *(continued)*
    with Revelations, 560:15
    your family history e. with you, 76:14

Endurance and courage, 603:5

Endure accent of coming Foot, 511:13
    all deaths I could e., 259:12
    all that human hearts e., 307:14
    courage to e., 476:13
    days go I e., 643:19
    for ages to come, 349:15
    his name shall e. for ever, 17:14
    if I e. you a little longer, 287:6
    knows how to e. poverty, 97:15
    man will not merely e., 714:5
    men must e. their going, 213:7
    misfortunes of others, 263:15
    my heart, 54:7
    Negroes will e., 713:14
    neither evils nor cures, 99:9
    no picture made to e., 665:12
    not e. husband with beard, 190:21
    not yet a breach, 229:16
    nought e. but Mutability, 401:12
    philosopher e. toothache, 191:13
    so long shall your honor e., 94:7
    testing whether nation e., 446:5
    then pity then embrace, 295:2
    we are here to e. it, 625:15
    weeping may e. for a night, 16:1
    what Malherbe writes will e., 162:25
    youth's a stuff will not e., 204:26

Endured, moon hath her eclipse e., 222:10
    much e. little enjoyed, 307:10
    remembers all that he wrought and e., 53:23
    something more dreadful, 54:7
    sufferings of troops, 668:7

Endures, fearlessness which e., 791:7
    heaven e., 576:4
    man in love e. more, 548:26
    moment or day, 594:13
    nothing e. but change, 61:27

Endureth, blessed the man that e. temptation, 45:21
    his mercy e. for ever, 12:22
    his truth e., 18:3
    word of the Lord e., 45:37

Enduring monument, 403:20
    opposing and e. forces, 421:12

Endymion, in E. leaped headlong, 413:7

Enemies called for peace, 608:7
    careful in choice of e., 560:1
    defend in assaults of our e., 48:13
    die not hating e., 300:8
    disposed of foreign e., 75:22
    eminence engenders e., 728:9
    fourth glass for mine e., 288:12
    friends close but e. closer, 795:10
    give e. means of our destruction, 59:18
    giving e. aid and comfort, 339:13
    giving e. the slip, 313:24
    great woe to their e., 53:3
    have made us one people, 579:4
    his e. shall lick the dust, 17:13
    I can defend myself from e., 367:*n*1
    in the presence of mine e., 15:23
    in war in peace friends, 336:2
    intelligent and corrupt, 738:5

Enemies *(continued)*
    just friends and brave e., 337:14
    keep our e., 600:1
    knew their e. in hell, 663:17
    learn from our e., 102:14
    look e. in face, 277:6
    love your e., 32:21
    make my e. ridiculous, 299:24
    makes peace with one's e., 786:13
    may e. live here in summer, 284:12
    naked to mine e., 226:6
    no liberty for e. of liberty, 364:7
    no perpetual e., 392:21
    of free institutions, 444:6
    of persecuted blacks, 433:3
    old friends become bitter e., 234:10
    saved from our e., 37:14
    secret history of e., 437:5
    soften to us our e., 556:12
    ten jokes an hundred e., 313:23
    treat words as e., 755:3
    trophies unto e. of truth, 247:13
    wise learn from e., 73:3

Enemigo, el cadáver de su e., 898:8
    que huye, 898:4

Enemy and friend hurt you to heart, 524:18
    art hath e. Ignorance, 231:18
    be able for thy e., 205:30
    be taken by Turkish e., 898:2
    best is e. of good, 299:21
    cannot be hidden, 30:39
    care's an e. to life, 204:13
    cruel and unrelenting e., 328:6
    dashed in pieces the e., 8:6
    death is the e., 654:19
    defeat e. in one battle, 333:11
    distinction between friend and e., 682:4
    drive e. beyond frontier, 365:10
    every admirer is potential e., 734:4
    every man his greatest e., 248:15
    eye neighbor as e., 614:4
    faints not nor faileth, 479:12
    goes over to e., 323:19
    happiness e. to pomp, 288:5
    hast thou found me O mine e., 12:6
    here shall he see no e., 194:11
    if thine e. be hungry, 21:34
    in their mouths, 208:31
    kisses of e. deceitful, 22:1
    last e. is death, 43:2
    let no e. haul colors down, 644:9
    man with bellyful of classics e., 690:16
    met e. and he is us, 393:*n*1
    met e. they are ours, 393:11
    mightest still the e., 15:5
    my e. is dead, 487:11
    my vision's greatest e., 354:15
    nearest and dearest e., 183:5
    nearly slew ye, 884:6
    no man's e., 748:5
    no potential e. to establish authority, 692:7
    nobody's e. but own, 465:31
    not how many e. are but where, 70:1
    of clear language is insincerity, 735:12
    of conventional wisdom not ideas, 753:6
    one e. is too much, 244:10
    places ship alongside e., 355:11
    principal e. of moral progress, 614:12

Enemy *(continued)*
    punished as e. of country, 363:14
    reason greatest e. faith has, 144:9
    rejoice not over thy e., 30:29
    Roosevelt no e. of entrenched privilege,
      685:4
    see your e. and know him, 670:2
    there is no little e., 302:3
    Thyself may be Thine E., 509:2
    to native every stranger an e., 660:1
    treat friend as if he might become e., 100:8
    turns to flee, 898:4
    we shall meet the e., 393:n1
    wherever e. goes our troops go, 498:3
    will meet one e. everywhere, 117:10
    you my e. and I yours, 303:10
Enemy's, by e. beak gouged, 836:2
    easier to get into e. toils, 59:17
    encounter with e. main force, 420:9
    mine e. dog, 213:3
    stand aside from e. onset, 72:4
    watch e. corpse go by, 898:8
Energies, give away e. and life, 789:10
    of cosmos into cultural manifestation,
      737:1
    self-circling e., 378:24
Energy and sleepless vigilance, 446:2
    atomic e. lead to bombs, 638:1
    atomic e. menace, 638:4
    cannot control atomic e., 611:10
    crime naught but undirected e., 604:12
    equals mass times speed of light squared,
      637:n4
    government want e. to preserve itself,
      337:9
    horse supplies locomotive e., 563:18
    of thought, 421:9
    power wielded by abnormal e., 532:3
    public life situation of e., 323:19
    release of atomic e., 661:4
    silent e. of nature, 420:18
    source of e. like a battery, 847:4
    two problems e. and malaise, 805:15
    uranium new source of e., 637:14
Enfants de la patrie, 361:3
    terribles, 430:22
Enfer, chaud comme l'e., 348:n1
    l'e. c'est les Autres, 743:n1
    l'e. des femmes, 266:n2
Enfin Malherbe vint, 278:n2
Enfold, how many perils do e., 160:6
Enforce, tongues of dying e. attention, 176:20
Enforced from our quiet sphere, 188:17
    it useth e. ceremony, 193:6
    obedience, 211:3
Enforcement, gentleness my strong e.,
    194:22
Enfranchisement, liberty freedom e., 192:17
Engaged in great civil war, 446:5
Engagement, get loose from honorable e.,
    323:17
    positive e. to marry, 420:11
Engenders, shudder in loins e., 594:16
    so much more, 713:17
Engine, clock not steam-e., 708:4
    human e. waits, 676:12
    power alone, 601:7
    steam e. in trousers, 375:4

Engine *(continued)*
    two-handed e. at door, 253:11
    which drives Enterprise, 656:13
    wit's an unruly e., 242:11
Engineer, give me the e., 481:3
    happens because you e. it, 878:1
    sometimes striking the e., 242:11
    story of brave e., 608:n1
Engineers of human souls, 636:15
    of soul, 602:3
Enginer hoist with own petar, 201:15
Engines, feeble e. of despotism, 338:15
    O you mortal e., 209:13
England, always be an E., 775:11
    an empire, 417:2
    and Saint George, 189:9
    at this door E. stands sentry, 535:7
    awake, 354:14
    be E. what she will, 326:6
    became top nation, 718:9
    bound with triumphant sea, 176:25
    breeds valiant creatures, 189:16
    cliffs of E. stand, 496:16
    corner of field forever E., 669:10
    expects, 355:12
    from old E. they set sail, 898:1
    further off from E., 515:4
    gentlemen of E., 247:4
    Greece Italy and E. did adorn, 274:7
    has no name for prairies, 405:8
    hath given warning, 333:2
    hath need of thee, 370:9
    high road to E., 309:3
    I am in E. everywhere, 248:14
    if E. to itself true, 176:7
    in E. I've mate, 468:1
    in E. now, 460:18
    in E. thought not catching, 559:20
    Ireland gives E. generals, 505:19
    keep my bones, 175:31
    know Kings of E., 526:6
    knuckle-end of E., 374:21
    let not E. forget precedence, 254:2
    light candle in E., 144:13
    many a peer of E. brews, 575:12
    mariners of E., 384:8
    men of E. wherefore plow, 402:15
    middle class in E., 497:21
    middle class safety of E., 459:17
    model to inward greatness, 189:2
    navy of E., 318:18
    neck wrung like chicken, 621:1
    never at foot of conqueror, 176:6
    nor E. did I know, 360:13
    of a king of E. too, 151:7
    oh to be in E., 460:18
    old E. to adorn, 589:24
    one of charms of E., 612:21
    one of stately homos of E., 752:3
    or E. breed again, 167:10
    paradise of women, 161:11
    poorest he in E., 239:4
    rightwise king of E., 138:2
    roast beef of E., 304:9
    roast beef of old E., 304:n3
    sea once made E. secure, 627:4
    shower of curates on E., 472:12
    slaves cannot breathe in E., 326:21

England *(continued)*
    stately homes of E., 405:7, 654:6
    such night in E., 419:16
    there I find flag of E., 365:14
    think about defense of E., 599:8
    this realm this E., 176:24
    what is left of E., 422:n1
    who dies if E. live, 590:6
    who only E. know, 588:8
    whoever wakes in E., 460:18
    wins last battle, 621:2
    with all thy faults, 326:n2
    wont to conquer others, 176:26
    world where E. dead, 627:5
    youth of E. are on fire, 189:1
England's green and pleasant land, 354:8
    mountains green, 354:8
    no future in E. dreaming, 874:12
    old E. winding sheet, 354:6
    pleasant pastures, 354:8
    song forever, 582:10
    stay no more on E. shore, 898:3
English, among E. Poets after death, 413:8
    anyone been to E. public school, 736:6
    attain E. style, 307:15
    can't think of E., 515:17
    Chaucer well of E., 160:16
    close wall with E. dead, 189:7
    department of the spirit, 810:3
    father of E. criticism, 307:17
    for suppressing other, 496:6
    gentleman after a fox, 561:7
    God had never spoken anything but E.,
      622:5
    Good Soldier finest French novel in E.,
      616:13
    his E. sweete upon his tonge, 133:20
    in an E. lane, 461:3
    in favor of boys learning E., 619:2
    king's E., 187:4
    kissed by E. dead, 699:8
    language of E. poet, 677:11
    most beautiful words in E. language,
      545:10
    not accessible even to Englishmen, 565:19
    not Turkish court, 188:26
    one pair of E. legs, 189:14
    or American lawyer, 433:12
    principle of E. constitution, 318:20
    tongue I love, 829:4
    trick of our E. nation, 187:34
    up with which not put, 622:3
    we E. nation of brutes, 567:n2
    white as angel E. child, 350:14
    winter ending in July, 399:1
    worst E. ever encountered, 645:6
Englishman, blood of an E., 897:3
    content to say nothing, 311:1
    either for E. or Jew, 354:18
    every E. paid his way, 319:n1
    hangdog look of E. about to talk French,
      648:15
    he is an E., 526:3
    if I were American as I am E., 306:5
    impossible for E. to open mouth, 565:19
    last great E., 454:15
    rights of E., 339:4
    stirred heart of E., 603:5

Error *(continued)*
  ignorance preferable to e., 336:4
  in endless e. hurled, 295:1
  is immense, 290:4
  love truth pardon e., 299:4
  no e. fails to find defenders, 518:9
  no effort without e., 571:13
  not afraid to tolerate e., 338:13
  nothing more damaging than old e.,
    344:21
  of 1848 and 1849, 470:6
  of opinion tolerated, 337:8
  old and gray-headed e., 248:21
  only e. to be exposed, 645:9
  opponent weaned from e., 604:4
  prophecy gratuitous e., 480:17
  reformers of e., 338:1
  religion not popular e., 500:14
  show a man he is in an e., 275:6
  sink of uncertainty and e., 269:25
  to consider children innocent, 341:11
  to expect favors, 329:4
  to marry with poets, 773:15
  trial and e., 562:14
  truth to one e. to other, 604:4
  very e. of the moon, 210:15
Errors, amusing with numerous e., 322:6
  correct e. when shown e., 445:12
  if to her female e. fall, 293:5
  in religion dangerous, 311:20
  not in art but in artificers, 279:13
  reasoned e., 502:12
  stratagems which e. seem, 292:11
  volitional, 650:16
  wanderings mists and tempests, 89:*n*12
Errs if he hopes to do deed without God's
    knowledge, 63:23
  man e. as long as he strives, 343:27
'Erse's, 'ear 'e. legs, 455:25
Erump, evade e., 87:*n*4
Erupit, abiit excessit evasit e., 87:*n*4
Eruption, strange e. to our state, 196:12
Eruptions, strange e., 182:32
Esau, hands are hands of E., 6:39
  sold his birthright, 6:38
  was a cunning hunter, 6:37
Escalier, l'esprit de l'e., 313:15
Escapades of death, 642:7
Escape, better ten guilty e., 318:21
  cannot e. history, 446:1
  good thing to e. death, 65:17
  immortals cannot e. love, 65:25
  into calm regions, 312:1
  less evil that some e., 539:6
  let no guilty e., 498:6
  me never, 461:6
  not e. my iambics, 92:1
  of all e. mechanisms, 645:16
  poetry e. from emotion, 675:19
  those who dream at night, 448:12
  thou shalt not e. calumny, 199:26
  urge to e. is appetite of soul, 702:16
  what struggle to e., 410:14
  whipping, 199:14
Escaped auction block, 468:19
  from the deep, 128:4
  I only am e., 12:38
  what speech e. your teeth, 51:5

Escaped *(continued)*
  with skin of my teeth, 13:37
Escapes, hair-breadth e., 207:37
  rarely e. injuring own hands, 58:4
  virtue e. not calumnious strokes, 197:19
Escaping left Death's scraping, 641:6
Eschewed, one that e. evil, 12:34
Escurial, Tom Jones will outlive E., 332:12
Eskimo Ootah had explanation, 564:11
Espaces infinis, 269:*n*4
Espagnol, je parle e. a Dieu, 148:*n*16
Espoir, un peu d'e., 519:*n*3
Espoused, saw my late e. saint, 255:1
Esprit, l'e. de l'escalier, 313:15
  l'e. de son âge, 300:*n*2
  une allure de nôtre e., 152:*n*9
Esprits, ne favorise que les e. préparés, 499:*n*1
Essay loose sally of mind, 306:25
  no room for impurities in e., 654:8
Essays, my e. come home, 165:10
Essence, fellowship with e., 409:9
  his glassy e., 206:28
  of gravity was design, 313:22
  knows e. of beauty, 74:5
  not disclose e. of phenomena, 662:2
Essences, combined e. of heaven and earth,
    86:16
Essential concept and first truth, 770:1
  disarmament is e., 653:16
  facts of life, 474:29
  four e. freedoms, 653:4
  gaudiness of poetry, 642:19
  give up e. liberty, 303:6
  great expense may be e., 325:13
  is invisible to eye, 726:18
  knowledge, 469:6
  natural e. rights, 336:*n*1
  poet is after e. you, 630:12
  poetry, 379:1
  relationship to existence, 469:6
  service to country, 285:1
  thing in form, 642:20
  things e. or things circumstantial, 271:16
Essentially, objects e. fixed and dead, 379:6
  what I e. did, 785:2
Essentials, six e. in painting, 122:11
Establish justice, 339:11
  ordain and e. Constitution, 339:11
  peace spare conquered, 94:35
  thou the work of our hands, 17:27
Established for prevention of crime, 78:24
  he hath e. it upon the floods, 15:24
  hope to see peace e., 653:15
  incompatibility e. between them, 616:1
  liberal institutions cease when e., 548:24
  our Constitution is now e., 303:20
Establishes tyranny establishes democratic
    regime, 142:9
Establishing, way of e. grievance for the day,
    680:11
Establishment and the Movement, 428:16
  based on White-Anglo Saxon-Protestant
    ~class, 777:19
  by the E. I do not mean, 806:1
  in Palestine of home for Jewish people,
    551:7
  military e., 686:16
  of religion, 340:1

Establishment *(continued)*
  of revolutionary-democratic dictatorship,
    607:10
  of system of security, 653:16
Establishments, nations stumbled upon e.,
    319:11
Estate, distressed in mind body or e., 48:15
  fallen from his high e., 274:18
  Fourth E., 406:9
  fourth e. in politics, 385:13
  good fame, 424:14
  how fleeting the e. of man, 112:7
  low e. of his handmaiden, 37:10
  real e., 431:16
  who not offended with his e., 117:3
  wish e. o' world undone, 217:24
Estates degrees and offices, 185:8
Esteem everything esteem nothing, 267:19
  give to get e., 322:1
  to all, 328:4
  what obtain cheap e. lightly, 333:6
Esteemed, better vile than vile e., 222:19
  medicine least e. of arts, 71:2
  wonder that gold e., 143:3
Esteems, everything man e., 594:13
  man worth as he e. himself, 145:12
Estimate, thou knowest thy e., 221:27
Estranged faces, 577:4
  lovers e. or dead, 596:3
E.T. phone home, 869:4
Et cum spiritu tuo, 47:18
  in Arcadia ego, 120:20
  tu Brute, 89:*n*3, 192:16
État, l'é. c'est moi, 278:*n*4
Eternal, abode where E. are, 404:3
  ancient houses not e., 583:6
  art alone e., 458:3
  assert e. Providence, 255:5
  attributes of God are e., 275:17
  boy e., 223:9
  dying yet fancy ourselves e., 115:18
  Fame's e. beadroll, 160:16
  Father strong to save, 503:1
  feast in thine e. cell, 202:34
  feel and know we are e., 276:18
  Feminine draws us on, 344:15
  fitness of things, 304:19
  Footman snicker, 675:3
  gift of God e. life, 41:16
  God is thy refuge, 9:33
  gone to e. rest, 448:2
  heaven's e. year, 273:19
  hope springs e., 294:19
  hostility against tyranny, 337:7
  importance like baseball, 664:3
  in whom standeth e. life, 48:13
  justice temporary but conscience e., 144:3
  lay hold on e. life, 44:36
  lids apart, 412:10
  mystery of world, 637:11
  new and e. covenant, 47:25
  no e. truth, 692:3
  note of sadness, 496:17
  now does always last, 265:11
  our e. home, 289:12
  outside of time, 818:2
  pain short joy e., 360:10
  quantity of force e., 494:5

Evening *(continued)*
  housewife ply e. care, 315:16
  in the e. it is cut down, 17:23
  is come rise up, 91:19
  isolation of sky at e., 640:22
  it was a summer e., 381:6
  light first light of e., 642:13
  like an e. gone, 289:13
  love morning and e. star, 664:6
  morning incense e. meal, 347:8
  must usher night, 403:19
  now came still e. on, 257:24
  of their lives, 500:5
  open house in e., 618:14
  quickly come as the E. Star, 87:4
  quiet-colored end of e., 461:1
  rainy e. to read this discourse, 244:34
  red light of e., 891:13
  rest at pale e., 730:15
  shades of e. drew on, 448:8
  shades prevail, 287:21
  shadow at e. rising, 676:6
  shadows of the e., 519:1
  slight sound at e., 472:22
  some enchanted e., 706:12
  soup of the e., 515:6
  spread out against sky, 674:17
  star love's harbinger, 259:24
  star you shine on dead, 403:*n*1
  sunset and e. star, 456:4
  to his labor until e., 18:11
  twilight and e. bell, 456:5
  until e. comes, 421:5
  walks at e. on three feet, 66:*n*3
  welcome peaceful e. in, 327:1
  when it is e. fair weather, 34:34
  withhold not thine hand in the e., 23:28
Evenings, we have had summer e., 666:2
Evensong, at last ring to e., 148:18
  at length ringeth to e., 148:*n*9
  dead ere e., 890:5
Event, caprice of minutest e., 483:11
  divine e., 454:12
  greatest e. in war, 72:9
  haunt spot of great e., 431:5
  Holocaust central e., 831:9
  how much the greatest e., 342:8
  men labels that name e., 506:15
  one e. happeneth to all, 22:29
  prophets make sure of e., 317:6
  thinking too precisely on e., 201:20
  unveil third e. to me, 511:9
  verity is an e., 542:9
Eventful, strange e. history, 194:25
Eventide, fast falls e., 405:8
Events, all e. bear relationship, 85:10
  cast shadows before, 384:10
  controlled me, 446:7
  course of human e., 336:1
  great e. make me calm, 485:2
  it turns out are almost always, 876:5
  my dear boy e., 703:7
  names deeds legends e., 411:15
  national e. decided by power elite, 782:12
  signs should prefigure e., 88:1
  some great e. some mean hypocrisies, 330:6
  spirits of great e., 384:*n*3

Events *(continued)*
  three e. in life, 280:26
  we will never forget, 871:6
Eventual domination over all, 765:14
Ever-during dark surrounds me, 257:6
  power, 372:7
  sleep one e. night, 226:20
Everest, square root of E., 795:6
  because [E.] is there, 668:7
Ever-fixed mark, 222:15
Everglades, no other E. in the world, 686:12
Ever-increasing wonder and awe, 320:2
Everlasting, achievements of intellect e., 92:10
  bonfire, 215:25
  composed to be e. possession, 71:12
  condemned into e. redemption, 191:9
  deprived of e. bliss, 168:18
  doors, 15:25
  Father, 25:16
  first last e. day, 229:9
  from e. to e. thou art God, 17:23
  funeral marches round your heart, 780:10
  God the E. Refuge, 119:20
  had not fixed canon, 196:29
  here set up my e. rest, 181:14
  hills, 7:21
  his mercy is e., 18:3
  life, 39:11
  no, 406:18
  open ye e. gates, 258:28
  stood from e. to e., 278:11
  the e. arms, 9:33
  yea, 406:21
Everlastingness, bright shoots of e., 268:10
Ever-living, our e. poet, 220:*n*2
Evermore, probing through you O e., 720:9
Ever-nearing circle weaves shade, 496:15
Ever-returning spring, 487:12
Ever-rolling, time like e. stream, 289:14
Evers, Tinker to E. to Chance, 646:12
Ever-whirling wheel, 160:22
Every, assimilates e. thing to itself, 314:9
  day a little death, 829:1
  day a wilderness, 871:2
  day in every way, 568:8
  day's news, 207:5
  feature works, 382:17
  inch a king, 212:26
  man architect of his fortune, 92:13
  man for himself, 148:24
  new idea, 790:4
  over and over e. year, 382:1
  sooner e. party breaks up, 382:19
  war of e. man against e. man, 239:9
Everybody, almost e. had troubles, 582:15
  everything happens to e., 565:26
  goes Awww, 799:3
  hard to please e., 100:30, 479:15
  he who praises e., 334:6
  Here Comes E., 650:20
  if e. minded business, 514:8
  lies about sex, 873:4
  looks like e. is down on me, 857:9
  most e. climbs into graves married, 715:6
  on this planet, 844:9
  suspect e., 464:30
  wants to be Cary Grant, 737:13
Everybody's business nobody's business, 245:3

Everyday, refinement of e. thinking, 637:12
Everyman I will go with thee, 880:18
Everyone, Future something e. reaches, 717:13
  has one sermon, 886:7
  has something to hide, 578:13
  in world is Christ, 632:15
  is a moon has dark side, 524:20
  love come to e., 697:9
  not e. can get to Corinth, 98:7
  understandable by e. not just scientists, 854:3
  went over e. nobody's missing, 773:9
  when e. is somebodee, 528:6
  will say, 526:11
  world breaks e., 721:7
Everyone's tired of turmoil, 787:18
  true worship, 73:24
Everything, a bore to tell e., 299:3
  about her was vigorous, 582:12
  as resulting from laws, 440:7
  autumn in e., 461:16
  begins in mysticism ends in politics, 617:5
  belongs to fatherland, 359:4
  conscience in e., 314:8
  costing not less than e., 679:13
  custom reconciles to e., 323:13
  deed e. glory nothing, 344:12
  detail is e., 723:12
  don't tell her e., 53:16
  else is about something, 864:9
  else is still, 351:7
  esteem e. esteem nothing, 267:19
  exists nothing has value, 638:12
  fearlessness of those who lost e., 791:7
  feeling not always e., 493:7
  for e. missed gained something, 426:27
  for poetry idea e., 497:20
  glory of e., 724:7
  god is present in everything, 754:8
  God not willing to do e., 142:6
  good for something, 273:11
  good in e., 193:37
  grows old under power of Time, 77:15
  had e. I wanted, 710:10
  happens to everybody, 565:26
  hard to attain easily assailed, 111:5
  has an end, 889:4
  he is superior to e. he possesses, 299:12
  hear voices talking about e., 865:13
  I could prove e., 828:4
  I have e. yet nothing, 86:7
  I touch mean and farcical, 505:3
  if you win you win e., 269:17
  in its place, 525:13
  in relation to nothing, 269:9
  includes itself in power, 203:8
  is A-OK, 800:4
  is for the best, 299:8
  is gratuitous, 742:19
  is sterilized, in cellophane, 691:4
  is up to date in Kansas City, 706:10
  know e. forgive e., 362:*n*5
  lived in me, 501:14
  man esteems, 594:13
  man grows used to e., 492:6
  mean between nothing and e., 269:9
  men ask for e., 792:13
  moments when e. goes well, 585:13

Evils *(continued)*
two e. monstrous either one, 681:18
weak e. age and hunger, 194:24
when e. most free, 192:3
which leave no home untouched, 694:4
yield not to e., 94:26
Evolution, cultural e., 607:18
Darwin's theory of e., 873:14
from vague to definite, 534:16
have they discovered e. yet, 850:10
leisure class in social e., 569:7
nothing makes sense except e., 725:6
of thought, 496:1
progress of E. from Washington to Grant, 531:22
Evolutionary epic is probably the best myth, 825:13
Evolved, endless beautiful forms e., 440:5
universe e. from unfamiliar, 836:4
Ev'rythin's up to date in Kansas City, 706:10
Ewe, lilting at e. milking, 321:8
tupping your white e., 207:27
Ewes, milk my e. and weep, 223:33
Ewig-Weibliche, das E. zieht uns hinan, 344:*n6*
Ex pede Herculem, 69:*n6*
ungue leonem, 120:21
Exact, aim of e. science, 513:1
equal and e. justice, 337:12
knowledge of the past, 71:12
set e. wealth of states, 183:11
writing maketh an e. man, 166:18
Exactitude is not truth, 605:12
judgment and e. enter him, 3:3
l'e. la politesse des rois, 349:*n3*
Exaggerated, love of the e., 835:17
stress on not changing mind, 626:16
Exaggeration, chargeable with no e., 385:8
report of my death an e., 524:21
Exalt him above all, 31:30
himself shall be abased, 35:14
will to live, 632:13
Exaltation from proximity of disaster, 618:19
highest pitch of e., 348:17
in chanting of Muses, 67:15
Exalted above his fellows, 383:2
both will be e., 638:10
every valley shall be e., 26:25
God an e. father, 563:8
no very e. opinion, 323:21
Satan e. sat, 256:6
them of low degree, 37:11
whoso humble himself be e., 35:14
Exalteth, righteousness e. a nation, 20:29
wisdom e. her children, 30:17
Exalts, not what man does e., 462:7
uniform humiliates and e., 637:1
Examination, decent and manly e., 381:2
of acts of government, 381:2
on minute e., 382:24
Examine, crime to e. laws of heat, 533:1
Examined, ought to have head e., 650:1
Examining what is within our reach, 298:22
Example, annoyance of good e., 524:3
from others take e., 86:15
from the monkey, 126:6
Homer is my e., 595:16
if lower orders don't set good e., 560:18
more efficacious than precept, 307:12

Example *(continued)*
profit by their e., 331:8
salutary influence of e., 307:16
Examples, be patterns be e., 270:3
no longer able to provide bad e., 264:4
Exasperated, American mind e. European, 531:16
Excalibur, so fell the brand E., 451:7
Exceed, never e. your rights, 312:13
reach e. grasp, 461:18
Exceedeth, wisdom and prosperity e. the fame, 11:34
Exceeding, grind e. small, 247:10
honest e. poor man, 184:35
wise fair-spoken, 226:12
Exceeds, far e. all earthly bliss, 154:*n8*
man's might, 203:19
Excel bees for government, 154:11
discredit what they do not e. in, 80:9
not e. because they labor, 386:14
teach who themselves e., 292:9
thou shalt not e., 7:19
Excellence, activity in accordance with e., 78:13
bearing on e. of character, 78:12
fair divided e., 175:9
fame of her e., 54:9
in front of e. gods put sweat, 54:21
mental e. a splendid possession, 92:3
not exchange e. for riches, 55:12
not only know e. but use it, 78:15
stewards of their e., 222:2
to few men comes e., 59:20
Excellencies, smaller e. of conversation, 334:8
true critic dwell on e., 288:13
Excellent dumb discourse, 224:34
everything that's e., 526:18
fancy, 202:12
first e. second good, 142:4
foppery of the world, 211:3
hard to be truly e., 60:8
how e. is thy lovingkindness, 16:9
how e. is thy name, 15:6
I cried, 573:17
if you were a village, 628:3
man of understanding is of e. spirit, 20:43
most e. canopy the air, 199:5
parts of it are e., 550:6
situation e. I am attacking, 557:1
so e. a king, 196:31
so so is e. good, 195:33
thing in woman, 213:13
things difficult as rare, 276:19
things in counsels, 21:20
things that are more e., 41:10
to have giant's strength, 206:27
well a fishmonger, 198:31
what actions most e., 495:13
wretch, 208:35
Excellently, goddess e. bright, 232:2
Excellest, thou e. them all, 22:20
Excelleth, light e. darkness, 22:28
wisdom e. folly, 22:28
Excelling, cunningest pattern of e. nature, 210:14
Excels dunce kept at home, 326:11
quirks of blazoning pens, 208:12
Excelsior, 436:15
Excelsis, gloria in e. Deo, 47:22

Except a man be born again, 39:8
it die, 43:4
the Lord build the house, 19:4
the Lord keep the city, 19:4
the present company, 342:4
thou bless me, 7:3
Exception, in your case make e., 707:12
no rule admits not some e., 234:17
proves rule, 234:*n3*
Exceptional, thing that makes you e., 827:8
Exceptionally fine writing, 584:1
Excess, blasted with e. of light, 316:13
desire of power in e., 165:24
don't regret a single e., 545:6
give me e. of it, 204:10
in charity no e., 165:22
nothing in e., 121:1
of glory obscured, 255:24
of wealth cause of covetousness, 168:9
reform carried to e. needs reforming, 379:2
reproach to religion, 280:8
road of e. leads to palace of wisdom, 351:11
such e. of stupidity, 309:7
surprise by fine e., 413:1
wasteful and ridiculous e., 175:24
when love is in e., 67:19
Excessit, abiit e. evasit erupit, 87:*n4*
Excessive, bail nor e. fines, 340:7
dark with e. bright, 257:8
if national debt not e., 349:2
laughter, 31:8
Exchange, atheist-laugh's a poor e., 356:20
by just e. one for other, 162:14
cross for crown, 615:5
excellence for riches, 55:12
Exchequer of the poor, 176:30
Excise hateful tax, 307:1
those to whom e. paid, 307:1
Excitabat enim fluctus in simpulo, 88:*n6*
Excite my amorous propensities, 308:14
Excited abnormal condition, 565:16
passions not at will e., 449:2
reverie, 593:11
Excitement, beyond e. into anguish, 833:17
spiritual e., 497:5
Excites us to arms, 273:24
Exciting, found it less e., 528:1
politics almost e. as war, 619:1
Excluded, law of e. middle, 795:6
places women are e., 458:17
Excludes, kitsch e. everything, 824:5
Excommunicate, [corporations] cannot e., 158:25
Excrement, as if earth were e., 658:13
place of e., 596:1
Excremental bound up with sexual, 563:7
Excursion same for sorrow as joy, 761:1
Excuse, any e. will serve tyrant, 59:8
came prologue, 259:13
denial vain and coy e., 253:2
fault worse by e., 175:25
for the glass, 346:11
I will not e., 433:5
my dust, 699:19
never e., 179:16
play needs no e., 179:16

Excused from it as against my conscience, 317:9

Excuses himself accuses himself, 151:3
 ignorance e. no man, 238:12
 must be made, 706:3

Excusing, love shows by e. nothing, 267:23
 make fault worse, 175:25

Execrable shape, 256:26
 sum of all villainies, 301:16

Execute, by contraries e., 224:19
 villainy you teach me, 185:13

Executed, successfully e., 343:10

Execution of final solution of Jewish question, 697:14
 projected in reverse, 789:8
 seeing evildoers taken to e., 149:8

Executioner, hire e. to throw switch, 709:15
 I victim and e., 491:7
 man his own e., 248:15
 mine own e., 231:5
 the master e., 58:4

Executioners would be most learned, 143:13

Executions far from useful examples, 360:25
 for the master executioner, 58:4

Executive, judicial distinct from e., 330:4
 legislative nominated by e., 332:3
 of modern state, 478:9

Executors, let's choose e., 177:7

Exegi monumentum aere perennius, 97:n8

Exemplary, our lives in acts e., 163:18

Exemplum de simia, 126:n3

Exempt from public haunt, 193:37
 true nobility e. from fear, 170:12

Exercise, bodily e. when compulsory, 75:15
 free e. of religion, 332:1
 gratuitous e. every day, 540:21
 is yuppie version of, 852:2
 prohibiting free e. thereof, 340:1
 reading to mind as e. to body, 287:19
 sad mechanic e., 453:12
 their constitutional right, 445:5
 wise for cure on e. depend, 274:24

Exercises his mind with suffering, 80:6

Exertions, what people attained with e., 335:7

Exhalation, bright e. in evening, 225:23

Exhaled, sighs infrequent e., 676:7

Exhaust the little moment, 783:8

Exhausted, my body infirm and e., 140:1
 resources of civilization not e., 442:15
 Time winds th' e. chain, 357:20
 worlds imagined new, 306:9

Exhaustive, give accurate e. account, 612:16

Exhausts and murders itself, 330:15

Exhilarating to be shot at without result, 618:18

Exhilaration, enjoyed perfect e., 425:21

Exigencies, great e. of government, 470:15
 pressure of e. of life, 563:9

Exile, king in e., 663:7
 kiss long as my e., 220:2
 men in e. feed on dreams, 63:10
 sleep in e., 559:3
 to e. friends everything, 615:15
 universal truth of e., 841:2

Exiled on ground in jeers, 491:2

Exile's life is no life, 83:2

Exiles, band of e. moored bark, 405:5

Exist, criterion for being allowed to e., 843:8
 God is in me or does not e., 643:7
 how would man e. if God did not need him, 634:8
 if God did not e., 299:27
 pathos piety courage e., 638:12
 rather believe God not e., 432:15
 saint if God does not e., 770:4
 seeing stars that ceased to e., 645:23
 since earth began to e., 327:12
 sir I e., 609:3
 time did not e. previously, 125:1
 true democracy never will e., 312:18
 we e. alone, 611:3
 why we and universe e., 854:3

Existed, true democracy never e., 312:18

Existence and world eternally justified, 547:11
 anxiety belongs to e., 668:19
 believing in his e., 645:23
 brief crack of light, 723:3
 ceased to notice e. of students, 723:10
 conscious of our own e., 78:11
 culture no prospect of continued e., 563:15
 determination to develop own e., 633:11
 essential relationship to e., 469:6
 every species come into e., 501:3
 fret of e., 725:11
 knowledge enlarges sphere of e., 363:10
 life hollow e. burden, 522:7
 lived purely airborne e., 850:8
 more beloved e., 396:3
 mystery of universal e., 416:16
 nature owes me another e., 343:23
 one way of tolerating e., 493:19
 posthumous e., 413:18
 precedes essence, 743:4
 precisely an e., 511:8
 real and ratified e., 477:n2
 saw him spurn reign, 306:9
 spoke herself into e. as nation, 363:3
 Struggle for E., 440:1
 struggle for e., 630:2
 teach men sense of e., 547:18
 truth find e., 568:4
 unacceptable in human e., 824:5
 woman's whole e., 398:6

Existential, enslavement and e. death, 816:1

Existing like light around body, 811:5

Exists a great chasm, 757:14
 everything e. nothing has value, 638:12
 language for something that already e., 378:17
 nowhere but in yourself, 604:8

Exit pursued by a bear, 223:19
 strategy, 806:5
 wheresoever called to make e., 341:10

Exits and their entrances, 194:25
 doors for men to take their e., 237:7

Exodus, mysterious E. of death, 437:8

Expand, passions we feel e. time, 610:17

Expanding conflict to all China, 661:12
 in summer fires, 867:1

Expanse, green and brown e., 686:12
 oft of one wide e. had I been told, 408:17

Expansion, not a breach but an e., 229:16

Expansive, containment of Russian e. tendencies, 738:8

Ex-parrot, this is an e., 879:8

Expatiate free o'er scene of man, 294:14

Expect Saint Martin's summer, 169:12
 something for nothing, 557:9

Expectantly, folded her hair e., 488:4

Expectation, better bettered e., 190:11
 oft e. fails, 206:2
 whirls me round, 203:15

Expected, least e. happens, 429:22

Expects, blessed man who e. nothing, 294:10
 England e., 355:12

Expediency determines form, 671:4
 evil on ground of e., 571:3

Expedient, all things not e., 42:21
 as lighting by gas, 442:12
 that one die, 39:35

Expedition, so ended Sicilian e., 72:9

Expeditionary, Allied E. Force, 686:13

Expelled, Asia and Africa e. freedom, 333:2
 Bourbons twice e., 477:n2
 or worse e., 879:3

Expend, silkworm e. her yellow labors, 234:4

Expendable, we were e., 803:14

Expende Hannibalem, 109:n14

Expense, at the e. of man, 706:3
 dog is item of e., 569:6
 great e. may be essential, 325:13
 of spirit in waste of shame, 222:20
 pretend to restrain e., 319:4

Expenses, consider my traveling e., 699:1
 work stops e. run on, 85:2

Expensive, nothing so e. as glory, 374:23
 politics e., 640:8
 sleek e. girls I teach, 814:14

Experience, accumulated e., 630:2
 an arch, 451:13
 arch to build upon, 531:7
 arranged in order, 532:18
 believe one who has e., 95:n4
 causes of future e., 541:15
 Court bows to e., 562:14
 customs shape e., 669:3
 effects of past e., 541:15
 encounter reality of e., 650:13
 expression of human e., 602:4
 gladly beyond any e., 701:15
 gone to end in e., 631:18
 has given no access, 549:10
 home where small e. grows, 173:8
 ignorant in spite of e., 305:11
 keeps dear school, 302:23
 knowledge not personal e., 75:3
 lamp of e., 331:11
 Liberal tempered by e., 497:9
 life of law, 538:3
 make me sad, 195:24
 mind heavy with useless e., 824:15
 Mother of Sciences, 156:12
 my own meandering e., 871:12
 name for mistakes, 560:11
 no knowledge beyond e., 275:5
 not fruit of e. but e., 534:7
 of this sweet life, 130:9
 Old Age and E., 281:4
 optimist never had much e., 635:8
 pushed beyond facts, 567:n1
 relations between aspects of e., 662:2
 substitute for e. is art and literature, 791:8

Experience *(continued)*
  teaches dangerous moment, 434:9
  tells in every soil, 322:4
  travel part of e., 165:28
  triumph of hope over e., 309:13
  what e. and history teach, 367:9
  whole past e. in consciousness, 534:17
  wisdom acting upon e., 308:6
  write from e. only, 544:9
Experienced, nothing real till e., 413:13
Experiences, evidence for God in inner e.,
  542:7
  in solitude, 541:18
  shared e., 365:6
  strong man digests e., 548:18
  way full of adventures and e., 583:11
Experiencing suffering to full, 611:5
Experiment, all life is e., 538:22
  convinced of imbecility by e., 307:25
  entrusted to American people, 328:11
  every e. like weapon, 145:2
  in anarchy, 874:1
  mad and lamentable e., 584:2
  reason and e. indulged, 336:6
  to me every one I meet, 510:10
  treacherous, 71:6
  we are not the only e., 705:16
Experimental, all poetry e. poetry, 643:4
  philosophy, 279:12
  youth is wholly e., 556:13
Experimentation active science, 468:11
  bold persistent e., 651:15
Experimented with marijuana, 863:2
Experiments, eclipses of moon and other e.,
  139:12
  I love fools' e., 441:2
  novel social and economic e., 562:12
  sure e. and demonstrated arguments,
  155:7
Expert, believe an e., 95:11
  knows more about less, 581:3
Expertly beaten up, 798:7
Experto credite, 95:*n*4
Experts, divine right of e., 703:4
Expire, clever hopes e., 748:16
  lamps e., 599:16
Expires, unawares Morality e., 297:6
Explain, can't e. myself said Alice, 514:3
  his explanation, 397:18
  law is but let me e. once more, 749:8
  owe it to e. why, 782:9
  spoil it by trying to e., 346:8
  till all men doubt, 297:5
  time will e. all, 68:17
  we may touch love e., 815:4
  you e. nothing O poet, 601:10
Explained, not die before we have e. ourselves,
  330:14
  shut up he e., 662:9
  simplicity itself once e., 573:15
Explainer, Ezra Pound was village e., 628:3
Explaining, surrender e. not acting, 617:4
Explanation, explain his e., 397:18
  inaccuracy saves e., 608:9
Expletives their feeble aid do join, 292:17
Explicable, beauties more palpable and e.,
  301:7
  thanks to poet things e., 601:10

Explode, or does it e., 731:9
Exploit my opponent's youth and inexperience,
  765:15
Exploitation, ultimate sanction of e., 698:4
Exploits, capitalism system where man e. man,
  792:3
  fond of relating own e., 276:8
Exploration, not cease from e., 679:12
Explore, came to e. wreck, 825:8
  falter or e., 797:14
  unconscious, 572:7
Explorers, old men ought to be e., 679:2
  scientists detectives and e., 780:4
Exploring, end of e. to arrive, 679:12
Exponent of Earth, 510:3
Exposed, intellect improperly e., 374:25
  left e. a Friend, 510:2
  on bare earth e. he lies, 274:18
Exposition of sleep upon me, 178:33
Expounding, it is a constitution we are e.,
  349:14
Express, don't dare to e. it, 797:6
  flowery tale, 410:13
  hand may e. more than face, 431:19
  it in numbers, 501:11
Expressed even such a beauty, 222:9
  monitor e., 372:7
  ne'er so well e., 292:13
  not e. in fancy, 197:23
Expresses, this young man e. himself, 526:10
Expressing emotion in art, 675:20
Expression, borrow shape to find e., 675:8
  freedom of e. matrix, 607:4
  freedom of speech and e., 653:4
  impassioned e., 369:3
  individuality of e. end of art, 344:20
  natural e. of villainy, 522:6
  neutral e. she wore, 809:7
  of mediocrity of apparatus, 643:15
  of working of mind, 502:3
  scream e. of vestige of human dignity,
  722:15
  setting aside e. in words, 569:1
  spirit cries for e., 703:10
Expunge, fool enough to e., 310:23
Expunged, Nature's works to me e., 257:6
Exquisite passions, 534:4
  vigorous and e., 582:12
Extend freedom to everyone, 697:2
  system to this hemisphere, 355:7
Extended to display its patterns, 62:21
Extent, full e. of its own value, 364:9
Extenuate, it is vain sir to e., 331:13
  nothing e., 210:20
Exterminate all the brutes, 567:16
Exterminating one another to last man, 563:17
Extermination camps intimated, 728:15
  of the Jewish race, 684:14
  threat of common e., 794:11
External artistries in circumstance, 536:14
  differ in e. forms, 309:15
  falseness in impressions of e., 484:7
  reimpressed by e. ordinances, 307:16
  these e. regions, 642:7
  world super-ego and id, 563:19
Extinct, aristocracy becomes e., 364:12
  Dodo invented for becoming e., 659:11
  our name not become e., 507:12

Extinction, continual e. of personality, 675:18
  from apathy, 722:14
  universe faces future e., 836:4
Extinguish hope from soul, 559:8
Extinguished, his soul, 444:11
  nature seldom e., 166:11
  prey of fear he e., 671:14
  theologians, 502:2
Extol, how shall we e. thee, 580:19
Extolling past, 375:13
Extra, add some e. just for you, 799:15
Extracted from many objects, 195:23
Extracting sunbeams of cucumbers, 285:2
Extraordinary, results of idealism e., 562:15
  youth the time for e. toil, 75:14
Extravagance, beauty without e., 71:15
  calls his e. generosity, 322:19
  if e. but little is left, 85:1
  of her evil, 53:15
Extravagant and erring spirit, 196:18
  flaunting e. quean, 346:11
Extreme, all evils equal when e., 249:12
  fear neither fight nor fly, 172:33
  for e. diseases e. strictness, 71:7
  in quest to have e., 222:20
  justice extreme injustice, 121:18
  justice often injustice, 86:*n*3
  law often extreme injustice, 86:3
  of wickedness or folly, 445:7
  perplexed in the e., 210:20
  political good carried to e., 360:24
  reformers have been bachelors, 557:8
  savage e. rude cruel, 222:20
Extremes, change of fierce e., 256:25
  meet, 334:9
Extremism in defense of liberty, 758:10
Extremist, what kind of e. we will be, 823:5
Extremity, daring pilot in e., 272:16
Exuberance, irrational e., 812:17
Exult, be secret and e., 592:11
  O shores ring O bells, 487:17
Exultantly, walk not on earth e., 118:14
Exultations agonies, 370:8
Exulting, people all e., 487:16
Eye, adds precious seeing to the e., 174:22
  affection beaming in one e., 464:34
  altering all, 756:15
  an unforgiving e., 346:12
  apple of the e., 15:13
  Athens the e. of Greece, 260:2
  beam in thine own e., 33:13
  beauty bought by judgment of e., 174:8
  beauty in e. of beholder, 561:12
  beginnings of things not distinguished by
  e., 89:14
  begins to see, 756:11
  beholding beauty with e. of mind, 74:6
  bigger than belly, 244:26
  cast cold e., 597:11
  cast longing e. on offices, 337:6
  casts a sheep's e., 157:9
  chips fall in e., 880:9
  close e. of day, 253:17
  connections of ear closer than e., 572:16
  corn high as elephant's e., 706:9
  cursed me with his e., 376:12
  defiance in their e., 322:2
  divorced from e. and bone, 713:4

Eye *(continued)*

drunkard's e., 595:6
dust hath closed Helen's e., 227:6
easier to go through e. of needle, 35:4
equal e. as God, 294:18
essential is invisible to e., 726:18
every old man's e., 180:18
evil e. that looks to mood apart, 624:16
far as human e. see, 452:2
fettered to her e., 266:1
for eye, 8:17
fringed curtains of thine e., 224:15
glad me with soft black e., 388:3
glittering e., 375:17
God caught e., 714:17
gray e. glances, 448:7
great e. of heaven, 160:5
had but one e., 464:14
half hidden from the e., 369:7
harmony in her bright e., 265:16
harvest of a quiet e., 369:11
hath not seen, 42:6
hearing ear seeing e., 21:11
I have good e. uncle, 190:24
I have only one e., 355:9
if thy right e. offend, 32:18
ignorant e., 641:20
in my mind's e. Horatio, 197:8
intent on mazy plan, 358:2
interest unborrowed from e., 368:10
inward e., 371:13
is not satisfied with seeing, 22:23
jaundiced e., 292:24
lack-luster e., 194:15
language in her e., 204:4
lend e. terrible aspect, 189:7
less than meets e., 733:13
lifting up a fearful e., 167:1
light of the body is e., 33:3
like Mars, 201:5
locked and frozen in e., 749:5
locked up from mortal e., 263:4
looked into e. of day, 595:1
looks with threatening e., 175:21
love comes in at e., 592:6
made quiet by power, 368:9
many an e. danced, 443:3
mild and magnificent e., 460:12
moist e. dry hand, 187:31
Monet is only an e., 533:18
mote in brother's e., 33:13
my e. and God's are one, 127:14
my face in thine e., 228:8
my great Taskmaster's e., 250:17
my striving e. dazzles, 269:1
Nature's walks, 294:15
negotiate for itself, 190:26
neighbor as possible enemy, 614:4
nothing situate under heaven's e.,
    172:15
now mine e. seeth thee, 14:38
of childhood, 215:23
of heaven shined bright, 160:5
of heaven to garnish, 175:24
of lip of e. of brow, 222:9
of man hath not heard, 179:4
of newt toe of frog, 216:27
of saint, 595:6

Eye *(continued)*

of trilobite, 435:23
one auspicious e., 196:22
places e. of heaven visits, 176:16
poet's e. in fine frenzy, 179:6
putting mind's e. in book, 795:6
rude e. of rebellion, 176:1
sail with unshut e., 494:13
saw through glass e. darkly, 524:6
see e. to e., 27:4
see for hand not mind, 474:5
see with e. serene, 371:7
see with half an e., 157:31
see with not through e., 354:17
seeing seven and seventy divils, 611:14
seller needs not one e., 244:6
set honor in one e., 191:23
smile in her e., 415:12
smile on lips tear in e., 373:12
sober coloring from e., 371:5
soul fix intellectual e., 415:16
still-soliciting e., 210:30
such a wistful e., 561:1
such beauty as woman's e., 174:20
tender e. of pitiful day, 216:13
that sun thine e., 221:14
thoughts legible in the e., 169:9
to a discerning E., 509:4
tongue sword, 200:2
twinkling of e., 43:8
vacant heart hand e., 374:11
vanquished by space, 158:18
view with hollow e., 186:7
wearing-stone or open e., 623:3
wet e. dhry heart, 600:11
what immortal hand or e., 353:1
when first your e. I eyed, 222:8
which girls hath merriest e., 169:15
wishing his foot equal with e., 170:27
with my little e., 893:9
Eyeball, I become transparent e., 425:22
    to eyeball, 888:17
Eye-beams, our e. twisted, 229:18
Eyebrow, mistress' e., 194:25
Eyed, when first your eye I e., 222:8
Eye-deep in hell, 665:8
Eyeless in Gaza, 260:8
Eyelids a little weary, 534:4
    from e. dripped love, 54:15
    from e. wiped tear, 194:22
    heavy and red, 418:8
    of the morn, 253:3
    slumber to mine e., 19:9
    take thee with her e., 20:2
    tinged e. and hands, 534:5
    tired e. upon tired eyes, 450:17
    weigh e. down, 188:9
Eyes, all things flourish where you turn e.,
    292:6
ancient glittering e., 596:11
and back turn upward, 676:12
and see not, 27:25
as in a theater e. of men, 177:21
asked him with e. to ask again, 650:18
attentive e., 308:3
avenged for my two e., 10:25
before streaming e., 516:7
began to roll, 296:26

Eyes *(continued)*

beheld God nature through their e.,
    425:19
bleared with tears, 122:8
blood-hot e., 704:16
bright e. of danger, 556:5
burning e., 819:12
burnt fire of thine e., 353:1
buyer needs a hundred e., 244:6
candid brow pure e., 567:11
cast mine e. and see, 241:14
cast one's e. so low, 212:24
close e. with holy dread, 377:23
close up his e. and draw curtain, 170:9
closed e. in endless night, 316:13
confess secrets of heart, 115:13
craters of my e. gape, 836:2
crossed with direct e., 676:20
cry my e. out, 156:30
cynosure of neighboring e., 251:3
death come close e., 882:2
deeper than depth, 505:23
desires in e. that looked at you, 583:12
die before our own e., 552:13
dreaming e. of wonder, 515:10
drink to me only with thine e., 232:16
dry e. laugh at fall, 461:7
dust thrown in my e., 623:17
eagle e., 408:17
elves whose little e. glow, 241:7
eternity was in our e., 218:7
eyelids upon tired e., 450:17
face facts with both e. open, 142:13
fields have e. woods have ears, 134:15
fix e. on greatness of Athens, 72:4
foe with fearless e., 582:8
fortune and men's e., 221:5
fountains fraught with tears, 163:7
from kindness cannot take e., 593:15
from starlike e. seek, 245:18
from those great e., 438:6
from women's e. this doctrine, 174:24
full of e. within, 46:28
gasp and stretch e., 606:12
gather to the e., 452:21
get thee glass e., 212:31
get weary head turns grey, 673:2
gone under earth's lid, 665:9
good for sore e., 285:14
had I your tongues and e., 213:12
hands only serve e., 472:19
hath not a Jew e., 185:11
have seen glory, 481:1
have their silence, 701:15
have they but see not, 18:22
having e. see not, 331:10
he has ears and two e., 467:5
he turned up his e., 352:4
Heaven before mine e., 251:23
her aspect and her e., 397:1
her e. were wild, 412:3
him who has e. to see, 502:6
his e. are blue, 794:6
his e. are in his mind, 178:*n*1
his e. were enlightened, 10:42
his flashing e., 377:23
I will lift up mine e., 18:30
I will not give sleep to mine e., 19:9

F

Face *(continued)*
  pardoned all except f., 398:24
  Pity has a human f., 351:4
  placid f. upon the pillow, 513:7
  plain as nose in f., 146:2
  poor lean lank f., 444:9
  prism and silent f., 368:16
  round jolly fruitful f., 444:*n*1
  sages have seen in thy f., 326:17
  saw manners in f., 308:3
  sea's f. and gray dawn, 635:15
  see another f. so frail, 817:6
  sees other's umbered f., 189:18
  set my ten commandments in your f.,
    169:24
  shining morning f., 194:25
  smiling f. dream of Spring, 378:14
  smiling in my f., 215:5
  socialism with human f., 796:5
  soft f. of a girl, 65:25
  sorrows of changing f., 591:6
  strong men f. to f., 587:8
  surrenders his f. to God, 119:4
  take a good look at my f., 849:4
  that launched a thousand ships, 168:21
  this fair f. the cause, 168:*n*5
  this sunburnt f., 350:15
  thou canst not see my f., 8:21
  thy classic f., 447:12
  touched f. of God, 800:1
  truth showing its f. undisguised, 64:3
  turn your f. toward past, 568:9
  turned f. with ghastly pang, 376:12
  visit her f. too roughly, 196:31
  was a chipped chunk, 836:6
  wear one face to himself, 431:9
  whole f. of world changed, 269:13
  why bidest thou thy f. from me, 17:22
  wish I loved silly f., 579:15
  with twain he covered his f., 25:8
  worst thing about him, 206:23
Faced, history f. with courage, 817:14
Face's, viewed in her fair f. field, 172:30
Faces all gather blackness, 29:6
  bid them wash their f., 219:27
  draw living f. from marble, 94:35
  dusk f. with silken turbans, 259:34
  estranged f., 577:4
  fools' names like fools' f., 883:11
  grind the f. of the poor, 24:37
  hearts do in the f. rest, 228:8
  in the crowd, 665:1
  lords and owners of their f., 222:2
  millions of f. none alike, 105:*n*2
  of coffee-pickers, 662:6
  of Negro school-children, 788:2
  old familiar f., 383:3
  put on two several f., 277:6
  sea of upturned f., 374:9
  sweat of other men's f., 447:1
  Thracian ships foreign f., 529:12
  worldly f. never look so wordly, 480:1
Facets, iceberg cuts f. from within, 762:12
Facias ipse quod faciamus suades, 84:*n*3
Facile, plus f. de faire la guerre, 537:*n*2
Facilis descensus Averni, 94:*n*12
Facing fearful odds, 419:19
  man who sits f. you, 56:5

Façon, je veux qu'on m'y voit en ma f., 151:*n*6
Fact, belief help create f., 541:14
  Caspian F., 510:16
  death ugly f. Nature hides, 512:11
  falsehood more miraculous than f., 311:24
  fatal futility of F., 544:18
  firm ground of F., 618:16
  frontiers wherever man fronts f., 473:25
  idea is the f., 497:20
  impressive f. about American women,
    800:8
  irritable reaching after f., 412:15
  knife-edge of mere f., 824:15
  natural f. spiritual f., 425:24
  of the Everglades, 686:12
  slaying of hypothesis by ugly f., 502:8
  state one f. belie another, 426:13
  superiority in f. of conservatism, 427:18
  that great f., 439:11
  thought counterparts in f., 490:13
  yesterday f. today doctrine, 339:3
Fact-finding more effective than fault-finding,
  615:4
Faction a number of citizens, 345:8
  danger of f., 345:10
Factions, old religious f., 325:11
Factor, timing is most important f., 54:27
Factories may make end of war, 518:8
Factors, gods as psychic f., 630:5
  women economic f. in society, 579:1
Factory windows always broken, 639:12
Facts alarm more than principles, 339:10
  all f. when come to brass tacks, 677:4
  alone wanted in life, 466:14
  are counterrevolutionary, 730:9
  are fitted round afterwards, 663:19
  are sacred, 550:10
  are stubborn things, 286:18, 329:11
  at first seem improbable, 167:17
  collection of f. not science, 558:8
  drop cloak stand forth naked, 167:17
  emphatic f. of history, 426:12
  front essential f. of life, 474:29
  if Lord knew f. iv case, 600:12
  ignorance inert f., 532:2
  ignore f. of history, 765:14
  imagination baffled by f., 620:4
  imagination for f., 346:20
  inert f., 532:2
  judges of f. not laws, 291:6
  large collections of f., 441:3
  looking toward f., 542:6
  of life do not penetrate, 610:12
  passions cannot alter f., 329:11
  personages appear twice, 477:14
  politics ignoring f., 532:1
  power most serious of f., 532:3
  science built with f., 558:8
  we poor passing f., 788:14
  what I want is F., 466:14
Faculties, borne his f. so meek, 214:24
  each according to his f., 469:14
  men free to develop f., 562:8
  t' affections and to f., 229:19
  whose f. can comprehend, 168:2
Faculty, infinite in f., 199:5
  of continuing to improve, 327:12
  of dying or adapting, 521:7

Faculty *(continued)*
  unshackled exercise of every f., 422:2
Fade as a leaf, 27:18
  burn out than to f. away, 862:7
  far away, 410:5
  first to f. away, 388:3
  into light of common day, 370:18
  loveliness f., 387:9
  lovely things f. and die, 683:4
  may flourish or may f., 322:22
  nothing of him that doth f., 224:14
  old soldiers f. away, 644:11, 887:4
  thy eternal summer not f., 221:3
Faded and gone, 387:11
  but still lovely woman, 710:14
  care sat on his f. cheek, 255:26
  flowers of friendship f., 627:20
  friendship f., 627:20
  insubstantial pageant f., 225:1
  oldest colors f., 587:12
  on crowing of the cock, 196:19
Fades glimmering landscape, 315:12
  out from kiss to kiss, 591:19
Fadeth, crown of glory that f. not, 46:2
  flower f., 26:27
Fading, bestows the f. rose, 245:14
  down the river, 582:10
  fading, 677:15
  in music, 185:16
  order is rapidly f., 851:5
Faery, Land of F., 591:7
  lands forlorn, 410:10
Faery's child, 412:3
Faggot, flames no f. feeds, 595:11
Faggots, some burn damp f., 592:17
Fagots, diadems and f., 424:23
Fags are great immoralists, 761:11
Fail, again f. better, 745:3
  audience never f. to laugh, 73:13
  desire shall f., 23:31
  from eternity shall not f., 575:15
  if we should f., 215:6
  let no man's heart f., 10:45
  mission continue to f., 556:11
  not ashamed to f., 306:14
  not f. that rendezvous, 682:7
  not flag or f., 619:14
  old stories when we f., 861:1
  possible to f. in many ways, 78:7
  sooner f. than not among greatest,
    413:7
  this could not f., 446:1
  we'll not f., 215:6
Failed, fluttered f. for breath, 495:20
  if cannot use talent, 727:14
  most editors f. writers, 679:16
  therefore turn critics, 378:20
  tried a little f. much, 556:3
Faileth, enemy faints not nor f., 479:12
  forsake me not when strength f., 17:11
Failing, bulwark never f., 143:16
  from f. hands we throw torch, 614:7
  tell aloud greatest f., 285:7
  that the rest of the city, 75:5
Fails, if heart f. climb not, 159:*n*3
  my voice f. me, 323:20
  oft expectation f., 206:2
  persuades when speaking f., 223:15

Faith (*continued*)

he who has courage and f., 822:4
holy f., 469:15
humor prelude to f., 696:5
if f. o'ercomes doubt, 461:24
illogical belief in improbable, 645:10
in result makes result, 541:12
in this f. I will live and die, 139:1
is sight and knowledge, 472:19
is the substance of things hoped for, 45:11
kept the f., 45:2
living f. of the dead, 803:12
man's seeming need for f., 780:13
many a man's soul and f., 857:5
martyrs create f., 586:3
more f. in honest doubt, 454:5
mystery of f., 47:25
no f. in immortality, 439:5
no more despair or loss of f., 791:5
nonviolence article of f., 604:3
nor love nor law, 402:1
not create martyrs, 586:3
not f. but philosophy, 248:11
not for all his f. see, 424:4
now abideth f., 42:29
O thou of little f., 34:29
O ye of little f., 33:29
of our fathers, 469:15
pin f. in things not seen, 112:23
plain and simple f., 193:6
Punic f., 92:12
reaffirm f. in human rights, 661:16
reason greatest enemy f. has, 144:9
sanctified by reason blest by f., 369:2
saved by f., 696:6
sea of f., 496:19
shell universe is to ear of F., 372:7
shines equal arming me, 476:14
show doubt prove f., 461:24
simple f. than Norman blood, 451:3
staff of f. to walk upon, 159:10
stand fast in f., 43:10
still by f. he trod, 639:10
that could remove mountains, 42:27
that yields to none, 101:21
thy f. hath saved thee, 37:28
walk by f. not sight, 43:15
want of enterprise and f., 475:12
wears f. as fashion of hat, 190:15
welcome home discarded f., 176:1
when f. lost honor dies, 438:6
where f. in reason timid, 614:4
without risk no f., 469:7
without works, 45:26
you call for f., 461:24
Faithful Achates, 94:28
action f. honor clear, 294:9
among the faithless f., 258:21
are the wounds of a friend, 22:1
at all times f. husband, 288:22
Christian f. man, 171:27
elephant's f. one hundred per cent, 739:11
ever f., 121:15
falling out of f. friends, 85:*n*10
fierce wars and f. loves, 160:2
friend is medicine, 30:26
friend is strong defense, 30:25
good and f. servant, 35:26

Faithful (*continued*)

in least faithful in much, 38:16
in love, 373:10
long and f. service, 468:19
love is f., 137:11
O come all ye f., 120:5
Penelope, 54:9
three f. friends, 302:17
to conviction to old age, 76:13
to his superiors, 60:17
to thee Cynara, 599:14
to what exists in yourself, 604:8
unto death, 46:22
women all alike, 649:14
Faithfully to serve State, 246:15
Faithfulness, His infinite f., 283:2
to duty, 420:8
Faithless, among the f. faithful, 258:21
arm, 748:10
as a smile, 675:14
be not f., 40:12
in friendship but f. haven, 65:7
Faith's Defender, 297:18
Faiths, fighting f., 538:22
men's f. wafer-cakes, 189:6
old f. loosen and fall, 530:9
Fakes, windpipe throttled in f. of death, 486:10
Fakir, powers of levitation make f. stare, 678:12
Falcon, dapple-dawn-drawn F., 546:9
gentle as f., 141:2
like a f. swooping, 3:11
not hear falconer, 593:9
towering in her pride, 216:3
Falconer, falcon not hear f., 593:9
Falconer's, O for a f. voice, 180:13
Falklands, the F. thing, 719:9
Fall, a thousand shall f. at thy side, 17:28
Anarch lets curtain f., 297:6
baseball leaves you face f. alone, 844:8
benison to f., 241:15
bigger they come harder f., 69:*n*7
both f. into ditch, 34:32
by dividing we f., 328:1
can't f. into love, 824:14
cradle will f., 550:7
decline and f. of Rome, 332:19
desire of power caused angels to f., 165:24
divided we f., 328:*n*1
down can f. no lower, 262:14
dying f., 204:10
fain climb yet fear to f., 159:6
fear no f., 271:25
flat on your face, 704:10
flower displayed doth f., 205:1
forts of folly f., 497:3
glass f. forever, 751:2
good to gain day good to f., 486:2
half to rise half to f., 295:1
harder they come harder they f., 866:2
haughty spirit before a f., 20:37
he that trusteth in riches shall f., 20:15
hero perish or sparrow f., 294:18
Humpty Dumpty had f., 895:1
I f. into Charybdis, 185:25
if Freedom f., 590:6
if you stay price will f., 166:2
in love with Athens, 72:4
in with what asked to accept, 625:10

Fall (*continued*)

into hands of Carl Sandburg, 708:16
into Scylla to avoid Charybdis, 185:*n*1
leaves f. early, 664:18
let f. the curtains, 327:1
let sword of France f., 686:7
lie talking of f. of man, 475:32
like a bright exhalation, 225:23
like one of the princes, 17:17
liquid siftings f., 676:2
not a sparrow f., 34:4
O what a f. was there, 193:1
of a sparrow, 202:26
one by one, 323:16
out and chide and fight, 289:7
pride will have a f., 66:*n*2
Satan as lightning f., 37:34
silence f. like dews, 666:3
since Adam's f., 592:1
soar not too high to f., 237:16
some by virtue f., 206:20
some rain must f., 436:14
stars begin to f., 898:24
take heed lest he f., 42:20
things f. apart, 593:9
though china f., 294:4
though heaven f. thy will be done, 121:14
through air of true wise friend, 764:1
to doom a long way, 609:1
to reprobation, 210:17
to the base earth, 177:2
tyrants f. in every foe, 358:17
universe must one day f., 795:5
unless billboards f., 732:8
upon gilded eaves, 453:1
upon thorns of life, 402:12
water reach rest and f., 713:5
what if sky were to f., 86:2
wide arch of ranged empire f., 218:3
wit on other souls may f., 273:14
woods decay and f., 455:5
Fall, die Welt ist alles was der F. ist, 685:*n*1
Fallacy, Pathetic F., 484:7
Fallen at length that tower, 454:16
Babylon is f., 25:27, 47:5
be forever f., 255:18
by the edge of the sword, 31:13
by the tongue, 31:13
cold and dead, 487:17
fallen fallen fallen, 274:18
from grace, 43:29
from his high estate, 274:18
how are mighty f., 11:9
how art thou f., 25:22
imagined despair f. upon me, 415:1
in love with world, 764:15
into the sere, 217:18
lines are f. unto me, 15:12
moon stars f. on me, 661:1
on evil days, 258:25
prince and great man f., 11:12
so f. so lost, 438:5
soldier's pole is f., 219:5
speak for f. and weak, 481:9
strength like f. angel, 409:4
what will I do when you f., 772:10
Fallest a blessed martyr, 226:5
if thou f. O Cromwell, 226:5

Fallible men governed by bad passions, 336:7
    will of another f. being, 360:18
Falling, adjusted to beams f., 702:7
    catch a f. star, 228:9
    cruelty to load f. man, 225:*n*2
    dropped like f. star, 256:5
    gently f. on thy head, 289:10
    in love at first sight, 587:2
    in melody back, 378:2
    of a leaf, 483:11
    on dark central plain, 650:9
    out of faithful friends, 85:*n*10
    press not f. man, 225:24
    salmon jumping f. back, 788:5
    softly on Bog of Allen, 650:9
    what's this am I f., 506:13
    when heaven f., 575:20
    with f. oars kept time, 267:7
Falling-off, what a f. was there, 198:9
Fallow, came a f. doe, 890:4
Falls, as long divorce of steel f., 225:15
    brightness f. from the air, 227:6
    Coliseum Rome fall, 396:14
    force without wisdom f. of own weight,
      96:28
    howls hoo and f., 642:2
    into abatement, 204:11
    like Lucifer, 225:25
    nature f. into revolt, 188:21
    nips his root then he f., 225:25
    ripest fruit first f., 176:27
    splendor f. on castle, 452:19
    the Shadow, 677:1
    thy shadow Cynara, 599:16
    with leaf in October, 236:5
False Achitophel was first, 272:16
    ambition drove men to become f., 92:5
    and hollow, 256:11
    as air as water, 203:20
    as common fame, 281:5
    as Cressid, 203:20
    as dicers' oaths, 201:3
    as tears of crocodiles, 163:*n*4
    as water, 210:16
    betrayed by f. within, 505:10
    burn out f. shames, 663:13
    by philosopher equally f., 332:2
    creation from brain, 215:13
    distinguish true from f., 276:1
    face dress voice all f., 341:12
    face must hide, 215:8
    fictions only and f. hair, 242:18
    framed to make women f., 208:10
    from f. to f., 203:20
    gallop of verses, 195:8
    history must be f., 290:3
    how f. the argument, 90:*n*1
    idea of what true and f., 276:1
    idle and f. imposition, 208:29
    idol or noble true birth, 76:5
    if I be f. or swerve, 203:20
    in friendship f., 272:19
    little better than f. knaves, 191:7
    maids in love, 203:20
    man does easy, 216:2
    never be f., 465:26
    never say I was f. of heart, 222:11
    not f. to others, 166:4

False *(continued)*
    or honest dreaming, 797:11
    philosophy, 256:22
    prophet, 696:2
    prophets, 33:20
    proved true before prove f., 262:21
    punishment if one swears f. oath, 52:10
    ring out the f., 454:8
    sea shows f. alluring smile, 90:6
    shoot f. Love, 881:11
    that which accepted f., 612:11
    to any man, 197:24
    to object, 748:7
    to two or three, 228:11
    understanding is f. mirror, 164:20
    what f. heart doth know, 215:8
    witness against thy neighbor, 8:14
    witness by their own mouth, 31:31
    words infect the soul, 74:16
Falsehood, flattery and f., 339:8
    God's mouth knows not f., 63:19
    goodly outside f. hath, 184:27
    has to be invented, 649:2
    history belief in f., 496:*n*1
    let her and F. grapple, 254:14
    Mississippi of f., 496:11
    more miraculous than fact, 311:24
    no f. lingers to old age, 66:25
    no word to express lying and f., 285:3
    not veil truth with f., 117:12
    of the tongue, 336:11
    stick the heart of f., 203:20
    strife of Truth with F., 481:12
    time's glory to unmask f., 172:35
    truth f. to world beyond, 152:21
    upbraid my f., 203:20
    your bait of f., 198:23
Falsehoods, we know how to speak f., 54:12
    which interest dictates, 307:5
Falsely, deal f. with God, 239:16
    paint f. and add accent of nature, 519:7
    science f. so called, 44:38
Falseness in impressions of external, 484:7
Falser than vows made in wine, 195:22
    tomorrow's f. than former day, 272:11
Falstaff in Arthur's bosom, 189:4
    sweats to death, 182:12
Falter life away, 495:15
    neither to change nor f. nor repent, 402:5
    or explore, 797:14
    when the Sun, 509:18
Fama volat, 94:*n*8
Fame created something of nothing, 250:6
    enjoying timeless f., 60:12
    estate good f., 424:14
    fair F. inspires, 295:13
    fool to f., 295:10
    foolish and false as f., 281:5
    for his f. the ocean sea, 233:13
    for pot of ale, 189:10
    from zone to zone, 539:19
    give me bitter f., 683:6
    great heir of f., 250:15
    Hall o' F. when you croaks, 681:4
    heard of the f. of Solomon, 11:33
    if not double-faced, 260:18
    is ephemeral, 112:3
    is food dead men eat, 535:9

Fame *(continued)*
    is no plant, 253:7
    is only sum of misunderstandings, 631:16
    is the spur, 253:6
    lives in f. died in virtue's cause, 172:42
    lost to f., 93:17
    love and f. to nothingness, 412:9
    nor F. I slight, 292:7
    nor yet fool to f., 295:10
    of her excellence, 54:9
    or country least their care, 483:21
    over living head bent, 403:20
    poets' food love and f., 402:8
    rather than love money f., 475:22
    Riches F. and Pleasure, 276:20
    ruins of another's f., 291:14
    thirst of youth, 395:22
    to fortune and f. unknown, 316:6
    trust to common f., 425:17
    was noised throughout the country, 10:1
    what is end of f., 398:7
    while f. elates thee, 387:5
    wisdom and prosperity exceedeth the f.,
      11:34
Famed in song famous Athens, 64:7
    Troy walls f. in battle, 94:13
Fame's eternal beadroll, 160:16
Familiar acts beautiful, 402:3
    as his garter, 188:33
    as rose in spring, 112:6
    be thou f., 197:22
    more f. with Africa, 834:12
    new things are made f., 307:21
    old and f. objects, 379:13
    old f. faces, 383:3
    sit at feet of the f., 426:7
    style f. but not coarse, 307:15
    things are made new, 307:21
    wine a good f. creature, 208:32
    with tragedies of antiquity, 843:6
Familiarity breeds contempt, 58:19
    breeds contempt and children, 58:*n*7
Families, best-regulated f., 465:32
    God setteth the solitary in f., 17:10
    happy f. alike, 507:3
    I hate you, 604:7
    lie together, 801:17
    rooks in f. go, 537:3
Familles je vous hais, 604:*n*3
Family, about man that left f., 523:3
    children of one f., 289:7
    church and private school, 498:7
    father of a f., 110:20
    greatest thing in f. life, 625:9
    history begins with me, 76:14
    in our f. no clear line, 731:16
    join the f., 623:18
    nobody not in f., 382:18
    of Man, 636:11
    party tribe or clan, 885:13
    refuse to help f., 600:2
    root of the state, 79:17
    stamped character on child, 630:8
    supporting f. paying taxes, 537:7
    unhappy f. unhappy in own way, 507:3
Famine Pestilence Destruction Death, 646:5
    seven years of f., 7:9
Famisht, I hear a f. howl, 773:4

Fam'ly, refuse to help f., 600:2
Famous Athens divine city, 64:7
  awoke and found myself f., 396:23
  by my sword, 262:24
  by their birth, 176:24
  day and year, 437:15
  earth sepulcher of f. men, 72:4
  forgotten for want of writers, 97:n11
  found that f. country, 695:2
  good time had by all, 752:6
  Hanover city, 460:6
  harmony of leaves, 591:4
  high top-hat, 639:16
  island descending, 619:7
  let us praise f. men, 31:26
  maiden f. to all time, 97:4
  make thee f. by my pen, 262:n2
  most f. event in biology, 821:n1
  to all ages, 254:4
  too f. too young, 720:14
  victory, 381:9
  world-f. for fifteen minutes, 817:1
Famoused, painful warrior f. for fight, 221:4
Fan, brain him with lady's f., 182:14
  cool gales f. the glade, 292:6
  like an injured f., 670:18
  with her f. spread, 287:3
Fanatic can't change mind, 621:17
  does what Lord wud do, 600:12
Fanatical, my f. will power, 684:16
Fanaticism redoubling efforts, 584:4
  to barbarism one step, 313:16
Fancies, high region of f., 253:19
  lay earthly f. down, 454:17
  our f. are more giddy, 204:34
  realities less dangerous than f., 615:4
Fanciful, no test which is not f., 66:11
Fancy, ever let f. roam, 411:3
  excellent f., 202:12
  from flower bell, 461:22
  full of shapes is f., 204:11
  hopeless f. feigned, 452:22
  I f. the face I face, 711:14
  is mode of memory, 379:7
  motives of more f., 206:12
  not expressed in f., 197:23
  not to f. what fair in life, 461:21
  now f. passes by, 574:17
  prose style, 723:6
  sweet and bitter f., 195:32
  where is f. bred, 185:17
  whispers of f., 307:8
  work of the brain and f., 277:28
  young man's f., 451:21
Fancy-free, maiden meditation f., 178:16
Fancy's, impediments in f. course, 206:12
  more witnesseth than f. images, 179:7
  Shakespeare F. child, 251:8
Faneuil Hall cradle of liberty, 390:21
Fangs, beware my f., 185:24
Fantasies, mingling of two f., 335:1
  thousand f. begin to throng, 252:12
  where gay f. come true, 849:7
Fantastic, light f. round, 252:11
  light f. toe, 250:22
  plays such f. tricks, 206:28
  reveries, 534:4
  summer's heat, 176:18

Fantastic (continued)
  tripped light f., 581:2
Fantastical, high f., 204:11
  old f. duke of dark corners, 207:11
Fantasy, begot of vain f., 179:26
  end this island f., 724:6
  goes for walk returns with bride, 775:7
  master of f., 559:10
  neurotic possessed by f., 743:15
  poet in command of f., 743:15
  suspicion rumor f., 824:15
  world writer takes seriously, 563:3
Far and few, 467:11
  and near unite, 332:20
  as coin would stretch, 181:24
  away from heart and eye, 405:1
  be it from God, 14:14
  brother f. off, 22:3
  do not peer too f., 63:24
  down within dim West, 448:2
  fair and softly goes f., 132:n5
  forward since we have come so f., 173:23
  from fiery noon, 411:12
  from madding crowd's, 316:3
  from old folks at home, 503:12
  from the sun, 316:11
  how f. candle throws beams, 186:18
  in the pillared dark, 624:9
  in western brookland, 575:8
  much too f. out all my life, 732:16
  o'er hills and f. away, 452:12
  on ringing plains of Troy, 451:13
  over hills and f. away, 291:17, 894:10
  peace to him that is f. off, 27:13
  side of baldness, 590:16
  slight not what's near by aiming f., 67:17
  so f. only should we hate, 65:7
  so f. trust thee Kate, 182:15
  so near yet so f., 454:6
  too f. bad as not f. enough, 61:8
  whistles f. and wee, 701:5
  why art thou so f. from helping me,
    15:21
Far East, those who brought war to F., 661:3
Far West, seek gold in F., 499:3
Farce, facts personages appear second as f.,
  477:14
  is played, 146:7
  Prologue to F. or Tragedy, 346:1
Farced title 'fore king, 189:23
Farcical, everything I touch f., 505:3
Fardels, who would f. bear, 199:21
Fare, bread and Gospel good f., 282:17
  delicate f. in another's house, 31:14
  forward, 84:n8
  forward voyagers, 679:6
  good-bye f. you well, 897:22
  last of Romans f. thee well, 193:20
  like my peers, 462:25
  thee well if forever, 397:6
Fares, how f. it with happy dead, 453:16
  ill f. the land, 322:22
Farewell all joys, 882:2
  also called F., 506:6
  and then forever, 357:8
  bid f. to every fear, 289:16
  bid joys f., 409:2
  content, 209:13

Farewell (continued)
  dear paintings, 247:7
  distracting town f., 293:20
  fair cruelty, 204:23
  fear farewell remorse, 257:13
  forever f. Cassius, 193:17
  goes out sighing, 203:24
  hail and f. my brother, 91:30
  hope, 257:13
  king, 177:9
  Leicester Square, 628:20
  lobster-nights f., 293:21
  Monsieur Traveler, 195:25
  Morning Star, 87:4
  my bok and my devocioun, 133:6
  neighing steed, 209:13
  only feel f., 394:8
  Othello's occupation's gone, 209:13
  plumed troop, 209:13
  renowned Eretria, 74:2
  rewards and fairies, 237:14
  sadness, 705:8
  sweets to the sweet f., 202:17
  the tranquil mind, 209:13
  thou art too dear, 221:27
  thou child of my right hand, 232:10
  to all my greatness, 225:25
  to college joys, 656:19
  to the Highlands, 357:14
  to thee farewell, 532:17
Farewells, as many f. as stars, 204:1
  should be sudden, 399:8
Far-flung battle line, 589:7
Farfrae, Elizabeth-Jane F. not told of my death,
  536:3
Farm, best business father's f., 458:4
  is like a man, 85:1
  keep 'em down on f., 664:1
  Middlesex village and f., 437:16
  snug little f. the world, 381:18
  spiritual dangers in not owning f., 668:3
  that is no more a f., 624:12
Farmer in the dell, 896:20
  sowing the corn, 897:8
Farmer's boy, 882:11
  wife, 892:10
Farmers, ah too fortunate f., 93:16
  embattled f. stood, 424:17
  founders of civilization, 390:15
  mechanics and laborers, 364:3
  pray that summers be wet, 93:11
  prison inmates than full-time f., 875:8
Farmhand, apple-faced f., 884:n3
Farmhouse, stop without f. near, 623:7
Farms, destroy f. grass will grow in streets,
  577:17
  houses and f. pillaged, 328:6
  what spires what f., 575:6
Far-off curfew sound, 251:17
  divine event, 454:12
  spies a f. shore, 170:27
Farquhar, Peyton F. was dead, 540:1
Far-reaching ancestry, 500:5
Farrier, Felix Randal the f., 546:15
Farrow, Ireland old sow that eats f., 650:10
Far-stretched, all the f. greatness, 159:15
Farther away on either hand, 695:6
  off from heaven, 418:3

Farthest Thule, 93:9
  Thulè, 301:1
  way home's the f. way, 242:4
Farthing, every f. of cost, 748:11
  hold f. candle to sun, 235:*n*5
  two sparrows sold for f., 34:4
Farthings, Latin word for three f., 174:12
  owe me five f., 893:6
Fas est et ab hoste doceri, 102:*n*10
Fascinate, blandishments not f. us, 341:10
Fascinates, work f. me, 576:7
Fascinating, when listen find noise f., 767:1
Fascination of what's difficult, 592:5
  war regarded wicked will have f., 559:22
  which expression exerts on us, 685:15
Fascist, no f. minded people drive me, 718:8
  woman adores F., 833:9
Fascists, This Machine Kills F., 768:6
Fashion born by facts trends politics, 688:14
  does not exist unless down streets, 655:2
  faithful in my f., 599:14
  glass of f. mould of form, 200:3
  guards secret well, 740:12
  high Roman f., 219:6
  is architecture, 655:3
  is made to become unfashionable, 655:1
  like rusty mail, 203:22
  mayest f. thyself in whatever shape, 141:3
  of these times, 194:6
  of this world passeth, 42:16
  seen in my natural f., 151:16
  true to you in my f., 691:16
  wears faith as f. of hat, 190:15
  wears out more apparel, 191:2
  worn-out poetical f., 678:16
Fashionable east seventies, 867:1
  New York Society, 504:2
  time like f. host, 203:24
Fashioned, gods f. by men, 584:12
  of water f. every living thing, 118:20
  so slenderly, 418:13
Fashion's word is out, 596:7
Fashions in proud Italy, 176:22
  not cut conscience to fit f., 741:12
  old f. please best, 173:15
Fast and furious, 358:8
  bound below the surface, 582:14
  driveth onward f., 450:19
  hit f. hit often, 650:4
  how f. shadows fall, 606:18
  ill weed groweth f., 147:20
  life in the f. lane, 865:14
  men die f. enough, 281:9
  not so f. we might arrive on time, 617:2
  now he is dead should I f., 11:20
  or come he f., 373:8
  ship that does not sail f., 342:1
  stumble that run f., 180:19
  they follow, 201:*n*2
  thick and f. came at last, 516:3
  thine arrows stick f. in me, 16:14
  wit speeds too f., 174:10
Fasted forty days and nights, 32:11
Fasten him as a nail, 25:30
  your seatbelts bumpy night, 759:4
Fastened me flesh, 546:5
  to dying animal, 594:3
  Venus f. to prey, 278:21

Faster, beat to follow f., 218:20
  faster, 515:15
  speed far f. than light, 618:1
  than speeding bullet, 777:1
  travel f. than stagecoach, 323:1
  walk a little f., 515:2
  world would go round f., 514:8
Fastest, travels f. alone, 587:6
Fastidiousness, unconscious f., 671:7
Fasting, lives on hope die f., 303:1
  thank heaven f., 195:20
  when full talk of f. easy, 115:16
Fat, all of us are f., 516:5
  and bean-fed horse, 178:12
  and greasy citizens, 194:2
  and sleek a true hog, 98:1
  black bucks, 639:13
  church ain't out till f. lady sings, 886:16
  contentions, 254:3
  duller than f. weed, 198:7
  eat the f. of the land, 7:16
  feast of f. things, 26:1
  feed f. the ancient grudge, 184:24
  geese are getting f., 884:7
  if to be f. be hated, 182:28
  in every f. man a thin one, 734:7
  is in the fire, 146:15
  Jack Sprat eat no f., 892:15
  Jeshurun waxed f., 9:31
  laugh and grow f., 191:*n*1
  men about me that are f., 191:28
  no sweeter f. than sticks to bones,
    486:3
  of others' works, 234:7
  one is f. and grows old, 182:19
  outside every f. man an even fatter man,
    734:*n*2
  Seymour's F. Lady, 793:12
  sharp names never f., 715:18
  should himself be f., 311:12
  take f. with lean, 466:6
  who drives f. oxen, 311:12
Fatal and perfidious bark, 253:8
  bellman, 215:17
  bowels of deep, 171:34
  complaint, 725:12
  embrace, 482:12
  entrance of Duncan, 214:17
  futility of Fact, 544:18
  gift of beauty, 396:5
  vision, 215:13
  Waterloo, 395:16
Fatality of seeing things too well, 642:10
  there is a f. in it, 314:25
Fate and character same conception, 380:11
  can be director of opponent's f., 80:19
  cannot harm me, 375:9
  certain of his f., 209:3
  complex f. being American, 544:1
  coughed and called it f., 605:21
  death milder f. than tyranny, 63:7
  determines or indicates f., 474:9
  eagle's f. and mine are one, 59:*n*5
  eccentric propositions of its f., 641:19
  fixed f. free will, 256:21
  forced by f., 274:13
  foulness of their f., 668:14
  gave his sad lucidity, 494:14

Fate *(continued)*
  had imagination about, 623:15
  hanging breathless on f., 436:23
  has cursed you, 67:14
  have conquered F., 494:16
  heart for any f., 436:7
  heart for every f., 397:13
  hung on razor's edge, 60:13
  I feel my f., 756:5
  I thy f. shall overtake, 241:18
  is being kind to me, 720:14
  is handspike, 483:8
  lead me Zeus and F., 82:3
  man identifies with his f., 719:3
  man's character is his f., 62:14
  man's f., 728:24
  master of f., 455:11, 685:6
  master of my f., 552:8
  masters of our own f., 718:3
  meet f. among clouds, 592:20
  men cannot suspend f., 282:9
  my f. cries out, 198:2
  no armor against f., 246:13
  no f. misunderstand me, 622:19
  nobly born must nobly meet f., 68:18
  of architect, 343:13
  of idealists, 614:14
  of nation in own power, 420:7
  of nation riding, 437:17
  of new truths, 502:13
  of unborn millions, 328:6
  Providence will and f., 256:21
  rave no more 'gainst f., 528:13
  read book of f., 188:12
  seize f. by the throat, 366:16
  sits on dark battlements, 362:2
  slave to f., 230:23
  so enviously debars, 267:4
  stronger than anything, 67:15
  summons monarchs obey, 273:13
  take a bond of f., 216:33
  take F. by throat, 513:9
  thy f. and mine sealed, 453:4
  torrent of his f., 306:19
  why know their f., 315:8
Fateful lightning, 481:1
Fates have given a patient soul, 52:18
  if the F. allow, 775:8
  impose that men abide, 170:32
  masters of their f., 191:26
  of dread death, 52:14
  spinning our own f., 540:23
Father Abraham, 457:3
  alone is God, 388:7
  and I went to camp, 883:*n*4
  and mither gae mad, 357:16
  answered never word, 436:9
  antichrist denieth the F., 46:9
  author of play, 584:18
  baptizing in the name of F., 36:23
  bed fell on my f., 704:7
  bosom of his F., 316:8
  called brother's f. dad, 175:10
  cannot teach the son, 807:19
  child f. of man, 369:14
  cold mad f., 651:3
  dear f. come home, 517:12
  deny thy f., 180:2

Father *(continued)*

  disappointed in monkey, 524:24
  eternal F. strong to save, 503:1
  far greater than his f., 51:14
  fear was my f., 756:1
  fell back behind Christ, 564:4
  foolish son calamity of f., 21:7
  forgive my injuries, 787:17
  full fathom five thy f. lies, 224:14
  gave f. forty-one, 885:22
  glorify your F. in heaven, 32:16
  glory be to the F., 48:8
  God an exalted f., 563:8
  God F. even more Mother, 768:12
  Great F. building forts among us, 499:3
  Great Spirit is my f., 365:1
  greatness in f. overwhelms son, 233:10
  happy to be f. unto many sons, 170:26
  hath chastised you, 11:37
  have we not all one f., 29:18
  heard my f. say, 330:13
  held out golden scales, 52:14
  honor thy f. and thy mother, 8:14
  I love you, 844:3
  in my youth said f., 514:5
  into thy hands, 38:37
  liar and f. of it, 39:26
  liked village in Ukrainia, 703:14
  lived his soul, 701:19
  mad feary f., 651:3
  man shall leave f. and mother, 5:17
  many talks from great f., 325:21
  more than hundred schoolmasters, 244:15
  moved through dooms, 701:18
  my f. paints summer, 797:9
  my f. sold me, 351:2
  my f. wept, 353:6
  name called everlasting F., 25:16
  no one like one's f. ever lived, 788:8
  not God for f. if not Church for mother,
    114:2
  of a family, 110:20
  of all in every age, 296:20
  of English criticism, 307:17
  of lights, 45:22
  of mankind, 438:18
  of many nations, 6:32
  of such as dwell in tents, 6:10
  of such as handle harp, 6:11
  of Waters unvexed to sea, 446:3
  of your country, 328:n3
  old f. antick the law, 181:25
  old f. old artificer, 650:13
  old F. William, 381:10, 514:4
  omnipotent F. with his thunder, 53:n3
  our F. the Sky, 891:12
  please world and f., 266:12
  prince subject F. Son, 230:15
  resembled my f. as he slept, 215:19
  ruffian, 182:27
  Scylla your f., 185:25
  seek f. who need son, 781:9
  serving f. and mother, 60:16
  smile at his f., 91:18
  Son and Holy Ghost, 36:23, 278:8
  Time and Mother Earth, 813:8
  to corruption thou art my f., 13:35
  told me businessmen sons of bitches, 786:6

Father *(continued)*

  true-begotten f., 184:34
  used to say, 671:5
  was a butcher, 270:12
  we don't need to escalate, 845:4
  which art in heaven, 32:25
  will of my F., 33:23
  wise son maketh a glad f., 20:10
  wish f. to thought, 188:22
  withered when my f. died, 201:31
  without f. bred, 251:10
  would strangle f., 313:13
  you think your f. does not, 67:9
  your f. the devil, 39:26
Fathered, so f. and so husbanded, 192:9
Fatherland, die for friends or f., 97:15
  everything belongs to f., 359:4
  no danger thine, 484:25
  O f. O Ilium, 94:13
  pressing needs of f., 356:1
Fatherless, judge the f., 24:32
Father-Mother God, 493:4
Father's, about my F. business, 37:21
  daughters of my f. house, 205:5
  desire f. death, 492:16
  drink in my F. kingdom, 36:3
  grave, 99:2
  house not house of merchandise, 39:7
  in my f. house, 39:40
  joy mother's pride, 374:5
  lean in joy upon F. knee, 351:1
  looked into f. heart, 727:11
  must be about His F. business, 710:4
  my f. theory, 552:5
  my land my f. land, 507:12
  sword girded on, 387:12
  we're going to our F. land, 861:8
Fathers, ashes of his f., 419:19
  brought forth nation, 446:5
  desire not merely what f. had, 78:22
  faith of our f., 469:15
  God of f. known of old, 589:7
  have eaten a sour grape, 28:6
  iniquity of the f., 8:12
  land where f. died, 439:9
  lie with my f., 7:18
  pardon old f., 592:9
  provoke not your children, 44:13
  scenes f. loved, 734:10
  sins of f. upon children, 69:2
  sojourner as all my f. were, 16:20
  sons similar to their f., 52:25
  that begat us, 31:26
  victory hundred f., 734:1
  worshipped stocks and stones, 254:23
  your f. where are they, 29:10
Fathers-forth whose beauty past change,
    546:13
Fathom, full f. five, 224:14
  line could never touch, 182:6
  scarcely f. their depths, 549:11
Fathomed, beauty not been f., 492:8
  the fathomable, 344:23
Fathoms, down f. down, 484:4
  fifty f. deep, 889:17
Fatigue of judging for themselves, 346:17
  of supporting freedom, 333:10
  without f. of traveling, 157:12

Fatling, lion and f. together, 25:19
Fatness of these pursy times, 201:11
Fatted calf, 38:11
Fattening, immoral illegal or f., 672:14
Fatter, outside fat man f. man trying to close in,
    734:n2
Fatti maschii parole femine, 244:n2
Fatuus, ignis f. of mind, 281:2
Faucet, love is just like a f., 779:8
  writing f. upstairs, 625:8
Faulkner sole owner, 714:1
Faulkner's, based on William F. idea, 843:15
Fault, all f. who hath no f., 455:14
  artist is his own f., 742:10
  by her f. dropped like flower, 91:8
  condemn f. and not actor, 206:24
  every man has his f., 213:23
  faultless to f., 463:4
  feed on for f. not mine, 399:10
  fellow f. came to match, 195:16
  find not f. with one another, 119:10
  great f. of our politicians, 472:1
  grows two thereby, 242:8
  if f. only on one side, 264:30
  if sack and sugar be f., 182:28
  just hint a f., 295:13
  knows how to confess f., 302:20
  no f. or flaw, 526:18
  not in our stars, 191:26
  O happy f., 47:26
  one f. at first, 242:n4
  only f. that he has no f., 110:22
  seeming monstrous, 195:16
  talk and find f., 155:19
  through my f., 47:17
  weariness and f., 623:10
  worse by excuse, 175:25
Fault-finding, fact-finding more effective than
    f., 615:4
Faultily faultless, 454:26
Faultless, to a fault, 463:4
Faults, all his f. observed, 193:12
  all men make f., 221:11
  best men molded of f., 207:18
  better occasional f. of government, 652:8
  cleanse me from secret f., 15:18
  frees all f., 225:9
  greatest of f. to be conscious of none,
    110:n14
  if no f. of our own, 263:18
  lie gently on him, 226:9
  love to f. always blind, 352:5
  man must have f., 105:19
  mum dad fill you with f. they had,
    799:15
  persuade ourselves we have no great f.,
    264:21
  pleasure in f. of others, 263:18
  see lover's f. as virtues, 345:2
  to f. a little blind, 283:12
  vile ill-favored f., 187:13
  who covers f., 210:31
  with all her f., 326:6
  with all thy f. I love thee, 326:n2
Fauna, flora f. geography, 763:5
Faustian, we are a F. age, 803:10
Faustus must be damned, 169:4
Faut, il f. cultiver notre jardin, 299:n5

Faute, pire qu'un crime c'est une f., 361:4
Favor, flattery in return for f., 366:19
   found f. in thy sight, 6:33
   from Fortune easier to get, 100:3
   in that same way grant f., 84:11
   increased in f., 37:22
   is deceitful, 22:20
   like a lady's f., 795:4
   look with f. on bold beginning, 93:10
   men f. deceit, 272:11
   nor f. to men of skill, 23:23
   render praise and f., 434:14
   those who f. fire, 623:4
   to this f. she must come, 202:12
   truths in and out of f., 622:16
   when f. of gods was equal, 69:4
   with God and man, 37:22
Favorite, a few of my f. things, 706:16
   has no friend, 315:10
   that f. subject Myself, 334:3
Favorites, all Kings and their f., 229:9
   heaven gives its f., 81:n4
Favors, conferring rather than accepting f.,
   72:n1
   error to expect f., 329:4
   fortune f. the brave, 86:n5, 95:10
   hangs on princes' f., 225:25
   lively sense of future f., 264:n2
   nor for her f. call, 292:7
   not by accepting f., 72:2
   not won by trifling f., 388:6
   rime into ladies' f., 190:8
   shower f. alike, 364:4
Fawning greyhound did proffer, 182:7
   publican, 184:23
   thrift may follow f., 200:10
Fawns, when lion f. upon lamb, 170:36
FBI, less training from the F., 780:2
Fe fi fo fum, 897:3
Fear, act of f., 197:13
   afraid of f., 366:9
   age of f., 724:4
   all-powerful should f. everything, 249:14
   and bloodshed, 371:21
   and danger of violent death, 239:10
   and distrust the people, 338:17
   and I were born twins, 239:15
   and Loathing in Las Vegas, 843:12
   angels f. to tread, 292:25
   arming me from f., 476:14
   as children f. in darkness, 90:10
   at my heart as at cup, 376:10
   be just and f. not, 226:5
   be not afraid of sudden f., 19:27
   better is little with the f. of the Lord, 20:32
   bid farewell to every f., 289:16
   birds of prey, 206:18
   bound subjected to better sway, 483:22
   by beauty and by f., 368:13
   came upon me, 13:7
   cannot be without hope, 276:10
   conquer f. beginning of wisdom, 615:1
   cornered-animal f., 840:3
   death as children fear dark, 165:13
   death feel fog, 462:24
   doth Job f. God for nought, 12:37
   encamps around thy home, 404:21
   endures for so long as f., 826:1

Fear *(continued)*
   every infant's cry of f., 353:3
   extreme f. neither fight nor fly, 172:33
   fain climb yet f. to fall, 159:6
   farewell f., 257:13
   Father F., 756:1
   feel fate in what I cannot f., 756:5
   for f. very stones prate, 215:15
   foundation of most governments, 330:3
   freedom from f., 653:4, 653:15
   frighted out of f., 218:35
   glad to brink of f., 425:21
   go in f. of abstractions, 665:3
   God, 119:15
   God and keep his commandments, 24:2
   God and take own part, 423:7
   God honor the king, 45:39
   Greeks even when they bring gifts, 94:10
   hair stand up in panic f., 66:21
   I am not in perfect mind, 213:5
   I cannot taint with f., 216:n1
   I will f. no evil, 15:23
   imagining some f., 179:6
   in handful of dust, 676:6
   is the mind-killer, 794:9
   is sharp-sighted, 156:6
   it would make me conservative, 624:4
   let them hate so long they f., 86:17
   littlest doubts are f., 200:19
   livid loneliness of f., 718:6
   living in f. but desperate, 813:2
   look f. in the face, 660:7
   love and f. hardly together, 141:14
   love is to f. life, 614:16
   made without f., 14:36
   mercy toward them that f. him, 18:6
   my heart shall not f., 15:28
   natural f. increased with tales, 165:13
   never f. to negotiate, 785:11
   never negotiate out of f., 785:11
   no fall, 271:25
   no f. is felt, 440:2
   no f. stand up to hunger, 567:15
   no more heat o' the sun, 220:26
   nor courage saves us, 675:23
   not I bring good tidings, 37:17
   not to touch the best, 159:9
   not well-fed long-haired men I f., 89:8
   nothing terrible except f. itself, 165:4
   nothing to be feared as f., 473:3
   nothing you carry Caesar, 89:3
   O word of f., 174:32
   of Acheron be sent packing, 90:8
   of censure, 665:8
   of change, 255:25
   of death more dreaded than death, 100:15
   of having to cry, 327:15
   of ignominious death, 360:25
   of kings, 186:1
   of little men, 501:4
   of separation unites, 668:9
   of suffering injustice, 263:25
   of the Lord, 25:18
   of the Lord is beginning of wisdom, 18:19
   of the Lord is wisdom, 14:5
   of violence and destruction, 722:16
   of weakness, 665:8
   only thing to f. is f., 652:2

Fear *(continued)*
   pale hungry-looking men, 89:8
   perfect love casteth out f., 46:12
   pine with f. and sorrow, 160:26
   possess them not with f., 189:24
   prey of f., 671:14
   punishment increases f., 548:16
   Puritanism haunting f. someone happy,
      645:19
   repentance is f. of consequence, 264:10
   shuddering f. green-eyed jealousy, 185:21
   source of superstition cruelty, 615:1
   spirit of f., 44:39
   strange that men f., 192:11
   tastes like rusty knife, 767:3
   that defeats and dreams are one, 641:19
   thee ancient Mariner, 376:13
   theoretic and visionary f., 337:9
   therefore will we not f., 16:26
   thief doth f. each bush, 171:5
   thing I f. most is f., 152:1
   thy skinny hand, 376:13
   to appear weak, 270:15
   to be we know not what, 272:10
   to f. worst cures worse, 203:17
   to him in f. everything rustles, 66:24
   to prevent war not f. it, 381:4
   to speak for fallen, 481:9
   to whom f. due, 41:38
   true nobility exempt from f., 170:12
   walk in f. and dread, 376:21
   was my father, 756:1
   watch not one another out of f., 228:7
   waves of anger and f., 748:16
   we f. in the light, 90:10
   we must travel in direction of f., 773:3
   we will not be driven by f., 754:12
   weapon to generate f., 839:21
   what others do from f. of law, 77:11
   what we f. of death, 207:1
   where angels f. to tread, 292:25
   whom shall I f., 15:27
   whom they f. they hate, 84:20
   work out salvation with f., 44:2
   yet do I f. thy nature, 214:16
Feared, better to be loved than f., 141:14
   by their breed, 176:24
   just as I f., 467:3
   nothing to be f. as fear, 473:3
   one that f. God, 12:34
   safer to be f. than loved, 141:14
   tread underfoot what too much f., 90:19
   witches, 562:9
Fearest nor sea rising, 545:12
Feareth, woman that f. the Lord, 22:20
Fearful, be f. when others are greedy, 826:13
   frame thy f. symmetry, 353:1
   goodness never f., 207:3
   how f. and dizzy, 212:24
   innocence, 370:4
   lifting up a f. eye, 167:1
   not a more f. wild-fowl, 178:25
   odds, 419:19
   our f. trip is done, 487:16
   saw a thousand f. wracks, 171:28
   snatch a f. joy, 315:5
   summons, 196:16
   why are ye f., 33:29

Fearfully and wonderfully made, 19:15
    o'ertrip the dew, 186:14
Fearing, I'm not f. any man, 823:16
    respect strength without f., 337:4
    stood there f., 449:7
    to attempt, 206:17
    to be spilt, 201:22
Fearless, foe with f. eyes, 582:8
Fearlessness of those who lost everything,
    791:7
Fears a painted devil, 215:23
    bondage of irrational f., 562:9
    dishonor worse than death, 97:15
    do make us traitors, 217:3
    dreams are made of desires and f., 801:9
    hopes and f. of all years, 521:2
    humanity with all f., 436:23
    I had no human f., 369:8
    less than imaginings, 214:11
    may be liars, 479:12
    more pangs and f., 225:25
    not mine own f., 222:10
    past Regrets future F., 441:15
    prosperity not without f., 165:16
    saucy doubts and f., 216:15
    tenderness its joys and f., 371:5
    that I may cease to be, 412:7
    that which it f. to lose, 221:19
    tie up thy f., 243:1
    trembling cold in ghastly f., 352:3
    when little f. grow great, 200:19
Fearsome banality of evil, 744:6
Feary, mad f. father, 651:3
Feast, bare imagination of f., 176:18
    beginning of a f., 183:19
    Belshazzar made a great f., 28:24
    Despair not f. on thee, 547:3
    drest as going to a f., 232:6
    enough as good as f., 148:27
    for eyes, 416:13
    good conscience continual f., 235:18
    great f. of languages, 174:26
    is made for laughter, 23:24
    is set, 375:18
    moveable f., 722:8
    nourisher in life's f., 215:21
    of Crispian, 189:26
    of fat things, 26:1
    of joy a dish of pain, 163:11
    of moon and men, 704:16
    of nectared sweets, 252:19
    of reason flow of soul, 296:6
    of Stephen, 479:1
    of wines on the lees, 26:1
    outcast from life's f., 650:8
    pomp and f. and revelry, 251:8
    riseth from f. with keen appetite, 184:39
    sat at good man's f., 194:22
    small cheer makes merry f., 172:19
    to the Lord, 7:41
    what f. is toward, 202:34
    when f. finished, 599:16
Feasting, good dinner and f., 277:13
    house of f., 23:9
Feasts, movable f., 47:27
    O nights and f. of gods, 95:25
    shown in courts at f., 252:25
Feat of Tell the archer, 360:14

Feather, a wit's a f., 295:5
    as f. wafted downward, 436:16
    birds of a f., 235:14
    for each wind, 223:17
    in hand better than bird in air, 108:*n*3
    in his cap, 314:15
    my foot my each f., 827:12
    never moults f., 464:26
    pluck out flying f., 530:13
    pun pistol not f., 383:22
    sharpened f., 483:11
    stuck f. in hat, 883:15
Featherbed, despotism to liberty in f., 337:1
Feathered, divide into featherless and f., 77:*n*1
    his nest well, 236:14
    with eagle's plumes, 59:18
Feather-footed through plashy fen, 736:9
Featherless, divide into f. and feathered, 77:*n*1
Feathers, brain of f., 296:27
    cover thee with his f., 17:28
    crow beautified with our f., 164:3
    field of f. for strife of love, 101:*n*10
    great wing f. swooping darkness, 891:8
    hope the thing with f., 508:12
    not only fine f. make fine birds, 59:3
    owl for all f., 409:18
    plumes her f., 252:17
    thing with f. my nephew, 839:12
    with our own f., 59:*n*5
Featly, foot it f., 224:12
Feats, 'twas one of my f., 399:11
Feature, every f. works, 382:17
    not single f. he actually values, 525:7
    show virtue her own f., 200:8
Featureless, more f. commonplace a crime,
    573:11
Features, double helix has novel f., 821:4
    homely f. to keep home, 252:25
    human f. composed of ten parts, 105:6
Feblit, and f. with infermite, 141:6
February, excepting F. alone, 150:*n*1
Fecund, searcher for f. minimum, 640:13
Fecundity, cringed before laws of f.,
    657:17
Fed, bite hand that f., 325:14
    dead who f. the guns, 668:14
    fish that hath f. of worm, 201:17
    grown by what it f. on, 197:1
    look up and are not f., 253:11
    man's resinous heart f., 594:14
    of dainties bred of a book, 174:15
    on fullness of death, 530:9
    on honeydew hath f., 377:23
    purely upon ale, 290:6
    those former bounty f., 274:18
    to be happy be well f., 645:11
    world on dreaming f., 590:20
Federal, happy incidents of f. system, 562:12
    our F. Union, 364:2
Federalists, we are all F., 337:8
Federation of the world, 452:3
Fee bestow upon foul disease, 210:28
    doctor for nauseous draught, 274:24
    for small f. in America, 828:14
    gorgeous east in f., 370:7
    set life at pin's f., 197:35
Feeble, and f. with infirmity, 141:6
    assist f. and friendless, 329:6

Feeble *(continued)*
    earthworm, 269:25
    engines of despotism, 338:15
    expletives f. aid join, 292:17
    help f. up, 213:17
    if Virtue f. were, 252:28
    religion of f. minds, 325:8
    we have become f. plant, 355:15
Feebler, nothing f. than a man, 54:4
Feed among the lilies, 24:13
    animals f. themselves men eat, 348:14
    Church sleep and f. at once, 675:24
    cloy appetites they f., 218:21
    cow and bear shall f., 25:19
    fat the ancient grudge, 184:24
    gave thee life bid thee f., 350:12
    He that doth ravens f., 194:3
    him with bread of affliction, 12:10
    his flock like a shepherd, 26:29
    his sacred flame, 378:3
    men in exile f. on dreams, 63:10
    nor f. the swine, 894:17
    on bitter fruit, 730:1
    on Death, 223:5
    on for fault not mine, 399:10
    on her damask cheek, 205:4
    on hope, 160:26
    people who will f. me, 814:5
    sleep and f., 201:19
    this mind of ours, 368:4
    till you f. us, 716:8
    upon strawberries, 894:17
    upon what meat Caesar f., 191:27
    where thou wilt, 171:9
    worm shall f. sweetly, 13:45
    you cannot f. capons so, 200:14
Feeds, Death that f. on men, 223:5
    mock meat it f. on, 209:3
    upon burrs of life, 409:4
Feel amid city's jar, 495:1
    and know we are eternal, 276:18
    as if top of head off, 511:15
    as if we were free, 541:20
    ask me how do I f., 762:3
    by turns bitter change, 256:25
    can Sporus f., 295:14
    did these f. earth move, 721:17
    dream happiness you may never f., 609:8
    first we f., 651:2
    fog in throat, 462:24
    happier in passion we f., 264:14
    heavy as yonder stone, 650:22
    hell within myself, 248:12
    how does it f., 851:14
    how swift how secretly, 695:1
    I can look East End in face, 725:7
    I f. your pain, 863:1
    I must f. it as a man, 217:9
    it and am in torment, 91:28
    it so like myself, 769:14
    my fate, 756:5
    my heart new opened, 225:25
    not f. the crowd, 327:2
    now does he f. his title, 217:15
    old as yonder elm, 650:22
    only f. farewell, 394:8
    passions we f. expand time, 610:17
    piercing cold I f., 316:18

Feel (*continued*)

rather to f. than reason, 360:20
see me f. me, 861:16
see not f. how beautiful, 378:6
speak what we f., 213:16
steady candle flame, 460:22
stir press f. with fingers, 486:11
strike so he may f. is dying, 104:11
sufferings of millions, 822:7
thing that could not f., 369:8
thy finger and find thee, 546:5
tragedy to those that f., 317:5
understand think and f., 757:14
we are greater, 372:12
what wretches feel, 211:33
whether you f. it or not, 826:14

Feeling, a f. and a love, 368:10

comfortable f. of superiority, 645:11
deepest f. in silence, 671:6
disputation, 182:39
fellow-f., 234:6
for single good action, 343:16
formal f. comes, 508:20
gives greater f. to the worse, 176:18
gratifying f. duty done, 528:5
has force of doom, 431:5
high mountains a f., 395:21
his cold strength, 670:5
I got beautiful f., 706:8
imprecision of f., 678:22
in all its nakedness, 417:14
intensity of f., 743:10
I've f. not in Kansas anymore, 764:5
makes us eloquent, 106:3
no f. of his business, 202:5
not always everything, 493:7
of my real life having passed, 413:18
one f. falsely disdained, 404:5
permanent contract on temporary f., 536:7
petrifies the f., 356:19
poetry presents thing to convey f., 123:7
profound or vehement, 379:13
push of cosmos, 542:5
religious f. part of consciousness, 490:15
religious f. towards life, 605:10
retains triumphant f., 563:11
sensible to f. as to sight, 215:13
shows in words, 123:7
what a glorious f., 702:4
whole of you transformed into f., 583:13
you've been cheated, 874:13

Feeling's dull decay, 397:4

Feelings, art transmission of highest f., 507:8

beings books events battles, 739:5
burial of my rosy f., 810:18
consideration for wives' f., 781:16
depth bitterness of f. about modern life, 767:8
my f. are too intense, 758:15
of women, 654:18
overflow of powerful f., 369:5
pass into friend, 535:1
permanently in race, 495:13
violent f. produce falseness, 484:7

Feels, do it so f. like hell, 833:3

heroism f. never reasons, 427:12
ne'er f. retiring ebb, 209:20
never f. wanton stings, 206:16

Fees, contrive our f. to pilfer, 72:16

flowing f., 254:3

Feet, able to draw with their f., 60:5

and did those f., 354:8
and his f. not be burned, 20:3
are always in water, 355:2
ask Alice when ten f. tall, 846:5
at her f. he bowed, 10:12
at the f. of Gamaliel, 40:42
beneath her petticoat, 261:5
broken by passing f., 590:23
chase hours with flying f., 395:14
come meet dancing f., 689:9
die on f. not live on knees, 653:5
die on f. than live on knees, 643:10
dreams under your f., 591:13
dust of your f., 33:39
fell at his f. as dead, 46:18
fog comes on cat f., 636:3
four white f. go without him, 886:5
gliding near with soft f., 487:15
heaven under our f., 475:14
if it is well with your f., 98:4
in ancient time, 354:8
keep thou my f., 421:4
lamp by which f. guided, 331:11
lamp unto my f., 18:28
landed on my f., 785:2
like unto fine brass, 46:17
liked getting f. wet, 598:7
little snow-white f., 590:21
locked upon rough bark, 827:12
make noise with my f., 775:12
making a tinkling with their f., 25:1
more instant than F., 576:14
nimble f. dance on air, 561:4
of clay, 28:21
of him that bringeth good tidings, 27:3
old shoes easiest for his f., 238:10
over whose acres blessed f., 181:19
patter of little f., 437:13
pretty f. like snails, 241:6
regards what is before his f., 84:19
rising and falling, 678:14
roll in ecstasy at your f., 655:17
scatter words at your feet, 765:6
Scots lords at his f., 889:17
seem to be saying, 833:5
shalt thou trample under f., 17:29
silver-sandaled f., 559:18
six f. of land, 507:7
take a walk I will tax your f., 856:11
teach f. a measure, 530:13
to the lame, 14:7
tremble under her f., 455:3
unstable, 639:13
walks in morning on four f., 66:n3
washed f. in soda water, 676:11
what flowers at my f., 410:7
wind's f. shine along sea, 530:2
with goat f. dance antic hay, 168:12
with twain he covered his f., 25:8
with your shoes on your f., 7:40

Feign thyng or fynde wordes new, 134:10

Feigned, by f. deaths to die, 229:2

hopeless fancy f., 452:22
necessities, 246:18

Felicities, close the circle of f., 337:11

Felicitous phenomenon, 671:21

Felicity, absent thee from f., 202:31

and flower of wickedness, 463:5
human f., 304:2
on far side of baldness, 590:16
or Doom, 511:13
perfect bliss and sole f., 168:2
possession without obligation, 505:14
we make or find, 307:14
what more f. to creature, 160:27

Feline, trying to control f. delinquency, 727:8

Felix culpa, 47:26

qui potuit cognoscere causas, 93:n5

Fell, all of us f. down, 193:1

among thieves, 37:36
at his feet as dead, 46:18
at one f. swoop, 217:8
bolt of Cupid f., 178:16
by that sin f. the angels, 226:4
clutch of circumstance, 552:7
epitaph of those who f., 621:7
from morn to noon he f., 256:5
great Caesar f., 193:1
help me when I f., 389:11
house f. not, 33:24
I do not love thee Doctor F., 282:23
I f. as a dead body, 128:20
in the great victory, 381:7
lash Magic Creature till it f., 510:17
men f. out knew not why, 261:17
mightiest Julius f., 196:15
my f. of hair, 217:22
of dark not day, 547:7
scales f. from eyes, 40:25
seeds f. by way side, 34:14
sergeant death, 202:28
shake my f. purpose, 214:17
some f. into good ground, 34:16
spirits that f. with Lucifer, 168:17
the wall f. down flat, 9:38
there he f. down dead, 10:12
thy shadow Cynara, 599:14
thy tempests f. all night, 243:7
Time's f. hand, 221:18
to earth knew not where, 436:19
upon his brother Benjamin's neck, 7:15
upon knees blessed God, 240:2
when stars shot and f., 624:15

Felled, hand that signed f. city, 777:5

Feller, met a city f., 887:6

sweetes' li'l' f., 569:3

Fellow, covetous sordid f., 298:7

damned in fair wife, 207:21
every sword against his f., 10:41
fault came to match, 195:16
Filipinos our f.-men, 545:11
folly has not f., 574:16
good hay hath no f., 178:32
hail f. well met, 286:12
has this f. no feeling, 202:5
have such a f. whipped, 200:6
he was a good f., 133:28
hook-nosed f. of Rome, 188:19
I shot his f., 184:11
laughing f. rover, 635:17
love my f. creatures, 527:6
loves his f. men, 392:18
make f. creatures happy, 333:18

Fellow (*continued*)
> met a city f., 887:6
> narrow F. in the Grass, 510:5
> never met this F., 510:6
> no f. in firmament, 192:14
> of infinite jest, 202:12
> robustious periwig-pated f., 200:6
> savage-creating f., 73:15
> sweetes' li'l' f., 569:3
> travelers of Revolution, 643:11
> use money for good of f. man, 535:4
> want of it the f., 295:4
> when man can help f. man, 716:14

Fellow-citizens, first in hearts of f., 350:*n*2
Fellow-feeling, 234:6
Fellowman, assist reduced f., 124:11
Fellow's got to swing, 561:2
> wise enough to play fool, 205:11

Fellows, club assembly of good f., 306:24
> good f. get together, 585:6
> it hurts to think, 575:12
> lewd f., 40:31
> man knows f. in himself, 611:3
> of infinite tongue, 190:8
> such f. as I crawling, 199:25

Fellowship divine, 409:9
> neither honesty nor good f., 181:31
> right hands of f., 43:26
> such a f. of good knights, 138:11
> with essence, 409:9

Felon, lets greater f. loose, 881:23
Felony to drink small beer, 170:13
Felt, darkness which may be f., 7:36
> he f. bad, 798:7
> how awful goodness is, 258:8
> I like watcher of skies, 408:17
> jests that never f. wound, 179:31
> knowing what really f., 721:12
> life in work of art, 544:16
> like planets fallen on me, 661:1
> ne'er saw I never f., 370:3
> never deeply f. nor willed, 495:15
> never f. I were American, 830:14
> no fear is f., 440:2
> through all this fleshy dress, 268:10
> touch scarcely f. or seen, 297:9
> writer must be everywhere f., 493:18

Female, adult American Negro f., 817:12
> child of Eve a f., 174:5
> despite they cast on f. wits, 261:10
> difference of education between male and f., 340:15
> elegance of f. friendship, 307:13
> fantasy onto the f. figure, 853:2
> if to her f. errors fall, 293:5
> male and f. created he, 5:7
> male and f. fuse into one solid, 71:9
> of sex it seems, 260:16
> of the species, 590:4
> patriotism in f. most disinterested of virtues, 341:5
> subtle and profound f., 57:2
> tell f. she's thin she's yours, 887:*n*5
> there is no f. mind, 579:2
> warriors, 299:22
> what f. heart gold despise, 315:9

Femaled, they maled and f. you jealously, 659:6
Females, trifling narrow education of f., 340:16

Femina, varium et mutabile f., 94:*n*10
Feminine, Eternal F. draws us on, 344:15
> research into f. soul, 564:5

Feminism, never able to find out what F. is, 697:1
Feminist, people call me a F., 697:1
Femme, cherchez la f., 422:*n*3
> ne naît pas f. le devient, 751:*n*1

Femmes, l'enfer des f., 266:*n*2
Fen, feather-footed through plashy f., 736:9
> of stagnant waters, 370:9

Fence, only f. against the world, 275:14
> Tom surveyed thirty yards of board f., 522:7

Fenced in piece of land, 312:12
> strangers who f. off meadows, 709:15

Fences, come to look after f., 501:1
> good f. good neighbors, 622:11

Fere libenter homines, 88:*n*12
Feri ut se mori sentiat, 104:*n*7
Ferlie he spied wi' his e'e, 889:27
Ferment, space in which soul in f., 409:6
Fermi, work by F. and Szilard, 637:14
Fern, pastures deep in f., 724:2
> sparkle out among f., 454:24

Ferocity, courage without f., 394:9
Ferry, back and forth all night on f., 695:9
Fertile hypothesis, 779:1
> metaphor f. power, 657:14
> miles of f. ground, 377:17
> to be so f., 732:6

Fertility begins to diminish, 837:4
Fervent, effectual f. prayer, 45:34
Fervet opus, 93:*n*9
Fervor, maintenance of first f., 144:17
Fester like a sore, 731:9
> lilies that f., 222:3

Festina lente, 99:*n*3
Festively she puts forth, 371:25
Festivity, Two Lands are in f., 4:6
Fetch pail of water, 893:18
> poor dog a bone, 895:6
> the Age of Gold, 250:12

Fettered, poetry f. fetters race, 354:12
> to her eye, 266:1

Fetters, no f. in Bay State, 438:3
> poetry fettered f. race, 354:12
> reason Milton wrote in f., 351:10

Fettle for great gray drayhorse, 546:16
Feuds, rent with civil f., 390:9
Fever called Living, 449:20
> is Nature's instrument, 270:8
> life's fitful f., 216:11
> of chills and f. died, 681:20
> of life over, 421:5
> of temptation, 688:7
> of the bone, 675:26
> weariness f. fret, 410:5
> youth bent by wintry f., 777:2

Feverish selfish little clod, 565:3
Fever-trees, set about with f., 589:17
Few admired by own households, 153:10
> are chosen, 35:11
> companions f. in serious business, 59:19
> condemn men because f., 475:24
> could know when Lucy ceased, 369:7
> days precious f., 673:1

Few (*continued*)
> err grossly as the f., 273:5
> far and f., 467:11
> give but f. thy voice, 197:23
> happy f., 190:1
> if bees are f., 511:12
> immortal names, 400:13
> in hands not of f. but many, 71:14
> join f. if any, 623:18
> join special f. at top, 831:6
> know how to be old, 264:27
> laborers are f., 33:36
> let thy words be f., 23:4
> many admire f. know, 71:8
> men of f. words best, 189:11
> much in f. words, 31:19
> philosophy is for the f., 155:6
> small country with f. people, 58:6
> so much owed to so f., 619:17
> some f. books to be chewed, 166:17
> the f. and the many, 349:4
> there be that find, 33:19
> to f. men comes excellence, 59:20
> very f. to love, 369:7
> ye are many they are f., 402:22
> yellow leaves or none or f., 221:24

Fewest, having f. wants, 70:3
Fezziwig, Mrs. F. one vast Smile, 465:9
ffinch-ffarrowmere corrected the visitor, 648:12
Fiamma, conosco i segni dell' antica f., 129:*n*4
Fiat justitia pereat coelum, 363:1
> justitia ruat coelum, 120:22
> lux, 5:*n*4
> ruat coelum f. voluntas tua, 121:14

Fiber, show food in minutest f., 380:2
Fibers, made of multitude of f., 422:15
Fibs, I'll tell you no f., 323:6
Fickle, whatever is f. freckled, 546:13
> woman always a f. thing, 94:23

Fico, a f. for the phrase, 187:1
Fiction, biography is ultimately f., 775:6
> concern of f. writer, 809:14
> house of f. has not one window, 544:17
> if woman is to write f., 654:14
> in disguise, 813:10
> lags after truth, 324:1
> poetry supreme f., 640:17
> that is what F. means, 843:*n*2
> tongue to deal in f., 291:11
> truth stranger than f., 399:5, 618:3
> work of f. affords aesthetic bliss, 723:9
> writing f. developed respect for unknown, 761:3

Fictional, work of history in f. form, 844:10
Fictions only and false hair, 242:18
> supreme f. of life, 642:21
> truth about reality is in the f., 835:8

Fictitious election results, 872:8
Fiddle, cat and f., 893:16
> de-dee, 468:4
> master's lost f. stick, 892:9
> music plays second f. to no one, 720:16
> play on f. in Dooney, 591:14
> robes riche or f., 133:23
> we know is diddle, 531:3

Fiddle-dee-dee, French for f., 516:18

Fiddler, in came a f., 465:9
  statesman and buffoon, 273:2
Fiddlers three, 892:13
Fide, Punica f., 92:*n*9
Fidelity, gossamer f. of Man, 448:16
  think of f. not husbands, 649:14
Fidus Achates, 94:*n*13
Fie fie upon her, 204:4
  foh and fum, 212:9
  my lord fie, 217:11
  upon this quiet life, 182:17
Field, accidents by flood and f., 207:37
  as a flower of the f., 18:7
  betokened tempest to f., 171:11
  consider lilies of f., 33:8
  cow a good animal in f., 309:20
  crop of corn a f. of tares, 163:11
  dedicate portion of f., 446:5
  dignity in tilling f., 566:4
  Esau was a man of the f., 6:37
  fair f. full of folk, 131:7
  gigantic f. of soya beans, 843:8
  goodliness as the flower of the f., 26:26
  Goya of the bare f., 836:2
  happy f. mossy cavern, 411:5
  has sight, 134:*n*2
  hath eyen wode eres, 134:15
  hi-hi-yee for f. artilleree, 639:3
  in league with stones of f., 13:13
  lay f. to f., 25:4
  life is not like crossing f., 897:11
  little f. well tilled, 302:8
  man for the f., 453:3
  man tills f. lies beneath, 455:5
  market economy's f. is world, 648:7
  not a f. but a cause, 333:11
  not that fair f. of Enna, 257:17
  not wholly reap corners of f., 8:26
  of grain, 775:11
  of human conflict, 619:17
  of ripe corn, 675:10
  potter's f., 36:12
  Prussia hurried to the f., 346:*n*4
  ring with importunate chink, 325:7
  roamed from f. to f., 350:7
  she is as in a f., 624:6
  shepherds abiding in f., 37:17
  six Richmonds in the f., 172:12
  so Truth be in the f., 254:14
  thy beauty's f., 220:31
  to live not as simple as cross f., 688:3
  viewed in her fair face's f., 172:30
  what though f. be lost, 255:10
Fields, as long as f. green, 403:19
  babbled of green f., 189:4
  battle won on playing f., 366:14
  carrying you into f. of light, 67:6
  dream of battled f., 373:21
  fight in f. and streets, 619:14
  flowering of His f., 455:17
  happy autumn f., 452:21
  have eyes woods have ears, 134:*n*2
  here lies W. C. F., 644:3
  hills and valleys dales and f., 168:*n*1
  hunt in f. for health, 274:24
  in Flanders f., 614:7
  in those holy f., 181:19
  lie with nothing at work in them, 757:3

Fields *(continued)*
  little tyrant of his f., 316:1
  of air, 327:11
  of corn where Troy was, 102:8
  once tall with wheat, 724:2
  out of olde f. newe corn, 132:8
  over f. all withered, 280:4
  plows in the f., 662:6
  they have not sown, 730:1
  unshorn f. boundless, 406:3
  valleys groves hills f., 168:4
Fiend, foul F. Apollyon, 271:15
  frightful f., 376:21
  like a f. in a cloud, 350:9, 353:6
  long spoon eat with f., 136:3
  marble-hearted f., 211:10
Fiendishness of business competition, 666:12
Fiends, juggling f., 217:29
  lore of f., 430:23
  that plague thee thus, 375:25
Fierce and accustomed to woods, 142:8
  change of f. extremes, 256:25
  composition and f. quality, 210:33
  contending nations know, 288:1
  extremes by change more f., 256:25
  four champions f. strive, 257:1
  fur soft to face, 798:1
  generous true and f., 619:4
  grew more f. and wild, 243:2
  lion not so f. as they paint him, 243:27
  look not so f. on me, 169:5
  more f. and inexorable far, 181:9
  no beast so f. but knows pity, 171:20
  Spirit f., 402:13
  though little she is f., 178:30
  wars and faithful loves, 160:2
  wretchedness that glory brings, 213:27
Fierceness, swalloweth the ground with f., 14:28
Fiercer, now f. by despair, 256:7
Fiercest, strongest and f. spirit, 256:7
Fiery, bathe in f. floods, 206:38
  far from f. noon, 411:12
  furnace, 28:22
  mind very f. particle, 398:29
  Pegasus, 183:14
  soul, 272:16
Fiery-footed steeds, 180:31
Fife, ear-piercing f., 209:13
  Elephant practiced on f., 517:8
  play f. lowly, 890:16
  Thane of F. had a wife, 217:13
  wry-necked f., 184:38
Fifteen apparitions seen, 597:6
  I was f. f., 639:1
  Jewish man remain f.-year-old boy, 835:5
  maiden of bashful f., 346:11
  men on Dead Man's Chest, 555:4
  until I was f., 834:12
  wild Decembers, 476:11
Fifth Amendment old friend, 716:18
  column, 670:13
  never walked down F. Avenue, 471:14
  of November, 882:18
  shall close drama, 291:9
  smote him under the f. rib, 11:11
Fifths, three f. genius, 481:19

Fifties, tranquilized F., 787:10
  word appreciated by man in love, 392:7
Fiftieth, hallow f. year, 9:1
Fifty, at f. chides delay, 290:23
  at f. everyone has face he deserves, 735:23
  corpulent man of f., 392:12
  dread f. above more than f. below, 623:11
  forty till f. man stoic or satyr, 561:15
  here's to the widow of f., 346:11
  million Frenchmen, 887:8
  not care to live after f., 600:10
  not have children after f., 126:8
  only leaves me f. more, 574:11
  Sleeping Beauty f. years old, 808:9
  springs little room, 574:11
  wise at f., 244:5
  years of Europe, 452:11
Fifty-four forty or fight, 423:3
Fifty-fourth Regiment, 519:10
Fifty-score strong, 460:4
Fifty-second, on F. Street, 748:16
Fig bear fruit then ripen, 108:18
  call f. a f., 81:10
  every man under his f. tree, 11:28
  for care fig for woe, 146:10
  land of vines and f. trees, 9:20
  sewed f. leaves together, 5:20
Fig leaf, democracy is the f., 841:14
Figments, de longs f. violets, 559:*n*1
Fight, African f. for emancipation, 690:9
  against his brother, 25:25
  against moralism feminism, 633:7
  aloud very brave, 508:5
  and conquer again, 316:20
  and not heed wounds, 144:16
  back from eyes tears, 682:12
  between two bald men, 719:9
  beyond your strength, 51:28
  cannot f. future, 442:13
  don't f. forces use them, 705:9
  don't want to f., 503:17
  Duke great f. did win, 381:9
  end crowns us not f., 240:13
  end of f. tombstone white, 587:11
  extreme fear neither f. nor fly, 172:33
  fall out and chide and f., 289:7
  fifty-four forty or f., 423:3
  fire and ice within me f., 575:3
  first rule of f. club, 877:9
  for love and glory, 702:12
  for one's country, 51:24
  fought a good f., 45:2
  fought the better f., 258:23
  gods f. against necessity, 55:9
  good fight of faith, 44:36
  harder matter to f., 455:24
  her till she sinks, 389:6
  how you f. as much as why, 802:1
  I will f. no more forever, 537:4
  in fields and streets, 619:14
  in France and on seas, 619:14
  it out on this line, 498:2
  like devils, 189:17
  like hell for living, 511:17
  love as much as good f., 651:13
  man who runs may f. again, 81:12

Fire *(continued)*

tongued with f. beyond living, 679:8
tongues of f., 40:15
tree is cast into f., 32:8
true love a durable f., 159:4
two irons in the f., 238:1
until latter f. shall heat deep, 450:6
view what f. was near, 167:1
what hand dare seize f., 353:1
what of faith and f., 536:19
when ready Gridley, 529:1
whether in sea or f., 196:18
while I was musing the f. burned, 16:16
world is ever-living F., 62:4
worthy of nothing but to be cast into f.,
    301:11
years steal f. from mind, 395:11
youth of England on f., 189:1
Firebell, like f. in the night, 338:10
Firebrand to smoke, 139:9
Fire-breathing Catholic C.O., 787:10
Fired another Troy, 274:20
don't fire unless f. upon, 325:19
if not f. shouldn't be hanging there, 578:*n*2
not who f. the shot, 757:12
shot heard round world, 424:17
third prize is you're f., 865:8
Firefly, life flash of f. in night, 492:1
wakens, 453:5
Fire-folk sitting in the air, 546:7
Firelit, think of f. homes, 668:12
Fire-red cherubynnes face, 134:7
Fire's, wore f. center, 760:6
Fires, death f. danced, 376:5
fuel to maintain his f., 245:18
keep home f. burning, 616:17
late when the f. out, 555:10
open f. on the hearth, 586:12
out by gas f. of the refinery, 868:5
passing through dark f., 811:5
thought-executing f., 211:24
true Genius kindles, 295:13
veils her sacred f., 297:6
violent f. soon burn out, 176:23
Fireside, Englishman's f., 361:6
king by your own f., 155:8
Firesides, protect health homes f., 554:5
Firing, if no one thinking of f. it, 578:5
no f. till you see whites of eyes, 312:5
to-morrow have what to do after f., 776:12
Firkin, meal in the f., 426:7
Firm and stable earth, 240:2
Catullus be resolved and f., 91:7
fly from f. base, 374:2
ground of Result, 618:16
heart f. as stone, 14:34
my f. nerves never tremble, 216:20
priests stood f. on dry ground, 9:36
office boy to Attorney's f., 525:22
stands watch along Rhine, 484:25
Firmament, brave o'erhanging f., 199:5
buzzing world lisping f., 641:18
Christ's blood streams in f., 169:4
fall to base earth from f., 177:2
no fellow in f., 192:14
now glowed the f., 257:25
payntit with sternis cleir, 143:12
planets and the f., 230:15

Firmament *(continued)*

showeth his handiwork, 15:15
spacious f. on high, 287:20
starry f. for roof, 533:12
Firmer, tired ox treads with f. step, 115:21
Firm-footed by sea unchanging, 419:1
Firmness, in the right, 447:2
Firm-set earth, 215:15
Firs, pointed f. darkly cloaked, 552:11
First, absurd is the f. truth, 770:1
after f. death no other, 777:7
Amendment has erected wall, 666:16
among equals, 121:9
and foremost I am individual, 504:10
and great commandment, 35:13
and second class citizens, 697:3
appearance of new beings, 439:11
bead of sweat, 829:6
best country is at home, 321:13
between acting and f. motion, 192:2
blow half battle, 323:4
born as children, 805:12
came the seen, 665:13
cannot be f. in everything, 59:6
cast a stone, 39:22
chance to build Great Society, 753:15
come first served, 125:*n*6
comes f. eats f., 125:8
descry the big canoe, 482:12
evening and morning were f. day, 5:4
fine careless rapture, 460:19
for which f. made, 462:13
get that f. take, 827:1
get there f., 494:4
God f. planted garden, 166:15
good die f., 372:6
Great F. Cause, 327:12
guarantee of F. Amendment, 667:2
He is the f. and the last, 119:14
him f. last midst, 258:15
hundred days, 785:12
in hearts of countrymen, 350:6
in past man has been f., 566:1
in war first in peace, 350:6
is deep love, 57:22
last everlasting day, 229:9
last shall be f., 35:5
light of evening, 642:13
looking away from f. things, 542:6
loved at f. sight, 168:14
man among these than second in Rome,
    89:1
man who said This is mine, 312:12
men f. subjects afterward, 473:13
moment of atomic age, 774:13
nothing be done for f. time, 622:4
office of government splendid misery, 337:5
one now will later be last, 851:5
pay for it f. or last, 471:15
saved because you were the f., 806:8
say what you would be, 109:5
seed de f. en last, 713:12
seems to Comprehend Whole, 509:9
shall be last, 35:5
step is hardest, 300:11
sweet sleep of night, 402:17
that ever burst, 376:1
that found famous country, 695:2

First *(continued)*

the f. and the last, 47:15
thing let's kill lawyers, 170:14
things the f. poets had, 167:13
thousands of f. responders, 853:13
time in city's long history, 724:6
thy f. love, 46:20
we feel, 651:2
we practice to deceive, 373:15
what are we f., 505:9
Who's on f., 705:3
women and children f., 885:5
youth tested to old age, 494:9
Zeus f. cause, 63:8
Firstborn among many brethren, 41:22
brought forth f. son, 37:16
offspring of heaven f., 257:5
smite all the f., 7:40
First-class fightin' man, 587:18
second-class intellect f. temperament, 539:11
travel f. and with children, 683:13
Firstfruits of them that slept, 43:1
Firstling of the infant year, 246:1
Fish, a poor f. peddler, 682:11
all f. that cometh to net, 147:31
and guests in three days, 83:*n*9
army is like f., 698:12
biggest f. got away, 553:17
cannot live in fields, 90:11
cars nose forward like f., 788:3
dart before you, 4:7
dies because he opens mouth, 898:7
disputants put me in mind of skuttle f.,
    288:16
dominion over f. of the sea, 5:8
eat f. that fed of worm, 201:17
fiddle de-dee, 468:4
flesh or fowl, 594:1
formal as scales on f., 670:17
I let f. go, 762:14
in troubled waters, 282:15
it's no f. ye're buying, 374:7
Jonah was in the belly of the f., 29:4
kettle of f., 527:1
know the places to f., 844:3
little F. swam, 467:13
needs a bicycle, 888:20
nor flesh nor good red herring, 147:15
not with melancholy bait, 184:9
one f. ball, 500:3
say they have stream, 669:8
son of first f. ashore, 816:9
teaching a f. to swim, 121:6
this f. will bite, 190:35
thou deboshed f. thou, 224:29
to f. and to seals, 762:16
we are f. and meat, 598:10
what cat's averse to f., 315:9
wise men f. here, 682:8
with F. questing Snail, 756:15
with worm that eat king, 201:17
Fishbone in city's throat, 787:19
Fished by obstinate isles, 665:5
Fisher, Kitty F. found it, 896:5
Fisherman's, well for f. boy, 452:15
Fishermen that walk upon the beach, 212:24
Fishers of men, 32:13
of song, 569:12

Flight *(continued)*
  black f. of crows, 891:*n*1
  fellow of selfsame f., 184:11
  flown his cloistered f., 216:12
  his wild airy f., 260:18
  life like f. of sparrow, 122:1
  never-ending f. of days, 256:14
  puts Stars to f., 441:5
  single f. of planes, 724:6
  struggle and f., 496:19
  Sun scattered into f., 441:4
  through sky thy certain f., 405:14
  time and world in f., 591:10
  time arrest f., 400:14
Flights and perchings, 540:25
  four f. Thursday, 601:7
  grand f. Sunday baths, 641:14
  of angels sing thee, 202:33
Flinch, we did not f., 60:13
Flinders, little Polly F., 895:3
Fling away ambition, 226:4
  garment of Repentance f., 441:7
Flint, behold man of f., 891:19
  firmest f. doth in continuance wear, 89:*n*9
  weariness snore upon f., 220:22
Flirtation, significant word f., 898:18
Flit on wings of borrowed wit, 239:19
Flits by on leathern wing, 317:13
Flitter dip and soar, 797:14
Flitting, Raven never f., 449:11
Float, how sweetly did they f., 252:15
  iron in water f., 882:15
  like a butterfly, 853:10
Floated into inmost soul, 482:20
  web f. wide, 451:6
Floating bulwark of our island, 318:18
  hair, 377:23
  ice mast-high came f. by, 375:23
  like vapor on air, 503:14
  many bells down, 701:17
  o my f. life, 734:16
  on the floor, 449:12
  spar to men that sink, 695:18
Floats, chicken hawk f. over, 817:8
  on high o'er vales, 371:9
  though unseen among us, 401:9
Flock, feed his f. like a shepherd, 26:29
  keeping watch over their f., 37:17
  of bridges bleating, 643:17
  shun the polluted f., 666:4
  silent f. in fold, 409:18
Flocks, bad herdsmen ruin their f., 53:25
  battening our f., 253:3
  bells of the f., 764:15
  casual f. of pigeons, 640:22
  or herds or human face, 257:6
  while shepherds watched f., 281:13
Flogged, man never f. never taught, 81:7
Flogging, habit of f. me constantly, 472:3
Flood, accidents by f. and field, 207:37
  arched the f., 424:17
  carriest them away as with a f., 17:23
  decay no f., 591:8
  enchafed f., 208:11
  giant race before the f., 274:11
  half our sailors swallowed in f., 171:1
  land of mountain and f., 373:4
  Milton Proteus of f., 379:15

Flood *(continued)*
  of mortal ills, 143:16
  of remembrance, 662:15
  of words drop of reason, 302:13
  taken at the f., 193:13
  ten years before the F., 266:21
  thorough f. thorough fire, 178:10
  throw things to the f., 734:16
  torn Naiad from f., 447:11
  when just cause reaches f. tide, 572:14
Floods, bathe in fiery f., 206:38
  haystack in f., 520:4
  he hath established it upon the f., 15:24
  neither can f. drown it, 24:26
  passions like f. and streams, 159:7
  rimless f., 720:2
  stood upright as an heap, 8:7
  that are deepest, 882:8
Floor, careless on granary f., 411:7
  cleaned windows swept f., 525:22
  forest's ferny f., 616:6
  mystery on bestial f., 592:12
  of heaven is inlaid, 186:15
  scratching at the f., 578:19
  starry f., 352:11
  sunk beneath watery f., 253:14
  two jars on f. of Zeus, 52:19
  wrought ghost upon f., 449:4
Floors of silent seas, 675:1
Flopsy Mopsy Cottontail Peter, 598:5
Flora and country green, 410:4
  fauna geography, 763:5
  Lady F. lovely Roman, 506:3
Florida, Everglades of F., 686:12
  weighted with regret, 819:15
Flots, léger j'ai dansé sur les f., 558:*n*9
Floundered enjoyed suffered, 545:6
Flouris, fair up sprang the f., 141:9
Flourish, almond tree shall f., 23:31
  may f. or may fade, 322:22
  men f. only for a moment, 54:5
  nations are destroyed or f., 354:12
  poetry painting music f., 354:12
  righteous shall f., 17:30
  set on youth, 221:17
  those which most admirably f., 222:*n*1
  where you turn eyes, 292:6
Flourished, bloody treason f., 193:1
  hoop unbroken people f., 583:5
Flourishes, society where moderation f., 614:1
Flourisheth as flower of the field, 18:7
  in the morning it f., 17:23
Flourishing like a green bay tree, 16:*n*1
  of the arts, 698:13
Flours, no f. on grave, 536:3
Flout, banners f. the sky, 213:32
  'em and scout 'em, 224:31
Flow, all pleasant fruits do f., 227:3
  ebb and f. by the moon, 213:8
  from discord f., 288:1
  from my lips would f., 403:6
  from whom all blessings f., 278:8
  gently sweet Afton, 357:19
  I within did f., 278:13
  its one will f., 720:6
  of soul, 296:6
  salt tides seaward f., 494:12
  streams f. with ambrosia, 68:3

Flow *(continued)*
  words to say it f., 278:3
Flower, age will fade beauty's f., 150:10
  as a f. of the field, 18:7
  bee does not hurt f., 64:19
  blue forked torch of f., 663:22
  crimson-tipped f., 356:17
  culture in finest f., 580:17
  displayed doth fall, 205:1
  fadeth, 26:27
  fancy from f. bell, 461:22
  from every opening f., 289:8
  from milky f., 822:11
  full many a f., 315:23
  glory in the f., 371:4
  glory of man as f. of grass, 45:37
  goodliness as the f. of the field, 26:26
  he cometh forth like a f., 13:29
  heaven in wild f., 353:14
  herself a fairer f., 257:17
  in crannied wall, 455:27
  in hand when he awoke, 378:18
  in the f. of their age, 10:33
  let black f. blossom, 431:6
  little f. if I understand, 455:27
  little western f., 178:16
  London f. of Cities all, 141:4
  look like innocent f., 214:20
  loved tree or f., 388:3
  masterpiece appear as f., 520:15
  meanest f. that blows, 371:5
  merry Margaret as midsummer f., 141:2
  moon like a f., 351:6
  my love dropped like a f., 91:8
  nipt my f. sae early, 358:13
  of kings and knights destroyed, 138:14
  of knyghthod and of fredom f., 136:14
  of wickedness, 463:5
  of wyfly pacience, 135:21
  or wearing-stone, 623:3
  prized beyond sculptured f., 406:1
  prove a beauteous f., 180:11
  safety, 182:13
  say yes my mountain f., 650:18
  seize the f., 358:6
  summer's f. to summer sweet, 222:2
  that smiles today, 241:4
  thou tree I f., 526:16
  through green fuse drives f., 777:2
  time cracks in furious f., 783:12
  torch of a f., 663:22
  wearing learning like f., 454:11
  when knighthood was in f., 392:15
  winds creep from f. to f., 401:9
  without fragrance, 590:18
  you are like a f., 415:2
Floweret, meanest f. of vale, 316:9
Flowering in lonely word, 456:1
  of His fields, 455:17
  wantons thro' f. thorn, 357:6
Flower-like, love is f., 378:13
Flowers, all its twined f., 411:7
  all the f. were mine, 448:6
  Alphabet of f., 230:8
  and fruits of love, 399:16
  and that f. gynnen sprynge, 133:6
  appear on the earth, 24:9
  April showers May f., 151:2

Flowers *(continued)*
are lovely, 378:13
as in causes sleep, 245:14
be sure to smell f. along way, 693:10
begotten, 529:13
buds of barren f., 530:16
choke them amid f., 90:17
cover with leaves and f., 237:3
fairy fruits and f., 448:6
foam of f., 530:2
for thee earth puts forth f., 89:10
glass f. at Harvard, 671:5
here's f. for you, 223:26
I like to press wild f., 879:9
in garden meat in hall, 133:*n*2
in the fields appear, 83:3
leaves and f. in sun, 592:7
let f. be crushed, 432:2
letting hundred f. blossom, 698:13
love I most f. white and rede, 133:7
lulled in these f., 178:19
madeleine soaked in lime f., 610:13
near his nose, 772:5
no f. on grave, 536:3
no hothouse f., 658:4
nosegay of culled f., 153:19
of all hue, 257:16
of forest a' wede away, 321:8
of friendship faded, 627:20
on chaliced f. that lies, 220:15
play with f. and smile, 189:4
relationships between f. and convicts,
   761:12
summer with f. that fell, 529:14
sweetest f. in forest, 160:11
that bloom in spring, 527:20
that do not wilt, 671:20
through grass, 125:6
to strew Thy way, 242:17
what f. are at feet, 410:7
where have all the f. gone, 793:13
where Proserpin gathering f., 257:17
where will I find f., 367:17
where'er you tread f. rise, 292:6
with what f. and shoots of glory,
   268:12
withered while I spent my days, 122:9
Flowery, crops f. food, 294:17
meads in May, 239:17
tale more sweetly, 410:13
walk f. way, 526:11
Floweth, sea itself f. in veins, 278:10
Flowing, every sluice of knowledge set a-f.,
   329:10
fees, 254:3
from rocky breasts forever f., 762:17
land f. with milk and honey, 7:28
robes loosely f., 232:7
Flown, black bat night f., 455:1
flowing and f., 762:17
his cloistered flight, 216:12
with insolence and wine, 255:20
Flows, as water f. downwards, 79:18
in scrolls of toga, 833:5
methinks how sweetly f., 241:14
thence f. all that charms, 378:10
Fluctuat nec mergitur, 120:25
Flügeln, auf F. des Gesanges, 414:*n*5

Fluidity of self-revelation, 545:4
solid for f., 619:5
Flumina, altissima f. minimo sono, 159:*n*4
Flung, doors are widely f., 755:10
roses roses riotously, 599:15
us on windy hill, 669:5
Flush as May, 200:33
roses for f. of youth, 512:7
Flushed, ethereal f. and like throbbing star,
   409:23
Flushing his brow, 409:21
Fluster, accept f. of lost, 763:7
Flute, distraction music of f., 677:15
soft complaining f., 273:25
violin bassoon, 455:2
Flutes, dance to f., 561:4
Dorian mood of f., 255:23
sound of lyres and f., 534:5
tune of f. kept stroke, 218:20
Fluttered, draft f. flame, 688:7
failed for breath, 495:20
round the lamp, 517:10
your Volscians, 220:6
Fluttering empty sleeves, 641:8
ghost fled like f. breeze, 94:18
sets my heart to f., 56:5
Flutterings, innumerable f. agitate mind,
   152:13
Flux, all is f., 61:26
of the senses, 378:24
Fluxions, what are these f., 291:7
Fly, all things on earth f., 443:1
as arrows f. to one mark, 188:36
as the sparks f. upward, 13:11
away breath, 205:3
away home, 893:2
away Jack, 897:7
beasts f. to wilderness, 79:18
busy curious thirsty f., 300:9
but little way to f., 441:7
creep swim or f., 278:6
down Death, 771:18
encountering a F., 511:6
extreme fear neither fight nor f., 172:33
forgotten as a dream, 289:14
from not hate mankind, 395:20
gilded f. does lecher, 212:27
have to f. more missions, 802:9
human race born to f. upward, 129:21
I can f. or I can run, 252:27
I said the f., 893:9
in greatness of God, 543:2
joys as dreams f., 881:8
let me to Thy bosom f., 305:8
like love can't compel or f., 749:9
little Birds f., 467:12
little birds that f., 290:10
little F., 352:15
long-legged f. upon stream, 597:4
make fur f., 262:13
my words f. up, 201:1
neglect God for noise of a f., 231:11
no longer wings to f., 677:13
on bat's back I do f., 225:5
riches f. away as an eagle, 21:26
rode upon a cherub and did f., 15:14
seem to f. it, 232:14
show f. way out of f. bottle, 685:14

Fly *(continued)*
soon cut off and we f. away, 17:25
sounds too blue to f., 804:1
Spider to F., 418:16
stir her lawn canapie, 154:12
that sips treacle, 291:19
this rock shall f., 374:2
to her, 453:1
to others we know not of, 199:21
to war and arms I f., 265:17
up above world you f., 514:15
upon the wings of the wind, 15:14
way I f. is hell, 257:12
when me they f., 425:5
which way shall I f., 257:12
white sails f. seaward, 677:19
willingly as kill a f., 173:3
with arms outstretched would f., 203:24
with twain he did f., 25:8
Flyin' fishes play, 588:2
Flying art of not falling, 627:8
banner torn but f., 396:10
chariot through air, 327:11
fishes play, 588:2
hoping lingering, 293:2
mind f. abroad, 76:6
old Time still a-f., 241:4
pluck out f. feather, 530:13
sea-crow, 487:19
seaward f., 677:19
snow came f., 545:13
time f. never to return, 93:23
trapeze, 532:16
wild echoes f., 452:19
Foal, likeness of filly f., 178:12
Foam, born and die like f., 125:5
copulate in f., 597:3
is not cruel, 484:7
like f. on river, 373:23
now I f. to wheat, 833:11
oceans white with f., 673:11
of flowers, 530:2
opening on the f., 410:10
poetry new as f., 425:12
sea folk turn into f., 432:18
too full for sound and f., 456:4
trails in the sea, 630:11
weeds and f., 424:3
white f. flew, 376:1
Foam-bell no consequence, 496:11
Foaming out their own shame, 46:13
Foams, my sad heart f. at stern, 558:16
Focis, pro aris atque f., 92:*n*6
Focus, mantras f. and simplicity, 873:11
of evil, 765:14
Fodder's in the shock, 553:10
Foe, angry with my f., 353:7
at another gate let in the f., 260:14
avowed erect manly f., 367:3
comes with fearless eyes, 582:8
foils f. by effusion of ink, 318:12
friend to her f., 363:14
grim Death my son and f., 256:27
heat not furnace for f., 225:12
idleness sorrow friend f., 699:10
laughter has no greater f. than emotion,
   572:6
meet insulting f., 346:23

Foe *(continued)*

met dearest f. in heaven, 197:7
never made a f., 455:15
Olympian a difficult f., 50:19
overcome but half his f., 256:2
perhaps a jealous f., 403:11
scratch lover find f., 699:12
someday to prove our f., 65:7
sternest knight to f., 138:15
support friend oppose f., 785:10
take up quarrel with f., 614:7
thou that seemest f., 143:*n*5
timorous f., 295:13
tyrants fall in every f., 358:17
wolf that's f. to men, 237:4
Foeman bares steel tarantara, 526:7
Foemen at morn friends at eve, 483:21
worthy of steel, 374:3
Foes, ah my f., 695:8
beat down baffling f., 495:8
learning's barbarous f., 306:9
man that makes character makes f., 290:16
not know friends from f., 473:19
now have neither f. nor friends, 695:*n*1
our f. press on, 127:3
so far only hate our f., 65:7
will provide with arms, 94:16
Fog and filthy air, 213:31
comes on cat feet, 636:3
feel f. in throat, 462:24
gleams through f., 314:28
London particular a f., 466:10
of war, 782:10
woodthrush singing through f., 677:20
yellow f. swirls down streets, 573:4
Foggy foggy dew, 884:15
Fogs, his rising f. prevail, 273:14
retiring f. revealed an army, 608:12
Foh a fico for the phrase, 187:1
Fie f. and fum, 212:9
Foiled, after thousand victories f., 221:4
Foils foe by effusion of ink, 318:12
Fold, all driven into same f., 96:21
flock in woolly f., 409:18
hands and wait, 528:13
home fast f. thy child, 547:2
sheep not of this f., 39:32
sheep to f., 575:17
star that bids shepherd f., 252:6
tents like Arabs, 436:18
to their bosoms the viper, 482:12
wolf in f. sad thing, 92:19
Folded her hair expectantly, 488:4
lord of f. arms, 174:14
Folding of the hands to sleep, 20:1
Folds, lost f. of damasked gown, 150:9
lull distant f., 315:12
of bright girdle furled, 496:19
rippling in breeze, 459:2
Foliage, children in f., 678:11
Folio, whole volumes in f., 174:7
Folk, ancient f. with evil spells, 891:20
best literature becomes f. literature, 743:17
black f. say America been stronger, 756:24
dance like wave of sea, 591:14
fair field full of f., 131:7
messenger with language of his f., 118:10
queerest f. of all, 579:3

Folk *(continued)*

songs from soul sounds, 704:16
we are plain quiet f., 696:12
Folks, as long as colored man look to white f., 862:3
O yonge fresshe f., 133:4
there's where old f. stay, 503:11
think you lack, 708:8
Folk-song, Negro f., 602:4
Follies and misfortunes of mankind, 332:5
cease with youth, 305:11
of town crept slowly, 323:1
perished by their own f., 52:21
that themselves commit, 185:1
vices and f. of human kind, 286:24
woes because of their own f., 52:22
Follow a shadow, 232:14
admire virtue f. not her lore, 259:29
after peace, 42:3
and will not see its back, 57:7
as night the day, 197:24
beat to f. faster, 218:20
even if disobedient I shall f., 82:3
good to fire but not into it, 153:8
goodness and mercy shall f. me, 15:23
grasp subject words will f., 85:7
him who sets you right, 112:17
I f. but myself, 207:25
if thou f. thy star, 129:2
knowledge like star, 451:15
lamb will never cease to f., 170:36
let who loves country f., 435:25
loves me let him f. me, 130:16
me fishers of men, 32:13
me let dead bury dead, 33:28
nature, 106:11
so fast they f., 201:*n*2
spirit of men who f., 664:11
still changes of the moon, 209:5
the Gleam, 456:3
the money, 829:13
the King, 455:9
things which make for peace, 42:3
this city going to f. you, 583:10
thrift may f. fawning, 200:10
truth wherever it may lead, 338:13
us disquietly to graves, 211:2
your bliss, 737:2, 766:16
your desire, 3:5
your spirit, 189:9
Followed, first f. it hymselve, 134:5
him honored him, 460:12
me since black womb held, 772:2
mercenary calling, 575:20
through all world she f. him, 452:12
Followeth, he that f. me, 39:24
not after me, 34:6
Following, in f. him I follow myself, 207:25
plow along mountainside, 369:16
the roe, 357:15
Follows but for form, 211:18
Folly, according to his f., 568:1
alone stays fugue of Youth, 141:11
and presumption, 319:6
answer a fool according to his f., 21:37
brood of F., 251:10
cannot remedy f. of people, 143:5
Catullus you should cease f., 91:6

Folly *(continued)*

centuries of f. noise sin, 461:2
every f. but vanity, 313:2
fool returneth to his f., 21:38
forts of f., 497:3
has not fellow, 574:16
Heaven itself we seek in our f., 96:3
in all of every age, 278:5
in king no f. or weakness, 318:17
joys to this are f., 234:5
lovely woman stoops to f., 322:16, 676:13
nights wherein you spend f., 236:9
noise of f., 251:15
of being comforted, 591:16
profit by f. of others, 105:9
rememberest not slightest f., 194:8
reveals to man own f., 713:13
rid of f. beginning of wisdom, 97:18
shakes rooted f. of age, 278:7
shielding from effects of f., 490:8
shoot f. as it flies, 294:15
to be wise, 315:8
uses f. like stalking horse, 196:8
who lives without f., 264:11
wickedness or f., 445:7
wisdom excelleth f., 22:28
Folly's all they taught me, 387:16
Fond, ae f. kiss, 357:8
and wayward thoughts, 369:6
foolish f. old man, 213:5
grow too f. of war, 436:1
I'm f. of lobsters, 439:7
lover, 261:2
prove so f., 213:21
too f. to rule alone, 295:13
trivial f. records, 198:15
Fonder, absence makes heart grow f., 101:17
Fondest hope decay, 388:3
Fondle, every salesman can f. her breasts, 626:6
Fondling she saith since I hemmed thee here, 171:9
Fondness, habitual hatred or f., 329:1
moderate f. for your children, 297:10
Fons Bandusiae splendidior vitro, 97:*n*4
Font, porphyry f., 453:5
Food as luscious as locusts, 208:9
bring your own f., 869:3
crops the flowery f., 294:17
eat f. not too much, 873:16
fame is f. dead men eat, 535:9
for worms, 301:20
gathereth her f. in the harvest, 19:32
glum urge for f. to fill us, 752:7
government see that people have f., 484:23
if music f. of love, 204:10
man merely a passage for f., 140:2
many companions for f. and drink, 59:19
moody f. of love, 218:24
music f. of love, 204:*n*1
my life my joy my f., 155:*n*3
of fancy, 195:32
of fools, 284:21
of love, 204:10
people have no f., 537:4
poets' f. love and fame, 402:8
seeking the f. he eats, 194:13
sharing f. is intimate act, 752:10
starving because f. isn't available, 765:16

Food *(continued)*
struggle for f., 440:*n1*
sweeping rain that leaveth no f., 278:9
sweet f. of knowledge, 162:17
that does not exist, 878:2
thousand tables wanted f., 368:1
to one poison to others, 90:16
Tom's f. for seven year, 212:6
too fine for angels, 280:18
Fool all people all the time, 447:5
almost at times the F., 675:4
and his money, 881:10
answer a f. according to his folly, 21:37
at forty fool indeed, 290:14
at his end shall be a f., 28:2
big f. says push on, 793:14
busy old f. unruly Sun, 228:15
called her his lady fair, 589:5
Don Quixote's a muddled f., 157:21
dullness of f. whetstone of wits, 193:25
enough to expunge, 310:23
every f. will be meddling, 21:10
every inch not f. is rogue, 273:8
gilded f., 228:3
great and sublime f., 522:11
greatest f. is man, 278:6
has feathered his nest, 236:14
hath said in his heart, 15:9
he that trusteth in his own heart is a f., 22:7
hold tongue and pass for sage, 101:5
how ill white hairs become f., 188:27
I am Fortune's f., 180:30
I have played the f., 11:6
invented kissing, 286:4
laughter of the f., 23:11
learned f. more foolish, 268:4
lies here, 587:11
life time's f., 183:30
love's not Time's f., 222:15
made serviceable, 568:1
me to top of my bent, 200:27
merciful to me a f., 539:17
met a f. i' the forest, 194:14
more hope of a f., 21:38
motley f., 194:14
multitude choose by show, 185:6
my poor f. is hanged, 213:14
need to f. ourselves, 601:4
no f. like old f., 148:2
nor yet f. to fame, 295:10
now and then right, 326:12
O f. I shall go mad, 211:23
old doting f., 108:6
old man who will not laugh is f., 584:14
once harm done even f. understands, 52:4
one draught above heat makes him f., 204:19
patriot a f. in every age, 296:9
play the Roman f., 217:26
politician who steals is a f., 543:14
poor f. with all my lore, 344:1
rather have f. make me merry, 195:24
relenting f., 172:3
remains f. his life long, 346:21
resolved to live a f., 237:20
returneth to his folly, 21:38
said my muse to me, 162:20
some people all the time, 447:5
strumpet's f., 218:1

Fool *(continued)*
suspects himself a f., 290:23
talk sense to a f., 68:10
the more f. I, 194:7
there was made his prayer, 589:5
think he is wise, 195:34
this night thy soul, 38:4
though he be a f., 277:7
to fame, 295:10
uttereth all his mind, 22:9
way of a f., 20:19
when he holdeth his peace, 20:43
when we play the f., 384:2
wise enough to play f., 205:11
wise man dieth as the f., 22:30
wise man knows himself f., 195:34
wisest f. in Christendom, 161:14
with f. no companionship, 64:14
with judges, 106:*n4*
yourself about love, 824:14
Fooled, don't get f. again, 861:18
nature cannot be f., 790:5
with hope, 272:11
Foolery governs whole world, 238:16
that wise men have, 193:26
walk about like sun, 205:10
Fool-gudgeon opinion, 184:9
Fooling, adapted to my f., 625:1
Foolish, an' f. notion, 356:16
and false as fame, 281:5
consistency, 426:19
fond old man, 213:5
fool calls you f., 68:10
forgive f. ways, 438:18
frantic boast f. word, 589:11
gets f. or wife does, 600:14
God hath chosen f. things, 42:5
hold that mortal f., 68:14
I being young and f., 590:21
learned fool more f., 268:4
man built house on sand, 33:25
man who trusts woman, 94:*n10*
men who accuse a woman, 281:7
never said a f. thing, 280:27
newspaper marries f., 600:16
old and f. king, 23:3
passionate man, 596:7
penny wise pound f., 234:11
people without understanding, 27:25
seem f. among wise, 106:4
son heaviness of his mother, 20:10
son is calamity of his father, 21:7
studied in my f. youth, 138:18
thing but a toy, 205:29
thing well done, 309:22
things to confound wise, 42:5
to make long prologue, 31:32
virgins, 35:25
when he had not pen, 311:3
wrath killeth the f., 13:10
Fool's errand, 313:25
mouth is his destruction, 21:1
paradise, 880:12
Fools, a little wise best f. be, 229:1
all f. on our side, 523:7
amongst f. a judge, 106:*n4*
are my theme, 394:11
but f. caught it, 592:13

Fools *(continued)*
by follies they perished the f., 52:21
by heavenly compulsion, 211:3
children and f. cannot lie, 147:30
crabbed as dull f. suppose, 252:19
discourse of f. is irksome, 31:12
displeasing ten thousand f., 124:13
do not imitate successes, 85:4
do not know how much more is half than
    whole, 54:18
dreading e'en f., 295:13
effect of coercion to make f., 336:8
fill world with f., 490:8
flanneled f. at wicket, 589:15
food of f., 284:21
great stage of f., 213:1
heart of f., 23:10
hundred f. not make wise man, 684:9
I am two f. I know, 228:21
illusion of f., 713:13
in all tongues called f., 196:3
in idle wishes f. stay, 347:9
laugh at men of sense, 280:25
learn in no other, 302:23
let f. use talents, 204:18
lighted f. way to dusty death, 217:23
make a mock at sin, 20:24
more f. than wise, 882:2
ninety-nine percent of people f., 715:12
no more I'll tease, 293:20
of fortune, 213:25
of nature, 197:34
old men know young men f., 163:13
Paradise of F., 257:9
play the f. with time, 188:5
poems made by f. like me, 668:1
poor f. decoyed, 277:14
rush in, 292:25
shoal of f. for tenders, 287:3
so deep-contemplative, 194:17
some made coxcombs nature meant f.,
    292:10
suckle f., 208:17
suffer f. gladly, 43:21
tedious old f., 198:38
the stop to busy f., 269:2
too green and only good for f., 58:*n5*
we f. of nature, 197:34
what f. these mortals be, 103:8, 178:28
who came to scoff, 322:26
wise men profit more from f., 85:4
wise men speak f. decide, 56:3
wish to appear wise among f., 106:4
words are money of f., 239:5
young men think old men f., 163:13
Fools' experiments, 441:2
names like f. faces, 883:11
Foos, my f. won't moos, 650:22
Foot, accent of coming F., 511:13
and hand go cold, 151:4
beat earth with unfettered f., 96:17
beggar on f., 596:16
better f. before, 175:28
cannot put shoe on every f., 100:26
crown to sole of f., 190:37
dash f. against stone, 37:24
dash thy f. against a stone, 17:29
for foot, 8:17

Foot *(continued)*
　　from the f. Hercules, 69:15
　　her f. speaks, 204:4
　　her f. was light, 412:3
　　here men first set f. on moon, 888:18
　　I hold Creation in my f., 827:12
　　in front of the other, 785:2
　　in the stirrup, 890:12, 890:13
　　it featly, 224:12
　　lived like f. for thirty years, 833:7
　　my f. on my native heath, 374:10
　　no f. of unfamiliar men, 496:12
　　no f. slide, 887:15
　　noiseless f. of time, 206:10
　　of hand of f. of lip, 222:9
　　one f. already in grave, 108:6
　　one f. in sea one on shore, 190:33
　　one white f. try him, 886:5
　　print of naked f., 282:11
　　proud f. of conqueror, 176:6
　　rest for the sole of her f., 6:20
　　silver f. in mouth, 834:15
　　stamped f. and cried, 508:21
　　suffer thy f. to be moved, 18:30
　　thy soul the fixt f., 229:17
　　wear steps of his door, 30:27
　　who cleft Devil's f., 228:9
　　wishing his f. equal with eye, 170:27
　　with naked f. stalking my chamber, 149:4
Foot-and-a-half-long words, 98:20
Football combines two worst features, 853:8
　　in life as in f., 571:4
Footfalls echo in memory, 678:7
Foothold tenoned and mortised in granite, 486:4
Footing, 'twixt his stretched f., 203:9
Foot-in-the-grave young man, 526:14
Footless halls of air, 800:1
Footman, eternal F. snicker, 675:3
Footnotes to Plato, 580:11
Footpads, when f. quail, 527:23
Footpath, jog on the f. way, 223:24
Footprints of gigantic hound, 573:19
　　on the sands of time, 436:6
Footstep, where thy f. gleams, 448:7
Footsteps, distant f. echo, 436:17
　　home his f. turned, 373:3
　　plants his f. in the sea, 326:9
　　someone follow in my f., 807:14
Footstool, earth as f., 599:5
　　earth is his f., 32:19
Foppery, excellent f. of the world, 211:3
Fops, whole tribe of f., 210:33
Forbade me to put off my hat, 270:5
Forbear and persevere, 556:12
　　be not too bold, 160:*n*6
　　cruel mother, 97:11
　　to dig dust enclosed here, 226:17
　　to judge, 170:9
Forbearance ceases to be virtue, 323:14
　　practice Christian f., 332:1
Forbid, God f., 7:13
　　it Almighty God, 331:13
　　them not, 36:38
Forbidden by Constitution, 349:11
　　tree whose mortal taste, 255:3
　　wanted apple because was f., 523:16
　　whatever not f. is permitted, 359:21

Forbids, my mind f. to crave, 154:10
　　rich as well as poor, 546:2
Force, abandonment of f., 653:16
　　acceleration proportional to applied f., 279:*n*3
　　adaptation of form to resist f., 484:22
　　Allied Expeditionary F., 686:13
　　and beauty of process, 545:8
　　change from liberty to f., 363:4
　　citizens to confess faith, 694:2
　　Conservation of F., 494:5
　　constant f. for muddlement, 544:19
　　eastward I go only by f., 475:28
　　elemental f. freed, 680:5
　　Expeditionary F., 517:16
　　from which sun draws power, 661:3
　　in Nature not increased, 494:5
　　knowledge more than f., 164:*n*3
　　language into meaning, 677:7
　　love f., 604:4
　　may the F. be with you, 859:10
　　moment to its crisis, 675:2
　　no motion has she no f., 369:8
　　no place where need of skill, 69:14
　　nobody really possesses it, 760:11
　　not by f. or violence, 332:1
　　not remedy, 457:14
　　of his own merit, 225:11
　　of righteousness, 604:4
　　of temporal power, 186:1
　　oppressor to commit brutality openly, 823:14
　　paralyzed f., 676:20
　　passion spent novel f., 451:22
　　produce according to f., 478:*n*2
　　proportional to motive f., 279:15
　　question of brute f., 663:18
　　secret f. driving me, 442:24
　　soul f., 604:4
　　spiritual f. stronger, 428:28
　　terror and f., 684:8
　　that through green fuse, 777:2
　　too revolutionary for old ideas, 661:4
　　tribalism strongest f., 834:4
　　uncomprehended which was his life, 506:17
　　use of f. but temporary, 324:4
　　when one by f. subdues, 79:14
　　who overcomes by f., 256:2
　　without wisdom falls of own weight, 96:28
　　world f. not presence, 643:8
　　worship God not constrained by f., 106:5
Forced by fate, 274:13
　　gait of shuffling nag, 182:36
　　to surrender truth, 248:1
　　wedlock f. a hell, 169:22
Forces, Armed F. in control, 692:7
　　avoid perils by united f., 276:14
　　by which nature animated, 345:3
　　deliberative f., 562:8
　　don't fight f. use them, 705:9
　　imagination one of f. of nature, 643:6
　　impressed upon it, 279:14
　　in the difficult are friendly f., 632:9
　　irresistible f. for uniformity, 667:5
　　man who f. opportunity, 348:9
　　natural and moral f., 494:6
　　one to repeat No, 549:12

Forces *(continued)*
　　opposing and enduring f., 421:12
　　our f. stand on Philippine soil, 644:8
　　politics struggle of f., 532:4
　　these f. met master, 652:10
Forcible, how f. are right words, 13:15
Forcibly if we must, 380:*n*2
Ford, I'm a F. not a Lincoln, 770:17
　　John F., 781:8
Fordoes, makes me or f. me quite, 210:12
Forearmed, forewarned f., 157:17
Forecast, others f. the rising stars, 94:35
Foredoomed, innocent and f., 739:9
Forefathers, contemplate our f., 318:4
　　had no books but score, 170:17
　　met the boat, 640:9
　　never forget laws of f., 106:6
　　rude f. of hamlet, 315:14
　　worked hard fought hard died hard, 567:1
Forefinger, agate on f. of alderman, 179:25
　　of all Time, 452:17
Forefront, fighting in f. of the Greeks, 60:10
　　set Uriah in f. of battle, 11:17
Foregoing generations beheld God nature, 425:19
Foregone conclusion, 209:18
Forehead, drops of blood form on f., 687:1
　　of humanity, 409:10
　　of the age to come, 408:18
　　of the morning sky, 253:14
　　right in middle of her f., 438:2
　　smooth f. suggests insensitivity, 716:13
Foreheads of defamers, 518:2
　　villainous low, 225:2
Foreign, apprenticehood to f. passages, 176:15
　　avoid f. collision, 384:16
　　banners of f. independence, 363:4
　　boys not sent into f. wars, 653:2
　　corner of f. field, 669:10
　　disposed of f. enemies, 75:22
　　gear of f. dead men, 679:4
　　intercourse with f. nations, 386:17
　　levy, 216:11
　　life is a f. language, 688:2
　　nations and the next age, 166:21
　　no f. sky protected me, 683:7
　　rule of conduct with f. nations, 329:2
　　the past a f. country, 707:7
　　things f. or things at home, 271:16
　　troop in my country, 306:5
　　wandering on f. strand, 373:3
Foreigner in country of birth, 862:11
　　no f. do business here, 139:10
Foreigners spell better than pronounce, 522:4
Foreknow, for whom he did f., 41:22
Foreknowledge absolute, 256:21
Forelock, by f. take time, 161:4
Foremost files of time, 452:9
Forensic, aim of f. oratory, 87:20
Forepangs, pangs schooled at f., 547:5
Foresee a considerable revolution, 440:3
Forest, beasts of the f. creep forth, 18:11
　　beautiful changes as f., 797:10
　　cutting through the f., 639:14
　　enchanted place on top of F., 651:10
　　every beast of the f. is mine, 16:29
　　flowers of the f., 321:8

Forest *(continued)*
    I believe in the f., 475:30
    lyre even as f. is, 402:13
    met a fool i' the f., 194:14
    midnight moment's f., 827:10
    primeval, 436:20
    vast wastes of f. verdure, 500:5
    waving f. of sea-growth, 694:13
    way into Universe through f., 533:9
    wild f. green mansions, 539:13
Foresters, Diana's f., 181:21
Forest's ferny floor, 616:6
Forests, helmets gleamed in f., 500:5
    in the f. of the night, 353:1
    Pelion with its leafy f., 53:12
Foretold that danger lurks within, 170:34
Forever, ae farewell and then f., 357:8
    and a day, 195:28
    and it lasted f., 828:11
    boot stamping on human face f., 735:22
    can't sleep with the river f., 866:11
    corner of field f. England, 669:10
    diamond lasts f., 698:9
    do you want to live f., 312:*n*2
    fare thee well, 397:6
    farewell Cassius, 193:17
    good jest f., 182:11
    I go on f., 454:25
    live f. or die in attempt, 802:8
    man has F., 461:13
    On a Clear Day You Can See F., 790:15
    piping songs, 410:17
    same yesterday today and f., 45:17
    segregation now segregation f., 794:2
    stranger and alone, 727:11
    thought love would last f., 748:14
    time will not be ours f., 232:5
    wild to be wreckage f., 801:16
    would you live f., 312:6
Forevermore, adieu f., 357:12
    glory gone f., 438:5
Forewarned forearmed, 157:17
Forfeit confidence of citizens, 447:5
    fair renown, 373:3
    to a confined doom, 222:10
Forgave, coward never f., 313:17
    hugged offender f. offense, 274:28
    took kindness f. theft, 463:1
Forge in smithy of soul, 650:13
    practice and thought f. art, 93:12
    random grim f., 546:16
Forged, chain I f. in life, 465:7
Forgeries, these are the f. of jealousy, 178:14
Forges, what his breast f., 219:32
Forget, abortions will not let you f., 783:6
    and forgive, 156:34, 213:6
    and if thou wilt f., 512:3
    and smile, 512:5
    better by far f. and smile, 512:5
    can I f. you for eternity, 788:9
    dissolve and f., 410:5
    don't f. from Virginia, 502:15
    events we will never f., 871:6
    happy f. what cannot be changed, 499:10
    how long wilt thou f. me, 15:8
    I must f. you first, 329:17
    I never f. a face, 707:12
    if I f. thee O Jerusalem, 19:11

Forget *(continued)*
    learn hateful art how to f., 241:20
    lest we f., 589:7
    live so long that I'll f. her, 781:3
    love to friends and brethren, 29:23
    my own name, 156:29
    never f. horror of moment, 515:11
    never f. it is a constitution, 349:14
    never f. laws of forefathers, 106:6
    never f. what they did, 446:5
    new-made honor doth f. men's names, 175:3
    not to do good and communicate, 45:19
    not yet tried intent, 149:2
    so many things I'd like to f., 738:16
    teach unforgetful to f., 506:7
    the best sometimes f., 208:26
    the He and She, 228:14
    till Future dares f. Past, 403:13
    what I have been, 177:11
    when image is effaced, 76:7
    womb shall f. him, 13:45
    women and elephants never f., 608:5
    women remember what don't want to f., 690:3
Forgetful, blessed are f., 548:10
    of his horsemanship, 52:3
Forgetfulness, complete f. that one is alive, 633:5
    not in entire f., 370:17
    of affliction, 30:37
    of all ills, 52:32
    space engenders f., 630:15
    steep senses in f., 188:9
    to dumb f. a prey, 316:4
Forgets dying bird, 333:15
    he f. not his own, 882:4
    man f. to live, 280:26
Forgetting, sleep and a f., 370:17
    struggle of memory against f., 824:1
    those things behind, 44:4
Forgive, as we f. our debtors, 32:25
    as we f. those who trespass, 32:*n*2
    being with the right to f., 492:11
    blindness we may f., 605:14
    close eyes to f., 582:6
    cursed be tribe if I f., 184:25
    Father f. them, 38:34
    forget and f., 156:34, 213:6
    give thanks and f., 531:1
    God f. you but I never, 151:11
    he will never f. you, 360:13
    I f. you you f. me, 353:11
    if Death knew how to f., 93:25
    know everything f. everything, 362:*n*5
    man who forces opportunity, 348:9
    me my injuries, 787:17
    me they were delicious, 658:19
    O Lord my little jokes, 624:19
    of course God will f. me, 415:10
    only brave know how to f., 313:17
    our foolish ways, 438:18
    person displaying feeling, 417:14
    public seldom f. twice, 335:4
    some sinner, 645:7
    sometimes children f. parents, 560:5
    them as a Christian, 382:11
    those I have injured, 787:17

Forgive *(continued)*
    those who bore us, 264:18
    Thy great big one on me, 624:19
    to f. divine, 292:23
    us all our trespasses little creatures, 654:3
    us our debts, 32:25
    us our trespasses, 32:*n*2
    wilt thou f. that sin, 231:3
    wrongs darker than death or night, 402:5
    you'll f. him, 856:3
Forgiven, her sins are f., 37:27
Forgiveness, after knowledge what f., 675:22
    ask of thee f., 213:8
    of sins, 47:25, 48:11
    to injured does belong, 103:*n*10
Forgives, God f. me for it., 805:14
Forgiving, enemy f. all, 748:5
Forgo, never in such slavery as to f. kindred, 106:6
Forgot, auld acquaintance be f., 357:17
    copperheads and assassin, 636:6
    cry of gulls, 676:14
    don't let it be f., 790:14
    Father Son are things f., 230:15
    for which he toiled, 221:4
    honey I just f. to duck, 705:5
    little town that time f., 854:11
    much Cynara, 599:15
    time hath f. itself, 203:20
    to wind clock, 313:20
Forgotten aim, 584:4
    all I have done for him, 278:15
    as a dead man out of mind, 16:2
    eagle f., 639:11
    fly f. as a dream, 289:14
    for want of writers, 97:*n*11
    glimpses of f. dreams, 450:11
    grief f., 529:13
    I am all f., 218:9
    I have f. your name, 530:19
    if you would not be f., 302:18
    learned nothing f. nothing, 348:6
    Man, 537:7
    man, 651:14
    memory of them is f., 23:21
    mornings, 777:8
    not f. inside of church, 183:7
    O mother what have I f., 812:15
    old times not f., 470:16
    through lapse of Time, 77:15
    undeservedly f., 749:18
    volume of f. lore, 449:3
    wars, 678:8
    you have f. my kisses, 530:19
Fork, come to f. in road take it, 807:8
    everyone sees what on end of f., 774:2
Forked mountain or blue promontory, 218:39
    poor bare f. animal, 212:3
    torch of a flower, 663:22
Forks and hope, 517:6
    fingers made before f., 286:2
Forlorn, faery lands f., 410:10
    glimpses make me less f., 371:24
    Stygian cave f., 250:19
Form, all must love human f., 351:5
    all-f. only f. rational, 542:10
    and frame from thinking, 642:12
    and pressure, 200:8

Forty, at f. reforms plan, 290:23
  cannot live on f. pound, 242:10
  centuries look down, 365:4
  days and forty nights, 6:19
  difference of f. thousand men, 366:8
  fasted f. days and f. nights, 32:11
  fool at f. fool indeed, 290:14
  I am f., 787:10
  life begins at f., 635:19
  men at f. learn, 807:21
  Moses was there f. days, 8:22
  nor rich at f., 244:5
  not enter government after f., 126:8
  rather than f. shillings, 186:26
  round earth in f. minutes, 178:17
  stripes save one, 43:22
  thousand brothers, 202:20
  thousand men, 892:14
  till fifty man stoic or satyr, 561:15
  understand life at f., 585:12
  wander in the wilderness f. years, 9:4
  whacks, 885:22
  winters besiege brow, 220:31
  work of men above f., 553:3
Forty-second, gang at F. Street, 634:11
  street, 689:9
Forum, allow women in F., 99:13
Forward, ever f. but slowly, 335:6
  expression was steady, 809:7
  fare f., 84:n8
  fare f. voyagers, 679:6
  life must be lived f., 469:2
  look f. to posterity, 325:2
  nothing to look f. to, 622:13
  since we have come so far, 173:23
  some a f. motion love, 268:11
  sons of France, 361:3
  the Light Brigade, 454:19
Fossil, language is f. poetry, 427:20
Fossils, God hid f. in rocks, 552:5
  thin layer of our f., radioactive, 773:2
  we are all potential f., 750:7
Foster child of silence, 410:13
  went to Gloucester, 896:10
Fostered alike by beauty and fear, 368:13
Foster-nurse of nature is repose, 212:23
Fou for weeks thegither, 358:5
  wasna f., 357:1
Fought a good fight, 45:2
  all wars f. by boys, 483:19
  and bled in Freedom's cause, 367:19
  battle not even f., 713:13
  battles won only to be f. again, 796:9
  better to have f. and lost, 453:n2
  Black Hawk f. against white men, 363:13
  dogs killed cats, 460:7
  each other for, 381:8
  for life, 760:6
  I f. the law, 842:9
  lie f. with outright, 455:24
  like pagan, 608:16
  man who never f. pilfers, 72:16
  Michael and angels f., 47:1
  spirit that f. in heaven, 256:7
  stars f. against Sisera, 10:10
  street by street, 619:16
  the better fight, 258:23
  to crown Greece with freedom, 60:12

Fought *(continued)*
  under whose colors he f. so long, 177:14
  war prepared for eventually f., 738:9
  witness that I have f., 271:27
  work they who f. advanced, 446:5
Foul and pestilent, 199:5
  and ugly mists, 181:33
  as Vulcan's stithy, 200:13
  bird that filleth own nest, 141:n1
  blood nipped and ways be f., 174:33
  contagion spread, 253:11
  deed which she plotted, 53:14
  deeds will rise, 197:18
  fair and f. near kin, 595:19
  fair is f. and f. is fair, 213:31
  fee bestow upon f. disease, 210:28
  Fiend Apollyon, 271:15
  from f. to fair, 166:27
  goat-head, 597:3
  I doubt some f. play, 197:17
  limbecks f. as hell, 222:16
  murder most f., 198:6
  pearl in your f. oyster, 196:5
  play, 197:17
  rag-and-bone shop, 597:8
  shapes of f. disease, 454:9
  so f. and fair a day, 214:4
Fouled-up, old-type natural f. guys, 799:14
Foulness of their fate, 668:14
Found crooked sixpence, 895:17
  death in life, 380:8
  dove f. no rest, 6:20
  empire for raising customers, 319:7
  favor in thy sight, 6:33
  fresh Rhodora, 424:9
  fun where I f. it, 589:3
  has f. out thy bed, 352:14
  hast thou f. me O mine enemy, 12:6
  Him in shining of stars, 455:17
  I could extinguish hope, 559:8
  I f. a new world, 261:16
  I f. my wits you lost yours, 239:2
  I have f. it, 83:4
  I oft f. both, 184:11
  I once was lost now am f., 320:13
  in that town dog was f., 322:13
  in whose hand the cup is f., 7:14
  it is f. again, 559:5
  lack of what is f. there, 659:8
  looked inwards f. Nature, 272:7
  lost in America shall be f., 727:15
  lost time never f., 302:27
  man who has f. himself out, 577:13
  one man among a thousand, 23:17
  rebellion in way he f. it, 183:22
  Rome city of bricks, 99:6
  sense beneath rarely f., 292:14
  sheep which was lost, 38:9
  someone else can always be f., 583:7
  sought but f. him not, 24:12
  struggle to f. Roman state, 93:30
  that famous country, 695:2
  was lost and is f., 38:12
  weighed in the balances and f. wanting,
    28:25
  when f. make note, 465:17
  where shall wisdom be f., 14:2
  who loveliness within hath f., 228:13

Found *(continued)*
  woman have I not f., 23:17
  you as a morsel, 218:33
Foundation consisting of confusion, 822:7
  fear f. of most governments, 330:3
  good order f. of good things, 325:9
  is love, 823:10
  new government laying f., 336:1
  no f., 756:18
  no sure f. on blood, 175:27
  of our faith, 125:1
  order our f., 416:7
Foundations, earth's f. fled, 575:20
  earth's f. stand, 576:4
  loosen old f., 636:8
  of knowledge in mathematics, 126:7
  of states laws and arms, 141:15
  when I laid f. of earth, 14:18
  wished to lay f. of kindness, 716:14
Founded, earth and heaven f. strong, 575:7
  government f. on compromise, 324:10
  he hath f. it upon the seas, 15:24
  principle on which society not f., 315:1
  securely f., 343:10
  upon a rock, 33:24
Founder, supinely enjoyed gifts of f., 332:13
  true f. of civil society, 312:12
Founders, newspapers did that which F. hoped,
    667:3
Founding, since the f. of the city, 119:28
Fount Bandusian more sparkling than glass,
    97:5
Fountain and a shrine, 448:6
  dying of thirst by the f., 137:12
  from f. wells up bitter taste, 90:17
  like bubble on f., 373:23
  pitcher broken at the f., 23:31
  rise like f. for me, 455:20
  the f. overflows, 351:15
  troubled like f. stirred, 203:27
  woman moved like f. troubled, 173:25
Fountain's silvery column, 378:2
Fountains, Afric's sunny f., 391:5
  are within, 378:7
  fraught with tears, 163:7
  mountains are f. of men, 533:10
  silver f. have mud, 221:11
  under f. and graves, 882:8
  where the pleasant f. lie, 171:9
Founts, old f. dried up, 672:4
Four, age best in f. things, 165:8
  and twenty tailors, 894:5
  angels to my bed, 265:3
  freedoms, 653:4
  Horsemen rode again, 646:5
  intimate equality of the F., 656:10
  looking over f.-leaf clover, 693:8
  not f. friends in world, 269:10
  snakes gliding, 425:8
  spend in prayer, 159:1
  things better without, 699:11
  things wiser to know, 699:10
  3 or f. families in Country Village, 382:25
  what F. Freedoms establish, 629:5
  winds of the heaven, 29:11
Fourfold, threefold f. tomb, 240:6
Four-in-hand, fiery f., 380:5
Fours, crawling on all f., 299:16

Free *(continued)*

if you can't be f., 871:3
in historical sense not f., 506:15
in my soul am f., 266:2
in whatever form used, 642:20
Indian f. in Nature, 472:20
information wants to be f., 843:18
Jesu set me f., 154:8
land in beloved home, 489:8
land of the f., 386:19
like spirit animating universe, 415:14
live hair shining and f., 669:9
living word set soul f., 644:5
love Virtue she alone is f., 252:28
maids that weave thread, 205:2
majestic f., 370:10
man abide with honor, 473:18
man is born f., 312:15
me from this turbulent priest, 124:10
men by nature equally f., 320:7
men citizens of Berlin, 786:13
mother of the f., 580:19
my lines and life are f., 242:26
nation ignorant and f., 338:7
neither bond nor f., 44:12
no such thing as f. lunch, 767:16
no woman can call herself f., 657:16
not happy unless f., 400:11
nothin' ain't worth nothin' but it's f.,
  841:15
nothing-withholding and f., 543:1
now f. I once more weave, 418:21
only educated are f., 109:1
only f. men can negotiate, 790:19
open-minded adjustment, 566:16
ourselves subdue our masters, 340:12
personal identity and f. will, 781:12
press necessity, 685:5
principle of f. thought, 539:7
principles of f. constitution lost, 332:3
private enterprise, 652:19
protection of f. speech, 538:21
pure in life f. from sin, 96:14
reason left f. to combat, 337:8
Russian speech, 479:8
servitude can pierce hearts, 672:6
set bodily f. from surroundings, 630:15
set my poor heart f., 207:*n*2
should himself be f., 311:*n*2
soil free men, 885:7
solitude unsponsored f., 640:22
soul in prison I am not f., 561:11
speech in repulsive form, 621:8
suppression of f. speech, 562:9
take away our f. will and glory, 142:6
that anchor and chain, 83:3
that moment they are f., 326:21
the human will, 296:21
thenceforward and forever f., 445:13
they bring it to you f., 798:8
think they ought to be f., 323:20
thou art f., 494:10
though thrall, 158:17
thought, 539:7
thought is f., 224:31
thus so cleanly I myself can f., 167:11
'tis the gift to be f., 885:3
to regulate industry, 337:11

Free *(continued)*

to think speak write, 338:17
trade in ideas, 538:22
trade unpopular, 419:6
truth shall make you f., 39:25
truth will set you f., 877:12
unreproved pleasures f., 250:24
was he f. was he happy, 749:11
we must be f. or die, 370:11
we will die f. men, 341:10
westward I go f., 475:28
when evils most f., 192:3
white and somewhat more f., 731:10
who would be f. strike blow, 395:7
wish all men everywhere f., 445:12
within ourselves, 730:12
woods more f. from peril, 193:36
yearning to breathe f., 552:16
your mind and your ass will, 850:5
Freed capacity of thought, 572:15
elemental force f., 680:5
no man's pie f. from his finger, 225:10
Freedom, abridging f. of speech, 340:1
abridgment of f., 345:13
African conditioned to f., 690:9
all solace to man gives, 131:4
all who love f., 686:13
altar of f., 446:12
and democracy, 765:13
another man's f., 823:3
associate democracy with f. of action,
  572:15
assure f. to the free, 446:1
battle cry of F., 489:9
black f. jeopardized, 808:18
born to f., 653:5
born to give you your name F., 705:7
brought independence and rationality,
  725:8
crown Greece with f., 60:12
cultural f., 633:11
cure is f., 419:10
deliver us from f., 827:5
deny f. to others, 444:13
deny participation of f., 324:12
deprived of f. by authorities, 692:6
deserving of f. and life, 344:13
economic f., 633:11
every man who lives without f., 741:10
fight for f. and truth, 504:17
fight to maintain f., 653:5
fills space 'twixt marsh, 543:2
flame of f. in souls, 537:9
for experimentation necessary, 708:12
for one who thinks differently, 608:1
for thought we hate, 539:7
free form not assure f., 642:20
friends of f. doubt our sincerity, 444:6
from every B.V.D. f. ring, 701:9
from fear, 653:4, 653:15
from mountain height, 408:12
from violence and lies, 578:3
from want, 653:4, 653:15
greater f. for average man, 652:5
greatest gift f. of will, 130:5
having my f. boast of nothing, 176:15
history is f. and necessity, 689:13
history progress of f., 367:12

Freedom *(continued)*

hunted round the globe, 333:2
idea of F., 457:9
if F. fall, 590:6
if I have f. in my love, 266:2
in a commons brings ruin, 779:7
in economic arrangements, 767:14
in highest position least f., 92:7
indispensable condition of f., 607:4
indivisible word, 697:2
infringement of human f., 359:7
intellectual f. only guarantee, 797:5
is slavery, 735:17
lack of belief in f., 767:15
law can only bring f., 344:17
let f. ring, 439:9, 823:9
liberal institutions enemies of f., 548:24
liberty f. enfranchisement, 192:17
life pure transparent f., 751:4
love not f. but license, 254:17
made man isolated anxious powerless,
  725:8
means never arriving on time, 617:2
murder never argument for f., 364:13
my story ends with f., 469:1
nation which enjoys most f., 363:5
new birth of f., 446:5, 877:1
none love f. but good men, 254:17
not conceived simply, 809:11
obedience bane of f., 401:8
of choice and with honor, 141:3
of expression matrix, 607:4
of f. he only is deserving, 344:13
of knyghthod and of f. flour, 136:14
of navigation, 566:16
of person, 337:12
of press, 337:12
of press bulwarks of liberty, 320:9
of press guaranteed those who own one,
  738:12
of religion, 337:12
of speech and expression, 653:4
of speech freedom of conscience, 524:14
of speech may be taken, 328:10
of thought, 318:6
of worship, 653:4
oh f. over me, 899:1
only f. gods grant us is this, 681:15
people f. light, 688:10
political f., 633:11
political f. business of Government, 652:6
private property guaranty of f., 720:17
reap blessings of f., 333:10
regardless of form, 642:20
religious f., 633:11
rhymes suggest wildest f., 425:9
safeguards of individual f., 721:1
secret of f. a brave heart, 72:4
secret of happiness, 72:4
seven-pillared house, 680:7
shall awhile repair, 317:11
slaves fought for f., 421:16
so celestial article as F., 333:6
spirit of truth and f., 504:6
state exists is no f., 607:15
striking blow for f., 670:15
system based on courage, 617:6
taken away from me, 790:20

Frightened, crept like f. girl, 559:18
    don't be f. it won't last, 585:13
    little mouse under chair, 895:7
    Miss Muffet away, 895:14
Frightening, many f. sights abroad, 555:11
Frightful fiend, 376:21
    vice a monster of f. mien, 295:2
Frights, it f. the isle, 208:25
Frigid, beat down f. Rome, 596:8
Fringe, lunatic f., 571:18
Fringed curtains of thine eye, 224:15
Fringes be falling rain, 891:13
Frippery, a little f. necessary, 341:3
Frisk i' the sun, 223:10
Frisson nouveau, 422:*n6*
Fritter my wig, 517:1
Frittered away by detail, 475:1
Frittering away his age, 375:1
Frivolity, irresponsible f., 430:20
Frivolous, one who is f. all day, 3:6
Frizzled stale and small, 787:8
Fro, going to and f. in the earth, 12:36
    many shall run to and f., 28:30
    reel to and f., 18:16
Frocks and Curls, 509:20
Frog better'n any other frog, 522:2
    eye of newt toe of f., 216:27
    has drink enough to spare, 82:15
    how public like a F., 508:14
    leaping in, 280:2
    outjump any f., 522:3
    thus use your f., 245:8
    would a-wooing go, 892:11
Frog's life is most jolly, 82:15
Frogs die in earnest, 82:9
    drone their lament, 93:14
    eat butterflies, 641:3
    in the marsh mud, 93:14
Frogs', spawning islands like f. eggs, 763:5
Frog-spawn of ditch, 595:4
Frolic wine, 241:9
Front, cannon in f., 454:22
    of Jove himself, 201:5
    one foot in f. of the other, 785:2
    only essential facts, 474:29
    see f. o' battle lour, 358:16
    smoothed his wrinkled f., 171:17
Frontier from Atlantic to Pacific, 619:9
    grave far away, 582:9
    has gone, 580:5
    New F., 785:5
    outer edge of wave, 580:4
    Rhine where f. lies, 599:8
    space the final f., 797:3
Frontiers, aggression outside f., 653:16
    economy not respect political f., 648:7
    wherever man fronts fact, 473:25
Frost, curdied by f. from snow, 220:3
    fell death's untimely f., 358:13
    is on the punkin, 553:10
    itself doth burn, 201:7
    performs secret ministry, 377:14
    prime of youth a f. of cares, 163:11
    secret ministry of f., 377:15
    snow congealed with biting f., 53:*n1*
    third day comes a f., 225:25
    was specter-gray, 536:10
    which binds so dear head, 403:12

Frosted September, 663:22
Frosts are slain, 529:13
Frost-wind, meantime the f. blows, 409:23
Frosty, blessings on your f. pow, 357:13
    but kindly, 194:5
    Caucasus, 176:18
    wind made moan, 512:6
Frothy, hopping through f. waves, 516:3
Froward, life like a f. child, 271:30
Frowned, Critic you have f., 372:16
    fair Science f. not, 316:6
Frowning, behind f. providence, 326:10
Frowns, sits on battlements and f., 362:2
Frowsy couch in sorrow steep, 359:2
Froze genial current, 315:22
    hunched in belly till wet fur f., 774:14
Frozen, children walk on f. toes, 606:2
    corpse was he, 436:9
    grass, 409:18
    incarnation of its f. woe, 582:14
    milk comes f. home in pail, 174:33
    music, 343:24
    Naked Lunch a f. moment, 774:2
    sea inside us, 655:10
    toes, 606:2
    torrid or f. zone, 245:17
    which thy f. bosom bears, 207:*n2*
    wind off f. peak, 623:19
    your tiny hand is f., 550:14
Fructify in lives of others, 84:*n8*
Frugal, how f. the Chariot, 510:14
    wise and f. government, 337:11
Frugality, second is f., 57:22
Fruit, bound as f. to tree, 499:2
    bringeth forth his f. in season, 14:40
    brought forth f., 34:16
    cease from yielding f., 27:39
    earth bringeth forth f., 36:29
    feed on bitter f., 730:1
    forth reaching to the f. she plucked, 259:11
    hang like f. my soul, 220:29
    husbandman waiteth for precious f., 45:32
    I bore was sun, 108:*n7*
    its f. sweet its shade delightful, 4:14
    man is not piece of f., 780:7
    man stole the f., 242:16
    of action not be motive, 84:9
    of experience, 534:7
    of her hands, 22:20
    of sense beneath, 292:14
    of Spirit, 43:31
    of that forbidden tree, 255:3
    of the vine, 36:3
    of thy womb, 37:8
    plant vineyards and eat the f., 27:22
    reach ripest f. of all, 168:2
    restore with cordial f., 242:26
    ripest f. first falls, 176:27
    southern trees bear strange f., 733:12
    that your seasons bring, 111:19
    tree bringeth not forth f., 32:8
    tree known by f., 34:11
    tree whose f. threw death, 230:21
    weakest f. drops earliest, 185:30
Fruited, above f. plain, 572:5
Fruitful, be f. and multiply, 5:8
    of golden deeds, 257:7
    vineyard in a very f. hill, 25:3

Fruitful (*continued*)
    was she not f., 107:23
Fruition, prospects more pleasing than f.,
    110:*n10*
    sweet f. of earthly crown, 168:2
Fruitless, cold f. moon, 177:26
    weak and f. words, 446:12
Fruits, all pleasant f. do flow, 227:3
    by their f. know them, 33:22
    Dead Sea f., 388:4
    descendants shall gather your f., 93:3
    eat his pleasant f., 24:16
    fairy f. and flowers, 448:6
    green f. of world, 640:16
    judge but by f., 399:10
    kindly f. of the earth, 49:2
    know them by f., 33:21
    let not f. of action be motive, 84:9
    no f. no flowers, 418:15
    of earth are for everyone, 361:1
    of life and beauty, 352:6
    of love gone, 399:16
Fruit-tree, tips with silver f. tops, 180:8
Frumious Bandersnatch, 515:12
Frustrate, not f. of his hope, 253:22
Fry in owene grece, 135:8
    me or Fritter my wig, 517:1
Frying, out of f. pan into fire, 113:14
Fuck, if men could f. with warm hearts, 663:11
    you up your mum and dad, 799:15
    zipless f. is absolutely pure, 854:9
Fucked, constantly getting f., 865:5
Fudge, two fifths sheer f., 481:19
Fuel, adding f. to the flame, 260:22
    to maintain his fires, 245:18
Fugit inreparabile tempus, 93:*n8*
Fugitive and cloistered virtue, 254:9
    from law of averages, 796:11
    receive the f., 333:2
    shalt thou be, 6:6
    what was so f., 370:20
Fugue, folly alone stays f. of Youth, 141:11
Fulfill desires of thy servants, 48:17
    not to destroy but f., 32:16
    to f. lusts, 41:40
Fulfilled, till all be f., 32:17
Fulfilling, love is f. of law, 41:39
Fulfillment, all men's plans to f., 52:9
    bring all his words to f., 52:11
    deferred f. of prehistoric wish, 563:4
    give each moment f., 631:11
Fulfills, God f. in many ways, 455:19
    great Nature's plan, 356:12
Full, age f. of care, 881:17
    bloody f. of blame, 222:20
    cause of weeping, 211:23
    earth is f. of his glory, 25:9
    earth is f. of thy riches, 18:11
    extent of its own value, 364:9
    fathom five, 224:14
    hell f. of good intentions, 123:13
    I am f. of matter, 14:12
    isle is f. of noises, 224:33
    little knowest that hast not tried, 160:26
    man that hath quiver f., 19:6
    meridian of my glory, 225:23
    moon throw shadow, 662:6
    night f. of ugly sights, 171:27

Full *(continued)*

not the f. four seasons, 695:11
o' milk of human kindness, 214:16
of artless jealousy, 201:22
of direst cruelty, 214:17
of few days and f. of trouble, 13:29
of grace and truth, 38:48
of high sentence, 675:4
of number of things, 555:13
of quarrels as egg of meat, 180:26
of shapes is fancy, 204:11
of smiles in early days, 75:21
of sound and fury, 217:23
of spirit as month of May, 183:12
of strange oaths, 194:25
of wiles full of guile, 73:4
of wise saws, 194:25
pursuit of the uneatable, 561:7
reading maketh a f. man, 166:18
sea is not f., 22:22
sea of faith at f., 496:19
someone not f. of herself, 856:8
speed ahead, 421:1
streets f. of water, 683:14
supped f. with horrors, 217:22
that your joy may be f., 40:4
to be empty is to be f., 57:10
too f. for sound and foam, 456:4
wasna f. but had plenty, 357:1
wheel is come f. circle, 213:11
woods are f. of them, 884:14
youth f. of pleasance, 881:17
Full-blown rose, 409:21
Full-dazzling, all his beams f., 487:10
Fullness, earth and f. thereof, 15:24, 42:22
of all things, 51:26
of perfection in him, 175:9
Full-throated ease, 410:3
Full-voiced choir below, 251:23
Fulmen, eripuit coelo f., 301:*n3*
eripuitque Jovi f., 104:*n5*
Fum, Fie foh and f., 212:9
Fumble with the sheets, 189:4
Fume of poppies, 411:7
Fumes, coiling in thousand f. of smoke, 805:*n*1
Fun, ain't we got f., 667:12
allowed himself f. and relaxation, 69:11
always seemed to leave you at loss, 763:9
are we having f. yet, 859:7
has the mostest f., 553:7
mirth and f. fast furious, 358:8
sex most f. without laughing, 839:15
she'll have f. f. f., 856:1
taken f. where found it, 589:3
to match sorrow, 519:8
What jolly f., 579:15
Function, form follows f., 565:27
intuitive in f., 456:14
judicial f., 562:14
of citizen, 694:6
of intellectuals, 689:12
to live is to f., 539:8
Functional capacity, 341:8
Functions, man in divers f., 188:34
Fund of good sense, 339:5
Fundamental article of political creed, 330:16
human rights, 661:16
law of life, 312:3

Fundamental *(continued)*

principle of constitution, 318:20
question of philosophy, 769:15
things apply, 702:11
Funeral baked meats, 197:7
behold his f. appears, 285:5
everlasting f. marches round your heart, 780:10
I didn't go to f. of poetry, 772:8
I walked at f. of tenderness, 773:11
if we see a f., 149:7
into silent f., 678:20
marches to grave, 436:5
mirth in f., 196:22
misbehaved once at f., 383:5
nobody's f., 678:20
nor celebrate f. with weeping, 84:17
present at your f., 703:*n*1
rejoice at birth grieve at f., 523:20
walks to own f. drest in shroud, 486:17
Funerals, go to other men's f., 622:6
Funnier, nothing f. than unhappiness, 744:22
Funny, if happening to somebody else, 640:5
you're certainly a f. girl, 718:10
Fur, err on some other f., 886:18
fierce f. soft to face, 798:1
hunched in belly till wet f. froze, 774:14
make f. fly, 262:13
oh my f. and whiskers, 514:2
Furey, churchyard where Michael F. buried, 650:9
Furious anger, 30:34
brother hard and f., 819:12
fast and f., 358:8
to be frighted out of fear, 218:35
vast and f. ocean, 240:2
winter blowing, 681:18
winter's rages, 220:26
wise amazed temperate f., 216:1
Furiously, green ideas sleep f., 817:15
Jehu driveth f., 12:17
Furled, battle flags were f., 452:3
bright girdle f., 496:19
Furlongs, thousand f. of sea, 224:2
Furnace, burning fiery f., 28:22
feet as if burned in a f., 46:17
heat not f. for foe, 225:12
in what f. thy brain, 353:2
lover sighing like f., 194:25
of affliction, 26:36
Furnish forth marriage tables, 197:7
means of acquiring knowledge, 363:10
you f. pictures I f. war, 583:14
you with argument and intellects, 322:9
Furnished, live in f. souls, 701:8
me from mine own library, 224:9
Furniture, don't bump into f., 719:17
Furrow followed free, 376:1
half-reaped f., 411:7
Furrows, smite sounding f., 451:18
Furs to touch, 669:9
Furside is outside, 610:9
Further, get a little f. you are too near, 325:21
hitherto shalt thou come but no f., 14:20
nearer to church f. from God, 147:8
Furtive, crept look of f. shame, 648:15
Fury, allaying their f., 224:13
blind F. with abhorred shears, 253:6

Fury *(continued)*

civil f. first grew high, 261:17
cunning old F., 514:1
full of sound and f., 217:23
in your words, 210:1
like woman scorned, 287:2
ne'er spend f. on child, 171:3
provides arms, 93:33
Queen crimson with f., 514:18
slinging flame, 453:18
stronger than afterthoughts, 67:21
swells in his f., 672:5
trample them in my f., 27:17
Fuse, through green f. drives flower, 777:2
war and music not have to f., 847:8
Fusion, complete f. with the world, 807:18
Fust in us unused, 201:19
Fustest, git thar f. with mostest, 494:*n*2
Fustian's so sublimely bad, 295:12
Fustilarian, you rampallian you f., 188:2
Futile, we need a f. gesture, 837:1
Futility, fatal f. of Fact, 544:18
Future, ages shall talk, 284:16
aid to interpretation of f., 71:12
all concerned about f., 633:3
Arthur the once and f. king, 138:16
as past would be present, 345:3
been into f. and it works, 598:9
belongs to crowds, 841:4
cannot fight f., 442:13
democracy shuts past opens f., 434:2
dipped into the f., 452:2
divine sign indicates f., 70:5
door opens and lets f. in, 737:14
education will determine f. life, 75:7
enters into us, 632:6
flight of f. days, 256:14
formula of management for f., 727:18
generations, 782:9
I am pleading for the f., 568:9
imagining a bright f., 860:2
imagining f. years come, 593:11
in f. everyone world-famous, 817:1
in f. light will shine, 620:14
in f. System must be first, 566:1
instruct as to f., 414:2
is somehow sending messages, 858:12
lays down law of today, 547:12
lively sense of f. favors, 264:*n*2
most in league with f., 504:14
Negro remake past to make f., 627:10
net nailed on futureless f., 788:10
never plan f. by past, 325:10
new building of the f., 655:8
no f. no f. no f. for you, 874:12
no past or f. in art, 647:13
no way of judging f., 331:11
not even the f., 871:1
O f. Vigor, 559:3
of human race, 634:5
one tip for the f., 871:12
orgiastic f. that recedes before us, 710:7
party of the F., 428:16
philosophy triumphs over f. evils, 263:16
picture of f., 735:22
Present Past F. sees, 352:10
prospect of f. war unendurable, 739:6
scaffold sways f., 481:13

Future *(continued)*
  security for the f., 306:*n*1
  seen f. and it works, 598:*n*2
  serve the f. hour, 372:11
  shock, 821:3
  smells of Russian leather, 415:8
  something everyone reaches, 717:13
  spend rest of lives in f., 633:3
  those who talk about f., 700:19
  till F. dares forget Past, 403:13
  time f. in time past, 678:6
  transform itself in us, 632:6
  wave of f. is coming, 746:10
  wings of the f., 670:4
  with equal blindness to f., 319:11
Future's, Heaven and f. sakes, 624:1
  poor old Past the F. slave, 483:18
Futurity, shadows f. casts upon present, 404:15
Fuzzy-Wuzzy, 'ere's to you F., 587:18

G

Gab, gift of g., 401:2
Gaberdine, Jewish g., 184:28
Gabrielle, long way to see G., 766:15
Gadire, bound for Javan or G., 260:16
Gaelic, cornet solo of G. islands, 694:12
Gaels of Ireland, 618:10
Gaffe is when a politician, 869:11
Gage, one for all we g., 172:31
Gai, toujours g., 635:6
Gaiety, based on foundation of realism, 712:8
  courage g. and quiet mind, 556:12
  eclipsed g. of nations, 307:20
Gain, don't lose head to g. minute, 887:12
  every way makes my g., 210:10
  for everything g. lose something, 426:27
  good to g. day, 486:2
  individual intends his own g., 319:5
  little patch of ground, 201:18
  my good vain hope of g., 163:11
  necessity to glorious g., 371:21
  seen hungry ocean g. advantage, 221:18
  serves and seeks for g., 211:18
  set down as g. each day, 96:10
  strength by experience, 660:7
  the whole world, 34:39
  timely inn, 216:14
  to die is g., 44:1, 74:9
  tragedy to g. heart's desire, 565:8
Gained, boisterously maintained as g., 175:22
  for everything missed g. something,
    426:27
  from Heaven all he wished, 316:7
  no title lost no friend, 294:9
  this by philosophy, 77:11
Gaining, something might be g. on you, 747:6
  trust and betraying, 838:5
Gains, do not seek evil g., 54:23
  evil g. equivalent of disaster, 54:23
  light g. make heavy purses, 163:14
  spirit that g. victory, 664:11
Gait, excessive laughter and g., 31:8
  forced g. of shuffling nag, 182:36
Gaiters, gas and g., 464:23
Gal, every g. born into world, 526:22
Galactic, evil g. empire, 859:11

Gale of creative destruction, 657:21
  note that swells g., 316:9
  of life blew high, 575:4
  sun and summer g., 316:11
  that sweeps from north, 331:13
  waters God has brewed into g., 482:22
  yell for yell to g., 567:6
Galeed, name of it called G., 7:1
Galen, more than G. cured, 243:26
Galeotto was the book, 128:19
Galère, dans la g. d'un Turc, 268:*n*2
  que diable allait-il faire dans cette g., 268:*n*2
Gales, cool g. fan the glade, 292:6
Galilean, O pale G., 530:9
  Pilot of the G. lake, 253:9
  you have conquered G., 114:9
Galilee, miracles in Cana of G., 39:5
  wave rolls nightly on deep G., 397:2
Gall, enough in thy ink, 205:18
  I am g. I am heartburn, 547:8
  lack g., 199:18
  of bitterness, 40:20
  take my milk for g., 214:17
  wormwood and the g., 28:12
Gallant, in g. trim vessel goes, 316:15
Gallanter I know, 508:5
Gallantly streaming, 386:19
Gallantry, what men call g., 397:21
Galled, let g. jade wince, 200:22
Galleon, moon ghostly g., 646:1
Gallery of works turned to wall, 502:1
Galley, on board a Turk's g., 268:*n*2
  slave to pen, 417:13
  what doing in that g., 268:2
Gallia est omnis divisa in partes tres, 88:*n*10
Gallio cared for none of those things, 40:36
Gallon, pint of sweat save g. of blood, 664:13
Gallop apace fiery-footed steeds, 180:31
  beggar will ride a g., 170:*n*1
  false g. of verses, 195:8
  go sit g., 365:5
  why does he g. and g., 555:10
Galloped, I g. Dirck g., 460:16
Galloping after a fox, 561:7
Gallops, who Time g. withal, 195:15
Gallows, complexion is perfect g., 224:1
  hanged Haman on the g., 12:33
  under the g. tree, 236:6
Galls, canker g. infants of spring, 197:19
  his kibe, 202:11
Gallup Poll feeling pulse, 620:11
Galoot's, till last g. ashore, 532:11
Gals, buffalo g. come out tonight, 885:4
Galumphing back, 515:13
Gamaliel, at feet of G., 40:42
Gambling is going on here, 758:7
Gambols, your g. your songs, 202:12
Game, back of bar in solo g., 627:12
  baseball is g. of skill, 688:16
  begins in the spring, 844:8
  can't anybody play this g., 689:1
  confidence g., 865:6
  gunless g., 569:12
  how you played g., 646:4
  in which my name was, 662:6
  is afoot, 573:20
  is being played, 269:17
  is done I've won I've won, 376:8

Game *(continued)*
  is up, 220:19
  love g. beyond prize, 582:8
  play up and play g., 582:11
  poetry mug's g., 677:22
  puzzling is not a solitary g., 842:4
  rigor of the g., 383:10
  rules of g. laws of Nature, 502:5
  start g. on lone heaths, 386:10
  take me out to ball g., 640:1
  that must be played, 605:16
  this g. is life, 727:4
  war's a g., 327:3
  was empires, 399:14
  woman is his g., 453:2
Game's afoot, 189:9
Games, humans playing at children's g., 618:2
  shows g. sports guns, 330:1
  victor in Olympic g. or announcer, 62:23
Gamesmanship, what is g., 726:8
Gammon and spinach, 892:12
  and spinnage, 465:30
Gamut of emotions, 699:18
Gander, goosey g., 894:6
Gane, nane sall ken where he is g., 890:6
Gang aft a-gley, 356:6
  grisly g., 620:9
  tell g. at Forty-second Street, 634:11
  That Couldn't Shoot, 826:8
Ganglion in nerves of society, 538:11
Gang's, hail hail g. all here, 526:*n*1
Gangs, don't join too many g., 623:18
Gangsters, conventions of g. film, 789:2
Gangway for de Lawd, 686:3
Gap appeared in the mountain, 59:7
  this great g. of time, 218:10
Gape, craters of my eyes g., 836:2
Gapes for drink again, 265:9
Gaping, love not a g. pig, 185:26
Garb, words in reason's g., 256:15
Garbage, prey on g., 198:10
Garbo, one sees in G. sober, 816:17
Garcia, message to G., 564:10
Garde meurt mais ne se rend pas, 366:*n*6
Garden, blow upon my g., 24:16
  cherubims east of the g., 6:2
  come into g. Maud, 455:1
  cultivate our g., 299:14
  died, 594:15
  earthly ball a peopled g., 343:2
  fairies at bottom of g., 634:3
  flowers in g. meat in hall, 133:*n*2
  full of weeds, 892:7
  ghost of g. fronts sea, 530:25
  God first planted g., 166:15
  God the first g. made, 265:15
  his heart was in his g., 494:7
  his own image walking in g., 401:15
  how does g. grow, 893:5
  Hyacinth G. wears, 441:14
  in her face, 227:3
  in this delightful g. grows, 160:12
  into the rose g., 678:7
  its end comes in the g., 4:14
  last gathered roses in g., 239:2
  lean on g. urn, 675:13
  let my beloved come into his g., 24:16
  lodge in a g. of cucumbers, 24:30

Garden *(continued)*
Lord God planted a g., 5:11
lovesome thing, 508:1
maid in g., 894:7
man and woman in g., 560:15
mind attached like g., 544:6
Mr. McGregor's g., 598:6
Never Promised You a Rose G., 818:10
of cucumbers, 24:30
over grass in West g., 664:18
piece of land with a g., 95:24
small house and large g., 265:8
snake stood up for evil in G., 623:2
suffer them and they'll o'ergrow g., 170:5
this g. city and myself, 742:19
tree of life in midst of the g., 5:12
turn her out of a g., 309:20
voice of Lord God walking in g., 5:20
we've got to get back to g., 858:2
who loves a g., 326:24, 417:7
Gardener Adam and his wife, 451:2
Adam was a g., 170:16, 590:5
though old man young g., 338:2
Gardener's, half proper g. work, 590:5
Gardeners ditchers and grave-makers, 202:3
gardens were before g., 166:*n*2
our wills are g., 208:7
Gardening, what man needs in g., 507:15
Garden's, river at my g. end, 296:7
Gardens, Babylon's G., 886:14
down by salley g., 590:21
Hanging G. were a dream, 628:17
imaginary g. with real toads, 671:2
our bodies are our g., 208:7
these g. of desert, 406:3
trim g., 251:14
were before gardeners, 166:*n*2
Garfield, James G. sat on other, 512:*n*2
Garish, pay no worship to g. sun, 180:32
Garland and singing robes, 253:19
green willow my g., 146:8
race where immortal g., 254:9
withered is the g. of war, 219:5
Garlands, bring flowering g. to me, 60:1
dead, 388:1
flanks with g., 410:18
gather g. there, 374:6
no g. for imitators, 359:18
Garlic and sapphires in mud, 678:8
eat no onions nor g., 179:5
wel loved he g. oynons lekes, 134:8
Garment, hardship our g., 620:1
left his g. in her hand, 7:8
of praise, 27:16
of Repentance fling, 441:7
she caught him by his g., 7:8
twitch Nymph's g. off, 460:21
weave g. of brightness, 891:13
Garments, agonies one of my changes of g.,
486:16
blood sprinkled upon g., 27:17
of gladness, 29:29
part my g. among them, 15:22
purses proud g. poor, 173:22
stuffs out vacant g., 175:19
takes off respect with g., 69:6
trailing g. of Night, 436:3
Garnish, eye of heaven to g., 175:24

Garp, world according to G., 854:8
Garret, speech I wrote in a g., 305:*n*5
Garrulous geese, 724:7
old men g. by nature, 88:16
Garter, Cluett Shirt Boston G., 701:9
familiar as his g., 188:33
Garters, scarfs g. gold, 295:3
Gary looked at ceiling hesitated, 803:11
Gas and gaiters, 464:23
expedient as lighting by g., 442:12
or steam or table turning, 491:18
smells awful, 699:14
Gash, be it g. or gold, 783:8
Gasoline cause of international conflict, 760:10
Gasp and stretch eyes, 606:12
at the last g., 31:33
fight till last g., 169:11
Gate, at one g. to make defense, 260:14
by the g. of breath, 530:6
come here to this g., 765:18
drops on g. hang in row, 537:3
here at g. alone, 455:1
lark at heaven's g. sings, 220:15
leant upon coppice g., 536:10
longest part of journey passing of g., 86:19
of subtle and profound female, 57:2
spears of little g., 650:9
starved at master's g., 353:16
strait is the g., 33:19
street before the water g., 12:29
this g. made only for you, 655:13
this is the g. of heaven, 6:43
we pass the g., 599:17
wide is the g., 33:19
willow cabin at your g., 204:21
Gatepost, you me and g., 463:10
Gates, at heaven's g. claps wings, 162:9
Chicago at northwest g., 605:13
dreams have two g., 54:6
enter into his g. with thanksgiving, 18:3
hateful as g. of Hades, 51:18
her own works praise her in the g., 22:20
husband is known in the g., 22:17
lift up your heads O ye g., 15:25
lion on old stone g., 451:1
of bird always open, 694:11
of dark Death stand wide, 94:27
of hell shall not prevail, 34:37
of Hercules, 539:14
of horn and of ivory, 54:6, 95:2
open ye everlasting g., 258:28
open ye the g., 26:3
Piper at the G. of Dawn, 574:8
sprouting at area g., 675:9
unbarred the g. of light, 258:22
Gateways of the stars, 576:15
Gath, tell it not in G., 11:7
Gather, descendants shall g. your fruits, 93:3
garlands there, 374:6
honey all the day, 289:8
knoweth not who shall g. them, 16:19
let me g. after the reapers, 10:31
me into artifice of eternity, 594:3
Rose whilst prime, 160:9
roses of life today, 150:8
shalt not g. every grape, 8:26
shalt not g. the gleanings, 8:26
tears g. to the eyes, 452:21

Gather *(continued)*
the lambs with his arm, 26:29
themselves together, 18:11
time to g. stones together, 22:31
up the fragments, 39:17
we g. together, 882:4
we'll g. and go, 367:15
ye rosebuds, 241:4
Gathered, all safely g. in, 456:9
by gloomy Dis was g., 257:17
cannot be g. up again, 11:21
into Armageddon, 47:7
last g. roses in garden, 239:2
Medea g. enchanted herbs, 186:14
nations g. before him, 35:29
together in my name, 34:42
together in thy name, 48:17
Gatherer of other men's stuff, 153:*n*6
Gathereth her food in the harvest, 19:32
Gathering brows like storm, 358:3
Gatherings of people thought educated,
743:12
Gathers, one that g. samphire, 212:24
rolling stone g. no moss, 100:16
Gatsby believed in the green light, 710:7
Jay G. of West Egg Long Island, 710:4
Gat-toothed I was, 135:12
Gaudeamus igitur, 120:26
Gaudier, cheaper crook g. patter, 702:8
Gaudiness of poetry, 642:19
Gaudy blabbing and remorseful day,
170:10
day denies, 397:1
night, 218:34
rich not g., 197:23
Gauged, never g. your cruelty recklessness,
689:5
Gaul divided into three parts, 88:21
Gaunt, city of G., 889:22
Gave bodies to commonwealth, 72:4
his honors to the world, 226:8
me for my pains, 208:3
only begotten Son, 39:11
she g. me of the tree, 5:21
the Lord g., 12:39
thee clothing of delight, 350:12
thee life bid thee feed, 350:12
to misery all he had, 316:7
up the ghost, 38:38
what Chance shall not control, 494:14
what other women gave, 596:5
Gavest, woman whom thou g., 5:21
Gawd, go to your G. like a soldier, 588:13
livin' G. that made you, 587:19
Gay apparel, 177:12
bedecked ornate and g., 260:16
deceiver, 361:9
goodnight and quickly turn away, 595:1
in halls in g. attire, 373:2
life earnest art g., 359:20
Lothario, 289:3
poet could not but be g., 371:12
some of them are g., 877:5
their ancient eyes are g., 596:11
we're not g., 874:3
where g. fantasies come true, 849:7
Gaza, brought Samson to G., 10:24
eyeless in G., 260:8

Girl *(continued)*
    gun and a g., 827:6
    Heaven protect working g., 569:2
    I can't get no g. reaction, 857:1
    I love the g. I'm near, 711:13
    leaves home at eighteen, 609:5
    little g. had making of poet, 572:4
    little g. my stringbean, 820:12
    need park policeman pretty g., 683:17
    needs good parents, 661:17
    nice g. won't give an inch, 107:12
    no g. ever ruined by book, 648:9
    soft face of a g., 65:25
    Spearmint G., 701:9
    sweetest g. I know, 628:20
    then spoke I to my g., 240:14
    there was a little g., 438:2
    unlessoned g. unschooled, 185:22
    wink at homely g., 645:7
    you're certainly a funny g., 718:10
Girlish glee, 527:12
Girl's, diamonds g. best friend, 726:14
    stumbling blocks in g. education, 616:4
Girls, all g. he can please, 532:16
    all the g. walk by, 861:12
    are all giggling, 755:7
    boys and g. level with men, 219:5
    boys and g. together, 581:2
    Dust was Lads and G., 509:20
    Glos'ter g. they have no combs, 897:21
    golden lads and g., 220:26
    hear what servant g. said, 611:13
    little g. made of, 895:12
    little g. recognize your prime, 791:17
    of all g. so smart, 292:1
    sleek g. I teach, 814:14
    thank heaven for little g., 790:13
    three giggling g., 821:2
    twelve g. in two straight lines, 715:16
    what shall I do for pretty g., 597:5
    which g. hath merriest eye, 169:15
    who wear glasses, 699:13
    will be boys, 859:3
    with g. be handy, 883:15
    wretched un-ideaed g., 308:16
Git thar fustest with mostest, 494:*n2*
Gitche Gumee, shores of G., 437:2
Give a little love to child, 484:18
    a man enough rope, 146:*n3*
    a new commandment, 39:39
    all that a man hath will he g., 13:1
    all thou canst, 372:14
    all to love, 424:14
    an inch take an ell, 148:*n12*
    and not count cost, 144:16
    Aztecs by no means would g. up, 144:12
    can't g. me love and peace, 683:6
    countries g. themselves to you, 662:7
    country back to Indians, 716:4
    cried G. Me, 508:21
    crowns pounds guineas, 574:14
    delight and hurt not, 224:33
    enemies means of our destruction, 59:18
    eternal rest g. them, 47:19
    every man thy ear, 197:23
    fame for pot of ale, 189:10
    freely received freely g., 33:38
    great meals of beef, 189:17

Give *(continued)*
    hand and heart, 390:3
    hautboys breath he comes, 274:16
    haves of g., 701:18
    him a little earth, 226:7
    him death by inches, 220:5
    his angels charge, 17:29
    I generally had to g. in, 365:16
    I will g. you rest, 34:9
    I will not g. sleep to mine eyes, 19:9
    in life did harbor g., 232:13
    it an understanding, 197:16
    kiss better than you g., 204:3
    lady what she wants, 519:11
    me a kiss, 241:3
    me a look, 232:7
    me a thousand kisses, 91:5
    me a torch, 663:22
    me ae spark, 356:11
    me again my hollow tree, 296:8
    me an ounce of civet, 212:28
    me another horse, 172:7
    me back my heart, 394:17
    me back my legions, 99:3
    me back my young brother, 819:12
    me bitter fame, 683:6
    me burning blue and burnt sea-weed,
        667:9
    me but that, 156:13
    me excess of it, 204:10
    me handfuls of lilies, 95:1
    me health and a day, 425:23
    me John Baptist's head, 34:24
    me liberty or give me death, 331:13
    me liberty to know, 254:13
    me more love or more disdain, 245:17
    me my scallop shell, 159:10
    me ocular proof, 209:14
    me quoth I, 213:33
    me that man, 200:12
    me that old-time religion, 884:19
    me the daggers, 215:23
    me to drink mandragora, 218:10
    me today take tomorrow, 119:24
    me truth, 475:22
    me where to stand, 83:5
    me your answer do, 598:3
    me your arm old toad, 799:12
    me your tired your poor, 552:16
    meanest flower can g., 371:5
    more blessed to g., 40:40
    mother g. me sun, 504:13
    my regards to Broadway, 634:11
    name to every fixed star, 174:1
    Nature a chance, 153:23
    never g. all heart, 591:17
    never g. in never, 620:12
    no more g. the people straw, 7:32
    no more to every guest, 285:12
    not a windy night rainy morrow, 221:29
    oh g. me a home, 890:20
    peace I g. unto you, 39:44
    peace in our time, 49:22
    reason on compulsion, 182:22
    sop to Cerberus, 119:23
    sorrow words, 217:7
    thee peace, 9:2
    them meat in due season, 18:11

Give *(continued)*
    these delights if thou canst g., 251:9
    thy thoughts no tongue, 197:21
    thy worst of thoughts, 209:1
    to a thief, 756:19
    to get esteem, 322:1
    to the poor, 35:3
    up verse my boy, 665:10
    up whole idea of life, 824:14
    us a song to cheer, 520:1
    us grace and strength, 556:12
    us grace to accept, 695:20
    us our daily bread, 32:25
    us peace, 47:23
    us rest or death, 450:20
    us taste of your quality, 199:11
    us the tools, 620:3
    warning to world, 221:23
    we g. what we have, 544:12
    we receive but what we g., 378:8
    what shall I g. my children, 783:7
    what we g. and preserve, 446:1
    what you command, 116:8
    while we have praise to g., 232:19
    world assurance of a man, 201:5
    world the lie, 159:9
    you all the pussy, 887:2
    you some violets, 201:31
Given, as if Checks g., 510:9
    ask and it shall be g., 33:16
    gladly not to be standing here, 753:10
    God has g. you one face, 200:1
    hast thou g. the horse strength, 14:26
    heart change of mood, 623:5
    heaven alone g. away, 481:15
    I have g. suck and know, 215:5
    much g. much required, 38:6
    not have g. it for monkeys, 185:14
    nothing g. nothing required, 304:12
    of thine own have we g. thee, 12:25
    our hearts away, 371:23
    pay for what gods g., 612:19
    take what is g., 625:10
    thee till break of day, 352:11
    them the slip, 282:19
    thou hast g. him his heart's desire,
        15:20
    too dear for what's g. freely, 223:8
    unto every one that hath be g., 35:27
    what scanted in hair g. in wit, 172:18
Giver, cheerful g., 43:19
    keep modest as g., 548:1
Givers, when g. prove unkind, 199:23
Gives, blesseth him that g., 186:1
    blessing love g., 815:16
    but for another g. ease, 352:12
    but greater feeling to worse, 176:18
    doubly benefits who g. quickly, 99:15
    'er all she needs, 589:2
    he that lends g., 244:18
    heart and soul away, 574:16
    lovely light, 695:8
    no man a sinecure, 665:10
    sternest good-night, 215:17
    thoughts nature g. way to, 215:11
    time takes all g. all, 158:16
    to airy nothing, 179:6
    twice who gives promptly, 120:7

Giveth his beloved sleep, 19:5
   land the Lord g. thee, 8:14
   life and breath, 40:33
   man g. up the ghost, 13:30
   not as world g., 39:44
   unto the poor, 22:8
Giving enemies the slip, 313:24
   heart to dog to tear, 589:25
   in g. we receive, 125:12
   insure position by g. generously, 4:10
   manner of g. worth more, 249:15
   not g. life but risking life, 751:6
   not in g. vein today, 171:35
   stealing and g. odor, 204:10
Gizzard, something in her g., 277:24
Glacier knocks in cupboard, 748:9
   woman, 720:7
Glad, almost g. we have been bombed, 725:7
   did I live gladly die, 555:16
   heart too soon g., 460:2
   kindness, 593:15
   let us live and be g., 120:26
   make g. the city of God, 16:27
   me with soft black eye, 388:3
   moments of g. grace, 591:6
   New Year, 450:15
   not born before tea, 375:12
   of other men's good, 195:6
   Olaf g. and big, 701:11
   sad g. brother's name, 530:24
   show ourselves g., 48:6
   tidings of great joy, 281:14
   to be of use, 675:4
   to brink of fear, 425:21
   to sleep with Aphrodite, 53:9
   weep for what could make them g., 624:13
   when they said unto me, 19:1
   wine that maketh g. the heart, 18:9
   wise son maketh a g. father, 20:10
   with all my heart, 167:11
   you like adverbs, 545:5
Glade, bee-loud g., 591:2
   cool gales fan the g., 292:6
   crown the watery g., 315:4
Gladly, be your wife g., 468:1
   beyond any experience, 701:15
   die, 555:16
   lerne and gladly teche, 133:24
   suffer fools g., 43:21
Gladness, begin in g., 369:16
   garments of g., 29:29
   I that in heill wes and g., 141:6
   notes of g., 384:15
   of the heart, 31:5
   serve the Lord with g., 18:3
   teach me half g., 403:6
   wealth small aid for daily g., 68:6
Gladsome light of jurisprudence, 158:22
Glamis hath murdered sleep, 215:22
   thou art and Cawdor, 214:16
Glamour, moment of romance of g., 567:10
   of childish days, 662:15
Glance from heaven to earth, 179:6
   glum, 527:25
   O brightening g., 594:17
   of the Lord, 397:3
   ten thousand saw I at a g., 371:11
   without a g. my way, 509:12

Glances, casting backward g., 488:17
   gray eye g., 448:7
Glare, rockets' red g., 386:19
   sunburnt by g. of life, 434:21
   surrounds king hides him, 153:14
Glareth, not all gold that g., 125:n2
Glasgerion swore great oath, 889:24
Glass, bishop kick hole in stained g. window, 674:7
   break bloody g., 751:2
   dome of many-colored g., 404:2
   drink not the third g., 242:7
   excuse for the g., 346:11
   failing hour by hour, 751:2
   first g. for myself, 288:12
   Fortune like g. easily broken, 100:2
   fount more sparkling than g., 97:5
   get thee g. eyes, 212:31
   grief with g. that ran, 529:14
   if your windows g., 302:16
   made mouths in a g., 211:27
   obscured or broken, 798:2
   of fashion mould of form, 200:3
   people in g. houses, 243:n2
   pride is his own g., 203:14
   satire a sort of g., 284:4
   saw through g. eye darkly, 524:6
   see through g. darkly, 42:29
   shown g. flowers, 671:5
   swift sandy g., 233:17
   third g. thou canst not tame, 242:7
   thou art thy mother's g., 220:32
   Time turn up his g., 233:17
   turn down empty G., 442:10
   wherein noble youth dress, 188:6
   whose house is g., 243:25
Glasses, girls who wear g., 699:13
   itself in tempests, 396:20
   on nose autumn in heart, 700:17
Glasses', peeps over g. edge, 461:20
Glassy cool translucent wave, 252:26
   his g. essence, 206:28
Glaze, bare trees above snow g., 658:8
   on katydid-wing, 671:19
Glazed with rain water, 658:14
Glazen, upon the g. shelves, 675:11
Gleam, bright g. of noble deeds, 64:5
   fled visionary g., 370:16
   follow the G., 456:3
   in midst of long night, 558:10
   of a thousand lights, 609:6
Gleamed upon my sight, 371:6
Gleaming, twilight's last g., 386:19
Gleams, light g. and is gone, 496:16
   of remoter world, 401:11
   on whom pale moon g., 549:13
   through fog, 314:28
   thy footstep g., 448:7
   untraveled world, 451:13
Glean, let me g. after the reapers, 10:31
   shalt not g. thy vineyard, 8:26
Gleaned my teeming brain, 412:7
Gleaning of grapes of Ephraim, 10:16
Gleanings, shalt not gather the g., 8:26
Glee, girlish g., 527:12
   piping songs of pleasant g., 350:10
Glen, down the rushy g., 501:4
Glenartney's, lone G. hazel shade, 373:18

Glib and oily art, 210:29
Glide, in sunny beams did g., 350:7
   leisurely we g., 513:10
   safe into haven g., 305:8
   soul into boughs does g., 267:2
   to wind tossing water, 659:1
Glided, mourns that day has g. by, 408:16
Glideth at own sweet will, 370:3
Gliding, dark mother always g. near, 487:15
   snakes g. up hollow, 425:8
Glimmer, women have g. of loyalty to Truth, 552:2
Glimmering, gone g., 395:5
   hold g. tapers to sun, 235:n5
   mere g. and decays, 268:17
   now fades g. landscape, 315:12
   river lake g. pool, 500:5
Glimpse, nor g. divine, 297:6
   same old g. of Paradise, 576:9
Glimpses make me less forlorn, 371:24
   of forgotten dreams, 450:11
   revisitest g. of the moon, 197:34
   thousand g. wins, 495:2
Glistering grief, 225:17
Glisters, all that g. not gold, 125:n2
Glitter of seas, 833:11
Glittered when he walked, 605:18
Glittering, ancient g. eyes, 596:11
   eye, 375:17
   how that g. taketh me, 241:14
Glitters, all that g. is not gold, 125:n2
Gloamin', roamin' in the g., 607:8
Global, my wars g. from the start, 776:13
   village, 764:12
Globally, think g., 727:18
Globe, common air bathes g., 486:1
   country spread over half g., 443:1
   distracted g., 198:15
   doubled g. of dead, 777:5
   flames have spread over g., 338:15
   freedom hunted round the g., 333:2
   great g. itself, 225:1
   interior of solid g., 415:14
   sop of all this solid g., 203:7
   sway destinies of half the g., 434:1
Glocca Morra, how are things in G., 711:15
Gloire, le jour de g. est arrivé, 361:3
Gloom, convent's solitary g., 293:23
   counterfeit a g., 251:18
   deep thicket's g., 342:15
   encircling g., 421:4
   moral g. of world, 430:25
   nor g. of night, 69:n8
   tempted her out of g., 449:17
Glooms, welcome kindred g., 300:15
Gloomy, deep and g. wood, 368:10
   view of future, 634:5
Gloria in excelsis Deo, 47:22
   mundi, 137:3
Gloriam, ad maiorem Dei g., 149:n1
Gloried and drank deep, 441:13
Glories, common g. in past, 500:15
   conquests g. triumphs spoils, 192:19
   Heaven's g. shine, 476:14
   my g. and state depose, 177:18
   of our blood and state, 246:13
   strung like beads, 487:1
   with their triumphs and their g., 461:2

Glorieth, let him that g. glory in me, 27:33
Glorified, whom he justified he g., 41:22
Glorify all sorts of bravery, 480:20
    Father in heaven, 32:16
    we wish to g. war, 633:7
Glorious blood-red, 460:20
    by my sword, 262:n2
    circumstance of g. war, 209:13
    crowded hour of g. life, 326:1
    full many a g. morning, 221:10
    gifts of the gods, 50:27
    heaven's g. sun, 174:1
    honorable and g., 328:9
    institution, 324:13
    king's daughter all g. within, 16:25
    made g. summer by sun of York, 171:16
    make thee g. by my pen, 262:24
    making city g. and great, 62:15
    mirror, 396:20
    mission of trade unions, 554:5
    morning for America, 318:5
    most g. city of God, 116:17
    most g. to victors, 72:9
    necessity to g. gain, 371:21
    place glorious age, 831:3
    right hand is become g., 8:6
    shadow of g. name, 106:10
    song of old, 457:11
    sun in Heaven, 377:16
    sunshine a g. birth, 370:15
    the g. Ninety-two, 331:6
    the more g. the triumph, 333:6
    thing to be Pirate King, 526:5
    things g. had no glory, 721:6
    things of thee are spoken, 321:1
    war's g. art, 290:15
Gloriously, he hath triumphed g., 8:4
    perjured, 97:4
    succeeded, 727:14
Glory, a light a g., 378:9
    and danger alike, 72:1
    and freshness of a dream, 370:13
    and nothing of a name, 397:5
    and shame of universe, 269:25
    and the dream, 370:16
    be the Perfect One, 509:18
    be to the Father, 48:8
    cataract leaps in g., 452:19
    crown of g., 46:2
    day of g. has come, 361:3
    days of youth days of g., 399:7
    deed everything g. nothing, 344:12
    desire for g. clings, 110:10
    die in g. never old, 575:2
    doesn't mean argument, 516:15
    drowned G. in Cup, 442:7
    excess of g. obscured, 255:24
    fight for love and g., 702:12
    flowers and shoots of g., 268:12
    for country's g. fast, 373:6
    from gray hairs gone, 438:5
    from the earth, 370:15
    full meridian of my g., 225:23
    go where g. waits thee, 387:5
    heavens declare the g. of God, 15:15
    hoary head a crown of g., 20:38
    Homer herald of your g., 80:21
    hope of g., 48:16

Glory *(continued)*
    in His bosom, 481:2
    in the flower, 371:4
    is departed from Israel, 10:37
    is in their shame, 44:5
    jest and riddle of world, 295:1
    King of g. shall come in, 15:25
    land of hope and g., 580:19
    like a circle in water, 169:13
    like a shooting star, 177:2
    long hair g. to woman, 42:23
    my gown of g., 159:10
    myn the travaille thyn the g., 134:21
    no more Hope no more G., 616:16
    nothing so expensive as g., 374:23
    O what joy and g. must be, 123:9
    of Christian religion, 139:10
    of coming of Lord, 481:1
    of Europe extinguished, 325:4
    of everything, 724:7
    of Him who moves everything, 130:2
    of his country, 390:2
    of honors beauties wits, 229:9
    of Lord shone, 37:17
    of old story is forever, 95:6
    of the Lord is risen, 27:14
    of their times, 31:27
    of thy people Israel, 37:20
    of war moonshine, 489:15
    of woman who occasions least talk, 72:5
    Old G., 423:15
    one star differeth in g., 43:5
    or grave, 384:11
    paths of g., 315:18
    pomp and g. of this world, 225:25
    power and g., 38:29
    power and the g., 12:24
    precious forever, 68:12
    pride of peacock g. of God, 351:14
    race of g. run, 260:15
    rainbow's g. is shed, 404:10
    search their own g., 21:36
    set stars of g. there, 408:12
    shone around, 281:13
    sing tongue the Savior's g., 126:12
    sittest throned in g., 517:11
    so passes g. of world, 137:3
    Solomon in all his g., 33:9
    such g. over everything, 490:9
    sudden g. maketh laughter, 239:7
    summers in a sea of g., 225:25
    take away our free will and g., 142:6
    that was Greece, 447:12
    they to g. ride therein, 280:16
    thine is the g., 32:25
    things glorious had no g., 721:6
    time's g. calm contending kings, 172:35
    to God for dappled things, 546:12
    to God in highest, 37:18, 47:22
    to newborn King, 305:10
    to the greater g. of God, 149:1
    trailing clouds of g., 370:17
    trembles before your g., 65:25
    triumph without g., 249:9
    'twas my one G., 510:8
    uncertain g. of April day, 173:29
    vain pomp and g., 49:11
    walked in g. and joy, 369:16

Glory *(continued)*
    walking in an air of g., 268:17
    was I had such friends, 597:2
    who is this King of g., 15:26
    wonder and g. of universe, 440:10
    words such as g. obscene, 721:6
    wretchedness that g. brings, 213:27
Gloss, all the g. of art, 322:27
    over my whole life story, 874:9
Glosses, write g. about each other, 153:20
Glossy, not for fine g. surface, 322:7
Gloucester, Doctor Foster went to G., 896:10
    girls they have no combs, 897:21
Glove, hand-and-g., 286:8
    iron hand in velvet g., 148:28
    O that I were a g., 180:1
Gloves, cat in g. catches no mice, 302:30
    not make revolution with silk g., 636:18
Glow has warmed the world, 660:n1
    of early thought declines, 397:4
Glowed, now g. the firmament, 257:25
Glowered, as Tammie g., 358:8
Glowing axle doth allay, 252:7
    chase g. hours, 395:14
    desires g. openly, 583:12
    embers through the room, 251:18
Glows, gold orange g., 342:15
    in every heart, 290:12
    intense atom g., 403:17
Glowworm, eyes the g. lend thee, 241:7
    shows matin to be near, 198:14
Glue and lime of love, 240:10
Glum, glance g., 527:25
Glut sorrow on rose, 411:10
Gluts twice ten thousand caverns, 412:6
Glutton, drunkard and g. shall come to
    poverty, 21:28
Gluttonous, behold a man g., 34:8
Gluttony, like adultery or g., 626:22
Glynn, marshes of G., 543:2
Gnarling sorrow hath less power, 176:17
Gnashing, weeping and g. of teeth, 33:26
    what g. is not a comfort, 231:9
Gnat, strain at g., 35:16
Gnats, small g. mourn, 411:8
Gnawed, thousand men that fishes g., 171:28
Gnawing, what g. of worm not tickling, 231:9
GNP, man does not live by G. alone, 780:12
Go a-angling, 245:10
    about woodlands I g., 574:11
    a-fishing, 475:4
    a-hunting we will g., 304:11
    all g. together when we g., 819:8
    all systems g., 800:4
    and catch a falling star, 228:9
    and do thou likewise, 37:38
    and listen as thou goest, 129:16
    and look behind Ranges, 589:21
    and see for ourselves, 761:9
    and sin no more, 39:23
    and the Lord be with thee, 10:46
    as cooks g. she went, 608:4
    as you g., 630:11
    ask Alice, 846:5
    at once, 216:22
    back to great sweet mother, 530:7
    beyond those of poor skill, 238:8
    burrow underground, 666:5

Go *(continued)*

by way wherein no ecstasy, 678:21
clear as you g., 525:14
come and trip it as you g., 250:22
don't know where to g., 490:11
don't want to g. no furder, 481:21
down again to the depths, 18:15
down Death, 610:7
down Moses, 898:18
down to the sea in ships, 18:14
dressed up nowhere to g., 603:12
easy to g. down into Hell, 94:27
for refuge to Buddha, 64:20
for they call you, 495:14
forth under open sky, 405:11
forward give us victories, 446:2
from strength to strength, 17:19
gentle into that good night, 777:15
hang yourselves critics, 146:4
home and get sleep, 604:1
home in dark, 582:4
I can't g. on like this, 744:18
I die as often as from thee I g., 229:5
I g. on forever, 454:25
I g. to prepare a place, 39:40
I will arise and g. now, 591:2
if g. high use own legs, 548:4
if I could g. through all again, 788:11
I'll g. on, 745:1
I'll g. to hell, 523:9
in peace, 37:28, 121:23
in the name of God g., 246:17
into night g. one and all, 552:6
into the house of the Lord, 19:1
know where'er I g., 370:15
learn to creep ere learn to g., 147:27
let my people g., 7:31
let us g. then, 674:17
let world g., 146:10
like Wind I g., 441:19
litel bok litel myn tragedye, 133:3
long way to g., 628:20
love without the help, 354:10
lovely rose, 249:24
mark him well, 373:3
men may come and g., 454:25
miles to g. before I sleep, 623:8
needs g. whom devil drive, 148:15
no g. my honey love, 751:2
no more a-roving, 397:14
nor sit nor stand but g., 462:15
not for every grief to physician, 244:1
not into every way, 30:21
not like quarry-slave, 405:13
not to Lethe, 411:9
not try to g. at all, 622:15
nowhere to run nowhere to g., 868:5
off with you where you want to g., 133:*n2*
once let ripe moment g., 352:7
out see Nature's riches, 254:6
out there and love people, 876:9
out to swim, 887:17
over rolling waters g., 452:18
poor devil, 314:6
returning as tedious as g. o'er, 216:25
rifle absolutely must g. off, 578:*n2*
season to come and g., 296:18
second best to g. back quickly, 66:19

Go *(continued)*

shopping, 859:6
side that I must g. withal, 175:15
since I needs must die, 159:9
sir gallop, 365:5
softly all my years, 26:22
Soul the body's quest, 159:9
Sun don't g., 814:10
sweetest love I do not g., 229:2
tell the Spartans, 60:11
tell those who sent you, 345:6
they all g. into dark, 678:19
they'd immediately g. out, 354:5
through world safely g., 354:2
till the end, 515:7
Time stays we g., 535:8
to bed by day, 555:8
to boldly g. where no man gone before, 797:3
to encounter reality, 650:13
to get along g. along, 651:12
to get where he has to g., 775:5
to grandfather's house we g., 421:17
to it with delight, 218:36
to lost sheep of Israel, 33:37
to restaurants, 859:6
to pot, 323:10
to the ant, 19:32
travel to g., 554:11
try to g. it sole alone, 624:17
turn and g., 817:6
up and down as a talebearer, 8:27
waiting for you g., 589:21
walk it slow where you g., 836:11
we know not where, 206:38
we shall g. on to end, 619:14
we'll gather and g., 367:15
west young man, 471:2
when half-gods g., 424:15
where glory waits thee, 387:5
where money is, 455:26
where did we g. right, 811:10
where we will on surface, 473:24
where you belong, 643:14
who will g. for us, 25:11
will not let thee g., 7:3
with anyone to death, 622:15
with drift of things, 622:8
with me like good angels, 225:15
with night will g., 350:9
women come and g., 674:18
write it before them, 26:11
ye and teach, 36:23
ye into all the world, 37:5
year going let him g., 454:8
Goä wheer munny is, 455:26
Goads them on behind, 590:23
words of wise are as g., 24:1
Goal, do not turn back at g., 100:23
good final g. of ill, 453:21
grave not life's g., 436:4
is living in agreement with nature, 82:1
progress our g., 416:7
rider deciding on g., 563:18
riders not stop at g., 539:8
same g. I've had, 875:6
the sky, 887:16
Goals, black people define g., 850:3
muddied oafs at g., 589:15

Goat, aimless g. paths, 830:12
lion could be g., 663:20
lust of g. bounty of God, 351:14
one girl remembers the wild g., 755:7
with g. feet dance antic hay, 168:12
Goat-head, foul g., 597:3
Goats, divideth sheep from g., 35:29
eat ivy, 896:4
lecherous g., 230:21
you herd g., 56:11
Gobbledygoo, your Luftwaffe your g., 833:8
Gobbler, black turkey g., 891:16
Gobble-uns 'at gits you, 553:7
Goblin, hag and hungry g., 881:22
Goblins 'at gits you, 553:7
sprites and g., 223:14
God, a G. ready to pardon, 12:30
a sea of infinite substance, 122:2
abhors you, 301:11
accept him, 454:17
act as if G. exist, 586:2
act as if there were G., 541:20
afraid to look upon G., 7:27
all mercy is God unjust, 291:1
Almighty has hung sign, 390:22
Almighty's gentlemen, 273:4
am I a g. I see so clearly, 344:2
and angels as surety, 118:16
and attributes eternal, 275:17
and devil fighting, 492:9
and imagination one, 642:14
and man decree, 575:16
and nature do nothing uselessly, 78:*n3*
and sinners reconciled, 305:10
announced selves descended from a g.,
    391:10
answering G. in every one, 270:3
any G. I ever felt in church, 860:8
Appears and God is Light, 354:7
argue not concerning G., 485:10
arm's too short to box with G., 610:3
as G. alone Jesus not saved us, 734:15
as G. gives us to see right, 447:2
as if G. wrote bill, 424:22
assumes the g., 274:15
atheist half believes G., 291:2
attribute to G. himself, 186:1
author should be like G., 493:10
be good to the man, 791:1
be merciful, 38:24
be praised Georges ended, 629:*n3*
be still and know that I am G., 16:28
be thanked, 669:11
be thanked I have proved it, 662:11
beauty the gift of G., 77:8
behold your G., 26:28
being with thee, 370:6
believe in one G. and no more, 333:18
believes he eats G., 315:2
bequeath my soul to G., 166:21
bless America, 673:10, 673:11
bless Captain Vere, 484:3
bless the child, 779:9
bless the Pretender, 297:18
bless us every one, 465:12
bless you, 884:7
bless you my dear, 311:17
body Nature G. soul, 294:22

God *(continued)*

brewed waters into gale, 482:22
brooding on G., 756:13
but for grace of G., 149:8
by G. Mr. Chairman, 320:5
by G. she'd better, 456:*n*4
by grace of G. forces on Philippine soil, 644:8
Cabots talk only to G., 577:15
Cabots walk with G., 577:*n*2
cast all cares on G., 455:22
caught his eye, 714:17
caused a deep sleep, 5:15
changes and man and form, 530:20
changes not people until they change, 118:9
charged with grandeur of G., 546:6
chide G. for countenance, 195:25
chosen people of G., 336:10
Christ came from G. and a woman, 416:2
circumvent G., 202:7
city of G., 116:17
closer walk with G., 326:7
comes as sun at noon, 231:10
comes G. behind them, 462:26
committed themselves to G., 240:1
confirms those who believe, 118:11
conscience a g. to all mortals, 81:13
contempt of G. love of G., 116:19
could have made a better berry, 245:7
course of Nature art of G., 248:*n*1
created heaven and earth, 5:3
created woman and boredom ceased, 549:1
curse for G., 819:12
curse G. and die, 13:2
damn you, 586:*n*4
darkness of G., 678:20
dazzled by ways of G., 639:10
dear G. the very houses, 370:3
dear G. who loveth us, 377:6
dear to G. famous to all ages, 254:4
death of one g. death of all, 641:21
deem himself g. or beast, 295:1
defend the right, 170:3
depth of all being is G., 668:17
did G. Care, 508:21
die adoring G. loving friends, 300:8
die young like kissing G., 807:11
died before g. of love was born, 229:21
discovered I was not G., 539:9
discussing duty to G., 486:14
does not leave us, 864:13
does what He will, 118:11
don't believe in G. or Mother Goose, 568:11
doth G. exact day-labor, 254:21
ef you want to take in G., 482:1
either a beast or a g., 78:18
electrical display of G., 681:7
Enoch walked with G., 6:13
enter into kingdom of G., 35:4
equal to a g. sitting opposite you, 91:16
erects house of prayer, 282:4
eternal G. is thy refuge, 9:33
every g. set his seal, 201:5
every man G. or Devil, 273:3
evidence for G. in inner experiences, 542:7

God *(continued)*

except for G. our only lord, 167:8
face of G. shine through, 695:6
far be it from G., 14:14
Father-Mother G., 493:4
favor with G. and man, 37:22
fear G., 119:15
fear G. and keep commandments, 24:2
fear G. and take own part, 423:7
fear G. honor the king, 45:39
fear G. nothing else, 470:12
fell upon knees and blessed G., 240:2
finger of G., 7:35
first planted garden, 166:15
for G. sake hold your tongue, 228:18
for Harry, 189:9
for us all, 148:24
forbid it Almighty G., 331:13
foregoing generations beheld G., 425:19
forgive you but I never, 151:11
forgives me for it, 805:14
forgotten all I have done, 278:15
formed matter, 279:17
formed vile creature woman, 136:22
from the machine, 81:9
from whom blessings flow, 278:8
fulfills in many ways, 455:19
gave every people cup of clay, 892:3
gave Loaf to Bird, 509:19
gave me my money, 535:4
gave Noah rainbow sign, 804:14
gave the increase, 42:7
give him blood to drink, 431:12
give them wisdom, 204:18
give us grace to accept, 695:20
giver of breath and bread, 546:5
gives artist in abundance, 551:5
giveth both mouth and meat, 146:*n*16
glory to G., 37:18, 47:22
good fortune is g. among men, 63:11
good G. prepare me, 277:27
grace is given of G., 479:9
granted it, 299:24
grants liberty, 390:13
great G. I'd rather be, 371:24
great G. our King, 439:10
great G. to thee we tend, 117:5
greater than G. cannot be conceived, 123:6
greatness of G., 543:2
guideth whom He will, 119:2
ha' mercy on such as we, 588:6
had I but studied, 138:18
had never spoken anything but English, 622:5
hand of G. spirit of G., 485:17
handiwork you give G., 557:4
Hannah G. and me, 518:7
has brought us this peace, 92:14
has given you one face, 200:1
has G. sent a mortal as messenger, 118:16
has no real style, 647:15
has pity on kindergarten children, 804:5
has written all the books, 521:13
hates bray of bragging, 65:10
hath chosen foolish things, 42:5
hath given liberty, 345:7
hath made man upright, 23:18
hath made them so, 289:5

God *(continued)*

hath no better praise, 545:14
hath not given spirit of fear, 44:39
hath not one G. created us, 29:18
hath numbered thy kingdom, 28:25
hath said there is no G., 15:9
hath sifted a nation, 275:2
have mercy on sinner, 682:1
have mercy on such as we, 588:6
he for G. only, 257:19
he was a son of G., 710:4
heirs of G., 41:19
help us we knew worst too young, 588:7
helps them that help selves, 302:15
helps those who get up early, 898:5
herdsman goads, 590:23
here I stand G. help me, 143:14
hid fossils in rocks, 552:5
Himself can't kill words, 98:*n*3
himself from G. not free, 424:5
himself scarce seemed to be, 377:4
his Father and his G., 316:8
hitting spitting poison at G., 301:9
honest G. noblest work, 518:3
honest man noblest work of G., 295:5, 356:10
how would man exist if G. did not need him, 634:8
I accuser G. accused, 821:5
I am a G., 401:17
I am a jealous G., 8:12
I am part or particle of G., 425:22
I am the Lord thy G., 8:10
I bless G. in libraries, 318:11
I don't need G. to love neighbor, 743:9
I hope there is no G., 843:1
I think it pisses G. off, 860:9
I who saw face of G., 168:18
I wretch wrestling with G., 547:4
if find answer know mind of G., 854:3
if G. be for us, 41:23
if G. did not exist, 299:27
if G. died, 828:7
if G. is male, 818:1
if G. will, 118:17
if he is not the word of G., 834:11
if it be of G., 40:18
if soul knows G., 127:13
if triangles had g., 297:12
I'll leap up to my G., 169:4
in all his werkis wittie is., 143:12
in apprehension like a g., 199:5
in G. dazzling darkness, 269:3
in G. is our trust, 387:1
in the image of G., 6:24
in Three Persons, 391:8
in youth remembered my G., 381:11
inclines to think there is G., 479:11
insult to G., 460:14
invite G. and his angels, 231:11
is a concept, 847:13
is a verb, 705:10
is an exalted father, 563:8
is an in order to, 586:7
is and is not voice of G., 296:12
is aware of things you do, 119:15
is day night winter summer, 62:5
is dead, 547:16

God *(continued)*

is G. blunder of man, 548:22
is G. dead, 415:19
is in heaven, 23:4
is in me or does not exist, 643:7
is in the details, 887:14
is in the midst of her, 16:27
is light, 46:6
is love, 46:11
is Love I dare say, 521:14
is man blunder of G., 548:22
is no respecter of persons, 40:27
is not a because, 586:7
is not a man, 9:9
is not mocked, 43:33
is or He is not, 269:17
is our refuge and strength, 16:26
is seen God, 462:5
is stupidity and cowardice, 450:5
is swift at the reckoning, 118:24
is their belly, 44:5
is there and man is not, 417:12
is they are, 462:20
it is a g. who gave you this gift, 50:13
it's not G. I don't accept, 492:11
jealous G., 8:12
just are the ways of G., 260:13
justify ways of G. to men, 255:5
keeps thee from G., 421:9
Kingdom of G. within you, 38:20
kissing carrion, 198:33
know what G. and man is, 455:27
know ye that the Lord he is G., 18:3
knowledge and love of G., 49:8
knowledge makes G. of me, 411:15
lamb of G., 47:23
land G. gave to Cain, 144:15
laws of G. are forever, 65:18
laws of G. laws of man, 575:16
laws of nature and nature's G., 336:1
lay me on anvil O G., 636:8
leads astray evildoers, 118:11
let not G. speak with us, 8:15
let us worship G., 356:9
life of ease not for a g., 407:26
light is shadow of G., 249:6
light of heavens and earth, 118:23
light prime work of G., 257:*n*2
live innocently G. is here, 305:5
livin' G. that made you, 587:19
living G., 16:21
looks up to Nature's G., 295:6
Lord G. Almighty, 391:8
Lord G. formed man, 5:10
Lord G. is subtle, 638:6
Lord G. made them all, 476:4
Lord G. of Hosts, 589:7
Lord G. planted a garden, 5:11
Lord G. send high wave, 611:14
Lord G. walking in garden, 5:20
Lord our G. is one Lord, 9:14
love of G. had blessed, 392:19
loveth cheerful giver, 43:19
lust of goat bounty of G., 351:14
made him let him pass for man, 184:18
made integers, 500:2
made the country, 326:19
made the world, 40:33

God *(continued)*

make me strong, 888:2
make straight a highway for our G., 26:24
man g. in ruins, 425:25
man proposes G. disposes, 137:5
man sent from G., 38:46
man with G. always in majority, 150:2
man with G. strive, 396:4
man's word G. in man, 455:7
Masai House of G., 721:16
men G. made mad, 618:10
mighty fortress is our G., 143:16
mills of G. grind slowly, 247:10
most glorious city of G., 116:17
moved upon face of the waters, 5:3
moves in mysterious way, 326:9
music sent up to G., 462:11
must think it exceedingly odd, 680:4
my G. and King, 243:9
my G. have mercy, 154:1
my G. look not so fierce, 169:5
my G. why hast thou forsaken me, 15:21, 36:20
my soul thirsteth for G., 16:21
nakedness of woman work of G., 351:14
name called the mighty G., 25:16
name of G. upon lips, 312:22
nation is chosen by G., 862:13
nature is the art of G., 248:6
Nature's G., 295:6
near and hard to grasp, 367:18
nearer my G. to thee, 432:16
nearer to church further from G., 147:8
nest on greatness of G., 543:2
never made work for man to mend, 274:24
never spoke with G., 510:9
next to of course g., 701:10
no g. higher than truth, 604:5
no G. stronger than death, 530:10
no man hath seen G., 38:49
no more Aurora Leighs thank G., 442:11
no society bring Kingdom of G., 648:6
noblest work of G., 295:5
none other but the house of G., 6:43
nor G. nor man, 609:1
not alone G. is within, 108:17
not even G. is wise enough, 889:11
not G. for father if not Church for mother, 114:2
not G. of dead, 38:27
not only no G., 839:11
not serve G. if devil bid, 207:28
not willing to do everything, 142:6
O G. that bread so dear, 418:12
O G. that it were possible, 233:17
O Lamb of G., 47:23
of battles, 189:24
of Clotilda grant victory, 116:25
of fathers known of old, 589:7
of God, 48:12
of my idolatry, 180:9
of Nature, 243:3
of Nature placed in power, 331:12
of such is kingdom of G., 36:38
of the Congo, 639:15
of truth, 9:30
of universal laws, 542:2
on right hand of G., 48:11

God *(continued)*

on seventh day G. ended his work, 5:9
on side of big squadrons, 265:5
one G. even the Father, 388:7
one g. greatest among gods, 60:6
one G. law element, 454:12
one G. one principle of being, 112:14
One God the Everlasting Refuge, 119:20
one sinks in on G., 591:15
one nation under G., 562:6
one that feared G., 12:34
only another artist, 647:15
only G. and angels lookers on, 164:16
only G. can make tree, 668:1
only G. had for asking, 481:15
only G. my dear, 595:7
only knows which is which, 531:2
our help in ages past, 289:12
out of me G. and man, 530:20
owe G. a death, 188:16
pairs off like with like, 53:24
peace of G. passeth understanding, 44:6
Peace of G. which passeth all understanding, 49:8
people are annoyed I believe in G., 754:8
perfect blessedness vision of G., 127:7
plays dice with world, 638:5
pleased G. to visit us with death, 240:4
plots of G. are perfect, 449:18
poet is a little g., 698:1
poor Mexico so far from G., 508:2
praise belongs to G., 117:11
presume not G. to scan, 295:1
pride of peacock glory of G., 351:14
put hand to ark of G., 11:14
rather believe G. not exist, 432:15
read New Yorker trust in G., 749:16
reason in man like G. in world, 127:9
rebellion obedience to G., 883:21
reflect that G. is just, 336:9
register of G., 249:2
reigns Government lives, 512:14
religion between man and G., 337:13
remains dead, 547:*n*4
render unto G., 35:12
rest you merry, 883:4
rib which Lord G. had taken, 5:15
rise and shine give G. glory, 898:23
said I am tired, 424:19
said Let Newton be, 296:23
said Let there be light, 5:3
said Let us make man, 5:6
saint if G. does not exist, 770:4
save the king, 10:39, 292:2
save the king say amen, 177:16
save the mark, 182:2
save the people, 389:4
save thee ancient Mariner, 375:25
saw that it was good, 5:5
say first of G. above, 294:16
says there is no G., 312:22
Scourge of G., 168:3
secluded from sight of G., 231:9
see G. made and eaten, 460:22
seek G. in old quiet places, 828:7
seen G. face to face, 7:4
sees G. in clouds, 294:20
sees the truth in us, 591:15

God *(continued)*

self-reliance is reliance on G., 428:2
send every gentleman, 890:5
sends meat Devil sends cooks, 146:*n*16
servant of G. well done, 258:23
servant of Living G., 318:14
served my G. with half the zeal, 226:6
service greater than the g., 203:13
set not up with G. another g., 118:13
sets nothing but riddles, 492:8
setteth the solitary in families, 17:10
shall any teach G., 13:43
shall smite thee, 40:44
shall wipe away tears, 47:12
she for G. in him, 257:19
shed grace on thee, 572:5
shield us, 178:25
shows sufficient light, 463:3
so commanded, 259:10
so loved the world, 39:11
so near is G. to man, 424:21
sole G. beside whom is none, 4:8
something beautiful for G., 762:9
Son of the living G., 34:36
sons of G. shouted for joy, 14:19
sons of the living G., 28:31
Soul of each G. of all, 375:16
souls are in the hand of G., 29:34
souls mounting up to G., 506:1
Spirit of G. descending, 32:9
spirit shall return unto G., 23:31
standeth G. within shadow, 481:13
stands winding horn, 591:10
stay with me G., 888:2
stepped out on space, 610:5
stern daughter of voice of G., 371:14
strengthen me to bear myself, 512:9
strong brown g., 679:3
subject to G. and Justice, 124:8
sufficeth me, 118:5
surrenders his face to G., 119:4
sways G. nearby, 773:4
take in G., 482:1
tempers wind, 151:6, 314:26
temple of G. is holy, 42:10
thank G. Almighty, 898:19
thank G. Almighty free at last, 823:9
thank G. for tea, 375:12
thank G. I have done duty, 355:13
thanked G. Beth was well, 513:7
the Father a school-divine, 296:13
the Father fell back behind Christ, 564:4
the first garden made, 265:15
the herdsman goads, 590:23
the unknown g., 40:32
the way of G., 261:16
the word spake it, 151:14
the world the book of G., 227:8
there G. is dwelling too, 351:5
there is no G. but He, 118:5
these old men, 67:8
they shall be called children of G., 32:14
they shall see G., 32:14
think not G. at all, 260:13
this nation under G., 446:5
this only is denied to G., 73:21
those G. loves do not live long, 81:*n*4
those G. wishes to destroy, 69:3

God *(continued)*

those whom G. hath joined to gether, 49:18
thou art the Son of G., 34:30
thou great democratic G., 482:24
thought and thought, 610:6
three-personed G., 230:26
through darkness up to G., 453:24
throws himself on G., 461:15
thy G. shall be my G., 10:30
'tis G. gives skill, 480:23
to begin new and great period, 254:11
to kirk nearer from G. more far, 160:1
to the greater glory of G., 149:1
to whom G. assigns no light, 118:24
too full of G. to speak, 590:19
took spinning-jenny, 594:15
touched face of G., 800:1
towards G. the other towards Satan, 491:16
trust in G. hope for best, 374:24
trust in G. keep powder dry, 385:6
twenty gods or no G., 336:5
two halves of, 422:7
two not without G., 113:19
unchanging law of G., 457:9
unpredictability of G., 802:2
unto G. is the sequel, 119:4
very G. of very G., 48:12
vindicate ways of G. to man, 294:15
voice of people is voice of G., 122:5
walk humbly with thy G., 29:5
wanted me to be Czech, 841:8
wants nothing of a g. but eternity, 220:4
war blood-swollen g., 608:13
Was Here but He Left Early, 772:9
was it G. was it man, 530:21
was the holy Lamb of G., 354:8
ways of G. justificate, 260:13
we believe in G., 117:13
we praise thee O G., 48:9
what G. do you pray to, 853:13
what G. hath joined, 35:2
what hath G. wrought, 9:10
what is G. everything, 64:9
what kind of g. art thou, 189:22
what man not know of G., 737:9
what we have instead of G., 721:4
when angels talk of praising G., 666:10
where G. built church, 144:5
where was He jealous vengeful G., 739:13
whispers to us in our pleasures, 717:14
who brought over ocean, 240:2
who could discover us, 104:10
who gave life gave liberty, 335:22
who G. doth late and early pray, 227:10
who is able to prevail, 244:30
who is not we see, 531:3
who is our home, 370:17
who made him sees, 590:5
who made thee mighty, 580:19
whole armor of G., 43:39
whom G. wishes to destroy, 121:11
whom science recognizes, 542:2
whom we see not is, 531:3
why did G. make me an outcast, 602:1
why St. Augustine thanked G., 630:7
will of G. prevail, 497:13
will provide himself a lamb, 6:35

God *(continued)*

will put an end to these, 93:34
will recognize his own, 126:2
will take you to task for your hearts, 118:2
wills it, 120:16
wisdom by awful grace of G., 63:2
with G. nothing impossible, 37:7
with strongest battalions, 312:8
with thousand voices praises G., 378:4
with us, 31:35
word of G. is quick, 45:7
word of our G. shall stand, 26:27
Word was with G., 38:44
words of G. not be spent, 119:5
worketh in you, 44:3
works in mysterious way, 675:24
worship G. according to own inclinations, 106:5
worship G. in own way, 653:4
would G. this flesh might be, 530:2
would have three sides, 297:12
wrath of G., 47:9
wrath of lion wisdom of G., 351:14
writer must be like G., 493:18
wrongs not men, 118:7
wrote it, 458:18
wrote of Angels and G., 351:10
yearning like G., 409:19
you need G. G. needs you, 634:8
your false g. dim rememoring, 682:12
Yours Faithfully G., 680:*n*2
Zion city of our G., 321:1
God-breathing machines, 468:19
Goddam precious American rights, 834:1
Goddamm, Lhude sing G., 665:2
Goddess, bitch-g. Success, 542:4
consult concerning great g., 366:18
Demeter or Earth, 68:9
excellently bright, 232:2
moves a g., 293:17
night sable g., 290:19
of Grecian woes O g. sing, 293:16
of the silver lake, 252:26
to thy shrine we come, 359:10
walk revealed her as true g., 94:2
White G., 706:5
write about it G., 297:5
Goddesses, even if g. too should be looking, 53:9
sweets of Fairies Peris G., 409:13
take hold ye gods and g., 51:16
Godfathers of heaven's lights, 174:1
God-fearing, signs for a g. people, 118:6
God-given rights, 433:7
Godhead, Buddha the G. resides, 820:1
God-intoxicated man, 275:*n*4
Godiva, white G. I unpeel, 833:10
Godlessness, future smells of g., 415:8
Godlike, capability and g. reason, 201:19
erect, 257:18
man with g. intellect, 440:13
Godliness, cheerful g., 370:10
cleanliness next to g., 301:18
Godly, old and g. and grave, 591:7
God's above all, 208:24
abusing of G. patience, 187:4
arrest, 280:20
blessing said Sancho Panza, 158:*n*3

God's (*continued*)

    capricious hand, 742:1

    crucible, 586:9

    dare ask just G. assistance, 447:1

    Devil is ever G. ape, 144:5

    do deed without G. knowledge, 63:23

    earthly power then likest G., 186:1

    elect, 41:24

    first creature light, 257:*n*2

    first temples, 405:15

    fool, 522:11

    for G. sake sit upon ground, 177:8

    gifts put dreams to shame, 434:16

    great Judgment Seat, 587:8

    greatest gift to us, 876:14

    greenwood chapel, 640:*n*1

    hand folks over to G. mercy, 480:8

    heaven is G. throne, 32:19

    help and their valor, 365:10

    here is G. plenty, 274:26

    I'm under G. arrest, 280:20

    in G. wildness hope of world, 533:6

    in his heaven, 459:19

    issue is in G. hands, 63:27

    justify G. ways to man, 575:12

    last Put out the Light, 623:13

    light G. eldest daughter, 250:3

    look in my G. right hand, 898:25

    love G. ultimate gift, 462:6

    man's bedevilment and G., 575:17

    mill grinds slow, 244:17

    mouth knows not falsehood, 63:19

    not G. not beasts', 462:20

    one on G. side majority, 458:11

    Park specimen of G. handiwork, 498:14

    reason G. crowning gift, 65:23

    sometimes it seems G. gone, 673:2

    supply of tolerable husbands, 706:3

    spies, 213:8

    things which are G., 35:12

    thy country's thy G. and truth's, 226:5

    to Indian all days are G., 570:8

    voice of G. creatures, 448:*n*1

    want to do G. will, 823:16

    ways to man, 575:12

    we are in G. hand, 189:15

    we are on G. side, 775:3

    woman G. second mistake, 549:1

    works are wide, 242:25

    written in G. book, 118:8

    ye are G. husbandry, 42:8

Gods, all ages believed in g., 630:5

    all men have need of g., 52:28

    altars to unknown g., 540:18

    angels would be g., 165:*n*4

    are just, 213:10

    are on side of stronger, 110:11

    arrive, 424:15

    as flies to boys we to g., 212:17

    as psychic factors, 630:5

    believe in g. of state, 74:7

    built against will of g., 51:23

    call the g. to witness, 213:18

    calling on the g., 71:10

    contend in vain, 360:9

    convenient that there be g., 102:4

    darling of men and g., 89:9

    daughter of g., 450:23

Gods (*continued*)

    dish fit for g., 192:4

    do not give all men gifts, 53:7

    do not answer letters, 833:17

    dwells with g. above, 203:19

    even if g. should be looking, 53:9

    execute judgment against g. of Egypt, 7:40

    fashioned by men, 584:12

    fight against necessity, 55:9

    glorious gifts of the g., 50:27

    go in various disguises, 54:3

    good g. how he will talk, 281:15

    grant me this, 91:27

    graven images of her g., 25:27

    hail to you g., 3:10

    happy who knows rural g., 93:19

    have neither age nor death, 66:17

    have their own rules, 102:16

    help them that help themselves, 59:14

    immortal g. I crave no pelf, 213:21

    in lap of the g., 52:*n*2

    in likeness of men, 40:28

    kings it makes g., 172:5

    knees of the g., 52:23

    laughter among the g., 50:20

    leave all else to the g., 96:9

    life in which g. are not, 849:12

    Little Tin G. on Wheels, 586:17

    live with the g., 112:11

    love rules the g., 66:10

    machine for making of g., 572:11

    make G. to whom to impute ills, 495:7

    makes g. by the dozen, 152:20

    may g. grant you all things, 53:3

    men determine g. dispose, 235:*n*3

    men that strove with g., 451:17

    might of g. slow but sure, 68:11

    minds of g. not changed, 52:29

    mortals are blaming the g., 52:22

    most beautiful among the immortal g., 54:14

    mother of g. and men, 4:3

    nearest to g., 70:3

    no other g. before me, 8:11

    not fit that men be compared with g., 91:22

    not know much about g., 679:3

    not similar are immortal g. and men, 51:8

    now g. stand up for bastards, 211:1

    O nights and feasts of g., 95:25

    of the Congo, 639:15

    Olympus abode of the g., 53:2

    only freedom g. grant us, 681:15

    opinion that there are no g., 76:13

    pay for what g. given, 612:19

    right idea of the g., 76:12

    search out purposes of g., 64:6

    sent not corn for rich men only, 219:20

    spun the thread for mortals, 52:19

    take hold ye g. and goddesses, 51:16

    temples of his g., 419:19

    that wanton in the air, 266:1

    themselves throw incense, 213:9

    thought otherwise, 94:17

    two g. Persuasion and Compulsion, 62:20

    victor had g. the vanquished had Cato, 106:9

    visit sins of fathers upon children, 69:2

Gods (*continued*)

    voice of g. makes heaven drowsy, 174:23

    what ailed us O g., 529:20

    what men or g. are these, 410:14

    when favor of g. was equal, 69:4

    whoever obeys the g., 50:15

    whom the g. love, 81:6

    whom the G. would destroy, 69:*n*3

    woman a dish for g., 219:11

    would draw g. like horses, 60:5

    would g. made thee poetical, 195:18

    ye shall be as g., 5:19

Gods' custom to bring low greatness, 69:16

Goes, anything g., 691:11

    down with great shout, 557:7

    from great deep he g., 455:21

    in and out with me, 555:12

    much against my stomach, 195:4

    naked to naked g., 596:5

    no one g. and comes back, 3:2

    nobody g. there anymore, 708:1

    one but g. abreast, 203:23

    one never g. so far, 343:17

    Rainbow comes and g., 370:14

    see how world g., 212:29

    so it g., 801:3

    the further one g. the less one knows, 57:16

    where tooth point g., 586:18

Goest, whither g. thou, 40:3

    whither thou g. I will go, 10:30

    with thee whithersoever thou g., 9:35

Goeth forth and weepeth, 19:3

    he g. after her straightway, 20:5

    light from wisdom never g. out, 30:7

    man g. forth unto his work, 18:11

    on to meet the armed men, 14:27

    pride g. before a fall, 66:*n*2

    whither it g., 39:9

Goethe, read G. or Rilke, 825:12

Gogol's Overcoat, 493:3

Going a journey, 386:7

    a-milking sir, 894:12

    down the wind, 277:3

    endure their g. hence, 213:7

    from g. to and fro, 12:36

    from rising of the sun unto g. down, 18:20

    his g. forth is from end of the heaven, 15:16

    if don't know where g., 793:8

    I'm g. all along, 508:19

    I'm g. to get what's mine, 866:2

    know world without g. outdoors, 57:16

    learn by g., 756:5

    long and loath at g., 681:18

    order of your g., 216:22

    out to clean spring, 622:9

    out with tide, 465:35

    preserve thy g. out and coming in, 18:30

    sage knows without g. about, 57:16

    sun knoweth his g. down, 18:11

    the way of all the earth, 10:5

    to St. Ives, 892:22

    to the fair, 893:12

    true order of g., 74:5

    way of all flesh, 237:2

    we're g. to our Father's land, 861:8

    what's it g. to be then eh, 783:14

Going *(continued)*
   when the g. gets weird, 843:16
   Where Are We G., 551:8
   year is g. let him go, 454:8
Gold, accurst craving for g., 94:19
   age of g., 97:12
   Age of G., 250:12
   all g. goose could give, 59:12
   all that glisters not g., 125:*n*2
   almighty g., 232:15
   and frankincense, 31:37
   and love affairs difficult to hide, 898:12
   and silver ivory and apes, 11:35
   and silver light, 591:12
   and the lust, 708:6
   apples of g. in pictures of silver, 21:33
   as good as American g., 553:14
   bar of Heaven, 505:23
   barbaric pearl and g., 256:6
   be it gash or g., 783:8
   beauty provoketh sooner than g., 193:34
   becomes her object, 188:21
   blazing in G., 508:11
   blue and g. mistake, 508:6
   bow of burning g., 354:8
   cemented with g., 886:13
   centuries roll back to age of g., 97:12
   cross of g., 577:18
   eyes of g. and bramble dew, 556:8
   fairy g., 223:20
   fin in porphyry font, 453:5
   fire is test of g., 103:25
   gateways of stars, 576:15
   gild refined g., 175:24
   gleaming in purple and g., 397:2
   good as g., 465:11
   great horse of g., 701:4
   hair turned quite g. from grief, 560:19
   hairy g. crown on 'ead, 587:20
   hammered g., 594:4
   harps of g., 457:11
   if g. ruste what shal iren do, 134:4
   in itself useless, 143:3
   in phisik is a cordial, 134:1
   jewel of g. in swine's snout, 20:14
   locks yellow as g., 376:7
   lust of g., 454:9
   man's the g. for all that, 358:18
   more to be desired than g., 15:17
   names written in letters of g., 145:1
   not all that shines as g., 125:4
   old man's g., 607:6
   orange glows, 342:15
   path of g. for him, 460:17
   patines of bright g., 186:15
   plate sin with g., 212:30
   poop was beaten g., 218:20
   potable g., 235:12
   purer than purest g., 232:9
   purse of g. resolutely snatched, 181:22
   quantity of g. temperate carry, 74:3
   rarer gifts than g., 669:12
   realms of g., 408:17
   robe of g. and pearl, 189:23
   roofs of g., 188:35
   saint-seducing g., 179:20
   scarfs garters g., 295:3
   shines like fire, 63:21

Gold *(continued)*
   shower of g., 407:3
   silver and g. have I none, 40:16
   speak silver reply g., 889:9
   still as a g. piece, 820:14
   that I never see, 575:5
   therefore lovede g. in special, 134:1
   thombe of g., 134:6
   to airy thinness beat, 229:16
   trodden g., 256:3
   troops pass through seek g., 499:3
   truth with g. she weighs, 296:25
   what female heart g. despise, 315:9
   what is g. doing in holy place, 105:13
   what's become of g., 462:4
   wisdom never comes g., 505:7
   wonder that g. esteemed, 143:3
Gold-bearing, crushed the g. Medes, 60:10
Golden Age before us not behind, 553:15
   age exists in imagination, 420:3
   all in g. afternoon, 513:10
   Aphrodite, 53:9, 55:3
   apples of sun, 591:11
   as they did in g. world, 193:24
   bindest in wreaths thy g. hair, 96:6
   bough, 594:4
   bought g. opinions, 215:1
   bowl be broken, 23:31
   care, 188:20
   chain from heaven, 51:16
   circle of g. year, 451:10
   crown like a deep well, 177:17
   days fruitful of golden deeds, 257:7
   door, 552:16
   every g. scale, 513:15
   father held out g. scales, 52:14
   fretted with g. fire, 199:5
   friends I had, 575:9
   goose with g. eggs, 59:12
   hanging in a g. chain, 257:4
   host of g. daffodils, 371:9
   hours on angel wings, 358:12
   in mercy of his means, 777:11
   Jerusalem the g., 479:2
   keep g. mean, 96:*n*16
   key, 252:1
   kings in g. suits ride elephants, 767:7
   lads and girls, 220:26
   lamps in a green night, 267:6
   like untuned g. strings women are, 168:15
   locks to silver turned, 163:3
   Love in a g. bowl, 351:9
   mean, 96:22
   miller hath g. thumb, 134:*n*1
   million g. birds, 559:3
   mind stoops not, 185:3
   mottoes in the mouth, 483:20
   nap before dinner g., 506:12
   on g. chair seated prince of Wales, 647:4
   ope their g. eyes, 220:15
   opes the iron shuts, 253:9
   pear, 894:18
   returns the G. Age, 92:22
   Rule, 33:*n*1
   rule will fit everybody, 520:7
   sands and crystal brooks, 229:14
   seven g. candlesticks, 46:16
   Silence g., 406:23

Golden *(continued)*
   sleep with g. Aphrodite, 53:9
   stretches out my g. wing, 350:8
   sun in g. cup, 596:4
   track, 639:14
   tree of life, 344:5
   two g. hours, 414:5
   Vanity, 898:2
   we are g., 858:2
   wear a g. sorrow, 225:17
   what delight without g. Aphrodite, 55:3
   years return, 403:8
Goldengrove unleaving, 546:17
Goldenrod, bent g., 677:19
Gold-feathered bird sings in palm, 642:18
Goldfish in glass bowl, 608:6
Goldsmith, here lies Nolly G., 316:21
Goldsmiths, Grecian g. make, 594:4
Golf is a good walk spoiled, 525:12
   links lie so near mill, 632:18
Golgotha, place called G., 36:17
   wherein all things rot, 234:1
Gondola, carries me quietly like a g., 814:8
   swam in a g., 195:25
Gone, all all are g., 383:3
   and never must return, 253:4
   and past help, 223:18
   aye ages long ago, 410:1
   coon, 393:16
   dead and g. lady, 201:24
   down drain of eternity, 67:11
   everything else was g., 747:10
   far away into silent land, 512:4
   glimmering, 395:5
   good old cause g., 370:4
   goodness lives though they are g., 68:20
   he has departed withdrawn g. away, 87:7
   he will know it's g., 772:5
   heaviness that's g., 225:7
   heavy change now thou art g., 253:4
   here and there, 222:13
   here today g. tomorrow, 279:9
   home art g., 220:26
   I am g. like the shadow, 18:17
   I shall be g., 622:21
   I shan't be g. long, 622:9
   I would have thee g., 180:15
   if she's not g., 896:11
   I'll be g., 851:4
   into world of light, 268:16
   line is g. out through all the earth, 15:16
   mischief past and g., 208:5
   my life has g., 814:13
   not lost but g. before, 103:17
   odds is g., 219:5
   Othello's occupation's g., 209:13
   Poets dead and g., 411:5
   romantic Ireland's dead and g., 592:10
   sea-discoverers to new worlds have g., 228:7
   she's g. forever, 213:12
   soon as she was g. from me, 352:3
   sweet cheat g., 616:8
   these things are past and g., 91:4
   they are all g. away, 605:17
   they're all g. now, 611:12
   they've g. about as fur as c'n go, 706:10
   thou art g. and forever, 373:23

Gone *(continued)*

Thursday come and week g., 244:12
to her death, 418:13
under earth's lid, 665:9
where have you g. Joe DiMaggio, 855:8
wind passeth over it and it is g., 18:7
with the wind, 599:15
yes thou art g., 496:15
Gonfalon bubble, 646:12
Gong, after great cathedral g., 595:10
Gong-tormented sea, 595:13
Gonna, what are you g. do, 762:8
Gonzo journalism, 843:15
Good, a little fun and g. morrow, 519:8
a little work and g. day, 519:8
a thing moderately g., 333:17
abroad for g. of country, 290:8
all g. men, 885:18
all g. to me is lost, 257:13
Americans die go to Paris, 560:13
amiable or sweet, 259:14
and bad angel, 234:14
and faithful servant, 35:26
any g. thing I can do, 884:21
any g. thing out of Nazareth, 39:1
apothecary, 212:28
apprehension of the g., 176:18
arrived in a g. harbor, 240:2
as all no better than any, 743:7
as gold, 465:11
as g. almost kill man as g. book, 254:7
as g. in the dark, 241:2
as g. luck would have it, 187:15
as I can be, 554:4
as seems beforehand, 480:13
ask not g. fortune, 486:24
atom's weight of g., 119:19
bad book as much labor as g., 702:13
bad end happily the g. unluckily, 843:7
bad indifferent, 276:12, 314:10
bad worst best, 448:2
be g. and be lonesome, 524:8
be g. and happy today, 375:14
be of g. cheer, 34:28, 40:5
because it's awful, 835:17
befriend themselves, 66:16
best is enemy of g., 299:21
best is g. enough, 343:7
book lifeblood of spirit, 254:8
bringer of g. tidings, 118:4
bringeth thee into a g. land, 9:19
but not religious-good, 535:12
by evil and g. report, 43:17
by quiet natures understood, 593:17
cannot come to g., 197:5
can't say anything g., 659:15
captive g. attending captain ill, 221:22
catches mice g. cat, 737:7
cause can become bad, 802:1
character remembered, 3:9
charm to make bad g., 207:9
cheer is best physician, 64:1
chief g. and market, 201:19
cigar is a smoke, 587:1
circumstance makes action g. or bad, 73:23
club assembly of g. fellows, 306:24
commodity of g. names, 181:27
constantly doing G., 60:21

Good *(continued)*

corn wood boards to sell, 425:17
counselors lack no clients, 206:13
crown g. with brotherhood, 572:5
day's work, 304:3
deed in naughty world, 186:18
deed to say well, 225:21
demean themselves as g. citizens, 328:12
deny us for our g., 218:17
depart from evil and do g., 16:7
devil have all g. tunes, 341:7
die early bad late, 282:9
die first, 372:6
digestion wait on appetite, 216:16
dinner and feasting, 277:13
do all the g. I can, 527:6
do all the g. you can, 301:19
do g. purify mind, 64:13
do g. to them that hate you, 32:21
do more g. with money, 543:15
doing g. one of professions full, 474:22
easy for us to do g., 805:13
eating is a small g. thing, 844:2
ended happily, 843:*n*2
enough for me, 884:19
enough to shed blood, 571:8
Epicurus set forth highest g., 90:21
evening Mr. Mrs. America, 715:15
every creature of God is g., 44:28
every evil hath g., 426:26
every g. gift, 45:22
everything in world g. for something, 273:11
evil be thou my g., 257:13
evil is absence of g., 116:20
evil reward punishment, 275:11
fair and learned and g. as she, 240:7
fair is by nature g., 161:8
faith toward nations, 329:1
fell into g. ground, 34:16
fellows get together, 585:6
fences make good neighbors, 622:11
fight of faith, 44:36
five-cent cigar, 558:6
follow g. side to fire, 153:8
for a man that he bear the yoke, 28:13
for country good for General Motors, 689:6
for sore eyes, 285:14
fortune is god among men, 63:11
fought a g. fight, 45:2
friend for Jesus' sake, 226:17
general g. is plea of scoundrel, 354:13
gentle beast of a g. conscience, 179:11
glad of other men's g., 195:6
go gentle into that g. night, 777:15
go with me like g. angels, 225:15
God saw that it was g., 5:5
gods do not give all men g. looks, 53:7
gods how he will talk, 281:15
greed is g. greed is right, 864:1
growing g. of world, 480:22
half so g. a grace, 206:25
hand that made you g., 207:2
hanging too g. for him, 271:18
happiness the only g., 518:6
hard beginning g. ending, 147:1

Good *(continued)*

have no need of advocate, 76:16
hay sweet hay, 178:32
he our g. will sever, 232:5
he who would do g., 354:13
hell full of g. intentions, 123:13
hell full of g. meanings, 243:23
hell paved with g. intentions, 123:*n*7, 243:*n*1
hey g. lookin', 804:3
highest g., 88:6, 90:*n*7
him that bringeth g. tidings, 27:3
hold fast that which is g., 44:22
hold thou the g., 453:20
honest painful sermon, 277:5
how g. and how pleasant, 19:10
human beings g. and evil, 555:14
I am the g. shepherd, 39:31
I have g. eye uncle, 190:24
I will be g., 485:1
if g. why do I yield, 214:11
if he had not been born, 36:2
ill wind bloweth no man g., 148:21
imaginary g. is boring, 760:14
in congruity of thing, 378:23
in everything, 193:37
in which mind at rest, 129:23
is it g. friend, 608:19
jest forever, 182:11
joke cannot be criticized, 618:12
keep g. tongue in head, 224:30
King Arthur, 896:23
King Wenceslas, 479:1
kissing carrion, 198:*n*1
know g. as g., 56:13
know what were g. to do, 184:14
knowing g. and evil, 5:19
lad of mettle a g. boy, 182:16
lady be g. to me, 710:21
largest universe of g., 541:16
law is g., 44:23
law is good order, 78:32
laws lead to better, 312:20
laws where state armed, 141:15
leave while looking g., 698:8
left country for country's g., 290:*n*1
lie and humbug for general G., 598:14
life neither g. nor bad., 580:1
life of battle g., 582:8
like a g. thing die, 557:14
line between g. and evil, 791:12
live in world g. or bad, 473:16
Lord deliver us, 48:19, 884:8
Lord is g., 18:3
lose g. we oft might win, 206:17
loser, 682:2
love as much as g. fight, 651:13
love g. pursue the worst, 102:*n*11
love sought is g., 205:16
luck in odd numbers, 187:19
maintain g. government, 349:4
make g. thing too common, 187:34
maketh sun rise on evil and g., 32:22
man and a just, 38:39
man's fortune, 211:15
man's g. knowing he is bad, 462:29
man's love, 195:20
man's sin, 314:*n*2

Good *(continued)*

man's treasure, 57:20
many g. men are poor, 55:12
marriage, 631:14
Master of All G. Workmen, 587:12
meaning g. or bad, 273:7
men and true, 190:40
men desire the g., 78:22
men eat that they may live, 70:7
men of g. will, 47:22
men of ill judgment ignore g., 65:8
men to do nothing, 325:15
mingled yarn g. and ill, 206:5
moral what you feel g. after, 721:11
Morning Midnight coming Home,
    509:3
morning sadness, 705:8
morrow to our waking souls, 228:7
mouth-filling oath, 183:2
music g. to melancholy, 276:12
must associate, 323:16
my g. vain hope of gain, 163:11
my religion is to do g., 333:16
name better than precious ointment, 23:8
name in man and woman, 209:2
name is rather to be chosen, 21:16
name like precious ointment, 165:21
nature in conversation, 288:11
neighbor is great blessing, 54:22
neighbor policy, 652:3
neighbors, 661:16
neither honesty nor g. fellowship, 181:31
never g. to bring bad news, 218:25
never g. war or bad peace, 303:16
news baits, 260:23
night and g. luck, 754:15
no evil can happen to g. man, 74:10
no g. can come of association, 648:14
no physician considers own g., 74:19
noble be man helpful and g., 342:12
noble to be g., 451:3
noble type of g., 437:11
not enough to have g. mind, 246:5
not g. for swarm not g. for bee, 112:13
not g. that man should be alone, 5:14
not three g. men unhanged, 182:19
not to make g. place to live, 473:16
nothing either g. or bad, 199:2
nothing g. alone, 424:2
nothing g. makes complete sense, 696:6
obstinacy in bad cause constancy in g.,
    248:7
of moral evil and of g., 368:6
oft interred with bones, 192:28
old age, 6:30
old Boston, 577:15
old paths where is the g. way, 27:28
old times are gone, 399:13
one g. custom corrupt, 455:19
one g. knowledge, 70:4
one g. turn deserves another, 105:18
or bad names, 314:1
or evil side, 481:12
orator a g. man skilled in speaking, 85:8
out of g. find evil, 255:12
overcome evil with g., 41:36
panics produce as much g., 333:7
Parent of g., 258:14

Good *(continued)*

partial evil universal g., 294:23
people are g. at heart, 822:7
people's g. the highest law, 88:10
perseverance in g. cause, 313:26
philosophy a g. horse, 322:18
phrase g. and bad at same time, 700:15
poet's made as well as born, 233:5
political g. carried to extreme, 360:24
portion of g. man's life, 368:7
poverty parts g. company, 374:15
prospect of distant g., 274:4
provoke to harm, 207:9
public g., 121:10
public g. and private rights, 345:10
pun may be admitted, 334:8
put on g. behavior, 398:23
really a very g. man, 562:5
recognize g. but be barred, 63:30
relinquish life for g. of country, 365:12
reputation valuable, 99:19
rewarded evil for g., 7:12
rewardeth evil for g., 20:41
rich in g. works, 44:37
right reader of g. poem, 623:12
ripe and g. scholar, 226:12
sat at g. man's feast, 194:22
sat too long for any g., 246:17
Scots lords, 889:16
second class of intellect g., 142:4
see your g. works, 32:16
seize g. fortune, 344:16
sense equally distributed, 246:4
sense in country, 339:5
seven g. kine, 7:9
seven hundred pounds g. gifts, 186:25
shall not see when g. cometh, 27:39
shepherd, 39:31
smell of old clothes, 669:9
smiled and said G. Night, 606:16
so so is g., 195:33
Soldier finest French novel, 616:13
some g. some so-so, 107:6
some said It might do g., 271:6
soul remembering my g. friends, 176:29
speech more hidden than malachite, 3:4
speed to your youthful valor, 95:9
spinning fates g. or evil, 540:23
strong and of g. courage, 9:35
strong thick stupefying, 460:22
substantial world pure and g., 372:1
sum of g. government, 337:11
sustain g. fortune, 263:17
taste and see that the Lord is g., 16:6
tendency to g. like water, 79:27
the g. I do not, 41:17
the G. lies so near, 344:16
them g. old boys, 861:11
them that call evil g., 25:7
thing when an't woman's, 463:23
things not had singly, 383:23
things strive to dwell, 224:17
third glass for g. humor, 288:12
this time like all times g., 426:6
this world's g., 46:10
thought to aim at some g., 78:3
to be merry and wise, 146:12, 359:3,
    884:12

Good *(continued)*

to do g. and to communicate, 45:19
to gain day good to fall, 486:2
today better tomorrow, 433:15
too much of g. thing, 155:15
tree of knowledge of g. and evil, 5:13
trust that somehow g., 453:21
undefined g. thirsted for, 388:9
value it next to g. conscience, 245:9
very little to govern g. people, 834:10
vote and act to bring g., 541:16
walk spoiled, 525:12
want power, 401:16
war slays g. man always, 66:14
we had all g. songs, 819:9
we know the g., 67:22
what a g. boy am I, 892:19
what do I care you are g., 491:12
what g. came of it, 381:9
whatsoever things are of g. report, 44:7
when all men's g., 451:10
when Fortune means most g., 175:21
when g. men die, 68:20
when g. very g. when bad better, 700:10
when she was g., 438:2
when were g. in majority, 475:24
whether it be g. or evil, 24:2
whosoever performs g. deeds, 119:4
wine a good creature, 208:32
wine needs no bush, 101:*n*1
without three g. friends, 195:5
wits jump, 158:3
woman if five thousand a year, 459:7
words worth much, 243:22
work together for g., 41:21
works better in sight of Lord, 118:18
world imagined ultimate g., 642:13
world kills the g., 721:7
write g. in dust, 143:8

Good-bye and keep cold, 623:11
brothers, 567:6
can scarcely bid g., 413:19
fare you well, 897:22
I am not saying g., 811:14
I have kissed it, 732:13
leave them laughing when say g., 634:10
like saying g. to statue, 721:9
Night Goodbye, 567:10
Old Paint, 890:12
Piccadilly, 628:20
proud world, 424:1
reap sowing and so g., 519:8
to bar and moaning, 481:6
to the war, 488:14
we now must say g., 716:10

Goodbyes, say my g. finish dying, 744:19
Good-humored stomach, 103:24
Goodliest, Adam the g. man, 257:21
Goodliness is as the flower of the field, 26:26
Good lookin', hey g., 804:3
Good-looking, Lake Wobegon where men are
    g., 854:10
Goodly apple rotten at heart, 184:27
how g. are thy tents, 9:11
I have a g. heritage, 15:12
outside falsehood hath, 184:27
states and kingdoms, 408:17
this g. frame earth, 199:5

Government (*continued*)

is best which governs least, 469:10
it deserves, 347:5
kept sheep rather than undertaken g., 246:19
keynote of g. is injustice, 604:13
lawful foundations of g., 363:3
legitimate object of g., 337:15
legitimate powers of g., 336:5
like big baby, 765:11
looked to G. for bread, 325:14
loyalty to G. when it deserves it, 524:23
luxury of liberal g., 470:8
made for people, 390:8
maintain good g., 349:4
maintain in emergencies, 446:10
make alter constitutions of g., 328:14
make it an article of faith, 336:6
man not enter g. after forty, 126:8
most dangerous moment for bad g., 434:9
necessary evil, 333:1
newspapers without g., 336:12
no administration injure g., 445:7
no g. by divine right, 381:1
no g. can do anything except, 810:8
no g. provides for termination, 445:3
no necessary evils in g., 364:4
not at war with rights, 336:17
not endure half slave, 444:8
not too strong for liberties, 446:10
object of British g., 349:3
of by and for people, 446:5, 457:9
of cities failure of United States, 532:10
of eternal justice, 457:9
of laws not men, 329:14
of nations, 564:2
of others, 337:10
of people, 404:17
of statesmen or clerks, 430:1
of the sage, 56:14
old forms of g. oppressive, 490:4
only maxim of free g., 329:12
organize civil g. of community, 363:9
petition g. for redress, 340:1
petticoat g., 391:11
play ignoble part, 539:6
political freedom business of G., 652:6
poverty a reproach to g., 280:8
power in g. sovereign, 349:10
power of making laws, 349:7
powers of g. reach actions, 337:13
programs never disappear, 765:10
proper function of g., 805:13
relaxing pressure, 434:8
republican model of g., 328:11
resting on property, 75:17
result of shared experiences, 365:6
secrecy and free g., 661:15
shackles and restraints of g., 604:14
shake off existing g., 444:4
shall be upon his shoulder, 25:16
sharp attacks on g., 745:9
sovereign control over g., 652:18
Soviet g. plus electrification, 607:16
spirit and form of popular g., 345:10
strong enough to protect, 652:18
sum of good g., 337:11
the less g. the better, 427:22

Government (*continued*)

this g. best hope, 337:9
to first class share in g., 349:4
trip on G. ship, 898:3
virtue of paper g., 323:21
watch and control g., 435:14
we live under a g. of men, 458:8
weary of existing g., 445:5
which imprisons unjustly, 473:18
which kept us free, 337:9
whose object is to elevate, 445:9
why g. at all, 349:8
will ever maintain good g., 349:4
wise and frugal g., 337:11
without newspapers, 336:12
women without share in g., 360:22
workings of g. that led to Vietnam War, 667:3

Governmental, right to be free from g. intrusion, 745:11

Governments, climates councils g., 451:13
concerned about conduct of man, 383:2
fear is foundation of most g., 330:3
instituted among men, 336:1
liberty is in moderate g., 349:5
never learned from history, 367:9
old tyrannical g. of Europe, 374:19
result of nature of governed, 286:21
whose independence acknowledged, 355:7

Governor, contempt for g. who is afraid, 65:12
governing g., 391:11
of New York not an acrobat, 617:12
of South Carolina said, 555:20

Governors, consent of g. and governed, 329:15
supreme g. the mob, 317:1

Governs, foolery g. whole world, 238:16
government best which g. least, 469:10
law which g. all law, 324:20
like a king, 313:10
opinion g. world, 566:7

Gowd, man's g. for a' that, 358:18

Gower, O moral G., 133:5

Gown, chose wife as she wedding g., 322:7
my g. of glory, 159:10
on g. appeared letter A, 431:3
smell fire whose g. burns, 243:18
tough guys who tear my g., 707:2
unclose damask g. to sun, 150:9

Gowns, furred g. hide all, 212:30
some in velvet g., 896:21

Goya of the bare field, 836:2

Grace a summer queen, 374:6
abound, 41:13
action of g., 809:13
amazing g. how sweet the sound, 320:13
and music of her face, 265:16
and strength to forbear, 556:12
appears most purely in human form, 385:4
as smart ship grew in stature g., 536:17
awful g. of God, 63:2
beauty without g., 428:13
because it is like g., 858:11
but for g. of God, 149:8
cheap g. is deadly enemy of Church, 745:7
comely g., 882:1
courage to live by g., 584:15
does it with better g., 204:27
fallen from g., 43:29

Grace (*continued*)

full of g. and truth, 38:48
get wealth with g., 296:11
given of God, 479:9
God shed g. on thee, 572:5
gods do not give all men gifts of g., 53:7
great g. with little gift, 82:16
half so good a g., 206:25
heart that lives in g., 129:14
heaven such g. did lend her, 173:34
her strong toil of g., 219:19
ideal G., 434:17
inward and spiritual g., 49:12
little g. my cause, 207:34
love brings bewitching g., 67:25
makes simplicity a g., 232:7
me no grace, 176:31
ministers of g. defend us, 197:32
moments of glad g., 591:6
more of his g. than gifts, 227:10
no spring beauty hath such g., 230:9
not an Attic g., 665:6
of day that is dead, 452:16
of Lord Jesus Christ, 43:25
renown and g. is dead, 215:30
seated on this brow, 201:5
silence gives proper g. to women, 65:2
speech be alway with g., 44:14
splendid g. of flanks, 149:11
strikes when in pain, 668:18
sways in wicked g., 783:12
sweet attractive g., 169:9, 257:19
tender g. of day dead, 452:16
thanks for means of g., 48:16
under pressure, 721:10
unshy beautiful full of g., 767:6
yield with g. to reason, 622:8

Graced, proud to have memory g., 683:10

Graces, lead these g. to grave, 204:20
mourn ye G. and Loves, 91:2
speech lacking in artificial g., 87:17

Gracing, either other sweetly g., 226:23

Gracious, a God g. and merciful, 12:30
and be g. unto thee, 9:2
and courteous to strangers, 165:23
evening star, 469:12
God save our g. king, 292:2
good g. loser, 682:2
heaven's all-g. King, 457:11
Lord bomb Germans, 745:5
my g. silence hail, 219:25
remembers me his g. parts, 175:19
seasoned with g. voice, 185:18
so hallowed and so g., 196:19
swear by thy g. self, 180:9
this is our g. will, 142:11

Gradual and silent encroachments, 345:13
road to Hell g., 717:12

Gradually extricate babe from fire, 433:4
let go earth, 715:7

Grain, amber waves of g., 572:5
beside a field of g., 775:11
cheeks of sorry g., 252:25
Demeter gave nourishment of g., 68:9
of mustard seed, 34:18
of poetry season a century, 557:11
say which g. will grow, 214:5
see world in g. of sand, 353:14

Grain *(continued)*
    send g. into wilderness, 275:2
    spirits of land and g., 80:8
    with a g. of salt, 105:10
Grains, two g. of wheat in chaff, 184:10
Grainy wood, 669:9
Grammar control even kings, 268:3
    corrupted youth in erecting g.-school, 170:17
    I am above g., 268:*n*3
    lesson on g. impertinence, 500:1
    prefer geniality to g., 569:14
Grammarian rhetorician geometrician, 109:14
Grammars, all g. leak, 660:11
Grammaticam, rex et supra g., 268:*n*3
Grammatici certant sub iudice lis est, 98:*n*6
Gramophone, puts record on g., 676:13
Grampa, one day bachelor next g., 732:12
Granary, sitting on g. floor, 411:7
Grand, dumb inscrutable g., 497:4
    hooded phantom, 482:20
    O Ireland g. you look, 551:3
    seek a g. perhaps, 146:7
    statues and pictures g., 520:10
    style, 496:2
    they said it would be g., 516:1
    this g. book the universe, 167:15
    'tis g. 'tis solemn, 400:8
Grand Army, between G. and dominion, 537:5
Grandam, soul of g. inhabit a bird, 185:*n*2
    to cub, 813:12
Grandchild heir of the first, 233:10
Grandchildren come into world with thick skin, 415:8
Grandest lesson On sail on, 539:15
    of all sepulchers, 72:4
Grandeur, bad that sort of g. creeps in, 645:6
    hear with disdainful smile, 315:17
    in this view of life, 440:5
    of God, 546:6
    of the dooms, 409:8
    remains without intensity, 107:3
    Scotia's g. springs, 356:10
    size is not g., 502:10
    so nigh g. to dust, 424:21
    that was Rome, 447:12
Grandfather, ape for his g., 502:14
Grandfather's house, 421:17
    rule was safer, 482:3
Grandmother, ape as his g., 502:*n*1
    child of our g. Eve, 174:5
    sings to stove, 762:20
Grandmother's long and faithful service, 468:19
Grandmothers, our mothers and g., 860:7
Grandsire cut in alabaster, 184:5
    proverbed with g. phrase, 179:23
Grandsires', sires' age worse than g., 97:1
Grange, moated g., 207:4, 450:7
Granite into which it reaches, 679:4
    tenoned and mortised in g., 486:4
Grant, everybody wants to be Cary G., 737:13
    Evolution from Washington to G., 531:22
    half g. what I wish, 622:19
    how could anyone be Cary G., 853:6
    I may never prove so fond, 213:21
    may gods g. you all things, 53:3
    me old man's frenzy, 596:14

Grant *(continued)*
    me this last labor, 93:6
    O gods g. me this, 91:27
    of power from governed, 381:1
    us safe lodging, 421:5
    youth's heritage, 462:17
Granted, and God g. it, 299:24
    to behold you again, 556:9
Gran'ther's rule safer, 482:3
Granting our wish one of Fate's jokes, 59:*n*4
Grants, each day that Fortune g., 96:10
Grape, a little more g., 393:1
    burst Joy's g., 411:11
    eaten a sour g., 28:6
    first from out the purple g., 252:4
    for one g. the vine destroy, 172:32
    peel me a g., 700:8
    rich g. juice of good sense, 115:22
    shalt not gather every g., 8:26
Grapes are sour, 58:16
    gleaning of the g. of Ephraim, 10:16
    of thorns, 33:21
    our vines have tender g., 24:10
    where g. of wrath stored, 481:1
    year the g. were growing, 877:8
Grapeshot, whiff of g., 407:4
Grapple, let her and Falsehood g., 254:14
    them to thy soul, 197:22
Grappling in central blue, 452:2
Grasp it like a man of mettle, 291:21
    reach should exceed g., 461:18
    subject words will follow, 85:7
    this Sorry Scheme, 442:9
    what dread g., 353:2
    what they do not know, 80:9
Grasping, a really g. imagination, 543:16
    by g. at the shadow, 59:9
    capable of earnest g., 412:1
    Scrooge g. covetous, 465:5
Grasps in the comer, 203:24
Grass, all flesh is as g., 45:37
    all flesh is g., 26:26
    as long as g. grow, 892:4
    below above vaulted sky, 404:19
    blade of g. is blade of g., 235:*n*2
    child said What is the g., 485:18
    dripping snow on g., 681:19
    eateth g. as an ox, 14:31
    Elfin from green g., 447:11
    entwined fall on the grass, 776:4
    essence of small people is of g., 61:10
    from heaps of couch g., 536:22
    green g. above me, 512:3
    grow from g. I love, 486:20
    grow in streets, 625:18
    grows on weirs, 590:22
    grows wherever land water is, 486:1
    Guests Star-scattered on G., 442:10
    happy as g. was green, 777:9
    hear g. as it grows, 480:18, 786:17
    his days are as g., 18:7
    I am the g., 636:4
    it dies but in vernal rain lives again, 483:24
    kissed the lovely g., 669:5
    know g. beyond the door, 506:8
    like drop of dew upon blade of g., 595:2
    like g. which groweth up, 17:23
    like rain upon mown g., 17:12

Grass *(continued)*
    may g. grow at door, 611:*n*5
    narrow Fellow in the G., 510:5
    Nebuchadnezzar did eat g., 28:23
    no less than stars, 486:13
    observing spear of summer g., 485:15
    over g. in West garden, 664:18
    paler than g., 56:5
    pigeons on g. alas, 627:19
    river of g., 686:12
    roots, 581:1
    roots marsh g. sends, 543:2
    snake in the g., 92:20
    splendor in the g., 371:4
    stoops not, 171:15
    through frozen g., 409:18
    tides of g., 530:2
    trembling g. quakes from human foot, 404:21
    two blades of g. grow, 285:1
    vaulter in sunny g., 392:13
    when elephants fight g. suffers, 889:5
    wind on buffalo g., 891:10
    withereth flower fadeth, 26:27
    withereth flower falleth, 45:37
Grass-blade's no easier than oak, 481:17
Grasses of forest's floor, 616:6
Grass-green turf, 201:24
Grasshopper, ant and the g., 59:5
    shall be a burden, 23:31
Grasshoppers make field ring, 325:7
Grate, fire dying in g., 505:7
Grated to dusty nothing, 203:20
Grateful, elderly mistress so g., 303:4
    evening mild, 258:1
Gratiano, but as the world G., 184:4
    speaks infinite deal of nothing, 184:10
Gratification from each component part, 379:10
    of every passion, 493:11
Gratified, Desire g. plants fruits, 352:6
    lineaments of G. Desire, 352:9
    sorry if wishes were g., 59:15
    to answer promptly, 522:14
Gratify some astonish rest, 524:22
Gratifying feeling duty done, 528:5
Grating, nor harsh nor g., 368:11
    roar of pebbles, 496:17
Gratitude, children's g. woman's love, 595:14
    desire for benefits, 264:17
    fruit of great cultivation, 308:2
    quiet humor in Yiddish and g., 740:3
    shall our g. sleep, 367:4
    soon grows old, 77:7
Gratuities and privileges, 364:3
Gratuitous, everything is g., 742:19
    exercise every day, 540:21
Grave, airs martial brisk or g., 327:4
    Alcestis from the g., 255:1
    Alice, 437:14
    almost as go into g., 277:27
    a-moldering in the g., 521:1
    approach thy g., 405:13
    between cradle and g., 300:13, 687:4
    botanize upon mother's g., 369:9
    buries empires in common g., 332:10
    but she is in her g., 369:7
    come to thy g. in full age, 13:14

Grave *(continued)*
conclude on edge of g., 531:8
coyotes howl o'er my g., 890:18
cradle to g., 553:13
defiled his father's g., 99:2
dig g. and let me lie, 555:16
Duncan is in his g., 216:11
earth and g. and dust, 159:16
earth is only grave, 234:1
expect of man this side g., 462:29
fall in g. like old dog, 780:5
from cradle to g., 402:4
from g. to light, 278:1
frontier g. far, 582:9
funeral marches to g., 436:5
Ghost sitting crowned upon g., 239:12
glory or g., 384:11
gone with old world to g., 552:9
hides things beautiful, 401:17
hungry as the g., 300:16
ignominy sleep with thee in g., 183:32
I'll be buried in g., 899:1
in law's g. study six, 159:1
in the air, 794:6
in the dark and silent g., 159:16
is not life's goal, 436:4
jealousy is cruel as the g., 24:25
lead but to g., 315:18
lead these graces to g., 204:20
learned secrets of g., 534:5
little g. an obscure g., 177:13
mummers, 297:1
natural philosophy deep moral g., 166:19
Nature a g., 416:6
no flours on g., 536:3
no wisdom in the g., 23:22
none shed tear at g., 611:*n*5
not g. nor bed denied, 595:19
now with love now in colde g., 134:23
O g. I will be thy destruction, 28:40
old and godly and g., 591:7
one foot already in the g., 108:6
peace is in g., 401:17
pompous in the g., 249:4
ransom them from the power of the g., 28:40
renowned be thy g., 220:27
rest profound as g., 531:26
rotting g. ne'er get out, 354:3
scalding g., 611:14
secret as the g., 158:7
secrets of the g., 534:5
seeking nothing but g., 691:18
send to g. in Y-shaped coffin, 834:13
shown Longfellow's g., 671:5
soldier's g. for thee best, 399:17
something beyond the g., 101:18
strewed thy g., 202:18
things holy profane g. and light, 239:8
this verse g. for me, 555:16
unto a soul, 175:17
where Laura lay, 159:11
with O'Leary in g., 592:10
with sorrow to the g., 7:10
without a g., 396:18
you shall find me g. man, 180:28
Zeus grant g. restraint, 63:28
Graved inside of it Italy, 461:4

Gravel, mouth filled with g., 21:13
pick about G., 412:14
shadow over g. of drive, 662:6
Grave-makers, gardeners ditchers and g., 202:3
Grave-making, he sings at g., 202:5
Graven image, 8:11
images of her gods, 25:27
Grave's a fine and private place, 266:23
Graves, beautiful uncut hair of g., 485:19
climbs into g. married, 715:6
dishonorable g., 191:26
follow disquietly to g., 211:2
from g. of our slain, 417:5
if we walk among g., 149:7
let's talk of g., 177:7
sacred g. plowed for corn, 499:3
sleep sweetly in humble g., 506:9
stood tenantless, 196:15
under fountains and g., 882:8
watch from their g., 460:13
Graveyard, friends have no place in g., 473:23
like g. marble sculpture, 624:12
of buried hopes, 627:6
Graveyards, no white or colored signs on g., 786:12
Gravitation, Newtonian principle of g., 336:6
Gravity, body subject to forces of g., 778:15
breaks law of g., 678:12
essence of g. was design, 313:22
fixed law of g., 440:5
out of his bed, 182:24
settled g., 221:14
sometimes man of g., 143:11
Gravy, no g. no grub, 682:1
person who disliked g., 268:*n*1
Gray, all cats g. when candles out, 108:*n*5
all theory is g., 344:5
amice, 260:7
beginning of years, 530:21
behind lay g. Azores, 539:14
bring down my g. hairs, 7:10
changing from brown suit to g., 664:3
cheerless over hills of g., 438:15
cold g. stones O Sea, 452:15
comb g. hair, 592:18
dawn breaking, 419:5, 635:15
dawn of morning after, 597:18
death's g. land, 668:11
dogs shame the g. head, 52:13
flannel suit, 796:2
friar of orders g., 881:7
glory from g. hairs gone, 438:5
great g. drayhorse, 546:16
handful of g. ashes at rest, 499:9
head grown g. in vain, 403:23
iniquity, 182:27
little g. cells, 686:1
locks left are g., 381:10
long g. beard, 375:17
mist on sea's face, 635:15
name was Dapple G., 896:16
night is growing g., 536:19
old and g. full of sleep, 591:5
pilgrim g., 317:11
sad last g. hairs, 410:5
set g. life, 451:9
spirit yearning, 451:15
still evening and twilight g., 257:24

Gray *(continued)*
Truth her painted toy, 590:20
where thy g. eye glances, 448:7
wing upon every tide, 592:10
withered cheek tresses g., 372:20
world g. from thy breath, 530:9
Gray-eyed Athena, 52:26
Gray-fly winds her sultry horn, 253:3
Gray-green greasy Limpopo, 589:17
Gray-haired Saturn, 411:12
Gray-headed, old and g. error, 248:21
Graze, as long as stars g., 94:7
neither g. nor pierce, 209:28
on my lips, 171:9
Grazes, work way cow g., 601:1
Grazing, men like satyrs g., 168:12
lust melted him in own g., 135:*n*3
servility slides by on g., 788:3
wheel that squeaks gets g., 476:8
Greased worm, 787:2
Greasy, fat and g. citizens, 194:2
gray-green g. Limpopo, 589:17
Joan doth keel pot, 174:33
top of g. pole, 430:10
Great, a g. g. man, 802:15
age begins anew, 403:8
Amen, 502:17
American Novel, 503:8
and original writer, 372:4
and wide sea, 18:11
Architect of Universe mathematician, 634:6
army of pointed firs, 552:11
artificer made my mate, 556:8
Babel, 327:2
ball of fire, 680:5
be g. be misunderstood, 426:20
Beginning produced emptiness, 86:16
Birnam wood, 216:34
black men once were g., 670:3
blew g. guns, 466:8
book that made g. war, 458:*n*4
build a G. Society, 753:15
burden upon his back, 271:8
Caesar fell, 193:1
ceremony that to g. ones 'longs, 206:25
chasm, 757:14
compare g. things with small, 92:15, 257:2
cost g. deal to make, 582:12
creatures g. and small, 476:4
crime look dull, 778:11
death, 608:17
deeds wrought at great risks, 69:20
deep to great deep, 455:21
desire to bottle of hay, 178:32
dissolved into something g., 615:12
do business in g. waters, 18:14
do g. right do little wrong, 186:2
duration of g. sentiments makes g. men, 548:6
Elizabeth, 450:22
empire and little minds, 324:14
Father building forts among us, 499:3
fault of our politicians, 472:1
feast of languages, 174:26
fell g. oaks, 302:29
finds pang as g., 206:35
First Cause, 327:12

Great *(continued)*

fortune great slavery, 104:2
Gaels of Ireland, 618:10
geniuses, 693:4
globe itself, 225:1
God our King, 439:10
gray-green greasy Limpopo, 589:17
Gromboolian plain, 468:2
gulf fixed, 38:18
have seen the wicked in g. power, 16:12
he is a g. observer, 191:29
hedgehog knows one g. thing, 55:2
heir of fame, 250:15
here thou g. Anna, 293:7
historical ideals, 757:15
horse of gold, 701:4
how g. that darkness, 33:4
ice also g. would suffice, 623:4
ill can he rule the g., 160:18
in admiration as herself, 226:14
indispensable unique g., 583:7
interests at stake, 78:29
is Diana, 40:39
is glory of the woman, 72:5
is truth, 29:24
leap in the dark, 239:14
let us mock at g., 594:10
lives of g. men remind us, 436:6
making city glorious and g., 62:15
malefactors of g. wealth, 571:10
man does not lose child's-heart, 79:25
man does not think beforehand, 79:24
man's memory, 200:16
many dull ugly people, 582:12
many talks from g. father, 325:21
manye smale maken a g., 136:18
mast of some g. ammiral, 255:16
matter or small, 30:23
meals of beef iron steel, 189:17
men are not always wise, 14:11
men can't be ruled, 742:15
men great nations not boasters, 428:3
men texts of Revelation, 406:20
names as these, 883:13
nature's second course, 215:21
Neptune's ocean wash, 215:24
nice customs curtsy to g. kings, 190:10
none unhappy but g., 289:2
nose great man, 603:4
not g. pleasure to bring death, 65:17
nothing g. accomplished without passion,
   367:13
nothing g. created suddenly, 108:18
O God thy sea is so g., 884:9
O that I were as g., 177:11
office not filled by great men, 532:9
ones eat up little ones, 220:12
Original proclaim, 287:20
our hearts are g., 455:10
packs and sets of g. ones, 213:8
pay g. deal too dear, 223:8
pearl of g. price, 34:19
persons great kindnesses, 157:32
pith and moment, 199:21
poet writes his time, 677:8
poets great audiences, 488:16
prince and a g. man fallen, 11:12
Prince in prison lies, 229:19

Great *(continued)*

quaint g. figure, 639:16
rats small rats, 460:8
rightly to be g., 201:21
rough diamond, 298:11
rudely g., 295:1
seekest thou g. things, 28:8
sleep out this g. gap, 218:10
small and g. beasts, 18:11
small thing analogy of g. things, 90:4
so clear in his g. office, 214:24
so g. is his mercy, 18:6
Society, 800:2
society big complicated, 685:5
society on earth, 369:1
some are born g., 205:8
souls suffer in silence, 359:15
sphere thou movest in, 219:3
stage of fools, 213:1
suffer g. destruction, 440:2
sweet mother, 530:7
that g. fact, 439:11
that he is grown so g., 191:27
the g. story, 864:8
thereby the g. is achieved, 57:12
things are done, 354:9
things both g. and small, 377:6
things made of little, 462:26
those who were truly g., 760:6
to do thing that ends all other, 219:7
truth g. and shall prevail, 500:9
whales sailing by, 494:13
when little fears grow g., 200:19
where love is g., 200:19
White Way, 579:14
winds shoreward blow, 494:12
wink of eternity, 720:2
with child and longing for prunes, 206:21
with young, 890:4
Great Spirit appointed place for us, 364:17
   gave ancestors lands we possess, 365:3
   is my father, 365:1
   make them all for his children, 365:2
Greater, Brutus makes mine g., 193:11
   far g. than his father, 51:14
   ignorance greater dogmatism, 553:1
   love false to object, 748:7
   love hath no man, 40:1
   more strong far g., 222:18
   none beneath Sun, 589:24
   out of small beginnings g. things, 240:5
   punishment g. than I can bear, 6:7
   risk g. faith, 469:7
   service g. than the god, 203:13
   than God cannot be conceived, 123:6
   than Solomon, 34:13
   than we know, 372:12
   the g. the more humble, 30:11
   thy necessity g. than mine, 162:23
   to the g. glory of God, 149:1
Greatest, artist embodied g. ideas, 484:5
   bears g. names, 260:18
   empty vessel g. sound, 190:2
   event in war, 72:9
   fool is man, 278:6
   generation, 847:1
   griefs those we cause, 66:5
   happiness for greatest numbers, 298:20

Greatest *(continued)*

happiness of g. number, 342:5
how much the g. event, 342:8
I am the g., 853:9
man ever seen, 323:*n*2
men women greatest city, 487:2
minds capable of g. vices, 246:6
my vision's g. enemy, 354:15
of these is charity, 42:29
pass days in that where skill g., 101:14
question ever debated, 329:18
scandal waits on greatest state, 172:36
service or greatest injury, 74:17
sooner fail than not among g., 413:7
tell aloud g. failing, 285:7
two g. most important events, 319:8
vicissitude of things, 166:20
well-wrought urn becomes g. ashes, 228:20
Great-grandfather was but a waterman, 271:19
Greathearted gentlemen, 460:4
Great-hearted Stentor, 51:9
Greatly, they shall be g. rewarded, 29:34
   to find quarrel in straw, 201:21
Greatness, abuse of g., 191:35
   all the far-stretched g., 159:15
   be not afraid of g., 205:8
   boy my g., 219:10
   changed to empty name, 419:*n*4
   farewell to all my g., 225:25
   France not France without g., 686:9
   gods' custom to bring low all things of g.,
      69:16
   Great Society lost its g., 800:2
   highest point of my g., 225:23
   honor and g. of his name, 226:15
   instruments of European g., 349:6
   inward g., 189:2
   is a-ripening, 225:25
   is spiritual condition, 497:11
   knows itself, 183:20
   moment of g. flicker, 675:3
   nurse into g., 75:20
   of Athens, 72:4
   of God, 543:2
   of name in the father, 233:10
   political g. and wisdom meet, 75:9
   rough road leads to g., 103:19
   some achieve g., 205:8
   thine O Lord is the g., 12:24
   within range of marshes, 543:2
   won by men with courage, 72:4
Great-rooted blossomer, 594:17
Grecian goldsmiths make, 594:4
   sighed soul toward G. tents, 186:14
   Urn worth old ladies, 714:8
   woes O goddess sing, 293:16
Greece, all G. the monument of Euripides,
   67:*n*1
   Athens the eye of G., 260:2
   bulwark of G. famous Athens, 64:7
   city is education to G., 72:3
   gave our lives to save G., 60:13
   glory that was G., 447:12
   isles of G., 398:15
   Italy England did adorn, 274:7
   might still be free, 398:17
   of China and of G., 737:8
   wounds me, 727:3

Greed all right healthy, 864:*n*1
    infectious g. seemed to grip, 812:18
    is good greed is right, 864:1
    no greater disaster than g., 57:15
    satisfy your g., 589:*n*1
    will save the U.S.A., 864:1
Greedy, can be g. feel good, 864:*n*1
    hands, 444:*n*1
    not for needy but g., 653:8
    of filthy lucre, 44:26
    the sinful and lewd, 708:6
    when others are fearful, 826:13
Greedy-gut, put on pot says G., 894:4
Greedy-gut, put on pot says G., 894:4
Greek, carve in Latin or in G., 249:26
    flower G. ecstasy, 667:8
    he G. and Latin speaks, 262:*n*1
    hungry little G., 109:14
    illusion of G. necessity, 833:5
    learn G. as treat, 619:2
    neither G. nor Jew, 44:12
    small Latin and less G., 233:1
    speak G. naturally as pigs squeak, 262:1
    thought and life, 504:3
    to me, 191:31
    turn pages of G. models, 98:28
Greeks, fear G. even when they bring gifts,
    94:10
    had modesty we have cant, 393:10
    have dreamt dream of life best, 344:28
    knew how to live, 547:14
    known what G. did not uncertainty, 719:7
    let G. be G., 261:11
    seeking land of G., 343:4
    were right, 560:26
    when G. joined G., 281:16
Green, all a g. willow, 146:8, 210:8
    all in g. went my love, 701:4
    among thy g. braes, 357:19
    and dying, 777:14
    and pleasant land, 354:8
    and yellow melancholy, 205:4
    as anything, 821:2
    as emerald, 375:23
    babbled of g. fields, 189:4
    banks of Shannon, 384:7
    bay tree, 16:12
    be the g. grass above me, 512:3
    be turf above thee, 400:12
    beechen g., 410:3
    casque has outdone elegance, 665:14
    colorless g. ideas sleep, 817:15
    crammers of green fruits, 640:16
    devouring g. azures, 558:18
    do these things in g. tree, 38:32
    doors of heaven both g., 656:8
    drives my g. age, 777:2
    dry smooth-shaven g., 251:16
    Elfin from g. grass, 447:11
    Flora and country g., 410:4
    Gatsby believed in the g. light, 710:7
    girl, 197:26
    golden lamps in g. night, 267:6
    Greta woods are g., 374:6
    groves of the blest, 94:32
    grow the rashes O, 356:23
    happy as grass was g., 777:9
    heads g. hands blue, 467:11
    heard on the g., 351:7

Green *(continued)*
    how much I want you green, 717:2
    in hamlets dances on g., 373:2
    in judgment, 218:16
    in thy g. lap, 316:11
    isle in sea, 448:6
    it's not easy bein' g., 879:15
    keep memory g., 387:7
    laid him on the g., 890:7
    Lantern's light, 888:5
    laurel g. for season, 530:9
    lavender's g., 896:13
    leaf shall be g., 27:39
    learn of g. world, 665:14
    legend of g. chapels, 777:8
    lie down in g. pastures, 15:23
    little Johnny G., 893:13
    little vaulter, 392:13
    making the g. one red, 215:24
    mansions, 539:13
    mantle of standing pool, 212:5
    Meander's margent g., 252:14
    memory be g., 196:21
    moon made of g. cheese, 148:19
    o'er g. corn-field did pass, 196:2
    on ilka g. loaning, 321:8
    out of hopeful g. stuff woven, 485:18
    pastures, 15:23
    sea's g. crying towers, 720:5
    sing all a g. willow, 210:8
    snow on g. grass, 681:19
    soul bright invisible g., 473:21
    swell in havens dumb, 546:3
    the golden tree of life, 344:5
    thought in a green shade, 267:1
    through g. fuse drives flower, 777:2
    to what g. altar, 410:18
    too much and only good for fools, 58:*n*5
    tossing g. water, 659:1
    U blue O, 559:4
    underwood and cover, 529:13
    wearin' o' the G., 884:4, 884:5
    when all trees g., 481:7
    with boughs, 557:7
Greenery, get all the g. one wishes, 814:1
Greenery-yallery, 526:14
Greenest of our valleys, 448:9
Green-eyed jealousy, 185:21
    monster, 209:3
Greenhouse, loves a g. too, 326:24
Greenland's icy mountains, 391:5
Greenly, we have done but g., 201:28
Greenness, clothe general earth with g., 377:15
    heart recovered g., 243:6
Greensleeves all my joy, 881:5
Green-walled by hills of Maryland, 438:12
Greenwood chapel, 640:*n*1
    must to g. go, 880:13
    under the g. tree, 194:11
Greet, in every angle g., 267:4
    it gars me g., 358:4
    me with that sun thine eye, 221:14
    offspring from camps, 742:7
    two solitudes g., 632:5
Gregor Samsa awoke from uneasy dreams,
    655:14
Gregory, John Synge and Augusta G.,
    597:1

Grenadier, British G., 883:13
    she strode like g., 567:11
Grenadiers, captain of Hampshire g., 332:18
Greta woods are green, 374:6
Greville Servant to Queen Elizabeth, 161:16
Grew, as ship g. in stature grace and hue,
    536:17
    autumn that g. by reaping, 219:8
    lean assailed seasons, 605:20
    miles around wonder g., 574:17
    together like double cherry, 178:29
    up fostered by beauty, 368:13
    where one g. before, 285:1
    within this learned man, 169:7
Greybeards, love which g. call divine, 171:6
Greyhound, fawning g. did proffer, 182:7
    puppies, 442:21
Greyhound's gentle tautness, 787:19
Greyhounds, stand like g. in slips, 189:9
Gridley, fire when ready G., 529:1
Grief, acquainted with g., 27:5
    age or g. or sickness, 241:18
    aggravates loss, 881:8
    and constant anxiety kill women, 499:8
    at not wanting to call dead back, 631:9
    beguile you from g., 446:12
    between g. and nothing I take g., 714:2
    but for g. as if not been, 403:18
    can honor take away g., 183:25
    can I see another's g., 351:8
    develops mind, 611:6
    divine radiance, 422:11
    drug which takes away g., 52:32
    each substance of a g., 176:28
    everyone can master g., 190:39
    fills room of absent child, 175:19
    for every g. to physician, 244:1
    forethought of g., 837:2
    forgotten, 529:13
    glistering g., 225:17
    great as my g., 177:11
    hair turned quite gold from g., 560:19
    hopeless g. passionless, 434:13
    I am g., 836:2
    in much wisdom is much g., 22:27
    is proud, 175:13
    itself be mortal, 403:18
    journeyman to g., 176:15
    make carnival of g., 602:16
    makes owner stoop, 175:13
    melts away, 243:5
    mortals live in, 52:19
    my joy my g., 249:23
    past help should be past g., 223:18
    pitched past pitch of g., 547:5
    plague of sighing and g., 182:25
    put in words g., 453:11
    reason unhinged by g., 484:7
    returns with revolving year, 403:16
    sees into bottom of my g., 181:4
    smiling at g., 205:4
    sure to come to g., 624:17
    teaches to waver, 65:19
    that does not speak, 217:7
    to weep make less depth of g., 170:20
    unmanly g., 196:28
    was ever g. like mine, 242:14
    what greater g., 67:20

Grief *(continued)*
 with glass that ran, 529:14
 worm canker and g., 399:16
 you must first feel g., 98:21
Griefs, drinking my g., 177:17
 even his g. are a joy, 53:23
 griping g., 881:6
 he hath borne our g., 27:6
 my state depose but not my g., 177:18
 patch g. with proverbs, 191:11
 private g., 193:2
 some g. are med'cinable, 220:17
 sufferest mortal g., 189:22
 that harass distressed, 306:7
 we cause ourselves, 66:5
Grievance, no g. redress by mob law,
  444:3
 way of establishing g. for the day,
  680:11
Grievances, clod of ailments and g., 565:3
 inferior g. lose force, 339:7
 redress of g., 340:1
Grieve at funeral, 523:20
 his heart, 217:1
 not for what past, 881:8
 not g. over inevitable, 84:7
 one suffer than nation g., 272:21
 though I g. there is no help, 121:26
 woman to be over-mastered, 190:23
Grieved, by wind g. ghost, 727:12
 forsaken g. at heart, 347:11
Grieving, Margaret are you g., 546:17
Grievous burden was thy birth, 171:37
 gossip is g. to bear, 54:28
 my most g. fault, 47:17
 remembrance of them is g., 49:5
Grievously, sins most g. committed, 49:5
Grim and ancient Raven, 449:8
 Death my son and foe, 256:27
 hushed in g. repose, 316:15
 king's dog, 67:6
 me with my g. techniques, 801:19
 shape towered up, 368:15
 wolf with privy paw, 253:11
Grimace, accelerated g., 665:6
Grimaces called laughter, 239:7
Grim-visaged comfortless Despair, 315:7
 war smoothed his front, 171:17
Grin, all Nature wears one g., 304:7
 ending with the g., 514:12
 how cheerfully seems to g., 513:15
 remained after rest gone, 514:12
 universal g., 304:7
Grind, ax to g., 389:1
 bones to make bread, 897:3
 demd horrid g., 464:24
 exceeding small, 247:10
 faces of the poor, 24:37
 in mill of truism, 426:10
 in the prison house, 10:24
 laws g. the poor, 322:5
 mills of God g. slowly, 247:10
 with water that's past, 243:21
Grinders cease, 23:30
Grinding, sound of the g. is low, 23:30
Grinds, God's mill g. slow, 244:17
Grindstone, hold noses to g., 147:6
 tightfisted hand at g., 465:5

Grinning, mock your own g., 202:12
 you just stood there g., 851:17
Grins, undermine 'em with g., 774:9
Griot, when a g. dies, 796:10
Griping griefs heart wound, 881:6
Gripping, piece of life g. baseball, 845:1
Grisilda, in trust to fynde G., 135:23
Grisly gang, 620:9
Gristle, a people still in the g., 324:2
Grizzled, his beard was g., 197:15
Groan, condemned alike to g., 315:8
 hear each other g., 410:5
 scarcely howl or g., 517:4
 sinks with bubbling g., 396:18
 spirit fled with g., 95:12
 weep no more nor g., 236:7
Groaned, my mother g., 353:6
Groaneth, whole creation g., 41:20
Groans, cackles g. and dies, 404:20
 of love like those of dying, 759:2
 shrieks and g. of wounded, 489:15
 sovereign of sighs and g., 174:14
Groceries, like you buy your g., 826:10
 shopped for g., 796:7
Grocery, eyeing the g. boys, 812:9
Groined aisles of Rome, 424:5
Grok, I am all that I g., 750:13
Grolle, ich g. nicht, 414:*n*6
Gromboolian, great G. plain, 468:2
Groove, freight proportioned to g., 511:14
Grooves, ringing g. of change, 452:10
Gross and scope of my opinion, 196:12
 flesh sinks downward, 177:25
 gratitude not among g. people, 308:2
 not g. to sink but light, 171:8
 scarce so g. as beetles, 212:24
 things rank and g., 196:30
 two g. broken statues, 665:9
Grossest iridescence of ocean, 642:2
 superstitions, 440:12
Grossly, decay doth g. close it in, 186:15
 err as g. as the few, 273:5
Gross-out, go for the g., 865:2
Grosvenor Gallery young man, 526:14
Grotesque, what is not g. and why, 809:9
Grotesques, all had become g., 632:14
Grotius, celebrities such as G., 518:9
Ground, accustomed to way g. opens up, 836:9
 acre of barren g., 224:2
 all seated on the g., 281:13
 another man's g., 187:9
 as water spilt on the g., 11:21
 beat the g., 252:11
 between two stools sits on g., 146:*n*11
 Cain was tiller of g., 6:3
 cannot dedicate this g., 446:5
 cast it to g. regardlessly, 236:15
 choose g. take thy rest, 399:17
 colored man occupies, 477:2
 crushed to g. diffuse sweets, 165:*n*3
 dark and bloody g., 489:7
 drops earliest to g., 185:30
 exiled on g. in jeers, 491:2
 fell into good g., 34:16
 gain little patch of g., 201:18
 gazes on the g., 557:3
 grow on Irish g., 884:4
 hallowed g., 697:11

Ground *(continued)*
 haunted holy g., 395:8
 into the sea upon dry g., 8:3
 kings sat down upon the g., 30:36
 lion on the g., 887:3
 lose g. won today, 495:15
 me on the g., 829:2
 miles of fertile g., 377:17
 more malign with bad seed, 129:26
 my tail go to the g., 146:14
 not buried in consecrated g., 536:3
 of all being God, 668:17
 passion that left g., 462:11
 place whereon thou standest is holy g.,
  7:26
 plat of rising g., 251:17
 rope just above g., 655:16
 solid g. to build house on, 431:16
 stand your g., 325:19
 stood firm on dry g., 9:36
 swalloweth g. with fierceness, 14:28
 till thou return unto the g., 6:1
 to own a bit of g., 507:14
 tract of inland g., 372:7
 vantage g. of truth, 89:*n*12
 vapors weep burthen to g., 455:5
 where sorrow holy g., 561:6
Groundlings, split ears of g., 200:6
Grounds, fight on landing g., 619:14
Group genocide destruction of nation ethnic
 g., 726:1
Grouping, free g. of individuals, 604:14
Grove, but cloud and like shady g., 350:15
 court the camp the g., 373:2
 Jemmy G. on deathbed lay, 889:25
 meadow g. and stream, 370:13
 olive g. of Academe, 260:3
 shade which g. of myrtles made, 233:14
 spicy g. cinnamon tree, 734:10
Groves are of laurel, 342:15
 God's first temples, 405:15
 green g. of the blest, 94:32
 o'er shady g. they hover, 237:3
 of Academe, 98:12
 valleys g. hills fields, 168:4
Grow, asked how pearls did g., 240:14
 cannot g. by inch, 596:10
 consider lilies how they g., 33:8
 corn and taters g., 558:1
 enter to g. in wisdom, 519:9
 from grass I love, 486:20
 grass will g. in streets, 625:18
 green g. the rashes O, 356:23
 hatched would g. mischievous, 192:1
 heads g. beneath shoulders, 208:2
 in Flanders fields, 614:7
 in place of one, 285:*n*1
 into likeness of bad men, 76:9
 learn but not wiser g., 283:20
 like a cedar in Lebanon, 17:30
 like savages, 190:7
 love's mysteries in souls g., 229:20
 makes not fresh nor g. again, 236:7
 my wrath did g., 353:7
 oaks from acorns g., 121:4
 old along with me, 462:13
 on Irish ground, 884:4
 out at heels, 211:15

H

Hand (*continued*)

death lays icy h. on kings, 246:13
died by the h. of the Lord, 8:8
do not saw air with h., 200:6
dry h. yellow cheek, 187:31
dyer's h., 222:14
each army hath a h., 175:15
East with richest h., 256:6
every man's h. against him, 6:31
eye see for h. not mind, 474:5
farther away on either h., 695:6
fear thy skinny h., 376:13
findeth to do, 23:22
foot and h. go cold, 151:4
for hand, 8:17
from h. no worthy action, 883:18
gods' capricious h., 742:1
handle toward my h., 215:13
hard h. of war, 489:13
having put h. to plow, 37:30
heart in h., 457:13
heaving up my either h., 241:15
her h. on her bosom, 210:8
here's my h., 224:28
his hat in his h., 308:10
hold fire in his h., 176:18
hold infinity in palm of h., 353:14
hold your h. victorious, 68:12
hop a little from her h., 180:15
hour is at h., 36:7
hurts my h., 209:25
I want to hold your h., 848:4
if they stamp your h., 800:11
if thy right h. offend thee, 32:18
in every honest h. a whip, 210:6
in hand Americans all, 328:1
in hand on edge of sand, 467:10
in hand with wandering, 259:28
in her left h. riches and honor, 19:25
in his h. are the deep places, 17:32
in one h. a stone, 83:10
individual led by invisible h., 319:5
infection and h. of war, 176:24
iron h. in velvet glove, 148:28
kingdom of heaven is at h., 32:4
kissing h. may feel good, 698:9
leans her cheek upon her h., 180:1
left h. know what right h. doeth, 32:24
left his garment in her h., 7:8
length of days in her right h., 19:25
lifted h. in awe, 290:15
like base Indian, 210:20
living from h. to mouth, 155:1
made all to prosper in his h., 7:7
man himself lend a h., 71:10
man's h. not able to taste, 179:4
medieval h., 526:11
mortality's strong h., 175:26
my right h. hasn't seen left h., 747:4
my thoughtless h., 352:15
my times are in thy h., 16:3
nature's sweet cunning h., 204:20
need of some stranger's h., 858:5
never had blister in h., 72:16
nonchalance of h., 593:6
not h. but understanding, 157:3
of all that hate us, 37:14
of God promise of my own, 485:17

Hand (*continued*)

of h. of foot of lip, 222:9
of Potter shake, 442:5
Old Age and Experience h. in h., 281:4
on the horn, 890:13
orders in his h., 608:11
our times in his h., 462:13
phrase men pass h. to mouth, 829:7
prentice h. tried on man, 356:22
put in his h. by the hole of the door, 24:17
raised to shed blood, 294:17
rash h. in evil hour, 259:11
right h. bigger than head, 815:8
right h. forget her cunning, 19:11
right h. is become glorious, 8:6
right h. of God, 48:11
scepter snatched with unruly h., 175:22
separate as fingers one as h., 566:3
shake of the h., 675:14
shakes parting guest by h., 203:24
sheep of his h., 17:32
shut when thou shouldest repay, 30:19
souls of righteous in h. of God, 29:34
stretched out to receive, 30:19
sweet Roman h., 205:20
sweeten this little h., 217:14
sword sleep in my h., 354:8
take my h. lead me home, 720:12
taking in h. a city, 62:15
ten thousand at thy right h., 17:28
that held dagger struck, 653:1
that I were glove upon that h., 180:1
that made you fair, 207:2
that mocked them, 401:13
that rocks cradle, 485:7
that rounded Peter's dome, 424:5
that signed the paper, 777:5
there shall thy h. lead me, 19:13
this living h., 412:1
thou openest thine h., 19:17
three lilies in her h., 505:23
thy h. great Anarch, 297:6
thy h. presseth me sore, 16:14
thy right h. shall hold me, 19:13
time hath taming h., 421:3
Time's fell h., 221:18
touch of vanished h., 452:15
unfriendly to tyrants, 268:7
Uzzah put forth his h., 11:14
vacant heart h. eye, 374:11
wash blood from my h., 215:24
we are in God's h., 189:15
what immortal h. or eye, 353:1
what thy right h. doeth, 32:24
whatsoever thou takest in h., 30:28
when love has h. in things, 320:10
with other h. held weapon, 12:28
with your staff in your h., 7:40
withhold not thine h. in the evening, 23:28
work of thy h., 27:19
your tiny h. is frozen, 550:14
Hand-and-glove, 286:8
Handclasp's a little stronger, 615:16
Handed in his checks, 528:9
   me my Being's worth, 511:8
Handel scarcely fit to hold candle, 297:19
Handful of dust, 676:6
   of gray ashes, 499:9

Handful (*continued*)

of meal in a barrel, 11:41
of silver, 460:11
until h. of earth stops mouths, 415:9
with quietness, 23:1
Handfuls, give me h. of lilies, 95:1
Handiwork, artist remains within behind h.,
   650:11
   firmament showeth his h., 15:15
   Park specimen of God's h., 498:14
   you give to God, 557:4
Handkerchief, black h. washed clean, 812:14
   holding pocket-h., 516:7
Handle, grasped the surest h., 119:4
   jug without h., 467:15
   lie a h. fits all tools, 443:11
   of big front door, 525:22
   such as h. harp and organ, 6:11
   touch not h. not, 44:10
   toward my hand, 215:13
Handlebar moustaches on Czar, 787:6
   wringing h. for speed, 801:16
Handled, vessels oft h. brightly shine, 168:15
   with a Chain, 509:4
Handler, nation's freight h., 636:2
Handles, vandals took the h., 851:16
Handling, tuning lyre and h. harp, 62:15
Handmaid, Nature's h. Art, 272:5
   riches good h. worst mistress, 165:5
Handmaiden, low estate of his h., 37:10
Hands and hearts, 170:33
   and then take h., 224:12
   as bands, 23:16
   bear thee up in their h., 17:29
   believe in fairies clap h., 577:11
   blue, 467:11
   by fairy h. knell rung, 317:11
   children join h. and sing, 823:9
   clasps with crooked h., 454:13
   clean h. and pure heart, 15:24
   come knit h., 252:11
   Country defended by h., 456:7
   dead h. dead stringencies, 833:10
   diadems and fagots in h., 424:23
   do what you're bid, 593:5
   entergraft our h., 229:18
   establish the work of our h., 17:27
   Father into thy h., 38:37
   fold h. and wait, 528:13
   folding of the h. to sleep, 20:1
   from failing h. we throw, 614:7
   fruit of her h., 22:20
   gilt comes off on our h., 493:15
   greedy h., 444:n1
   hath not a Jew h., 185:11
   held heart in h., 608:19
   his h. formed the dry land, 17:32
   horny h. of toil, 481:8
   idle h., 289:9
   in h. not of few but many, 71:14
   into thy h. I commend my spirit, 38:37
   issue is in God's h., 63:27
   I've only got three h., 766:14
   kills Scots washes his h., 182:17
   large and sinewy h., 436:11
   little h. make pretense, 513:10
   little h. never made, 289:6
   lives in h. of Great Spirit, 365:3

Hands *(continued)*
   looked at h. see if I was same, 490:9
   lover threw wild h. toward sky, 609:2
   made before knives, 286:2
   man's fortune in own h., 166:13
   many h. make light work, 148:10
   musket molds in his h., 554:2
   my own fair h., 284:9
   nobody has such small h., 701:16
   not hearts, 209:21
   not without men's h., 480:23
   of Esau, 6:39
   of ghostly confessors, 448:11
   of sisters Death and Night, 487:11
   only serve eyes, 472:19
   pale h. I loved, 586:15
   Pilate washed h., 36:15
   plunge h. in water, 748:9
   predatory human h., 574:6
   pure of h., 3:10
   rarely escapes injuring own h., 58:4
   right h. of fellowship, 43:26
   rosy h. in steam, 797:13
   shake h. forever, 167:11
   something from our h., 372:11
   sore laborers have hard h., 261:14
   soul clap h. and sing, 594:2
   speak h. for me, 192:15
   strength without h. to smite, 529:14
   temples made with h., 40:33
   that rod of empire, 315:21
   that work on us, 632:9
   that wove shirt of flame, 679:11
   union of h., 423:2
   union of h. and hearts, 265:1
   with Pilate wash your h., 177:19
   without dirtying your h., 824:14
   work h. from day to day, 751:2
   wounds in thine h., 29:17
Handsaw, know hawk from h., 199:8
Handsome as bull that kidnapped Europa, 87:24
   big-boned and hardy-h., 546:15
   house to lodge friend, 296:7
   in three hundred pounds, 187:13
   is that handsome does, 322:8
   Jesus he was a h. man, 701:7
   man but gay deceiver, 361:9
   not h. at twenty, 244:5
   rather a h. pig, 514:11
   some women h. without adornment, 87:17
   strong rich or wise, 244:5
   wee thing, 358:11
   with my mourning very h., 277:20
Handsomely, have merit h. allowed, 311:5
Handspike, Fate is h., 483:8
Handy, with girls be h., 883:15
Handy-dandy which is the justice, 212:29
Hang by your thumbs, 802:3
   calf's-skin on limbs, 175:14
   caps on horns o' the moon, 219:21
   clothes on hickory limb, 887:17
   decided to h. himself, 821:8
   enough rope h. himself, 146:*n*3
   feel his title h. loose, 217:15
   go h. yourselves critics, 146:4
   I h. around in bars, 879:9
   in their own straps, 204:14

Hang *(continued)*
   let it all h. out, 852:14
   let him h. there, 807:16
   like drop of dew, 595:2
   like icicle on beard, 205:17
   loop to h. doubt on, 209:15
   my harp on willow-tree, 885:15
   on to your name, 830:13
   out our banners, 217:21
   pearl in cowslip's ear, 178:11
   she would h. on him, 197:1
   so fretted you would h. yourself, 309:19
   sorrow, 191:*n*1
   that jurymen may dine, 293:9
   them up in silent icicles, 377:15
   there like fruit my soul, 220:29
   together or hang separately, 303:11
   up philosophy, 180:35
   upon his pent-house lid, 214:1
   us every mother's son, 178:7
   when icicles h. by the wall, 174:33
   yellow leaves do h., 221:24
   you may h. these boys, 568:9
   your head over, 884:2
Hangdog, shifty h. look, 648:15
Hanged by dictionaries, 398:12
   house of a man h., 156:28
   I'll be h., 182:9
   knows he is to be h., 310:12
   longed to see him h., 606:14
   millstone h. about neck, 38:19
   my poor fool is h., 213:14
   our harps upon willows, 19:11
   they h. Haman, 12:33
   went out to see Harrison h., 277:4
Hangin' Danny Deever, 587:15
   men and women there, 884:5
Hanging and wiving by destiny, 146:*n*14
   around till you've caught on, 625:12
   breathless on thy fate, 436:23
   Danny Deever, 587:15
   in a golden chain, 257:4
   likewise destiny, 146:19
   men and women there, 884:5
   no man h. deserve h., 153:17
   shadow h. over me, 848:6
   too good for him, 271:18
   worst use for man, 227:13
Hangout, it's a limited h., 844:6
   talking about certain h., 708:1
Hangs as mute on Tara's walls, 387:8
   blossom h. on bough, 225:5
   bodiless as false dawn, 797:12
   goose h. high, 884:3
   he h. between in doubt, 295:1
   in shades the orange bright, 267:6
   in uncertain balance, 164:4
   on Dian's temple, 220:3
   on princes' favors, 225:25
   tail h. down behind, 588:17
   thereby h. a tale, 194:16
   upon cheek of night, 179:28
Hank of hair, 589:5
Hannah, amount to H. Cook, 886:11
   God and me, 518:7
Hannibal is at the gates, 120:28
   know how to win victory H., 84:6
   put H. in the scales, 109:25

Hanover, famous H. city, 460:6
Hansom, helped to h. outside, 745:4
Hap, from better h. to worse, 166:27
   my hope my h. my love, 155:3
Ha'penny will do, 884:7
Haply I think on thee, 221:6
Happen, it can't h. here, 664:8
   know what will h. next, 722:6
   lies at last letting it h., 798:1
   melting pot did not h., 586:*n*2
   things you do not hope h., 84:3
   we's nuts and things h., 681:3
   what would h. if one woman told truth, 771:19
Happened, nothing ever h. at all, 523:2
   put down what really h., 721:12
   remember anything whether h. or not, 525:9
   show what actually h., 414:2
Happening, being and h., 749:20
   funny if h. to somebody else, 640:5
Happens, don't want be there when h., 839:13
   future in us before it h., 632:6
   music of what h., 845:12
   too much h., 713:17
   truth h. to idea, 542:9
   unexpected always h., 84:*n*2
Happier, envy of less h. lands, 176:24
   I am h. than I know, 258:31
   in passion we feel, 264:14
   people capable of becoming h., 685:6
   Pobbles h. without toes, 468:5
   remembering h. things, 451:23
Happiest day happiest hour, 447:9
   intellection, 797:14
   man alive, 690:17
   martini one of h. marriages, 713:10
   of all men, 299:12
   time of New Year, 450:15
   treatise of natural education, 312:25
   women nations have no history, 480:12
Happily may I walk, 891:18
Happiness activity in accordance with excellence, 78:13
   avarice and h., 302:7
   beauty that comes from h., 493:14
   beneficial for body, 611:6
   best recipe for h., 382:14
   beyond h. is bliss, 691:2
   care of life and h., 337:15
   ceases like dream, 247:3
   conditions that make h., 615:6
   consume h. without producing it, 564:19
   contributes to h. of country, 380:14
   counting upon H., 412:14
   dream h. you may never feel, 609:8
   enjoy h., 100:*n*10
   envy no man's h., 195:6
   find the h. I seek, 673:8
   flushed sense of h., 857:13
   freedom secret of h., 72:4
   greatest degree of h., 320:8
   greatest h. for greatest numbers, 298:20
   greatest h. for thinking man, 344:23
   greatest h. of greatest number, 342:5
   Greatest H. Principle, 435:15
   hairbreadth missings of h., 304:24
   health foundation of h., 430:16

Happiness *(continued)*

hope for h. beyond life, 333:18
how simple and frugal is h., 656:5
in married estate, 250:5
is new idea in Europe, 364:8
is of retired nature, 288:5
jealous possessions of h., 604:7
liberty secret of h., 562:8
lifetime of h. hell, 565:4
look into h. through another's eyes, 196:1
made of minute fractions, 380:6
make ourselves worthy of h., 320:3
makes up in height, 624:8
man mistakes evil for h., 360:15
new dish does more for human h., 348:16
no h. like mine, 838:15
no h. where no wisdom, 66:1
no one can arrange another's h., 738:2
not in multitude of friends, 232:1
of peoples, 545:18
of society end of government, 330:2
on earth no sure h., 160:21
only one h. in life, 432:13
pastime and our h., 372:1
principles to effect h., 336:1
produced by good tavern, 310:7
pursuing and obtaining h., 320:7
pursuit of h., 336:1
regret or secret h., 552:12
result h., 465:24
secret of h. freedom, 72:4
she does not find, 306:20
sole object of government, 332:4
take life-lie away take h., 505:1
that makes heart afraid, 418:4
the only good, 518:6
the only sanction of life, 584:2
thirst after h., 313:9
to be dissolved into something great, 615:12
to crave h. is revolt, 504:11
too swiftly flies, 315:8
two foes of human h., 400:4
what right have we to h., 504:11
wherein lies h., 409:9
without looking into h., 61:4
Happy a man as any in world, 277:10
accident, 236:19
age when idle with impunity, 391:15
all the while I was h., 856:9
and I wrote my h. songs, 350:11
as grass was green, 777:9
as heart was long, 777:13
as kings, 555:13
as we imagine, 263:20
ask yourself whether h., 435:21
autumn fields, 452:21
be and have immortal bliss, 160:12
be good and h. today, 375:14
breed of men, 176:24
bridegroom Hesper brings, 575:19
call that man h., 63:5
Christmas to all, 387:3
combination of circumstances, 374:13
created you while h., 583:13
days here again, 697:4
deep down, 680:12
description of h. state, 275:10

Happy *(continued)*

don't worry be h., 700:14
duty of being h., 555:1
families alike, 507:3
fault, 47:23
few, 190:1
field mossy cavern, 411:5
genius of my household, 658:5
good to be just plain h., 691:2
good-night air, 536:12
had Vietnam instead of h. childhoods, 847:7
hail Columbia h. land, 367:19
he of calm and h. nature, 74:18
high majestical, 402:7
highways where I went, 575:6
horse to bear Antony, 218:11
hour wherein man might be h., 244:28
house shelters friend, 427:5
how h. he who crowns, 322:24
how we make ourselves h., 320:3
if all h. as we, 353:5
if ever wife h. in man, 261:15
I'm h. again, 702:4
I'm h. tonight, 823:16
in arms of chambermaid, 310:21
in being and knowing, 691:2
in even bad movie, 783:1
in nothing else so h., 176:29
in small ways, 583:4
in sorrow, 158:17
is be aware without fright, 692:10
is he born and taught, 227:9
is he who can forget, 499:10
Isles, 451:18
Jerusalem h. home, 881:18
keep talkin' h. talk, 706:15
laugh before we are h., 280:24
liking what they do, 315:1
little h. if say how much, 190:28
little needed to make h. life, 112:16
living things, 376:17
lucid intervals and h. pauses, 165:3
make fellow creatures h., 333:18
make two lovers h., 294:12
man be his dole, 146:*n*15
man happy dole, 146:20
man that hath his quiver full, 19:6
man who could search out causes, 93:18
man who works ancestral acres, 95:27
man's without a shirt, 146:9
master of himself a h. man, 97:8
mindful of h. time in misery, 128:18
never was so h., 884:17
no lad so h. as I, 384:7
no man h. who does not think so, 100:24
not h. unless free, 400:11
not to seem too h., 462:22
O h. fault, 47:26
object of making men h., 492:12
old man, 92:16
pair, 257:23
people whose annals blank, 408:9
persons with torn bodies h., 608:14
place green groves of blest, 94:32
place to be h. here, 518:6
policeman's lot not h., 526:8
ports and h. havens, 176:16

Happy *(continued)*

prologues to swelling act, 214:10
prospects more pleasing than fruition, 110:*n*10
Puritanism haunting fear someone h., 645:19
rarely find a h. life, 95:18
realize been h. was h. still, 769:14
ring h. bells, 454:8
secrets of a h. life, 755:*n*1
so h. as America, 333:8
survive and multiply, 440:2
that we are not over happy, 199:1
the man and happy he alone, 273:17
the man whose wish, 292:4
they h. are and love, 249:25
thing to be father unto many sons, 170:26
this h. country, 318:6
this the h. morn, 250:9
those early days when I, 268:9
those who plant cabbages, 145:14
those whose walls already rise, 94:3
time to be h. is now, 518:6
to be alone last work done, 760:7
to be h. be well fed, 645:11
to be h. make others so, 518:6
to have been h. most unhappy, 117:2
tragedy with h. ending, 529:4
'twere now to be most h., 208:19
until dead not call man h., 55:17
Warrior, 371:20, 617:*n*4
was he free was he h., 749:11
when am I h., 830:12
where h. wing-beats are, 359:10
where one is h. there's homeland, 121:21
which of us h. in world, 459:8
who hath this only, 55:6
who in verse steer, 278:1
who knows rural gods, 93:19
who uses blessings with wisdom, 97:15
whoever h. make others h., 822:4
whom unbroken bond unites, 96:12
world not making you h., 565:3
world of h. days, 171:27
would never be so h. again, 710:10
Harangue, telling nothing in great h., 267:20
Harbinger, evening star love's h., 259:24
Harbingers are come, 243:8
to heaven, 250:1
Harbor, age the h. of all ills, 82:6
arrived in a good h., 240:2
bar be moaning, 481:5
cleared, 375:20
in life did h. give, 232:13
looking over h. and city, 636:3
run into a safe h., 55:21
ship of state safely to h., 65:11
Hard as a piece of nether millstone, 14:34
as nails, 464:8
beginning good ending, 147:1
brother h. and furious, 819:12
cause that makes these h. hearts, 212:12
Christ ain't a-going to be too h., 532:12
curst h. reading, 346:19
dealing teaches them suspect, 184:31
for women to keep counsel, 192:13
forefathers worked h., 567:1
gemlike flame, 534:8

Harvest *(continued)*
  reap the h. of your land, 8:26
  seedtime and h., 6:23
  shalt not gather the gleanings of h., 8:26
  time of h., 678:14
  truly is plenteous, 33:36
  your hour, 150:10
Harvests, wholesome h. reaps, 417:7
Harwich, steamer from H., 527:4
Has, what man h. he's sure of, 158:4
Hasard, coup de dés n'abolira le h., 543:*n*4
  l' h. ne favorise que les esprits préparés,
    499:*n*1
Haste, always in h., 301:17
  away so soon, 241:5
  brings failures, 69:17
  come time and h. day, 346:24
  eat it in h., 7:40
  I said in my h., 18:23
  in wikked h. no profit, 146:*n*8
  make h. better foot before, 175:28
  make h. my beloved, 24:27
  maketh waste, 146:11
  married in h. repent at leisure, 286:23
  more h. less speed, 99:4
  now to my setting, 225:23
  still pays haste, 207:17
  thee Nymph, 250:21
  this sweaty h., 196:14
  without h. but without rest, 344:31
  wooed in h. wed at leisure, 173:16
Hasten, minutes h. to their end, 221:16
Hastening, to h. ills a prey, 322:22
Hastens, midnight strikes and h., 576:1
Hastily, no werkman may werke wel and h.,
    136:2
  nothing can be done h. and prudently,
    100:20
Hasty, common sense takes h. view, 473:26
  man in his h. days, 545:14
  marriage seldom proveth well, 170:31
  orisons, 699:6
  Pudding, 347:8
  pudding, 883:*n*4
  start awa sae h., 356:4
Hat, cat in the h., 739:12
  cockle h. and staff, 201:23
  he can't think without h., 744:16
  his h. in his hand, 308:10
  lightly doffed h., 584:19
  Lord forbade me to put off my h., 270:5
  my h. upon my head, 308:10
  not worse for wear, 326:18
  off with your h., 561:10
  penny in old man's h., 884:7
  purple with a red h., 832:4
  runcible h., 467:6
  stuck feather in h., 883:15
  wears faith as fashion of h., 190:15
Hatched, count chickens before h., 58:15
  silent when eggs h., 250:5
  would grow mischievous, 192:1
Hatchet, I did cut it with my h., 328:*n*3
Hatching vain empires, 256:17
Hate, all people your relatives h., 706:14
  cherish hearts that h. thee, 226:5
  common herd, 96:25
  counsels not in such quality, 185:15

Hate *(continued)*
  creative h., 615:10
  do good to them that h. you, 32:21
  dumpy woman, 397:20
  envy calumny h. pain, 403:23
  envy dared not h., 396:28
  families I h. you, 604:7
  fear h. surrender defiance, 840:3
  fly from not h. mankind, 395:20
  for arts, 295:13
  freedom for thought we h., 539:7
  gods h. the obvious, 50:3
  hand of all that h. us, 37:14
  him for a Christian, 184:23
  how much men h. them, 845:7
  I dont h. it, 713:20
  I h. and I love, 91:28
  I h. babies, 608:10
  I h. definitions, 429:17
  I h. nobody, 285:16
  I h. quotation, 425:14
  I h. slavery, 444:6
  I h. the day, 161:1
  I h. too bitterly, 758:15
  I h. war, 652:9
  I know enough of h., 623:4
  I shall h. all women, 229:6
  immortal h., 255:10
  implacable in h., 272:19
  in white men, 809:1
  inaccuracy, 521:15
  ingratitude, 205:25
  Juno's unrelenting h., 274:13
  let them h. so long they fear, 86:17
  love and desire and h., 599:17
  love as though someday h., 65:*n*3
  love can conquer h., 845:4
  love commingled with h., 844:12
  love treason but h. traitor, 88:23
  loved him too much not to h., 278:17
  making other Englishman h. him, 565:19
  mankind, 213:28
  never bother with people I h., 707:3
  nor love thy life nor h., 259:22
  nought I did in h., 210:19
  of those below, 395:17
  one and love other, 33:5
  one another and know it, 277:25
  only love sprung from only h., 179:29
  only those who h. Negro, 557:15
  owe no man h., 195:6
  Persian luxury I h., 96:18
  rage and h. from Adam down, 483:3
  religion enough to make us h., 284:14
  scourge laid upon your h., 181:16
  skins not like your own, 477:1
  smile to those who h., 397:13
  so far only should we h., 65:7
  strength erect against her h., 687:12
  the tree, 116:13
  things we ought, 78:12
  those I fight I do not h., 592:20
  those who h. and destroy, 557:13
  those who h. you don't win, 771:10
  time to h., 22:31
  to be unquiet at home, 277:26
  to leave world, 721:18
  to see evenin' sun go down, 616:20

Hate *(continued)*
  traitors and treason love, 274:5
  tyrants, 485:10
  war, 652:9
  was failure of imagination, 737:16
  were why men breathe, 701:19
  where guile and h. never rise, 476:16
  whom they fear they h., 84:20
  whom they have injured they h., 103:27
  why do you h. the South, 713:20
Hated, everything he h. was here, 835:10
  for my name's sake, 34:2
  if to be fat be h., 182:28
  past reason h., 222:20
  the approximate, 631:19
  to be h. needs but be seen, 295:2
  way she had of waking him, 680:11
  with scabby hatred, 836:8
Hateful art how to forget, 241:20
  as the gates of Hades, 51:18
  pride is h. before God, 30:32
  second wife h. to children, 67:4
  self is h., 269:26
  what h. to you do not to neighbor, 102:27
  woman once loved h., 612:18
Hater, very good h., 308:5
Hates, anyone who h. babies, 644:*n*1
  children can't be all bad, 644:2
  God h. bray of bragging, 65:10
  him that would stretch him, 213:15
  himself in others, 335:14
  tell him he h. flatterers, 192:5
  thing he would not kill, 185:28
Hath, unto everyone that h., 35:27
Hating, die not h. enemies, 300:8
Hatred, all h. driven hence, 593:18
  carried in my heart, 804:6
  ceases by love, 64:22
  comes from heart, 399:21
  envy h. and malice, 48:19
  habitual h. or fondness, 329:1
  hate Negro see h. in him, 557:15
  hated with scabby h., 836:8
  healthy h. of scoundrels, 408:7
  I must have no h., 586:11
  I welcome their h., 652:11
  if no h. in mind, 593:16
  if one succeeds, 299:2
  intellectual h. worst, 593:17
  love to h. turned, 287:2
  not cease by h., 64:22
  of bourgeois beginning of wisdom, 493:20
  renders votaries credulous, 313:7
  stalled ox and h. therewith, 20:32
  stirreth up strifes, 20:12
  systematic organization of h., 531:4
  through h. borne apart, 67:1
  unanimous in h. for me, 652:11
  where h. let me sow love, 125:12
Hatreds, old h. shall pass, 877:4
Hats off gentlemen a genius, 457:10
  Seraphs swing snowy H., 508:10
  war their h. aboon, 889:16
Hatter, can't take less said H., 514:16
Hatteras, walked the waves off H., 856:10
Haughtiness of the terrible, 25:21
Haughty, discountenance h. and lawless, 329:6
  Juno's unrelenting hate, 274:13

Haughty *(continued)*
 nation proud in arms, 252:2
 spirit before a fall, 20:37
Hauling, crazy as h. timber into woods, 95:22
Haunch and hump is Obey, 588:20
Haunches, sits on silent h., 636:3
Haunt, breed and h., 214:21
 exempt from public h., 193:37
 ghostlike the spot, 431:5
 murmurous h. of flies, 410:8
 so h. thy days, 412:1
Haunted, beneath waning moon h., 377:18
 by ghost of innocent convicted, 613:16
 by ghosts, 177:8
 by waters, 731:18
 holy ground, 395:8
 me like a passion, 368:10
 passage in Lear h. me, 412:*n*2
 summer eves by h. stream, 251:8
Haunters of cavern lake waterfall, 409:13
Haunting black air, 820:9
 Puritanism h. fear someone may be happy,
  645:19
 Haunts about thy shape, 410:13
 of coot and hem, 454:24
 suspicion h. guilty mind, 171:5
 tempest laughs at archer, 491:2
Hautboys, give h. breath he comes, 274:16
Have, all I h. would h. given gladly, 753:10
 curtsied when you h., 224:12
 desire what we ought not to h., 100:21
 everything yet nothing, 86:7
 House of H., 534:1
 in quest to h. extreme, 222:20
 more than thou showest, 211:8
 that which it fears to lose, 221:19
 thee not yet see thee still, 215:13
 their Affliction by drops, 278:9
 these for yours, 576:4
 to h. and to hold, 49:16
 to h. to hold and let go, 586:14
 to h. what we would h., 206:30
 try to h. and use excellence, 78:15
 what she's having, 852:5
 what we h. we prize not, 191:6
 where ask is h., 318:9
 you can h. it, 819:12
Haven, in friendship but faithless h., 65:7
 safe into h. glide, 305:8
 under the hill, 452:15
Have-nots, Haves and H., 157:22
Havens, in h. dumb, 546:3
 ports and happy h., 176:16
Haves and have-mores, 862:12
 and Have-Nots, 157:22
 of give, 701:18
Having, are we h. fun yet, 859:7
 fewest wants, 70:3
 had h. and in quest to have, 222:20
 love not h. to say sorry, 843:5
 not a h. and resting, 497:12
 nothing possessing all, 43:18
Havoc, cry H., 192:23
Hawk, chicken h. floats over, 817:8
 gentle as falcon or h. of tower, 141:2
 know h. from handsaw, 199:8
 sooner kill man than h., 670:6
Hawked, by mousing owl h. at, 216:3

Hawks, dark h. hear us, 650:22
 such hounds such h., 890:5
 which h. flies higher pitch, 169:15
Hawthorn in the dale, 251:2
Hawthorne says NO in thunder, 482:17
Hay, antic h., 168:12
 bottle of h., 178:32
 came creaking to barn, 787:3
 first bucked h., 828:10
 from fields comes breath of h., 568:15
 good h. sweet h., 178:32
 make h. when sun shineth, 146:16
 needle in bottle of h., 157:18
 new-mown h., 609:10
 work and pray live on h., 639:4
Haystack in the floods, 520:4
 needle in h., 157:*n*4
 under h. asleep, 893:11
Hazard, men that h. all, 185:3
 nice h. of doubtful hour, 183:11
 of concealing, 356:19
 of new fortunes, 175:5
 of the die, 172:12
Hazel, lone Glenartney's h. shade, 373:18
Hé Dieu si j'eusse étudié, 138:*n*3
He for God only, 257:19
 forget the H. and She, 228:14
 if you build it h. will come, 840:5
 is risen, 37:4, 47:28
 is the Rock, 9:30
 poorest h. in England, 239:4
 was h. and I was I, 152:8
Head and hoof of Law, 588:20
 anointest my h. with oil, 15:23
 at his h. a grass-green turf, 201:24
 bare Ben Bulben's h., 597:10
 behold my h., 243:8
 bending low, 503:15
 binds so dear a h., 403:12
 black wires grow on her h., 223:1
 blessings upon the h. of the just, 20:11
 bloody but unbowed, 552:7
 bullet through his h., 605:19
 call in thy death's h., 243:1
 chop off her h., 514:9
 chop off your h., 393:7
 crotchets in thy h., 187:6
 crown in my heart not on h., 170:25
 crown of h. to sole, 190:37
 dark hole of the h., 827:11
 desolate and bowed h., 599:14
 dogs shame the gray h., 52:13
 don't lose your h., 887:12
 eat my h., 464:10
 feel as if top of h. off, 511:15
 four angels round my h., 265:3
 from heels up to h., 555:12
 from the fair h. forever, 293:12
 full of quarrels, 180:26
 gently falling on thy h., 289:10
 grown gray in vain, 403:23
 guts in his h., 203:11
 hairs of h. numbered, 34:4
 hang your h. over, 884:2
 heap coals of fire upon his h., 21:34
 heart runs away with h., 361:7
 heaven to weary h., 418:7
 her h. on her knee, 210:8

Head *(continued)*
 here rests his h., 316:6
 hers is the h., 534:4
 hide h. under his wing, 895:5
 hitteth nail on h., 148:26
 hoary h. a crown of glory, 20:38
 if she'd but turn her h., 591:16
 imperfections on my h., 198:12
 in heart and h., 829:1
 in heart or in h., 185:17
 in lion's mouth, 774:9
 incessantly stand on h., 514:4
 it shall bruise thy h., 5:23
 Jezebel tired her h., 12:18
 John Baptist's h., 34:24
 keep good tongue in h., 224:30
 keep h. up high, 706:11
 King Charles's h., 465:28
 lay sleeping h. my love, 748:10
 make you shorter by the h., 151:9
 man with the h., 453:3
 meet and not see its h., 57:7
 more than churches bibles creeds, 486:8
 my h. is a city, 867:1
 my hat upon my h., 308:10
 my ho h. halls, 650:22
 no bigger than his h., 212:24
 no roof to shroud his h., 233:19
 not sound the rest not well, 157:*n*2
 not yet has heart or h., 734:11
 of a pin, 850:7
 off with her h., 514:18
 off with his h., 171:33, 287:14
 on horror's h. horrors, 209:16
 ought to have h. examined, 650:1
 over h. and heels, 91:9
 picked up poker hit him in h., 894:1
 precious jewel in his h., 193:37
 right hand bigger than h., 815:8
 root of family is person of its h., 79:17
 sacred h. of thine, 253:8
 shake of his poor little h., 527:21
 shot it through the h., 896:12
 show my h. to the people, 359:6
 singe my white h., 211:24
 slide into lover's h., 369:6
 so young body with so old h., 185:32
 some once lovely H., 441:14
 Son of man nowhere to lay h., 33:27
 stone of the corner, 18:25
 strike stars with my exalted h., 96:1
 stuff the h. with reading, 297:5
 sudden if thing comes in his h., 171:4
 that wears crown, 188:11
 this old gray h., 438:13
 threw back fierce young h., 629:8
 thudding in his h., 798:7
 to contrive, 261:1
 trickled through h., 516:17
 turns no more his h., 376:21
 useful lesson to h., 327:5
 very staid h., 185:*n*3
 well-made rather than well-filled h.,
  152:7
 when the h. aches, 157:4
 whole h. is sick, 24:29
 wisdom of h. and heart, 466:16
 with its h. went galumphing, 515:13

Head (*continued*)
　your h. concerned with outer weather, 623:15
Headache, dismal h., 527:3
Head-down tail-up hunt, 845:11
Headings, good reduced to three h., 276:20
Headlines, black h. of the latest edition, 724:6
Headlong down an immutable course, 761:8
　hurled h. flaming, 255:7
Headpiece filled with straw, 676:19
Heads, beast of many h., 97:*n*13
　beast with many h., 220:1
　blood be on your h., 40:35
　brains of better h., 248:2
　day fate put h. together, 623:15
　diminished h., 257:11
　erect instead of bowing necks, 115:17
　green hands blue, 467:11
　grow beneath shoulders, 208:2
　heaven over our h., 475:14
　hills whose h. touch heaven, 208:1
　houseless h., 211:33
　lift up your h. O ye gates, 15:25
　monster with uncounted h., 187:21
　not seat on others' h., 548:4
　o'ertaxed, 495:17
　old men's h. bare, 687:4
　or tails will turn up, 269:17
　revolutions begin in best h., 381:3
　saw h. black and gold in water, 767:6
　so many h. so many wits, 86:*n*6
　tossing in sprightly dance, 371:11
　two h. better than one, 147:12
　when trees bow h., 512:8
　within secrecy of our own h., 865:13
Headstones, crooked crosses and h., 650:9
Headstrong liberty lashed with woe, 172:15
Heal, physician h. thyself, 37:25
　time to h., 22:31
　touch me h. me, 861:16
　wound h. by degrees, 208:34
Healed of suffering by experiencing it, 611:5
Healer, Plato h. of soul, 74:*n*1
Healing in his wings, 29:21
　matter of time, 70:16
Health and a day, 425:23
　and quiet breathing, 409:7
　and wealth missed me, 392:20
　best physic to preserve h., 166:10
　blessing money cannot buy, 245:9
　double h. to thee, 397:13
　foundation of happiness, 430:16
　greatest of blessings, 71:5
　I swear by H., 70:14
　I that in h. was and gladness, 141:6
　in h. and mind's content, 277:18
　in sickness and in h., 49:16
　innocence and h., 322:23
　intelligence talent, 578:3
　is a human right, 805:16
　is infinite and expansive, 835:12
　physical mental h. of country, 796:8
　protect h. homes firesides, 554:5
　recover h. through contentment, 70:18
　taken from you for your better h., 236:15
　that mocks doctor's rules, 438:8
　trusts in horse's h., 212:10
　unbought, 274:24

Health (*continued*)
　unto all nations, 48:14
　wait on both, 216:16
　war is h. of state, 667:5
Healthful, sober h. with his wits, 265:2
Healthy and happy survive, 440:2
　and wealthy and dead, 704:9
　breath of morn, 411:12
　free the world before me, 486:24
　-mindedness is inadequate, 541:21
　sick danger for h., 548:17
　wealthy wise, 302:12
Heap coals of fire, 21:34
　o' livin', 647:8
　of broken images, 676:6
　of loose sand, 598:10
　of stones not a house, 558:8
　on more wood, 373:13
　worn out before thrown on scrap h., 565:3
Heap, ash h. of history, 765:13
Heapeth, he h. up riches, 16:19
Hear a little song, 343:1
　all ye Angels, 258:20
　angels sing, 457:11
　at back from time to time h., 676:11
　at my back I always h., 266:22
　be silent that you may h., 192:24
　bronze Negroes breathe, 787:19
　by tale or history, 177:27
　can't h. with bawk of bats, 650:22
　conclusion of the whole matter, 24:2
　destroyer and preserver h., 402:10
　did ye not h. it, 395:14
　dust h. her and beat, 455:3
　each other groan, 410:5
　'erse's legs, 455:25
　ever approaching thunder, 822:7
　every child may joy to h., 350:11
　falcon cannot h. falconer, 593:9
　far-off curfew sound, 251:17
　few love to h. sins they act, 220:10
　friend do you h., 891:*n*1
　hate enough to h. your prayers, 59:*n*4
　have ears and h. not, 27:25
　have ears but h. not, 18:22
　having ears h. not, 331:10
　he wept to h., 350:10
　heart h. her and beat, 455:3
　hungry stomach cannot h., 266:16
　I h. America singing, 485:14
　I h. you I will come, 575:1
　in chamber above me, 437:13
　incline thine ear and h., 26:21
　it not Duncan, 215:16
　know the man that must h. me, 377:3
　lady sing in Welsh, 183:1
　let him h., 34:7
　listen and do not h. it, 57:6
　listen and you shall h., 437:15
　Lord h. me out, 756:14
　me for my cause, 192:24
　me now Mighty One, 505:5
　mermaids singing, 228:9
　mind-forged manacles I h., 353:3
　music everyone should h., 643:23
　my voice approach, 486:23
　never merry when h. sweet music, 186:16
　no evil, 882:7

Hear (*continued*)
　none h. beside the singer, 384:3
　not my steps, 215:15
　now this, 27:2
　now this foolish people, 27:25
　O Israel, 9:14
　old Triton, 371:24
　one to speak another h., 473:22
　only one you ever h., 850:7
　other side, 116:9
　public does not h. what I say, 626:4
　replication of your sounds, 191:21
　rogues talk of court news, 213:8
　Shenandoah I long to h. you, 897:19
　still stood fixed to h., 258:29
　strike but h. me, 62:17
　sudden cry of pain, 654:2
　surly sullen bell, 221:23
　swift to h., 45:23
　that lonesome whippoorwill, 804:1
　the word of the Lord, 28:4
　the words of the wise, 21:19
　therefore h. now this, 27:2
　those things ye h., 37:35
　through midnight streets I h., 353:4
　thy shrill delight, 403:4
　Time's winged chariot, 266:22
　to see moves more than to h., 172:37
　us when we cry to Thee, 503:1
　voice in every wind, 315:5
　voice of the Bard, 352:10
　whatsoever I shall see or h., 70:14
　wind blow, 884:2
　wooden dialogue and sound, 203:9
　word culture reach for pistol, 687:5
　you or you hear him, 288:24
　you this Triton, 219:30
Heard, ain't h. nothing yet, 667:10
　by each let this be h., 561:3
　cannot be h. so high, 212:24
　chimes at midnight, 188:15
　eye of man hath not h., 179:4
　have ye not h., 26:31
　heavens fill with shouting, 452:2
　her massive sandal, 695:14
　I have h. key turn, 676:17
　I h. nothing, 366:17
　I will be h., 433:5
　in ancient days, 410:10
　it on the Aegean, 496:18
　laugh h. when nobody else laughing, 770:15
　laughing h. on hill, 351:7
　long after h. no more, 370:12
　loud bassoon, 375:21
　melodies are sweet, 410:15
　music h. so deeply, 679:7
　music I h. with you, 683:3
　never h. so musical discord, 179:2
　nor ear h., 42:6
　not regarded, 183:4
　of thee by hearing of the ear, 14:38
　of wonderful one-hoss shay, 443:12
　of your paintings, 200:1
　old old men say, 592:2
　other side, 68:4
　people who never h. of Jesus Christ, 683:18

Heard *(continued)*

putter as though I had not h., 817:7
shot h. round the world, 424:17
sing songs not h. before, 96:25
sweetest song ever h., 397:9
the mermaids singing, 675:6
then is h. no more, 217:23
trumpet be h. on high, 273:26
voice cry Sleep no more, 215:21
voices of children h. on the green, 351:7
we should certainly have h., 749:11
whether there be Holy Ghost, 40:38
wise man say, 574:14
wished she had not h. it, 208:3
Hearers, convince h. of own assertions, 74:15
not h. only, 45:24
Hearest thou hardly a breadth, 344:19
why h. thou music sadly, 220:33
Heareth, thy servant h., 10:35
Hearing ear and the seeing eye, 21:11
grass grow, 480:18
heard of thee by h. of the ear, 14:38
make passionate my h., 174:11
mentioned in your h., 382:11
nor ear filled with h., 22:23
of a voice, 483:11
vision spectator h. participator, 572:16
Hearings, smallest sights and h., 487:1
Hearken, will not h. to voice of charmers, 16:39
Hearkened, old men h. when he was young, 99:8
to my commandments, 26:37
Hears different drummer, 475:20
ear of him that h., 174:31
him in the wind, 294:20
man h. what he wants to hear, 855:9
monarch h., 274:15
neither h. nor sees, 369:8
step to music he h., 475:20
sun which h. all things, 51:4
you nearby sweetly speaking, 56:5
Hearse, attend progress of his h., 285:5
gilded h., 677:16
marriage h., 353:4
underneath this sable h., 240:7
why h. horse snicker, 636:7
Heart, a man's h. deviseth his way, 20:36
absence makes h. grow fonder, 101:17
abundance of the h., 34:12
all that mighty h., 370:3
all thy h. open, 453:6
although my h. is torn, 414:11
and mind of America, 749:22
and voice oppressed, 479:2
apple rotten at the h., 184:27
apply h. unto my knowledge, 21:19
as he thinketh in his h., 21:27
as long as human h. strong, 503:3
Atman dwells within our h., 50:8
baseball breaks your h., 844:8
batter my h., 230:26
battlefield h. of man, 492:9
beats so I can hardly speak, 673:8
because it is my h., 608:19
because my h. is pure, 452:13
begins to bleed, 892:8
betray h. that loved her, 368:12

Heart *(continued)*

black spot in any h., 504:5
blessed are the pure in h., 32:14
blood around men's h., 67:2
book and h. never part, 283:4
bread strengthens man's h., 282:16
break into flaws, 211:23
bring my aching h. to rest, 86:18
broken and contrite h., 16:35
brute h. of brute like you, 833:9
buildeth on vulgar h., 187:38
bullets seek out where h. lies, 739:2
burn within us, 38:42
bury my h. at Wounded Knee, 715:19
by sorrow of the h. the spirit is broken, 20:31
can push sea and land, 695:6
candle of understanding in thine h., 29:27
caused the widow's h. to sing, 14:6
change of h., 748:6
clean hands and a pure h., 15:24
command my h. and me, 263:3
committed adultery in his h., 32:18
committed adultery in my h., 805:14
congenial to my h., 322:27
consume my h. away, 594:3
counsel of thine own h., 31:22
create in me a clean h., 16:32
Cruelty has human h., 353:8
cry of Absence in h., 681:18
cutting the h. asunder, 654:16
darkness of man's h., 764:1
darling of my h., 292:1
day breaks not it is my h., 882:3
deep in h. believe, 888:15
departeth from the Lord, 27:39
destroy a piece of his own h., 791:12
dispossessed had stopped, 544:14
distant h. creates wilderness, 116:21
do not submit in h., 79:14
don't eat your h., 58:9
each h. to pierce, 285:5
East and West will pinch h., 695:6
endure my h., 54:7
even in laughter the h. is sorrowful, 20:26
everlasting funeral marches round your h., 780:10
every h. prepare room, 289:15
executions hardening the h., 360:25
faint h. ne'er won fair lady, 157:16
faint h. never won fair lady, 527:5
falsehood of the h., 336:11
fear at my h. as at cup, 376:10
fed on truth, 380:2
find Calais lying in my h., 150:5
fire that in h. resides, 494:17
firm as stone, 14:34
followed delight with h. unsatisfied, 122:6
fool hath said in his h., 15:9
for any fate, 436:7
for every fate, 397:13
foul rag-and-bone shop of h., 597:8
fresh complexion and h., 223:34
getting rid of work breaks h., 576:7
give a loving h. to thee, 240:11
give lesson to head, 327:5
give me back my h., 394:17
give world another h., 408:18

Heart *(continued)*

given h. change of mood, 623:5
gives h. and soul away, 574:16
giving h. to dog to tear, 589:25
glad with all my h., 167:11
gladness of the h., 31:16
glows in every h., 290:12
got you deep in h. of me, 691:14
grant all things your h. desires, 53:3
Greensleeves my h. of gold, 881:5
grieve his h., 217:1
grown cold in vain, 403:23
habitation large enough, 431:4
happiness makes h. afraid, 418:4
happy as h. was long, 777:13
hardened Pharaoh's h., 7:34
has hidden treasures, 472:8
has its reasons, 269:18
hatred carried in my own h., 804:6
he that is of a merry h., 20:32
hear her and beat, 455:3
held h. in hands, 608:19
hid in h. of love, 591:3
hide what false h. know, 215:8
high as my h., 195:14
high-erected thoughts in h. of courtesy, 162:12
his h. was going like mad, 650:18
his sad and usual h., 775:1
history begins in h. of man or woman, 615:8
hold me in thy h., 202:31
hope deferred maketh h. sick, 20:20
hot within me, 16:16
how dear to this h., 393:12
how h. grows weary, 503:12
human h. by which we live, 371:5
I am sick at h., 196:9
I have h. of a king, 151:7
I told her all my h., 352:3
if h. fails climb not, 159:*n3*
imagination of man's h., 6:22
in h. and head, 829:1
in h. cold December, 881:11
in h. voice said I want, 778:8
in his pained h., 409:21
in my h. of h., 200:12
in peril truth drawn from h., 90:9
in the h. or in the head, 185:17
into h. air that kills, 575:6
is a lonely hunter, 562:1
is a treasury, 417:14
is deceitful, 28:1
is harder than stone, 54:8
is Highland, 417:4
is like a viper, 301:9
is lying still, 370:3
is wounded within me, 18:17
keep thy h. with all diligence, 19:30
keeps open house, 755:10
kindnesses makes h. run over, 334:7
knock at my ribs, 214:11
know truth by the h., 269:19
knoweth own bitterness, 20:25
laid h. open to indifference, 769:14
language of the h., 296:3
lay h. out for my board, 787:5
leaps up, 369:14

Heart (*continued*)

let no man's h. fail, 10:45
let not h. be troubled, 39:40, 39:44
level in her husband's h., 204:34
lies open unto me, 453:6
like music on my h., 376:23
like singing bird, 512:1
little body mighty h., 189:2
look in thy h. and write, 162:20
look into your h., 359:17
looked into father's h., 727:11
Lord Christ's h., 425:6
Lord looketh on the h., 10:43
lost h. stiffens, 677:19
love Lord with h. soul and mind, 35:13
love the Lord with all thine h., 9:15
make a stone of h., 593:8
make glad h. of childhood, 533:19
make h. stop beating, 631:2
man after his own h., 10:40
man who's pure in h., 732:15
man's own resinous h. fed, 594:14
May when lusty h. blossom, 138:9
meditation of my h., 15:19
mend the h., 293:13
Mercy has a human h., 351:4
merry h. doeth good, 20:42
merry h. goes all day, 223:24
merry h. maketh cheerful countenance,
    20:31
mind is dupe of the h., 264:5
Mind lives on the H., 264:*n1*
mine with my h. in it, 224:28
momentary anesthesia of h., 572:6
more knowledge of h. in Richardson's,
    309:18
mortality touches the h., 94:4
moved more than with trumpet, 162:19
music in h. I bore, 370:12
must pause to breathe, 397:14
my crown is in my h., 170:25
my h. aches, 410:2
my h. consumed in fire, 122:10
my h. in my mouth, 105:22
my h. is at rest, 351:7
my h. is heavy, 344:8
my h. is not here, 357:15
my h. is pure, 452:13
my h. is sick and sad, 537:4
my h. leaps up, 369:14
my h. rose, 261:16
my h. says yes indeed, 813:6
my h. shall not fear, 15:28
my sad h. foams at stern, 558:16
my true-love hath my h., 162:14
naughtiness of thine h., 10:44
ne'er within him burned, 373:3
never give all h., 591:17
never given in vain, 574:15
never more hollowness of h., 488:11
never say I was false of h., 222:11
new opened, 225:25
no island but continent, 165:23
no matter from the h., 204:7
no nor for constant h., 882:1
no wider than h. wide, 695:6
nor h. to report, 179:4
not with Club H. broken, 510:17

Heart (*continued*)

not yet has h. or head, 734:11
not your h. away, 574:14
now cracks a noble h., 202:33
O h. if she'd but turn, 591:16
O h. O troubled h., 594:5
obey thy h., 424:14
o'er-fraught h., 217:7
of a king, 151:7
of a lion, 119:25
of an old youngster, 761:6
of animals, 236:1
of bronze, 50:25
of criminal, 581:8
of fools, 23:10
of form, 756:9
of man changeth countenance, 31:3
of knight, 61:17
of lead, 296:27
of my mystery, 200:24
of oak our ships, 316:20
of Russia not forget, 429:15
of Son of man, 490:16
of stone to read death of Little Nell, 561:8
of uncorrupted good man, 757:15
of wise, 23:10
oh h. oh blood that freezes, 461:2
old brag of my h., 832:13
old darky's h., 558:1
once woman has given h., 283:16
one jot of h. or hope, 254:24
only with h. one can see, 726:18
open my h. and see, 461:4
open unto me, 453:6
out of h. rapture, 550:3
peace at h. of endless agitation, 372:7
penknife in your h., 892:8
pent-up love of h., 551:3
people are good at h., 822:7
Pharaoh's h., 7:34
piece of my h., 822:1
pierce h. with languor, 549:17
plunges lower than night, 659:3
poor h. would fain deny, 217:18
possessing h. of woman, 610:14
pourest thy full h., 403:2
preaching down daughter's h., 451:25
prithee send back my h., 261:6
quanch my h. trobling, 682:12
razors to my wounded h., 172:41
recoiled at war, 701:11
records of h. in pain, 418:17
recovered greenness, 243:6
replies, 327:4
revolting and rebellious h., 27:26
rise in the h., 452:21
rises I've gladdened lifetime, 788:10
room my h. keeps empty, 241:18
rose in deeps of h., 591:9
runs away with head, 361:7
sad h. of Ruth, 410:10
savage indignation lacerate h., 286:15
seal upon thine h., 24:25
seared and blighted h., 447:9
secret anniversaries of h., 437:22
secret of freedom a brave h., 72:4
sesoun priketh every gentil h., 134:11
set my poor h. free, 207:*n2*

Heart (*continued*)

set not h. upon goods, 30:20
sets my h. a-clickin', 553:10
sets my h. to fluttering, 56:5
Shakespeare unlocked h., 372:16
shaped like valentine, 780:14
Shot straighter to H., 510:2
sick at h., 196:9
simple frugal h., 656:5
sound as bell, 190:38
soured kindness in my h., 214:*n1*
spring of love gushed from h., 376:17
squirrel's h. beat, 480:18
stick the h. of falsehood, 203:20
stirred h. of Englishman, 603:5
stop H. from breaking, 510:4
strike mine eyes but not my h., 232:7
strong and diverse h., 716:1
stubborn h. shall fare evil, 30:15
stuff which weighs upon h., 217:19
summer to your h., 695:11
Sweeping up the H., 510:11
take beak from out my h., 449:10
that fed, 401:13
that loveth nought in May, 132:4
there will your h. be also, 33:2
there's where h. turning, 503:11
thing that eats h., 742:2
thinks tongue speaks, 190:38
though h. still as loving, 397:14
thou'll break my h., 357:6
through fire for kind h., 187:14
thy breast encloseth my h., 171:21
tickleth me aboute myn h. roote, 135:7
tiger's h. in player's hide, 164:3
tiger's h. in woman's hide, 170:19
to mind shameful to h. beauty, 492:9
too soon made glad, 460:2
took all h. for speech, 592:19
trusteth in his own h., 22:7
turned to stone, 209:25
unchristened h., 595:16
unfortified, 196:28
unquiet h. and brain, 453:12
untraveled turns to thee, 321:12
vacant h. hand eye, 374:11
venting a heavy h., 488:2
verities and truths of h., 714:3
visit my sad h., 192:8
war in his h., 16:38
warm and gay, 706:7
warm h. within, 327:7
was in his garden, 494:7
waters of the h., 777:3
way to h. through stomach, 458:2
weaned h. from low desires, 143:1
wear h. upon my sleeve, 207:26
weeping in my h., 549:18
wet eye dhry h., 600:11
what dungeon dark as h., 431:15
what female h. gold despise, 315:9
what missing at the man's h., 773:17
what stronger breastplate than h., 170:7
when my h. hath 'scaped, 221:29
when to h. of man, 622:8
whole h. is faint, 24:29
wine that maketh glad the h., 18:9
wisdom of head and h., 466:16

Heart *(continued)*
  wise and understanding h., 11:26
  with h. in hand, 457:13
  with my whole h., 28:7
  with rue h. laden, 575:9
  with whole h. listen, 643:23
  withered h., 737:8
  woman whose h. is snares, 23:16
  woman with the h., 453:3
  words shall be in thine h., 9:15
  work with all one's h., 552:14
  world will break your h., 816:13
  wounded is wounding h., 263:8
Heartache, by sleep we end h., 199:21
Heartbreak, better chiding than h., 187:20
  Hotel, 840:12
Heartburn, I am h., 547:8
Hearth, by this still h., 451:11
  clean-winged h., 438:16
  clear fire clean h., 383:10
  cricket on the h., 251:18
  no more blazing h., 315:16
  woman for the h., 453:3
Hearths, their country their h., 92:8
Hearthstone, fox build nest on h., 611:*n*5
  of hell best bed, 611:*n*5
Heartily know when half-gods go, 424:15
Heart-leaves of lilac all over New England,
  626:15
Heart-revealing intimacy, 593:12
Heart's affections, 412:11
  burst hot h. shell, 483:3
  desire, 15:20
  Desire, 442:9, 591:8
  desires be with you, 193:28
  his h. his mouth, 219:32
  lose h. desire, 565:8
  my h. in the Highlands, 357:15
  my h. right there, 628:20
  my h. undoing, 387:15
  red h. core, 409:12
  wear him in my h. core, 200:12
Hearts, affect h. and minds, 692:4
  all that human h. endure, 307:14
  and minds, 49:8
  apply our h. unto wisdom, 17:26
  beauty that breaks h., 631:10
  blind h., 90:1
  cash-boxes for h., 417:18
  cause that makes hard h., 212:12
  cheerful h. now broken, 387:17
  cherish h. that hate thee, 226:5
  cleanse thoughts of our h., 49:3
  come not to steal away h., 193:3
  Country cherished in h., 456:7
  day star arise in your h., 46:4
  dry as summer dust, 372:6
  find agonies strife of human h., 409:2
  finite h. that yearn, 461:5
  first in h. of countrymen, 350:6
  given our h. away, 371:23
  high in people's h., 191:34
  hoard little h. great, 455:10
  hugest h. that break, 511:2
  human h. to chew, 402:21
  in imagination of their h., 37:11
  in love use own tongues, 190:26
  itch grows old in sick h., 109:22

Hearts *(continued)*
  keep your h. and minds, 44:6
  keeps their h. vacuous, 56:14
  kind h. more than coronets, 451:3
  Knave of H., 894:2
  Lord dwelt in people's h., 270:4
  Lord searcheth all h., 12:23
  mercy enthroned in h. of kings, 186:1
  neither have h. to stay, 262:23
  new heraldry hands not h., 209:21
  not had as gift are earned, 593:14
  not their h. that roam, 589:1
  of controversy, 191:25
  of oak, 146:3
  of the noble may be turned, 51:32
  palsied h., 495:17
  pluck their h. from them, 189:24
  queen in people's h., 876:9
  Queen of H., 894:2
  servitude can pierce our h., 672:6
  shutting away of loving h., 695:17
  somewhere h. are light, 585:1
  steel my soldiers' h., 189:24
  that roam, 589:1
  their bursting h. despond, 398:12
  their h. not grown old, 592:16
  though stout and brave, 436:5
  thousand h. beat happily, 395:13
  tight hot cell of h., 713:3
  touched with fire, 538:6
  true plain h., 228:8
  union of hands and h., 265:1
  union of h., 423:2
  unto whom all h. are open, 49:3
  what we do not doubt in h., 534:15
  what your h. have amassed, 118:2
  while your h. are yearning, 616:17
  wine unto those of heavy h., 22:15
  with your hands your h., 170:33
  wore at h. the fire's center, 760:6
  write upon h. of men, 359:11
Heartsease, infinite h., 189:22
Heart-sick hand workers, 520:8
Heartstrings are a lute, 448:*n*1
  though jesses my dear h., 209:7
Heart-whole, warrant him h., 195:26
Hearty, humble and h. thanks, 48:16
  old man, 381:19
Heat as mode of motion, 490:12
  burden and h. of day, 35:6
  cannot pass from colder, 497:23
  cold and h., 6:23
  crime to examine laws of h., 533:1
  fantastic summer's h., 176:18
  fear no more h. o' the sun, 220:26
  flow from hot to cold object, 497:*n*1
  he makes h. as he wishes, 4:3
  if you can't stand h., 661:7
  I'll shade him from h., 351:1
  mechanical equivalent of h., 542:12
  neither h. affection limb, 206:34
  neither sun light on them nor h., 46:37
  not furnace for foe, 225:12
  not see when h. cometh, 27:39
  not snow nor rain nor h., 69:21
  one draught above h., 204:19
  one h. drive out another, 163:16
  Promethean h., 210:14

Heat *(continued)*
  race not without h., 254:9
  surprised was I with sudden h., 167:1
  there is nothing hid from the h., 15:16
  which made my heart to glow, 167:1
Heath and harebells, 476:18
  best felt not clearly seen, 535:14
  brown h. and shaggy wood, 373:4
  foot on my native h., 374:10
  in the desert, 27:39
Heathcliff, I am H., 476:17
Heathen Chinee is peculiar, 528:10
  human form in h. turk or jew, 351:5
  in his blindness, 391:7
  pore benighted h., 587:18
  why do the h. rage, 15:1
Heather, know how H. looks, 510:9
Heaths, game on these lone h., 386:10
Heat-oppressed brain, 215:13
Heave away heave away, 897:21
Heaven about to confer great office, 80:6
  above road below, 556:4
  all H. before mine eyes, 251:23
  all hell that is not h., 168:20
  all I ask h. above, 556:4
  all places distant from h. alike, 235:10
  all things in h., 44:9
  all this and h. too, 282:22
  alone given away, 481:15
  and earth quilt and pillow, 122:3
  and earth pass away, 35:23
  and earth to witness, 9:13
  and future's sakes, 624:1
  and nature sing, 289:15
  angels in H. above, 449:23
  as it is in h., 32:25
  as the h. is high, 18:6
  ascended into h., 48:11
  attacking h. and earth, 827:14
  band in h. they play, 870:8
  blazing into head, 596:10
  bottom line is in h., 758:16
  bread of h., 18:12
  brightest h. of invention, 188:29
  brilliant glorious eternal h., 663:17
  by h. I do love, 174:19
  call h. and earth to witness, 9:13
  clear religion of h., 409:9
  combined essences of h. and earth,
    86:16
  confess yourself to h., 201:10
  confines of h. and earth, 119:13
  could not be happy in h., 663:17
  court it in shape of h., 198:10
  crawling between h. and earth, 199:25
  dances in sight of h., 797:13
  did recompense send, 316:7
  doors of h. adjacent identical, 656:8
  each goes own byway to h., 282:6
  earth and high h., 575:7
  earth nigher h. than now, 459:21
  endures, 576:4
  enter into kingdom of h., 33:23, 34:40
  eye of h. to garnish, 175:24
  farewells as stars in h., 204:1
  farther off from h., 418:3
  finds means to kill joys, 181:16
  floor of h. is inlaid, 186:15

Heaven *(continued)*

four winds of the h., 29:11
gained from H., 316:7
gate of h., 6:43
gems of h. starry train, 258:1
gentle rain from h., 186:1
getting to H. at last, 508:19
gives its favorites, 81:*n*4
glance from h. to earth, 179:6
God created h. and earth, 5:3
God is in h., 23:4
God's in his h., 459:19
going forth is from the end of the h., 15:16
gold bar of H., 505:23
great eye of h., 160:5
had made her such a man, 208:3
harbingers to h., 250:1
has no rage, 287:2
have ye souls in h., 411:4
hell I suffer seems a h., 257:12
helps not men who will not act, 59:*n*3
hills whose heads touch h., 208:1
his blessed part to h., 226:8
hours to which H. chime, 269:2
how long permit to H., 259:22
humbler h., 294:20
husbandry in h., 215:10
if earth be shadow of h., 258:19
if H. looked on riches, 284:23
if I ascend up into h., 19:13
if I cannot bend H., 95:5
I'm in h., 673:8
in h. perfect round, 462:10
in Hell's despair, 352:12
in which no horses, 557:2
is above all yet, 225:20
is he in h., 590:10
is love, 373:2
it saves going to H., 511:3
it smells to h., 200:31
itself we seek in our folly, 96:3
itself would stoop to her, 252:28
keys of kingdom of h., 34:37
kingdom of h. is at hand, 32:4
kingdom of h. like a net, 34:20
kingdom of h. like mustard seed, 34:18
kingdom of H. within you, 114:1
knows how to put price, 333:6
lay up treasures in h., 33:1
leave her to h., 198:13
leave the rest to h., 249:11
leaving mercy to h., 304:18
let justice be done though h. fall, 120:22
lies about us in infancy, 370:17
lift my soul to h., 225:15
like egg earth like yolk, 111:3
look down from h., 567:1
Lord of h. and earth, 40:33
love is h., 373:2
made h. and earth, 18:30
made thee neither of h. nor of earth, 141:3
majesty of H., 301:8
make a h. of hell, 255:14
make face of h. so fine, 180:32
Maker of h. and earth, 48:11
makes h. drowsy with harmony, 174:23
man is as H. made him, 157:7
marriages made in h., 162:11

Heaven *(continued)*

matches made in h., 146:*n*14
measuring earth and h., 76:6
met my dearest foe in h., 197:7
more things in h. and earth, 198:19, 693:11
mount up to h., 18:15
near h. by sea as by land, 154:3
needs such men more than H. does, 335:10
new h. and new earth, 47:11
no humor in h., 524:12
not enter into kingdom of h., 34:40
not h. itself upon past has power, 273:18
nurseries of H., 576:11
of whales in waters, 663:21
offspring of h. firstborn, 257:5
on earth, 257:15
open face of h., 408:15
or near it, 403:2
our Father which art in h., 32:25
parting all we know of h., 511:9
peep through blanket, 214:18
places eye of h. visits, 176:16
plays such tricks before h., 206:28
presents the solid hue, 623:3
prove that I and she ride together, 461:12
puts all H. in rage, 353:15
rains pennies from H., 751:15
reach port of h., 443:9
rejects the lore, 372:14
remembrance fallen from h., 529:14
same world hell h., 425:7
see h. in wildflower, 353:14
see h. open, 39:2
sends love of her, 3:11
serve in h., 255:15
short prayer pierces h., 136:21
sincerity the way of h., 79:21
single Dram of H., 511:8
smells to h., 200:31
so he goes to h., 200:32
some call it Tree of H., 740:5
spark from h., 495:15
spark from H. immortal, 359:10
spirit that fought in h., 256:7
starry cope of h., 258:11
stay the bottles of h., 14:25
steep and thorny way to h., 197:20
strange interesting astonishing grotesque, 525:7
such grace did lend her, 173:34
summons thee to h. or hell, 215:16
Sun drives Night from H., 441:4
swear neither by h. nor earth, 32:19
symbol of power of H., 671:21
take my soul, 175:31
tasted eternal joys of H., 168:18
tell little Greek to go to h., 109:14
thank h. fasting, 195:20
thank h. for little girls, 790:13
that leads men to hell, 222:20
theirs is the kingdom of h., 32:14
then Summer Then H. of God, 509:9
therefore doth h. divide, 188:34
things are sons of h., 306:23
though h. fall thy will be done, 121:14
though h. may perish, 363:1
till h. and earth pass, 32:17
to be young was very h., 368:18

Heaven *(continued)*

to gaudy day denies, 397:1
to h. being gone, 230:1
to throne in, 220:4
toward H. advancing, 359:10
treasure in h., 35:3
treasures in h., 33:1
trouble deaf h., 221:5
under feet as well as over heads, 475:14
understand will of H., 61:25
unextinguishable laugh in h., 249:5
unfolds both h. and earth, 177:28
vain war with h., 256:6
visited in H., 510:9
war in h., 47:1
watered h. with tears, 353:2
way to h. of like length, 154:*n*2
what's a h. for, 461:18
when h. was falling, 575:20
wherever bright sun of h., 226:15
which giant Atlas upholds, 68:3
who know h. save by heaven's gift, 104:10
who sword of h. will bear, 207:6
will most incorrect to h., 196:28
will protect working girl, 569:2
wind from blue h. blows, 342:15
winds of h. visit face roughly, 196:31
winged seraphs of H., 449:22
wished Hell for ease from H., 354:11
with all splendors lie, 481:14
with the company of h., 49:6
words never to h. go, 201:1
Heaven-born band, 367:19
    child, 250:10
Heaven-gates not so arched, 237:8
Heaven-kissing hill, 201:5
Heavenly blessings without number, 289:10
    can h. minds yield, 93:29
    caught my h. jewel, 162:22
    city formed by love of God, 116:19
    connection, 812:13
    Father disappointed in monkey, 524:24
    fools by h. compulsion, 211:3
    gift of poesy, 273:20
    harmony, 273:22
    paradise is that place, 227:3
    Powers, 342:14
    princes like to h. bodies, 166:1
    refuse h. mansion, 595:9
    remove weight from h. bodies, 801:11
    Rosalind, 193:32
    things h. or things earthly, 271:16
Heaven-rescued land, 387:1
Heaven's, against h. hand, 254:24
    all-gracious King, 457:11
    at h. gates claps wings, 162:9
    breath smells wooingly, 214:21
    cherubin horsed, 214:24
    command, 301:3
    despite, 352:13
    eternal King, 250:9
    eternal year is thine, 273:19
    glories shine, 476:14
    godfathers of h. lights, 174:1
    great lamps do dive, 226:20
    in h. high bower, 351:6
    lark at h. gate sings, 220:15
    last best gift, 258:13

Heaven's *(continued)*
    light forever shines, 404:2
    my destination, 715:3
    net is indeed vast, 58:3
    nothing situate under h. eye, 172:15
    own sweet will H. will, 593:18
    patio h. watercourse, 718:14
    riches of h. pavement, 256:3
    study like h. glorious sun, 174:1
    success found, 461:14
    sugar cake, 280:18
    vaults should crack, 213:12
    wide pathless way, 251:16
Heavens, ancient h., 371:17
    and earth a mass sewn up, 118:20
    clothed with h., 278:10
    declare glory of God, 15:15
    distorts the h., 354:17
    fill with commerce, 452:2
    fill with shouting, 452:2
    flaming walls of h., 89:11
    God light of h. and earth, 118:23
    hung be h. with black, 169:10
    let justice be done though h. fall, 120:*n*6
    new h. and a new earth, 27:21
    offered this trust to h., 119:6
    potentates blazing in h., 62:27
    pure as naked h., 370:10
    show h. more just, 211:33
    sing ye h. earth reply, 305:7
    spangled h., 287:20
    starry h. above me, 320:2
    themselves blaze forth, 192:10
    themselves the planets, 203:5
    when I consider thy h., 15:5
Heavens' embroidered cloths, 591:12
Heaviest ore of the body, 663:13
Heaviness, drama not of h. but of lightness, 824:4
    foolish son the h. of his mother, 20:10
    garment of praise for spirit of h., 27:16
    that's gone, 225:7
Heaving up my either hand, 241:15
Heavy, advance of a h. truck, 809:7
    as yonder stone, 650:22
    change now thou art gone, 253:4
    eyelids h. and red, 418:8
    laden, 34:9
    light gains make h. purses, 163:14
    light wife h. husband, 186:21
    my heart is h., 344:8
    steps of plowman, 591:9
    toward school with h. looks, 180:12
    venting a h. heart, 488:2
    weight of world, 368:8
    wine unto those of h. hearts, 22:15
Hebrew, aside from few odd words in H., 622:5
    blessing before eating bread, 703:13
    called in H. Armageddon, 47:7
Hebrides, in dreams behold H., 417:4
    stormy H., 253:12, 301:1
Hecate's, black H. summons, 216:12
    pale H. offerings, 215:14
Hector is dead, 204:8
Hecuba, what's H. to him, 199:16
Hedge, divinity cloth h. a king, 201:29
    over h. before stile, 156:2

Hedge *(continued)*
    pull not down your h., 243:19
Hedge-crickets sing, 411:8
Hedgehog knows one great thing, 55:2
Hedgehogs, belongs to the h., 757:14
    thorny h., 178:22
Heed, I will take h. to my ways, 16:15
    rumble of distant Drum, 441:11
    take h. lest he fall, 42:20
    take h. of loving me, 230:3
    ye who lead take h., 605:14
Heedless, earth's h. sons, 709:6
    ran my h. ways, 777:13
Heejous, creature of h. mien, 600:9
Heel, bedroom under my h., 316:18
    coat from h. to throat, 592:13
    Europe under his h., 620:8
    of courtier, 202:11
    of Northeast Trade, 588:12
    on throat of my song, 699:2
    pain of bone spur in h., 722:3
    thou shalt bruise his h., 5:23
    tread upon another's h., 201:*n*2
Heels, at his h. a stone, 201:24
    follow truth too near h., 159:14
    fortune grow out at h., 211:15
    from h. up to head, 555:12
    horses' h. over paving, 677:21
    out at h., 187:2
    over head and h., 91:9
    small war on h. of small war, 788:6
    took to my h., 86:12
Heft of Cathedral Tunes, 508:13
Hegemony protected by armor of coercion, 689:14
Heifer, if ye had not plowed with my h., 10:20
    lowing at skies, 410:18
Heifer's, false as wolf to h. calf, 203:20
Heigho the derry oh, 896:20
Height, asks of us certain h., 624:18
    depths of h., 701:18
    happiness makes up in h., 624:8
    my soul can reach, 434:17
    nor depth, 41:26
    worth's unknown although h. taken, 222:15
Heights, topped wind-swept h. with grace, 800:1
    towering h. of hills, 468:3
Heill, I that in h. wes and gladness, 141:6
Heine, Heinrich H. loosened corsets of German, 626:6
Heir as great in admiration as herself, 226:14
    grandchild h. of the first, 233:10
    great h. of fame, 250:15
    of all the ages, 452:9
    of mongrel bitch, 211:13
    that flesh is h. to, 199:21
    to the throne, 836:12
    yourself sole h. of world, 278:10
Heirs, joint h. with Christ, 41:19
    of all eternity, 173:39
    of God, 41:19
Held, things she h. against missionaries, 802:6
Helen brought her dowry destruction, 63:3
    did not board the ships, 55:18
    Leda mother of H., 534:5
    like another H., 274:20

Helen *(continued)*
    sweet H. make me immortal, 168:21
    threw into wine a drug, 52:32
    thy beauty is to me, 447:12
Helen's beauty in brow of Egypt, 179:6
    dawn in H. arms, 596:2
    dust hath closed H. eye, 227:6
Helicon, muses of H., 54:10
    shepherding below holy H., 54:11
    watered our horses in H., 164:1
Helix, double h. structure, 821:4
Hell, agreement with h., 433:6
    all h. broke loose, 258:9
    all h. stir for this, 190:5
    all we need of h., 511:9
    better to reign in h., 255:15
    black as h., 223:7
    catch the same h., 808:13
    city much like London, 402:18
    cunning livery of h., 206:37
    curse of h. frae me, 889:19
    deep in h., 763:11
    do it so feels like h., 833:3
    each bears his own H., 94:34
    easy to go down into H., 94:27
    England h. of horses, 161:11
    entertained great scorn of H., 128:24
    even with h. in your head, 868:11
    failure in great object, 409:5
    fight like h. for living, 511:17
    followed with him, 46:32
    full of good intentions, 123:13
    full of good meanings, 243:23
    full of musical amateurs, 565:6
    gates of h. not prevail, 34:37
    give 'em h., 392:22
    God holds you over pit of h., 301:11
    got a h. of a beating, 658:2
    halls of h., 665:13
    hath no limits, 168:19
    hearthstone of h. best bed, 611:*n*5
    heaven that leads men to h., 222:20
    hot as h., 348:5
    I love this cultured h., 687:12
    I myself am h., 787:16
    I oft wished for H., 354:11
    I raised h. all over, 511:18
    I shall move H., 95:5
    I suffer seems a heaven, 257:12
    I'm mad as h., 801:14
    in Heaven's despite, 352:13
    in most literal sense, 744:3
    into mouth of h., 454:23
    is he in h., 590:10
    is other people, 743:3
    is to love no longer, 673:16
    itself breathes out, 200:29
    keys of h. and death, 46:19
    lead apes in h., 173:12
    liberated the h. out of place, 888:3
    limbecks foul as h., 222:16
    madness risen from h., 529:14
    make a heaven of h., 255:14
    make my bed in h., 19:13
    more devils than h. hold, 179:6
    myself am h., 257:12
    name of this land is h., 759:1
    never married that's his h., 235:7

Hell *(continued)*

no fury like woman scorned, 287:2
of a good universe, 702:2
of nuclear destruction, 823:13
old age is woman's h., 266:4
on earth, 565:4
out of h. leads to light, 256:19
passage broad to h., 82:*n*3
paved with good intentions, 123:*n*7,
    243:*n*1
paved with priests' skulls, 115:25
pour milk of concord into h., 217:6
print news and raise h., 885:9
procuress to Lords of H., 453:20
Puritan's idea of H., 519:*n*1
raise less corn more h., 554:6
rebellious h., 201:7
reign in h., 255:15
riches grow in h., 256:4
rising from thousand thrones, 448:5
road to H. gradual, 717:12
same world h. heaven, 425:7
served my time in h., 888:1
spinach and the h. with it, 723:17
summons thee to heaven or h., 215:16
tell him to go to h., 393:2
this is h. nor am I out, 168:18
though h. bar way, 646:2
till H. freezes, 888:7
to h. with badges, 689:4
tyranny like h., 333:6
very respectable H., 601:11
walked eye-deep in h., 665:8
war is h., 489:15
way I fly is h., 257:12
we make ourselves, 540:22
wedlock forced a h., 169:22
what h. in suing long, 160:26
what in h. have i done, 635:9
when one is in h., 299:10
where h. is there must we be, 168:19
where we are is h., 168:19
whip all h. yet, 489:*n*5
whole body not be cast into h., 32:18
with h. are we at agreement, 26:8
with work which bores you life is h.,
    602:10
within him, 257:10
within myself, 248:12
wrote of Devils and H., 351:10
Hellas, confounded H., 72:10
of Hellas, 67:*n*1
Hellenes, boy is most powerful of H., 62:18
Hellespont, Propontic and H., 209:20
Hell-kite, O h., 217:8
Hello darkness my old friend, 855:6
had me at h., 875:2
sucker, 659:12
Hell's broke loose in Georgia, 715:17
broken loose, 164:5
concave, 255:22
despair, 352:12
Hells, tormented with ten thousand h., 168:18
Helm, everyone prepared to take h., 504:15
hold h. when sea calm, 100:6
Pleasure at the h., 316:15
Helmet and the plume, 451:6
for h. the hope of salvation, 44:20

Helmet *(continued)*

now hive for bees, 163:4
Helmets gleamed in forests, 500:5
Help, a little h. from my friends, 848:13
a very present h. in trouble, 16:26
between hindrance and h., 369:12
cannot h. or pardon, 748:8
encumbers him with h., 308:17
feeble up, 213:17
for living hope for dead, 518:5
from whence cometh my h., 18:30
George can't h. it, 834:15
go love without the h., 354:10
God our h. in ages past, 289:12
God's h. and their valor, 365:10
her and that right early, 16:27
here I stand God h. me, 143:14
I ask for your h. and God's, 753:8
into Macedonia and h. us, 40:30
man is without h., 742:22
me down Cemetery Road, 799:12
my h. cometh from the Lord, 18:30
nothing will h., 704:2
of the helpless, 405:8
one fainting Robin, 510:4
only h. her to know, 771:14
others out of fellow-feeling, 234:6
past hope past cure past h., 181:5
since there's no h., 167:11
them that help themselves, 59:14
there is no h., 121:26
thou mine unbelief, 36:37
thyself, 59:*n*3
to half-a-crown, 536:13
to h. or do no harm, 70:15
use treatment to h. sick, 70:14
what's gone past h., 223:18
when no h. in truth, 66:3
with h. of surgeon recover, 179:15
Helped every one his neighbor, 26:33
to hansom outside, 745:4
Helper, Lord is my h., 45:16
mother's little h., 857:3
Helpers fail and comforts flee, 405:8
Helpful, noble be man h. and good, 342:12
Helping, God h. me I can do no other, 143:*n*4
men to practice virtue, 79:15
so far from h. me, 15:21
Helpless before the iron, 771:14
justice without strength is h., 269:20
man in ignorance sedate, 306:19
naked piping loud, 353:6
Helpmeet, make him an h., 5:14
Helps, art h. old ladies across street, 824:12
fortune h. the brave, 86:13
God h. them that help selves, 302:15
God h. those who get up early, 898:5
Hemisphere, extend system to this h., 355:7
Hemispheres, where find two better h., 228:8
Hemlock I had drunk, 410:2
snow from h. tree, 623:5
Hemlocks, murmuring pines and h., 436:20
Hemmed, since I have h. thee here, 171:9
Hemp, molders h. and steel, 374:8
Hempen, sing in a h. string, 236:6
Hen, as h. gathereth chickens, 35:18
cackles as if laid asteroid, 524:9
egg's way of making egg, 521:4

Hen *(continued)*

eggs do not teach h., 897:12
homely h. lays one, 886:4
laid an egg, 654:4
marsh h. secretly builds, 543:2
my black h., 895:13
my white h., 895:*n*1
two owls and h., 467:3
Hence all you vain delights, 236:9
endure their going h., 213:7
horrible shadow, 216:21
loathed Melancholy, 250:19
stay far h. you prudes, 102:1
these tears, 85:14
vain deluding joys, 251:10
with denial vain, 253:2
Henna hackles halt, 640:23
Henpecked, fraternity of h., 288:17
you all, 397:19
Henroosts, defend ourselves and h., 475:26
Henry, never did H. end anyone, 773:9
pried open for all to see, 773:6
unappeasable H. sulked, 773:5
Hens, milk-white H. of Dorking, 467:16
Hent, merrily h. the stile-a, 223:24
Heraclitus, told me H. dead, 499:9
your death H., 83:1
Herald, hark the h. angels sing, 305:10
Homer h. of your glory, 80:21
lark h. of the morn, 181:1
Morning Star h. of dawn, 87:4
owl night's h., 171:12
silence perfectest h. of joy, 190:28
station like h. Mercury, 201:5
three years we waited for h., 727:1
Herald Square, remember me to H., 634:11
Heraldry, boast of h., 315:18
new h. hands not hearts, 209:21
Herb, dew bespangling h. and tree, 241:11
Herba, latet anguis in h., 92:*n*15
Herbs and trees flourish in May, 138:9
better is a dinner of h., 20:32
bitter h., 7:39
Medea gathered enchanted h., 186:14
men with h. to smoke, 139:9
of every joyous kind, 118:21
Hercules and Goth bequeathed us, 535:7
behind Gates of H., 539:14
from the foot H., 69:15
let H. do what he may, 202:22
not H. but Superman, 831:3
snakes beside cradle of H., 502:2
Herd, avoid reeking h., 666:4
groups individuals lack h. sense, 667:5
hate the common h., 96:25
Hesperus you h. homeward, 56:11
imitators you slavish h., 98:11
lowing h. wind slowly, 315:11
of elephant traveling, 662:5
ran into sea, 36:32
Herds, flocks or h. or human face, 257:6
Herdsman, God the h. goads, 590:23
Herdsmen, bad h. ruin flocks, 53:25
Here a little child I stand, 241:15
a little there a little, 26:7
am I, 10:34
am I send me, 25:11
and h. I am, 814:9

Here *(continued)*
  and now cease to matter, 679:2
  and now is happiness, 656:5
  but I'm h., 860:10
  Comes Everybody, 650:20
  comes the trout, 205:6
  from h. to Eternity, 588:6
  gone h. and there, 222:13
  he lies where he longed, 555:16
  I am and here I stay, 439:2
  I have been h. before, 506:8
  I stand, 143:14
  is God's plenty, 274:26
  is my space, 218:3
  is no water, 676:15
  it can't happen h., 664:8
  just for saying, 632:3
  Lafayette we are h., 576:10
  lies a King that ruled, 245:13
  lies lady of beauty, 681:20
  lies my wife let her lie, 275:1
  lies W. C. Fields, 644:3
  no intelligent life down h., 888:19
  reason can decide nothing h., 269:17
  rests his head, 316:6
  today gone tomorrow, 279:9
  where wind north-northeast, 606:2
  where world is quiet, 530:15
Hereafter, she should have died h., 217:23
  what is love 'tis not h., 204:26
  what may come h., 530:16
Hereditary, virtue is not h., 333:4
Here's looking at you kid, 758:5
Heresies, truths begin as h., 502:13
Heresy, no h. so abhorrent, 650:6
  overcome h. with fire, 143:13
Heretic that makes the fire, 223:16
  they will proclaim me h., 141:12
Heritage, I have a goodly h., 15:12
  of woe, 396:29
  proud of ancient h., 785:10
  what thou lovest thy true h., 665:13
  youth's h., 462:17
Hermeneutics, in place of a h. we need,
    835:15
Hermit crab whale's backbone, 679:4
  dwell a weeping h., 317:11
  old h. of Prague, 205:26
  poor in place obscure, 159:2
  shall I like a h. dwell, 159:12
Hermitage, give palace for h., 177:12
  take that for h., 266:2
Hern, coot and h., 454:24
Hero, A H. of Our Time, 469:16
  basic of books labor, 603:1
  conquering h. comes, 301:13
  Conqueror Worm, 448:15
  every h. becomes bore, 427:27
  killed h. in man, 742:16
  millions of murders makes h., 683:15
  must drink brandy, 310:24
  of course Alexander h., 442:20
  perish or sparrow fall, 294:18
  show me a h., 710:18
  to his valet, 249:8
  Truth h. of my tale, 506:10
  unhappy land that needs h., 716:12
  working class h., 848:2

Herod, born in the days of H., 31:36
  out-herods H., 200:6
  Salome pleased H., 34:23
  should not return to H., 31:37
Herodias, daughter of H. danced, 34:23
Heroes as well as idealists, 538:7
  blood of our h., 337:12
  hail ye h., 367:19
  hand in hand with my h., 442:23
  if we will, 494:11
  many valiant souls of h., 50:9
  peers h. of old, 462:25
  seeds of patriots and h., 321:*n*2
  statesmen philosophers, 340:14
  thanks to our fallen h., 769:10
  thin red h., 587:16
  thin red line of h., 489:*n*4
  world's brave h., 883:13
Heroic decision not from cowards, 684:9
  for earth too hard, 462:11
  little monkey, 440:12
  poem a biography, 407:14
  systematically h., 540:21
  womanhood, 437:11
Heroically mad, 273:7
Heroism, dandyism last spark of h., 491:13
  feels never reasons, 427:12
  vices fathered by h., 675:23
Héros pour les valets de chambre, 249:*n*1
Herring, fish nor flesh nor good red h., 147:15
Herrings, not stored in barrel like salt h., 769:8
  red h., 893:1
Herself, show me someone not full of h., 856:8
Herz, mein H. ist schwer, 344:*n*3
  und wenn das H. auch bricht, 414:*n*6
Hesiod, Homer and H. attributed to gods,
    60:4
  might have kept his breath, 55:5
  taught H. beauteous song, 54:11
Hesitate and falter life away, 495:15
  dislike, 295:13
Hesitation, wager without h. that He is, 269:17
Hesper loves to lead home, 575:19
Hesperian, apple-bearing H. coast, 68:3
Hesperides, we shall find H., 662:14
Hesperus entreats thy light, 232:2
  it was schooner H., 436:8
  that led the starry host, 257:25
  you herd homeward, 56:11
Hessians, yonder are the H., 323:11
Hew, not h. as carcass, 192:4
  somebody to h. and hack, 262:12
Hewers of wood, 10:2
Hewing wood for master carpenter, 58:4
Hewn on Norwegian hills, 255:16
  tree is h. down, 32:8
  wisdom hath h. out her seven pillars,
    20:7
Hexameter, in the h. rises, 378:2
Hey for boot and horse, 481:7
  ho the wind and the rain, 205:29,
    211:31
  Mr. Tambourine Man, 851:12
  nonino, 196:2
Heyday in the blood is tame, 201:6
Hi, answer to H. or loud cry, 517:1
  ni ya behold man of flint, 891:19
Hibernated in my past, 643:20

Hic est enim calix Sanguinis mei, 47:25
  jacet Arthurus rex quondam rexque
    futurus, 138:16
  narrow words H., 159:15
Hick, sticks nix h. pix, 725:10
Hickety pickety, 895:13
Hickory, clothes on h. limb, 887:17
  dickory dock, 893:3
Hid, city set on hill cannot be h., 32:16
  fiend h. in a cloud, 353:6
  half as well as he did, 528:3
  hallowed relics h., 250:15
  he run and h., 833:16
  himself among women, 248:27
  I h. behind a tree, 814:9
  I h. from Him, 576:13
  in heart of love, 591:3
  in her interlunar cave, 260:10
  love and a cough cannot be h., 243:14
  Moses h. his face, 7:27
  Nature and Nature's laws h., 296:23
  there is nothing h. from the heat, 15:16
  wheat h. in two bushels of chaff, 184:10
  wherefore these things h., 204:16
  which is to keep that h., 228:12
Hidden, America of poverty is h., 819:1
  beauties commonly greatest, 301:7
  cause h. result well known, 102:13
  growths in mind, 480:14
  half h. from the eye, 369:7
  he who lives well lives h., 102:23
  investigation of h. causes, 155:7
  lived faithfully a h. life, 480:22
  motion of h. fire, 372:19
  nature often h., 166:11
  noise like h. brook, 376:19
  player on other side h., 502:5
  reveal what should remain h., 821:6
  something h. behind things, 638:9
  something h. go and find, 589:21
  treasures, 472:8
  try to speak h. self, 495:12
Hide, everyone has something to h., 578:13
  furred gowns h. all, 212:30
  he can run but can't h., 775:4
  head under his wing, 895:5
  it under his tongue, 13:41
  let me h. myself in thee, 334:13
  lies to h. it, 242:*n*4
  me O my Savior, 305:8
  me under the shadow of thy wings, 15:13
  nature wont to h. herself, 62:2
  one talent death to h., 254:20
  owest beast no h., 212:3
  rude stream that must forever h. me, 225:25
  shame from every eye, 322:17
  stars h. their diminish'd heads, 257:11
  their diminish'd heads, 257:11
  those hills of snow, 207:*n*2
  thou wear lion's h., 175:14
  thyself for a little moment, 26:5
  tiger's heart in player's h., 164:3
  tiger's heart in woman's h., 170:19
  us from each other's sight, 241:17
  what false heart know, 215:8
  what may man within h., 207:7
  world to h. virtues in, 204:17
  your diminished rays, 257:*n*3

Hideous, making night h., 197:34
　　more h. in a child, 211:10
　　notes of woe, 399:4
　　phantasma or h. dream, 192:2
　　ruin and combustion, 255:7
　　vice a creature of h. mien, 600:9
Hides, death fact Nature h., 512:11
　　glare surrounds king h. him, 153:14
　　God h. in smallest pieces, 887:*n6*
　　night that h. things from us, 130:11
　　not visage from cottage, 223:32
　　one thing speaks another, 51:18
　　smiling face, 326:10
　　what plighted cunning h., 210:31
Hidest, why h. thou thy face from me, 17:22
Hiding, dark and lonely h. place, 377:16
　　place from the wind, 26:15
Hier stehe ich ich kann nicht anders, 143:*n4*
Hierarchies, old h. of whales, 663:21
Hierarchy, authority h. and domination, 817:16
　　in h. employee tends to rise, 793:7
Hierophants of inspiration, 404:15
Hies to his confine, 196:18
Higgledy-piggledy my white hen, 895:*n1*
High and boastful neighs, 189:18
　　and low rich and poor, 364:4
　　and palmy state of Rome, 196:15
　　art and pure science, 723:12
　　as my heart, 195:14
　　as the heaven is h., 18:6
　　backwards and in h. heels, 834:16
　　be yours to hold torch h., 614:7
　　birth vigor of bone, 203:25
　　cannot be heard so h., 212:24
　　characters cries one, 261:4
　　corn h. as elephant's eye, 706:9
　　crimes and misdemeanors, 339:12
　　death makes equal h. and low, 146:10
　　diddle diddle, 893:16
　　earth and h. heaven, 575:7
　　for contempt too h., 265:6
　　full of h. sentence, 675:4
　　gale of life h., 575:4
　　get h. with a little help, 848:13
　　hew not too h., 880:9
　　how h. that highest candle, 642:14
　　in azure steeps, 719:19
　　in heavens' h. bower, 351:6
　　in people's hearts, 191:34
　　instincts, 371:1
　　killed calf in h. style, 270:12
　　know how h. we are, 510:12
　　man aiming at million, 461:15
　　mountains are a feeling, 395:21
　　no bird soars too h., 351:13
　　no higher than soul h., 695:6
　　object strange and h., 267:3
　　office teaches decision-making, 802:12
　　on throne of royal state, 256:6
　　road that leads to England, 309:3
　　Roman fashion, 219:6
　　shore of world, 189:23
　　shores of H. Barbaree, 898:1
　　soar not too h. to fall, 237:16
　　spacious firmament on h., 287:20
　　spiritual wickedness in h. places, 43:40
　　that proved too high, 462:11

High *(continued)*
　　thinking, 370:4
　　thoughts must have high language, 73:16
　　wall must be kept h., 666:16
　　where he got that h. brow, 109:7
　　ye'll tak' the h. road, 884:13
High-blown pride broke under me, 225:25
High school, all the crap I learned in h., 855:11
Higher, draw powers into h. classes, 338:17
　　move h. and h., 831:6
　　no h. than soul high, 695:6
　　rock that is h. than I, 17:3
　　than the sphery chime, 252:28
High-erected thoughts, 162:12
Highest, dispose of h. Wisdom, 260:26
　　Epicurus set forth h. good, 90:21
　　glory to God in h., 37:18, 47:22
　　good, 88:6, 90:*n7*
　　in h. position least freedom, 92:7
　　people's good the h. law, 88:10
　　point not Knowledge, 656:7
　　point of my greatness, 225:23
　　stand on h. pavement, 675:13
　　this is the very h. of all, 76:12
Highland, between lowland and h., 530:25
　　heart is H., 417:4
　　my sweet H. Mary, 358:12
Highlands, farewell to the H., 357:14
　　my heart's in the H., 357:15
　　ye H. and Lawlands, 890:7
Highness', I am his H. dog, 296:22
Highnesses, as their h. traveled, 317:2
Highway, broad h. of world, 403:11
　　I traveled each and ev'ry h., 849:11
　　make straight a h. for our God, 26:24
　　novel a mirror that strolls along h., 392:5
　　pull of the blue h., 846:1
　　quietly along king's h., 313:21
Highwayman came riding, 646:1
Highways, happy h. where I went, 575:6
Hi-hi-yee, 639:3
Hill, all all sleeping on h., 605:3
　　and house live together, 606:5
　　ascend into the h. of the Lord, 15:24
　　below the kirk below the h., 375:20
　　city set on an h., 32:16
　　city upon a h., 239:16
　　cloud-topped h., 294:20
　　dancers all gone under h., 678:18
　　flung us on windy h., 669:5
　　haven under h., 452:15
　　heaven-kissing h., 201:5
　　high Dunsinane h., 216:34
　　house should be of h., 606:5
　　hunter home from h., 555:16
　　hunts on lonely h., 562:1
　　is this the h., 376:22
　　Jack and Jill went up h., 893:18
　　King of France up h., 892:14
　　laughing heard on h., 351:7
　　like snow on craggy h., 231:20
　　lived under a h., 896:11
　　over h. over dale, 178:10
　　Pillicock h., 212:1
　　round it was upon a h., 641:2
　　ruin decay in House on H., 605:17
　　shall be made low, 26:25
　　some liken fame to climbing up h., 398:7

Hill *(continued)*
　　they call you Shepherd from the h., 495:14
　　vineyard in a very fruitful h., 25:3
　　who shall dwell in thy holy h., 15:10
　　yon high eastern h., 196:20
Hills, alter when H. do, 509:18
　　and valleys dales and fields, 168:*n1*
　　army stretched out on h., 608:12
　　as old as h., 374:14
　　blue remembered h., 575:6
　　brown h. melted into spring, 476:11
　　cattle upon thousand h., 16:29
　　empty h., 122:4
　　everlasting h., 7:21
　　far-off h. mirrored, 361:14
　　fight in the h., 619:14
　　great shout upon h., 557:7
　　hewn on Norwegian h., 255:16
　　hide h. of snow, 207:*n2*
　　if those h. be dry, 171:9
　　Israel scattered upon the h., 12:9
　　lift up mine eyes unto the h., 18:30
　　little h. like lambs, 18:21
　　ocean of h. and hollows, 83:3
　　o'er h. and far away, 452:12
　　o'er vales and h., 371:9
　　of Chankly Bore, 468:3
　　of Habersham, 543:3
　　of Highlands, 357:14
　　of home, 556:9
　　of Maryland, 438:12
　　out of h. thou mayest dig brass, 9:20
　　over h. and everywhere, 898:17
　　over h. and far away, 291:17, 894:10
　　reverberate h., 204:22
　　rock-ribbed and ancient, 405:12
　　shine forth upon clouded h., 354:8
　　snow on treeless h., 650:9
　　strength of h. is his, 17:32, 48:7
　　vales woodland plain, 293:14
　　valleys groves h. fields, 168:4
　　whose heads touch heaven, 208:1
　　ye too changed ye h., 496:12
Hillside's dew-pearled, 459:19
Hilltops, o'er all the h. is quiet, 344:19
Him first him last, 258:15
　　President's spouse I wish h. well, 807:14
Himself, black man not by h., 808:18
　　ech man for h., 134:12
　　every man for h., 148:24
　　got the better of h., 158:10
　　he h. said it, 120:30, 526:3
　　his mother his wife or h., 382:24
　　into h. Eternity changed him, 543:7
　　knows universe not h., 266:15
　　lives unto h., 241:21
　　lord of h., 227:11, 396:29
　　man count on no one but h., 742:22
　　man lost nothing if he has h., 152:10
　　master of h., 237:17
　　no man born unto h., 241:21
　　no man dieth to h., 42:2
　　no man wise by h., 84:1
　　none liveth to h., 42:2
　　savage he who saves h., 140:8
　　special people unto h., 9:17
　　witness against h., 340:4

Holy *(continued)*
in those h. fields, 181:19
Lamb of God, 354:8
Land of Ireland, 880:*n*2
land of Irlonde, 880:7
land of Walsinghame, 159:3
let him be h. still, 47:14
Mother Earth, 63:20, 891:9
mouth of h. prophets, 37:14
my h. mountain, 25:19
my h. of holies, 578:3
neither h. nor Roman, 299:7
odd old ends stolen of h. writ, 171:25
pebbles of h. streams, 777:12
place whereon thou standest is h. ground, 7:26
places of private universe, 750:9
proofs of h. writ, 209:10
remember sabbath to keep it h., 8:13
revered h. simplicity, 115:15
Roman Empire, 299:7
sages once did sing, 250:9
shall come again win H. Cross, 138:16
silent night h. night, 401:5
simplicity, 137:1
stand in his h. place, 15:24
take not thy h. spirit from me, 16:33
temple of God is h., 42:10
text of pike and gun, 262:10
things h. profane clean obscene, 239:8
time quiet as nun, 370:5
tradition becomes h., 547:13
what is gold doing in h. place, 105:13
where sorrow h. ground, 561:6
who shall dwell in thy h. hill, 15:10
Holy Ghost, communion of H., 43:25
conceived by the H., 48:11
Father Son and H., 36:23, 278:8
filled with H., 40:15
glory be to the H., 48:8
I believe in the H., 48:11
incarnate by the H., 48:12
whether there be any H., 40:38
Holystone decks scrape cable, 470:13
Homage, lesser stars do h., 60:18
owes no h. unto sun, 248:19
vice pays to virtue, 264:12
won by lavish h., 388:6
Homard a l'Américaine, 616:4
Home, about h. and run, 772:14
afraid to go h. in dark, 582:*n*2
again jiggety-jig, 896:9
all the way h., 893:10
and being washing-day, 277:16
art gone and ta'en wages, 220:26
artist no h. save Paris, 549:8
best be getting h. he said, 517:10
best country is at h., 321:13
better h. a-waiting in sky, 689:8
call cattle h., 481:4
charity begins at h., 85:16, 248:15
Christmas, 601:7
come h. to roost, 381:14
coming for to carry me h., 898:21
daddy left h., 833:16
dunce kept at h., 326:11
eaten out of house and h., 188:3
father come h. with me, 517:12

Home *(continued)*
fear encamps around h., 404:21
fly away h., 893:2
give you husband and h., 53:3
go h. in dark, 582:4
God who is our h., 370:17
Good Morning Midnight coming H., 509:3
harvest-h., 181:35, 456:9
hate to be unquiet at h., 277:26
Hesper loves to lead h., 575:19
hills of h., 556:9
his footsteps turned, 373:3
homely features to keep h., 252:25
homely h. simple pleasures, 576:6
hotel refuge from h. life, 565:1
house is not a h., 724:10
how can tyrants govern h., 170:29
hunter h. from hill, 555:16
I am far from h., 421:4
I came h. forever, 383:15
I keep Sabbath staying at H., 508:18
I'm going h., 424:1
in minds of men, 72:4
in our own beloved h., 489:8
is home, 400:*n*3
is not a place, 804:11
is on the deep, 384:9
is safest refuge, 158:*n*7
is so sad, 799:8
is the sailor, 555:16
is where one starts from, 679:1
it was his rightful h., 805:8
Jerusalem happy h., 881:18
knock as you please nobody h., 294:11
longest way round shortest h., 242:*n*2
lost that love or h., 841:2
made of blue clouds, 891:15
make house h., 647:8
man goeth his long h., 23:31
merriest when from h., 188:37
my h. sweet h., 673:11
my songs draw Daphnis h., 93:1
Naiad airs brought h., 447:12
never change when love has found h., 101:12
never felt myself from h., 334:4
no h. like raft, 523:4
no place like h., 400:16, 562:4
of bean and cod, 577:15
of lost causes, 496:8
of love, 222:12
of the brave, 386:19
of wild mirth, 430:25
old Kentucky h., 503:13
our eternal h., 289:12
outlives day and comes safe h., 189:26
Paris my h. town, 628:6
place they have to take you in, 622:14
pleasure never at h., 411:3
returned h. previous night, 618:1
seek fortunes further than h., 173:8
send h. my long strayed eyes, 229:10
shall men come, 618:14
show piety at h., 44:30
sick for h., 410:10
song of h. and friends, 520:1
stayed h. and baked cookies, 864:4

Home *(continued)*
stranger has h. in arms, 691:18
sweet h. Alabama, 867:10
tavern for friends, 601:13
they'll come h., 895:2
things foreign or things at h., 271:16
this pig stayed h., 893:10
till boys come h., 616:17
till the cow comes h., 238:3
to a lie, 665:8
to my Lord and be free, 899:1
toddle safely h., 668:13
turns again h., 456:4
welcome h. discarded faith, 176:1
what does it leave at h., 470:1
what is more agreeable than h., 87:23
when you knock it never is h., 326:13
where buffalo roam, 890:20
wherever that may be, 762:18
with no direction h., 851:14
Wyoming will be your new h., 890:11
Home-keeping youth homely wits, 173:27
Homeland of patience, 429:16
where happy there's h., 121:21
wherever he prospers, 73:20
who no longer has h., 733:11
Homeless, job is home to h. man, 747:1
near thousand homes, 368:1
tempest-tost, 552:16
Homely beauty of good old cause, 370:4
conversational or h. type, 607:2
definitions, 380:3
features to keep home, 252:25
hen lays one, 886:4
home be it never so h., 400:*n*3
home simple pleasures, 576:6
home-keeping youth h. wits, 173:27
joys, 315:17
men who charmed women, 581:15
person attract by charm, 667:4
slighted shepherd's trade, 253:6
wink at h. girl, 645:7
Homemade but aren't we all, 763:4
Homer and Hesiod attributed to the gods, 60:4
and Whitman roared in pines, 605:5
deep-browed H. ruled as demesne, 408:17
even good old H. nods, 98:30
found H. herald of your glory, 80:21
is my example, 595:16
learned root of H., 233:*n*3
liken H. to setting sun, 107:3
living H. begged bread, 233:*n*3
nods, 98:30, 292:11
our poets steal from H., 234:8
there were poets before H., 87:19
think of Bible and H., 628:10
translator of H., 496:1
warred for H. being dead, 233:19
with single exception of H., 565:15
Homerus, quandoque dormitat H., 98:*n*13
Home's, way h. the farthest way, 242:4
Homes, homeless near thousand h., 368:1
introduce philosophy into h., 88:5
protect health h. firesides, 554:5
shut-in h. closed doors, 604:7
stately h. of England, 405:7, 654:6
think of firelit h., 668:12

Hopes *(continued)*
of future years, 436:23
remnants of childhood h. of adulthood, 730:6
shadowy shared h., 861:2
stirred up with high h., 254:4
tender leaves is h., 225:25
that resemble regrets, 479:6
that St. Nicholas, 387:2
vanity of human h., 306:22
wholly h. to be, 462:20
Hoping, trembling h. lingering, 293:2
Hopkins, Mark H. on one end, 512:15
Hopping, meager shriveled h., 325:7
through frothy waves, 516:3
Horace, studied spontaneity of H., 105:24
Horatii curiosa felicitas, 105:*n*11
Horatio, I knew him H., 202:12
in my mind's eye H., 197:8
more things in heaven H., 198:19
speak to it H., 196:11
thrift thrift H., 197:7
to what base uses we may return H., 202:13
Horde, society one polished h., 399:2
Horizon, dusk on eastern h., 704:14
of his homing, 679:9
our h. never at our elbows, 475:8
Horizon's edge, 487:19
Horizontal one, 748:4
Horn, barter that h., 593:17
beetle winds sullen h., 317:13
blow wreathed h., 371:24
come blow h., 893:11
cow with crumpled h., 897:8
Dinah blow your h., 884:22
gate of h., 54:6, 95:2
God winding lonely h., 591:10
gray-fly winds sultry h., 253:3
hand on h., 890:13
honey in the h., 884:17
hounds and h., 251:1
huntsman winds his h., 304:11
lusty h., 195:31
mouth of Plenty's h., 593:17
of hunter on hill, 419:5
one blast upon bugle h., 374:4
Roland sound your h., 124:2
sound of h. at night, 416:4
sound upon bugle h., 451:20
with his hounds and h., 408:13
Horned Moon with one bright star, 376:11
Horner, little Jack H., 892:19
Hornets, bees for flies and h. for bees, 143:15
cobwebs let h. through, 284:6
Horns, hang caps on h. o' the moon, 219:21
like Kyloe cow, 894:5
of Elfland, 452:20
of my dilemma, 314:14
sound of h. and motors, 676:11
Horny hands of toil, 481:8
Horresco referens, 94:*n*5
Horrible, hence h. shadow, 216:21
imaginings, 214:11
that lust and rage, 596:17
voice, 72:12
Horribly, I will h. revenge, 190:4
stuffed with epithets of war, 207:20

Horrid, blow h. deed in every eye, 214:24
dream h. dreams, 483:12
hideous notes of woe, 399:4
image doth unfix hair, 214:11
life demd h. grind, 464:24
shapes and shrieks, 250:19
when bad she was h., 438:2
Horridly to shake our disposition, 197:34
Horrify, I will try to h., 865:2
Horror fell upon Christian, 271:22
grades of incredible h., 537:8
irony seldom absent, 687:9
no effect on me as h., 397:16
lived through this h., 660:7
of bourgeois is bourgeois, 585:9
of outer darkness, 517:15
of that moment, 515:11
of Twentieth Century, 803:9
screams of h. rend, 293:12
soul of plot, 448:14
the h. the h., 567:17
this h. is ours, 761:5
universal h. unbend, 648:5
Horror's, on h. head horrors, 209:16
Horrors accumulate, 209:16
congenial h. hail, 300:15
of half known life, 483:5
sunset stained with mystic h., 559:1
supped full with h., 217:22
waked by h. in night, 347:11
Horrorshow, shut her up h. and lovely, 783:15
Horse stood near stable door, 881:*n*3
a dog a h. a rat, 213:14
and his rider hath he thrown, 8:4
bean-fed h. beguile, 178:12
beggars mounted run h. to death, 170:18
body my h. my hound, 772:10
boot saddle to h. and away, 460:5
brewer's h., 183:7
bring h. to water, 147:24
call me h., 182:21
cart before h., 148:16
dark h., 429:20
dearer than his h., 451:22
death on his pale h., 259:20
difference of opinion makes h.-races, 524:4
ego's relation to id as rider to h., 563:18
fine lady upon white h., 894:9
flung himself on h., 605:2
foot an' artillery, 660:5
for want of h. rider lost, 244:8, 303:3
for want of shoe h. lost, 244:8, 303:3
give me another h., 172:7
great h. of gold, 701:4
guide h. along path it wants to go, 563:18
happy h. to bear Antony, 218:11
hast thou given the h. strength, 14:26
hey for boot and h., 481:7
horsewhip you if had a h., 659:13
I am not so poor a h., 446:8
in silence champed, 616:6
in the mountain, 717:2
knows the way, 421:17
leene as is a rake, 133:22
love and marriage like h. and carriage, 769:11
more rational than infant, 342:6
must think it queer, 623:7

Horse *(continued)*
my h. my wife my name, 429:13
my kingdom for a h., 172:11
nation, 891:11
never look gift h. in mouth, 115:24
noblest conquest of man, 304:4
nothing but talk of his h., 184:16
O for a h. with wings, 220:18
of different color, 204:*n*2
of our courage, 798:2
of that color, 204:31
old h. stumbles and nods, 536:22
pale h., 46:32, 259:20
philosophy a good h., 322:18
shoe the h., 897:5
sits on h. at hostess' door, 175:8
uses folly like stalking h., 196:8
when h. stolen fool shuts stable, 147:*n*6
Horseback, beggar on h., 170:*n*1
beggar upon h., 596:16
man on h., 885:11
on h. through dreary tract, 448:8
Horsed upon sightless couriers, 214:24
Horseman pass by, 597:11
Horsemanship, forgetful of his h., 52:3
witch world with noble h., 183:14
Horsemen, chariot and h. of Israel, 12:12
Horsemill, desire a h., 234:21
Horse's, 'ear h. legs, 455:25
trusts in h. health, 212:10
Horses, all the king's h., 895:1
and poets not overfed, 158:20
as fed h. in the morning, 27:24
black are the h., 717:4
carriages without h. go, 882:12
chariot and h. of fire, 12:11
don't do it and frighten h., 586:10
England hell of h., 161:11
handling of blooded h., 493:11
heaven in which no h., 557:2
if cattle and h. had hands, 60:5
if wishes were h., 271:2
more careful of breed of h. than children, 280:10
not swap h., 446:8
oats in England given to h., 307:4
of instruction, 351:17
price of thousand h., 611:11
run slowly h. of night, 101:24
slowly run O h. of night, 169:4
they shoot h. don't they, 715:1
they tend, 468:19
watered our h. in Helicon, 164:1
which h. bear him best, 169:15
wild white h. play, 494:12
women h. economic factors in society, 579:1
would draw gods like horses, 60:5
Horses' heels over paying, 677:21
Horseshoes, laws flung like h., 690:14
Horsewhip, I'd h. you if had a horse, 659:13
Hose, washed me out of turret with h., 774:14
youthful h. well saved, 194:25
Hospitable, in peace generous h., 400:7
on h. thoughts intent, 258:17
Hospital, first requirement in H., 489:6
road to contagious h., 658:9
this life is a h., 491:14

Hospital *(continued)*
   tray of narcotics, 766:8
   world not inn but h., 248:18
Hospitality, given to h., 41:32
Host, Hesperus led starry h., 257:25
   many an old h. damned, 182:28
   of golden daffodils, 371:9
   praise Him heavenly h., 278:8
   though an h. should encamp, 15:28
   tie of h. and guest, 63:14
   time like fashionable h., 203:24
   with angelic h. proclaim, 305:10
Hostage, you are eternity's h., 688:4
Hostages to fortune, 165:19
Hostel, five or six days same h., 612:21
Hostess', sits on horse at h. door, 175:8
Hostesses make parties as ministers cabinets, 480:24
Hostile, not that it is h., 819:2
Hostilities, victory when opponent surrenders before h., 80:18
Hostility, eternal h. against tyranny, 337:7
   sorrow to disarm h., 437:5
Host's Canary wine, 411:5
Hosts, holy is the Lord of h., 25:9
   Lord God of H., 589:7
   Lord of h. King of glory, 15:26
   of Error, 577:16
Hot and bothered, 590:8
   and cold and moist and dry, 257:*n*1
   and rebellious liquors, 194:4
   as hell, 348:5
   blow h. and cold, 59:11
   boiling-h. days, 488:9
   can one go upon h. coals, 20:3
   cold and h. moist and dry, 273:22
   cold moist and dry, 257:1
   conscience seared with h. iron, 44:27
   cross buns, 894:15
   fair h. wench in taffeta, 181:20
   for certainties, 505:11
   ginger h. i' the mouth, 204:29
   hammer iron when h., 99:23
   heat flow from h. to cold object, 497:*n*1
   I would thou wert cold or h., 46:26
   in my h. youth, 97:6
   Just Add H. Water, 701:9
   little pot and soon h., 173:18
   my heart was h. within me, 16:16
   neither cold nor h., 46:26
   pease-porridge h., 894:16
   sleep is cold for the h., 158:8
   snake came on h. h. day, 663:6
   so h. that it singe yourself, 225:12
   stink of fox, 827:11
   temper leaps over, 184:15
   time in old town tonight, 585:5
   w'en stew smokin' h., 613:15
   when iron is h. strike, 99:*n*13
   why sea boiling h., 516:4
   your wit's too h., 174:10
Hotel, back to h. in rain, 721:9
   born in goddam h. room dying in h. room, 681:12
   Heartbreak H., 840:12
   instead of hymns, 642:11
   queen of this summer h., 820:8
   refuge from home life, 565:1

Hotel *(continued)*
   smoke-filled room in h., 578:17
   terrible strange-looking h., 805:8
Hothouse, no h. flowers, 658:4
Hotness, day in its h., 495:9
Hotspur of the North, 182:17
Hotter, pass from colder to h., 497:23
Hound dog cryin' all the time, 834:6
   footprints of gigantic h., 573:19
   hold with hare run with h., 147:14
   mongrel puppy whelp h., 322:13
   my horse my h., 772:10
   single H., 510:1
Hounds and horn, 251:1
   carcass fit for h., 192:4
   join in glorious cry, 304:11
   moon men and barking h., 704:16
   noise like questing of thirty h., 138:3
   of spring, 529:12
   such h. such hawks, 890:5
   with his h. and horn, 408:13
Hour before dawn silent, 635:3
   books of the h., 484:16
   childhood's h., 388:3, 447:10
   Children's H., 437:12
   cometh and now is, 39:13
   crowded h. of glorious life, 326:1
   dark h. or twain, 216:4
   destined H., 441:12
   eternity in an h., 353:14
   every h. a miracle, 488:1
   every h. that passes O, 356:21
   fall that very h., 205:1
   fluster of h. badly spent, 763:7
   for one short h. see, 455:4
   from h. to h. we ripe, 194:16
   had I died h. before, 215:30
   happiest day happiest h., 447:9
   hazard of doubtful h., 183:11
   I have had my h., 273:18
   I was born, 884:17
   improve each shining h., 289:8
   inevitable h., 315:18
   is at hand, 36:7
   is not yet come, 39:3
   its h. come round at last, 593:10
   last h. of my life, 301:5
   laugh an h. by his dial, 194:17
   lengthy cocktail h., 827:7
   living at this h., 370:9
   look on you when last h. comes, 101:19
   Lord through this h., 887:15
   matched us with His h., 669:11
   met me in evil h., 356:17
   more desirable than fortunate h., 91:20
   nighing his h., 575:18
   not an h. more or less, 213:5
   not showpiece of an h., 71:12
   nothing can bring back h., 371:4
   now's the h., 358:16
   of departure has arrived, 74:11
   of thoughtless youth, 368:11
   one bare h. to live, 169:3
   one dead deathless h., 506:4
   rash hand in evil h., 259:11
   ripe, 188:23
   serve the future h., 372:11
   stay longer in h., 529:5

Hour *(continued)*
   struts and frets his h., 217:23
   takes away things, 310:11
   that turns back longing of seafarers, 129:18
   the wished the trysted h., 358:15
   this was their finest h., 619:15
   thou the day I the h., 526:16
   time and the h., 214:13
   two hundred fifty words every quarter h., 472:5
   uncertain h. before morning, 679:9
   violet h., 676:12
   watch with me one h., 36:6
   wherein man might be happy, 244:28
   who drowsy at that h., 249:7
   wonder of an h., 395:6
Hour's, never spent h. talk withal, 174:9
   sleep before midnight, 244:22
Hours and minutes dollars cents, 303:*n*1
   arrest your course, 400:14
   better three h. too soon, 187:10
   creeping h. of time, 194:22
   entertain lag-end with quiet h., 183:21
   few h. more agreeable than tea, 544:5
   golden h. on angel wings, 358:12
   his brief h. and weeks, 222:15
   I once enjoyed, 326:8
   life short quiet h. few, 484:15
   mournful midnight h., 342:14
   nor h. days months, 228:16
   redeem these h., 233:17
   seven h. to law, 159:*n*1
   six h. in sleep, 159:1
   sixteen h. ago Hiroshima, 661:3
   sorrow breaks reposing h., 171:30
   steal h. from night, 387:13
   success unexpected in common h., 475:19
   sweetest h. e'er I spend, 356:23
   three h. a day what man ought to write, 472:4
   Time in h. days years, 268:14
   to which Heaven doth chime, 269:2
   two golden h., 414:5
   unless h. cups of sack, 181:20
   waked by circling h., 258:22
   weary of days and h., 530:16
   what h. O what black h., 547:7
   Woman in our h. of ease, 373:16
House, a h. no more a h., 624:12
   all the h. of Israel played, 11:13
   all through the h., 387:2
   appointed for all living, 14:8
   bear witness to his piety, 363:7
   blessings on this h., 330:12
   body my h. my horse my hound, 772:10
   built on sand, 33:25
   Bustle in a H. Morning after Death, 510:11
   by the side of the road, 51:10, 569:13
   call upon my soul within the h., 204:21
   chief benefit of the h., 659:10
   child draws inscrutable h., 762:20
   children's h. of make believe, 624:13
   civilized man's h. prison, 472:20
   clergyman so much about h., 521:9
   covet thy neighbor's h., 8:14
   crooked h., 895:17
   daughter in mother's h., 589:6
   daughters of my father's h., 205:5

Hum (*continued*)

> still steeples h., 575:1
> thousand instruments h., 224:33

Human, Adam was but h., 523:16

> all h. life in monkeys and cats, 544:4
> all h. must retrograde, 332:11
> all must love h. form, 351:5
> all right for woman to be h., 735:1
> all that h. hearts endure, 307:14
> as I am if I am, 788:12
> bears stamp of h. condition, 153:11
> being crushed by books, 774:13
> being h. born alone, 666:7
> being more or less, 778:9
> beings are flying overhead, 735:8
> beings are good and evil, 555:14
> beings ever realize life, 715:8
> beings in underground den, 75:11
> beings into machines, 478:3
> beings live and progress, 602:11
> bellyful of classics enemy to h. race, 690:16
> benefit and enjoyment, 324:10
> best work the h. mind, 358:2
> biggest h. ever lived, 720:15
> body best picture of h. soul, 685:12
> body politic like h. body, 312:19
> body sacred, 486:21
> burn books burn h. beings, 415:3
> Chariot that bears H. Soul, 510:14
> city is never more fully h., 865:9
> civilization scarcely h., 609:7
> combination or society, 247:8
> community, 653:12
> condition, 153:11
> conspiracy of h. beings, 598:14
> contrivance of h. wisdom, 325:3
> couple find true form, 751:8
> course of h. events, 336:1
> creatures' lives, 418:11
> crises of h. affairs, 349:15
> Cruelty has h. heart, 353:8
> December 1910 h. character changed, 654:4
> dignity, 862:11
> distances between h. beings, 631:15
> earth's h. shores, 412:10
> engine waits, 676:12
> every h. is archaeological, 873:2
> everything h. pathetic, 524:12
> evil is always h., 748:15
> execution of h. design, 319:11
> face divine, 257:6
> features composed of ten parts, 105:6
> felicity produced by little advantages, 304:2
> field of h. conflict, 619:17
> fighting for h. rights, 808:17
> figure interests me most, 605:10
> Form Display, 354:7
> four essential h. freedoms, 653:4
> free the h. will, 296:21
> fundamental h. rights, 661:16
> future of h. race, 634:5
> greater than h. intelligence, 860:5
> he served h. liberty, 595:8
> health is a h. right, 805:16
> heart by which we live, 371:5
> heart has treasures, 472:8

Human (*continued*)

> hearts to chew, 402:21
> hope springs in h. breast, 294:19
> hum of h. cities, 395:21
> I had no h. fears, 369:8
> identify myself with something h., 774:16
> if h. beings were to disappear, 825:14
> in course of h. nature, 349:9
> in h. life much endured, 307:10
> inextinguishable rights of h. nature, 363:3
> informer poor weak h. being, 712:6
> infringement of h. freedom, 359:7
> intelligence would grace the replay, 852:6
> Jealousy has a h. face, 353:8
> kind not bear much reality, 678:5
> king's might greater than h., 69:22
> knowledge of h. nature, 382:21, 531:15
> life a Mansion, 413:5
> life might be pure freedom, 751:4
> life transient, 580:9
> live in h. imagination, 818:1
> Love the h. form divine, 351:4
> march of h. mind slow, 324:9
> Mercy has a h. heart, 351:4
> milk of h. kindness, 214:16
> more than h. arms, 648:5
> my Treatise of H. Nature, 312:2
> nature finer, 413:3
> nature is such that, 838:4
> nature seeming born again, 368:17
> nature weak in bookstore, 468:7
> no h. being understand another, 738:2
> no h. creature give orders to love, 432:6
> no h. thing of importance, 75:24
> nor h. spark is left, 297:6
> nothing h. is alien, 85:17
> observer of h. nature, 463:20
> on my faithless arm, 748:10
> ought be satisfied with tranquility, 472:10
> Peace the h. dress, 351:4
> Pity has a h. face, 351:4
> position in universe as h. being, 556:17
> power cannot remove, 679:11
> predatory h. hands, 574:6
> primary h. affections, 495:13
> provide for h. wants, 325:3
> questions make us h., 790:16
> race born to fly upward, 129:21
> race has means for annihilating itself, 649:1
> race never have rest from evils, 75:9
> race playing children's games, 618:2
> reason is beautiful, 764:16
> recognition as h. beings, 808:17
> result of h. action, 319:11
> reverence h. nature, 388:8
> rights, 661:16
> rights are women's rights, 864:5
> rights to which committed, 785:10
> ruler having h. body as subject, 74:19
> Secrecy the h. dress, 353:8
> shambles that follows it, 798:12
> so long as h. heart strong, 503:3
> socialism with h. race, 796:5
> solitude at depth of h. condition, 776:2
> species of two races, 383:8
> speech like cracked kettle, 493:13
> stares from every h. face, 749:5
> stories repeating selves, 615:7

Human (*continued*)

> subtlety never devise more than nature, 140:11
> Terror the h. form divine, 353:8
> things subject to decay, 273:13
> thought or form, 401:10
> three words for h. race, 561:16
> till H. nature came, 510:15
> to err is h., 108:15, 120:19, 292:23
> to step aside is h., 357:3
> too profound for h. intellect, 440:7
> understanding is false mirror, 164:20
> vanity of h. hopes, 306:22
> vast empire of h. society, 369:4
> voices wake us, 675:7
> weakness of h. mind, 276:3
> wisdom of h. contrivances, 324:3
> wish I loved h. race, 579:15
> woman behave like full h. being, 838:12
> world began without h. race, 754:1

Humane, heaven and earth are not h., 57:1

Humani nil a me alienum puto, 85:*n*12

Humanité, il n'y a de réel que l'h., 416:*n*3

Humanity, address ourselves not to their h., 318:22

> assumptions of h. over h., 483:14
> can there be any study of h., 730:3
> common h. shall reveal itself, 877:4
> common right of h., 444:12
> exalts delights adorns h., 393:10
> experience fate of h., 627:7
> first thing that h. has built, 874:1
> forehead of h., 409:10
> history life of h., 507:2
> idiom of frightened hopeful h., 740:3
> imitated h. so abominably, 200:9
> justice equity, 324:20
> law of h., 324:20
> nothing real except h., 416:8
> one can't love h., 737:17
> only three days old, 634:5
> robbed of their h., 790:20
> science and art unite h., 809:3
> silence real crime against h., 722:15
> slavery of half of h., 751:8
> still sad music of h., 368:11
> wearisome condition of h., 161:15
> with all its fears, 436:23

Humanized, deep distress hath h. my Soul, 371:19

Humanizes, liberal arts study h., 102:26

Humanizing, power of h. nature, 379:18

Humankind, lords of h. pass by, 322:2

> not bear much reality, 678:5
> of all tyrannies on h., 274:1
> porcelain clay of h., 274:8
> vices and follies of h., 286:24

Humble and hearty thanks, 48:16

> are usually envious, 276:11
> be it ever so h., 400:16
> frowned not on h. birth, 316:6
> help h. and strengthen soul, 150:3
> heyday in blood is h., 201:6
> himself shall be exalted, 35:14
> honor shall uphold the h., 22:11
> if economists thought of as h., 656:16
> livers in content, 225:17
> members of society, 364:3

I

I *(continued)*

can no more, 547:3
can't get no respect, 796:4
cleave wood there am I, 113:19
did cut it with hatchet, 328:*n3*
do it exceptionally well, 833:3
Don't Know's on third, 705:3
even as you and I, 589:5
fashioned myself sorcerer, 559:12
feel it and am in torment, 91:28
get a kick out of you, 691:10
have a dream, 823:7, 823:8
have found it, 83:4
have liberated my soul, 123:12
have not begun to fight, 342:2
have somewhat against thee, 46:20
he was he and I was I, 152:8
hear America singing, 485:14
heir of all ages, 452:9
here am I, 10:34
hid from Him, 576:13
in twelve thousand none, 177:16
infinite I Am, 379:5
is an other, 558:15
it is I, 34:28
John, 46:14
knew him when, 609:12
know not the man, 36:11
know thee not old man, 188:27
letting I dare not, 215:2
longed to see him hanged, 606:14
Lord is it I, 36:1
man in the moon, 179:12
Muses' priest sing, 96:25
myself am hell, 787:16
not basic I that poet is after, 630:12
one alone I am with him, 113:19
reader I married him, 472:11
red I green U, 559:4
rock fly as soon as I, 374:2
said the sparrow, 893:8
say it's spinach, 723:17
says the Quarterly, 399:11
shall return, 644:7
sing of brooks, 240:9
sleep alone, 56:8
stand at the door and knock, 46:27
stranger and afraid, 575:17
struck the board, 242:26
survived, 342:7
the more fool I, 194:7
the sole unbusy thing, 378:14
then Roman now I, 575:4
think therefore I am, 246:9
Tiresias, 676:12
to die and you to live, 74:11
told you so, 399:4
want to be alone, 741:7
wasted time now doth time waste me,
    177:23
went to Taffy's house, 894:1
went to the woods, 474:29
when I am for myself what am I, 102:29
who saw face of God, 168:18
will be good, 485:1
will be heard, 433:5
will move the earth, 83:5
would prefer not to, 483:15

I *(continued)*

yam what I yam that's all I yam, 704:1
you and I are suddenly, 815:4
Iacta alea est, 89:*n1*
Iago, delight in conceiving I., 413:9
    pity of it I., 209:27
Iam ver egelidos refert tepores, 91:*n6*
Iambics, not escape my i., 92:1
    what little i., 605:5
Ibycus, cranes of I., 58:*n2*
Ice age is coming, 871:9
    and iron not be welded, 556:10
    between Eliza and pursuer, 458:13
    caves of i., 377:21, 377:23
    chaste as i., 199:26
    fire and i. within fight, 575:3
    for destruction would suffice, 623:4
    into eternal darkness fire and i., 128:12
    mast-high, 375:23
    on hot stove, 625:5
    seek i. in June, 394:15
    skating over thin i., 427:11
    smooth the i., 175:24
    thick-ribbed i., 206:38
    trust not one night's i., 244:7
    was here ice was there, 375:24
    will burn, 424:6
Ice cream, emperor of i., 640:18
    enjoy i. while it's on plate, 715:11
Iceberg cuts facets from within, 762:12
    in shadowy silent distance grew I., 536:17
Icebergs behoove the soul, 762:13
Icebox, plums that were in the i., 658:19
Iceland, from Rome to I., 278:6
Ich am of Irlonde, 880:7
    bin ein Berliner, 786:13
    grolle nicht, 414:*n6*
    weiss nicht was soll es bedeuten, 415:*n1*
Ichabod, named the child I., 10:37
Icicle, chaste as the i., 220:3
    on Dutchman's beard, 205:17
Icicles, silent i., 377:15
    when i. hang by the wall, 174:33
Icily regular, 454:26
Icumen, sumer is i. in, 880:5
    winter is i. in, 665:2
Icy arms hold hidden charms, 708:6
    bound in i. chains, 207:*n2*
    current compulsive course, 209:20
    death lays i. hand on kings, 246:13
    reason's i. intimations, 418:17
    silence of tomb, 412:1
Id, ego's relation to i. as rider to horse, 563:18
    external world super-ego and i., 563:19
    where i. was ego shall be, 563:20
Idaho, your own private I., 870:2
Idea, a good i., 633:6
    absolute i. of knowledge, 76:1
    abstracted from m. doesn't exist, 737:11
    angry opposition to i., 630:13
    antiquated was once modern, 616:18
    between i. and reality, 677:1
    Christianity is an i., 415:5
    clarity of a general i., 852:7
    dangerous when only one, 601:9
    does not belong to soul, 534:13
    due to individual, 647:7
    every i. an incitement, 539:3

Idea *(continued)*

every new i., 790:4
every thing has determinate i., 76:2
for poetry i. everything, 497:20
give up whole i. of life, 824:14
grant artist his i., 544:10
he has been reborn as an i., 597:14
is the fact, 497:20
is not banal, 778:11
it's the i. behind me Ignatz, 644:4
made true by events, 542:9
nothing more dangerous than i., 601:9
of Freedom, 457:9
of genius, 778:11
of sun, 641:20
of what true and false, 276:1
one i. and that wrong, 309:12
original i. animate nation, 456:15
pain of a new i., 503:6
right i. of the gods, 76:12
see clearly in i. of it, 641:20
sends us back to first i., 642:1
teach young i. to shoot, 300:19
truth happens to i., 542:9
very i. embraces people, 705:4
when i. new custodians have fervor, 580:16
whose time come, 422:8
with image, 379:13
Ideal, cherished i. for which prepared to die,
    790:18
    Christian i. found difficult, 618:8
    higher than ordinary man, 496:3
    I see only the i., 634:2
    Milton attracts into his i., 379:15
    polity, 75:10
    to be right by instinct, 65:24
Idealism, spark of i. fanned, 562:15
Idealists, heroes as well as i., 538:7
Idealize, secondary imagination struggles to i.,
    379:6
Ideals, altars of great historical i., 757:15
    dropped all my i., 822:7
    form which destroys their i., 614:14
    higher i. revolutionary, 541:15
    tell i. by advertisements, 601:12
    two warring i. in body, 602:3
Ideas are intellectual instruments, 468:13
    best i. common property, 103:11
    colorless green i. sleep, 817:15
    dead i. and beliefs, 504:12
    does away with i. of things, 76:2
    free trade in i., 538:22
    greatest artist greatest i., 484:5
    having even slightest importance, 745:8
    hold two opposed i. at same time, 710:12
    I go to bed with i., 557:12
    make best i. prevail, 496:5
    man of nasty i., 284:19
    matter and i., 496:1
    new i. must use old buildings, 782:5
    of mise-en-scène, 820:4
    poem words not i., 543:11
    ruling i. of each age, 478:14
    say it no i. but in things, 658:16
    soldier of i., 811:14
    too revolutionary for old i., 661:4
    won't keep, 580:16
    world of i. world of practice, 496:6

Ill *(continued)*
 things are not so i., 480:22
 things i. got had bad success, 170:22
 to have been born in these times, 568:16
 took i. on Thursday, 895:10
 unquiet meals make i. digestions, 172:27
 weary and i. at ease, 502:16
 weed groweth fast, 147:20
 wind bloweth no man good, 148:21
Ill-advised, quotations i., 570:1
Ill-born, amphibious i. mob, 282:5
Ill-bred as audible laughter, 322:*n*5
 scenes, 582:20
 this age how i., 91:13
Ill-clad, ill-housed i., 652:12
Illegal, immoral i. or fattening, 672:14
 when President does it not i., 771:12
Ill-favored thing but mine own, 196:4
 vile i. faults, 187:13
Ill-housed ill-clad ill-nourished, 652:12
Illiberal as audible laughter, 322:*n*5
Illinois not control feline delinquency, 727:8
Ill-natured, vain i. Englishman, 282:5
Illness is night-side of life, 835:19
 psychoanalysis is mental i., 626:8
 to be too conscious is i., 492:3
 with which smitten, 418:20
Illnesses, benefit from i., 71:5
Ill-nourished, ill-housed ill-clad i., 652:12
Illogical belief in improbable, 645:10
 doctrine so i. and dull, 656:12
Ills, age the harbor of all i., 82:6
 bear those i. we have, 199:21
 flood of mortal i. prevailing, 143:16
 forgetfulness of all i., 52:32
 medicos marveling on i., 681:20
 mighty i. done by woman, 281:11
 no sense of i. to come, 315:6
 scholar's life assail, 306:16
 to hastening i. a prey, 322:22
 we ought to bear, 495:7
 what i. you are free from, 89:20
Ill-seeming, muddy i. thick, 173:25
Ill-spenders, borrowers i., 484:17
Ill-spirit sob in blood cell, 787:16
Ill-tempered and queer, 467:4
Illuminate, Smokey the Bear will i., 828:12
Illuminatio, dominus i. mea, 15:*n*2
Illumination of ignorant, 329:8
Illuminations, bonfires and i., 330:1
Illumine, sunset i. rolling waves, 559:1
 what in me is dark i., 255:5
Illumines, history i. reality, 87:13
Ill-used, hardest knife i., 222:4
Illusion by which cheated, 611:3
 certainty generally i., 538:8
 Clemenceau had one i., 656:9
 in love i. reaches zenith, 548:26
 life is an i., 247:1
 of philosophers, 713:13
 only in i. of freedom freedom exist, 681:15
 religion an i., 564:1
 what I have seen is not an i., 581:8
 world of divine i., 497:20
Illusions, attachment fabricator of i., 760:12
 dupe to i. all one's life, 556:19
 most dangerous calculations we call i., 673:19

Illusions *(continued)*
 natural to indulge in i., 331:10
 poetry purged of i., 612:8
Illusory, reality reveals itself to be i., 601:4
Illustrate all shadows, 231:10
Illustrious acts high raptures infuse, 249:20
 name i. and revered, 106:15
 predecessors, 304:17
Ilych, Ivan I. dying, 507:6
Ilych's, Ivan I. life most simple, 507:5
I'm mad as hell, 801:14
 not a Jew I'm Jew-ish, 838:7
Image, age demanded an i., 665:6
 comparing i. of him in imagination, 507:4
 constant i. of the creature, 204:33
 consumed in i. if not in usage, 778:1
 graven i., 8:11
 his own i. walking in garden, 401:15
 horrid i. doth unfix hair, 214:11
 idea with i., 379:13
 in the i. of God, 6:24
 make man in our i., 5:6
 man is God's i., 242:13
 man's i. and his cry, 591:4
 of Eternity, 396:21
 of his own eternity, 29:33
 of revolution, 4:11
 of splitting apart, 4:10
 of war without guilt, 289:19
 of what we actually see, 533:15
 scorn her own i., 200:8
 speech is i. of actions, 55:15
 that blossoms a rose, 591:9
 thrice tried to clasp her i., 53:11
 time the i. of eternity, 113:1
Images, both i. regard, 242:13
 deposits of accumulated experience, 630:2
 draw from ourselves i., 728:13
 everything is made through i., 348:3
 find mirror in every mind, 307:19
 graven i. of her gods, 25:27
 heap of broken i., 676:6
 more witnesseth than fancy's i., 179:7
 no graven i. worshipped, 479:13
 of beauty, 74:6
 of collective unconscious, 630:2
 on reverse side of eyes, 583:15
 prisoners tattoo, 727:5
 receives i. without absorbing, 531:20
 reflect before throwing i., 684:2
 visual or auditory i., 612:9
 what i. return O my daughter, 677:20
Imaginary gardens with real toads, 671:2
 necessities, 246:18
 relish is so sweet, 203:15
Imagination, a really grasping i., 543:16
 abandoned by Reason, 341:*n*4
 abhorred in my i., 202:12
 Adam's dream, 412:12
 as i. bodies forth, 179:6
 audacity of i., 572:17
 baffled by facts, 620:4
 bare i. of feast, 176:18
 cold and barren, 324:1
 colors of i., 379:8
 comparing image of him in her i., 507:4
 creates reality, 767:17
 dwell most on woman won or lost, 594:6

Imagination *(continued)*
 failure of i., 853:14
 fate had i. about her, 623:15
 gifted with egotistical i., 430:19
 God and i. one, 642:14
 I believe in i., 733:8
 in balance or reconciliation, 379:13
 in i. of their hearts, 37:11
 incalculable debt to i., 630:1
 indebted to i. for facts, 346:20
 instrument of moral good is i., 404:13
 judgment and i., 378:23
 lady's i. rapid, 382:5
 literalists of the i., 671:2
 live in human i., 818:1
 living power prime agent, 379:5
 loose i., 596:13
 makes us eloquent, 106:3
 man without i., 657:15
 master of art, 568:4
 of boy healthy, 409:6
 of i. all compact, 179:6
 of man's heart, 6:22
 one of forces of nature, 643:6
 political ideas and i., 743:16
 primary i. living power, 379:5
 reconciling mediatory power, 378:24
 regulate i. by reality, 308:7
 resemblance striking i., 333:15
 secondary i. dissolves, 379:6
 such tricks hath strong i., 179:6
 suspend i., 722:1
 swallowing up all thought and i., 301:10
 sweeten my i., 212:28
 synthetic and magical i., 379:12
 takes abundance of i., 626:9
 trace dust of Alexander, 202:13
 truth of I., 412:11
 truth only in i., 568:4
 were it not for i., 310:21
Imaginations, Lord understandeth all the i., 12:23
 my i. are as foul, 200:13
Imaginative awe, 749:20
Imagine a man in a ditch, 755:6
 himself pleasing to all, 276:6
 midnight moment's forest, 827:10
 more felicity than can i., 590:16
 people i. a vain thing, 15:1
 then by miracle with me, 745:17
 to i. is everything, 545:17
 too bold to i., 327:12
 writing these poems i., 814:9
 you are creating human destiny, 492:12
Imagined, each i. pinnacle, 411:16
 exhausted worlds i. new, 306:9
 land, 641:15
 live life he has i., 475:19
 one chose person one loved, 611:1
 republics and principalities, 142:1
 round earth's i. corners, 230:19
 way world i. determines what men do, 685:3
 world i. ultimate good, 642:13
Imagining in excited reverie, 593:11
 some fear, 179:6
Imaginings, horrible i., 214:11
Imbeciles, three generations of i., 539:4
Imbecility, convinced of i., 307:25

Impossible, analysis third of i. professions, 564:2
    can't believe i. things, 516:13
    certain because i., 113:13
    dream i. dream, 784:8
    eliminate i. truth remains, 573:5
    in reality, 507:4
    looked on as i. until effected, 105:5
    love those who yearn for i., 344:11
    loyalties, 496:8
    most i. of conclusions, 584:3
    not to love all things, 375:15
    nothing i. to willing heart, 147:4
    nothing unnatural that is not i., 346:18
    past them into the i., 784:2
    peace i. war improbable, 740:6
    pure and complete sorrow i., 507:1
    takes longer, 887:18
    that not i. she, 263:3
    these i. women, 73:10
    to be silent, 324:18
    to live pleasurably without living wisely, 81:16
    to love and be wise, 99:*n*11
    to please all the world, 266:12
    to write a novel, 815:13
    to write history i., 507:2
    who is set up for the i., 835:11
    with God nothing i., 37:7
    word i. not French, 365:8
Im-possible, in two words i., 649:16
Impostors, treat two i. same, 590:1
Impotence in face of armed evil, 863:10
Impotent, all-powerful to be i., 619:5
    lame and i. conclusion, 208:17
Impoverished stock of harmless pleasure, 307:20
Impoverishment in symbolism, 630:5
Imprecise determination of velocity, 728:3
Imprecision of feeling, 678:22
Impress, humans want to i. others, 648:17
    themselves our minds i., 368:4
Impressed, line in which force i., 279:15
Impression as from seal of ring, 76:7
    be not swept off feet by i., 109:4
Impressionable, girl at i. age, 791:16
Impressions, did not trust my own i., 71:12
    early i. hard to eradicate, 115:19
    falseness in i. of external, 484:7
    of American manners, 389:2
Impressive, poetry most i. mode, 496:9
Imprinted, remember what is i., 76:7
Imprison, allow it to i. us, 830:18
    gifts in such calling, 599:3
Imprisoned in every fat man, 734:7
    in viewless winds, 206:38
    millions of innocent i., 336:8
Imprisonment, age ache penury and i., 207:1
Improbable, absurd not the i., 469:4
    facts at first seem i., 167:17
    truth sometimes i., 399:*n*1
    what remains however i., 573:5
Impropriety, indulge in without i., 527:3
Improve each shining hour, 289:8
    shining tail, 513:15
    town that decades cannot i., 854:11
Improvement, diversion or i. of country, 288:3
    makes straight roads, 351:19

Improvements by generation, 327:12
Improver of natural knowledge, 502:4
Improving, middle age time of i., 261:12
Improviste, le courage de l'i., 365:*n*5
Impulse, blot out pomp check i., 112:20
    faction united by common i., 345:8
    household of I. mourns, 749:7
    lonely i. of delight, 593:1
    natural i. God gave me, 281:8
    one i. from vernal wood, 368:6
    prolongs the i., 822:9
    to perpetuate fine writing, 584:1
    to see it tried, 447:3
Impulses, instinctual wishful i., 564:1
    of all evil empires, 765:14
    primitive i. of heart, 449:*n*1
Impunity, no one provokes me with i., 120:34
Impure, although it passes among i., 77:*n*4
Impurify all our precious bodily fluids, 819:5
Impurities, no room for i. in essay, 654:8
Impute, make Gods to whom i., 495:7
In and out the Eagle, 885:6
    birds without despair to get i., 153:12
    harm's way, 342:1
    hoc signo vinces, 114:*n*5
    marriage wish to get out, 428:1
    when age i. wit out, 191:3
    who's i. who's out, 213:8
Inability of mind to correlate all contents, 687:7
Inaccessible, desert i., 194:22
    tower of past, 482:9
    valley of reveries, 616:19
Inaccuracy, not mind lying hate i., 521:15
    saves explanation, 608:9
Inaction, moment not of action or i., 84:*n*8
    nor be thy attachment to i., 84:9
    saps vigor of mind, 140:7
Inactivity, wise and masterly i., 362:4
Inadvertently said some evil thing, 76:15
Inalienable rights, 336:*n*1
Inarticulate, raid on i., 678:22
Inartistic, Thoreau i., 544:3
Inattention, patient i., 505:20
Inattentive, brave man i. to duty, 364:1
Inaudible and noiseless foot, 206:10
    its name is The I., 57:6
Inauspicious stars, 181:14
Incandescent, suffused with an i. glow, 819:8
Incantations of defeats, 641:19
Incapable, noble and i. of deceit, 374:17
Incarnadine, seas i., 215:24
Incarnate by the Holy Ghost, 48:12
    Well I told you so, 437:18
Incarnation of its frozen woe, 582:14
Incense, gods themselves throw i., 213:9
    my morning i., 347:8
    soft i. hangs, 410:7
    stupefying i. smoke, 460:22
Incense-breathing Morn, 315:15
Incensed, blows and buffets have i., 216:7
    most fragrant when i., 165:18
Incertainties now crown themselves, 222:10
Incessant, war of nature is not i., 440:2
    what boots it with i. care, 253:6
Incessantly stand on head, 514:4
    weeps i. for my sin, 353:10
    work i. to the last, 343:23

Incessantly *(continued)*
    world joked i., 528:7
Inch, cannot grow by i., 596:10
    cubic i. of space a miracle, 488:1
    every i. a king, 212:26
    every i. not fool is rogue, 273:8
    give an i. take an ell, 148:22
    I'll not budge an i., 173:4
    no painful i. to gain, 479:12
    paint an i. thick, 202:12
    queen it no i. further, 223:33
Inchcape Rock, 381:13
Inches, death by i., 220:5
    we're dyin' by i., 746:13
Incident, curious i. of dog in nighttime, 573:14
Incidents, so many i. so many details, 583:13
Incidis in Scyllam cupiens, 185:*n*1
Incipit Vita Nova, 127:15
Incisions, underneath fine i., 508:3
Incisors, writers divided into i. and molars, 503:2
Incite people to learn from past, 821:6
Incited, pseudo-event someone i., 773:21
Incitement, every idea an i., 539:3
Inciters of servile insurrection, 519:10
Incivility and procrastination, 393:7
Inclement, raw i. summers, 285:2
Inclination, read as i. leads, 309:4
    to hear you, 288:24
Inclinations cannot alter evidence, 329:11
    worship God according to own i., 106:5
Incline thine ear O Lord, 26:21
    to which side shall we i., 269:17
Inclined, as to embrace me she i., 255:2
    as twig bent tree's i., 293:24
    to notice ruin in things, 780:11
    to snap like vixens, 666:9
Inclines to think there is God, 479:11
Include me out, 649:15
    things that included whole, 642:6
Included in We the people, 841:12
Includes itself in power, 203:8
Income, annual i. twenty pounds, 465:24
    decent fall cloths over high i., 773:16
    devote i. labor to others, 485:10
    good i. of no avail, 590:13
    he has i. she pattable, 732:11
    however great i., 85:1
    just man will pay more i. tax, 74:20
    large i. is the best recipe, 382:14
    live beyond i., 521:12
    small but adequate i., 708:11
    solvency not matter of i., 590:12
    twenty expenditure nineteen, 465:24
Incommunicable, burden of i., 393:4
Incomparable, Clemens sole i., 529:3
Incompatibility established between them, 616:1
    spice of life, 732:11
Incompetence, reached their level of i., 793:9
    rise to level of i., 793:7
Incompetent, though competent appear i., 80:16
Incomplete and unfit for view, 520:14
Incomprehension, mutual i., 743:11
Inconceivable idea of sun, 641:20
Incongruous moonlight shines, 687:11
    with intelligence, 490:14

Industries, solemnest of i., 510:11
Industry, arms i., 686:16
    avarice spur of i., 311:22
    bring i. into competition, 319:10
    captains of i., 408:3
    free to regulate i., 337:11
    life without i. guilt, 484:20
    particular talent or i., 331:4
    proletariat product of i., 478:11
    without art brutality, 484:20
Inebriate, of Air am I, 508:9
Inebriated with verbosity, 430:19
Ineffable, my wickedness appeared perfectly i.,
    301:10
Ineffective, though effective appear i., 80:16
Ineffectual angel, 497:22
    armed neutrality i., 566:13
Inequality effect of brutalizing, 497:19
Inert facts, 532:2
Inescapable animal walks with me, 772:2
    wide water i., 640:22
Inestimable, thine i. love, 48:16
Inevitable, arguing with i., 482:8
    awaits alike i. hour, 315:18
    French Revolution i., 434:7
    not grieve over i., 84:7
    war is i., 638:2
    war regarded as i. or probable, 738:9
Inexactitude, terminological i., 618:20
Inexhaustible depth of all being God, 668:17
    Paris i., 691:5
Inexorable boredom at core of life, 270:16
    more fierce and i. far, 181:9
Inexplicable dumbshows, 200:6
    poetry search for i., 643:9
Inexterminate, man's practically i., 624:20
Inextinguishable passion of woman, 286:17
    rights of human nature, 363:3
Infallible all-pervasiveness, 542:14
    symptom of liberty, 332:6
Infâme, écrasez l'i., 299:*n*6
Infamous, crush the i. thing, 299:17
    delay, 290:23
Infamy, answer thee without fear of i.,
    129:7
    date live in i., 653:6
Infancy, heaven about us in i., 370:17
    nations like men have i., 290:5
    not only around our i., 481:14
    perish in their i., 882:3
    shined in my angel-i., 268:9
    tetchy and wayward thy i., 171:37
Infant, compared to an i., 57:17
    crying in night, 453:22
    firstling of the i. year, 246:1
    horse or dog more rational than, 342:6
    mewling and puking, 194:25
    murder i. in cradle, 351:20
    of three, 681:20
    phenomenon, 464:19
Infantryman's, look at i. eyes, 796:12
Infant's, in every i. cry of fear, 353:3
    newborn i. tear, 353:4
    reasoning, 313:13
Infants begin to see by noticing, 868:9
    canker galls i. of spring, 197:19
    damnation of unbaptized i., 532:15
    nuclear giants ethical i., 697:5

Infect, false words i. the soul, 74:16
    to north star, 190:27
Infected, all seems i. that i. spy, 292:24
Infection and hand of war, 176:24
    love whatever it was an i., 820:11
Infectious greed seemed to grip, 812:18
Infelicity, her i. years too many, 237:9
    sense of constant i., 264:32
Inferior grievances, 339:7
    no one make you feel i., 660:6
Inferiority, acknowledgment of i., 389:9
    feeling of i., 692:4
    rancor feeling of i., 657:5
    Senator seldom proclaims i., 531:10
    women have i. complexes, 688:15
Inferiors revolt to be equal, 78:28
Infernal serpent whose guile, 255:6
Infidel I have thee on the hip, 186:10
    worse than an i., 44:31
Infidelity, neither loses through i., 578:1
    tempt geologists into i., 552:5
Infidels, Jews kiss and i. adore, 293:4
    sleep with Turks and i., 177:15
Infinite chaos which separated us, 269:17
    climbing after knowledge i., 168:2
    day excludes the night, 289:17
    deal of nothing, 184:10
    debt through eternity, 343:11
    deluge or mountains, 301:10
    depth of all being God, 668:17
    echo of i., 538:9
    evil has i. forms, 269:23
    fellow of i. jest, 202:12
    fellows of i. tongue, 190:8
    genius i. capacity for taking pains,
        528:11
    God a sea of i. substance, 122:2
    Goodness has wide arms, 129:13
    he cannot bury under Finite, 406:22
    health is i. and expansive, 835:12
    heart's ease, 189:22
    ignorance must be i., 732:4
    in faculty, 199:5
    Infinitesimal and the I., 813:7
    king of i. space, 199:3
    nature's i. book of secrecy, 218:4
    nothing in relation to i., 269:9
    passion and the pain, 461:5
    power wisdom goodness, 283:2
    riches in little room, 168:8
    silence of i. spaces, 269:14
    though i. can never meet, 267:4
    variety, 218:21
    vicissitudes and calamities, 416:16
    virtue comest smiling, 218:37
    what can not see over is i., 406:16
    while men believe in i., 475:15
    wrath and infinite despair, 257:12
Infinitesimals, countless i. of feeling, 380:6
Infinities, numberless i. of souls, 230:19
    of islands, 763:3
Infinity, hold i. in palm of hand, 353:14
Infirm, Minstrel i. and old, 372:20
    my body i. and exhausted, 140:1
    of purpose, 215:23
    poor i. weak old man, 211:26
Infirmities, bear his friend's i., 193:11
    bear i. of weak, 42:4

Infirmity, feblit with i., 141:6
    first i. of weak minds, 253:*n*1
    last i. of noble mind, 253:6
    of his age, 210:32
    of will, 426:23
Inflamed with mutual animosity, 345:9
    with study of learning, 254:4
Inflections, beauty of i., 641:7
Inflexible, important principles i., 447:4
    we must be i., 620:1
Influence, Anxiety of I., 826:5
    cock has great i. on own dunghill, 100:5
    corrupt i., 324:15
    deprives republican example of just i.,
        444:6
    naked people have little i., 525:10
    planetary i., 211:3
    rain i. and judge prize, 251:7
    salutary i. of example, 307:16
    teacher's i. never stops, 531:23
    unwarranted i., 686:16
    win friends i. people, 674:1
Influences, servile to all skyey i., 206:33
    sweet i. of Pleiades, 14:23
    wide world-embracing i., 406:9
Influenza, much reduced by i., 612:21
Infolded, tongues of flame i., 679:13
Inform, occasions i. against me, 201:19
    press home Christmas, 601:7
    their discretion, 338:12
Information, can find i., 310:5
    knowledge we have lost in i., 679:14
    popular Government without popular i.,
        346:1
    vegetable animal mineral, 526:6
    wants to be free, 843:18
    wealth of i., 783:2
    woman of little i., 382:4
Informed, correctly i. as to past, 420:3
    people well enough i., 652:18
Informer poor weak human being, 712:6
Infrequent, sighs short and i., 676:7
    worshipper of gods, 96:16
Infringement of human freedom, 359:7
Infuse, illustrious acts high raptures i., 249:20
    souls of animals i. into men, 185:31
Infuses that liberal obedience, 324:13
Infusing thoughts and passions, 379:18
Infusion, sticky i., 815:15
Ingiuria, chi fa i. non perdona, 103:*n*10
Inglorious arts of peace, 266:17
    mute i. Milton, 316:1
Ingrateful man, 211:24
Ingratitude, hate i. more than lying, 205:25
    man's i., 195:1
    thou marble-hearted fiend, 211:10
Inhabit, build houses and i. them, 27:22
    country belongs to people who i. it,
        445:5
    house and all that i. it, 330:12
    parched places, 27:39
    soul of grandam i. bird, 185:*n*2
Inhabitant, Indian is Nature's i., 472:20
Inhabitants, Californians a race not i., 582:1
    not only i. of field, 325:7
    number of portraits as great as i., 645:23
    of some sequestered island, 482:12
    proclaim liberty to all i., 9:1

Inhabits our frail blood, 205:25
Inhale, I didn't i., 863:2
Inherent, decay i. in all component things, 64:16
   purpose i. in art so in nature, 77:14
   rights, 320:7
Inherit, all which it i. dissolve, 225:1
   looking uncomfortably to world we i., 888:16
   meek shall i. the earth, 16:10, 32:14
   the wind, 20:16
   tonight doth i., 495:20
   with pain purchased i. pain, 173:40
Inheritance, divided an i. with him, 335:3
   not be destroyed, 339:6
Inherited total lot of parents, 842:7
   tradition cannot be i., 675:17
Inheritor, president is i., 764:4
Inhuman of the veritable ocean, 641:8
   reign of lie, 688:8
Inhumanity, indifferent is essence of i., 565:2
   man's i. to man, 356:8
Inimies, keep our i., 600:1
Iniquities, judge allow i., 539:6
Iniquity, bond of i., 40:20
   draw i. with cords of vanity, 25:6
   gray i., 182:27
   I was shapen in i., 16:30
   is pardoned, 26:24
   of oblivion, 249:1
   of the fathers, 8:12
   punish wicked for their i., 25:21
   reaped i., 28:37
   religious know more about i., 587:4
Initial of Creation, 510:3
Initiative in creating the Internet, 866:7
Iniuria, volenti non fit i., 121:25
Injured, forgiveness to i. does belong, 103:n10
   like i. fan, 670:18
   minds i. by hunger and thirst, 80:7
   no one i. save by himself, 115:n13
   those I have i., 787:17
   whom they have i. they hate, 103:27
Injures, never pardons those he i., 103:n10
Injuries, forgive me my i., 787:17
   saints in your i., 208:13
Injuring, kill time without i. eternity, 474:10
   rarely escapes i. own hands, 58:4
   restrain men from i., 337:11
Injurious, beauty though i., 260:19
Injury, add insult to i., 103:6
   adding insult to i., 312:10
   fear of serious i., 562:9
   greatest service or greatest i., 74:17
   it does me no injury, 336:5
   never forget i., 608:5
   never use treatment with view to i., 70:14
   returns on him who began, 90:20
   sooner forgotten than insult, 298:4
   such i. vex a saint, 173:17
   where i. let me sow pardon, 125:12
Injustice, complain of i. of government, 364:3
   conscience with i. corrupted, 170:7
   extreme justice extreme i., 121:18
   extreme justice often i., 86:n3
   extreme law often extreme i., 86:3
   fear of suffering i., 263:25
   keynote of government is i., 604:13

Injustice (continued)
   makes democracy necessary, 696:3
   man ever in darkness of i., 119:6
   mankind censure i., 75:1
   no i. to person who consents, 121:25
   nothing so felt as i., 466:24
   put a halt to i., 808:18
   sometimes service to public, 339:10
Injustices, heaped i. upon us, 603:9
Ink, effusion of i., 318:12
   essential in painting, 122:11
   gall enough in thy i., 205:18
   galley slave to i., 417:13
   hath not drunk i., 174:15
   it uses is human blood, 757:13
   never saw pen and i., 205:26
   runs from mouth, 838:15
Inky, not alone my i. cloak, 196:26
Inlaid with patines of bright gold, 186:15
Inland island, 530:25
   though i. far we be, 371:3
Inn, gain timely i., 216:14
   happiness produced by i., 310:7
   make my house your i., 671:6
   no room in the i., 37:16
   take mine ease in mine i., 147:5
   up to old i.-door, 646:1
   warmest welcome at an i., 310:n1
   world not i. but hospital, 248:18
Inner light will shine forth, 345:n1
   man, 43:35
   mine with i. weather, 623:15
   slight i. adjustments, 860:3
   Temple's i. shrine, 370:6
   weather, 623:15
Innisfail, harp of I., 384:15
Innisfree, go to I., 591:2
Innocence and health, 322:23
   ceremony of i., 593:9
   changed i. for i., 223:10
   fearful i., 370:4
   has nothing to dread, 279:1
   her i. a child, 273:21
   ignorance not i., 463:11
   murderous i. of sea, 593:11
   never blossom into license, 279:2
   never such i. again, 799:9
   of love, 205:2
   of our neighbors, 475:16
   our peace our i., 370:4
   possessing i. above suspicion, 784:10
   Ralph wept for end of i., 764:1
   recovered i., 475:16
   silence often of pure i., 223:15
   soul recovers i., 593:18
   what is our i., 671:8
Innocent and foredoomed, 739:9
   are so few, 719:10
   as new-laid egg, 525:17
   calm quiet i. recreation, 245:7
   changed to protect the i., 796:1
   children's souls not i., 115:28
   condemn an i. person, 299:6
   coursed down his i. nose, 194:1
   haunted by i. man convicted, 613:16
   I seek an i. country, 682:9
   look like i. flower, 214:20

Innocent (continued)
   merriment, 527:16
   millions of i. burnt tortured, 336:8
   minds i. and quiet, 266:2
   no i. wit be suppressed, 334:8
   of the blood, 36:15
   officious i. sincere, 311:7
   Parry was i., 784:11
   skin of i. lamb parchment, 170:15
   sleep, 215:21
   taking toll of many i. lives, 728:7
   than one i. suffer, 318:21
   who perished being i., 13:6
   women i. and pure, 224:19
   won by blood and sweat of i., 852:10
Innocently, live i. God here, 305:5
Innocents, we are the flawed ones the i., 841:3
Innovation, restructuring combines continuity i., 830:3
   scientific i. rarely converts opponents, 570:10
Innovator, time the greatest i., 166:7
Inns not residences, 671:6
   of Molten Blue, 508:9
Innuendoes, beauty of i., 641:7
Innumerable bees, 453:7
   caravan which moves, 405:13
   things creeping i., 18:11
Inoffensive, smooth easy i. down to Hell, 82:n3
   untitled aristocracy, 443:14
Inoperative, others are i., 846:6
Inordinate interest in animals and athletes, 672:1
Input, differences in i. overwhelming, 872:5
Inquiries about events following birth, 111:6
   suspended religious i., 332:14
Inquiry, do not block way of i., 534:12
   thought to aim at some good, 78:3
   undismayed unintimidated i., 614:3
Inquisition, committee i., 638:7
   nobody expects Spanish I., 879:10
Inquisitive, acute i. dexterous, 324:7
Inquisitor of structures, 642:12
Inquisitors, whom will you make your i., 336:7
Insane, all the children are i., 858:6
   delusion can't be held, 820:3
   most i. of passions, 565:16
   root, 214:8
Insanity, delusion it is called i., 820:n1
   often logic, 443:6
Insatiable intellectual curiosity, 583:4
   sexually i. both naked, 834:14
Insatiate to pursue war with heaven, 256:6
Inscape is what I aim at, 547:10
Inscription, altar with i., 40:32
Inscriptions, lapidary i., 310:6
Inscrutable, dark i. workmanship, 368:14
   dumb i. grand, 497:4
   jest unseen i., 173:30
Insect, I am that i. brother, 492:8
   transformed into gigantic i., 655:14
   vile i. that has risen up, 301:8
Insects, loud and troublesome i., 325:7
   move and men like i., 813:2
   of the hour, 325:7
   to whom God gave lust, 492:8
Insensate care of mortals, 90:n1
Insensibility, stark i., 308:12

Insensible, honor i. then, 183:25
    to freedoms of Constitution, 649:10
Inseparable, nonviolence and truth i., 604:5
    one and i., 390:10
    sex and beauty i., 663:16
Inshallah, say only I., 118:17
Inside, not forgotten i. of church, 183:7
Insight, give me i. into to-day, 426:7
Insignificant book, 654:18
    chatter of the world, 471:13
    vice-presidency most i. office, 330:10
Insisture course proportion, 203:5
Insolence, above i. and triviality, 671:2
    flown with i. and wine, 255:20
    of office, 199:21
    strength without i., 394:9
    surfeit begets i., 59:21
Insolent menaces of villains, 331:6
Inspector of snowstorms rainstorms, 473:1
Inspiration, cleanse by the i. of thy Holy Spirit,
    49:3
    descends only in flashes, 769:8
    genius one percent i., 550:13
    hierophants of i., 404:15
    lasting i. sanctified by reason, 369:2
    love and freedom, 578:3
    of the names, 314:1
    shining star and i., 710:24
    whatever poet writes with divine i., 70:10
Inspirations of people and time, 717:9
Inspire, passions we i. contract time, 610:17
    two qualities i. affection, 78:19
    we do not i. conduct, 264:25
Inspires, fair Fame i., 295:13
Inspiring bold John Barleycorn, 358:7
Instances, wise saws and modern i., 194:25
Instancy, majestic i., 576:14
Instant, for each ecstatic i., 508:4
    in season, 45:1
    made eternity, 461:12
    more i. than Feet, 576:14
Instantaneous, miracles are i., 688:11
Instinct, civilized i. find subtler pleasure,
    582:13
    collectors people with tactical i., 692:13
    men should be right by i., 65:24
    no longer guided by i., 609:7
    of self-preservation, 569:5
    sensation i. intelligence, 415:15
Instinctive, pursuing i. course, 413:12
Instinctively, rats i. have quit it, 224:8
Instincts, cost of satisfaction of i., 563:9
    heed no i. but our own, 266:6
    high i., 371:1
    plant himself on i., 426:8
    uncivilized Eastern i., 587:2
Instinctual wishful impulses, 564:1
Institute and digest of anarchy, 325:1
Instituted, governments i. among men, 336:1
Institution, glorious i., 324:13
    lengthened shadow of one man, 426:21
Institutions cease being liberal, 548:24
    enemies of free i., 444:6
    liberal i. enemies of freedom, 548:24
    mind soul of self-perpetuating i., 789:3
    on point of collapse, 760:2
    reject racist i., 850:3
    this country with its i., 445:5

Instruct how mind of man more beautiful,
    369:2
    sorrows to be proud, 175:13
Instructing, delighting and i. at same time,
    98:29
Instruction, I will better the i., 185:13
    no i. book came with it, 705:13
    text of civil i., 337:12
    tygers of wrath wiser than horses of i.,
    351:17
Instructions for well-being, 4:13
Instructive to take woman's view, 431:13
Instructor, age not qualified as i., 474:14
Instructors, practice best of i., 100:11
Instructs, delights reader i. too, 278:7
Instrument, fever is Nature's i., 270:8
    in shape of a woman, 825:3
    law not i. of any kind, 804:16
    of moral good is imagination, 404:13
    of slavery, 317:9
    of your peace, 125:12
    pen excellent i., 329:7
    sweeter than sound of i., 248:17
    tune the i. here at the door, 231:1
    writer's work is optical i., 611:7
Instruments, electrical i. for musical purposes,
    766:19
    find fit i. of ill, 293:11
    fit i. to make slaves, 305:13
    genius and mortal i., 192:2
    intellectual i., 468:13
    looking with familiar i., 799:5
    of darkness, 214:9
    of European greatness, 349:6
    played before the Lord on i., 11:13
    stringed i. and organs, 19:21
    thousand twangling i., 224:33
    to plague us, 213:10
Insubstantial pageant faded, 225:1
Insufficient, seven years would be i., 382:2
Insular Tahiti full of peace, 483:5
Insulate, television used to amuse i. us, 754:14
Insult, add i. to injury, 103:6
    adding i. to injury, 312:10
    injury sooner forgotten than i., 298:4
    to God, 460:14
Insulting, rushed to meet i. foe, 346:23
Insults my painting has won me, 479:15
    of Fortune, 304:24
Insure domestic tranquillity, 339:11
Insurrection, never did i. want such water-
    colors, 183:23
    revolution is i., 698:10
    servile i., 519:10
    suffers nature of an i., 192:2
Intangible, world i. we touch, 577:3
Integer vitae scelerisque purus, 96:*n*9
Integers, God made i., 500:2
Integration, not fighting for i., 808:17
Integrity, does one's i. lie, 809:11
    in silence preserve i., 127:10
    territorial i., 566:17
    were we men of i., 785:9
Intellect, achievements of i. everlasting, 92:10
    adduces authority uses not i., 140:6
    character higher than i., 426:3
    conformity of object and i., 124:9
    feather to tickle i., 383:22

Intellect *(continued)*
    find no i. comparable to my own, 456:16
    forced to choose, 595:9
    improperly exposed, 374:25
    interpretation is revenge of i., 835:14
    is to emotion as clothes, 580:18
    light between truth and i., 129:17
    man with godlike i., 440:13
    marks of God in liberal i., 388:8
    mugwump educated beyond i., 529:9
    of narrow normal amount, 400:5
    restless versatile i., 502:14
    scepticism chastity of i., 584:13
    scholar is delegated i., 425:26
    second-class i. first-class temperament,
    539:11
    too profound for human i., 440:7
    unaging i., 594:1
    weakness of i., 527:21
    Will and I. the same, 276:2
    with i. or with conscience, 450:3
Intellection, happiest i., 797:14
Intellects, argument and i. too, 322:9
    three classes of i., 142:4
Intellectual all-in-all, 369:10
    before committees, 638:7
    being, 256:12
    dandyism, 505:13
    desolation, 478:3
    disgrace, 749:5
    enjoyment, 577:7
    freedom only guarantee, 797:5
    greater sense of i. degradation, 552:3
    hatred worst, 593:17
    lords of ladies i., 397:19
    neutralize i. element, 584:10
    Northwest Passage to i. world, 314:17
    ought to refuse to testify, 638:7
    passion drives out sensuality, 140:3
    product judged from age produced, 534:3
    responsibility, 692:3
    take i. possession, 545:1
    throne, 495:16
    virile courageous, 603:4
Intellectuals, all men are i., 689:12
    at one pole, 743:11
    better governed by man in street than by i.,
    72:6
    characterize themselves as i., 789:6
    deserve intended slavery, 638:7
    I'm one of the i., 712:10
    Treachery of the I., 599:9
Intelligence, controlling i. understands, 112:12
    gods do not give all men i., 53:7
    greater than human i., 860:5
    highest i. in the freest body, 634:1
    human i. would grace the replay, 852:6
    incongruous with i., 490:14
    lost money underestimating i. of people,
    645:15
    making artificial objects, 572:9
    overwhelms i. of all gods, 54:14
    School I. make it a soul, 413:15
    sensation instinct i., 415:15
    talent inspiration, 578:3
    test of a first-rate i., 710:12
    vast enough to comprehend all forces,
    345:3

Intelligence *(continued)*
    which goes with sex, 663:16
Intelligences, first animals then i., 505:9
Intelligent, all i. thoughts already thought,
    344:26
    beam me up no i. life down here, 888:19
    enemies i. and corrupt, 738:5
    impossible for i. people, 836:5
    life might develop, 854:4
    life on a planet, 850:10
    may begin a movement, 568:2
    Mr. Toad, 574:9
    perception of least i., 684:11
    perfection in becoming i. being, 124:14
    pleasing one i. man displeasing fools,
    124:13
    so elegant so i., 676:9
    woman, 612:10
Intelligibly, speak i. to world, 590:19
Intend, what evil I i. to do, 67:21
Intended, take hint when i., 625:9
    years damp my i. wing, 259:6
Intending to build tower, 38:8
Intense moment isolated, 679:1
Intensely, soul listened i., 372:7
Intensity, all I care about is i., 537:11
    full of passionate i., 593:9
    grandeur remains without i., 107:3
    moving into another i., 679:2
    of feeling, 743:10
Intent, eye i. on mazy plan, 358:2
    forget not yet tried i., 149:2
    his first avowed i., 271:26
    is al, 133:2
    love come with murderous i., 67:25
    night of dark i., 623:13
    not criminal unless i. criminal, 120:3
    on hospitable thoughts i., 258:17
    prick sides of my i., 214:24
    truth told with bad i., 354:1
Intention, no i. to write atheistically, 440:6
    stabs the center, 223:12
Intentional, abstain from i. wrongdoing, 70:14
    Petersburg most i. town, 492:4
Intentions, hell full of good i., 123:13
    hell paved with good i., 123:*n*7, 243:*n*1
Intents are savage-wild, 181:9
    discerner of thoughts and i., 45:7
    wicked or charitable, 197:33
Inter, in hugger-mugger i. him, 201:28
    in peace children i. parents, 69:7
Intercourse, avoid sexual i., 847:2
    hold i. with roots of trees, 666:5
    in her i. with foreign nations, 386:*n*2
    lived in social i., 309:16
    open and friendly in private i., 71:14
    sexual i. began, 799:13
    supremest of delights sexual i., 525:7
    with foreign nations, 386:17
Interest, art makes life makes i., 545:8
    duty and i., 329:1
    exceed in i. knock at door, 383:13
    features of biological i., 821:4
    I du believe in i., 482:2
    impulse of passion or i., 345:8
    it wouldn't i. anybody, 849:3
    of the producer, 319:9
    promote public i., 319:5

Interest *(continued)*
    pursue his own i. his own way, 319:10
    regard to their own i., 318:22
    take personal i. in well-drawn character,
    522:18
    unborrowed from the eye, 368:10
Interested in big things, 583:4
    know one's self is i., 534:10
    not i. in defeat, 485:4
    what American people are i. in, 863:3
Interesting because unimportant, 686:2
    other people, 534:10
    statements i. but tough, 523:3
Interest's on dangerous edge, 461:23
Interests, eternal and perpetual i., 392:21
    great i. at stake, 78:29
    human figure i. me most, 605:10
    of community, 345:8
    politicians have i. aside from people's,
    444:1
    various powerful i., 389:8
Interfered in behalf of rich, 419:2
Interfused, something far more i., 368:11
Intergraft our hands, 229:18
Interim like a phantasma, 192:2
Interlude, strange i., 681:7
Interludes, strange dark i., 681:7
Interlunar, vacant i. cave, 260:10
Intermeddle, stranger doth not i., 20:25
Interminable night, 679:9
Intermission, laugh sans i., 194:17
Internal domestic empire, 713:9
    environment, 468:14
International, bring order to i. affairs, 638:4
    nuclear control, 786:14
Internationally, bring suit in court i., 661:2
Internet, initiative in creating the I., 866:7
    invented the I., 866:*n*2
    Is for Porn, 880:3
    is the first thing that humanity, 874:1
Interpose, who in quarrels i., 291:13
Interpret interpretatons, 153:20
Interpretation, aid to i. of future, 71:12
    is revenge of intellect, 835:14
    of dreams road to knowledge, 563:1
    this is the i. of the thing, 28:25
Interpreter hardest understood of the two,
    346:15
    in marriage room for i., 742:4
    perfect i. of life, 666:11
Interpreters, for crowd they need i., 63:25
Interred, good oft i. with bones, 192:28
    life is shrunk dead and i., 229:12
Interrupt with such silly question, 313:20
Interstellar, vacant i. spaces, 678:19
Interstitially, judges legislate i., 538:18
Intertissued robe of gold, 189:23
Interval, enjoy i., 584:11
    lucid i., 273:14
Intervals, full of lucid i., 157:21
    lucid i. and happy pauses, 165:3
Interview, after i. with a doctor, 552:3
    not train wreck earthquake but i.,
    773:21
Intimacy cannot be trapped, 859:15
    gay i. of slums, 736:6
    heart-revealing i., 593:12
Intimate equality of the Four, 656:10

Intimates are predestined, 531:17
Intimation of mortality part of New York,
    724:6
Intimations, reason's icy i., 418:17
Intimidate human race into order, 638:4
    threats of halter i., 341:10
Intolerable, burden of them is i., 49:5
    deal of sack, 182:31
    in worst state i., 333:1
    music falls, 597:3
    shirt of flame, 679:11
    wrestle with words and meanings, 678:16
Intoxicate the brain, 292:12
Intoxication, best of life i., 398:11
Intractable, sullen untamed i., 679:3
Intricate as death, 231:12
Intricated, poor i. soul, 231:13
Intrinsic value of knowledge, 298:11
Introduce philosophy into homes, 88:5
    please allow me to i. myself, 857:5
Introduced, cut anyone i. to, 516:19
    when I'm i. to one, 579:15
Introibo ad altare Dei, 47:16
Introspection, prone to i., 672:2
Introversion, tendency to i., 428:17
Introverts, society where none i., 396:16
Intrusion, right to be free from governmental
    i., 745:11
Intuition is intelligence which goes with sex,
    663:16
    more subtle than premise, 538:15
    passionate i., 372:8
    reliance on i., 629:11
Intuitive, beautiful always i., 378:23
    calculation transcended mathematics,
    629:11
Inurned, weep a people i., 419:*n*4
Invade, lobsters don't i. our privacy, 439:7
Invaded, France is i., 365:10
Invalid, invaluable permanent i. Bunbury,
    560:20
Invasion can be resisted, 422:8
    l'i. des idées, 422:*n*4
    waiting for i. so are fishes, 620:2
Invent boat of your flesh, 839:4
    lies you can i., 354:1
    necessary to i. him, 299:27
    the world i. reality, 723:13
    would children i. game, 662:6
Invented an invaluable invalid, 560:20
    Dodo i. for becoming extinct, 659:11
    falsehood i., 649:2
    first i. sleep, 158:8
    first i. war, 167:19
    first i. work, 383:16
    fool i. kissing, 286:4
    history, 300:10
    the Internet, 866:*n*2
    time someone i. plot, 654:20
Invention, brightest heaven of i., 188:29
    equal license in bold i., 98:16
    greatest i. of nineteenth century, 580:8
    is unfruitful, 324:1
    man is an i., 812:4
    necessity mother of i., 105:*n*7, 120:32
    of method of invention, 580:8
    scaled i., 665:14
    stomach dispenser of i., 105:12

Island (*continued*)
  misty i., 417:4
  no man is an i., 231:8
  no owls in whole i., 310:*n*2
  of England, 189:16
  sad dark i. Cythera, 491:9
  savages in unknown i., 429:21
  snug little i., 372:18
  solitude unsponsored free, 640:22
  some sequestered i., 482:12
  tight little i., 372:18
  watched famous i. descending, 619:7
Islanded in stream of stars, 673:22
  place remote and i., 552:12
Island's, take my way along i. edge, 488:2
Islands, looked seaward among i., 552:11
  nightmares of other i., 763:5
  realms and i. as plates, 219:8
  round many western i., 408:17
  what gray rocks what i., 677:20
  whose raving skies opened, 559:3
Isle, cause or men of Emerald I., 347:14
  green i. in sea, 448:6
  in far-off seas, 459:20
  is full of noises, 224:33
  it frights the i., 208:25
  sceptered i., 176:24
  that is called Patmos, 46:14
Isled, wound with thee in thee i., 547:2
Isles, fished by obstinate i., 665:5
  moving i. of winter, 451:7
  naked melancholy i., 301:1
  of Greece, 398:15
  throned on her hundred i., 396:1
  touch Happy I., 451:18
Isness of man's nature, 823:12
Isn't, as it i. it ain't, 515:19
Isolated, Chinese not remain i., 771:6
  freedom made man i., 725:8
  on promontory stood i., 488:5
  with no before and after, 679:1
Isolates, silence i., 631:7
Isolation of sky at evening, 640:22
  robbed of i. that is life, 638:10
Israel, ancient nations Egypt and I., 769:10
  arose a mother in I., 10:8
  blessed be Lord God of I., 37:13
  captive I., 479:3
  chariot of I., 12:12
  glory departed from I., 10:37
  glory of thy people I., 37:20
  he that keepeth I., 18:30
  hear O I., 9:14
  in I. believe in miracles, 666:13
  Judah and I. dwelt safely, 11:28
  lost sheep of house of I., 33:37
  no king in I., 10:29
  of our time, 482:15
  scattered upon the hills, 12:9
  sweet psalmist of I., 11:24
  thy tabernacles O I., 9:11
  to your tents O I., 11:38
Israel's body drifted as smoke, 691:17
Israelis, no more war between Arabs I., 791:5
Israfel, dwell where I. dwelt, 448:1
  whose heartstrings a lute, 448:*n*1
Issue is in God's hands, 63:27
  judged in light of final i., 79:8

Issues, contrived corridors and i., 675:22
  debate on public i. uninhibited, 745:9
  out of it are the i. of life, 19:30
  when i. are joined, 58:1
Isthmus of a middle state, 295:1
  took the I. started the Canal, 571:16
It can't happen here, 664:8
  is finished, 40:10
  it's just I., 589:23
  let's do i., 803:11
  strong magnetism called i., 585:4
  takes a village, 864:6
Ita in maxima fortuna minima licentia, 92:*n*5
Italia who hast fatal gift, 396:5
Italian, I speak I. to women, 148:31
  operas translated into I., 582:18
  perhaps I., 526:4
  proletariat, 657:1
Italien, je parle i. aux femmes, 148:*n*16
Italy, beyond Alps lies I., 99:12
  far from I. I lie, 83:2
  fashions in proud I., 176:22
  graved inside of it I., 461:4
  Greece I. and England did adorn, 274:7
  had warfare terror murder, 781:4
  notice ruin because born in I., 780:11
Itch, incurable i. for writing, 109:22
  of disputing, 227:15
  Seven Year I., 798:9
Itching palm, 193:7
Iteration, damnable i., 181:28
Ithaca, fill I. full of moths, 219:22
  setting out on voyage to I., 583:11
Ithers, see ourselves as i. see us, 356:16
Itself, illness which regards i. as therapy, 626:8
  is it true in and for i., 367:14
  love is most nearly i., 679:2
  thou art the thing i., 212:3
Itylus, half assuaged for I., 529:12
Iucundior, quae est domestica sede i., 87:*n*12
Iudex damnatur ubi nocens absolvitur, 100:*n*4
Iudicaret, ne supra crepidam sutor i., 81:*n*2
Iura, sunt superis sua i., 102:*n*12
Ius est ars boni et aequi, 120:31
  summum saepe summa est malitia, 86:*n*3
Ivan Ilych dying, 507:6
  Ilych's life most simple, 507:5
Ives, going to St. I., 892:22
Ivory apes and peacocks, 11:35
  bit of i. on which I work, 383:1
  cross through gates of i., 439:4
  gate of i., 54:6, 95:2
  neck is as a tower of i., 24:22
  tower, 493:9
  tower of i., 432:3
Ivy, goats eat i., 896:4
  holly and the i., 883:5
  myrtle and i., 399:7
  not hang i. over wine, 101:6
  pluck i. branch for me, 512:7
  with i. never sere, 252:29

J

Jabal father of such as dwell in tents, 6:10
Jabberwock, beware J., 515:12
J'accuse, 537:16

Jack and Jill, 893:18
  banish plump J., 182:29
  be nimble, 895:16
  house that J. built, 897:8
  joke poor potsherd, 547:9
  little J. Horner, 892:19
  makes J. a dull boy, 245:12
  of Spades, 660:*n*2
  one named J. fly away J., 897:7
  Sprat eat no fat, 892:15
Jack Benny's, even J. overrated, 736:18
Jack Daniel's, a bottle of J., 780:13
Jackass can kick barn down, 651:11
Jackknife, just a j. has Macheath, 716:7
Jackson standing like stone wall, 501:5
  Stonewall J. wrapped in beard, 716:3
  who didst pick up Andrew J. from pebbles, 482:24
Jacky have new master, 893:19
Jacob called the place Peniel, 7:4
  gave Esau bread and pottage, 6:38
  God of J. not philosophers, 270:2
  served seven years, 6:44
  sold his birthright unto J., 6:38
  that which has been sent down on J., 117:13
  thy tents O J., 9:11
  was a plain man, 6:37
  was left alone, 7:2
  wrestled as Angel with J., 244:30
Jacob's voice is J. voice, 6:39
Jade, arrant j. on a journey, 322:18
  let galled j. wince, 200:22
Jael brought forth butter, 10:11
  took a nail, 10:7
J'ai vécu, 342:7
Jail, can't be sint to j. for it, 600:17
  git little drunk land in j., 706:6
  like living in j., 756:22
  little stealin' gits you in j., 681:4
  patron and the j., 306:16
  with chance of being drowned, 309:1
Jailer another kind of captive, 439:3
  inexorable as self, 431:15
Jam, Calico J., 467:13
  every other day, 516:9
  tomorrow jam yesterday, 516:10
Jamaicas of Remembrance, 511:6
Jambs, unscrew doors from j., 486:7
James could almost hear the bronze Negroes, 787:19
  Councillor to King J., 161:16
  James Morrison Morrison, 651:6
  King J. used to call for old shoes, 238:10
  let J. rejoice, 318:12
Jamshyd gloried drank deep, 441:13
Jane, from J. to Elizabeth, 382:7
  John Thomas marryin' Lady J., 663:12
  me Tarzan you J., 629:*n*4
Jangled, sweet bells j., 200:4
Jangling, keep juices flowing by j. around, 747:6
January, a Fly this J. Day, 511:6
Japan, forces of Empire of J., 653:6
  from Paris to J., 278:6
Japanese reliance on intuition, 629:11
  toilet place of spiritual repose, 668:16
Japheth, Noah begat J., 6:15

Jar, feel amid city's j., 495:1
    in Tennessee, 641:2
    strings untouched will harshly j., 168:15
    to the person in the bell j., 832:14
    wine j. when molding began, 98:17
Jardin, il faut cultiver notre j., 299:*n5*
Jargon of the schools, 283:10
Jars, two j. on floor of Zeus, 52:19
Jasper of jocundity, 141:5
Jaundiced eye, 292:24
Jaunts, Jorrocks' j. and jollities, 429:12
Javan, bound for J. or Gadire, 260:16
Jaw, muscular strength to j., 514:5
Jawbone of an ass, 10:22
Jaw-jaw better than to war-war, 621:16
Jaws, gently smiling j., 513:15
    of darkness do devour it, 177:28
    of death, 155:2, 454:23
    that bite, 515:12
Jay Gatsby of West Egg Long Island, 710:4
    new j. born every day, 886:*n5*
    poor Jim J., 616:10
Jaybird don't rob own nes', 551:11
Jazz, ask what j. is, 724:11
    misunderstood utterance of prayer, 703:10
    right seasoning for j., 664:9
    swift j. poem of success, 799:4
    we j. June, 783:10
Je connais tout fors moi-même, 139:*n3*
Jealous, art j. mistress, 428:7
    confirmations, 209:10
    for they are jealous, 209:22
    I am a j. God, 8:12
    in honor, 194:25
    law a j. mistress, 388:6
    not j. for the cause, 209:22
    of every word and action, 238:23
    one not easily j., 210:20
    possessions of happiness, 604:7
    scornful yet j. eyes, 295:13
    souls not answered, 209:22
    venom clamors of j. woman, 172:26
Jealousies, surmises j. conjectures, 187:21
Jealousy, beware my lord of j., 209:3
    born with love, 264:24
    ear of j. heareth all, 29:30
    full of artless j., 201:22
    green-eyed j., 185:21
    has a human face, 353:8
    in j. more self-love, 264:20
    is cruel as the grave, 24:25
    is the rage of a man, 20:4
    life of j., 209:5
    moral indignation j. with halo, 598:15
    of rivals near throne, 340:15
    these are the forgeries of j., 178:14
Jeanie with light brown hair, 503:14
Jeanne d'Arc and Bonaparte, 686:10
Jedi, old J. mind-trick, 867:9
Jeers, exiled on ground in j., 491:2
Jefferson, celebrities such as J., 518:9
    Thomas J. still surv—, 330:18
    when J. dined alone, 786:5
    Yoknapatawpha County, 714:1
Jehovah, in name of great J., 334:1
    is my strength, 25:20
    Jove or Lord, 296:20
    Lawd God J., 686:3

Jehovah *(continued)*
    tell them I Am J. said, 318:7
Jehu, the driving of J., 12:17
Jell-O, like J. on springs, 748:2
Jelly, distilled almost to j., 197:13
    out vile j., 212:14
Je-ne-sais-quoi young man, 526:13
Jenny kissed me, 392:20
Jeoffrey, consider my Cat J., 318:14
Jeopardized, black freedom j., 808:18
Jeopardy, nor be twice put in j., 340:4
    went in j. of their lives, 11:25
Jeremy, Mr. J. liked feet wet, 598:7
Jericho, from Jerusalem to J., 37:36
    Joshua fit battle of J., 898:15
    tarry at J. until beards be grown, 11:16
Jerusalem, Athens to do with J., 113:18
    daughters of J., 24:4
    from J. to Jericho, 37:36
    I saw the new J., 47:11
    I will wipe J., 12:21
    if I forget thee O J., 19:11
    liberating J. and the holy shrines, 842:12
    meet in sweet J., 171:2
    my happy home, 881:18
    speak comfortably to J., 26:24
    that killest prophets, 35:18
    the golden, 479:2
    thy sister calls, 354:14
    was J. builded here, 354:8
    wise men came to J., 31:36
Jeshurun waxed fat, 9:31
Jessamine, casement j. stirred, 455:2
Jesse, David the son of J., 11:24
    rod out of the stem of J., 25:18
Jesses my dear heart-strings, 209:7
Jessica, sit J. look, 186:15
Jest and youthful jollity, 250:21
    best to use myself in j., 229:2
    between j. and earnest, 156:26
    breaks no bones, 311:6
    fellow of infinite j., 202:12
    glory j. and riddle, 295:1
    good j. forever, 182:11
    I j. to Oberon, 178:12
    life is a j., 291:20
    most bitter is scornful j., 306:7
    put his whole wit in a j., 237:20
    rather lose friend than j., 238:23
    unseen inscrutable, 173:30
Jester, fool and j., 188:27
Jesting, what is truth said j. Pilate, 165:11
Jest's prosperity lies in ear, 174:31
Jests, he j. at scars, 179:31
    indebted to memory for j., 346:20
Jesu, by will of J. into another place, 138:16
    Christ and seiynte Benedight, 134:25
    Lord J. blessed Pelican, 127:4
    my dearest one, 154:8
Jesus, accept J. as Savior, 805:12
    age of good sans-culotte J., 361:2
    as J. sat at meat, 35:32
    author and finisher, 45:12
    came to save sinners, 44:24
    Cross of J., 518:14
    died for somebody's sins, 863:14
    gentle J. meek and mild, 305:9
    Incarnate saved us, 734:15

Jesus *(continued)*
    increased in wisdom, 37:22
    keep your hearts through Christ J., 44:6
    king of Jews, 36:18
    lover of my soul, 305:8
    loves me this I know, 504:4
    man who says he is J., 315:2
    miracles did J. in Cana, 39:5
    most scientific man, 493:5
    nobody knows but J., 898:14
    none but J. heard, 416:1
    parsons preaching J. a revolutionary, 802:7
    saith give me to drink, 39:12
    stand up stand up for J., 477:11
    sure this J. will not do, 354:18
    that which was given to J., 117:13
    took bread, 36:3
    was born in Bethlehem, 31:36
    went to them walking on the sea, 34:27
    wept, 39:34
    we're more popular than J. now, 847:12
    with J. we worship Father, 388:7
Jesus Christ, advocate with the Father J., 46:8
    Don Quixote and I, 391:4
    her little child, 476:5
    I believe in J., 48:11
    kingdom and patience of J., 46:14
    our Lord, 49:8
    people who never heard of J., 683:18
    redemption by our Lord J., 48:16
    testimony of J., 46:14
    that J. is born, 898:17
    the same yesterday today and for ever,
      45:17
Jesus', feel just like J. son, 855:2
    good friend for J. sake, 226:17
Jets, sound of j. overhead, 724:6
Jeunesse, au temps de ma j. folle, 138:*n3*
    cueillez cueillez votre j., 150:*n9*
    qu'as-tu fait de ta j., 549:*n6*
    si j. savait, 151:5
Jew, because I wasn't J., 696:7
    either for Englishman or J., 354:18
    hated like a J., 836:8
    hath not a J. eyes, 185:11
    human form in heathen turk or j., 351:5
    hurt Negro avoid J. is curriculum,
      772:6
    I'm not a J. I'm Jew-ish, 838:7
    judges neither J. nor Gentile, 649:10
    much kindness in the J., 184:30
    neither Greek nor J., 44:12
    of Tarsus, 40:41
    only J. in Danville looking for matzoh,
      808:3
    wandering J., 889:23
    what one J. does, 822:5
    yes I am a J., 429:21
Jewel, caught my heavenly j., 162:22
    immediate j. of souls, 209:2
    no j. like Rosalind, 195:7
    of gold in swine's snout, 20:14
    of the just, 268:18
    precious j. in his head, 193:37
    rich j. in Ethiop's ear, 179:28
Jeweled unicorns, 677:16
Jewelry, just rattle your j., 847:11
    like j. from a grave, 762:12

Jewels five-words-long, 452:17
  give j. for set of beads, 177:12
  unclasps warmed j., 409:22
Jewish, being J. trouble enough, 778:10
  difficulty of being J., 768:10
  establishment of home for J. people, 551:7
  final solution of J. question, 697:14
  gaberdine, 184:28
  genius on a par with, 835:9
  living in middle of J. joke, 835:4
  man with parents alive, 835:5
  Mankind rather than J., 819:14
  no J. blood in my veins, 836:8
  take risks essence of J. life, 562:11
Jew-ish, I'm not a Jew I'm J., 838:7
Jews, Jesus king of J., 36:18
  King of the J., 31:36
  kiss and infidels adore, 293:4
  Papists Protestants J. Turks in one ship,
    247:8
  refuse till conversion of J., 266:21
  right and status of J. in any country, 551:7
  thrown back at all J., 822:5
  what have I in common with J., 655:12
Jezebel, dogs shall eat J., 12:7
  painted her face, 12:18
Jiggety-jig, home again j., 896:9
Jigsaw, Rosebud missing piece in j. puzzle,
    714:16
Jill, Jack and J., 893:18
  other named J. fly away J., 897:7
Jim, poor J. Jay, 616:10
  simple child dear brother J., 368:n1
Jimmie crack corn, 884:18
Jingle, little j. little chimes, 291:22
  triumph and the j., 654:5
Jingling of guinea, 452:1
Jingly, Lady J. Jones, 467:16
Jingo, by j. if we do, 503:17
Joan as my Lady, 241:2
  greasy J. keel pot, 174:33
Job, blessed the latter end of J., 14:39
  doth J. fear God for nought, 12:37
  fall into it like a soft j., 824:14
  give tools finish j., 620:3
  hypocrisy is whole-time j., 626:22
  is home to homeless man, 747:1
  more than one way to do j., 888:n4
  patience of J., 45:33
  poor as J., 187:29
  that's my j., 855:15
Jobs have been gone for 25 years, 877:3
Jockey of Norfolk not too bold, 160:n6
Jocosity, coarse j. catches the crowd, 635:11
Jocund, cocks and lions j. be, 230:5
  day stands tiptoe, 181:2
  rebecks sound, 251:4
  such a j. company, 371:12
  then be thou j., 216:12
Jocundity, jasper of j., 141:5
Joe, G.I. J., 887:22
  Old Black J., 503:15
  say it ain't so J., 887:9
  set 'em up J., 759:7
  where have you gone J. DiMaggio, 855:8
Joe's, Sloppy J., 749:13
Jog on the footpath way, 223:24
Johannes, absolute J. fac totum, 164:3

John Anderson my jo, 357:13
  awake my St. J., 294:14
  Baptist's head, 34:24
  Barleycorn got up again, 357:2
  Bull or Englishman's fireside, 361:6
  Donne Anne Donne Un-done, 228:n2
  I J., 46:14
  I J. saw the holy city, 47:11
  inspiring bold J. Barleycorn, 358:7
  Matthew Mark Luke and J., 265:3
  my son J., 896:1
  now I'm J., 848:1
  or Shaun, 650:22
  Peel with coat so gay, 408:13
  shut the door good J., 295:9
  some said J. print it, 271:6
  speak for yourself J., 437:7
  Stuart Mill, 629:3
  there St. J. mingles, 296:6
  Thomas marryin' Lady Jane, 663:12
  who killed J. Keats, 399:11
  whose name was J., 38:46
John Brown, in what balance weigh J., 716:2
John Brown's body, 716:2
John Henry told his captain, 885:12
Johnny, Frankie and J., 886:3
  I hardly knew ye, 884:6
  leave her J. leave her, 897:23
  little J. Green, 893:13
  when J. goes out, 867:11
  whiskey J., 897:15
John's, bounded by St. J., 456:7
Johnson, great Cham of literature Samuel J.,
    318:2
  Kennedy and J. administrations, 782:9
  no arguing with J., 323:8
Joie de vivre, distaste for spectacle of j., 857:13
Join, children j. hands and sing, 823:9
  choir invisible, 480:16
  don't j. too many gangs, 623:18
  few gangs if any, 623:18
  hand in hand Americans, 328:1
  now j. your hands and hearts, 170:33
  the family, 623:18
  them that j. house to house, 25:4
  triumph of skies, 305:10
  union and say Equal Pay, 488:22
  United States, 623:18
  will you j. dance, 515:3
Joined, he has j. great majority, 105:16
  lawfully j. together, 49:14
  make third j. former two, 274:7
  my name j. to theirs, 102:7
  rogue and whore together, 285:13
  what God hath j., 35:2
  when issues are j., 58:1
  whom God hath j., 49:18
Joint, every j. and motive, 204:4
  heirs with Christ, 41:19
  remove the j., 516:19
  time is out of j., 198:22
Joint-laborer, night j. with day, 196:14
Joints, dividing j. and marrow, 45:7
  of all gin j. in all towns in world, 758:3
Joke, ain't no j., 835:4
  dirty j. not attack upon morality, 735:9
  every j. long ago made, 528:7
  forgive Thy j. on me, 624:19

Joke *(continued)*
  funniest j. in world, 565:12
  good j. not criticized, 618:12
  housekeeping ain't no j., 513:6
  it's our only j., 577:14
  Jack j. poor potsherd, 547:9
  laughter over dirty j., 722:18
  life is but a j., 852:1
  living in middle of Jewish j., 835:4
  loses everything when joker laughs, 359:8
  treat woman as dirty j., 838:12
  worth laughing at, 735:7
Joked about every prominent man, 640:10
  world j. incessantly, 528:7
Joker, joke loses everything when j. laughs,
    359:8
Jokes, crack any of these old j., 73:13
  difference of taste in j., 480:25
  Fate's saddest j., 59:n4
  little j. on Thee, 624:19
  ten j. an hundred enemies, 313:23
Joking, my way of j. is tell truth, 565:12
Jollities, Jorrocks' jaunts and j., 429:12
Jollity, jest and youthful j., 250:21
  tipsy dance and j., 252:8
  upon my yowthe and my j., 135:7
Jolly and easy in minds, 459:5
  miller, 330:19
  swagman, 585:8
  three j. huntsmen, 896:6
  What j. fun, 579:15
Jonah was in the belly of the fish, 29:4
Jonathan heard not his father's oath, 10:42
  loved him as his own soul, 11:4
Jones, Casey J., 608:11
  Lady Jingly J., 467:16
  this is the army Mr. J., 673:13
Joneses, keeping up with J., 670:14, 886:10
Jonson, Ben J. his best poetry, 232:11
  O rare Ben J., 231:n2
Jonson's learned sock, 251:8
Jordan, I looked over J., 898:20
  stood in midst of J., 9:36
  that's the river of J., 898:26
Joris, and he, 460:16
Jorrocks' jaunts and jollities, 429:12
Joseph, king which knew not J., 7:22
  stript J. of his coat, 7:6
Joshua fit battle of Jericho, 898:15
  like J. commanded sun, 303:14
Jostle, though Philistines may j., 526:11
Jostling, no man lives without j., 407:15
  not done by j. in street, 354:9
Jot, one j. of former love retain, 167:11
  one j. of heart or hope, 254:24
  or tittle, 32:17
Jour, le j. de gloire est arrivé, 361:3
Journal will be disadvantageous, 499:6
Journalism, confuse television news with j.,
    852:4
  Gonzo j. is a style, 843:15
  no higher law in j., 685:2
  Rock j. is people who can't, 849:9
Journalist, historian is j. facing backwards, 626:11
  knows is morally indefensible, 838:5
Journalists, diplomats lie to j., 626:12
Journey, arrant jade on a j., 322:18
  back to seek my kindred, 672:4

Judea, Bethlehem of J., 31:36

Judeo-Christian, ancient rival against J. heritage, 782:8

Judge above his last, 81:3
    allow iniquities, 539:6
    amongst fools a j., 106:*n*4
    by sample we j. whole, 155:13
    children j. parents, 560:5
    condemned when criminal absolved, 100:10
    do not j. us too harshly, 716:14
    forbear to j., 170:9
    I'll be j. I'll be jury, 514:1
    impartial guardian of rule of law, 795:12
    impartial j., 325:12
    law says j. as looks down nose, 749:8
    learn from books we cannot j., 343:21
    listening like j. supreme, 418:18
    my witness and my j., 236:4
    never j. until other side heard, 68:4
    no king can corrupt, 225:20
    no one should j. own case, 100:18
    none blessed, 30:38
    not according to appearance, 39:20
    not play before done, 242:5
    not that we be not judged, 447:1
    not that ye be not judged, 33:12
    of all things, 269:25
    of authors' names, 292:21
    out of thy mouth will I j., 38:25
    people seldom j. right, 349:4
    quick and the dead, 48:11
    rain influence and j. prize, 251:7
    right j. judges wrong, 65:15
    setting yourself up as j., 76:11
    should not be young, 75:3
    sober as j., 304:10
    sole j. of truth, 295:1
    taste is best j., 533:14
    the fatherless, 24:32
    upright j. learned j., 186:9

Judged in light of final issue, 79:8
    intellectual product j. from age produced, 534:3
    judge not that we be not j., 447:1
    judge not that ye be not j., 33:12
    not to have lived, 538:5
    should be j. as a captain, 139:13

Judge's robe, 206:25

Judges, a fool with j., 106:*n*4
    as j. neither Jew nor Gentile, 649:10
    common j. of property, 307:1
    Constitution what j. say, 582:5
    do and must legislate, 538:18
    hungry j. sentence sign, 293:9
    in every state bound thereby, 339:14
    of facts not laws, 291:6
    right judge j. wrong, 65:15
    unelected life-tenured j., 842:5

Judgest, thou j. another, 41:8

Judging for themselves, 346:17
    no way of j. future, 331:11
    people by appearances, 266:13

Judgment, accurate in his j., 329:*n*1
    and exactitude enter him, 3:3
    and imagination, 378:23
    beauty bought by j. of eye, 174:8

Judgment *(continued)*
    bounded by Day of J., 456:*n*1
    bring every work into j., 24:2
    complains of his j., 264:3
    Daniel come to j., 186:3
    Day of J., 656:1
    difficult, 71:6, 343:3
    do not wait for last j., 770:8
    ever awake, 379:13
    execute j. against gods of Egypt, 7:40
    fled to brutish beasts, 192:31
    God's great J. Seat, 587:8
    green in j., 218:16
    hard to found j. on man, 151:17
    he looked for j., 25:4
    his ways are j., 9:30
    I suspend my j., 152:18
    men of ill j. ignore good, 65:8
    nor people's j. always true, 273:5
    or intuition more subtle, 538:15
    power out of thy soul's j., 141:3
    practical j. of Americans, 433:11
    private j., 318:6
    prophet under j. he preaches, 696:2
    reserve thy j., 197:23
    seek j., 24:32
    shallow spirit of j., 169:15
    we thought it J. Day, 536:20
    were we men of j., 785:9
    young in limbs in j. old, 185:4

Judgments, men's j. parcel of their fortunes, 218:32
    of Lord righteous, 15:17, 447:2
    with j. as watches, 292:8

Judicial, duty of j. department, 349:13
    function, 562:14
    power distinct from legislative, 330:4
    types of j. writing, 607:2

Judiciary, Imperial J. lives, 842:5
    safeguard of liberty, 582:5

Judicious, a little j. levity, 555:19
    swearin' keeps temper, 600:15
    wales portion with j. care, 356:9

Judy's in the bedroom, 870:7

Jug of Wine Loaf of Bread, 441:10
    one old j. without handle, 467:15

Jugement, je suspends mon j., 152:*n*11

Juggler of Day is gone, 508:11
    threadbare j. fortune-teller, 172:28

Juggling fiends no more believed, 217:29

Jug-jug, cuckoo j. pu-we, 227:4

Jugular, nearer unto him than his j. vein, 119:12

Juice, write until still have j., 722:6

Juices, keep j. flowing by jangling around, 747:6

Jukebox roars just like thunder, 861:12

Julia, in silks my J. goes, 241:14

Julian, remembered poor J., 721:15
    year of J. Calendar 710, 237:13

Julia's, where my J. lips smile, 240:12

Juliet and her Romeo, 181:17
    is the sun, 179:31
    unless philosophy make a J., 180:35

Julius Caesar thou art mighty yet, 193:19
    mightiest J. fell, 196:15

July, born on Fourth of J., 634:12
    English winter ending in J., 399:1

July *(continued)*
    in her eyes, 881:11
    June and J. flowers, 240:9
    March J. October May, 150:*n*1
    second day of J. 1776, 330:1
    swarm of bees in J., 882:16
    what to slave your Fourth of J., 476:21

July's day short as December, 223:13

Jumblies, lands where J. live, 467:11

Jump, good wits j., 158:3
    I cut down trees skip and j., 879:9
    I see him j. before me, 555:12
    not j. with common spirits, 185:7
    over the candlestick, 895:16
    thought j. sea and land, 221:13
    we'd j. life to come, 214:22

Jumped into bramble bush, 897:6

Jumping, chinook salmon j. falling back, 788:5
    from chair she sat in, 392:20

Jumps over lazy dog, 885:19

June and July flowers, 240:9
    as cuckoo is in J., 183:4
    knee-deep in J., 553:8
    leafy month of J., 376:19
    newly sprung in J., 357:4
    rare as day in J., 481:16
    seek ice in J., 394:15
    sophistries of J., 508:6
    swarm of bees in J., 882:16
    tell one's name livelong J., 508:14
    tenth day of J. 1940, 653:1
    thirty days hath J., 149:12
    this moment in J., 654:5
    we jazz J., 783:10
    when J. is past the fading rose, 245:14

Jungle, in j. too little to be killed, 588:16
    Law of the J., 588:18
    Laws of the J., 588:20
    like a j. sometimes, 875:4
    never get out of j. that way, 780:6
    Pack meets Pack in J., 588:19

Junk is not a kick, 774:1

Junkie's, every j. like a setting sun, 862:6

Junkies, our mothers all are j., 828:15

Junkyard, soul of j., 801:16

Juno's unrelenting hate, 274:13

Junto, power in oligarchical j., 330:16

Jupiter aligns with Mars, 846:4
    knows how to sugarcoat, 267:27
    laughs at perjuries of lovers, 101:20
    not bring back opportunity, 103:7
    singing vespers in Temple of J., 332:19
    what you see and touch, 106:16
    wresting from J. his thunder, 104:9

Jupiter's Statue by Phidias, 886:14

Juridical safeguards of individual freedom, 721:1

Juries, trial by j., 337:12

Jurisprudence, gladsome light of j., 158:22

Jury, I'll be judge I'll be j., 514:1
    passing on prisoner's life, 206:19
    trial by impartial j., 340:5
    trial by j., 340:6
    trial by j. a delusion, 386:18

Jurymen, that j. may dine, 293:9
Just, a j. war, 303:*n*3, 333:13
    actions of the j., 246:12
    Add Hot Water, 701:9
    and lasting peace, 447:2
    are the ways of God, 260:13
    be j. and fear not, 226:5
    be j. before you're generous, 346:13
    blessing upon head of j., 20:11
    blood of this j. person, 36:15
    cause it is j., 387:1
    company of j. and righteous, 68:15
    friends and brave enemies, 337:14
    gods are j., 213:10
    good man and j., 38:39
    how should man be j., 13:19
    if all men were j., 73:22
    in J.-spring, 701:5
    jewel of the j., 268:18
    let him be j., 394:3
    made what is strong j., 269:20
    man will pay more income tax, 74:20
    memory of the j. is blessed, 20:11
    merely j. is severe, 299:5
    not a j. man upon earth, 23:15
    nothing to do with that j. man, 36:13
    path of the j. as shining light, 19:29
    place for j. man prison, 473:18
    play fair j. and patient, 502:5
    rain on j. and unjust, 32:22
    reflect that God is j., 336:9
    shall man be more j. than God, 13:9
    show heavens more j., 211:33
    spirits of j. men, 45:14
    thrice armed that hath quarrel j., 170:7
    unjust peace before j. war, 303:*n*3
    upright man laughed to scorn, 13:24
    way is plain peaceful j., 446:1
    whatsoever things are j., 44:7
Justice, ancient j. overflows our crimes, 242:25
    art of good and fair, 120:31
    blind deaf an' dumb, 600:6
    confidence in j. of people, 445:6
    delayed justice denied, 442:18
    do j., 3:8
    doing j. loving mercy, 333:18
    equal and exact j., 337:12
    equal j. for all, 71:14
    establish j., 339:11
    even-handed j., 214:23
    extreme j. extreme injustice, 121:18
    extreme j. often injustice, 86:*n*3
    get out of way of j., 758:19
    government of eternal j., 457:9
    great interest of man, 390:17
    in fair round belly, 194:25
    in j. none should see salvation, 186:1
    inviolability founded on j., 797:2
    is the first virtue of social, 797:1
    is the only worship, 518:6
    lance of j. hurtless breaks, 212:30
    law of humanity j. equity, 324:20
    let j. be done though heaven fall, 120:22
    let j. be done though heaven perish, 363:1
    liberty plucks j., 206:14
    longed-for tidal wave of j., 845:14
    love of j. simply fear, 263:25
    machine rolls of itself, 600:20

Justice (*continued*)
    made for sake of peace, 144:2
    man's capacity for j., 696:3
    marriage placed under rule of equal j., 435:20
    mercy seasons j., 186:1
    military j. is to j., 538:2
    mirage of social j., 721:1
    model to the world of j., 862:13
    moderation in pursuit of j., 758:10
    no such thing as j., 568:12
    not charity wanting in world, 360:21
    not to be taken by storm, 606:19
    not violate laws of j., 319:10
    peace a disposition for j., 275:15
    peace more important than j., 144:2
    penetrates Eternal J. as eye into sea, 130:8
    Poetic J., 296:25
    rails upon thief, 212:29
    reason and j., 349:8
    returns, 92:22
    revenge a wild j., 165:14
    strength without j., 269:20
    strong lance of j., 212:30
    subject to God and J., 124:8
    superhighway of j., 823:11
    sword of j. has no scabbard, 347:6
    temper j. with mercy, 259:17
    temporary but conscience eternal, 144:3
    terror nothing but stern j., 356:1
    the law my ducats, 185:5
    there is none, 125:7
    though j. be thy plea, 186:1
    thunders condemnation, 472:16
    Thwackum was for doing j., 304:18
    to none sell j., 126:5
    toward all nations, 329:1
    uncompromising as j., 433:4
    want j. for all human beings, 808:3
    was done, 536:5
    where j. denied, 477:9
    which is the j., 212:29
    white moderate less devoted to j., 823:3
    with liberty and j. for all, 562:6
    without j. courage weak, 302:4
    without strength, 269:20
    work for tolerance for j., 682:10
Justices, current j. read the Constitution, 745:13
Justifiable, inconsistencies often j., 390:18
    ways of God j. to men, 260:13
Justification, work of art carry j., 567:2
Justified, existence and world justified, 547:11
    not j. doing evil for expediency, 571:3
    whom he called he j., 41:22
    wisdom j. of her children, 34:8
Justifieth, it is God that j., 41:24
Justify, end must j. the means, 283:11
    God's ways to man, 575:12
    he will not j. you without you, 116:16
    thought to j. wrongdoings, 299:23
    ways of God to men, 255:5
Justifying means by the end, 115:6
Justitia, fiat j. ruat coelum, 120:22
Justly, do j. and love mercy, 29:5
Just-spring, in J., 701:5
Jutty, no j. frieze buttress, 214:21
J'y suis j'y reste, 439:*n*2

K

Kaleidoscope, no law of history than of k., 484:14
Kane man who got everything wanted, 714:16
Kansas and Colorado have quarrel, 661:2
    I've feeling not in K. anymore, 764:5
    what is matter with K., 603:10
Kansas City, ev'rythin's up to date in K., 706:10
Karamazovs, all we K. such insects, 492:8
    they have Hamlets we K., 493:1
Kaspar's, old K. work was done, 381:6
Kat, I ain't a K., 644:4
Kate, kiss me K., 173:14
    O K. nice customs curtsy to great kings, 190:10
    some alas with K., 749:13
    trust thee gentle K., 182:15
Kathleen Mavourneen, 419:5
Kathryn, or Mabelle or K., 648:14
Katydid, glaze on k.-wing, 671:19
Kayak, I was out in my k., 892:6
Keats, who killed John K., 399:11
Kedar, tents of K., 24:4
Keel, drinks water her k. plows air, 163:20
    greasy Joan doth k. pot, 174:33
    in politics keep afloat on even k., 729:7
    ship sink on even k., 103:20
    thrill of life along k., 436:22
Keen and hard like wedge, 662:14
    and quivering ratio, 508:4
    dull fighter and k. guest, 183:19
    love's k. arrows, 195:19
    polished razor k., 297:9
    with k. appetite he sits down, 184:39
Keener with constant use, 391:14
    with his k. eye, 266:18
Keep and pass and turn again, 425:4
    another thing hidden, 53:16
    bid them k. teeth clean, 219:27
    breath's a ware will not k., 574:12
    cold young orchard, 623:11
    coming back and coming back, 642:11
    company he is wont to k., 68:22
    cool, 427:30
    corner in thing I love, 209:9
    easier to get than k. Fortune, 100:3
    'em down on the farm, 664:1
    England k. my bones, 175:31
    except the Lord k. the city, 19:4
    eyes open before marriage, 302:19
    fear God and k. his commandments, 24:2
    golden mean, 96:*n*16
    good tongue in head, 224:30
    goodbye and k. cold, 623:11
    guard and k. them, 57:22
    he may k. that will and can, 575:16
    home fires burning, 616:17
    how to k. is there any, 546:21
    ideas won't k., 580:16
    in adversity k. an even mind, 96:20
    in despite of light k. us together, 229:8
    let it k. one shape, 206:18
    like love seldom k., 749:9
    Lord bless thee and k. thee, 9:2
    many to k., 481:5

Keep *(continued)*
  me as the apple of the eye, 15:13
  on truckin', 856:7
  our Christmas merry still, 373:13
  own appointed limits k., 503:1
  promises to k., 623:8
  republic if you can k. it, 303:19
  right to k. and bear arms, 340:2
  Sabbath going to Church, 508:18
  shop and shop keep thee, 163:14
  six honest servingmen, 589:16
  soul bought by one able to k. it,
    458:16
  state in wonted manner k., 232:2
  stiff upper lip, 501:6
  stop hole to k. wind away, 202:14
  strong in any case keep cool, 707:11
  sunny side up, 697:10
  talk from getting overwise, 623:17
  thee in all thy ways, 17:29
  thee in the way, 8:18
  thee only unto her, 49:15
  them within thee, 21:19
  thou my feet, 421:4
  thy friend under own key, 205:30
  thy heart with all diligence, 19:30
  thy tongue from evil, 16:7
  time to k., 22:31
  to moderation, 106:11
  up appearances, 464:36
  up your bright swords, 207:30
  we are going to k. dog, 771:2
  wolf from door, 140:*n6*
  word of promise to our ear, 217:29
  wrong to k. guest back, 53:22
  yet I k. them, 822:7
  you shall k. the key, 197:25
  your hearts and minds, 44:6
  your powder dry, 385:6
  yourself to yourself, 463:27
Keeper, Abel was k. of sheep, 6:3
  brother's k., 6:4
  of warm lights, 65:25
  the Lord is thy k., 18:30
Keepers of the house shall tremble, 23:30
Keepest ports of slumber open, 188:20
Keepeth, he that k. Israel, 18:30
  he that k. thee will not slumber, 18:30
Keeping, time keeping rhythm, 678:14
  time time time, 449:25
  up with Joneses, 670:14, 886:10
  up with yesterday, 635:7
Keeps, bond which k. me pale, 216:13
  end from being hard, 624:2
  his house in hand, 65:21
  known by company he k., 68:*n8*
  money movin' around, 600:14
  on windy side of care, 190:29
  perseverance k. honor bright, 203:22
  self-made laws, 491:21
  thee from thy God, 421:9
  truly k. his first last day, 229:9
  warm her note, 245:15
Keg, fizz like wine in k., 635:10
Kelly, slide K. slide, 885:21
Kelson of creation is love, 485:17
Ken, nane sall k. where he is gane, 886:10
  swims into his k., 408:17

Kennedy and Johnson administrations, 782:9
  gave world vision, 788:17
  on the assassination of K., 809:1
  you are no Jack K., 796:3
Kennel, truth's a dog must to k., 211:7
Kennin', gang a k. wrang, 357:3
Kennst du das Land, 342:*n6*
Kenny, they killed K., 879:13
Kentuck, hurrah for old K., 392:22
Kentucky, long ago in K. I stood, 744:2
  old K. home, 503:13
Kept breath to cool his pottage, 55:5
  by transgressing k. law, 254:15
  falling oars k. time, 267:7
  I have not k. my square, 218:22
  I k. my word he said, 616:7
  the faith, 45:2
  watch Matthew and Waldo, 675:11
  when no proportion k., 177:22
Kernel, if it contain K., 510:10
Kestrels dear to kestrels, 82:14
Kettle, faces as blackness of a k., 29:*n1*
  how agree the k. and pot, 30:41
  of fish, 527:1
  Polly put k. on, 896:17
  pot calls k. black, 158:5
  speech like cracked k., 493:13
Kew, his Highness' dog at K., 296:22
Key, door to which no K., 441:20
  each in prison thinking of k., 676:17
  golden k., 252:1
  I have heard k. turn, 676:17
  in a bondman's k., 184:29
  out of k. with his time, 665:4
  to keep back beauty, 546:21
  to life's significance, 541:21
  under thy own life's k., 205:30
  used k. always bright, 302:24
  who was a k. a man, 783:11
  with this k. Shakespeare, 372:16
  you shall keep the k., 197:25
Key-machine of modern industrial age,
    708:4
Keynote of government is injustice, 604:13
Keys, fingers on these k., 641:4
  fluster of lost door k., 763:7
  of hell and death, 46:19
  of kingdom of heaven, 34:37
  of Paradise O opium, 393:6
  over the noisy k., 502:16
  shining k. took from her, 536:2
  two massy k. he bore, 253:9
Khrushchev, I call upon Chairman K., 786:8
Kibe, galls his k., 202:11
Kick against pricks, 40:23, 63:9
  I get k. out of you, 691:10
  jackass can k. barn down, 651:11
  wheel's k., 635:15
  won't have Nixon to k., 771:4
  you downstairs, 514:6
Kicked and torn and beaten out, 404:20
  waxed fat and k., 9:31
Kicks dust, 474:21
  on Route Sixty-six, 792:2
Kid, here's looking at you k., 758:5
  leopard shall lie down with the k., 25:19
Kiddo, take it from me k., 701:9
Kidney, man of my k., 187:16

Kids, come on k., 690:15
  loved the dog, 771:2
  playing game in rye, 793:11
  thank you k., 732:13
Kike, make sure not a guinea or k., 709:14
Kilimanjaro highest mountain, 721:16
Kill, almost k. man as k. book, 254:7
  and bliss me, 881:14
  basilisk is sure to k., 291:19
  be my brother or I k. you, 335:2
  best to k. him right away, 344:10
  bullet that will k. me, 365:11
  cankers in musk-rose buds, 178:20
  care k. a cat, 191:*n1*
  cure disease k. patient, 166:8
  do not k., 3:8
  establishes tyranny k. Brutus, 142:9
  flea though he k. none, 231:6
  gonna k. me., 762:8
  hates thing he would not k., 185:28
  him in the shell, 192:1
  himself or someone else, 756:21
  human beings trying to k. me, 735:8
  if they move k. 'em, 841:6
  in artificial manner, 407:6
  joys with love, 181:16
  kill kill kill kill kill, 213:2
  killing beast that cannot k., 672:5
  learn him or k. him, 522:17
  let's k. all the lawyers, 170:14
  mockingbird, 813:4
  nor yet canst thou k. me, 230:22
  not alive enough to know how to k. self,
    793:2
  one admiral to encourage others, 299:11
  one to save hundred thousand, 364:15
  reverence you've killed hero, 742:16
  sooner k. man than hawk, 670:6
  strike at king must k. him, 429:10
  them all, 126:2
  things they do not love, 185:28
  thou shalt not k., 8:14
  thy physician, 210:28
  time to k., 22:31
  time without injuring eternity, 474:10
  to know to k. to create, 491:17
  to wear fox have to k. it, 671:22
  us for their sport, 212:17
  when you have to k., 621:14
  where I please, 827:12
  why k. her policeman asked, 715:1
  wife with kindness, 173:20
  willingly as k. a fly, 173:3
  you can k. anyone, 795:11
  you if you quote it, 598:1
Killed, books not k. by fire, 653:7
  by overwork, 587:7
  calf in high style, 270:12
  care k. a cat, 191:15
  dragons have to be k., 773:19
  effort nearly k. her, 606:12
  fought dogs k. cats, 460:7
  hawked at and k., 216:3
  I'm k. sire, 459:23
  many times in politics, 619:1
  more k. by suppers, 243:26
  only once in war, 619:1
  scotched snake not k. it, 216:10

Killed *(continued)*
some sleeping k., 177:8
the rat, 897:8
they k. Kenny, 879:13
too little to be k., 588:16
two thirds of people k., 638:3
we could all have been k., 879:3
we have k. God, 547:*n*4
who k. Cock Robin, 893:8
who k. John Keats, 399:11
who k. the pork chops, 812:9
you first time off base, 721:8
you who are k. and wasted, 703:12
you've k. all our leaders, 869:7
Killeth, letter k., 43:12
wrath k. the foolish man, 13:10
Killing as canker to rose, 253:5
by simply exerting will, 492:*n*4
defenseless black people, 809:1
eternity essence of tragedy, 586:6
frost, 225:25
medal for k. two men, 857:14
no qualms at all about k., 843:14
time essence of comedy, 586:6
treat for Ossete, 690:14
Kills, air that k., 575:6
destroys book k. reason, 254:7
shadow k. the growth, 233:10
six or seven dozen Scots, 182:17
superiority to sex that k., 751:6
thing he loves, 561:3
world k. the good, 721:7
Kiltartan, my country K. Cross, 592:20
Kiltartan's poor, 592:20
Kimono, woman in k., 738:7
Kin, fair and foul near k., 595:19
little more than k., 196:24
makes whole world k., 203:25
Kind, adieu k. friends, 885:15
as kings upon coronation, 274:2
be to her virtues k., 283:12
be too k. to be k. enough, 292:3
blundering k. of melody, 273:7
charity is k., 42:27
consorteth according to k., 31:1
could not ourselves be k., 716:14
cruel only to be k., 201:14
Fortune more k. than her custom,
186:7
had it been early had been k., 308:17
hearts more than coronets, 451:3
human k. not bear much reality, 678:5
I am a k. of burr, 207:12
I have been her k., 820:10
less than k., 196:24
love is k., 42:27
not seek for k. relief, 351:8
serve country and thy k., 519:9
talk about this be k., 783:4
thief said last k. word, 463:1
through fire for k. heart, 187:14
two almost divide the k., 294:1
war is k., 609:2
were all thy children k., 189:2
where each of us belongs, 819:9
you've got to be k., 801:2
Kinder, a little k. than necessary, 577:8
gentler nation, 805:4

Kindergarten, God has pity on k. children,
804:5
Kindle, cannot k. when will, 494:17
soft desire, 274:21
truths k. light for t., 89:19
Kindled, anger of Lord k., 11:14
at taper of conwiviality, 464:26
light here k., 240:5
man like light k. and put out, 62:10
world Fire k., 62:4
Kindles, fires true Genius k., 295:13
in clothes a wantonness, 240:15
love kindled by virtue k. another, 129:24
Kindleth, how great a little fire k., 45:27
Kindliness of sheets, 669:9
Kindling her undazzled eyes, 254:12
Kindly, be k. affectioned, 41:31
earth slumber, 452:4
frosty but k., 194:5
fruits of the earth, 49:2
had we never loved sae k., 357:9
Light, 421:4
Nature's k. law, 295:3
stopped for me, 509:17
to his fellow men, 51:10
Kindness, a God of great k., 12:30
acts of k. and of love, 368:7
always depended on k. of strangers, 766:7
and lies, 738:1
begets kindness, 65:5
Christ took k., 463:1
cup o' k. yet, 357:18
glad k., 593:15
in women not looks, 173:21
kill wife with k., 173:20
lose natural k., 593:12
milk of human k., 214:16
much k. in the Jew, 184:30
no act of k. ever wasted, 58:17
not free from ridicule, 446:4
practice random k., 871:5
to fellow creature, 884:21
tongue is the law of k., 22:19
wished to lay foundations of k., 716:14
Kindnesses, great persons great k., 157:32
of k. one makes heart run over, 334:7
thought of k. done, 91:25
Kindred, friends k. days, 424:14
journey back to see k., 672:4
never in such slavery as to forgo k., 106:6
welcome k. glooms, 300:15
Kindreds, all nations and k., 46:35
Kinds, absolute natures or k., 76:1
birds are k. of knowledge, 76:8
material objects of two k., 89:17
Kine, learn from k. ruminating, 548:3
Pharaoh's lean k. loved, 182:28
seven good k., 7:9
seven thin k., 7:9
King, a' for our rightfu' K., 357:10
a new k. over Egypt, 7:22
and god in world he knew, 701:1
Arthur is not dead, 138:16
balm from an anointed k., 177:4
but thou the k. did banish, 176:16
by your own fireside, 155:8
Cambyses' vein, 182:26
can do no wrong, 318:20

King *(continued)*
cat may look on k., 148:13
catch conscience of k., 199:19
Charles's head, 465:28
chief defect of Henry K., 606:11
cometh unto thee lowly, 29:14
contrary to k. built paper-mill, 170:17
Cophetua loved beggarmaid, 179:30
cotton is k., 422:3
divinity doth hedge a k., 201:29
earth receive her K., 289:15
every inch a k., 212:26
every man a K., 698:6
exists only as such, 153:14
farced title 'fore k., 189:23
farewell k., 177:9
follow the K., 455:9
George be a k., 459:18
glare surrounds k. hides him, 153:14
glorious to be Pirate K., 526:5
glory to newborn K., 305:10
God bless the K., 297:18
God save the k., 10:39, 292:2
God save the k. say amen, 177:16
good K. Wenceslas, 479:1
governs like a k., 313:10
great God our K., 439:10
great K. above all gods, 17:32
greater than K. himself, 306:2
half the zeal I served my k., 226:6
heart and stomach of a k., 151:7
heaven's all-gracious k., 457:11
here lies a K. that ruled, 245:13
here lies the k., 280:27
honor the k., 45:39
I am the Lizard K., 858:8
I am the Roman k., 268:*n*3
I was a K. in Babylon, 552:9
if chance will have me K., 214:12
impossible to discharge duties as K., 705:2
in country of blind one-eyed man is k.,
141:10
in exile, 663:7
in sleep a k., 221:28
incapable of doing wrong, 318:17
is the k. dead, 172:4
it's good to be the k., 811:11
Jesus K. of Jews, 36:18
kings did k. to death, 777:5
let there be one k., 50:23
little profits idle k., 451:11
love is my lord and k., 454:10
made for quietness' sake, 238:21
Madness wholesome even for K., 511:1
mine eyes have seen the K., 25:10
mockery k. of snow, 177:20
more royalist than k., 890:22
mortal temples of k., 177:8
my God and K., 243:9
niece of K. Gorboduc, 205:26
no k. in Israel, 10:29
not every year a k. born, 111:4
of a k. of England too, 151:7
of all kings, 880:11
of Babylon stood at the parting, 28:16
of France went up hill, 892:14
of glory shall come in, 15:25

King *(continued)*
of infinite space, 199:3
of kings, 47:8, 305:*n*4
of pain, 530:13
of shreds and patches, 201:8
of Spain's daughter, 894:18
of terrors, 13:36
of the Jews, 31:36
of the world, 872:2
offends no law is k. indeed, 163:19
old and foolish k., 23:3
old k. to sparrow, 616:9
old mad blind despised k., 402:19
once and future k., 365:*n*1
once asked a poet, 781:5
over children of pride, 14:37
Ozymandias k. of kings, 401:13
pageantry of k., 339:9
passing brave to be a k., 168:1
Pirate K., 526:5
reigns but not govern, 154:9
rightwise k. of England, 138:2
ruthless K., 316:14
seemed to me like k., 663:7
shall reign in righteousness, 26:14
sits in Dunfermline, 889:13
so excellent a k., 196:31
Son of Heaven's eternal K., 250:9
still I am k. of those, 177:18
stomach of a k., 151:7
strike at k. must kill him, 429:10
such a K. Harry, 167:10
the K. went on, 515:11
think not k. did banish thee, 176:16
this hath not offended k., 143:10
to be k. not within prospect, 214:6
tomorrow shall die, 30:33
true beggar true k., 325:18
was in countinghouse, 894:7
was pregnant, 824:8
wash balm from an anointed k., 177:4
whatsoever k. reign, 883:12
who is this K. of glory, 15:26
who Pretender or who K., 297:18
whom the k. delighteth to honor, 12:32
winter k., 720:7
without woman I love, 705:2
world is a k., 366:19
worm that eat of a k., 201:17
year's pleasant k., 227:4
King Lear, impressed by reading K., 335:21
Kingdom, and patience of Jesus Christ, 46:14
by the sea, 449:22
Childhood Is K. Nobody Dies, 695:19
death's other K., 676:20
drink in my Father's k., 36:3
enter into k. of heaven, 33:23
fit for k. of God, 37:30
given them isn't worth ruling, 513:8
God hath numbered thy k., 28:25
good mind possesses k., 104:8
is divided, 28:25
keys of k. of heaven, 34:37
large k. for little grave, 177:13
man like little k., 192:2
my k. for a horse, 172:11
my mind to me a k. is, 154:10
no society bring K. of God, 648:6

Kingdom *(continued)*
not enter into k. of heaven, 34:40
of daylight's dauphin, 546:9
of God within you, 38:20
of heaven is at hand, 32:4
of heaven like a net, 34:20
of heaven like mustard seed, 34:18
of Heaven within you, 114:1
of perpetual night, 171:29
of such is k. of God, 36:38
of the shore, 221:18
of well kingdom of sick, 835:19
remember me when in thy k., 38:35
rich man enter into k., 35:4
root of the k., 79:17
teach order to peopled k., 188:34
theirs is k. of heaven, 32:14
thine is the k., 12:24, 32:25
thy k. come, 32:25
who draw us to k., 114:1
Kingdoms, all the k. of world, 37:23
are but cares, 138:17
are clay, 218:3
did shake k., 25:23
goodly states and k., 408:17
kissed away k., 218:30
of this world, 46:39
sifted three k., 275:*n*1
Kingfishers, as k. catch fire, 546:20
Kingly, his state is k., 254:22
King's, all the k. horses, 895:1
daughter is all glorious within, 16:25
daughter o' Noroway, 889:14
English, 187:4
First Minister, 621:4
grim k. dog, 67:6
marched by k. name, 695:2
might greater than human, 69:22
name a tower of strength, 172:6
not the k. crown nor sword, 206:25
our only lord, 167:8
rides hobbyhorse along k. highway, 313:21
subject's duty is k., 189:21
Kings, all be happy as k., 555:13
all K. and their favorites, 229:9
all k. mostly rapscallions, 523:6
and counselors of the earth, 13:4
and princes have philosophy, 75:9
angels in forms of k., 337:10
barrel-house k., 639:13
cabbages and k., 516:4
calm contending k., 172:35
captains and k. depart, 589:8
change state with k., 221:7
crown that seldom k. enjoy, 170:25
death beats at palaces of k., 96:4
death lays icy hand on k., 246:13
descended of so many k., 219:18
did king to death, 777:5
divine right of k., 444:12
dread and fear of k., 186:1
flower of k. and knights, 138:14
glory to King of k., 305:*n*4
grammar control k., 268:3
happy as k., 704:11
have sat down, 30:36
he shall stand before k., 21:23
heart's ease must k. neglect, 189:22

Kings *(continued)*
in golden suits ride elephants, 767:7
it makes gods, 172:5
kind as k. upon coronation day, 274:2
king of all k., 880:11
King of k., 47:8, 305:*n*4
know K. of England, 526:6
laws or k. cause or cure, 307:14
like stars, 403:7
mad world mad k., 175:11
may love treason but traitor hate, 88:*n*13
meaner creatures k., 172:5
mercy enthroned. in hearts of k., 186:1
Nature's little k., 227:16
nice customs curtsy to great k., 190:10
not k. and lords but nations, 389:3
overthrown divine right of k., 703:4
Ozymandias king of k., 401:13
pale k. and princes, 412:5
peasants born k. of earth, 432:10
plucker down of k., 170:23
politeness of k., 349:12
pretend to watch over economy, 319:4
pride of k., 294:14
princes but breath of k., 356:10
prophets and k., 37:35
Right Divine of K., 297:4
royal throne of k., 176:24
sad stories of death of k., 177:8
setter up of k., 170:23
showers on her k. barbaric pearl, 256:6
slave to fate chance k., 230:23
spirit of Zeus-fostered k., 50:22
sport of k., 289:19
tax heavier than k., 303:7
teeming womb of royal k., 176:24
tired of k., 424:19
tyrants from policy, 325:5
until philosophers are k., 75:9
vain the ambition of k., 237:11
walk with K., 590:2
what have k. that privates have not, 189:22
would not play at, 327:3
Kinship with the stars, 505:7
Kinsmen, as K. met a Night, 509:7
Kirk, below the k., 375:20
is this the k., 376:22
nearer God more far, 160:1
Kiss, ae fond k., 357:8
afresh, 241:3
after k. comes throttle, 748:7
and cling, 517:*n*1
and tell, 286:29
being tired she bade me k., 168:13
blow the k., 817:6
come k. me, 881:14
come let us k. and part, 167:11
coward does it with k., 561:3
darling k. me, 779:10
fades out from k. to k., 591:17
first k. is magic, 674:12
gin a body k. a body, 883:*n*1
give me a k., 241:3
is still a kiss, 702:11
Jews k. infidels adore, 293:4
keep k. in refrigerator, 713:10
Kiss Bang Bang, 792:9
last lamenting k., 230:4

Kiss (*continued*)
 leave a k. but in the cup, 232:16
 long as my exile, 220:2
 make me immortal with a k., 168:21
 me and be quiet, 297:8
 me Hardy, 355:14
 me Kate, 173:14
 me sweet and twenty, 204:26
 not a k. nor look be lost, 748:11
 not k. your f.ing flag, 701:12
 of death, 617:10
 on hand might feel good, 746:6
 part without k., 520:4
 place to make well, 389:11
 rough male k. of blankets, 669:9
 so k. on, 241:3
 soldier's k. dwells on lips, 487:9
 some that shadows k., 185:9
 these secret stones with me, 739:3
 till the cow comes home, 238:3
 what is a k., 240:10
 while I k. the sky, 854:5
 with one long k. my soul, 168:*n6*
 you take is better, 204:3
Kissed by white paper, 839:6
 came to Jesus and k. him, 36:8
 curtsied when you have and k., 224:12
 good-bye I have k. it, 732:13
 here hung lips I have k., 202:12
 in field of white, 726:7
 Jenny k. me, 392:20
 lovely grass, 669:5
 maiden all forlorn, 897:8
 not k. in forty years, 688:13
 O sad k. mouth, 530:3
 pacified Psyche k. her, 449:17
 righteousness and peace have k. each other,
  17:21
 stones k. by English dead, 699:8
 them and put them there, 554:2
 we have k. away kingdoms, 218:30
 what lips my lips have k., 695:12
Kisses, between k. and wine, 599:14
 bring again bring again, 207:8
 from female mouth, 397:17
 give me a thousand k., 91:5
 I understand thy k., 182:39
 joy as it flies, 352:8
 many thousand k., 219:4
 more than k. letters mingle souls, 230:14
 of enemy deceitful, 22:1
 played cards for k., 162:8
 remembered k. after death, 452:22
 stolen k. much completer, 392:14
 you have forgotten my k., 530:19
Kissing, die young like k. God, 807:11
 fool invented k., 286:4
 god k. carrion, 198:33
 had to stop, 462:3
 hand may feel good, 698:9
 no more k. after, 517:*n1*
Kit, your old k.-bag, 643:22
Kitchen, get out of k., 661:7
 long and ghastly k., 468:12
 scrub k. pavement, 591:18
 set around the k. fire, 553:7
Kitchens, wildcats in your k., 208:13
Kites, chronicle the wars of k., 260:28

Kits cats sacks wives, 892:22
Kitsch causes two tears to flow, 824:6
 excludes everything, 824:5
 is epitome of all spurious, 758:13
Kitten, rather be k. and cry mew, 182:35
 trouble with a k., 732:10
Kittens, deserve all these k., 635:9
 whiskers on k., 706:16
Kitty, I don't wants tips from k., 747:3
Kitty Fisher found it, 896:5
Klug, und bin so k. als wie zuvor, 344:*n1*
Knapsack, marshal's baton in k., 366:4
Knave, arrant k., 198:18
 himself a k., 291:8
 how absolute the k. is, 202:10
 of Hearts, 894:2
 playing the k., 277:6
 rascally yea-forsooth k., 187:25
 surname epithet for k., 141:*n7*
Knavery, picture requires k. trickery deceit,
  519:7
 religion k. and change, 279:4
Knaves arrant k. all, 199:25
 called them untaught k., 181:36
 little better than false k., 191:7
 thieves and treachers, 211:3
Kneaded, a k. clod, 206:38
Knee, banjo on my k., 503:9
 bowed patient k., 395:23
 her head on her k., 210:8
 lean in joy upon Father's k., 351:1
 pregnant hinges of the k., 200:10
Knee-deep in June, 553:8
Kneel before Lord our maker, 17:32
 down and ask forgiveness, 213:8
Kneels, not one k., 486:14
Knees, bringing to his k., 695:16
 down on your k., 195:20
 fell upon k. and blessed God, 240:2
 live on k., 643:10, 653:5
 man-at-arms now serve on k., 163:4
 of the gods, 52:23
 they that enter must go on k., 237:8
 to thee all k. bent, 517:11
 work done upon his k., 590:5
Knell, by fairy hands k. rung, 317:11
 curfew tolls k., 315:11
 of Union, 338:10
 strikes like rising k., 395:13
 that summons, 215:16
Knew, Achilles whom we k., 451:18
 anguish of marrow, 675:26
 anybody else I k. as well, 474:7
 been a bell and never k. it, 860:12
 changed from him they k., 622:7
 he nothing k., 260:5
 I k. him Horatio, 202:12
 I k. him when, 609:12
 if youth but k. if old age but could, 151:5
 Johnny I hardly k. ye, 884:6
 life the old Sabines k., 93:20
 man was coming to my house, 474:24
 my son was mortal, 73:26
 never k. so young a body, 185:32
 none k. color of the sky, 608:18
 not Astrophil, 169:8
 not Joseph, 7:22
 phoenix in my youth, 593:4

Knew (*continued*)
 taught me all I k., 589:16
 that life was fiction, 813:10
 they were pilgrims, 239:20
 things that were and would be, 50:12
 thy face or name, 229:7
 who k., 835:2
 worst too young, 588:7
Knickknacks, Beulah patient among k., 871:2
Knife, chasing you down street with k., 814:4
 cut off tails with k., 892:10
 fear tastes like rusty k., 767:3
 hardest k. ill-used, 222:4
 how cut without k., 893:14
 I the wound and k., 491:7
 like eating soup with a k., 680:8
 other men are the carving k., 598:10
 put a k. to thy throat, 21:24
 sharpening my oyster k., 689:16
 smylere with k., 134:19
 war even to k., 395:4
 watering pot pruning k., 456:17
 when they take k., 508:3
 wind's like whetted k., 635:17
Knife-edge of mere fact, 824:15
Knight, ail thee k.-at-arms, 412:2
 gentle k. pricking on plain, 160:3
 like young Lochinvar, 373:10
 not worthy to be called k., 61:13
 of the Sorrowful Countenance, 156:4
 parfit gentil k., 133:10
 plumed k., 518:2
 prince can mak belted k., 358:19
 there lived a k., 392:15
 to be their wooer, 890:2
 who has heart of k., 61:17
Knighthood, of k. and of freedom flour,
  136:14
 so full of k., 138:5
 when k. was in flower, 392:15
Knightly years were gone, 552:9
Knights, armorers accomplishing k., 189:18
 death of most noblest k., 138:13
 flower of kings and k. destroyed,
  138:14
 ladies dead and lovely k., 222:9
 let others sing of k., 167:4
Knit, come k. hands, 252:11
Knits a bolder One, 509:1
 up ravelled sleave of care, 215:21
Knitters in the sun, 205:2
Knitting loose train of thy hair, 252:26
Knives, hands made before k., 286:2
 men with k. in brain, 428:17
Knock and it shall be opened, 33:16
 as you please nobody home, 294:11
 'em out pick round, 853:11
 first to k. first admitted, 778:7
 heart k. at my ribs, 214:11
 sounds exceed k. at door, 383:13
 stand at the door and k., 46:27
 to wail or k. the breast, 260:25
 when you k. it never is home, 326:13
 where k. is open wide, 318:9
 you but k. breathe shine, 230:26
Knockdown argument, 274:9, 516:15
Knocked, when Luftwaffe k. down buildings,
  866:1

Knocker, tie up the k., 295:9
Knocking, come k. at my door, 505:4
   on moonlit door, 616:6
Knocks, apostolic blows and k., 262:11
   open locks whoever k., 216:29
   opportunity k. once, 103:*n4*
   you down with butt end, 323:8
Knolled, bells k. to church, 194:22
Knolling departing friend, 187:23
Knot, crowned k. of fire, 679:13
   Gordian k. unloose, 188:33
   subtle k. which makes us man, 229:19
   thrice tie up true love's k., 227:2
Knots, pokers into true-love k., 378:12
Knotted and combined locks part, 198:5
Know a subject ourselves, 310:5
   all I k. is I am not Marxist, 478:6
   all there is to be knowed, 574:9
   all ye k. on earth, 410:20
   arrive at what not k., 678:21
   as I am known, 42:29
   as if to k. became fatality, 642:10
   as much as possible, 545:6
   be still and k. that I am God, 16:28
   better be ignorant than half k., 101:3
   better k. nothing than half-k., 476:*n2*
   better k. nothing than what ain't so, 476:9
   blaspheme what they do not k., 269:27
   both act and k., 266:19
   by their fruits k. them, 33:22
   dancer from dance, 594:17
   determined to k. beans, 475:11
   disciplines of wars, 189:13
   disposition of women, 86:11
   do not k. much about gods, 679:3
   do you k. me my lord, 198:31
   do you want to k. who you are, 737:12
   do your thing & I shall k. you, 423:19
   does one really want to k., 775:6
   doesn't k. what he likes, 704:5
   don't k. where go better, 622:19
   dost k. who made thee, 350:12
   dost thou k. me fellow, 211:5
   enough who k. how to learn, 531:25
   every wise man's son k., 204:25
   everything forgive everything, 362:*n5*
   for whom bell tolls, 231:8
   four things wiser to k., 699:10
   gallanter I k., 508:5
   go we k. not where, 206:38
   God with thee k. it not, 370:6
   greater than we k., 372:12
   have the gift to k. it, 194:19
   hawk from handsaw, 199:8
   he will k. it's gone, 772:5
   heartily k., 424:15
   how in your darkness k., 610:4
   how should I k. what I'll be, 681:14
   how should I true love k., 201:23
   how tender 'tis to love babe, 215:5
   how to grow old, 490:18
   how to speak falsehoods, 54:12
   I am but summer, 695:11
   I am happier than I k., 258:31
   I k. a bank, 178:19
   I k. all worth knowing in America, 456:16
   I k. and world knows, 421:13
   I k. it when I see it, 780:15

Know *(continued)*
   I k. myself a man, 227:17
   I k. not seems, 196:26
   I k. not the man, 36:11
   I k. that is poetry, 511:15
   I k. thy pride, 10:44
   I k. what I like, 612:17
   I k. you all, 181:33
   I said I didn't k., 522:14
   I shall meet fate, 592:20
   if cuckold may not k., 662:4
   if don't k. where going, 793:8
   if find answer k. mind of God, 854:3
   if to do as easy as to k., 184:14
   if you gotta ask you'll never k., 724:11
   if you want to k. yourself, 359:17
   I'm farther from heaven, 418:3
   in baseball don't k. nothing, 807:3
   in Boston ask how much does he k., 524:5
   in mathematics never k. what about, 614:8
   in part prophesy in part, 42:29
   in truth we k. nothing, 70:11
   it no more, 18:7
   Jesus loves me this I k., 504:4
   less than all unknown, 236:2
   less understand more, 654:1
   let him not k. 't, 209:12
   let not left hand k., 32:24
   liberty to k., 254:13
   like love don't k. where or why, 749:9
   living k. no bounds, 246:11
   lucky to die and k. it, 485:20
   make me to k. mine end, 16:17
   man not k. of God, 737:9
   many admire few k., 71:8
   men k. so little of men, 602:2
   much say little, 312:23
   my methods Watson, 573:16
   my soul hath power to k., 227:16
   neither shall his place k. him, 13:17
   never k. how high we are, 510:12
   never k. what is enough, 351:18
   never prophesy onless k., 482:3
   never see nor k. nor miss me, 651:3
   no such liberty, 266:1
   none of them k. one half as much, 574:9
   not enough to k., 78:15
   not k. I am a woman, 195:12
   not subtle ways, 425:4
   not utter what dost not k., 182:15
   not what they do, 38:34
   not what they mean, 452:21
   not what we may be, 201:25
   nothing except my ignorance, 70:6
   oh do I k. them, 718:11
   only broken images, 676:6
   only k. we loved in vain, 394:8
   only that he nothing knew, 260:5
   others that we k. not of, 199:21
   parting all we k. of heaven, 511:9
   people you k. yet can't name, 799:16
   place for first time, 679:12
   pleasure none but madmen k., 273:9
   pools I used to k., 575:8
   power to k. all things, 227:16
   reason from what we k., 294:16
   rest who does not k., 101:22
   safer to k. too little, 521:6

Know *(continued)*
   say not you k. another, 335:3
   she thinks o' me, 588:1
   something of own country, 314:19
   strive to grasp what they do not k., 80:9
   study great deal to k. little, 297:16
   subject of knowledge is to k., 76:8
   tell me what you k., 425:14
   that age to age succeeds, 450:10
   that I may k. how frail I am, 16:17
   that man might k. end, 193:18
   that my redeemer liveth, 13:39
   that the Lord is God, 18:3
   that you do not know, 58:2
   the best thought and said, 497:7
   the right moment, 55:10
   them by their fruits, 33:21
   there is cause for her to k., 771:14
   they k. and do not k., 678:2
   this I k. full well, 282:23
   thought so now I k. it, 291:20
   thyself, 55:4, 295:1
   till then what love I bore thee, 369:13
   to k. is nothing, 545:17
   to k. to kill to create, 491:17
   to k. to k. to love her so, 627:18
   to k. well involves ignorance, 484:6
   trick worth two of that, 182:8
   we all k. Anna Livia, 650:21
   we are eternal, 276:18
   we k. the good, 67:22
   we k. what we are, 201:25
   what do I k., 152:19
   what false heart doth k., 215:8
   what God and man is, 455:27
   what I know and write it, 776:9
   what I like, 612:17
   what I read in papers, 640:3
   what is past I k., 29:25
   what is to come I k. not, 29:25
   what no other man can k., 567:14
   what other people don't know, 573:12
   what should it k. of death, 368:2
   what should they k. of England, 588:8
   what 'tis to pity, 194:22
   what to do with this time, 426:6
   what you don't k. make book, 375:10
   when did he k. it, 806:9
   when one doesn't k. where going, 343:17
   when you k. your name, 830:13
   where'er I go, 370:15
   where I am I don't k., 745:1
   which way wind blows, 851:15
   who only England k., 588:8
   who speaks does not k., 57:18
   who we are enlist again, 816:5
   whose prayers make whole, 587:10
   whose woods I think I k., 623:6
   with complete certainty, 795:12
   world unknowable we k., 577:3
   world without going outdoors, 57:16
   worst and provide for it, 331:10
   wot lays afore us, 465:3
   ye not there is a prince fallen, 11:12
   you k. as well as we, 72:7
   you k. how it always is, 790:4
   you know more than you think, 736:4
   you k. we French, 459:22

L

Latin, all their botany L., 424:16
    carve in L. or in Greek, 249:26
    he Greek and L. speaks, 262:n1
    learn L. as honor, 619:2
    small L. and less Greek, 233:1
    soft bastard L., 397:17
    speke no word but L., 134:9
    was no more difficile, 262:1
    word for three farthings, 174:12
Latina, wise L. woman, 873:5
Latin-American, not only L. nation, 811:13
Latitude, use longitude and l. for seine, 522:12
Latrine, mouth used as a l., 798:7
Latter and former rain, 28:34
    blessed the l. end of Job, 14:39
    early and l. rain, 45:32
    end of a fray, 183:19
    shall stand at the l. day, 13:39
Lattice, cried through the l., 10:13
Laud and magnify thy Name, 49:6
    more l. than gilt o'er-dusted, 203:26
Laudable things, 253:22
Laudamus, te deum l., 48:9
Laudanum, whipping and abuse are like l.,
    458:15
Laudator temporis acti, 98:n12
Laugh and grow fat, 191:n1
    and shake, 296:24
    and world laughs, 556:16
    anything awful makes me l., 383:5
    at a play to l. or cry, 285:6
    at any mortal thing, 398:20
    at gilded butterflies, 213:8
    at need for beauty and romance, 736:14
    at them in our turn, 382:12
    audience never fail to l., 73:13
    before we are happy, 280:24
    dry eyes l. at fall, 461:7
    folks l. at you scorn you, 708:8
    fools l. at men of sense, 280:25
    for fear of having to cry, 327:15
    if you tickle us do we not l., 185:12
    make her l. at that, 202:12
    men that l. and weep, 530:16
    Merlin had strange l., 770:15
    my bitter l., 443:2
    myself to death, 224:25
    never granted before fortieth day, 105:2
    not thing to l. to scorn, 195:31
    nothing more silly than silly l., 91:12
    sans intermission, 194:17
    seas l. when rocks near, 237:5
    siege to scorn, 217:21
    that spoke vacant mind, 322:25
    they l. that win, 209:24
    time to l., 22:31
    to l. proper to man, 145:5
    to memory of those who made us l.,
      718:12
    to scorn power of man, 216:32
    too badly hurt to l., 445:14
    unextinguishable l. in heaven, 249:5
    we must l. and sing, 595:5
    when you want a good l., 98:1
    where we must, 294:15
    yet all these seem to l., 229:12
    you will l., 320:10
    yourselves into stitches, 205:19

Laughable, your looks are l., 707:4
Laughed, day on which not l., 334:14
    he l. because knew what next, 770:15
    in the sun, 669:5
    little dog l., 893:16
    no man who l. bad, 406:12
    upright man l. to scorn, 13:24
    when he l. senators burst, 749:12
Laughing Allegra, 437:14
    at yourselves, 442:22
    bee on stalk, 820:8
    fellow rover, 635:17
    he l. said to me, 350:10
    heard on the hill, 351:7
    in your sleeve, 346:4
    leave them l., 634:10
    read death of Little Nell without l., 561:8
    sets a wise man to l., 53:21
    sex most fun without l., 839:15
    somewhere men are l., 585:1
    split sides with l., 156:31
    sports and plays, 350:8
    sweetly speaking and softly l., 56:5
    up her sleeve, 267:13
    Water, 437:3
Laughingstock, make myself l., 157:11
Laughs at archer, 491:2
    best who laughs last, 283:18
    fair l. the morn, 316:15
    joke loses everything when joker l., 359:8
    Jove l. at lovers' perjuries, 180:5
    Jupiter l. at perjuries of lovers, 101:20
    laugh and world l., 556:16
Laughter, a little time for l., 517:n1
    against assault of l. nothing stand, 525:3
    and ability and Sighing, 509:20
    and joy of poetry, 405:3
    arose among gods, 50:20
    beginning of prayer, 696:5
    better last smile than first l., 283:n5
    born with gift of l., 632:11
    can blow it to rags atoms, 525:3
    edges of l. and anguish, 654:16
    enjoy l. at right moment, 82:18
    excessive l., 31:8
    feast is made for l., 23:24
    for a month, 182:11
    has no greater foe than emotion, 572:6
    heart is sorrowful even in l., 20:26
    hidden l. of children, 678:11
    holding both his sides, 250:22
    I'll use you for my l., 193:9
    ill-bred as audible l., 322:n5
    love and l., 517:15
    myriad l. of ocean waves, 63:15
    no one died of l., 613:1
    no time for mirth and l., 597:18
    note short of scream of fear, 726:10
    of her heart, 706:7
    of the fool, 23:11
    over a dirty joke, 722:18
    present l., 204:26
    seriously scribbling to excite l., 522:1
    sudden glory maketh l., 239:7
    that all can see, 442:23
    tinkled among teacups, 675:12
    tired of tears and l., 530:16
    under running l., 576:13

Laughter *(continued)*
    weeping and the l., 599:17
    wine women mirth l., 398:10
    with pain fraught, 403:5
Laughter-silvered wings, 800:1
Launched, face that l. a thousand ships, 168:21
    forth filament, 488:5
Laundry, dreamed dream called L., 813:9
    nothing but l., 797:13
Laura, grave where L. lay, 159:11
    if L. Petrarch's wife, 398:14
    rose-cheeked L. come, 226:23
Laurea, concedat l. laudi, 88:n3
Laurel and myrtle and rose, 342:15
    burned is Apollo's l. bough, 169:7
    crown yield to praise, 88:7
    crowned with l., 695:17
    for perfect prime, 512:7
    green for a season, 530:9
    outlives not May, 530:9
    poison from Caesar's l. crown, 354:4
Laurels all are cut, 499:5
    Northern l. not change, 327:13
    worth all your l., 399:7
    yet once more O ye l., 252:29
Lavender in the windows, 245:4
    mints savory marjoram, 223:26
Lavender's blue dilly dilly lavender's green,
    896:13
Laver son linge sale, 365:n4
Lavish, liar always l. of oaths, 249:16
    no calamity greater than l. desires, 57:15
Law agin wearin' o' Green, 884:4
    all things by l. divine, 402:16
    and the prophets, 33:18, 35:13
    bloody book of l., 207:32
    book of the l., 12:29
    born under one l. to another bound,
      161:15
    broken every human l., 678:12
    by transgressing kept l., 254:15
    can only bring freedom, 344:17
    common l. not omnipresence, 538:19
    common l. nothing but reason, 158:21
    Congress shall make no l., 340:1
    curses in Book of L., 275:n4
    delight is in l. of the Lord, 14:40
    despair l. chance hath slain, 230:20
    do as adversaries in l., 173:11
    do what thou wilt whole of L., 629:10
    due process of l., 340:4, 340:8
    dusty purlieus of l., 454:4
    embodies nation's development, 538:4
    embody the L., 526:18
    ends Tyranny begins, 275:9
    equal before l., 518:1
    extreme l. often extreme injustice, 86:3
    faith nor love nor l., 402:1
    first l. for historian, 87:14
    for man law for thing, 424:13
    for rulers and people, 470:15
    fugitive from l. of averages, 796:11
    future lays l. of today, 547:12
    good l. is good order, 78:32
    great cases make bad l., 538:13
    great l. of culture, 407:12
    hath not been dead, 206:26
    having not the l., 41:9

Law *(continued)*

head and hoof of L., 588:20
hint of universal l., 538:9
hocus-pocus science, 300:12
I am the l., 632:19
I fought the l., 842:9
I my Lords embody L., 526:18
ignorance of the l., 238:12
in his l. doth he meditate, 14:40
in l. what plea so tainted, 185:18
in majestic equality, 546:2
is a ass a idiot, 464:13
is a jealous mistress, 388:6
is good, 44:23
is order, 78:32
is The Law, 749:8
is whatever is boldly asserted, 350:5
justice the l. my ducats, 185:5
lapped in universal l., 452:4
last result of wisdom, 308:6
lesser breeds without L., 589:10
life of l. is experience, 538:3
live outside the l., 851:19
locks up man and woman, 881:23
love is fulfilling of l., 41:39
love l. to itself, 117:6
make no l. respecting religion, 337:13
master after my disappearance, 64:17
mighty mightier necessity, 344:9
mob l., 444:3
moral l. within me, 320:2
more l. in policeman's nightstick, 535:5
murder by the l., 290:15
Murphy's L., 888:11
mysterious l. true source, 258:5
natural l. old nonsense, 392:6
Nature's kindly l., 295:3
nature's l. man made to mourn, 356:7
necessity has no l., 116:11
necessity hath no l., 246:18
necessity knows no l. except prevail, 100:19
nice sharp quillets of l., 169:15
no l. more binding than custom, 572:13
no l. of history, 484:14
no such thing as natural l., 392:6
nor l. bade me fight, 593:1
not a light to see by, 804:16
not come to destroy l., 32:16
not concerned with trifles, 120:15
not exempted from power of l., 161:17
not l. so much as right, 473:13
not make scarecrow of l., 206:18
not one jot pass from l., 32:17
of excluded middle, 795:6
of gravity, 440:5
of humanity, 324:20
of life, 648:17
of musical world, 582:18
of nature and nations, 324:20
of our Creator, 324:20
of the Jungle, 588:18
of the land, 126:4
of the Medes and Persians, 28:26
of the Yukon, 627:11
old father antick the l., 181:25
one God l. element, 454:12
one l. and one truth, 112:14
one l. for all, 324:20

Law *(continued)*

one L. for Lion and Ox, 352:1
ordinance of reason for common good, 127:6
others will plead at l., 94:35
ought to weed it out, 165:14
our reason is our l., 259:10
people fight for their l., 62:12
people's good the highest l., 88:10
perfection of reason, 158:21
perpetual constitution or perpetual l., 336:16
Poetry not matured by l., 413:7
possession eleven points in l., 287:13
precedents constitute l., 339:3
primary l. of every work of art, 498:13
protection by l., 364:3
Proust's L., 813:11
public opinion in advance of l., 600:21
reason the life of the l., 158:21
remoter aspects of l., 538:9
rich men rule the l., 322:5
rule nations under l., 94:35
rule of l. not l. of jungle, 805:6
same l. shapes earth-star and snow-star, 473:9
say what l. is, 349:13
says judge as looks down nose, 749:8
seat of l. bosom of God, 161:17
seven hours to l., 159:*n*1
so general a study, 324:7
sociability l. of nature, 542:15
stable but not stand still, 608:3
stands mute in midst of arms, 87:9
Supreme L. of the land, 339:14
sword of war or of l., 338:9
this is l. I maintain, 883:12
tongue is the l. of kindness, 22:19
took to the l., 514:5
translating into living l., 666:15
true embodiment, 526:18
universal l., 320:4
unto themselves, 41:9
voice of l. harmony of world, 161:17
what others do from fear of l., 77:11
where no l. no transgression, 41:11
which governs all law, 324:20
who to himself is l., 163:19
windy side of the l., 190:*n*1
write in books of l., 753:11
Lawd, gangway for de L., 686:3
Lawful, all things l. for me, 42:21
guns aren't l., 699:14
is it not l., 35:7
without some l. recreation, 157:2
Lawfully, if a man use it l., 44:23
Lawlands, ye Highlands and L., 890:7
Lawless attack upon liberty, 318:4
discountenance haughty and l., 329:6
linsey-woolsey brother, 262:15
winged unconfined, 352:5
Lawlessness, world l., 652:17
Lawn, rivulets through l., 453:7
sisters crab grass in l. of life, 800:10
white as driven snow, 223:30
Lawns, like satyrs grazing on the l., 168:12
Law's delay, 199:21
in l. grave study six, 159:1

Law's *(continued)*

to take care o' raskills, 480:9
Laws, abhor makers and their l. approve, 274:5
acting around us, 440:4
and arms foundations of states, 141:15
are like cobwebs, 284:6
are sand customs rock, 525:1
bad l. bring about worse, 312:20
base l. of servitude, 272:9
best l. teach to trample bad l., 458:10
breathing household l., 370:4
city better off with bad fixed l., 72:6
conflict courts decide, 349:13
Constitution and l. of U.S., 339:14
crime to examine l. of heat, 533:1
devise l. for blood, 184:15
doing what l. permit, 297:13
end tyranny begins, 306:1
equal protection of the l., 340:8
fewer l. less power, 427:22
flung at head, 690:14
for themselves not me, 575:16
forms all produced by l., 440:4
found state and give it l., 142:7
give little Senate l., 295:13
God of universal l., 542:2
good l. lead to better, 312:20
government free where l. rule, 280:6
government of l. not men, 329:14
grind the poor, 322:5
grinding general l. out, 441:3
human and divine, 131:3
in which we have no voice, 340:11
judges of facts not l., 291:6
language manners l. customs, 369:4
like spiders' webs, 56:2
Nature and Nature's l. hid, 296:23
never forget l. of forefathers, 106:6
not assume physical l. exist, 570:9
not care who make l., 282:2
not good l. where not armed, 141:15
not violate l. of justice, 319:10
obedient to their l. we lie, 60:11
of God are forever, 65:18
of God laws of man, 575:16
of its own freedom, 705:4
of nature and nature's God, 336:1
of the Jungle, 588:20
one by one forging l., 690:14
or kings cause or cure, 307:14
ought not to remain unaltered, 78:21
physical l. and l. of numbers, 513:1
power of making l., 349:7
removal of unwise l. from books, 615:3
resulting from designed l., 440:7
right from which l. derive authority, 339:7
rules of game l. of Nature, 502:5
secure equal justice, 71:14
self-made l., 491:21
sweeps a room as for thy l., 243:10
the more l. are made prominent, 57:19
three l. of righteousness, 62:25
true friendship's l., 293:19
two l. discrete, 424:13
unequal l. to savage race, 451:11
useless l. weaken necessary l., 297:14
which ran like drinking songs, 72:10
Lawsuit machine you go into, 540:10

Less *(continued)*
    is more, 461:17
    more and more about l., 581:3
    more matter with l. art, 198:27
    nicely calculated l. or more, 372:14
    no man shall have, 571:8
    not that I loved Caesar l., 192:25
    of two evils, 52:*n*1
    rather than be l. cared not to be, 256:8
    small Latin and l. Greek, 233:1
    than kind, 196:24
    than meets the eye, 733:13
    the l. one knows, 57:16
    weep to make l. depth of grief, 170:20
Lessened, one pain l. by another's, 179:21
Lessening, little things go l., 462:26
Lesser breeds without Law, 589:10
    than my name, 177:11
    woman l. man, 452:7
Lesson, draw from others the l., 85:18
    grandest l. On sail on, 539:15
    harder l. how to die, 152:*n*3
    heart give l. to head, 327:5
    on grammar impertinence, 500:1
    you should heed, 389:10
Lessons, three l. I would write, 359:11
Let all her ways be unconfined, 283:12
    another man praise thee, 21:41
    at another l. in the foe, 260:14
    dead bury dead, 33:28
    evening come, 864:13
    every thing that hath breath praise, 19:21
    face of God shine through, 695:6
    freedom ring, 439:9
    go l. go, 484:1
    Greeks be Greeks, 261:11
    her not walk in the sun, 198:33
    him be just and deal kindly, 394:3
    him look to his bond, 185:10
    him now speak, 49:14
    him pass for a man, 184:18
    it all hang out, 852:14
    it be l. it be, 80:11
    it be let it pass, 298:*n*4
    it begin here, 325:19
    justice be done though heaven fall, 120:22
    me die death of righteous, 9:8
    me have no lying, 223:35
    me love, 228:18
    me not to marriage of true minds, 222:15
    me tell the world, 183:27
    my people go, 7:31, 898:18
    never curtain drawn, 623:14
    never l. me go, 840:13
    no dog bark, 184:7
    no man's heart fail, 10:45
    no such man be trusted, 186:17
    not heart be troubled, 39:40, 39:44
    not poor Nelly starve, 272:2
    not the sun go down, 43:37
    sleeping dogs lie, 466:2
    slip dogs of war, 192:23
    thame say, 161:9
    the toast pass, 346:11
    the words of my mouth, 15:19
    them eat cake, 313:8
    them have their day, 593:4
    this cup pass, 36:5

Let *(continued)*
    thy words be few, 23:4
    us all to meditation, 170:9
    us alone, 450:19
    us begin, 785:12
    us do something beautiful, 762:9
    us go into the house of the Lord, 19:1
    us go singing as far as we go, 93:5
    us go then, 674:17
    us have peace, 498:5
    us have tongs and bones, 178:31
    us live and love, 91:5, 226:20
    us now praise famous men, 31:26
    us reason together, 24:32
    us then be up, 436:7
    what will be said or done, 337:2
    will not l. thee go, 7:3
    your light shine, 32:16
Lethal, turn underground passages into l.
    chambers, 724:6
Lethe, cup that brings sleep of L., 95:28
    go not to L., 411:9
    river of oblivion, 256:24
    rots in ease on L. wharf, 198:7
    time is L., 630:15
Lethean, drunken of things L., 530:9
Lethe-wards had sunk, 410:2
Let's carve him as a dish, 192:4
    choose executors, 177:7
    contend no more Love, 460:23
    do it, 803:11
    kill all the lawyers, 170:14
    look at the record, 617:11
    Pretend and we did, 836:10
    roll, 879:7
    talk of graves, 177:7
Lets, make ghost of him that l. me, 198:3
Letter and spirit of constitution, 349:16
    broke spell of dead l., 688:8
    killeth, 43:12
    last till you write your l., 228:11
    longer than usual, 269:5
    not l. but spirit, 43:12
    on gown appeared l. A, 431:3
    one l. of Richardson's, 309:18
    read in the bitter l., 207:32
    scarlet l. passport, 431:8
    to the World, 509:5
Lettered, locked l. collar, 356:14
Lettering, stripped of l. and gilding, 301:20
Letters, graven with diamonds in l. plain, 149:5
    in your l. speak of me, 210:20
    like writin' anonymous l., 600:17
    man of l., 270:17
    men of l., 433:13
    mingle souls, 230:14
    no arts no l. no society, 239:10
    republic of l., 304:25
    sensitive ear detecting capital l., 648:12
    should not be known, 224:19
    you bid me burn l., 329:17
Letter-writing, the great art o' l., 463:29
Letting hundred flowers blossom, 698:13
    I dare not, 215:2
Levee, drove my Chevy to the l., 861:11
Level, boys and girls l. with men, 219:5
    in her husband's heart, 204:34
    levelers wish to l. down, 309:6

Levelers wish to level down, 309:6
Leveling, cannot bear l. up, 309:6
    rancorous mind, 595:6
    wind, 594:10
Lever you can only turn once, 700:15
Leviathan, draw out l. with a hook, 14:32
    hugest of creatures, 258:27
    that crooked serpent, 26:6
    whom thou hast made to play, 18:11
Levitation, evil emissions fled l., 803:7
    powers of l. would make fakir stare,
      678:12
Levity, a little judicious l., 555:19
    say it with utmost l., 564:18
    soul ruled by l. pure, 778:15
    there should be no l., 307:27
Levy, foreign l., 216:11
Levying war, 339:13
Lewd fellows, 40:31
    the sinful and l., 708:6
Lewdness, though l. court it, 198:10
Lewinsky, that woman Miss L., 863:5
Lex, de minimis non curat l., 120:15
    salus populi suprema l., 88:*n*5
Lexicographer writer of dictionaries, 307:3
Lexicography, not yet so lost in l., 306:23
Lexington and Bunker Hill, 390:7
Lhude sing cuccu, 880:5
    sing Goddamm, 665:2
Liable, all men are l. to error, 275:7
Liar always lavish of oaths, 249:16
    and the father of it, 39:26
    doubt truth to be l., 198:30
    either l. or madman, 312:22
    of first magnitude, 286:27
    should have good memory, 106:2
    show me a l., 244:14
    they answered Little l., 606:13
Liars, all Cretans are l., 58:7
    all men are l., 18:23
    drunkards l. adulterers, 211:3
    fears may be l., 479:12
    may photograph, 625:14
    when they speak truth, 77:5
Libelous statements about dog, 653:9
Liber, vade salutatum pro me l., 133:*n*2
Liberal arts study humanizes, 102:26
    central l. truth, 816:14
    education, 282:21
    I am a L., 497:9
    infuses that l. obedience, 324:13
    institutions cease being liberal, 548:24
    little L., 526:22
    luxury of l. government, 470:8
    tempered by experience, 497:9
    who has been mugged, 795:2
Liberalism is sole intellectual tradition,
    743:14
Liberals, foxy white l., 808:12
    understand everything but, 807:9
Liberality in gifts well timed, 280:22
Liberated, I have l. my soul, 123:12
    the hell out of place, 888:3
Liberates, neither shoots nor l. me, 475:25
Liberation, madness potentially l., 816:1
    of Europe, 686:13
    of human mind, 604:14
Liberavi animam meam, 123:*n*6

Liberis, pro patria pro l., 92:*n*6
Libertas, in dubiis l., 265:*n*2
Libertate, sub l. quietem, 268:*n*4
Liberté, je suis né pour te nommer L., 705:*n*3
Liberties, dramatist wants l., 545:2
    liberty above all l., 254:13
    not too strong for l., 446:10
    science and l. of Europe, 338:15
    we bear ark of l. of world, 482:15
Libertine, chartered l., 188:33
    I am a l., 334:10
    puffed and reckless l., 197:20
Libertines, self-love makes more l., 313:1
Liberty, Americans love l., 306:3
    and glory of his country, 390:2
    and Union, 390:10
    arduous struggle for l., 331:10
    as end and means, 562:8
    assert and maintain l. and virtue, 329:6
    back stairs to l., 555:3
    basis of democratic state is l., 78:31
    brightest in dungeons L., 397:8
    bulwark of continuing l., 652:18
    bulwarks of l., 320:9
    by accident got its l., 142:8
    cannot be preserved without knowledge,
        329:9
    Captivity is Consciousness so's L., 509:2
    change from l. to force, 363:4
    claim their l. but not their duty, 842:1
    condition upon which given l., 345:7
    contending for l., 328:5
    corruption symptom of l., 332:6
    cost of l., 602:5
    courage secret of l., 562:8
    cradle of l., 390:21
    crust of bread and l., 296:8
    deprive of life l. or property, 340:8
    deprived of life l. or property, 340:4
    despotism of l. against tyranny, 356:2
    doing what laws permit, 297:13
    doing what one desires, 435:12
    enjoy delight with l., 160:27
    enjoy such l., 266:2
    enjoyment of life and l., 320:7
    equality fraternity, 891:2
    establish our real l., 152:11
    extremism in defense of l., 758:10
    freedom enfranchisement, 192:17
    from despotism to l. in featherbed, 337:1
    give me l. or death, 331:13
    give up essential l., 303:6
    God who gave life gave l., 335:22
    hail L. hail, 417:5
    he served human l., 595:8
    he that commands sea is at l., 166:16
    headstrong l., 172:15
    highest political end, 518:12
    history of l. history of safeguards, 649:9
    history of progress of human l., 477:3
    I must have l. withal, 194:20
    if l. found in democracy, 78:25
    if l. means anything, 735:10
    in doubtful things l., 265:4
    in moderate governments, 349:5
    in mouth of Webster, 425:16
    in proportion to restraint, 390:19
    individual l. individual power, 363:5

Liberty *(continued)*
    interfering with l., 435:1
    judiciary safeguard of l., 582:5
    know no such l., 266:1
    lawless attack upon l., 318:4
    life l. pursuit of happiness, 336:1
    little is achieved through L., 463:15
    love of l. love of others, 385:12
    man establish reign of l., 751:9
    mocks my loss of l., 350:8
    mountain nymph sweet l., 250:23
    my Soul at L., 509:1
    nation conceived in L., 446:5
    natural l. establishes itself, 319:10
    neither l. nor safety, 303:6
    no l. for enemies of l., 364:7
    not between order and l., 846:*n*1
    of conscience, 247:8
    of individual, 435:8
    of thought life of soul, 300:5
    only to those who love it, 390:13
    peace l. and safety, 337:12
    people so dead to l., 305:13
    placid repose under l., 268:7
    plucks justice by nose, 206:14
    power to endanger public l., 329:12
    precious must be rationed, 607:17
    price of l., 345:*n*4
    proclaim l. throughout land, 9:1
    property no stamps, 883:14
    proud monuments of l., 383:2
    putrid corpse of l., 657:3
    right to death or l., 490:10
    sacred fire of l., 328:11
    safeguards of l., 649:11
    secret of happiness, 562:8
    secure blessings of l., 339:11
    seeking l. which is so dear, 129:10
    so loving-jealous of his l., 180:15
    soul of journey is l., 386:9
    spirit of l., 324:3
    survival of l., 785:10
    sweet land of l., 439:9
    this country to preserve l., 338:15
    to know, 254:13
    to think feel do, 386:9
    Tree, 332:20
    tree of l. refreshed, 336:15
    tree of l. watered by blood, 348:12
    what crimes in thy name, 348:4
    where Slavery is L. cannot be, 459:1
    with l. and justice for all, 562:6
    wrote at l. when of Devils, 351:10
Liberty's in every blow, 358:17
Librarian analogous to a god, 719:1
Libraries, I bless God in l., 318:11
    meek young men grow up in l., 426:1
Library, as if l. burned to ground,
        796:10
    furnished me from mine own l., 224:9
    Paradise as kind of l., 719:8
    public l. affords conviction, 306:22
    turn over half a l., 310:3
    was dukedom large enough, 224:7
    whereon I look, 241:16
Libre, l'homme est né l., 312:*n*3
Libri, cave ab homine unius l., 120:8
Lice tethered, 755:16

License, equal l. in bold invention, 98:16
    innocence never blossom into l., 279:2
    love not freedom but l., 254:17
    poetic l., 87:15
Licensing and prohibiting, 254:14
Licentiae, poetarum l. liberiora, 87:*n*9
Licentious soldiery, 324:17
Lick absurd pomp, 200:10
    ill cook that cannot l. fingers, 181:6
    the dust, 17:13
    Valleys up, 509:10
Licked platter clean, 892:15
    soup from ladies, 460:7
Licks hand raised to shed blood, 294:17
    pride that l. the dust, 296:2
Lid, earth's l., 665:9
    pent-house l., 214:1
Lids, drops blue-fringed l., 377:16
    eternal l. apart, 412:10
Lie a thought more nigh, 240:6
    abroad for commonwealth, 227:14
    all the Dead l. down, 509:8
    asked lady to l. her down, 352:4
    asks no questions isn't told l., 323:*n*1
    at proud foot of conqueror, 176:6
    athwart noses as they l. asleep, 179:25
    becomes habitual, 336:11
    before us like land of dreams, 496:19
    big l., 684:12
    by emperor's side, 209:25
    can't pray a l., 523:8
    children and fools cannot l., 147:30
    circumstantial, 196:6
    climb when I l. down, 268:13
    contrive one noble l., 75:5
    countenance cannot l., 169:9
    credit his own l., 224:5
    deep buried, 59:23
    differences between cat and l., 523:18
    dig grave let me l., 555:16
    direct, 196:6
    dost thou l. so low, 192:19
    down because 'twas night, 229:8
    down for eon or two, 587:12
    down in green pastures, 15:23
    down like tired child, 401:14
    down till leaders spoken, 588:19
    down where ladders start, 597:8
    every word she writes is l., 768:14
    fain wald l. down, 890:9
    families l. together, 801:17
    faults l. gently on him, 226:9
    give the world the l., 159:9
    half a truth blackest, 455:24
    handle which fits all, 443:11
    has seven endings, 889:7
    heaven with splendors l., 481:14
    here let her l., 275:1
    here obedient to their laws we l., 60:11
    home to a l., 665:8
    how l. through centuries, 460:22
    how still we see thee l., 521:2
    I can't tell a l., 328:*n*3
    I l. down alone, 576:1
    I shall l. in the dust, 52:8
    I their map l. flat, 231:2
    if I l. spit in my face, 182:21
    in cold obstruction, 206:38

Lie (*continued*)

in cowslip's bell I l., 225:5
in dark weep for sins, 486:14
in your throat, 187:26
inhuman reign of l., 688:8
is a dream a l., 868:3
leads you to believe a l., 354:17
lightly gentle earth, 238:5
like bill on Nature's Reality, 407:2
nicer to l. in bed, 607:9
not a man that he should l., 9:9
not know what it is to l., 420:2
nothing can need a l., 242:8
on knees of the gods, 52:23
on Mother's bed, 787:12
one daiquiri told the other a l., 773:8
permits himself to tell l., 336:11
rather l. in woollen, 190:21
shall rot, 500:9
sleep will never l., 180:18
sleeping dogs l., 466:2
still and slumber, 289:10
still ye thief, 183:1
stone tell where I l., 292:5
sweet compulsion in music l., 250:18
sweets compacted l., 242:20
talking of fall of man, 475:32
tangled in her hair, 266:1
the old l., 699:5
truth in masquerade, 398:28
underneath this stone doth l., 232:13
unless statistics l., 701:14
upon the daisies, 526:10
violence intertwined with l., 791:10
what is a l., 398:28
where'er she l., 263:4
which is all a lie, 455:24
who loves to l. with me, 194:11
with a purpose worst, 600:4
with my fathers, 7:18
yonder all before us is l., 266:22
young shall l. down together, 25:19

Liebchen with whom should I quarrel, 742:3
Lieben und arbeiten, 564:*n*4
Lied, never seen anybody but l., 523:1
Lief not be as be in awe, 191:24
Liege of loiterers, 174:14
we are men my l., 216:6

Lies are mortar, 598:14

at last as always, 798:1
believe her though she l., 223:2
believe l. when in print, 626:12
Bible has thousand l., 525:8
bodyguard of l., 621:6
cruelest l. told in silence, 554:13
dalliance in wardrobe l., 189:1
death l. on my tongue, 183:30
everybody l. about sex, 873:4
exposed he l., 274:18
Fool l. here, 587:11
freedom from l., 578:3
full fathom five thy father l., 224:14
great Prince in prison l., 229:19
half truth blackest of l., 455:24
he entered territory of l., 738:3
heaven l. about us, 370:17
here again he l., 487:8
here food for worms, 301:20

Lies (*continued*)

here l. a King that ruled, 245:13
here l. my wife, 275:1
here l. one who meant well, 556:3
here l. one whose name, 414:1
here l. W. C. Fields, 644:3
Hope l. to mortals, 575:21
in his bed walks with me, 175:19
in the rude manger l., 250:10
kindness and l., 738:1
long time l. in one word, 176:13
make l. sound truthful, 735:13
Matilda told dreadful l., 606:12
matters I relate are true l., 684:4
music on spirit l., 450:17
now l. he there, 192:32
old men's l., 665:8
on chaliced flowers that l., 220:15
poets tell many l., 55:13
religion of slaves, 602:14
speaking l. in hypocrisy, 44:27
steep my speech in l., 63:26
tells l. without attending, 336:11
that way madness l., 211:32
to hide it, 242:*n*4
truth to cover l., 286:26
uneasy l. head that wears crown, 188:11
where he longed to be, 555:16
with dogs riseth with fleas, 244:4
you can invent, 354:1

Life a battle and sojourning, 111:13

a Fury slinging flame, 453:18
a man's real l., 567:20
academic l., 233:15
accept Jesus new l., 805:12
account of her l. to clod, 190:23
actuality of thought is l., 78:1
admits not of delays, 310:11
adore my l. with Bird, 756:15
affirmation of l., 632:13
after l. is death, 530:14
aim of l. is to live, 691:3
ain't all beer and skittles, 464:*n*1
all a man hath will he give for l., 13:1
all his l. in the wrong, 281:4
all human l. in monkeys and cats, 544:4
all I care about is l., 537:11
all l. an experiment, 538:22
all l. is a dream, 247:1
all l. 6 to 5 against, 660:9
all my l. I was a bride, 840:10
American l. solvent, 584:10
and memory of it, 763:8
and power of increase, 275:3
anyone whose l. married to sea, 617:15
anythin' for a quiet l., 464:4
anything for a quiet l., 237:1
art long l. short, 343:3
art makes l., 545:8
art of drawing conclusions, 521:11
as for future l. man judge, 441:1
as much as my l. was worth, 314:13
as to bed's-feet l. shrunk, 229:12
as to breathe were l., 451:14
at no point in l. felt American, 830:14
at the door of l., 530:6
bagatelle of transient experience, 580:9
bankrupt of l., 272:17

Life (*continued*)

be it l. or death crave reality, 475:3
be not afraid of l., 541:14
bear a charmed l., 217:27
beg delinquents for l., 788:4
begins at forty, 635:19
begins perpetually, 599:5
being what it is, 551:9
believe in l., 602:11
believe in l. to come, 744:21
best of l. intoxication, 398:11
best portion of man's l., 368:7
best things in l. free, 697:9
birth l. and death, 280:26
birthday of my l., 512:2
bitterness of feelings about modern l., 767:8
bitterness of L., 517:8
blot out of book of l., 46:25
boat of l. be light, 576:6
Book of L. begins, 560:15
book of l. opened, 47:10
books substitute for l., 554:15
boredom at core of l., 270:16
bread called staff of l., 282:16
bread of l., 39:18
breath of l., 5:10
breathed by Creator, 440:5
brisking about the l., 318:15
broad margin to my l., 475:7
broken l. up for bread, 530:5
buried l., 495:11
burrs and thorns of l., 409:4
but a span, 283:8
C Major of this l., 462:12
calamity of so long l., 199:21
can be great, 662:11
cannot tear out page of l., 432:8
care of l. and happiness, 337:15
careless of single l., 453:23
care's an enemy to l., 204:13
cast cold eye on l. on death, 597:11
chain of l., 795:15
change we think we see in l., 622:16
chaos breeds l., 531:18
charmed l., 217:27
chief business of my l., 320:11
clock stops time come to l., 713:11
closed twice before close, 511:9
comes a time in every man's l., 689:2
comes to end in prosperity, 63:5
compared l. to a dream, 153:1
compel philosophy to inquire about l., 88:5
conduct three-fourths of l., 497:16
consists of what man is thinking, 425:13
consists with wildness, 475:31
contraction of l., 630:4
control nature and human l., 558:2
controlling circumstances of l., 489:3
cool sequestered vale of l., 316:3
count l. of battle good, 582:8
crowded hour of l., 326:1
crown of l., 45:21, 46:22
crown of l. as it closes, 529:19
Culprit L., 508:2
daily beauty in his l., 210:11
dancing is l. itself, 574:4
dead husks of l., 750:1
dear as light and l., 358:12

Life *(continued)*

death after l. does please, 160:7
death makes l. live, 463:7
death nor l. nor angels, 41:26
death of each day's l., 215:21
death part of l., 631:3
death side of l. away from us, 632:4
defeat my l., 210:7
demd horrid grind, 464:24
deprive of l. liberty or property, 340:8
deprived of l. liberty or property, 340:4
destroys single l. rescues single l., 117:9
difficult to write good l. as live one, 646:10
digressions l. of reading, 314:3
dim origins of l., 750:1
disease of modern l., 495:17
does thy l. destroy, 352:14
doesn't imitate art, 839:19
dost thou love l., 302:26
dream is second l., 439:4
dream of l., 403:22
dreamed l. was beauty, 472:15
dreams necessary to l., 735:2
drink l. to lees, 451:12
each l. touches other lives, 687:2
earnest art gay, 359:20
ease one L. the Aching, 510:4
echo undermine hold on l., 638:12
ecstasy that marks summit of l., 633:5
education not preparation for l. is l., 573:2
education will determine future l., 75:7
elevate l. by conscious endeavor, 474:28
empty dream, 436:4
end in itself, 538:10
end of l. cancels bands, 183:6
enjoyment of l. and liberty, 320:7
enlarge my l., 306:18
enough for my l., 30:20
entrusts l. to one hole, 83:11
envy and wrath shorten l., 31:17
eternal l. gift of God, 41:16
eternal l. in knowledge of God, 48:13
everlasting l., 39:11
everything in political l., 497:15
exempt from public haunt, 193:37
exile's l. no l., 83:2
experience of this sweet l., 130:9
fabric of l., 750:5
facts of l. do not penetrate, 610:12
fall upon thorns of l., 402:12
falter l. away, 495:15
fear of Acheron which troubles l., 90:8
feels l. in every limb, 368:2
felt l. in producing art, 544:16
fever of l. over, 421:5
fie upon this quiet l., 182:17
for l. six hundred pounds, 296:7
for l. to come, 223:23
for me no crystal stair, 731:2
for why my l. at end, 889:20
force uncomprehended was his l., 506:17
fought for l., 760:6
friend is medicine of l., 30:26
frittered away by detail, 475:1
from this cup they drank their l., 892:3
front essential facts of l., 474:29
fruits of l. and beauty, 352:6
fundamental law of l., 312:3

Life *(continued)*

gale of l. high, 575:4
game is l., 727:4
game that must be played, 605:16
gave thee l. bid thee feed, 350:12
give to eat of the tree of l., 46:21
give up whole idea of l., 824:14
giveth his l. for sheep, 39:31
giving l. by death of others, 140:2
gloss over my whole l. story, 874:9
God gave l. gave liberty, 335:22
goes by so swiftly, 139:5
golden tree of l., 344:5
good death does honor to whole l., 130:18
great business of l., 533:3
great l. if you don't weaken, 629:7
greater price than l., 726:15
greatest thing in family l., 625:9
Greek thought and l., 302:3
Greeks have dreamt dream of l. best, 344:28
growth only evidence of l., 421:7
half a l. asunder, 515:10
half spent before we know, 244:25
happy all his l., 244:28
harder toward summit, 549:2
have the light of l., 39:24
have you found l. distasteful, 463:12
he giveth l., 40:33
he that findeth l., 34:6
he that loveth her loveth l., 30:17
he who knows l., 281:9
here find l. in death, 380:8
hidden l., 480:22
his l. was gentle, 193:22
honor dearer than l., 156:32
hope for happiness beyond l., 333:18
horrors of half known l., 483:5
hot for certainties in l., 505:11
human l. a large Mansion, 413:5
human l. a state in which much endured,
    307:10
human l. priceless, 726:15
hungry for l. and death, 776:9
I am in mourning for my l., 578:6
I am the bread of l., 39:18
I believe in l. everlasting, 48:11
I burned my l., 713:4
I have painted my l., 672:7
I have wasted my l., 817:8
if anything in l. is certain, 795:11
if it be l. to pitch, 595:4
if l. bitter pardon, 531:1
if one had courage l. livable, 505:2
if woman told truth about her l., 771:19
if you haven't had l., 544:15
ills scholar's l. assail, 306:16
imagination master of l., 568:4
imitates art, 559:21
immortal Death has taken mortal l., 90:13
in fast lane, 865:14
in internal environment, 468:14
in l. as in football, 571:4
in l. did harbor give, 232:13
in London all l. can afford, 310:13
in middle of journey of l., 128:3
in our l. Nature live, 378:8
in sea of l. enisled, 495:10

Life *(continued)*

in the midst of l. death, 49:19
in which gods are not invited, 849:12
in whom standeth eternal l., 48:13
Indian summer of l., 532:7
inseparable like l. and consciousness,
    663:16
intelligent l. might develop, 854:4
intelligent l. on a planet, 850:10
intend to lead new l., 49:4
interest in death interest in l., 631:6
into each l. rain fall, 436:14
involves self between contradictions,
    746:1
is a foreign language, 688:2
is a jest, 291:20
is action and passion, 538:5
is all beer and skittles, 464:*n*1
is an incurable disease, 265:13
is banquet, 779:12
is boring, 773:7
is bowl of cherries, 697:8
is but a joke, 852:1
is but a span, 283:8
is glorious cycle of song, 699:17
is great surprise, 723:11
is made of sobs sniffles and smiles, 581:13
is interweaving of freaks and irrelevancies,
    712:13
is its own journey, 747:11
is l. so dear, 331:13
is made up of single moment, 719:2
is neither good nor bad, 580:1
is not a spectacle, 770:12
is not l. more than meat, 33:6
is painting picture, 538:16
is real life is earnest, 436:4
is short art long, 71:6
is stage to play fool upon, 555:3
is supremely easy for men, 53:1
is the other way round, 840:7
is the thing, 590:15
is thorny, 377:13
is trouble Zorba continued, 656:6
is unfair, 786:4
is warfare against malice of others, 247:6
is what we make it, 541:13
is worth saving, 568:9
isn't all beer and skittles, 498:11
it takes l. to love l., 605:6
it would be L., 509:14
it's alright Ma it's l., 851:11
joy of l. is variety, 307:6
jump the l. to come, 214:22
jury passing on l., 206:19
keep pure both l. and art, 70:14
keep way of the tree of l., 6:2
lag-end of my l., 183:21
large as l. twice as natural, 516:16
Last Abode is L., 119:3
last hour of my l., 301:5
last of l. best, 462:13
lasted the rest of my l., 514:5
later l. flings itself faster, 631:2
lay down his l., 60:16
lay down l. for friends, 40:1
lay down your l. Perkins, 837:1

Life *(continued)*

lay hold on eternal l., 44:36
Leaves of L. falling, 441:8
left behind a real l., 819:15
length of l. leading among inquiries, 111:6
let thy l. be sincere, 30:22
liberty pursuit of happiness, 336:1
light l. pleasure pain, 517:15
light of l., 39:24
like a dome of many-colored glass, 404:2
like a froward child, 271:30
like living l. over, 303:21
like runners pass on torch of l., 90:3
little l. rounded with sleep, 225:1
little needed to make happy l., 112:16
live all days of your l., 286:6
live l. he has imagined, 475:19
live l. not simple, 688:3
live l. through not like crossing field, 897:11
lived in scene it composes, 642:22
lived l. talking at street corners, 682:10
lively form of death, 163:7
living someone else's l., 873:12
Lolita light of my l., 723:5
London this moment, 654:5
long disease my l., 295:11
long littleness of l., 667:6
looking out from eyes of doe, 695:16
lose l. shall find it, 34:39
love an episode in man's l., 362:13
Love anterior to L., 510:3
love l. of their parents, 723:4
love long l. better than figs, 218:5
love of wisdom guide of l., 355:3
love only business in l., 392:11
love the history of woman's l., 362:13
loveth her loveth l., 30:17
man lives l. of epoch, 631:1
mankind fleet of l. like leaves, 73:5
man's l. cheap as beast's, 211:21
many-colored l. he drew, 306:9
married to sea, 617:15
married to single l., 263:6
may perfect be, 233:8
meaning of his own l., 841:9
meaningful events in his l., 878:1
measured l. with coffee spoons, 674:21
medicine for l. which has fled, 58:11
memory without pain, 66:8
messed up l. for nothing, 677:22
might have brought end of my l., 366:17
mine honor is my l., 176:9
miserable mortals flame with l., 52:12
mission in l. is not to succeed, 556:11
money as means to l., 656:15
more abundant l., 652:4
more lost than l., 106:13
more sweet than painted pomp, 193:36
more than he slew in his l., 10:26
most loathed worldly l., 207:1
much too far out all my l., 732:16
my l. has gone, 814:13
my l. is preserved, 7:4
my l. my joy, 155:3
my l. my real l. in danger, 804:6
my l. poem I would have writ, 474:1
my lines and l. are free, 242:26

Life *(continued)*

my poems naughty my l. pure, 107:4
my way of l. is fallen, 217:18
near bone sweetest, 475:21
never know what l. means till you die, 463:7
never to have drawn breath of l., 595:1
new era in l. from book, 475:6
new l. begins, 127:15
nightmare L.-in-Death was she, 376:7
no life but death, 163:7
no l. by others' death, 175:27
no l. can be recaptured wholly, 775:6
no l. moves in empty passageways, 66:2
no man loses other l. than that he lives, 111:10
no man loves l. like old, 66:26
no no no l., 213:14
no wealth but l., 484:12
nobody write l. of man, 309:16
nor love thy l. nor hate, 259:22
not a matter of painting l., 599:13
not cheap but sacred, 428:10
not doing a sum, 538:16
not giving l. but risking l., 751:6
not l. alone makes man, 728:15
not L. for which they stand, 520:10
not long l. by fire, 579:13
not take his own l., 74:12
not to fancy what fair in l., 461:21
not totally regret l., 814:1
nothing but our present l., 119:9
nothing give up l., 755:13
nothing in his l., 214:14
nothing much to lose, 576:2
novel attempt to represent l., 544:8
now I live now l. is done, 163:11
now is immortal l., 552:4
O Death in L., 452:22
O for L. of Sensations, 412:13
o' the building, 215:28
occupations few tranquil l., 112:1
ocean of l., 437:19
of jealousy, 209:5
of law not logic, 538:3
of l. he only is deserving, 344:13
of little value, 803:14
of man heroic poem, 407:14
of man solitary, 239:10
of peoples and humanity, 507:2
of poor man in mean cottage, 31:14
of simplicity independence magnanimity, 474:16
of soul, 300:5
old age crown of l., 88:17
one Draught of L., 511:8
one entrance into l., 30:6
one in l. and death are we, 526:16
one l. to lose for country, 349:1
one long struggle in dark, 90:2
only one happiness in l., 432:13
our l. is changed, 672:6
out of ashes l. again, 550:3
out of it are the issues of l., 19:30
outlive his l. half a year, 200:16
over my long l., 580:3
over there behind Shelf, 509:14
part with l. cheerfully, 112:7

Life *(continued)*

pass them for nobler l., 409:2
perceivers of terror of l., 428:3
perfect interpreter of l., 666:11
perfected by death, 434:11
perfection of l. or work, 595:9
permission to know death, 692:9
period in l. when work comes first, 601:1
philosophy you leader of l., 88:4
piece of buffoonery, 601:4
poem ends in clarification of l., 625:3
poet gives l. to fictions, 642:21
present l. a diversion and sport, 119:3
present l. like flight of sparrow, 122:1
pressure of exigencies of l., 563:9
price l. exacts for peace, 718:6
progress from want to want, 310:9
progress to fuller l., 602:11
protracted is protracted woe, 306:18
protracting l. not deduct from death, 90:15
public l. situation of power, 323:19
pulse of l. stood still, 290:20
pure in l. free from sin, 96:14
Purpose Driven L., 873:6
ran gaily as Thames, 495:17
rarely find a happy l., 95:18
realize l. while live it, 715:8
reason the l. of the law, 158:21
religion reaction upon l., 541:19
religious feeling toward l., 605:10
relinquish l. for good of country, 365:12
respect for human l., 795:1
rest of his dull l., 237:20
resurrection and the l., 39:33
resurrection unto eternal l., 49:20
Reverence for L., 632:12
rights to a better l., 554:5
rounded with a sleep, 225:1
rule of l. from tonight, 577:8
sated with banquet of l., 90:14
save l. shall lose it, 34:39
saw l. steadily saw it whole, 494:9
science of l. superb hall, 468:12
scraped l. with fine-tooth comb, 783:5
seas of l. like wine, 278:13
secret l. of belly and bone, 772:2
secrets of a happy l., 755:n1
see how very strange it is, 579:16
see into l. of things, 368:9
seek not l. of immortals, 63:29
sense of what l. means, 542:5
set before you l. and death, 9:29
set gray l., 451:9
set l. at pin's fee, 197:35
set my l. on any chance, 216:8
set my l. upon cast, 172:12
sex pattern of process of l., 573:23
shadow of death, 249:6, 529:14
shape that l. takes, 826:9
she is mine for l., 791:16
sheltered l. can be daring l., 761:4
short l. in saddle, 579:13
short quiet hours few, 484:15
shouldn't be printed on dollar, 746:14
sin to prefer l. to honor, 109:23
slits the thin-spun l., 253:6
smiling aspects of l., 529:2
smooth road of l., 314:24

Life *(continued)*

so short craft so long, 132:7
so was it when l. began, 369:14
somebody taken lid off l., 702:6
soul the captain of l., 92:9
space of l. between, 409:6
spare all I have take l., 290:9
spend l. your own way, 688:1
spirit giveth l., 43:12
staff of l. bread, 282:*n*4
staff of my l., 156:19
stands brunt of l., 67:23
State have possibility of l., 75:9
stir within another's l., 801:15
story of my l., 207:36
stream of subjective l., 540:24
strenuous l., 570:12
struck on death, 434:19
struggle is my l., 790:17
struggling for l. in the water, 308:17
suicide is about l., 828:8
sunny side of l., 648:11
sunset of l. gives lore, 384:10
surging immensity of l., 442:23
sweet courtesies of l., 314:24
take honor and my l. is done, 176:9
take l. easy, 590:22
take vows of organization l., 789:3
taking l. by throat, 625:7
taking l. without blood, 582:20
tatty wreckage of my l., 832:15
teaches us to be less harsh, 343:6
teaching for l., 4:13
tedious as twice-told tale, 175:20
that breathes with breath, 450:12
that dares send challenge, 263:5
that they might have l., 39:30
that which men call death, 69:1
the L. that feeling, 831:2
the Lord is the strength of my l., 15:27
the old Sabines knew, 93:20
the only sanction of l., 584:2
the way the truth and the l., 39:42
theater of man's l., 164:16
therefore choose l., 9:29
they were busy dreaming about, 792:10
think l. too long, 281:9
thin-spun l., 253:6
this is alone L. Joy Empire Victory, 402:5
this is my l. my only l., 835:4
this is your l. and mine, 746:13
thought's slave of l., 183:30
threatened with suffocation, 708:5
thrill of l. along keel, 436:22
till storm of l. past, 305:8
time of l. is short, 183:28
time stuff l. made of, 302:26
time's fool, 183:30
tired of London tired of l., 310:13
to be misunderstood is cross of l., 490:16
to fear love is to fear l., 614:16
to neighbor's creed lent, 424:2
to seek out new l. new civilizations, 797:3
to sovereign power, 450:14
tomorrow's l. is too late, 107:5
too short to bore ourselves, 548:11
too strong for you, 605:6
tough proposition, 633:8

Life *(continued)*

treasured up to l. beyond l., 254:8
Tree of Knowledge not that of l., 397:15
tree of l. in garden, 5:12
Tree of L. middle tree, 257:14
trifles make sum of l., 466:7
tugging at perverse l., 755:14
twenty years in woman's l., 75:8
two things aim at in l., 590:11
understand l. at forty, 585:12
understood backward lived forward, 469:2
unexamined not worth living, 74:8
useless l. is early death, 343:5
uttered part of man's l., 407:16
vagrant gypsy l., 635:17
vale of l., 316:3
variety's spice of l., 326:22
veil those who live call L., 402:*n*1
voyage of their l., 193:13
warmed hands before fire of l., 384:4
was fiction in disguise, 813:10
was so new so real so right, 711:11
way that leadeth to l., 33:19
way they do my l., 845:5
weathered storms of l., 576:8
web of our l., 206:5
weight and pain of l., 66:20
welcome O l., 650:13
well spent is long, 140:4
well-written L. rare, 407:11
what is l., 492:1
what is l. a madness, 247:1
what is l. if full of care, 609:4
what is the prime of l., 75:8
what is your l., 45:31
what l. is there without Aphrodite, 55:3
what makes l. so sweet, 511:10
what signifies l. o' man, 356:21
what you think of this l., 191:24
when I consider l., 272:11
when l. and mind are broken, 591:15
when l. is burdensome, 69:18
when Love and L. fair, 561:4
when we come to end of l., 703:8
wherever l. ends it is all there, 152:5
while l. there's hope, 86:5, 87:22
whose l., 801:15
why l. all labor be, 450:18
why should a dog have l., 213:14
win passion and l., 378:7
wine of l. is drawn, 215:30
winged l. destroy, 352:8
wish human l. pure freedom, 751:4
with dull bits cut out, 722:9
with work which bores you l. hell,
  602:10
within us and abroad, 375:15
without him live no l., 259:12
without industry guilt, 484:20
woke found l. duty, 472:15
words have longer l. than deeds, 64:2
worth living, 584:3
would not be worth living, 558:12
wrung l. dry for your lips, 530:5
you must change your l., 632:10
you take my l., 186:12
young l. is before us, 120:26
your carriage and l. may preach, 270:3

Lifeblood, book l. of master spirit, 254:8
of our enterprise, 183:10
seemed to sip, 376:10
Life-in-Death, nightmare L. was she, 376:7
Life-lie, take l. away take happiness, 505:1
Life's a tough proposition, 633:8
brief span forbids us, 96:5
business terrible choice, 463:6
but a walking shadow, 217:23
common way, 370:10
dim windows of soul, 354:17
dull round, 310:*n*1
enchanted cup, 395:11
fitful fever, 216:11
here at l. end, 596:13
I know my l. a pain, 227:17
nourisher in l. feast, 215:21
our l. star, 370:17
outcast from l. feast, 650:8
page, 395:9
pay glad l. arrears, 462:25
poor play is o'er, 295:3
spirit that on l. rough sea, 163:20
travel on l. common way, 370:10
uncertain voyage, 213:29
under thy own l. key, 205:30
Lifetime burning in every moment, 679:1
great event given color to l., 431:5
human l. reduced to a brevity, 830:9
in my l. I have seen Frenchmen, 347:4
knotting undoing fishnet, 788:10
lamps not lit in our l., 581:10
love wakes men once a l., 500:7
not l. of one man only, 679:1
nothing completed in l., 696:6
of happiness hell, 565:4
respect for unknown in human l., 761:3
Liffeying waters of, 650:22
Lift and loosen old foundations, 636:8
her with care, 418:13
him into my arms, 817:7
lamp beside golden door, 552:16
me as wave leaf cloud, 402:12
my soul to heaven, 225:15
not painted veil, 402:*n*1
people from dust, 424:20
people who l., 556:15
thou up the light of thy countenance, 15:3
up mine eyes, 18:30
up your heads O ye gates, 15:25
us as he goes, 505:15
waters l. their bosoms, 203:7
Lifted, hath not l. his soul unto vanity, 15:24
moment I was l. and struck, 860:12
nevermore, 449:12
Light a glory a fair cloud, 378:9
a little warmth a little l., 519:8
a little while is l., 39:37
afraid of l. all of us, 504:12
all was l., 296:23
and life pleasure pain, 517:15
and silence make sound, 734:17
and will aspire, 171:8
Angels progeny of l., 258:20
appareled in celestial l., 370:13
armor of l., 41:40
around the body, 811:5
a-roving by l. of moon, 397:14

Light *(continued)*

at end of tunnel, 788:13
be not darkened, 23:30
be the earth, 67:7
because it lendeth l., 161:1
better to l. one candle, 660:*n1*
black as if bereaved of l., 350:14
body changed to l., 892:5
breaks where no sun shines, 777:3
bringeth to l. the shadow of death, 13:27
broke upon brain, 397:9
buried under chains, 717:8
burning and shining l., 39:14
by her own radiant l., 252:17
by l. of moon, 891:*n2*
candle and put it under bushel, 32:16
candle of understanding, 29:27
candle to the sun, 268:8
carrying you into fields of l., 67:6
certain Slant of l., 508:13
children of l., 38:15, 496:10
children of l. and day, 44:19
cities have kind of l., 867:12
come on baby l. my fire, 858:4
comes from thine eyes, 882:3
consider how l. is spent, 254:20
danced by l. of moon, 467:10
darkness and l. alike to thee, 19:14
dawn's early l., 386:19
dear as l. and life, 358:12
dies before thy word, 297:6
dim religious l., 251:23
doth trample on my days, 268:17
echo and l. unto eternity, 403:13
enough for wot I've to do, 464:12
everlasting L., 521:2
exact day-labor l. denied, 254:21
excelleth darkness, 22:28
excess of l., 316:13
existence brief crack of l., 723:3
fade from eyes, 611:*n5*
fade into l. of common day, 370:18
fantastic round, 252:11
fantastic toe, 250:22
flash of l. cut across sky, 774:12
former l. restore, 210:14
forward the L. Brigade, 454:19
freedom's holy l., 439:10
from grave to l., 278:1
gains make heavy purses, 163:14
garmented in l., 403:1
gates of l., 258:22
Gatsby believed in the green l., 710:7
gives a lovely l., 695:8
gives l. in darkness, 170:2
gladsome l. of jurisprudence, 158:22
gleams and is gone, 496:16
God Appears and God is L., 354:7
God guideth to His l., 118:23
God is l., 46:6
God l. of heavens and earth, 118:23
God shows sufficient l., 463:3
God's eldest daughter, 250:3
God's first creature l., 257:*n2*
gold and silver l., 591:12
gone into world of l., 268:16
guide by l. of reason, 562:13
hail holy l., 257:5

Light *(continued)*

half l. half shade, 451:8
half-believers, 495:15
have l. of life, 39:24
he is angel of l., 475:27
heaven to day denies, 397:1
heaven's l. forever shines, 404:2
here kindled, 240:5
Hesperus entreats thy l., 232:2
how weak and little is the l., 636:20
I am l. of the world, 39:24
I see my l. come shining, 851:20
if l. in thee be darkness, 33:4
if once we lose this l., 232:5
imperishable Name in registry of L., 550:8
in despite of l. keep us together, 229:8
in present l. flames, 620:14
in room by artificial l., 797:9
in sound sound-like power in light, 375:15
in the dust lies dead, 404:10
infant crying for l., 453:22
inner l. will shine forth, 345:*n1*
is left hand of darkness, 824:9
is lion comes to drink, 641:11
is shadow of God, 249:6
it giveth l. unto all, 32:16
judged in l. of final issue, 79:8
law not a l. to see by, 804:16
lead kindly L., 421:4
lead me from darkness to l., 50:1
let perpetual l. shine, 47:19
let there be l., 5:3
let your l. shine, 32:16
lift up the l. of thy countenance, 15:3
live and love in God's l., 143:2
lived l. in spring, 495:8
Lolita l. of my life, 723:5
long l. shakes, 452:19
made l. of it, 35:10
man like l. kindled and put out, 62:10
many hands make l. work, 148:10
mass times speed of l. squared, 637:*n4*
mocks at it and sets it l., 176:17
moralists put tale in edifying l., 726:11
more l., 345:1
my burden is l., 34:9
my fire, 858:4
neither joy nor love nor l., 496:19
night shadow of l., 529:14
no l. but darkness visible, 255:8
no l. propitious shone, 327:10
Noose of L., 441:5
of Light, 48:12
of light beguile, 173:41
of my understanding, 281:8
of oncoming train, 788:13
of setting suns, 368:11
of the body, 33:3
of the world, 32:16, 39:24
of things, 368:5
of thy sword, 417:5
on dark theme trace verses of l., 89:18
once set is our little l., 226:20
one small candle l. a thousand, 240:5
out of hell leads to l., 256:19
people have seen a great l., 25:15
people in darkness saw great l., 32:12
place void of all l., 128:14

Light *(continued)*

pleasing dreams slumbers l., 373:17
prime work of God, 257:*n2*
progeny of l., 258:20
pure and endless l., 268:14
purple l. of Love, 316:10
put out the l., 210:14, 572:2
Put out the L., 623:13
radiant l. rests on men, 63:31
rage against dying of l., 777:15
rather l. candles than curse darkness, 660:*n1*
river of crystal l., 554:1
roving by l. of moon, 397:14
sadder l. than moon, 438:15
seeking light, 173:41
shaft of l. in darkness, 786:14
she be made all of light, 226:21
she treads on it so l., 171:15
shines over land and sea, 620:14
shineth in darkness, 38:45
shower of l. is poesy, 409:3
solarium a rage of l., 871:2
something of angelic l., 371:8
speed far faster than l., 618:1
stand in your own l., 148:6
strikes Sultan's Turret with L., 441:4
strong shadow where much l., 342:9
suffusion from that l., 378:10
sun gives l. soon as he rises, 303:18
sweetness and l., 284:5, 497:13
teach l. to counterfeit a gloom, 251:18
that cometh from her wisdom, 30:7
that green l. that lingers, 378:7
that lies in woman's eyes, 387:15
that loses night that wins, 529:13
that never was, 371:18
that shineth more and more, 19:29
the first light of evening, 642:13
the Lord is my l., 15:27
the true L., 38:47
there is only the l., 789:11
thickens and crow makes wing, 216:13
things holy profane grave and l., 239:8
this is the l. of the mind, 832:12
those that rebel against the l., 13:44
thousand points of l., 805:2
threshold of waking l., 814:13
thy l. is come, 27:14
thy l. relume, 210:14
time's glory bring truth to l., 172:35
to guide, 371:15
to lighten Gentiles, 37:20
to them in darkness, 37:15
to those in darkness, 145:1
to whom God assigns no l., 118:24
tracings of eternal l., 359:11
travel l., 750:10
trifles l. as air, 209:10
tripped l. fantastic, 581:2
truth will come to l., 136:*n2*
truths kindle l. for truths, 89:19
unto my path, 18:28
unveiled her peerless l., 257:25
upon them hath the l. shined, 25:15
us down in honor or dishonor, 446:1
Vesper now raising his l., 91:19
void of l., 255:13
waited for the l., 605:19

Light *(continued)*
walk while ye have l., 39:37
wave of l. breaks into darkness, 668:18
we fear in the l., 90:10
we shall need no other l., 345:*n*1
what l. through yonder window, 179:31
when daylight comes comes in l., 479:12
when my l. low, 453:17
when our brief l. has set, 91:5
which lighteth every man, 38:47
white l. of morning, 891:13
why rise because 'tis l., 229:8
wife make heavy husband, 186:21
winning make prize light, 224:16
withdrawn which once he wore, 438:5
world but thickened l., 429:8
Lighted fools way to dusty death, 217:23
old is having l. rooms in head, 799:16
Lighten our darkness, 48:18
Lightened, thundered and l., 72:10
weight of world l., 368:8
Lightens, cease to be ere it l., 180:10
Lighter than cork danced on waves, 558:17
town is l. than vanity, 271:17
Lightest, movements of l. atom, 345:3
sovereign is the l., 80:8
word harrow soul, 198:5
Lightfoot, many a l. lad, 575:9
Light-hearted, afoot and l., 486:24
Lighthouse, below the l. top, 375:20
took sitivation at l., 464:4
Lighting is director's philosophy, 727:7
Lightland, rise in heaven's l., 4:4
set in western l., 4:5
Lightly draws its breath, 368:2
earth rest l. on you, 121:17
entered into unadvisedly or l., 49:13
lie l. gentle earth, 238:5
rest, 67:7
tread l. she is near, 559:15
we esteem too l., 333:6
Lightness, drama not of heaviness but of l., 824:4
Lightning, bottled l., 464:22
countenance like l., 36:22
does the work, 525:2
done like l., 231:17
fateful l., 481:1
flashed the living l., 293:12
flash of l. in summer cloud, 112:26
he's a l. pilot, 522:16
in collied night, 177:28
in thunder l. or in rain, 213:30
like writing history with l., 566:18
makes awful l., 434:19
mirth like flash of l., 288:15
outstare the l., 218:35
Satan as l. fall, 37:34
scratch head with l., 522:12
strikes mountaintop, 96:23
Superman the l., 547:18
too like the l., 180:10
vain to look for defense against l., 101:1
zigzag l. stands high, 891:17
Lightnings, four l. zigzag from me, 891:19
in the splendor of the moon, 451:7
veiling l. of song, 403:20
Light-o'-love lady known as Lou, 627:12

Lights around the shore, 506:8
Father of l., 45:22
fled garlands dead, 388:1
godfathers of heaven's l., 174:1
highest candle l. dark, 642:14
love is keeper of warm l., 65:25
moon l. up the earth, 56:6
Northern L. seen sights, 627:13
that do mislead the morn, 207:8
turn up l., 582:4
water closing over sleepy l., 765:4
your l. burning, 38:5
Light-winged Dryad, 410:3
Ligislachure, newspaper conthrols l., 600:16
Like a winter my absence, 222:5
ape how l. to us, 84:18
can afford to l. them, 838:13
doth quit like, 207:17
find their l. again, 373:7
God pairs with l., 53:24
how do you l. your blueeyed boy, 701:7
I didn't l. it, 863:2
I don't l. you Sabidius, 107:7
I know what I l., 612:17
I l. to be in America, 828:14
I would l. to be the air, 844:16
look upon his l. again, 197:9
me from heels to head, 555:12
more ye see better l. it, 600:9
never met one I didn't l., 640:10
not fair terms, 184:32
of each thing, 174:2
one that stands on promontory, 170:27
people like priest, 28:32
poor cat i' the adage, 215:2
tell me what you l., 484:19
those who admire us, 264:16
to an hermit poor, 159:2
to see it lap Miles, 509:10
upon earth there is not his l., 14:36
very l. a whale, 200:26
very l. me, 555:12
want it most l. it least, 298:8
we don't l. it, 814:11
what he loves never l. too much, 232:11
will to like, 147:2
you l. me, 863:9
Liked, all people need be l. by some people, 760:4
book the better, 323:5
it not and died, 227:12
several women, 224:27
way it walks, 579:15
Likely impossibility preferable, 79:6
man in preference to rich, 62:19
we are all l. to go astray, 65:24
Likeness, devil created in man's l., 492:10
gods in l. of men, 40:28
grow into l. of bad men, 76:9
let us make man after our l., 5:6
of filly foal, 178:12
very l. of roasted crab, 178:12
Likes, are cured by l., 348:19
doesn't know what he l., 704:5
nobody l. man who brings bad news, 65:13
Likewise, go and do l., 37:38
Liking, all love all l. all delight, 241:13
grounds other than l., 480:24

Liking *(continued)*
happy l. what they do, 315:1
saves me trouble of l., 382:23
Lilac all over New England, 626:15
and brown hair, 677:15
lost l., 677:19
Lilacs last in dooryard bloomed, 487:12
out of dead land, 676:5
Lilies and languors of virtue, 529:16
beauty of the l., 481:2
crowned with l., 695:17
feed among the l., 24:13
handfuls of l. to scatter, 95:1
of the field, 33:8
peacocks and l., 484:9
roses and white l. grow, 227:3
silent war of l., 172:30
that fester, 222:3
three l. in her hand, 505:23
twisted braids of l., 252:26
wheat set about with l., 24:21
Lilting house, 777:9
I've heard them l., 321:8
Lily maid of Astolat, 455:13
of the valleys, 24:6
paint the l., 175:24
poppy or a l., 526:11
Shanghai L., 679:17
water l. bloom, 451:6
Lily-livered boy, 217:17
Lima, curious traveler from L., 317:4
Limb, feels life in every l., 368:2
neither heat affection l., 206:34
sound wind and l., 157:27
Limbecks foul as hell, 222:16
Limbo large and broad, 257:9
Limbs, gentle l. undress, 377:10
his l. cold in death, 95:12
I the l. and wheel, 491:7
lopped l., 755:11
melter of l., 54:14
of a dismembered poet, 95:20
recreant l., 175:14
ruddy l. flaming hair, 352:6
these l. her provinces, 230:1
young in l. judgment old, 185:4
Lime, madeleine soaked in l. flowers, 610:13
of love, 240:10
Limestone quarried near spot, 597:11
Limit, fixes solemn l. of Heaven, 68:3
of becoming mirth, 174:9
quiet l. of world, 455:6
use me to the l., 571:2
Limitations, in l. the master, 344:17
no man climb beyond l., 533:4
Limited, it's a l. hang-out, 844:6
Limitless night, 609:1
swelling and l. billows, 378:1
Limits, hell hath no l., 168:19
of my language and world, 685:10
of own field limits of world, 400:1
own appointed l. keep, 503:1
stony l. cannot hold love, 180:4
truth has its l., 153:21
Limns on water writes in dust, 166:23
Limousine, one perfect l., 699:15
Limp and damp as tendrils, 756:4
into scalding grave, 611:14

Lips *(continued)*
    wrung life dry for your l., 530:5
Lipstick, hockey mom and pit bull l., 878:9
Liquefaction of her clothes, 241:14
Liquid, bedewed with l. odors, 96:6
    dew of youth, 197:19
    inventing l. wine, 68:9
    lapse of murmuring streams, 258:30
    notes close eye of day, 253:17
    siftings fall, 676:2
Liquidate labor stocks farmers real estate,
    561:14
Liquidation evaporation precedes l., 568:6
    of British Empire, 621:4
Liquidity of investment, 656:18
Liquids, alcohol is prince of l., 348:17
Liquor, can't hold my l. either, 844:3
    claret the l. for boys, 310:24
    drank l. straight, 749:13
    is one way out, 766:9
    is quicker, 732:5
    lips that touch l., 597:15
    livelier l. than Muse, 575:12
    never brewed, 508:8
Liquor's out why clink cannikin, 460:9
Liquors, hot and rebellious l., 194:4
Lisp and wear strange suits, 195:25
    of leaves, 529:12
Lisped, I l. in numbers, 295:10
    somewhat he l., 133:20
List, have l. of members of Communist Party,
    754:6
    he's making a l., 680:2
    I've got a little l., 527:10
    then the L. is done, 509:9
'Listed, legion never was 'l., 588:10
Listen all day to such stuff, 514:6
    and save, 252:26
    as I am listening now, 403:6
    awhile ye nations, 408:18
    but l. it's not finished, 715:5
    do not l. simply wait, 655:17
    for dear honor's sake, 252:26
    go and l. as thou goest, 129:16
    gods to him particularly l., 50:15
    good music people don't l., 560:21
    heath slowly awake and l., 535:15
    here is the law, 632:19
    my children, 437:15
    not l. to reason, 457:2
    remain sitting and l., 655:17
    there's a hell of good universe, 702:2
    to it and do not hear, 57:6
    to little bird's voice, 73:1
    to Muse when unhappy, 732:17
    to the Revolution, 643:23
    to them children of the night, 551:6
    where thou art sitting, 252:26
    wind is rising, 666:2
    wise to l. to the Word, 62:1
    wish him to l., 540:5
    you hear the grating roar, 496:17
Listened and looked sideways up, 376:10
    soul l. intensely, 372:7
    things most l. for, 488:8
Listening, are you l., 813:11
    disease of not l., 187:28
    mood seemed to stand, 373:19

Listening *(continued)*
    nightly to l. earth, 287:21
    planets in stations l., 258:28
    voice say to everything l., 860:10
Listens, he l. well who takes notes, 129:4
    like three years' child, 375:19
Listeth, wind bloweth where it l., 39:9
Lit, lamps not l. in our lifetime, 581:10
    upon gentle sensitive mind, 593:6
Literalists of the imagination, 671:2
Literary accomplishments in women, 340:14
    attempt unfortunate, 312:2
    culture is held hostage, 835:7
    fellow travelers, 643:11
    flatting and sharping, 524:7
    German dives into sentence, 523:14
    intellectuals at one pole, 743:11
    lock words in l. storehouse, 578:7
    nature and civilization l. field, 543:16
Literature, all else is l., 550:1
    analysis of character, 740:2
    apocalyptic l., 826:2
    best l. becomes folk l., 743:17
    Bible l. not dogma, 584:9
    books not American l., 456:15
    Borges can weave l., 719:6
    classicist in l., 677:9
    clear and cold, 664:7
    Clemens the Lincoln of l., 529:3
    complete statement l., 654:9
    continue to have a function, 801:13
    defect of modern l., 495:22
    gives no man sinecure, 665:10
    great l. is simply language, 665:17
    had call to l. of low order, 522:1
    imaginary l., 760:14
    impurities of l., 654:8
    is fragment of fragments, 343:20
    is mostly about having sex, 840:7
    Johnson great Cham of l., 318:2
    little or great L., 552:15
    lose oneself in l., 493:19
    masterwork of l., 496:4
    modern American l. from one book, 721:14
    must aim at the maximum, 801:12
    my mistress, 578:1
    news that stays news, 665:19
    of l. as work, 778:4
    once l. is contrived as, 847:5
    or chickens, 723:18
    place we can hear everything, 865:13
    reduced to essence, 612:8
    remarks are not l., 628:2
    reward to be expected from l., 299:2
    sanity virtue of ancient l., 495:22
    substitute for experience, 791:8
    this is what l. is, 871:7
    to produce a little l., 544:2
    turn woman into l., 767:11
    with noble sentiments bad l., 604:10
Literatures, knowledge of different l., 557:10
Lithe, I asked a l. lady, 352:4
Litigious terms fat contentions, 254:3
Littérature, beaux sentiments mauvaise l.,
    604:*n4*
    tout le reste est l., 550:*n1*
Little, a l. I can read, 218:4
    a l. more than kin, 196:24

Little *(continued)*
    advantages every day, 304:2
    better is l. with the fear of the Lord, 20:32
    better than one of wicked, 181:29
    bitter l. embryos, 723:4
    black sheep, 588:6
    body with mighty heart, 189:2
    Bo-peep, 895:2
    boy blue, 893:11
    Boy Blue kissed them, 554:2
    boys made of, 895:11
    but l. at a time, 285:12
    candle throws beams, 186:18
    cargo boats, 589:2
    child shall lead them, 25:19
    country retreat, 279:10
    Cousins called back, 511:16
    creature formed of joy, 354:10
    creatures everywhere, 654:3
    dear l. Buttercup, 525:18
    death of L. Nell without laughing, 561:8
    do great right do l. wrong, 186:2
    do or can the best of us, 463:15
    dogs and all, 212:11
    every day a l. death, 829:1
    every l. makes a mickle, 157:15
    fall by l. and l., 31:6
    fire quickly trodden out, 170:35
    Fly, 352:15
    foxes that spoil the vines, 24:10
    friend of all the world, 589:13
    gain l. patch of ground, 201:18
    girls made of, 895:12
    goodness in l. finger, 286:3
    great empire and l. minds, 324:14
    great grace with l. gift, 82:16
    great ones eat up l. ones, 220:12
    happy if say how much, 190:28
    having been a l. chastised, 29:34
    here a l. and there a l., 26:7
    here a l. child I stand, 241:15
    hills like lambs, 18:21
    hoard l. hearts great, 455:10
    horse think it queer, 623:7
    how l. one knows oneself, 686:10
    how l. room we take in death, 246:11
    if thou have but a l., 29:28
    infinite riches in l. room, 168:8
    is never lacking, 90:18
    Jack Horner, 892:19
    Johnny Green, 893:13
    Lamb who made thee, 350:12
    lame balloonman, 701:5
    learning dangerous thing, 292:12
    life rounded with a sleep, 225:1
    like l. mice stole in and out, 261:5
    like some l. woman, 856:*n1*
    little grave, 177:13
    love me l. love me long, 241:1, 881:2
    man had a little gun, 896:12
    man like l. kingdom, 192:2
    man little man, 151:15
    man wants but l., 290:25, 322:10
    Miss Muffet, 895:14
    monstrous l. voice, 178:5
    more than kin, 196:24
    more than little is too much, 183:3
    mother's l. helper, 857:3

Little *(continued)*

much drinking l. thinking, 284:13
Namby Pamby's l. rhymes, 291:22
nameless acts, 368:7
Nature's l. kings, 227:16
needed to make happy life, 112:16
nourishment I get, 666:7
nut tree, 894:18
O thou of l. faith, 34:29
O ye of l. faith, 33:29
old lady from Dubuque, 696:*n*1
old New York, 582:2
one l. room an everywhere, 228:7
one l. word, 176:13
one shall become a thousand, 27:15
philosophy inclineth to atheism, 165:27
pig went to market, 893:10
Polly Flinders, 895:3
pot and soon hot, 173:18
profits that idle king, 451:11
put even l. on l., 54:24
safer to know too l., 521:6
shall I grace my cause, 207:34
shrunk to this l. measure, 192:19
snug l. island, 372:18
strokes fell great oaks, 302:29
Sunshine stayed on, 805:8
sweeten this l. hand, 217:14
there is no l. enemy, 302:3
things affect little minds, 430:5
things go lessening, 462:26
think too l., 273:1
this l. world, 176:24
those who have too l., 652:13
though l. I'll work, 882:11
though l. she is fierce, 178:30
tight l. island, 372:18
Tin Gods on Wheels, 586:17
tiny boy, 205:29
tiny wit, 211:31
to earn, 481:5
to have l. is to possess, 57:10
Tom Tucker, 893:14
Tommy Tittlemouse, 896:19
too l. to be killed, 588:16
touch of Harry, 189:19
town of Bethlehem, 521:2
toy dog covered with dust, 554:2
wanton boys that swim on bladders, 225:25
we see in Nature, 371:23
when l. fears grow great, 200:19
while is the light, 39:37
who are a l. wise, 229:1
who knows only his side knows l., 435:6
with a l. pin, 177:9
woman who wrote the book, 458:*n*4
work a little play, 519:8
world made cunningly, 230:18
world of childhood, 630:8
wretched creature, 301:8
yield when taken l. by l., 108:2
Little Dorrit, let us read L. again, 736:8
Littleness, assemblage of sloth sleep and l., 330:6
long l. of life, 667:6
Littlenesses, disdaining l., 76:6
Little's, Mrs. L. second son, 724:1
Live a barren sister all your life, 177:26
a little too wise ne'er l. long, 171:*n*1

Live *(continued)*

actual writing is what you l. for, 674:11
after so many deaths I l., 243:7
age youth not l. together, 881:17
alive while thy book l., 232:19
all days of your life, 286:6
all that l. must die, 196:25
all you can, 544:15
alone in bee-loud glade, 591:2
and die in Aristotle's works, 168:16
and die in Dixie, 471:1
and die r-r-rich, 466:30
and die wi' Charlie, 367:15
and learn, 283:20
and let live, 883:2
and love in God's light, 143:2
as an animal, 690:18
as if God beheld you, 103:10
as long as you please, 152:4
as men not ostriches, 653:12
as we can, 81:4
at home at ease, 247:4
because I l. here, 841:8
begins to l. that day, 510:13
better l. rich, 310:20
better to l. alone, 64:14
bid me to l., 240:11
blindly and upon the hour, 628:16
by squeezing from stone, 666:7
can these bones l., 28:18
can't l. with them or without, 73:10
can't l. without or with you, 102:2
ceases to l. unreflectively, 632:13
converse and l. with ease, 295:13
courage to l., 406:11
date l. in infamy, 653:6
dead l. the living die, 273:26
decided to l. forever, 802:8
deeds by which we l., 163:18
deliberately, 474:29
desire to l. again, 549:4
desire to l. beyond income, 521:12
difficult to write good life as l. one, 646:10
do not l. but linger, 234:20
do you want to l. forever, 312:*n*2
easy l. quiet die, 374:11
eat to l. not l. to eat, 302:1
evil manners l. in brass, 226:11
exalt will to l., 632:13
for more than one century, 91:1
for what l. but make sport, 382:12
glad l. and gladly die, 555:16
good to l. it again, 734:13
gray dawn, 814:13
Greeks knew how to l., 547:14
hair shining and free, 669:9
haven't knowledge how to l., 560:23
his shame would l. on after him, 656:2
Hope without object not l., 378:15
how to l. well on nothing, 459:6
how we l. far from how we ought, 142:1
human heart by which we l., 371:5
I cannot l. with You, 509:14
I cannot l. without books, 338:6
I cannot l. without brainwork, 573:4
I still l., 391:1
I sure did l. in this world, 830:10
I to die and you to l., 74:11

Live *(continued)*

I would not l. alway, 13:18
if I l. I will fight, 686:8
if I should l. to be, 443:15
if man die shall he l. again, 13:31
ill report while you l., 199:13
in fragments no longer, 638:10
in him we l., 40:34
in house by side of road, 569:13
in human imagination, 818:1
in old chaos of sun, 640:22
in our life Nature l., 378:8
in restricted circle, 542:3
in small circle as we will, 343:14
in the time of your life l., 756:16
in this faith I will l. and die, 139:1
in world as spectator, 288:2
in world good or bad, 473:16
innocently God is here, 305:5
isn't fit to l., 823:6
it all again, 595:4
known going to l. this long, 654:21
leave sack l. cleanly, 183:37
let me l. unseen unknown, 292:5
let us l. and love, 91:5, 226:20
life he has imagined, 475:19
life through not like crossing field, 897:11
like stoic bird, 666:4
like to l. a long life, 823:16
like velvet mole, 666:5
like wretch and die rich, 234:22
long l. our noble king, 292:2
long l. the strike, 815:11
love wisdom l. accordingly, 474:16
loves to l. i' the sun, 194:13
mad to l. mad to be saved, 799:3
make war to l. in peace, 78:14
man desires to l. long, 284:18
man does not l. by GNP alone, 780:12
man forgets to l., 280:26
martyrdom to l., 248:24
marvel how fishes l. in sea, 220:12
means be divinely aware, 691:3
merrily shall I l. now, 225:5
mirth with thee I mean to l., 251:9
more virtue than doth l., 232:13
name shall l. behind me, 202:31
no man shall see me and l., 8:21
no picture made to l. with, 665:12
nobly to l., 65:3
not both l. and utter it, 474:1
not in myself, 395:21
not l. by bread only, 9:18
not l. if England finished, 627:5
not l. unto oneself, 81:8
not l. with living, 183:25
not three good men unhanged, 182:19
not to l. but to make war, 760:10
now I l. now life is done, 163:11
on crusts we call bread, 681:16
on knees, 643:10, 653:5
one bare hour to l., 169:3
only by risking we l., 541:12
or die, 390:3
peaceably, 41:34
pleasurably without living wisely, 81:16
power to l. and act, 372:11

Locust of soul unshelled, 798:2
   tossed up and down as the l., 18:17
Locusts and wild honey, 32:6
   food as luscious as l., 208:9
   like in Bible with l., 741:9
Lodge, house to l. friend, 296:7
   in garden of cucumbers, 24:30
   in some vast wilderness, 326:20
   not l. thee by Chaucer, 232:19
   thorns that in bosom l., 198:13
   where thou lodgest I will l., 10:30
Lodged with me useless, 254:20
Lodges, where care l. sleep never lie, 180:18
Lodgest, where thou l. I will lodge, 10:30
Lodging, grant us safe l., 421:5
   Phoebus' l., 180:31
   place of wayfaring men, 27:32
Loftier race than known, 537:9
   raise somewhat l. strain, 92:21
Loftiest peaks most wrapt, 395:17
Loftiness of thought surpassed, 274:7
Lofts of jaw-loss, 867:1
Lofty and sour, 226:12
   build the l. rhyme, 253:1
   scene be acted o'er, 192:18
   sky immeasurably l., 506:13
   towers I see down-rased, 221:18
Log hut with simple bench, 512:15
   Mark Hopkins at end of l., 512:*n*2
   roll my l. I roll yours, 104:4
   tough wedge for tough l., 100:31
   will never be crocodile, 889:12
Logan's, enter L. cabin hungry, 320:6
Logic and rhetoric able to contend, 166:19
   and sermons never convince, 486:12
   doctrinaire l., 694:5
   is logic, 443:13
   of mind overtasked, 443:6
   page of history worth volume of l., 539:2
   that's l., 515:19
Logical, built in such l. way, 443:12
Logicians are wrong, 722:13
Logs, Tom bears l. into the hall, 174:33
Loins, gird up thy l. like a man, 14:17
   he girded up his l., 12:3
   let your l. be girded, 38:5
   Lolita fire of my l., 723:5
   shudder in l., 594:16
   with your l. girded, 7:40
Loiterers, liege of all l., 174:14
Loitering, alone and palely l., 412:2
Lola, shook up world except for L., 859:3
Lolita, immortality you and I share L., 723:8
   light of my life, 723:5
Loman never made money, 780:5
Lomond, bonnie banks of Loch L., 884:13
London Bridge falling down, 581:2, 892:20
   broken arch of L. Bridge, 419:17
   don't send poet to L., 415:4
   flower of Cities all, 141:4
   foggy day in L. town, 711:7
   great cesspool, 573:3
   hell city much like L., 402:18
   in ruins rather than enslaved, 619:16
   is drowning, 871:9
   Lord Mayor of L., 881:20
   loved life L., 654:5
   mind is city like L., 772:3

London *(continued)*
   particular a fog, 466:10
   sea at best at L., 617:14
   this is L., 754:9
   tired of L. tired of life, 310:13
   to L. to look at queen, 895:7
   vilest alleys of L., 573:13
Lone Glenartney's hazel shade, 373:18
   lorn creetur, 465:20
   not in l. splendor, 412:10
   poor l. woman, 188:1
   sheiling, 417:4
   walking by wild l., 589:19
   worker makes first advance, 647:7
Loneliness, beside the clock's l., 827:10
   die of l., 597:13
   is an aspect of the land, 838:9
   no one discovers depths of own l., 673:17
   people's ignorance or l., 838:5
   swoops down upon you, 679:15
   ultimate in l., 803:14
   when l. attacks world, 769:1
   who knows what true l. is, 567:21
Lonely, all the l. people, 848:7
   and poor of old, 669:12
   and swift like planet, 567:5
   as in metropolitan crowd, 572:3
   dark and l. hiding place, 377:16
   down at end of l. street, 840:12
   flowering in l. word, 456:1
   God winding l. horn, 591:10
   hunts on l. hill, 562:1
   I'm l. I'll make world, 610:5
   impulse of delight, 593:1
   I've seen l. times, 866:12
   more l. among men, 475:9
   must also make you l., 827:8
   nation turns its l. eyes to you, 855:8
   no matter how l. you get, 869:6
   rapture on l. shore, 396:16
   sea and sky, 635:15
   so l. 'twas that God, 377:4
   sun in l. lands, 454:13
   thing that shone, 595:17
   those whose lives are l., 781:1
   tramp l. fellow, 683:16
   to l. it wears mask, 567:21
   wandered l. as a cloud, 371:9
Lonelyhearts, Miss L., 736:11
Lonesome, be good and be l., 524:8
   like one that on l. road, 376:21
   October, 449:14
   place against sky, 557:7
   road, 376:21
   whippoorwill, 804:1
Lonesomeness, starlight lit l., 535:11
Lonesome's a bad place, 765:8
Long ago in Kentucky, 744:2
   and faithful service, 468:19
   and ghastly kitchen, 468:12
   and lank and brown, 376:13
   and loath at going, 681:18
   and steep is the way, 54:21
   and terrible way, 756:14
   apprenticehood, 176:15
   arm of coincidence, 577:19
   art l. life short, 343:3
   as l. as ever you can, 301:19

Long *(continued)*
   as l. as moon rise, 892:4
   be day never so l., 148:18
   calamity of so l. life, 199:21
   day's journey into night, 681:11
   day's task is done, 219:1
   deliberate derangement, 558:14
   divorce of steel, 225:15
   for imperishable quiet, 756:9
   for l. time used to go to bed early, 610:11
   from l. to l. in solemn sort, 378:11
   gray beard glittering eye, 375:17
   hair glory to woman, 42:23
   happy as heart was l., 777:13
   his arm is very l., 69:22
   how l. a time in one word, 176:13
   how l. to obtain vote, 800:8
   how l. wilt thou forget me, 15:8
   I have lived l. enough, 217:18
   I learned l. time ago, 864:7
   I loved you once l. ago, 56:7
   I speak not loud or l., 161:*n*3
   in l. run all dead, 656:11
   it shan't be l., 298:19
   it wont be l. now, 635:12, 635:14
   kiss l. as my exile, 220:2
   labor l. workers idle, 117:8
   lane knows no turnings, 460:10
   life how l. or short, 259:22
   life is short art l., 71:6
   life well spent is l., 140:4
   light shakes, 452:19
   littleness of life, 667:6
   live our noble king, 292:2
   live the strike, 815:11
   long thoughts, 437:9
   long wintry nights, 468:2
   Lord how l., 25:12
   love me little love me l., 241:1, 881:2
   may land be bright, 439:10
   mechanic pacings, 451:9
   melancholy l. withdrawing roar, 496:19
   merry as day is l., 190:22
   never make l. visits, 671:5
   nor that little l., 290:25
   nor wants that little l., 322:10
   not l. life by fire, 579:13
   not l. the weeping and the laughter, 599:17
   poem does not exist, 450:1
   pray that way be l., 583:11
   pull strong pull, 465:34
   run misleading guide to affairs, 656:11
   see so much nor live so l., 213:16
   seven l. year, 212:6
   short and l. of it, 187:8
   short meaning of l. speech, 360:3
   small showers last l., 176:23
   Tail, 876:6
   that thy days may be l., 8:14
   think life too l., 281:9
   three l. mountains, 695:5
   time between drinks, 555:20
   time coming, 829:10
   to talk with lover's ghost, 229:21
   trick's over, 635:17
   Trochee trips from l. to short, 378:11
   vainly l. to see her, 121:26
   way l. wind cold, 372:20

Long *(continued)*

way to Tipperary, 628:20
ways from home, 898:16
what a l. strange trip, 852:8
within no power to live l., 103:12
words Bother me, 651:8

Long Island, Jay Gatsby of West Egg L., 710:4
Long-drawn aisle, 315:19
Longed, lies where l. to be, 555:16
to embrace mother's ghost, 53:11
truly l. for death, 450:12

Longer, impossible takes l., 887:18
letter l. than usual, 269:5
no l. stay with you, 885:15
smile dwells l., 615:16
some days l., 621:15
song had been l., 893:17
stretch him out l., 213:15
words have l. life than deeds, 64:2

Longest fifty-nine minutes, 601:7
journey go, 403:11
journey inwards, 741:8
journey to oblivion, 663:23
nights are l. there, 206:22
part of the journey, 86:19
way round shortest home, 242:n2

Longest-lived and shortest-lived die same, 111:12
Longeth, my flesh l. for thee, 17:6
Longevity has its place, 823:16
Longfellow's, shown L. grave, 671:5
Long-haired, not these l. men I fear, 89:8
Longing, cast l. eye on offices, 337:6
for stewed prunes, 206:21
for that lovely lady, 86:18
for them will kill you, 859:4
leans and beckons, 482:9
lingering look behind, 316:4
more l. wavering, 204:34
on a large scale, 841:5
what sweet thoughts what l., 128:17

Longings, I have immortal l. in me, 219:13
Longitude, in l. tho' scanty, 358:9
use l. and latitude for seine, 522:12
Long-legged fly upon stream, 597:4
Long-leggety beasties, 884:8
Long-lost, I can be your l. pal, 855:13
Longmans', it's still in L. shop, 369:n1
Long-strayed eyes, 229:10
Long-suffering and very pitiful, 30:10
fruit of Spirit is l., 43:31
love is l., 137:11

Longtemps je me suis couché de bonne heure, 610:n3
Longue, je n'ai fait celle-ci plus l., 269:n1
Look about us and die, 294:14
afraid to l. upon God, 7:27
after all it is a poor land, 491:9
after our people, 603:8
after souls in labor, 76:5
all world here to l. on me, 178:18
and pass on, 128:10
angel of backward l., 438:17
around choose ground, 399:17
as they run l. behind, 315:5
ashamed to l. next morning, 245:5
astronomy compels soul to l. upwards, 75:12

Look *(continued)*

at all the fire-folk, 546:7
at the stars, 546:7
at things in bloom, 574:11
away Dixie Land, 470:16
before time to l. round, 343:14
before you leap, 262:20
behind the Ranges, 589:21
clean starved for a l., 221:25
direct him where to l. for it, 230:15
do it with bitter l., 561:3
don't l. back, 747:6
down on hate, 395:17
ere ye leap, 146:13
eyes l. your last, 181:14
fear in the face, 660:7
for circumstances, 564:15
for me in nurseries, 576:11
for me under boot-soles, 486:20
for truth but not find it, 313:14
fortress-like l. of it, 850:8
forty centuries l. down, 365:4
forward to posterity, 325:2
forward to with hope, 622:13
give me a l., 232:7
goose l., 217:16
her quick l., 756:4
her wanton spirits l. out, 204:4
homeward Angel, 253:13
how floor of heaven, 186:15
how others do it, 359:17
how ring encompasseth thy finger, 171:21
I could not l. on Death, 590:7
I had fixed my l. on his, 128:24
I'll not l. for wine, 232:16
in almanack find out moonshine, 178:26
in my God's right hand, 898:25
in thy heart and write, 162:20
into happiness through another's eyes, 196:1
into lives as into mirror, 86:15
into oneself, 582:6
into seeds of time, 214:5
into your heart, 359:17
lean and hungry l., 191:28
learned to l. on nature, 368:11
let him l. to his bond, 185:10
let it l. like perfect honor, 218:8
library whereon I l., 241:16
lift their heavy lids and l., 500:7
like innocent flower, 214:20
lingering l. behind, 316:4
look up at skies, 546:7
make man l. sad, 179:14
making crime l. dull, 778:11
morn in russet mantle clad, 196:20
my God l. not so fierce, 169:5
ne'er l. back, 209:20
nine out of ten will stay and l., 722:11
no more upon't, 236:15
not down but up, 462:18
not thou upon the wine, 21:30
of bay mare shames silliness out of me, 485:21
on both indifferently, 191:23
on my works ye Mighty, 401:13
on you when last hour comes, 101:19
only a l. and voice, 437:19

Look *(continued)*

out here comes Master Race, 811:9
out where yr going, 811:17
out your window, 851:4
reader l., 232:18
see monument l. around, 276:21
shifty hangdog l., 648:15
somebody let him l. at works, 702:6
soul l. body touch, 596:12
Stein does not l. like portrait, 628:1
straight at a film, 854:7
take a backward l., 508:6
things fairer when we l. back, 482:9
through a millstone, 162:5
to it, 445:8
upon a little child, 305:9
upon his like again, 197:9
upon world as parish, 301:15
upward l. of caution, 624:15
we l. at each other, 815:16
we l. before and after, 403:5
westward l. land is bright, 479:12
when will I l. at it, 772:5
who comes here, 175:17
with favor on bold beginning, 93:10
with thine ears, 212:29
ye there, 304:n4
you could l. it up, 704:12

Looked again found it was, 517:8
and sighed again, 274:19
as she did love, 412:4
before thou leapt, 146:n10
down to Camelot, 451:6
God l. around and said, 610:5
into eye of day, 595:1
Lot's wife l. back, 6:34
love to eyes which spake, 395:13
no sooner l. but loved, 195:35
on better days, 194:22
on women with lust, 805:14
out of eye of saint, 595:6
sideways up, 376:10
to Government for bread, 325:14
up in perfect silence, 487:6
with such a wistful eye, 561:1
with wild surmise, 408:17

Looker-on, patient l., 242:5
Lookers-on, only God and angels l., 164:16
Looketh, Lord l. on the heart, 10:43
on the outward appearance, 10:43
well to ways of her household, 22:19

Lookin' eastward to sea, 588:1
Looking, act of l. back, 825:11
as if alive, 460:1
as like one pea does another, 146:5
at self through others, 602:3
at significant work of art, 639:6
conscience warns somebody l., 645:18
eastward to sea, 588:1
even if gods should be l., 53:9
for honest man, 77:2
hand to plow and l. back, 37:30
here's l. at you kid, 758:5
leave them while l. good, 698:8
one way rowing another, 271:19
outward together, 726:16
over harbor and city, 636:3

Looking (*continued*)

pleasure in l. has been split, 853:2
seaman l. for something else, 672:3
see without l. through windows, 57:16
well can't move her, 261:2

Looking Backward was written, 553:15
Looking-glass, no use to blame l., 442:19
Looking-glasses, women l. reflecting man, 654:17
Looks, assurance given by l., 169:9

commercing with the skies, 251:13
dispatchful l., 258:17
everybody's l. of death, 277:12
gigantically down, 448:4
gods do not give all men good l., 53:7
in the clouds, 191:36
kindness not beauteous l., 173:21
love l. not with eyes, 178:1
modest l. cottage adorn, 322:28
more elder than thy l., 186:4
never l. nor 'eeds, 589:2
not deep-searched with saucy l., 174:1
old man l. before and after, 50:28
on alike, 223:32
on tempests, 222:15
patron l. with unconcern, 308:17
poet l. at world as man at woman, 643:2
puts on his pretty l., 175:19
quite through deeds of men, 191:29
she l. with threatening eye, 175:21
she needs good l., 661:17
stolen l. nice in chapels, 392:14
through Nature up, 295:6
toward school with heavy l., 180:12
war of l. between them, 171:10
were free, 376:7
whole world in face, 436:12

Loom, I cannot ply the l., 56:9
left the web left the l., 451:6
Loon, thou cream-faced l., 217:16
Loop to hang doubt on, 209:15
Looped and windowed raggedness, 211:33
Loophole, from her cabined l. peep, 252:10
Loopholes of retreat, 386:5
Loose, all hell broke l., 258:9

as the wind, 242:26
feel his title hang l., 217:15
hell's broken l., 164:5
imagination, 596:13
lips sink ships, 887:19
the bands of Orion, 14:23

Loosed, arrows l. several ways, 188:36
blood-dimmed tide l., 593:9
fateful lightning, 481:1
silver cord be l., 23:31
Loosen, old faiths l. and fall, 530:9
old foundations, 636:8
Loosened, Heine l. corsets of German language, 626:6
Loosens fragrant bodice, 409:22
Loot, difference between yield and l., 685:7
Lopped limbs, 755:11
Lord, all ye works of the L., 31:30

am an attendant l., 675:4
among wits, 308:18
and Father of mankind, 438:18
angel of L. came down, 281:13
angel of L. came upon them, 37:17

Lord (*continued*)

anger of L. kindled, 11:14
answered Job out of the whirlwind, 14:17
be thankit, 358:14
be with you, 47:18
better is little with the fear of the L., 20:32
bless thee and keep thee, 9:2
bless ye the L., 31:30
blessed be L. God, 37:13
blessed the latter end of Job, 14:39
bringeth thee into good land, 9:19
Cain went out from presence of the L., 6:9
Christ the L. risen today, 305:7
Christ's heart, 425:6
climb tree L. to see, 283:7
come quickly sweetest L., 226:24
coming of the L., 481:1
Dark Maid and her L., 67:6
day of the L., 44:18
day which the L. hath made, 18:26
dead which die in the L., 47:6
decreed not serve any but Him, 118:13
died by the hand of the L., 8:8
directeth his steps, 20:36
disciples of the L., 40:21
do if He knew facts, 600:12
eternal rest give them O L., 47:19
fear of the L. is beginning of wisdom, 18:19
fear of the L. is wisdom, 14:5
feast to the L., 7:41
forbade me to put off my hat, 270:5
forgive O L. my jokes, 624:19
from winter plague L. deliver us, 227:5
gangway for L., 686:3
gave and hath taken away, 12:39
glory of the L. is risen, 27:14
go and the L. be with thee, 10:46
go home to my L. and be free, 899:1
God Almighty, 46:28
God caused a deep sleep, 5:15
God formed man, 5:10
God is subtle, 638:6
God L. of all Being, 117:11
God made them all, 476:4
God of Hosts, 589:7
God planted a garden, 5:11
God send high wave, 611:14
God walking in garden, 5:20
good L. deliver us, 48:19, 884:8
good works better in sight of L., 118:18
Gracious L. bomb Germans, 745:5
great and dreadful day of the L., 29:22
hath chosen thee, 9:17
have mercy on us, 47:21, 227:6
hear me out, 756:14
hear word of the L., 28:4
holy is the L. of hosts, 25:9
how discourse is of death, 277:12
how long, 25:12
how world given to lying, 183:36
I am the L. thy God, 8:10
I believe, 36:37
I heard the voice of the L., 25:11
I replied My L., 243:2
I want to be in that number, 899:5
I were l. in May, 530:12
I will sing unto the L., 8:4
in glance of the L., 397:3

Lord (*continued*)

is a man of war, 8:5
is come, 289:15
is good, 18:3
is in his holy temple, 29:9
is in this place, 6:42
is it I, 36:1
is my helper, 45:16
is my light, 15:27
is my rock, 11:23
is my shepherd, 15:23
is my strength and shield, 15:29
is my strength and song, 8:4
is nigh unto them that call, 19:18
is risen, 47:28
is risen indeed, 38:43
is the strength of my life, 15:27
is thy keeper, 18:30
is thy shade, 18:30
is with thee, 37:6
Jehovah Jove or L., 296:20
kingdoms of our L., 46:39
King's our only l., 167:8
know ye that the L. he is God, 18:3
land which the L. giveth thee, 8:14
lendeth unto the L., 21:8
lift up his countenance, 9:2
listens with special pleasure, 666:10
looketh on the heart, 10:43
love is my l. and king, 454:10
love the L. with all thine heart, 9:15
made all to prosper, 7:7
make a joyful noise unto the L., 18:3
make his face shine upon thee, 9:2
make me an instrument, 125:12
make my enemies ridiculous, 299:24
Mayor of London, 881:20
mercy on Thy People L., 589:11
methought what pain to drown, 171:28
my help cometh from the L., 18:30
my L. what a morning, 898:24
my soul doth magnify L., 37:9
name of the L. in vain, 8:12
neat and trimly dressed, 181:35
not everyone that saith L., 33:23
not in wind earthquake fire, 12:4
not tempt the L. your God, 9:16
not the weight of an ant escapes the L., 118:8
O L. if there is a L., 500:13
O L. my God I have trusted, 154:8
of all Being, 117:11
of all yet prey to all, 295:1
of far-flung battle line, 589:7
of folded arms, 174:14
of heaven and earth, 40:33
of himself, 227:11, 396:29
of hosts he is the King of glory, 15:26
of living and dead, 546:5
of lords, 47:8
of the Ocean, 68:3
of yourself, 274:23
oure l. dooth with youre owene thing, 135:19
patient unto coming of L., 45:32
peace in our time O L., 49:22

Lord *(continued)*
praise L. pass ammunition, 687:10
pray L. soul to keep, 283:9
precious in the sight of the L., 18:24
precious L. take my hand, 720:12
prepare way of L., 26:24, 32:5
preserve thee, 18:30
raise me up I trust, 159:16
reason L. makes so many, 446:6
reigneth, 18:2
replied O L. Thou art, 318:7
reserves reward for who serve, 150:3
rib which L. God had taken, 5:15
Savior which is Christ the L., 37:17
searcheth all hearts, 12:23
secret things belong unto the L., 9:28
seeth not as man, 10:43
servant in love l. in marriage, 136:7
servant not above l., 34:3
serve the L. with gladness, 18:3
serves good l. lives in luxury, 124:6
set a mark upon Cain, 6:8
shall preserve thy going and coming, 18:30
short life in saddle L., 579:13
showed me so I did see, 270:4
sitting upon a throne, 25:8
soul is the concern of my L., 118:15
Spirit of the L. shall rest upon him, 25:18
support us all day long, 421:5
sword of the L. and of Gideon, 10:15
taste and see that the L. is good, 16:6
taught Man that he knew not, 119:18
through this hour, 887:15
thy God is with thee, 9:35
thy L. the most generous, 119:18
'twant me 'twas the L., 490:11
wait upon the L., 26:32
watch between me and thee, 7:1
we battle for the L., 571:17
went before them, 8:2
what fools these mortals be, 178:28
who created Man, 119:18
who was Future died long ago, 628:16
whom the L. loveth he chasteneth, 45:13
whose hope the L. is, 27:39
will wipe away tears, 26:2
with me abide, 405:8
woman that feareth the L., 22:20
won't you buy me a Mercedes-Benz, 857:10
word of the L. endureth, 45:37
worship the L. in beauty of holiness, 15:30
Lordly, butter in a l. dish, 10:11
cedar green with boughs, 557:7
darkness, 795:4
name is, 449:8
Lord's anointed temple, 215:28
ask the L. blessing, 882:4
earth is the L., 15:24, 42:22
it is the L. passover, 7:40
name is to be praised, 18:20
sing the L. song, 19:11
who is on the L. side, 8:20
Lords and ladies of Byzantium, 594:4
and owners of their faces, 222:2
but breath of kings, 356:10
gude Scots l., 889:16
Lord of l., 47:8

Lords *(continued)*
masters l. and rulers, 557:4
not kings and l., 389:3
o' the creation, 356:15
of Hell, 453:20
of humankind pass by, 322:2
of ladies intellectual, 397:19
princes and l., 322:22
Scots l. at his feet, 889:17
seemed l. of all, 257:18
who lay ye low, 402:15
wit among L., 308:18
Lordship, plant man's l., 537:10
Lordships sold to maintain ladyships, 234:4
Lordships', dance attendance on l. pleasures, 226:13
Lore, admire virtue follow not her l., 259:29
Cristes l. and his apostles twelve, 134:5
gives me mystical l., 384:10
Heaven rejects the l., 372:14
poor fool with all my l., 344:1
volume of forgotten l., 449:3
Lorn, lone l. creetur, 465:20
Lose a campaign than l. a war, 842:2
and neglect creeping hours, 194:22
convictions to win or l., 614:4
don't l. your head, 887:12
every day we l. something, 417:1
for everything gain l. something, 426:27
gain world l. soul, 34:39
good we oft might win, 206:17
have what it fears to l., 221:19
having nothing nothing l., 170:30
he that findeth life shall l. it, 34:6
his child's-heart, 79:25
I would not l. you, 185:15
if once we l. this light, 232:5
if you l. you l. nothing, 269:17
it that buy it with care, 184:3
itself in sky, 462:11
knife ill-used l. edge, 222:4
life nothing much to l., 576:2
managing to l. presidency, 810:11
more of yourself than redeem, 845:13
mos peoples gonna l., 773:13
myself in a mystery, 248:3
myself in other minds, 383:18
name of action, 199:21
natural kindness, 593:12
never l. touch of the one, 580:2
nobly save meanly l., 446:1
nor l. common touch, 590:2
not courage l. not faith, 670:3
nothin' left to l., 841:15
nothing to l. but chains, 478:15
one life to l. for country, 349:1
oneself in literature, 493:19
our ventures, 193:14
some day l. them all, 468:4
something every day, 763:7
substance by grasping at shadow, 59:9
sweets grown common l. delight, 222:7
thee lose myself, 259:16
this intellectual being, 256:12
time to l., 22:31
tomorrow ground won today, 495:15
tragedy to l. heart's desire, 565:8
what a waste to l. one's mind, 888:*n*9

Lose *(continued)*
what he never had, 245:6
whosoever l. life shall find it, 34:39
Loser, identity of l. perfectly clear, 795:12
I'll show you l., 682:*n*1
show me good l., 682:2
turned Big L. into perfect triumph, 810:11
Losers, both should l. be, 243:3
Loses, army l. if it does not win, 802:14
both itself and friend, 197:24
light that l., 529:13
what one l. one l., 544:15
who l. and who wins, 213:8
Loseth, he that l. life shall find it, 34:6
Losing, art of l. not hard, 763:7
my religion, 876:3
profit by l. our prayers, 218:17
tense for first l., 773:18
Loss, black as our l., 672:12
grief aggravates l., 881:8
mocks my l. of liberty, 350:8
new thinking is about l., 852:7
of all I sing, 814:13
of Eden, 255:3
of native land, 67:20
profit and l., 676:14
so overwhelming, 446:12
unexpected unwelcome l., 841:2
unknown no loss, 99:18
Losses, all l. are restored, 221:9
tosses up our l., 679:4
wrought by nature, 341:8
Lost, all good to me is l., 257:13
all is not l., 255:10
all l. save honor, 145:3
all l. wild America, 716:5
all was l., 259:11
and by wind grieved ghost, 727:12
and waiting for you go, 589:21
Angel of ruined Paradise, 403:15
are you l. daddy, 662:9
battles l. in spirit in which won, 486:2
become a l. name, 771:18
behind the Ranges, 589:21
better to have loved and l., 453:15
books by which printers have l., 250:4
Bo-peep has l. sheep, 895:2
but ane twa behin', 358:21
defaced deflowered, 259:14
every other friend, 446:11
for him I am not l., 84:12
for want of nail shoe l., 244:8, 303:3
found my wits you l. yours, 239:2
found sheep which was l., 38:9
France not l. war, 686:5
friends I have l. a day, 107:21
generation, 627:17
haven't l. battle yet, 773:18
he is not l. for Me., 84:12
heart stiffens, 677:19
her honest name, 887:6
holding anchor l., 171:1
I have l. my reputation, 208:28
I once was l. now am found, 320:13
in America shall be found, 727:15
in convent's gloom, 293:23
in Roman wilderness of pain, 858:6

Love *(continued)*

curiosity freckles doubt, 699:11
dare l. that and say so too, 228:14
dark secret l., 352:14
deep as first l., 452:22
demanded of genius l. of truth, 344:24
desire more l. and knowledge, 193:31
die for l., 205:32
died before god of l. was born, 229:21
diminution of l. of truth, 307:5
dinner of herbs where l. is, 20:32
distills desire, 67:25
do justly and l. mercy, 29:5
do not trifle with l., 457:6
does not consist in gazing, 726:16
doesn't l. a wall, 622:10
dooms of l., 701:18
draw as l. with thread, 235:15
drew them with bands of l., 28:38
dropped like a flower, 91:8
dull sublunary lovers', 229:15
each other without l., 761:11
earth sun animals, 485:10
earth's place for l., 622:19
end of l. or season, 622:8
endureth all things, 42:28
envieth not, 42:27
episode in man's life, 362:13
eternity in l. with production of time,
   351:12
faith nor l. nor law, 402:1
faithful in l., 373:10
fall in l. with Athens, 72:4
falling out renewing is of l., 85:*n*10
false maids in l., 203:20
false or true, 591:6
few l. to hear sins they act, 220:10
first is deep l., 57:22
first learned in lady's eyes, 174:21
fitter l. for me, 229:2
flies out window, 882:17
food of l., 204:10
fool yourself about l., 824:14
for l. I make characters in plays, 766:12
for l. lead apes in hell, 173:12
for l. of Barbara Allen, 889:25
for Love's sake, 756:15
for sale, 691:8
forbearance l. charity, 332:1
force, 604:4
forever lost, 414:11
forever wilt thou l., 410:16
forget l. to friends and brethren, 29:23
forgive us, 409:14
forspent with l. and shame, 543:4
foundation is l., 823:10
freedom in my l., 266:2
freely serve because we freely l., 258:18
friendship charity, 203:25
from eyelids dripped l., 54:15
fruit of Spirit is l., 43:31
fruits of l. gone, 399:16
fullness even of l., 51:26
game beyond prize, 582:8
gather Rose of l., 160:9
gilds the scene, 346:9
give a little l. to child, 484:18
give all to l., 424:14

Love *(continued)*

give me more l. or more disdain, 245:17
go l. without the help, 354:10
go out and l. people, 876:9
God is l., 46:11
God is L. I dare say, 521:14
gods l. the obscure, 50:3
goes toward love, 180:12
gold and l. affairs difficult to hide, 898:12
good man's l., 195:20
great l. grows there, 200:19
great secret of morals is l., 404:13
greater l. hath no man, 40:1
greater l. the more false, 748:7
greatest is l., 42:29
greatness worthy to excite l., 497:11
groans of l. like those of dying, 759:2
grown old in l., 354:11
grows bitter with treason, 530:9
gude to be off with old l., 884:12
guided by strong feelings of l., 818:11
hail wedded l., 258:5
half in l. with Death, 410:9
happiness to l. and be loved, 432:13
hardly worth thinking of, 591:17
harmony is pure l., 167:7
hate as though someday l., 65:*n*3
hate foes as far as we soon might l. them,
   65:7
hate one and l. other, 33:5
hate traitors treason l., 274:5
hath an end, 530:8
hath so long possessed me, 128:1
hatred as well as l., 313:7
hatred ceases by l., 64:22
he will then l. me, 351:1
hearts in l. use own tongues, 190:26
heaven is l., 373:2
heaven sends l. of her, 3:11
hell is to l. no longer, 673:16
hid in heart of l., 591:3
Highlands for ever I l., 357:14
him who in l. of Nature, 405:10
himself in others, 335:14
his banner over me was l., 24:8
hiss of l., 742:3
hold your tongue and let me l., 228:18
hope nor l. nor friend, 556:4
hopeth all things, 42:28
how do I l. thee, 434:17
how should I true l. know, 201:23
how they could l., 886:3
how to l. this world, 840:8
human l. seen at its height, 638:10
hunt down l. together, 530:13
I am glad you l. the Blossoms, 511:3
I am sick of l., 24:8
I both l. and do not l., 60:2
I do not l. thee Doctor Fell, 282:23
I don't think we don't l. each other, 828:6
I hate and I l., 91:28
I lived for l., 551:1
I l. a lassie, 607:7
I l. broad margin to life, 475:7
I l. everything old, 323:2
I l. sound of bone, 850:8
I taught thee to l., 230:7

Love *(continued)*

I told my l., 352:3
I was in l. with the whole world, 872:4
I'd l. to get you on slow boat, 762:1
idea of two sexes, 704:4
if ever thou shalt l., 204:33
if l. were what rose is, 530:11
if music food of l., 204:10
if no l. is what feel I so, 132:12
if she will not l., 261:3
if world and l. were young, 159:5
if you can't give me l., 683:6
if you l. him, 856:3
if you l. it not, 636:20
I'm savin' my l. for you, 708:7
impossible not to l. all things, 375:15
in a golden bowl, 351:9
in a hut, 409:14
in it was l. and desire, 51:29
in l. and charity with neighbors, 49:4
in l. illusion reaches zenith, 548:26
in l. two solitudes touch, 632:5
in l. with American names, 715:18
in l. with loving, 116:2
in l. with the world, 764:15
in l. woman more barbarous, 548:7
in my bosom like a bee, 163:9
in others they l. l., 264:29
in our will to l. or not, 258:18
in spite of darkness, 229:8
inestimable l., 48:16
innocence of l., 205:2
inspiration l. and freedom, 578:3
instill l. of you into world, 3:9
is a boy, 262:17
is agreement, 167:7
is all there is, 511:14
is best, 461:2
is blind, 185:1
is blynd, 135:25
is dead, 162:15
is enough, 520:6
is flower-like, 378:13
is fulfilling of law, 41:39
is heaven, 373:2
is here to stay, 711:8
is holy, 858:11
is just a ghost, 816:2
is just like a faucet, 779:8
is kind, 42:27
is lovelier second time around, 769:12
is most beautiful among gods, 54:14
is most nearly itself, 679:2
is not all, 695:18
is not love which alters, 222:15
is strong as death, 24:25
is the whole, 701:19
is then our duty, 291:18
is thing that can't go wrong, 699:17
it's lack of l. we die from, 844:17
itself have rest, 397:14
itself slumber on, 404:4
iz like meazles, 476:6
jealousy born with l., 264:24
Joy and L. triumphing, 257:7
joy nor l. nor light, 496:19
joy of l. too short, 138:7
jumps from admiration to l., 382:5

Love (*continued*)

keep corner in thing I l., 209:9
kelson of creation is l., 485:17
kill things they do not l., 185:28
kill your joys with l., 181:16
kindled by virtue, 129:24
kindness shall win my l., 173:21
King without the woman I l., 705:2
know the l. betwixt us, 265:14
knowledge and l. of God, 49:8
known l. how bitter, 530:4
knows nothing of order, 114:13
labor of l., 44:16
laggard in l., 373:11
land that I l., 673:10
last not least in l., 192:21
law to itself, 117:6
lay aside long-cherished l., 91:26
learn to bear beams of l., 350:15
lease of my true l., 222:10
least that let men know, 173:28
leave me O L., 162:16
leaving L. behind, 510:2
lest thy l. prove variable, 180:8
let l. who never loved, 180:8
let me l. river and woodland, 93:17
let thy l. be younger, 205:1
let us be true, 496:19
let us live and l., 91:5, 226:20
let us surrender to l., 93:8
let warm L. in, 411:2
life of their parents, 723:4
like everybody not in l., 611:1
like l. don't know where or why, 749:9
live and l. in God's light, 143:2
live with me and be my l., 168:4, 229:14
live with thee and be thy l., 159:5
long life better than figs, 218:5
long l. doth so, 180:25
look at enemies with l., 277:6
looked as she did l., 412:4
looks not with eyes, 178:1
Lord with all thy heart, 35:13
lore of l. deep learned, 409:12
lost to L. and Truth, 588:7
lovers' quarrels renewal of l., 85:15
Lyric L. half angel, 462:28
makes world go round, 527:5, 891:4
man in l. endures more, 548:26
man in l. with suffering, 492:5
man is in l., 594:8
mankind except American, 310:18
man's l. apart from life, 398:6
many waters cannot quench l., 24:26
marriage without l., 302:6
martyrs honor slain, 492:15
may perfectly l. thee, 49:3
me and keep my commandments, 8:12
me and my true l., 884:13
me little love me long, 241:1, 881:2
me not for grace, 882:1
me sure to die, 388:3
me tender, 840:13
means not having to say sorry, 843:5
medicines to make me l. him, 182:9
men died but not for l., 195:27
Mercy Pity Peace and L., 351:3
mercy unto them that l. me, 8:12

Love (*continued*)

met you not with my true L., 159:3
mie l. ys dedde, 346:22
mighty pain to l., 265:10
ministers of L., 378:3
mischievous devil, 521:14
moderately, 180:25
money rage and l., 742:1
money the sinew of l., 88:*n*8
moody food of l., 218:24
more libertines than l., 313:1
more l. less we flatter, 267:23
more than love, 449:22
more true than L. to me, 881:16
morning and evening star, 664:6
most important business, 392:11
music food of l., 218:24
musick thing I l. most, 277:17
my home of l., 222:12
my hope my hap my l., 155:3
my hope my l., 249:23
my lord and king, 454:10
my l. and I did meet, 590:21
my l. he purloined away, 532:16
my l. is come to me, 512:2
my L. like red red rose, 357:4
my L. like the melodie, 357:4
my l. of birth as rare, 267:3
my whole course of l., 207:34
mysterious by this l., 228:19
need someone to l. me, 719:11
ne'er ebb to humble l., 209:20
neighbor as thyself, 8:28
neighbor yet pull not down hedge, 243:19
never any that could escape l., 114:6
never change when l. has found home,
    101:12
never doubt I l., 198:30
never faileth, 42:28
never knew what l. was before, 662:11
never see what you l., 611:*n*5
never seek to tell thy l., 352:3
never seeketh own, 137:11
never sick old dead, 159:4
never taint my l., 210:7
never told her l., 205:4
no concern with art, 520:16
no creature give orders to l., 432:6
no disguise conceal l., 263:22
no go my honey l., 751:2
no l. lost, 157:26, 231:19
no more dear l., 453:4
no season knows, 228:16
noght oold as whan newe, 135:20
none but L. find me out, 159:2
none knew thee but to l., 400:12
nor l. thy life nor hate, 259:22
not a gaping pig, 185:26
not Death but L., 434:15
not enough religion to make us l., 284:14
not found thing to l., 632:16
not freedom but license, 254:17
not l. thee dear so much, 265:18
not man the less, 396:16
not my l. to see, 161:1
not puffed up, 42:27
not to be loved but to l., 125:12
not to eat not for l., 425:8

Love (*continued*)

not to l. when we l., 156:9
not wise who buffet against l., 66:10
nothing l. as much as fight, 651:13
nothing in l., 217:15
now abideth l., 42:29
now l. is over, 590:17
now warm in l., 293:23
now who never loved before, 290:11
now with l. now in colde grave, 134:23
O ye that l. mankind, 333:2
obedience troops of friends, 217:18
of a brute, 448:16
of British people, 324:13
of gentle woman, 767:3
of God, 43:25
of God in Christ, 41:26
of justice simply fear, 263:25
of learning, 437:20
of money as possession, 656:15
of money the root of evil, 44:35
of old for old, 576:8
of pleasure, 294:1
of praise, 290:12
of self love of God, 116:19
of slaughter, 665:8
of spiders, 724:7
of sway, 294:1
of the exaggerated, 835:17
of wisdom guide of life, 355:3
of you has entrapped me, 3:12
of young for young, 576:8
offender detest offense, 274:*n*4
on l. request for money chilling, 493:16
one another, 39:39, 41:38
one can only l. people, 737:17
one jot of former l. retain, 167:11
one of best things about l., 616:3
only l. sprung from only hate, 179:29
open rebuke better than secret l., 22:1
our l. hath no decay, 229:9
our occupations, 465:16
our principle, 416:7
out of l. cheat others, 611:3
out of l. with your nativity, 195:25
pain to l. in vain, 265:10
pains of l. sweeter far, 272:8
pangs of disprized l., 199:21
pardon to extent we l., 264:22
passed muse appeared, 418:21
passing the l. of women, 11:10
perfect l. casteth out fear, 46:12
physicians by their l. grown
    cosmographers, 231:2
pitched his mansion, 596:1
Platonic l., 156:27
pleasure drives l. away, 594:13
pleasure of l. in loving, 264:14
pleasure of l. lasts moment, 348:18
poets' food l. and fame, 402:8
possesses heart fall in l., 610:14
pray that l. may never come, 67:25
prophet of soul, 424:4
prosperity's very bond of l., 223:34
purple light of L., 316:10
Pussy my l., 467:7
putting L. away, 510:11
quaint figure men l., 639:16

Love *(continued)*

quantity of l., 202:20
quarrels in concord end, 260:20
quick-eyed L., 243:11
radiant with splendor, 125:10
rather than l. than money than fame, 475:22
regain l. once possessed, 260:19
regent of l.-rimes, 174:14
rekindled by absence, 307:6
resembleth April day, 173:29
respect or natural l., 567:20
right true end of l., 230:10
rose of our l., 798:2
ruined l. when built anew, 222:18
rules the court, 373:2
rules the gods, 66:10
satisfied, 677:14
saved by l., 696:6
scenes of first l., 750:9
seals of l., 207:8
see how Christians l. one another, 113:6
seeketh not itself to please, 352:12
seeketh self to please, 352:13
seized this man for fair form, 128:16
separate us from l. of Christ, 41:25
servant in l. lord in marriage, 136:7
shadow of power, 630:10
shall know no quarrels, 96:12
shoot false L., 881:15
sigh to those who l. me, 397:13
sighed for l. of lady, 527:25
silence in l. bewrays woe, 159:8
sit down says L., 243:12
sleep on my L., 241:18
smell of napalm, 845:3
smile of l., 353:13
so dear I l. him, 259:12
so full in my nature, 462:6
so long as we l. we serve, 556:1
someone to l. and l. you, 576:6
something tells me but not l., 185:15
sorrow of l. dureth overlong, 138:7
sought is good, 205:16
speak low if you speak l., 190:25
spirit all compact of fire, 171:8
spirit of l., 44:39
spirit of l. how quick and fresh, 204:11
sports of l., 232:5
spring of l. gushed from heart, 376:17
steer stars, 846:4
stony limits cannot hold l., 180:4
struck dumb by l., 821:1
study way to l. each other, 241:20
such I believe my l., 142:16
suffereth long, 42:27
swears she is made of truth, 223:2
sweet as l., 348:5
sweet for a day, 530:9
sweet lovers l. spring, 196:2
sweetest l. I do not go, 229:2
take l. away no art, 570:3
takes life to l. life, 605:6
tell the world you l. him, 856:2
that can be reckoned, 218:2
that comes too late, 206:11
that dare not speak its name, 607:5
that endures for breath, 529:14

Love *(continued)*

that L. is all is all we know of L., 511:14
that moves sun and other stars, 130:13
that my l. were in my arms, 881:1
that never told can be, 352:3
that winged seraphs coveted, 449:22
that word is l., 66:20
the brotherhood, 45:39
the girl I'm near, 711:13
the good pursue the worst, 102:*n*11
the human form divine, 351:4
the Lord with all thine heart, 9:15
the only meaning, 715:2
the only priest, 518:6
thee better after death, 434:18
thee to the depth, 434:17
them that love me, 20:6
there are those who l. it, 389:14
they do not l. that do not show, 173:28
they happy are and l., 249:25
they l. a train, 201:*n*2
this bud of l., 180:11
this cultured hell, 687:12
those I guard I do not l., 592:20
those who always loved l. more, 290:11
those who l. and create, 557:13
those who l. want wisdom, 401:16
those who love you, 299:17
those who wrong him, 112:15
those who yearn for impossible, 344:11
thou wast all to me l., 448:6
thousands have lived without l., 749:17
through l. come together into one, 67:1
through our l. is my lord slain, 138:13
throw away l. on conceited, 480:*n*2
thy first l., 46:20
thy honesty and l., 208:27
thy l. to me was wonderful, 11:10
thy neighbor, 8:28
thy neighbor as thyself, 35:13
thy sweet l. remembered, 221:7
thyself last, 226:5
till I prince of l. beheld, 350:7
time to l., 22:31
time weakens l., 280:23
tired of L., 606:15
to be wise and l., 203:19
to be worst of company, 284:11
to begin journey on Sundays, 286:7
to faults always blind, 352:5
to fear l. is to fear life, 614:16
to hatred turned, 287:2
to know to know to l. her so, 627:18
to lose myself, 383:18
to lose myself in a mystery, 248:3
to l. and to cherish, 49:16
to l. and to work, 564:7
to matrimony in a moment, 382:6
to say how much l. is little l., 130:19
to see her was to l. her, 357:9
took all my l., 597:7
trace visionary company of l., 720:10
trade you have learned, 112:2
tragedy of l. indifference, 626:21
treason but hate traitor, 88:23
true l. a durable fire, 159:4
true l. differs from gold and clay, 403:11
true l. is like ghosts, 263:24

Love *(continued)*

true l. sits him down, 885:14
truth pardon error, 299:4
tunes shepherd's reed, 373:2
turns to thoughts of l., 451:21
unconditional l., 823:13
unconquerable waster, 65:25
unfamiliar Name, 679:11
unsatisfied, 677:14
unsought is better, 205:16
up groweth with youre age, 133:4
vaunteth not, 42:27
vegetable l. grow, 266:21
vegetable l. not suit me, 526:11
very ecstasy of l., 198:25
very few to l., 369:7
Virtue she alone is free, 252:28
visible world formed in l., 483:4
waft her l. to Carthage, 186:14
wakes men once a lifetime, 500:7
wants to enjoy in other ways, 806:2
warm-hearted in l., 663:11
was a star a song unsung, 711:11
we may touch l. explain, 815:4
we must l. one another or die, 749:1
weathered storms of life, 576:8
what I l. near at hand, 756:10
what is l., 664:6
what is l. 'tis not hereafter, 204:26
what l. I bore to thee, 369:13
whatever it was an infection, 820:11
when I l. thee not, 208:35
when I was in l. with you, 574:17
when L. and Life fair, 561:4
when l. begins to sicken, 193:6
when l. has a hand in things, 320:10
when l. is in excess, 67:19
when L. speaks, 174:23
when my l. swears, 223:2
when we love not, 156:9
when you l. someone, 763:15
where I and my L. wont to gae, 890:8
where is l. beauty truth, 402:7
where l. and need one, 624:1
where l. is great, 200:19
where l. of man l. of art, 70:18
where l. rules no will to power, 630:10
where Mercy L. and Pity dwell, 351:5
where power predominates l. lacking, 630:10
which greybeards call divine, 171:6
which us doth bind, 267:4
whom the gods l., 81:6
why is all l. speak, 511:2
why L. needs be blind, 178:*n*1
will find out way, 882:8
will you l. me tomorrow, 845:6
winter l. in dark corner, 233:9
wisdom live accordingly, 474:16
wish I were in l. again, 707:5
with all thy faults I l. thee, 326:*n*2
with delight discourses, 128:2
with you l. to live, 97:3
without dissimulation, 41:30
without his wings, 394:6
without marriage, 302:6
without power destroyed, 696:1
women l. lovers, 264:29

Love *(continued)*

    word l. in mouth of courtesan, 425:16
    words of l. then spoken, 387:17
    work is l. made visible, 655:6
    world in l. with night, 180:32
    world outlasts l., 494:15
    worms eaten but not for l., 195:27
    would be dried up, 492:7
    write of hunger writing about l., 752:9
    wroth with one we l., 377:13
    wrought new alchemy, 229:13
    ye do me wrong, 881:4
    years grow cold to l., 93:22
    yields to business, 102:20
    you as New Englanders love pie, 635:4
    you for yourself alone, 595:7
    you l. me so much, 662:12
    you l. the daylight, 67:9
    you take is equal, 849:1
    you ten years before the Flood, 266:21
    your enemies, 32:21
    your solitude, 632:7
    youth gave l. and roses, 388:2
    Zeus's bed of l., 68:3
Loved a shade of you so hard, 725:5
    alas that all we l. of him, 403:18
    Alcuin my name learning I l., 122:7
    and lost, 446:12, 453:15
    and thought himself beloved, 593:15
    as l. we are indispensable, 556:1
    at first sight, 168:14
    at home revered abroad, 356:10
    betray heart that l. her, 368:12
    better to have l. and lost, 453:15
    burning Sappho l., 398:15
    country as no other man, 498:10
    cursed floundered, 545:6
    did till we l., 228:6
    each other and were ignorant, 596:3
    God so l. world, 39:11
    had somebody l. him, 802:15
    happiness to love and be l., 432:13
    him because he was he, 152:8
    him like a brither, 358:5
    him so followed him, 460:12
    him too much not to hate him, 278:17
    I have l. beauty, 413:17
    I have l. thee Ocean, 396:22
    I l. her that she did pity, 208:3
    I l. Ophelia, 202:20
    I not honor more, 265:18
    I saw and l., 332:15
    if ever man l. by wife, 261:15
    if I had a friend that l. her, 208:3
    Jonathan l. him as his own soul, 11:4
    King Cophetua l. beggarmaid, 179:30
    know we l. in vain, 394:8
    knowing I l. my books, 224:9
    life London this moment, 654:5
    love and be l. by me, 449:21
    love now who never l., 290:11
    love of being l., 536:8
    mansionry, 214:21
    memory of l. and lost, 446:12
    moments of glad grace, 591:6
    Muses l. me, 83:2
    never l. tree or flower, 388:3
    never time place l. one, 463:14

Loved *(continued)*

    never to have l., 453:15
    no man ever l., 222:15
    no sooner looked but l., 195:35
    not l. world nor world me, 395:23
    not that I l. Caesar less, 192:25
    not wisely but too well, 210:20
    one blotted from page, 395:9
    out upon it I have l., 261:8
    pale hands I l., 586:15
    passing well, 199:10
    Pharaoh's lean kine l., 182:28
    pilgrim soul in you, 591:6
    produces motion through being l., 77:19
    remember not only how l., 583:12
    Rome more, 192:25
    safer to be feared than l., 141:14
    scenes his fathers l., 734:10
    see souls we l., 455:4
    she l. me for dangers, 208:3
    she l. much, 37:27
    sighed to many l. one, 395:2
    so much cost me so much, 247:7
    Solomon l. many strange women, 11:36
    some we l. loveliest, 441:16
    the man and honor memory, 233:11
    those who always l. love more, 290:11
    thou hast not l., 194:8
    to be l. be lovable, 102:5
    to have l. to have thought, 495:8
    too late I l. you, 116:7
    too much hope of thee l. boy, 232:10
    twice or thrice had I l. thee, 229:7
    use him as though you l. him, 245:8
    we never l. sae kindly, 357:9
    wish I l. human race, 579:15
    with more than love, 449:22
    woman once l. hateful, 612:18
    you once long ago, 56:7
    you so I drew tides of men, 680:7
Love-darting eyes, 252:25
Love-gift of fairy tale, 515:10
Love-in-idleness, 178:16
Loveliest and best, 441:16
    and best said Good Night, 606:16
    despairing songs l., 457:7
    not yet come into world, 650:12
    of lovely things, 406:1
    of trees, 574:10
    village of the plain, 322:21
    woman born, 593:17
Loveliness, its l. increases, 409:7
    lay down in her l., 377:10
    let thy l. fade, 387:9
    portion of the l., 404:1
    this Adonis in l., 392:12
    within, 228:13
    your L. and my death, 413:16
Lovely, a single l. action, 482:11
    all l. things have ending, 683:4
    amiable l. death, 175:18
    and pleasant in their lives, 11:8
    apparition sent, 371:6
    April of her prime, 220:32
    as l. so be various, 706:1
    as woman so be l., 706:1
    billboard l. as a tree, 732:8
    come l. soothing death, 487:14

Lovely *(continued)*

    corpse, 465:2
    devours all l. things, 695:10
    diminutives, 756:3
    everything that's l. is, 591:17
    faded but still l. woman, 710:14
    flowers are l., 378:13
    gentleman-like man, 178:9
    gives a l. light, 695:8
    go l. rose, 249:24
    he is altogether l., 24:18
    honest labor bears a l. face, 228:4
    in her bones, 756:6
    is the Rose, 370:14
    ladies dead and l. knights, 222:9
    loveliness he made more l., 404:1
    more l. and more temperate, 221:2
    more l. than Pandora, 258:3
    Nature swears l. dears, 356:22
    never a l. so real, 757:9
    poem l. as a tree, 667:13
    Richard sweet l. rose, 182:3
    see cloud appear, 891:14
    shut her up horrorshow and l., 783:15
    so l. fair, 210:5
    some once l. Head, 441:14
    two l. berries on one stem, 178:29
    virtue how l., 258:8
    whatsoever things are l., 44:7
    wise and the l., 695:17
    woman stoops to folly, 322:16, 676:13
    woods l. dark and deep, 623:8
Lover all as frantic, 179:6
    and praiser of himself, 238:23
    as l. you reach forward, 868:10
    dividing l. and l., 529:13
    easier to be l. than husband, 417:10
    every l. a warrior, 101:23
    faithless l., 398:12
    fond l., 261:2
    give repentance to her l., 322:17
    I am l., 632:16
    it was a l. and his lass, 196:2
    Jesus l. of my soul, 305:8
    love a l., 427:2
    lunatic the l. the poet, 179:6
    music sent up by l. and bard, 462:11
    my truant l. has come, 488:4
    night that joined beloved and l., 154:6
    no l. and no adventurer, 567:8
    of concord, 48:13
    of men the sea, 530:7
    of swamps, 404:21
    scratch l. find foe, 699:12
    sighed as l. obeyed as son, 332:16
    sighing like furnace, 194:25
    threw wild hands toward sky, 609:2
    true l. therefore had good end, 138:10
    wild Jack for a l., 595:18
    without indiscretion no lover, 535:13
    woman loves her l., 398:13
    woman wailing for demon-l., 377:18
    Wotton a most dear l., 245:1
    you l. of trees, 461:3
Loverly, wouldn't it be l., 790:7
Lover's, death as l. pinch, 219:15
    quarrel with world, 624:10
    run into it as to l. bed, 219:2

Luckiest, people in the world, 800:3
Lucky, do I feel l., 791:3
    enough to know, 761:8
    not call man happy but l., 55:17
    sixpence in shoe, 886:16
    them that die'll be l. ones, 555:7
    to be born, 485:20
    to die and I know it, 485:20
    to have lived in Paris, 722:8
Lucre, filthy l., 44:26
Lucrece swears he did her wrong, 172:39
Lucy, if L. should be dead, 369:6
    Locket lost her pocket, 896:5
    when L. ceased to be, 369:7
Luddington's my dwelling place, 715:3
Luftwaffe, give this much to the L., 866:1
    your L. your gobbledygoo, 833:8
Lugged, melancholy as l. bear, 181:26
Lui, parce que c'était l., 152:*n*5
Lui-Même, tel qu'en L. l'éternité le change,
    543:*n*3
Luke beloved physician, 44:15
    Matthew Mark L. and John, 265:3
Lukewarm, because thou art l., 46:26
Lull distant folds, 315:12
    my senses, 780:1
Lullaby, dreamy l., 527:7
Lulled in these flowers, 178:19
Lumbering, creak of l. cart, 591:9
Luminescence growing more intense, 859:16
Luminous, beating l. wings in vain, 497:22
    fair l. cloud, 378:9
    joy the l. cloud, 378:10
Lump, leaveneth the whole l., 42:13
    of same l. make one vessel, 41:27
Lumpenprole tenants, 831:1
Lunatic fringe, 571:18
    optimism in l. asylum, 574:5
    padded l. asylums, 654:6
    the lover the poet, 179:6
Lunatics, crowd treat great as l., 104:*n*1
Lunch, ladies who l., 828:18
    Naked L. a frozen moment, 774:2
    no such thing as free l., 767:16
Lune, au clair de l., 891:7
Lung, Randolph Churchill to have l. removed,
    736:10
Lungful, some must sing l. of psalm, 769:7
Lungs, if l. receive our air, 326:21
    my l. began to crow, 194:17
    rooted to air through l., 528:17
Lure it back to cancel, 442:2
    of the real in their hearts, 643:1
    this tassel-gentle back, 180:13
Lurk I in gossip's bowl, 178:12
    we l. late, 783:10
Lurks, foretold that danger l. within, 170:34
    under every stone l. politician, 73:11
Luscious, food as l. as locusts, 208:9
    lot of me and all so l., 486:9
    woodbine, 178:19
    world is mud-l., 701:5
Luscus, in regione caecorum rex est l., 141:*n*6
Lush life in some small dive, 781:1
    weeds shoot long lovely and l., 546:8
Lust a species of madness, 276:15
    and rage, 596:17
    buys them in marriage, 398:12

Lust *(continued)*
    for blood and plunder, 620:8
    for power, 652:10
    gold and the l., 708:6
    in action, 222:20
    into ashes all my l., 266:23
    is perjured murderous, 222:20
    looked on women with l., 805:14
    looketh to l. after her, 32:18
    melted him in own grease, 135:*n*3
    morning L. is furtive, 806:2
    narrowing l. of gold, 454:9
    not after her beauty, 20:2
    of goat bounty of God, 351:14
    power of fright and l., 706:5
    sensual l. tempest, 492:8
    so l. will sate itself, 198:10
Luster, shine with such a l., 327:8
    shone with preeminent l., 110:3
Lustily, swans sing more l., 74:14
Lusts, fleshly l., 45:38
    not to fulfill l., 41:40
Lusty horn, 195:31
    month of May, 138:9
    my age l. winter, 194:5
    sails filled with l. wind, 163:20
    stealth of nature, 210:33
    yet I am strong and l., 194:4
Lute, heartstrings a l., 448:*n*1
    lascivious pleasing of a l., 171:18
    musical as bright Apollo's l., 174:23
    musical as is Apollo's l., 252:19
    my l. awake, 149:3
    Orpheus with his l., 225:19
    rift within l., 455:12
    star-studded l. wears black sun, 439:6
Lutes, dance to l., 561:4
Luther's day expand to Darwin's year, 483:23
Luve, my L. is like a red red rose, 357:4
    my L. is like the melodie, 357:4
Lux, fiat l., 5:*n*4
Luxe calme et volupté, 491:*n*4
Luxuries, hindrances, 474:15
    two l. in my walks, 413:16
Luxurious lobster-nights, 293:21
    society as l. as can be, 310:16
Luxury, blesses his stars and thinks it l., 287:23
    morality private costly l., 531:27
    more deadly than war, 109:20
    of liberal government, 470:8
    Persian l. I hate, 96:18
    wealth the parent of l., 75:6
    who serves good lord lives in l., 124:6
Lycidas, for L. sorrow not dead, 253:14
    sunk low but mounted high, 253:14
Lydian, soft L. airs, 251:8
Lying, African moon l. on back, 662:6
    awake with headache, 527:3
    days of my youth, 592:7
    done as easily as l. down, 839:14
    essence of l. not in words, 484:8
    let me have no l., 223:35
    lovers l. two and two, 574:13
    mighty heart l. still, 370:3
    no word to express l., 285:3
    not mind l. hate inaccuracy, 521:15
    now on his side now on back, 52:17
    settling and loosely l., 545:13

Lying *(continued)*
    till noon, 308:1
    vainness drunkenness, 205:25
    when asserts contrary is l., 611:3
    world given to l., 183:36
Lynching, high-tech l. for uppity blacks, 866:13
Lyonnesse, set out for L., 535:11
Lyre, a god has given l. and song, 51:27
    idle to play l. for ass, 115:5
    lacking neither honor nor l., 96:15
    living l., 315:21
    make me thy l., 402:13
    minstrel's l., 610:4
    tuning l. and handling harp, 62:15
    within the sky, 448:1
Lyres, sound of l. and flutes, 534:5
Lyric Love half angel, 462:28
    name me among l. bards, 96:1

M

M, drew everything begins with M, 514:17
Ma, it's alright M., 851:11
Mab, Queen M. hath been with you, 179:25
Mabelle or Kathryn, 648:14
Macaroni, called it m., 883:15
MacArthur, victory M. had in mind, 661:12
Macavity Macavity no one like Macavity,
    678:12
Macbeth does murder sleep, 215:21
    none shall harm M., 216:32
    shall never vanquished be, 216:34
    shall sleep no more, 215:22
Macdonald, wherever M. sits, 426:5
Macduff from mother's womb untimely ripped,
    217:28
    lay on M., 217:31
Mace, sword the m. the crown, 189:23
Macedon, Euripides' grave lies in M., 67:*n*1
Macedonia, come into M., 40:30
MacGregor, my name is M., 374:10
Macgregor, wherever M. sits, 426:*n*1
MacGuffin is the term, 722:13
Macheath, just a jackknife has M., 716:7
Machiavel, every Country hath its M., 141:*n*7
    much beholden to M., 164:17
Machiavellis, reign of the Mayberry M., 875:9
Machina, deus ex m., 81:9
Machinations hollowness treachery, 211:2
Machine, bathing m., 527:4
    beauty of great m., 669:9
    becomes so odious, 855:4
    body statue or m. made of earth, 246:3
    created to serve us, 753:2
    for grinding general laws, 441:3
    for living in, 670:12
    for the making of gods, 572:11
    for turning wine into urine, 662:3
    god from the m., 81:9
    I want to be a m., 817:2
    justice is a m., 600:20
    like a sex m., 837:7
    man is a m., 311:18
    no unnecessary parts, 606:3
    poem is small (or large) m. of words, 659:4
    pulse of the m., 371:7
    slaughtering m. went on, 636:12

Machine *(continued)*
  slavery of the m., 560:26
  This M. Kills Fascists, 768:6
Machine-à-habiter, 670:*n*1
Machinery, my m. can't be fixed, 746:15
  of night, 812:13
Machines, can m. think, 769:5
  God-breathing m. are no more, 468:19
  human beings into m., 478:3
  slaves not masters, 574:3
  soul paints itself in our m., 347:15
  speak of m. thinking, 769:6
Mächte, ihr himmlischen M., 342:*n*5
Mackerel, stinks like rotten m., 381:5
Mackerel-crowded seas, 594:1
Macrocosm, microcosm and m. atoned,
  501:14
Macte nova virtute puer, 95:*n*2
Mad, all poets are m., 234:13
  am m. and am not m., 60:2
  and lamentable experiment, 584:2
  as Bedlam, 465:25
  as hell, 801:14
  as March hare, 140:*n*4
  bad and dangerous, 393:8
  cold m. father, 651:3
  dogs and Englishmen, 719:12
  don't call a man m., 315:2
  don't get m. get even, 680:3
  father and mither gae m., 357:16
  go m. or unstable, 69:11
  half m. with beauty, 520:3
  he first makes m., 69:3
  heroically m., 273:7
  I am not m., 60:2, 737:3
  idolatry, 203:13
  if they behold a cat, 185:26
  I'm m. as hell, 801:14
  in pursuit, 222:20
  laid to make taker m., 222:20
  makes men m., 210:15
  March hare, 140:18
  men God made m., 618:10
  more deadly than m. dog's tooth, 172:26
  much learning make m., 41:4
  naked summer night, 486:6
  nobly wild not m., 241:8
  north-northwest, 199:8
  O fool I shall go m., 211:23
  old m. blind despised king, 402:19
  pleasure in being m., 273:9
  practice drives m., 881:3
  prose run m., 295:12
  provided man not m., 313:2
  pursuit, 410:14
  sad and bad and m., 462:23
  sad m. brother's name, 530:24
  sense that world was m., 632:11
  some born m. some remain so, 744:17
  that he is m. 'tis true, 198:28
  that trusts in wolf, 212:10
  to live mad to be saved, 799:3
  we all go a little m, 800:14
  we are m. nationally, 103:23
  went m. and bit the man, 322:14
  whom God wishes to destroy he makes m.,
    69:3, 121:11
  why will you say I am m., 448:17

Mad *(continued)*
  world, 465:25
  world mad kings, 175:11
Madam is there nothing else, 509:12
Madame Bovary had beauty, 493:14
  hell M. is to love no longer, 673:16
  I am M. Bovary, 494:3
  poetry the supreme fiction m., 640:17
Madcap, once in my days be a m., 181:32
Maddens, all that m. torments, 483:3
Madder music stronger wine, 599:16
Maddest merriest day, 450:15
Madding, far from m. crowd's strife, 316:3
Made a rural pen, 350:11
  and loveth all, 377:6
  annihilating all that's m., 267:1
  begotten not m., 48:12
  by whom all things m., 48:12
  Christians not born but m., 115:20
  confusion m. masterpiece, 215:28
  day which the Lord hath m., 18:26
  did he who m. Lamb, 353:2
  fearfully and wonderfully m., 19:15
  friends born not m., 531:11
  God m. and eaten, 460:22
  God m. him let him pass for man, 184:18
  him a little lower than angels, 15:5
  his pendent bed, 214:21
  in wisdom hast thou m. all, 18:11
  incarnate and was m. man, 48:12
  it is he that hath m. us, 18:3
  little Lamb who m. thee, 350:12
  Lord God m. them all, 476:4
  marriages m. in heaven, 162:11
  men and not made them well, 200:9
  mouths in a glass, 211:27
  my song a coat, 592:13
  myself a motley, 222:13
  of sterner stuff, 192:30
  poet's m. as well as born, 233:5
  sea is his and he m. it, 17:32
  stuff as dreams are m. on, 225:1
  swears she is m. of truth, 223:2
  the best of this, 359:1
  this parting well m., 193:17
  us with large discourse, 201:19
  what man has m. of man, 368:3
  when or you or I are m., 241:13
  without fear, 14:36
  world I never m., 575:17
  world m. safe for democracy, 566:14
  you've got it m., 799:4
Madeleine soaked in lime flowers, 610:13
Mademoiselle from Armenteers, 688:13
Madest, creature that thou m., 576:3
Madly, stars shot m. from spheres, 178:15
  twirled fingers m., 468:1
Madman, difference between m. and myself,
    737:3
  either liar or m., 312:22
  if he like m. lived, 158:14
  is not man who has lost reason, 618:7
  that is the m., 179:6
  truth of a m., 821:6
Madmen, which none but m. know, 273:9
Madness, a little M. in Spring, 511:1
  anger a short m., 97:23
  avarice a piece of m., 276:*n*1

Madness *(continued)*
  destroyed by m., 812:13
  everything is form of m., 822:8
  from breakfast to m., 820:8
  great wits to m. allied, 272:16
  harmonious m. flow, 403:6
  in brain, 377:13
  let us have m. openly, 765:3
  life is a m., 247:1
  midsummer m., 205:21
  moon-struck m., 259:21
  much M. divinest Sense, 509:4
  much of M., 448:14
  need not be all breakdown, 816:1
  no genius without touch of m., 104:1
  one that achieves m., 837:8
  risen from hell, 529:14
  Sense starkest M., 509:4
  species of m., 276:15
  sudden m. came upon Orpheus, 93:25
  that fine m., 167:14
  that way m. lies, 211:32
  the rest is m. of art, 544:12
  though this be m., 198:37
  'tis m. to defer, 290:21
  to live like wretch, 234:22
  various forms of religious m., 434:4
  what m. has caught you, 92:17
Madrigals, melodious birds sing m., 168:5
Madruga, al que m. Dios ayuda, 898:5
Madrugar, no por mucho m., 898:10
Mads, music m. me, 177:24
  second m. him, 204:19
Maecenas, how comes it M., 95:15
Maggots, breed m. in dead dog, 198:33
  make speech to m., 700:19
Magic, argosies of m. sails, 452:2
  casements, 410:10
  first kiss is m., 674:12
  I want m., 766:6
  indistinguishable from m., 784:2
  lash M. Creature, 510:17
  must not let daylight in upon m., 503:5
  of a face, 246:2
  of the sea, 437:10
  old black m., 759:6
  painting form of m., 648:1
  preservation in books, 407:20
  still m. abroad, 740:12
  sweet m. brings together, 359:10
  swirlin' ship, 851:13
  this rough m., 225:3
  thought and m. sound, 418:21
  with a m. like thee, 397:10
Magical, I am m. mouse, 765:7
  power imagination, 379:12
  purely m. object, 778:1
Magician Merlin had strange laugh, 770:15
  rope-dancer physician m., 109:14
Magick, strange kind of m. bias, 314:1
Magister artis ingenique largitor venter,
  105:*n*7
Magisterial or imperative type, 607:2
Magistrate, by m. equally useful, 332:2
  no name of m., 224:19
Magma, volumes of m. risen, 861:10
Magna Carta will have no sovereign,
  158:26

Magna est veritas et praevalet, 29:*n*3
Magnanimity and trust, 474:16
   in politics, 324:14
   in victory m., 621:12
   marks of God in m., 388:8
Magnetic nourishing night, 486:6
Magnetism, strong m., 585:4
Magnificence, pristine m., 414:6
Magnificent, battle most m. competition,
   664:12
   blond beast, 548:15
   but not war, 456:11
   desolation, 825:18
   from work returned m., 258:28
   mild and m. eye, 460:12
   most m. movement of all, 329:13
Magnificently unprepared, 667:6
Magnify, laud and m. thy Name, 49:6
   my soul doth m. Lord, 37:9
   thy holy Name, 49:3
Magnitude, liar of first m., 286:27
   star of smallest m., 257:4
Magnus ab integro saeclorum nascitur ordo,
   92:*n*17
   inter opes inops, 97:*n*6
Magus Zoroaster my dead child, 401:15
Mahomet, sanctity truth of revelation of M.,
   332:8
Maid, Abyssinian m., 377:22
   a-roving with you fair m., 897:20
   as with m. so with mistress, 25:32
   beggar m. be queen, 452:14
   chariest m. prodigal, 197:19
   Dark M. and her Lord, 67:6
   fair m. dwellin', 889:25
   lily m. of Astolat, 455:13
   many a youth and many a m., 251:4
   my pretty m., 894:12
   neither m. widow nor wife, 207:16
   not dead but sleepeth, 33:35
   nut-brown m., 880:12
   of Athens, 394:17
   slain by fair cruel m., 205:3
   still as a m., 352:4
   was in garden, 894:7
   way of man with m., 22:14, 588:12
   wedded m. virgin mother, 250:9
   whom none to praise, 369:7
   widow or wife, 141:1
   yonder a m. and wight, 536:22
Maiden, do not weep m., 609:2
   famous to all time, 97:4
   fleshed thy m. sword, 183:35
   I sing of a m., 880:11
   kissed m. all forlorn, 897:8
   marrying left m. name disused, 799:7
   meditation fancy-free, 178:16
   never bold, 207:35
   of bashful fifteen, 346:11
   phoenix ashes new-create, 226:14
   presence, 197:29
   rare and radiant m., 449:5
   rose-lipped m., 575:9
   wilt thou go with me, 405:2
   with no other thought, 449:21
Maidens call it Love-in-idleness, 178:16
   loth, 410:14
   not human but nymphic, 723:7

Maids are May when maids, 195:29
   dance in a ring, 227:4
   false m. in love, 203:20
   pretty m. in row, 893:5
   seven m. with seven mops, 516:1
   that weave with bones, 205:2
   three little m., 527:12
Maidservant, not covet neighbor's m., 8:14
Mail, gentlemen do not read other's m., 601:5
   on time with southbound m., 608:*n*1
   rusty m., 203:22
Maimed, he that wants anger hath m. mind,
   250:7
   poor and m., 38:7
Main, arose from out azure m., 301:3
   beams bemocked sultry m., 376:16
   came silent flooding in the m., 479:12
   chance, 162:1, 262:20
   part of the m., 231:8
   street on August afternoon, 788:16
   to cross raging m., 898:3
Maine, as M. so goes nation, 885:20
   if row comes Remember the M., 886:*n*2
   remember the M., 886:2
Mains, dorure en reste aux m., 493:*n*5
Mainstay, workers m. of civilization, 554:5
Maintain, fuel to m. his fires, 245:18
   his argument, 189:12
   lordships sold to m. ladyships, 234:4
   the sublime, 665:4
Maintained, boisterously m. as gained, 175:22
Maintaining constitutional shield, 666:15
Mair, cantie wi' m., 357:5
Maître, qui que tu sois voici ton m., 300:*n*3
   tel m. tel valet, 151:*n*1
Maîtresse des maîtresses, 491:*n*3
Maize, rose with m. to die, 720:7
Majestic free, 370:10
   instancy, 576:14
   law in m. equality, 546:2
   motion, 396:2
   though in ruin, 256:16
Majestical, happy high m., 402:7
   laid in bed m., 189:23
   roof, 199:5
Majesties, purple mountain m., 572:5
   rebellions m. voices agonies, 411:15
Majesty, against thy Divine M., 49:5
   attribute to awe and m., 186:1
   beauty and m. of ships, 437:10
   clad in naked m., 257:18
   dignity m. sublimity, 329:13
   moon rising in clouded m., 257:25
   next in m. surpassed, 274:7
   of gods is revealed, 53:*n*1
   of Heaven, 301:8
   rayless m., 290:19
   sight so touching in m., 370:2
   tender M., 509:5
   thine O Lord is the m., 12:24
   this earth of m., 176:24
Majesty's, His M. dominions, 321:*n*3
Major, minor fall the m. lift, 837:11
   model of M.-General, 526:6
   twelve years in the m. leagues, 844:7
Majorities, decision by m. expedient,
   442:12
   not entirely wrong, 490:5

Majority deprive minority of right, 445:4
   divine M., 508:16
   doesn't abide by m. rule, 813:5
   fools big enough m., 523:7
   he has joined great m., 105:16
   man with God always in m., 150:2
   never replace man, 684:9
   not leave right to m., 473:15
   of one, 473:17
   one man with courage a m., 364:5
   one on God's side m., 458:11
   power in m. of popular assembly, 330:16
   questions not decided by m., 470:6
   silent m., 771:5
   'tis M. prevail, 509:4
   when were good and brave in m., 475:24
Make a joyful noise, 17:8, 18:3
   angels weep, 206:28
   be and m. new nations, 226:15
   can't find circumstances m. them, 564:15
   conscience m. cowards, 199:21
   content with his fortunes, 211:31
   equal to the love you m., 849:1
   fault worse by excuse, 175:25
   fears m. us traitors, 217:3
   felicity we m. or find, 307:14
   ghost of him that lets me, 198:3
   haste better foot before, 175:28
   he himself his quietus m., 199:21
   her laugh at that, 202:12
   I could not well m. out, 381:8
   I shall m. reckless choice, 622:21
   if I can m. it there, 818:6
   it do or do without, 886:15
   it look ordinary, 778:11
   it over your way, 625:10
   life what we m. it, 541:13
   me a fixed figure, 210:3
   me a willow cabin, 204:21
   me conservative when old, 624:4
   me immortal with a kiss, 168:21
   me to know mine end, 16:17
   men m. the city, 72:8
   money by any means, 97:19
   most of what may spend, 441:17
   my bed in hell, 19:13
   my bed soon, 890:9
   my house your inn, 671:6
   my seated heart knock, 214:11
   my small elves coats, 178:20
   not m. can not mar, 495:1
   not m. graven image, 8:11
   not m. scarecrow of law, 206:18
   of your prayers one sacrifice, 225:15
   only God can m. tree, 668:1
   other people not at ease, 504:2
   right to m. alter constitutions, 328:14
   so much of fragmentary blue, 623:3
   soul is form and doth body m., 161:7
   straight a highway for our God, 26:24
   sudden sally, 454:24
   the Lord m. his face shine upon thee, 9:2
   the most of it, 331:8
   the phrase to m. money, 742:18
   thee an ark, 6:17
   thee mightier yet, 580:19
   thick my blood, 214:17
   unless philosophy m. a Juliet, 180:35

Make *(continued)*
  up my sum, 202:20
  us do what we can, 428:11
  us heirs of all eternity, 173:39
  war to live in peace, 78:14
  waves m. towards pebbled shore, 221:16
  world safe for diversity, 786:10
  worse appear the better, 72:13
  yourselves another face, 200:1
Make-believe, children's house of m., 624:13
  wouldn't be m. if you believed, 711:10
Makeless, maiden that is m., 880:11
Maker, as though m. and molder of thyself,
    141:3
  Lord our m., 17:32
  more pure than his m., 13:9
  of Heaven and earth, 48:11
  reproacheth his M., 20:39
  rests in lightland, 4:6
  tool m., 636:2
Makers, abhor m. and their laws approve, 274:5
Makes, another which m., 75:23
  heaven drowsy with harmony, 174:23
  heretic that m. the fire, 223:16
  me or fordoes me quite, 210:12
  me poor indeed, 209:2
  men mad, 210:15
  night hideous, 197:*n2*
  one little room an everywhere, 228:7
  or mars us, 210:9
  swanlike end, 185:16
  sweet music with stones, 173:31
  thinking m. it so, 199:2
  tongue of him that m. it, 174:31
  whole world kin, 203:25
Makest, thou m. darkness, 18:11
  what m. thou, 26:35
Maketh clouds his chariot, 18:8
  he m. me to lie down, 15:23
  the deep to boil, 14:35
Making green one red, 215:24
  many books, 24:2, 647:2
  news better than taking it, 618:17
  night hideous, 197:34
  shaping and controlling life, 489:3
Mal, honi soit qui m. y pense, 131:1
Malachite, good speech more hidden than m.,
    3:4
Maladies, soul with all its m., 534:4
Maladministration, secured against m., 320:8
Malady, he smiles it is a m., 91:11
  medicine worse than m., 100:*n1*
  of not marking, 187:28
Malaise, two problems energy and m., 805:15
Malcontents, liege of m., 174:14
  Mars of m., 187:3
Male and female created he, 5:7
  and female fuse into one solid, 71:9
  cannot tolerate living with equal, 435:18
  clothes keep m. and female likeness, 654:12
  determining m. gaze projects, 853:2
  difference of education between m. and
    female, 340:15
  especially m. of species, 663:14
  healthy wealthy and dead, 704:9
  if God is m., 818:1
  kiss of blankets, 669:9
  more deadly than m., 590:4

Maled, they m. and femaled you jealously,
    659:6
Malefactors of great wealth, 571:10
Malfi, I am Duchess of M. still, 237:6
Malfunction, wardrobe m., 880:4
Malherbe, at last comes M., 278:2
  what M. writes will endure, 162:25
Malheur, de son âge tout le m., 300:*n2*
Malice domestic, 216:11
  from envy hatred and m., 48:19
  life is warfare against m. of others, 247:6
  much m. little wit, 274:3
  never was his aim, 285:9
  no m. or ill will, 363:8
  no rampart against m., 267:11
  no suspicion of m. in his writing, 87:14
  nor set down aught in m., 210:20
  ridicule without m., 446:4
  toward none, 447:2
  truth with m. in it, 483:3
  we've got a lot of m., 837:6
Malicious, he is not, 638:6
  wisdom entereth not in m. mind, 145:10
Malignant and turbaned Turk, 210:21
  so m. so devastating, 694:3
  trouble was not m., 736:10
Maligners of his honor, 518:2
Malignity, motiveless m., 378:21
  practical m. of man, 386:16
Malitia, ius summum saepe summa est m.,
    86:*n3*
Mallecho, miching m., 200:17
Malorum, radix m. est cupiditas, 44:*n1*
Malt, ate the m., 897:8
  does more than Milton can, 575:12
Maltreat, shouldn't m. our idols, 493:15
Mama, we've lost good old m., 716:10
Mamas, last of red-hot m., 661:*n2*
Mammon, cannot serve God and m., 33:5
  is like fire, 407:*n3*
  the least erected spirit, 256:3
Man, a certain m. went down, 37:36
  a clear proof against himself, 119:17
  a great great m., 802:15
  a little worse than a m., 184:19
  a m. like me, 352:15
  a m. zealous for nothing, 310:23
  a social animal, 276:13
  Adam the goodliest m., 257:21
  after all he's just a m., 856:3
  after his own heart, 10:40
  aged m. paltry thing, 594:2
  ah for m. to arise, 454:27
  ah when to heart of m., 622:8
  ain't nothin' but a man, 885:12
  all that a m. hath will he give, 13:1
  all that may become a m., 215:3
  alone abandoned on earth, 742:22
  alone can enslave man, 760:16
  always tell Harvard m., 886:8
  am I not a m. and brother, 326:2
  ambitious m. have no satisfaction,
    231:14
  an ape or angel, 430:9
  and bird and beast, 377:5
  and brother, 326:2
  and his fate, 637:10
  and I ain't together, 703:3

Man *(continued)*
  and woman in garden, 560:15
  animal which devours own, 336:13
  apparel oft proclaims m., 197:23
  arms and the m. I sing, 93:28, 274:13
  Art mediatress between nature and m.,
    379:18
  as a m. wipeth a dish, 12:21
  as happy a m. as any, 277:10
  as M. alone Jesus not saved us, 734:15
  as m. looks at woman, 643:2
  as nature made him, 313:4
  assurance of a m., 201:5
  at expense of m., 706:3
  at thirty m. suspects himself fool, 290:23
  average m., 652:5
  baker's m., 892:17
  battered wrecked old m., 488:2
  battlefield heart of m., 492:9
  be a friend to m., 569:13
  be m. be nonconformist, 426:16
  bears stamp of lowly origin, 440:13
  beautiful thing raises m., 142:16
  became a living soul, 5:10
  become ignorant m. again, 641:20
  been mother's undisputed darling, 563:11
  before you trust a m., 880:15
  behold m. of flint, 891:19
  behold the m., 40:8
  being his own physician, 77:14
  being reasonable must get drunk, 398:11
  belief woman made for m., 471:7
  believe in equality of m., 333:18
  Benedick the married m., 190:20
  best m. like water, 57:3
  better governed by m. in street, 72:6
  better m. than I Gunga Din, 587:19
  better spared better m., 183:33
  beware m. of one book, 120:8
  bites dog, 550:2
  blessings on thee little m., 438:7
  blest m. that spares these stones, 226:17
  blood of a British m., 212:9
  blow the m. down, 897:16
  bold bad m., 160:4, 225:16
  bold m. first eat oyster, 285:21
  born dies and does not come again, 889:1
  boyhood changing into m., 595:3
  brave m. inattentive to duty, 364:1
  brave m. with a sword, 561:3
  breathes there the m., 373:3
  bronzed lank m., 639:16
  Brutus is an honorable m., 192:29
  but be a m., 495:3
  by m. came death, 43:1
  by m. came resurrection, 43:1
  by m. shall his blood be shed, 6:24
  by nature political animal, 78:16
  Caius is a m., 507:6
  came to making of m., 529:14
  can a m. take fire in his bosom, 20:3
  can die but once, 188:16
  can raise thirst, 588:3
  cannot emerge from himself, 611:3
  can't hold m. down without staying, 566:5
  can't love m. till baby with him, 561:18
  capable of becoming true m., 685:6
  cause of work, 612:5

Man (*continued*)

caverns measureless to m., 377:17
cease ye from m., 24:35
century of the common m., 683:1
certain way to hold a m., 791:15
certainly crazy, 152:20
child conceived, 13:3
child father of m., 369:14
childhood shows the m., 260:1
Christian faithful m., 171:27
city is teacher of the m., 60:9
civilized m. has habits of house, 472:20
clothed with rags, 271:8
come through door with gun in hand, 674:9
common m. has triumphed, 548:14
composed of all men, 743:7
concern for m. himself, 637:10
concrete m. has one interest, 540:17
conference maketh a ready m., 166:18
confidence in tall m. merited, 753:1
connection of individual m., 885:13
control the wind, 495:6
count on no one but himself, 742:22
country turns out, 428:19
coupling of m. and woman, 678:14
created M. of blood clot, 119:18
crime of being young m., 305:11
crooked m., 895:17
cruelty to load falling m., 225:*n*2
daring young m. on trapeze, 532:16
dark as world of m., 672:12
dark cloud m., 547:18
delights not me, 199:6
desire for desire of m., 380:4
desire of knowledge caused m. to fall, 165:24
diapason closing in M., 273:22
did not make can not mar, 495:1
dies in all who keep silent, 838:11
dieth and wasteth away, 13:30
dignity of m. capacity to despise self, 584:8
dispute it like a m., 217:9
do not bet that m., 660:*n*2
does not live by GNP alone, 780:12
doth not live by bread only, 9:18
dream past wit of m., 179:3
drest in brief authority, 206:28
drove out the m., 6:2
drowsed off, 633:6
dull ear of drowsy m., 175:20
ear of m. hath not seen, 179:4
end of m. is knowledge, 744:1
end of that m. is peace, 16:13
endeavoring to turn m. into beast, 728:15
errs as long as he strives, 343:27
Esau was a m. of the field, 6:37
escape from rope and gun, 291:19
establish reign of liberty, 751:9
even such a m. so faint, 187:22
every cry of every m., 353:3
every m. a piece of the continent, 231:8
every m. architect of his fortune, 92:13
every m. at his best state, 16:18
every m. for himself, 148:24
every m. has his fault, 213:23
every m. hath a good and bad angel, 234:14

Man (*continued*)

every m. his greatest enemy, 248:15
every m. is wanted, 427:24
every m. own architect, 463:9
every m. satisfied there is truth, 534:14
every m. under his vine, 11:28
every m. was God or Devil, 273:3
every m. will do duty, 355:12
expatiate o'er scene of m., 294:14
eye of m. hath not heard, 179:4
false m. does easy, 216:2
false to any m., 197:24
Family of M., 636:11
fashion wears out more than m., 191:3
favor with God and m., 37:22
first m. among these than second in Rome, 89:1
first-class fightin' m., 587:18
fit night for m. or beast, 644:1
foolish fond old m., 213:5
foolish passionate m., 596:7
foot-in-the-grave young m., 526:14
for all seasons, 143:11
for the field, 453:3
for the sword, 453:3
forgotten as a dead m. out of mind, 16:2
Forgotten M., 537:7
forgotten m., 651:14
formed for society, 318:16
formed m. of dust, 5:10
free as Nature made m., 272:9
frees himself from bonds, 432:7
Friday, 282:12
frontiers wherever m. fronts fact, 473:25
gently scan brother m., 357:3
get a new m., 224:26
girl up thy loins like a m., 14:17
give every m. thy ear, 197:23
giveth up the ghost, 13:30
go west young m., 471:2
goal of landing m. on moon, 786:1
God above or m. below, 294:16
God and m. decree, 575:16
god in ruins, 425:25
God is not a m., 9:9
God is there and m. is not, 417:12
God's ways to m., 575:12
goes riding by, 555:10
goeth forth unto his work, 18:11
goeth to his long home, 23:31
good for a m. that he bear the yoke, 28:13
good m. and just, 38:39
good name in m. and woman, 209:2
great m. great ganglion, 538:11
great nose great m., 603:4
greatest fool is m., 278:6
greatest m. ever seen, 323:*n*2
greatness of work inside m., 794:10
grew within this learned m., 169:7
ground colored m. occupies, 477:2
grows beyond his work, 733:2
grows used to everything, 492:6
half part of blessed m., 175:9
hand of a mighty m., 19:6
hand will be against every m., 6:31
happy m. be his dole, 146:*n*15
happy m. happy dole, 146:20
happy m. works ancestral acres, 95:27

Man (*continued*)

happy old m., 92:16
happy the m. and he alone, 273:17
hardly a m. now alive, 437:15
harrowing clods, 536:22
has Forever, 461:13
has two primal passions, 553:2
has will woman way, 443:7
hath penance done, 376:20
having put hand to plow, 37:30
he created m., 889:1
he was a m., 608:17
he was a m. take him for all in all, 197:9
he was her m., 886:3
heard wise m. say, 574:14
hears what he wants to hear, 855:9
heart of m. place devil dwells in, 248:12
hearty old m., 381:10
her wit was more than m., 273:21
himself important creation, 725:9
himself lend a hand, 71:10
his own executioner, 248:15
honest exceeding poor m., 184:35
honest m. close-buttoned, 327:7
honest m. noblest work of God, 295:5, 356:10
honest m. sent to lie abroad, 227:14
horse noblest conquest m.-made, 304:4
how dieth the wise m., 22:30
how many heads m. walk down, 851:1
how marvelous is M., 602:15
how proud word M. rings, 602:15
how would m. exist if God did not need him, 634:8
humiliation by white m., 802:6
hungry sinner, 399:3
I am cease to be, 454:27
I am first a m., 297:15
I am free m., 824:11
I am the m., 486:15
I appeal to any white m., 320:6
I declare I never met m., 347:4
I got my m., 710:23
I have been a m., 343:19
I know thee not old m., 188:27
I loved the m. and honor memory, 233:11
I must feel it as a m., 217:9
I never writ nor no m. loved, 222:15
I the m. in the moon, 179:12
identifies with his fate, 719:3
if a m. die shall he live, 13:31
if a m. finishes a poem, 839:6
if a m. has talent, 727:14
if a m. publicly denounces poetry, 839:5
if not wedding day absolutely fixed on, 305:1
I'll make me a m., 610:6
I'm m. of wealth and taste, 857:5
improvable reason of M., 415:15
in armor slave, 463:8
in arms wish to be, 371:20
in body of violent beast, 641:13
in every fat m. a thin one, 734:7
in every m. two postulations, 491:16
in gray flannel suit, 796:2
in his hasty days, 545:14
in love endures more, 548:26
in love with suffering, 492:5

Man *(continued)*

in midst of a crowd, 431:21
in mind of m. a motion, 368:11
in our town, 897:6
in past m. has been first, 566:1
in subjection to white Saxon m., 471:6
in whose hand cup is found, 7:14
in wilderness, 893:1
in wit a m., 294:13
incarnate and was made m., 48:12
ingrateful m., 211:24
inner m., 43:35
intellect of m. choose, 595:9
invented m. because disappointed in
  monkey, 524:24
invisible m., 774:8
is a machine, 311:18
is a prisoner, 74:12
is a reasoning animal, 103:14
is a thinking reed, 269:21
is an invention, 812:4
is as Heaven made him, 157:7
is born free, 312:15
is born unto trouble, 13:11
is child of customs used to, 131:10
is cooking animal, 334:5
is creature that can get used to anything,
  492:2
is everywhere disturbing agent, 421:2
is God blunder of m., 548:22
is man and master, 455:11
is m. blunder of God, 548:22
is m. no more than this, 212:3
is not piece of fruit, 780:7
is not so good a Christian, 555:18
is not so great a coward, 555:18
is one soul many tongues, 113:8
is origin of his action, 78:9
is raised above animal, 751:6
is the hunter, 453:2
is useless passion, 743:1
je-ne-sais-quoi young m., 526:13
Jewish m. with parents alive, 835:5
joked about every prominent m., 640:10
killed hero in m., 742:16
killed one m. to save hundred thousand,
  364:15
kills thing he loves, 561:3
know how to defy opinion, 362:14
know myself a m., 227:17
know the m. that must hear me, 377:3
know what God and m. is, 455:27
knoweth not his time, 23:23
known by company he keeps, 68:*n*8
lame m. leap as an hart, 26:18
large-hearted m., 434:10
last strands of m., 547:3
laugh to scorn power of m., 216:32
law for m., 424:13
laws of God beyond m., 65:18
laws of God laws of m., 575:16
leave his father and mother, 5:17
lengthened shadow of one m., 426:21
less no m. have, 571:8
let each m. hope and believe, 440:7
let end try the m., 188:4
let him pass for a m., 184:18
let m. outlive his wealth, 186:7

Man *(continued)*

let no such m. be trusted, 186:17
let us make m. in our image, 5:6
life of m. solitary, 239:10
lightning out of cloud m., 547:18
like light kindled and put out, 62:10
little difference between m. and m., 541:17
little m. had little gun, 896:12
lives life of epoch, 631:1
living-dead m., 172:28
long as colored m. look to white folks,
  862:3
look no way but downwards, 271:24
looketh on the outward appearance, 10:43
looking for honest m., 77:2
Lord is a m. of war, 8:5
Lord seeth not as m. seeth, 10:43
lose what he never had, 245:6
love not m. the less, 396:16
lovely gentleman-like m., 178:9
loves what vanishes, 594:8
low m. seeks little thing, 461:15
made for joy and woe, 354:2
made her such a m., 208:3
made the town, 326:19
made to mourn, 356:7
majority never replace m., 684:9
makes gods by the dozen, 152:20
making deserts of earth, 635:12
manners maketh m., 131:5
man's inhumanity to m., 356:8
man's word God in m., 455:7
marks earth with ruin, 396:17
master of fate, 455:11, 685:6
master of himself a happy m., 97:8
may fish with worm, 201:17
measure of all things, 69:25
mere M., 448:16
merely a passage for food, 140:2
metaphysical m. is dead, 537:14
middle-aged m. build woodshed, 473:6
military m., 189:12
mind's the standard of m., 289:4
misfortunes of m. occasioned by m., 105:4
mistakes evil for happiness, 360:15
Mr. Tambourine M., 851:12
Moby Dick whale or m., 696:9
mollusk cheap edition of m., 428:26
more no m. entitled to, 571:8
more right than neighbors, 473:17
more sinned against, 211:29
muffin m., 896:8
must have faults, 105:19
my m. of men, 218:15
my quietness has a m. in it, 814:8
Nature formed one such m., 397:7
nature has given m. into woman's hands,
  528:12
necessarily a m., 297:15
ne'er left m. i' mire, 213:20
negations of m., 807:17
neither angel nor beast, 269:22
neither m. nor woman but author, 472:14
never is blest, 294:19
never met one I didn't like, 640:10
never saw m. who looked, 561:1
new m. raised up in him, 49:23
nice m., 284:19

Man *(continued)*

no benefit in gifts of bad m., 67:18
no indispensable m., 652:1
no m. born an angler, 244:33
no m. born unto himself, 241:21
no m. content with lot, 95:15
no m. deserved less at country's hands,
  498:10
no m. do for your sake, 530:5
no m. hero to his valet, 249:8
no m. is an island, 231:8
no m. not deserve hanging, 153:17
no m. remember me, 536:3
no m. see me more, 225:23
no m. takes with him wealth, 59:24
no m. useless who has friend, 556:1
no m. worth having true, 283:17
no sin for m. to labor in vocation, 181:30
no such thing as honest m., 291:8
noble animal, 249:4
noble be m. helpful and good, 342:12
noblest work of m., 518:3
none more wonderful than m., 65:16
not a just m. upon earth, 23:15
not a m. but cloud, 698:16
not good that m. be alone, 5:14
not happy unless free, 400:11
not lifetime of one m. only, 679:1
not passion's slave, 200:12
not sum of what he has, 742:20
not take goods with him, 3:2
not what kind of paper but m., 474:6
nothing feebler than a m., 54:4
nothing more wretched than a m., 52:6
nothing to do with just m., 36:13
nothing wears clothes but M., 242:23
O that m. might know end, 193:18
of action forced into thought, 600:22
of an unbounded stomach, 226:10
of comfort no m. speak, 177:7
of dust, 5:10
of genius had to pay, 612:19
of honor regrets discreditable act, 645:13
of letters, 270:17
of many resources, 52:20
of many wiles, 293:18
of my kidney, 187:16
of my peculiar weakness, 645:11
of nasty ideas, 284:19
of powerful character, 431:20
of sorrows, 27:5
of strife and contention, 27:37
of unclean lips, 25:10
of understanding, 30:27
of understanding is of excellent spirit,
  20:43
of understanding lost nothing, 152:10
of words not deeds, 892:7
old age in universal m., 164:*n*5
old m. broken, 226:7
old m. had so much blood, 217:12
old m. in dry month, 675:21
old m. to whom old men hearkened, 99:8
old m. twice a child, 199:9
old m. who will not laugh, 584:14
Old M. with beard, 467:3
old m. with something of young, 88:15
old m. wouldn't say prayers, 894:6

Man *(continued)*

on horseback, 885:11
once a man who said God, 680:4
once to every m. and nation, 481:12
one m. among a thousand, 23:17
one m. born one m. died, 719:4
one m. crossing bridge, 640:11
one m. one film, 713:7
one m. one vote, 888:8
one m. plays many parts, 194:25
one m. with courage a majority, 364:5
one more wrong to m., 460:14
one small step for m., 825:20
one-book m., 375:7
only animal that blushes, 524:16
only feels alone, 776:2
only m. harrowing clods, 536:22
only m. is vile, 391:6
only one that knows nothing, 105:3
organization m., 789:3
organized by labor, 603:1
out of me God and m., 530:20
out of one m. a race, 258:26
outrage a brave m. dead, 65:9
outside every fat m., 734:*n*2
owes not any m., 436:12
palms greater no m. made them, 829:5
Parliament of m., 452:3
particularly pure young m., 526:11
partly is, 462:20
people arose as one m., 10:28
perceives it die away, 370:18
perhaps this is the m., 792:12
picked out of ten thousand, 198:32
pig edible to m., 540:7
pious m. not less a m., 267:16
place and means for every m., 206:6
plain blunt m., 193:3
Plato's m., 76:18
play is tragedy M., 448:15
play the m. Master Ridley, 144:13
poor despised old m., 211:26
poor m. accustomed to small things, 768:13
poor m. being down, 31:2
poor m. had nothing, 11:18
poor m. is Christ's stamp, 242:13
poor m. poor mankind, 713:15
poor m. that has loved, 593:15
poorest m. in his cottage, 305:12
power of m. and moment, 496:4
powers superior to m., 558:2
prayer of righteous m., 45:34
prejudiced unreasonable m., 466:9
prentice han' tried on m., 356:22
press not falling m., 225:24
primitive and civilized m., 569:10
proper m. as see in summer's day, 178:9
proper study of mankind is m., 295:1
proposes God disposes, 137:5
prosperity comes to bad m., 59:21
proud yet wretched thing, 227:17
prudent m. looketh well to his going, 20:27
rather be worm than son of m., 670:10
reading maketh a full m., 166:18
ready money makes the m., 289:18
ready to believe what is told, 105:17

Man *(continued)*

really a very good m., 562:5
rebounds whole aeons back in nature, 483:22
rebuke a wise m., 20:8
recovered of the bite, 322:15
register of God not record of m., 249:2
rejoice O young m. in youth, 23:29
rejoiceth as a strong m., 15:16
result of purposeless natural process, 732:14
rich in things he can let alone, 474:27
rich m. beginning to fall, 31:2
rich m. enter into kingdom, 35:4
richest pleasures cheapest, 473:10
righteous m. regardeth the life of his beast, 20:18
righteous m. to make fall, 160:6
Rights of M., 325:1
rope between animal and Superman, 547:17
rousing like strong m., 254:12
ruins of the noblest m., 192:22
rule will show the m., 55:11
sabbath made for m., 36:27
said to universe, 609:3
savage in m. never eradicated, 473:11
savage individual m., 598:14
says what he knows, 313:3
scholar is M. Thinking, 425:26
screaming is not dancing bear, 770:12
seeks for what is remote, 79:20
seen how m. made slave slave made m., 476:20
sent from God, 38:46
serve time to every trade, 394:13
setting m. free from men, 742:14
seven women shall take hold of one m., 25:2
shall m. be more pure than maker, 13:9
shall man no longer crush, 346:24
shall mortal m. be more just, 13:9
she knows her m., 235:*n*4
sight make old m. young, 451:8
single sentence for modern m., 770:9
singularly deep young m., 526:10
slothful m. saith, 21:38
smiteth a m. so that he die, 8:16
so can any m., 182:34
so frail a thing m., 283:8
so in way in house, 457:1
so is it now I am a m., 369:14
so much one m. can do, 266:19
so near is God to m., 424:21
so unto m. woman, 437:4
so various, 273:2
social friendly honest m., 356:12
social world work of m., 286:20
something m. will die for, 823:6
son of m. that thou visitest him, 15:5
sooner kill m. than hawk, 670:6
soul of m. imperishable, 75:25
spares neither m. nor his works, 332:10
spirit stands by naked m., 881:22
stage where every m. play part, 184:4
stagger like a drunken m., 18:16
stand by your m., 856:2
standing by my m., 856:*n*1
state of m. like kingdom, 192:2

Man *(continued)*

stole the fruit, 242:16
strives for someone to worship, 492:13
strong m. digests experiences, 548:18
strongest m. stands alone, 504:18
style is the m., 304:5
subtle knot which makes us m., 229:19
successful animal, 570:5
such a disagreeable m., 527:6
such master such m., 151:1
survives earthquakes, 507:9
system where m. exploits m., 792:3
teach you more of m., 368:6
tempt not desperate m., 181:10
that died for men, 532:12
that hangs on favors, 225:25
that hath his quiver full, 19:6
that hath no music, 186:17
that hath tongue no man, 173:32
that is a worm, 14:1
that is born of a woman, 13:29
that makes character, 290:16
that m. to man the world o'er, 358:20
that mocks and sets it light, 176:17
that trusteth in man, 27:39
that trusteth in the Lord, 27:39
that which m. is made of, 320:1
that's marred, 206:4
that's the m. of today, 666:14
there did meet another m., 308:10
there is a m. child conceived, 13:3
thin m., 702:10
think mortal thoughts, 67:12
thinking or working is alone, 475:9
third beast had a face as a m., 46:28
this is Plato's m., 76:18
this is the state of m., 225:25
this m. shall be myself, 313:4
this was a m., 193:22
thou art the m., 11:19
though old m. young gardener, 338:2
thought young m. brings forth, 76:5
tills field lies beneath, 455:5
time whereof memory of m., 318:19
Time you old gypsy m., 609:14
to a wise m. ports, 176:16
to command, 453:3
to every m. a damsel or two, 10:14
to every m. according to his work, 17:5
to every m. upon earth, 419:19
to laugh proper to m., 145:5
to man so oft unjust always to women, 398:12
to match mountains, 557:5
to men m. is mind, 540:2
to the young m. knowledge and discretion, 19:22
tool-using animal, 406:14
totality of what he might have, 742:20
tragedy of modern m., 841:9
tree of m. never quiet, 575:4
trust m. on his oath or bond, 213:21
try fortunes to last m., 188:18
two words for m., 561:16
tyranny over mind of m., 337:7
unaccommodated m., 212:3
uncorrupted good m., 757:15
unfinished m. and his pain, 595:3

Man *(continued)*

use every m. after desert, 199:14
use money for good of fellow m., 535:4
vain diverse undulating, 151:17
various M., 358:2
vertical m., 748:4
very unclubable m., 309:10
victory shifts from m. to m., 51:13
vindicate ways of God to m., 294:15
want anything said ask m., 810:9
wants but little, 290:25, 322:10
war as is of every m. against every m., 239:9
war is to m. as motherhood to woman, 657:2
was it God was it m., 530:21
was there m. dismayed, 454:19
way of m. with maid, 22:14, 588:12
We created M., 119:12
wealth even to a wicked m., 59:20
well-bred m. knows how to confess, 302:20
well-favored m., 190:41
went mad and bit the m., 322:14
went to Bar as very young m., 526:21
what a chimera is m., 269:25
what a piece of work is m., 199:5
what is American this new m., 331:2
what is m. in nature, 269:9
what is m. that thou art mindful, 15:5
what is m. what is he not, 63:31
what m. dare I dare, 216:20
what m. has made of m., 368:3
what m. not know of God, 737:9
what manner of m., 36:30
what may m. within hide, 207:7
what signifies life o' m., 356:21
what treaty white m. kept, 513:4
when honor dies m. dead, 438:6
when I search for m., 807:17
when m. can help fellow m., 716:14
when m. of rank an author, 311:5
when m. of real talent dies, 335:10
when right m. rings them, 556:7
where love of m. love of art, 70:18
whiskey life of m., 897:15
white m. warmed before Indians' fire, 325:20
who brings bad news, 65:13
who craves more is poor, 103:9
who expects nothing, 294:10
who had been promised, 695:3
who had folly and presumption, 319:6
who has city obedient, 75:10
who has found himself out, 577:13
who is not himself mean, 674:10
who laughs hasn't heard news, 716:13
who never fought pilfers, 72:16
who runs may fight again, 81:12
who said This is mine, 312:12
who sits facing you, 56:5
who touches this touches a m., 488:6
who was a key a m., 783:11
who wasn't there, 631:12
who wert once despot, 402:4
whole duty of m., 24:2
whom Fortune scratched, 206:8
whom king delighteth to honor, 12:32
who's master who's m., 286:12
who's pure in heart, 732:15

Man *(continued)*

whose blood is snow-broth, 206:16
whose blood warm within, 184:5
why can't woman be more like m., 790:11
will cleave to like, 31:1
will no m. say amen, 177:16
will not merely endure, 714:5
wind sweep m. away, 495:6
wine a peep-hole on a m., 55:20
wise and moral m., 64:19
wise in his own conceit, 21:38
wise m. is strong, 21:31
wise m. knows himself fool, 195:34
wise m. not leave right to chance, 473:15
wise old m. wise old woman, 873:5
with God always in majority, 150:2
with God strive, 396:4
with great thing to pursue, 461:15
with seven wives, 892:22
with the head, 453:3
without a flaw, 95:21
without imagination, 657:15
without money rather than money without man, 62:19
wolf to man, 682:12
woman lesser m., 452:7
woman more barbarous than m., 548:7
woman needs m. like fish needs bicycle, 888:20
woman not depend on protection of m., 489:1
woman without m. cannot meet m., 792:12
women looking-glasses reflecting m., 654:17
wonder and glory of universe, 440:10
words guard shape of m., 727:6
work for m. to mend, 274:24
work from sun to sun, 883:17
world without God and m., 821:5
worst use a m. could be put to, 227:13
worth makes the m., 295:4
wovon m. nicht sprechen kann, 685:*n*3
wrathful m. stirreth up strife, 20:33
writing maketh exact m., 166:18
writing master to world, 671:12
you don't need a weather m., 851:15
you drop from chamber, 474:6
you shall find me grave m., 180:28
you'll be a M. my son, 590:3
young m. I think I know you, 487:8
young m. in whom something of old, 88:15
young m. married is marred, 206:4
young m. there is America, 323:22
young m. who has not wept, 584:14
Manacles, mind-forged m., 353:3
Manage this matter to a T, 145:*n*10
Management, formula of ecological m., 727:18
of change, 758:2
Man-at-arms now serve on knees, 163:4
Mandalay, back to M., 588:1
road to M., 588:2
Mandarin, my thirty-third m., 492:*n*4
Manderley, dreamt I went to M. again, 750:6
Mandragora, give me to drink m., 218:10
not poppy nor m., 209:11
Mandrake, get with child a m. root, 228:9

Manes, whirlwind home in m., 443:1
Mangent, qu'ils m. de la brioche, 313:*n*1
Manger, cold and not cleanly m., 263:11
dog in the m., 59:4
for his bed, 476:5
in the rude m. lies, 250:10
laid in a m., 37:16
not live as dogs in m., 653:12
One born in a m., 268:15
Mangled by the bronze spear, 52:13
naked poor m. Peace, 190:6
Manhattan, we'll have M., 707:1
Whitman of M. the son, 486:7
Man-hero not exceptional monster, 642:8
Manhood, bone of m., 324:2
conspiracy against m., 426:15
do what m. bids thee, 491:21
honesty m. nor fellowship, 181:31
my m. is cast down, 662:15
nothing of poetry about m., 405:3
shouldered a kind of m., 845:10
Mania for saying things are well, 299:10
of owning things, 486:14
Maniac scattering dust, 453:18
Manic statement, 787:10
Manière, seulement une m. de le dire, 800:*n*3
Manifest destiny, 469:11
himself, 818:2
nothing is secret that shall not be m., 37:29
plainness, 57:8
work be made m., 42:9
Manifestation of unfriendly disposition, 355:7
Manifestations of curvature of space, 766:3
Manifesto, this m. more than theory, 539:3
Manifold, how m. are thy works, 18:11
our m. sins, 49:5
sins and wickedness, 48:1
Manikin, what an eloquent m., 91:17
Mankind, all m. done in books, 407:20
all m. of one Author, 231:7
at war with rights of m., 336:17
by thee less bored, 245:*n*1
calamities shared by m., 282:10
censure injustice, 75:1
composed of two sorts, 557:13
creations of mind blessing to m., 637:10
crucify m., 577:18
custom despot of m., 418:19
deserve better of m., 285:1
divided m. into parties, 345:9
doings of m. subject of my book, 109:11
entitled to respect of m., 390:16
expand the destiny of m., 820:2
Father of m., 438:18
fleet of life like leaves, 73:5
fly from not hate m., 395:20
furnishing m. with two noblest things, 284:5
giant leap for m., 825:20
hate m., 213:28
he lived from all m. apart, 347:11
hindrances to elevation of m., 474:15
histories of m. are of higher class, 362:8
history of m., 319:8
history of m. history of injuries to woman, 471:4
I love m., 800:12
in charity to all m., 363:8

Mankind *(continued)*

in conscious virtue bold, 293:13
involved in m., 231:8
is dream of a shadow, 63:31
lay out ourselves in service of m., 341:1
love a lover, 427:2
love m. except American, 310:18
make little adjustment in face of new, 694:10
minus one of one opinion, 435:2
mother of m., 255:6
must put an end to war, 786:2
no history of m., 732:2
O ye that love m., 333:2
of all m. I love but you, 880:12
one disillusion m., 656:9
our countrymen m., 433:2
plagues with which m. cursed, 282:7
poor man poor m., 713:15
possesses two blessings, 68:9
prepare asylum for m., 333:2
proper study of m. is man, 295:1
rather than Jewish, 819:14
spectator of m., 288:2
surpasses or subdues m., 395:17
survey m., 306:15
things ride m., 424:12
to you and all m., 281:14
we came in peace for all m., 888:18
will remain damned, 450:5

Mankind's epitome, 273:2
motto, 266:8

Manly, avowed erect m. foe, 367:3
deeds womanly words, 244:*n*2
his big m. voice, 194:25
love is m., 137:11

Manna, give us this day m., 129:19
it is m., 8:9

Manner, after m. of men, 41:15
after this m. pray ye, 32:25
all m. of thing shall be well, 131:14
all m. of thing well, 679:13
ease in Casey's m., 584:19
gay and delicious, 722:18
no m. of doubt, 528:4
of giving worth more, 249:15
pleasant shy m. of mouse, 724:1
remains intact after morale cracks, 710:11
state in wonted m. keep, 232:2
subordinates m. to matter, 379:13
to the m. born, 197:31
vulgar m., 72:12
what m. of man is this, 36:30

Mannerly, behave m. at table, 555:9

Manners, bewrayed by his m., 160:20
catch the m. living, 294:15
climates councils, 451:13
contact with m. is education, 101:11
corrupt good m., 43:3
evil m. live in brass, 226:11
happy ways of doing, 428:9
impressions of American m., 389:2
language m. laws customs, 369:4
maketh man, 131:5
mirror which shows portrait, 344:25
must adorn knowledge, 298:11
new world and new m., 261:16
not men but m., 304:13

Manners *(continued)*

of undertaker, 603:13
old m. books wines, 323:2
our nation limps after, 176:22
savage men uncouth m., 323:22
saw m. in face, 308:3

Mannish cowards, 193:35

Man-of-war, in well-conducted m., 525:*n*2

Manor, as if a m. washed away, 231:8

Man-o'-War's 'er 'usband, 589:2

Man's, a m. worth something, 462:1
always been m. world, 751:5
any m. death diminishes me, 231:8
bad m. refuge, 57:20
bedevilment and God's, 575:17
best portion of m. life, 368:7
blind m. ditch, 595:4
brown m. burden, 589:*n*1
character is his fate, 62:14
cloud like m. hand, 12:2
Dead M. Chest, 555:4
deceiver never mine, 575:21
desire is for woman, 380:4
desiring this m. art, 221:6
discovery genitalia a weapon, 839:21
distinctive mark, 462:20
every m. Cleopatra, 272:13
every old m. eye, 180:18
every true m. apparel, 207:10
every wise m. son know, 204:25
fate, 728:14
first disobedience, 255:3
fortune in own hands, 166:13
good m. feast, 194:22
good m. fortune, 211:15
good m. love, 195:20
good m. sin, 314:*n*2
good m. treasure, 57:20
gowd for a' that, 358:18
great m. memory, 200:16
grown m. passion, 313:13
hand not able to taste, 179:4
honest m. aboon his might, 358:19
honest m. noblest work, 295:5, 356:10
idea of sexual rights, 471:7
image and his cry, 591:4
imagination of m. heart, 6:22
imperial race ensnare, 293:6
in theater of m. life, 164:16
ingratitude, 195:1
inhumanity to man, 356:8
life allegory, 413:11
life cheap as beast's, 211:21
love an episode in m. life, 362:13
love of man's life apart, 398:6
nature cultural product, 725:9
no m. enemy, 748:5
no m. pie is freed, 225:10
old m. eagle mind, 596:15
old m. frenzy, 596:14
old m. gold, 607:6
one m. will all men's misery, 161:18
own resinous heart, 594:14
plant m. lordship, 537:10
practically inexterminate, 624:20
print of m. foot, 282:11
proud m. contumely, 199:21
reach exceed grasp, 461:18

Man's *(continued)*

rising to a m. work, 112:8
skill built cities, 87:2
stain my m. cheeks, 211:22
take each m. censure, 197:23
thirty years in m. life, 75:8
truly sorry m. dominion, 356:5
unconquerable mind, 370:8
watch o'er m. mortality, 371:5
way to m. heart, 458:2
White M. burden, 589:12
word God in man, 455:7
work portrait of himself, 521:8
young m. fancy, 451:21

Manservant, not covet neighbor's m., 8:14

Mansion, back to its m. call, 315:20
human life a M., 413:5
Jove's Court my m., 251:24
Love has pitched his m., 596:1
refuse heavenly m., 595:9

Mansionry, approve by his loved m., 214:21

Mansions, build more stately m., 443:10
green m., 539:13
his m. deathless, 52:31
in Father's house many m., 39:40
in the skies, 289:16

Manslaughter, check m. but what of war, 103:23

Mantle, green m. of standing pool, 212:5
like a standing pond, 184:6
morn in russet m. clad, 196:20
of Elijah, 12:13
of wind and chill and rain, 137:13
silver m. threw, 257:25
twitched his m. blue, 253:15

Manual on uses of new metal, 815:3

Manufactures, monopoly same as secret in m., 319:1

Manunkind, busy monster m., 702:1

Manure, natural m., 336:15

Manus haec inimica tyrannis, 268:*n*4

Manuscript, before sending m. to press, 584:1

Manuscripts don't burn, 689:7

Many a one for him maks mane, 890:6
admire few know, 71:8
and mighty are they, 588:20
are called, 35:11
as the sand by the sea, 11:27
beast with m. heads, 220:1
beguile m. beguiled by one, 209:23
can brook the weather, 174:16
conceive the m. without one, 76:3
daughters have done virtuously, 22:20
done because we are too m., 536:9
hands make light work, 148:10
here among us who feel, 852:1
in hands not of few but m., 71:14
inventions, 23:18
I've had m. of them, 689:2
must labor for one, 396:27
mutable rank-scented m., 219:29
not how m. enemy are but where, 70:1
not m. but much, 121:2
one composed of m., 95:13
play of the m., 580:2
reason Lord makes so m., 446:6
receive advice few profit, 99:20
shall run to and fro, 28:30

Memory *(continued)*

of Boatswain a dog, 394:9
of loved and lost, 446:12
of Paris inexhaustible, 691:5
of the just is blessed, 20:11
of them is forgotten, 23:21
of those who made us laugh, 718:12
out of sight and of m., 636:12
outlive his life, 200:16
pluck from m. rooted sorrow, 217:19
poor m. that only works backwards, 516:11
pray bring me to men's m., 128:22
proud to have m. graced, 683:10
sinner of his m., 224:5
some women stay in m., 589:23
struggle of m. against forgetting, 824:1
table of my m., 198:15
tablet a gift of M., 76:7
that serves no purpose, 770:5
their very m. is fair, 268:16
throng into my m., 252:12
'tis in my m. locked, 197:25
to m. nothing really lost, 761:3
ventricle of m., 174:18
vibrates in m., 404:4
viol of her m., 641:6
warder of the brain, 215:7
while m. holds a seat, 198:15
wit at expense of m., 286:16

Memory's, confusing beams from m. lamp, 732:12

Men, a few honest m., 246:14

about me that are fat, 191:28
above reach of ordinary m., 369:17
act and women appear, 811:1
advantage women have over m., 688:12
adversity test of strong m., 103:25
all are m. condemned, 315:8
all honorable m., 192:29
all m. and women had become grotesques, 632:14
all m. are liars, 18:23
all m. be free, 447:3
all m. born are my brothers, 485:17
all m. born free, 254:18
all m. by nature give praise, 659:9
all m. created equal, 336:1, 446:5
all m. hate wretched, 415:18
all m. liable to error, 275:7
all m. make faults, 221:11
all m. of a size, 427:26
all m. would be tyrants, 282:8, 340:11
all sorts and conditions of m., 48:14
all the king's m., 895:1
all the sad young m., 816:3
all the same, 627:2
and boys thick as hasty pudding, 883:*n4*
and women affirm brotherhood, 751:9
and women created equal, 471:3
and women merely players, 194:25
and women with conventional upbringing, 614:15
animals infuse into trunks of m., 185:31
April when they woo, 195:29
are grown mechanical, 406:7
are like earth and we are moon, 561:17
are like plants, 331:3
are men, 208:26

Men *(continued)*

are my teachers, 295:*n1*
are quick to flare up, 53:6
are we not M., 598:11
are where they are, 475:12
are yielding to animal nature, 614:15
arm and burgonet of m., 218:12
as in a theater eyes of m., 177:21
ask for everything, 792:13
at forty learn to close softly, 807:21
at point of death, 181:12
attend m. and not women, 76:5
bad cause bad means bad m., 333:9
become brothers, 359:10
becoming m. we wanted to marry, 838:14
believe what pornography says, 863:7
below and saints above, 373:2
best m. molded of faults, 207:18
best of m., 218:19
black m. are pearls, 173:36
blaspheme what they do not know, 269:27
bodies of unburied m., 237:3
boldly speak and have hearts of m., 347:13
books are not m., 488:19
books like m., 284:1
boys and girls level with m., 219:5
brave m. and worthy patriots, 254:4
brave m. lived before Agamemnon, 97:14
brave m. living and dead, 446:5
bribed by loyalties and ambitions, 694:7
busy hum of m., 251:6
by nature desire knowledge, 77:18
by nature equally free, 320:7
capable of wickedness, 568:3
captain of m. of death, 271:29
capture of m. by women, 459:*n1*
cause or m. of Emerald Isle, 347:14
cheerful ways of m., 257:6
children of M. full of wiles, 73:4
circumstances rule m., 69:19
cities of m. and manners, 451:13
condemn m. because few, 475:24
Constitution for all m., 470:15
creep not walk, 438:9
cunning m. pass for wise, 166:3
darling of m. and gods, 89:9
day is for honest m., 68:8
dead m. tell no tales, 273:12
deal with m. as equals, 838:13
Death that feeds on m., 223:5
decay, 322:22
deceivers ever, 190:33
decent easy m., 332:13
desire the good, 78:22
Destiny with M. for Pieces plays, 441:22
determine gods dispose, 235:*n3*
die like m., 17:17
die miserably every day, 659:8
die nightly in beds, 448:11
die to make m. free, 481:2
died to make m. holy, 481:2
difference between m. and women, 729:3
difference of forty thousand m., 366:8
dine with some m., 629:2
done with roofs and m., 579:12
doors for m. to take their exits, 237:7
duration of great sentiments makes great m., 548:6

Men *(continued)*

dying m. enforce attention, 176:20
eat hogs, 641:3
eat m. like air, 833:4
Education is Making M., 512:*n2*
elevate condition of m., 445:9
England is purgatory of m., 161:11
equal right of m. and women, 661:16
evil m. do lives after them, 192:28
evils draw m. together, 79:1
fair women and brave m., 395:13
fallible m. governed by bad passions, 336:7
fear of little m., 501:4
feared witches, 562:9
fell out knew not why, 261:17
fifteen m. on Dead Man's Chest, 555:4
fight between two bald m., 719:9
Filipinos our fellow-m., 545:11
filthy dirty pigs, 627:2
finds too late m. betray, 322:16
first subjects afterward, 473:13
fishers of m., 32:13
flourish only for a moment, 54:5
foolery wise m. have, 193:26
foolish m. who accuse a woman, 281:7
fools laugh at m. of sense, 280:25
foot of unfamiliar m., 496:12
forty thousand m., 892:14
free m. free speech, 885:7
gear of foreign dead m., 679:4
get there first with most m., 494:4
given to m. of middle age, 223:26
God justifiable to m., 260:13
God made mad, 618:10
God these old m., 67:8
God wrongs not m., 118:7
gods fashioned by m., 584:12
gods in likeness of m., 40:28
goeth on to meet the armed m., 14:27
good m. and true, 190:40
good m. eat that they may live, 70:7
good m. to do nothing, 325:15
good will to m., 457:11
good will toward m., 37:18
government of laws not m., 329:14
great city greatest m. women, 487:2
great m. are not always wise, 14:11
great m. can't be ruled, 742:15
great m. not boasters, 428:3
great m. texts of Revelation, 406:20
grow into likeness of bad m., 76:9
hangin' m. and women, 884:5
happiest of all m., 299:12
happy breed of m., 176:24
harmony between m. and land, 668:6
hate in white m., 809:1
have died from time to time, 195:27
have lost their reason, 192:31
have their price, 290:2
heard old old m. say, 592:2
heart of oak our m., 316:20
heaven that leads m. to hell, 222:20
His ways with m., 455:17
history biography of great m., 407:17
hit only what they aim at, 474:18
hollow m., 676:19, 676:20
homely m. charmed women, 581:15
honor all m., 45:39

Men *(continued)*

how much m. hate them, 845:7
if all m. were just, 73:22
if m. are destroyed, 65:1
if m. could get pregnant, 782:7
if m. knew how women pass time, 581:11
impossible m., 706:3
in catalogue ye go for m., 216:6
in m. we various passions find, 294:1
indulge themselves in abuse, 741:3
inflation few m. remit, 781:16
is there view for enlisted m., 796:13
know so little of men, 602:2
labels that give name to event, 506:15
Lake Wobegon where m. are good-
    looking, 854:10
lead lives of quiet desperation, 474:11
led me to him blindfold and alone, 590:7
let us die like m., 439:8
let us praise famous m., 31:26
let your light shine before m., 32:16
like m. undergo fatigue, 333:10
like satyrs grazing, 168:12
live as m. not ostriches, 653:12
lived like fishes, 220:*n1*
lives of great m. remind us, 436:6
lodging place of wayfaring m., 27:32
looks quite through deeds of m., 191:29
love is waster of rich m., 65:25
love wakes m. once a lifetime, 500:7
made m. and not made them well, 200:9
made spectacle to m., 42:11
make the city, 72:8
make their own history, 477:15
man that died for m., 532:12
masters of their fates, 191:26
may come men may go, 454:25
may read strange matters, 214:19
melancholy m. eat no beans, 234:15
merriest when from home, 188:37
merry m. all, 889:20
mice and m., 356:6
mighty m. of valor, 9:37
mighty m. which were of old, 6:16
mocks married m., 174:32
moon m. and barking hounds, 704:16
more lonely among m., 475:9
more m. killed by overwork, 587:7
mountains are fountains of m., 533:10
must be decided, 79:23
must endure their going, 213:7
must work women weep, 481:5
my man of m., 218:15
natives of rain rainy m., 640:14
naturally in two parties, 338:17
need of world of m., 460:17
never be beloved by m., 353:17
never knew so many m. alive, 589:14
no common m., 427:26
no compacts between lions and m., 52:15
no country for old m., 594:1
no two m. cannot be distinguished, 105:6
no worse husband than best of m., 218:19
nor blame the writings but the m., 292:21
not descended from fearful m., 754:12
not fit that m. be compared with gods,
    91:22
not m. but manners, 304:13

Not m. but measures, 323:17
not m. you took them for, 191:1
not similar are gods and m., 51:8
not three good m. unhanged, 182:19
O m. in the harbor lane, 83:3
O miserable minds of m., 90:1
O what m. dare do, 191:4
object of making m. happy, 492:12
of Athens, 40:32
of courtly nurture, 500:5
of culture true apostles, 497:14
of despised race, 519:10
of England wherefore plow, 402:15
of few words best, 189:11
of good will, 47:22
of ill judgment ignore good, 65:8
of less value than gold, 143:3
of like passions, 40:29
of my generation, 765:3
of polite learning, 282:21
of renown, 6:16
of the South, 643:10
of understanding, 23:23
old m. are all dead, 537:4
old m. are children, 72:15
old m. from chimney corner, 162:18
old m. garrulous by nature, 88:16
old m. know young m. fools, 163:13
old m. ought to be explorers, 679:2
old m. shall dream dreams, 28:41
older m. declare war, 625:19
our m. live all in one house, 499:7
peace to m. of good will, 47:22
persuade eyes of m. without orator, 172:29
phrase m. pass hand to mouth, 829:7
place where m. can pray, 618:13
port liquor for m., 310:24
praise famous m., 31:26
private m. enjoy, 189:22
prize the thing ungained, 203:3
proper m. as ever trod, 191:20
proud m. in old age, 66:1
put enemy in their mouths, 208:31
quit you like m., 43:10
quit yourselves like m., 10:36
real half-horse half-alligator breed, 393:15
reject prophets, 492:15
rich m. rule the law, 322:5
rivalship of wisest m., 288:23
roll of common m., 182:33
room for honest m., 333:12
rooted out of kindly parts of life, 555:15
sailors but m., 184:21
saints aid if m. call, 377:12
sandwich m. shuffling, 654:5
savage m. uncouth manners, 323:22
search land of living m., 373:7
see m. as trees walking, 36:36
seldom make passes, 699:13
sensible conscientious m., 309:*n1*
setting man free from m., 742:14
should be what they seem, 208:36
shut doors against setting sun, 213:22
sit and hear each other groan, 410:5
slain a thousand m. with jawbone, 10:22
slave to fate chance desperate m., 230:23
sleek-headed m., 191:28

small m. afraid of writings, 327:17
small things make base m. proud, 170:11
so many m. so many opinions, 86:14
some m. killed wounded never leave, 786:4
some m. love not a pig, 185:26
some to pleasure take, 294:2
sons of m. and angels say, 305:7
sons of m. snared in evil time, 23:23
speak with tongues of m., 42:26
spirit of m. who follow, 664:11
spirits of just m., 45:14
strange that m. fear, 192:11
strength of twenty m., 181:8
strong m. shall bow themselves, 23:30
such as sleep o' nights, 191:28
such m. are dangerous, 191:28
take best they can get, 310:16
talk of crabbed old m., 91:5
talking of fall of man, 475:32
text of M. and Women, 574:1
that hazard all, 185:3
that laugh and weep, 530:16
that sow and reap, 530:16
that strove with gods, 451:17
that you could work with m., 865:4
themselves m. wrong, 118:7
there before us, 473:24
there He makes m., 390:22
there is danger from all m., 329:12
think all men mortal but themselves, 290:24
thoughts of m. decay, 160:25
thoughts of m. widened, 452:5
thousand m. that fishes gnawed, 171:28
three merry m. be we, 236:*n2*
tide in affairs of m., 193:13
tides of m., 680:7
to match mountains, 557:*n3*
to m. a man is a mind, 540:2
tongues of m. and of angels, 42:26
tracings upon the hearts of m., 359:11
traveled among unknown m., 369:13
tread underfoot what feared, 90:19
trivial attentions m. pay women, 360:19
trust ears less than eyes, 69:5
truth on lips of dying m., 495:21
truths not for all m., 299:15
twelve honest m., 291:6
twenty m. crossing bridge, 640:11
two m. went up to pray, 38:22
two sorts of m., 557:13
two strong m. face to face, 587:8
uselessness of m. above sixty, 553:4
wars won by m., 664:11
watch the m. at play, 632:18
ways of God to m., 255:5
we are m. my liege, 216:6
we are the stuffed m., 676:19
we petty m., 191:26
we will die free m., 341:10
were deceivers ever, 190:33
we've got the m., 503:17
what is it m. in women require, 352:9
what mothers made them, 428:4
what you and other m. think, 191:24
whatsoever ye would m. do, 33:18
when bad m. combine, 323:16
when force subdues m., 79:14

Merit *(continued)*
makes his way, 225:11
of perpetuity, 249:1
oft got without m., 208:29
patient m. takes, 199:21
purchased by m. of wearer, 185:8
to particularize is m., 353:9
unassisted m., 306:*n*2
whoever rescues single life earns m., 117:9
Merits, goodness result of one's own m., 124:1
original m. of case disappeared, 466:11
seek his m. to disclose, 316:8
Merlin had strange laugh, 770:15
I am M., 456:3
Mermaid on dolphin's back, 178:15
Tavern, 411:5
what things done at the M., 237:20
Mermaids, heard the m. singing, 675:6
singing, 228:9
Merrier man never spent talk withal, 174:9
the more the m., 148:17
Merriest, maddest m. day, 450:15
when they are from home, 188:37
Merrily did we drop, 375:20
die all die m., 183:16
fly after summer m., 225:5
hent the stile-a, 223:24
shall I live now, 225:5
Merriment, flashes of m., 202:12
innocent m., 527:16
Merry, all their wars m., 618:10
as cricket, 147:22
as day is long, 190:22
as marriage bell, 395:13
eat drink be m., 23:20, 38:3
God rest you m. gentlemen, 883:4
good to be m. and wise, 146:12
gude to be m. and wise, 884:12
guid to be m. and wise, 359:3
he that is of a m. heart, 20:32
heart doeth good, 20:42
heart goes all the day, 223:24
heart maketh cheerful countenance, 20:31
I am not m., 208:15
if to be old and m. be sin, 182:28
keep our Christmas m. still, 373:13
Margaret, 141:2
may'st hear the m. din, 375:18
measure, 404:9
men all, 889:20
men at point of death m., 181:12
merry merry roundelay, 163:2
monarch scandalous and poor, 281:1
month of May, 233:14
never m. when hear sweet music, 186:16
obstinate pliant m. morose, 107:18
old soul, 892:13
playing of m. organ, 883:5
rather have fool make me m., 195:24
small cheer makes m. feast, 172:19
three m. boys are we, 236:6
turn his m. note, 194:11
tu-who a m. note, 174:33
wanderer of the night, 178:12
we were very m., 695:9
wine maketh m., 23:24
wives may be m., 187:18
yarn from fellow rover, 635:17

Merryman, Doctor M., 286:5
moping mum, 527:25
Mescalin, what rest of us see with m., 702:15
Meshach, Shadrach M. and Abednego, 28:22
Meshes, though its m. are wide, 58:3
Mess, Benjamin's m., 7:11
let other people clean up m., 710:6
of imprecision of feeling, 678:22
Message, ask me to take m. to Albert, 430:21
knowing how to reply to m., 4:13
many a m. from skies, 358:1
medium is m., 764:10
messenger makes m. clear, 118:10
to Garcia, 564:10
Messages, future is somehow sending m., 858:21
Messed up life for nothing, 677:22
Messenger, bisy lark m. of day, 134:13
don't shoot the m., 65:*n*5
has God sent a mortal as m., 118:16
I will send my m., 29:19
with language of his folk, 118:10
Messenger-boy Presidency, 788:18
Messiah come only when no longer necessary, 655:15
Messing about in boats, 574:7
up your nice clean soul, 824:14
Met dearest foe in heaven, 197:7
guests are m., 375:18
hail fellow well m., 286:12
he had m. him before, 757:8
man who wasn't there, 631:12
me in evil hour, 356:17
mercy and truth are m. together, 17:21
never m. one I didn't like, 640:10
never m. or never parted, 357:9
no sooner m. but looked, 195:35
part of all I have m., 451:13
true when you m. her, 228:11
we have m. enemy, 393:11
you not with my true Love, 159:3
Metal, as m. keeps fragrance, 625:5
manual on uses of new m., 815:3
no use of m., 224:19
sonorous m. blowing, 255:22
Metals, keys of m. twain, 253:9
Metamorphosis separated me from day before, 616:5
Metaphor fertile power, 657:14
Holocaust m. for century, 831:9
mistaking m. for proof, 612:4
Metaphysical man is dead, 537:14
Mete and dole laws, 451:11
with what measure ye m., 33:13
Meteor of ocean air, 443:3
streamed like a m., 255:*n*1
streaming to the wind, 255:21
Meter ballad-mongers, 182:35
prose opposed to m., 378:19
Meter-making, not meters but m., 427:19
Method by which unconscious studied, 563:12
careful disorderliness is true m., 483:6
in man's wickedness, 238:4
invention of m. of invention, 580:8
madness yet m. in't, 198:37
new psychoanalytic m. irreplaceable, 562:16
of drawing up indictment, 324:8

Method *(continued)*
of making a fortune, 316:17
of scientific investigation, 502:3
take m. and try it, 651:15
what pragmatic m. means, 542:6
which rejects revenge, 823:10
Methods, know my m. Watson, 573:16
Methought I heard one calling Child, 243:2
I saw late espoused saint, 255:1
I saw the grave, 159:11
Methuselah, days of M., 6:14
Meticulous, politic cautious and m., 675:4
Métier, c'est son m., 415:10
mon m. et mon art c'est vivre, 152:*n*10
Metropolis, all great art born of the m., 664:15
has symptoms of mind gone berserk, 740:1
Metternich, Pope Czar M. Guizot, 478:7
Mettle enough to kill care, 191:15
grasp it like a man of m., 291:21
lad of m. a good boy, 182:16
Metuant, oderint dum m., 86:*n*8
Meum est propositum in taberna mori, 125:*n*1
Meurs, je m. de soif auprès de la fontaine, 137:*n*6
Meurt, la Garde m. mais ne se rend pas, 366:*n*6
Mew, cat m. and dog have day, 202:22
kitten and cry m., 182:35
Me-wards, to m. your affection's strong, 241:1
Mewing her mighty youth, 254:12
Mewling and puking, 194:25
Mexico, a Virgil at M., 317:4
not M. of course but in heart, 759:1
poor M. so far from God so close to U.S., 508:2
U.S. M. border, 818:7
Micawber's favorite expression, 465:22
Mice and men, 356:6
and rats and such small deer, 212:6
cat catches m. good cat, 737:7
cat in gloves catches no m., 302:30
desert building about to fall, 105:8
fishermen appear like m., 212:24
like little m. stole in and out, 261:5
three blind m., 892:10
Michael and his angels fought, 47:1
face like hoosier M. Angelo, 488:10
row the boat ashore, 898:22
Michelangelo, Italy produced M. Leonardo, 781:4
talking of M., 674:18
Miching mallecho, 200:17
Mickle, every little makes a m., 157:15
Microcosm and macrocosm atoned, 501:14
heart sun of their m., 236:1
Mid-air, you in m., 829:2
Midday, kindling eyes at m. beam, 254:12
Middle age time of improving, 261:12
beware the m. mind, 666:9
class best political community, 78:26
class in America the nation, 497:21
class the safety of England, 459:17
dead vast and m. of night, 197:11
enchantments of M. Age, 496:8
flowers of m. summer men of m. age, 223:26
in politics m. way none at all, 329:16
in the m. be sparing, 54:25
isthmus of a m. state, 295:1

Middle *(continued)*
   law of excluded m., 795:6
   of the night, 515:20
   ones of m. class who left home, 789:3
   safest in the m., 102:11
   station fewest disasters, 282:10
   vulgarizing m. class, 497:19
   wheel in the m. of a wheel, 28:14
   whole has beginning m. and end, 79:4
   wives companions for m. age, 165:20
Middle-aged build woodshed, 473:6
Middles are nowhere to be found, 829:9
Middlesex village and farm, 437:16
Midnight, cease upon the m., 410:9
   Cerberus and blackest M., 250:19
   clear, 457:11
   deep m. lair made, 373:18
   dreary, 449:3
   Good Morning M. coming Home, 509:3
   gravity out of bed at m., 182:24
   bags, 216:30
   he was my m., 748:14
   heard chimes at m., 188:15
   hour's sleep before m., 244:22
   iron tongue of m., 179:17
   it is m. and time passes, 56:8
   moan upon m. hours, 411:1
   moment's forest, 827:10
   mournful m. hours, 342:14
   Ninth-month m., 487:5
   on Emperor's pavement, 595:11
   once upon m. dreary, 449:3
   owl songs or m. blast, 399:4
   ride of Paul Revere, 437:15
   shout and revelry, 252:8
   strikes and hastens, 576:1
   through m. streets, 353:4
   time cease and m. never come, 169:3
   train whining low, 804:1
   troubled m. and noon's repose, 675:15
   wrote it is m., 744:20
   year's m., 229:11
Midshipmite, bo'sun tight and m., 525:16
Midst, him first last m., 258:15
   I am in m. of eternity, 552:4
   I am in the m. of them, 34:42
   in m. of life we are in death, 49:19
   in the m. of things, 98:25
   into the m. of the sea upon dry ground, 8:3
   stood in m. of Jordan, 9:36
Midsummer, gorgeous as sun at m., 183:12
   madness, 205:21
   merry Margaret as m. flower, 141:2
Midwest, lot of small towns in M., 877:3
Midwife, she is the fairies' m., 179:25
Midwifery, my m. like theirs, 76:5
Midwinter, bleak m., 512:6
Mien, monster of frightful m., 295:2
Mieux, je vais de m. en m., 568:*n*1
   le m. est l'ennemi du bien, 299:*n*7
   tout est au m., 299:*n*1
Might, dear m. of him that walked, 253:14
   do it with thy m., 23:22
   exceeds man's m., 203:19
   half slumbering, 409:3
   honest man's aboon his m., 358:19
   is right, 125:7
   it m. be so, 706:3

Might *(continued)*
   it m. have been, 438:10
   king's m. greater than human, 69:22
   love the Lord with all thy m., 9:15
   mighty man not glory in m., 27:33
   not by m. nor by power, 29:12
   of gods slow but sure, 68:11
   of the Gentile, 397:3
   protect us by thy m., 439:10
   right makes m., 444:16
   sadness of her m., 411:11
   shining with all m., 515:20
   spend her blood and m., 566:15
   spirit of counsel and m., 25:18
Might-have-been, name is M., 506:6
Mightier, cometh one m. than I, 36:25
   make thee m. yet, 580:19
   pen m. than sword, 423:13
   than the noise of many waters, 17:31
   than they in arms, 258:23
Mightiest in the mightiest, 186:1
   Julius fell, 196:15
Mightily, lay m. in whirl of dust, 52:3
   strive m. eat as friends, 173:11
Mighty above all things, 29:24
   all proud and m. have, 300:13
   all that m. heart lying still, 370:3
   Caesar thou art m. yet, 193:19
   dead, 300:17
   each a m. voice, 372:3
   eagle mewing her m. youth, 254:12
   fortress is our God, 143:16
   God who made thee m., 580:19
   hand of m. man, 19:6
   he that is slow to anger is better than the
     m., 20:38
   how are the m. fallen, 11:9
   I am m. world-destroying Time, 84:14
   in the Scriptures, 40:37
   lak' a rose, 569:3
   law m. mightier necessity, 344:9
   let m. babe alone, 263:12
   little body m. heart, 189:2
   look on my works ye M., 401:13
   man not glory in might, 27:33
   many and m. are they, 588:20
   Marlowe's m. line, 232:20
   maze not without plan, 294:14
   men of valor, 9:37
   men which were of old, 6:16
   Merchant sneered, 509:12
   Merciful and M., 391:8
   minds of old, 381:15
   name shall be called the m. God, 25:16
   O m. Caesar, 192:19
   pain to love, 265:10
   poets in misery dead, 370:1
   put down the m., 37:11
   scourge of war, 447:2
   so m. a Redeemer, 47:26
   some have called thee m., 230:22
   sound of m. wind, 40:14
   states characterless, 203:20
   things from small beginnings grow, 272:5
   to produce m. book choose m. theme,
     483:7
   true free Russian speech, 479:8
   weak things to confound m., 42:5

Mighty One, splendor of M. Krishna, 84:13
Mignonne allons voir si la rose, 150:*n*8
Migrate, come Muse m. from Greece, 487:3
Migration of the soul, 74:9
Migratory, unperplexed like m. birds,
   631:21
Mild and magnificent eye, 460:12
   gentle Jesus meek and m., 305:9
   grateful evening m., 258:1
   he is meek he is m., 350:13
   Mary was mother m., 476:5
   peace on earth mercy m., 305:10
Milder fate than tyranny is death, 63:7
   term to governments, 336:13
Mildewed day in August, 787:3
Mildness, ethereal m. come, 300:18
Mile, crooked m., 895:17
   miss as good as m., 374:18
Mile-a, your sad tires in a m., 223:24
Miles around wonder grew, 574:17
   of fertile ground, 377:17
   sed m. sed pro patria, 582:9
   see it lap the M., 509:10
   six m. from earth, 774:14
   to go before I sleep, 623:8
Milestones, counting m. count on, 443:1
   road to Hell without m., 717:12
Milieu, un m. entre rien et tout, 269:*n*2
Milishy, newspaper commands m., 600:16
Militarism, greatest bulwark of capitalism is m.,
   605:1
Militaristic stairway, 823:13
Military, civilian control of m., 661:11
   establishment, 686:16
   justice is to justice as m. music is to music,
     538:2
   man, 189:12
   mind, 599:3
   no adequate m. defense, 661:5
   now close m. career fade away, 644:11
   operation involves deception, 80:16
   war too serious for m., 348:11
   when I was in the m., 857:14
Military-industrial complex, 686:16
Militia, newspaper commands m., 600:16
   place dependence upon m., 328:8
   well-regulated m. necessary, 340:2
Milk, adversity's sweet m. philosophy,
   180:34
   and honey blest, 479:2
   black m. of daybreak, 794:6
   comes frozen home in pail, 174:33
   find trout in m., 473:2
   gin was mother's m. to her, 565:23
   in the pan, 426:7
   land flowing with m. and honey, 7:28
   money is mother's m., 801:1
   my ewes and weep, 223:33
   of human kindness, 214:16
   of Paradise, 377:23
   skim m. masquerades as cream, 526:2
   sweet m. of concord, 217:6
   take my m. for gall, 214:17
   white curd of ass's m., 295:14
Milked cow with crumpled horn, 897:8
Milking, going a-m. sir she said, 894:12
   lilting at ewe m., 321:8
   time of m., 678:14

Milks, love babe that m. me, 215:5
Milk-white, before m. now purple, 178:16
　　Hens of Dorking, 467:16
Milky, all the m. sky, 591:4
Milky Way, never look now at the M., 784:1
　　over Sado the M. Way, 280:3
　　penetrates M. without contact, 658:11
　　sister in whiteness, 643:21
　　solar walk or m., 294:20
　　twinkle on m., 371:10
Mill, at the m. with slaves, 260:8
　　cannot grind with water that's past, 243:21
　　God's m. grinds slow, 244:17
　　golf links so near m., 632:18
　　John Stuart M., 629:3
　　much water goeth by m., 148:14
　　of the mind, 596:13
　　of truism, 426:10
Milldams o' Binnorie, 890:2
Mille, plus de souvenirs que si m. ans, 491:*n5*
Millennial, give vent to m. anger, 793:1
Millennium, war usher in new m., 684:17
Miller, honest m. hath golden thumb, 134:*n1*
　　knoweth not of water, 148:14
　　sees not all the water, 148:*n8*
　　Stuhldreher M. Crowley Layden, 646:5
　　there was a jolly m., 330:19
Milliard-headed throng, 294:*n1*
Milliner, perfumed like a m., 181:35
Million, bought St. Louis for six m. dollars, 522:19
　　earth's five m. years old, 828:5
　　eight m. stories in naked city, 754:4
　　golden birds, 559:3
　　high man aiming at m., 461:15
　　eight m. stories in naked city, 754:4
　　make that thousand up a m., 241:3
　　multitude of m. divided by m., 741:16
　　play pleased not the m., 199:12
　　second m., 312:14
Millionaire, I am a M. that is my religion, 565:14
　　right of m. to millions, 521:16
Millions, cremate the m., 724:6
　　fate of unborn m., 328:6
　　for defense, 362:3
　　of debt, 324:15
　　of murders makes a hero, 683:15
　　of spiritual creatures, 258:2
　　of tongues record, 395:16
　　right of millionaire to m., 521:16
　　sufferings of m., 822:7
　　tear-wrung m., 619:*n3*
　　there's m. in it, 522:5
　　we mortal m. live alone, 495:10
　　with m. under his care, 4:2
　　yearly multiplying m., 469:11
　　yet unborn, 318:4
Millionth, encounter for m. time, 650:13
Mills, dark Satanic m., 354:8
　　of God grind slowly, 247:10
Millstone hanged about neck, 38:19
　　hard as a piece of nether m., 14:34
　　look through a m., 162:5
Millwheel, sight of m. depresses me, 468:17
Milton aggravated dissociation, 676:4
　　attracts into unity of ideal, 379:15
　　faith hold which M. held, 370:11

Milton *(continued)*
　　function as M., 645:8
　　malt does more than M., 575:12
　　mute inglorious M., 316:1
　　reason M. wrote in fetters, 351:10
　　test of M. to function as M., 645:8
　　thou shouldst be living, 370:9
　　was for us, 460:13
Miltonic, balanced and M. style, 547:10
Milton's wormwood words, 254:*n1*
Miltons, no mute inglorious M., 645:8
Miltown, tamed by M., 787:12
Mimic motion made cry, 641:8
Mimics, we are the m., 642:3
Miming, different m. performed by body, 136:23
Mimsy were borogoves, 515:12
Mince, not to m. the matter, 155:9
　　this matter, 208:27
Mincing poetry, 182:36
　　walking and m. as they go, 25:1
Mind, a certain unsoundness of m., 419:9
　　absence of m. we have borne, 383:21
　　accurate m. overtasked, 443:6
　　acts of m. itself, 379:17
　　all comes from the m., 64:12
　　allus on yer m., 647:8
　　and soul according, 453:10
　　as a dead man out of m., 16:2
　　as m. pitched ear pleased, 327:4
　　as we observe it, 802:2
　　aspire to higher things, 162:16
　　aware of own rectitude, 94:6
　　balloon of the m., 593:5
　　beauty exists in m., 311:23
　　beauty momentary in m., 641:5
　　become aware of itself, 428:17
　　beholding beauty with eye of m., 74:6
　　beings of m. are not of clay, 396:3
　　benevolence is man's m., 80:3
　　best work the human m., 358:2
　　beware the middle m., 666:9
　　block of wax, 76:7
　　body filled and vacant m., 189:23
　　bonds only in m., 611:3
　　breaks chains from every m., 352:5
　　bright child of m., 701:3
　　celestial Wisdom calms m., 306:20
　　chance favors prepared m., 499:1
　　changeful m. of mortals, 64:10
　　characteristics of vigorous m., 306:21
　　chaste breast quiet m., 265:17
　　clap padlock on her m., 283:12
　　clear your m. of cant, 311:11
　　clothed and in right m., 36:33
　　companion none like unto m., 149:9
　　complicated state of m., 526:10
　　concentrates his m. wonderfully, 310:12
　　conjunction of the m., 267:4
　　conscious m. trained like parrot, 630:7
　　courage gaiety quiet m., 556:12
　　cover the defects of the m., 313:22
　　creations of m. be blessing, 637:10
　　dagger of the m., 215:13
　　daylight in the m., 288:15
　　disdaining littlenesses, 76:6
　　distressed in m. body or estate, 48:15
　　dupe of the heart, 264:5

Mind *(continued)*
　　education forms common m., 293:24
　　employ m. to rule, 92:2
　　enabled to number worlds, 415:14
　　essay a loose sally of m., 306:25
　　exercises his m. with suffering, 80:6
　　eye see for hand not m., 474:5
　　face the mirror of the m., 115:13
　　fanatic can't change m., 621:17
　　farewell the tranquil m., 209:13
　　feed this m. of ours, 368:4
　　fiery particle, 398:29
　　first destroys their m., 69:*n3*
　　first from m. banish understanding, 69:*n3*
　　fool uttereth all his m., 22:9
　　free your m. and your ass will, 850:5
　　gentle m. by gentle deeds, 160:20
　　gentle sensitive m., 593:6
　　gentleness of spirit serenity of m., 245:*n2*
　　golden m. stoops not, 185:3
　　good in which m. at rest, 129:23
　　good m. possesses kingdom, 104:8
　　great fortitude of m., 308:12
　　greatest powers of m., 382:21
　　grief develops m., 611:6
　　had such burdens on m., 594:10
　　has mountains cliffs, 547:6
　　he that wants anger hath maimed m., 250:7
　　heart and m. of America, 749:22
　　heavy with useless experience, 824:15
　　her m. to be attached like garden, 544:6
　　his eyes are in his m., 178:*n1*
　　his m. is the nigger, 832:1
　　his own business, 156:16
　　household in oneness of m., 53:3
　　I am not in perfect m., 213:5
　　I had thee least in m., 880:17
　　if find answer know m. of God, 854:3
　　if I am to know may not m., 662:4
　　if no hatred in m., 593:16
　　impatient, 196:28
　　in adversity keep an even m., 96:20
　　in another Zeus puts a good m., 51:27
　　in m. of man a motion, 368:11
　　in my m. of mankind, 880:12
　　in purest play like bat, 797:14
　　in the m. ever burning, 159:4
　　inability of m. to correlate, 687:7
　　inaction saps vigor of m., 140:7
　　Indian whose untutored m., 294:20
　　is an aviary, 76:8
　　is an enchanting thing, 671:19
　　is city like London, 772:3
　　is its own place, 255:14
　　is stayed on thee, 26:3
　　is teeming with ideas, 669:2
　　know what going on in baby's m., 712:7
　　knowledge of unconscious activities of m., 563:1
　　known m. of the Lord, 41:28
　　labyrinthine ways of m., 576:13
　　last infirmity of noble m., 253:6
　　laugh that spoke vacant m., 322:25
　　let dauntless m. still ride, 170:28
　　let m. awake and revive, 139:5
　　leveling rancorous m., 595:6
　　liberation of the human m., 604:14
　　live on little with contented m., 90:18

Mind *(continued)*

lives on the Heart, 264:*n*1
look clean through the m., 162:5
love looks with the m., 178:1
love Lord with all thy m., 35:13
make up my m., 432:2
makes body rich, 173:22
man's unconquerable m., 370:8
marble index of a m., 368:16
march of human m. slow, 324:9
Marxism product of bourgeois m., 657:19
measure my mind against Shakespeare's, 565:15
military m., 599:3
mill of the m., 596:13
mingles with whole frame, 94:33
minister to m. diseased, 217:19
mirror in every m., 307:19
mode of working of human m., 502:3
moldering like wedding-cake, 824:15
movement so wandering as that of m., 152:13
moves upon silence, 597:4
my m. forbids to crave, 154:10
my m. is going, 784:4
my m. is my church, 333:19
my m. is troubled, 203:27
nature of m. mortal, 90:12
nature with equal m., 495:6
never brought to m., 357:17
noble m. here o'erthrown, 200:2
nobler in m. to suffer, 199:21
not body enough to cover m., 374:25
not enough to have good m., 246:5
not sex-typed, 729:4
not to be changed, 255:14
not yet of Percy's m., 182:17
of individual thinker, 757:15
of man becomes more beautiful, 369:2
of own beauty m. diseased, 396:12
old in body but never m., 88:15
old man's eagle m., 596:15
opinionated m., 593:17
oppressions of body and m., 338:8
or body to prefer, 295:1
our concern be peace of m., 82:13
out of sight out of m., 137:8
over matter, 415:15
painter's m. with viewer, 416:11
palm at end of m., 642:18
passion wholly of m., 713:4
peace is a state of m., 275:15
perfect body with your m., 837:9
persecutes the m., 274:1
persuaded in his m., 42:1
poem of act of m., 379:*n*2
poetry fine-spun from m. at peace, 102:21
power lies in m. and body, 92:2
presence of m. in danger, 276:9
prudent m. can see room, 66:9
purify the m., 64:13
quiet m. cureth all, 235:19
quiet m. richer than crown, 164:2
raise and erect the m., 164:14
reading to m. as exercise to body, 287:19
reason ignis fatuus of m., 281:2
reclothe us in our rightful m., 438:18
responds and connects, 123:7

Mind *(continued)*

rest to m. cheerer of spirits, 245:1
seek for the lost m., 80:4
seems to have become a machine, 441:3
serene for contemplation, 287:*n*3
so fine no idea could violate it, 675:16
sound m. in sound body, 109:26, 275:10
sound of body and m., 96:15
speculate on the m. of Newton, 440:7
Spirit of chainless M., 397:8
spirit of a sound m., 44:39
stations in a single M., 818:3
steal fire from m., 395:11
stops and steps of m., 677:15
stress on not changing m., 626:16
sublimity the echo of a noble m., 107:2
submitting things to desires of m., 164:14
subsoil of the m., 572:7
Sumner's m. contained itself, 531:20
suspicion haunts guilty m., 171:5
sweet to let m. unbend, 97:16
terrible thing to waste, 888:21
the music and the step, 883:15
the music breathing, 265:*n*5
this is the light of the m., 832:12
time out of m., 155:11
to me a kingdom is, 154:10
to men man is m., 540:2
to m. shameful to heart beauty, 492:9
torpid in old age, 310:14
tranquil m. a m. well ordered, 111:15
traveled crooked streets, 830:12
trick, 867:9
tumors of a troubled m., 260:12
tyranny over m. of man, 337:7
universal frame without m., 165:26
unsuitability of m. and purpose, 466:5
untutored m., 294:20
vacant is mind distressed, 326:14
villain's m., 184:32
was still unpledged, 68:1
water never formed to m., 641:8
weakness of human m., 276:3
weapon of oppressor m. of oppressed, 862:10
wet m. and say something clever, 72:11
what is M. No matter, 550:5
where is love but in m., 402:7
wisdom entereth not in malicious m., 145:10
words are physicians of m. diseased, 63:17
writing drains and supplies m., 724:9
your m. and you, 664:19
your m. tossing on ocean, 183:38
Minded what they were about, 313:19
Mind-forged manacles I hear, 353:3
Mindful of unhonored dead, 316:5
  what is man that thou art m., 15:5
Mindfulness, right m., 64:18
Mindless of its just honors, 372:16
Mind's, find the m. construction, 214:15
  in my m. eye Horatio, 197:8
  my m. not right, 787:16
  opaque depths of m. folds, 152:13
  putting m. eye in book, 795:6
  the standard of man, 289:4
Minds, admiration only of weak m., 259:31
  affect hearts and m., 692:4

Minds *(continued)*

all their m. transfigured, 179:7
all to have aspiring m., 168:2
balm of hurt m., 215:21
becks m. to fellowship, 409:9
best m. of my generation, 812:13
can heavenly m. yield, 93:29
comfortable m., 701:8
great empire and little m., 324:14
greatest m. capable of greatest vices, 246:6
grow in spots, 542:8
hearts and m., 49:8
hobgoblin of little m., 426:19
home in m. of men, 72:4
injured by hunger and thirst, 80:7
innocent and quiet, 266:2
keep your hearts and m., 44:6
let our m. be bold, 562:13
little things affect little m., 430:5
lose self in other m., 383:18
made better by presence, 480:16
marriage of true m., 222:15
me o' departed joys, 357:6
mighty m. of old, 381:15
naturally affirmative, 528:16
never do more than imperfectly reach, 709:1
O miserable m. of men, 90:1
of American women, 796:7
of gods not changed, 52:29
reason freed men's m., 104:9
record of best m., 404:14
refuge of weak m., 298:13
religion of feeble m., 325:8
show how myths operate in m., 754:2
so many men so many m., 86:*n*6
speak m. of others to speak my own better, 152:6
stay our m. be staid, 624:18
steadiest m. to waver, 65:19
strongest m. world hears least, 372:5
themselves our m. impress, 368:4
to different m., 425:7
young men's m. are changeable, 50:28
Mine, because it is all mine, 827:12
every beast of the forest is m., 16:29
eyes have seen glory, 481:1
fatal words M. and Thine, 155:17
I am Tarzan I am yours you are m., 629:9
I'm going to get what's m., 866:2
lives ye led were m., 586:16
mother o' m., 587:10
she is m. for life, 791:16
was always like that, 744:21
was ever grief like m., 242:14
what is yours is m., 83:8
what's m. is yours, 207:19
why shouldst thou have m., 261:6
will defend what's m., 158:*n*7
with my heart in it, 224:28
Mineola, track star for M. Prep, 814:4
Mineral, information vegetable animal m., 526:6
Minerals, poisonous m. and that tree, 230:21
Minerva, owl of M. spreads wings, 367:8
Mingle blood with blood of children, 419:3
in one spirit meet m., 402:16
letters m. souls, 230:14
not want to m. in the fray, 386:5

Misery *(continued)*
  too much m. in world, 440:6
Misfit, good woman The M. said, 809:6
Misfortune, bad neighbor is m., 54:22
  brought me to edge of despair, 366:17
  in other countries poverty m., 423:11
  it's your m. none of my own, 890:11
  lose one parent m., 560:22
  made throne her seat, 289:2
  never delight in another's m., 100:13
  not to be born, 534:2
  of our best friends, 264:31
  remembrance of former m., 156:21
  shows who not really friends, 79:7
  to have been happy is most unhappy m.,
    117:2
Misfortune's, sour m. book, 181:11
Misfortunes, crimes and m., 299:25
  delight in real m. of others, 323:12
  endure m. of others, 263:15
  follies and m. of mankind, 332:5
  not unacquainted with m., 53:19
  of man occasioned by man, 105:4
Misgiving, room for m., 66:9
Misgivings, not view process with m., 619:18
Misgovernment, augur m., 324:7
Mislead, lights that m. morn, 207:8
Misleading, long run m. guide, 656:11
Misled, simplicity no longer m., 339:8
Mislike me not for complexion, 184:33
  not my speeches you m., 169:23
Misprint, poet not survive m., 559:19
Mispronounce, all men m. it, 688:2
Misquote, enough learning to m., 394:14
Miss as good as mile, 374:18
  I m. kisses I m. bites, 707:5
  many-splendored thing, 577:4
  march of retreating world, 699:9
  mine he cannot m., 162:14
  Nature cannot m., 274:27
  pain that pain to m., 265:10
  see nor know nor m. me, 651:3
Miss Lonelyhearts priests of twentieth-century,
    736:12
Miss T., whatever M. eats, 616:11
Missed, for everything m. gained something,
    426:27
  I wouldn't have m. it, 732:13
  never would be m., 527:10
  stars might not have m., 624:15
  woman much m., 536:18
  whatever we m. we possessed, 615:14
  wonder what you've m., 748:9
Misses an unit, 461:15
  Heaven's net m. nothing, 58:3
  man who m. opportunity, 348:9
Missing, I am what is m., 839:1
  nobody is ever m., 773:9
  Rosebud m. piece in jigsaw puzzle, 714:16
  what m. at the man's heart, 773:17
Mission, glorious m. of unions, 554:5
  in life is not to succeed, 556:11
  to come down alive, 802:8
Missionaries, things she held against m., 802:6
Missionary leave China convert Christians,
    525:4
  not be confused with m. work, 802:11
  not visited our planet, 482:16

Missionary *(continued)*
  stew, 677:3
Mississippi, commence travels in M. steamboat,
    389:2
  Delta, 855:14
  of falsehood called History, 496:11
  rolling mile-wide tide along, 522:13
Missouri, 'cross the wide M., 897:19
  I am from M., 559:14
  sound of rampaging M., 811:6
Misspelled, Nothing but Sex M., 837:15
Mist, came both m. and snow, 375:23
  gray m. on sea's face, 635:15
  in my face, 462:24
  of tears, 576:13
  only m. is real, 776:8
  swoln with rank m., 253:11
  white in blue m. on foam, 470:1
Mistake, admit m. and amend ways, 60:17
  America giant m., 564:6
  biggest damfool m., 686:17
  blue and gold m., 508:6
  first m. of Art, 865:15
  is has been shall be no m., 366:12
  last man to die for a m., 857:11
  man found way into life by mistake, 579:16
  never overlooks m., 502:5
  not to close eyes, 582:6
  of enclosing envelope, 662:10
  of my life, 522:19
  pardon Thy M., 745:5
  pray make no m., 527:13
  to suppose only five senses, 500:10
  when I make m. it's a beaut, 651:5
  woman God's second m., 549:1
Mistaken, I pronounce m., 264:n3
  intuitive calculation, 629:11
  think that we may be m., 614:2
  think that you may be m., 246:16
Mistakes, experience name for m., 560:11
  making m. in centuries, 866:9
  man of genius no m., 650:16
  physician can bury m., 606:6
  we all make m., 782:10
Mistaking paradox for discovery, 612:4
Mister Death, 701:7
  never apologize, m., 755:1
Mistress, art a jealous m., 428:7
  as with maid so with her m., 25:32
  court a m. she denies you, 232:14
  in my own, 589:6
  law a jealous m., 388:6
  literature my m., 578:1
  my m. the open road, 556:5
  necessity m. of nature, 140:10
  no casual m. but wife, 454:2
  no legal slaves except m. of house, 435:19
  O m. mine, 204:24
  of herself, 294:4
  of mistresses, 491:4
  or a friend, 403:11
  riches good handmaid worst m., 165:5
  should be like a country retreat, 279:10
  such m. such Nan, 151:1
  teeming m. barren bride, 293:26
Mistress' eyebrow, 194:25
  my m. eyes nothing like the sun, 223:1
  orders to perform, 297:2

Mistresses, mistress of m., 491:4
  others go to bed with m., 557:12
  wives young men's m., 165:20
Mistrust, more ignominious to m., 264:2
Mists, errors wanderings m. and tempests,
    89:n12
  foul and ugly m., 181:33
  mothlike in m., 659:1
  season of m., 411:6
  the Apennine, 508:7
Misty moisty morning, 897:1
  mountaintops, 181:2
  out of m. dream, 599:17
  sheiling of m. island, 417:4
Misunderstand, no fate willfully m., 622:19
Misunderstanding, culture a m. if not French,
    549:6
Misunderstandings, fame is only sum of m.,
    631:16
Misunderstands, how often he m. others, 343:15
Misunderstood, He is the great m., 490:16
  he throws to be m., 728:1
  to be great to be m., 426:20
Misuse, oft happeth to m. wit, 136:15
Misused, sweet poison of m. wine, 252:4
Mite, can't make m. makes gods, 152:20
Mites, widow threw in two m., 37:2
Mither, father and m. gae mad, 357:16
  leave to m. dear, 889:18
Mithridates he died old, 575:13
Mitte sectari rosa, 96:n13
Mixed, elements so m. in him, 193:22
  in wrong that's all, 681:3
Mixing memory and desire, 676:5
Mixture, good things come in m., 383:23
  that strange m. of blood, 331:2
Mizpah, name of it called M., 7:1
Moab is my washpot, 17:2
Moan, delicious m., 411:1
  frosty wind made m., 512:6
  made sweet m., 412:4
  of doves in elms, 453:7
  paid with m., 576:12
Moananoaning, moyles of it m., 651:3
Moaning, harbor bar m., 481:5
  no m. of the bar, 456:4
  now they are m., 321:8
Moans, amid no earthly m., 448:5
  round with many voices, 451:18
Moat defensive to a house, 176:24
  of risotto, 850:8
Moated grange, 207:4, 450:7
Mob, amphibious ill-born m., 282:5
  at times m. swayed, 624:18
  begin to think and reason, 347:3
  damned m. of scribbling women, 431:22
  honor depends on opinion of m., 276:16
  hungry m. is angry m., 861:6
  I am the m., 636:1
  is varied and inconstant, 276:16
  not ask better only different, 143:15
  of gentlemen, 296:14
  redress of m. law, 444:3
  supreme governors the m., 317:1
Mobile, donna è m., 94:n10
Mobilized, when armies are m., 58:1
Moby Dick whale or man, 696:9
  evil assailable in M., 483:3

Mock, after I have spoken m. on, 13:42
   air with idle state, 316:14
   at the great, 594:10
   fools make a m. at sin, 20:24
   meat it feeds on, 209:3
   on Voltaire Rousseau, 353:12
   spirits of wise m. us, 188:5
   their own presage, 222:10
   their useful toil, 315:17
   time with fairest show, 215:8
   Turtle, 514:21, 514:22
   your own grinning, 202:12
Mocked, God is not m., 43:33
   my sense is m., 227:17
   smiles as if he m. himself, 191:30
Mocker, wine is a m., 21:9
Mockery king of snow, 177:20
   monumental m., 203:22
   of monumental stone, 403:21
   of sham of m. of travesty, 839:9
   religion is dream and m., 421:8
   unreal m. hence, 216:21
Mocketh, whoso m. the poor, 20:39
Mockingbird, sin to kill a m., 813:4
Mockingbird's, out of m. throat, 487:5
Mocks, man that m. and sets it light, 176:17
   married men, 174:32
   my loss of liberty, 350:8
Model, Americans may become m., 321:9
   British government best m., 349:3
   little m. was Benjamin, 663:4
   of Deportment, 466:13
   of modern Major-General, 526:6
   republican m. of government, 328:11
   small m. of barren earth, 177:8
   to thy inward greatness, 189:2
Models, turn pages of Greek m., 98:28
Moderate, give m. alarm, 433:4
   liberty is in m. governments, 349:5
   that fondness for your children, 297:10
   white m. devoted to order, 823:3
Moderately, a thing m. good, 333:17
   love m., 180:25
   rescue wife, 433:4
Moderation, astonished at my own m., 320:5
   gone no court can save, 614:1
   in all things, 85:13
   in justice no virtue, 758:10
   in principle a vice, 333:17
   in pursuit of justice no virtue, 758:10
   in temper a virtue, 333:17
   keep to m., 106:11
   spirit of m. flourishes, 614:1
   stoutness in m., 526:15
   urge me not to m., 433:4
Moderator of passions, 245:1
Modern, all history m., 643:3
   American literature from one book, 721:14
   disease of m. life, 495:17
   evil in the m. world, 765:14
   feelings about m. life, 767:8
   idea antiquated once m., 616:18
   in love with m. world, 870:1
   inconveniences, 522:21
   key-machine of m. industrial age, 708:4
   man invents museum, 708:5
   old or m. bard, 252:3
   one must be absolutely m., 559:13

Modern *(continued)*
   single sentence for m. man, 770:9
   something for m. stage, 665:6
   to be m. is to find ourselves, 846:7
   wise saws and m. instances, 194:25
Moderns only have opinions, 415:6
   speak of m. without contempt, 298:9
Modest and commonly chaste, 400:7
   coy submission m. pride, 257:20
   doubt, 203:12
   keep m. as giver, 548:1
   looks cottage adorn, 322:28
   no more m. than immodest, 486:7
   quip m., 196:6
   stillness and humility, 189:7
   wee m. crimson-tipped, 356:17
Modesty a species of nobility, 276:9
   ancient sculpture true m., 393:10
   blushing m., 101:21
   o'erstep not m. of nature, 200:7
Modification, bad plan admits no m., 100:14
Modified limited hang-out, 844:*n*1
   single substance variously m., 311:18
Modifying colors of imagination, 379:8
Modum, servare m., 106:*n*9
Modus, est m. in rebus, 95:*n*7
Möglichen, Politik ist die Lehre von M., 470:*n*4
Moi, le m. est haïssable, 269:*n*10
   l'état c'est m., 278:*n*4
   pretentious m., 845:2
Moider, I'll m. de bum, 761:10
Moi-même, je suis m. la matière de mon livre, 151:*n*6
Moist, cold and hot m. and dry, 273:22
   eye dry hand, 187:31
   hot cold m. and dry, 257:1
   in mystical m. night-air, 487:6
   unpleasant body, 464:21
Moisty morning, 897:1
Mojo, I got my m. working, 840:2
Molar to molecular motions, 538:18
Molars, writers divided into incisors and m., 503:2
Mold, made him and then broke m., 142:14
   of form, 200:3
   splashing wintry m., 591:9
Molded, best men m. of faults, 207:18
   changing lineaments, 534:5
   two berries m. on one stem, 178:29
Moldering, a-m. in grave, 521:1
   mind m. like wedding-cake, 824:15
Molders hemp and steel, 374:8
Molding, wine jar when m. began, 98:17
Molds, crack nature's m., 211:24
   musket in his hands, 554:2
Mole is deep penetration agent, 830:6
   live like velvet m., 666:5
   wilt thou go ask the M., 351:9
Molecular motions, 538:18
Molecule, propensity to unite even in m., 648:3
Molecules, preserve m. known as genes, 850:9
   simple and indivisible m., 339:1
Moles, cast his idols to m., 24:34
Molle atque facetum, 95:*n*11
Mollify it with tears, 619:*n*3
Mollusk cheap edition of man, 428:26
Molly Stark a widow, 323:11
Moloch sceptered king, 256:7

Molten, inns of M. Blue, 508:9
   tears scald like m. lead, 213:4
Moly, flickers in grass the m., 822:11
Mome raths outgrabe, 515:12
Moment, brief shining m. Camelot, 790:14
   culture m. of clarity, 657:8
   endures m. or day, 594:13
   eternity was in that m., 286:22
   exhaust the little m., 783:8
   first m. of atomic age, 774:13
   force m. to its crisis, 675:2
   from the impulse of the m., 382:6
   great pith and m., 199:21
   hide thyself for a little m., 26:5
   hold every m. sacred, 631:11
   I cut his throat, 805:11
   I live in m. in unmortal space, 731:15
   in a m. of time, 37:23
   intense m. isolated, 679:1
   knew precise m. to say nothing, 560:3
   know the right m., 55:10
   last m. belongs to us, 682:11
   lifetime burning in m., 679:1
   loyal and neutral in m., 216:1
   men flourish only for a m., 54:5
   not of action or inaction, 84:*n*8
   nothing startles beyond M., 412:14
   of difficulty and danger, 339:8
   of greatness flicker, 675:3
   of strength of romance, 567:10
   of time fleeting by, 533:15
   only a m., 567:10
   only m. here and m. there, 625:6
   perfection but m., 221:1
   power of man and m., 496:4
   present m. of time, 541:6
   psychological m., 560:3
   quick wild lovely m., 704:8
   she is introduced, 458:17
   that his face I see, 377:3
   the Decisive M., 752:1
   this m. in June, 654:5
   this which you deem of no m., 76:12
   time of death every m., 84:*n*8
   to decide, 481:12
   trap m. before ripe, 352:7
   when man finds out who he is, 719:2
   when the bird sings, 845:12
   your m. of Zen, 877:10
Momentariness, take your delight in m., 706:2
Momentary, beauty m. in mind, 641:5
Moment's, midnight m. forest, 827:10
   monument, 506:4
   seem a m. thought, 591:18
   sent to be m. ornament, 371:6
Moments, art gives quality to m., 534:9
   best and happiest m., 404:14
   hardly dared pass, 725:11
   practiced at spare m., 626:22
   when everything goes well, 585:13
   young have no m., 568:7
Momentum, psychological m., 560:*n*1
Mom's, never eat at place called M., 757:11
Mona Lisa, you're the smile on M., 691:12
Monan's, moon on M. rill, 373:18
Monarch, becomes throned m. better than crown, 186:1
   but would give his crown, 249:22

Monarch *(continued)*
   hears, 274:15
   merry m. scandalous and poor, 281:1
   morsel for a m., 218:14
   of all I survey, 326:16
   of the vine, 218:27
   richest m. in world, 359:16
Monarchs, fate summons m. obey, 273:13
   perplexes m., 255:25
Monarchy, British m. mystery is life, 503:5
   is a merchantman, 355:2
   universal m. of wit, 245:13
Monastery, years in a Japanese m., 781:2
Monastic aisles, 424:4
Monday, born on a M., 895:10
   snatched on M. night, 181:22
   unromantic as M. morning, 472:13
Monday's child fair of face, 895:9
Monde, l'amour fait tourner le m., 891:4
   tard dans m. trop vieux, 457:*n*2
Mondes, ce meilleur des m. possibles, 299:*n*1
Monet is only an eye, 533:18
Money, a little wanton m., 143:6
   and goods best references, 466:28
   and room of her own, 654:14
   answereth all things, 23:24
   beautiful as roses, 427:23
   begets money, 271:3
   bet my m. on bobtail nag, 503:10
   billion here there talking real m., 709:13
   blessing m. cannot buy, 245:9
   business may bring m., 382:20
   business other people's m., 501:8
   corporate m. in politics, 795:13
   counting out m., 894:7
   disease called lack of m., 145:11
   doänt marry for m., 455:26
   doesn't talk it swears, 851:10
   follow the m., 829:13
   fool and his m., 881:10
   forget how the m. was made, 803:6
   Friendship last if not asked to lend m., 523:19
   gives me pleasure, 606:15
   goä wheer m. is, 455:26
   government consists in taking m., 299:19
   hired the m. didn't they, 613:9
   honey and plenty of m., 467:7
   how painful to keep m., 277:23
   is like muck, 165:25
   is mother's milk, 801:1
   is not an infantile wish, 563:4
   is power, 543:15
   it turned out was exactly like, 804:13
   keeps m. movin' around, 600:14
   knowledge m. power, 766:4
   lawyers can steal more m., 795:8
   like sixth sense, 626:18
   love of m. as possession, 656:15
   love of m. root of evil, 44:35
   love of m. taken hold, 433:9
   make m. by any means, 97:19
   making m. like bee, 64:19
   man without m. rather than m. without man, 62:19
   may rub off on you, 660:8
   means and content, 195:5
   much m. as 'twill bring, 262:16

Money *(continued)*
   never without thinking of m., 471:14
   no m. no resources no hopes, 690:17
   no one ever lost m., 645:15
   no trick to make a lot of m., 714:15
   not good unless spread, 165:25
   nothing lost but m., 752:13
   nothing so demoralizing as m., 65:14
   old wife old dog ready m., 302:17
   on love request for m. chilling, 493:16
   only sick music makes m., 548:20
   pays m. takes choice, 550:4
   power to make m. is gift from God, 535:4
   pretty to see what m. will do, 277:19
   prose of life, 427:23
   put m. in thy purse, 208:8
   put m. in trust, 443:8
   rage and love, 742:1
   ready m. makes the man, 289:18
   reputation more valuable than m., 99:19
   retreated back into m., 710:6
   rich have more m., 721:*n*4
   rub up against m., 660:8
   seed of money, 312:14
   sets world in motion, 100:28
   sex is like m., 833:18
   show me the m., 875:1
   silk suit cost much m., 277:1
   sinew of love, 88:*n*8
   sinews of business, 88:*n*8
   sinews of war, 88:18
   society for previntion of croolty to m., 535:*n*1
   speaks sense, 279:6
   they have more m., 721:15
   thy m. perish with thee, 40:19
   time is m., 303:5, 422:*n*1
   times hard m. scarce, 428:23
   to even get beat with, 640:8
   use m. for good of fellow man, 535:4
   voice is full of m., 710:5
   war begun without m., 145:7
   way the m. goes, 885:6
   we're in or out of m., 759:9
   we're in the m., 689:10
   we've got the m. too, 503:17
   Willy Loman never made m., 780:5
   with lent m. evil done, 484:17
   words are m. of fools, 239:5
   world his who has m., 428:6
   wrote except for m., 310:8
   you never give me your m., 848:18
Moneybag, Aristocracy of M., 407:9
Moneychanger, morals of m., 603:13
Moneychangers, tables of the m., 35:8
Moneymaker, not a mere m., 74:19
Money's, stand aghast at m. significance, 568:17
Mongrel puppy whelp hound, 322:13
   son and heir of m. bitch, 211:13
Monism thinks all-form only form, 542:10
Monitor expressed, 372:7
Monk, cowl does not make m., 120:12
   I said to this m., 828:3
   only connect beast and m., 638:10
Monkey, as soon be descended from m., 440:12
   disappointed in m., 524:24
   heroic little m., 440:12

Monkey *(continued)*
   higher m. climbs more see of behind, 126:6
   in the tree, 887:2
   never look long on m., 440:*n*2
   thirty-five pound m. on his back, 757:8
Monkeys, army of m. strumming on typewriters, 649:6
   cats and m. m. and cats, 544:4
   New and Old World m., 440:10
   people are all m. to me, 663:8
   they remind me of m., 608:10
   wilderness of m., 185:14
Monks, sit like m. in London, 830:5
Monogamy, at its best m. may be, 872:9
Monopoly has same effect as trade secret, 319:1
   no m. of war powers, 694:8
   no single nation have m., 661:5
Monotonous languor, 549:17
Monotony, bleats articulate m., 372:*n*1
   time consequent upon m., 631:2
Monroe Doctrine, 355:5
   will go far, 571:5
Monsieur, farewell M. Traveler, 195:25
Monster begot upon itself, 209:22
   green-eyed m., 209:3
   I had created, 415:17
   I have lived in the m., 557:16
   man-hero not exceptional m., 642:8
   manunkind, 702:1
   many-headed m. of pit, 296:17
   marriage must ceaselessly combat m., 417:11
   more hideous than sea m., 211:10
   not encountered in private life, 770:10
   of wickedness, 620:8
   queer m. the artist, 545:7
   see to it not become m., 548:8
   universe suspended on tooth of m., 578:14
   vice m. of frightful mien, 295:2
   what a m. is man, 269:25
   with uncounted heads, 187:21
Monsters, America goes not abroad in search of m., 363:2
   from the Id, 725:13
   Imagination abandoned by Reason produces m., 341:*n*4
   sleep of reason produces m., 341:13
   thinking woman sleeps with m., 825:1
   whoever fights m., 548:8
Monstrosity and miracle myself, 153:18
   more prodigious than Hydra, 97:*n*13
Monstrous anger of guns, 699:6
   big river down there, 523:5
   bottom of m. world, 253:12
   every fault seeming m., 195:16
   little voice, 178:5
   O m., 182:31
   regiment of women, 150:1
   two evils m. either, 681:18
Monstruos, sueño de la razón m., 341:13
Montague, fair M. I am too fond, 180:6
Montaigne, in his tower, 737:8
Montes, parturient m. nascetur mus, 98:*n*9
Montesquieu, celebrities such as M., 518:9
   thanks to M., 347:4
Montezuma, halls of M., 885:2
Montgomery to Oslo, 823:11
Month, April cruellest m., 676:5
   follow month with woe, 403:19

Moral *(continued)*
everything's got a m., 514:19
find m. in narrative be banished, 522:22
flabbiness, 542:4
gloom of world, 430:25
grandeur, 782:1
law within me, 320:2
natural and m. forces, 494:6
natural philosophy deep m. grave, 166:19
no m. or immoral book, 559:23
of m. evil and of good, 368:6
perception of beauty m. test, 473:5
point a m. or adorn tale, 306:17
positive m. sense, 531:6
real progress is m. progress, 491:15
regeneration of mankind, 435:20
saintliness a m. procedure, 761:15
satire ever m. ever new, 278:7
sense of work of art, 544:16
soil for aesthetic growth, 618:9
spark out of stone easier than m., 528:18
things m. or things evangelical, 271:16
thinks is m. when uncomfortable, 565:7
true war story is never m., 863:11
what is beautiful is m., 494:2
what you feel good after, 721:11
will ends by settling m., 531:6
wise and m. man, 64:19
Moralists, come from set of m., 726:11
tampering to put in edifying light, 726:11
Moralities, never mind about m., 524:19
Morality, conventionality not m., 472:9
dirty joke not attack upon m., 735:9
enliven m. with wit, 288:4
for morality's sake, 400:17
I who dispensed with m., 559:12
ignorance of m., 269:8
intimation of m. part of New York, 724:6
not doctrine of how we make ourselves
happy, 320:3
of common man, 548:14
periodical fits of m., 419:13
private costly luxury, 531:27
taste is the only m., 484:19
temper wit with m., 288:4
true m. takes no heed of m., 269:6
unawares M. expires, 297:6
Moralize my song, 160:2
Moralized his song, 160:*n*1
Morally, journalist m. indefensible, 838:5
Morals, book on m. attacking women, 136:22
code of modern m., 403:11
conventional m., 614:17
faith and m. hold, 370:11
great secret of m. is love, 404:13
have you no m. man, 565:21
if your m. make you dreary, 556:2
of moneychanger, 603:13
time legalizer of m., 645:1
Moravians, no M. in Moon, 482:16
Morbidity, somewhat disgusting m., 656:15
Morbus, senectus insanabilis m. est, 427:*n*1
Mordecai rent his clothes, 12:31
More and more about less and less, 581:3
and more and more, 516:3
cantie wi' m., 357:5
Cawdor shall sleep no m., 215:22
celebrities such as M., 518:9

More *(continued)*
come through alive, 52:1
easy to take m. than nothing, 514:16
for I have m., 231:3
grow from m. to m., 453:10
how much m. is half than whole, 54:18
is man of angel's wit, 143:11
know what is m. than enough, 351:18
little m. than kin, 196:24
loved Rome m., 192:25
Macbeth shall sleep no m., 215:22
matter with less art, 198:27
meant than meets ear, 251:22
nicely calculated less or m., 372:14
no man entitled to, 571:8
no m. dear love, 453:4
no m. of that, 210:20
Oliver asked for m., 464:6
say m. than this rich praise, 221:26
sleep no m., 215:21
the m. the merrier, 148:17
there isn't any m., 637:3
to be desired than gold, 15:17
to say when I am dead, 606:1
Mores, O tempora O m., 87:6
Mori, pro patria m., 96:*n*18
ut se m. sentiat, 104:*n*7
Moriarty Napoleon of crime, 573:18
Morir, mejor m. a pie, 643:*n*1
Morituri, ave Caesar m. te salutamus, 111:*n*1
Morn and liquid dew of youth, 197:19
approach of even or m., 257:6
as yet 'tis early m., 451:20
cock trumpet to m., 196:17
day's at m., 459:19
each M. a thousand Roses, 441:9
fair laughs the m., 316:15
from m. to noon he fell, 256:5
healthy breath of m., 411:12
in russet mantle clad, 196:20
incense-breathing M., 315:15
lark herald of the m., 181:1
lights that mislead m., 207:8
lived the space of a m., 162:24
not waking till she sings, 162:9
on the Indian steep, 252:10
opening eyelids of the m., 253:3
peeping in at m., 418:2
red m. betokened wrack, 171:11
rose the morrow m., 377:7
rouse the slumbering m., 251:1
September m., 438:11
sweet is breath of m., 257:26
this the happy m., 250:9
tresses like the m., 252:25
ushers in the m., 304:11
waked by circling hours, 258:22
Morne plaine, 422:*n*5
Mornin', hangin' Danny Deever in m., 587:15
nice to get up in m., 607:9
top o' the m., 551:3
Morning after, 597:18
after Death, 510:11
air awash with angels, 797:12
all whom m. sends to roam, 575:19
almost at odds with m., 216:24
as Adam early in the m., 486:23
as fed horses in the m., 27:24

Morning *(continued)*
as m. shows the day, 260:1
a-walking one m. for pleasure, 890:10
birdsong at m., 556:6
breaks, 127:13
dissolutely spent Tuesday m., 181:22
early in m., 897:17
early in the m. our song, 391:8
evening and m. were first day, 5:4
fair came forth, 260:7
farewell M. Star, 87:4
forehead of the m. sky, 253:14
fresh as the m., 487:13
full many a glorious m., 221:10
give him the m. star, 46:24
glorious m. for America, 318:5
glut sorrow on m. rose, 411:10
Good M. Midnight coming Home, 509:3
good m. sadness, 705:8
hangin' Danny Deever in m., 587:15
if they take you in the m., 804:15
in Bowl of Night, 441:5
in m. we remember them, 603:14
in the m. it flourisheth, 17:23
in the m. like grass, 17:23
in the m. of the times, 164:*n*5
in the m. we drink, 794:6
it was whole m. world, 761:2
joy cometh in the m., 16:1
looketh forth as the m., 24:19
love m. and evening star, 664:6
matter for May m., 205:22
misty moisty m., 897:1
my Lord what a m., 898:24
my m. incense, 347:8
napalm in the m., 845:3
nice to get up in m., 607:9
of the world, 459:21
oh what a beautiful m., 706:8
penitence next m., 464:28
praise at m. blame at night, 292:22
quintessence of life, 400:6
shadow at m. striding, 676:6
shining m. face, 194:25
singing each m., 701:18
some m. unaware, 460:18
son of the m., 25:22
sorrow makes night m., 171:30
sow thy seed in the m., 23:28
star you shone among living, 403:*n*1
stars drift away in invisible m., 816:7
stars sang together, 14:19
they that watch for m., 19:8
think in the m., 351:16
this m. came home cloak, 277:1
till m. in the land of Nod, 555:11
tonight no m. star, 828:13
two o'clock in m. courage, 365:18
uncertain hour before m., 679:9
when m. sun lights up, 803:13
white light of m., 891:13
wings of the m., 19:13
woe to them that rise early in m., 25:5
womb of m. dew, 160:10
work at Auschwitz in m., 825:12
would God it were m., 9:27
Morning's at seven, 459:19
early m. strangely silent, 750:4

Morning's *(continued)*
  minion, 546:9
Mornings, forgotten m., 777:8
Morose, obstinate pliant merry m., 107:18
  view of present, 420:3
Morphine, steeped amid honeyed m., 486:10
Morrison, James James M. M., 651:6
Morrow, a little fun and good m., 519:8
  cease to ask what m. will bring, 96:10
  desire of night for the m., 404:6
  good m. to our waking souls, 228:7
  good night till it be m., 180:16
  man's yesterday ne'er like m., 401:12
  misty m. a myrie someris day, 132:17
  night urge the m., 403:19
  put no trust in the m., 96:11
  rainy m., 221:29
  rash who reckons on m., 66:12
  rose the m. morn, 377:7
  take no thought for m., 33:11
Mors, nil igitur m. est ad nos, 90:*n4*
  ultima ratio, 120:33
Morsel for a monarch, 218:14
  I found you as a m., 218:33
  under tongue sweet m., 282:13
Morsels, tough m. to swallow, 548:18
Mort, Ô m. vieux capitaine, 491:*n9*
  que la m. me trouve plantant mes choux,
    152:*n2*
Mortal arm and nerve feel, 374:8
  behind m. Bone, 509:1
  coil, 199:21
  disgraced and m., 742:6
  dreams no m. dared, 449:7
  element bearable to no m., 762:16
  every tatter in m. dress, 594:2
  frame, 378:3
  genius and m. instruments, 192:2
  grief itself be m., 403:18
  grows on m. soil, 253:7
  has God sent m. as messenger, 118:16
  I sing with m. voice, 258:25
  immortal Death has taken m. life, 90:13
  knew my son was m., 73:26
  laugh at m. thing, 398:20
  locked up from m. eye, 263:4
  made thee neither m. nor immortal, 141:3
  melody, 448:1
  millions live alone, 495:10
  moon eclipse endured, 222:10
  nature did tremble, 371:1
  nature of mind m., 90:12
  no m. could vie with Zeus, 52:31
  not m. what you desire, 102:10
  O you m. engines, 209:13
  only m. sounds can awake, 815:16
  purest treasure m. times afford, 176:8
  put on immortality, 43:8
  quit this m. frame, 293:2
  raised a m. to the skies, 274:22
  reason immortal all else m., 58:10
  shall m. man be more just, 13:9
  shuffled off this m. coil, 199:21
  sins of commission m., 311:19
  stakes, 624:1
  struck a deep m. blow, 63:6
  sufferest m. griefs, 189:22
  temples of king, 177:8

Mortal *(continued)*
  tend on m. thoughts, 214:17
  therefore Caius is m., 507:6
  things doth sway, 160:22
  think all men m. but themselves, 290:24
  think m. thoughts, 67:12
  tree whose m. taste, 255:3
  what m. heard good of George the Third,
    629:*n3*
Mortalem vitam mors cum immortalis, 90:*n5*
Mortality, nothing serious in m., 215:30
  pilgrims of m., 673:22
  to frail m. trust, 166:23
  touches the heart, 94:4
  watch o'er man's m., 371:5
  weighs on me like sleep, 411:16
Mortality's strong hand, 175:26
Mortals are blaming the gods, 52:22
  changeful mind of m., 64:10
  fellow m. accepted as they are, 480:2
  Hope lies to m., 575:21
  make earth bitter, 407:5
  miserable m. like leaves, 52:12
  no ascent too steep for m., 96:3
  not in m. to command success, 287:22
  what all m. may correct, 285:9
  what fools these m. be, 103:8, 178:28
  when to mischief m. bend, 293:11
Mortar, as if chest a m., 483:3
  lies m. that bind, 598:14
Mortgaged, they m. off their lives, 857:4
Mortification, live in continual m., 301:6
Mortify a wit, 296:17
Mortifying reflections, 440:*n2*
  when woman considers difference of
    education, 340:15
Mortis, Timor M. conturbat me, 141:6
Mortised, tenoned and m. in granite, 486:4
Mortuis, de m. nil nisi bonum, 55:*n7*
Moscas, en boca cerrada no entran m., 898:9
Moscow, to M. to M., 578:11
Moses, go down M., 898:18
  greeted M. from Pisgah, 414:6
  hid his face, 7:27
  smote the rock twice, 9:5
  that which was given to M., 117:13
  was there forty days, 8:22
Moses' sepulcher, 9:34
Moslems, ask M. to execute them, 725:14
Moss, rolling stone gathers no m., 100:16
  until M. reached lips, 509:7
Moss-covered bucket, 393:13
Mosses, addled m. dank, 664:17
  greenest m. cling, 438:4
Mossy cavern, 411:5
  violet by the, 369:7
Most enjoy contented least, 221:6
  fails where m. it promises, 206:2
  make the m. of it, 331:8
  may err grossly as few, 273:5
  thing they m. do show, 222:1
  who is it that says m., 221:26
Mostest, git thar fustest with m., 494:*n2*
Mot, pour écrire m., 891:7
Mote in thy brother's eye, 33:13
Motes, thikke as m. in sonne-beem, 135:14
Moth and rust doth corrupt, 33:1
  desire of m. for star, 404:6

Mother accursed the night she bore me, 67:13
  actor pregnant with part, 584:18
  and lover the sea, 530:7
  are you in pain dear m., 466:15
  arose a m. in Israel, 10:8
  as m. so her daughter, 28:15
  blessed m. of us all, 338:20
  boy's best friend is m., 800:13
  call me early m., 450:15
  came and caught her, 895:3
  Charybdis your m., 185:25
  child to m. sheep to fold, 575:19
  choose whether she will be a m., 657:16
  Church, 113:9
  cruel m. of sweet loves, 97:11
  dark m. always gliding near, 487:15
  Death m. of beauty, 640:21
  despise not thy m., 21:29
  died today, 769:13
  earth is my m., 365:1
  earth no more a m., 104:*n10*
  experience M. of Sciences, 156:12
  fairer daughter of fair m., 96:13
  father and m. gae mad, 357:16
  Father-M. God, 493:4
  Father Time and M. Earth, 813:8
  first you are wife and m., 504:10
  foolish son the heaviness of his m., 20:10
  from one m. both draw breath, 64:4
  gave m. forty whacks, 885:22
  give me the sun, 504:13
  God Father even more M., 768:12
  his m. his wife or himself, 382:24
  holy M. Earth, 63:20
  Holy M. Earth, 891:9
  honor thy father and thy m., 8:14
  if writer rob m., 714:8
  in sin did my m. conceive me, 16:30
  laid her baby, 476:5
  leave to m. dear, 889:18
  make my bed soon, 890:9
  man shall leave father and m., 5:17
  Mary was that m. mild, 476:5
  may I go out to swim, 887:17
  Memory m. of Muses, 76:7
  my m., 389:11
  my m. bore me, 350:14
  my m. groaned, 353:6
  myself commanded by boy's m., 62:18
  Named is m. of all things, 56:12
  nature by her m. wit, 160:17
  Nature called m., 416:6
  Nature tender and benignant m., 140:14
  necessity m. of invention, 105:*n7*, 120:32
  no one like one's m. ever lived, 788:8
  not God for father if not Church for m.,
    114:2
  o' mine, 587:10
  O m. what have I left out, 812:15
  of Aeneas and his race, 89:9
  of all living, 6:1
  of All Living, 706:5
  of arts and eloquence, 260:2
  of five sons who died, 446:12
  of gods and men, 4:3
  of mankind, 255:6
  of memories, 491:4
  of months, 529:12

Mountainside, following plow along m., 369:16
    from every m., 439:9
Mountaintop, lightning strikes m., 96:23
    standing alone on m., 533:12
Mountaintops, stands tiptoe on misty m., 181:2
    that freeze, 225:19
    who ascends to m., 395:17
Mountebank, mere anatomy a m., 172:28
Mountebanks, motley m., 718:12
Mounted, beggars m. run horse to death, 170:18
    to his cabin, 608:11
    Troilus m. Troyan walls, 186:14
Mounteth, courage m. with occasion, 175:6
Mounting at break of day, 371:25
    lives not m. and unfolding, 630:4
    souls m. to God, 506:1
Mounts, in war m. warrior's steed, 373:2
Mourn, all beings thou shouldst not m., 84:8
    blessed are they that m., 32:14
    can children of bridechamber m., 33:33
    countless thousands m., 356:8
    how shall we m. you, 703:12
    I will not m., 414:11
    man was made to m., 356:7
    Margaret you m. for, 546:18
    mischief past and gone, 208:5
    music bad to those who m., 276:12
    must m. the deepest o'er fatal truth, 397:15
    no longer m. for me, 221:23
    small gnats m., 411:8
    the dead, 797:11
    time to m., 22:31
    ye Graces and Loves, 91:2
Mourned at birth not death, 297:11
    I m. and shall mourn, 487:12
Mourners go about the streets, 23:31
    no m. walk behind me, 536:3
Mournful ditty to merry measure, 404:9
    I with m. tread, 487:17
    midnight hours, 342:14
    numbers, 436:4
Mourning becomes Electra, 681:8
    don't waste time m., 639:5
    grief at not wanting to call back, 631:9
    house of m., 23:9
    I am in m. for my life, 578:6
    in such very deep m., 382:24
    in the house of m., 23:10
    let m. shows be spread, 162:15
    music in m., 31:9
    oil of joy for m., 27:16
    through night of m., 611:2
    with my m. very handsome, 277:20
Mourns his yet unbroken chains, 346:24
    household of Impulse m., 749:7
    that day has glided by, 408:16
Mourra, on m. seul, 269:*n*5
Mouse, baby looked like m., 724:1
    cat watch m., 286:9
    caught crooked m., 895:17
    consider the little m., 83:11
    frightened m. under chair, 895:7
    I am magical m., 765:7
    I am m. among elephants, 752:11

Mouse *(continued)*
    in a trappe if deed or bledde, 133:15
    mountains brought forth m., 98:23
    not a m. stirring, 196:10
    not even a m., 387:2
    pleasant shy manner of m., 724:1
    ran up clock, 893:3
    that hath one hole, 83:*n*8
    tiny m. came forth, 59:7
    town m. country m., 59:1
Mouse's, holde a m. herte nat worth leek, 83:*n*8
Mousetrap, build a better m., 425:*n*2
Mousetraps moon memory muchness, 514:17
Mousing, by m. owl hawked at, 216:3
Mouth, bread from m. of labor, 337:11
    brown hair over m. blown, 677:15
    butter not melt in m., 147:19
    cane-lipped scented m., 704:16
    closed m. swallows no flies, 898:9
    cold hard m. of world, 762:17
    false witness by their own m., 31:31
    filled with dust, 231:14
    filled with gravel, 21:13
    find m. a rein, 530:13
    fish dies because he opens m., 898:7
    fool's m. is his destruction, 21:1
    from m. flow gentle words, 54:13
    ginger hot i' the m., 204:29
    God's m. knows not falsehood, 63:19
    head in the lion's m., 774:9
    heart in my m., 105:22
    her m. is smoother than oil, 19:31
    his heart's his m., 219:32
    his m. is most sweet, 24:18
    impossible for Englishman to open m., 565:19
    in cannon's m., 194:25
    in her m. was an olive leaf, 6:21
    ink runs from m., 838:15
    it as many players do, 200:6
    kisses from female m., 397:17
    living from hand to m., 155:1
    most beautiful m. in world, 298:18
    my m. shall show forth thy praise, 16:34
    nay an thou'lt m., 202:21
    never look gift horse in m., 115:24
    not that which goeth into m., 34:31
    not thine own m., 21:41
    O sad kissed m., 530:3
    of hell, 454:23
    of his holy prophets, 37:14
    of one just dead, 635:3
    of Plenty's horn, 593:17
    ope his m. out flew trope, 262:4
    opened the m. of the ass, 9:7
    out of the m. of babes, 15:5
    out of thine own m., 38:25
    phrase men pass hand to m., 829:7
    proceedeth out of the m. of the Lord, 9:18
    pure of m., 3:10
    purple-stained m., 410:4
    sendeth m. sendeth meat, 146:21
    silver foot in m., 834:15
    silver spoon in m., 158:11
    smiling at the good m., 665:9
    speaketh out of abundance, 34:12
    spew thee out of my m., 46:26

Mouth *(continued)*
    strange m., 488:10
    that which cometh out of m., 34:31
    tongue cleave to the roof of my m., 19:11
    used as a latrine, 798:7
    violence covereth the m. of the wicked, 20:11
    was a quick stroke, 836:6
    wear not my dagger in my m., 220:25
    which dogs hath deeper m., 169:15
    wickedness sweet in his m., 13:41
    wine comes in at m., 592:6
    words of his m. were smoother than butter, 16:38
    words of my m. be acceptable, 15:19
Mouth-honor breath, 217:18
Mouths, blind m., 253:10
    enemy in their m., 208:31
    had I a hundred m., 94:31
    handful of earth stops m., 415:9
    have m. but speak not, 18:22
    made m. in a glass, 211:27
    not if I had ten m., 50:25
Moutons, revenons à nos m., 890:21
Movable feasts, 47:27
    impenetrable m. particles, 279:17
Move, aim of oratory to m., 87:20
    but if the other do, 229:17
    but it does m., 167:16
    did thee feel earth m., 721:17
    doubt that sun doth m., 198:30
    gentle wind does m., 352:3
    great affair is to m., 554:11
    I by backward steps m., 268:11
    I shall m. Hell, 95:5
    I will m. the earth, 83:5
    if they m. kill 'em, 841:6
    on m. Americans feel anchored, 803:8
    only in command, 217:15
    pretty pleasures might me m., 159:5
    social conscience of nation, 823:14
    stars m. still time runs, 169:4
    stones known to m., 216:23
    stones of Rome to mutiny, 193:5
    times change and m. continually, 160:24
    we live and m., 40:34
    when looking well can't m. her, 261:2
Moveable feast, 722:8
Moved, have not m. from there to here, 780:10
    how nice to be m., 824:6
    I shall not be m., 17:4
    like a vast shadow m., 268:14
    more ways than one, 756:6
    not m. with concord, 186:17
    not suffer thy foot to be m., 18:30
    she shall not be m., 16:27
    through dooms of love, 701:18
    to smile at anything, 191:30
    virtue never will be m., 198:10
    we shall not be m., 899:4
    woman m. like fountain troubled, 173:25
Movement, electrical in m., 456:14
    Establishment and the M., 428:16
    most magnificent m., 329:13
    out of dream into codification, 815:9
    retard the m., 569:7
    so wandering as that of mind, 152:13
    they's m. now, 733:1

Movements of the largest bodies, 345:3
  over one action is grace, 578:10
Mover, Zeus prime m., 63:8
Movers and shakers, 549:13
Moves a goddess, 293:17
  and mates and slays, 441:22
  curst be he that m. my bones, 226:17
  glory of Him who m. everything, 130:2
  God m. in mysterious way, 326:9
  look how she m., 748:2
  Love that m. sun and other stars, 130:13
  no life m. in empty passageways, 66:2
  she stirs she starts she m., 436:22
  sits looking then m. on, 636:3
  to see sad sights m. more, 172:37
  where I move, 772:2
  whole creation m., 454:12
Movest, great sphere thou m. in, 219:3
Movie, all you need for a m., 827:6
  fact of entire m. industry, 829:14
  happy in even bad m., 783:1
  hot medium like m., 764:11
  life in the m. business, 865:5
  moonbeams of m. projector, 820:5
Moviegoers, for m. to get idea of combat, 763:18
Movies are like predigested food, 757:6
  at m. the only modern mystery, 709:10
  basic appeal of m., 792:9
  Chinese tradition and what is m., 847:10
  watch same m. over and over, 792:10
  way things happen in the m., 817:5
Movin' 'cause they want somepin better, 733:1
  up and down again, 589:22
Moving accidents by flood and field, 207:37
  always m. as restless Spheres, 168:2
  finger writes, 442:2
  forward to greater freedom, 652:5
  his slow and m. finger, 210:3
  in m. how express, 199:5
  into another intensity, 679:2
  others themselves as stone, 222:1
  tide as m. seems asleep, 456:4
  up and down again, 589:22
  waters at priestlike task, 412:10
  we won't quit m., 837:6
Mown, like rain upon m. grass, 17:12
  we multiply whenever m. down, 113:7
Moyles and moyles of it, 651:3
Mozart last chord of European taste, 548:12
  when M. was my age, 819:11
  when u are M., 813:14
Much, and this is m., 395:16
  by m. too m., 183:3
  don't say too m., 751:3
  drinking little thinking, 284:13
  enough or too m., 351:22
  faithful in m., 38:16
  given much required, 38:6, 785:9
  have I seen and known, 451:13
  have I traveled, 408:17
  I do not ask you m., 176:5
  in few words, 31:19
  lady doth protest too m., 200:21
  learning doth make thee mad, 41:4
  learning not teach understanding, 62:3
  little happy if I could say how m., 190:28
  no man wanted m., 427:24

Much *(continued)*
  not many but m., 121:2
  nothing too m., 55:7
  of a muchness, 283:19, 514:17
  of Madness, 448:14
  once that seemed too m., 623:9
  safer too little than too m., 521:6
  see so m. nor live so long, 213:16
  so m. depends upon, 658:14
  so m. for him, 196:23
  so m. owed by so many, 619:17
  talk too m., 273:1
  those who have too m., 652:13
  too m. of good thing, 155:15
  unjust in m., 38:16
  what he loves never like too m., 232:11
  wrested from sure defeat, 680:9
Muck, all of a m. of sweat, 322:11
  know when to stop raking m., 571:9
  money is like m., 165:25
  whole world is m., 571:9
Muckle, twice as m. 's a' that, 358:21
Muckrake in his hand, 271:24
Muckrakes, men with m. indispensable, 571:9
Mud, fragrance of salt marsh shore m., 487:19
  frogs in the marsh m., 93:14
  garlic and sapphires in m., 678:8
  in m. eel is, 896:4
  nostalgia for the m., 489:4
  silk stocking filled with m., 366:2
  silver fountains have m., 221:11
Muddied oafs at goals, 589:15
Muddle through, 458:1
Muddled, Don Quixote's a m. fool, 157:21
  state sharpest of realities, 544:19
Muddlement, constant force for m., 544:19
Muddy ill-seeming thick, 173:25
  mastodons like m. buses, 821:1
  vesture of decay, 186:15
  waist deep in Big M., 793:14
Mud-luscious, world is m., 701:5
Mudville, no joy in M., 585:1
Muffet, little Miss M., 895:14
Muffin man, 896:8
Muffled and dumb, 424:23
Muffler, Fortune painted blind with m., 166:*n*1
Mugged, liberal who has been m., 795:2
Mug's, poetry m. game, 677:22
Mugwump educated beyond intellect, 529:9
Muhammad, I M. am only a warner, 118:4
Mulatto, incontestably m., 782:13
Mulattoes, resemble the white children, 499:7
Mule, Democratic Party like m., 512:13
  nigger woman m. uh de world, 690:4
Multa, non m. sed multum, 121:2
Multeity in Unity, 378:22
Multifold, dying m., 510:7
Multiplication is vexation, 881:3
Multiplied, deviation from truth is m., 77:16
  entities not m. unnecessarily, 130:15
  visions, 28:39
Multiplieth words without knowledge, 14:15
Multiplicity, contradictory m. of events, 692:8
Multiply, be fruitful and m., 5:8
  in us a brighter ray, 396:3
  survive and m., 440:2
  thanks to art see world m., 611:8
  thoughts, 758:17

Multiply *(continued)*
  we m. whenever mown down, 113:7
Multitude a Hydra, 97:*n*13
  as the sand by the sea in m., 11:27
  barbarous m., 185:7
  beast of many heads, 97:*n*13
  charity creates m. of sins, 560:27
  charity shall cover m. of sins, 46:1
  could not name the m., 50:25
  discordant wavering m., 187:21
  efforts of busy m., 500:4
  every step and movement of m., 319:11
  many-headed m., 97:*n*13, 219:26
  of counsellors, 20:13
  of days, 306:18
  of friends, 232:1
  of million divided by million, 741:16
  of rulers, 50:23
  of sins, 46:1
  rude m. call afternoon, 174:27
  swinish m., 325:6
  that choose by show, 185:6
Multitudes, against revolted m., 258:23
  I am large contain m., 486:18
  in the valley of decision, 28:42
  pestilence-stricken m., 402:9
  vast m. of Russia, 620:8
Multitudinous seas incarnadine, 215:24
Multiversity, university become m., 764:4
Mum, cry m., 158:*n*2
  merryman moping m., 527:25
  they fuck you up your m. and dad, 799:15
Mumbo-Jumbo God of the Congo, 639:15
Mumbo-jumbos, soot-smeared M., 406:8
Mummers, grave m., 297:1
Mummy, yesterday embryo tomorrow a m., 112:7
Mum's the word, 158:6
Munch your good dry oats, 178:32
Munched and munched and munched, 213:33
Mundi, flammantia moenia m., 89:*n*6
Mundus, fiat justitia et pereat m., 120:*n*6
  quantilla prudentia m. regatur, 144:*n*2
Munich, wave M. all thy banners, 384:11
Munny, doänt marry for m., 455:26
  goä wheer m. is, 455:26
Muove, e pur si m., 167:*n*3
Murder and misdeeds, 163:7
  brother's m., 200:31
  can smell like honeysuckle, 748:1
  cannot be hid, 136:*n*2
  contrived husband's m., 53:14
  describing m., 786:18
  from battle and m., 48:21
  get the curse out of m., 778:11
  how easily m. discovered, 136:*n*2
  I'll m. de bum, 761:10
  indulges himself in m., 393:7
  infant in cradle, 351:20
  lesson in the m., 837:14
  Macbeth does m. sleep, 215:21
  make m. respectable, 735:13
  met M. on the way, 402:20
  most foul, 198:6
  one m. makes a villain, 683:15
  one to destroy is m., 290:15
  sacrilegious m., 215:28
  shrieks out, 136:*n*2, 237:10

Music *(continued)*
  wherever there is harmony, 248:17
  why hearest thou m. sadly, 220:33
  with silver sound, 881:6
  with thy beauty's silent m., 226:23
  yearning like a God, 409:19
  you are m. while m. lasts, 679:7
Musical as bright Apollo's lute, 174:23
  as is Apollo's lute, 252:19
  law of m. world, 582:18
  most m. most melancholy, 251:15
  shuttle, 487:5
  so m. a discord, 179:2
Musically, so m. wells, 449:25
Music-makers, we are the m., 549:13
Music's power obey, 273:22
Musing there an hour alone, 398:17
  while I was m. the fire burned, 16:16
Muslim, individual duty of every M., 874:14
  no Hindu no M., 142:10
Musk, cankers in m.-rose buds, 178:20
  sweet m.-roses and eglantine, 178:19
Musket molds in his hands, 554:2
Mussel, crow-blue m. shells, 670:18
Must a word to be addressed to princes,
    151:15
  die we m., 170:37
  if we can we m., 575:15
  it m. be, 366:20
  shoot if you m., 438:13
  Thou m., 424:21
  to greenwood go, 880:13
  She-Who-M.-Be-Obeyed, 564:9
  you m. go on, 745:1
Mustache, neat m. and Aryan eye, 833:8
Mustaches, doodle m. on last Czar, 787:6
Mustard, heaven like to m. seed, 34:18
  Johnson's conversation was m., 335:5
Muster, three quarks for M. Mark, 651:1
Mutabile, varium et m. femina, 94:*n*10
Mutability in large republics, 391:2
  nought endure but M., 401:12
Mutable rank-scented many, 219:29
Mute, by and by music m., 455:12
  hangs as m., 387:8
  inglorious Milton, 316:1
  law stands m. in midst of arms, 87:9
  melancholy landscape, 582:14
  thou alone and m. sitteth, 404:21
  unchanged to hoarse or m., 258:25
Mutilated, praise m. world, 862:8
Mutilators of collections, 383:9
Mutine in matron's bones, 201:7
Mutinous and quarrelsome, 304:3
  Shannon waves, 650:9
Mutiny, move stones of Rome to m., 193:5
  of preverts, 819:7
Mutter, blessed m. of Mass, 460:22
  unmentionable thoughts, 483:12
Mutual aid law of animal life, 542:15
  and partaken bliss, 252:24
  guarantees of independence, 566:17
  in marriage dependence m., 405:9
  incomprehension, 743:11
  inflamed with m. animosity, 345:9
  prevention of m. crime, 78:24
Muzzle, not m. ox when treadeth corn, 9:25
  self-expression, 765:13

My, I did it m. way, 849:11
  Lord what a morning, 898:24
Myriad laughter of ocean waves, 63:15
  there died a m., 665:9
Myriad-minded Shakespeare, 379:16
Myriads of rivulets hurrying, 453:7
Myrrh, gold and frankincense and m.,
    31:37
Myrtle and ivy of two-and-twenty, 399:7
  and turkey part, 382:14
  laurel and m. and rose, 342:15
Myrtles, once more ye m. brown, 252:29
  which a grove of m. made, 233:14
Myself, all by m., 137:14
  am hell, 257:12
  answer questions about m., 741:11
  awe of such thing as m., 191:24
  coming down shift for m., 143:9
  commanded by boy's mother, 62:18
  feel it so like m., 769:14
  first glass for m., 288:12
  garden city and m., 742:19
  hell within m., 248:12
  I am m. and what is around me, 657:6
  I celebrate m. sing m., 485:15
  I contradict m., 486:18
  I live not in m., 395:21
  I m. am hell, 787:16
  I pray for no man but m., 213:21
  I was at last becoming m., 743:6
  if not for m. who is, 102:29
  it is m. I portray, 151:16
  it is m. I remake, 592:3
  know all except m., 139:4
  know how to kill m., 793:2
  monstrosity and miracle m., 153:18
  must I remake, 596:14
  not least honored of all, 451:13
  not talk so much about m., 474:7
  quite m. again, 574:17
  sacred duty to m., 504:9
  taken better care of m., 654:21
  that favorite subject M., 334:3
  this man shall be m., 313:4
  understanding of m., 504:8
  when young, 441:18
  with Yesterday's Years, 441:15
Mysteries are revealed unto the meek,
    30:12
  lie beyond thy dust, 268:18
  love's m. in souls grow, 229:20
  power in m. of thought, 67:15
  talk of m., 473:12
  wingy m. in divinity, 248:2
Mysterious, be m. to point of soundlessness,
    80:19
  beauty m. as well as terrible, 492:9
  by this love, 228:19
  don't take serious it's too m., 697:8
  God moves in m. way, 326:9
  God works in m. way, 675:24
  law true source, 258:5
  O m. priest, 410:18
  past of sea, 750:1
  source of art and science, 637:8
  that this thing should be is m., 542:13
  thing in soul, 483:12
  union with native sea, 372:7

Mysterium fidei, 47:25
Mystery as it is incarnated, 809:14
  at movies the only modern m., 709:10
  be a m., 871:3
  beauty is a m., 663:15
  blessings of Great M., 603:9
  British monarchy m. is life, 503:5
  burthen of the m., 368:8
  I had m., 699:9
  I show you a m., 43:8
  in m. soul abides, 494:17
  inside enigma, 619:10
  is that we deny our nothingness, 728:13
  it's all a m., 625:15
  key to m. of great artist, 789:10
  lose myself in a m., 248:3
  marked by ruins and m., 834:8
  miracle m. authority, 492:14
  no antiquity no m., 431:18
  now comes the m., 468:10
  of faith, 47:25
  of language revealed to me, 644:5
  of Man's life, 413:11
  of mysteries, 439:11
  of things, 213:8
  on bestial floor, 592:12
  perhaps this is m. they speak of, 681:13
  pluck out heart of my m., 200:24
  riddle wrapped in m., 619:10
  sense of m., 567:3
  stupendous and frightening m., 416:16
  tear the heart out of every m., 740:12
  ultimate m. works sadly, 541:11
  world turned into m., 824:3
  you must not touch, 230:1
Mystic too full of God, 590:19
  walk your m. way, 526:10
  wonderful, 455:8
Mystical, gives me m. lore, 384:10
  in m. moist night-air, 487:6
Mysticism, begins in m. ends in politics, 617:5
Mystics, scientists artists and m., 780:4
Mystifies, something simply m. me, 691:7
Myth, best m. we will ever have, 825:13
  dreams boil up from ring of m., 737:1
  is secret opening, 737:1
  no bloodless m. will hold, 832:2
Mythologies, embroideries out of old m.,
    592:13
Mythology, favorite breeding place of m.,
    756:20
Myths, show how m. operate in minds, 754:2
  that actually touched you, 831:3

N

Na poo finny, 616:16
Nabobs, nattering n. of negativism, 789:7
Nächte, wer nie die kummervollen N., 342:*n*5
Naebody, I care for n., 331:*n*1
Nag, bobtail n., 503:10
  forced gait of shuffling n., 182:36
Naiad airs brought me home, 447:12
  guardian N. of strand, 373:19
  torn N. from flood, 447:11
Nail, Dick the shepherd blows his n., 174:33
  fasten him as a n., 25:30

Nail *(continued)*
> for want of n. shoe lost, 244:8, 303:3
> hitteth n. on head, 148:26
> Jael smote n. into his temples, 10:7
> parted from others as n. from flesh, 124:5
> taller by breadth of n., 284:24

Nailed colors to the mast, 373:6
> for our advantage, 181:19
> if you hadn't n. parrot to perch, 879:8

Nails, blind as n. upon Cross, 672:12
> come near your beauty with n., 169:24
> fastened by masters, 24:1
> hard as n., 464:8
> with broad flat n., 76:18
> with n. he'll dig them up again, 237:4

Naître, la peine de n., 327:*n*5
naïve domestic Burgundy, 704:6
Naked, all are n., 671:8
> and he clothed him, 320:6
> and ye clothed me, 35:30
> as a worm was she, 132:5
> bedizened or stark n., 671:12
> born n. and falls a-whining, 105:*n*1
> came I out, 12:39
> cast n. upon n. earth, 105:1
> city, 754:4
> clad in n. majesty, 257:18
> clothe my n. villainy, 171:25
> condemned to never being n., 811:2
> creature n. bestial, 608:19
> enterprise in walking n., 592:13
> every day he clad, 322:12
> facts drop cloak stand forth n., 167:17
> find out who is swimming n., 826:11
> helpless n. piping loud, 353:6
> in death on unknown shore, 94:25
> in n. beauty more adorned, 258:3
> lash the rascals n., 210:6
> Lunch a frozen moment, 774:2
> mad n. summer night, 486:6
> man in book of Moons, 881:22
> melancholy isles, 301:1
> outcries call me from n. bed, 163:6
> people have little influence, 525:10
> pity like n. new-born babe, 214:24
> poor mangled Peace, 190:6
> poor n. wretches, 211:33
> print of n. foot, 282:11
> pure as n. heavens, 370:10
> sexually insatiable both n., 834:14
> shall he return, 23:7
> shall I return thither, 12:39
> shingles of the world, 496:19
> sometimes must have to stand n., 851:9
> soul pale stiff and n., 111:2
> starving hysterical n., 812:13
> stood n. in open air, 556:20
> they enter world n., 658:10
> they were both n., 5:17
> though locked in steel, 170:7
> to go n. best disguise, 286:26
> to mine enemies, 226:6
> to naked goes, 596:5
> truth is I have no shirt, 174:30
> truths, 411:14
> unshy beautiful full of grace, 767:6
> wallow n. in December snow, 176:18
> with n. foot stalking my chamber, 149:4

Naked *(continued)*
> woman closest to n. when well dressed, 655:4
> woods, 406:2

Nakedness all joys due to thee, 230:13
> dogs shame n. of old man, 52:13
> feeling in all its n., 417:14
> not in utter n., 370:17
> of woman work of God, 351:14
> toil hunger n., 414:7

Namby Pamby's little rhymes, 291:22
Name, age without a n., 326:1
> at which world grew pale, 306:17
> become a lost n., 771:18
> behind hands that wove, 679:11
> bless his n., 18:3
> blessed be the n. of the Lord, 12:39
> blot out his n., 46:25
> breathe not his n., 387:6
> builds his n., 291:14
> call his n. Immanuel, 25:13
> called his wife's n. Eve, 6:1
> cometh in the n. of the Lord, 18:27
> crimes committed in thy n., 348:4
> deed without a n., 216:31
> forever sad forever dear, 293:22
> forget my own n., 156:29
> frailty thy n. is woman, 197:2
> game in which my n. was, 662:6
> gathered in thy N., 48:17
> gathered together in my n., 34:42
> George Brush is my n., 715:3
> give each figure living n., 788:14
> give n. to every fixed star, 174:1
> glory and nothing of n., 397:5
> good n. better than precious ointment, 23:8
> good n. in man and woman, 209:2
> good n. is rather to be chosen, 21:16
> good n. like precious ointment, 165:21
> great in story, 399:7
> greatness of n. overwhelms son, 233:10
> hang on to your n., 830:13
> hallowed be thy n., 32:25
> he is called by thy n., 350:13
> his n. shall endure for ever, 17:14
> holla your n. to hills, 204:22
> honor and greatness of his n., 226:15
> hopes no more change n., 371:16
> how excellent is thy n., 15:6
> I have forgotten your n., 530:19
> I remember your n., 549:16
> illustrious and revered, 106:15
> is Might-have-been, 506:6
> is The Invisible Inaudible Subtle, 57:6
> king's n. a tower of strength, 172:6
> knew thy face or n., 229:7
> lashed vice spared n., 285:9
> leave a living n., 237:11
> led all the rest, 392:19
> left a n. behind them, 31:27
> lesser than my n., 177:11
> liveth for evermore, 31:28
> local habitation and n., 179:6
> Lord blot out his n., 275:*n*4
> Lord's n. is to be praised, 18:20
> lose the n. of action, 199:21
> lost her honest n., 887:6

Name *(continued)*
> Love that dare not speak its n., 607:5
> love unfamiliar N., 679:11
> marched by king's n., 695:2
> marrying left maiden n. disused, 799:7
> murder takes specious n., 290:15
> my n. and memory I leave, 166:21
> my n. is Legion, 36:31
> my n. is MacGregor, 374:10
> my n. joined to theirs, 102:7
> my n. survives me, 83:2
> my 'oss my wife my n., 429:13
> no n. of magistrate, 224:19
> no one knows real n., 550:8
> no profit but the n., 201:18
> not the eternal n., 56:12
> object take away pleasure of poem, 543:9
> of friendless n. the friend, 311:7
> of God upon lips, 312:22
> of late deceased, 587:11
> of one was Obstinate, 271:9
> of scorn, 455:16
> of the beast, 47:3
> of the Lord thy God in vain, 8:12
> of the star is Wormwood, 46:38
> of the wicked shall rot, 20:11
> our n. not become extinct, 507:12
> people you know yet can't quite n., 799:16
> problem that has no n., 796:8
> proud his n., 373:3
> refuse thy n., 180:2
> rose by any n. as sweet, 180:3
> rouse at n. of Crispian, 189:26
> Sacco's n. live, 682:12
> sad bad brother's n., 530:24
> see n. in print, 394:12
> shadow of glorious n., 106:10
> shall be called Wonderful, 25:16
> shall live behind me, 202:31
> sing praises to his N., 882:4
> single nature's double n., 202:35
> so long shall your n. endure, 94:7
> somewhere a rare n., 73:6
> synonym for devil, 141:*n*7
> teach but to n. tools, 262:5
> tell one's n. livelong June, 508:14
> that can be named, 56:12
> that will not perish, 381:16
> thy n. shall be Abraham, 6:32
> to all ages cursed, 272:16
> weak witness of thy n., 250:15
> what a wounded n., 202:31
> what n. Achilles assumed, 248:27
> what the dickens his n. is, 187:11
> what thy lordly n. is, 449:8
> what's in a n., 180:3
> writ in water, 414:1
> writing is a n. for conversation, 314:5

Named, a tip-toe when day n., 189:26
> constitution n. a democracy, 71:15
> is mother of all things, 56:12
> thee but to praise, 400:12
> you n. him not I, 278:20

Nameless deed, 362:2
> the N. is the origin, 56:12
> unremembered acts, 368:7

Name's, for his n. sake, 15:23
> hated for my n. sake, 34:2

Naught but care on ev'ry han', 356:21
  but vast sorrow there, 616:8
  by spreading disperse to n., 169:13
  carry on dread n., 619:11
  doth Job fear God for n., 12:37
  enters there, 204:11
  it is n. saith the buyer, 21:12
  it will come to n., 40:18
  shall make us rue, 176:7
  so sweet as melancholy, 234:5
  stitching and unstitching n., 591:18
  venture nought have, 147:29
Naughtiness of thine heart, 10:44
Naughty, gonna find out who's n. and nice,
    680:2
  good deed in n. world, 186:18
  my poems n. but life pure, 107:4
  night to swim in, 212:4
Nausea, that's n., 742:19
Nauseate, I n. walking, 287:4
Nauseous, fee doctor for n. draught, 274:24
Naval, study n. architecture, 330:7
  without n. force nothing, 328:9
Navee, Ruler of Queen's N., 525:22
Navies, airy n., 452:2
Navigation commerce agriculture, 330:7
  freedom of n., 566:16
  truce to n., 526:9
Navigators, winds on side of ablest n., 332:9
Navy but rotten timber, 324:13
  came the n. of Tharshish, 11:35
  gives you army and n., 324:13
  load would sink a n., 226:2
  of England, 318:18
  Royal N. watchword, 619:11
  Ruler of Queen's N., 525:22
  thoroughly efficient n., 571:5
Nay I have done, 167:11
Nazarene, he shall be called a N., 32:3
Nazareth, good thing out of N., 39:1
  Jesus of N. scientific, 493:5
  pulled into N., 858:9
Nazarite, bee shall be called a N., 184:*n*1
  your prophet the N., 184:22
Nazi concentration camp system, 793:4
  tyranny, 620:10, 653:15
Nazis, camps perfected by N., 744:3
  comparison involving N., 874:4
Ne quid nimis, 121:*n*1
Neaera's, tangles of N. hair, 253:6
Near, better a neighbor that is n., 22:3
  duty lies in what is n., 79:20
  far and n. unite, 332:20
  peace to him that is n., 27:13
  slight not what's n., 67:17
  so n. is God to man, 424:21
  so n. yet so far, 454:6
  to heaven by sea, 154:3
  what I love n. at hand, 756:10
Nearer my God to thee, 432:16
  to church further from God, 147:8
Nearest and dearest enemy, 183:5
  catch the n. way, 214:16
  friends can go, 622:15
  to gods, 70:3
Nearness of rats, 724:7
Neat, lord n. and trimly dressed, 181:35
  still to be n., 232:6

Neatly, bury for nothing do it n., 465:1
  spreads his claws, 513:15
Neatness a duty not sin, 301:18
  no text condemns n., 301:18
  plain in thy n., 96:6
Neat's, trod upon n. leather, 191:20
Nebuchadnezzar did eat grass, 28:23
Nebulae, path to other n., 643:21
Necessaries, not subdued for want of n., 106:7
Necessarily, I am n. a man, 297:15
  it ain't n. so, 711:3
Necessary, a little frippery n., 341:3
  a little kinder than n., 577:8
  and fundamental principle, 318:20
  conclusions, 447:7
  death a n. end, 192:11
  for triumph of evil, 325:15
  Government a n. evil, 333:1
  harmless n. cat, 185:27
  if dhrink evil not n., 600:18
  in n. things unity, 265:4
  make yourself n., 428:12
  marriage a n. evil, 81:11
  Messiah come when no longer n., 655:15
  most n. of assumptions, 584:3
  never say more than n., 346:3
  no n. evils in government, 364:4
  rebellion n., 336:14
  the superfluous n., 299:1
  that unnoticed & that n., 844:16
  to burn out false shames, 663:13
  to dissolve political bands, 336:1
  to invent him, 299:27
  to try to think them again, 344:26
  useless laws weaken n. laws, 297:14
  war only art n., 141:16
  World of Pains and troubles, 413:15
Necessities, art of n. strange, 211:30
  feigned n. imaginary n., 246:18
  great n. call out great virtues, 341:2
  looking away from supposed n., 542:6
  soil of people's n., 581:1
Necessity, absolute n. in mathematics, 614:10
  argument of tyrants, 359:7
  brings him not pleasure, 129:1
  calamitous n. of going on, 333:20
  creed of slaves, 359:7
  find alone N. Supreme, 520:12
  give n. praise of virtue, 106:1
  has no law, 116:11
  hath no law, 246:18
  history is freedom and n., 689:13
  illusion of Greek n., 833:5
  knows no law except prevail, 100:19
  law mighty mightier n., 344:9
  mistress of nature, 140:10
  mother of invention, 105:*n*7, 120:32
  nature must obey n., 193:15
  never good bargain, 302:9
  no virtue like n., 176:16
  not even gods fight n., 55:9
  of being ready, 445:8
  of the times, 318:4
  of treating Negroes, 321:2
  plea for infringement of freedom, 359:7
  strives against stress of n., 68:14
  teach thy n. to reason, 176:16
  thy n. greater than mine, 162:23

Necessity *(continued)*
  to glorious gain, 371:21
  to which world conform, 614:10
  villains by n., 211:3
Necessity's sharp pinch, 211:20
Neck, arms about n. crossed and rested, 487:9
  chain fastened about own n., 477:8
  clothed his n. with thunder, 14:26
  fell upon Benjamin's n., 7:15
  is as a tower of ivory, 24:22
  millstone about n., 38:19
  or nothing, 461:14
  some chicken some n., 621:1
  take eloquence wring n., 549:20
  thrice thrown arms about her n., 94:18
  would that Roman people had single n.,
    104:12
  written her fair n. round about, 149:5
  yield not n. to fortune's yoke,, 170:28
Neckcurls limp and damp, 756:4
Necks, heads erect instead of bowing n.,
    115:17
  walk with stretched forth n., 25:1
Nectar in a sieve, 378:15
  of Jove's n. sup, 232:16
Nectared, feast of n. sweets, 252:19
Need, all men have n. of gods, 52:28
  all we n. of hell, 511:9
  all ye n. to know, 410:20
  consume according to n., 478:*n*2
  deserted at utmost n., 274:18
  distribution according to n., 40:17
  England hath n. of thee, 370:9
  everywhere we have n. of Zeus, 82:11
  France has more n. of me, 365:9
  friend in n., 84:2
  how many things no n. of, 70:2
  I had most n. of blessing, 215:20
  in thy n. go by thy side, 880:18
  na start awa sae hasty, 356:4
  no n. for tongue, 755:10
  no n. of valor, 73:22
  no n. to get out of bed, 798:8
  nothing can n. a lie, 242:8
  of world of men, 460:17
  people who n. people, 800:3
  pray in distress and n., 655:7
  somebody to love me, 719:11
  someone we can lean on, 857:7
  thy n. greater than mine, 162:*n*5
  to know to stay alive, 830:12
  we shall n. no other light, 345:*n*1
  what is natural is n., 392:6
  where love and n. one, 624:1
  you don't n. weather man, 851:15
  you get what you n., 857:7
  you n. God God needs you, 634:8
Needed, all n. by each, 424:2
  Harlem n. something to smash, 804:7
  six feet all he n., 507:7
Needful, one thing is n., 38:1
Needle, for the n. she, 453:3
  go through eye of n., 35:4
  in bottle of hay, 157:18
  in haystack, 157:*n*4
  lean as compass-n., 787:19
  my hand a n. better fits, 261:10
  plying n. and thread, 418:8

Never apologize mister, 755:1
  be mean false cruel, 465:26
  better late than n., 99:11
  blows so red, 441:14
  came back to me, 467:12
  come back to me, 452:16
  contradict, 755:n1
  despair, 96:7
  do what can put off, 500:11
  everywhere felt but n. seen, 493:18
  excuse, 179:16
  give all the heart, 591:17
  give in never never, 620:12
  go to sea, 526:1
  has almost always meant N., 823:4
  if is means is and n. has been, 863:6
  in field of human conflict, 619:17
  less idle than wholly idle, 88:8
  love means n. having to say sorry, 843:n1
  man spake like this, 39:21
  never never never never, 213:14
  no n. what n., 525:20
  now or n., 314:16
  saw wild thing sorry, 663:5
  seek to tell thy love, 352:3
  shake thy gory locks, 216:17
  story of more woe, 181:17
  thinks of me, 885:14
  this will n. do, 372:n2
  time to make up mind about people, 709:4
  to be disquieted, 241:18
  to have lived is best, 595:1
  to hope again, 225:25
  too late to give up prejudices, 474:13
  tried marijuana again, 863:2
  twain meet, 587:8
  we may n. know, 795:12
  whispered she, 431:7
  you can n. leave, 864:11
  you n. give me your money, 848:18
Never-ending flight of future days, 256:14
Nevermore, door marked n., 759:12
  quoth Raven N., 449:8, 449:10
  shall be lifted n., 449:12
New, adversity blessing of N. Testament,
    165:15
  all the glad N. Year, 450:15
  all the n. thinking, 852:7
  always something n. out of Africa, 105:7
  Aurora, 881:13
  be and make n. nations, 226:15
  beings on this earth, 439:11
  birth of freedom, 446:5
  blood of the n. testament, 36:3
  brave n. world, 225:6
  change old love for n., 163:2
  commandment I give, 39:39
  cost little less than n., 287:17
  deal for American people, 651:16
  direction of Time, 662:13
  draw n. mischief on, 208:5
  embrace the n., 761:8
  era in life from reading, 475:6
  exhausted worlds imagined n., 306:9
  familiar things made n., 307:21
  first by whom n. is tried, 292:16
  force too revolutionary, 661:4
  fresh woods and pastures n., 253:15

New *(continued)*
  friend is as new wine, 30:31
  Frontier, 785:5
  generation descends from on high, 92:22
  generation of Americans, 785:10
  has a n. master get a n. man, 224:26
  hazard of n. fortunes, 175:5
  heaven and new earth, 47:11
  heavens and a new earth, 27:21
  heraldry hands not hearts, 209:21
  how strange it seems and n., 461:8
  Jerusalem, 47:11
  leisure class replaced by N. Class, 752:17
  life begins, 127:15
  love noght oold as whan n., 135:20
  man raised up in him, 49:23
  meet the n. boss, 862:1
  nation conceived in Liberty, 446:5
  no n. acquaintance, 311:16
  No N. Taxes, 805:3
  no n. thing under the sun, 22:24
  not criticize N. Testament, 581:5
  nothing more perilous than n. order,
    141:13
  nothing quite n. is perfect, 87:18
  off with old love before on with n., 884:12
  off with Old Woman before N., 564:13
  old lamps for n., 883:7
  old offenses of affections n., 222:13
  old woes n. wail, 221:8
  only thing n. in world, 661:14
  opinions always suspected, 275:4
  order in Europe, 636:16
  pain of n. idea, 503:6
  philosophy calls all in doubt, 230:15
  piping songs forever n., 410:17
  plants still awkward, 756:3
  regions we call New World, 140:16
  reproduction to n. individuals, 341:8
  ring in the n., 454:8
  satire ever moral ever n., 278:7
  sea-discoverers to n. worlds, 228:7
  so various so beautiful so n., 496:19
  something n., 886:16
  stand upon threshold of the n., 249:28
  terms between old and n. world, 349:6
  things are made familiar, 307:21
  time to begin a n., 274:25
  time was when toy dog n., 554:2
  tomorrow a n. day, 157:30
  turn over a n. leaf, 157:20
  wail my dear times' waste, 221:8
  way to pay old debts, 237:19
  what is n. not valuable what valuable not n.,
    385:7
  what's the n. news at n. court, 193:23
  wine in old bottles, 33:34
  world and n. manners, 261:16
  world order, 805:6
  Year's Day in morning, 896:3
  years ruin and rend, 530:9
  yielding place to n., 455:19
  you will see something n., 739:12
New England, Brahmin caste of N., 443:14
  growth of N., 500:4
  heart-leaves of lilac all over N., 626:15
  iron N. dark, 713:20
  weather, 522:10

New England *(continued)*
  wild N. shore, 405:5
New Englanders, as N. love pie, 635:4
New France, expansion of N., 500:4
New Hampshire, up in mountains of N.,
    390:22
New Hampshiremen, two N., 716:4
New Orleans, no architecture in N., 522:20
New York, a Xenophon at N., 317:4
  autumn in N., 734:13
  butterfly in Peking storm systems in N.,
    872:5
  dawn has mud, 717:7
  from California to N. island, 768:5
  Governor of N. not an acrobat, 617:12
  has symptoms of mind gone berserk, 740:1
  homeward bound for N. town, 897:22
  I like streets of N., 703:14
  in N. ask how much worth, 524:5
  intimation of mortality part of N., 724:6
  is city that will be replaced, 859:8
  it is 12:20 in N., 814:5
  it's a helluva town, 784:6
  it's up to you N., 818:6
  little old N., 582:2
  makes one think of collapse, 778:12
  never leave confines of N., 814:1
  only credential N. asked, 738:6
  present in N. powerful, 581:7
  sidewalks of N., 581:2
  was heaven to me, 809:2
  way of taking life, 582:20
New Yorker not edited for old lady, 696:8
  read the N. trust in God, 749:16
  you are a N. when, 879:16
New York's ghosts are the unresting, 873:1
  one sight of N. skyline, 742:17
New Zealand, traveler from N., 419:17
Newborn, glory to n. King, 305:10
  infant's tear, 353:4
  pity like naked n. babe, 214:24
New-create another heir, 226:14
Newest, oldest sins n. ways, 188:24
Newfangled, May's n. mirth, 174:2
  theories, 430:9
Newfangledness, men loven n., 136:4
New-found, America my n. land, 230:12
New-laid, innocent as n. egg, 525:17
New-lighted on heaven-kissing hill, 201:5
New-made clouds, 777:13
  honor doth forget, 175:3
New-mown hay, 609:10
New-reaped, chin n., 181:35
New-risen, sits as n. from dream, 173:19
News, all n. fit to print, 570:7
  best way to get the n., 862:16
  better making n. than taking it, 618:17
  bitter n. to hear, 499:9
  bringer of unwelcome n., 187:23
  confuse television n. with journalism,
    852:4
  evil n. rides post, 260:23
  get the n. from poems, 659:8
  good n. baits, 260:23
  good n. from a far country, 21:35
  hear talk of court n., 213:8
  literature n. that stays n., 665:19
  man bites dog that's n., 550:2

Night *(continued)*

listen to them children of n., 551:6
lives here or passes n., 656:3
long day's journey into n., 681:11
lovers' tongues by n., 180:14
machinery of n., 812:13
made for loving, 397:14
makes n. enter into day, 119:7
makes no difference, 241:2
making n. hideous, 197:34
many a watchful n., 188:20
meditate day and n., 14:40
merry wanderer of the n., 178:12
middle of the n., 515:20
moonless n. in small town, 777:17
morning and noontide night, 171:30
mother of Day, 438:4
motions of spirit dull as n., 186:17
mystical moist n.-air, 487:6
Nature's laws hid in n., 296:23
naughty n. to swim in, 212:4
night my ho head halls, 650:22
no moon outlives n., 814:13
not only a n. an age, 623:13
not snow nor rain nor heat nor n., 69:21
not spend another such n., 171:27
nothing but the n., 575:11
now tell me elm, 650:22
of cloudless climes, 397:1
of dark intent, 623:13
of memories and sighs, 383:26
of time surpasseth day, 249:3
offends the September n., 748:16
oft in the stilly n., 387:17
on marge of Lake Lebarge, 627:13
one calm summer n., 605:19
only for a n. and away, 279:10
out of n. that covers me, 552:7
perpetual n., 91:5, 232:5
Portals alternate N. and Day, 441:12
praise at morning blame at n., 292:22
preceding twenty third day of October,
    237:13
proof through the n., 386:19
resonance recedes, 595:10
returned home previous n., 618:1
revelry by n., 395:13
round me too the n., 496:15
run slowly horses of n., 101:24
sable goddess, 290:19
sash lowered when n., 623:14
says his prayers at n., 732:15
screaming n. away, 891:8
set the n. on fire, 858:4
shadow of light, 529:14
shadow of n. comes on, 695:1
ships that pass in n., 437:19
show dangerous brow by n., 192:3
shrouds remote antiquity, 286:20
silent n. holy n., 401:5
silver lining on the n., 252:13
singeth all n. long, 196:19
sits and smiles on the n., 351:6
sleep in the n., 351:16
sleep neither n. nor day, 214:1
sleep of perpetual n., 91:5
sleep one ever-during n., 226:20
slowly run O horses of n., 169:4

Night *(continued)*

smiled and said Good N., 606:16
snatched on Monday n., 181:22
soft stillness and the n., 186:15
sorrow makes n. morning, 171:30
specter n. and day, 353:10
Spirit of N., 404:7
Stars from Field of n., 441:4
starshine at n., 556:6
steal hours from n., 387:13
stilly n., 387:17
such a n. as this, 186:14
such n. in England, 419:16
suffocating n., 575:3
sweat with terror, 594:7
tell me elm n. n., 650:22
tender and growing n., 486:6
tender is the n., 410:6
that hides things from us, 130:11
that joined beloved and lover, 154:6
that makes or fordoes me, 210:12
that n. that year, 547:4
that wins, 529:13
there shall be no n., 47:13
thief in the n., 44:18
this n. of no moon, 122:10
those poor Souls who dwell in N.,
    354:7
those who dream at n., 448:12
thou be black as n., 226:21
thou makest darkness and it is n., 18:11
thought is gleam in midst of long n.,
    558:10
thy tempests fell all n., 243:7
tired with one spend n. with other, 578:1
trailing garments of N., 436:3
try to set the n. on fire, 858:4
turn by n. or day, 370:13
unto n. showeth knowledge, 15:15
unwept in eternal n., 97:14
urge the morrow, 403:19
walks n. in silver shoon, 616:12
war's annals cloud into n., 536:22
watch in the n., 17:23
watch that ends n., 289:13
watches of n., 438:1
we are not of the n., 44:19
we drink you at n., 794:6
weepeth sore in the n., 28:10
weeping may endure for a n., 16:1
what hath n. to do with sleep, 252:9
what is the n., 216:24
what of the n., 25:28
whatever flames upon n., 594:14
when no man can work, 39:27
when she deserts the n., 260:10
where kings in golden suits ride, 767:7
who art dark as n., 223:7
windy n. rainy morrow, 221:29
wings of N., 436:16
witching time of n., 200:29
with n. we banish sorrow, 233:18
with n. will go, 350:9
womb of uncreated n., 256:12
world in love with n., 180:32
world's last n., 230:25
year plunges into n., 659:3
yield day to n., 169:10

Night-bird's wail, 527:23
Nightdress, black plunge-line n., 845:11
Nightingale, brown bright n. amorous, 529:12
no music in n., 173:33
roar you as any n., 178:8
sing like a n., 108:20
sing of hope, 432:20
that on yon bloomy spray, 253:16
wakeful n., 257:25
when May is past, 245:15
Nightingales are singing near Convent, 676:2
silent when eggs hatched, 250:5
thy N. awake, 499:9
Nightly on deep Galilee, 397:2
owl that n. hoots, 178:21
shore, 449:8
sings the staring owl, 174:33
to listening earth, 287:21
Nightmare from which trying to awake, 650:15
in n. of the dark, 749:4
Life-in-Death, 376:7
making the n. real, 804:9
national n. over, 770:18
on brain of living, 477:15
see an American n., 808:15
vexed to n., 593:10
woke to flak n. fighters, 774:14
Nightmares of other islands, 763:5
Night's candles are burnt out, 181:2
owl n. herald, 171:12
piercing n. dull ear, 189:18
Plutonian shore, 449:8
rung n. yawning peal, 216:12
starred face, 412:8
sweet bird, 403:25
trust not one n. ice, 244:7
Nights and feasts of gods, 95:25
are longest there, 206:22
are very damp, 517:10
are wholesome, 196:19
Checkerboard of N. and Days, 441:22
chill thy dreaming n., 412:1
days and n. to Addison, 307:15
delights as short as n., 236:9
fasted forty days and n., 32:11
fled Him down the n., 576:13
forty days and forty n., 6:19
in bottomless n. you sleep, 559:3
long wintry n., 468:2
luxurious lobster-n., 293:21
men such as sleep o' n., 191:28
Moses was there forty days and forty n.,
    8:22
no more profit of shining n., 174:1
of waking, 373:21
revels long o' n., 192:12
shorten tedious n., 227:1
two n. to every day, 242:22
waste n. in discontent, 160:26
Night-side, illness is n. of life, 835:19
Nighttime, dog did nothing in n., 573:14
Night-walkers' song, 595:10
Nihil nimis, 121:1
nos haec novimus esse n., 107:*n8*
Nihilist man who does not bow, 479:5
spring abhorrent to n., 640:13
Nil desperandum, 96:*n4*
habet infelix paupertas, 109:*n7*

Nil *(continued)*
    humani n. a me alienum puto, 85:*n*12
    igitur mors est ad nos, 90:*n*4
    posse creari de nilo, 89:*n*8
    tam difficile est, 86:*n*1
    terribile nisi ipse timor, 165:*n*1
Nile, dogs drink running at the N., 103:3
    outvenoms worms of N., 220:20
    serpent of old N., 218:13
    waters of the N., 513:15
    you're the N., 691:12
Nimble airy servitors, 253:23
    in calling of selling, 664:2
    Jack be n., 895:16
    thought can jump, 221:13
    with n. feet dance on air, 561:4
    words so n., 237:20
Nimbly and sweetly, 214:21
    he capers n. in lady's chamber, 171:18
Nimis, ne quid n., 121:*n*1
Nimrod the mighty hunter, 6:26
Nine and fifty swans, 592:15
    and sixty ways, 588:11
    bean-rows have there, 591:2
    days old, 894:16
    lives like a cat, 148:3
    most terrifying words, 765:17
    she-camel hairs aid memory, 671:20
    some say there are n. muses, 56:*n*3
    stitch in time saves n., 105:*n*8
    then there were n., 896:22
    thrice again to make up n., 214:3
Nineteen, average n.-year-old American boy,
    850:2
    intercourse began in n. sixty-three, 799:13
Ninety and nine went not astray, 34:41
Ninety-nine percent of people fools, 715:12
Ninety-two, the glorious N., 331:6
Nineveh, one with N. and Tyre, 589:9
Ninny, compared to Handel's a n., 297:19
Ninth beatitude, 294:10
    part of a hair, 182:37
Ninth-month midnight, 487:5
Niobe, like N. all tears, 197:3
Nipped, blood is n. and ways foul, 174:33
    my flower sae early, 358:13
Nipping, winter with wrathful n. cold, 170:4
Nipple, plucked n. from his gums, 215:5
Nips his root then he falls, 225:25
Nix, sticks n. hick pix, 725:10
Nixon, tin soldiers and N. coming, 862:5
    won't have N. to kick, 771:4
No comment is splendid expression, 621:10
    continuing city, 45:18
    cross no crown, 242:1
    Day But Today, 875:13
    dignity will make you say n., 863:10
    discharge in that war, 23:19
    effects, 407:2
    everlasting n., 406:18
    forces one to repeat N., 549:12
    future n. future n. future, 874:12
    go not to Lethe, 411:9
    Hawthorne says N. in thunder, 482:17
    I was out for stars, 624:9
    in him is n. darkness, 46:6
    let me taste the whole, 462:25
    love lost, 157:26

No *(continued)*
    man content with lot, 95:15
    man is an island, 231:8
    man see me more, 225:23
    more trusting in women, 53:17
    New Taxes, 805:3
    new thing under the sun, 22:24
    nice girl won't say n., 107:12
    no no life, 213:14
    oh Caroline n., 855:16
    one about in the Quad, 680:4
    one can return from there, 3:1
    one cares for me, 331:1
    one goes and comes back, 3:2
    one means all he says, 532:6
    one should judge own case, 100:18
    others said N., 271:6
    remembrance of former things, 22:25
    retreat baby n. surrender, 868:4
    time like present, 283:1
    to think is say n., 601:8
No pasarán, 707:9
Noah begat Shem Ham Japheth, 6:15
    God gave N. rainbow sign, 804:14
    often said to wife, 618:15
Nobility, betwixt wind and n., 181:36
    idleness an appendix to n., 234:18
    in their natures, 208:20
    of style, 392:10
    species of n., 276:9
    true n. exempt from fear, 170:12
    war alone brings n., 657:4
Nobility's, mercy is n. true badge, 172:40
Nobis pereunt et imputantur, 107:*n*5
Noble and incapable of deceit, 374:17
    and most sovereign reason, 200:4
    and puissant nation, 254:12
    army of Martyrs, 48:10
    be man helpful and good, 342:12
    bright gleam of n. deeds, 64:5
    British sentence n. thing, 619:2
    contrive one n. lie, 75:5
    cookery a n. science, 234:16
    dust of Alexander, 202:13
    efforts in last war, 306:3
    eightfold path, 64:18
    eminently n., 496:1
    false idol or n. true birth, 76:5
    he shall have a n. memory, 220:8
    hearts of the n. may be turned, 51:32
    horsemanship, 183:14
    in reason, 199:5
    is he no more, 65:5
    last infirmity of n. mind, 253:6
    Living and noble Dead, 369:1
    long live our n. king, 292:2
    man a n. animal, 249:4
    mind here o'ethrown, 200:2
    nature passion not shake, 209:28
    nature poetically gifted, 496:2
    nature too n. for world, 219:32
    negligences teach, 283:15
    not rebellion which is n., 770:3
    now cracks a n. heart, 202:33
    quiet us in death so n., 260:25
    repressed their n. rage, 315:22
    savage, 272:9
    sentiments, 604:10

Noble *(continued)*
    silence n. till end, 529:15
    society exists for n. actions, 78:24
    to be good, 451:3
    train n. natures, 78:20
    type of good, 437:11
    work is alone n., 407:26
    work of n. note, 451:17
Nobleman, nature's own N., 457:13
    underrated n., 528:2
    when n. writes book, 311:*n*1
Noblemen, in America no n. or men of letters,
    433:13
Nobler in mind to suffer, 199:21
    pass them for n. life, 409:2
    two of far n. shape, 257:18
    yet in his own worth, 273:6
Nobles by earlier creation, 419:7
Noblesse oblige, 361:16
Noblest deed will die if unsung, 64:8
    horse n. conquest of man, 304:4
    lives and noblest dies, 491:21
    prospect a Scotchman sees, 309:3
    Roman of them all, 193:21
    ruins of the n. man, 192:22
    time's n. offspring, 291:9
    two n. of things, 284:5
    work of God, 295:5, 356:10
    work of man, 518:3
    work she classes O, 356:22
Nobly born must nobly meet fate, 68:18
    Cape Saint Vincent, 460:20
    deeds die however n. done, 160:25
    perfect woman n. planned, 371:8
    save or meanly lose, 446:1
    to be n. born now crime, 237:18
    to die, 65:3
    to live, 65:3
    too difficult to think n., 313:6
    wild not mad, 241:8
    within reach to live n., 103:12
    work they so n. advanced, 446:5
Nobody, are you N. too, 508:14
    asked you, 894:14
    can rule guiltlessly, 364:6
    cares for me, 331:*n*1
    come because nobody does, 536:6
    comes nobody goes, 744:15
    does anything about weather, 525:11
    expected me to be President, 444:9
    expects the Spanish Inquisition, 879:10
    gets old and crafty, 591:7
    give a war and n. come, 636:9
    goes there anymore, 708:1
    helps me over puddles, 416:1
    I care for n., 331:1
    I hate n., 285:16
    I'm N. who are you, 508:14
    is ever missing, 773:9
    knock as you please n. home, 294:11
    knows anything, 829:14
    knows trouble I've seen, 898:14
    knows you, 839:3
    likes man who brings bad news, 65:13
    more space where n. than anybody, 628:8
    never made me, 458:14
    not even the rain, 701:16
    praises everybody praises n., 334:6

Nose *(continued)*

Cleopatra's n., 269:13
entuned in hir n. ful semely, 133:14
European n., 798:3
following advice of his n., 860:4
gave pouncet-box his n., 181:35
great n. great man, 603:4
innocent n., 194:1
law says judge as looks down n., 749:8
liberty plucks justice by n., 206:14
like loving woman with broken n., 757:9
Marian's n. looks red, 175:1
often wipe bloody n., 291:13
plain as n. in face, 146:2
putting mind's eye or n. in book, 795:6
red n. makes me ashamed, 277:22
ring at end of n., 467:8
which direction to point n., 749:19
with spectacles on n., 194:25

Nosegay of culled flowers, 153:19

Noses, athwart n. as asleep, 179:25
hold n. to grindstone, 147:6

Nosing up to impossible stone, 788:5

Nostalgia for the mud, 489:4
last n., 641:16

Nostrils, blast of thy n., 8:7
breathed into his n., 5:10
clouds of smoke issue from n., 334:2
whose breath is in his n., 24:35

Not an Attic grace, 665:6
as I will but thou, 36:5
as the world giveth, 39:44
for love, 195:27
going to take this anymore, 801:14
I not I, 662:13
in vain, 621:7
lost but gone before, 103:17
my will but thine, 38:31
so wild a dream, 431:4
that I loved Caesar less, 192:25
to eat not for love, 425:8

Note and enjoy noting, 545:7
bolder n. than this, 448:1
deed of dreadful n., 216:12
dreadful n. of preparation, 189:18
eternal n. of sadness, 496:17
it in a book, 26:11
living had no n., 882:2
make sure one n. follows another, 789:10
silent n. Cupid strikes, 248:17
take n. O world, 209:17
that swells gale, 316:9
tu-who a merry n., 174:33
when found make n., 465:17
work of noble n., 451:17
world little n., 446:5
wrapped in five-pound n., 467:7
you in book of memory, 169:16

Notebook, set in a n., 193:12

Noted down and remembered, 830:13

Notes as warbled to the string, 251:20
curls done up with bank n., 471:11
flute in dying n., 273:25
he listens well who takes n., 129:4
liquid n. close day, 253:17
of gladness, 384:15
rough n. and dead bodies, 603:5
simply too many n., 814:12

Notes *(continued)*

thrill deepest n. of woe, 357:7
through all compass of n., 273:22
trills thick-warbled n., 260:3
with many a winding bout, 251:8
write N. from Olympus, 656:10

Nothing, a man zealous for n., 310:23
a worm a mere n., 301:8
a year, 459:6
ain't heard n. yet, 667:10
ain't worth nothin' but it's free, 841:15
airy n., 179:6
all for love n. for reward, 160:8
before and nothing behind, 378:1
begins and nothing ends, 576:12
begot of n. but vain fantasy, 179:26
beside remains, 401:13
better know useless things than n., 103:22
blessed man who expects n., 294:10
book's a book though n. in 't, 394:12
bring peace but yourself, 426:25
brought n. into world, 44:34
but hath been said, 234:8
but our present life, 119:9
but pack of cards, 515:9
but talk of his horse, 184:16
but the night, 575:11
but the truth, 156:35
call our own but death, 177:8
can be accomplished alone, 696:6
can be created from nothing, 89:13
can be done hastily and prudently, 100:20
can bring back hour, 371:4
can come of this, 801:19
can need a lie, 242:8
can rescue me, 169:2
can touch him further, 216:11
cannot create when n. to say, 728:12
certain except death and taxes, 303:20
comes amiss so money comes, 173:10
comes out, 426:10
common law n. but reason, 158:21
constant but inconstancy, 284:7
could stop you, 839:2
death in itself is n., 272:10
death is n. to us, 81:14, 90:12
deed everything glory n., 344:12
did n. in particular, 527:2
do much harm, 704:2
done merely for beauty, 888:4
done while anything remained, 106:12
dusty n., 203:20
easier than self-deceit, 79:9
easy to take more than n., 514:16
either good or bad, 199:2
else is, 228:17
emboldens sin as mercy, 213:24
endures but change, 61:27
esteem everything esteem n., 267:19
everything in relation to n., 269:9
except battle lost, 366:7
except empty curved space, 766:3
exists without some effect, 275:18
expect something for n., 557:9
extenuate, 210:20
eyes n. like the sun, 223:1
fair alone, 424:2
fame created something of n., 250:6

Nothing *(continued)*

fear God n. else, 470:12
fear n. you carry Caesar, 89:3
for sale in Stupidity Street, 609:13
funnier than unhappiness, 744:22
give your services for n., 70:18
given nothing required, 304:12
glory and n. of a name, 397:5
good men to do n., 325:15
goodness had n. to do with it, 700:5
grated to dusty n., 203:20
great without enthusiasm, 427:15
greater than one's self, 486:17
had n. can't take more, 514:16
half so sweet in life, 387:10
happens nobody comes, 744:15
happens which he is not fitted to bear, 112:10
has value, 638:12
have value but object of utility, 478:2
having n. n. can he lose, 170:30
having n. possessing all, 43:18
he who believes n., 336:4
heaven's net misses n., 58:3
her wishes and ways be as n., 536:2
hold on to n. expect n., 690:18
human is alien, 85:17
I am n., 42:27
I am n. I see all, 425:22
I do n. upon myself, 231:5
I had seen n. sacred, 721:6
I have everything yet n., 86:7
I know these are n., 107:20
I love as good fight, 651:13
I regret n., 744:*n*1
if not critical, 208:14
if you lose you lose n., 269:17
important is regional, 835:21
in baseball don't know n., 807:3
in desert there is all and n., 417:12
in excess, 121:1
in his life, 214:14
in nature's inventions n. lacking, 140:11
in n. else so happy, 176:29
in relation to infinite, 269:9
in the pot, 613:15
in truth we know n., 70:11
in world single, 402:16
indolent but agreeable doing n., 110:21
infinite deal of n., 184:10
is had for nothing, 479:10
is here for tears, 260:25
is it n. to you, 28:11
is secret, 37:29
it profiteth me n., 42:27
it's about n., 864:9
knew moment to say n., 560:3
know n., 476:9
know n. except my ignorance, 70:6
know only that he n. knew, 260:5
lack for n., 821:1
learned n. forgotten n., 348:6
left remarkable, 219:5
left to lose, 841:15
less will content me, 324:5
like a dame, 706:13
like the sun, 223:1
lost but money, 752:13

O

Obey (*continued*)
  voice at eve, 425:3
  weight of time o., 213:16
  woman to o., 453:3
Obeyed at prime, 425:3
  nature to be commanded must be o., 165:1
  parents insist on being o., 360:23
  She-Who-Must-Be-O., 564:9
  sighed as lover o. as son, 332:16
  sun and moon o. him, 303:14
  Truth o. his call, 596:14
Obeys, bends him but o. him, 437:4
  has humor when she o., 294:3
  whoever o. the gods, 50:15
Object all sublime, 527:15
  conformity of o. and intellect, 124:9
  consideration of public o., 71:13
  first o. looked upon that o. became, 487:18
  Hope without o., 378:15
  in living to unite, 624:1
  in possession seldom retains charm, 110:18
  legitimate o. of government, 337:15
  marriage had always been her o., 382:9
  obligation to o. possessed, 505:14
  of British government, 349:3
  of war is peace, 489:14
  only of war honorable, 333:13
  paramount o. save Union, 445:11
  perceived harmony of o., 378:23
  purely magical o., 778:1
  strange and high, 267:3
  take an o., 827:15
  to carry terror and destruction, 420:10
  to division of society, 423:10
  when gold becomes her o., 188:21
  worthiness of its o., 858:11
Objective and subjective united, 379:4
  Church and State demand, 652:4
  correlative, 675:20
  most o. sources I have, 862:16
Objectivity and again objectivity, 664:17
  subjectivity and o., 709:8
Objects, all o. of all thought, 368:11
  all visible o. are pasteboard masks, 483:2
  are nothing, 789:11
  classified, 343:16
  earnest about these o., 664:3
  extended in space, 642:22
  extracted from many o., 195:23
  material o. are of two kinds, 89:17
Oblations, bring no more vain o., 24:31
Obligation, not created sense of o., 609:3
  to object possessed, 505:14
Obligations, in marriage o. reciprocal, 405:9
  rank has its o., 361:16
Oblige, noblesse o., 361:16
Obliged, so obliging he ne'er o., 295:13
  wealthy and relieved poor, 51:*n*1
  whatever o. to do whatever not o. to do,
    522:8
Obliging, so o. he ne'er obliged, 295:13
Oblique, as lines so loves o., 267:4
Oblivion, alms for o., 203:21
  blind o. swallowed cities, 203:20
  blindly scattereth poppy, 249:1
  commend to cold o., 403:11
  diffuses senses with o., 95:28
  formless ruin of o., 204:5

Oblivion (*continued*)
  Lethe the river of o., 256:24
  longest journey to o., 663:23
  my o. is a very Antony, 218:9
  not to be hired, 249:2
  of a day, 505:8
  razure of o., 207:14
  sacred to o., 234:2
  second childishness and o., 194:25
  six months' o., 531:26
Oblivioni sacrum, 234:2
Oblivious, sweet o. antidote, 217:19
Oblomovism, 466:32
Obnoxious to each carping tongue, 261:10
Obscene, abstract words o., 721:6
  as cancer bitter as cud, 699:5
  live without duties o., 429:5
  sailing on o. wings, 377:16
  things holy profane clean o., 239:8
Obscenity, Bible has wealth of o., 525:8
  rejection of o., 745:8
Obscure, cloud o. science, 338:15
  destiny o., 315:17
  gods love the o., 50:3
  hermit poor in place o., 159:2
  little grave an o. grave, 177:13
  regions of philosophy, 312:1
  the palpable o., 256:18
  unconscious mental processes, 562:16
  when brief I become o., 98:18
Obscured, excess of glory o., 255:24
Obscurely, body to be buried o., 166:21
Obscures show of evil, 185:18
Obscurities, I choose o. of tongue, 812:20
Obscurity, origin involved in o., 391:10
Obsequies, come to these sorrowful O., 91:29
  solemnized their o., 248:23
Obsequious and conciliating abroad, 391:13
Observance, more honored in breach than o.,
    197:31
Observation, bearings of this o., 465:18
  in o. chance favors prepared mind, 499:1
  know evil from long o., 75:3
  let o. observe, 306:*n*3
  love you for speed of o., 626:14
  man's own o. best physic, 166:10
  passive science, 468:11
  with extensive view, 306:15
Observations, return to soundness of o.,
    277:28
Observe, can o. a lot by watching, 807:5
  degree priority and place, 203:5
  due measure, 54:27
  physician with diligence, 231:4
  pleasant to o. how free, 284:16
  see but not o., 573:7
  so naturalists o. a flea, 285:11
  the opportunity, 30:18
  what we o. not nature itself, 728:5
Observed, all his faults o., 193:12
  of all observers, 200:3
  single carrot freshly o., 533:16
Observer, he is a great o., 191:29
  measuring device constructed by o., 728:5
  of human nature, 463:20
Observers, observed of all o., 200:3
Observes, artist o. selects guesses, 578:4
Observeth, he that o. the wind, 23:27

Observing anything new, 378:17
  him in action, 712:7
  quick-eyed Love o. me, 243:11
  wrongdoing and righteousness, 54:3
Obsessed, beware the politically o., 869:5
Obsessing our private lives, 748:16
Obsession, in sorrow's o., 154:8
Obsolescence, planned o. of people, 769:2
Obsolescent, conserve what is o., 569:7
Obsolete, clarity punctuation other o. stuff,
    740:4
Obstacle, I shatter every o., 417:19
  Napoleon sole o. to peace, 365:12
  to every o. oppose patience, 337:2
Obstacles, combat o. to get repose, 532:5
  knows what o. there, 797:14
  of civilization, 432:5
  ride over o. win race, 465:33
Obstinacy in bad cause, 248:7, 313:26
Obstinate condolement, 196:28
  fished by o. isles, 665:5
  name of one was O., 271:9
  pliant merry morose, 107:18
  virtue, 267:26
Obstruction, lie in cold o., 206:38
Obtain, they shall o. mercy, 32:14
  what they have struggled for, 614:14
Obtained, with great sum o. freedom, 40:43
Obtaining, pursuing and o. happiness, 320:7
Obvious, gods hate the o., 50:3
  grand and impressive to mistrust o.,
    112:23
  material and o. things, 277:28
  there's no real problem, 790:4
Occam's Razor, 130:*n*7
Occasion, bent on evil never want o., 100:12
  courage mounteth with o., 175:6
  delivered upon mellowing of o., 174:18
  ecstasy affords o., 671:4
  ill ne'er wants o., 243:17
  rough torrent of o., 188:17
  to true o. true, 454:16
Occasionem cognosce, 55:*n*8
Occasions, all o. invite his mercies, 231:10
  and causes why, 190:3
  do inform against me, 201:19
  woman who o. least talk, 72:5
Occupation, absence of o. not rest, 326:14
  future o. of all moppets, 760:5
  idleness and lack of o., 71:4
  never found any o. more important,
    320:11
  no o. all men idle, 224:19
  only o. left to men of science, 513:2
  pride in o., 522:15
Occupation's, Othello's o. gone, 209:13
Occupations, let us love o., 465:16
  let your o. be few, 112:1
  pause in the day's o., 437:12
  woman's normal o. counter creative life,
    746:11
Occupied territories, 620:10
Occur, accidents o. in best-regulated families,
    465:32
  as they occur, 641:14
Occurred, ought never to have o., 629:4
Occurrence, any o. of special good fortune,
    425:21

Ocean, abandon the o., 384:16
    appalling o. surrounds land, 483:5
    biddest mighty o. deep, 503:1
    caves of o. bear, 315:23
    Cybele fresh from o., 396:2
    dark secrets of o., 415:14
    for his fame the o. sea, 233:13
    grossest iridescence of o., 642:2
    his legs bestrid the o., 219:8
    hungry o. gain advantage, 221:18
    I have loved thee O., 396:22
    is ever sending gusts, 53:1
    laughter of o. waves, 63:15
    loose chains of things, 104:7
    Lord of the O., 68:3
    men want o. without roar, 477:3
    meteor of o. air, 443:3
    mind is tossing on the o., 183:38
    more than o. water broken, 623:13
    Neptune's o. wash blood, 215:24
    Northern o. in vast whirls, 301:1
    not the o. rocking, 839:2
    nothing but sky and the o., 378:1
    of hills and hollows, 83:3
    of life, 437:19
    of truth undiscovered, 279:18
    painted o., 376:2
    post o'er land and o., 254:22
    roll on thou deep and dark blue o., 396:17
    round o. and living air, 368:11
    sinks day-star in o. bed, 253:14
    soul fall into the o., 169:5
    source of all, 51:31
    tomorrow we sail the O. Sea, 96:8
    vast and furious o., 240:2
    veritable o., 641:8
Ocean's, in o. bosom unespied, 267:5
Oceans, fight on seas and o., 619:14
    white with foam, 673:11
    wilderness o., 500:5
Oceanus the ocean river, 750:1
O'clock, always three o. in morning, 710:13
    it's now ten o., 457:4
    says wisely it is ten o., 194:15
    two o. in morning courage, 365:18
O'Connor, Justice O. has often been cited, 873:5
October, falls with leaf in O., 236:5
    lonesome O., 449:14
    March July O. May, 150:*n*1
    now for O. eves, 666:2
    something in O., 579:11
    twenty third day of O., 237:13
Octopus, adopt character of o., 59:22
Ocular, give me o. proof, 209:14
Odd, and this was o., 515:20
    as can be, 616:11
    choose the o., 749:16
    divinity in o. numbers, 187:19
    good luck in o. numbers, 187:19
    luck in o. numbers, 415:13
    must think it exceedingly odd, 680:4
    numbers are most effectual, 105:11
    old ends stolen of holy writ, 171:25
    people's voice o., 296:12
    this was scarcely o., 516:8
    volumes, 383:9
Oddness, my poetry errs on side of o., 547:10

Odds, almost at o. with morning, 216:24
    facing fearful o., 419:19
    is gone, 219:5
    of man's bedevilment, 575:17
    what is the o., 464:26
Oderint dum metuant, 86:*n*8
Odes, quoted o. and jewels, 452:17
Odi et amo, 91:*n*9
Odious, comparisons are o., 137:16
    vermin, 284:26
Odor, no o. so bad as goodness tainted, 474:23
    of corruption, 650:7
    of death, 748:16
    stealing and giving o., 204:10
Odorous, amber scent of o. perfume, 260:16
Odors, bedewed with liquid o., 96:6
    of ointments more durable, 165:21
    virtue like precious o., 165:18
    when violets sicken, 404:4
Odysseus, soon as he had seen O., 54:2
Odysseus', matter of O. wanderings, 487:3
Oedipus solved riddle of Sphinx, 66:7
O'ercast, sun's o. with blood, 175:15
O'erdoing Termagant, 200:6
O'erdusted, more laud than gilt o., 203:26
O'erfraught heart, 217:7
O'er-informed tenement of clay, 272:16
O'erleaps, ambition which o. itself, 214:24
O'erthrown, noble mind here o., 200:2
O'ertrip, fearfully o. the dew, 186:14
O'erwhelm, though all earth o. them, 197:18
Oeufs, ne saurait faire omelette sans casser des o., 891:5
Off, camp the love of the o., 835:17
    on bus or o. bus, 840:4
    with her head, 514:18
    with his head, 171:33, 287:14
    with Old Woman, 564:13
    with you where you want to go, 133:*n*2
    you lendings, 212:3
Offend, he who dares not o., 333:5
    if thy right hand o. thee, 32:18
    not o. you by speaking truth, 142:5
Offended, brother o. is harder to be won, 21:3
    Deity o., 356:20
    devils being o., 208:13
    him have I o., 192:27
    if anybody not o. I apologize, 517:14
    if we shadows have o., 179:18
    this hath not o. king, 143:10
    with his estate, 117:3
Offender, hugged o. forgave offense, 274:28
    love o. detest offense, 274:*n*4
    never pardons, 103:*n*10
Offenders, mercy on us miserable o., 48:4
    society o., 527:10
Offending Adam, 188:31
    most o. soul alive, 189:25
Offends me to the soul, 200:6
    no law is king indeed, 163:19
    the September night, 748:16
Offense, conscience void of o., 41:1
    dire o. from amorous causes, 293:3
    every desire a punishable o., 700:20
    giving and receiving o., 407:15
    hugged offender forgave o., 274:28
    let punishment match o., 88:12
    love offender detest o., 274:*n*4

Offense *(continued)*
    my o. is rank, 200:31
    pardon one o. encourage many, 100:32
    real o. was having mind, 544:6
    rock of o., 25:14
    scorn to take o., 292:20
    would appear o. in us, 191:34
Offenses, enemies for small o., 234:10
    old o. of affections new, 222:13
Offensive, didn't replace with anything more o., 866:1
Offer he can't refuse, 795:7
    I o. hunger thirst battles, 435:25
    itself to be unmasked, 655:17
    not o. to people but ask, 785:5
    nothing to o. but blood, 619:12
    you only one tip, 871:12
    yourselves to sea, 543:1
Offered, I o. Being for it, 509:12
Offering, a lamb for a burnt o., 6:35
Offerings, knowledge of God more than burnt o., 28:35
    pale Hecate's o., 215:14
Office and affairs of love, 190:26
    and custom, 203:5
    boy to Attorney's firm, 525:22
    Circumlocution O., 466:18
    great o. not filled by great men, 532:9
    Heaven about to confer great o., 80:6
    high o. teaches decision-making, 802:12
    I shall return to the o., 288:21
    insolence of o., 199:21
    never ask refuse resign o., 304:1
    prisidincy highest o., 600:17
    public o. public trust, 528:*n*3
    serves it in o. of a wall, 176:24
    so act toward o. so toward wealth, 109:6
    so clear in his great o., 214:24
    unfit to hold an o., 83:6
    vice-presidency most insignificant o., 330:10
    vice-prisidincy next highest an' lowest o., 600:17
    which false man does easy, 216:2
Officeholder, president is o., 764:4
Officer, drunken o. of British rule, 829:4
    fear each bush an o., 171:5
Officers, behind o. government people, 498:9
    civil o. removed on impeachment, 339:12
    make o. but not scholars, 235:4
    white o. cast lot, 519:10
Offices acceptable as elsewhere, 337:6
    cast longing eye on o., 337:6
    estates degrees and o., 185:8
    female sex excluded from honors and o., 341:5
    people I cannot win with o., 270:7
    post o. and cabinet appointments, 444:*n*1
Official, centers of o. power, 806:1
    no o. high or petty, 694:2
    not just an elected o., 791:2
Officials, sharp attacks on public o., 745:9
Officious innocent sincere, 311:7
Offspring, moral virtues are political o., 287:11
    of heaven firstborn, 257:5
    terrible from camps, 742:7
    time's noblest o., 291:9
    true source of human o., 258:5

One (*continued*)

alone I am with him, 113:19
among a thousand, 14:13
and inseparable, 390:10
and the same thing, 276:12
born in a manger, 268:15
by one two by two, 402:21
clear call for me, 456:4
composed of many, 95:13
conceive many without the o., 76:3
country one constitution, 390:14
crowded hour, 326:1
dead deathless hour, 506:4
each hath o. and is o., 228:7
enemy is too much, 244:10
ere herde at tothir oii, 132:20
fair daughter and no more, 199:10
fall o. by o., 323:16
far-off divine event, 454:12
fire burns out another's, 179:21
fish ball, 500:3
flew over cuckoo's nest, 896:15
food to o. poison to others, 90:16
foot in sea one on shore, 190:33
for all, 172:31, 422:4
for my master, 893:4
for o. sweet grape vine destroy, 172:32
found truth in all but o., 177:16
from all, 114:5
from all things o. and from o. all things,
   62:8
god greatest among gods, 60:6
God law element, 454:12
good knowledge, 70:4
good turn deserves another, 105:18
hundred years of solitude, 818:9
I am party of o., 724:4
if by land, 437:16
if ever two were o., 261:15
in life and death, 526:16
is fat and grows old, 182:19
is or is not, 76:4
just o. of those things, 691:13
less than tenth part of o., 203:18
little o. shall become a thousand, 27:15
live as two, 677:5
lost but o. twa behin', 358:21
low man adding o. to o., 461:15
majority of o., 473:17
man among a thousand, 23:17
man of o. book, 120:8
man one vote, 888:8
man's meat another's poison, 90:n6
man's will all men's misery, 161:18
minute with him, 660:4
more river, 898:26
more unfortunate, 418:13
my little o. pretty o., 452:18
nature o. and continuous, 474:2
never do merely o. thing, 779:5
never lose touch of the o., 580:2
not o. for putting off proof, 623:17
on God's side majority, 458:11
our two souls which are o., 229:16
pain lessened by another's, 179:21
parted between twelve and o., 189:4
pay for o. by o., 588:9
people arose as o. man, 10:28

One (*continued*)

perfect limousine, 699:15
perfect rose, 699:15
road up and road down o. and same, 62:9
shock of recognition, 482:14
small o. a strong nation, 27:15
small step for man, 825:20
spot where I made O., 442:10
striking at root of evil, 474:25
swallow not a summer, 78:5
sweet sacrifice, 225:15
that loved not wisely, 210:20
the o. and the many, 75:26
the other will contain, 509:13
Thing O. and Thing Two, 739:12
third of a nation, 652:12
this o. thing I do, 44:4
three centuries removed, 734:10
to succeed possible only o. way, 78:7
touch of nature, 203:25
two and third in your bosom, 180:20
two one two, 515:13
two three strikes you're out, 640:2
twothreefourfive pigeons, 701:7
we are o. flesh, 259:16
who died for Truth, 509:6
word frees us, 66:20
word Plastics, 827:9
world's life and mine o., 501:14
One-and-a-half, aphorism o. truths, 626:7
One-and-twenty, when I was o., 574:14
One-book man, 375:7
One-eyed, in country of blind o. man is king,
   141:10
One-hoss shay, 443:12, 443:13
Oneness, household in o. of mind, 53:3
Ones, great o. eat up little o., 220:12
Oneself, belong to o., 152:12
   idea of o. as cause, 276:7
   little one knows o., 686:10
   look better into o., 582:6
   mistaking o. for oracle, 612:4
   not live unto o., 81:8
One's-Self I sing, 485:12
One-third of a nation, 652:12
One-woman waterfall, 823:1
Onion, thumb instead of o., 833:6
   will do well for such shift, 173:5
Onions, eat no o. nor garlic, 179:5
   wel loved he garleek o. lekes, 134:8
Onlie begetter of insuing sonnets, 220:n2
Online, as an o. discussion grows, 874:4
Only for a night and away, 279:10
   I o. am escaped, 12:38
   I'm o. sleeping, 848:10
   love sprung from only hate, 179:29
   one you ever hear, 850:7
   that it is your o. one, 78:19
   two people who count, 864:7
   winning isn't everything o. thing, 888:12
Onset, stand aside from enemy's o., 72:4
Ontogenesis recapitulation of phylogenesis,
   519:12
Ontogeny recapitulates phylogeny, 519:n5
Onward Christian soldiers, 518:14
   half a league o., 454:18
   steer right o., 254:24
Ootah, Eskimo O. had explanation, 564:11

Oozy weeds about me twist, 484:4
Ope his mouth out flew trope, 262:4
   their golden eyes, 220:15
   when I o. my lips, 184:7
Open and friendly in private, 71:14
   covenants of peace, 566:16
   door, 532:14
   doors of his face, 14:33
   ear the o. vowels tire, 292:17
   ever-o. door, 51:n1
   eyes o. before marriage, 302:19
   face facts with both eyes o., 142:13
   free and o. encounter, 254:14
   locks whoever knocks, 216:29
   my heart, 461:4
   my mistress the o. road, 556:5
   no right to o. door, 74:12
   page of book carelessly o., 820:11
   ports of slumber o., 188:20
   rebuke better than secret love, 22:1
   road, 556:5
   sentence is for o. war, 256:9
   sesame, 883:8
   this gate, 765:18
   thou my lips, 16:34
   Time and let him pass, 579:12
   unto whom all hearts are o., 49:3
   war, 256:9
   where knock is o. wide, 318:9
   with o. arms stand ready, 482:12
   ye everlasting gates, 258:28
   ye the gates, 26:3
Opened, door we never o., 678:7
   eyes o. to the sea, 761:8
   he o. us, 783:11
   knock and it shall be o., 33:16
   Lord o. mouth of the ass, 9:7
   my heart new o., 225:25
   your eyes shall be o., 5:19
Openest, thou o. thine hand, 19:17
Open-eyed Conspiracy, 224:21
Opening eyelids of the morn, 253:3
   myth is secret o., 737:1
   of a Door, 511:13
Open-minded impartial adjustment, 566:16
Opens, production o. a demand, 364:9
Opera ain't over till fat lady sings, 886:n8
Operas, German text of French o., 582:18
Operate, show how myths o. in minds, 754:2
Operation, crucial dangerous o., 812:3
   military o. involves deception, 80:16
   preparing us for fatal o., 766:8
Operations, enjoy both o. at once, 674:2
   no plan of o., 420:9
   we perform without thinking, 580:6
Operative statement, 846:6
Ophelia, I loved O., 202:20
Opiate, emptied dull o., 410:2
Opinion, backed o. with quotations, 283:13
   basis of government o., 336:12
   custom supported by popular o., 572:13
   difference of o., 247:12
   difference of o. makes horse-races, 524:4
   endeavoring to stifle, 435:3
   error of o. tolerated, 337:8
   governs world, 566:7
   gross and scope of my o., 196:12
   having no o. at all, 335:8

Overrefines argument brings self to grief, 130:17

Overseer, no guide o. or ruler, 19:32

Overserious, reindeer seem o., 671:23

Overstep not modesty of nature, 200:7

Overt, two witnesses to o. act, 339:13

Overtake, death will o. you, 118:3
    I thy fate shall o., 241:18

Overthrew the tables of moneychangers, 35:8

Overthrow, forcible o. of social conditions, 478:15
    linger out a purposed o., 221:29
    revolutionary right to o., 445:5
    whom thou thinkest thou o., 230:22
    ye cannot o. it, 40:18

Overwhelm myself in poesy, 409:1

Overwhelming, let it be o., 623:17
    loss so o., 446:12
    tiny differences in input o., 872:5

Overwhelms, greatness of name o. son, 233:10

Overwise in doing thy business, 30:35
    keep talk from getting o., 623:17

Overwork, killed by o., 587:7

Overworked, neither idle nor o., 520:8

Ovid, Venus clerk O., 132:3

Ovo, ab o., 98:n10

Owe, duty we o. Creator, 332:1
    God a death, 188:16
    I o. a cock, 70:9
    if I can't pay I can o., 146:10
    it to future generations, 782:9
    it to posterity, 339:6
    me five farthings, 893:6
    no man anything, 41:38
    no man hate, 195:6
    Shallow I o. thousand pound, 188:28
    sum married people o., 343:11
    to this place I o. everything, 445:1

Owed, so much o. by so many, 619:17
    throw away dearest thing he o., 214:14

Owedst, sleep which thou o., 209:11

Owes, duty subject o. prince, 173:26
    me another existence, 343:23
    no homage unto sun, 248:19
    not any man, 436:12

Owest, lend less than thou o., 211:8
    worm no silk, 212:3

Owl and Pussycat, 467:7
    by mousing o. hawked at, 216:3
    clamorous o., 178:21
    Creek bridge, 540:1
    for all his feathers, 409:18
    in Douglas fir turn head, 811:6
    is endlessly hungry, 840:11
    nightly sings the staring o., 174:33
    night's herald, 171:12
    of Minerva spreads wings, 367:8
    Pussy said to O., 467:8
    sadder than o. songs, 399:4
    that shrieked, 215:17
    to moon complain, 315:13

Owlet Atheism, 377:16
    whoops to wolf below, 377:1

Owls, ancient o. of the earth, 822:2
    bringing o. to Athens, 73:2
    companion to o., 14:9
    couch when o. do cry, 225:5
    court for o., 26:16

Owls *(continued)*
    no o. in whole island, 310:n2
    two o. and hen, 467:3

Own a bit of ground, 507:14
    he forgets not his o., 882:4
    if any provide not for his o., 44:31
    ill-favored thing but mine o., 196:4
    my o. my native land, 373:3
    my o. shall come to me, 528:13
    of thine o. have we given, 12:25
    poor thing but mine o., 196:n1
    room of her o., 654:14
    thing that is your o., 78:19
    to be on your o., 851:14
    you break it you o. it, 843:2

Owned, dearest thing he o., 214:14
    I was o. of Thee, 510:8

Owner of the sphere, 425:6
    ox knoweth his o., 24:28

Owners, faithful service to her o., 468:19
    lords and o. of their faces, 222:2

Owning, mania of o. things, 486:14

Ox, as an o. goeth to the slaughter, 20:5
    eateth grass as an o., 14:31
    knoweth his owner, 24:28
    lion eat straw like the o., 25:19
    makes difference whose o. gored, 144:11
    not covet neighbor's o., 8:14
    not muzzle o. when treadeth corn, 9:25
    one Law for Lion and O., 352:1
    stalled o. and hatred therewith, 20:32
    stands on my tongue, 63:1
    tired o. treads with firmer step, 115:21

Oxen, draw more than hundred pair of o., 235:n4
    of his own breeding, 95:27
    man whose talk is of oxen, 393:3
    who drives fat o., 311:12
    years like great black o., 590:23

Oxford, clever men at O., 574:9
    from O. up pathway strays, 496:12
    interpretation of Koran taught at O., 332:8
    Street stony-hearted, 393:5

Oxlips and nodding violet grows, 178:19

Oxymoron, sound like an o., 873:15

Oyster, bold man first eat o., 285:21
    pearl in your foul o., 196:5
    sharpening my o. knife, 689:16
    solitary as o., 465:5
    unseasonable to eat an o., 154:2
    world's mine o., 187:7

Oyster-bank, shelving in o., 428:26

Oysters come walk with us, 516:2
    wait a bit the O. cried, 516:5

Ozymandias king of kings, 401:13

P̄

Pace, creeps in this petty p., 217:23
    moving to faster p., 811:9
    not keep p. with companions, 475:20
    requiescat in p., 121:12
    thoughts with violent p., 209:20
    unperturbed p., 576:14

Paced into the hall, 375:22

Pacem, desiderat p. praeparet bellum, 115:n14
    in terris, 647:9

Paces about room again alone, 676:13
    three p. through room, 451:6
    time travels in divers p., 195:15

Pacific, frontier from Atlantic to P., 619:9
    in his name to great P., 639:17
    leans on the land, 670:5
    olive leaf p. sign, 259:27
    stared at the P., 408:17

Pacified Psyche and kissed her, 449:17

Pacify stomach with cool thoughts, 747:6
    touchy tribe of poets, 98:15

Pacis, nunc patimur longae p. mala, 109:n10

Pack clouds away, 233:18
    hear baying of p., 688:10
    meets with Pack in Jungle, 588:19
    nothing but p. of cards, 515:9
    relations a tedious p., 560:23
    up your troubles, 643:22
    we'll face murderous cowardly p., 687:14
    when it begins to rain, 211:18

Packard, first P. had whipstock, 694:10

Packs and sets of great ones, 213:8

Padded lunatic asylums, 654:6

Paddle, doves p. in putrescent waters, 717:7
    in cold streams, 592:16
    own canoe, 401:4

Paddling palms and pinching fingers, 223:11

Paddocks, cold as p., 241:15

Paddy dear did ye hear, 884:4

Padlock, clap p. on her mind, 283:12

Padua, come to wive it wealthily in P., 173:9

Pagan, poor p. planet of ours, 482:16
    suckled in creed outworn, 371:24
    tenets admitted into p. creed, 532:15
    who defends religion, 608:16

Page, blank p., 827:10
    cannot tear out p. of life, 432:8
    don't know which writing this p., 719:6
    excels at title p., 321:10
    history's purchased p., 395:19
    is printed, 827:11
    knowledge her ample p., 315:22
    life's p., 395:9
    of book carelessly open, 820:11
    of prancing Poetry, 510:14
    refine her sterling p., 278:7
    shone not on poet's p., 97:n11
    what one sweet p. can teach, 500:7

Pageant, became like piece of p., 578:15
    insubstantial p. faded, 225:1

Pageantry, mask and antique p., 251:8
    of a king, 339:9

Pages, take volume of blank p., 431:10
    title p. and spines, 719:8
    turn p. of Greek models, 98:28

Pagoda, old Moulmein P., 588:1

Paid, attention must be p., 780:5
    debt to Nature's quickly p., 242:3
    in his own coin, 156:3
    shoot murderer without asking to be p., 825:17
    soul bought and p. for, 458:16
    tell you what I p., 511:8
    well p. that is satisfied, 186:13
    who p. for the bullet, 757:12
    with moan, 576:12
    with sighs aplenty, 574:15

Pail, milk comes frozen home in p., 174:33

Pain, after great p. formal feeling, 508:20
  and anguish wring brow, 373:16
  and boredom foes of happiness, 400:4
  and evil in life of worms, 501:15
  and pleasure rudders, 275:*n*3
  antidote to mental suffering is physical p.,
    478:1
  are you in p. dear mother, 466:15
  aromatic p., 294:21
  as readily blisses as p., 535:10
  assuage unforgotten p., 506:7
  beauty pierce like p., 630:14
  bitterest p. among men, 69:23
  born in other's p., 576:12
  cease upon midnight with no p., 410:9
  cool one P., 510:4
  cry of p. that could have got worse, 763:3
  cure not worth the p., 100:*n*1
  darkness and cold, 462:25
  dashed with p., 623:10
  despite history's wrenching p., 817:14
  die of rose in aromatic p., 294:21
  doomed to company with p., 371:21
  draw thy breath in p., 202:31
  envy calumny hate p., 403:23
  equal ease unto my p., 245:17
  feast of joy a dish of p., 163:11
  feel no p., 861:3
  for leaven, 529:14
  foresight of bodily p., 315:3
  full of p. this intellectual being, 256:12
  great p. and restlessness, 668:18
  has Element of Blank, 509:16
  heart rapture then p., 550:3
  history of wound beguiles p., 314:4
  I feel your p., 863:1
  I know my life's a p., 227:17
  joys three parts p., 462:15
  king of p., 530:13
  labor we delight in physics p., 215:27
  laughter with p. fraught, 403:5
  life a memory without p., 66:8
  light life pleasure p., 517:15
  man dies in p., 280:26
  marriage has more joy than p., 67:3
  mighty p. to love, 265:10
  narcotics numbing p., 453:12
  neither any more p., 47:12
  occasional enjoyments lighting p., 580:9
  of a new idea, 503:6
  of bone spur in heel, 722:3
  of finite hearts, 461:5
  oh the p. the bliss, 293:2
  older connotation of p., 752:17
  one p. lessened by another's, 179:21
  Our Lady of P., 529:17
  painful pleasure to pleasing p., 160:13
  peace nor help for p., 496:19
  pleasure recalled gives p., 139:5
  pleasures banish p., 289:17
  records of heart in p., 418:17
  Roman wilderness of p., 858:6
  sense of pity beauty p., 567:3
  short joy eternal, 360:10
  still in the middle distance, 772:5
  sudden cry of p., 654:2
  sweet pleasure after p., 274:17
  tender for another's p., 315:8

Pain *(continued)*
  that cannot forget, 63:2
  time cancels young p., 67:16
  'tis p. that p. to miss, 265:10
  to the bear, 420:4
  tongueless vigil and all the p., 529:12
  travaileth in p., 41:20
  turns with ceaseless p., 321:12
  unfinished man and his p., 595:3
  wanders through bones, 756:13
  we measure our p., 847:13
  weight and p. of life, 66:20
  what p. it was to drown, 171:28
  which cost Ceres all that p., 257:17
  with p. purchased inherit p., 173:40
  words of p. tones of anger, 128:8
  world p., 361:*n*4
  yearning like God in p., 409:19
  you purchase p., 293:27
Painful, good honest p. sermon, 277:5
  how p. to keep money, 277:23
  pleasure to pleasing pain, 160:13
  seem no p. inch to gain, 479:12
  truth, 331:10
  warrior famoused for fight, 221:4
Painless, face full of p. peace, 513:7
Pains, capacity for taking p., 528:11
  delight in real p. of others, 323:12
  disciplined state of pleasures and p., 275:*n*3
  have taken up residence, 867:1
  marriage has many p., 307:11
  members partake of p., 157:4
  nothing but labor for p., 155:10
  nothing without p., 155:*n*7
  numbness p. sense, 410:2
  of all p. the greatest, 265:10
  of love be sweeter far, 272:8
  she gave me for my p., 208:3
  stings you for your p., 291:21
Paint an inch thick, 202:12
  capture its reality in p., 533:15
  good-bye Old P., 890:12
  I believe in optimism and white p., 586:12
  lily, 175:24
  lion not so fierce as they p. him, 243:27
  live to p. not p. to live, 551:5
  meadows with delight, 174:32
  my picture truly like me, 246:20
  vices and follies, 286:24
Painted, angels are p. fair, 281:12
  child of dirt, 295:15
  death, 4:9
  Duchess p. on wall, 460:1
  Earth's last picture, 587:12
  fears a p. devil, 215:23
  gourds on a shelf, 810:19
  I have p. my life, 672:7
  love things we see p., 462:8
  not so black as p., 163:10
  not so young as p., 612:15
  players and p. stage, 597:7
  pomp, 193:36
  ship upon painted ocean, 376:2
  veil call Life, 402:*n*1
  winged Cupid p. blind, 178:1
Painter, canvas appeared to American p., 747:7
  I am a p., 639:7
  quality of p. depends on past, 647:12

Painter *(continued)*
  trainer soothsayer, 109:14
Painter's brush consumes dreams, 594:13
  mind with that of viewer, 416:11
Painters and poets have equal license, 98:16
  modern p. work from within, 768:16
Painting, Action P. has to do with self-creation,
    747:8
  all the insults p. has won me, 479:15
  as in p. so in poetry, 99:1
  bridge linking painter's mind, 416:11
  contains divine force, 137:17
  feast for eyes, 416:13
  from today p. is dead, 414:9
  give children right to study p., 330:7
  gives form to terrors, 648:1
  I want to assassinate p., 699:3
  is silent poetry, 60:14
  man that has taste of p., 288:7
  mediator between world and us, 648:1
  my instinct about p. says, 817:3
  not a matter of p. life, 599:13
  not done to decorate apartments, 647:14
  poetry is p. that speaks, 60:14
  poetry p. and music, 354:12
  six essentials in p., 122:11
  that lends joyousness, 539:16
Paintings, farewell dear p., 247:7
  heard of your p., 200:1
  in a room with p., 865:1
Pair, are we a p., 829:2
  no burial this pretty p., 880:14
  nor build nor sing, 378:14
  of ragged claws, 675:1
  of star-crossed lovers, 179:19
  of very strange beasts, 196:3
  one p. of English legs, 189:14
  then there's a p. of us, 508:14
  yet happy p., 257:23
Paired butterflies yellow, 664:18
Pairing suggests copying mechanism, 821:4
Paisley, cutty sark o' P. harm, 358:9
Paix, plus facile de faire la guerre que la p.,
    537:*n*2
Pajamas fresh from washer, 787:9
  how got into p. never know, 708:9
  I in p. for heat, 663:6
  shot elephant in my p., 708:9
Pal, long lost p., 855:13
Palace and prison on each hand, 395:25
  Beautiful, 271:13
  chalice from the p., 775:10
  cypress in p. walk, 453:5
  fair and stately p., 448:9
  give p. for hermitage, 177:12
  golden mean avoids envy of p., 96:22
  of Cyrus, 886:14
  of Eternity, 252:1
  road of excess leads to p. of wisdom,
    351:11
  think upon the pleasure of the p., 234:3
Palaces, cottages princes' p., 184:14
  Death beats at p. of kings, 96:4
  gorgeous p., 225:1
  'mid pleasures and p., 400:16
  my body parks and p., 555:17
  not so arched as princes' p., 237:8
  prosperity within thy p., 19:2

Pard, bearded like the p., 194:25
  false as p. to hind, 203:20
Pardon, a God ready to p., 12:30
  beg death's p. now, 797:11
  cannot help or p., 748:8
  for too much loving you, 209:6
  if life bitter to thee p., 531:1
  love truth p. error, 299:4
  me thou bleeding piece of earth, 192:22
  old fathers, 592:9
  one offense encourage many, 100:32
  pity though not p., 172:14
  remorseful p., 206:11
  to spirit of liberty, 324:3
  virtue of vice p. beg, 201:11
  we p. to extent we love, 264:22
Pardoned all except her face, 398:24
  her iniquity is p., 26:24
Pardoning, in p. we are pardoned, 125:12
Pardonner, tout comprendre tout p., 362:n5
Pardonnera, bien sûr il me p., 415:10
Pardons, never p. those he injures, 103:n10
Paree, after they've seen P., 664:1
Parent, lose one p. misfortune, 560:22
  Nature a kind p., 104:15
  of good, 258:14
  poverty is p. of meanness, 75:6
  wealth is p. of luxury, 75:6
Parental, mild p. sway, 500:5
Parents, be good to p., 118:13
  behave well to p. and elders, 60:15
  bore their children, 565:18
  children begin loving p., 560:5
  girl needs good p., 661:17
  in peace children inter p., 69:7
  in Philadelphia ask who were p., 524:5
  insist on being obeyed, 360:23
  introduces me to her p., 826:15
  Jewish man with p. alive, 835:5
  meek-eyed p., 742:7
  reverence for p., 62:25
  sometimes disappoint children, 742:11
  spying on love life of p., 723:4
  was the same, 887:6
  who weighed measured priced, 466:17
Pares, primus inter p., 121:9
Parfums, les p. les couleurs, 491:n2
Paring, artist indifferent p. fingernails, 650:11
Paris, after they've seen P., 664:1
  Americans die go to P., 560:13
  artist no home save P., 549:8
  from P. to Japan, 278:6
  I shall die in P., 696:16
  il n'est bon bec que de P., 139:n1
  in old house in P., 715:16
  is a moveable feast, 722:8
  is P. burning, 684:18
  is well worth a Mass, 161:13
  last time I saw P., 706:7
  last time I see P., 691:5
  mighty P. when he found, 596:2
  my home town, 628:6
  no good speech save in P., 139:2
  vaut bien une messe, 161:n4
  week in P. will ease, 780:16
  we'll always have P., 758:6

Parish, look upon world as p., 301:15
  plain as way to p. church, 194:21
Park, come out to ball p., 807:6
  I'll be a p. thou shalt be my deer, 171:9
  need p. policeman pretty girl, 683:17
  over p. over pale, 178:10
Parked, motorcycle p. like soul of junkyard, 801:16
Parker, digging Charlie P., 781:2
Parking, paved paradise put up p. lot, 858:1
Parks, I'm world-famous Dr. P. said, 830:17
  my body p. and palaces, 555:17
Parley, no truce or p., 620:9
Parley-voo, hinky dinky p., 688:13
Parliament, coach through Act of P., 883:9
  government is p. of whores, 865:10
  of man, 451:25
  Three Estates in P., 406:n1
Parliaments, kings and p., 303:7
Parlor, queen in p., 894:7
  walk into p., 418:16
Parlors, bells in your p., 208:13
Parlous boy, 171:31
Parmigianino did it, 815:8
Parnassus, rocks of your snowy P., 487:3
Parochial, worse than provincial p., 544:3
Parodies, like p. of themselves, 824:7
Parole humaine comme chaudron fêlé, 493:n4
Parrot, conscious mind trained like p., 630:7
  this p. is no more, 879:8
Parry was innocent, 784:11
Parsimony not economy, 325:13
Parsnips, words butter no p., 374:12
Parson's, coughing drowns p. saw, 175:1
Parsons, white p. preaching Jesus, 802:7
Part, art too precise in every p., 240:16
  beginning most important p., 75:2
  better p. of valor, 183:34
  book and heart never p., 283:4
  come let us kiss and p., 167:11
  death p. of life, 631:3
  each play p. in memorable days, 620:13
  every man must play a p., 184:4
  from yours will not p., 261:6
  half p. of blessed man, 175:9
  his blessed p. to heaven, 226:8
  I am p. of all met, 451:13
  immortal p. of myself, 208:28
  know in p., 42:29
  love's passives his activest p., 263:8
  maid of Athens ere we p., 394:17
  Mary hath chosen good p., 38:1
  my garments among them, 15:22
  my hair behind, 675:6
  myrtle and turkey p., 382:14
  Nature hath done her p., 259:4
  ninth p. of a hair, 182:37
  none shall p. us, 526:16
  of mute melancholy landscape, 582:14
  of solution or part of problem, 839:23
  prophesy in p., 42:29
  read p. all through, 649:17
  some p. of day I had rued, 623:5
  some p. of me contradicts the rest, 468:16
  take my own p., 423:7
  that which is in p., 42:29
  thou and nature so gently p., 219:15
  till death us do p., 49:16

Part (continued)
  we sadly in troublous world, 171:2
  which laws or kings cause, 307:14
  without kiss, 520:4
  you and I must p., 882:3
  you're really p. of me, 691:14
Partaken, banquet p. in anxiety, 59:1
  mutual and p. bliss, 252:24
Parted between twelve and one, 189:4
  fool and money p., 881:10
  from others as nail from flesh, 124:5
  never be p. bliss or woe, 259:15
  never met or never p., 357:9
Partes, Gallia est omnis divisa in p. tres, 88:n10
Parteth the hoof, 8:23
Parthenope nourished me, 93:26
Partial evil universal good, 294:23
  Nature wherefore thus p., 140:14
Partiality, no p. in his writing, 87:14
Participate in America's growth, 756:24
Participated in decisions on Vietnam, 782:9
Participation, deny them p. of freedom, 324:12
  hot media low in p. cool media high, 764:11
Particle, mind very fiery p., 398:29
  part or p. of God, 425:22
Particles, impenetrable movable p., 279:17
  straining at p. of light, 413:12
Particular, each p. erases, 852:7
  each p. hair to stand, 198:5
  London p. a fog, 466:10
  love a bright p. star, 205:31
Particularize, to p. is merit, 353:9
Particularly Gwladys, 648:14
Particulars, do good in minute p., 354:13
  flies from p. to axioms, 164:18
  minutely organized p., 354:13
Parties, all tomorrow's p., 855:1
  always two p., 428:16
  divided mankind into p., 345:9
  men naturally in two p., 338:17
  not built up by deportment, 507:11
Parting all we know of heaven, 511:9
  at p. we will be as when we met, 232:12
  foretaste of death, 400:2
  if not this p. well made, 193:17
  is such sweet sorrow, 180:16
  king stood at p. of way, 28:16
  shakes p. guest by hand, 203:24
  speed the p. guest, 293:19
  speeds the p. guest, 594:11
Partisan cares nothing about rights, 74:15
Partition, union in p., 178:29
Partitions, thin p., 272:16
Partner, when a man's p. is killed, 702:9
Partners, our property subject to control of p., 341:5
  set to p. change lobsters, 515:1
  we are p. in this land, 742:5
Partridge sitteth on eggs, 28:2
Parts, Gaul divided into three p., 88:21
  here the p. shift, 462:6
  no small p. only small actors, 584:16
  of good natural p., 156:15
  of it are excellent, 550:6
  one man plays many p., 194:25
  only Christian come to these p., 139:10
  remembers me his gracious p., 175:19

Peace *(continued)*

commerce honest friendship, 337:12
Constitution law in war and p., 470:15
contributions to p. of world, 661:9
corrupt, 259:26
crimes against p., 694:3
crowned with smiles, 268:15
crust eaten in p., 59:1
cultivate p. and harmony, 329:1
dangerous to p. and safety, 355:7
deep dream of p., 392:16
depart in p., 394:2
easier to make war than p., 537:17
end of that man is p., 16:13
enemies called for p., 608:7
enemies in war in p. friends, 336:2
face full of painless p., 513:7
first in war first in p., 350:6
follow after p., 42:3
fool when he holdeth p., 20:43
for our time, 604:1
fruit of Spirit is p., 43:31
gentlemen may cry P., 331:13
give citizens little p., 803:8
give to all nations p., 49:1
give us p., 47:23
go in p., 37:28, 121:23
go sleep with Turks, 177:15
god has brought this p., 92:14
God is war p. surfeit hunger, 62:5
guide planets, 846:4
habits of p. and patience, 245:1
hard and bitter p., 785:10
hath her victories, 254:19
hope to see p. established, 653:15
I am for p., 18:29
I give unto you, 39:44
I leave with you, 39:44
if you can't give me love and p., 683:6
if you want p., 482:5
imperishable p., 576:4
impossible war improbable, 740:6
in His will is our p., 130:4
in our time, 49:22
in p. children inter parents, 69:7
in p. goodwill, 621:12
in p. just generous, 400:7
in p. Love tunes, 373:2
in p. nothing so becomes man, 189:7
in p. thinks of war, 235:11
in p. ye critics dwell, 293:20
in their hearts, 791:7
in what p. a Christian can die, 288:19
indivisibility of p., 633:n2
indivisible, 633:4
inglorious arts of p., 266:17
is in grave, 401:17
is not absence of war, 275:15
is p. so sweet, 331:13
is poor reading, 536:16
it's wonderful, 649:4
just and lasting p., 447:2
justice made for sake of p., 144:2
keep him in perfect p., 26:3
keep p. within yourself, 137:10
lay me down in p., 15:4
let us have p., 498:5
liberty and safety, 337:12

Peace *(continued)*

live together in p., 661:16
make a desert call it p., 110:13
make war to live in p., 78:14
makes solitude calls it p., 396:25
may he rest in p., 121:12
means of preserving p., 328:13
Mercy Pity P. and Love, 351:3
more important than justice, 144:2
more precious than piece of land, 791:4
my p. is gone, 344:8
naked poor mangled P., 190:6
Napoleon sole obstacle to p., 365:12
never good war or bad p., 303:16
no p. unto the wicked, 26:38
no triumph of p. great as of war, 570:11
nor help for pain, 496:19
nor shall this p. sleep with her, 226:14
not made for justice, 144:2
not p. but a sword, 34:5
not take atomic weapons to want p., 739:6
nothing bring p. but self, 426:25
nothing contributes more to p. of soul,
  335:8
object of war p., 489:14
of all countries connected, 647:9
of God which passeth all understanding,
  49:8
of p. there shall be no end, 25:16
of wild things, 837:2
on earth mercy mild, 305:10
on earth p. and good will, 37:18
on the earth, 457:11
one does not make p. with, 800:5
order security and p., 647:9
our concern be p. of mind, 82:13
our p. our innocence, 370:4
passes into Anesthesia, 580:14
pattern of celestial p., 169:22
perpetual p., 250:9
perpetual p. is dream, 420:8
poetry fine-spun from mind at p., 102:21
price life exacts for p., 718:6
Prince of P., 25:16
proclaims olives of age, 222:10
publisheth p., 27:3
rest in soft p., 232:11
righteousness and p. have kissed each
  other, 17:21
running wild all over, 716:15
seek p. and pursue it, 16:7
separate p., 721:2
servant depart in p., 37:19
slept in p., 226:8
snow said p., 683:5
soft phrase of p., 207:33
speak or forever hold his p., 49:14
suffering evils of long p., 109:20
Tahiti full of p. and joy, 483:5
take chances for p., 674:16
the charm's wound up, 214:3
the human dress, 351:4
there is no p., 331:13
they are in p., 29:34
though make this marriage for my p.,
  218:23
thousand years of p., 454:9
time of p., 22:31

Peace *(continued)*

to him that is far off, 27:13
to men of good will, 47:22
to our children when they fall, 788:6
to this house, 37:32
universal p., 451:10
unjust p. before just war, 303:n3
until I come in p., 12:10
uproar the universal p., 217:6
war is p., 735:17
we came in p. for all mankind, 888:18
we now to p. and darkness, 576:3
we shall find p., 578:9
weak piping time of p., 171:19
what hast thou to do with p., 12:16
what kind of p. do we seek, 786:11
when there is no peace, 27:27
when there was p. he was for p., 749:10
where p. neither anxiety nor doubt, 125:11
which America treasured, 566:15
which passeth understanding, 44:6
who desires p. prepare for war, 115:27
with honor, 430:17, 604:1
without honor not peace, 401:6
without sorrow, 671:15
without victory, 566:12
work us a perpetual p., 250:9
world p. or destruction, 606:7
Peaceably along highway, 313:21
if we can, 380:n2
live p., 41:34
to assemble, 340:1
Peaceful abodes of the gods, 53:n1
as old age tonight, 461:19
coexistence, 741:4
generous just, 446:1
sloth, 256:15
welcome p. evening in, 327:1
what p. hours enjoyed, 326:8
Peacemaker, if is the only p., 196:7
Peacemakers, blessed are the p., 32:14, 170:1
Peach, asked thief to steal me p., 352:4
dare to eat a p., 675:6
once bitter almond, 523:17
ripest p. highest, 553:5
Peacock Pie, 616:9
pride of p. glory of God, 351:14
Peacocks and lilies, 484:9
ivory apes and p., 11:35
Pea-green boat, 467:7
Peak, dwindle p. and pine, 214:2
frozen p., 623:19
in Darien, 408:17
Peaks most wrapt in clouds, 395:17
Peal, rung night's yawning p., 216:12
Pealing anthem swells, 315:19
let the p. organ blow, 251:23
Peanut butter, ate p. sandwiches, 796:7
Peanuts, buy p. and cracker-jack, 640:1
Pear, go to p. tree for pears, 100:29
golden p., 894:18
Pearl, barbaric p. and gold, 256:6
hang p. in cowslip's ear, 178:11
in your foul oyster, 196:5
of great price, 34:19
quarelets of p., 240:14
robe of gold and p., 189:23
Tankards scooped in P., 508:8

Pearl *(continued)*
　threw a p. away, 210:20
Pearls, asked how p. did grow, 240:14
　black men are p., 173:36
　cast p. before swine, 33:15
　string p. strung on, 544:13
　that were his eyes, 224:14
Pearly, shows teeth p. white, 716:7
Pears, go to pear tree for p., 100:29
Peas, tame pigeons p., 262:*n*1
Peasant have chicken in pot, 161:12
　rogue and p. slave, 199:15
　toe of p., 202:11
Peasantry, bold p., 322:22
　dictatorship of proletariat and p., 607:10
Peasants born kings of earth, 432:10
　call bachelors' prayer, 662:4
　carry honor in their hands, 238:22
　you're still fucking p., 848:3
Pease-porridge hot, 894:16
Pebble, finding smoother p., 279:18
　is a perfect creature, 806:4
Pebbled, waves make towards p. shore, 221:16
Pebbles, didst pick up Andrew Jackson from p., 482:24
　grating roar of p., 496:17
　of holy streams, 777:12
　unnumbered idle p., 212:24
Peccata, qui tollis p. mundi, 47:23
Peck, for daws to p. at, 207:26
　of pickled peppers, 895:8
　truly a p. of provender, 178:32
Pecks, three p. of barley meal, 896:23
Pecksniff, said Mr. P. tenderly, 464:35
Pectus est enim quod disertos facit, 106:*n*3
Peculiar deposit for virtue, 336:10
　God's p. light, 143:2
　heathen Chinee is p., 528:10
Pedagogues, clouds are p., 642:3
Pedantical, figures p., 174:28
Pedants, learned p. much affect, 262:6
Peddler, lives of shoemaker and fish p., 682:11
Pede, ex p. Herculem, 69:*n*6
Pedestal, on p. these words appear, 401:13
　women put not on p. but in cage, 745:12
Pedigree of Honey, 511:5
Peel, d'ye ken John P., 408:13
　me a grape, 700:8
　set sharp racks to pinch and p., 409:17
Peeled patched and piebald, 297:1
Peep about to find graves, 191:26
　and botanize, 369:9
　at such a world, 327:2
　from her cabined loophole p., 252:10
　heaven p. through blanket, 214:18
　treason can but p., 201:29
Peep-hole, wine is a p., 55:20
Peeping in at morn, 418:2
Peeping Tom, instincts of a p., 816:16
Peeps over glasses' edge, 461:20
　primrose p. beneath thorn, 322:28
Peer, do not p. too far, 63:24
　many a p. of England brews, 575:12
Peereth, honor p. in meanest habit, 173:22
Peering, into darkness p., 449:7
Peerless, unveiled her p. light, 257:25
Peers, drunk delight of battle with p., 451:13
　heroes of old, 462:25

Peers *(continued)*
　House of P. throughout war, 527:2
　judgment of his p., 126:4
　powerful amidst p., 546:16
Peg, square p. in round hole, 374:*n*2
Pegasus, turn and wind a fiery P., 183:14
Peignoir, complacencies of p., 640:20
Peine, la p. de naître, 327:*n*5
Pejorist, not pessimist but p., 574:*n*1
Peking, butterfly stirring air in P., 872:5
　improved relations with P., 771:6
Peleus', wrath of P. son, 50:9, 293:16
Pelf, I crave no p., 213:21
　titles power and p., 373:3
Pelican, Lord Jesu blessed P., 127:4
Pelion, from Ossa hurled P., 53:*n*3
　pile Ossa on P., 93:13
　with its leafy forests, 53:12
Pellet with poison, 775:10
Pellinore followed questing beast, 138:3
Peloponnesians, war between P. and Athenians, 71:11
Pelops', Thebes or P. line, 251:19
Pelting of pitiless storm, 211:33
Pembroke's mother, 240:7
Pen, and I made a rural p., 350:11
　antique p. would have expressed, 222:9
　cold words of tongue or p., 609:12
　excellent instrument, 329:7
　galley slave to p., 417:13
　gleaned teeming brain, 412:7
　I don't use a p., 763:13
　in hand, 311:3
　lend me your p., 891:*n*2
　Lord taught by the P., 119:18
　make famous by my p., 262:*n*2
　make glorious by my p., 262:24
　mightier than sword, 423:13
　my tongue is the p. of a ready writer, 16:24
　need far less brilliant p. than mine, 612:16
　never saw p. and ink, 205:26
　nose as sharp as p., 189:4
　poet's p. turns to shapes, 179:6
　preferable to sword, 156:39
　rob you with a fountain p., 768:3
　sad words of tongue or p., 438:10
　squat p. rests, 845:9
　through every other word, 375:11
　whether chisel p. brush, 593:6
　with such acts fill a p., 167:10
　words as with burning p., 359:11
　worse than the sword, 235:5
　write p. for I am volumes, 174:7
　written with a pen of iron, 27:38
Penal, chains and p. fire, 255:7
Penalty, death p., 770:10
　greatest p. of evildoing, 76:9
Penance, hath p. done, 376:20
　more will do, 376:20
Pence, for thirty p. my death, 242:15
　take care of p., 298:7
　three hundred p., 39:36
Pencil-sketches that pass behind original's back, 431:13
Pendent, blown about p. world, 206:38
　made his p. bed, 214:21
　towered citadel p. rock, 218:39
　world as a star, 257:4

Penelope, constant as P., 881:19
　faithful P., 54:9
　true P. was Flaubert, 665:5
Penetrable to shower of gold, 407:3
Penetrates Eternal Justice as eye into sea, 130:8
　non-being p. no space, 57:14
　sun p. privies, 77:3
Peniel, called the place P., 7:4
Peninsula, whole p. of Florida, 819:15
Penitence, vague kind of p., 464:28
Penitentiary, down in shadow of the p., 868:5
Penknife in your heart, 892:8
Pennies, rains p. from Heaven, 751:15
Penniless, forgive man for being p., 417:14
Pennsylvania, some small towns in P., 877:3
Penny, beg p. by and by, 683:4
　for your thought, 148:4
　in for p. in for pound, 527:5
　in old man's hat, 884:7
　Jacky have a p. a day, 893:19
　not a p. in it, 896:5
　one a p. two a p., 894:15
　postage stamp, 517:10
　wise pound foolish, 234:11
Pens are too light, 724:16
　natural right to use p., 299:20
　of diplomats not ruin, 335:7
　quirks of blazoning p., 208:12
　skewered with office p., 466:3
　though trees in earth were p., 119:5
Pensant, un roseau p., 269:*n*7
Pense, honi soit qui mal y p., 131:1
　je p. donc je suis, 246:9
Pension never enriched young man, 244:9
Pensive Eve, 317:12
Pent by sea and dark brows, 488:2
　long in city p., 408:15
　long in populous city p., 259:9
Pentagon turn orange and vibrate, 803:7
Pentameter, in p. aye falling, 378:2
Penthouse, hang upon his p. lid, 214:1
Pent-up, drain p. rivers of myself, 486:22
　love of my heart, 551:3
Penuries, to fill all p., 231:10
Penury, age ache p., 207:1
　chill p., 315:22
　talk tendeth only to p., 20:28
People, a stiffnecked p., 8:19
　absolved of history, 829:8
　aging college p., 723:10
　all exulting, 487:16
　all p. and tongues, 46:35
　all p. need be liked by some p., 760:4
　all sorts of p., 215:1
　all the lonely p., 848:7
　Americans a P., 695:4
　Americans are chosen p., 482:15
　are all monkeys to me, 663:8
　are like water, 698:12
　are trapped in history, 804:10
　arose as one man, 10:28
　attentive unto book of law, 12:29
　be nice to p. on way up, 633:9
　beat my p. to pieces, 24:37
　behind p. the country, 498:9
　believe p. are really good, 822:7
　believe these p. from sky, 139:11
　black p. unite, 850:3

People *(continued)*

brave new world that has such p., 225:6
British p. like to be told worst, 620:5
capable of becoming happier, 685:6
change what is in themselves, 118:9
chief business of American p., 613:6
chosen p. children of light, 496:10
chosen p. of God, 336:10
colored p. understand white p., 610:1
come to church good p., 575:1
come ye thankful p., 456:9
comfort ye my p., 26:23
common-looking p. best, 446:6
complained of long voyage, 139:7
conceited p. carry comfort, 480:11
conditioned p. of Africa to humiliation,
    802:6
confidence in justice of p., 445:6
considered by p. equally true, 332:2
contracts with the p., 661:10
country belongs to p., 445:5
dangerous who make no noise, 266:14
descend to meet, 427:4
difference between rich and other p.,
    721:n4
difficult to believe p. starving, 765:16
dull and ugly p., 582:12
easily becomes prey, 142:8
economics as if p. mattered, 766:2
experiment of American p., 328:11
eyes of all p. upon us, 239:16
fear and distrust the p., 338:17
find p. have good sense, 264:23
fool some p., 447:5
freedom light, 688:10
gift iv the p., 600:17
given over in troops to disease and death,
    90:22
glory of thy p. Israel, 37:20
God save the p., 389:4
good tidings to all p., 37:17
government for benefit of p., 384:17
government for the p., 390:8
government of by for p., 446:5, 457:9
Government of p. Congress is p., 404:17
greater part of rich p., 319:3
grudge what they cannot enjoy, 59:4
have always some champion, 75:20
have right to knowledge, 329:9
have right to rise up, 444:4
hell is other p., 743:3
his p. were his temple, 270:4
hoop unbroken p. flourished, 583:5
how you are to govern p., 323:20
I am the p., 636:1
I don't eat p., 798:11
I know all p. worth knowing in America,
    456:16
I loathe p. who keep dogs, 553:11
I see dead p., 880:1
if p. don't want to come, 807:6
imagine a vain thing, 15:1
in a boat, 874:6
in fashionable New York Society, 504:2
in glass houses, 243:n2
in old times had convictions, 415:6
included in We the p., 841:12
indictment against whole p., 324:8

People *(continued)*

is a great beast, 97:n13
it's P. I can't stand, 800:12
judging p. by appearances, 266:13
known by p. never heard of Jesus Christ,
    683:18
land of Russian p., 429:16
laughed cried most silent, 739:8
law for rulers and p., 470:15
leader and commander to the p., 27:10
let go hold of p., 715:7
let my p. go, 7:31, 898:18
let p. think they govern, 280:14
lie during sex, 873:4
lift p. from dust, 424:20
like p. like priest, 28:32
look after our p., 603:8
love of British p., 324:13
made the Constitution, 350:2
maintain control of government, 652:18
many p. unable to find work, 613:10
many-headed beast, 97:20
masses of p. not qualified, 657:12
may grow old without visiting, 58:6
may walk but not throw stones at birds,
    307:27
mediocre p. have answer for everything,
    416:12
mercy on my poor p., 154:1
mercy on Thy P. Lord, 589:11
more dead p. than living, 768:8
more than half p. right, 724:3
most important element, 80:8
most p. my age are dead, 689:3
multitude of the gross p., 97:n13
must look to themselves, 810:8
muzzle self-expression of p., 765:13
my p. are Americans, 717:9
my p. would increase, 507:12
naked p. have little influence, 525:10
never learned from history, 367:9
new deal for American p., 651:16
ninety-nine percent of p. fools, 715:12
no doubt but ye are the p., 13:23
no more give the p. straw, 7:32
not always what seem, 325:17
numerous and warlike, 139:13
O stormy p., 135:22
oats supports p., 307:4
of his pasture, 17:32
of p. by p. for p., 446:5, 457:9
of that flow are new, 755:4
of unclean lips, 25:10
of Western Europe, 686:13
old p. are square, 814:11
on whom nothing lost, 544:9
on world not in it, 533:11
one man die for p., 39:35
one should like to drop, 311:4
only p. for me mad, 799:3
only the little p. pay taxes, 794:8
only two p. who count, 864:7
our land before we her p., 624:5
our p. never had it so good, 703:5
our sovereign the p., 390:n4
people have for friends, 579:3
people marry, 579:3
planned obsolescence of p., 769:2

People *(continued)*

power from the p., 429:19
protection of p., 320:8
put up with oppressive rule, 434:8
relation between white and colored p.,
    477:5
religion opium of p., 477:12
remove weight from p., 801:11
representatives of p., 400:15
resemble wild beast, 142:8
retain virtue and vigilance, 445:7
right of p. to make alter constitutions,
    328:14
right of trampling on p., 421:15
Sacco's name in hearts of p., 682:12
safe depository of powers, 338:12
say life is the thing, 590:15
seldom judge right, 349:4
sensed by p. expressed by p., 500:14
separated by six other p., 844:9
should be beautiful, 578:8
should be taught what is, 807:10
should fight for their law, 62:12
shouted with a great shout, 9:38
show my head to the p., 359:6
showed thy p. hard things, 17:1
signs for a god-fearing p., 118:6
small country with few p., 58:6
so dead to liberty, 305:13
special p. unto himself, 9:17
spoil lives of better p., 556:2
still in the gristle, 324:2
strange p. who have courage to be
    unhappy, 552:1
struggled on with troubles, 582:15
such tongue to great p., 479:8
sum married p. owe, 343:11
talebearer among thy p., 8:27
talk sense to American p., 727:9
tell p. what they don't want to hear,
    735:10
that once bestowed commands, 109:24
that p. may require leader, 75:22
the p. will live on, 636:10
there is a p. risen, 270:7
thy p. shall be my p., 10:30
to all the p. you can, 301:19
to these p. I owe everything, 445:1
tricked and sold, 636:10
turn to benevolent rule, 79:18
two kinds of p., 556:15
two p. miserable instead of four, 521:5
two thirds of p. killed, 638:3
under violent passions, 565:16
underestimating intelligence of p., 645:15
visited and redeemed his p., 37:13
voice of p. is voice of God, 122:5
watch over economy of private p., 319:4
we are his p., 18:3
we are one p., 579:4
we p. will get to promised land, 823:16
we the p., 339:11
were passed clean over Jordan, 9:36
we're the p. we go on, 733:4
what is the city but p., 219:31
what kind of p. do they think we are,
    620:15
what p. are like here, 342:11

People *(continued)*
where no vision the p. perish, 22:10
which sat in darkness, 32:12
who eat the earth, 741:9
who know little, 312:23
who lift people who lean, 556:15
who need people, 800:3
who will feed me, 814:5
win friends influence p., 674:1
wish p. to think well of you, 269:7
witness to the p., 27:10
would die for my p., 513:4
would that Roman p. had single neck, 104:12
you know yet can't name, 799:16
Peopled, earthly ball a p. garden, 343:2
teach order to p. kingdom, 188:34
world must be p., 190:36
People's good is highest law, 88:10
in p. eyes life, 654:5
nor p. judgment always true, 273:5
not seat self on other p. backs, 548:4
other p. money, 501:8
queen in p. hearts, 876:9
reforming other p. habits, 523:23
she was the P. Princess, 871:10
sits high in p. hearts, 191:34
soil of p. necessities, 581:1
state worst of all states, 249:13
this is a p. contest, 445:9
voice odd, 296:12
Peoples, domination over all p., 765:14
English-speaking p., 557:17
happiness of p., 545:18
history life of p., 507:2
mos p. gonna lose, 773:13
of United Nations, 661:16
sink or swim together, 607:3
who have courage to face war, 657:4
wishes of p. concerned, 653:14
Peopling the void air, 495:7
Peor and Baalim, 250:14
Peoria, it'll play in P., 807:15
Peppercorn, I am a p., 183:7
Peppered two of them, 182:21
Peppers, peck of pickled p., 895:8
Per caputque pedesque, 91:n5
Perceive differently than one sees, 812:8
here a divided duty, 208:4
what he is intending to say, 524:7
ye are too superstitious, 40:32
yourself sole heir of world, 278:10
Perceived harmony of object, 378:23
Perceivers of terror of life, 428:3
Perceives, artist p. more than fellows, 613:11
it die away, 370:18
Perceiving, conscious that we are p., 78:11
genius p. in unhabitual way, 541:7
Percent, eighty p. of success, 839:20
produce 80 p. of the sales, 795:14
Perception, imagination agent of p., 379:5
of beauty moral test, 473:5
pale colorless, 541:9
Perch, custom make it their p., 206:18
if you hadn't nailed parrot to p., 879:8
where eagles dare not p., 171:23
Perches in the soul, 508:12
Perchings, flights and p., 540:25

Percy, old song of P. and Douglas, 162:19
Percy's, not yet of P. mind, 182:17
Perdition, bottomless p., 255:7
catch my soul, 208:35
Perdu, tout p. fors l'honneur, 145:n4
Perdue, une génération p., 627:n1
Pereant qui nostra ante nos dixerunt, 121:5
Pereat, fiat justitia et p. mundus, 120:n6
Perennial pleasures plants, 417:7
spring of prodigality, 324:15
Perestroika combines continuity innovation, 830:3
Perfect and entire, 45:20
be ye therefore p., 32:23
circle and vicious circle, 768:7
every p. gift, 45:22
form a more p. Union, 339:11
Glory be the P. One, 509:18
his work is p., 9:30
I am not in p. mind, 213:5
in bud as in bloom, 520:15
in heaven p. round, 462:10
interpreter of life, 666:11
keep him in p. peace, 26:3
let patience have her p. work, 45:20
life may p. be, 233:8
love casteth out fear, 46:12
made p. in weakness, 43:24
mark the p. man, 16:13
move in p. phalanx, 255:23
nothing quite new is p., 87:18
one p. limousine, 699:15
pebble is a p. creature, 806:4
practice makes p., 100:n5
really p. poem, 810:2
shineth unto the p. day, 19:29
spirits of just men made p., 45:14
then if ever p. days, 481:16
to be p. is to have changed often, 421:6
touched her p. body, 837:9
visit p. in being too short, 382:16
when that which is p., 42:29
woman nobly planned, 371:8
Perfected, woman is p., 833:5
Perfectest, silence p. herald of joy, 190:28
Perfectibility of man, 433:15
Perfection as culture conceives it, 497:12
culture study of p., 497:10
dead p., 454:26
fullness of p. in him, 175:9
holds in p. but moment, 221:1
law is p. of reason, 158:21
little concerned with p., 537:11
of form and beauty, 142:12
of life or of work, 595:9
of mathematics, 614:9
of planned layout, 760:2
pink of p., 323:3
right praise true p., 186:19
spiritual p. of man, 124:14
stern p. as greatest art, 614:9
vowing p. of ten, 203:18
Perfections, discovers p. in beloved, 391:20
Perfectly, I remember your name p., 549:16
loser is p. clear, 795:12
Perfidious Albion, 366:5
fatal and p. bark, 253:8

Perform, ability they never p., 203:18
every act as though it were your last, 111:9
his wonders to p., 326:9
never promise more than p., 100:17
Performance, desire outlive p., 188:8
lovers swear more p., 203:18
only p. that makes it, 837:8
takes away the p., 215:26
Performed, rites simple decisive, 810:18
to a T, 145:15
Performs, man p. engenders, 713:17
Perfume, amber scent of odorous p., 260:16
feel my breasts all p., 650:18
not like you buy your p., 826:10
owest cat no p., 212:3
throw p. on violet, 175:24
Perfumed like milliner, 181:35
old women should not be p., 55:1
sea, 447:12
so p. that winds love-sick, 218:20
Perfumes, all the p. of Arabia, 217:14
colors sounds echo, 491:3
like a dancer amid her p., 493:9
Perhaps, seek a grand p., 146:7
Pericles, in wrath the Olympian P., 72:10
Periclum ex aliis facito, 85:n13
Periculum in mora, 161:n6
Periit, qui ante diem p., 582:9
Peril, in p. mask is off, 90:9
those in p. on sea, 503:1
use our pens at our p., 299:20
woods more free from p., 193:36
Perilous, cleanse bosom of p. stuff, 217:19
fight, 386:19
nothing more p. than new order, 141:13
seas in faery lands forlorn, 410:10
turns to p. waters, 128:4
unsifted in p. circumstance, 197:26
Perils, avoid p. by united forces, 276:14
defend us from all p., 48:18
how many p. do enfold, 160:6
of camp march and battle, 519:10
when our p. are past, 367:4
Period at the right moment, 700:16
new and great p. in His Church, 254:11
of effectiveness of generation, 657:13
Periphrastic study, 678:16
Peris, sweets of Fairies P. Goddesses, 409:13
Perish, beauty so soon to p., 654:16
city to p. if it finds buyer, 92:11
drink unto him that is ready to p., 22:15
fame of her excellence will never p., 54:9
hero p. or sparrow fall, 294:18
if it had to p. twice, 623:4
if we must p. in fight, 439:8
in our own, 576:12
in their infancy, 882:3
let justice be done though world p., 120:n6
let the day p., 13:3
may they p. who used our words, 121:5
name not p. in dust, 381:16
or catch up, 607:13
shall not p. from earth, 446:5
should not p., 39:11
spirit of moderation will p., 614:1
surely weak p., 627:11
survive or p., 390:3
that one of thy members should p., 32:18

Perish *(continued)*
the thought, 287:15
their goodness does not p., 68:20
those most likely to p., 321:5
though heaven may p., 363:1
thy money p., 40:19
truths wake to p. never, 371:2
twice, 623:4
weakly p. at another moment, 52:12
where no vision the people p., 22:10
with the sword, 36:9
Perished as they had never been, 31:27
by own follies they p., 52:21
in his pride, 369:16
the weapons of war p., 11:10
we p. each alone, 327:10
who p. being innocent, 13:6
Perishes, everything p., 891:3
Periuria ridet amantum Iupiter, 101:*n*8
Periwig, new p. make a great show, 277:20
Periwig-pated, robustious p. fellow, 200:6
Perjured, gloriously p., 97:4
murderous bloody, 222:20
Perjuries, at lovers' p. Jove laughs, 180:5
of lovers, 101:20
Perked up in glistering grief, 225:17
Perkins, lay down your life P., 837:1
Permanence, from days of old no p., 4:9
sea cannot claim, 535:16
Permanent alliances, 329:3
and certain characteristics, 306:21
and the same, 495:13
contract on temporary feeling, 536:7
disuse of any organ, 341:8
feeling towards people, 663:8
feelings p. and the same, 495:13
interests of community, 345:8
more p. than fish or weed, 825:9
nothing ought to be p., 433:15
share in government, 349:4
system of security, 653:16
Permission, life p. to know death, 692:9
nobody without Count's p., 656:3
place of first p., 792:5
Permit base contagious clouds, 181:33
doing what laws p., 297:13
how long p. to Heaven, 259:22
Permitte divis cetera, 96:*n*6
Permitted, whatever not forbidden is p.,
359:21
Pernicious consequences, 470:15
race of odious vermin, 284:26
Perpetual, constitution or p. law, 336:16
desire a p. rack, 234:21
devotion to business, 554:16
feast of nectared sweets, 252:19
kingdom of p. night, 171:29
let p. light shine, 47:19
move around in p. motion, 790:2
neglect of other things, 554:16
night, 91:5, 232:5
orgy, 493:19
our interests eternal and p., 392:21
scoured with p. motion, 187:35
sleep of p. night, 91:5
speculators about p. motion, 140:13
summary court in p. session, 656:1
work us a p. peace, 250:9

Perpetually, life begins p., 599:5
nation p. to be conquered, 324:4
one hour then damned p., 169:3
saves itself p., 762:12
Perpetuate, any way to p. the World, 248:16
piece of fine writing, 584:1
Perpetuity, merit of p., 249:1
Perplexed in the extreme, 210:20
labyrinthical soul, 231:13
to have plenty is to be p., 57:10
Perplexes and affronts, 772:2
monarchs, 255:25
Perplexity of radical evil, 744:9
Persecute, despitefully use and p. you, 32:21
you for my sake, 32:14
Persecuted church of God, 42:32
for righteousness' sake, 32:14
most p. minority, 649:10
Persecutes the mind, 274:1
Persecutest, why p. thou me, 40:22
Persecution bad way to plant religion, 248:8
gives p. no assistance, 328:12
object of p. is p., 735:21
Persecutions have made Church grow, 113:*n*4
Persephone, even where P. goes, 663:22
Persepolis, ride in triumph through P., 168:1
Persever in obstinate condolement, 196:28
Perseverance and soothing language, 337:2
fortitude and p., 318:4
in good cause, 313:26
keeps honor bright, 203:22
more prevailing than violence, 108:2
Persevere, forbear and p., 556:12
Persia, past first sleep in P., 249:7
Persian luxury I hate, 96:18
Persians accustomed to deliberate when drunk,
69:8
law of the Medes and P., 28:26
taught three things, 399:6
Persicos odi puer apparatus, 96:*n*12
Person, aging p. give attention to self, 630:4
agreeable p. agrees with me, 430:13
attention must be paid to p., 780:5
beggared all description, 218:20
blood of this just p., 36:15
commanding p. suddenly to die, 431:20
dignity and worth of p., 661:16
don't believe no sich p., 465:4
France a p., 417:2
freedom of p., 337:12
get up so white p. could sit, 771:16
may have many thousand selves, 654:13
no agent more effective than other p.,
799:1
no more a p. now, 749:6
no p. must have to, 325:16
no sich p., 465:4
not p. involved, 523:20
of contrary opinion, 435:2
of its head root of family, 79:17
produce the p., 120:27
really hope no white p., 856:9
seize p. next to you, 874:6
show you hungry p., 856:8
simple separate p., 485:12
touch my p. to someone else's, 486:11
very umble p., 465:27
who seizes two things, 889:6

Person *(continued)*
young p. occupied with self, 630:4
Personages, facts p. appear twice, 477:14
Personal considerations in public duty, 498:6
inner p. experiences, 542:7
knowledge not p. experience, 75:3
none can regard it as p., 444:1
perspective only kind of history, 844:10
politics of p. destruction, 863:3
Personalities, meeting of p. chemical contact,
630:3
trivial p. decomposing, 654:7
Personality, continual extinction of p., 675:18
cult of p., 702:18
intellectual and artistic p., 757:14
needs a good p., 661:17
poetry escape from p., 675:19
taint of p., 505:16
Personified, evil to Ahab p., 483:3
Personne, celui que p. ne peut imiter, 364:*n*6
Persons About to Write History, 518:11
all p. born in U.S. citizens, 340:8
all p. share in government, 78:25
divers paces with divers p., 195:15
God in Three P., 391:8
God no respecter of p., 40:27
great p. great kindnesses, 157:32
neither p. nor property safe, 477:9
respect of place p. time, 204:28
without respect of p., 45:36
Person's, majority rule is p. conscience, 813:5
Perspective, cylinder sphere cone in p., 533:17
personal p. only kind of history, 844:10
youth forge central p., 730:6
Perspicuity, we praise thee for p. of language,
123:8
Perspiration, ninety-nine percent p., 550:13
Persuade a man to believe, 843:11
beauty doth of itself p., 172:29
even if you p. me, 73:19
if possible the rulers, 75:5
impossible to p. a man, 792:1
tongue to p., 261:1
Persuaded, burnt each other quite p., 398:1
cannot be p. by gun or lariat, 895:*n*1
in his own mind, 42:1
none could advise thou p., 159:15
Persuader, president is p., 764:4
Persuaders, Hidden P., 775:9
Persuades, truth p. by teaching, 113:10
when speaking fails, 223:15
Persuadest, almost p. me to be a Christian, 41:7
Persuading, fair-spoken and p., 226:12
Persuasion and belief, 372:8
companion's words of p., 51:22
hung upon his lips, 314:2
in it was blandishing p., 51:29
two gods P. and Compulsion, 62:20
whatever race creed or p., 666:15
Persuasive, demonstrative or p. type, 607:2
Pert as schoolgirl can be, 527:12
Perturbation, polished p., 188:20
Perturbed, rest p. spirit, 198:21
Peru, a Newton at P., 317:4
mankind from China to P., 306:15
there lies P., 414:7
Perverse, art selfish and p., 366:19
imp of the p., 449:13

Perverse *(continued)*
 tugging at p. life, 755:14
 widows most p. creatures, 288:14
 wood so crooked and p., 320:1
Perverseness primitive impulse, 449:*n*1
Perversion, Christianity enormous p., 549:3
Perversions, most unnatural of sexual p., 702:14
Pervert, use novel not for art you p. it, 809:8
Pessary, will not give woman p., 70:14
Pessimism agreeable as optimism, 599:11
Pessimist fears this is true, 637:6
 looks at glass, 646:8
 not p. but pejorist, 574:*n*1
Pestered with a popinjay, 182:1
Pestilence, Famine P. Destruction Death, 646:5
 noisome p., 17:28
 power like desolating p., 401:8
 that walketh in darkness, 17:28
 winter plague and p., 227:5
Pestilence-stricken multitudes, 402:9
Pestilent, foul and p., 199:5
Pestle, vessel with the p., 775:10
Petal, now sleeps crimson p., 453:5
Petal's, from p. edge a line starts, 658:11
Petals on wet black bough, 665:1
Petar, hoist with his own p., 201:15
Peter denied Lord and cried, 283:5
 Flopsy Mopsy Cottontail P., 598:5
 give not Saint P. so much, 147:*n*8
 Piper picked peck, 895:8
 Pumpkin-Eater, 895:15
 remembered word of Jesus, 36:11
 rob P. pay Paul, 147:23
 thou art P., 34:37
 wept bitterly, 36:11
Peterkin, quoth little P., 381:9
Peter's, blessing of Saint P. Master, 245:10
 dome, 424:5
Petersburg I still possess list of addresses, 690:12
 most theoretical town, 492:4
Petite, oh my P., 787:13
Petition government for redress, 340:1
Petitions, desires and p. of thy servants, 48:17
Petrarch's, if Laura P. wife, 398:14
Petrel, waters of p. and porpoise, 679:2
Petrifies the feeling, 356:19
Petrol more likely than wheat, 760:10
Petticoat, feet beneath her p., 261:5
 government, 391:11
 tempestuous p., 240:16
 turned out of Realm in my p., 151:8
Petty, creeps in this p. pace, 217:23
 makes each p. artery, 198:2
 never be p., 771:10
 official high or p., 694:2
 we p. men, 191:26
Peuple, pitié de mon pauvre p., 154:*n*1
Peur, de p. d'en pleurer, 327:*n*4
 le plus de p. que la p., 152:*n*1
Peut-être, chercher un grand p., 146:*n*5
Pewter, no p. no pub, 682:1
Pez muere por la boca, 898:7
Phalanx, move in perfect p., 255:23
Phantasma, like p. or hideous dream, 192:2
Phantom deer arise, 716:5
 flickering lamp p. dream, 112:26

Phantom *(continued)*
 of delight, 371:6
 one grand hooded p., 482:20
Pharaoh, one more plague upon P., 7:37
 tell old P., 898:18
Pharaoh's, he hardened P. heart, 7:34
 lean kine loved, 182:28
 wise men cast down rods, 7:34
Pharisee, one a P. the other a publican, 38:22
 the son of a P., 40:46
Pharisees, scribes and P., 35:15
Pharisees', drowns in P. hypocrisy, 688:3
Pharos of Egypt, 886:13
Phases, definite historical p. of production, 477:16
Phenomena, concepts call p. to mind, 338:22
 new p. lead to bombs, 638:1
 not deduced from p. is hypothesis, 279:12
 not disclose essence of p., 662:2
 predict p., 406:6
 same circumstances same p., 286:19
 sequence of p., 338:22
Phenomenon, felicitous p., 671:21
 infant p., 464:19
 portray p. concept needed, 338:22
Phidias, by P. done, 886:14
 unable to reach all the material, 112:24
Philadelphia, in P. ask who were parents, 524:5
 rather be in P., 644:3
Philanthropist, masterpiece delusion to p., 520:15
Philanthropy of Captain Brown, 475:25
 only virtue appreciated, 474:26
 which forgives, 388:8
 which neither shoots nor liberates, 475:25
Philippine, our forces stand on P. soil, 644:8
Philistia triumph thou because of me, 17:2
Philistine, David prevailed over the P., 11:2
 strong dogged unenlightened, 496:10
 what is called a p., 400:5
Philistines, avenged of P., 10:25
 Barbarians P. Populace, 497:8
 be upon thee, 10:23
 put out Samson's eyes, 10:24
 though P. may jostle, 526:11
Phillips, was it Wendell P., 438:21
Philosopher, anything implausible already said by p., 246:8
 endure toothache, 191:13
 great poet profound p., 379:14
 guide p. and friend, 295:7, 647:2
 not aloof to gain reputation, 76:6
 nothing so ridiculous but p. said it, 88:2
 thinks like a p., 313:10
 to be p. to love wisdom, 474:16
 was a p. yet hadde but litel gold, 133:23
 weeping p. when old, 184:17
 what are sinews of p., 109:2
 worship considered by p., 332:2
Philosopher's stones, 235:12
Philosophers come down from mountains, 533:10
 discovered unconscious, 563:12
 God of Abraham not p., 270:2
 great economists called worldly p., 792:7
 heroes statesmen p., 340:14
 illusion of p., 713:13
 interpreted world in various ways, 477:13

Philosophers *(continued)*
 not all atheists, 723:16
 not from p. but nature, 236:3
 until p. are kings, 75:9
Philosophers' Syndrome mistaking a failure, 853:14
Philosopher-scientists, there are p., 780:4
Philosophia biou kybernetes, 355:*n*2
 O vitae p. dux, 88:*n*1
Philosophic ideals altars to unknown gods, 540:18
 poetry more p., 79:5
Philosophical, European p. tradition footnotes to Plato, 580:11
 healthy-mindedness as p. doctrine, 541:21
 speculators of common sort, 155:7
Philosophize on vanity of life, 149:7
 to ridicule philosophy is to p., 269:24
Philosophy, adversity's sweet milk p., 180:34
 as we use the word, 685:15
 bladders of p., 281:3
 call p. down from heavens, 88:5
 can only describe language, 685:13
 clip angel's wings, 409:16
 Comte's p., 502:7
 defense of p., 723:16
 depth in p. bringeth to religion, 165:27
 divine p., 252:19
 divine P., 453:20
 dreamed of in any p., 693:11
 dreamt of in your p., 198:19
 errors in p. ridiculous, 311:20
 experimental p., 279:12
 false p., 256:22
 fundamental question of p., 769:15
 gained this by p., 77:11
 good horse in stable, 322:18
 guide of life, 355:3
 hang up p., 180:35
 hast any p. in thee, 195:4
 history is p. learned from examples, 101:11
 I have no p. myself, 693:11
 if p. could find it out, 199:7
 in p. most worldly of activities, 792:7
 is comprehended in thoughts, 367:6
 is for the few, 155:6
 little p. inclineth to atheism, 165:27
 make a Juliet, 180:35
 my sons ought to study p., 330:7
 natural p. deep moral grave, 166:19
 Natural P. embodied in mathematical beauty, 579:8
 new p. calls all in doubt, 230:15
 new p. proceeds from world, 227:8
 no p. so abhorrent, 650:6
 not faith but mere p., 248:11
 not pretend to doubt in p., 534:15
 not technical matter, 542:5
 obscure regions of p., 312:1
 pieced thoughts into p., 594:7
 remains true, 822:12
 right in saying life understood backward, 469:2
 sense of what life means, 542:5
 spirit and power of p., 75:9
 stares but brings no solution, 542:13
 to get rid of self-conceit, 109:3
 to ridicule p., 269:24

Pig, buy a fat p., 896:9
  dear P. are you willing, 467:9
  eat Tom beat, 894:11
  I am only guinea p. I have, 705:15
  in a poke, 148:25
  in as p. out as sausage, 540:10
  little p. to market, 893:10
  love not a gaping p., 185:26
  rather a handsome p., 514:11
  snake edible to p., 540:7
Pigeon-livered, I am p., 199:18
Pigeons, casual flocks of p., 640:22
  on grass alas, 627:19
  onetwothreefourfive p., 701:7
  tame p. peas, 262:n1
Piggy, said P. I will, 467:9
  true wise friend called P., 764:1
Piggy-wig stood, 467:8
Pigments, secret of durable p., 723:8
Pigmy's straw does pierce it, 212:30
Pigs, men filthy p., 627:2
  speak Greek naturally as p. squeak, 262:1
  whether p. have wings, 516:4
Pigtail, seized him by little p., 527:18
Pike, holy text of p. and gun, 262:10
Pilate, Pontius P., 110:6
  saith what is truth, 40:6
  suffered under Pontius P., 48:11
  washed his hands, 36:15
  what is truth said jesting P., 165:11
  with P. wash your hands, 177:19
Pile bodies at Austerlitz, 636:4
  on brown man's burden, 589:n1
  Ossa on Olympus, 53:12
  Ossa on Pelion, 93:13
Piled, labor of an age in p. stones, 250:15
Pilfer, contrive our fees to p., 72:16
Pilgrim came forth with p. steps, 260:7
  craves p. here to pause, 506:9
  gray, 317:11
  intent to be a p., 271:26
  my first p. has shown his face, 133:n2
  of Eternity, 403:20
  soul in you, 591:6
Pilgrimage, blisses about my p., 535:10
  comforts of weary p., 311:8
  succeed me in my p., 271:27
  thus I'll take my p., 159:10
Pilgrimages, longen folk to goon on p., 133:9
Pilgrim's Progress about man left family,
  523:3
Pilgrims of mortality, 673:22
  they knew they were p., 239:20
  we p. passing to and fro, 134:24
Pilgrims', land of p. and so forth, 701:10
  land of p. pride, 439:9
Pill, little yellow p., 857:3
  one p. makes you larger, 846:5
  outlived doctor's p., 291:19
  sugarcoat the p., 267:27
Pillage, slaughter p. devastation, 620:8
Pillaged, houses and farms p., 328:6
Pillar of cloud by day, 8:2
  of fire by night, 8:2
  of salt, 6:34
  of state, 256:16
  triple p. of the world, 218:1
Pillared dark, 624:9

Pillars of society, 504:6
  of Western prosperity, 702:17
  wisdom hath hewn out her seven p., 20:7
Pillicock sat on Pillicock-hill, 212:1
Pillow, heaven and earth our quilt and p., 122:3
  placid face upon the p., 513:7
  sloth finds down p. hard, 220:22
  stone better p. than visions, 670:7
Pilot cares about nothing but river, 522:15
  daring p. in extremity, 272:16
  great p. sail with canvas rent, 103:13
  he's a lightning p., 522:16
  in calm sea every man p., 271:1
  lives our p. still, 171:1
  no chance to p. Union, 445:2
  of the Galilean lake, 253:9
  see P. face to face, 456:6
  that weathered storm, 367:4
  unstable p. steers leaking ship, 115:7
Pilots man bombers to kill babies, 824:10
  of purple twilight, 452:2
Pimpernel, demmed elusive P., 590:10
Pimples warts and everything, 246:20
Pin, angels on head of a p., 850:7
  Taffy stole silver p., 894:1
  with a little p., 177:9
Pinafore, Captain of the P., 525:19
Pinch, death as lover's p., 219:15
  East and West will p. heart, 695:6
  hungry lean-faced villain, 172:28
  necessity's sharp p., 211:20
  set sharp racks to p., 409:17
Pinched, complains of having p. finger, 563:2
Pinches, none tell where shoe p. me, 107:23
Pinching, paddling palms and p. fingers,
  223:11
Pindar, flying abroad as P. says, 76:6
Pine because they lost virtue, 105:14
  dwindle peak and p., 214:2
  for what is not, 403:5
  for which soul did p., 448:6
  into waves p. needles, 280:1
  palm and p., 589:7
  scent of p., 677:20
  shall I ever sigh and p., 242:26
  shattered dishes underneath p., 624:13
  tall p. of the forest, 355:15
  tallest p., 255:16
  with fear and sorrow, 160:26
  yonder p. that sings, 82:12
Pined and wanted food, 368:1
  she p. in thought, 205:4
Pines, cones under his p., 622:11
  keep shape of wind, 727:6
  murmuring p. hemlocks, 436:20
  roared in the p., 605:5
  watching p. shore and stars, 727:1
Pining pining, 546:15
'Pinions, tell you what his 'p. is, 525:5
Pink, Bacchus with p. eyne, 218:27
  moon is on its way, 866:4
  of perfection, 323:3
  twenty-nine p. shades, 560:12
Pinker, girls I teach younger p. every year,
  814:14
Pinkham, land of Lydia E. P., 701:9
Pinks that grow, 207:n2
Pinnacle, imagined p. and steep, 411:16

Pinpoint, Yiddish words p. individuals, 739:10
Pin's, set life at p. fee, 197:35
Pint of plain is your only man, 765:1
  of sweat save blood, 664:13
Pioneers, disillusioned colored p., 842:7
  O pioneers, 487:4
Pious action sugar o'er, 199:20
  Bernard rarther p., 647:3
  feeling of gratitude, 390:2
  fraud as with bad action, 333:20
  love is p., 137:11
  man not less a man, 267:16
  not p. longer than rod behind, 144:1
  thoughts as harbingers, 250:1
  times ere priestcraft, 272:14
Pipe but as linnets, 453:14
  called for p., 892:13
  cat dog p. or two, 576:6
  easier played on than p., 200:25
  for fortune's finger, 200:12
  me to pastures still, 546:4
  piped silly p., 413:7
  rumor is a p., 187:21
  song about a Lamb, 350:10
  three-p. problem, 573:9
Piped silly pipe, 413:7
  with merry cheer, 350:10
Piper at the Gates of Dawn, 574:8
  followed the P., 460:8
  he who pays p., 286:n3
  pay the p., 286:28
  Peter P. picked peck, 895:8
  pipe song again, 350:10
Piper's son, 894:10
Pipers, wi' a hundred p. an' a', 362:11
Pipes and timbrels, 410:14
  and whistles in his sound, 194:25
Piping, cicadas pour out their p. voices, 50:29
  down valleys wild, 350:10
  helpless naked p. loud, 353:6
  songs forever new, 410:17
  songs of pleasant glee, 350:10
  weak p. time of peace, 171:19
Piracee, vary p., 526:9
Piracy, let's vary p., 526:9
Pirate King, 526:5
  more fun to be a p., 873:10
Pisa, you're the Tower of P., 691:12
Piscem natare doces, 121:6
Pisgah, greeted Moses from P., 414:6
Piss off he said to me, 828:3
  vice-presidency not worth pitcher of warm
  p., 602:12
Pisses, I think it p. God off, 860:9
Pistol, hear word culture reach for my p., 687:5
  if his p. misses fire, 323:8
  pun a p. not feather, 383:22
Pistols, fire p. for new century, 631:4
  put on p. went riding, 681:17
  words are loaded p., 743:5
Pit, black as the P., 552:7
  Eagle know what is in p., 351:9
  many-headed monster of p., 296:17
  they'll fill a p., 183:18
  whoso diggeth a p., 21:39
Pit bull, hockey mom and a p., 878:9
Pitch, daubed with slime and p., 7:23
  he that toucheth p., 30:40

Pocket full of rye, 894:7
  learning in private p., 298:10
  Lucy Locket lost p., 896:5
  neither picks p. nor breaks leg, 336:5
  never alone with poet in p., 330:8
  plates dropped from his p., 219:8
  put me in your p., 662:12
  save their own p., 71:13
Pocket-handkerchief, holding p., 516:7
Pockets, contents of his p., 664:3
  slithered and too ample pockets, 719:18
Pod, seeds in dry p. tick, 605:5
Poe with his raven, 481:19
Poem a poem and nothing more, 450:2
  bathed in P. of Sea, 558:18
  begins as lump in throat, 622:22
  change is the only p., 825:4
  dignity in writing p., 566:2
  does P. not merely says P., 408:5
  don't make p. with ideas, 543:11
  epic is p. including history, 665:16
  everything truly seen must become p.,
    631:13
  feeling for single good p., 343:16
  figure a p. makes, 625:3
  for poem's sake, 450:2
  heroic p. a biography, 407:14
  if a man finishes a p., 839:6
  immediate object pleasure not truth,
    379:10
  is a response to a p., 826:7
  is small (or large) machine of words, 659:4
  language touched by poetry is p., 776:6
  lovely as a tree, 667:13
  means just what it says it means, 625:13
  metermaking argument makes p., 427:19
  my life p. I would have writ, 474:1
  never finished only abandoned, 612:14
  of any length not all poetry, 379:11
  of the act of the mind, 379:n2
  of world, 737:9
  ought himself to be true p., 253:22
  phrase long p. contradiction, 450:1
  pleasure of p. guessing, 543:9
  poetry subject of p., 641:9
  read a good p., 343:1
  really perfect p., 810:2
  ride on own melting, 625:5
  right reader of good p., 623:12
  rooted in awe, 749:20
  should not mean, 694:15
  that took place of mountain, 642:15
  to read a p., 776:5
  to which we return, 379:1
  true p. an invocation, 706:5
  United States greatest p., 485:8
  way to tell if p. lasting, 623:12
  who wants to understand p., 343:18
  write p. for money, 742:1
Poème, baigné dans le P., 558:n10
  supprimer la jouissance du p., 543:n5
Poem's, poem for p. sake, 450:2
Poems by water-drinkers, 98:10
  dictionaries and temporary p., 307:2
  get the news from p., 659:8
  here I am writing these p., 814:9
  I'm sick of good p., 810:19
  made by fools like me, 668:1

Poems *(continued)*
  more p. produced, 623:1
  my p. naughty but life pure, 107:4
  no less makings of the sun, 642:16
  plum survives its p., 640:15
  possess origin of all p., 485:16
  that's how book of p. made, 107:6
  you provide p. I'll provide war, 714:12
Poena, noxiae p., 88:n7
Poesis, ut pictura p., 99:n1
Poesy, heavenly gift of p., 273:20
  overwhelm myself in p., 409:1
  participation of divineness, 164:14
  should be friend, 409:4
  shower of light is p., 409:3
Poet, all p. can do is warn, 699:4
  beneath this sod p. lies, 380:8
  binds together by passion, 369:4
  born not made, 111:n4
  brings soul into activity, 379:12
  comic p. paint follies, 286:24
  could not but be gay, 371:12
  creates world, 642:21
  don't send p. to London, 415:4
  even when p. seems most himself, 597:14
  every p. in his kind, 285:11
  flourished here disheveled, 836:3
  force language into meaning, 677:7
  gives life to fictions, 642:21
  great p. writes his time, 677:8
  had no p. and died, 296:19
  he was a true p., 351:10
  he was p. and hated approximate, 631:19
  I the p. still do Thank God, 836:10
  if surgeon is like p., 820:6
  in command of fantasy, 743:15
  is a little god, 698:1
  is priest of invisible, 643:5
  is response to p., 826:7
  king once asked a p., 781:5
  language of English p., 677:11
  like an acrobat, 792:6
  like prince of clouds, 491:2
  limbs of a dismembered p., 95:20
  looks at world, 643:2
  lunatic the lover the p., 179:6
  makes himself seer, 558:14
  man that lies in Bedlam, 762:21
  most unpoetical, 413:10
  never alone with p. in pocket, 330:8
  never sure of value, 677:22
  never trust p. who can drive, 867:2
  no p. without unsoundness, 419:9
  not every year a p. born, 111:4
  not survive misprint, 559:19
  of Body poet of Soul, 486:5
  our ever-living p., 220:n2
  potent figure, 642:21
  priest soldier p., 491:17
  profound philosopher, 379:14
  proof of a p., 485:11
  retired in Tower of Ivory, 432:n1
  skilled p. through natural gift, 63:25
  soaring in high region, 253:19
  they lack a sacred p., 97:14
  this truth p. sings, 451:23
  to p. nothing useless, 307:9
  wasted time for nothing, 677:22

Poet *(continued)*
  whatever p. writes with enthusiasm, 70:10
  who wishes to understand p., 343:18
  who writes down whatever in his head,
    735:25
  whole race is a p., 641:19
  worthy name of P., 408:5
  you explain nothing p., 601:10
Poeta nascitur non fit, 111:n4
Poetarum licentiae liberiora, 87:n9
Poète semblable au prince, 491:n1
Poetic faith, 379:9
  Justice, 296:25
  license, 87:15
  meet nurse for p. child, 373:4
  pleasure in p. pains, 273:n2
Poetical character, 413:9
  worn-out p. fashion, 678:16
  would gods made thee p., 195:18
Poetically, noble nature p. gifted, 496:2
Poetics, old p. in my alchemy, 559:11
Poetry about the existence of childhood, 405:3
  actual is rarest p., 473:26
  administers to effect, 404:13
  after Auschwitz is barbarisch, 733:10
  aim at inscape in p., 547:10
  all p. difficult, 463:2
  all p. experimental p., 643:4
  antithesis to science, 378:19
  as in painting so in p., 99:1
  atrophies when too far from music, 665:18
  Ben Jonson his best p., 232:11
  best words in best order, 380:3
  Bible has noble p., 525:8
  book not concerned with P., 699:4
  boom in petroleum but not in p., 776:10
  breath of knowledge, 369:3
  by which I lived, 815:15
  circumscribe p. by definition, 307:22
  cleanses, 786:15
  comes naturally as Leaves to tree, 413:2
  communicate before understood, 677:10
  communication of pleasure, 378:19
  dead art of p., 665:4
  do a hundred things, 749:20
  does not matter, 678:16
  emptied of its p., 749:3
  enters deeply into us, 123:7
  escape from emotion, 675:19
  essential p., 379:1
  fettered fetters race, 354:12
  fine-spun from mind at peace, 102:21
  for p. idea everything, 497:20
  gaudiness of p., 642:19
  Genius of P., 413:7
  give children right to study p., 330:7
  grain of p. season a century, 557:11
  grand style in p., 496:2
  great and unobtrusive, 412:16
  hate p. with design on us, 412:16
  he sees in manner of p., 755:6
  homely definitions of p., 380:3
  I have been eating p., 838:15
  I know that is p., 511:15
  I too dislike p., 671:1
  if a man publicly denounces p., 839:5
  if this is p. very easy, 520:2
  in unconscious fastidiousness, 671:7

Poetry *(continued)*
   is in the pity, 699:4
   is mediation of life, 808:4
   is painting that speaks, 60:14
   is redemption from pessimism, 842:11
   is what is lost in translation, 625:13
   journey to unknown, 699:1
   knew well how to write p., 82:18
   language is fossil p., 427:20
   language touched by p., 776:6
   learned about p. from Dante, 677:11
   less subtle and fine, 254:5
   literature reduced to essence, 612:8
   makes nothing happen, 749:2
   maximum concentration of p., 801:12
   mincing p., 182:36
   more philosophic than history, 79:5
   most beautiful mode, 496:9
   must be new and old, 425:12
   must be well written as prose, 664:16
   must go to land of p., 343:18
   my p. errs on oddness, 547:10
   no man ever talked p., 463:28
   no one listens to p., 810:4
   not antithesis to prose, 378:19
   not p. but prose run mad, 295:12
   not purpose but passion, 449:2
   of earth never dead, 408:19
   of Natural Philosophy, 579:8
   of speech, 396:8
   Orpheus' voice and p., 67:6
   painting and music, 354:12
   painting is silent p., 60:14
   phrase men pass, 829:7
   plied myself to fruitless p., 163:8
   poem of any length not all p., 379:11
   praise for being, 749:20
   prancing P., 510:14
   purpose of p. to remind us., 764:14
   record of best moments, 404:14
   religion unconscious p., 497:20
   reminds of limitations, 786:15
   rhythmical creation, 450:3
   search for inexplicable, 643:9
   simple sensuous, 254:5
   skin bristles at p., 576:5
   spontaneous overflow, 369:5
   subject matter of p. life, 642:22
   subject of poem, 641:9
   supreme fiction, 640:17
   surprise by excess, 413:1
   sympathy with the p., 379:13
   that which is worth translating, 868:7
   this p., 126:3
   two cardinal points of p., 379:8
   vein of p. in all men, 407:18
   way of taking life by throat, 625:7
   we all scribble p., 98:22
   we campaign in p., 831:12
   whining p., 228:21
   wit flock to aid, 426:10
Poetry's unnat'ral, 463:28
Poet's dream, 371:18
   eye in fine frenzy, 179:6
   joy conceals despair, 633:1
   made as well as born, 233:5
   must go to the p. land, 343:18
   pen turns to shapes, 179:6

Poet's *(continued)*
   possess a p. brain, 167:14
   shone not on p. page, 97:*n*11
Poets, among English P. after death, 413:8
   among us can be literalists, 671:2
   are mad, 234:13
   begin in gladness, 369:16
   Catullus worst of all p., 91:15
   clever young p., 380:3
   come down from mountains, 533:10
   creatures most absurd, 296:18
   die of loneliness, 597:13
   discovered unconscious, 563:12
   error to marry with p., 773:15
   first P. Then Sun, 509:9
   great p. great audiences, 488:16
   hallucinations of p., 645:8
   hierophants, 404:15
   horses and p. not overfed, 158:20
   I write P. All, 509:9
   if p. and writers set themselves, 801:13
   immature p. imitate, 676:3
   Irish p. learn trade, 597:9
   legislators of world, 404:16
   let mad p. say whate'er please, 409:13
   lose half the praise, 249:27
   mature p. steal, 676:3
   mighty p. in misery dead, 370:1
   mirrors of gigantic shadows, 404:15
   must be difficult, 677:7
   pacify touchy tribe of p., 98:15
   painters and p. have equal license,
      98:16
   pleasure only p. know, 273:*n*2
   puff p. of other days, 107:15
   reviewers would have been p., 378:20
   sometimes seem businesslike, 623:1
   souls of P. dead and gone, 411:5
   steal from Homer, 234:8
   tell many lies, 55:13
   that lasting marble seek, 249:26
   there were p. before Homer, 87:19
   things the first p. had, 167:13
   three p. in three ages, 274:7
   we P. in youth, 369:16
   witty mathematics subtile, 166:19
   your p. have said, 40:34
   youthful p. dream, 251:8
Poets' food love and fame, 402:8
   wares harder to get rid of, 623:1
Poet-scientists, there are p., 780:4
Poignant, few sorrows however p., 590:13
Point, at highest p. in arc of bridge, 767:8
   at no p. in life felt American, 830:14
   except for p. no dance, 678:10
   highest p. not Knowledge, 656:7
   highest p. of my greatness, 225:23
   men at p. of death, 181:12
   moral or adorn tale, 306:17
   of a diamond, 27:38
   on which soul fix eye, 415:16
   picked up broken p., 686:7
   put too fine a p., 158:15
   slow and moving finger, 210:3
   where tooth p. goes, 586:18
Pointed firs, 552:11
Pointless, universe more comprehensible more
   p., 836:4

Points, armed at p. exactly, 197:12
   beaten at all p., 72:9
   possession eleven p., 287:13
   thousand p. of friendly light, 805:*n*1
   thousand p. of light, 805:2
Poirot tapped his forehead, 686:1
Poison, all that lasts of love is p., 166:25
   destined to p. all their joys, 482:12
   food to one p. to others, 90:16
   from Caesar's laurel crown, 354:4
   hissing and spitting p. at God, 301:9
   if you p. us do we not die, 185:12
   instead of dirt and p., 284:5
   more deadly than mad dog's tooth, 172:26
   neither will administer p., 70:14
   one man's meat another man's p., 90:*n*6
   one man's p., 90:*n*6
   pellet with the p., 775:10
   some sentences release p. after years,
      740:9
   steel nor p., 216:11
   sweet p. for age's tooth, 175:4
   sweet p. of misused wine, 252:4
   turning to p., 411:11
   whispering tongues can p. truth, 377:13
   whole blood stream fills, 745:16
Poisoned rat in hole, 285:8
   some p. by their wives, 177:8
   with blood of both, 829:4
Poisoning, slow process of p., 649:1
Poisonous, curse this p. bunch-backed toad,
   171:24
   minerals and that tree, 230:21
   wolf's-bane for p. wine, 411:9
Poke, drew dial from his p., 194:15
   pig in a p., 148:25
Poker, picked up p. hit him in head, 894:1
Pokers into true-love knots, 378:12
Poland, Hungary P. doing it their way,
   849:*n*1
Polar bear with stuffing missing, 821:1
Pole, beloved from p. to p., 376:18
   black as Pit from p. to p., 552:7
   embrace P. as Frenchman, 153:16
   heavens from p. to p., 354:17
   intellectuals at one p., 743:11
   so tall to reach p., 289:4
   soldier's p. is fallen, 219:5
   top of greasy p., 430:10
   truth from p. to p., 287:21
Poles, North P. and Equators, 517:2
Pole-star remains in place, 60:18
Police, beaten up by secret p., 798:7
   fear in presence of secret p., 722:16
   newspaper runs p. foorce, 600:16
   only easy in a p. state, 781:6
   so I quit the p. department, 848:17
   walked in she surprised, 802:7
   who are the brain p., 849:10
Policeman cannot be improvised, 647:11
   electric light most efficient p., 562:7
   need park p. pretty girl, 683:17
   terrorist and p. from same basket, 567:19
Policeman's job is only easy, 781:6
   lot not happy one, 526:8
   more law in p. nightstick, 535:5
Policemen, not enough p. to control thoughts,
   758:17

Poor *(continued)*

die not p. death, 230:22
dog Tray, 384:7
every desire of p. man punishable, 700:20
exchequer of the p., 176:30
few save p. feel for p., 422:20
fools decoyed, 277:14
freedom to rich or p., 697:2
George, 834:15
get poorer, 667:12
give me your tired your p., 552:16
give to the p., 35:3
giveth unto the p., 22:8
grind the faces of the p., 24:37
hear p. rogues talk of news, 213:8
heart would fain deny, 217:18
high and low rich and p., 364:4
honest exceeding p. man, 184:35
I am even p. in thanks, 199:4
I am p. and needy, 18:17
if p. whenever you can, 77:1
if we not make somebody p., 353:5
I'm p. I'm black, 860:10
in behalf of despised p., 419:3
infirm weak old man, 211:26
intricated soul, 231:13
Jim Jay, 616:10
Kiltartan's p., 592:20
last I lay upon thy lips, 219:4
law forbids rich as well as p., 546:2
laws catch the weak and p., 56:2
laws grind the p., 322:5
lean lank face, 444:9
leave them for the p. and stranger, 8:26
little lambs lost way, 588:6
lo the p. Indian, 294:20
lone woman, 188:1
lonely and p. of old, 669:12
makes me p. indeed, 209:2
man accustomed to small things, 768:13
man being down, 31:2
man deprived of power, 75:17
man had nothing, 11:18
man is Christ's stamp, 242:13
man poor mankind, 713:15
man that hangs on favors, 225:25
man who craves more is p., 103:9
many a p. man that loved, 593:15
many good men are p., 55:12
men's cottages palaces, 184:14
my children who are p., 783:7
my p. fool is hanged, 213:14
my wife p. wretch, 277:8
naked p. mangled Peace, 190:6
naked wretches, 211:33
neither rich nor p., 520:8
none so p. to do him reverence, 192:32
not p. who has enough to use, 98:4
obliged wealthy and relieved p., 51:*n*1
one of the undeserving p., 565:22
outrage of p., 424:19
pity upon the p., 21:8
player that struts, 217:23
prey of rich on p., 336:13
purses proud garments p., 173:22
relation irrelevant, 383:17
rich gifts wax p., 199:23
rich honesty in p. house, 196:5

Poor *(continued)*

rich rob p., 416:3
rob not the p., 21:21
rob one another, 416:3
scandalous and p., 281:1
scandals of th' p., 600:7
shall never cease, 9:23
Shine Shine save p. me, 887:2
slipping out of consciousness, 819:1
so p. he could not keep a dog, 114:7
sold the p. for a pair of shoes, 29:1
solitary p. nasty, 239:10
sort of memory, 516:11
soul sat sighing, 210:8
soul the center, 223:4
splendid wings, 530:23
strength to the p., 25:33
that have not patience, 208:34
thing but mine own, 196:*n*1
Tom's a-cold, 212:8
too p. for bribe, 316:17
two nations the rich and p., 430:3
unhappy brains for drinking, 208:22
we know we're p., 712:8
what will p. robin do, 895:5
when anything to eat, 77:*n*2
whoso mocketh the p., 20:39
why not given to p., 39:36
with hunger rich and p. as one, 68:6
world said I, 263:11
wot gets blame, 887:7
ye have p. always, 35:34

Poorer, for richer for p., 49:16

Poorest he that is in England, 239:4
in p. thing superfluous, 211:21
man in his cottage, 305:12
nor p. receive contentment, 231:14
this Traverse p. take, 510:14

Pop goes the weasel, 885:6

Pope and emperor, 422:7
anybody can be p., 647:11
better err with P., 394:16
Czar Metternich Guizot, 478:7
definition which shall exclude P., 307:22
how many divisions has P. got, 636:17

Popery, inclines a man to P., 165:*n*5

Popinjay, pestered with a p., 182:1

Popinjays, reverences gilt P., 406:8

Pop'lar, dead always p., 600:2

Poplar of water, 776:3

Poplars stand and tremble, 575:8

Poppet, no go my p., 751:2

Poppies, fume of p., 411:7
grow in Flanders fields, 614:7
pleasures like p. spread, 358:6

Poppy, not p. nor mandragora, 209:11
oblivion blindly scattereth p., 249:1
or a lily, 526:11

Populace, Barbarians Philistines P., 497:8
man to whom p. is entrusted, 50:21
revolutions run steadily down to p., 381:3

Popular, addressing p. audiences, 79:2
characteristics of p. politician, 72:12
conscience, 649:12
custom supported by p. opinion, 572:13
dead always p., 600:2
government without p. information, 346:1
power in majority of p. assembly, 330:16

Popular *(continued)*

propaganda has to be p., 684:11
spirit and form of p. government, 345:10
truth not so p. as fiction, 399:*n*1
war will cease to be p., 559:22
we're more p. than Jesus now, 847:12
when Fortune on our side, 99:26

Population unchecked increases, 362:7

Populi, salus p. suprema lex, 88:*n*5
vox p. vox Dei, 122:5

Populous and smoky city, 402:18
long in p. city pent, 259:9

Porcelain clay of humankind, 274:8
give children right to study p., 330:7
precious p. of human clay, 274:*n*1

Porches of mine ears, 198:11

Porcupine, quills upon fretful p., 198:5

Pore benighted 'eathen, 587:18
I'm p. I'm black, 860:10

Pork, yes to smell p., 184:22

Pork chops, who killed the p., 812:9

Porn, Internet Is for P., 880:3

Pornography, I know it when I see it, 780:15
is the theory, 853:1
what p. says about women, 863:7

Porpentine, quills upon fretful p., 198:5

Porphyry font, 453:5

Porpoise close behind us, 515:2
waters of petrel and p., 679:2

Porridge, comfort like cold p., 224:18
pease p. hot, 894:16
spare breath to cool p., 55:*n*5

Porsches, my friends all drive P., 857:10

Port after stormy seas, 160:7
bomb might destroy whole p., 638:1
is near bells I hear, 487:16
liquor for men, 310:24
pride in their p., 322:2
Scylla to p., 185:*n*1

Portable, get hold of p. property, 466:26

Portal, fitful tracing of p., 641:5
opens to receive me, 362:2

Portals alternate Night Day, 441:12
errors p. of discovery, 650:16
of church and school, 614:2

Portas, Hannibal ad p., 120:28

Portent of fate awaiting Nazi tyranny, 620:10
of new atomic age, 606:7

Portentous phrase I told you so, 399:4
sight, 377:16

Porter, all p. and skittles, 464:3
decompose in a barrel of p., 812:2
Mrs. P. in the spring, 676:11

Portion, best p. of man's life, 368:7
dedicate p. of field, 446:5
equal p. for who lingers, 51:19
fill certain p. of uncertain paper, 398:7
he wales a p., 356:9
is to have Affliction by drops, 278:9
no p. in us after, 599:17
of that around me, 395:21

Portions and parcels of Past, 450:19

Portofino, mountains of P., 547:15

Portrait, Hero of Our Time a p., 469:16
manners mirror which shows p., 344:25
man's work p. of himself, 521:8
of Gertrude Stein, 628:1
of person one knows, 343:12

Poverty *(continued)*

greatest of our evils, 565:13
I pay thy p. not thy will, 181:7
is no sin, 244:20
knows how to endure p., 97:15
neither p. nor riches, 22:12
no disgrace to acknowledge p., 71:15
of the incapable, 490:2
Panama and its p., 414:7
parent of meanness, 75:6
parts good company, 374:15
qualities thwarted by p., 109:16
reproach to government, 280:8
rich in p., 158:17
riches p. and use of service, 224:19
sat in p. hunger dirt, 418:8
stepmother ov genius, 476:7
the America of p., 819:1
the greatest p., 641:17
to the very lips, 210:2
view age of p., 186:7
we live in ambitious p., 109:17
where p. and joy, 125:11
where p. enforced, 477:9
worth by p. depressed, 306:8
Pow, blessings on your frosty p., 357:13
Powder, food for p., 183:18
keep p. dry, 385:6
Power a trust, 429:19
absolute p. corrupts absolutely, 518:10
absolute p. in majority, 330:16
absolute p. over wives, 340:12
abuse of p. no surprise, 869:1
accord women equal p., 489:3
action nor p. of speech, 193:4
and beauty of lyre, 610:4
and publicity, 531:13
and the glory, 12:24
balance of p., 330:9
beauty hath strange p., 260:19
believe source of p. is sky, 139:11
between equals in p., 72:7
bicycle fleshed with p., 801:16
black p., 850:3
Bureaucracy giant p. wielded by pygmies, 417:17
by Thy p. no foot slide, 887:15
corrupts poetry cleanses, 786:15
critical p. creative, 496:5
deep p. of joy, 368:9
defy P. which seems omnipotent, 402:5
desire of p. in excess, 165:24
destroy p. of reasoning, 76:2
disjoins remorse from p., 191:35
during time men live without common p., 239:9
earthly p. then likest God's, 186:1
educator wielder of p., 764:4
effect of p. on men, 531:13
elite decide national events, 782:12
empire p. in trust, 272:20
encroachments of those in p., 345:13
equate p. with virtue, 741:6
ever-during p., 372:7
everything includes itself in p., 203:8
extent of beauty and p., 419:11
eye made quiet by p., 368:9
fate in own p., 420:7

Power *(continued)*

fewer laws less p., 427:22
force from which sun draws p., 661:3
force of temporal p., 186:1
forces of lust for p., 652:10
friend in p. friend lost, 531:12
from the people, 429:19
good want p., 401:16
goodness armed with p., 696:1
greater than people, 389:8
had chained him for a time, 347:12
hath not potter p., 41:27
have joy or p., 425:10
have seen the wicked in great p., 16:12
hope of pride and p., 447:9
human p. cannot remove, 679:11
if women submit to p., 360:18
imagination reconciling p., 378:24
immensity of first p., 362:7
in government sovereign, 349:10
in mysteries of thought, 67:15
in our p. to begin world again, 333:3
in p. unpleased, 272:16
in spite of variety and p., 495:22
includes right to means, 349:10
individual is product of p., 812:7
individual liberty individual p., 363:5
influence of sea p., 537:5
into will, 203:8
Jove for 'is p. to thunder, 219:32
judicial p. distinct from legislative, 330:4
just cause overwhelming p., 572:14
knowledge but no p., 69:23
knowledge is p., 164:8
knowledge money p., 766:4
laugh to scorn p. of man, 216:32
lay down reins of p., 446:11
lead life to p., 450:14
lies in mind and body, 92:2
like pestilence pollutes, 401:8
lively p. of mind prevailed, 89:11
living p. prime agent, 379:5
love of p. love of selves, 385:12
love without p. destroyed, 696:1
means not to have to give in, 767:10
meet inner p. with inner p., 61:16
metaphor fertile p., 657:14
money is p., 543:15
monuments of wit survive monuments of p., 164:7
Music's p. obey, 273:22
my fanatical will p., 684:16
my p. Green Lantern's light, 888:5
nations possessing great p., 638:2
new source of p. and beauty, 821:9
nonviolence paralyzed p. structures, 823:14
not by might nor by p., 29:12
not means is end, 735:21
not now in fortune's p., 262:14
object of p. is p., 735:21
obtained by weakness, 360:20
of fright and lust, 706:5
of making laws, 349:7
of man and moment, 496:4
of one fair face, 143:1
of public plunder, 389:*n*3

Power *(continued)*

of surplus in banks, 389:8
of the atom, 638:8
of visible is invisible, 671:9
of world works in circles, 583:5
once we have p., 714:9
only prize for powerful is p., 538:17
over man's subsistence, 349:9
over man's will, 349:9
over the clay, 41:27
passing from the earth, 372:2
plants will stop generating, 740:1
poesy supreme of p., 409:3
political p. out of barrel of gun, 698:11
pomp of p., 315:18
possesses the genuine p., 379:1
pre-eminence and p., 345:9
pride of p. sink, 324:3
proud Edward's p., 358:16
public life situation of p., 323:19
ransom them from the p. of the grave, 28:40
rather in p. than use, 205:30
relations within which p. is exercised, 806:1
rich have p. and poor deprived, 75:17
riches and p. gifts of fate, 124:1
right hand is glorious in p., 8:6
rise of misplaced p., 686:16
shadow of love, 630:10
shadow of unseen P., 401:9
some p. giftie gie us, 356:16
sorrow hath less p. to bite, 176:17
spare thee past my p., 356:17
spirit of p., 44:39
strange p. of speech, 377:3
struggle against p., 824:1
surpassed others but had no more p., 99:7
symbol of p. of Heaven, 671:21
tends to corrupt, 518:10
that regards individuals, 812:5
the great aphrodisiac, 802:10
thine is the p., 32:25
thou shalt have p. to degenerate, 141:3
titles p. and pelf, 373:3
to add or detract, 446:5
to be silent, 276:4
to build black institutions, 850:*n*1
to cancel his captivity, 191:33
to chasten and subdue, 368:11
to do me ill, 226:*n*1
to drink or rise, 393:9
to hurt and will do none, 222:1
to impose boredom, 778:14
to know all things, 227:16
to live and act, 372:11
to say Behold, 177:28
to tax not power to destroy, 539:5
to tax power to destroy, 350:1
to undo the past, 73:21
transfiguring p., 548:26
true p. that subdues everything, 832:5
trust no man with p. to endanger liberty, 329:12
unlimited p. corrupt, 306:1
unlimited p. into hands of husbands, 340:11
upon the past has p., 273:18
villains in p., 331:6

Power *(continued)*
　we here hold the p., 446:1
　we should read for p., 666:1
　weird p. in spoken word, 567:7
　where love rules no will to p., 630:10
　where p. predominates love lacking, 630:10
　which men call Chance, 252:22
　wielded by abnormal energy, 532:3
　will and p., 203:8
　will to p., 630:10
　wisdom goodness, 283:2
　witch hath p. to charm, 196:19
　with p. and glory, 38:29
　witty beauty a p., 505:17
　woman's place of p., 838:2
　word after a word is p., 844:15
Powerful amidst peers, 546:16
　black is p., 731:11
　boy is most p. of Hellenes, 62:18
　goodness want, 401:16
　has power over self, 145:n8
　humblest peer of most p., 518:1
　impulse to punish p., 548:2
　invisible and all-p., 493:18
　make potent more p., 364:3
　more p. than locomotive, 777:1
　more p. than love or hate, 844:12
　nation which enjoys most freedom most p.,
　　363:5
　nobody's as p., 860:6
　only prize for p. is power, 538:17
　outlive this p. rime, 221:15
　overflow of p. feelings, 369:5
　will to abolish conscience, 778:11
　word of God is p., 45:7
Powerless, dead are not p., 394:3
　freedom made man anxious p., 725:8
　to be born, 495:23
Powerlessness, basic personal p., 878:1
　to have no cash means p., 432:11
Powers, accumulation of p. in same hands,
　345:11
　against principalities and p., 43:40
　colonization by European p., 355:5
　cultivation of her p., 405:9
　deem that there are P., 368:4
　deny us for our good, 218:17
　depository of ultimate p., 338:12
　desires dreams and p., 530:16
　doing Goodness beyond your p., 61:14
　draw p. into higher classes, 338:17
　evils avoided p. exercised, 109:2
　just p. from consent, 336:1
　knows you not Heavenly P., 342:14
　lay waste our p., 371:23
　men fear p. principalities of air, 645:14
　merciful p., 215:11
　of augury, 50:26
　Princedoms Virtues P., 258:20
　principalities nor p., 41:26
　specified p., 349:11
　superior to man, 558:2
　tempt frailty of our p., 204:2
　that be, 41:37
　wars of European p., 355:6
　what is use of having p. Doctor, 573:4
Practical politics, 442:14
　politics ignoring facts, 532:1

Practicality never even suggested, 488:15
Practice and thought forge art, 93:12
　best of instructors, 100:11
　childish ways, 52:24
　Christian forbearance, 332:1
　drives me mad, 881:3
　he fell mightily in his p., 270:9
　helping men p. virtue, 79:15
　humility all preach none p., 238:11
　is everything, 100:n5
　makes perfect, 100:n5
　selfish in p. not principle, 382:13
　to deceive, 373:15
　what you preach, 84:5, 115:7
　world of p., 496:6
Practicer, frequent p. of angling, 245:1
Practices, fair p. to fair notions, 74:5
Practitioner in panegyric, 346:16
Praevalet, magna est veritas et p., 29:n3
Pragmatic method attitude of orientation,
　542:6
Prague, as old hermit of P. said, 205:26
　in P. stories aren't simply stories, 835:7
Prairie, bury me not on lone p., 890:17
　bury me out on p., 890:18
　last night as I lay on p., 890:14
　to make a p., 511:12
Prairie-lawyer master of all, 639:16
Prairies for which speech no name, 406:3
　from mountains to p., 673:11
Praise, all men by nature give p., 659:9
　ask criticism want p., 626:17
　at morning blame at night, 292:22
　belongs to God, 117:11
　boldness certain to win p., 101:15
　book people p. don't read, 524:15
　bury Caesar not p. him, 192:28
　damn with faint p., 295:13
　dispraised no small p., 259:32
　famous men, 31:26
　for being and happening, 749:20
　forms no part of beauty, 111:18
　garment of p., 27:16
　God from whom all blessings flow, 278:8
　God hath no better p., 545:14
　he fathers-forth p. him, 546:13
　her own works p. her, 22:20
　him and exalt him, 31:30
　I p. the Frenchman, 326:15
　if there be any p., 44:7
　in country you p. city, 95:26
　in deeper reverence p., 438:18
　in p. of ladies dead, 222:9
　into his courts with p., 18:3
　kind of strife man might p., 54:16
　laurel crown yield to p., 88:7
　let another man p. thee, 21:41
　let every thing p. the Lord, 19:21
　lived without disgrace without p., 128:9
　Lord pass ammunition, 687:10
　love of p., 290:12
　maid whom none to p., 369:7
　my mouth shall show forth thy p., 16:34
　named thee but to p., 400:12
　never p. sister to sister, 587:3
　nor blame the writings, 292:21
　nourish agues, 183:15
　only to be praised, 264:9

Praise *(continued)*
　or blame momentary, 413:6
　or blame too far, 624:18
　poets lose half the p., 249:27
　Power that hath made, 387:1
　right p. and true perfection, 186:19
　sacrament of p., 641:6
　say more than this rich p., 221:26
　scarce could p., 306:10
　see how man receives p., 103:16
　sing thee a song in thy p., 357:19
　solid pudding empty p., 296:25
　swells note of p., 315:19
　that will never die, 72:4
　those who follow other paths, 95:15
　to give, 232:19
　try to p. mutilated world, 862:8
　verses but read something else, 107:11
　we p. thee for perspicuity of language, 123:8
　we p. thee O God, 48:9
　your p. not worth dying for, 107:15
Praise-all, Blame-all and P. blockheads, 302:5
Praised, honesty is p. and starves, 109:9
　Lord's name is to be p., 18:20
　praise only to be p., 264:9
　the dead already dead, 22:32
　woman that feareth the Lord shall be p.,
　　22:20
Praiser, great lover and p. of himself, 238:23
　of past time, 98:26
Praises, earth with voices p. God, 378:4
　everybody praises nobody, 334:6
　might be reported, 31:27
　sing p. to his Name, 882:4
　so long shall your p. endure, 94:7
　with enthusiastic tone, 527:11
Praising, advantage of p. oneself, 521:10
　lean and sallow abstinence, 252:23
　what is lost, 206:9
Pram enemy of good art, 734:3
Prancing Poetry, 510:14
Prate, stones p. of whereabout, 215:15
Prates, all she p. has nothing in it, 285:6
Prattle, nor do children p. about his knees, 51:7
　thinking his p. tedious, 177:21
Praxed, Saint P. in a glory, 460:21
Praxiteles unable to reach all the material, 112:24
Pray, after this manner p. ye, 32:25
　all p. in their distress, 351:3
　as if to die tomorrow, 302:31
　can't p. a lie, 523:8
　farmers p. that summers be wet, 93:11
　for dead fight like hell for living, 511:17
　for me and come not, 169:2
　for no man but myself, 213:21
　for repose of his soul, 578:16
　for them which despitefully use you, 32:21
　God absolve us all, 139:3
　God to keep me from being proud, 276:24
　goes to bed and does not p., 242:22
　how they p. for death, 67:8
　I p. you in your letters, 210:20
　in distress and need, 655:7
　in fullness of joy, 655:7
　late and early p., 227:10
　Lord soul to keep, 283:9
　make me able to pay for it, 277:1
　make no mistake, 527:13

Pretty *(continued)*
>   only p. ring time, 196:2
>   pleasures might me move, 159:5
>   puts on his p. looks, 175:19
>   state of things, 527:14
>   to see what money will do, 277:19
>   to think so, 721:5
>   what do for p. girls, 597:5
>   young wards, 526:19

Prevail against human reason, 764:16
>   evening shades p., 287:21
>   fair words p., 588:19
>   gates of hell not p., 34:37
>   God who is able to p., 244:30
>   his rising fogs p., 273:14
>   make best ideas p., 496:5
>   man will p., 714:5
>   masculine values that p., 654:18
>   necessity knows no law except p., 100:19
>   'tis the Majority p., 509:4
>   truth shall p. when none cares, 500:9
>   will looking ill p., 261:2

Prevailed, David p. over the Philistine, 11:2
>   the dragon p. not, 47:1
>   with double sway, 322:26

Prevails, when vice p., 287:28

Prevarication, last dike of p., 324:19

Prevent, enjoy religion p. others, 519:5
>   lower from getting more, 78:20
>   me from carrying you up, 67:6
>   surest way to p. war, 381:4

Prevention, anthology used for p., 706:4
>   of mutual crime, 78:24
>   society for p. of croolty to money, 535:*n1*

Prevents our being natural, 264:28

Preverts, mutiny of p., 819:7

Previous, calling to mind p. benefaction, 70:18
>   result of p. study, 382:6
>   returned home p. night, 618:1

Prey, animals and athletes not p., 672:1
>   at fortune, 209:7
>   beast of p. in aristocratic races, 548:15
>   eagle seeketh p., 14:29
>   expects his evening p., 316:15
>   fear birds of p., 206:18
>   great lord yet p. to all, 295:1
>   have they not divided the p., 10:14
>   of fear, 671:14
>   of rich on poor, 336:13
>   of rival imperialisms, 690:9
>   on garbage, 198:10
>   people easily becomes p., 142:8
>   smaller fleas on him p., 285:11
>   to dumb forgetfulness a p., 316:4
>   to hastening ills a p., 322:22
>   universal p., 203:8
>   Venus fastened to p., 278:21
>   where eagles dare not perch, 171:23
>   young lions roar after p., 18:11

Preying on people's vanity ignorance, 838:5

Priam's curtain, 187:22

Priapus, it is I P. crying, 83:3
>   made of marble, 92:23

Price, abatement and low p., 204:11
>   great p. for wisdom, 505:7
>   greater p. than life, 726:15
>   greet cheep holde at litel p., 135:11
>   heaven put p. upon goods, 333:6

Price *(continued)*
>   is far above rubies, 22:16
>   life exacts for peace, 718:6
>   market p. they said, 511:8
>   men have their p., 290:2
>   natural and market p., 380:13
>   of everything, 560:10
>   of liberty, 345:*n4*
>   of thousand horses, 611:11
>   of wisdom is above rubies, 14:4
>   pay any p., 785:10
>   pearl of great p., 34:19
>   too high p. for harmony, 492:11
>   waiting to find out what p., 851:18
>   weighed for my p., 29:16
>   what p. bananas, 812:9
>   will fall, 166:2
>   words beyond p., 838:8

Priced, weighed measured p. everything, 466:17

Priceless, human life p., 726:15

Prices, contrivance to raise p., 319:2

Prick and sting her, 198:13
>   if you p. us do we not bleed, 185:12
>   it mark it with B, 892:17
>   sides of my intent, 214:24

Pricking, gentle knight p. on plain, 160:3
>   gonfalon bubble, 646:12
>   of my thumbs, 216:29

Pricks, honor p. me on, 183:25
>   kick against the p., 40:23, 63:9
>   to subsequent volumes, 203:10

Pride, age that will p. deflower, 160:9
>   aiming at blest abodes, 165:*n4*
>   all the p. cruelty and ambition, 159:15
>   and courage of patriot, 519:10
>   bold peasantry country's p., 322:22
>   chastening in hour of p., 444:15
>   coy submission modest p., 257:20
>   Democratic Party without p. of ancestry, 512:13
>   Envy Avarice three sparks, 128:21
>   fell with my fortunes, 193:30
>   flattery begot upon p., 287:11
>   from p. vainglory and hypocrisy, 48:19
>   goeth before destruction, 20:37
>   he that is low no p., 271:25
>   I know thy p., 10:44
>   idleness and p., 303:7
>   in Casey's bearing, 584:19
>   in occupation, 522:15
>   in their port, 322:2
>   is hateful before God, 30:32
>   is his own glass, 203:14
>   is therefore pleasure, 276:5
>   king over children of p., 14:37
>   land of pilgrims' p., 439:9
>   look backward with p., 622:13
>   mother's p. father's joy, 374:5
>   my high-blown p. broke under me, 225:25
>   nature's p. is withered daffodil, 231:20
>   not p. selves on actual achievements, 648:17
>   of country, 459:2
>   of kings, 294:14
>   of peacock glory of God, 351:14
>   of power sink, 324:3
>   of those who have survived, 621:7

Pride *(continued)*
>   perished in his p., 369:16
>   plume here buckle, 546:11
>   pomp and circumstance, 209:13
>   rid earth of him in my p., 605:15
>   shall bring him low, 22:11
>   soldier's p., 459:23
>   solemn p. yours, 446:12
>   speak with p. of our doings, 670:15
>   stoic's p., 295:1
>   tasted all the summer's p., 350:7
>   that licks the dust, 296:2
>   that puts country down, 881:9
>   touched to quick, 459:23
>   towering in p. of place, 216:3
>   true to his profit and his p., 285:5
>   tyrant is child of P., 66:4
>   vain the sage's p., 296:19
>   was not made for men, 30:34
>   will have a fall, 66:*n2*

Priest all shaven and shorn, 897:8
>   free me from turbulent p., 124:10
>   God's high p., 40:45
>   I the Muses' p. sing, 96:25
>   like people like p., 28:32
>   love the only p., 518:6
>   no difference 'twixt P. and Clerk, 241:2
>   no man can serve ten years as p., 531:9
>   O mysterious p., 410:18
>   of most authentic creed, 518:4
>   soldier poet, 491:17
>   still is Nature's p., 370:18
>   the true God's p., 245:13
>   well ought p. example give, 197:*n1*
>   while runnin' for p., 660:4

Priestcraft, pious times ere p., 272:14

Priestlike, waters at p. task, 412:10

Priestly vestments in dens, 500:5

Priests, ancestors p. in temple, 429:21
>   bless her when she is riggish, 218:21
>   by mightier hand, 419:7
>   High P. of America, 874:8
>   Miss Lonelyhearts p., 736:12
>   stood firm on dry ground, 9:36

Priests', hell paved with p. skulls, 115:25

Priez Dieu que tous nous veuille absoudre, 139:*n2*

Primal eldest curse, 200:31

Primary, great p. human affections, 495:13
>   imagination, 379:5

Prime, buried him before p., 890:5
>   gather Rose whilst p., 160:9
>   give him always of p., 285:12
>   laurel for perfect p., 512:7
>   light the p. work of God, 257:*n2*
>   lovely April of her p., 220:32
>   obeyed at p., 425:3
>   of youth a frost of cares, 163:11
>   one's p. elusive, 791:17
>   rose up in his p., 681:17
>   what is the p. of life, 75:8
>   Zeus p. mover, 63:8

Prime Minister returned, 604:1
>   what war said P., 736:7

Primeval, forest p., 436:20
>   mountains in p. sleep, 500:5

Primitive impulses of heart, 449:*n1*
>   people not waken sleeper, 558:3

Primitive *(continued)*
    unattached state, 630:15
Primordial images of collective unconscious,
    630:2
Primrose path of dalliance treads, 197:20
    sweet as the p., 322:28
    way, 215:25
Primum non nocere, 70:*n*5
Primus inter pares, 121:9
Prince, advise the p., 675:4
    can mak belted knight, 358:19
    duty subject owes p., 173:26
    first servant of state, 312:7
    good night sweet p., 202:33
    great P. in prison lies, 229:19
    have no study but war, 141:16
    I am not P. Hamlet, 675:4
    I warn you, 742:8
    imitate fox and lion, 142:2
    must be lion, 108:*n*1
    not propose it to my p., 297:15
    of apple towns, 777:10
    of Aquitaine, 439:6
    of clouds haunts tempest, 491:2
    of darkness a gentleman, 212:7
    of Peace, 25:16
    of Wales in small but costly crown, 647:4
    of Wales is not a position, 836:*n*3
    Rasselas P. of Abyssinia, 307:8
    semblable au p. des nuées, 491:*n*1
    subject Father Son, 230:15
    there is a p. fallen, 11:12
    till I p. of love beheld, 350:7
Princedoms Virtues Powers, 258:20
Princely counsel in his face, 256:16
Princerple, don't believe in p., 482:2
Princes, all p. I, 228:17
    ancestors p. of earth, 429:*n*3
    and lords may flourish, 322:22
    blaze forth death of p., 192:10
    but breath of kings, 356:10
    contentment in being equal to p., 231:14
    fall like one of the p., 17:17
    gilded monuments of p., 221:15
    hate traitor but love treason, 88:*n*13
    kings and p. have philosophy, 75:9
    like to heavenly bodies, 166:1
    must a word to be addressed to p.,
      151:15
    orgulous, 398:*n*1
    pale kings and p., 412:5
    put not your trust in p., 19:19
    sweet aspect of p., 225:25
    Three P. of Serendip, 317:2
    whose merchants are p., 25:31
Princes', cottages p. palaces, 184:14
    hangs on p. favors, 225:25
    not so arched as p. palaces, 237:8
Princess descended of kings, 219:18
    felt pea through mattresses, 432:17
    People's P., 871:10
    thoughtless saying of p., 313:8
    three days afterwards p. buried, 506:14
Principal, wisdom is the p. thing, 19:28
Principalities, against p. and powers, 43:40
    men fear power p. of air, 645:14
    never known to exist, 142:1
    nor powers, 41:26

Principle, active p. of literature, 612:8
    but a cold p., 245:*n*1
    don't believe in p., 482:2
    general p. gives no help, 367:10
    Greatest Happiness P., 435:15
    love our p., 416:7
    moderation in p. a vice, 333:17
    necessary and fundamental p., 318:20
    nihilist takes no p. on trust, 479:5
    of Conservation of Force, 494:5
    old but true as fate, 88:*n*13
    on which society not founded, 315:1
    one God one p. of being, 112:14
    one p. make universe single creature, 114:5
    precedent embalms p., 430:7
    rebels from p., 325:5
    same p. in whatever shape, 444:12
    strange p. as first requirement, 489:6
Principles and traditions of nation, 782:9
    are conventions and definitions, 558:9
    elements or p. of bodies, 339:1
    facts alarm more than p., 339:10
    first p. take deepest root, 340:14
    guide his life by true p., 90:18
    important p. inflexible, 447:4
    less than chaff, 567:15
    looking away from p., 542:6
    normal p. may have to bend, 846:3
    of Political Economy, 629:3
    restless unfixed in p., 272:16
    that gave America birth, 566:15
    to effect safety, 336:1
Print, all news fit to p., 570:7
    eternity of p., 654:7
    I love a ballad in p., 223:31
    news and raise hell, 885:9
    of a man's naked foot, 282:11
    see name in p., 394:12
    sharpest weapon, 636:14
    some said John p. it, 271:6
Printed, that they were p. in a book, 13:38
    page is p., 827:11
Printer, Benjamin Franklin P., 301:20
Printers, books by which p. have lost, 250:4
Printing and Protestant religion, 407:13
    caused p. to be used, 170:17
    invented art of p., 406:13
Priority, degree p. and place, 203:5
Prisidincy highest office, 600:17
Prism and silent face, 368:16
    prunes and p., 466:19
Prison, beast brought up in p., 142:8
    born black born in p., 808:11
    civilized man's house p., 472:20
    come let's away to p., 213:8
    die in the streets or in p., 607:19
    each confirms a p., 676:17
    each in his p., 676:17
    Europe p. of nations, 636:16
    feel at home in p., 736:6
    great Prince in p. lies, 229:19
    grind in the p. house, 10:24
    in p. and ye came unto me, 35:30
    more p. inmates than, 875:8
    of nations, 636:16, 636:*n*2
    one wall is the avant-garde, 803:4
    only house in slave State, 473:18
    open door of p. and run away, 74:12

Prison *(continued)*
    outside p. in Leningrad, 683:8
    palace and p., 395:25
    Russia is a p., 400:10
    scream reaches remotest p. cell, 722:15
    soul in p. I am not free, 561:11
    stone walls do not p. make, 266:*n*1
    to sit in silence is pestilential p., 527:8
    true place for just man, 473:18
    wake up and find myself in p., 247:3
    wear out in a walled p., 213:8
Prisoner in his twisted gyves, 180:15
    man is a p., 74:12
    stone walls a p. make, 266:*n*1
    takes the reason prisoner, 214:8
    to white man, 363:12
Prisoner's, jailer envious of p. dreams, 439:3
    jury passing on p. life, 206:19
Prisoners call the sky, 561:1
    cannot enter into contracts, 790:19
    images p. tattoo, 727:5
    in Bastille couldn't have touched them,
      770:14
    of hope, 29:15
    of starvation, 472:16
    sorrow of p. and exiles, 770:5
    we degraded p. destined to hunger, 658:13
Prison-house of Language, 838:1
    shades of the p., 370:17
Prison-pent, forever p., 727:11
Prisons, archipelagoes of South p., 829:7
    little reform needed in p., 484:13
Pristine magnificence, 414:6
Prithee pretty maiden, 526:12
Privacy, civilization progress toward p.,
    742:14
    goldfish for p. I got, 608:6
    lobsters don't invade our p., 439:7
    right of p. encompass woman's decision,
      751:10
    right of p. means anything, 745:11
    suffocate for p., 787:19
    tumultuous p. of storm, 424:8
Private, abolition of p. property, 478:12
    beneficence inadequate, 577:6
    dog to gain p. ends, 322:14
    enterprise not yet tried, 652:19
    equal justice in p. disputes, 71:14
    grave's a fine p. place, 266:23
    griefs, 193:2
    judgment, 318:6
    men enjoy, 189:22
    men governed by p. reasons, 336:7
    morality p. luxury, 531:27
    nor public flame nor p., 297:6
    obsessing our p. lives, 748:16
    open and friendly in p., 71:14
    post of honor is p. station, 287:28
    property fruit of labor, 633:11
    public good and p. rights, 345:10
    served no p. end, 294:9
    sets p. friendship above public, 65:12
    sin in p. not sin, 267:17
    sin not so prejudicial, 157:25
    system of p. property, 720:17
    takes no p. road, 295:6
    vices public benefits, 287:10
    your own p. Idaho, 870:2

Privates, what have kings that p. have not, 189:22

Privations, cheerful amid p., 519:10
   dull p. and lean emptiness, 229:13

Privies, sun penetrates p., 77:3

Privilege, let others enjoy p. too, 300:*n*4
   my right and my p., 852:10
   of absurdity, 239:6
   of early youth, 568:7
   Roosevelt no enemy of entrenched p., 685:4

Privileges, age of p., 364:12
   claim none of the rights or p., 385:5
   do not make common law, 115:23
   laws add exclusive p., 364:3
   or immunities of citizens, 340:8

Privilegia paucorum non faciunt legem, 115:*n*11

Privy, grim wolf with p. paw, 253:11
   to do gentil dedes, 135:16

Prize above my dukedom, 224:9
   at three hundred pence ointment p., 242:15
   decline the Pulitzer P., 664:5
   first p. is Cadillac Eldorado, 865:8
   for powerful is power, 538:17
   humble hen we p., 886:4
   in war no second p., 697:6
   light winning make p. light, 224:16
   love game beyond p., 582:8
   men p. the thing ungained, 203:3
   one receiveth p., 42:19
   rain influence and judge the p., 251:7
   we sought is won, 487:16
   what we have we p. not, 191:6
   world within I doubly p., 476:16

Prized beyond sculptured flower, 406:1
   something he p., 658:4

Pro aris atque focis, 92:*n*6
   bono publico, 121:10
   patria pro liberis, 92:*n*6

Probabilities, judge between p., 441:1
   theory of p., 345:4

Probable, no warrants but upon p. cause, 340:3
   possible shadow of doubt, 528:4
   war regarded as inevitable p., 738:9

Probing through you toward me, 720:9

Probitas laudatur et alget, 109:*n*3

Problem, common p. yours mine everyone's, 461:21
   easy solution to every human p., 645:5
   every p. is worldwide, 835:21
   Houston we've had a p., 819:13
   lay buried, 796:7
   never be solved by science, 440:9
   obvious there's no real p., 790:4
   of creative writer, 563:16
   of twentieth century is color line, 601:14
   part of solution or of p., 839:23
   philosophical p., 769:15
   that has no name, 796:8
   there is only an American p., 753:13
   three-pipe p., 573:9

Problems, great p. of life, 630:2
   of complex civilization, 652:14
   of dog versus cat bird versus bird, 727:8
   of our country, 805:15

Procedural, history of p. safeguards, 649:9

Proceed ad infinitum, 285:11
   from impulse of the moment, 382:6
   nature not p. by leaps, 305:3
   so they resolved to p., 240:1

Proceedeth, every word that p., 9:18
   wickedness p. from the wicked, 11:5

Proceeding from heat-oppressed brain, 215:13

Process, due p. of law, 340:4, 340:8
   in creative p. father mother child, 584:18
   inexorable inner p. contraction of life, 630:4
   not view p. with misgivings, 619:18
   of the suns, 452:5
   verity is a p., 542:9

Processes, obscure unconscious mental p., 562:16

Procession, stay with p., 597:17
   systematic p. of universe, 142:13

Processions, endless p. of the whale, 482:20

Proclaim, great Original p., 287:20
   liberty throughout land, 9:1
   no shame, 201:7
   they will p. me heretic, 141:12
   with angelic host p., 305:10

Proclaiming peace and good will to men, 340:12

Proclaims, apparel oft p. the man, 197:23
   peace p. olives of age, 222:10

Proconsuls, each year new p., 111:4

Procrastination, incivility and p., 393:7
   is thief of time, 290:22
   keeping up with yesterday, 635:7
   no idleness no p., 500:*n*1

Procreant cradle, 214:21

Procreate, that we might p. like trees, 248:16

Procul hinc procul este severi, 102:*n*1

Procurer of contentedness, 245:1

Procuress to Lords of Hell, 453:20

Prodigal, Catiline p. of own possessions, 92:4
   chariest maid p. enough, 197:19
   enemy be p., 748:5
   how p. the soul, 197:28
   of ease, 272:17
   son, 38:10

Prodigality, spring of p., 324:15

Prodigies, all Africa and her p., 248:5

Prodigy, what a p. is man, 269:25

Produce according to aptitudes, 478:*n*2
   but not take possession, 57:4
   eating p. of the land, 52:12
   laboring to p. bons mots, 267:22
   my foot my feather, 827:12
   sacrificed to p. her, 582:12
   the person, 120:27
   things and to rear them, 57:4

Produced, after they p., 56:12
   intellectual product judged from age p., 534:3

Producer, promoting interest of p., 319:9

Producers, can't p. ever be wrong, 710:15

Produces, final cause p. motion, 77:19

Producing, consume without p., 564:19

Product, book is p. of different self, 611:9
   man's nature cultural p., 725:9

Production, belief that increased p. is worthy, 753:4
   consumption sole end of all p., 319:9
   entrepreneur contributes to p., 657:18

Production (*continued*)
   eternity in love with p. of time, 351:12
   improvement of instruments of p., 478:10
   means of social p., 478:*n*5
   opens demand for products, 364:9
   practice and theory of p., 764:3
   utility or cost of p., 543:12

Products, demand for p., 364:9
   of art and science, 693:4

Profanation to keep in, 241:12

Profane and old wives' fables, 44:29
   and vain babblings, 44:38
   for me to p. it, 404:5
   things holy p. clean obscene, 239:8
   things sacred or things p., 271:16

Profaned heavenly gift of poesy, 273:20
   one word too often p., 404:5

Profaning, joy brought by certainty of p. beauty, 713:2

Profess not the knowledge, 30:15

Profession, hold up Adam's p., 202:3
   is to disguise, 143:4
   most ancient p., 587:5

Professions, analysis third of impossible p., 564:2
   one of p. which are full, 474:22
   satisfied to have two p., 578:1

Professor encouraging clever pupil, 305:4
   of art of puffing, 346:16
   profit p. naught, 163:8

Professors like literature dead, 664:7
   of Dismal Science, 408:6

Proffer, fawning greyhound did p., 182:7

Profit, and the p. and loss, 676:14
   between the p. and the loss, 677:18
   by folly of others, 105:9
   by losing our prayers, 218:17
   by their example, 331:8
   engine of Enterprise, 656:13
   entrepreneurial p., 657:18
   few p. by advice, 99:20
   in all labor there is p., 20:28
   no more p. of shining nights, 174:1
   no p. but the name, 201:18
   no p. where no pleasure, 173:6
   private enterprise for p., 652:19
   professor naught, 163:8
   title and p. I resign, 287:*n*3
   true to his p. and his pride, 285:5
   truth as opposeth no p., 239:13
   what p. of all his labor, 22:21
   winds blow p., 751:2
   wise men p. more from fools, 85:4

Profitable, lie with purpose most p., 600:4

Profited, age not p. so much as lost, 474:14
   what is a man p., 34:39

Profits, civilization and p. hand in hand, 613:5
   keeping p. up by keeping wages down, 380:15
   little p. that idle king, 451:11

Profound, both may be called p., 56:12
   in his view, 329:*n*1
   man thinks woman p., 549:*n*2
   naked silence and p. quiet, 416:16
   subtle and p. female, 57:2
   whole subject is too p., 440:7

Profoundness of yearning for more vivid world, 767:8

Publish *(continued)*
  yourselves to sky, 543:1
Published, what should not be p. abroad, 70:14
Publisher, Barabbas a p., 399:18
  no author genius to p., 415:11
Publisheth peace, 27:3
Pudding, hasty p., 883:*n*4
    proof of p. in eating, 156:38
    solid p. empty praise, 296:25
    sweets of Hasty P., 347:8
    to make bag p., 896:23
Pudding-bag string, 897:4
Puddle, stepped in a p., 896:10
    world is p.-wonderful, 701:6
Puddles, novel reflects mud p. underfoot, 392:5
Puddle-wonderful, world is p., 701:6
Puffed and reckless libertine, 197:20
    charity not p. up, 42:27
    love not p. up, 42:27
Puffeth, knowledge p. up, 42:17
Puffing, professor of art of p., 346:16
Puffins razorbills guillemots and kittiwakes, 365:*n*1
Puissance, between corn-rows held old p., 645:14
Puissant nation rousing herself, 254:12
Pukes, sea passenger p. in, 398:22
Puking, mewling and p., 194:25
Pulitzer, decline the P. Prize, 664:5
Pull all together, 465:34
    chestnuts out of fire, 267:8
    door called p., 886:3
    down thy vanity, 665:14
    long p. strong p., 465:34
    not down your hedge, 243:19
    opportunities around for political p., 543:14
    Paquin p. down, 665:14
    weight, 571:6
Pulled into Nazareth, 858:9
    our ploughs and borne our loads, 672:6
Puller down of kings, 170:*n*2
Pulleth sword out of stone, 138:2
Pulleys, cry of p., 797:12
Pullin', you do de p. Sis Cow, 551:15
Pullman, ten years on P. cars, 681:4
Pulls, who p. me down, 169:4
Pulping, no p. of books, 764:16
Pulpit drum ecclesiastic, 261:18
Pulpits, some to common p., 192:17
Pulsations, translate p. into images, 825:3
Pulse, my p. like soft drum, 241:19
    of life stood still, 290:20
    of the machine, 371:7
    poll feeling p., 620:11
    scene beat like a p., 798:7
Pulses, axioms proved upon p., 413:4
    give world other p., 408:18
Pumice, smoothed with dry p. stone, 90:23
Pump don't work, 851:16
    president is p., 764:4
Pumpkin, frost is on p., 553:10
    put her in p. shell, 895:15
Pumpkins, where early p. blow, 467:15
Pun, good p. may be admitted, 334:8
    pistol not feather, 383:22

Punctual as a Star, 509:11
    rape of every day, 797:13
Punctuality politeness of kings, 349:12
Punic faith, 92:12
Punica fide, 92:*n*9
Punish, distrust impulse to p., 548:2
    the world for evil, 25:21
    to p. they answer prayers, 59:*n*4
Punished as enemy of country, 363:14
    big words always p., 66:1
    in the sight of men, 29:34
Punishing anyone between them, 375:8
    beware of p. wrongfully, 3:8
Punishment, broad effects of p., 548:16
    could not name all types of p., 94:31
    cruel and unusual p., 340:7
    Erinyes exact p. underground, 52:10
    failure not only p. for laziness, 585:10
    fit the crime, 527:15
    good evil reward p., 275:11
    is greater than I can bear, 6:7
    let p. match offense, 88:12
    makes us obey orders, 733:16
    no p. prevent crimes, 744:7
    of petty crimes, 694:4
    pleasing p. women bear, 172:13
    reward rather than p., 419:2
    servitude p. of guilt, 345:7
    tames man, 548:16
    transgressed custom brings p., 525:1
Punishments, for great wrongdoing great p., 69:10
Punk, do you p., 791:3
Punkin, frost is on p., 553:10
Punks, natcherly we're p., 828:15
Pup, remember when he was p., 624:3
Pupil, encouraging clever p., 305:4
Pupils, true teacher defends p., 417:6
Puppet, in the p. or in the god, 385:4
    making President czar making him p., 788:18
Puppets, shut up box and p., 459:8
Puppies, greyhound p., 442:21
Puppy dogs' tails, 895:11
    mangled under a screaming wheel, 772:5
    mongrel p. whelp hound, 322:13
Pur comme un ange, 348:*n*1
Purblind Doomsters, 535:10
    wimpled whining p., 174:14
Purchase a little temporary safety, 303:6
    unless abroad p. alliance, 170:29
    you p. pain, 293:27
Purchased at price of chains, 331:13
    by merit of the wearer, 185:8
    history's p. page, 395:19
    with pain p. inherit pain, 173:40
Purchaser, new p. of country place, 739:9
    worth what p. will pay, 101:2
Pure and complete sorrow impossible, 507:1
    and disposed to mount to stars, 130:1
    and eloquent blood, 230:16
    and endless light, 268:14
    as an angel, 348:5
    as driven slush, 733:14
    as naked heavens, 370:10
    as snow, 199:26
    beauty of mathematics, 614:9

Pure *(continued)*
    blessed are the p. in heart, 32:14
    clean hands and a p. heart, 15:24
    clear as crystal, 466:32
    harmony is p. love, 167:7
    I will keep p. and holy, 70:14
    immortals cannot escape, 65:25
    in high art and p. science, 723:12
    in life free from sin, 96:14
    land of p. delight, 289:17
    literature p. and dead, 664:7
    live p. speak true, 455:9
    love without power, 696:1
    lovers' souls descend, 229:19
    man who's p. in heart, 732:15
    mathematics original, 580:7
    my heart is p., 452:13
    my poems naughty my life p., 107:4
    of mouth pure of hands, 3:10
    particularly p. young man, 526:11
    religion breathing laws, 370:4
    shall man be more p. than maker, 13:9
    silence of p. innocence, 223:15
    sleep from p. digestion bred, 258:12
    so sweet and p. and fair, 415:2
    soul unto captain Christ, 177:14
    stars are not p. in his sight, 14:1
    substantial world p. and good, 372:1
    thy truth so p. of old, 254:23
    unclouded brow, 515:10
    unto p. all things p., 45:4
    whatsoever things are p., 44:7
    whether his work be p., 21:11
    women innocent and p., 224:19
    young man, 526:11
Purer than purest gold, 232:9
Purest, frost from p. snow, 220:3
    purer than p. gold, 232:9
    ray serene, 315:23
    treasure mortal times afford, 176:8
    virgin p. lipped, 409:12
Purgatory, England is p. of men, 161:11
    in erthe I was his p., 135:9
Purge and leave sack, 183:37
    me with hyssop, 16:31
    melancholy, 223:36
    rottenness out of system, 561:14
Purified, every creature p., 168:20
Purify dialect of tribe, 679:10
    the mind, 64:13
Puritan, devil a p. that he is, 204:30
    hated bear-baiting, 420:4
Puritanism haunting fear someone may be happy, 645:19
Puritans founded to give thanks, 600:8
    great artists never P., 645:4
    nobly fled, 519:5
    thanks we are presarved fr'm P., 600:8
Purity ability to contemplate difilement, 760:15
    ore of body into p., 663:13
Purlieus, dusty p. of law, 454:4
Purloined, love he p. her away, 532:16
Purple, beyond utmost p. rim, 452:12
    blossom in p. and red, 455:3
    cow, 597:19
    first from out the p. grape, 252:4
    gleaming in p. and gold, 397:2

Q

Qualified, I am q., 211:6
  masses are not q., 657:12
Qualify, my flame to q., 222:11
Qualis artifex pereo, 106:*n*6
Qualities, chose on various q., 611:1
  such q. as would wear, 322:7
Quality, composition and fierce q., 210:33
  draw inward q. after, 218:32
  hate counsels not in such a q., 185:15
  of mercy not strained, 186:1
  not quantity but q., 121:*n*2
  rather than quantity, 103:15
  royal banner and all q., 209:13
  taste of your q., 199:11
  true-fixed and resting q., 192:14
Quanch my heart trobling, 682:12
Quantities, determination of q. by numbers,
    513:1
  ghosts of departed q., 291:7
  such q. of sand, 516:1
Quantity, not q. but quality, 121:*n*2
  of force in Nature eternal, 494:5
  of love, 202:20
  of matter unalterable, 494:5
  quality rather than q., 103:15
Quantum, waive q. o' the sin, 356:19
Quantum Mechanics, no one understands Q.,
    790:3
Quarantine aggressors, 652:*n*3
  to protect community, 652:17
Quarelets of pearl, 240:14
Quarks, three q. for Muster Mark, 651:1
Quarrel, beware entrance to q., 197:23
  find q. in a straw, 201:21
  how they behave in q., 564:14
  lover's q. with world, 624:10
  make of q. with others rhetoric, 592:14
  no q. with Viet Cong, 853:12
  nor for every q. to lawyer, 244:1
  over water, 661:2
  pretty q. as it stands, 346:8
  sudden and quick in q., 194:25
  take up our q. with the foe, 614:7
  thrice armed that hath q. just, 170:7
  with bread and butter, 285:18
  with whom should I q., 742:3
Quarreling, set them a-q., 312:1
Quarrels, dove loves when it q., 116:14
  full of q. as egg of meat, 180:26
  love know no sundering q., 96:12
  love-q. in concord end, 260:20
  lovers' q. renewal of love, 85:15
  who in q. interpose, 291:13
  would not last long, 264:30
Quarrelsome, countercheck q., 196:6
  little words are q., 80:10
  mutinous and q., 304:3
Quarried, limestone q. near spot, 597:11
Quarry, go not like q.-slave, 405:13
  mine blessed am I, 892:1
Quartered, see Harrison hanged drawn q.,
    277:4
Quarterly, I says the Q., 399:11
Quarter-tone, discover value of q., 626:3
Que sais-je, 152:*n*12
Quean, flaunting extravagant q., 346:11
Queen and huntress, 232:2
  be the battle q. of yore, 535:3

Queen (*continued*)
  beggar maid my q., 452:14
  come not near our fairy q., 178:22
  every lass a q., 481:7
  grace a summer q., 374:6
  I am your anointed Q., 151:8
  I would not be a q., 225:18
  in people's hearts, 876:9
  it no inch further, 223:33
  Mab hath been with you, 179:25
  mathematics q. of sciences, 385:3
  moves a goddess looks a q., 293:17
  must not bring Q. into politics, 503:5
  now now cried the Q., 515:15
  o' the May, 450:15
  of Hearts, 894:2
  of pleasure, 530:13
  of Sheba heard of Solomon, 11:33
  of this summer hotel, 820:8
  poor memory the Q. remarked, 516:11
  to London to look at q., 895:7
  turned crimson with fury, 514:18
  unveiled peerless light, 257:25
  was in parlor, 894:7
  you shall be q., 896:13
  you will though Q. said, 515:11
Queen's, Ruler of Q. Navee, 525:22
Queens, have died young and fair, 227:6
  women called q. a long time, 513:8
Queer, horse must think it q., 623:7
  how strange and q., 461:*n*1
  ill-tempered and q., 467:4
  monster the artist, 545:7
  Northern Lights seen q. sights, 627:13
  putting q. shoulder to wheel, 812:12
  you look so q., 884:6
Queerer, universe q. than we suppose, 693:11
Queerest folk of all, 579:3
  they ever did see, 627:13
Quell, music raise and q., 273:23
Quelle est cette île triste et noire, 491:*n*8
Quem deus vult perdere, 121:11
Quench, fire rivers cannot q., 170:35
  if I q. thee, 210:14
  many waters cannot q. love, 24:26
  smoking flax shall he not q., 26:34
Quenched in most cold repose, 403:17
Quenching in Purple, 508:11
Querulous, newspapers q. and bellicose, 645:3
  usual q. serenity, 382:10
Quest, go Soul the body's q., 159:9
  in q. to have extreme, 222:20
  things they were not in q. of, 317:2
  whither and what thy q., 545:12
Questing, passes the q. vole, 736:9
  Pellinore followed q. beast, 138:3
  Snail, 756:15
Question, ask yourself one q., 791:3
  between equals of power, 72:7
  broach q. begin to quote, 425:14
  consider q. can machines think, 769:5
  final solution of Jewish q., 697:14
  fundamental q. of philosophy, 769:15
  greatest q. ever debated, 329:18
  he would not ask any q., 534:14
  if His Glory, 509:18
  in that case what is the q., 628:15
  includes every great q. of Being, 646:6

Question (*continued*)
  interrupt with silly q., 313:20
  is absurd, 749:11
  is not whether we will be, 823:5
  is this all, 796:7
  is which is to be master, 516:15
  let history answer q., 337:10
  momentous q. like firebell, 338:10
  most momentous q. on continent, 500:6
  not been able to answer, 564:5
  not harm nor q. much, 230:1
  others abide our q., 494:10
  settle q. discuss it, 419:12
  that is the q., 199:21
  there is only one q., 840:8
  two sides to every q., 69:26
  what q. you desire to answer, 617:3
  why did you do that, 563:2
  why we and universe exist, 854:3
  wisdom of novel q. for everything, 824:3
  young embarrassed to q. older, 52:27
Questionable, comest in such q. shape, 197:33
Questioned me story of my life, 207:36
Questioning, drew nearer sweetly q., 243:11
  is piety of thought, 684:7
  nature exposed to method of q., 728:5
  needs no q. before he speaks, 68:17
  warned prior to q., 692:6
Questions, answer q. about myself, 741:11
  answer q. intelligently, 518:4
  answered three q., 514:6
  arise that can't be answered, 832:6
  ask me no q., 323:6
  attempt to answer q., 617:3
  came to prove him with hard q., 11:33
  get you asking the wrong q., 843:4
  heard you asking q., 812:9
  make us human, 790:16
  no q. unanswerable, 425:20
  them that asks no q., 323:*n*1
  though puzzling q. not beyond conjecture,
    248:27
  you might want to ask, 850:7
Qui ante diem periit, 582:9
  procul hinc legend's writ, 582:9
  s'excuse s'accuse, 151:*n*2
Quibbles, in q. angel and archangel, 296:13
Quick and dead, 48:11
  brown fox, 885:19
  even in death, 158:17
  eyes gone, 665:9
  her q. look, 756:4
  how did I get old so q., 732:12
  how q. and fresh art thou, 204:11
  intake of air, 874:6
  Jack be q., 895:16
  now here now always, 678:11
  so q. bright things come to confusion,
    177:28
  sudden and q. in quarrel, 194:25
  to arm, 665:8
  to flare up, 53:6
  true apothecary thy drugs q., 181:15
  word of God is q., 45:7
Quicken, live within sense they q., 404:4
Quickened, not q. except it die, 43:4
Quickeneth, spirit that q., 39:19
Quickens to rebel, 677:19

Rainbow *(continued)*
    rainbow rainbow, 762:14
    somewhere over r., 711:12
Rainbow's glory shed, 404:10
Rainbows, poisoned with r., 837:10
Rain-drenched hair, 660:13
Raindrop, down names r. plows, 537:1
Raindrops on roses, 706:16
Rained ghastly dew, 452:2
Raineth drop staineth slop, 665:2
    rain it r. every day, 205:29, 211:31
Rainfall, West begins where r. drops, 713:8
Rain's, out of wind's and r. way, 647:6
Rains, ev'ry time r. r. pennies from Heaven,
    751:15
    long r. were falling, 122:9
    return in rivers, 750:1
    winter's r. and ruins, 529:13
Rainstorms, inspector of r., 473:1
Rainwater, glazed with r., 658:14
Rainy evening to read this discourse, 244:34
    eyes, 177:7
    love world and all in its r. arms, 872:4
    morrow, 221:29
    natives of rain r. men, 640:14
    Pleiads wester, 576:1
    weary of wench guest weather r., 302:2
Raise, Death old captain r. anchor, 491:10
    didn't r. boy to be soldier, 887:5
    joys and triumphs high, 305:7
    less corn more hell, 554:6
    Lord shall r. me up I trust, 159:16
    man can r. a thirst, 588:3
    Music r. and quell, 273:23
    print news and r. hell, 885:9
    somewhat loftier strain, 92:21
    song of harvest-home, 456:9
    stone cleave wood, 113:19
    the genius, 293:13
    what is low r. and support, 255:5
Raised a mortal to the skies, 274:22
    dead shall be r., 43:8
    in incorruption, 43:6
    me up when I was little, 118:13
    new man r. up in him, 49:23
Raiseth, cross that r. me, 432:16
Raisin in the sun, 731:9
Raising, empire for r. customers, 319:7
Raisons, le coeur a ses r., 269:*n*6
Rake among scholars, 420:1
    every woman at heart r., 294:2
    hors leene as is a r., 133:22
    stop to r. leaves away, 622:9
Rake's progress, 459:10
Rakes, scholar among r., 420:1
Raking, know when to stop r. muck, 571:9
Rally round the flag boys, 489:9
Ralph wept for end of innocence, 764:1
Ram, black r. tupping your ewe, 207:27
    caught in a thicket, 6:36
    how wind doth r., 665:2
Ramble, always we r. that river and I, 768:4
Rambles, Hamlet r., 596:10
Ramblin', he made a r. man, 804:2
Ramm, how wind doth r., 665:2
Rampallian, away you r., 188:2
Rampant for spoil and victory, 548:15
Rampart, no r. against malice, 267:11

Ramparts we watched, 386:19
Ramps, hasten down r., 742:7
Rams, mountains skipped like r., 18:21
Ran a hundred years to a day, 443:12
    before Ahab, 12:3
    dismayed away, 186:14
    grief with glass that r., 529:14
    my heedless ways, 777:13
    neighing canyons, 720:7
    sunset r. one glorious blood-red, 460:20
Rancor outpouring of inferiority, 657:5
    will out, 169:23
Rancorous rational mind, 595:6
Randal, Felix R. the farrier, 546:15
    Lord R. my son, 890:9
Randolph Churchill went into hospital, 736:10
Random grim forge, 546:16
    I am writing at r., 413:12
    practice r. kindness, 871:5
    we thrown down here at r., 728:13
Rang, sabbath r. slowly, 777:12
    them while touring Timbucktoo, 823:2
Range with humble livers, 225:17
Ranged his tropes, 283:13
    if I have r., 222:12
    wide arch of r. empire fall, 218:3
Ranges, something lost behind the r., 589:21
Rank, battle of the first r., 422:13
    black r. and file, 519:10
    but guinea's stamp, 358:18
    flavor of blood, 815:15
    great beautifier, 423:12
    has its obligations, 361:16
    keep no r. nor station, 787:8
    me with barbarous multitude, 185:7
    my offense is r., 200:31
    swoln with r. mist, 253:11
    things r. and gross, 196:30
    when man of r. an author, 311:5
Rankers, gentlemen r., 588:6
Ranks, for adoration all the r., 318:8
    I belong in r. of religious men, 637:9
    of death, 387:12
Rank-scented many, 219:29
Ransom captive Israel, 479:3
    them from the power of the grave,
    28:40
Rant, I'll r. as well as thou, 202:21
    when you r. and swear, 235:*n*4
Rap is black America's CNN, 875:*n*1
    music is the invisible, 875:12
Rapacious and licentious soldiery, 324:17
Rape an insurrectionary act, 839:22
    another name for date r., 874:11
    of every day, 797:13
    theory and r. the practice, 853:1
Raphael made a century of sonnets, 462:9
Rapid, drive the r. car, 327:11
    Homer eminently r., 496:1
    lady's imagination r., 382:5
Rapidly, order is r. fadin', 851:5
Rapping at chamber door, 449:3
Rapscallions, all kings mostly r., 523:6
Rapt ship run on side so low, 163:20
    soul sitting in thine eyes, 251:13
Rapture, first fine careless r., 460:19
    on lonely shore, 396:16
    then a pain, 550:3

Raptures and roses of vice, 529:16
    illustrious acts high r. infuse, 249:20
    no Minstrel r. swell, 373:3
Rara avis in terris, 109:*n*8
Rare and bloodless week of repose, 73:*n*2
    and radiant maiden, 449:5
    are solitary woes, 201:*n*2
    as day in June, 481:16
    Beaumont, 240:6
    Ben Jonson, 231:*n*2
    bird on earth, 109:18
    delicate and r., 561:4
    detachment of spirit, 626:22
    excellent things r., 276:19
    few rid selves of friendship, 520:13
    my love of birth as r., 267:3
    somewhere a r. name, 73:6
    to meet man outdoors, 474:4
    tobacco divine r., 235:12
Rarely rarely comest thou, 404:8
Rarer gifts than gold, 669:12
    the living are getting r., 768:8
Rarity of Christian charity, 418:14
Rascal, biggest r. that walks, 110:16
    if r. have not given medicines, 182:9
Rascally yea-forsooth knave, 187:25
Rascals, lash the r. naked, 210:6
    law's to take care o' r., 480:9
    one of most unscrupulous r., 573:22
    would you live forever, 312:6
Rase, slowly r. she up, 889:26
Rash hand in evil hour, 259:11
    not splenetive and r., 202:19
    too r. too unadvised, 180:10
    who reckons on morrow, 66:12
Rash-embraced despair, 185:21
Rashes, green grow the r. O, 356:23
Rashly charged troops of error, 247:13
    importune, 418:13
Rashness, beware of r., 446:2
Raskills, law's to take care o' r., 480:9
Rasselas Prince of Abyssinia, 307:8
Rat, a dog a horse a r., 213:14
    begin to smell a r., 156:37
    how now a r., 201:2
    is in the trap, 827:14
    killed the r., 897:8
    poisoned r. in hole, 285:8
Raths, mome r. outgrabe, 515:12
Ratified, real and r. existence, 477:*n*2
Ratio, increase in geometrical r., 440:2
    keen and quivering r., 508:4
    population increases in geometrical r.,
    362:7
    subsistence in arithmetical r., 362:7
Ratiocination, pay with r., 262:3
Rational consciousness as we call it, 542:1
    ethics, 584:6
    I am r. therefore sing hymns, 108:20
    one r. voice dumb, 749:7
    rancorous r. mind, 595:6
    with men he can be r., 382:17
    world presents r. aspect, 367:11
Rationalism adventure in clarification of
    thought, 580:10
Rationality, freedom brought independence r.,
    725:8
    if r. were criterion, 843:8

Rationality (*continued*)
  will not save us, 782:11
Rationally, him who looks on world r., 367:11
  live r. for time assigned, 112:7
  till women more r. educated, 360:17
Rationed, so precious must be r., 607:17
Rations, live upon daily r., 465:16
Ratisbon, stormed R., 459:22
Rats came tumbling, 460:8
  desert sinking ship, 105:*n4*
  have quit it, 224:8
  land-r. and water-r., 184:21
  mice r. and such small deer, 212:6
  nearness of r., 724:7
  they fought dogs, 460:7
Rats' alley, 676:8
Rattle, just r. your jewelry, 884:10
  pleased with a r., 295:3
  rifles' rapid r., 699:6
Rattling good history, 536:16
  he was as r. thunder, 219:8
  o'er stony street, 395:14
  of a coach, 231:11
Ravages, irreparable r. of time, 279:3
Rave at close of day, 777:15
  no more 'gainst time, 528:13
Raved, but as I r., 243:2
Raveled sleave of care, 215:21
Raven, censure pardons r., 109:12
  grim and ancient R., 449:8
  himself is hoarse, 214:17
  locks were like the r., 357:13
  never flitting, 449:11
  Poe with his r., 481:19
  smoothing the r. down, 252:15
Ravening, inwardly are r. wolves, 33:20
Ravens brought him bread, 11:40
  He that doth r. feed, 194:3
  three r. on a tree, 890:3
Ravine, threw dead dog down the r., 759:3
Raving skies opened to voyager, 559:3
Ravished ears, 274:15
Raw, give them r. truth, 581:6
  inclement summers, 285:2
  Marian's nose red and r., 175:1
  material of opinion, 566:7
Ray, multiply a brighter r., 396:3
  purest r. serene, 315:23
  Shadwell's night admits no r., 273:14
Rayless majesty, 290:19
Rays, hide your diminished r., 257:*n3*
  in vain produced all r. return, 424:6
  your r. in midst of sea, 4:7
Raze out troubles of brain, 217:19
Razed, from books of honor r., 221:4
  Nature's works to me r., 257:6
Razón, sueño de la r. monstruos, 341:13
Razor, each holds locked r., 787:7
  Occam's R., 130:*n7*
  satire like polished r., 297:9
Razor's, fate hung on r. edge, 60:13
Razors to my wounded heart, 172:41
Razure of oblivion, 207:14
Reach, above r. of ordinary men, 369:17
  apple pickers not r. it, 56:10
  bloom gradually out of r., 814:14
  enjoy resources within thy r., 63:29
  fool to follow what is out of r., 108:7

Reach (*continued*)
  I cannot r. it, 269:1
  man's r. exceed grasp, 461:18
  me a gentian, 663:22
  never more than imperfectly r., 709:1
  not condescending to anything within r.,
    76:6
  of wisdom and of r., 198:23
  unreachable star, 784:8
  until we r. ripest fruit, 168:2
Reaches five hundred thousand readers, 531:21
  thoughts beyond r. of souls, 197:34
Reaching forth unto things before, 44:4
  irritable r. after fact, 412:15
Reaction, attack is the r., 310:1
  I can't get no girl r., 857:1
  if any r. both transformed, 630:3
  religion r. upon life, 541:19
  to every action equal r., 279:16
Reactivates object reproduced, 693:3
Read a good poem, 343:1
  a little I can r., 218:4
  a silly fairy tale, 317:2
  as deliberately as written, 475:5
  as inclination leads, 309:4
  aught I could ever r., 177:27
  best company when you r., 375:5
  better neither r. nor write, 386:1
  blockheads r. what blockheads wrote,
    298:16
  book of fate, 188:12
  book people praise don't r., 524:15
  both r. the Bible, 354:16
  children don't r. to find identity, 740:4
  damn authors they never r., 326:5
  gentlemen do not r. other's mail, 601:5
  he that runs may r., 327:8
  history in nation's eyes, 316:2
  I have r. all the books, 543:6
  I have time to r. my books, 116:22
  in the bitter letter, 207:32
  know what I r. in papers, 640:3
  many benefits from good r., 769:7
  mark learn, 49:10
  my lips No New Taxes, 805:3
  my title clear, 289:16
  never learned to r., 811:4
  never r. book not year old, 428:14
  not poem we have r., 379:1
  old authors to r., 165:8
  only books that wound us, 655:10
  part all through, 649:17
  poetry difficult to r., 463:2
  rather r. what famous author cut, 335:13
  sins scarlet books r., 606:17
  strange matters, 214:19
  take up r., 116:5
  that day we r. no farther, 128:19
  timetable than nothing, 627:3
  to by a boy, 675:21
  to r. comes by nature, 190:41
  very few to r., 369:*n1*
  we should r. for power, 666:1
  what do you r. my lord, 198:35
  whoso that kan r. hem as they write,
    132:11
  with joy then shut the book, 500:7
  wits to r., 232:19

Read (*continued*)
  youngsters r. men understand, 157:5
Readable, book chief need is be r., 472:6
Reader, birth of the r., 778:3
  delighting and instructing r., 98:29
  delights r. instructs too, 278:7
  exciting sympathy of r., 379:8
  good r. makes good book, 428:24
  hypocrite r., 491:1
  I married him, 472:11
  look, 232:18
  make r. no longer consumer, 778:4
  my story ends with freedom, 469:1
  no tears in r., 625:4
  of his own self, 611:7
  poetry strike R. as own thoughts, 413:1
  right r. of good poem, 623:12
  take them not for mine, 133:*n2*
  wise r. quote wisely, 417:8
Readers, five hundred thousand r., 531:21
  new books are for r., 297:17
  of Boston Evening Transcript, 675:10
  parts that r. tend to skip, 808:10
Reader's Bill of Rights, 859:13
Readest, thou r. black, 354:16
Readeth, he may run that r. it, 29:7
Readiness, in state of r. in mind and body,
    566:20
  is all, 202:26
Reading, after r. your work, 299:16
  basis of their r. experience, 846:8
  contemplation more than r., 270:10
  creative r. creative writing, 426:2
  curst hard r., 346:19
  digressions sunshine of r., 314:3
  it with perfect contempt, 671:1
  life the thing but I prefer r., 590:15
  maketh a full man, 166:18
  my own writings, 809:13
  new era in life from r., 475:6
  no r. more fascinating than catalogue,
    545:16
  Peace makes poor r., 536:16
  point of writing and r., 869:9
  such r. as never read, 297:5
  theologian not born by r., 144:8
  to mind as exercise to body, 287:19
  valueless books, 484:15
  who abstains from r. abuse of self, 472:2
  write things worthy r., 302:18
Reads as task, 309:4
  but one book, 244:29
  he r. much great observer, 191:29
Ready, a God r. to pardon, 12:30
  completely r. state, 470:8
  conference maketh a r. man, 166:18
  fire when r. Gridley, 529:1
  for war way to avoid it, 281:10
  in defense, 324:7
  minds to fellowship, 409:9
  money makes the man, 289:18
  my tongue is the pen of a r. writer, 16:24
  necessity of being r., 445:8
  no r. way to virtue, 248:13
  old wife old dog r. money, 302:17
  rough sir but r., 465:19
  to embrace the strangers, 482:12
  to ride spread alarm, 437:16

Ready *(continued)*
  to try our fortunes, 188:18
  we always are r., 316:20
  with every nod to tumble, 171:34
  with you be r. to die, 97:3
Ready-made, critics all r., 394:13
Real, a man's r. life, 567:20
  coming back to r., 642:11
  do it so feels r., 833:3
  lead me from unreal to r., 50:1
  life r. life earnest, 436:4
  lure of the r., 643:1
  margin between r. and unreal, 282:1
  never fit for r. work, 806:10
  no r. problem, 790:4
  nothing r. except humanity, 416:8
  nothing r. till experienced, 413:13
  only mist is r., 776:8
  producing r. social wealth, 604:14
  spirit r. and eternal, 493:6
  that is moral, 491:15
  thing which made the emotion, 721:12
  this is the r. me, 540:16
  War Will Never Get in Books, 488:14
  what is r. is reasonable, 367:7
  you r. me, 703:8
Realism, I don't want r., 766:6
Realist, in Israel to be r., 666:13
Realities and creators, 426:15
  less dangerous than fancies, 615:4
  muddled state sharpest of r., 544:19
  not images of beauty but r., 74:6
Reality attained only by detached, 760:12
  between idea and r., 677:1
  capture its r. in paint, 533:15
  ceases to be r. of my life, 431:1
  final word in r., 823:13
  fine r. of hunger satisfied, 752:9
  history illumines r., 87:13
  human kind not bear much r., 678:5
  I have more faith in r., 733:8
  in r. atoms and space, 70:12
  is in the reader's mind, 385:11
  is that which, 818:4
  is things as they are, 642:22
  lose our sense of r., 860:1
  make credible much of American r., 835:3
  mask off r. remains, 90:9
  misunderstandings with r., 681:16
  must take precedence, 790:5
  no humbling of r. to precept, 810:16
  of distress, 333:15
  of experience, 650:13
  regulate imagination by r., 308:7
  scientific statement speaks about r., 732:3
  the more threatening r. appears, 648:5
  three mirror same r., 338:22
  truth about r., 835:8
  use r. rather than know it, 776:1
  we crave only r., 475:3
  we create our own r., 875:10
  your own r. for yourself, 567:14
Reality-based community, 875:10
Realize bitterness of Life, 517:8
  earth too wonderful to r. you, 715:8
  I'd been happy, 769:14
  Mrs. Pontellier to r. position, 556:17
  suddenly I r., 817:9

Realized, design of all his words r., 642:12
  they and I civilized, 734:11
Realm, invade borders of my r., 151:7
  mysterious r., 405:13
  riding o'er azure r., 316:15
  this r. this England, 176:24
  turned out of R. in my petticoat, 151:8
Realms above, 377:13
  and islands as plates, 219:8
  Anna whom three r. obey, 293:7
  of gold, 408:17
  those who Dwell in R. of day, 354:7
  whatever r. to see, 321:12
Reap an act, 885:17
  as you sow ye r., 262:20
  blessings of freedom, 333:10
  harvest of your land, 8:26
  he that regardeth the clouds not r., 23:27
  in joy, 19:3
  men that sow and r., 530:16
  not wholly r. the corners, 8:26
  sow not neither r., 33:6
  that shall he also r., 43:33
  the whirlwind, 28:36
  we r. our sowing, 519:8
Reaped, all the harvest I r., 441:19
  iniquity, 28:37
  wheat never r. nor sown, 278:11
Reaping, autumn that grew by r., 219:8
Reappraisal, agonizing r., 787:11
Reaps, wholesome harvests r., 417:7
Rear my dusky race, 452:8
  tender thought, 300:19
  to produce and to r. them, 57:4
Reared arm crested the world, 219:8
  himself a throne, 448:2
Rearward of a conquered woe, 221:29
Reason and experiment have been indulged, 336:6
  and will of God prevail, 497:13
  argument needs no r., 58:12
  art has r. for being, 428:20
  asked one another the r., 195:35
  beast that wants discourse of r., 197:4
  but from what we know, 294:16
  by r. of strength, 17:25
  can decide nothing here, 269:17
  capability and godlike r., 201:19
  common law nothing but r., 158:21
  destroys book kills r., 254:7
  discourse of r., 197:4
  feast of r. flow of soul, 296:6
  flood of words drop of r., 302:13
  freed men's minds, 104:9
  give r. on compulsion, 182:22
  God's crowning gift, 65:23
  greatest enemy faith has, 144:9
  guide by light of r., 562:13
  have I not r. to lament, 368:3
  human r. is beautiful, 764:16
  ignis fatuus of mind, 281:2
  I'm trav'lin' on, 851:4
  Imagination abandoned by R., 341:*n*4
  immortal all else mortal, 58:10
  improvable r. of Man, 415:15
  in images of sense, 378:24
  in itself confounded, 202:36
  in man like God in world, 127:9

Reason *(continued)*
  is of no use to us, 328:10
  is past care, 223:6
  is slave of passions, 311:21
  keep r. under control, 112:20
  know truth not only by r., 269:19
  knows nothing of, 269:18
  law is perfection of r., 158:21
  law ordinance of r. for common good, 127:6
  left free to combat error, 337:8
  left free to combat it, 338:13
  let my will take place of r., 109:19
  let us r. together, 24:32, 753:9
  lies between spur and bridle, 244:16
  life of the law, 158:21
  madman is not man who has lost r., 618:7
  make worse appear better r., 72:13
  men have lost their r., 192:31
  Milton wrote in fetters, 351:10
  most sovereign r., 200:4
  noble in r., 199:5
  not listen to r., 457:2
  not yet guided by r., 609:7
  one considers r. a quality, 380:7
  our r. is our law, 259:10
  panders will, 201:7
  passions not conform to r., 349:8
  past r. hunted, 222:20
  psychological r., 544:11
  pursue my R. to O altitudo, 248:3
  rather to feel than r., 360:20
  reaching after fact and r., 412:15
  rhyme nor r., 161:10
  right deed for wrong r., 678:4
  ruling passion conquers r., 294:8
  sanctified by r. blest by faith, 369:2
  shall enforce her sway, 346:24
  since everything has its r., 493:9
  sleep of r. produces monsters, 341:13
  takes the r. prisoner, 214:8
  teach thy necessity to r., 176:16
  tell me the r. I pray, 381:10
  theirs not to r. why, 454:21
  themselves out again, 190:8
  victory over r., 684:8
  we bicker creates war, 152:17
  what someone else has to say, 457:2
  where faith in r. timid, 614:4
  why I cannot tell, 282:23
  worse appear better r., 256:11
  yield with grace to r., 622:8
Reasonable good ear in music, 178:31
  holy and living sacrifice, 49:7
  man being r. must get drunk, 398:11
  nothing r. from pure reason, 618:9
  speak a few r. words, 343:1
  what is real is r., 367:7
Reasoned errors, 502:12
Reasoning but to err, 295:1
  destroy power of r., 76:2
  infant's r., 313:13
  like all Holmes's r., 573:15
  man is a r. animal, 103:14
  mathematician capable of r., 75:13
  self-sufficing thing, 369:10
Reasonings, versed in r. of men, 67:15

Reason's icy intimations, 418:17
  in erring r. spite, 294:23
  words clothed in r. garb, 256:15
Reasons, and he had r., 605:20
  as two grains of wheat, 184:10
  everybody has his r., 703:11
  find of settled gravity, 221:14
  heart has its r., 269:18
  heroism never r., 427:12
  man always has two r., 529:6
  one wants decisions the other r., 433:12
  plenty as blackberries, 182:22
  private as well as public r., 336:7
  so long as human r. is weak, 503:3
Rebecks, jocund r. sound, 251:4
Re-begot, ruined me and I am r., 229:13
Rebel, aspiring to angels men r., 165:*n*4
  I'm a good old r., 529:10
  in act and deed, 585:2
  learn from past and r., 821:6
  quickens to r., 677:19
  spaceships, 859:11
  those that r. against the light, 13:44
  without a cause, 775:2
Rebellion, a little r. a good thing, 336:14
  against United States, 445:13
  century and half without r., 336:15
  determined to foment r., 340:11
  lay in his way, 183:22
  not r. which is noble, 770:3
  now and then good, 336:14
  rude eye of r., 176:1
  Rum Romanism R., 463:17
  to tyrants, 883:21
Rebellions, legends events r. majesties, 411:15
Rebellious, dark r. brows, 488:2
  hell, 201:7
  hot and r. liquors, 194:4
  revolting and r. heart, 27:26
  stubborn and r. generation, 17:15
Rebelliousness, culture drives to r., 563:15
Rebels from principle, 325:5
  our countrymen again, 498:4
Rebirth, of Union, 566:9
Reborn, power to be r. into highest forms, 141:3
Rebounds, hit hard it r., 310:1
Rebuff, welcome each r., 462:15
Rebuffs, confront accidents r., 485:13
Rebuke a wise man, 20:8
  is better than secret love, 22:1
  recoils, 622:2
Rebus, cedit amor r., 102:*n*14
  est modus in r., 95:*n*7
Recall a stone thrown, 98:*n*3
Recalled, word cannot be r., 98:8
Recant, if I do not r., 141:12
Recapitulation, ontogenesis r. of phylogenesis, 519:12
Recapture, never could r., 460:19
Recede, unpurged images r., 595:10
Recedes, orgiastic future that r. before us, 710:7
Receipt of little bit of paper, 483:11
  sitting at r. of custom, 33:30
Receive, ask and ye shall r., 40:4
  Christ r. him, 454:17
  hand stretched out to r., 30:19

Receive (*continued*)
  if lungs r. our air, 326:21
  more blessed to give than r., 40:40
  my soul at last, 305:8
  the fugitive, 333:2
  we r. but what we give, 378:8
Received, freely ye have r., 33:38
Receives comfort like cold porridge, 224:18
  reproach of being, 222:19
Receiveth, one r. prize, 42:19
Reciprocal in marriage obligations r., 405:9
Recirculation, commodius vicus of r., 650:19
Recite In the name of thy Lord, 119:18
Reck the rede, 197:*n*1
Reckless, make r. choice, 622:21
  puffed and r. libertine, 197:20
  what I do to spite world, 216:7
Recklessness, never gauged your cruelty r., 689:5
Reckon I got to light out for the Territory, 523:10
  ill who leave me out, 425:5
  when I count at all, 509:9
Reckoned, love that can be r., 218:2
Reckoning, day of great r., 3:10
  God swift at the r., 118:24
  honor a trim r., 183:25
  no r. made, 198:12
  sense of r., 189:24
  truth to the end of r., 207:15
Reckons, rash who r. on morrow, 66:12
  up by dozens, 525:21
Recks not his own rede, 197:20
Reclothe us in rightful mind, 438:18
Recognition of evil, 56:13
  of ugliness, 56:13
  shock of r., 482:14
Recognize a wise man, 60:7
  did not r. me by my face, 472:3
  gods' hand, 742:1
  good but be barred, 63:30
  relations to world, 556:17
Recognizes my book in me, 153:13
Recognizing man's step, 616:3
Recoiled, warmest heart r. at war, 701:11
Recoils, rebuke r., 622:2
Recollect, cannot r. ignorance in which born, 314:27
  cannot r. when it begun, 509:16
  that Almighty gave dog, 374:17
Recollected, emotion r. in tranquillity, 369:5
Recollection, fond r. presents them, 393:12
  like living life over, 303:21
Recommencée, la mer toujours r., 612:*n*2
Recommends, nimbly and sweetly r. itself, 214:21
Recompense as largely send, 316:7
  no evil for evil, 41:33
  service beyond all r., 249:18
Reconciled, become partially r., 416:15
  God and sinners, 305:10
Reconciles, custom r. to everything, 323:13
  discordant elements, 368:14
  forgotten wars, 678:8
  good dinner r., 277:13
  world easily r. to death, 431:17
Reconciliation of opposite qualities, 379:13
Reconciling mediatory power, 378:24

Reconstructed, won't be r., 529:11
Reconstruction, demand in R. suffrage, 471:8
Record, dreadful r. of sin, 573:13
  let's look at the r., 617:11
  poetry r. of best happiest moments, 404:14
  puts r. on gramophone, 676:13
  register of God not r. of man, 249:2
  weep to r., 314:*n*2
Recorded, by Muses live for ay, 160:25
  greatest and most important events r., 319:8
  last syllable of r. time, 217:23
Recorders, flutes and soft r., 255:23
Recording Angel dropped a tear, 314:18
  make ourselves r. plate, 533:15
  man shaving, 738:7
Records that defy tooth of time, 290:17
  trivial fond r., 198:15
Recount, such bickerings to r., 260:28
Recover and prove an ass, 179:15
  hair that grows bald, 172:17
  health through contentment, 70:18
  that I may r. strength, 16:20
Recovered innocence, 475:16
  man r. of the bite, 322:15
  virtue if lost seldom r., 275:13
Recreant limbs, 175:14
Recreation, calm quiet innocent r., 245:7
  without some lawful r., 157:2
Recruits in worldly warfare, 261:*n*2
Rectitude, marks of God in r., 388:8
  mind aware of own r., 94:6
Recure, woes time cannot r., 159:2
Recurrent end of unending, 679:9
Red animal war, 608:13
  as a rose is she, 375:22
  as stones kissed by dead, 699:8
  badge of courage, 608:14
  beauty whose r. and white, 204:20
  blossom in purple and r., 455:3
  China not seeking to dominate world, 697:7
  coat r. breeches blue, 381:19
  coral is far more r., 223:1
  fair weather for sky is r., 34:34
  heart's core, 409:12
  her lips were r., 376:7
  herrings, 893:1
  I green U blue O, 559:4
  in him the r. earth, 557:6
  in r. cloth appeared letter A, 431:3
  in tooth and claw, 454:1
  Lantern and his undersea folk, 836:10
  leaf r. and sear, 373:5
  life stream again, 412:1
  lips not so red, 699:8
  making the green one r., 215:24
  Marian's nose looks r., 175:1
  men scalped each other, 419:18
  morn that betokened, 171:11
  my Luve like a r. r. rose, 357:4
  my sin is r., 280:20
  my skin is r., 513:4
  nose makes me ashamed, 277:22
  pale and hectic r., 402:9
  plague rid you, 224:11
  purple with a r. hat, 832:4
  remember R. River Valley, 890:19

Red *(continued)*
rise with my r. hair, 833:4
Rose proud Rose, 591:1
roses r. and violets blue, 160:11
sap make cherry r., 671:17
shadow under r. rock, 676:6
slayer, 425:4
so r. the Rose, 441:14
soldier r. with rust, 554:2
States and Blue States, 876:12
still and awful r., 376:16
sun pasted in sky, 608:15
swift r. flesh, 720:7
tape, 466:3
thin r. 'eroes, 587:16
thin r.-line streak, 489:10
thoughts were r. thoughts, 608:7
tigers in r. weather, 640:19
wheel barrow, 658:14
when last r. man has vanished, 394:3
wine when it is r., 21:30
Redbreast, call for robin r., 237:3
robin r. in cage, 353:15
Robin R. piously, 880:14
sit and sing, 377:15
whistles from garden-croft, 411:8
Reddens, as an apple r., 56:10
Rede, reck the r., 197:*n1*
recks not his own r., 197:20
Redeem, lose more of yourself than r., 845:13
the time, 677:16
them from death, 28:40
these hours, 233:17
unread vision, 677:16
us from virtue, 529:20
Redeemed of the Lord shall return, 26:39
visited and r., 37:13
Redeemer, know that my r. liveth, 13:39
my strength and my r., 15:19
such and so mighty a R., 47:26
Redeeming, past never past r., 797:11
Redemption, condemned into everlasting r.,
191:9
from above did bring, 250:9
from Wilderness, 812:14
inestimable in r., 48:16
poetry is r. from pessimism, 842:11
Redemptorem, tantum meruit habere R.,
47:26
Red-handed, 120:24
Red-hot, last of r. mamas, 661:*n2*
Rediscover gods as psychic factors, 630:5
Red-letter days, 383:7
Red-line streak, 489:10
Redoubling efforts, 584:4
Redress, music send r., 881:6
no r. by mob law, 444:3
of grievances, 340:1
procure r. of wrongs, 329:6
things past r. now past care, 177:1
Reduce selfishness, 57:8
Redwood, from r. forest to Gulf Stream waters,
768:5
Redwoods, I'm going down like r., 830:10
Reed, be merciful to broken r., 165:2
bruised r. shall he not break, 26:34
Love tunes shepherd's r., 373:2
man is a thinking r., 269:21

Reed *(continued)*
staff of this broken r., 26:20
Reeds, bending r. again and again, 811:6
Reedy shore, 882:2
Reef of Norman's Woe, 436:10
Reeking herd, 666:4
into Cadiz Bay, 460:20
Reel, about in r. and rout, 376:5
to and fro, 18:16
Réel, il n'y a de r. que l'humanité, 416:*n3*
Reeled, sagged and r., 639:13
Reeling, send me r. in, 511:6
through summer days, 508:9
Reenactments of something that happened,
757:6
Re-enter, I r. world, 825:2
Reference to one consent, 188:36
References, money and goods best r., 466:28
Refine, cannot r. war, 489:11
if good sense r. her page, 278:7
it ne'er so much, 232:9
Refined, artist r. out of existence, 650:11
gild r. gold, 175:24
or artificial type, 607:2
pleasures too r., 293:27
thee but not with silver, 26:36
Refinement of everyday thinking, 637:12
Refinery, out by gas fires of the r., 868:5
Reflect before throwing images, 684:2
how you are to govern, 323:20
on struggle for life, 440:2
Reflecting man twice natural size, 654:17
Reflection, dispense with necessity of r., 558:7
Liberal tempered by r., 497:9
on acts of mind, 379:17
remembrance and r. allied, 272:*n1*
Reflections, except r. escapades of death, 642:7
mortifying r., 440:*n2*
Reflects, novel r. blue of skies, 392:5
who r. too much, 360:12
Reform carried to excess needs reforming,
379:2
is not to equalize property, 78:20
let us r. schools, 484:13
Reformation, reforming of R. itself, 254:11
revolution and r., 337:12
Reformer is guy who rides through sewer,
648:10
Reformers, all r. are bachelors, 557:8
of error, 338:1
Reforming of Reformation itself, 254:11
other people's habits, 523:23
reform carried to excess needs r., 379:2
Reforms, at forty r. plan, 290:23
Refrain from setting yourself judge, 76:11
from unholy pleasure, 606:9
time to r. from embracing, 22:31
tonight, 201:13
Refreshed, as Adam r. with sleep, 486:23
tree of liberty r., 336:15
Refreshes, presence of wildness r., 475:31
Refrigerator, keep martini in r., 713:10
Refuge and abode of evil and vice, 136:22
bad man's r., 57:20
be r. unto yourselves, 64:15
death become sought-after r., 69:18
eternal God is thy r., 9:33
go for r. to Buddha, 64:20

Refuge *(continued)*
God is our r. and strength, 16:26
God the Everlasting R., 119:20
he is my r. and fortress, 17:28
home is safest r., 158:*n7*
hotel r. from home life, 565:1
idleness r. of weak minds, 298:13
patriotism last r. of scoundrel, 310:4
studies a r. in adversity, 87:11
Refugium, domus rutissimum r., 158:23
Refuse, creeds that r., 529:20
heavenly mansion, 595:9
I would r. to get up, 771:16
make offer he can't r., 795:7
never ask r. resign office, 304:1
nothing r., 424:14
profane fables, 44:29
thy name, 180:2
till conversion of Jews, 266:21
wretched r. of shore, 552:16
Refused, stone which the builders r., 18:25
Refuses, what one r. in a minute, 359:13
Refutable, charm of theory r., 548:5
Refute, who can r. a sneer, 339:2
Regain love once possessed, 260:19
Regard, strict r. to conscience, 331:6
two qualities inspire r., 78:19
well-assured place in men's r., 569:6
without remedy without r., 216:9
Regarded, heard not r., 183:4
Regardeth, he that r. the clouds, 23:27
Regardez c'est une pauvre terre, 491:*n8*
Regardless, alas r. of their doom, 315:6
Regards to Broadway, 634:11
what is before his feet, 84:19
Regeneration, moral r. of mankind, 435:20
suffering may be r., 480:7
Regent, of love-rimes, 174:14
Regime based on bayonets and blood, 693:9
establishes democratic r. kill sons of Brutus,
142:9
no r. ever loved great writers, 791:6
Regiment, half the r. dead, 787:19
led r. from behind, 528:1
monstrous r. of women, 150:1
warring within for r., 168:2
Regio, cuius r. eius religio, 120:13
Region, calm r. where no night, 241:17
poet soaring in high r., 253:19
thrilling r. of ice, 206:38
Regional, nothing important is r., 835:21
Regions, double-lived in r. new, 411:4
in soft r. born soft men, 69:24
obscure r. of philosophy, 312:1
of sorrow doleful shades, 255:9
these external r., 642:7
Register, history r. of crimes, 332:5
of God, 249:2
Regret, Florida weighted with r., 819:15
I have but one life, 349:1
I must say I r. nothing, 744:*n1*
my seedtime, 787:10
only r. is all so terribly true, 566:18
or secret happiness, 552:12
possibilities I didn't embrace, 545:6
trifling education of females, 340:16
vain desire vain r., 506:7
wild with all r., 452:22

Regret *(continued)*
you will r. both, 469:3
Regrets, congratulatory r., 430:18
past R. future Fears, 441:15
that resemble hopes, 479:6
Regrette l'Europe aux anciens parapets, 559:*n*2
Regretted speech never silence, 101:9
Regrow, dragons r. their parts, 773:19
Regular, be r. and orderly in your life, 494:1
everything's so awful r., 522:9
icily r., 454:26
Regulate, free to r. industry, 337:11
imagination by reality, 308:7
my room, 307:23
use of property, 571:15
Rehearse as ny as evere he kan, 134:10
Reign, awful darkness r., 468:2
come to r. over us, 123:4
existence saw him spurn r., 306:9
in hell, 255:15
king shall r. in righteousness, 26:14
of the good Cinara, 97:11
to r. is worth ambition, 255:15
to r. to be omnipotent but friendless,
402:1
what is pomp rule r., 170:37
where saints immortal r., 289:17
Reigned, I have r. with your loves, 151:12
Reigneth, the Lord r., 18:2
Reigns but does not govern, 154:9
God r. Government lives, 512:14
if censorship r., 327:17
no crude surfeit r., 252:19
of terror, 490:4
Reimpressed by external ordinances, 307:16
Rein, find his mouth a r., 530:13
give free r. to women, 99:13
not give dalliance r., 224:35
rung upon r., 546:9
Rein, so hold und schön und r., 415:*n*2
Reindeer seem over-serious, 671:23
Reins, gae his bridle r. a shake, 357:12
of power, 446:11
Reintegrated, reduce elements can no longer be
r., 754:1
Reject, ignoring all you r., 429:6
men r. prophets, 492:15
that they r. is wrong, 531:6
world of Freud, 723:4
Rejected, despised and r. of men, 27:5
Rejects, consciousness r. object, 541:2
Heaven r. the lore, 372:14
Rejoice at birth grieve at funeral, 523:20
desert shall r., 26:17
for I have found sheep, 38:9
in ancestral Jove Troy's sons r., 95:4
in thy youth, 23:29
let James r., 318:12
let the earth r., 18:2
not over thy enemy, 30:29
we in ourselves r., 378:10
Rejoices in the lost lilac, 677:19
Rejoiceth as a strong man, 15:16
in his strength, 14:27
more of that sheep, 34:41
Rejoicing, come again with r., 19:3
see riches partake in r., 254:6
Relate, these unlucky deeds r., 210:20

Relation, all just supply and all r., 230:15
enjoy original r. to universe, 425:19
poor r. irrevelant, 383:17
Relations between aspects of experience, 662:2
candor and amicable r., 355:7
fundamental of social r., 435:20
lift coffins of dead r., 845:10
public r., 790:5
renewal of r. nervous, 531:19
sexual r. with that woman, 863:5
squire and his r., 465:16
tedious pack of people, 560:23
with intellect only collateral r., 450:3
Relationship, all events bear r., 85:10
between flowers and convicts, 761:12
essential r. to existence, 469:6
friendly and charming r., 144:7
is like a shark, 839:17
Relative, set out in r. way, 618:1
that r. pronoun, 570:2
Relatives, choosing one's r., 774:10
Relativism, dictatorship of r., 816:15
Relaxation, allowed himself fun and r., 69:11
maturity sacred to r., 553:12
there may be r., 307:27
Release, deadly forfeit should r., 250:9
ensured r., 576:4
from little things, 718:6
from loneliness, 679:15
of atomic energy, 661:4
Released, I shall be r., 851:20
Relent, shall make him once r., 271:26
Relenting fool, 172:3
Relentless, Hades is r., 51:17
war r., 607:13
Relents, my rigor r., 324:3
Reliability, shifts of Fortune test r. of friends,
88:13
Reliance on divine providence, 336:3
self-reliance r. on God, 428:2
Relics, hallowed r. should be hid, 250:15
unhonored his r. laid, 387:6
Relief, cricket no r., 676:6
for greedy, 653:8
for this r. much thanks, 196:9
hold out r. coming, 489:*n*5
not seek for kind r., 351:8
sea-sharp wash of r., 825:10
to dig him up throw stones at him, 565:15
too proud for r., 624:17
Relieve the oppressed, 24:32
what wealth r. conscience, 235:19
Relieved, by desperate appliance r., 201:16
obliged wealthy and r. poor, 51:*n*1
unless I be r. by prayer, 225:9
Religio, tantum r. potuit suadere malorum,
89:*n*7
Religion, airy subtleties in r., 248:2
Anglo-Catholic in r., 677:9
any r. keeping masses satisfied, 685:6
behold clear r., 409:9
blunderbuss against r., 308:19
blushing veils fires, 297:6
breathing household laws, 370:4
but a childish toy, 168:7
called in to construct r., 799:11
Christian r. as organized in churches,
614:12

Religion *(continued)*
Christian r. attended with miracles, 311:25
Christianity r. of the son, 564:4
cult is a r., 831:7
decency is not derived from r., 867:6
delusion it is called R., 820:*n*1
depth in philosophy bringeth to r., 165:27
different opinions concerning r., 345:9
duty we owe Creator, 332:1
enjoy r. prevent others, 519:5
enough to make us hate, 284:14
enterprise for glory of Christian r., 139:10
errors in r. dangerous, 311:20
establishment of r., 340:1
every form of r. degraded women, 471:9
evil deeds r. prompt, 89:12
excess a reproach to r., 280:8
feelings in solitude, 541:18
for religion's sake, 400:17
free exercise of r., 332:1
free for r., 694:9
freedom of r., 337:12
he who controls area controls r., 120:13
hypothesis grounded in r., 873:14
I am a Millionaire that is my r., 565:14
in r. so uneven, 282:6
inconsistent with Christian r., 317:9
is an illusion, 564:1
is dream and mockery, 421:8
is matter between man and God, 337:13
Judaism r. of the father, 564:4
knavery and change, 279:4
leave him for r., 791:15
leave r. to family, 498:7
liberation from dominion of r., 604:14
lies r. of slaves, 602:14
line between r. and fly fishing, 731:16
losing my r., 876:3
made honest woman, 750:11
my r. is to do good, 333:16
no part of r. to compel r., 113:16
not popular error, 500:14
of feeble minds, 325:8
of well-doing and daring, 309:*n*1
of which rewards distant, 307:16
one r. true as another, 235:17
one's r. neither harms nor helps another,
113:15
opium of people, 477:12
orthodox in r., 694:2
pagan who defends r., 608:16
persecution bad way to plant r., 248:8
politics like r., 338:1
poverty a reproach to r., 280:8
powerless to bestow, 428:27
printing and Protestant r., 407:13
propitiation of powers, 558:2
restores man to dignity, 584:15
rum and true r., 398:8
self-righteousness not r., 472:9
slovenliness no part of r., 301:18
stands on tiptoe, 243:13
superstition incongruous r., 490:14
that old-time r., 884:19
then it's a r., 820:3
total reaction upon life, 541:19
we too have our r., 518:5
wonders of Christian r., 283:2

Religions, neurotics founded r., 610:18
    thirty-two r. one dish, 348:8
    vicissitude of sects and r., 166:20
Religious, appeals to r. prejudice, 502:14
    dim r. light, 251:23
    do evil from r. conviction, 270:1
    duties consist in justice, 333:18
    feeling a verity, 490:15
    feeling toward life, 605:10
    freedom, 633:11
    guarantee of r. pluralism, 867:4
    intelligent people to be r., 836:5
    nothing delights truly r. people so much,
      367:16
    old r. factions, 325:11
    people suspicious, 587:4
    rather political than r., 309:2
    suspended r. inquiries, 332:14
    various forms of r. madness, 434:4
    vision our ground for optimism, 580:9
    waves of r. emotion, 672:2
    way to think of death, 631:3
    whole life of r. bodies, 144:17
Religious-good, good but not r., 535:12
Religiousness, this knowledge center of all r.,
    637:9
Relish him more in soldier, 208:18
    imaginary r. is so sweet, 203:15
    love of gentle woman, 767:3
    no r. of those arts, 288:7
    of saltness of time, 187:27
    versing, 243:7
Relished, taste by which r., 372:4
Reluctant sweet r. amorous delay, 257:20
Reluctantly, difficult when you do it r., 86:4
Relume, Promethean heat thy light r., 210:14
Rem tene verba sequentur, 85:*n*4
Remain, if our loves r., 461:3
    laws ought not to r. unaltered, 78:21
    my thoughts r. below, 201:1
    nothing will r., 574:17
    shall France r. here, 500:6
    sitting at your table, 655:17
    some born mad some r. so, 744:17
    thou shalt r., 410:20
    until death do part, 565:16
    with unavenged suffering, 492:11
Remained to pray, 322:26
Remaineth, while the earth r., 6:23
Remains, the One r., 404:2
    what r. is bestial, 208:28
    what thou lovest well r., 665:13
    women cut up what r., 588:13
Remake, it is myself I r., 592:3
    myself must I r., 596:14
Remark, Frenchman r. shrewd, 326:15
    which I wish to r., 528:10
Remarkable, nothing r. beneath moon, 219:5
Remarks are not literature, 628:2
    Hegel r. somewhere, 477:14
Remedies, die of r. not illnesses, 268:6
    he that will not apply new r., 166:7
    worse than disease, 100:4
Remedy against consumption of purse, 187:36
    cannot r. folly of people, 143:5
    force not r., 457:14
    Fortune leaves door to r., 155:21
    is to inform discretion, 338:12

Remedy *(continued)*
    sought the r., 195:35
    things without all r., 216:9
    tobacco sovereign r., 235:12
    too strong for disease, 66:22
    worse than disease, 100:*n*1
Remember, all it is about to r., 797:13
    and be sad, 512:5
    cannot r. past, 584:5
    children you did not get, 783:6
    Christ our Savior, 883:4
    die on day I already r., 696:16
    distinctly I r., 449:4
    easier to die than r., 724:14
    everything, 822:8
    fifth of November, 882:18
    gentlemen r. blondes, 698:7
    God is place where I do not r. rest, 348:1
    house where I was born, 418:2
    if I do not r. thee, 19:11
    if row comes R. the Maine, 886:*n*2
    if thou wilt r., 512:3
    in sweet pangs r. me, 204:33
    let dozing soul r., 139:5
    little note nor r., 446:5
    Lot's wife, 38:21
    me to Herald Square, 634:11
    me when I am gone, 512:4
    me when in thy kingdom, 38:35
    no man r. me, 536:3
    not only how much loved, 583:12
    not r. what I must be, 177:11
    now thy Creator, 23:30
    oh still r. me, 387:5
    pleasant to r. even this, 93:35
    Red River Valley, 890:19
    sweet Alice Ben Bolt, 480:26
    that We created him, 118:19
    that we die all, 30:29
    the Alamo, 433:8
    the end, 30:28
    the ladies, 340:11
    the Maine, 886:2
    the neckcurls, 756:4
    the sabbath day, 8:13
    thee, 198:15
    things that were precious, 217:9
    this day in which ye came out, 8:1
    time to r., 567:10
    to pay the debt, 70:9
    us if at all not as lost, 676:20
    we will r. them, 603:14
    what is imprinted, 76:7
    what we say here, 446:5
    who commended yellow stockings, 205:9
    who will r. unheroic dead, 668:14
    who you are, 515:17
    women forget all don't want to r., 690:3
    you must r. this, 702:11
    your name perfectly, 549:16
Remembered, be all my sins r., 199:22
    blue r. hills, 575:6
    he shall be no more r., 13:45
    how often you and I, 499:9
    I was owned of Thee, 510:8
    in spite of ourselves, 446:1
    kisses after death, 452:22
    knolling departing friend, 187:23

Remembered *(continued)*
    my God, 381:11
    name noted down and r., 830:13
    no books undeservedly r., 749:18
    not r. in thy epitaph, 183:32
    poor Julian, 721:15
    thy sweet love r., 221:7
    time r., 529:13
    when we r. Zion, 19:11
    would have made self r., 413:17
Rememberest not slightest folly, 194:8
Remembering happier things, 451:23
    soul r. my good friends, 176:29
    this he wept bitterly, 52:17
    with twinklings and twinges, 783:9
Remembers all that he wrought, 53:23
    me his gracious parts, 175:19
    nature yet r., 370:20
    who r. Armenians, 684:15
    who r. famous day, 437:15
Remembrance, absence doth breed continual
    r., 137:*n*5
    and reflection allied, 272:*n*1
    do this in r. of me, 42:24
    fallen from heaven, 529:14
    flood of r., 662:15
    Jamaicas of R., 511:6
    let his r. rest, 31:24
    makes r. dear, 206:9
    of a guest, 30:3
    of former things, 22:25
    of prosperity, 30:37
    of them is grievous, 49:5
    of things past, 221:8
    of things to come, 22:25
    poetry appears as R., 413:1
    rosemary for r., 201:30
    this do in r. of me, 38:30
    writ in r., 176:21
Remembrances, burden our r., 225:7
Remembreth, whan that it r. me upon my
    yowthe, 135:7
Rememoring, false god dim r., 682:12
Remind, foolish things r. me of you, 729:1
    him of glory of country, 390:2
    lives of great men r. us, 436:6
    us of everything lost, 764:15
Reminiscences, hysterical patients suffer from
    r., 563:5
Remission, shed for r. of sins, 36:3
    without shedding of blood no r., 45:10
Remnant of Spartan dead, 398:18
Remnants, deal in r. of r., 287:7
    of childhood hopes of adulthood, 730:6
Remold it nearer to Heart's Desire, 442:9
R-e-m-o-r-s-e, 597:18
Remorse, access and passage to r., 214:17
    betraying them without r., 838:5
    disjoins r. from power, 191:35
    farewell r., 257:13
    is nothing than foresight of pain, 315:3
    sleeps, 313:5
    such as I cast r., 595:5
    that precedes sin, 809:4
Remorseful, gaudy blabbing r. day, 170:10
    pardon, 206:11
Remote, do in that r. spot, 365:15
    from wrangling world, 333:8

Republican, deprives r. example of just
    influence, 444:6
  eternal importance like R. Party, 664:3
  forming a r. government, 349:5
  model of government, 328:11
  only form of government, 336:17
Republicans, Red States for R., 876:12
  we are R., 337:8, 463:17
Republics appeal to understanding, 503:3
  destiny of r. settled, 482:10
  in small r. is stability, 391:2
  never known to exist, 142:1
Repulsive, free speech in r. form, 621:8
Reputation an idle imposition, 208:29
  at every word r. dies, 293:8
  better than my r., 360:8
  bubble r., 194:25
  gain forever r. among men, 70:14
  I have lost my r., 208:28
  men who survive their r., 153:2
  more valuable than money, 99:19
  not aloof in order to gain r., 76:6
  not carefully preserved, 276:16
  part of man's Self, 541:4
  reputation reputation, 208:28
  sold R. for Song, 442:7
  spotless r., 176:8
  until you've lost your r., 726:2
Repute, sink present r. for freedom, 481:18
  thing of good r., 569:6
Reputed wise for saying nothing, 184:8
Request deed in silence, 129:5
Requiem aeternam dona eis, 47:19
  to thy high r., 410:9
Requiescat in pace, 121:12
Require, that people may r. leader, 75:22
  what is it men in women r., 352:9
Required, much given much r., 38:6, 785:9
  nothing given nothing r., 304:12
  of us a song, 19:11
  of us mirth, 19:11
  this night soul shall be r., 38:4
Requirement, first r. in Hospital, 489:6
Requisite, first r. of good citizen, 571:6
  Meat r. to Squirrels, 510:10
  right to means r., 349:10
Rere-mice, some war with r., 178:20
Re-resolves then dies, 290:23
Rerum, sunt lacrimae r., 94:*n2*
Res iudicata pro veritate habetur, 121:13
Rescind, voted not to r., 331:6
Rescue me protect me, 3:10
  my soul from their destructions, 16:8
  nothing can r. me, 169:2
  trump of r. sound, 424:20
Rescued, we r. beg you, 691:19
Rescues, whoever r. single life earns merit,
    117:9
Research, steal from many authors is r., 633:10
Researchers into Public Opinion, 749:10
Resemblance neglects spirit of objects, 123:1
  showy r. of distress, 333:15
Resemblances, our r. to the savage, 558:5
Resembled my father as he slept, 215:19
Resembleth, love r. April day, 173:29
Resentment consumes a man, 549:5
  meet r. with upright dealing, 61:16
  whim envy or r., 326:5

Reserve back shop all our own, 152:11
  side of last r., 265:*n3*
  thy judgment, 197:23
Reservedly, read books as r. as written, 475:5
Réserver une arrière boutique toute notre,
    152:*n7*
Reside in thrilling region, 206:38
Residence, forted r., 207:14
  pains have taken up r., 867:1
Residences, inns not r., 671:6
Resides, fire that in heart r., 494:17
Resign, never ask refuse r. office, 304:1
  title and profit I r., 287:*n3*
Resignation is confirmed desperation, 474:11
  please accept r., 707:13
Resigned, I am not r., 695:17
  pleasing being e'er r., 316:4
  to shutting away, 695:17
  trees more r. than other things, 615:9
Resinous heart has fed, 594:14
Resist beginnings, 102:19
  boots not to r. wind and tide, 170:32
  easier to r. at beginning, 140:9
  everything except temptation, 560:7
  not evil, 32:20
  strength not adequate to r., 79:14
  the devil, 45:30
  nonviolent r. paralyzed, 823:14
  or abject submission, 328:6
  Passive R., 604:4
  planning better plan than opposite, 729:8
  spirit of r., 339:5
Resistance, French r. must not die, 686:6
Resistances, breaking down halfhearted r., 493:11
Resisted, rejoice that America r., 305:13
Resolute, be bloody bold and r., 216:32
  imperturbable r. tree-like, 61:12
  think beforehand that actions be r., 79:24
Resolutely, purse most r. snatched, 181:22
Resolution, in war r., 621:12
  native hue of r., 199:21
  passed without dissenting, 329:18
  road to r., 242:4
Resolutions, careful r. unerring decisions, 109:2
  keep r., 307:25
Resolve is not to seem but be, 62:26
  itself into a dew, 196:29
  not shaken from his firm r., 96:27
  pushes his purpose to r., 290:23
  to conquer or die, 328:6
  we here highly r., 446:5
Resolved, Catullus be r. and firm, 91:7
  is once to be r., 209:5
  so they r. to proceed, 240:1
  to be irresolute, 619:5
  to die in last dike, 324:19
  to live a fool, 237:20
  to ruin or rule state, 272:19
  to take Fate by throat, 513:9
Resolves and re-resolves, 290:23
Resonance, sinister r., 567:*n1*
Resort of mirth, 251:18
Resound in another street, 776:8
Resources, enjoy r. within thy reach, 63:29
  full of r., 324:7
  greater vital r. than supposed, 542:3
  man of many r., 52:20
  of civilization not exhausted, 442:15

Resources (*continued*)
  oneness of r., 795:15
  rock of national r., 390:12
  small portion of soul's r., 542:3
  wagers sum of r., 799:*n1*
  waste natural r., 571:12
Respect, but you lose their r., 142:5
  decent r. to opinions, 336:1
  developed r. for unknown in lifetime,
    761:3
  for human life, 795:1
  have his son r. him, 275:12
  I can't get no r., 796:4
  idle wind which I r. not, 193:10
  little r. when I come home, 853:3
  man who wears air of r., 60:16
  mingled with surprise, 374:3
  neighborly r., 619:9
  not law so much as right, 473:13
  of place persons time, 204:28
  or natural love, 567:20
  strength without fearing, 337:4
  that makes calamity of life, 199:21
  those equal in any r., 78:27
  three worthy of r., 491:17
  to acquire growing and lasting r., 737:4
  too much r. upon world, 184:3
  woman takes off claim to r., 69:6
  you in my r. are world, 178:18
Respectable, all get r. if last long enough, 839:7
  great artists seldom r., 645:4
  Hell, 601:11
  highly r. tribe, 885:16
  make murder r., 735:13
  more ashamed more r., 565:5
  not one r. or unhappy, 486:14
  Professors of Dismal Science, 408:6
  since when genius r., 434:22
  turkey a more r. bird, 303:17
Respectables, n'existe que trois êtres r., 491:*n13*
Respecter, God no r. of persons, 40:27, 419:3
Respectfully return Him ticket, 492:11
Respite from long year's watch, 62:27
  to be dead, 510:7
Responders, thousands of first r., 853:13
Responding, successfully r. to challenges, 685:8
Response to a poem, 826:7
Responsibilities, fulfilled r. to state, 785:9
  infinite r. of man, 742:22
  who has many r., 50:21
Responsibility, at summit r. increases, 549:2
  in dreams begins r., 592:8
  intellectual r., 692:3
  no r. at other end, 765:11
  without woman I love, 705:2
  writer's only r., 714:8
Responsible, belief r. for the slaughter, 757:15
  for each other, 703:9
  for what we are, 742:21
  no snowflake in avalanche feels r., 758:18
  not r. for dreams, 630:7
  through time and eternity, 445:15
Rest, absence of occupation not r., 326:14
  and be thankful, 884:10
  and faith we need it, 587:12
  body continues in state of r., 279:14
  cannot r. for seeing countries, 889:23
  choose ground and take r., 399:17

Rest *(continued)*
    choose their place of r., 259:28
    cities never have r. from evils, 75:9
    could r. anywhere would be in Arkansaw,
      393:15
    die or r. at last, 403:9
    dove found no r., 6:20
    embrace r. that knows no care, 90:14
    eternal r. give them, 47:19
    failing that the r. of the city, 75:5
    far far better r., 466:23
    from their labors, 47:6
    gets him to r., 189:23
    God r. you merry, 883:4
    gone to eternal r., 448:2
    good in which mind at r., 129:23
    grant us holy r., 421:5
    he was my Sunday r., 748:14
    hearts do in the faces r., 228:8
    her soul she's dead, 202:9
    here set up my everlasting r., 181:14
    I will give you r., 34:9
    if England r. but true, 176:7
    I'll r. but thou walk, 889:23
    in doubt to act or r., 295:1
    in Nature not God, 243:3
    in soft peace, 232:11
    is dross, 665:13
    is silence, 202:32
    let his remembrance r., 31:24
    lightly r., 67:7
    long long ago at r., 499:9
    long r. or death, 450:20
    may he r. in peace, 121:12
    much veneration but no r., 166:1
    my heart is at r., 351:7
    of my days, 815:15
    peace and r. never dwell, 255:9
    perturbed spirit, 198:21
    profound as grave, 531:26
    said Good Night gone to r., 606:16
    shall shortly be at r., 260:15
    she's at r. and so am I, 275:1
    sing thee to thy r., 202:33
    so may he r., 226:9
    soldier r., 373:21
    Swift sailed into his r., 595:8
    then had I been at r., 13:4
    then would I fly away and be at r., 16:36
    there the weary be at r., 13:5
    thou too shalt r., 344:19
    to mind cheerer of spirits, 245:1
    toil and not seek r., 144:16
    under the trees, 501:10
    unto your souls, 34:9
    water rush to r. in air, 713:5
    wear ourselves and never r., 168:2
    where peace and r. can never dwell, 255:9
    where's r. of me, 736:1
    who does not know, 101:22
    who sink to r., 317:10
    William Yeats laid to r., 749:3
    without haste but without r., 344:31
    ye brother mariners, 450:21
Restaurant, at Alice's R., 864:10
    I walked into this r., 831:15
Restaurants, go to r., 859:6
Reste, j'y suis j'y r., 439:*n2*

Rested, arms about neck crossed and r., 487:9
Restful, for r. death I cry, 221:20
Resting, army on the hills r., 608:12
    history knows no r. places, 802:13
    not a having and r., 497:12
    place for those who gave lives, 446:5
    true-fixed and r. quality, 192:14
Restless, blown with r. violence, 206:38
    tenacious but r., 672:2
    unfixed in principles, 272:16
Restlessness, great pain and r., 668:18
Restore, thy former light r., 210:14
    to earth and thee r., 576:3
Restored, all losses are r., 221:9
    Chaos is r., 297:6
    civilization could be r., 638:3
    O divinely r., 417:5
Restorer, tired nature's sweet r., 290:18
Restoreth, he r. my soul, 15:23
Restrain, creeds that r., 529:20
    in me cursed thoughts, 215:11
    men from injuring, 337:11
Restraint, acknowledge r. of reverence, 71:14
    charisma inner determination inner r.,
      586:8
    not silence but r., 671:6
    systems of preference or r., 319:10
    wholesome r., 390:19
    Zeus grant grave r., 63:28
Restraints, shackles and r. of government,
    604:14
Restricted circle of potential, 542:3
Restructuring combines continuity innovation,
    830:3
Rests and nodding places, 288:9
    here r. his head, 316:6
    mountain r. on earth, 4:10
Resty sloth finds down pillow hard, 220:22
Result, cause hidden r. well known, 102:13
    faith in r. makes r., 541:12
    firm ground of R., 618:16
    happiness, 465:24
    misery, 465:24
    of previous study, 382:6
    shot at without r., 618:18
Results, good r. beyond estimation, 569:9
    sure of unsatisfying r., 564:2
Resurrection and the life, 39:33
    books symbol of his r., 611:2
    by man came r., 43:1
    foretaste of r., 400:2
    in doubt as to the R., 118:21
    my subscription to r., 858:7
    newspaper r. rare, 531:26
    of dry sticks, 755:11
    of the body, 48:11
    of the dead, 43:1
    unto eternal life, 49:20
Resuscitate dead art, 665:4
Retail, God who does wholesale not r., 542:2
Retailer of phrases, 287:7
Retain, not r. all rare works, 610:16
Retake, go back and r. Burma, 658:2
Retire, anecdotage sign to r., 430:11
    like guest sated, 90:14
    like satisfied guest, 95:18
Retired, happiness of r. nature, 288:5
    Leisure, 251:14

Retired *(continued)*
    sweet r. solitude, 252:17
Retirement, end of world want to be living in r.,
    626:5
    Plato's r., 260:3
    rural quiet friendship, 300:20
    Sleeping Beauty planning r., 808:9
    urges sweet return, 259:8
Retiring at high speed toward Japanese, 650:5
    ne'er feels r. ebb, 209:20
Retort courteous, 196:6
Retreat, friend in my r., 326:15
    honorable r., 195:9
    little country r., 279:10
    loopholes of r., 327:2
    my soul's calm r., 269:2
    not r. a single inch, 433:5
Retreated back into money, 710:6
Retreating to the breath, 496:19
    we're not r., 700:1
    world, 699:9
Retrograde if not advance, 332:11
Retrouvée, l'Éternité r., 559:*n5*
Return, all things r. to you Nature, 111:19
    bid time r., 177:5
    departed never to r., 357:6
    dust shall r. to earth, 23:31
    gone and never must r., 253:4
    he shall not r. to me, 11:20
    I ask to be allowed to r., 507:12
    I shall r., 644:7
    like him that travels I r., 222:12
    may r. if dissatisfied, 625:2
    naked shall he r., 23:7
    naked shall I r. thither, 12:39
    no eternity will r., 359:13
    no more to his house, 13:17
    no one r. from there, 3:1
    O Shulamite, 24:20
    once dead never r., 441:21
    only dead who do not r., 348:13
    redeemed of the Lord shall r., 26:39
    retirement urges sweet r., 259:8
    snatch me not to r., 622:19
    spirit shall r. unto God, 23:31
    their thankfulness, 351:3
    till thou r. unto the ground, 6:1
    unto dust r., 6:1
    with the greatest pleasure, 379:1
    with the year seasons r., 257:6
    ye children of men, 17:23
Returned home previous night, 618:1
    I have r., 644:8
    just r. from Boston, 700:12
    when her aunt r., 606:13
Returneth, dog r. to his vomit, 21:38
    fool r. to his folly, 21:38
    to dust again, 517:15
Returning as tedious as go o'er, 216:25
Returns, all r. to sea, 750:1
    earth's r., 461:2
    Justice r., 92:22
    no traveler r., 199:21
    not to me r. day, 257:6
    road whence no one r., 91:3
    the Golden Age, 92:22
Réussit, rien ne r. comme le succès, 422:*n2*
Rêve, un peu de r., 519:*n3*

Rhein, die Wacht am R., 484:*n2*
Rhetoric able to contend, 166:19
    for r. he could not ope, 262:4
    obscure by aimless r., 502:14
    of rule of Plato, 254:5
    we make of quarrel with others r., 592:14
Rhetorician, grammarian r. geometrician,
        109:14
    sophisticated r., 430:19
Rhetorician's rules, 262:5
Rhine frontier of England, 599:8
    watch along the R., 484:25
Rhinoceros, armed r., 216:20
Rhodes, Colossus of R., 886:14
Rhodora, fresh R. in woods, 424:9
Rhyme, beauty making beautiful old r., 222:9
    hope and history r., 845:14
    into ladies' favors, 190:8
    it hath taught me to r., 174:19
    lofty r., 253:1
    many a mused r., 410:9
    more sweetly than r., 410:13
    nor reason, 161:10
    outlive this powerful r., 221:15
    Runic r., 449:25
    tired of Love more tired of R., 606:15
    unattempted yet in prose or r., 255:4
Rhymed dogerel, 136:12
Rhymes, Namby Pamby's little r., 291:22
    regent of love-r., 174:14
    suggest freedom, 425:9
    that r. with P, 733:6
Rhyming planet, 191:16
Rhythm essential in painting, 122:11
    I got r., 710:23
    in all thought, 375:15
    keeping r. in dancing, 678:14
    poor as dirt don't get r., 836:11
Rhythmical creation of Beauty, 450:3
Rhythms measureless and wild, 67:25
    of American popular music, 717:10
    we tap crude r. for bears, 493:13
Rialto, what news on R., 184:22
Rib, smote him under the fifth r., 11:11
    which Lord God had taken, 5:15
Riband in cap of youth, 202:1
    to stick in coat, 460:11
Ribbed sea sand, 376:13
Ribbon, a R. at a time, 508:17
    in cap of youth, 202:1
    road r. of moonlight, 646:1
    round it, 896:5
Ribs, he took one of his r., 5:15
    heart knock at my r., 214:11
    of Death, 252:21
Rice, same old r., 576:9
Rich, abundance of the r., 23:6
    America in which people still get r., 765:12
    and poor all as one, 68:6
    are different from you and me, 710:9
    as easy to marry r. woman, 459:11
    attire creeps rustling, 409:22
    beauty too r. for use, 179:28
    better live r. than die r., 310:20
    beyond dreams of avarice, 312:11
    blow bugles over r. dead, 669:12
    can't be too r. or too thin, 712:11
    choose likely man in preference to r., 62:19

Rich *(continued)*
    company of just men better than r. estate,
        68:15
    dies r. dies disgraced, 521:18
    difference between r. and other people,
        721:*n4*
    different from you and me, 721:15
    dull and drank, 721:15
    few are r. and wellborn, 349:4
    flames and hired tears, 248:23
    freedom to r. or poor, 697:2
    get rich, 667:12
    gifts wax poor, 199:23
    greater part of r. people, 319:3
    had I interfered for r., 419:2
    have more money, 721:*n4*
    have power and poor deprived, 75:17
    high and low r. and poor, 364:4
    honesty dwells like miser, 196:5
    if r. and a woman, 785:1
    if r. gets foolish, 600:14
    if r. whenever you please, 77:1
    in good works, 44:37
    in loss of all I sing, 814:13
    in poverty, 158:17
    in things he can let alone, 474:27
    is better, 662:1
    isn't it r., 829:2
    it is your duty to get r., 543:15
    jewel in Ethiop's ear, 179:28
    joys fall not to r. alone, 98:6
    knowledge a r. storehouse, 164:13
    labor not to be r., 21:25
    law forbids r. as well as poor, 546:2
    laws broken by mighty and r., 56:2
    let him be r. and weary, 243:4
    live and die r-r-r., 466:30
    live like a wretch and die r., 234:22
    make r. richer, 364:3
    maketh haste to be r., 22:6
    man beginning to fall, 31:2
    man not glory in riches, 27:33
    man to enter into kingdom, 35:4
    many evil men are r., 55:12
    men rule the law, 322:5
    mind r. with suspicion, 824:15
    moral soil for aesthetic growth, 618:9
    neither r. nor poor, 520:8
    no woman can be too r. too thin, 887:13
    nor r. at forty, 244:5
    not gaudy, 197:23
    poor and content is r., 209:4
    rob poor, 416:3
    say more than this r. praise, 221:26
    seems it r. to die, 410:9
    sent empty away, 37:12
    sent not corn for r. men only, 219:20
    something r. and strange, 224:14
    the treasure, 274:17
    'tis mind makes body r., 173:22
    to hear wooden dialogue, 203:9
    two nations the r. and poor, 430:3
    waster of r. men, 65:25
    we are r. and beautiful, 712:8
    when he is hungry, 77:*n2*
    when men drink they are r., 72:12
    when thou art old and r., 206:34
    with corn, 438:11

Rich *(continued)*
    with spoils of Nature, 248:4
    with spoils of time, 315:22
    wot gets pleasure, 887:7
    you'll never get r., 633:12
Richard Cory one summer night, 605:19
    sweet lovely rose, 182:3
Richardson, if you read R. for story, 309:19
Richardson's, one letter of R., 309:18
Richer, for r. for poorer, 49:16
    love's r. than my tongue, 210:22
    make rich r., 364:3
    man held to be holier, 114:14
    quiet mind r. than crown, 164:2
    than all his tribe, 210:20
Riches and power gifts of fate, 124:1
    are for spending, 166:9
    are ready snares, 138:17
    best r. ignorance of wealth, 322:23
    by theft will not stay, 5:2
    cover multitude of woes, 81:5
    deceitfulness of r., 34:17
    despise r., 485:10
    earth is full of thy r., 18:11
    embarrassment of r., 300:2
    enjoyment of r. parade of r., 319:3
    Fame and Pleasure, 276:20
    full of days r. and honor, 12:27
    good handmaid worst mistress, 165:5
    good name rather than r., 21:16
    grow in hell, 256:4
    he heapeth up r., 16:19
    he that getteth r. not by right, 28:2
    he that trusteth in his r., 20:15
    house field and wife great r., 302:8
    if r. valuable to Heaven, 284:23
    in her left hand r. and honor, 19:25
    infinite r. in little room, 168:8
    make themselves wings, 21:26
    neither poverty nor r., 22:12
    no r. above a sound body, 31:15
    nor r. to men of understanding, 23:23
    not exchange our excellence for r., 55:12
    not profit the sluggish, 3:5
    of heaven's pavement, 256:3
    Peru with its r., 414:7
    poverty and use of service, 224:19
    renown which r. or beauty confer, 92:3
    rich man not glory in r., 27:33
    see her r. partake in rejoicing, 254:6
    to live on little with contented mind, 90:18
    to make gifts to friends, 68:6
    to make thy r. pleasant, 206:34
    to such a scoundrel, 284:23
    watching for r., 31:18
Richesses, l'embarras des r., 300:*n1*
Richest alchemy, 191:34
    East with r. hand, 256:6
    man r. pleasures cheapest, 473:10
    monarch in Christian world, 359:16
    Spain is become r. of countries, 139:13
Richly, storied windows r. dight, 251:23
Richmonds, six R. in the field, 172:12
Richness, much r. in lytell space, 168:*n3*
    of soul, 77:4
    quietness and pleasure, 491:5
    warmth r. reality of hunger satisfied,
        752:9

Right *(continued)*

thy r. hand shall hold me, 19:13

to be free from governmental intrusion, 745:11

to be let alone, 562:10

to be r. is art of arts, 540:17

to keep and bear arms, 340:2

to make alter constitutions, 328:14

to means requisite, 349:10

to remain silent, 692:6

to say what one pleases, 667:2

to speedy and public trial, 340:5

to strike, 613:4

to vote denied, 489:2

to vote not denied on account of sex, 340:10

to vote not denied or abridged, 340:9, 340:10

transforms strength into r., 312:16

true end of love, 230:10

views, 64:18

wars for r. thing, 661:12

what thy r. hand doeth, 32:24

whatever is is r., 294:23

when r. man rings them, 556:7

where did we go r., 811:10

wrong follow King, 455:9

Righteous are bold as a lion, 22:5

armor of r. cause, 577:16

be not r. over much, 23:14

company of just and r., 68:15

die the death of the r., 9:8

flourish like palm, 17:30

have not seen the r. forsaken, 16:11

I am not come to call r., 33:32

judgments of Lord r., 15:17, 447:2

let him be r. still, 47:14

man regardeth the life of his beast, 20:18

man to make fall, 160:6

nation which keepeth the truth, 26:3

prayer of r. man, 45:34

sold the r. for silver, 29:1

souls of the r. are in hand of God, 29:34

where were the r. cut off, 13:6

Righteousness and peace have kissed, 17:21

as waves of sea, 26:37

exalteth a nation, 20:29

force of r., 604:4

found in the way of r., 20:38

he looked for r., 25:4

his straight path, 79:19

hunger and thirst after r., 32:14

is man's path, 80:3

king shall reign in r., 26:14

leadeth me in paths of r., 15:23

not infused from without, 80:2

not r. to outrage man dead, 65:9

three laws of r., 62:25

wrath worketh not r., 45:23

wrongdoing and r. of men, 54:3

Righteousness', persecuted for r. sake, 32:13

Righteousnesses are as filthy rags, 27:18

Rightful, tenacious of purpose in r. cause, 96:27

Rightly to be great, 201:21

Rights, at war with r. of mankind, 336:17

become accumulated wrong, 585:2

Bill of R. into suicide pact, 694:5

Rights *(continued)*

black man within his r., 808:18

certain unalienable r., 336:1

civil r. citizens equal, 518:1

claim none of r. and privileges, 385:5

equal in r. and in cultivation, 435:20

essential unalienable r., 336:*n*1

fighting for human r., 808:17

fundamental human r., 661:16

God-given r., 433:7

halve r. double duties, 399:20

inextinguishable r. of human nature, 363:3

inherent in human being, 433:7

inherent r., 320:7

make real the Bill of R., 629:5

man's idea of sexual r., 471:7

never exceed your r., 312:13

no more suffering or denial of r., 791:5

of Englishman, 339:4

of existing non-Jewish communities, 551:7

of man, 325:1

of Nation's citizens, 828:2

partisan cares nothing about r., 74:15

preserve entire r., 339:6

public good and private r., 345:10

refuses to defend r., 363:14

reparation for r. at home, 306:4

slow undoing of human r., 785:10

sovereign has three r., 503:4

surrender r. for common good, 561:13

talked long enough about equal r., 753:11

women have as much r. as man, 416:2

women's r. are human r., 864:5

Right-wing conspiracy, 864:8

Rightwise king of England, 138:2

Rigor, my r. relents, 324:3

of the game, 383:10

Rill, moon on Monan's r., 373:18

Rim, beyond utmost purple r., 452:12

sun over mountain's r., 460:17

sun's r. dips, 376:9

Rime, beauty making beautiful old r., 222:9

into ladies' favors, 190:8

it hath taught me to r., 174:19

outlive this powerful r., 221:15

was on the spray, 535:11

Rimes, regent of love-r., 174:14

Riming planet, 191:16

Rimini miminy piminy, 526:13

Rimless floods, 720:2

Ring at end of nose, 467:8

at last r. to even-song, 148:18

becomes thin by wearing, 89:15

bright the r. of words, 556:7

curfew not r. tonight, 556:14

dance in r. and suppose, 624:11

impression as from seal of r., 76:7

let freedom r., 439:9

maids dance in a r., 227:4

my r. encompasseth thy finger, 171:21

O bells, 487:17

of convulsive rubber, 801:19

of pure and endless light, 268:14

one R. to rule one R. to find them, 696:14

only pretty r. time, 196:2

out the old, 454:8

out wild bells, 454:7

out your bells, 162:15

Ring *(continued)*

what shall we do for r., 467:8

when we let freedom r., 823:9

with importunate chink, 325:7

with this r. I thee wed, 49:17

woods answer and Echo r., 161:5

Ring-a-rosie, tots sang R., 581:2

Ringed with azure world, 454:13

Ringing grooves of change, 452:10

just like r. a bell, 811:4

plains of Troy, 451:13

Rings, postman r. twice, 693:6

when right man r. them, 556:7

Riot is at bottom, 823:15

purple r., 409:21

spent waves' r., 530:15

woods in r., 575:4

Rioting, not in r. and drunkenness, 41:40

Riotous living, 38:10

Riotously, flung roses riotously, 599:15

Ripe and good scholar, 226:12

cherry r. I cry, 240:12

Crops are r., 616:9

field of r. corn, 675:10

from hour to hour we r., 194:16

hour r., 188:23

once let r. moment go, 352:7

trap moment before it's r., 352:7

Ripeness is all, 213:7

Ripening, his greatness is a-r., 225:25

summer's r. breath, 180:11

Riper, amuse his r. stage, 295:3

Ripest fruit first falls, 176:27

fruit of all, 168:2

peach highest, 553:5

Ripped, from mother's womb untimely r., 217:28

Ripple of rain, 529:12

Rippling, folds r. in breeze, 459:2

Rip-tooth of sky's acetylene, 720:4

Rire de tout, 327:*n*4

est le propre de l'homme, 145:*n*6

Rise alone and drink more, 393:9

and fight again, 81:*n*9

and shine give God glory, 898:23

and walk with him, 67:8

at six dine at ten, 422:18

bad moon on the r., 860:14

by sin, 206:20

caused himself to r., 295:13

constellations when they r., 62:27

created half to r., 295:1

early to r., 302:12, 704:9

evening is come r. up, 91:19

foul deeds will r., 197:18

happy those whose walls already r., 94:3

in heaven's lightland, 4:4

in roaring he shall r and on surface die, 450:6

in the heart, 452:21

joyful all ye nations r., 305:10

kings r. and set, 403:7

light to r. by and I r., 463:3

like dust I'll r., 817:13

like fountain for me, 455:20

like Lions after slumber, 402:22

maketh sun r. on evil and good, 32:22

move stones of Rome to r., 193:5

Rise *(continued)*
    my Shakespeare r., 232:19
    not r. early never do good, 308:1
    out of ash I r., 833:4
    out of wreck r., 463:13
    people have right to r. up, 444:4
    stoop to r., 237:16
    sun sets to r. again, 463:12
    suns that set may r. again, 232:5
    then we shall r., 241:17
    though war should r. against me, 15:28
    till we are called to r., 510:12
    to feet as He passes by, 587:13
    to r. love stoops, 462:19
    truth crushed will r. again, 406:4
    up at the voice of the bird, 23:30
    up my love, 24:9
    up so early in morn, 884:22
    we die and r. the same, 228:19
    why r. because 'tis light, 229:8
    wilt thou therefore r. from me, 229:8
    with lark, 162:3
    woe unto them that r. up early, 25:5
Risen, Christ r. from dead, 43:1
    Christ the Lord today, 305:7
    He is r., 37:4, 47:28
    Lord is r. indeed, 38:43
    the Lord is r., 47:28
    there is a people r., 270:7
Riser, dawn comes no sooner for early r.,
    898:10
Rises, everything that r. must converge, 648:2
    hidden laughter, 678:11
    hooray up she r., 897:18
    howls hoo and r., 642:2
    my gorge r. at it, 202:12
    soul that r. with us, 370:17
    sun gives light soon as he r., 303:18
    unspeakable desire, 495:11
Riseth from feast with keen appetite, 184:39
    late trot all day, 302:22
    with fleas, 244:4
Rising, beating way for r. sun, 730:2
    before the r. sun, 289:13
    every land rejoices at his r., 4:3
    fogs prevail upon day, 273:14
    from r. of the sun unto going down, 18:20
    I see them r., 651:3
    listen the wind is r., 666:2
    more worship r. than setting sun, 88:19
    of the sun, 883:5
    plat of r. ground, 251:17
    Proteus r. from sea, 371:24
    shadow r. to meet you, 676:6
    warm cheek and r. bosom, 316:10
    wind is r., 612:7
Risk, conquer without r., 249:9
    I had to take and took, 624:15
    of reigns of terror, 490:4
    t'other half for freedom, 481:18
    without r. no faith, 469:7
Risking, not giving life but r. life, 751:6
    only by r. we live, 541:12
Risk-management, this modern r. paradigm,
    812:19
Risks, great deeds wrought at great r., 69:20
    to take r. is essence of Jewish life, 562:11
Risotto, moat of r., 850:8

Rites, performed r. simple decisive, 810:18
Ritz, puttin' on the R., 673:7
Rival, remains to r. what they have done, 72:4
Rivalry of aim, 531:24
Rivals, jealousy of r. near throne, 340:15
Rivalship of wisest men, 288:23
River, Alph the sacred r., 377:17
    among r. sallows, 411:8
    at my garden's end, 296:7
    can't sleep with the r. forever, 866:11
    cross r. rest under trees, 501:10
    down around the r., 703:2
    drifting down r., 523:2
    Eliza across r., 458:13
    glideth at own sweet will, 370:3
    great r. take me to main, 453:4
    I was born by the r., 829:10
    lake glimmering pool, 500:5
    let me love r. and woodland, 93:17
    Lethe the r. of oblivion, 256:24
    like foam on r., 373:23
    like snow falls in r., 358:6
    lived on R. Dee, 330:19
    met character on r., 522:18
    monstrous big r. down there, 523:5
    not step twice into same r., 62:*n*2
    Oceanus the ocean r., 750:1
    of crystal light, 554:1
    of grass, 686:12
    of oblivion, 256:24
    Ol' Man R., 706:6
    on a tree by a r., 527:21
    one more r. to cross, 898:26
    over r. through wood, 421:17
    passage over the r., 487:1
    peace as a r., 26:37
    pilot cares about nothing but r., 522:15
    runs through it, 731:17
    see one r. and see all, 235:6
    she's fading down r., 582:10
    spreadeth out her roots by the r., 27:39
    strong brown god, 679:3
    swap horses crossing r., 446:8
    there is a r., 16:27
    time a r. of strong current, 112:5
    time r. without banks, 888:6
    tirra lirra by r., 451:5
    water of r. never the same, 125:5
    way-hay you rolling r., 897:19
River City, trouble here in R., 733:6
Rivering, beside r. waters of, 650:22
Riverrun past Eve and Adam's, 650:19
Rivers, as long as r. flow, 892:4
    as long as r. shall run, 94:7
    at their source, 666:5
    by shallow r. birds sing, 168:5
    by the r. of Babylon, 19:11
    deepest r. least sound, 159:*n*4
    drain pent-up r. of myself, 486:22
    fire r. cannot quench, 170:35
    I've known r., 730:13
    my soul deep like r., 730:13
    not step twice into same r., 62:6
    of water in a dry place, 26:15
    rains return in r., 750:1
    run into the sea, 22:22
    shallow brooks and r. wide, 251:3
    tree planted by r., 14:40

Rivets, busy hammers closing r., 189:18
Rivulets hurrying through lawn, 453:7
    meadow r. overflow, 537:3
R'lyeh, in house at R., 687:8
Road, backward glances over traveled r.,
    488:17
    broad hard-beaten r., 425:17
    but one r. leads to Corinth, 98:*n*2
    butterfly upon r., 586:18
    by r. his ever-open door, 51:*n*1
    by r. to the contagious hospital, 658:9
    come to fork in r. take it, 807:8
    dark r. whence no one returns, 91:3
    divils in twists of r., 611:14
    free as the r., 242:26
    from Montgomery, 823:11
    heaven above r. below, 556:4
    help me down Cemetery R., 799:12
    high r. to England, 309:3
    house by side of r., 51:10, 569:13
    if r. could not make it out, 615:11
    I'm ten years burning down the r., 868:5
    in middle of r. a stone, 730:5
    is smooth, 54:21
    lonesome r., 376:21
    matrimony r. to wealth, 471:12
    no r. or ready way to virtue, 248:13
    no royal r. to geometry, 82:5
    no smooth r. into the future, 663:10
    of excess leads to palace of wisdom, 351:11
    on r. to destiny of damned, 488:13
    open r., 556:5
    poor slaves tread, 403:11
    ribbon of moonlight, 646:1
    right r. to Ireland, 731:14
    rough r. leads to greatness, 103:19
    smooth r. of life, 314:24
    take to open r., 486:24
    takes no private r., 295:6
    to City of Emeralds, 562:3
    to Hades easy to travel, 82:8
    to Hell gradual, 717:12
    to resolution, 242:4
    to stars through atom, 649:7
    up and down City R., 885:6
    up and road down one and same, 62:9
    virtue demands thorny r., 152:15
    when find r. narrow, 124:13
    which leads to peace, 337:12
    will be less tedious, 93:5
    winding r. before me, 386:10
    with bread and wine walk r., 898:6
    ye'll take the high r., 884:13
Roads, crooked r. are r. of genius, 351:19
    how many r., 851:1
    improvement makes straight r., 351:19
    lie with nothing to use them, 757:3
    old r. return to sky some color, 846:1
    open when you rise, 4:7
    two r. diverged, 622:18
Roadway, cry of child by r., 591:9
Roam, all morning sends to r., 575:19
    dunce sent to r., 326:11
    ever let fancy r., 411:3
    ev'rywhere I r., 503:12
    home where buffalo r., 890:20
    long wont to r., 447:12
    not their hearts that r., 589:1

Roam (*continued*)
   though we may r., 400:16
   where'er I r., 321:12
   wish to r. farther, 344:16
Roamed, how sweet I r., 350:7
   with my Soul, 449:16
Roamin' in the gloamin', 607:8
Roaming, ceaseless thoughts of r., 279:20
   mistress mine where r., 204:24
Roar, grating r. of pebbles, 496:17
   hiss now becoming r., 683:5
   melancholy long withdrawing r., 496:19
   men want ocean without r., 477:3
   music in its r., 396:16
   of only beast in arena, 599:12
   other side of silence, 480:18
   set table on a r., 202:12
   swinging low with sullen r., 251:17
   think lion sleeping because he didn't r.,
     359:9
   welkin r., 188:7
   you as any nightingale, 178:8
   you gently as sucking dove, 178:8
   young lions r. after prey, 18:11
Roared, cracked growled r. howled, 375:24
   Declamation r., 306:11
   Homer and Whitman r., 605:5
   well r. Lion, 179:13
Roaring, devil as r. lion, 46:3
   empty tigers or r. sea, 181:9
   words of my r., 15:21
Roars it through the hall, 500:3
Roast beef of England, 304:9
   rules the r., 140:*n*5
   set house on fire to r. eggs, 166:5
   with fire, 7:39
Roasted crabs hiss in bowl, 175:1
   very likeness of r. crab, 178:12
Roasts, newspaper buries dead r. thim
     aftherward, 600:16
Rob, could steal but she could not r., 848:17
   if writer r. mother, 714:8
   jaybird don't r. own nes', 551:11
   lady by marriage, 304:23
   neighbor he promised to defend, 419:18
   not the poor, 21:21
   Peter pay Paul, 147:23
   rich r. poor, 416:3
   some will r. you with six-gun, 768:3
   starve ere I'll r. further, 182:10
   words r. Hybla bees, 193:16
Robbed, he's not r. at all, 209:12
   not wanting what stolen, 209:12
   of their humanity, 790:20
   that smiles, 208:6
   we wuz r., 711:17
Robber, Barabbas a r., 40:7
Robbers, the more r. there will be, 57:19
   what makes r. bold but lenity, 170:24
Robbing, live by sharping and r., 303:17
   think little of r., 393:7
Robe, giant's r., 217:15
   intertissued r. of gold, 189:23
   judge's r., 206:25
   sa r. de pourpre au soleil, 150:*n*8
Robert, believe R. who has tried it, 95:*n*4
Robes and furred gowns, 212:30
   garland and singing r., 253:19

Robes (*continued*)
   loosely flowing, 232:7
   mountain in azure hue, 384:6
   riche or fithele, 133:23
   sky-r. spun of Iris' woof, 252:5
   washed r. in blood, 46:36
Robespierre sea-green Incorruptible, 407:8
Robin, call for r. redbreast, 237:3
   fainting R., 510:4
   redbreast in a cage, 353:15
   redbreast piously, 880:14
   what will poor r. do., 895:5
   who killed Cock R., 893:8
Robinson Crusoe, 282:10, 312:25
Robinson in Glen plaid jacket, 775:1
Robot vehicles blindly programmed, 850:9
Robots, Rossum's Universal R., 685:16
Robs me of that which not enriches him, 209:2
Robust, debate on public issues r., 745:9
Robustious periwig-pated fellow, 200:6
Rock, cradle will r., 550:7
   crag of the r., 14:29
   dwell on r. or in cell, 159:12
   eagle dwelleth on r., 14:29
   eagle of the r., 666:4
   founded upon r., 33:24
   he is the R., 9:30
   he only is my r., 17:4
   it is the Inchcape R., 381:13
   journalism, 849:9
   knew the perilous r., 381:12
   laws are sand customs r., 525:1
   living as black r. star, 813:14
   Lord is my r., 11:23
   Moses smote r. twice, 9:5
   no water only r., 676:15
   of Ages, 334:13
   of offense, 25:14
   of our salvation, 17:32
   poetry old as r., 425:12
   sails well but strike r., 355:2
   shadow under red r., 676:6
   shadows of a great r. in a weary land, 26:15
   small r. holds back great wave, 52:30
   takes on appearance of nearby r., 59:22
   that is higher than I, 17:3
   the tall r. the mountain, 368:10
   this r. shall fly, 374:2
   towered citadel pendant r., 218:39
   upon this r. I will build, 34:37
   was landed on us, 808:16
   way of a serpent upon a r., 22:14
   which Hercules bequeathed, 535:7
   will split, 662:14
Rock-a-bye-baby, 550:7
Rock and roll, ain't gonna r. no more, 834:7
   not tell Vietnam from r. veterans, 847:8
   sex and drugs and r., 854:1
   which go first r. or Christianity, 847:12
Rockbound, stern and r. coast, 405:4
Rocked in cradle of deep, 394:5
Rockets, once r. are up, 819:10
Rockets' red glare, 386:19
Rockies, applies west of R., 795:6
   ghost train in R. buried in snow, 811:6
   may crumble, 711:8
Rocking, cradle endlessly r., 487:5
   in your r. chair by window, 609:8

Rock-ribbed, hills r., 405:12
Rocks and stones and trees, 369:8
   before your mind like r., 828:9
   cries of cicadas sink into r., 279:21
   hand that r. cradle, 485:7
   marriage on the r., 813:8
   nor can sap be in r., 90:11
   older than r., 534:5
   over r. wood and water, 420:18
   seas laugh when r. near, 237:5
   soften r. or bend oak, 287:1
   Soundings quicksands r., 413:7
   that are steepest, 882:8
   the r. rent, 36:21
   trees wind, 473:12
   walled round with r., 530:25
   what gray r., 677:20
Rocky Raccoon, 848:15
   shore beats back siege, 176:25
Rod, a chief a r., 295:5
   Aaron's r., 7:34
   and blows not much good, 144:1
   cast thy r. before Pharaoh, 7:33
   he that spareth his r., 20:23
   Jonathan put forth the r., 10:42
   not pious longer than r., 144:1
   of empire, 315:21
   of iron, 46:23
   out of the stem of Jesse, 25:18
   spare r. and spoil child, 81:*n*5, 262:17
   thy r. and thy staff, 15:23
   to check the erring, 371:15
   Wisdom be put in silver r., 351:9
Rode him through mire, 896:16
   off in all directions, 605:2
   the six hundred, 454:18
   upon a cherub, 15:14
Roderick, Saxon I am R. Dhu, 374:1
   where was R. then, 374:4
Rodillas, mejor morir que vivir en r., 643:*n*1
Roe, be thou like to a r., 24:27
   following the r., 357:15
Roes, breasts like two young r., 24:13
Rogers, Ginger R. did everything, 834:16
Rogue and peasant slave, 199:15
   every inch not fool is r., 273:8
   joined this r. and whore, 285:13
Rogues, hear r. talk of court news, 213:8
Roi, plus royaliste que le r., 890:22
Rois, l'exactitude la politesse des r., 349:*n*3
Roland, a R. for an Oliver, 124:*n*2
   Child R. to dark tower, 212:*n*2
   est preux et Oliver est sage, 124:*n*2
   sound your horn, 124:2
   valorous Oliver wise, 124:3
Role, child r. to be born, 584:18
   your r. is played out, 643:14
Roles, self-interest plays all r., 263:19
Roll, centuries r. back to age of gold, 97:12
   confirm tidings as they r., 287:21
   darkling down torrent, 306:19
   'em up, 884:16
   eyes began to r., 296:26
   in ecstasy at your feet, 655:17
   it, 879:*n*1
   jest r. to your rifle, 588:13
   let's r., 879:7
   me over fair, 484:4

S

Sabachthani, Eli Eli lama s., 36:20
Sabbath, child born on S., 895:9
    keep S. going to Church, 508:18
    made for man, 36:27
    rang slowly, 777:12
    remember the s. day, 8:13
Sabbath-breaking, drinking and S., 393:7
Sabbath-day, abhor detest S., 523:11
Sabbaths, endless s. blessed ones see, 123:9
Sabidius, I don't like you S., 107:7
Sabine, bounded by S., 456:7
Sabines, life the old S. knew, 93:20
Sable cloud, 252:13
    it was a s. silvered, 197:15
    night s. goddess, 290:19
    Sleep son of s. Night, 167:3
    underneath this s. hearse, 240:7
Sables, suit of s., 200:15
Sabrina fair, 252:26
Sacco and Vanzetti must not die, 812:10
Sacco's name will live, 682:12
Sack, each S. had seven cats, 892:22
    if s. and sugar be fault, 182:28
    intolerable deal of s., 182:31
    leave s. live cleanly, 183:37
    unless hours cups of s., 181:20
Sackcloth, put on s. with ashes, 12:31
Sacked the holy citadel of Troy, 52:20
Sacks, seven s., 892:22
Sacrament, men pregnant abortion a s., 782:7
    of praise, 641:6
    virtue of s. like light, 77:*n*4
Sacred, Alph the s. river, 377:17
    Awe, 656:7
    cod, 577:*n*2
    cows make tastiest hamburger, 841:11
    drama heaved, 596:8
    duty to myself, 504:9
    even bad books are s., 815:14
    facts are s., 550:10
    feed his s. flame, 378:3
    fire of liberty, 328:11
    hair dissever, 293:12
    head of thine, 253:8
    history a s. thing, 157:6
    hold every moment s., 631:11
    hoop of the nation, 583:5
    human body s., 486:21
    let there be s. silence, 96:25
    life not cheap but s., 428:10
    lips touch s. fire, 610:4
    nothing s., 721:6
    our s. honor, 336:3
    sane and s. death, 487:13
    they lack a s. poet, 97:14
    things s. or things profane, 271:16
    to departed spirit, 120:17
    to oblivion, 234:2
    veils her s. fires, 297:6
Sacredness of property, 521:16
Sacrifice acceptable to God, 41:29
    coming to s., 410:18
    living s., 41:29, 49:7

Sacrifice (*continued*)
    make one sweet s., 225:15
    mercy and not s., 28:35
    spirit of s., 420:8
    too long a s., 593:8
Sacrificed, certainty precedent not lightly s., 607:1
    Christ our Passover s., 42:14
    more significant art had to be s., 639:6
    to produce her, 582:12
Sacrifices like stockyards, 721:6
    of friendship, 608:8
    such s. my Cordelia, 213:9
    with such s. God is pleased, 45:19
Sacrilegious murder hath broke ope, 215:28
Sacrum, oblivioni s., 234:2
Sad, a little sunny a little s., 532:7
    all their songs s., 618:10
    all world s. dreary, 503:12
    and bad and mad, 462:23
    and weary I go back, 651:3
    as angels, 314:*n*2
    augurs mock own presage, 222:10
    bad brother's name, 530:24
    be beautiful and be s., 491:12
    companion dull-eyed melancholy, 220:11
    created you while s., 583:13
    cypress, 205:3
    experience make me s., 195:24
    flesh is s. alas, 543:6
    heart foams at stern, 558:16
    heart of Ruth, 410:10
    home is so s., 799:8
    is Eros builder of cities, 749:7
    kissed mouth, 530:3
    last gray hairs, 410:5
    lucidity of soul, 494:14
    make man look s., 179:14
    mechanic exercise, 453:12
    mine a s. one, 184:4
    name forever s., 293:22
    no s. songs for me, 512:3
    or singing weather, 530:11
    remember and be s., 512:5
    Rose of all my days, 591:1
    say I'm s., 392:20
    soul s. glance glum, 527:25
    sound of horn, 416:5
    still s. music of humanity, 368:11
    stories of death of kings, 177:8
    sullen and s., 300:14
    tale's best for winter, 223:14
    tires in a mile-a, 223:24
    to see s. sights moves, 172:37
    'twas s. by fits, 317:14
    uncertain rustling, 449:6
    vicissitude of things, 313:18
    visit my s. heart, 192:8
    weight of this s. time, 213:16
    when am I s., 830:12
    words of tongue or pen, 438:10
    young men drifting, 816:3
Sadder and wiser man, 377:7
    few things s. than monstrous, 736:14
    light than waning moon, 438:15
    than owl songs, 399:4

Saddest are these, 438:10
    of the year, 406:2
    story ever heard, 616:14
    sweetest songs s. thought, 403:5
Saddle, boot s. to horse, 460:5
    put Germany in s., 470:9
    short life in s., 579:13
    things are in s., 424:12
Sadie stayed home, 783:5
    Thompson answer, 627:2
Sadist, forty-nine masochists to one s., 734:2
Sadly, part we s. in troublous world, 171:2
    why hearest thou music s., 220:33
Sadness, diverter of s., 245:1
    eternal note of s., 496:17
    farewell s., 705:8
    humorous s., 195:23
    more prevailing s., 384:15
    of a vale, 411:12
    of conviction, 538:7
    soul taste s. of might, 411:11
    sweet though in s., 402:13
    touches me with a prayer, 415:2
    unmannerly in youth, 184:17
    where s. let me sow joy, 125:12
    wraps me in humorous s., 195:23
Sado, over S. the Milky Way, 280:3
Safe, compulsion to become s., 664:5
    depository of public interests, 338:17
    direct and honest not s., 209:17
    he that's secure is not s., 302:28
    none is s., 671:8
    run into a s. harbor, 55:21
    see me s. up, 143:9
    shall wooden wall continue, 62:*n*3
    world s. for democracy, 566:14
    world s. for diversity, 786:10
Safeguard against prurient curiosity, 646:9
    judiciary s. of liberty, 582:5
    of the west, 370:7
Safeguards, history of procedural s., 649:9
    of liberty forged in controversies, 649:11
Safely, but to be s. thus, 216:5
    citizen may walk s. on law, 804:16
    Judah and Israel dwelt s., 11:28
    ship of state s. to harbor, 65:11
    toddle s. home, 668:13
Safer to be feared than loved, 141:14
    world s. for children, 824:10
Safest, home is s. refuge, 158:*n*7
    in the middle, 102:11
    just when s. sunset touch, 461:22
    road to Hell, 717:12
Safety, as if s. in stupidity, 475:18
    concern for s. in face of dangers, 802:9
    dangerous to peace and s., 355:7
    fame for ale and s., 189:10
    greatest degree of s., 320:8
    in multitude of counsellors, 20:13
    in s. within boundaries, 653:15
    in skating s. is speed, 427:11
    no s. here below, 143:*n*5
    no strike against public s., 613:4
    obtaining happiness and s., 320:7
    peace liberty and s., 337:12
    pluck this flower s., 182:13
    principles to effect s., 336:1
    purchase little temporary s., 303:6

Safety *(continued)*
to hope not safety, 94:15
unite for public s., 365:13
with which error tolerated, 337:8
Sagacious bold and turbulent of wit, 272:16
how s. the mouse, 83:11
Sagacity, by accidents and s., 317:2
Sage, by saint by savage by s., 296:20
daughters of Muses, 64:1
government of the s., 56:14
hoary S. replied, 308:4
hold tongue pass for s., 101:5
knows without going about, 57:16
lengthened s. advices, 358:4
Milton's wormwood words, 254:*n*1
never strives for the great, 57:12
who delights in bringing success is not s.,
80:14
Sage, que m'importe que tu sois s., 491:*n*11
Sager sort our deeds reprove, 226:20
Sage's, vain the s. pride, 296:19
Sages, have seen in thy face, 326:17
holy s. once did sing, 250:9
than all the s. can, 368:6
wisdom of our s., 337:12
Sagged and reeled, 639:13
Sags like heavy load, 731:9
Sahara dies, 510:16
Said, by and by easily s., 200:28
death has something to be s. for it, 798:8
didn't say everything I s., 807:1
fool hath s. in his heart, 15:9
he himself has s. it, 526:3
he was against sin, 613:8
I kept my word he s., 616:7
I meant what I s. s. what I meant, 739:11
I s. in my haste, 18:23
I to myself said I, 526:21
in grief or pride, 695:15
inadvertently s. some evil thing, 76:15
least s. soonest mended, 156:*n*4
let no more be s., 497:1
let what will be s., 337:2
little s. soon amended, 156:24
much s. on both sides, 288:8
never to himself hath s., 373:3
no sooner s. than done, 84:15
nothing s. that has not been s., 86:6
so Sancho Panza s., 647:2
the best thought and s., 497:7
thing that is s. is s., 136:17
thing which was not, 285:3
things most listened for are things
least s., 488:8
'tis well s. again, 225:21
to my soul be still, 678:20
too late to say anything not s., 280:21
want anything s. ask man, 810:9
well as if I had s. it, 286:1
when all is s. and done, 558:5
who s. Peacock Pie, 616:9
word dead when s., 510:13
Sail, all s. no anchor, 420:5
at break of day, 656:19
beyond sunset and stars, 451:18
cried A s. a s., 376:6
even with canvas rent, 103:13
here she comes full s., 287:3

Sail *(continued)*
hoist s. while gale, 146:*n*12
more s. than ballast, 280:12
on, 539:15
on O Ship of State, 436:23
out on your trades again, 83:3
sea-mark of my utmost s., 210:18
shallow bauble boats dare s., 203:4
solitary s. that rises, 470:1
time to take in s., 425:2
tomorrow s. the Ocean Sea, 96:8
two lofty ships set s., 898:1
we must s. not drift, 443:9
weather-beaten s., 226:24
wet seas roun', 589:2
with unshut eye, 494:13
Sailed away year and day, 467:8
off in wooden shoe, 554:1
Swift s. into rest, 595:8
Sailing celestial spaces, 533:12
denies voyager further s., 68:3
great whales s. by, 494:13
like a stately ship, 260:16
on obscene wings, 377:16
ship a-s. with the wind, 896:7
Sailor, drunken s. on mast, 171:34
here and there old s., 640:19
home is the s., 555:16
staring s. that shakes watch, 762:21
well for s. lad, 452:15
what shall we do with drunken s., 897:17
Sailor's wife had chestnuts, 213:33
Sailors but men, 184:21
half our s. swallowed, 171:1
images s. tattoo, 727:5
rough lot as s. mostly are, 555:15
show world how American s. fight, 886:*n*2
soldiers s. airmen, 621:9
Spanish s. with bearded lips, 437:10
won't believe it, 374:16
Sail's shaking, 635:15
Sails, argosies of magic s., 452:2
biased by full s., 720:5
broad bellying s., 659:1
filled streamers waving, 260:16
filled with lusty wind, 163:20
handed all s. and set treo, 139:8
purple the s., 218:20
swell full, 423:4
thy white s. crowding, 545:12
vessel of my genius now hoists s., 129:9
well but strike rock, 355:2
white s. fly seaward, 677:19
Sail-yards tremble masts crack, 163:20
Saint and Martyr rule from tomb, 678:3
become a s., 824:14
by s. by savage by sage, 296:20
corrupt a s., 181:28
dead sinner revised, 540:13
Doctor and S., 441:18
history puts s. in every dream, 868:6
if God does not exist, 770:4
lips would temp a s., 395:*n*1
looked out of eye of s., 595:6
neither s.- nor sophist-led, 495:3
old s. in forest, 547:16
saw my late espoused s., 255:1
seem s. when most play devil, 171:25

Saint *(continued)*
strained so much, 755:11
such injury vex a s., 173:17
threadbare s., 228:3
Saint Agnes' Eve, 409:18
moon hath set, 409:23
Saint Anne mother of Mary, 534:5
yes by S., 204:29
Saint Augustine thanked God, 630:7
Saint Clement's, bells of S., 893:6
Saint George, England and S., 189:9
that swinged dragon, 175:8
Saint Ives, going to S., 892:22
Saint John, ancient animal symbols of S., 415:7
awake my S., 294:14
there S. mingles, 296:6
Saint John's, whether bounded by the S.,
456:7
Saint Louis bought it for six million dollars,
522:19
Saint Martin's, expect S. summer, 169:12
Saint Nicholas soon would be there, 387:2
Saint Paul's, designing S., 629:2
ruins of S., 317:4, 419:17
Saint Peter's, blessing of S. Master, 245:10
Saint Theresa in wild lament, 737:8
Saint Vincent, nobly Cape S., 460:20
Sainted, thing enskyed and s., 206:15
Sainte-Terrer, there goes a S., 472:*n*2
Saintliness not a state, 761:15
Saintly, woman's normal occupations counter s.
life, 746:11
Saints aid if men call, 377:12
all the sinners s., 857:6
choir of s., 231:1
Communion of S., 48:11
four s. prepare for s., 627:18
happiness of s. may be more delightful,
127:8
heroes if we will, 494:11
in your injuries, 208:13
men below and s. above, 373:2
precious is the death of his s., 18:24
rarely married women, 746:11
should be guilty until proven innocent,
735:24
slaughtered s., 254:23
sweetly sing, 280:16
take your s. and virgins, 481:3
to windows run, 508:10
when s. go marching in, 899:5
where s. immortal reign, 289:17
Saint-seducing gold, 179:20
Saintship of an anchorite, 395:3
Sairey, oh S. S. little do we know, 465:3
Sais, que s.-je, 152:*n*12
Saisons, O s. O châteaux, 559:*n*6
Saith, he s. among the trumpets, 14:28
Sake, for God's s. sit upon ground, 177:8
for his name's s., 15:23
good friend for Jesus' s., 226:17
hated for my name's s., 34:2
love for Love's s., 756:15
persecute you for my s., 32:14
poem for poem's s., 450:2
wine for thy stomach's s., 44:33
Sakes, Heaven and future's s., 624:1
Saki, O S. you pass, 442:10

Salad, crazy s. with meat, 593:13
    days, 218:16
Salads, ho 'tis time of s., 314:20
Salaputium disertum, 91:*n*7
Salary depends on his not understanding,
    636:13
Sale, base s. of chapmen's tongues, 174:8
    city for s., 92:11
    love for s., 691:8
Sales, produce 80 percent of s., 795:14
Salesman, every s. can fondle her breasts, 626:6
    for s. no rock bottom, 780:8
    is got to dream, 780:9
    percent of group of s., 795:14
Salesmen, nation of used car s., 843:14
Salley, down by s. gardens, 590:21
Sallied flesh, 196:*n*2
Sallow, lean and s. abstinence, 252:23
Sallows, among river s., 411:8
Sally in our alley, 292:1
    loose s. of mind, 306:25
    make a sudden s., 454:24
    none like pretty S., 292:1
Salmon, like chinook s. jumping, 788:5
    wasn't wine was s., 463:21
Salmon-falls, 594:1
Salome danced, 34:23
Saloon, all s. keepers Democrats, 458:5
Salt, became a pillar of s., 6:34
    drift in laboring s., 839:4
    eat peck of s. with him, 880:15
    eaten your bread and s., 586:16
    fragrance of s. marsh, 487:19
    how s. is another's bread, 130:6
    if s. have lost savor, 32:15
    land and not inhabited, 27:39
    no joy but lacks s., 623:10
    not worth his s., 105:21
    of the earth, 32:15
    one s. sea, 188:36
    speech seasoned with s., 44:14
    tides seaward flow, 494:12
    upon their tails, 284:3
    water and s. and darkness, 874:6
    water unbounded, 589:20
    with a grain of s., 105:10
Salted, wherewith shall it be s., 32:15
Saltness of time, 187:12
Saltsick, seasilt s., 651:3
Salt-water, I have become s. man, 723:19
Saltus, natura non facit s., 305:*n*2
Salus extra ecclesiam non est, 114:*n*3
    populi suprema lex, 88:*n*5
Salutary influence of example, 307:16
    wise and s. neglect, 324:3
Salute, we about to die s. you, 111:1
Salutes everyone in early days, 75:21
Salvage, no end to the work of s., 769:1
Salvaged, ships s. and retiring, 650:5
Salvation, concern temporal s., 331:10
    for helmet the hope of s., 44:20
    for him there is s., 344:14
    for our s. came down, 48:12
    Genius work out s., 413:7
    he is become my s., 8:4, 25:20
    he only is my rock and s., 17:4
    in union, 607:3
    my bottle of s., 159:10

Salvation (*continued*)
    my light and my s., 15:27
    no more s. by society, 758:1
    no s. outside Church, 114:3
    none should see s., 186:1
    rock of our s., 17:32
    three things necessary for s., 127:5
    waited for thy s., 7:20
    work out own s., 44:2
    work out s. with diligence, 64:16
Sam, play it S., 758:4
Samaria, woman of S., 39:12
Samaritan had compassion, 37:37
Samarra, appointment in S., 627:1
Same, always s. old story, 813:8
    descent to Hades is s., 64:11
    ever the s., 151:13
    looking outward in s. direction, 726:16
    men all the s., 627:2
    permanent and the s., 495:13
    precisely s. rocks, 439:12
    repose that ever is the s., 371:16
    self was not the s., 202:35
    the more they remain s., 439:1
    the s. as everywhere, 342:11
    think and hit s. time, 807:2
    whole world over, 887:7
    yesterday today and for ever, 45:17
Sameness of sheep, 724:7
    with difference, 379:13
Sames of am, 701:18
Samite, arm clothed in white s., 138:4
    clothed in white s. mystic, 455:8
Sammy, What Makes S. Run, 776:14
Samphire, one that gathers s., 212:24
Sample, by s. we judge whole, 155:13
Sampler, serve to ply the s., 252:25
Sam's, nephew of my Uncle S., 634:12
Samsa, Gregor S. awoke from uneasy dreams,
    655:14
Samson, Philistines be upon thee S., 10:23
    Philistines brought S. to Gaza, 10:24
San Francisco Bay center of prosperity, 470:14
    carry me home to S., 719:11
    is where gay fantasies, 849:7
    West is S., 582:1
San Quentin, he was taken to S., 784:11
San Salvador, island called S., 139:8
Sancho Panza, God's blessing said S., 158:*n*3
    so S. said so say I, 647:2
Sanctified by reason blest by faith, 369:2
Sanction, gives bigotry no s., 328:12
    happiness the only s. of life, 584:2
    laws with s., 349:7
Sanctity and truth of revelation of Mahomet,
    332:8
    untrespassed s. of space, 800:1
Sanctuary, wild s., 616:19
Sand, abstinence sows s. all over, 352:6
    as the s. by the sea, 11:27
    blood of Ignacio on s., 717:6
    heap of loose s., 598:10
    house built on s., 33:25
    laws are s. customs rock, 525:1
    line has been drawn in the s., 805:5
    number the s. of the sea, 30:8
    on edge of s., 467:10
    ostrich with head in s., 566:11

Sand (*continued*)
    ribbed sea s., 376:13
    roll down golden s., 391:5
    see world in grain of s., 353:14
    such quantities of s., 516:1
    sun s. wild uproar, 424:3
    throw s. against the wind, 353:12
    weaving s., 429:7
Sandal, battering s., 546:16
    heard her massive s., 695:14
    shoon, 201:23
Sandburg, fall into hands of Carl S., 708:16
Sands and shores, 252:12
    come unto these yellow s., 224:12
    footprints on s. of time, 436:6
    ghosts countless as s., 504:12
    golden s. crystal brooks, 229:14
    lone level s. stretch, 401:13
    of Dee, 481:4
    of time, 436:6
    steer too nigh s., 272:16
    suffice, 510:16
Sandwich men shuffling, 654:5
Sandwiches, ate peanut butter s., 796:7
Sandy, false as s. earth, 203:20
    swift s. glass, 233:17
Sane and had to fly, 802:9
    and sacred death, 487:13
    assent you are s., 509:4
    only s. thing to do if up there [Boston],
      700:12
Saner to be rebel, 585:2
Sang, all we said or s., 597:1
    beyond genius of sea, 641:8
    bonny bonny Biscay O, 883:22
    from morn till night, 330:19
    ful weel s. service dyvyne, 133:14
    his didn't, 701:17
    in my chains like sea, 777:14
    morning stars s. together, 14:19
    perhaps it may turn out s., 356:18
    Sir Lancelot, 451:5
    summer s. in me, 695:13
    Tilly-loo, 467:12
    to small guitar, 467:7
    what song the Sirens s., 248:27
    when a lark I s., 756:7
    where late sweet birds s., 221:24
    Willow titwillow, 527:21
    within bloody wood, 676:2
Sang, qu'un s. impur, 361:3
Sangfroid, preserve your s., 337:2
Sanglots longs des violons, 549:*n*4
Sangreal, noble history of S., 138:1
Sanguinis, hic est enim calix S. mei, 47:22
Sanitary, give me s. reformer, 481:3
Sanity, reassure selves of s., 760:8
    virtue of ancient literature, 495:22
Sank my boat, 785:4
    sighted sub s. same, 771:1
Sans teeth eyes everything, 194:25
    Wine Song Singer, 441:17
Santa Anas, one of those hot dry S., 674:3
Santa Claus is comin' to town, 680:2
    yes Virginia there is a S., 533:19
Sap, dried s. out of veins, 592:5
    make cherry red, 671:17
    material s., 212:19

Sap *(continued)*
nor can s. be in rocks, 90:11
world's whole s. is sunk, 229:12
Sapless, earth s. as bone, 635:14
Sapphire bracelet lasts forever, 698:9
heaven's deep repose, 409:23
the s. blaze, 316:13
Sapphires, garlic and s., 678:8
glowed with living s., 257:25
Sappho, burning S., 398:15
of Lesbos tenth muse, 56:*n*3
would speak openly, 626:14
Sarah, blossomed S. and I blossom, 773:4
Sarcasm language of Devil, 406:17
Sargasso of the imagination, 736:13
your mind and you S. Sea, 664:19
Sash lowered night comes, 623:14
Sat among the cinders, 895:3
at good man's feast, 194:22
by the fleshpots, 8:8
like a cormorant, 257:14
like Patience on monument, 205:4
on a tuffet, 895:14
on Pillicock-hill, 212:1
Satan exalted s., 256:6
so Tiberius might have s., 497:4
you have s. too long, 246:17
Satan as lightning fall, 37:34
came also, 12:35
exalted sat, 256:6
finds mischief, 289:9
get thee behind me S., 34:38
old serpent called S., 47:2
that waiteth to bigile, 135:6
towards God the other towards S., 491:16
you have given me the shell, S., 720:3
Satanic, dark S. mills, 354:8
Satanic Verses, author of S., 725:14
Satchel, whining school-boy with s., 194:25
Sate itself in celestial bed, 198:10
Sated with banquet of life, 90:14
Satire a sort of glass, 284:4
be my song, 394:11
ever moral ever new, 278:7
hard not to write s., 109:8
like polished razor, 297:9
or sense can Sporus feel, 295:14
points at no defect, 285:7
what closes Saturday, 684:19
Satire's my weapon, 296:5
Satirist describes things as they are, 752:4
Satisfaction, ambitious man have no s., 231:14
cost of s. of instincts, 563:9
I can't get no s., 857:1
in making it possible for others, 771:15
previous benefaction or present s., 70:18
that I have not lived in vain, 288:3
work brings, 602:10
Satisfactory, plant seeds most s., 507:14
Satisfied, charm makes us more s., 490:17
fine reality of hunger s., 752:9
I can't be s., 731:1
love s. greater torment, 677:14
nature of desire not to be s., 78:20
retire like s. guest, 95:18
to live in hunger, 685:6
well paid that is well s., 186:13

Satisfies, makes hungry where most s., 218:21
not that this notion s. me, 440:7
Satisfiest desire of every living thing, 19:17
Satisfy your greed, 589:*n*1
Satisfying, comfortable and s. sleep, 633:6
curiosity of young, 546:1
Saturam, difficile est s. non scribere, 109:*n*2
Saturday, died on S., 895:10
mornings we listened to Red Lantern, 836:10
satire closes S., 684:19
Saturday's child, 895:9
Saturn, connection between spider and S., 298:22
gray-haired S., 411:12
Revolution like S., 468:15
Saturnians through life's Tempe led, 483:20
Satya truth, 604:5
Satyagraha, term S. coined by me, 604:4
Satyr, forty till fifty man a s., 561:15
Hyperion to a s., 196:31
Satyrs, men like s. grazing, 168:12
nymphs and s., 597:3
Sauce, cloyless s., 218:18
no s. like hunger, 157:8
Saucy doubts and fears, 216:15
not deep-searched with s. looks, 174:1
Saul and Jonathan were lovely and pleasant, 11:8
becomes Paul, 570:10
hath slain his thousands, 11:3
is S. among the prophets, 10:38
why persecutest thou me, 40:22
yet breathing slaughter, 40:21
Saunders, a bed Clerk S. said, 890:1
Saunter, great art to s., 472:21
Sauntering from à la Sainte Terre, 472:*n*2
Sausage, in as pig out as s., 540:10
Savage and Tartarly, 399:11
breast, 287:1
bull bear the yoke, 190:19
by saint by s. by sage, 296:20
contemplates mother-in-law, 558:4
delights to torture, 440:12
dole laws unto s. race, 451:11
extreme rude cruel, 222:20
half s. country, 665:4
if little s. left to himself, 313:13
in man never eradicated, 473:11
indignation, 286:15, 595:8
individual man, 598:14
is he who saves himself, 140:8
men and uncouth manners, 323:22
noble s., 272:9
our resemblances to the s., 558:5
place as holy and enchanted, 377:18
ruled s. hordes, 500:5
servility slides by, 788:3
soothe a s. breast, 287:1
take some s. woman, 452:8
thrown on s. shore, 488:2
young man who not wept s., 584:14
Savage-creating fellow, 73:15
Savageness, sing s. out of a bear, 209:26
Savagery, meeting-point between s. and civilization, 580:4
Savages, grow like s., 190:7
in unknown island, 429:21

Savage-wild, time and intents are s., 181:9
Save, assist him to s. face, 707:11
came to s. sinners, 44:24
conquer but to s., 384:13
destroy Ben Tre in order to s., 847:9
destroy village in order to s., 847:*n*1
eternal Father strong to s., 503:1
God s. the king, 10:39, 177:16, 292:2
God s. the mark, 182:2
greed will s. the U.S.A., 864:1
himself he cannot s., 36:19
it all, 822:13
killed one to s. hundred thousand, 364:15
listen and s., 252:26
me from Candid Friend, 367:3
me from therrble prongs, 651:3
my soul if I have soul, 500:13
nobly s. or meanly lose, 446:1
not s. it it not s. me, 657:6
one drop would s. my soul, 169:4
Shine Shine s. poor me, 887:1
thee ancient Mariner, 375:25
what is around me, 657:6
whosoever s. life shall lose it, 34:39
wish to s. their own pocket, 71:13
Saved by hope faith love, 696:6
harvest is past and we are not s., 27:30
he s. others, 36:19
I have s. myself, 54:29
I would have s. them if I could, 397:16
part of day rued, 623:5
there be souls must be s., 208:24
you were s. because you were, 806:8
youthful hose well s., 194:25
Saves, humor s. a few steps, 671:13
itself perpetually, 762:12
savage he who s. himself, 140:8
soul in new French books, 461:23
where danger lies grows that which s., 367:3
Savin', I'm s. love for you, 708:7
Savings, not by s. and capital, 753:3
Savior at his sermon on mount, 460:21
Christ our S., 883:4
men that compare selves with s., 438:21
of 'is country, 587:17
which is Christ, 37:17
Savior's birth celebrated, 196:19
sing tongue the S. glory, 126:12
Savoir être à soi, 152:*n*8
tuer et créer, 491:*n*13
Savor, filths s. but themselves, 212:20
fleeting delights, 400:14
if salt have lost s., 32:15
joyously s. one single instant, 682:9
seeming and s. all winter, 223:25
thoughts that s. of content, 164:2
Savory, lavender mints s. marjoram, 223:26
Saw, all at once I s. a crowd, 371:9
coughing drowns parson's s., 175:1
do not s. the air, 200:6
expanse of s. grass and water, 686:12
first one another s., 229:9
heavens fill, 452:2
I at a glance, 371:11
I came I s. I conquered, 89:6
I came s. and overcame, 188:19
I s. and loved, 332:15

Saw *(continued)*
last time I s. Paris, 706:7
life steadily saw it whole, 494:9
man clothed with rags, 271:8
manners in face, 308:3
ne'er s. I never felt, 370:3
never s. a man who looked, 561:1
never s. a Moor, 510:9
never s. purple cow, 597:19
not seen as others s., 447:10
on a cloud I s. a child, 350:10
skull beneath skin, 675:25
spiders marching, 787:3
then I s. the Congo, 639:14
three ships, 896:3
through glass eye darkly, 524:6
water lily bloom, 451:6
who was that lady I s., 601:6
young Harry with beaver on, 183:13
Saws, full of wise s., 194:25
Sawyer, Adventures of Tom S., 523:1
Saxa, in spatio pertundere s., 89:*n*9
Saxon I am Roderick Dhu, 374:1
in subjection to white S. man, 471:6
Saxophone, learn to work the s., 868:8
Say, cannot create when nothing to s., 728:12
canst not s. I did it, 216:17
can't s. anything good, 659:15
defend right to s. it, 300:7
didn't s. everything I said, 807:1
disapprove of what you s., 300:7
Do as I s. not as I do, 238:20
don't s. too much, 751:3
everything interestingly, 554:8
find right thing to s., 564:18
first of God above, 294:16
good deed to s. well, 225:21
good night till it be morrow, 180:16
I don't s. what public wants, 626:4
I shall have less to s., 622:21
I want to s., 840:10
I'd like to s. a few words, 879:2
it ain't so Joe, 887:9
It Loud, 837:6
it no ideas but in things, 658:16
it with utmost levity, 564:18
know much s. little, 312:23
love not having to s. sorry, 843:5
more to s. when dead, 606:1
never know what I'm going to s., 126:3
never s. I was false of heart, 222:11
never s. more than necessary, 346:3
not struggle nought availeth, 479:12
not what we ought to s., 213:16
nothin' without compelled, 482:6
nothin' you can be held to, 482:6
nothing but what said, 234:8
nothing to s. s. nothing, 388:12
nothing you couldn't actually s., 664:17
one may s. what one thinks, 110:8
one word Plastics, 827:9
remember what we s. here, 446:5
right to s. what one pleases, 667:2
secure within can s., 273:17
see what I s., 572:4
shame s. what it will, 202:2
shudder to s. it, 94:12
so long as we can s., 212:16

Say *(continued)*
some s. I'm impatient impetuous uppity, 794:3
some s. world end in fire, 623:4
style of what man has to s., 497:5
tale as said to me, 373:1
temple bells they s., 588:1
that's all I s., 443:13
there is no more to s., 204:8
there is nothing more to s., 605:17
things I did not do or s., 595:15
this again, 863:5
to all the world, 193:22
to the fleet, 355:*n*3
too late to s. anything not said, 280:21
way they s. it, 733:3
wet mind and s. something clever, 72:11
what everyone else does not s., 548:25
what law is, 349:13
what more is there to s., 594:8
what others s. of them, 269:10
what will Mrs. Grundy s., 362:1
what you mean, 514:13
what you would be, 109:5
which can s. more, 221:26
which grain will grow, 214:5
you can have it, 819:12
Sayer, always seer is a s., 426:9
Saying, for loving and for s. so, 228:21
good-bye to statue, 721:9
is one thing, 153:6
mode of s. things, 496:9
reputed wise for s. nothing, 184:8
thoughtless s. of princess, 313:8
wise and old, 160:*n*6
Says, no one means all he s., 532:6
she speaks yet s. nothing, 179:32
what he s. least important, 533:5
who is it that s. most, 221:26
who s. it what he s., 533:5
Scab of churches, 227:15
Scabbard, sword of justice has no s., 347:6
Scabby, hated with s. hatred, 836:8
Scabies, disputandi pruritus ecclesiarum s., 227:*n*4
Scaffold sways the future, 481:13
Truth forever on s., 481:13
Scaffoldage, 'twixt footing and s., 203:9
Scald, tears s. like molten lead, 213:4
Scalding grave, 611:14
Scale, every golden s., 513:15
he by geometric s., 262:7
in equal s. weighing, 196:22
lapping scale with regularity, 671:11
Poetic Justice with lifted s., 296:25
so shall you s. the stars, 95:9
society without objective legal s., 791:14
Scaled invention or artistry, 665:14
Scales are his pride, 14:33
father held out golden s., 52:14
fell from his eyes, 40:25
put Hannibal in the s., 109:25
waves as formal as s. on fish, 670:17
Scallop shell of quiet, 159:10
Scalped each other, 419:18
Scan, gently s. brother man, 357:3
presume not God to s., 295:1

Scandal, dreaded s. more than disease, 582:20
greatest s. waits on greatest state, 172:36
love and s., 304:16
public s. is wicked, 267:17
tea and s., 286:25
treatment of Negro greatest s., 718:5
Scandalous and poor, 281:1
Scandals of th' poor, 600:7
short an' simple s., 600:7
Scanted, what s. in hair given in wit, 172:18
Scanter of your maiden presence, 197:29
Scanty, in longitude tho' s., 358:9
'Scape, who should 's. whipping, 199:14
'Scaped, heart 's. this sorrow, 221:29
Scapegoat, let him go for a s., 8:25
'Scapes, hair-breadth 's., 207:37
Scar, not really border but s., 818:7
virtue or vice leaves s., 540:23
wound heals s. disappears, 474:2
Scarcely greet me with that sun, 221:14
Scarceness, eat bread without s., 9:20
Scarcity, on first s. will turn, 325:14
Scare, don't let them s. you, 686:4
white clouds on, 622:21
Scarecrow, not make s. of law, 206:18
Scared, always been s. of you, 833:8
to go to brink, 674:16
Scarf up tender eye of day, 216:13
Scarfs garters gold, 295:3
Scarlet, in S. town, 889:25
letter her passport, 431:8
line slender rigid exact, 489:*n*4
of maples shake me, 579:10
passion for a s. coat, 285:6
sins s. books read, 606:17
though your sins be as s., 24:32
Scars, he jests at s., 179:31
I carry with me, 271:27
inveterate s., 678:8
of others teach caution, 115:14
you have made, 820:6
Scatter plenty o'er smiling land, 316:2
Scattered, he hath s. the proud, 37:11
Israel s. upon the hills, 12:9
when cloud s., 404:10
Scattering, maniac s. dust, 453:18
Scatters, anarchy s. armies, 65:22
deep surmise s., 474:3
rear of darkness thin, 251:1
Scene before him beat like pulse, 798:7
dreamer is dream s., 630:9
last s. of all, 194:25
live o'er each s., 293:13
lofty s. be acted o'er, 192:18
love gilds the s., 346:9
not ask to see distant s., 421:4
play one s. of excellent dissembling, 218:8
speaks a new s., 242:5
start a s. or two, 675:4
Scenery essential in painting, 122:11
fine human nature finer, 413:3
Scenes, from s. like these, 356:10
his fathers loved, 734:10
ill-bred s., 582:20
no more behind your s. David, 308:14
of my childhood, 393:12
Scent, amber s. of perfume, 260:16
of arm-pits aroma finer than prayer, 486:8

Scent (continued)
    of pine, 677:20
    of roses hang round it, 387:14
Scepter, balm s. and ball, 189:23
    leaden s., 290:19
    shows force of power, 186:1
    snatched with unruly hand, 175:22
Sceptered, in s. pall sweeping by, 251:19
    isle, 176:24
    mercy above s. sway, 186:1
    Moloch s. king, 256:7
    what avails the s. race, 383:25
Schedule no more than half time, 757:16
Scheldt, lazy S. or wandering Po, 321:11
Scheme, Sorry S. of Things, 442:9
    yields no revenue, 323:20
Schemes, best laid s., 356:6
Scholar among rakes, 420:1
    he was a s., 226:12
    is delegated intellect Man Thinking,
      425:26
    more in soldier than s., 208:18
    showed him gentleman an' s., 356:14
    ten o'clock s., 896:14
    thou art a s., 196:11
Scholar's, courtier's soldier's s., 200:2
    ills s. life assail, 306:16
Scholars, danger makes apt s., 386:2
    dispute and case still before courts, 98:19
    God of Abraham not s., 270:2
    land of s., 322:3
    make mayors but not s., 235:4
    Pythagoras said to his s., 234:15
Schön, so hold und s. und rein, 415:n2
School, anyone been to English public s., 736:6
    corrupted youth in erecting s., 170:17
    creeping like snail to s., 194:25
    experience keeps dear s., 302:23
    in joyful s. days, 383:3
    in my s.-days, 184:11
    in which nothing harsh, 117:1
    Intelligence make it a soul, 413:15
    leave religion to private s., 498:7
    of Stratford atte Bowe, 133:14
    tales out of s., 147:13
    threadbare saint in wisdom's s., 228:3
    three little maids from s., 527:12
    time the s. in which we learn, 772:1
    to s. not to travel, 165:28
    toward s. with heavy looks, 180:12
    we left s., 783:10
Schoolboy, every s. knows it, 264:33
    whining s. with satchel, 194:25
Schoolboy's tale, 395:6
Schoolboys, as s. from books, 180:12
School-children, Negro s., 788:2
School-divine, God the Father a s., 296:13
Schoolgirl, pert as s. can be, 527:12
Schooling, in and outdoor s., 625:1
Schoolman's subtle art, 296:3
Schoolmaster, becoming a s. sir, 736:5
    no man can serve ten years as s., 531:9
Schoolmasters, bankers s. clergymen, 591:19
    father more than hundred s., 244:15
Schools, hundred s. of thought contend,
    698:13
    jargon of the s., 283:10
    knowledge never learned of s., 438:8

Schools (continued)
    let us reform s., 484:13
    maze of s., 292:10
    nurseries of vice, 304:15
    old maxim in the s., 284:21
Schooner Hesperus, 436:8
    ladder close to s., 825:7
Schweigen, darüber muss man s., 685:n3
    ist golden, 406:23
Science achieve perfect knowledge, 494:6
    advance in s. audacity of imagination, 572:17
    aim of exact s., 513:1
    and applications together, 499:2
    and opinion, 71:3
    and technology multiply, 826:3
    and technology unite humanity, 809:3
    applied s. not exist, 499:2
    art and s. in particulars, 354:13
    astrology disease not s., 124:12
    built with facts, 558:8
    challenge of rootless s., 717:8
    cloud obscure s., 338:15
    communication of truth, 378:19
    cookery a noble s., 234:16
    countenance of all S., 369:3
    cradle of every s., 502:2
    Dismal S., 408:6
    dissociate language from s., 338:22
    experimentation active s., 468:11
    fair S. frowned not, 316:6
    falsely so called, 44:38
    God whom s. recognizes, 542:2
    great achievements of s., 836:5
    great tragedy of S., 502:8
    in high art and pure s., 723:12
    is no illusion, 563:14
    law a hocus-pocus s., 300:12
    mysterious is source of art and s., 637:8
    natural s. involves three things, 338:22
    not safe for S. to divulge causes, 228:2
    numerical precision soul of S., 579:7
    object of s. truth, 378:19
    observation passive s., 468:11
    of life superb hall, 468:12
    of Nature, 277:28
    only occupation left to men of s., 513:2
    out of olde bokes newe s., 132:8
    physical s. not console me, 269:8
    poem opposed to works of s., 379:10
    poetry antithesis to s., 378:19
    politics is not exact s., 470:7
    products of art and s., 693:4
    promote progress of s., 698:13
    pronouncements of history or s., 757:15
    proud S., 294:20
    refinement of everyday thinking, 637:12
    scarcely advanced to s., 501:11
    shalt not commit a social s., 749:15
    this or that problem never solved by s.,
      440:9
    thought to aim at some good, 78:3
    treating Psychology like natural s., 541:10
    true s. teaches doubt, 586:1
    typical triumph of modern s., 736:10
    waves of s. beat in vain, 490:15
    which draws conclusions, 447:7
    without conscience ruin, 145:10
Science fiction is apocalyptic literature, 826:2

Sciences, experience Mother of S., 156:12
    mathematical s. founded, 513:1
    mathematics queen of s., 385:3
    mechanics paradise of mathematical s.,
      140:12
Scientia potestas est, 164:8
Scientific, ideals altars to unknown gods,
    540:18
    innovation rarely converts opponents,
     570:10
    Jesus most s. man, 493:5
    method by which unconscious studied,
     563:12
    method of s. investigation, 502:3
    mind asks right questions, 754:3
    plunges into s. questions, 502:14
    theory cannot yet render, 873:14
Scientific-democratic, intellectual freedom s.
    approach, 797:5
Scientist does not study nature because useful,
    558:12
    independent s., 705:1
    wiser not to withhold, 343:25
Scientists at other pole, 743:11
    collectors classifiers tidiers-up, 780:4
    during revolutions s. see, 799:5
    illiteracy of s., 743:12
    understandable by everyone not just s.,
     854:3
Scintillant in cloudless days, 659:1
Scissors, two halves of pair of s., 375:n1
    upper or under blade of s., 543:12
Scoff, fools who came to s., 322:26
Scolded, nobody ever s. him, 598:7
Scooped, Tankards s. in Pearl, 508:8
Scope had not been so short, 226:n1
    of my opinion, 196:12
    this man's art that man's s., 221:6
    within s. of constitution, 349:16
Score, from seventy springs a s., 574:11
    give me a kiss and to that a s., 241:3
    no books but s. and tally, 170:17
Scored, our days are s. against us, 107:13
Scorer, One Great S., 646:4
Scorn, bright creatures not one, 372:17
    child of s., 605:20
    dangers make us s., 358:7
    delights, 253:6
    figure for time of s., 210:3
    folks s. you too, 708:8
    foul s. that prince invade, 151:7
    her own image, 200:8
    laugh a siege to s., 217:21
    laugh to s. power of man, 216:32
    looks beautiful, 205:15
    mine ever name of s., 455:16
    not the sonnet, 372:16
    not thing to laugh to s., 195:31
    of mankind down centuries, 620:6
    sound of public s., 259:19
    to change state with kings, 221:7
    to take offense, 292:20
    under solemn fillet saw s., 425:1
    upright man laughed to s., 13:24
Scorned his spirit, 191:30
    woman s., 287:2
Scorner, contemner and s. of others, 238:23
    reprove not a s., 20:8

Scornful, most bitter is s. jest, 306:7
    sitteth in the seat of the s., 14:40
    yet jealous eyes, 295:13
Scorning base degrees, 191:36
Scorns, whips and s. of time, 199:21
Scorpion, under every stone a s., 73:*n3*
Scorpions, ants centipedes and s., 635:12
    I will chastise with s., 11:37
    whips and scorpions, 341:6
Scotch, bourbon s. and beer, 777:18
    drink s. whiskey all night long, 868:8
Scotched, we have s. the snake, 216:10
Scotchman, beggarly S., 308:19
    if caught young, 309:21
    noblest prospect S. sees, 309:3
Scotia's grandeur springs, 356:10
Scotland, be in S. before ye, 884:13
    in S. oats supports people, 307:4
Scotland's, left fair S. strand, 357:10
Scots, gude S. lords, 889:16
    kills six or seven dozen S., 182:17
    lords at his feet, 889:17
    wha hae wi' Wallace bled, 358:16
Scott, beam us up Mr. S., 888:*n8*
    no eminent writer not even S., 565:15
Scottsboro, I am the S. boys, 812:10
Scotty, beam me up S., 888:19
Scoundrel, A is a s., 645:17
    and coward, 308:19
    hypocrite flatterer, 354:13
    man the s., 492:6
    patriotism last refuge of s., 310:4
Scoundrels, healthy hatred of s., 408:7
    never again think tramps drunken s., 735:5
    often the refuge of s., 852:3
    talk about future are s., 700:19
Scoured with perpetual motion, 187:35
Scourge laid upon your hate, 181:16
    mighty s. of war, 447:2
    of God, 168:3
    of small cords, 39:6
    of war, 661:16
Scourged to his dungeon, 405:13
Scout, blabbing eastern s., 252:10
    flout 'em and s. 'em, 224:31
Scouts, chauffered Cub S., 796:7
Scouts' motto is founded on my initials, 566:20
Scramble, great s. and big divide, 537:7
Scrambling to the shore, 516:3
Scrap, worn out before on s. heap, 565:3
Scrape cable, 470:13
Scraping, Death's ironic s., 641:6
Scraps, on s. of learning dote, 290:13
    stolen the s., 174:26
Scratch it with a hoe, 507:14
    lover find foe, 699:12
Scratched, expect to be s., 156:17
    head kept thinking, 605:21
    man whom Fortune s., 206:8
    out both eyes, 897:6
Scratching at the floor, 578:19
Scrawls, few hundhred s., 660:5
Scrawny cry was a chorister, 642:17
Scream, better to s., 722:15
    laughter note short of s. of fear, 726:10
    not a shriek not a s., 517:4
    suddenly s. pierced the air, 800:9
Screamed, Mrs. Hutchinson s., 782:3

Screaming, buttons stamped with s. eagle, 709:14
    night away, 891:8
Screams message to outside world, 722:15
    of horror rend, 293:12
Screeches, mouthful of s. like torn tin, 827:14
Screen, world vast s. of snow, 683:5
Screw, atomic bomb turn of s., 739:6
    your courage, 215:6
Scribble scribble scribble, 335:20
    we all s. poetry, 98:22
Scribbled, parchment s. o'er undo a man, 170:15
Scribbling, damned mob of s. women, 431:22
    seriously s. to excite laughter, 522:1
Scribes and Pharisees, 35:15
Scrip and scrippage, 195:9
    nor s. nor shoes, 37:31
    of joy immortal diet, 159:10
Scrippage, scrip and s., 195:9
Script, never all in the s., 765:9
    next thing is get good s., 711:16
Scripture, devil can cite S., 184:26
    dream is a s., 831:13
    moveth us, 48:1
Scriptures, let us look at the s., 238:9
    mighty in S., 40:37
    search S., 39:15
Scrolls, flows in s. of toga, 833:5
Scrollwork, cut that s. or ornament out, 722:7
Scrooge, bah said S. humbug, 465:6
    covetous old sinner, 465:5
    Ghost of Christmas Yet to Come said S., 465:13
Scrub kitchen pavement, 591:18
Scrunch or be scrunched, 466:31
Scrunched, scrunch or be s., 466:31
Scruple, some craven s., 201:20
Scrutamini scripturas, 238:9
Scud, low s. slick street, 821:2
Scullion, away you s., 188:2
Sculptor well those passions read, 401:13
Sculpture, like graveyard marble s., 624:12
Scum of the earth, 366:10
    Okie means s., 733:3
    wash s. off the streets, 863:12
Scurvy politician, 212:31
'Scuse me while I kiss the sky, 854:5
Scutcheon, blot in thy s., 158:2
    honor a mere s., 183:25
Scuttlefish, disputants like s., 288:16
    rejoice with S., 318:12
Scuttling across floors of seas, 675:1
Scylla guards right side, 185:*n1*
    to port, 185:*n1*
    when I shun S., 185:25
Scythe, iron s. in grass, 703:12
    work the s. of time, 365:15
Scythian, Barbarian S. bond nor free, 44:12
Sea, all our s. our own, 249:21
    all returns to s., 750:1
    all the rivers run into the s., 22:22
    all went to s., 896:2
    alone on wide wide s., 376:14
    as long as rivers run to s., 94:7
    as near by s. as by land, 154:3
    as the sand by the s., 11:27
    Atlanta to the s., 517:13

Sea *(continued)*
    bark is on s., 397:13
    bathed in Poem of S., 558:18
    beetles o'er base into s., 198:1
    being smooth, 203:4
    best in chair before fire, 617:14
    better cast into s., 38:19
    beyond genius of s., 641:8
    born across the s., 481:2
    bottom of s. is cruel, 720:1
    bound with triumphant s., 176:25
    bred to the s., 401:2
    by the deep s., 396:16
    changed Egdon remained, 535:16
    cold gray stones O S., 452:15
    creation of Omnipotence, 617:15
    crept into bosom of the s., 170:10
    dance like wave of s., 591:14
    deep s. swell, 676:14
    delicate algae and s. anemone, 679:4
    demons down under s., 449:23
    depths congealed in heart of s., 8:7
    desert of the s., 25:26
    do you not hear s., 412:*n2*
    dolphin-torn s., 595:13
    dragon that is in the s., 26:6
    earth fire s. air, 537:10
    eastward to the s., 588:1
    edge of s. strange beautiful place, 750:2
    empty tigers or roaring s., 181:9
    ever renewing s., 612:6
    eyes opened to the s., 761:8
    far-heard whisper o'er the s., 376:9
    Father of Waters unvexed to s., 446:3
    firm-footed by s., 419:1
    fishes of the s. shall declare, 13:25
    from s. to shining s., 572:5
    frozen s. inside us, 655:10
    ghost of garden fronts s., 530:25
    go down to the s. in ships, 18:14
    God a s. of infinite substance, 122:2
    goes to s. for nothing, 230:10
    gone with the sun, 559:5
    grasped eastern and western s., 325:20
    great and wide s., 18:11
    great shroud of s. rolled on, 483:9
    green isle in s., 448:6
    grew civil at her song, 178:15
    half-held by night, 486:6
    has many voices, 679:4
    hast thou entered into the springs of the s., 14:21
    he that commands s. is at liberty, 166:16
    herd ran into s., 36:32
    hold helm when s. calm, 100:6
    houses all gone under s., 678:17
    how many strawberries in s., 893:1
    hurt not the s., 46:34
    I beneath a rougher s., 327:10
    if we gang to s. master, 889:15
    in calm s. every man pilot, 271:1
    in flat s. sunk, 252:17
    in peril on the s., 503:1
    influence of s. power, 537:5
    into the s. upon dry ground, 8:3
    iridescent and dark, 767:6
    is both friend and enemy, 729:7
    is calm tonight, 496:16

Securely founded, 343:10
Security against future violations, 306:4
    culture moment of s., 657:8
    for average man, 652:5
    for the future, 306:*n*1
    maintain peace and s., 661:16
    militia necessary to s. of free State, 340:2
    of all countries connected, 647:9
    of people, 320:8
    order s. and peace, 647:9
    public strength individual s., 349:3
    system of general s., 653:16
    to democracies against despots, 345:*n*4
Sed haec prius fuere, 91:*n*3
Sedate, ignorance s., 306:19
Sedated, I wanna be s., 869:12
Sedge withered from lake, 412:2
Seductive, voice of sea is s., 556:18
Sedulously cultivate free speech, 621:8
See a fine picture, 343:1
    all could s. was sky water birds, 761:2
    all we s. or seem, 447:8
    and be seen, 102:3
    bachelor of threescore again, 190:18
    best not to s. beams of sun, 59:23
    blind now I s., 39:28
    bosom I must not s., 267:15
    both things to eat and things to s., 555:11
    but not observe, 573:7
    can I s. another's woe, 351:8
    cannot s. as plainly as others, 440:6
    change we think we s., 622:16
    cherry hung with snow, 574:11
    church by daylight, 190:24
    dagger I s. before me, 215:13
    direction which thou canst not s., 294:23
    dwarf on giant s. farther, 234:9
    eye begins to s., 756:11
    eye to eye, 27:4
    eyes and s. not, 27:25
    eyes have they but s. not, 18:22
    eyes weep but never s., 383:26
    from where I stood, 695:5
    full plain I s., 377:2
    go and s. for ourselves, 761:9
    God made and eaten, 460:22
    God whom we s. not is, 531:3
    gold that I never s., 575:5
    have thee not yet s. thee still, 215:13
    hear read or understand, 314:9
    Heaven's glories shine, 476:14
    here it is, 412:1
    here shall he s. no enemy, 194:11
    how she leans her cheek, 180:1
    how they run, 892:10
    how world goes, 212:29
    how world wags, 194:15
    how yond justice rails, 212:29
    I don't s. said Caterpillar, 514:3
    I know it when I s. it, 780:15
    I s. dead people, 880:1
    I s. it all perfectly, 469:3
    I s. not feel how beautiful, 378:6
    I s. only the ideal, 634:2
    I s. what I eat, 514:13
    I'll s. you again, 719:13
    image of what we actually s., 533:15
    in all things thee to s., 243:9

See *(continued)*
    in my flesh shall I s. God, 13:39
    in small proportions beauties s., 233:8
    into life of things, 368:9
    it clearly in the idea, 641:20
    it lap the Miles, 509:10
    it shining plain, 575:6
    it yet remains to s., 511:9
    kings have desired to s., 37:35
    let mine eyes not s., 204:12
    lofty towers I s. down-rased, 221:18
    little Tippler, 508:10
    lovers cannot s. follies, 185:1
    me feel me, 861:16
    me safe up, 143:9
    Mediterraneans s. clearly, 657:7
    meet and not s. its head, 57:7
    more ye s. better like it, 600:9
    never s. nor know nor miss me, 651:3
    never s. tree at all, 732:8
    no evil, 882:7
    no man s. me more, 225:23
    none should s. salvation, 186:1
    none so blind as not s., 282:18
    not my love to s., 161:1
    not s. me stopping here, 623:6
    not the bottom of it, 203:27
    not worth going to s., 310:25
    O can't you s. it, 704:14
    oh say can you s., 386:19
    one mountain and see all, 235:6
    one-third of nation ill-housed, 652:12
    only their own shadows, 75:11
    only with heart one can s., 726:18
    other whole against sky, 631:15
    oursels as ithers see us, 356:16
    people refuse to s. me, 774:8
    really do not s. signal, 355:9
    sad sights moves, 172:37
    see their mark, 243:8
    seem to s. things thou dost not, 212:31
    she stirs, 436:22
    Shelley plain, 461:8
    smile his work to s., 353:2
    so much nor live so long, 213:16
    sons what things you are, 188:21
    sun with ignorant eye, 641:20
    taste and s. that the Lord is good, 16:6
    the conquering hero, 301:13
    the Way of Heaven, 57:16
    there shall no man s. me, 8:21
    they bark at me, 212:11
    they shall s. God, 32:14
    things as they are, 308:7
    things seen I s. no more, 370:13
    things through his eyes, 707:11
    think I shall never s., 667:13, 732:8
    those things ye see, 37:35
    thou canst not s. my face, 8:21
    through glass darkly, 42:29
    to s. her was to love her, 357:9
    Veil through which not s., 441:20
    was blind but now I s., 320:13
    we are as much as we s., 472:19
    what a rent, 192:34
    what can not s. over is infinite, 406:16
    what I say, 572:4
    what I see, 200:5

See *(continued)*
    what s. elsewhere not here, 137:6
    what you s. is what you s., 842:6
    whatever you s. is Jupiter, 106:16
    whatsoever I shall s. or hear, 70:14
    where Christ's blood streams, 169:4
    where it flies, 168:21
    where she comes apparelled like spring,
      220:9
    Winter comes, 300:14
    with half an eye, 157:31
    with not through the eye, 354:17
    world in grain of sand, 353:14
    you s. things and say Why, 565:25
    you s. what I am, 774:15
    young men shall s. visions, 28:41
    your good works, 32:16
Seed, bearing precious s., 19:3
    blood of Christians is s., 113:4
    blood of martyrs s. of Church, 113:*n*4
    broadcast catch somewhere, 457:8
    de first en last s. de beginnin, 713:12
    enmity between thy s. and her s., 5:23
    ground more malign with bad s., 129:26
    groweth s., 880:5
    heaven like to mustard s., 34:18
    money the s. of money, 312:14
    nor his s. begging bread, 16:11
    searching to rediscover first s., 727:2
    sow thy s. in the morning, 23:28
    wonder the s. of knowledge, 164:9
    work is s. sown, 406:10
Seeds in dry pod tick, 605:5
    of godlike power, 494:11
    of patriots and heroes, 321:*n*2
    of time, 214:5
    plant s. watch renewal, 507:14
    some s. fell by way side, 34:14
    sowing s. crooked in furrow, 815:5
    treason sows secret s., 125:7
Seedtime and harvest, 6:23
    fair s. had my soul, 368:13
    regret my s., 787:10
Seeing, adds precious s. to the eye, 174:22
    eye is not satisfied with s., 22:23
    eyes made for s., 424:10
    fatality of s. too well, 642:10
    hearing ear s. eye, 21:11
    individual way of s., 542:5
    my head is worth s., 359:6
    the root of the matter, 13:40
    understands without s., 57:16
    what everybody seen nobody thought,
      700:3
    with fresh eyes, 825:11
    worth s. not going to see, 310:25
Seek all day ere you find them, 184:10
    and adore them, 545:14
    and ye shall find, 33:16
    beauteous eye of heaven to garnish, 175:24
    by trophies and dead things, 237:11
    carry with us wonders we s., 248:5
    empty world again, 476:12
    flee from me that did me s., 149:4
    for Eldorado, 449:19
    for the lost mind, 80:4
    for truth in groves of Academe, 98:12
    fortunes further than home, 173:8

Seek *(continued)*
    going to s. grand perhaps, 146:7
    Heaven itself in our folly, 96:3
    I shall not s. nomination, 753:17
    it in My arms, 577:2
    judgment, 24:32
    knock breathe and s. to mend, 230:26
    labored for them that s. learning, 31:20
    never s. to tell thy love, 352:3
    newer world, 451:18
    no farther s. his merits, 316:8
    not life of immortals, 63:29
    not out things that are too hard, 30:13
    not s. for kind relief, 351:8
    out soldier's grave, 399:17
    peace and pursue it, 16:7
    poets that lasting marble s., 249:26
    some dew drops here, 178:11
    that which thou dost s., 404:2
    their meat from God, 18:11
    they s. a sign, 38:2
    those that s. me early, 20:6
    to bring largest good, 541:16
    to s. her through the world, 257:17
    to strive s. find, 451:19
    we s. him here we s. him there, 590:10
    we s. no wider war, 753:14
    where s. is find, 318:9
    why s. living among dead, 38:40
    with fear and trembling, 541:16
    world was not to s. me, 311:10
    ye first the kingdom of God, 33:10
Seekest thou great things, 28:8
Seeketh, love never s. own, 137:11
    love s. not itself to please, 352:12
    love s. self to please, 352:13
Seeking bubble reputation, 194:25
    light s. light, 173:41
    may be found by s., 86:1
    symbolical language, 378:17
    the food he eats, 194:13
    unperplexed s. find Him, 461:15
    what leopard was s., 721:16
    whom he may devour, 46:3
    with the soul, 343:4
Seeks abroad may find, 411:7
    man s. for what is remote, 79:20
    serves and s. for gain, 211:18
    Wisdom's self oft s., 252:17
    with the sword repose, 268:7
Seeling, come s. night, 216:13
Seem a saint when most play devil, 171:25
    all uses of this world, 196:29
    all we see or s., 447:8
    earth to me did s., 370:13
    finale of s., 640:18
    grow to what they s., 322:1
    men should be what they s., 208:36
    not always what they s., 325:17
    not to s. but be best, 62:26
    things not always what they s., 103:5
    things not what they s., 436:4
    things seldom what s., 526:2
    though I die old, 596:7
    to fly it, 232:14
    to see things thou dost not, 212:31
Seemed, absence s. my flame to qualify, 222:11
    but a few days, 6:44

Seemed *(continued)*
    part of the landscape, 582:14
    scarce s. there to be, 377:4
    that which once s. he, 380:8
    they s. to die, 29:34
    to me like king, 663:7
Seeming and savor all winter, 223:25
    beguile by s. otherwise, 208:15
Seemly for young man to lie mangled, 52:13
Seems, I know not s., 196:26
    madam Nay it is, 196:26
    no bigger than his head, 212:24
    she hangs on cheek of night, 179:28
    such s. your beauty still, 222:8
    to shake the spheres, 274:15
Seen, after they've s. Paree, 664:1
    artist records more than s., 613:11
    best of our time, 211:2
    better days, 194:23, 213:26
    better days who has not, 399:12
    ear of man hath not s., 179:4
    ere I had s. that day, 197:7
    everything s. must become poem, 631:13
    everywhere felt but never s., 493:18
    evidence of things not s., 45:11
    eye hath not s., 42:6
    first came the s., 665:13
    future and it works, 598:*n*2
    hungry ocean gain advantage, 221:18
    I have s. better faces, 211:14
    I have s. further, 279:11
    I have s. God face to face, 7:4
    I have s. the sunset, 559:1
    I have s. the wicked in great power, 16:12
    known me had he s. me, 472:3
    moment of greatness flicker, 675:3
    nature of things s. only once, 815:10
    no man hath s. God, 38:49
    not s. as others saw, 447:10
    not s. the righteous forsaken, 16:11
    not s. yet believed, 40:13
    nothing yet, 156:25
    on our way, 764:15
    one city slum seen all, 789:5
    pin faith in things not s., 112:23
    promised land, 823:16
    starry archipelagoes, 559:3
    thee oft amid store, 411:7
    things not s. eternal, 43:14
    things s. are temporal, 43:14
    to be hated needs but be s., 295:2
    too early s. unknown, 179:29
    touch scarcely felt or s., 297:9
    war hate war, 652:9
    we have not s. him since, 603:7
    what I have seen, 200:5
Seer is a sayer, 426:9
    must make oneself a s., 558:14
    poet makes himself a s., 558:14
Sees, care not who s. your back, 182:20
    doubts from what he s., 354:5
    God who made him s., 590:5
    into bottom of my grief, 181:4
    it and does it, 461:15
    man control wind, 495:6
    Me in all, 84:12
    nature s. all her sons at play, 495:6
    neither hears nor s., 369:8

Sees *(continued)*
    never s. a whole, 495:2
    perceive differently than one s., 812:8
    Present Past Future s., 352:10
    some morning unaware, 460:18
    sun which s. all things, 51:4
    things as they are, 540:6
Seesaw Margery Daw, 893:19
Seest, what thou s. write, 46:15
Seeth, Lord s. not as man s., 10:43
    now mine eye s. thee, 14:38
Seethe a thousand men in troubles, 409:17
Segregated, rigidly s. precincts, 782:13
Segregation now segregation tomorrow, 794:2
Seine, torn s. shattered lobsterpot, 679:4
    under Pont Mirabeau flows S., 643:18
Seize fate by the throat, 366:16
    good fortune, 344:16
    maybe person next to you, 874:6
    ruin s. thee, 316:14
    the day, 96:11
    the flower, 358:6
    what hand dare s. fire, 353:1
Seized, love s. me so strongly, 128:16
Seizures, unreasonable searches and s., 340:3
Seldom he smiles, 191:30
Selection, Natural S., 439:13
    natural s., 490:7
Selects, artist observes s. guesses, 578:4
    Soul s. her own Society, 508:16
Self, applause from none but s., 491:21
    concentered all in s., 373:3
    earthly city formed by love of s., 116:19
    for my single s., 191:24
    friend is a second s., 88:14
    his s. and the sun were one, 642:16
    is hateful, 269:26
    is honey of all beings, 50:2
    love seeketh s. to please, 352:13
    not mine but ours, 810:17
    nothing greater than one's s., 486:17
    One's-S. I sing, 485:12
    product of a different s., 611:9
    swear by thy gracious s., 180:9
    through eyes of others, 602:3
    to thine own s. be true, 197:24
    toll me back from thee to my sole s.,
        410:11
    total of all he can call his, 541:4
    try to speak hidden s., 495:12
    was not the same, 202:35
    what jailer inexorable as s., 431:15
Self-affrighting, learns it is s., 593:18
Self-appeasing, learns it is s., 593:18
Self-appointed inspector of snowstorms, 473:1
Self-balanced, O to be s. for contingencies,
    485:13
Self-blinding, nothing so s., 707:11
Self-canceling, democracy s., 407:10
Self-circling energies, 378:24
Self-complacency is pleasure, 276:7
Self-conceit, philosophy to get rid of s., 109:3
Self-conscious, not make us s., 672:1
Self-constituted, Americans first s. People,
    695:4
Self-contained, placid and s., 486:14
Self-control, self-knowledge s., 450:14
    which enhances self-respect, 733:16

Senses *(continued)*
  lull my s., 780:1
  mistake to suppose only five s., 500:10
  our gentle s., 214:21
  steep s. in forgetfulness, 188:9
Sensibilities, do double dose as s. decline,
    458:15
Sensibility, dissociation of s., 676:4
  inexhaustible s., 545:7
  soil of subject, 544:16
Sensible and conscientious men, 309:*n*1
  this s. warm motion, 206:38
  to feeling as to sight, 215:13
Sensitive, gentle s. mind, 593:6
Sensitivity, chief area of s., 760:4
Sensual, caught in s. music, 594:1
  lust a tempest, 492:8
  this wisdom is s., 45:29
  turbulent fleshy s. eating drinking, 486:7
Sensuality, intellectual passion drives out s.,
    140:3
Sensuous, simple s. and passionate, 254:5
Sent, him that s. me, 39:27
  thee late a rosy wreath, 232:17
  to my account, 198:12
  to spy out the land, 9:3
Sentence, death s. of Versailles, 684:16
  first true simple declarative s., 722:7
  first verdict afterwards, 515:8
  full of high s., 675:4
  German dives into s., 523:14
  hungry judges s. sign, 293:9
  I catch every s., 578:7
  my s. is for open war, 256:9
  no s. of banishment, 764:16
  no unnecessary words, 606:3
  not understand words apart from s.,
    506:17
  originator of good s., 429:1
  single s. for modern man, 770:9
  structure of British s., 619:2
  true in all times, 444:15
  waiting s. in bull pen, 787:10
Sentenced, author sentenced to death, 725:14
Sentences, paragraph no unnecessary s., 606:3
  say in ten s. what others in book, 548:25
  shall quips and s. awe, 190:36
  some s. release poison after years, 740:9
Sententiae, quot homines tot s., 86:*n*6
Sententious, laconic or s. type, 607:2
Sentest, thou s. forth thy wrath, 8:7
Sentient, boil a s. creature alive, 878:3
Sentiment and alliteration, 520:15
  in s. public crude, 392:3
  living s. and dying s., 390:4
  read Richardson for s., 309:19
Sentimental, aspect of American s. life,
    784:10
  carry body for s. value, 750:10
Sentimentalist, no s. no stander above, 486:7
Sentimentality, piece of idle s., 435:5
Sentiments, duration of great s., 548:6
  precluded from offering s., 328:10
  them's my s., 459:4
  to which bosom echo, 307:19
  weigh less than action, 482:11
  with noble s. bad literature, 604:10
Sentinels almost receive, 189:18

Sentry are you there, 484:4
  at this door England stands s., 535:7
  stands a winged s., 268:15
Separate and equal station, 336:1
  and unequal, 753:18
  but equal, 692:4
  church and State s., 498:7
  dying ember, 449:4
  educational facilities unequal, 692:4
  from forces to repeat No, 549:12
  he shall s. them, 35:29
  like marbles touching but s., 533:11
  peace, 721:2
  people s. rigidly alone, 533:11
  quite quite s., 507:6
  simple s. person, 485:12
  to s. because of race, 692:4
  us from love of Christ, 41:25
Separated by only six people, 844:9
  infinite chaos which s. us, 269:17
Separately, hang together or hang s., 303:11
Separateness of all things, 756:3
Separateth, he that repeateth a matter s. friends,
    20:40
Separation between Church and State, 337:13
  causes which impel s., 336:1
  fear of s. is all that unites, 668:9
  not fighting for s., 808:17
  prepare definitely for s., 380:12
  six degrees of s., 844:9
  yield who will to s., 624:1
September 11 2001 thousands of, 853:13
  from frosted S. to sightless realm, 663:22
  morn, 438:11
  offends the S. night, 748:16
  thirty days hath S., 149:12
  when you reach S., 672:15
  within bosom S., 881:11
Sepulcher, night dome of vast s., 402:11
  no man knoweth of his s., 9:34
  there by the sea, 449:24
  whole earth s. of famous men, 72:4
Sepulchers, grandest of all s., 72:4
  shrouds and s. delight, 409:4
  whited s., 35:17
Sequel, unto God is the s., 119:4
Sequence, natural s. of unnatural beginning,
    382:22
  of phenomena, 338:22
Sequestered nooks, 437:20
  vale of life, 316:3
Seraphically, song s. free, 505:16
Seraphim, bright s. in burning row, 253:18
Seraphims, above it stood the s., 25:8
Seraphs swing snowy Hats, 508:10
  winged s. of Heaven, 449:22
Sere, fallen into the s., 217:18
  leaf red and s., 373:5
  leaves crisped and s., 449:14
  meadows brown and s., 406:2
  with ivy never s., 252:29
Serendipity, now do you understand s., 317:2
Serene before direst death, 500:5
  I fold my hands, 528:13
  mind s. for contemplation, 287:*n*3
  pure s., 408:17
  purest ray s., 315:23
  see with eye s., 371:7

Serene *(continued)*
  true friendship never s., 270:13
Serenely eternity waits at crossway of stars,
    718:14
  full epicure would say, 375:9
Serenity, gentleness of spirit s. of mind, 245:*n*2
  grace to accept with s., 695:20
  state of wonder and s., 831:14
  steady and perpetual s., 288:15
  sweet s. of books, 437:20
  usual querulous s., 382:10
Serf, labor as another's s., 53:18
  patrician plebeian lord and s., 478:8
Serfdom, abolish s. from above, 476:3
  African not accept s. forever, 690:9
Serfs, spending lives like s., 475:12
  vassals and s., 414:4
Sergeant, back to Army again s., 588:14
  Color-S. said, 587:14
  this fell s. death, 202:28
Serious and alarming consequences, 328:10
  and the smirk, 464:16
  annuity is a s. business, 382:1
  assume that it's s., 865:15
  audience takes him s., 640:7
  Cervantes' s. air, 296:24
  comedian takes himself s., 640:7
  companions few in s. business, 59:19
  don't take life s., 697:8
  everything one does with s. face, 335:12
  I am a very s. woman, 794:3
  imitation of action that is s., 79:3
  insisted always on being s., 69:11
  marriage damnably s. business, 698:14
  no human thing of s. importance, 75:24
  nothing s. in mortality, 215:30
  one who is s. all day, 3:6
  philosophical problem, 769:15
  strenuous and s., 680:12
  war too s. for military, 348:11
Sermon, calls it a s., 374:22
  good honest painful s., 277:5
  in the suicide, 837:14
  perhaps turn out a s., 356:18
  verse find who s. flies, 242:6
  whole of her s., 638:10
Sermons and soda water, 398:10
  in stones, 193:37
  logic and s. never convince, 486:12
  no s. in stones, 528:18
Serpent, be the s. under 't, 214:20
  beguiled me, 5:22
  biteth like a s., 21:30
  infernal s. whose guile, 255:6
  Leviathan that crooked s., 26:6
  more s. than dove, 168:10
  of old Nile, 218:13
  old s. called Devil, 47:2
  rod shall become a s., 7:33
  sharpened their tongues like a s., 19:16
  sting thee twice, 185:29
  subtlest beast, 259:7
  was more subtile, 5:18
  way of a s. upon a rock, 22:14
Serpent's egg, 192:1
  sharper than s. tooth, 211:11
Serpents, all the s. bite, 4:6
  be wise as s., 34:1

Serpents *(continued)*
    envious, 230:21
    plays with the s., 794:6
    rods became s., 7:34
    there's no pleasing them, 514:7
Servant, accuse not a s. unto his master, 22:13
    borrower is s. to the lender, 21:18
    good and faithful s., 35:26
    he shall be my s., 7:14
    hear what s. girls said, 611:13
    in love lord in marriage, 136:7
    is thy s. a dog, 12:15
    lettest thy s. depart, 37:19
    not above lord, 34:3
    of God well done, 258:23
    of Living God, 318:14
    prince first s. of state, 312:7
    thy s. heareth, 10:35
    unprofitable s., 35:28
    virtues expected of s., 327:14
    with this clause, 243:10
Servants, desires and petitions of thy s., 48:17
    fire best of s., 407:25
    frantic among thy s., 30:19
    gods s. of human interest, 584:12
    of the machine, 753:2
    reveal Himself to His s., 254:11
Servants', never equality in s. hall, 577:9
Servare modum, 106:*n*9
Serve, also s. who only stand, 254:22
    and obey passions, 311:21
    as Thou deservest, 144:16
    as we love we s., 556:1
    because we freely love, 258:18
    cannot s. God and mammon, 33:5
    country and thy kind, 519:9
    employ body to s., 92:2
    faithfully to s. State, 246:15
    future hour, 372:11
    how can you s. ghosts, 61:7
    if elected I will not s., 490:*n*1
    in heaven, 255:15
    long apprenticehood, 176:15
    my nation ruin another, 297:15
    no man can s, two masters, 33:5
    not s. God if devil bid, 207:28
    the Lord with gladness, 18:3
    they also s., 254:22
    'tis enough 'twill s., 180:28
    whom should we s., 341:1
Served, first come first s., 125:*n*6
    God with half zeal, 226:6
    human liberty, 595:8
    my time in hell, 888:1
    no private end, 294:9
    public will be s., 280:13
    youth will be s., 423:8
Serves it in office of a wall, 176:24
    sit which s. and seeks for gain, 211:18
    take current when it s., 193:14
Serveth not another's will, 227:9
Service beyond all recompense, 249:18
    desert in s., 203:25
    do a friend s., 65:7
    done the state some s., 210:20
    essential s. to country, 285:1
    ful weel soong s. dyvyne, 133:14
    greater than the god, 203:13

Service *(continued)*
    greatest s. or greatest injury, 74:17
    high and anthems clear, 251:23
    in purer lives s., 438:18
    injustice sometimes s. to public, 339:10
    is perfect freedom, 48:13
    lay out ourselves in s. of mankind, 341:1
    long and faithful s., 468:19
    of his prince, 60:16
    of vast meretricious beauty, 710:4
    pressed into s., 622:17
    riches poverty and use of s., 224:19
    shrink from s. of country, 333:6
    small s. is true s., 372:17
    weary and old with s., 225:25
    yeoman's s., 202:25
Serviceable, fool be made s., 568:1
    substitute for masturbation, 626:9
Services, give your s. for nothing, 70:18
Servile, inciters of s. insurrection, 519:10
    to all skyey influences, 206:33
Servility, savage s. slides by, 788:3
Serving, cumbered with s., 37:39
    duly and daily s. him, 318:14
Servingmen, six honest s., 589:16
Servitors, airy s., 253:23
Servitude, base laws of s. began, 272:9
    beast brought up in s., 142:8
    consequence of crime, 345:7
    previous condition of s., 340:9
Sesame, open s., 883:8
Sesquipedalia verba, 98:*n*7
Session, court in perpetual s., 656:1
Sessions of sweet silent thought, 221:8
Set about with fever-trees, 589:17
    born to s. it right, 198:22
    candle in the sun, 235:16
    cause above renown, 582:8
    children's teeth s. on edge, 28:6
    down aught in malice, 210:20
    exact wealth of states, 183:11
    forth for somewhere, 622:21
    god seem to s. his seal, 201:5
    gray life, 451:9
    have s. before you life and death, 9:29
    he s. a tabernacle for the sun, 15:16
    himself doggedly to it, 308:15
    honor in one eye, 191:23
    I'd s. my ten commandments in face,
      169:24
    in a notebook, 193:12
    in western lightland, 4:5
    is our little light, 226:20
    kings rise and s., 403:7
    life at pin's fee, 197:35
    me as a seal, 24:25
    minutely s. ingenious machine, 662:3
    moon has s., 56:8
    my life on any chance, 216:8
    my life upon a cast, 172:12
    my poor heart free, 207:*n*2
    noisy s., 591:19
    out one day, 618:1
    precious stone s. in silver sea, 176:24
    suns that s. may rise again, 232:5
    table on a roar, 202:12
    the night on fire, 858:4
    thine house in order, 12:20

Set *(continued)*
    when our brief light has s., 91:5
    wild echoes flying, 452:19
Setebos Setebos and Setebos, 462:21
Sets, packs and s. of great ones, 213:8
    sun in dominions never s., 359:16
    sun never s. on empire, 359:*n*4
    sun s. to rise again, 463:12
Setter up of kings, 170:23
Setteth the solitary in families, 17:10
Setting endeavor in continual motion, 188:34
    gather round s. sun, 371:5
    had elsewhere its s., 370:17
    haste now to my s., 225:23
    hush with s. moon, 455:2
    it up to fear birds, 206:18
    light of s. suns, 368:11
    more worship rising than s. sun, 88:19
    shut doors against s. sun, 213:22
    sun and music at close, 176:21
    with the s. sun, 256:5
    yourself up as judge, 76:11
Settle, though there he s. young, 500:8
Settled by precedent, 607:1
    gravity, 221:14
    I have s. in short, 809:13
Settlement, consider s. of America with
    reverence, 329:8
Settlers, children swarmed like s., 749:14
Settling, stealthily perpetually s., 545:13
Seul, on mourra s., 269:*n*5
Seven ages, 194:25
    churches in Asia, 46:15
    cities warred, 233:19
    days shall ye eat unleavened bread, 7:42
    empty ears, 7:9
    everything left at six and s., 132:*n*4
    fourscore and s. years, 446:5
    from s. till s. times s., 354:11
    golden candlesticks, 46:16
    good kine, 7:9
    hours to law, 159:*n*1
    hundred pounds and possibilities, 186:25
    Jacob served s. years, 6:44
    lie has s. endings, 889:7
    long year, 212:6
    maids with seven mops, 516:1
    morning's at s., 459:19
    pounds tenpence a man, 323:11
    sealed with s. seals, 46:30
    sette world on six and s., 132:21
    seventy times s., 35:1
    sleepers' den, 228:6
    stars in hair s., 505:23
    thin kine, 7:9
    wisdom hath hewn out her s. pillars, 20:7
    Year Itch, 798:9
    years of famine, 7:9
    years would be insufficient, 382:2
Seven-pillared, Freedom s. house, 680:7
Seventeen times high as moon, 895:4
Seventeenth century dissociation, 676:4
Seventh day thou shalt not work, 8:13
    Harlem was S. Heaven, 809:2
    hour, 779:3
    on s. holystone decks, 470:13
Seventy, oh to be s. again, 539:10
    times seven, 35:1

Shadows *(continued)*
how fast s. fall, 606:18
if we s. have offended, 179:18
illustrate all s., 231:10
not substantial things, 246:13
numberless, 410:3
of a great rock, 26:15
of living, 249:6
of plumbing left of city, 816:10
of the evening, 519:1
see only their own s., 75:11
some that s. kiss, 185:9
substance of grief hath twenty s., 176:28
unsubstantial as s., 73:5
until s. lengthen, 421:5
upon a sea obscure, 118:24
we watch the show of s., 777:4
Shadowy, boundaries s. and vague, 448:18
in s. silent distance grew Iceberg,
536:17
Shadrach Meshach and Abednego, 28:22
Shadwell never deviates into sense, 273:14
Shadwell's genuine night, 273:14
Shady, but cloud and like s. grove, 350:15
cypress tree, 512:3
leaves of destiny, 263:4
Lily O'Grady silly and s., 672:11
o'er s. groves they hover, 237:3
Olympus, 53:*n3*
sadness of vale, 411:12
sunshine in s. place, 160:5
Shaft of light across land, 451:10
when I had lost one s., 184:11
Shaftoe's, Bobby S. gone to sea, 897:2
Shafts, spend s. spare not, 881:15
Shaggy, brown heath and s. wood, 373:4
Shake and shake catsup bottle, 744:11
boughs which s. against cold, 221:24
caper and s. leg, 635:10
darling buds of May, 221:2
did Hand of Potter s., 442:5
gae his bridle reins a s., 357:12
hands forever, 167:11
laugh and s., 296:24
living out of Fate, 513:9
man that did s. kingdoms, 25:23
my fell purpose, 214:17
never s. thy gory locks, 216:17
of poor little head, 527:21
of the hand, 675:14
off dust of your feet, 33:39
off this downy sleep, 215:29
our disposition, 197:34
out the ruffle, 817:6
quail and s. the orb, 219:8
saintship of anchorite, 395:3
seems to s. the spheres, 274:15
superflux to them, 211:33
this war s. world, 684:17
whom passion could not s., 209:28
yoke of inauspicious stars, 181:14
Shaked, when degree is s., 203:6
Shaken, looks on tempests never s., 222:15
Martini s. and not stirred, 752:12
neither s. by winds nor wet, 53:2
not s. from his firm resolve, 96:27
so s. as we are, 181:18
Shakers, movers and s., 549:13

Shakes across the lakes, 452:19
his dewy wings, 249:19
out rain-drenched hair, 660:13
parting guest by hand, 203:24
rooted folly of age, 278:7
Shake-scene, only S. in country, 164:3
Shakespeare and I are often low browed,
635:11
belongs to second category, 757:14
born at Stratford, 270:12
darts himself forth, 379:15
despise S. when I measure my mind, 565:15
Fancy's child, 251:8
had largest soul, 272:6
immortal S. rose, 306:9
is happy hunting ground, 650:17
life of Allegory, 413:11
may appear once, 820:5
my S. rise, 232:19
myriad-minded S., 379:16
never blotted line, 233:11
room for S. in your tomb, 240:6
think of S. and think of me, 628:10
tongue S. spake, 370:11
unlocked heart, 372:16
was naturally learned, 272:7
was of us, 460:13
what needs my S., 250:15
Shakespeare's, acrostics in S. work, 723:4
have you read work of S., 743:12
strain, 425:6
Shakespeherian Rag, 676:9
Shaking her invincible locks, 254:12
sail's s., 635:15
Shale, early days of the Burgess S., 852:6
Shalimar, pale hands beside S., 586:15
Shall, all that is and s. be, 65:20
mark you his absolute s., 219:30
Shallow bauble boats, 203:4
brooks and rivers wide, 251:3
by s. rivers birds sing, 168:5
changing woman, 172:3
draughts intoxicate, 292:12
I owe thousand pound, 188:28
in himself, 260:6
murmur but deep are dumb, 159:7
spirit of judgment, 169:15
weeds are s.-rooted, 170:5
woman not even s., 549:*n2*
Shallows, bound in s. and miseries, 193:13
Shalott, Lady of S., 451:6
Sham, Fourth of July celebration a s., 476:21
Shaman is healer and psychopomp, 750:8
Shame, avoid s. but not seek glory, 374:23
bloomin' s., 887:7
cast s. when cast off smok, 135:13
cometh behind, 66:*n2*
crept look of furtive s., 648:15
Despair her teachers, 431:8
doff it for s., 175:14
everything that is a s. among men, 60:4
forspent with love and s., 543:4
glory and s. of universe, 269:25
he was not born to s., 180:33
hide s. from every eye, 322:17
is ashamed to sit, 180:33
on herself and all women, 53:15
proclaim no s., 201:7

Shame *(continued)*
put him to open s., 45:9
quit quit for s., 261:3
race of s., 260:15
say what it will, 202:2
secret thoughts without s., 239:8
speak truth and s. Devil, 146:1
tell truth and s. devil, 685:2
them derides, 210:31
transgression brings admitted s., 71:14
waste of s., 222:20
waves foaming out their s., 46:13
where is thy blush, 201:7
whose glory is in their s., 44:5
Shameful conquest of itself, 176:26
to mind s. to heart beauty, 492:9
Shameless, nothing more s., 53:14
nothing worse than s. woman, 73:12
Shame's, thy tongue thy s. orator, 172:23
Shames, burn out false s., 663:13
hold candle to my s., 185:2
look of bay mare s. silliness, 485:21
Shamest to show dangerous brow, 192:3
Shamrock by law forbid, 884:4
Thistle S. Rose entwine, 511:19
Shanghai Lily, 679:17
Shangri-La, serenity of S., 725:11
Shank, shrunk s., 194:25
Shannon, green banks of S., 384:7
mutinous S. waves, 650:9
Shanti, 50:7
Shanty, come up to town a S. Town, 850:12
Shape, always same s. very numerous, 578:18
Attic s., 410:19
borrow every changing s., 675:8
cloud in s. of a camel, 200:26
collects motions into s., 823:1
court it in s. of heaven, 198:10
execrable s., 256:26
grim s. towered up, 368:15
haunts about thy s., 410:13
let it keep one s., 206:18
may be summoning itself, 810:17
no bigger than agate-stone, 179:25
of Things to Come, 599:6
one's queer bodily s. in darkness, 542:13
pressed out of s., 622:17
questionable s., 197:33
take any s. but that, 216:20
two of far nobler s., 257:18
without form, 676:20
words guard s. of man, 727:6
Shapen, I was s. in iniquity, 16:30
Shapes, behind outside pattern dim s., 578:18
bright container can contain, 756:6
calling s. and beckoning shadows, 252:12
divinity that s. our ends, 202:23
full of s. is fancy, 204:11
horrid s. and shrieks, 250:19
of foul disease, 454:9
poet's pen turns to s., 179:6
ring out old s., 454:9
Shard-borne beetle, 216:12
Share, all persons s. in government, 78:25
bear own s. with courage, 501:15
friends s. all things, 58:8
passion and action of time, 538:5
threatened with railway s., 517:6

Shillings, rather than forty s., 186:26
Shin, give kick to right s. of society, 737:4
Shine, all thou dost s. upon, 401:10
    as sure as sun will s., 866:2
    by side of path we tread, 327:8
    continuous as stars that s., 371:10
    face of God s. through, 695:6
    for thy light is come, 27:14
    forth upon clouded hills, 354:8
    full alchemized and free, 409:9
    Heaven's glories s., 476:14
    inner light will s. forth, 345:n1
    let your light s., 32:16
    make his face s. upon thee, 9:2
    nor public flame dares s., 297:6
    not to s. in use, 451:14
    perpetual light s. upon them, 47:19
    rise and s. give God glory, 898:23
    S. S. save poor me, 887:1
    vessels oft handled brightly s., 168:15
    wherever bright sun shall s., 226:15
    wind's feet s. along sea, 530:2
    wit will s., 273:16
    with Pye, 394:16
    you but knock breathe s., 230:26
Shined, eye of heaven s. bright, 160:5
    in my angel-infancy, 268:9
    upon them hath the light s., 25:15
Shines and stinks, 381:5
    faith s. equal arming me, 476:14
    foolery s. everywhere, 205:10
    gold s. like fire, 63:21
    good deed, 186:18
    incongruous moonlight s., 687:11
    light where no sun s., 777:3
    moon s. bright, 186:14
    simile that solitary s., 296:15
    upon court and cottage, 223:32
    wise moral man s. like fire, 64:19
    wit s. at expense of memory, 286:16
Shineth everlasting Light, 521:2
    light s. in darkness, 38:45
    light that s. unto perfect day, 19:29
    when sun s. make hay, 146:16
Shingle and waving forest of sea-growth, 694:13
Shingles, naked s. of world, 496:19
Shining Big-Sea-Water, 437:2
    burning and s. light, 39:14
    death loves s. mark, 291:4
    eyes s. for me, 680:7
    I see my light come s., 851:20
    improve each s. hour, 289:8
    improve s. tail, 513:15
    like a National guitar, 855:14
    live hair s. and free, 669:9
    look s. at architecture, 748:6
    morning face, 194:25
    no more profit of s. nights, 174:1
    nowhere but in the dark, 268:18
    of the stars, 455:17
    on broken fragments, 390:9
    on the sea, 515:20
    only one s. in sky, 369:7, 647:2
    path of the just is as s. light, 19:29
    sea to s. sea, 572:5
    see it s. plain, 575:6
    spangled heavens s. frame, 287:20

Shining *(continued)*
    through dark cloud s., 616:17
    to the quiet moon, 377:15
    with all his might, 515:20
Shins, break s. against wit, 194:10
Ship, anchor heaves s. swings free, 423:4
    and I took off suddenly, 731:13
    as the smart s. grew, 536:17
    being in s. is being in jail, 309:1
    build s. of death, 663:23
    came from north country, 898:2
    community like s., 504:15
    don't give up the s., 389:n2
    fragment from earth, 567:5
    I wouldn't get back on s., 704:8
    idle as painted s., 376:2
    land to which s. must go, 371:25
    me east of Suez, 588:3
    my being stranger to the s., 568:5
    name of s. Golden Vanity, 898:2
    never sink except on even keel, 103:20
    not to give up s., 389:6
    of state, 65:11
    of State, 436:23
    of Union, 445:2
    Papists Protestants Jews Turks in one s., 247:8
    places s. alongside enemy, 355:11
    rapt s. run on side so low, 163:20
    rats desert sinking s., 105:n4
    sailing like a stately s., 260:16
    tall s. and star to steer, 635:15
    though my s. was on the way, 814:3
    trip on Government s., 898:3
    unstable pilot steers leaking s., 115:1
    upon the sea, 717:2
    was cheered, 375:20
    way of a s. in the sea, 22:14
    weathered every rack, 487:16
    whither O splendid s., 545:12
    whose weal and woe is common, 247:8
    wish to have no connection with any s., 342:1
Shipped, and this is what ye have s. for, 483:1
Ship's huge shadow, 376:16
    way upon the sea, 588:12
Ships are but boards, 184:21
    are only hulls, 66:2
    are swift as a bird, 53:5
    beauty and majesty of s., 437:10
    believe these s. from sky, 139:11
    board the well-benched s., 55:18
    by s. lies a dead man, 52:16
    distant storm-beaten s., 537:5
    face that launched a thousand s., 168:21
    fare north fare south, 4:7
    go down to the sea in s., 18:14
    guarded with s., 249:21
    heart of oak our s., 316:20
    how many s. my presence worth, 79:12
    loose lips sink s., 887:19
    Mr. Mrs. America all s. at sea, 715:15
    salvaged and retiring, 650:5
    saw three s. come sailing, 896:3
    season of s. is here, 83:3
    shoes s. sealing wax, 516:4
    stately s. go on, 452:15
    that pass in night, 437:19

Ships *(continued)*
    there go the s., 18:11
    there were two lofty s., 898:1
    Thracian s. foreign faces, 529:12
    we've got the s., 503:17
    wooden wall is your s., 62:16
Shipwreck, delivered from s. of blood, 717:8
Shipwrecked before I got aboard, 103:21
Shiraz, wine of S. into urine, 662:3
Shirt, happy man's without s., 146:9
    land of the Cluett S., 701:9
    naked truth is I have no s., 174:30
    of flame, 679:11
    of Nessus upon me, 218:38
    Song of the S., 418:9
Shirtless, sleeveless some s. others, 297:1
Shirtsleeves, three generations s. to s., 521:19
Shit, built-in shock-proof s. detector, 722:5
    where stink s. smell of being, 709:3
Shiver runs down spine, 706:5
    sunset breezes s., 582:10
Shivering, stood s. in snow, 167:1
Shoal, bank and s. of time, 214:22
    of fools for tenders, 287:3
Shock and Awe, 853:7
    culture s., 729:9
    disturbing delicate balance, 756:23
    fodder's in the s., 553:10
    future s., 821:3
    like s. of corn cometh, 13:14
    of recognition, 482:14
    strikes with shivering s., 381:13
    we shall s. them, 176:7
    you must s. bourgeois, 491:20
Shocked if I put on something comfortable, 723:1
    to find gambling, 758:7
Shocking, glimpse of stocking s., 691:11
Shocks, thousand natural s., 199:21
Shod, worse s. than shoemaker's wife, 147:32
Shoe, cannot put s. on every foot, 100:26
    dame has lost s., 892:9
    for want of nail s. lost, 244:8, 303:3
    none tell where s. pinches me, 107:23
    not do any more black s., 833:7
    old s. for good luck, 147:9
    old woman lived in s., 894:8
    one s. off one s. on, 896:1
    over Edom will I cast out my s., 17:2
    sailed in wooden s., 554:1
    sixpence in her s., 237:15, 886:16
    the horse, 897:5
Shoemaker, lives of s. and fish peddler, 682:11
Shoemaker's, worse shod than s. wife, 147:32
Shoes and ships and sealing wax, 516:4
    blue suede s., 832:11
    dance fire dance in iron s., 820:13
    eats soles offen s., 715:17
    good tailor and comfortable s., 844:18
    heard you got stock of s., 828:3
    him that makes s. go barefoot, 147:n13
    King James used to call for old s., 238:10
    latchet of whose s., 36:25
    nor scrip nor s., 37:31
    put off thy s., 7:26
    put yourself in his s., 707:11
    sold the poor for a pair of s., 29:1
    surgeon to old s., 191:19

Shout *(continued)*
    made universal s., 191:21
    midnight s. and revelry, 252:8
    out your numbers, 639:3
    people shouted with a great s., 9:38
    somewhere children s., 585:1
    that tore hell's concave, 255:22
Shouted, sons of God s. for joy, 14:19
Shouting battle cry of Freedom, 489:9
    chased s. wind along, 800:1
    heavens fill with s., 452:2
    their emulation, 219:21
    thunder of the captains and the s., 14:28
    tumult and s. dies, 589:8
Shouts, with sister at play, 452:15
Shovel under let me work, 636:4
Shoveled into the tombs, 636:6
Show an unfelt sorrow, 216:2
    and gaze o' the time, 217:30
    authority and s. of truth, 191:5
    contain and nourish all world, 174:24
    dangerous brow by night, 192:3
    doubt prove faith, 461:24
    every man walketh in vain s., 16:19
    his eyes, 217:1
    I s. you doubt, 461:24
    let's put on a s., 690:15
    look a needless S., 509:9
    love people and s. it, 876:9
    man as nature made him, 313:4
    man who keeps his house, 65:21
    me a greater evil, 65:22
    me a hero, 710:18
    me a liar, 244:14
    me but thy worth, 189:22
    me dear Christ Thy spouse, 230:27
    me good loser, 682:2
    me steep and thorny way, 197:20
    me the money, 875:1
    mock time with fairest s., 215:8
    more fair, 370:2
    multitude that choose by s., 185:6
    my head to the people, 359:6
    my mouth shall s. forth thy praise, 16:34
    new periwig make great s., 277:20
    no business like s. business, 673:14
    not love that do not s. love, 173:28
    nothing else We can s. Today, 509:12
    obscures the s. of evil, 185:18
    something different from either, 676:6
    swine s. you where truffles are, 817:11
    that is really a s., 709:12
    that within which passeth s., 196:27
    thing they most do s., 222:1
    virtue her own feature, 200:8
    virtue that possession would not s., 191:6
    what actually happened, 414:2
    whole world a Freeman, 328:5
    you have got to s. me, 559:14
    you have one, 298:10
    your confidence, 859:6
    you're not afraid, 859:6
Showed him gentleman an' scholar, 356:14
    Lord s. me so I did see, 270:4
    more s. than men understand, 30:14
Shower, arrowy s., 316:16
    drainless s. of light, 409:3
    favors alike, 364:4

Shower *(continued)*
    of curates, 472:12
    of gold, 407:3
    rain s. of commanded tears, 173:5
Showers and dewdrops wet, 512:3
    April s. May flowers, 151:2
    Aprille with his s. soote, 133:8
    as s. that water the earth, 17:12
    barbaric pearl, 256:6
    drying after bracing s., 708:13
    nor clouds soak with s., 53:*n*1
    small s. last long, 176:23
Showest, have more than thou s., 211:8
Showeth, firmament s. his handiwork, 15:15
    night unto night s. knowledge, 15:15
Showing, success is s. up, 839:20
    truth s. face undisguised, 64:3
Shown, worlds on worlds have s., 228:7
Showpiece, not s. of an hour, 71:12
Shows, dark side never s. to anybody, 524:20
    games sports guns, 330:1
    let mourning s. be spread, 162:15
    purrs and never s. tooth, 666:9
    scepter s. force of power, 186:1
Shreds, king of s. and patches, 201:8
    thing of s. and patches, 527:7
Shrewd, Frenchman remark s., 326:15
    guess valuable, 779:1
Shrewdly, air bites s., 197:30
Shrews, under s. at home, 391:13
Shriek, not a s. not a scream, 517:4
    short shrill s., 317:13
    solitary s., 398:9
Shrieked, it was the owl that s., 215:17
Shrieking, hooting and s., 191:32
Shrieks and groans of wounded, 489:15
    horrid shapes and s., 250:19
    murder s. out, 237:10
Shrill, farewell the s. trump, 209:13
    hear thy s. delight, 403:4
    short s. shriek, 317:13
Shrine, fountain and s., 448:6
    goddess to thy s. we come, 359:10
    Melancholy has sovran s., 411:11
    Temple's inner s., 370:6
Shrink from service of country, 333:6
    not because they s. from it, 75:1
Shriveled heart recovered greenness, 243:6
    meager hopping, 325:7
Shroud, great s. of sea, 483:9
    me and please me, 163:5
    no roof to s. his head, 233:19
    of thoughts, 395:24
    stiff dishonored s., 676:2
    walks to own funeral drest in s., 486:17
    wear it like banner not s., 731:7
    whoever comes to s. me, 230:1
Shrouds, darkness worms and s., 409:4
Shrunk, as to bed's-feet life s., 229:12
    shank, 194:25
    to this little measure, 192:19
    vanished and s. away, 167:2
Shudder, hands over with s., 656:15
    in loins, 594:16
    to say it, 94:12
    when I think earth takes day to rotate, 468:17
Shuddering fear green-eyed jealousy, 185:21

Shuffle, patience and s. cards, 157:28
Shuffled off this mortal coil, 199:21
Shuffling, forced gait of s. nag, 182:36
    sandwich men s., 654:5
Shulamite, return O S., 24:20
Shun, frumious Bandersnatch, 515:12
    heaven that leads men to hell, 222:20
    let me s. that, 211:32
    polluted flock, 666:4
    studies in which work dies with worker, 140:5
    when I s. Scylla, 185:25
    who doth ambition s., 194:13
    wise men s. mistakes of fools, 85:4
Shuns, weather shepherd s., 537:2
Shut, am now going to s. gate, 655:13
    be charming and s. up, 491:11
    doors against setting sun, 213:22
    doors s. in the streets, 23:30
    eyes against painful truth, 331:10
    her up horrorshow and lovely, 783:15
    in from world without, 438:16
    no door is s., 580:2
    shut the door, 295:9
    them in with their triumphs, 461:2
    up box and puppets, 459:8
    up he explained, 662:9
    up in measureless content, 215:12
    when thou shouldest repay, 30:19
Shut-in homes closed doors, 604:7
Shuts up story of our days, 159:16
Shutter, body borne before her on s., 459:14
    camera with s. open, 738:7
    it may be in the s., 472:22
Shutters, close s. fast, 327:1
Shutteth up bowels of compassion, 46:10
Shutting away of loving hearts, 695:17
Shuttle, musical s., 487:5
    swifter than weaver's s., 13:16
Shy, we are not s., 527:13
Sibboleth, he said S., 10:17
Sibyl, as David and the S. say, 47:20
Sic semper tyrannis, 121:16, 532:8
    sic iuvat ire sub umbras, 94:*n*11
    transit gloria mundi, 137:3
Sicilian, so ended S. expedition, 72:9
Sicilians never want to improve, 712:4
Sick and tired, 785:3
    and ye visited me, 35:30
    at heart, 196:9
    became tired and s., 487:6
    danger for the healthy, 548:17
    do s. no harm, 489:6
    enterprise is s., 203:6
    for home, 410:10
    hope deferred maketh heart s., 20:20
    I am s. at heart, 196:9
    I am s. I must die, 227:6
    I am s. of both, 310:10
    I'm s. of good poems, 810:19
    in fortune, 211:3
    kingdom of s., 835:19
    love never s. old dead, 159:4
    make me s. discussing duty, 486:14
    need physician, 33:31
    never never s. at sea, 525:20
    night but daylight s., 186:20
    nothing but to make him s., 230:10

Sick *(continued)*
    O Rose thou art s., 352:14
    of an old passion, 599:14
    of love, 24:8
    only s. music makes money, 548:20
    say I'm s. I'm dead, 295:9
    superintend s., 70:18
    that surfeit with too much, 184:12
    use treatment to help s., 70:14
    whole head is s., 24:29
    with desire, 594:3
Sicken, appetite may s. and die, 204:10
    when love begins to s., 193:6
Sickened and nigh to death, 488:2
Sickle, crowned with the s., 300:21
    never thrust s. in another's corn,
      100:25
    not move s. unto neighbor's corn, 9:24
Sickle's, bending s. compass, 222:15
Sicklied o'er with thought, 199:21
Sickness, age or grief or s., 241:18
    as regards my long s., 548:21
    enlarges dimension of self, 383:20
    in s. and in health, 49:16
    trublit now with gret s., 141:6
Sickness-broken body, 250:1
Sidcup, if only I could get to S., 828:4
Side, a thousand shall fall at thy s., 17:28
    angel on outward s., 207:7
    back and s. go bare, 151:4
    cooperative on my upper west s., 867:1
    cracked from s. to s., 451:6
    curse angel from his s., 210:17
    East S. West S., 581:2
    far s. of baldness, 590:16
    God on s. of big squadrons, 265:5
    good or evil s., 481:12
    hear other s., 116:9
    heard other s., 68:4
    history is on our s., 702:19
    house by s. of road, 51:10, 569:13
    on that s. toil hunger, 414:7
    proneness to s. with beauty, 631:10
    spinning-jenny out of s., 594:15
    stands out on either s., 695:6
    to which s. shall we incline, 269:17
    trumpets on other s., 271:28
    which s. that I must go, 175:15
    who is on the Lord's s., 8:20
    windy s. of care, 190:29
    windy s. of law, 190:*n*1
    with pouch on s., 194:25
    wrong s. of thirty, 285:19
Sidelong pickerel smile, 756:4
Sides, god would have three s., 297:12
    Laughter holding both his s., 250:22
    much said on both s., 288:8
    prick s. of my intent, 214:24
    split s. with laughing, 156:31
    thorns in your s., 10:6
    two s. to every question, 69:26
    unfed s., 211:33
Sidewalk contacts are small change, 782:4
    Tom appeared on s., 522:7
Sidewalks of New York, 581:2
Sideways, listened and looked s. up, 376:10
Sidney, Friend to Sir Philip S., 161:16
Sidney's sister Pembroke's mother, 240:7

Siege, envious s. of watery Neptune, 176:25
    how cam'st to be s. of this moon calf,
      224:24
    laugh a s. to scorn, 217:21
    of city of Gaunt, 889:22
    there was a s. going on, 802:4
Sieges, battles s. fortunes, 207:36
Sienta, el que s. en la puerta, 898:8
Sierras, crossed the s., 695:2
    people who live in s., 139:13
Sieve, nectar in a s., 378:15
    to sea in s., 467:11
    water through a s., 516:17
Sifted, God hath s. a nation, 275:2
Siftings, liquid s. fall, 676:2
Sigh back at them, 756:6
    is just a sigh, 702:11
    lack of many a thing, 221:8
    like Tom o' Bedlam, 211:4
    no more ladies, 190:33
    shall I ever s. and pine, 242:26
    some a light s., 423:5
    telling this with s., 622:18
    time for a s., 567:10
    to those who love me, 397:13
    very beadle to humorous s., 174:13
    weep no more nor s., 236:7
Sighed and looked and sighed again, 274:19
    as lover obeyed as son, 332:16
    for love of lady, 527:25
    no sooner loved but s., 195:35
    soul toward Grecian tents, 186:14
    to many though he loved one, 395:2
    when small birds s., 756:6
Sighing by a sycamore tree, 210:8
    farewell goes out s., 203:24
    laughter ability S., 509:20
    lover s. like furnace, 194:25
    plague of s. and grief, 182:25
    shall flee away, 26:19
    sound lights around shore, 506:8
    that Nature formed but one, 397:7
    through all her works, 259:11
    with s. and crying, 154:8
Sighs, before my s. did dry it, 242:26
    Bridge of S., 395:25
    lamentations and wailings, 128:8
    most s. edited, 758:20
    night of memories and s., 383:26
    paid with s. aplenty, 574:15
    short and infrequent, 676:7
    sovereign of s. and groans, 174:14
    still breathed in s., 293:22
    vaudeville audiences give loudest s., 770:14
    world of s., 208:3
Sight, be acceptable in thy s., 15:19
    buried out of s. and memory, 636:12
    earth and every common s., 370:13
    faith s. and knowledge, 472:19
    falling in love at first s., 587:2
    field has s., 134:*n*2
    for sore eyes, 285:*n*3
    found favor in thy s., 6:33
    gleamed upon my s., 371:6
    half so fine a s., 261:5
    hide us from each other's s., 241:17
    in s. of their masters, 468:19
    islands in s. of each other, 439:12

Sight *(continued)*
    lecher in my s., 212:27
    loved at first s., 168:14
    near s. of mere size of him, 651:3
    no shade in s., 871:2
    of means to do ill deeds, 175:30
    of Proteus rising, 371:24
    of salt water unbounded, 589:20
    out of s. out of mind, 137:8
    portentous s., 377:16
    precious in the s. of the Lord, 18:24
    secluded from s. of God, 231:9
    see such s. in life, 892:10
    sensible to feeling as s., 215:13
    so touching in majesty, 370:2
    spotted s. or sound, 666:5
    stars not pure in his s., 14:1
    to dream of not to tell, 377:11
    to make old man young, 451:8
    two eyes one in s., 624:1
    visionary anger cleansing s., 825:5
    walk by faith not s., 43:15
    we shall live in his s., 28:33
Sightless couriers of the air, 214:24
    realm where darkness awake, 663:22
Sights as youthful poets dream, 251:8
    love of other s. controls, 228:7
    night full of ugly s., 171:27
    Northern Lights seen s., 627:13
    shrieks and s. unholy, 250:19
    smallest s. and hearings, 487:1
    to see sad s. moves, 172:37
    what s. of ugly death, 171:28
Sign, divine s. indicates future, 70:5
    first s. of beginning of knowledge, 656:4
    he dies and makes no s., 170:8
    hungry judges sentence s., 293:9
    in this s. conquer, 114:8
    know him by this S., 284:15
    of old age, 375:13
    of weakness, 755:1
    olive leaf pacific s., 259:27
    outward and visible s., 49:12
    that something's wrong with you, 715:14
    they seek a s., 38:2
    to know gentle blood, 161:8
    V s. symbol, 620:10
    you must not touch, 230:1
Signal, death loves s. blow, 291:4
    only a s. shown, 437:19
    really do not see s., 355:9
Signals, hackneyed phrases danger s., 569:15
    neither seen or understood, 355:11
    recognize s. of ancient flame, 129:25
    white and aimless s., 810:4
Signature, scratches on deed, 739:9
Signed, hand that s. the paper, 777:5
    with their honor, 760:6
Significance, best key to life's s., 541:21
    death gives life s., 463:7
    no personal s. spare us, 446:1
Signifies, what s. life o' man, 356:21
Signify, doesn't s. whom one marries, 361:13
Signifying nothing, 217:23
Signposts, without s., 717:12
Signs, all things full of s., 114:4
    in what God has created, 118:6
    men hang out s., 390:22

Signs *(continued)*
    merely conventional s., 517:2
    of the times, 34:35
    should prefigure events, 88:1
Silas, good for Paul and S., 884:20
Silence, and slow time, 410:13
    baring tatty wreckage of my life, 832:15
    be checked for s., 205:30
    calumnies answered best with s., 232:4
    cruelest lies told in s., 554:13
    darkness again and s., 437:19
    deep as death, 384:12
    deepest feeling in s., 671:6
    die by negligence and s., 311:8
    dust and s. of shelf, 419:8
    elected S. sing to me, 546:4
    envious tongues, 226:5
    expressive s., 301:2
    fall like dews, 666:3
    fell with waking bird, 455:2
    float upon wings of s., 252:15
    free of networks of dead speech, 700:2
    genre of s., 700:18
    gives consent, 322:20
    gives proper grace to women, 65:2
    golden, 406:23
    great souls suffer in s., 359:15
    horse in s. champed, 616:6
    icy s. of tomb, 412:1
    in love bewrays woe, 159:8
    in s. hushed his very soul, 372:7
    in s. preserve integrity, 127:10
    in s. you don't know, 745:1
    is best tactic, 264:1
    is contempt, 432:4
    isolates, 631:7
    kept by ourselves in s., 437:22
    let all the earth keep s., 29:9
    let there be sacred s., 96:25
    listening to s., 418:6
    living with us even in s., 343:2
    looked up in perfect s. at stars, 487:6
    loves s. platonically, 406:*n2*
    mind moves upon s., 597:4
    my gracious s. hail, 219:25
    naked s. and profound quiet, 416:16
    night and s. who is here, 178:23
    night in her s., 495:9
    no worse than cheers, 574:18
    noble till the end, 529:15
    not s. but restraint, 671:6
    of history must be made to speak, 417:3
    of infinite spaces, 269:14
    of those who do not react, 822:3
    often of pure innocence, 223:15
    perfectest herald of joy, 190:28
    pit against death and s., 844:11
    real crime against humanity, 722:15
    regretted speech never s., 101:9
    request deed in s., 129:5
    rest is s., 202:32
    roar other side of s., 480:18
    rushed me to sleep, 832:15
    sank like music, 376:23
    sit in solemn s. in dull dark dock, 527:8
    small things and s., 768:13
    sounds of s., 855:7
    speech after long s., 596:3

Silence *(continued)*
    stunned by s. everywhere, 813:1
    supreme, 517:4
    swung high in sunlit s., 800:1
    that dreadful bell, 208:25
    then a lark, 550:3
    time to keep s., 22:31
    treasures in s. sealed, 472:8
    was pleased, 257:25
    what cannot speak about pass over in s., 685:11
    white s. below, 666:3
    widening slowly s. all, 455:12
    wings of s., 252:15
    wisest thing to heed, 64:3
    woman hold to keeping s., 432:7
    work in s. and with all one's heart, 552:14
    wrapped in beard and s., 716:3
    your eyes have their s., 701:15
Silenced man not converted, 533:2
Silences, three s. there are, 437:21
Silencing, not justified in s. one, 435:2
Silent as the moon, 260:10
    be s. as to his works, 310:22
    be s. that you may hear, 192:24
    center of s. Word, 677:17
    Chamber for most part s., 783:16
    chew cud and are s., 325:7
    church, 426:22
    counsel of the Unseen and S., 408:2
    dumb and s. be led, 328:10
    dust, 315:20
    enim leges inter arma, 87:*n6*
    evening mild s. night, 258:1
    flock in woolly fold, 409:18
    floors of s. seas, 675:1
    give me splendid s. sun, 487:10
    gone into s. land, 512:4
    gradual and s. encroachments, 345:13
    halls of death, 405:13
    haunches, 636:3
    icicles, 377:15
    impossible to be s., 324:18
    in face of tyranny, 838:11
    in shadowy s. distance grew Iceberg, 536:17
    in the dark and s. grave, 159:16
    into the s. funeral, 678:20
    lark that soars singing then s., 130:10
    long and s. street, 559:18
    majority, 771:5
    my tongue falls s., 56:5
    night holy night, 401:5
    note Cupid strikes, 248:17
    painting is s. poetry, 60:14
    power in men to be s., 276:4
    prism and s. face, 368:16
    question is this all, 796:7
    right to remain s., 692:6
    sea, 376:1
    slow and s. stream Lethe, 256:24
    spectator of scene, 386:3
    spring, 750:5
    stars go by, 521:2
    sweet s. thought, 221:8
    the truly s. who keeps apart, 4:14
    these three s. things, 635:3
    to be s. better than to speak, 108:5

Silent *(continued)*
    upon peak in Darien, 408:17
    used to be in s. pictures, 693:5
    war of lilies, 172:30
    what s. still and s. all, 398:19
    when eggs hatched, 250:5
    with s. delight, 351:6
    wound deep in her breast, 94:22
Silently, falls through clear ether s., 408:16
    how s. with how wan face, 162:21
    invisibly, 352:3
    now the moon, 616:12
    steal away, 436:18
Silk, not make revolution with s. gloves, 636:18
    owest worm no s., 212:3
    soft as s. remains, 291:21
    sound of her s. skirt, 86:18
    stocking filled with mud, 366:2
    stockings and white bosoms, 308:14
    suit which cost me much, 277:1
    that thing of s., 295:14
Silken dalliance, 189:1
    flanks, 410:18
    in field s. tent, 624:6
    lines silver hooks, 229:14
    sad uncertain, 449:6
    terms precise, 174:28
    ties of love, 624:7
    white s. turbans wreathed, 259:34
Silks, in s. my Julia goes, 241:14
Silk-sack clouds, 546:14
Silkworm expend her yellow labors, 234:4
    size or immense, 671:21
Silliness, look of bay mare shames s. out of me, 485:21
Sillons, abreuve nos s., 361:3
Silly, envy slayeth the s., 13:10
    fairy tale, 317:2
    joy at silly things, 322:*n5*
    Lily O'Grady s. and shady, 672:11
    loved its s. face, 579:15
    nothing more s. than s. laugh, 91:12
    question, 313:20
    sooth, 205:2
Silver and gold have I none, 40:16
    answer rang, 434:15
    apples of gold in pictures of s., 21:33
    apples of moon, 591:11
    bells cockleshells, 893:5
    buckles on knee, 897:2
    cord be loosed, 23:31
    foot in his mouth, 834:15
    for handful of s. he left, 460:11
    fountains have mud, 221:11
    give him s. bridge, 898:4
    goddess of the s. lake, 252:26
    gold and s. ivory and apes, 11:35
    gold and s. light, 591:12
    hooks, 229:14
    into s. dawn, 701:4
    lining on the night, 252:13
    lining through cloud, 616:17
    look for s. lining, 705:6
    mantle threw, 257:25
    moon in s. bag, 596:4
    nap after dinner s., 506:12
    nutmeg, 894:18
    oars were s., 218:20

Silver *(continued)*
    precious stone set in s. sea, 176:24
    refined thee but not with s., 26:36
    seated in thy s. chair, 232:2
    shoon, 616:12
    sixpence in shoe, 886:*n*7
    sold the righteous for s., 29:1
    speak s. reply gold, 889:9
    spoon in mouth, 158:11
    stroke his s. hair, 351:1
    swan who living, 882:2
    Taffy stole s. pin, 894:1
    thirty pieces of s., 29:16, 35:35
    tips with s. fruit-tree tops, 180:8
    Wisdom be put in s. rod, 351:9
Silvered, it was a sable s., 197:15
Silvern, Speech is s., 406:23
Silver-sandaled, dawn with s. feet, 559:18
Silver-sweet sound lovers' tongues, 180:14
Silver-white, lady-smocks all s., 174:32
Silvia, be by S. in the night, 173:33
    who is S. what is she, 173:34
Simia, exemplum de s., 126:*n*3
    quam similis nobis, 84:*n*11
Simiadae branched off, 440:10
Similar, not s. are race of gods, 51:8
    sons s. to their fathers, 52:25
    to mortals neither in shape nor thought, 60:6
Simile a like perfection, 797:14
    that solitary shines, 296:15
Similitudes, I have used s., 28:39
Simon, Simple S., 893:12
Simple, a s. child, 368:2
    analyses grow beautifully s., 800:6
    and faithless as smile, 675:14
    as false dawn, 797:12
    back in a time made s., 624:12
    can be harder than complex, 873:11
    facts in naked s. beauty, 167:17
    faith than Norman blood, 451:3
    great swindles s., 581:12
    how s. and frugal is happiness, 656:5
    Ivan Ilych's life most s., 507:5
    justice rails upon yon s. thief, 212:29
    my s. natural fashion, 151:16
    natural s. affecting, 323:7
    no vice so s., 185:19
    ordinary therefore terrible, 507:5
    performed rites s. and decisive, 810:18
    plain and s. faith, 193:6
    real s. soul-moving poetry, 405:3
    sensuous and passionate, 254:5
    separate person, 485:12
    short and s. annals, 315:17
    Simon, 893:12
    'tis gift to be s., 389:14, 885:3
    to give subtilty to the s., 19:22
    truth his utmost skill, 227:9
    truth miscalled simplicity, 221:22
Simple-minded modes of discrimination, 649:8
Simpler, better and s. people, 556:2
Simples, compounded of many s., 195:23
Simplest note that swells gale, 316:9
Simplex munditiis, 96:*n*3
Simplicitas, O sancta s., 137:*n*2
    venerationi sancta s., 115:*n*7

Simplicity and charm, 95:23
    complete s., 679:13
    embrace s., 57:8
    in wit man s. child, 294:13
    independence magnanimity, 474:16
    makes s. a grace, 232:7
    makes uneducated effective, 79:2
    mantras focus and s., 873:11
    mine is unadorned s., 101:21
    no longer misled, 339:8
    O holy s., 137:1
    pity my s., 305:9
    revered holy s., 115:15
    seemed s. itself once explained, 573:15
    simple truth miscalled s., 221:22
    since clarity suggests s., 812:20
    Spartan s., 888:4
    treats with s. or severity, 496:2
Simplify simplify, 475:1
Simulacrum, sun the dark s. of God, 249:6
Simulate, no disguise can s. love, 263:22
Sin, against s., 613:8
    be ye angry and s. not, 43:37
    before polygamy made a s., 272:14
    behoved that there should be s., 131:14
    blossoms of my s., 198:12
    by that s. fell the angels, 226:4
    cunning s. cover itself, 191:5
    draw s. with cart rope, 25:6
    dreadful record of s., 573:13
    folly noise and s., 461:2
    fools make a mock at s., 20:24
    go and s. no more, 39:23
    good man's s., 314:*n*2
    guilty of dust and s., 243:11
    has many tools, 443:11
    he that is without s., 39:22
    hold it half a s., 453:11
    human sympathy for s., 430:24
    if old and merry be s., 182:28
    ignorance not innocence but s., 463:11
    in private not sin, 267:17
    in s. did my mother conceive me, 16:30
    in this be free from s., 413:12
    is Behovely, 131:*n*5
    much of Madness more of S., 448:14
    my s. is red, 280:20
    my s. my soul, 723:5
    neatness a duty not s., 301:18
    no s. but ignorance, 168:7
    no s. to labor in vocation, 181:30
    nothing emboldens s. as mercy, 213:24
    of Judah, 27:38
    original s., 491:18
    physicists have known s., 739:7
    plate s. with gold, 212:30
    pleasure's a s., 398:5
    poverty is no s., 244:20
    private s. not so prejudicial, 157:25
    pure in life free from s., 96:14
    remorse that precedes s., 809:4
    some rise by s., 206:20
    sure your s. will find you out, 9:12
    taketh away s. of world, 38:50
    that I s. not with my tongue, 16:15
    'tis s. nay profanation, 241:12
    to covet honor, 189:25
    to prefer life to honor, 109:23

Sin *(continued)*
    usura s. against nature, 665:12
    wages of s. is death, 41:16
    waive quantum o' the s., 356:19
    was too much hope, 232:10
    we sing s., 783:10
    weeps incessantly for my s., 353:10
    where s. abounded, 41:13
    wilt thou forgive that s., 231:3
    without s. without guilt, 3:10
    worst s. towards fellow creatures, 565:2
    ye do by two and two, 588:9
Sinai, Wilson write Notes from S., 656:10
Sinais, we S. climb, 481:14
Sincere flattery, 327:17
    friend person with whom s., 427:6
    his soul s., 316:7
    let thy life be s., 30:22
    love is s., 137:11
    not s. even when saying not s., 585:11
    of soul s., 294:9
    officious innocent s., 311:7
    prayer soul's s. desire, 372:19
    think beforehand that words be s., 79:24
Sincerely from author's soul, 702:13
Sincerest, our s. laughter, 403:5
Sincerity, friends of freedom doubt our s., 444:6
    panics touchstones of s., 333:7
    tell young men with great s., 308:1
    way of heaven, 79:21
    wrought in sad s., 424:5
Sinecure, gives no man a s., 665:10
Sinew, money the s. of love, 88:*n*8
Sinews, coin is s. of war, 145:7
    cracks s. cakes brain, 483:3
    exercises s. with toil, 80:6
    money s. of war, 88:18
    of soul, 250:7
    stiffen s. summon blood, 189:7
    wealth the s. of affairs, 82:7
    what are s. of philosopher, 109:2
Sinewy, youthful s. races, 487:4
Sinful, center of my s. earth, 223:4
    desires of the flesh, 49:11
    greedy the s. and lewd, 708:6
Sinfulness, any other cause their own s., 521:7
Sing, a little time to s., 517:*n*1
    all a green willow, 210:8
    ancient ways, 591:1
    and build the lofty rhyme, 253:1
    and louder sing, 594:2
    arms and the man I s., 93:28, 274:13
    awake and s., 26:4
    because I must, 453:14
    bid soul of Orpheus s., 251:20
    bow themselves when he did s., 225:19
    caused the widow's heart to s., 14:6
    charmingly sweet you s., 467:8
    dance and drink and s., 352:15
    do not think they s. to me, 675:6
    eagle suffers little birds to s., 173:2
    elected Silence s. to me, 546:4
    for Horse nation, 891:11
    Grecian woes goddess s., 293:16
    hark the herald angels s., 305:10
    hear angels s., 457:11
    hear lady s. in Welsh, 183:1

Sing *(continued)*
heaven and nature s., 289:15
heigh-ho says Rowley, 892:11
holy sages once did s., 250:9
I am Rose and when I s., 628:13
I s. as bird sings, 342:13
I s. myself, 485:15
I s. of brooks, 240:9
I s. with mortal voice, 258:25
I will s. unto the Lord, 8:4
in a hempen string, 236:6
let others s. of knights, 167:4
lhude s. cuccu, 880:5
Lhude s. Goddamm, 665:2
lift into my arms and s., 817:7
like birds i' the cage, 213:8
loss of all I s., 814:13
me your song O, 527:24
nightingale came to s., 432:20
no birds s., 412:2
no sad songs for me, 512:3
nor pair nor build nor s., 378:14
of a maiden, 880:11
of Olaf glad and big, 701:11
of thee I s., 439:9
of thee I s. baby, 710:24
of you i s., 701:9
one of the songs of Zion, 19:11
One's-Self I s., 485:12
or cease to sing, 296:18
pipe as linnets s., 453:14
praises to his Name, 882:4
pretty birds do s., 227:4
saints sweetly s., 280:16
savageness out of a bear, 209:26
set upon bough to s., 594:4
sit and hear me s., 350:8
so we'll live pray s., 213:8
so wildly well, 448:1
song of cheer again, 697:4
song of sixpence, 894:7
songs not heard before, 96:25
still wouldst thou s., 410:9
strange that death should s., 176:3
the Lord's song, 19:11
thee a song in thy praise, 357:19
thee to thy rest, 202:33
thou smoothly, 226:23
tongue of the dumb shall s., 26:18
tongue the Savior's glory, 126:12
unto him a new song, 16:5
unto the Lord a new song, 18:1
we must laugh and s., 595:5
we s. sin, 783:10
what shall I s., 897:4
whatever well made, 597:9
when birds do s., 196:2
willow willow willow, 210:8
wrath of Achilles, 50:9
ye heavens earth reply, 305:7
Singe, flame that cannot s. sleeve, 595:12
my white head, 211:24
so hot that it s. yourself, 225:12
Singe, ich s. wie der Vogel singt, 342:*n*4
Singer, none bear beside the s., 384:3
sans Wine Song S., 441:17
thou s. I song, 526:16
Singers, long ago was one of the s., 467:5

Singest of summer, 410:3
soaring ever s., 403:3
Singeth all night long, 196:19
quiet tune, 376:19
Singin' in the rain, 702:4
this'll be day I die, 861:11
Singing and making melody, 43:38
come before his presence with s., 18:3
come with s. unto Zion, 26:39
comes deer to my s., 892:1
dancing and s. performed by body, 136:23
delight in s., 384:3
each morning, 701:18
garland and s. robes, 253:19
go s. as far as we go, 93:5
hear mermaids s., 228:9
heard the mermaids s., 675:6
heart like s. bird, 512:1
hollaing and s. of anthems, 187:33
I hear America s., 485:14
in the choir, 883:5
in the Wilderness, 441:10
locust of soul, 798:2
masons building roofs, 188:35
of Mount Abora, 377:22
sad or s. weather, 530:11
secret s. when lawyer cashes in, 636:7
sets even a wise man s., 53:21
still dost soar, 403:3
till his heaven fills, 505:15
time of the s. of birds, 24:9
we are nest of s. birds, 308:13
with muses of Helicon begin s., 54:10
woodthrush s. through fog, 677:20
Single, beauty draws with s. hair, 293:6
best augury is to fight, 51:24
Dram of Heaven, 511:8
draw you with s. hair, 235:*n*4
eternity only a s. night, 74:9
every s. one is right, 588:11
flight of planes, 724:6
for my s. self, 191:24
from s. crime know nation, 94:11
Hound, 510:1
man in possession of fortune, 382:3
married to s. life, 263:6
must begin with a s. step, 57:21
nature's double name, 202:35
no s. nation have monopoly, 661:5
no such creature as s. individual, 772:17
not a s. kind of strife, 54:16
nothing in world s., 402:16
out aristocratic pretensions, 631:10
soul in two bodies, 77:10
spies, 201:27
Single-minded like migratory birds, 631:21
Sings at grave-making, 202:5
below inveterate scars, 678:8
church ain't out till fat lady s., 886:17
each song twice, 460:19
for his supper, 893:14
he that s. lasting song, 596:6
in boat on bay, 452:15
in summer song s. itself, 658:18
know why caged bird s., 613:13
lark at heaven's gate s., 220:15
like an angel s., 186:15
moment when the bird s., 845:12

Sings *(continued)*
morn not waking till she s., 162:9
nightly s. the staring owl, 174:33
on orchard bough, 460:18
this truth poet s., 451:23
thus s. he Cuckoo, 174:32
tune without the words, 508:12
yonder pine that s., 82:12
Singularity almost invariably a clue, 573:11
poetry surprise not by S., 413:1
Singulars, statements of history are s., 79:5
Sinister resonance, 567:*n*1
Sink downward to darkness, 640:22
heart and voice oppressed, 479:2
hold you as I s., 101:19
load would s. a navy, 226:2
loose lips s. ships, 887:19
Neptune's ship on even keel, 103:20
not gross to s. but light, 171:8
of uncertainty and error, 269:25
or swim, 182:4
or swim live or die, 390:3
or swim together, 607:3
present repute for freedom, 481:18
pride of power s., 324:3
raft which will never s., 355:2
to nothingness do s., 412:9
tosses but doesn't s., 120:25
who s. to rest, 317:10
Sinking into inferiority, 389:9
knowledge like s. star, 451:15
rats desert s. ship, 105:*n*4
Sinks and I am ready to depart, 384:4
day-star in ocean bed, 253:14
gross flesh s. downward, 177:25
one s. in on God, 591:15
with bubbling groan, 396:18
Sinn, das kommt mir nicht aus dem S., 415:*n*1
Sinned against my brother the ass, 126:1
in Adam's fall s., 283:3
more s. against than sinning, 211:29
we have s. against thee, 27:35
Sinner, dead s. revised and edited, 540:13
desireth not death of s., 48:5
forgive some s., 645:7
merciful to me a s., 38:24
of his memory, 224:5
too weak to be a s., 213:20
whether he be s., 39:28
who write with no dinner, 682:1
Sinners, all the s. saints, 857:6
call s. to repentance, 33:32
came to save s., 44:24
God and s. reconciled, 305:10
if s. entice thee, 19:23
miserable s., 49:9
old s. have brawny consciences, 261:14
publicans and s., 34:8
Son of man betrayed to s., 36:7
standeth in the way of s., 14:40
we are s. all, 170:9
Sinning, more sinned against than s., 211:29
Sin's, sometimes s. a pleasure, 398:5
Sins, acknowledge our manifold s., 49:5
are attempts to fill voids, 760:13
be all my s. remembered, 199:22
charity creates multitute of s., 560:27
don't make up for s. in church, 855:5

Sins *(continued)*

double for all her s., 26:24
few love to hear s. they act, 220:10
forgiveness of s., 47:25
Forgiveness of s., 48:11
forgiveth s. and saveth, 30:10
guilt about s. unable to commit, 726:12
her s. which are many, 37:27
lie in dark weep for s., 486:14
love covereth all s., 20:12
manifold s. and wickedness, 48:1
multitude of s., 46:1
of commission mortal, 311:19
of fathers upon children, 69:2
of omission venial, 311:19
of the world, 47:23
oldest s. newest ways, 188:24
other s. only speak, 136:*n2*
other s. speak murder shrieks, 237:10
scarlet books read, 606:17
shed for remission of s., 36:3
snows and s., 529:13
somebody's s. not mine, 863:14
takes away s. of the world, 47:23
though your s. be as scarlet, 24:32
weep for her s. at other, 674:2
Sion, never climbed Mount S., 787:17
Sioux owned the world, 513:4
Sip, can't be tasted in s., 464:29
lifeblood seemed to s., 376:10
Sipped no sup, 527:25
Sir Oracle, 184:7
Siren, listen to song of s., 331:10
song of s. nor voice of hyena, 163:15
tears, 222:16
Sirens, what song the S. sang, 248:27
Sires' age worse than grandsires', 97:1
Sisera, mother of S. looked out window, 10:13
stars fought against S., 10:10
Sister Anne do you see, 883:6
art my mother and my s., 13:35
Caroline, 610:7
Jerusalem thy s. calls, 354:14
live a barren s. all your life, 177:26
Milky Way s. in whiteness, 643:21
ministering angel my s., 202:16
never praise s. to s., 587:3
shouts with s., 452:15
Sidney's s. Pembroke's mother, 240:7
still gentler s. woman, 357:3
Sister's husband's niece, 517:9
Sisters, all s. virtuous, 882:9
big s. are crab grass, 800:10
Brothers and S. beware, 589:25
cousins and aunts, 525:21
Death and Night, 487:11
twa s. sat in bour, 890:2
under skins, 589:4
wayward s. depart, 394:2
weird s. hand in hand, 214:3
we're s. under the mink, 751:14
women born my s. and lovers, 485:17
Sisyphus, believe S. happy, 770:2
Sit and hear me sing, 350:8
around so much doing nothing, 628:11
bird of night did s., 191:32
dicky-bird why do you s., 527:21
down says Love, 243:12

Sit *(continued)*

get up so white person could s., 771:16
here will we s., 186:15
I s. in one of the dives, 748:16
in a barn, 895:5
in darkness, 37:15, 256:17
in solemn silence, 527:8
Jessica look, 186:15
let us s. upon the ground, 177:8
like grandsire in alabaster, 184:5
nor s. nor stand but go, 462:15
not s. on throne of bayonets, 579:6
on a cushion, 894:17
on our own bottom, 153:22
right here by me, 659:15
shalt not s. with statisticians, 749:15
shame is ashamed to s., 180:33
so I did s. and eat, 243:12
such as s. in darkness, 18:13
teach us to s. still, 677:13
thee down sorrow, 174:6
their strength is to s. still, 26:11
them that s. in darkness, 37:15
thou a patient looker-on, 242:5
though I s. down now, 429:23
trees where you s., 292:6
unable to s. still, 269:12, 773:1
Sit tibi terra levis, 121:17
Sits and smiles on the night, 351:6
as one new-risen from dream, 173:19
high in people's hearts, 191:34
looking over harbor, 636:3
on horse at hostess' door, 175:8
Secret s. in middle, 624:11
truth s. on lips of dying, 495:21
watching for omens, 73:8
wind in that corner, 190:34
with keen appetite he s. down, 184:39
Sittest throned in glory, 517:11
Sitteth in the seat of the scornful, 14:40
Sittin' on the dock of the bay, 853:4
Sitting, as cheap s. as standing, 285:15
by desolate streams, 549:13
careless on floor, 411:7
equal to a god s. opposite you, 91:16
here like some little woman, 856:*n1*
in a pleasant shade, 233:14
in catbird seat, 704:13
in the sun, 381:6
listen where thou art s., 252:26
no pity s. in clouds, 181:4
remain s. at your table, 655:17
still is s., 449:11
well in order smite, 451:18
Situation excellent I am attacking, 557:1
inwardness of s., 542:12
marines landed and s. well in hand, 585:3
normal all fucked up, 887:21
Situations, there are two possible s., 469:3
Six Characters in Search of an Author, 601:2
days shalt thou labor, 8:13, 470:13
essentials in painting, 122:11
everything left at s. and seven, 132:*n4*
feet of land, 507:7
honest servingmen, 589:16
hours in sleep, 159:1
hundred pounds a year, 296:7
impossible things before breakfast, 516:13

Six *(continued)*

of one half-dozen other, 401:1
or seven dozen Scots, 182:17
Richmonds in the field, 172:12
rode the s. hundred, 454:18
separated by s. people, 844:9
sette world on s. and sevene, 132:21
snowed s. days and s. nights, 777:16
Sixes, things go at s. and sevens, 132:*n4*
whole world's at s. and sevens, 715:10
Sixpence, found crooked s., 895:17
I give thee s., 367:1
in her shoe, 237:15, 886:16
not a s. sir, 362:*n1*
song of s., 894:7
Sixteen hours ago Hiroshima, 661:3
you load s. tons, 789:1
Sixth, every s. man a slave, 374:19
Sixties made so many casualties, 847:8
Sixty, man should not travel after s., 126:8
minutes an hour, 717:13
Sixtyfold, brought forth fruit s., 34:16
Sixty-four, when I'm s., 848:11
Sixty-six, Route S., 792:2
Sixty-three, intercourse began in nineteen s.,
799:13
Size, all men are of a s., 427:26
near sight of mere s. of him, 651:3
not grandeur, 502:10
silkworm s. or immense, 671:21
take s. of pots of ale, 262:7
those of largest s., 516:7
Sizzle, sell s. s. sells steak, 747:12
Skating, burnt match s. in a urinal, 720:8
in s. safety is speed, 427:11
Skeleton, ague of s., 675:26
Skeptic, too much knowledge for s., 295:1
Skepticism chastity of intellect, 584:13
highest of duties, 502:4
more clearly understood, 152:19
Skeptics' way of speaking, 152:18
Sketch ruins of St. Paul's, 419:17
Skewered with office pens, 466:3
Skies above clear again, 697:4
as long as s. are blue, 403:19
ashen and sober, 449:14
change s. above them, 589:1
cloudless climes starry s., 397:1
common sun air s., 316:9
danced the s., 800:1
distant deeps or s., 353:1
fear can see more in s., 156:6
heifer lowing at s., 410:18
islands whose raving s. opened, 559:3
join triumph of the s., 305:10
keep watching the s., 746:5
ladder to s., 161:2
look up at s., 546:7
looks commercing with the s., 251:13
mansions in the s., 289:16
many a message from s., 358:1
molded and melted across s., 546:14
moon climbest s., 162:21
no matter how many s. have fallen, 663:10
not cloudy all day, 890:20
raised mortal to the s., 274:22
rend the affrighted s., 293:12
resume sophistries of June, 508:6

Skies *(continued)*
    spacious s., 572:5
    statures touch s., 510:12
    watcher of the s., 408:17
    wings across canceled s., 694:14
Skill, a little s. in antiquity, 165:*n*5
    baseball is game of s., 688:16
    force no place where need of s., 69:14
    honor hath no s. in surgery, 183:25
    man's s. built cities, 87:2
    nor favor to men of s., 23:23
    oars plied with little s., 513:10
    pass days in that where s. greatest, 101:14
    simple truth his utmost s., 227:9
    'tis God gives s., 480:23
    to conceal skill, 264:13
    to him that can get it, 271:27
Skilled in works of both languages, 97:2
    orator a good man s. in speaking, 85:8
    poet through natural gift, 63:25
Skillful, all s. in the wars, 268:15
Skillfully, play s. with a loud noise, 16:5
Skim milk masquerades, 526:2
Skimble-skamble stuff, 182:38
Skin, after my s. worms destroy, 13:39
    beauty's but s. deep, 226:18
    because my s. is red, 513:4
    born with black s., 808:11
    calf's-s. on recreant limbs, 175:14
    can the Ethiopian change his s., 27:34
    chameleon's tuning s., 797:10
    color loves and s., 228:13
    come into world with thick s., 415:8
    come off with whole s., 156:5
    for skin, 13:1
    got you under my s., 691:14
    like dusk on horizon, 704:14
    Negro's s. prima facie evidence, 471:6
    no matter color of s., 697:2
    nor s. nor hide nor fleece, 667:7
    not judged by color of s., 823:8
    of innocent lamb parchment, 170:15
    patch lion's s. with fox's, 108:1
    rip off s., 886:*n*4
    skull beneath the s., 675:25
    snake throws enamelled s., 178:19
    white as leprosy, 376:7
    with the s. of my teeth, 13:37
    worth not related to color of s., 798:6
Skinny, fear thy s. hand, 376:13
Skins not colored like your own, 477:1
    sisters under s., 589:4
Skinside is inside, 610:9
Skip, I cut down trees s. and jump, 879:9
    readers tend to s., 808:10
Skipped, mountains s. like rams, 18:21
Skipper had taken daughter, 436:8
Skirmish of wit, 190:14
Skirt, shortening or lengthening of s., 688:14
    sound of her silk s., 86:18
Skirts you could run and dance in, 838:10
Skittish, unstaid and s. in motions, 204:33
Skittles, beer and s., 464:*n*1, 498:11
    porter and s., 464:3
Skugg, here S. lies, 303:9
Skull beneath the skin, 675:25
    of a lawyer, 202:8
    place of s., 36:17

Skull *(continued)*
    some poor fellow's s., 381:7
Skulls, hell paved with priests' s., 115:25
    leaden they don't weep, 717:4
    place of s., 395:12
Skuttle-Fish, rejoice with S., 318:12
Sky, above the vaulted s., 404:19
    above world stretched the s., 695:6
    all could see was s. water birds, 761:2
    all the milky s., 591:4
    and sea and land, 576:4
    at end of storm golden s., 706:11
    banners flout the s., 213:32
    beautiful as the s., 487:11
    believe power and goodness in s., 139:11
    believe these ships from s., 139:11
    blue ethereal s., 287:20
    blue s. bends over all, 377:12
    blue s. over my head, 386:10
    bluebird carries s., 473:4
    Brain wider than S., 509:13
    bridal of earth and s., 242:19
    broad and peaceful s., 805:2
    changes when wives, 195:29
    daily bread of eyes, 425:11
    diamond in the s., 389:12
    dusky night rides down s., 304:11
    Eagle looking at s., 411:16
    ethereal s., 255:7
    fair weather for s. is red, 34:34
    forehead of morning s., 253:14
    go forth under open s., 405:11
    goal the s., 887:16
    guides through s. thy flight, 405:14
    home a-waiting in s., 689:8
    immeasurably lofty, 506:13
    inverted Bowl we call S., 442:3
    isolation of s., 640:22
    lingered under benign s., 476:18
    living air and blue s., 368:11
    lonely sea and s., 635:15
    lonesome place against s., 557:7
    lose itself in s., 462:11
    lyre within s., 448:1
    mauve and rosy s., 710:10
    measure pathways of s., 94:35
    membrane of bright blue s., 772:18
    moving moon went up s., 376:15
    Music shall untune s., 273:26
    no foreign s. protected me, 683:7
    none knew color of the s., 608:18
    nothing but hath bound in s., 172:15
    nothing but s. and the ocean, 378:1
    November's s., 373:5
    old and true as s., 588:18
    only one shining in s., 369:7, 647:2
    our Father the S., 891:12
    peopling earth waters s., 278:6
    pie in s., 639:4
    prisoners call the s., 561:1
    publish yourselves to s., 543:1
    pulling blanket off eastern s., 891:8
    rainbow in the s., 369:14
    ring out to wild s., 454:7
    robes spun of Iris' woof, 252:5
    sea rising nor s. clouding, 545:12
    sent him down the s., 499:9
    shoulder s. drink ale, 575:15

Sky *(continued)*
    slope down which s. flows, 718:14
    somewhere S. touches Earth, 889:2
    sparkling with diamonds, 578:9
    split the s. in two, 695:6
    spread out against s., 674:17
    squired glacier woman down s., 720:7
    stand at Judgment Seat, 587:8
    star drooped in western s., 487:12
    star that burns forever in s., 892:5
    steal across the s., 519:1
    sweep cobwebs from s., 895:4
    teatray in the s., 514:15
    threw wild hands toward s., 609:2
    tree cannot grow in s., 90:11
    tree struggles to reach s., 740:5
    under wide and starry s., 555:16
    went out under s. Muse, 558:13
    what if s. were to fall, 86:2
    while I kiss the s., 854:5
    will cave in on him, 695:6
    wrote across s. in stars, 680:7
Skyey, servile to s. influences, 206:33
Skylark have you seen valley green, 759:5
Skyline, one sight of New York's s., 742:17
Skyscrapers, send s. toppling, 756:23
Sky's, rip-tooth of s. acetylene, 720:4
    whatever s. above me, 397:13
Slack, observing me grow s., 243:11
Slacker, you're a s., 870:4
Slain a thousand men with jawbone, 10:22
    all whom war hath s., 230:20
    by fair cruel maid, 205:3
    crippled palsied s., 627:11
    death ere thou s. another, 240:7
    Earl of Murray, 890:7
    from graves of our s., 417:5
    frosts are s., 529:13
    her own eyes see him s., 520:4
    honor those they have s., 492:15
    if s. thinks he is s., 50:5
    Jabberwock, 515:13
    more come through alive than are s., 52:1
    time has s. desire, 813:11
    Saul hath s. his thousands, 11:3
    some s. in war, 177:8
    think he is slain, 425:4
    through our love is my lord s., 138:13
    where s. are there is she, 14:29
    with him beauty s., 171:14
    wounded but not s., 889:*n*1
Slam, Emily set doors ajar and s. them, 626:14
Slander, give lie to s., 394:1
    influenced neither by s. nor denunciation,
      61:9
    lives upon succession, 172:22
    one to s. other to get news to you, 524:18
    protest discrimination and s., 629:6
    vindication against s., 446:9
    whose edge sharper than sword, 220:20
Slanderous, death by s. tongues, 191:18
Slanged, acquaintance sneered and s., 606:14
Slant, certain S. of light, 508:13
Slanting-eyed, lame wrinkled and s., 51:21
Slashed, she s. him, 896:16
Slaughter, as an ox goeth to the s., 20:5
    as lamb to the s., 27:8
    like sheep to s., 328:10

Sleep *(continued)*

miles to go before s., 623:8
most gentle s., 188:*n*1
most things s. lying, 242:24
mountains in primeval s., 500:5
nature's soft nurse, 188:9
neither night nor day, 214:1
neither slumber nor s., 18:30
never s. with women, 757:11
nice quiet s., 604:1
no more, 215:21
no s. till morn, 395:14
nor shall this peace s. with her, 226:14
not dream not, 476:10
not hypocrites in s., 386:15
not my design to s., 246:21
nothing s. in that cellar, 755:12
of a laboring man, 23:6
of death, 199:21
of Lethe, 95:28
of perpetual night, 91:5
of reason produces monsters, 341:13
off to death, 633:6
old and gray full of s., 591:5
on my Love in thy cold bed, 241:18
one ever-during night, 226:20
one short s. past, 230:24
only s., 460:23
out the thought of it, 223:23
out this great gap, 218:10
past first s. in Persia, 249:7
perchance to dream, 199:21
quiet s. when trick's over, 635:17
rounded with a s., 225:1
rude forefathers s., 315:14
sets fool and wise even, 158:8
shake off this downy s., 215:29
shall our gratitude s., 367:4
shall we s. after all, 530:9
silence rushed me to s., 832:15
six hours in s., 159:1
sleeping wake and waking s., 153:1
snow said s., 683:5
softly eagle forgotten, 639:11
some must watch some s., 200:23
son of sable Night, 167:3
sooner over sooner to s., 481:6
soundly as wretched slave, 189:23
spirited from s., 797:12
strong man after s., 254:12
sun is laid to s., 232:2
sweetly in your humble graves, 506:9
sword is s. in my hand, 354:8
task done we must s., 219:1
that knits up ravelled sleave, 215:21
that knows not breaking, 373:21
that masters all, 65:6
the sleep of death, 354:14
they are as a s., 17:23
they s. and it is lifted, 402:2
time enough to s., 574:12
time for s., 53:13
to die to s., 199:21
turned aside to s., 229:4
two gates of S., 95:2
under bridges beg and steal, 546:2
unseasonable immoderate s., 307:24
upon golden bed, 596:2

Sleep *(continued)*

visit soul in s., 401:11
voices that make me s. again, 224:33
wake to s., 756:5
waked after long s., 224:33
was airy light, 258:12
we shall not all s., 43:8
we shall not s., 614:7
weary of everything but s., 530:16
weighs like unwilling s., 411:16
what hath night to do with s., 252:9
why wilt thou s., 354:14
will never lie, 180:18
with golden Aphrodite, 53:9
with Turks and infidels, 177:15
without wink of s., 155:20
would s. with his mother, 313:13
ye harlots s. at ease, 293:20
yet a little s., 20:1
Sleeper, primitive people not waken s., 558:3
Sleepers in that quiet earth, 476:18
numb nudgers, 755:16
Sleepers', seven s. den, 228:6
Sleepeth, not dead but s., 33:35
peradventure he s., 12:1
Sleeping, all all s. on hill, 605:3
and the dead as pictures, 215:23
at last, 512:10
Beauty wakes up, 808:9
dogs lie, 466:2
he find you s., 37:3
I'm only s., 848:10
is a wool blanket, 73:17
like s. with elephant, 794:1
some s. killed, 177:8
think lion s. because he didn't roar, 359:9
wake and waking sleep, 153:1
wakened us from s., 669:11
woods all night, 376:19
Sleepless Eremite, 412:10
soul that perished, 369:16
through suburbs s. people, 717:8
vigilance, 446:2
watches of night, 438:1
Sleeps, after life's fever s., 216:11
creation s., 290:20
moonlight s. upon this bank, 186:15
now s. crimson petal, 453:5
on watch, 323:19
remorse s., 313:5
there s. Titania, 178:19
till tired he s., 295:3
while my little one s., 452:18
Sleepwalker, assurance of s., 684:13
Sleepy and proud, 681:19
I am s. and weeds twist, 484:4
I'm not s., 851:12
Sleepyhead, let's to bed says S., 894:4
Sleet, iron s., 316:16
pattering sharp s., 409:23
Sleeve, flame that cannot singe s., 595:12
laughing in your s., 346:4
laughing up her s., 267:13
ravelled s. of care, 215:21
wear heart upon my s., 207:26
Sleeveless some shirtless others, 297:1
Sleeves, fluttering empty s., 641:8
Sleigh, carry the s., 421:17

Slender debt to Nature's, 242:3
thy s. stem, 356:17
waist confined, 249:22
Slenderly, fashioned so s., 418:13
Slept, and then I s., 814:10
dreamed life beauty, 472:15
I should have s., 13:4
I s. in a bed, 865:1
in peace, 226:8
law not dead though it s., 206:26
one wink, 220:21
Passion s., 306:11
resembled my father as he s., 215:19
Slew, as ambitious I s. him, 192:26
dead which he s. at his death, 10:26
death s. not him, 161:2
enemy nearly s. ye, 884:6
who s. warriors, 513:4
Slice, no matter how thin s. it, 617:13
Slices of quince, 467:10
Slick, low scud s. street, 821:2
Slide into lover's head, 369:6
Kelly slide, 885:21
let world s., 146:10
no foot shall s., 887:15
Slight, nor Fame I s., 292:7
not what's near, 67:17
Slightest, rememberest not s. folly, 194:8
Slightly shakes parting guest, 203:24
Slime, daubed with s. and pitch, 7:23
Slimy things did crawl with legs, 376:4
Sling, my s. the s. of David, 557:16
prevailed with a s. and with a stone, 11:2
Slinging, fury s. flame, 453:18
Slings and arrows of fortune, 199:21
Slinks out of race, 254:9
Slip away before they're up, 651:3
given them the s., 282:19
giving enemies s., 313:24
let it s. useless away, 408:10
let s. dogs of war, 192:23
slidin' away, 855:12
'twixt cup and lip, 235:*n*3
Waring gave us all the s., 461:9
Slipcover, matched s. material, 796:7
Slipped surly bonds of Earth, 800:1
thrice it s. through my hands, 53:11
Slippered, lean and s. pantaloon, 194:25
Slippers, same old s., 576:9
Slippery, he that stands on s. place, 175:22
words s. thought viscous, 532:6
Slippy-sloppy, water s. in larder, 598:7
Slips, greyhounds in s., 189:9
remember black wharves and s., 437:10
seizes two things one s., 889:6
Slit, tongue be s., 892:21
Slithy toves, 515:12
Slits the thin-spun life, 253:6
Sliver and disbranch, 212:19
Slogan, Party s., 735:18
earned s. yanks go home, 708:18
Slop Over, 519:4
staineth s., 665:2
Slope, patio s. down which sky flows, 718:14
through darkness to God, 453:24
Sloppy Joe's, 749:13

Smile, affliction s. again, 174:6
and be a villain, 198:17
as I do now, 443:15
at claims of descent, 451:2
better last s., 283:*n*5
did he s. work to see, 353:2
disdainful s., 315:17
dwells longer, 615:16
faithless as a s., 675:14
forget and s., 512:5
horror unbend and s. at us, 648:5
if we meet we shall s., 193:17
in her eye, 415:12
in spite of it, 780:16
jest to Oberon make him s., 178:12
loving s. surely hail, 515:10
make the learned s., 292:15
of accomplishment, 833:5
of deceit, 353:13
of love, 353:13
of smiles, 353:13
on Casey's face, 584:19
on lips tear in eye, 373:12
on the Mona Lisa, 691:12
once more turn thy wheel, 211:16
one vast substantial s., 465:9
riding on s. and shoeshine, 780:8
sea shows false alluring s., 90:6
secret of sad and melancholy s., 490:16
sidelong pickerel s., 756:4
smile smile, 643:22
sweet s. at his father, 91:18
to those who hate, 397:13
upon fingers' ends, 189:4
vehicle for ambiguities, 483:13
we s. and touch arms, 815:16
we would aspire to, 225:25
when only dead could s., 683:9
when world begins to s. upon him, 416:15
when you call me that s., 579:9
where my Julia's lips s., 240:12
world seems to s. upon me, 277:10
you make me s. with heart, 707:4
Smiled and said Good Night, 606:16
at the dame, 352:4
of darkness till it s., 252:15
through their tears, 513:7
Smiler with knyf, 134:19
Smiles, all s. stopped together, 460:3
and soap, 517:6
as if he mocked himself, 191:30
does not disagree but s., 792:1
full of s. in early days, 75:21
he s. it is a malady, 91:11
in which two s. meet, 353:13
kindling s. in ladies' eyes, 418:18
Peace crowned with s., 268:15
quiet-colored evenings., 461:1
same flower that s. today, 241:4
seldom he s., 191:30
sits and s. on the night, 351:6
smile of s., 353:13
sobs sniffles and s., 581:13
sweet strains pensive s., 424:4
tears of boyhood's years, 387:17
the robbed that s., 208:6
welcome ever s., 203:24
wreathed s., 250:21

Smilest and art still, 494:10
Smiling at grief, 205:4
at the good mouth, 665:9
damned villain, 198:17
from world's snare, 218:37
gently s. jaws, 513:15
hides s. face, 326:10
in my face, 215:5
scatter plenty o'er s. land, 316:2
the boy fell dead, 459:23
through tears, 51:15
wish granted to a s. ghost, 813:11
Smirk, serious and the s., 464:16
Smite all the firstborn, 7:40
baseness we will s., 605:14
God shall s. thee, 40:44
once and smite no more, 253:11
sounding furrows, 451:18
the sun shall not s. thee, 18:30
thee on thy right cheek, 32:20
without hands to s., 529:14
Smiteth so that he die, 8:16
Smith mighty man, 436:11
Sydney S. a molar, 503:2
Smithsonian, to found S. Institution, 362:6
Smithy of soul, 650:13
village s. stands, 436:11
Smitten, illness with which s., 418:20
with our own feathers, 59:*n*5
Smock, cast shame when cast off s., 135:13
Smoke and stir of this dim spot, 251:25
clouds of s. issue from nostrils, 334:2
days are consumed like s., 18:4
days gone up in s., 577:1
gets in your eyes, 617:1
good cigar is a s., 587:1
good strong incense s., 460:22
herbs to smother s. thereof, 139:9
in yon s. concealed, 479:12
no fire without s., 148:12
thin s. without flame, 536:22
w'at do wid de s., 551:12
Smoked, whole world s., 873:3
Smoke-filled room, 578:17
Smokey the Bear will illuminate, 828:12
Smoking flax shall he not quench, 26:34
gun to be a mushroom cloud, 872:11
one stops s. only when, 846:2
Smoky, populous and s. city, 402:18
Smooth as monumental alabaster, 210:13
away trouble, 669:9
billows s. and bright, 515:20
block s. and well fitting, 665:11
chose him five s. stones, 11:1
easy inoffensive down to Hell, 82:*n*3
road is s., 54:21
road of life, 314:24
runs water where brook deep, 159:*n*4
sea being s., 203:4
the ice, 175:24
true love never did run s., 177:27
Smoothed his wrinkled front, 171:17
Smoother, finding s. pebble, 279:18
her mouth is s. than oil, 19:31
words were s. than butter, 16:38
Smoothest, stream s. water deepest, 159:*n*4
Smooth-faced gentleman Commodity,
175:12

Smoothing the raven down, 252:15
Smooth-lipped, convolutions of s. shell,
372:7
Smoothly, my task is s. done, 252:27
Smoothness, temperance may give it s., 200:6
turns s. rough, 462:15
Smooths hair with automatic hand, 676:13
oil s. what is rough, 104:14
Smooth-shaven, dry s. green, 251:16
Smote him thus, 210:21
him under the fifth rib, 11:11
Jael s. the nail into his temples, 10:7
them hip and thigh, 10:21
Smother up his beauty, 181:33
Smothered, I should die there s., 662:12
Smothery, cramped up and s., 523:4
SNAFU, 887:21
Snail, creeping like s. to school, 194:25
questing S., 756:15
turn not pale beloved s., 515:4
went to kill s., 894:5
whiting to a s., 515:2
Snail's on the thorn, 459:19
Snails, pretty feet like s., 241:6
snips and s., 895:11
Snake came to water trough, 663:6
eagle or s., 588:12
earth like s. renew, 403:8
in the grass, 92:20
like a wounded s., 292:18
no s. can live there, 121:27
stood up for evil, 623:2
things are of the s., 424:11
throws enamelled skin, 178:19
toad edible to s., 540:7
we have scotched the s., 216:10
Snakes eat frogs, 641:3
gliding up hollow, 425:8
hogs eat s., 641:3
no s. to be met with, 310:15
spotted s. with double tongue, 178:22
strangled s. beside Hercules, 502:2
Snakeskin titles of claims, 715:18
Snap like vixens at truth, 666:9
Snapper-up of unconsidered trifles, 223:22
Snare of the fowler, 17:28
rabbit in a s., 654:2
trial by jury a s., 386:18
world's great s., 218:37
Snares, heart is s. and nets, 23:16
riches are ready s., 138:17
traps gins pitfalls, 459:*n*1
Snark was a Boojum, 517:7
Snatch a fearful joy, 315:5
me away not to return, 622:19
Snatched from all effectual aid, 327:10
purse most resolutely s., 181:22
scepter s. with unruly hand, 175:22
spear but left shield, 346:*n*4
Snatches, ballads songs s., 527:7
Snatching victuals from table, 619:8
Snaw, locks are like the s., 357:13
Sneer at me for leaning, 442:5
of cold command, 401:13
who can refute a s., 339:2
without sneering teach to s., 295:13
Sneered, acquaintance s., 606:14
Mighty Merchant s., 509:12

Sneering, born s., 527:9
   without s. teach to sneer, 295:13
Sneezed, not to be s. at, 361:5
Sneezes, beat him when he s., 514:10
Snicker, eternal Footman s., 675:3
   why does hearse horse s., 636:7
Snicker-snack, blade went s., 515:13
Snickersnee, I drew my s., 527:18
Sniff, I s. the mothproof air, 821:1
Sniffles, sobs s. and smiles, 581:13
Snips and snails, 895:11
Snob, admires mean things is S., 459:9
   after that be a s., 737:4
Snobbish, camels are s., 671:23
Snobs, effete corps of impudent s., 789:6
Snodgrass, murmured Mr. S., 463:21
Snore, weariness s. upon flint, 220:22
Snorted we in seven sleepers' den, 228:6
Snout, jewel of gold in a swine's s., 20:14
Snow, arrives the s., 424:7
   bells across the s., 454:8
   birds sit brooding in s., 175:1
   buck in the s., 695:16
   came both mist and s., 375:23
   came flying, 545:13
   chaste as unsunned s., 220:16
   cherry hung with s., 574:11
   dripping s. on grass, 681:19
   dust of s., 623:5
   fallen s. on s., 512:6
   falling faintly through universe, 650:9
   falling s. silent, 635:3
   fare wel s. of ferne yere, 133:1
   fleece white as s., 399:19
   frost from purest s., 220:3
   geese like s. cloud, 681:19
   general over Ireland, 650:9
   hide hills of s., 207:*n*2
   I shall be whiter than s., 16:31
   if s. be white, 223:1
   lay round about, 479:1
   like s. falls in river, 358:6
   like s. hill in the air, 482:20
   like s. in May, 243:5
   locks are like s., 357:13
   melted s., 397:3
   mockery king of s., 177:20
   no s. is there, 53:1
   nor does s. come near it, 53:2
   not s. nor rain nor heat, 69:21
   pure as s., 199:26
   raiment white as s., 36:22
   said peace cold sleep, 683:5
   she is near under s., 559:15
   sins shall be white as s., 24:32
   something crabwise across s., 808:6
   step softly under s., 618:13
   stood shivering in s., 167:1
   swept world end to end, 688:6
   swooned as he heard s., 650:9
   try s. of heaven, 704:2
   tufts of s. on bare branch, 377:15
   wallow naked in December s., 176:18
   we shall have s., 895:5
   white and drifted s., 421:17
   white as driven s., 223:30
   wish s. in May's mirth, 174:2
   woods fill with s., 623:6

Snow *(continued)*
   world vast screen of s., 683:5
   wrapt in clouds and s., 395:17
Snow-broth, man whose blood is s., 206:16
Snowed, it s. of mete amd drynke, 133:27
   six days and six nights, 777:16
   whole world over, 688:6
Snowflake in avalanche, 758:18
   not a s. escapes fashioning hand, 473:8
Snowflakes, words like winter s., 51:3
Snows and sins, 529:13
   of the year 1941, 836:2
   where are s. of yesteryear, 138:19
   where s. of yesteryear, 506:3
Snow-star, earth-star and s., 473:9
Snowstorms, inspector of s., 473:1
Snow White, I used to be S., 700:9
Snow-white, little s. feet, 590:21
Snowy, Seraphs swing s. Hats, 508:10
   summits old in story, 452:19
Snub, hard to s. beautiful woman, 622:2
Snuff approach of tyranny, 324:7
Snuff-colored, Doctor Franklin s. little man, 663:4
Snuffed out by article, 398:29
Snug as bug in rug, 303:9
   little farm the world, 381:18
   little island, 372:18
So can any man, 182:34
   if it was s. it might be, 515:19
   if she be not s. to me, 239:17
   it goes, 801:3
   it has been, 695:17
   life boring must not say s., 773:7
   much for him, 196:23
   runs world away, 200:23
Soakers, old s., 277:11
Soaking in comfortable baths, 708:13
Soap dishes or mirrors or Coke bottles, 810:1
   smiles and s., 517:6
Soar, angels alone that s. above, 266:2
   flitter dip and s., 797:14
   not too high to fall, 237:16
   singing still dost s., 403:3
Soaring ever singest, 403:3
   in high region of fancies, 253:19
Soars, if he s. with own wings, 351:13
   no bird s. too high, 351:13
Sober as a judge, 304:10
   be s. be vigilant, 46:3
   certainty of waking bliss, 252:16
   healthful and with his wits, 265:2
   in s. livery clad, 257:24
   plain in dress s. in diet, 297:8
   skies ashen and s., 449:14
   sleep with s. cannibal, 482:21
   steadfast and demure, 251:12
   studious days, 293:21
   take s. coloring from eye, 371:5
   to bed go s., 236:5
Sobering thought when Mozart my age, 819:11
Soberly, entered into s., 49:13
Soberness, speak truth and s., 41:5
Sobers, drinking s. again, 292:12
Sobriety a species of courage, 276:9
   courtesy cleanliness s. and order, 458:17
   something said for s., 773:12

Sobs of violins of autumn, 549:17
   sniffles and smiles, 581:13
   with s. and tears sorted out, 516:7
Sociability law of nature, 542:15
Sociable, society no comfort to one not s., 220:24
Social, capitalism creates s. unrest, 657:22
   chaos serves no s. end, 694:1
   conscience of nation, 823:14
   Contract vast conspiracy, 598:14
   friendly honest man, 356:12
   fundamental of s. relations, 435:20
   in things purely s. separate, 566:3
   leisure class in s. evolution, 569:7
   lies mortar that bind man into s. masonry, 598:14
   lived in s. intercourse, 309:16
   man is a s. animal, 276:13
   mirage of s. justice, 721:1
   Nature's s. union, 356:5
   order and thirsty aspiration, 756:23
   overthrow of s. conditions, 478:15
   process of s. change, 694:10
   producing real s. wealth, 604:14
   progress of each country, 647:9
   ramble ain't restful, 747:6
   self-love and s. be made the same, 363:9
   self-love and s. the same, 295:8
   shalt not commit a s. science, 749:15
   state natural to man, 435:16
   Statics, 538:14
   world work of man, 286:20
Socialism, combines Bolshevism s., 830:3
   inherent virtue of s., 621:18
   Marxian S. portent to historians, 656:12
   what I mean by S., 520:8
   with human face, 796:5
Socialist culture to thrive, 698:13
   democracy may be sham, 658:1
   proceed to construct s. order, 607:11
Socializing, conversation s. instrument, 657:10
Socially invisible, 819:1
Societies, two s. one black one white, 753:18
Society, armed s. is polite s., 750:12
   build a Great S., 753:15
   care of poor incumbent on s., 276:17
   cling together in one s., 368:14
   complicated urban s., 685:5
   conspiracy against manhood, 426:15
   dead or dying, 792:11
   democratic s. like ours, 649:12
   distributes itself, 497:8
   division of s. into two classes, 423:10
   exists for noble actions, 78:24
   fashionable New York S., 504:2
   for previntion of croolty to money, 535:*n*1
   formation of classless s., 477:16
   full of women who remained thirty-five, 560:25
   governed by first two thousand, 807:13
   Great S. lost greatness, 800:2
   great s. on earth, 369:1
   happiness of s. end of government, 330:2
   human combination or s., 247:8
   humble members of s., 364:3
   ideal of democratic free s., 790:18
   in our factitious s., 432:11

Society *(continued)*
>individual not accountable to s., 435:11
>individual promotes interest of s., 319:5
>is a blessing, 333:1
>is no comfort, 220:24
>love as it exists in s., 335:1
>man was formed for s., 318:16
>naked people little influence in s., 525:10
>nerves of s., 538:11
>no arts no letters no s., 239:10
>no one would talk much in s., 343:15
>no s. bring Kingdom of God, 648:6
>no s. can make perpetual constitution, 336:16
>no such thing as s., 810:8
>of neither rich nor poor, 520:8
>offenders, 527:10
>one polished horde, 399:2
>Open S. and Its Enemies, 731:19
>part of S. and traditions, 831:4
>pillars of s., 504:6
>principle on which s. not founded, 315:1
>protection of s., 435:10
>revolutionary reconstitution of s., 478:8
>so riven that moderation gone, 614:1
>solitude best s., 259:8
>Soul selects her S., 508:16
>state = political s. + civil s., 689:14
>state not a mere s., 78:24
>taxes pay for civilized s., 538:12
>three chairs for s., 475:10
>till s. differently constituted, 360:23
>true founder of civil s., 312:12
>unable to live in s., 78:18
>vanilla of s., 375:2
>vast empire of human s., 369:4
>where none intrudes, 396:16
>without aristocracy not society, 657:9
>without objective legal scale, 791:14
>women horses economic factors in s., 579:1
>wonderfully delightful, 560:16

Sociology, children detest s., 740:4
Sock, Jonson's learned s., 251:8
Socket, burn to the s., 372:6
Socrates and two great disciples, 584:6
>corrupts the youth, 74:7
>first to call philosophy down, 88:5
>is a doer of evil, 74:7
>not because S. said so, 153:16
>wisest of men, 260:4

Sod, beneath s. poet lies, 380:8
>builds on watery s., 543:2
>lay s. o'er me, 890:16
>roots grass sends in s., 543:2
>to thy requiem a s., 410:9

Soda, sermons and s. water, 398:10
>wash feet in s. water, 676:11
>water the day after, 398:10

Sodom, is there beauty in S., 492:9
>pitched his tent toward S., 6:29

Soeur, voie lactée ô s. lumineuse, 643:*n9*
Sofa, wheel s. round, 327:1
Soft answer turneth away wrath, 20:30
>bastard Latin, 397:17
>complaining flute, 273:25
>everyone in America s., 581:6
>eyes looked love, 395:13

Soft *(continued)*
>face of a girl, 65:25
>flutes and s. recorders, 255:23
>her voice was ever s., 213:13
>in s. regions born s. men, 69:24
>like a s. job, 824:14
>Lydian airs, 251:8
>makes them s. where we are hard, 710:9
>nature's s. nurse, 188:9
>phrase of peace, 207:33
>rest in s. peace, 232:11
>stillness and the night, 186:15
>summer air, 503:14
>summer season when s. was sun, 131:6
>underbelly of Axis, 621:5
>what s. incense, 410:7
>zephyr blows, 316:15

Soften rocks or bend oak, 287:1
>to us our enemies, 556:12

Softened, cultivation of taste s. me, 761:14
Softer, words were s. than oil, 16:38
Softest clothing woolly bright, 350:12
>music to attending ears, 180:14
>overcome the hardest, 57:14

Soft-lifted by winnowing wind, 411:7
Softly, fair and s. goes far, 132:*n5*
>go s. all my years, 26:22
>she was going up, 376:15
>sleep s. eagle forgotten, 639:11
>speak s. carry big stick, 571:5
>step s. under snow, 618:13
>sweet Thames run s., 161:9
>sweetly speaking and s. laughing, 56:5
>tread s. on dreams, 591:13

Softness, she for s. formed, 257:19
Soil, awkward in their s., 756:3
>contact with s., 597:1
>deserve precious bane, 256:4
>difference of s. and climate, 369:4
>for aesthetic growth, 618:9
>free s. free men, 885:7
>grows on mortal s., 253:7
>itself begins to flee, 837:4
>nation that destroys its s., 652:16
>not every s. can bear all, 93:15
>of experimental physics, 585:7
>of people's necessities, 581:1
>our forces stand on Philippine s., 644:8
>roots of lilac under s., 626:15
>weed that grows in every s., 324:11

Soiled, poor wings so s., 530:23
>truth impossible to be s., 77:*n4*
>wash s. world, 487:11

Soi-même, si l'homme a s., 152:*n6*
Soir, voici le s. charmant, 491:*n7*
Sojourner as all my fathers were, 16:20
Sojourners, we are s. on planet, 415:14
Sojourning, life a battle and s., 111:13
Solace, freedom all s. to man gives, 131:4
Solar walk or milky way, 294:20
Solarium, the s. a rage of light, 871:2
Sold cheap what is most dear, 222:13
>Dickon thy master s., 160:*n6*
>Esau s. his birthright, 6:38
>even to cloak I wore, 140:1
>for endless rue, 574:15
>for old man's gold, 607:6
>goodness s. itself, 889:8

Sold *(continued)*
>my father s. me, 351:2
>neither bought nor s., 838:8
>Reputation for Song, 442:7
>righteous for silver, 29:1
>virtue now is s., 232:15

Soldat, tout s. français porte le bâton, 366:*n3*
Soldier, a s. and afeard, 217:11
>as s. for his country, 290:*n1*
>come back British s., 588:1
>devotion of patriot s., 519:10
>didn't raise boy to be a s., 887:4
>French s. carries marshal's baton, 366:4
>full of strange oaths, 194:25
>gallant old s., 381:*n1*
>gives his life, 420:8
>go to your Gawd like a s., 588:13
>Good S. finest French novel, 616:13
>in s. is flat blasphemy, 206:29
>no s. in gallant band, 528:3
>of ideas, 811:14
>priest s. poet, 491:17
>relish him more in s., 208:18
>rest, 373:21
>stool pigeon when cannot be s., 493:8
>summer s. sunshine patriot, 333:6
>tells his wounds, 101:13
>toy s. red with rust, 554:2

Soldier's, ambition s. virtue, 218:28
>courtier's s. scholar's, 200:2
>grave best, 399:17
>history of s. wound, 314:4
>kiss dwells on bearded lips, 487:9
>many a s. loving arms, 487:9
>pole is fallen, 219:5
>pride touched to quick, 459:23
>sound of white s. axe, 499:3

Soldiers are dreamers, 668:12
>bore dead bodies by, 181:36
>by two and by three, 889:22
>Christian s., 518:14
>citizens of death's land, 668:11
>French s. with artilleryman, 506:13
>grow like savages as s. will, 190:7
>Ireland gives England s., 505:19
>old s. never die, 644:11, 887:4
>regarded wounded s. in envious way, 608:14
>sailors and airmen, 621:9
>tin s. and Nixon coming, 862:5

Soldiers', steel my s. hearts, 189:24
Soldiery, Emperor's drunken s., 595:10
>licentious s., 324:17

Sole arbiter is taste, 450:3
>crown of head to s., 190:37
>go it s. alone, 624:17
>God beside whom is none, 4:8
>rest for the s. of her foot, 6:20
>unbusy thing, 378:14

Soleil bas taché d'horreurs mystiques, 559:*n1*
Solemn drifting down river, 523:2
>fillet, 425:1
>gorgeous palaces s. temples, 225:1
>he says with s. air, 356:9
>pride yours, 446:12
>stillness lay, 457:11
>suits of s. black, 196:26
>this her s. bird, 258:1

Solemnest of industries, 510:11
Solemnities, feasts and high s., 252:25
Solemnized their obsequies, 248:23
　with pomp and parade, 330:1
Soles, eats s. offen shoes, 715:17
Soliciting, still s. eye, 210:30
Solid earth actual world, 473:12
　for fluidity, 619:5
　heaven presents s. hue, 623:3
　massy hard particles, 279:17
　nothing s. is its s. self, 641:18
　pudding empty praise, 296:25
　sop of all this s. globe, 203:7
　this too too s. flesh, 196:29
　virtue, 209:28
Solidarity, family and clan s., 598:10
　forever, 669:14
　independent of differences, 809:3
Solidity, atoms preserved by absolute s., 89:17
　give appearance of s. to pure wind, 735:13
Solitary and cannot impart it, 308:17
　as oyster, 465:5
　be not s. be not idle, 235:20
　convent's s. gloom, 293:23
　God setteth the s. in families, 17:10
　how doth the city sit s., 28:9
　if idle be not s. if s. be not idle, 310:26
　impossible for two s. men, 612:21
　love all s. places, 402:6
　men know friendship, 615:15
　only artist who must be s., 552:14
　poor nasty brutish, 239:10
　puzzling is not a s. game, 842:4
　quite still and s., 655:17
　rare are s. woes, 201:*n*2
　sail that rises, 470:1
　shriek, 398:9
　simile that s. shines, 296:15
　stirred by s. cloud, 279:20
　took their s. way, 259:28
Solitude, artist judged by resonance of s., 734:8
　as if two in deepest s., 431:21
　at depth of human condition, 776:2
　bliss of s., 371:13
　companionable as s., 475:9
　each guardian of other's s., 631:14
　friend to genius, 428:8
　honorable pact with s., 818:8
　how sweet is s., 326:15
　independence of s., 426:18
　is sweet, 326:15
　island s. unsponsored free, 640:22
　love your s., 632:7
　makes s. calls it peace, 396:25
　moral force never dwells in s., 61:3
　not exchange s. for anything, 771:13
　nurse of souls s., 481:11
　O S. where are charms, 326:17
　of his own heart, 434:3
　one chair for s., 475:10
　one hundred years of s., 818:9
　religion experiences in s., 541:18
　safeguard to mediocrity, 428:8
　sometimes best society, 259:8
　Soul to S. retires, 441:6
　steady view of moral s., 567:21
　sweet retired s., 252:17
　teach us to die, 396:4

Solitude *(continued)*
　wander in abysses of s., 556:18
Solitudes, in love two s. touch, 632:5
　pierced our s., 424:9
Solo, cornet s. of Gaelic islands, 694:12
　game, 627:12
Solomon, behold a greater than S., 34:13
　curtains of S., 24:4
　Grundy, 895:10
　in all his glory, 33:9
　loved many strange women, 11:36
　priests in temple of S., 429:21
　Proverbs of S., 465:17
　wisdom of S., 11:30
Solomon's, song of songs which is S., 24:3
Solon was under a delusion, 75:14
Solution, dissatisfaction with other s., 425:18
　easy s. to every human problem, 645:5
　final s., 757:15
　final s. of Jewish question, 697:14
　for world peace, 644:12
　part of s. or of problem, 839:23
Solutions for insoluble problems, 696:4
　two equally convenient s., 558:7
Solvency a matter of temperament, 590:12
Solvent, American life powerful s., 584:10
Somber, I am the s. one, 439:6
　not as s. as December, 821:2
Some are born great, 205:8
　born mad some remain so, 744:17
　born posthumously, 549:9
　come to take their ease, 226:16
　day you'll know, 814:10
　for adventure, 665:8
　gave white bread, 892:18
　must watch some sleep, 200:23
　of you with Pilate, 177:19
　quick to arm, 665:8
　said John print it, 271:6
　say world will end in fire, 623:4
　talk of Alexander, 883:13
　that shadows kiss, 185:9
　the portion of s., 278:9
　to kill cankers, 178:20
　war with rere-mice, 178:20
　will smart for it, 191:14
Somebody, could've had class been s., 776:17
　had s. loved him, 802:15
　how dreary to be S., 508:14
　may be looking, 645:18
　necessary to s., 428:12
　to hew and hack, 262:12
　when everyone is s., 528:6
Somebody's always throwing bricks, 639:12
Someday I must go into that, 624:20
　inner light shine forth, 345:*n*1
　love as though s. hate hate as though s.
　　love, 65:*n*3
　to prove our foe, 65:7
Someone better be prepared, 623:13
　else's freedom, 790:20
　find next morning it was s. else, 361:13
　gently rapping, 449:3
　had blundered, 454:20
　someone else begat, 624:20
　to love and someone to love you, 576:6
　touch my person to s. else's, 486:11
　we can lean on, 857:7

Someone *(continued)*
　while s. else is eating, 748:12
Something about a Martini, 732:9
　attempted something done, 436:13
　beautiful for God, 762:9
　bright and alien, 731:*n*2
　cool s. flowing over hand, 644:5
　crabwise across snow, 808:6
　dead in each of us, 561:5
　death has s. to be said for it, 798:8
　else is alive, 827:10
　ere the end, 451:17
　everything else is about s., 864:9
　everything good for s., 273:11
　expect s. for nothing, 557:9
　fame created s. of nothing, 250:6
　far more interfused, 368:11
　for modern stage, 665:6
　had greater price than life, 726:15
　have all wanted to do s., 472:1
　have in me s. dangerous, 202:19
　he prized and is known by, 658:4
　hidden behind things, 638:9
　hidden go and find it, 589:21
　if s. can go wrong it will, 888:11
　in her gizzard, 277:24
　in the wind, 172:20
　in this more than natural, 199:7
　in us never dies, 358:1
　like a star, 624:18
　lost behind Ranges, 589:21
　might be gaining on you, 747:6
　must be left to chance, 355:10
　nasty in woodshed, 730:7
　old something new, 886:16
　one must be s. to do s., 343:22
　rich and strange, 224:14
　right in world something we trust, 789:10
　rotten in state of Denmark, 198:4
　tells me but not love, 185:15
　that doesn't love a wall, 622:10
　that doth live, 370:20
　time for a little s., 651:9
　'tis s. nothing, 209:2
　to do, 481:20
　too much of this, 200:12
　try do s. for my country, 841:8
　very like Him, 479:11
　what is that s., 726:15
　wrong with something human, 774:16
　you do s. to me, 691:7
　you have to get through, 674:11
　you will see s. new, 739:12
Sometime, come up and see me s., 700:*n*3
　come up s. and see me, 700:7
　did me seek, 149:4
　lofty towers down-rased, 221:18
　woman a s. thing, 711:1
Sometimes, arriving s. at profundity, 830:12
　I feel like a motherless child, 898:16
Somewhat, I have s. against thee, 46:20
Somewhere ages hence, 622:18
　beyond the curtain, 595:17
　end up s. else, 793:8
　Hegel remarks s., 477:14
　in favored land, 585:1
　over the rainbow, 711:12
　people freedom light, 688:10

Sonorous metal blowing, 255:22
Son's son till he gets wife, 503:7
Sons, all her s. at play, 495:6
    anchors of mother's life, 66:23
    bears all its s. away, 289:14
    brother's s. gathering stalk and root, 730:1
    businessmen s. of bitches, 786:6
    degenerate s. and daughters, 605:6
    earth's heedless s., 709:6
    five s. died gloriously, 446:12
    forward s. of France, 361:3
    give them to your s., 894:15
    guide Arcturus with his s., 14:24
    happy to be father unto many s., 170:26
    kill s. of Brutus, 142:9
    more worthless than sires, 97:1
    now we are all s. of bitches, 739:n3
    of Atreus, 583:6
    of Belial, 255:20
    of bitches do you want to live forever, 312:n2
    of dark and bloody ground, 489:7
    of Edward sleep, 171:36
    of former slaves, 823:7
    of God shouted for joy, 14:19
    of men and angels say, 305:7
    of the living God, 28:31
    of toil, 500:5
    see s. what things you are, 188:21
    similar to their fathers, 52:25
    that my s. may have liberty to study, 330:7
    things are s. of heaven, 306:23
    who Shem and Shaun s. of, 650:22
Soon as once set is our little light, 226:20
    better three hours too s., 187:10
    late and s., 371:23
    little pot and s. hot, 173:18
    said to eve Be s., 576:16
    shall thy arm, 327:11
Sooner every party breaks up, 382:19
    it's over sooner to sleep, 481:6
    kill man than hawk, 670:6
    product is no s. created, 364:9
Soonest, least said s. mended, 156:n4
Soot, in s. I sleep, 351:2
Sootfall, stirred by s. of your things, 845:11
Sooth, silly s., 205:2
Soothe a savage breast, 287:1
    cares lift thoughts, 409:4
    flattery s. ear of death, 315:20
    songs s. with their touch, 64:1
    thine ear, 317:12
    what charm s. melancholy, 322:16
Soothed by unfaltering trust, 405:13
Soothing, come lovely s. death, 487:14
    language like Irish for s., 612:3
    language, 337:2
    music, 780:1
Soothsayer, painter trainer s., 109:14
Soothsayers make better living than truthsayers, 335:11
Sop, give s. to Cerberus, 119:23
    of all this solid globe, 203:7
Sophist, saint- nor s.-led, 495:3
Sophisters, age of s., 325:4
Sophisticated modes of discrimination, 649:8
    three on 's are s., 212:3
Sophistries, old old s. of June, 508:6

Sophocles drew men as they ought to be, 65:n1, 67:n1
    long ago, 496:18
Sorbonne, straight one day at S., 642:9
Sorcerer, I who fashioned myself s., 559:12
Sorcery of hot embraces, 688:5
Sordid boon, 371:23
    covetous s. fellow, 298:7
Sore, good for s. eyes, 285:14
    laborers have hard hands, 261:14
    labor's bath, 215:21
    stiff with toils, 488:2
    task, 196:13
    thy hand presseth me s., 16:14
Sores, vile incurable s. on tongues, 699:5
Sorrow, a little fun to match s., 519:8
    abandon learning and no s., 57:9
    and barrenness wrought in my life, 568:17
    and sighing shall flee away, 26:19
    bitterest cup of s., 611:n5
    bread in s. ate, 342:14
    breaks seasons, 171:30
    bring forth children in s., 5:24
    by s. of the heart the spirit is broken, 20:31
    calls no time that's gone, 236:7
    comes in great waves, 544:7
    death and s. our companions, 620:1
    down thou climbing s., 211:17
    enough to disarm, 437:5
    ere s. comes with years, 434:12
    excursion same for s. as joy, 761:1
    for angels, 460:14
    for lost Lenore, 449:5
    for Lycidas s. not dead, 253:14
    frowsy couch in s. steep, 359:2
    give s. words, 217:7
    glut s. on rose, 411:10
    hang s. care'll kill cat, 191:n1
    happy in s., 158:17
    hath less power to bite, 176:17
    he that increaseth knowledge increaseth s., 22:27
    I have known s., 94:8
    idleness s. friend foe, 699:10
    is knowledge, 397:15
    keep thy s. to thyself, 29:26
    legacy alleviates s., 158:13
    more beautiful, 411:13
    more in s. than anger, 197:14
    naught but vast s. there, 616:8
    never comes too late, 315:8
    no great s. dammed up in soul, 689:16
    no more s., 47:12
    no old age only s., 583:3
    not be in s. too, 351:8
    of all prisoners and exiles, 770:5
    of love dureth overlong, 138:7
    of love lasts all life long, 348:18
    parting is such sweet s., 180:16
    pine with fear and s., 160:26
    pure and complete s. impossible, 507:1
    regions of s., 255:9
    rooted s., 217:19
    Russian people make s. a diversion, 602:16
    see if there be s. like unto my s., 28:11
    shall we never have peace without s., 671:15
    sing away s., 156:14

Sorrow *(continued)*
    sit thee down s., 174:6
    sorrow's crown of s., 451:23
    source of Humor not joy but s., 524:12
    sphere of our s., 404:6
    stranger to s., 67:14
    to think full of s., 410:5
    unfelt s., 216:2
    unspeakable s. you bid me renew, 94:9
    veiling song in s., 403:20
    we are not sure of s., 530:17
    wear a golden s., 225:17
    when my heart 'scaped this s., 221:29
    where s. is holy ground, 561:6
    why should s. last, 881:8
    wilt Thou live with me, 454:2
    with night we banish s., 233:18
    with s. to the grave, 7:10
    write s. on bosom of earth, 177:7
    year wake year to s., 403:19
    yet is their strength labor and s., 17:25
Sorrowful, even in laughter the heart is s., 20:26
    O sad kissed mouth how s., 530:3
    soul s. unto death, 36:4
    they were exceeding s., 36:1
Sorrow's crown of sorrow, 451:23
Sorrows, carried our s., 27:6
    come not single spies, 201:27
    disease or s. strike him, 479:11
    few s. in which income no avail, 590:13
    instruct s. to be proud, 175:13
    losses restored and s. end, 221:9
    man of s., 27:5
    of your changing face, 591:6
    when gods bring s., 54:4
    when s. have end, 881:18
    women plunged into s., 360:20
Sorry, cheeks of s. grain, 252:25
    feel s. because we cry, 541:9
    heartily s. for misdoings, 49:5
    if our wishes were gratified, 59:15
    love not having to say s., 843:5
    man who is s. will win, 58:1
    now I wrote it, 598:1
    Scheme of Things, 442:9
    truly s. man's dominion, 356:5
    union of very s. men, 51:25
    wild thing s. for itself, 663:5
Sort, ambition of meaner s., 169:18
    sager s. our deeds reprove, 226:20
    two of every s., 6:18
Sorted out largest size, 516:7
Sorts, all s. and conditions of men, 48:14
    all s. of people, 215:1
So-so is good, 195:33
    some good some s., 107:6
Soudan, home in the S., 587:18
Sought, by night on my bed I s. him, 24:12
    he s. the storms, 272:16
    I never s. world, 311:10
    it with thimbles, 517:6
    less often s. than found, 399:17
    love s. is good, 205:16
    many a thing I s., 221:8
    out many inventions, 23:18
    the remedy, 195:35

Sought *(continued)*

to men that s. him sweet, 226:12

Soul, adventure most unto itself S., 510:1

all the agonies of the s., 507:9

America save s. rather than face, 660:14

and in my s. am free, 266:2

architect expends s., 343:13

art work of body and s., 484:10

astounded s., 797:12

astronomy compels s. to look upwards, 75:12

beauty in inward s., 74:3

belongs to the idea, 534:13

bequeath my s. to God, 166:21

bitterness of my s., 26:22

body brevity wit s., 378:5

body Nature is and God the s., 294:22

brevity the s. of wit, 198:26

call upon my s., 204:21

calm S. of all things, 495:1

can split sky in two, 695:6

captain of his s., 685:6

captain of life, 92:9

captain of my s., 552:8

chainless s., 476:13

charge not s. save to its ability, 118:22

Chariot that bears Human S., 510:14

clap hands and sing, 594:2

cold waters to a thirsty s., 21:35

condemned to be, 510:1

damned of body and s., 587:10

damp of night drives deeper into s., 486:12

dare call s. my own, 434:20

dark night of the s., 154:5

dead that slumbers, 436:4

deep distress humanized my S., 371:19

digressions s. of reading, 314:3

discipline s. of army, 328:4

dissever my s. from s. of Annabel Lee, 449:23

dividing s. and spirit, 45:7

dull would he be of s., 370:2

dusty answer gets s., 505:11

engineers of s., 602:17

eternally unslayable, 84:8

even-balanced s., 494:9

extinguish hope from s., 559:8

extinguished his s., 444:11

fair seedtime had my s., 368:13

false words infect the s., 74:16

fates have given a patient s., 52:18

fiery s., 272:16

find prison s. destroying, 736:6

floated into my inmost s., 482:20

flow of s., 296:6

folk songs from s. sounds, 704:16

for which s. did pine, 448:6

force, 604:4

from out that shadow, 449:12

gain world lose s., 34:39

genial current of s., 315:22

gives heart and s. away, 574:16

go S. the body's quest, 159:9

God changes I am the s., 530:20

grapple them to thy s., 197:22

grave unto a s., 175:17

half conceal S. within, 453:11

half of my own s., 96:2

Soul *(continued)*

hang like fruit my s., 220:29

harrow up thy s., 198:5

has fled, 438:6

has many motions, 756:12

has to itself decreed, 409:1

hath been alone, 377:4

hath elbow-room, 176:4

hath not lifted his s. unto vanity, 15:24

hath power to know all things, 227:16

he restoreth my s., 15:23

he shall preserve thy s., 18:30

he whose s. is flat, 695:6

heaven take my s., 175:31

height my s. can reach, 434:17

her lips suck forth my s., 168:21

him whom my s. loveth, 24:12

his s. sincere, 316:7

honor belongs to s., 111:7

Horror s. of plot, 448:14

human body best picture human s., 685:12

humble and strengthen s., 150:3

I am world's s., 364:16

I have liberated my s., 123:12

I hope his s. be in glorie, 135:9

icebergs behoove the s., 762:13

idea does not belong to s., 534:13

if s. knows God in creatures, 127:13

if you would keep s., 666:5

immortal because has s., 714:6

immortal s. and all, 663:4

in bliss, 213:4

in mystery s. abides, 494:17

in prison I am not free, 561:11

in s. of man one insular Tahiti, 483:5

in the s. and the clod, 462:5

into boughs does glide, 267:2

inviting s. to wander for a spell, 556:18

iron entered into his s., 49:21

is form and doth body make, 161:7

is his own, 189:21

is in a ferment, 409:6

is marching on, 521:1

is the concern of my Lord, 118:15

its body off, 596:5

Jesus lover of my s., 305:8

Jonathan loved him as his own s., 11:4

joy's s. lies in doing, 203:2

kindled at conwiviality, 464:26

kiss my whole s., 168:*n*6

knows no release, 718:6

largest and most comprehensive s., 272:6

lay not unction to s., 201:9

lends tongue vows, 197:28

let dozing s. remember, 139:5

life meets all motion becomes its s., 375:15

life of s., 300:5

lift my s. to heaven, 225:15

listened intensely, 372:7

little s. wandering guest, 111:2

loafe and invite my s., 485:15

locust of s. unshelled, 798:2

look and body touch, 596:12

love the Lord with all thy s., 9:15

made up of wants, 480:10

man became a living s., 5:10

many a man's s. and faith, 857:5

means of soothing s., 605:11

Soul *(continued)*

measured by my s., 289:4

meeting s. may pierce, 251:8

merry old s., 892:13

migration of the s., 74:9

mind and s. according, 453:10

mirroring s., 495:2

more stately mansions O s., 443:10

most offending s. alive, 189:25

motorcycle parked like s. of junkyard, 801:16

mount mount my s., 177:25

my father lived his s., 701:19

my sin my s., 723:5

my s. an't yours Mas'r, 458:16

my S. at Liberty, 509:1

my s. breaks and buds, 268:12

my s. bright invisible green, 473:21

my s. deep like rivers, 730:13

my s. doth magnify the Lord, 37:9

my s. there is a country, 268:15

my s. thirsteth for thee, 17:6

my s. waiteth for the Lord, 19:8

my unconquerable s., 552:7

mysterious thing in s., 483:12

nature shows inner images of s., 583:15

never did I harm living s., 551:1

never taught to stray, 294:20

new depths broken in s., 388:9

nice clean s., 824:14

no coward s. mine, 476:14

no higher than s. high, 695:6

no s. shall be wronged, 119:8

Northland s., 708:6

not bruised to pleasure s., 594:17

not more than body, 486:17

not spoken of the s., 436:4

nothing contributes more to peace of s., 335:8

numerical precision s. of science, 579:7

O my prophetic s., 198:8

O my s. is white, 350:14

O s. be changed to waterdrops, 169:5

of Adonais like star, 404:3

of business, 298:15

of each God of all, 375:16

of goodness in things evil, 189:20

of grandam inhabit a bird, 185:*n*2

of man immortal, 75:25

of music shed, 387:8

of sleeper away, 558:3

of s. sincere, 294:9

of the age, 232:19

of the plot, 448:14

of wit, 198:26

offends me to the s., 200:6

one of principal appetites of s., 702:16

one s. though many tongues, 113:8

owe s. to company store, 789:1

paints itself in our machines, 347:15

perches in the s., 508:12

perdition catch my s., 208:35

pilgrim s. in you, 591:6

Plato healer of s., 74:*n*1

pledge s. had been there, 378:18

poet brings s. into activity, 379:12

poet of Body poet of S., 486:5

poetry should enter one's s., 412:16

Soul *(continued)*

poor intricated s., 231:13
poor s. sat sighing, 210:8
poor s. the center, 223:4
possess s. with patience, 274:6
pouring forth s., 410:9
pray for repose of his s., 578:16
pray Lord my s. keep, 283:9
preserve one's s. alive, 568:16
prophet of the s., 424:4
prophetic s. of world, 222:10
Psyche my S., 449:16
pure and clear as crystal, 466:32
rapt s. in thine eyes, 251:13
receive my s. at last, 305:8
recovers radical innocence, 593:18
rejoices in truth uttered, 471:7
remembering my good friends, 176:29
rescue my s. from their destructions, 16:8
research into feminine s., 564:5
rest her s. she's dead, 202:9
richness of s., 77:4
riddling perplexed s., 231:13
roamed with my S., 449:16
ruled by levity pure, 778:15
sad glance glum, 527:25
sad lucidity of s., 494:14
said to s. be still, 678:20
same in all creatures, 71:9
save my s. if I have s., 500:13
saves s. in new French books, 461:23
School Intelligence make it a s., 413:15
science without conscience ruin of s., 145:10
seeking with s. land of Greeks, 343:4
selects her Society, 508:16
shall be required of thee, 38:4
shorten stature of s., 505:8
shrinks from all to remember, 797:13
sighed s. toward Grecian tents, 186:14
sincerely from author's s., 702:13
sinews of s., 250:7
single s. in two bodies, 77:10
sleepless s. that perished, 369:16
smithy of s., 650:13
so dead, 373:3
so panteth my s. after thee, 16:21
sorrowful unto death, 36:4
speech a mirror of s., 101:10
stirred s. to inmost depths, 420:18
strains that might create a s., 252:21
strong is the s., 494:11
sun steadies my s., 671:14
sweet and virtuous s., 242:21
swell the s. to rage, 274:21
swooned slowly, 650:9
take my s. to rest, 226:24
takes nothing with her, 74:17
taste sadness of might, 411:11
terror is of the soul, 448:10
that rises with us, 370:17
the hungry s., 22:2
thirst that from s. doth rise, 232:16
thirsteth for God, 16:21
this that oppresses s., 517:5
thou hast much goods, 38:3
thoughtful S. to Solitude, 441:6
thy s. the fixt foot, 229:17
time the s. of this world, 108:16

Soul *(continued)*

'tis my outward s., 230:1
to dare, 373:20
to find its proper body, 775:12
two to bear my s. away, 265:3
unconscious s. of country, 581:8
unlettered small-knowing s., 174:4
unto captain Christ, 177:14
upon my s. between kisses, 599:14
variety s. of pleasure, 279:5
wake s. by tender strokes, 293:13
was like a star, 370:10
wears out breast, 397:14
weddings of the s., 641:14
what Fortitude S. contains, 511:13
what of s. left I wonder, 462:3
what s. without flaws, 559:6
whispereth within him, 119:12
whose s. is sense, 229:15
why art thou cast down O my s., 16:22
why castest thou off my s., 17:22
windows of the s., 354:17
with all its maladies, 534:4
with all thy heart and s., 35:13
with my whole s., 28:7
witness of s. naturally Christian, 113:5
yet my s. drew back, 243:11
Soul-hungry, worse to be s., 886:12
Soul-making, vale of S., 413:14
Soul's dark cottage, 249:28
for s. good do things disliked, 626:19
my s. calm retreat, 269:2
prayer s. sincere desire, 372:19
whole s. tasking, 481:15
Souls are in the hand of God, 29:34
beams of wit on other s., 273:14
beyond reaches of our s., 197:34
boundless as we wish our s., 402:6
corporations have no s., 158:25, 551:2
damp s. of housemaids, 675:9
departed shadows of living, 249:6
engineers of human s., 636:15
essential American s. is hard, 663:3
flame of freedom in s., 537:9
great s. suffer in silence, 359:15
have sight of sea, 371:3
hear me ambitious s., 605:4
immediate jewel of their s., 209:2
in s. sympathy with sounds, 327:4
jealous s. not answered, 209:22
left your s. on earth, 411:4
letters mingle s., 230:14
live in furnished s., 701:8
look after s. in labor, 76:5
love's mysteries in s. grow, 229:20
many valiant s. of heroes, 50:9
memory green in our s., 387:7
miserable state wretched s., 128:9
mounting up to God, 506:1
must not be saved, 208:24
numberless infinities of s., 230:19
nurse of full-grown s., 481:11
of animals infuse themselves, 185:31
of emperors and cobblers, 152:17
of Poets dead, 411:5
our selves our s. and bodies, 49:7
our s. survive death, 101:*n*6
our two s. which are one, 229:16

Souls *(continued)*

patent leather s., 717:4
possess s. in patience, 38:28
prosperity tries s. even of wise, 92:6
pure lovers' s. descend, 229:19
see s. we loved, 455:4
sit close and silently, 155:*n*1
such harmony in immortal s., 186:15
sucks two s., 230:4
that cringe and plot, 481:14
there be s. must be saved, 208:24
those poor S. who dwell in Night, 354:7
through such s. God shows light, 463:3
times that try men's s., 333:6
to believing s. gives light, 170:2
unbodied, 230:13
violent s., 676:20
waking s., 228:7
wounded by such things, 267:15
Sound as of rushing wind, 40:14
believeth it is s. of trumpet, 14:28
bells s. on Bredon, 575:1
bitter joy hear s. of wings, 718:6
came o'er my ear like sweet s., 204:10
chief s. of life is hiss, 483:17
come back s., 157:27
deeper than plummet s., 225:4
empty vessel greatest s., 190:2
far-off curfew s., 251:17
full of s. and fury, 217:23
hearest the s. thereof, 39:9
heart s. as bell, 190:38
let it s. no more, 177:24
let s. of it flee, 332:20
light in s. s.-like power in light, 375:15
mind in sound body, 109:26, 275:10
music with silver s., 881:6
must seem echo to sense, 292:19
my barbaric yawp, 486:19
nature without voice or s., 318:7
no riches above s. body, 31:15
no s. of planes, 774:12
no s. of water, 676:6
no war or battle's s., 250:11
noght but eyr ybroken, 132:2
of body and mind, 96:15
of bone against plate, 850:8
of great Amen, 502:17
of her silk skirt, 86:18
of horn at night, 416:4
of horns and motors, 676:11
of jets overhead, 724:6
of public scorn, 259:19
of revelry by night, 395:13
of the grinding is low, 23:30
of thunder heard remote, 256:20
of voice that is still, 452:15
silver-sweet s. lovers' tongues, 180:14
slight s. at evening, 472:22
sweet is every s., 453:7
thought and magic s., 418:21
too full for s., 456:4
trump of rescue s., 424:20
trumpet beat drums, 301:13
trumpet give uncertain s., 42:30
trumpet shall s., 43:8
trumpets beat drums, 274:16
upon bugle horn, 451:20

Species *(continued)*
    in every individual, 774:7
    in propagating the s., 614:15
    not individual but s., 304:13
    one s. of superstition, 312:1
    origin of s., 440:3
    preservation of s., 360:26
    strange s. we are, 733:5
    variety among individuals of species, 321:5
Specified, localized and s., 582:15
Specious, murder takes s. name, 290:15
Spectacle, life is not a s., 770:12
    unto the world, 42:11
Spectacles, finest s. in nature, 303:8
    immense accumulation of s., 829:12
    of books, 272:7
    on nose pouch on side, 194:25
Spectator, live as s. of mankind, 288:2
    of mighty scene, 386:3
Spectators, pleasure to s., 420:4
    some must be s., 233:12
    we are only s., 672:10
Spectatum veniunt veniunt spectentur, 102:*n*3
Specter bark, 376:9
    haunting Europe, 478:7
    my s. around me, 353:10
Specter-gray, when Frost was s., 536:10
Specters' holiday, 527:23
Specter-thin, pale and s., 410:5
Speculate, dog might as well s., 440:7
Speculating, theologian not born by s., 144:8
Speculation, everybody watches s., 464:38
    rouse s. about dangerous things, 770:16
Speculators about perpetual motion, 140:13
    philosophical s., 155:7
Speech, abridging freedom of s., 340:1
    after long silence, 596:3
    be alway with grace, 44:14
    day unto day uttereth s., 15:15
    dead had no s. for, 679:8
    finely framed, 31:34
    first silence of s., 437:21
    free men from bondage, 562:9
    free s. Frémont, 885:7
    free s. in repulsive form, 621:8
    freedom of s. and expression, 653:4
    freedom of s. freedom of conscience,
      524:14
    freedom of s. taken, 328:10
    from him never real s., 408:2
    good s. more hidden than malachite, 3:4
    I am slow of s., 7:30
    I wrote in a garret, 305:*n*5
    impelled us, 679:10
    in substaunce ys but air, 132:2
    is civilization, 631:7
    is image of actions, 55:15
    is like tapestries, 62:21
    is serious, 764:2
    let thy s. be short, 31:19
    like cracked kettle, 493:13
    make s. to maggots, 700:19
    many harmed by s., 149:9
    mend your s. a little, 210:25
    mighty true free Russian s., 479:8
    mirror of soul, 101:10
    never taxed for s., 205:30
    no good s. save in Paris, 139:2

Speech *(continued)*
    nowhere is s. freer, 621:8
    our concern was s., 679:10
    plainness of s., 43:13
    poetry of s., 396:8
    protection of free s., 538:21
    regretted s. never silence, 101:9
    right s., 64:18
    rude am I in my s., 207:33
    rude in s., 43:20
    short meaning of long s., 360:3
    Silence golden S. silvern, 406:23
    speak the s. I pray you, 200:6
    steep my s. in lies, 63:26
    strange power of s., 377:3
    subtle s. delights us, 87:17
    suppression of free s., 562:9
    sweeter than honey, 50:16
    Tennysonianness of s., 664:17
    thy s. bewrayeth thee, 36:10
    to conceal thoughts, 299:23
    to stir men's blood, 193:4
    took all heart for s., 592:19
    what s. escaped your teeth, 51:5
Speeches, men's charitable s., 166:21
    no one hears our s., 690:13
    not my s. you mislike, 169:23
    questions not decided by s., 470:6
Speed, all deliberate s., 692:*n*4
    at rate of six miles an hour, 388:14
    be wise with s., 290:14
    deliberate s., 576:14
    far faster than light, 618:1
    full s. ahead, 421:1
    good s. to your youthful valor, 95:9
    his plow, 163:17
    in skating safety is s., 427:11
    mass times s. of light squared, 637:*n*4
    more haste less s., 99:4
    of my desire, 502:18
    retiring at high s. toward Japanese, 650:5
    the parting guest, 293:19
    the plow, 163:*n*5
    thousands at his bidding s., 254:22
    through the antiseptic tunnel, 820:8
    today put back tomorrow, 160:26
    wrong to s. a guest, 53:22
Speeding, Rus whither are you s., 443:1
    unreeling tirelessly s. them, 488:5
Speeds, dawn s. a man, 54:26
    parting guest, 594:11
    tale s. best plainly told, 172:1
    wit s. too fast, 174:10
Speedy and public trial, 340:5
Spell, foreigners s. better than pronounce,
    522:4
Spells, all civil charms and priestly s., 483:22
Spencer, expression used by S., 439:14
Spencer's, Mr. S. Social Statics, 538:14
Spend life your own way, 688:1
    mind business s. less, 277:9
    ne'er s. fury on child, 171:3
    not s. another such night, 171:27
    not then his gifts in vain, 232:5
    shafts and spare not, 881:15
    sweetest hours e'er I s., 356:23
    that shortness basely, 183:28
    time most valuable thing man can s., 81:17

Spend *(continued)*
    we s. our years as a tale that is told, 17:24
    wealth at once you are ruined, 417:14
    what we yet may s., 441:17
    whatever you have s. less, 311:9
Spending, getting and s., 371:23
    lives like serfs, 475:12
    old age time of s., 261:12
    riches are for s., 166:9
    youth now bravely s., 683:4
Spendthrifts, kings and ministers greatest s.,
    319:4
Spens, gude Sir Patrick S., 889:17
Spenser, not lodge thee by S., 232:19
    renowned S., 240:6
Spent, all passion s., 260:27
    but one day thoroughly well, 137:9
    confess this world's s., 230:15
    consider how light is s., 254:20
    days are s. without hope, 13:16
    dissolutely s. Tuesday morning, 181:22
    life half s. before we know, 244:25
    life well s. is long, 140:4
    never s. hour's talk withal, 174:9
    under belly, 236:12
    waves' riot, 530:15
Sperm, created you of s. drop, 118:21
Spes, dum anima est s. est, 87:*n*11
Spew thee out of my mouth, 46:26
Sphere, enforced from quiet s., 188:17
    great s. thou movest in, 219:3
    in which our beliefs are cherished, 610:12
    motion in one s., 183:29
    nature in terms of s., 533:17
    owner of s., 425:6
    storm-troubled s., 476:14
Spheres, driven by the s., 268:14
    ever-moving s. of Heaven, 169:3
    invisible s. formed in fright, 483:4
    moving as the restless S., 168:2
    music from the s., 205:12
    music of the s., 248:17
    prefers live music to humdrum s., 813:14
    seems to shake the s., 274:15
    stars shot madly from their s., 178:15
    start from their s., 198:5
    tuned s., 219:8
Spherical, body perfectly s., 467:6
    predominance, 211:3
    read that world was s., 139:12
Sphery chime, 252:28
Sphinx, riddle of the S., 66:7
Spice, sugar and s., 895:12
    variety's s. of life, 326:22
Spices thereof may flow out, 24:16
    young hart upon mountains of s., 24:27
Spicy grove cinnamon tree, 734:10
    no s. fragrance while they grow, 165:*n*3
    nut-brown ale, 251:5
    Phoenix builds s. nest, 245:16
Spider, almost like a s., 154:12
    along came a s., 895:14
    confined in web's center, 154:12
    connection between s. and Saturn, 298:22
    much as one holds s., 301:11
    noiseless patient s., 488:5
    spend time like spider spinning entrails,
      499:6

Spider *(continued)*
    subtle s., 155:*n*1
    to Fly, 418:16
Spider-like we feel the touch, 155:*n*1
Spider's net is heavy, 757:3
    touch how fine, 155:*n*1
Spiders, like s. across stars, 799:3
    love of s., 724:7
    marching through air, 787:3
    none of new s. took her place, 724:8
    preserved in amber, 107:*n*4
Spiders', laws like s. webs, 56:2
Spielvogel, Doctor S. this is my life, 835:4
Spies a far-off shore, 170:27
    God's s., 213:8
    single s., 201:27
    what do you think s. are, 830:5
Spill, all germens s. at once, 211:24
Spilled, as water s. on the ground, 11:21
    fearing to be s., 201:22
Spills in fearing to be spilt, 201:22
Spin, great world s. forever, 452:10
    set by fire and s., 893:15
    toil not neither s., 33:8
    webs from entrails s., 155:*n*1
Spinach and the hell with it, 723:17
    gammon and s., 465:30, 892:12
Spinnage, gammon and s., 465:30
Spinning our own fates, 540:23
Spinning-jenny and railroad, 481:3
    out of side, 594:15
Spinning-wheel, make me O Lord thy s., 280:17
Spinoza, atheism like that of S., 584:12
Spins, hither and thither s., 495:2
Spinsters and knitters in the sun, 205:2
Spiral down militaristic stairway, 823:13
Spires, dreaming s., 496:13
    what s. what farms, 575:6
    ye distant s., 315:4
Spirit, absent in body present in s., 42:12
    Accusing S., 314:18
    actions must be his s., 79:10
    against flesh, 43:30
    all compact of fire, 171:8
    and with your s., 47:18
    animating universe, 415:14
    be thou S. fierce, 402:13
    Big Blue Mountain S., 891:15
    blessed are poor in s., 32:14
    blithe s., 403:2
    bloweth and is still, 494:17
    body and s. twins, 531:2
    body without s. is dead, 45:26
    born of the S., 39:9
    by my s. saith the Lord, 29:12
    by sorrow s. broken, 20:31
    cabined ample s., 495:20
    capable of compassion, 714:6
    Chinese not have national s., 598:10
    cries for expression, 703:10
    decides issue, 644:14
    delighted s., 206:38
    descending like dove, 32:9
    dividing soul and s., 45:7
    English department of the s., 810:3
    erring s., 196:18
    essential in painting, 122:11
    eternal S. of chainless Mind, 397:8

Spirit *(continued)*
    everything that emancipates s., 344:29
    expense of s. in waste of shame, 222:20
    fled indignant to the shades, 95:12
    follow your s., 189:9
    fruit of the S., 43:31
    full of s. as month of May, 183:12
    gentleness of s. serenity of mind, 245:*n*2
    gentlier on s. lies, 450:17
    giveth life, 43:12
    haughty s. before a fall, 20:37
    he that ruleth his s., 20:38
    holiday-rejoicing s., 383:16
    humble in s., 22:11
    I commend my s., 38:37
    ill s. have so fair a house, 224:17
    immortal s. grows, 368:14
    in one s. meet mingle, 402:16
    in s. and truth, 39:13
    invisible s. of wine, 208:30
    is departed, 31:24
    is willing, 36:6
    letter and s. of constitution, 349:16
    lifeblood of master s., 254:8
    lively understandable s., 756:2
    Mammon least erected s., 256:3
    man of understanding is of excellent s.,
      20:43
    meek and quiet s., 45:40
    motion and a s., 368:11
    motions of his s. dull, 186:17
    my s. too weak, 411:16
    naught so much s. calms, 398:8
    no longer ruler of own s., 363:4
    no s. can walk abroad, 196:19
    not letter but s., 43:12
    of age, 300:3
    of Beauty that dost consecrate, 401:10
    of counsel and might, 25:18
    of Delight, 404:8
    of fear, 44:39
    of God brother of my own, 485:17
    of God moved upon face of the waters, 5:3
    of knowledge and fear of the Lord, 25:18
    of liberty, 324:3
    of love how quick and fresh, 204:11
    of men who follow, 664:11
    of moderation, 614:1
    of Night, 404:7
    of party, 328:15
    of popular government, 345:10
    of prophecy in me, 74:14
    of repose, 420:18
    of suspicion and distrust, 614:3
    of the valley never dies, 57:2
    of wisdom and understanding, 25:18
    of youth in everything, 222:6
    of Zeus-fostered kings, 50:22
    original creation of s., 580:7
    passed before my face, 13:8
    perturbed s., 198:21
    poetry finer s. of knowlege, 369:3
    proud and chivalrous s., 79:10
    rare detachment of s., 626:22
    real and eternal, 493:6
    renew a right s. within me, 16:32
    resemblance neglects s. of objects, 123:1
    revenge delight of mean s., 110:1

Spirit *(continued)*
    rules secretly alone, 868:11
    sacred to departed s., 120:17
    scorned his s., 191:30
    self-same sounds on s., 641:4
    shall rest upon him, 25:18
    shall return unto God, 23:31
    shallow s. of judgment, 169:15
    slave s. below, 666:12
    slumber did my s. seal, 369:8
    so still and quiet, 207:35
    spur the clear s. cloth raise, 253:6
    strongest and fiercest s., 256:7
    that always denies, 344:4
    that on life's rough sea, 163:20
    that quickeneth, 39:19
    that stands by naked man, 881:22
    thy s. walks abroad, 193:19
    too much s. to be at ease, 293:27
    tool carries s. by which created, 728:4
    travail and vexation of s., 23:1
    truth shows s. and substance, 123:1
    vanity and vexation of s., 22:26
    vital s., 572:10
    weak s. quickens, 677:19
    whatever anguish of s., 331:10
    whither shall I go from thy s., 19:13
    wild S. moving everywhere, 402:10
    within me constraineth me, 14:12
    within nourishes, 94:33
    wounded s. who can bear, 21:2
    yearning in desire, 451:15
    yet a S. still and bright, 371:8
Spirit-voice, 268:13
Spiriting, do my s. gently, 224:10
Spiritless, man so faint so s., 187:22
Spirit's, clown of s. motive, 772:2
Spirits, all s. and melted into air, 225:1
    blast drives wicked s., 128:15
    by our own s. defied, 369:16
    call s. from vasty deep, 182:34
    can either sex assume, 255:19
    cheerer of s., 245:1
    day of s., 269:2
    good s. when well dressed, 464:33
    her wanton s. look out, 204:4
    I summoned up, 343:9
    in the material world, 870:3
    insult to s. of ancestors, 499:3
    like two s. suggest me, 223:3
    maketh his angels s., 45:6
    master s. of this age, 192:20
    not jump with common s., 185:7
    of great events, 384:*n*3
    of just men, 45:14
    of land and grain, 80:8
    of the damned, 444:11
    of wise mock us, 188:5
    other s. standing apart, 408:18
    that fell with Lucifer, 168:17
    that tend thoughts, 214:17
    throng with returning s., 394:3
    tribe of s. and of men, 119:13
    unclean s. entered swine, 36:32
    unhappy s. fell with Lucifer, 168:17
    vanish like evil s., 338:8
    we are s. not animals, 620:7
    who live in twilight, 571:1

Spirits *(continued)*
    wonders at quaint s., 178:21
Spirit-stirring drum, 209:13
Spiritu, et cum s. tuo, 47:18
Spiritual excitement, 497:5
    found s. cause, 493:5
    highest s. authority, 647:10
    in tendency, 456:14
    inward and s. grace, 49:12
    millions of s. creatures, 258:2
    natural fact symbol of s., 425:24
    Negro s. free at last, 823:9
    perfection of man, 124:14
    psalms hymns and s. songs, 43:38
    single s. heritage of nation, 602:4
    stronger than material, 428:28
    wickedness in high places, 43:40
Spirochete, without little s., 798:3
Spit, if I lie s. in my face, 182:21
    on us for luck, 82:13
    upon my Jewish gaberdine, 184:28
Spite, in erring reason's s., 294:23
    O cursed s., 198:22
    of cormorant devouring Time, 173:38
    the world, 216:7
Spiteful envious animal the Public, 386:4
Splashing wintry mold, 591:9
Spleen, in a s. unfolds heaven and earth, 177:28
    that scourge of Britain, 418:20
Splendid abilities utterly corrupt, 381:5
    and sterile Dolores, 529:17
    by the vision s., 370:18
    give me s. silent sun, 487:10
    in ashes, 249:4
    little war, 532:13
    misery, 337:5
    poor s. wings, 530:23
    you rise, 4:4
Splendide mendax, 97:*n2*
Splendidly null, 454:26
Splendor falls on castle walls, 452:19
    in the grass, 371:4
    not in lone s., 412:10
    of the Mighty One Krishna, 84:13
    your s. like heaven's s., 4:2
Splendors, heaven with s. lie, 481:14
Splenetive and rash, 202:19
Split ears of groundlings, 200:6
    mountains with thunderbolt, 93:13
    sides with laughing, 156:31
    the sky in two, 695:6
    world would s. open, 771:19
Splits, who s. wood warms twice, 475:*n1*
Splitting, image of s. apart, 4:10
    warmed while s. stumps, 475:13
Spoil it by trying to explain, 346:8
    little foxes that s. the vines, 24:10
    lives of better people, 556:2
    no more s. upon my face, 190:9
    rampant for s. and victory, 548:15
    spare rod and s. child, 81:*n3*, 262:17
    villainous company s. of me, 183:8
Spoiled, good walk s., 525:12
Spoiling nice new clothes, 895:3
Spoils, conquests glories triumphs s., 192:19
    of time, 315:22
    rich with s. of Nature, 248:4
    to victor belong s., 393:17

Spoils *(continued)*
    treasons stratagems and s., 186:17
    victor belongs to s., 710:1
Spoke, never s. with God, 510:9
    of disastrous chances, 207:37
    town-crier s. my lines, 200:6
Spoken, glorious things of thee s., 321:1
    God had never s. anything but English,
      622:5
    God's last Put out Light s., 623:13
    lie down till leaders s., 588:19
    not s. of soul, 436:4
    Rome has s. case closed, 116:15
    speak when s. to, 555:9
    weird power in s. word, 567:7
    word comes not back, 98:*n3*
Spokesmen have all the loudspeakers, 764:2
Spondee, slow S. stalks, 378:11
Sponges, string of wet s., 645:6
Spontaneity, studied s. of Horace, 105:24
Spontaneous joy and natural content, 592:5
    overflow of feelings, 369:5
Spoon, dish ran away with s., 893:16
    hire long s. eat with feend, 136:3
    runcible s., 467:10
    silver s. in mouth, 158:11
Spoonful, everybody fightin' about s., 779:4
Spoons, faster counted s., 419:*n3*
    guard our s., 419:15
    let us count our s., 309:5
    measured life with coffee s., 674:21
    woman with silver s., 473:19
Sport, boys throw stones in s., 82:9
    ended his s. with Tess, 536:5
    make s. for neighbors, 382:12
    of kings, 289:19
    present life a diversion and s., 119:3
    that wrinkled Care derides, 250:22
    they kill us for their s., 212:17
    to have enginer hoist, 201:15
    with Amaryllis, 253:6
    would be tedious, 181:33
Sported on the green, 381:6
Sports and plays with me, 350:8
    joy of youthful s., 396:22
    of love, 232:5
    shows games s. guns, 330:1
Sporus, let S. tremble, 295:14
Spot, black s. to keep concealed, 504:5
    certain am I of s., 510:9
    dim s. men call earth, 251:25
    do in that remote s., 365:15
    earth one mighty blood s., 430:24
    out damned s., 217:10
    stand on right s., 343:10
    there is no s. in thee, 24:14
    what is Black S., 555:5
Spotless reputation, 176:8
Spots, leopard change his s., 27:34
    minds grow in s., 542:8
Spotted sight or sound, 666:5
    snakes with double tongue, 178:22
Spouse, President's s. I wish him well, 807:14
    so bright and clear, 230:27
Spout till you have drenched, 211:24
Spouted arms, 720:7
Spouts black blood and rolls fin out, 483:1
    trunk s. out a sea, 258:27

Sprang to the stirrup, 460:16
Sprat, Jack S. eat no fat, 892:15
Sprawl is bad aesthetics, 789:4
Spray, never a s. of yew, 495:19
    nightingale on bloomy s., 253:16
    rime was on the s., 535:11
    toss in the s., 494:12
Spread alarm, 437:16
    dreams under your feet, 591:13
    masters s. yourselves, 178:3
    money not good unless s., 165:25
    out against sky, 674:17
    truth from pole to pole, 287:21
    with her fan s., 287:3
Spreading, by broad s. disperse, 169:13
    chestnut tree, 436:11
    himself like a green bay tree, 16:12
Spreads, wrath s. through hearts of men, 52:7
Sprechen ist silbern, 406:23
    wovon man nicht s. kann, 685:*n3*
Spree, gentlemen rankers on s., 588:6
Sprightly, tossing heads in s. dance, 371:11
Spring, a little Madness in S., 511:1
    absent in the s., 222:6
    apparelled like the s., 220:9
    blossom by blossom s. begins, 529:13
    breaks through again, 719:13
    brings back balmy warmth, 91:14
    brown hills melted into s., 476:11
    can really hang you up, 816:2
    can s. be far behind, 402:14
    clean pasture s., 622:9
    come gentle S., 300:18
    comes slowly up this way, 377:8
    comes unheralded by birds, 750:4
    comes with rustling shade, 682:6
    direful s., 293:16
    disturbance of the s., 678:15
    ever-returning s., 487:12
    flowers that bloom in s., 527:20
    from her may violets s., 202:15
    full of sweet days, 242:20
    game begins in the s., 844:8
    hounds of s., 529:12
    in Just-s., 701:5
    in s. young man's fancy, 451:21
    in the fire of S., 441:7
    infants of s., 197:19
    last leaf in s., 443:15
    lived light in s., 495:8
    makest a s. to gush forth, 118:16
    Mrs. Porter in s., 676:11
    no season such delight as s., 240:8
    no s. nor summer beauty, 230:9
    not as in bud of s., 231:10
    nothing so beautiful as S., 546:5
    of ever-flowing water, 95:24
    of love gushed from heart, 376:17
    of love resembleth April day, 173:29
    of prodigality, 324:15
    Pierian s., 292:12
    ran canyons all s., 720:7
    season of s. comes on, 51:11
    silent s., 750:5
    starless and bible-black, 777:17
    stirring roots with s. rain, 676:5
    summer autumn winter, 701:17
    sunshine streamed in, 513:7

Spring *(continued)*
    sweet lovers love the s., 196:2
    targeted trod like S., 595:17
    that brims and ripples, 154:4
    time abhorrent to nihilist, 640:13
    'tis s. and weeds shallow-rooted, 170:5
    where are songs of S., 411:8
    Winter mother of S., 438:4
    year's at s., 459:19
    year's pleasant king, 227:4
Springes to catch woodcocks, 197:27
Springs, beside the s. of Dove, 369:7
    entered into s. of sea, 14:21
    every thought that s., 372:15
    fifty s. little room, 574:11
    from seventy s. a score, 574:11
    hope s. eternal, 294:19
    of behavior hidden, 617:15
    root from which tyrant s., 75:20
    Scotia's grandeur s., 356:10
    steeds to water at those s., 220:15
Springth the wude nu, 880:5
Springtime, birds warble sweet in s., 558:1
    for Hitler and Germany, 811:9
    fragrance of all s., 780:14
    in s. every day growths, 480:14
    only pretty ring time, 196:2
Sprinkled, blood s. upon my garments, 27:17
Sprite, angelic s., 230:18
    my weary s. longs to fly, 226:24
Sprites and goblins, 223:14
Sprouting despondently at gates, 675:9
    no cabbages s. out, 444:9
Spruce affectation, 174:28
    cone regularity, 671:11
Sprung, vile dust whence he s., 373:3
Spun, gods have s. the thread, 52:19
    of Iris' woof, 252:5
    yarn s. in Ulysses' absence, 219:22
Spur, avarice s. of industry, 311:22
    between s. and bridle, 244:16
    fame is the s., 253:6
    me into song, 596:17
    my dull revenge, 201:19
    no s. to my intent, 214:24
    pain of bone s. in heel, 722:3
    reward and punishment s., 275:11
    studies a s. to young, 87:11
Spurn, existence saw him s. reign, 306:9
Spurned, youth s. in vain, 163:3
Spurns that patient merit takes, 199:21
Spurred boldly on and dashed, 273:7
Spurs, let boy win his s., 131:2
    now s. lated traveler, 216:14
Spy, prettiest little parlor you did s., 418:16
    sent to s. out the land, 9:3
Spying, bitter little embryos s., 723:4
Squabbling nationalities, 571:19
Squadrons, God on side of big s., 265:5
Squads, undisciplined s. of emotion, 678:22
Squalid cash interpretation, 542:4
Squander, do not s. time, 302:26
Square, damned thick s. book, 335:20
    deal, 571:8
    everything upon the s., 157:10
    gathered on public s., 583:9
    I have not kept my s., 218:22
    old people are s., 814:11

Square *(continued)*
    person in round hole, 374:20
    root of Everest, 795:6
    triangular person in s. hole, 374:20
Squared, mass times speed of light s., 637:*n*4
Squat like toad at ear of Eve, 258:6
    pen rests, 845:9
    toad work s. on my life, 799:6
Squatting upon ground held heart in hands, 608:19
Squeak and gibber, 196:15
    speak Greek naturally as pigs s., 262:1
Squeaking Cleopatra, 219:10
Squeaks, wheel that s. gets grease, 476:8
Squealing of wry-necked fife, 184:38
Squeezing from a stone, 666:7
Squired glacier woman, 720:7
Squirmed and struggled, 527:18
Squirmers in bogs, 755:16
Squirrel's heart beat, 480:18
Squirrels, requisite to S. and to Me, 510:10
Squirt cider in your ear, 660:*n*2
Sredni Vashtar went forth, 608:7
Stability in small republics, 391:2
Stable earth proper element, 240:2
    good horse in s., 322:18
    its own s. door, 509:11
    law s. but not stand still, 608:3
    steed stolen shut s. door, 147:18
Stabs, every word s., 190:27
    intention s. the center, 223:12
Stack or the barn door, 251:1
Stacker of wheat, 636:2
Staff, bread called s. of life, 282:16
    cockle hat and s., 201:23
    I'll break my s., 225:4
    of faith to walk upon, 159:10
    of life bread, 282:*n*4
    of life ease of burdens, 156:19
    of this broken reed, 26:20
    resting upon broken s., 328:8
    stay and the s., 24:36
    thy rod and thy s., 15:23
    very s. of my age, 184:36
    with your s. in your hand, 7:40
Stag at eve, 373:18
Stage, all the world's a s., 194:25
    dreamer is s. manager, 630:9
    earth a s., 194:*n*2
    frets his hour upon s., 217:23
    great s. of fools, 213:1
    meet disease at first s., 105:15
    not put loaded rifle on s., 578:5
    on s. always now, 715:9
    on the s. he was natural, 323:7
    players and painted s., 597:7
    something for modern s., 665:6
    to play the fool upon, 555:3
    Tragic Muse trod s., 293:13
    well-graced actor leaves s., 177:21
    well-trod s., 251:8
    where every man play part, 184:4
    wonder of our s., 232:19
    world's a s., 194:*n*2
Stagecoach, travel faster than s., 323:1
Stages, hundred thousand s., 596:10
Stagger but not with strong drink, 26:10
    like a drunken man, 18:16

Staggered and terrible-eyed, 745:4
Stagnant, fen of s. waters, 370:9
    water loses purity, 140:7
Stagnate, without war world would s., 420:8
Staid, stay our minds be s., 624:18
    very s. head, 185:*n*3
Stain all my raiment, 27:17
    both moon and sun, 221:11
    crave s. of tears, 623:10
    in thine honor, 31:21
    my man's cheeks, 211:22
    national s. washed clean, 686:8
    stiff dishonored shroud, 676:2
    world's slow s., 403:23
Stained, and I s. the water clear, 350:11
    bishop kick hole in s. glass window, 674:7
    with mystic horrors, 559:1
Staineth slop, 665:2
Stainless, conscience upright and s., 129:11
Stains white radiance of eternity, 404:2
Stair, as I was going up s., 631:12
    climbing the third s., 677:15
    pausing on final s., 823:1
Staircase, palms on s., 745:4
    wit, 313:15
Stairs, down darker and darker s., 663:22
    great world's altar s., 453:24
    how hard the way up another's s., 130:6
    of concepts, 733:2
    recognizing man's step when climbs s., 616:3
    threw him down the s., 894:6
Stairway leads to dark gulf, 619:7
    militaristic s., 823:13
    of surprise, 424:18
Stake, great interests at s., 78:29
    I am tied to the s., 212:13
    in glorious institution, 324:13
    when honor's at the s., 201:21
Stakes, mortal s., 624:1
    value of s. at issue, 743:10
    were thrones, 399:14
Stale, bread ever more s. rags, 665:12
    dull s. tired bed, 210:33
    frizzled s. and small, 787:8
    how weary s. flat, 196:29
    nor custom s., 218:21
    winter hangs on till s., 615:13
Stalemate, mired in s., 781:13
Stalin, guilt of S. and entourage, 830:2
    millions whom S. imprisoned, 739:13
    rose to his position, 643:15
Stalk, corn ear on tip of s., 891:14
    gathering s. and root, 730:1
    half asleep as they s., 536:22
    of death, 820:8
Stalking, uses folly like s. horse, 196:8
    with naked foot s. my chamber, 149:4
Stalks, slow Spondee s., 378:11
Stalled ox and hatred therewith, 20:32
Stallion, like a s. on the track, 3:11
    shod with fire, 502:18
    watersmooth-silver s., 701:7
Stalls above like elephant, 787:15
Stamp, change s. of nature, 201:13
    if they s. your hand, 800:11
    man bears s. of lowly origin, 440:13
    of human condition, 153:11

Stirred *(continued)*
- casement jessamine s., 455:2
- heart of Englishman, 603:5
- Martini shaken and not s., 752:12
- troubled like fountain s., 203:27
- up with envy and revenge, 255:6
- up with high hopes, 254:4

Stirring, always s. up some war, 75:22
- butterfly s. air in Peking, 872:5
- dull roots, 676:5
- it was a strange s., 796:7
- not a creature s., 387:2
- not a mouse s., 196:10

Stirrup, foot in s., 890:12, 890:13
- sprang to s., 460:16

Stirs, blood more s. to rouse lion, 182:5
- Culprit Life, 508:3
- of discontented strife, 233:15
- see she s., 436:22
- this mortal frame, 378:3

Stitch in time saves nine, 105:*n*8
- stitch stitch, 418:8

Stitches, laugh yourselves into s., 205:19

Stitching and unstitching naught, 591:18

Stithy, foul as Vulcan's s., 200:13

Stock of Barabbas, 186:8
- see how his s. went on, 381:18

Stockholm Syndrome, 872:6

Stocking, glimpse of s. shocking, 691:11
- silk s. filled with mud, 366:2

Stockings, commended yellow s., 205:9
- hung by chimney, 387:2
- silk s. and white bosoms, 308:14
- to bed with s. on, 896:1

Stocks, buy s. like you buy, 826:10
- worshipped s. and stones, 254:23

Stockyards, sacrifices like s., 721:6

Stoic, every S. was a S., 426:24
- forty till fifty man a s., 561:15
- live like s. bird, 666:4

Stoic's pride, 295:1

Stole, like little mice s. in and out, 261:5
- man s. the fruit, 242:16
- memory of all he s., 296:26
- pig and away run, 894:11
- tarts and took them away, 894:2
- thence life o' building, 215:28

Stolen be your apples, 392:14
- ducats s. by my daughter, 185:5
- many a man's soul and faith, 857:5
- my three-and-twentieth year, 250:16
- not wanting what is s., 209:12
- odd old ends s. of holy writ, 171:25
- pants to my dinner jacket, 704:8
- steed s. shut stable door, 147:18
- sweets are best, 287:18
- the scraps, 174:26
- waters are sweet, 20:9

Stomach, army marches on s., 366:3
- dispenser of invention, 105:12
- disputes you, 747:6
- full talk of fasting easy, 115:16
- goes much against my s., 195:4
- good-humored s., 103:24
- hungry s. cannot hear, 266:16
- loathing to s. brings, 178:24
- man of an unbounded s., 226:10
- no patriot on empty s., 366:*n*2

Stomach *(continued)*
- no s. for such meat, 535:9
- seat of sensation s., 576:5
- teacher of arts, 105:12
- thought depends on s., 299:26
- way to heart through s., 458:2

Stomachaches, tuned like fifty s., 465:9

Stomach's, wine for thy s. sake, 44:33

Stomachs, rooted to soil through our s., 528:11
- who have best s. not best thinkers, 299:26

Stone, ask bread and give s., 33:17
- at his heels a s., 201:24
- better pillow than visions, 670:7
- bows to wood and s., 391:7
- bronze stone steel, 677:21
- cold as any s., 189:5
- conscious s. to beauty grew, 424:5
- dash foot against s., 37:24
- dash thy foot against a s., 17:29
- dripping water hollows s., 89:15
- dry s. no water, 676:6
- flung S. puts Stars to flight, 441:5
- he that rolleth a s., 21:39
- head s. of the corner, 18:25
- heart firm as s., 14:34
- heart harder than s., 54:8
- heart of s. to read death of Little Nell, 561:8
- heart turned to s., 209:25
- heavy as yonder s., 650:22
- house of good s., 665:11
- if any have s. to throw, 666:8
- in middle of road a s., 730:5
- in one hand a s., 83:10
- Jackson like s. wall, 501:5
- leaf unfound door, 727:10
- leave no s. unturned, 68:5
- legs of s., 401:13
- let him first cast s., 39:22
- like a rolling s., 851:14
- live by squeezing from s., 666:7
- make s. of heart, 593:8
- mark with white or black s., 157:19
- mockery of monumental s., 403:21
- moving others themselves as s., 222:1
- no bigger than agate-s., 179:25
- nosing up to impossible s., 788:5
- not to conclude against s., 797:14
- not with Club nor S., 510:17
- of stumbling, 25:14
- precious s. set in silver sea, 176:24
- pulleth sword out of s., 138:2
- quiet as s., 411:12
- raise s. cleave wood, 113:19
- rolling s. gathers no moss, 100:16
- shall cry out of wall, 29:8
- sleep softly eagle under s., 639:11
- spark out of s. easier than moral, 528:18
- star s. flesh soul, 462:5
- stem as s., 650:22
- strength of past, 670:4
- tell where I lie, 292:5
- that puts Stars to flight, 441:5
- turn s. start wing, 577:4
- under every s. a politician, 73:11
- underneath this s. lie, 232:13
- violet by mossy s., 369:7

Stone *(continued)*
- walls do not prison make, 266:2
- water like a s., 512:6
- which the builders refused, 18:25
- written of me on my s., 624:10
- youth s. dead, 668:13

Stone Age, bomb them into S., 746:7

Stone-deaf fishes, 755:16

Stonefence sherry cobbler, 391:12

Stone's, within a s. throw, 156:20

Stones are iron, 9:20
- blest man that spares these s., 226:17
- boys throw s. at frogs, 82:9
- chose him five smooth s., 11:1
- cold gray s. O Sea, 452:15
- cry out, 38:26
- dig him up throw s. at him, 565:15
- don't throw s. if your windows glass, 302:16
- have been known to move, 216:23
- heap of s. a witness, 7:1
- heap of s. not house, 558:8
- his look drained s., 756:1
- house glass not throw s., 243:25
- in league with s. of field, 13:13
- kissed by English dead, 699:8
- labor of an age in piled s., 250:15
- makes music with enamelled s., 173:31
- move s. of Rome, 193:5
- no sermons in s., 528:18
- not decked with Indian s., 170:25
- not throw s. at birds, 307:27
- of Troy, 203:20
- philosopher's s., 235:12
- prate of my whereabout, 215:15
- rocks and s. and trees, 369:8
- roots of trees and s., 666:5
- scrub pavement or break s., 591:18
- sermons in s., 193:37
- shows that wood s. are one, 75:26
- that cannot be deciphered, 679:1
- time to cast away s., 22:31
- trees and s. will teach you, 123:11
- worshipped stocks and s., 254:23
- you are men of s., 213:12

Stonest them sent unto thee, 35:18

Stonewall, want you to s. it, 771:8

Stony British stare, 454:28
- limits cannot hold love out, 180:4

Stony-hearted stepmother, 393:5

Stood against world, 192:32
- among them not of them, 395:24
- apart studiously neutral, 566:10
- for country's glory, 373:6
- from everlasting to everlasting, 278:11
- graves s. tenantless, 196:15
- hair of my flesh s. up, 13:8
- in tears amid alien corn, 410:10
- in whirling summer, 737:8
- long I s. there, 449:7
- naked in open air, 556:20
- not Death for I s. up, 509:8
- see from where I s., 695:5
- should of s. in bed, 712:1
- snake s. up for evil, 623:2
- that night against fire, 213:3

Stool pigeon when cannot be soldier, 493:8

Stools, between two s., 146:14

Strange *(continued)*
but true, 399:5
capers, 194:9
dark interludes, 681:7
disease of modern life, 495:17
eruption to our state, 196:12
eruptions, 182:32
eventful history, 194:25
force in s. steeds, 443:1
how s. it seems and new, 461:8
how s. it seems and queer, 461:*n*1
interlude, 681:7
isn't it, 687:2
kind of magick bias, 314:1
lips of a s. woman drop as honeycomb, 19:31
lisp and wear s. suits, 195:25
Lord's song in s. land, 19:11
more cunning to be s., 180:7
most s. that men fear, 192:11
Nature hath framed s. fellows, 184:2
object s. and high, 267:3
pair of very s. beasts, 196:3
read s. matters, 214:19
seas of thought, 368:16
soldier full of s. oaths, 194:25
Solomon loved many s. women, 11:36
something howsoever s. and admirable, 179:7
something rich and s., 224:14
stranger in a s. country, 66:15
stranger in a s. land, 7:24
that death should sing, 176:3
that desire outlive performance, 188:8
things come out, 360:7
throne in s. city, 448:2
truth always s., 399:5
'twas passing s., 208:3
what a long s. trip, 852:8
world is a s. affair, 267:10
Strangely pass, 221:14
Strangeness, addition of s. to beauty, 534:11
some s. in proportion, 166:14
Stranger across crowded room, 706:12
and afraid, 575:17
and alone, 727:11
and ye took me in, 35:30
as we grow older world s., 679:1
doth not intermeddle, 20:25
entertain this starry s., 263:11
Europe regards her like s., 333:2
has homeland in arms, 691:18
he that is surety for a s., 20:13
I am a s. with thee, 16:20
I pass a willful s., 556:5
in a strange country, 66:15
in a strange land, 7:24
in financial straits, 70:18
leave them for poor and s., 8:26
my being s. to the ship, 568:5
never fight fair with s., 780:6
nothing s. ever happened, 763:2
than fiction, 399:5
to a native every s. is enemy, 660:1
to myself, 568:5
to sorrow, 67:14
why did God make me a stranger, 602:1
Stranger's, need of some s. hand, 858:5

Strangers, always depended on kindness of s., 766:7
America beaten by s., 709:15
and beggars are from Zeus, 53:4
desire we may be better s., 195:13
entertain s., 45:15
gods likening themselves to s., 54:3
gracious and courteous to s., 165:23
I am writing for myself and s., 627:15
ready to embrace the s., 482:12
Strangest, fate of architect s., 343:13
things are there for me, 555:11
Strangle, vapors seem to s. him, 181:33
would s. his father, 313:13
Strangled snakes beside Hercules, 502:2
Strapped noosed nighing hour, 575:18
Straps, hang in their own s., 204:14
Stratagems, treasons s. and spoils, 186:17
which errors seem, 292:11
Strategy, exit s., 806:5
involve us in wrong war, 697:7
Stratford, Shakespeare was born at S., 270:12
Straw dogs, 57:1
find quarrel in a s., 201:21
headpiece filled with s., 676:19
I don't care one s., 86:9
lion shall eat s., 25:19
no more s. to make brick, 7:32
pigmy's s. does pierce it, 212:30
see which way wind is, 238:14
stumbles at a s., 160:1
tickled with a s., 295:3
turkey in the s., 884:16
Strawberries, feed upon s., 894:17
great s. at mouth of pot, 165:7
how many s. in sea, 893:1
melts on vine, 553:8
of angling as of s., 245:7
Strawberry, like s. wives, 165:7
Straws, as s. that blow, 552:6
oaths are s., 189:6
Stray, if with me fondly s., 291:17
lower where the pleasant fountains lie, 171:9
never taught to s., 294:20
wishes never learned to s., 316:3
Strayed like lost sheep, 48:2
Streak, red-line s., 489:10
Stream, at certain stations he would view s., 347:12
bashful s. hath seen God, 263:*n*1
bubble in s., 112:26
by thy murmuring s., 357:19
ever-rolling s., 289:14
fish have their s., 669:8
islanded in s. of stars, 673:22
meadow grove and s., 370:13
mercy of a rude s., 225:25
no striving against s., 157:1
of consciousness, 540:25
of time run, 188:17
red life s. again, 412:1
slow and silent s. Lethe, 256:24
smoothest water deepest, 159:*n*4
steep Atlantic s., 252:7
strove against s. in vain, 453:4
summer eves by haunted s., 251:8
time s. I go a-fishing in, 475:4

Streamed like a meteor to air, 255:*n*1
spring sunshine s. in, 513:7
Streamer of the northern morn, 451:7
Streamers, her fan spread s. out, 287:3
sails filled s. waving, 260:16
Streaming, before his s. eyes, 516:7
meteor s. to the wind, 255:21
Streams and woods belong, 569:12
cold companionable s., 592:16
flow with ambrosia, 68:3
lapse of murmuring s., 258:30
like thunderstorm, 396:10
may valley s. content me, 93:17
meet in one salt sea, 188:36
passions like floods and s., 159:7
pebbles of holy s., 777:12
sitting by desolate s., 549:13
what eternal s., 448:7
whereof make glad city of God, 16:27
Strebend, wer immer s. sich bemüht, 344:*n*5
Street, art tells where a s. is, 824:12
ballad in the s., 426:7
car rattling o'er s., 395:14
dives on Fifty-second S., 748:16
don't do it in s., 586:10
down at end of lonely s., 840:12
down long and silent s., 559:18
Forty-second S., 689:9
fought s. by s., 619:16
harlot's cry from s. to s., 354:6
main s. on August afternoon, 788:16
my steps along s., 776:8
not done by jostling in s., 354:9
Old Lady of Threadneedle S., 355:1
once walked down s., 589:23
Second Avenue is a dismal s., 805:7
slick s., 821:2
walk in the s., 487:1
works both sides of s., 653:11
Streets, die in the s. or in prison, 607:19
doors shut in the s., 23:30
down mean s. man must go, 674:10
fashion does not exist unless it goes down s., 655:2
fight in fields and s., 619:14
full of water, 683:14
gibber in Roman s., 196:15
grass will grow in s., 577:17, 625:18
her mind traveled crooked s., 830:12
in thy dark s. shineth, 521:2
lion is in the s., 21:38
mourners go about the s., 23:31
of Laredo, 890:15
publish it not in the s. of Askelon, 11:7
through midnight s., 353:4
through negro s., 812:13
truth never fell dead in s., 457:8
world's most crowded s., 495:11
Strength, all your s. in union, 437:1
all your s. is weakness, 65:18
alone of Muses born, 409:4
ancient and natural s., 318:18
and honor are her clothing, 22:18
as thy days so thy s., 9:32
beyond hope and despair, 677:15
by experience with fear, 660:7
castle's s. will laugh, 217:21
collected s. and struck, 575:18

Studied a minute, 523:9
   in my foolish youth, 138:18
   method by which unconscious s., 563:12
   one s. in his death, 214:14
Studies, air of delightful s., 253:21
   in which work dies with worker, 140:5
   spur to the young, 87:11
Studious, sober s. days, 293:21
   there s. let me sit, 300:17
   to please, 306:14
Studiously neutral, 566:10
Studium, eigentliche S. der Menschheit, 295:*n*1
Study a great deal to know little, 297:16
   but litel on the Bible, 133:29
   commonwealth affairs his s., 188:32
   culture s. of perfection, 497:10
   give children right to s. painting, 330:7
   I am slow of s., 178:6
   in brown s., 161:21
   in law's grave s. six, 159:1
   labor and intent s., 253:20
   law so general a s., 324:7
   like heaven's glorious sun, 174:1
   lives on a leaf, 755:16
   much s. is a weariness, 24:2
   my sons ought to s. mathematics, 330:7
   of revenge immortal hate, 255:10
   periphrastic s., 678:16
   politics and war, 330:7
   prince have no s. but war, 141:16
   result of previous s., 382:6
   secret of s. of nature, 432:14
   to be quiet, 44:17
   we that did nothing s., 241:20
   what you most affect, 173:6
Stuff, ale's the s. to drink, 575:12
   ambition of sterner s., 192:30
   as dreams are made on, 225:1
   everything of one hidden s., 427:1
   he is writing bad s., 569:15
   listen all day to such s., 514:6
   neither starve nor s., 285:12
   of various s. various Man, 358:2
   out of hopeful green s. woven, 485:18
   precious as s. they sell, 442:8
   Right S., 831:6
   skimble-skamble s., 182:38
   stuffed bosom of perilous s., 217:19
   the head with reading, 297:5
   written volumes of s., 467:4
   youth's a s. will not endure, 204:26
Stuffed bosom of perilous stuff, 217:19
   men, 676:19, 676:20
   with epithets of war, 207:20
Stuffing, polar bear with s. missing, 821:1
Stuffs out vacant garments, 175:19
Stuhldreher Miller Crowley Layden, 646:5
Stultitia, tanta s. mortalium est, 103:*n*6
Stumble, designed to make people s., 655:16
   men that s. at threshold, 170:34
   that run fast, 180:19
Stumbles at a straw, 160:1
   old horse s. and nods, 536:22
   upon them by chance, 615:6
Stumbling blocks in girl's education, 616:4
   Negro's great s. block, 823:3
   stone of s., 25:14
Stump, they dying like a s., 830:10

Stupefaction, death releases aura of s., 493:17
   that passing s., 615:17
Stupefying incense smoke, 460:22
Stupendous, parts of one s. whole, 294:22
Stupid, be as s. as one wants, 612:10
   clown of spirit's motive, 772:2
   dastardly Public, 386:4
   it's the economy s., 859:1
   stand up for s. and crazy, 485:10
   you can afford to be s., 423:17
Stupidity, against s. gods contend, 360:9
   as if safety in s., 475:18
   God is s. and cowardice, 450:5
   nature equals s. of man, 659:3
   Street, 609:13
   such excess of s., 309:7
   with s. man may front much, 406:19
Sturdy and staunch he stands, 554:2
Sturm und Drang, 347:1
Stuttering rifles' rapid rattle, 699:6
Stygian cave forlorn, 250:19
Style, attain English s., 307:15
   camp a vision in terms of s., 835:17
   Cobbett s. stuns readers, 385:13
   definition of s., 284:22
   dress of thought, 298:14
   fancy prose s., 723:6
   God has no real s., 647:15
   grand s., 496:2
   honorable s. of Christian, 247:11
   is a recasting and heightening, 497:5
   is the man, 304:5
   is the thought itself, 348:2
   killed calf in high s., 270:12
   labored nothings in strange s., 292:15
   of Europe, 807:17
   Racine will go out of s., 270:14
   radical Chic only radical in s., 831:4
   tell me in good old s., 110:17
   turns revolt into a s., 822:9
   vigor it will give s., 375:11
   will make writers unreadable, 392:10
Suades, facias ipse quod faciamus s., 84:*n*3
Suage, words have power to s., 260:12
Sub, sighted s. sank same, 771:1
Sub rosa, 248:*n*2
Subconscious, colonized our s., 862:2
Subdue appetites my dears, 464:15
   force may s. for moment, 324:4
   free ourselves s. our masters, 340:12
   power to chasten and s., 368:11
   replenish the earth and s. it, 5:8
Subdued, be s., 50:4
   eyes, 210:20
   my nature is s., 222:14
   not s. for want of necessaries, 106:7
Subdues, surpasses or s. mankind, 395:17
   when one by force s., 79:14
Subduing, necessity of s. again, 324:4
Subject, any s. taught to any child, 779:2
   being good neighbor bad s., 652:*n*2
   duty s. owes prince, 173:26
   everything is a s., 416:10
   fanatic won't change s., 621:17
   grant artist his s., 544:10
   grasp s. words will follow, 85:7
   her s. her slave her toy, 528:12
   honor the s. of my story, 191:24

Subject *(continued)*
   idea donnée, 544:10
   know a s. ourselves, 310:5
   matter of poetry life, 642:22
   my s. in fiction, 809:13
   of all verse, 240:7
   of it is War, 699:4
   of knowledge is to know, 76:8
   poetry s. of poem, 641:9
   prince s. Father Son, 230:15
   ruler having human body as s., 74:19
   sensibility soil of s., 544:16
   that favorite s. Myself, 334:3
   treats serious s. with simplicity, 496:2
   unlike s. I frame song, 298:19
   whole s. is too profound, 440:7
Subjection to white Saxon man, 471:6
Subjective, all history s., 426:12
   creation, 630:9
   objective and s. united, 379:4
   stream of s. life, 540:24
Subjectivity and objectivity, 709:8
Subject's duty is king's, 189:21
Subjects, free and loyal s., 883:14
   men first s. afterward, 473:13
   of which soul speaks same everywhere, 113:8
   rebels from principle, 325:5
   were their s. wise, 327:3
Sublime, aim at something more s., 361:1
   bards s., 436:17
   boundless endless and s., 396:21
   dashed to pieces, 380:5
   from s. to ridiculous, 365:7
   great and s. fool, 522:11
   lieth s., 449:1
   maintain the s., 665:4
   make our lives s., 436:6
   object all s., 527:15
   second line s. third bombast, 107:1
   sense s., 368:11
   tobacco, 399:15
   when authors talk of s., 333:21
Sublimely, fustian's so s. bad, 295:12
Sublimity echo of a noble mind, 107:2
   in effort of patriots, 329:13
Sublunary lovers' love, 229:15
Submarine, in our yellow s., 848:9
Submission, bear his share with s., 501:15
   Christ's s. to humiliation, 802:6
   no wisdom but in s., 66:1
   resistance or abject s., 328:6
   yielded with coy s., 257:20
Submit because strength not adequate, 79:14
   courage never to s., 255:10
   I s. let it be done, 419:3
   to be oppressed, 339:5
   woman know how to s., 362:14
   yourself to destructive element, 567:9
Submits, man in love s. to everything, 548:26
Submitted and joined the church, 261:16
Submitting, by s. sways, 294:3
Subordinates art to nature, 379:13
Subscription, cancel my s. to the resurrection, 858:7
Subsequent, pricks to s. volumes, 203:10
Subsist, beg leave to s., 585:2
Subsistence in arithmetical ratio, 362:7
Subsoil of the mind, 572:7

Suffereth, charity s. long, 42:27
  love s. long, 42:27
Suffering, about s. they were never wrong,
    748:12
  acting is s., 678:2
  Christian principle of s., 432:7
  decisive criterion for real s., 878:4
  end the s. of our people, 840:1
  exercises his mind with s., 80:6
  extremity of city's s., 131:3
  healed of s. by experiencing it, 611:5
  incomprehensibility of s., 835:11
  knowledge by s., 434:11
  man consume own smoke, 407:22
  man in love with s., 492:5
  may be called baptism, 480:7
  miserable doing or s., 255:11
  no more s. or denial of rights, 791:5
  only one antidote to mental s., 478:1
  relieve s. of brother, 125:2
  truth by s., 604:4
  unavenged s., 492:11
  weak helpless in s., 712:6
  what is insufferable, 728:7
Sufferings, allowed to see s. of damned, 127:8
  are as nothing compared to reward, 150:4
  I can feel s. of millions, 822:7
  indifferent to s. of fellow creatures, 321:2
  of the troops, 668:7
  to each his s., 315:8
Suffers, eagle s. little birds to sing, 173:2
  then nature of insurrection, 192:2
Suffice, ice also would s., 623:4
  O when may it s., 593:8
  Sands s., 510:16
Sufficeth, God s. me, 118:5
Sufficiency, elegant s., 300:20
Sufficient, beauty s. end, 593:12
  ocean sea not s. room, 233:13
  unto the day is evil thereof, 33:11
  virtue s. of herself, 245:*n1*
  whether s. to finish, 38:8
Suffocate for privacy, 787:19
Suffocating night, 575:3
Suffocation, life threatened with s., 708:5
Suffrage for all citizens, 471:8
Suffuses all with blackness of death, 90:8
Suffusion from that light, 378:10
Sugar and spice, 895:12
  Heaven's s. cake, 280:18
  if sack and s. be fault, 182:28
  in the gourd, 884:17
  my hair, 515:5
  not made of s. candy, 620:16
  pious action s. o'er, 199:20
Sugarcoat the pill, 267:27
Sugarplums, decorating with s., 569:15
Suggest, like two spirits s. me, 223:3
  to s. is ideal of poem, 543:9
Suggested, minutiae of deeds never s., 488:15
Suggestion, yield to that s., 214:11
Suicide, Bill of Rights into s. pact, 694:5,
    846:*n1*
  book is postponed s., 763:12
  Constitution is not a s. pact, 846:3
  despair and s., 439:5
  is about life, 828:8
  is confession, 390:11

Suicide *(continued)*
  live through time or die by s., 444:2
  never democracy that did not commit s.,
    330:15
  philosophical problem is s., 769:15
  sermon in the s., 837:14
  supplied by the S. Club, 555:3
  thermonuclear war means to universal s.,
    797:4
  thought of s. consolation, 548:9
Suis, j'y s. j'y reste, 439:*n2*
Suit action to the word, 200:7
  bring s. in Supreme Court, 661:2
  certainly not s. me, 526:11
  changing from brown s. to gray, 664:3
  Man in Gray Flannel S., 796:2
  of ancient black, 639:16
  of sables, 200:15
  shall I be still in s., 242:26
  silk s. which cost much, 277:1
Suits, kings in golden s. ride elephants, 767:7
  of solemn black, 196:26
  out of s. with fortune, 193:29
  these but s. of woe, 196:27
  wear strange s., 195:25
Sukey take it off again, 896:18
Sulky, our s. sullen dame, 358:3
Sullen and sad, 300:14
  beetle winds s. horn, 317:13
  hear the surly s. bell, 221:23
  our sulky s. dame, 358:3
  swinging low with s. roar, 251:17
  tongue sounds as s. bell, 187:23
  untamed intractable, 679:3
  winter hangs on till s., 615:13
Sullenness against Nature, 254:6
Sullied, crown s. in the winning, 360:1
  flesh, 196:*n2*
Sulphur, Calvin oatcakes and s., 374:21
Sulphureous torture-lake away below, 663:17
Sulphurous and thought-executing, 211:24
Sultan after Sultan with his Pomp, 441:12
Sultan's Turret, 441:4, 441:5
Sultry, common where climate's s., 397:21
  gray-fly winds her s. horn, 253:3
  main, 376:16
Sum, life not doing s., 538:16
  make up my s., 202:20
  man not s. of what he has, 742:20
  married people owe, 343:11
  of all villainies, 301:16
  of earthly bliss, 259:2
  of good government, 337:11
  of human achievement, 553:3
  of things ever being renewed, 90:3
  with a great s. obtained freedom, 40:43
Sumer, dô der s. komen was, 125:*n4*
  is icumen in, 880:5
Summary, contained in a five-line s., 819:4
  court in perpetual session, 656:1
  fair s. of history, 649:11
Summer, after many a s. dies the swan, 455:5
  after s. barren winter, 170:4
  afternoon most beautiful words, 545:10
  and winter shall not cease, 6:23
  baseball blossoms in s., 844:8
  being done, 240:3
  capriciousness of s. air, 624:7

Summer *(continued)*
  clothe general earth, 377:15
  commend all s. long, 594:1
  dream beneath tamarind, 447:11
  ends now, 546:14
  eternal s. gilds them, 398:16
  eves by haunted stream, 251:8
  expanding in s. fires, 867:1
  expect Saint Martin's s., 169:12
  fight if it takes all s., 498:2
  flies on s. eves, 410:8
  flowers of middle s., 223:26
  fly after s. merrily, 225:5
  God is day night winter s., 62:5
  grace a s. queen, 374:6
  hath his joys, 227:1
  hearts dry as s. dust, 372:6
  in s. song sings itself, 658:18
  in s. the other way, 555:8
  Indian s. of life, 532:7
  is ended, 27:30
  is icumen in, 880:5
  it was a s. evening, 381:6
  last rose of s., 387:11
  mad naked s. night, 486:6
  made s. by sun of York, 171:16
  my father paints s., 797:9
  no season such delight as s., 240:8
  no spring nor s. beauty, 230:9
  now s. came to pass, 125:6
  observing spear of s. grass, 485:15
  one swallow makes a s., 78:*n2*
  one swallow not a s., 78:5
  pleasures they are gone, 405:1
  provideth her meat in the s., 19:32
  reeling through s. days, 508:9
  sang in me, 695:13
  season when soft was the sun, 131:6
  singest of s., 410:3
  soldier sunshine patriot, 333:6
  summer's flower to s. sweet, 222:2
  sun and s. gale, 316:11
  sweet as s., 226:12
  that I was ten, 772:12
  then S. Then Heaven of God, 509:9
  this guest of s., 214:21
  thy eternal s. not fade, 221:3
  to your heart, 695:11
  we have had s. evenings, 666:2
  welcome s. with sonne softe, 132:10
  when had not been a member, 788:15
  whirling s., 737:8
  with flowers that fell, 529:14
  within me invincible s., 770:7
  words in winter articulated next s., 108:10
Summer's, all on s. day, 894:2
  compare thee to s. day, 221:2
  day and with setting sun, 256:5
  fantastic s. heat, 176:18
  flower to summer sweet, 222:2
  lease too short, 221:2
  proper man as see in s. day, 178:9
  ripening breath, 180:11
  tasted all the s. pride, 350:7
  thy s. play, 352:15
  vernal bloom or s. rose, 257:6
Summers, farmers pray that s. be wet, 93:11
  in a sea of glory, 225:25

Summers *(continued)*
raw inclement s., 285:2
Summertime and the livin' is easy, 662:8
Summit, dreadful s. of the cliff, 198:1
from s. of pyramids, 365:4
life harder toward s., 549:2
lost in vapor, 398:7
Summits, snowy s. old in story, 452:19
Summon up remembrance of things past,
221:8
up the blood, 189:7
Summoned, miracles cannot be s., 688:11
spirits I s. up, 343:9
Summons, black Hecate's s., 216:12
Black Spot a s., 555:5
fate s. monarchs obey, 273:13
fearful s., 196:16
thee to heaven or hell, 215:16
when s. comes to join, 405:13
Summum bonum, 88:*n*2, 90:*n*7
ius summa iniuria, 121:18
Sumner, was it Charles S., 438:21
Sumner's mind contained itself, 531:20
Sumptuous variety about New England
weather, 522:10
Sun, again the s., 671:14
all except s. is set, 398:16
also ariseth, 22:21
and moon in flat sea sunk, 252:17
and moon should doubt, 354:5
and with the setting s., 256:5
ariseth they gather themselves, 18:11
as if s. blackamoor, 641:1
as long as s. shine, 892:4
as sure as s. will shine, 866:2
at going down of s., 603:14
at mercy of s., 556:20
at noon, 231:10
aweary of the s., 217:24
be not darkened, 23:30
beating way for rising s., 730:2
before the rising s., 289:13
best not to see beams of s., 59:23
born dies comes again, 888:22
born of the s., 760:6
born over and over, 777:13
breaks through darkest clouds, 173:22
Brother S. who brings us day, 125:9
burn the great sphere, 219:3
cast in brass to S., 886:13
chaos of the s., 640:22
clear as the s., 24:19
common s. air skies, 316:9
dark simulacrum of God, 249:6
day past and yet I saw no s., 163:11
die with face to s, 557:14
distilled by the s., 535:16
don't go, 814:10
don't know why no s. in sky, 703:3
doubt that s. doth move, 198:30
duty to worship s., 533:1
evenin' s. go down, 616:20
eyes behold s. last time, 390:9
face downward in s., 695:1
far from the s., 316:11
fear no more heat o' the s., 220:26
first Poets Then S., 509:9
follow thy fair s., 226:21

Sun *(continued)*
foolery about orb like s., 205:10
force from which s. draws power, 661:3
frisk i' the s., 223:10
from rising of the s. unto going down,
18:20
fruit I bore was the s., 108:*n*7
gather round setting s., 371:5
give me splendid silent s., 487:10
gives light soon as he rises, 303:18
glorious s. in Heaven, 377:16
go out in midday s., 719:12
golden apples of s., 591:11
gorgeous as s. at midsummer, 183:12
greater none beneath S., 589:24
he set a tabernacle for the s., 15:16
heap o' s. and shadder, 647:8
heart s. of their microcosm, 236:1
himself at center of universe, 142:13
himself fair hot wench, 181:20
his self and the s. were one, 642:16
hold farthing candle to s., 235:*n*5
hold glimmering tapers to s., 235:*n*5
hot s. cool fire, 163:5
I saw under the s., 23:23
if s. breed maggots, 198:33
images where s. beats, 676:6
imitate the s., 181:33
in bowling alley bowled s., 280:15
in dim eclipse, 255:25
in dominions never sets, 359:16
in front s. climbs slow, 479:12
in golden cup, 596:4
in lonely lands, 454:13
inconceivable idea of s., 641:20
is but a morning star, 475:23
is gone down while it was day, 27:36
is laid to sleep, 232:2
is lost and the earth, 230:15
itself which makes times, 229:9
Juliet is the s., 179:31
junkie's like a setting s., 862:6
knitters in s., 205:2
knoweth his going down, 18:11
laughed in the s., 669:5
leaning against S., 508:10
leaves and flowers in s., 592:7
let not the s. go down, 43:37
light candle to the s., 268:8
light where no s. shines, 777:3
like ball of fire, 363:12
like Joshua commanded s., 303:14
liken Homer to setting s., 107:3
little window where s., 418:2
livery of burnished s., 184:33
looked over mountain's rim, 460:17
love earth s. animals, 485:10
Love that moves s. and other stars, 130:13
loves to live i' the s., 194:13
low descending s., 883:18
made summer by s. of York, 171:16
make guilty the s., 211:3
make our s. stand still, 266:24
maketh s. rise on evil and good, 32:22
man work s. to s., 883:17
marigold goes to bed wi' the sun, 223:26
maturing s., 411:6
moon or s. or what you please, 173:23

Sun *(continued)*
moon stars sweet, 423:6
more worship rising than setting s., 88:19
morning s. lights up, 803:13
mother give me s., 504:13
my mistress' eyes nothing like the s., 223:1
neither shall s. light on them, 46:37
never sets on empire, 359:*n*4
no better thing under the s., 23:20
no new thing under the s., 22:24
no s. its day, 814:13
no s. upon an Easter-day, 261:5
of righteousness arise, 29:21
only you under s., 691:9
out of God's blessing into s., 148:11
owes no homage unto s., 248:19
part of the colossal s., 642:17
pasted in sky, 608:15
pay no worship to garish s., 180:32
penetrates privies, 77:3
protects dewdrop from s., 372:17
question if His Glory, 509:18
raisin in the s., 731:9
ran s. down with talk, 83:1
remains pure through pollutions, 77:*n*4
rising of the s., 883:5
rose and set on Sioux land, 513:4
sand and wild uproar, 424:3
sea gone with s., 559:5
see s. with ignorant eye, 641:20
seemed a sheet of s., 774:12
self-same s. on court and cottage, 223:32
set a candle in the s., 235:16
sets to rise again, 463:12
setting s. and music at close, 176:21
setting s. set to rights, 412:14
shall not smite thee, 18:30
shineth upon dunghill, 77:*n*4
shone on nothing new, 744:13
show us your s. gradually, 691:19
shut doors against setting s., 213:22
sitting in the s., 381:6
somewhere s. is shining, 585:1
Son of the S., 79:13
stain both moon and s., 221:11
stand a little out of my s., 76:17
stand still upon Gibeon, 10:3
steadies my soul, 671:14
study like heaven's glorious s., 174:1
summer season when soft was s., 131:6
tell you how S. rose, 508:17
that brief December day, 438:15
that is young once only, 777:11
that s. thine eye, 221:14
tired s. with talking, 499:9
to have enjoyed s., 495:8
to me is dark, 260:10
traveled short while towards s., 760:6
unruly S., 228:15
walk in the s., 198:33
was shining on the sea, 515:20
was warm wind chill, 623:19
when s. goes down, 704:14
when s. out wind still, 623:19
when s. shineth make hay, 146:16
wherever bright s. of heaven, 226:15
which sees all things, 51:4
who scattered into flight, 441:4

Sun *(continued)*
    wing subdivided by s., 671:19
    wishes lengthen as our s. declines, 291:3
    works done under the s., 22:26
    worse than s. in March, 183:15
    would have disappeared, 574:6
    yesternight s. went hence, 229:3
Sunbeam impossible to be soiled, 77:*n*4
    in winter's day, 300:13
    thikke as motes in s., 135:14
Sunbeams, chances like s. pass, 302:*n*2
    out of cucumbers, 285:2
    stream forward, 891:16
Sunburnt by glare of life, 434:21
    mirth, 410:4
    this s. face, 350:15
Sunday, buried on S., 895:10
    chicken in pot every S., 161:12
    different from another day, 307:27
    eight o'clock on S. morning, 864:3
    grand flights S. baths, 641:14
    he was my S. rest, 748:14
    not divide S. from week, 196:13
    we will be married o' S., 173:14
Sundays, begin journey on S., 286:7
Sundered, as if birth s., 474:2
Sundering, love know no s. quarrels, 96:12
Sundown, elected between s. and sunup, 640:6
    we drink you at s., 794:6
Sundry contemplation of my travels, 195:23
    moveth us in s. places, 48:1
Sung, by forms unseen dirge s., 317:11
    first and last sung no more, 882:2
    guardian angels s. this strain, 301:3
    her amorous descant s., 257:25
    Sappho loved and s., 398:15
    strongest sweetest songs to be s., 488:18
Sunk, all s. beneath waves, 327:9
    beneath watery floor, 253:14
    in flat sea s., 252:17
    Lethe-wards had s., 410:2
    so low that sacred head, 253:8
    world's whole sap is s., 229:12
Sunless sea, 377:17
Sunlight best of disinfectants, 562:7
    has never heard of trees, 810:13
    late s. enters deep wood, 122:4
    moonlight unto s., 452:7
    parables of s., 777:8
    sudden in shaft of s., 678:11
    weave s. in hair, 675:13
Sunlit arch, 623:19
Sunnier side of doubt, 456:2
Sunny, a little s. a little sad, 532:7
    dome, 377:23
    in s. beams did glide, 350:7
    lazing on a s. afternoon, 859:2
    pleasure dome, 377:21
    side of life, 648:11
    side of the street, 740:14
    side up, 697:10
    web of s. air, 472:7
Sunrise, lives in eternity's s., 352:8
    lost between s. and sunset, 414:5
Sun's o'ercast with blood, 175:15
    rim dips, 376:9
Suns, light of setting s., 368:11
    process of the s., 452:5

Suns *(continued)*
    radiance of a thousand s., 84:13
    that set may rise again, 232:5
Sunscreen, wear s., 871:12
Sunset and evening star, 456:4
    between sunrise and s., 414:5
    breezes shiver, 582:10
    I have seen s., 559:1
    life little shadow in s., 492:1
    of life gives me lore, 384:10
    ran one glorious blood-red, 460:20
    sail beyond the s., 451:18
    stained with horrors, 559:1
    touch, 461:22
Sunsets, I eat s. and trees, 765:7
Sunshine and shade of earth, 367:17
    comforteth like s. after rain, 171:13
    digressions s. of reading, 314:3
    eternity about me in s., 552:4
    fill sky with cloudless, 97:8
    glorious birth, 370:15
    holiday, 251:4
    if opened in s., 431:10
    in the shady place, 160:5
    Little S. stayed on, 805:8
    on strange shore, 567:10
    patriot, 333:6
    spring s. streamed in, 513:7
    white town drowsing in s., 522:13
Sun-split, tumbling mirth of s. clouds, 800:1
Sunt lacrimae rerum, 94:*n*2
Sun-thaw, thatch smokes in s., 377:15
Sunup, elected between sundown and s., 640:6
Sunward I've climbed, 800:1
Sup at six sleep at ten, 422:18
    before we go, 894:4
    of Jove's nectar s., 232:16
    sipped no s., 527:25
Super Bowl, halftime at the S., 880:4
Superannuated idol, 288:6
Supercilious hypocrisy of bishop, 339:9
Superego, external world s. and id, 563:19
Superexcellent, tobacco divine rare s., 235:12
Superficial, common sense hasty s., 473:26
Superfluity sooner white hairs, 184:13
Superfluous, in nature's inventions nothing s.,
    140:11
    in poorest thing s., 211:21
    to demand time of day, 181:20
    to point out this is war, 435:22
    totalitarianism system where men are s.,
    744:4
    very necessary thing, 299:1
Superflux, shake s. to them, 211:33
Superhighway of justice, 823:11
Superhuman, daily struggle for s. beauty,
    845:8
Superintend sick, 70:18
Superior, educated men s., 77:9
    equals revolt to be s., 78:28
    man will not manifest narrow mindedness,
    79:16
    no attribute of s. man greater, 79:15
    people never make long visits, 671:5
    powers s. to man, 558:2
    someone whom we consider s., 838:4
    to slavish mercenary, 328:5
Superiorities, age of s., 364:12

Superiority, feeling of s., 645:11
    of their women, 434:5
    Senate s. invisible, 531:10
    to sex that kills, 751:6
Superiors, faithful to his s., 60:17
Superman, it's a bird plane S., 777:1
    lightning out of dark cloud, 547:18
    not Hercules but S., 831:3
    rope between animal and S., 547:17
Supernatural, honest woman of s., 750:11
Superstition ain't the way, 869:8
    constructive religion, 490:14
    die detesting s., 300:8
    fear source of s., 615:1
    has ample wages, 144:4
    infamous thing, 299:17
    less than chaff, 567:15
    opposing one s. to another, 312:1
    pernicious s. temporarily suspended, 110:6
    religion of feeble minds, 325:8
    will drag him down, 834:9
Superstitions, haunted by grossest s., 440:12
    truths end as s., 502:13
Superstitious atheist, 461:23
    in all things too s., 40:32
    modest chaste, 400:7
    valuation of Europe, 544:1
Supinely enjoyed gifts of founder, 332:13
    fools s. stay, 347:9
Supped full with horrors, 217:22
Supper, hope good breakfast bad s., 165:6
    nourishment which is called s., 174:3
    sings for his s., 893:14
    when s. things is done, 553:7
Suppers, more killed by s., 243:26
Suppliant, thus the s. prays, 306:18
Supplied, can never be s., 322:22
    charm by thought s., 368:10
    with visual or auditory images, 612:9
Supply, all just s. and all relation, 230:15
    eating air on promise of s., 187:37
Supply-side economics, 871:11
Support Caledonia's cause, 359:3
    that renders independent, 328:7
    to s. him after, 213:17
    visible means of s., 540:12
    what is low raise and s., 255:5
Supporting, fatigue of s. freedom, 333:10
Suppose, dance in ring and s., 624:11
    do you s. Walrus said, 516:1
    I could have stayed home, 864:4
    my daughters I s., 742:8
    they gave a war no one came, 636:*n*1
    universe queerer than we s., 693:11
Supposed as forfeit to confined doom,
    222:10
Supposing, no ground for s. it true, 614:13
Suppress nothing that is true, 87:14
Suppressed, neither world to be s., 496:6
    no innocent wit s., 334:8
Suppressing, French for s. one, 496:6
Suppression of bourgeois state by proletarian,
    607:14
    of free speech, 562:9
    patriotism means s. of truth, 668:15
Supramundane mushroom, 680:6
Suprema, salus populi s. est lex, 88:*n*5
Supremacy of the state, 765:14

Supreme, bring suit in S. Court, 661:2
    coort follows iliction, 600:3
    find alone Necessity S., 520:12
    governors the mob, 317:1
    Law of the land, 339:14
    poetry s. fiction, 640:17
    self-sacrifice, 705:1
    silence s., 517:4
    theme of Art and Song, 596:3
Surcease, catch with his s. success, 214:22
Surcingles, Gilt S., 511:4
Sure and firm-set earth, 215:15
    as death, 231:15
    as s. as sun will shine, 866:2
    be s. give ocular proof, 209:14
    be s. your sin will find you out, 9:12
    it may be so in Denmark, 198:17
    joy was never s., 530:17
    make assurance double s., 216:33
    more s. of all I thought, 622:7
    no s. foundation on blood, 175:27
    not s. there's no problem, 790:4
    nothing s. in sea fight, 355:10
    slow but s., 244:17
    slow but s. moves might, 68:11
    sweet cement of love, 240:10
    this Jesus will not do, 354:18
    visitor wept to be s., 636:12
    what man has he's s. of, 158:4
Surely, as s. as I am not free, 790:20
    every man walketh in a vain show, 16:19
    goodness and mercy shall follow me, 15:23
Surest way to get a thing, 420:16
Surety, he that is s. for a stranger, 20:13
Surface, fast bound below the s., 582:14
    fine glossy s., 322:7
    go where we will on s., 473:24
    material s. of things, 493:5
    stop courageously at s., 547:14
Surfeit begets insolence, 59:21
    God is war peace s. hunger, 62:5
    no crude s. reigns, 252:19
    of our own behavior, 211:3
    sick that s. with too much, 184:12
    when the Daffodil, 509:18
Surfeited with honey, 183:3
Surfeiting appetite may sicken, 204:10
Surge, booming s. of Aegean, 74:2
    laces just reveal s., 508:7
    murmuring s., 212:24
    Thulé and Atlantic s., 301:1
Surgeon, if s. is like poet, 820:6
    to old shoes, 191:19
    with help of s. recover, 179:15
Surgeons must be careful, 508:3
Surgery, honor hath no skill in s., 183:25
Surging immensity of life, 442:23
Surly bonds of Earth, 800:1
    hear the s. sullen bell, 221:23
Surmise, deep s. pierces, 474:3
    wild s., 408:17
Surmises jealousies conjectures, 187:21
Surname, his s. epithet for knave, 141:*n7*
Surpass today what you were yesterday, 238:8
Surpassed, loftiness of thought s., 274:7
    others but had no more power, 99:7
Surpasses, not to be born s. thought, 66:19
    or subdues mankind, 395:17

Surpasseth, night of time s. day, 249:3
Surplus, power of s. in banks, 389:8
    wealth sacred trust, 521:17
Surpluses, get off fat s., 754:14
Surprise, abuse of power no s., 869:1
    come as welcome s., 98:1
    meaning unfolded by s., 625:5
    poetry should s., 413:1
    respect mingled with s., 374:3
    stairway of s., 424:18
    that I landed on my feet, 785:2
    unfolded by s., 625:5
    was there no s., 829:6
Surprised by joy, 372:9
    guilty thing s., 371:1
    police walked in she s., 802:7
    sore s. them all, 357:2
    to find it done at all, 309:8
    was I with sudden heat, 167:1
    we were s. once long ago, 815:6
    you are ready to be s., 763:15
Surrealism, belief in superior reality, 709:7
Surrender, explaining instead of acting, 617:4
    fear hate s. defiance, 840:3
    Guards die but never s., 366:21
    let us s. to love, 93:8
    man may be forced to s., 248:1
    no retreat baby no s., 868:4
    of life nothing, 389:9
    shameful to s. to first comer, 584:13
    to Him we s., 117:13
    unconditional s., 498:1
    we shall never s., 619:14
Surrenders, victory when opponent s. before
    hostilities, 80:18
    whosoever s. his face to God, 119:4
Surrounding, how to explore vacant vast s.,
    488:5
Surrounds, ever-during dark s. me, 257:6
Survey mankind, 306:15
    monarch of all I s., 326:16
    time takes s. of world, 183:30
Survival, assure s. of liberty, 785:10
    love the only s., 715:2
    of Fittest, 439:14
    of fittest, 490:7
    of wildlife in Africa, 796:14
    re-vision an act of s., 825:11
    we are s. machines, 850:9
    without victory no s., 619:13
Survive and multiply, 440:2
    cannot s. wrongs repeated, 694:3
    monuments of wit s. monuments of power,
    164:7
    only the fit s., 627:11
    opinions not s. without fight, 631:5
    or perish, 390:3
    our souls s. death, 101:*n6*
    passions which yet s., 401:13
    you s. but there's less, 844:14
Survived, astonishing that some of us s., 722:17
    don't see how Henry s., 773:6
    I s., 342:7
    pride of those who have s., 621:7
Survives, classic s. circumstances, 779:11
    plum s. its poems, 640:15
    Thomas Jefferson still s., 330:18
Survivor of that time that place, 683:7

Survivors', dying more s. affair, 631:8
Susanna, O S., 503:9
Susanna's music, 641:6
Suspect everybody, 464:30
    once s. Caspian Fact, 510:16
    thoughts of others, 184:31
Suspected, new opinions always s., 275:4
    wished wife not so much as s., 88:24
Suspecting, without s. our abode, 511:7
Suspects himself of virtues, 710:2
    round up the usual s., 758:8
    yet soundly loves, 209:3
Suspend functioning of imagination, 722:1
    I s. my judgment, 152:18
    men cannot s. fate, 282:9
Suspended, I s. religious inquiries, 332:14
Suspense in news is torture, 260:24
Suspension of disbelief, 379:9
Suspicion always haunts guilty mind, 171:5
    Caesar's wife must be above s., 88:*n14*
    general s. and distrust, 614:3
    more than half right, 724:3
    no s. of partiality in his writing, 87:14
    rumor fantasy, 824:15
    stuck full of eyes, 183:26
Suspicions, fresh s., 209:5
Suspicious friend, 295:13
    religious people s., 587:4
Suspire, we only live only s., 679:11
Sustain, prop that doth s. house, 186:12
Sustenance, best adapted to s. and propagation,
    321:5
    White S. Despair, 509:15
Swagman, jolly s., 585:8
Swains, that all our s. commend her, 173:34
Swallow a camel, 35:16
    blow and s. at same moment, 84:4
    come before s. dares, 223:27
    flying South, 453:1
    gudgeons ere they're catch'd, 58:*n4*
    one s. makes a summer, 78:*n2*
    one s. not a summer, 78:5
    revenge s. them up, 209:20
    Swallow flying, 453:1
    up death in victory, 26:2
Swallowed, Aaron's rod s. their rods, 7:34
    as a s. bait, 222:20
    death s. up, 43:9
    easier s. than flap-dragon, 174:26
    half our sailors s., 171:1
    oblivion s. cities up, 203:20
    other books to be s., 166:17
    up and lost, 256:12
    up in death, 74:13
Swalloweth the ground with fierceness, 14:28
Swallowing, pity from s. wave, 266:3
    up all thought and imagination, 301:10
Swallow's, hope flies with s. wings, 172:5
Swallows twitter in the skies, 411:8
    west wind and the s., 83:3
Swam in a gondola, 195:25
    little Fish s., 467:13
Swamped, atoms cannot be s. by force, 89:17
Swamps, lover of s., 404:21
Swan, black s. rare bird, 109:18
    cygnet to pale faint s., 176:3
    dies the s., 455:5
    every goose s. lad, 481:7

Sweet *(continued)*

milk of concord, 217:6
mingles s. bitterness with her cares, 91:21
more s. than painted pomp, 193:36
mountain nymph s. liberty, 250:23
musk-roses and eglantine, 178:19
my Adonis hath a s. tooth, 162:6
my home s. home, 673:11
my lady s. arise, 220:15
my life smack s., 463:12
my s. Highland Mary, 358:12
nature's s. cunning hand, 204:20
naught so s. as melancholy, 234:5
neglect more taketh me, 232:7
never merry when hear s. music, 186:16
not s. to dance on air, 561:4
o' the year, 223:21
oblivious antidote, 217:19
of bitter bark, 623:10
one s. sacrifice, 225:15
Parthenope nourished me, 93:26
parting is such s. sorrow, 180:16
Peace is crowned, 268:15
plums so s. and so cold, 658:19
poison for age's tooth, 175:4
poison of misused wine, 252:4
pour s. dew on his tongue, 54:13
psalmist of Israel, 11:24
reluctant amorous delay, 257:20
retired solitude, 252:17
retirement urges s. return, 259:8
Richard s. lovely rose, 182:3
Roman hand, 205:20
rose by any name as s., 180:3
serenity of books, 437:20
silent thought, 221:8
singing in the choir, 883:5
sleep of laboring man s., 23:6
Slug-a-bed, 241:11
smell of success, 780:1
smell s. and blossom in dust, 246:12
smellest so s., 210:5
solitude is s., 326:15
sounds and s. airs, 224:33
sounds together, 591:19
spring full of s. days, 242:20
spring year's pleasant king, 227:4
stay O s., 882:3
stolen waters are s., 20:9
such fleet things s., 530:18
such s. thunder, 179:2
summer's flower to summer s., 222:2
swan of Avon, 233:6
sweets to the s., 202:17
sweets with s. war not, 220:33
tell not s. I am unkind, 265:17
Thames run softly, 161:9
the coming on of evening, 258:1
the moonlight sleeps, 186:15
then how it was s., 462:23
thing to revisit in dreams, 67:5
things s. to taste prove sour, 176:14
though in sadness, 402:13
though wickedness be s., 13:41
thoughts that savor of content, 164:2
thy s. love remembered, 221:7
to dance to violins, 561:4
to know eye will mark, 398:3

Sweet *(continued)*

to let mind unbend, 97:16
to look into fair, 408:15
to make the end most s., 176:11
took s. counsel together, 16:37
touches of s. harmony, 186:15
two-and-twenty, 399:7
utter s. breath, 179:5
wee wife o' mine, 358:11
what makes life so s., 511:10
where late s. birds sang, 221:24
world not s. in end, 530:9
your most s. voices, 219:28
Zeus grant s. delight, 63:28
Sweet Pea, poor little S., 720:15
Sweeten my imagination, 212:28
this little hand, 217:14
Sweeteners of tea, 304:16
Sweeter air where it was made, 671:18
no s. fat than sticks to bones, 486:3
pains of love be s. far, 272:8
rose is s. in bud, 162:7
speech s. than honey, 50:16
than honey and the honeycomb, 15:17
than sound of instrument, 248:17
world hath not a s. creature, 209:25
wrath s. than honeycomb, 52:7
Sweetes' li'l' feller, 569:3
Sweetest, canker lives in s. bud, 221:11
girl I know, 628:20
hours e'er I spend, 356:23
last taste s. last, 176:21
Lesbia, 226:20
life near bone s., 475:21
li'l' feller, 569:3
love I do not go, 229:2
melancholy, 236:9
rain makes not fresh, 236:7
Shakespeare Fancy's child, 251:8
song ear ever heard, 397:9
songs saddest thought, 403:5
strongest and s. songs remain, 488:18
surfeit of the s. things, 178:24
sweet Echo s. nymph, 252:14
vibrate s. pleasure, 357:7
voice of God's creatures, 448:*n*1
way to me, 588:12
Sweetheart come see if the rose, 150:9
stay my s. never go, 540:2
that old s. of mine, 553:6
Tray Blanch and S., 212:11
Sweetly, hears you nearby s. speaking, 56:5
how s. did they float, 252:15
marveling s. on ills, 681:20
methinks how s. flows, 241:14
more s. than rhyme, 410:13
nimbly and s. recommends, 214:21
played in tune, 357:4
so s. were forsworn, 207:8
worm feed s. upon me, 231:14
worm shall feed s. on him, 13:45
Sweetness and light, 284:5, 497:13
by convention s., 70:12
flows into breast, 595:5
sweetness infinite s., 268:12
keeps with perfect s., 426:18
linked s. long drawn out, 251:8
loathe taste of s., 183:3

Sweetness *(continued)*

out of the strong came s., 10:19
through mine ear, 251:23
waste s. on desert air, 315:23
Sweets, brought'st Thy s. along, 242:17
compacted lie, 242:20
diffuse balmy s. around, 165:*n*3
feast of nectared s., 252:19
grown common lose delight, 222:7
into your list, 392:20
last taste of s., 176:21
lost in the s., 291:19
of Hasty Pudding, 347:8
stolen s. are best, 287:18
stolen s. are sweeter, 392:14
to the sweet, 202:17
wilderness of s., 258:16
with sweet war not, 220:33
Swell a progress, 675:4
bosom with thy fraught, 209:19
deep sea s., 676:14
drift in gradual s., 839:4
from lyre within sky, 448:1
ghosted you up a s. story, 731:4
green in havens dumb, 546:3
music with voluptuous s., 395:13
no Minstrel raptures s., 373:3
soul to rage, 274:21
Swelling and limitless billows, 378:1
prologues to the s. act, 214:10
Swells and s. in his fury, 672:5
note that s. gale, 316:9
pealing anthem s., 315:19
Swept, be not s. off feet by impression, 109:4
cleaned windows s. floor, 525:22
it for half a year, 516:1
with confused alarms, 496:19
Swerve a hair from truth, 203:20
from s. of shore to bend of bay, 650:19
Swift as a bird or thought, 53:5
as a shadow, 177:28
has sailed into rest, 595:8
how s. how secretly, 695:1
lonely and s. like planet, 567:5
love is s., 137:11
O time too s., 163:3
race is not to the s., 23:23
race is to the s., 568:13
red flesh, 720:7
sandy glass, 233:17
slow man catches up with s., 53:8
slow sweet sour, 546:13
terrible s. sword, 481:1
to hear, 45:23
too s. arrives as tardy, 180:25
true hope is s., 172:5
Swifter than eagles, 11:8
than weaver's shuttle, 13:16
Swiftest traveler goes afoot, 474:19
Swiftly, bright youth passes s., 59:25
happiness too s. flies, 315:8
most s. fester or putrefy, 222:*n*1
walk o'er wave, 404:7
Swiftness, O s. never ceasing, 163:3
Swill, I positively s. in their ale, 718:11
Swim, creep s. or fly, 278:6
mother may I s., 887:17
naughty night to s. in, 212:4

Swim *(continued)*
  sink or s., 182:4
  sink or s. live or die, 390:3
  sink or s. together, 607:3
  teaching a fish to s., 121:6
  wanton boys that s. on bladders, 225:25
  wherever wood can s., 365:14
  with bladders of philosophy, 281:3
Swimmer, strong s. in agony, 398:9
Swimmin', old s. hole, 553:9
Swimming, art of not drowning, 627:8
  find out who is s. naked, 826:11
  from tree to tree, 787:3
  my wife and sister were s., 767:6
Swims into his ken, 408:17
Swindles, great s. simple, 581:12
Swine, cast pearls before s., 33:15
  gotta have a s., 817:11
  is unclean, 8:24
  nor feed the s., 894:17
  unclean spirits entered s., 36:32
Swine's, jewel of gold in a s. snout, 20:14
Swing, don't mean thing if ain't got s., 720:13
  low sweet chariot, 898:21
  of the sea, 546:3
  Seraphs s. snowy Hats, 508:10
  that fellow's got to s., 561:2
  tramp and trudge, 654:5
Swing'd, Saint George that s. dragon, 175:8
Swinger of birches, 622:20
Swinging low with sullen roar, 251:17
Swings, lost on roundabouts pulls up on s., 613:3
Swinish, hoofs of s. multitude, 325:6
Switch, hire executioner to throw s., 709:15
Switzerland had love democracy, 781:4
Swiveller, here's a state cried Mr. S., 464:29
Swollen shadow, 772:2
Swoller, let 'em s. you, 774:9
Swoon, Locke sank into s., 594:15
Swooned, soul s. slowly, 650:9
Swoop, at one fell s., 217:8
Sword, another drawn with s., 447:2
  arm held fair s., 138:4
  brave man with s., 561:3
  deputed s., 206:25
  die on mine own s., 217:26
  every man's s. was against his fellow, 10:41
  eye tongue s., 200:2
  fallen by edge of the s., 31:13
  famous by my s., 262:24
  father's s. girded on, 387:12
  flaming s. which turned, 6:2
  fleshed thy maiden s., 183:35
  glorious by my s., 262:n2
  I gave them a s., 771:11
  I with s. will open, 187:7
  is the s. unswayed, 172:4
  leave s. in hands of child, 113:4
  let s. of France fall, 686:7
  light of thy s., 417:5
  man for the s., 453:3
  nation shall not lift s., 24:33
  nor s. nor age destroy, 102:18
  not peace but a s., 34:5
  of heaven will bear, 207:6
  of justice has no scabbard, 347:6
  of the Lord and of Gideon, 10:15

Sword *(continued)*
  of war or of law, 338:9
  outwears its sheath, 397:14
  pen mightier than s., 423:13
  pen preferable to s., 156:39
  pen worse than s., 235:5
  Pizarro traced line with s., 414:7
  pulleth s. out of stone, 138:2
  seeks with the s. repose, 268:7
  shall be against his brother, 28:20
  sharp as a two-edged s., 19:31
  sharper than two-edged s., 45:7
  slander whose edge sharper than s., 220:20
  sleep in my hand, 354:8
  take the s. perish with s., 36:9
  terrible swift s., 481:1
  the mace the crown, 189:23
  time rust sharpest s., 374:8
  to him that succeed me, 271:27
  united nations drew, 395:16
  unsmote by s., 397:3
Swords into plowshares, 24:33
  keep up your bright s., 207:30
  little after draw out s., 29:23
  play orators for us, 167:18
  sheathed s. for lack of argument, 189:8
  walks and turns our s., 193:19
  yet were they drawn s., 16:38
Swore, armies s. in Flanders, 314:11
  full great oath, 889:24
  in faith 'twas strange, 208:3
  my tongue s., 68:1
  to be true to each other, 886:3
Sworn, be but s. my love, 180:2
  had I so s. as you, 215:5
  hostility against tyranny, 337:7
  I have s. thee fair, 223:7
  in s. twelve have thief, 206:19
  to weed and pluck away, 176:32
  who hath not s. deceitfully, 15:24
Swound, noises in a s., 375:24
Sybil of Cumae hanging in a jar, 105:20
Sycamore seed twirling, 724:15
  sighing by a s. tree, 210:8
Sycamores, through s. candle lights are gleaming, 568:15
  through s. lights, 609:10
Syllable, built of just s., 511:2
  last s. of recorded time, 217:23
  men's names, 252:12
Syllables, equal s. require, 292:17
  govern the world, 238:18
Syllabub sea, 467:13
Syllogism from Kiezewetter's Logic, 507:6
Syllogisms, army of six hundred s., 141:12
Sylvan historian, 410:13
Symbol, books s. of his resurrection, 611:2
  of power of Heaven, 671:21
Symbolism, impoverishment in s., 630:5
Symbols, ancient animal s. of Saint John, 415:7
  crankish quest for sexual s., 723:4
  discourses to us by s., 380:1
  from s. into truth, 421:11
  harmonious in themselves, 378:24
  of high romance, 412:8
Symmetry, frame thy fearful s., 353:1
  mysterious demand of eye and mind for s., 582:17

Symmetry *(continued)*
  of shelves, 383:9
Sympathetic wife best possession, 68:19
Sympathies, tumor killing s., 531:13
Sympathize, I deeply s., 516:7
Sympathy cold to distant misery, 332:7
  does not get s. he hoped for, 563:2
  exciting s. of reader, 379:8
  friend with whom I am in s., 535:1
  no conscious s. or relationship, 533:11
  patience and s., 604:4
  walks furlong without s., 486:17
  with sounds, 327:4
Symphony, revive her s. and song, 377:23
Syndrome, Philosophers' S. mistaking a failure, 853:14
  Stockholm S., 872:6
Syne, auld lang s., 357:17, 357:18
Synergy behavior of whole systems, 705:12
Synge, John S. and Augusta Gregory, 597:1
Syntax, both in s. and words, 496:1
Synthesizes, artist selects guesses s., 578:4
Synthetic magical power imagination, 379:12
Syracusans, eight victories over S., 69:4
System, extend s. to this hemisphere, 355:7
  in future S. must be first, 566:1
  of general security, 653:16
  purge rottenness out of s., 561:14
Systematic procession of universe, 142:13
Systems, all s. go, 800:4
  and creeds, 450:10
  atoms or s., 294:18
  butterfly can transform storm s., 872:5
  of preference or restraint, 319:10
  our little s. have day, 453:9
  perverted by selfishness, 648:6
  synergy behavior of whole s., 705:12
  that make black man foreigner, 862:11
Szilard, work by Fermi and S., 637:14

T

T, fitted him to a T, 145:n10
  performed to a T, 145:15
Tabernacle, cloudy t. parted, 414:6
  he set a t. for the sun, 15:16
  who shall abide in thy t., 15:10
Tabernacles, how amiable are thy t., 17:18
  how goodly thy t., 9:11
  of the most High, 16:27
Table, arose from t. sober, 265:2
  behave mannerly at t., 555:9
  candle burned on t., 688:6
  crumbs from masters' t., 34:33
  earth dice human bones, 399:14
  etherized upon a t., 674:17
  gas steam or t. turning, 491:18
  general joy of whole t., 216:19
  of my memory, 198:15
  remain sitting at your t., 655:17
  set t. on a roar, 202:12
  sit at t. of brotherhood, 823:7
  snatching from t., 619:8
  there is head of t., 426:5
  thou preparest a t. before me, 15:23
  with a stein on t., 585:6
  write it before them in a t., 26:11

Tableau, l'histoire t. des crimes, 299:*n*8

Tableaux, adieu chers t., 247:*n*4

Tables, he wrote upon t. words of covenant, 8:22

    make it plain upon t., 29:7

    marriage t., 197:7

    of moneychangers, 35:8

    thousand t. wanted food, 368:1

Tablet gift of Memory, 76:7

Taboo, I know it's strictly t., 813:6

Tabooed by anxiety, 527:3

Tackle, bravery on and t. trim, 260:16

Tacks, come to brass t., 677:4

Tactic, silence is best t., 264:1

Tactics, triumph over weapons and t., 629:11

Taffeta, fair hot wench in t., 181:20

    phrases, 174:28

Taffy came to my house, 894:1

    was a Welshman, 894:1

Tags, some in t., 896:21

Tahiti, in soul of man one insular T., 483:5

Tail and pointed ears, 440:11

    bear your blazing t., 641:1

    beginning with end of t., 514:12

    durst not touch t., 894:5

    hangs down behind, 588:17

    hole where t. came through, 381:19

    improve shining t., 513:15

    Long T., 876:6

    my t. go to ground, 146:14

    plaited t. brandished high, 334:2

    such little t. behind, 606:10

    tied to me as to dog's t., 594:5

    tips of his beautiful t., 891:16

    treading on my t., 515:2

    uninterrupted central t. row, 671:11

    waving wild t., 589:19

Tailor, good t. and comfortable shoes, 844:18

Tailors, four and twenty t., 894:5

Tails behind them, 895:2

    cut off t., 892:10

    heads or t. will turn up, 269:17

    puppy dogs' t., 895:11

    salt upon their t., 284:3

Tail-up, head-down t. hunt, 845:11

Taint, any t. of vice, 205:25

    I cannot t. with fear, 216:*n*1

    never t. my love, 210:7

    of personality, 505:16

Tainted, goodness t., 474:23

    tyranny in t. breeze, 324:7

    what plea so t., 185:18

Taj Mahal, flat that would flatten T., 762:2

Take a bond of fate, 216:33

    advantage get advantage, 480:6

    animal you t. for a walk, 439:7

    another station, 526:9

    any shape but that, 216:20

    arms against sea of troubles, 199:21

    arms t. your last embrace, 181:14

    beak from out heart, 449:10

    bread from mouth of labor, 337:11

    but degree away, 203:7

    care of the sense, 514:20

    chances for peace, 674:16

    come to fork in road t. it, 807:8

    each man's censure, 197:23

    eat this is my body, 36:3

Take *(continued)*

    form from off my door, 449:10

    from seventy springs score, 574:11

    from them sense of reckoning, 189:24

    get that first t., 827:1

    give an inch t. an ell, 148:*n*12

    give me today t. tomorrow, 119:24

    heaven t. my soul, 175:31

    heed of loving me, 230:3

    her up tenderly, 418:13

    him and cut him in stars, 180:32

    him for all in all, 197:9

    honor from me and life done, 176:9

    I believe and t. it, 151:14

    into air my breath, 410:9

    it from me, 582:3

    it from me kiddo, 701:9

    kiss you t. is better, 204:3

    life easy, 590:22

    love easy, 590:21

    love you t. is equal to, 849:1

    me into bright child of mind, 701:3

    my milk for gall, 214:17

    my waking slow, 756:5

    my wife please, 748:3

    my yoke, 34:9

    no thought for morrow, 33:11

    not able to t. the lead, 51:27

    not t. his own life, 74:12

    not t. this anymore, 801:14

    not thy holy spirit from me, 16:33

    note O world, 209:17

    nothing of his labor, 23:7

    nothing on looks, 466:27

    O take those lips away, 207:8

    passage we did not t., 678:7

    physic pomp, 211:33

    pray Lord soul t., 283:9

    risk I had to t. and took, 624:15

    some come to t. their ease, 226:16

    the wings of the morning, 19:13

    thee with her eyelids, 20:2

    them he cannot t., 499:9

    they can't t. that away from me, 711:5

    they have to t. you in, 622:14

    thine ease, 38:3

    thine old cloak about thee, 881:9

    this cannot t. her, 261:3

    thy rod, 7:33

    Time will t. my love away, 221:19

    to open road, 486:24

    triple ways to t., 588:12

    up our quarrel with the foe, 614:7

    up read, 116:5

    up thy bed, 36:26

    upon's mystery of things, 213:8

    we must t. the current, 193:14

    what course others may t., 331:13

    what is given, 625:10

    will for the deed, 145:16

    winds of March, 223:27

    you a button-hole lower, 174:29

    you t. my house, 186:12

    your delight in momentariness, 706:2

Taken, ark of God is t., 10:37

    at the flood, 193:13

    away that which he hath, 35:27

    better care of myself, 654:21

Taken *(continued)*

    from you for your better health, 236:15

    fun where found it, 589:3

    hath t. away thy blessing, 6:40

    home gone and t. thy wages, 220:26

    justice not to be t. by storm, 606:19

    no profit where no pleasure t., 173:6

    one t. the other left, 35:24

    the Lord hath t. away, 12:39

    to drink, 606:4

    worth's unknown although height t., 222:15

Taker, laid to make t. mad, 222:20

Takes away the performance, 215:26

    blesseth him that t., 186:1

    no fairy t., 196:19

    no man t. wealth with him, 59:24

    no private road, 295:6

    soul t. nothing with her, 74:17

    the reason prisoner, 214:8

    time t. all gives all, 158:16

Takest, bringing in secret whom thou t. away, 87:4

    whatsoever thou t. in hand, 30:28

Taketh away sin of world, 38:50

    he t. wise in craftiness, 13:12

    sweet neglect more t. me, 232:7

Taking away someone else's freedom, 790:20

    from one class to give to other, 299:19

    in hand a city, 62:15

Tale, as a t. that is told, 17:24

    every t. condemns me, 172:9

    every tongue brings in t., 172:9

    fair t. of a tub, 143:7

    flowery t. more sweetly, 410:13

    hear by t. or history, 177:27

    I could a t. unfold, 198:5

    love-gift of fairy t., 515:10

    moon takes up wondrous t., 287:21

    never heard in t. or song, 252:3

    of hardihood endurance, 603:5

    of Shaun or Shem, 650:22

    of Troy divine, 251:19

    out of season, 31:9

    plain t. put you down, 182:23

    point moral or adorn t., 306:17

    round unvarnished t., 207:34

    say t. as said to me, 373:1

    schoolboy's t., 395:6

    shepherd tells his t., 251:2

    silly fairy t., 317:2

    speeds best plainly told, 172:1

    tell t. tit, 892:21

    telle a t. after a man, 134:10

    thereby hangs a t., 194:16

    to him my t. I teach, 377:3

    told by an idiot, 217:23

    Truth hero of my t., 506:10

    twice-told t., 175:20

    which holdeth children from play, 162:18

    would cure deafness, 224:6

    yet often told a t., 384:15

Talebearer, go up and down as a t., 8:27

Talebearers as bad as tale-makers, 346:10

Tale-makers, tale-bearers as bad as t., 346:10

Talent, blessed who have no t., 425:15

    blessed with each t., 295:13

    contrast between genius and t., 617:16

Talent *(continued)*
  contribution according to t., 478:*n*2
  does what it can, 512:16
  extraordinary collection of t., 786:5
  formed in stillness, 343:8
  good thing if you possess great t., 737:4
  grieved when man of t. dies, 335:10
  has t. cannot use it, 727:14
  honors t. in every branch, 71:14
  inspiration love, 578:3
  of meat-packer, 603:13
  particular t. or industry, 331:4
  succeeded using whole t., 727:14
  to amuse, 719:14
  to see what under nose, 749:19
  to write in way hard to understand, 335:18
  which is death to hide, 254:20
Talents equal to business, 110:4
  grounds are virtue and t., 338:4
  la carrière ouverte aux t., 365:17
  let fools use t., 204:18
  reviewers tried t. failed, 378:20
Tale's, sad t. best for winter, 223:14
Tales already plainly told, 53:20
  dead men tell no t., 273:12
  natural fear increased with t., 165:13
  out of school, 147:13
  tell old t. and laugh, 213:8
  witch-t. Annie tells, 553:7
  words as idle t., 38:41
Talk a little wild, 225:13
  about washing machines, 771:3
  after-dinner t., 450:13
  always t. who never think, 233:*n*1
  and never think, 233:7
  bad music people don't t., 560:21
  Cabots t. only to God, 577:15
  can we t., 835:1
  cane leaves rusty with t., 704:15
  come after me let people t., 129:15
  create do not t., 344:18
  fishes t. like whales, 323:9
  from getting overwise, 623:17
  good gods how he will t., 281:15
  hear t. of court news, 213:8
  innocent of t. or action, 741:11
  I t. a lot I like to t., 628:4
  is of bullocks, 31:25
  I've come to t. with you again, 855:6
  let's t. of graves, 177:7
  let's t. of wills, 177:7
  living doll can t. t. t., 833:1
  loves to hear himself t., 180:23
  low talk slow, 751:3
  money doesn't t. it swears, 851:10
  never spent hour's t. withal, 174:9
  night crept upon our t., 193:15
  no one would t. much in society, 343:15
  not of other men's lives, 31:7
  not to me of name, 399:7
  nothing but t. of his horse, 184:16
  of crabbed old men, 91:5
  of degeneracy and decay, 420:3
  of many things, 516:4
  of mysteries, 473:12
  of nothing but business, 139:6
  of pushing their bones, 820:8
  of things heavenly, 271:16

Talk *(continued)*
  pleasant walk pleasant t., 516:2
  ran sun down with t., 83:1
  save us, 650:22
  sense to a fool, 68:10
  sense to American people, 727:9
  so much about myself, 474:7
  some little t. awhile, 441:20
  some t. of Alexander, 883:13
  tendeth only to penury, 20:28
  'tisn't beauty nor good t., 589:23
  tongues have their t., 155:*n*10
  too much, 273:1
  true I t. of dreams, 179:26
  two t. one hear, 427:8
  what common t. of town is, 277:7
  when you t. about this, 783:4
  with crowds keep virtue, 590:2
  with lover's ghost, 229:21
  with you walk with you, 184:22
  woman who occasions least t., 72:5
Talked between the Rooms, 509:7
  like poor Poll, 316:21
  long enough about rights, 753:11
  worse than being t. about, 559:25
Talker, time is a t., 68:17
Talkers, know little great t., 312:23
  no good doers, 171:26
Talkin', you t. to me, 863:13
Talking, Frenchman always t., 311:1
  he is t. or is pursuing, 12:1
  he will be t., 191:3
  bear voices t. about everything, 865:13
  don't say yes until I finish t., 733:7
  hydrant in yard, 625:8
  in mathematics never know what t., 614:8
  is passion of woman, 286:17
  keep people from t., 155:*n*10
  know what we are t. about, 545:6
  lived life t. at street corners, 682:10
  of axes, 514:9
  of fall of man, 475:32
  of Michelangelo, 674:18
  sound of someone t., 122:4
  tired sun with t., 499:9
  to Hens of Dorking, 467:16
  we're not actually t. about it, 865:3
Talks, wish I liked way it is, 579:15
Tall, ask Alice when ten feet t., 846:5
  confidence in t. man merited, 753:1
  divinely t., 450:23
  ship and star to steer, 635:15
  to reach the pole, 289:4
  yond t. anchoring bark, 212:24
Taller by breadth of nail, 284:24
  town than Rome, 618:14
Tallest pine, 255:16
Tally, no books but score and t., 170:17
Talmud, rather believe fables in T., 165:26
Tam lo'ed him like brither, 358:5
Tamarind, dream beneath t. tree, 447:11
Tambourine, Mr. T. Man, 851:12
Tamburlaine must die, 168:3
  the Scourge of God, 168:3
Tame, glass thou canst not t., 242:7
  heyday in the blood is t., 201:6
  of all t. a flatterer, 232:3
  though I seem t., 149:5

Tame *(continued)*
  tongue can no man t., 45:28
Tamed by Miltown, 787:12
Tamely, suffer t. lawless attack, 318:4
Tameness, trusts in t. of a wolf, 212:10
Tames, punishment t. man, 548:16
Tammie, as T. glowered, 358:8
Tammy, like T. Wynette, 856:*n*1
Tamper, where executives never want to t.,
    749:2
Tan, caftan of t., 640:23
  cheek of t., 438:7
Tangere, noli me t., 40:*n*3
  noli me t. for Caesar's I am, 149:5
Tangle of squabbling nationalities, 571:19
Tangled, lie t. in her hair, 266:1
  web we weave, 373:15
Tangles of Neaera's hair, 253:6
Tankards scooped in Pearl, 508:8
Tant, pour t., 148:*n*3
Tantum religio potuit suadere malorum, 89:*n*7
Tao, action of T., 57:13
  function of T., 57:13
  is storehouse of all things, 57:20
  look at T. and do not see it, 57:6
  takes no action, 57:13
  that can be told of, 56:12
  why it is so near to T., 57:3
Tape, red t., 466:3
  ticker t. ain't spaghetti, 651:4
Taper of conwiviality, 464:26
Taper-light, with t. garnish heaven, 175:24
Tapers, hold glimmering t. to sun, 235:*n*5
Tapestries, speech like embroidered t., 62:21
Tapestry, give children right to study t., 330:7
Tapping, suddenly there came t., 449:3
Tar, in fir t. is, 896:4
Tarantara tarantara, 526:7
Tarantula, inconspicuous as t. on angel food,
    674:6
Tara's halls, 387:8
Tar-baby ain't sayin' nuthin', 551:13
Tard dans un monde trop vieux, 457:*n*2
Tardy apish nation, 176:22
  as t. as too slow, 180:25
Tarentum, far from my native T., 83:2
Tares, crop of corn a field of t., 163:11
  of mine own brain, 248:9
Targeted trod like Spring, 595:17
Tarn, dank t. of Auber, 449:15
Tarnish late on Wenlock Edge, 575:5
Tarquin viewed in her face's field, 172:30
Tarried, too long we t., 467:8
Tarrieth, guest that t. but a day, 30:3
  tide t. no man, 146:17
  time nor tide t., 146:*n*12
Tarry at Jericho until beards be grown,
    11:16
  awhile says Slow, 894:4
  why t. the wheels of his chariots, 10:13
Tar's labor or Turkman's rest, 399:15
Tarsus, a Jew of T., 40:41
  stately ship of T., 260:16
Tartarly, savage and T., 399:11
Tarts, made some t., 894:2
Tarzan, I am T. of the Apes, 629:9
  me T. you Jane, 629:*n*4
  of the Apes, 629:8

Task before all is to make you see, 567:4
  delightful t., 300:19
  hardest t. in world, 423:18
  long day's t. is done, 219:1
  my t. is smoothly done, 252:27
  of pure ablution, 412:10
  of twentieth century to explore
    unconscious, 572:7
  remaining before us, 446:5
  sore t., 196:13
  there's the rub the t., 94:27
  though hard be t., 501:6
  what he reads as t., 309:4
  worldly t. hast done, 220:26
Tasking, whole soul's t., 481:15
Taskmaster's, my great T. eye, 250:17
Taskmasters, lies religion of t., 602:14
Tassel-gentle, lure this t. back, 180:13
Taste, all ashes to the t., 395:15
  and see that the Lord is good, 16:6
  arbiter of t., 110:7
  by which relished, 372:4
  constant exercise of good t., 835:16
  essence of t. is suitability, 582:17
  from fountain wells up bitter t., 90:17
  good strong thick smoke, 460:22
  is best judge, 533:14
  is the only morality, 484:19
  last t. of sweets, 176:21
  liquor never brewed, 508:8
  loathe t. of sweetness, 183:3
  man of wealth and t., 857:5
  man's hand not able to t., 179:4
  never t. who always drink, 233:*n*1
  not Pierian spring, 292:12
  of death but once, 192:11
  of your quality, 199:11
  refusing to have t., 761:14
  sans t. sans everything, 194:25
  sit down and t. my meat, 243:12
  sole arbiter is t., 450:3
  things sweet to t. prove sour, 176:14
  touch not t. not, 44:10
  tree whose mortal t., 255:3
  whole joys, 230:13
  whole of it, 462:25
  wild vicissitudes of t., 306:12
  willing to t. any drink once, 637:5
  your ware, 893:12
Tasted all the summer's pride, 350:7
  can't be t. in sip, 464:29
  eternal joys of Heaven, 168:18
  I t. careless then, 508:15
  of desire, 623:4
  some books to be t., 166:17
Tasteless, this age how t., 91:13
Tastes, no accounting for t., 120:14
  wit ne'er t., 295:15
  woman ruin meets, 291:19
Tastiest, sacred cows make t. hamburger,
    841:11
Tasting of Flora and country, 410:4
Tat, tit for t., 148:7
Taters, corn and t. grow, 558:1
Tatter in mortal dress, 594:2
Tattered coat upon stick, 594:2
  ears and battered head, 827:13
  ensign, 443:3

Tattered *(continued)*
  married man t. and torn, 897:8
  through t. clothes, 212:30
Tatters, tear a passion to t., 200:6
Tattlers and busybodies, 44:32
Tattoo, images prisoners t., 727:5
Tatty wreckage of my life, 832:15
Taught, character t. learnt, 497:6
  dream t. me this wisdom, 247:3
  first he wroghte afterward t., 134:3
  folly's all they t. me, 387:16
  genius never can be t., 274:12
  happy is he born and t., 227:9
  hearts t. to conceal, 398:12
  I t. thee to love, 230:7
  it hath t. me to rime, 174:19
  man never flogged never t., 81:7
  Man that he knew not, 119:18
  me all I knew, 589:10
  ruin hath t. me thus to ruminate, 221:19
  should be t. what is, 807:10
  three useful things, 399:6
  Tortoise because he t. us, 514:21
  wise words t. in numbers, 160:25
  you t. me language, 224:11
  you t. them, 838:6
  you've got to be t., 706:14
Taut, by going slightly t., 624:7
Tautness, greyhound's gentle t., 787:19
Tavern, happiness produced by t., 310:7
  I am come to t. alone, 288:21
  in the town, 885:14
  intend to die in t., 125:3
  Mermaid T., 411:5
  opened t. for friends, 601:13
Taverns, knew t. wel in every toun, 133:19
Tawny, gray rats t. rats, 460:8
Tax, excise hateful t., 307:1
  for being eminent, 284:17
  heavier than kings, 303:7
  I t. not you you elements, 211:25
  just man will pay more income t., 74:20
  man's taken all my dough, 859:2
  not t. bill but t. relief bill, 653:8
  power to t. not power to destroy, 539:5
  power to t. power to destroy, 350:1
  take a walk I will t. your feet, 856:11
  where no revenue found, 323:20
Taxation at beginning of dynasty, 131:11
  without representation, 321:4
Taxed, never t. for speech, 205:30
  without consent, 321:*n*3
Taxes, arrange affairs so that t. be low, 613:17
  death and t., 303:20
  death t. childbirth, 726:4
  I like to pay t., 539:12
  laying t. on the next age, 284:16
  No New T., 805:3
  only little people pay t., 794:8
  pay for civilized society, 538:12
  true as t., 465:29
  war certain to increase t., 333:14
Taxi throbbing waiting, 676:12
TB was a disease, 835:20
T-Bird, till her daddy takes the T. away, 856:1
Tchaikovsky, tell T. the news, 811:3
Te deum laudamus, 48:9
  spectem te teneam, 101:*n*7

Te Deum before battle begun, 420:17
Tea, after t. and cakes and ices, 675:2
  and comfortable advice, 413:7
  and scandal, 286:25
  and sometimes t., 293:7
  breakfasts at five-o'clock t., 517:3
  ceremony known as afternoon t., 544:5
  destruction of t. so bold, 329:13
  glad not born before t., 375:12
  honey still for t., 669:7
  put kettle on all have t., 896:17
  sweeteners of t., 304:16
  take some more t., 514:16
  thank God for t., 375:12
  way you sip your t., 711:5
Teach act of order to kingdom, 188:34
  aim of oratory to t., 87:20
  basest thing is to be afraid, 714:3
  beasts shall t. thee, 13:25
  child to doubt, 354:3
  crab to walk straight, 72:17
  eggs do not t. hen, 897:12
  gladly lerne and gladly t., 133:24
  go and t. all nations, 36:23
  he who shall t. child, 354:3
  him to tell my story, 208:3
  him what said in past, 3:3
  his feet a measure, 530:13
  I didn't t. them, 838:6
  learn from those who can t., 65:24
  learn what it had to t., 474:29
  let such t. others, 292:9
  me half the gladness, 403:6
  me my God and King, 243:9
  me to hear mermaids singing, 228:9
  men sense of existence, 547:18
  noble negligences t., 283:15
  nothing but Facts, 466:14
  nothing but to name tools, 262:5
  order to peopled kingdom, 188:34
  same prayer doth t. us all, 186:1
  shall any t. God, 13:43
  sleek girls I t., 814:14
  still pleased to t., 293:1
  the earth shall t. thee, 13:25
  them diligently unto thy children, 9:15
  thy necessity to reason, 176:16
  to him my tale I t., 377:3
  trees and stones will t. you, 123:11
  unforgetful to forget, 506:7
  us good Lord to serve Thee, 144:16
  us how to die, 396:4
  us to care, 677:13
  us to have aspiring minds, 168:2
  us to live again, 691:19
  us to number our days, 17:26
  us to sit still, 677:13
  villainy you t. me, 185:13
  without sneering t. to sneer, 295:13
  ye how to climb, 252:28
  you more of man, 368:6
  young idea to shoot, 300:19
Teacher affects eternity, 531:23
  city is t. of the man, 60:9
  leave them kids alone, 858:13
  Nature be your t., 368:5
  passed for a good t., 141:*n*6
  says every time bell rings, 687:3

Teacher *(continued)*
    success is a lousy t., 873:8
    true t. has no disciple, 417:6
    value of true t., 512:15
    who can arouse feeling, 343:16
Teachers, men are my t., 295:*n*1
    Shame Despair her t., 431:8
    their t. and precursors, 826:6
Teaches, grief t. to waver, 65:19
    hard dealing t. them suspect, 184:31
    he who cannot t., 565:9
    life t. us to be less harsh, 343:6
    nature t. beasts to know friends, 219:23
    nature t. more than preaches, 528:18
    standing on toes, 714:18
    such beauty as woman's eye, 174:20
    time t. all things, 63:18
Teaching a fish to swim, 121:6
    for life, 4:13
    for the day, 568:16
    hold fast to t. as a lamp, 64:15
    is awakening curiosity, 546:1
    nations how to live, 254:2
    only t. on Tuesdays, 787:9
    thank thee Jew for t. word, 186:11
    truth persuades by t., 113:10
    well-established truth, 124:13
    what t. is and was, 714:18
Teachings, Nature's t., 405:11
Teacup, crack in t. opens, 748:9
Teacups, tinkled among t., 675:12
Team of little atomies, 179:25
Teapot, storm in a t., 88:11
Tear a passion to tatters, 200:6
    all he had a t., 316:7
    cannot t. out page of life, 432:8
    down this wall, 765:18
    each other's eyes, 289:6
    from eyelids wiped t., 194:22
    heart to dog to t., 589:25
    never t. linnet from leaf, 593:16
    newborn infant's t., 353:4
    passage of angel's t., 408:16
    Recording Angel dropped a t., 314:18
    shed bitter t., 516:1
    smile on lips t. in eye, 373:12
    still ushered with t., 293:22
    tattered ensign, 443:3
    to pieces that great bond, 216:13
    we shed though secret, 387:7
Tearing up pea patch, 704:13
Tears, angry t. gone, 593:3
    are on her cheeks, 28:10
    before my t. did drown it, 242:26
    big round t. coursed down, 194:1
    bitter t. to shed, 499:9
    blood toil t. sweat, 619:12
    broomsticks and t., 593:3
    bucket full of t. am I., 177:17
    cannot bear a mother's t., 95:8
    crave stain of t., 623:10
    crocodile t., 163:*n*4
    crocodiles shed t. when would devour, 166:6
    dark with torment and t., 476:10
    drop t. as fast, 210:20
    eyes bleared with t., 122:8
    fight from eyes t., 682:12

Tears *(continued)*
    fountains fraught with t., 163:7
    from wrath-bearing tree, 675:23
    hence these t., 85:14
    here are the t. of things, 94:4
    hired t., 248:23
    idle tears, 452:21
    if you have t., 192:33
    in t. amid alien corn, 410:10
    iron t. down Pluto's cheek, 251:20
    kitsch causes two t., 824:6
    like Niobe all t., 197:3
    Lord God will wipe away t., 26:2
    mine own t. do scald, 213:4
    mist of t., 576:13
    no t. in writer no t. in reader, 625:4
    nor all your T. wash out, 442:2
    nor widows' sighs, nor orphans' t., 285:5
    not pay honor with t., 84:17
    nothing is here for t., 260:25
    now am full of t., 590:22
    of one tiny creature, 492:12
    of repentance you'll wipe, 352:7
    of things, 94:4
    rain shower of commanded t., 173:5
    shall drown the wind, 214:24
    Siren t., 222:16
    smiled through their t., 513:7
    smiles t. of boyhood's years, 387:17
    smiling through t., 51:15
    songs composed of t., 457:7
    such as angels weep, 256:1
    sweat or blood, 619:*n*3
    thaw not frost, 403:12
    they that sow in t., 19:3
    thoughts too deep for t., 371:5
    time to plant t., 762:20
    time with gift of t., 529:14
    tired of t. and laughter, 530:16
    trace the tracks of my t., 849:4
    unseen and unknown, 442:23
    watered heaven with t., 353:2
    way with t. watered, 609:15
    weep barren t., 401:16
    why should t. the pale cheek fret, 484:1
    wipe away all t., 47:12
    with sobs and t. sorted, 516:7
    your death brought me t., 83:1
Tear-wrung millions, 619:*n*3
Teas, baked cookies and had t., 864:4
Tease, fools no more I'll t., 293:20
    the huswife's wool, 252:25
Teases, he knows it t., 514:10
    mind over for years, 552:15
Teatray, like t. in sky, 514:15
Technique and style of Europe, 807:17
    of reproduction, 693:3
Techniques, me with my grim t., 801:19
Technology, creation by t. of entities, 860:5
    for a successful t., 790:5
    is indistinguishable from magic, 784:2
    knack of arranging world, 763:16
    science and t. multiply, 826:3
Tecum vivere amem tecum obeam libens, 97:*n*1
Tedious as twice-told tale, 175:20
    old fools, 198:38
    relations t. pack, 560:23

Tedious *(continued)*
    returning as t. as go o'er, 216:25
    road will be less t., 93:5
    shorten t. nights, 227:1
    sport would be t., 181:33
    thinking his prattle t., 177:21
    to tell tales already told, 53:20
Tedium is seasoned with terror, 778:14
    pretentious quotations t., 570:1
    rather abnormal shortening of time, 631:2
Teeming brain, 412:7
    mistress barren bride, 293:26
    refuse of t. shore, 552:16
    womb of kings, 176:24
Teenage, American T. Drive-In Life, 831:2
    angst has paid off well, 879:6
    wasteland, 861:17
Teenager, as t. you are at last stage, 869:2
Teeth, bid them keep t. clean, 219:27
    bitch gone in the t., 665:9
    children's t. set on edge, 28:6
    red thoughts t. white, 608:7
    sans t. sans eyes, 194:25
    shark has pretty t., 716:7
    terrible round about, 14:33
    truth may strike out his t., 159:14
    weeping and gnashing of t., 33:26
    what speech escaped your t., 51:5
    who made t. shall give bread, 146:*n*16
    with the skin of my t., 13:37
    writers like t. incisors molars, 503:2
Tehee quod she, 134:27
Tekel, Mene Mene T. Upharsin, 28:25
Telegraph, Cunard's liners and t., 481:3
Telemachus, mine own T., 451:16
Teleology is theology, 586:7
Telephone, cool medium like t., 764:11
Telephones, army no private baths or t., 673:13
Televised, revolution will not be t., 868:1
Television, confuse t. news with journalism, 852:4
    crouch to t. set, 788:2
    give us this day our t., 827:5
    imitates bad t., 839:19
    it's like watching t., 817:5
    parade of t. pictures, 821:11
    used to distract delude amuse insulate, 754:14
    vast wasteland, 813:15
    watched funeral of poetry on t., 772:8
Tell, a bore to t. everything, 299:3
    aloud greatest failing, 285:7
    can't t. him much, 886:8
    dead can t. you being dead, 679:8
    dead men t. no tales, 273:12
    don't t. they'd advertise, 508:14
    dream of not t., 377:11
    every word t., 606:3
    feat of T. the archer, 360:14
    fowls shall t. thee, 13:25
    her one thing and keep another, 53:16
    her that wastes her time, 249:24
    her what I tell to thee, 453:1
    him he hates flatterers, 192:5
    him to go to hell, 393:2
    if one but t. a thing well, 64:5
    I'll t. you no fibs, 323:6
    it like it is, 168:*n*4

Tell *(continued)*
  it not in Gath, 11:7
  it on the mountain, 898:17
  kiss and t., 286:29
  little Lamb I'll t. thee, 350:13
  me muse, 52:20
  me Muse, 293:18
  me not in mournful numbers, 436:4
  me not sweet I am unkind, 265:17
  me of John or Shaun, 650:22
  me tell me elm, 650:22
  me thy company, 157:29
  me what thy name is, 449:8
  me what you eat, 348:15
  me what you know, 425:14
  me what you like, 484:19
  me where all past years are, 228:9
  me where fancy bred, 185:17
  my story, 202:31
  never seek to t. thy love, 352:3
  O t. me all about Anna Livia, 650:21
  old tales and laugh, 213:8
  sad stories of death of kings, 177:8
  tale tit, 892:21
  tales already told, 53:20
  Tchaikovsky the news, 811:3
  teach him to t. my story, 208:3
  that I cannot t. said he, 381:9
  that to the marines, 374:16
  the crooked rose, 777:2
  the world, 183:27
  them I Am, 318:7
  them I came, 616:7
  those who sent you, 345:6
  truth and shame devil, 146:*n*1
  we t. ourselves stories, 837:13
  what and where they be, 455:4
  what thou art, 157:29
  wife all he knows, 250:2
  you a great secret, 770:8
  you my drift, 190:31
  you what you are, 348:15, 484:19
  young men, 308:1
Telleth number of the stars, 19:20
Telling, I am not arguing I am t., 520:17
  nothing in great harangue, 267:20
  off state and president, 787:10
  pity beyond all t., 591:3
  this with sigh, 622:18
Tells lies without attending, 336:11
  nobody t. me anything, 600:19
  of a nameless deed, 362:2
Telmetale of stem or stone, 650:22
Téméraire, Fighting T., 582:10
Tempe, through life's T. led, 483:20
Temper doctrinaire logic, 694:5
  hot t. leaps over, 184:15
  judicious swearin' keeps t., 600:15
  justice with mercy, 259:17
  made thee to t. man, 281:12
  moderation in t. a virtue, 333:17
  unless I mistake its t., 651:15
  which blades bears better t., 169:15
  wit with morality, 288:4
  woman of uncertain t., 382:4
Temperament, creation seen through t., 537:12
  harmony of t. and circumstances, 493:14

Temperament *(continued)*
  man not product of t., 131:10
  second-class intellect first-class t., 539:11
  solvency matter of t., 590:12
Temperamental atmosphere of Gallup Poll, 620:11
Temperance a species of courage, 276:9
  acquire and beget a t., 200:6
  as easy as t. difficult, 308:11
  fruit of Spirit is t., 43:31
Temperate affords me none, 245:17
  more lovely and more t., 221:2
  wise amazed t. furious, 216:1
Temperature, poll taking t., 620:11
Tempered, absolutism t. by assassination, 362:9
  by war, 785:10
Tempers wind to shorn lamb, 151:6, 314:26
Tempest, betokened t. to field, 171:11
  covert from the t., 26:15
  haunts t., 491:2
  in a teapot, 88:*n*6
  in the very torrent t., 200:6
  on me t. falls, 63:20
  seaman's story is of t., 101:13
  sensual lust t., 492:8
  still is high, 305:8
Tempested, thou shalt not be t., 132:1
Tempests, errors wanderings mists and t., 89:*n*12
  fell all night, 243:7
  glasses itself in t., 396:20
  looks on t., 222:15
Tempest-tost, send t. to me, 552:16
Tempestuous petticoat, 240:16
Temple bells they say, 588:1
  drove out of t., 39:6
  hangs on Dian's t., 220:3
  his people were his t., 270:4
  his train filled the t., 25:8
  Lord is in his holy t., 29:9
  Lord's anointed t., 215:28
  no sooner t. built to God, 144:*n*1
  nothing ill in such t., 224:17
  of Delight, 411:11
  of Dian, 886:14
  of God is holy, 42:10
  singing vespers in T. of Jupiter, 332:19
  two went into t. to pray, 38:22
  veil of t. rent, 36:21
Temple-haunting martlet, 214:21
Temple's inner shrine, 370:6
Temples, forsake their t. dim, 250:14
  God's first t., 405:15
  gorgeous palaces solemn t., 225:1
  made with hands, 40:33
  mortal t. of king, 177:8
  of his gods, 419:19
  shall my joyful t. bind, 249:22
  smote the nail into his t., 10:7
  we build t. for tomorrow, 730:12
  which men had commanded, 270:4
Tempora mutantur nos et mutamur, 121:19
  O t. O mores, 87:6
Temporal, concern t. salvation, 331:10
  force of t. power, 186:1
  matter unreal and t., 493:6
  things seen are t., 43:14

Temporary, dictionaries and t. poems, 307:2
  permanent contract on t. feeling, 536:7
  use of force but t., 324:4
Temps, au t. de ma jeunesse folle, 138:*n*3
  le t. a laissé son manteau, 137:*n*7
  O t. suspends vol, 400:*n*2
Tempt frailty of our powers, 204:2
  not desperate man, 181:10
  shall not t. the Lord, 9:16
  upper classes, 569:2
Temptation, beware t. to ignore facts, 765:14
  blessed the man that endureth t., 45:21
  cold and to t. slow, 222:1
  enter not into t., 36:6
  last t. greatest treason, 678:4
  lead us not into t., 32:25
  maximum of t., 565:10
  my t. is quiet, 596:13
  resist everything except t., 560:7
  to get rid of t. yield, 560:2
  to the editor, 662:10
  white fever of t., 688:7
Temptations, rid of t. by yielding, 417:16
  to belong to other nations, 526:4
Tempted her out of gloom, 449:17
Tempus edax rerum, 102:*n*13
  omnia t. revelat, 103:*n*9
Ten, and David his t. thousands, 11:3
  aren't no T. Commandments, 588:3
  ask Alice when t. feet tall, 846:5
  better t. guilty escape, 318:21
  Commandments, 835:9
  Council of T., 656:10
  death hath t. thousand doors, 237:7
  I'm t. years burning down the road, 868:5
  it's now t. o'clock, 457:4
  jokes an hundred enemies, 313:23
  little Indians, 896:22
  live t. times t., 422:18
  low words, 292:17
  not if I had t. tongues, 50:25
  o'clock scholar, 896:14
  only one summer that I was t., 772:12
  set my t. commandments in your face, 169:24
  strength as strength of t., 452:13
  thousand miles away, 898:3
  thousand saw I at a glance, 371:11
  thousand to go out of it, 284:1
  to the world allot, 159:*n*1
  vowing perfection of t., 203:18
  when angry count t., 338:19
  wrote words of t. commandments, 8:22
Tenacious but restless, 672:2
  of purpose in rightful cause, 96:27
Tenanted, by good angels t., 448:9
  differently t. islands, 439:12
Tenantless, graves stood t., 196:15
  save to wind, 395:18
Tend, great God to thee we t., 117:5
  no more than horses they t., 468:19
  on mortal thoughts, 214:17
Tendencies, containment of Russian expansive t., 738:8
Tendency to good like water, 79:27
Tender eye of pitiful day, 216:13
  for another's pain, 315:8
  grace of day dead, 452:16

Text *(continued)*
   you write must prove, 778:5
Thaïs, where is T., 506:3
Thalatta, 73:*n*5
Thames, life ran gaily as T., 495:17
   sweet T. run softly, 161:9
Thane, I am T. of Cawdor, 214:11
   of Fife had a wife, 217:13
Thank God Almighty, 898:19
   God Almighty free at last, 823:9
   God for tea, 375:12
   heaven fasting, 195:20
   how can I say t. you, 844:3
   me no thankings, 181:3
   thee I am not as other men, 38:23
   thee Jew for word, 186:11
   you for nothing, 155:22
   you for your voices, 219:28
Thanked, God be t., 669:11
   she t. me, 208:3
   when I'm not t., 304:8
Thankful, be t. unto him, 18:3
   come ye t. people, 456:9
   rest and be t., 884:10
Thankfulness, return their t., 351:3
Thankings, thank me no t., 181:3
Thankless arrant, 159:9
   child, 211:11
   meditate the t. Muse, 253:6
Thanks, angels yield eternal t., 318:8
   exchequer of poor, 176:30
   for this relief much t., 196:9
   his my special t., 494:9
   humble and hearty t., 48:16
   I am even poor in t., 199:4
   if life sweet give t., 531:1
   leave off wishing to deserve t., 91:24
   of man and woman, 333:6
   of Republic, 446:12
   Puritans founded to give t., 600:8
   taken with equal t., 200:11
   to give t. is good, 531:1
   to the human heart, 371:5
   we are preserved fr'm Puritans, 600:8
Thanksgiving, come before his presence with t., 17:32, 48:6
   enter into his gates with t., 18:3
   received with t., 44:28
Tharshish, came the navy of T., 11:35
That and which, 570:2
   for a' t., 358:20, 358:21
   relative pronoun, 570:2
   that is is, 205:26
   thou doest do quickly, 39:38
   which is grows, 112:25
   which is not becomes, 112:25
Thatch smokes in sun-thaw, 377:15
   weeded and worn ancient t., 450:7
Thatcher, you're right Mr. T., 714:14
That's all there is, 637:3
   the way it is, 781:14
   what you think, 744:18
   wot I am, 644:4
Thaw and resolve itself into dew, 196:29
The, every word a lie including t., 768:14
Theater, as in a t. eyes of men, 177:21
   dream is a t., 630:9
   how wide t. expands, 384:2

Theater *(continued)*
   I like t. but never come late, 707:3
   Idols of the T., 164:19
   in t. of man's life, 164:16
   needs reminders, 810:10
   shouting fire in t., 538:21
   without cruelty t. not possible, 709:2
   world's a t., 194:*n*2
Theatrical, apt to be most t., 774:11
Thebes or Pelops' line, 251:19
Thee, I to t. thou to me, 526:16
   no more of T. and Me, 441:20
   of t. I sing, 439:9
   of t. I sing baby, 710:24
   through t. and me kings destroyed, 138:14
Thee's, from me to T. long way, 756:14
Theft, Christ forgave t., 463:1
   from those who hunger, 686:15
   property is t., 450:4
   riches by t. will not stay, 5:2
Theirs but to do and die, 454:21
Them that die'll be lucky ones, 555:7
Theme, act of the imperial t., 214:10
   fools are my t., 394:11
   of Art and Song, 596:3
   on dark t. trace verses of light, 89:18
   saluting felicitously every t., 418:18
Them's my sentiments, 459:4
Themselves, God helps them that help t., 302:15
   help them that help t., 59:14
   judging for t., 346:17
   law unto t., 41:9
   must strike the blow, 395:7
   our minds impress, 368:4
   think all men mortal but t., 290:24
Then, as soon as t. supervenes, 868:10
   is now, 725:1
   That Was T., 866:10
Theologian born by living, 144:8
Theologians, extinguished t., 502:2
Theological notions are reflected, 824:7
Theology, persecution is used in t., 615:2
   teleology is t., 586:7
Theoretic and visionary fear, 337:9
Theoretical, Petersburg most t. town, 492:4
Theoric, bookish t., 207:22
Theories, newfangled t., 430:9
   takes stand upon economic t., 648:8
   test of true t. to predict, 406:6
Theorizing, all t. is flight, 793:6
Theory, all t. is gray, 344:5
   complete unified t. of universe, 854:3
   of description matters most, 641:18
   of probabilities, 345:4
   sea of Cause and T., 618:16
   trickle-down t., 753:7
Therapy, psychoanalysis regards itself as t., 626:8
There a little, 26:7
   because it is t., 668:7
   gone here and t., 222:13
   I suffered I was t., 486:15
   is no there there, 628:12
   over over t., 635:2
   tell gang I will be t., 634:11
   there is nothing but grace, 491:5
Truth Is Out T., 874:2

Thereby hangs a tale, 194:16
There's the rub, 199:21
Theresa, Saint T. in wild lament, 737:8
Thermodynamics, describe Second Law of T., 743:12
Thermonuclear war means to universal suicide, 797:4
Thermopylae, make a new T., 398:18
Therrble prongs, 651:3
Thersites was the ugliest man, 50:24
These are the arks, 167:5
   desolate dark weeks, 659:3
Thick and fast came at last, 516:3
   another damned t. book, 335:20
   as autumnal leaves, 255:17
   as hasty pudding, 883:*n*4
   blood t. water's thin, 527:5
   blushing honors t. upon him, 225:25
   butter's spread too t., 516:6
   dashed through t. and thin, 273:7
   inlaid with patines, 186:15
   lay it on t., 521:10
   make t. my blood, 214:17
   muddy ill-seeming t., 173:25
   paint an inch t., 202:12
   rotundity o' the world, 211:24
   stupefying incense smoke, 460:22
   thurgh t. and thenne, 135:2
Thickened, world but t. light, 429:8
Thickens, light t. and crow makes wing, 216:13
   plot t., 272:1
Thicker, blood t. than water, 271:4
Thicket, filled t. with honeyed song, 73:1
   in t. ahead danger or treasure, 772:11
   ram caught in a t., 6:36
Thicket's, deep t. gloom, 342:15
Thick-ribbed ice, 206:38
Thicks man's blood with cold, 376:7
Thick-sighted, ambition t., 409:6
Thick-warbled, trills her t. notes, 260:3
Thief, asked t. to steal me peach, 352:4
   death like a t. in night, 448:13
   doth fear each bush, 171:5
   dwarfish t., 217:15
   fits your t., 207:10
   give to a t., 756:19
   honest t. tender murderer, 461:23
   I'll show thee a t., 244:14
   in the night, 44:18
   in twelve have t. or two, 206:19
   justice rails upon yon simple t., 212:29
   lie still ye t., 183:1
   no longer a t., 756:19
   procrastination t. of time, 290:22
   said last kind word, 463:1
   steals something from t., 208:6
   Taffy was t., 894:1
   Time subtle t. of youth, 250:16
   time you t., 392:20
   which is the t., 212:29
   you cannot banish, 742:8
Thieves, beauty provoketh t., 193:34
   fell among t., 37:36
   knaves t. and treachers, 211:3
   land-t. and water-t., 184:21
   made it a den of t., 35:9
   night is for t., 68:8
   the more t. there will be, 57:19

Thieves *(continued)*
    where t. break through, 33:1
Thigh, smote them hip and t., 10:21
Thimbles, sought it with t., 517:6
Thin air, 225:1
    man, 702:10
    my wit is t., 136:1
    no matter how t. slice it, 617:13
    no woman can be too rich too t., 887:13
    one wildly signaling, 734:7
    partitions, 272:16
    red 'eroes, 587:16
    red-line streak, 489:10
    ring becomes t. by wearing, 89:15
    seven t. kine, 7:9
    smoke without flame, 536:22
    tell female she's t. she's yours, 887:n5
    through thick and t., 135:n1, 273:7
    thurgh thikke and t., 135:2
    water's t., 527:5
    we t. gin, 783:10
Thine, fatal words Mine and T., 155:17
    is the kingdom, 12:24
    not my will but t., 38:31
    wear both for both are t., 171:21
Thing, a little learning is a dangerous t., 292:12
    acting of dreadful t., 192:2
    aged man paltry t., 594:2
    asked no other t., 509:12
    awe of such t. as myself, 191:24
    come at last the Distinguished T., 545:9
    crush the infamous t., 299:17
    dejected t. of fortune, 212:15
    do not do t. they most do show, 222:1
    do your t. & I shall know you, 423:19
    doing is another t., 153:6
    don't mean t. if ain't got swing, 720:13
    dooth with your owene t., 135:19
    each t. is what it is, 875:3
    eating is a small good t., 844:2
    enskyed and sainted, 206:15
    every bitter t. is sweet, 22:2
    every t. that lives is Holy, 352:2
    excellent t. in woman, 213:13
    far far better t., 466:23
    fine t. needs laboring, 592:1
    foolish t. but a toy, 205:29
    goes dead once it has been said, 628:5
    good t. out of Nazareth, 39:1
    guilty t. surprised, 371:1
    hates t. he would not kill, 185:28
    having seen one t., 530:8
    hedgehog knows one great t., 55:2
    hope not t. with feathers, 839:12
    I am every dead t., 229:13
    I have done one braver t., 228:12
    I was born to do, 167:6
    ill-favored t. but mine own, 196:4
    is it so small a t., 495:8
    keep corner in t. I love, 209:9
    kills t. he loves, 561:3
    law for t., 424:13
    learn about one t. from another, 114:4
    life is the t., 590:15
    little learning dangerous t., 292:12
    make good t. too common, 187:34
    many a t. sought, 221:8
    many-splendored t., 577:4

Thing *(continued)*
    mastery of the t., 546:10
    meanest t. he ever did, 833:16
    men prize the t. ungained, 203:3
    mind terrible t. to waste, 888:21
    moderately good, 333:17
    motion like living t., 368:15
    necessary for triumph of evil, 325:15
    never do merely one t., 779:5
    never done single t. I wanted to, 664:4
    never said a foolish t., 280:27
    no new t. under the sun, 22:24
    no such cold t., 243:5
    no the t. I should be, 358:22
    not done in a corner, 41:6
    not t. to laugh to scorn, 195:31
    of beauty joy forever, 409:7
    of darkness, 225:8
    of evil, 449:9
    of shreds and patches, 527:7
    One and Thing Two, 739:12
    only t. to fear is fear, 652:2
    pleasant t. if thou keep them within thee,
        21:19
    poor t. but mine own, 196:n1
    quite another t., 297:18
    reasoning self-sufficing t., 369:10
    reward of t. to have done it, 427:25
    romantic a t. as one can imagine, 627:6
    said t. which was not, 285:3
    same t. good bad indifferent, 276:12
    saying is one t., 153:6
    sleep it is a gentle t., 376:18
    small t. analogy of great things, 90:4
    so neatly you never feel t., 798:4
    started like a guilty t., 196:16
    sudden if t. comes in his head, 171:4
    surest way to get a t., 420:16
    that eats the heart, 742:2
    that ends all other deeds, 219:7
    that hath been is that which shall be, 22:24
    that is one t., 863:6
    that is your own, 78:19
    the Falklands t., 719:9
    the play's the t., 199:19
    thou art the t. itself, 212:3
    throw away dearest t. owed, 214:14
    time least t. we have of, 722:2
    to every t. there is a season, 22:31
    to love, 632:16
    too much of good t., 155:15
    unfeathered two-legged t., 272:18
    very odd t., 616:11
    we may nat lightly have, 135:10
    what t. of sea and land, 260:16
    winning isn't everything only t., 888:12
    winsome wee t., 358:11
    with feathers, 508:12
    you start out with one t., 871:1
Things, admires mean t. is Snob, 459:9
    age best in four t., 165:8
    all these t. added unto you, 33:10
    all t. are artificial, 248:6
    all t. are one, 62:1
    all t. born through strife, 62:7
    all t. bright beautiful, 476:4
    all t. by law divine, 402:16
    all t. come of thee, 12:25

Things *(continued)*
    all t. great and small, 377:6
    all t. how small soever, 275:3
    all t. taken from us, 450:19
    all t. to all men, 42:18
    all thinking t., 368:11
    always best in beginning, 269:4
    are in saddle, 424:12
    are not what they seem, 436:4
    are of the snake, 424:11
    are sons of heaven, 306:23
    are what you have left, 822:13
    as language are attractive, 427:29
    as they are, 642:22
    as t. have been t. remain, 479:12
    authentic tidings of invisible t., 372:7
    beautiful and good, 401:17
    beginnings of t. not distinguished by eye,
        89:14
    best t. confused with ill, 401:16
    best t. in life free, 697:9
    bitterness of t., 372:15
    both great and small, 377:6
    by season seasoned, 186:19
    by whom all t. were made, 48:12
    calm Soul of all t., 495:1
    compare great t. with small, 92:15, 257:2
    counter original spare, 546:13
    dappled t., 546:12
    day of small t., 29:13
    desired and timely t., 575:19
    DiMaggio, does t. perfectly, 722:3
    does away with ideas of t., 76:2
    done a thousand dreadful t., 173:3
    dream strange t., 431:2
    dreaming on t. to come, 222:10
    drift of t., 622:8
    elemental t., 557:6
    eternal fitness of t., 304:19
    evidence of t. not seen, 45:11
    excellent t. in counsels, 21:20
    facts are stubborn t., 286:18, 329:11
    fair and flagrant t., 263:7
    fairer when we look back, 482:9
    fall apart, 593:9
    filled with intent to be lost, 763:7
    forms of t. unknown, 179:6
    four t. come not back, 98:n3
    friends share all t., 58:8
    from all t. one and from one all t., 62:8
    fundamental t. apply, 702:11
    glorious t. of thee spoken, 321:1
    good t. strive to dwell, 224:17
    great t. are done, 354:9
    great t. from neurotics, 610:18
    great t. made of little, 462:26
    greatest vicissitude of t., 166:20
    he can afford to let alone, 474:27
    he is before all t., 44:9
    here are the tears of t., 94:4
    holy profane clean obscene, 239:8
    how can these t. be, 39:10
    how many t. I have no need of, 70:2
    human t. subject to decay, 273:13
    I did not do or say, 595:15
    impossible t., 516:13
    in all t. thee to see, 243:9
    in the midst of t., 98:25

Thinking *(continued)*
high t., 370:4
highly of men or matrimony, 382:9
is dismissal of irrelevancies, 705:14
it ain't t. about it, 471:16
life consists of what man is t. all day, 425:13
love hardly seem worth t., 591:17
makes it so, 199:2
man t. or working is alone, 475:9
most unhealthy thing in world, 559:20
much drinking little t., 284:13
new t. is about loss, 852:7
of the key, 676:17
on fantastic summer's heat, 176:18
on frosty Caucasus, 176:18
on thinking, 78:2
operations we perform without t., 580:6
reed, 269:21
refinement of everyday t., 637:12
scholar is Man T., 425:26
scratched head kept t., 605:21
theologian not born by t., 144:8
through t. few or none harmed, 149:9
too highly of himself, 276:5
too much t. to have common thought, 293:27
too precisely on event, 201:20
what nobody has thought, 700:3
woman sleeps with monsters, 825:1
writing one way to go about t., 724:9
Thinkings, speak as to thy t., 209:1
Thinks better of gilded fool, 228:3
divine thought of itself, 78:2
evil to him who evil t., 131:1
freedom for one who t. differently, 608:1
he t. too much, 191:28
heart t. tongue speaks, 190:38
in a marrowbone, 596:6
know she t. o' me, 588:1
like a philosopher, 313:10
never t. of me, 885:14
not look to see what neighbor t., 111:17
think as native t., 641:10
to get a living, 313:6
too little or too much, 295:1
what a man t. of himself, 474:9
Thinness, gold to airy t. beat, 229:16
Thin-spun, slits the t. life, 253:6
Third and fourth generation of them that hate me, 8:12
day comes a frost, 225:25
day he will raise us up, 28:33
drink not the t. glass, 242:7
drowns him, 204:19
fire tolerable t. party, 473:7
I Don't Know's on t., 705:3
in your bosom, 180:20
is not to dare to be ahead, 57:22
of all people in world died, 131:12
to make t. she joined former two, 274:7
who walks beside you, 676:16
Thirst after happiness, 313:9
dangerous thing, 576:6
drank without t., 285:4
dying of t. by the fountain, 137:12
fame t. of youth, 395:22
goes away with drinking, 145:6
he that believeth on me shall never t., 39:18

Thirst *(continued)*
hunger and t. after righteousness, 32:14
man can raise t., 588:3
mouth and belly injured by t., 80:7
neither t. any more, 46:37
nor for every t. to pot, 244:1
that from soul doth rise, 232:16
this T. blister easier, 508:15
Thirsteth, everyone that t., 27:9
my soul t. for God, 16:21
my soul t. for thee, 17:6
Thirsty and ye gave drink, 35:30
busy curious t. fly, 300:9
cold waters to a t. soul, 21:35
earth soaks up the rain, 265:9
if thine enemy be t., 21:34
in a dry and t. land, 17:6
sleep is drink for the t., 158:8
Thirteen, clocks striking t., 735:15
month old baby, 869:8
Thirties, in t. want friends, 710:20
Thirty, at t. man suspects himself fool, 290:23
days hath November, 149:12
don't trust anybody over t., 849:6
for t. pence my death, 242:15
live enough before t., 600:10
man should not marry after t., 126:8
never admitted I am more than t., 560:12
no one would live out t. years, 755:2
nor strong at t., 244:5
on the wrong side of t., 285:19
once t. already old, 344:10
pieces of silver, 29:16, 35:35
years in man's life, 75:8
Thirty-five, from t. to fifty-five, 661:17
very attractive age, 560:25
Thirtyfold, brought forth fruit t., 34:16
Thirty-four, this day t. years old, 277:18
Thirty-one, all the rest have t., 149:12
This above all, 197:24
after t. therefore because of t., 121:8
do in remembrance of me, 38:30
hath not offended king, 143:10
is London, 754:9
is my beloved, 24:18
is my beloved Son, 32:10
is my body, 36:3
is my friend, 24:18
is my own my native land, 373:3
is our gracious will, 142:11
is the place, 421:14
is the real me, 540:16
is the way, 26:13
is the worst, 212:16
it is t. oh it is t., 882:6
that it should come to t., 196:30
too shall pass away, 444:15
was a man, 193:22
Thisbe fearfully o'ertrip dew, 186:14
Thisby, Pyramus and T., 178:2
Thistle Shamrock Rose entwine, 511:19
Thistles, figs of t., 33:21
Thither, hither and t. spins, 495:2
Thomas, John T. marryin' Lady Jane, 663:12
saith he to T., 40:12
true T., 889:27
Thompson, Sadie T. answer, 627:2
Thonx, Bronx no t., 732:7

Thor, da stehe ich nun ich armer T., 344:n1
Thoreau, living like T., 591:n1
unperfect unfinished, 544:3
Thoreau's, no question of T. genius, 544:3
Thorn in the flesh, 43:23
no harvest but a t., 242:26
oak and ash and t., 589:24, 889:24
plant this t. this canker, 182:3
primrose peeps beneath t., 322:28
snail's on t., 459:19
wantons thro' flowering t., 357:6
without t. the rose, 257:16
Thornbush, this t. my t., 179:12
Thorns and dangers of this world, 175:32
burrs and t. of life, 409:4
crown of t. on labor, 577:18
fall upon t. of life, 402:12
grapes of t., 33:21
in your sides, 10:6
noble crown is of t., 408:1
roses have t. fountains mud, 221:11
snow on barren t., 650:9
that in bosom lodge, 198:13
under a pot, 23:11
without roses, 341:6
Thorny hedge-hogs, 178:22
life is t., 377:13
undertaking to follow mind, 152:13
virtue demands t. road, 152:15
way to heaven, 197:20
Thou art the man, 11:19
beside me singing, 441:10
Duty whispers T. must, 424:21
holier than t., 27:20
shalt not sit with statisticians, 749:15
Though an host should encamp, 15:28
Thought, act like a man of t., 572:12
actuality of t. is life, 78:1
adorns nature with new thing, 427:19
adventure in clarification of t., 580:10
all I t. was true, 622:7
all objects of all t., 368:11
armor is his honest t., 227:9
as a child, 42:29
believe own t. genius, 426:14
beneath slight film, 508:7
best known and t., 496:7
beyond utmost bound of t., 451:15
brightest t. incomplete, 490:13
by t. word and deed, 49:5
can't bear the t., 824:14
chaos of t. and passion, 295:1
charm by t. supplied, 368:10
community of t., 531:24
concentration of poetry and of t., 801:12
depends on stomach, 299:26
divine t. thinks of itself, 78:2
divorced from eye, 713:4
energy of t., 421:9
essential in painting, 122:11
every t. that springs, 372:15
evolution of t., 496:1
flashes in world of t., 490:13
free t., 539:7
freed capacity of t., 572:15
freedom of t., 318:6
glow of early t. declines, 397:4
God t. and t., 610:6

Thought *(continued)*

gods t. otherwise, 94:17
Greek t. and life, 504:3
green t. in green shade, 267:1
he t. they were old friends, 773:10
her body t., 230:16
human t. or form, 401:10
I t. that love would last, 748:14
ideal conversation exchange of t., 617:7
in England t. is not catching, 559:20
in you boundless t. born, 442:24
independent of labor, 474:4
is as a death, 221:19
is free, 224:31
is gleam in midst of long night, 558:10
is simply vague shapeless mass, 569:1
lean upon the t., 495:5
liberty of t. life of soul, 300:5
lies like burden, 426:9
like full-blown rose, 409:21
lived with no other t., 449:21
loftiness of t. surpassed, 274:7
man of action forced into t., 600:22
near to be t. so shortly, 191:7
nimble t. can jump, 221:13
nor t. of leveling wind, 594:10
not a t. be lost, 748:11
not t. death undone so many, 676:7
not t. of own in head, 567:11
of China and Greece, 737:8
of kindnesses done, 91:25
often original, 443:5
old man had so much blood, 217:12
one t. in breast another on tongue, 92:5
pale cast of t., 199:21
passes swiftly as a t., 59:25
penny for your t., 148:4
perish the t., 287:15
plunged into sea of words, 654:10
power in mysteries of t., 67:15
practice and t. forge art, 93:12
principle of free t., 539:7
rear tender t., 300:19
rhythm in all thought, 375:15
Roman t. hath struck him, 218:6
seem a moment's t., 591:18
sense from t. divide, 272:*n*1
servants in t. as in action, 753:2
she pined in t., 205:4
sleep out the t. of it, 223:23
sow a t., 885:17
strange seas of t., 368:16
stream of t., 540:24
style is the t. itself, 348:2
sweet silent t., 221:8
sweetest songs saddest t., 403:5
swift as a bird or t., 53:5
take no t. for morrow, 33:11
taking t. add one cubit, 33:7
the best t. and said, 497:7
thee bright, 223:7
thinking what nobody t., 700:3
third silence of t., 437:21
to have loved t. done, 495:8
to justify wrongdoings, 299:23
too much thinking to have common t.,
    293:27
too much to stoop to action, 533:13

Thought *(continued)*

traversed universe in t., 89:11
tremble into t., 375:16
uffish t., 515:13
understandest my t. afar off, 19:12
unmeaning thing they call a t., 292:18
vitality of t., 580:16
we do not think we are t., 827:2
weave emotion t. sound, 418:21
what jolly fun, 579:15
what oft was t., 292:13
what was once t., 796:6
when t. takes breath away, 500:1
wish father to t., 188:22
words slippery t. viscous, 532:6
would destroy paradise, 315:8
young man brings forth, 76:5
Thoughtcrime, make t. literally impossible,
    735:19
Thought-executing fires, 211:24
Thoughtless, hour of t. youth, 368:11
    my t. hand, 352:15
    saying of great princess, 313:8
Thoughtlessness and optimism, 584:10
Thought's slave of life, 183:30
Thoughts, all intelligent t. already thought,
    344:26
    all t. all passions, 378:3
    and intents of heart, 45:7
    are function of ailments, 763:10
    assault of t. on unthinking, 656:17
    beautiful in t., 578:8
    beyond reaches of souls, 197:34
    calmer of t., 245:1
    ceaseless t. of roaming, 279:20
    discerner of the t., 45:7
    doubtful t., 185:21
    fat paunch never breeds fine t., 115:9
    fly in twinkling of eye, 882:13
    fond and wayward t., 369:6
    fresh t. along shores, 456:15
    give thy t. no tongue, 197:21
    give thy worst of t., 209:1
    gored mine own t., 222:13
    high t. must have high language, 73:16
    high-erected in heart of courtesy, 162:12
    holy profane clean obscene, 239:8
    in these t. myself despising, 221:6
    joy of elevated t., 368:11
    leave to think own t., 585:2
    legible in the eye, 169:9
    long long t., 437:9
    multiply t., 758:17
    my bloody t., 209:20
    my sad t. doth clear, 268:16
    my t. are minutes, 177:23
    my t. my trollops, 313:12
    my t. not your t., 27:12
    of a turtle turtles, 429:9
    of earthly men, 54:4
    of men decay, 160:25
    of men widened, 452:5
    of other men, 567:20
    of youth long, 437:9
    on hospitable t. intent, 258:17
    pansies for t., 201:30
    philosophy is comprehended in t., 367:6
    pieced t. into philosophy, 594:7

Thoughts *(continued)*

pious t. as harbingers, 250:1
quotations give good t., 619:3
remain below, 201:1
rule the world, 428:28
second t. are best, 67:24
secret t. run over all things, 239:8
Sensations rather than T., 412:13
shroud of t., 395:24
slumbering t., 249:7
so thy t. when thou gone, 404:4
soothe cares lift t., 409:4
speech to conceal t., 299:23
style the dress of t., 298:14
suspect the t. of others, 184:31
tend on mortal t., 214:17
that arise in me, 452:15
that nature gives way to, 215:11
that savor of content, 164:2
think mortal t., 67:12
to think great t. be heroes, 538:7
too deep for tears, 371:5
turns to t. of love, 451:21
understandeth all imaginations of the t.,
    12:23
unexpressed fall dead, 98:*n*3
unmentionable t., 483:12
unrighteous man forsake his t., 27:11
uplifting t. in baths, 708:13
wander through eternity, 256:12
were always downward bent, 256:3
were red thoughts, 608:7
what sweet t. what longing, 128:17
which were not their thoughts, 395:24
words without t., 201:1
wrapped in my t., 137:14
Thousand, a t. shall fall at thy side, 17:28
    actions once afoot, 188:36
    after t. victories foiled, 221:4
    ages in Thy sight, 289:13
    cattle upon t. hills, 16:29
    conscience hath t. tongues, 172:9
    day in thy courts better than a t., 17:20
    death hath ten t. doors, 237:7
    difference of forty t. men, 366:8
    done a t. dreadful things, 173:3
    doors that lead to death, 237:*n*1
    earth with t. voices, 378:4
    few t. battered books, 665:9
    first t. days, 785:12
    forty t. brothers, 202:20
    fragrant posies, 168:6
    furlongs of sea, 224:2
    give me a t. kisses, 91:5
    hacking at branches of evil, 474:25
    hearts beat happily, 395:13
    Hell rising from t. thrones, 448:5
    his songs were a t. and five, 11:29
    homeless near t. homes, 368:1
    hundhred t. thrained men, 660:5
    I in twelve t. none, 177:16
    journey of a t. miles, 57:21
    leagues a thousand years, 303:13
    little one shall become a t., 27:15
    man picked out of ten t., 198:32
    men that fishes gnawed, 171:28
    more memories than if t. years old, 491:6
    natural shocks, 199:21

Throne, Aphrodite on your rich-wrought t., 56:4

barge like burnished t., 218:20

besides circling the T., 850:7

Death reared t., 448:2

didst thunder him higher than t., 482:24

down to Gehenna up to T., 587:6

ebon t. in rayless majesty, 290:19

heaven is God's t., 32:19

heaven to t. in, 220:4

heir to t. is not a position, 836:12

intellectual t., 495:16

jealousy of rivals near t., 340:15

Lord sitting upon a t., 25:8

Misfortune made t. seat, 289:2

no brother near t., 295:13

nor tide of pomp, 189:23

of bayonets, 579:6

of royal state, 256:6

on highest t. we sit on our own bottom, 153:22

ready to descend t., 365:12

royal t. of kings, 176:24

something behind t., 306:2

the living t., 316:13

what is the t., 365:9

Wrong forever on t., 481:13

Throned, becomes t. monarch better, 186:1

in glory, 517:11

on hundred isles, 396:1

Thrones Dominations Princedoms, 258:20

Hell rising from thousand t., 448:5

not t. and crowns, 389:3

stakes were t., 399:14

Throng, flung roses with t., 599:15

into my memory, 252:12

thou idol I t., 526:16

Throttle, after kiss comes t., 748:7

Throttled, windpipe t. in fakes of death, 486:10

Through, muddle t., 458:1

Through-and-through universe, 542:14

Throw away dearest thing owed, 214:14

do not t. book about, 606:9

don't t. stones at neighbors', 302:16

from failing hands we t. torch, 614:7

gods themselves t. incense, 213:9

if any have stone to t., 666:8

myself down in my chamber, 231:11

of dice never abolish chance, 543:8

others t. to be comprehended, 728:1

people in glass houses shouldn't t. stones, 243:n2

people walk but not t. stones at birds, 307:27

physic to the dogs, 217:19

sand against the wind, 353:12

time t. dart at thee, 240:7

whole book in fire, 432:8

within a stone's t., 156:20

yourself into coach, 671:n2

Thrown on savage shore, 488:2

Throws himself on God, 461:15

holds rolls t. breakfalls, 776:13

little candle t. beams, 186:18

shadows which fire t., 75:11

snake t. enamelled skin, 178:19

up a steamy column, 327:1

Thrush frail gaunt small, 536:11

music went, 624:9

that's the wise t., 460:19

Thrust, greatness t. upon them, 205:8

into nature like wedge, 474:2

ivrybody but cut ca-ards, 600:13

man who knows when to t., 145:2

of cure, 820:8

spear to t. club to strike, 145:2

Thucydides wrote history of war, 71:11

Thudding, dusty t. in his head, 798:7

Thule, farthest T., 93:9, 301:1

ultima T., 93:n3, 104:n4

Thumb, between finger t. squat pen, 845:9

instead of onion, 833:6

miller hath golden t., 134:n1

O Tom T., 180:n1

of gold, 134:6

put in his t., 892:19

Thumbs, hang by your t. everybody, 802:3

if you reckon two t., 467:5

pricking of my t., 216:29

Thunder, clothed his neck with t., 14:26

comb me all to t., 522:9

dawn comes up like t., 588:2

didst t. him higher than throne, 482:24

good thunder impressive, 525:2

Hawthorne says NO in t., 482:17

he was as rattling t., 219:8

he who rules t., 285:13

I hear ever approaching t., 822:7

love for 'is power to t., 219:32

lightning or in rain, 213:30

men want rain without t., 477:3

moan of t. to song, 403:25

of the captains, 14:28

of your words, 214:n1

omnipotent Father with his t., 53:n3

purr to sleep with t., 522:12

sound of t. heard remote, 256:20

steal my t., 282:3

such sweet t., 179:2

thou all-shaking t., 211:24

wresting from Jupiter his t., 104:9

Thunderbolt, like t. he falls, 454:13

split mountains with t., 93:13

Thunderbolts and tyrants, 301:n3

oak-cleaving t., 211:24

Thundered and lightened, 72:10

volleyed and t., 454:22

Thundering Aeschylus, 233:2

shepherd hears their t., 51:6

Thunders condemnation, 472:16

Thunderstorm, no t. for new year, 631:4

streams like t., 396:10

Thurmond, Strom T. ran for president, 852:12

Thursday come and week gone, 244:12

die doubtless on a T., 696:16

took ill on T., 895:10

Thursday's child, 895:9

Thus joy to pass to world below, 94:24

to be t. is nothing, 216:5

Thwackum was for doing justice, 304:18

Thyme, bank whereon wild t. blows, 178:19

Thyrsis and I, 496:12

Thyself, know then t., 295:1

love thy neighbor as t., 8:28

love t. last, 226:5

Thyself (continued)

reule wel t., 136:19

so true to t., 166:4

Tiara, diamond t. lasts forever, 746:6

of proud towers, 396:2

Tiber, let Rome in T. melt, 218:3

not a drop of allaying T., 219:24

trembled underneath banks, 191:21

Tiberius, had T. been cat, 497:4

Tick, seeds in dry pod t., 605:5

Ticker tape ain't spaghetti, 651:4

Ticket, respectfully return Him t., 492:11

Tickle, if you t. us do we not laugh, 185:12

one's vanity, 493:11

your catastrophe, 188:2

Tickled with a straw, 295:3

Tickleth me aboute myn herte roote, 135:7

Tickling, trout caught with t., 205:6

what gnawing of worm not t., 231:9

Ticks, the clock t., 827:11

Tide, a-going out with t., 465:35

blood-dimmed t. loosed, 593:9

boots not to resist wind and t., 170:32

burnt sea-weed above t.-line, 667:9

call of running t., 635:16

dire gorge of salt sea t., 185:n1

full moon lies fair, 496:16

in affairs of men, 193:13

of pomp that beats, 189:23

of times, 192:22

rise and fall of pellucid t., 694:13

such t. as seems asleep, 456:4

swimming naked when t. goes out, 826:11

tarrieth no man, 146:17

time nor t. tarrieth, 146:n12

turning o' the t., 189:4

under the whelming t., 253:12

when just cause reaches flood t., 572:14

wind nor t. nor sea, 528:13

Tides, dread abysses unknown t., 542:14

of grass foam of flowers, 530:2

of men into my hands, 680:7

push in their t., 777:3

salt t. seaward flow, 494:12

Tidiers-up, scientists t., 780:4

Tidings, bringer of good t., 118:4

confirm t. as they roll, 287:21

glad t. of great joy, 281:14

good t. of great joy, 37:17

him that bringeth good t., 27:3

of invisible things, 372:7

Tie, careless shoestring in whose t., 240:16

of host and guest, 63:14

strangled by a t., 826:15

that binds, 831:11

up the knocker, 295:9

up thy fears, 243:1

Tied by chance bond together, 472:18

I am t. to the stake, 212:13

to me as to dog's tail, 594:5

Ties, no time at which t. do not matter, 648:13

Tiger, Hyrcan t., 216:20

imitate action of the t., 189:7

lady or t., 520:9

rides t. afraid to dismount, 619:n2

sin on a t. skin, 886:18

Tiger burning bright, 353:1

Tiger's heart in player's hide, 164:3
    heart in woman's hide, 170:19
    sinks into my throat t. tooth, 687:12
Tigers, catches t. in red weather, 640:19
    empty t. or roaring sea, 181:9
    getting hungry, 619:6
    not daughters, 212:21
    of wrath, 351:17
    they dare not dismount, 619:6
Tight hot cell, 713:3
    little island, 372:18
    suddenly you held me t., 759:10
Tighter, without t. breathing, 510:6
Tightfisted hand at the grindstone, 465:5
Tight-rooted, wolf's-bane t., 411:9
Tiles, as many devils in Worms as t., 144:10
Tillage begins other arts follow, 390:15
Tilled, little field well t., 302:8
Tiller, Cain was t. of ground, 6:3
Tilling, dignity in t. field, 566:4
Tills, man t. field lies beneath, 455:5
Tilly-loo, sang T., 467:12
Tilt at all I meet, 296:5
Tilth vineyard none, 224:19
Tilt-yard, charmed alike t. and bower, 392:15
Tim, Tiny T. last of all, 465:12
Timber, crazy as hauling t. into woods, 95:22
    navy would be rotten t., 324:13
    one old t. leg, 611:14
    seasoned t. never gives, 242:21
Timbrel, praise him with t., 19:21
Timbrels, pipes and t., 410:14
    played before the Lord on t., 11:13
Timbucktoo, rang them while touring T., 823:2
Time, a little t. for laughter, 517:*n*1
    a t. when it was not, 509:16
    abysm of t., 224:4
    age and body of the t., 200:8
    almighty t. disquiets, 66:17
    an endless song, 591:8
    and chance happeneth to all, 23:23
    and intents are savage-wild, 181:9
    and Patience strongest of warriors, 506:16
    and the hour, 214:13
    and world ever in flight, 591:10
    annihilate space and t., 294:12
    arrest your flight, 400:14
    Art long T. fleeting, 436:5
    art that tells t. of day, 824:12
    as one born out of t., 42:32
    as t. goes by, 702:11, 702:12
    ask for anything except t., 365:5
    at hands of T. and Chance, 536:1
    at same t. good bad indifferent, 276:12
    author of authors, 164:10
    ay fleeth t., 135:18
    bank and shoal of t., 214:22
    bears away all things, 93:4
    bid t. return, 177:5
    Bird of T. has little way, 441:7
    books of all t., 484:16
    born out of my due t., 520:5
    bounds of place and t., 316:13
    brief chronicles of the t., 199:13
    but little at a t., 285:12
    can slow as it nears, 821:10
    cancels young pain, 67:16

Time *(continued)*
    captive of t., 688:4
    cease and midnight never come, 169:3
    chinks that T. has made, 249:28
    chronicle of wasted t., 222:9
    coincident in t. with preexisting species, 501:3
    come t. and haste day, 346:24
    come unstuck in t., 801:4
    comes a t. in every man's life, 689:2
    condemned to kill t., 776:7
    consume strongest cord, 374:8
    convinced of imbecility by t., 307:25
    cormorant devouring T., 173:38
    corridors of T., 436:17
    could have had damned good t., 721:5
    cracks in furious flower, 783:12
    creeping hours of t., 194:22
    crumbles things, 77:15
    daughters of T., 424:23
    Death old captain it is t., 491:10
    defy tooth of t., 290:17
    destroyer time preserver, 679:5
    devourer of all things, 102:17
    did not exist previously, 125:1
    die for such a long t., 267:9
    died far away before his t., 582:*n*3
    discovers truth, 103:26
    do not squander t., 302:26
    done his best for his t., 359:19
    don't waste t. mourning, 639:5
    doth transfix flourish, 221:17
    driveth onward fast, 450:19
    duty beyond space and t., 620:7
    eases all things, 66:6
    engenders forgetfulness, 630:15
    enough for sleep, 574:12
    enough for that, 223:37
    envious and calumniating t., 203:25
    eternity in love with production of t., 351:12
    ever-flowing stream of t., 750:1
    falling oars kept t., 267:7
    famous good t. had by all, 752:6
    Father T. and Mother Earth, 813:8
    feet in ancient t., 354:8
    find ourselves in another t., 703:8
    fire in which we burn, 772:1
    fleet the t. carelessly, 193:24
    flying never to return, 93:23
    fool some people all the t., 447:5
    footprints on sands of t., 436:6
    for a change, 730:4
    for a little something, 651:9
    for all good men, 885:18
    for long t. used to go to bed early, 610:11
    for many words, 53:13
    for quick intake of air, 874:6
    for sleep, 53:13
    for such a word, 217:23
    for us to leave her, 897:23
    foremost files of t., 452:9
    future in time past, 678:6
    get me to church on t., 790:10
    goes you say, 535:8
    great legalizer, 645:1
    great poet writes his t., 677:8
    grown old before my t., 512:7

Time *(continued)*
    half as old as t., 468:18
    happiest t. of New Year, 450:15
    has come Walrus said, 516:4
    has no divisions, 631:4
    has passed like a courier, 806:7
    has slain desire, 813:11
    hath taming hand, 421:3
    hath to silver turned, 163:3
    hath wallet at his back, 203:21
    haven't t. to take our t., 768:9
    healing a matter of t., 70:16
    held me green and dying, 777:14
    history the witness to passing t., 87:13
    history triumphed over t., 159:13
    hold fast the t., 631:11
    holy t. quiet as nun, 370:5
    hot t. in old town, 585:5
    how angels pass eternal t., 850:7
    how long a t. in one word, 176:13
    hurry up please its t., 676:10
    I am mighty world-destroying T., 84:14
    I had lived a blessed t., 215:30
    I may be some t., 603:7
    idea whose t. come, 422:8
    image of eternity, 113:1
    in a moment of t., 37:23
    in a t. like this, 844:2
    in hours days years, 268:14
    irreparable ravages of t., 279:3
    is a very shadow, 29:31
    is dead, 713:11
    is elastic, 610:17
    is Lethe, 630:15
    is limited so don't waste it, 873:12
    is longest distance between two places, 766:5
    is money, 303:5, 422:*n*1
    is nothing but race to death, 116:18
    is on our side, 442:13
    is out of joint, 198:22
    is still a-flying, 241:4
    is that wherein is opportunity, 70:17
    it is t. it were t., 794:7
    it's only a matter of t., 866:11
    joyous t. not be stayed, 161:4
    keeping t., 678:14
    kill t. injuring eternity, 474:10
    killing t. essence of comedy, 586:6
    lack t. to make it short, 269:5
    last syllable of recorded t., 217:23
    last t. I see Paris, 691:5
    learned a long t. ago, 864:7
    least thing we have of, 722:2
    leave enough t. unscheduled, 757:16
    let me play, 777:11
    like ever-rolling stream, 289:14
    like fashionable host, 203:24
    liked by some people some of t., 760:4
    little town that t. forgot, 854:11
    long t. between drinks, 555:20
    lost t. never found, 302:27
    made me his numbering clock, 177:23
    made simple by loss of detail, 624:12
    makes these decay, 245:18
    man knoweth not his t., 23:23
    maniac scattering dust, 453:18
    market of his t., 201:19

Time *(continued)*

memory emancipated from t., 379:7
mock t. with fairest show, 215:8
moment of t. fleeting by, 533:15
most valuable thing, 81:17
must have stop, 183:30
my t. is at hand, 35:36
my t. is today, 717:9
my t. not come either, 549:9
never t. and place, 463:14
new direction of T., 662:13
night of t. surpasseth day, 249:3
no t. at which ties do not matter, 648:13
no t. like old t., 443:4
no t. like present, 283:1
nobody gave me greater thing than t., 734:17
noiseless foot of t., 206:10
nor tide tarrieth, 146:*n*12
nor t. nor place, 215:4
not of an age but for all t., 233:3
not so fast or we might arrive on t., 617:2
nothing but T. destroys us, 119:9
nothing should be done for first t., 622:4
nothing so precious as t., 81:*n*10
now is accepted t., 43:16
now is t. for drinking, 96:17
now near at hand, 328:6
nyl no man abyde, 135:18
O t. too swift, 163:3
of death every moment, 84:*n*8
of life is short, 183:28
of milking time of harvest, 678:14
of peace, 22:31
of scorn, 210:3
of the singing of birds, 24:9
of war, 22:31
old common arbitrator T., 204:6
on Johnny's own T., 867:11
on the geologic t. scale, 830:9
one is so lucky as to have, 544:15
one-way property of t., 649:5
one world at a t., 476:2
only pretty ring t., 196:2
open T. let him pass, 579:12
opportunity is that wherein is no t., 70:17
out of key with his t., 665:4
out of mind, 155:11, 695:17
out of Space out of T., 449:1
panting T. toiled after him, 306:9
pass the t. away, 884:22
past comes not back, 98:*n*3
peace for our t., 604:1
peace in our t. O Lord, 49:22
play the fools with t., 188:5
present and time past, 678:6
procrastination thief of t., 290:22
rags of t., 228:16
rave no more 'gainst t., 528:13
redeem the t., 677:16
remembered, 529:13
respect of place persons t., 204:28
reveals all, 103:*n*9
rider that breaks youth, 244:13
right more than half the t., 724:3
right t. and right place, 839:8
river of strong current, 112:5
river without banks, 888:6

Time *(continued)*

rolling T. hath pressed, 441:16
runs on cried she, 880:*n*2
runs the clock will strike, 169:4
rushes toward us, 766:8
rust sharpest sword, 374:8
saltness of t., 187:27
school in which we learn, 772:1
seas of space and t., 673:22
seeds of t., 214:5
seen the best of our t., 211:2
served my t. in hell, 888:1
shall throw a dart at thee, 240:7
shall unfold, 210:31
show and gaze o' the t., 217:30
silence and slow t., 410:13
so gracious is the t., 196:19
sons of men snared in evil t., 23:23
soul of this world, 108:16
speech shallow as T., 406:*n*2
spend t. like spider spinning entrails, 499:6
spoils of t., 315:22
stays we go, 535:8
stream I go a-fishing in, 475:4
stream of t. run, 188:17
strengthens friendship, 280:23
subtle thief of youth, 250:16
superfluous to demand t. of day, 181:20
take T. by the forelock, 161:*n*2
takes all gives all, 158:16
teaches all things, 63:18
that great eccentric T., 696:10
that I have had my world as in my t., 135:7
that takes in trust, 159:16
that takes survey of world, 183:30
that t. of year in me behold, 221:24
the greatest innovator, 166:7
thief you cannot banish, 742:8
think and hit same t., 807:2
this day T. winds, 357:20
this great gap of t., 218:10
this t. like all times good, 426:6
though t. be fleet, 515:10
till t. and times done, 591:11
time time, 449:25
'tis almost fairy t., 179:17
to be born, 22:31
to break down, 22:31
to build up, 22:31
to cast away stones, 22:31
to dance, 22:31
to die, 22:31
to embrace, 22:31
to every purpose, 22:31
to gather stones together, 22:31
to get, 22:31
to hate, 22:31
to heal, 22:31
to keep, 22:31
to keep silence, 22:31
to kill, 22:31
to laugh, 22:31
to lose, 22:31
to lose t. displeasing, 129:12
to love, 22:31
to make up mind about people, 709:4
to mourn, 22:31
to murder and create, 674:19

Time *(continued)*

to plant, 22:31
to plant tears, 762:20
to pluck up, 22:31
to refrain from embracing, 22:31
to remember, 567:10
to rend, 22:31
to sew, 22:31
to speak, 22:31
to stand and stare, 609:4
to weep, 22:31
to wonder Do I dare, 674:20
too much change too short t., 821:3
tooth of t., 207:14
travels in divers paces, 195:15
turn up swift sandy glass, 233:17
uncertain balance of proud t., 164:4
unconscionable t. dying, 272:3
unimaginable touch of T., 372:13
upset fighting faiths, 538:22
vague crepuscular t., 479:6
was when toy dog new, 554:2
waste sad t., 678:11
wasted t. now doth t. waste me, 177:23
wastes her t. and me, 249:24
wasting of t. an abomination, 3:5
weak piping t. of peace, 171:19
weaken love, 280:23
weight of this sad t., 213:16
what a waste of t., 468:17
what is t., 116:6
what's t., 461:13
when meadow grove stream, 370:13
when only dead smile, 683:9
when t. is broke, 177:22
when t. is old, 203:20
whereof memory of man, 318:19
which antiquates antiquities, 248:26
whips and scorns of t., 199:21
whirligig of t., 205:28
whole earth and all t., 369:4
will change your opinions, 76:11
will come take my love away, 221:19
will come you will hear me, 429:23
will doubt of Rome, 398:21
will explain all, 68:17
will not be ours forever, 232:5
will run back, 250:12
wisest of counselors T., 64:23
witching t. of night, 200:29
with gift of tears, 529:14
with thee I forget all t., 257:26
woes t. cannot recure, 159:2
woman's t. of opportunity short, 73:8
work expands to fill t., 760:1
work the scythe of t., 365:15
world enough and t., 266:20
writes no wrinkle, 396:19
wrong war at wrong t., 697:7
ylost may nought recovered be, 132:22
you have to spend dead, 152:4
you old gypsy man, 609:14
you thief, 392:20
youth 'gainst t. and age, 163:3
youth the t. for toil, 75:14

Timed, gifts well t., 280:22

Timely, desired and t. things, 575:19
gain t. inn, 216:14

Timeo Danaos et dona ferentis, 94:*n*4

Time-pleaser, anything constantly but a t.,
204:30

Time's fell hand, 221:18
    flies, 213:25
    glory calm contending kings, 172:35
    life t. fool, 183:30
    love's not T. fool, 222:15
    noblest offspring, 291:9
    winged chariot, 266:22

Times, all classes t. circumstances, 470:15
    all old t. good, 399:13
    all t. are his seasons, 231:10
    are in his hand, 462:13
    at all the t. you can, 301:19
    at t. almost ridiculous, 675:4
    background of the t., 359:14
    before you, 248:22
    best of t. worst of t., 466:21
    brisk and giddy-paced t., 204:32
    change and move continually, 160:24
    change and we change with them, 121:19
    cowards die many t., 192:11
    fashion of these t., 194:6
    glory of their t., 31:27
    go by turns, 166:27
    hard and wages low, 897:23
    hard money scarce, 428:23
    I live in dark t., 716:13
    ill to have been born in these t., 568:16
    in the morning of the t., 147:*n*14
    in which a genius would live, 341:2
    lived for all t., 359:19
    my t. are in thy hand, 16:3
    necessity of the t., 318:4
    O what fine t., 298:23
    of great Elizabeth, 450:22
    oh the t. the customs, 87:6
    old t. manners books, 323:2
    old t. not forgotten, 470:16
    past t. preserve themselves, 708:5
    people in old t. had convictions, 415:6
    purest treasure mortal t. afford, 176:8
    pursy t., 201:11
    signs of the t., 34:35
    sun itself which makes t., 229:9
    that try men's souls, 333:6
    these t. are ancient t., 164:12
    these unhappy t., 651:14
    they are a-changin', 851:5
    tide of t., 192:22
    till time and t. done, 591:11
    truth which cunning t. put on, 185:20
    truths not for all t., 299:15
    wild dark t. rumbling toward us, 415:7

Times', my dear t. waste, 221:8

Timetable, read t. than nothing, 627:3
    set t. for another's freedom, 823:3

Timid, State t. as lone woman, 473:19

Timing, circumstance and proper t., 73:23
    is most important factor, 54:27

Timon, till I am T. and Lear, 596:14

Timor Mortis conturbat me, 141:6
    nil terribile nisi ipse t., 165:*n*1

Timorous beastie, 356:4
    foe, 295:13

Timothy, O T. keep thy trust, 44:38

Tim'rous beastie, 356:4

Tin, cat on t. roof, 766:10
    in t. factory human being crushed, 774:13
    Little T. Gods, 586:17
    screeches like torn t., 827:14
    soldiers and Nixon coming, 862:5

Tincture, best virtue has t. of vice, 153:5

Tinged by what absorbs it, 542:8
    eyelids and hands, 534:5

Tinhorn politicians, 603:11

Tinker more than renew, 542:8
    to Evers to Chance, 646:12

Tinkled among teacups, 675:12

Tinkling with their feet, 25:1

Tinklings, drowsy t. lull, 315:12

Tintinnabulation musically wells, 449:25

Tiny, little t. boy, 205:29
    little t. wit, 211:31
    round bole in t. leaf, 460:18
    Tim last of all, 465:12
    your t. hand is frozen, 550:14

Tip, offer you only one t., 871:12
    star within nether t., 376:11

Tiphys disclose new worlds, 104:7

Tippecanoe and Tyler too, 381:*n*1
    iron-armed soldier of T., 381:*n*1

Tipped with line of steel, 489:10

Tippenny, wi' t. fear nae evil, 358:7

Tipperary, long way to T., 628:20

Tippled drink more fine, 411:5

Tippler, little T. leaning, 508:10

Tips, I don't want t. from kitty, 747:3
    with silver fruit-tree tops, 180:8

Tipsy dance and jollity, 252:8

Tiptoe on misty mountaintops, 181:2
    religion stands on t., 243:13
    stand a t. when day named, 189:26

Tirade, your old-fashioned t., 787:14

Tire, ear the open vowels t., 292:17
    speeds too fast 'twill t., 174:10

Tired, became t. and sick, 487:6
    being t. she bade me kiss, 168:13
    dull stale t. bed, 210:33
    eyelids upon tired eyes, 450:17
    give me your t. your poor, 552:16
    he was so t., 578:16
    nature's sweet restorer, 290:18
    of honest things, 695:15
    of kings, 424:19
    of London tired of life, 310:13
    of Love, 606:15
    of my turmoil, 787:18
    of ruling over slaves, 312:9
    of tears and laughter, 530:16
    sick and t., 785:3
    Sister Caroline t., 610:7
    sun with talking, 499:9
    till t. he sleeps, 295:3
    we were very t., 695:9
    with all these, 221:20

Tirelessly, unreeling t. speeding them, 488:5

Tirer les marrons du feu, 267:*n*1

Tires, sad t. in a mile-a, 223:24
    unchartered freedom t., 371:16

Tiresias, I T. though blind, 676:12

Tirlin' at the window, 457:4

Tirra lirra by the river, 451:5

Tit for tat, 148:7
    tell tale t., 892:21

Titan, like thy glory T., 402:5

Titania, ill met by moonlight proud T., 178:13
    there sleeps T., 178:19

Titanic, alley T., 449:16

Tithe of mint and anise, 35:15

Title and profit I resign, 287:*n*3
    excels at t. page, 321:10
    farced t. 'fore king, 189:23
    feel his t. hang loose, 217:15
    gained no t., 294:9
    read my t. clear, 289:16

Titles gratuities privileges, 364:3
    high though his t., 373:3
    of mining claims, 715:18
    power and pelf, 373:3
    such as Indispensable Unique, 583:7

Titter w'en stew smokin' hot, 613:15

Titters hailed groans of death, 719:20

Tittle, jot or t., 32:17

Tittlemouse, Tommy T., 896:19

Titwillow, willow t., 527:21

Tityrus, once sang of you T., 93:27

To, going t. and fro in earth, 12:36
    many shall run t. and fro, 28:30
    reel t. and fro, 18:16
    the unknown god, 40:32

Toad beneath harrow knows, 586:18
    curse this pois'nous bunch-backed t.,
        171:24
    give me your arm old t., 799:12
    I had rather be a t., 209:9
    intelligent Mr. T., 574:9
    like t. at ear of Eve, 258:6
    like t. ugly and venomous, 193:37
    preaches contentment to t., 586:18
    why should I let t. work, 799:6
    worm to a t., 540:7

Toads, imaginary gardens with real t., 671:2

Toast attributed to one of naval heroes, 363:1
    let the t. pass, 346:11

Tobacco crumbs vases fringes, 783:9
    custom loathsome to the eye, 226:19
    devilish and damned t., 235:12
    divine rare, 235:12
    nothing compared with t., 399:*n*2
    sublime t., 399:15

Tobacco's fragrance greet, 798:3

Toboggan, quick t. when you reach heights,
    707:5

Toby, my uncle T., 314:11

Toccatas, sat and played t., 462:2

Today a king, 30:33
    and yet is here t., 229:3
    be good and happy t., 375:14
    be wise t., 290:21
    call t. his own, 273:17
    flower that smiles t., 241:4
    future lays law of t., 547:12
    give me t. take tomorrow, 119:24
    he puts forth tender leaves, 225:25
    here t. gone tomorrow, 279:9
    here you come t., 729:12
    I have dined t., 375:9
    I have lived t., 273:17
    in t. walks tomorrow, 384:*n*3
    isn't any other day, 516:10
    live t., 107:5
    lose ground won t., 495:15

Tomorrow *(continued)*
    wait not till t., 150:8
    why T. I may be, 441:15
    will be dying, 241:4
    will repay, 272:11
    will you love me t., 845:6
Tomorrow's, all t. parties, 855:1
    falser than former day, 272:11
    life is too late, 107:5
Tom's food for seven long year, 212:6
    poor T. a-cold, 212:8
Tomtit, little t., 527:21
Tone, antediluvian t., 517:4
    deep autumnal t., 402:13
    licked clean over centuries, 813:12
    Robert Emmet and Wolfe T., 592:10
    take t. of company, 298:6
    testimony against slavery, 476:19
Tongs, let us have t. and bones, 178:31
Tongue at will yet never loud, 208:16
    can no man tame, 45:28
    candied t. lick pomp, 200:10
    cleave to the roof of my mouth, 19:11
    cold words of t. or pen, 609:12
    could scarcely cry, 351:2
    customs politics and t., 500:8
    death lies on my t., 183:30
    dove with flickering t., 679:9
    every t. brings in tale, 172:9
    eye t. sword, 200:2
    fair words never hurt t., 147:*n3*
    fallen by the t., 31:13
    falls silent, 56:5
    falsehood of the t., 336:11
    fellows of infinite t., 190:8
    flattering t. speeds guest, 594:11
    fool hold t. and pass for sage, 101:5
    from his t. flowed speech, 50:16
    give thy thoughts no t., 197:21
    great ox stands on my t., 63:1
    heart thinks t. speaks, 190:38
    his t. dropped manna, 256:11
    his t. must vent, 219:32
    hold your t. and let me love, 228:18
    hurteth not t. to give fair words, 147:11
    I am the t. of war, 836:2
    in mouth is root of yew, 741:14
    iron t. of midnight, 179:17
    is the clapper, 190:38
    is the law of kindness, 22:19
    keep good t. in head, 224:30
    keep thy t. from evil, 16:7
    keep t. and keep freend, 136:16
    live t. all dispelled, 798:2
    love's richer than my t., 210:22
    man that hath t. no man, 173:32
    murder though no t. speak, 136:*n2*
    my t. is the pen of a ready writer, 16:24
    my t. swore, 68:1
    never hold t. a minute, 285:6
    never in t. that makes it, 174:31
    never repented held t., 101:*n2*
    no need for t., 755:10
    no t. their beauty declare, 376:17
    not able to conceive, 179:4
    obnoxious to each carping t., 261:10
    of a slow t., 7:30
    of the dumb shall sing, 26:18

Tongue *(continued)*
    old and bitter of t., 591:7
    on his t. they pour sweet dew, 54:13
    one thought in breast another on t., 92:5
    outvenoms all worms of Nile, 220:20
    put a t. in every wound, 193:5
    rolls it under his t., 282:13
    sad words of t., 438:10
    Shakespeare spake, 370:11
    shall be slit, 892:21
    sharp t. grows keener, 391:14
    sing t. the Savior's glory, 126:12
    snakes with double t., 178:22
    soul lends t. vows, 197:28
    sounds as sullen bell, 187:23
    strenuous t., 411:11
    such t. to great people, 479:8
    that I sin not with my t., 16:15
    though he hide it under his t., 13:41
    thy own shame's orator, 172:23
    to deal in fiction, 291:11
    to persuade, 261:1
    trippingly on the t., 200:6
    truth in shepherd's t., 159:5
    understanding but no t., 197:16
    use of my oracular t., 346:5
    use our t. at our peril, 299:20
    wery good thing, 463:23
    when my t. blabs, 204:12
    with his t. win a woman, 173:32
    wool of bat t. of dog, 216:27
    would t. utter, 452:15
Tongued with fire beyond living, 679:8
Tongueless vigil, 529:12
Tongues, all people and t., 46:35
    and deeds, 450:10
    aspics' t., 209:19
    bray of bragging t., 65:10
    clocks the t. of bawds, 181:20
    conscience hath thousand t., 172:9
    evil days and evil t., 258:25
    from the strife of t., 16:4
    govern t. with difficulty, 276:4
    had I a hundred t., 94:31
    had I your t. and eyes, 213:12
    have their talk, 156:*n1*
    hearts in love use own t., 190:26
    in all t. called fools, 196:3
    in trees, 193:37
    mild old t., 813:12
    millions of t. record, 395:16
    not if I had ten t., 50:25
    not uttered by chapmen's t., 174:8
    of Douglas and myself, 444:12
    of dying men, 176:20
    of fire, 40:15
    of flame infolded, 679:13
    of men and angels, 42:26
    one soul though many t., 113:8
    self-interest speaks all t., 263:19
    separating my t. from the taste, 868:9
    sharpened their t. like a serpent, 19:16
    silence envious t., 226:5
    silver-sweet sound lovers' t., 180:14
    slanderous t., 191:18
    speak with other t., 40:15
    that syllable men's names, 252:12
    whispering t. can poison truth, 377:13

Tongues *(continued)*
    woods have t., 134:*n2*
Tongue-tied by authority, 221:21
Tonight, curfew not ring t., 556:14
    from Oxford strays, 496:12
    hot time in old town t., 585:5
    met in thee t., 521:2
    refrain t., 201:13
    tenting t. on campground, 520:1
    tonight won't be just any night, 828:13
    world may end t., 461:11
    you're mine completely, 845:6
Tonnage, damp t., 720:6
Tonsorial or agglutinative type, 607:2
Took all heart for speech, 592:19
    all which I t. from thee, 577:2
    by throat circumcised dog, 210:21
    great care of his Mother, 651:6
    not men you t. them for, 191:1
    one Draught of Life, 511:8
    one less traveled by, 622:18
    seen my opportunities and t. 'em, 543:13
    to my heels, 86:12
    to the law, 514:5
    wages and are dead, 575:20
Tool carries spirit, 728:4
    grows keener with use, 391:14
    maker, 636:2
    nor any t. of iron, 11:31
Too-late, also called T., 506:6
Tools, give us the t., 620:3
    Master's T. Will Never Dismantle, 838:3
    sin has many t., 443:11
    teach but to name t., 262:5
    to make tools, 572:9
    with t. he is all, 406:14
Tool-using animal, 406:14
Tooth, defy t. of time, 290:17
    for tooth, 8:17
    hadde alwey coltes t., 135:12
    more deadly than mad dog's t., 172:26
    my Adonis hath a sweet t., 162:6
    of time, 207:14
    one t. and it aching, 611:14
    poison for age's t., 175:4
    purrs and never shows t., 666:9
    red in t. and claw, 454:1
    sharper than serpent's t., 211:11
    sinks into throat tiger's t., 687:12
    where each t. point goes, 586:18
Toothache, philosopher endure t., 191:13
Toothpaste and dandruff ads, 720:9
Tootings at weddings of soul, 641:14
Top, die at the t., 286:13
    fool me to t. of my bent, 200:27
    o' the mornin', 551:3
    of head taken off, 511:15
    of sovereignty, 411:14
    special few at very t., 831:6
    struggle to reach t., 770:2
    you're the t., 691:12
Top-hat, famous high t., 639:16
Topics, only two serious t., 597:12
    two t. yourself and me, 310:10
    while serious t. disputing, 418:18
Topless towers of Ilium, 168:21
Toppling, send skyscrapers t., 756:23
Tops, tips with silver fruit-tree t., 180:8

Town *(continued)*
  another hill t., 781:10
  bear witness to his munificence, 363:7
  come up to t. a Shanty T., 850:12
  country in t., 107:19
  dear damned distracting t., 293:20
  defend village t. city, 619:16
  distressed and forsaken, 277:12
  down that t. settle hence, 448:5
  Dürer in a t. like this, 670:16
  faraway t. sleeping in valley, 523:13
  follies of t. crept slowly, 323:1
  he could see the t. below, 805:*n*1
  hot time in old t., 585:5
  hushing traffic of drowsy t., 545:13
  in Scarlet t., 889:25
  is lighter than vanity, 271:17
  little t. of Bethlehem, 521:2
  little t. that time forgot, 854:11
  man in our t., 897:6
  man made the t., 326:19
  many ways meet in one t., 188:36
  my old native t., 431:1
  never go down to end of t., 651:6
  Paris my home t., 628:6
  Petersburg theoretical intentional t.,
    492:4
  pretty how t., 701:17
  proud tower in t., 448:4
  rest in t. were bad, 141:*n*6
  sent them out of t., 892:18
  taller t. than Rome, 618:14
  tavern in the t., 885:14
  that is no more a t., 624:12
  what common talk of t. is, 277:7
  white t. drowsing in sunshine, 522:13
  Yankee Doodle came to t., 883:15
Town-crier spoke my lines, 200:6
Towns, away away from t., 404:12
  prince of apple t., 777:10
  seven t. contend for Homer, 233:*n*3
  winter too long in country t., 615:13
Toy dog covered with dust, 554:2
  foolish thing but a t., 205:29
  had not friend nor t., 482:7
  religion but a childish t., 168:7
  sells eternity to get t., 172:32
  soldier red with rust, 554:2
  Truth her painted t., 590:20
Toys, all is but t., 215:30
  enemies for t., 234:10
  for your delight, 556:6
  love and all his pleasures t., 227:1
  of age, 295:3
Trace, no single t. will remain, 416:16
  noble dust of Alexander, 202:13
  on dark theme t. verses of light, 89:18
Traces of original sin, 491:18
  winter's t., 529:12
Tracing, fitful t. of portal, 641:5
Tracings of eternal light, 359:11
Track down relations of aspects of experience,
    662:2
  golden t., 639:14
  narrow t. to highest good, 90:21
Tracks of my tears, 849:4
  show t. of knowledge, 90:4
Tract of inland ground, 372:7

Trade, came for t. unionists, 696:7
  commonly called Slave T., 301:16
  dreadful t., 212:24
  food of us that t. in love, 218:24
  free t., 419:6
  free t. in ideas, 538:22
  heel of Northeast T., 588:12
  homely slighted shepherd's t., 253:6
  Irish poets learn t., 597:9
  love t. you have learned, 112:2
  mission of t. unions, 554:5
  my t. and art is living, 152:14
  no nation ruined by t., 303:15
  nothing to do but t., 333:8
  people of the same t., 319:2
  secret, 319:1
  serve time to every t., 394:13
  Slave T., 301:16
  those who affected to t. for public good,
    319:5
  two of a t. never agree, 291:12
Trades, sail out on your t. again, 83:3
Tradesmen, bow ye t., 526:17
  lying becomes none but t., 223:35
Trading company, monopoly granted to t.,
    319:1
Tradition becomes holy, 547:13
  cannot be inherited, 675:17
  desert t., 426:10
  is living faith of dead, 803:12
  of all dead generations weighs, 477:15
  reverence due t. increases, 547:13
  tremendous shattering of t., 693:3
  true to its classic t., 822:12
  youth of America oldest t., 560:14
Traditionalism is dead faith of living, 803:12
Traditions, part of Society and its t., 831:4
  pattern of our t., 756:24
  principles and t. of nation, 782:9
Traduced the state, 210:21
Traffic, hushing t. of drowsy town, 545:13
  no kind of t., 224:19
Trafficked for strange webs, 534:5
Tragedies of antiquity, 843:6
  only two t. in world, 560:9
  two t. in life, 565:8
Tragedy, American t., 609:9
  denies us another chance, 834:3
  facts personages appear first as t., 477:14
  go litel bok litel myn t., 133:3
  gorgeous T., 251:19
  herein t. of age, 602:2
  imitation of action, 79:3
  killing eternity essence of t., 586:6
  Maxine said it was another t., 844:1
  of love indifference, 626:21
  of modern man, 841:9
  of Science, 502:8
  of the bedroom, 507:9
  of the Commons, 779:6
  out of stress and t. of it all, 598:13
  play is t. Man, 448:15
  public wants t. with happy ending, 529:4
  that is what t. means, 843:7
  to be out of society a t., 560:16
  who is set up for t., 835:11
  world is a t., 317:5
  write you a t., 710:18

Tragedy *(continued)*
  wrought to uttermost, 596:10
Tragic, in t. life no villain, 505:10
  Muse first trod stage, 293:13
  perform t. play, 596:9
Tragical mirth, 179:8
Tragically, I am not t. colored, 689:16
Trail, neither go from t., 588:19
  out of it is dark cloud, 891:17
Trailing clouds of glory, 370:17
  garments of Night, 436:3
Train, biggest electric t. set, 781:7
  filled the temple, 25:8
  freight t. whistle taught me to cry, 733:9
  ghost t. in Rockies, 811:6
  him to be semihuman, 832:3
  jump in front of a t., 821:8
  light of oncoming t., 788:13
  midnight t. whining low, 804:1
  miserable t., 371:21
  noble natures not to desire more, 78:20
  off on morning t., 898:3
  old t. rolling down the line, 804:2
  sensational to read in t., 560:24
  starry t., 258:1
  they love a t., 65:*n*3
  trees that would t., 639:17
  up child in way he should go, 21:17
  war t. of circumstances, 333:14
  world and all her t., 268:14
Trained, conscious mind t. like parrot, 630:7
  hundred thousand t. men, 660:5
Trainer, painter t. soothsayer, 109:14
Training, genius will live without t., 456:17
  is everything, 523:17
Train's, Gospel t. a-coming, 899:3
Trains, sigh of midnight t., 729:1
Traitor, love treason but hate, 88:23
  not put me to die like t., 557:14
Traitorously corrupted youth, 170:17
Traitors escape detection, 614:3
  fears make us t., 217:3
  hate t. and treason love, 274:5
  our doubts are t., 206:17
Trammel up the consequence, 214:22
Tramp gentleman poet dreamer, 683:16
  swing t. and trudge, 654:5
  that's why lady is a t., 707:3
  tramp tramp, 489:8
Trample bad laws under feet, 458:10
  light doth t. on my days, 268:17
  them in my fury, 27:17
  vices underfoot, 116:12
  young lion and dragon shalt thou t., 17:29
Trampling out the vintage, 481:1
  right of t. on people, 421:15
Tramplings of three conquests, 248:25
Tramp's, in t. clothes feel degraded, 735:4
Tramps like us were born to run, 868:2
  never think t. are drunken scoundrels, 735:5
Trances, days are t., 448:7
  heard in t. of the blast, 377:15
Tränen, wer nie sein Brod mit T. ass, 342:*n*5
Tranquil, benevolence t. habitation, 79:19
  cliffs vast in t. bay, 496:16
  farewell the t. mind, 209:13
  mind a mind well ordered, 111:15
  occupations few t. life, 112:1

Tranquility Base here, 825:19
  ought to be satisfied with t., 472:10
Tranquilize, steady purpose t. mind, 415:16
Tranquilized Fifties, 787:10
Tranquillity, emotion recollected in t., 369:5
  feeling of inward t., 428:27
  insure domestic t., 339:11
Transatlantic, control of t. force, 349:6
Transcendent, shun the t., 867:5
Transcendental kind, 526:10
Transcribed without acknowledgment, 104:13
Transcript, Boston Evening T., 675:10
Transfigured, all their minds t. together, 179:7
Transfigures, grief t. wretched, 422:11
  you and me, 481:2
Transfiguring power, 548:26
Transfix flourish set on youth, 221:17
Transform, future t. itself in us, 632:6
  ourselves into beasts, 208:31
Transformed, if any reaction both t., 630:3
  into gigantic insect, 655:14
  into strumpet's fool, 218:1
  joy t. in us, 632:1
  lover into beloved t., 154:6
  whole of you t. into feeling, 583:13
Transforms strength into right, 312:16
Transgressed custom brings punishment,
  525:1
Transgressing, by t. truly kept law, 254:15
Transgression brings admitted shame, 71:14
  no law no t., 41:11
Transgressors, way of t. is hard, 20:21
Transient, human life t., 580:9
  most t. of passions, 565:16
  opportunity t., 343:3
Transit where dreams cross, 677:18
Transitory, false world but t., 141:7
Translated, Bottom thou art t., 178:27
  from despotism to liberty, 337:1
Translates, speaking t. me into the universal,
  469:5
Translating into living law, 666:15
  poetry is that which is worth t., 868:7
Translation, poetry is what is lost in t., 625:13
Translator of Homer, 496:1
Translucent, glassy cool t. wave, 252:26
Translunary, those brave t. things, 167:13
Transparent, I become t. eyeball, 425:22
  pure t. freedom, 751:4
Trap moment before ripe, 352:7
  rat is in the t., 827:14
  you set for yourself, 674:13
Trapeze, daring young man on t., 532:16
Trappings, these but t. of woe, 196:27
Traps, be fox to recognize t., 142:2
  not fall into same t. twice, 115:12
  snares t. gins pitfalls, 459:n1
Trash, steals my purse steals t., 209:2
Trauma, freaks were born with their t., 801:8
Traurig, dass ich so t. bin, 415:n1
Travail and vexation of spirit, 23:1
  great t. so gladly spent, 149:2
  le t. éloigne de nous trois grands maux,
  299:n4
  my labor for my t., 203:1
  myn the t. thyn the glorie, 134:21
Travailed, thou shalt not be t., 132:1
Travaileth, groaneth and t., 41:20

Travel, beauties of t. due to strange hours,
  658:7
  dangerous to t. to known places, 240:3
  faster than stagecoach, 323:1
  first-class and with children, 683:13
  for travel's sake, 554:11
  from Dan to Beersheba, 314:23
  hopefully better than arrive, 555:2
  in direction of our fear, 773:3
  light, 750:10
  man should not t. after sixty, 126:8
  never t. without diary, 560:24
  not to go anywhere, 554:11
  on life's common way, 370:10
  part of education, 165:28
  prayers to preserve t., 286:7
  road to Hades easy to t., 82:8
  to home among dead, 403:11
  to school not to t., 165:28
  want to t. with her, 837:9
  wherever I t. Greece wounds me, 727:3
  youth who from east t., 370:18
Traveled a good deal in Concord, 474:8
  among unknown men, 369:13
  as their highnesses t., 317:2
  backward glances over t. road, 488:17
  her mind t. crooked streets, 830:12
  I t. each and ev'ry highway, 849:11
  much have I t., 408:17
  short while towards sun, 760:6
  somewhere i have never t., 701:15
  took one less t. by, 622:18
  whoe'er has t., 310:n1
Traveler, a t. came by, 352:3
  anybody there said T., 616:6
  farewell Monsieur T., 195:25
  from antique land, 401:13
  from cradle to grave, 402:4
  from New Zealand, 419:17
  hour pierces new t. with love, 129:18
  no t. returns, 199:21
  spurs lated t. apace, 216:14
  swiftest t. afoot, 474:19
  world-besotted t., 595:8
Travelers, fellow t. of Revolution, 643:11
  must be content, 194:7
  of eternity, 279:20
Traveleth before he hath language, 165:28
  poverty come as one that t., 20:1
Traveling, consider my t. expenses, 699:1
  in t. carry knowledge, 310:19
  through dense forest, 662:5
  to regulate imagination, 308:7
  without fatigue of t., 157:12
Travels, commence t. in Mississippi steamboat,
  389:2
  fastest travels alone, 587:6
  in strait so narrow, 203:23
  like him that t., 222:12
  sundry contemplation of t., 195:23
  time t. in divers paces, 195:15
Traverse, this T. poorest take, 510:14
Travesty of a mockery of a sham, 839:9
Trav'lin', reason I'm t. on, 851:4
Tray Blanch and Sweetheart, 212:11
  dog T., 384:7
Treacherous, dog never t., 512:12
  experiment t., 71:6

Treacherous *(continued)*
  generals, 738:17
  proneness to side with beauty, 631:10
Treachers by spherical predominance, 211:3
Treachery, in politics all terms conceal t., 728:8
  is all their trust, 398:12
  machinations hollowness t., 211:2
  of the Intellectuals, 599:9
  wedlock-t., 260:20
Treacle, fly that sips t., 291:19
Tread, close behind him t., 376:21
  Death with impartial t., 96:4
  don't t. on me, 883:19
  each other's heel, 201:n2
  endless road you t., 575:11
  ever so airy t., 455:3
  far-off shore where he would t., 170:27
  hungry generations t., 410:10
  I with mournful t., 487:17
  lightly she is near, 559:15
  men t. underfoot what feared, 90:19
  poor beetle we t. upon, 206:35
  shine by side of path we t., 327:8
  softly t. on dreams, 591:13
  them in mine anger, 27:17
  thou shalt t. upon the lion, 17:29
  upon another's heel, 201:n2
  upon brink of meaning, 307:18
  upon my patience, 181:34
  where angels fear to t., 292:25
  where'er we t. haunted, 395:8
  where'er you t., 292:6
  years like oxen t. world, 590:23
Treadeth, not muzzle ox when t. corn, 9:25
  winepress of wrath, 47:9
Treading on my tail, 515:2
Treadmill, set you on a t., 864:12
Treads, one who t. alone, 388:1
  primrose path of dalliance t., 197:20
  she t. on it so light, 171:15
Treason against the United States, 339:13
  bloody t. flourished, 193:1
  bribery or other high crimes, 339:12
  but trusted like fox, 183:26
  can but peep, 201:29
  corporations cannot commit t., 158:25
  cried the Speaker, 331:8
  doth never prosper, 166:26
  ever less than t., 622:8
  gunpowder t. and plot, 882:18
  has done his worst, 216:11
  hate traitors and t. love, 274:5
  if this be t., 331:8
  last temptation greatest t., 678:4
  love bitter with t., 530:9
  love t. but hate traitor, 88:23
  none dare call it t., 166:26
  sows secret seeds, 125:7
Treasons stratagems and spoils, 186:17
Treasure, buried t., 544:13
  chiefest t., 606:9
  danger or t., 772:11
  good man's t., 57:20
  great t. and trouble, 20:32
  hath found a t., 30:25
  purest t. mortal times afford, 176:8
  rich the t., 274:17
  thou shalt have t., 35:3

Treasure *(continued)*

where your t. is, 33:2

witty woman a t., 505:17

Treasured, embalmed and t. up, 254:8

Treasures, heart has hidden t., 472:8

I have three t., 57:22

lay not up t., 33:1

lay up t. in heaven, 33:1

sea-born t., 424:3

see t. that prevail, 825:9

Treasury, our heart is a t., 417:14

Treat as dogs do the Nile, 103:*n2*

friend as if he might become enemy, 100:8

killing t. for Ossete, 690:14

nature in terms of cylinder, 533:17

two impostors same, 590:1

you'd t. if met where bar, 536:13

Treaties under authority of U.S., 339:14

Treatise, at dismal t. rouse, 217:22

my T. of Human Nature, 312:2

of natural education, 312:25

Treatment, dark world present t., 602:9

extreme diseases extreme strictness of t., 71:7

of Negro greatest scandal, 718:5

stomach endure rough t., 103:24

use t. to help sick, 70:14

Treaty, what t. white man kept, 513:4

Treble, childish t., 194:25

Tree, almond t. shall flourish, 23:31

apple t. among the trees, 24:7

as twig bent t. inclined, 293:24

at my window, 623:14

beneath the tamarind t., 447:11

billboard lovely as t., 732:8

boughs off many a t., 242:17

but I must climb the t., 242:16

cannot grow in sky, 90:11

cinnamon t., 734:10

coolibah t., 585:8

corrupt word is as corrupt t., 118:11

cut cherry t., 328:*n3*

dead t. no shelter, 676:6

deep-rooted yet dancing still, 776:3

dew bespangling herb and t., 241:11

do these things in green t., 38:32

down to calico t., 467:12

easy as leaves grow on t., 590:21

elm t. bole, 460:18

fleet of life like t. leaves, 73:5

forbidden t. whose mortal taste, 255:3

friendship a sheltering t., 378:13

give me my hollow t., 296:8

give to eat of the t. of life, 46:21

go to pear t. for pears, 100:29

golden t. of life, 344:5

good word is as good t., 118:11

grows in Brooklyn, 740:5

had a peach from the t., 352:4

hang harp on willow t., 885:15

hang there till t. die, 220:29

hate the t., 116:13

I hid behind a t., 814:9

I shall be like t., 286:13

if t. dies plant another, 305:6

is hewn down, 32:8

is known by fruit, 34:11

keep way of the t. of life, 6:2

Tree *(continued)*

last leaf upon t., 443:15

Liberty T., 332:20

lighted from a blessed t., 118:23

like a t. planted by rivers, 14:40

like t. grown in meadow, 4:14

like t. standing by water, 899:4

little nut t., 894:18

loved t. or flower, 388:3

man plants t. for posterity, 85:*n5*

monkey in the t., 887:3

never see t. at all, 732:8

O chestnut t., 594:17

of Knowledge is not that of life, 397:15

of knowledge of good and evil, 5:13

of liberty refreshed, 336:15

of liberty watered by blood, 348:12

of life, 5:12

of Life, 257:14

of man never quiet, 575:4

on a t. by a river, 527:21

only God can make t., 668:1

planted by the waters, 27:39

poem lovely as a t., 667:13

poisonous minerals and that t., 230:21

possible for every person to own a t., 569:9

presents upon a T., 510:10

riding by Eildon T., 889:27

righteous like palm t., 17:30

shady cypress t., 512:3

she gave me of the t., 5:21

sighing by a sycamore t., 210:8

snow from hemlock t., 623:5

some call it T. of Heaven, 740:5

spreading chestnut t., 436:11

spreading himself like a green bay t., 16:12

swimming from t. to t., 787:3

tall slim t., 730:15

this t. continues to be, 680:4

thou t. I flower, 526:16

under the bamboo t., 677:5

under the gallows t., 236:6

under the greenwood t., 194:11

which did not know, 265:14

will continue to be, 680:*n2*

window t., 623:14

with ease from t. to t., 290:10

woodman spare beechen t., 384:14

woodman spare that t., 423:1

wrath-bearing t., 675:23

you have grown to be a mighty t., 355:15

Zaccheus climb t., 283:7

Tree's, as twig bent t. inclined, 293:24

Trees, all the t. green, 481:7

all t. in earth were pens, 119:5

amidst tall ancestral t., 405:7

among gusty t., 646:1

and all nature, 891:9

and fields tell nothing, 295:*n1*

and stones will teach you, 123:11

Arabian t. their med'cinable gum, 210:20

axe laid unto root of the t., 32:8

birds are asleep in t., 344:19

birds in the t., 594:1

blasts roots of t., 777:2

blue promontory with t., 218:39

bosomed high in tufted t., 251:3

cannot see wood for t., 148:5

Trees *(continued)*

cross river rest under t., 501:10

Dryad of the t., 410:3

grow up again quickly, 65:1

grown strong with forest t., 533:10

he that plants t. loves others, 85:*n5*

herbs and t. flourish in May, 138:9

herbs are sprouting, 4:7

hurt not the t., 46:34

I cut down t. skip and jump, 879:9

known to speak, 216:23

land of vines and fig t., 9:20

lemon t. bloom, 342:15

loveliest of t., 574:11

men as t. walking, 36:36

more resigned, 615:9

my apple t. never eat cones, 622:11

of all t. that grow so fair, 589:24

Orpheus with lute made t., 225:19

plum t. function gorgeously, 803:15

procreate like t., 248:16

rocks and stones and t., 369:8

roots of t. and stones, 666:5

seemed to march seaward, 552:11

set about with fever-t., 589:17

shall be my books, 195:2

southern t. bear strange fruit, 733:12

sunlight has never heard of t., 810:13

sunsets and tops of t., 765:7

that would march, 639:17

to benefit another generation, 85:9

tongues in t., 193:37

uptorn, 409:4

walked among ancient t., 352:10

we are walking t., 528:17

what t. tell us we are, 815:4

when t. bow down heads, 512:8

where you sit, 292:6

wind in t. a sad thing, 92:19

wind is in palm t., 588:1

you lover of t., 461:3

Treetop, baby on t., 550:7

Treetops, in all t. hardly a breath, 344:19

Trelawny, shall T. die, 429:11

Trellis, over the t. blow the kiss, 817:6

Tremble, afraid because we t., 541:9

army began to t. with eagerness, 608:12

at word of Lord, 270:6

begin to t. and cry, 772:5

enemies of blacks t., 433:3

I t. for my country, 336:9

into thought, 375:16

keepers of the house shall t., 23:30

let Sporus t., 295:14

like guilty thing surprised, 371:1

made the earth to t., 25:23

my firm nerves never t., 216:20

poplars stand and t., 575:8

Quakers because we bid them t., 270:6

sail-yards t. masts crack, 163:20

under her feet, 455:3

while they gaze, 316:13

Trembled, Tiber t. underneath banks, 191:21

Trembler, no t. in world's sphere, 476:14

Trembles before your glory, 65:25

in the breast, 372:19

to be so understood, 642:10

wild braid of creation t., 742:5

Trembling cold in ghastly fears, 352:3
    cup of t., 27:1
    fear came upon me and t., 13:7
    for you in voices, 583:12
    hare limped t., 409:18
    hoping lingering, 293:2
    in t. hope repose, 316:8
    seizes me all over, 56:5
    work out salvation with fear and t., 44:2
Tremulous cadence slow, 496:17
Trenchant blade Toledo trusty, 262:12
Trencher, dead Caesar's t., 218:33
Trencher-friends, 213:25
Trencherman, valiant t., 190:13
Trenches in beauty's field, 220:31
Treo, handed all sails and set t., 139:8
Trespass, those who t. against us, 32:*n*2
Trespasses against duty, 323:19
    forgive us all our t., 654:3
    forgive us our t., 32:*n*2
Tresses, fair t. race ensnare, 293:6
    like the morn, 252:25
    withered cheek t. gray, 372:20
Trial and error, 562:14
    by juries, 337:12
    by jury, 340:6
    by jury a delusion, 386:18
    cruelest t. reserved for self-devotion, 490:16
    fiery t. which we pass, 446:1
    for crimes against peace, 694:3
    right to speedy and public t., 340:5
    this t. is a travesty, 839:9
    truth the t. of itself, 232:9
Triangles and other geometrical figures, 167:15
    if t. had god, 297:12
Triangular person in square hole, 374:20
Tribal, constructing t. lays, 588:11
    I'm a t. chieftain, 791:2
Tribalism strongest force, 834:4
Tribe, abhorred senseless t., 285:9
    and all that t., 95:19
    cursed be my t., 184:25
    family party t. clan, 885:13
    highly respectable t., 885:16
    his t. were God Almighty's gentlemen, 273:4
    Idols of the T., 164:19
    may his t. increase, 392:16
    pacify touchy t. of poets, 98:15
    phylogenesis development of t., 519:12
    purify dialect of t., 679:10
    richer than all his t., 210:20
    whole t. of fops, 210:33
Tribes, all t. of birds sang, 125:6
    that which has been sent down on the T., 117:13
    two mighty t., 399:2
Tribu, mots de la t., 679:*n*1
Tribulation, brother and companion in t., 46:14
    came out of great t., 46:36
    gaze from shore on another's t., 89:20
    youth inherit t. of war, 625:19
Tribune, Roosevelt no t. of people, 685:4
Tribute, not one cent for t., 362:3
    to whom t. due, 41:38
Trice, change in a t., 529:16

Triche pour le beau, 633:*n*1
Trick, get the t., 523:15
    of our English nation, 187:34
    when in doubt win t., 288:20
    worth two of that, 182:8
Trickery, picture requires knavery t. deceit, 519:7
Tricking and stopping, 681:19
Trickle-down theory, 753:7
Trickled, hope has never t. down, 769:3
    through my head, 516:17
Trick's, long t. over, 635:17
Tricks, fox has many t., 55:*n*2
    his tenures and his t., 202:8
    no t. in faith, 193:6
    plays such fantastic t., 206:28
    such t. hath strong imagination, 179:6
    that are vain, 528:10
    wilderness seems full of t., 533:8
    Yahoo t., 639:12
Trident, flatter Neptune for t., 219:32
Tried a little failed much, 556:3
    accuracy t. by severe tests, 71:12
    and found wanting, 618:8
    first by whom new t., 292:16
    never t. marijuana again, 863:2
    private enterprise not yet t., 652:19
    their adoption t., 197:22
    thou that hast not t., 160:26
    to hustle the East, 587:11
    to live without him, 227:12
Tries everything before arms, 86:10
    no one knows till he t., 100:33
Trifle, at t. scorn to take offense, 292:20
    careless t., 214:14
    do not t. with love, 457:6
    Dying is a t., 510:7
    how love can t. with itself, 173:35
Trifles, dispense with t., 187:5
    irritate my nerves, 485:2
    law not concerned with t., 120:15
    light as air, 209:10
    make sum of life, 466:7
    think my t. worth something, 90:23
    unconsidered t., 223:22
    win us with honest t., 214:9
Trifling narrow education of females, 340:16
Trigger, draw t. after his death, 308:19
Trilling wire in blood, 678:8
Trills her thick-warbled notes, 260:3
Trilobite, eye of t., 435:23
Trim, April dressed in all his t., 222:6
    array, 371:25
    bravery on and tackle t., 260:16
    gardens, 251:14
    he that shot so t., 179:30
    honor a t. reckoning, 183:25
    in gallant t. vessel goes, 316:15
    meadows t. with daisies pied, 251:3
Trinity, Blessed T., 391:8
    unscriptural doctrine, 388:7
Trip, fearful t. is done, 487:16
    it as you go, 250:22
    taking t. on Government ship, 898:3
    upon your magic swirlin' ship, 851:13
    what a long strange t., 852:8
Triple, arm as with t. steel, 256:23
    pillar of the world, 218:1

Triple *(continued)*
    ways to take, 588:12
Tripods, flames of t. expired, 448:13
Tripoli, shores of T., 885:2
Tripped light fantastic, 581:2
Trippingly on the tongue, 200:6
Triste, la chair t. hélas, 543:*n*2
    le son du cor est t., 416:*n*2
    post coitum omne animal t., 121:7
    sois belle et sois t., 491:*n*11
Tristesse, adieu t. bonjour t., 705:*n*4
Trite, make murder look t., 778:11
Triton, hear old T., 371:24
    of the minnows, 219:30
Triumph and Disaster, 590:1
    and the jingle, 654:5
    Chief who in t. advances, 373:22
    few men know, 727:14
    join the t. of skies, 305:10
    learning's t. o'er foes, 306:9
    necessary for t. of evil, 325:15
    no t. of peace great as of war, 570:11
    of hope over experience, 309:13
    one more devils'-t., 460:14
    over scientific weapons, 629:11
    Philistia t. thou because of me, 17:2
    ride in t. over mischance, 170:28
    ride in t. through Persepolis, 168:1
    that agony our t., 682:11
    the more glorious the t., 333:6
    this is our career our t., 682:10
    turned Big Loser into perfect t., 810:11
    typical t. of modern science, 736:10
    without glory, 249:9
Triumphal procession air to marriage, 420:17
Triumphant, as one disembodied t. dead, 488:7
    bound in with t. sea, 176:25
    retains t. feeling, 563:11
Triumphed, he hath t. gloriously, 8:4
    history t. over time, 159:13
    morality of common man t., 548:14
    nothing but eternity t., 159:13
Triumphing, with Joy and Love t., 257:7
Triumphs, conquests glories t. spoils, 192:19
    raise joys and t. high, 305:7
    shut them in with their t., 461:2
Trivet, right as a t., 464:5
Trivial and political, 309:2
    attentions men think manly, 360:19
    in Nature nothing t., 124:15
    personalities decomposing, 654:7
    rise from t. things, 293:3
    wipe away t. fond records, 198:15
Trivialities, good sense about t., 613:2
Triviality, above insolence and t., 671:2
    of our lives, 824:7
Trochee trips from long to short, 378:11
Trod me in the very dirt, 817:13
    still by faith he t., 639:10
    upon neat's leather, 191:20
Trodden gold, 256:3
    little fire quickly t. out, 170:35
    the winepress alone, 27:17
    under hoofs of multitude, 325:6
    worm will turn being t. on, 170:21
Troika, Rus similar to nimble t., 443:1
    winged t. who invented you, 443:1

True *(continued)*

pessimist fears this is t., 637:6
pity 'tis 'tis t., 198:28
plain hearts, 228:8
poem an invocation, 706:5
proved t. before prove false, 262:21
right praise t. perfection, 186:19
right t. end of love, 230:10
ring in the t., 454:8
small service is t. service, 372:17
so t. to thyself, 166:4
so young my lord and t., 210:26
story you just heard is t., 796:1
strange but t., 399:5
such as I all t. lovers, 204:33
that he is mad 'tis t., 198:28
the blushful Hippocrene, 410:4
the t. Light, 38:47
theory of t. civilization, 491:18
Thomas, 889:27
'tis t. 'tis day, 229:8
'tis t. 'tis pity, 198:28
to his word, 60:16
to thee till death, 469:15
to thine own self be t., 197:24
to t. occasion t., 454:16
to you in my fashion, 691:16
trusty dusky vivid t., 556:8
way but yet untried, 164:18
way goes over rope, 655:16
what each wishes he believes t., 79:9
what is t. in the world, 830:12
what is t. of shopkeeper, 313:11
whatsoever things are t., 44:7
when you met her, 228:11
wit nature to advantage, 292:13
woman t. and fair, 228:10
worshippers shall worship, 39:13
writ your annals t., 220:6
writer has nothing to say, 800:7
True-begotten father, 184:34
True-born Englishman, 176:19
True-fixed and resting quality, 192:14
True-love, my t. hath my heart, 162:14
pokers into t. knots, 378:12
Truer, another and t. way, 815:7
to be rebel, 585:2
Truffles, swine show you where t. are, 817:11
Truism, not paradox but t., 75:26
Truly a peck of provender, 178:32
I am not t. free, 790:20
marvellous demonstration, 247:5
those who were t. great, 760:6
Trump, farewell the shrill t., 209:13
last t., 43:8
of rescue sound, 424:20
tell truth or t., 523:15
Trumpet, believeth that it is sound of the t., 14:28
blow t. to arms, 332:20
cock the t. to the morn, 196:17
first blast of the t., 150:1
give uncertain sound, 42:30
great sound of a t., 35:22
hear t. sound, 898:25
heart moved more than with t., 162:19
of his own virtues, 191:17
of prophecy O Wind, 402:14

Trumpet *(continued)*

praise him with t., 19:21
pride his own t., 203:14
shall be heard on high, 273:26
shall sound, 43:8
sound t. beat drums, 301:13
when people heard sound of t., 9:38
Trumpet's loud clangor, 273:24
Trumpets, blow your t. angels, 230:19
he saith among the t., 14:28
loud uplifted angel t., 253:18
no t. for new year, 631:4
of the sky, 424:7
sound t. beat drums, 274:16
sounded for him, 271:28
Trumpet-tongued, angels t., 214:24
Trumps, let spades be t. and t. they were, 293:10
Truncheon, marshall's t., 206:25
Trunk, joy up t. needles tingle, 801:15
so large a t. before, 606:10
spouts out a sea, 258:27
Trunkless legs of stone, 401:13
Trunks, animals infuse into t. of men, 185:31
Trust, a little t., 519:8
before you t. a man, 880:15
built absolute t., 214:15
did not t. own impressions, 71:12
don't t. anybody over thirty, 849:6
ears less than eyes, 69:5
empire power in t., 272:20
everybody but cut ca-ards, 600:13
government is a t., 384:17
hope for best t. in God, 374:24
husband doth safely t. in her, 22:16
in God is our t., 387:1
in God keep powder dry, 385:6
in Him I put my t., 118:5
in him will I t., 17:28
in Providence, 245:10
in the Lord, 767:3
life of magnanimity and t., 474:16
Lord shall raise me up I t., 159:16
love all t. a few, 205:30
man bore this t., 119:6
man on his oath or bond, 213:21
never t. artist, 663:2
never t. poet who can drive, 867:2
no agent, 190:26
none, 189:6
not one night's ice, 244:7
not t. in money, 443:8
old friends to t., 165:8
power a t., 429:19
public office public t., 528:*n*3
put no t. in the morrow, 96:11
put not your t. in princes, 19:19
put their t. in him, 30:1
read New Yorker t. in God, 749:16
rude cruel not to t., 222:20
something right in world we t., 789:10
soothed by unfaltering t., 405:13
surplus wealth sacred t., 521:17
that man in nothing, 314:8
that somehow good, 453:21
thee gentle Kate, 182:15

Trust *(continued)*

they that put their t. in him, 15:2
though he slay me yet will I t., 13:28
time that takes in t., 159:16
to frail mortality t., 166:23
tomorrow will repay, 272:11
treachery is all their t., 398:12
try to t. one another, 690:10
tyranny's disease to t. no friends, 63:16
under his wings shalt thou t., 17:28
wonder men t. themselves with men, 213:19
yourself, 344:6, 736:4
Trusted, Founders t. they would do, 667:3
I am not to be t., 724:12
I have t. in thee, 154:8
let no such man be t., 186:17
not in one bottom t., 184:1
treason but t. like fox, 183:26
where I t. I am beguiled, 880:10
with government of others, 337:10
Trustees, officers of government t., 384:17
Trustest in staff of this broken reed, 26:20
Trusteth, he that t. in his riches, 20:15
in his own heart, 22:7
in man, 27:39
in the Lord, 27:39
Trustful, makes them cynical where we are t., 710:9
Trusting, calls his t. benevolence, 322:19
no more t. in women, 53:17
Trusts, foolish man who t. woman, 94:*n*10
in tameness of wolf, 212:10
offices public t., 389:7
Trusty, ancient t. drouthy crony, 358:5
dusky vivid true, 556:8
Toledo t., 262:12
Truth, about reality, 835:8
absurd is the first t., 770:1
adherence to t. of nature, 379:8
affirm what seems to be t., 76:4
all we know for t., 592:6
always strange, 399:5
and nonviolence inseparable, 604:5
aphorism never coincides with t., 626:7
as opposeth no profit, 239:13
authority and show of t., 191:5
awoke and found it t., 412:12
be in the field, 254:14
beauty, 410:20
beauty adventure, 580:13
Beauty must be t., 412:11
being truth tell it, 146:*n*1
best test of t., 538:22
bright countenance of t., 253:21
bring t. to light, 172:35
call upon him in t., 19:18
carp of t., 198:23
certainty of the words of t., 21:20
comes like bastard, 254:1
crushed to earth, 406:4
demanded of genius love of t., 344:24
depository of t., 269:25
deviation from t. is multiplied, 77:16
dignity of t. lost with protesting, 232:8
diminution of love of t., 307:5
does not blush, 113:11
doubt t. to be liar, 198:30

Truth *(continued)*

draw bow ride and speak t., 399:6
dreadful knowledge of t., 66:3
dream is the t., 690:3
enemies of t., 247:13
every man satisfied there is t., 534:14
Exactitude Is Not T., 605:12
exists falsehood invented, 649:2
fiction lags after t., 324:1
fills me with astonishment, 850:9
follow t. too near heels, 159:14
follow t. wherever it may lead, 338:13
forever on scaffold, 481:13
found t. in all but one, 177:16
friend to t., 294:9
from his lips prevailed, 322:26
from shadows into t., 421:11
full of grace and t., 38:48
gate of horn for t., 95:2
give them raw t., 581:6
God of t., 9:30
goes a-begging, 144:4
great and shall prevail, 500:9
great is t., 29:24
habit with him test of t., 347:10
half t. blackest lie, 455:24
happens to idea, 542:9
has limits, 153:21
hath a quiet breast, 176:12
heart fed upon t., 380:2
help you by telling the t., 876:1
hero of my tale, 506:10
Him who is T. itself, 283:2
his t. endureth, 18:3
His t. is marching on, 481:1
his t. shall be thy shield, 17:28
holding on to t., 604:4
honor t. above friends, 78:4
hyest thyng men kepe, 136:9
I am very fond of t., 300:1
I tell what ought to be t., 766:6
I will be harsh as t., 433:4
if life be t., 247:2
image of inner t., 4:12
impossible to be soiled, 77:*n*4
in masquerade, 398:28
in peril t. drawn from heart, 90:9
in shepherd's tongue, 159:5
in spirit and t., 39:13
in the end t. will conquer, 131:9
in t. we know nothing, 70:11
in war-time t. is precious, 621:6
in wine is t., 55:*n*11, 120:29
is about life before death, 878:5
is at bottom of well, 797:7
is concrete, 367:5
is not in us, 46:7
Is Out There, 874:2
is there in t. no beauty, 242:18
is too multi-faceted, 819:4
is torch, 314:28
is truth to the end, 207:15
isn't always beauty, 802:5
kept strict regard for t., 606:12
language of t., 612:8
liars when they speak t., 77:5
lie which is half t., 455:24
lies in the depth, 70:11

Truth *(continued)*

light between t. and intellect, 129:17
like bastard comes into world, 254:*n*1
look for t. not find it, 313:14
lost to Love and T., 588:7
love t. pardon error, 299:4
loyalty to T. to yourself, 552:2
maintained cause of t., 258:23
make strange things look like t., 431:2
make the t. known, 596:13
map of t. in thy face, 170:6
marvelous T. confront us, 803:2
mathematics possesses t., 614:9
may strike out his teeth, 159:14
mercy and t. are met together, 17:21
more boring than the t., 794:5
most valuable thing economize it, 524:10
must be stranger than fiction, 618:3
my way of joking is to tell t., 565:12
naked t. is I have no shirt, 174:30
nation which keepeth the t., 26:3
never fell dead in streets, 457:8
never understood and not believed, 351:21
no concern with duty or t., 450:3
no eternal t., 692:3
no god higher than t., 604:5
no t. in him, 39:26
no t. to be discovered, 645:9
nor grave nor bed denied, 595:19
not better for showing face, 64:3
not conceal t. knowingly, 117:12
not offend you by speaking t., 142:5
not only by reason, 269:19
not veil t. with falsehood, 117:12
nothing but the t., 156:35
nothing more damaging to new t., 344:21
nothing so least as t., 701:19
now her painted toy, 590:20
nutritive or suggestive t., 544:16
obedience bane of t., 401:8
obeyed his call, 596:14
object of science t., 378:19
ocean of t. undiscovered, 279:18
of a MacGuffin, 722:13
of a madman, 821:6
of Imagination, 412:11
on march nothing can stop, 537:15
one law and one t., 112:14
one t. is clear, 294:23
One who died for T., 509:6
only in imagination, 568:4
only two ways of discovering t., 164:18
openers of eyes to t., 541:21
painful t., 331:10
peeps over glasses' edge, 461:20
persuades by teaching, 113:10
Plato and t. are dear, 78:4
Plato dear t. dearer, 78:*n*1
poet sings, 451:23
politician tells the t., 869:11
possession of t. as city, 248:1
put in possession of t., 275:6
put to the worse, 254:14
rather than love give me t., 475:22
religion instinctive t., 500:14
Satya t., 604:5
seek t. in groves of Academe, 98:12
shall be thy warrant, 159:9

Truth *(continued)*

shall make you free, 39:25
shows spirit and substance, 123:1
simple t. his utmost skill, 227:9
simple t. miscalled simplicity, 221:22
sits on lips of dying, 495:21
snap like vixens at t., 666:9
sole judge of t., 295:1
sometimes improbable, 399:*n*1
soul rejoices in t. uttered, 471:7
speak t. and shame Devil, 146:1
speak t. and soberness, 41:5
speak t. as much as I dare, 153:9
spirit of t. and freedom, 504:6
spread t. from pole to pole, 287:21
stranger than fiction, 399:*n*1
strife of T. with Falsehood, 481:12
suffers by heat of defenders, 280:7
swears she is made of t., 223:2
swerve a hair from t., 203:20
takes two to speak t., 473:22
teaching well-established t., 124:13
tell how t. may be, 373:1
tell t. and shame devil, 685:2
tell t. or trump, 523:15
the t. and the life, 39:42
thee shal delivere, 136:19
there are all kinds of t., 809:5
they shall understand the t., 30:1
thy t. so pure of old, 254:23
time discovers t., 103:26
to cover lies, 286:26
to one error to other, 604:4
told the t. mainly, 523:1
told with bad intent, 354:1
trial of itself, 232:9
twenty-four times per second, 827:3
unarmed t., 823:13
universally acknowledged, 382:3
vantage ground of t., 89:*n*12
vantage-ground of t., 165:12
vindication against slander, 446:9
vindication of t. by suffering, 604:4
was out, 657:17
we do not see the t., 591:15
what happen if one woman told t., 771:19
what is t., 40:6
what is t. said jesting Pilate, 165:11
what of t. bounded by mountains, 152:21
what remains must be t., 573:5
when no help in t., 66:3
where is t. we seek, 402:7
which cunning times put on, 185:20
which has been withheld, 825:10
whispering tongues can poison t.,
  377:13
will come to light, 136:*n*2
will set you free, 877:12
willing to know whole t., 331:10
wine dear boy and t., 55:19
with gold she weighs, 296:25
with malice in it, 483:3
wither into t., 592:7
within little compass, 290:4
without error, 126:7
Truthful, make lies sound t., 735:13
Truth's a dog must to kennel, 211:7
  thy country's thy God's and t., 226:5

Truths, all t. half-t., 580:15
    aphorism one-and-a-half t., 626:7
    art establishes t., 786:15
    bear all naked t., 411:14
    begin as blasphemies, 565:24
    begin as heresies, 502:13
    doubts more cruel than t., 267:24
    end as superstitions, 502:13
    in and out of favor, 622:16
    in flag government and t., 468:8
    instruments of darkness tell us t., 214:9
    irrationally held t., 502:12
    kindle light for truths, 89:19
    kindness and lies worth thousand t., 738:1
    mistaking verbiage for t., 612:4
    not for all men nor times, 299:15
    of the heart, 714:3
    old universal t., 714:3
    symbols conductors of t., 378:24
    treating half-truths as whole t., 580:15
    wake to perish never, 371:2
    we hold these t. self-evident, 336:1, 471:3
    we know many t., 298:22
    woman reveals by causing to suffer, 611:4
Truthsayers, soothsayers make better living
    than t., 335:11
Try, above all t. something, 651:15
    axe's edge did t., 266:18
    fair adventure of tomorrow, 176:2
    first thyself, 59:*n3*
    fortunes to last man, 188:18
    guiltier than him they t., 206:19
    if you t. sometimes you just might, 857:8
    let end t. the man, 188:4
    might as well not t., 622:15
    one white foot t. him, 886:5
    then worms shall t., 266:23
    times that h. men's souls, 333:6
    to be one on whom nothing lost, 544:9
    tropic for your balm, 704:2
    try again, 389:10
    whole cause condemn you, 514:1
Trying, God keeps on t. other things, 647:15
    to fool yourself about love, 824:14
Trysted, the wished the t. hour, 358:15
Tsarism, revolution's victory over t., 607:10
Tu, et t. Brute, 89:*n3*, 192:16
Tub, every t. stand upon bottom, 271:*n1*
    fair tale of a t., 143:7
    three men in a t., 896:2
Tubal-cain artificer in brass and iron, 6:12
Tubes twisted and dried, 587:12
Tuckahaw, high t., 884:16
Tucker, little Tom T., 893:14
Tucson and Deadwood, 715:18
Tuesday, christened on T., 895:10
    dissolutely spent T. morning, 181:22
Tuesday's child full of grace, 895:9
Tuesdays, only teaching on T., 787:9
Tuffet, sat on a t., 895:14
Tufted, bosomed high in t. trees, 251:3
Tug, then was the t. of war, 281:16
Tugged with fortune, 216:8
Tugging all day at perverse life, 755:14
Tulgey wood, 515:13
Tumble, anarchy why cities t., 65:22
    ready with every nod to t., 171:34
Tumbler, clean t. corkscrew, 464:22

Tumbling, Jill t. after, 893:18
    joined t. mirth, 800:1
Tumor ends by killing sympathies, 531:13
Tumors of a troubled mind, 260:12
Tumult and shouting dies, 589:8
    in the clouds, 593:1
    of mighty harmonies, 402:13
    whirling through air forever dark, 128:8
Tumultuous privacy of storm, 424:8
Tune, all t. he could play, 894:10
    droning drowsy syncopated t., 730:16
    he who pays piper calls t., 286:*n3*
    instrument here at the door, 231:1
    loveliest t. becomes vulgar, 551:16
    near the t. but not the t., 524:7
    of flutes kept stroke, 218:20
    out of t. and harsh, 200:4
    singeth a quiet t., 376:19
    sings t. without words, 508:12
    sweetly played in t., 357:4
    turn on t. in drop out, 795:3
    voices keep t. oars time, 387:4
Tuned like fifty stomachaches, 465:9
    spheres, 219:8
Tunes, Cathedral T., 508:13
    devil have all good t., 341:7
    in one of my earliest t., 664:9
    New Orleans Blues, 664:9
    Love t. shepherd's reed, 373:2
Tuning lyre and handling harp, 62:15
Tunnel, antiseptic t., 820:8
    end of t., 786:9
    light at end of t., 788:13
Tunnels that re-wind themselves, 720:8
Tupping your white ewe, 207:27
Turbaned, malignant and t. Turk, 210:21
Turbans, white silken t. wreathed, 259:34
Turbulent fleshy sensual eating drinking, 486:7
    free me from t. priest, 124:10
    freezing t. water, 874:6
    people t. and changing, 349:4
    sagacious and t. of wit, 272:16
Turc, la galère d'un T., 268:*n2*
Turf, bless t. that wraps clay, 317:11
    grass-green t., 201:24
    green be t. above thee, 400:12
    green t. beneath feet, 386:10
Turk, bear like the T., 295:13
    human form in heathen t. or jew, 351:5
    malignant and turbaned T., 210:21
    or Proosian, 526:4
    out-paramoured the T., 212:2
    work hard as T., 882:11
Turkey a more respectable bird, 303:17
    black t. gobbler, 891:16
    in the straw, 884:16
    it was a t., 465:15
    myrtle and t. part, 382:14
Turkish, be taken by T. enemy, 898:2
    English not T. court, 188:26
Turkman's rest, 399:15
Turk's, on board a T. galley, 268:*n2*
Turks, Papists Protestants Jews T. in one ship,
    247:8
    sleep with T. and infidels, 177:15
Turmoil, economic progress means t.,
    657:20
    tired of my t., 787:18

Turn again Whittington, 881:20
    away no more, 352:11
    currents t. awry, 199:21
    dark cloud inside out, 616:17
    do not hope to t. again, 677:12
    do not t. back at goal, 100:23
    down empty Glass, 442:10
    good t. asketh another, 147:33
    him to cause of policy, 188:33
    his merry note, 194:11
    I'd love to t. you on, 848:12
    if you want to, 810:6
    in door once turn once only, 676:17
    now t. different hue, 59:22
    on tune in drop out, 795:3
    one good t. deserves another, 105:18
    out your toes, 515:17
    over a new leaf, 157:20
    over half a library, 310:3
    pass and t. again, 425:4
    quickly t. away, 595:1
    smile once more t. thy wheel, 211:16
    stone start a wing, 577:4
    the other cheek, 32:20
    thee behind me, 12:16
    to t. you out t. you out, 587:14
    up the lights, 582:4
    where shall I t., 829:4
    wheresoe'er I may, 370:13
    why wilt thou t. away, 352:11
    worm will t., 170:21
Turned aside to sleep, 229:4
    dead and t. to clay, 202:14
    face with ghastly pang, 376:12
    from one's course by opinions, 83:6
    having once t. walks on, 376:21
    he t. up his eyes, 352:4
    heart is t. to stone, 209:25
    him right and round about, 357:12
    home his footsteps t., 373:3
    in case anything t. up, 465:22
    round and round in world, 483:8
    suddenly cried and t. away, 669:6
    sword which t. every way, 6:2
    them inside outside, 610:*n1*
    world t. upside downward, 234:12
Turnest, thou t. man to destruction, 17:23
Turning, from itself never t., 159:4
    gas steam or table t., 491:18
    in widening gyre, 593:9
    lady's not for t., 810:6
    neither shadow of t., 45:22
    o' the tide, 189:4
    wine into urine, 662:3
Turnings, long lane knows no t., 460:10
Turnips, true as t., 465:29
Turns again home, 456:4
    climber-upward t. face, 191:36
    earth's smoothness rough, 462:15
    giddy thinks world t. round, 173:24
    his necessity to gain, 371:21
    into Miss T., 616:11
    lightly t. to love, 451:21
    no more his head, 376:21
    poet's pen t. to shapes, 179:6
    times go by t., 166:27
    to thoughts of love, 451:21
    unto ladder t. his back, 191:36

U

United States *(continued)*
  bounded on north, 456:*n*1
  British Empire and U., 619:18
  Canada hunting preserve convenient to U., 708:17
  Constitution and laws of U., 339:14
  Constitution for U., 339:11
  Constitution of U. shield, 470:15
  curse be on the Constitution of U., 458:6
  declare unilaterally Vietnam war over, 692:7
  deliberately attacked, 653:6
  exists as idea history literature, 691:1
  gives bigotry no sanction, 328:12
  government of cities failure of U., 532:10
  has more prison inmates, 875:8
  has thirty-two religions, 348:8
  hollowness of heart in U., 488:11
  in U. more space, 628:8
  join U., 623:18
  land of free speech, 621:8
  monster the U., 557:16
  neutral in fact, 566:6
  next president of the U., 866:8
  not finished, 715:5
  pledge allegiance to flag of U., 562:6
  policy toward Soviet Union, 738:8
  poor Mexico so close to the U., 508:2
  President of the U. is from Texas, 880:2
  religious madness common in U., 434:4
  so happy as in U., 645:11
  students from U., 557:17
  themselves greatest poem, 485:8
  treason against the U., 339:13
  Ulysses admitted into U., 634:7
  unfriendly toward U., 355:7
  we the people of the U., 339:11
Unites, fear of separation in, 668:7
  happy whom unbroken bond u., 96:12
Unities sir are a completeness, 464:20
Uniting, by u. we stand, 328:1
Unity, can't impose u. on country, 686:11
  confound all u. on earth, 217:6
  doth enchant me, 158:17
  dwell together in u., 19:10
  give to all nations u., 49:1
  in necessary things u., 265:4
  Multeity in U., 378:22
  of German nation, 684:16
  of nation consists in being able to act, 740:11
  preserve u. of empire, 324:12
Universal and common bond, 153:16
  appetite a u. wolf, 203:8
  blank, 257:6
  books of u. appeal, 616:15
  cock, 641:1
  currents of U. Being, 425:22
  darkness buries all, 297:6
  dismal u. hiss, 259:19
  dove-tailedness, 464:20
  frame without mind, 165:26
  God of u. laws, 542:2
  grin, 304:7
  horror unbend, 648:5
  lapped in u. law, 452:4
  law, 320:4
  made u. shout, 191:21

Universal *(continued)*
  monarchy of wit, 245:13
  mystery of u. existence, 416:16
  nature say, 305:*n*4
  nuisance, 276:6
  old age in u. man, 164:*n*5
  partial evil u. good, 294:23
  peace like light, 451:10
  prey, 203:8
  quality is diversity, 153:7
  Rossum's U. Robots, 685:16
  seek u. in individual, 529:2
  thermonuclear war means to u. suicide, 797:4
  this u. frame began, 273:22
  threat of becoming u., 723:15
  truths, 714:3
  uproar the u. peace, 217:6
Universals, statements of poetry are u., 79:5
Universe and nature be no more, 416:16
  as great as vast u., 50:8
  author should be like God in u., 493:10
  beginning the U. was created, 870:5
  benign indifference of u., 769:14
  chess pieces phenomena of u., 502:5
  complete unified theory of u., 854:3
  connect subject with u., 538:9
  Creator of u., 275:3
  emptiness produced the u., 86:16
  enjoy original relation to u., 425:19
  evolved from unfamiliar, 836:4
  glory and shame of u., 269:25
  glory of the u., 440:10
  God created U. from nothing, 125:1
  Great Architect of U., 634:6
  harmony for you my U., 111:19
  hell of a good u. next door, 702:2
  hints for better ordering of u., 126:9
  hitched to everything in u., 533:7
  I accept the u., 456:18
  I don't want the u. to be, 843:1
  in harmony with u., 481:3
  in u. neither center nor circumference, 158:19
  is change, 111:16
  is a plot of God, 449:18
  know another's view of u., 611:8
  knows the u. not himself, 266:15
  largest u. of good, 541:16
  makes a u. for them to describe, 854:2
  man said to u., 609:3
  Masters of the U., 831:8
  must fall through black hole, 795:5
  no hint throughout U. of good or ill, 520:12
  nothing lowly in u., 810:14
  one u. made up of all that is, 112:14
  open to our gaze, 167:15
  queerer than we suppose, 693:11
  realize position in u., 556:17
  result of blind chance, 440:8
  shell u. itself is, 372:7
  single complex living creature, 114:5
  slip away across the u., 848:16
  snow falling faintly through u., 650:9
  spirit animating u., 415:14
  Sun himself at center of U., 142:13
  suspended on tooth of monster, 578:14

Universe *(continued)*
  systematic procession of U., 142:13
  terrifying fact about the u., 819:2
  things in u. are just there, 858:12
  this grand book the u., 167:15
  this is a big beautiful u., 811:15
  through-and-through u., 542:14
  traversed u. in thought, 89:11
  true piety towards u., 584:12
  unit and u. are round, 424:6
  way into U. through forest, 533:9
  whole u. is in Him, 50:8
Universities, housed now in u., 888:16
University a collection of books, 407:21
  become multiversity, 764:4
  faculty members of Harvard U., 807:13
  he who enters u., 697:11
  politics of the u., 743:*n*3
Unjoined, Frankie had become u. person, 788:15
Unjust, evil and u. ends, 668:7
  God all mercy is God u., 291:1
  in least unjust in much, 38:16
  let him be u. still, 47:14
  peace before just war, 303:*n*3
  sendeth rain on just and u., 32:22
  war protracted, 484:17
  will pay less tax, 74:20
Unkind, tell me not I am u., 265:17
  thou art not so u., 195:1
  when givers prove u., 199:23
Unkindest cut of all, 192:35
Unkindness, I tax not you with u., 211:25
  may defeat my life, 210:7
  may do much, 210:7
Unkissed, unknowe u. and lost, 132:13
Unknelled uncoffined, 396:18
Unknowable, world u. we know, 577:3
Unknown, accents yet u., 192:18
  affection hath u. bottom, 195:30
  altars to u. gods, 540:18
  behind dim u., 481:13
  black and u. bards, 610:4
  critics shouting He's u., 539:19
  developed respect for u. in lifetime, 761:3
  forms of things u., 179:6
  hardships we suffered, 695:2
  know less than all u., 236:2
  let me live unseen u., 292:5
  like a complete u., 851:14
  loss no loss, 99:18
  means of destruction hitherto u., 661:5
  naked in death on u. shore, 94:25
  nature is but art u., 294:23
  not lived ill who passed u., 98:6
  not to know me argues yourselves u., 258:7
  out of me unworthy u., 605:7
  poetry journey to u., 699:1
  she lived u., 369:7
  taken for marvelous, 110:12
  there are also u. unknowns, 833:13
  things standing thus u., 202:31
  to fortune and fame u., 316:6
  to the u. god, 40:32
  too early seen u., 179:29
  traveled among u. men, 369:13
  unkist and lost, 132:13
  unknelled uncoffined u., 396:18

Unknown *(continued)*
worth's u. although height taken, 222:15
Unlamented let me die, 292:5
Unlearned, amaze th' u., 292:15
Unleashed power of the atom, 638:8
Unleavened bread and bitter herbs, 7:39
seven days shall ye eat u. bread, 7:42
Unleaving, Goldengrove u., 546:17
Unless name is noted down, 830:13
statistics lie, 701:14
Unlessoned girl unschooled, 185:22
Unlettered small-knowing soul, 174:4
Unlimited power apt to corrupt, 306:1
rights will become u., 312:13
Unlived, history cannot be u., 817:14
Unlocked, Shakespeare u. heart, 372:16
silent throat, 882:2
Unloose, Gordian knot u., 188:33
not worthy to u., 36:25
Unlovely, keep u. things afar, 82:13
Unlucky, these u. deeds relate, 210:20
Unmake, people can u. Constitution, 350:2
Unmanageable, most u. of all animals, 76:10
our lives had become u., 708:10
Unmanliness, wisdom without u., 71:15
Unmanly, 'tis u. grief, 196:28
Unmannerly, called them untaught u., 181:36
sadness in youth, 184:17
Unmarried, writing is profoundly u., 781:17
Unmask her beauty to moon, 197:19
time's glory to u. falsehood, 172:35
Unmasked, offer itself to be u., 655:17
Unmatchable, mastiffs of u. courage, 189:16
Unmeaning thing they call a thought, 292:18
Unmentionable odor of death, 748:16
thoughts, 483:12
Unmortal, moment in strange u. space, 731:15
Unmoved cold and to temptation slow, 222:1
Unnat'ral, poetry's u., 463:28
Unnatural, most u. of sexual perversions,
702:14
nothing u. that is not impossible, 346:18
vices fathered by heroism, 675:23
Unnecessarily, entities not multiplied u.,
130:15
Unnecessary, curious in u. matters, 30:14
great guilt of u. war, 330:11
heroic in u. points, 540:21
in Nature nothing u., 124:15
sentence no u. words, 606:3
Unnerved and untrained, 540:21
Unnoticed, rather attacked than u., 310:22
that u. & that necessary, 844:16
Unnumbered idle pebbles, 212:24
Unobtrusive, poetry should be u., 412:16
Unofficial force Baker Street irregulars, 573:6
Unordered, Chaos a rough u. mass, 102:9
Unparalleled catastrophes, 638:8
lass u., 219:17
Unpassioned beauty of great machine, 669:9
Unpeel, white Godiva I u., 833:10
Unperiphrastic, 73:15
Unperplexed like migratory birds, 631:21
seeking find Him, 461:15
Unperturbed pace, 576:14
Unpitied sacrifice, 323:16
unrespited u. unreprieved, 256:13
Unpleasant, demd u. body, 464:21

Unpleasantest words that blotted paper,
185:23
Unpleased, in power u., 272:16
Unpleasing to a married ear, 174:32
Unpledged, mind was still u., 68:1
Unplottable, completely u. manner, 860:4
Unpoetical, poet u., 413:10
Unpolluted, fair and u. flesh, 202:15
Unpopular, free trade u., 419:6
names impossible loyalties, 496:8
Unpossessed, is empire u., 172:4
Unpracticed, unlessoned girl u., 185:22
Unpredictability, midway between the u. of
matter, 802:2
Unpremeditated art, 403:2
verse, 259:5
Unprepared courage, 365:18
magnificently u., 667:6
Unprofitable, how weary stale flat u., 196:29
servant, 35:28
Unpurged images of day, 595:10
Unqualified blessing, 364:4
Unquenchable, gleam of noble deeds ever u.,
64:5
Unquiet, hate to be u. at home, 277:26
heart and brain, 453:12
how imagine u. slumbers, 476:18
meals make ill digestions, 172:27
Unravel, what common language to u., 659:5
Unravished bride of quietness, 410:13
Unread his works, 369:*n*1
vision, 677:16
Unreadable forty years from now, 392:10
Unreal, lead me from u. to real, 50:1
margin between real and u., 282:1
matter u. and temporal, 493:6
mockery hence, 216:21
nothing more u. than we see, 687:15
way things happen in movies is u., 817:5
Unreality and loud music, 788:11
Unreason, age of u., 754:12
Unreasonable, perfectly u. man, 466:9
Unredeemed, unblighted u. wilderness, 533:6
Unreeling tirelessly speeding them, 488:5
Unreflectively, ceases to live u., 632:13
Unregarded time slips away, 631:11
Unregenerate, more about iniquity than u.,
587:4
Unrelated and contradictory ends, 757:14
Unrelenting, haughty Juno's u. hate, 274:13
our cruel and u. enemy, 328:6
Unremembered, nameless u. acts, 368:7
Unreprieved, unrespited unpitied u., 256:13
Unreproved pleasures free, 250:24
Unrequited, self-love seems so often u., 742:12
toil, 447:2
Unrespited unpitied unreprieved, 256:13
Unrest, capitalism creates social u., 657:22
frantic-mad with evermore u., 223:6
had a beating heart, 794:7
large part of current u., 563:17
men miscall delight, 403:23
Unrighteous man forsake his thoughts, 27:11
Unroll, page did ne'er u., 315:22
Unromantic as Monday morning, 472:13
Unruly, scepter snatched with u. hand, 175:22
Sun, 228:15
tongue an u. evil, 45:28

Unruly *(continued)*
wit's an u. engine, 242:11
Unsaid, something u., 820:11
Unsatisfied, culture leaves u. drives to
rebelliousness, 563:15
indignation, 492:11
love u., 677:14
under long shadow-on-snow, 667:9
Unschooled, unlessoned girl u., 185:22
Unscottified, most u. of your countrymen,
309:25
Unscrew locks from doors, 486:7
Unscrupulous, one of most u. rascals, 573:22
Unsearchable dispose, 260:26
Unseasonable and immoderate sleep, 307:24
to eat an oyster, 154:2
Unseasoned telling found in legends, 813:12
Unseemly, not u. to die in defense, 51:33
Unseen, all u. and unheeded, 636:12
born to blush u., 315:23
by forms u. dirge sung, 317:11
counsel of the U. and Silent, 408:2
down u. full of water, 177:17
I walk u., 251:16
jest u. inscrutable, 173:30
let me live u. unknown, 292:5
nature works by bodies u., 89:16
thou art u. yet I hear, 403:4
walk the earth u., 258:2
within thy airy shell, 252:14
Unselfish, absolutely u. friend is dog, 512:12
and intelligent begin movement, 568:2
love of brute, 448:16
Unsettled, precedent not u. overnight, 607:1
Unsex me here, 214:17
Unshackled exercise of every faculty, 422:2
Unshorn fields boundless beautiful, 406:3
Unshut eye, 494:13
Unsifted in perilous circumstance, 197:26
Unsightly noisome things, 424:3
Unslayable, soul eternally u., 84:8
Unsmiling, implacable u. men, 874:6
Unsmote by the sword, 397:3
Unsought, love u. is better, 205:16
Unsoundness of mind, 419:9
Unspeakable desire, 495:11
in pursuit of the uneatable, 561:7
is sorrow you bid me renew, 94:9
Unspoken problem for many years, 796:7
words which were better u., 53:21
Unsponsored, solitude u. free, 640:22
Unspotted from the world, 45:25
Unstable as water, 7:19
become u. without knowing it, 69:11
feet u., 639:13
woman always fickle u. thing, 94:23
Unstaid and skittish in motions, 204:33
Unsteadiness of second class, 349:4
Unstilled world whirled, 677:17
Unsubstantial as shadows, 73:5
Unsuccessful or successful war, 326:20
Unsung noblest deed will die, 64:8
unwept unhonored u., 373:3
Unsunned, chaste as u. snow, 220:16
Unsure, habitation giddy and u., 187:38
what's to come still u., 204:26
Unsuspected isle in far-off seas, 459:20
Unswayed, is the sword u., 172:4

Untainted, what stronger breastplate than
heart u., 170:7
Untamed continent, 500:5
sullen u. intractable, 679:3
Untaught, called them u. knaves, 181:36
Untell the days, 233:17
Untender, so young and so u., 210:26
Untented Kosmos my abode, 556:5
Unthinking, assault of thoughts on u., 656:17
Unthought, once thought never be u., 796:6
Unthread rude eye of rebellion, 176:1
Until the day break, 24:11
Untimely, from mother's womb u. ripped,
217:28
Untitled aristocracy, 443:14
Untouched, strings u. will harshly jar, 168:15
Untrained to stand test, 540:21
Untraveled, gleams u. world, 451:13
heart u. turns to thee, 321:12
Untrespassed sanctity of space, 800:1
Untried, found difficult left u., 618:8
Untrodden, dwelt among u. ways, 369:7
Untroubling and untroubled where I lie,
404:19
Untrue, cloth u. twisted cue, 527:17
might telle his tale u., 134:10
thy lovers were all u., 274:25
unsad and evere u., 135:22
Untruth, never dare utter u., 87:14
Untune, Music shall u. the sky, 273:26
that string, 203:7
Untuned, like u. strings women are,
168:15
Untutored, Indian whose u. mind, 294:20
Untwist last strands of man, 547:3
Unum, E pluribus u., 95:*n5*
Unus, E pluribus u., 95:*n5*
Unused, fust in us u., 201:19
to the melting mood, 210:20
Unusual, cruel and u. punishment, 340:7
Unuttered part of man's life, 407:16
Unvanquishable, in u. number, 402:22
Unvanquished, I u. and unyielding, 654:19
Unvarnished, round u. tale deliver, 207:34
Unveil, Immortality u. third event, 511:9
Unveiled her peerless light, 257:25
Unveiling, uprising u. affirm, 448:15
Unvexed to the sea, 446:3
Unvictorious, conscripted u. ones, 668:14
Unwashed, great u., 385:9
lean u. artificer, 175:29
platters ride, 720:9
Unwastefully, manage affairs u., 520:8
Unwearied still lover by lover, 592:16
Unwelcome, bringer of u. news, 187:23
Unwept in eternal night, 97:14
unburied Patroclus, 52:16
unhonored unsung, 373:3
Unwillingly I left your land, 94:30
to school, 194:25
Unwomanly rags, 418:8
Unworthy, merit of the u. takes, 199:21
out of me u. unknown, 605:7
Unwritten, history u. because yet to be enacted,
488:12
ordinances, 71:14
written and u. law, 113:2
Unwrung, our withers are u., 200:22

Unyielding, Hades is u., 51:17
I unvanquished and u., 654:19
Unyoked humor of idleness, 181:33
Up and down City Road, 885:6
cannot bear leveling u., 309:6
game is u., 220:19
go u. and down as a talebearer, 8:27
lad when journey's over, 574:12
look not down but u., 462:18
Looks Like U. to Me, 842:10
men to your posts, 502:15
nice to people on way u., 633:9
road u. and road down one and same, 62:9
roos sonne and up roose Emelye, 134:20
Satan walking u. and down, 12:36
so floating many bells, 701:17
success is showing u., 839:20
sunny side u., 697:10
you've got to get u., 673:4
Upbraid my falsehood, 203:20
Upbringing, children look after own u., 822:6
nun would envy, 834:12
who have had conventional u., 614:15
Upharsin, Mene Mene Tekel U., 28:25
Upholds, giant Atlas u., 68:3
Upkeep, annual u. of yacht, 529:7
Uplift, educate Filipinos u. civilize them,
545:11
Uplifted, from despair thus high u., 256:6
loud u. angel trumpets, 253:18
Uplifting, in u. get underneath, 597:16
thoughts in baths, 708:13
Upmost, attains u. round, 191:36
Upon, and then they were u. her, 782:3
Upper, materializing u. class, 497:19
part of mankind, 282:10
stiff u. lip, 501:6
Uppity, high-tech lynching for u. blacks,
866:13
I'm u. rude profane brash, 794:3
Upright, behold the u., 16:13
God hath made man u., 23:18
judge learned judge, 186:9
man is laughed to scorn, 13:24
these set our flesh u., 230:11
walks u. on a straight path, 119:16
Uprising, my downsitting and mine u., 19:12
unveiling affirm, 448:15
Uproar, in bellow and u., 654:5
sand and wild u., 424:3
universal peace, 217:6
Upset, progress of Evolution u. Darwin,
531:22
Upside, world turned u. downward, 234:12
Upstairs and downstairs, 457:4
downstairs in lady's chamber, 894:6
equal u., 577:9
Upstart crow beautified with our feathers,
164:3
Upswept angel wings, 688:7
Upturned, sea of u. faces, 374:9
Upward, as the sparks fly u., 13:11
human race born to fly u., 129:21
look of caution, 624:15
Upwards, astronomy compels soul to look u.,
75:12
Uranium new source of energy, 637:14
Uranus, it may be in U., 472:22

Urban, complicated u. society, 685:5
spirits of the u. wilderness, 873:1
Urbi et orbi, 121:22
Urge for destruction also creative u., 469:13
glum u. for food to fill us, 752:7
of a song, 625:2
to beware the temptation, 765:14
toward whiteness, 730:10
wrestle resurrection, 755:11
Urgent, Master is u., 117:8
Uriah, set ye U. in forefront of battle, 11:17
Urinal, burnt match skating in u., 720:8
Urine, shoes will fill with u., 839:5
turning wine into u., 662:3
Urn, bubbling loud-hissing u., 327:1
Grecian U. worth old ladies, 714:8
lean on garden u., 675:13
storied u., 315:20
well-wrought u. becomes greatest ashes,
228:20
U.S.A., greed will save the U., 864:1
Usage, consumed in image if not in u., 778:1
'Usband, Man-o'-War's 'er 'u., 589:2
Use a little wine for stomach's sake, 44:33
again until Eternity, 510:11
against the u. of nature, 214:11
all gently, 200:6
almost change nature, 201:13
any language you choose, 527:3
beauty too rich for u., 179:28
cannot u. talent, 727:14
come to deadly u., 212:19
doth breed habit, 173:37
every man after desert, 199:14
find but seldom u. them, 427:10
frequent u. of any organ, 341:8
glad to be of u., 675:4
him as though loved him, 245:8
I'll u. you for my mirth, 193:9
in measured language, 453:12
it and never wear it out, 57:2
it up wear it out, 886:15
know not how to u. victory, 84:6
living measured by u., 152:5
main thing is u. it well, 246:5
make proper u. of victories, 85:11
me to the limit, 571:2
no u. of metal, 224:19
not poor who has enough to u., 98:4
not to shine in u., 451:14
of force but temporary, 324:4
of him more than I see, 555:12
rather in power than u., 205:30
ring worn thin by u., 89:*n9*
speak daggers but u. none, 200:30
treatment to help sick, 70:14
try to have and u. excellence, 78:15
tyrannous to u. strength like giant, 206:27
want of u. mind torpid, 310:14
worship he found in u., 73:24
worst u. a man could be put to, 227:13
Used, I am u. to it, 446:4
I have u. similitudes, 28:39
key always bright, 302:24
man grows u. to everything, 492:6
mouth u. as a latrine, 798:7
my credit, 181:24
only witchcraft I have u., 208:3

Used *(continued)*
wine good if well u., 208:32
Useful, be u. where thou livest, 242:12
books you may carry most u., 308:9
by magistrate equally u., 332:2
lesson to head, 327:5
mock their u. toil, 315:17
nothing in houses not u., 520:7
use of the u., 80:13
Usefulness, power of u. gone, 571:9
Useless, art quite u., 559:24
better know u. things than nothing, 103:22
each without other, 437:4
gold in itself u., 143:3
if object u. labor u., 478:2
laws weaken necessary laws, 297:14
life is early death, 343:5
lodged with me u., 254:20
most beautiful most u., 484:9
no man u. who has friend, 556:1
second good third u., 142:4
slip u. away, 408:10
to poet nothing u., 307:9
Uselessly, nature does nothing u., 78:17
Uselessness, moved by spirit of u., 658:15
of men above sixty, 553:4
Uses, corner for others' u., 209:9
one art which u. things, 75:23
panics have u., 333:7
seem all u. of this world, 196:29
sweet are u. of adversity, 193:37
to what base u. return, 202:13
Usher, House of U., 448:8
Ushered, still u. with tear, 293:22
Ushers in the morn, 304:11
Usquebae, wi' u. face the devil, 358:7
Usual, not in the u. way, 469:1
Usura sin against nature, 665:12
with U., 665:11
Usurpations, violent and sudden u., 345:13
Usurpers, lay proud u. low, 358:17
Usury, from all u. free, 95:27
Utility, as foundation of morals U., 435:15
has u. as evidence of leisure, 569:8
in science seek immediate u. in vain, 494:6
nothing value but object of u., 478:2
or cost of production, 543:12
Utinam populus Romanus unam cervicem, 104:*n*8
Utmost bound of human thought, 451:15
bound of the everlasting hills, 7:21
Thule, 93:9
Utter, liberty to u., 254:13
not both live and u. it, 474:1
not in u. nakedness, 370:17
not u. what dost not know, 182:15
nothing for which not responsible, 445:15
sweet breath, 179:5
wise man u. vain knowledge, 13:32
would tongue u., 452:15
Utterance, action nor u., 193:4
if u. denied thought a burden, 426:9
Uttered, not u. by chapmen's tongues, 174:8
or unexpressed, 372:19
part of man's life, 407:16
Uttereth, day unto day u. speech, 15:15
fool u. all his mind, 22:9

Uttereth *(continued)*
wisdom u. her voice, 19:24
Uttering such dulcet breath, 178:15
Utterly destroy power of reasoning, 76:2
Uttermost parts of the sea, 19:13
Uzzah put forth his hand, 11:14

V

V sign is symbol and portent, 620:10
Vacant, body filled and v. mind, 189:23
heart hand eye, 374:11
interlunar cave, 260:10
interstellar spaces, 678:19
into the vacant, 678:19
laugh that spoke v. mind, 322:25
mind distressed, 326:14
stuffs out v. garments, 175:19
Vacationless, mothers and housewives v., 746:12
Vacillation from one sex to other, 654:12
Vacuous, keeps their hearts v., 56:14
Vacuum, nature abhors a v., 275:16
Vade in pace, 121:23
salutatum pro me liber, 133:*n*2
Vae victis, 121:24
Vagabond shalt thou be, 6:6
Vague, boundaries shadowy and v., 448:18
crepuscular time, 479:6
evolution from v. to definite, 534:16
The V. and Elusive, 57:7
Vagueness, poem best when tantalizing v., 622:22
Vain, a' is done in v., 357:11
all delights are v., 173:40
all Doric discipline, 594:12
ambition of kings, 237:11
beauty is v., 22:20
begot of v. fantasy, 179:26
blood pour in v., 568:14
bring no more v. oblations, 24:31
citadels not walled, 699:9
deluding Joys, 251:10
denial v. and coy excuse, 253:2
desire vain regret, 506:7
dreme of joye all but in v., 137:*n*8
every man walketh in a v. show, 16:19
hatching v. empires, 256:17
hence all you v. delights, 236:9
I have not lived in v., 288:3
I shall not live in V., 510:4
ill-natured Englishman, 282:5
in v. always in v., 568:14
in v. to wish for death, 66:13
know we loved in v., 394:8
labour and wounds are v., 479:12
man may become proud, 276:6
man pleased with effect on people, 612:20
man v. diverse undulating, 151:17
mock on 'tis all in v., 353:12
name of the Lord in v., 8:12
not in v., 621:7
oblations, 24:31
pain to love in v., 265:10
people imagine a v. thing, 15:1
pomp and glory, 49:11, 225:25
profane and v. babblings, 44:38

Vain *(continued)*
sealed in v., 207:8
spend not then his gifts in v., 232:5
the Present teaches in v., 613:14
they are disquieted in v., 16:19
they labor in v., 19:4
to look for defense against lightning, 101:1
tricks that are v., 528:10
war with heaven, 256:6
was the chief's pride, 296:19
watchman waketh but in v., 19:4
wisdom all, 256:22
wise man utter v. knowledge, 13:32
words in your oaths, 118:2
you're so v., 861:13
youth is v., 377:13
Vaine, la vie est v., 519:*n*3
Vainglory, from pride v. and hypocrisy, 48:19
humble through v., 153:4
pleasance here all v., 141:7
Vainness, lying v. drunkenness, 205:25
Vale, depart this v., 645:7
far sunken, 411:12
meanest floweret of v., 316:9
meet thee in hollow v., 241:18
of Soul-making, 413:14
of years, 209:8
sequestered v. of life, 316:3
violet-embroidered v., 252:14
Vale, ave atque v., 91:*n*10
Valentine, heart shaped like v., 780:14
my funny v., 707:4
Vales, hills v. woodland plain, 293:14
o'er v. and hills, 371:9
of meadowsweet, 724:2
Valet, hero to his v., 249:8
not aware of this, 79:13
Valets, masters worthy v., 327:14
Valets de chambre, héros pour les v., 249:*n*1
Valiant, as v. I honor him, 192:26
be v. not too venturous, 161:19
brothers v., 882:9
dust, 190:23
England breeds v. creatures, 189:16
if you are very v., 50:13
never taste of death but once, 192:11
reproof v., 196:6
souls of heroes, 50:9
trencher-man, 190:13
Validation, validity process of v., 542:9
Validity process of validation, 542:9
what v. and pitch, 204:11
Valley, all in the v. of death, 454:18
bicker down v., 454:24
down in the v., 884:2
every v. shall be exalted, 26:25
faraway town sleeping in v., 523:13
he paweth in the v., 14:27
his golden cup, 505:15
may v. streams content me, 93:17
of Ajalon, 10:3
of decision, 28:42
of dry bones, 28:17
of Humiliation, 271:14
of reveries, 616:19
of Shadow, 449:19
of shadow of death, 15:23
Skylark have you seen v. green, 759:5

Valley *(continued)*
    spirit of the v. never dies, 57:2
    take me to green v., 890:16
Valleys, greenest of our v., 448:9
    groves hills fields, 168:4
    hills and v. dales and fields, 168:*n*1
    lick V. up, 509:10
    lily of the v., 24:6
    of Hall, 543:3
    piping down v. wild, 350:10
Vallombrosa, strow the brooks in V., 255:17
Valor, better part of v. discretion, 183:34
    birthplace of v., 357:14
    brute beauty and v., 546:11
    constancy and v. our shield, 620:1
    deed whereat v. will weep, 220:7
    God's help and their v., 365:10
    good speed to your youthful v., 95:9
    he for v. formed, 257:19
    mighty men of v., 9:37
    no need of v., 73:22
    plucks dead lions, 175:7
    thy v. prevail, 417:5
    uncommon v. common virtue, 664:10
    who would true v. see, 271:26
Valorous, Roland v. Oliver wise, 124:3
Valuable coin of thinker, 779:1
    if riches v. to Heaven, 284:23
    reputation more v. than money, 99:19
    time most v. thing, 81:17
    what v. not new, 385:7
Valuation, government resting on v. of
        property, 75:17
    superstitious v. of Europe, 544:1
Value at a penny talk of old men, 91:5
    carry body for its sentimental v., 750:10
    cynic knows v. of nothing, 560:10
    dearness only gives v., 333:6
    full extent of its own v., 364:9
    governed by utility or cost, 543:12
    it next to good conscience, 245:9
    men of less v. than gold, 143:3
    none but horizontal, 748:4
    nothing has v., 638:12
    nothing v. but object of utility, 478:2
    of stakes at issue, 743:10
    of what entrepreneur contributes, 657:18
    of what poet has written, 677:22
    then we rack the v., 191:6
    things will come to have, 822:13
    what I say more lasting v., 820:2
Valueless, reading v. books, 484:15
Values, masculine v., 654:18
    not single feature in heaven he v., 525:7
Vampire, like v. dead many times, 534:5
Vanbrugh's, dead Sir John V. house of clay,
        283:*n*4
Vandals took the handles, 851:16
Vanessa extraordinary woman, 284:*n*2
Vanilla of society, 375:2
    suburbs, 850:6
Vanish like evil spirits, 338:8
    where did children v., 742:8
Vanished and shrunk away, 167:2
    Cheshire Cat v. slowly, 514:12
    touch of v. hand, 452:15
Vanishes, man loves what v., 594:8
Vanisheth, life a vapor that v., 45:31

Vanishing, keep beauty from v., 546:21
    photographers deal in v. things, 752:2
    race, 712:10
Vanitas vanitatum, 459:8
Vanities, age of v., 364:12
    guides us by v., 675:22
    man of my v., 645:11
Vanity, all is v., 22:21
    and vexation of spirit, 22:26
    beauty without v., 394:9
    conscience or v. appalled, 595:15
    cords of v., 25:6
    cured of every folly but v., 313:2
    dispel v. with v., 113:17
    every man at his best state is v., 16:18
    Fair, 271:17, 459:5
    give no hollow aid, 396:4
    Golden V., 898:2
    hath not lifted his soul unto v., 15:24
    in years, 182:27
    my days are v., 13:18
    of human hopes, 306:22
    of vanities, 22:21
    philosophize on v. of life, 149:7
    preying on people's v. ignorance, 838:5
    pull down thy v., 665:14
    repeyreth hom fro worldly v., 133:4
    tickle one's v., 493:11
    town is lighter than v., 271:17
Vanquished by desire, 56:9
    had Cato, 106:9
    Macbeth never v. be, 216:34
    one safety to v., 94:15
Vans, omnibuses and v., 654:5
    to beat the air, 677:13
Vantage, coign of v., 214:21
    ground of truth, 89:*n*12
Vapor, floating like v. on air, 503:14
    life a v. that vanisheth, 45:31
    like bear or lion, 218:39
    live upon v. of dungeon, 209:9
    summit lost in v., 398:7
Vapors both away, 230:4
    congregation of v., 199:5
    strangle him, 181:33
    weep their burthen, 455:5
Variable as the shade, 373:16
    lest thy love prove v., 180:8
Variableness, with whom is no v., 45:22
Variation if useful preserved, 439:13
Varied, mob is v. and inconstant, 276:16
    rule the v. year, 300:14
Variety about New England weather, 522:10
    among individuals, 321:5
    Democracy admits v., 638:14
    democracy full of v., 75:18
    in spite of v. and power, 495:22
    infinite v., 218:21
    joy of life is v., 307:6
    mother of Enjoyment, 429:18
    no pleasure unseasoned by v., 100:9
    order in v. we see, 293:14
    soul of pleasure, 279:5
Variety's spice of life, 326:22
Various, a man so v., 273:2
    as lovely so be v., 706:1
    as your land, 716:1
    constant as v., 706:1

Various *(continued)*
    distribution of property, 345:9
    of v. stuff the v. Man, 358:2
    so v. so beautiful so new, 496:19
    speaks a v. language, 405:10
Varium et mutabile femina, 94:*n*10
Varying shore o' the world, 219:3
Vase, shatter v. if you will, 387:14
Vases, beads dolls cloths v., 783:9
Vassal, God how fine a v., 124:4
    Muse I was your v., 558:13
Vassals and serfs at side, 414:4
Vast and furious ocean, 240:2
    dead v. and middle of night, 197:11
    deserts of v. eternity, 266:22
    edges drear, 496:19
    heaven's net is v., 58:3
    intelligence were v. enough, 345:3
    like a v. shadow moved, 268:14
    lodge in v. wilderness, 326:20
    mass of London itself, 619:16
    more devils than v. hell, 179:6
    plastic and v. one intellectual breeze,
        375:16
    right-wing conspiracy, 864:8
    slow-breathing unconscious, 542:14
    struggle to found Roman state, 93:30
    unbelievably small unbelievably v., 813:7
    wings across skies, 694:14
Vaster, grow v. than empires, 266:21
Vasty, call spirits from v. deep, 182:34
    hall of death, 495:20
Vat, every v. stand upon bottom, 271:11
Vaterland, lieb V. magst ruhig sein, 484:*n*2
Vats, cheeses out of v., 460:7
Vaudeville audiences give loudest sighs, 770:14
Vault, fretted v., 315:19
    left this v. to brag of, 215:30
Vaulter in sunny grass, 392:13
Vaulting ambition, 214:24
Vaults, heaven's v. should crack, 213:12
Vaunt-couriers to thunderbolts, 211:24
Vaunteth, charity v. not, 42:27
Vauntie, her best and she was v., 358:9
Vaward of our youth, 187:30
Vécu, j'ai v., 342:*n*2
    rose a v. ce que vivent les roses, 162:*n*7
Vegetable, information v. animal mineral,
        526:6
    love not suit me, 526:11
    my v. love should grow, 266:21
Vegetate the country, 386:8
Vehicles, robot v., 850:9
Veil, invisible new v. of finity, 821:2
    my v. no mortal ever took up, 108:14
    of temple rent, 36:21
    painted v. call Life, 402:*n*1
    through which not see, 441:20
Veiled Melancholy, 411:11
Veiling lightnings of song, 403:20
Veillons dormants et veillants dormons,
        153:*n*1
Veils, Religion v. her fires, 297:6
Vein, divided to the v., 829:4
    Ercles' v. a tyrant's v., 178:4
    King Cambyses' v., 182:26
    not in giving v. today, 171:35
    of poetry in all men, 407:18

Veins, bound bones and v. in me, 546:5
  dried sap out of v., 592:5
  in my v. red life, 412:1
  sea itself floweth in v., 278:10
Velocities of evanescent increments, 291:7
Velocity, determination of v., 728:3
Velvet, gilded and covered with v., 365:9
  iron hand in v. glove, 148:28
  live like v. mole, 666:5
  some in v. gowns, 896:21
  walk in v. shoes, 666:3
Venenum, ali cibus aliis v., 90:*n6*
Venerable, every tradition grows v., 547:13
  parts of constitution, 324:15
Veneration, much v. but no rest, 166:1
Venerationi sancta simplicitas, 115:*n7*
Venetian, Turk beat a V., 210:21
Vengeance, achieving their v., 804:9
  blood v. desolation, 489:15
  in the day of v., 20:4
  is mine, 41:35
  nor one feeling of v., 347:14
  of history terrible, 643:16
Veni vidi vici, 89:*n2*
Venial, sins of omission v., 311:19
Venice, at V. gave his body, 177:14
  commonwealth of V. this inscription,
    235:11
  more than any man in V., 184:10
  on Bridge of Sighs, 395:25
  sate in state, 396:1
Venienti occurrite morbo, 105:*n8*
Venizelos observed, 621:2
Venom clamors of jealous woman, 172:26
Venomous, like toad ugly and v., 193:37
  no means too v., 549:3
Vent, his tongue must v., 219:32
Vent, le v. se lève, 612:*n3*
Venting heavy heart, 488:2
Ventre affamé, 266:*n3*
Ventricle of memory, 174:18
Venture, each v. new beginning, 678:22
  nothing v. nothing win, 527:5
  nought v. nought have, 147:29
Ventured like wanton boys, 225:25
  neck or nothing, 461:14
Ventures, lose our v., 193:14
  not in one bottom trusted, 184:1
Venturous, be valiant not too v., 161:19
Venus, herself fastened to prey, 278:21
  mingles sweet bitterness with cares, 91:21
  nurturing V., 89:9
Vénus toute entière, 278:*n8*
Veracity which increases with age, 264:26
Verb, emerges with v. in mouth, 523:14
  God is a v., 705:10
  I think I am a v., 498:8
Verba, rem tene v. sequentur, 85:*n4*
Verbal agreement isn't worth paper written on,
  650:2
Verbiage, mistaking v. for truths, 612:4
Verbose, revolutions are always v., 643:13
Verbosity, not crude v. but holy simplicity,
  115:15
  thread of his v., 174:25
Verdant, ocean surrounds v. land, 483:5
Verdantly, entwine itself v., 387:9
Verdict afterwards, 515:8

Verdure, vast forest v., 500:5
Vere, God bless Captain V., 484:3
Vereker's secret, 544:13
Verge, ability to get to v., 674:16
  on very v. of her confine, 211:19
Verification, verity process of v., 542:9
Verisimilitude, artistic v., 527:19
Veritable ocean, 641:8
Veritas, amicus Plato sed magis amica v., 78:*n1*
  in vino, 55:*n11*, 120:29
  magna est v., 29:*n3*
  non erubescit, 113:*n6*
Veritatem dies aperit, 103:*n9*
Vérité que ces montagnes, 152:*n14*
Verities and truths of heart, 714:3
Verity is an event, 542:9
  religious feeling a v., 490:15
  verifying itself, 542:9
Vermeil-tinctured lip, 252:25
Vermin, race of odious v., 284:26
Vermont, as Maine so goes V., 885:*n8*
Vermouth, not the v., 732:9
  union of gin and v., 713:10
Vernal, one impulse from v. wood, 368:6
  seasons of the year, 254:6
  sight of v. bloom, 257:6
Verneint, der Geist der stets v., 344:*n2*
Versailles, death sentence of V., 684:16
  these palms greater than V., 829:5
Verse, able to bumbast out blank v., 164:3
  all not prose is v., 267:30
  art of Racine's v., 612:5
  as soon write free v., 625:11
  brings to his v. cadence, 278:2
  child with a taste for v., 852:13
  find him who sermon flies, 242:6
  give up v. my boy, 665:10
  happy who in v. steer, 278:1
  married to immortal v., 251:8
  read out my v., 150:7
  statues pictures v. grand, 520:10
  subject of all v., 240:7
  this v. grave for me, 555:16
  unpremeditated v., 259:5
  whatever I tried to write was v., 102:24
  yet write v. badly, 267:25
Versed, deep v. in books, 260:6
  in reasonings of men, 67:15
Verses, Appius says in v., 92:13
  doctrine hidden under strange v., 128:23
  false gallop of v., 195:8
  indignation will produce v., 109:10
  on dark theme trace v. of light, 89:18
  poverty drove me to writing v., 98:13
  praise v. but read something else, 107:11
  stop abusing my v. or publish, 107:8
  underneath the Bough, 441:10
  writes v. speaks holiday, 187:12
Versing, relish v., 243:7
Vertebrae, stiffening of v., 564:10
Vertical man, 748:4
Very beadle to humorous sigh, 174:13
  God of very God, 48:12
Vesper now raising his light, 91:19
Vespers, barefoot friars singing v., 332:19
Vesprée, a point perdu cette v., 150:*n8*
Vessel, a chosen v., 40:24
  empty v. greatest sound, 190:2

Vessel *(continued)*
  gilded v. goes, 316:15
  goodly v., 436:21
  I am like a broken v., 16:2
  of more ungainly make, 442:5
  of my genius now hoists sails, 129:9
  one v. unto honor, 41:27
  strikes with shivering shock, 381:13
  though masts be firm, 473:20
  wife the weaker v., 45:41
  with the pestle, 775:10
Vessels oft handled brightly shine, 168:15
  pass close to each other, 437:*n2*
Vest, casting the body's v., 267:2
Vestige, last v. of human dignity, 722:15
  no v. of a beginning, 321:6
  philosophy leaves not v., 149:7
Vestigia, agnosco veteris v. flammae, 94:*n9*
Vestments, priestly v. in dens, 500:5
Vesture, cast lots upon my v., 15:22
  muddy v. of decay, 186:15
Veterans, not tell Vietnam v. from rock v.,
  847:8
Veuf, le v. l'inconsolé, 439:*n4*
Vex and oppress each other, 345:9
  definition of oats meant to v., 307:*n1*
  not his ghost, 213:15
  such injury v. a saint, 173:17
Vexation, multiplication is v., 881:3
  only to understand the report, 26:9
  travail and v. of spirit, 23:1
  vanity and v. of spirit, 22:26
Vexed with mirth ear of night, 395:1
Vexing dull ear of drowsy man, 175:20
Vibrate, Pentagon turn orange and v., 803:7
  sweetest pleasure, 357:7
Vibrates in memory, 404:4
Vibration, brave v. each way free, 241:14
Vibrations of deathless music, 605:7
Vicar, of Bray, 883:12
Vice, accommodating v., 267:26
  amusements keep people from v., 309:17
  any taint of v., 205:25
  avarice not so much a v., 276:*n1*
  best virtue has tincture of v., 153:5
  boredom v. and poverty, 299:13
  bullied out of v., 429:14
  by action dignified, 180:17
  conceal dreary morals like v., 556:2
  creature of heejous mien, 600:9
  cruelty is virtue not v., 334:11
  discourage and abolish tyranny and v.,
    329:6
  distinction between virtue and v., 309:5
  extremism in defense of liberty no v.,
    758:10
  homage v. pays to virtue, 264:12
  hypocrisy is nerve-racking vice, 626:22
  hypocrisy v. of vices, 744:9
  inherent v. of capitalism, 621:18
  lashed v. spared name, 285:9
  moderation in principle a v., 333:17
  monster of frightful mien, 295:2
  no v. so simple, 185:19
  prosperity best discover v., 165:17
  raptures and roses of v., 529:16
  reverend v., 182:27
  schools nurseries of v., 304:15

W

Wafer, sun pasted like w., 608:15
Wafer-cakes, men's faiths w., 189:6
Waft her love to Carthage, 186:14
Wag, let world w., 147:5
Wage laborers having no means of production, 478:*n*6
Wägen, erst w. dann wagen, 420:*n*1
Wager, what will you w., 269:17
Wagers sum of resources, 799:*n*1
Wages are value expression, 657:18
   home gone and ta'en thy w., 220:26
   keeping profits up by keeping w. down, 380:15
   of sin is death, 41:16
   times hard and w. low, 897:23
   took w. and are dead, 575:20
Wagner's music better than it sounds, 554:9
Wagon, hitch your w. to star, 428:18
   storm like w. crossing bridge, 760:17
   water-w. place for me, 597:18
Wagons, honored among w., 777:10
Wags, see how world w., 194:15
   so w. the world, 194:*n*1
Wail, new w. times' waste, 221:8
   night bird's w., 527:23
   or knock the breast, 260:25
   to w. such woes, 159:2
   who buys mirth to w. a week, 172:32
Wailful choir, 411:8
Wailing winds naked woods, 406:2
   woman w. for demon-lover, 377:18
Wailings, sighs lamentations and w., 128:8
Waist deep in Big Muddy, 793:14
   slender w. confined, 249:22
Wait a bit Oysters cried, 516:5
   a man should w., 74:12
   all things come to who w., 426:*n*2
   be still w., 756:2
   digestion w. on appetite, 216:16
   do not listen simply w., 655:17
   do not w. be still, 655:17
   do not w. for last judgment, 770:8
   drift w. and obey, 590:9
   fold hands and w., 528:13
   for wisest of counselors, 64:23
   heard the word W., 823:4
   I almost had to w., 278:16
   labor and to w., 436:7
   right and wrong can w., 716:8
   stand and w., 254:22
   these w. all upon thee, 18:11
   times we can't w. for somebody, 840:4
   to watch water clear, 622:9
   upon I would, 215:2
   upon the Lord, 26:32
   who only stand and w., 254:22
Waited for billy-boil, 585:8
   for the light, 605:19
   for thy salvation, 7:20
   three years w. for herald, 727:1
Waiter roars it through hall, 500:3
Waitest for spark from heaven, 495:15
Waiteth, my soul w. for the Lord, 19:8
Waiting for invasion so are fishes, 620:2
   for rain, 675:21
   taxi throbbing w., 676:12
   what are we all w. for, 583:9
   worse things w. than death, 530:6

Waits, destiny w. alike, 63:12
   human engine w., 676:12
Waive quantum o' the sin, 356:19
Wake and call me early, 450:15
   and feel fell of dark, 547:7
   awake for night is flying, 162:26
   better to wake up after all, 556:19
   blank w. of passion, 839:6
   die before I w., 283:9
   Do I w. or sleep, 410:12
   eternally, 230:24
   for the Sun, 441:4
   him no not I, 893:11
   human voices w. us, 675:7
   in durance vile I w., 359:2
   nations underground, 898:25
   sleeping w. and waking sleep, 153:1
   thou wilt not w., 241:18
   to sleep, 756:5
   truths w. to perish never, 371:2
   unto me, 503:16
Waked after long sleep, 224:33
   by the circling hours, 258:22
   I w. she fled, 255:2
   priest all shaven, 897:8
   to ecstasy living lyre, 315:21
   you have w. me too soon, 289:11
Wakeful nightingale, 257:25
Waken, not w. sleeper soul is away, 558:3
   thou with me, 453:5
Wakened us from sleeping, 669:11
Wakens, firefly w., 453:5
Wakes, Maypoles Hock-carts wassails w., 240:9
   Sleeping Beauty w. up, 808:9
   whoever w. in England, 460:18
Waketh, watchman w. but in vain, 19:4
Waking bliss, 252:16
   hope is w. dream, 77:6
   morn not w. till she sings, 162:9
   nights of w., 373:21
   no such matter, 221:28
   silence with w. bird, 455:2
   sleeping wake and w. sleep, 153:1
   souls, 228:7
   take my w. slow, 756:5
   threshold of w. light, 814:13
   vision or w. dream, 410:12
   way she had of w. him, 680:11
Waldo, Matthew and W. guardians, 675:11
Wales, prince of W. in small but costly crown, 647:4
   Prince of W. is not a position, 836:*n*3
Walk a little faster, 515:2
   and not faint, 26:32
   and wot not what they are, 174:1
   ask for old paths and w. therein, 27:28
   away from it, 815:1
   before they dance, 296:10
   between dark and dark, 706:2
   by faith, 43:15
   can two w. together, 29:2
   cheerfully over the world, 270:3
   citizen may w. safely on law, 804:16
   closer w. with God, 326:7
   crust where I must w., 787:17
   cypress in palace w., 453:5
   deck my Captain lies, 487:17
   down Piccadilly, 526:11

Walk (*continued*)
   fantasy goes for w. returns with bride, 775:7
   fishermen that w. beach, 212:24
   foolery does w. about, 205:10
   for a walk's sake, 639:9
   from breakfast to madness, 820:8
   good w. spoiled, 525:12
   happily may I w., 891:18
   humbly with thy God, 29:5
   I w. back streets, 658:6
   I w. the line, 831:11
   I w. unseen, 251:16
   I'll rest but thou w., 889:23
   in fear and dread, 376:21
   in the street, 487:1
   in velvet shoes, 666:3
   into my parlor, 418:16
   it slow where you go, 836:11
   let her not w. in the sun, 198:33
   let us w. honestly, 41:40
   no spirit can w. abroad, 196:19
   not on earth exultantly, 118:14
   on eggs, 233:16
   on the Wild Side, 757:10
   Oysters come w. with us, 516:2
   people may w. but not throw stones, 307:27
   pleasant w. pleasant talk, 516:2
   race of men who w. upon earth, 51:8
   revealed her as true goddess, 94:2
   rise and w. with him, 67:8
   roads must man w. down, 851:1
   shall not w. in darkness, 39:24
   slow silent w., 536:22
   solar w. or milky way, 294:20
   take up bed and w., 36:26
   talk with you w. with you, 184:22
   teach crab to w. straight, 72:17
   the earth unseen, 258:2
   through valley of shadow, 15:23
   under water men w., 882:14
   upon England's mountains, 354:8
   upon the beach, 675:6
   where'er you w., 292:6
   which way they w., 215:15
   while ye have light, 39:37
   with Kings, 590:2
   with stretched forth necks, 25:1
   wood so wild, 880:10
   ye in it, 26:13
   your ghost will w., 461:3
   your mystic way, 526:10
Walked along the Strand, 308:10
   among ancient trees, 352:10
   Cat w. by himself, 589:18
   crowns and crownets, 219:8
   Enoch w. with God, 6:13
   eye-deep in hell, 665:8
   glittered when he w., 605:18
   him that w. the waves, 253:14
   in glory and in joy, 369:16
   in the search of the depth, 14:21
   people that w. in darkness, 25:15
   through wilderness of world, 271:7
   to hotel in rain, 721:9
   with his mother, 777:8
   without upward look, 624:15

War *(continued)*
relentless, 607:13
remember w. against Franco, 819:9
result of mistaken calculation, 629:11
scourge of w., 447:2, 661:16
seek no wider w., 753:14
send my ships off to w., 858:12
sentence is for open w., 256:9
Seven Years W., 644:15
silent w. of lilies, 172:30
sinews of w., 88:18
situation not to Japan's advantage, 728:6
small w. on heels of small w., 788:6
some slain in w., 177:8
Spanish-American W. splendid little w.,
    532:13
spares not the brave, 60:3
stand by country but not vote for w., 646:3
study politics and w., 330:7
subject of it is W., 699:4
suppose they gave a w., 636:n1
sweets with sweet w. not, 220:33
sword of w. or of law, 338:9
talk's spoiling fun, 689:15
tempered by w., 785:10
the w. is over, 498:4
there was w. in heaven, 47:1
thermonuclear w. means to suicide, 797:4
they could do with good w., 716:15
this is the W. Room, 819:6
this is w., 435:22
this w. one of elemental conflicts, 684:17
those who brought w. to Far East, 661:3
though w. should rise against me, 15:28
Thucydides wrote history of w., 71:11
time of w. time of peace, 22:31
to prevent w. not fear it, 381:4
to w. and arms I fly, 265:17
too serious for military, 348:11
train of circumstances, 333:14
true w. story never moral, 863:11
unjust peace before just w., 303:n3
unjust w. protracted, 484:17
unsuccessful or successful w., 326:20
upon rebellion was messy and slow, 680:8
vain w. with heaven, 256:6
vast aloof absentee, 843:3
victorious warriors win go to w., 80:17
warmest heart recoiled at w., 701:11
we wish to glorify w., 633:7
weapons of w. perished, 11:10
well that w. so terrible, 436:1
what is it good for, 849:8
what w. said Prime Minister, 736:7
when aggressions require w., 337:14
when I speak they are for w., 18:29
when w. he went, 749:10
when w. is done, 668:13
whenever we engage in w., 708:15
who desires peace prepare for w., 115:27
with rere-mice, 178:20
with rights of mankind, 336:17
woman cause of ten years' w., 281:11
world ruled and led to w., 626:12
wrong w. at wrong time, 697:7
you provide poems I'll provide w., 714:12
youth I love gone to w., 892:2
War-bonnet of Medicine Hat, 715:18

Warble child, 174:11
    native wood-notes wild, 251:8
    sweet in springtime, 558:1
Warbled to the string, 251:20
Warbler, Dan Chaucer first w., 450:22
Warblest at eve, 253:16
Warbling, thou w. bird, 357:6
Warden said do you have anything to say,
    803:11
Warder, memory the w. of brain, 215:7
Wardrobe, dalliance in w. lies, 189:1
    malfunction, 880:4
Wards, pretty young w. in Chancery, 526:19
Ware, taste your w., 893:12
    that will not keep, 574:12
Wares harder to get rid of, 623:1
Warfare against malice of others, 247:6
    is accomplished, 26:24
    Italy years of w. terror murder, 781:4
    love a kind of w., 101:n10
    thy w. o'er, 373:21
War-horse, didst hurl him upon a w., 482:24
Waring, what's become of W., 461:9
Warlike, people numerous and w., 139:13
Warm, all that was w. and sentient, 582:14
    and capable of grasping, 412:1
    cheek and rising bosom, 316:10
    heart within, 327:7
    her coat is so w., 389:13
    into the w. sun, 148:11
    keeper of w. lights, 65:25
    keeps w. her note, 245:15
    let me w. it in mine, 550:14
    let out to w. air, 285:2
    man whose blood is w., 184:5
    now w. in love, 293:23
    nursing wrath to keep it w., 358:3
    precincts of cheerful day, 316:4
    so cold no fire w., 511:15
    sun was w. wind chill, 623:19
    this sensible w. motion, 206:38
    weather in bed, 284:8
    wind the west wind, 635:18
Warm-blooded animals from one filament,
    327:12
Warmed, glow has w. the world, 660:n1
    hands before fire of life, 384:4
    neither harmed nor w., 813:11
    unclasps w. jewels, 409:22
    wood stumps w. me twice, 475:13
Warmest heart recoiled at war, 701:11
    welcome at an inn, 310:n1
Warming pretty little toes, 895:3
Warms, who splits wood w. twice, 475:n1
Warmth, a little w. a little light, 519:8
    no w. no cheerfulness, 418:15
    spring brings back balmy w., 91:14
    writing about w., 752:9
Warn, all poet can do is w., 699:4
    to comfort and command, 371:8
Warned in a dream, 31:37
    prior to questioning, 692:6
    woman be w., 838:12
Warner, I am only a w., 118:4
Warning, give w. to world, 221:23
    I bring you a w., 746:5
    with no w. at all, 874:6
Warp, may w. be light of morning, 891:13

Warrant, child was his w., 834:11
    him heart-whole, 195:26
    in most cases a death w., 582:15
    she'll prove an excuse, 346:11
    truth shall be thy w., 159:9
Warrants, no w. but upon probable cause,
    340:3
Warred for Homer dead, 233:19
Warring within breasts, 168:2
Warrior, better thing exists not for w., 84:8
    every lover a w., 101:23
    Happy W. of political battlefield, 617:n4
    like an armed w., 518:2
    of North America, 400:7
    painful w. famoused for fight, 221:4
    who is the happy W., 371:20
Warrior's, in war mounts w. steed, 373:2
Warriors, defeated w. go to war first, 80:17
    female w., 299:22
    pale w. death-pale, 412:5
    stern joy w. feel, 374:3
    Time and Patience strongest of w., 506:16
    victorious w. win first go to war, 80:17
    where are Sioux w., 513:4
War's a game, 327:3
    annals cloud into night, 536:22
    disciplinary function, 542:12
    glorious art, 290:15
Wars, all skillful in the w., 268:15
    all their w. merry, 618:10
    all w. boyish fought by boys, 483:19
    always the old to lead us to w., 849:2
    and alarums unto nations, 160:23
    and rumors of wars, 35:19
    boys not sent into foreign w., 653:2
    brought nothing about, 274:25
    chronicle the w. of kites, 260:28
    conflict it's all business, 683:15
    continual w. and wives, 827:13
    disciplines of w., 189:13
    fierce w. and faithful loves, 160:2
    for right thing, 661:12
    forgotten w., 678:8
    fought by babies, 801:5
    fought by human beings, 708:14
    global from the start, 776:13
    I don't oppose all w., 876:10
    more pangs than w. or women, 225:25
    of European powers, 355:6
    of interest and intrigue, 363:4
    that make ambition virtue, 209:13
    thousand w. of old, 454:9
    want end to beginnings of w., 653:13
    won by men, 664:11
    wrong from every standpoint, 661:12
    you masters of men plan the w., 743:18
War-time, in w. truth is so precious, 621:6
Warts and all, 246:n4
    pimples w. and everything, 246:20
War-war, jaw-jaw better than to w., 621:16
Was, he is or w. or has to be, 300:6
    which w. and is and is to come, 46:28
Wash, air w. leaves cover me, 530:2
    balm from anointed king, 177:4
    bid them w. their faces, 219:27
    Death and Night w. world, 487:11
    dirty linen at home, 365:9
    feet in soda water, 676:11

Wash (*continued*)

gulfs w. us down, 451:18
makes me w., 522:9
me and I shall be whiter than snow, 16:31
this blood from my hand, 215:24
what art w. guilt away, 322:16
with Pilate w. your hands, 177:19
Washed her with wine, 820:14
if clod w. away, 231:8
Pilate w. hands, 36:15
robes in blood, 46:36
when died w. me out of turret, 774:14
Washing-day, home and being w., 277:16
Washington, America furnished W., 390:16
bequeathed name of W., 396:28
Evolution from W. to Grant, 531:22
Government at W. lives, 512:14
if you want friend in W., 512:n1
in clear upper sky, 390:5
intrepid W. reporter, 878:7
Leonidas and W., 398:26
like Joshua of old, 303:14
never slopt over, 519:4
opened his eyes on sun, 422:21
task greater than W., 445:1
was city of Northern charm, 786:3
what posterity say of W., 303:13
Washpot, Moab is my w., 17:2
WASP upper class, 777:19
Waspish, when you are w., 193:9
Wasps and hornets break through, 284:6
Wassails, Maypoles Hock-carts w., 240:9
Waste and solitary places, 402:6
don't w. time mourning, 639:5
haste maketh w., 146:11
his flames must w. away, 245:18
lay w. our powers, 371:23
mind terrible thing to w., 888:21
my dear times' w., 221:8
natural resources, 571:12
nights in discontent, 160:26
now doth time w. me, 177:23
of seas, 417:4
of shame, 222:20
peace corrupt war w., 259:26
remains and kills, 745:16
sad time, 678:11
serious crisis to go to w., 875:7
sweetness on desert air, 315:23
to what purpose this w., 35:33
Wasted, barrel of meal w. not, 11:42
chronicle of w. time, 222:9
his substance, 38:10
I have w. my life, 817:8
love is w. on the young, 769:12
most w. day of all, 334:14
no act of kindness ever w., 58:17
they that w. us, 19:11
time now doth time waste me, 177:23
Wasteful and ridiculous excess, 175:24
not have mind very w., 888:n9
youth of pleasure w., 463:12
Wasteland, teenage w., 861:17
television vast w., 813:15
Waster of rich men, 65:25
Wastes exhausts and murders itself, 330:15
her time and me, 249:24
marble w. statue grows, 142:15

Wasteth, destruction that w. at noonday, 17:28
man dieth and w. away, 13:30
Wasting, shall I w. in despair, 239:17
Watch along the Rhine, 484:25
and control government, 435:14
and pray, 36:6
care keeps his w., 180:18
cat w. mouse, 286:9
could ye not w., 36:6
Ef you don't w. out, 553:7
from their graves, 460:13
I could w. I could w., 756:3
I w. and am as a sparrow, 18:5
in the night, 17:23
it all from outside, 598:13
keeping w. above own, 481:13
keeping w. over their flock, 37:17
kept w. Matthew and Waldo, 675:11
Lord w. between thee and me, 7:1
men at play, 632:18
not one another out of fear, 228:7
o'er man's mortality, 371:5
one to w. one to pray, 265:3
secret whispers of other's w., 189:18
sleeps upon w., 323:19
some must w. some sleep, 200:23
tells time of poet, 762:21
that basket, 524:1
that ends night, 289:13
they that w. for the morning, 19:8
this long year's w., 62:27
wear learning like w., 298:10
woods fill with snow, 623:6
ye stand fast, 43:10
ye therefore, 37:3
Watchdog's honest bark, 398:3
voice, 322:25
Watched, deaths ye died w. beside, 586:16
ramparts we w., 386:19
Watcher of the skies, 408:17
Watches, dictionaries are like w., 308:8
I know He w. me., 598:4
of night, 438:1
with judgments as w., 292:8
Watchful, many a w. night, 188:20
place of w. intentness, 535:15
stubbornly opposed by w. men, 724:4
Watching, Big Brother w., 735:16
can observe a lot by w., 807:5
for riches, 31:18
pines shore and stars, 727:1
sits w. for omens, 73:8
with eternal lids apart, 412:10
Watchmaker, it is the blind w., 850:11
Watchman waketh but in vain, 19:4
what of the night, 25:28
Watchmen on the heights are crying, 162:26
Watchword, Royal Navy w., 619:11
W-a-t-e-r cool something flowing over hand, 644:5
Water, all could see was sky w. birds, 761:2
and a crust, 409:14
as showers that w. the earth, 17:12
as the hart panteth after w. brooks, 16:21
as w. flows downwards, 79:18
as w. spilt on the ground, 11:21
as w. unto wine, 452:7
as wheel runs why w. pitcher, 98:17

Water (*continued*)

benison of hot w., 669:9
best man like w., 57:3
blood is thick w. thin, 527:5
blood thicker than w., 271:4
bridge over troubled w., 855:10
brimming w. among stones, 592:15
bring w. bring wine, 60:1
buffaloes neurasthenic, 671:23
burn everything or throw into w., 144:12
burned on the w., 218:20
but the desert, 396:11
came out abundantly, 9:5
charmed w. burnt alway, 376:16
conscious w. saw its God, 263:1
dark fingers of w., 765:4
don't care where w. goes, 618:15
don't go near w., 887:17
down unseen full of w., 177:17
drawers of w., 10:2
dreadful noise of w., 171:28
drink no longer w., 44:33
drinks w. her keel plows air, 163:20
dripping w. hollows stone, 89:15
drunk your w. and wine, 586:16
dry and thirsty land where no w. is, 17:6
dry stone no w., 676:6
earth and w. strive again, 293:14
earth hath bubbles as w., 214:7
earth not w. is unstable, 694:13
etched with waves, 670:17
false as w., 203:20, 210:16
feet are always in w., 355:2
fetch pail of w., 893:18
fire and w., 187:14
give thine enemy w., 21:34
glory like circle in w., 169:13
goodness more than w. and fire, 61:22
grass grows wherever land w. is, 486:1
grind with w. that's past, 243:21
he will infallibly lead you to w., 482:19
hears thy faintest word, 263:n1
heaven as near by w., 154:n2
honest w., 213:20
I came like W., 441:19
if British went by w., 331:7
into freezing turbulent w., 874:6
is best, 63:21
is good, 57:3
is victim of man's indifference, 750:3
Just Add Hot W., 701:9
know worth of w., 302:25
land-rats and w.-rats, 184:21
land-thieves and w.-thieves, 184:21
Laughing W., 437:3
leave log in w., 889:12
like a stone, 512:6
lily bloom, 451:6
limns on w. writes in dust, 166:23
little w. in stream fault of source, 115:3
more than ocean w. broken, 623:13
more w. glideth by mill, 148:n8
much w. goeth by mill, 148:14
name writ in w., 414:1
never formed to mind, 641:8
never hold w., 287:16
never miss w. till well dry, 302:n2
no more w., 804:14

Water *(continued)*
no sound of w., 676:6
no w. only rock, 676:15
not all w. in rough rude sea, 177:4
not one lived without w., 749:17
o'er the w. to Charlie, 367:15
of affliction, 12:10, 26:12
of river never the same, 125:5
of w. fashioned every living thing, 118:20
over rocks wood and w., 420:18
people are like w., 698:12
plunge hands in w., 748:9
quarrel over w. in Arkansas River, 661:2
reflects images, 531:20
rivers of w. in a dry place, 26:15
run through fire and w., 187:14
rush to rest in air, 713:5
salt w. unbounded, 589:20
saw grass and of w., 686:12
send down w. on earth, 118:21
should make use of w., 799:11
skuttle fish blackens w., 288:16
slippy-sloppy in larder, 598:7
snake came to w. trough, 663:6
sound of w., 280:2
spring of ever-flowing w., 95:24
stagnant w. loses purity, 140:7
stained the w. clear, 350:11
steeds to w. at those springs, 220:15
stream smoothest w. deepest, 159:*n4*
street before the w. gate, 12:29
streets full of w., 683:14
struggling for life in the w., 308:17
supposes mirage to be w., 118:24
through a sieve, 516:17
through fire and through w., 17:9
tossing green w., 659:1
tree planted by rivers of w., 14:40
under w. men walk, 882:14
unstable as w., 7:19
until Desert knows W., 510:16
virtues we write in w., 226:11
wait to watch w. clear, 622:9
was made wine, 39:4
wash feet in soda w., 676:11
water everywhere, 376:3
welling from earth, 673:20
what w. lapping bow, 677:20
which they beat, 218:20
whole stay of w., 24:36
wide w. inescapable, 640:22
without a flaw, 713:5
written in running w., 91:23
Watercolors to impaint his cause, 183:23
Watercourse, patio heaven's w., 718:14
Water-drinkers, no poems by w. please for long, 98:10
Waterdrops, soul be changed to w., 169:5
women's weapons w., 211:22
worn stones of Troy, 203:20
Watered, Apollos w., 42:7
by blood of tyrants, 348:12
heaven with tears, 353:2
our horses in Helicon, 164:1
with tears w., 609:15
Waterfall, from w. named her, 437:3
nosing up to bone-crushing w., 788:5
one-woman w., 823:1

Waterfall *(continued)*
sight of the stupendous w., 559:17
Waterfront, Cover the W., 723:2
Watering, a-w. last year's crops, 480:4
pot and pruning knife, 456:17
your waters and w. place, 624:14
Waterloo, Austerlitz and W., 636:4
battle of first rank, 422:13
dismal plain, 422:9
every man meets W., 458:12
from Marathon to W., 526:6
thou fatal W., 395:16
won on playing fields, 366:14
Waterman, great-grandfather was but a w., 271:19
Water's thin, 527:5
Waters and their powers, 396:2
at their priestlike task, 412:10
beams of his chambers in w., 18:8
beautiful drifts like w., 592:2
beside the still w., 15:23
cannot quench love, 24:26
cast thy bread upon the w., 23:26
cold w. to a thirsty soul, 21:35
come ye to the w., 27:9
cover the sea, 25:19
do business in great w., 18:14
Father of W. unvexed to sea, 446:3
fen of stagnant w., 370:9
fish in troubled w., 282:15
here are your w., 624:14
hitherandthithering w., 650:22
liffeying w., 650:22
like cataract descend from jaws, 334:2
like music on w., 397:10
music crept by upon w., 224:13
nearer roll, 305:8
noise of many w., 17:31
of beginning and end, 663:21
of petrel and porpoise, 679:2
of the heart, 777:3
once more upon w., 395:10
over great sea winds trouble w., 89:20
over rolling w. go, 452:18
peopling earth w. and sky, 278:6
pour w. of Nile, 513:15
rivering w., 650:22
rushing of many w., 25:24
secret w., 709:6
set it upon w., 839:4
should lift their bosoms, 203:7
Spirit of God moved upon w., 5:3
stilled at even, 505:23
stolen w. are sweet, 20:9
take heed of still w., 159:*n4*
tree planted by the w., 27:39
turns to perilous w., 128:4
voice as sound of many w., 46:17
voice of many w., 47:4
were a wall, 8:3
were gathered together, 8:7
were his winding sheet, 233:13
woe to him who seeks to pour oil upon w., 482:22
Watersmooth-silver stallion, 701:7
Water-wagon place for me, 597:18
Watery, crown the w. glade, 315:4
envious siege of w. Neptune, 176:25

Watery *(continued)*
nest, 249:19
shore, 352:11
sunk beneath w. floor, 253:14
Watson, know my methods W., 573:16
Mr. W. come here, 550:11
Wave, all sunk beneath the w., 327:9
as w. succeeds w., 201:*n2*
blue w. rolls nightly, 397:2
cry wind cry vast waters, 679:2
dance like w. of sea, 591:14
frontier outer edge of w., 580:4
glassy cool translucent w., 252:26
lift me as w. leaf cloud, 402:12
small rock holds back great w., 52:30
star-spangled banner w., 386:19
swiftly walk o'er w., 404:7
to wash him from world, 611:14
whose arm bind restless w., 503:1
wind or swallowing w., 266:3
winning w. deserving note, 240:16
wish you a w. o' the sea, 223:29
write woman's vows upon w., 66:27
Waved, long has it w. on high, 443:3
Waver, steadiest minds to w., 65:19
Wavering between profit and loss, 677:18
discordant w. multitude, 187:21
more longing w., 204:34
Waves, amber w. of grain, 572:5
bound as steed, 395:10
breaking w. dashed, 405:4
Britannia rule the w., 301:3
cypress in palace walk, 453:5
formal as scales on fish, 670:17
here shall thy proud w. be stayed, 14:20
him that walked the w., 253:14
hopping through frothy w., 516:3
I danced on the w., 558:17
into w. pine needles, 280:1
laughter of ocean w., 63:15
make towards pebbled shore, 221:16
march o'er mountain w., 384:9
mutinous Shannon w., 650:9
of anger and fear, 748:16
of religious emotion, 672:2
of science beat in vain, 490:15
on side of ablest navigators, 332:9
over mountains over w., 882:8
pebbles which w. fling, 496:17
raging w. of the sea, 46:13
righteousness as w. of sea, 26:37
sorrow comes in great w., 544:7
sunset illumine w., 559:1
that invited her, 556:20
tired w. vainly breaking, 479:12
we lived beneath the w., 848:9
whales in w. of sea, 663:21
when w. went high, 272:16
wild w. whist, 224:12
Waves', spent w. riot, 530:15
Waving, not w. but drowning, 732:16
sails filled streamers w., 260:16
wild tail, 589:19
Wax, fill hives with honey and w., 284:5
mind a block of w., 76:7
rich gifts w. poor, 199:23
shoes ships sealing w., 516:4

Wax *(continued)*
　　snapped like sealing w., 465:15
　　to flaming youth virtue w., 201:7
Waxed, Jeshurun w. fat, 9:31
Waxworks, if we're w. you pay, 515:18
Way, abode Hour and went his w., 441:12
　　all the w. home, 893:10
　　another and truer w., 815:7
　　broad is the w., 33:19
　　catch the nearest w., 214:16
　　come all the w. for this, 520:4
　　crow shook snow, 623:5
　　decent easy w. to quit stage, 555:3
　　down upon Swanee River, 503:11
　　every day in every w., 568:8
　　every one his own w., 86:14
　　every w. makes my gain, 210:10
　　everything's going my w., 706:8
　　for woman to hold a man, 791:15
　　go not into every w., 30:21
　　God moves in mysterious w., 326:9
　　going the w. of all the earth, 10:5
　　Great White W., 579:14
　　he should go, 21:17
　　heaven's wide pathless w., 251:16
　　home's the farthest way, 242:4
　　Hungary Poland doing it their w., 849:*n*1
　　I did it my w., 849:11
　　in dark wood where straight w. lost, 128:3
　　in morning hear the W., 61:1
　　in whatsoever w. any come to Me, 84:11
　　is plain peaceful just, 446:1
　　jog on the footpath w., 223:24
　　king stood at parting of w., 28:16
　　lambs who lost w., 588:6
　　let the wicked forsake his w., 27:11
　　life's common w., 370:10
　　like wild beast guards w., 353:10
　　long and steep is the w., 54:21
　　long is the w. and hard, 256:19
　　long w. to Tipperary, 628:20
　　long wind cold, 372:20
　　longest w. round shortest home, 242:*n*2
　　love find w., 882:8
　　make it over your w., 625:10
　　merit makes his w., 225:11
　　met you not my Love by the w., 159:3
　　my w. of life is fallen, 217:18
　　narrow is the w., 33:19
　　new w. to pay old debts, 237:19
　　no ready w. to virtue, 248:13
　　no w. out for me, 688:10
　　noiseless tenor of their w., 316:3
　　not pass this w. again, 884:21
　　of a fool, 20:19
　　of a man with a maid, 22:14, 588:12
　　of a serpent upon a rock, 22:14
　　of a ship in the sea, 22:14
　　of all flesh, 237:2
　　of an eagle in the air, 22:14
　　of coming into world, 284:1
　　of God, 261:16
　　of ignorance, 678:21
　　of the tree of life, 6:2
　　of transgressors is hard, 20:21
　　old paths where is the good w., 27:28
　　out of hell leads up, 256:19
　　out of wind's and rain's w., 647:6

Way *(continued)*
　　plods his weary w., 315:11
　　prepare the w. before me, 29:19
　　prepare the w. of the Lord, 26:24, 32:5
　　primrose w., 215:25
　　rebellion lay in his w., 183:22
　　roses all the w., 460:15
　　see the W. of Heaven, 57:16
　　set out in relative w., 618:1
　　ship's w. upon sea, 588:12
　　so plain we may lose way, 618:13
　　solar walk or milky w., 294:20
　　Spring comes slowly up this w., 377:8
　　such ever love's w., 462:19
　　sweetest w. to me, 588:12
　　that can be told of, 56:12
　　that w. madness lies, 211:32
　　that's the w. it is, 781:14
　　that's the w. to do it, 392:22
　　the money goes, 885:6
　　the truth and the life, 39:42
　　there is a lion in the w., 21:38
　　they say it, 733:3
　　this is w. world ends, 677:2
　　this the w. walk ye in it, 26:13
　　thorny w. to heaven, 197:20
　　though hell bar w., 646:2
　　thoughts nature gives w. to, 215:11
　　to bliss, 242:1
　　to draw new mischief, 208:5
　　to dusty death, 217:23
　　to keep thee in the w., 8:18
　　to man's heart, 458:2
　　to tell if poem lasting, 623:12
　　took their solitary w., 259:28
　　true w. but yet untried, 164:18
　　true w. goes over rope, 655:16
　　twinkle on milky w., 371:10
　　unlikely to be undone, 692:4
　　what counts is w. writer says it, 800:7
　　win my w. to the coast, 68:3
　　wisdom finds a w., 347:9
　　with tears watered, 609:15
　　world ends, 677:2
Wayfarer there is no way, 630:11
　　world renowned, 122:6
Wayfaring, lodging place of w. men, 27:32
Way-hay you rolling river, 897:19
Ways, amend your w., 27:29
　　blood nipped and w. be foul, 174:33
　　consider her w. and be wise, 19:32
　　dazzled by w. of God, 639:10
　　dwelt among untrodden w., 369:7
　　from cheerful w. of men, 257:6
　　God's w. to man, 575:12
　　her w. are w. of pleasantness, 19:26
　　his w. are judgment, 9:30
　　I will take heed to my w., 16:15
　　in all the w. you can, 301:19
　　in His w. found Him not, 455:17
　　just are the w. of God, 260:13
　　keep thee in all thy w., 17:29
　　labyrinthine w., 576:13
　　lots worse w. to die, 633:6
　　many w. meet in one town, 188:36
　　nine and sixty w., 588:11
　　of God justifiable, 260:13
　　of God to man, 294:15

Ways *(continued)*
　　of God to men, 255:5
　　oldest sins newest w., 188:24
　　possible to fail in many w., 78:7
　　practice childish w., 52:24
　　sing ancient w., 591:1
　　stand ye in the w., 27:28
　　that are dark, 528:10
　　to lengthen our days, 387:13
　　to make thy w. known, 48:14
　　triple w. to take, 588:12
　　your w. are not my w., 27:12
Wayside, seeds fell by w., 34:14
Wayward, clod of w. marl, 190:23
　　fond and w. thoughts, 369:6
　　fortune's w. tyranny, 65:4
　　purblind w. boy, 174:14
　　sisters depart, 394:2
　　terchy and w. thy infancy, 171:37
Wayworn, weary w. wanderer, 447:12
We about to die salute you, 111:1
　　are all Americans, 866:3
　　are Ancients of the earth, 164:*n*5
　　are as much as we see, 472:19
　　are his offspring, 40:34, 82:11
　　are his people, 18:3
　　are many, 36:31
　　are not amused, 485:5
　　are the hollow men, 676:19
　　are the world, 875:5
　　be brethren, 6:28
　　gather together, 882:4
　　happy few, 190:1
　　must needs die, 11:21
　　my ship and I, 731:13
　　real cool, 783:10
　　shall not be moved, 899:4
　　shall overcome, 888:15
　　that had loved him so, 460:12
　　the peoples of United Nations, 661:16
　　thought we would try, 731:13
　　were very tired, 695:9
　　would and would not, 207:13
Weak and beggarly elements, 43:27
　　and fruitless words, 446:12
　　and little is the light, 636:20
　　creatures of clay, 73:5
　　devouring w. by strong, 490:6
　　evils age and hunger, 194:24
　　fear to appear w., 270:15
　　flesh is w., 36:6
　　God hath chosen w., 42:5
　　infirmities of w., 42:4
　　men not changing mind, 626:16
　　my spirit too w., 411:16
　　not w. if we use means, 331:12
　　piping time of peace, 171:19
　　pondered w. and weary, 449:3
　　poor infirm w. old man, 211:26
　　refuge of w. minds, 298:13
　　shoulderings aside of w., 490:2
　　speak for fallen and w., 481:9
　　spirit quickens to rebel, 677:19
　　success to the w., 328:4
　　suffer what they must, 72:7
　　surely w. perish, 627:11
　　to be w. is miserable, 255:11
　　too w. to be a sinner, 213:20

Weary *(continued)*
  with disasters, 216:8
  world w. of past, 403:9
Weasel, as w. sucks eggs, 194:12
  methinks it is like a w., 200:26
  pop goes the w., 885:6
  tendency to use w. words, 572:1
Weasels fighting in a hole, 594:7
Weather, always fair w., 585:6
  born with anxiety about w., 528:14
  clear w. spreads cloudless, 53:2
  cloudy was the w., 897:1
  come wind come w., 271:26
  don't need a w. man, 851:15
  everybody talks about w., 525:11
  fair w. cometh out of the north, 14:16
  grumble about w., 525:n1
  if it prove fair w., 261:8
  in w. the Butterfly Effect, 872:5
  inner w., 623:15
  it will be fair w., 34:34
  like marble sculpture in the w., 624:12
  many can brook the w., 174:16
  mighty good w., 523:2
  mine with inner w., 623:15
  New England w., 522:10
  sad or singing w., 530:11
  shepherd shuns, 537:2
  stormy w., 703:3
  this w. for to slepen inne, 132:16
  tigers in red w., 640:19
  trying to get behind w., 567:12
  under oak in stormy w., 285:13
  waiting for w. to break, 828:4
  warm w. in bed, 284:8
  weary of wench guest w. rainy, 302:2
  winter and rough w., 194:11
  won't hold up the w., 751:2
Weather-beaten, all things stand with w. face, 240:3
Weatherby George Dupree, 651:6
Weathercock, unseen as w. on steeple, 173:30
Weathered, love w. storms of life, 576:8
  pilot that w. storm, 367:4
  ship w. every rack, 487:16
Weathervanes creak, 367:17
Weatherwise, some w. some otherwise, 302:14
Weave, Borges can w. literature, 719:6
  circle round him thrice, 377:23
  flitter dip and soar, 797:14
  garment of brightness, 891:13
  nets to catch wind, 237:11
  old England's winding sheet, 354:6
  sunlight in your hair, 675:13
  tangled web we w., 373:15
  their thread with bones, 205:2
Weaver's, swifter than w. shuttle, 13:16
Weaving sand, 429:7
Web, left the w. left the loom, 451:6
  of our life, 206:5
  of sunny air, 472:7
  out flew the w., 451:6
  subtle spider in w., 155:n1
  tangled w. we weave, 373:15
Web's, spider in w. center, 154:12
Webs from entrails spin, 155:n1
  laws are like spiders' w., 56:2
  trafficked for strange w., 534:5

Webster, Daniel W. steam engine, 375:4
  much possessed by death, 675:25
  word liberty in mouth of W., 425:16
Wed, December when they w., 195:29
  fair Ellen, 373:11
  love star and think to w. it, 205:31
  with this ring I thee w., 49:17
  wooed in haste w. at leisure, 173:16
Wedded, hail w. love, 258:5
  maid virgin mother, 250:9
  man assaille wyves pacience, 135:23
  medication and water w., 482:19
Wedding, chose wife as she her w. gown, 322:7
  dance barefoot on w. day, 173:12
  day after w. night, 616:5
  day fixed, 305:1
  Guest stood still, 375:19
  is destiny, 146:19
  O W. Guest, 377:4
  saw a w. in the church, 277:14
Wedding-cake, mind moldering like w., 824:15
Weddings of the soul, 641:14
Wede, flowers of the forest a' w. away, 321:8
Wedge, hard like tip of w., 662:14
  planes no bigger than w. of geese, 724:6
  thrust into nature like w., 474:2
  tough w. for tough log, 100:31
Wedlock compared to public feasts, 153:n3
  forced a hell, 169:22
Wedlock-treachery, 260:20
Wednesday, he that died o' W., 183:25
  married on W., 895:10
Wednesday's child, 895:9
Weds, old man w. tyrant, 68:21
Wee modest crimson-tipped flower, 356:17
  sleekit cow'rin beastie, 356:4
  sweet w. wife o' mine, 358:11
  wee wee, 893:10
  Willie Winkie, 457:4
  winsome w. thing, 358:11
Weed, anger is a w., 116:13
  duller than fat w., 198:7
  ill w. groweth fast, 147:20
  ill w. grows apace, 147:n7
  in wild w. a citizen, 783:13
  law ought to w. it out, 165:14
  O thou w., 210:5
  sworn to w. and pluck away, 176:32
  that grows in every soil, 324:11
  what is a w., 429:4
  wide to wrap a fairy, 178:19
Weeded and worn the ancient thatch, 450:7
Weeds and foam, 424:3
  are shallow-rooted, 170:5
  garden full of w., 892:7
  great w. grow apace, 147:n7
  in wheels shoot long and lovely, 546:8
  long live w. and wildness, 546:19
  of Athens he doth wear, 178:23
  of mine own brain, 248:9
  oozy w. about me twist, 484:4
  sleep beneath these w., 605:8
  smell far worse than w., 222:3
  subterranean w., 755:16
  winter w. outworn, 403:8
Week, argument for a w., 182:11
  he was my working w., 748:14
  is a long time in politics, 783:3

Week *(continued)*
  longer in hour than w., 529:5
  not divide Sunday from w., 196:13
  rare and bloodless w. of repose, 73:n2
  Thursday come and w. gone, 244:12
  who buys mirth to wail a w., 172:32
Weekends, try getting plumber on w., 839:11
Weeks, desolate dark w., 659:3
  his brief hours and w., 222:15
  to months, 455:16
Weel done Cutty Sark, 358:10
Weep a people inurned, 419:n4
  and you weep alone, 556:16
  at joy, 190:12
  away life of care, 401:14
  but never see, 383:26
  deed whereat valor will w., 220:7
  do not w. it's chronic, 464:35
  do not w. maiden, 609:2
  for Adonais, 403:12
  for her sins at the other, 674:2
  for what could make them glad, 624:13
  for you the Walrus said, 516:7
  he made them w., 285:5
  heart break ere I'll w., 211:23
  I do not w. at world, 689:16
  if she saugh mous kaught, 133:15
  if you wish me to w., 98:21
  in durance vile I w., 359:2
  laugh that I may not w., 398:20
  lie in dark w. for sins, 486:14
  like a child, 662:15
  like love often w., 749:9
  make the angels w., 206:28
  men that laugh and w., 530:16
  men work women w., 481:5
  milk my ewes and w., 223:33
  no more my lady, 503:13
  no more nor sigh, 236:7
  quanch heart to not w., 682:12
  stricken deer go w., 200:23
  strive nor w., 460:23
  tears such as angels w., 256:1
  time to w., 22:31
  to record, 314:n2
  to see you haste away so soon, 241:5
  to w. is to make less depth, 170:20
  vapors w. their burthen, 455:5
  what's Hecuba that he should w., 199:16
  you are Emperor yet w., 278:18
'Weep, scarcely cry 'w., 351:2
Weeper, calm the w., 3:8
Weepeth, goeth forth and w., 19:3
  sore in the night, 28:10
Weeping anarchic Aphrodite, 749:7
  and gnashing of teeth, 33:26
  and the laughter, 599:17
  do ye hear children w., 434:12
  dwell a w. hermit there, 317:11
  full cause of w., 211:23
  handkerchief washed clean by w., 812:14
  in my heart, 549:18
  joy at w., 190:12
  may endure for a night, 16:1
  nor celebrate funeral with w., 84:17
  philosopher when old, 184:17
  Rachel w. for her children, 32:2
  upon his bed has sate, 342:14

Weeping *(continued)*
wipe my w. eyes, 289:16
with him rises w., 223:26
without cease, 549:19
Weeps incessantly for my sin, 353:10
Weft, may w. be red light of evening,
891:13
Weib, was will das W., 564:*n*3
Wein W. und Gesang, 346:*n*1
Weigh eyelids down, 188:9
let us not w. them, 226:20
things w. me down, 595:15
Weighed in the balances, 28:25
me Dust by Dust, 511:8
measured priced everything, 466:17
thirty pieces of silver, 29:16
Weighing delight and dole, 196:22
Weighs, mortality w. like sleep, 411:16
stuff which w. upon heart, 217:19
truth with gold she w., 296:25
Weight and pain of life, 66:20
bear w. of Antony, 218:11
force without wisdom falls of own w.,
96:28
heaviest w. of all to bear, 512:9
I have tried to remove w., 801:11
of another's burthen, 244:21
of centuries, 557:3
of chance desires, 371:16
of learning, 454:11
of this sad time, 213:16
of unintelligible world, 368:8
pull his w., 571:6
Weights, equal rate with unequal w., 90:5
lift artificial w. from shoulders, 445:9
Wein Weib und Gesang, 346:*n*1
Weir, woodland of W., 449:15
Weird power in spoken word, 567:7
sisters hand in hand, 214:3
when the going gets w., 843:16
wild w. clime, 449:1
Weirs, grass grows on w., 590:22
Weiss, ich w. nicht, 415:*n*1
Welcome, advice is seldom w., 298:8
all wonders, 263:13
be thou faire fresshe May, 134:14
chanted chant of fullest w., 487:15
come as w. surprise, 98:1
coming guest, 293:19
deep-mouthed w., 398:3
dog first to w., 394:10
each rebuff, 462:15
ever smiles, 203:24
great w. makes merry feast, 172:19
home discarded faith, 176:1
kindred glooms, 300:15
love bade me w., 243:11
make w. the present guest, 53:22
marriage an evil most men w., 81:*n*8
O life, 650:13
pack clouds away and w. day, 233:18
peaceful evening in, 327:1
say W. friend, 263:5
such truth to all men w., 239:13
to your gory bed, 358:16
warmest w. at an inn, 310:*n*1
Welcomes, consciousness w. object, 541:2
little fishes in, 513:15

Welcomest, unbidden guests w. when gone,
169:14
Welded, ice and iron not w., 556:10
Welfare, indifferent to public w., 341:5
promote general w., 339:11
public w., 571:15
sets friendship above public w., 65:12
Welkin, hark how w. rings, 305:*n*4
let the w. roar, 188:7
Well, all is not w., 197:17
all shall be w. all manner of thing w.,
131:14
all w. that ends w., 147:16
all's w. that ends w., 206:7
bed-time Hal and all w., 183:24
begun is half done, 78:30
bucket which hung in w., 393:13
cannot wish w. love w. sleep w., 654:15
Chaucer w. of English, 160:16
content to entertain lag-end of my life,
183:21
do w. what not worth doing, 810:10
done and fitting for a princess, 219:18
done Cutty Sark, 358:10
done good and faithful servant, 35:26
done is quickly done, 99:5
don't speak w. of self, 269:7
every day the bucket go a w., 861:5
foolish thing w. done, 309:22
for fisherman's boy, 452:15
golden crown like a deep w., 177:17
good deed to say w., 225:21
hope all will yet be w., 445:1
I feel happy all is w., 680:12
it were done quickly, 214:22
kingdom of w., 835:19
kiss place to make w., 389:11
learn to do w., 24:32
loved not wisely but too w., 210:20
mania for saying things are w., 299:10
moments when everything goes w., 585:13
not so deep as a w., 180:28
paid that is satisfied, 186:13
poetry must be w. written as prose,
664:16
preaches w. that lives w., 157:23
pussy's in w., 893:21
roared Lion, 179:13
servant of God w. done, 258:23
sing so wildly w., 448:1
spent but one day thoroughly w., 137:9
till the w. runs dry, 302:*n*2
to do w. is what matters, 247:2
truth is at bottom of a w., 797:7
worth doing is worth doing w., 298:2
Well-a-day, youth cry W., 889:25
Well-behaved women, 844:13
Well-being dependent on well-being of others,
653:12
instructions for, 4:13
Well-beloved, my w. hath a vineyard, 25:3
Well-benched, board the w. ships, 55:18
Wellborn, few are rich and w., 349:4
Well-bred man knows how to confess,
302:20
very strange and w., 287:5
Well-chosen anthology, 706:4
book or friend, 227:10

Well-conducted, like a w. person, 459:14
Well-doing, be not weary in w., 43:34
religion of w. and daring, 309:*n*1
Well-drawn, find w. character, 522:18
Well-dressed, sense of being perfectly w.,
428:27
Well-educated young women, 382:9
Well-favored man, 190:41
Well-fed, not these w. men I fear, 89:8
Well-filled, well-made rather than w. head,
152:7
Well-graced actor leaves, 177:21
Well-greaved Achaeans, 51:2
Well-housed well-warmed well-fed, 483:14
Wellington's army, 319:*n*1
Well-knownness, celebrity person known for
w., 773:22
Well-made rather than well-filled head, 152:7
Well-read, writer to show he is w., 570:1
Well's, when the w. dry, 302:25
Wells, buckets into empty w., 326:23, 375:1
Well-spent, rare as w. life, 407:11
Well-trod stage, 251:8
Well-wishing adventurer, 220:*n*2
Well-written life rare, 407:11
Well-wrought urn becomes greatest ashes,
228:20
Welsh, hear lady sing in W., 183:1
Welshman, Taffy was a W., 894:1
Welt, die W. ist alles was der Fall ist, 685:*n*1
Weltering in his blood, 274:18
Weltgeschichte ist das Weltgericht, 359:*n*3
Weltschmerz, 361:10
Wenceslas, good King W., 479:1
Wench, besides the w. is dead, 168:11
fair hot w. in taffeta, 181:20
one w. in the house, 238:*n*1
weary of w. guest weather, 302:2
Wenlock, tarnish late on W. Edge, 575:5
Went, as cooks go she w., 608:4
in jeopardy of their lives, 11:25
Lord w. before them, 8:2
ne'er w. up again, 892:14
same door wherein I w., 441:18
to bed with stockings on, 896:1
to woods to live deliberately, 474:29
Wept as I remembered, 499:9
he w. to hear, 350:10
I w. and I believed, 364:10
I w. for I longed to see him hanged, 606:14
Jesus w., 39:34
like anything to see, 516:1
my father w., 353:6
Peter w. bitterly, 36:11
remembering he w. bitterly, 52:17
that he was born, 605:20
when the poor cried Caesar w., 192:30
when we remembered Zion, 19:11
young man who has not w., 584:14
Were, Euripides drew men as they w., 65:*n*1
now you are not as you w., 536:18
Werewolf's painful change, 798:1
Wernher, not my department says W. von
Braun, 819:10
West, at the wild wild w., 878:6
begins where rainfall drops, 713:8
bosom of urgent W., 545:12
Cincinnatus of W., 396:28

Where *(continued)*
not how many but w. they are, 70:1
was Roderick then, 374:4
wast thou when I laid the foundations, 14:18
we are is hell, 168:19
who are we w. are we, 473:12
your treasure is, 33:2
Whereabout, stones prate of my w., 215:15
Whereas I was blind, 39:28
Where'er she lie, 263:4
you walk, 292:6
Wherefore are these things hid, 204:16
art thou Romeo, 180:2
causes why and w., 190:3
every why hath a w., 172:16
stopp'st thou me, 375:17
Wherein lies happiness, 409:9
Where's my serpent of old Nile, 218:13
rest of me, 736:1
Wheresoever called to make exit, 341:10
Wherever, home w. that may be, 762:18
I am, 839:1
there's a cottage small, 775:11
they burn books, 415:3
you may be, 798:8
Whether he hears my song or not, 817:7
Whetstone of wits, 193:25
Whetted, wind's like w. knife, 635:17
Whey, curds and w., 895:14
Which, at odds with morning w. is w., 216:24
God only knows w. is w., 531:2
is the justice, 212:29
of us has known brother, 727:11
that and w., 570:2
who why w. what, 467:14
Whiff of grapeshot, 407:4
Whiffling through tulgey wood, 515:13
Whiggery, what is W., 595:6
Whigs, caught the W. bathing, 430:6
While there's life there's hope, 86:5, 87:22
Whilst planet has gone cycling on, 440:5
Whim envy or resentment, 326:5
Whimper, not bang but w., 677:2
Whine, sweat and w. about condition, 486:14
Whining at threshold, 578:19
born naked and falls a-w., 105:*n*1
of a door, 231:11
poetry, 228:21
school-boy with satchel, 194:25
wimpled w. purblind, 174:14
Whip all hell yet, 489:*n*5
in every honest hand a w., 210:6
so small you could not see, 510:17
Whipped for overdoing Termagant, 200:6
he must be w. out, 211:7
her little daughter, 895:3
offending Adam, 188:31
she w. him, 896:16
them all soundly, 894:8
Whipping and abuse like laudanum, 458:15
future smells of w., 415:8
who should 'scape w., 199:14
Whippoorwill, hear that lonesome w., 804:1
Whips and scorns of time, 199:21
and scorpions, 341:6
my father chastised you with w., 11:37

Whipstock, first Packard had w. on dashboard, 694:10
Whirl asunder and dismember me, 175:15
lay mightily in w. of dust, 52:3
Whirled in an arch, 451:7
unstilled world w., 677:17
Whirligig of time, 205:28
Whirling summer, 737:8
Whirls, expectation w. me round, 203:15
Northern ocean in vast w., 301:1
Whirlwind, Elijah went up by a w., 12:11
home in your manes, 443:1
Lord answered Job out of the w., 14:17
of passion, 200:6
reap the w., 28:36
Whirlwind's, sweeping w. sway, 316:15
Whirlwinds in the south, 25:26
Whiskers, oh my fur and w., 514:2
Whiskey and Rye, 861:11
for my Johnny, 897:15
gimme a w. ginger ale on side, 681:2
must have w. you know why, 716:10
on your breath, 755:15
prayers in hall w. afterwards, 647:3
Whisper, breathed the husky w., 556:14
far-heard w. o'er the sea, 376:9
not a w. be lost, 748:11
Whispered, Devil w. behind leaves, 588:4
in sounds of silence, 855:7
into your brain, 864:12
voice behind me w. low, 561:2
Whispereth, soul w. within him, 119:12
Whispering ambitions, 675:22
bayed the w. wind, 322:25
from Oxford towers, 496:8
humbleness, 184:29
I will ne'er consent, 398:2
maid and wight w. by, 536:22
music of yonder pine, 82:12
tongues can poison truth, 377:13
Whisperings, keeps eternal w., 412:6
Whispers, Duty w. low, 424:21
listen to w. of fancy, 307:8
o'er-fraught heart, 217:7
of each other's watch, 189:18
what good author w., 590:14
Whist, wild waves w., 224:12
Whistle and I'll come to you, 357:16
and she'll come to you, 238:7
blackbird 'tis to w., 262:1
don't you hear w. blowing, 884:22
go w. for the rest, 156:10
hir joly w. wel ywet, 135:3
I love to w., 724:2
I'd w. her off, 209:7
let it w. as it will, 373:13
maybe just w., 680:1
pay too much for w., 303:12
quail w. about us, 640:22
train w. taught me to cry, 733:9
Whistles far and wee, 701:5
pipes and w. in his sound, 194:25
thrice, 376:8
Whistling, blackbird w. or just after, 641:7
to bear courage up, 274:*n*2
to keep from being afraid, 274:10
White, a moment w., 358:6
and drifted snow, 421:17

White *(continued)*
as angel English child, 350:14
as driven snow, 223:30
as leprosy, 376:7
as long as colored man look to w. folks, 862:3
beard decreasing leg, 187:31
beautiful when it helps, 798:6
beauty whose red and w., 204:20
black and w. separate as fingers, 566:3
Black Hawk fought against w. men, 363:13
black where I read w., 354:16
bosoms of actresses, 308:14
bread and butter, 893:14
candle in holy place, 647:5
chickens, 658:14
Citizen's Counciler, 823:3
cliffs of Dover, 627:4
clothed in w. samite, 138:4, 455:8
colored people understand w. people, 610:1
consternation throughout w. race, 839:22
crimson petal now w., 453:5
dreaming of w. Christmas, 673:12
end of fight tombstone w., 587:11
fever of temptation, 688:7
fleece w. but 'tis too cold, 160:*n*6
foam flew, 376:1
fought against w. domination, 790:18
get up so w. person could sit, 771:16
Goddess, 706:5
Godiva I unpeel, 833:10
Great W. Way, 579:14
hair become very w., 514:4
happens to be a w. man, 808:13
hate in w. men, 809:1
how ill w. hairs become fool, 188:27
humiliation by w. man, 802:6
I appeal to any w. man, 320:6
if snow be w., 223:1
I'm ashamed of being w., 731:12
if you w. should be all right, 716:17
in subjection to w. Saxon man, 471:6
in w. black and green, 882:14
is their color, 243:8
little missionary stew, 677:3
made w. in blood, 46:36
majority of w. people want, 808:3
man warmed before Indians' fire, 325:20
man will never be alone, 394:3
Man's burden, 589:12
moderate devoted to order, 823:3
not neutralize black, 463:6
O my soul is w., 350:14
o'er his w. banes, 890:6
officers cast lot, 519:10
one w. foot try him, 886:5
or colored signs, 786:12
parsons preaching Jesus, 802:7
prisoner to w. man, 363:12
radiance of eternity, 404:2
radiance stretches above it, 53:2
raiment w. as snow, 36:22
really hope no w. person, 856:9
red thoughts teeth w., 608:7
relation between w. and colored people, 477:5
roses and w. lilies grow, 227:3

Wicked *(continued)*
    war regarded as w., 559:22
    wealth even to a w. man, 59:20
    wickedness proceedeth from the w., 11:5
    Witch of the East, 562:2
    work your w. will, 620:9
Wickedness appeared perfectly ineffable, 301:10
    did sell himself to work w., 12:8
    dwell in the tents of w., 17:20
    far be it from God that he should do w., 14:14
    flower of w., 463:5
    Hitler monster of w., 620:8
    manifold sins and w., 48:1, 49:5
    men capable of every w., 568:3
    method in man's w., 238:4
    my beautiful w., 764:9
    never have a chance, 60:21
    of a woman, 31:11
    or folly, 445:7
    plowed w. reaped iniquity, 28:37
    proceedeth from the wicked, 11:5
    spiritual w. in high places, 43:40
    though w. be sweet, 13:41
    turn from w. and live, 48:5
Wicket, flanneled fools at w., 589:15
Wicklow, chink in floor of W. house, 611:13
Widder eats by bell, 522:9
Widders, be wery careful o' w., 463:24
Wide and starry sky, 555:16
    arch of ranged empire fall, 218:3
    capable and w. revenge, 209:20
    dark world and w., 254:20
    enough to wrap a fairy, 178:19
    gates of dark Death stand w., 94:27
    great and w. sea, 18:11
    is the gate, 33:19
    no wider than heart w., 695:6
    nor so w. as church door, 180:28
    shallow brooks and rivers w., 251:3
    though its meshes are w., 58:3
    too w. for shrunk shank, 194:25
    water inescapable, 640:22
    wide sea, 376:14
    womb of uncreated night, 256:12
    world dreaming on things to come, 222:10
    world w. enough to hold both, 314:6
Widely, doors are w. flung, 755:10
Widened, thoughts of men w., 452:5
Widening, ever w. slowly silence, 455:12
    turning in w. gyre, 593:9
Wider and permanent system, 653:16
    no w. than heart wide, 695:6
    seek no w. war, 753:14
    still and wider, 580:19
Wide-sounding Zeus, 51:27, 54:1
Wide-watered shore, 251:17
Wide-waving wings, 327:11
Widow, a certain poor w., 37:2
    at Windsor, 587:20
    Black W. death, 787:4
    care for w. and orphan, 447:2
    do not oppress w., 3:8
    eats by bell, 522:9
    here's to the w. of fifty, 346:11
    how is she become as a w., 28:9
    maid w. nor wife, 207:16

Widow *(continued)*
    maid w. or wife, 141:1
    Molly Stark a w., 323:11
Widower, unconsoled w., 439:6
Widow's, caused the w. heart to sing, 14:6
Widows, be wery careful o' w., 463:24
    most perverse creatures, 288:14
    when w. against second marriages, 305:1
Widows', devour w. houses, 37:1
    nor w. sighs nor orphans' tears, 285:5
Wie es eigentlich gewesen ist, 414:*n*2
Wife, all world and his w., 286:11
    and children are impediments, 165:19
    and children part of Self, 541:4
    and children stand afraid, 248:10
    argued each case with w., 514:5
    be your w. gladly, 468:1
    by degrees dwindle into a w., 287:6
    Caesar's w. must be above suspicion, 88:*n*14
    cleave unto his w., 5:17
    contentions of a w., 21:7
    contract of w. and her works, 781:16
    covet thy neighbor's w., 8:14
    damned in a fair w., 207:21
    debauch friend's w. genteelly, 310:2
    devil having trouble with w., 564:11
    don't be gentle to your w., 53:16
    eat no lean, 892:15
    eneugh for a' that, 358:21
    first you are w. and mother, 504:10
    gardener Adam and w., 451:2
    giving honor unto the w., 45:41
    had seven sacks, 892:22
    had w. couldn't keep her, 895:15
    here lies my w., 275:1
    his mother his w. or himself, 382:24
    husband and w. keep household in oneness, 53:3
    husband frae w. despises, 358:4
    I'd have no w., 263:6
    if ever man loved by w., 261:15
    if ever w. happy in man, 261:15
    in mountains of Hagai, 121:26
    kill w. with kindness, 173:20
    letter from his w., 517:8
    light w. make heavy husband, 186:21
    little w. well willed, 302:8
    Lot's w. looked back, 6:34
    maid widow or w., 141:1
    matched with aged w., 451:11
    medicine my lawful w., 578:1
    must be in want of w., 382:3
    my child-w., 466:4
    my 'oss my w. my name, 429:13
    my w. hath something in her gizzard, 277:24
    my w. is my plague, 55:6
    my w. poor wretch, 277:8
    neighed after his neighbor's w., 27:24
    neither maid widow nor w., 207:16
    no casual mistress but w., 454:2
    no man worth having true to w., 283:17
    of thy bosom, 9:22
    old w. old dog ready money, 302:17
    pixy w., 631:11
    Potiphar's w., 7:8
    ran after farmer's w., 892:10

Wife *(continued)*
    remember Lot's w., 38:21
    ruled roast, 391:11
    sailor's w. had chestnuts, 213:33
    says to w. Fie upon quiet life, 182:17
    second w. hateful to children, 67:4
    she ain't no lady she's my w., 601:6
    smiles and lets it go at that, 577:14
    so act toward children so toward w., 109:6
    son till he gets w., 503:7
    suburban w., 796:7
    sweet wee w. o' mine, 358:11
    sympathetic w. best possession, 68:19
    take my w. please, 748:3
    take w. or cowl, 155:*n*10
    tell w. all he knows, 250:2
    Thane of Fife had a w., 217:13
    true and honorable w., 192:8
    uncumbered with a w., 274:23
    understanding w., 237:12
    weds tyrant not w., 68:21
    whoso findeth a w., 21:4
    wished w. not so much as suspected, 88:24
    without e'er a w., 893:14
    worse shod than shoemaker's w., 147:32
Wig, Fritter my w., 517:1
Wight, blesse hous from wikked w., 134:25
    maid and her w., 536:22
Wights, descriptions of fairest w., 222:9
Wigwam of Nokomis, 437:2
Wilbur, best place thought W., 724:7
Wild, air w. with leaves, 666:2
    anarchy of drink, 233:7
    and fair, 374:6
    Ass stamps o'er his Head, 441:13
    at the w. w. west, 878:6
    bank whereon w. thyme blows, 178:19
    bore me in southern w., 350:14
    born to be w., 856:4
    by starts 'twas w., 317:14
    Caledonia stern and w., 373:4
    call and clear call, 635:16
    cataract leaps, 452:19
    civility, 240:16
    country available to us, 760:8
    creatures wild places natural resources, 796:14
    dark times rumbling toward us, 415:7
    Decembers, 476:11
    ducks plunging to bottom, 504:19
    echoes flying, 452:19
    ecstasy, 410:14
    for to hold though I seem tame, 149:5
    geese spread gray wing, 592:10
    grew more fierce and w., 243:2
    harp slung behind him, 387:12
    heaven in w. flower, 353:14
    her eyes were w., 412:3
    home of w. mirth, 430:25
    I'm w. again, 707:6
    in woods noble savage ran, 272:9
    it was the winter w., 250:10
    Jack for a lover, 595:18
    lament, 737:8
    let the w. rumpus start, 820:7
    like w. beast guards way, 353:10
    locusts and w. honey, 32:6
    native wood-notes w., 251:8

Wisdom *(continued)*

    to relieve suffering, 125:2
    unerring w. never below, 278:5
    use blessings with w., 97:15
    vain w. all, 256:22
    was mine, 699:9
    what is w., 68:12
    where shall w. be found, 14:2
    where w. neither fear nor ignorance, 125:11
    where w. we have lost in knowledge, 679:14
    whose w. brings him to power, 61:21
    wise man not glory in w., 27:33
    wit and w. born with man, 238:13
    with how little w. world governed, 238:*n*4
    with the ancient is w., 13:26
    without unmanliness, 71:15
    wrath of lion w. of God, 351:14
Wisdom's self oft seeks, 252:17
    threadbare saint in w. school, 228:3
Wise, a little too w. ne'er live long, 171:*n*1
    and beautiful, 494:11
    and frugal government, 337:11
    and masterly inactivity, 362:4
    and moral man, 64:19
    and salutary neglect, 324:3
    and the lovely, 695:17
    and understanding heart, 11:26
    and wonderful, 476:4
    answers make us w., 790:16
    arrows which speak to the w., 63:25
    art of being w., 541:8
    be w. as serpents, 34:1
    be w. today, 290:21
    be w. with speed, 290:14
    beacon of the w., 203:12
    better is a poor and w. child, 23:3
    both true both w., 265:8
    by nature w., 237:12
    consider her ways and be w., 19:32
    consider w. what they cleave to, 112:4
    cunning men pass for w., 166:3
    dare to be w., 97:21
    darkly w., 295:1
    enough to play fool, 205:11
    every w. man's son know, 204:25
    exceeding w. fair-spoken, 226:12
    father that knows child, 184:37
    folly to be w., 315:8
    fool counted w., 20:43
    fool doth think he is w., 195:34
    foolery w. men have, 193:26
    foolish things to confound w., 42:5
    full of w. saws, 194:25
    good to be merry and w., 146:12
    great men are not always w., 14:11
    gude to be merry and w., 884:12
    guid to be merry and w., 359:3
    he that kan hymselven knowe, 136:13
    he was wondrous w., 897:6
    healthy wealthy w., 302:12
    hear the words of the w., 21:19
    heard w. man say, 574:14
    heart of the w., 23:10
    histories make men w., 166:19
    holy fair and w. is she, 173:34
    honest and w. men rule, 330:12

Wise *(continued)*

    how dieth the w. man, 22:30
    if w. gets rich, 600:14
    in his own conceit, 21:38
    in old age learn to be w., 66:1
    in your own conceits, 41:33
    learn from enemies, 73:3
    like w. one died, 158:14
    love and be w., 99:17
    man is strong, 21:31
    man knows himself fool, 195:34
    man not glory in wisdom, 27:33
    man not leave right to chance, 473:15
    man seeks to minimize risks, 562:11
    man utter vain knowledge, 13:32
    men fish here, 682:8
    men from the East, 31:36
    men in great struggle, 331:10
    men know art of eating, 348:14
    men of Gotham, 893:17
    men profit more from fools, 85:4
    men refrain to meddle, 143:5
    men shun mistakes of fools, 85:4
    men speak fools decide, 56:3
    more fools than w., 882:2
    more w. master simpler work, 127:11
    neither yet bread to w., 23:23
    no man w. by himself, 84:1
    none is born w., 3:3
    nor ever did a w. one, 280:27
    nor w. at fifty, 244:5
    not even God is w. enough, 889:11
    not w. who buffet against love, 66:10
    not worldly w., 242:2
    old and crafty and w., 591:7
    on exercise depend, 274:24
    passiveness, 368:4
    pause from learning to be w., 306:16
    penny w. pound foolish, 234:11
    powers deny us for our good, 218:17
    prosperity tries souls even of w., 92:6
    rebuke a w. man, 20:8
    reputed w. for saying nothing, 184:8
    Roland valorous Oliver w., 124:3
    saying w. and old, 160:*n*6
    so w. so young, 171:32
    son maketh a glad father, 20:10
    spirits of w. mock us, 188:5
    steals mind even of the w., 51:29
    takes w. man to recognize w. man, 60:7
    taketh the w. in craftiness, 13:12
    thrush, 460:19
    to be w. and love, 203:19
    to listen to the Word, 62:1
    to w. man are ports and havens, 176:16
    virgins, 35:25
    want love, 401:16
    wealthy, 74:3
    were their subjects w., 327:3
    when he had pen in hand, 311:3
    who are a little w., 229:1
    who can be w. amazed, 216:1
    who knows others is w., 57:11
    who tries everything before arms, 86:10
    wine sets w. man singing, 53:21
    wish to appear w. among fools, 106:4
    without folly not so w., 264:11
    woman never yields, 392:1

Wise *(continued)*

    word to w. enough, 158:3, 302:32
    words are w. men's counters, 239:5
    words of the w. are as goads, 24:1
    words taught in numbers, 160:25
    wretch, 293:27
Wisely and slow, 180:19
    charming never so w., 16:39
    faire and softe, 132:23
    he who lives w. to himself, 386:5
    live pleasurably without living w., 81:16
    loved not w. but too well, 210:20
    worldly, 242:2
Wiser, four things w. to know, 699:10
    learn but not w. grow, 283:20
    no w. than a daw, 169:15
    no w. than before, 344:1
    sadder and w. man, 377:7
    scientist w. not to withhold, 343:25
    than children of light, 38:15
    than our ordinary selves, 497:15
    tygers of wrath w., 351:17
    without books, 327:5
    women w. than men, 654:1
Wisest, days to come are w. witnesses, 63:22
    fool in Christendom, 161:14
    of counselors Time, 64:23
    of mankind enjoy life, 590:11
    prophets make sure, 317:6
    rivalship of w. men, 288:23
    seeming truth to entrap w., 185:20
    silence w. thing to heed, 64:3
    Socrates w. of men, 260:4
    these are w., 68:13
    virtuousest discreetest, 259:3
Wish all men everywhere free, 445:12
    deferred fulfillment of prehistoric w., 563:4
    each w. of my heart, 387:9
    every man in arms w. to be, 371:20
    father to thought, 188:22
    half grant what I w., 622:19
    happy whose w. and care, 292:4
    heart dry of blood, 412:1
    I knew how to quit you, 840:14
    I liked way it talks, 579:15
    I loved human race, 579:15
    I thought What jolly fun, 579:15
    I was in land of cotton, 470:16
    I w. he'd stay away, 631:12
    I'd said that, 520:18
    in vain to w. for death, 66:13
    men believe what they w., 88:22
    my days to be, 369:14
    of some is to avenge, 71:13
    snow in May's mirth, 174:2
    things were otherwise, 735:9
    to save their own pocket, 71:13
    upon a star, 729:13
    what is it gentlemen w., 331:13
    you a wave o' the sea, 223:29
Wished heaven made her such a man, 208:3
    I oft w. for Hell, 354:11
    she had not heard it, 208:3
    the w. the trysted hour, 358:15
    to see thee cross-gartered, 205:9
Wishes, by country's w. blessed, 317:10
    cannot alter facts, 329:11
    expressed w. of people, 653:14

Wishes *(continued)*
  her w. and ways be as nothing, 536:2
  if w. were horses, 271:2
  in idle w. fools stay, 347:9
  lengthen as our sun declines, 291:3
  never learned to stray, 316:3
  sorry if w. were gratified, 59:15
  what each w. he believes, 79:9
  whom God w. to destroy, 69:3
Wishful, instinctual w. impulses, 564:1
Wishing his foot equal with eye, 170:27
Wishings, hell full of good w., 243:23
Wist ye not, 37:21
Wistful, such a w. eye, 561:1
Wit, a w. is a feather, 295:5
  all your Piety nor W., 442:2
  among Lords, 308:18
  and wisdom born with man, 238:13
  beams of w. on other souls, 273:14
  beauty w. high birth, 203:25
  boast his w., 272:16
  bold and turbulent of w., 272:16
  borrowed w., 239:19
  brevity the soul of w., 198:26
  cause w. in other men, 187:24
  craves a kind of w., 205:11
  devise w. write pen, 174:7
  does harm to my w., 204:15
  dream past the w. of man, 179:3
  drink goes in w. goes out, 243:24
  dronkenesse is sepulture of w., 136:10
  eloquent exhibition of w. or oratory, 617:7
  enliven morality with w., 288:4
  enough to run away, 262:23
  fancy w. will come, 294:11
  good nature more agreeable than w.,
    288:11
  her w. was more than man, 273:21
  hope flock to aid, 426:10
  in w. a man, 294:13
  invites you by his looks to come, 326:13
  is wall between us and dark, 704:17
  kind of senseless w., 797:14
  lasts two centuries, 392:9
  levels all distinctions, 429:3
  little tiny w., 211:31
  liveliest effusions of w., 382:21
  love paradox without losing w., 427:17
  makes its own welcome, 429:3
  men of w., 284:21
  monuments of w. survive monuments of
    power, 164:7
  mortify a w., 296:17
  much malice little w., 274:3
  my w. is thynne, 136:1
  nature by her mother w., 160:17
  ne'er tastes, 295:15
  no innocent w. suppressed, 334:8
  no man's w. can well direct him, 230:15
  nor words nor worth, 193:4
  Phoenix riddle hath more w., 228:19
  plentiful lack of w., 198:36
  put his whole w. in a jest, 237:20
  shines at expense of memory, 286:16
  shoots his w., 196:8
  skirmish of w., 190:14
  soul of epigram, 378:5
  soul of w., 198:26

Wit *(continued)*
  staircase w., 313:15
  temper w. with morality, 288:4
  that can creep, 296:2
  true w. is nature to advantage dressed,
    292:13
  universal monarchy of w., 245:13
  use w. as pitchfork, 799:6
  ware of mine own w., 194:10
  wears his w. in his belly, 203:11
  whan man hath over-greet a w., 136:15
  what scanted in hair given in w., 172:18
  when age in w. out, 191:4
  will shine, 273:16
  with dunces, 297:3
Witch, aroint thee w., 213:33
  hath power to charm, 196:19
  I have gone out a w., 820:9
  wicked W. of the East, 562:2
  world with noble horsemanship, 183:14
Witchcraft, 'cause it's w. wicked w., 813:6
  celebrates, 215:14
  only w. I have used, 208:3
  same old w., 759:6
Witches, feared w. burned women, 562:9
  wild w. noble ladies, 593:3
Witching time of night, 200:29
Witch-tales Annie tells about, 553:7
Withal, money comes w., 173:10
Withdrawing, melancholy long w. roar, 496:19
Withdrawn, he has departed w. gone away,
  87:7
Wither, age cannot w. her, 218:21
  and come to deadly use, 212:19
  his leaf shall not w., 14:40
  into the truth, 592:7
Withered because no root, 34:15
  before they be w., 29:32
  cheek tresses gray, 372:20
  flowers w. while I spent my days, 122:9
  hand capped w. heart, 737:8
  is garland of the war, 219:5
  sedge w. from lake, 412:2
  there it could not w. be, 232:17
  when my father died, 201:31
Withereth, grass w., 26:27, 45:37
Withering, leaves w. and sere, 449:14
  now w. in my bloom, 293:23
Withers, our w. are unwrung, 200:22
Withheld, truth which has been w., 825:10
Withhold not thine hand in the evening, 23:28
  others instinctively w., 813:11
  scientist wiser not to w., 343:25
Within, birds w. despair, 153:12
  consecration from w. himself, 705:1
  foretold that danger lurks w., 170:34
  fountains are w., 378:7
  I have that w., 196:27
  serious daring starts from w., 761:4
Without, birds w. despair to get in, 153:12
  can't live with them or w., 73:10
  can't live w. or with you, 102:2
  four things better w., 699:11
  prepared for doing w., 420:16
  princesses would never leave w. me,
    725:7
Withstand in the evil day, 43:40
Withstood, little tyrant of fields w., 316:1

Witness against himself, 340:4
  call heaven and earth to w., 9:13
  call the gods to w., 213:18
  false w. by their own mouth, 31:31
  for me that I have fought, 271:27
  heap of stones a w., 7:1
  heaven and earth to w., 9:13
  history the w. to passing time, 87:13
  I stand w. to common lot, 683:7
  no w. so dreadful, 85:12
  of soul naturally Christian, 113:5
  shalt not bear false w., 8:14
  single w. is no w., 121:20
  to the people, 27:10
  weak w. of thy name, 250:15
  without w. against me, 3:10
  your eyes my w., 236:4
Witnesses, cloud of w., 45:12
  days to come are wisest w., 63:22
  to same overt act, 339:13
  trees and all nature w., 891:9
  victims become w., 821:7
Wit's, a w. a feather, 295:5
  an unruly engine, 242:11
  at their w. end, 18:16
  your w. too hot, 174:10
Wits, dunce with w., 297:3
  from table with his w., 265:2
  good w. jump, 158:3
  great w. to madness allied, 272:16
  home-keeping youth homely w., 173:27
  honors beauties w., 229:9
  I found my w. you lost yours, 239:2
  Lord among w., 308:18
  so many heads so many w., 86:*n6*
  summoned w. from woolgathering,
    236:13
  to read, 232:19
  were fresh and clear, 495:17
  whetstone of w., 193:25
Witticism, to fail in w. is worst, 384:1
Wittily, old hermit very w. said, 205:26
Witty beauty a power, 505:17
  buzz w. and fair annoys, 295:15
  difficult to be w. every day, 417:10
  it shall be w., 298:19
  not only w. in myself, 187:24
  poets w. mathematics subtile, 166:19
  to be rude, 285:7
  woman a treasure, 505:17
  words though ne'er so w., 159:8
Wive, I come to w. it wealthily in Padua, 173:9
Wives, absolute power over w., 340:12
  continual wars and w., 827:13
  gifted energetic w. of writers, 781:15
  like strawberry w., 165:7
  live with w. and concubines, 499:7
  man with seven w., 892:22
  may be merry, 187:18
  sky changes when w., 195:29
  some poisoned by their w., 177:8
  think of homes and w., 668:12
  to be paid in consideration, 781:16
  young men's mistresses, 165:20
Wives', old w. fables, 44:29
Wiving, hanging and w. go by destiny,
  146:*n14*
Wizard, very bad W., 562:5

Wobegon, that's the news from Lake W.,
   854:10
Woe, can I see another's w., 351:8
   Cavalry of W., 508:5
   come weal come w., 367:15
   conquered w., 221:29
   fig for w., 146:10
   great w. to their enemies, 53:3
   heritage of w., 396:29
   hideous notes of w., 399:4
   Ho told story of w., 517:4
   howling w., 350:9
   if love good whennes cometh w., 132:12
   incarnation of frozen w., 582:14
   is me for I am undone, 25:10
   is me to have seen, 200:5
   is me Winter come, 403:16
   liberty lashed with w., 172:15
   man made for joy and w., 354:2
   month follow month with w., 403:19
   never parted bliss or w., 259:15
   never was a story of more w., 181:17
   never wipe off tears of w., 352:7
   one w. tread upon another's heel, 201:*n2*
   protracted w., 306:18
   proved a very w., 222:20
   reef of Norman's W., 436:10
   silence in love bewrays w., 159:8
   succeeds a woe, 201:*n2*
   suits of w., 196:27
   thrill deepest notes of w., 357:7
   to him that reads but one book, 244:29
   to him who seeks to pour oil upon waters,
     482:22
   to the conquered, 121:24
   unto them that call evil good, 25:7
   unto them that draw iniquity, 25:6
   unto them that join house to house, 25:4
   unto them that rise up early, 25:5
   unto you scribes and Pharisees, 35:15
   unto you when men speak well, 37:26
   weal and w. is common, 247:8
   with loss of Eden, 255:3
   world but thurghfare of w., 134:24
Woebegone, so dead in look so w., 187:22
Woeful ballad, 194:25
Woes as time cannot recure, 159:2
   beyond their share, 52:22
   cluster, 201:*n2*
   for such a woman they suffer w., 51:2
   Grecian w., 293:16
   he suffered in his heart many w., 52:20
   of hopeless lovers, 273:25
   rare are solitary w., 201:*n2*
   riches cover multitude of w., 81:5
   upon Achaeans myriad w., 50:9
   what is worst of w., 395:9
   with old w. new wail, 221:8
Wohnet, der in den Zweigen w., 342:*n4*
Woke and found life was duty, 472:15
Wolf, appetite a universal w., 203:8
   boy cried W., 58:20
   cloud that looked like w., 72:14
   committing lamb to custody of w., 330:9
   false as w. to heifer's calf, 203:20
   from door, 140:20
   grim w. with privy paw, 253:11
   hates when it flatters, 116:14

Wolf *(continued)*
   in fold sad thing, 92:19
   in sheep's clothing, 58:13
   is at the door, 578:19
   keep the w. far thence, 237:4
   like w. on the fold, 397:2
   live with wolves howl like w., 897:13
   man w. to man, 682:12
   may become a w., 732:15
   neither yield to howling of w., 163:15
   owlet whoops to w. below, 377:1
   shall dwell with lamb, 25:19
   that keep it prosper, 588:18
   that's foe to men, 237:4
   trusts in tameness of w., 212:10
   we have w. by ear, 338:11
   who's afraid of big bad w., 817:*n1*
Wolfe, Robert Emmet and W. Tone, 592:10
Wolf's-bane tight-rooted, 411:9
Wolves and lambs have no concord, 52:15
   eat like w. fight like devils, 189:17
   inwardly ravening w., 33:20
   live with w. howl like wolf, 897:13
Woman a contradiction, 294:5
   a foreign land, 500:8
   a sometime thing, 711:1
   adores Fascist, 833:9
   always fickle thing, 94:23
   aren't I a w., 416:1
   as easy to marry rich w., 459:11
   as man looks at w., 643:2
   as you are w., 706:1
   behave like full human being, 838:12
   behold thy son, 40:9
   being w. hard beset, 666:7
   belief w. made for man, 471:7
   believe w. or epitaph, 394:15
   body of weak and feeble w., 151:7
   brawling w. in a wide house, 21:15
   cast shame away, 135:13
   Christ came from God and a w., 416:2
   constant but yet a w., 182:15
   coupling of man and w., 678:14
   created w. boredom ceased, 549:1
   debility to which Nature condemned w.,
     334:12
   destructive damnable w., 281:11
   did ever w. since creation, 313:20
   discovering that w. has brain, 726:3
   dissimulation innate in w., 400:3
   easier for a w. to lead, 847:2
   enmity between thee and w., 5:23
   every colored w. is dying, 830:10
   every w. knows that, 577:14
   excellent thing in w., 213:13
   faded but still lovely w., 710:14
   fair w. without discretion, 20:14
   finest w. in nature, 288:23
   first loves lover, 398:13
   foolish men who accuse w., 281:7
   for such a w. they suffer, 51:2
   for the hearth, 453:3
   for thy understanding a w., 174:5
   frailty thy name is w., 197:2
   frumpy old w., 583:2
   give w. comfortable clothes, 655:4
   glacier w., 720:7
   God's second mistake, 549:1

Woman *(continued)*
   good name in man and w., 209:2
   good w. if five thousand a year, 459:7
   good w. The Misfit said, 809:6
   hard to snub beautiful w., 622:2
   has her way, 443:7
   has revenge ready, 267:14
   hate a dumpy w., 397:20
   have I not found, 23:17
   he that tastes w. ruin meets, 291:19
   heart of w. he loves, 610:14
   I am a very serious w., 794:3
   I am a w. first, 735:1
   I am w., 853:5
   if one is rich and one's a w., 785:1
   in argument with men a w. worse, 260:17
   in hours of ease, 373:16
   in kimono, 738:7
   in this humor wooed, 171:22
   instrument in shape of a w., 825:3
   is a dish for gods, 219:11
   is at heart a rake, 294:2
   is goddess poetess muse, 736:17
   is his game, 453:2
   is only a woman, 587:1
   is perfected, 833:5
   just because I am a w., 131:13
   know how to submit, 362:14
   large-brained w., 434:10
   last thing civilized, 505:6
   lesser man, 452:7
   let w. into Paradise, 897:9
   let w. then go on, 405:9
   like some little w., 856:*n1*
   like that not woman quite, 820:10
   like w. stooping down creeping about,
     578:18
   lips of a strange w. drop as honeycomb,
     19:31
   Little Girl My Stringbean My Lovely W.,
     820:12
   little w. who wrote the book, 458:*n4*
   lived in shoe, 894:8
   lone w. with silver spoons, 473:19
   long hair glory to w., 42:23
   look for the w., 422:6
   loveliest w. born, 593:17
   lovely in her bones, 756:6
   lovely w. stoops to folly, 322:16, 676:13
   made he a w., 5:15
   made mouths in a glass, 211:27
   man and w. in garden, 560:15
   man that is born of a w., 13:29
   man's desire for w., 380:4
   mighty ills done by w., 281:11
   more barbarous than man, 548:7
   mortifying when w. considers difference of
     education, 340:15
   mountainous w. not breaks will bend,
     773:4
   moved like fountain troubled, 173:25
   much missed, 536:18
   must have money and a room, 654:14
   nakedness of w. work of God, 351:14
   needs man like fish needs bicycle, 888:20
   neither man nor w. but author, 472:14
   nigger w. mule uh de world, 690:4
   no animal more invincible than w., 73:9

Women *(continued)*

hate all w. when thou art gone, 229:6
have as much rights as man, 416:2
have glimmer of loyalty to Truth, 552:2
have inferiority complexes, 688:15
have no characters, 293:25
have no wilderness, 713:3
have positive moral sense, 531:6
have very little idea, 845:7
haven't any depths, 549:11
hid himself among w., 248:27
homely men charmed w., 581:15
how can you shoot w. children, 847:6
how hard for w. to keep counsel, 192:13
I know disposition of w., 86:11
if men knew how w. pass time, 581:11
impressive fact about American w., 800:8
in w. two divide, 294:1
innocent and pure, 224:19
kindness in w. not looks, 173:21
know less understand more, 654:1
knowledge of w. of his own family, 435:17
labor of w. in house, 579:1
Lake Wobegon where w. are strong,
854:10
let w. into your life, 565:20
like to be conquered, 459:15
like untuned golden strings, 168:15
liked several w., 224:27
literary accomplishments in w., 340:14
looking-glasses reflecting man, 654:17
love lovers, 264:29
make public judge, 392:3
man always unjust to w., 398:12
married beneath me all w. do, 637:2
men and w. affirm brotherhood, 751:9
men and w. created equal, 471:3
men and w. merely players, 194:25
men w. and clergymen, 375:3
men work w. weep, 481:5
minds of American w., 796:7
monstrous regiment of w., 150:1
more pangs than wars or w., 225:25
musick and w. give way to, 277:15
must try things men have tried, 718:7
my deceptions of w., 320:10
my sisters and lovers, 485:17
no more trusting in w., 53:17
not so young as painted, 612:15
not w. or Negroes but citizens, 471:8
of Nation still control destinies, 751:12
old w. should not be perfumed, 55:1
one sees in other w., 816:17
other w. cloy appetites, 218:21
ought to have representatives, 360:22
passing the love of w., 11:10
passionate w., 591:17
pleasing punishment w. bear, 172:13
plunged into cares and sorrows, 360:20
pursuit of loose w., 493:11
put not on pedestal but in cage, 745:12
remember what don't want to forget,
690:3
saints were rarely married w., 746:11
seven w. take hold of one man, 25:2
sexual life of adult w., 563:13
silence gives grace to w., 65:2
Solomon loved many strange w., 11:36

Women *(continued)*

some w. charm all, 577:12
some w. handsome without adornment,
87:17
some w. stay in memory, 589:23
spare w. for Thy Sake, 745:5
superiority of their w., 434:5
text of Men and W., 574:1
that men have warned us about, 852:14
that's the nature of w., 156:9
these impossible w., 73:10
thou fairest among w., 24:5
till w. more rationally educated, 360:17
trained to place others' needs first, 771:15
under control of men, 99:13
upset everything, 565:20
watch themselves, 811:1
watched naked w. walk out of sea, 767:6
we should have learned w., 340:14
wear the breeches, 234:12
well-behaved w., 844:13
what a woman thinks of w., 505:18
what is it men in w. require, 352:9
what pornography says about w., 863:7
when candles out all w. fair, 108:11
who remained thirty-five, 560:25
wine and w. go together, 235:1
wine w. and song, 346:21
wine w. mirth laughter, 398:10
wonder so many w. die, 499:8
words are w. deeds men, 244:19
young w. of small fortune, 382:9
Women's, from w. eyes this doctrine, 174:24
I put on w. clothing, 879:9
rights are human rights, 864:5
sooner lost than w. are, 204:34
weapons waterdrops, 211:22
Won, battles lost in spirit in which w., 486:2
battles that should been w., 796:9
by captain of second rank, 422:13
by men with courage, 72:4
game is done I've w., 376:8
lose ground w. today, 495:15
not that you w. or lost, 646:4
on playing fields of Eton, 366:14
other palms are w., 371:5
prize we sought is w., 487:16
small have plodders w., 174:1
so melancholy as battle w., 366:7
the ear of Pluto, 251:9
things w. are done, 203:2
though he w. all battles, 819:9
wars w. by men, 664:11
was woman in this humor w., 171:22
when battle's lost and w., 213:30
woman therefore to be w., 169:21
woman w. or woman lost, 594:6
wooed and not unsought be w., 259:1
world made to be w. by youth, 619:4
Wonder, a w. I haven't dropped ideals, 822:7
all knowledge and w. is pleasure, 164:9
all w. that would be, 452:2
and glory of universe, 440:10
and wild desire, 462:28
at so grotesque a blunder, 629:4
at the workmanship, 252:25
bird of w. dies, 226:14
capacity for w., 567:3

Wonder *(continued)*

construction of a state of w., 831:14
Do I dare, 674:20
dreaming eyes of w., 515:10
ever-increasing w. and awe, 320:2
how I w. what you're at, 514:15
I w. by my troth, 228:6
men trust themselves, 213:19
miles around w. grew, 574:17
of an hour, 395:6
of our stage, 232:19
so many women die, 499:8
to have w. steal over detail, 542:13
what I was begun for, 883:1
what you are, 389:12
what you've missed, 748:9
Wonderer, way for the W., 812:14
Wonderful, all things wise and w., 476:4
mystic w., 455:8
name shall be called W., 25:16
none more w. than man, 65:16
one-hoss shay, 443:12
peace it's w., 649:4
's w. 's marvelous, 710:22
three things which are too w., 22:14
thy love to me was w., 11:10
to get out of bed, 814:6
what a w. world, 797:8
wonderful most wonderful, 195:10
Wonderfully, fearfully and w. made, 19:15
Wondering fearing doubting dreaming, 449:7
Wonders, America land of w., 433:16
at our quaint spirits, 178:21
carry with us w. we seek, 248:5
his w. to perform, 326:9
numberless are world's w., 65:16
of all w. I have heard, 192:11
of Christian religion, 283:2
welcome all w., 263:13
Wonder Woman, she is known as W., 698:15
Wonder-working earth puts forth sweet
flowers, 89:10
Wondrous Architecture of world, 168:2
days have been w. free, 290:10
he was w. wise, 897:6
it grew w. cold, 375:23
moon takes up w. tale, 287:21
'twas w. pitiful, 208:3
Wont, more near earth than w., 210:15
Won't, when you will they w., 86:11
will you w. you, 515:3
Woo, men April when they w., 195:29
that would w. her, 208:3
Wood, an ark of gopher w., 6:17
beyond these a bit of w., 95:24
Birnam w. to Dunsinane, 216:34
Birnam W. to Dunsinane, 639:17
bows to w. and stone, 391:7
brings dark w. to life, 871:2
brown heath and shaggy w., 373:4
burgeoning w. brings forth, 51:11
cannot see w. for tree, 148:5
children in the w., 880:14
cleave w. there am I, 113:19
crow makes wing to rooky w., 216:13
dark w. where straight way lost, 128:3
deep and gloomy w., 368:10
feeld hath eyen w. eres, 134:15

Wood *(continued)*

go walk the w. so wild, 880:10
grainy w., 669:9
has a sharp ear, 134:*n2*
heap on more w., 373:13
hewers of w., 10:2
hewing w. for master carpenter, 58:4
in w. a Piggy-wig, 467:8
in w. furious winter blowing, 681:18
into a different w., 760:7
land set out to plant w., 296:7
late sunlight enters deep w., 122:4
mountains and a w., 695:5
Norwegian w., 848:5
old w. to burn, 165:8
one impulse from vernal w., 368:6
out of w. so crooked and perverse, 320:1
over river through w., 421:17
red herrings in w., 893:1
sang within bloody w., 676:2
stumps warmed me twice, 475:13
throne is bit of w. gilded, 365:9
to wild w. and downs, 404:12
tulgey w., 515:13
two roads diverged in w., 622:18
wherever w. can swim, 365:14
who splits w. warms twice, 475:*n1*

Woodbine, luscious w., 178:19
Woodcocks, springes to catch w., 197:27
Wooden dialogue and sound, 203:9
float easy as w. boat, 882:15
justice has w. leg, 600:6
O, 188:30
wall is your ships, 62:16
Woodland, hills vales w. plain, 293:14
let me love river and w., 93:17
of Weir, 449:15
Woodlands, about w. I will go, 574:11
Woodman spare beechen tree, 384:14
spare that tree, 423:1
Wood-notes, native w. wild, 251:8
Woods against stormy sky, 405:4
are full of them, 884:14
are the w. for me, 709:5
crazy as hauling timber into w., 95:22
cut down w. for pulp, 709:15
decay and fall, 455:5
fierce and accustomed to w., 142:8
fill up with snow, 623:6
for hunters of dreams, 569:12
fresh w. and pastures new, 253:15
Greta w. are green, 374:6
have ears, 134:*n2*
have tongues, 134:*n2*
horn in depths of w., 416:4
I am for the w., 709:5
in riot, 575:4
in w. Yongby-Bonghy-Bò, 467:15
into the w. my Master went, 543:4
lovely dark deep, 623:8
more free from peril, 193:36
more in w. than in books, 123:11
naked w., 406:2
of Arcady dead, 590:20
or steepy mountain yields, 168:4
pleasure in pathless w., 396:16
Rhodora in the w., 424:9
shall to me answer, 161:5

Woods *(continued)*

to sleeping w. singeth, 376:19
to w. to live deliberately, 474:29
we'll to w. no more, 499:5
wet wild w., 589:19
when all w. are still, 253:16
whose w. these are, 623:6
wild in w. noble savage, 272:9
wind through w. in riot, 575:4
Woodshed, middle-aged build w., 473:6
something nasty in w., 730:7
Woodside, lived under my w., 246:19
Woodspurge has cup of three, 506:2
Woodstock, by the time we got to W., 858:3
Woodthrush singing through fog, 677:20
Woodwork, crawled out of the w., 864:12
Wooed and not unsought be won, 259:1
beautiful therefore to be w., 169:21
by slow advances, 606:19
I w. her in wintertime, 884:15
in haste wed at leisure, 173:16
woman in this humor w., 171:22
world made to be w. by youth, 619:4
Wooer, knight to be their w., 890:2
Woof, Iris' w., 252:5
Wooing, if I am not worth w., 437:6
women are angels w., 203:2
Wooingly, heaven's breath smells w., 214:21
Wool, bending to your w., 150:7
have you any w., 893:4
much cry and no w., 137:15
of bat tongue of dog, 216:27
owest sheep no w., 212:3
restore to whiteness w. dyed purple, 115:19
sleeping is a w. blanket, 73:17
tease the huswife's w., 252:25
Woolen, rather lie in w., 190:21
Woolf, who's afraid of Virginia W., 817:10
Woolgathering, summoned wits from w.,
236:13
Woolly, flock in w. fold, 409:18
softest clothing w. bright, 350:12
Word a lamp unto my feet, 18:28
after a w. after a w., 844:15
against W. unstilled world, 677:17
alchemy of the w., 559:11
almost-right w. and right w., 523:12
and a blow, 180:27
answer me in one w., 195:11
any w. can explain man's life, 714:16
as good as bond, 158:1
better than a gift, 31:4
blotted w. out forever, 314:18
brings to pass every w., 63:19
burned like a lamp, 31:29
but a w. and a blow, 274:9
by His firm W., 118:11
by thought w. and deed, 49:5
cannot be recalled, 98:8
center of silent W., 677:17
choice w. measured phrase, 369:17
choleric w., 206:29
conscience but w. cowards use, 172:10
corrupt w. like corrupt tree, 118:11
dead when it is said, 510:13
deals destruction, 567:7
Democracy is a great w., 488:12
doers of the w., 45:24

Word *(continued)*

done for least w. said, 530:5
ears have heard Holy W., 352:10
eaten thee for a w., 174:26
every w. she writes is lie, 768:14
every w. stabs, 190:27
every w. tell, 606:3
every w. that proceedeth, 9:18
fashion's w. is out, 596:7
finest w. Frenchman ever uttered,
366:*n6*
fitly spoken, 21:33
flowering in lonely w., 456:1
frantic boast foolish w., 589:11
freed from world, 760:7
freedom indivisible w., 697:2
God the w. spake it, 151:14
good w. is as good tree, 118:11
guileless w. is folly, 716:13
hear the w. of the Lord, 28:4
his w. was Fie foh fum, 212:9
how proud w. Man rings, 602:15
I catch every w., 578:7
I kept my w. he said, 616:7
I to my pledged w. true, 682:7
ill deeds doubled with evil w., 172:24
impossible not French, 365:8
in beginning the W., 38:44
keep w. of promise to our ear, 217:29
Latin w. for three farthings, 174:12
let w. go forth, 785:10
lightest w. harrow soul, 198:5
like a bell, 410:11
living w. awakened my soul, 644:5
love which greybeards call divine, 171:6
making of a world, 641:18
man's w. God in man, 455:7
meaning of the w. is is, 863:6
mightier than they in arms, 258:23
mum's the w., 158:6
must a w. to be addressed to princes, 151:15
needed for concept, 338:22
never break w. or lose self-respect, 111:14
O w. of fear, 174:32
of Caesar stood, 192:32
of earth in ears of world, 530:21
of gentleman and Christian, 156:33
of God is quick, 45:7
of our God shall stand, 26:27
of the Lord endureth, 45:37
one little w., 176:13
one w. for woman, 561:16
one w. frees us, 66:20
one w. plastics, 827:9
one w. too often profaned, 404:5
over all, 487:11
pen through every other w., 375:11
preserves contact, 631:7
seldom heard discouraging w., 890:20
shadow of deed, 70:13
some with flattering w., 561:3
spoken in due season, 20:34
spoken w. comes not back, 98:*n3*
struggles against divine W., 144:9
suit action to the w., 200:7
thank thee Jew for teaching me that w.,
186:11
theory of the w., 641:18

Work *(continued)*

comes first, 601:1
contrariously, 188:36
dawn speeds him in his w., 54:26
day's wages for day's w., 407:24
debasing w. to do what not worth doing, 810:10
did sell himself to w. wickedness, 12:8
dirty w. at crossroads, 885:10
dregs of artist's w., 798:12
end crowns the w., 120:23
entire land sets to w., 4:7
Equal Pay for Equal W., 488:22
establish the w. of our hands, 17:27
expands to fill time, 760:1
from sun to sun, 883:17
good day's w., 304:3
greatness of w. inside man, 794:10
grows beyond his w., 733:2
half proper gardener's w., 590:5
hands from day to day, 751:2
hands that w. on us, 632:9
harder yet thought idler, 591:19
he can w. no faster, 893:19
his six days' w. a world, 258:28
his w. is perfect, 9:30
how the hell can I w., 886:1
I am rising to a man's w., 112:8
I don't like w., 567:14
I like what is in w., 567:14
I like w. it fascinates me, 576:7
I want w., 182:17
if this w. be of men, 40:18
in silence with all one's heart, 552:14
incessantly to the last, 343:23
is done by those, 793:9
is less boring than pleasure, 491:19
is seed sown, 406:10
it is not hard to w., 632:17
job of w. which I enjoyed, 702:3
judgeth according to w., 45:36
Kaspar's w. was done, 381:6
keeps us from three evils, 299:13
labor and do all thy w., 8:13
leave w. sit at temple, 655:6
let patience have her perfect w., 45:20
light prime w. of God, 257:*n*2
like madness in brain, 377:13
live splendidly if w. and love, 506:11
love made visible, 655:6
lovely dears her noblest w., 356:22
made it w. again, 870:7
man goeth forth unto his w., 18:11
many hands make light w., 148:10
men w. women weep, 481:5
more wise master simpler w., 127:11
nakedness of woman w. of God, 351:14
never fit for real w., 806:10
never made w. for man to mend, 274:24
nice w. if you can get it, 711:6
night when no man can w., 39:27
no immortal w. behind me, 413:17
no substitute for hard w., 550:12
no werkman may w. wel and hastily, 136:2
no w. nor device nor knowledge, 23:22
no w. to do, 886:1
noblest w. of God, 295:5, 356:10
noblest w. of man, 518:3

Work *(continued)*

none of older connotation of pain, 752:17
nor fire nor age shall destroy, 102:18
of art corner of creation, 537:12
of noble note, 451:17
of thy hand, 27:19
on seventh day God ended his w., 5:9
others w. better with bronze, 94:35
out own salvation, 44:2
partly done, 671:14
people unable to find w., 613:10
perfection of life or w., 595:9
play for mortal stakes, 624:1
portrait of self, 521:8
posterity of w. of art, 610:15
put us to w. anew, 587:12
race over w. never done, 539:8
reproduction of w. of art, 693:1
scythe of time, 365:15
seventh day thou shalt not w., 8:13
shall not be lost, 301:20
shovel under let me w., 636:4
slaves to do ugly w., 560:26
smile his w. to see, 353:2
so w. the honeybees, 188:34
social world w. of man, 286:20
soon as your day's w. done, 517:12
sport tedious as to w., 181:33
spur whereby mankind w., 275:11
stops expenses run on, 85:2
strive on to finish w., 447:2
studies in which w. dies with worker, 140:5
that aspires to art, 567:2
that you could w. with men, 865:4
they w. and despise their w., 792:11
those who w. with joy, 655:6
to every man according to his w., 17:5
to love and to w., 564:7
to pray is to w., 121:3
to w. to w. wolf at door, 578:19
together for good, 41:21
unfinished w. they advanced, 446:5
until our w. done, 421:5
us a perpetual peace, 250:9
we are w. of thy hand, 27:19
we have corrected Thy w., 492:14
we have undertaken, 239:16
we w. in the dark, 544:12
what a piece of w. is man, 199:5
whatever body obliged to do, 522:8
whether his w. be pure, 21:11
which bores you, 602:10
who first invented w., 383:16
why don't you w., 886:1
why should I let toad w., 799:6
with materials I have, 739:5
with one hand wrought in w., 12:28
with so fine a brush, 383:1
without Hope, 378:15
woman's w. never done, 883:17
work work, 418:10
world's need of w., 602:10
write if you get w., 802:3
writer's w. optical instrument, 611:7
your wicked will, 620:9
Worked and sang, 330:19
and waited for light, 605:19

Worker, art for intellectual w., 605:11
lone w. makes first advance, 647:7
studies in which work dies with w., 140:5
to w. God lends aid, 59:*n*3
value of what w. produces, 657:18
Workers, as w. not as women, 488:21
brain-sick brain w., 520:8
heart-sick hand w., 520:8
idle reward great, 117:8
mainstay of civilization, 554:5
of world unite, 479:*n*1
Park to supply w. God's handiwork, 498:14
Worketh, wrath w. not righteousness, 45:23
Working class hero is something, 848:2
Heaven protect w. girl, 569:2
man thinking or w. is alone, 475:9
men of all countries unite, 478:15
necessary mode of w. of mind, 502:3
on the railroad, 884:22
Working-day world, 193:33
Workings, hum of mighty w., 408:18
Workman, by work one knows w., 266:9
no w. may werke wel and hastily, 136:2
that needeth not to be ashamed, 44:40
Workmanship, dark inscrutable w., 368:14
most may wonder at w., 252:25
skill of w. or design, 149:11
Workmen, Master of All Good W., 587:12
Works, all ye w. of the Lord, 31:30
authors' names not w., 292:21
be silent as to his w., 310:22
been into future it w., 598:9
best of all God's w., 259:14
both sides of street, 653:11
done under the sun, 22:26
every feature w., 382:17
faith without w., 45:26
fat of others' w., 234:7
for sweetness and light, 497:13
God's w. are wide, 242:25
good w. better in sight of Lord, 118:18
her own w. praise her, 22:20
how manifold are thy w., 18:11
I know thy w., 46:26
live and die in Aristotle's w., 168:16
look on my w. ye Mighty, 401:13
man is son of own w., 92:*n*11
move immediately upon your w., 498:1
Nature's w. expunged, 257:6
neurotics created great w. of art, 610:18
not retain rare w., 610:16
of art products of danger, 631:18
of darkness, 41:40
of him that sent me, 39:27
of unbelievers a mirage, 118:24
our w. do not ennoble us, 127:12
part of man's Self, 541:4
renounce the devil and his w., 49:11
reward according to his w., 45:3
rich in good w., 44:37
see your good w., 32:16
seen future and it w., 598:*n*2
sighing through all her w., 259:11
skilled in w. of both languages, 97:2
spares man nor his w., 332:10
subdued to what it w. in, 222:14
these are thy glorious w., 258:14

World (continued)

is wonderful and beautiful and good, 662:11
it is a w. to see, 162:2
it must have been a wonderful old w., 663:20
it was whole morning w., 761:2
joy to pass to w. below, 94:24
joy to the w., 289:15
justice is wanting in w., 360:21
kill babies make w. safer, 824:10
king of the w., 872:2
knew w. would not be same, 739:8
knowledge of w. acquired in w., 298:3
lash rascals through w., 210:6
laugh and w. laughs, 556:16
law of musical w., 582:18
lawlessness, 652:17
learn of green w., 665:14
leave the w. no copy, 204:20
leave w. by natural door, 557:14
leaves w. to darkness, 315:11
let justice be done though w. perish, 120:n6
let the w. mind him, 461:15
let us possess one w., 228:7
let w. slide, 146:10
let w. wag, 147:5
letter to W., 509:5
lie on bosom of infinite w., 364:16
light of the w., 32:16, 39:24
limits of vision limits of w., 400:1
listen then as I now, 403:6
little friend of all w., 589:13
little note nor long remember, 446:5
little w. made cunningly, 230:18
little w. of childhood, 630:8
live in w. as spectator, 288:2
look upon w. as parish, 301:15
looking uncomfortably to w. we inherit, 888:16
looks at busy w. through loop-holes, 386:5
looks on w. rationally, 367:11
looks whole w. in face, 436:12
love all things in w. so filled, 375:15
love beyond w., 280:9
Love makes w. go round, 527:5
love makes w. go round, 891:4
lover's quarrel with w., 624:10
loves w. as his body, 57:5
luckiest people in the w., 800:3
mad as Bedlam, 465:25
mad w. mad kings, 175:11
made in six days, 365:5
made safe for democracy, 566:14
made to be won by youth, 619:4
make w. within the w., 568:16
makes whole w. kin, 203:25
margent of w., 576:15
market economy's field is w., 648:7
mass of public wrongs, 163:7
may end tonight, 461:11
mere anarchy loosed on w., 593:9
money sets w. in motion, 100:28
more overwork than w. justifies, 587:7
morning of the w., 459:21
most people on w. not in it, 533:11
movers and shakers of w., 549:13

World (continued)

mud-luscious, 701:5
must be peopled, 190:36
must conform to necessity, 614:10
my all the w., 155:n3
my country is the w., 333:16
naked shingles of w., 496:19
native in this w., 641:10
nature too noble for w., 219:32
needs men of real talent, 335:10
never enjoy w. aright, 278:10
new w. order, 599:7, 805:6
next w. as closely apprehended, 248:24
no world but wrongs, 163:7
noisy set martyrs call w., 591:19
Northwest Passage to intellectual w., 314:17
not a joy the w. can give, 397:4
not as w. giveth, 39:44
not be queen for all w., 225:18
not inn but hospital, 248:18
not loved w. nor w. me, 395:23
not sweet in the end, 530:9
not to live but die in, 248:18
not to live in physical w., 641:17
not worth while to go round the w., 475:17
November's w., 821:2
now bubble burst now w., 294:18
O w. invisible intangible, 577:3
O w. w. w., 204:9
of compensations, 444:13
of dew is w. of dew, 361:15
of Freud, 723:4
of happy days, 171:27
of ideas, 496:6
of light, 268:16
of men for me, 460:17
of nuclear giants, 697:5
of Pains and troubles, 413:15
of sighs, 208:3
of this bad w., 606:16
of twentieth century, 718:1
of vile faults, 187:13
of words, 643:6
on back burden of w., 557:3
on dreaming fed, 590:20
on w. to turn thine eyes, 306:16
one custom corrupt w., 455:19
one w. at a time, 476:2
only fence against the w., 275:14
only thing new in w., 661:14
opinion governs w., 566:7
our country the w., 433:2
outlasts aversion outlasts love, 494:15
pain, 361:n4
part we sadly in troublous w., 171:2
pass through w. once, 884:21
peace or world destruction, 606:7
peace reversal of record, 644:12
peep at such a w., 327:2
pendant w., 206:38, 257:4
place I do not care to be, 773:14
Playboy of the Western W., 612:1
please w. and father, 266:12
pleases w. cannot please himself, 278:4
poet creates w., 642:21
poet looks at w., 643:2

World (continued)

poets legislators of w., 404:16
point is to change it, 477:13
poor w. said I, 263:11
power of w. works in circles, 583:5
praise the mutilated w., 862:8
presents rational aspect, 367:11
puddle-wonderful, 701:6
quiet limit of w., 455:6
rack of this tough w., 213:15
read that w. was spherical, 139:12
reared arm crested the w., 219:8
rebellion in political w., 336:14
recognize relations to w. within, 556:17
regions we call New W., 140:16
remote from wrangling w., 333:8
retire from w. satisfied, 95:18
retreating w., 699:9
richest monarch in w., 359:16
riddle of the w., 295:1
ringed with azure w., 454:13
rivers ancient as w., 730:13
rocks cradle rules w., 485:7
roofs of w., 486:19
round w. forever and aye, 494:13
sad and dreary, 503:12
safe for diversity, 786:10
same whole w. over, 887:7
same w. a hell a heaven, 425:7
say to all the w., 193:22
see how w. goes, 212:29
see w. in grain of sand, 353:14
seek a newer w., 451:18
seek empty w. again, 476:12
seem all uses of this w., 196:29
seems to smile upon me, 277:10
sense that w. was mad, 632:11
separate us from invisible w., 439:4
serpent deceiveth whole w., 47:2
shore of the wide w., 412:9
shot heard round w., 424:17
should he need next w., 461:15
should wide w. roll away, 609:1
show contain and nourish all w., 174:24
shut in w. without, 438:16
sins of whole w., 46:8
sins of w., 47:23
slumbering w., 290:19
smother up beauty from w., 181:33
snow swept w. end to end, 688:6
snug little farm the w., 381:18
so hopeless is w. without, 476:16
so it was I entered broken w., 720:10
so passes glory of w., 137:3
so runs w. away, 200:23
so wags the w., 194:n1
social w. work of man, 286:20
solid earth actual w., 473:12
spectacle unto w., 42:11
spirits in the material w., 870:3
stands out, 695:6
start w. all over at, 624:20
steady patriot of w. alone, 367:2
still point of turning w., 678:9
stood against w., 192:32
story and byword through w., 239:16
strongest force in w. today, 834:4
strongest minds w. hears least, 372:5

World *(continued)*
syllables govern the w., 238:18
take note O w., 209:17
taketh away sin of w., 38:50
technology knack of arranging w., 763:16
tell the w., 183:27
ten hours to w. allot, 159:*n*1
terms between old and new w., 349:6
terrible in mass, 536:4
that I have had my w. as in my tyme, 135:7
the w. the book of God, 227:8
their words to end of w., 15:16
they enter the w. naked, 658:10
thick rotundity o' the w., 211:24
think of this fleeting w., 112:26
this is great and terrible w., 589:14
this little w., 176:24
this war shake w., 684:17
thorns and dangers of w., 175:32
thoughts rule w., 428:28
through all w. she followed him, 452:12
through art w. multiply, 611:8
time and w. in flight, 591:10
time takes survey of w., 183:30
time the soul of this w., 108:16
to hide virtues in, 204:17
to seek her through the w., 257:17
to succeed in the w., 263:21
to the city and the w., 121:22
to win, 478:15
today sick, 673:20
too much misery in the w., 440:6
too much respect upon w., 184:3
too much with us, 371:23
too old, 457:5
too wide for shrunk shank, 194:25
triple pillar of the w., 218:1
turned round in w., 483:8
turned upside downward, 234:12
two classes of people in w., 683:12
undulate round the w., 487:14
United States of W., 422:19
unknowable we know, 577:3
unspotted from the w., 45:25
unstilled w. whirled, 677:17
up above w. fly, 514:15
up above w. so high, 389:12
varying shore o' the w., 219:3
vast screen of snow, 683:5
visible poem of w., 737:9
visible w. abstract and mysterious, 770:20
visible w. formed in love, 483:4
Vision of the w., 452:2
visits his dinners not him, 267:21
void the w. can never fill, 326:8
wags, 194:15
walk cheerfully over the w., 270:3
wants to be deceived, 140:17
was all before them, 259:28
was not to seek me, 311:10
was there ever such a dreary w., 573:4
wash soiled w., 487:11
wave to wash him from w., 611:14
way of coming into w., 284:1
way w. ends, 677:2
way w. imagined determines what men do, 685:3
we are the w., 875:5

World *(continued)*
we desire more real, 767:17
weary of past, 403:9
weight of unintelligible w., 368:8
what a wonderful w., 797:8
what an age what a w., 277:6
what I do to spite w., 216:7
what is this w., 134:23
what is true in the w., 830:12
when all the w. dissolves, 168:20
when all w. young lad, 481:7
when Don Quixote when out into w., 824:3
when end of w. comes, 626:5
when Rome falls the w., 396:14
where England dead, 627:5
where is any author in w., 174:20
where much to be done, 307:26
where nothing for nothing, 479:10
where owl is hungry, 840:11
which seems before us, 496:19
whole face of w. changed, 269:13
whole w. at sixes and sevens, 715:10
whole w. is made to end in book, 543:10
whom w. flattered thou despised, 159:15
whose w. or mine or theirs, 665:13
wide enough to hold both, 314:6
widest outlook on the w., 552:14
wilderness of this w., 271:7
will beat a path to your door, 425:*n*2
will break your heart, 816:13
will freely offer itself, 655:17
will welcome lovers, 702:12
wish estate o' w. undone, 217:24
with old w. to the grave, 552:9
without end, 48:8, 327:12
without God and man, 821:5
without spilling blood of whole w., 482:13
wondrous Architecture of w., 168:2
word freed from w., 760:7
word making of a w., 641:18
word of earth in ears of w., 530:21
work of w. done through me, 636:1
workers of w. unite, 479:*n*1
working-day w., 193:33
would be field of soya beans, 843:8
would go round faster, 514:8
would split open, 771:19
writing master to this w., 671:12
yearning for vivid simple peaceable w., 767:8
years like oxen tread w., 590:23
you in my respect are w., 178:18
yourself sole heir of w., 278:10
World-besotted traveler, 595:8
World-destroying, I am mighty w. Time, 84:14
World-famous all over Canada, 830:17
for fifteen minutes, 817:1
World-historic facts personages appear twice, 477:14
World-losers and world-forsakers, 549:13
Worldly, all his w. goods, 467:15
faces never look so w. as at funeral, 480:1
great economists called w. philosophers, 792:7
most loathed w. life, 207:1
never desire w. ease, 301:6
renown naught but wind, 129:20
task hast done, 220:26
wisely w., 242:2

Worldly *(continued)*
with all my w. goods, 49:25
Worldly-Wise-Man, Mr. W., 271:12
World-mothering air, 547:2
World-renowned, wayfarer w., 122:6
World's a bubble, 166:22
a stage, 194:*n*2
all the w. a stage, 194:25
better w. in birth, 472:16
brave heroes, 883:13
character formed in w. torrent, 343:8
confess this w. spent, 230:15
course will not fail, 500:9
government w. best hope, 337:9
great age begins anew, 403:8
great snare, 218:37
great w. altar-stairs, 453:24
hath this w. good, 46:10
in state o' chassis, 660:3
last night, 230:25
live after w. opinion, 426:18
mine oyster, 187:7
most crowded streets, 495:11
Night this w. defeat, 269:2
numberless are w. wonders, 65:16
she that was w. delight, 530:1
slow stain, 403:23
storm-troubled sphere, 476:14
strand, 546:5
what all w. alarms, 596:2
whole sap is sunk, 229:12
wore it in w. eyes, 592:13
world history is w. court, 359:12
Worlds, as many w. as artists, 611:8
best of all possible w., 299:8, 637:6
beyond ken of eye, 415:14
both w. at once they view, 249:28
exhausted w. imagined new, 306:9
not w. undone, 398:26
on worlds have shown, 228:7
sea-discoverers to new w., 228:7
so many w., 454:3
Tiphys disclose new w., 104:7
to explore strange new w., 797:3
wandering between two w., 495:23
World-transforming Charlemagne, 596:8
World-wearied flesh, 181:14
Worldwide, problem destined to become w., 835:21
Worl's in state o' chassis, 660:3
Worm, a w. a mere nothing, 301:8
canker and grief, 399:16
catch Christ with w., 787:2
Conqueror W., 448:15
fish that hath fed of w., 201:17
i' the bud, 205:4
I wish you joy of the w., 219:12
in the wheat, 609:13
invisible w., 352:14
man edible to w., 540:7
man that is a w., 14:1
nakid as a w. was she, 132:5
owest w. no silk, 212:3
rather be w. in apple, 670:10
shall feed sweetly on him, 13:45
shall feed sweetly upon me, 231:14
that hath eat of a king, 201:17
to a toad, 540:7

Worm (continued)
to the w. thou art my mother, 13:35
tough w. in your inside, 527:21
vessel bears w., 473:20
what gnawing of w., 231:9
when I was a w., 756:7
will turn, 170:21
Worms, as many devils in W. as tiles, 144:10
darkness w. and shrouds, 409:4
destroy this body, 13:39
filled with ends of w., 696:11
food for w., 301:20
graves w. and epitaphs, 177:7
have eaten them, 195:27
more flesh more w., 103:1
outvenoms w. of Nile, 220:20
pain woven in life of w., 501:15
then w. shall try, 266:23
with vilest w. to dwell, 221:23
Worms', made w. meat of me, 180:29
Worm's-eye point of view, 726:13
Wormwood and the gall, 28:12
her end is bitter as w., 19:31
Milton's w. words, 254:*n*1
name of the star is W., 46:38
wormwood, 200:20
Worn, all things w. out and old, 591:9
out before on scrap heap, 565:3
sooner lost and w., 204:34
to be w. out is to be renewed, 57:10
weeded and w. ancient thatch, 450:7
Worn-out poetical fashion, 678:16
Worried, I'm not w. about anything, 823:16
the cat, 897:8
Worries, I am leaving you with w., 747:9
Worry away our lives, 773:1
did not w. about it afterward, 661:8
don't hurry don't w., 693:10
don't w. be happy, 700:14
I should w. and fret, 635:6
leave w. on doorstep, 740:14
more possessions more w., 103:1
not w. about what is far off, 61:18
two days about which not w., 545:15
what me w., 888:13
Worrying over them will kill you, 859:4
we are w. animal, 773:1
what's use of w., 643:22
Worse, a little w. than a man, 184:19
approve better but follow w., 102:15
as Heaven made him and sometimes w.,
157:7
bad laws bring about w., 312:20
bark w. than bite, 244:27
better day w. deed, 236:*n*5
fault w. by excuse, 175:25
for better for w., 49:16
gives greater feeling to the w., 176:18
hat not w. for wear, 326:18
lots w. ways to die, 633:6
make w. appear the better, 72:13
medicine w. than malady, 100:*n*1
most are w. than their fathers, 52:25
no better, but often w., 313:22
no w. a husband than best, 218:19
nothing w. than shameless woman, 73:12
on Friday, 895:10
or w. expelled, 879:3

Worse (continued)
pen w. than the sword, 235:5
pray gods they change for w., 163:2
remedies w. than disease, 100:4
than an infidel, 44:31
than be swinger of birches, 622:20
than being talked about, 559:25
than crime it is blunder, 361:4
than sun in March, 183:15
things waiting than death, 530:6
to fear worst cures w., 203:17
you have suffered w. things, 93:34
Worship bitch-goddess Success, 542:4
come to w. him, 31:36
compelled from their w., 247:8
duty to w. sun, 533:1
everyone's true w., 73:24
Father in spirit, 39:13
freedom of w., 653:4
God according to own inclinations, 106:5
in Roman world, 332:2
justice the only w., 518:6
let us w. and bow down, 17:32
let us w. God, 356:9
man strives for someone to w., 492:13
more w. rising than setting sun, 88:19
of Opinion is established religion, 422:21
of world but no repose, 403:7
pay no w. to garish sun, 180:32
stated calls to w., 307:16
the Lord in beauty of holiness, 15:30
true worshippers shall w., 39:13
what thou hast burned, 116:24
Worshipped, burn what thou hast w., 116:24
fell down and w. him, 31:37
neither w. with hands, 40:33
no graven images w., 479:13
stocks and stones, 254:23
Worshipper, grudging w. of the gods, 96:16
Worshippers, sufferest more than thy w.,
189:22
true w. shall worship, 39:13
Worst and best inclined to snap, 666:9
are full of passionate intensity, 593:9
best and w. of this is, 530:19
bottom of the w., 203:12
British like to be told w., 620:5
Catullus w. of all poets, 91:15
comes to the worst, 236:11
death not the w., 66:13
do your w. we our best, 620:9
ecclesiastic tyranny's w., 282:7
give thy w. of thoughts, 209:1
good bad w. best, 448:2
his face the w. thing, 206:23
intellectual hatred w., 593:17
is better than none, 308:8
is death, 177:6
is not, 212:16
is yet to come, 455:23
knew w. too young, 588:7
know w. and provide for it, 331:10
love good pursue the w., 102:*n*11
no w. there is none, 547:5
of all states, 249:13
of the company, 284:11
of words, 209:1
perhaps w. most of all, 841:7

Worst (continued)
persecutes the mind, 274:1
race and nation judged by best not w.,
610:2
things present w., 187:39
this is the w., 212:16
to fear w. cures worse, 203:17
tomorrow do thy w., 273:17
treason has done his w., 216:11
use a man could be put to, 227:13
when w. little better than beast, 184:19
where best like w., 588:3
Worth a thousand men, 374:4
an age without a name, 326:1
as much as my life was w., 314:13
conscience of her w., 259:1
country of w., 357:14
dignity and w. of person, 661:16
doing is worth doing well, 298:2
good words w. much, 243:22
how many ships my presence w., 79:12
in New York ask how much w., 524:5
in the w. and choice, 232:1
little more than coward, 364:1
makes the man, 295:4
man w. as he esteems himself, 145:12
my Being's w., 511:8
never knew w. of him, 605:15
nobler yet in his own w., 273:6
not w. going to see, 310:25
not w. his salt, 105:21
not w. the search, 184:10
not w. wooing not w. winning, 437:6
nothing w. doing completed, 696:6
Paris well w. a Mass, 161:13
show me but thy w., 189:22
slow rises w., 306:8
trick w. two of that, 182:8
what is w. in anything, 262:16
what purchaser will pay, 101:2
wit nor words nor w., 193:4
you are not w. the dust, 212:18
Zeus takes away half a man's w., 54:1
Worthies, than all the W. did, 228:12
Worthily, write w. of American things, 543:16
Worthiness, change to virtue and w., 191:34
love in excess brings nor w., 67:19
Worthless, sons more w. than sires, 97:1
Worth's unknown although height taken, 222:15
Worthwhile, worrying never w., 643:22
Worthy, brave men and w. patriots, 254:4
foemen of steel, 374:3
I am not w. to unloose, 36:25
laborer w. of hire, 37:33
no w. action done, 883:18
of great DiMaggio, 722:3
of nothing but to be cast into fire, 301:11
proved them and found them w., 29:34
taketh not cross is not w., 34:6
valets, 327:14
who looks for right time not w., 80:14
Wot, knows wot's w., 464:2
walk and w. not what they are, 174:1
Wotton a most dear lover, 245:1
Would God I had died for thee, 11:22
God it were even, 9:27
God it were morning, 9:27
he had blotted a thousand, 233:11

Would (*continued*)
 that I did too, 495:19
 thou hadst ne'er been born, 210:5
 wait upon I w., 215:2
 we w. and we w. not, 207:13
Wound, earth felt the w., 259:11
 he will never get over, 623:12
 heal by degrees, 208:34
 heals scar disappears, 474:2
 history of soldier's w., 314:4
 honor take away grief of w., 183:25
 I the w. and knife, 491:7
 immortal w., 623:12
 jests that never felt w., 179:31
 purple with love's w., 178:16
 put a tongue in every w., 193:5
 read only books that w. us, 655:10
 red badge of courage, 608:14
 silent w. deep in her breast, 94:22
 what missing so he does not w., 773:17
 willing to w., 295:13
 with mercy round, 547:1
 with thee in thee isled, 547:2
 with touch scarcely felt, 297:9
Wounded and left on Afghanistan's plains,
  588:13
 but not slain, 889:*n*1
 in house of my friends, 29:17
 is the wounding heart, 263:8
 like a w. snake, 292:18
 my heart is w. within me, 18:17
 razors to my w. heart, 172:41
 regarded w. soldiers in envious way, 608:14
 shrieks and groans of w., 489:15
 situation of the walking w., 810:5
 souls w. by such things, 267:15
 spirit who can bear, 21:2
 what a w. name, 202:31
 you're w., 459:23
Wounded Knee, bury my heart at W., 715:19
Wounding, wounded is the w. heart, 263:8
Wounds, bind up my w., 172:7
 bind up nation's w., 447:2
 faithful are w. of friend, 22:1
 fight and not heed w., 144:16
 Greece w. me, 727:3
 in thine hands, 29:17
 invisible, 195:19
 labour and w. are vain, 479:12
 soldier tells his w., 101:13
Wove shirt of flame, 679:11
Woven, out of hopeful green stuff w., 485:18
Wovon man nicht sprechen kann, 685:*n*3
Wow, Oh wow, 873:13
Woyzeck I shudder, 468:17
Wrack, betokened w. to seaman, 171:11
 blow wind come w., 217:25
Wracks, thousand fearful w., 171:28
Wraggle-taggle gypsies O, 884:1
Wrang, may gang a kennin w., 357:3
Wrangling, remote from w. world, 333:8
Wrap baby bunting in, 894:3
 thousand onward years, 486:22
 wide enough to w. a fairy, 178:19
Wrapped, child all meanly w., 250:10
 in clouds and snow, 395:17
 in five-pound note, 467:7
 in swaddling clothes, 37:16

Wrapped (*continued*)
 tiger's heart w. in woman's hide, 170:19
Wraps me in humorous sadness, 195:23
Wrath, between dragon and w., 210:27
 day of w., 47:20
 did grow, 353:7
 envy and w. shorten life, 31:17
 flee from w. to come, 32:7
 grapes of w., 481:1
 in w. the Olympian Pericles, 72:10
 infinite w. and despair, 257:12
 killeth the foolish man, 13:10
 let not sun go down on w., 43:37
 matter of Troy and Achilles' w., 487:3
 my w. did end, 353:7
 neither w. of love nor fire, 102:18
 nursing w., 358:3
 of Almighty God, 47:9
 of lion wisdom of God, 351:14
 of Peleus' son, 50:9, 293:16
 provoking most justly thy w., 49:5
 sentest forth thy w., 8:7
 slow to w., 45:23
 soft answer turneth away w., 20:30
 sweeter than honeycomb, 52:7
 towards you burns like fire, 301:11
 tygers of w., 351:17
 winepress of w., 47:9
 worketh not righteousness, 45:23
Wrath-bearing, tears from w. tree, 675:23
Wrathful man stirreth up strife, 20:33
 winter with w. nipping cold, 170:4
Wreath, hanging the w. over the vane, 505:5
 rosy w., 232:17
 subtle w. of hair, 230:1
Wreathe iron pokers into knots, 378:12
Wreathed, blow w. horn, 371:24
 smiles, 250:21
 with fairy fruits, 448:6
 with silken turbans w., 259:34
Wreaths, bindest in w. thy golden hair, 96:6
 no w. please, 658:4
Wreck, came to explore w., 825:8
 decay of colossal w., 401:13
 Hope creates from its own w., 402:5
 out of the w. I rise, 463:13
Wreckage, tatty w. of my life, 832:15
 wild to be w. forever, 801:16
Wrecked, battered w. old man, 488:2
 on lee shore of age, 552:10
Wren, four larks and w., 467:3
 goes to 't, 212:27
 hurt the little w., 353:17
 robin redbreast and w., 237:3
 Sir Christopher W., 629:2
Wrenlike vigilance, 787:19
Wrens make prey where eagles dare not, 171:23
Wrested from sure defeat, 680:9
Wresting from Jupiter his thunder, 104:9
Wrestle, this urge w. resurrection, 755:11
 we w. not against flesh, 43:40
 with words and meanings, 678:16
Wrestled as Angel with Jacob, 244:30
 until breaking of day, 7:2
Wrestling for world axeth a fal, 136:20
 with my God my God, 547:4
Wretch, concentered all in self, 373:3
 excellent w., 208:35

Wretch (*continued*)
 hollow-eyed sharp-looking w., 172:28
 I beheld the w., 415:17
 I w. lay wrestling, 547:4
 live like a w., 234:22
 my wife poor w., 277:8
 saved a w. like me, 320:13
 wise w., 293:27
Wretched, all men hate w., 415:18
 companions consolation to w., 101:7
 despicable creature, 301:8
 grief transfigures w., 422:11
 have no friends, 272:12
 learned to aid w., 94:8
 learning how to be w., 431:14
 man outlive wealth, 186:7
 nothing more w. than a man, 52:6
 of the earth, 472:16
 poor man that hangs on princes' favors,
  225:25
 proud yet w. thing, 227:17
 refuse of teeming shore, 552:16
 sleep soundly as w. slave, 189:23
 un-ideaed girls, 308:16
Wretchedness, consigned to state of w., 328:6
 that glory brings, 213:27
Wretches, feel what w. feel, 211:33
 hang that jurymen dine, 293:9
 hired, 307:1
 poor naked w., 211:33
 who never were alive, 128:11
Wrigley, Spearmint Girl With W. Eyes, 701:9
Wring his bosom, 322:17
 pain and anguish w. brow, 373:16
 pangs wilder w., 547:5
Wringing bread from sweat, 447:1
 handlebar for speed, 801:16
Wrings, wearer knows where shoe w.,
  107:*n*11
Wrinkle, no w. on azure brow, 396:19
 stamps w. deeper, 395:9
Wrinkled Care derides, 250:22
 lame w. and slanting-eyed, 51:21
 sea, 454:13
 smoothed his w. front, 171:17
 view with w. brow, 186:7
Wrinkles, eyes mid many w., 596:11
Wrist, ease darbies at w., 484:4
 hands in up to w., 748:9
Writ, having w. moves on, 442:2
 I never w., 222:15
 in remembrance, 176:21
 name w. in water, 414:1
 odd old ends stolen of holy w., 171:25
 proofs of holy w., 209:10
 with me in misfortune's book, 181:11
 your annals true, 220:6
Write about it Goddess, 297:5
 all books in British Museum, 649:6
 anyone allowed to w. like that, 655:*n*3
 as much as man ought to w., 472:4
 as soon w. free verse, 625:11
 baseness to w. fair, 202:24
 better neither read nor w., 386:1
 born to w., 295:13
 can't w. can review, 481:20
 casts to w. living line, 233:4
 devise wit w. pen, 174:7

Write *(continued)*
  difficult to w. good life as live one, 646:10
  evil in marble, 143:8
  faster than people who w. better, 738:15
  finely upon broomstick, 284:*n*2
  free to think speak w., 338:17
  from worm's-eye view, 726:13
  good in dust, 143:8
  History Don't, 518:11
  I detest what you w., 300:*n*4
  I did not w. it, 458:18
  I do not think I can w. more, 603:8
  I live and w., 243:7
  I w. nothing other than images, 727:5
  I w. Poets All, 509:9
  I w. wonders of religion, 283:2
  if I started to w. elaborately, 722:7
  if she is to w. fiction, 654:14
  if you get work, 802:3
  impossible to w. a novel, 815:13
  in books of law, 753:11
  in de blotter I was born, 681:5
  instruction manual, 815:3
  it or tell it is to spoil it, 765:2
  know what I know and w. it, 776:9
  last till you w. your letter, 228:11
  look in thy heart and w., 162:20
  man may w. at any time, 308:15
  me as one that loves, 392:18
  me down an ass, 191:10
  never learned to w., 811:4
  no intention to w. atheistically, 440:6
  nothing to w. about, 110:17
  of hunger, 752:9
  poem for money, 742:1
  poetry very easy to w., 520:2
  sorrow on bosom of the earth, 177:7
  speak associate, 754:12
  the next chapter, 753:11
  the vision, 29:7
  things worthy reading, 302:18
  three lessons I would w., 359:11
  to w. and read comes by nature, 190:41
  until still have juice, 722:6
  virtues we w. in water, 226:11
  well in laudable things, 253:22
  well of American things, 543:16
  whatever I tried to w. was verse, 102:24
  with ease to show breeding, 346:19
  with no dinner, 682:1
  with watch before me, 472:5
  woman's vows upon wave, 66:27
  yet w. verse badly, 267:25
  you a tragedy, 710:18
Writer, all w. had known become grotesques,
      632:14
  American w. in the middle, 835:3
  concealed beauties of w., 288:13
  creative w. like child at play, 563:3
  every w. creates own precursors, 719:5
  excels at title page, 321:10
  fit to be a w., 806:10
  great and original w., 372:4
  great w. second government, 791:6
  I'm a good w. honest, 710:15
  in his work must be like God, 493:18
  main concern of fiction w., 809:14
  moment here and there w. has, 625:6

Writer *(continued)*
  most essential gift for good w., 722:5
  must refuse to let himself be transformed,
      743:8
  must pretend to be w. to be w., 737:10
  my tongue is the pen of a ready w., 16:24
  no eminent w. whom I can despise, 565:15
  no tears in w. no tears in reader, 625:4
  nodding places in w., 288:9
  of dictionaries, 307:3
  one thing w. can write about, 774:3
  original w. one nobody can imitate, 364:11
  paperback w., 848:8
  problem of creative w., 563:16
  someone true friend good w., 724:8
  Southern w. adept at recognizing
      grotesque, 809:9
  teach basest thing to be afraid, 714:3
  true w. has nothing to say, 800:7
  unmistakable animal a w., 819:16
  who came from sheltered life, 761:4
  who shuts himself up in a room, 871:7
  writing make us chase the w., 862:9
Writer's only responsibility is to art, 714:8
  that is w. lot, 552:14
  understand w. ignorance, 379:3
Writers, all w. are vain selfish lazy, 735:14
  ancient w. say, 595:1
  are always selling somebody out, 837:12
  compulsion put upon w., 664:5
  dissatisfied with books they could buy,
      692:12
  divided into incisors and molars, 503:2
  editors are failed w. but so are w., 679:16
  forgotten for want of w., 97:*n*11
  gifted energetic wives of w., 781:15
  habit of accurate w., 518:13
  if poets and w. set themselves, 801:13
  make mistake of enclosing envelope, 662:10
  of small histories, 307:2
  Southern w. have penchant, 809:10
  strong w. will rise, 826:6
  transcribed from former works, 104:13
  two kinds of w., 626:10
Writes, as happens when one w., 847:4
  great poet w. his time, 677:8
  limns on water w. in dust, 166:23
  Moving Finger w., 442:2
  verses speaks holiday, 187:12
  very well for a gentleman, 289:*n*4
  whatever poet w. with enthusiasm, 70:10
Writing a name for conversation, 314:5
  all w. is profoundly unmarried, 781:17
  becomes place to live, 733:11
  book is horrible struggle, 735:14
  books praiseworthy method, 692:12
  creative reading creative w., 426:2
  didn't require real work, 806:10
  do things worth the w., 302:18
  faucet upstairs, 625:8
  for myself and strangers, 627:15
  good w. takes concentration, 800:9
  I'd do no w. here, 757:2
  in book of gold, 392:17
  in w. himself writes his time, 677:8
  incurable itch for w., 109:22
  is easy, 687:1
  is what you live for, 674:11

Writing *(continued)*
  it isn't w. it's typing, 805:10
  judicial w., 607:2
  least of recorded w. has survived, 343:20
  make us chase the writer, 862:9
  maketh an exact man, 166:18
  master to this world, 671:12
  much w. many opinions, 254:10
  my daughter is w., 798:5
  no harder prison than w. verse, 829:7
  no partiality in his w., 87:14
  not a profession, 736:3
  one way to go about thinking, 724:9
  piece of exceptionally fine w., 584:1
  point of w. and reading, 869:9
  precautions against disease of w., 123:10
  putting it down in w., 303:21
  rid of things by w. them, 721:13
  that was written, 28:25
  these poems, 814:9
  true ease in w., 292:19
  vigorous w. concise, 606:3
  weakest thing you can do in w., 845:15
  would have started w. long ago, 655:*n*3
Writing's, easy w. curst hard reading, 346:19
Writings, praise nor blame w., 292:21
  small men afraid of w., 327:17
Written and unwritten law, 113:2
  as it is w., 42:6
  biography of man himself cannot be w.,
      525:6
  books well w. or badly w., 559:23
  censure who have w. well, 292:9
  isn't worth paper w. on, 650:2
  of me on my stone, 624:10
  poetry well w. as prose, 664:16
  read books as deliberately as w., 475:5
  sonnets all his life, 398:14
  that mine adversary had w. a book, 14:10
  that my words were w., 13:38
  troubles of the brain, 217:19
  what woman says w. in wind, 91:23
  words w. on subway walls, 855:7
Wrong, accumulated w., 585:2
  all his life in the w., 281:4
  always in the w., 273:2
  citizens clamoring for what is w., 96:27
  difficult for us to do w., 805:13
  do great right do little w., 186:2
  do w. to none, 205:30
  done my credit w., 442:7
  dreary morals w., 556:2
  even if I were w., 492:11
  fashioning characters w. way, 540:22
  forever on throne, 481:13
  Frenchmen can't be w., 887:8
  friends have it I do w., 592:3
  from the start, 665:4
  gloomy w., 431:18
  had anything been w., 749:11
  he done her w., 886:3
  he who believes what is w., 336:4
  I know I've done wrong, 890:16
  I was w., 748:14
  if end brings me out w., 447:6
  if I called w. number, 704:3
  if something can go w. it will, 888:11
  if w. to be set right, 507:13

Z